CHAMBERS EVERYDAY DICTIONARY

CHAMBERS
EVERYDAY
DICTIONARY

Edited by
A M Macdonald OBE BA
and E M Kirkpatrick MA

Chambers

© W & R Chambers Ltd Edinburgh 1975

Published in paperback under the title
Chambers Everyday Paperback Dictionary
and also in a school edition under the title
Chambers Students' Dictionary

Latest reprint 1977

Edited by A M Macdonald OBE BA and E M Kirkpatrick MA

ISBN 0 550 10612 X

Set in the Netherlands by Eltrac-Infonet n.v. and
printed in Great Britain by T & A Constable Ltd Edinburgh.

Contents

Contents

Introduction

Chambers Everyday Dictionary is a welcome addition to the Chambers range of dictionaries. Here is a handy, medium-size English dictionary—as reliable, though obviously not as comprehensive, as **Chambers Twentieth Century Dictionary**.

It provides in a compact easy-to-read form a wide-ranging selection of words likely to be encountered by the modern reader and speaker of English in his day-to-day activities. There is also good coverage of literary vocabulary and special attention has been given to technical words and meanings, which are of increasing importance in the modern world.

We have included a large number of colloquial and figurative expressions which play an important and colourful part in the English language. This dictionary is therefore an invaluable vocabulary guide for the modern user of English, bearing in mind the diversity of interests common today.

Derivations of most of the words have been included to allow fuller understanding of the words. Where the derivation is absent it is either self-evident or of unknown or uncertain origin.

One note on spelling is necessary. We have throughout adopted the spelling *-ise* for verbs corresponding to French verbs ending in *-iser*, Latin ending in *-izāre*, Greek ending in *-izein* (eg *realise*, *baptise*, *catechise*, *bowdlerise*). The spelling *-ize* is also correct and is indeed preferred by some.

Pronunciation is mainly indicated by respelling, which is simpler for the general reader than a system of phonetic symbols. A full pronunciation guide is given on pages viii and ix.

Pronunciation guide

Accented syllables are marked thus ´, e.g. *ban'dit, as-ton'ish-ing*

Vowels and diphthongs in accented syllables

Sound		Examples	Pronunciation
ā	as in (1) fate	name, aid, rein	*nām, ād, rān*
	(2) bare	tare, wear, hair, heir	*tār, wār, hār, ār*
ä	as in (1) father	grass, path	*grāss, pāth*
	(2) far	harm, heart, palm	*härm, härt, päm*
a	as in sat	bad, have	*bad, hav*
ē	as in (1) me	lean, keel, chief, sieze	*lēn, kēl, chēf, sēz*
	(2) fear	gear, sheer, here, bier	*gēr, shēr, hēr, bēr*
e	as in pet	red, thread, said, bury	*red, thred, sed, ber'i*
ī	as in (1) mine	side, shy, dye, height	*sīd, shī, dī, hīt*
	(2) sire	hire, byre	*hīr, bīr*
i	as in bid	pin, busy, hymn	*pin, biz'i, him*
ō	as in (1) mote	bone, road, foe, dough	*bōn, rōd, fō, dō*
	(2) more	fore, soar, floor	*fōr, sōr, flōr*
o	as in got	shot, shone	*shot, shon*
ö	as in (1) all	haul, lawn, fall, bought	*höl, lön, föl, böt*
	(2) for	swarm, horn	*swörm, hörn*
ōō	as in (1) moon	fool, sou	*fōōl, sōō*
	(2) poor	boor, tour	*bōōr, tōōr*
ōō	as in foot	good, full, would	*gōōd, fōōl, wōōd*
ū	as in (1) mute	tune, due, newt, view	*tūn, dū, nūt, vū*
	(2) pure	endure	*en-dūr'*
u	as in bud	run, love	*run, luv*
û	as in her	heard, bird, world, absurd	*hûrd, bûrd, wûrld, ab-sûrd'*
ow	as in (1) house	mount, frown	*mownt, frown*
	(2) hour	sour	*sowr*
oi	as in boy	toy, buoy, soil	*toi, boi, soil*

Certain acceptable variations in pronunciation of vowels before *r* are not allowed for in the table above. For instance, especially in the south of England, the *o* in *port* is often pronounced *ö*.

Vowels of Unaccented Syllables

Sound		Examples	Pronunciation
à	as in (1) signal	mental, infant, desperate	*men'tàl, in'fànt, des'per-àt*
	(2) beggar	altar	*ölt'àr*
è	as in (1) moment	potent	*pō'tènt*
	(2) silver	never	*nev'èr*
i	as in perish	merit, minute, mountain, silly	*mer'it, min'it, mownt'in, sil'i*
ò	as in (1) abbot	faggot, bishop	*fag'òt, bish'òp*
	(2) doctor	sailor, rigour	*sāl'òr, rig'òr*
ù	as in (1) circus	nimbus, bulbous	*nim'bùs, bul'bùs*
	(2) figure	treasure	*trezh'ùr*
	(3) tenure	adventure	*ad-ven'tyùr* (or *ad-ven'chùr* see below)

Consonants

Sound		Examples	Pronunciation
ch	as in cheap	church, feature, match	*chûrch, fē'chûr* (or *fē'tyûr*), *mach*
f	as in fate	fell, phone, laugh	*fel, fōn, läf*
g	as in good	game, mitigate, guard, ghastly	*gām, mit'i-gāt, gärd, gäst'li*
gw	as in penguin	linguist	*ling'gwist*
gz	as in example	exist	*egz-ist'*
н	as in loch	pibroch, leprechaun	*pē'broн, lep'rĕ-нōn*
hw	as in where	what	*hwot*
j	as in just	jade, gentle, midge, rigid, region	*jād, jen'tl, mij, rij'id, rē'jŏn*
k	as in keel	kite, cold, chorus	*kit, kōld, kō'rus* (or *kŏ'rus*)
ks	as in axe	explain	*eks plān'*
kw	as in queen	quite, choir, coiffeur	*kwīt, kwīr, kwäf-œr'*
ng	as in sing	rang, rank, longer	*rang, rangk, long'gĕr*
s	as in see	sole, cede, scent, mass	*sōl, sēd, sent, mas*
sh	as in shine	shape, machine, sugar, pressure, precious, mention	*shāp, ma-shēn', shoog'ár presh'ûr, presh'ûs, men'sh(ó)n*
th	as in thin	theme, health	*thēm, helth*
тн	as in then	though, bathe	*тнō, bāтн*
y	as in yet	young, super, feature	*yung, s(y)oo'pêr, fē'tyûr* (or *fē'chûr*)
z	as in zone	zero, maze, muse, xylem, roads	*zē'rō, māz, mūz, zī'lem, rōdz*
zh	as in azure	measure, vision, rouge	*mezh'ûr, vizh'(ó)n, roozh*

Additional sounds in foreign words

Sound		Examples	Pronunciation
o	as in père	maître	*metr'*
œ	as in deux	douloureux	*doo-loo-rœ*
œ	as in œuvre	fauteuil, fleur	*fō tœ y', flœr*
ü	as in Führer	Führer	*fü'rêr*

Nasalised vowels

ã	as in blanc	outrance, mélange	*oo-trãs, mã-läzh*
ɛ̃	as in vin	poussin, timbre	*poos-ɛ̃, tɛ̃br'*
ɔ̃	as in mon	accompli, convenance	*a-kɔ̃-plē, kɔ̃'ve-näs*
œ̃	as in lundi	un	*œ̃*

An apostrophe is used to mark such pronunciations as t'h
(where the sound is two separate consonants). It is also used in
such words as timbre (*tɛ̃br'*).

Abbreviations used in the dictionary

abbrev.	abbreviation	*E.*	East
abl.	ablative	*econ.*	economics
acc.	accusative	*e.g.*	(L. *exempli gratia*)
adj(s).	adjective(s)		for example
adv(s).	adverb(s)	*elect.*	electricity
aero.	aeronautics	*erron.*	erroneous(ly)
alg.	algebra	*esp.*	especially
anat.	anatomy	*ety.*	etymology
anc.	ancient(ly)		
anthrop.	anthropology		
aor.	aorist	*facet.*	facetiously
app.	apparently	*fem.*	feminine
approx.	approximately	*fig.*	figuratively
arch.	archaic	*foll.*	followed
archeol.	archeology		following
archit.	architecture	*freq.*	frequentative
arith.	arithmetic	*fut.*	future
astrol.	astrology		
astron.	astronomy		
at. no. or	atomic number	*gen.*	genitive
at. numb.		*geog.*	geography
		geol.	geology
		geom.	geometry
B.	Bible (Authorised Version)	*gram.*	grammar
biol.	biology		
book-k.	book-keeping		
bot.	botany	*her.*	heraldry
		hist.	history
c.	(L. *circa*) about		
cap.	capital	*i.e.*	(L. *id est*)
cent.	century		that is
cf.	(L. *confer*) compare	*imit.*	imitative
chem.	chemistry	*imper.*	imperative
cog.	cognate	*impers.*	impersonal(ly)
coll.	colloquial(ly)	*incl.*	including
comp.	comparative	*indic.*	indicative
conj.	conjunction	*infin.*	infinitive
conn.	connected	*inten.*	intensive
	connection	*interj.*	interjection
contr.	contracted	*interrog.*	interrogative(ly)
	contraction	*intrans.*	intransitive
cook.	cookery		
corr.	corruption		
	corresponding	*lit.*	literal(ly)
dat.	dative	*mach.*	machinery
demons.	demonstrative	*masc.*	masculine
der.	derived	*math.*	mathematics
	derivation	*mech.*	mechanics
derog.	derogatory	*med.*	medicine
	derogatorily	*mil.*	military
dial.	dialectal	*min.*	mineralogy
Dict.	Dictionary	*mod.*	modern
dim.	diminutive	*mus.*	music
dub.	dubious, doubtful	*myth.*	mythology

Abbreviations used in etymologies

N.	North	*pron(s).*	pronoun(s)
n(s).	noun(s)	*pron.*	pronounced
naut.	nautical		pronunciation
neg.	negative	*pros.*	prosody
neut.	neuter	*psych.*	psychology
nom.	nominative		
n.pl.	noun plural		
n.sing.	noun singular		
N.T.	New Testament	*q.v.*	(L. *quod vide*)
	(Authorised Version)		which see
		R.C.	Roman Catholic
obs.	obsolete	*reflex.*	reflexive
opp.	opposed	*rel.*	related, relative
orig.	original(ly)		
	origin		
O.T.	Old Testament	*S.*	South
	(Authorised Version)	*Shak.*	Shakespeare
		sing.	singular
		subj.	subjunctive
p.	participle	*suffx.*	suffix
p.adj.	participial adjective	*superl.*	superlative
pa.p.	past participle		
part.	participle		
pass.	passive	*theat.*	theatre
pa.t.	past tense	*theol.*	theology
perf.	perfect	*trans.*	transitive
perh.	perhaps		translation
pers.	person(al)	*trig.*	trigonometry
pfx.	prefix	*TV*	television
phil(os).	philosophy		
phonet.	phonetics		
phot.	photography	*ult.*	ultimately
phys.	physics	*usu.*	usually
pl	plural		
poet.	poetical		
pop.	popular(ly)	*vb(s).*	verbs
poss.	possessive	*v(s).i.*	verb(s) intransitive
	possibly	*voc.*	vocative
Pr. Bk.	Book of Common	*v(s).t.*	verb(s) transitive
	Prayer	*vulg.*	vulgar(ly)
pr.p.	present participle		
prep.	preposition		
pres.	present	*W.*	West
print.	printing		
priv.	privative		
prob.	probably	*zool.*	zoology

For abbreviations used in etymologies see next page.

Abbreviations used in etymologies

A.F.	Anglo-French	*L.*	Latin
Afrik.	Afrikaans	*L. Ger.*	Low German
Amer.	American	*L.L.*	Late Latin
Angl.	Anglian	*Low L.*	Low Latin
Ar.	Arabic		
Austr.	Australian		
		M.E.	Middle English
		Mex.	Mexican
Beng.	Bengali		
		Norm.	Norman
Celt.	Celtic	*Norw.*	Norwegian
Chin.	Chinese		
		O.E.	Old English
Dan.	Danish	*O.Fr.*	Old French
Du.	Dutch	*O.H.G.*	Old High German
		O.N.	Old Norse
Eng.	English		
		Pers.	Persian
		Pol.	Polish
Fr.	French	*Port.*	Portuguese
Gael.	Gaelic	*Russ.*	Russian
Ger.	German		
Gmc.	Germanic		
Gr.	Greek	*S. Afr.*	South African
		Sans.	Sanskrit
		Scand.	Scandinavian
		Scot.	Scottish
Heb.	Hebrew	*Sp.*	Spanish
Hind.	Hindi	*Sw.*	Swedish
Icel.	Icelandic (Modern)	*Turk.*	Turkish
Ir.	Irish		
Ind.	Indian	*U.S.*	United States
It.	Italian		
		W.	Welsh
Jap.	Japanese	*W.S.*	West Saxon

A

a, *a* (when emphatic sometimes *ā*), *adj.* the indefinite article, a broken-down form of **an,** used before words beginning with the sound of a consonant: one: any.

a, *á, prep.,* derived from the prep. *on,* still used as a prefix, as in *a*foot, twice *a* day, *a*-going. [Short for O.E. *an,* a dialectic form of *on,* on, in, at.]

A-bomb, *ā'bom, n.* atomic bomb; **A-level,** *a'lev'l,* advanced level, an examination at the end of a school course demanding an advanced knowledge of a subject: a pass in an A-level.

A1, *ā wun,* classed as A1 in Lloyd's (q.v.) Register: (*coll.*) first-rate.

aardvark, *ärt'färk'* (S. Afr.), *ärd'värk, n.* the ant-bear, an edentate of South Africa. [Du. *aarde,* earth, *vark* (now *varken*), pig.]

aardwolf, *ärt'volf* (S. Afr.), *ärd'w̅o̅o̅lf, n.* the earth-wolf of South Africa, a carnivore near akin to the hyenas. [Du. *aarde,* earth, *wolf,* wolf.]

abaca, *ä-bä-kä, n.* a plantain grown in the Philippine Islands: its fibre, called *Manila hemp.* [Native name.]

aback, *a-bak', adv.* (*naut.*) (of sails) pressed backward against the mast by the wind— hence (*fig.*) **taken aback,** taken by surprise. [O.E. *on bæc.* **on** and **back.**]

abacus, *ab'a kus, n.* a counting frame or tablet (*archit.*) a level tablet on the capital of a column:—*pl.* **ab'aci**(-sī). [L.,—Gr.*abax, -akos,* a board for reckoning on.]

abaft, *a-bäft', adv.* and *prep.* on the aft; hind, or stern part of a ship: behind. [Pfx. *a-* (O.E. *on*), on, and *bæftan,* after, behind; itself made up of pfx. *be-,* and *æftan.* See **aft.**]

abandon, *a-ban'don, v.t.* to give up: to desert: to yield (oneself) without restraint (to).—*n.* **aban'don** (sometimes *ä-bä-dõ,* as Fr.), careless freedom of action.—*adj.* **aban'doned,** completely deserted: given up, as to a vice: very wicked. *ns.* **abandonee',** (*law*) an insurer to whom a wreck has been abandoned; **aban'donment,** act of abandoning: state of being given up: complete surrender of self (to an influence or to a cause): abandon. [O.Fr. *à bandon,* at one's disposal, and *abandoner,* to leave to one's discretion or mercy—*bandon,* ban, control.]

abase, *a-bās',* (*arch.*) to cast down, lower: to humble: to degrade.—*n.* **abase'ment,** state of humiliation. [O.Fr. *abaissier,* to bring low— L. *ad,* to, and L.L. *bassus,* low.]

abash, *a-bash', v.t.* to disconcert, discomfit, mortify.—*n.* **abash'ment,** confusion from shame. [O.Fr. *esbahir,* to be amazed—L. *ex,* out, and Fr. interj. *bah,* expressive of astonishment.]

abate, *a-bāt', v.t.* to lessen: to mitigate: to deduct: (*obs.*) to blunt.—*v.i.* to grow less.—*n.* **abate'ment,** the act of abating: the sum or quantity abated: (*her.*) a mark of dishonour on a coat

of arms. [O.Fr. *abatre,* to beat down—L. *ab,* form, and *batēre,* popular form of *batuēre,* to beat: conn. with **beat.**]

abatis, abattis, *a-bat'ē, -is, n. sing.* and *pl.* (*fort.*) a rampart of trees felled and laid side by side, with the branches towards the enemy. [Fr. See **abate.**]

abattoir, *ab'a-twär, n.* a public slaughter-house. [Fr. See **abate.**]

Abba, *ab'a, n.* Father, applied to God the Father. [Aramaic word *abbā* retained in the Greek New Testament and its translations.]

abbacy, *ab'a-si, n.* the office of an abbot: the establishment under an abbot: an abbey.—*adj.* **abbatial** (*ab-ā'shàl*). [App. orig. a Scottish form for older *abbatie*—see **abbey.**]

abbé, *ab'ā, n.* originally the French name for an abbot, but often used in the general sense of a priest or clergyman.

abbess, *ab'es, n.* the female head of an abbey. [Fr. *abesse*—L.L. *abbātissa;* cf. **abbot.**]

abbey, *ab'i, n.* a convent under an abbot or abbess: the church now or formerly attached to it:—*pl.* **abb'eys.** [O.Fr. *abaïe*—L.L. *abbātia.*]

abbot, *ab'ot, n.* the male head of an abbey:—*fem.* **abb'ess.** [L. *abbās, abbātis*—**Abba.**]

abbreviate, *a-brē'vi-āt, v.t.* to make brief: to shorten, to abridge.—*n.* **abbrevia'tion,** an act of shortening: a shortened form: a part of a word written or printed for the whole.—*adj.* **abbrē'viatory.** [L. *abbreviāre, -ātum—ab, intens.* and *brevis,* short. See **brief.**]

ABC, abcee, *ā-bē-sē', n.* the alphabet, hence (*fig.*) the rudiments of anything: anything arranged alphabetically, as a railway guide.

abdicate, *ab'di-kāt, v.t.* and *v.i.* formally to renounce or give up (office or dignity).—*n.* **abdica'tion.** [L. *ab,* from or off, *dicāre, -ātum,* to proclaim.]

abdomen, *ab'dō-men, ab-dō'men, n.* the belly: in mammals, the part between diaphragm and pelvis: in arthropods, the hind part of the body.—*adj.* **abdominal** (*-dom'-*). [L.]

abduct, *ab-dukt', v.t.* to take away by fraud or violence: to kidnap.—*ns.* **abduc'tion,** the carrying away, esp. of a person by fraud or force; **abduc'tor,** one guilty of abduction: a muscle that draws away. [L. *abdūcēre—ab,* from, *dūcēre, ductum,* to draw, lead.]

abeam, *a-bēm', adv.* (*naut.*) on the beam, or in a line at right angles to a vessel's length. [Pfx. *a-* (O.E. *on*), on, and **beam.**]

abed, *a-bed', adv.* in bed. [Pfx. *a-* (O.E. *on*), on, and **bed.**]

Aberdonian, *ab-ér-dō'ni-án, n.* a native or citizen of Aberdeen, (traditionally) mean. Also *adj.*

aberrant, *ab-er'ánt, adj.* deviating from what is usual, normal, or right.—*n.* **aberra'tion,** a wandering from the right path: deviation from truth or rectitude: mental lapse: deviation from the type: non-convergence of rays, owing to difference in refrangibility or different colours (*chromatic aberration*), or to difference of focus of the marginal and central parts of a lens or mirror (*spherical aberration*). [L. *aberrāre, -ātum—ab*, from, *errāre*, to wander.]

abet, *a-bet′, v.t.* to incite by encouragement or aid (used chiefly in a bad sense):—*pr.p.* abett′ing; *pa.p.* abett′ed.—*n.* abett′er, abett′or, one who abets. [O.Fr. *abeter—à* (L. *ad*), to, and *beter*, to bait, from root of **bait.**]

abeyance, *a-bā′áns, n.* a state of suspension or temporary inactivity. [O.Fr. *abeance—à* (L. *ad*), to, and *beer, baer*, to gape.]

abhor, *ab-hör′, v.t.* to shrink from with horror: to detest, loathe:—*pr.p.* abhorr′ing; *pa.p.* abhorred′.—*n.* abhorr′ence (*-hor′*), extreme hatred.—*adj.* abhorr′ent, detesting; repugnant (often with *to*): out of keeping with (with *from*).—*n.* abhorr′ing (*arch.*), object of abhorrence. [L. *abhorrēre—ab*, from, and *horrēre*. See **horror.**]

abide, *a-bīd′, v.t.* to bide or wait for: to endure: to tolerate.—*v.i.* to remain in a place, dwell or stay: to remain, continue, endure: to conform to, adhere to (with *by*):—*pa.t.* and *pa.p.* abode′. [O.E. *ābīdan*—pfx. *ā-*, inten., and *bīdan*, to wait.]

abide, *a-bīd′, v.t.* (*Shak.* and *Milton*) to pay the penalty for, suffer for. [M.E. *abyen*, confounded with **abide.**]

abigail, *ab′i-gāl, n.* a lady's-maid. [From *Abigail* in Beaumont and Fletcher's *Scornful Lady*, or 1 Sam. xxv.]

ability, *a-bil′i-ti, n.* quality of being able: power (physical or mental): strength: skill.—*n.pl.* abil′ities, the powers of the mind. [O.Fr. *ableté* (Fr. *habileté*)—L. *habilitās—habilis*, apt—*habēre*, to have, hold.]

abject, *ab′jekt, adj.* cast down (*arch.*): worthless: cowering: miserable.—*ns.* abjec′tion, ab′jectness, a mean or low state.—*adv.* ab′jectly. [L. *abjectus*, cast away—*ab*, away, *jacĕre*, to throw.]

abjure, *ab-jōōr′, v.t.* to renounce on oath or solemnly: to recant.—*n.* abjurā′tion. [L. *ab*, from, *jurāre, -ātum*, to swear.]

ablative, *ab′lat-iv, adj.* (*gram.*) in or belonging to a case which in Indo-Germanic languages originally expressed *direction from* or *time when*.—*n.* the ablative case. [L. *ablātīvus—ab*, from, *ferre, lātum*, to bear.]

ablaut, *ab′lowt*, (Ger.) *ap′, n.* (*philol.*) a variation of root vowel, as in s*i*ng, s*a*ng, s*o*ng, distinct from the phonetic influence of a succeeding vowel (cf. *umlaut*); also called *gradation*. [Ger. from *ab*, off, and *laut*, sound.]

ablaze, *a-blāz′, adj.* in a blaze, on fire. [Pfx. *a-* (O.E. *on*), on, and **blaze** (1).]

able, *ā′bl, adj.* having enough strength, power or means (to do a thing): skilful.—*adv.* a′bly.—*adj.* a′ble-bod′ied, of a strong body: robust.—**able seaman, able-bodied seaman** (abbrev. A.B.), one able to perform all the duties of seamanship and having a higher rating than the ordinary sailor. [O.Fr. *(h)able*—L. *habilis*; see **ability.**]

-able, *-á-bl, adj. suff.* capable of being.—Also **-ible.**

ablution, *á-blōō′sh(ó)n, n.* (often *pl.*) act of washing, esp. the body, in the ordinary course or preparatory to religious rites. [L. *ablūtiō, -ōnis—ab*, away, *luĕre*, to wash.]

abnegate, *ab′ni-gāt, v.t.* to deny, to renounce.—*n.* abnegā′tion, renunciation: denial: (usu. with **self-**) self-sacrifice. [L. *ab*, away, *negāre*, to deny.]

abnormal, *ab-nör′mál, adj.* not normal or according to rule: irregular.—*n.* abnormal′ity (*-nor-*).—*adv.* abnor′mally. [From root of **anomalous;** influenced by **normal.**]

aboard, *a-bōrd′, -börd, adv.* or *prep.* on board: in, or into, a ship, a railway train, &c. [Pfx. *a-* (O.E. *on*), on, and **board.**]

abode, *a-bōd′, n.* a dwelling-place: stay (as, *make one's abode*). [From **abide** (1).]

abode, *a-bōd′, pa.t.* and *pa.p.* of **abide.**

abolish, *ab-ol′ish, v.t.* to put an end to: to annul.—*ns.* aboli′tion, the act of abolishing; aboli′tionist, one who seeks to abolish anything, esp. slavery. [Fr. *abolir, abolissant*—L. *abolescĕre—abolēre, -itum.*]

abominate, *ab-om′in-āt, v.t.* to abhor, to detest extremely.—*adj.* abom′inable, hateful, detestable.—*n.* abom′inableness.—*adv.* abom′inably.—*n.* abominā′tion, extreme aversion: anything disgusting or detestable.—**abominable snowman,** a mythical hairy manlike creature supposed to live in the snows of Tibet. [L. *abōminārī, -ātus*, to turn from as of bad omen. See **omen.**]

aborigines, *ab-o-rij′in-ēz, n.pl.* the original or native inhabitants of a country (a *sing.* **aborig′inē,** formed by dropping *s*, is used, esp. of aboriginal Australians).—*adj.* aborig′inal, earliest, primitive, indigenous.—*n.* one of the aborigines. [L. *aborīgines—ab orīgine*, from the beginning. See **origin.**]

abort, *ab-ört′, v.i.* to miscarry in birth: to be arrested in development: to come to nothing.—*v.t.* to cause to abort: to stop (e.g. flight of rocket) in emergency before completion of mission.—*n.* an instance of abortion (esp. of rocket).—*adj.* abort′ed.—*n.* abor′tion, premature delivery, or the procuring of such: arrest of development: failure: anything that does not reach maturity.—*adj.* abort′ive, born untimely: unsuccessful, vain, fruitless: rudimentary.—*adv.* abort′ively.—*n.* abort′iveness. [L. *aborīrī, abortus—ab*, from (reversing meaning), *orīrī*, to rise.]

abound, *ab-ownd′, v.i.* to overflow, be in great plenty: to be rich (in): to teem (with). [O.Fr. *abunder*—L. *abundāre*, to overflow—*ab*, from, *unda*, a wave.]

about, *a-bowt′, prep.* round on the outside of: all round: here and there in: on (one's person): near (place, time, size, &c.): concerning: engaged in.—*adv.* around: near: nearly: here and there: (*naut.*) on the opposite tack: in the opposite direction (e.g. *to face about*).—**be about to,** to be on the point of; **bring about,** to cause to take place; **come about,** to take place; **go about,** to prepare to do; **put about,** disturbed, distressed: (also see **put**); **time, turn about,** alternately: in rotation; **week** (&c.) **about,** every second period of seven days (&c.). [O.E. *on būtan—on*, in, *būtan*, without—*be*, by, and *ūtan*, locative of *ūt*, out.]

Neutral vowels in unaccented syllables: *em′pér-ór*; for certain sounds in foreign words see p. ix.

2

above, *a-buv′, prep.* on or to the upside of: higher than: more than: too proud or too good to descend to.—*adv.* overhead: in a higher position, order, or power: at an earlier point in a writing.—*adjs.* **above′-board,** open, honourable; **above′-ground,** alive, [O.E. *ābūfan—on,* on, *bufan,* above—*be,* by, *ufan,* high, upwards, prop. the locative of *uf,* up.]

abracadabra, *ab-ra-ka-dab′ra, n.* a magic word written so that the letters form a triangle—worn as a charm: any unintelligible spell or formula. [L., origin unknown.]

abrade, *ab-rād′, v.t.* to scrape or rub off (skin, &c.): to wear down by friction.—*n.* **abrasion** *(ab-rā′zh(ò)n),* the act of rubbing off: an abraded place.—*adj.* **abra′sive** *(-ziv, -siv),* tending to abrade.—*n.* something that abrades (as *emery*). [L. *ab,* off, *rādĕre, rāsum,* to scrape.]

abreaction, *ab-rē-ak′sh(ò)n, n.* a method of curing a neurosis or emotional trouble by reviving forgotten or repressed memories of the experience that first caused the trouble. *v.t.* **abreact′.** [L. *ab,* from, and **reaction.**]

abreast, *a-brest′, adv.* with fronts in a line: side by side: (keeping) up with (e.g. the times—with *with, of*).—*prep.* (*naut.*) opposite to. [Pfx *a-* (O.E. *on*), on, and **breast.**]

abridge, *a-brij′, v.t.* to shorten: to epitomise: to curtail, as privileges or authority. *n.* **abridg′-ment** (sometimes **abridge′ment**), the act of abridging. shortening of time or labour: curtailment of privileges: a shortened form of a larger work made by omitting details. [O.Fr. *abregier*—L. *abbreviāre.* See **abbreviate.**]

abroad, *a-bröd′, adv.* over a wide area: out of doors: at large: in or to another country. —Also *n.,* as in *from abroad.* [Pfx. *a-* (O.E. *on*), on, and **broad.**]

abrogate, *ab′ro-gāt, v.t.* to annul.—*n.* **abrogā′-tion,** act of repealing or setting aside. [L. *ab-rogāre—ab,* away, *rogāre, -ātum,* to ask, or to propose a law.]

abrupt, *ab-rupt′, adj.* the opposite of gradual, as if broken off: precipitous: sudden, hasty: (of style) passing from one thought to another with sudden transitions: (of manners) ungracious, rude.—*adv.* **abrupt′ly.**—*n.* **abrupt′-ness.** [L. *abruptus—ab,* off, *rumpĕre, ruptum,* to break.]

abscess, *ab′ses, n.* a collection of pus localised within some tissue of the body. [L. *abscessus—abs,* away, *cēdĕre, cessum,* to go, to retreat.]

abscisson, *ab-sizh′(ò)n, n.* act of cutting off: state of being cut off: (*bot.*) the shedding of a part by means of an **absciss layer,** tissue whose disorganisation causes a leaf, a branch, or a scale of bark, to separate off.—*n.* **abscissa** *(ab-sis′a),* for rectilineal axes, the distance of a point from the axis of ordinates (*y*-axis) measured in a direction parallel to the axis of abscissae (*x*-axis):—*pl.* **absciss′ae** (*-ē*), **abss-sciss′as.** [L. *abscindĕre, abscissum—ab,* from, *scindĕre,* to cut.]

abscond, *ab-skond′, v.i.* to hide, or get out of the way, esp. in order to escape a legal process. [L. *abscondĕre abs,* from or away, *condĕre,* to hide.]

abseil, *ap′zīl, ab-sīl′ v.i.* to lower oneself down a rock face using a double rope.—*n.* **abseiling.**

[Ger. *-ab,* down, *seil,* a rope.]

absent, *ab′sént, adj.* away, not present: not existing: inattentive.—*adv.* **ab′sently,** in an inattentive, abstracted manner.—*v.t.* **absent′,** to keep (oneself) away.—*ns.* **ab′sence,** the state of being away or not present: want: non-existence: inattention; **absentee′,** one who is absent: one who makes a habit of living away from his estate or his office; **absentee′-ism,** the practice of absenting oneself from duty, station, or esp. estate.—*adj.* **ab′sent-mind′ed,** inattentive to surroundings: preoccupied. [L. *absens, -entis,* pr.p. of *abesse—ab,* away from, *esse,* to be.]

absinth, absinthe, *ab′sinth, n.* wormwood: a liqueur containing (orig. at all events) extract of wormwood. [Fr.,—L. *absinthium*—Gr. *apsinthion,* wormwood.]

absolute, *ab′sòl-(y)ōōt, adj.* free from limits or conditions: complete: certain, positive: free from mixture: independent of relations to other things: not relative or comparative: unalterable: (of a ruler or his government) despotic, not restricted: (*gram.*) out of ordinary syntactic relation to the other parts of the sentence (as *ablative absolute*).—*adv.* **ab′sol-utely,** independently, unconditionally: positively: completely: (*gram.*) without the part of speech that usually accompanies it, as a transitive verb without an object, or an adjective without a noun.—*ns.* **ab′soluteness; ab′solut-ism,** government where the ruler is without restriction.—**the absolute,** that which is absolute, self-existent, uncaused; **absolute alcohol,** water-free alcohol; **absolute music,** music that does not attempt to illustrate or describe—opp. to *programme music;* **absolute pitch,** the actual pitch of a sound (determined by the number of vibrations per sec.), not its pitch in relation to that of other notes in a scale: a sense of, or memory for, absolute pitch; **absolute temperature,** temperature measured from absolute zero; **absolute zero,** the temperature at which (ideally) a gas kept at constant volume would exert no pressure—approx. −273° C. [L. *absolūtus,* pa.p. of *absolvĕre.* See **absolve.**]

absolution, *ab-sol-(y)ōō′sh(ò)n, n.* release from punishment: acquittal: remission of sins declared officially by a priest. [O.Fr.,—L. *absolūtiō, -ōnis*—*absolvĕre.* See **absolve.**]

absolve, *ab-zolv′,* or *-solv′, v.t.* to set free, release (from e.g. an obligation, blame): to pardon: to acquit.—*n.* **absolv′itor** (*Scots law*), a legal decision in favour of a defendant. [L. *absolvĕre—ab,* from, *solvĕre;* see **solve.**]

absorb, *ab-sörb′, v.t.* to suck in: to take in: to swallow up: to incorporate: to take up and transform (energy) instead of transmitting or reflecting it: to engage wholly.—*adj.* **absorb′-able.**—*n.* **absorbabil′ity.**—*advs.* **absorb′edly; absorb′ingly.**—*adj.* **absorb′ent,** absorbing: able to absorb.—*n.* that which absorbs.—*ns.* **absorb′er,** that which absorbs: material for absorbing neutrons without generating more neutrons; **absorp′tion,** the act of absorbing: entire occupation of mind.—*adj.* **absorp′tive,** having power to absorb. [Fr.,—L. *absorbĕre—ab,* from, *sorbēre, sorptum,* to suck in.]

abstain, *ab-stān′, v.i.* to hold or refrain

---

fāte, fär; mē, hûr (her); *mīne; mōte, för; mūte; mōōn, fŏŏt;* ᴛʜᴇn (then)

(from).—*ns.* **abstain′er**, used esp. of one who does not take alcoholic drinks; **absten′tion**, a refraining. [Fr. *abstenir*—L. *abstinēre*—*abs*, from, *tenēre*, to hold.]

abstemious, *ab-stēm′i-us*, *adj.* temperate: sparing in food, drink or enjoyments.—*adv.* **abstem′iously.**—*n.* **abstem′iousness.** [L. *abstēmius*—*abs*, from, *tēmētum*, strong wine.]

abstersion, *ab-stûr′sh(ó)n*, *n.* act of cleansing or washing away impurities.—*adj.* **abstergent** (*ab-stûr′jent*), serving to cleanse. [L. *abstergēre, -tersum*—*abs*, from, *tergēre*, to wipe.]

abstinent, *ab′stin-ént*, *adj.* abstaining from: temperate.—*ns.* **ab′stinence, ab′stinency**, an abstaining or refraining, esp. from some indulgence. [Fr.,—L. *abstinens, -entis*—*abstinēre.* See **abstain.**]

abstract, *ab-strakt′*, *v.t.* to draw away: to separate: to remove quietly: to purloin: to summarise: to form a general concept from consideration of particular instances.—*adj.* **abstract′ed**, absent-minded.—*adv.* **abstract′edly**, in the abstract: absentmindedly.—*ns.* **abstract′edness; abstrac′tion**, act of abstracting: state of being abstracted: absence of mind: the operation of the mind by which certain qualities or attributes of an object are considered apart from the rest: that which exists only in theory.—*adj.* **abstract** (*ab′strakt*), considered apart from actual material instances, existing only as a mental concept—opp. to *concrete*: theoretical: (of terms) denoting the qualities of an object apart from the object itself.—*n.* summary, abridgment: essence.—*adv.* **ab′stractly.**—*n.* **ab′stractness.**—**in the abstract**, in theory: as an abstraction. [L. *abstrahēre*—*abs*, away from, *trahēre, tractum*, to draw.]

abstruse, *ab-strōōs′*, *adj*, (*obs.*) hidden: remote from apprehension, difficult to understand.—*adv.* **abstruse′ly.**—*n.* **abstruse′ness.** [L. *abstrūsus*, thrust away (from observation)—*abs*, away from, *trūdēre, trūsum*, to thrust.]

absurd, *ab-sûrd′*, *adj.* obviously unreasonable or false: ridiculous.—*ns.* **absurd′ness; absurd′ity**, the quality of being absurd: anything absurd.—*adv.* **absurd′ly.** [L. *absurdus*—*ab*, inten., *surdus*, deaf, dull.]

abundance, *ab-und′áns*, *n.* ample sufficiency: great plenty.—*adj.* **abund′ant**, plentiful: rich (in).—*adv.* **abund′antly.** [See **abound.**]

abuse, *ab-ūz′*, *v.t.* to use wrongly: (*arch.*) to maltreat: to revile: to violate.—*n.* **abuse** (*ab-ūs′*), ill use: misapplication: an unjust or corrupt usage: vituperation.—*adj.* **abusive** (*-ūs-*), involving, characterised by, misuse or misapplication: coarsely reproachful, vituperative.—*adv.* **abus′ively.**—*n.* **abus′iveness.** [L. *ab*, away (from what is right), *ūtī, ūsus*, to use.]

abut, *a-but′*, *v.i.* to end or lean (on, upon, against): to border (on):—*pr.p.* abutt′ing; *pa.p.* abutt′ed.—*n.* **abut′ment** (*archit.*), what a limb of an arch ends or rests on. [O.Fr. *abouter*, to touch by an end, and O.Fr. *abuter*, to touch at the end (*à*, to, *bout*, end).]

abysm, *a-bizm′*, *n.* (*arch.* and *poet.*) abyss.—*adj.* **abys′mal**, bottomless: unfathomable.—*adv.* **abys′mally.** [O.Fr. *abisme*—L. *abyssimus*, superl. of *abyssus*, bottomless.]

abyss, *a-bis′*, *n.* a bottomless depth: a deep mass of water: a chasm. [Gr. *abyssos*, bottomless—*a-*, priv., *byssos*, bottom.]

Abyssinian cat, *ab-i-sini′-in*, a small domestic cat, of African origin, greyish or brownish ticked with darker colour.

acacia, *a-kā′sh(y)a*, *n.* a genus of thorny leguminous plants with pinnate leaves. [L.,—Gr. *akakia*—*akē*, a sharp point.]

academic. See **academy.**

academy, *a-kad′em-i*, *n.* (*orig.*) the school of philosophy of Plato: a higher school, a university: a society for the promotion of science or art.—*adj.* **academ′ic**, of an academy: scholarly: theoretical as opposed to practical.—*n.* a Platonic philosopher: one studying or teaching at university, esp. one who has scholarly tastes.—*adj.* **academ′ical**, academic.—*n.* (in *pl.*) university garb.—*adv.* **academ′ically.**—*n.* **academician** (*á-kad-é-mish′n*), member of academy, esp. of French Academy (letters) or Royal Academy, London (painting, &c.). [Gr. *Akadēmia*, name of garden orig. outside Athens where Plato taught.]

acanthus, *a-kan′thus*, *n.* a genus of prickly-leaved plants: (*archit.*) an ornament resembling their leaves used in the capitals of the Corinthian and other orders. [L.,—Gr. *akanthos*—*akantha*, thorn, conn. with *akē*, point.]

acarpous, *a-kär′pus*, *adj.* (*bot.*) without fruit. [Gr. *a-*, priv., and *karpos*, fruit.]

accede, *ak-sēd′*, *v.i.* to approach (*rare*): to come into some office or dignity: to adhere (to a party): to agree or assent (with *to*). [L. *accēdere, accessum*, to go near to—*ad*, to, *cēdēre*, to go.]

accelerando, *ak-sel-ér-an′dō*, *adv.* (*mus.*) with gradual increase in speed. [It.]

accelerate, *ak-sel′ér-āt*, *v.t.* to increase the speed of: to hasten the progress or occurrence of.—*v.i.* to move faster.—*n.* **accelera′tion**, the act of hastening: increase of speed: rate of change of velocity.—*adj.* **accel′erative**, quickening.—*n.* **accel′erator**, one who or that which accelerates, esp. a substance that increases the speed of a chemical action or an apparatus for regulating the speed of a machine, or one for accelerating elementary particles to high energies (e.g. cyclotron). [L. *accelerāre, -ātum*—*ad*, to, *celer*, swift.]

accent, *ak′sént*, *n.* modulation of the voice: tone of the voice: stress on a syllable or word: a mark used to direct this stress: any mode of utterance characteristic of a region, a class, or an individual: (*pl.*) speech, language.—*v.t.* **accent′**, to express or note the accent: to accentuate.—*adj.* **accent′ual**, relating to accent.—*v.t.* **accent′uate**, to mark or pronounce with accent: to make prominent, emphasise.—*n.* **accentua′tion**, the act of marking or of pronouncing or of playing accents: emphasis. [Fr.,—L. *accentus*, accent—*ad*, to, *cantus*, song.]

accentor, *ak-sent′ór*, *n.* the so-called 'hedge-sparrow' (q.v.) or other bird of its genus. [LL. *accentor*, one who sings with another—*ad*, to, *cantor*, singer.]

accept, *ak-sept′*, *v.t.* (also—*arch.* or formal—*v.i.* with *of*) to take (something offered): to receive (e.g. one's fate) without demur: to take upon oneself (e.g. a task, responsibility): to

Neutral vowels in unaccented syllables: *em′pér-ór*; for certain sounds in foreign words see p. ix.

4

take in respect of meaning: to receive with approval or favour: to receive as adequate or true: to agree to: to undertake to pay.—*adj.* **acceptable** (*ak-sept'a-bl*, or *ak'-*), worth accepting, pleasing, agreeable.—*ns.* **accept'ableness, acceptabil'ity.**—*adv.* **accept'ably.**—*ns.* **accept'ance,** act of accepting or state of being accepted: acceptableness: a favourable reception: assent: received meaning of a word, &c.: an accepted bill of exchange; **accepta'tion,** a favourable reception: assent: received meaning.—*adj.* **accep'ted,** generally approved or believed in.—*ns.* **accept'er; accept'or,** one who accepts: an impurity in semiconductor material which increases the conductivity of the material. [L. *acceptāre—accipěre, acceptum—ad,* to *capěre,* to take.]

access, *ak'ses,* or *ak'ses',* *n.* approach: means or opportunity of approach: entrance: addition, increase: onset, attack (of illness): a fit or outburst. *adj.* **access'ible,** able to be reached: open (to). *n.* **accessibil'ity.** *adv.* **access'ibly.** [See **accede.**]

accessary, *ak-ses'ár-i,* or *ak'ses-ár-i.* Same as **accessory.**

accession, *ak-sesh'(ó)n, n.* act of acceding: an onset, as of illness, folly: addition: an addition: (*law*) addition by nature or industry of something new to an existing property. [See **accede.**]

accessory, *ak-ses'ór-ι,* or *ak'ses-or-ι, adj.* additional: contributory: aiding: (*law*) participating in a crime but not as principal: adventitious.—*n.* anything additional: an additional item of equipment: one who aids or gives countenance to a crime.—*adj.* **accessōr'ial.** [See **accede.**]

accidence, *ak'si-déns, n.* the part of grammar treating of accidents (i.e. inflections) of words. [For *accidents,* or perh. directly from *accidentia,* neut. pl. of pr.p. of *accidēre,* treated as noun of first declension. See **accident.**]

accident, *ak'si-dént, n.* that which happens: an unforeseen or unexpected event: a mishap or disaster: chance: an unessential quality or property.—*adj.* **accident'al,** happening by chance: not essential.—*n.* anything not essential: (*mus.*) a sharp, flat, or natural not in the key-signature.—*adv.* **accident'ally.**—**chapter of accidents,** the unforeseen course of events: a series of unfortunate happenings [L. *accidēre,* to happen—*ad,* to, *caděre,* to fall.]

acclaim, *a klām' v.t.* to applaud: to hail as.—*v.i.* to shout applause.—*n.* a shout of applause or assent: enthusiastic approbation or assent. *n.* **acclamā'tion,** acclaim: shouted assent without recourse to voting.—*adj.* **acclam'atory,** expressing acclamation. [L. *acclāmāre—ad,* to, *clāmāre, -ātum,* to shout.]

acclimatise, *a-klīm'a-tιz, v.t.* to inure to a new climate.—Also **acclim'ate.**—*n.* **acclimatisā'tion,** the act of acclimatising: the state of being acclimatised.—Also **acclimā'tion, acclimatā'tion.** [Fr. *acclimater,* from *à,* to, and *climat.* See **climate.**]

acclivity, *a-kliv'i-ti, n.* a slope upwards—opp. to *declivity,* a slope downwards. [L. *acclīvitās—acclīvis,* uphill—*ad,* to, *clīvus,* a slope.]

accolade, *ak-ol-ād', -ăd', n.* the mark used in conferring knighthood, now a light touch on

each shoulder with the flat of a sword: high honour or praise publicly given. [Fr.,—L. *ad,* to, *collum,* neck.]

accommodate, *a-kom'od-āt, v.t.* to adapt: to make suitable: to adjust: to bring to settlement or agreement: to furnish or supply (with): to oblige: to lodge.—*p.adj.* **accomm'-odating,** willing to make adjustment: obliging: easily corrupted.—*n.* **accommodā'tion,** adaptation: adjustment: obligingness: an arrangement or compromise: space or room: lodging: a loan of money.—*adj.* **accomm'od-ative,** furnishing accommodation: of the nature of an accommodation: obliging. —**accommodation address,** an address to which mail may be sent but which is not that of the addressee's home or office. [L. *accommodāre, -ātum—ad,* to, *commodus,* fitting. See **com-modious.**]

accompany, *a-kum'pan-i, v.t.* to go with: to attend, escort: to supplement (with something): to go along with or to characterise: to perform an accompaniment to or for.—*ns.* **accom'pani-ment,** that which accompanies: (*mus.*) a subsidiary part or parts supporting a solo; **ac-com'panist,** one who performs an accompaniment. [Fr. *accompagner—à,* to *compagne,* companion. See **company.**]

accomplice, *a-kom'plis,* or *kum'-, n.* an associate, esp. in crime. [L. *complex, -icis,* joined; pfx. unexplained.]

accomplish, *a-kum'plish, v.t.* to complete: to effect, fulfil: (*arch.*) to equip.—*adjs.* **accom'-plishable,** that may be accomplished; **accom'-plished,** complete in acquirements, esp. graceful acquirements: polished.—*n.* **accom'plish-ment,** completion, fulfilment: acquirement, esp. one regarded as primarily of social value. [O.Fr. *acomplir—* L. *ad,* to, *complēre,* to fill up. See **complete.**]

accord, *a-körd', v.i.* to agree: to be in correspondence (with).—*v.t.* to grant, give to (a person). *n.* agreement: harmony. *n.* **accord'-ance,** agreement: conformity.—*adj.* **accord'-ant,** agreeing: corresponding.—*adv.* **accord'-antly.**—*p.adj.* **accord'ing,** in accordance: agreeing.—*adv.* **accord'ingly,** in agreement (with what precedes): consequently.—**accord-ing as,** precisely as: in proportion as: in a manner depending on whether; **according to,** in accordance with: as asserted by.—**of one's own accord,** of one's own free will, spontaneously. [O.Fr. *acorder—* L. *ad,* to, *cor, cordis,* the heart.]

accordion, *a kör'di on, n.* a musical instrument consisting of folding bellows, keyboard, and free metal reeds.—*n.* **accordion-pleating,** pleating with very narrow folds like the bellows of an accordion. [From **accord.**]

accost, *a-kost', v.t.* to speak first to: to address: (of a prostitute) to solicit. [O.Fr. *acoster—* L. *ad,* to, *costa,* a side.]

accouchement, *a-kōōsh'mä, -ment, n.* delivery in childbed. [Fr.,—*accoucher—à,* to, *coucher,* bed. See **couch.**]

accoucheur, *ă-kōō-shœr', n.* a man who assists women in childbirth.—*fem.* **accoucheuse** (*ă-kōō-shœz').* [Fr.; see previous word.]

account, *a-kownt', v.t.* to place to one's account or credit (with *to*): to judge, consider.—*v.i.* to give reason (for): to serve as a reason (for): to give an account of money held in trust: to kill or otherwise dispose of (with *for*).—*n.* a counting: statement: narrative: value: sake: a statement of money due.—*adj.* **account′able**, liable to account, responsible (*for* something; *to* someone): explicable.—*ns.* **account′able-ness, accountabil′ity**, liability to give account, responsibility to fulfil obligations.—*adv.* **account′ably**.—*ns.* **account′ant**, one who keeps, or is skilled in, accounts; **account′ancy**, the office or work of an accountant; **account′ant-ship**, the employment of an accountant.—**make account of**, to set value upon; **on account of**, because of; **on no account**, not for any reason or consideration; **take into account**, to consider; **take no account of**, to disregard; **turn to account**, to turn to advantage. [O.Fr. *acconter*—L. *ad*, to, *computāre*, to reckon.]

accoutre, *a-kōō′tér*, *v.t.* to dress or equip (esp. a warrior):—*pr.p.* accoutring (*a-kōō′tér-ing*); *pa.p.* accoutred (*a-kōō′térd*).—*n.pl.* **accoutre-ments** (*a-kōō′tér-ments*), dress: military equipment. [Fr. *accoutrer*, earlier *accoustrer*.]

accredit, *a-kred′it*, *v.t.* to give credit, authority, or honour to: to show to be true or correct: to accept as true: to furnish with credentials (with *to, at*): to ascribe or attribute to (with *with*).—*adj.* **accred′ited**, certified officially: accepted as valid: (of livestock) certified free from a particular disease, e.g. brucellosis. [Fr. *accréditer*—à, to, *crédit*, credit—L. *crēdĕre*, to believe.]

accretion, *a-krē′sh(ó)n*, *n.* process of growing continuously: the growing together (e.g. of separate particles) into one: that which has grown in such a way: any extraneous addition. [L. *accrētiō, -ōnis*—*accrescĕre*—*ad*, in addition, *crescĕre*, to grow.]

accrue, *a-krōō′*, *v.i.* to spring or grow as a natural result (from): to be added (to a person) by way of advantage. [O.Fr. *acrewe*, what grows up in a wood to the profit of the owner—*acreistre*—L. *accrescĕre*—*ad*, in addition, *crescĕre*, to grow.]

accumulate, *a-kūm′ūl-āt*, *v.t.* to heap or pile up, to amass.—*v.i.* to increase greatly: to go on increasing.—*n.* **accumulā′tion**, a heaping up: a heap, mass, or pile.—*adj.* **accum′ulative**, heaping up.—*n.* **accum′ulator**, a thing or person that accumulates, esp. an electric battery that can be recharged by sending a reverse current through it: in a computer, &c., a device that performs arithmetical operations and stores the results. [From L. *accumulātus*, pa.p. of *accumulāre*—*ad*, to, *cumulus*, a heap.]

accurate, *ak′ūr-át*, *adj.* done with care (*obs.*): exact.—*n.* **acc′uracy**, correctness: exactness.—*adv.* **acc′urately**.—*n.* **acc′urateness**. [L. *accūrātus*, performed with care—*ad*, to, *cūra*, care.]

accursed, *a-kûrs′id, -kûrst*, *adj.* subjected to a curse: ill-fated, doomed: worthy of a curse: extremely wicked. [O.E. pfx. *ā-*, inten., and *cursian*, to curse.]

accusative, *a-kūz′a-tiv*, *adj.* accusing: (*gram.*) in, or belonging to, the case that expresses the direct object of transitive verbs (in English, the *objective*). [Fr. *accusatif*—L. *accūsātīvus*.]

accuse, *a-kūz′*, *v.t.* to bring a charge against: to blame (with *of* before the thing charged).—*n.* **accusā′tion**, the act of accusing: the charge brought against anyone.—*adj.* **accus′atory**, containing accusation.—*p.adj.* **accused** (*a-kūzd′*), charged with a crime: usu. as *n.*, the person accused.—*n.* **accus′er**, one who accuses or brings a charge against another. [O.Fr. *acuser*—L. *accūsāre, -ātum*—*ad*, to, *causa*, cause.]

accustom, *a-kus′tóm*, *v.t.* to make familiar by custom, habituate (to).—*p.adj.* **accus′tomed**, usual: habituated (to). [O.Fr. *acostumer* (Fr. *accoutumer*)—à, to, *co(u)stume*. See **custom**.]

ace, *ās, n.* the one in dice, cards, dominoes, &c.: a single point: a hair's-breadth (e.g. *within an ace of*): a crack airman, &c.—*adj.* of highest quality: outstanding. [Fr.,—L. *as*, unity—*as*, a dialectal form of Gr. *heis*, one.]

acephalous, *a-sef′a-lus*, *adj.* without a head. [Gr. *a-*, priv., *kephalē*, the head.]

acerbity, *a-sûr′bi-ti*, *n.* bitterness, sourness: harshness, severity. [Fr.,—L. *acerbitās*—*acerbus*, bitter—*acer*, sharp.]

acetic, *a-sēt′ik, a-set′ik*, *adj.* of the nature of vinegar: sour.—Also **ac′etous**.—*n.* **ac′etate**, a salt of **acetic acid**, which is the sour principle in vinegar. [L. *acētum*, vinegar—*acēre*, to be sour.]

acetify, *a-set′i-fī, a-sēt′i-fi*, *v.t.* or *v.i.* to turn into vinegar.—*n.* **acetificā′tion**. [L. *acētum*, vinegar, *facĕre*, to make.]

acetylene, *a-set′i-lēn, n.* a gas formed by the action of water on carbide of calcium which burns with oxygen in a hot flame; used for welding, lighting, &c. [**acetic**, and Gr. *hylē*, matter.]

ache, *āk, n.* a continued pain.—*v.i.* to be in continued pain:—*pr.p.* āch′ing; *pa.p.* āched.—*n.* **ach′ing**, continued pain or distress. [The verb was properly *ake*, the noun *ache* (as in *speak* and *speech*)—O.E. vb. *acan* and its derivative n. *æce*.]

achieve, *a-chēv′*, *v.t.* to bring to a head or end: to perform, accomplish: to gain, win.—*adj.* **achiev′able**.—*n.* **achieve′ment**, a performance: an exploit: an escutcheon, esp. a hatchment. [Fr. *achever*, from à *chief* (*venir*)—Low. L. *ad caput*, to a head. See **chief**.]

achromatic, *a-krōm-at′ik*, *adj.* (of a lens or telescope) transmitting light without much colour due to aberration (q.v.).—*n.* **achrom′atism**, the state of being achromatic. [Gr. *a-*, priv., *chrōma*, gen. *chrōmatos*, colour.]

acicular, *as-ik′ū-lár*, *adj.* needle-shaped: slender and sharp-pointed.—Also **acic′ulate, acic′u-lated**. [L. *acicula*, dim. of *acus*, a needle.]

acid, *as′id*, *adj.* sharp: sour: (*geol.*) containing a large proportion of silica.—*n.* a sour substance: in chemistry, variously considered as:—any of a class of substances which redden litmus and combine with bases, certain metals, &c., to form salts; any of a class of substances that dissolve in water with the formation of ions; any of a class of substances that can transfer a proton to another substance: (*slang*) LSD or other hallucinogenic drug.—*v.t.* **acid′ify**, to make acid: to convert into an acid.—*v.i.* to become acid.—*pr.p.* acid′ifying; *pa.p.* acid′ified.—*ns.* **acidifica′tion**;

Neutral vowels in unaccented syllables: *em′pér-ór*; for certain sounds in foreign words see p. ix.

6

acid'ity, ac'idness, quality of being acid or sour: degree of sourness; **acidō'sis,** the presence of acids in the blood beyond normal limits.—*v.t.* **acid'ulate,** make slightly acid.—*adj.* **acid'ulous,** slightly sour: containing carbonic acid, as mineral waters.—**acid salt,** salt in which only part of the replaceable hydrogen is replaced by a metal or basic radical, e.g. potassium bicarbonate ($KHCO_3$) as compared with normal potassium carbonate (K_2CO_3); **acid test,** a test for gold by acid: (*fig.*) a searching test. [L. *acidus*—*acēre,* to be sour.]

acknowledge, ak-nol'ij, *v.t.* to own a knowledge of: to own as true: to confess: to intimate receipt of.—*n.* **acknow'ledg(e)ment,** recognition: admission: confession: thanks: a receipt. [Pfx. *a-* (O.E. *on*), on, and **knowledge.**]

acme, ak'mē, *-mi, n.* the top or highest point: the culmination or perfection: crisis, as of a disease. [Gr. *akmē,* a point, the highest point—*akē,* a point.]

acne, ak'nē, *-ni, n.* a pimple: a common skin disease, often occurring on the face, inflammation of sebaceous glands due to a bacillus. [Perh. Gr. *akmē.* See **acme.**]

acolyte, ak'o-līt, *n.* an inferior church officer: an attendant or assistant: a novice. [Gr. *akolouthos,* an attendant.]

aconite, ak'o-nīt, *n.* a genus of plants of the buttercup family, including monkshood or wolfsbane: a poison from monkshood. [L. *aconītum*—Gr. *akonīton.*]

acorn, ā'körn, *n.* the fruit of the oak.—*adj.* **a'corned.** [O.E. *æcern,* prob.—*æcer,* field, hence meaning 'the fruit of the unenclosed land': confused with *oak* (O.E. *āc*) and *corn.*]

acotyledon, *a kot i lē'don, n.* a plant without cotyledons or seed-lobes. [Gr. *a-,* priv., and *kotylēdōn.* See **cotyledon.**]

acoustic, a-kōōs'tik, *adj.* pertaining to the sense of hearing or to the theory of sounds: used in hearing, auditory: operated by sound (as an *acoustic mine*).—*n.pl.* **acous'tics,** properties (e.g. of a room or hall) determining whether accurate hearing in it is easy or difficult: (treated as *sing.*) the science of sound. [Fr.,—Gr. *akoustikos*—*akouein,* to hear.]

acquaint, a-kwānt', *v.t.* to make (oneself) familiar (with): to inform (a person) of a thing (with *with*).—*ns.* **acquaint'ance,** knowledge falling short of intimacy: a person known slightly; **acquaint'anceship,** slight knowledge.—*p.adj.* **acquaint'ed** (*with*), having personal knowledge of. [O.Fr. *acointer*—L.L. *accognitāre*—L. *ad,* to, *cognitus,* known.]

acquiesce, ak-wi-es', *v.i.* to rest satisfied with, or make no opposition to (with *in*): to assent.—*n.* **acquiesc'ence,** acceptance: assent.—*adj.* **acquiesc'ent,** resting satisfied, submissive. [L. *acquiescēre*—*ad,* and *quiēs,* rest.]

acquire, a-kwīr', *v.t.* to gain: to attain to.—*adj.* **acquir'able,** that may be acquired.—*ns.* **acquire'ment,** something learned or got by effort, not by a gift of nature; **acquisi'tion,** the act of acquiring: that which is acquired: something worth acquiring, a useful gain.—*adj.* **acquis'itive,** desirous of, or directed towards, acquiring (possessions).—*n.* **acquis'itiveness.** [O.Fr. *aquerre*—L. *acquīrēre, -quīsītum*—*ad,*

to, and *quaerēre,* to seek.]

acquit, a-kwit', *v.t.* to free: to settle, as a debt: to behave or conduct (oneself): to declare innocent:—*pr.p.* acquitt'ing; *pa.p.* acquitt'ed.—*ns.* **acquitt'al,** a judicial discharge from an accusation; **acquitt'ance,** a discharge from an obligation or debt: a receipt. [O.Fr. *aquiter*—L. *ad,* to, *quiētāre.* See **quit.**]

acre, ā'kėr, *n.* prob. orig. unenclosed land, then a field: now a measure of land containing 4840 sq. yards: (*pl.*) lands, estates generally.—*n.* **acreage** (ā'kėr-ij), the number of acres in a piece of land.—*adj.* **a'cred,** possessing land. [O.E. *æcer,* cognate with Ger. *acker,* L. *ager,* Gr. *agros,* Sans. *ajra.*]

acrid, ak'rid, *adj.* biting to the taste, pungent: bitter: also *fig.*—*ns.* **acrid'ity, ac'ridness.** [L. *ācer, acris,* sharp.]

acrimony, ak'ri-mŏn-i, *n.* bitterness of feeling or language.—*adj.* **acrimō'nious,** sharp, bitter. [L. *acrimōnia*—*ācer,* sharp.]

acritude, ak'ri-tūd, *n.* the quality of being acrid: a sharp bitter taste: bitterness of temper or language. [L. *acritūdō*—*ācer,* sharp.]

acrobat, ak'ro-bat, *n.* a rope-dancer: one who performs gymnastic feats.—*adj.* **acrobat'ic.** —*n.pl.* **acrobat'ics,** acrobatic performances, esp. *fig.* [Gr. *akrobatos,* walking on tiptoe—*akron,* point, *batos*—*bainein,* to go.]

acronym, ak'rō-nim, *n.* a word formed from the initial letters of other words (as *radar*). [Gr. *akron,* tip, point, *onoma,* name.]

acrophobia, ak-rō-fō'bi-ä, *n.* fear of heights. [Gr. *akron,* tip, *phobos,* fear.]

acropolis, a-krop'ol-is, *n.* a citadel, esp. (*cap.*) that of Athens. [Gr. *akropolis*—*akros,* the highest, *polis,* a city.]

across, a-kros', *prep.* from side to side of: on or to the other side of.—Also *adv.* [Pfx. *a-* (O.E. *on*), on, and **cross.**]

acrostic, a-kros'tik, *n.* a poem or puzzle in which the first, the middle, or the last letters of each line (or a combination of two or of all three of these), when taken in order, spell a word or a sentence: an acronym. [Gr. *akros,* extreme, and *stichos,* a line.]

act, akt, *v.i.* to exert force or influence: to produce an effect: to conduct oneself: to perform, as on the stage: to feign.—*v.t.* to perform: to imitate or play the part of.—*n.* something done, a deed: an exploit: the very process of doing something: a law or decision of a legislative body: a distinct section of a play.—*r.* **act'ing,** action: act of performing an assumed or a dramatic part.—*adj.* performing some duty temporarily, or for another.—*n.* **act'or,** one who acts: a stage-player:—*fem.* **act'ress.**—**act of God,** a result of forces beyond the control of human foresight. [L. *agēre, actum*; Gr. *agein,* to put in motion; Sans. *aj,* to drive.]

actinism, ak'tin-izm, *n.* the chemical action of radiant energy (as that of the green, blue, and ultraviolet rays of the spectrum).—*adj.* **ac'tinic** (or *-tin'-*). [Gr. *aktīs, aktīnos,* a ray.]

actinium, ak-tin'i-um, *n.* a radioactive metal (atomic no. 89; symbol Ac). [Gr. *aktīs,* a ray.]

action, ak'sh(ŏ)n, *n.* a state of acting: a deed: operation: a gesture: a battle: a lawsuit: the movement of events in a drama, novel, &c.: in a musical instrument, the mechanism operated by the keyboard: mode of moving (of a horse, &c.).—*adj.* **ac′tionable,** liable to a law-suit.—**action committee,** or **group,** members of an organisation who are chosen to take active measures; **action painting,** splashing paint and other substances on canvas so that the unconscious may be free to initiate a work of art—a style originating in America; **action station,** a post to be manned during or in preparation for a battle (also *fig.*). [L. *actiō, -ōnis—agĕre.* See **act.**]

active, *akt′iv, adj.* that acts: energetic: busy: nimble: effective: (*gram.*) of that voice in which the subject of the verb represents the doer of the action.—*adv.* **act′ively.**—*ns.* **act′iveness; activ′ity,** state of being active: exertion of energy: nimbleness: diligence: process of organism: occupation or recreation.—**act′ivate,** *v.t.* to make more active: to make radioactive. [L. *actīvus—agĕre.* See **act.**]

actual, *ak′tū-ál, ak′chōō-ál, adj.* real: existing in fact and now, as. opp. to an imaginary or past state of things.—*v.t.* **act′ualise,** to realise in action: to represent realistically.—*n.* **actual′ity.**—*adv.* **act′ually,** in fact, really: even (implying surprise or disapproval). [L. *actuālis—agĕre.* See **act.**]

actuary, *ak′tū-ár-i, n.* a registrar or clerk: one who makes the calculations connected with an insurance office.—*adj.* **actuā′rial.** [L. *actuārius* (*scriba*), an amanuensis, a clerk.]

actuate, *ak′tū-āt, v.t.* to put in motion: to incite to action, or inspire the conduct of (a person): to be the motive of (an action). [L. *actus,* action. See **act.**]

acuity, *a-kū′i-ti, n.* sharpness. [L.L. *acuitās*—L. *acus,* needle.]

acumen, *a-kū′men, a′-, n.* sharpness, quickness of perception, penetration. [L. See **acute.**]

acute, *a-kūt′, adj.* sharp-pointed: keen: opposite of dull: shrewd: shrill: critical: (of a disease) coming to a crisis (opp. to *chronic*).—*adv.* **acute′ly.**—*n.* **acute′ness.**—**acute accent,** a mark (′) originally indicating a rising pitch, now used for various purposes; **acute angle,** an angle less than a right angle. [L. *acūtus,* pa.p. of *acuĕre,* to sharpen, from root *ak,* sharp.]

ad., short for **advertisement**—whence *ns.* **ad′-man,** one who takes part in advertising that reaches a large public (as through television); **ad′-mass′, ad′mass′** (also *cap.*), the large group of people unduly influenced by such advertising.—Also *adj.*

adage, *ad′ij, n.* an old saying, a proverb. [Fr.,—L. *adagium—ad,* to, and root of *aio,* I say.]

adagio, *ä-dä′j(y)ō, adv.* (*mus.*) slowly.—*n.* a slow movement. [It. *ad agio,* at ease.]

adamant, *ad′a-mánt, n.* a very hard stone: (*obs.*) the diamond: (*obs.*) the lodestone.—*adj.* **aman′tine** (also **adamant**), made of or like adamant: that cannot be broken, penetrated, or forced to yield. [O.Fr. through L.,—Gr. *adamas, -antos—a-,* priv., and *damaein,* to break, tó tame.]

Adam's-apple, *ad′amz-ap′l, n.* the hard projection in front of the throat.

adapt, *a-dapt′, v.t.* to make apt or fit, to accommodate (with *to*—e.g. circumstances, environ-ment—or *for*—e.g. purpose): to alter, modify to suit.—*adj.* **adapt′able,** that may be adapted: changing readily.—*ns.* **adaptabil′ity; adaptā′-tion,** the act, process, or result of adapting; **adapt′er, adapt′or,** an attachment or accessory enabling a piece of apparatus to be used for some purpose other than that for which it was intended. [Fr. *adapter*—L. *adaptāre—ad,* to, *aptāre,* to fit.]

add, *ad, v.t.* to put (one thing) to (another): to find the sum of: to say in continuation, to remark further.—*v.i.* to increase (with *to*): to perform the operation of summing up.—*n.* **addi′tion,** the act of adding: the thing added: the rule in arithmetic for adding numbers together: title, honour.—*adj.* **addi′tional,** that is added.—**add-to system,** a hire-purchase arrangement by which a customer obtains a series of articles, making a down payment on the first only; **add up,** to find the sum of: to amount (to) on adding (*lit.* and *fig.*): to point to a reasonable conclusion. [L. *addĕre, ad-ditum—ad,* to, *dăre,* to put.]

addend, *ad′end, ∂-dend′, n.* a number or quantity added. [See **addendum.**]

addendum, *a-den′dum, n.* a thing to be added:—*pl.* **adden′da.** [L., gerundive of *addĕre.* See **add.**]

adder, *ad′ér, n.* the only venomous British snake, a viper. [O.E. *nædre;* cf. Ger. *atter* for *natter.* An adder was orig. *a nadder.* For reverse development see **newt.**]

addict, *a-dikt′, v.t.* to give (oneself) up to (generally in a bad sense).—*n.* (*ad′ikt*) a slave to a habit or vice, esp. drugs.—*adj.* **addict′ed,** given up (to).—*n.* **addic′tion.** [L. *addicĕre, addictum,* to consent, devote—*ad,* to, *dicĕre,* to declare.]

additive, *ad′i-tiv, adj.* of the nature of an addition: characterised by addition: to be added.—Also *n.* [L. *additivus—addĕre.* See **add.**]

addle, *ad′l, adj.* putrid: barren, empty: muddled.—*v.t.* to make putrid: to confuse.—*adjs.* **add′le-head′ed, add′le-pat′ed,** having addled or unsound brains. [M.E. *adele*—O.E. *adela,* mud.]

address, *a-dres′, v.t.* to direct (to): to speak or write to: to court: to direct in writing: (*refl.*) to turn one's skill or energies (to).—*n.* a formal communication in writing: a speech: manner, deportment: dexterity: the place to which a letter is directed (also *ad′res*): a place of residence:—*pl.* **address′es,** attentions of a lover.—*n.* **addressee′,** the person to whom a letter is addressed. [Fr. *adresser*—L. *ad, to, directum,* straight.]

adduce, *a-dūs′, v.t.* to bring forward, to cite or quote.—*adj.* **adduc′ible.**—*n.* **adduct′or,** a muscle that draws one part towards another. [L. *adducĕre—ad,* to, *ducĕre,* to bring.]

adenine, *ad′én-ēn, n.* substance found in all glandular tissues. [Gr. *adēn,* a gland.]

adenoid, -al, *ad′en-oid, -ál, adj.* of a gland-like shape: glandular: affected by, or as if by, adenoids (as a voice).—*n.* (*pl.*) **ad′enoids,** swollen tissue at the back of the nose. [Gr. *adēn,* a gland, *eidos,* form.]

adept, *ad-ept′, ad′ept, adj.* completely skilled.—*n.* an expert. [L. *adeptus* (*artem*), having attained (an art), pa.p. of *adipisci—ad,* to, *apisci,*

Neutral vowels in unaccented syllables: *em′pér-ór;* for certain sounds in foreign words see p. ix.

to reach, obtain.]

adequate, *ad'e-kwāt*, *adj.* sufficient: equal to (requirements—with *to, for*).—*adv.* **ad'equately**.—*ns.* **ad'equateness, ad'equacy**, state of being adequate: sufficiency. [L. *adaequātus*, made equal—*ad*, to, and *aequus*, equal.]

adhere, *ad-hēr'*, *v.i.* to stick: to remain fixed or attached (with *to*).—*n.* **adhēr'ence**, state of adhering: steady attachment.—*adj.* **adhēr'ent**, sticking (to)—*n.* one who adheres, a follower, a partisan. [L. *ad*, to, *haerēre, haesum*, to stick.]

adhesion, *ad-hē'zh(ó)n*, *n.* the act of adhering or sticking: steady attachment (to): (*med.*) abnormal union of parts that have been inflamed: a band of fibrous tissue joining such parts.—*adj.* **adhēs'ive**, sticky: apt to, or intended to, adhere.—*n.* a substance (as glue, gum) used to make objects adhere to each other.—*adv.* **adhes'ively.**—*n.* **adhes'iveness.** [See **adhere**.]

ad hoc, *ad hok, adj.* (of a committee or other body) constituted for this purpose. [L., to this.]

adiabatic, *ad-i-a-bat'ik, adj.* without gain or loss of heat. [Gr. *adiabatos*, not to be passed—*a-*, not, *dia*, through, *bainein*, to go.]

adieu, *a-dū', interj.* (I commend you) to God: farewell.—*n.* a farewell:—*pl.* **adieus or adieux** (*a-dūz'*). [Fr. *à Dieu*, to God.]

ad infinitum, *ad in-fin- īt'um, -ēt' ŏŏm*, to infinity. [L.]

adipose, *ad'i-pōs, adj.* fatty. [L. *adeps, adipis*, soft fat.]

adit, *ad'it, n.* an opening or passage, esp. into a mine. [L. *adītus—ad*, to, *īre*, to go.]

adjacent, *a-jās'ent, adj.* lying near (to): contiguous.—*n.* **adjac'ency.**—*adv.* **adjac'ently.** [L. *ad*, to, *jacēre*, to lie.]

adjective, *aj'ek-tiv, n.* a word added to a noun to qualify it, or to limit it by reference to quality, number, or position.—*adj.* , **adjectīv'al.**—*advs.* **adjectīv'ally, ad'jectively.** [L. *adjectīvum* (*nomen*), an added (word)—*adjicere, -jectum* to throw to, to add—*ad*, to, *jacĕre*, to throw.]

adjoin, *a-join', v.t.* to lie next to.—*v.i.* to be contiguous.—*adj.* **adjoin'ing**, near, adjacent. [Through Fr. from L. *adjungĕre—ad*, to, *jungĕre*. See **join**.]

adjourn, *a-jûrn', v.t.* to put off to another day, to postpone: to discontinue (a meeting) in order to resume it at another time or place.—*v.i.* to suspend proceedings and disperse for any time specified, or *sine die* (q.v.).—*n.* **adjourn'ment**, the act of adjourning: the interval it causes. [O.Fr. *ajorner*—L.L. *adiurnāre*, L. *ad*, to, L.L. *jurnus*—L. *diurnus*, daily.]

adjudge, *a-juj', v.t.* to decide judicially: to assign judicially (to): to condemn (to). [O.Fr. *ajuger*—L. *adjūdicāre—ad*, to, inten., *jūdicāre*.]

adjudicate, *a-jōō'di-kāt, v.t.* to determine judicially: to pronounce (someone to be).—*v.i.* to pronounce judgment: to act as judge in a competition between amateurs in one of the arts, e.g. music.—*ns.* **adjū'dicator; adjudica'tion** (*Eng. law*), an order of the Bankruptcy Court, adjudging the debtor to be a bankrupt, and transferring his property to a trustee. [L. *adjūdicāre, -ātum—ad*, to, inten., *jūdicāre*. See **judge**.]

adjunct, *a'jungkt, adj.* joined or added.—*n.* a thing joined or added: a person joined to another in some office or service: (*gram.*) any word or clause enlarging the subject or predicate: (*logic*) any non-essential attribute.—*adj.* **adjunct'ive**, joining: forming an adjunct.—*advs.* **adjunct'ively; adjunct'ly**, in connection (with). [L. See **adjoin**.]

adjure, *a-jōōr', v.t.* to charge on oath or solemnly.—*n.* **adjurā'tion**, the act of adjuring: the charge or oath used in adjuring. [L. *adjūrāre—ad*, to, *jūrāre, -ātum*, to swear.]

adjust, *a-just', v.t.* to arrange properly: to regulate, bring the parts (of a mechanism) into correct relation: to adapt (to)· to settle (e.g. differences of opinion).'—*adj.* **adjust'able.**—*n.* **adjust'ment.** [O.Fr. *ajouster*—L.L. *adjuxtāre*, to put side by side—L. *juxta*, near.]

adjutant, *a'jōō-tánt, n.* an officer, not above the rank of major, specially appointed to assist a commanding officer: a large stork found in India.—*ns.* **ad'jutancy**, the office of an adjutant: assistance; **ad'jutant-gen'eral**, the head of a department of the general staff of the army: the executive officer of a general. [L. *adjūtāre*, freq. of *adjūvāre—ad*, inten., *jūvāre*, to assist.]

ad-lib, *ad'-lib, v.t.* and *v.i.* to extemporise, esp. to fill up time. [L. *ad libitum*, at pleasure.]

admeasure, *ad-mezh'ur, v.t.* to measure: to apportion.—*n.* **admeas'urement.** [Fr.,—L. *ad*, to, *mensūra*, measure.]

administer, *ad-min'is-tér, v.t.* to manage as a steward, substitute, or executor: to conduct or execute (as offices of religion): to tender (an oath—with *to*): to apply, give (e.g. a remedy, a rebuke—with *to*).—*n.* **administrā'tion**, the act of administering: management: the government (legislative, executive, and judicial, or executive and judicial only): the Government: the period during which a particular person controls the government or management of a state, region, or concern.—*adj.* **admin'istrative**, that administers.—*n.* **admin'istrator**, one who manages or directs: the person to whom is committed the administration of the estate of a deceased person who has appointed no executor:—*fem.* **administrā'trix.**—*n.* **admin'istratorship.** [Through Fr.,—L. *administrāre—ad*, to, *ministrāre*, to minister.]

admiral, *ad'mir-ál, n.* a naval officer of the highest rank. In the British navy, **ad'mirals of the fleet** rank first; then **ad'mirals, vice'-ad'mirals**, and **rear'-ad'mirals**: a butterfly of certain species.—*n.* **ad'miralty**, former board of commissioners for administration of naval affairs (unified Ministry of Defence set up 1964). [Through Fr.,—Ar. *amīr*, a lord, a chief—*d* introduced through confusion with L. *admīrarī*, to wonder at.]

admire, *ad-mīr', v.t.* to regard with wonder or surprise: to esteem highly: to regard with enthusiastic approval. *adj.* **admirable** (*ad'-mir-à-bl*), worthy of being admired.—*n.* **ad'mirableness.**—*adv.* **ad'mirably.**—*n.* **admirā'tion**, the act of admiring: wonder, together with esteem, love, or veneration: (*arch.*) astonishment.—*n.* **admīr'er**, one who admires: a lover.—*adv.* **admīr'ingly.** [Fr. *admirer*—L. *ad*, at, *mīrārī*, to wonder.]

---

fāte, fär; mē, hûr (her); *mīne, mōte, för; mūte; mōōn, fŏŏt;* THen (then)

admit, *ad-mit', v.t.* to allow to enter: to have room for: to concede: to acknowledge: to be capable of, leave room for (also *v.i.* with *of*):—*pr.p.* admitt'ing; *pa.p.* admitt'ed.—*adj.* **admiss'ible,** that may be admitted or allowed.—*ns.* **admissibil'ity; admitt'ance,** the act of admitting: leave to enter: (*elect.*) the property of an electric circuit by virtue of which an alternating current flows under the action of an alternating potential difference; **admiss'ion,** admittance: anything acknowledged or conceded.—*adv.* **admitt'edly,** without question or debate. [Through Fr. from L. *admittĕre, -missum—ad,* to, *mittĕre,* to send.]

admixture, *ad-miks'tyŭr, -chŭr, n.* what is added to the chief ingredient of a mixture: act of mixing: mixture. [L. *ad,* to, and **mix.**]

admonish, *ad-mon'ish, v.t.* to warn: to counsel: to reprove mildly. [O.Fr. *amonester—*L.L. *admonestāre—admonēre—ad,* inten., *monēre,* to warn.]

admonition, *ad-mon-ish'(ó)n, n.* reproof, warning: counsel, advice: ecclesiastical censure.—*adj.* **admon'itory,** containing admonition. [L. *admonitiō, -ōnis—admonēre, -itum.*]

ad nauseam, *ad nö'shi-am, now'si-,* to the point of producing disgust. [L.]

ado, *a-dōō', n.* a to-do: bustle, trouble, fuss. [Contr. of *at do=to do,* a form of the infin. borrowed from the Scandinavian.]

adobe, *a-dō'bi, n.* a sun-dried brick: a house made of such bricks. [Sp. *adobar,* to plaster.]

adolescent, *ad-o-les'ént, adj.* growing from childhood to maturity.—Also *n.*—*n.* **adolesc'ence,** the period of youth, between childhood and maturity. [Through Fr. from L. *adolēscēns, -entis—adolescĕre,* to grow up.]

adopt, *a-dopt', v.t.* to choose: to take up, embrace (e.g. an opinion, a practice): to take as one's own what is another's, as a child, &c.—*n.* **adop'tion,** the act of adopting: the state of being adopted.—*adj.* **adopt'ive,** that adopts or is adopted. [L. *adoptāre—ad,* inten., *optāre,* to choose.]

adore, *a-dōr', -dör', v.t.* to worship: to love intensely.—*adj.* **ador'able,** worthy of being adored.—*n.* **ador'ableness.**—*adv.* **ador'ably.**—*ns.* **adōrā'tion,** divine worship, homage: profound regard; **ador'er,** one who adores: lover.—*adv.* **ador'ingly.** [L. *ad,* to, *ōrāre.*]

adorn, *a-dörn', v.t.* to deck or dress: to embellish.—*n.* **adorn'ment,** ornament: decoration. [O.Fr. *aörner, adorner—*L. *adornāre—ad,* to, *ornāre,* to furnish.]

adrenal, *ad-rē'nál, adj.* beside the kidneys.—*n.* **adrĕn'aline,** a substance obtained from glands above the kidney, or prepared artificially, used to increase blood pressure, &c. [L. *ad,* to, *rēnes,* kidneys.]

adrift, *a-drift', adj.* or *adv.* floating as driven by wind or tide (*lit.* and *fig.*): moving at random. [Pfx. *a-* (O.E. *on*), on, and **drift.**]

adroit, *a-droit', adj.* dexterous, skilful.—*adv.* **adroit'ly.**—*n.* **adroit'ness.** [Fr. *à droit,* according to right—L. *directus,* straight. See **direct.**]

adscititious, *ad-si-tish'ús, adj.* added or assumed: additional. [L. *adscīscĕre, -scītum,* to take or assume—*ad,* to, *scīscĕre,* to inquire—*scīre,* to know.]

adscript, *ad'skript, adj.* attached, esp. to the soil,

as feudal serfs—in this sense also used as a noun. [L. *adscriptus—ad,* to, *scrībĕre,* to write.]

adsorb, *ad-sörb', v.t.* of a solid, to take up a vapour on its surface.—*n.* **adsorption.** [L. *ad* to, *sorbēre,* to suck in.]

adulation, *ad-ū-lā'sh(ó)n, n.* fawning: flattery. —*adj.* **adulatory** (*ad'ū-la-tór-i*). [L. *adūlārī, adūlātus,* to fawn upon.]

adult, *ad'ult, ad-ult', adj.* grown: mature.—*n.* a grown-up person. [L. *adultus—adolēscĕre, adultum,* to grow.]

adulterate, *a-dul'tér-āt, v.t.* to corrupt: to make impure (by mixing).—*adj.* (*-āt*) defiled by adultery: spurious: corrupted by base elements.—*ns.* **adul'terant,** a substance used to adulterate (also *adj.*); **adulterā'tion,** the act of adulterating: the state of being adulterated. [L. *adulterāre, -ātum,* to corrupt—*adulterium.* See **adultery.**]

adultery, *a-dul'tér-i, n.* sexual intercourse between a married man and a woman not his wife, or between a married woman and a man not her husband.—*n.* **adul'terer,** a man guilty of adultery:—*fem.* **adul'teress.**—*adjs.* **adul'terine,** resulting from adultery: spurious; **adul'terous,** guilty of adultery. [O.Fr. *avoutrie,* adultery—L. *adulterium,* prob. from *ad,* to, *alter,* another. The modern form is due to a later reintroduction of Latin spelling.]

adumbrate, *ad-um'brāt,* or *ad'-, v.t.* to give a faint shadow of: to sketch the outline of.—*n.* **adumbrā'tion.** [L. *adumbrāre, adumbrātus—ad,* inten., *umbra,* a shadow.]

ad valorem, *ad va-lō'rem, -lö'-, adv.* and *adj.* according to, in proportion to, the value. [L.]

advance, *ad-väns', v.t.* to put forward: to promote to a higher office: to encourage the progress of: to propose: to supply or pay beforehand.—*v.i.* to move or go forward: to make progress: to rise in rank or in value.—*n.* progress: improvement: a rise in price or value: payment beforehand: a loan: approach: overture with a view to an understanding.— *adj.* supplied, &c., in advance.—*n.* **advance'ment,** promotion: improvement.—**in advance,** beforehand.—**advance factory,** one built to encourage development, in the belief that a firm will take it over. [O.Fr. *avancer—*L. *abante—ab ante,* from before; the pfx. was later refashioned as if it were from L. *ad.*]

advantage, *ad-vänt'ij, n.* superiority over another: gain or benefit: a favouring condition: (*lawn tennis*) first point gained after *deuce* (also **vantage**).—*v.t.* to benefit, profit.—*adj.* **advantā'geous,** of advantage: useful (with *to* and *for*).—*adv.* **advantā'geously.**—*n.* **advanta'geousness.**—**have the advantage of anyone,** to recognise him without oneself being recognised. [Fr. *avantage—avant,* before—L. *ab ante.* See **advance.**]

advent, *ad'vent, n.* a coming or arrival: the first or the second coming of Christ: (*cap.*) a period including four Sundays before Christmas. [Through Fr. from L. *adventus—advenīre—ad,* to, *venīre,* to come.]

adventitious, *ad-ven-tish'ús, adj.* coming from outside: added by chance: (*bot.*) developed out of the usual order or place.—*adv.* **adventi'tiously.** [Low L. *adventitius—*L. *adventīcius—advenīre.* See **advent.**]

Neutral vowels in unaccented syllables: *em'pér-ór*; for certain sounds in foreign words see p. ix.

adventure, ad-ven′tyůr, -chůr, n. a risk: a strange or exciting experience: an enterprise.—v.i. to attempt or dare.—v.t. to risk or hazard.—n. **adven′turer,** one who engages in hazardous enterprises: one who seeks to better his fortune by bold and discreditable means:—fem. **adven′turess.**—adjs. **adven′turous, adven′turesome,** enterprising: ready to incur risk.—adv. **adven′turously.**—n. **adven′turousness.**—**adventure playground,** one with objects that can be used by children for building, to climb on, &c. [O.Fr. aventure—L. adventūrus, about to happen, fut. part. of ad venīre. See **advent.**]

adverb, ad′vėrb, n. a word added to a verb, adjective, or other adverb to express some modification of the meaning or an accompanying circumstance.—adj. **adver′bial,** pertaining to an adverb.—adv. **adver′bially.** [L. adverbium—ad, to, verbum, a word.]

adversary, ad′vér-sár-i, n. an opponent: an enemy: (cap.) Satan, as the enemy of mankind. [O.Fr. adversier—L. adversārius—adversāri. See **adverse.**]

adverse, ad′vérs, adj. acting in a contrary direction (to): opposed (to): injurious (to): unfortunate.—adv. **ad′versely.**—ns. **ad′verseness; advers′ity,** adverse circumstances: affliction, misfortune.—adj. **advers′ative,** denoting opposition or contrariety. [Through Fr. from L. adversus—advertĕre—ad, to, and vertĕre, versum, to turn.]

advert, ad-vůrt′, v.i. to turn the mind (to): to refer (to). [O.Fr. avertir, avertissant—L. advertĕre—ad, to, vertĕre, to turn.]

advert. Coll. abbrev. for **advertisement.**

advertise, ad′vér-tiz, or -tiz′, v.t. to bring (something) to public notice, esp. by a printed (often illustrated) account of its real or alleged good qualities: to notify, inform.—ns. **advertisement** (-iz-, -īs-), the act of advertising or making known: a public notice: any device for obtaining public notice or notoriety; **adver′tiser,** one who advertises: a paper carrying advertisements. [Fr.,—L. advertĕre. See **advert.**]

advice, ad-vīs′, n. counsel: skilled opinion: intelligence, information (usually in pl.): a formal notice. [O.Fr. a(d)vis—L. ad vīsum, according to what is seen.]

advise, ad-vīz′, v.t. to give advice or counsel to: to recommend: to inform (usu. with of).—v.i. to consult (with):—pr.p. advīs′ing; pa.p. advīsed (-vīzd′).—adj. advīs′able, prudent, expedient.—ns. **advisabil′ity, advis′ableness.**—adv. **advis′ably.**—adjs. **advis′ory,** giving advice; **advised′,** deliberate: directed, guided (as in well-advised and ill-advised).—adv. **advis′edly,** after due consideration.—n. **advis′er,** one who advises. [O.Fr. a(d)viser, from a(d)vis. See **advice.**]

advocacy, ad′vo-ká-si, n. the function of an advocate: a pleading in support (of). [Fr. advocacie—L. advocāre. See **advocate.**]

advocate, ad′vo-kát, n. an intercessor: one who pleads the cause of another, esp. in a court of law in Scotland and France: a supporter.—v.t. (-āt) to plead in favour of, recommend. **Lord Advocate,** the first law-officer of the crown and public prosecutor of crimes for Scotland.

[O.Fr. a(d)vocat—L. advocātus—advocāre, -ātum, to summon, esp. for help—ad, to, vocāre, to call.]

advowson, ad-vow′zón, n. the right of patronage or presentation to a church benefice. [O.Fr. avoëson—L. advocātiō, -ōnis, right of the patron—advocātus, a patron.]

adze, adz, adz, n. a carpenter's tool consisting of a thin arched blade with its edge at right angles to the handle. [O.E. adesa.]

aedile, edile, ē′dīl, n. a magistrate in ancient Rome whose duties included the charge of public buildings.—n. **ae′dileship.** [L. aedīlis—aedēs, -is, a building.]

aegis, ē′jis, n. (orig.) a shield belonging to Zeus, or to Pallas: anything that protects: patronage. [L.,—Gr. aigis.]

Aeolian, ē-ō′li-án, adj. pertaining to, or acted on by, the wind: aerial.—**Aeo′lian harp,** a stringed instrument sounded by currents of air. [L. Aeolus—Gr. Aiolos, god of winds.]

aeon, eon, ē′on, n. a long period of time, an age: in one of a series of ages eternity. [Gr. aiōn.]

aerate, ā′ér-āt, v.t. to put air into: to charge with carbonic acid or other gas, as **aerated waters.**—n. **aera′tion,** exposure to the action of air: mixing with air.—**aerated concrete,** lightweight concrete made by a process which traps gas bubbles in the mix. [L. āēr, air.]

aerial, ā-ēr′i-ál, adj. belonging to the air: existing in the air: ethereal.—n. (often ā′ér-i-ál, ār-), a system of electrical conductors designed to transform oscillatory currents into electromagnetic radiation, e.g. radio waves, (transmitter), or vice versa (receiver). [L. āēr, air.]

aerie, ā′ri, also ē′ri, ī′ri, n. the nest of any bird of prey, esp. an eagle.—Also **aery, eyrie, eyry.** [O.Fr. aire; origin unknown. The form **eyry** seems to have been originally due to a confusion with M.E. ey, an egg.]

aeriform, ā′ér-i-förm, adj. having the form or nature of air or gas. [L. āēr, air, and forma, form.]

aerobatics, ā-ér-ō-bat′iks, n. evolutions performed by an aircraft at the will of the pilot, usually excluding those needed for normal flight—stunts. [Formed from Gr. āēr, air, and acrobatics.]

aerodrome, ā′ér-ō-drōm, n. a reserved area of land or water, with the necessary buildings, used for the landing, taking-off, re-fuelling, repair, &c., of aircraft. [Gr. āēr, air, dromos, running.]

aerodynamics, ā-ér-ō-di-nam′iks, n. the dynamics of gases, particularly the study of forces acting on bodies in motion in the air.—adj. **aerodynam′ic.** [Gr. āēr, air, and dýnamis, power.]

aerofoil, ār′ō-foil, n. a body shaped so as to produce lift perpendicular to its direction of motion—a wing, aileron, &c. [Gr. āēr, air, and foil.]

aerolite, ā′ér-o-līt, n. a stony, as distinct from an iron, meteorite. [Gr. āēr, air, lithos, a stone.]

aeronaut, ā′ér-o-nöt, n. one who sails in a balloon or airship.—n. **acronaut′ics,** the science or art of aerial navigation. [Gr. āēr, air, nautēs, sailor.]

---

aeroplane, *ā'ér-ō-plān, n.* a flying machine, heavier than air, with planes or wings. [Gr. *āēr,* air, and **plane** (1).]

aerosol, *ā'ér-ō-sol, n.* a suspension of fine particles in a gas, e.g. fog: a liquid in a container under pressure: the container. [Gr. *āēr,* air.]

aerospace, *ā'ér-ō-spās, n.* the earth's atmosphere together with space beyond.—Also *adj.* pertaining to, capable of operating in, air and space. [Gr. *āēr,* air, and **space.**]

aery, *ā'ér-i, adj.* aerial, visionary. [L. *āērius—āēr,* air.]

Aesculapian, *ēs-kū-lā'pi-án,* or *es-,* pertaining to the art of healing.—Also **Esculapian.** [L. *Aesculapius—*Gr. *Asklēpios,* god of healing.]

aesthetics, *es-thet'iks,* or *ēs-thet'iks, n.* the principles of taste and of art: the philosophy of the fine arts.—*n.* **aesthete** (*es'thēt,* or *ēs'-*), one who affects an extravagant love of art.—*adjs.* **aesthet'ic, aesthet'ical,** pertaining to aesthetics.—*adv.* **aesthet'ically.**—*n.* **aesthet'icism,** the cult of the beautiful, or susceptibility to artistic influences, esp. when carried to excess.— Also **esthetics, esthete,** &c. [Gr. *aisthētikos,* perceptive—*aisthanesthai,* to feel.]

aether. Same as **ether.**

aetiology, etiology, *ē-ti-ol'o-ji, n.* the study of causation, esp. of the causes of a disease. [L. *aetiologia*—Gr. *aitiologia—aitia,* cause, *logos,* discourse.]

afar, *a-fär, adv.* from, at, or to, a distance—usu. **from afar, afar off.** [Pfx. *a-* (O.E. *on* or *of*), on, or from, and **far.**]

affable, *af'a-bl, adj.* easy to speak to, approachable: courteous or condescending (used with *to*).—*ns.* **affabil'ity, aff'ableness.**—*adv.* **aff'ably.** [Fr.,—L. *affābilis—affārī,* to speak to—*ad,* to, and *fārī,* to speak.]

affair, *a-fār', n.* that which is to be done: business: a concern: a love affair (also **affaire**): a minor battle: (vaguely) a happening or a proceeding: (*coll.*) a material thing: (*pl.*) transactions in general.—**affair of honour,** a duel. [O.Fr. *afaire—à* (L. *ad*) *faire* (L. *facĕre*), to do. Cf. **ado.**]

affect, *a-fekt', v.t.* to act upon: to produce a change in: to move the feelings of.—*adj.* **affect'ed,** touched with a feeling (see also next word).—*adv.* **affect'edly.**—*n.* **affect'edness.**— *adj.* **affect'ing,** having power to move the feelings: pathetic.—*adv.* **affect'ingly.** [L. *afficĕre, affectum—ad,* to, *facĕre,* to do.]

affect, *a-fekt', v.t.* to make a show or pretence of: to have, show a preference for.—*n.* **affecta'tion,** a striving after, or an attempt to assume, what is not natural or real: pretence.—*adj.* **affect'ed,** full of affectation: feigned. [L. *affectāre,* freq. of *afficĕre.* See **affect** (1).]

affection, *a-fek'sh(ó)n, n.* act of affecting or having an effect on: a disposition of mind: (*arch.*) any strong feeling: kindness or love, attachment (with *for* or *towards*): an attribute or property: a malady.—*adj.* **affectionate,** full of affection, loving.—*adv.* **affec'tionately.**—*n.* **affec'tionateness.**—*adj.* **affec'tioned** (*B.*), disposed. [L. *affectiō, -ōnis—afficĕre.* See **affect** (1).]

afferent, *af'ér-ént, adj.* (*anat.*) bringing inwards, applied to the nerves that convey impulses to the central nervous system. [L. *afferens,* *-entis—ad,* to, and *ferre,* to carry.]

affiance, *a-fī'áns, n.* pledging of faith: marriage contract: trust (*in, on*).—*v.t.* to pledge faith to: to betroth. [O.Fr. *afiance, afier—*L. *ad,* to, *fides,* faith.]

affidavit, *af-i-dā'vit, n.* a written declaration on oath. [*Affīdāvit,* 3rd pers. sing. perf. of a L.L. *affīdāre,* to pledge one's faith.]

affiliate, *a-fil'i-āt, v.t.* to receive into a family as a son, or into a society as a member: to attach (to), connect (with), as minor colleges to a university.—*n.* an affiliated person: a subsidiary of an organisation.—*n.* **affilia'tion,** the act of receiving into a family or society as a member: (*law*) the assignment of an illegitimate child to its father. [L. *affīliāre, -ātum,* to adopt—*ad,* to, *fīlius,* a son.]

affine geometry, *a-fīn',* the geometry associated with affine transformations; **affine transformation,** the composition of a reversible linear mapping followed by a translation. [L. *affīnis.* See **affinity.**]

affinity, *a-fin'i-ti, n.* relationship by marriage— opp. to *consanguinity* (relationship by blood): nearness of kin: structural resemblance: similarity, likeness: attraction, liking: (*chem.*) the force that binds atoms together in molecules, enabling elements to form compounds. [Fr. *affinité*—L. *affīnitās—affīnis,* neighbouring—*ad,* at, *fīnis,* boundary.]

affirm, *a-fûrm', v.t.* to assert confidently or positively: (*law*) to make a formal declaration or affirmation, without an oath: to ratify (a judgment).—*adj.* **affirm'able,** that may be affirmed (followed by *of*).—*n.* **affirma'tion,** act of affirming: that which is affirmed.—*adj.* and *n.* **affirm'ative,** that affirms or asserts: not negative.—*adv.* **affirm'atively.** [O.Fr. *afermer*—L. *affirmāre—ad,* to, *firmus,* firm.]

affix, *a-fiks', v.t.* to fix (to): to add: to attach (with *to, on, upon*).—*n.* **aff'ix,** a prefix or a suffix. [L. *affīgĕre, -fixum—ad,* to, *fīgĕre,* to fix.]

afflatus, *a-flā'tus, n.* inspiration (with emphasis on its divine source). [L.—*afflāre—ad,* to, *flāre,* to breathe on.]

afflict, *a-flikt', v.t.* to crush by pain, distress, or grief: to harass or vex.—*n.* **afflic'tion,** state or cause of distress: an ailment, disease.—*adj.* **afflic'tive,** causing distress. [L. *afflīgĕre, -flictum—ad,* to, *flīgĕre,* dash to the ground.]

affluent, *af'loo-ént, adj.* abounding: wealthy: rich (in).—*n.* a stream flowing into a river or lake.—*n.* **aff'luence,** abundance: wealth.—**affluent society,** a society in which the ordinary person can afford many things once regarded as luxuries. [L. *affluens, -entis—affluĕre—ad,* to, *fluĕre,* to flow.]

afford, *a-förd', -förd', v.t.* to yield, produce: (with *can*) to bear the expense of (also *fig.,* as we can't afford, it is not expedient for us). [M.E. *aforthen—*O.E. *geforthian* or *forthian,* to further or to cause to come forth.]

afforest, *a-for'est, v.t.* to turn into forest by planting young trees.—*n.* **afforesta'tion.** [L.L. *afforestāre—ad,* to, *forestis.* See **forest.**]

affranchise, *a-fran'chiz,* or *-chīz, v.t.* to free from slavery, or from some obligation. [O.Fr. *afranchir, affranchissant,* ·from *à,* to, *franchir,* to free—*franc,* free.]

Neutral vowels in unaccented syllables: *em'pèr-ör*; for certain sounds in foreign words see p. ix.

12

affray, *a-frā'*, *n.* a fight causing alarm: a brawl. [O.Fr. *afrayer*, *esfreer*—L.L. *exfrīdiāre*, to break the king's peace—L. *ex*, and O.H.G. *fridu* (Ger. *friede*), peace.]

affright, *a-frīt'*, *v.t.* to frighten.—*n.* sudden terror. [O.E. *āfyrhtan*—*ā-*, inten., and *fyrhtan*. See **fright**.]

affront, *a-frunt'*, *v.t.* to meet face to face: to insult openly.—*n.* an open insult. [O.Fr. *afronter*—L.L. *affrontāre*—L. *ad*, to, *frons*, *frontis*, forehead.]

affusion, *a-fū'zh(ò)n*, *n.* the act of pouring upon. [L. *affūsiō*, *-ōnis*—*affundĕre*—*ad*, to, *fundĕre*, *fūsum*, to pour.]

afield, *a-fēld'*, *adv.* to, in, or on the field. [Pfx. *a-* (O.E. *on*), on, and **field**.]

afire, *a-fīr'*, *adj.* (*predicative*) and *adv.* on fire. [Pfx. *a-* (O.E. *on*), on, and **fire**.]

aflame, *a-flām'*, *adj.* (*predicative*) and *adv.* flaming: glowing. [Pfx. *a-* (O.E. *on*), on, and **flame**.]

afloat, *a-flōt'*, *adv.* or *adj.* (*predicative*) floating: at sea: in circulation. [O.E. *on flote*. See **float**.]

afoot, *a-fŏŏt'*, *adv.* on foot: astir: in progress, operation. [Pfx. *a-* (O.E. *on*), on, and **foot**.]

afore, *a-fōr'*, *-för'*, *prep.*, *adv.* (*arch.*) before.—*adv.* **afore'hand**, beforehand.—*adjs.* **afore'said**, aforementioned, said or named before; **afore'thought**, premeditated.—*adv.* **afore'time**, in former or past times. [O.E. *on-foran*—*on*, prep. and adv. *foran*, in front (dat. of adj. and n. *for*). See **fore**.]

afraid, *a-frād'*, *adj.* struck with fear: frightened (of): reluctantly inclined to think (that): admit with regret. [Pa.p. of obs. vb. *affray*, to startle, frighten. See **affray**.]

afreet. Same as **afrit**.

afresh, *a-fresh'*, *adv.* anew. [O.E. pfx. *a-* (*of*, off, from), and **fresh**.]

Africanise, *af'rik-ản-īz*, *v.t.* to make African: to exclude people of other races from, replacing them by Africans. Also *vb.* *n.* **Africanisa'tion**.

Afrikaner, *af-ri-kän'ér*, *n.* one born in South Africa of white parents (esp. of Dutch descent).—*n.* **Afrikaans** (*af-ri-käns'*), one of the two official languages of S. Africa; it developed from 17th-cent. Dutch. [Du; earlier S. African *afrikander*, influenced by Hollander.]

afrit, *a-frēt'*, *n.* an evil demon in Arabian mythology. [Ar. *'ifrīt*.]

aft, *äft*, *adj.* and *adv.* behind: near or towards the stern of a vessel. [O.E. *æftan*.]

Afro, *af'rō*, *adj.* slang abbrev. for African.—**Af'ro-**, in composition, African (and).—*adj.* **Afro-Asian**, of, consisting of, Africans and Asians: of Asian origin but African citizenship: of mixed Asian and African blood.

after, *äft'ér*, *prep.* and *adv.* behind in place: later, later than: following in search of: in imitation of: according to: subsequently.—*adj.* behind in place: later in time: more toward the stern of a vessel (as in *after part*).—*ns.* **aft'erbirth**, the placenta and membranes which are expelled from the womb after birth; **af'tercare**, care following a period of treatment; **aft'ercrop**, a second crop in the same year; **aft'er-damp**, choke-damp, arising in coal-mines after an explosion of fire-damp; **aft'erglow**, the glow often seen in the sky after sunset; **aft'ermath** (O.E. *mæth*, mowing), a second mowing of

grass in the same season: later consequences (esp. if bad).—*adj.* **aft'ermost**, hindmost.—*n.* **afternoon** (*aft-ér-nōōn'*), the time between noon and evening—also *adj.* (*aft'-*).—*ns.* **aft'erpiece**, a farce or other minor piece performed after a play; **aft'erthought**, thought or reflection after an action: a later thought or the action resulting from it.—*adv.* **aft'erwards**, in aftertime, later, subsequently. [O.E. *æfter*, comp. of *af* or of, the primary meaning being 'more off', 'farther away'; *-ter* is the comparative affix seen as *-ther* in **other**.]

aga, **agha**, *ä-gä'*, or *a'ga*, *n.* a Mohammedan (esp. a Turkish) commander or chief officer. [Turk. *aghā*, Pers. *ak*, *aka*, a lord.]

again, *a-gen'*, also *a-gān'*, *adv.* once more: in addition: moreover: in return: back. [O.E. *ongēan*, again, opposite; Ger. *entgegen*.]

against, *a-genst'*, also *a-gānst'*, *prep.* opposite to: in opposition to: in contact or in collision with: in provision for: in exchange for. [Formed from *again*, with genitive ending *-es*, as *whilst* from *while*—the *-t* being a later addition.]

agape, *ag'a-pē*, *n.* a love-feast, held by the early Christians in connection with the Lord's Supper. [Gr. *agapē*, love.]

agape, *a-gāp'*, *adj.* or *adv.* gaping from wonder, expectation or attention. [Pfx. *a-* (O.E. *on*), on, and **gape**.]

agar-agar, *ä'gär-ä'gär* (or *ä'gär-ä'gär*), *n.* one of various seaweeds used in cooking, medicine, bacteria-culture, &c.: a jelly made from one of these. [Malay.]

agaric, *ag'ar-ik*, *ag'ar'ik*, *n.* a fungus, properly one of the mushroom family, but loosely applied. [Gr. *agarikon*.]

agate, *ag'ät*, *n.* a precious stone composed of more or less concentric layers of quartz of different tints. [Gr. *achātēs*, said to be so called because first found near the river *Achates* in Sicily.]

agave, *a-gā'vi*, *n.* an American genus of aloe-like plants, one species of which is a source of sisal. [L.,—Gr. *Agauē*, a woman in Greek legend.]

age, *āj*, *n.* the time during which a person or thing has lived or existed: a stage of life: later years of life: mature years: legal maturity: a period of time: any great division of world history: a generation of men: (*coll.*) a long time (often *pl.*)—*v.i.* to grow old.—*v.t.* to make old:—*pr.p.* aging (*āj'ing*); *pa.p.* aged (*ājd*).—*adj.* **aged** (*āj'id*), advanced in age: (*ājd*) of the age of.—*n.pl.* (*āj'id*) old people.—*adj.* **age'less**, never growing old. [O.Fr. *aage*, *edage*—L. *aetās* = *aevitās*—L. *aevum*, age; cog. with **ever**.]

agenda, *a-jen'da*, *n.* things to be done, as items of business to be considered: a memorandum-book. [L. ncut. pl. of *agendus*, gerundive of *agĕre*, to do.]

agent, *ā'jént*, *n.* a person or thing that acts or exerts power: any natural force acting on matter: one authorised to transact business for another: a paid political party worker: a spy.—*n.* **ag'ency**, the office or business of an agent: instrumentality.—**agency shop**, one in which the union represents all workers, whether they are union members or not. [L. *agĕre*, to do. See **act**.]

agglomerate, *a-glom′ér-āt, v.t.* to make into a ball: to collect into a mass.—*v.i.* to grow into a mass.—*ns.* **agglom′erate** (-*āt*), volcanic rock consisting of irregular fragments; **agglomerā′tion,** a growing or heaping together: a cluster. [L. *agglomerāre, -ātum*—*ad,* to, L. *glomus, glomeris,* a ball.]

agglutinate, *a-glōōt′in-āt, v.t.* to cause to adhere, as by glue or cement.—*n.* **agglutinā′tion,** the act of uniting, as by glue: adhesion of parts: the clumping of bacteria, blood corpuscles, protozoa, &c.—*adj.* **agglut′inative,** tending to, or having power to, cause adhesion: (of languages) in which complex ideas are expressed by words composed of simpler words, the elements retaining their independence and their original form and meaning. [L. *agglūtināre, -ātum*—*ad,* to, *glūten,* glue. See **glue.**]

aggrandise, *ag′rand-īz, v.t.* to make greater in power, rank, honour, &c.: to exaggerate the greatness of.—*n.* **aggrandisement** (*a-gran′-diz-ment*). [Fr.,—L. *ad,* to, *grandis,* large.]

aggravate, *ag′ra-vāt, v.t.* to make more grievous or worse: (*coll.*) to provoke, irritate.—*n.* **aggravā′tion,** a making worse: any quality or circumstance which makes a thing more grievous or worse. [L. *aggravāre, -ātum*—*ad,* to, *gravis,* heavy.]

aggregate, *ag′re-gāt, v.t.* and *v.i.* to collect into a mass: to accumulate.—*v.i.* (*coll.*) to amount to.—*adj.* (-*āt*) formed of parts collected in a mass.—*n.* the sum total: (*geol.*) a mass consisting of rock or mineral fragments: any material mixed with cement to form concrete: (*math.*) a collection of elements having a common property that identifies the collection.—*adv.* **agg′regately.**—*n.* **aggregā′tion,** act of aggregating: state of being collected together: an aggregate.—**in the aggregate,** collectively, as a whole. [L. *aggregāre, -ātum,* to bring together, as a flock—*ad,* to, *grex, gregis,* a flock.]

aggress, *a-gres′, v.i.* to attack first.—*v.t.* to attack.—*adj.* **aggress′ive,** making the first attack: prone to do so, self-assertive: offensive as opposed to defensive.—*ns.* **aggression** (*a-gresh′(ó)n*), first act of hostility; **aggress′iveness; aggress′or.** [L. *aggredī, -gressus*—*ad,* to, *gradī,* to step.]

aggrieve, *a-grēv′, v.t.* to press heavily upon, hence (*fig.*) pain or injure (usu. passive). [O.Fr. *agrever*—L. *ad,* to, *gravis,* heavy.]

aghast, *a-gäst′, adj.* stupefied with horror. [Properly *agast*; M.E. *agasten,* to terrify—O.E. inten. pfx. *ā-,* and *gæstan,* to terrify.]

agile, *aj′īl, aj′il, adj.* active, nimble.—*n.* **agility** (*a-jil′i-ti*), quickness of motion, nimbleness, [Fr.,—L. *agilis*—*agĕre,* to do or act.]

agio, *a′ji-ō, ä′ji-ō, n.* the percentage charged for exchanging money from one currency into another. [The corresponding It. word is *aggio,* a variant of *agio,* convenience.]

agitate, *aj′i-tāt, v.t.* to shake, set in motion: to stir violently: to disturb, excite: to keep up the discussion of, esp. with a view to reform.—*v.i.* to make an agitation (for).—*ns.* **agitā′tion,** commotion: perturbation of mind: discussion: continued stirring up of public feeling; **ag′itator,** one who excites or keeps up a public agitation. [L. *agitāre,* freq. of *agĕre,* to put in

motion. See **act.**]

aglet, aiglet, aiguillette, *ag′let, āg′let, ā-gwi-let′, ns.* the tag or point of a lace or string for passing through the eyelet-holes: (**aiguillette**) a tagged point of braid hanging from the shoulder in some uniforms. [Fr. *aiguillette,* dim. of *aiguille,* a needle—from L. *acūcula* = *acicula,* dim. of *acus,* a needle.]

aglow, *a-glō′, adj.* and *adv.* very warm: red-hot. [Pfx. *a-* (O.E. *on*), on, and **glow.**]

agnate, *ag′nāt, adj.* related on the father's side: allied.—*n.* a relative of this kind. [L. *agnātus*—*ad,* to, *(g)nasci* (*g)nātus,* to be born.]

agnomen, *ag-nō′men, n.* a surname added to the family name, as *Africanus* to P. Cornelius Scipio. [L.,—*ad,* to, *(g)nōmen,* name.]

agnostic, *ag-nos′tik, n.* one who holds that we know (and apparently can know) nothing of God, or of an unseen world beyond material phenomena.—*n.* **agnos′ticism.** [Coined by T. H. Huxley in 1869—Gr. *a-,* priv., *gnōstikos,* good at knowing. See **gnostic.**]

Agnus Dei, *ag′nus dē′ī,* a part of the Mass beginning with the words *Agnus Dei*: a figure of a lamb emblematic of Christ: a round cake of wax stamped with such a figure and blessed by the Pope. [L., 'lamb of God'.]

ago, *a-gō′,* **agone,** *a-gon′, advs.* past: since. [Pa.p. of O.E. *āgān,* to pass away—inten. pfx. *ā-,* and *gān,* to go.]

agog, *a-gog′, adj.* (*predicative*), or *adv.* eager: astir. [Ety. doubtful.]

à gogo, à go-go, *a-gō-gō,* (Fr.) in abundance; used in names of discothèques, &c.—**gogo, go-go,** used loosely, *adj.,* active, alert.

agoing, *a-gō′ing, adv.* going on: in motion. [Pfx. *a-* (O.E. *on*), on, and **going.**]

agony, *ag′o-ni, n.* a violent struggle: extreme suffering: the death struggle in particular.—*v.i.* and *v.t.* **ag′onise,** to suffer, or subject to, agony.—*adj.* **ag′onising** (or *-īz′-*), causing agony.—*adv.* **ag′onisingly** (or *-īz′-*).—**agony column,** the part of a newspaper containing advertisements for missing friends, advice on personal problems, &c. [Gr. *agōnia*—*agōn,* contest.]

agoraphobia, *ag′or-à-fō′bi-a, n.* morbid fear of (crossing) squares or open places. [Gr. *agora,* market-place, *phobos,* fear.]

agrarian, *ag-rā′ri-án, adj.* relating to land, or its management.—*n.* **agrā′rianism,** a political movement in favour of change in the conditions of property in land. [L. *agrārius*—*ager,* a field.]

agree, *a-grē′, v.i.* to get on with one another: to come to an understanding: to consent (to): to assent (to): to concur (with): to be consistent, to harmonise (with): to suit (with *with*—e.g. *heat does not agree with him*): (*gram.*) to be in concord with—taking the same gender, number, case, or person:—*pr.p.* agree′ing; *pa.p.* agreed′.—*adj.* **agreed′,** used loosely, as if *pa.p.* of *v.t.,* for agreed upon, accepted (e.g. *agreed syllabus*).—*adj.* **agree′able,** pleasant: pleasing (to): in favour of (with *to*): willing: consistent with (with *to*).—*n.* **agree′ableness.**—*adv.* **agree′ably.**—*n.* **agree′ment,** concord: conformity: a bargain or contract. [O.Fr. *agréer*—L. *ad,* to, *grātus,* pleasing.]

agriculture, *ag′ri-kul-tyùr, -chùr, n.* art or prac-

Neutral vowels in unaccented syllables: *em′pér-ór*; for certain sounds in foreign words see p. ix.

14

tice of cultivating land.—*adj.* **agricult′ural.**—*n.* **agricult′urist,** one skilled in agriculture—also **agricult′uralist.** [L. *agricultūra*—*ager*, a field, *cultūra*, cultivation. See **culture.**]

aground, *a-grownd′, adv.* stranded. [Pfx. *a-* (O.E. *on*), on, and **ground.**]

ague, *ā′gū, n.* a fever coming in periodical fits, accompanied with shivering: chilliness.—*adjs.* **a′gued; aguish** (*ā′gū-ish*). [O.Fr. *aigue* (Fr. *aigu*, sharp)—L. *acūta* (*febris*). See **acute.**]

ahead, *a-hed′, adv.* farther on: in advance: on: onward. [Pfx. *a-* (O.E. *on*), on, and **head.**]

ahoy, *a-hoi′, interj.* a nautical call used in hailing. [Form of interj. **hoy.**]

ahull, *a-hul′, adv.* (*naut.*) with sails furled, and helm lashed to the lee-side. [Pfx. *a-* (O.E. *on*), on, and **hull** (2).]

aid, *ād, v.t.* to help, assist.—*n.* help: anything that helps: a helper: an apparatus, &c. that gives help, e.g. hearing-aid: a subsidy.—*n.* **aid′er,** one who brings aid: a helper.—*adj.* **aid′less.—in aid of** (*slang*), intended to achieve. [O.Fr. *aider*—L. *adiūtāre*, freq. of *adjūvāre*—*ad*, intens. *jūvāre*, *jūtum*, to help.]

aide-de-camp, *ā′de-kā, n.* an officer who carries the orders of a general and acts as his secretary: an officer attending a king, governor, &c.:—*pl.* **aides′-de-camp** (pron. as *sing.*). [Fr., assistant on the field.]

aide-mémoire, *cd , ād mā mwär, n.* aid to the memory: a memorandum: a memorandum book: a written summary of the items of a diplomatic document (e.g. an agreement) in course of preparation. [Fr.]

aiglet. Same as **aglet.**

aigrette, *ā′gret, n.* a small white heron (also **egret**): a plume composed of feathers, or of gems, like a heron's crest. [Fr.]

aiguillette. Same as **aglet.**

ail, *āl, v.i.* to feel pain, be ill.—*v.t.* to trouble, afflict—*obs.* except in such impers. phrases as, 'What ails you?'—*n.* **ail′ment,** pain: indisposition: disease. [O.E. *eglan*, to pain.]

aileron, *ā′lér-on, el′é-rō n.* a flap on aeroplane wing-tips for lateral balancing. [Fr., dim. of *aile*—L. *āla*, a wing.]

aim, *ām, v.i.* (with *at*), to try to hit with a missile: to direct the intention or endeavour towards (with *at*).—*v.t.* to point or direct towards a mark.—*n.* the action or manner of aiming: the mark aimed at: design, intention.—*adj.* **aim′less,** without purpose or object.—*adv.* **aim′lessly.** [O.Fr. *esmer*, to reckon—L. *aestimāre*, to estimate.]

ain't, *ānt,* (*coll.*) contracted form of *are not, am* or *is not*: also *has not, have not.*

air, *ār, n.* the mixture of gases we breathe: the atmosphere: any special condition of atmosphere: a light breeze: outward appearance, manner, look: (*mus.*) a rhythmical melody: the soprano part in a harmonised composition: (*pl.*) affectation.—*adj.* of, pertaining to the air: affecting (the) air: by means of air or aircraft.—*v.t.* to expose to the air: to dry: to bring to public notice.—*n.* **air′ing,** exposure to air or heat: a short excursion in the open air.—*adj.* **air′y,** consisting of or relating to air: open to the air: like air: unsubstantial: light of heart, sprightly.—*adv.* **air′ily.**—*n.* **air′iness.**—*adj.* **air′less,** without air: without wind: without free communication with the open air.—*ns.* **air arm,** that branch of the fighting services which uses aircraft; **air′-bladd′er,** a sac containing gas, as those that buoy up certain seaweeds, or the swim-bladders in fishes serving to regulate buoyancy and in some cases acting as a lung.—*adj.* **air′borne,** transported by air: borne up in the air.—*ns.* **air′brake,** a vehicle brake worked by compressed air; **air′brush,** any of several devices for spraying paint by compressed air; **air-cav′ity, air′-cell** (*bot.*), an intercellular space containing air; **air chief-marshal,** an officer of the Royal Air Force ranking with an admiral or general; **air commodore,** an officer of the Royal Air Force ranking with a commodore or brigadier; **air′-condi′tioning,** (means of) bringing air to the desired state of purity, temperature and humidity; **air′-corr′idor,** in an area where flying is restricted, a narrow strip along which flying is allowed; **air′craft** (*sing.* and *pl.*), any structure or machine for navigating the air; **aircraft carrier,** a vessel from which aircraft can take off and on which they may alight; **air′-cush′ion,** an inflatable cushion: protective barrier, e.g. between hovercraft and land or water, formed by downdriven air; **air′-en′gine,** an engine driven by heated or compressed air; **air force,** a force organised for warfare in the air; **air′gun,** a gun that discharges missiles by compressed air; **air-host′ess, -stew′ardess,** young woman who looks after the comfort of passengers in an aircraft; **air′-jack′et,** a casing containing air to reduce loss or gain of heat: a garment with airtight cavities to buoy up in water; **air′-lift,** a transportation operation carried out by air; **air′-line,** a route, or system of traffic, by aircraft: an organisation operating such a system; **air′-lin′er,** a large passenger aircraft plying in an air-line; **air′-lock,** a small chamber in which pressure of air can be raised or lowered: a bubble in a pipe obstructing flow of liquid; **air mail,** system of transporting mail by air: mail carried by air; **air′man,** an aviator, pilot; **air-mar′shal,** officer of the Royal Air Force ranking with a vice-admiral or lieutenant-general.—*adj.* **air′-mind′ed,** alive to the importance of aviation.—*ns.* **air′plane** (*U.S.*), an aeroplane; **air′-pock′et,** a region of rarefied air, in which aircraft drop; **air′port,** an aerodrome where commercial aircraft arrive and depart; **air′-pump,** an instrument for pumping the air out of a vessel; **air′-raid,** a raid by hostile aircraft; **air′-sac,** an outgrowth of the lung in birds, helping respiration and lightening the body; **air′screw,** the propeller of an aircraft; **air′-shaft,** a passage for air into a mine; **air′ship,** a navigable balloon, or dirigible; **air′space,** cubic content of air available for respiration; **air′-stop,** a stopping-place for helicopters; **air′-strip,** a temporary or emergency landingplace for aircraft: a runway; **air terminal,** a terminus to or from which passengers are conveyed from or to an aircraft.—*adj.* **air′tight,** so tight as not to admit air: affording no opening to an opponent.—*ns.* **air′-trap,** a device to prevent the escape of foul air; **air vice-mar′shal,** an officer of the Royal Air Force ranking with a rear-admiral or major-general; **air′way**, a passage for air: organised route for air travel.—*adj.* **air′worthy**, in a fit condition for safe flying.—**air-sea res′cue**, combined use of aircraft and high-speed launches in sea rescue; **air-traffic control**, system of regional centres and airport units which instruct aircraft exactly about route to follow, height at which to fly, &c.; **(go) up in the air**, (to become) excited or angry; **in the air**, without firm foundation: vague: exercising a pervasive influence on general opinion; **off the air**, not broadcasting, or being broadcast, for a period of time; **on the air**, broadcast by wireless: in the act of _broadcasting. [Fr.,—L. *äer*—Gr. *āēr*, air.]

aisle, *īl*, *n.* the wing or side of a church: the side passages in a church: (loosely) any passage in a church.—*adj.* **aisled** (*īld*), having aisles. [O.Fr. *ele*, *aisle*—L. *axilla*, *āla*, wing.]

aitchbone, *āch′bōn*, *n.* the bone of the rump: the cut of beef over this bone. [Orig. *nache*- or *nage*-bone—O.Fr. *nache*, *nage*—L. *natis*, buttock; *a nache* became *an aitch.*]

ajar, *a-jär′*, *adv.* partly open. [Pfx. *a*- (O.E. *on*), on, *cerr*, a turn.]

akimbo, *a-kim′bō*, *adv.* or *adj.* (*predicative*) with hand on hip and elbow bent outward.

akin, *a-kin′*, *adj.* related by blood: having the same or similar characteristics, allied in nature. [O.E. prep. *of*, and **kin**.]

à la, *a la*, *prep.* in the manner of. [Fr.]

alabaster, *al′a-bäs-tér*, or *-bäs′-*, *n.* a semitransparent massive gypsum.—*adj.* made of alabaster. [Gr. *alabastros*,- said to be derived from *Alabastron*, a town in Egypt.]

à la carte, *ä lä kärt′*, *adv.* according to the bill of fare.—Also *adj.* as in an *à-la-carte* dinner, one chosen dish by dish, each dish being paid for at the price stated on the menu; cf. *table d′hôte*. [Fr.]

alack, *a-lak′*, *interj.* an exclamation denoting sorrow. [Interj. *ah*, and **lack**.]

alacrity, *a-lak′ri-ti*, *n.* briskness, cheerful readiness, promptitude. [L. *alacritās*—*alacer*, gen. *alacris*, brisk.]

à la mode, **alamode**, *a-lä-mōd′*, *adv.* and *adj.* according to the fashion. [Fr.]

alarm, *a-lärm′*, *n.* a call to arms: notice of danger: sudden surprise with fear: vivid apprehension: a mechanical contrivance to arouse from sleep or to attract attention.— *v.t.* to call to arms: to give notice of danger: to fill with dread.—*adv.* **alarm′ingly.**—*n.* **alarm′ist**, one who excites alarm: one given to prophesying danger.— Also *adj.* [Fr. *alarme*— It. *all′ arme*, to arms.]

alarum, *al-ä′rum*, *n.* and *v.t.* Same as **alarm**.

alas, *a-läs′*, *interj.* expressive of grief. [O.Fr. *(h)a las* (mod. Fr. *hélas*); *ha!* ah! *las(se)*, wretched, weary—L. *lassus*, wearied.]

alate, *āl′āt*, *adj.* winged, or having wing-like appendages.—Also **al′ated**. [L. *ālātus*—*āla*, a wing.]

alb, *alb*, *n.* in R.C. churches, a white linen vestment reaching to the feet, worn by priests at the celebration of the eucharist, under the chasuble, cope, or dalmatic. [O.E. *albe*—L. *albus*, white.]

albatross, *al′ba-tros*, *n.* any of several large, web-footed sea-birds of the Southern Ocean.

[Corr. from Sp. *alcatraz*, perh. with reference to L. *albus*, white, from their colour.]

albeit, *öl-bē′it*, *conj.* although: notwithstanding. [All be it (that) = all though it be that.]

albert, *al′bért*, *n.* a short watch-chain. [Prince *Albert*, husband of Queen Victoria.]

albino, *al-bē′no*, *n.* a human being or animal whose skin and hair are abnormally white, and the pupil of the eye of pink colour: a plant lacking chlorophyll:—*pl.* **albi′nos**. [Port. or Sp. *albino*, whitish—L. *albus*, white.]

Albion, *al′bi-ón*, *n.* the island of Great Britain, or England or Scotland. [L.—Celt.]

album, *al′bum*, *n.* among the Romans, a white tablet or register: a blank book for the insertion of portraits, autographs, &c.: a booklike container for gramophone records. [L.,—*albus*, white.]

albumen, *al-bū′men*, *n.* white of egg: the nutritive material surrounding the yolk in the eggs of higher animals, a mixture of proteins.—*n.* **albū′min**, one of the classes of proteins soluble in water, the solutions coagulable by heat.—*adjs.* **albū′minous**, like or containing albumen; **albū′minoid**, like albumen.—*n.* one of a class of insoluble proteins. [L.,—*albus*, white.]

alburnum, *al-bûr′num*, *n.* in trees, the white and soft parts of wood between the inner bark and the heart-wood. [L.,—*albus*, white.]

alchemy, **alchymy**, *al′ki-mi*, *n.* the infant stage of chemistry, as astrology was of astronomy—its chief aims being to transmute the other metals into gold, and to discover the elixir of life: (*fig.*) transmuting power.—*n.* **al′chemist**. [Ar. *al-kīmīā*—*al*, the, *kīmīā* (late Gr. *chēmeiā*), 'transmutation'; confused with Gr. *chÿmeiā*, pouring, from *cheein*, to pour, hence the old spellings *alchymy*, *chymistry*.]

alcohol, *al′kō-hol*, *n.* pure spirit, a liquid generated by the fermentation of sugar and other saccharine matter, and forming the intoxicating element of fermented liquors: a general name for a class of compounds analogous to common alcohol (ethanol).—*adj.* **alcohol′ic**, of or like alcohol: caused by alcohol.—*n.* one addicted to excessive drinking of alcohol.—*v.t.* **al′coholīse**, to convert into alcohol: to rectify.—*n.* **al′coholism**, alcoholic poisoning: condition suffered by an alcoholic. [Ar. *al-kohl′*—*al*, the, *koh′l*, fine powder of antimony used in the East to stain the eyelids.]

Alcoran, *al-ko-rän′*, *n.* the Koran. [Ar. *al*, the, and **Koran.**]

alcove, *al′kōv*, *al-kōv′*, *n.* a recess in a room: any recess: a shady retreat. [Sp. *alcoba*, a place in a room railed off to hold a bed—Ar. *al*, the, *qobbah*, a vault.]

aldehyde, *al′di-hīd*, *n.* one of a large class of compounds differing from alcohols in having two atoms less of hydrogen. [From *al. dehyd.*, a contr. for *alcohol dehydrogenatum*, alcohol deprived of hydrogen.]

alder, *öl′dér*, *n.* genus of trees related to the birch, usually growing in moist ground. [O.E. *alor*; Ger. *erle*; L. *alnus*.]

alderman, *öl′dér-man*, *n.* in English boroughs, a civic dignitary next in rank to the mayor.—*adj.* **alderman′ic**. [O.E. (Anglian) *aldor* (*ald*, old), senior, chief; *aldorman*, ruler.]

Neutral vowels in unaccented syllables: *em′pér-ór*; for certain sounds in foreign words see p. ix.

Aldine, al'dīn, adj. applied to books printed by Aldus Manutius of Venice, in 16th century.

ale, āl, n. a beverage made from an infusion of malt by fermentation: (arch.) a festival, so called from the liquor drunk.—n. **ale'-house,** a house in which ale is sold. [O.E. (Anglian) alu; O.N. öl.]

alec, a-lĕc', adv. on the lee-side. [Pfx. a (O.E. on), on, and **lee.**]

alembic, a-lem'bik, n. a vessel used in distillation by the old chemists. [Ar. al, the, anbīq, a still—Gr. ambix, a cup.]

alert, a-lûrt', adj. watchful: brisk.—n. a sudden attack or surprise: a danger warning.—v.t. to forewarn, put on the alert.—adv. **alert'ly.**—n. **alert'ness.**—**on the alert,** on the watch. [Fr.—It. all' erta, on the erect—erto, erect—L. ērectus.]

Alexandrine, al-egz-an'drīn, n. a rhyming verse of twelve syllables, six iambic feet, perh. so called from its use in old French poems on Alexander the Great.

alfa, al'fa, n. an African name for esparto grass.

alfalfa, al-fal'fa, n. lucerne. [Sp.,—Ar. alfaçfaçah.]

alfresco, al-fres'ko, adv. and adj. in the fresh or cool air. [It. al fresco.]

Algae, al'jē, n. (bot.) a division of plants, embracing seaweeds and allied forms. [L., pl. of alga, seaweed.]

algebra, al'je-bra, n. a method of calculating by means of letters employed to represent numbers, and signs to represent their relations: the branch of mathematics concerned with operations on symbols, involving reasoning about their relationships.—adjs. **algebrā'ic, -al,** pertaining to algebra.—n. **algebrā'ist,** one skilled in algebra. [It. and Sp., from Ar. al-jebr, the resetting of anything broken, hence combination—jabara, to reunite.]

alginic acid, al-jin'ik as'id, acid obtained from certain seaweeds, used in plastics, &c. [L. alga, seaweed.]

algorithm, al'go-ridhm, n. rule for solving mathematical problem in a finite number of steps.

algum, al'gum. Same as **almug.**

alias, ā'li-as, adv. otherwise.—n. an assumed name:—pl. **a'liases.** [L. aliās, at another time, otherwise alius, other.]

alibi, al'i-bī, n. the plea that a person charged with a crime was elsewhere when it was committed: (loosely; coll.) an excuse. [L., elsewhere—alius, other, ibi, there.]

alien, āl'yen, or ā'li-en, adj. foreign: different in nature: repugnant (to).—n. one belonging to another country: one of foreign birth who has not qualified for, and not obtained, naturalisation. [L. aliēnus—alius, other.]

alienate, āl'yen-āt, ā'li-en-āt, v.t. to transfer to another: to estrange: to divert (from).—adj. **āl'ienable,** capable of being transferred to another.—ns. **alienabil'ity; alienā'tion.** [L. aliēnāre, -ātum—aliēnus. See **alien.**]

alienist, āl'yen-ist, ā'li-en-ist, n. one who specially treats mental diseases. [Fr. aliéniste.]

alight, a-līt', v.i. to come down, as from a horse: to descend: to fall (upon). [O.E. ālīhtan, to come down—a-, inten., and līhtan.]

alight, a-līt', adj. on fire: lighted up. [Pfx a- (O.E. on), on, and **light** (1).]

align, a-līn', v.t. to arrange in line, as troops: to bring into line: to array (on a particular side in a controversy).—n. **align'ment,** a laying out by a line: state of being aligned: taking of side, or side taken, politically, &c.: the ground-plan of a railway or road. [Fr. aligner—L. ad, to, and līnea, a line.]

alike, a-līk', adj. like one another, having resemblance.—adv. in the same manner or form: similarly. [O.E. gelīc, anlīc, onlīc—ge, together, an, on, on, and līc. See **like** (1).]

aliment, al'i-mėnt, n. nourishment: food: provision for maintenance.—adjs. **aliment'al,** supplying food; **aliment'ary,** pertaining to aliment: nutritive.—ns. **alimentā'tion,** the act or state of nourishing or of being nourished; **al'imony,** an allowance for support made to a wife when legally separated from her husband.—**alimentary canal,** the principal part of the digestive apparatus of animals, extending from the mouth to the anus—including the gullet, stomach, intestines, &c. [L. alimentum—alēre, to nourish.]

aliphatic, al-i-fat'ik, adj. (chem.) fatty: pertaining to fatty acids derived from the paraffins and to other compounds of similar structural formula—opp. to aromatic. [Gr. aleiphar, oil.]

aliquot, al'i-kwot, adj. used of a part which is contained in the whole an exact number of times. [L. aliquot, some, several—alius, other, quot, how many.]

alive, a-līv', adj. in life: brisk: alert: full of activity.—**alive to,** conscious of, susceptible to. [O.E. on līfe—līfe, dat. of līf, life.]

alkali, al'ka-li, or -lī, n. (chem.) a substance that dissolves in water to form an alkaline solution, esp. the hydroxides of sodium and potassium. Alkalis are often spoken of as bases, but the term base has wider signification: pl. **al'kali(e)s.**—adj. **alkaline** (al'kalīn, or -lin), having the properties of an alkali.—n. **alkali'nity** (-lin'), quality of being alkaline: extent of this quality.—**alkaline solution,** an aqueous solution, with strong basic properties, containing more hydroxyl ions than hydrogen ions.—**caustic alkalis** (see **caustic**). [Ar. al-qalīy, ashes, the term having been originally applied to salts, chiefly potassium carbonate and sodium carbonate, got from plant ashes.]

alkaloid, al'ka-loid, n. any one of a number of organic bases found in plants and often important in medicine on account of their physiological action.—adj. pertaining to or resembling alkali. [alkali, Gr. eidos, form.]

Alkoran. Same as **Alcoran.**

all, öl, adj. the whole of: every one of.—adv. wholly: completely: entirely.—n. the whole: everything.—**all at once,** suddenly; **all but,** everything short of, almost; **all in,** everything included: (coll.) exhausted; **all in all,** taking everything into account: the chief object of affection or desire; **all right,** a colloquial phrase expressing assent or approbation; **all one,** just the same; **all out,** (coll.) with maximum effort.—**at all,** in the least degree or to the least extent; **for good and all,** finally; **once for all,** once and once only, finally. [O.E. all, eall; Ger. all, Gael. uile, W. oll.]

Allah, ä'la, n. the Arabic name of God. [Ar. contr. of al-ilāh, 'the worthy to be adored'.]

fāte, fär; mē, hûr (her); *mīne; mōte, för; mūte; mōōn, fŏŏt;* ᴛʜen (then)

allay, a-lā′, v.t. to lighten, relieve: to make quiet or calm. [M.E. forms, *aleggen, aleyen* (O.E. *alecgan*—*ā*-, inten., *lecgan*, causal of *licgan*, to lie); identical in form, and accordingly confounded in meaning, with two M.E. words of Latin origin from which came **alloy** and an obs. verb *allege*, to alleviate.]

allege, a-lej′, v.t. to produce as an argument or plea: to assert.—*n.* **allegātion** (al-e-gā′-sh(ö)n), an assertion, esp. without proof. [Through O.Fr. forms from L.L. *exlītigāre*, to clear at law.]

allegiance, a-lē′j(y)áns, n. the duty of a subject to his liege or sovereign: loyalty. [L. *ad*, to, and **liege**.]

allegory, al′e-gor-i, n. a description of one thing under the image of another.—*adjs.* **allegor′ic**, -al, in the form of an allegory: figurative.—*adv.* **allegor′ically**.—*v.t.* **all′egorise**, to put in form of an allegory.—*v.i.* to use allegory. [Gr. *allēgoriā*; *allos*, other, and *agoreuein*, to speak.]

allegro, a-lā′grō, or -le′-, adv. adj., n. (mus.) a word denoting a brisk movement.—*adv., adj., n.* **allegrett′o**, (a) somewhat brisk (movement). [It.,—L. *alacer*, brisk.]

alleluia(h), al-e-lōō′ya. Same as **halleluiah**.

allergy, al′ér-ji, n. an altered or acquired state of sensitivity: abnormal reaction of the body to substances normally harmless: (coll.) antipathy.—*adj.* **aller′gic**, (with *to*) adversely affected by, supersensitive to (certain substances): (coll.) feeling distaste, dislike for. [Gr. *allos*, other, *ergon*, work.]

alleviate, a-lē′vi-āt, v.t. to make light: to mitigate.—*ns.* **alleviā′tion**; **allev′iātor**. [L. *alleviāre*, *-ātum*—*ad*, inten., *levis*, light.]

alley, al′i, n. a walk in a garden or shrubbery: a passage in a city narrower than a street: a long narrow enclosure for skittles, &c.:—*pl.* **all′eys**. [O.Fr. *alee*, passage—*aller*, to go.]

All Fools′ Day, öl fōölz′ dā, n. April first. [From sportive deceptions practised then.]

all-hail, öl-hāl′, interj. all health! a phrase of salutation. [**all** and **hail**, interj.]

All-hallow, öl-hal′ō, **All-hallows**, öl-hal′ōz, n. the day of all the holy ones. Same as **All Saints′ Day**. [**all** and **hallow**.]

alliance, a-lī′áns, n. state of being allied: union by marriage or treaty: any union for a common purpose: (bot.) a subclass, or group of families. [O.Fr. *aliance*—*alier*. See **ally**.]

alligator, al′i-gā-tór, n. a reptile of the crocodile group found mainly in America. [Sp. *el lagarto*—L. *lacerta*, a lizard.]

alliteration, a-lit-ér-ā′sh(ö)n, n. the recurrence of the same *sound* (not necessarily the same *letter*) at the beginning of two or more words in close succession, as 'seven grave and stately cedars': the regular recurrence of the same initial sound characteristic of O.E. and other Gmc. verse.—*v.i.* **allit′erate**, to begin with the same sound.—*adj.* **allit′erative**. [Fr.,—L. *ad*, to, *lītera*, a letter.]

allo-, in composition, other: denoting one of a group constituting a structural unit. [Gr. *allos*, other.]

allocate, al′o-kāt, v.t. to divide into shares: to assign as a share.—*n.* **allocā′tion**, act of allocating: share allocated: allowance made

upon an account. [L. *allocāre*—*ad*, to, and *locāre*, *-ātum*—*locus*, a place.]

allocution, al-o-kū′sh(ö)n, n. a formal address, esp. of the Pope to his clergy. [L. *allocūtiō*, *-ōnis*—*ad*, to and *loquī*, *locūtus*, to speak.]

allot, a-lot′, v.t. to divide as by lot, distribute in portions: to assign as one's share (lit. and fig.):—*pr.p.* allott′ing; *pa.p.* allott′ed.—*n.* **allot′ment**, the act of allotting: part or share allotted: a piece of ground let out for spare-time cultivation. [O.Fr. *aloter*; *lot* is Gmc., seen in O.E. *hlot*.]

allotropy, a-lot′ro-pi, n. (chem.) the property in some elements, as carbon, of existing in two or more forms—each called an **allotrope** (al′o-trōp).—*adj.* **allotrŏp′ic**. [Gr. *allotropia*, variety—*allos*, another, and *tropos*, turn.]

allow, a-low′, v.t. to permit: to acknowledge, admit, concede: to give, grant (sum of money at regular intervals): to add or deduct in estimating.—*v.i.* to admit (of).—*adj.* **allow′-able**, not forbidden: permissible.—*n.* **allow′-ance**, that which is allowed: a limited portion: a stated quantity: a concession.—**allow for**, take into the reckoning; **make allowance for**, to allow for, esp. mitigating circumstances. [O.Fr. *alouer*, to grant, to approve, which combines meanings derived from L. *adlocare* (*ad*, to, *locāre*, to place), and L. *allaudare* (*ad*, to, *laudāre*, to praise).]

alloy, a-loi′, v.t. to mix one metal with another: to reduce the purity of a metal by mixing a baser one with it: (fig.) to temper, moderate.—*n.* (a′loi, a-loi′) a mixture of two or more metals (cf. **amalgam**): a baser metal mixed with a finer: anything that impairs quality. [O.Fr. *aleier* (Fr. *aloyer*), to combine—L. *alligāre*, to bind.]

all-round, öl-rownd′, adj. competent in all branches. [**all, round**.]

All Saints′ Day, öl sānts′ dā, n. November 1, a feast of the Church in honour of all the saints collectively. Same as **All-hallows**.

All Souls′ Day, öl sōlz′ dā, n. November 2, a day of prayer for the repose of the souls of all the faithful departed.

allspice, öl′spīs, n. pimento or Jamaica pepper, supposed to combine the flavour of cinnamon, nutmeg, and cloves. [**all, spice**]

allude, a-l(y)ōōd′, v.i. to make reference (to) indirectly or in passing: to have reference (to).—*n.* **allū′sion**, an indirect reference.—*adj.* **allus′ive**, containing an allusion: containing many allusions.—*adv.* **allus′ively**. [L. *allūdēre*—*ad*, at, *lūdēre*, *lūsum*, to play.]

allure, a-l(y)ōōr′, v.t. to draw on as by a lure or bait: to entice.—*n.* ability to fascinate, charm.—*n.* **allure′ment**, act of alluring: enticement: charm.—*adj.* **allur′ing**, enticing: charming.—*adv.* **allur′ingly**. [O.Fr. *al(e)urer*—à, to, *loerre*, a lure.]

alluvium, a-l(y)ōō′vi-um, n. earth, sand, gravel, &c., carried along by rivers and deposited on lower lands:—*pl.* **allū′via**.—*adj.* **allū′vial**. [L.—*alluĕre*, to wash to or on—*ad*, to, *luĕre*, to wash.]

ally, a-lī′, v.t. to join in relation of marriage, friendship, treaty, co-operation, or assimilation:—*pa.p.* and *adj.* **allied′**, united by contract or agreement: related.—*n.* **ally** (a-lī′, or a′lī), a

Neutral vowels in unaccented syllables: em′pér-ór; for certain sounds in foreign words see p. ix.

18

confederate: a state or ruler united by treaty or league: a person or thing giving aid: a person, animal, or plant akin to another:—*pl.* **allies', all'ies** (-*īz*). [O.Fr. *alier*—L. *alligāre—ad*, to, *ligāre*, to bind.]

Alma Mater, *al'ma mā'ter, n.* one's university or school. [L. benign mother.]

almanac, *al', ŏl', ma-nak, n.* a register of the days, weeks, and months of the year, &c. [Most prob. the original of the word as in Fr., It., and Sp. was a Spanish-Arabic *al-manākh.*]

almighty, *öl-mīt'ĭ, adj.* possessing all might or power, omnipotent: very powerful generally: (*slang*) great.—*adv.* **almight'ily.**—*n.* **almight'iness.—the Almighty,** God; **the almighty dollar,** a phrase of Washington Irving's, expressive of the greatness of the power of money. [O.E. *ælmeahtig—eal,* all, *mihtig,* mighty.]

almond, *ä'mŏnd, n.* the fruit, and esp. the kernel, of the almond-tree, akin to the peach, but having a dry husk instead of flesh. [O.Fr. *almande*—L. *amygdala*—Gr. *amygdalē.*]

almoner, *al'mŏn-ėr, ä'm(ŏ)n-ėr, n.* a distributer of alms: (**hospital almoner**) a medical social worker (no longer official title).—*n.* **al'monry,** the place where alms are distributed. [O.Fr. *aumoner, aumonier*—L.L. *eleēmosynārius* (adj.). See **alms.**]

almost, *öl'mōst, adv.* nearly, all but, very nearly. [**all** and **most** (adv.).]

alms, *ämz, n.* (*sing.* and *pl.*) relief given out of pity to the poor.—*n.* **alms'house,** a house endowed for the support and lodging of the poor. [O.E. *ælmysse,* through L.L., from Gr. *eleēmosynē cleos,* compassion.]

almug, *al'mug, n.* the wood of a tree brought from Ophir in the time of Solomon—probably the red sandalwood of India. [Heb. *almūg, algūm.*]

aloe, *al'ō, n.* a genus of plants of the lily family of considerable medicinal importance:—*pl.* **aloes,** also used as *sing.* as the name of a purgative bitter drug, the juice of the leaves of several species of aloe.—**American aloe,** the agave—of the same order, but not the same family, as the aloes.—**The aloes wood** of the Bible was the heart-wood of two large spreading trees not of the same order as aloes and American aloes. [O.E. *aluwan*—L. *aloē*—Gr. *aloē.*]

aloft, *a-loft', adv.* on high: overhead: at a great height: (*naut.*) above the deck, at the masthead. [O.N. *ā lopt* (pron. *loft*), expressing motion; *ā lopti,* expressing position—O.N. *ā*—O.E. *on,* in. See **loft.**]

alone, *a-lōn', adj.* by oneself: solitary: unique.—*adv.* singly, by oneself.—**leave, let alone** (see **leave, let**). [**all** (adv.), and **one.**]

along, *a-long', adv.* in the direction of the length: onward: (followed by *with*) in company of.—*prep.* by the side of: near.—*prep.* and *adv.* **along'side,** beside: side by side: close to a ship's side.—**all along,** all the time. [O.E. *and-lang*—pfx. *and-,* against, and *lang,* long.]

aloof, *a-lōōf', adv.* at a distance: apart—*adj.* showing aloofness.—*n.* **aloof'ness,** reluctance to associate freely with others. [Pfx. *a-* (O.E. *on*), on, and **luff.**]

alopecia, *al-o-pē'si-a,* or *-sha, n.* baldness: a scalp-disease producing this. [Gr. *alōpekia,*

fox-mange.]

aloud, *a-lowd', adv.* with a loud voice, loudly: not in a whisper or undertone, not silently. [Pfx. *a-* (O.E. *on*), on, and *hlūd,* noise; Ger. *laut.*]

alp, *alp, n.* a high mountain:—*pl.* **alps,** specially applied (*cap.*) to the lofty ranges of Switzerland.—*adj.* **alpine** (*alp'in,* or *alp'īn*), pertaining to the Alps (*cap.*), or to any lofty mountains: very high: characteristic of mountain tops.—*n.* **alp'enstock,** a long stick or staff used by travellers in climbing the Alps. [L.; of Celtic origin; cf. Gael. *alp,* a mountain; allied to L. *albus,* white (with snow).]

alpaca, *al-pak'a, n.* a domesticated quadruped, a species of llama, having long silken wool: cloth made of its wool. [Sp. *alpaca* or *al-paco.*]

alpha, *al'fa, n.* the first letter of the Greek alphabet: the first, chief (e.g. the brightest star of a constellation): the beginning.—**alpha and omega,** the beginning and the end: the chief purpose; **alpha particles,** one of the products of the spontaneous disintegration of radioactive substances; they have been identified as the nuclei of helium atoms; **alpha rays,** streams of alpha particles. [Gr. *alpha*—Heb. *aleph,* an ox, the name of the first letter of the Phoenician and Hebrew alphabets.]

alphabet, *al'fa-bet, n.* the letters of a language arranged in conventional order.—*adjs.* **alphabet'ic, -al,** relating to, or in the order of, an alphabet.—*adv.* **alphabet'ically.** [Gr. *alpha, beta,* the first two Greek letters.]

already, *öl-red'ĭ, adv.* previously or before the time specified. [**all** (adv.), and **ready.**]

Alsatian, *al-sā'sh(y)án, adj.* of, pertaining to Alsatia or Alsace.—*n.* a large wolf-like dog, often used as a guard dog.

also, *öl'sō, adv.* in addition.—*n.* **als'o-ran',** a horse that is not placed in a race. (*fig.*) an undistinguished person. [**all** (adv.), and **so.**]

alt, *alt, n.* a high tone in voice or instrument.—**in alt,** in the octave above the treble stave beginning with G. [L. *altum.*]

altar, *ölt'ár, n.* an elevated place or structure, block or stone, or the like, on which sacrifices were anciently offered: in Christian churches, the table on which the officiating priest consecrates the eucharist.—*n.* **alt'arpiece,** a work of art placed above and behind an altar. [L. *altāre—altus,* high.]

alter, *öl'tér, v.t.* to make different: to change—*v.i.* to become different: to vary.—*adj.* **al'terable,** that may be altered.—*adv.* **al'terably.**—*n.* **altera'tion,** change.—*adj.* **al'terative,** having power to alter.—*n.* a medicine that alters favourably the processes of nutrition. [L. *alter,* the other—*al* (root of *alius,* other) and the old comp. suffix *-ter*= Eng. *-ther.*]

altercate, *öl'tér kāt, v.i.* to dispute or wrangle.—*n.* **alterca'tion,** contention, controversy. [L. *altercārī, -cātus,* to bandy words from one to the other (*alter,* other).]

alter ego, *al'tér eg'o, öl'tér ēg'ō, n.* second self, counterpart, double: a bosom friend. [L. *alter,* other, *ego,* I.]

alternant, *öl-tûr'nánt, n.* (*math.*) a type of determinant. [L. *alternāre, ātum alter.* See **alter.**]

alternate, *öl'tér-nāt, v.t.* to cause to follow each other by turns (properly of two things).—*v.i.*

fāte, fär; mē, hûr (her); *mīne; mōte, för; mūte; mōōn, fōōt;* тнen (then)

to happen by turns: to follow, or interchange with, each other (with *with*).—*adj.* **alter′nate** (-nát), (of two things) coming or following by turns: of leaves, placed singly with change of side at each node.—*adv.* **alter′nately.**—*n.* **alterna′tion.**—*adj.* **alter′native**, offering a choice of two things: (*wrongly*) other.—*n.* a choice between two (or, *loosely*, more) things: one of two things between which there is a choice.—*adv.* **alter′natively.**—*n.* **alt′ernator**, a generator of alternating current.—**alternating current**, an electric current that periodically reverses its direction; **alternation of generations** (*biol.*), the occurrence in a life-cycle of two or more different forms in successive generations, the offspring being unlike the parents. [L. *alternāre, -ātum—alter.* See **alter.**]

although, öl-тнō′, *conj.* admitting that: notwithstanding that. [**all** (adv.), and **though.**]

altimeter, al-tim′e-tér, *n.* an aneroid barometer used for measuring altitude by decrease in atmospheric pressure with height: an instrument for measuring altitude by means of the time taken by a radio wave sent out from an aircraft to be reflected back from the ground (**radio altimeter**; also, for high altitudes, **radar altimeter**). [L. *altus*, high, and **meter.**]

altitude, al′ti-tūd, *n.* height: a high point or position: angle of elevation above horizon: high rank or eminence. [L. *altitūdō—altus*, high.]

alto, al′tō, *n.* (*mus.*) properly the same as counter-tenor, the male voice of the highest pitch (now principally *falsetto*), and not the lowest female voice, which is properly *contralto*, though in printed music the second part in a quartet is always called *alto.* [It.,—L. *altus*, high.]

altogether, öl-tó-ge′тнér, *adv.* wholly: completely. [**all, together.**]

alto-relievo, al′tō-re-lē′vō, *n.* high relief. [It. *alto-rilievo.* See **relief.**]

altruism, al′trōō-izm, *n.* the principle of living and acting for the interest of others.—*adj.* **altruis′tic.** [Fr. *altruisme*, formed from It. *altrui*—L. *alter*, the other.]

alum, al′um, *n.* a mineral salt, the double sulphate of aluminium and potassium, used as a mordant in dyeing. [L. *alūmen.*]

alumina, a-l(y)ōō′min-a, *n.* the oxide of aluminium.—*adj.* **alū′minous**, containing alum or alumina. [L. *alūmen*, alum.]

aluminium, a-l(y)ōō-min′i-um, *n.* a silvery metal (atomic no. 13; symbol Al) remarkable for its lightness and good electrical conductivity.—Also (*U.S.*) **alū′minum.** [**alumina.**]

alumnus, al-um′nus, *n.* a pupil or student of a school or university:—*pl.* **alum′ni.** [L.,—*alĕre*, to nourish.]

always, öl′wāz, **alway** (*arch.*) öl′wā, *adv.* at all times: continually: in any case. [**all, way.**]

am, am, the 1st pers. sing. pres. indic. of the verb **to be.** [O.E. *eom*; Gr. *eimi* (orig. *esme*); L. *sum* (orig. *esum*); Sans. *asmi.*]

amain, a-mān′, *adv.* with main force or strength. [Pfx. *a-* (O.E. *on*), on, **main** (1).]

amalgam, a-mal′gam, *n.* a mixture of metals in which one is mercury: any soft mixture: (*fig.*) a combination of various elements.—*v.t.* **amal′gamate**, to mix mercury with another

metal: to combine, unite (e.g. business firms).—*v.i.* to unite: to blend.—*n.* **amalgamā′tion**, the blending of different things: a close union. [L. and Gr. *malagma*, an emollient—Gr. *malassein*, to soften.]

amanuensis, a-man-ū-en′sis, *n.* one who writes to dictation: a copyist: a secretary:—*pl.* **amanuen′ses** (-sēz). [L.,—*ab*, from, and *manus*, the hand.]

amaranth, am′ár-anth, *n.* a genus of plants with richly-coloured flowers, long in withering, and early employed as an emblem of immortality.—*adj.* **amaranth′ine**, pertaining to amaranth: unfading. [Through Fr. and L. from Gr. *amarantos*, unfading—*a-*, priv., and root *mar*, to waste away; allied to L. *mori*, to die.]

amass, a-mas′, *v.t.* and *v.i.* to gather in large quantity: to accumulate. [Fr. *amasser*—L. *ad*, to, and *massa*, a mass.]

amateur, am′a-tyùr, or am-a-tûr′, *n.* one who cultivates a particular activity for the love of it, and not for professional gain.—*adj.* **amateur′ish**, lacking professional skill: immature. [Fr.,—L. *amātor*, a lover—*amāre*, to love.]

amatory, am′a-tór-i, *adj.* relating to love, causing love. [L. *amātōrius—amāre*, to love.]

amaze, a-māz′, *v.t.* to confound with surprise or wonder.—*n.* (*poet.*) amazement.—*n.* **amaze′ment**, surprise mingled with wonder: astonishment.—*p.adj.* **amaz′ing**, causing amazement: astonishing.—*adv.* **amaz′ingly.** [O.E. *āmasian* (preserved in the pa.p. *āmasod*).]

Amazon, am′a-zón, *n.* one of a fabled nation of female warriors: a masculine woman: a virago.—*adj* **Amazō′nian.** [Popular Gr. ety. from *a-*, priv., *mazos*, a breast—the Amazons being fabled to cut off the right breast that they might draw the bow to its full stretch.]

ambassador, am-bas′a-dòr, *n.* a diplomatic minister of the highest order: (*fig.*) an intermediary, messenger:—*fem.* **ambass′adress.**—*adj.* **ambassadō′rial.** [Fr. *ambassadeur*—L. *ambactus*, a vassal.]

amber, am′bér, *n.* ambergris (*obs.*): a yellowish fossil resin, used for ornaments, &c.—*adj.* made of amber: amber-hued. [Fr. *ambre*—Ar. *anbar*, ambergris.]

ambergris, am′bér-grēs, *n.* a fragrant substance of an ash-grey colour, found floating on the sea, cast on the seacoast of warm countries, and in the intestines of the spermaceti whale. [Fr. *ambre gris*, grey amber.]

ambidexter, am-bi-deks′tér, *adj.* and *n.* (one) able to use both hands with equal facility: double-dealing, or a double-dealer.—*n.* **am′bidexter′ity.**—*adj.* **ambidex′trous.** [L. *ambo*, both, *dexter*, right hand.]

ambient, am′bi-ént, *adj.* going round: surrounding: investing.—*ns.* **am′bience, am′biance**, surroundings, environment: surrounding influence, atmosphere. [L. *ambiens, -entis*, pr.p. of *ambīre*—pfx. *ambi-*, about, *īre*, to go.]

ambiguous, am-big′ū-us, *adj.* admitting of more than one meaning, equivocal: capable of being placed in any of two or more categories: indistinct: uncertain.—*n.* **ambigū′ity**, dubiousness of meaning (also **ambig′uousness**): an ambiguous expression.—*adv.* **ambig′uously.** [L. *ambiguus—ambigĕre*, to go about—pfx.

Neutral vowels in unaccented syllables: *em′pér-òr*; for certain sounds in foreign words see p. ix.

ambi-, about, *agĕre*, to drive.]

ambit, *am'bit*, *n.* a circuit: space included: scope. [L. *ambitus—ambīre*. See **ambient**.]

ambition, *am-bish'(ó)n*, *n.* desire for power, honour, fame, excellence—*adj.* **ambi'tious**, full of ambition: desirous (of): showing ambition, pretentious.—*adv.* **ambi'tiously**.—*n.* **ambi'tiousness**. [Fr.,—L. *ambitiō, -ōnis*, the canvassing for votes practised by candidates for office in Rome—pfx. *ambi-*, about, and *īre, itum*, to go.]

ambivalence, *am-biv'ä-léns*, *n.* (*psych.*) the coexistence in one person of opposing emotional attitudes (e.g. love and hate) towards the same object.—*adj.* **ambiv'alent**, characterised by ambivalence. [L. *ambo*, both, *valens*, *-entis*, pr.p. of *valēre*, to be strong.]

amble, *am'bl*, *v.i.* (of a horse, &c.) to move at an easy pace.—*n.* a pace of a horse between a trot and a walk.—*n.* **am'bler**. [Fr. *ambler*—L. *ambulāre*, to walk about.]

ambrosia, *am-brō'z(h)i-a*, *n.* the fabled food of the gods which gave immortal youth and beauty to those who ate it.—*adj.* **ambrō'sial**, fragrant: divine. [L.,—Gr. *ambrosios—ambrotos*, immortal—*a-*, priv., *brotos*, mortal.]

ambry, *am'bri*, *n.* a niche in churches in which the sacred utensils, &c., are kept. [O.Fr. *armarie* (Fr. *armoire*), a cupboard—L. *armārium*, a chest for arms *arma*, arms.]

ambulance, *am'būl-áns*, *n.* a special conveyance for the sick or injured: a movable field hospital.—Also *adj.—adjs.* **am'bulant**, moving from place to place, shifting: **am'bulatory**, having the power or faculty of walking: moving: movable: (*fig.*) temporary, mutable.—*n.* any part of a building intended for walking in, the cloisters of a monastery. [Fr.,—L. *ambulans, -antis*, pr.p. of *ambulāre, -ātum*, to walk about.]

ambuscade, *am'bus-kad*, *n.* and *v.t.* ambush. [Fr. *embuscade*, O.Fr. *embusche*. See **ambush**.]

ambush, *am'bŏŏsh*, *n.* a concealment of assailants to make a surprise attack: a band of assailants so hidden: the bushes or other cover in which they are hidden.—*v.t.* to set an ambush for: to attack from an ambush. [O.Fr. *embusche, embuscher*—L.L. *emboscāre in-*, in, *boscus*, a bush.]

ameer, *a-mēr'*, *n.* Same as **emir**.

ameliorate, *a-mēl'yór-āt*, *v.t.* to make better, to improve.—*v.i.* to grow better.—*n.* **ameliorā'tion**. [L. *ad*, to, *melior*, better.]

amen, *ä'men'*, or *ä'men'*, *interj.* so let it be! [Gr.,—Heb. *āmēn*, firm, true.]

amenable, *ä-mēn'a-bl*, *adj.* easy to lead, tractable: liable (to): subject (to).—*ns.* **amenabil'ity**, **amen'ableness**.—*adv.* **amen'ably**. [Fr. *amener*, to lead—*à* (L. *ad*), and *mener*, to lead—L.L. *mināre*, to lead, to drive (as cattle) —L. *mināri*, to threaten.]

amend, *a-mend'*, *v.t.* to correct: to improve: to alter in detail.—*v.i.* to grow or become better.—*adj.* **amend'able**.—*n.* **amend'ment**, correction: improvement: an alteration proposed on a motion under consideration.—*n.pl.* **amends**, as in **make amends**, to make reparation, give compensation, make good a loss. [Fr. *amender* for *émender*—L. *ēmendāre*, to remove a fault—*ē* (*ex*), out of, *menda*, a fault.]

amende, *ä-mād'*, *n.* a fine, penalty.—**amende honorable** (*on-o-rä-bl'*), a public apology and amends to one who has been wronged. [Fr. See **amend**.]

amenity, *a-mēn'i-ti*, *n.* pleasantness, as regards situation, climate, manners, or disposition: (*pl.*) agreeable characteristics—now esp. attractive features of a locality (e.g. parks, playgrounds), a residence, &c. [Fr. *aménité*—L. *amoenĭtās—amoenus*, pleasant, from root of *amāre*, to love.]

amenorrhoea, *a-, ä-men-ō-rē'a*, *n.* failure of menstruation. [Gr. *a-*, 'priv., *mēn*, month, *rhoiā*, a flowing.]

amerce, *a-mûrs'*, *v.t.* to punish by a fine.—*n.* **amerce'ment**, a penalty inflicted. [O.Fr. *amercier*, to impose a fine—L. *ad*, to, *mercēs*, reward, punishment.]

American, *a-mer'i-kán*, *adj.* pertaining to America, esp. to the United States.—*n.* a native of America.—*n.* **Amer'icanism**, a custom, word, phrase, or idiom peculiar to Americans. **American organ**, a kind of harmonium (q.v.) in which the air is drawn through the reeds. [From *America*, named after *Amerigo* (L. *Americus*) Vespucci, in the belief that he was the first explorer to reach the American mainland.]

americium, *am or ish'i um*, *n.* a transuranic element (atomic number 95; symbol Am) first obtained artificially in *America*.

amethyst, *am'e-thist*, *n.* a bluish-violet variety of quartz of which drinking cups used to be made, which the ancients supposed prevented drunkenness.—*adj.* **amethyst'ine**. [Gr. *amethystos—a-*, priv., *methyein*, to be drunken—*methy*, wine.]

amiable, *ām'i-abl*, *adj.* lovable: likable: of sweet disposition.—*ns.* **amiabil'ity**, **am'iableness**, quality, or instance, of being good-natured or likable.—*adv.* **am'iably**. [O.Fr. *amiable*, friendly—L. *amīcābilis—amīcus*, a friend; there is confusion in meaning with O.Fr. *amable*, lovable—L. *amābilis—amāre*, to love.]

amicable, *am'i-ka-bl*, *adj.* friendly.—*ns.* **amicabil'ity**, **am'icableness**.—*adv.* **am'icably**. [L. *amīcābilis—amīcus*, a friend—*amāre*, to love.]

amice, *am'is*, *n.* a flowing cloak formerly worn by priests and pilgrims: a strip of fine linen worn on the shoulders by R.C. priests in the service of the mass. [O.Fr. *amit*—L. *amictus—amicĕre*, to wrap about—*ambi-*, about, and *jacĕre*, to throw.]

amid, *a-mid'*, **amidst**, *a-midst'*, *prep.* in the middle or midst: among.—Also *adv.—adv.* **amid'ships**, half-way between the stem and stern of a ship. [Pfx. *a-* (O.E. *on*), on, and **mid**; for *-st*, see **against**.]

amino, *a-mē'nō, am'in-ō, adj.* and *pfx.* pertaining to, or containing, the group NH_2, united to a radical other than an acid radical.—**amino acid**, any of a group of fatty acids formed in the body from proteins. [*Ammonia, -ine*, and *-o*.]

amir, *a-mēr'*, *n.* Same as **emir**.

amiss, *a-mis'*, *adj.* wrong: out of place, out of order, inappropriate.—*adv.* in a faulty manner, ill, improperly.—*adj.* **amiss'ing**, wanting, lost.—**come amiss**, come inconveniently, be unacceptable: **take amiss**, take ill, resent. [Pfx.

a- (O.E. *on*), on, and **miss**, failure.]

amity, *am'i-ti, n.* friendship: good-will. [Fr. *amitié*—L. *amīcitia*, friendship—*amīcus*, a friend—*amāre*, to love.]

ammeter, *am'e-tér*, an instrument for measuring the current in an electric circuit. [*am*pere (q.v.), and **meter**.]

ammonia, *a-mō'ni-a, n.* a pungent gas, a compound of nitrogen and hydrogen, very soluble in water: (loosely) a solution of ammonia in water: a name for a large series of compounds analogous to ammonia.—*adj.* **ammon'iac**, pertaining to, or having the properties of, ammonia.—*adj.* **ammōn'iated**, containing ammonia.—*n.* **ammon'ium**, the hypothetical base of ammonia, the radical NH$_4$, which behaves in many ways like the atom of a metal of valency 1. [From **salammoniac** (q.v.) traditionally first obtained in Libya, near the temple of *Ammon.*]

ammonite, *am'on-īt, n.* the fossil of an extinct mollusc, so called because it resembled the horns on the statue of *Ammon*, worshipped as a ram.

ammunition, *am-ū-nish'(ò)n, n.* military stores, formerly of all kinds, now esp. shells, bullets, bombs, &c.: (*fig.*) any material that may be used to discomfit opponents in a controversy. [O.Fr. (*l'*) *amunition*, for (*la*) *munition*—L. *munīre*. See **munition**.]

amnesia, *am-nē'zh(y)a*, or *-si-a, n.* loss of memory. [Gr. *amnēsia*—*a-*, priv., and root of *mnaesthai*, to remember.]

amnesty, *am'nest-i, n.* a general pardon of political or other offenders. [Gr. *amnēstia*—*amnē-stos*, not remembered—*a-*, priv., and *mnēstis*, memory.]

amnion, *am'ni-ón, n.* the innermost membrane enveloping the embryo of reptiles, birds and mammals.—*adj.* **amniot'ic**.—**amniotic fluid**, the fluid within the amnion in which the embryo is suspended. [Gr.]

amoeba, *a-mē'ba, n.* one of the simplest animals or Protozoa, of indeterminate and variable shape:—*pl.* **amoebae** (*-bē*). [Gr. *amoibē*, change, alteration.]

amok, *a-mok', adv.* in a frenzy: with a furious impulse to attack all comers.—Also **amuck**. [Malay *amoq*, frenzied.]

among, *a-mung', **amongst**, *a-mungst', prep.* of the number of: amidst. [O.E. *on(ge)mang*—(*ge*)*mengan*, to mingle; for *-st,'* see **against**.]

amoral; *a-mor'ál*, or *ā-, adj.* such that no moral responsibility can be imputed: incapable of distinguishing between right and wrong. [Gr. *a-*, priv., and **moral**.]

amorous, *am'or-us, adj.* easily inspired with love: fondly in love (with *of*): relating to love.—*adv.* **am'orously**.—*n.* **am'orousness**. [O.Fr. *amorous*—L.L. *amōrōsus*—L. *amor*, love.]

amorphous, *a-mōr'fus, adj.* without regular shape, shapeless: uncrystallised. [Gr. *a-*, priv., *morphē*, form.]

amortise, *a-mört'īz*, or *-īz, v.t.* to wipe out (as a debt).—*n.* **amortisā'tion**, reduction of a debt through a sinking-fund. [A.Fr. *amortir*—L.L. *admortīre*—L. *ad*, to, *mors, mortis*, death.]

amount, *a-mownt', v.i.* to come in total (to): to be equivalent in meaning or substance

(to).—*n.* the whole sum: a quantity: (*fig.*) value: a principal sum together with the interest on it. [O.Fr. *amonter*, to ascend—L. *ad*, to, *mons, montis*, a mountain.]

amour, *am-ōōr', n.* a love intrigue, or illicit affection.—**amour propre**, self-esteem ready to take offence at slights. [Fr.,—L. *amor*, love.]

ampere, *am'pār, am'pēr, n.* the SI-unit by which an electric current is measured. Often abbrev. **amp**. [From *Ampère*, a French physicist (1775-1836).]

ampersand, *am'pér-sand, n.* a name for the character &, 'and'. [A corr. of *and per se and*—i.e. '& standing by itself means *and*'.]

amphetamine, *am-fet'á-mēn, -min, n.* synthetic drug used to stimulate the central nervous system. [*a*lpha *m*ethyl *phe*net*hyl* + *amine*.]

Amphibia, *am-fib'i-a, n.pl.* one of the main divisions of vertebrates, a class of animals between fishes and reptiles, including frogs, toads, &c.—*n.* **amphib'ian**, one of the Amphibia: an amphibious plant: an aeroplane designed to alight on land or water: a vehicle for use on land or water.—*adj.* **amphib'ious**, adapted to life, or to use, on land and in water.—**amphibious operations**, military operations in which troops are conveyed across the sea or other water in landing barges, assault craft, &c., and land on enemy-held territory. [L.,—Gr.,—*amphi*, on both sides, *bios*, life.]

amphibrach, *am'fi-brak, n.* (*pros.*) a foot of three syllables—a short, a long, and a short, as *ămārĕ*, or an unaccented, an accented, and an unaccented, as *amuse'ment*. [L.,—Gr.,—Gr. *amphi*, on both sides, *brachys*, short.]

amphitheatre, *am-fi-thē'a-tér, n.* an oval or circular edifice having rows of seats, one behind and above another, round an open space, called the arena, in which public spectacles are exhibited: anything like an amphitheatre in form. [Gr. *amphi*, round about, *theātron*. See **theatre**.]

amphora, *am'fo-ra, n.* a two-handled jar used by the Greeks and Romans for holding liquids. [Gr. *amphoreus, amphiphoreus*—*amphi*, on both sides, *pherein*, to bear.]

amphoteric, *am-fo-ter'ik, adj.* capable of showing properties either of a base or of an acid. [Gr. *amphoteros*, both.]

ample, *am'pl, adj.* spacious: large enough: copious.—*n.* **am'pleness**.—*adv.* **am'ply**. [Fr.,—L. *amplus*, large.]

amplify, *am'pli-fī, v.t.* to express more fully: to enlarge, make greater: to increase loudness of (sound), strength of (current), &c.—*n.* **amplificā'tion**.—*adj.* **amplifica'tory**.—*n.* **am'plifier**, one who amplifies: a lens that enlarges the field of vision: a device for increasing the power-level of electric currents in a communication channel, e.g. an apparatus used in a wireless set to increase the volume of the sound. [L. *amplificāre*—*amplus*, large, and *facĕre*, to make.]

amplitude, *am'pli-tūd, n.* largeness: breadth (*lit.* and *fig.*): extent (of vibratory movement): wide range (of mind): the angular distance from the east point of a horizon at which a heavenly body rises, or from the west point at which it sets.—**amplitude modulation**, modu-

Neutral vowels in unaccented syllables: *em'pér-ór*; for certain sounds in foreign words see p. ix.

lation in radio transmission by varying the amplitude of the carrier wave—cf. **frequency modulation**. [Fr.,—L. *amplitūdō*.]

ampoule, *am-pōōl′, n.* a small, sealed, glass capsule for holding measured quantities of medical preparations. [Fr.,—L. *ampulla*, a flask.]

ampulla, *am-pul′a, n.* a small two-handled flask. [L.; made up of *amb*-, on both sides, and *olla*, a jar; or an irregular dim. of *amphora*; see **amphora**.]

amputate, *am′pū-tāt, v.t.* to cut off, as a limb.—*n.* **amputā′tion**. [L. *amputāre—amb-*, round about, *putāre*, to cut.]

amuck, *a-muk′.* Same as **amok**.

amulet, *am′ū-let, n.* a gem, scroll, or other object carried about the person, as a charm against sickness, harm, or witchcraft. [Fr. *amulette*—L. *amulētum*, a word of unknown origin.]

amuse, *a-mūz′, v.t.* to occupy or entertain pleasantly: to divert: to excite mirth in.—*n.* **amuse′ment**, that which amuses: pastime.—*adj.* **amus′ing**, affording amusement: entertaining.—*adv.* **amus′ingly**. [Fr. *amuser.*]

an, *an, adj.* one: the indefinite article, used before words beginning with the sound of a vowel. [O.E. *ān*. See **one**.]

an, *an, conj.* if. [A form of **and**.]

anabaptist, *an-a-bapt′ist, n.* one who holds that baptism ought to be administered only to adults, and therefore that those baptised in infancy ought to be baptised again. [Gr. *ana*, again, *baptizein*, to dip in water, to baptise.]

anabolism, *an-ab′ol-izm, n.* the constructive processes within the protoplasm, by which food or other material passes through an ascending series of ever more complex and unstable combinations, until it is finally worked up into living matter. Cf. **katabolism** and see **metabolism**. [Gr. *anabolē*, rising up.]

anachronism, *an-a′kron-izm, n.* an error in chronology, whereby a thing is assigned to a period to which it does not belong (orig. too early a time, now also too late): anything out of keeping with the time.—*adj.* **anachronist′ic**. [Gr. *ana*, backwards, *chronos*, time.]

anacoluthon, *an-a-ko-lū′thon, n.* want of sequence in the construction of a sentence, when the latter part does not correspond grammatically with the former. [Gr. *anakolouthos—an-*, priv., and *akolouthos*, following.]

anaconda, *an-a-kon′da, n.* a large South American water-snake akin to the boa-constrictor. [Perh. a Cingalese name for a different snake.]

anacoustic zone, *an-a-kōōs′tik zōn*, zone of absolute silence in space. [Gr. *an-*, priv., and **acoustic**.]

anacreontic, *an-a-kre-on′tik, adj.* after the manner of the Greek poet *Anacreon*: convivial, erotic.—*n.* a poem in this vein.

anaemia, *a-nē′mi-a, n.* bloodlessness, lack of red blood corpuscles or of haemoglobin—a condition marked by pallor and debility.—*adj.* **anae′mic**, suffering from anaemia: (*fig.*) sickly, feeble. [Gr. *an-*, priv., *haima*, blood.]

anaesthetic, *an-es-thet′ik,* or *-es-thē′tik, adj.* producing insensibility to external impressions.—*n.* a substance, as chloroform or cocaine, that produces insensibility, whether general or local.—*n.* **anaesthē′sia**, loss of feeling, insensibility.—*v.t.* **anaes′thetise.**—*n.*

anaes′thetist, one who administers anaesthetics. [Gr. *anaisthētos*, without feeling—*an-*, priv., *aisthēsis*, sensation.]

anaglyph, *an′a-glif, n.* an ornament carved in low relief.—*adj.* **anaglypt′ic**. [Gr. *anaglyphē—ana*, up, *glyphein*, to carve.]

anagram, *an′a-gram, n.* a word or sentence formed by rewriting in a different order the letters of another word or sentence: as, 'live' for 'evil', 'Flit on, cheering angel' for 'Florence Nightingale'.—*adjs.* **anagrammat′ic, anagrammat′ical**. [Gr. *ana*, again, *gramma*, letter—*graphein*, to write.]

anal, *ān′al, adj.* pertaining to or near the **anus**.

analects, *an′a-lekts, n.pl.* collections of literary fragments.—Also **analec′ta**. [Gr. *analektos—ana*, up, *legein*, to gather.]

analgesia, *an-al-jē′zi-a, n.* painlessness: insensibility to pain.—*n.* **analgē′sic**, a pain-relieving drug.—*adj.* that dispels pain. [Gr.—*an-*, priv., *algeein*, to feel pain.]

analogy, *an-al′o-ji, n.* an agreement or correspondence in certain respects between things otherwise different: likeness: reasoning from similar, or apparently similar cases: (*philol.*) a resemblance by virtue of which a word may be altered on the model of another class of words, for instance, the verb *to strive*, borrowed from O.Fr., was supplied with a new *pa.t.* and *pa.p. strove, striven* on the analogy of the O.E. verbs *drive*, &c.—*adj.* **analog′ical**.—*adv.* **analog′ically**.—*adj.* **anal′ogous**, having analogy: corresponding with or resembling: similar in certain respects (to).—*n.* **an′alogue**, a word or thing bearing analogy to, or resembling, another: (*biol.*) an organ that performs the same function as another, though differing from it in structure or origin, e.g. (*a*) the gill of a fish and the lung of an animal; (*b*) tendrils of different plants, which may be modified leaves, or branches, or inflorescences; cf. **homologue**.—**analogue computer**, type of computer in which variable electrical currents or voltages, &c. are used to represent proportionally other quantities (e.g. forces, speeds) in working out problems about these quantities. [Gr. *ana*, according to, and *logos*, ratio.]

analysis, *an-al′i-sis, n.* a resolving or separating a whole into its elements or component parts as opp. to *synthesis*: a statement of the results of this process: (*gram.*) the separation into its logical and grammatical elements of a sentence or part of a sentence: analysing a complex experience or mental process, determining the elements of which it is made up: psychoanalysis:—*pl.* **anal′yses**.—*v.t.* **an′alyse** (*-īz*), to resolve (a whole) into elements: to separate into component parts.—*adj.* **analys′able**.—*n.* **an′alyst** (*-ist*), one skilled in analysis, esp. chemical analysis: a psycho-analyst.—*adjs.* **analytic** (*-it′ik*), **-al**, pertaining to analysis: resolving into first principles.—*adv.* **analyt′ically**.—**analytical geometry**, geometry treated by reference to a system of co-ordinates.—**in the last analysis**, when all inessentials are excluded from the problem, or the situation. [Gr. *analysis—analyein*, to unloose—*ana*, up, *lyein*, to loose.]

ananas, *a-nä′nas, n.* the pineapple.—Also

anan′a. [Peruvian.]

anapaest, anapest, *an′a-pēst, -pest, n.* (*pros.*) a foot consisting of two short syllables before a long, so named because an anapaest (e.g. *pŭĕ-rī*) is the *reverse* of a dactyl (e.g. *fīlĭă*): (in Eng.) two unaccented syllables before an accented, e.g. 'wĭth ă smile' ŏn hĕr lip'.—*adjs.* **anapaes′tic, -al.** [Gr. *anapaistos,* reversed—*ana,* back, *paiein,* to strike.]

anarack, anarak. Spellings of **anorak.**

anarchy, *an′ärk-i, n.* the absence or failure of government in a state: political confusion.—*adjs.* **anarch′ic, anarch′ical.**—*ns.* **an′archism,** the theory that all government is an oppressive restriction of freedom; **an′archist,** one who strives to create anarchy, esp. by violence. [Gr. *an-, priv., archē,* government.]

anathema, *an-ath′em-a, n.* a solemn ecclesiastical curse or denunciation: any person or thing anathematised.—*v.t.* **anath′ematise,** to pronounce accursed. [The classical Gr *anathēma* meant a votive offering set up in a temple—*ana,* up, *tithenai,* to place; the *anathĕma* of the New Testament meant something specially devoted to evil.]

anatomy, *an-a′tom-i, n.* the art of dissecting any organised body: the science of the structure of the body learned by dissection: the detailed analysis of anything: (loosely) the human body: structure.—*adjs.* **anatom′ic, -al,** relating to anatomy.—*adv.* **anatom′ically.**—*v.t.* **anat′-omise,** to dissect: (*fig.*) to lay open minutely.—*n.* **anat′omist,** one who practises dissection of bodies, or who analyses minutely. [Gr. *ana,* up, asunder, *temnein,* to cut.]

anbury, *an′bŭr-i, n.* a disease in turnips, produced by one of the slime-fungi, commonly termed *finger-and-toe.* [Perh. for *angberry*—O.E. *ang-,* pain.]

ancestor, *an′ses-tór,* or *an′sis-, n.* one from whom a person is descended, a forefather—*fem.* **an′cestress.**—*adj.* **ances′tral.**—*n.* **an′-cestry,** a line of ancestors: lineage. [O.Fr. *ancestre*—L. *antecēssor*—*ante,* before, *cēdĕre, cēssum,* to go.]

anchor, *ang′kór, n.* a hooked implement that sticks into the bed of a sea or river and thus holds a ship in position: (*fig.*) anything that gives stability or security.—*v.t.* to fix by an anchor: to fasten.—*v.i.* to cast anchor: to stop, or rest.—*n.* **anch′orage,** a place for anchoring: duty imposed for anchoring: (*fig.*) rest or support to the mind.—**at anchor,** anchored; **cast anchor,** to let down the anchor, to take a position; **weigh anchor,** to take up the anchor: to sail away. [O.E. *ancor*—L. *ancora*; cf. Gr. *ankȳra*—*ankos,* a bend; conn. with **angle.**]

anchoret, *ang′kór-et,* **anchorite,** *ang′kór-ī, n.* one who has withdrawn from the world: a hermit.—*n.* **anch′oress,** a female anchorite. [Gr. *anachōrētēs*—*ana,* apart, *chōreein,* to withdraw.]

anchovy, *an′cho-vi,* also *an-chō′vi, n.* a small Mediterranean fish of the herring family, used for pickling, and for making sauce, paste, &c. [Sp. and Port. *anchova.*]

ancient, *ān′shént, adj.* very old: belonging to, or relating to, times long past, esp. before the downfall of the Western Roman Empire A.D. 476.—*n.* an aged man: one who lived in an-

cient times.—*adv.* **an′ciently,** in ancient times.—*n.* **an′cientness.**—*n.pl.* **an′cients,** those who lived in remote times, esp. the Greeks and Romans of classical times: (*B.*) elders.—**Ancient Monument,** building of historical interest scheduled for preservation, in many cases under the care of a government department.—**The Ancient of days,** the Almighty. [Fr. *ancien*—L.L. *antiānus,* former—L. *ante,* before.]

ancient, *ān′shént, n.* (*obs.*) a flag: a standard-bearer: an ensign. [Corr. of Fr. *enseigne.* See **ensign.**]

ancillary, *an-sil′ár-i, an′, adj.* subservient, subsidiary (to). [L. *ancilla,* maid-servant.]

and, *and, conj.* signifies addition, repetition, or consequence, and is used to connect words, phrases, clauses, and sentences: in M.E. (but not O.E.) it was used for *if,* and often also with added *if,* as in Luke xii. 45. [O.E., and other Gmc. languages; prob. allied to L. *ante,* before, Gr. *anti,* against.]

andante, *an-dan′tā, adv., adj.,* and *n.* (*mus.*) moving with moderately slow, even expression: a movement or piece composed in andante time. [It.—pr.p. of *andare,* to go.]

andiron, *and′ī-érn, n.* an iron bar to support the end of a log in a wood fire, a fire-dog. [O.Fr. *andier*—L.L. *anderius, andena*; further ety. uncertain; early confused with *iron.*]

androecium, *an-drē′s(h)i-um, n.* the whole of the stamens in one flower. [Gr. *anēr,* gen. *andros,* a man, *oikos,* a house.]

androgynous, *an-droj′i-nus, adj.* hermaphrodite: (*bot.*) having an inflorescence consisting of both male and female flowers. [Gr.; *anēr,* gen. *andros,* a man, and *gynē,* woman.]

anecdote, *an′ek-dōt, n.* (*orig.,* in *pl.*) details of history hitherto unpublished: a brief account of any curious or interesting incident.—*adj.* **an′ecdotal,** in the form of an anecdote.—*n.* **an′ecdotage,** the age at which one is addicted to anecdotes (cf. *dotage*). [Gr. *an-,* priv., *ek-dotos,* published—*ek,* out, *didonai,* to give.]

anele, *an-ēl′, v.t.* (*arch.*) to anoint: to administer extreme unction to. [O.E. pfx. *an-,* on, and *ele,* oil.]

anemometer, *an-e-mom′it-ér, n.* an instrument for measuring the speed of the wind. [Gr. *anemos,* wind, *metron,* measure.]

anemone, *a-nem′ó-ne, n.* a genus of the crowfoot family, the wind-flowers: a sea-anemone (q.v.). [Gr. *anemōnē*—*anemos,* wind.]

anent, *a-nent′, prep.* and *adv.* in regard to, concerning, about. [From O.E. *on efen,* on even, on a level with.]

aneroid, *an′é-roid, adj.* of a barometer in which the pressure of the air is measured without the use of mercury or other fluid.—*n.* an 'aneroid barometer'. [Fr. *anéroide*—Gr. *a,* priv., *nēros,* wet, *eidos,* form.]

aneurysm, aneurism, *an′ūr-izm, n.* the dilatation of an artery; any abnormal enlargement. [Gr. *aneurysma*—*ana,* up, *eurys,* wide.]

anew, *a-nū′, adv.* afresh: again. [O.E. prep. *of,* and **new.**]

anfractuous, *an-frakt′ū-us, adj.* winding, tortuous.—*n.* **anfractuos′ity.** [L. *anfractuōsus*—*ambi-,* about, *frangĕre, fractum,* to break.]

angel, *ān′jél, n.* a divine messenger: a minister-

Neutral vowels in unaccented syllables: *em′pér-ór*; for certain sounds in foreign words see p. ix.

24

ing or guardian spirit: (*fig.*) a person of extraordinary beauty or virtue: (*slang*) financial backer: an old Eng. gold coin bearing the figure of an angel: radar echo of unknown origin.—*adjs.* **angel'ic** (*an-*), **angel'ical**—*adv.* **angel'ically**. [Gr. *angelos*, a messenger.]

angelus, *an'ji-lus*, *n.* a short devotional exercise in honour of the Incarnation: the bell rung in Roman Catholic countries at morning, noon, and sunset, the times for this exercise. [From its first words. '*Angelus domini nuntiavit Mariae*' (Luke i. 28).]

anger, *ang'gėr*, *n.* hot displeasure, often involving a desire to retaliate: wrath.—*v.t.* to make angry: to irritate.—*adj.* **ang'ry**, excited with anger: inflamed: of sullen aspect (e.g. of the sky).—*n.* an angry young man.—*adv.* **ang'rily**. —*n.* **ang'riness.**—**angry young man**, a young man loud in disgust at what his elders have made of society (from *Look Back In Anger* (1956), a play by John Osborne, one of a group of writers of the period to whom the term was applied). [O.N. *angr*, allied to **anguish**.]

Angevin, *an'je-vin*, *adj.* pertaining to Anjou, a province of France, or to the Plantagenet kings, descendants of a Count of Anjou.

angina, *an-jī'na*, *n.* angina pectoris: any inflammatory affection of the throat, as quinsy, croup.—**angina pec'toris**, a disease of the heart marked by paroxysms of intense pain. [L. *angīna*, conn. with L. *ang(u)ĕre*, to strangle.]

angiogram, *an'ji-ō-gram*, *n.* a photograph made by angiography.—*n.* **angio'graphy**, art or process of making X-ray photographs of blood-vessels by injecting the vessels with a substance opaque to the rays. [Gr. *angeion*, case, vessel, *gramma*, that which is written.]

angiosperm, *an'ji-o-spėrm*, *n.* a plant of the **Angiosperm'ae** (*-ē*), a large and important division of flowering plants, in which the seeds are in a closed ovary. [Gr. *angeion*, case, *sperma*, seed.]

angle, *ang'gl*, *n.* a corner: the point from which lines or surfaces diverge: (*geom.*) the inclination of two straight lines which meet in a point: (*fig.*) awkward trait: point of view.—*v.t.* to present (e.g. news), not objectively, but in such a way as to serve a particular end.—*adj.* **ang'ular**, having an angle or angles: forming an angle: measured by an angle: (*fig.*) stiff and awkward in manner, apt to seem disagreeable: bony and lean in figure.—*n.* **angular'ity.**—**angle iron**, an L-shaped iron used to support corners in building, &c. [Fr.,—L. *angulus*; cog. with Gr. *ankylos*; both from root *ank*, to bend, seen also in **anchor**, **ankle**.]

angle, *ang'gl*, *n.* a hook or barb: a fishing-rod with line and hook.—*v.i.* to fish with an angle: (often with *for*) to cast about for, scheme to obtain.—*ns.* **ang'ler**, one who fishes with an angle: a voracious fish found on British shores; **ang'ling**, the art or practice of fishing with a rod and line. [O.E. *angul*, a hook.]

Angles, *ang'glz*, *n.pl.* the Low German tribe who founded settlements in eastern and central Britain, from whom the country took the name of England, i.e. land of the Angles. [L. *Angli*, Angles or English.]

Anglian, *ang'gli-ån*, *adj.* of or pertaining to the

Angles (q.v.).—*n.* the dialect of Old English spoken by the Angles (divided into Northumbrian, that of the Angles north of the Humber, and Mercian, that of the Angles farther south). [From L. *Angli*. See **Angles**.]

Anglican, *ang'glik-ån*, *adj.* belonging to, or characteristic of, the Church of England: English.—*n.* **Ang'licanism**, attachment to English institutions, esp. the English Church: the principles of the English Church.—*adv.* **anglice** (*ang'gli-sē*), in English.—*v.t.* **Ang'licise** (*-sīz*), to adapt to English standards and practice.—*n.* **Ang'licism**, an English idiom or peculiarity.—*v.t.* **Ang'lify**, to make English. [L. *Anglicānus—Angli*, English.]

Anglo-, *ang'glo*, *pfx.* English—as in *Anglo-Saxon*, &c.—*n.* (and *adj.*) **Ang'lo-Cath'olic**, one who calls himself a Catholic of the Anglican pattern, refusing the name of 'Protestant'.—*n.* **Ang'lo-Cathol'icism**.—*n.* (and *adj.*) **Ang'lo-Nor'man**, the French dialect of the Normans in England: also **Ang'lo-Fr'ench** (sometimes used for the French—influenced by central French—spoken in England under the Angevin kings).—*adj.* and *n.* **Ang'lo-Sax'on**, applied to the earliest form of the English language—better termed Old English: to all the Germanic settlers of England and southern Scotland and their descendants: to the English-speaking world generally. [L.— *Anglus*, English.]

anglomania, *ang'glō-mān'i-a*, *n.* a mania for English institutions. [**Anglo-**, and **mania**.]

anglophil(e), *ang'glō-fīl*, *n.* and *adj.* (one who is) well disposed towards England and things English. [**Anglo-**, and Gr. *phileein*, to love.]

anglophobe, *ang'glō-fob*, *n.* and *adj.* (one) fearing or disliking England.—*n.* **anglophobia** (*ang-glōfō'bi-a*; see **phobia**). [Fr. *anglophobe*—L. *Anglo* (see **Anglo**), and Gr. *phobos*, fear.]

Angora, *ang-gō', -gö', ra*, *n.* a goat with long white silky hair: mohair: a cat or a rabbit with long silky hair. [*Angora*, now Ankara, Asia Minor, famous for its breed of goats.]

angry. See **anger**.

angst, *angst*, *n.* fear, anxiety. [Ger.]

angström, *ang'strom* (or *ong'strum*) *n.* the obsolescent unit employed in expressing wavelengths of light, ultra-violet radiations, X-rays, molecular and atomic distances—equal to 10^{-10} metres. Formerly, but not now usu., **Ång-**, **angstrom unit**. [A. J. Ångström (1814-74), Swedish physicist.]

anguish, *ang'gwish*, *n.* excessive pain of body or mind, agony. [O.Fr. *angoisse*—L. *angustia*, a strait, straitness—*ang(u)ĕre*, to press tightly, to strangle.]

anhydrous, *an-hī'drus*, *adj.* (a term applied to a chemical substance) free from water. [Gr. *an-*, priv., *hydōr*, water.]

anil, *an'il*, *n.* a plant from whose leaves and stalks indigo is made.—*n.* **aniline** (*an'il-īn*, *-ēn*, or *-in*), a product of coal-tar, first obtained from anil, extensively used in dyeing and other industrial arts. [Port. *anil*; Ar. *an-nīl*, for *al-nīl*, the indigo plant.]

anile, *an'īl*, *ān'īl*, *adj.* old-womanish: imbecile. [L. *ānus*, *-ūs*, an old woman.]

animadvert, *an-im-ad-vûrt'*, *v.i.* (with *on*) to

express criticism of, usu. to censure.—*n.* **animadver'sion**, criticism, censure, or reproof. [L., to turn the mind to—*animus*, the mind, *ad*, to, *vertĕre*, to turn.]

animal, *an'im-ăl, n.* an organised being, having life, sensation, and voluntary motion, typically distinguished from a plant, which is organised and has life, but apparently not sensation or voluntary motion: one of the lower animals as opp. to man.—*adj.* of, of the nature of, derived from, or belonging to, an animal or animals: sensual.—*n.* **an'imalism**, the state of being actuated by animal appetites only: sensuality.—**animal spirits**, exuberance of health and life: boisterous behaviour. [L. *animal—anima*, air, breath, life.]

animalcule, *an-im-al'kūl, n.* a small animal: now one that cannot be seen by the naked eye:—*pl.* **animal'cules**, **animal'cula**. [L. *animaloulum*, dim. of *animal.*]

animate, *an'im-āt, v.t.* to give life to: to enliven: to actuate.—*adj.* (-*ăt*) living: possessing animal life.—*p.adj.* **an'imated**, lively: full of spirit: endowed with life: moving as if alive.—*n.* **animā'tion**, liveliness: vigour. [L. *animāre, -ātum*, to make alive—*anima*, life.]

animism, *an'im-izm, n.* the belief of primitive races that natural objects and phenomena have souls. [L. *anima*, life, the soul.]

animosity, *an-im-os'i-ti, n.* strong dislike: enmity. [L. *animōsitās—animōsus*, full of spirit; cf. *animus.*]

animus, *an'im-us, n.* intention: feeling of like or dislike: ill-will. [L. *animus*, spirit, soul.]

anise, *an'is, n.* an umbelliferous plant whose aromatic seeds are used in making cordials.—*n.* **an'iseed**, the seed of anise: a cordial prepared from it. [Gr. *anīson.*]

anker, *angk'ĕr, n.* an old measure for wines and spirits used in Northern Europe, varying considerably—that of Rotterdam = 8¼ imperial gallons. [Du.]

ankle, *angk'l, n.* the joint connecting the foot and leg.—*n.* **ank'let**, an ornament for the ankle. [O.E. *anclēow*; cf. Ger. *enkel*, and **angle**.]

anna, *an'ä, n.* an obsolescent coin worth one-sixteenth of a rupee. (Decimal coinage introduced India, 1957, Pakistan, 1961.) [Hindustani *ānā*.]

annals, *an'ălz, n.pl.* records of the events of successive years; historical records generally. —*n.* **ann'alist**, a writer of annals. [L. *annālis*, yearly—*annus*, a year.]

annat, *an'at, n.* **annates**, *an'āts, n.pl.* one year's income, or a specified portion of such, paid to the Pope by an ecclesiastic appointed to a new benefice. [L. *annāta*—L. *annus*, a year.]

anneal, *an-ēl', v.t.* to subject (glass or metals) to heat and gradual cooling: to heat in order to fix colours on (e.g. glass). [O.E. pfx. *an-*, on, *œlan*, to burn.]

annelid, *an'el-id, n.* any one of the **Annel'ida**, a class of animals comprising the red-blooded worms, having a long body composed of numerous rings. [L. *annellus, ānellus*, dim. of *ānulus*, a ring.]

annex, *a-neks', v.t.* to add to the end: to affix: to attach, as a penalty, &c.: to take possession of, esp. by virtue of superior might: (*coll.*) to appropriate.—*n.* (*an'eks*) something added: a

supplementary building—usually with the Fr. spelling **annexe**.—*ns.* **annexā'tion; annex'ure**, something added, esp. an addition to a document. [Fr. *annexer*—L. *annectĕre, annex-um—ad*, to, *nectĕre*, to tie.]

annihilate, *a-nī'hil-āt, v.t.* to reduce to nothing: to put out of existence: (*fig.*) to crush by look or word.—*ns.* **annihilā'tion**, reduction to nothing: utter destruction; **annihilā'tionism**, the theory that the soul (esp. of the unrepentant wicked) dies with the body. [L. *annihilāre, -ātum—ad*, to, *nihil*, nothing.]

anniversary, *an-i-vŭrs'ár-i, adj.* returning, happening, or commemorated, about the same date every year: pertaining to annual recurrence or celebration.—*n.* the day of the year on which an event occurred or is commemorated. [L. *anniversārius—annus*, a year, *vertĕre, versum*, to turn.]

anno Domini, *an'ō dom'in-ī, -ē*, in the year of our Lord (used as *n.* for 'advancing old age'). [L.]

annotate, *an'ō-tāt, v.t.* to make notes on, provide with notes.—*ns.* **annota'tion**, a note of explanation: comment; **ann'otator**, a writer of notes, a commentator. [L. *annotāre—ad*, to, *notāre, -ātum*, to mark.]

announce, *a-nowns', v.t.* to give public notice of: to intimate: to make known, be evidence of (e.g. *a familiar smell announced the goat's arrival*).—*ns.* **announce'ment; announc'er**, one who announces, esp. who introduces items of a radio or television programme. [O.Fr. *anoncer*—L. *annuntiāre—ad*, to, *nuntiāre*, to deliver news.]

annoy, *a-noi', v.t.* to molest: to vex: to tease: to harm, esp. in military sense:—*pr.p.* annoy'ing; *pa.p.* annoyed'.—*n.* **annoy'ance**, that which annoys: state of being annoyed. [O.Fr. *anoier*; noun, *anoi* (mod. *ennui*) perh. from L. phrase, *in odio*, as in 'est mihi *in odio*', 'it is to me hateful'.]

annual, *an'ū-ăl, adj.* yearly: coming every year: requiring to be renewed every year: performed in a year.—*n.* a plant that lives only one year: a series of books published yearly: any volume of the series.—*adv.* **ann'ually**. [L.L. *annuālis—annus*, a year.]

annuity, *a-nū'i-ti, n.* a payment falling due in each year during a given period, the capital sum not being returnable.—*n.* **annū'itant**, one who receives an annuity. [Fr. *annuité*—L.L. *annuitās, -ātis*—L. *annus*, year.]

annul, *a-nul', v.t.* to make null, to reduce to nothing: to cancel:—*pr.p.* annull'ing; *pa.p.* annulled'.—*n.* **annul'ment**, the act of annulling. [Fr. *annuler*—L.L. *annullāre*, to make into nothing—L. *ad*, to, *nullus*, none.]

annular, *an'ūl-ăr, adj.* ring-shaped: (of a tool) cutting in a ring.—*adj.* **ann'ulate(d)**, formed or divided into rings.—*n.* **ann'ulus** (*biol.*), a ring-shaped structure.—**annular eclipse**, an eclipse of the sun during which a ring-shaped part of its surface encircles the portion obscured by the moon. [L. *annulāris*, or *ānulāris—ānulus*, a ring—dim. of *ānus*, a rounding or ring.]

annunciation, *a-nun-si-ā'sh(ó)n, n.* the act of announcing: the Angel's salutation to the Virgin Mary (Luke i. 28): (*cap.*) the 25th of March,

Neutral vowels in unaccented syllables: *em'pér-ór*; for certain sounds in foreign words see p. ix.

Lady-day. [Fr. *annonciation*—L. *annuntiātiō, -ōnis*—*annuntiāre*. See **announce**.]

anode, *an'ōd, n.* the positive electrode by which an electric current enters an electrolytic cell, gas discharge tube, or thermionic valve—opp. to *cathode*: the electrode to which electrons flow.—*v.t.* **an'odise,** to give a protective or decorative coat to a metal by using it as an anode in electrolysis. [Gr. *anodos,* a way up—*ana,* up, *hodos,* way.]

anodyne, *an'ō-dīn, n.* a medicine allaying pain. [Gr. *anōdynos*—*an-,* priv., *odynē,* pain.]

anoint, *an-oint', v.t.* to smear with ointment or oil: to consecrate with oil.—**The Lord's Anointed** (*B.*), the Messiah: a king by divine right. [Fr. *enoint,* pa.p. of *enoindre*—L. *in,* on, *ung(u)ĕre,* to smear.]

anomaly, *a-nom'á-li, n.* irregularity: deviation from rule: something that deviates from rule.—*adj.* **anom'alous,** irregular: deviating from rule. [Gr. *anōmalos*—*an-,* priv., and *homalus,* even—*homos,* same.]

anon, *an-on', adv.* immediately: in a short time. [O.E. *on,* in, *ān,* one (instant).]

anon., *a-non',* a contr. of **anonymous.**

anonymous, *a-non'im-us, adj.* lacking a name: without the name of the author.—*n.* **anonym'ity,** the quality or state of being anonymous.—*adv.* **anon'ymously.** [Gr. *anōnymos*—*an-,* priv., and *onoma,* name.]

anorak, *an'ō-rak, n.* a Greenlander's fur coat: a hooded waterproof outer jacket. [Greenland word.]

anorexia, *an-ōr-ek'si-a, n.* want of appetite, esp. the pathological condition *anorexia nervosa.* [Gr. *an-,* priv., *orexis,* longing—*oregein,* to reach out.]

another, *an-uтн'ér, adj.* a different or distinct (thing or person): one more of the same kind: any other.—Also *pron.*—**one another,** each other. [Orig. **an other.**]

anserine, *an'sér-in,* or *-īn, adj.* relating to the goose or goose-tribe: stupid, silly. [L. *anserinus*—*anser,* goose.]

answer, *än'sér, n.* a reply or response: retaliation: the solution of a problem.—*v.t.* to reply or respond: to satisfy (e.g. one's requirements) or to correspond to (e.g. a description): to comply with or obey.—*v.i.* to reply: to act in response (to): to be accountable (for): to suffer (for—e.g. a fault): to yield a sufficiently good result: to correspond (to).—*adj.* **an'swerable,** able to be answered: accountable: correspondent (to), or proportionate (to).—*adv.* **an'swerably.** [O.E. *andswaru* (n.), *andswarian* (vb.)—*and-,* against, *swerian,* to swear.]

ant, *ant, n.* any of a family of small insects (belonging to the same order as bees, wasps, &c.) of proverbial industry, the emmet or pismire.—*ns.* **ant'-bear,** the largest species of ant-eater; **ant'-eat'er,** a family of edentate S. American quadrupeds, feeding chiefly on ants.—*n.pl.* **ant'-eggs,** pupae of ants.—*n.* **ant'-hill,** the hillock raised as nest by ants or by termites.—**white ant,** the termite (of a different order from the ant). [A contr. of **emmet.**]

antacid, *ant-as'id, n.* medicine that counteracts acidity. [Gr. *anti,* against, and **acid.**]

antagonist, *ant-ag'on-ist, n.* one who strives against another: an opponent: something that

has an opposite effect.—*v.t.* **antag'onise,** to counteract the action of: to arouse opposition in.—*n.* **antag'onism,** opposition: hostility.—*adj.* **antagonist'ic.**—*adv.* **antagonist'ically.** [Gr. *anti,* against, *agōn,* a contest.]

Antarctic, *ant-ärk'tik, adj.* opposite the Arctic: of, near, or relating to, the south pole or to south polar regions.—Also *n.* (usu. with **the**). [O.Fr. *antartique*—L. *antarcticus*—Gr. *antarktikos*—*anti,* opposite, and *arktikos.* See **Arctic.**]

ante-, *an-ti, pfx.* before (in place or time):—e.g. **an'tedor'sal** (*zool.*), situated in front of the dorsal fin; **an'te-Christ'ian,** before the days of Christianity. [L. *ante*; allied to Gr. *anti,* against.]

antecedent, *an-ti-sēd'ent, adj.* going before in time: prior (to).—*n.* that which precedes in time: (*gram.*) the noun or its equivalent to which a relative pronoun refers: (*math.*) the first of two terms that compose a ratio: (*pl.*) previous principles, conduct, history, &c.—*adv.* **anteced'ently.** [L. *antecēdens, -entis*—*ante,* before, *cēdĕre, cessum,* to go.]

antechamber, *an'ti-chām-bér, n.* an anteroom. [Fr. *antichambre*—*ante,* before, *camera,* a vault.]

antedate, *an'ti-dāt, v.t.* to date before the true time: to be previous to: to anticipate. [L. *ante,* before, and **date** (1).]

antediluvian, *an-ti-di-l(y)ōō'vi-án, adj.* existing or happening before Noah's Flood: antiquated.—*n.* one who lived before the Flood: one who has long survived a notable event. [L. *ante,* before, and *dīlūvium,* flood.]

antelope, *an'ti-lōp, n.* one of a group of swift and graceful ruminant quadrupeds, akin to the goat, but differing from it and resembling the deer in certain respects. [O.Fr. *antelop*—L. *antalopus*—Late Gr. *antholops.*]

antemeridian, *an-ti-me-ri'di-án, adj.* before midday or noon. [L. *antemeridiānus*—*ante meridiem,* before noon. See **meridian.**]

antenatal, *an-ti-nā'tál, adj.* before birth. [L. *ante,* before, and *natal.*]

antenna, *an-ten'a, n.* a feeler or horn in insects, crustaceans, and myriapods: a system of conductors used for the transmission and/or reception of electromagnetic waves: an aerial:—*pl.* **antenn'ae** (*-ē*), (*radio*) **antenn'as.** [L. the yard of a sail.]

antenuptial, *an-ti-nup'shál, adj.* before marriage. [L. *ante,* before, and **nuptial.**]

antepenult, *an-ti-pen-ult', n.* the syllable before the penult, i.e. the last syllable but two of a word, as *ag* in ant-*ag*-on-ist. [L. *ante,* before, and **penult.**]

anterior, *an-tē'ri-ór, adj.* before, in time or place: in front. [L. *anterior,* comp. of *ante,* before.]

anteroom, *an'ti-rōōm, n.* a room leading into another. [L. *ante,* before, and **room.**]

anthelmintic, *an-thel-mint'ik, adj.* and *n.* (a drug) destroying or expelling worms. [Gr. *anti,* against, and *helmins, -inthos,* a worm.]

anthem, *an'thém, n.* an antiphon (*obs.*): a musical composition for a church choir, commonly with solo passages, usually set to words from Scripture: any song of praise or gladness. [O.E. *antefn*—Gr. *antiphōna*—*anti,* in return, *phōnē*, the voice.]

anther, *an'thêr*, *n.* that part of the stamen in a flower which contains the pollen. [L. *anthēra*, a medicine extracted from flowers—Gr. *anthēros*, flowery—*anthos*, a flower.]

anthology, *an-thol'oj-i*, *n.* (*lit.*) a gathering or collection of flowers: a collection of Greek epigrams: any collection of choice pieces of poetry or prose.—*n.* **anthol'ogist**, one who makes, or has made, an anthology or anthologies. [Gr. *anthos*, a flower, *legein*, to gather.]

anthracite, *an'thra-sīt*, *n.* a kind of coal, rich in carbon, that burns nearly without flame, smell, or smoke. [Gr. *anthrakītēs*, coal-like—*anthrax*, coal.]

anthrax, *an'thraks*, *n.* a deadly disease, from which man is not immune, common among sheep and cattle, caused by a bacillus.—*adjs.* **anthracic** (*-thras'ik*), **anthracoid** (*an'thrakoid*). [L.,—Gr. *anthrax*, *-ăkos*, coal, a carbuncle.]

anthropo-, *an-thrō-po-* (or *-pō-*), in composition, man. [Gr. *anthrōpos*, man.]:—e.g. **anthropography** (*an-thrō-pog'ra-fi*), *n.* the branch of anthropology treating of the geographical distribution of man (*graphein*, to write).

anthropocentric, *an-thrō-pō-sent'rik*, *adj.* regarding man as the centre of the universe. [Gr. *anthrōpos*, man, and *kentron*, centre.]

anthropoid, *an'thrō-oid*, or *-thrōp'-*, *adj.* man-like: applied esp. to the highest apes.—*n.* an anthropoid ape. [Gr. *anthrōpos*, man, *eidos*, form.]

anthropology, *an-thrō-pol'oj-i*, *n.* the science of man in its widest sense, treating of his relation to the brutes, his evolution, the different races, &c.—*adj.* **anthropolog'ical.**—*n.* **anthropol'ogist**, one versed in anthropology. [Gr. *anthrōpos*, man, *logos*, discourse.]

anthropomorphism, *an-thrōp-o-mörf'izm*, *n.* the representation of a god in the form of man or with bodily parts: the ascription of human characteristics to other beings or to things.—*adj.* **anthropomorph'ic.** [Gr. *anthrōpos*, man, *morphē*, form.]

anthropophagy, *an-thrō-pof'a-ji*, *n.* cannibalism.—*n.* **anthropoph'agi**, cannibals.—*adj.* **anthropoph'agous** (*-a-gus*). [Gr. *anthrōpos*, man, *phagein*, to eat.]

anti-, *ant'i-*, *pfx.* against, in opposition to: rival: unlike, the reverse of like. It is used to form nouns and adjectives, as *antipole*, the opposite pole, *antipopular*, opposed to the popular cause, *anti-aircraft*, *anti-tank*, *anti-Fascist*, *anti-king*; **anticyclone**, **anticlimax** (see below). See also **antagonist**. [Gr. *anti*, against, instead of, &c.]

antibiotic, *an-ti-bī-ot'ik*, *adj.* and *n.* (a chemical compound) usu. of microbiological origin, e.g. penicillin, used to inhibit the growth of bacteria and other micro-organisms (particularly those causing disease). [Gr. *anti*, against, *biōtikos*, pertaining to life—*bios*, life.]

antibody, *an'ti-bod-i*, *n.* a defensive substance produced in an organism in response to the action of a foreign body such as the toxin of a parasite. [Gr. *anti*, against, and **body**.]

antic, *ant'ik*, *adj.* grotesque.—*n.* a fantastic figure: (*arch.*) a buffoon: (usu. in *pl.*) a fantastic action or trick, a caper.—*v.i.* to cut capers.

[It. *antico*, ancient—L. *antīquus*; orig. used of the fantastic decorations found in the remains of ancient Rome.]

Antichrist, *an'ti-krīst*, *n.* the great enemy of Christ, who, the early church believed, would soon appear: variously identified in later times with Mohammed, the Pope, Luther, Napoleon, and many others.—*adj.* **antichristian** (*-krist'-*). [Gr.; *anti*, against, and *Chrīstos*.]

anticipate, *an-tis'ip-āt*, *v.t.* to be beforehand with (another person or thing), to forestall: to use, spend, deal with, in advance: to foresee: to count upon as certain, to expect.—*v.i.* to speak, act, before the appropriate time.—*n.* **anticipa'tion**, act of anticipating: foretaste: previous notion: expectation.—*adj.* **antic'ipatory**. [L. *anticipāre*, *-ātum*—*ante*, before, *capĕre*, to take.]

anticlerical, *an-ti-kler'i-kál*, *adj.* opposed to the clergy or their power. [Gr. *anti*, against, and **clerical**. See **clergy**.]

anticlimax, *an-ti-klī'maks*, *n.* a sequence of words or phrases arranged in ascending order of emphasis, which, but for a ludicrously inappropriate final term, would form a climax: an ineffective or disappointing ending to a story or series of events. [Gr. *anti*, against (in this case = the reverse of), and **climax**.]

anticoagulant, *an-ti-kō-ag'ū-lánt*, *n.* drug that hinders clotting of blood.

anticyclone, *an-ti-sī'klōn*, *n.* a rotatory outflow of air from an area of high atmospheric pressure. [Gr. *anti*, against (in this case = the reverse of), and **cyclone**.]

antidote, *an'ti-dōt*, *n.* that which is given to counteract poison: (*fig.*) anything that prevents evil (with *against*, *for*, *to*).—*adj.* **anti'dotal**. [Gr. *antidotos*—*anti*, against, *didonai*, to give.]

antifreeze, *an'ti-frēz*, *n.* substance with low freezing point put into the radiator of an internal-combustion engine to prevent freezing up.

antigen, *an'ti-jen*, a substance that stimulates the production of an antibody. [Gr. *anti*, against, *gennoein*, to produce.]

anti-hero, *an'ti-hē'rō*, *n.* a principal character who lacks noble qualities and whose experiences are without tragic dignity.—*adj.* **anti-hero'ic.**

antihistamine, *an-ti-hist'á-mēn*, *n.* any of a group of drugs that prevent the action of histamines in allergic conditions.

antilog, *an'ti-log*, **antilogarithm**, *an-ti-log'arithm*, *n.* the numbers corresponding to a given logarithm, e.g. 50 is the antilog of 1.69897, which is the logarithm of 50 to the base 10. [Gr. *anti*, against (the reverse of), **logarithm**.]

antimacassar, *an-ti-ma-kas'ár*, *n.* a covering to protect chair-backs, &c., from Macassar oil or other grease, or for ornament. [Gr. *anti*, against, and **Macassar**.]

antimony, *an'ti-món-i*, *n.* a brittle, bluish-white metallic element (symbol S♭, see **stibium**; atomic no. 51), used in the arts and in medicine. [Through Fr. from L.L. *antimonium*.]

antineutron, *an-ti-nū'trón*, *n.* an uncharged particle that combines with the neutron, both particles being annihilated with much energy

Neutral vowels in unaccented syllables: *em'pér-ór*; for certain sounds in foreign words see p. ix.

released.

antinomian, *an-ti-nōm'i-án, n.* one who believes that Christians are emancipated by the gospel from the obligation to keep the moral law—also *adj.—n.* **antinom'ianism.** [Gr. *anti,* against, *nomos,* a law.]

antiparticle, *an'ti'pär'ti-kl, n.* the 'pair' of an elementary particle. (The elementary particles can occur in mutually destructive 'pairs'—particle and antiparticle.)

antipathy, *an-tip'ath-i, n.* opposition in feeling: rooted dislike (with *to, against, between*): incompatibility.—*adjs.* **antipathet'ic, -al.** [Gr. *anti,* against, *pathos,* feeling.]

anti-personnel, *an'ti-pér-són-el', adj.* intended to destroy military personnel (q.v.) or other persons. [**anti-, personnel.**]

antiphon, *an'tif-on, n.* a form of church music sung by two groups, each responding to the other—also **antiph'ony.**—*adj.* **antiph'onal,** pertaining to antiphony.—*n.* a book of antiphons or of anthems. [Gr.,—*anti,* against, in return, and *phōnē,* voice.]

antipodes, *an-tip'od-ēz, n.pl.* (also *sing.*) the inhabitants of the other side of the globe: places on the earth's surface diametrically opposite each other: the exact opposite of a person or thing.—*adj.* **antip'odal.** [Gr. *antipōdēs*—*anti,* opposite to, *pous, podos,* a foot.]

Antipope, *an'ti-pop, n.* a rival set up in opposition to the Pope held to be elected according to church law. [Gr. *anti,* against, and **Pope.**]

antiproton, *an-ti-prō'ton, n.* a negative proton.

antipyretic, *an-ti-pī-ret'ik, adj.* counteracting fever.—*n.* a remedy for fever. [Gr. *anti,* against, *pyretos,* fever.]

antiquary, *an'ti-kwăr-i, n.* one who studies or collects monuments and relics of the past.—*adj.* **antiquăr'ian,** connected with the study of antiquities.—*n.* an antiquary.—*n.* **antiquăr'ianism,** study of, or devotion to the study of, antiquities. [L. *antiquarius*—*antiquus,* old.]

antique, *an-tēk', adj.* ancient: old-fashioned: after the manner of the ancients.—*n.* anything very old: a piece of old furniture or other object sought by collectors.—*adj.* **an'tiquated,** grown old, or out of fashion: obsolete.—*ns.* **antique'ness; antiq'uity,** ancient times, esp. the times of the ancient Greeks and Romans: great age: (*pl.*) manners, customs, relics of ancient times.—**the antique,** ancient work in art: the style of ancient art. [L. *antīquus,* old—*ante,* before; influenced by Fr. *antique.*]

antirrhinum, *an-ti-rī'num, n.* the genus of plants to which snapdragon belongs. [Latinised from Gr. *antirrhinon*—*anti,* like, mimicking, *rhis,* gen. *rhīnos,* nose.]

antiscorbutic, *an-ti-skör-būt'ik, adj.* acting against scurvy.—*n.* a remedy for, preventive of, scurvy.

anti-semite, *an'ti-sem'īt,* or *-sēm'īt, n.* one who cherishes hatred of Jews or their influence.—*adj.* **anti-semit'ic.**—*n.* **anti-sem'itism.**

antiseptic, *an-ti-sept'ik, adj.* counteracting putrefaction (or, more accurately, infection with bacteria), esp. in a wound, by chemical agents.—*n.* a substance that destroys bacteria or prevents their growth.—*adv.* **antisept'ically.**—*n.* **antisep'sis,** antiseptic treatment. [Gr. *anti,* against, and *septikos,* rotten.]

antisocial, *an-ti-sō'shál, adj.* opposed to, or subversive of, the welfare of society.

antistrophe, *an-tis'trŏ-fe, n.* in ancient Greek drama, a stanza in the same metre as the strophe (q.v.), in singing which the chorus repeated the movements of the strophe in reverse order: the stanza of a choral ode alternating with, and exactly corresponding to, the strophe. [Gr. *antistrophē*—*anti,* against, and **strophe.**]

antithesis, *an-tith'i-sis, n.* a figure in which thoughts or words are balanced in contrast: opposition (with *between, of*): the direct opposite (with *of, to*):—*pl.* **antith'esēs** (*-sēz*).—*adjs.* **antithetic, -al** (*-thet'-*).—*adv.* **antithet'ically.** [Gr. *anti,* against, *tithenai,* to place.]

antitoxin, *an-ti-tok'sin, n.* a substance formed in the body that neutralises the action of toxins or bacterial poisons.—*adj.* **antitox'ic.**

anti-trade, *an'ti-trād, n.* a wind that blows in the opposite direction to the prevailing tradewind. [Gr. *anti,* against (here – the reverse of), and **trade.**]

antitype, *an'ti-tīp, n.* that which is pre-figured by the *type* (q.v.). [Gr. *anti,* against, like, and **type.**]

antler, *ant'lèr, n.* a bony outgrowth from the frontal bone of a deer: a branch of a stag's horn.—*adj.* **ant'lered.** [O.Fr. *antoillier.*]

antonym, *ant'ō-nim, n.* either of two words that have opposite meanings, as 'long' and 'short'. [Gr. *anti,* against, *onoma,* a name.]

antrum, *an'trum, n.* (anat.) a cavity, sinus. [L.,—Gr. *antron.*]

anus, *ān'us, n.* the lower orifice of the alimentary canal. [L. *ānus,* a ring.]

anvil, *an'vil, n.* an iron block on which smiths hammer metal into shape. [O.E. *anfilte.*]

anxious, *angk'shús, adj.* agitated by mingled hope and fear; uneasy; solicitous; causing anxiety.—*n.* **anxiety** (*ang-zī'i-ti*), state of being anxious: state of chronic apprehension as a symptom of mental disorder.—*adv.* **an'xiously.**—*n.* **an'xiousness.** [L. *anxius*—*ang(u)ĕre,* to press.]

any, *en'i, adj.* and *pron.* one indefinitely: some: whichever, no matter which.—*adv.* at all, to an appreciable extent.—*pron.* and *n.* **an'ybody,** any single person: a person of any account.—*adv.* **an'yhow,** in any way whatever: in any case, at least.—*ns.* and *prons.* **an'yone,** (or **any one**), anybody; **an'ything,** a thing indefinitely, as opposed to nothing—also *adv.,* any whit, to any extent.—*advs.* **an'yway, an'yways,** in any manner: anyhow: in any case; **an'ywhere,** in any place whatever; **an'ywise,** in any manner, to any degree.—**at any rate,** whatever may happen or have happened, at all events. [O.E. *ǣnig*—*ān,* one.]

Anzac, *an'zak, n.* an Australasian expeditionary soldier (1914-18). [Coined from initials of *Australian-New-Zealand Army Corps.*]

aorist, *ā'or-ist, n.* a tense, esp. in Greek, expressing simple past time. [Gr. *aoristos,* indefinite—*a-,* priv., and *horistos,* limited.]

aorta, *ā-ör'ta, n.* the great artery that rises from the left ventricle of the heart. [Gr. *aortē*—*aeirein,* to raise up.]

apace, *a-pās', adv.* at a quick pace: swiftly. [Pfx. *a-* (O.E. *on*), on, and **pace.**]

fāte, fär; mē, hûr (her); *mīne; mōte, för; mūte; mōōn, fŏŏt;* ᴛʜᴇn (then)

Apache, ä-pä′chā, *n.* a Red Indian of a group of tribes in Arizona, New Mexico, &c.: (*á-pash*) a ruffian in Paris or elsewhere.—**apache dance**, a dance showing brutality, real or simulated. [Fr., perh.—Amer. Indian *apachu*, enemy.]

apart, ɐ-pärt′, *adv.* separately: aside: asunder.—**apart from**, leaving out of consideration: **set apart**, to separate, consecrate. [Fr. *à part*—L. *à parte*, from the part or side.]

apartheid, ä-pärt′hāt, -pär′tīd, *n.* segregation of races. [Afrikaans.]

apartment, ɐ-pärt′ment, *n.* a separate room in a house: (usu. in *pl.*) a suite or set of rooms. [Fr. *appartement*, a suite of rooms forming a complete dwelling—L. *ad*, and *partīre*, to divide—*pars*, a part.]

apathy, ap′ath-i, *n.* want of feeling: absence of passion: indifference.—*adj.* **apathet′ic.**—*adv.* **apathet′ically.** [Gr. *a-*, priv., *pathos*, feeling.]

ape, āp, *n.* a monkey, esp. a large monkey without a tail or with a very short one and with many human traits—hence termed *anthropoid*: one who foolishly copies the behaviour of another as apes imitate men.—*v.t.* to imitate as an ape. [O.E. *apa*; Ger. *affe*.]

apeak, apeek, a-pēk′, *adv.* (*naut.*) vertical—the anchor is apeak when a ship's bow is directly over the spot where the anchor is embedded and the cable is, consequently, vertical. [Pfx. *a-* (O.E. *on*), on, and **peak**.]

aperient, a-pē′ri-ent, *adj.* opening: mildly purgative.—*n.* any laxative medicine. [L. *aperiens*, *-entis*, pr.p. of *aperīre*, to open.]

apéritif, ä-pär-i-tēf, *n.* an appetiser, esp. alcoholic. [Fr.,—L. *aperīre*, to open.]

aperture, a′pér-tyúr, -chúr, *n.* an opening: a hole. [L. *apertūra*—*aperīre*, *apertum*, to open.]

apetalous, a-pet′al-us, *adj.* (*bot.*) without petals. [Gr. *a-*, priv., and *petalon*, a petal.]

apex, ā′peks, *n.* the summit, climax, culminating point: the vertex of a triangle:—*pl.* **ā′pexes**, **apices** (ap′i-sēz, or āp′-). [L.]

aphaeresis, apheresis, a-fēr′i-sis, *n.* (*gram.*) the taking away of a letter or syllable at the beginning of a word, as in *adder* = *nadder* (see **adder**). [Gr. *aphairesis*, a taking away—*apo*, away, and *haireein*, to take.]

aphasia, a-fā′zi-a, *n.* loss of power to use or to interpret spoken language, caused by disease of the brain, or by emotional disturbance. [Gr. *a-*, priv., *phasis*, speech.]

aphelion, a-fē′li-on, *n.* the point of a planet's orbit farthest away from the sun:—*pl.* **aphē′lia.** [Gr. *apo*, from, *hēlios*, sun.]

apheresis. See **aphaeresis.**

aphesis, af′es-is, *n.* a special form of aphaeresis, in which an unaccented vowel at the beginning of a word is gradually lost, as in *squire* = *esquire.*—*adj.* **aphet′ic.** [Coined from Gr. *apo*, from, *hienai*, to send.]

aphis, af′is, ā′fis, **aphid**, *ns.* a plant-louse or greenfly, any of a large number of small insects that suck the juice of plants:—*pl.* **aphides** (af′i-dēz, ā′fi-dēz). [Ety. unknown.]

aphorism, af′or-izm, *n.* a brief, pithy saying, an adage.—*adj.* **aphoris′tic.** [Gr. *aphorizein*, to mark off by boundaries—*apo*, from, and *horos*, a limit.]

aphrodisiac, af-rō-diz′-i-ák, *adj.* exciting sexually.—Also *n.* [Gr. *aphrodīsiakos*—*Aphrodītē*,

the goddess of love.]

apiary, āp′i-ár-i, *n.* a place where bees are kept.—*n.* **ap′iarist**, one who keeps bees. [L. *apiārium*—*apis*, a bee.]

apices. See **apex.**

apiculture, ā′pi-cul-tyúr, -chúr, *n.* bee-keeping. [L. *apis*, bee, *cultura*, keeping—*colĕre*, *cultum*, to keep.]

apiece, a-pēs′, *adv.* to or for each one. [**a**, indefinite article, **piece**.]

apish, āp′ish, *adj.* ape-like. [**ape.**]

aplomb, a-plō′, *n.* perpendicularity: self-possession, coolness. [Fr. *aplomb*, perpendicular position—*à plomb*, according to plummet.]

apocalypse, a-pok′al-ips, *n.* (*cap.*) last book of the New Testament containing the 'revelation' granted to St John: any revelation or disclosure of the future.—*adjs.* **apocalypt′ic, -al.** [Gr., a revelation, an uncovering—*apo*, from, *kalyptein*, to cover.]

apocope, a-pok′o-pe, *n.* the cutting off of the last letter or syllable of a word as *th′* for *the*, *I* for O.E. *ic.* [Gr. *apo*, off, *koptein*, to cut.]

apocrypha, a-pok′rif-a, *n.* religious writings suitable for the initiated only, esp. those of unknown date and origin: (*cap.*) fourteen books included in the Septuagint but subsequently excluded from the Old Testament.—*adj.* **apoc′ryphal**, of doubtful authority: spurious: fabulous. [Gr., 'things hidden'—*apo*, from, *kryptein*, to hide.]

apodosis, a-pod′o-sis, *n.* (*gram.*) the principal clause in a conditional sentence, as opp. to the *protasis.* [Gr.—*apo*, back, *didonai*, to give.]

apogee, ap′o-jē, *n.* the greatest distance of the earth from any of the heavenly bodies, now restricted to the sun and moon, the sun's apogee corresponding to the earth's aphelion, and the moon's being the point of its orbit farthest from the earth.—opp. to *perigee.* [Gr. *apogaion*—*apo*, from, *gē*, the earth.]

apolitical, ā-pol-it′ik-ál, *adj.* indifferent to political affairs: uninvolved in politics.—*n.* **apol′iticism.** [Gr. *a-*, priv., and **political.**]

apologetic, -al, a-pol-o-jet′ik, -ál, *adj.* excusing: penitently acknowledging: said or written in defence.—*adv.* **apologet′ically.**—*n.* **apologet′ics**, the defensive argument, esp. the defence of Christianity. [See **apology.**]

apologue, ap′o-log, *n.* a fable, a short allegorical tale intended to convey a moral, esp. one in which the characters are animals or inanimate things. [Fr.,—Gr. *apologos*, a fable—*apo*, from, *logos*, speech.]

apology, a-pol′oj-i, *n.* a defence or justification: an expression of penitence: a poor substitute (with *for*).—*v.i.* **apol′ogīse**, to make excuse: to express regret for a fault.—*n.* **apol′ogist**, one who makes an apology: one who defends (a person or cause) by argument. [Gr. *apologia*—*apo*, from, *logos*, speech.]

apophthegm, apothegm, a′po-them, *n.* a pithy saying, more terse than an aphorism need be. [Gr. *apophthegma*—*apo*, forth, and *phthengesthai*, to utter.]

apoplexy, a′po-pleks-i, *n.* sudden loss of sensation and of motion, generally the result of haemorrhage in the brain or of thrombosis—also figuratively.—*adjs.* **apoplec′tic, -al**, pertaining to or causing apoplexy: suffering from,

Neutral vowels in unaccented syllables: em′pér-ór; for certain sounds in foreign words see p. ix.

30

or having the symptoms of, apoplexy. [Gr. *apoplēxia—apo*, away (with notion of completeness), *plēssein*, to strike.]

apostasy, apostacy, *a-pos'ta-si, n.* abandonment or desertion of one's religion, principles, or party.—*n.* **apost'ate**, one guilty of apostasy: a renegade from his faith.—*adj.* false: traitorous.—*v.i.* **apost'atise** (from, to). [Gr. *apostasis*, a revolt or 'standing away'—*apo, from, histanai*, to stand.]

a posteriori, *ā pos-te-ri-ō'rī, -ō'rī, adj.* applied to reasoning from experience, from effect to cause, as opposed to *a priori* reasoning (from cause to effect). [L. *a = ab*, from, *posteriori*, abl. of *posterior*, comp. of *posterus*, after.]

apostle, *a-pos'l, n.* one sent to preach the gospel: specially, one of the twelve disciples of Christ: the principal champion or supporter of a new system or cause.—*n.* **apos'tleship**, the office or dignity of an apostle.—*adjs.* **apostol'ic, -al** (*ap-os-tol'ik, -ál*).—*n.* **apostolic'ity** (*-is'i-ti*), the quality of being apostolic. **Apostles' Creed**, the oldest form of Christian creed that exists, early ascribed to the apostles; **apostle spoons**, silver spoons with handles ending in figures of the apostles; **Apostolic See**, that of Rome.—**apostolical succession**, the derivation of holy orders by continuous transmission from bishop to bishop from the time of the apostles to the present day. [Gr., one sent away—*apo*, away, *stellein*, to send.]

apostrophe, *a-pos'trof-e, n.* (*rhet.*) a sudden turning away from the ordinary course of a speech to address some person or object present or absent.—*v.t.* **apos'trophise**, to address by apostrophe. [Gr. *apostrophē.*]

apostrophe, *a-pos'trof-e, n.* a mark (') showing the omission of a letter or letters in a word, also a sign of the modern Eng. genitive or possessive case. The final *e* is sounded by confusion with preceding word. [Gr. *apostrophos*, turned away.]

apothecary, *a-poth'ek-ár-i, n.* (*arch.*) one who dispenses drugs and medicines: (*obs.*) a medical practitioner.—**apothecaries' weight**, the system of weights used before 1969 in dispensing drugs. [Through Fr. and L., from Gr. *apothēkē*, a storehouse—*apo*, away, *tithenai*, to place.]

apothegm. See **apophthegm**.

apotheosis, *a-po-the-ō'sis, n.* deification: the glorification of a principle or person: (loosely) release from earthly life. [Gr. *apotheōsis—apo*, away from (what he was), *theos*, a god.]

appal, *a-pöl', v.t.* to terrify, dismay:—*pr.p.* appal'ling; *pa.p.* appalled'.—*p.adj.* **appall'ing**, shocking.—*adv.* **appall'ingly**. [Perh. from O.Fr. *apal-(l)ir*, to wax pale, also to make pale.]

appanage, apanage, *ap'an-ij, n.* the assignment of lands as a provision for younger sons of kings and nobles: any perquisite: an adjunct or attribute. [Fr. *apanage*—L. *ad*, to, *panis*, bread.]

apparat, *ä'pa-rät*, the political machine of the Communist party. [Russ., apparatus.]

apparatus, *ap-ar-ā'tus* (also *-a'tus*), *n.* things prepared or provided, material: set of tools: equipment. [L.—*ad*, to, *parātus* (*parāre*), prepared.]

apparel, *a-par'él, n.* covering for the body,

dress.—*v.t.* to dress, adorn:—*pr.p.* appar'elling; *pa.p.* appar'elled. [O.Fr. *apareiller*—L. *par*, equal, like.]

apparent, *a-pār'ent, a-par'ént, adj.* that may be seen: evident: seeming.—*adv.* **appar'ently**. [Through Fr., from L. *appārens, -entis*, pr.p. of *appārēre*, to appear.]

apparition, *a-par-ish'(ó)n, n.* an appearance or manifestation: a visionary appearance, a ghost.—*adj.* **appari'tional**. [Fr.,—L. *appāritiō, -ōnis—appārēre*; see **appear**.]

apparitor, *a-par'it-ór, n.* an officer who attends on a court, or on a magistrate, to execute orders [L. See **appear**.]

appeal, *a-pēl', v.i.* to call, make application, have recourse (with *to*): to refer (to a witness or superior authority): to make earnest request: to be pleasing (with *to*): to transfer a lawsuit to a higher court.—*n.* act of appealing: an earnest request: transference of a lawsuit: attractive power.—*adj.* **appeal'able**. [O.Fr. *apeler* L. *appellāre, ātum*, to address, call by name; also to appeal to.]

appear, *a-pēr', v.i.* to become visible: to come into view: to be published: to present oneself formally: to be manifest: to seem, esp. as opp. to *to be*.—*n.* **appear'ance**, the act of appearing: that which appears: form, aspect: outward look or show: an apparition. [Through Fr., from L. *appārēre—ad*, to, *pārēre, pāritum*, to come forth.]

appease, *a-pēz', v.t.* to pacify, esp. by granting demands: to propitiate: to allay.—*n.* **appease'ment**, the action of appeasing: the state of being appeased. [O.Fr. *apeser*, to bring to peace—L. *pax, pācis*, peace.]

appellant, *a-pel'ánt, n.* one who makes an appeal from a lower court of justice to a higher: a suppliant.—*adj.* **appell'ate**, relating to appeals. [See **appeal**.]

appellation, *ap-el-ā'sh(ó)n, n.* that by which anything is called: a distinctive name or title.—*n.* **appell'ative**, a common, as distinguished from a proper, name.—*adj.* common, as distinguished from proper: of or pertaining to the giving of names. [Fr.,—L. See **appeal**.]

append, *a-pend', v.t.* to hang (one thing) to another: to add.—*n.* **append'age**, something appended.—*ns.* **appendec'tomy**, more commonly **appendicec'tomy** (*-dis-*), removal of the vermiform appendix; **appendici'tis**, inflammation of the vermiform appendix; **append'ix**, something appended or added: supplementary information at the end of a book or document: (*anat.*) a prolongation, projection, esp. the vermiform appendix:—*pl.* **append'ixes, append'ices**.—**appendix vermiformis, or vermiform appendix**, a tubular prolongation of the large intestine in man and some other animals. [L. *ad*, to, *pendēre*, to hang.]

apperception, *ap-er-sep'sh(ó)n, n.* the mind's perception of itself as a conscious agent. [L. *ad*, to, and **perception**.]

appertain, *ap-ér-tān', v.i.* to belong (to): to be the property or attribute of (with *to*).—*p.adj.* **appertain'ing**, proper, appropriate (to). [Through Fr., from L. *ad*, to, *pertinēre*, to belong. See **pertain**.]

appetency, *ap'et-ens-i, n.* a seeking after: desire,

fāte, fär; mē, hûr (her); *mīne, mōte, för; mūte; mōōn, fŏŏt;* THEN (then)

appetite

approve

especially sensual desire.—Also **app′etence.** [L. *appetens, -entis,* pr.p. of *appetĕre.* See **appetite.**]

appetite, *ap′et-īt, n.* sensation of physical need and desire: natural desire: desire for food: hunger (with *for*).—*v.t.* **app′etise,** to create or whet appetite.—*n.* **appetis′er,** something that whets the appetite. [Through Fr., from L. *appetītus*—*appetēre*—*ad,* to, *petĕre, petītum,* to seek.]

applaud, *a-plöd′, v.t.* to praise by clapping the hands: to praise loudly: to extol.—*n.* **applause′,** praise loudly expressed, esp. by clapping: acclamation.—*adj.* **applaus′ive.**—*adv.* **applaus′ively.** [L. *applaudĕre*—*ad,* to, *plaudĕre, plausum,* to clap.]

apple, *ap′l, n.* the fruit of the **app′le-tree,** any of a genus of trees of the rose order: extended to other fruits, as *pineapple, oak apple*: a pome.—**apple of the eye,** the pupil of the eye: something especially dear; **apple-pie order,** complete order. [O.E. *æppel*; cf. Ger. *apfel, O.N. epli,* Ir. *abhal, W. afal.*]

Appleton layer, *ap′l-tón lā′ér,* an ionised region in the atmosphere that acts as a reflector of radio waves. [From the physicist Sir Edward *Appleton.*]

appliqué, *a-plē′kā, n.* work applied to, or laid on, another material, either of metal-work or of lace or the like. [Pa.p. of Fr. *appliquer.*]

apply, *a-plī′, v.t.* to set, place, bring close (to): to bring to bear on: to devote (oneself, to a pursuit).—*v.i.* to have reference (to): to have recourse (to): to make request (for an office, &c.): to be relevant:—*pr.p.* apply′ing; *pa.p.* applied (*-plīd′*).—*n.* **appli′ance,** anything applied: means used, as a piece of apparatus.—*adj.* **app′licable,** that may be applied: appropriate, relevant (to).—*adv.* **app′licably.**—*ns.* **applicability** (*ap-li-ka-bil′iti*), **app′licableness.**—*ns.* **app′licant,** a candidate: a petitioner; **applica′tion,** the act of applying, as the administration of a remedy: diligent effort: attentive study: the process of bringing a general truth to bear on a particular case: the conclusion thus deduced: relevancy: a request (for office, &c.).—**applied science,** science put to use, generally industrial, not studied simply for its own sake—opp. to *pure science.* [O.Fr. *aplier*—L. *applicāre, -ātum*—*ad,* to, *plicāre, -ātum,* to fold.]

appoggiatura, *a-pod-jä-tōō′ra, n.* (*mus.*) a grace-note taking its time at the expense of the following note. [It. *appoggiare,* to lean.]

appoint, *a-point′, v.t.* to fix: to prescribe: to assign: to select for an office or situation.—*p.adj.* **appoint′ed,** fixed: furnished (as in *well-appointed*).—*n.* **appoint′ment,** settlement: engagement, rendezvous: situation, office: (*pl.*) equipment. [O.Fr. *apointer*—L.L. *appunctāre*—L. *ad,* to, *punctum,* a point. See **point.**]

apportion, *a-pōr′, -pör′-, sh(ó)n, v.t.* to portion out: to divide in due proportion.—*n.* **appor′tionment.** [L. *ad,* to, and **portion.**]

apposite, *ap′oz-it, adj.* suitable, appropriate.—*adv.* **app′ositely.**—*ns.* **app′ositeness; apposi′tion,** the act of adding: state of being placed beside or against: (*gram.*) the placing of one noun beside another, in the same case or relation, in order that the second may explain

or limit the first. [L. *appositus,* pa.p. of *apponĕre*—*ad,* to, *pōnĕre,* to put.]

appraise, *a-prāz′, v.t.* to set a price on: to value, esp. with a view to sale: (*fig.*) to estimate the amount and quality of (anything).—*ns.* **apprais′al, appraise′ment,** a valuation, estimation of quality; **apprais′er.** [Late in appearing: for some time used in the same sense as *praise.*]

appreciate, *a-prē′shi-āt, v.t.* to estimate justly: to esteem highly: to raise the price of.—*v.i.* to rise in value.—*adj.* **appre′ciable,** capable of being estimated: perceptible.—*adv.* **appre′ciably.**—*n.* **apprecia′tion,** appraisement: generous esteem: a sympathetic literary essay: increase in value.—*adjs.* **appre′ciative, appre′ciatory,** implying appreciation. [L. *appretiātus,* pa.p. of *appretiāre*—*ad,* to and *pretium,* price.]

apprehend, *ap-re-hend′, v.t.* to lay hold of: to arrest: to perceive by the senses: to grasp by the intellect: to understand: to fear.—*adj.* **apprehens′ible**—*n.* **apprehen′sion,** act of apprehending: arrest: mental grasp: ability to understand: fear.—*adj.* **apprehen′sive,** pertaining to sensuous and mental apprehension: timid: anxious.—*n.* **apprehens′iveness.** [L. *apprehendĕre*—*ad,* to, *prehendĕre, -hensum,* to lay hold of.]

apprentice, *a-prent′is, n.* one bound to another to learn a trade or art: a novice.—*v.t.* to bind as an apprentice.—*n.* **apprent′iceship,** the state of an apprentice: the term for which he is bound. [O.Fr. *aprentis*—*aprendre,* to learn—L. *apprehendĕre.* See **apprehend.**]

apprise, *a-prīz′, v.t.* to give notice to, to inform. [Fr. *apprendre,* pa.p. *appris*—L. *apprehendĕre.* See **apprehend.**]

approach, *a-prōch′, v.i.* to draw near: to draw near (to): to approximate (to).—*v.t.* to come near to: to come near in quality, value, &c.: to be nearly equal to: to open discussion with, address (a person) with the purpose of getting him to act in a particular way.—*n.* a drawing near (*lit.* and *fig.*): a means of access (to), way leading (to—*lit.* and *fig.*): approximation: (usually *pl.*) advances, overtures.—*adj.* **approach′able.** [O.Fr. *aprochier*—L.L. *adpropiāre*—L. *ad,* to, *prope,* near.]

approbation, *ap-rob-ā′sh(ó)n, n.* formal sanction: approval.—**sent on approbation,** sent without obligation to buy unless the article is approved as satisfactory. [Fr.,—L. *approbātiō, -ōnis*—*approbāre.* See **approve.**]

appropriate, *a-prō′pri-āt, v.t.* to take as one's own: to set apart for a purpose.—*adj.* (*-āt*) set apart for a particular purpose: peculiar (to): suitable.—*adv.* **appro′priately.**—*ns.* **appro′priateness; appropria′tion,** the act of appropriating: assignment (of revenue) to a specified purpose.—**appropriation bill, clause,** a parliamentary bill, or clause, allotting revenue to some special purpose. [L. *appropriāre, -ātum*—*ad,* to, *proprius,* one's own.]

approve, *a-prōōv′, v.t.* to show, demonstrate (also reflexively, e.g. *to approve oneself a liar*): to sanction or ratify: to commend.—*v.i.* to be satisfied with (with *of*).—*n.* **approv′al,** the act of approving: approbation.—*adv.* **approv′ingly.**—**approved school** (1933—Scotland

---

Neutral vowels in unaccented syllables: *em′pér-ór*; for certain sounds in foreign words see p. ix.

1937—to 1969), a state boarding school for young law-breakers or for young people pronounced to be in need of care and protection.—**on approval**, on approbation. [O.Fr. *aprover*—L. *approbāre*—*ad*, to, and *probāre*, to test or try—*probus*, good.]

approximate, *a-proks'im-āt*, *adj.* nearest or next: approaching correctness.—*v.t.* to bring very near.—*v.i.* to come very near, to approach closely. *adv.* **approx'imately.**—*n.* **approximā'tion**, an approach: a result in mathematics not rigorously exact, but so near the truth as to be sufficient for a given purpose. [L. *approximāre*, *-ātum*—*ad*, to, *proximus*, nearest, superl. of *prope*, near.]

appurtenance, *a-pûr'ten-äns*, *n.* that which appertains (to something else) as an appendage or accessory.—*adj.* and *n.* **appur'tenant**. [Anglo-Fr. *apurtenance*, through L.L. from L. *ad*, *pertinēre*. See **appertain**.]

après-ski, apres-, *a-pre-skē*, *-prā-*, *n.* (evening period of) amusements after skiing—Also *adj.* [Fr.]

apricot, *ā'* or *a'pri-kot*, *n.* an orange-coloured fruit of the plum kind—older form **a'pricock**. [Port. *albricoque* (Fr. *abricot*)—Ar. *al-birqūq*—*birqūq* is a corr. of Late Gr. *praikokion*—L. *praecoquum* or *praecox*, early ripe: the form is perh. due to a fancied connection with L. *aprīcus*, sunny.]

April, *ā'pril*, *n.* the fourth month of the year.—*n.* **A'pril-fool**, the victim of a hoax on the 1st of April, All Fools' Day. [Fr. *Avril*—L. *Aprīlis*.]

a priori, *ā prī-ō', -ō', rī*, a term applied to reasoning from what is prior, logically or chronologically, e.g. reasoning from cause to effect, from a general principle to its consequences: presumptive. See **a posteriori**. [L. *a*, *ab*, from *priōri*, abl. of *prior*, preceding.]

apron, *ā'pron*, *n.* a cloth or piece of leather worn before one to protect the dress: a short cassock, part of the official dress of a bishop, &c.: applied to a number of things resembling an apron in shape or use, including things made by man from hard material, as a hard surface in an airfield, a concrete or other surface in a river, &c.: (also **apron stage**) a stage or part of a stage projecting into the auditorium.—*adj.* **a'proned**, wearing an apron. [O.Fr. *naperon*—*nappe*, cloth, tablecloth—L. *mappa*, a napkin. *A napron* became an *apron*: cf. **adder**.]

apropos, *a-pro-pō'*, *adv.* appropriately: in reference to (with *of*, sometimes to).—*adj.* to the purpose: opportune. [Fr. *à propos*—*à*, to, *pro-pos*, purpose. See **purpose**.]

apse, aps, *n.* an arched recess, esp. at the east end of the choir of a church.—*adj.* **ap'sidal.** [From **apsis**.]

apsis, *ap'sis*, *n.* one of the two extreme points in the orbit of a planet, one at the greatest, the other at the least distance from the sun: one of the two corresponding extreme points in the orbit of a satellite round its planet:—*pl.* **apsides** (*ap'si-dēz*).—*adj.* **ap'sidal**. [L. *apsis*—Gr. *hapsis*, a connection, an arch—*haptein*, to connect.]

apt, apt, *adj.* liable, ready, or prone (to): suitable, appropriate: quick, clever (at).—*n.* **apt'itude**, fitness: readiness: capacity, talent (for).—*adv.* **apt'ly**.—*n.* **apt'ness.** [L. *aptus*, fit;

cog. with Gr. *haptein*, to connect.]

apterous, *ap'tér-us*, *adj.* without wings. [Gr. *a-*, priv., *pteron*, a feather, wing.]

apteryx, *ap'tér-iks*, *n.* the kiwi of New Zealand, a wingless bird about the size of a large hen. [Gr. *a-*, priv., *pteryx*, wing.]

aqua fortis, *a'kwa för'tis* (or *ā'*), *n.* nitric acid.—**a'qua vi'tae** (*vītē*), an old name for alcohol, used of brandy, whisky, &c.; cf. Fr. *eau de vie* (brandy), and *usquebaugh* (q.v.). [L. *aqua*, water, *fortis*, strong, *vītae*, of life.]

aqualung, *ak'wa-lung*, *n.* a light-weight self-contained diving apparatus with compressed-air supply carried on the back. [L. *aqua*, water, and **lung**.]

aquamarine, *a-kwa-ma-rēn'* (or *ā-*), *n.* a pale green beryl.—*adj.* bluish-green, sea-coloured. [L. *aqua*, water, *marīna*—*mare*, the sea.]

aquaplane, *ak'wa-plān*, *n.* a board on which one stands and is towed behind a motor-boat.—Also *v.i.* [L. *aqua*, water, and **plane** (1).]

aquarium, *a-kwā'ri-um*, *n.* a tank or series of tanks for keeping aquatic animals: a building in which such tanks are exhibited:—*pl.* **aquā'riums, aquā'ria**. [L.—*aqua*, water.]

Aquarius, *a-kwā'ri-us*, *n.* the water-bearer, the eleventh sign of the zodiac. [L.—*aqua*, water.]

aquatic, *a-kwat'ik*, *adj.* relating to water: living or growing in water.—*n.pl.* **aquat'ics**, amusements, sports, or exercises on or in the water. [L. *aquāticus*—*aqua*, water.]

aquatint, *a'kwa-tint*, or *-ēn*, *adj.* a mode of etching on copper with aqua fortis (q.v.), by which imitations are produced of drawings in Indian ink, &c. [It. *acqua tinta*—L. *aqua*, water, *tingēre*, *tinctum*, to wet, to colour.]

aqueduct, *ak'we-dukt*, *n.* an artificial channel for conveying water: a bridge conveying such a channel, or a canal, across a valley. [L. *aqua*, water, *ducēre*, *ductum*, to lead.]

aqueous, *ā'kwe-us*, *adj.* watery: deposited by water. [L. *aqua*, water.]

aquiline, *ak'wil-in*, or *-īn*, *adj.* relating to or like the eagle: curved or hooked, like an eagle's beak. [L. *aquila*, eagle.]

Arab, *ar'ab*, *n.* one of the Semitic inhabitants of Arabia and adjacent countries: an Arabic-speaking Muslim: an Arabian horse.—*adj.* of or belonging to Arabia.—*adj.* **Arāb'ian**, relating to Arabia.—*n.* a native of Arabia.—*adj.* **Ar'abic**, relating to Arabia, or to its language.—*n.* language of Arabia.—**Arabic numerals**, the characters 0, 1, 2, 3, etc.—**street Arab**, neglected or homeless child. [L. *Arabs*, *Arabis*—Gr. *Araps*.]

arabesque, *ar'ab-esk*, *adj.* after the manner of Arabian designs.—*n.* a fantastic style of decoration, used by the Spanish Moors, consisting of foliage and other parts of plants curiously intertwined: a posture in ballet dancing in which one leg is stretched out backwards parallel with the ground and the body is bent forward from the hips. [Fr.,—It. *arabesco*; *-esco* corresponding to Eng. *-ish*.]

arable, *ar'a-bl*, *adj.* fit for ploughing or tillage: under cultivation. [L. *arābilis*—*arāre*, cog. with Gr. *aroein*, to plough, O.E. *erian*, Ir. *araim*.]

Aramaic, *ar-a-mā'ik*, *adj.* relating to *Aramaea*, or *Aram* (roughly modern Syria) or its language—also **Aramean** (*-mē'án*).—*n.* any of

fāte, fär; mē, hûr (her); *mīne, mōte, för; mūte, mōōn, fŏŏt;* THen (then) a group of Semitic languages (including that spoken by Christ) once used in this and neighbouring areas in commerce and government. [Gr. *Aramaios*.]

Araucaria, *ar-ö-kā′ri-a*, *n.* the monkey-puzzle genus, coniferous trees of S. America and Australasia. [*Arauco*, a province in S. Chile.]

arbiter, *är′bit-ér*, *n.* one chosen by parties in controversy to decide between them: a judge: an umpire: anyone having absolute power of decision or absolute control (with *of*):—*fem.* **ar′bitress**.—*n.* arbit′rament, -rement, decision by an arbiter: a decision.—*v.i.* **ar′bitrate**, to act as an arbiter: to decide.—*ns.* **arbitrā′tion; ar′bitrātor** (same as **arbiter**):—fem. **ar′bitrātrix**. [L.—*ar* = ad, to, *bitēre* (cog. with Gr. *bainein*), to go or come; signifying one who comes to look on, a witness, a judge.]

arbitrary, *är′bi-trár-i*, *adj.* not bound by rules: despotic, absolute: capricious, unreasonable.—*adv.* **ar′bitrarily**.—*n.* **ar′bitrariness.** [L. *arbitrārius*, arbiter.]

arboreal, *är-bōr′, -bōr′i-ál*, *adj.* living in trees: of tree-like character.—*adj.* **arboresc′ent**, growing or formed like a tree.—*ns.* **arboresc′ence**, tree-like growth; **arborē′tum**, a place in which specimens of trees and shrubs are cultivated:—*pl.* **arborē′ta.**—*n.* **ar′boriculture**, forestry, the culture of trees, esp. timbertrees.—*adj.* **arboricul′tural.**—*n.* **arboricul′turist.** [L. *arbor*, a tree.]

arbour, *är′bór*, *n.* an enclosed seat in a garden, covered with branches of trees, plants, &c.: a bower. [L. *herbārium*—*herba*, grass, herb; confused with L. *arbor*, tree.]

arbute, *är′būt*, **arbutus**, *är′būt-us*, *n.* a genus of evergreen shrubs of the heath family, one of which is known as the strawberry-tree. [L. *arbūtus*, akin to *arbor*, tree.]

arc, *ärk*, *n.* a part of the circumference of a circle or other curve: angular measurement (e.g. 60 *seconds of arc*): (*elect.*) a luminous discharge of electricity across a gap between two conductors or terminals.—*v.i.* to form an electric arc.—*ns.* **arc-lamp, arc-light**, a lamp in which the source of light is an electric arc between carbon electrodes. [O.Fr.,—L. *arcus*, a bow.]

arcade, *ärk-ād′*, *n.* a walk arched over: a covered passageway lined with shops on both sides. [Fr.,—L.L. *arcāta*, arched—L. *arcus*, a bow.]

Arcadian, *är-kād′i-án*, *adj.* pertaining to *Arcadia* (*poet.* **Ar′cady**), a rural district in Greece: pastoral: simple, innocent.

arcanum, *ärk-ān′um*, *n.* a secret: a mystery:—*pl.* **arcan′a.** [L.—*arcānus*—*arca*, a chest.]

arch, *ärch*, *n.* a curved structure so built that the stones or other component parts support each other by mutual pressure and can sustain a load: of the foot, the part from heel to toes of the body structure, normally having an upward curve.—*v.t.* to cover with an arch: to curve, raise in an arch.—*n.* **arch′way**, an arched or vaulted passage, esp. that leading into a castle.—**dropped, fallen, arch**, a flattened foot arch. [O.Fr.,—L. *arca*, chest, and *arcus*, bow.]

arch, *ärch*, *adj.* clever, sly: mischievous, roguish.—*adv.* **arch′ly.**—*n.* **arch′ness.** [Derived from the prefix *arch-*, in its use in words such as *arch*-rogue, &c.]

arch-, *ärch* (*ärk* in words directly from Greek), a prefix, now chiefly as an intensive in an odious sense: the first or chief, as **arch′en′emy; arch′-fiend; arch′-traitor**, a chief traitor, sometimes applied esp. to the devil, or to Judas. [O.E. *arce, ærce*, through L. from Gr. *archi*, cog. with *archein*, to begin, be first, rule.]

Archaean, *är-kē′án*, *adj.* belonging to the earliest geological period, or the earliest known group of rocks—either the Pre-Cambrian, or the lowest part of the Pre-Cambrian. [Gr. *archaios*, ancient—*archē*, beginning.]

archaeology, *ärk-e-ol′oj-i*, *n.* a knowledge of ancient art, customs, &c.: the science that studies the extant relics of ancient times.—*adj.* **archaeolog′ical.**—*adv.* **archaeolog′ically**.—*n.* **archaeol′ogist.** [Gr. *archaios*, ancient—*archē*, beginning, *logos*, discourse.]

archaic, -al, *ärk-ā′ik, -ál*, *adj.* ancient: oldfashioned, no longer in common use, esp. of language.—*n.* **arch′aism**, an archaic word or phrase. [Gr. *archaikos*—*archaios*, ancient—*archē*, beginning.]

archangel, *ärk-ān′jél*, *n.* an angel of the highest order.—*adj.* **archangel′ic.** [**arch-**, chief, and **angel.**]

archbishop, *ärch-bish′óp*, *n.* a chief bishop: a metropolitan bishop who superintends the other bishops in his province, and also exercises episcopal authority in his own diocese.—*n.* **archbish′opric.** [**arch-**, chief, and **bishop.**]

archdeacon, *ärch-dē′kón*, *n.* a chief deacon: the ecclesiastical dignitary next under the bishop in the supervision of a diocese or part of it.—*ns.* **archdeac′onry**, the office, jurisdiction, or residence of an archdeacon; **archdeac′onship**, the office of an archdeacon.—*adj.* **archidiaconal** (*är-ki-dī-ak′ón-ál*), pertaining to an archdeacon. [**arch-**, chief, and **deacon.**]

archdiocese, *ärch-dī′o-sēz*, *n.* the diocese of an archbishop. [**arch-**, chief, and **diocese.**]

archduke, *ärch-dūk′*, *n.* the title of certain early reigning dukes of importance, and of princes of the imperial house of Austria:—*fem.* **archdūch′ess**.—*adj.* **archdū′cal**.—*ns.* **archdüch′y, archdūke′dom**, the territory of an archduke or archduchess. [**arch-**, chief, and **duke.**]

archer, *ärch′ér*, *n.* one who shoots with a bow and arrows:—*fem.* **arch′eress**.—*n.* **arch′ery**, the art of shooting with the bow. [O.Fr. *archier*—L. *arcārium*—*arcus*, a bow.]

archetype, *ärk′e-tīp*, *n.* the original pattern or model, a prototype.—*adj.* **archetyp′al.** [Gr. *archetypon*—*archi-*, first, *typos*, a model.]

archiepiscopal, *ärk-i-ep-is′kop-ál*, *adj.* belonging to an archbishop.—*ns.* **archiepis′copacy, archiepis′copate**, dignity or province of an archbishop. [L.L. *archiepiscopus*—*archi-*, chief. See **episcopal**.]

archimandrite, *är-ki-man′drīt*, *n.* in the Greek Church, the superior of a monastery. [Late Gr. *archimandritēs*—pfx. *archi-*, first, and *mandra*, an enclosure, a monastery.]

Archimedian, *ärk-i-mē-dē′an*, or *-mē′di-án*, *adj.* pertaining to *Archimedes*, a celebrated Greek mathematician of Syracuse (c. 287-212 B.C.).

Neutral vowels in unaccented syllables: *em′pér-ór*; for certain sounds in foreign words see p. ix.

34

archipelago, ärk-i-pel′a-gō, *n.* the chief sea of the Greeks, i.e. the Aegean Sea: a sea abounding in small islands: a group of such islands:—*pl.* **archipel′ago(e)s.** [An Italian compound from Gr. *archi-,* chief, *pelagos,* sea.]

architect, ärk′i-tekt, *n.* one who designs buildings and superintends their erection: a maker: (*cap.*) the Creator.—*adj.* **architectonic** (*ärk-i-tek-ton′ik*), pertaining to architecture: constructive· controlling: pertaining to the systematisation of knowledge.—*n.* **architec′ture** (*-tyūr, -chūr*), art or science of building: structure: distinctive style of building (e.g. *Gothic architecture*).—*adj.* **architec′tural.** [Gr. *architektōn—archi-,* chief, and *tektōn,* a builder.]

architrave, ärk′i-trāv, *n.* (*archit.*) the lowest division of the entablature (q.v.): collective name for the jambs, lintels, and other parts surrounding a door or window. [It., from Gr. *archi-,* chief, and L. *trabs, trabis,* a beam.]

archives, ärk′īvz, *n.pl.* the place in which government records are kept: public records.—*n.* **arch′ivist** (*-iv-*), a keeper of archives or records. [Fr.,—Gr. *archeion,* magisterial residence—*archē,* beginning, power, government.]

archon, ärk′on, *n.* one of nine chief magistrates of ancient Athens. [Gr. *archōn—archein,* to be first, to rule.]

Arctic, ärk′tik, *adj.* relating to the constellation the Great Bear: of, near, or relating to the north pole or to north polar regions: extremely cold.—*n.* (usu. *cap.* and with **the**) the area lying north of the Arctic Circle or north of the timber line.—**Arctic Circle,** an imaginary circle round the north pole, at a distance of about 23½ degrees. [O.Fr. *artique*—L. *arcticus*—Gr. *arktikos—arktos,* a bear.]

ardent, ärd′ent, *adj.* burning· fiery: passionate; zealous: fervid.—*adv.* **ard′ently.**—*n.* **ard′our,** warmth of passion or feeling: eagerness.—Also **ard′ency.**—**ardent spirits,** distilled alcoholic liquors, whisky, brandy, &c. [L. *ardens, -entis,* pr.p. of *ardēre,* to burn.]

arduous, ärd′ū-us, *adj.* steep: difficult to accomplish: laborious.—*adv.* **ard′uously.**—*n.* **ard′uousness.** [L. *arduus,* high; cog. with Celt. *ard,* high.]

are, är, *n.* the unit of the metric land measure, equals 100 sq. metres. [Fr.,—L. *ārea.*]

are, är, the plural of the present indicative of the verb *to be.* [Old Northumbrian *aron,* of Scand. origin. This form ousted the older, O.E. *sind, sindon.* Both are cog. with Gr. *eisin,* L. *sunt,* &c.]

area, ā′rē-a, *n.* a surface or an enclosed space: (*geom.*) the superficial extent of any figure: the sunken space around the basement of a building: (*fig.*) extent or scope. [L. *ārea.*]

areca, ar′e-ka, ar-ē′ka, *n.* a genus of palm, one species of which bears the so-called betel-nut (q.v.). [Port.,—Dravidian (q.v.) *adekka.*]

arena, a-rē′na, *n.* part of the ancient amphitheatre strewed with sand and used for the combats of gladiators and wild beasts: a place or sphere of contest or action of any kind.—*adj.* **arenaceous** (*a-re-nā′shŭs*), sandy.—**arena stage,** a stage which can have the audience all around it. [L. *arēna,* sand.]

Areopagus, ar-e-op′ag-us, *n.* 'Mars' Hill', on which the supreme court of ancient Athens was held: the court itself.—*n.* **Areop′agite,** a member of the Areopagus. [Gr. *Areios pagos,* hill of Ares or Mars.]

argent, ärj′ent, *adj.* and *n.* silver, or like silver, silvery-white. [Fr.,—L. *argentum,* silver.]

argil, är′jil, *n.* clay, esp. potter's.—*adj.* **argilla-ceous** (*är-jil-ā′shŭs*), of the nature of clay. [L. *argilla*—Gr. *argilos,* white clay—*argēs,* white.]

argol, är′gol, *n.* a hard crust formed on the sides of wine-vessels, yielding cream of tartar and tartaric acid. [Prob. conn. with Gr. *argos,* white.]

argon, är′gon, *n.* a rare gaseous element (symbol A; atomic no. 18), discovered in the atmosphere in 1894, so named from its chemical inactivity. [Gr. *argon* (neut.), inactive—*a-,* priv., *ergon,* work.]

Argonaut, är′go-nöt, *n.* one of those who sailed in the ship *Argo* in search of the golden fleece: (*ar′gonaut*) the paper-nautilus. [Gr. *Argō,* and *nautēs,* a sailor.]

argosy, är′go-si, *n.* a large merchant-vessel richly laden, esp. one of Ragusa or Venice: also figuratively. [Prob. from It. *Ragusea,* a ship belonging to Ragusa on the Adriatic.]

argot, är′got, *n.* slang, cant, originally that of thieves and vagabonds. [Fr.]

argue, ärg′ū, *v.t.* to prove, or to maintain, by reasoning: to discuss, dispute: to persuade (into, out of): to be evidence of, imply.—*v.i.* to offer reasons: to dispute:—*pr.p.* arg′üing; *pa.p.* arg′üed.—*adj.* **arg′üable,** capable of being argued.—*v.i.* **arg′ufy** (*-fī*; *coll.*), to wrangle.—*n.* **arg′ument,** a reason put forward in support of an assertion or opinion: a series of such reasons: discussion, dispute: theme of discourse: an outline of the substance of a book: (*math.*) a quantity upon which another depends (e.g. an independent variable upon which the value of a function depends): the value in a mathematical or similar table against which a dependent value is to be found.—*n.* **argumentā′tion,** an arguing or reasoning.—*adj.* **argu-ment′ative,** characterised by argument: addicted to arguing.—*adv.* **argument′atively.**—*n.* **argument′ativeness.** [O.Fr. *arguer*—L. *argūtāre,* frequentative of *arguĕre,* to prove.]

Argus, ärg′us *n.* a person as vigilant as *Argus,* who in fable had a hundred eyes. [Gr.—*argos,* bright.]

aria, ä′ri-a, *n.* an air, in a cantata, oratorio, or opera, for one voice supported by instruments. [It., from root of **air.**]

Arian, ā′ri-àn, *adj.* pertaining to *Arius* of Alexandria (died 336), who denied the divinity of Christ, and whose doctrine was condemned as heresy by the Church under the leadership of Athanasius (296-373).—*n.* one who adheres to the doctrines of Arius: a Unitarian.—*n.* **A′rianism,** the doctrines of the Arians.

arid, ar′id, *adj.* dry, parched (*lit.* and *fig.*): barren.—*ns.* **arid′ity, ar′idness.** [L. *āridus.*]

Aries, ā′ri-ēz, *n.* the Ram, the first of the signs of the zodiac. [L.]

aright, a-rīt′, *adv.* in a right way, rightly. [Pfx. *a-* (O.E. *on*), on, and **right.**]

arise, a-rīz′, *v.i.* to rise up: to come into view: to come into being, or into notice: to spring,

aristocracy

around

originate (from):—*pa.t.* arose'; *pa.p.* arisen (*a-riz'n*). [O.E. *ārīsan*—pfx. *ā-*, inten., and *rīsan*. See **rise**.]

aristocracy, *ar-is-tok'ras-i, n.* government by a privileged class: the nobility, the upper classes generally: persons noted for exceptional distinction in any sphere.—*n.* **aristocrat** (*ar'is-to-krat,* or *ar-is'-*), one who belongs to, or has the characteristics of, or favours, an aristocracy.—*adjs.* **aristocrat'ic, -al,** belonging to aristocracy: characteristic of an aristocrat.—*adv.* **aristocrat'ically.** [Gr. *aristos,* best, and *kratos,* power.]

Aristotelian, *ar-is-to-tē'li-an, adj.* relating to *Aristotle,* the Greek philosopher, or to his philosophy.

arithmetic, *ar-ith'met-ik, n.* the science of numbers: the art of reckoning by figures: a treatise on reckoning: a book of number problems to be worked.—*adj.* **arithmet'ical.**—*adv.* **arithmet'ically.**—*n.* **arithmetician** (*-ish'an*), one skilled in arithmetic.—**arithmetical progression,** a series of numbers that increase or diminish by a common difference, e.g. 7, 10, 13, 16 . . ., or 12, 10½, 9, 7½ . . . . [Gr. *arithmētikē* (*technē*), (art) relating to numbers—*arithmos,* number.]

ark, *ärk, n.* a chest or coffer: (*B.*) the sacred chest in which the Tables of the Law were kept (Ex. xxv. 10-16): the vessel in which Noah escaped the Deluge (Gen. vi.-viii.). [O.E. *arc*—L. *arca,* a chest—*arcēre,* to guard.]

arles, *ärlz,* or *ärlz, n.* part payment made in confirmation of a bargain or engagement. [Scot. and northern Eng.; M.E. *erles*—prob. through O.Fr. from L. *arrha.*]

arm, *ärm, n.* the limb extending from the shoulder to the hand: anything projecting from the main body, as an inlet of the sea, a rail or support on a chair: (*fig.*) power.—*n.* **arm'-chair,** a chair with arms.—*adj.* (of a critic, &c.) without practical knowledge, doctrinaire.—*ns.* **arm'ful,** as much as the arms can hold; **arm'-hole,** the hole in a garment through which the arm is put.—*adj.* **arm'-less.**—*ns.* **arm'let,** a band round the arm; **arm'-pit, arm'pit** (see **pit**).—**at arm's length,** at a distance (*lit.* and *fig.*), not showing friendliness or familiarity; **with open arms,** with hearty welcome. [O.E.; cognate with L. *armus,* the shoulder-joint, Gr. *harmos,* a joint.]

arm, *ärm, n.* a weapon: a branch of the military service:—*pl.* **arms,** weapons of offence and defence: war, hostilities: heraldic bearings.—*v.t.* **arm,** to furnish with weapons: to fortify.—*v.i.* to take arms.—*adj.* **armed** (*ärmd,* or *ärm'-id*).—*n.* **small'-arm** (see **small**).—**arms race,** competition among nations in building up armaments.—**College of Arms,** the Heralds' College; **to lay down arms,** to surrender; **up in arms,** armed for combat: defiant, protesting hotly. [Through Fr., from L. *arma*; cog. with **arm** (1).]

armada, *är-mä'da, är-mä'da, n.* a fleet of armed ships, esp. the Spanish Armada of 1588. [Sp., —L. *armāta*—*armāre,* to arm.]

armadillo, *ärm-a-dil'ō, n.* a family of small American quadrupeds, having the body armed with bony plates:—*pl.* **armadill'os.** [Sp., dim. of *armado,* armed.]

Armageddon, *är-ma-ged'ón, n.* the great symbolical battlefield of the Apocalypse (Rev. xvi. 16)—also **Har-Magedon:** any momentous struggle between the powers of good and evil. [Heb.—(*H*)*ar* (of doubtful meaning), and *Megiddo,* a famous battlefield (Judges v. 19; 2 Kings xxiii. 29, 30).]

armament, *ärm'a-mént, n.* forces armed or equipped for war: munitions of war, esp. the guns with which a ship is armed. [L. *armāmenta*—*arma.*]

armature, *är'ma-tyùr, n.* armour: anything serving as a defence: a piece of iron connecting the two poles of a permanent magnet to reduce demagnetisation: a moving part in a magnetic circuit to indicate the presence of electric current: that part of a direct-current machine in which, in the case of a generator, the electromotive force is produced, or, in the case of a motor, the torque is produced. [L. *armātūra*—*armāre,* to arm.]

Armenian, *ar-mē'ni-án, adj.* belonging to *Armenia* in Western Asia.—*n.* a native of Armenia: a member of the Armenian branch of the Christian Church: the language of Armenia.

Arminian, *ar-min'yán, n.* a follower of *Arminius* (1560-1609), a Dutch divine, who denied the Calvinistic doctrine of predestination.—*adj.* holding the doctrines of Arminius.—*n.* **Armin'ianism.**

armistice, *ärm'ist-is, n.* a suspension of hostilities, a truce. [Fr.,—L. *armistitium.* from L. *arma,* arms, *sistěre,* to stop.]

armour, *ärm'ór, n.* defensive arms or dress: defensive steel- or iron-plating on a ship of war or a military vehicle: collectively, vehicles, esp. tanks, with armour and guns, and the forces that fight in them.—*adjs.* **arm'oured,** protected by armour: fought by armoured vehicles (e.g. *armoured battle*); **armō'rial,** belonging to armour, or to the arms of a family.—*ns.* **arm'our-bear'er,** one who carried a superior's armour; **arm'ourer,** a maker or reparer of, or one who has the charge of, armour.—*adj.* **arm'our-plat'ed.**—*n.* **arm'oury,** the place in which arms are made or kept: a collection of ancient armour.—**armorial bearings,** the design in a coat of arms. [O.Fr. *arm-(e)ure*—L. *armātūra*—*arma,* arms.]

army, *ärm'i, n.* a large body of men armed for war and under military command: a body of men banded together in a special cause: a great number.—*ns.* **army ant,** any of several kinds of stinging ants which move about in vast numbers; **arm'y-corps** (*-kōr*), a large division of the army in the field. [Fr. *armée*—L. *armāta,* fem. pa.p. of *armāre,* to arm.]

aroma, *a-rō'ma, n.* sweet smell: the odorous principle of plants: (*fig.*) flavour or peculiar charm.—*adj.* **aromat'ic,** fragrant: spicy: (*chem.*) said of a large class of compounds having a nucleus similar to that of benzene, many of which are odorous. [Through Fr. and L., from Gr. *arōma, -atos,* spice.]

arose, *a-rōz', pa.t.* of **arise.**

around, *a-rownd', prep.* on all sides of: (*U.S.*) round about.—*adv.* on every side: in a circle: (*U.S.*) round, all about.—**get around to** (*coll.*), to reach the point of (doing something); **have**

Neutral vowels in unaccented syllables: *em'pér-ór*; for certain sounds in foreign words see p. ix.

been around (*coll.*), to be experienced, sophisticated. [Pfx. *a-* (O.E. *on*), on, and **round**.]

arouse, *a-rowz′, v.t.* to rouse: to waken into activity (e.g. *to arouse suspicion, resentment*). [Pfx. *ā-*, inten., and **rouse** (1).]

arpeggio, *är-pej-(y)ō, n.* (*mus.*) a chord of which the notes are given, not simultaneously, but in rapid succession. [It. *arpeggiare*, to play upon the harp—*arpa*, harp.]

arquebus, *är′kwi-bus, n.* an old-fashioned hand-gun.—Also **har′quebus**. [Fr. *arquebuse* Du. *haakbus—haak*, hook, and *bus*, box, barrel of a gun.]

arrack, *ar′ak, n.* an intoxicating spirit used in the East. [Ar. *'araq*, juice.]

arraign, *a-rān′, v.t.* to call (one) to account: to put (a prisoner) on trial: to accuse publicly.— *n.* **arraign′ment**. [O.Fr. *aresnier*—Low L. *arrationāre*—L. *ad*, to, *ratiō, -ōnis*, reason.]

arrange, *a-rānj′, v.t.* to set in a rank or row: to put in order: to settle: (*mus.*) to adapt (a composition) for performance by instruments or voices other than those for which it was originally written.—*v.i.* to come to an agreement (with a person).—*n.* **arrange′ment**, act of arranging: classification: settlement: a piece of music arranged as described above. [O.Fr. *arangier—à* (L. *ad*, to), and *rangier, rengier—rang*, rank.]

arrant, *ar′ant, adj.* downright, notorious (used in a bad sense). [A variant of **errant**, which acquired an abusive sense from its use in phrases like 'arrant thief'.]

arras, *ar′as, n.* tapestry, esp. a screen hung round the walls of rooms. [From *Arras* in Northern France, where it was first made.]

array, *a-rā′, n.* order: dress: equipage: (*math.*) an arrangement of terms in rows and columns, (esp. if square) a matrix: *v.t.* to put in order, to arrange: to dress, adorn, or equip. [O.Fr. *arei*, array, equipage—L. *ad*, and a Gmc. root found in Eng. **ready**.]

arrear, *a-rēr′, n.* (*arch.*) that which is in the rear: that which remains unpaid or undone (usu. *pl.*): (*sing.* or *pl.*) condition of being behindhand. [O.Fr. *ar(i)ere*—L. *ad*, to, *retro*, back, behind.]

arrest, *a-rest′, v.t.* to stop: to seize: to catch the attention of: to apprehend by legal authority.—*n.* stoppage: seizure by warrant.—**arrester gear**, shock-absorbing transverse cables on an aircraft carrier's deck for the **arrester hook**, put out by an alighting aircraft, to catch on. [O.Fr. *arester*—L. *ad*, *restāre*, to stand still.]

arrière pensée, *ar-yer′ pä′sā′, n.* mental reservation. [Fr.]

arrive, *a-rīv′, v.i.* to reach any place: to attain to (any object, *lit.* or *fig.*, e.g. a conclusion, a solution with *at*): (*coll.*) to achieve success, recognition.—*n.* **arriv′al**, the act of arriving: a person or thing that arrives. [O.Fr. *ariver*—L. *ad*, to, *rīpa*, a bank.]

arriviste, *a-rē-vēst′, n.* a person 'on the make', a parvenu, a self-seeker. [Fr.]

arrogate, *ar′og-āt, v.t.* to claim as one's own: to claim proudly or unduly: to ascribe, attribute, or assign (to another).—*ns.* **arr′ogance**, **arr′ogancy**, undue assumption of importance.—*adj.* **arr′ogant**, claiming too much: overbearing.—

adv. **arr′ogantly**. [L. *arrogāre*—*ad*, to, *rogāre*, *-ātum*, to ask, to claim.]

arrondissement, *a-rō-dēs′mä, n.* a subdivision of a French department, comprising a number of communes. [Fr.—*arrondir*, to make round.]

arrow, *ar′ō, n.* a straight, pointed weapon, made to be shot from a bow: any arrow-shaped object.—*n.* **arr′ow-head**, the head or pointed part of an arrow: an aquatic plant native to England.—*adj.* **arr′ow-head′ed**, shaped like the head of an arrow. *n.* **arr′ow-shot**, the distance traversed by an arrow.—*adj.* **arr′owy**, of, or like, arrows. [O.E. *earh, arwe*; cog. with L. *arcus.*]

arrowroot, *ar′ō-rōōt, n.* a starch obtained from the roots of certain tuberous tropical plants, much used as food for invalids and children. [From its use by South American Indians as an antidote to arrow-poisoning.]

arsenal, *är′se-nál, n.* a magazine or manufactory for naval and military weapons and ammunition: (*fig.*) a storehouse. [It. *arzenale, arsenale* (Sp., Fr. *arsenal*)—Ar. *dār açcinā'ah*, workshop.]

arsenic, *ärs′(e-)nik, n.* a metallic element (symbol As; atomic no. 33): a highly poisonous compound of this metal and oxygen (also **white arsenic**).—*adjs.* **arsen′ic, -al**, **arse′nious**, composed of or containing arsenic— *arsenical* has the most general meaning; *arsenic* properly denotes compounds in which the valency of the arsenic is 5, *arsenious* those in which it is 3, but *arsenic* is often used less exactly, e.g. *arsenic trioxide* (As_2O_3 arsenious oxide), *arsenic pentoxide* (As_2O_5—arsenic oxide). [Gr. *arsenikon*, yellow orpiment (q.v.) fancifully associated with *arsēn*, male, and the alchemists' notion that metals have sex.]

arsis, *är′sis, n.* the accented syllable in English metre:—*pl.* **ar′ses**. [L.,—Gr. *arsis—airein*, to lift.]

arson, *ärs′on, n.* the crime of wilfully setting fire to houses or other inflammable property. [O.Fr. *arson*—L. *ardēre, arsum*, to burn.]

art, *ärt*, 2nd pers. sing. of the present tense of the verb *to be*. [O.E. *eart*.]

art, *ärt, n.* human skill as opposed to natural agency (e.g. *produced by art not by nature*): skill, knack acquired by study and practice (e.g. *the art of making a little go a long way*): taste and skill, artistry (e.g. *the art of the painter, dramatist, in creating this effect*): the rules, methods, general principles of a branch of learning or an activity (e.g. *the art of war*): (*arch.*) learning as opposed to natural ability: a branch of learning, esp. (in *pl.*) used of certain departments or faculties of academic studies, as in the phrase 'Master of Arts': a trade or craft: contrivance, cunning.—*adj.* of, for, concerned with, painting, &c.: intended to be decorative: produced with studied artistry, not spontaneously.—*adj.* **art′ful**, cunning: showing art.—*adv.* **art′fully**.—*n.* **art′fulness**.—*adj.* **art′less**, simple, guileless.—*adv.* **art′lessly**.—*n.* **art′lessness**.—*adj.* **art′y** (*coll.*), aspiring to be artistic.—*n.* **art form**, a set arrangement in poetry or music: an accepted medium of artistic expression.—*adj.* **art′y-craft′y**, self-consciously artistic.—**art and part**

(e.g. *to be art and part in*), orig. legal, as, 'to be concerned in either by *art* (in contriving) or by *part* (in actual execution)': now (loosely) participating, sharing. For **fine arts, useful arts,** see **fine.** [L. *ars, artis.*]

artery, är′tėr-i, *n.* a tube or vessel that conveys blood from the heart: any main channel of communication.—*adj.* **artēr′ial.** [L.,—Gr. *artēr-ia,* orig. the windpipe most probably.]

artesian, är-tē′zhȧn, -zi-ȧn, *adj.* pertaining to a type of well in which water rises of itself in a borehole by internal pressure—in early use at *Artois* (L. *Artesium*) in the north of France.

arthritis, är-thrī′tis, *n.* inflammation of a joint.—*adj.* **arthritic** (-thrit′ik). [Gr. *arthritikos*—*arthron,* a joint.]

Arthropoda, är-throp′od-a, *n.pl.* a phylum (q.v.) of the animal kingdom, with bodies consisting of segments bearing jointed appendages—including crustaceans, spiders, insects, &c.—*n.* **ar′thropod,** one of the Arthropoda. [Gr. *arthron,* joint, *pous,* gen. *podos,* a foot.]

Arthurian, är-thū′ri-ȧn, *adj.* relating to King *Arthur,* a ruler of the Britons.

artichoke, är′ti-chōk, *n.* a thistle-like plant with large scaly heads, parts of which are succulent and edible.—**Jerusalem artichoke,** a totally different plant, a species of sunflower, bearing tubers like those of the potato, Jerusalem being a corr. of It. *girasole* ('turn-sun') sunflower. [Old It. *articiocco*—Old Sp. *alcarchofa*—Ar. *al-kharshōfa, al-kharshūf.*]

article, är′ti-kl, *n.* a separate element, member, or part of anything: a particular object or commodity: a single clause or term: (*pl.*) an agreement made up of such clauses, as 'articles of apprenticeship', &c.: a section of any document: a literary composition in a newspaper, magazine, encyclopaedia, &c., dealing with a particular subject: (*gram.*) the name given to the adjectives *the* (**definite article**) and *a* or *an* (**indefinite article**).—*v.t.* to draw up, or bind by, articles.—**in the article of death,** at the point of death; **the Thirty-nine Articles,** the articles of religious belief finally agreed upon by the bishops and clergy of the Church of England in 1562. [L. *articulus,* a little joint—*artus,* a joint.]

articular, är-tik′ū-lär, *adj.* of, belonging to, the joints. [L. *articulāris*—*artus,* a joint.]

articulate, är-tik′ūl-āt, *adj.* jointed: capable of speech, or of expressing one's thoughts clearly: distinct, clear, intelligible.—*v.t.* (-āt) to joint: to form into distinct sounds, syllables, or words.—*v.i.* to speak distinctly.—*adv.* **artic′ulately.**—*ns.* **artic′ulateness; articulā′tion,** a joining as of the bones: part between two joints: distinctness, or distinct utterance: a consonant; **articulated vehicle,** one made easier to manoeuvre by having a detachable cab section which, when attached, can move at an angle to the rest. [L. *articulāre, -ātum,* to furnish with joints, to utter distinctly.]

artifact, artefact, är′ti-fakt, *n.* (*archaeology*) a product of human workmanship, esp. a very simple one, as opposed to an object shaped by natural agency. [L. *ars, artis,* art, *facěre, factum,* to make.]

artifice, är′ti-fis, *n.* a contrivance: a trick: contrivance: trickery.—*n.* **artificer** (ar-tif′is-ér) a

workman: an inventor.—*adj.* **artificial** (ärt-i-fish′ȧl), made by art: not natural: feigned: not natural in manner.—*n.* **artificial′ity**—*adv.* **artific′ially.**—*ns.* **artificial kidney,** apparatus used in cases where the kidney functions badly to remove, by dialysis, harmful substances from the blood; **àrtificial respiration,** stimulation of respiration manually or mechanically by forcing air in and out of the lungs. [L. *artificium*—*ars, artis,* art, *facěre,* to make.]

artillery, är-til′ér-i, *n.* offensive weapons of war, esp. cannon, &c.: the men who manage them, a branch of the military service: gunnery.—*ns.* **artill′erist,** one skilled in artillery; **artill′eryman,** a soldier of the artillery. [O.Fr. *artillerie*—*artiller,* to arm; through a supposed L.L. *artillāre*—L. *ars, artis,* art.]

artisan, ärt-i-zan′, or ärt′-, *n.* one skilled in any art or trade: a mechanic. [Fr.,—It. *artigiano*—L. *artītus,* skilled in arts—*ars, artis,* art.]

artist, ärt′ist, *n.* one who practises an art, esp. one of the fine arts, as painting, sculpture, engraving, or architecture.—*adjs.* **artist′ic, -al,** showing skill and taste.—*adv.* **artist′ically.**—*n.* **art′istry,** artistic occupation or quality or ability. [Fr. *artiste,* It. *artista*—L. *ars, artis,* art.]

artiste, är-tēst′, *n.* a public performer: an adept in a manual art. [Fr.]

arum, ā′rum, *n.* a genus of monocotyledons—represented in Britain by the cuckoo-pint.—**arum lily** (or **calla lily**), a decorative house plant of the same family as the arums. [L.,—Gr. *aron.*]

Aryan, ä′ri-ȧn, är′yȧn, *adj.* relating to the family of peoples otherwise called Indo-European, or Indo-Germanic (q.v.), or to their languages; now usu. confined to the Indian and Persian branch of these peoples and languages: (as used by the Nazis—q.v.) non-Jewish. [L. *ariānus,* belonging to *Ariana* or *Aria* (Gr. *Areia*), the east part of Ancient Persia—Sans. *Arya* (cf. *Irān,* Persia), often traced to a root *ar,* plough.]

as, az, *adv.* and *conj.* (denoting comparison or consequence) in that degree, so far, e.g. *as* (adv.) good *as* (conj.) new, *as* (adv.) soon *as* (conj.) I can, *as* (adv.) much *as* (conj.) to say, so good *as* (conj.) to do.—*conj.* since, because: when, while: for instance: in like manner.—*rel. pron.* (correctly used only after *such, same*), that, who, whom, which, e.g. such a man *as* I, do the same *as* he did.—**as concerning, as regards, as to, as for,** so far as concerns; **as from,** from (a specified time); **as it were,** as if it were; **as well,** besides, too; **as well as,** equally with: in addition to. [A worndown form of *all-so,* O.E. *all-swā,* wholly so.]

asafoetida, as-a-fēt′i-da, *n.* an evil-smelling medicinal gum-resin, procured by drying the juice of the root of a Persian plant. [Pers. *aza,* mastic, and L. *foetida,* stinking.]

asbestos, az-best′os, *n.* an incombustible siliceous mineral, of a fine fibrous texture, resembling flax and capable of being woven: also, commercially, a serpentine. [Gr., unquenchable—*a-,* priv., *sbestos*—*sbennunai,* to quench; used as noun for various substances including asbestos.]

ascend, a-send′, *v.i.* to climb or mount up: to rise

Neutral vowels in unaccented syllables: *em′pér-ór*; for certain sounds in foreign words see p. ix.

(*lit.* or *fig.*): to go backwards in the order of time.—*v.t.* to climb or go up: to mount.—*adj.* **ascend'ant, -ent,** rising: above the horizon: predominant.—*n.* (*astrol.*) the part of the ecliptic rising above the horizon at the time of one's birth—it was supposed to have commanding influence over one's life (hence, **in the ascendant,** supreme, in a dominating position): great influence.—*ns.* **ascend'ancy,** controlling influence—also **ascend'ency; ascen'sion,** a rising or going up; **Ascen'sion-day,** the festival held on Holy Thursday, ten days before Whitsunday, to commemorate Christ's ascension to heaven; **ascent',** act, or way, of ascending: rise (*lit.* and *fig.*): slope or gradient. [L. *ascendĕre, ascensum*—*ad,* to, *scandĕre,* to climb.]

ascertain, *as-ér-tān',* *v.t.* to find out, obtain certain knowledge of.—*adj.* **ascertain'able.**—*n.* **ascertain'ment.** [O.Fr. *acertener*—*à,* to; see **certain.**]

ascetic, *a set'ik, n.* one who trains himself to endure severe bodily hardship as a religious discipline: any extremely abstemious person.—*adjs.* **ascet'ic, -al,** excessively rigid: austere.—*n.* **ascet'icism.** [Gr. *askētikos*—*askētēs,* one who trains himself by exercises—*askeein,* to work, take exercise, (*eccles.*) to mortify the body.]

ascribe, *a-skrīb', v.t.* to attribute, impute: to assign.—*adj.* **ascrib'able.**—*n.* **ascrip'tion,** act of imputing: any expression of ascribing, or any formula for such. [L. *ascrībĕre, -scriptum*—*ad,* to, *scrībĕre,* to write.]

asepsis, *a-sep'sis, n.* (*med.*) the exclusion of putrefying bacteria from the field of surgical operation by the use of sterilised dressings and instruments.—*adj.* **asep'tic,** not liable to decay or putrefaction: conducive to asepsis.—*n.* **asepticism** (*a-sep'tis-izm*) aseptic principle, *sēpsis*—*sēpein,* cause to decay.]

asexual, *a-seks'ū-ál, adj.* without sex: (*bot.,* of reproduction) of any type not depending on a sexual process or a modified sexual process—including cell-division, spore-formation, &c. [Gr. *a-,* priv., and **sexual.**]

ash, *ash, n.* a well-known timber tree, or its wood, which is white, tough, and hard.—*adj.* **ash'en.** [O.E. *æsc;* Ger. *esche,* O.N. *askr.*]

ash, *ash, n.* (often in *pl.*) the dust or remains of anything burnt: (in *pl.*) the remains of the human body when burnt: a symbol of repentance or of sorrow: an emblem of pallor (e.g. *pale as ashes*).—*adjs.* **ash'en, ashy.**—*ns.* **ashblonde,** a person with fair hair the colour of ashes (also *adj.*); **Ash-Wednesday** (*ash-wenz'dā*), the first day of Lent, so called from the R.C. custom of sprinkling ashes on the head.—**the Ashes,** the ashes of English cricket, which, according to a mock 'In Memoriam' notice in the *Sporting Times* in 1882, the Australians, having beaten England, carried home with them—supposed ever since to be fought over by the two teams. [O.E. *asce;* O.N. *aska.*]

ashamed, *a-shāmd', adj.* affected with shame. [Pa.p. of old verb *ashame*—pfx. *a-,* **shame.**]

ashlar, *ash'lár,* or **ashler,** *n.* stone accurately hewn or squared to given dimensions: a thin

facing of squared stones to cover brick or rubble walls. [O.Fr. *aiseler*—L. *axillāris*—*axilla,* dim. of *axis, assis,* axle, plank.]

ashore, *a-shōr', shōr', adv.* on shore. [Pfx. *a-* (O.E. *on*), on, and **shore.**]

Asiatic, *ā-zhi-at'ik,* or *āsh-i-at'ik, adj.* belonging to *Asia.*—*n.* a native or inhabitant of *Asia.*—Also **Asian** (*āzh'yán,* or *āsh'i-án*).

aside, *a-sīd', adv.* on or to one side: privately.—*n.* words spoken in an undertone: words spoken by an actor which the other persons on the stage are supposed not to hear.—**set aside,** to quash (a judgment). [Pfx. *a-,* (O.E. *on*), on, and **side.**]

asinine, *as'in-īn, adj.* of or like an ass.—*n.* **asininity** (*-in'i-ti*). [L. *asinīnus*—*asinus,* ass.]

ask, *äsk, v.t.* to request, beg: inquire: inquire of: invite.—*v.i.* to make request or inquiry (for, about).—**asking price,** that set by the seller of an article before bargaining has begun. [O.E. *āscian, ācsian.*]

askance, *a skans', **askant,** a skant', adv.* sideways: awry: obliquely.—**eye, look at,** or **view askance,** to look at with suspicion.

askew, *a-skū', adv.* and *adj.* obliquely: aside: awry. [Prob. conn. with **skew.**]

aslant, *a-slänt', adv.* or predicative *adj.* oblique-(ly). [Pfx. *a-* (O.E. *on*), on, and **slant.**]

asleep, *a-slēp', adv.* or predicative *adj.* sleeping: dead: (of limbs) numbed. [Pfx. *a-* (O.E. *on*), on, and **sleep.**]

aslope, *a-slōp', adv.* or predicative *adj.* on the slope. [O.E. *āslopen,* pa.p. of *āslūpan,* to slip away.]

asp, *äsp, n.* a venomous snake of various kinds. [L.,—Gr. *aspis.*]

asparagus, *as-par'a-gus, n.* a genus of plants some species of which is cultivated for its young shoots, esteemed as a table delicacy. [L.,—Gr. *asparagos.*]

aspect, *as'pekt, n.* look: view: appearance: position in relation to the points of the compass: the situation of one planet with respect to another, as seen from the earth: (*aircraft*) attitude.—**aspect ratio,** (*TV*) ratio of the width to the height of a reproduced image: ratio of the span of an aerofoil to its mean chord. [L. *aspectus*—*ad,* at, *specĕre,* to look.]

aspen, *äsp'en, n.* the trembling poplar.—*adj.* made of, or like, the aspen: tremulous. [O.E. *æspe,* Ger. *espe.*]

asperity, *as-per'i-ti, n.* roughness: harshness: bitter coldness. [L. *asperitās*—*asper,* rough.]

asperse, *as pûrs', v.t.* bespatter: to slander or calumniate.—*n.* **asper'sion,** calumny, slander. [L. *aspergĕre, aspersum*—*ad,* to, *spargĕre,* to sprinkle.]

asphalt, *as'falt,* now more usu. *-fölt, n.* a dark, hard, bituminous substance, anciently used as a cement, and now for paving, roadmaking, damp-proof courses, &c. [Gr. *asphaltos,* from an Eastern word.]

asphodel, *as'fo-del, n.* a genus of plants of the same order as the daffodil, which in Greece flower luxuriantly during winter and early spring: in mythology and poetry, a flower said to bloom in the Elysian fields: the daffodil. [Gr. *asphodelos;* cf. Homer's *asphodelos* (*leimōn*), (the meadow) of the dead.]

asphyxia, *as-fik'si-a, n.* (*lit.*) stoppage of the

pulse: suspended animation due to deficiency of oxygen in the blood from any cause: suffocation.—*v.t.* **asphyx'iāte,** to cause to suffer asphyxia, to suffocate.—*n.* **asphyxiā'tion.** [Gr.,—*a,* neg., *sphyxis,* the pulse.]

aspic, *as'pik, n.* a savoury meat-jelly containing fish, game, hard-boiled eggs, &c. [Fr.]

aspidistra, *as-pid-ist'ra, n.* a genus of plants with large leaves, often grown in pots. [Perh. Gr., *aspis, -idos,* a shield.]

aspirant, *as-pīr'ant,* or *as'pir-ant, n.* one who aspires: a candidate. [See **aspire.**]

aspirate, *as'pir-āt, v.t.* to pronounce with a full breathing, as *h* in *house.*—*n.* (*-āt*) sound of the letter *h*: (in Sanskrit, &c.) a consonant sound consisting of a stop followed by an audible breath: a mark of aspiration ('): a letter representing an aspirate.—*ns.* **aspirā'tion,** pronunciation of a letter with a full breathing: an aspirated sound: the act of drawing a gas or liquid in, out, or through, by suction; **as'pirātor,** a device for drawing a stream of air or liquid through an apparatus by suction. [See **aspire.**]

aspire, *as-pīr', v.i.* with *to* or *after,* or an infinitive) to desire eagerly: to aim at high things.—*n.* **aspiration** (*as-pir-ā'sh(ó)n*), eager desire: ambition.—*adj.* **aspīr'ing.**—*adv.* **aspīr'ingly.** [Fr.,—L. *aspīrāre, -ātum*—*ad,* to, *spīrāre,* to breathe.]

aspirin, *as'pir-in, n.* a sedative drug used for relieving rheumatic pains, neuralgia, &c. [Originally a trademark.]

asquint, *a-skwint', adv.* or predicative *adj.* towards the corner of the eye: obliquely.

ass, *as, n.* any of several species of quadrupeds of the same genus as the horse, a donkey: (*fig.*) a dull, stupid fellow.—**asses' bridge,** or **pons asinorum,** a humorous name for the fifth proposition of the first book of Euclid. [O.E. *assa,* the earlier Gmc. form being *esol, esil*—L. *asinus*; Gr. *onos,* ass.]

assagai. Same as **assegai.**

assail, *a-sāl', v.t.* to attack suddenly or repeatedly (often *fig.*).—*n.* **assail'ant,** one who assails or attacks. [O.Fr. *asaillir*—L. *assilīre*—*ad,* upon, and *salīre,* to leap.]

assassin, *as-as'in, n.* one of a fanatical Moslem sect whose creed sanctioned the murder of prominent adversaries: one who takes the life of another by treacherous violence.—*v.t.* **assass'inate,** to murder (esp. a prominent person) violently, often publicly: (*fig.*) to destroy treacherously.—*n.* **assassinā'tion.** [Through Fr. or It. from Ar. *hashshāshīn,* 'hashisheaters', because the assassins drugged themselves with hashish in preparation for their crimes.]

assault, *a-sölt', n.* a sudden onslaught: a storming, as of a town: an attack of any sort.—*v.t.* to make an assault or attack upon.—**assault at arms,** a display of attack and defence in fencing. [O.Fr. *asaut*—L. *ad,* upon, *saltus,* a leap—*salīre,* to leap.]

assay, *a-sā', v.t.* to determine the proportions of a metal in an ore or alloy: to test critically.—*v.i.* to attempt, essay.—*n.* the determination of the quantity of metal in an ore or alloy: a trial, test: an attempt or endeavour. [O.Fr. *assayer,*

n. assai, essai. See **essay.**]

assegai, *as'é-gī, n.* a spear or javelin used in S. Africa. [Ar. *azzaghāyah.*]

assemble, *a-sem'bl, v.t.* to call or bring together: to collect: to put together (the parts of a machine).—*v.i.* to meet together.—*ns.* **assem'blage,** a collection of persons or things: (also *a-sä-bläzh*), (putting together) a sculptural or other work of art consisting in whole or in part of selected objects, usu. objects made for another purpose; **assem'bly,** the act of assembling: the company so assembled: a gathering of persons for a particular purpose; **assembly line,** the machines and workers necessary for the manufacture of an article, arranged in such a way that individual articles can follow each other without break through successive processes; **assem'blyroom,** a room in which persons assemble, especially for dancing.—**General Assembly,** in Scotland, Ireland, and the United States, the highest court of the Presbyterian Church: the main body of the United Nations, on which all members are represented; **House of Assembly,** the lower house of the parliament of the Republic of South Africa. [Fr. *assembler*—L.L. *assimulāre,* to bring together—*ad,* to, *similis,* like.]

assent, *a-sent', v.t.* to agree in thought: to indicate agreement.—*n.* concurrence or acquiescense: compliance. [O.Fr. *asenter,* assent—L. *assentāre*—*assentīre*—*ad,* to, *sentīre,* to think.]

assert, *a-sûrt', v.t.* to vindicate or defend (e.g. rights): to declare strongly, affirm.—*n.* **asser'tion,** the act of asserting: confident affirmation or demand.—*adj.* **assert'ive,** inclined to assert: dogmatic.—*adv.* **assert'ively.**—*n.* **assert'iveness.**—**assert oneself,** to insist strongly on one's rights or opinions: to refuse to be ignored. [L. *asserēre* (supine *assertum*) *aliquem manu in libertatem,* to lay a hand on one (a slave) in token of manumission, hence to protect, affirm, declare—*ad,* to, and *serēre,* to join.]

assess, *a-ses', v.t.* to fix the amount of, as a tax: to tax or fine: to value, for taxation: to estimate.—*adj.* **assess'able.**—*ns.* **assess'ment,** act of assessing: a valuation for the purpose of taxation: a tax; **assess'or,** an adviser associated with a magistrate or a deliberative body: one who assesses taxes.—*adj.* **assessō'rial.**—*n.* **assess'orship.** [Fr.,—L. *assessāre,* freq. of *assidēre, assessum,* to sit by, esp. of judges in a court—*ad,* to, at *sedēre,* to sit.]

assets, *as'ets, n.pl.* (orig. *sing.*) the property of a deceased or insolvent person, considered as chargeable for all debts, &c.: the entire property of all sorts belonging to a merchant or to a trading association.—*false sing.* **ass'et,** an item of property: something advantageous. [From the Anglo-Fr. law phrase *aver assetz,* to have enough—O.Fr. *asez,* enough—L. *ad,* to, *satis,* enough.]

asseverate, *a-sev'ér-āt, v.t.* to declare solemnly.—*n.* **asseverā'tion,** any solemn affirmation or confirmation. [L. *assevērāre, -ātum*—*ad,* to, *sevērus,* serious.]

assiduity, *as-id-ū'i-ti, n.* constant application or diligence: (*pl.*) constant attentions, as to a

Neutral vowels in unaccented syllables: *em'pér-ór*; for certain sounds in foreign words see p. ix.

40

lady.—*adj.* **assid'uous,** constant or unwearied in application: diligent.—*adv.* **assid'uously.**—*n.* **assid'uousness.** [L. *assiduitās*—*assiduus,* sitting close at—*ad,* to, at, *sedēre,* to sit.]

assiento, *as-ē-en'to, n.* an exclusive contract formerly made with the King of Spain for the supply of African slaves for his American possessions. [Sp. (now *asiento*), a seat, a seat in a court, a treaty.]

assign, *a-sīn', v.t.* to award by a sign: to 'allot: to appoint: to ascribe.—*n.* one to whom any property or right is made over. *adj.* **assign'-able,** that may be assigned.—*ns.* **assignation** (*as-ig-nā'sh(ó)n*), an appointment to meet, used chiefly of love-trysts: (*Scots law*) the making over of any right to another, assignment; **assignee** (*as-in-ē',* or *-sīn-*), one to whom a right or property is assigned: (*pl.*) trustees of a sequestrated estate; **assign'ment** (*-sīn-*), act of assigning: anything assigned: the writing by which a transfer is made: (orig. *U.S.*) a task allotted. [Fr.,—L. *assignāre,* to mark out—*ad,* to, *signum,* a mark or sign.]

assimilate, *a-sim'il-āt, v.t.* to make similar or like (to): to compare (to): (of plants and animals) to take in (food) and convert into living substance—also *fig.* (with knowledge, experience, &c., as object).—*v.i.* (of food) to be, or be capable of being, absorbed and incorporated.—*adj.* **assim'ilable.**—*ns.* **assimilabil'ity; assimila'tion.**—*adj.* **assim'ilative,** having the power or tendency to assimilate. [L. *assimilāre, -ātum*—*ad,* to, *similis,* like.]

assist, *a-sist', v.t.* to help.—*v.i.* (*Gallicism*) to be present at a ceremony.—*n.* **assist'ance,** help: relief.—*adj.* **assist'ant,** helping or lending aid.—*n.* one who assists: a helper. [L. *assistere,* to stand by—*ad,* to, and *sistere* (Gr. *histanai*), to cause to stand.]

assize, *a-sīz', n.* a statute settling the weight, measure, or price of anything: (*Scot.*) a trial by jury: (*pl.*) the sessions or sittings of a court held periodically in English counties, at which causes are tried by judges on circuit and a jury.—*n.* **assiz'er,** an officer who inspects weights and measures. [O.Fr. *assise,* an assembly of judges, a set rate—*asseoir*—L. *assidēre*—*ad,* to *sedēre,* to sit.]

associate, *a-sō'shi-āt, v.t.* to join in friendship or partnership, to bring together: to unite in the same body: to connect in thought.—*v.i.* to keep company (with): to combine or unite.—*adj.* (*-āt*) allied or connected.—*n.* one joined or connected with another: a companion, friend, partner, or ally.—*n.* **associa'tion** (*-si-*), act of associating: union or combination: a society of persons joined together to promote some object: (*football*) the game played under the rules of the Football Association with eleven a side, 'soccer'—cf. *Rugby*: connection of thoughts, of feelings: (usu. in *pl.*) thought, feeling, &c. more or less permanently connected with e.g. a place, an occurrence.—*adj.* **asso'ciative,** tending to association: (*math.*) such that $(a*b)*c = a*(b*c)$—where $*$ denotes a binary operation. [L. *associāre, -ātum*—*ad,* to, *socius,* a companion.]

assoil, *a-soil', v.t.* (*arch.*) to absolve or acquit.—*v.t.* (*Scots*) **assoilzie** (*ä-soil'(y)i*), to assoil.

[Through Fr. from L.—L. *ab,* from, *solvēre,* to loose.]

assonance, *as'on-áns, n.* a correspondence in sound: a kind of rhyme, consisting in the coincidence of the vowels of the corresponding syllables, without regard to the consonants as in *mate* and *shape, feel* and *need.*—*adj.* **ass'onant,** resembling in sound. [Fr.,—L. *assonāre*—*ad,* to, *sonāre,* to sound.]

assort, *a-sort', v.t.* to separate into classes: to arrange.—*v.i.* to agree, to match, be suitable (with).—*p.adj.* **assort'ed,** arranged in sorts: miscellaneous.—*n.* **assort'ment,** act of assorting: that which is assorted: a variety. [Fr. *assortir*—L. *ad,* to, *sors, sortis,* a lot.]

assuage, *a-swāj', v.t.* to soften, mitigate, or allay.—*v.i.* to abate or subside.—*n.* **assuage'ment,** abatement: mitigation.—*adj.* **assua'sive,** softening, mild. [O.Fr., formed as if from a L. *assuāviāre*—*ad,* to, *suāvis,* mild.]

assume, *a-sūm', or -sōōm', v.t.* to take up, put on: to adopt: to take upon oneself: to take for granted: to pretend to possess.—*v.i.* to claim unduly: to be arrogant.—*adjs.* **assumptive** (*as-um(p)'tiv*), that may be assumed; **assumed',** appropriated, usurped: pretended: taken as the basis of argument; **assum'ing,** presumptuous, arrogant. [L. *assūmēre*—*ad,* to, *sūmēre, sumptum,* to take.]

assumption, *a-sum'sh(ó)n, n.* act of assuming: that which is taken for granted, supposition.—**Assumption of the Virgin,** a church festival, 15th of August (the tradition, dating from the 3rd century A.D., that after death the soul and body of Mary were taken up to heaven by Christ and His angels, became R.C. dogma, 1950). [L. *assumptiō, -ōnis*—*assūmēre.* See **assume.**]

assure, *ä-shōōr', v.t.* to make sure or certain: to give confidence: to tell positively: to insure.—*n.* **assur'ance,** feeling of certainty: confidence: effrontery: a solemn declaration or promise: insurance, as applied to a life.—*adj.* **assured',** certain: without doubt: insured: confident.—*adv.* **assur'edly** (*-id-li*), certainly.—*n.* **assur'edness.** [O.Fr. *aseürer*—L.L. *adsēcūrāre*—*ad,* to, *sēcūrus,* safe.]

asswage. A form of **assuage.**

aster, *as'tér, n.* a genus of composite plants with flowers like little stars, mostly perennial, flowering in late summer and autumn, hence called Michaelmas daisies: extended to a summer annual of kindred species, brought from China in 18th century and much improved and varied by culture. [Gr. *astēr,* a star.]

asterisk, *as'tér-isk, n.* a star-shaped mark, used in printing as a sign of reference to a note, or of the omission of words, &c., thus*. [Gr. *asteriskos,* dim. of *astēr,* a star.]

astern, *a-stûrn', adv.* in the stern: towards the hinder part of a ship: behind. [Pfx. *a-* (O.E. *on*), on, and **stern** (2).]

asteroid, *as'tér-oid, n.* one of the minor planetary bodies, most of which revolve between the orbits of Mars and Jupiter.—*adj.* **asteroid'al.** [Gr. *astēr,* a star, *eidos,* form.]

asthma, *as(th)'ma* (also *ast'ma, az'ma), n.* a chronic disorder of the organs of respiration, characterised by paroxysms in which the sufferer gasps painfully for breath.—*adjs.*

fāte, fär; mē, hûr (her); mīne, mōte, för; mūte; mōōn, fŏŏt; тнen (then)

asthmat′ic, -al, pertaining to or affected by asthma: puffing.—*adv.* **asthmat′ically.** [Gr. *asthma, -atos—aazein,* to breathe hard.]

astigmatism, *a-stig′ma-tizm, n.* a defective condition of the eye, in which rays proceeding to the eye from one point are not correctly brought to a focus at one point.—*adj.* **astigmat′ic.** [Gr. *a-,* priv., and *stigma, -atos,* a point.]

astir, *a-stûr, adv.* on the move: out of bed: in motion or excitement. [Pfx. *a-* (O.E. *on*), on, and **stir.**]

astomatous, *as-tom′a-tus, adj.* having no mouth.—Also **as′tomous.** [Gr. *a-,* priv., *stoma, -atos,* mouth.]

astonish, *as-ton′ish, v.t.* to impress with sudden surprise or wonder, to amaze—older form **aston′y,** whence the *p.adj.* **aston′ied,** dazed, bewildered.—*adj.* **aston′ishing,** very wonderful, amazing.—*adv.* **aston′ishingly.**—*n.* **aston′ishment,** amazement: wonder. [From the earlier *astony*—M.E. *aston(i)en*—O.Fr. *estoner*—L. *ex,* out, *tonāre,* to thunder.]

astound, *as-townd′, v.t.* to amaze, to strike dumb with astonishment:—*pa.p.* **astound′ed;** *pr.p.* **astound′ing.**—*p.adj.* **astound′ing.** [M.E. *aston-(i)en;* a doublet of **astonish.**]

astraddle, *a-strad′l, adv.* sitting astride. [Pfx. *a-* (O.E. *on*), on, and **straddle.**]

astragal, *as′tra-gal, n.* (*archit.*) a small semicircular moulding or bead encircling a column. [Gr. *astragalos,* one of the vertebrae, a moulding.]

astrakhan, *as-tra-kan′, n.* lambskin with a curled wool: a fabric made in imitation of it. [From *Astrakhan* on the Caspian Sea.]

astral, *as′trál, adj.* belonging to the stars: starry: in theosophy, descriptive of an impalpable essence supposed to pervade all space and enter into all bodies.—**astral body,** a living form composed of astral fluid, a wraith or ghost. [L. *astrālis—astrum,* a star.]

astray, *a-strā′, adv.* out of the right way. [Pfx. *a-* (O.E. *on*), on, and **stray.**]

astriction, *as-trik′sh(ó)n, n.* a binding or contraction. [L. *astrictiō, -ōnis—astringĕre.* See **astringent.**]

astride, *a-strīd′, adv.* predicative *adj.,* and *prep.* with legs on each side (of): with the legs apart: with legs on each side of. [Pfx. *a-* (O.E. *on*), on, and **stride.**]

astringent, *as-trin′jént, adj.* binding, contracting (organic tissues—e.g. so as to stop bleeding): (of manner, quality, &c.) austere, sharp.—*n.* medicine, &c., that draws the tissues together.—*n.* **astrin′gency.**—*adv.* **astrin′gently.** [L. *astringens, -entis,* pr.p. of *astringĕre—ad,* to, *stringĕre,* to bind.]

astrolabe, *as′trō-lāb, n.* an instrument formerly used for measuring the altitudes of the sun or stars. [Gr. *astron,* a star, and root of *lambanein,* to take.]

astrology, *as-trol′o-ji, n.* the study of the positions and motions of the heavenly bodies (out of which grew astronomy) to determine their supposed influence on the destinies of men.—*n.* **astrol′oger,** one versed in astrology.—*adjs.* **astrolog′ic, -al.**—*adv.* **astrolog′ically.** [Gr. *astrologia—astron,* star, *logos,* discourse.]

astronaut, *as′trō-nöt, n.* one engaged in space

travel.—*adj.* **astronaut′ical.**—*n.* **astronaut′ics,** the science of travel in space. [Gr. *astron,* a star, *nautēs,* a sailor.]

astronomy, *as-tron′öm-i, n.* the laws or science of the stars or heavenly bodies.—*n.* **astron′omer,** one versed in astronomy.—*adj.* **astronom′ic, -al,** of, or pertaining to, astronomy: (of numbers) very large.—*adv.* **astronom′ically.**—**astronomical unit,** the earth's mean distance from the sun, about 92.9 million miles (1.496×10^{11}m), used as a measure of distance within the solar system. [Gr. *astronomia—astron,* star, *nomos,* a law.]

astrophysics, *as-trō-fiz′iks, n.* that branch of astronomy which deals with the physical constitution and properties of the stars. [Gr. *astron,* star, and **physics.**]

astute, *ast-ūt′, adj.* crafty, cunning: shrewd, sagacious.—*adv.* **astute′ly.**—*n.* **astute′ness.** [L. *astūtus—astus,* craft.]

asunder, *a-sun′dér, adv.* apart: into parts. [Pfx. *a-* (O.E. *on*), on, and **sunder.**]

asylum, *a-sīl′um, n.* a place of refuge for debtors and for fugitives from justice: an institution for the care or relief of the unfortunate, such as the blind or (old-fashioned) mentally ill: any place of refuge. [L.,—Gr. *asylon—a-,* priv., *sylē,* right of seizure.]

asymptote, *a′sim-tōt, n.* (*math.*) a line that continually approaches nearer to some curve without ever meeting it.—*adjs.* **asymptot′ic, -al.** [Gr. *asymptōtos,* not coinciding—*a-,* priv., *syn,* with, *ptōtos,* apt to fall—*piptein,* to fall.]

at, *at, prep.* denoting precise position in space or time or some kindred relation. [O.E. *æt;* cog. with O.N. *at,* L. *ad;* Sans. *adhi,* on.]

atavism, *at′av-izm, n.* appearance of ancestral, as distinguished from parental, characteristics: reversion to a more primitive type.—*adj.* **atavis′tic.** [L. *atavus,* a great-great-grandfather—*avus,* a grandfather.]

ataxia, *a-tak′si-a,* **ataxy,** *a-tak′si, at′aks-i, n.* (*med.*) inability to co-ordinate voluntary movements of the limbs. [Gr., disorder—*a-,* priv., *taxis,* order.]

ate, *et,* or *āt, pa.t.* of **eat.**

atelier, *at-él-yā′, n.* a workshop, esp. an artist's studio. [Fr.]

Athanasian, *ath-a-nāz′yán, adj.* relating to *Athanasius* (296-373), the leader of the party that induced the Church to adopt the orthodox doctrine of the divinity of Christ.

atheism, *ā′the-izm, n.* disbelief in the existence of God.—*n.* **a′theist,** one who disbelieves in the existence of God.—*adjs.* **atheist′ic, -al.**—*adv.* **atheist′ically.** [Fr. *athéisme*—Gr. *a-,* priv., and *theos,* God.]

atheling, *ath′el-ing, n.* (O.E. *hist.*) a member of a noble family, latterly a prince of the blood royal. [O.E. *ætheling;* Ger. *adel.*]

Athenaeum, Atheneum, *ath-e-nē′um, n.* a temple of Athena at Athens, in which scholars and poets read their works: (not *cap.*) a public institution for lectures, reading, &c. [Gr. *Athēnaion—Athēna* or *Athēnē.*]

Athenian, *a-thē′ni-án, adj.* relating to *Athens,* the capital of Greece.—*n.* a native of Athens.

athirst, *a-thûrst′, adj.* thirsty: eager (for). [O.E. *ofthyrst(ed),* pa.p. of *ofthyrstan—thyrstan,* to thirst.]

Neutral vowels in unaccented syllables: *em′pér-ór;* for certain sounds in foreign words see p. ix.

42

athlete, *ath'lēt*, *n.* a competitor in contests of strength: one vigorous in body.—*adj.* **athlět'ic**, relating to athletics: strong, vigorous.—*n.pl.* **athlet'ics**, the art of wrestling, running, &c.: athletic sports. [Gr. *athlētēs—athlos*, contest.]

at-home. See **home**.

athwart, *a-thwört'*, *prep.* across.—*adv.* sidewise: wrongly: perplexingly. [Pfx. *a-* (O.E. *on*), on, and **thwart**.]

atlantes, *at-lan'tēz*, *n.pl.* figures of men used as columns. [Gr. *Atlas, -antos*. See **Atlas**.]

Atlantic, *at-lan'tik*, *adj.* pertaining to Atlas, or to the Atlantic Ocean.—*n.* the ocean between Europe, Africa, and America. [From Mount *Atlas*, in the north-west of Africa, named from *Atlas, -antos*. See **Atlas**.]

Atlas, *at'las*, *n.* the leader of the Titans in their unsuccessful war with Zeus; he was condemned to bear heaven on his head and hands. [Gr. *Atlas, -antos*.]

atlas, *at'las*, *n.* a book of maps. [Gr. *Atlas* (see **Atlas**) whose figure used to be shown on the title-page of atlases.]

atmosphere, *at'mos-fēr*, *n.* the gaseous envelope that surrounds the earth or any of the heavenly bodies: any gaseous medium: a conventional unit of atmospheric pressure, 101325 N m^{-2} or 14·7 lbf. in.$^{-2}$ (under this pressure—other conditions being standard—the height of the mercury barometer is 760 millimetres): (*fig.*) any surrounding influence.—*adjs.* **atmosphěr'ic, -al**, of or depending on the atmosphere.—*n.pl.* **atmospher'ics**, in radio reception, interfering or disturbing signals due to atmospheric conditions. [Gr. *atmos*, air, *sphaira*, a sphere.]

atoll, *a-tol'*, or *at'ol*, *n.* a coral island formed by a circular belt of coral enclosing a central lagoon. [A Dravidian (q.v.) word.]

atom, *at'óm*, *n.* the smallest particle of an element that can take part in a chemical reaction thought by nineteenth century chemists to be indivisible, but now known to be a complex system of electrons, protons, and neutrons: anything very small.—*adjs.* **atomic, -al**, pertaining to atoms.—*ns.* **atomic'ity** (-*is-*), number of atoms contained in the molecule of an element; **atomisā'tion**, the reduction of liquids to the form of spray.—*v.t.* **at'omise**, to reduce to atoms: to reduce to a fine spray or minute particles: to destroy by bombing.—*ns.* **atomi'ser**, an instrument for discharging liquids in a fine spray; **at'omy**, an atom or mote: a pygmy.—**atom(ic) bomb**, a bomb in which the explosion is caused by a sustained neutron chain reaction (i.e. a self-propagating reaction) resulting from the fission of nuclei of atoms of uranium or its derivatives; **atomic aircraft-carrier, icebreaker, submarine**, &c., an aircraft-carrier, icebreaker, submarine, &c., driven by atomic power; **atomic energy**, nuclear (q.v.) energy; **atomic number**, the number of an element when arranged with others in the periodic chemical classification, equal to the number of protons in the nucleus of its atom; **atomic pile** (see **pile**); **atomic power**, power for making electricity or for other purpose obtained by means of a nuclear reaction; **atomic radiator**, one heated by atomic power; **atomic weight** (*obs.*), now re-lative **atomic mass**, the inferred weight of an atom of an element, relatively to that of carbon 12 as 12 units or (formerly, now *obs.*) oxygen as 16 units; **at'om-smasher**, an apparatus for breaking up atoms, an accelerator. [Gr. *atomos*, indivisible—*a-*, priv., *temnein*, to cut.]

atonal, *a-tōn'ál*, *adj.* (*mus.*) not referred to any scale or tonic.—*n.* **atōnal'ity**.—*adj.* **atŏn'ic** (*pros.*), unaccented. [Gr. *a-*, priv., *tonos*, tone. See **tone**.]

atone, *at-ōn'*, *v.i.* (formerly also *v.t.*) to give satisfaction or make reparation: to make up (for deficiencies): to harmonise.—*n.* **atone'ment**, the act of atoning: expiation: reparation: esp. (*theol.*) the reconciliation of God and man by means of the incarnation and death of Christ. [**at** and **one**, as if to set at one, reconcile.]

atrabiliar, *at-ra-bil'i-àr*, *adj.* of a melancholy temperament: acrimonious.—Also **atrabil'iary, atrabil'ious**. [L. *atra* (masc. *ater*), black, *bilis*, gall, bile.]

atrium, *ā'tri-um*, *n.* entrance-hall or chief apartment of Roman house:—*pl.* **a'tria**. [L.]

atrocious, *a-trō'shús*, *adj.* extremely cruel or wicked: abominable.—*adv.* **atrō'ciously**.—*ns.* **atrō'ciousness**, gross cruelty; **atrocity** (*a-tros'it-i*), atrociousness: an atrocious act. [L. *ātrox, ātrocis*, cruel—*āter*, black.]

atrophy, *at'rof-i*, *n.* (*med.*) wasting of a cell or of an organ of the body: (*zool.*) degeneration, i.e. diminution in size, complexity, or function, through disuse.—Also *v.t.* and *v.i.* [Gr. *a-*, priv., and *trophē*, nourishment.]

atropin(e), *at'ro-pin*, *n.* a poisonous alkaloid existing in the deadly nightshade. [Gr. *Atropos*, the one of the Fates who cut the thread of life.]

attach, *a-tach'*, *v.t.* to bind or fasten (to something): to append: to join (oneself): to associate as an adjunct (e.g. to attach a condition): to attribute (e.g. importance): to gain or win over (to): to seize by legal process.—*v.i.* to be attributable, incident (to—e.g. *no blame, interest, attaches to*).—*adj.* **attach'able**.—*p.adj.* **attached'**, fastened, fixed: joined by taste or affection, devoted (to).—*n.* **attach'ment**, act or means of fastening: something attached, esp. an extra part attached to a machine to enable it to do special work: a tie of fidelity or affection: the seizure of anyone's goods or person by virtue of a legal process. [O.Fr. *atachier*, from *à* (L. *ad*), and perh. the root of **tack** (1) (q.v.).]

attaché, *a-tash'ā*, *n.* a junior member of an ambassador's suite.—*n.* **attach'é-case**, a small rectangular leather hand-bag for documents, &c. [Fr., attached.]

attack, *a-tak'*, *v.t.* to fall upon violently, to assault: to assail in speech or writing: to begin to affect (of a disease).—*n.* an assault, onset: an access or fit of illness: severe criticism or calumny: mode of beginning a performance. [Fr. *attaquer*. See **attach**, of which it is a doublet.]

attain, *a-tān'*, *v.t.* to reach or gain by effort: to arrive at.—*v.i.* (with *to*) to come to or arrive at.—*adj.* **attain'able**, that may be reached.—*ns.* **attain'ableness, attainabil'ity; attain'ment,**

act of attaining: the thing attained: acquisition: (*pl.*) acquirements in learning. [O.Fr. *ataindre*—L. *attingĕre*—*ad*, to, *tangĕre*, to touch.]

attainder, *a-tān'dèr, n.* act of attainting: (*law*) loss of civil rights through conviction for high treason.—*v.t.* **attaint'**, to convict: to deprive of rights for being convicted of treason. [O.Fr. *ataindre.* See **attain.**]

attar, *at'ár, n.* a very fragrant essential oil made chiefly from the damask rose.—Also **ott'o.** [Pers. *atar.*]

attempt, *a-temt', v.t.* to try or endeavour: to try to do: to make an attack upon.—*n.* a trial, endeavour, or effort: an attack (e.g. *an attempt on one's life*). [O.Fr. *atempter*—L. *attentāre*—*ad*, to, *temptāre, tentāre*, to try.]

attend, *a-tend', v.t.* to wait on or accompany: to be present at: to wait for.—*v.i.* to give heed: to act as an attendant: to wait.—*n.* **attend'ance,** act of attending: presence: the number of persons attending.—*adj.* **attend'ant,** giving attendance: accompanying.—*n.* one who attends or accompanies, esp. in order to render service. [O.Fr. *atendre*—L. *attendĕre*—*ad*, to, *tendĕre*, to stretch.]

attention, *a-ten'sh(ó)n, n.* act or faculty of taking notice of or giving heed: notice, heed (as in *attract, call, pay, give attention*): steady application of the mind: care: civility, courtesy: position of standing rigidly erect with hands by the sides and heels together.—*adj.* **attent'ive,** full of attention: courteous: mindful.—*adv.* **attent'ively.**—*n.* **attent'iveness.** [L. *attentiō, -ōnis*—*attendĕre.* See **attend.**]

attenuate, *a-ten'ū-āt, v.t.* to make thin or lean: to reduce in strength or value.—*v.i.* to become thin or fine.—*adjs.* **attenuate(d)** (*a-ten'ū-āt, -id*), made thin or slender: reduced: dilute, rarefied.—*n.* **attenua'tion,** reduction in density, force, magnitude, amplitude or intensity. [L. *attenuāre, -ātum*—*ad*, to, *tenuis*, thin.]

attest, *a-test', v.t.* to testify or bear witness to: to authenticate (a document) officially: to give proof of, manifest: to put on oath.—*v.i.* to bear witness (to).—*n.* **attesta'tion,** act of attesting.—*adj.* **attest'ed,** certified free from the tubercle baccillus. [L. *attestārī*—*ad*, to, *testis*, a witness.]

Attic, *at'ik, adj.* pertaining to Attica, characteristic of Athens: refined, elegant.—*n.* **att'ic,** a low storey above the cornice that terminates the main part of an elevation, usu. in a style supposed to have prevailed in Athens: a room in the roof of a house.—**Attic salt** (or **Attic wit**), wit of a dry, delicate, and refined quality. [Gr. *Attikos,* Attic, Athenian—*Attikē,* Attica.]

attire, *a-tīr, v.t.* to dress, array, or adorn.—*n.* dress, clothing. [O.Fr. *atirer,* put in order—*à tire,* in a row—*à* (L. *ad*), to, *tire, tiere,* order.]

attitude, *at'i-tūd, n.* posture: position: state of thought or feeling: of an aircraft in flight, or on the ground, the angles made by its axes with the relative airflow, or with the ground, respectively.—*v.i.* **attitud'inise,** to assume affected attitudes.—**strike an attitude,** to attitudinise. [Fr. or It. from L.L. *aptitūdō, -inis*—*aptus,* fit.]

attorney, *a-tûr'ni, n.* one legally authorised to act for another: one legally qualified to man-

age cases in a court of law (in full, **attorney-at-law**)—now known in Britain as a solicitor:—(*pl.*) **attor'neys.**—*ns.* **Attor'ney-Gen'eral,** the first ministerial law-officer of the state in England, Eire, &c.; **attor'neyship.**—**district attorney** (*U.S.*), a public prosecutor for a district; **power of attorney,** the formal warrant by one person authorising another to perform certain acts for him. [O.Fr. *atorné*—L.L. *atornāre,* to commit business to another—*ad,* to, *tornāre.* See **turn.**]

attract, *a-trakt', v.t.* to draw (to): to cause to approach: to allure: to draw forth (e.g. attention).—*adj.* **attract'able.**—*ns.* **attractabil'ity; attract'ant,** something that attracts; **attrac'tion,** act of attracting: the force that draws or tends to draw bodies or their particles to each other: that which attracts.—*adj.* **attract'ive,** having the power of attracting: alluring.—*adv.* **attract'ively.**—*n.* **attract'iveness.** [L. *attrahĕre, attractum*—*ad,* to, *trahĕre,* to draw.]

attribute, *a-trib'ūt, v.t.* to consider as belonging (to): to ascribe, impute (to).—*adj.* **attrib'utable.**—*ns.* **att'ribute,** that which is attributed: a quality or property inseparable from anything: that which can be predicated of anything; **attribu'tion,** act of attributing: that which is attributed.—*adj.* **attrib'utive,** expressing an attribute: (of an adjective or its equivalent) standing before the qualified noun (e.g. a *loud* noise)—cf. **predicative.**—Also *n.* [L. *attribuĕre, -tribūtum*—*ad,* to, *tribuĕre,* to give.]

attrition, *a-tri'sh(ó)n, n.* the rubbing of one thing against another: a wearing by friction: (*fig.*) the wearing down of resources, resistance. [L. *attrītus*—*atterĕre*—*ad,* inten., and *terĕre, trītum,* to rub.]

attune, *a-tūn', v.t.* to put (an instrument) in tune: to make melodious: to harmonise with (with *to*—lit., *fig.*). [L. *ad,* to, **tune.**]

aubade, *ō-bäd', n.* a sunrise song. [Fr. *aube,* dawn.]

auburn, *ö'bûrn, adj.* reddish brown. [The old meaning was a light yellow, or lightish hue; L.L. *alburnus,* whitish—L. *albus,* white.]

auction, *ök'sh(ó)n, n.* a public sale in which articles are sold to the person who 'bids' or offers a higher price than any other is willing to pay.—*v.t.* to sell by auction.—*n.* **auctioneer',** one who is licensed to sell by auction.—**auc'tion bridge,** a development of the game of bridge in which the players bid for the privilege of choosing trump suit or no-trumps.—**Dutch auction,** a kind of auction at which the salesman starts at a high price, and comes down till he meets a bidder. [L. *auctiō, -ōnis,* an increasing—*augēre, auctum,* to increase.]

audacious, *ö-dā'shús, adj.* daring, bold: impudent.—*adv.* **auda'ciously.**—*ns.* **auda'ciousness, audacity** (*ö-das'i-ti*). [Fr. *audacieux*—L. *audax*—*audēre,* to dare.]

audible, *öd'i-bl, adj.* able to be heard.—*ns.* **aud'ibleness, audibil'ity.**—*adv.* **aud'ibly.**—*n.* **aud'ience,** the act of hearing: admittance to a hearing: a ceremonial interview: an assembly of hearers.—*n.* **aud'it,** an examination of accounts by one or more duly authorised persons.—*v.t.* to examine and verify by reference to vouchers, &c.—*ns.* **audi'tion,** the sense of

Neutral vowels in unaccented syllables: *em'pér-òr*; for certain sounds in foreign words see p. ix.

44

hearing: the act of hearing: a hearing to test a performer; **aud′itor,** a hearer: one who audits accounts; **aud′itorship; auditōr′ium,** space allotted to the audience in a public building.— *adj.* **aud′itory,** relating to the sense of hearing.—*n.* an audience: a place where lectures, &c., are heard.—**audience participation,** drawing audience into a theatrical performance by direct appeal to its members. [L. *audīre,* -*ītum,* to hear.]

audio, *ōd′i-ō, adj.* pertaining to sound esp. broadcast sound: using audio-frequencies.—*n.* an acoustic device by which an airman returning to an aircraft-carrier knows when he is at a proper speed for landing.—*ns.* **aud′io-engineer′,** one concerned with the transmission and reception of broadcast sound; **aud′io-fre′quency,** a frequency of the same order as those of normally audible sound waves; **aud′io-typ′ist,** typist able to type directly material reproduced by a Dictaphone.—*adj.* **audio-vis′ual,** concerned simultaneously with both seeing and hearing (**audio-visual aids,** material such as pictures, closed-circuit TV, teaching machines, used in the classroom). [L. *audīre,* to hear.]

au fait, *ō fā,* predicative *adj. phrase,* conversant (with): familiar with the facts (of). [Fr.]

Augean, *ô-jē′án, adj.* (of a task, &c.) so repulsively filthy as to demand superhuman effort. [From *Augeas,* a fabled king, whose stalls, containing 3000 oxen, and uncleaned for thirty years, were swept out by Hercules in one day.]

auger, *ō′gér, n.* a carpenter's tool used for boring holes in wood. [M.E. *nauger* (*an auger* for *a nauger*)—O.E. *nafugār—nafu,* a nave of a wheel, *gār,* a piercer.]

aught, *ōt, n.* a whit: ought: anything: a part. [O.E. *ā-wiht,* contr. to *aht—ā, ō,* ever, *wiht,* creature; cf. **ought.**]

augment, *ōg-ment′, v.t.* and *v.i.* to increase.—*n.* **aug′ment,** increase: (*gram.*) prefixed or lengthened vowel in the past tenses of verb in Sanskrit and Greek.—*adj.* **augment′ative,** having the quality or power of augmenting.—*n.* (*gram.*) a word formed from another to express increase of its meaning.—*n.* **augmentā′tion.**—*adj.* **augment′ed** (*mus.*), of an interval, greater by a semitone than the perfect or the major.—**Augmented Roman Alphabet,** earlier name for Initial Teaching Alphabet. [L. *augmentum,* increase.]

augur, *ō′gur, n.* among the Romans, one who gained what was believed to be knowledge of future things by observing the flight and the cries of birds: a soothsayer.—*v.t.* to foretell, as from signs: (of things) to forebode, betoken.—*v.i.* to conjecture: (of things) to promise (well, ill). —*adj.* **au′gural.** — *n.* **augury** (*ō′gū-ri*), the art or practice of auguring: an omen. [L.; prob. from *avis,* bird.]

august, *ō-gust′, adj.* venerable: imposing: majestic.—*adv.* **august′ly.**—*n.* **august′ness.** [L. *augustus—augēre,* to increase, honour.]

August, *ō′gust, n.* the eighth month of the year, so called after the first Roman emperor *Augustus* Caesar.—*adj.* **Augus′tan,** pertaining to the Emperor Augustus, or to his reign (31 B.C.-A.D. 14) which was the most brilliant age

in Roman literature: extended to any similar age, esp. to the reign of Queen Anne or that of Louis XIV: classic: refined.

Augustine, *ō′gust-in, ō-gust′in,* **Augustinian,** *ō-gus-tin′i-án, n.* one of an order of monks who derive name and rule from St *Augustine* (A.D. 354-430).—*adj.* **Augustin′ian.**

auk, *ōk, n.* a family of web-footed sea-birds, with short wings, found in northern seas. [O.N. *ālka.*]

auld, *ōld, adj.* (*Scot.*) old.—**auld lang syne** (*lang sīn*), the dear and distant past (*lit.* old long since). [Variant of **old**; cf. Ger. *alt.*]

aulic, *ōl′ik, adj.* pertaining to a royal court. [L. *aulicus—aula*—Gr. *aulē,* a royal court.]

au naturel, *ō nat-ü-rel, adv. phrase,* in the nude: (cooked) in the simplest way. [Fr.]

aunt, *änt, n.* a father's or a mother's sister: an uncle's wife.—**Aunt Sally,** a game in which missiles are aimed at a pipe placed in the mouth of a wooden head set on a pole: the wooden head: (*fig.*) a target for abuse. [O.Fr. *ante* (Fr. *tante*)—L. *amita,* a father's sister.]

au pair, *ō per, adj.* orig. by mutual service without payment: used of arrangement whereby girls perform light domestic duties in exchange for board and lodging and pocket-money—*n.* an au pair girl.

aura, *ōr′a, n.* a supposed subtle emanation from any source, esp. the essence that is alleged to emanate from all living things and to afford an atmosphere for occult phenomena:—*pl.* **aur′ae** (-*ē*). [L. *aura,* a breeze.]

aural, *ōr′ál, adj.* pertaining to the ear.—*adv.* **aur′ally.** [L. *auris,* ear.]

aureola, *ōr-ē′o-la,* **aureole,** *ōr′i-ōl, n.* in early pictures, the gold disc round the head symbolising glory: (*fig.*) a glorifying halo.—*adj.* **aur′eoled,** encircled with an aureole. [L. *aureolus,* dim. of *aureus,* golden,]

au revoir, *ō re-vwär,* (goodbye) until we meet again. [Fr.]

auric, *ōr′ik, adj.* pertaining to gold: (*chem.*) applied to compounds in which gold has a valency of 3. [L. *aurum,* gold.]

auricle, *ōr′i-kl, n.* the external ear: either of the two upper cavities of the heart.—*n.* **auric′ula,** dusty-miller, a species of primula.—*adj.* **auric′ular,** pertaining to the ear: known by hearing: told in the ear (i.e. privately).—*adv.* **auric′ularly.** [L. *auricula,* dim. of *auris,* the ear.]

auriferous, *ōr-if′ér-us, adj.* bearing or yielding gold. [L. *aurifer—aurum,* gold, *ferre,* to bear.]

auriform, *ōr′i-förm, adj.* ear-shaped. [L. *auris,* ear, and suffx. -*form.*]

aurist, *ōr′ist, n.* one skilled in diseases of the ear. [L. *auris,* ear.]

aurochs, *ōr′oks, n.* the extinct urus or wild ox: (erroneously) the European bison. [O.H.G. *ūr-ohso,—ūr* (adopted into L. as *ūrus,* into Gr. as *ouros*), and *ochs,* ox.]

aurora, *ō-rō′, -rō′, ra, n.* the dawn: (*cap.*) the goddess of dawn: a luminous meteoric phenomenon of electrical character seen in and towards the polar regions, polar lights.—**aurora borealis** (*bō-re-ā′lis*), the northern aurora or 'northern lights'; **aurora australis** (*os-tra′lis*), the 'southern lights', a similar phenomenon in the southern hemisphere:—*pl.* **auro′ras, -rae** (-*rē*). [L. *Aurōra,* goddess of the dawn; from a root seen in Sans. *ush,* to burn.]

auscultation, *ös-kult-ā'sh(ó)n, n.* the act of discovering the condition of the lungs and heart by applying the ear or the stethoscope to the part.—*adj.* **auscult'atory,** relating to auscultation. [L. *auscultāre, -ātum,* to listen.]

auspice, *ö'spis, n.* an omen: augury: (*pl.*) protection, patronage (*under the auspices of*): (*pl.*) prospects (*under good auspices*).—*adj.* **auspi'cious,** having good auspices or omens of success, favourable, fortunate, propitious.—*adv.* **auspi'ciously.**—*n.* **auspi'ciousness.** [Fr.,—L. *auspicium,* divination by watching birds, omen—*auspex, auspicis,* a bird-seer—*avis,* a bird, *specĕre,* to observe.]

austere, *ös-tēr', adj.* harsh: stern: strictly upright: severely simple.—*adv.* **austere'ly**—*ns.* **austere'ness, austĕr'ity,** quality of being austere: severity of manners or life: abstemiousness: severe simplicity. [L. *austērus*—Gr. *austēros—auein,* to dry.]

austral, *ös'trál, adj.* southern. [L. *austrālis—auster,* the south wind.]

autarchy, *öt'är-ki, n.* absolute power. [Gr. *autos,* self, *archein,* to rule.]

autarky, *öt'är-ki, n.* self-sufficiency. [Gr. *autarkeiă—autos,* self, *arkeein,* to suffice.]

authentic, -al, *ö-thent'ik, -ál, adj.* not spurious or counterfeit: genuine, original: certified by valid evidence: unquestionably true.—*adv.* **authent'ically.**—*v.t.* **authent'icate,** to make or prove authentic: to give legal validity to: to certify the authorship of.—*ns.* **authenticā'tion,** act of authenticating: confirmation; **authentic'ity** (*-is-*), quality of being authentic: state of being in accordance with fact: genuineness. [Fr. and L. from Gr. *authentēs,* one who does anything with his own hand—*autos,* self.]

author, *öth'ór, n.* one who brings anything into being: a beginner of any action or state of things: the writer of a book, article, &c.: elliptically for an author's writings: one's authority for something, an informant:—*fem.* **auth'oress.**—*v.t.* **auth'orise,** to give authority to: to sanction: to establish by authority.—*ns.* **authorisā'tion; auth'orship,** state or quality of being an author.—**Authorised Version,** the translation of the Bible completed in 1611 and appointed to be read in churches. [Through Fr. from L. *auctor—augēre, auctum,* cause to increase, produce.]

authority, *öth-or'i-ti, n.* legal power or right: power derived from office or character: opinion, testimony, carrying weight: a book containing, or a person delivering, such opinion or testimony: permission: precedent: justification: a body or board in control: (in *pl.*) persons in power:—*pl.* **author'ities.**—*adj.* **authorĭtā'rian,** setting authority above liberty.—Also *n.*—*adj.* **author'itative,** having the sanction or weight of authority: dictatorial.—*adv.* **author'itatively.**—*n.* **author'itativeness.** [L. *auctoritās, -ātis—auctor,* author, authority.]

autism, *öt'izm, n.* absorption in fantasy and in imaginative activity directed by the thinker's wishes, with loss of contact with reality.—*adj.* **autist'ic.** [Gr. *autos,* self.]

auto-, aut-, auth-, *ö'tō-, öt-, öth-,* (in composition) pertaining to oneself, for oneself, by oneself, independently. [Gr. *autos,* self.]

auto, *ö'tō, n.* (*coll.*) an automobile.—*ns.* **au'tobus, au'to-car, au'to-cycle,** a motor-bus, car, or cycle. [Contr. of **automobile.**]

autobahn, *ow'tō-bän,* an arterial double road for motor traffic only. [Ger.]

autobiography, *ö-to-bī-og'raf-i, n.* the biography or life of a person written by himself.—*n.* **autobiog'rapher.**—*adjs.* **autobiograph'ic, -al.** [Gr. *autos,* self, *bios,* life, *graphein,* to write.]

autochthon, *ö-tok'thon, n.* one of the primitive inhabitants of a country, an aboriginal.—*adj.* **autoch'thonous.** [Gr. *autochthōn—autos,* self, *chthōn,* the soil.]

autocrat, *ö'to-krat, n.* an absolute sovereign: one whose word is law.—*n.* **autoc'racy,** an absolute government by one man, despotism.—*adj.* **autocrat'ic.**—*adv.* **autocrat'ically.** [Gr. *autokrātes—autos,* self, *kratos,* power.]

autocross, *ö-tō-kros', n.* a motor race round a grass field. [Gr. *autos,* self, and **cross.**]

auto-da-fé, *ö'to-dä-fā, n.* the publication of the judgment passed on heretics by the Inquisition: the infliction of the punishment, esp. the public burning of the victims:—*pl.* **autos-da-fé.** [Port. *auto da fé* (Sp. *auto de fe*)—*auto* (L. *actum*), act, *da* (L. *dē*), of, *fé* (L. *fidēs*), faith.]

autodigestion, *ö-tō-dī-jes'ch(ó)n, n.* Same as **autolysis.** [Gr. *autos,* self, and **digestion.**]

autodyne, *ö'tō-dīn, adj.* in radio, of an electrical circuit in which the same elements and valves are used both as oscillator and detector. [Gr. *autos,* self, and **(hetero)dyne.**]

autograph, *ö'to-gräf, n.* one's own handwriting: a signature: an original manuscript.—*v.t.* to write with one's hand: to write one's signature in or on.—*adj.* **autograph'ic.** [Gr. *autos,* self, *graphē,* writing.]

autolysis, *ö-tol'is-is, n.* the breaking down of dead tissue by the organism's own ferments.—*v.t.* and *v.i.* **aut'olyse.** [Gr. *autos,* self, *lysis,* loosening.]

automaton, *ö-tom'a-ton, n.* a self-moving machine, or one that moves by concealed machinery: a human being who acts mechanically and without intelligence:—*pl.* **autom'atons, autom'ata.**—*v.t.* **au'tomate,** to apply automation to.—*adjs.* **automat'ic, -al,** acting like an automaton, self-acting: involuntary, unconscious.—*n.* an automatic pistol which reloads itself from an internal magazine, or a firearm that goes on firing as long as there is pressure on the trigger.—*adv.* **automat'ically.** —*n.* **automation** (*-mā'sh(ó)n*), a high degree of mechanisation in manufacture, the handling of material between processes being automatic, and the whole being automatically controlled.—**automatic transmission,** power transmission in which gear-changing is automatic. [Gr. *automatos,* self-moving.]

automobile, *ö-to-mō-bēl',* or *ö'-, n.* a motor-car. [Gr. *autos,* self; L. *mōbilis,* mobile.]

autonomy, *ö-ton'om-i, n.* the power or right of self-government.—*adj.* **auton'omous,** having autonomy. [Gr. *autos,* self, *nomos,* law.]

autopsy, *ö'top-si,* or *-top'-, n.* personal inspection, esp. examination of a body after death. [Gr. *autopsia—autos,* self, *opsis,* sight.]

auto-suggestion, *ö'to-su-jes'ch(ó)n, n.* a mental process similar to suggestion, but originating in a belief in the subject's own mind. [Gr.

Neutral vowels in unaccented syllables: *em'pér-ór*; for certain sounds in foreign words see p. ix.

autos, self, and **suggestion**.]

autumn, *ö'tum*, *n.* the season of the year when fruits are gathered in, generally (in the northern hemisphere) from August or September to October or November: astronomically, the three months immediately before the winter solstice, 21st December: a period in which growth ceases and decay sets in.—*adj.* **autum′nal**, pertaining to autumn: beyond the prime. [L. *autumnus*.]

auxiliary, *ög-zil'yär-i*, *adj.* helping: subsidiary.—*n.* a helper: an assistant: (*gram.*) a verb that helps to form the moods, tenses, and voices of other verbs: (esp. in *pl.*) a soldier serving with another nation. [L. *auxiliāris—auxilium*, help—*augēre*, to increase.]

avail, *a-vāl′*, *v.t.* to be of value or service to, to benefit: to take the benefit of (e.g. *avail oneself of*).—*v.i.* to be of use: to answer the purpose.—*n.* benefit, use (e.g. *of no avail*).—*adj.* **avail′able**, that can be obtained or used: accessible.—*ns.* **avail′ableness**, **availabil′ity**, quality of being available.—*adv.* **avail′ably**. [Through Fr., from L. *ad*, to, *valēre*, to be strong, to be worth.]

avalanche, *av'al-änsh, -önsh, n.* a mass of snow, ice, and rock sliding down from a mountain: (*fig.*) an overwhelming influx: a shower of particles resulting from the collision of a high-energy particle with matter. [Fr. *avaler*, to slip down—L. *ad*, to, *vallis*, valley.]

avant-courier, *av-ä-kōō′ri-ér, n.* one who runs before to give notice:—*pl.* scouts, skirmishers. [Fr.,—*avant*, before, and **courier**.]

avant-garde, *av-ä-gärd, n.* (*fig.*) those who create or support the newest ideas and techniques in an art, &c. Also *adj.* [Fr.]

avarice, *av'ar-is, n.* eager desire for wealth, covetousness.—*adj.* **avaricious** (*av-är-i'shús*), extremely covetous, greedy.—*adv.* **avari'cious-ly**, *n.* **avari'ciousness**. [Fr., L. *avāritia—avārus*, greedy—*avēre*, to pant after.]

avast, *a-väst′, interj.* (*naut.*) hold fast! stop! [Du. *houd vast*, hold fast.]

avatar, *a-va-tär′, n.* the descent of a Hindu deity in a visible form: incarnation. [Sans.—*ava*, away, down, root *tar-*, pass over.]

avaunt, *a-vönt′, interj.* move on! begone! [Fr. *avant*, forward—L. *ab*, from, *ante*, before.]

ave, *ā′vē, interj.* and *n.* hail: an address or prayer to the Virgin Mary—in full, **ave Maria** (*ā′vē Ma-rī′a, ävä Ma-rē′a*), hail Mary (Luke i. 28). [Imper. of L. *avēre*, to be well.]

avenge, *a-venj′, -venzh′, v.t.* to exact due penalty or reparation for (an injury—often followed by *on, upon*): to exact due penalty on behalf of (a person).—*n.* **aveng′er**. [O.Fr. *avengier*—L. *vindicāre*.]

avenue, *av'én-ū, n.* the main approach to a country-house, usually bordered by trees: a double row of trees: a street: (*fig.*) means of access or attainment. [Fr.,—L. *ad*, to, *venīre*, to come.]

aver, *a-vûr′, v.t.* to declare to be true: to affirm or declare positively:—*pr.p.* aver'ring; *pa.p.* averred'.—*n.* **aver'ment**, positive assertion: (*law*) a formal offer to prove a plea: the proof offered. [Fr. *avérer*—L. *ad*, and *vērus*, true.]

average, *av'ér-ij, n.* the mean value of a number of quantities, as obtained by dividing the sum of the quantities by their number: assessment of compensation in the same proportion as amount insured bears to actual worth.—*adj.* containing a mean value: midway between extremes: ordinary.—*v.t.* to fix the average of.—*v.i.* to exist as, or form, an average. [The word first appears, in various forms, about 1500 in conn. with Mediterranean sea-trade; prob.—It. *avere* (L. *habēre*, to have), goods, the orig. sense being a 'charge on property or goods'.]

averse, *a-vûrs′, adj.* having a disinclination or hatred (with *to*; *from* is preferred by some). —*ns.* **averse′ness**; **aver′sion**, dislike, hatred: the object of dislike.—*v.t.* **avert′**, to turn from or aside (e.g. eyes, thoughts): to prevent, ward off.—*adj.* **avert′ible**, capable of being averted. [L. *avertěre, aversum—ab*, from, *vertěre*, to turn.]

aviary, *ā′vi-ár-i, n.* a place for keeping birds. [L. *aviārum—avis*, a bird.]

aviation, *ā-vi-ā′sh(ö)n, n.* the art or practice of mechanical flight.—*n.* **aviation spirit**, a motor fuel with a low boiling-point for use in aeroplanes. [L. *avis*, a bird.]

avidity, *a-vid′i-ti, n.* eagerness: greediness.—*adj.* **av′id**, greedy: eager.—*adv.* **av′idly**. [L. *avidi tās—avidus*, greedy—*avēre*, to pant after.]

avitaminosis, *ā-vīt-à-min-ō′sis*, or *-vit-, n.* deficiency of vitamins or disease resulting from it. [Gr. *a-*, priv., **vitamin**, and *-osis*, indicating diseased state.]

avizandum, *av-iz-an′dum, n.* (*Scots law*) private consideration of a case by a judge before giving judgment.—Also **avisan′dum**. [Gerund of L.L. *avisāre*, to advise.]

avocation, *a-vo-kā′sh(ö)n, n.* properly, a diversion or distraction from one's regular employment—improperly—*vocation*: business that calls for one's time and attention. [Through Fr from L. *āvocātiō, -ōnis*, a calling away—*ab*, from, *vocāre*, to call.]

avoid, *a-void′, v.t.* to escape, keep clear of: to shun: (*law*) to make void.—*adj.* **avoid′able**.—*n.* **avoid′ance**, the act of avoiding or shunning: act of annulling. [Pfx. *a* = Fr. *es* = L. *ex*, out, and **void**.]

avoirdupois, *av-ér-dé-poiz′*, or *av′-, adj.* or *n.* (according to) the system of weights in which the lb. equals 16 oz. [O.Fr. *aveir de pes* (*avoir du pois*), to have weight—L. *habēre*, to have, *pensum*, that which is weighed.]

avouch, *a-vowch′, v.t.* to avow, assert or own positively. [O.Fr. *avochier*—L. *advocāre*, to call to one's aid—*ad*, to, *vocāre*, to call.]

avow, *a-vow′, v.t.* to declare openly: to own or confess.—*pa.p.* as *adj.* **avowed** (*-vowd′*), self-acknowledged.—*adv.* **avow′edly** (*-id-li*).—*adj.* **avow′able**.—*n.* **avow′al**, a positive declaration: a frank confession. [O.Fr. *avouer*, orig. to swear fealty to—L. *ad*, and L.L. *vōtāre—vōtum*, a vow—*vovēre*, to vow.]

avuncular, *a-vung′kū-lär, adj.* pertaining to an uncle. [L. *avunculus*, an uncle.]

await, *a-wāt′, v.t.* to wait or look for: to be in store for. [Through Fr. from the common Gmc. root of Ger. *wacht*, Eng. **wait**.]

awake, *a-wāk′, v.t.* to rouse from sleep: to rouse from inaction.—*v.i.* to cease sleeping: to rouse oneself:—*pa.t.* awoke', awaked'; *pa.p.* awaked',

fāte, *fär*; *mē*, *hûr* (her); *mīne*; *mōte*, *för*; *mūte*; *mōōn*, *fŏŏt*; *ᴛʜen* (then) or awoke'.—*adj.* not asleep: vigilant.—*v.t.* and *v.i.* **awak'en,** to awake: to rouse into interest or attention.—*n.* **awak'ening,** the act of awaking or ceasing to sleep: an arousing from indifference.—**awake to,** fully aware of. [O.E. *āwæcnan* (pa.t. *āwōc,* pa.p. *āwacen*) confused with *āwacian* (pa.t. *āwacode.*). See **wake, watch.**]

award, *a-wörd', v.t.* to adjudge, bestow: to assign legally.—*n.* judgment: final decision: esp. of arbitrators: portion, payment, prize, assigned. [O.Fr. *ewarder, eswarder*—*es* (L. ex, in sense of thoroughly), and *guarder,* watch. See **ward, guard.**]

aware, *a-wār', adj.* (used predicatively) informed, conscious (of).—*n.* **aware'ness.** [O.E. *gewær*—pfx. *ge*-, and *wær,* cautious. See **wary.**]

awash, *a-wosh', adv.* on a level with the surface of the water so that the waves wash over it (e.g. of a deck): floating at the mercy of the waves. [Pfx. *a*- (O.E. *on*), on, and **wash.**]

away, *a-wā', adv.* onward, along, continuously: at once, forthwith: from a place: absent: gone, dead, fainted.—*interj.* begone! (e.g. *away with you!*)—**away with him,** take him away; **I cannot away with,** I cannot bear or endure; **make away with,** to steal and escape with: to squander: to destroy; **do away with,** to make an end of; **fall away,** to desert (with *from*), to diminish, decline. [O.E. *aweg*—*on,* on, *weg,* way, *lit.* 'on one's way'.]

awe, *ö, n.* reverential fear, or wonder: dread.—*v.t.* to strike with, or influence by, fear.—*adjs.* **awe'some,** full of awe: inspiring awe: weird, dreadful; **awe'struck,** struck or affected with awe; **aw'ful,** full of awe: dreadful: inspiring respect: expressive of awe: (*slang*) fearful, excessive.—*n.* **aw'fulness.** [O.N. *agi* (O.E. *ege*), fear; cog. with Gael. *eaghal;* Gr. *achos,* anguish.]

aweary, *a-wē'ri, adj.* weary (of).—*adj.* **awea'ried,** weary. [Pfx. *a*- (O.E. *on*), on, and **weary.**]

a-week, *a-wēk', adv.* in the week, per week. [Prep. *a,* and **week.**]

awhile, *a-hwīl', adv.* for some time: for a short time. [O.E. *āne hwīle,* a while.]

awkward, *ök'ẃard, adj.* clumsy: ungraceful: embarrassing: difficult to deal with.—*adv.* **awk'wardly.**—*n.* **awk'wardness.** [Prob. O.N. *afug,* turned wrong way, and suffix. -*ward,* expressing direction.]

awl, *öl, n.* a pointed instrument for boring small holes in leather. [O.E. *æl;* cog. with O.N. *alr,* Ger. *ahle.*]

awn, *ön, n.* the beard of certain grasses, as barley: any similar growth.—*adjs.* **awned; awn'less.** [O.N. *ögn;* Ger. *ahne.*]

awning, *ön'ing, n.* a covering above or in front of

a place to afford shelter from the sun or weather. [Ety. uncertain.]

awoke, *a-wōk', pa.t.* and *pa.p.* of **awake.**

awry, *a-rī', adj.* (used predicatively) twisted to one side: crooked.—*adv.* crookedly, obliquely: perversely. [Pfx. *a*- (O.E. *on*), on, **wry.**]

axe, ax, *aks, n.* a tool or instrument for hewing or chopping:—*pl.* **ax'es.**—*v.t.* to use an axe on: (*fig.*) to cut down, reduce: (*fig.*) to dispense with.—**axe to grind,** a private purpose to serve. [O.E. *æx;* L. *ascia;* Gr. *axinē.*]

axil, *aks'il, n.* (*bot.*) the upper angle between leaf and stem or between branch and trunk. [L. *axilla,* the armpit.]

axiom, *aks'i-òm, aks'yóm, n.* a self-evident truth: a universally received principle in an art or science.—*adjs.* **axiomat'ic, axiomat'ical.**—*adv.* **axiomat'ically.** [Gr. *axiōma*—*axioein,* to think worth, to take for granted—*axios,* worthy.]

axis, *aks'is, n.* a line about which a body rotates, or about which a figure is conceived to revolve: a straight line about which the parts of a figure, body or system are symmetrically arranged: a fixed line adopted for reference in co-ordinate geometry: an alliance of powers, around which other powers are supposed to revolve:—*pl.* **axes** (*aks'ēz*).—*adj.* **ax'ial.** [L. *axis;* cf. Gr. *axōn,* Sans. *aksa,* O.E. *eax.*]

axle, *aks'l,* **axle-tree,** *aks'l-trē, n.* the pin or rod in the nave of a wheel on which the wheel turns. [From O.N. *öxull.*]

Axminster, *aks'min-stér, adj.* applied to a variety of pile carpet. [*Axminster* in Devon, where it used to be made.]

ay, aye, *ī, adv.* yea: yes: indeed.—*n.* **aye** (*ī*), a vote in the affirmative: (*pl.*) those who vote in the affirmative. [Perh. a dial. form of *aye,* ever; perh. a variant of *yea.*]

ayah, *ī'ya, n.* an Indian waiting-maid or nurse-maid. [Hindustani *āya;* Port. *aia,* nurse.]

aye, ay, *ā, adv.* ever: always: for ever. [O.N. *ei,* ever; conn. with O.E. *ā,* always; also with **age, ever.**]

azalea, *a-zā'li-a, n.* a genus of shrubby plants, closely allied to the rhododendrons. [Gr. *azaleos,* dry—reason for name uncertain.]

azimuth, *az'im-uth, n.* the arc of the horizon between the meridian of a place and a vertical circle passing through any celestial body.—*adj.* **az'imuthal.** [Ar. *as-sumūt*—*as*=*al,* the, *sumūt,* pl. of *samt,* direction. See **zenith.**]

Aztec, *az'tek, adj.* relating to or descended from the Aztecs, the dominant tribe in Mexico at the time of the arrival of the Spaniards.—*n.* a member of that tribe: the language of the Aztecs.

azure, *azh'ÿur,* or *ā'zyÿur, adj.* of a faint blue, sky-coloured: clear, cloudless.—*n.* a delicate blue colour: the sky. [O.Fr. *azur*—through L.L. and Ar. from Pers. *lājward,* lapis lazuli.]

Neutral vowels in unaccented syllables: *em'pér-òr;* for certain sounds in foreign words see p. ix.

B

baa, *bä*, *n.* the cry of a sheep.—*v.i.* to cry or bleat as a sheep. [From the sound.]

Baal, *bā'ál*, *n.* a god of the Phoenicians: a false god generally:—*pl* **Bā'alim**. [Heb.]

babble, *bab'l*, *v.i.* to speak like a baby: to make a babbling noise: to talk incessantly or incoherently: to tell secrets (to).—*v.t.* to prate: to utter.—*ns.* **babb'le**, **babb'lement**, idle senseless talk, prattle: confused murmur; **babb'ler**, one who babbles. [Prob. imit.; cf. Ger. *pappelen*, Fr. *babiller*.]

babe, *bāb*, *n.* form of **baby**.

babel, *bā'bėl*, *n.* a lofty structure; a confused combination of sounds: a scene of confusion. [Heb. *Babel*, explained in Gen. xi. as confusion.]

baboo, **babu**, *bä'bōō*, *n.* orig. a title in Bengal corresponding to our *Mr*: an Indian clerk: an Indian with a pretentious and defective knowledge of English. [Hindustani *bābū*.]

baboon, *ba-bōōn'*, *n.* a large monkey of various species, having a long face, dog-like tusks, large lips, and a short tail. [Fr. *babouin*.]

baby, *bā'bi*, *n.* an infant or child: a thing small of its kind: an inexperienced person: (*coll.*) one's pet project: (*coll.*) responsibility.—Also *adj.*—*n.* **bā'byhood.**—*adj.* **bā'byish.**—*n.* **bā'bysitter**, someone who remains in the house with a baby while its mother or usual guardian goes out.—*v.i.* **bā'by-sit.** [Prob. imitative; cf. **babble**.]

baccalaureate, *bak a lö're át*, *n.* the university degree of bachelor. [Low L. *baccalaureus*.]

baccarat, **baccara**, *bak'är-ä*, *n.* a French gambling card-game. [Fr.]

bacchanal, *bak'a-nál*, *n.* a worshipper, priest, or priestess of Bacchus: one who indulges in drunken revels.—*adj.* relating to drinking or drunken revels—also **bacchanā'lian.**—*ns.pl.* **bacchanā'lia**, **bacch'anals**, drunken revels.—*n.* and *adj.* **bacchant** (*bak'ant*), a priest or worshipper of Bacchus: a reveller.—*n.* **bacchante** (*bak-ant'*, *bak'ant*, *ba-kant'i*), a priestess of Bacchus: a female bacchanal:—*pl.* **bacchant'es.** [L. *Bacchus*—Gr. *Bakchos*, the god of wine.]

bachelor, *bach'el-ór*, *n.* (*hist.*) a young knight who followed the banner of another: an unmarried man: one who has taken his or her first degree at a university.—*ns.* **bach'elorhood**, **bach'elorship.**—**bach'elor-girl**, a young unmarried woman who supports herself; **bach'elor's-butt'on**, a kind of buttercup. [O.Fr. *bacheler*—Low L. *baccalārius*, a small farmer.]

bacillus, *ba-sil'us*, *n.* a rod-shaped member of the **bacteria**: (loosely) any bacterium, esp. one causing disease:—*pl.* **bacill'i.** [Low L. *bacillus*, dim. of *baculus*, a rod.]

back, *bak*, *n.* the hinder part of the body in man, and the upper part in beasts: the hinder part: the convex surface of anything curved, as the convex part of a book: the thick edge of a knife or the like: (*football*) one of the players behind the forwards. *adj.* rearward: in arrears or out of date: reversed: (*phonet.*) made by raising the back of the tongue.—*adv.* to the place from which the person or thing came: to a former state or condition: behind: in return: again.—*v.t.* to get upon the back of: to force back: to furnish with a back: to form the back of: to help, as if standing at one's back: to support one's opinion by a wager or bet: to countersign (a warrant), endorse (e.g. a cheque).—*v.i.* to move or go back (of the wind) to change counter-clockwise.—*adj.* **backed**, having a back (as in *humpbacked*).—*v.t.* **back'bite**, to speak evil of anyone behind his back or in his absence.—*n.* **back'biter.**—*n.pl.* **back'-blocks** (*Austr.*), the interior parts of a station (q.v.), far from the riverfront.—*ns.* **back'-board**, a board placed at the back of a cart, boat, &c.: a board fastened across the back to straighten the body; **back'bone**, the spine or vertebral column: mainstay: firmness; **back'-chat**, answering back, impertinence; **back'-cloth**, **back'-drop**, the painted cloth at the back of a stage: **back'(-)country**, districts not yet thickly peopled; **back'-door**, a door in the back part of a building.—*adj.* unworthily secret, clandestine.—*ns.* **back'-end**, the rear end: (*Scot.*) the late autumn; **back'er**, one who backs or supports another in a contest or undertaking—e.g. with money: a punter; **back'fire**, ignition of gas in an internal combustion engine's cylinder at the wrong time, or *within* a gasburner instead of at the outlet.—Also *v.i.* (*bak-fīr'*).—*ns.* **back'-forma'tion**, (the coining of) a word from one that is in error or jocularly taken to be a derivative, as the verb *burgle* from *burglar*; **back'-ground**, ground at the back: a place of obscurity: the space behind the principal figures of a picture (also *fig.*): (*fig.*) upbringing, environment; **back'-hand**, the hand turned backwards in making a stroke; a stroke so made: handwriting with the letters sloped backwards.—*adj.* **back'-hand'(ed)**, made with the hand turned backward (of a blow or stroke): (*fig.*) indirect.—*ns.* **back'-hand'er**, a blow with the back of the hand: a bribe; **back'-lash** (*fig.*), reaction or consequence, esp. if violent; **backlog** (*fig.*), reserve or accumulation of business, stock, &c.—*adj.* **back'most**, farthest to the back.—*n.* **back'-num'ber**, a copy or issue of a newspaper or magazine of a bygone date: (*fig.*) a person, thing, out of date or past usefulness.—*v.i.* **back'-pedal**, to hold back: to reverse one's course of action. *ns.* **back'-scratching** (*fig.*), doing favours in return for favours: servile flattery; **back'side**, the back or hinder side or part of anything (also **back side**): the hinder part of an animal.—*v.i.* **backslide'**, to slide or fall back in faith or morals:—*pa.p.* backslid', or backslidd'en.—*ns.* **backslid'er**; **backslid'-ing**.—*n.pl.* **back'stairs**, servants' or private stairs of a house.—*adj.* secret or under-hand.—*n.pl.* **back'stays**, ropes to support the mast, sloping backwards from the mast-head to the ship's sides.—*v.i.* **back'track**, to go back on one's course.—*ns.* **back'-wash** (*lit.* and *fig.*), a backward current, as of a receding wave; **back'water**, water turned back by an obstacle such as a waterwheel, paddles, oars, &c.: a river pool not in the main channel: a place unaffected by the movements of the day.—*n.pl.* **back'-woods**, the forest or uncul-tivated part of a country beyond the cleared land, as in North America.—*n.* **back-woods'man**—**back**! go back, turn back (*im-peratively*); **back of** (*U.S.*), behind; **back down,** to abandon one's opinion or position; **back out,** to move out backwards: to recede from an engagement or promise; **back up,** to give support to; **back-seat driver**, one free of responsibility but full of advice; **back water,** to keep a boat steady or make it move back-wards by reversing the action of the oars; **break the back of,** to overburden: to complete the hardest part of (a task); **put one's back into,** to do with might and main; **put one's back up,** to arouse one's resentment; **take a back seat,** (*fig.*), to take a subordinate or in-conspicuous place. [O.E. *bæc,* Swed. *bak,* Dan. *bag.*]

backgammon, *bak-gam'ón, n.* a game played by two persons on a board with dice and fifteen men or pieces each. [Perh. O.E. *bæc,* back, and M.E. *gamen,* game.]

backsheesh, backshish. See **baksheesh.**

backward, *bak'wárd, adv.* and *adj.* towards the back: on the back: towards the past: from a better to a worse state.—*adv.* also **back'-wards**.—*adj.* **back'ward,** slow: late: dull or stu-pid: bashful.—*n.* **back'wardness.**—**bend, fall, lean, over backwards** (*coll.*), to go up to the point of personal discomfort (to be accommodat-ing). [**back,** and affix. *-ward, -wards,* in the direction of.]

bacon, *bā'kón, n.* swine's flesh (now the back and sides) salted or pickled and dried.—**to bring home the bacon** (*coll.*), to achieve an object: provide material support; **to save one's bacon,** to come off unharmed, though with difficulty. [O.Fr. *bacon,* of Gmc. origin; cf. Ger. *bache.*]

Baconian, *bā-kōn'i-án, adj.* pertaining to Lord *Bacon* (1561-1626), or to his philosophy, or to the theory that he wrote Shakespeare's plays.

bacteria, *bak-tē'ri-a, n.pl.* microscopic organ-isms (name orig. applied to those that were rod-shaped) found in countless numbers wherever organic matter is in process of de-composition and abundantly present in the air, the soil and its products, and in living bodies. Their manifold activities are essential to plant and animal life, but some are the germs of disease.—*sing.* **bactēr'ium.**—*ns.* **bac-teriol'ogy,** the study of bacteria; **bacteriol'-ogist; bactē'riophage** (*-fāj, -fäzh*), any of a number of virus-like agents, present in soil,

water, &c., which destroy bacteria. [Gr. *baktē-rion,* dim. of *baktron,* a stick.]

bad, *bad, adj.* wicked: hurtful: rotten (e.g. egg): incorrect, faulty: worthless: spurious: un-favourable: painful: unwell: severe:—*comp.* **worse,** *superl.* **worst.**—*adv.* **bad'ly.**—*n.* **bad'-ness.—bad blood,** ill-feeling; **bad coin,** false coin; **bad debt,** debt that cannot be recovered; **bad form** (see **form**).—**go bad,** to decay; **go to the bad,** to go to moral ruin; **with bad grace,** ungraciously. [M.E. *badde.*]

bade, *bad, pa.t.* of **bid.**

badge, *baj, n.* a distinguishing mark or emblem. [M.E. *bage;* origin obscure.]

badger, *baj'ér, n.* a genus of burrowing, hiber-nating animals of the weasel family.—*v.t.* to pursue with eagerness, as dogs hunt the badger, to pester or worry. [Prob. from **badge** and suffix. *-ard,* from the white mark like a badge on the badger's forehead.]

badinage, *bad'in-äzh, n.* light playful talk, ban-ter. [Fr. *badinage—badin,* playful.]

badminton, *bad'min-ton, n.* a cooling summer drink compounded of claret, sugar, and sodawater: a game played with shuttlecocks. [From *Badminton,* a seat of the Duke of Beaufort.]

baffle, *baf'l, v.t.* to check or make ineffectual: to bewilder.—*n.* **baffle plate,** a device for regulat-ing the flow of liquids, gas, &c. [Prob. Scottish; but cf. Fr. *beffler,* from O.Fr. *befe,* mockery.]

baffy, *baf'i, n.* (*golf*) a club like a brassy, but with a shorter shaft and a more sloping face.

bag, *bag, n.* a sack, pouch: a measure of quantity for produce: the quantity of fish, game, &c., secured: (*slang*) an unattractive or immoral woman.—*v.t.* to put (especially game) into a bag, hence to kill (game): to seize, secure, or steal:—*pr.p.* bagg'ing; *pa.p.* bagged.—*n.* **bagg'-ing,** cloth or material for bags.—*adj.* **bagg'y,** loose like a bag.—*ns.* **bag'man,** a commercial traveller; **bag'-wig,** an 18th-century wig, the back-hair of which was enclosed in an orna-mental bag.—**bag and baggage** (originally a military expression), entire equipment; **let the cat out of the bag,** to disclose the secret. [M.E. *bagge.*]

bagatelle, *bag-a-tel', n.* a trifle: a piece of music in a light style: a game played on a board with nine balls and a cue. [Fr.,—It. *bagatella,* a conjurer's trick, a trifle.]

baggage, *bag'ij, n.* the tents, provisions, and other necessaries of an army: traveller's luggage: a worthless or saucy woman. [O.Fr. *bagage—baguer,* to bind up.]

bagnio, *ban'yō, n.* a bathing house, esp. one with hot baths: an oriental prison: a brothel. [It. *bagno*—L. *balneum,* a bath.]

bagpipe, *bag'pīp, n.* (often in *pl.*) a wind-instrument, consisting of a bag fitted with pipes.—*n.* **bag'piper.** [**bag, pipe.**]

bail, *bāl, n.* one who procures the release of an accused person by becoming security for his appearing in court: the security given.—*v.t.* to set a person free by giving security for him (with *out*): to release on the security of another (but more commonly to **accept, allow, admit to, bail**): to deliver (goods) in trust upon a contract.—*n.* **bailee',** one to whom goods are entrusted on bail.—**go bail,** to be-

Neutral vowels in unaccented syllables: *em'pér-òr;* for certain sounds in foreign words see p. ix.

50

come surety (for). [O.Fr. *bail*, jurisdiction— *baillier*, to have in custody; the word became associated with Norm. Fr. *bailler*, to deliver— L. *bajulus*, a carrier.]

bail, *bāl*, *n*. one of the cross pieces laid on the top of the wicket in cricket. [M.E.,—O.Fr. *baile*, perh. from *baillier*, to enclose; cf. **bail**(1).]

bail, *bāl*, *v.t.* to clear (a boat) of water with shallow buckets, &c.; to scoop (water out) from a boat.—Also **bale.—to bale (bail) out,** to escape from an aeroplane by parachute or (*fig.*) from a potentially difficult situation. [Fr. *baille*, a bucket, perh. from Low L. *bacula*, dim. of *baca*, a basin.]

bailey, *bāl'i*, *n*. the outer court of a feudal castle. [Fr. *baille*, palisade, enclosure.]

Bailey bridge, *bā'li-brij*, a bridge prefabricated for rapid erection. [Inventor's name.]

bailie, *bāl'i*, *n*. in Scotland, title of magistrate who presides in borough or police court. [O.Fr. *bailli*, earlier *baillis*, land-steward, officer of justice. See **bailiff.**]

bailiff, *bāl'if*, *n*. a sheriff's officer: an agent or land-steward.—*n*. **bail'iwick,** the jurisdiction of a bailiff. [O.Fr. *baillif*, acc. of *baillis*—Low L. *bājulīvus*—*bājulus*, carrier, administrator; cf. **bail** (1).]

bairn, *bārn*, *n*. (*Scot.*) a child. [O.E. *bearn*— *beran*, to bear.]

bait, *bāt*, *n*. food put on a hook to allure fish or make them bite: any allurement: a refreshment taken on a journey.—*v.t.* to set food as a lure: to give refreshment on a journey: to set dogs on (a bear, badger, &c.): to worry, persecute, harass.—*v.i.* to take refreshment on a journey. [M.E. *beyten*—Scand. *beita*, to cause to bite—*bita*, to bite.]

baize, *bāz*, *n*. a coarse woollen cloth. [Fr. *baies*, pl. of *bai*—L. *badius*, bay-coloured.]

bake, *bāk*, *v.t.* to dry, harden, or cook by the heat of the sun or of fire: to prepare food in an oven.—*v.i.* to work as a baker: to become firm through heat:—*pa.p.* baked (*bākt*); *pr.p.* bāk'ing.—*ns.* **bake'house,** a house or place used for baking in; **bake'meat** (*B.*), pastry, pies; **bak'er,** one who bakes bread, &c.; **baker's dozen** (see **dozen**); **bak'ery,** a bakehouse; **bak'ing,** the process by which bread is baked: the quantity baked at one time.— **baking powder,** a powder containing a carbonate (such as *baking soda*) and an acid substance (such as *cream of tartar*) used to make cakes, &c., rise; **baking soda,** sodium bicarbonate. [O.E. *bacan*; cog. with Ger. *backen*, to bake, Gr. *phōgein*, to roast.]

baksheesh, bakhshish, backsheesh, backshish, *buk'shēsh*, or *bak'shēsh*, *n*. a present of money in the East: a tip. [Pers. *bakhshīsh*.]

balalaika, *bä-lä-lī'kä*, *n*. a Russian musical instrument with a triangular body and normally three strings. [Russ.]

balance, *bal'ans*, *n*. an instrument for weighing, usually formed of two dishes or scales hanging from a beam supported in the middle: act of weighing (*lit.* and *fig.*): equality or just proportion of weight or power (as *the balance of power*): state of mental or emotional equilibrium: harmony among the parts of anything (as in a work of art): the sum required to make the two sides of an account equal,

hence the surplus, or the sum due on an account: a counterpoise.—*v.t.* to weigh in a balance: to counterpoise: to compare: to bring into, or keep in, equilibrium: to make the debtor , and creditor sides of an account agree.—*v.i.* to have equal weight or power, &c.: to be or come to be in equilibrium: to hesitate or fluctuate.—*ns.* **bal'ance-sheet,** a sheet of paper showing a summary and balance of accounts; **bal'ance-wheel,** a wheel in a watch which regulates the beat or rate.—**balance of payments,** difference over a period between a nation's total receipts from foreign countries and its total payments to foreign countries; **on balance,** having taken everything into consideration. [Fr.,—L. *bilanx*, having two scales—*bis*, double, *lanx, lancis*, a dish or scale.]

balata, *bal'a-ta*, *n*. the gum of the bullet or bully tree of South America, used as a substitute for rubber and gutta-percha. [Sp., from South American Indian.]

balcony, *balk'on-i*, *n*. a stage or platform projecting from the wall of a building within or without. [It. *balcōne*—*balco*, of Gmc. origin; O.H.G. *balcho*, Eng. **balk.**]

bald, *böld*, *adj.* without hair (or feathers, &c.) on the head (or on other parts of the body): bare, unadorned.—*n*. **bald'head,** a person bald on the head.—*adj.* and *adv.* **bald'-headed** (*slang*), impetuous(ly), reckless(ly).—*adj.* **bald'ing,** growing bald.—*adv.* **bald'ly.**—*n*. **bald'ness.** [Orig. 'shining', 'white'—Ir. and Gael. *bàl*, 'white' spot.]

balderdash, *böl'dėr-dash*, *n*. senseless confused talk or writing. [Origin unknown.]

baldric, baldrick, *böld'rik*, *n*. a warrior's belt or shoulder-sash. [O.Fr. *baldrei*—Low L. *baldringus*, perh. from L. *balteus*, a belt.]

bale, *bāl*, *n*. a bundle or package of goods.—*v.t.* to make into bales. [M.E. *bale*, perh. from O.Fr. *bala*—O.H.G. *balla, palla*, ball.]

bale, *bāl*, *v.t.* same as **bail** (3).

bale, *bāl*, *n*. evil, injury: woe.—*adj.* **bale'ful,** full of evil, malignant, sorrowful, sad.—*adv.* **bale'fully.**—*n*. **balefulness.** [O.E. *bealu*; O.H.G. *balo*; O.N. *böl*.]

bale, *bāl*, *n*. (*arch.*) a fire, funeral pyre.—*n*. **bale-fire,** a blazing fire: a beacon-fire: a bonfire. [O.E. *bǣl*; Scand. *bàl*; cog. with Gr. *phalos*, bright.]

baleen, *ba-lēn'*, *n*. whalebone. [O.Fr. *baleine*—L. *bālaena*, whale.]

balk, baulk, *bök*, *n*. an unploughed ridge of turf: squared timber: hindrance, disappointment.—*v.t.* to avoid, shirk: to check, disappoint, or elude.—*v.i.* to swerve, pull up. [O.E. *balca*, ridge; O.H.G. *balcho*, beam.]

ball, *böl*, *n*. anything spherical or nearly so: a globular body to play with in tennis, football, &c.: (*pl.*) testicles: a bullet: any rounded protuberant part of the body.—*n.pl.* **ball'-bearings,** in machinery, a device for lessening friction by making a revolving part turn on loose steel balls.—*ns.* **ball'-cart'ridge,** a cartridge containing both powder and ball; **ball'-cock,** a valve in a cistern, shut or opened by the rise or fall of a ball floating in the water.—*adjs.* **ball'-point,** of a fountain pen, having a tiny ball rotating against an inking car-

ball

tridge as its writing tip; **ball'-proof,** proof against balls discharged from firearms.—**no ball** (*cricket*), a delivery adjudged contrary to rule.—**have the ball at one's feet,** to have success in one's reach; **keep the ball up** or **rolling,** to keep things going. [M.E. *bal,* Scand. *böllr.*]

ball, *böl, n.* an entertainment of dancing.—*n.* **ball'room.—open the ball,** to begin the dancing: to begin operations. [O.Fr. *bal*—*baller,* to dance—Low L. *ballāre,* referred by some to Gr. *ballizein.*]

ballad, *bal'ád, n.* a simple narrative poem in stanzas of two or four lines: a simple song, usually of a sentimental nature.—*n.* **ball'ad-monger,** a dealer in, or composer of, ballads.—**ballad opera,** an opera with spoken dialogue and songs set to existing popular tunes. [O.Fr. *balade,* from Low L. *ballāre.* to dance.]

ballade, *bä-läd', n.* a poem of one or more triplets of stanzas, each of seven or eight lines, including a refrain, usually concluding with an envoy: now frequently used of any poem in stanzas of equal length: a form of instrumental music (not strictly defined). [An earlier spelling of **ballad.**]

ballast, *bal'ást, n.* heavy matter placed in a ship to keep it steady when it has no cargo: that which renders anything steady.—*v.t.* to load with ballast: to make or keep steady.—**in ballast,** without cargo. [Probably Old Swed. *barlast*—*bar,* bare, and *last,* load.]

ballerina, *bal-ler-ēn'ä, n.* a female ballet-dancer:—*pl.* **ballerin'as, balleri'ne.** [It.]

ballet, *bal'ā, n.* a theatrical exhibition of dancing and pantomimic action: the troupe that performs it.—*ns.* **balletomane** (*-et'ō-mān*)*;* ballet enthusiast; **balletomā'nia.** [Fr.; dim. of *bal,* a dance.]

ballista, balista, *bä-lis'tä, n.* a Roman military engine, in the form of a crossbow, which propelled large and heavy missiles.—*adj.* **ballistic,** of or pertaining to forcible throwing of missiles: relating to projectiles (**ballistic missile,** a missile guided for only part of its course and falling as an ordinary projectile).—*n.* **ballis'tics,** the science of projectiles. [L.—Gr. *ballein,* to throw.]

balloon, *ba-lōōn', n.* a large bag, made of light material and filled with a gas lighter than air so as to be able to ascend—often with car attached: a toy of similar form: anything inflated and empty: balloon-shaped drawing enclosing words spoken in a strip cartoon.—*v.i.* to travel in a balloon: to puff out like a balloon.—**when the balloon goes up,** when proceedings begin or trouble starts. [It. *ballone,* augmentative of *balla,* ball.]

ballot, *bal'ót, n.* a little ball or ticket or paper used in voting: a method of secret voting by putting a ball or ticket or paper into an urn or box.—*v.i.* to vote by ballot: to draw lots (*for*):—*pr.p.* ball'oting; *pa.p.* ball'oted.—*n.* **ball'ot-box,** a box to receive ballots. [It. *ballotta,* dim. of *balla,* ball.]

ballyhoo, *bal-i-hōō'* (or *bal'-*)*, n.* (*slang*) noisy or sensational propaganda.

ballyrag, *bal'i-rag, v.t.* to bullyrag (q.v.).

balm, *bäm, n.* an aromatic substance: a fragrant

band

and healing ointment: anything that heals or soothes pain.—*adj.* **balm'y,** fragrant: soothing: bearing balm: (*slang*) mad, crazy. [O.Fr. *basme* (*baume*)—L. *balsamum.* See **balsam.**]

balmoral, *bal-mor'ál, n.* a flat Scottish bonnet: a figured woollen petticoat: a kind of boot lacing in front. [*Balmoral,* royal castle in Aberdeenshire built by Queen Victoria.]

balsa, *bäl'sa, n.* a raft or float: a tropical American tree with very light, porous wood: its wood (also *cork-wood*). [Sp., raft.]

balsam, *böl'sam, n.* the common name of a genus of herbaceous plants: a liquid resin or resinous oily substance derived from various trees of the East or of America.—*adj.* **balsam'ic,** soothing. [L. *balsamum*—Gr. *balsamon;* prob. of Semitic origin.]

baluster, *bal'us-tér, n.* a small pillar supporting a stair rail, &c.—*adj.* **bal'ustered.**—*n.* **bal'ustrade,** a row of balusters joined by a rail. [Fr. *balustre*—Low L. *balaustium*—Gr. *balaustion,* the pomegranate flower, from the similarity of form.]

bambino, *bam-bē'no, n.* a child: representation of the child Jesus. [It.]

bamboo, *bam-bōō', n.* a genus of gigantic tropical and subtropical grasses, with hollow, jointed, woody stem.—**bamboo curtain,** the impenetrable barrier of Asiatic, esp. Chinese, communism. [Malay *bambu.*]

bamboozle, *bam-bōō'zl, v.t.* to deceive: to confound or mystify. [Origin unknown; first appears about 1700.]

ban, *ban, n.* a proclamation: a denunciation: a curse: a prohibition.—*v.t.* to proscribe: to forbid or prohibit. [O.E. *bannan,* to summon.]

banal, *bān'ál, ban'ál, ban-äl',* adj. commonplace, trivial.—*n.* **banality** (*ban-al'-i-ti*). [Fr.]

banana, *bá-nä'nä, n.* a gigantic herbaceous plant of which there are many varieties: its nutritious fruit. [Sp. or Port., from the native name on the Guinea coast.]

band, *band, n.* that by which loose things are held together. [M.E. *band, bond*—O.N. *band.*]

band, *band, n.* a strip of cloth, &c., to bind round anything, as a hat-band, &c.: a stripe crossing a surface, distinguished by its colour or appearance: (*pl.*) the pair of linen strips hanging down in front from the collar, worn by clergymen and barristers: (*radio*) a group or range of frequencies: a group of wavelengths.—*n.* **band'age,** a strip to bind up a wound or fracture, &c.—*v.t.* to bind with such.—*ns.* **band'box,** a thin box for holding millinery, &c. (orig. for bands or ruffs); **band-saw,** an endless saw, a toothed steel belt. [M.E. *bande*—O.Fr. *bande,* of Gmc. origin; cf. **band** (1).]

band, *band, n.* a number of persons bound together for any common purpose: a troop of conspirators, &c.: a body of musicians.—*v.t.* to bind (together).—*v.t.* and *v.i.* to associate, unite.—*ns.* **band'master,** conductor of a band of musicians; **bands'man,** member of a band of musicians; **band'-stand,** a platform for accommodating a band of musicians; **band'-wagon,** the car that carries the band in a procession (**climb, jump on the bandwagon,** to join the popular or winning side, support the candidate who is obviously going to be

Neutral vowels in unaccented syllables: *em'pér-ór;* for certain sounds in foreign words see p. ix.

52

successful, &c.).—**Band of Hope**, a temperance association for children. [Fr. *bande*, but with changed sense; cf. **band** (2).]

bandana, bandanna, *ban-dän′ä, n.* a kind of silk or cotton coloured handkerchief, originally from India. [Hindustani *bāndhnū,* a mode of dyeing.]

bandeau, *ban-dō′, n.* a fillet or band to bind the hair:—*pl.* **bandeaux** (*ban-dōz′*). [Fr.]

banderol, banderole, *ban′de-rōl, n.* a small banner or streamer, as that borne on the shaft of a lance. [Fr.]

bandicoot, *ban′di-kōōt, n.* a very large rat found in India and Ceylon: a genus of small marsupials in Australia, &c. [Dravidian (q.v.) *pandikokku,* pig-rat.]

bandied, *ban′did, pa.t.* and *pa.p.* of **bandy** (2).

bandit, *ban′dit, n.* an outlaw: a brigand:—*pl.* **ban′dits, banditti** (*ban-dit′ē*).—**one-armed bandit**, a fruit machine, from the similarity to an arm of the lever pulled to operate it, and the heavy odds against the user. [It. *bandito*—Low. L. *bannīre, bandīre,* to proclaim.]

bandoleer, bandolier, *ban-do-lēr′, n.* a shoulder belt, esp. for holding cartridges. [O.Fr. *bandouillere*—It. *bandoliera*—*banda,* a band.]

bandy, *ban′di, n.* a club bent at the end for striking a ball: (also **bandy-ball**) hockey. [Origin obscure.]

bandy, *ban′di, v.t.* to beat to and fro: to give and take (blows or reproaches):—*pa.t.* and *pa.p.* ban′died.—*n.* **ban′dying.** [Origin obscure.]

bandy, *ban′di, adj.* (of legs) bent outward at the knee.—*adj.* **ban′dy-legged′.** [Origin obscure.]

bane, *bān, n.* destruction, mischief, woe: poison: source or cause of evil.—*adj.* **bane′ful,** destructive.—*adv.* **bane′fully.**—*n.* **bane′fulness.** [O.E. *bana,* a murderer; O.N. *bani,* death.]

bang, *bang, n.* a heavy blow: a sudden loud noise.—*v.t.* to beat: to strike violently: to slam.—*n.* **bang′er** (*slang*), an explosive fire work: a sausage.—**bang on,** on the mark; **bang up to,** right up to. [Scand. *banga,* to hammer; cf. Ger. *bengel,* a cudgel.]

bang. Same as **bhang.**

bangle, *bang′gl, n.* a ring worn on arms or legs. [Hindustani *bangrī.*]

banian, banyan, *ban′yan, n.* an Indian fig-tree with vast rooting branches: a native Indian broker or financier.—**banian days** (*naut.*), meatless days. [Port. *banian,* perh. through Ar. and Hindustani, from Sans. *vaṇija,* a merchant.]

banish, *ban′ish, v.t.* to condemn to exile: to drive away.—*n.* **ban′ishment,** exile. [Fr. *banir*—Low L. *bannīre,* to proclaim; of same origin as **ban**.]

banister, *ban′istér, n.* a corr. of **baluster.**

banjo, *ban′jō, n.* a musical instrument of the guitar kind [Negro pronunciation of Fr. *bandore* or *pandore*—L. *pandūra*—Gr. *pandoura.*]

bank, *bangk, n.* a mound or ridge: the margin of a river, lake, &c.: rising ground in the sea.—*v.t.* (often with *up*) to enclose, strengthen, fortify with a bank: to pile up: to cover (a fire) so as to lessen the rate of combustion.—*v.t.* and *v.i.* (of aircraft) to tilt in turning. [M.E. *banke,* of Scand. origin; cog. with **bank** (2 and 3), **bench.**]

bank, *bangk, n.* a bench in a galley: a tier or rank of oars. [O.Fr. *banc,* of Gmc. origin, cog. with **bank** (1).]

bank, *bangk, n.* a place where money or other valuable material, e.g. blood, data (**blood, data bank**) is deposited until required: an institution for the keeping, lending, exchanging, &c., of money.—*v.t.* to deposit in a bank, as money.—*ns.* **bank-ā′gent,** formerly the head of a branch-bank in Scotland (now *bank manager*); **bank′-book,** a book in which record is kept of money deposited in, or withdrawn from, a bank; **bank′er,** one who keeps a bank: one employed in banking business: the stakeholder in certain gambling games; **banker's card,** a card issued by a bank guaranteeing the honouring of any cheque up to a specified value; **bank hol′iday,** a day on which banks are legally closed; **bank′ing,** the business of a banker.—*adj.* pertaining to a bank.—*ns.* **bank′-note,** a note issued by a bank, which passes as money, being payable to bearer on demand; **bank′-rate,** the minimum lending rate, the rate at which the Bank of England is prepared to discount bills; **bank′-stock,** a share or shares in the capital stock of a bank.—**joint-stock bank,** one whose capital is subscribed by a large number of shareholders.—**bank on,** to rely implicitly on, reckon on; **break the bank,** to win from the casino management a sum fixed as the limit it is willing to lose on any one day. [Fr. *banque,* of Gmc. origin, cog. with **bank** (1), (2).]

bankrupt, *bangk′rupt, n.* one who fails in business, an insolvent person.—*adj.* insolvent: destitute (of).—*n.* **bank′ruptcy,** the state of being, or act of becoming, bankrupt. [Fr. *banqueroute,* It. *banca rotta*—L. *ruptus,* broken.]

banner, *ban′ér, n.* a military standard: a flag or ensign.—*adj.* **bann′ered,** furnished with banners.—**banner headline,** a large-type headline running right across a newspaper page. [O.Fr. *banere*—Low L. *bandum, bannum*; cog. with **band** and **bind.**]

bannerol, *ban′ér-ōl, n.* Same as **banderol.**

bannock, *ban′ok, n.* a flat home-made cake of oatmeal, barley, or pease-meal. [O.E. *bannuc.*]

banns, *banz, n.pl.* a proclamation of intention to marry.—**forbid the banns,** to make formal objection to a proposed marriage. [From **ban**.]

banquet, *bangk′wet, -wit, n.* a feast; a ceremonial dinner, with speeches. *v.t.* to give a feast to.—*v.i.* to fare sumptuously.—*ns.* **banq′ueter; banq′ueting; banqueting-hall.** [Fr.,—*banc,* bench, like It. *banchetto,* from *banco.*]

banshee, *ban′shē, n.* a female fairy in Ireland and elsewhere, who wails and shrieks before a death in the family to which she is attached. [Ir. *bean sidhe*—Old Ir. *ben side,* woman of the fairies.]

bantam, *ban′tam, n.* a small variety of the common domestic fowl, notable for courage.—*adj.* of bantam-breed: little and combative.—*n.* **ban′tam-weight,** a boxer of over 8 st. but not more than 8 st. 6 lb. (amateur 8 st. 7 lb.). [Prob. *Bantam* in Java.]

banter, *bant′ér, v.t.* assail with good-humoured raillery.—*n.* humorous raillery: jesting.

bantling *bant′ling, n.* a child. [Prob. Ger. *bänkling,* bastard—*bank,* bench.]

fāte, fär; mē, hûr (her); *mīne; mōte, för; mūte; mōōn, fōōt;* ᴛʜen (then)

53

Bantu, *ban'tōō, n.* a name for a large group of South African languages and the peoples speaking them. [African, meaning 'people'.]

banyan. See **banian.**

baobab, *bā'o-bab, n.* a magnificent tree, native to tropical western Africa. [African.]

baptise, *bap-tīz', v.t.* to administer baptism to: to christen, give a name to.—*n.* **bap'tism,** immersion in, or sprinkling with, water as a religious ceremony.—*adj.* **baptis'mal.**—*adv.* **baptis'mally.**—*ns.* **bap'tist,** one who baptises: (*cap.*) one of a sect that approves of adult baptism only; **bap'tist(e)ry,** a place where baptism is administered.—**baptism of fire,** martyrdom by fire: (*fig.*) any trying ordeal, as a young soldier's first experience of being under fire. [Gr. *baptizein*—*baptein,* to dip in water.]

bar, *bär, n.* a rod of any solid substance: a bolt: a hindrance or obstruction: a bank of sand or other matter at the mouth of a river or a harbour: a counter across which drinks are served: a public-house: a counter at which one particular article of food, clothing, &c., is sold, or one particular service is given: the wooden rail dividing off the judge's seat, at which prisoners are placed for arraignment or sentence: any tribunal: the pleaders in a court as distinguished from the judges: a division in music.—*v.t.* to fasten or secure, as with a bar: to hinder or exclude:—*pr.p.* **barr'ing;** *pa.p.* **barred.**—*prep.* excluding, excepting (e.g. **bar none**).—*ns.* **bar'graph,** a diagram representing quantities by means of rectangles of different sizes; **bar'maid,** a waitress at the bar of a tavern or hotel; **bar'-man, -tend'er,** a man who serves at the bar of a public-house &c.—*prep.* **barr'ing,** excepting, saving.—**bar (-)sin'ister** (see **baton**); **called to the bar,** admitted as a barrister or advocate. [O.Fr. *barre*—Low L. *barra.*]

bar, *bar, n.* a unit of pressure or stress (one bar equals 10^5 newtons per square metre). [Gr. *baros,* weight.]

barb, *bärb, n.* the beard-like jag near the point of a fish-hook, &c.: (*fig.*) a wounding or pointed remark.—*v.t.* to arm with barbs.—*adjs.* **barbed,** furnished with a barb or barbs (e.g. **barbed-wire** used for fences); **barb'ate,** bearing a hairy tuft or tufts. [Fr. *barbe*—L. *barba,* a beard.]

barb, *bärb, n.* a swift kind of horse, the breed of which came from *Barbary* (see **Barbary ape**).

barbarous *bär'bär-us, adj.* uncivilised: uncultured: brutal.—*adj.* **barbār'ian,** uncivilised: without taste or refinement: foreign.—*n.* an uncivilised man (but usu. not a savage): a cruel, brutal man.—*adj.* **barbār'ic,** uncivilised: of art or taste, like that of barbarians.—*v.t.* **bar'barise,** to make barbarous.—*ns.* **bar'barism,** uncivilised life: rudeness of manners: a word or expression offensive to scholarly taste; **barbār'ity,** barbaric style: cruelty.—*adv.* **bar'barously.**—*n.* **bar'barousness.** [L.,—Gr. *barbaros,* foreign, lit. stammering, from the unfamiliar sound of foreign tongues.]

Barbary ape, *bär'bär-i äp, n.* the magot, or small tailless ape found in Africa and Gibraltar. [*Barbary,* the country of the Berbers in N. Africa, and **ape.**]

barbecue, *bärb'e-kū, v.t.* to roast whole: to cure flesh by exposing it on a barbecue.—*n.* a framework for drying and smoking meat: an animal roasted whole: an open-air party at which food is cooked over a charcoal fire. [Sp. *barbacoa*—Haitian (q.v.) *barbacôa,* a framework of sticks set upon posts.]

barbel, *bärb'el, n.* a fresh-water fish of the carp family, with beard-like appendages at its mouth. [O.Fr.,—Low L. *barbellus*—L. *barba,* a beard.]

barber, *bärb'èr, n.* one who shaves faces and dresses hair. [O.Fr. *barbeor*—L. *barba,* a beard.]

barberry, *bär'bèr-i, n.* a genus of thorny shrubs with yellow flowers and usu. red berries. [Low L. *berberis*; not from *berry.*]

barbette, *bär-bet', n.* a platform from which heavy guns are fired: the parapet protecting such a platform. [Fr.]

barbican, *bär'bi-kan, n.* a watch-tower over the gate of a fortress, esp. the outwork defending the drawbridge. [O.Fr. *barbacane*; perh. of Ar. or Pers. origin.]

barbital, *bär'bi-tál,* **barbitone,** *bär'bi-tōn, ns.* veronal, one of the soporific derivatives (**barbiturates**) of **barbituric acid.**

barcarol(l)e, *bär'ka-rōl, n.* a Venetian boat-song: a musical composition of similar character. [It. *barcarōla,* boat-song—*barca,* a boat.]

bard, *bärd, n.* a poet and singer among the ancient Celts: a poet.—*adj.* **bard'ic.** [Gael. and Ir. *bàrd.*]

bare, *bār, adj.* uncovered: naked: open to view: poor, scanty: unadorned: mere or by itself.—*v.t.* to strip or uncover.—*adjs.* **bare'backed,** with bare back: unsaddled; **bare'faced,** with the face uncovered: impudent.—*adv.* **bare'facedly.**—*n.* **bare'facedness.**—*adjs.* **bare'foot, -ed,** having the feet bare; **bare'headed; bare'legged.**—*adv.* **bare'ly,** scantily: only just: scarcely.—*n.* **bare'ness.** [O.E. *bær;* Ger. *baar,* *bar.*]

bare, *bār,* old *pa.t.* of **bear.**

bargain, *bär'g(i)n, n.* a contract or agreement: a (usu. favourable) transaction: a (usu. advantageous) purchase.—*v.i.* to make a contract or agreement: to chaffer.—*n.* **bar'gainer.**—**into the bargain,** over and above; **strike a bargain,** to come to terms, make an agreement. [O.Fr. *bargaigner*—Low L. *barcāniāre*; perh. from *barca,* a boat.]

barge, *bärj, n.* a flat-bottomed freight boat, used on rivers and canals: a large pleasure or state boat.—*v.i.* to move clumsily: to bump (into) like a barge.—*n.* **bar'gee,** a bargeman.—**barge in,** to intrude: to interfere. [O.Fr. *barge*—Low L. *barga.*]

barge-board, *bärj'-bōrd, börd, n.* a board extending along the edge of the gable of a house to cover the rafters and keep out the rain. [Perh. from Low L. *bargus,* a gallows.]

barilla, *bär-il'a, n.* an impure sodium carbonate obtained by burning certain seaside plants, used in making soap, glass, &c. [Sp.]

baritone, barytone, *bar'i-tōn, n.* a deep-toned male voice between bass and tenor: a singer with such a voice. [Through Fr.,—Gr. *barys,* heavy, deep, and *tonos,* tone.]

barium, *bā'ri-ùm, n.* a metallic element (atomic

Neutral vowels in unaccented syllables: *em'pér-ór*; for certain sounds in foreign words see p. ix.

54

no. 56; symbol Ba) present in baryta.—*adj.*
bar'ic. [From **baryta.**]

bark, *bärk, n.* the abrupt cry of a dog, wolf, &c.:
any similar sound.—*v.i.* to yelp like a dog: to
clamour: to advertise wares noisily: (*slang*) to
cough.—**bark up the wrong tree,** (*fig.*) to be
on the wrong scent, esp. to try to lay the
blame on the wrong person. [O.E. *beorcan.*]

bark, barque, *bärk, n.* technically, a three-
masted vessel whose mizzen-mast is fore-
and-aft rigged: (*poet.*) any boat or sailing
ship. [Fr. *barque*—Low L. *barca.*]

bark, *bärk, n.* (*bot.*) strictly, all tissues external
to the cork cambium (q.v.): popularly, the
corky and other material that can be peeled
from a woody stem.—*v.t.* to strip or peel the
bark from. [Scand. *börkr*; Dan. *bark.*]

barley, *bär'li, n.* a hardy grain used for food and
for making malt liquors and spirits.—*ns.*
bar'ley-su'gar, sugar candied by melting and
cooling (formerly by boiling with a decoction
of barley); **bar'ley-wat'er,** a decoction of
pearl-barley; **pearl'-bar'ley,** the grain ground
small; **pot'-bar'ley,** the grain deprived by
milling of its outer husk, used in making
broth, &c. [O.E. *bærlic* (*adj.*), from the same
root as *bere* (**bear,** 3), with suffix *-lic.*]

barm, *bärm, n.* froth of beer or other fermenting
liquor: yeast: leaven.—*adj.* **barm'y,** containing
barm or yeast, frothy. [O.E. *beorma*; Dan.
bärme, Ger. *bärme.*]

Barmecide, *bär'mē-sīd, n.* one who offers an
imaginary or pretended banquet or other benefit.—*adjs.* **bar'mecide, barmeci'dal.** [From
an imaginary feast given to a beggar in the
Arabian Nights by one of the *Barmecide*
family.]

barn, *bärn, n.* a building in which grain, hay,
&c., are stored.—*v.t.* to store in a barn.—*ns.*
and *adjs.* **barn'-door, barn'-yard.**—*ns.* **barn'-
owl,** a species of owl, generally buff-coloured
above, white below; **barn'-stormer,** a strolling
player. [O.E. *bere-ern,* contracted *bern,* from
bere, barley; *ern,* a house.]

barnacle, *bär'na-kl, n.* any of numerous shellfish
that, in the adult stage, adhere to rocks and
ship bottoms: a companion who sticks closely—*n.* **bar'nacle-goose,** a species of wild
goose. [O.Fr. *bernaque*—Low L. *bernaca.*]

barnacle, *bär'na-kl, n.* an instrument put on a
restless horse's nose to keep him quiet:
(*pl.—coll.*) spectacles. [O.Fr. *bernac,* muzzle, of
which *bernacle* seems to be a dim. form.]

barograph, *bar'o-gräf, n.* a barometer that records automatically variations of atmospheric
pressure. [Gr. *baros,* weight, *graphein,* to
write.]

barometer, *bar-om'et-ér, n.* an instrument by
which the pressure of the atmosphere is
measured, and changes of weather indicated:
(*fig.*) an indicator of change (e.g. in public
opinion).—*adj.* **baromet'ric.**—*adv.* **baro-
metrically** [Gr. *baros,* weight, *metron,* measure.]

baron, *bar'on, n.* a title of rank, the lowest in the
House of Peers: a foreign noble of similar
grade: formerly a title of the judges of the
Court of Exchequer: (*pl.*) in feudal times the
tenants-in-chief of the Crown, later the peers
or great lords of the realm generally: an
industrial magnate (e.g. *a press baron*).—*ns.*
bar'onage, the whole body of barons: a list or
book of barons; **bar'oness,** a baron's wife, or a
lady holding a baronial title in her own
right.—*adj.* **barōn'ial,** pertaining to a baron:
befitting a baron: (*archit.*) of a modern pretentious style imitating that of old castles.—*n.*
bar'ony, the territory of a baron: in Ireland, a
division of a county: in Scotland, a large manor: the rank of baron.—**baron of beef,** a joint
consisting of two sirloins left uncut at the
backbone. [O.Fr. *barun, -on*—Low L. *barō,
-ōnis,* in the Romance tongues the word
meant a man as opposed to a woman, a strong
man, a warrior.]

baronet, *bar'on-et, n.* the lowest British hereditary title.—*ns.* **bar'onetage,** the whole body
of baronets: a list of such; **bar'onetcy,** the
rank of baronet; **baronetess,** a woman who
succeeds to a Scottish baronetcy. [Dim. of
baron.]

baroque, *bar-ōk', adj.* originally a jeweller's term
applied to a rough pearl: now applied in art
generally to a vigorous, exuberant style—
grotesque, extravagant, whimsical—in vogue
from the mid 16th to the late 18th century:
sometimes used as equivalent to *rococo*
(q.v.).—Also *n.* [Fr. *baroque*; ety. uncertain.]

baroscope, *bar'o-skōp, n.* an instrument for indicating changes in the density of the air. [Gr.
baros, weight, *skopeein,* to look at.]

barouche, *ba-rōōsh', n.* a double-seated four-
wheeled carriage with a falling top. [Ger. *bar-
utsche*—It. *baroccio*—L. *bis,* twice, *rota,* a
wheel.]

barque. Same as **bark** (2).

barrack, *bar'ak, n.* a building for soldiers, esp. in
garrison (generally in *pl.*). [Fr. *baraque* (It.
baracca, Sp. *barraca,* a tent).]

barrack, *bar'ak, v.i.* to make a hostile demonstration, esp. by cheering ironically—Also
v.t. -n. and *adj.* **barr'acking.** [Austr. *borak.*]

barracuda, -coota, -couta, *bar-a-kōō'dä, -kōō'tä,
n.* a voracious West Indian fish. (**barracouta**
only) snoek. [Sp. *baracuta.*]

barrage, *bar-äzh', bar'äzh,* or *bar'ij, n.* an artificial bar across a river: the forming of such a
bar: a barrier formed by a continuous shower
of projectiles along a fixed or a moving line, or
by captive balloons &c. [Fr. *barrage*—*barre,*
bar.]

barrel, *bar'él, n.* a round wooden vessel made of
curved staves bound with hoops: the quantity
which such a vessel contains: anything long
and hollow, as the barrel of a gun.—*v.t.* to put
in a barrel.—*p.adj.* **barr'elled,** having a barrel
or barrels: placed in a barrel.—*n.* **barr'el-
or'gan,** a mechanical instrument for playing
tunes by means of a revolving barrel or cylinder set with pins which operate keys and thus
open the valves and admit air to the pipes. [Fr.
baril—Low L. *barile, barillus,* possibly from
barra, bar.]

barren, *bar'én, adj.* incapable of bearing offspring: unfruitful: dull, stupid: unprofit-
able.—*adv.* **barr'enly.**—*n.* **barr'enness.** [O.Fr.
barain, brahain, brehaing, perh. from *bar,*
man, as if 'male-like, not producing offspring'.]

barricade, *bar'ik-ād, n.* a temporary fortification
raised to block a street: an obstruction.—*v.t.* to

obstruct: to fortify.—Earlier form **barricā'do**. [Fr. *barricade*, or Sp. *barricada*—perh. Fr. *barrique* or Sp. *barrica*, a cask, the first street barricades being of casks filled with stones, &c.]

barrier, *bar'i-ėr, n.* a defence against attack: a limit or boundary: a fence or other structure to bar passage, prevent access, control crowds, &c.—*ns.* **barrier cream,** a dressing for the skin used to prevent dirt from entering the pores and as a protection against oils and solvents; **barr'ier-reef,** a coral-reef surrounding an island or fringing a coast with a navigable channel inside. [O.Fr. *barrière*—Low L. *barrāria*—*barra*, bar.]

barrister, *bar'is-tér, n.* one who is qualified to plead at the bar in an English or Irish law-court. [From *barra*, bar, the suffix being unexplained.]

barrow, *bar'ō, n.* a small hand or wheeled vehicle used to bear or convey a load.—*n.* **barr'ow-boy,** a street-trader who sells goods from a barrow. [M.E. *barewe*, from an assumed O.E. form *bearwe*—*beran*, to bear.]

barrow, *bar'ō, n.* a mound raised over graves in former times. [O.E. *beorg*; cog. with Ger. *berg*.]

barter, *bär'tér, v.t.* to give (one thing) in exchange (for another): to give (away for some unworthy gain).—*v.i.* to traffic by exchanging.—*n.* traffic by exchange of commodities. [Prob. from O.Fr. *barat*, deceit.]

bartisan, bartizan, *bär'ti-zan, n.* a parapet or battlement. [Apparently an adaptation by Sir Walter Scott of Scot. *bertisene*, for *bratticing*. See **brattice**.]

barton, *bär'ton, n.* a farm-yard. [O.E. *bere*, barley, *tun*, enclosure.]

baryon, *bar'i-on, n.* any one of the heavier class of subatomic particles, which includes protons and neutrons.—Opp. to *lepton*. [Gr. *barys*, heavy.]

baryta, *bä-rī'ta, n.* an oxide of barium.—*n.* **barytes** (*bä-rī'tēz*), heavy-spar, native barium sulphate. [From Gr. *barys*, heavy.]

barytone *bar'i-tōn.* Same as **baritone.**

basalt, *bas'ölt, bas-ölt', n.* name for certain dark-coloured rocks of igneous origin.—*adj.* **basalt'ic.** [L. *basaltes*—an African word.]

base, *bās, n.* that on which a thing rests: bottom, foundation, support: the chief or essential ingredient: an ingredient of a mixture not contributing directly to its essential purpose but playing an important subsidiary part, e.g. a constituent that chiefly gives bulk: a place from which operations are conducted: a fixed station in games such as baseball: the line or surface on which a plane or solid figure is regarded as standing: (*chem.*) a substance that reacts with an acid to form a salt: the part of a pillar below the shaft: (*her.*) the lower portion of a shield: the number on which a system of numeration or of logarithms is founded.—*v.t.* to found (on):—*pr.p.* bās'ing; *pa.p.* based (*bāst*).—*adjs.* bās'al, pertaining to or situated at the base, esp. of the skull; **base'-less,** without a base: (*fig.*) unfounded.—*ns.* **base'ball,** American team game, a development of rounders, played nine-a-side with bat and ball; **base'ment,** the lowest storey of a building, below street level; **base'-plate,** bed-

plate (q.v.).—*adj.* **bās'ic,** belonging to, or of the nature of, a base: containing excess of a base: (*geol.*) poor in silica—opposed to *acid*: (loosely) fundamental.—*n.* **basic-slag,** a by-product in the manufacture of steel, used as manure.—**Basic English,** English employing a limited, carefully selected, vocabulary, designed for use by foreigners: (without *cap.*) English using few and simple words; **basic salt,** a salt having one or more hydroxyl groups in place of an acid radical or radicals, as in basic lead nitrate, Pb(OH)NO$_3$, compared with normal lead nitrate, Pb(NO$_3$)$_2$. [Fr.,—L. *basis*—Gr., *ba-*, in *bainein*, to go.]

base, *bās, adj.* low in place, value, estimation, or principle: mean, vile, worthless: counterfeit.—*adj.* **base'-born,** low-born: illegitimate.—*adv.* **base'ly.**—*n.* **base'ness.**—**base metal,** any metal other than the precious metals. [Fr. *bas*—Low L. *bassus*, thick, fat—L., a vulgar word, found in name *Bassus*.]

base, *bās, n.* an old game played by two sides occupying contiguous spaces, called *bases* or *homes*. Forms of this are *Prisoner's Base* or *Bars*, and *Rounders*. [Perh. *bars*, pl. of **bar**.]

baseball, *bās'böl.* See **base** (1).

basecourt, *bās'kört, kört, n.* the outer court of a castle or mansion. [Fr. *basse-court*.]

bash, *bash, v.t.* to beat or smash in.—*n.* a heavy blow: a dint.—**have a bash** (*slang*), to have a try. [Prob. Scand.]

bashaw, *ba-shö', n.* usu. written **pasha** (q.v.) or **pacha.**

bashful, *bash'fōōl, -fl, adj.* easily confused, shy, wanting confidence.—*adv.* **bash'fully.**—*n.* **bash'fulness.** [Obs. *bash* for **abash,** and suffx. *-ful*.]

bashi-bazouk, *bash-i-ba-zōōk', n.* a Turkish irregular trooper: a brutal ruffian. [Turk. *bashi-bozuq*, wild head.]

basil, *baz'il, n.* a genus of aromatic plants, the leaves of which are used to season food. [O.Fr. *basile*—L. *basilisca*—Gr. *basilikon*, royal.]

basilica, *baz-il'ik-a, n.* among the Romans, a large oblong hall for judicial and commercial purposes—many of them were afterwards converted into Christian churches: a magnificent church built after the plan of the ancient basilica.—*adj.* **basil'ican.** [L. *basilica*—Gr. *basilikē* (*oikia*), a royal (house), from *basileus*, a king.]

basilisk, *baz'il-isk, n.* a fabulous creature with fiery death-dealing eyes and breath, so named from its crown-like crest: in modern zoology, a kind of crested lizard. [Gr. *basiliskos*, dim of *basileus*, a king.]

basin, *bās'n, n.* a wide open vessel or dish, usu. not so deep as wide (cf. **bowl**): any hollow place containing water, as a dock: the area drained by a river and its tributaries.—**have a basinful** (*slang*), to have an excess of. [O.Fr. *bacin*—Low L. *bachīnus*, perh. from *bacca*, a vessel.]

basinet, *bas'i-net, n.* a light helmet worn with a visor.—Also **bas'net.** [Dim. of **basin.**]

basis, *bās'is, n.* the foundation, or that on which a thing rests: a pedestal: the groundwork or first principle: the fundamental ingredient:—*pl.* **bas'es** (*bās'ēz*). [L.; see **base** (1).]

bask, *bäsk, v.i.* to lie in warmth or sunshine.—

Neutral vowels in unaccented syllables: *em'pêr-ór*; for certain sounds in foreign words see p. ix.

56

Also *fig.* [O.N. *bathask,* to bathe oneself.]

basket, *bäs'két, n.* a receptacle made of plaited twigs, rushes, or other flexible materials.—*ns.* **bas'ket-ball,** a game in which goals are scored by throwing a ball into a raised net (originally a basket); **bas'ketful,** as much as fills a basket; **bas'ket-hilt,** a sword hilt with a protective covering wrought like basketwork; **bas'ketwork,** any structure of interlaced twigs or the like. [Origin obscure.]

basque, *bäsk, n.* (*cap.*) one of a people inhabiting the western Pyrenees, in Spain or France, or their language: kind of short-skirted jacket worn by women: a continuation of the bodice a little below the waist.—*adj.* relating to the Basques or their language or country. [Fr. *Basque*—Low L. *Vasco,* an inhabitant of *Vasconia,* whence *Gascony.*]

bas-relief, bass-relief, *bas'-re-lēf',* or (*Ital.*) **basso-relievo,** *bäs'sō-rēl-yā'vo, n.* sculptures in which the figures do not stand far out from the ground on which they are formed. [Fr. *bas relief.* See **base** (2), and **relief.**]

bass, *bās, n.* the lowest part assigned to a voice or instrument in a piece of concerted music: a bass singer: a bass instrument, esp. (*coll.*) a double bass, *adj.* low, deep —n **thorough-bass** (see **thorough**). [From **base** (2).]

bass. Same as **bast.**

bass, basse, *bas, n.* a marine fish allied to the perches. [O.E. *bærs*; cf. Ger. *bars,* perch.]

basset, *bas'ét, n.* a hound like a dachshund, but bigger.—*n.* **bass'et-horn** [It. *corno di bassetto*], the richest and softest of all wind-instruments, similar to a clarinet in tone. [Fr. *bas,* low.]

bassinet, bassinette, *bas'i-net, n.* a kind of basket with a hood, used as a cradle: a similarly shaped perambulator. [Fr., dim. of *bassin,* a basin.]

basso, *bäs'sō, n.* a bass singer. [It.]

bassoon, *bas-ōōn', n.* (It. *fagotto*) a wood-wind instrument of a bass or very low note—the **double bassoon** (It *contrafagotto*) sounds an octave lower. [It. *bassone,* augmentative of *basso,* low, from root of **base** (2), **bass** (1).]

bass-viol, *bās-vī'ol, n.* a musical instrument with four strings, used for playing the bass in concerted music: the violoncello. [See **bass** (1), and **viol.**]

bast, *bast, n.* the phloem (q.v.) of stems, esp. of the lime-tree: fibre: matting. [O.E. *bæst*; Ger. *bast.*]

bastard, *bas'tård, n.* a child born of parents not married.—*adj.* born out of wedlock: not genuine: false.—*v.t.* **bas'tardise,** to prove or declare to be a bastard: to reduce to a lower state or condition.—*n.* **bas'tardy,** the state of being a bastard. [Fr. *bâtard*; O.Fr. *fils de bast,* son of the pack-saddle.]

bastard, *bas'tård,* Afrik. **baster,** *bas'tér,* (*S. Africa*), *n.* a person of mixed white and coloured parentage, whether legitimately born or not. [Du. *bastaard,* bastard.]

baste, *bāst, v.t.* to beat with a stick.—*n.* **bast'ing.** [Prob. conn. with O.N. *beysta,* Dan. *böste,* to beat.]

baste, *bast, v.t.* to drop fat or butter over (roasting meat, &c.). [Ety. unknown.]

baste, *bāst, v.t.* to sew slightly or with long stitches. [O.Fr. *bastir,* from O.H.G. *bestan,* to sew.]

Bastille, *bast-ēl', n.* an old fortress in Paris long used as a state prison, and demolished at the French Revolution. [O.Fr. *bastir,* to build.]

bastinado, *bast-in-ād'ō,* **bastinade,** *bast-in-ād', vs.t.* to beat with a baton or stick, esp. on the soles of the feet (an Eastern punishment):—*pr.p.* bastinād'oing or bastinād'ing; *pa.p.* bastinād'oed or bastinād'ed.—*ns.* **bastinäde', bastinād'o.** [Sp. *bastonada,* Fr. *bastonnade*—*baston, bâton.* See **baton.**]

bastion, *bast'yón, n.* a kind of tower at the angle of a fortification: (*fig.*) a defence.—*adj.* **bast'ioned.** [O.Fr. *bastir,* to build.]

bat, *bat, n.* a heavy stick: a flat club for striking the ball in cricket: a club for baseball: a batsman: a piece of brick: a blow: (*slang*) a spree.—*v.i.* to use the bat in cricket:—*pr.p.* batt'ing; *pa.p.* batt'ed.—*ns.* **batt'er, bats'man,** one who wields the bat at cricket, &c.; **batt'ing,** management of a bat in cricket: cotton fibre prepared in sheets.—**bat around** (*slang*), to wander: to go on a spree; **off one's own bat** (*fig.*), on one's own initiative. [Perh. from O.E. *bat* (a doubtful form), prob. Celt. *bat,* staff.]

bat, *bat, n.* any of an order of flying mammals, with body like a mouse and wings attached mainly to arms and hands.—*adj.* **bat'like:** bat-infested: (*slang*) crazy. [M.E. *bakke,* apparently from Scand.]

bat, *bat, v.i.* to flutter, wink.—**not to bat an eyelid,** not to sleep a wink: to show no emotion [Prob. O.F. *batre,* to beat.]

batch, *bach, n.* the quantity of bread baked, or of anything made or got ready, at one time: a set. [M.E. *bacche* **bakc.**]

bate. Same as **abate.**

hath, *hāth n* water for immersing the body: a bathing: a receptacle or a house for bathing: the act of exposing the body to vapour, mud, sunlight, &c.: (*chem.*) a liquid or other material (as sand), or a receptacle, in which anything is immersed for heating, washing, &c.—*pl.* **baths** (*bäTHz, baths*).—*v.t.* to subject to a bath.—*n.* **bath'room.**—**Order of the Bath,** an English order of knighthood, so named from the bath before installation. [O.E. *bæth,* cog. with Ger. *bad.*]

Bath, *bāth,* a famous city in Somerset, with Roman *baths.*—*ns.* **Bath'-bun,** a rich sweet bun; **Bath'-chair,** a large wheeled chair for invalids; **Bath'-brick,** a siliceous substance manufactured (at Bridgwater) in the form of bricks, and used in cleaning knives.

bathe, *bāTH, v.t.* to wash as in a bath: to wash or moisten with any liquid.—*v.i.* to take a bath.—*n.* the act of taking a bath: a swim or dip.—*ns.* **bath'er; bath'ing-box,** a box for bathers to undress and dress in; **bath'ing-cost'ume, -dress, -suit; bath'ing-machine',** a small carriage to carry a bather into water of the depth desired. [O.E. *bathian.*]

bathometer, *bath-om'et-ér, n.* an instrument for ascertaining depth. [Gr. *bathos,* depth, *metron,* measure.]

bathos, *bā'thos, n.* a ludicrous descent from the elevated to the mean in writing or speech.—*adj.* **bathetic** (*ba-thet'ik*; irregularly formed on the analogy of *pathos, pathetic*). [Gr., depth.]

bathymeter, *bath-im′et-êr, n.* a bathometer. [Gr. *bathys*, deep, *metron*, measure.]

bathyscaphe, *bath′i-skāf,* **bathyscope**, *-skōp, ns.* observation chambers of later type than the **bathysphere**. [Gr. *bathys*, deep, *skaphē*, boat, *skopeein*, to look at.]

bathysphere, *bath′i-sfēr, n.* a submersible observation chamber for natural history work. [Gr. *bathys*, deep, *sphaira*, sphere.]

batik, *bat′ik, n.* an East Indian method of producing designs on cloth by covering with wax, for each successive dipping, those parts that are to be protected from the dye. [Malay.]

bating, *bāt′ing, prep.* excepting. [abate.]

batiste, *ba-tēst′, n.* a fine fabric of linen and cotton. [Perh. from *Baptiste*, the original maker; perh. from its use in wiping the heads of children after baptism.]

batlet, *bat′let, n.* a wooden mallet used for beating clothes. [Dim. of **bat**.]

batman, *bat′, bä′,* or *bö′man, n.* a man who has charge of a bathorse (a horse carrying an officer's baggage): an officer's servant. [Fr. *bât*, a pack-saddle.]

baton, *bat′ón, n.* a staff or truncheon, esp. of policeman, conductor, or marshal.—*v.t.* to strike with a baton.—*n.* **bat′on(-)sin′ister**, a well-known heraldic indication of illegitimacy, improperly called **bar(-)sinister**. [Fr. *bâton*—Low L. *basto*, a stick; of unknown origin.]

Batrachia, *ba-trā′ki-a, n.pl.* the order of Amphibia which includes the frogs and toads: the class Amphibia.—*adj.* and *n.* **batrā′chian**. [From Gr. *batrachos*, a frog.]

battalion, *bat-al′yón, n.* a body of soldiers consisting of several companies: a body of men drawn up in battle array. [Fr.; from root of **battle**.]

batten, *bat′n, v.i.* to grow fat: to feed abundantly (on; *lit.* and *fig.*). [O.N. *batna*, to grow better.]

batten, *bat′n, n.* sawn timber used for flooring: in ships, a strip of wood used to fasten down the hatches.—*v.t.* to fasten with battens. [Same as **baton**.]

batter, *bat′êr, v.t.* to beat with successive blows: to wear out by beating or by use: to attack with artillery.—*n.* ingredients beaten along with liquid into a paste: paste for sticking.—*n.* **batt′ering-ram**, a large beam with a metal head sometimes like that of a ram, formerly used in war as an engine for battering down walls.—**battered baby syndrome**, collection of symptoms found in a baby, caused by violence on the part of the parent or other adult. [O.Fr. *batre*—L.L. *battĕre* (L. *batuĕre*), to beat.]

battery, *bat′êr-i, n.* a number of cannon with their equipment: the place on which cannon are mounted: the unit of artillery or its personnel: a series of two or more electric cells arranged to produce a current, or store charge: a similar arrangement of other apparatus: an arrangement of cages in which hens are kept, usu. one in each cage, and treated in such a way that they will produce the maximum number of eggs: (*law*) an assault by beating or wounding. [Fr. *batterie*—*battre*

(O.Fr. *batre*); see **batter**.]

battle, *bat′l, n.* a contest between opposing armies: a fight or encounter.—*v.i.* to contend: to fight: to struggle (with, against).—*ns.* **batt′le-axe, -ax,** a kind of axe once used in battle: (*fig.*) a formidable woman; **batt′le-cruis′er**, a heavily armed but lightly armoured warship, faster but more vulnerable than a battleship; **batt′le-cry**, a war-shout; **batt′le-field**, the place on which a battle is fought; **batt′le-piece**, a passage, or a painting, describing a battle.— *adj.* **batt′le-scarred**, scarred in battle.—*n.* **batt′le-ship**, a heavily armed, heavily armoured warship.—**battle royal**, a general mêlée: a notable contest of great fierceness; **half the battle**, anything that brings one well on the way to success; **line of battle**, position of troops or ships ready for battle; **to join, do battle**, to fight. [O.Fr. *bataille*—*batre*, to beat. See **batter**.]

battledore, **battledoor**, *bat′l-dōr, -dör, n.* a wooden bat used for washing, &c.: a light bat for striking a ball or shuttlecock. [Perh. Sp. *batidor*, a beater, a washing beetle.]

battlement, *bat′l-mént, n.* a wall or parapet with embrasures, an indented parapet.—*adj.* **batt′lemented**, fortified with battlements. [O.Fr. *batailles*, movable defences on a wall.]

battue, *bä-tōō′,* or *tū′, n.* a method of hunting in which animals are driven into some place for the convenience of the shooters: indiscriminate slaughter. [Fr.—*battre*, to beat.]

bauble, *bö′bl, n.* a trifling piece of finery: a child's plaything: a stick surmounted by a head with ass's ears, the mock emblem of the court-jester. [O.Fr. *babel*, prob. from the root seen in L. *babulus*, a babbler.]

baudrick, *böd′rik.* Same as **baldric**.

baulk. See **balk**.

bauxite, *bök′sīt, -zit, bö′zīt, n.* an important aluminium ore found at Les *Baux*, near Arles, and elsewhere.

bawbee, *bö-bē′, n.* a halfpenny: originally a silver coin worth three pennies Scots. [Prob. from a 16th-century Scottish mint-master, the laird of *Sillebawby*; others identify with 'baby'.]

bawd, *böd, n.* a woman who keeps a house of prostitution.—*adj.* **bawd′y**, obscene, unchaste (e.g. talk).—*ns.* **bawd′ry**; **bawd′y-house**, a brothel. [Perh. abbrev. from **bawd′strot**, a word for a pander, now obsolete.]

bawl, *böl, v.i.* to shout or cry out loudly.—*n.* a loud cry or shout.—*ns.* **bawl′er, bawl′ing**. [Perh. Low L. *baulāre*, to bark like a dog; but cf. O.N. *baula*, to low like a cow.]

bay, *bā, adj.* reddish brown inclining to chestnut.—*n.* elliptical for bay horse. [Fr. *bai*—L. *badius*, chestnut-coloured.]

bay, *bā, n.* an inlet of the sea: an inward bend of the shore. [Fr. *baie*—Low L. *baia*, a harbour.]

bay, *bā, n.* the space between two columns: any recess: a compartment (e.g. bomb bay) or section of an aircraft.—*n.* **bay′-win′dow**, any window forming a recess. [O.Fr. *baée*—*baer*, to gape, be open; prob. conn. with **bay** (2).]

bay, *bā, n.* a laurel-tree (q.v.): (*pl.*) an honorary garland or crown of victory, originally of laurel: literary renown.—*ns.* **bay leaf**, dried laurel leaf used as a flavouring agent; **bay′-rum**, an

Neutral vowels in unaccented syllables: *em′pér-ór*; for certain sounds in foreign words see p. ix.

aromatic liquid originally prepared from leaves of the **bay′berry**, a tree akin to allspice. [O.Fr. *baie*, a berry—L. *bāca*.]

bay, *bā, n.* barking, baying (esp. of a dog in pursuit): the combined cry of hounds in conflict with a hunted animal: used often of the last stand of a hunted animal.—*v.i.* to bark (esp. of large dogs).—*v.t.* to bark at: to follow with barking.—**bay at the moon**, to make a futile gesture; **hold, keep at bay**, (*lit.* and *fig.*) to show fight against, fight off, said of the hunted animal; **stand, be, at bay**, to be at close quarters: (*lit.* and *fig.*) to be in a position where further retreat is impossible and a fight must be made. [A confusion of two distinct words: (1) to hold at bay = O.Fr. *tenir a bay* = It. *tenere a bada* —where *bay, bada,* denote suspense indicated by an open mouth; (2) in 'to stand at bay', *bay* is prob. O.Fr. *abai,* barking—*bayer,* to bark.]

Bayard, *bā′ärd, n.* a brave and honourable gentleman [After the Chevalier Bayard (1476–1524).

bayonet, *bā′on-et, n.* a stabbing instrument of steel fixed to the muzzle of a musket or rifle.—*v.t.* to stab with a bayonet. [Fr. *baionnette,* perh. from *Bayonne,* in France; or from O.Fr. *bayon,* arrow.]

bayou, *bī′ōō, n.* the marshy offshoot of a lake or river, esp. in North America. [Perh. corrupted from Fr. *boyau,* gut.]

bay-salt, *bā′-sölt, n.* salt obtained by slow evaporation, originally from sea-water. [Prob. from **bay,** an inlet, and **salt.**]

bazaar, bazar, *ba-zär′, n.* an Eastern marketplace or exchange: a fancy fair in imitation of an Eastern bazaar. [Pers. *bāzār,* a market.]

bazooka, *bá-ōō′ka, n.* a weapon, used chiefly against tanks, consisting of a long tube that launches a projectile with an explosive head: a rocket launcher situated on the wing of an aeroplane. [From the name of a musical instrument used for comic purposes.]

bdellium, *del′i-ùm, n.* a kind of gum. [Gr. *bdellion,* used to translate, but prob. unconnected with, Heb. *b′dōlakh,* Gen. ii. 12.]

be, *bē, v.i.* to live: to exist: to have a specified state or quality:—*pr.p.* be′ing; *pa.p.* been. [O.E. *bēon;* Ger. *bin;* Gael. *bi,* to exist; &c.]

beach, *bēch, n.* the shore of the sea or of a lake, esp. when sandy or pebbly, the strand.—*v.t.* to drive or haul (a boat) up on the beach.—*ns.* **beach′head,** a position on a seashore in enemy territory seized by an advance force and held to cover the main landing; **beach′comber,** a long rolling wave: a drunken loafer in Pacific seaports: a settler on a Pacific island; **beach′-mas′ter,** an officer in charge of disembarking troops. [Orig. a dial. Eng. word for shingle.]

beacon, *bē′kón, n.* a fire on an eminence, used as a sign of danger: anything that warns of danger, esp. an erection, with or without a light, marking a rock or shoal in navigable waters: a sign marking a street crossing—e.g. a Belisha (*bé-lē′sha*) beacon, named after the Minister of Transport (1934): a wireless transmitter that sends forth signals to guide shipping or aircraft.—*v.t.* to act as a beacon to: to light up: to mark by beacons. [O.E. *bēacn,* a beacon, a sign.]

bead, *bēd, n.* a little ball strung with others in a rosary, for counting prayers: any small ball of glass, amber, &c., strung e.g. to form a necklace: bead-like drop of liquid: the small knob of metal forming the foresight of a gun— whence **to draw a bead upon,** to take aim at: (*archit.*) a narrow moulding with semicircular section.—*v.t.* to furnish with beads.—*v.i.* to form a bead or beads.—*adjs.* **bead′ed,** having beads or a bead: in beadlike form; **bead′y,** bead-like, small and bright (of eyes): covered with beads or bubbles.—*ns.* **bead′ing,** bead-moulding: work in beads; **bead′-roll,** orig. a list of the dead to be prayed for, hence a list of names, a long series: a rosary; **beads′man, bedes′man,** one bound or endowed to pray for others: (*Scot.*) a licensed beggar:—*fem.* **beads′woman.—say, tell, count one's beads,** to offer prayers. [O.E. *bed, gebed,* prayer. See **bid.**]

beadle, *bēd′l, n.* a mace-bearer: a petty officer of a church, college, parish, &c.: in Scotland, used the 'church-officer' attending on the clergyman. [O.E. *bydel—bēodan,* to proclaim, to bid; affected by O.Fr. form *bedel.*]

beagle, *bē′gl, n.* a small hound tracking by scent, formerly much used in hunting hares.

beak, *bēk, n.* the bill of a bird: anything pointed or projecting: the nose: in the ancient galley, a pointed iron fastened to the prow for piercing the enemy's vessel.—*adj.* **beaked** (*bēkt*). [O.Fr. *bec*—Low L. *beccus,* of Celt. (Gaulish) origin.]

beaker, *bēk′ér, n.* a large drinking-bowl or cup, or its contents: a deep glass or other vessel used by chemists. [Scand. *bikarr,* prob. from Low L. *bioārium,* a drinking bowl.]

beam, *bēm, n.* a large and straight piece of timber or iron forming one of the main structural members of a building, &c.: (*fig.*) a great fault (from the metaphor of the mote and the beam, Matt. vii. 3): any of the transverse pieces of framing extending across a ship's hull: the greatest width of a ship or boat: the part of a balance from which the scales hang: the pole of a carriage: a cylinder of wood in a loom: a shaft of rays of light or other radiation.—*v.t.* to send forth (light) in a beam: to place on a beam.—*v.i.* to shine: to smile radiantly.—*adjs.* **beam′less,** without beams: emitting no rays of light; **beam′y,** shining.—**a beam sea,** one rolling against the ship's side; **lee** or **weather beam,** the side away from or towards the wind; **on the beam,** in the direction of a ship's beams, at right angles to her course: on the course shown by a radio beam: (*fig.*) on the mark (opp. **off the beam**); **abaft,** or **before, the beam,** behind, or before, the direction indicated by *on the beam*; **on her beam ends,** the position of a ship so much inclined to one side that the beams become nearly vertical—whence **on one's beam ends,** at the end of one's resources; **on the port,** or **starboard, beam,** applied to any distant point out at sea, at right angles to the keel, and on the left, or right, side of the ship. [O.E. *bēam,* a tree, stock of a tree, a ray of light; Gmc.]

bean, *bēn, n.* the name of several kinds of leguminous plants and their seeds: applied also to the seeds of some other plants, from their bean-like form, as coffee: (*slang*) a coin: (*slang*) the head.—*ns.* **bean'-feast**, an annual dinner given by employers to their hands, at which beans used to be prominent: a celebration; **bean'o** (*slang*), a disturbance, a jollification.—**full of beans**, in high spirits; **old bean**, a familiar, disrespectful form of address; **give one beans**, to treat one severely. [O.E. *bēan*; Ger. *bohne*.]

bear, *bār*, *v.t.* to carry (*lit.* and *fig.*): to support: to endure: to admit of (e.g. an interpretation): to behave or conduct (oneself): to bring forth or produce.—*v.i.* to be patient: to have reference to (with *upon*): to press (with *on* or *upon*): to be situated:—*pr.p.* bear'ing; *pa.t.* bōre; *pa.p.* bōrne (*bōrn, bōrn*), born (*bōrn*)—the latter referring to something brought forth.—*adj.* **bear'able**, that may be endured.—*adv.* **bear'ably.**—*ns.* **bear'er**, one who or that which bears, esp. one who assists in carrying a body to the grave: a carrier, messenger, or (India) body-servant; **bear'ing**, demeanour: direction, situation (of one object with regard to another): relation to, significance in relation to (e.g. *has no bearing on this question*): a device borne on an escutcheon (usu. *pl.*) the part of a machine that bears friction; **bear'ing-cloth**, the mantle or cloth in which a child was carried to the font; **bear'ing-rein**, a fixed rein between the bit and the saddle, by which a horse's head is held up in driving and its neck made to arch.—**bear a hand**, to give assistance; **bear away**, to sail away; **bear down**, to press down by weight, overthrow: (with *upon* or *towards*) to sail with the wind towards: to swoop upon; **bear hard, heavily (up)on** (*lit.* and *fig.*), to press heavily on: oppress; **bear in mind**, remember, think of, take into consideration; **bear out**, to corroborate; **bear up**, to keep up one's courage; **bear up for** (a place), to sail towards; **bear with**, to make allowance for, be patient with; **be borne in upon one**, to be forcibly impressed on one's consciousness (that); **bring to bear**, to bring into operation (with *against, upon*); **lose one's bearings**, to become uncertain of one's position. [O.E. *beran*; L. *ferre*, Gr. *pherein*.]

bear, *bār*, *n.* a family of heavy quadrupeds with shaggy hair and hooked claws: a rough or ill-bred fellow: one who sells stocks for delivery at a future date, anticipating a fall in price so that he may buy first at an advantage: (*astron.*; *cap.*) the name of two northern constellations, the Great and the Little Bear, also known as *Ursa Major* and *Ursa Minor.*—*ns.* **bear'-bait'ing** (see **bait**); **bear'-gar'den**, an enclosure where bears are kept: a rude, turbulent company.—*adj.* **bear'ish**, like a bear.—*ns.* **bear'ishness; bear'-lead'er**, a person who leads about a bear for exhibition: the tutor or governor of a youth at the university or on travel; **bear'skin**, the skin of a bear: a shaggy woollen cloth for overcoats: the high fur cap worn by the Guards in England; **bear'ward**, a warden or keeper of bears. [O.E. *bera*; Ger. *bär*; Du. *beer.*]

bear, bere, *bēr, n.* kind of barley grown in Scotland. [O.E. *bere*.]

beard, *bērd, n.* the hair that grows on the chin and adjacent parts of the face: prickles on the ears of corn: the barb of an arrow: the gills of oysters, &c.—*v.t.* to take by the beard: to oppose to the face.—*adjs.* **beard'ed**, having a beard: prickly: barbed; **beard'less**. [O.E. *beard*; W. *barf*, Ger. *bart*.]

beast, *bēst, n.* an irrational animal, as opposed to man: a four-footed animal: a brutal person.—*dim.* **beast'ie.**—*adj.* **beast'ly**, like a beast in actions or behaviour: coarse: obscene: (*coll.*) disagreeable, irksome.—*n.* **beast'liness**. [O.Fr. *beste*—L. *bestia*.]

beat, *bēt, v.t.* to strike repeatedly: to strike, as bushes, in order to rouse game: to thrash: to overcome: to be too difficult for: to mark (time) with a baton, &c.: to spread (a metal) flat and thin by beating with a tool.—*v.i.* to move with regular strokes: to pulsate, throb: to dash (on, against), as a flood or storm:—*pr.p.* beat'ing; *pa.t.* beat; *pa.p.* beat'en.—*n.* a recurrent stroke, or its sound, or its moment, as of a watch or the pulse: a round or course: a place of resort.—*adj.* weary, fatigued.—*adj.* **beat'en**, made smooth or hard by beating or treading: worn by use: shaped by hammering.—*ns.* **beat'er**, one who rouses or beats up game: an instrument for beating; **beat'ing**, the act of striking: thrashing: pulsation or throbbing: rousing of game.—**beaten work**, metal shaped by hammering; **beat music**, popular music with a very pronounced rhythm; **beat'nik**, one of the **beat generation**, a group of unconventional poets, &c. (orig. in U.S.) who, in the 1950s, refused to accept the aims and standards of contemporary society and led a bohemian existence: later used loosely for a young person whose behaviour, dress, &c. were unconventional.—*adj.* **beat'-up**, dilapidated through excessive use.—**beat about the bush**, to approach a subject in an indirect way; **beat a retreat**, to retreat, originally to beat the drum as a signal for retreat; **beat down**, to reduce (the price of goods) by haggling: to force (a person) down to a lower price; **beat off**, to drive back; **beat the bounds**, to trace out boundaries of a parish in a periodic survey or perambulation; **beat one's brains**, to make a great mental effort; **beat up**, to attack suddenly: to make way against wind or tide: to collect by diligence and determination (e.g. recruits, helpers): (*slang*) to thrash, knock about, severely.—**dead beat**, completely exhausted. [O.E. *bēatan*, pa.t. *bēot*.]

beatify, *bē-at'i-fī, v.t.* to make blessed or happy: to declare to be in eternal bliss or heaven.—*adjs.* **beatif'ic, -al**, making supremely happy: expressing and communicating happiness (e.g. *beatific smile*).—*n.* **beatifica'tion**, act of beatifying: (*R.C. Church*) a declaration by the Pope that a person is blessed in heaven, the first step to canonisation. [L. *beātus*, blessed, and *facĕre*, to make.]

beatitude, *bē-at'i-tūd, n.* heavenly happiness, or happiness of the highest kind: (*pl.*) sayings of Christ in Matt. v., declaring certain classes of persons to be blessed. [L. *beātitūdō*—*beātus*, blessed.]

beau, *bō, n.* a man attentive to dress or fashion: a lover:—*pl.* **beaux** (*bōz*):—*fem.* **belle.**—*ns.*

Neutral vowels in unaccented syllables: *em'pér-òr*; for certain sounds in foreign words see p. ix.

beau´-īdē´al, ideal beauty: (loosely) a person in whom the highest excellence is embodied; **beau´-monde** (*bō´-mŏd*), the gay or fashionable world. [Fr. *beau, bel* (fem. *belle*) — L. *bellus*, fine, gay, as if for *benulus*, dim. of *benus* = *bonus*, good.]

Beaune, *bōn, n.* a wine of Burgundy. [From the town of *Beaune*.]

beauty, *bū´ti, n.* a pleasing combination of qualities in a person or object: a particular grace or excellence: a beautiful person, esp. a woman: a beautiful object (sometimes ironical). — *adj.* **beauteous** (*-ti-ùs, -tyús; poet.*), full of beauty, fair. — *adv.* **beau´teously.** — *n.* **beau´teousness.** — *adj.* **beau´tiful**, fair, with qualities that give delight to the senses (esp. the eye or ear) or to the mind. — *adv.* **beau´tifully.** — *v.t.* **beau´tify**, to make beautiful: to grace: to adorn. — *ns.* **beautician** (*bū-tish´an*), one engaged in women's hairdressing, facial make-up, manicuring, &c.; **beautifica´tion; beau´tifier**, one who or that which beautifies or makes beautiful, **beau´ty-queen**, a girl who is voted the most attractive or best-proportioned in a competition; **beau´ty-sleep**, the sleep before midnight, considered the most refreshing; **beau´ty-spot**, a patch placed on the face to heighten beauty: a birthmark resembling such a patch: a place of outstanding beauty. [O.Fr. *biaute, beaute* — Low L. *bellitās, ātis* — L. *bellus*. See **beau.**]

beaver, *bēv´ér, n.* a genus of amphibious rodents valuable for their fur: the fur of the beaver: a hat made of the beaver's fur or a substitute — a top-hat. — *n.* **beav´er-board**, a building board of wood fibre. [O.E. *befer, beofor*; Du. *hever*, Ger. *biber*, Gael. *beabhar*, L. *fiber.*]

beaver, *bēv´ér, n.* in mediaeval armour, the covering for the lower part of the face. [So called from a fancied likeness to a child's bib. O.Fr. *bavière*, from *bave*, slaver.]

bebop, *bē´bop, n.* a style of jazz in the 1940s — forerunner of *bop* (q.v.).

becalm, *bi-käm´, v.t.* to make calm, still, or quiet. — *p.adj.* **becalmed´**, motionless from want of wind. [Pfx. *be-*, inten., and **calm.**]

became, *bi-kām´, pa.t.* of **become.**

because, *bi-koz´, bi-köz´, conj.* and *adv.* for the reason that: on account (of). [Prep. *by*, and **cause.**]

bechance, *bi-chäns´, v.i.* to happen by chance. — *v.t.* to befall. — *adv.* by chance: accidentally. [O.E. *be-*, by, and **chance.**]

beck, *bek, n.* a brook. [O.N. *bekkr*; Ger. *bach.*]

beck, *bek, n.* a sign with the finger or head: a nod. — *v.i.* to make such a sign. — *v.t.* to call by a nod. — **at one's beck**, subject to one's will. [A contraction of **beckon.**]

beckon, *bek´on, v.t.* and *v.i.* to nod or make a sign (to), esp. to summon by this means. [O.E. *bīecnan — bēacn*, a sign.]

becloud, *bi-klowd´, v.t.* to obscure by clouds: to dim. [Pfx. *be-*, around, and **cloud.**]

become, *bi-kum´, v.i.* to come to be: to be the fate (of — e.g. *What has become of it? What is to become of me?*). — *v.t.* to suit or befit: — *pa.t.* **became´**; *pa.p.* **become´.** — *adj.* **becom´ing**, suitable (to): that adorns fittingly. — *adv.* **becom´ingly.** [O.E. *becuman* — pfx. *be-*, and *cuman*, to come.]

bed, *bed, n.* a couch or place to sleep on: the marriage-bed: the channel of a river: a plot in a garden: a place in which anything rests: a layer. — *v.t.* to place in bed: to sow or plant: to set in layers: — *pr.p.* bedd´ing; *pa.p.* bedd´ed. — *ns.* **bed´chamber** (see **bed´room**); **bedd´ing**, mattress, bed-clothes, &c.: litter for cattle. — *adj.* **bed´fast**, confined to bed. — *ns.* **bed´fellow**, a sharer of the same bed: (*fig.*) a colleague; **bed´-key**, a tool for tightening a bedstead; **bed´-pan**, a vessel for use in sick-bed: a warming-pan; **bed´-plate** (*mech.*), the foundation plate of an engine, lathe, &c.; **bed´post**, a post forming an angle of a bedstead. — *adj.* **bed´rid(den)**, confined to bed by age or sickness. — *n.* **bed´-rock**, the solid rock underneath superficial formations. — *adj.* **bottom**, lowest. — *ns.* **bed´room**, a sleeping apartment — *bed-chamber* was the earlier form; **bed´side**, position by a bed — also *adj.* as a *bedside book*, &c. — *ns.* **bed´-sitt´er, bed´-sitt´ing-room**, a combined bedroom and sitting room (abbrev. **bed´-sit**); **bed´sore**, one of the painful ulcers that often arise in a long confinement to bed; **bed´spread**, a coverlet put over a bed during the day, **bed´stead**, a frame for supporting a bed; **bed´tick**, the case in which feathers, hair, chaff, &c., are put for bedding; **bed´time**, the hour for going to bed at night. — *adv.* **bed´ward**, in the direction of bed: towards bedtime. — **bed and board**, food and lodging: full connubial relations; **bed of down**, or **roses**, any easy or comfortable place. — **be brought to bed**, to be confined in childbirth (with *of*); **keep one's bed**, to remain in bed; **lie in the bed one has made**, to have to accept the consequences of one's own acts; **make a bed**, to put a bed in order. [O.E. *bod(d)*; Ger. *bett*, O.N. *bethr.*]

bedad, *bi-dad´, interj.* an Irish form of **begad.**

bedaub, *bi-döb´ v.t.* to daub over or smear. [Pfx. *be-*, and **daub.**]

bede, same as **bead**, a prayer.

bedeck, *bi-dek´, v.t.* to deck or ornament. [Pfx. *be-*, and **deck.**]

bedesman. Same as **beadsman** (q.v. under **bead**)

bedevil, *bi-dev´l, v.t.* to 'play the devil' with: to torment with devilish malignity: to muddle, spoil. — *pass.* to be possessed of a devil. [Pfx. *be-*, and **devil**, n.]

bedew, *bi-dū´, v.t.* to moisten gently, as with dew. [Pfx. *be-*, and **dew.**]

bedight, *bi-dīt´, adj.* (*poet.*) adorned. [Pfx. *be-*, and **dight.**]

bedim, *bi-dim´, v.t.* to make dim or dark. — *pa.p.* **bedimmed´.** [Pfx. *be-*, and **dim**, adj.]

bedizen, *bi-dīz´n, bi-diz´n, v.t.* to dress gaudily. [Pfx. *be-*, and **dizen.**]

bedlam, *bed´lám, n.* an asylum for lunatics: a place of uproar. — *adj.* fit for a madhouse. — *n.* **bed´lamite**, a madman. [From the priory of St Mary of *Bethlehem* in London, afterwards a madhouse (*Bethlehem* Royal Hospital).]

bedouin, *bed´ōō-in, n.* a tent-dwelling nomad Arab (properly *pl.*). [Fr. — Ar. *badāwīn*, dwellers in the desert.]

bedraggle, *bi-drag´l, v.t.* to soil by dragging in the wet or dirt. [Pfx. *be-*, and **draggle.**]

bee, *bē, n.* a four-winged insect that makes honey, the honey bee: any of a group of in-

fāte, fär; mē, hûr (her); *mīne; mōte, för; mūte; mōōn, fŏŏt;* ᴛʜᴇn (then)

sects of the same order as wasps and ants: (orig. *U.S.*) a social gathering for common work or entertainment (from the bee's habit of combined labour).—*ns.* bee'-house; bee'-keeper; bee'-mas'ter; bee'-bread, the pollen of flowers collected by bees as food for their young; bee'-eat'er, a brightly plumaged family of birds that feed on bees, nearly allied to the kingfishers; bee'-glue, the soft glutinous matter by which bees fix their combs to the hive; bee'hive, a case or box in which bees are kept, of straw-work, wood, &c.—*adj.* shaped like an old-fashioned beehive, dome-shaped.—*ns.* bee'-line, the most direct road from one point to another, like the honey-laden bee's way home to the hive; bee'-skep, a beehive, properly of straw; bees'wax, the wax secreted by bees, and used by them in constructing their cells.—*v.t.* to polish with bees-wax.—*n.* bees'wing, a filmy crust of tartar formed in port and some other wines after long keeping.—a bee in one's bonnet, a persistent whimsical or crazy notion: an obsession. [O.E. *bēo*; Ger. *biene*.]

beech, *bēch, n.* a genus of forest trees with smooth silvery bark and small edible nuts.—*adj.* beech'en.—*ns.* beech'-mast, the mast or nuts of the beech-tree, which yield a valuable oil, beech'-oil.—copper beech, a variety of the common beech with purplish-brown foliage. [O.E. *bēce* (and related noun *bōc*); Ger. *buche*, L. *fāgus*, Gr. *phēgos* (oak).]

beef, *bēf, n.* the flesh of an ox or cow: (*slang*) muscular force: (*slang*) a complaint, an argument:—*pl.* beeves (used in original sense, oxen).—*adj.* consisting of beef.—*v.i.* (*slang*) to grumble.—*ns.* beef'-eat'er (*bēf´-ēt´ér*), a yeoman of the sovereign's guard, also a warder of the Tower of London (the obvious ety. is the right one); beef'iness; beef'-steak, a thick slice of beef for broiling or frying; beef'tea, the juice of chopped beef, prepared as a beverage for invalids.—*adj.* beef'y, like beef: fleshy: stolid. [O.Fr. *boef*—L. *bōs, bovis*; cf. Gr. *bous*, &c.]

Beelzebub, *bē-el´ze-bub, n.* a form of Baal worshipped by the Philistines at Ekron: the prince of the evil spirits. [Heb. *ba'al z'būb*, fly-lord.]

been, *bēn, bin, pa.p.* of be.

beer, *bēr, n.* an alcoholic beverage made by fermentation, in which the yeast settles to the bottom, from malted barley and hops.—*ns.* beer'-garden, a garden with tables where beer and other refreshments are supplied; beer'-house, a house where beer or malt liquors are sold.—*adj.* beer'y, of, or affected by, beer.—*n.* beer'iness.—beer and skittles, idle enjoyment; small beer, weak beer: hence, trivial affairs: (an) unimportant, uninfluential (person). [O.E. *bēor*; Ger. and Du. *bier*, O.N. *bjorr*.]

beestings, *bēst´ingz, n.* the first milk drawn from a cow after calving. [O.E. *bȳsting, bēost*; Ger. and Du. *biest*.]

beet, *bēt, n.* a small genus of plants with carrot-shaped succulent root used as food and as a source of sugar.—*n.* beet'root, the root of the beet. [O.E. *bēte*—L. *bēta*.]

beetle, *bē´tl, n.* any insect of the Coleoptera (q.v.): a game in which a drawing of a beetle

is made up gradually of its parts, body, head, &c., according to the throw of a dice, the aim being to produce a completed drawing.—*n.* beet'le-drive, a progressive game of beetle.—beetle off (*slang*), to scuttle off.—black beetle (see black). [M.E. *bityl*—O.E. *bitula, bitela*—*bītan*, to bite.]

beetle, *bē´tl, n.* a heavy wooden mallet used for driving wedges, or the like: a wooden pestle-shaped utensil for mashing potatoes, beating linen, &c. [O.E. *bīetl*—*bēatan*, to beat.]

beetle-browed, *bē´tl-browd, adj.* with overhanging or prominent brow: scowling.—*v.i.* bee'tle, to jut, to hang over. [The word is first found in the 14th century in the form *bitel*-browed, probably meaning 'with eyebrows like a beetle's'—i.e. projecting.]

beeves, *bēvz.* See beef.

befall, *bi-föl´, v.t.* to fall or happen to.—*v.i.* to happen or come to pass:—*pr.p.* befall'ing; *pa.t.* befell'; *pa.p.* befall'en. [O.E. *befeallan*—*be-*, inten., *feallan*, to fall.]

befit, *bi-fit´, v.t.* to be suitable to: to be right for:—*pr.p.* befitt'ing; *pa.p.* befitt'ed.—*adj.* befitt'ing.—*adv.* befitt'ingly. [Pfx. *be-*, intensive, and fit.]

befog, *bi-fog´, v.t.* (*lit.* and *fig.*) to envelop in fog: to obscure. [Pfx. *be-*, and fog, *n.*]

befool, *bi-fōōl´, v.t.* to make a fool of, or deceive: to treat as a fool. [Pfx. *be-*, and fool, *n.*]

before, *bi-fōr´, -för´, prep.* in front of: in presence or sight of: previous to: in preference to: superior to.—*adv.* in front: earlier.—*conj.* previous to the time when (*arch.* with *that*): rather than.—*advs.* before'hand, before the time: by way of preparation; before'time, in former time.—be beforehand with (e.g. a person), to forestall (him) in any action. [O.E. *beforan*—*be-*, and *foran*, *adv.* See fore.]

befoul, *bi-fowl´, v.t.* to make foul: to soil. [Pfx. *be-*, and foul, *adj.*]

befriend, *bi-frend´, v.t.* to act as a friend to, to favour. [Pfx. *be-*, and friend, *n.*]

beg, *beg, v.i.* to ask alms or charity, esp. habitually.—*v.t.* to ask earnestly: to beseech: to take for granted what ought to have been proved, esp. in the phrase in logic, 'to beg the question':—*pr.p.* begg'ing; *pa.p.* begged.—*n.* beggar (*beg´ár*), one who begs: one who lives by begging: a mean fellow, a poor fellow.—*v.t.* to reduce to beggary: (*fig.*) to go beyond the resources of (e.g. *its beauty beggars description*).—*adj.* begg'arly, poor: mean: worthless.—*ns.* begg'arliness; begg'ar-my-neigh'bour, a game at cards which goes on till one of the players has gained all the other's cards; begg'ary, extreme poverty.—beg off, to obtain release for (another), or for oneself, by entreaty; go a-begging, to find no claimant or purchaser. [Ety. very obscure; the words *beg* and *beggar* first appear in the 13th century.]

begad, *bi-gad´, interj.* a minced oath, softened from 'By God.'

began, *bi-gan´, pa.t.* of begin.

beget, *bi-get´, v.t.* (of a male parent) to procreate, generate: to produce as an effect, to cause:—*pr.p.* begett'ing; *pa.t.* begot' (or begat'); *pa.p.* begott'en (or begot').—*n.* begett'er, one who begets: a father. [O.E. *begitan*, to acquire—*be-*, inten., *gitan*, to get.]

Neutral vowels in unaccented syllables: *em´pér-ór*; for certain sounds in foreign words see p. ix.

begin, *bi-gin'*, *v.i.* to take rise: to enter on something new: to commence: to start to speak: to do in the smallest degree (e.g. *not to begin to understand*).—*v.t.* to enter on: to commence, start:—*pr.p.* beginn'ing; *pa.t.* began'; *pa.p.* begun'.—*ns.* **beginn'er**, one who begins: one who is beginning to learn or practise anything; **beginn'ing**, origin or commencement: rudiments. [O.E. *beginnan* (more usually *onginnan*), from *be-* and *ginnan*, to begin.]

begird, *bi-gûrd'*, *v.t.* to gird or bind with a girdle: to surround or encompass (with):—*pa.t.* begirt', begird'ed; *pa.p.* begirt'. [O.E. *begyrdan*. See **gird**.]

begone, *bi-gon'*, *interj.* lit. be gone! be off! get away!—For **woe'-begone'**, see **woe**.

begonia, *bi-gōn'ya*, *n.* a genus of plants cultivated in greenhouses for their (usually) pink flowers and their remarkable unequal sided and often coloured leaves. [Named from Michel *Bégon*, patron of botany, 1638-1710.]

begot, *bi-got'*, *pa.t.* and *pa.p.*, **begotten**, *bi-got'n*, *pa.p.*, of **beget**.

begrime, *bi-grīm'*, *v.t.* to grime or soil deeply. [Pfx. *be-*, and **grime**.]

begrudge, *bi-gruj'*, *v.t.* to grudge, envy (e.g. *to begrudge him his success*). [Pfx. *be-*, inten., and **grudge**.]

beguile, *bi-gīl'*, *v.t.* to cheat (with *of*, *out of*): to wile (into): to divert attention from (anything tedious or painful).—*ns.* **beguile'ment**; **beguil'er**.—*adv.* **beguil'ingly**. [Pfx. *be-*, inten., and obs. vb. *guile*, related to **guile**, n.]

beguine, *bé-gēn'*, *n.* a dance of French West Indian origin or its music, in bolero rhythm. [Fr.]

begum, *bē'gum*, *n.* a Moslem princess or lady of rank: a deferential title given to any Moslem lady. [Fem. of *beg*, or **bey** (q.v.).]

begun, *bi-gun'*, *pa.p.* (sometimes *pa.t.*) of **begin**.

behalf, *bi-häf'*, *n.* (*arch.*) favour or benefit: sake, account, part—in phrases 'on', 'in behalf of', [M.E. *behalve*—O.E. *be healfe*, by the side. See **half**.]

behave, *bi-hāv'*, *v.t.* to bear or carry, to conduct (oneself).—*v.i.* to conduct oneself, also to conduct oneself well: to act, esp. in response to specified treatment or stimuli: to function:—*pa.t.* and *pa.p.* behaved'.—*n.* **behaviour** (*bi-hāv'yór*), conduct (of persons, things): manners or deportment, esp. good manners; response to treatment or stimuli.—**behavioural science**, a science, e.g. psychology, sociology, which studies the behaviour of human beings or other organisms; **behaviour therapy**, treating a neurotic symptom, e.g. a phobia, by gradually conditioning the patient to react normally.—**be (up)on one's (good) behaviour**, to be so placed that watchfulness over one's conduct is required: to be making an effort to behave very well. [Probably formed in 15th century from *be-* and **have**; apparently unconnected with O.E. *behabban*.]

behead, *bi-hed'*, *v.t.* to cut off the head of.—*n.* **behead'ing**, the act of cutting off the head. [O.E. *behēafdian*—*be-*, privative, *hēafod*, head.]

beheld, *bi-held'*, *pa.t.* and *pa.p.* of **behold**.

behemoth, *bi-hē'moth*, also *bē'i-moth*, *n.* an animal described in the Book of Job, prob. the hippopotamus: a great beast. [Either pl. of Heb. *b'hēmāh*, a beast, or a Heb. form of Egyptian *p-ehe-mout*, 'water-ox'.]

behest, *bi-hest'*, *n.* a command, charge. [O.E. *behǣs*, a promise.]

behind, *bi-hīnd'*, *prep.* at the back of: at the far side of: in support of, encouraging or initiating: in a direction backward from: later than: inferior to.—*adv.* at the back, in the rear: backward: past (e.g. *things that are behind*).—*adv.* or predicative *adj.* **behind'(-hand)**, tardy, or in arrears. [O.E. *behindan*—*be-*, and *hindan*. See **hind** (3).]

behold, *bi-hōld'*, *v.t.* to see, observe: to contemplate.—*v.i.* to look:—*pa.t.* and *pa.p.* beheld.—*imper.* or *interj.* see! lo! observe!—*adj.* **behold'en**, bound in gratitude, obliged.—*n.* **behold'er**, one who beholds: an onlooker. [O.E. *behealdan*, *behaldan*, to hold, observe—pfx. *be-*, and *h(e)aldan*, to hold.]

behoof, *bi-hōōf'*, *n.* benefit, convenience. [O.E. *behōf*.]

behove, **behoove**, *bi-hōōv'*, *v.t.* now only in phrase **it beho(o)ves** (with *n.* or *pron.*), it is right or necessary for. [O.E. *behōfian*, to be fit.]

beige, *bāzh*, *n.* a woollen fabric made of undyed wool: the colour of this, or a similar colour.—Also *adj.* [Fr.]

being, *bē'ing*, *n.* existence: any person or thing existing: substance, essence.—*adj.* **bē'ing**, existing, present. [From *pr.p.* of **be**.]

bel, *bel*, *n.* a measure for comparing intensity of noises, electric currents, &c., the number of bels being the logarithm to the base 10 of the ratio of one to the other. [From Alexander Graham Bell (1847-1922), telephone inventor.]

belabour, *bi-lā'bór*, *v.t.* (*obs.*) to ply: to beat soundly: to assail with words. [Pfx. *be-*, and **labour**.]

belate, *bi-lāt'*, *v.t.* (*obs.*) to make late. *pa.adj.* **belāt'ed**, made too late: benighted. [Pfx. *be-*, and **late**, adj.]

belay, *bi-lā'*, *v.t.* (*naut.*) to fasten (a running rope) by coiling it round a cleat or a **belay'ing-pin**: to make fast.—**belay there** (*naut. slang*), hold! that is enough. [O.E. *belecgan*—*be-*, and *lecgan*. See **lay** (2).]

belch, *belch*, *belsh*, *v.t.* and *v.i.* to emit wind from the stomach by the mouth: to eject violently.—*n.* eructation. [O.E. *bealcian*; Du. *balken*.]

beldam, **beldame**, *bel'dam*, *n.* an old woman, esp. an ugly one: a virago: (*obs.*) a grandmother [Formed from *dam*, mother, and *bel-*, used like *grand-*.]

beleaguer, *bi-lēg'ér*, *v.t.* to lay siege to. [Du. *belegeren*, to besiege—*leger* a camp.]

belfry, *bel'fri*, *n.* the part of a steeple or tower in which bells are hung. [Orig. a watch-tower—O.Fr. *berfroi*; cf. Middle High German *berchfrit*—*bergan*, to protect, *frid*, *frit*, tower.]

Belgian, *bel'ji-án*, *-ján*, *adj.* belonging to *Belgium*, a country of Europe.—*n.* a native or citizen of Belgium.

Belial, *bēl'yál*, *n.* the devil: in Milton, one of the fallen angels. [Heb. *b'li-ya'al*—*b'li*, without, *ya'al*, usefulness.]

belie, *bi-lī'*, *v.t.* to give the lie to: fail to justify or act up to (hope, promise): to present in a false character:—*pr.p.* bely'ing; *pa.p.* belīed'. [Pfx. *be-*, and **lie** (1).]

believe, bi-lēv′, v.t. to regard as true: to accept as true what is said by (a person): to think or suppose.—v.i. to be firmly persuaded: to have faith (with in, on).—n. belief′, persuasion of the truth of anything: faith: the opinion or doctrine believed.—adj. believ′able, that may be believed.—n. believ′er, one who believes: a professor of Christianity.—p.adj. believ′ing, trustful.—make believe (see make). [M.E. bileven—bi-, be-, and leven. The O.E. form was gelēfan; the present compound appears in the 12th century.]

belike, bi-līk′, adv. (arch.) probably: perhaps. [Pfx. be-, and like, adj.]

Belisha beacon. See beacon.

belittle, bi-lit′l, v.t. to make small: to represent as small, to depreciate. [Pfx. be-, little, adj.]

bell, bel, n. an instrument for giving a ringing sound, typically a hollow vessel of metal struck by a tongue or clapper suspended inside, but taking many other forms: anything bell-shaped, as in diving-bell, &c.: the sound of a bell: a signal by bell.—v.t. to furnish with a bell, esp. in **to bell the cat**, to take the leading part in any hazardous movement, from the ancient fable of the mice who proposed to hang a warning bell round the cat's neck.—adj. **bell′bottomed**, widening towards the ankle.—ns. **bell′-buoy**, a buoy carrying a bell, which is rung by the waves; **bell′-hang′er**, one who hangs and repairs bells; **bell′man**, a town-crier, who rings a bell to attract attention; **bell′-met′al**, metal of which bells are made—an alloy of copper and tin; **bell′-pull**, a cord or handle used in ringing a bell; **bell′-rope**, the rope by which a bell is rung.—adj. **bell′-shaped**.—ns. **bell′-tent**, a bell-shaped tent; **bell′-tow′er**, a tower built to contain one or more bells, a campanile; **bell′-weth′er**, the leading sheep of a flock, on whose neck a bell is hung: (fig.) a ringleader.—**bear or carry off the bell**, to have or gain the first place. [O.E. belle; cog. with Du. bel.]

bell, bel, v.i. to bellow, roar: to utter loudly.—n. the cry of a stag at rutting time. [O.E. bellan, to roar; cf. Ger. bellen.]

belladonna, bel-a-don′a, n. the deadly nightshade or dwale, all parts of which are narcotic and poisonous from the presence of atropine: the drug prepared from it. [It. bella donna, fair lady; one property of belladonna is to enlarge the pupil, and so add a brilliance to the eyes.]

belle, bel, n. the most charming lady of a company: a fair lady generally. [Fr. belle—L. bella, fem. of bellus.]

belles-lettres, bel-let′r, n.pl. polite or elegant literature, including poetry, fiction, criticism, aesthetics, &c. [Fr., lit. 'fine letters'.]

bellicose, bel′ik-ōs, adj. contentious, warlike. [L. bellicōsus—bellum, war.]

belligerent, bel-ij′ér-ént, adj. carrying on regular war: pertaining to a nation, &c., that is doing so (e.g. belligerent rights): warlike, bellicose (e.g. a belligerent attitude).—n. a party or person waging regular war.—n. **bellig′erency**. [For belligerant—L. belligerans, -antis, pr.p. of belligerāre, to wage war.]

bellow, bel′ō, v.i. to roar like a bull: to make any violent outcry.—v.t. to utter very loudly.—n. the roar of a bull: any deep sound or cry. [M.E.

belwen; O.E. bylgian, to roar; there is an O.E. bellan, to roar—see bell (2).]

bellows, bel′ōz, or old-fashioned bel′us, n.pl. (often treated as sing.) an instrument for producing and directing a current of air. [Same as belly; now used only in pl.]

belly, bel′i, n. the part of the body between the breast and the thighs: the interior of anything: the bulging part of anything.—v.i. to swell or bulge out:—pr.p. bell′ying; pa.p. bell′ied.—n. **bell′y-ache′**, a pain in the belly: (slang) a persistent complaint, whine.—v.i. (slang) to complain in a whining fashion.—ns. **bell′y-band**, a saddle-girth: a band fastened to the shafts of a vehicle, and passing under the belly of the horse drawing it; **bell′y-dance**, a solo dance with very pronounced movement of abdominal muscles; **bell′y-flop**, a dive in which one lands in the water on one's stomach; **bell′yful**, a sufficiency; **bell′y-god**, a glutton; **bell′y-landing**, of an aircraft, a landing without using the landing-wheels; **bell′y-laugh**, a deep unrestrained laugh. [M.E. bali, bely—O.E. bæl(i)g, bel(i)g, bag.]

belong, bi-long′, v.i. to go along (with), to pertain (to), as a characteristic, right, duty, &c.: to be the property of (with to): to be a native, member, &c., of (with to).—n.pl. **belong′ings**, possessions: relatives. [M.E. bi-, be-longen—pfx. be-, inten., longen obs. vb. to pertain (to).]

belove, bi-luv′, v.t. obs. except in pa.p. beloved (bi-luvd′), loved.—p.adj. beloved (bi-luv′id), much loved, very dear.—n. one who is much loved. [Pfx. be-, and love.]

below, bi-lō′, prep. beneath in place, rank, or quality: underneath: not worthy of.—adv. in a lower place: (fig.) on earth, or in hell, as opposed to heaven. [Pfx. be-, and low, adj.]

belt, belt, n. a girdle, zone, or band: a zone of country, a district.—v.t. to surround with a belt: to thrash with a belt.—v.i. (slang) to hurry.—p.adj. belt′ed, wearing a belt, of a knight: marked with a belt.—n. **belt′ing**, flexible belts for the transmission of motion from one wheel of a machine to another: a thrashing.—**hit below the belt**, to hit an opponent's body lower than the waist: (fig.) to attack unfairly; **tighten one's belt**, to reduce one's demands or expenditures. [O.E. belt; O.N. belti, Gael. balt, L. balteus.]

beltane, bel′tān, n. an ancient Celtic festival, held in the beginning of May, when bonfires were lighted on the hills: the first day of May (Old Style). [Gael. bealltainn, beilteine, apparently 'bright fire'.]

belvedere, bel′ve-dēr, n. a raised turret on the top of a house, open for the view: a summerhouse on an eminence. [It. belvedere—bel, beautiful, vedere, a view.]

bemoan, bi-mōn′, v.t. to moan at, to lament. [O.E. bemǣnan—pfx. be-, mǣnan, to moan.]

bemuse, bi-mūz′, v.t. to stupefy.—p.adj. bemused′, dazed, fuddled: absorbed (with). [Pfx. be-, inten., and muse (1).]

ben, ben, n. a mountain peak. [Geal. beann.]

ben, ben, prep. and adv. (Scot.) in or toward the inner apartment of a house.—n. the inner apartment of a house of two rooms. See but. [M.E. binne—O.E. binnan, within.]

bench, bench, -sh, n. a long seat or form: a

Neutral vowels in unaccented syllables: em′pér-ór; for certain sounds in foreign words see p. ix.

64

mechanic's work-table: a judge's seat: the body or assembly of judges, bishops, &c.—*ns.* **bench′er**, a senior member of an inn of court; **bench′-mark**, a surveyor's mark cut on a rock, or the like, into which a crooked iron is set so as to form a bench for the levelling instrument. [O.E. *benc*; cog. with Ger. and Du. *bank*.]

bend, *bend*, *v.t.* to curve or bow: to make crooked: to subdue: to apply closely, to strain (e.g. energies): to turn, direct (e.g. steps, eyes): (*naut.*) to tie, make fast.—*v.i.* to be crooked or curved: to stoop: to lean: to bow in submission (with *to*, *before*, *towards*):—*pa.t.* and *pa.p.* bent, also bend′ed (in *bended knees*).—*n.* a curve or crook: (in *pl.*) caisson disease (q.v.).—*ns.* **bend′er** (*slang*), a spree; **bent′wood**, wood artificially curved for chair-making, &c.—Also *adj.*—**round the bend**, crazy, mad. See **bent**. [O.E. *bendan*, to bind, to string (a bow).]

beneath, *bi-nēth′*, *prep.* under, or lower in place than: unworthy the dignity of, unbecoming to. Also *adv.* [O.E. *beneothan*—*be*- and *neothan*, under.]

benedicite, *ben-e-dis′i-te*, *n.* the canticle beginning '*Benedicite* omnia opera Domini' ('*Bless ye*, O all ye works of the Lord'): the blessing before a repast.

benedick, *ben′i-dik*, or (erroneously) **benedict**, *-dikt*, *n.* a newly married man, esp. one who has long disdained marriage—from *Benedick* in Shakespeare's *Much Ado*.

Benedictine, *ben-i-dik′tin*, *adj.* pertaining to St Benedict or his monastic rule.—*n.* a Black Friar or monk or nun of the order founded by St *Benedict* (480–543): a cordial or liqueur resembling Chartreuse—once distilled by Benedictine monks.

benediction, *ben-i-dik′sh(ò)n*, *n.* a solemn invocation of the divine blessing on men or things: blessedness.—*adj.* **benedic′tory**. [L. *benedictiō*, *-onis*—*bene*, well, and *dīcĕre*, *dictum*, to say.]

benefaction, *ben-i-fak′sh(ò)n*, *n.* the act of doing good: a good deed done or benefit conferred: a grant or endowment.—*n.* **ben′efactor**, one who confers a benefit:—*fem.* **ben′efactress**. [L. *benefactiō*, *-ōnis*—*bene*, well, and *facĕre*, *factum*, to do.]

benefice, *ben′i-fis*, *n.* a church living, such as a rectory, vicarage, or other parochial cure, as distinct from a bishopric, deanery, &c.—*adj.* **ben′eficed**, possessed of a benefice. [Through Fr.—L. *beneficium*—*bene*, well, *facĕre*, to do.]

beneficence, *bi-nef′i-sèns*, *n.* active goodness, kindness, charity: a gift, benefaction.—*adj.* **benef′icent**.—*adv.* **benef′icently**. [L. *beneficentia*.]

beneficial, *ben-i-fish′àl*, *adj.* useful, advantageous.—*adv.* **benefic′ially**.—*n.* **benefic′iary**, a holder of a benefice: one who enjoys a gift or advantage. [L. *beneficium*. See **benefice**.]

benefit, *ben′i-fit*, *n.* a kindness, favour: an advantage: a performance at a theatre, or the like, at which the receipts are used for the *benefit* of one of the performers: a right under insurance schemes.—*v.t.* to do good to.—*v.i.* to gain advantage (from, by):—*pr.p.* ben′efiting; *pa.t.* and *pa.p.* ben′efited.—*n.* **ben′efit-of-clergy**, the privilege (abolished in 1827) of

being tried by an ecclesiastical rather than a secular court—for long claimed by any who could read.—**benefit society**, a Friendly (q.v.) Society. [M.E. *benfet*, through Fr. from L. *benefactum*.]

benevolence, *ben-ev′ol-éns*, *n.* disposition to do good: an act of kindness: generosity: (*Eng. hist.*) a forced loan, ostensibly a gift, levied by kings without legal authority.—*adj.* **benev′olent**, charitable, generous, well disposed.—*adv.* **benev′olently**. [Through Fr. from L. *benevolentia*, goodwill—*bene*, well, *volens*, *-entis*, pr.p. of *velle*, to wish.]

Bengali, *ben-gö′lē*, *adj.* of or belonging to *Bengal*.—*n.* a native of Bengal: the language of Bengal.—*n.* **bengal′-light**, a species of firework producing a very vivid blue light, used for signals by ships.

benighted, *bi-nīt′id*, *adj.* overtaken by night: (*fig.*) involved in darkness, ignorant. [Pa.p. of obs. verb—pfx. *be*-, and **night**.]

benign, *bin-īn′*, *adj.* favourable—opp. to *malign*, *unwholesome*: kindly (*med.*) of a tumour, disease, &c., of a mild type—opp. to *malignant*.—*adv.* **benign′ly**.—*adj.* **benignant** (*bi-nig′nànt*), kind: gracious.—*n.* **benig′nancy**.—*adv.* **benig′nantly**.—*n.* **benig′nity**, goodness of disposition: kindness and graciousness. [O.Fr. *benigne*—L. *benignus*, for *benigenus*—*bene*, well, and root of *genus*, birth.]

benison, *ben′izn*, *n.* benediction, blessing. [O.Fr. *beneicun*—L. *benedictiō*. See **benediction**.]

Benjamin, *ben′ja-min*, *n.* a favourite youngest son. [Gen. xlii.–xlv.]

benjamin, *ben′ja-min*, *n.* gum benjamin or **benzoin**. [A corr. of **benzoin**.]

bent, *bent*, *pa.t.* and *pa.p.* of **bend**.—*n.* leaning or bias, tendency, natural inclination of the mind: the extent to which a bow may be bent—whence, **to the top of one's bent**, to the full measure of one's inclination.—*adj.* curved: intent, set (upon doing something), determined (as *bent on going*, *bent on reform*): morally crooked or criminal: (*slang*) of goods, stolen. [From **bend** (q.v.).]

bent, *bent*, *n.* any stiff or wiry grass. [O.E., *beonnet*, found in place-names; a Gmc. word.]

benthoscope, *ben′thō-skōp*, *n.* a submersible sphere from which to study deep-sea life. [Gr. *benthos*, depth, *skopeein*, to look at.]

benumb, *bi-num′*, *v.t.* to make numb or powerless: to deaden (the feelings).—*p.adj.* **benumbed′**. [Pfx. *be*-, and **numb**.]

benzene, *ben′zēn*, *n.* simplest of the aromatic series of hydrocarbons, discovered by Faraday in 1825, now mostly prepared by destructive distillation of coal tar—formerly called benzine, benzol (see below).—*ns.* **benzine** (*ben′zēn*), a mixture of hydrocarbons got by destructive distillation of petroleum, used as a solvent of grease, &c., and for motor fuel, &c.: improperly, benzene; **ben′zol(e)**, crude benzene, used as a motor spirit: improperly, benzene. [From **benzoin**.]

benzoin, *ben′zō-in*, or *-zoin*, *n.* gum benjamin, the aromatic and resinous juice of the benjamin-tree of Java and Sumatra, the source of Friar's Balsam.—*adj.* **benzo′ic**. [Most prob. through It. from Ar. *lubān jāwī*, frankincense of Jawa (i.e. Sumatra).]

bequeath, *bi-kwēth',* *v.t.* to leave (personalty) by will (cf. *devise*): to transmit to posterity. [O.E. *becwethan*—pfx. *be-,* and *cwethan,* to say.]

bequest, *bi-kwest',* *n.* act of bequeathing: that which is bequeathed, a legacy. [M.E. *biqueste*—O.E. pfx. *bi-, be-, cwethan,* to say.]

Berber, *bûr'bér, n.* a member of one of the Hamitic peoples of Barbary (North Africa): the language of the Berbers.—Also *adj.* [Ar. *barbar*; connection with Gr. *barbaros,* foreign, is doubtful.]

berceuse, *ber-sœz', n.* a cradle-song. [Fr.]

bereave, *bi-rēv', v.t.* to deprive (of): to leave desolate:—*pa.t.* and *pa.p.* bereaved'—the latter also **bereft'.**—*adj.* **bereaved',** robbed by death.—*n.* **bereave'ment.** [O.E. *berēafian,* to plunder—*be-,* inten., *rēafian,* to rob.]

beret, *ber'ā,* **berret,** *ber'et, n.* a flat, round, woollen cap. [Fr. *béret.*]

berg, *bûrg, n.* a hill or mountain: short for iceberg. [Ger., Du., Swed. *berg,* hill; cog. with **barrow** (2).]

bergamot, *bûr'ga-mot, n.* a kind of citron or orange whose aromatic rind yields oil of bergamot. [Perh. from *Bergamo,* a town in Italy.]

bergamot, *bûr'ga-mot, n.* a fine pear. [Fr.,—Turk., *begarmūdi,* the prince of pears.]

beriberi, *ber'i-ber'i, n.* an Eastern disease, due to lack of vitamin B. [Sinhalese *beri,* weakness.]

berkelium, *bér-kē'li-um,* earlier *bûrk'li-ùm, n.* a transuranium element (atomic number 97; symbol Bk) made at *Berkeley,* California.

berlin, *bûr'lin, bér-lēn', n.* a four-wheeled covered carriage, with a hood-covered seat behind—also **berline.** [From the city of *Berlin.*]

Bermuda shorts, *bér-mū'da,* shorts, for men or women, reaching to just above the knees.

berry, *ber'i, n.* any small succulent fruit: restricted in botanical language to simple fruits with pericarp succulent throughout: a coffeebean: the egg of a lobster or crayfish.—*adj.* **berr'ied,** bearing berries. [O.E. *berie.*]

berserk, -er, *bér-sûrk'(ér), -zûrk'(ér), n.* a Norse warrior filled with a frenzied and resistless fury—the 'berserker rage'.—*adj., adv.* in a violent frenzy. [O.N. *berserker,* prob. bearsark.]

berth, *bûrth, n.* a ship's station at anchor or in port: a room or sleeping-place in a ship, &c.: a situation or place of employment.—*v.t.* to moor a ship at a berth.—**give a wide berth to,** to keep well away from. [Ety. obscure.]

bertha, *bûr'tha,* **berthe,** *bûrth, n.* a woman's falling collar. [From the name *Bertha.*]

beryl, *ber'il, n.* a silicate of beryllium and aluminium, a precious stone of which emerald and aquamarine are varieties, once esteemed as a magic crystal.—*n.* **beryllium,** a light steely metallic element (symbol Be; atomic no. 4) used in nuclear reactors and to harden alloys, &c.—also called glucinum. [O.Fr. *beryl*—L. *bēryllus*—Gr. *bēryllos.*]

beseech, *bi-sēch', v.t.* to entreat, to implore: to beg, pray earnestly for:—*pa.t.* and *pa.p.* besought'.—*adv.* **beseech'ingly.** [Pfx. *be-,* inten., and M.E. *sechen,* to seek.]

beseem, *bi-sēm', v.t.* to be seemly or fit for, to suit. [Pfx. *be-,* inten., and **seem.**]

beset, *bi-set', v.t.* to surround (with—now only in *pa.p.*): to besiege: to assail, perplex:—*pr.p.*

besett'ing; *pa.t.* and *pa.p.* beset'.—**besett'ing sin,** the sin that most often assails or tempts one. [O.E. *besettan*—pfx. *be-,* and **set.**]

beshrew, *bi-shrōō', v.t.* curse. [Pfx. *be-,* and **shrew,** n.]

beside, *bi-sīd', prep.* by the side of, near: over and above: apart from.—Also *adv.*—**beside the mark, point, question,** ill aimed, irrelevant.—**be beside oneself,** to be distraught with anxiety, fear, or anger. [M.E. *bi siden*—O.E. *be sīdan,* by the side (dat.).]

besides, *bi-sīdz', prep.* over and above, in addition to.—Also *adv.* [**beside,** with the *s* of the adverbial gen.]

besiege, *bi-sēj', v.t.* to lay siege to: to throng round: to assail (with requests).—*n.* **besieg'er.** [M.E. *besegen*—pfx. *be-,* and *segen,* through O.Fr. and L.L.—L. *sedēre,* to sit.]

beslobber, *bi-slob'ér, v.t.* to slaver or slobber upon: to cover with drivelling kisses: to flatter fulsomely. [Pfx. *be-,* and **slobber,** vb.]

besmear, *bi-smēr', v.t.* to smear, or be smeared, over. [O.E. *bismierwan*—pfx. *be-,* inten., and *smierwan,* to anoint.]

besmirch, *bi-smûrch', v.t.* to soil: to sully. [Pfx. *be-,* and **smirch.**]

besom, *bē'zóm, bez'óm, n.* a bunch of twigs for sweeping, a broom. [O.E. *besema*; a common Gmc. word: Ger. *besen,* Du. *bezem.*]

besom, *biz'óm, bēz'óm, n.* (*Scot.* and *dial.*) an impudent woman. [Perh. the same word as the preceding; perh. connected with O.E. *bysn, bisn,* example, or O.N. *bysn,* wonder.]

besot, *bi-sot', v.t.* to make sottish, dull, or stupid: to infatuate (with):—*pr.p.* besott'ing; *pa.p.* besott'ed. [Pfx. *be-,* and **sot,** n.]

besought, *bi-söt', pa.t.* and *pa.p.* of **beseech.**

bespangle, *bi-spang'gl, v.t.* to adorn with spangles. [Pfx. *be-,* and **spangle.**]

bespatter, *bi-spat'ér, v.t.* to spatter or sprinkle with dirt or anything moist: to defame. [Pfx. *be-,* and **spatter.**]

bespeak, *bi-spēk', v.t.* to speak for or engage beforehand: to betoken:—*pa.t.* bespoke'; *pa.p.* bespōke' and bespōk'en. [O.E. *besprecan*—pfx. *be-,* and *sprecan,* to speak.]

bespoke(n), *bi-spōk'(-n), pa.p.* of **bespeak,** ordered (as boots, clothes, &c.).

besprinkle, *bi-spring'kl, v.t.* to sprinkle over. [M.E. *besprengil*—*be-,* inten., and *sprenkel,* freq. of *sprengen,* to sprinkle.]

Bessemer, *bes'ém-ér, adj.* derived from the name of the inventor, Sir H. *Bessemer* (1813-1898), applied to the method of making steel from pig-iron by forcing a blast of air through the molten metal, and to steel thus produced.

best, *best, adj.* (serving as *superl.* of **good**) good in the highest degree, first, highest, most excellent.—*n.* one's utmost endeavour: the highest perfection: the best part.—*adv.* (*superl.* of **well**) in the highest degree: in the best manner.—*v.t.* (*coll.*) to get the better of.—**best man** and **best maid,** the groomsman and brīdesmaid at a wedding; **best part,** greater part; **best'seller,** a book that has had one of the biggest sales of the season: the writer of such a book.—**at best,** on the most favourable supposition; **for the best,** with the best intentions: with the best results all things considered; **I**

Neutral vowels in unaccented syllables: *em'pér-ór*; for certain sounds in foreign words see p. ix.

66

had best, I were best, it were best *for me* (for earlier *me were best*); **have the best of it**, to prevail in a contest; **make the best of one's way**, to go as well as one can; **put one's best foot foremost**, to make one's best effort; **with the best**, as successfully as anyone.[O.E. *betst, betest*. See **better**.]

bestead, bested, *bi*-sted', *p.adj.* beset (by): situated—usually with *ill, hard,* &c. [M.E. *bistad*—pfx. *be-,* and *stad,* placed.]

bestial, *best'i-ăl, adj.* like a beast: brutally sensual.—*n.* **bestial'ity.** [L. *bestiālis.*]

bestiary, *best'i-ăr-i, n.* a book of a class popular in the Middle Ages, a mixture of natural and unnatural history of animals, allegorised. [L.L. *bestiārium,* a menagerie.]

bestir, *bi*-stûr', *v.t.* to put into lively action: to rouse (oneself). [O.E. *bestyrian*—*be-,* inten., *styrian,* to stir.]

bestow, *bi*-stō', *v.t.* to stow, place, or put by: to give or confer.—*n.* **bestow'al**, disposal: act or fact of conferring as a gift. [M.E. *bistowen*—*be-,* inten., *stowen.* See **stow.**]

bestrew, *bi*-strōō', *v.t.* to strew or scatter over:—*pa.p.* bestrewed', bestrown', bestrewn' (followed by *with*). [O.E. *bestrēowian*—*be-,* and *strēowian.* See **strew.**]

bestride, *bi*-strīd', *v.t.* to stride over: to sit or stand across:—*pa.t.* bestrid', bestrode'; *pa.p.* bestrid', bestridd'en. [O.E. *bestrīdan*—pfx. *be-,* and *strīdan,* to stride.]

bet, *bet, n.* a wager, something staked to be lost or won on an uncertain issue.—*v.t.* and *v.i.* to lay or stake, as a bet:—*pr.p.* bett'ing: *pa.t.* and *pa.p.* bet or bett'ed.—*ns.* **bett'er**, one who bets; **bett'ing**, act of betting or proposing a wager.—**an even bet**, an equal chance; **you bet** (*slang*), certainly. [Possibly from **abet.**]

beta, *bē'ta, n.* the second letter of the Greek alphabet.—**beta rays**, streams of **beta particles**, one of the products emitted from the atomic nuclei of certain radioactive substances; they have been shown to be electrons, moving with high velocities, prob. coming from neutrons (converted by their loss into protons).

betake, *bi*-tāk', *v.t.* to take (oneself), i.e. to go (with *to*): to apply (oneself to) or have recourse (to):—*pa.t.* betook'; *pa.p.* betak'en. [Pfx. *be-,* and **take.**]

betel, *bē'tl, n.* the leaf of the betel-pepper, which is chewed in the East along with the areca-nut and lime.—*ns.* **betel-nut**, a name used for the areca nut; **betel palm**, properly the areca palm. [Through Port. from Dravidian (q.v.) *vettila.*]

bête noir, *bet nwär,* (*lit.* black beast) one's bugbear, pet abomination. [Fr.]

bethel, *beth'el, n.* a hallowed spot: a place of worship. [Heb. *Bēth-ēl,* house of God.]

bethink, *bi*-thingk', *v.t.* (followed by a reflexive pronoun and *of*) to think on or call to mind:—*pa.t.* and *pa.p.* bethought (*bi*-thöt'). [O.E. *bithencan*—pfx. *be-,* and **think.**]

betide, *bi*-tīd', *v.i.* and *v.t.* to befall, to happen to—now little used except in **woe betide** (**him,** &c.). [M.E. *betīden*—pfx. *be-,* and **tide.**]

betimes, *bi*-tīmz', *adv.* in good time: seasonably. [Pfx. *be-,* and **time,** with adverbial gen. *-s*; like *besides* from beside.]

betoken, *bi*-tō'kn, *v.t.* to show by a sign, signify: foreshow. [M.E. *bitacnien*—pfx. *be-,* and **token.**]

betony, *bet'on-i, n.* a woodland plant, once valued as a medicinal herb. [Fr.,—L. *betonica, vettonica.*]

betook, *bi*-tōōk', *pa.t.* of **betake.**

betray, *bi*-trā', *v.t.* to give up treacherously: to disclose in breach of trust: to deceive: to lead (into a course of action): to reveal unintentionally: to show signs of.—*ns.* **betray'al**, **betray'er.** [M.E. *betraien*—pfx. *be-,* and O.Fr. *traïr*—L. *tradēre,* to deliver up.]

betroth, *bi*-trōTH' (or *-troth*), *v.t.* to promise in marriage, to affiance.—*n.* **betroth'al.**—*n.* and *adj.* **betroth'ed.** [M.E. *bitreuthien*—pfx. *be-,* and **truth** or **troth.**]

better, *bet'ér, adj.* (serves as *comp.* of **good**) good in a greater degree: preferable: improved: stronger in health.—*adv.* (*comp.* of **well**) well in a greater degree: more fully or completely: with greater advantage.—*n.* a superior (esp. in *pl.*).—*v.t.* to make better, to improve: to surpass.—*n.* **bett'erment.**—**better half**, a jocose term for a wife.—**I had better**, it would be better for me to; **be better off**, to be in more desirable circumstances; **be better than one's word**, to do more than one had promised; **get the better of**, to gain the advantage over; **think better of**, to revise one's decision about; to have a better opinion of. [O.E. *bet* (adv.), *betera* (adj.), *betst*; Ger. *besser.*]

between, *bi*-twen', *prep.* and *adv.* in, to, through, or across an interval of space, time, &c.: to and from: connecting: by combined action of: part to (one), part to (the other). *n.* **between'-decks**, the space between any two decks of a ship.—*advs.* **between times, between'-whiles**, at intervals.—**between the devil and the deep sea**, in a desperate dilemma; **between our selves, between you and me**, in confidence.—**go between**, to act as a mediator (*n.* go-between—see go). [O.E. *betwēonum, betwēonan*—*be,* and *twēgen,* neut. *twā,* twain, two.]

betwixt, *bi*-twikst', *prep.* and *adv.* between.—**betwixt and between**, in a middling position. [O.E. *betweox*—*twā,* two, and the suffix. *-ix,* *-ish,* with added *-t* as in *against.*]

Bev, BeV, (*obs.*) a billion electron volts (see **MeV**). Because the value of a billion in Europe is different from that in U.S.A. a term **GeV** (q.v.) was introduced.

bevel, *bev'l, n.* a slant or inclination of a surface: an instrument, opening like a pair of compasses, for measuring angles.—*adj.* having the form of a bevel: slanting.—*v.t.* to form with a bevel or slant:—*pr.p.* bev'elling; *pa.p.* bev'elled.—*ns.* **bev'el-gear, bev'el-wheels**, wheels with bevelled cogs, working on each other in different planes. [Fr. *biveau,* an instrument for measuring angles.]

beverage, *bev'ér-ij, n.* any liquid for drinking, esp. tea, coffee, milk, &c. [O.Fr. *bevrage*—*beivre*—L. *bibēre,* to drink.]

bevy, *bev'i, n.* a brood or flock of birds, esp. of quails: a company, esp. of ladies. [M.E. *bevey,* prob. the same as O.Fr. *bevee, buvee,* drink; the transference of sense being perh. from a drink to a drinking-party.]

bewail   bid

bewail, *bi-wāl'*, *v.t.* to lament. [Pfx. *be-*, and **wail**.]

beware, *bi-wār'*, *v.i.* and *v.t.* to be on one's guard (against—*v.i.* with *of*)—now used only in imperative and infinitive, and with auxiliaries *shall, must, let*; often followed by clause with *lest, that not,* or *how.* [From the words **be** and **ware** (2), run together. Cf. **wary**.]

bewilder, *bi-wil'dèr*, *v.t.* to perplex or lead astray.—*n.* **bewil'derment**, perplexity. [Pfx. *be-*, and obs. Eng. *wildern*—O.E. *wilddēoren*, wilderness—*wild*, wild, *deor*, beast.]

bewitch, *bi-wich'*, *v.t.* to affect by witchcraft: to fascinate or charm.—*ns.* **bewitch'ery**, **bewitch'ment.**—*adj.* **bewitch'ing**, charming, enchanting.—*adv.* **bewitch'ingly.** [M.E. *biwicchen*—*be-*, inten., O.E. *wiccian*—*wicca, wicce,* witch.]

bewray, *bi-rā'*, *v.t. (obs.)* to accuse: to reveal. [M.E. *bewreien*—*be-*, and O.E. *wrēgan*, to accuse.]

bey, *beg, bā*, *n.* a Turkish governor of a town or province. [Turk. *bey*, pronounced *bā*, a governor.]

beyond, *bi-yond'*, *prep.* on the farther side of: farther onward than: out of reach of.—*adv.* farther away.—*n.* the unknown: the hereafter.—**the back of beyond**, a very remote place.—**be beyond one**, to pass one's comprehension; **go beyond**, to surpass: to circumvent. [O.E. *begeondan*—pfx. *be-*, and *geond*, across, beyond.]

bezel, *bez'él*, *n.* the oblique side or face of a cut gem: the grooved rim in which a gem or watch-glass is set: the slope at the edge of a chisel or plane (usu. **bas'il**). [From O.Fr. (Fr. *biseau*); of uncertain origin.]

bezique, *be-zēk'*, *n.* a game at cards, in which *bezique* denotes the combination of the knave of diamonds and queen of spades. [Fr. *bésigue*, of obscure origin.]

bhang, *bang*, *n.* the leaves and shoots of hemp used as a narcotic and intoxicant. [Hindustani *bhāng*; Pers. *bang*.]

bi-, *bī, pfx.* twice, double. [L. *bis*, twice, *bīnī*, two by two, for *duis, duīnī*.]

biannual, *bī-an'ū-ál*, *adj.* half-yearly. [L. *bi-*, twice, *annus*, a year.]

bias, *bī'as*, *n.* a bulge or greater weight on one side of a bowl which prevents it from rolling in a straight line: a slant or leaning to one side: a one-sided inclination of the mind, prejudice.—*v.t.* to give a bias to: to prejudice or prepossess:—*pa.t.* and *pa.p.* bi'ased or bī'assed.—*adj.* (of material) cut on the cross.—*n.* **bias binding**, a long narrow folded piece of material cut slantwise and used for finishing hems, seams, &c., in sewing. [Fr. *biais*, slant; of unknown origin.]

bib, *bib*, *n.* a cloth or plastic shield put under a child's chin: of an apron, overalls, &c., the front part extending above the waist.—*v.t.* and *v.i.* to drink, to tipple.—*n.* **bibb'er** (as in *wine-bibber*).—**best bib and tucker** (*coll.*) best clothes. [M.E. *bibben*, most prob. from L. *bibēre*, to drink.]

bib, *bib*, *n.* the pout, a fish of the same genus as the cod and haddock. [**bib** (1).]

Bible, *bī'bl*, *n.* the sacred writings of the Christian Church, consisting of the Old and

New Testaments: any authoritative book.—*adj.* **biblical** (*bib'li-kl*), of or relating to the Bible: scriptural.—*adv.* **bib'lically.** [Fr.,—Low L. *biblia*, from Gr. *ta biblia*, lit. 'the books', esp. the canonical books, sing. *biblion*, a book, dim. of *biblos*, papyrus, paper.]

bibliography, *bib-li-og'raf-i*, *n.* the description or knowledge of books, in regard to their authors, subjects, editions, and history: a descriptive list of books.—*n.* **bibliog'rapher.**—*adjs.* **bibliograph'ic**, **bibliograph'ical.** [Gr. *biblion*, a book, *graphein*, to write.]

bibliolatry, *bib-li-ol'at-ri*, *n.* a superstitious reverence for a book, esp. the Bible.—*n.* **bibliol'ater.**—*adj.* **bibliol'atrous.** [Gr. *biblion*, a book, *latreia*, worship.]

bibliomania, *bib-li-ō-mān'i-a*, *n.* a mania for collecting rare books: love of books.—*n.* **bibliomān'iac.** [Gr *biblion*, a book. and **mania.**]

bibliophile, *bib'li-ō-fil*, *n.* a lover of books, esp. a collector of rare books. [Fr.,—Gr. *biblion*, a book, *philos*, friend.]

bibliopole, *bib'li-ō-pōl*, *n.* a bookseller.—Also **bibliŏp'olist.**—*n.* **bibliop'oly.** [Gr. *biblion*, a book, *pōleein*, to sell.]

bibulous, *bib'ū-lus*, *adj.* drinking or sucking in, spongy: addicted to drink: of, pertaining to, drinking. [L. *bibulus*—*bibēre*, to drink.]

bicameral, *bī-kam'ér-ál*, *adj.* having two legislative chambers. [L. *bi-*, twice, and *camera*, chamber.]

bicarbonate, *bī-kär'bon-át*, *n.* an acid salt of carbonic acid. [L. *bi-*, twice, and **carbonate.**]

bice, *bīs*, *n.* a pale blue or green paint. [Fr. *bis.*]

bicentenary, *bī-sen'ten-ár-i*, or *-tēn'-*, or *-ten'-*, *adj.* pertaining to two hundred years.—*n.* the two hundredth anniversary. [L. *bi-*, twice, *centēnārius*, pertaining to a hundred—*centum*, a hundred.]

bicentennial, *bī-sen-ten'i-ál*, *adj.* pertaining to two hundred years.—*n.* a two hundredth anniversary. [L. *bi-*, twice, *centum*, a hundred, *annus*, year.]

biceps, *bī'seps*, *n.* the muscle with two heads in front of the upper arm. [L. *biceps*, two-headed—*bis*, twice, and *caput*, head.]

bicker, *bik'ér*, *v.i.* to contend in a petty way: to quiver, as flame: to brawl, as running water.—*n.* a fight, a quarrel. [Perh. *bicker* = *picker*, or *pecker*, to *peck* repeatedly with the beak.]

bicuspid, *bī-kus'pid*, *adj.* having two cusps.—*n.* a premolar tooth. [L. *bi-*, twice, and **cusp.**]

bicycle, *bī'si-kl*, *n.* a vehicle, driven by pedals or a motor, consisting of two wheels, arranged one before the other, and a seat for the driver—also **bike** (*coll.*).—*v.i.* to ride a cycle.—*n.* **bī'cyclist.** [Formed from L. *bi-, bis,* twice, and Gr. *kyklos*, wheel.]

bid, *bid*, *v.t.* to command: to invite (e.g. *to bid one to a feast*): to wish, utter as a greeting (e.g. *to bid one good-morning*): to proclaim (e.g. *defiance*): to offer, esp. at an auction or in card games.—*v.i.* to make an offer:—*pr.p.* bidd'ing; *pa.t.* bade (pron. *bad*, sometimes *bād*), bid; *pa.p.* bidd'en, bid.—*n.* an offer of a price: a venture.—*adj.* **bidd'able**, obedient, docile.—*ns.* **bidd'er**; **bidd'ing**, offer: invitation: command.—**bid fair**, to seem likely (to). [Part-

Neutral vowels in unaccented syllables: *em'pér-ór*; for certain sounds in foreign words see p. ix.

68

ly O.E. *bēodan* (Ger. *bieten*), to offer; partly
O.E. *biddan* (Ger. *bitten*), to pray, ask.]
bide, *bīd, v.t.* and *v.i.* to wait for: to dwell: to
endure. [O.E. *bīdan*; but sometimes for **abide**.]
biennial, *bī-en'i-al, adj.* lasting two years: happening once in two years.—*n.* a plant that
flowers and fructifies only in its second year,
then dies.—*adv.* **bienn'ially.** [L. *biennālis*—*bi*-,
twice, and *annus*, a year.]
bier, *bēr, n.* a carriage or frame of wood for
bearing the dead to the grave. [O.E. *bǣr*; Ger.
bahre, L. *feretrum*—*fērre*, to bear. From root
of verb **bear**.]
biestings. Same as **beestings.**
bifacial, *bī-fā'shàl, adj.* two-faced: having two
unlike sides. [L. *bi-*, twice, and **facial**.]
bifocal, *bī-fō'kàl, adj.* having two foci, used of
spectacles adapted for near, or for distant,
vision. [L. *bi-*, twice, **focal.** See **focus.**]
bifurcate, *bī'fur-kāt,* or *-fūr'-*, **bifurcated,** *-id,
adj.* two-forked: having two prongs or
branches.—*n.* **bifurca'tion.** [L. *bifurcus bi ,
bis*, twice, *furca*, a fork.]
big, *big, adj.* large or great: important: pompous
(esp. *to talk big, to look big*).—*adj.*
bigg'ish, rather big.—*ns.* **big'ness,** bulk, size;
big'wig (*coll*), a person of importance.—**Big
Brother,** a dictator as in George Orwell's
Nineteen Eighty Four (1949); **big business,**
large business enterprises and organisations,
esp. collectively; **big end,** in an internal-
combustion engine, the larger end of the connecting rod; **big game,** the larger and more
formidable beasts of chase; **big money,** money
in large sums; **big name,** a person who is well
known and influential; **big noise** (*slang*), person important (esp.) in small circle; **big shot**
(*slang*), an important person; **big-time,** the
top level in any pursuit; **big top,** the main
circus tent. [M.E. *big*; origin very obscure.]
bigamy, *big'àm-i, n.* the crime of having two
wives or two husbands at once.—*n.* **big'-
amist.**—*adj.* **big'amous.**—*adv.* **big'amously.** [L.
bi-, twice; Gr. *gamos*, marriage.]
bight, *bīt, n.* a wide bay: a bend or coil of a rope.
[O.E. *byht*; cf. Dan. and Swed. *bugt*, Du. *bocht*.]
bigot, *big'ot, n.* one blindly and obstinately devoted to a particular creed or party.—*adj.*
big'oted.—*n.* **big'otry.** [O.Fr.; of uncertain
origin.]
bijou, *bē'zhoo, n.* a trinket: a jewel: a little
box:—*pl.* **bijoux** (*bē'zhōō*).—*adj.* small and
elegant.—*n.* **bijou'terie,** jewellery. [Fr.]
bike. See **bicycle.**
bikini, *bi-kē'nē, n.* a very scanty form of bathing
dress in two parts. [Said to be from *Bikini*, an
atoll in the Marshall Islands in the Pacific,
partly denuded by atom-bomb experiments.]
bilabiate, *bī-lā'bi-āt, adj.* having two lips, as
some corollas. [L. *bi-*, twice, and **labiate.**]
bilateral, *bī-lat'ér-àl, adj.* having two sides.—
adv. **bilat'erally.** [L. *bi-*, twice, and **lateral.**]
bilberry, *bil'ber-i, n.* a whortleberry or blaeberry
shrub: its dark blue berry. [Cf. Dan. *bøllebær*.]
bilbo, *bil'bō, n.* a rapier or sword. [From *Bilbao*,
in Spain.]
bile, *bīl, n.* a thick bitter fluid secreted by the
liver: (*fig.*) ill-humour.—*adj.* **bilious** (*bil'-yùs*),
pertaining to or affected by bile.—*n.* **bil'iousness.** [Fr.,—L. *bīlis*.]

bilge, *bilj, n.* the bulging part of a cask: the
broadest part of a ship's bottom: filth such as
collects there.—*n.* **bilge'-wat'er,** the foul water
in a ship's bilge. [Most prob. conn. with **bulge**.]
bilingual, *bī-ling'gwàl, adj.* expressed in two
languages: speaking two languages, esp.
native or habitual (e.g. English and Welsh). [L.
bilinguis—*bi-*, twice, *lingua*, language.]
bilk, *bilk, v.i.* to elude: to cheat.—*n.* **bilk'er.**
[Perh. a form of **balk**.]
bill, *bil, n.* a kind of battle-axe: a hatchet with a
long blade, used in cutting hedges or in pruning.—*ns.* **bill'hook,** a bill having a hooked
point; **bill'man,** a soldier armed with a bill.
[O.E. *bil*; Ger. *bille*.]
bill, *bil, n.* the beak of a bird, or anything like it:
a sharp promontory.—*v.i.* to join bills as
doves: to caress fondly. [O.E. *bile*, most prob.
the same word as the preceding.]
bill, *bil, n.* a draft of a proposed law: an account
of money owed to a creditor for merchandise,
&c : a written engagement to pay a sum of
money at a fixed date (*U.S.*) a bank note: a
placard or advertisement: any written statement of particulars: a written accusation of
serious crime preferred before a grand jury
(see **grand**).—*v.t.* to announce by bill.—*ns.*
bill'-board, a board on which placards are
posted; **bill'-brok'er,** one who deals in bills of
exchange and promissory notes; **bill'-stick'er,
-post'er,** one who sticks or posts up bills or
placards.—**bill of costs,** a detailed account of
the sums due by a client to his solicitor; **bill of
exchange,** a written order from one person
(the *drawer*) to another (the *drawee*), desiring the latter to pay to some specified person
a sum of money on a certain future date; **bill
of fare,** a list of dishes or articles of food; **bill
of health,** an official certificate of the state of
health on board ship before sailing; **bill of
indictment,** a statement of a criminal charge
against a person; **bill of lading,** a paper signed
by the master of a ship, by which he makes
himself responsible for the safe delivery of
the goods specified therein; **bill of mortality,**
an official return of births and deaths; **bill of
sale,** in English law, a formal deed assigning
personal property. [Through Low L. *billa*, a
seal—L. *bulla*, a knob. Cf. **bull** (2).]
billabong, *bil'a-bong, n.* (*Austr.*) an effluent
from a river: a water-hole, pond, or small lake.
[Native words *billa*, river, *bung*, dead.]
billet, *bil'ét, n.* a note (*arch.*) or notice (*obs.*): a
ticket assigning quarters to soldiers: quarters:
(*coll.*) a post, job.—*v.t.* to quarter or lodge, as
soldiers, evacuees:—*pr.p.* **bill'eting;** *pa.p.*
bill'eted. [Fr.; dim. of **bill** (3).]
billet, *bil'ét, n.* a small log of wood used as fuel.
[Fr. *billette*—*bille*, the young stock of a tree;
prob. of Celt. orig.]
billet-doux, *bil'e-dōō', n.* a love letter:—*pl.*
billets-doux (*bil'e-dōōz'*). [Fr. *billet*, a letter,
doux, sweet.]
billiards, *bil'yàrdz, n.* a game played with a cue
and balls on a table with pockets at the sides
and corners.—*adj.* **bill'iard.** [Fr. *billard*—*bille*,
a stick, hence a cue.]
billingsgate, *bil'ingz-gāt, n.* foul and abusive
language like that used at *Billingsgate* (the
London fish-market).

billion, *bil'yŏn, n.* a million millions (1,000,000,000,000): in U.S.A., one thousand millions (1,000,000,000) or a milliard. [L. *bi-,* twice, and **million.**]

billow, *bil'ō, n.* a great wave of the sea swelled by the wind.—*v.i.* to roll as in large waves.— *adjs.* **bill'owed, bill'owy.** [Scand.; O.N. *bylgja*; Swed. *bölja,* Dan. *bölge,* a wave.]

billy, billie, *bil'i, n.* a comrade: an Australian bushman's boiling-pan or tea-pot (also **billycan**):—*pl.* **bill'ies.**—*n.* **bill'y-goat,** a he-goat. [Prob. from *Bill,* abbrev. of William.]

billycock, *bil'i-kok, n.* a hard felt hat. [Said to be from William *Coke,* nephew of Earl (1837) of Leicester.]

biltong, *bil'tong, n.* (*S. Africa*) sun-dried lean meat in tongue-shaped strips. [Du. *bil,* buttock, *tong,* tongue.]

bimetallism, *bī-met'ăl-izm, n.* a monetary system in which gold and silver are on precisely the same footing as regards mintage and legal tender.—*adj.* **bimetall'ic,** adapted to that standard.—*n.* and *adj.* **bimet'allist,** (one) advocating bimetallism. [L. *bi-,* twice, and **metal.**]

bimonthly, *bī-munth'li, adj.* once in two months: also twice a month. [L. *bi-,* twice, and **month.**]

bin, *bin, n.* a receptacle for corn, wine, dust, &c. [O.E. *binn,* a manger.]

binary, *bī'năr-i, adj.* twofold.—**binary operation** (*math.*), the combining of two elements in a collection of elements in such a way as to give another element (as addition or multiplication in the ordinary number system); **binary star** (see **binary system**); **binary system,** two stars revolving about their centre of gravity (also **binary star**): system in which numbers are expressed by using two digits only, viz. 1 and 0. [L. *bīnārius*—*bīnī,* two by two—*bis.*]

bind, *bīnd, v.t.* to tie or fasten together with a band or bandage: to make fast (to): to encircle (with): to sew a border on: to fasten together and put a cover on (a book): to impose an obligation, by oath or promise, on (one to do something): to indenture: to render hard:— *pa.t.* and *pa.p.* bound (also **bounden,** q.v.).—*n.* (*slang*) a bore.—*n.* **bind'er,** one who binds, as books or sheaves: a reaping-machine with an attachment for binding the grain into sheaves as it cuts.—*adj.* **bind'ing,** restraining: obligatory.—*n.* the act of binding: anything that binds: the covering of a book.—*ns.* **bind'weed,** the convolvulus, a genus of plants that entwine the stems of other plants; **bine, bind,** the slender stem of a climbing plant.—**I dare** or **will be bound,** I will be responsible for the statement; **be bound up in,** to be wholly devoted to; **bind over,** to subject to legal obligation; **bound to** (see **bound**). [O.E. *bindan*; cog. with Ger. *binden,* Sans. *bandh.*]

bingo, *bing'gō, n.* game played by covering on a card each number called until all numbers are covered.

binnacle, *bin'ä-kl, n.* (*naut.*) the box in which a ship's compass is kept. [Formerly *bittacle* — Port. *bitácola*—L. *habitāculum,* a dwelling-place—*habitāre,* to dwell.]

binocular, *bin-ok'ūl-ár, adj.* having two eyes: suitable for two eyes.—*n.* (usu. *pl.*) a field-glass having two tubes, one for each eye. [L. *bīnī,* two by two, *oculus,* an eye.]

binomial, *bī-nōm'i-ăl, adj.* and *n.* (*alg.*) a quantity consisting of two terms, as *a + b.* [L. *bi-, bis,* twice, and *nōmen,* a name.]

bio-, *bī-ō,* in composition, life: living organisms: living tissue. [Gr. *bios,* life.]

biochemistry, *bī-ō-kem'is-tri, n.* the chemistry of living substances, physiological chemistry.—*adj.* **biochem'ical.**—*n.* **biochem'ist.** [Gr. *bios,* life, and **chemistry.**]

biogenesis, *bio-jen'es-is, n.* the theory that life can come only from living things. [Gr. *bios,* life, and **genesis.**]

biography, *bī-og'raf-i, n.* a written account of history of the life of an individual: the art of writing such accounts.—*n.* **biog'rapher.**—*adjs.* **biograph'ic, -al.**—*adv.* **biograph'ically.** [Gr. *bios,* life, *graphein,* to write.]

biology, *bī-ol'oj-i, n.* the science that treats of living things (animals and plants).—*adj.* **biolog'ical.**—*adv.* **biolog'ically.**—*n.* **biol'ogist.**— **biological control,** method of reducing the numbers of a pest—plant, animal or parasite—by introducing or fostering one of its enemies; **biological warfare,** methods of fighting involving the use of disease bacteria. [Gr. *bios,* life, *logos,* a discourse.]

biophysics, *bi-o-fiz'iks, n.* the application of physics to the study of living things. [Gr. *bios,* life, and **physics.**]

biopsy, *bī'op-si, n.* removal of tissue or fluid from a living body for diagnostic examination: such examination. [Gr. *bios,* life, *opsis,* appearance.]

bipartite, *bī-pärt'īt, adj.* in two parts: having two corresponding parts (as a document): affecting two parties (as a treaty or agreement). [L. *bi-, bis,* twice, *partītus,* divided—*partīre,* or *-īrī,* to divide.]

biped, *bi'ped, n.* an animal with two feet.—*adj.* having two feet. [L. *bipēs*—*bi-, bis,* twice, *pēs, pedis,* foot.]

biplane, *bī'plān, n.* an aeroplane with two sets of wings, one above the other. [L. *bi-,* twice, and **plane.**]

birch, *bûrch, n.* a genus of forest trees, with smooth white bark and very durable wood: a rod for punishment, consisting of a birch twig or twigs.—*v.t.* to flog.—*adjs.* **birch, birch'en.** [O.E. *berc, bierce*; O.N. *björk,* Sans. *bhūrja.*]

bird, *bûrd, n.* a general name for feathered animals: (*arch., dial.*; later *slang*) a girl or woman.—*ns.* **bird'-call,** an instrument used by fowlers to call or allure birds to them, by imitating their notes; **bird'-fan'cier** (see **fancier**); **bird'ie** (*dim.*), a little bird: (*golf*) a hole in one stroke less than par; **bird'-lime,** a sticky substance for catching birds; **bird'-nesting,** searching for birds' nests and taking the eggs; **bird'-seed,** seed (hemp, &c.) for cage-birds: (*slang*) something trifling in amount; **bird's-eye,** a kind of primrose, of speedwell, or of tobacco; **bird'-strike',** collision of a bird with an aircraft resulting in aircraft damage.—**bird's-eye view,** a general view from above, as if seen by a bird on the wing: a general view or résumé of a subject.—**bird of paradise** (see **paradise**); **for the birds** (*slang*), not to be taken seriously, of little value. [O.E. *brid,* the young of a bird, a bird.]

bireme, *bī'rēm, n.* an ancient vessel with two

Neutral vowels in unaccented syllables: *em'pér-ôr*; for certain sounds in foreign words see p. ix.

70

tiers of oars. [Fr.,—L. *birēmis—bi-*, twice, and *rēmus*, an oar.]

biretta, *bir-et'a*, *n.* a square cap worn by ecclesiastics. [It. *berretta*—Low L. *birretum*, a cap.]

birth, *bûrth*, *n.* a ship's station. [**berth**.]

birth, *bûrth*, *n.* the act of bearing or bringing forth: coming into the world: the offspring born: lineage: dignity of family: beginning or origin.—*ns.* **birth'-control**, the control of reproduction by contraceptives; **birth'day**, the day on which one is born, or the anniversary of that day.—*adj.* relating to the day of one's birth.—*ns.* **birth'-mark**, a peculiar mark on one's body at birth; **birth'place**, the place of one's birth; **birth'-rate**, the ratio of births to population; **birth'right**, the right or privilege to which one is entitled by birth. [Prob. O.N. *byrthr*.]

bis, *bis*, *adv.* twice: (*mus.*) a direction for repetition. [L.]

biscuit, *bis'kit*, *n.* a small thin crisp cake made of unleavened dough: (*I/G.*) a soft unglazed pottery that has undergone the first firing before being glazed.—*adj.* pale brown in colour.—**to take the biscuit**, to surpass all others (*ironically*). [O.Fr. *bescoit*—L. *bis*, twice, *coquĕre*, *coctum*, to cook or bake.]

bisect, *bī-sekt'*, *v.t.* to cut into two equal parts.—*ns.* **bisec'tion**; **bisec'tor**, a line that bisects. [L. *bi-*, twice, and *secāre*, *sectum*, to cut.]

bisexual, *bī-seks'ū-ál*, *adj.* hermaphrodite: attracted sexually to both sexes. [L. *bi-*, twice, and **sexual**.]

bishop, *bish'op*, *n.* a clergyman consecrated for the spiritual oversight of a group of churches: a spiritual overseer in the early Christian Church: one of the pieces in chess.—*n.* **bish'opric**, the office and jurisdiction of a bishop: a diocese. [O.E. *biscop* L. *episcopus*—Gr. *episkopos*, an overseer—*epi*, upon, *skopein*, to look at.]

bismuth, *biz'muth*, or *his'-*, *n.* a brittle reddish-white element (symbol Bi; atomic no. 83). [Ger. *bismuth*, *wissmuth* (now *wismut*).]

bison, *bī'són*, *n.* a large wild ox, of which there are two species, the European, now almost extinct, and the American, commonly called buffalo. [From L. *bisōn*, prob. of Gmc. origin; cf. O.H.G. *wisunt*, O.E. *wesend*.]

bisque, *bisk*, *n.* unglazed white porcelain. [Corr. of **biscuit**.]

bisque, *bisk*, *n.* a handicap whereby the recipient chooses the time at which to claim the concession allowed. [Fr.]

bistable, *bī'stā'bl*, *adj.* (of a valve or transistor circuit) having two stable states. [L. *bi-*, twice, and **stable**.]

bistre, **bister**, *bis'tér*, *n.* a warm brown pigment made from the soot of wood. [Fr. *bistre*; origin unknown.]

bit, *bit*, *n.* a bite, a morsel (of food): a small piece: a coin: the smallest degree: a brief space of time: a small tool for boring: the part of the bridle that the horse holds in his mouth—hence **take the bit in one's teeth**, to be beyond restraint.—*v.t.* to put the bit in the mouth: to curb or restrain:—*pr.p.* bitt'ing;*pa.p.* bitt'ed.—*adj.* bitt'y, scrappy, disjointed.—*n.*

bit'-part, a small part in acting.—**bit by bit**, piecemeal, gradually.—**do one's bit**, do one's due share. [From **bite**.]

bit, *bit*, *n.* the smallest unit of information in computers and communications theory. [Contracted binary digit.]

bitch, *bich*, *n.* the female of the dog, wolf, and fox: (abusively) a woman. [O.E. *bicce*; O.N. *bikkja*.]

bite, *bīt*, *v.t.* and *v.i.* to seize or tear with the teeth: to puncture with the mouth parts, as an insect: to eat into chemically: to cause pain like that inflicted by teeth: to wound by reproach: to grip (of an implement):—*pa.t.* bit; *pa.p.* bit or bitt'en.—*n.* a grasp by the teeth: a puncture by an insect: something bitten off: a mouthful: (*fig.*) grip, pungency.—*v.t.* **bite in**, to eat into chemically.—*n.* **bit'er**.—*n.* and *adj.* **bit'ing**.—**bite the dust**, to fall, to die: to be humbled, discomfited. [O.E. *bītan*; O.N. *bīta*, Ger. *beissen*.]

bitt, *bit*, *n.* a post on a ship's deck for fastening cables (usu. in *pl.*)—*v.t.* to fasten round the bitts. [Perh. O.N. *biti*, a cross beam.]

bitter, *bit'ér*, *adj.* biting or acrid to the taste: sharp: painful: acrimonious.—*n.* any substance having a bitter taste.—*adv.* **bitt'erly**.—*n.* **bitt'erness**.—*n.pl.* **bitt'ers**, a liquid prepared from bitter herbs or roots, and used as a stomachic.—*n.* **bitt'er-sweet**, the woody nightshade, a climbing hedge-plant, whose stems when chewed taste first bitter then sweet. [O.E. *biter*—*bītan*, to bite.]

bittern, *bit'érn*, *n.* a genus of birds of the heron family. [M.E. *bittour*, *botor*—O.Fr. *butor*.]

bitumen, *bi-tū'men*, or *bit'-*, *n.* a name applied to various inflammable mineral substances consisting mainly of hydrocarbons, as certain kinds of naphtha, petroleum, asphalt.—*adj.* **bitūminous**.—**bituminous coal**, coal containing a high proportion of bituminous substances. [L.]

bivalent, *bī-vā'lént*, or *biv'a-lént*, *adj.* having a valency of two (chem.): pertaining to one of a pair of homologous chromosomes (also *n.*).—*ns.* **bivalence**, **bivalency**. [L. *bi-*, twice, and **valent**.]

bivalve, *bī'valv*, *n.* an animal having a shell in two valves or parts, like the oyster: a seedvessel of like kind.—*adj.* having two valves.—*adj.* **bivalv'ular**. [L. *bi-*, twice, *valva*, a leaf of a door.]

bivouac, *biv'ōō-ak*, *n.* the resting at night of soldiers in the open air instead of under cover in camp.—*v.i.* to pass the night in the open air:—*pr.p.* biv'ouacking; *pa.p.* biv'ouacked. [Fr.,—Ger. *beiwacht*, an additional watch—*bei*, by, *wachen*, to watch.]

bi-weekly, *bī'wēk'li*, *adj.* occurring once in two weeks, or twice a week.—*n.* a periodical issued twice a week, or fortnightly. [L. *bi-*, twice, and **weekly**.]

bizarre, *bi-zär'*, *adj.* odd, fantastic, extravagant. [Fr.,—Sp. *bizarro*, gallant.]

blab, *blab*, *v.i.* to talk much: to tell tales.—*v.t.* to let out (a secret):—*pr.p.* blabb'ing; *pa.p.* blabbed.—*n.* a tell-tale, a tattler: tattling.—*n.* **blabb'er**. [M.E. *blabbe*, a chatterer, also *blabber*, to babble.]

black, *blak*, *adj.* of the darkest colour: without

fāte, fär; mē, hûr (her); *mīne, mōte, för; mūte; mōōn, fōōt;* THen (then)

71

colour: obscure: dismal: sullen: horrible: foul: illicit: under trade-union bar.—*n.* black colour: absence of colour: a Negro: a smut: black clothes.—*v.t.* to make black: to soil or stain.— *n.* **black′amoor,** a black Moor: a Negro.—*adj.* **black′-and-tan,** having black hair on the back, and tan or yellowish-brown elsewhere, esp. of a terrier.—*n.* an auxiliary policeman in Ireland about 1920 (from his khaki uniform with black cap and armlet).—*adj.* **black′-a-vised** (*blak′ä-vīst* or -*vīzd*), swarthy in complexion (probably originally *black-à-vis*).—*v.t.* **black′ball,** to reject in voting by putting a black ball into a ballot-box.—*ns.* **black′balling; black′-band,** iron ore containing enough of coal to calcine it; **black′-bee′tle,** a cockroach (not a true beetle); **black′berry,** the fruit of the bramble; **black′bird,** a dark-coloured species of thrush; **black′board,** a board painted black for writing in chalk; **blackcap,** a warbler with a black crown: (**black cap**) the cap put on by English judges to pronounce sentence of death; **black′cock,** the male of the **black′-grouse** or **black′game,** a species of grouse, common in the north of England and in Scotland; **black′-curr′ant,** a garden shrub of the gooseberry genus with black fruit used in making preserves.—*v.t.* **black′en,** to make black: to defame.—*ns.* **black′fellow,** a native in Australia; **black′flag,** the flag of a pirate; **Black Friar,** a Dominican friar, so called from his black mantle; **blackguard** (*blag′ärd*), originally applied to the lowest menials about a court, who took charge of the pots, kettles, &c.: a low scoundrel.—*adj.* low: scurrilous.— *v.t.* to vituperate, abuse.—*n.* **black′guardism.**—*adj.* **black′guardly.**—*n.* **black′ing,** a substance used for blacking leather, &c.—*adj.* **black′ish.**—*ns.* **black′-lead,** a black mineral (graphite, not lead) used in making pencils, blacking grates, &c.; **black′leg,** a low, gambling fellow: a man willing to work during a strike; **black′-lett′er,** the Old English (also called Gothic) type (**black letter**); **black′-list,** a list of defaulters or offenders; **black′mail,** (*hist.—mail* = rent) tribute levied by robbers for immunity: now, hush-money.—*v.t.* to extort money by threat of revealing something discreditable in the victim's life: to coerce (into doing something) by threats.—*ns.* **blackmail′er; black′-Mari′a,** a prison van; **black mar′ket,** illicit buying and selling, at extortionate prices, of goods that are in short supply and subject to control.—Also *adj.*— *ns.* **Black Monk,** a monk of the order of St Benedict, from his garments; **black′ness; black′out,** the darkness produced by total extinction or concealment of lights: temporary loss of memory or of sight: suppression (of news, &c.).—Also *adj.*—*ns.* **black-pudding,** a sausage containing suet, blood, and other materials; **Black′-Rod,** the usher of the chapter of the Garter and of the House of Lords, so called from his black wand; **black′-sheep,** a disreputable member of a family or group; **Black′shirt,** a member of a Fascist organisation, esp. in the Nazi SS and in Italy during World War II; **black′smith,** a smith who works in iron, as opposed to a *white-smith,* who works in tin; **black′thorn,** a dark-

coloured thorn bearing sloes: a stick made from its stem.—**black and blue,** with the livid colour of a bruise; **black art,** necromancy, magic (perh. a translation of Low L. *nigromantia,* erroneously used for Gr. *nekromanteia*—see **necromancy**—as if derived from L. *niger,* black); **black body,** one that absorbs all incident radiation, reflecting none; **black book,** a book recording the names of offenders; **black box,** a type of seismograph for registering underground explosions: a unit of electronic equipment in package form which can be put into, or removed from, aircraft, spacecraft, &c.; **black bread,** rye-bread; **Black Country,** the industrial Midland counties of England; **black eye,** a discoloration around the eye due to a blow or fall; **black frost,** frost without rime; **black humour,** humour which laughs at the tragedy of the human lot.—**in black and white,** in writing or in print: (in art) in no colours but black and white; **to be black in the face,** to have the face purple through strangulation, passion, or effort; **to be in anyone's black books,** to be out of favour with him or her; **to black out,** to obliterate: to darken by an opaque screen: to suppress. [O.E. *blæc,* black.]

bladder, *blad′ér, n.* a thin bag distended with liquid or air: the receptacle for the urine.—*ns.* **bladd′erwort,** a genus of aquatic insectivorous plants with bladders to catch their prey; **bladd′er-wrack,** a common brown seaweed covered with air-bladders. [O.E. *blǣdre*—*blawan,* to blow; O.H.G. *blâ(h)en, blâgen;* cf. L. *flātus,* breath.]

blade, *blād, n.* the flat part of a leaf or petal, esp. a leaf of grass or corn: the cutting part of a knife, sword, &c.: the flat part of an oar: the free outer part of the tongue: a dashing fellow.—*n.* **blade′bone,** the shoulder-blade.—*adj.* **blad′ed.** [O.E. *blæd;* O.N. *blath;* Ger. *blatt.*]

blague, *blag, n.* blustering humbug, bounce. [Fr.]

blain, *blān, n.* a boil or blister. [O.E. *blegen.*]

blame, *blām, v.t.* to censure: to attribute the responsibility to.—*n.* imputation of a fault: censure.—*adjs.* **blam′able,** deserving of blame or censure; **blame′ful,** meriting blame: criminal.—*adv.* **blame′fully.**—*adj.* **blame′less,** without blame: innocent.—*adv.* **blame′lessly.**—*n.* **blame′lessness.**—*adj.* **blame′worthy,** worthy of blame.—*n.* **blame′worthiness,** culpability.—**be to blame (for),** to be responsible (for). [Fr. *blâmer*—O.Fr. *blasmer*—Gr. *blasphēmeein,* to speak ill. See **blaspheme.**]

blanch, *blänch* or -*sh, v.t.* to whiten.—*v.i.* to grow white. [Fr. *blanchir*—*blanc,* white.]

blanc-mange, *blä-man(g)zh′, n.* a white jelly prepared with milk. [Fr. *blancmanger*—*blanc,* white, *manger,* food.]

bland, *bland, adj.* smooth: gentle, mild: polite, suave.—*adv.* **bland′ly.**—*n.* **bland′ness.** [L. *blandus.*]

blandish, *bland′ish, v.t.* to flatter and coax, to cajole.—*n.* **bland′ishment.** [Fr. *blandir,* pr.p. *blandissant*—L. *blandīrī.*]

blank, *blangk, adj.* of paper, without writing or marks: empty: expressionless: nonplussed: sheer.—*n.* a paper without writing: a lottery-ticket that brings no prize: an empty space: (*archery*) the white mark in the centre of a

---

Neutral vowels in unaccented syllables: *em′pér-ór*; for certain sounds in foreign words see p. ix.

target (see **point-blank**).—*adv.* **blank′ly.**—*n.* **blank′ness.**—**blank cart′ridge,** one without a bullet; **blank cheque,** a cheque on which the sum to be paid has not been entered; **blank verse,** unrhymed verse, usually written in lines of five iambic feet. [Fr. *blanc,* from root of Ger. *blinken,* to glitter.]

blanket, *blang′ket, n.* originally a white woollen fabric: an oblong sheet, generally woollen, for covering in bed, or used as a garment by American Indians, &c.: a covering generally.—*adj.* applying generally or covering all cases.—*v.t.* to cover, interrupt, or extinguish, with, or as with, a blanket: to toss in a blanket: (*naut.*) to cut off from the wind.—*n.* **blank′eting,** cloth for blankets: punishment of being tossed in a blanket.—**wet blanket,** a person who, or a thing which, quenches cheerfulness as fire is quenched by a wet blanket. [O.Fr. *blankete,* dim. of *blanc,* white.]

blare, *blār, v.i.* to roar, to sound loudly, as a trumpet. *n.* roar, noise. [M.E. *blaren.*]

blarney, *blär′ni, n.* pleasant talk or flattery.—*v.t.* to beguile with such. [*Blarney* Castle, near Cork, where a stone, difficult to reach, confers the gift on those who kiss it.]

blasé, *blä-zā, adj.* fatigued with, and so indifferent to, pleasures. [Fr., pa.p. of *blaser,* to cloy.]

blaspheme, *blas-fēm′, v.t.* and *v.i.* to speak impiously of, as of God: to curse and swear.—*n.* **blasphem′er.**—*adj.* **blasphemous** (*blas′fem us*), profane: impious.—*adv.* **blas′phemously.**—*n.* **blas′phemy,** profane speaking: contempt or indignity offered to God. [Gr. *blasphēmia*—*blasphēmeein.* See **blame.**]

blast, *bläst, n.* a blowing or gust of wind: a forcible stream of air: the sound of a wind-instrument: an explosion or detonation: a hammer-like blow progressing through the air, caused by the build-up of the wave-front from an explosion: any pernicious influence acting suddenly.—*v.t.* to strike with some pernicious influence, to blight; to affect with sudden violence or calamity: to rend asunder by an explosion.—*adj.* **blast′ed,** blighted: cursed, damned.—*ns.* **blast′-fur′nace,** a smelting furnace into which hot air is blown; **blast′ing,** the separating of masses of stone by an explosion; **blast′-off,** the (moment of) launching of a rocket-propelled missile or space capsule (*v.t.* and *v.i.* **blast off**). [O.E. *blæst;* cf. O.N. *blása;* Ger. *blasen.*]

blatant, *blāt′ant, adj.* noisy: obtrusive: glaring: egregiously vulgar.—*adv.* **blat′antly.** [Prob. a coinage of Spenser.]

blaze, *blāz, n.* a rush of light or of flame: an active display, outburst: intense light, splendour.—*v.i.* to burn with a strong flame: to throw out a brilliant light.—*n.* **blaz′er,** a light sports jacket of bright colour.—**blazes,** the fires of hell, in imprecations like **to blazes;** also **like blazes,** with fury.—**blaze away,** to fire continuously. [O.E. *blæse,* a torch.]

blaze, *blāz, n.* a white mark on a beast's face: a mark made on a tree by chipping the bark.—*v.t.* to mark a tree with a blaze: to indicate a forest track by trees so marked. [Perh. Du. *bles* or O.N. *blesi;* or blaze (1).]

blaze, *blāz, v.t.* to proclaim, to spread abroad. [Connected with O.N. *blása,* to blow; confused

with **blazon.**]

blazon, *blā′zn, v.t.* to make public: to display: to depict, or to explain in proper terms, the figures, &c., in armorial bearings.—*n.* the science or rules of coats-of-arms: a heraldic shield: a coat-of-arms: a record.—*n.* **blaz′onry,** the art of drawing or of deciphering coats-of-arms, heraldry: brilliant display. [Fr. *blason,* shield, confused with M.E. *blasen,* infin., **blaze** (3).]

bleach, *blēch, v.t.* to make pale or white: to whiten, as textile fabrics.—*v.i.* to grow white.—*ns.* **bleach′ing,** the process of whitening or decolourising; **bleach′ing-pow′der,** a compound of calcium, chlorine, and oxygen, commonly known as chloride of lime. [O.E. *blǣcan,* from root of **bleak.**]

bleak, *blēk, adj.* colourless: dull and cheerless: cold, unsheltered.—*adv.* **bleak′ly.**—*n.* **bleak′ness.** [Apparently O.N. *bleikr,* answering to O.E. *blǣc, blāc,* pale, shining, black.]

blear, *blēr, adj.* (as in **blear eyed**) sore or inflamed: blurred with inflammation.—Also *v.t.* [Cf. Low Ger. *bleer-oged,* 'blear-eyed'.]

bleat, *blēt, v.i.* to cry as a sheep: to complain: to talk nonsense.—*n.* the cry of a sheep: any similar cry.—*n.* **bleat′ing,** the cry of a sheep. [O.E. *blǣtan;* L. *balāre,* Gr. *blēchē,* a bleating; root *bla-;* imit.]

bled, *bled, pa.t.* and *pa.p.* of **bleed.**

bleed, *blēd, v.i.* to lose blood: to die by slaughter: to issue forth as blood (*life bleeds away*): to lose sap: to be filled with grief or sympathy.—*v.t.* to draw blood or sap from: to extort money from: to trim a page so as to cut into (an illustration):—*pa.t.* and *pa.p.* bled.—*ns.* **bleed′er,** one who is liable to discharge of blood: an extortioner; **bleed′ing,** a discharge of blood: the operation of letting blood. [O.E. *blēdan.*]

bleep, *blēp, v.i.* to give out a high sound or radio signal. [Imit.]

blemish, *blem′ish, n.* a stain or defect.—*v.t.* to mark with any deformity, to tarnish. [O.Fr. *blesmir, blemir,* pr.p. *blemissant,* to stain.]

blench, *blench* or *-sh, v.i.* to shrink or start back, to flinch. [O.E. *blencan.*]

blend, *blend, v.t.* to mix together: to mix so that the elements cannot be distinguished.—*v.i.* to be mingled or mixed: to harmonise:—*pa.p.* blend′ed, blent (*poet.*).—*n.* a mixture.—*ns.* **blend′er; blend′ing.** [M.E. *blenden;* c.f. O.E. *blandan,* O.N. *blanda.*]

blende, *blend, n.* a mineral, zinc sulphide. [Ger. *blende*—*blenden,* deceive, from its resemblance to lead sulphide.]

Blenheim, *blen′em, n.* a kind of spaniel. [*Blenheim,* Duke of Marlborough's seat.]

blent, *blent, pa.p.* (*poet.*) of **blend.**

bless, *bles, v.t.* to consecrate: to extol as holy: to pronounce holy or happy: to invoke divine favour upon: to wish happiness to: to make happy:—*pa.p.* blessed (*blest*), or blest.—*adj.* **bless′ed** (*-id*), happy, prosperous: happy in heaven.—*adv.* **bless′edly.**—*ns.* **bless′edness; bless′ing,** a wish or prayer for happiness or success: any cause of happiness.—**single blessedness,** the unmarried state. [O.E. *blēdsian, blētsian,* to bless, prob. from *blōd,* blood. The word was used as equivalent to *benedīcĕre.*]

blest, *blest, pa.p.* of **bless.**

blether, *bleʈʜ'er, v.i.* to chatter foolishly.—*n.* one who blethers: (often in *pl.*) foolish chatter.— Also **blath'er.**—*ns.* **bleth'erskate,** (*U.S.*) **blath'erskite,** a loquacious fool. [M.E. *blather*—O.N. *blathra,* to talk foolishly, *blathr,* nonsense. *Blether* is the Scots form.]

blew, *blōō, pa.t.* of **blow.**

blight, *blīt, n.* a disease in plants that blasts or withers them: anything that injures or destroys.—*v.t.* to affect with blight: to blast: to frustrate.—*n.* **blight'er,** a scamp, beggar, wretch. [First appears in literature in the 17th century; prob. of Scand. origin.]

blighty, *blī'ti, n.* home, Britain: a wound necessitating return home. [Hindustani *bilāyatī,* foreign, European.]

blimp, *blimp, n.* an incurably conservative elderly military officer, as Colonel *Blimp* of the cartoonist David Low, or any other person of similar views: soundproof housing for a sound-film camera.

blind, *blīnd, adj.* without sight: dark: ignorant or undiscerning: not directed, or affording no possibility of being directed, by sight or by foresight: concealed: without an opening.—*n.* something to mislead: a window-screen, a shade.—*v.t.* to make blind: to darken, obscure: to dazzle: to deceive:—*pa.t.* and *pa.p.* blīnd'ed.—*adj.* **blind'ing,** tending to make blind.—*pr.p.* making blind.—*adv.* **blind'ly.**—*ns.* **blind'ness,** want of sight: (*fig.*) failure or inability to perceive and understand; **blind'coal,** anthracite (as burning without flame). —*adj.* **blind'fold,** having the eyes bandaged, so as not to see: thoughtless, reckless.—*v.t.* to cover the eyes of; to mislead (M.E. *blindfallen,* to strike blind; pa.p. *felled* confused with *fold*).—*ns.* **blind'-side,** the side on which a person fails to see: weak point; **blind'worm,** a small reptile, like a snake, having eyes so small as to be supposed blind.— **blind alley,** a passage without an exit: employment with no prospect of permanence or of promotion; **blind date,** an appointment with someone, usu. a member of the opposite sex, whom one has not seen; **blind flying, blind landing,** flying, landing, by instruments alone, without seeing the course or receiving directions from wireless; **blind gut,** the caecum; **blind spot,** the point on the retina that is insensitive to light and on which no images are formed: any sphere within which perception or understanding fails.—**blind-man's buff,** a game in which one of the party is blindfolded and tries to catch the others; **blind to,** unaware of, unable to appreciate. [O.E. *blind;* O.N. *blindr.*]

blink, *blingk, v.i.* to twinkle, or wink: to see obscurely, or with the eyes half-closed.—*v.t.* to shut out of sight, to avoid or evade.—*n.* a glimpse, glance: a momentary gleam.—*n.pl.* **blink'ers,** leather flaps on a bridle which prevent the horse from seeing sideways.—**on the blink,** (of electrical or electronic device) (going) out of order. [M.E. a variant of *blenk,* prob. the same as **blench.**]

blip, *blip, n.* the image of an object on a radar screen.

bliss, *blis, n.* the highest happiness: heaven.— *adj.* **bliss'ful.**—*adv.* **bliss'fully.**—*n.* **bliss'fulness.** [O.E. *blītho*—*blīthe,* joyful.]

blister, *blis'ter, n.* a thin bubble or bladder on the skin, containing watery matter: a similar raised spot on any other surface: a plaster applied to raise a blister.—*v.t.* to raise a blister.—*adj.* **blis'tering,** of criticism, savage, cruel.—*ns.* **blister beetle, blister fly,** various beetles used for blistering. [M.E.; most prob. O.Fr. *blestre,* conn. with O.N *blāstr, blāsa,* to blow.]

blithe, *blīʈʜ, adj.* happy, gay, sprightly.—*adv.* **blithe'ly.**—*n.* **blithe'ness.**—*adj.* **blithe'some,** joyous.—*adv.* **blithe'somely.**—*n.* **blithe'someness.** [O.E. *blīthe,* joyful.]

blitz, *blits, n.* (short for Ger. *blitzkrieg,* lightning war), any sudden and overwhelming attack: heavy aerial bombardment, such as that of London in 1940-41.—*v.t.* to make a heavy and destructive attack on with aircraft.—Also (*fig.*).

blizzard, *bliz'ard, n.* a blinding storm of wind and snow. [Most prob. onomatopoeic, on the analogy of *blow, blast,* &c.]

bloat, *blōt, v.t.* to swell or puff out: to dry by smoke (applied to fish).—*v.i.* to swell, dilate, grow turgid.—*p.adj.* **bloat'ed.**—*n.* **bloat'er,** a herring partially dried in smoke. [Scand., as in Swed. *blöt,* soft.]

blob, *blob, n.* a drop of liquid: a round spot: zero.—*v.i.* to form into a blob. [Imit.]

bloc, *blok, n.* a combination of parties, nations, &c., to achieve a common purpose. [Fr.]

block, *blok, n.* a mass of wood or stone, &c., usu. flat-sided: the piece of wood on which a person to be beheaded laid his neck: a piece of wood or other material used as a support (for chopping, &c.), or as a mould (for hats), or for printing (illustrations), or as a toy (for building): (*mech.*) a pulley with its framework, or the framework alone: a connected group of houses: an obstruction: a stolid, stupid, or unfeeling person: (*cricket*) the place where a batsman rests his bat.—*adj.* comprising a number grouped and dealt with together: in a lump.—*v.t.* to enclose or shut up: to obstruct: to shape: to shape or sketch out roughly (often with *out, in*): to stop (a ball) with bat resting upright on the ground.—*ns.* **blockade',** the isolation of a place by blocking every approach by land and sea (*v.t.* to isolate by blockade); **block'age,** act or instance of obstructing or state of being obstructed.—*ns.* **blockade-runn'er,** a person or ship that passes through a blockading force; **block'-chain',** an endless chain made so as to work on cogwheels, as on a bicycle; **block'head,** a stupid fellow; **block'-house,** a small temporary fort generally made of logs; **block'-sys'tem,** a system of signalling by which no train can enter a block or section of the railway till the previous train has left it; **block'-tin,** tin in the form of blocks or ingots.—**block capital, block letter,** a capital letter written in imitation of type. [Fr. *bloc,* prob. Gmc. in origin.]

bloke, *blōk, n.* (*coll.*) a fellow, a man.

blond, (*fem.*) **blonde,** *blond, n.* a person of fair complexion and light-coloured hair—opp. to *brunette.*—*adj.* (of hair) between golden and light chestnut in colour: of a fair complexion: fair. [Fr.]

Neutral vowels in unaccented syllables: *em'pėr-ór*; for certain sounds in foreign words see p. ix.

blood, *blud, n.* the red fluid in the arteries and veins: descent: kindred: elliptically for a blood-horse: a swaggering dandy: temper, anger: bloodshed or murder: the juice of anything, esp. if red: a sensational tale.—*adj.* **blood′y,** stained with blood: murderous, cruel: vulgarly, as an expletive (*adj.* or *adv.*).—*v.t.* to make bloody.—*adv.* **blood′ily.**—*adj.* **blood-and-thunder,** sensational.—*n.* **blood′-bath,** a massacre.—*adjs.* **blood′-bought,** bought at the expense of blood or life; **blood′-curd′ling,** exciting horror with a physical sensation as if the blood had curdled.—*ns.* **blood′-feud,** a feud arising out of an act of bloodshed; **blood′-group,** any one of the four kinds (designated O, A, B, AB) into which human blood is classified for transfusion; **blood′-guilt′iness,** the guilt of shedding blood, as in murder.—*adj.* **blood′-guil′ty.**—*ns.* **blood′-heat,** the temperature of the human blood (about 98° Fahr.); **blood′-horse,** a horse of the purest blood, origin, or stock, **blood′-hound,** a large, keen-scented hound, noted for its powers of tracking: (*fig.*) a detective.—*adj.* **blood′less,** without blood, anaemic: without spirit: without the shedding of blood.—*ns.* **blood′lessness,** anaemia; **blood′-lett′ing,** the act of letting blood, or bleeding by opening a vein; **blood′-mon′ey,** a reward for co-operation in action by which the life of another is endangered: money paid to next of kin as reparation for manslaughter; **blood′-pois′oning,** one of several diseases due to the presence of bacteria or poisonous matter in the blood; **blood′-pudd′ing,** a black-pudding (q.v.); **blood′-rela′tion,** one related by common ancestry; **blood-royal,** royal descent; **blood′shed,** the shedding of blood: slaughter.—*adjs.* **blood′shot** (of the eye), red or inflamed with blood; **blood′-stained,** stained with blood: guilty of murder.—*ns.* **blood′-stone,** a green chalcedony with blood-like spots of red jasper: haematite; **blood′-suck′er,** an animal that sucks blood, esp. a leech: an extortioner; **blood′-thirst′iness,** thirst or desire for shedding blood.—*adj.* **blood′-thirst′y.**—*ns.* **blood′-vess′el,** a vessel in which blood flows, a vein or artery; **blood′y-flux,** dysentery (q.v.).—*adj.* **bloody-mind′ed,** liking bloodshed: inclined to be aggressively obstinate.—*n.* **blood′y-sweat,** a sweat accompanied with the discharge of blood.—**blood bank,** a supply of blood plasma, or the place where it is kept; **blood count,** the number of red or white corpuscles in the blood; **blood donor,** one who gives blood for use in transfusion; **blood orange,** an orange with red or red-streaked pulp; **blood pressure,** the pressure of the blood on the walls of the blood-vessels, varying with age and physical condition; **blood sports,** those involving the killing of animals, as fox-hunting and the like; **blood test,** a medical examination of a specimen of the blood of an individual;′ **bad blood,** (see **bad**); **in hot,** or **cold, blood,** under, or free from, excitement or sudden passion. [O.E. *blōd*; Old Frisian *blōd,* Ger. *blut.*]

bloom, *blōōm, n.* a blossom or flower: the state of being in flower: the first freshness, the highest perfection of anything: rosy colour:

the delicate powder on the rind of fresh fruits.—*v.i.* to flower: to flourish.—*n.* **bloom′er** (*slang*), an egregious blunder.—*p.adj.* **bloom′ing,** flourishing: (*slang*) a euphemism for bloody. [O.N. *blōm*; cf. Ger. *blume.*]

bloomer, *blōōm′ér, n.* and *adj.* a masculine dress for women, devised by Mrs *Bloomer* of New York about 1849: (in *pl.*) bloomer trousers or any similar garment.

blossom, *blos′óm, n.* a flower, esp. one that precedes edible fruit.—*v.i.* to put forth blossoms or flowers: to flourish and prosper. [O.E. *blōstm, blōstma,* from the same root as **bloom.**)

blot, *blot, n.* a spot or stain: a stain in reputation.—*v.t.* to spot or stain: to obliterate: to disgrace: to dry with blotting-paper:—*pr.p.* blott′ing; *pa.p.* blott′ed.—*ns.* **blott′er,** a pad or book of blotting-paper; **blott′ing-pad,** a pad of blotting-paper; **blott′ing-pā′per,** unsized paper, used for absorbing ink. [Possibly Scand., cf. Dan. *plet,* O.N. *blettr,* a spot.]

blotch, *bloch, n.* an irregular discoloration: a pustule.—*v.t.* to mark or cover with blotches.—*adjs.* **blotched, blotch′y.** [Prob. formed from **blot.**]

blouse, *blowz, n.* a loose outer garment, like the smock-frock: a loose-fitting bodice for women, usu. tucked in at the waist. [Fr.]

blow, *blō, n.* a stroke or knock: a sudden misfortune or calamity.—**at a blow, by a single stroke; come to blows,** to fight. [Prob. from vb. **blow** (3)—O.E. *blāwan.*]

blow, *blō, v.i.* to bloom or blossom:—*pr.p.* blōw′ing; *pa.t.* blew (*blōō*); *pa.p.* blown (*blōn*). [O.E. *blōwan*; Ger. *blühen.*]

blow, *blō, v.i.* to produce a current of air: to drive air (upon or into): to move, as air or the wind (often *impers.*): to breathe hard or with difficulty: to spout, as whales: to emit a sound produced by a current of air: of an electric fuse, to melt (also *v.t.*): (*slang*) to boast.—*v.t.* to drive by a current of air: to sound, as a wind-instrument: to drive air into: to fan or kindle: (of insects) to deposit eggs on: to curse: (*slang*) to squander:—*pa.t.* blew (*blōō*); *pa.p.* blown (*blōn*).—*ns.* **blow′er** (*slang*), a telephone or similar means of sending messages: a communication system; **blow′-fly,** or *flesh-fly,* any of various flies of the family to which the house-fly and bluebottle belong; **blow′-hole,** a hole in ice to which whales, &c., come to breathe: a whale's spiracle (q.v.): a vent for the escape of gas.—*p.adj.* **blown,** out of breath, tired: swelled: tainted (see **fly-blown**).—*ns.* **blow-out′** (*slang*), a feast: a tyre burst; **blow′-pipe,** a pipe through which air is blown on a flame, to increase its heat: a long straight tube from which an arrow is blown by the breath.—*adj.* **blow′y,** windy.—**blow hot and cold,** to be favourable and unfavourable by turns: to be irresolute; **blow off** (steam, &c.), to allow to escape, esp. forcibly; **blow one's own trumpet,** to sound one's own praises; **blow one's top,** to lose one's temper; **blow over,** to abate, pass over or away; **blow up,** to shatter, or be shattered, by explosion: to inflate: to enlarge, as an illustration: to allow one's anger to burst forth: to scold; **blow upon,** to take the bloom, freshness, or the interest off anything, to bring into discredit: to inform upon. [O.E. *blāwan*; Ger. *blähen, blasen*; L. *flāre*.]

blowzy, *blowz'i, adj.* fat and ruddy: dishevelled.—Also **blowzed**. [Perh. related to **blush** or **blow**; or of cant (q.v.) origin.]

blubber, *blub'ér, n.* the fat of whales and other sea animals.—*v.i.* to weep effusively. [M.E. *blo-ber, bluber*; most likely onomatopoeic.]

blucher, *blōōch'ér,* or *blōōk'-, n.* a strong leather half-boot or high shoe, from Prussian Field-Marshal *Blücher* (1742-1819).

bludgeon, *bluj'ón, n.* a short stick with a heavy end for striking.—Also *v.t.* [First in 18th century; origin very obscure.]

blue, *blōō, adj.* of the colour of the sky or the deep sea: livid: dismal: depressed: (of a story) indecent: dressed in blue.—*n.* one of the colours of the rainbow: the sky: the sea: a blue pigment: a blue powder or liquid used in laundries: a member of a group or team whose badge is blue: badge or distinction given to one who has represented his university in athletics, &c.: one who has won such a distinction: blue clothes.—*ns.* **blue'bell**, in S. England the wood hyacinth: (usu. *-bel'*) in Scotland and N. England the harebell; **blue'berry**, the berry of any of several plants, including the whortleberry (q.v.); **blue-bonn'et**, a round flat woollen cap—hence a Scottish peasant or soldier; **blue-book**, a parliamentary report (from its blue paper wrapper); **blue'bott'le**, the blue cornflower: a large fly with metallic blue abdomen; **blue'coat**, a pupil of Christ's Hospital or other **bluecoat school**, whose garb is blue; **blue'ing, blu'ing**, the process of imparting a blue colour; **bluegrass**, a permanent grass of North America and Europe, slightly blue-green in colour; **blue'-jacket**, a seaman in the navy; **blue-mould**, any of a genus of fungi (*Penicillium*), esp. one that turns bread, cheese, &c., blue; **blueness; blue-pen'cil**, a pencil for making blue marks of correction or censorship (also *v.t.*); **blue'pill**, a mercurial pill; **blue'print**, a white photographic print, on blue sensitised paper, made from a photographic negative or from a drawing on transparent paper: a preliminary sketch of proposed reforms: a plan of work to be done or a guide or model provided by agreed principles; **blue'-stock'ing**, a learned lady, esp. one inclined to pedantry: one who cultivates learning to the neglect of feminine charm; **blue'stone, blue vitriol**, hydrated copper sulphate; **bluey** (*blōō'i*), an Australian bushman's bundle (because often wrapped in a blue cloth).—*adj.* **blū'ish**, slightly blue.—**blue baby**, a baby suffering from congenital cyanosis; **blue blood**, aristocratic blood; **blue-eyed boy**, favourite who can do no wrong; **blue funk** (*slang*), great terror; **Blue Peter**, a blue flag with white rectangle hoisted on a ship ready to sail; **blue ribbon**, the blue ribbon worn by Knights of the Garter: any great prize; **blue water**, the deep sea.—**from (out of) the blue**, without warning, as a thunderbolt from a clear sky; **once in a blue moon**, exceedingly seldom; **The Blues**, the Royal Horse Guards; **the blues**, low spirits: a very slow dismal song, of American Negro origin; **true blue**, unswervingly faithful, esp. to the political party wear-

ing blue as its colour, often identified with Conservative: steadfast (*n.* **true'-blue**). [M.E. *blew*—O.Fr. *bleu*, of Gmc. origin.]

bluff, *bluf, adj.* rough and hearty in manner: outspoken: steep: (of the shape of a body) such that, when it moves through air or other fluid, it leaves behind it a large disorderly wake and experiences a large drag.—opp. of *streamlined.*—*n.* a high steep bank overlooking the sea or a river.—*n.* **bluff'ness**. [Prob. Du.]

bluff, *bluf, v.t.* and *v.i.* (*obs.*) to blindfold: to deceive or seek to deceive by a pretence of superiority, e.g. in card games.—*n.* such pretence: a horse's blinkers.—**call one's bluff**, to expose or challenge one's bluff. [Perh. Du. *bluffen*, to brag.]

blunder, *blun'dér, v.i.* to make a gross mistake: to flounder about.—*n.* a gross mistake. [M.E. *blondren*; prob. conn. with obs. *bland*, to mix; perh. from O.N. *blunda*, to doze.]

blunderbuss, *blun'dér-bus, n.* a short hand-gun with a wide bore. [Corr. of Du. *donderbus—donder*, thunder, *bus*, a box, barrel of a gun, a gun.]

blunt, *blunt, adj.* having a dull edge or point: rough, outspoken: dull, insensitive, stupid:—*v.t.* to dull the edge or point of (*lit.* and *fig.*).—*adv.* **blunt'ly.**—*n.* **blunt'ness**. [Orig. sleepy, dull; prob. conn. with O.N. *blunda*, to doze.]

blur, *blûr, n.* a smudge, smear: a confused impression.—*v.t.* to blot: to obscure, dim:—*pr.p.* blurr'ing; *pa.p.* blurred. [**blear**.]

blurb, *blûrb, n.* a publisher's descriptive notice of a book, usually printed on the jacket. [Attributed to an American writer and illustrator, Gelett Burgess.]

blurt, *blûrt, v.t.* to utter suddenly or unadvisedly (with *out*). [From sound.]

blush, *blush, n.* a red glow on the skin caused by shame, modesty, &c.: any reddish colour (e.g. of sunset, a rose).—*v.i.* to show shame, confusion, joy, &c., by growing red in the face (often with *for*): to grow red.—*adv.* **blush'-ingly.**—**at the first blush**, at the first glance or appearance: off-hand; **put to the blush**, to make ashamed. [M.E. *blusche, blysche*; origin obscure, but cf. O.E. *blysa*, a blaze.]

bluster, *blus'tér, v.i.* to make a noise like a blast of wind: to bully or swagger.—*n.* a blast or roaring as of the wind: bullying or boastful language.—*adv.* **blus'teringly**. [Prob. conn. with **blast**.]

bo, *bō, interj.* a word used to frighten the timid.—**cannot say bo to a goose**, is silent from extreme meekness.

boa, *bō'ä, n.* a genus of snakes, including the large species of snake (the **boa-constric'tor**), that kill their prey by constriction or pressure: a long serpent-like coil of fur, feathers, or the like, worn round the neck by ladies. [L. *bŏa*, a kind of snake.]

boar, *bōr, bör, n.* the male of swine, esp. of wild swine, or its flesh.—**boar'hound**, a powerful dog, esp. the Great Dane, used for hunting the wild boar. [O.E. *bār*; Du. *beer*.]

board, *bōrd, börd, n.* a broad and thin strip of timber: a table to put food on: meals, or meals and lodging: a council-table: a body of persons who direct or supervise: the side (*seaboard*,

Neutral vowels in unaccented syllables: *em'pér-ór*; for certain sounds in foreign words see p. ix.

over board): (*pl.*) the stage: a sheet of stiff material prepared for a special use, esp. for binding books: a surface for an indoor game, a notice, &c.—*v.t.* to cover with boards: to supply with board at fixed terms: to enter a ship, &c., esp. by force: to accost.—*v.i.* to receive meals—usu. to lodge and take meals.—*ns.* **board′er**, one who receives board (meals, &c.), esp. at a boarding-school: one who boards a ship; **board′ing**, a structure of boards; **board′ing-house**, a house where residents pay for their board; **board′ing-school**, a school in which board is given as well as instruction; **board′-school**, a school under control of a school-board.—*n.pl.* **board′-wā′ges**, payment to a servant in lieu of food.—**above board**, open(ly); **board out**, to place (children from undesirable homes, &c.) in the care of paid foster-parents; **by the board**, over the side of a ship; **go by the board**, to be lost or destroyed or discarded; **on board**, aboard; **sweep the board**, to win every point in a game or contest. [O.E. *bord*, a board, the side of a ship; O.N. *borth*.]

boast, *bōst*, *v.i.* to talk vaingloriously: to brag (of, about).—*v.t.* to brag of, speak proudly of: to possess with pride (also *v.i.* with *of*).—*n.* a brag: a subject of pride, a cause of boasting.—*n.* **boast′er**.—*adj.* **boast′ful**.—*adv.* **boast′fully**.—*n.* **boast′fulness**. [M.E. *bost*.]

boat, *bōt*, *n.* a small open craft usually moved by oars: a ship: a dish shaped like a boat.—*v.i.* to sail about in a boat.—*ns.* **boat′er**, a straw hat; **boat′-hook**, an iron hook fixed to a pole used for pulling or pushing a boat into position; **boat′-house**, a shed for (a) boat(s); **boat′ing**, the art or practice of sailing in boats; **boat′-man**, a man who has charge of a boat: a rower; **boat′-train**, a train conveying passengers to or from a ship in dock—**in the same boat**, in the same plight. [O.E. *bāt*; Du. *boot*; Fr. *bateau*.]

boatswain, *bō′sn*, *n.* an officer (warrant-officer in the navy) who looks after a ship's boats, rigging, flags, &c.—*ns.* **boatswain's mate**, boatswain's assistant: boatswain's whistle, &c. (see **whistle**). [**boat**, **swain**.]

bob, *bob*, *v.i.* to move quickly up and down: to curtsey: to fish with a bob.—*v.t.* to move in short jerks: to dock (a tail): to cut (hair) so that it does not fall beyond the neck—*pr.p.* **bobb′ing**; *pa.p.* **bobbed**.—*n.* a short jerking motion: a slight blow: the weight on a pendulum, plumb-line, &c.: a pendant: horse's docked tail: bobbed hair: a knot of hair, as in **bob′-wig** (one with the ends turned up into short curls).—*n.* **bob′sled**, **bob′sleigh**, a short sledge: a sleigh made up of two smaller sledges coupled together. [Perh. Celt., Gael. *babhan*, *babag*.]

bob, *bob*, *n.* (*slang*) a shilling (5p):—*pl.* **bob**. [Origin uncertain.]

bobbin, *bob′in*, *n.* a reel or spool for winding yarn, wire, &c. [Fr. *bobine*, prob. Celt.; cf. Gael. *baban*, a tassel.]

bobby, *bob′i*, *n.* (*slang*) a policeman. [Familiar form of *Robert*, from Sir Robert Peel, who reorganised the London Police in 1829; cf. **peeler**.]

bobolink, *bob′ō-lingk*, *n.* a North American

song-bird. [At first *Bob Lincoln*, from the song of the bird.]

bobstays, *bob′stāz*, *n.pl.* (*naut.*) ropes or stays for holding the bowsprit down. [*bob* (meaning uncertain), **stay**.]

bobtail, *bob′tāl*, *n.* a short or cut tail: the rabble, as in 'rag-tag and bobtail'.—Also *v.t.* [**bob**, and **tail**.]

bode, *bōd*, *v.t.* to portend: (*arch.*) to prophesy.—*v.i.* to be an omen: to promise (well or ill).—*adj.* **bode′ful**, ominous. [O.E. *bodian*, to announce—(*ge*)*bod*, a message; allied to **bid**.]

bodega, *bo-dē′ga*, *n.* a wine-shop. [Sp.]

bodice, *bod′is*, *n.* the close-fitting body of a woman's dress: a vest worn over the corset. [A form of *bodies*, pl. of **body**.]

bodkin, *bod′kin*, *n.* a small dagger: a small instrument for pricking holes, for dressing the hair, &c.: a large blunt needle. [Perh. conn. with W. *bidog*, a dagger.]

body, *bod′i*, *n.* the whole frame of a man or animal: a corpse: the trunk of an animal, as distinguished from the limbs: the main part of anything: the part of a vehicle which carries the passengers: matter, as opposed to spirit: substance, substantial quality, fullness, solidity: a mass: a piece of matter: a substance: (*coll.*) a person: a group of persons united by a common tie: *pl.* **bod′ies**.—*v.t.* to give form to: to embody—*pr.p.* **bod′ying**; *pa.p.* **bod′ied**.—*adjs.* **bod′iless**; **bod′ily**, relating to or affecting the body, esp. as opp. to the mind.—*adv.* as one whole and completely (e.g. *to remove bodily*).—*ns.* **bod′y-build′er**, a maker of vehicle bodies: an apparatus for exercising muscles: a nutritious food; **bod′y-col′our**, a pigment or paint that has enough substance to be opaque; **bod′yguard**, a guard to protect the person, esp. of a sovereign; **bod′y-ser′vant**, a personal attendant; **bod′y-snatch′er**, one who secretly removes dead bodies from their graves—**body pol′itic**, the people as a political unit. [O.E. *bodig*.]

Boeotian, *bē-ō′shyan*, *adj.* pertaining to *Boeotia* in Greece, noted for the dullness of its inhabitants—hence stupid, dull.

Boer, *bōōr*, *n.* a South African of Dutch descent.—Also *adj.* [Du., a farmer. See **boor**.]

boffin, *bof′in*, *n.* (*slang*) a scientist.

bog, *bog*, *n.* soft spongy ground, a marsh or quagmire: (*slang*) a latrine.—*v.t.* to submerge, as in a bog: to entangle.—*adj.* **bogg′y**.—*ns.* **bog′-moss**, the sphagnum genus; **bog′-myr′tle**, sweet-gale, a plant growing in bogs; **bog′-oak**, trunks of oak embedded and preserved in bogs; **bog′-trott′er**, one who lives in a boggy country, hence an Irishman.—**bog down** (*fig.*), to make, or to be made, feel helpless through amount of work required or the difficulty of a task. [Ir. and Gael. *bogach*; bog, soft.]

bogey, *bō′gi*, *n.* (*golf*) the score, for a given hole or for the full round, of an imaginary good player, Colonel *Bogey*, fixed as a standard. [Perh. **bogy**.]

boggle, *bog′l*, *v.i.* to start back in fear or agitation as at a bogie: to hesitate: to make difficulties (about—or with *at*). [From **bogle**.]

bogie, **bogey**, *bō′gi*, *n.* a low truck so constructed as to turn easily: a four- or six-wheel truck that forms a pivoted support at one or both ends of a long rigid vehicle such as a locomotive. [Ety. unknown.]

bogle, *bōg'l, n.* a spectre or goblin: a scarecrow: a bugbear. [Scot.; perh. conn. with **bug** (1).]

bogus, *bō'gus, adj.* counterfeit, spurious. [An American cant (q.v.) word, of doubtful origin.]

bogy, bogey, *bō'gi, n.* a goblin: a bugbear or special object of dread: the devil.—*n.* **bo'gyman.** [Ety. uncertain.]

bohea, *bō-hē', n.* the lowest quality of black tea: tea generally. [Chinese.]

Bohemian, *bō-hē'mi-án, n.* a Czech: a gipsy: one who defies social conventions.—Also *adj.* [Fr. *bohémien,* a gipsy, from the belief that these wanderers came from *Bohemia.*]

boil, *boil, v.i.* to pass rapidly from the liquid state into vapour, with violent evolution of bubbles: to bubble up: to be heated in boiling liquid: to be hot: to be excited, esp. with anger.—*v.t.* to heat to a boiling state: to cook by boiling.—*ns.* **boil'er,** one who boils: a vessel in which water is heated or steam is generated; **boil'er-suit,** a workman's overall garment; **boil'ing-point,** the temperature at which a liquid boils, esp. at standard atmospheric pressure.—**boil down,** to reduce, or be reduced, in bulk by boiling: to epitomise: to reduce itself; **boil over,** to bubble over the sides of the containing vessel: to burst into passion. [O.Fr. *boillir*—L. *bullīre*—*bulla,* a bubble.]

boil, *boil, n.* an inflamed swelling. [O.E. *bȳl;* Ger. *beule.*]

boisterous, *bois'tér-us, adj.* wild, noisy, turbulent, stormy.—*adv.* **bois'terously.**—*n.* **bois'terousness.** [M.E. *boistous.*]

bolas, *bō'las, n.* (properly *pl.*) a thong, weighted with stones or balls, which South American gauchos can throw so as to curl round the legs of an animal and hobble it. [Sp., balls.]

bold, *bōld, adj.* daring or courageous: forward, impudent, presumptuous: executed with spirit: striking to the sight, well-marked.—*adj.* **bold'-faced,** impudent.—*adv.* **bold'ly.**—*n.* **bold'ness.**—**make bold,** to take the liberty (to). [O.E. *bald;* O.H.G. *bald.*]

bole, *bōl, n.* the round stem or body of a tree. [Scand. *bolr;* Ger. *bohle,* a plank.]

bolero, *bo-lā'ro,* or *bo-lē'ro, n.* Spanish national dance: the music to which it is danced: a jacket-like bodice coming barely to the waist. [Sp.]

boll, *bōl, n.* a swelling: a knob: a round seed-vessel as in cotton, flax, poppy, &c.—*p.adj.* **bolled** (*bōld*), swollen, podded.—*ns.* **boll'wee'vil,** a weevil whose larvae infest cotton-bolls; **boll'-worm,** a moth caterpillar that destroys cotton-bolls, &c. [A form of **bowl;** O.E. *bolla.*]

bollard, *bol'árd, n.* a short post on a wharf or ship round which ropes are secured: one of a line of short posts barring the passage of motor vehicles. [Prob. **bole.**]

bolshevik, *bol'shé-vik, bol-shev'ik, n.* (*pl.* **bol'sheviks, bolshev'iki**), (*cap.*) a member of the Russian Majority (or Extreme) Socialist party (opp. to *Menshevik,* one of the less radical party): a violently revolutionary Marxian communist: often used loosely, an anarchist, agitator, causer of trouble.—Also *adj.*—coll.

contr. **bol'shie, bol'shy.**—*v.t.* **bol'shevise.**—*ns.* **bol'shevism; bol'shevist,** a Bolshevik: a revolutionary communist (of any country).—Also *adj.* [Russ. *bolshe,* greater.]

bolster, *bōl'stér, n.* a long round pillow or cushion: a pad: a prop.—*v.t.* to support as with a bolster: to prop up: to aid, countenance.—Also **bolster up.** [O.E. *bolster;* from root of **bowl.**]

bolt, *bōlt, n.* a bar used to fasten a door, &c.: an arrow, esp. for a crossbow: a thunderbolt: a stout pin: a roll of cloth of indefinite measure: a rush.—*v.t.* to fasten with a bolt: to swallow hastily.—*v.i.* to rush away (like a bolt from a bow): to escape from control or custody.—*adv.* **bolt'-up'right, -upright',** upright and straight as an arrow.—**bolt from the blue,** an unexpected event; **have shot one's bolt,** to be unable to do more than one has done. [O.E. *bolt;* O.H.G. *bolz.*]

bolt, *bōlt, v.t.* (better spelling, **boult**), to sift through coarse cloth: to examine by sifting.—*ns.* **bolt'er,** a sieve: a machine for separating bran from flour; **bolt'ing-hutch,** a large box into which flour falls when bolted. [O.Fr. *bulter,* or *buleter*=*bureter,* from *bure*—L.L. *burra,* a coarse reddish-brown cloth—Gr. *pyrrhos,* reddish.]

bolus, *bō'lus, n.* a rounded mass of anything: a large pill. [L. *bōlus*—Gr. *bōlos,* a lump.]

bomb, *bom, n.* a hollow case containing explosive, incendiary, or other offensive material, thrown, deposited, dropped, or shot from a mortar.—*v.t.* to drop bombs on.—*v.t.* **bombard',** to attack with artillery: to batter or pelt: (*fig.*) to assail (as with questions): (*phys.*) to subject, as the atom, to a stream of particles at high speed.—*ns.* **bombardier** (*-bár-dēr'*), the lowest non-commissioned officer in the British artillery: the bomb aimer in a bombing aeroplane; **bombard'ment; bomber** (*bom'ér*), one who bombs: an aeroplane designed for bombing.—*adjs.* **bomb'-happ'y,** shocked into insouciance by shell or bomb explosions; **bomb'-proof,** proof or secure against the force of bombs.—*n.* **bomb'shell,** (*obs.*) a bomb: now (*fig.*) startling news.—**atomic bomb** (see **atom**); **fission bomb,** one deriving its energy from atomic fission; **fusion bomb,** one deriving its energy from the conversion of simpler atoms into more complex, as the conversion of hydrogen into helium in the **hydrogen bomb; H-bomb,** hydrogen bomb. [Fr. *bombe*—L. *bombus*—Gr. *bombos,* a humming sound.]

bombasine, bombazine, *bom'-,* *bum'ba-zēn,* or *-zēn', n.* a twilled or corded fabric of silk and worsted, or of cotton and worsted. [Fr. *bombasin,* through Low L.—Gr. *bombyx,* silk.]

bombast, *bom'-,* *bum'bast, n.* pompous language: originally cotton or any soft material used for stuffing.—*adj.* **bombas'tic.**—*adv.* **bombas'tically.** [Low L. *bombax,* cotton—Gr. *bombyx,* silk.]

Bombay-duck, *bom-bā'-duk', n.* an Indian fish, which is salted, dried, and eaten as a relish.

bombe, *bōb, n.* a dessert, usu. ice-cream, frozen in a round mould. [Fr.]

bon, *bɔ', adj.* good—used in phrases such as: **bon accord** (*bon a-körd'*), good-will, agreement; **bon mot** (*mō*), a witty saying:—*pl.* **bons mots**

Neutral vowels in unaccented syllables: *em'pér-ór;* for certain sounds in foreign words see p. ix.

($b\bar{o}$ $m\bar{o}$); **bon ton** ($t\bar{o}$), good style, the fashionable world; **bon vivant** ($v\bar{e}$-$v\ddot{a}$), one who lives well or luxuriously. [Fr.]

bona fide, $b\bar{o}'na$ $f\bar{\imath}d'\bar{a}$, adv. and adj. in good faith: genuine. [L.]

bonanza, bon-$an'z\ddot{a}$, n. a rich mass of gold: any mine of wealth or stroke of luck. [Sp., good weather.]

bonbon, $b\bar{o}$-$b\bar{o}$, n. a sweetmeat. [Fr., 'very good'—bon, good.]

bond, $bond$, n. that which binds: link of connection or union: a written obligation to pay a sum or to perform a contract: a debenture: method of overlapping stones in masonry: (pl.) imprisonment, captivity: the condition of goods retained in a warehouse till the duties on them are paid—hence **bonded stores** or **warehouses, to take out of bond**, &c.—v.t. to put imported goods in the customs' warehouses: to cause to adhere (e.g. metal to glass or plastic).—ns. **bond'er**, a binding stone or brick; **bond'-hold'er**, one who holds bonds of a private person or public company, **bonds'-man**, a surety on a bond: see also **bond** (2).—**bonded debt**, the debt of a corporation represented by the bonds it has issued; **bond paper**, a superior kind of paper orig. intended for bonds. [A variant of band—O.E. bindan, to bind.]

bond, $bond$, adj. in a state of servitude, esp. as prefix in **bond(s)'man**, &c.—n. **bond'age**, captivity: slavery. [O.E. bonda, a peasant, a householder—O.N. bóndi; meaning affected by association with **bond** (1).]

bone, $b\bar{o}n$, n. a hard substance forming the skeleton of higher animals: a piece of the skeleton: (pl.) the skeleton: (pl.) any framework.—v.t. to take the bones out of, as meat.—adjs. **boned**, having bones: used in composition, as high-boned; having the bones removed; **bon'y**, full of, or consisting of, or like, bones: having large bones or little flesh.—ns. **bone'-ash**, **bone'-earth**, the remains when bones are burnt in an open furnace; **bone'-black**, the remains when bones are heated in a close vessel.—adj. **bone'-dry'**, absolutely dry.—ns. **bone china**, china made with bone-ash as a constituent; **bone'-dust**, pulverised bones, used in agriculture.—adj. **bone'less**.—n. **bone'-sett'er**, one who treats broken or displaced bones without being a duly qualified surgeon; **bone'-shāk'er** (slang), a bicycle, esp. any of the earlier types.—a **bone of contention**, a subject of dispute, a cause of strife; **a bone to pick with**, a grievance against, a subject of dispute with (a person); **bone up on** (slang), to study or collect information about (a subject); **make no bones of, about**, to have no scruples about: to make no difficulty about; **near the bone**, mean: on the verge of the indecent; **to the bone**, to the inmost part. [O.E. bān.]

bonfire, $bon'f\bar{\imath}r$, n. a large fire in the open air, esp. on occasions of public rejoicing—originally a fire burning bones. [**bone**, **fire**.]

bonhomie, $bon'o$-$m\bar{e}$, n. easy good-nature. [Fr.—bon homme, a good fellow.]

bonne, bon, n. a French maidservant, nursemaid. [Fr.; fem. of bon, good.]

bonne-bouche, bon-$b\bar{oo}sh$, n. a delicious morsel.

[Fr. bonne, good, and bouche, mouth.]

bonnet, $bon'\acute{e}t$, n. a covering for the head: a feminine head-dress fastened by strings: (Scot.) a cap, esp. a broad, round, flat, dark-blue cap with a tuft on the top: the cover of a chimney-top, of a motor-car engine, &c.—v.t. to put a bonnet on. [O.Fr.—Low L. bonnetum, orig. the name of a stuff.]

bonny, bonnie, $bon'i$, adj. beautiful: comely, pretty: healthy-looking: as a general term of appreciation, often ironically.—adv. **bonn'ily**. [Possibly connected with Fr. bon, bonne.]

bonus, $b\bar{o}n'us$, n. a voluntary addition to the sum due as interest, dividend, or wages. [L. bonus, good.]

bonze, $bonz$, n. a Buddhist priest. [Jap. bonzô or bonzi, a priest.]

boo, booh, $b\bar{oo}$, interj. expressive of disapprobation or contempt.—v.t. and v.i. to utter 'boo!', to hoot.—v.t. **boo'-hoo'**, to weep noisily. [Imit.]

boob, $b\bar{oo}b$, v.t. to bungle.—v.i. to blunder.—n. a blunder; a stupid fellow (U.S.), [**booby**,]

booby, $b\bar{oo}'bi$, n. a simpleton: any of several sea-birds, species of gannets, notorious for their apparent stupidity.—ns. **boo'by-prize**, a prize for the lowest score; **boo'by-trap**, a device for playing a practical joke on a guileless victim: an apparently harmless mechanical contrivance which, if touched unwarily, automatically injures the finder. [Perh. Sp. bobo.]

boogie-woogie, $b\bar{oo}g'i$-$w\bar{oo}g'i$, n. a style of fast jazz for the piano, with a persistent rhythm in the bass. [From U.S. slang boogie, a Negro performer, and woogie, invented to rhyme.]

book, $b\bar{oo}k$, n. a collection of sheets of paper bound together, either printed, written on, or blank: a literary composition: a division of such: a libretto: a record of bets: six tricks gained by a side at whist: (fig.) any source of information: (pl.) formal records of transactions.—v.t. to note in a book: to engage in advance: of police, to take the name of, for an alleged offence.—v.i. to buy a ticket (for).—ns. **book'binding**, the art or practice of putting the covers on books; **book'binder**; **book'-case**, a case with shelves for books; **book'-club**, a society (esp. mail order) that produces books for its members; **book'-end**, a prop for the end of a row of books; **book'ie** (coll.), a bookmaker; **book'ing-off'ice**, an office where tickets are sold.—adj. **book'ish**, fond of books: acquainted only with books.—ns. **book'ishness**; **book'-keep'er**; **book'-keep'ing**, the art of keeping accounts in a regular and systematic manner; **book'-learn'ing**, learning got from books, as opposed to practical knowledge; **book'let**, a small book; **book'-mak'er**, one who makes money by inducing others to bet with him on the terms he offers and notes in a book the bets he accepts; **book'man**, a scholar, student; **book'-mark**, something placed in a book to mark a particular page; **book'-plate**, a label, usually pasted inside the cover of a book, bearing the owner's name, crest, coat-of-arms, or peculiar device; **book'-stall**, a stall or stand where books are sold; **book'-worm**, a grub that eats holes in books: one who reads assiduously, esp. if without profit.—**be in another's good** (or **bad**) **books**, to be in his

$f\bar{a}te$, $f\ddot{a}r$; $m\bar{e}$, $h\hat{u}r$ (her); $m\bar{\imath}ne$; $m\bar{o}te$, $f\ddot{o}r$; $m\bar{u}te$; $m\bar{oo}n$, $f\bar{oo}t$; THen (then)

79

favour (disfavour); **book of words**, directions for use; **bring to book**, to bring to account; **get one's books** (*slang*), to be dismissed; **take a leaf out of another's book**, to follow the example of someone; **talk like a book**, to talk with precision and readiness; **without the book**, from memory: unauthorisedly. [O.E. *bōc*, book, the beech; Ger. *buche*, the beech, *buch*, a book, because the Germanic peoples first wrote on beechen boards.]

Boolean algebra, *bōō'lē-an al'ji-bra*, an algebra closely related to logic in which the symbols used do not represent arithmetical quantities. [Named after George *Boole* (1815-64).]

boom, *bōōm*, *n.* a pole by which a sail is stretched: a chain or bar stretched across a harbour. [Du. *boom*, beam, tree.]

boom, *bōōm*, *v.i.* to make a hollow sound or roar.—*n.* a hollow sound, as of the sea: the cry of the bittern: the buzz of a beetle. [From a Low Ger. root found in O.E. *byme*, a trumpet, Du. *bommen*, to drum.]

boom, *bōōm*, *v.i.* to become suddenly active or prosperous.—*v.t.* to push into sudden prominence.—*n.* a sudden increase of activity in business, or the like: a sudden rise in price or value.—**boom town**, a town that booms and enjoys abnormal economic prosperity. [Prob. from **boom** (2).]

boomerang, *bōōm'e-rang*, *n.* a curved hardwood missile used by the natives of Australia, so balanced that, when thrown to a distance, it returns towards the thrower: (*fig.*) an act that recoils on the agent. [Australian.]

boon, *bōōn*, *n.* a petition; a gift, favour. [O.N. *bón*, prayer; O.E. *bēn*.]

boon, *bōōn*, *adj.* gay, merry, congenial (of a companion): kind (e.g. *boon nature*). [Fr. *bon*—L. *bonus*, good.]

boondoggle, *bōōn'dog-l*, *n.* a Scout's plaited cord, worn round the neck: an article of simple handcraft: work of little or no practical value. [Scout coinage.]

boor, *bōōr*, *n.* a peasant: a coarse or awkward person.—*adj.* **boor'ish.**—*adv.* **boor'ishly.**—*n.* **boor'ishness.** [Du. *boer*; Ger. *bauer*; O.E. *ge-būr*, a farmer.]

boose. See **booze.**

boost, *bōōst*, *v.t.* to help forward: to raise: to advertise fervently: to supplement voltage of: to increase supply of air to, or pressure.—*n.* a push.—*n.* **boost'er**, any device which increases the effect of another mechanism (also *fig.*): an auxiliary motor in a rocket, usu. breaking away after delivery of its impulse. [Orig. U.S.; origin unknown.]

boot, *bōōt*, *n.* a covering for the foot and lower part of the leg, generally made of leather: also **boot'ikin:** a box or receptacle in a coach or motorcar: (*slang*) unceremonious dismissal.—*v.t.* to put boots on: to kick.—*ns.* **boot'black**, a shoeblack; **boot'jack**, an instrument for taking off boots; **boot'lace**, a lace for fastening boots; **boot'last, boot'tree**, the last or foot-like mould on which boots or shoes are made, or stretched to keep their shape; **boot'leg**, the leg of a high boot; **boot'legger**, one who smuggles alcoholic liquor in a boot-leg, or elsewhere: an illicit dealer (*slang*—also *v.t.,*

v.i. and *adj.* **boot'leg**); **boots**, servant in a hotel who may clean the boots, &c.—**boot and saddle** (a corruption of Fr. *boute-selle*, place saddle—*bouter*, to place, *selle*, saddle), the signal to cavalry to mount.—**the boot is on the other leg**, it is the other way round: the responsibility lies with the other party; **get the boot** (*slang*), to be dismissed; **have one's heart in one's boots**, to be in terror. [O.Fr. *bote*—Low L. *botta*, *bota*.]

boot, *bōōt*, *v.t.* to profit or advantage.—*n.* advantage, profit.—*adj.* **boot'less** (of an action) useless.—*adv.* **boot'lessly.**—*n.* **boot'lessness.**—**to boot**, in addition. [O.E. *bōt*, compensation, amends, whence *bētan*, to amend, to make **better.**]

bootee, *bōōt-ē'*, *n.* a woollen boot for infants. [Dim. of **boot.**]

booth, *bōōᴛʜ*, or *-th*, *n.* a temporary erection formed of slight materials: a covered stall: a polling place. [O.N. *būth*; Ger. *bude.*]

booty, *bōōt'i*, *n.* spoil, plunder: a prize. [O.N. *bȳti*, share—*bȳta*, to divide.]

booze, boose, *bōōz*, **bouse**, *bowz*, *v.i.* to drink deeply or excessively.—*n.* intoxicating liquor: a drinking bout.—*n.* **booz'er** (*slang*), public house. [Apparently Middle Du. *bûsen*, to drink deeply.]

bop, *bop*, *n.* a style of jazz in the 1950s, the earliest form of 'cool' jazz, a development of *bebop.*

bo-peep, *bo-pēp'*, *n.* a children's game in which one peeps from behind something and cries 'Bo!'

borax, *bō'raks*, *n.* a mineral compound of sodium, boron, and oxygen, found as a saline incrustation on the shores of certain lakes, used in various industries, as a substitute for soap, and in antiseptic preparations.—*adjs.* **boric, boracic** (*bō-ras'ik*), of or relating to borax.—**boracic acid**, a weak acid obtained by dissolving borax. [Through Fr. and Low L. *borax, boracis,* from Ar. *bûraq.*]

Bordeaux, *bōr-dō'*, *n.* claret, wine of *Bordeaux.*

border, *bōrd'ér*, *n.* the edge or margin of anything: the boundary of a country, esp. that between England and Scotland: (*cap.* and *pl.*) the part of Scotland nearest to the boundary with England, and vice versa: a row of plants lining a plot or path in a garden.—*v.i.* to come near, to adjoin (with *on, upon*).—*v.t.* to adorn with a border: to adjoin: to be a border to.—*ns.* **bord'erer**, one who dwells on the border of a country; **bord'erland.**—*adj.* **bord'erline**, marginal, hardly or doubtfully coming within the definition (as of insanity).—Also *n.* [O.Fr. *bor-dure*; from root of **board.**]

bore, *bōr*, *bôr*, *v.t.* to pierce so as to form a hole: to thrust against (as one racehorse against another): to weary, to fail to interest.—*n.* a hole made by boring: the size of the cavity of a gun: a tiresome person or thing.—*n.* **bore'dom**, tedium. [O.E. *borian*, to bore; cf. Ger. *bohren*; allied to L. *forāre*, to bore, Gr. *pharynx*, the gullet.]

bore, *bōr*, *bôr*, *pa.t.* of **bear.**

bore, *bōr*, *bôr*, *n.* a tidal flood which rushes violently up the estuaries of certain rivers. [O.N. *bāra*, a wave or swell.]

boreas, *bō're-as*, *n.* the north wind.—*adj.* **bō'real,**

Neutral vowels in unaccented syllables: *em'pér-ór*; for certain sounds in foreign words see p. ix.

of boreas: northern. [L. and Gr.]

boric. Same as **boracic** (q.v. under **borax**).

born, *börn, pa.p.* of **bear,** to bring forth.

borne, *börn, börn, pa.p.* of **bear,** to carry.

boron, *bō′ron, n.* non-metallic element (symbol B; at. no. 5), found in borax, &c. [See **borax.**]

borough, *bur′ō, n.* a town with a municipal corporation: a town that is represented in parliament.—*n.* **bor′oughmonger,** one who bought or sold the right of nominating the member of parliament for a close or rotten borough.— **close** or **pocket borough,** a borough in which the election of a member of parliament was controlled by an individual; **county borough,** a borough of 100 000 inhabitants or more; **rotten borough,** one of the boroughs disfranchised in 1832, where the electorate had almost disappeared through depopulation. See also **burgh.** [O.E. *burg, burh,* a city, akin to *beorgan,* to protect.]

borrow, *bor′ō, v.t.* to obtain on loan or trust: to adopt from a foreign source. *n.* **borr′ower.** [O.E. *borgian borg, borh,* a pledge, security.]

borsch, *börsh(t), n.* Russian soup made with beetroot, &c. Also **bortsch.** [Russ. *borshch.*]

borstal, *bör′stál, adj.* applied to a system of reforming youthful delinquents by residential training, named from the first institution of the kind at *Borstal* in Kent.—Also *n.*

borzoi, *bör′zoi, n.* the Russian wolf-hound. [Russ. *borzoy,* swift.]

boscage, *bosk′ij, n.* thick foliage: woodland. [Fr. *boscage, bocage*—Low L. *boscus*; conn. with Ger. *busch,* Eng. **bush.**]

bosh, *bosh, n.* nonsense.—Also *interj.* [Turk. *bosh,* worthless.]

bosky, *bosk′i, adj.* woody or bushy: shady. [Prob. M.E. *bosk,* a bush; cf. **boscage.**]

bosom, *bŏŏz′-, bŏŏz′óm, n.* the breast of a human being, or the part of the dress that covers it: *(fig.)* the seat of the passions and feelings, the heart: the midst. *adj.* confidential: intimate. [O.E. *bōsm*; Ger. *busen.*]

boson, *bō′son, n.* any of a class of subatomic particles whose behaviour is governed by **Bose–Einstein statistics,** according to which, under certain conditions, particles of the same kind will accumulate in each low-energy quantum mechanical state. [S.N. *Bose,* physicist.]

boss, *bos, n.* a knob or stud: a raised ornament.—*v.t.* to ornament with bosses. [O.Fr. *boce,* from Old Ger. *bōzan,* to beat.]

boss, *bos, n.* the master, manager, or foreman: the person who pulls the wires in political intrigue. *v.t.* to manage: to keep in subjection. [New York Dutch *baas,* master.]

bosun. Common spelling of **boatswain.**

bot, bott, *bott, n.* the maggot of the **bot′fly,** a name for various flies parasitic in the intestines of the horse and other animals: (in *pl.*) the disease caused by them.

botany, *bot′án-i, n.* the science of plants.—*adjs.* **botan′ic, -ical.**—*n.* **botan′ical,** a vegetable drug.—*adv.* **botan′ically.**—*v.i.* **bot′anise,** to gather plants for study.—*n.* **bot′anist,** one skilled in botany.—**botanic garden(s),** a park stocked with indigenous and exotic plants, frequented by students of botany and by the public. [Gr. *botanē,* grass; cf. *boskein,* to feed,

L. *vescī,* to feed.]

botch, *boch, n.* a swelling on the skin: a clumsy patch: ill-finished work.—*v.t.* to patch or mend clumsily: to put together unsuitably or unskilfully. [Perh. from root of **boss** (1).]

botfly. See **bot.**

both, *bōth, adj.* and *pron.* the two: the one and the other.—*conj.* (or *adv.*) as well, equally. *Both ... and* is nearly equivalent to *not only ... but also* (e.g. *both the cat and the dog, both wise and learned*). [O.N. *bāthar*; O.E. *bā*; Ger. *beide*; cf. L. *ambo,* Gr. *amphō.*]

bother, *boȟ′ér, v.t.* to perplex or tease.—*ns.* **both′er, botherā′tion.**—*adj.* **both′ersome.** [Poss. Anglo-Irish for **pother.**]

bothy, bothie, *both′i, n.* a barely furnished hut, esp. one shared by farm-servants, or fishermen, &c.—**bothy ballad,** a folk-song dealing with country matters, sometimes bawdy. [Cf. **booth,** and Gael. *both,* a hut.]

bo-tree, *bō′-trē, n.* the sacred fig-tree, planted close by Buddhist temples in Ceylon. [Sinhal *ēsa ba.*]

botryoid, -al, *bot′ri-oid, -oid′al, adjs.* resembling a bunch of grapes. [Gr. *botrys,* a bunch of grapes, *eidos,* form.]

bottle, *bot′l, n.* a bundle (of hay). [O.Fr. *botel.*]

bottle, *bot′l, n.* a hollow narrow-necked vessel for holding liquids: the contents of such a vessel.—*v.t.* to enclose in bottles.—*p.adj.* **bott′led,** enclosed in bottles: shaped like a bottle: kept in restraint.—*ns.* **bott′le gas,** butane (q.v.) in liquid form; **bott′le-glass,** a coarse green glass used in the making of bottles.—*adj.* **bott′le-green,** dark green in colour, like bottle-glass.—*ns.* **bott′le-head, bott′le-nose,** a genus of toothed whales; **bott′le-neck,** a narrow section of a road where traffic is apt to be congested: *(fig.)* any stage of a process at which facilities for progress are inadequate; **bott′le-party** one to which everyone brings a bottle; **bott′le wash′er,** one who washes bottles: a factotum.—**bottle up,** to confine, repress. [O.Fr. *bouteille,* dim. of *botte,* a vessel for liquids—Low L. *butis.*]

bottom, *bot′om, n.* the lowest part of anything: that on which anything rests or is founded: the sitting part of the body: the seat of a chair: the hull of a ship, hence the vessel itself: the bed of the sea, &c.: the portion of a wig hanging down over the shoulders: the basis of anything.—*v.t.* to found or rest upon.—*adj.* **bott′omless.**—*n.* **bott′omry,** a contract by which money is borrowed on the security of a ship.—**at bottom,** in reality; **be at the bottom of,** to be the real cause, originator, of; **to get to the bottom of,** to discover the explanation of, or real facts of. [O.E. *botm*; Ger. *boden*; L. *fundus,* bottom.]

bouclé, *bŏŏ′klā, n.* a yarn having the threads looped to give a bulky effect. [Fr.]

boudoir, *bŏŏd′wär, n.* a lady's private room. [Fr.—*bouder,* to pout, to be sulky.]

bouffant, *bŏŏf′ā, adj.* puffed out, in dressmaking and hair-dressing. [Fr.]

Bougainvillaea, *bŏŏg-ān-vil-ē′ä,* or *-vil′-, n.* a genus of herbaceous plants of tropical America, conspicuous for the beauty of their rosy or purple bracts—also **Bougainvil′ia.** [French explorer de *Bougainville* (1729–1811).]

fāte, fär; mē, hûr (her); *mīne, mōte, för; mūte; mŏŏn, fŏŏt;* THen (then)

bough, *bow, n.* a branch of a tree. [O.E. *bōg, bōh,* an arm, the shoulder; *būgan,* to bend.]

bought, *bôt, pa.t.* and *pa.p.* of **buy.**

bouillon, *bōō-yō n.* a strong broth. [Fr., from same root as **boil.**]

boulder, *bōld'ér, n.* a large stone rounded by the action of water: (*geol.*) a mass of rock transported by natural agencies from its native bed.—*adj.* containing boulders.—*n.* **bould'er-clay** (*geol.*), an unstratified stony clay formed by glaciation. [Prob. from Swed. *bullra,* Dan. *buldre,* to roar like thunder, as large pebbles do.]

boulevard, *bōōl'e-vär, n.* a promenade on the dismantled fortifications of a town: any broad road lined by trees. [Fr.,—Ger. *bollwerk*; same root as **bulwark.**]

bounce, *bowns, v.i.* to jump or spring suddenly: to rebound like a ball: to come back to one, as a cheque that cannot be cashed: to boast, to exaggerate.—*v.t.* (*slang*) to reprimand: to bring to book.—*n.* a thud: a leap or spring: a boast.—*n.* **bounc'er,** one who bounces: a liar: something big.—*adj.* **bounc'ing,** lusty. [Du. *bonzen,* strike, *bons,* a blow.]

bound, *bownd, pa.t.* and *pa.p.* of **bind.**—In composition, restricted to or by, as *housebound, stormbound.*—**bound to,** obliged to: sure to.

bound, *bownd, n.* the limit of a definite area: (*pl.*) the area so defined: (*pl.—fig.*) the limits (of what is reasonable or what is permitted).—*v.t.* to set bounds to: to limit, restrain, or surround.—*n.* **bound'ary,** the line by which an area is defined.—*adj.* **bound'less,** having no limit: vast. [O.Fr. *bonne*—Low L. *bodina*; cf. Breton *bonn,* a boundary.]

bound, *bownd, v.i.* to spring or leap.—*n.* a spring or leap.—*n.* **bound'er,** one who bounds: a boisterous, vulgar person. [Fr. *bondir,* to spring, in O.Fr. to resound—L. *bombitāre.*]

bound, *bownd,* predicative *adj.* ready to go to, on the way to (e.g. *bound for the North, outward bound*). [O.N. *būinn,* pa.p. of *būa,* to prepare.]

bounden, *bownd'n, adj.* obligatory (*bounden duty*). [Archaic pa.p. of **bind.**]

bounty, *bown'ti, n.* liberality in bestowing gifts: the gifts bestowed: money paid to a recruit on enlisting: a state subsidy to encourage the production of a commodity.—*adjs.* **bounteous** (*-ti-ús*), **boun'tiful,** liberal in giving: generous.—*advs.* **boun'teously, boun'tifully.** [O.Fr. *bontet,* goodness—L. *bonitās -ātis*—*bonus,* good.]

bouquet, *bōōk'-ā,* or *-ā', n.* a bunch of flowers, a nosegay: the perfume exhaled by wine.—**bouquet garni** (*gär'nē*), a bunch of herbs used in cooking, removed before serving. [Fr. *bosquet,* dim. of *bois,* a wood; cf. It. *bosco.*]

bourgeois, *bōōrzh'wä, n.* one of the **bourgeoisie** (*bōōrzh'wä-zē* or *-zē'*), or middle class of citizens: a merchant or shopkeeper.—*adj.* middle class: conventional: humdrum. [Fr. *bourgeois,* citizen.]

bourgeon, *bûr'jón, v.i.* to put forth sprouts or buds: to grow: to flourish. [Fr. *bourgeon,* a bud, shoot.]

bourn, bourne, *bōrn, börn, bōōrn, n.* a boundary, a limit, a goal. [Fr. *borne,* a limit.]

bourn, bourne, *bōōrn, n.* variant of **burn** (1).

bourse, *bōōrs, n.* an exchange where merchants meet for business. [Fr. *bourse.* See **purse.**]

bouse. See **booze.**

bout, *bowt, n.* a turn, spell, fit (of): a contest. [Doublet of **bight**; from root of **bow** (1).]

boutique, *bōō-tēk', n.* a small shop, or a department in a shop, selling one type of goods, esp. clothing. [Fr.]

bovine, *bō'vīn, adj.* pertaining to cattle: dull, unemotional. [L. *bōs, bovis,* an ox or cow.]

bow, *bow, v.i.* to bend the neck, body, in saluting a person, &c.: to submit.—*v.t.* to bend, incline downwards: to weigh down, crush: to usher with a bow: to express by a bow.—*n.* a bending of the neck or body in salutation.—**make one's bow,** to retire ceremoniously. [O.N. *būgan,* to bend; akin to L. *fugĕre,* to flee, to yield.]

bow, *bō, n.* anything in the shape of an arch, as the rainbow: a tough, flexible curved rod by which arrows are shot from a string: the instrument by which the strings of a violin or the like are sounded: a looped knot of ribbon, &c.—*adj.* **bow'-backed,** with bent back.—*n.* **bow'-leg,** a leg crooked like a bow.—*adj.* **bow'legged.**—*ns.* **bow'man,** an archer; **bow'shot,** the distance to which an arrow can be shot from a bow; **bow'string,** the string by which a bow is drawn: a string with which the Turks strangled offenders; **bowstring bridge,** a bridge supported by an arch strengthened by a horizontal tie corresponding to a bowstring; **bow'-win'dow,** a window projecting in a curve.—*adj.* **bow'-win'dowed.**—**draw the long bow** (see **longbow**); **have two** (or more) **strings to one's bow,** to have another alternative or other resources. [O.E. *boga*; cog. with Ger. *bogen.*]

bow, *bow, n.* the fore-part of a ship—often used in *pl.*—*ns.* **bow'er, bow'er-anch'or,** an anchor at the bow or forepart of a ship. [From a Low Ger., Du., or Scand. word for shoulder. Cf. **bough.**]

bowdlerise, *bowd'lér-īz, v.t.* to purge (a book) by altering or omitting indelicate expressions, esp. to do so unnecessarily. [From Dr T. *Bowdler,* who thus edited Shak. in 1818.]

bowel, *bow'él, n.* an interior part of the body: (in *pl.*) the entrails, the intestines: (*pl.*) the interior part of anything: (*pl.—fig.*) the heart, pity, tenderness. [O.Fr. *boel*—L. *botellus,* a sausage, also an intestine.]

bower, *bow'ér, n.* an arbour: an inner room, a boudoir.—*n.* **bow'er-bird,** an Australian bird that makes a bower ornamented with gay feathers, shells, &c.—*adj.* **bow'ery,** containing bowers: shady. [O.E. *būr,* a chamber; root O.E. *būan,* to dwell.]

bowie-knife, *bō'i-nīf, n.* an American dagger-knife, designed by Colonel *Bowie* in 1827.

bowl, *bōl, n.* a wooden ball used for rolling along the ground: (*pl.*) a game played on a green with bowls having a bias.—*v.t.* and *v.i.* to play at bowls: to speed smoothly (along) like a bowl: to deliver a ball, in cricket: to put (a batsman) out thus.—*ns.* **bowl'er,** one who bowls; **bowl'ing-all'ey,** a long narrow covered rink for skittles; **bowl'ing-green,** a smooth grassy plot for bowls.—**bowl over,** to knock down: (*fig.*) to overwhelm. [Fr. *boule*—L. *bulla.*]

bowl, *bōl, n.* a basin for holding liquids, formerly

Neutral vowels in unaccented syllables: *em'pér-ór*; for certain sounds in foreign words see p. ix.

restricted to one nearly hemispherical in shape: the round hollow part of anything. [O.E. *bolla.*]

bowler, *bō'ler, n.* a hard round felt hat.—Also **bow'ler-hat'.**—*v.t.* **bow'ler-hat'** (*slang*), to discharge, dismiss in civil dress. [Name of manufacturer.]

bowline, *bō'lin, n.* a rope to keep a sail close to the wind.—**bowline (knot)**, a knot used to tie a bowline so that it will not slip or jam. [M.E.; of doubtful origin.]

bowsprit, *bō'sprit, n.* a strong spar projecting over the bows of a ship. [Apparently Du. *boegspriet.*]

box, *boks, n.* a genus of evergreen shrubs and small trees with very compact habit of growth and hard, strong, heavy wood: a case or receptacle for holding anything: the contents of a box: a (Christmas) present: a hut or cabin: a compartment: in a theatre, a group of enclosed seats: the driver's seat on a carriage: a predicament —*v.t.* to put into or furnish with, boxes: to enclose.—*ns.* **box-bed**, a bed closed in on all sides except the front, which may also be shut by sliding doors; **Box'ing-day**, in England, the day after Christmas, when boxes or presents are given; **box'-number**, a number to which replies to advertisements may be sent; **box-office**, in a theatre, &c., the office at which seats are booked: receipts from a play, &c.: ability to draw an audience: an attraction as judged by the box-office (also adj.); **box'-pleat**, a double fold of cloth; **box'wood**, wood of the box tree: the dwarf box-tree, used to border garden walks and plots.—**box the compass**, to name the 32 points in their order and backwards, hence to adopt successively every phase of opinion. [O.E. *box*—L. *buxus*—Gr. *pyxos*, a box-tree.]

box, *boks, n.* a blow on the head or ear with the hand.—*v.t.* to strike with the hand or fist.—*v.i.* to fight with the fists.—*ns.* **box'er**, one who boxes; **box'ing-glove**, a padded glove worn in boxing. [Possibly connected with Gr. *pyx* (adv.), 'with the fist'.]

box-calf, *boks'kāf, n.* a chrome-tanned calfskin. [Possibly Joseph *Box*, shoemaker.]

boy, *boi, n.* a male child: a lad: a servant.—*n.* **boy'hood**, time, or state, of being a boy.—*adj.* **boy'ish.**—*adv.* **boy'ishly.**—*n.* **boy'ishness.**—**Boys' Brigade**, an organisation of boys for the promotion of habits of obedience, reverence, discipline, and self-respect (founded in 1883); **Boy Scout** (now **Scout**), a member of an organisation of boys formed in 1908 to develop mental and physical alertness and strong character. [M.E. *boi, boy*; Ger. *bube.*]

boycott, *boi'kot, v.t.* to shut out from all social and commercial intercourse. [From Captain *Boycott*, who was so treated by his Irish neighbours in 1880.]

bra, *brä, n.* short for **brassière.**

brace, *brās, n.* anything that draws together and holds tightly: a rod or bar connecting two parts of a structure for stiffening purposes: an instrument for turning boring tools: in printing, a mark connecting two or more words or lines (|): a pair, couple: (*pl.*) straps for supporting the trousers: ropes for turning the yards of a ship.—*v.t.* to tighten or to strength-

en.—*adj.* **brac'ing**, invigorating. [O.Fr. *brace*, the arm, power—L. *brachium*—Gr. *brachiōn*, the arm, that which holds.]

bracelet, *brās'let, n.* an ornament for the wrist: (*coll.*) a handcuff. [Fr.,—L. *brachiāle—brachium*, the arm.]

brach, *brach, n.* a dog for the chase, esp. a bitch hound. [O.Fr. *brachet*, pl. *brachès*, dim. of *brac*—Low L. *bracco*, of Gmc. origin.]

brachial, *brāk'-* or *brak'i-ăl, adj.* belonging to the arm. [L. *brachiālis—brachium*, arm.]

brachycephalic, *brak-i-sef-al'ik* (also -*sef'-*), **brachycephalous**, *brak-i-sef'al-us, adj.* short-headed, applied to skulls of which the breadth is at least four-fifths of the length—opp. to *dolichocephalic.* [Gr. *brachys*, short, *kephalē*, head.]

bracken, *brak'en, n.* a fern, esp. the commonest British fern. [Ety. obscure.]

bracket, *brak'et, n.* a support for a shelf, &c., projecting from a wall: a small shelf: a bracketed group, as of people classified according to income (e.g. *in the lower, middle, upper income bracket*): (*pl.*) in printing, the marks [ ] used to enclose one or more words.—*v.t.* to support by brackets: to enclose by brackets: to group together, as implying equality. [Fr. *braguette*—L. *brācae*, breeches.]

brackish, *brak'ish, adj.* of water, saltish.—*n.* **brack'ishness.** [Du. *brak*, and suffx. *ish.*]

bract, *brakt, n.* a leaf (often modified) that bears a flower in its axil.—*adj.* **brac'teal** (-*ti-ăl*). [L. *bractea*, gold-leaf.]

brad, *brad, n.* a small nail having a slight projection at the top on one side instead of a head.—*n.* **brad'awl**, an awl to pierce holes. [O.N. *broddr*, a pointed piece of iron.]

Bradshaw, *brad'shô, n.* a noted railway-guide (1839-1961), named after first compiler.

brae, *brā, n.* (*Scot.*) the slope above a river bank: a hill-slope. [O.N. *brá.*]

brag, *brag, v.i.* to boast or bluster:—*pr.p.* **bragg'ing**; *pa.p.* **bragged.**—*n.* a boast or boasting: the thing boasted of: a game at cards. [Most prob. Celt.]

braggadocio, *brag-a-dō'shi-ō, n.* a braggart or boaster: empty boasting.—Also *adj.* [From *Braggadochio*, a boastful character in Spencer's *Faerie Queene.*]

braggart, *brag'ärt, adj.* boastful.—*n.* a vain boaster. [Fr. *bragard*, vain, bragging.]

Brahman, -min, *brä'man, -min, n.* (also without *cap.*) a person of the highest or priestly caste among the Hindus.—*n.* **Brah'manism, -minism**, the worship of **Brah'ma**, an impersonal supreme spirit, and also (pronounced *brä-mä'*) the supreme deity and creator.

braid, *brād, v.t.* to plait or entwine.—*n.* a narrow band made by plaiting thread, &c.: entwined hair. [O.E. *bregdan*; O.N. *bregtha*, to weave.]

braille, *brāl, n.* printing for the blind, using a system of dots in relief.—Also *adj.* [From Louis *Braille*, the inventor (1809-52).]

brain, *brān, n.* the part of the central nervous system which is contained within the skull: the seat of the intellect and of sensation: the intellect: a person of exceptional intelligence—often used in *pl.*—*v.t.* to dash out the brains of.—*ns.* **brain'-child**, an original thought or work; **brain'-fe'ver**, any one of several fevers in which the brain is affected; **brain'-pan**, the skull; **brain'-storm**, a sudden and severe mental disturbance: sudden inspiration; **brain'-wash'ing**, a systematic attempt to change what a person thinks and believes by methods, not necessarily violent, which applied persistently, usu. over a long period, shake his faith in his accepted views (*v.t.* **brain'-wash**); **brain'-wave**, a sudden bright idea.—*adj.* **brainy**, intellectual.—**brain drain**, continuing loss of citizens of high intelligence and creativity through emigration; **brains trust**, a committee of experts: a number of reputedly well-informed persons chosen to answer questions of general interest in public and without preparation. [O.E. *bRÆgen*; Du. *brein*.]

braird, *brārd*, *n.* the first shoots of corn or other crop.—*v.i.* to appear above ground. [Orig. Scot.; O.E. *brerd*, edge, *brord*, point.]

braise, *brāz*, *v.t.* to stew in a closed vessel. [Fr. *braiser*.]

brake, *brāk*, obsolete *pa.t.* of **break** (1).

brake, *brāk*, *n.* a fern: bracken. [Perh. **bracken**.]

brake, *brāk*, *n.* a thicket.—*adj.* **brak'y**. [Ety. uncertain.]

brake, *brāk*, *n.* an instrument to break flax or hemp: a harrow: a contrivance for retarding the motion of a wheel by friction: a kind of vehicle—see **break** (1).—*ns.* **brake'man**, the man whose business it is to manage the brake of a railway-train; **brake'-van**, the carriage from which the brake is worked. [From root of **break**.]

bramble, *bram'bl*, *n.* the blackberry bush: any rough prickly shrub: (*Scot.*, &c.) a blackberry. [O.E. *brēmel*; Du. *braam*; Ger. *brom-beere*.]

bran, *bran*, *n.* the refuse of grain: the inner husks of grain sifted from the flour. [O.Fr. *bran*, bran; perh. Celt.]

branch, *brānch*, or *-sh*, *n.* a shoot or arm-like limb of a tree: any offshoot from a parent stem: a department of a business or enterprise: a subdivision, section of a subject.—*v.i.* to spread out as a branch (with *out, off, from*), or in branches.—Also *v.t.*—**branch'-off'icer**, *n.* (*navy*) officer holding warrant. [Fr. *branche*—Low L. *branca*, paw.]

branchia, *brangk'i-a*, *n.* a gill:—*pl.* **branchiae** (*brangk'i-ē*). [L.,—Gr.]

brand, *brand*, *n.* a piece of wood burning or partly burned: a mark stamped with a hot iron: such a mark inflicted on the person as a sign of guilt or disgrace: particular quality (of goods): a trademark: a sword.—*v.t.* to mark with a hot iron: to fix a mark of infamy upon.—*n.* **brand'er**, a gridiron.—*v.t.* to cook on the gridiron.—*adj.* **bran(d)'-new**, quite new (as if newly from the fire). [O.E. *brand, brond*, from root of **burn** (2).]

brandish, *brand'ish*, *v.t.* to wave or flourish as a brand or weapon.—*n.* a waving or flourish. [Fr. *brandissant*—*brandir*, from root of **brand**.]

brandy, *brand'i*, *n.* an ardent spirit distilled from wine.—*ns.* **brand'y-ball**, a kind of sweetmeat; **brand'y-snap**, a gingerbread biscuit orig. flavoured with brandy. [Formerly *brandwine*—Du. *brandewijn*—*branden*, to burn, to distil, and *wijn*, wine.]

bran-new. See **brand**.

brant-goose. Same as **brent-goose**.

brash, *brash*, *adj.* impetuous: bumptious: bold.

brass, *bräs*, *n.* an alloy of copper and zinc: (*fig.*) effrontery: (*slang*) money: (usu. in *pl.*) monumental plates or fixtures of brass.—*ns.* **brass'-found'er**, a maker of articles in brass; **brass'-hat** (*mil. slang*), a staff officer; **brass'-plate**, a plate on a door, &c., with the tenant's name, &c.; **brass'y** (or **brassie**), a wooden golf-club with a brass sole.—*adj.* of or like brass: impudent: pitiless: harsh in tone.— **brass band**, a band of players of (mainly) brass wind instruments; **brass tacks**, fundamental principles.—**top brass**, brass-hats: those in authority at the top. [O.E. *bRÆs*.]

brassard, *bras'ärd*, *n.* an arm-band or armlet. [Fr.—*bras*, arm.]

brassière, *bras'i-er*, *n.* a woman's undergarment supporting the breasts. [Fr.]

brat, *brat*, *n.* a contemptuous name for a child: an apron. [O.E. *bratt*; of Celt. origin.]

brattice, *brat'is*, *n.* (in mediaeval siegecraft) a tower of wood, a covered gallery on a castle wall, &c.: a wooden partition or lining, esp. to control ventilation in a mine.—Also **bratt'ic-ing**.—*v.t.* to furnish with a brattice.—*n.* **bratt'ice-cloth**, strong tarred cloth used for brattices in mines. [O.Fr. *breteshe*—Low L. *bretachia*; prob. Gmc.]

bravado, *brav-ä'dō*, *brav-ā'dō*, *n.* a defiant display of bravery: a boastful threat:—*pl.* **brava'do(e)s**. [Sp. *bravada*—*bravo*, brave.]

brave, *brāv*, *adj.* courageous: noble: finely dressed, handsome; a general word for excellent.—*v.t.* to meet boldly: to defy: to face (it out).—*n.* a brave soldier, esp. a North American Indian warrior.—*adv.* **brave'ly.**—*n.* **brav'ery**, heroism: finery. [Fr. *brave*; It. and Sp. *bravo*; perh. from Celt.]

bravo, *brä'vō*, *n.* a daring villain: a hired assassin:—*pl.* **bravo(e)s** (*brä'vōz*). [It., Sp.]

bravo, *brä'vō*, *interj.* well done! excellent! [It.]

bravura, *bräv-ōōr'a*, *n.* (*mus.*) bold and spirited execution: a passage requiring such execution. [It.]

brawl, *bröl*, *n.* a noisy quarrel.—*v.i.* to quarrel noisily: to murmur or gurgle (as a running stream). [M.E. *bralle*; perh. conn. with Du. *brallen*, Ger. *prahlen*, to boast.]

brawn, *brön*, *n.* muscle, esp. of the arm or leg: muscular strength: flesh of a boar: potted meat made from pig's head and ox-feet.—*adj.* **brawn'y**, muscular. [O.Fr. *braon*, flesh (for roasting); of Gmc. origin.]

braxy, *brak'si*, *n.* and *adj.* a Scottish name for several sheep diseases. [Prob. the original form is *bracks*, the sing. of which is a variant of **break**.]

bray, *brā*, *v.t.* to break, pound, or grind small. [O.Fr. *breier*.]

bray, *brā*, *n.* the cry of the ass: any harsh grating sound.—*v.i.* to utter such sounds. [O.Fr.·*brai*, *brait*—*braire*—Low L. *bragīre*; perh. of Celt. origin.]

braze, *brāz*, *v.t.* to cover with or make like brass.—*adj.* **brā'zen**, of or belonging to brass: impudent.—*v.t.* to face (a situation) with impudence (as in *to brazen it out*).—*n.* **brazier** (*brāz'yér*, *brāzh'(y)ér*), a worker in brass. [O.E. *bRÆsian*—*bRÆs*, brass.]

Neutral vowels in unaccented syllables: *em'pér-ór*; for certain sounds in foreign words see p. ix.

braze, *brāz, v.t.* to join with hard solder.—*n.* **brazier** (*brāz'yér, brāzh'(y)ér*), a pan for hot coals. [O.Fr. *braser,* to burn; perh. influenced by **brass.**]

brazil, *bra-zil', n.* usu. **brazil'(-)wood** (or *cap.*), hard red wood used in dyeing.—*n.* **Brazil'ian,** a native of Brazil, in South America.—*adj.* belonging to Brazil.—*n.* **Brazil'-nut,** the edible seed of a large tree, native to Brazil. [O.Fr. *bresil;* Sp., Port., *brasil*—Low L. *brasilium,* a red dyewood brought from the East. When a similar wood was discovered in South America the country became known as *terre de brasil,* whence *Brasil,* Brazil.]

breach, *brēch, n.* an act of breaking: a break or gap, as in the walls of a fortress: a breaking of law, contract, covenant, promise, &c.: a quarrel.—*v.t.* to make a breach or opening in.— **breach of promise,** often used for breach of promise of marriage; **breach of the peace,** a violation of the public peace, e.g. by riot or improper behaviour. [O.E. *bryce, brice,* related to **break.**]

bread, *bred, n.* food made of flour or meal baked: livelihood (also **bread-and-butt'er**): food: (*slang*) money.—*adj.* **bread-and-butter,** youthfully insipid.—*ns.* **bread'fruit-tree,** a tree of the South Sea Islands, whose fruit, when roasted, forms a good substitute for bread; **bread'-winn'er,** one who earns a living for a family.—**bread-and-butter letter,** written thanks for hospitality.—**on the breadline,** at subsistence level, with just enough to make ends meet (from **breadline,** a queue of poor waiting for free bread). [O.E. *brēad,* prob. from a Gmc. root meaning a fragment, like the Scot. and North country use of 'a *piece',* for a bit of bread. The usual O.E. word was *hlāf.*]

breadth, *bredth, n.* extent from side to side, width: liberality (*e.g.* of mind): in art, subordination of details to the harmony of the whole. [O.E. *brædu;* Ger. *breite;* same root as **broad.**]

break, *brāk, v.t.* to sever forcibly: to divide: to shatter: to crush: to tame: to violate: to fail to fulfil: to check, as a fall: to interrupt (e.g. silence): to discontinue: to cure (of a habit): to make bankrupt: to impart (news, esp. with delicacy).—*v.i.* to fall asunder: to pass suddenly (into a condition or action): to force a passage: to dawn or come into view: to become bankrupt: to crack (as the voice): to burst into foam: to sever a connection: to change direction (as a cricket-ball on pitching): (of news, &c.) suddenly and sensationally to become public:—*pa.t.* brōke, (*arch.*) brāke; *pa.p.* brok'en (q.v.).—*n.* state of being broken: an opening: a pause or interruption: (*billiards*) a consecutive series of successful strokes: (*cricket*) the deviation of a ball on striking the pitch: (*U.S. slang*) a stroke of luck (good or ill): also a chance or opportunity.—*adj.* **break'able.**—Also *n.,* in *pl.*—*ns.* **break'age,** the action of breaking, or its consequences; **break'away,** revolt, secession; **break'down,** collapse: an accidental stoppage: an analysis; **break'er,** a wave broken on rocks or the beach; **break'ing** (*phonet.*), change of a vowel to a diphthong by the influence of following sounds.—*adj.* **break'-neck,** reckless.— *ns.* **break'through,** action of breaking through

an obstruction (*lit.* and *fig.*): the sensational solving of a scientific or other problem, usu. after much effort; **break'water,** a barrier to break the force of the waves.—**break cover,** to burst forth from concealment, as a fox; **break down,** to crush: to collapse: to fail completely: to separate into component parts, analyse; **break'-down gang,** a squad of men to remove wreckage, e.g. after a railway accident; **break in,** to train to labour, as a horse; **break in,** or **into,** to enter violently or unexpectedly; **break out,** to appear suddenly: to break through all restraint: to become covered with (a rash &c.—with *in*): to begin abruptly to say; **break the heart,** to cause, or feel, crushing sorrow; **break the ice** (*fig.*), to overcome initial difficulties, esp. reserve or restraint; **break up,** to break open: to break in pieces: to go to pieces: to decay: to disperse; **break on the wheel,** to punish by stretching a criminal on a wheel and breaking his bones; **break with,** to quarrel with: to cease adherence to (tradition, a habit, &c.). [O.E. *brecan;* Ger. *brechen.*]

break, brake, *brāk, n.* a large wagonette: a carriage used in breaking in horses. [**break,** *v.t.*]

breakfast, *brek'fast, n.* a *break* or breaking of a *fast*—the first meal of the day.—*v.i.* to take breakfast.

bream, *brēm, n.* a fresh-water fish of the carp family: various salt-water fishes. [O.Fr. *bresme,* from O.H.G.; Ger. *brassen.*]

breast, *brest, n.* the forepart of the human body between the neck and the belly: one of the two mammary glands: the corresponding part of any animal: (*fig.*) conscience, disposition, affections.—*v.t.* to bear the breast against: to oppose: to mount.—*ns.* **breast'plate,** a plate or piece of armour for the breast: (*B.*) part of the dress of the Jewish high-priest; **breast'work,** a hastily constructed low earthwork.—**make a clean breast,** to make a full confession. [O.E. *brēost;* Ger. *brust;* Du. *borst.*]

breath, *breth, n.* the air drawn into and then expelled from the lungs: power of breathing: life: a single act of breathing: a very slight breeze: an exhalation: (*phonet.*) sound produced by breathing without vibrating the vocal chords (e.g. *p, t, f,* opp. to *b, d, v*).—*adj.* **breath'less,** out of breath: dead: excessively eager.—*n.* **breath'lessness.**—**catch the breath,** to stop breathing for an instant; **with bated breath,** with breath restrained through awe or suspense. [O.E. *bræth;* Ger. *brodem,* steam, breath.]

breathe, *brēTH, v.i.* to draw in and expel breath or air from the lungs: to take breath, to rest or pause: to live.—*v.t.* to draw in or expel from the lungs, as air: to infuse (into): to give out as breath: to whisper: to exercise: to let (a horse) recover breath.—*ns.* **breathalyzer** (in Britain, usu. **breathalyser;** *breth'á-lī-zer*), a device which indicates the amount of alcohol in a person's breath, and so in his blood; **breath'er,** a spell of exercise: a rest to recover breath; **breathing,** the act of breathing: respite: one or other of two signs used in Greek to signify presence or absence of the aspirate; **breath'ing-time,** time to breathe or rest.—*adj.* **breath'-tak'ing,** astounding, startling. [M.E. *brethen,* from O.E. *bræth,* breath.]

breccia, *brech'yä, n.* a rock composed of angular fragments. [It.]

bred, *bred, pa.t.* and *pa.p.* of **breed.**

breech, *brēch, n.* (*arch.*) the lower part of the body behind: the hinder part of anything, esp. of a gun.—*v.t.* (*brich, brēch*) to put into breeches.—*n.pl.* **breeches** (*brich'ez*), a garment worn by men on the lower limbs of the body—strictly, as distinguished from trousers, coming just below the knee.—*ns.* **breeching** (*brich'-, brēch'-*), part of a horse's harness that comes round the breech; **breech'es-buoy,** a life-saving apparatus enclosing the person like a pair of breeches; **breech'load'er,** a fire-arm loaded by introducing the charge at the breech instead of the muzzle.—**breech birth, breech delivery,** one in which the breech comes first. [O.E. *brēc;* found in all Gmc. languages; cf. Ger. *bruch,* Du. *brock.*]

breed, *brēd, v.t.* to generate or bring forth: to train or bring up: to propagate, raise (e.g. *he breeds horses*): to cause or occasion.—*v.i.* to be with young: to produce offspring: to be produced (e.g. *trouble breeds there*):—*pa.t.* and *pa.p.* bred.—*n.* progeny or offspring: kind or race.—*ns.* **breed'er; breed'ing,** act of producing: education and training: good manners resulting from good training.—**breeder reactor,** a nuclear reactor capable of creating more fissile material than it consumes in maintaining the chain reaction. [O.E. *brēdan,* to cherish, keep warm; Ger. *brüten,* to hatch.]

breeze, *brēz, n.* a gentle gale: a wind: a disturbance or quarrel.—*adj.* **breez'y,** fanned with or subject to breezes: bright, lively. [Old Sp. *briza,* It. *brezza.*]

breeze, *brēz, n.* furnace refuse used by brick-makers. [Perh. O.Fr. *brese.*]

bren gun, *bren gun, n.* a light portable machine-gun. [*Br*no in Moravia; *En*field in England.]

brent-goose, *brent'-gōōs, n.* a small wild goose with black, white, and grey feathers.—Also **brant'-goose.** [Prob. *branded* = brindled.]

brer, *brér, n.* a Negro pronunciation of **brother.**

brethren, *breTH'ren, pl.* of **brother** (q.v.).

Breton, *bret'on, n.* a native of Brittany (*Bretagne*), France: the Celtic tongue of Brittany.—*adj.* pertaining to Brittany.

brettice. Same as **brattice.**

bretwalda, *bret-wöl'dä, n.* a title of supremacy borne by certain Old English kings. [Lit. 'Lord of the *Britons',* or 'of Britain'—O.E. *walda,* a ruler.]

breve, *brēv, n.* an obsolescent note, ⊫, twice as long as the longest now used (**semibreve**); originally the shortest of the three notes used in early music. [It. *breve*— L. *brevis,* short.]

breviary, *brēv'i-ár-i* (also *brev'-*) *n,* book containing the daily service of the R.C. Church. [L. *breviārium—brevis,* short.]

brevity, *brev'it-i, n.* shortness: conciseness. [L. *brevitās—brevis,* short.]

brew, *brōō, v.t.* to prepare a liquor, as from malt, and other materials: to contrive or plot.—*v.i.* to perform, or undergo, the operation of brewing: to be in preparation.—*n.* something brewed.—*ns.* **brew'er,** one who brews; **brew'ery,** a place for brewing. [O.E. *brēowan,* cf. Ger. *brauen.*]

briar. Same as **brier** (1).

briar-root. See **brier** (2).

bribe, *brīb, n.* something offered to influence the judgment unduly or corrupt the conduct.—*v.t.* to influence by a bribe.—*n.* **brib'ery,** the act of giving or taking bribes. [O.Fr. *bribe,* a lump of bread; origin uncertain.]

bric-à-brac, *brik'a-brak, n.* curios, treasured odds and ends [Fr.]

brick, *brik, n.* baked or 'burned' clay: a block of burned clay for building: a similar block of other material often compressed: (*slang*) a person who stands up cheerfully to his own troubles or supports others in theirs.—*v.t.* to lay or pave with brick.—*ns.* **brick'bat,** a piece of brick, esp. as a missile; **brick'-field,** a place where bricks are made; **brick'layer,** one who lays or builds with bricks; **brick'-tea,** tea-leaves pressed into cakes; **brick'-work,** a structure formed of bricks.—**drop a brick,** to make a shocking and tactless blunder. [Fr. *brique,* from root of **break.**]

bridal, *brīd'ál, n.* a marriage feast: a wedding.—*adj.* belonging to a bride or a wedding, nuptial. [**bride,** and **ale,** a feast.]

bride, *brīd, n.* a woman about to be married or newly married.—*ns.* **bride'-cake, bride's'-cake,** the cake distributed at a wedding; **bride'-groom,** a man about to be married: a man newly married; **bride'maid, bride's'-maid,** and **bride'man, bride's'-man,** unmarried people who attend the bride and bridegroom at a wedding. [O.E. *brŷd;* O.N. *brūthr,* Ger. *braut,* a bride.]

bridewell, *brīd'wel, n.* a house of correction: a gaol. [From such a place, once a palace, near St *Bride's Well* in London.]

bridge, *brij, n.* a structure by which traffic is conveyed over a river or intervening space: the narrow raised platform whence the captain of a ship gives directions: the bony part of the nose: the support of the strings of a violin: (*fig.*) anything that connects across a gap.—*v.t.* to be, or to build, a bridge over (also *fig.*): to make an electrical connection between.—*n.* **bridge'head,** a fortification covering the end of a bridge nearest to the enemy's position: any advanced position seized in enemy territory.—**bridging loan,** provision of credit necessary for a business transaction. [O.E. *brycg;* Ger. *brücke.*]

bridge, *brij, n.* a modification of whist in which the dealer has the option of declaring which suit shall be trumps—the original form being superseded by *auction bridge* and *contract bridge.* [Ety. uncertain.]

bridle, *brī'dl, n.* the head-gear to which a horse's reins are attached: any restraint.—*v.t.* to put a bridle on: to manage by a bridle: to restrain.—*v.i.* to toss the head proudly like a restive horse (often with *up* and *at*).—*ns.* **bri'dle-hand,** the left-hand; **bri'dle-path, -road,** a path or way for horsemen. [O.E. *brīdel;* O.H.G. *brittel.*]

brief, *brēf, n.* a short account of a client's case for the instruction of counsel: a writ: a short statement of any kind.—*v.t.* to furnish with instructions.—*adj.* short: concise.—*adv.* **brief'ly.**—*n.* **brief'ness.**—*adj.* **brief'less,** without a brief.—*n.* **brief'-case,** a small case for carrying documents.—**hold a brief for,** to be, or assume

Neutral vowels in unaccented syllables: *em'pér-ór;* for certain sounds in foreign words see p. ix.

86

the attitude of, an advocate for, of; **in brief**, in few words. [Fr. *bref* — L. *brevis*, short.]

brier, briar, brī'ér, *n.* a prickly shrub: a wild rose-bush.—*adj.* **brī'ery, brī'ary**. [O.E. (Anglian) *brēr*.]

brier, briar, brī'ér, *n.* the white heath, a shrub grown in France, from whose root tobacco-pipes are made: a pipe of this wood.—*n.* **brier-, briar-root**, the root of the brier or white heath. [Fr. *bruyère*, heath.]

brig, brig, *n.* a two-masted, square-rigged vessel. [Shortened from **brigantine**.]

brigade, brig-ād', *n.* a body of troops consisting of two or more regiments, battalions or batteries, and commanded by a general officer: an organised troop.—*ns.* **brigade'-ma'jor**, a staff-officer attached to a brigade; **brigadier'**, formerly **brigadier'-gen'eral**, a general officer of the lowest grade, who has command of a brigade. [Fr. *brigade* — It. *brigata* — Low L. *briga*, strife.]

brigand, brig'ánd, *n.* a freebooter. *n.* **brig'and age**, plundering. [Fr.,—It. *brigante* — *briga*, strife.]

brigantine, brig'án-tēn, *n.* a brig with fore-and-aft sails on the main mast. [Fr. *brigantin* — It. *brigantino*, a pirate ship.]

bright, brīt, *adj.* shining: clear: (*arch.*) beautiful: cheerful: clever: illustrious.—*adv.* brightly: clearly.—*v.t.* **bright'en**, to make bright or brighter.—*v.i.* to grow bright or brighter.—*adv.* **bright'ly**.—*n.* **bright'ness**—**bright and early**, in good time. [O.E. *byrht*, *beorht*; cog. with L. *flagrāre*, to flame.]

Bright's-disease, brīts'-diz-ēz', *n.* a generic name for a group of diseases of the kidneys. [From Dr Richard *Bright* (1789-1858).]

brill, bril, *n.* a flat-fish allied to the turbot, spotted with white. [Ety. unknown.]

brilliant, bril'yánt, *adj.* sparkling: splendid: talented.—*n.* a diamond of the finest cut.—*adv.* **brill'iantly**.—*ns.* **brill'iance**, **brill'iancy**, brightness: splendour: great cleverness: one of the three attributes of colour—white having the highest brilliance and black having zero brilliance, and light, medium, and dark grey representing respectively high, medium, and low brilliance; **brilliantine** (*bril'yán-tēn*), a dressing to make the hair glossy. [Fr. *brillant*, pr.p. of *briller*, to shine—Low L. *beryllus*, a beryl.]

brim, brim, *n.* the edge of a river, lake, or hollow vessel: the rim of a hat.—*v.t.* to fill to the brim.—*v.i.* to be full to the brim:—*pr.p.* brimm'ing;*pa.p.* brimmed.—*adj.* **brim'ful, brim'full**, full to the brim: completely full.—**brim over**, to overflow. [M.E. *brymme*.]

brimstone, brim'stōn, *n.* roll sulphur. [Lit. burning stone; from O.E. *brȳne*, a burning—*byrnan*, to burn, and **stone**.]

brinded, brin'did, **brindle(d)**, brin'dl(d), *adj.* brownish or grey, marked with darker spots or streaks. [Prob. connected with **brand**.]

brine, brīn, *n.* very salt water: the sea.—*ns.* **brine'-pan, -pit**, a pan or pit in which brine is evaporated, leaving salt: a salt spring.—*adj.* **brin'y**, pertaining to brine or to the sea: salt.—**the briny** (*coll.*), the sea. [O.E. *brȳne*, a burning; applied to salt liquor, from its burning, biting quality.]

bring, bring, *v.t.* to fetch, to lead or carry hither—opp. to *take*, to convey: (*fig.*) to cause to come (e.g. rain, relief), to result in: to induce: to adduce or institute (e.g. an argument, a charge):—*pa.t.* and *pa.p.* brought (*brawt*).—*n.* **bringer**.—**bring about**, to bring to pass, to effect; **bring down**, to humble: to cause to fall; **bring down the house**, to cause tumultuous applause; **bring forth**, to give birth to, to produce; **bring home to**, to prove to, to impress upon; **bring in**, to introduce: to yield: to pronounce (a verdict); **bring low**, to humble; **bring off**, to rescue: to achieve; **bring on**, to cause to happen or to advance; **bring oneself to**, to induce oneself to; **bring out**, to make clear or prominent: to put before the public: to introduce formally into society; **bring round**, to restore from illness or unconsciousness: to win over; **bring to**, to restore to consciousness: (*naut.*) to bring to a standstill; **bring up**, to rear or educate: to introduce to notice; **bring up the rear**, to come last. [O.E. *bringan*, to carry, to bring; allied perh. to **bear**.]

brink, bringk, *n.* the edge or border of a steep place or of a river (often *fig.*).—*n.* **brink'man**, one who practises **brink'manship**, the action or art of going to the very edge of, but not into, war or other disaster, in pursuit of a policy. (First used in 1956 following a statement by J. Foster Dulles, U.S. Secretary of State, that U.S. diplomacy had three times walked to the brink of war.) [Prob. Dan. *brink*, declivity.]

briony. Same as **bryony**.

briquette, bri-ket', *n.* a brick-shaped block of fuel made of coal-dust. [Fr. *briquette*, dim. of *brique*, a **brick**.]

brisk, brisk, *adj.* full of life and spirit: active, energetic: effervescent (of liquors).—*adv.* **brisk'ly**. *n.* **brisk'ness**. [Perh. Celtic; perh. Fr. *brusque*.]

brisket, brisk'ét, *n.* the part of the breast next to the ribs [Perh. Fr. *brechet*, *brichet*.]

brisling, bris'ling, *n.* a Norwegian sprat. [Norw., sprat.]

bristle, bris'l, *n.* a short, stiff hair.—*v.i.* to stand erect, as bristles: to have the bristles erect (*lit.* and *fig.*) showing anger or desire to resist:—*pr.p.* brist'ling, *pa.p.* brist'led.—*adj.* **brist'ly**, set with bristles: rough.—**bristle with**, to be full of, beset with. [Conn. with O.E. *byrst*, a bristle.]

bristol-board, bris'tól bōrd. -bōrd. *n.* a smooth pasteboard. [From the town *Bristol*, England.]

Britannia, brit-an'i-a, *n.* Britain: female figure personifying it.—*adj.* **Britann'ic**.—**Britannia metal**, an alloy of tin with antimony and a little copper or zinc. [L. *Britannia*.]

British, brit'ish, *adj.* pertaining to Britain, to its former or present inhabitants or citizens, or to the empire or commonwealth of nations of which it is the nucleus.—*n.* the language of the ancient Britons, Welsh.—**British Standard Time** (1968-70), time one hour ahead of Greenwich Mean Time. [O.E. *Brettisc* — *Bret*, a Briton, Welshman.]

Briton, brit'ón, *n.* one of the Brythonic inhabitants of Britain, or one of their descendants: a native or citizen of Great Britain or of any of the associated states. [L. *Britto*, from root of

Brython.]

brittle, *brit'l*, *adj.* easily broken: frail.—*n.*
britt'leness. [O.E. *brēotan*, to break.]

broach, *brōch*, *n.* an instrument for boring: a
spit.—*v.t.* to pierce, as a cask, to tap: to open
up or begin (a subject). [Fr. *broche*; cf.
brooch.]

broad, *brōd*, *adj.* wide: large, free or open:
coarse, indelicate: strongly marked in pronunciation or dialect: tolerant: giving prominence
to main elements, or harmony of the whole,
without insisting on detail.—*n.* the broad part:
(in Norfolk) a lake-like expansion of a river:
(*slang*) a woman, a prostitute.—*advs.* **broad**,
broad'ly.—*ns.* **broad'-arr'ow**, a mark (↑)
stamped on British government property;
broad'-brim, a hat with a broad brim, such as
those worn by Quakers: (*coll.*) a Quaker.—*adj.*
broad'cast, scattered or sown by hand: wide-
spread: brought to general notice, esp. by
radio or television.—*adv.* in all directions.—*n.*
sowing by broadcasting: general dissemina-
tion: transmission by radio or television for
public reception: the matter so transmitted.—
v.t. to scatter broadcast: to publish widely: to
transmit by radio or television:—*pa.t.* and
pa.p. broadcast.—*ns.* **broad'caster**; **broad'-
cloth**, a fine kind of woollen fulled cloth, used
for men's garments.—*v.t.* and *v.i.* **broad'en**, to
make or grow broad or broader.—*ns.* **broad'-
gauge** (see **gauge**); **broad'ness**; **broad'side**,
the side of a ship: all the guns on one side of
a ship of war, or their simultaneous discharge:
a large sheet of paper with matter (often
popular) printed on one side only (also **broad-
sheet**).—*adj.* **broad'-spectrum**, of antibiotics,
effective against a wide range of bacteria.—*n.*
broad'sword, a cutting sword with a broad
blade.—**broad jump**, (*U.S.*) long jump; **broad
Scots** or **Scotch**, Scottish dialect. [O.E. *brād.*]

brobdingnagian, *brob-ding-nag'i-àn*, *n.* (*cap.*)
an inhabitant of the fabulous region of *Brob-
dingnag* (in *Gulliver's Travels*), where everything was gigantic: hence, a giant.—*adj.*
gigantic.

brocade, *brok-ād'*, *n.* a silk stuff on which figures are wrought.—*adj.* **brocad'ed**, woven,
worked, or dressed in brocade. [It. *broccato*,
Fr. *brocart*, from It. *broccare*, Fr. *brocher*, to
prick, stitch.]

broccoli, *brok'o-li*, *n.* a hardy variety of cauliflower. [It.; pl. of *broccolo*, a sprout, dim. of
brocco, a skewer, a shoot.]

broch, *broħ*, *n.* an ancient dry-built circular
castle, chiefly found in the north of Scotland.—Also **brogh** and **brough**. [Scot.—O.N.
borg; O.E. *burh.*]

brochure, *bro-shōōr'*, *n.* a pamphlet. [Fr., lit. a
small book, stitched—*brocher*, to stitch.]

brock, *brok*, *n.* a badger. [O.E. *brocc*, from Celt.]

broderie anglaise, *brod-rē ā-glāz*, openwork
embroidery. [Fr., English embroidery.]

brog, *brog*, *n* (*Scot.*) an awl.—*v.t.* to prick.

brogue, *brōg*, *n.* a stout shoe: a manner of pronunciation, esp. the Irish (perh. a different
word). [Ir. *bróg*, Gael, *bròg*, a shoe.]

broider, *broid'ér*, **broidery**, *broid'ér-i.* Same as
embroider, **embroidery**.

broil, *broil*, *n.* a noisy quarrel: a confused disturbance. [Fr. *brouiller*, to entangle, disorder.]

broil, *broil*, *v.t.* to cook over hot coals: to grill.—
v.i. to be greatly heated.—*n.* **broil'er**, a quickly
reared young chicken sold ready for broiling:
(*slang*) a very hot day. [Ety dub.]

broke, *brōk*, *pa.t.* and old *pa.p.* of **break**, surviving as *pa.p.* chiefly in sense of hard up.

broken, *brō'kn*, *pa.p.* of **break**.—*pa.adj.* incomplete, interrupted, intermittent: irregular: imperfect (e.g. *he speaks broken English*):
humbled: ruined.—*adv.* **brok'enly**.—*adjs.*
brok'en-heart'ed, crushed with grief;
brok'en-wind'ed, having short breath or disordered respiration, as a horse.—**broken
home**, the home of children whose parents
are divorced or have separated; **broken man**,
an outlaw (*hist.*): a bankrupt: one whose
spirits have been crushed.

broker, *brōk'ér*, *n.* one employed to buy and sell
for others: a second-hand dealer.—*n.* **brok'erage**, the business of a broker; the commission
charged by a broker. [M.E. *brocour*—Anglo-Fr.
brocour.]

bromine, *brō'mēn*, *-min*, *-mīn*, *n.* a non-metallic
element (symbol Br; atomic no. 35), named
from its pungent fumes.—*n.* **brō'mīde**, a compound of bromine and another element or
radical, esp. those used as medicinal sedatives.—**bromide paper**, in photography, paper
with a highly sensitive surface containing
bromide of silver, used in printing from a
negative. [Gr. *brōmos*, a stink.]

broncho, **bronco**, *brong'ko*, *n.* (*U.S.*) a half-
tamed horse. [Sp. *bronco*, rough, sturdy.]

bronchus, *brongk'us*, *n.* either of the main forks
of the windpipe:—*pl.* **bronch'ī**.—*n.pl.* **bron-
ch'ia**, erroneously **bronch'iae**, the ramifica-
tions of the bronchi.—*adjs.* **bronch'ial**; **bron-
chit'ic**, pertaining to bronchitis.—*n.* one suffering from bronchitis.—*n.* **bronchitis**
(*brongk-ī'tis*), inflammation of the lining of
the bronchial tubes. [Gr. *bronchos*, windpipe.]

brontosaurus, *bron-to-sō'rus*, *n.* a genus of
dinosaurs, found fossil in U.S.A. [Gr. *brontē*,
thunder, *sauros*, lizard.]

bronze, *bronz*, *n.* an alloy of copper and tin used
in various ways since prehistoric times: a
copper alloy without tin: anything cast in
bronze: the colour of bronze.—*adj.* made of, or
coloured like, bronze.—*p.adj.* **bronzed**, coated
with bronze: bronze-coloured, sunburned.—
Bronze Age or **Period**, the prehistoric period
between the Stone and Iron Ages, in which
tools and weapons were made from bronze.
[Fr.,—It. *bronzo*—L. *Brundusium*, Brindisi.]

brooch, *brōch*, *n.* an ornamental clasp with an
attached pin fitting into a hook. [Fr. *broche*, a
spit. Cf. **broach**.]

brood, *brōōd*, *v.i.* to sit as a hen on eggs: to hang
or hover (over): to meditate silently (on,
over): to think anxiously for some time.—*n.*
something bred: offspring: a race, kind: the
number hatched at once.—*adj.* for breeding,
as in *brood*-mare, &c.—*adj.* **brood'y**, inclined
to sit or incubate. [O.E. *brōd*; Du. *broed*; from
the same root as **breed**.]

brook, *brŏŏk*, *n.* a small stream.—*n.* **brook'let**, a
little brook. [O.E. *brōc*, water breaking forth;
Du. *broek*, Ger. *bruch.*]

brook, *brŏŏk*, *v.t.* (*arch.*) to enjoy: to bear or
endure. [O.E. *brūcan*, to use, enjoy; Ger.

Neutral vowels in unaccented syllables: *em'pér-ór*; for certain sounds in foreign words see p. ix.

brauchen, L. *frui, fructus.*]

brooklime, *brŏŏk'līm*, *n.* a speedwell that grows in brooks and ditches. [**brook**, and O.E. *hleomoc*, brooklime.]

broom, *brōōm*, *n.* a wild evergreen shrub of the pea family with yellow flowers: any of various kindred shrubs: a besom—orig. made of its twigs: a long-handled sweeping brush.—*ns.* **broom'staff**, **broom'stick**, the handle of a broom. [O.E. *brōm.*]

brose, *brōz*, *n.* a food made by pouring boiling water or milk on meal, esp. oatmeal. [Scot.]

broth, *broth*, *n.* a soup, esp. one containing vegetables and barley or rice: (*bacteriology*) a fluid culture medium. [O.E. *broth*—*brēowan*, to brew.]

brothel, *broth'-*, *brŏTH'él*, *n.* a house of prostitution. [M.E. *brothel*, a worthless person—O.E. *brothen*, ruined—*brēothen*, to go to ruin.]

brother, *bruTH'ér*, *n.* the name applied to a male child by the other children of his parents: anyone closely united with or resembling another: a fellow member of any group or association:—*pl.* **broth'ers** and **breth'ren** (the latter esp. used in the sense of fellowmembership of guilds, religious communities, &c.). *ns.* **broth'er-ger'man**, a brother having the same father and mother, in contradistinction to a *half-brother*, by one parent only; **broth'erhood**, the state of being a brother: an association of men for any purpose; **broth'er-in-law**, the brother of a husband or wife: a sister's husband:—*pl.* **brothers-in-law.**—*adj.* **broth'erly**, like a brother: kind: affectionate.—*n.* **broth'erliness.** [O.E. *brōthor*; cog. with Ger. *bruder*, Gael, *brathuir*, L. *frater*, &c.]

brougham, *brōō'ám*, *brō'ám*, *brōōm*, *n.* a one-horse close carriage, named after Lord *Brougham* (1778–1868): types of motor-car of similar construction.

brought, *bröt*, *pa.t.* and *pa.p.* of **bring.**

brouhaha, *bruhaha*, *brōō'hä-hä*, *n.* fuss, clamour. [Fr.; perh. from Heb.]

brow, *brow*, *n.* the eyebrow, the ridge over the eyes: the forehead: the edge of a hill.—*v.t.* **brow'beat**, to cow by stern looks or speech, to bully. [O.E. *brū*; O.N. *brún.*]

brown, *brown*, *adj.* of a dark or dusky colour, inclining to red or yellow: sunburnt.—*n.* a dark-reddish colour.—*v.t.* to give a brown colour to: to roast brown.—*ns.* **brown'-bread**, bread made of unbolted flour; **brown'-coal**, lignite—*adj.* **brown'ish.**—*n.* **Brown'shirt**, a member of Hitler's organisation of storm-troopers: a Nazi.—**brown study**, a reverie, orig. a gloomy one; **brown sugar**, unrefined or partially refined sugar. [O.E. *brūn*; Du. *bruin*, Ger. *braun.*]

brownie, *brown'i*, *n.* in Scottish folklore, a friendly domestic goblin: (*cap.*) a junior Girl Guide in brown garb. [**brown.**]

browse, *browz*, *v.t.* and *v.i.* to feed on the rough shoots or leaves of plants: to read desultorily. [O.Fr. *brouster*—*broust*, a sprout.]

brucellosis, *brōō-sél-ō'sis*, *n.* a bacterial disease in animals communicable to man as a relapsing fever. [Sir David *Bruce*, bacteriologist.]

bruin, *brōō'in*, *n.* a bear, so called from the name of the bear in the famous beast epic *Reynard*

the Fox. [Du. *bruin*, **brown.**]

bruise, *brōōz*, *v.t.* to crush or injure by violent impact (also *fig.*).—*n.* an injury with discoloration of the skin usu. made by anything heavy and blunt.—*n.* **bruis'er**, one that bruises: a prize-fighter. [O.E. *brȳsan*, to crush.]

bruit, *brōōt*, *n.* noise: a rumour.—*v.t.* to noise abroad: to make famous. [Fr. *bruit*—Fr. *bruire*; *cf.* Low L. *brugītus*; prob. imit.]

brummagem, *brum'a-jem*, *adj.* showy but worthless. [Another form of *Birmingham.*]

brunette, *brŏŏn-et'*, *n.* a woman with brown or dark hair. [Fr. dim. of *brun*, brown.]

brunt, *brunt*, *n.* the shock of an onset, the force of a blow: the chief shock or strain of anything (*bear the brunt of*). [Origin obscure.]

brush, *brush*, *n.* an instrument set with bristles or the like for cleansing or for applying friction or a coating of some material: a painter's hair pencil: a bushy tail: a grazing contact: a skirmish: **an area covered with thickets**: (*Australia*) a forest, the backwoods.—*v.t.* to pass a brush over: to remove by a sweeping motion.—*v.i.* to pass with light contact.—*ns.* **brush'-off**, a rebuff: a curt setting aside or dismissal; **brush'wood**, loppings and broken branches: underwood or stunted wood.—**brush turkey**, a gallinaceous bird of eastern Australia that builds a mound of decaying matter in which to hatch its eggs; **to brush up**, to brighten: to revive in the memory. [O.Fr. *brosse*, brushwood.]

brusque, *brŏŏsk*, *brusk*, *adj.* blunt and abrupt in manner.—*adv.* **brusque'ly.**—*ns.* **brusque'ness**, **brusquerie** (*brŏŏs'ke-rē*). [Fr.]

Brussels, *brus'lz*, *n.* contracted from **Brussels-carpet**, a kind of carpet having a woollen surface on a foundation of linen.—*n.pl.* **Bruss'els-sprouts**, a variety of the common cabbage with sprouts like miniature cabbages. [Named from *Brussels* in Belgium.]

brute, *brōōt*, *adj.* belonging to, or as if belonging to, the lower animals: soulless: irrational: stupid: cruel: material, without consciousness.—*n.* one of the lower animals: a brutal man.—*adj.* **brut'al**, like a brute: unfeeling: inhuman.—*v.t.* **brut'alise**, to make like a brute, to degrade.—*n.* **brutal'ity.**—*adv.* **brut'ally.**—*adj.* **brut'ish**, brutal: stupid.—*adv.* **brut'ishly.**—*n.* **brut'ishness.**—**brute force**, sheer strength. [Fr. *brut*—L. *brūtus*, dull, irrational.]

bryony, *brī'o-ni*, *n.* a wild climbing plant, common in English hedgerows. [Through L.—Gr. *bryōnia.*]

Brython, *brith'on*, *n.* a Celt of the group to which Welsh, Cornish, and Bretons belong—distinguished from Gadhel or Goidel.—*adj.* **Brython'ic.** [W. *Brython*, Briton.]

bubble, *bub'l*, *n.* a bladder of liquid or solidified liquid blown out with gas: anything empty: an unsound or fraudulent scheme—*adj.* unsubstantial.—*v.i.* to rise in bubbles: to show great joy, rage, &c.:—*pr.p.* **bubb'ling**; *pa.p.* **bubb'led.**—*adj.* **bubb'ly.**—*n.* (*slang*) champagne.—*ns.* **bubb'le-car**, a midget motor-car resembling a bubble in its rounded line and windowed top; **bubb'le-cham'ber**, device for showing the path of a charged particle by the string of bubbles left in its track—variant of the cloud chamber; **bubble and squeak**, meat

fāte, fär; mē, hûr (her); *mīne; mōte, för; mūte; mōōn, fŏŏt;* THen (then)

and cabbage fried together. [Cf. Swed. *bubbla,* Du. *bobbel.*]

bubo, *bū'bo, n.* an inflammatory swelling of the glands in the groin or armpit.—*adj.* **bubon'ic,** accompanied by buboes. [L.,—Gr. *boubōn,* the groin, a bubo.]

buccaneer, buccanier, *buk'an-ēr', n.* one of the pirates in the West Indies during the seventeenth century: a sea-robber: an adventurer. —*v.i.* to act as a buccaneer. [Fr. *boucaner,* to smoke meat—Carib *boucan,* a wooden gridiron. The French settlers in the West Indies cooked their meat on a *boucan* in native fashion, and were hence called *boucaniers.*]

buck, *buk, n.* the male of the deer, goat, hare, and rabbit: a male fallow-deer: a dashing fellow: a counter, marker, in poker: (*U.S.*) a dollar.—*v.i.* (of a horse or mule—a **buck'-jumper**) to attempt to throw the rider by rapid jumps into the air: (*coll.*) to resist.— *p.adj.* **bucked** (*slang*), cheered, invigorated.— *ns.* **buck'-shot,** a large kind of shot, used in shooting ducks; **buck'skin,** a soft leather made of deerskin or sheepskin: (*pl.*) breeches or suit of buckskin.—*adj.* made of or like the skin of a buck.—*n.* **buck'-tooth,** a projecting tooth.—**buck up** (*slang*), to bestir oneself: to cheer up.—**pass the buck** (see **pass**). [O.E. *buc, bucca;* Du. *bok,* Ger. *bock,* he-goat.]

buckboard, *buk'bōrd, -bord, n.* a board or rail projecting over cart wheels. [O.E. *būc,* body, and **board.**]

bucket, *buk'et, n.* a vessel for drawing or holding water, &c.: one of the compartments on the circumference of a water-wheel, or one of the scoops of a dredging machine: a leather socket for holding a whip, &c.—*n.* **buck'et-shop,** the office of an outside broker—mere agent for bets on the rise or fall of prices of stock, &c.—**bucket seat,** a round-backed, often forward-tipping, seat for one in a motor-car, aeroplane. [Prob. conn. with O.E. *būc,* a pitcher; or O.Fr. *buket,* a pail.]

buckle, *buk'l, n.* a fastening for a strap or band, consisting of a rim and a tongue: a curled or warped condition.—*v.t.* to connect with a buckle: to join closely: to prepare (oneself) for action.—*v.i.* to apply oneself zealously (to).—*v.t.* and *v.i.* to warp: to bend or crumple (of a metal object—e.g. a wheel, a girder).—*n.* **buck'ler,** a small shield used for parrying. [Fr. *boucle,* the boss of a shield, a ring—Low L. *buccula.*]

buckram, *buk'ram, n.* a coarse open-woven fabric of jute, cotton, or linen, stiffened with size: stiffness in manners and appearance.—*adj.* made of buckram: stiff: precise. [O.Fr. *boquerant.*]

buckshish. Same as **backsheesh.**

buckwheat, *buk'hwēt, n.* a kind of grain having triangular seeds like the kernels of beech-nuts. [Prob. Du. *boekweit,* or Ger. *buchweizen,* beech-wheat.]

bucolic, -al, *bū-kol'ik, -ál, adj.* pertaining to the tending of cattle: rustic.—*n.* **bucol'ic,** a pastoral poem: a rustic. [L.,—Gr. *boukolikos—boukolos,* a herdsman.]

bud, *bud, n.* an undeveloped stage of a branch, consisting of a shoot bearing undeveloped leaves, and sometimes one or more young flowers.—*v.i.* to put forth buds: to begin to grow.—*v.t.* to graft by inserting a bud under the bark of another tree:—*pr.p.* budd'ing; *pa.p.* budd'ed.—*n.* **budd'ing,** the production of daughter cells in the form of rounded outgrowths, characteristic of yeasts, &c.: (*zool.*) a primitive method of asexual reproduction by growth, specialisation, and separation of part of the parent.—**in bud,** in a budding condition; **nip in the bud,** to destroy at its very beginning. [M.E. *budde;* perh. related to Du. *bot,* a bud.]

Buddha, *bōŏd'ä, n.* a title applied to Sakyamuni or Gautama, the founder of the Buddhist religion or **Budd'hism:** a general name for any of a series of teachers of which he is one.—*n.* **Budd'hist,** a believer in Buddhism. [Sans. *buddha,* wise, from *budh,* to know.]

budge, *buj, v.i.* and *v.t.* to move or stir. [Fr. *bouger*—It. *bulicare,* to boil—L. *bullīre.*]

budgerigar, *buj-er-i-gär', n.* a favourite aviary and cage bird, an Australian parrakeet.—Also (*coll.*) **budgie.** [Austr. native *budgeri,* good, *gar,* cockatoo.]

budget, *buj-et, n.* a sack with its contents: a collection, stock: a financial statement and programme put before parliament by the Chancellor of the Exchequer: any plan of expenditure.—*v.i.* to prepare a budget or plan of revenue and expenditure: to allow (for) in a budget.—Also *v.t.* [Fr. *bougette,* dim. of *bouge,* a pouch—L. *bulga.*]

buff, *buf, n.* white leather from which the grain surface has been removed, used for army accoutrements: a military coat: the colour of buff, a light yellow: (*pl.—cap.*) certain regiments in the British army, so named from their former buff-coloured facings: (*coll.*) bare skin. [Fr. *buffle,* a buffalo.]

buffalo, *buf'a-lō, n.* a name for certain large animals of the ox kind, esp. the tame Asiatic buffalo and the wild Cape buffalo: (*U.S.*) the American bison:—*pl.* **buff'aloes.**—*n.* **buff'alo-robe,** a bison-hide rug. [It. *buffalo,* through L. from Gr. *boubalos.*]

buffer, *buf'ér, n.* a mechanical apparatus for deadening the force of a concussion, as on railway carriages: (*chem.*) a substance or mixture which opposes change of hydrogen-ion concentration in a solution.—*v.t.* to treat with a buffer.—*n.* **buff'er-state,** a neutral country lying between two rival states. [Prob. from obs. *buff,* to strike.]

buffet, *buf'et, n.* a blow with the fist, a slap.—*v.t.* to strike with the hand or fist: to contend against.—*v.i.* to contend (with).—*n.* **buffet'ing,** repeated blows: irregular oscillation of any part of an aircraft, caused by an eddying wake from some other part. [O.Fr. *buffet*—*buffe,* a blow, esp. on the cheek.]

buffet, *buf'et, n.* a kind of sideboard: a low stool: a refreshment-bar (in this sense usu. pronounced *būf'ā*).—**buffet car,** railway coach providing a light meal service. [Fr. *buffet.*]

buffoon, *buf-ōōn', n.* one who amuses by jests, grimaces, &c.: a clown: a fool.—*n.* **buffoon'ery,** ludicrous or vulgar jesting. [Fr. *bouffon*—It. *buffone; buffare,* to' jest.]

bug, *bug, n.* an object of terror.—*ns.* **bug'aboo,** a bogy; **bug'bear,** an object of terror (generally

Neutral vowels in unaccented syllables: *em'pér-ór*; for certain sounds in foreign words see p. ix.

imaginary) or of abhorrence. [M.E. *bugge*, prob. W. *bwg*, a hobgoblin.]

bug, *bug, n.* a name applied loosely to certain insects,. esp. to one that infests houses and beds: in America applied to any insect or to a disease germ: (*U.S.*) a crazy idea: a crazy person: a hidden microphone: a lunar excursion module.—*v.t.* to plant a concealed listening device in: (*slang*) to annoy.—**big bug,** (*coll.*) an important person.

bug, *bug, v.i.* (*U.S.*) to start or bulge.—*adjs.* **bug'-eyed',** with eyes protruding in astonishment, &c.

buggy, *bug'i, n.* a light one-horse vehicle of various kinds. [Ety. unknown.]

bugle, *bū'gl,* **bugle-horn,** *bū'gl-horn, ns.* a hunting-horn, orig. a buffalo-horn: a wind instrument, with or without keys, used chiefly for military signals.—*n.* **bū'gler,** one who plays upon the bugle. [O.Fr. *bugle*—L. *būculus,* dim. of *bōs,* an ox.]

buhl, *bōōl, n.* unburnished gold, brass, or mother-of-pearl worked in patterns for inlaying: furniture ornamented with such. [From André Charles *Boulle* (1642-1732), the inventor.]

build, *bild, v.t.* to erect: to form or construct.—*v.i.* to depend (with *on, upon*):—*pa.p.* built (*arch.* build'ed).—*n.* construction: make.—*ns.* **build'er; building,** the art of erecting houses, &c.: anything built; **build'-up,** a building up, strengthening: a working up of favourable publicity: preliminaries leading up to a climax in a story, &c.—*adjs.* **built'-in,** formed as part of a main structure, esp. if recessed (as *built-in wardrobe*): present as part of one's genetic inheritance (as *built-in aptitude*): firmly fixed; **built'-up,** of an area, covered with buildings.—**building society,** a society that advances money to its members towards providing them with dwelling-houses, against periodical subscriptions; **build up,** to close up by building: to cover with buildings: to establish gradually (as a reputation). [O.E. *gebyld,* pa.p. of an assumed *byldan,* to build—*bold,* a dwelling.]

bulb, *bulb, n.* a subterranean bud with swollen leaf bases in which reserve materials are stored, as in onions, narcissi, &c.: any similar protuberance: the globe of an electric light.—*adjs.* **bulbed, bul'bous.** [L. *bulbus*—Gr. *bolbos,* an onion.]

bulbul, *bōōl'bōōl, n.* the 'Persian nightingale': any of several birds of Asia and East Africa. [Ar.]

bulge, *bulj, n.* the widest part of a cask: a swelling: a rounded projecting part: a temporary increase.—*v.i.* to swell out.—*adj.* **bul'gy.** [O.Fr. *boulge,* prob. L. *bulga,* a leather knapsack; cf. **bilge.**]

bulk, *bulk, n.* magnitude or size: great size: large quantity: the greater part: the whole cargo in the hold.—*v.i.* to be in bulk: to be of weight or importance.—*adj.* **bulk'y,** having bulk: unwieldy.—*n.* **bulk'iness.**—**bulk carrier,** vessel carrying cargo which is not in package form.—**load in bulk,** to put cargo in loose; **sell in bulk,** to sell cargo as it is in the hold: to sell in large quantities. [Prob. Scand.; O.N. *bulki,* a heap.]

bulkhead, *bulk'hed, n.* a partition separating one part of a ship's interior from another.

bull, *bōōl, n.* the male of bovine and certain other animals, as the whale, walrus, elephant, moose: (*cap.*) *Taurus* (sign of the zodiac or constellation): one who seeks to raise the price of stocks and speculates on a rise (cf. **bear**): a bull's-eye: (*slang*) nonsense: (*U.S. slang*) policeman.—*adj.* male. *ns.* **bull'-bait'ing,** the sport of baiting or exciting bulls with dogs; **bull'dog,** a breed of dogs of great courage, formerly used for baiting bulls; **bull'-fight,** a popular spectacle in Spain, in which a bull is goaded to fury by mounted men with lances, and finally despatched by a swordsman on foot; **bull'finch,** a species of red-breasted finch; **bull'-frog,** a large North American frog.—*adj.* **bull'-head'ed,** impetuous and obstinate.—*ns.* **bull'ock,** an ox or castrated bull; **bull'-ring,** the enclosure in which a bull-fight takes place; **bull roarer,** a primitive magic device consisting of a serrated strip of wood on the end of a cord which rotates when swung round, emitting a low musical note; **bull's-eye,** the centre of a target, of a different colour from the rest, and usually round: a thick lump of coloured or striped candy; **bull'-terr'ier,** a cross-breed between the bulldog and the terrier; **bull'-trout,** a name applied in different localities to different varicties of trout, also to salmon.—**take the bull by the horns,** to take the initiative boldly. [M.E. *bole,* prob. Scand. *bole, boli*; most prob. related to **bellow.**]

bull, *bōōl, n.* an edict of the pope which has his seal affixed. [L. *bulla,* a knob, a leaden seal.]

bull, *bōōl, n.* a ludicrous inconsistency in speech. [Prob. O.Fr. *boul,* cheat.]

bulldoze, *bōōl'dōz, v.t.* (*U.S.*) to intimidate: to clear by bulldozer.—*n.* **bull'dozer,** tractor with horizontal ram for clearing and levelling ground. [Origin obscure.]

bullet, *bōōl'et, n.* the ball fired from any kind of small-arm.—*n.* **bull'et-head,** a head round like a bullet: (*U.S.*) an obstinate fellow.—*adjs.* **bull'ct-head'ed; bull'et-proof,** proof against bullets. [Fr. *boulette,* dim. of *boule,* a ball—L. *bulla.*]

bulletin, *bōōl'e-tin, n.* an official report of public news, or of a patient's progress. [Fr.,—It. *bullettino.*]

bullion, *bōōl'yon, n.* gold and silver in the mass and uncoined. [Ety. uncertain, app. related to L.L. *bullio,* a boiling, melting.]

bullock. See **bull** (1).

bully, *bōōl'i, n.* a cruel and boastful oppressor of the weak.—*adj.* blustering: brisk: (*U.S.*) excellent.—*v.t.* to treat with persistent petty cruelty: to domineer over: to coerce (into).—*pr.p.* bull'ying; *pa.p.* bull'ied.—*v.t.* **bull'y-rag** (*coll.*), to overawe by threats and taunts. [Perh. Du. *boel,* a lover; cf. Ger. *buhle.*]

bully, *bōōl'i,* **bully-beef,** *bōōl'i-bēf, ns.* canned or pickled beef. [Prob. Fr. *bouilli,* boiled beef, influenced by **bull** (1).]

bulrush, *bōōl'rush, n.* a tall strong rush. [Perh. **bull** (1), in sense of great, and **rush** (2).]

bulwark, *bōōl'wark, n.* a fortification or rampart: the side of a ship projecting above the deck: any means of defence or security.—*v.t.* to defend: to fortify. [Cf. Ger. *bollwerk*.]

bum, *bum, n.* the buttocks.—*n.* **bum'(-)bailiff,** a bailiff who comes behind to make an arrest. [Apparently from *bump* in sense of swelling.]

bum, *bum, n.* (*slang*) a sponger: a tramp.

bum, *bum, v.i.* to hum:—*pr.p.* bumm'ing; *pa.p.* bummed.—*n.* a humming sound.—*n.* **bum'bee** (*Scot.*), a bumble-bee. [Imit.]

bumble, bummle, *bum'(b)l, v.i.* to utter indistinctly: to bungle.—*n.* **bum'ble-bee,** a large wild loud-humming bee, a humble-bee. [Freq. of **bum** (2).]

bumble, *bum'bl, n.* a beadle: a self-important minor official.—*n.* **bum'bledom.** [From Mr *Bumble* in Dickens's *Oliver Twist.*]

bum-boat, *bum'bōt, n.* a boat bringing provisions for sale to ships. [Origin doubtful.]

bumf, *bumf, n.* lavatory paper: (*disparagingly*) papers, official papers, documents.

bump, *bump, v.i.* to knock dully: to jolt.—*v.t.* to strike against or on: to jolt.—*n.* a dull, heavy blow, a thump: a lump or swelling: one of the protuberances on the surface of the skull supposed to indicate certain mental characteristics, hence (*coll.*) faculty: the cry of the bittern.—*n.* **bump'er,** a bar on a motor-car to lessen the shock of collision: a cup or glass filled to the brim: anything large or generous in measure.—Also *adj.*—**bump off** (*slang*), to murder; **bump up** (*slang*), to raise (as prices): to increase size of. [Onomatopoeic.]

bumpkin, *bump'kin, n.* an awkward, clumsy rustic: a clown. [Prob. Du. *boomken,* a log.]

bumptious, *bump'shus, adj.* offensively self-assertive.—*adv.* **bump'tiously.**—*n.* **bump'tiousness.** [Prob. formed from **bump.**]

bun, *bun, n.* a kind of sweet cake: a rounded mass of hair. [Prob. from O.Fr. *bugne,* a swelling.]

bun, *bun, n.* a playful name for a rabbit or a squirrel.—*n.* **bunn'y,** a rabbit.

buna, *bōō'na, n.* one form of synthetic rubber. [From parts of the names of its chemical constituents; orig. trademark.]

bunch, *bunch* or *-sh, n.* a lump (*rare*): a number of things fastened together: a cluster: something in the form of a tuft or knot: a group.—*v.i.* to cluster.—*v.t.* to make a bunch of, to concentrate.—*adj.* **bunch'y,** growing in bunches or like a bunch: bulging.

bundle, *bun'dl, n.* a number of things bound together: a loose package: (*biol.*) a strand of conducting vessels, fibres, &c.—*v.t.* to make into bundles: to put, push hastily or unceremoniously.—*v.i.* to go hurriedly or in confusion (away, off, out). [Conn. with **bind** and **bond.**]

bung, *bung, n.* the stopper of the hole in a barrel: a large cork.—*v.t.* to stop up with a bung.—*n.* **bung'-hole,** a hole for a bung.

bungalow, *bung'ga-lō, n.* a lightly built house of one storey occupied by Europeans in India: any similar house of one storey. [Hindi *bangla,* (house) in the style of Bengal house.]

bungle, *bung'gl, n.* anything clumsily done: a gross blunder.—*v.i.* to act in a clumsy awkward manner.—*v.t.* to make or mend clumsily: to manage awkwardly.—*n.* **bung'ler.** [Ety. obscure; prob. onomatopoeic.]

bunion, *bun'yon, n.* a lump or inflamed swelling

on the first joint of the great toe.

bunk, *bungk, n.* a box or recess in a ship's cabin: a sleeping-berth anywhere.—*n.* **bunk'er,** a large bin or chest, esp. for stowing coals: a sand-pit in a golf-links.—*v.t.* and *v.i.* to fuel.—*adj.* **bunk'ered,** in a bunker: in difficulties.—*n.* **bunk'ering,** loading fuel of any kind into a ship, aeroplane, motor-vehicle, &c. [Prob. of Scand. origin; cf. O.N. *bunki,* Dan. *bunke,* a heap.]

bunk, *bungk, n.* (*slang*) flight (esp. in phrase **do a bunk**).—*v.i.* to flee.

bunkum, *bung'kum, n.* shallow pretentious oratory, humbug: pretentious nonsense—also (*slang*) **bunk.** [From *Buncombe,* U.S.A., whose member in Congress confessed that he was talking simply to please Buncombe.]

bunny. See **bun** (2).

bunsen, *bōōn'sen,* or *bun'sen, adj.* applied to some of the inventions of the great chemist R. W. *Bunsen* (1811–1899).—*n.* **bun'sen-burn'er,** a gas-burner in which air mingles with the gas and produces a smokeless flame of great heating power.

bunt, *bunt, n.* a disease of wheat or the fungus that causes it. [Ety. unknown.]

bunting, *bunt'ing, n.* a thin worsted stuff for ships' colours: flags, cloth decorations.

bunting, *bunt'ing, n.* a genus of finches nearly allied to the crossbills. [Ety. uncertain.]

buntline, *bunt'lin, n.* a rope passing from the foot-rope of a square sail, led up to the masthead and thence on deck, to help in hauling up the sail. [*bunt,* part of a sail, and **line** (2).]

bunyip, *bun'yip, n.* an Australian swamp monster invisible to whites: an impostor. [Native word.]

buoy, *boi, n.* a floating secured mark, serving as a guide or as a warning for navigation, or as a mooring point.—*v.t.* to fix buoys or marks to: to keep afloat, or sustain: to raise the spirits of—in last two meanings usu. with *up.*—*n.* **buoy'ancy,** capacity for floating lightly on water or in the air: (*fig.*) cheerfulness, elasticity of spirit.—*adj.* **buoy'ant,** tending to float: cheerful.—*n.* **life-buoy** (see **life.**) [Du. *boei,* buoy, fetter, through Romance forms, from Low L. *boia,* a collar of leather.]

bur, burr, *bûr, n.* the prickly adhesive seed-case or head of certain plants: rough edge to a line on a dry-point plate.—*n.* **bur'dock,** a plant with a bur or prickly head and docklike leaves. [Cog. with Dan. *borre,* a bur.]

bur, burr, *bûr, n.* the rough sound of *r* pronounced in the throat, as in Northumberland. [Prob. preceding, but perh. from the sound.]

burble, *bûrb'l, v.i.* to talk incoherently, esp. from excitement: to gurgle.—*n.* **burb'ling,** separation of the flow of air from the upper surface of a moving aerofoil. [Prob. onomatopoeic.]

burbot, *bûr'bot, n.* a fish having a longish beard on its lower jaw, the only fresh-water species of the cod family. [Fr. *barbote.*—L. *barba,* a beard.]

burden, *bûrd'n, n.* a load: cargo: tonnage (of a ship): that which is oppressive or difficult to bear: responsibility.—*v.t.* to load: to oppress: to encumber.—*adj.* **bur'densome,** heavy, oppressive. [O.E. *byrthen*—*beran,* to bear.]

burden, *bûrd'n, n.* part of a song repeated at the

Neutral vowels in unaccented syllables: *em'pêr-ôr*; for certain sounds in foreign words see p. ix.

end of every stanza, a refrain: the leading idea (of anything). [Fr. *bourdon,* a humming tone in music—Low L. *burdo,* a drone bee; confused with **burden** (1).]

bureau, *bū-rō′, bū′rō, bū′rō, n.* a combined writing-table and chest of drawers: a chest of drawers: an office or department for collecting and supplying information (e.g. *a labour bureau or exchange*): a government department:—*pl.* **bureaux, bureaus** (-*ōz*). [Fr. *bureau*—O.Fr. *burel,* russet cloth—L. *burrus,* red.]

bureaucracy, *bū-rok′ra-si,* or -*rōk′-, n.* a system of government by officials, responsible only to their chiefs.—*n.* **bur′eaucrat,** one who practises or favours bureaucracy.—*adj.* **bureaucrat′ic.** [bureau, and Gr. *krateein,* to govern.]

burette, *bū-ret′, n.* graduated glass tube, usu. with a tap, for measuring the volume of liquids. [Fr.]

burgeon, *bûr′jon, n.* and *v.i.* Same as **bourgeon.**

burgess, *bûr′jĕs, n.* a freeman or citizen of a borough. [O.Fr. *burgeis.*]

burgh, *bur′ō, n.* another spelling of **borough,** used for Scottish burghs, otherwise archaic.—*ns.* **burg** (same as **borough**), **burgher** (*bûrg′ér*), an inhabitant of a borough: a citizen or freeman.—*adj.* **burghal** (*bûrg′ál*).

burglar, *bûrg′lar, n.* one who enters a building (before 1969, by night) to commit a felony, e.g. to steal.—*adj.* **burglār′ious.**—*adv.* **burglār′iously.**—*v.t.* **burg′le** (a back-formation).—*n.* **burg′lary.** [Ety. uncertain.]

burgomaster, *bûr′gō-mäs-tér, n.* the chief magistrate of a Dutch, Flemish, or German town. [Du. *burgemeester;* Gr. *bürgermeister,* lit. borough-master.]

burgundy, *bûr′gun-di, n.* a French wine, so called from *Burgundy,* the district where it is made

burial, *ber′i-ál, n.* the act of burying. [O.E. *byrgels,* a tomb—*byrgan,* to bury.]

burin, *bū′rin, n.* a chisel used in copper engraving. [Fr.; from root of **bore** (1).]

burke, *bûrk, v.t.* to murder, esp. by stifling: hence (*fig.*) to stifle, to suppress. [From *Burke* (hanged 1829), who committed this crime in order to sell the bodies of his victims for dissection.]

burlesque, *bûr-lesk′, n.* a ludicrous and exaggerated imitation.—*adj.* of the nature of burlesque.—*v.t.* to mock by burlesque. [It. *burlesco;* prob. from Low L. *burra,* a flock of wool, a trifle.]

burly, *bûr′li, adj.* big and sturdy.—*n.* **bur′liness.** [M.E. *borlich;* perh. the same as O.H.G. *burlîh,* high—*bor,* a height.]

Burmese, *bûr′mēz, -mēz′, adj.* relating to Burma or its language.—*n.* a native of Burma, or the language of Burma.

burn, *bûrn, n.* a small stream or brook. [O.E. *burna;* cog. with Du. and Ger. *born.*]

burn, *bûrn, v.t.* to consume or injure by fire: to expose to great heat: to oxidise.—*v.i.* to be on fire: to consume through fire: to feel excess of heat: to be inflamed with passion:—*pa.t.* and *pa.p.* burned, burnt.—*n.* a hurt or mark caused by fire.—*n.* **burn′ing,** conflagration: controlled expenditure of rocket propellant for course adjustment purposes.—Also *adj.*—*ns.* **burn′er,** in a lamp or gas-jet, the part from which the

flame arises, or the whole fixture; **burn′ing-glass,** a convex lens concentrating the sun's rays at its focus and causing ignition; **burnt′-off′ering,** something offered and burned upon an altar as a sacrifice; **burnt′-sienn′a** (see **sienna**).—**burning bush,** the emblem of the Presbyterian churches of Scotland, adopted from Ex. iii. 2: any of several plants; **burning question,** one being hotly discussed; **burn one's boats,** to destroy all means of retreat, to stake everything on success; **burn one's fingers,** to suffer through rash action; **burn up,** to consume by fire: to increase in activity of burning: to make short or easy work of. [O.E. weak trans. verb. *bærnan* confused with strong intrans. *beornan.*]

burnish, *bûrn′ish, v.t.* to make bright by rubbing.—*n.* polish: lustre. [Fr. *burnir, burnissant,* to burnish—*brun,* brown.]

burnous, *bûr-nōōs′, n.* a mantle with a hood much worn by the Arabs. [Fr.—Ar. *burnus.*]

burnt, *pa.t.* and *pa.p.* of **burn.**

burp, *bûrp, v.i.* (*coll.*) to belch.—Also *n.*—*v.t.* to pat a baby's back to cause it to belch.

burr. Same as **bur** (1) and (2).

burrow, *bur′ō, n.* a hole excavated by certain animals for shelter: a refuge.—*v.i.* to make, live in, holes underground, as rabbits: to dwell in a concealed place.—*v.i.* and *v.t.* to tunnel. [Prob. a variant of **borough**—O.E. *beorgan,* to protect.]

bursar, *bûrs′ar, n.* one who keeps the purse, a treasurer: in Scotland, a student assisted by the funds of an endowment.—*n.* **burs′ary,** in Scotland, the grant paid to a bursar. [Low L. *bursa,* a purse -Gr. *byrsa,* skin or leather.]

burst, *bûrst, v.t.* to break into pieces: to break open suddenly or by violence.—*v.i.* to fly open or break in pieces: to break forth or away: to force one's way (into): to break (into some sudden expression of feeling, condition, or activity):—*pa.t.* and *pa.p.* burst.—*n.* a sudden outbreak: a spurt: a drunken bout. [O.E. *berstan;* Ger. *bersten.*]

burthen, *bûr′thn, n.* and *v.t.* For **burden.**

bury, *ber′i, bûr′i, v.t.* to hide in the ground: to cover: to consign to the grave, the sea, &c., as a dead body: to hide or blot out of remembrance—*pr.p.* bur′ying; *pa.p.* bur′ied.—**bury the hatchet,** to renounce enmity. [O.E. *byrgan,* to bury; Ger. *bergen,* to hide.]

bus, 'bus, *bus, n.* an omnibus: (*slang*) a car, aeroplane, &c.:—*pl.* buses.—*n.* **bus′man,** the driver or conductor of a bus.—**busman's holiday,** a holiday spent in activities similar to one's work; **miss the bus,** to lose an opportunity. [Short for **omnibus.**]

busby, *buz′bi, n.* a tall fur head dress worn by hussars. [Prob. Hungarian.]

bush, *bŏŏsh, n.* a shrub thick with branches: anything of bushy tuft-like shape: forest: wild uncultivated country: a bunch of ivy formerly hung up as a tavern sign (as in *good wine needs no bush,* i.e. needs nothing to advertise it).—*adj.* **bush′y,** full of bushes: thick and spreading.—*ns.* **bush′iness; bush′-man,** a settler in uncleared land, a woodsman: one of an almost extinct aboriginal race in S. Africa; **bush′-ranger** (-*rānj′-*), in Australia, one who leads a lawless life in the bush: (*fig.*) a rapacious person.—**bush pilot,** airline pilot operating over uninhabited country; **bush shirt, jacket,** a garment, often of cotton, with four patch pockets and a belt; **bush telegraph,** the obscure and rapid transmission of news through a country or population.—**beat about the·bush,** to talk without coming to the point. [M.E. *busk, busch*; from a Gmc. root found in Ger. *busch,* Low L. *boscus,* Fr. *bois.*]

bush, *bŏŏsh, n.* the metal box or lining of any cylinder in which an axle works. [Du. *bus*—L. *buxus,* the box-tree.]

bushel, *bŏŏsh'l, n.* a dry measure of 8 gallons, no longer official. [O.Fr. *boissiel,* from the root of **box.**]

Bushido, *bŏŏ'shi-dō, n.* a Japanese code of chivalry. [Jap.]

business, *biz'nis, n.* (*obs.*) busyness (q.v.): trade, profession, or occupation: one's concern or affair: one's duty: a matter or affair: (*theat.*) the details of action, as distinguished from dialogue, that make up a part.—*adj.* **bus'i-ness-like,** methodical, systematic, practical.—**mean business,** to be in earnest; **mind one's own business,** to avoid meddling with the affairs of others; **no business,** no right; **send about one's business,** to dismiss abruptly. [**busy.**]

busk, *busk, v.t.* or *v.i.* to prepare: to dress. [O.N. *būa,* to prepare, and *-sk,* contr. of *sik,* the refl. pron. *self.*]

busk, *busk, n.* the piece of bone, wood or steel in the front of a corset: a corset. [Fr. *busc.*]

busker, *busk'er, n.* a wandering musician or actor who depends on money voluntarily given him by his audience. [Perh. Sp. *buscar,* to seek.]

buskin, *busk'in, n.* a half-boot, esp. one with thick soles worn in ancient times by actors of tragedy—hence, the tragic drama as distinguished from comedy.—*adj.* **busk'ined,** tragic: dignified. [Ety. uncertain.]

buss, *bus, n.* a rude or playful kiss, a smack.—*v.t.* to kiss, esp. rudely or playfully. [M.E. *bass*; cf. Old Ger. *bussen,* to kiss, Fr. *baiser.*]

bust, *bust, n.* a sculpture representing the head and breast of a person: the upper front part of the human body, esp. a woman's. [Fr. *buste*; It. and Sp. *busto.*]

bust, *bust, n.* and *v.* a vulgar form of **burst.**—**go bust** (*slang*), become bankrupt.

bustard, *bus'tard, n.* a genus, or a family, of large heavy birds, related to cranes. [Fr. *bistard,* corr. of L. *avis tarda,* slow bird (a misnomer).]

bustle, *bus'l, v.i.* to busy oneself noisily or fussily.—*n.* hurried activity, stir, tumult. [M.E. *bustelen.*]

bustle, *bus'l, n.* a frame or pad for causing a skirt to hang back from the hips.

busy, *biz'i, adj.* fully employed: active: diligent: meddling: of a design or picture, having too much detail.—*v.t.* to make busy: to occupy (esp. oneself)—*pr.p.* busying (*biz'i-ing*); *pa.p.* busied (*biz'id*).—*adv.* **bus'ily.**—*ns.* **bus'yness,** state of being busy; **bus'ybody,** a meddling person. [O.E. *bysig.*]

but, *but, prep.* only: except: (*Scot.*) in or towards the outer room of.—*conj.* on the other hand: in contrast: nevertheless: except that (merging

in *prep.*—e.g. *they had all left but he, him*): that not (developing into negative *rel. pron.*—e.g. *there is none of them but thinks*).—*adv.* only: (*Scot.*) in or to the outer room.—*n.* (*Scot.*) the outer apartment of a house of two rooms. See **ben.** [O.E. *be-ūtan, būtan,* without—*be,* by and *ūtan,* out, i.e. near and yet outside.]

butane, *bū'tān, n.* a colourless inflammable gas, usu. obtained from petroleum, supplied for domestic purposes.

butch, *bŏŏch, n.* a very short haircut: (*slang*) an aggressively tough man: (*slang*) the 'male' partner in a lesbian relationship. [Amer. boy's nickname.]

butcher, *bŏŏch'er, n.* one whose business is to kill cattle for food, or who deals in their flesh: one who delights in slaughter.—*v.t.* to kill·for food: to put to a bloody death, to kill cruelly: (*fig.*) to spoil by bad acting, reading, &c.—*ns.* **butch'er-bird** (see under **shrike**); **butch'er-meat, butch'er's-meat,** the flesh of animals killed by butchers, as distinguished from fish, fowls, and game; **butch'ery,** great or cruel slaughter: a slaughter-house or shambles. [O.Fr. *bochier, bouchier,* one who kills he-goats—*boc,* a he-goat.]

butler, *but'ler, n.* a servant who has charge of the liquors, plate, &c. [Norm. Fr. *butuiller*—Low L. *buticulārius*—*butis.* See **bottle.**]

butt, *but, v.i.* and *v.t.* to strike with the head, as a goat, &c.—*n.* a push with the head.—**butt in,** to intervene: to intrude. [O.Fr. *boter,* to push, strike.]

butt, *but, n.* a large cask. [Cf. Fr. *botte,* Sp. *bota,* Low L. *butta.*]

butt, *but, n.* a mark for archery practice: a mound behind targets: a victim of ridicule: (*pl.*) a shooting range. [Fr. *but,* goal.]

butt, *but, n.* the thick and heavy end: the stump.—*n.* **butt'-end.** [Ety. uncertain.]

butter, *but'er, n.* an oily substance obtained from cream by churning.—*v.t.* to spread over with butter.—*ns.* **butt'ercup,** a genus of plants (*Ranunculus*), esp. one of those with a cup-like flower of a golden yellow; **butt'er-fing'ers,** one who lets a ball, &c., he ought to catch slip through his fingers; **butt'erfly,** a general name for any of the beautiful daylight Lepidoptera (q.v.), roughly distinguished from moths by their clubbed antennae: (*fig.*) a gay, flighty person: butterfly breast-stroke:—*pl.* **butt'er-flies.**—Also *adj.*—*ns.* **butt'er-milk,** the milk that remains after the butter has been separated from the cream by churning; **butt'er-scotch,** a kind of toffee containing a large admixture of butter; **butt'erwort,** a genus of insectivorous plants with glistening leaves.—*adj.* **butt'ery,** like, containing, or with, butter: (*fig.*) offensively flattering; **butterfly (breast-) stroke,** in swimming, a faster variation of the breast-stroke in which the arms are recovered out of the water and there is a different kick.—**butterflies in the stomach,** nervous tremors in the stomach. [O.E. *butere*; Ger. *butter*; both from L. *būtyrum*—Gr. *boutyron*—*bous,* ox, *tyros,* cheese.]

buttery, *but'er-i, n.* a storeroom for provisions, esp. liquors. [Fr. *bouteillerie,* lit. 'place for bottles'.]

Neutral vowels in unaccented syllables: *em'per-or*; for certain sounds in foreign words see p. ix.

buttock, *but'ók, n.* either half of the rump or protuberant part of the body behind. [Dim. of **butt,** end.]

button, *but'n, n.* a knob or disk of metal, bone, &c., used as a fastening, ornament, or badge: any similar knob or disk.—*v.t.* to fasten by means of buttons: to close (up) tightly.—*v.i.* to admit of buttoning.—*adj.* **butt'oned-up** (*slang*), uncommunicative.—*n.* **butt'onhole,** the hole or slit into which a button is passed: a flower or flowers therein.—*v.t.* to work with a stitch (*buttonhole stitch*) suitable for defence of edges: to detain in talk (orig. *buttonhold*).—*n.* **butt'on-hook,** a hook for pulling the buttons of gloves and shoes through the buttonholes.—**buttoned up** (*slang*), successfully fixed up: safe in hand: ready for action; **boy in buttons,** or **buttons,** a boy servant in livery, a page. [Fr. *bouton,* any small projection, from *bouter,* to push.]

buttress, *but'res, n.* a projecting support built on to the outside of a wall: any support or prop.—*v.t.* to prop or support. [Apparently from O.Fr. *bouterez* (*bouteret*)—*bouter,* to push, bear against.]

butyl, *bū'til, n.* an alcohol radical C_4H_9.

buxom, *buks'óm, adj.* yielding, elastic: plump and comely. [M.E. *buhsum,* pliable, obedient—O.E. *būgan,* to bow, yield, and affix *-some.*]

buy, *bī, v.t.* to purchase (for money): to bribe: to obtain in exchange for something not necessarily concrete: (*slang*) to accept, believe:—*pr.p.* buy'ing; *pa.t.* and *pa.p.* bought (*bawt*).—Also *n.*—*n.* **buy'er.—buyer's market,** one in which, because the supply exceeds the demand, the buyers control the price. [O.E. *bycgan,* pa.t. *bohte, boht.*]

buzz, *buz, v.i.* to make a noise like that of insects' wings: to murmur: to hover (about). —*v.t.* to whisper or spread secretly: (*aero.*) to fly very low over or very close to: to interfere with in flight by flying very close to.—*n.* the noise of bees and flies: a whispered report.—*n.* **buzz'er,** an electrical or other apparatus producing a buzzing sound. [Imit.]

buzzard, *buz'árd, n.* a genus of large hawks: extended to some other birds of prey, as the *honey-buzzard, turkey-buzzard.* [Fr. *busard;* prob. conn. with L. *buteo,* a kind of hawk.]

by, *bī, prep.* at the side of: near to: along a route passing through, via: past: through denoting the agent, cause, means, &c.: to the extent of (e.g. *short by three inches*): measured in terms of (e.g. *by the yard, by this standard*): of time, at or before: during, or under specified conditions (*by day, by candle-light*).—*adv.* near: in reserve: past: aside.—*adv.* **by'-and-by,** at some future time.—*ns.* **by'-elec'tion,** an election during the sitting of parliament to fill a vacant seat; **by'form,** a parallel form (of a word), a variant.—*adj.* **by'gone,** past.—*n.* (*in pl.*) past causes of ill-will.—*ns.* **by'name,** a nickname: **by'pass,** a side track to avoid an obstruction or a congested area (also *fig.*).—*v.t.* to avoid by means of a by-pass.—*ns.* **by'path,** a secluded or indirect path; **by'play,** action apart from the main action: dumbshow aside on the stage; **by'-pro'duct,** a product formed in the process of making something else; **by'road,** a side road; **by'stander,** one who stands near—hence a spectator; **by'way,** a private and obscure way; **by'word,** a common saying: a proverb: an object of common reproach.—**by and large,** on the whole; **by the way** (see way); **let bygones be bygones,** let the past be forgotten. [O.E. *bi, big;* Ger. *bei,* L. *ambi-.*]

bye, by, *bī, n.* anything of minor importance: the state of one who has not drawn an opponent and passes without contest to the next round: in golf, the holes played after the match is won: in cricket, a run made from a bowled ball not struck by the bat.—*adj.* and *pfx.* subsidiary.—**by(-)the(-)bye,** or (-)**by,** incidentally. [by.]

bylaw, bye-law, *bī'lö, n.* the law of a local authority: a supplementary law or regulation. [From O.N. *byjar-lög,* Dan. *by-lov,* town-law; from O.N. *būa,* to dwell.]

byre, *bīr, n.* a cowhouse. [O.E. *bȳre.*]

Byronic, *bī-ron'ik, adj.* possessing the characteristics, or alleged characteristics, of Lord *Byron* (1788-1824), or of his poetry, esp. overstrained in sentiment, cynical and libertine.

Byzantine, *biz-an'tīn, biz'-, adj.* relating to *Byzantium* or Constantinople (now Istanbul). —**Byzantine Empire,** the Eastern or Greek Empire from A.D. 395 to 1453.

fāte, fär; mē, hûr (her); *mīne; mōte, för; mūte; mōōn, fŏŏt;* THen (then)

C

ca′, *kö*, v.t. and v.i. to call: to drive, to propel: to knock.—**ca′ canny**, deliberately to restrict output or effort (see **canny**). [Scots form of **call**.]

cab, *kab*, *n*. a public carriage, horse-drawn or motor-driven: a taxi-cab: a driver's shelter on a vehicle.—*ns.* **cabb′y**, familiar dim. of **cab′-man**, one who drives a cab for hire; **cab′-rank**, **cab′-stand**, a place where cabs stand for hire. [Shortened from **cabriolet**.]

cabal, *ka-bal′*, *n*, a small party united for some secret design: a conspiracy. [Fr. *cabale*; from Heb.; see **cabbala**.]

cabaret, *kab′a-rā*, *n*, a restaurant with variety turns: an entertainment of the type given in such a restaurant. [Fr., tavern; prob. for *cabanaret—cabane*, a hut.]

cabbage, *kab′ij*, *n*. a vegetable of the Cruciferae, of many varieties. [Fr. *caboche*, head; from L. *caput*, the head.]

cabbala, cabala, *kab′ä-la*, *n*. a secret science of the Jewish rabbis for the interpretation of the hidden sense of Scripture.—*n.* **cabb′alist**, one versed in the cabbala.—*adj.* **cabbalist′ic**, relating to the cabbala: having a hidden meaning. [Heb. *qabbālāh*, tradition—*qibbēl*, to receive.]

caber, *käb′ér*, *käb′ér*, *n*. a long, heavy pole tossed by Highland athletes. [Gael. *cabar*.]

cabin, *kab′in*, *n*. a hut or cottage: a small room, esp. in a ship: a compartment for passengers in an aircraft.—*v.t.* to shut up in a cabin.—*n.* **cab′in-boy**, a boy who serves the occupants of a ship's cabin; **cab′in-cruis′er**, a power-driven boat with full provision for living on board. [Fr. *cabane*—Low L. *capanna*.]

cabinet, *kab′in-et*, *n*. a small room, closet, or private apartment; a case for storing articles of value.—**the cabinet**, a select number of the chief ministers who govern a country.—*n.* **cab′inet-mak′er**, a maker of cabinets and other fine furniture. [Dim. of **cabin**.]

cable, *kā′bl*, *n*. a strong rope or chain for hauling or tying anything, esp. a ship's anchor: a wire for carrying electric current: a cablegram.—*v.t.* and *v.i.* to telegraph by cable.—*n.* **ca′blegram**, a telegram sent by cable; **ca′ble-stitch**, (a series of stitches producing) a pattern resembling cables; **ca′ble-tram′way**, **-rail′way**, one along which cars or carriages are drawn by an endless cable. [Fr.,—Low L. *caplum*, a halter—*capēre*, to hold.]

caboose, *ka-boos′*, *n*. a ship's kitchen: an open-air cooking stove: (*U.S.*) the van on a freight train for the train crew: a hut. [Du. *kombuis*; cf. Ger. *kabuse*.]

cabriolet, *kab-ri-ō-lā′*, *n*. a light carriage with two wheels: a cab. [Fr.]

cacao, *ka-kā′o*, or *ka-kā′o*, *n*. the tropical American tree from whose seeds cocoa and chocolate are made. [Mexican *cacauatl*.]

cachalot, *kash′a-lot*, *-lö*, *n*. sperm-whale. [Fr.]

cache, *kash*, *n*. a hiding-place for treasure, stores, &c.: treasure, stores, &c., hidden. [Fr. *cacher*, to hide.]

cachet, *kash′ā*, *n*. a seal: any distinctive stamp (*fig.*), esp. something showing or conferring prestige.—**lettre de cachet** (*hist.*), a letter under the private seal of the King of France. [Fr.]

cachinnate, *kak′in-āt*, *v.i.* to laugh loudly.—*n.* **cachinna′tion**. [L. *cachinnāre*, to laugh loudly.]

cachou, *kash′oo*, *n.* a sweetmeat, used to perfume the breath. [Fr.]

cacique, *ka-sēk′*, *n*. a West Indian chief. [Sp.—native word in Haiti.]

cackle, *kak′l*, *n*. the sound made by a hen or goose: talk or laughter of similar sound.—*v.i.* to make such a sound.—Also *v.t.*—**cut the cackle**, to stop the useless talk. [M.E. *cakelen*.]

cacophony, *ka-kof′o-ni*, *n*. a disagreeable sound: discord of sounds.—*adj.* **cacoph′onous**. [Gr. *kakos*, bad, *phōnē*, sound.]

cactus, *kak′tus*, *n*. any one of a family of prickly plants whose stems store water and do the work of leaves:—*pl.* **cac′tī** or **cac′tuses**. [L.,—Gr. *kaktos*, a prickly plant found in Sicily.]

cad, *kad*, *n*. one who lacks the instincts of a gentleman.—*adj.* **cadd′ish**. [Short for **cadet**.]

cadastral, *ka-däs′tral*, *adj.* pertaining to a **cadas′tre** (*-tér*) or public register of lands of a country. [Fr.—Low L. *capitastrum*, register for a poll-tax—L. *caput*, the head.]

cadaverous, *ka-dav′ér-us*, *adj.* looking like a dead body: sickly-looking, esp. gaunt, haggard. [L. *cadāver*, a dead body—*cadĕre*, to fall dead.]

caddie, *kad′i*, *n*. one who carries clubs for a golfer.—Also *v.t.*—**caddie car**, a device on two wheels for taking a bag of golf clubs round the course. [Scot., from **cadet**.]

caddis, caddice, *kad′is*, *n*. the larva of the **caddis-fly**, which lives in water in a silken sheath or **caddis-case**. [Ety. uncertain.]

caddy, *kad′i*, *n*. a small box for holding tea. [Malay *kati*, the weight of a small packet of tea.]

cadence, *kā′dens*, *n*. the fall of the voice: rise and fall of sound: modulation: rhythm: a succession of chords closing a musical period.—*n.* **caden′za** (*kä-dent′sä*, *kä-den′zä*), a flourish given by a solo voice or instrument. [Fr.,—L. *cadĕre*, to fall.]

cadet, *ka-det′*, *n*. a younger son: a member of the younger branch of a family: a student in a military or naval school.—*n.* **cadet′ship**. [Fr. *cadet*, formerly *capdet*—dim. of L. *caput*, the head.]

cadge, *kaj*, *v.t.* and *v.i.* to beg, or to go about begging: to sponge.—*n.* **cadg′er**, a carrier who collects country produce: a hawker: a sponge. [Prob. conn. with **catch**.]

Neutral vowels in unaccented syllables: *em′pér-ór*; for certain sounds in foreign words see p. ix.

cadi, *kä′di, kā′di, n.* a magistrate in Mohammedan countries. [Ar. *qādī*, a judge.]

cadmium, *kad′mi-úm, n.* a metallic element (symbol Cd; atomic no. 48) occurring in zinc ores. [Gr. *kadmeia*, calamine.]

cadre, *kad′r, n.* a nucleus, framework, esp. the officers of a military unit. [Fr.]

caducous, *ka-dū′kus, adj.* falling early, as leaves. [L. *cadūcus—cadĕre*, to fall.]

caecum, *sē′kum, n.* a sac or bag, having only one opening, connected with the intestine of an animal:—*pl.* **cae′ca**. [L.—*caecus*, blind.]

caerulean. See **cerulean.**

Caesar, *sē′zär, n.* the title assumed by the Roman Emperors as heirs of Julius *Caesar,* an absolute monarch.—**Caesar′ean operation,** the delivery of a child by cutting through the walls of the abdomen, as is (improbably) said to have been the case with Julius Caesar or one of his ancestors.

caesium, *sēz′i-úm, n.* a metallic element (symbol Cs; atomic no. 55); used in form of compounds or alloys in photoelectric cells. [L. *caesius*, bluish grey.]

caesura, cesura, *sē-zū′rä, n.* (*pros.*) division of a foot between two words: a pause in a line of verse (generally near the middle).—*adj.* **caesū′ral.** [L. *caedĕre, caesum*, to cut off.]

café, *kaf′ā, n.* a coffee-house, a restaurant.—**café au lait, café-noir,** (the colour of) white, black, coffee. [Fr.]

cafeteria, *ka-fe-tēr′i-a, n.* a coffee-stall: a restaurant with a counter. [Cuban Spanish *cafetería*, a tent in which coffee is sold.]

caffeine, *kaf′e-in, -īn, -ēn, n.* theine, an alkaloid present in coffee and tea. [Fr. *caféine*—ultimately from Turkish *qahveh*. See **coffee.**]

caftan, *kaf′tan, n.* a long-sleeved Persian or Turkish garment. [Turk. *qaftān.*]

cage, *kāj, n.* a place of confinement: a box made of wire and wood for holding captive birds or animals: any similar structure.—*v.t.* to imprison in a cage. [Fr.,—L. *cavea*, a hollow place.]

cagey, cagy, *kāj′i, adj.* (*coll.*) wary, not frank.

Cain, *kān, n.* a murderer, from *Cain*, who killed his brother Abel (Gen. iv.).—**to raise Cain,** to make a violent disturbance.

Cainozoic, *kī-no-zō′ik, adj.* and *n.* (*geol.*) Tertiary plus Quaternary, or Tertiary alone. [Gr. *kainos*, new, *zōē*, life.]

caique, *kä-ēk′, n.* a light skiff used on the Bosporus. [Fr.,—Turk. *kaik*, a boat.]

cairn, *kārn, n.* a heap of stones: a small variety of Scottish terrier.—*n.* **cairngorm′-stone,** or simply **cairngorm′,** brown or yellow quartz found in Cairngorm Mts. [Celt. *carn.*]

caisson, *kās′on, kä-sōōn′, n.* an ammunition chest or wagon: a strong case for keeping out the water while the foundations of a bridge are being built: an apparatus for lifting a vessel out of the water for repairs or inspection.—**caisson disease,** pain in the joints, paralysis, &c., caused by a too sudden change from a higher to a lower pressure, suffered by caisson-workers, divers, pilots, &c. [Fr., from *caisse*, a case or chest.]

caitiff, *kā′tif, n.* a mean despicable fellow.—*adj.* mean, base. [O.Fr. *caitif* (Fr. *chétif*)—L. *captīvus*, a captive—*capĕre*, to take.]

cajole, *ka-jōl′, v.t.* to coax: to cheat by flattery. [Fr. *cajoler*, to chatter; ety. uncertain.]

cake, *kāk, n.* a piece of dough that is baked: a small loaf of fine bread, flavoured with spices, &c.: any flattened mass baked hard.—*v.t.* and *v.i.* to form into a cake or hard mass.—**a piece of cake,** a thing easy to do. [O.N. *kaka*; cog. with Ger. *kuche.*]

calabash, *kal′a-bash, n.* a tree of tropical America bearing a large melon-like fruit, the shell of which, called a calabash, is dried and used for holding liquids, &c. [Fr. *calebasse*—Sp. *calabaza*—Pers. *kharbuz*, melon.]

calamary, *kal′a-mär-i, n.* See **squid.**

calamine, *kal′a-mīn, -min, n.* a mineral, zinc carbonate: (*U.S.*) hydrous zinc silicate. [Fr.—Low L. *calamīna.*]

calamity, *kal-am′i-ti, n.* a great misfortune: affliction.—*adj.* **calam′itous,** disastrous.—*adv.* **calam′itously.** [Fr. *calamité*—L. *calamitās, -ātis.*]

calamus, *kal′a-mus, n.* the traditional name of the sweet flag, an aromatic plant: the reed pen used by the ancients:—*pl.* **calamī.** [L.—Gr. *kalamos*, reed, cane.]

calash, *ka-lash′, n.* a light low-wheeled carriage with a folding top: a hood formerly worn by ladies. [Fr. *calèche*; of Slavonic origin.]

calcareous, *kal-kā′re-us, adj.* like or containing chalk or lime [L. *calcārius*, from *calx*, a stone, lime.]

calceolaria, *kal-se-o-lā′ri-a, n.* a South American plant with slipper-like flowers. [L. *calceolus*, dim. of *calceus*, a shoe.]

calcium, *kal′si úm, n.* the metal (symbol Ca; atomic no. 20) present in chalk and lime.—*adj.* **calcif′erous,** containing lime.—*v.t.* and *v.i.* **cal′cify,** to make or become limy.—*v.t.* and *v.i.* **cal′cine** (*kal′sīn, -sin*) to reduce to, or to become, a *calx* (q.v.) by prolonged heating at fairly high temperatures. [Formed from L. *calx*, a stone, lime.]

calculate, *kal′ku-lāt, v.t.* to count or reckon: to think out, esp. mathematically: (*U.S.*) to think, purpose, suppose.—*v.i.* to make a calculation: to rely, base one's plans or forecasts (on).—*adj.* **cal′culable.**—*p.adjs.* **cal′culated,** fitted (to), likely(to): deliberate; **cal′culating,** given to forethought: selfish and scheming.—*n.* **calculā′tion,** the art or process of calculating: estimate: forecast.—*adj.* **cal′culative.**—*n.* **cal′culātor.** [L. *calculāre, -ātum,* to reckon by help of little stones—*calculus* (dim. of *calx*), a little stone.]

calculus, *kal′kū-lus, n.* a stone-like concretion which forms in certain parts of the body (*pl.* **cal′culi**): (*math.*) the study of the changes of a continuously varying function (*pl.* **cal′culuses**).—**differential calculus,** the investigation of the *rate* at which a given function is changing for a specified value of its argument; **integral calculus,** the investigation of the *amount* by which a function changes for a specified change in its argument when the rate of change is known. [L.]

caldron. Same as **cauldron.**

Caledonian, *kal-e-dō′ni-än, adj.* pertaining to ancient *Caledonia*, the Highlands, or Scotland generally.—*n.* a Scot. [L. *Calēdōnia.*]

calefactory, *kal-e-fak′tor-i, adj.* warming.—*n.* a

fāte, fär; mē, hûr (her); mīne; mōte, för; mūte; mōōn, fŏŏt; тнеn (then) room in which monks warmed themselves. [L. *calēre*, to grow hot, *facēre*, to make.]

calendar, *kal'en-dàr*, *n.* an almanac or table of months, days, and seasons (see **Gregorian, Julian**): any list or record. [O.Fr. *calendier*—L. *calendārium*, an account-book—*kalendae*, calends.]

calender, *kal'en-dér*, *n.* a press with rollers for finishing the surface of cloth, paper, &c.—*v.t.* to press in a calender. [Fr. *calandre*—L. *cylindrus*—Gr. *kylindros*, roller.]

calends, *kal'endz*, *n.* among the Romans, the first day of each month.—Also **kalends**. [L. *kalendae*—*calāre*, to call (because the beginning of the month was proclaimed).]

calenture, *kal'en-tyùr*, *n.* a kind of fever or delirium occurring on board ship in hot climates. [Fr. and Sp.—L. *calens*, *-entis*, pr.p. of *calēre*, to be hot.]

calf, *käf*, *n.* the young of the cow, elephant, whale, and certain other mammals: calf-skin leather:—*pl.* **calves** (*kävz*).—*ns.* **calf'-love**, immature affection of a boy for a girl; **calf's-foot, calves'-foot**, the foot of the calf, used in making a palatable jelly. [O.E. *cealf*; Ger. *kalb*.]

calf, *käf*, *n.* the thick fleshy part of the leg behind. [O.N. *kālfi*; perh. the same word as the preceding.]

calibre, caliber, *kal'i-bér*, *n.* the size of the bore of a tube: diameter: (*fig.*—of a person) degree of excellence or importance.—*v.t.* **cal'ibrāte**, to determine the calibre of: to mark the scale on a measuring instrument. [Fr. *calibre*, the bore of a gun.]

calico, *kal'i-kō*, *n.* a cotton cloth first brought from *Calicut* in India.

calif. Same as **caliph.**

californium, *kal-i-fōr'-ni-ùm*, *n.* a transuranium element (atomic no. 98; symbol Cf), made at the University of *California*.

caliph, *kal'if*, or *kā'lif*, *n.* the name assumed by the successors of Mohammed.—*n.* **cal'iphate**, the office, rank, or government of a caliph. [Fr. *calife*—Ar. *khalīfah*, a successor.]

calisthenics. Same as **callisthenics.**

calk. See **caulk.**

calk, *kök*, *n.* a spike in a horse-shoe to prevent slipping.—Also **calkin**.—*v.t.* to provide with a calk. [L. *calx, calcis*, a heel.]

call, *köl*, *v.i.* to cry aloud: to make a short visit.—*v.t.* to name: to summon: to appoint or proclaim: to describe as: to declare (trump suit, &c.).—*n.* a summons or invitation: a sense of vocation: a demand: a short visit: a telephone connection or conversation or a request for one: a cry, esp. of a bird: need, occasion.—*ns.* **call'-boy**, a boy who calls the actors when wanted on the stage; **call'er**, one who pays a short visit; **call'ing**, vocation, trade, profession.—**call in question**, to challenge, dispute; **call out**, to instruct (members of a trade union) to come out on strike; **call to account**, to demand an explanation from; **call up**, to summon from beneath or from another world: to summon to a tribunal or to the colours: to bring into the memory; **on call**, ready to answer summons. [O.E. *ceallian*; O.N. *kalla*, Du. *kallen*.]

calligraphy, *kal-ig'ra-fi*, *n.* fine penmanship: characteristic style of writing. [Gr. *kallos*,

beauty, *graphein*, to write.]

callipers, calipers, *kal'i-pérz*, *n.pl.* compasses with legs suitable for measuring the inside or outside diameter of bodies. [Corr. of **caliber**.]

callisthenics, *kal-is-then'iks*, *n.pl.* exercises for promoting gracefulness and strength of body.—*adj.* **callisthen'ic**. [Gr. *kallos*, beauty, *sthenos*, strength.]

callous, *kal'us*, *adj.* hardened: unfeeling.—*n.* **cal'losity**, a hard thickening of the skin.—*adv.* **call'ously.**—*n.* **call'ousness**. [L. *callōsus*—*callus*, hard skin.]

callow, *kal'ō*, *adj.* not covered with feathers, unfledged: immature. [O.E. *calu*; Ger. *kahl*, L. *calvus*. bald.]

calm, *käm*, *adj.* still or quiet: serene, tranquil.—*n.* absence of wind: repose: serenity.—*v.t.* to make calm: to quiet.—*adv.* **calm'ly.**—*n.* **calm'ness**. [Fr. *calme*, from Low L. *cauma*—Gr. *kauma*, noonday heat.]

calomel, *kal'ō-mel*, *n.* the popular name of one of the compounds of mercury and chlorine, much used in medicine. [Fr.]

Calor gas, *kal'ór gas*, trademark name of a bottle gas.

calorie, calory, *kal'or-i*, *n.* the amount of heat needed to raise the temperature of a gram of water from 15° C. to 16° C., equal to 4.186 **joules**, q.v.: (loosely, for *kilocalorie*) a heat unit 1000 times as great as this (also **large, great, calorie**), used in measuring the heat- or energy-producing value of food.—*adj.* **calorif'ic**, causing heat: heating.—*ns.* **calorifica'tion; calorim'eter**, an instrument for measuring quantities of heat (not temperature); **calorim'etry**, the art or process of measuring heat. [L. *calor*, heat.]

caltrop, *kal'trop*, *köl'trop*, *n.* an instrument armed with four spikes so arranged that one always stands upright, used to obstruct the progress of an enemy.—Also **cal'trap**. [O.E. *coltetræppe, calcatrippe*—L. *calx, calcis*, heel.]

calumet, *kal'ū-met*, *n.* a tobacco-pipe smoked by North American Indians as a symbol of peace. [Fr.,—L. *calamus*, a reed.]

calumny, *kal'um-ni*, *n.* false accusation: slander.—*v.t.* **calum'niāte**, to accuse falsely: to slander.—*v.i.* to spread evil reports.—*ns.* **calum'niātion; calum'niātor.**—*adj.* **calum'nious**, of the nature of calumny, slanderous.—*adv.* **calum'niously**. [L. *calumnia*.]

Calvary, *kal'va-ri*, *n.* the name of the place where Christ was crucified: a representation of Christ's crucifixion, or a series of scenes connected with it. [L. *calvāria*, a skull.]

calve, *käv*, *v.t.* and *v.i.* to bring forth (a *calf*).

calves. See **calf.**

Calvinism, *kal'vin-izm*, *n.* the doctrines of the great Genevan religious reformer, John *Calvin* (1509-64). The distinguishing doctrine of his system is predestination, coupled with the irresistibility of God's grace.—*n.* **Cal'vinist.**—*adjs.* **Calvinist'ic, -al.**

calx, *kalks*, *n.* the substance of a metal or mineral that remains after strong heating (an oxide or oxides):—*pl.* **calxes** (*kalk'sēz*), or **calces**, (*kal'sēz*). [L. *calx*, a stone, lime.]

calypso, *kä-lip'sō*, *n.* a West-Indian folk song, usu. a commentary on a current happening, made up as the singer goes along.

Neutral vowels in unaccented syllables: *em'pér-ór*; for certain sounds in foreign words see p. ix.

calyx, *kal'iks*, or *kā'liks*, *n.* the outer covering or cup of a flower, its separate leaves being termed *sepals*:—*pl.* **calyces**, or **calyxes**. [Gr. *kalyx*, a covering—*kalyptein*, to cover.]

camaraderie, *kam-a-räd'ér-ē*, *n.* the spirit of comradeship. [Fr.]

camarilla, *kam-ar-il'ä*, *n.* a body of secret intriguers. [Sp. dim of *cámara*, a chamber.]

camber, *kam'bér*, *n.* a slight convexity upon an upper surface, as of a deck, a bridge, an aeroplane wing, a road surface.—*v.t.* and *v.i.* to arch slightly. [Fr. *cambrer*— L. *camerāre*, to vault.]

cambium, *kam'bi-úm*, *n.* the layer between the wood and the bark (q.v.) of a stem, in which the annual growth of new phloem and xylem takes place. [L. *cambīre*, to change.]

cambrel, *kam'brel*, *n.* a bent piece of wood or iron on which butchers hang carcasses. [Prob. conn. with **camber**.]

Cambrian, *kam'bri-án*, *adj.* Welsh.—*n.* the period of the Primary geological era following the Archaean.—**Cambrian System**, the rocks formed during this period. [Formed from *Cymry*, Welshmen, or *Cymru*, Wales.]

cambric, *kām'brik*, *n.* a fine white linen, orig. manufactured at *Cambrai* (then Flanders, now France).

came, *kām*, *pa.t.* of **come**.

camel, *kam'él*, *n.* an animal of Asia and Africa with one or two humps on its back, used as a beast of burden and for riding.—**camel('s) hair**, the hair of the camel: the hair of the squirrel's tail used for paint-brushes. [L. *camēlus*—Gr. *kamēlos*—Heb. *gāmāl*.]

camellia, *ka-mēl'ya*, -*mel'*, *n.* a genus of evergreen shrubs, natives of eastern Asia, grown for the singular beauty of their flowers. [Named from *Camellus*, a Jesuit botanist.]

camelopard, *kam-el'ō-pärd*, or *kam'el-ō-pärd*, *n.* the giraffe. [Gr. *kamēlopardālis*—*kamēlos*, camel, *pardālis*, panther.]

Camembert, *kam-ā-ber'*, *n.* a soft rich cheese made near *Camembert*, in Normandy.

cameo, *kam'ē-ō*, *n.* an engraved gem in which the figure or subject is carved in relief:—*pl.* **cam'eos** [It. *cammeo* (Fr. *camée*)—Low. L. *cammaeus*.]

camera, *kam'ér-a*, *n.* a vaulted room: a judge's private chamber (**in camera**, of a case, tried in secret): the apparatus in which a photographer exposes a sensitive plate or film: (*TV*) the apparatus that forms the image of the scene and converts it into electrical impulses for transmission.—**cam'era-obscu'ra**, an instrument for throwing the images of external objects on a white surface placed within a dark chamber or box. [L.]

camisole, *kam'is-ōl*, *n.* a loose underbodice with or without sleeves.—*n.pl.* **cami-knickers**, combined camisole and knickers. [Sp. *camisa*—L. *camisia*.]

camomile, **chamomile**, *kam'ō-mīl*, *n.* a name for several plants, or their dried flowers, used in medicine, affording a bitter stomachic and tonic. [Fr.,—L.—Gr. *chamaimēlon*, lit. earth-apple, from the apple-like smell of the blossoms—*chamai*, on the ground, *mēlon*, an apple.]

camouflage, *ka'mōō-fläzh*, *n.* any device (esp. deceptive colouring) for deceiving an adversary.—*v.t.* and *v.i.* to disguise. [Fr. *camouflet*, a whiff of smoke blown in the face, &c.]

camp, *kamp*, *n.* the ground on which tents are pitched: a permanent military station: any temporary quarters for travellers, &c.: a party or side.—*v.i.* to encamp or pitch tents.—*ns.* **camp'-bed**, **camp'-chair**, **camp'-stool**, a bed, chair, or stool that can be folded up when not in use; **camp'er**, one who camps: a motor vehicle converted for use as temporary living accommodation; **camp'-foll'ower**, a noncombatant who follows in the rear of an army; **camp'-meet'ing**, a religious gathering held in the open air. [Fr. *camp*, a camp—L. *campus*, a plain.]

camp, *kamp*, *adj.* theatrical, affected, exaggerated: homosexual.—Also *n.*

campaign, *kam-pān'*, *n.* the time during which an army keeps the field: the operations of that time: organised action in support of a cause.—*v.i.* to serve in a campaign.—*n.* **campaign'er** [Fr. *campagne*—L. *campania*—*campus*, a field.]

campanile, *kam-pan-ē'lā*, *n.* a bell-tower, esp. one detached from the church: (*pl.*) usually **campaniles** (*ē'lēz*), sometimes the It. **campanili**, (*-ē'lē*) [It., from *campana*, a bell.]

campanology, *kam-pan-ol'ō-ji*, *n.* the subject or science of bells or bell-ringing. [It. *campana*, a bell, and Gr. *logos*, a discourse.]

campanula, *kam-pan'ū-la*, *n.* a genus of flowers, commonly known as bell-flowers or bells.—*adj.* **campan'ulate**, bell-shaped. [It. *campana*, a bell.]

campestral, *kam-pes'trál*, *adj.* growing in, or pertaining to, fields. [L. *campestris*, from *campus*, a field.]

camphor, *kam'fór*, *n.* a solid essential oil, obtainable from the camphor laurel of India, China, and Japan (or manufactured), having a peculiar aromatic taste and smell.—*adj.* **cam'phorated**, impregnated with camphor. [Fr. *camphre*—Low L. *camphora*—Malay, *kāpūr*, chalk.]

campus, *kam'pús*, *n.* (*U.S.*) college or school grounds (and buildings): a college or self-contained division of a university: a university: the academic world. [L., a field.]

can, *kan*, *v.t.* (*obs.*) to know, to have skill in: to be able, to have sufficient power:—*pa.t.* **could**. [O.E. *cunnan*, to know (how to do), to be able; pres. indic. (orig. past) *can*.]

can, *kan*, *n.* a vessel for holding or carrying liquids: a chimney-pot: a vessel of tin-plate in which meat, fruit, &c., are preserved: a container for various things, as film in quantity: a jacket in which a fuel rod is sealed in an atomic reactor.—*v.t.* to put up for preservation in cans.—*adj.* **canned**, of music, recorded for reproduction.—*n.* **cann'ery**, a place where goods are canned.—**carry the can** (*slang*), to take the blame. [O.E. *canne*.]

Canadian, *ka-nā'di-án*, *adj.* and *n.* pertaining to *Canada*: a native of Canada.

canaille, *ka-nā'e*, *n.* the mob, the vulgar rabble. [Fr.,—L. *canis*, a dog.]

canal, *kan-al'*, *n.* an artificial watercourse, esp. for navigation: a duct in the body for conveying fluids.—*v.t.* **can'alise**, to convert into a canal: to direct into a channel (*lit.* and *fig.*). [L. *canālis*, a water-pipe.]

canard, *ka-när(d)′*, *n.* a false rumour. [Fr., *lit.* 'duck'.]

canary, *ka-nā′ri*, *n.* a light sweet wine from the Canary Islands: a song-bird (finch) found in the Canary Islands, bright yellow in domestic breeds.—*adj.* canary-coloured.

can-can, *kan-kan*, *n.* a dance of French origin, orig. considered immodest. [Ety. obscure.]

cancel, *kan′sel*, *v.t.* to strike out by crossing with lines: to annul or suppress: to countermand: to counterbalance or compensate for: to remove like quantities from opposite sides of an equation or like factors from numerator and denominator of a fraction:—*pr.p.* can′celling; *pa.p.* can′celled.—*n.* a printed page, &c., cancelled, or substituted for one cancelled.—*n.* **cancellā′tion**. [Fr. *canceller*—L. *cancellāre*, from *cancelli*, railings, lattice-work.]

cancelled, *kan′sel-ā-tid*, crossed by bars or lines. [L. *cancelli*, railings.]

cancer, *kan′sér*, *n.* a malignant growth or tumour: (*fig.*) any corroding evil: (*cap.*) the Crab, a sign of the zodiac whose first point marks the limit of the sun's course northward.—*adj.* **can′cerous**, of or like a cancer. [L. *cancer*; cog. with Gr. *karkinos*, a crab.]

candela, *kan-del′a*, *n.* SI unit of luminous intensity such that the luminous intensity of a black body radiator at the temperature of solidification of platinum is 60 candela per sq. cm. [**candle**.]

candelabrum, *kan-de-lā′brum*, *n.* a branched and ornamented candlestick or lampstand:—*pl.* **candelā′bra**—also used as *sing.* with *pl.* **candelā′bras.** [L.]

candid, *kan′did*, *adj.* frank, ingenuous: free from prejudice, impartial.—*adv.* **can′didly.**—*n.* **can′didness.**—**candid camera**, a type of small camera for taking unposed photographs of people engaged in their ordinary daily occupations. [Fr. *candide*—L. *candidus*, white.]

candidate, *kan′di-dát*, *n.* one who offers himself for any office or honour, so called because, at Rome, the applicant used to dress in white.—*ns.* **can′didature**, **can′didacy.** [L. *candidātus—candidus*, white.]

candied. See **candy.**

candle, *kan′dl*, *n.* a cylinder of wax, tallow, or like substance surrounding a wick: a light.—*adj.* **can′dle-end**, niggardly.—*ns.* **can′dlepow′er**, illuminating power in terms of a standard candle; **can′dlestick**, portable stand for holding a candle.—**burn the candle at both ends**, to exhaust one's strength by taxing it in two directions (e.g. by working early and late); **not fit to hold a candle to**, utterly inferior to; **the game is not worth the candle**, the thing is not worth the cost. [O.E. *candel*—L. *candēla*, from *candēre*, to shine, to glow.]

Candlemas, *kan′dl-mas*, *n.* the R.C. festival of the purification of the Virgin Mary, on 2nd February, when candles are blessed: a quarter-day in Scotland. [**candle** and **mass.**]

candour, *kan′dór*, *n.* freedom from prejudice: sincerity: frankness. [L. *candor*, whiteness, from *candēre*, to shine.]

candy, *kan′di*, **sugar-candy**, *shoog′ár-kan′di*, *n.* a sweetmeat made of sugar: anything preserved

in sugar.—*v.t.* to preserve or dress with sugar: to congeal or crystallise as sugar.—*v.i.* to become crystallised:—*pr.p* can′dying; *pa.t.* and *pa.p.* can′died.—**candy floss**, a fluffy ball of spun coloured and flavoured sugar sold on the end of a stick. [Fr. *candi*, from Ar. *qandah*, candy.]

candytuft, *kan′di-tuft*, *n.* a genus of plants with flowers in tufts. [*Candia* (or Crete) and **tuft.**]

cane, *kān*, *n.* the stem of one of the smaller palms, or larger grasses: any slender rod: a walking-stick.—*v.t.* to beat with a cane.—*n.* **cane′-su′gar**, sugar obtained from the sugarcane. [Fr. *canne*—L. *canna*—Gr. *kannē*, a reed.]

canine, *kan′īn*, *kān′īn*, *kan-īn′*, *adj.* like or pertaining to a dog.—**canine teeth**, in man, four sharp-pointed teeth between the incisors and premolars. [L. *canīnus—canis*, a dog.]

canister, *kan′ist-tér*, *n.* a box or case, usu. metal, for holding tea, shot, &c.—*v.t.* **can′isterise**, to store in a canister.—*n.* **canisterisā′tion.**—*n.* **can′ister-shot**, a case containing shot, which bursts on being discharged. [L. *canistrum*, a wicker basket—Gr. *kanastron—kannē*, a reed.]

canker, *kang′kér*, *n.* an ulcerous sore: any of several fungus diseases in trees: inflammation in horses' feet: eczema of dogs' ears: anything that corrupts or consumes—*v.t.* to eat into, corrupt, or destroy: to infect or pollute.—*v.i.* to grow corrupt: to decay.—*adj.* **cank′ered**, corroded: malignant: crabbed.—*adj.* **cank′erous**, corroding like a canker.—*n.* **cank′er-worm**, a worm that cankers or eats into plants. [L. *cancer*, a crab, gangrene.]

cannabis, *kan′ábis*, *n.* a narcotic drug variously known as hashish, bhang, marihuana, &c: (*cap.*) the hemp genus. [Gr. *kannabis.*]

cannel, *kan′él*, *n.* a bituminous coal that burns with a bright flame.—Also **cann′el-coal**, **can′dle-coal.** [Prob. **candle.**]

cannibal, *kan′i-bál*, *n.* an eater of the flesh of his own species.—*adj.* relating to, or indulging in, cannibalism.—*v.t.* **cann′ibalise**, to repair (a vehicle) with parts taken from other vehicles.—*n.* **cann′ibalism**, the practice of eating one's own kind. [Sp., a corr. of *Canibal*, *Caribal* (Eng. *Carib*—q.v.), a people who formerly ate human flesh.]

cannikin, *kan′i-kin*, *n.* a small can. [Dim. of **can.**]

cannon, *kan′ón*, *n.* a general name for a firearm discharged from a carriage or mount (now oftener *gun*): a great gun: a stroke in billiards—an oblique hit from one ball to another.—*v.i.* to hit and rebound as a ball in a cannon at billiards.—*n.* **cannonade′**, an attack with cannon.—*v.t.* to attack or batter with cannon.—*ns.* **cann′on-ball**, a ball to be shot from a cannon; **cann′on-shot**, a cannon-ball: the distance to which a cannon will throw a ball.—**cannon fodder**, men regarded merely as material to be consumed in war. [Fr. *canon*—L. *canna*, a reed.]

cannot, *kan′ot*, am, is, or are, unable to. [Neg. form of pres. indic. of **can.**]

canny, *kan′i*, *adj.* (*Scot.*) shrewd: cautious: comfortable: gentle.—*adv.* **cann′ily.** [Apparently connected with **can.**]

canoe, *ka-nōō′*, *n.* a skiff driven by paddling.—*n.*

Neutral vowels in unaccented syllables: *em′pér-ór*; for certain sounds in foreign words see p. ix.

canoe′ist. [Sp. *canoa* – Haitian.]

cãnon, canyon, *kan′yón, n.* a deep gorge or ravine between high and steep banks, worn by watercourses. [Sp. *cañon,* a hollow, from root of **cannon.**]

canon, *kan′ón, n.* a law or rule, esp. in ecclesiastical matters: a standard: the books of the Bible accepted by the Christian Church: the recognised genuine works of any author: a clerical dignitary belonging to a cathedral: a list of saints canonised: a species of musical composition constructed according to a rule, one part following another in imitation. – *adj.* **canon′ical,** according to, or included in, a canon: authoritative: ecclesiastical. – *adv.* **canon′ically.** – *n.pl.* **canon′icals,** the official dress esp. of the clergy. – *v.t.* **can′onise,** to enrol in the canon, or list of saints. – *ns.* **canonisã′tion; can′on-law,** a code of ecclesiastical law based on the canons of the early church; **can′onry,** the benefice of a canon. [O.E. *canon* – L. *canon* – Gr. *kanōn,* a straight rod.]

canopy, *kan′o-pi, n.* a covering hung over a throne or bed: any similar covering: the transparent cover over the cockpit of an aircraft. – *v.t.* to cover as with a canopy: – *pr.p.* can′opying, *pa.p.* can′opied. [Fr. *canapé* – Low L. *canopeum* – Gr. *kōnōpeion,* a (*cap.*) curtain – *kōnōps,* a mosquito.]

cant, *kant, v.i.* to talk in an affectedly solemn or hypocritical way. – *n,* a hypocritical or affected style of speech: the language peculiar to a class (e.g. to thieves): conventional talk of any kind. [L. *cantãre,* freq. of *canēre,* to sing.]

cant, *kant, n.* an inclination from the level: a toss or jerk: a sloping or tilted position. – *v.t.* and *v.i.* to turn on the edge or corner: to tilt or toss suddenly. [Prob. conn. with Du. *kant;* Ger. *kante,* corner.]

can′t, *känt,* coll. contraction for **cannot.**

Cantab, *kan′tab,* for **Cantabrigian,** *adj* of or pertaining to the Cambridge University. [L. *Cantabrigia,* Cambridge.]

cantabile, *kän-täb′ē-lā, adj.* easy and flowing. [It.]

cantaloup, *kan′ta-lōōp, n.* a small, ribbed variety of musk-melon. [Fr., – It. *Cantalupo,* a town near Rome, where it was first grown in Europe.]

cantankerous, *kan-tang′kėr-us, adj.* perverse in temper, quarrelsome. – *adv.* **cantan′kerously.** – *n.* **cantan′kerousness.** [M.E. *contek,* strife.]

cantata, *kan-tä′tä, n.* a short oratorio or opera intended for concert performance only. – *n.* **cantatrice** (*kän-tä-trē′chā*), a female singer. [It., – L. *cantãre,* freq. of *canēre,* to sing.]

canteen, *kan-tēn′, n.* a vessel used by soldiers for holding liquors: a refreshment room in barracks, factory, &c.: a case for cutlery. [Fr. *cantine* – It. *cantina,* a cellar.]

canter, *kan′tér, n.* an easy gallop. – *v.i.* to move at an easy gallop. – *v.t.* to make to canter. [Orig. *Canterbury-gallop,* from the easy pace at which the pilgrims rode to Canterbury.]

Canterbury bell, *kan′tér-ber-i bel, n.* a variety of campanula. [Supposed to resemble the bells on the horses of pilgrims to Canterbury.]

cantharides, *kan-thar′i-dēz, n.pl.* a preparation used in medicine made from dried blister beetles, esp. those known as Spanish flies.

[L., – Gr. *kantharis,* a blister beetle, pl. *kantharidēs.*]

canticle, *kan′ti-kl, n.* a song: a non-metrical hymn: (*pl., cap.*) the Song of Solomon. [L. *canticulum,* dim. of *canticum* – *cantus,* a song.]

cantilever, *kan′ti-lēv-ér, n.* a large bracket for supporting cornices, balconies, and stairs. – **cantilever bridge,** one composed of self-supporting projecting arms built inwards from the piers and meeting in the middle of the span, where they are connected together. [**cant,** angle, and **lever.**]

cantle, *kan′tl, n.* a corner, edge, or slice of anything. [**cant** (2).]

canto, *kan′tō, n.* a division of a long poem: (*mus.*) the part that carries the melody: – *pl.* **can′tos.** [It., – L. *cantus* – *canēre,* to sing.]

canton, *kan′ton, kan-ton′, n.* a district: one of the Swiss federal states. – *v.t.* to divide into cantons: (mil. pron. *kan-tōōn′*) to allot quarters to troops. – *n.* **canton′ment** (mil. pron. *kan-tōōn′-ment*), the temporary quarters of troops: in India, a permanent military town. [O.Fr. *canton;* It. *cantone,* corner, district – *canto,* a corner; cf. **cant** (2).]

cantor, *kan′tor,* the leader of the singing in church. [L., singer – *canēre,* to sing.]

Canuck, Kanuck, *kan-uk′, n.* a Canadian: a French Canadian.

canvas, *kan′vas, n.* a coarse cloth made of hemp or other material, used for sails, tents, &c., and for painting on: the sails of a ship. – **under canvas,** with sails spread: living in tents. [O.Fr. *canevas* – L. *cannabis* – Gr. *kannabis,* hemp.]

canvass, *kan′vas, v.t.* (*obs.*) to toss in a canvas sheet: to discuss: to examine: to solicit the votes, custom, &c., of. – *v.i.* to solicit votes, &c. – *n.* close examination: a solicitation. – *n.* **can′vasser.** [From **canvas.**]

canyon. Same as **cãnon.**

canzone, *kant-sō′nä, n.* a song or air resembling a madrigal but less strict. – (*dim.*) **canzonet, canzonette** (*kan-zō-net′*). [It., a song – L. *cantiō, -ōnis* – *canēre,* to sing.]

caoutchouc, *kow′chōōk, n.* raw rubber, gum-elastic, the latex or juice of rubber trees. [Fr. – Carib (q.v.) *cahuchu.*]

cap, *kap, n.* an unbrimmed covering for the head: a cover: the top. – *v.t.* to cover with a cap: to confer a degree or distinction on: to outdo or surpass: – *pr.p.* capp′ing; *pa.p.* capped. – *n.* **capp′ing,** a covering: a graduation ceremony. – **cap and bells,** the characteristic marks of a professional jester; **cap in hand,** submissively. – **set one's cap at,** of a woman, to try to win the admiration of (a man); **the cap fits,** the allusion is felt to apply. [O.E. *cæppe* – Low L. *cappa,* a cape or cope.]

capable, *kāp′a-bl, adj.* having ability or skill to do (often with *of*): competent: susceptible (of): suitable for, adapted to. – *n.* **capabil′ity,** quality or state of being capable: (usu. in *pl.*) feature capable of being used or developed. – *adv.* **cap′ably.** [Fr., – Low L. *capãbilis* – L. *capēre,* to hold, take.]

capacity, *kap-as′i-ti, n* power of holding, containing, absorbing, or grasping: volume: ability: power of mind: character (e.g. *in his* *capacity as leader*): legal competence: maximum possible content, or output.—*adj.* **capā′cious,** roomy, wide.—*adv.* **capā′ciously.** —*n.* **capā′ciousness.**—*n.* **capăc′itance,** property that allows a system or body to store an electric charge: the value of this expressed in farads.—*v.t.* **capăc′itate,** to make capable, to qualify.—*n.* **capăc′itor,** an electric device having capacitance. [Fr.,—L. *capăcitās*—*capěre,* to take, hold.]

cap-à-pie, *kap-a-pē′, adv.* from head to foot (e.g. *armed cap-à-pie*—of a knight). [O.Fr. *cap a pie* (mod. *de pied en cap*)—L. *caput,* head, *pēs,* foot.]

caparison, *ka-par′is-ón, n.* the covering of a horse: a rich cloth laid over a war-horse: dress and ornaments.—*v.t.* to cover with a cloth, as a horse: to dress very richly. [Fr. *caparaçon*—Sp. *caparazón*—*capa,* a cape, cover—Low L. *cappa.*]

cape, *kāp, n.* a covering for the shoulders attached as to a coat or cloak: a sleeveless cloak. [O.Fr. *cape*—Low L. *cappa.*]

cape, *kāp, n.* a head or point of land running into the sea.—**Cape Coloured,** a person of mixed race, mainly in the W. Cape area; **the Cape,** Cape of Good Hope: Cape Province, Capetown and Cape Peninsula. [Fr. *cap*—L. *caput,* the head.]

caper, *kā′pér, n.* the pickled flower-bud of the caper-shrub, much used in sauces. [L. *capparis*—Gr. *kapparis.*]

caper, *kā′pér, v.i.* to leap or skip like a goat: to dance in a frolicsome manner.—*n.* a leap: a prank.—**to cut a caper,** to frisk. [Shortened form of **capriole.**]

capercailzie, *kā-pér-kāl′yi, n.* a large species of grouse. [Gael. *capull coille,* 'horse of the wood'.]

capillary, *ka-pil′ár-i, kap′il-àr-i, adj.* as fine or minute as a hair: having a very small bore, as a tube.—*n.* a tube with a fine bore: (*pl.*) the minute vessels that unite the veins and arteries in animals.—*n.* **capillar′ity,** a phenomenon depending on surface tension and angle of contact, of which the rise of liquids in capillary tubes and the action of blotting paper and wicks are examples. [L. *capillāris*—*capillus,* hair, akin to *caput.*]

capital, *kap′it-ál, adj.* relating to the head: involving the loss of the head or of life: fatal: chief, principal: (*coll.*) excellent.—*n.* the chief or most important thing: the chief town or seat of government: a large letter: capitalists collectively: the stock or money for carrying on any business: any advantage used as a means of gaining further advantage.—*v.t.* **cap′italīse,** to convert into capital or money: to furnish with capital: to turn to advantage: to write with capital letters.—*ns.* **capitalisā′tion; cap′italism,** condition of possessing capital: the economic system controlled by capitalists; **cap′italist,** one who has capital or money: one who derives income from invested capital.—*adv.* **cap′itally,** chiefly, principally: (*coll.*) excellently.—**capital gains,** profit from the sale of bonds or other assets: **capital goods,** producers' (q.v.) goods; **capital levy,** an exaction by a state, for a specific purpose, of a proportion of the capital of its members; **capital murder,** one for which the punishment is death; **capital ship,** a warship of the largest and strongest class.—**make capital out of,** to turn to advantage. [O.Fr. *capitel*—L. *capitālis*—*caput,* the head.]

capital, *kap′it-ál, n.* the head or top part of a column, &c. [L. *capitellum*—*caput,* head.]

capitation, *kap-it-ā′sh(ó)n, n.* numbering heads or individuals: a poll-tax.—**capitation grant,** a grant of a fixed sum per head. [L. *capitātus,* headed, *capitātiō,* poll-tax—*caput,* head.]

Capitol, *kap′it-ol, n.* the temple of Jupiter at Rome, built on the *Capitoline* hill: (*U.S.*) the building where Congress meets. [L. *Capitōlium*—*caput,* the head.]

capitulate, *kap-it′ūl-āt, v.i.* to yield or surrender on certain conditions or heads.—*n.* **capitulā′tion.** [Low L. *capitulātus,* pa.p of *capitulāre,* to arrange under heads—*capitulum,* a chapter.]

capon, *kā′pón, n.* a castrated cock. [O.E. *capun*; L. *capō, -ōnis*—Gr. *kapōn*—*koptein,* to cut.]

capote, *ka-pōt′, n.* a long kind of cloak or mantle. [Fr., dim. of *cape,* a cloak.]

caprice, *ka-prēs′, n.* a change of humour or opinion without reason, a freak: disposition or mood inclining to such changes: a fanciful and sprightly work in music, &c.—*adj.* **capri′cious** (*-ri′-shús*), full of caprice: changeable.—*adv.* **capri′ciously.**—*n.* **capri′ciousness.** [Fr. *caprice* and It. *capriccio*; perh. from L. *caper,* a goat.]

Capricorn, *kap′ri-körn, n.* a constellation and a sign of the zodiac, represented as a horned goat, which marks the limit of the sun's course southward. [L. *capricornus*—*caper,* a goat, *cornu,* a horn.]

caprine, *kap′rin, adj.* like a goat. [L. *caprīnus*—*caper,* a goat.]

capriole, *kap′ri-ōl, n.* a caper: a leap without advancing.—*v.i.* to leap: to caper. [O.Fr. *capriole*—It. *capriola*—L. *caper, capra,* a goat.]

capsicum, *kap′si-kùm, n.* a genus of tropical shrubs yielding cayenne pepper. [Perh. L. *capsa,* a case—*capěre,* to take, hold.]

capsize, *kap-sīz′, v.t.* to upset.—*v.i.* to be upset.

capstan, *kap′stan, n.* an upright machine turned by bars, used for winding e.g. a ship's cable. [Fr. *cabestan, capestan,* through Low L. forms from L. *capěre,* to take, hold.]

capsule, *kap′sūl, n.* a dry, dehiscent seed-vessel consisting of two or more carpels: (*zool.*) a fibrous or membraneous covering: a gelatine case for holding a dose of medicine: a metal or other container: a self-contained spacecraft or a part of one, manned or unmanned, recoverable or non-recoverable.—*adj.* **cap′sular.** [Fr.,—L. *capsula,* dim. of *capsa,* case.]

captain, *kap′tin, n.* a head or chief officer: the commander of a troop of horse, a company of infantry, or a ship: the leader of a team or club.—*v.t.* to be captain of.—*n.* **cap′taincy,** the rank or commission of a captain. [O.Fr. *capitaine*—Low L. *capitāneus,* chief—L. *caput,* head.]

caption, *kap′sh(ó)n, n.* the act of taking: an arrest: a newspaper heading, or a note accompanying an illustration, cinematograph picture, &c.—*v.t.* to give a caption (heading, &c.) to.—*adj.* **cap′tious,** ready to catch at faults or to take offence, carping.—*adv.* **cap′tiously.**—*n.* **cap′tiousness.** [L. *captiō, -ōnis*—*capěre,* to take.]

Neutral vowels in unaccented syllables: *em′pér-ór*; for certain sounds in foreign words see p. ix.

captivate, *kap'tiv-āt*, *v.t.* to charm: to engage the affections of. [L. *captīvāre*, *-ātum*, to take captive.]

captive, *kap'tiv*, *n.* a prisoner: one kept in confinement.—*adj.* confined: kept in bondage: restrained by a rope (as a balloon): (*fig.*) charmed, captivated by (with *to*)—*ns.* **captiv'ity; cap'tor**, one who takes a captive or a prize; **cap'ture**, the act of taking: the thing taken: an arrest.—*v.t.* to take as a prize: to take by force: to take possession of (e.g. attention, imagination). [L. *captīvus—capĕre, captum*, to take.]

Capuchin, *kap'ū-chin* or *kap-ōō-shēn'*, *n.* a friar of a branch of the Franciscan order, so called from the hood he wears: a hooded pigeon. [Fr. *capuchin*, It. *cappucino*, a cowl—Low L. *cappa*.]

capybara, *kap-i-bär'a*, *n.* the largest living rodent, a native of S. America, allied to the guinea-pig. [Brazilian.]

car, *kär*, *n.* a vehicle moved on wheels, as an automobile, a tramway car, &c.: a railway carriage: the part of a balloon or airship that carries passengers and cargo.—*n.* **car'-port**, a covered parking space, esp. a space under a roof projecting from a building. [Norm. Fr. *carre*—Low L. *carra*, itself a Celt. word.]

carabine. See **carbine.**

caracal, *kar'a-kàl*, *n.* the Persian lynx. [Fr., prob. from Turk. *qara-qulaq*, black ear.]

caracole, *kar'a-kōl*, *n.* a half-turn or wheel made by a horseman: a winding stair.—*v.i.* to turn half-round: to prance about. [Fr. *caracole*—It. *caracollo*—Sp. *caracol*, a spiral snail-shell.]

carafe, *ka-räf'*, *n.* a bottle holding water or wine for the table. [Fr. *carafe*, prob. from Ar. *gharafa*, to draw water.]

caramel, *kar'a-mėl*, *n.* a dark-brown substance produced by heating sugar above its melting-point, used for colouring or flavouring: a confection made with sugar, butter, &c.—*adj.* made of or containing caramel: of the colour of caramel.—*v.t.* and *v.i.* **car'amelise.** [Fr.—Sp. *caramelo.*]

carat, *kar'át*, *n.* a measure of weight for gems: a twenty-fourth part, taken as a unit in stating the fineness of gold, so that e.g. 18-carat gold means an alloy in which 18 out of 24 parts are pure gold. [Fr. *qīrāt*, perh. from Gr. *keration*, a carob seed used as a weight.]

caravan, *kar'a-van, -van'*, *n.* a company travelling together for security, esp. in crossing the desert: a covered van: a house on wheels.—*n.* **caravanserai**, *kar-a-van'ser-ī*, a kind of unfurnished inn or extensive enclosed court where caravans stop.— Also **caravansarai, -sary.** [Pers. *kārwānsarāī—kārwān*, caravan, *sarāī*, inn.]

caravel, *kar'av-el*, *n.* a kind of light sailing-vessel. [Fr.,—It. *caravella*; cf. Low L. *carabus*, Gr. *karabos*, a bark.]

caraway, *kar'a-wā*, *n.* a plant with aromatic seeds, used as a tonic and condiment. [Prob. Sp. *alcaravea* (*carvi*)—Ar. *karwiyā*; cf. Gr. *karon*.]

carbide, *kär'bīd*, *n.* a compound of carbon with another element: calcium carbide, used to generate acetylene. [**carbon.**]

carbine, *kär'bīn*, *n.* a short light musket—also

carabin(e), *kar'a-bin.—ns.* **carbineer', carabineer'**, a soldier armed with a carbine. [Fr. *carabine.*]

carbohydrate, *kär-bō-hī'drāt*, *n.* a compound of carbon, hydrogen, and oxygen, the last two being in the same proportion as in water—e.g. sugars, starch, cellulose. [See **carbon, hydrate.**]

carbolic acid, *kar-bol'ik as'id*, *n.* an acid produced from coal-tar, used as a disinfectant. [L. *carbō*, coal, *oleum*, oil.]

carbon, *kär'bon*, *n.* a non-metallic element (symbol C; at. no. 6) widely diffused, occurring as pure charcoal, diamond and graphite: a carbon copy.—*adj.* **carbona'ceous**, pertaining to, or composed of, carbon.—*n.* **car'bonate**, a salt of carbonic acid.—*adj.* **carbonif'erous**, producing carbon or coal.—*n.* (*cap.*) the period of the Primary geological era between the Devonian and the Permian.—*v.t.* **car'bonise**, to impregnate with, or combine with, carbon.—*n.* **carbonisā'tion.—Carboniferous System**, the rocks (containing great coal-measures) formed during this period.—**carbon-14**, a radioactive isotope of carbon u.ed as a tracer element in biological studies; **carbon black**, a fine carbon used in the manufacture of rubber and in other industries; **carbon copy**, a duplicate of writing made by means of **carbon paper**, a paper coated with lamp black, &c.; **carbon dating**, estimating the date of death of prehistoric organic material from the amount of carbon-14 still present in it; **carbon disulphide**, a poisonous, inflammable liquid used as a solvent for rubber, &c.; **carbonic acid**, a weak acid formed by the solution in water of **carbon dioxide**, a gas evolved by respiration and combustion. [Fr. *carbone*—L. *carbō, -ōnis*, coal.]

Carborundum, *kär-bòr-un'dum*, *n.* a proprietary name for a compound of silicon and carbon used as an abrasive.

carboy, *kär'boi*, *n.* a large bottle with a frame of basket-work. [Pers. *qarābah.*]

carbuncle, *kär'bung-kl*, *n.* a fiery-red precious stone (a garnet): an inflamed ulcer.—*adj.* **carbun'cular.** [L. *carbunculus*, dim. of *carbō*, coal.]

carburettor, *kär'bū-ret-ôr* (or *-ret'-*), **carburetter**, *n.* part of an internal-combustion engine in which air is mixed with volatile fuel. [Fr. *carbure*—L. *carbō*, coal.]

carcanet, *kär'ka-net*, *n.* a collar of jewels. [*Carcan*, an obsolete word for an iron collar used for punishment—Low L. *carcannum.*]

carcass, carcase, *kär'kás*, *n.* a dead body: (*disrespectfully*) a live human body: the framework of anything.—**carcass meat, carcase meat**, raw meat as prepared for the butcher's shop, not tinned. [O.Fr. *carquois.*]

carcinoma, *kär-si-nō'ma*, *n.* a cancer.—*n.* **carcin'ogen**, a substance that encourages the growth of cancer.—*adj.* **carcinogen'ic.** [Gr. *karkinōma—karkinos*, crab.]

card, *kärd*, *n.* a small piece of pasteboard: one with figures for playing a game, with a person's name and address, with a greeting, invitation, message, or programme: (*pl.*) game(s) played with cards: a wag, an eccentric.—*ns.* **card'board**, a stiff, finely finished pasteboard; **card'-sharp'er**, one who systematically cheats at cards; **card'-vote**, a voting system that gives each delegate's vote a value proportionate to the number of persons he represents.—**get one's cards** (*slang*), to be dismissed; **on the cards**, not improbable. [Fr. *carte*—L. *c(h)arta*—Gr. *chartēs*, a leaf of papyrus.]

card, *kärd*, *n.* an instrument for combing wool and flax.—*v.t.* to comb (wool, &c.). [Fr. *carde*—L. *carduus*, a thistle.]

cardiac, *kär'di-ak*, *adj.* belonging to the heart.—*ns.* **car'diograph**, an instrument for recording movements of the heart; **car'diogram**, a tracing obtained from a cardiograph; **cardiol'ogy**, the science dealing with the structure, function and diseases of the heart. [Gr. *kardia*, the heart.]

cardigan, *kär'di-gan*, *n.* a knitted woollen jacket. [Lord *Cardigan* (1797-1868).]

cardinal, *kär'din-äl*, *adj.* denoting that on which a thing hinges or depends, fundamental.—*n.* one of the dignitaries next to the Pope in the R.C. Church hierarchy.—*ns.* **car'dinalate**, **car'dinalship**, the office or dignity of a cardinal.—**cardinal numbers**, numbers expressing how many (1, 2, 3, &c.—1st, 2nd, 3rd, &c., being *ordinals*); **cardinal points**, the four chief points of the compass—north, south, east, and west; **cardinal virtues**, justice, prudence, temperance, fortitude, so called because the whole of human nature was supposed to hinge or turn on them. [Fr.,—L. *cardinālis*—*cardō*, *cardinis*, a hinge.]

care, *kär*, *n.* affliction: anxiety: heedfulness: charge, keeping: the cause or object of anxiety.—*v.i.* to be anxious (for, about): to be disposed, willing (to): to have a liking or fondness (for): to provide (for).—*adjs.* **care'-free'**, light-hearted; **care'ful**, full of care: heedful: (*B.*) anxious.—*adv.* **care'fully.**—*n.* **care'fulness.**—*adj.* **care'less**, without care: heedless, unconcerned.—*adv.* **care'lessly.**—*ns.* **care'lessness**; **care'tak'er**, one put in charge of anything, esp. a building.—*adj.* exercising temporary control or supervision (as *caretaker government*).—*adj.* **care'-worn**, worn or vexed with care.—**take care**, to be cautious; **take care of**, to look after with care: (*coll.*) to make the necessary arrangements regarding. [O.E. *caru*; O.N. *kæra*, to lament.]

careen, *ka-rēn'*, *v.t.* to lay a ship on her side to repair her bottom and keel.—*v.i.* to heel over. [Fr. *carène*—L. *carīna*, the bottom of a ship, the keel.]

career, *ka-rēr'*, *n.* a race: a rush: progress through life, esp. advancement in calling or profession.—*adj.* having a professional career: dedicated to a career.—*v.i.* to move or run rapidly. [Fr. *carrière*, a racecourse.]

caress, *kä-res'*, *v.t.* to touch endearingly, to fondle.—*n.* an endearing touch. [Fr. *caresser*—It. *carezza*, an endearment; Low L. *cāritia*—*cārus*, dear.]

caret, *kar'et*, *n.* a mark, ∧, to show where to insert something omitted. [L., 'there is wanting'.]

cargo, *kär'gō*, *n.* the goods a ship carries: its load:—*pl.* **car'goes**. [Sp. from root of **car.**]

Carib, *kar'ib*, *n.* one of a native race inhabiting parts of Central America and the north

of South America, or their language.—*adj.* **Caribbē'an.** [From Sp.; cf. **cannibal.**]

caribou, *kar-i-bōō'*, *n.* the American reindeer. [Canadian Fr.]

caricature, *kar'i-kä-tyùr, -chòōr, n.* a likeness or imitation so exaggerated or distorted as to appear ridiculous.—*v.t.* to make ridiculous by an absurd likeness or imitation.—*n.* **caricatur'ist.** [It. *caricatura*—*caricare*, to load, from root of **car.**]

caries, *kā'ri-ēz*, *n.* decay, esp. of teeth.—*adj.* **cā'rious**, decayed. [L.]

carillon, *kar'il-yon*, *ka-ril'yon*, *n.* a set of bells for playing tunes: a melody played on them. [Fr.,—Low L. *quadrilliō, -ōnis*, a quaternary, because carillons were formerly rung on four bells.]

cariole, **carriole**, *kar'i-ōl*, *n.* a small open carriage: a light cart. [Fr. *carriole*—root of **car.**]

cark, *kärk*, *n.* (*arch.*) anxiety.—*v.t.* to burden, harass.—*adj.* **cark'ing**, distressing. [Norm.Fr. *kark(e)*—Low L. *carcāre*—*carricāre*, to load.]

carl, *kärl*, *n.* a man: a fellow.—*n.* **carline** (*kär'lin*), an old woman: a witch. [O.N. *karl*, a man, a male. Cf. **churl.**]

Carmelite, *kär'mel-īt*, *n.* a friar of the order of Our Lady of Mount *Carmel*, in Syria, founded about 1156: a variety of pear.

carminative, *kär-min'ä-tiv, kär'min-ä-tiv, n.* a medicine to relieve flatulence.—Also *adj.* [L. *carmināre*, to card or cleanse (wool).]

carmine, *kär'mīn, -min, n.* the red colouring matter of the kermes insect. [Fr. *carmin*, through Sp. from Ar.; cf. **crimson.**]

carnage, *kär'nij*, *n.* slaughter. [Fr.,—It. *carnaggio*, carnage—L. *carō, carnis*, flesh.]

carnal, *kär'näl*, *adj.* fleshly: sensual: unspiritual.—*ns.* **car'nalist**, a sensualist; **carnal'ity**, state of being carnal.—*adv.* **car'nally.** [L. *carnālis*—*car(ō), carnis*, flesh.]

carnation, *kär-nā'sh(ò)n, n,* flesh-colour: a garden flower, a variety of the clove pink. [L. *carnātiō*, fleshiness.]

carnelian. See **cornelian.**

carnival, *kär'ni-väl, n.* a feast observed by Roman Catholics just before the fast of Lent: any season of revelry or indulgence: a fairlike entertainment. [It. *carnevale*—Low L. *carnelevārium*, apparently from L. *carnem levāre*, to put away flesh.]

Carnivora, *kär-niv'ō-ra, n.pl.* an order of flesh-eating animals.—*adj.* **carniv'orous**, flesh-eating.—*adv.* **carniv'orously.**—*ns.* **carniv'orousness**; **car'nivore**, a carnovorous animal. [L. *carō, carnis*, flesh, *vorāre*, to devour.]

carob, *kar'ob, n.* a leguminous Mediterranean tree, one of those known as the 'locust tree'. [Through Fr. from Ar. *kharrūbah*; cf. **carat.**]

carol, *kar'ol, n.* a song of joy or praise.—*v.i.* to sing a carol: to sing or warble.—*v.t.* to praise or celebrate in song:—*pr.p.* **car'olling**; *pa.p.* **car'olled.** [O.Fr. *carole*; It. *carola*, orig. a ring-dance.]

carotid, *ka-rot'id*, *adj.* relating to the two great arteries of the neck. [Gr. *karōtidĕs* (pl.)—*karos*, sleep, the ancients supposing that deep sleep was caused by compression of them.]

carouse, *kar-owz', n.* a drinking-bout: a noisy revel.—*v.i.* to hold a drinking-bout: to drink

Neutral vowels in unaccented syllables: *em'pèr-òr*; for certain sounds in foreign words see p. ix.

freely and noisily.—*n.* **carous'al**, a carouse: a feast. [O.Fr. *carous*, Fr. *carrousse*—Ger. *gar aus*, quite out!—that is, empty the glass.]

carousel, kar-ōō-sel', -zel, *n.* a tournament: a merry-go-round: a rotating conveyor, e.g. for luggage at an airport. [Fr. *carrousel.*]

carp, kärp, *v.i.* to catch at small faults or errors (with *at*).—*n.* **carp'er**. [Most prob. Scand., O.N. *karpa*, to boast, modified in meaning through likeness to L. *carpĕre*, to pluck, deride.]

carp, kärp, *n.* a fresh-water fish common in ponds. [O.Fr. *carpe*—Low L. *carpa*; perh. Gmc.]

carpal, kär'pál, *adj.* pertaining to the wrist.— *n.* a carpal bone. [Gr. *karpos*, wrist.]

carpel, kär'pêl, *n.* a modified leaf forming the whole or part of the pistil of a flower. [Gr. *karpos*, fruit.]

carpenter, kär'pent-ér, *n.* a worker in timber as used in building houses, &c.—*v.i.* to do the work of a carpenter.—*n.* **car'pentry**, the trade or work of a carpenter. [O.Fr. *carpentier*—Low L. *carpentārius*—*carpentum*, a wagon, car, from root of **car**.]

carpet, kär'pét, *n.* the woven or felted covering of floors, stairs, &c.: an expanse of growing flowers, &c.: a smooth, or thin, surface or covering.—*v.t.* to cover with, or as with, a carpet: to have (someone) up for reprimand:—*pr.p.* car'peting; *pa.p.* car'peted.—*ns.* **car'pet-bag**, a travelling-bag made of carpeting; **car'pet-bagg'er**, a new-comer, esp. a political candidate for a constituency in which he does not reside; **car'peting**, material of which carpets are made; **car'pet-knight**, a knight who has not proved his valour in action: an effeminate person.—**on the carpet**, under discussion: up before someone in authority for reprimand; **sweep under the carpet**, to hide from notice, put out of mind (unpleasant problems or facts); **to be carpeted**, to be reprimanded. [O.Fr. *carpite*—Low L. *carpeta*, a coarse fabric made from rags pulled to pieces—L. *carpěre*, to pluck.]

carrack, kar'ak, *n.* (*hist.*) an armed merchant vessel.—Also **car'ack**. [O.Fr. *carraque*.]

carrag(h)een, kar-a-gēn', *n.* an edible seaweed from which size is made—also known as *Irish moss*. [Prob. Ir. *carraigín*, little rock.]

carriage, kar'ij, *n.* act, or cost, of carrying: a vehicle for carrying: behaviour, bearing: (*B.*) baggage.—*n.* **carr'iage-way**, road or part of a road used by vehicles.—**carriage and pair**, a turn-out of a carriage and two horses; **carriage free**, free of charge for carrying; **carriage paid**, **carriage forward**, phrases indicating that the charge for conveying goods is, or is not, prepaid. [From **carry**.]

carrier. See **carry**.

carriole. See **cariole**.

carrion, kar'i-ón, *n.* the dead and putrid body or flesh of any animal: anything vile.—*adj.* relating to, or feeding on, putrid flesh. [Fr. *carogne*—L. *carō*, *carnis*, flesh.]

carronade, kar-ón-ād', *n.* a short cannon of large bore, first made at *Carron* in Stirlingshire.

carrot, kar'ót, *n.* a vegetable with a sweet and edible tapering root of reddish or yellowish colour.—*adj.* **carr'oty**, carrot-coloured (applied to the hair). [Fr. *carotte*—L. *carōta*.]

carry, kar'i, *v.t.* to convey or transport: to bear: to support, sustain: to bear (oneself): to extend: to take by force: to gain: to gain by a majority of votes: to do the work of, or perform in sport or entertainment well enough to cover up the deficiencies of (another).—*v.i.* (of a voice, a gun, &c.) to reach, indicating its range:—*pr.p.* carr'ying; *pa.p.* carr'ied—*n.* the distance over which anything is carried.—*ns.* **carr'ier**, one who carries, esp. for hire: a receptacle or other device for carrying: one who transmits an infectious disease without himself suffering from it: (*radio*, &c.) a steady current by modulations of which signals are transmitted: non-active material mixed with, and chemically identical to, a radioactive compound; **carr'ier-pig'eon**, a pigeon with homing instinct, used for carrying messages.—**carry all before one**, to overcome all resistance; **carry on**, to promote: to manage: (*coll.*) to misbehave (*ns.* **carr'y-on**, **carr'ying-on**): (*mil.*) to continue: to proceed; **carry one's point**, to make one's plan or view prevail; **carry out**, **through**, to accomplish; **carry the day**, to gain the victory.—**be carried away**, to be highly excited: to be misled. [O.Fr. *carier*—Low L. *carricāre*, to cart—L. *carrus*, a car.]

cart, kärt, *n.* a two-wheeled vehicle for conveying heavy loads.—*v.t.* to convey in a cart.—*ns.* **cart'age**, the act, or cost, of carting; **cart'er**, one who drives a cart; **cart'wright**, a carpenter who makes carts.—**put the cart before the horse**, to reverse the natural order of things. [Ety. uncertain; O.E. *cræt*, or O.N. *kartr.*]

carte, kärt, *n.* Same as **quarte**.

carte, kärt, *n.* a bill of fare.—*adv.* **à la carte**, (of a meal) according to the bill of fare, chosen dish by dish.—*ns.* **carte-blanche** (*bläsh*), a blank paper, duly signed, to be filled up at the recipient's pleasure: freedom of action; **cart'el**, a challenge: an agreement for exchange of prisoners: (*kär-tel'*) a combination of business firms to gain monopoly. [Fr.,—L. *c(h)arta*. See **card** (1).]

Cartesian, kar-tē'zi-án, -zhyán, *adj.* relating to the French philosopher *Descartes* (1596–1650), or to his philosophy or mathematical methods.

Carthusian, kär-thū'zi-án, *n.* a monk of an order founded in 1086, noted for its strictness: a scholar of the Charterhouse (q.v.) School.—*adj.* of or pertaining to the order. [L. *Cartusiānus*; from a village (now *La Grande Chartreuse*) near Grenoble near which their first monastery was founded.]

cartilage, kär'ti-lij, *n.* in vertebrate animals, a firm elastic substance, often converted later into bone: gristle.—*adj.* **cartilaginous** (-*laj'*-). [Fr.,—L. *cartilāgō*; cf. *crātis* (see **crate**).]

cartography, kär-tog'ra-fi, *n.* map-making.—*ns.* **cartog'rapher**; **car'togram**, a map presenting statistical information in diagrammatic form. [L. *c(h)arta*—Gr. *chartēs*, a leaf of papyrus, and Gr. *graphein*, to write.]

cartology, kär-tol'ó-ji, *n.* the science of maps and charts.—*adj.* **cartolog'ical**. [L. *c(h)arta*—Gr. *chartēs*, a leaf of papyrus, and Gr. *logos*, discourse.]

carton, kär'tón, *n.* a thin pasteboard or a box made from such. [Fr. See **cartoon**.]

fāte, fär; mē, hûr (her); *mīne; mōte, för; mūte; mōōn, fŏŏt;* ᴛʜᴇɴ (then)

cartoon, *kär-tōōn′*, *n.* a preparatory drawing on strong paper to be transferred to frescoes, tapestry, &c.: any large sketch or design on paper: a comic or satirical drawing: a cinematograph film made by photographing a succession of drawings. [Fr. *carton* (It. *cartone*)—*carte*; see **carte** (2).]

cartouche, *kär-tōōsh′*, *n.* a case for holding cartridges: (*archit.*) an ornament resembling a scroll of paper with the ends rolled up: an oval figure on ancient Egyptian monuments or papyri enclosing characters expressing royal or divine names.—Also **cartouch′**. [Fr.,—It. *cartoccio*—L. *c(h)arta*. See **card** (1).]

cartridge, *kär′trij*, *n.* a case containing the charge for a gun.—**blank cartridge** (see **blank**).—*n.* **car′tridge-pā′per**, a light-coloured strong paper, originally manufactured for making cartridges. [A corr. of **cartouche**.]

cartulary, *kär′tū-lär-i*, *n.* a register-book of a monastery, &c. [Low L. *c(h)artularium*—L. *c(h)arta*, a leaf of papyrus.]

carve, *kärv*, *v.t.* to cut into forms, devices, &c.: to make or shape by cutting: to cut up (meat) into slices or pieces.—*v.i.* to exercise the trade of a sculptor.—*p.adj.* **carv′en**, carved.—*ns.* **carv′er**, one who carves: a sculptor: a carving-knife; **carving**, the act or art of carving: the device or figure carved.—**carve out**, to hew out: to gain by one's exertions; **carve up**, to subdivide, apportion. [O.E. *ceorfan*, to cut; Du. *kerven*; Ger. *kerben*, to notch.]

carvel, *kär′vel*, *n.* older form of **caravel**.—*adj.* **car′vel-built**, built with planks meeting flush at the seams; opp. to *clinker-built*.

caryatid, *kar-i-at′id*, *n.* a female figure used instead of a column to support an entablature:—*pl.* **caryat′ides** (-*id-ēz*). [Gr. *Karyātis*.]

Casanova, *kas-ä-nō′va*, *n.* (*coll.*) a person conspicuous for his amorous adventures, as was Giovanni Jacopo *Casanova* de Seingalt (1725-1798), whose Memoirs, written in French, tell a tale of adventure, roguery, intrigue, scandal, of many kinds.

cascade, *kas-kād′*, *n.* a waterfall: connection of apparatus in series.—*v.i.* to fall in cascades. [Fr.,—It.—L. *cadĕre*, to fall.]

cascara, *kas-kä′ra*, or *käs′ka-ra*, *n.* a Californian bark used as a tonic aperient. [Sp. *cáscara*, bark.]

case, *kās*, *n.* a covering, box, or sheath: the boards and back of a book: the tray in which a compositor has his types before him.—*v.t.* to enclose in a case.—*v.t.* **case′-hard′en**, to harden on the surface, as by carbonising iron.—*adj.* **case-hardened** (*fig.*), callous: incorrigible.—*ns.* **case′-knife**, a large knife kept in a sheath; **case′ment**, the frame of a window: a window that opens on hinges: a hollow moulding; **case′ment-cloth**, a plain cotton fabric; **case′-shot**, canister-shot; **cas′ing**, the act of the verb *case*: an outside covering of boards, plaster, &c. [O. North Fr. *casse*—L. *capsa*—*capĕre*, to take.]

case, *kās*, *n.* that which falls or happens, event: state or condition: subject of question or inquiry: a person under medical treatment: a legal statement of facts: (*gram.*) the grammatical relation of a noun, pronoun, or adjective to other words in a sentence, &c.:

(*slang*) an odd character.—*v.t.* (*slang*) to reconnoitre with a view to burglary.—*ns.* **case′-law**, law as decided in previous cases; **case′-work**, study of maladjusted individuals or families; **case′-work′er**.—**in case**, in the event that: lest; **make out a case**, to argue convincingly. [O.Fr. *cas*—L. *cāsus*, from *cadĕre*, to fall.]

casein, caseine, *kā′sē-in*, *n.* the principal albuminous constituent of milk or cheese.—*adj.* **cā′sēous**, pertaining to cheese. [Fr.,—L. *caseus*, cheese.]

casemate, *kās′māt*, *n.* (*orig.*) a loopholed gallery within the thickness of a wall, from which the garrison of a fort could fire upon an enemy: a heavily protected chamber or compartment, esp. one in which a gun is mounted.—*adj.* **case′mated**. [Fr.; ety. uncertain.]

casern(e), *kä-zern′*, *n.* a barrack. [Fr.,—Sp. *caserna*.]

cash, *kash*, *n.* coin or money: ready money.—*v.t.* to turn into or exchange for money.—*ns.* **cashier′**, one who has charge of the receiving and paying of money; **cash′-reg′ister**, a till that automatically and visibly records the amount put in.—**cash down**, immediate payment; **cash in on**, to profit by; **hard cash, spot cash**, ready money; **out of cash**, or **in cash**, without, or with, money: out of, or in, pocket. [O.Fr. *casse*, a box.]

cashier, *kash-ēr′*, *v.t.* to dismiss from a post in disgrace: to discard or put away. [Du. *casseren*, to cashier—L. *cassāre*—*cassus*, void, empty.]

cashmere, *kash′mēr*, *n.* (a shawl or fabric made from) fine soft *Kashmir* goats' hair: any similar product.

casino, *ka-sē′no*, *n.* a building with public dance halls, gaming tables, &c. [It.; from L. *casa*, a cottage.]

cask, *käsk*, *n.* a hollow round vessel for holding liquor, made of staves bound with hoops. [Fr. *casque*—Sp. *casco*, skull, helmet, cask.]

casket, *käsk′et*, *n.* a little cask or case: a small case for holding jewels, &c.: a coffin. [Ety. uncertain: hardly a dim. of **cask**.]

casque, *käsk*, *n.* a cover for the head: a helmet. [A doublet of **cask**.]

cassava, *ka-sä′vä*, *n.* the West Indian name of the manioc, and its product, tapioca.

casserole, *kas′e-rōl*, *n.* a stew-pan: a vessel in which food is both cooked and served: the food itself. [Fr.]

cassette, *kas-et′*, *n.* a light-tight container for an X-ray film, or one for film in a miniature camera: a holder with reel of magnetic tape, esp. tape on which there is pre-recorded material. [Fr. dim. of *casse*, case.]

cassia, *kas(h)′ya*, *n.* a coarser kind of cinnamon: the tree that yields it: a fragrant plant mentioned in Ps. xlv. 8: a shrub yielding senna. [L. *casia*—Gr. *kasia*—Heb.]

cassimere, *kas′i-mēr*, *n.* a twilled cloth of the finest wools.—Also **ker′seymere**. [Corr. of **cashmere**.]

cassock, *kas′ok*, *n.* a long black robe worn by clergy and choristers: a shorter garment, usually of black silk, worn under the pulpit gown by Scottish ministers. [Fr. *casaque*—It. *casacca*.]

Neutral vowels in unaccented syllables: *em′pér-ór*; for certain sounds in foreign words see p. ix.

cassowary, *kas'ō-wár-i*, *n.* a genus of running birds, found esp. in New Guinea, nearly related to the emus. [Malay *kasuārī* or *kasavārī*.]

cast, *kást*, *v.t.* to throw or fling: to shed, drop: to reckon: to mould or shape:—*pa.t.* and *pa.p.* cast.—*n.* act of casting: a throw: the thing thrown: the distance thrown: a motion, turn, or squint, as of the eye: matter ejected by an earthworm, or by a hawk, &c.: fly, hook, and gut: a mould: the form received from a mould: type or quality: a tinge: the assignment of the various parts of a play to the several actors: the company of actors playing rôles.—*n.* cast'away, one shipwrecked in a desolate place: an outcast.—*adj.* cast'-down, dejected. -*ns.* cast'ing, act of casting or moulding: that which is cast: a mould; cast'ing-vote, the vote by which the president of a meeting decides the issue when the other votes are equally divided; cast'-i'ron, an iron-carbon alloy distinguished from steel by the presence of impurities which make it unsuitable for working.—*adj.* rigid: unyielding, inflexible.— *adj.* cast'-off, laid aside or rejected.—*n.* cast'-steel, steel that has been cast, not shaped by mechanical working.—cast about, to look round enquiringly: to search; cast in the teeth of, to fling as a reproach against; cast off, to throw off: to set aside as useless: to unmoor: to eliminate stitches: to disown; cast on, to make stitches; cast up, to add up: to bring up as a reproach. [O.N. *kasta*, to throw.]

castanets, *kas'ta-nets*, *n.pl.* two hollow shells of ivory or hard wood, joined by a band passing round the thumb, and struck by the fingers to produce an accompaniment to dances and guitars. [Sp. *castañeta*—L. *castanea*, a chestnut.]

caste, *kást*, *n.* a social class in India: any exclusive social class.—lose caste, to descend in social rank. [Port. *casta*, breed, race—L. *castus*, pure, unmixed.]

castellan, castellated. See castle.

caster. Same as castor (2).

castigate, *kas'tig-āt*, *v.t.* to chastise: to criticise severely.—*ns.* castiga'tion; cas'tigator. [L. *castīgāre*, *-ātum*, from *castus*, pure.]

castle, *käs'l*, *n.* a fortified house or fortress: the residence of a prince or nobleman: anything built in the likeness of such: a piece in chess (also called *rook*).—*n.* castellan (*kas'tel-an*), governor or captain of a castle.—*adj.* cas'tellated, having turrets and battlements like a castle.—castles in the air, or in Spain, visionary projects. [O.E. *castel*—L. *castellum*, dim. of *castrum*, a fortified place.]

castor, *käs'tor*, *n.* the beaver: a hat made of its fur. [L., —Gr. *kastōr*.]

castor, *käs'tor*, *n.* a small wheel on the legs of furniture: a small vessel with perforated top for pepper, sugar, &c.—Also cas'ter. [cast.]

castor-oil, *käs'tor-oil*, *n.* a medicinal and lubricating oil obtained from a tropical plant.

castrate, *kas'trāt*, *v.t.* to deprive of the power of generation by removing the testicles, to geld: to take from or render imperfect.—*n.* castra'tion. [L. *castrāre*, *-ātum*.]

casual, *kaz(h)'ū-ál*, *adj.* accidental: unforeseen: occasional: careless: unceremonious.—*n.* a chance or occasional visitor, labourer,

pauper, &c.—*adv.* cas'ually.—*n.* cas'ualty, that which falls out: an accident: a misfortune: (*mil.*) a loss by wounds, death, desertion, &c.: a person injured or killed: a thing damaged or destroyed. [L. *cāsuālis*—*cāsus*. See case (2).]

casuarina, *kas-ū-a-rī'na*, *n.* a genus of trees, mainly Australian. [Named from their resemblance to cassowary plumage.]

casuistry, *kaz'ū-is-tri* (or *kazh'-*), *n.* the reasoning that enables a man to decide in a particular *case* between conflicting duties: in the R.C. Church, the science that examines the nature of actions, determining whether any particular action is sinful or innocent and distinguishing between duties that are obligatory and those that are not: sophistical reasoning about conduct, quibbling.—*n.* cas'uist, one who practises casuistry.—*adjs.* casuist'ic, -al, relating to casuistry: subtle: specious. [Fr. *casuiste*—L. *cāsus*. See case (2).]

cat, *kat*, *n.* a wild or domesticated animal of genus *Felis*: a spiteful woman: short for the cat-o'-nine tails, a whip with nine lashes: (*slang*) a jazz musician or enthusiast: (*slang*) a man, a fellow: a caterpillar tractor.—*ns.* cat'amount, a wild cat: a puma; cat'amoun'tain, or cat o' mountain, a leopard, wild cat, or ocelot: a wild mountaineer.—*adj.* ferocious, savage.—*adj.* cat-and-dog, quarrelsome.—*ns.* cat'-call, a squeaking instrument once used in theatres to express disapprobation: a shrill whistle; cat'gut, a kind of cord made from the intestines of sheep and other animals, and used for violin strings, surgical ligatures, &c.; cat'kin, a spike or tuft of small flowers, as in the willow, hazel, &c.—*adj.* cat-like, noiseless, stealthy.—*ns.* cat's'-cra'dle, a pastime in which a string looped about the fingers and passed from player to player is transformed from one pattern to another; cat's'-eye, a beautiful variety of quartz: a reflector set in a frame fixed in a road surface; cat's'-paw (*naut.*), a light breeze: a dupe or tool—from the fable of the monkey who used the paws of a cat to draw the roasting chestnuts out of the fire; cat's'-tail, a catkin: a genus of aquatic reeds; cat'-suit, a type of one-piece trouser suit; catt'ery, a place where cats are bred or cared for.—*adj.* catt'y, like a cat: spiteful.—*n.* cat'-walk, a narrow footway, as on a bridge.—bell the cat (see bell). [O.E. *cat*; found in many languages; Low L. *cattus*, prob. Celt.]

cataclysm, *kat'a-klizm*, *n.* a flood of water: a debacle: a great revolution.—*adj.* cataclys'mic. [Gr. *kataklysmos*—*kata*, downward, *klyzein*, to wash.]

catacomb, *kat'a-kōm*, *n.* a subterranean burial place, esp. the famous Catacombs near Rome, where many of the early Christian victims of persecution were buried. [It. *catacomba*—through Late L., prob. from Gr. *kata*, downward, and *kymbē*, a hollow.]

catafalque, *kat'a-falk*, *n.* a temporary structure representing a tomb placed over the coffin during a lying-in-state: the stand on which the coffin rests. [Fr.,—It. *catafalco*.]

catalectic, *kat-a-lek'tik*, *adj.* incomplete—applied to a verse wanting one syllable at the end. [Gr. *katalēktikos*, incomplete—*kata-*

lēgein, to stop.]

catalepsy, *kat′a-lep-si, n.* a state of insensibility with bodily rigidity.—*adj.* **catalep′tic.** [Gr. *kata,* down, *lēpsis,* seizure.]

catalogue, *kat′a-log, n.* a classified list of names, books, &c.—*v.t.* to put in a catalogue: to make a catalogue of:—*pr.p.* cat′aloguing; *pa.p.* cat′alogued. [Fr. through L.L.—Gr. *katalogos—kata,* down, *legein,* to choose.]

catalysis, *ka-tal′i-sis, n.* the acceleration or retardation of a chemical reaction by a substance which itself undergoes no permanent chemical change.—*n.* **cat′alyst** (or **catalyt′ic agent**), a substance acting as the agent in catalysis.—*v.t.* **cat′alyse.** [Gr. *katalysis—kata,* down, *lyein,* to loosen.]

catamaran, *kat-a-mär-an′,* or *kat-am′är-an, n.* a raft of logs lashed together: a boat with two hulls. [From Tamil (q.v.), 'tied wood'.]

catamount. See **cat.**

catapult, *kat′a-pult, n.* anciently an engine of war for throwing stones, arrows, &c.: a small forked stick with an elastic string fixed to the prongs, used by boys for throwing small missiles: any similar device, as for launching aeroplanes. [L. *catapulta*—Gr. *katapeltēs.*]

cataract, *kat′a-rakt, n.* a waterspout: a waterfall: an opaque condition of the lens of the eye causing blindness. [L. *cataracta*—Gr. *kataraktēs,* a waterfall (*kata,* down).]

catarrh, *kat-är′, n.* a discharge of fluid due to the inflammation of a mucous membrane, esp. of the nose: a cold.—*adj.* **catarrh′al.** [L. *catarrhous*—Gr. *katarrhous—kata,* down, *rhein,* to flow.]

catastrophe, *kat-as′trō-fe, n.* an overturning: a final event, dénouement: an unfortunate conclusion: a calamity.—*adj.* **catastroph′ic.** [Gr., *kata,* down, *strophē,* a turn.]

cat-call. See **cat.**

catch, *kach, v.t.* to take hold of, esp. a thing in motion: to seize after pursuit: to trap or ensnare: to be in time for: to surprise, detect: to take (a disease) by infection: to grasp (e.g. a meaning).—*v.i.* to be contagious: to be entangled or fastened:—*pa.t.* and *pa.p.* caught (*kōt*).—*n.* seizure: anything that seizes or holds: that which is caught: anything worth catching: a snare: a song in which the parts are successively caught up by different voices.—*n.* **catch′-as-catch′-can′,** a style of wrestling in which any hold is allowed.—Also *adj.* and *adv.*—*n.* **catch′er.**—*adj.* **catch′ing,** infectious: captivating, attractive.—*ns.* **catch′-ment-a′rea, -bas′in,** the area from which a river or a reservoir draws its water-supply, and from which, therefore, it is fed (also *fig.*); **catch′penny,** any worthless thing, esp. a publication, intended merely to gain money (also *adj.*); **catch′-phrase,** a phrase that becomes popular and is much repeated: a slogan; **catch′word,** among actors, the last word of the preceding speaker—the cue: any word or phrase taken up and repeated, esp. the watchword or symbol of a party.—*adj.* **catch′y,** attractive: deceptive: readily caught up, as a tune, &c.—**catch fire,** to become ignited: to become inspired by passion or zeal; **catch it,** to get a scolding or the like; **catch on,** to comprehend: to catch the popular fancy; **catch**

out, to put out at cricket by catching the ball: (*fig.*) to detect in error; **catch up,** to overtake; **catch up,** or **away,** to snatch or seize hastily. [From O.Fr. *cachier*—Late L. *captiāre* for *captāre,* inten. of *capĕre,* to take.]

catchpole, -poll, *kach′pōl, n.* a constable. [Through, O.Fr. from Low L. *cachepolus, chassipullus,* one who chases fowls.]

catchup, catsup. See **ketchup.**

cat-cracker, *kat′-krak′ér, n.* (in full **catalytic cracker**) a plant in which the cracking of petroleum is speeded up by the use of a catalyst.

catechise, *kat′e-kīz, v.t.* to instruct by question and answer: to question, examine searchingly.—*adjs.* **catechĕt′ic, -al,** relating to a catechism or to oral instruction.—*adv.* **catechĕt′ically.**—*ns.* **cat′echīser; cat′echīsm,** a summary of instruction in the form of question and answer; **cat′echist,** one who catechises: a native teacher in a mission church. [L. *catēchismus,* formed from Gr. *katēchizein, katēcheein,* to din into the ears, teach—*kata,* down, *ēchē,* a sound.]

catechumen, *kat-e-kū′men, n.* one who is being taught the rudiments of Christianity. [Gr. *katēchoumenos,* being taught, pr.p. pass. of *katēcheein,* to teach.]

category, *kat′e-gor-i, n.* what may be affirmed of a class: a class or order.—*adj.* **categor′ical,** positive: absolute, without exception.—*adv.* **categor′ically.**—*n.pl.* **cat′egories** (*phil.*), the highest classes under which objects of philosophy can be systematically arranged.—**categorical imperative,** in the ethics of Kant, the absolute unconditional command of the moral law. [Gr. *katēgoria; katēgoros,* an accuser.]

cater, *kā′tér, v.i.* to provide food, entertainment, &c. (with *for*).—*n.* **cā′terer.** [Lit. to act as a *cater,* the word being orig. a noun (spelled *catour*)—O.Fr. *acateor, achetour*—L.L. *acceptāre,* to acquire.]

cateran, *kat′er-án, n.* a Highland robber. [Gael. *ceathairne,* peasantry, Ir. *ceithern,* a band of soldiers.]

caterpillar, *kat′ér-pil-ár, n.* a butterfly grub: extended to other larvae: a tractor or other vehicle running on endless articulated tracks consisting of flat metal plates (from **Caterpillar,** trademark). [Prob. O.Fr. *chatepelose,* 'hairy cat'.]

caterwaul, *kat′ér-wöl, n.* the shriek or cry of the cat.—*v.i.* to make such a noise. [The second part is prob. imit.]

cates, *kāts, n.pl.* dainty food. [O.E. *acates*—O.Fr. *acat* (sing.), purchase; cf. **cater.**]

catgut. See **cat.**

cathartic, -al, *kath-ärt′ik, -ál, adj.* having the power of cleansing: purgative.—*ns.* **cathar′sis,** purification of the emotions, as by the drama according to Aristotle: purging of the effects of a pent-up emotion and repressed thoughts, by bringing them to the surface of consciousness; **cathart′ic,** a purgative medicine. [Gr. *kathartikos,* fit for cleansing—*katharos,* clean.]

cathedral, *kath-ēd′rál, n.* the principal church of a diocese, in which is the seat or throne of a bishop.—*adj.* belonging to a cathedral. [L. *cathēdra*—Gr. *kathēdra,* a seat.]

Neutral vowels in unaccented syllables: *em′pér-ór;* for certain sounds in foreign words see p. ix.

Catherine-wheel, kath′é-rin-hwēl, n. (archit.) an ornamented window of a circular form: a kind of firework which in burning rotates like a wheel. [St. Catherine of Alexandria (4th cent.), who escaped torture on a wheel.]

catheter, kath′e-tér, n. a tube for admitting gases or liquids through the channels of the body, or for removing them, esp. for removing urine from the bladder. [Through L.—Gr. kathetēr—kathienai, to send down.]

cathode, kath′ōd, n. the negative terminal of an electrolytic cell at which positively charged ions are discharged into the exterior electric circuit: in valves and tubes, the source of electrons.—opposed to anode.—adjs. cath′odal; cathod′ic.—cathode rays, streams of negatively charged particles (electrons) emitted normally from the surface of the cathode during an electrical discharge in a rarefied gas; cathode ray tube, a device in which a narrow beam of electrons strikes against a screen, as in a television set. [Gr. kata, down, hodos, a way.]

catholic, kath′ol-ik, adj. universal: general, embracing the whole body of Christians: liberal, the opposite of exclusive: relating to the Roman Catholic Church.—n. (cap.) an adherent of the R.C. Church.—ns. Cath′olicism, (tenets of the R.C. Church: (without cap.) catholicity (rare): catholic′ity, (-is′-), universality: liberality or breadth of view: Catholicism (rare).—Catholic or General Epistle, epistle addressed to the Church universal or to a large and indefinite circle of readers. [Gr. katholikos, universal—kata, throughout, holos, the whole.]

catkin. See cat.

cattle, kat′l, n.pl. beasts of pasture, esp. oxen, bulls, and cows: sometimes also horses, sheep, &c.—ns. cattle-grid, a grid-covered trench used instead of a gate to keep hooved animals in a field; catt′le-lift′ing, the stealing of cattle; catt′le-plague, disease among cattle, esp. rinderpest. [O.Fr. catel, chatel—Low L. captāle, orig capital, property in general, then esp. animals—L. capitalis, chief—caput, the head.]

Caucasian, kö-kā′z(h)i-án, adj. pertaining to the Caucasus.—n. the name used by anthropologists for a member of the white race: now in some places by law, a white person.

caucus, kö′kus, n. a meeting of delegates to direct the policy of a political party: any too-influential small group, esp. in a constituency. [Ety. uncertain.]

caudal, kö′dál, adj. pertaining to the tail.—adj. cau′date, tailed. [L. cauda, a tail.]

caudle, kö′dl, n. a warm drink given to the sick. [O.Fr. chaudel—L. calidus, hot.]

caught, köt, pa.t. and pa.p. of catch.

caul, köl, n. a net or covering for the head: the membrane covering the head of some infants at their birth. [O.Fr. cale, a little cap, prob. Celt.]

cauldron, caldron, köl′drón, n. a large kettle for boiling or heating liquids. [O Fr. caudron—L. caldārium—calidus, hot.]

cauliflower, kol′i-flow(é)r, n. a variety of cabbage whose young inflorescence is eaten. [Earlier cole-florye, colie-florie—Low L. cauli flora—L. caulis, cabbage.]

caulk, calk, kök, v.t. to render watertight by pressing oakum, &c., into the seams.—n. caulk′er. [O.Fr. cauquer, to press—L. calcāre, to tread—calx, heel.]

cause, köz, n. that which produces an effect: ground, motive, justification: a legal action: the aim proposed, or the opinions advocated, by an individual or party.—v.t. to produce: to bring about: to induce.--adj. caus′al, relating to a cause or causes.—ns. causal′ity, the relation of cause and effect; causā′tion, the operation of cause and effect.—adj. caus′ative, producing an effect, causing.—adv. caus′atively.—adj. cause′less, without cause: without just cause.—adv. cause′lessly.—n. cause′lessness.—final cause, the end or object for which a thing is done, or operates, esp. the design, purpose of the universe; make common cause (with), to unite for common action. [Fr.,—L. causa.]

cause célèbre, köz sā-leb-r′, a legal case that excites much public interest. [Fr.]

causerie, kōz-er-ē, n. a talk or gossip: a short and informal essay. [Fr.]

causeway, köz′wā, **causey**, köz′i, n. a pathway raised and paved with stone.—v.t. to pave. [M.E. causee—O.Fr. caucie—Low L. (via) calciata—L. calx, heel; and way.]

caustic, kös′-, kos′tik, adj. burning: (fig.) severe, cutting.—n. a substance that burns or wastes away the skin and flesh.—adv. caus′tically.—n. caustic′ity, quality of being caustic.—caustic potash, soda, potassium, sodium hydroxide, also known as caustic alkalis—a term which sometimes includes in addition certain other hydroxides. [L.,—Gr. kaustikos—kaiein, kausein, to burn.]

cauterise, kö′ter-īz, v t. to burn with a caustic or a hot iron: (fig.) to sear.—ns. cau′tery, a burning with caustics or a hot iron: an iron or caustic used for burning tissue; cauterisā′tion, cau′terism. [Fr cautériser—Low L. cautēri-zāre—Gr. kautēr, a hot iron—kaiein, to burn.]

caution, kö′sh(ô)n, n. heedfulness: security (e.g. caution money): warning.—v.t. to warn.—adj cau′tionary, containing caution: cau′tious, possessing or using caution: watchful: prudent.—adv. cau′tiously.—n. cau′tiousness. [Fr.,—L. cautiō, -ōnis—cavēre, to beware.]

cavalcade, kav-ál-kād′, n. a procession of persons on horseback: any procession. [Fr., through It. and Low L.—L. caballus, a horse.]

cavalier, kav-ál-ēr′, n. a knight: a Royalist in the Civil War: a swaggering fellow: a gallant or gentleman.—adj. like a cavalier: gay: haughty, off-hand, disdainful.—adv. cavalier′ly. [Fr.,—It. cavallo—L. caballus, a horse.]

cavalry, kav′ál-ri, n. horse-soldiers: a troop of horse or horsemen. [Fr. cavallerie—It. cavalleria—L. caballārius, horseman.]

cave, kāv, n. a hollow place in a rock: any small faction of dissentients from a political party.—n. cave′-man, one, esp. of the Stone Age, who lives in a cave: (coll.) one who acts with primitive violence.—to cave in, to slip, to fall into a hollow: (fig.) to give way, collapse. [Fr.,—L. cavus, hollow.]

caveat, kā′ve-at, n. a notice or warning: a notice to stay proceedings in a court of law. [L., 'let him take care'—cavēre, to take care.]

fāte, fär; mē, hûr (her); mīne, mōte, för; mūte; mōōn, fōōt; ʀнen (then)

cavendish, *kav'en-dish, n.* tobacco moistened and pressed into quadrangular cakes. [Poss. from the name of original manufacturer.]

cavern, *kav'ern, n.* a deep hollow place in rocks.—*adj.* **cav'ernous,** hollow: full of caverns. [Fr.,—L. *caverna*—*cavus,* hollow.]

caviare (often **caviar,** esp. in *U.S.*), *kav'i-är, kav-i-är'* (originally four syllables), *n.* salted roe of the sturgeon, &c.: (*fig.*) something too fine for the vulgar taste. [Prob. the 16th-cent. It. *caviale.*]

cavil, *kav'il, v.i.* to make empty, trifling objections:—*pr.p.* cav'illing; *pa.p.* cav'illed.—*n.* a frivolous objection.—*n.* **cav'iller.** [O.Fr. *caviller*—L. *cavillārī,* to practise jesting—*cavilla,* jesting.]

cavity, *kav'it-i, n.* a hollow: a hollow place.—**cavity wall,** a wall consisting of two layers with a space between. [L. *cavitās, -ātis*—*cavus,* hollow.]

cavort, *kav-ört', v.i.* to curvet, frolic, bound. [Explained as a corr. of **curvet.**]

cavy, *kāv'i, n.* a genus of rodents, to which the guinea-pig belongs. [*cabiai,* the native name in French Guiana.]

caw, *kö, v.i.* to cry as a crow.—*n.* the cry of a crow. [From the sound.]

cayenne, *kā-en', n.* a very pungent red pepper, made from several species of capsicum. [Usually referred to *Cayenne* in French Guiana; but prob. the word is Brazilian.]

cayman, *kā'man, n.* an alligator, esp. of South American kinds:—*pl.* **caymans.** [Sp. *caimán,* most prob. Carib (q.v.).]

cease, *sēs, v.t.* and *v.i.* to give over, to stop.—*v.i.* to be at an end.—*adj.* **cease'less,** without ceasing: incessant.—*adv.* **cease'lessly.** [Fr. *cesser*—L. *cessāre,* to give over—*cēdĕre,* to yield, give up.]

cedar, *sē'där, n.* any of a number of large coniferous evergreen trees remarkable for the durability and fragrance of their wood.—*adj.* made of cedar—also (*poet.*) **cē'darn.** [L. *cedrus*—Gr. *kedros.*]

cede, *sēd, v.t.* to yield or give up to another.—*v.i.* to give way. [L. *cēdĕre, cessum,* to yield, give up.]

cedilla, *se-dil'a, n.* a mark placed under the letter *c* (thus *ç*) to show that it is to have the sound of *s.* [Sp. (Fr. *cédille,* It. *zediglia*), all from *zēta,* the Greek name of *z.*]

ceil, *sēl, v.t.* to overlay the inner roof of: to provide with a ceiling—*n.* **ceil'ing,** the inner roof of a room: the upper limit: the limiting height for a particular aircraft. [Prob. conn. with Fr. *ciel,* It. *cielo,* Low L. *caelum,* a canopy.]

ceilidh, *kā'li, n.* an informal evening of song and story. [Gael., a visit.]

celandine, *sel'an-dīn, n.* swallow-wort (*greater celandine*), a plant of the poppy family, supposed to flower when the swallows appeared, and to perish when they departed: also a species of ranunculus (*lesser celandine*). [O.Fr. *celidoine*—Gr. *chelīdonion*—*chelīdōn,* a swallow.]

celebrate, *sel'e-brāt, v.t.* to make famous: to honour with solemn ceremonies: to perform with proper rites and ceremonies.—*n.* **cel'e-brant,** one who performs a rite.—*adj.* **cel'e-**

brated, distinguished, famous.—*ns.* **celebrā'tion,** act of celebrating; **celeb'rity,** the condition of being celebrated, fame: a notable person. [L. *celebrāre, -ātum*—*celeber,* much visited, renowned.]

celerity, *sel-er'it-i, n.* quickness, rapidity of motion. [L. *celeritās*—*celer,* quick.]

celery, *sel'er-i, n.* a kitchen vegetable with long succulent stalks. [Fr. *célerie*—Gr. *selīnon,* parsley.]

celestial, *sel-est'yəl, adj.* heavenly: dwelling in heaven: in the visible heavens.—*n.* an inhabitant of heaven: a Chinese.—**the Celestial Empire,** an old name for China. [Through Fr. from L. *caelestis*—*caelum,* heaven.]

celibacy, *sel'i-bas-i,* or *se-lib'as-i, n.* the unmarried state.—*adj.* **cel'ibate,** living single.—*n.* one unmarried, or bound by vow not to marry. [L. *caelebs,* single.]

cell, *sel, n.* a small room in a prison, &c.: a hermit's one-roomed dwelling: a small cavity: a unit-mass of living matter: a unit-group within a larger organisation: the unit of an electrical battery, in which chemical action takes place between an anode and a cathode both separately in contact with an electrolyte: (*meteor.*) a part of the atmosphere that behaves as a unit: unit of storage in computing.—*n.* **cell'ule,** a little cell—whence:—*adj.* **cell'ular,** consisting of, or containing, cells.—*ns.* **cell'uloid,** a hard elastic substance made from gun-cotton and camphor, &c.; **cell'ulose,** the chief component of cell membrane of plants and of wood—cotton down, linen fibre, wood pulp being almost pure cellulose. [O.Fr. *celle*—L. *cella,* conn. with *celāre,* to cover.]

cellar, *sel'ár, n.* any underground room or vault, esp. one where stores are kept.—*ns.* **cell'arage,** cellars: charge for storing in cellars; **cell'arer,** the caretaker of a cellar; **cell'aret,** a case for holding bottles. [O.Fr. *celier*—L. *cellārium*—*cella*; see **cell.**]

cello, 'cello, *chel'ō, n.* for **violoncello.**—**cellist, 'cellist,** for **violoncellist.**

cellophane, *sel'ō-fān, n.* a tough transparent paper-like wrapping material made from viscose. [Orig. trademark—**cell(ul)o(se),** and Gr. *phainein,* to show.]

Celsius. See centigrade.

celt, *selt, n.* a prehistoric axe-like instrument. [Ety. uncertain.]

Celt, *kelt, selt, n.* a Gaul: extended to include members of other Celtic-speaking peoples.—*adj.* **Celt'ic,** pertaining to the Celts.—*n.* a branch of the Indo-Germanic family of languages, including Breton, Welsh, Cornish, Irish, Gaelic, Manx. [L. *Celtae*; Gr. *Keltoi* or *Keltai.*]

cement, *se-ment', n.* anything that makes two bodies stick together: mortar: a bond of union.—*v.t.* to unite with cement: to join firmly.—*n.* **cementā'tion,** the act of cementing: the process of impregnating the surface of one substance with another, as in the case-hardening of iron: the setting of a plastic: process of injecting fluid cement mixture for strengthening purposes. [O.Fr. *ciment*—L. *caementum,* chip of stone used to fill up in building a wall.]

Neutral vowels in unaccented syllables: *em'pér-ór*; for certain sounds in foreign words see p. ix.

110

cemetery, *sem'e-tér-i* (or *-tri*), *n.* a burying-ground. [Low L. *coemētērium* — Gr. *koi-mētērion.*]

cenobite. Same as **coenobite.**

cenotaph, *sen'ō-täf, n.* a sepulchral monument to one who is buried elsewhere. [Fr., — L. — Gr. *kenotaphion* — *kenos*, empty, and *taphos*, a tomb.]

Cenozoic, *sē-no-zō'ik, adj.* Same as **Cainozoic.**

censer, *sens'ér, n.* a pan in which incense is burned. [O.Fr. *censier, encensier* — Low L. *in-censorium* — L. *incendēre, incensum,* to burn.]

censor, *sen'sôr, n.* a Roman magistrate with authority to regulate the moral conduct of the citizens: any of several university officials: an officer who examines written and printed matter or films with power to delete or suppress the contents or to forbid publication or showing: a stern critic: (*psych.*) an unconscious inhibitive mechanism in the mind that prevents what is painful from emerging into consciousness. — *v.t.* to subject to censorial examination: to delete, suppress as a censor might. — *adjs.* **censo'rial,** belonging to a censor, or to the correction of public morals; **censō'rious,** expressing censure: fault-finding. — *adv.* **censō'riously.** — *ns.* **censō'rious-ness; cen'sorship,** office or action of a censor: time during which a Roman censor held office. [L.; cf. **censure.**]

censure, *sen'shúr, n.* an unfavourable judgment, blame, reproof. — *v.t.* to blame: to condemn as wrong. — *adj.* **cen'surable.** [L. *censūra* — *censēre,* to estimate or judge.]

census, *sen'sus, n.* an official enumeration of inhabitants with statistics relating to them. [L. *census*, a register.]

cent, *sent, n.* a coin = the hundredth part of dollar, rupee, rand, &c. — **per cent** (see **per**). [L. *centum,* a hundred.]

centaur, *sen'tör, n.* a fabulous monster, half man, half horse. [L. *Centaurus* — Gr. *Kentauros.*]

centenary, *sen-tēn'ár-i,* or *-ten'-,* or *sen'tin-,* *n.* a hundred: a century or hundred years: a hundredth anniversary. — *adj.* pertaining to a hundred. — *n.* **centenā'rian,** one a hundred years old. [L., — *centenī,* a hundred each — *centum.*]

centennial, *sen-ten'i-ál, adj.* happening once in a hundred years. — *n.* a hundredth anniversary. [Coined from L. *centum,* and *annus,* a year.]

centesimal, *sen-tes'i-mál, adj.* hundredth. [L. *centēsimus* — *centum.*]

centi-, *sen-ti-,* in composition 1/100 of the unit named. [L. *centum,* a hundred.]

centigrade, *sen'ti-grād, adj.* divided into a hundred degrees, as the *centigrade thermometer* (first constructed by Celsius, 1701-44), in which freezing-point (of water) is zero and boiling-point (of water) is 100°. *Celsius* is now the prefered term. [L. *centum, gradus,* a step.]

centigram(me), *sen'ti-gram, n.* the hundredth part of a gram(me). [Fr., — L. *centum,* a hundred, and **gram(me).**]

centilitre, *sen'ti-lē-tér, n.* the hundredth part of a litre, 10 cubic centimetres. [Fr., — L. *centum,* a hundred, and **litre.**]

centime, *sä-tēm, n.* the hundredth part of anything, esp. of a franc. [Fr., — L. *centēsimus,*

hundredth.]

centimetre, *sen'ti-mē-tér, n.* a lineal measure, the hundredth part of a metre. — **centimetre-gram(me)-second** (contr. **C.G.S., CGS**) **system,** a system of scientific measurement with centimetre, &c. as units of length, mass, time. [Fr., — L. *centum,* a hundred, and **metre.**]

centipede, *sen'ti-pēd, n.* a general name for a class of flattened animals with many joints, most of the joints bearing one pair of legs. [L. *centum,* and *pēs, pedis,* a foot.]

cento, *sen'tō, n.* a literary composition made up of scraps from various sources: — *pl.* usually **cen'tos.** [L. *cento,* Gr. *kentrōn,* patchwork.]

centre, center, *sen'tér, n.* the middle point of anything, esp. a circle or sphere: the middle: men of moderate political opinions. — *v.t.* to place in, or collect to, the centre. — *v.i.* to lie, move, be concentrated (on, in, round, about — a centre): — *pr.p.* cen'tring, cen'tering; *pa.p.* cen'tred, cen'tered. — *adj.* **central,** belonging to the centre, principal, dominant. — *n.* **centralisā'tion,** the tendency to administer affairs by a central rather than a local authority. — *v.t.* **cen'tralise,** to draw to a centre. — *adv.* **cen'trally.** — *ns.* **cen'tre-bit,** a joiner's boring tool; **cen'tre-piece,** an ornament for the middle of a table, ceiling, &c. — **central heating,** a system of heating a building by conducting heat from one source; **central nervous system,** the brain and spinal cord; **centre of gravity,** the point at which the weight of a body may be supposed to act, and at which the body may be supported in equilibrium. [Fr. — L. *centrum* — Gr. *kentron,* a sharp point.]

centrifugal, *sen-trif'ū-gál, adj.* tending away from the centre, as in *centrifugal force.* — *n.* **centrifuge** (*sen'tri-fūj*), an apparatus that separates liquids, &c. of different density by rotating them at very high speed. [L. *centrum,* centre, *fugēre,* to flee from.]

centripetal, *sen-trip'et-ál, adj.* tending towards the centre. [L. *centrum,* centre, *petēre,* to seek.]

centuple, *sen'tū-pl, adj.* hundredfold. [L. *centu-plex* — *centum,* hundred, *plicāre,* to fold.]

century, *sen'tū-ri, n.* a band of a hundred Roman soldiers: a period of a hundred years: any sequence of a hundred, as runs in cricket. — *n.* **centū'rion,** the commander of a *century.* [L. *centuria* — *centum,* hundred.]

ceorl, *kāorl, chāorl, n.* before the Norman Conquest, an ordinary freeman not of noble birth. [O.E. See **churl.**]

cephalic, *se-fal'ik, adj.* belonging to the head. — *adj.* **ceph'alous,** having a head. — **cephalic index,** the ratio of the breadth to the length of the skull expressed as a percentage. [Gr. *kephalē,* head.]

Cephalopoda, *sef-al-op'od-a, n.pl.* the highest class of molluscs, exclusively marine, with the foot modified into arms surrounding the mouth — cuttlefish, &c. — *n.* and *adj.* **ceph'alo-pod,** (pertaining to) one of the Cephalopoda. [Gr. *kephalē,* head, *pous,* gen. *podos,* foot.]

Cepheid, *sē'fē-id, n.* any of a class of stars whose characteristic is that over a short period (in most cases less than three weeks) they dim and brighten again; they are used in the

---

fāte, fär; mē, hûr (her); *mīne; mōte, för; mūte; mōōn, fŏŏt;* тнen (then)

estimation of distances in outer space. [Gr.]

ceraceous. See **cere.**

ceramic, se-ram'ik, adj. pertaining to a ceramic or to ceramics: made of a ceramic.—n. any product that is first shaped and then hardened by means of heat, or the material from which it is formed—including not only traditional potter's clays, but also a large range of new dielectric materials: (in pl.; treated as sing.) the potter's art: articles made of ceramic material. [Gr. keramos, potter's earth.]

cere, sēr, v.t. to cover with wax.—adj. **cērā'ceous** (-shùs), of or like wax.—ns. **cere'cloth, cere'-ment,** a cloth dipped in melted wax in which to wrap a dead body: a shroud. [L. cēra, wax.]

cereal. See **Ceres.**

cerebrum, ser'e-brum, n. the front and larger part of the brain.—n. **cerebell'um,** the hinder and lower part of the brain.—adj. **cer'ebral,** pertaining to the cerebrum.—n. **cerebrā'tion,** action of the brain, esp. unconscious.—**cer'ebrospīn'al fever,** meningitis.—adj. **cer'ebrovas'cular,** relating to the cerebrum and its blood vessels; **cerebrovascular accident,** a paralytic stroke. [L. cerebrum, the brain; prob. cog. with Gr. kara, the head, kranion, the cranium.]

ceremony, ser'e-mo-ni, n. a sacred rite: a formal act: pomp or state.—adj. **ceremō'nial,** relating to ceremony.—n. outward form: a system of ceremonies.—adv. **ceremō'nially.**—adj. **ceremō'nious,** full of ceremony: precise.—adv. **ceremō'niously.**—**Master of Ceremonies,** the person who directs the form and order of a ceremonial; **stand on ceremony,** to be unduly formal and precise. [Fr.—L. caerimōnia, sanctity.]

Ceres, sē'rēz, n. the Roman goddess of tillage and corn.—adj. **ce'real,** relating to corn or edible grain.—n. (usu. pl.) a grain used as food, as wheat, barley, &c.: a food prepared from such grain. [L. prob. from root of creāre, to create.]

cerise, ser-ēz', also -ēs', n. and adj. a light and clear red colour. [Fr., 'cherry'.]

cerium, sē'ri-ùm, n. a rare metallic element (symbol Ce; at. no. 58). [Named from planet Ceres discovered about the same time.]

certain, sûr'tin, -tn, adj. sure, convinced: unerring: sure to happen: regular, inevitable: sure (to do): indisputable: some: one.—adv. **cer'tainly.**—ns. **cer'tainty,** that which is undoubted: that which is inevitable: assurance of a truth or of a fact; **cer'titude,** freedom from doubt. [O.Fr.—L. certus—cernēre, to decide.]

certes, sûr'tez, adv. certainly: in sooth. [Fr.]

certificate, sér-tif'i-kát, n. a written declaration of some fact: a testimonial of character.—v.t. to give a certificate to.—n. **certificā'tion.**—adj. **certifi'able,** that can, or must, be certified (esp. as insane).—v.t. **cer'tify,** to declare formally or in writing, and usu. with authority: to inform:—pr.p. cer'tifying; pa.p. cer'tified.—**certified milk,** milk certified as having been obtained from tuberculin-tested herds. [Fr. certificat.—L. certificāre—certus, certain, facēre, to make.]

cerulean, caerulean, si-rōō'li-än, adj. sky-blue: dark blue: sea-green. [L. caeruleus.]

ceruse, sē'rōōs, or si-rōōs', n. white-lead used as a pigment. [Fr.,—L. cērussa, conn. with cēra, wax.]

cervical, sûr'vi-kál, sér-vī'kál, adj. belonging to the neck. [Fr.,—L. cervix, cervīcis, the neck.]

cervine, sûr'vīn, adj. relating to deer: like deer: fawn-coloured. [L. cervīnus—cervus, a stag.]

cess, ses, n. a tax, a local rate.—v.t. to impose a tax. [Shortened from assess.]

cessation, ses-ā'sh(ó)n, n. a ceasing or stopping: a pause. [Fr.,—L. cessātiō, -ōnis—cessāre. See **cease.**]

cession, sesh'(ó)n, n. a yielding up, a surrender. [Fr.,—L. cessiō, -ōnis—cēdēre. See **cede.**]

cesspool, ses'pōōl, n. a pool or pit for collecting filthy water. [Origin obscure.]

cestus, ses'tus, n. a girdle, esp. of Venus. [L.—Gr. kestos.]

cestus, ses'tus, n. an ancient boxing-glove loaded with lead or iron. [L. caestus.]

cesura. See **caesura.**

Cetacea, se-tā'shi-a, n.pl. an order of mammals of aquatic habit and fish-like form, including whales, dolphins, and porpoises.—n. **cetā'cean.**—adj. **cetā'ceous.** [L.,—Gr. kētos, any sea-monster.]

cetane, sē'tān, n. a paraffin hydrocarbon found in petroleum.—**cetane number,** a measure of the ignition quality of diesel engine fuel.

cha-cha (-cha), chä-chä (-chä), n. a Latin American dance.

chafe, chāf, v.t. to make hot by rubbing: to fret or wear by rubbing: to cause to fret or rage.—v.t. to fret or rage.—n. heat: anger.—n. **chaf'ing-dish,** a dish or vessel in which anything is heated by hot coals, &c.: a dish for cooking on the table. [Fr. chauffer—L. calefacēre—calēre, to be hot, facēre, to make.]

chafer, chāf'ér, n. a beetle. [O.E. cefer; cog. with Du. kever, Ger. käfer.]

chaff, chäf, n. the husks of corn as threshed or winnowed: cut hay and straw: worthless matter: light banter.—v.t. to banter. [O.E. ceaf; cf. Du. kaf.]

chaffer, chaf'ér, v.i. to bargain: to haggle about the price.—n. **chaff'erer.** [M.E. chapfare, a bargain, from O.E. cēap, price, barter, faru, way.]

chaffinch, chaf'inch, -sh, n. a little song-bird of the finch family. [Said to delight in chaff.]

chagrin, shä-grēn', -grin', shag'rin, n. that which wears or gnaws the mind: vexation: annoyance.—v.t. (shä-grēn') to vex or annoy. [Fr. chagrin, shagreen, rough skin, ill-humour.]

chain, chān, n. a series of links or rings passing through one another: any continuous series: anything that binds: a measure of 100 links, 66 feet long: (pl.) fetters, bonds, confinement: (pl.) metal links fitted to the wheels of a car in icy conditions to prevent skidding.—v.t. to fasten: to fetter.—ns. **chain'-arm'our,** chainmail; **chain'-bridge,** a suspension-bridge; **chain drive,** transmission of power by **chaingear(ing),** gearing consisting of an endless chain and (generally) sprocket wheels; **chain'-gang,** a gang of convicts chained together; **chain'-mail,** mail or armour made of iron links; **chain reaction,** chemical, atomic, or other process in which each reaction is in turn the stimulus of a similar reaction, e.g. ordinary combustion, or nuclear fission; **chain**

Neutral vowels in unaccented syllables: em'pér-ór; for certain sounds in foreign words see p. ix.

reactor, a nuclear reactor; **chain'-shot,** two cannon balls chained together, formerly fired to destroy rigging, &c., in a naval action; **chain'-smo'ker,** a non-stop smoker; **chain'-stitch,** a peculiar kind of stitch resembling the links of a chain; **chain store,** one of a number of shops closely linked under the same ownership. [Fr. *chaîne* — L. *catēna*.]

chair, *chār, n.* a movable seat for one, with a back to it: the seat or office of one in authority: the office of a professor: the instrument, or punishment, of electrocution: a railchair (q.v.). — *v.t.* to carry publicly in triumph. — *ns.* **chair'-lift,** a set of seats suspended from overhead wires for taking skiers up a hill; **chair'-man, -woman,** one who takes the chair, or presides at a meeting; **chair'manship.** [Fr. *chaire* — L. — Gr. *kathedra*.]

chaise, *shāz, n.* a light open carriage for one or more persons. [Fr., from *chaire*. See **chair.**]

chalcedony, *kal-sed'o-ni,* or *kal'-, n.* a beautiful translucent mineral composed of silica, generally white or bluish-white. [Gr. *chalkēdōn,* possibly from *Chalcedon,* in Asia Minor.]

chalet, *shal'ā, n.* a summer hut used by Swiss herdsmen in the Alps: a wooden villa: a small dwelling forming a unit in a holiday camp, &c. [Fr.]

chalice, *chal'is, n.* a cup or bowl: a communion-cup. — *adj.* **chal'iced,** cup-like. [Fr. *calice* — L. *calix, calisis;* cf. Gr. *kylix,* a cup.]

chalk, *chök, n.* the well-known white rock, a soft limestone, composed of calcium carbonate: a substitute for this used for writing. — *v.t.* to rub or to manure with chalk: to mark or write with chalk. — *adj.* **chalk'y.** — *n.* **chalk'iness.** — **chalk up,** to make a note of: to record. — **by a long chalk,** by far; **the Chalk,** the uppermost part of the Cretaceous System in England. [O.E. *cealc* — L. *calx,* limestone.]

challenge, *chal'enj,* or *-inj, v.t.* to summon to a combat or contest: to defy: to accuse (of — with *with*): to object to: to claim (as due). — *n.* a summons to a contest of any kind: a calling of anyone or anything in question: a difficulty which stimulates interest or effort. — *n.* **chall'enger.** [O.Fr. *chalenge,* a dispute, a claim — L. *calumnia,* a false accusation.]

chalybeate, *ka-lib'e-āt, adj.* containing iron. — *n.* a water or other liquor containing iron. [Gr. *chalyps,* gen. *chalybos,* steel, so called from the *Chalybes,* a nation famous for steel.]

cham, *kam, n.* (*obs.*) a Khan: (*fig.*) an autocrat. [khan.]

chamber, *chām'bér, n.* an apartment: the place where an assembly meets: a legislative or deliberative assembly: a hall of justice: a compartment: the back end of the bore of a gun. — *v.i.* to be wanton. — *adj.* **cham'bered.** — *ns.* **cham'ber-maid,** a female servant in charge of bedrooms; **cham'ber-mu'sic,** music suitable for a room as opposed to a theatre or a large hall, now almost confined to music for strings, with or without piano or wind. — **chamber of commerce,** an association formed in a town or district to promote the interests of commerce. [Fr. *chambre* — L. *camera* — Gr. *kamara,* a vault.]

chamberlain, *chām'bér-lin, n.* an officer in charge of the private apartments of a king or

nobleman: the treasurer of a corporation. — *n.* **cham'berlainship.** [O.Fr. *chambrelenc;* O.H.G. *chamerling* — L.. *camera,* a chamber, and affix *-ling* or *-lenc.*]

chameleon, *ka-mēl'yón,* or *-i-ón, n.* a small lizard famous for changing its colour: (*fig.*) an inconstant person. [L. *chamaeleon* — Gr. *chamaileōn* — *chamai* (= L. *humi*), on the ground (i.e. dwarf), and *leōn,* a lion.]

chamfer, *cham'fér,* or *sham', n.* a bevel or slope: a groove, channel, or furrow. — *v.t.* to groove or bevel. [Fr. *chanfrein* — O.Fr. *chanfraindre.*]

chamois, *sham'wä, n.* an Alpine antelope: (*pron. sham'i*) a soft kind of leather originally made from its skin (also **shammy**). [Fr., perh. from Romansh (q.v.).]

champ, *champ, v.i.* to make a snapping noise with the jaws in chewing. — *v.t.* to chew, munch. [Older form *cham,* most prob. from Scand.]

champagne, *sham-pān', n.* a white or red, sparkling or still, wine from *Champagne* in France.

champaign, *cham'pān,* also *sham-pān', adj.* level, open. — *n.* an open, level country. [A doublet of **campaign,** from O.Fr. *champaigne* — L. *campānia,* a plain.]

champion, *cham'pi-ón, n.* one who fights in single combat for himself or for another: one who defends a cause: in games, a competitor who has excelled all others. — *adj.* first-class. — *v.t.* to defend, to support. — *n.* **cham'pionship.** [Fr. — Low L. *campiō, -ōnis* — L. *campus.* a plain, a place for games.]

chance, *chäns, n.* that which falls out or happens without assignable cause: an unexpected event: risk: opportunity: possibility: (esp. in *pl.*) probability. — *v.t.* to risk. — *v.i.* to happen. — *adj.* happening accidentally, without assignable cause, without design. — *adj.* **chanc'y** (*coll.*), lucky: risky, uncertain. — **chance one's arm,** to take a chance, often recklessly; **even chance,** equal probability for and against; **stand a good chance,** to have a reasonable expectation; **the main chance,** the chief object, self-enrichment. [O.Fr. *cheance* — Low L. *cadentia* — L. *cadēre,* to fall.]

chancel, *chän'sl, n.* eastern part of church, orig. separated from nave by lattice-work screen. [O.Fr. — L. *cancelli,* lattice.]

chancellery, *chän'sé-lé-ri, -slé-ri, n.* office attached to embassy: — *pl.* **-ies.** [Same as next.]

chancellor, *chän'sel-ór, n.* a chief minister: the president of a court of chancery or other court. — *n.* **chan'cellorship.** — **Chancellor of the Exchequer,** the chief minister of finance in the British government; **Lord Chancellor, Lord High Chancellor,** the speaker of the House of Lords, presiding judge of the Chancery Division, keeper of the great seal, and first lay person of the state after the blood-royal. [Fr. *chancelier* — Low L. *cancellārius,* orig. an officer who had charge of records, and stood near the *cancelli* (L.), the crossbars that surrounded the judgment-seat.]

chance-medley, *chäns'-med-li, n.* unintentional homicide in which the killer is not entirely without blame: action with an element of chance. [O.Fr. *chance medlée,* mingled chance.]

chancery, *chän'sér-i, n.* formerly the highest

court of justice next to the House of Lords, presided over by the Lord High Chancellor: now a division of the High Court of Justice.— **in chancery**, in litigation, as an estate; in a helpless position. [Fr. *chancellerie*.]

chandelier, *shan-dé-lēr'*, *n.* a frame with branches for holding lights.—*n.* **chandler** (*chand'lēr*), a candle maker: a dealer in candles: a dealer generally. [Fr.,—Low L. *candelāria*, a candlestick.—L. *candēla*, a candle.]

change, *chānj*, *v.t.* to alter or make different: to make to pass from one state (into another): to put, give, take, put on, in place of another or others: to exchange: to give or get smaller coin for.—*v.i.* to suffer alteration, become different: to put on different clothes.—*v.t.* and *v.i.* to leave one station, train, &c., and take one's place in another.—*n.* the act of changing: alteration or variation of any kind: variety: small coins, esp. those given to adjust a payment: an exchange (now usu, '**Change**).—*adj.* **change'able**, subject or prone to change: fickle: inconstant.—*adv.* **change'ably.**—*ns.* **changeabil'ity**, **change'ableness**, fickleness: power of being changed.—*adj.* **change'ful.**—*adv.* **change'fully.**—*n.* **change'fulness.**—*adj.* **change'less**, unchanging, constant.—*n.* **change'ling**, a child taken or left in place of another.—**change hands**, to pass into different ownership; **change one's mind**, to adopt a different opinion or purpose; **change one's tune**, to change one's manner.—**ring the changes** (see **ring**). [Fr. *changer*—Late L. *cambiāre*—L. *cambīre*, to barter.]

channel, *chan'l*, *n.* the bed of a stream of water: a navigable passage: a strait or narrow sea: means of communication: a path for information in a computer: a narrow range or group of frequencies, part of a frequency band, assigned to a particular station so that it may transmit radio or television programmes without interference from other transmissions.—*v.t.* to make a channel: to furrow: to direct (into a particular course; *lit.* and *fig.*).—**the Channel**, the English Channel. [O.Fr. *chanel, canel*—L. *canālis*, a canal.]

chant, *chänt*, *v.t.* to sing: to celebrate in song: to recite in a singing manner.—*n.* song: a kind of sacred music in which a number of syllables are recited to one tone: a manner of singing or speaking in a musical monotone.—*ns.* **chant'er**, a singer: a precentor: the tenor or treble pipe of a bagpipe, on which the melody is played; **chant'ry**, an endowment, or chapel, for the chanting of masses; **chanty** (see **shanty** (2)). [Fr. *chanter*—L. *cantāre*—*canēre*, to sing.]

chanticleer, *chant'i-klēr*, *n.* a cock. [From the name of the cock in the old beast epic of Reynard the Fox. O.Fr. *chanter*, to sing, *cler*, clear.]

chaos, *kā'os*, *n.* disorder: the state of matter before it was reduced to order by the Creator.—*adj.* **chaot'ic**, confused.—*adv.* **chaot'ically.** [L.—Gr., the first unformed state of the universe.]

chap, *chap*, *v.i.* to crack, as soil in dry weather or the skin in cold weather.—*n.* a crack: an open fissure in the skin. [M.E. *chappen*; cog. with Du. and Ger. *kappen*.]

chap, *chap*, *n.* a fellow, originally a customer, from **chapman**.—*n.* **chapp'ie**, a familiar diminutive.

chap, *chap*, *n.* a jaw: a cheek.—*adj.* **chap'fall'en**, a variant of chop-fallen (q.v.). [Northern Eng. and Scot. *chaft*; O.N. *kjaptr*, the jaw.]

chap-book. See **chapman**.

chapel, *chap'él*, *n.* a place of worship inferior or subordinate to a regular church, or attached to a house or institution: a cell of a church containing its own altar: a dissenters' place of worship. [O.Fr. *capele*—Low L. *cappella*, dim. of *cappa*, a cloak or cope.]

chaperon, (now often **chaperone**), *shap'e-rōn*, *n.* a lady under whose care a girl appears in society.—*v.t.* to act as chaperon to. [Fr., a large hood—*chappe*, a hooded cloak—Low L. *cappa*, a cloak.]

chapiter, *chap'i-tér*, *n.* the head or capital of a column. [Fr. *chapitre*—L. *caput*, the head.]

chaplain, *chap'lin*, *n.* a clergyman attached to a ship of war, a regiment, a public institution, or private family.—*n.* **chap'laincy.** [O.Fr. *chapelain*—Low L. *cappellānus*—*cappella.* See **chapel**.]

chaplet, *chap'let*, *n.* a garland or wreath for the head: a circlet of gold, &c.: a string of beads used in counting prayers, one-third of a rosary in length. [O.Fr. *chapelet*—*chape*, a head-dress.]

chapman, *chap'man*, *n.* one who buys or sells: a pedlar:—*pl.* **chapmen.**—*n.* **chap'-book**, a book or pamphlet of the popular type formerly sold by chapmen. [O.E. *cēap-mann*—*cēap*, price, barter, *mann*, man. See **cheap**.]

chapter, *chap'tér*, *n.* a main division of a book: a subject or category generally: an assembly of the canons of a cathedral (see **chapterhouse**), or the members of a religious or military order: an organised branch of some society or fraternity.—*n.* **chap'ter-house**, a house or room where a chapter meets—formerly (in the case of canons or monks) in order to read a *chapter* of their rule.—**chapter of accidents**. See **accident**. [O.Fr. *chapitre*—L. *capitum*, dim. of *caput*, the head.]

char, *chär*, *n.* a small red-bellied fish of the salmon kind. [Prob. Celt.; cf. Gael, *ceara*, red, blood-coloured.]

char, *chär*, *v.t.* to reduce to carbon.—*v.t.* and *v.i.* to scorch:—*pr.p.* **charr'ing**; *pa.p.* **charred**. [Origin obscure.]

char, *chär*, **chare**, *chār*, *n.* an occasional piece of work, an odd job: (*pl.*) household work—now usually **chores** (*chōrz*).—*v.i.* to do odd jobs: to do house-cleaning.—*n.* **char'woman**, a casual domestic servant hired to do rough work. [O.E. *cerran, cierran*, to turn.]

char-à-banc, *shar'-a-bang*, *n.* a long open vehicle with transverse seats, for excursions:—*pl.* **char'-à-bancs** or (as in French) **chars-à-bancs**. [Fr. *char à bancs*, carriage with benches.]

character, *kar'ak-tér*, *n.* a letter or distinctive mark: writing generally, handwriting: a secret cipher: any essential feature or peculiarity: the aggregate of peculiar qualities which constitutes personal or national individuality: a formal statement of such qualities: a person of remarkable individuality: a personality as

Neutral vowels in unaccented syllables: *em'pér-ór*; for certain sounds in foreign words see p. ix.

114

created in a play or novel: (*slang*) a person.—
v.t **char′acterise**, to describe by (its or his)
peculiar qualities: to describe (as): to distinguish, be characteristic of.—*ns.* **character.isā′-
tion; characteris′tic**, that which marks or constitutes the character: the integral part of a
logarithm.—*adjs.* **characteris′tic, -al**, marking
or constituting the peculiar nature.—*adv.*
characteris′tically.—character actor, one who
makes a specialty of portraying eccentricities;
character part, the part (in a play) of a person
of marked eccentricity; **character sketch**, a
short description of the main traits in a person's character.—**in character**, appropriate: in
keeping with the person's usual conduct or
attitudes; **out of character**, not in character,
unlike what one would expect from the person
concerned. [Fr. *caractère*—L. *character*—Gr.
charaktēr, *charassein*, to engrave.]
charade, *shar-ād′, n.* an acted riddle in which
the syllables of the word proposed and the
whole word are represented in successive
scenes: a similar riddle with written clues.
[Fr.; ety. uncertain.]
charcoal, *chär′kōl, n.* the carbonaceous residue
from the partial combustion of wood or animal matter. [char (2), coal.]
charge, *chärj, v.t* to load, to fill (with): to burden, to lay a task, trust upon (one): to exhort:
to accuse: to ask as the price: to attack at a
rush.—*v.i.* to make an onset.—*n.* that which is
laid on: cost or price: the load of powder, &c.,
for a gun: care, custody: the object of care: an
accumulation of electricity: command: exhortation: accusation: attack or onset: (*pl.*) expenses.—*adj.* **charge′able**, liable to be
charged: blamable.—*n.* **charg′er**, a flat dish
capable of holding a large joint, a platter: a
war-horse: an instrument or device for charging.—**charge account**, an account in which
goods obtained were entered to be paid for
later.—**give in charge**, to hand over to the
police. [Fr. *charger*—Low L. *carricāre*, to
load—L. *carrus*, a wagon.]
chargé-d′affaires, *shär′zhā-dä-fer′, n.* a minor
diplomatic agent: an ambassador's deputy.
[Fr.]
charily, chariness. See **chary**.
chariot, *chari′-ŏt, n.* a pleasure or state carriage:
a car used in ancient warfare or racing.—*n.*
charioteer′, one who drives a chariot. [Fr.,
dim. of *char*, a car.]
charisma, *kar-is′mä, n.* a spiritual power given
by God: personal quality that enables an individual to influence his fellows: a similar
quality felt to reside in an office or position.—*adj.* **charismat′ic**. [Gr. *charis*, -*itos*,
grace.]
charity, *char′i-ti, n.* (*N.T.*) universal love: benevolence: the disposition to think favourably
of others, and do them good: almsgiving: a
benevolent fund or institution.—*adj.* **char′it-
able**, of or relating to charity: lenient, kindly:
liberal to the poor.—*n.* **char′itableness.**—*adv.*
char′itably. [Fr. *charité*—L. *cāritās*—*cārus*,
dear.]
charivari, *shär′i-vär′i, n.* a disorderly and derisive demonstration of displeasure. [Fr.]
charlatan, *shär′la-tän, n.* a mere talking pretender: a quack.—*n.* **char′latanry**. [Fr.,—It. *ciar-*

latano—*ciarlare*, to chatter.]
Charles's Wain, *chärlz′ez wān, n.* the Plough
(q.v.). [O.E. *Carles wægn*, Carl being Charlemagne.]
charlock, *chär′lok, n.* wild mustard, a common
weed with yellow flowers. [O.E. *cerlic*.]
charlotte, *shär′lot, n.* a kind of tart containing
fruit: a moulded dessert enclosed in sponge
fingers. [From the name *Charlotte*.]
charm, *chärm, n.* a spell: something thought to
possess occult power, as words in metrical
form or an amulet or trinket: attractiveness:
personal attractions.—*v.t.* to influence by a
charm: to enchant: to delight.—*adj.* **charmed**,
protected, as by a spell: delighted.—*n.*
charm′er.—*adv.* **charm′ingly.** [Fr. *charme*—L.
carmen, a song.]
charnel, *chär′nel, adj.* of, or pertaining to, a
charnel or burial place.—*n.* **char′nel (-house)**,
a place where the bones thrown up by
gravediggers are put. (O Fr. *charnel*—L. *carnālis*—*carō, carnis, flesh*.]
chart, *chärt, n.* a map of part of the sea, with its
coasts, shoals, &c., for the use of sailors: an
outline map: a tabular statement. [O.Fr.
charte—L. *c(h)arta*; see **card** (1).]
charter, *chärt′er, n.* any formal writing conferring or confirming titles, rights, or privileges,
or the like, esp. one granted by the sovereign
or government: a deed or conveyance: privilege.—*v.t.* to establish by charter: to let or
hire, as a ship, on contract.—*adj.* hired, as
a *charter plane*: made in a hired aeroplane, as
charter flight.—*ns.* **chartered accountant**, one
qualified under the regulations of the Institute of Accountants; **chartered company**, a
trading company acting under a charter from
the crown. [O.Fr. *chartre*—L. *c(h)artula*, dim.
of *c(h)arta*; see **card** (1).]
Charterhouse, *chär′ter-hows, n.* the famous hospital and school, the first premises of which
stood on the site of a *Carthusian* (q.v.)
monastery in London.
charter-party, *chärt′er pär′ti, n.* a mutual charter or compact for the hire of a ship. [Fr.
charte partie, lit. a divided charter.]
Chartism, *chärt′izm, n.* a movement in support
of the reforms demanded by the People's
Charter of 1838.—*n.* **Chart′ist**.
chartreuse, *shär-trœz′, n.* a famous liqueur first
manufactured by the monks of the monastery
of La Grande *Chartreuse*. [See **Carthusian**.]
charwoman. See **char**.
chary, *chär′i, adj.* sparing (of, in): unwilling to
risk (with *of*): cautious.—*adv.* **char′ily.**—*n.*
char′lness. [O.E. *cearig*—*cearu*, care.]
chase, *chās, v.t.* to pursue: to hunt: to drive
away.—*n.* pursuit: a hunting: that which is
hunted: an unenclosed game preserve.—*n.*
chas′er.—wild-goose chase, futile pursuit of
the unattainable. [O.Fr. *chacier, chasser*—L.
captāre, freq. of *capĕre*, to take.]
chase, *chās, v.t.* to decorate with engraving.—*n.*
chas′er. [Short for **enchase**.]
chase, *chās, n.* a frame for holding printing
types: a groove. [Fr. *châsse*, a shrine, a setting—L. *capsa*, a chest. See **case** (1).]
chasm, *kazm, n.* a yawning or gaping hollow: a
gap or opening in void space. [Gr. *chasma*,
from *chainein* (pr. indic. *chaskō*), to gape.]

chassé, *shas'ā, n.* a gliding step in dancing. [Fr.]

chassis, *shas'ē, n.* the frame of a motor-car, &c. to which the wheels, engine, &c. are affixed: an aeroplane's landing-carriage:—*pl.* **chassis** (*shas'ez*). [Fr. *châssis,* frame.]

chaste, *chāst, adj.* modest: virtuous: virgin: pure in taste and style.—*adv.* **chaste'ly.**—*ns.* **chaste'ness; chăs'tity,** sexual purity: virginity: refinement of style. [O.Fr. *chaste*—L. *castus,* pure.]

chasten, *chās'n, v.t.* to free from faults by punishing—hence, to punish or correct. [**chaste,** with suffix. *-en.*]

chastise, *chas-tīz', v.t.* to punish for the purpose of correction: to reduce to order or to obedience.—*n.* **chas'tisement.** [Related to *chasten;* exact history of word unknown.]

chasuble, *chaz'-* or *chas'ū-bl, n.* a sleeveless vestment worn by the priest celebrating mass. [Fr.,—Low L. *casubula*—L. *casula,* dim. of *casa,* a hut.]

chat, *chat, v.i.* to talk easily or familiarly:—*pr.p.* chatt'ing; *pa.p.* chatt'ed.—*n.* familiar, easy talk.—*adj.* **chatt'y,** inclined to talk much and in familiar style.—**chat up,** to talk to lightly and informally but with a purpose, e.g. in order to cajole. [Short for **chatter.**]

chat, *chat, n.* a genus of small birds of the thrush family. [From the sound of their voice.]

château, *shä'tō, n.* a castle, a great country-seat: a vineyard estate around a castle, esp. in Bordeaux, France (common in names of wines):—*pl.* **châ'teaux** (*-tōz*).—*ns.* **chatelain** (*shat'e-lā*), a castellan; **chat'elaine** (*-len*), a female castellan: an ornamental bunch of short chains bearing keys, scissors, &c. [O.Fr. *chastel* (Fr. *château*)—L. *castellum,* dim. of *castrum,* a fort.]

chattel, *chat'él, n.* any kind of property that is not freehold.—**goods and chattels,** all movable property. [O.Fr. *chatel*—Low L. *captāle*—L. *capitāle,* &c., property, goods.]

chatter, *chat'ér, v.i.* to talk idly or rapidly: (of birds) to utter a succession of rapid short notes: to sound as the teeth when one shivers.—*n.* idle talk.—*ns.* **chatt'erbox,** one who chatters or talks incessantly; **chatt'erer.** [From the sound.]

Chaucerian, *chô-sē'ri-án, adj.* pertaining to, or like, *Chaucer* (1345-1400).—*n.* a student or a follower of Chaucer.

chauffeur, *shō'fér, shō-fœr', n.* one employed to drive a motor-car:—*fem.* **chauffeuse,** (*shō-fœz'*). [Fr.]

chauvinism, *shō'vin-izm, n.* excessive national pride and contempt for other countries: excessive attachment to any group, cause, &c.—*n.* **chau'vinist.**—*adj.* **chauvinist'ic.** [From *Nicolas Chauvin,* ardent Napoleonic veteran.]

chaw, *chö, v.t.* to chew, as tobacco. [By-form of **chew.**]

cheap, *chēp, adj.* low in price: charging low prices: of small value: paltry: inferior.—*v.t.* **cheap'en,** to lower the price or reputation of.—*adv.* **cheap'ly.**—*ns.* **cheap'ness; cheap-jack,** a pedlar of cheap wares. [Originally *good cheap,* i.e. a good bargain; O.E. *cēap,* price, barter; O.E. *cēapian,* O.N. *kaupa,* Ger. *kaufen,* to buy—all from L. *caupo,* a huckster.]

cheat, *chēt, v.t.* to deceive: to defraud.—*v.i.* to practise deceit.—*n.* a fraud: one who cheats.—*n.* **cheat'er.** [M.E. *cheten,* a form of *escheten,* to escheat.]

check, *chek, v.t.* to bring to a stand: to restrain or hinder: to rebuke: to scrutinise: to verify: to mark with a pattern of squares.—*n.* in chess, a threat to the king: anything that checks: a sudden stop or repulse: a mark put against items in a list: an order for money (usually written **cheque**): a token or counter: a pattern of small squares.—*ns.* **check'er; check'-key,** a latch-key; **check'-mate,** in chess, a position from which the king cannot escape: disaster that cannot be retrieved.—*v.t.* in chess, to make a move that causes checkmate: to frustrate.—**hold in check,** to restrain, keep back. [O.Fr. *eschec, eschac,* through Low L. and Ar. from Pers. *shāh,* king—**checkmate** being O.Fr. *eschec mat*—Ar. *shāh māt(a),* 'the king is dead'.]

checker. See **chequer.**

checkers, *chek'érz, n. pl.* the game of draughts.

cheddar, *ched'ár, n.* a kind of cheese first made at *Cheddar* in Somersetshire.

cheek, *chēk, n.* the side of the face below the eye: the side of a door, &c.: (*coll.*) effrontery, impudence.—*adj.* **cheek'y,** insolent, saucy.—**cheek by jowl,** side by side. [O.E. *cēce, céace,* the cheek, jaw; cf. Du. *kaak.*]

cheep, *chēp, v.i.* to chirp, as a young bird.—*n.* any chirping sound. [From the sound.]

cheer, *chēr, n.* disposition, frame of mind: joy: a shout of approval or welcome: entertainment: fare, food.—*v.t.* to comfort: to encourage: to applaud.—*adjs.* **cheer'ful,** in good spirits: lively: ungrudging; **cheer'y,** cheerful, lively, merry.—*advs.* **cheer'fully; cheer'ily.**—*ns.* **cheer'fulness; cheer'iness.**—*adj.* **cheer'less,** without comfort, gloomy.—*n.* **cheer'lessness.** [O.Fr. *chiere,* the face—Low L. *cara,* the face.]

cheese, *chēz, n.* the curd of milk coagulated and pressed into a hard mass.—*n.* **cheese'par'ing,** miserly economy.—*adj.* miserly, niggardly.—*adj.* **chees'y,** cheese-like. [O.E. *cēse, cȳse,* curdled milk—L. *cāseus.*]

cheetah, *chē'tä, n.* an Eastern animal like the leopard, used in hunting. [Hindustani *chītā.*]

chef, *shef, n.* a master-cook (**chef de cuisine,** *dé kwē-zēn'*).—*n.* **chef d'œvre** (*shä dœvr'*), masterpiece:—*pl.* **chefs d'œvre** (pron. as *sing.*): [Fr. See **chief.**]

cheiromancy, *kī'rō-man-si, n.* fortune-telling by the hand. [Gr. *cheir,* the hand, *manteia,* prophecy.]

Cheiroptera, *kī-rop'tér-a, n.pl.* the order of mammals consisting of the bats. [Gr. *cheir,* the hand, *pteron,* a wing.]

chemise, *she-mēz', n.* a woman's smock-like undergarment. [Fr. *chemise*—Low L. *camisia,* a nightgown, surplice.]

chemistry, *kem'is-tri,* formerly **chymistry** (*kim'-*), *n.* the science that treats of the properties of substances both elementary and compound, and of the laws of their combination and action one upon another.—*adjs.* **chem'ic, -al** (**chem'ico-, chem'o-,** in compound words).—*adv.* **chem'ically.**—*n.pl.* **chem'icals,** substances used in chemical processes.—*n.* **chem'ist,** one skilled in chemistry: a druggist.—**chemical engineering,** design,

---

Neutral vowels in unaccented syllables: *em'pér-ór;* for certain sounds in foreign words see p. ix.

construction, and operation of chemical plant and works, esp. in industrial chemistry; **chemical warfare**, warfare involving the use of irritating or asphyxiating gases, oil, flames, &c. [From **alchemy** (q.v.).]

chemotherapy, *kem-ō-ther'ă-pi*, *n.* treatment of a disease by means of a chemical compound having a specific effect on the micro-organisms involved (either destroying them or inhibiting their growth) but no harmful effect on the patient's tissues. [**chemo-** (see **chemistry**), and **therapy**.]

chemurgy, *kem'ûr-ji*, *n.* the application of chemistry to agriculture: agriculture prosecuted for chemical purposes, e.g. potato-growing for the purpose of making industrial alcohol by fermentation.—*adj.* **chemur'gic**. [Coined in U.S.A. in 1934.]

chenille, *she-nēl'*, *n.* a velvety cord of silk or wool (resembling a caterpillar), used in ornamental sewing: a velvet-like material used for table-covers. &c. [Fr., a caterpillar.]

cheque, check, *chek*, *n.* a money order on a banker.—*ns.* **cheque'-book**, a book of cheque forms; **chequ'-, check'er**, (*obs.*) a chessboard.—*v.t.* to mark in squares of different colours: to diversify.—*adj.* **cheq'uered**, variegated, like a chess-board. **check'ered**, variegated, like a chess-board. varying in character: eventful, with alternations of good and bad fortune. [A variant of **check**.]

cheralite, *cher'ă-līt*, *n.* a radioactive mineral rich in thorium and uranium. [*Chera*, ancient name of Travancore, where discovered, Gr. *lithos*, a stone.]

cherish, *cher'ish*, *v.t.* to protect and treat with affection: to entertain in the mind, hold in the heart, to nurse. [Fr. *chérir*, *chérissant*—*cher*, dear—L. *cārus*.]

cheroot, *she-rōōt'*, *n.* a cigar not pointed at either end. [Fr. *cheroute*—Tamil (q.v.) *shuruttu*, roll.]

cherry, *cher'i*, *n.* any of several species of trees of the same genus as the plum: the small stone-fruit, usually bright red, which they bear.—*adj.* like a cherry in colour: ruddy.—*n.* **cherr'y-brand'y**, a liqueur made by steeping cherries in brandy. [O.E. *ciris*—L. *cerasus.*—Gr. *kerasos*, a cherry-tree.]

chert, *chûrt*, *n.* a compact rock, consisting of silica, occurring in limestone formations older than the Chalk (q.v.). [Ety. doubtful.]

cherub, *cher'ub*, *n.* a winged creature with human face: a celestial spirit: a beautiful child—*pl.* **cher'ubs**, **cher'ubim** (*-y ōō-bim*), **cher'ubims.**—*adjs.* **cheru'bic** (*-ōō'bik*), **-al.** [Heb. *k'rūb*, pl. *k'rūbīm.*]

chess, *ches*, *n.* a game played by two persons with figures or 'men', which are moved on a chequered board.—*n.pl.* **chess'men**, pieces used in chess. [Fr. *échecs*; It. *scacchi*; Ger. *schach*. Orig. from Pers. *shāh*, a king.]

chest, *chest*, *n.* a large strong box: a treasury: the part of the body between the neck and the abdomen, the thorax.—**chest of drawers**, a set of drawers fitted in a single piece of furniture. [O.E. *cyst*; Scot. *kist.*—L. *cista.*]

chesterfield, *chest'ér-fēld*, *n.* a long overcoat: a heavily padded sofa. [A 19th century Lord Chesterfield.]

chestnut, chesnut, *ches'nut*, *n.* a common edible nut enclosed in a prickly husk (the *Spanish* or *sweet chestnut*): the tree that bears it, or other tree of the same genus: the *horse chestnut* (q.v.) or its fruit: (*slang*) a stale joke.—*adj.* of chestnut colour, reddish-brown.—**pull the chestnuts out of the fire**, to take control and rescue someone from a difficult situation. [O.Fr. *chastaigne*—L. *castanea.*]

cheval-de-frise, *she-val'-de-frēz*, *n.* a spiky defensive structure, used esp. to stop cavalry (often in *pl.* form): *-pl.* **chevaux-de-frise** (*she-vō'-*). [Fr.,—*cheval*, horse, *de*, of, *Frise*, Friesland.]

cheval glass, *shĕ-val' gläs*, *n.* a large glass or mirror supported on a frame. [Fr. *cheval*, horse, stand.]

chevalier, *shev-a-lēr'*, *n.* a cavalier: a knight: a gallant. [Fr.,—*cheval*—L. *caballus*, a horse.]

cheviot, *chē'vi-ot*, or *chev'i-ot*, *n.* a breed of sheep reared on the *Cheviot Hills*: a cloth made from their wool.

chevron, *shev'ron*, *n.* a rafter: the V-shaped band on the sleeve of a non-commissioned officer's coat. [Fr. *chevron*, a rafter—L. *capreolus*, dim. of *caper*, a goat.]

chevy, chivy, *chev'i*, *chiv'i*, *n.* a cry, shout: a hunt.—*v.t.* and *v.i.* to chase. [Perh. 'Chevy Chase', a well-known ballad relating the story of a Border battle.]

chew, *chōō*, *v.t.* to bruise and grind with the teeth, to masticate.—*n.* action of chewing: a quid of tobacco.—*n.* **chew'ing-gum**, a preparation made from chicle, or other gum, sweetened and flavoured.—**chew the cud**, to masticate a second time food already swallowed: to ponder. [O.E. *cēowan*; Ger. *kauen.*]

chez, *shā*, *prep.* at the home or establishment of [Fr.]

Chianti, *kē-an'ti*, *n.* a wine (usu. red) of Tuscany. [Named from the *Chianti Mts.*]

chiaroscuro, *kyär-o-skōō'ro*, *n.* management of light and shade in a picture. [It.,—L. *clārus*, clear, *obscurus*, dark.]

chic, *shēk*, *n.* style, fashion.—*adj.* stylish. [Fr.]

chicane, *shi-kān'*, *v.i.* to use shifts and tricks.—*v.t.* to deceive.—*n.* (also **chica'nery**), trickery or artifice, esp. in legal proceedings. [Fr. *chicane*, sharp practice at law.]

chiccory. See **chicory**.

chichi, chi-chi, *shē-shē*, *adj.* pretentious: fussy: affected: stylish, self-consciously fashionable.—*n.* something that is, or the quality of being, chichi: red tape: fuss. [Fr.]

chick, chik, *n.* the young of a fowl, esp. of the hen: a child, as a term of endearment: (*slang*) a girl or a young woman.—*ns.* **chick'en**, a chick: flesh of a fowl: a child: a coward; **chick'en-feed**, poultry food: (*slang*) small change: (*slang*) something of little value; **chick'en-heart**, cowardly person.—*adj.* **chick'-en-heart'ed.**—*ns.* **chick'en-pox**, a contagious febrile disease, chiefly of children, not unlike a very mild form of smallpox: **chick'weed**, a species of stitchwort, much relished by fowls and cage-birds.—**no chicken**, no longer young. [O.E. *cicen*; cf. Du. *kieken*, Ger. *küken.*]

chicle, *chik'l*, *chik'li*, *n.* the gum of the sapodilla tree. [Sp.,—Mex. ...]

chicory, chiccory, *chik'o-ri*, *n.* a plant with blue

flowers: its carrot-like root (ground to mix with coffee).—Also **succ′ory**. [Fr. *chicorée*—L. *cichorium*—Gr. *kichōrion*.]

chide, *chīd*, *v.t.* to scold, rebuke, reprove by words:—*pr.p.* chīd′ing; *pa.t.* chīd, sometimes chīd′ed; *pa.p.* chīd, chidd′en. [O.E. *cīdan*.]

chief, *chēf*, *adj.* head: principal, most important.—*n.* the head of a clan or tribe: a leader: the head of a department or business.—*adv.* **chief′ly**, in the first place, principally: for the most part.—*ns.* **chief′tain** (-*tin*), the head of a clan: a leader; **chief′taincy, chief′tainship**. [Fr. *chef*—L. *caput*, the head.]

chiffon, *shē′fō, shif′on*, *n.* a thin gauzy material used as a trimming.—*n.* **chiffonier** (*shif-on-ēr*), an ornamental cupboard or cabinet. [Fr., rag, adornment—*chiffe*, rag.]

chignon, *shē′nyō*, *n.* a fold or roll of hair worn on the back of the head and neck. [Fr.]

chigoe, *chig′ō*, **chigre, chigger**, *chig′ér*, *n.* a flea of the West Indies, South America, &c. which buries itself, esp. beneath the toe-nails, and causes sores.—Also **jigg′er**. [Fr. *chique*.]

chihuahua, *chi-wä′-wä*, *n.* a very small dog with pointed ears. [*Chihuahua* in Mexico.]

chilblain, *chil′blān*, *n.* a painful red swelling, esp. on hands and feet, in cold weather. [**chill** and **blain**.]

child, *chīld*, *n.* a very young person: a son or daughter: one connected with a person, place, or state by resemblance or origin (e.g. *a child of the devil, of the East, of shame*): a youth of gentle birth, esp. in ballads, &c. (sometimes **childe** and **chylde**):—*pl.* **chil′dren**, offspring: descendants: inhabitants.—*ns.* **child′-bear′ing**, the act of bringing forth children; **child′bed**, the state of a woman brought to bed with child; **child′birth**, parturition; **child′hood**, state of being a child.—*adj.* **child′ish**, of or like a child—silly, trifling.—*adv.* **child′ishly.**—*n.* **child′ishness.**—*adjs.* **child′less**, without children; **child′-like**, like a child—docile, innocent.—**child's play**, an easy task; **second childhood**, childishness sometimes characterising old age; **with child**, pregnant. [O.E. *cild*, pl. *cild*, later *cildru*, -*ra*.]

Childermas, *chil′dér-mas*, *n.* Innocents′ Day, a festival (Dec. 28) to commemorate the slaying of the children by Herod. [O.E. *cildra*, gen. pl. of *cild*, child, *mæsse*, mass.]

chiliad, *kil′i-ad*, *n.* the number 1000: 1000 of anything. [Gr. *chīlioi*, 1000.]

chill, *chil*, *n.* coldness: a cold that causes shivering: anything that damps or disheartens.—*adj.* shivering with cold: slightly cold: opposite of *cordial.*—*v.i.* to grow cold.—*v.t.* to make chill or cold: to blast with cold: to discourage.—*adj.* **chill′y**, chill.—*ns.* **chill′ness, chill′iness**. [O.E. *cele, ciele*, cold.]

chilli, *chil′i*, *n.* the pod of some of the capsicums, pungent and stimulant, used in sauces, pickles, &c., and dried and ground to form the spice Cayenne pepper. [Mexican.]

Chiltern Hundreds, *chil′térn hund′redz*, a district in the *Chiltern* Hills, by accepting the stewardship of which, a nominal office under the crown, a member of parliament can vacate his seat. [See **hundred**.]

chimaera, chimera, *ki-mē′ra*, *n.* (*cap.*) a fabulous fire-spouting monster: any idle or wild fancy.—*adj.* **chimĕr′ical**, wild: fanciful.—*adv.* **chimer′ically.** [L.,—Gr. *chimaira*, a she-goat.]

chime, *chīm*, *n.* a set of bells tuned in a scale: the ringing of such bells in succession: a definite sequence of bell-like notes sounded as by a clock: the harmonious sound of bells, &c.: harmony.—*v.i.* **·t**o sound in harmony: to jingle: to accord or agree.—*v.t.* to strike, or cause to sound in harmony. [M.E. *chimbe*, prob. O.Fr. *cymbale*—L. *cymbalum*, a cymbal.]

chimney, *chim′ni*, *n.* a passage for the escape of fumes, smoke, or heated air from a fireplace or furnace: anything of a like shape.—*v.t.* to climb a narrow crevice with back against one wall and feet against the other.—*ns.* **chim′ney-can**, or **-pot**, a cylindrical pipe at the top of a chimney; **chim′ney-cor′ner**, the fireside, esp. as a place of warmth and comfort; **chim′ney-piece**, a shelf over the fireplace; **chim′ney-shaft**, the stalk of a chimney which rises above the building; **chim′ney-stack**, a group of chimneys carried up together; **chim′ney-stalk**, a very tall chimney; **chim′ney-sweep, chim′ney-sweep′er**, one who sweeps or cleans chimneys. [Fr. *cheminée*—L. *camīnus*; Gr. *kamīnos*, a furnace.]

chimpanzee, *chim-pan-zē′*, also *chim′-*, *n.* an African ape, the most manlike of the anthropoid apes. [West African.]

chin, *chin*, *n.* the jutting part of the face below the mouth.—*n.* and *v.i.* **chin′wag** (*slang*), talk. [O.E. *cin*; Ger. *kinn*, Gr. *genys.*]

china, *chīn′ä*, *n.* fine kind of earthenware originally made in *China*, porcelain.—*ns.* **chin′a-clay**, a fine white clay used in making porcelain, kaolin; **chin′a-grass**, ramie; **Chin′a-man**, a native of China (slightly derogatory): (*cricket*) off-break bowled by a left-handed bowler to a right-handed batsman; **chin′a-shop**, a shop in which china, crockery, &c., are sold; **chin′a-ware**, porcelain-ware; **Chinese′**, a native of China (*pl.* **Chinese′**): the language of China.—Also *adj.*—**Chinese lantern**, a paper lantern; **Chinese white**, a zinc oxide pigment.

chinchilla, *chin-chil′a*, *n.* a small rodent of South America valued for its soft grey fur: the fur itself: (*cap.*) a breed of rabbit or of cat with soft grey fur. [Sp.]

chine, *chīn*, *n.* the spine or backbone: a piece of the backbone and adjoining parts for cooking. [O.Fr. *eschine*, prob. from O.H.G. *scina*, a pin, thorn.]

chine, *chīn*, *n.* a ravine. [O.E. *cinu*, a cleft.]

chink, *chingk*, *n.* a cleft, a narrow opening.—*v.i.* to crack. [M.E. *chine*, a crack.]

chink, *chingk*, *n.* the clink, as of coins.—*v.i.* to give forth a sharp sound. [From the sound.]

chinook, *chin-ook′*, *n.* a warm dry wind that blows down the eastern side of the Rocky Mountains. [*Chinook*, an Amer. Indian tribe.]

chintz, *chints*, *n.* cotton printed in several colours. [Orig. *pl.*—Hindustani *chīnt*, spotted cotton-cloth.]

chip, *chip*, *v.t.* to cut as with a chisel: to strike small pieces from the surface of:—*pr.p.* chipp′ing; *pa.p.* chipped.—*n.* a small piece chipped off: a games counter.—*n.* **chip′board**, reconstructed wood made by consolidation of chips from woodland trimmings, workshop waste, &c., with added resin: a wastepaper

Neutral vowels in unaccented syllables: *em′pér-ór*; for certain sounds in foreign words see p. ix.

cardboard used in box-making.—**chip in**, to interpose: to pay part of the cost of something.—**a chip of the old block**, one with the characteristics of his father; **have a chip on one's shoulder**, to be defiant and aggressive: to be ready to take offence; **have had one's chips**, to have died: to have had one's chance; **when the chips are down**, at a critical moment when it is too late to alter the situation. [M.E. *chippen*, to cut in pieces. Conn. with **chop**.]

chipmunk, *chip'mungk, n.* any of various kinds of small striped rodents of the squirrel family common in North America.

chipolata, *chip-ó-lä'tä, n.* a small sausage. [Fr.,—It. *cipolla*, onion.]

Chippendale, *chip'en-dāl, adj.* applied to a light style of drawing-room furniture, after the name of a well-known cabinet-maker of the 18th century.

chiropodist, *kī-rop'o-dist, n.* one who treats corns, bunions, warts, &c.—*n.* **chirop'ody**, the care and treatment of minor ailments of the feet. [Gr. *cheir*, hand, and *pous*, gen. *podos*, foot.]

chiropractic, *kī'rō-prak-tik, n.* method or practice of curing diseases by manipulating joints, esp. of the spine: one who carries out such treatment (also **chi'ropractor**). [Gr. *cheir*, the hand, *prāktikos*, fit for action.]

chirp, *chûrp, n.* the sharp, thin sound of certain birds and insects.—*v.i.* to make such a sound: to talk in a lively strain.—*adj.* **chirp'y**, lively: merry. [From the sound.]

chirur'geon, **chirur'gery**, **chirur'gical**, old forms of **surgeon**, **surgery**, **surgical**. [Fr. *chirurgien*—Gr. *cheirourgos*—*cheir*, the hand, *ergon*, a work.]

chisel, *chiz'él, n.* tool with the end bevelled to a cutting edge.—*v.t.* to cut, carve, &c., with a chisel:—*pr.p.* chis'elling; *pa.p.* chis'elled.—*adj.* **chis'elled**, cut with a chisel: (*fig.*) sharply defined. [O.Fr. *cisel*—L. *caedĕre*, to cut.]

chit, *chit, n.* a brief note: an order or pass.—Also **chitt'y**. [Hindustani *chitthī*.]

chit, *chit, n.* a child: (*slightingly*) a girl. [A contraction of **kitten**.]

chitin, *kī'tin, n.* the substance that forms most of the hard parts of crustaceans, insects, and spiders.—*adj.* **chi'tinous**. [Fr. *chitine*—Gr. *chiton*, a tunic.]

chivalry, *shiv'ál-ri* (orig. *chiv-'*), *n.* the usages and qualifications of chevaliers or feudal knights: bravery and courtesy.—*adjs.* **chival'ric**, **chiv'alrous**, pertaining to chivalry: showing the qualities of an ideal knight, generous, courteous, &c.—*adv.* **chiv'alrously**. [Fr. *chevalerie*—*cheval*—L. *caballus*, a horse.]

chive, *chīv, n.* a herb like the leek and onion, with tufts of leaves used as flavouring, and clustered bulbs: a small bulb.—Also **cive**. [Fr. *cive*—L. *coepa*, an onion.]

chivy, *chiv'i, n.* and *v.* See **chevy**.

chlorine, *klō'rēn, -rin, -rīn, n.* a chemical element (symbol Cl; at. no. 17), a yellow-green gas with a peculiar, suffocating odour—used in bleaching, disinfecting, and in industry.—*ns.* **chlor'al**, strongly narcotic substance obtained by the action of chlorine on alcohol; **chlō'rate**, a salt of chloric acid.—*adjs.* **chlō'ric**, **chlor'ous**, of or from chlorine.—*n.*

chlō'ride, a compound of chlorine with another element or radical.—*v.t.* **chlō'rinate**, to treat with chlorine (as in sterilisation of water, extraction of gold from ore).—*ns.* **chlo'rodyne**, a patent medicine—anodyne and hypnotic; **chloroform** (*klor'ō-fōrm*, or *klō'rōfōrm*), a colourless, volatile liquid used to induce insensibility (also *v.t.*); **chlō'rophyll**, the ordinary green colouring matter of vegetation; **chlorō'sis**, properly *green-sickness*, a peculiar form of anaemia. [Gr. *chlōros*, pale-green.]

chock, *chok, v.t.* to fasten as with a wedge.—*n.* a wedge to keep a cask from rolling: a log.—*adjs.* **chock-a-block'**, **chock'-full**, **choke'-full**, quite full. [Ety. obscure.]

chocolate, *chok'ō-lät, n.* a paste made of the pounded seeds of the cacao tree (cocoa) with sugar and flour or similar material: a beverage made by dissolving this paste in boiling water: a sweetmeat made of the paste.—*adj.* chocolate-coloured, dark reddish-brown: made of or flavoured with chocolate.—*adj.* **choc'olate-box**, pretty-pretty or oversentimental, esp. of a painting. [Sp. *chocolate*; from Mexican *chocólatl*.]

chode, *chōd,* an occasional *pa.t.* of **chide**.

choice, *chois, n.* act or power of choosing: the thing chosen: alternative: preference: the best (part).—*adj.* worthy of being chosen: select. [Fr. *choix*—*choisir*; from same Gmc. root as **choose**.]

choir, *kwīr, n.* a chorus or band of singers, esp. those belonging to a church: the part of a church appropriated to the singers: the part of a cathedral separated from the nave by a rail or screen.—*n.* **choir'-screen**, a screen of lattice-work, separating the choir from the nave. [Fr. *chœur*—L. *chorus*. See **chorus**.]

choke, *chōk, v.t.* to interfere with the breathing of: to throttle: to suffocate: to stop or obstruct.—*v.i.* to be choked.—*n.* the action of choking: the sound of choking: a device to prevent the passage of too much gas, electric current, &c.—*adj.* **chok'y**, tending to cause choking: inclined to choke, as with emotion.—*n.* **choke'-damp**, carbon dioxide or other non-explosive, suffocating gas in coalmines.—*adj.* **choke'-full** (see **chock-full**).—*n.* **chok'er**, one who chokes: a high collar: a high tight necklace.—**choke back**, to repress; **choke off**, to get rid of. [Ety. obscure.]

choler, *kol'ér, n.* the bile: anger: irascibility.—*adj.* **chol'eric**, irascible, prone to anger: angry. [Fr.,—L.,—Gr. *cholera*—*cholē*, bile.]

cholera, *kol'ér-a, n.* a highly infectious and deadly disease characterised by bilious vomiting and purging.—*adj.* **cholerā'ic**. [Gr. *cholera*—*cholē*, bile.]

choose, *chōōz, v.t.* to take (one thing) in preference to another: to select.—*v.i.* to will or determine, to think fit:—*pa.t.* chose; *pa.p.* chos'en.—*adj.* **choos'(e)y** (*coll.*), difficult to please, fastidious.—**I cannot choose but**, I must. [O.E. *cēosan*, Du. *kiesen*.]

chop, *chop, v.t.* to cut with a sudden blow: to cut into small pieces.—*n.* a piece cut off: a slice of mutton or pork containing a rib: a sharp downward blow.—*ns.* **chop'-house**, an eating house where chops are served; **chopp'er**, one who or that which chops: a cleaver: (*slang*) a helicopter.—*adj*. **chopp′y**, running in irregular waves. [A form of **chap** (1).]

chop, *chop*, *v.t.* and *v.i.* to barter or exchange: to change direction:—*pr.p.* **chopp′ing**; *pa.p.* **chopped**.—**chop and change**, to buy and sell: to change about; **chop logic**, to argue contentiously. [Connection with **chop** (1) is not clear.]

chop, *chop*, *n.* the chap or jaw, generally used in *pl.*—*adj.* **chop′-fall′en**, cast-down: dejected. [See **chap** (3).]

chop-sticks, *chop′-stiks*, *n.pl.* two small sticks of wood, ivory, &c., used by the Chinese instead of a fork. [Pidgin Eng. *chop-chop*, quick, and **stick**.]

choral, chorale. See **chorus**.

chord, *körd*, *n.* (*mus.*) a number of notes (formerly, in harmony) played together. See also **common**. [From **accord**.]

chord, *körd*, *n.* a string of a musical instrument: a cord (**spinal, vocal**): (*geom.*) a straight line joining any two points on a curve: (*aero.*) the straight line joining the leading and the trailing edges of an aerofoil section. [L. *chorda* — Gr. *chordē*, a gut string.]

chore, *chōr*, *chör*, *n.* a household task: an unenjoyable task. [Form of **char** (3).]

chorea, *ko-rē′ä*, *n.* St Vitus's dance, a nervous disease causing involuntary movements of the limbs or face. [L.,—Gr. *choreia*, a dancing.]

choreography, *kor-i-og′ra-fi*, *n.* the art or the notation of dancing: the art of arranging dances, esp. ballets: the arrangement of a ballet.—*adj.* **choreograph′ic**.—*n.* **choreog′rapher**. [Gr. *choreia*, dancing, *graphē*, description—*graphein*, to write. Cf. **chorus**.]

chortle, *chört′l*, *v.i.* to utter a low deep laugh. [Coined by Lewis Carroll in 1872, perh. from *chuckle* and *snort*.]

chorus, *kō′rus*, *kö′*, *n.* a band of singers and dancers: in Greek plays, a number of persons who commented, counselled, &c.: that which is sung by a chorus: a refrain: a combined utterance.—*v.t.* to sing or say together.—*adj.* **chōr′al**, pertaining to a chorus or a choir.—*n.* **chōrāl′** (often altered to **chorale′**), a simple harmonised composition with slow rhythm: a psalm or hymn tune.—*adv.* **chōr′ally**, in the manner of a chorus.—*adj.* **cho′ric**,—*n.* **chör′ister**, a member of a choir. [L.,—Gr. *choros*, dance.]

chose, chosen. See **choose**.

chough, *chuf*, *n.* the red-legged crow. [From its cry.]

chow, *chow*, *n.* a dog of probably Chinese breed.

chrism, *krizm*, *n.* consecrated or holy oil: unction.—*adj.* **chris′mal**, pertaining to chrism. [O.Fr. *chresme* —Gr. *chrisma*, from *chriein*, to anoint.]

Christ, *krīst*, *n.* the Anointed, the Messiah.—*v.t.* **christe·n** (*kris′n*), to baptise in the name of Christ: to give a name to.—*ns.* **Chris′tendom** (*kris′n-*), the part of the world in which Christianity is the received religion: the whole body of Christians; **Chris′tian** (*chän*), a follower of Christ.—*adj.* relating to Christ or His religion.—*v.t.* **chris′tianise**, to make Christian: to convert to Christianity.—*n.* **Christian′ity**, the religion of Christ: the spirit of this

religion.—*adj.* **Chrīst′ly**.—**Christian era**, the era counted from the birth of Christ; **Christian name**, the personal name given (as at christening), distinguished from the surname; **Christian Science**, a religion which includes the belief that healing, mental and physical, can be achieved without medicine by means of the patient's Christian faith—founded in 1866 by Mrs Eddy. [O.E. *Crist* — Gr. *Christos* — and *chriein*, to anoint.]

Christmas, *kris′mas*, *n.* an annual festival, originally a mass, in memory of the birth of Christ, held on the 25th of December.—*ns.* **Christ′mas-box**, a box containing Christmas presents: a Christmas gift; **Christ′mas-eve**, (evening of) Dec. 24.—*adj.* **Christ′ma(s)sy**, appropriate to Christmas.—*ns.* **Christ′mastide, -time**, the season of Christmas; **Christ′mas-tree**, a tree, usually fir, loaded with Christmas gifts. [**Christ** and **mass**.]

Christology, *kris-tol′o-ji*, *n.* that branch of theology which treats of the nature and person of Christ. [Gr. *Christos*, Christ, *logos*, a discourse.]

chromatic, *krō-mat′ik*, *adj.* relating to colours: coloured: (*mus.*) pertaining to or proceeding by semitones.—*ns.* **chromatic′ity**, the colour quality of light depending on hue and saturation (i.e. excluding brightness), one method of defining it being by its purity and dominant wavelength; **chrōmat′ics**, the science of colours; **chromatog′raphy**, methods of separating substances in a mixture which depend on the fact that different absorbents will take up different constituents of the mixture, that certain solvents will not mix but will be in layers one over the other, &c.—methods which finally present the substances as a **chromat′ogram**, such as a series of visible bands in a vertical tube; **chrōme, chrō′mium**, metallic element (symbol Cr; at. no. 24) remarkable for the colours of its compounds.—*adj.* **chrōm′ic**.—*ns.* **chrō′minance** (TV), difference between any colour and a reference colour (usu. a white of specified chromaticity) of equal luminance; **chrō′mosome**, that portion of a cell nucleus through which hereditary characters are believed to be transmitted; **chrō′mosphere**, a layer of incandescent gas surrounding the sun. [Gr. *chrōmatikos-chrōma*, colour.]

chronic, -al, *kron′ik, -ál*, *adj.* lasting a long time: of a disease, deep seated or long continued; as opposed to *acute*. [Gr. *chronikos—chronos*, time.]

chronicle, *kron′i-kl*, *n.* a record of events in order of time: a history.—*v.t.* to record.—*n.* **chron′icler**, a writer of a chronicle. [O.Fr. *chronique*, through L.—Gr. *chronika*, annals—*chronos*, time.]

chronograph, *kron′o-gräf*, *n.* an instrument for taking exact measurements of time, e.g. a *stop watch*. [Gr. *chronos*, time, *graphein*, to write.]

chronology, *kron-ol′o-ji*, *n.* the science of computing time: a scheme of time: order in time.—*ns.* **chronol′oger, chronol′ogist**.—*adjs.* **chronolog′ic, -al**.—*adv.* **chronolog′ically**. [Gr. *chronos*, time, *logos*, a discourse.]

chronometer, *kron-om′e-ter*, *n.* a very accurate

Neutral vowels in unaccented syllables: *em′pér-ór*; for certain sounds in foreign words see p. ix.

120

form of timekeeper. [Gr. *chronos*, time, *metron*, a measure.]

chronotron, *kron'ō-tron*, *n.* a device which measures very small time intervals by comparing the distance between electric pulses from different sources. [Gr. *chronos*, time.]

chrysalis, *kris'a-lis*, **chrysalid**, *kris'a-lid*, *n.* the golden-coloured resting stage in the life-history of many butterflies: any pupa:—*pl.* **chrysal'ides** (*-i-dēz*).—*adj.* **chrys'alid**. [Gr. *chrȳsallis*—*chrȳsos*, gold.]

chrysanthemum, *kris-an'thē-mum*, *n.* a genus of composite plants to which belong the corn marigold and oxeye daisy, esp. showy garden varieties. [Gr. *chrȳsos*, gold, *anthemon*, flower.]

chrysolite, *kris'ō-līt*, *n.* a yellow or green precious stone. [Gr. *chrȳsos*, gold, *lithos*, stone.]

chrysoprase, *kris'o-prāz*, *n.* a green chalcedony. [Gr. *chrȳsos*, gold, *prason*, a leek.]

chub, *chub*, *n.* a small fat river-fish of the carp family.—*adj.* **chubb'y**, short and thick, plump.—*n.* **chubb'iness**. [Origin unknown.]

Chubb, *chub*, *n.* a lock invented by *Chubb*, a locksmith in London. [Trademark.]

chuck, *chuk*, *n.* the call of a hen: a chicken: a word of endearment.—*v.i.* to call, as a hen. [A variety of **cluck**.]

chuck, *chuk*, *n.* a gentle blow (under the chin).—*v.t.* to pat gently (under the chin): to toss: to pitch.—*n.* **chuck'er-out**, one who expels undesirable people.—**chuck up**, to give up, to throw up (the sponge). [Fr. *choquer*, to jolt; allied to **shock**.]

chuck, *chuk*, *n.* a pebble: a device on a machine tool for gripping revolving work or a drill. [Ety. uncertain.]

chuckle, *chuk'l*, *n.* a quiet laugh: the cry of a hen.—*v.i.* to laugh quietly: to call as a hen does her chickens. [Akin to **chuck** (1).]

chuffed, *chuft*, *adj.* (*coll.*) very pleased. [**chuff** (*dial.*), chubby.]

chum, *chum*, *n.* a chamber-fellow: a close companion.—*v.i.* to share a room: to be a chum.—*adj.* **chumm'y**, sociable. [Perh. a mutilation of **chamber-fellow**.]

chump, *chump*, *n.* an end lump of wood: the head.—**off his chump**, (slang) out of his mind. [Perh. related to **chunk**.]

chunk, *chungk*, *n.* a thick piece of anything, as wood, bread, &c. [Perh. related to **chuck** (3).]

Chunnel, *chun'l*, *n.* proposed tunnel underneath the English Channel, connecting England and France. [**Ch**annel **tunnel**.]

church, *chûrch*, *n.* a house set apart for public worship: (usu. *cap.*) the whole body of Christians, or (with *adj.* Jewish) of those who hold the Jewish faith: (usu. *cap.*) the clergy, or the clerical profession (e.g. *to go into the Church*): (usu. *cap.*) any particular sect or denomination of Christians (e.g. *the Baptist Church*).—*v.t.* to bring to a church service on a special occasion.—*adj.* **church'less**, not belonging to a church.—*ns.* **church'man**, a clergyman or ecclesiastic: a member or upholder of the established church; **church'-rate**, an assessment for the upkeep of the parish church; **church-war'den**, a lay officer who looks after the interests of a parish or church:

a long clay-pipe; **church'yard**, the burial-ground round a church.—**Church Army**, an organisation of the Church of England, resembling the Salvation Army; **Church militant**, the Church on earth in its struggle against evil; **Church triumphant**, the Church in heaven, which has triumphed over evil. [O.E. *circe*—Gr. *kȳriakon*, belonging to the Lord—*Kȳrios*, the Lord.]

churl, *chûrl*, *n.* a rustic: an ill-bred, surly fellow.—*adj.* **churl'ish**.—*adv.* **churl'ishly**.—*n.* **churl'ishness**. [O.E. *ceorl*, a countryman; O.N. *karl*.]

churn, *chûrn*, *n.* a machine for the production of butter from cream or milk: a large milk can.—*v.t.* to agitate so as to obtain butter: to shake or beat violently, as milk in a churn: to turn over persistently (ideas in the mind).—*v.i.* to perform the act of churning.—**churn out**, to produce continuously with effort. [O.E. *cyrin*; O.N. *kirna*, a churn.]

chuse, *chōōz*, *v.t.* a form of **choose**.

chute, *shōōt*, *n.* a waterfall, rapid: a passage for sending down water, logs, rubbish, &c. [Fr. *chute*, a fall.]

chutney, **chutnee**, *chut'ni*, *n.* an East Indian condiment of mangoes, chillies, &c. [Hindustani *chatni*.]

chyle, *kīl*, *n.* a white fluid drawn from the food while in the intestines.—*adj.* **chyl'ous**. [Fr.,—Gr. *chȳlos*, juice—*cheein*, to pour.]

chyme, *kīm*, *n.* the pulp to which the food is reduced in the stomach. [Gr. *chȳmos*.]

chymical, **chymistry**, obsolete forms of **chemical**, **chemistry**.

cicada, *si-kā'da*, **cicala**, *si-kā'la*, *ns.* an insect remarkable for its chirping sound. [L. *cicāda*; It. *cicala*.]

cicatrix, *sik-ā'triks*, or *sik'a-triks*, **cicatrice**, *sik'a-tris*, *ns.* a scar over a wound that is healed.—*v.t.* **cic'atrise**, to help the formation of a cicatrix on.—*v.i.* to heal. [L. *cicatrix*, *-īcis*, a scar.]

cicerone, *chich-er-ō'nā*, *n.* one who shows strangers the curiosities of a place: a guide:—*pl.* **cicero'ni** (*-nē*). [It.,—L. *Cicero*, the Roman orator.]

Ciceronian, *sis-er-ō'ni-an*, *adj.* relating to or like *Cicero* (B.C. 106-43), Roman orator and essayist.

cider, *sī'der*, *n.* a drink made from apples. [Fr. *cidre*, through L.L.—Gr. *sikera*, strong drink—Heb. *shēkar*.]

ci-devant, *sē-de-vä*, *adj.* late, former (e.g. *the ci-devant ruler*). [Fr. formerly.]

cigar, *si-gär'*, *n.* a roll of tobacco-leaves for smoking.—*n.* **cigarette'**, finely cut tobacco rolled in thin paper. [Sp. *cigarro*.]

cilium, *sil'i-um*, *n.* a hair-like lash borne by a cell:—*pl.* **cil'ia**.—*adjs.* **cil'iary**; **cil'iated**, having cilia. [L. *cilium*, pl. *cilia*, eyelids, eyelashes.]

Cimmerian, *sim-ē'ri-an*, *adj.* relating to the *Cimmerii*, a tribe fabled to live in perpetual darkness: extremely dark.

cinch, *sinch*, *n.* saddle-girth: (*coll.*) a secure hold: (*coll.*) a certainty, something easy.—*v.t.* to tighten the cinch. [Sp. *cincha*—L. *cingula*.]

cinchona, *sing-kō'na*, *n.* a genus of trees, yielding the bark from which quinine is obtained: also called *Peruvian bark*. [Said to be

fāte, *fär*; *mē*, *hûr* (her); *mīne*; *mōte*, *för*; *mūte*, *mōōn*, *fŏŏt*; тнen (then)

121

so named from the Countess of *Chinchon*, who was cured of a fever by it in 1638.]

cincture, *singk'tyúr*, *n.* a girdle or belt: a moulding round a column.—*v.t.* to gird, encompass. [L. *cinctūra—cingĕre*, *cinctum*, to gird.]

cinder, *sin'dėr*, *n.* the refuse of burned coals: anything charred by fire.—*adj.* **cin'dery**. [O.E. *sinder*, slag.]

cine-, ciné-, *sin'ī-*, in composition, cinematograph, as *ns.* **cin'e-cam'era**, a camera for taking moving photographs; **cin'e-microg'raphy**, cinematographic recording of changes under the microscope.

cinema, *sin'é-má*, *n.* a cinematograph: a building in which motion pictures are shown: motion pictures collectively.—*adj.* **cinemat'ic**. [cinematograph.]

cinematograph, *sin-i-mat'ō-gräf*, *n.* an apparatus for projecting a series of instantaneous photographs or pictures so as to give a moving representation of a scene, with or without reproduction of sound: a camera for taking such photographs: an exhibition of such photographs: a building in which they are shown.—Also **kinemat'ograph** (*kin'-*, *kĭn-*).—*n.* **cinemato'grapher**.—*adjs.* **cinematograph'ic, -al**. [Fr. *cinématographe—*Gr. *kinēma, -atos*, motion, *graphein*, to write.]

cinerary, *sin'e-ra-ri*, *adj.* pertaining to ashes. [L. *cinereus*, ashy—*cinis, cineris*, ash.]

Cingalese. See **Sinhalese**.

cingulum, *sing'gū-lum*, *n.* a girdle: a structure like a belt. [L.]

cinnabar, *sin'a-bár*, *n.* sulphide of mercury, called vermilion when used as a pigment. [L.,—Gr. *kinnabari*, a dye, from Persian.]

cinnamon, *sin'a-món*, *n.* the spicy bark of a tree of the laurel family in Ceylon: the tree: a light yellowish-brown.—Also *adj.* [L. *cinnamomum—*Heb. *kinnamon*.]

cinque, *singk*, *n.* the number five as on dice. —*n.pl.* **cinque'-ports**, the five ancient ports on the south of England lying opposite to France—Sandwich, Dover, Hythe, Romney, and Hastings. [Fr.]

cipher, *sī'fér*, *n.* (*arith.*) the character 0: any of the Arabic numerals: anything of little value: a nonentity: an interweaving of the initials of a name: a secret mode of writing.—*v.i.* to work at arithmetic: to write in cipher. [O.Fr. *cifre* (Fr. *chiffre*)—Ar. *cifr*, empty.]

circa, *súr'ka*, *prep.* and *adv.* about. [L.]

circadian, *súr-ká-dē'án*, *adj.* pertaining to any biological cycle which is repeated, usu. approx. every 24 hours. [From L. *circa*, about, *di*(*em*), day, and suffix. -*an*.]

Circassian, *sér-kash'yán*, *adj.* belonging to *Circassia*, a region in the western Caucasus, or to certain tribes living there proverbial for their good looks.

Circean, *sér-sē'án*, *adj.* like, pertaining to, *Circe*, a sorceress who changed the companions of Ulysses into swine.

circle, *súr'kl*, *n.* a plane figure bounded by one line every point of which is equally distant from a certain point called the centre: the line which bounds the figure: a ring: a planet's orbit: a series ending where it began: a company or group (of people).—*v.t.* to move

round: to encompass.—*v.i.* to move in a circle.—*n.* **cir'clet**, a little circle: a circular head-band worn as an ornament.—**great circle**, a circle on the surface of a sphere whose centre is the centre of the sphere; **small circle**, one whose centre is not the centre of the sphere. [O.E. *circul—*L. *circulus*, dim. of *circus*.]

circuit, *súr'kit*, *n.* the way or path round: the path of an electric current: area, extent: a round made in the exercise of a calling, esp. the round made by judges for holding courts of law.—*adj.* **circū'itous**, round-about, not direct.—*adv.* **circū'itously**.—*n.* **circuitry**, detailed plan of a circuit, as in radio or television, or its components.—*n.* **cir'cuit-break'er**, a switch or other device for interrupting an electric circuit. [Fr.,—L. *circuitus—circuīre—circum*, round, *īre*, to go.]

circular, *súr'kū-lár*, *adj.* round: ending in itself: addressed to a circle of persons.—*n.* an intimation sent to a number of persons.—*n.* **circular'ity**.—*v.t.* **cir'cularise**, to send circulars to.—**circular function**, any of the trigonometrical (q.v.) functions with argument in radians; **circular saw**, a steel disk with teeth on its periphery, used for sawing wood, metal, &c., and generally power-driven. [O.Fr. *circulier—*L. *circulāris*.]

circulate, *súr'kū-lāt*, *v.t.* to make to go round as in a circle: to spread.—*v.i.* to move round: to be spread about.—*n.* **circulā'tion**, the act of moving in a circle or in a closed path (as the blood): the sale of a book or periodical: the money in use at any time in a country.—*adj.* **cir'culatory**, circulating.—**circulating library**, one where books are lent to subscribers in turn. [L. *circulāre, -ātum*.]

circumambient, *súr-kum-am'bi-ént*, *adj.* surrounding. [L. *circum*, about, *ambīre*, to go round.]

circumambulate, *súr-kum-am'bū-lāt*, *v.i.* to walk round about.—*n.* **circumambulā'tion**. [L. *circum*, about, *ambulāre, -ātum*, to walk.]

circumcise, *súr'kum-sīz*, *v.t.* to cut off the foreskin according to the Jewish law.—*n.* **circumci'sion**. [L. *circumcīdĕre, circumcīsum—circum*, about, *caedĕre*, to cut.]

circumference, *súr-kum'fér-éns*, *n.* the boundary line, esp. of a circle: the distance round.—*adj.* **circumferen'tial**. [L. *circum*, about, *ferre*, to carry.]

circumflex, *súr'kum-fleks*, *n.* an accent (∧) originally denoting a rising and falling of the voice on a vowel or syllable.—Also *adj.* [L. *circum*, about, *flectĕre*, *flexum*, to bend.]

circumfluence, *súr-kum'floō-éns*, *n.* a flowing round: (*zool.*) circumvallation (q.v.).—*adj.* **circum'fluent**. [L. *circum*, about, *fluĕre*, to flow.]

circumfuse, *súr-kum-fūz'*, *v.t.* to pour around—*n.* **circumfū'sion**. [L. *circum*, about, *fundĕre*, *fūsum*, to pour.]

circumjacent, *súr-kum-jā'sént*, *adj.* lying round: bordering on every side. [L. *circum*, about, *jacens*, lying—*jacēre*, to lie.]

circumlocution, *súr-kum-lō-kū'sh(ó)n*, *n.* roundabout and evasive speech: a roundabout phrase.—*adj.* **circumloc'utory**. [L. *circum*, about, *loquī*, *locūtus*, to speak.]

circumnavigate, *súr-kum-nav'i-gāt*, *v.t.* to sail

Neutral vowels in unaccented syllables: *em'pér-òr*; for certain sounds in foreign words see p. ix.

round.—*ns.* **circumnaviga′tion; circumnav′i-gator.** [L. *circum*, about, and **navigate.**]

circumscribe, *sûr-kum-skrīb′*, *v.t.* to draw a line round: to draw (one plane figure) so as to enclose another, the outer touching the inner at as many points as possible: (of a plane figure) to enclose (another) thus: to confine within limits, restrict.—*n.* **circumscrip′tion.** [L. *circum*, about, *scrībĕre*, to write.]

circumspect, *sûr′kum-spekt*, *adj.* looking round on all sides watchfully, cautious, prudent.—*n.* **circumspec′tion.**—*adv.* **cir′cumspectly.**—*n.* **cir′cumspectness.** [L. *circum*, about, *spicĕre*, *spectum*, to look.]

circumstance, *sûr′kum-stăns*, *n.* a fact or event, esp. in relation to others: a detail: ceremony: (*pl.*) time, place, and occasion, &c., of an act: the state of one's affairs.—*v.t.* to place in particular circumstances.—*adj.* **circumstantial** (-*stan′shăl*), consisting of details: minute.—*adv.* **circumstan′tially.**—*n.pl.* **circumstan′tials,** non-essentials.—*v.t.* **circumstan′tiate** (-*shi-*), to prove by circumstances: to describe exactly.—**circumstantial evidence,** evidence inferred from circumstances proved by direct evidence. [L. *circum*, about, *stans, stantis*, standing—*stāre.*]

circumvallate, *sûr-kum′val-āt*, *v.t.* to surround with a defensive rampart.—*n.* **circumvalla′tion,** a surrounding with a wall: an encircling rampart: (*zool.*) engulfing of food by surrounding it (as protozoa do). [L. *circum*, about, *vallum*, rampart.]

circumvent, *sûr-kum-vent′*, *v.t.* to go round: to surround so as to intercept or capture: to outwit (a person).—*n.* **circumven′tion.** [L. *circum*, about, *venīre, ventum*, to come.]

circumvolve, *sûr-kum-volv′*, *v.t.* to roll round.—*v.i.* to revolve:—*pr.p.* circumvolv′ing; *pa.p.* circumvolved′.—*n.* **circumvolu′tion.** [L. *circum*, about, *volvĕre, volūtum*, to roll.]

circus, *sûr′kus*, *n.* a circular building for the exhibition of games: a place for the exhibition of feats of horsemanship: a group of houses arranged in the form of a circle: a travelling show consisting of exhibitions of horsemanship, acrobatics, performances by animals, &c.: (usu. with *adj.*) a group of people giving a display, esp. in a number of places, as *tennis circus, flying circus*: a noisy entertainment or scene. [L. *circus*; cog. with Gr. *kirkos.*]

cirrhosis, *si-rō′sis*, *n.* a hardening of tissues of various organs, esp. a disease of the liver characterised by an increase of fibrous tissue and destruction of liver cells. [Gr. *kirros*, orange-tawny.]

cirrus, *sir′us*, *n.* the highest form of clouds consisting of curling fibres: (*bot.*) a tendril: (*zool.*) any curled filament:—*pl.* cirri (*sir′ī*).—*adjs.* **cirr′ate, cirr′ose, cirr′ous.** [L. a curl.]

cis-, sis-, a prefix signifying on this side, as in **cisalpine,** on this side—i.e. on the Roman side—of the Alps. [L. *cis*, on this side.]

cist, *sist*, *n.* a tomb consisting of a stone chest covered with stone slabs. [L. *cista*. See **chest.**]

Cistercian, *sis-tûr′shăn*, *n.* one of the order of monks established in 1098 in the forest of Cîteaux (*Cistercium*), in France—an offshoot of the Benedictines.

cistern, *sis′tern*, *n.* an artificial reservoir or tank

for storing water or other liquid: a natural reservoir. [L. *cisterna*, from *cista*, a chest.]

citadel, *sit′a-dél*, *n.* a fortress in or near a city. [It. *cittadella*, dim. of *città*, a city—L. *cīvitās.*]

cite, *sīt*, *v.t.* to call or summon: to summon to appear in court: to quote: to adduce.—*n.* **citā′-tion** (or *sī-*), an official summons to appear: the document containing it: the act of quoting: that which is quoted: official recognition of achievement. [L. *citāre, -ātum*, to call, inten. of *ciēre, cīre*, to make to go.]

cithara, *sith′a-ra*, *n.* an ancient Greek musical instrument differing from the lyre in its flat, shallow sound box—also **cith′er.**—*ns.* **cith′ern, citt′ern,** a metal-stringed musical instrument of the 16th and 17th centuries: the Tirolese zither. [L.,—Gr. *kitharā*; cf. **guitar, zither.**]

citizen, *sit′i-zén*, *n.* an inhabitant of a city: a member of a state: a townsman.—*n.* **cit′izenship,** rights and duties of a citizen. [M.E. *citesein*—O.Fr. *citeain*—*cité*. See **city.**]

citron, *sit′ron*, *n.* the fruit of the citron-tree, resembling a lemon.—*n.* **cit′rate,** a salt of citric acid.—*adj.* **cit′ric,** derived from the citron.—*ns.* **cit′rin,** the water-soluble vitamin P, found in citrus fruits, &c.; **cit′rus,** a citron-tree: a genus including the citron, lemon, lime, orange, &c.—**citric acid,** the acid to which lemons and certain other fruits owe their sourness. [Fr.,—L. *citrus*, a citron.]

cittern. Same as **cithern** (q.v. under **cithara.**)

city, *sit′i*, *n.* a large town: a town with a corporation or a cathedral: the business centre or original area of a large town.—**Eternal City,** Rome. [Fr. *cité*, a city—L. *civitās*, the state—*cīvis*, a citizen.]

civet, *siv′et*, *n.* a perfume obtained from the civet or **civ′et-cat,** a small carnivorous animal of Africa, India, &c. [Fr. *civette*—Ar. *zabād.*]

civic, *siv′ik*, *adj.* pertaining to a city or citizen.—*n.* **civics,** the science of citizenship. [L. *cīvicus*—*cīvis*, citizen.]

civil, *siv′il*, *adj.* pertaining to the community or to a citizen: having the refinement of city-bred people: polite: pertaining to ordinary, as opposed to military or ecclesiastical, life: (*law*) relating to actions or suits concerned not with crime but with private rights and the remedy of injuries other than criminal.—*ns.* **civil′ian,** one engaged in civil as distinguished from military and other pursuits; **civil′ity,** good-breeding: politeness.—*adv.* **civ′illy.**—**civil disobedience,** refusal to obey laws and regulations, pay taxes, &c.—a non-violent means of forcing concessions from government; **civil engineer** (see **engineer**); **civil list,** the expenses of the sovereign's household; **civil rights** (often *cap.*), rights of a citizen to personal freedom, political, racial, legal, social, &c.; **civil service,** the paid service of the state exclusive of navy, army, and air force; **civil war,** a war between citizens of the same state. [L. *cīvīlis*—*cīvis*, a citizen.]

civilise, *siv′il-īz*, *v.t.* to reclaim from barbarism: to instruct in arts and refinements.—*n.* **civilisā′tion,** state of being civilised: a making civilised: civilised peoples: culture.—*adj.* **civ′ilised,** beyond barbarism: refined: sophisticated. [**civil.**]

clachan, *klä′Han*, *n.* (*Scot.*) a small village.

[Gael. *clachan*—*clach*, stone.]

clack, *klak*, *v.i.* to make a noise as by striking wood with wood: to talk noisily.—*n.* a clacking sound: the clatter of voices. [Imit.]

clad, *klad*, *pa.t.* and *pa.p.* of **clothe**.—*adj.* clothed or covered.—*v.t.* to cover one material with another, e.g. one metal with another (as in nuclear reactor), or brick or stonework with a different material (in building).—*n.* **cladd'ing**.

claim, *klām*, *v.t.* to call for: to demand as a right: to maintain or assert.—*n.* a demand for something supposed due: right or ground for demanding: the thing claimed, esp. a piece of land appropriated by a miner or other.—*adj.* **claim'able**.—*n.* **claim'ant**, one who makes a claim. [O.Fr *claimer*—L. *clamāre*, to call out.]

clairschach, *klār'shä*ᶜʰ, *n.* the old Celtic harp strung with wire. [Gael. and Irish *clairseach*, the harp.]

clairvoyance, *klār-voi'áns*, *n.* the alleged power of seeing things not present to the senses.—*n.* and *adj.* **clairvoy'ant**. [Fr. *clair* (L. *clārus*), clear, *voir* (L. *vidēre*), to see.]

clam, *klam*, *n.* a bivalve shellfish.—**clam up** (*coll.*), to be silent. [O.E. *clam*, fetter.]

clam, *klam*, *v.t.* to clog: to smear: *pr.p.* **clamm'ing**; *pa.p.* **clammed**.—*adj.* **clamm'y**, moist and sticky: moist and cold.—*n.* **clamm'iness**. [O.E. *clæman*, to anoint.]

clamant, *klam'ánt*, *klām'ánt*, *adj.* calling loudly, insistently (*lit.* and *fig.*).—*n.* **clam'ancy**. [L. *clāmans*, *-antis*—*clāmāre*, to cry out.]

clamber, *klam'bér*, *v.i.* to climb with difficulty, grasping with the hands and feet.—*n.* a difficult climb. [From root of **climb**.]

clamour, *klam'ór*, *n.* a loud continuous outcry: uproar.—*v.i.* to cry out aloud in demand: to make a loud continuous outcry.—*adj.* **clam'orous**, noisy, boisterous.—*adv.* **clam'orously**.—*n.* **clam'orousness**. [L. *clāmor*.]

clamp, *klamp*, *n.* a piece of timber, iron, &c. used to fasten things together or to strengthen any framework.—*v.t.* to bind with a clamp.—**clamp down on**, to suppress, or suppress the activities of, firmly. [From a root seen in O.E. *clam*, fetter; Du. *klamp*, a clamp; akin to **clip** (2), **climb**.]

clan, *klan*, *n.* a tribe or collection of families subject to a single chieftain, commonly bearing the same surname, and supposed to have a common ancestor: a clique, sect, or group.—*adj.* **clann'ish**, closely united and holding aloof from others.—*adv.* **clann'ishly**.—*ns.* **clann'ishness**; **clan'ship**, association of families under a chieftain; **clans'man**, a member of a clan. [Gael. *clann*, offspring, tribe—L. *planta*, a shoot.]

clandestine, *klan-des'tin*, *adj.* concealed or hidden, private, sly.—*adv.* **clandes'tinely**. [L. *clandestīnus*—*clam*, secretly.]

clang, *klang*, *v.i.* to produce a loud, deep, ringing sound.—*v.t.* to cause to do so.—*n.* a ringing sound, like that made by metallic substances struck together.—*ns.* **clang'er**, a singularly ill-timed remark or comment: a stupid mistake; **clangour** (*klang'gór*), a clang: a loud, ringing noise.—*adj.* **clang'orous**.—*adv.* **clang'orously**. [L. *clangēre*, to sound.]

clank, *klangk*, *n.* a sound, less prolonged than a clang, such as is made by a chain.—*v.i.* or *v.t.*

to make or cause a clank. [Prob. formed under the influence of **clink** and **clang**.]

clap, *klap*, *n.* (*lit.* or *fig.*) a sudden blow or stroke: the noise made by the sudden striking together of two things, the hands: a burst of sound.—*v.t.* to strike together so as to make a noise: to thrust or drive together suddenly: (*Scot.*) to pat with the hand: to applaud with the hands: to put suddenly (e.g. *to clap one in prison*; *to clap eyes on*).—*v.i.* to strike together with noise: to applaud:—*pr.p.* **clapp'ing**; *pa.p.* **clapped**.—*ns.* **clapp'er**, one who claps: that which claps, as the tongue of a bell; **clap'trap**, flashy display: empty words.—**clap hold of**, to seize roughly; **like the clappers** (*slang*), at top speed. [O.N. *klappa*, to pat; Du. and Ger. *klappen*.]

clarendon, *klar'en-don*, *n.* (*print.*) a heavy seriphed type face as **cat, dog**.

claret, *klar'et*, *n.* originally applied to wines of a light-red colour, but now used in England for the dark-red wines of Bordeaux.—*n.* **clar'et-cup**, a drink made up of iced claret, brandy, sugar, &c. [Fr. *clairet*—*clair*—L. *clārus*, clear.]

clarify, *klar'i-fī*, *v.t.* to make clear or pure.—*v.i.* to become clear:—*pr.p.* **clar'ifying**; *pa.p.* **clar'ified**.—*ns.* **clarifica'tion**; **clar'ifier**. [L. *clārus*, clear, and *facĕre*, to make.]

clarinet, *klar-in-et'*, or *klar'-*, **clarionet**, *klar'i-on-et*, *ns.* a wind-instrument, usually of wood, in which the sound is produced by a single thin reed. [Fr.,—L. *clārus*, clear.]

clarion, *klar'i-ón*, *n.* a kind of trumpet whose note is clear and shrill: a thrilling note. [Fr. *clairon*—*clair*—L. *clārus*, clear.]

clarity, *klar'i-ti*, *n.* clearness. [M.E. *clarte*—L. *clāritās*.]

clarsach. Same as **clairschach**.

clash, *klash*, *n.* a loud noise, such as is caused by the striking together of weapons: opposition: contradiction.—*v.i.* to dash noisily (against, into): to meet in opposition: to disagree.—*v.t.* to strike noisily together. [Formed from the sound, like Ger. and Swed. *klatsch*.]

clasp, *kläsp*, *n.* a hinged fastening: a bar on the ribbon of a medal: an embrace.—*v.t.* to fasten with a clasp: to grasp in the hand: to hold in the arms, embrace.—*n.* **clasp'knife**, a knife whose blade folds into the handle.—**clasp one's hands**, to interlace the fingers. [M.E. *claspe*, *clapse*; ety. uncertain.]

class, *kläs*, *n.* a rank or order of persons or things: high rank or social standing: a number of students or scholars who are taught together: a group of things alike in some respect: in biological classification, a division above an *order*.—*v.t.* to form into a class or classes: to place in a class.—*adj.* **class'-con'scious**, acutely conscious of membership of a social class.—*ns.* **class'-fell'ow**, **class'-mate**, a pupil in the same class; **cläss'ic**, any standard writer or work: a student of the ancient classics: (*pl.*) Greek and Latin studies.—*adjs.* **class'ic**, **-al**, of the highest class or rank, esp. in literature—originally, and chiefly, used of the best Greek and Roman writers: (as opposed to *romantic*) like in style to the authors of Greece and Rome or to the old masters in music: traditionally accepted: standard, stock (as in *classic example*): (*slang*) excellent: of

Neutral vowels in unaccented syllables: *em'pér-ór*; for certain sounds in foreign words see p. ix.

clothes, made in simple tailored style that does not soon go out of fashion.—Also *n.—adv.* **class′ically.**—*ns.* **class′icism** (*-is-izm*), a classical idiom: principle, character, tendency such as is seen in Greek classical literature; **class′icist,** one versed in the classics: one supporting their use in education.—*adj.* **class′less,** having no class distinctions: not belonging obviously to any social class.—*n.* **class′war′,** antagonism between different social classes.—*adj.* **class′y** (*slang*), of or characteristic of high or upper class.—**class legislation,** legislation unduly favourable to one section of the community. [L. *classis,* a division of the Roman people.]

classify, *klas′i-fī, v.t.* to arrange in classes: to make secret for security reasons:—*pr.p.* **class′ifying;** *pa.p.* **class′ified.**—*n.* **classifica′tion.**—*adj.* **class′ified,** arranged in classes: on the secret list: of a road, in a class entitled to receive a government grant: of advertisements in a newspaper, grouped according to goods or services offered. [L. *classis,* a division of the Roman people, *facĕre,* to make.]

clatter, *klat′er, n.* a repeated rattling noise: a repetition of abrupt sharp sounds: noisy talk.—*v.i.* to make rattling sounds: to chatter noisily.—*v.t.* to cause to rattle. [O.E. *clatrung,* clattering (verbal noun).]

clause, *klöz, n.* a sentence: part of a sentence with subject and predicate: an article or part of a contract, will, &c. [Fr. *clause*—L. *clausus*—*claudĕre,* to shut.]

claustral. See **cloister.**

claustrophobia, *klö-strō-fō′bi-a, n.* a morbid dread of confined places. [L. *claustrum,* a barrier, Gr. *phobos,* fear.]

clave, *klāv, pa.t.* of **cleave** (2).

clavichord, *klav′i-körd, n.* an old keyboard stringed instrument. [L. *clāvis,* a key, *chorda,* a string.]

clavicle, *klav′i-kl, n.* the collar-bone, connecting the shoulder-blade and breast-bone.—*adj.* **clavic′ular.** [Fr. *clavicule*—L. *clāvicula,* dim. of *clāvis,* a key.]

clavier, *kla-vēr′, n.* a stringed keyboard instrument, esp. the pianoforte. [Fr.,—L. *clāvis,* a key.]

claw, *klö, n.* the hooked nail of a beast or bird: the leg of a crab, insect, &c. or its pointed end or pincer: anything like a claw.—*v.t.* to scratch or tear as with the claws or nails.—*n.* **claw′hammer,** a hammer fitted with a claw for drawing nails. [O.E. *clawu;* akin to **cleave,** to stick.]

clay, *klā, n.* a tenacious ductile earthy material, hydrated aluminium silicates more or less impure: earth in general: the human body.—*adj.* **clay′ey,** made of clay: covered with clay.—**feet of clay** (*fig.*), faults and weaknesses of character not at first suspected. [O.E. *clæg.*]

claymore, *klā-mōr′, -mör′, n.* a large sword formerly used by the Scottish Highlanders. [Gael. *claidheamh-mór*—Gael. and Ir. *claidheamh,* sword, *mór,* great.]

clean, *klēn, adj.* free from defilement (*lit.* and *fig.*): pure: guiltless: neat: complete: free of radioactive fall-out.—*adv.* quite: entirely: smoothly, neatly.—*v.t.* to make clean or free

from dirt.—*ns.* **clean′er,** one who, or that which, cleans; **cleanness** (*klēn′nes*).—*adj.* **cleanly** (*klen′li*), clean in habits or person: pure: neat.—*adv.* (*klēn′li*).—*n.* **cleanliness** (*klen′li-nes*), habitual cleanness or purity.—*adj.* **clean′-limbed,** well-proportioned, handsome.—**clean slate,** a fresh start; **clean up,** to make clean: to free from vice, corruption, &c.: to make (large profits); **have clean hands,** to be free from guilt; **make a clean breast of,** to own up frankly; **show a clean pair of heels,** to escape by running: to outstrip by a long distance. [O.E. *clǣne;* Ger. *klein,* small.]

cleanse, *klenz, v.t.* to make clean or pure.—*n.* **cleans′er,** one who, or that which, cleanses. [O.E. *clǣnsian.*]

clear, *klēr, adj.* pure, bright, undimmed: free from obstruction or difficulty: plain, distinct, obvious: without blemish, defect, drawback, or diminution.—*adv.* in a clear manner: plainly: wholly: apart from (e.g. *stand clear of the gates*).—*v.t.* to make clear: to empty: to free from obscurity or obstruction: to free from suspicion, acquit or vindicate: to declare free from security restrictions: to decode: to leap, or pass by or over: to make a profit of: to set free for sailing.—*v.i.* to become clear: to grow bright, transparent: to sail after satisfying demands and obtaining permission.—*adv.* **clear′ly,** in a clear manner: distinctly.—*ns.* **clear′ness; clear′ance,** act of clearing: a certificate that a ship has satisfied all demands of the custom-house and procured permission to sail: the distance between two objects, or between a moving and a stationary part of a machine.—*adj.* **clear′-cut,** sharp in outline: free from obscurity.—*ns.* **clear′ing,** the act of making clear: a tract of land cleared of wood, &c., for cultivation; **clear′ing-house,** an office in which banks, railway companies, &c. adjust their mutual claims; **clear-story** (see **clerestory**); **clear′way,** a stretch of road on which motor vehicles are not allowed to stop.—**clear out,** to get rid of: to empty: to go away; **clear up,** to make or become clear. [Fr. *clair*—L. *clārus,* clear.]

cleat, *klēt, n.* a wedge: a piece of wood nailed across a structure to keep it firm: a projection to which ropes are made fast. [From a supposed O.E. *clēat;* cf. Du. *kloot;* Dan. *klode;* Ger. *kloss.*]

cleave, *klēv, v.t.* to divide, to split: to make a way through.—*v.i.* to part asunder, or crack:—*pr.p.* **cleav′ing;** *pa.t.* **clōve** or **cleft;** *pa.p.* **clov′en** or **cleft.**—*ns.* **cleav′age,** a split: tendency to split; **cleav′er,** one who or that which cleaves: a butcher's chopper. [O.E. *clēofan.*]

cleave, *klēv, v.i.* to stick or adhere: to be united closely (to), remain faithful (to):—*pa.t.* **cleaved** or **clāve;** *pa.p.* **cleaved.** [O.E. *clifian;* cog. with Ger. *kleben.*]

cleek, *klēk, n.* a large hook: a narrow-faced iron-headed golf-club. [M.E. *kleken;* perh. related to **clutch.**]

clef, *klef, n.* a character placed on the stave by which the pitch of the notes is fixed. [Fr., from L. *clāvis;* Gr. *kleis,* a key.]

cleft, *kleft, pa.t.* and *pa.p.* of **cleave** (1).

cleft, *kleft, n.* an opening made by cleaving or

splitting: a crack, fissure, or chink.—Also **clift**
(*B.*). [Cf. Ger. *kluft*, Dan. *klyft*, a hole.]

cleg, *kleg*, *n.* gadfly, horsefly. [O.N. *kleggi*.]

clematis, *klem'a-tis*, *n.* a genus of creeping
plants including *Virgin's Bower* or *Traveller's
Joy*. [L.,—Gr. *klēmatis*, a plant, probably periwinkle—*klēma*, a twig.]

clement, *klem'ent*, *adj.* mild, gentle: kind, merciful.—*n.* **clem'ency.**—*adv.* **clem'ently.** [Fr.,—L.
clēmens.]

clench, *klench*, or *-sh*, *v.t.* to close tightly: to
grasp: to clinch. [See **clinch**.]

clepsydra, *klep'si-dra*, *n.* an instrument used by
the Greeks and Romans for measuring time
by the trickling of water. [L.,—Gr. *klep-
sydra*—*klepstein*, to steal, *hydōr*, water.]

clerestory, clear-story, *clēr-stō'ri*, *n.* the part of
a church wall that rises above the roof of the
aisle, and contains windows for lighting the
nave. [**clear** and **stor(e)y.**]

clergy, *klûr'ji*, *n.* the ministers of the Christian
religion, as holders of an allotted office, in
contradistinction to the laity.—*n.* **cler'gyman**,
one of the clergy, a regularly ordained minister.—*adjs.* **cler'ic, -al** (*kler'ik, -ál*), belonging
to the clergy: pertaining to a clerk.—*n.* **cler'ic**,
a clergyman.—**benefit of clergy** (see **benefit**).
[Fr. *clergé*—Late L. *clēricus*—Gr. *klērikos*,
from *klēros*, a lot, a heritage, then the clergy.]

clerihew, *kler'i-hū*, *n.* a jingle in two short
couplets purporting to give the quintessence
of the life and character of some notable person. [First used by E. *Clerihew* (Bentley) in
his *Biography for Beginners* (1905).]

clerk, *klärk* (U.S. *klûrk*), *n.* a clergyman or
priest: a scholar: one who leads the responses
in the English Church service: an official who
conducts the correspondence and records
the transactions of a court or corporation:
one who does written work in an office.—*adj.*
cler'ical, pertaining to a clerk or copyist, as in
'clerical error'.—*ns.* **clerk'ess**, a female clerk;
clerk'ship.—**clerk of works**, one who superintends the erection of a building, &c. [O.E.
clerc, a priest—Late L. *clēricus.*]

clever, *klev'ér*, *adj.* able or dexterous: ingenious:
skilful.—*n.* **clev'erness.**—*adv.* **clev'erly.** [Ety.
uncertain.]

clew, clue, *klōō*, *n.* a ball of thread, or the thread
in it: a thread that guides through a labyrinth:
anything that points to the solution of a
mystery (usu. *clue*): the corner of a sail. [O.E.
cliwen.]

cliché, *klē-shā*, *n.* the impression made by a die:
an electrotype or stereotype plate: a hackneyed phrase. [Fr.,—*clicher*, to stereotype.]

click, *klik*, *n.* a short, sharp ticking sound: anything that makes such a sound, as a small
piece of iron falling into a notched wheel: a
latch for a gate.—*v.i.* to make a light, sharp
sound. [Dim. of **clack**.]

client, *klī'ent*, *n.* one who employs a lawyer or
professional adviser: (*arch.*) a dependent: a
customer.—*ns.* **clientele** (*klī'en-tēl*), **clientèle**
(*klē-ä-tel'*), a group of clients; **cli'entship.** [L.
cliens, -entis, for *cluens*, one who listens (to
advice)—*cluēre*, to hear.]

cliff, *klif*, *n.* a high steep rock: the steep side of
a mountain.—*n.* **cliff'hanger**, a tense, exciting
adventure or contest: an ending line that

leaves one in suspense. [O.E. *clif*; Du. *clif*; O.N.
klif.]

clift. See **cleft** (2).

climacteric, *klī-mak-ter'ik*, or *klī-mak'tér-ik*, *n.*
a critical period in human life, in which some
great bodily change takes place.—*adj.* critical.—*adj.* **climacter'ical.**—**the grand climacteric**, the sixty-third year. [Gr. *klīmaktēr*—
klīmax, a ladder.]

climate, *klī'mát*, *n.* the average weather conditions of a region (temperature, moisture,
&c.)—*adjs.* **climat'ic, -al**,—*n.* **climatol'ogy**, the
science of the causes on which climate de-
pends.—**climate of opinion**, the critical atmosphere, complex of opinions present at a particular time or in a particular place. [O.Fr.
climat—Gr. *klima*, gen. *klimatos*, slope—*klinein*, to slope.]

climax, *klī'maks*, *n.* the arrangement of a series
of ideas, or of words or phrases, in ascending
order of emphasis: the last term of the arrangement: a culmination. [Gr. *klīmax*, a ladder—from *klinein*, to slope.]

climb, *klīm*, *v.i.* or *v.t.* to ascend or mount by
clutching with the hands and feet: to ascend
with effort: of plants, to ascend by clinging to
other objects:—*pa.t.* climbed (*arch.* clomb).
—*n.* an ascent.—*n.* **climb'er**, one who or that
which climbs.—**climb down**, to descend: to
take a lower place: to abandon a firmly stated
opinion or resolve. [O.E. *climban*; conn. with
clamber and **cleave**, to stick.]

clime, *klīm*, *n.* a country, region, tract. [A variant of **climate**.]

clinch, *klinch*, or *-sh*, *v.t.* to fasten a nail by
bending down the point: to settle or confirm
(an argument, a bargain).—*v.i.* to grapple.—*n.*
the act of clinching: in boxing, a holding grapple.—*n.* **clinch'er**, one that clinches: (*coll.*) a
decisive argument.—*adj.* **clinch'er-built** (same
as **clinker-built**). [Same as **clench**; causal
form of **clink**.]

cline, *klīn*, *n.* (*biol.*) a gradation of differences of
form, &c., seen e.g. within one species over a
specified area of the world. [Gr. *klīnein*, to
lean.]

cling, *kling*, *v.i.* to adhere or stick close: to adhere in interest or affection:—*pa.t.* and *pa.p.*
clung. [O.E. *clingan.*]

clinic, *klin'ik*, *n.* a private hospital or nursing-
home: an institution, or a department of one,
or a group of doctors, for treating or advising
out-patients: the teaching of medicine or surgery at the bedside of hospital patients (also
adj.).—*adj.* **clin'ical**, hospital-like: based on
observation: strictly objective.—*adv.* **clin'i-
cally.**—**clin'ical thermom'eter**, one for taking
the temperature of patients. [Gr. *klīnikos*—
klīnē, a bed.]

clink, *klingk*, *n.* a ringing sound made by
striking metal, glass, &c.—*v.t.* to cause to
make a ringing sound.—*v.i.* to ring or jingle.—*n.* **clink'er**, hard brick: the incombustible cinder or slag formed in furnaces.—*adj.*
clink'er-built, made of planks overlapping
those below (as distinguished from carvel-
built) and fastened with clinched nails. [A
form of **click** and **clank**.]

clink, *klingk*, *n.* (*coll.*) prison. [Name of a former
prison in Southwark, London.]

Neutral vowels in unaccented syllables: *em'pér-ór*; for certain sounds in foreign words see p. ix.

126

clinometer, *klin-, klīn-om'i-tér, n.* any of various instruments for measuring slope, elevation or inclination. [Gr. *klīnein,* to lean.]

clip, *klip, v.t.* to cut with shears: to trim: to pare down: to shorten (in indistinct utterance):—*pr.p.* clipp'ing; *pa.p.* clipped.—*n.* the thing clipped off, as wool shorn off sheep: a smart blow.—*ns.* **clip'-joint,** a place of entertainment, e.g. a night club, where customers are overcharged or cheated; **clipp'ie,** (*slang*) a woman bus or tram conductor; **clipp'er,** one that clips: a fast-sailing vessel with very sharp lines and great spread of canvas; **clipp'ing,** the act of cutting, esp. debasing coin by cutting off the edges: the thing clipped off.—**clip the wings,** (*fig.*) to restrict (a person's) power to realise (his) ambition. [Prob. from O.N. *klippa,* to cut.]

clip, *klip, v.t.* to hold firmly: to fasten with a clip.—*n.* an appliance for gripping and holding (e.g. loose papers) together. [O.E. *clyppan,* to embrace; O.N. *klȳpa,* to pinch.]

clique, *klēk, n.* an exclusive group of persons in union for a purpose, a faction, a gang—usu. in a bad sense.—*adj.* **cliqu'ish.** [Fr.]

cloaca, *klō-ā'kä, n.* a sewer: a privy: (*zool.*) the lower alimentary canal:—*pl.* **cloacae** (*klō-ā'sē*). [L.]

cloak, cloke, *klōk, n.* a loose outer garment: a covering: that which conceals, a disguise, pretext.—*v.t.* to put a cloak on: to cover: to conceal.—*adj.* **cloak'-and-dagg'er,** concerned with plot and intrigue.—*n.* **cloak'-room,** a room for keeping coats, hats, and personal luggage: a lavatory. [O.Fr. *cloke, cloque*—Low L. *cloca,* a bell, a horseman's bell-shaped cape.]

clobber, *klob'ér,* a paste used by shoemakers to hide the cracks in leather.

clobber, *klob'ér,* (*slang*) clothing, gear.

clobber, *klob'ér, v.t.* (*slang*) to strike very hard: to defeat overwhelmingly. [Origin unknown.]

clock, *klok, n.* a machine for measuring time—strictly, one marking the hours by strokes of a gong or bell.—*v.t.* to time by a clock or stop-watch: to achieve (a certain officially attested time for a race).—*adv.* **clock'wise,** in the direction of the hands of a clock.—*n.* **clock'work,** machinery as steady and regular as that of a clock.—*adj.* automatic.—**clock in, out, on, off,** to register the time of entering or leaving a workshop, &c. [M.E. *clokke,* prob. through O.Fr. from Low L.; Ger. *glocke.*]

clock, *klok, n.* an ornament worked on the side of a stocking. [Ety. uncertain.]

clod, *klod, n.* a thick round mass or lump that sticks together, esp. of earth or turf: the ground: a stupid fellow.—*n.* **clod'hopper,** a countryman, a peasant: a dolt.—*adj.* **clod-hopp'ing,** boorish. [A later form of **clot.**]

clog, *klog, n.* a block of wood: an impediment: a shoe with a wooden sole.—*v.t.* to accumulate in a mass and cause stoppage in: to obstruct: to encumber.—*v.i.* **clog'-dance,** a dance performed in clogs. [Ety. uncertain.]

cloister, *klois'tér, n.* a covered arcade forming part of a monastery or college: a place of religious retirement, a monastery or nunnery: an enclosed place.—*v.t.* to confine in a cloister: to confine within walls.—*adjs.* **clois'teral, clois'tral, claus'tral** (*klös'träl*), pertaining to,

or confined to, a cloister: secluded; **clois'tered,** dwelling in cloisters: solitary. [O.Fr. *cloistre* (O.E. *clauster*)—L. *claustrum—claudēre, clausum,* to shut.]

cloke, *klōk, n.* Same as **cloak.**

clomb, *klōm,* old *pa.t.* of **climb.**

close, *klōs, adj.* shut up: with no opening: hot and airless, stifling: narrow, confined: stingy: near, in time or place: intimate: compact, dense (e.g. of texture): hidden: reserved, secretive: (of argument, examination, &c.) careful, precise, with no weak spots: (of a vowel) pronounced with slight opening or with the tongue tense.—*adv.* in a close manner: nearly: densely.—*n.* an enclosed place: a narrow entry: the precinct of a cathedral.—*adv.* **close'ly.**—*ns.* **close'ness; close'-corporā'tion,** one that fills up vacancies in its membership by co-option.—*adjs.* **close'-fist'ed,** penurious; **close'-grained,** with the fibres, &c., close together, compact; **close'-hauled,** with sails trimmed for sailing as near as possible to the wind.—*ns.* **close'-sea'son,** the time of year when it is illegal to kill certain game or fish: a prohibited period; **close-up,** a photograph or film taken near at hand and thus detailed and big in scale: a close scrutiny.—**close call, close shave,** a narrow escape; **close harmony,** harmony in which the parts are grouped closely together, esp. in which the three upper voice parts are, within the compass of an octave. [Fr. *clos,* shut—L. *claudēre, clausum,* to shut.]

close, *klōz, v.t.* to make close: to draw together and unite: to shut: to end: to complete, conclude (e.g. a bargain).—*v.i.* to come together: to grapple (with): to agree (with): to come to an end.—*n.* the manner or time of closing: a pause or stop: the end.—*n.* **clos'ure,** the act of closing: the end: the stopping of a parliamentary debate by vote of the House.—**close down,** to cease operations; **closed circuit,** an electrical circuit in which there is a complete path, with no break, for the current to flow along: (*TV*) a system in which the showing is for restricted, not general, viewing; **closed community,** one having few contacts outside itself; **closed shop,** a phrase variously understood, as:—an establishment in which only members of (*a*) a trade union, or (*b*) a particular trade union, will be employed: the principle or policy implied in such a regulation. [M.E. *closen*—L. *claudēre, clausum.*]

closet, *kloz'ét, n.* a small private room: a recess off a room: a privy: the private chamber of a sovereign.—*v.t.* to shut up in or take into a closet: to conceal:—*pr.p.* clos'eting; *pa.p.* clos'eted. [O.Fr. *closet,* dim. of *clos.* See **close** *adj.*]

clot, *klot, n.* a mass of soft or fluid matter concreted, as blood.—*v.t.* and *v.i.* to form into clots, to coagulate:—*pr.p.* clott'ing; *pa.p.* clott'ed.—**clotted cream,** Devonshire dainty prepared by scalding milk. [O.E. *clott,* clod.]

cloth, *kloth, n.* woven material from which garments, coverings, &c., are made: a piece of such material: a table-cloth:—*pl.* **cloths** (*kloths, klōтнz*).—*v.t.* **clothe** (*klōтн*), to cover with a garment: to provide with clothes: (*fig.*) to invest as with a garment:—

pr.p. clōth′ing(TH); *pa.t., pap.* clōthed(TH), clad.—*n.pl.* **clothes** (*klō′THz*, coll. *klōz*), garments or articles of dress: coverings.—*ns.* **clothes′-horse,** frame for hanging clothes on to dry; **clothes′-pin, -peg,** forked piece of wood to secure clothes on a line; **clothier** (*klō′THi-ér*), one who makes or sells clothes; **clothing** (*klō′THing*), clothes, garments: covering.—**the cloth,** the clerical profession: the clergy. [O.E. *clāth,* cloth; Ger. *kleid,* a garment.]

cloud, *klowd, n.* a mass of fog, consisting of minute particles of water, often in a frozen state, floating in the atmosphere: (*fig.*) anything unsubstantial: a great number or multitude: a great volume (of dust or smoke): anything that obscures as a cloud: anything gloomy or ominous.—*v.t.* to overspread with clouds: to darken: to stain with dark spots or streaks.—*v.i.* to become clouded or darkened.—*p.adj.* **cloud′ed,** hidden by clouds: (*fig.*) darkened: indistinct.—*adj.* **cloud′y,** darkened with, or consisting of, clouds: obscure: gloomy: stained with dark spots.—*adv.* **cloud′ily.**—*n.* **cloud′iness.**—*adj.* **cloud′less.**—*ns.* **cloud′-berry,** a moorland plant, related to the bramble, with an orange-red berry of delightful flavour; **cloud′-burst,** a sudden flood of rain over a small area.—*adj.* **cloud′-capt** (*Shak.*), capped with or touching the clouds.—**cloud chamber,** an apparatus in which the path of charged particles is made visible by means of water-drops condensed on gas ions.—**under a cloud,** in trouble, disgrace, or disfavour. [O.E. *clūd,* a hill, then a cloud, the root idea being a mass or ball; **clod** and **clot** are from the same root.]

clough, *kluf,* or *klow, n.* a ravine: a valley. [Assumed O.E. *clōh*; Scot. *cleuch.*]

clout, *klowt, n.* a piece of cloth, esp. one used for mending, a patch: a rag: a blow, a cuff.—*v.t.* to mend with a patch: to cuff. [O.E. *clūt*; cf. O.N. *klūtr,* a kerchief.]

clove, *klōv,* pa.t. of **cleave.**—*n.* **clove′-hitch,** a kind of temporary knot that holds firmly round an object.

clove, *klōv, n.* the flower-bud of the *clove-tree,* dried as a spice, and yielding an essential oil: (*pl.*) a cordial · therefrom.—*ns.* **clove′-gill′y-flower, clove′-pink,** a variety of pink smelling of cloves. [Fr. *clou,* a nail—L. *clāvus.*]

cloven, *klōv′én, p.adj.* split: divided.—*adjs.* **clov′en-foot′ed, clov′en-hoofed,** having the hoof divided, as the ox or sheep.—**the cloven hoof,** a symbol of devilish agency or of evil character. [Pa.p. of **cleave,** to divide.]

clover, *klōv′ér, n.* a genus of three-leaved plants, growing among grass and affording rich pasturage.—*n.* **clov′erleaf,** a traffic arrangement in which one road passes over the top of another and the roads connecting the two are in the pattern of a four-leaved clover.—**live in clover,** to live luxuriously. [O.E. *clāfre*; Du. *klaver*; Dan. *klöver*; Ger. *klee.*]

clown, *klown, n.* a rustic or country fellow: one with the awkward manners of a countryman: a fool or buffoon.—*adj.* **clown′ish,** coarse and awkward: rustic.—*adv.* **clown′ishly.**—*n.* **clown′ishness.** [Prob. conn. with **clod.**]

cloy, *kloi, v.t.* to sate (esp. with sweetness): to weary with excess.—*pr.p.* cloy′ing; *pa.p.*

cloyed.—Also *v.i.* [For *accloy*—O.Fr. *encloyer,* to drive a nail into, to spike or stop, as a gun—L. *in,* in, *clāvus,* a nail.]

club, *klub, n.* a heavy tapering stick, knobby or massy at one end, used to strike with, a cudgel: an implement for striking a ball in golf and other games: an association of persons for social, political, athletic, or other ends: the premises occupied by a club: (*pl.*) one of the four suits of cards.—*v.t.* to beat with a club: to contribute to a common stock.—*v.i.* to combine (for a common end).—*adj.* **club(b)′able,** sociable.—*n.* **club′-foot,** a deformed foot.—*adj.* **club′-foot′ed.**—*ns.* **club′-house, club′-room,** a house or room occupied by a club; **club′-law,** government by violence; **club′-moss,** a moss with scaly leaves and club-like stems. [O.N. and Swed. *klubba*; same root as **clump.**]

cluck, *kluk, n.* the call of a hen to her chickens: any similar sound.—*v.i.* to make such a sound. [From the sound, like Du. *klokken,* Ger. *glucken,* Dan. *klukke.*]

clue, *klōō.* See **clew.**

clump, *klump, n.* a thick, short, shapeless piece of anything: a cluster (e.g. of trees or shrubs; see also **agglutination**): a blow.—*v.i.* to walk heavily.—*v.t.* to beat. [Prob. Scand.; Dan. *klump,* a lump.]

clumsy, *klum′zi, adj.* shapeless: ill-made: unwieldy: awkward in movement: without adroitness or tact.—*adj.* **clum′sily.**—*n.* **clum′siness.** [M.E. *clumsen,* to be stiff.]

clung, *klung,* pa.t. and *pa.p.* of **cling.**

cluster, *klus′tér, n.* a number of things of the same kind growing or joined together: a bunch: a group or crowd.—*v.i.* to grow, or gather, into clusters.—*v.t.* to collect into clusters. [O.E. *clyster*; prob. conn. with **clot.**]

clutch, *kluch, v.t.* to seize or grasp: to hold tightly in the hand.—*n.* a claw: (*fig.*) hand (often in *pl.*—e.g. *to fall into his clutches*): a grasp: a device by which two shafts or rotating members of a machine may be connected or disconnected. [O.E. *clyccan,* to clench.]

clutch, *kluch, n.* a brood of chickens, a 'sitting' of eggs.—Also **cletch.** [From *cleck* (now chiefly Scot.), to hatch—O.N.]

clutter, *klut′ér, n.* confusion: stir: noise: irregular interference on radar screen from echoes, rain, buildings, &c.—*v.i.* to crowd together: to go about in disorder.—*v.t.* to litter. [A variant of **clatter.**]

Clydesdale, *klīdz′dāl, n.* a cart horse of the breed originating in *Clydesdale.*

Co., *kō,* an abbreviation for **Company.**

co-, *kō-,* a prefix signifying jointness, accompaniment, connection. [L. *cum,* with.]

coach, *kōch, n.* a large, close, four-wheeled carriage: a railway carriage: a motor omnibus for tourists: a private tutor: a trainer in athletics.—*v.t.* to carry in a coach: to prepare (another), as for an examination or a contest.—*ns.* **coach′-box,** the driver's seat on a coach; **coach′man, coach′y,** the driver of a coach. [Fr. *coche*—Hungarian *kocsi,* from *Kocs,* a village in Hungary.]

coadjutor, *kō-ad-jōōt′ór,* or *-ad′-, n.* a helper or assistant, a co-worker.—*fem.* **coadju′trix** (or *-ad′-*). [L. *co-,* with, *adjūtor,* a helper—*ad.* to, *juvāre,* to help.]

Neutral vowels in unaccented syllables: *em′pér-ór*; for certain sounds in foreign words see p. ix.

coagulate, *kō-ag'ū-lāt*, *v.t.* to make to curdle or congeal.—*v.i.* to curdle or congeal.—*adj.* **coag'ulable.**—*ns.* **coag'ulant**, a substance that causes curdling, as rennet; **coagula'tion.**—*adj.* **coag'ulative.**—*n.* **coag'ulum**, what is coagulated. [L. *coāgulāre, -ātum—co-*, together, *agĕre*, to drive.]

coal, *kōl*, *n.* a solid, black, combustible mineral, derived from vegetable matter, used for fuel.—*v.i.* to take in coal.—*v.t.* to supply with coal.—*adj.* **coal'y**, of or like coal: blackened with coal.—*ns.* **coal'-bed**, a stratum of coal; **coal'-bunk'er**, a box or recess for holding coal; **coal'-face**, the exposed surface of coal in a mine; **coal'field**, a district containing coal strata; **coal'ite**, a smokeless fuel obtained by low-temperature carbonisation; **coal'-gas**, the mixture of gases produced by the distillation of coal, used for lighting and heating; **coal'-heav'er**, one employed in carrying coal; **coal'-mas'ter**, the owner or lessee of a coal-mine.—*n.pl.* **coal'-meas'ures**, the group of carboniferous strata in which coal is found.—*ns.* **coal'-mine, coal'-pit**, a mine or pit from which coal is dug; **coal'-own'er**, one who owns a coal-mine; **coal'-tar**, or *gas-tar*, a thick, black, opaque liquid formed when coal is distilled; **coal'-tit** (also **cole-**), a dark species of tit; **coal'-trimm'er**, one employed in storing or shifting coal on board vessels.—**coaling station**, a port at which steamships take in coal.—**haul** (or **call**) **over the coals**, to reprimand. [O.E. *col*; cog. with O.N. *kol*, Ger. *kohle*.]

coalesce, *kō-al-es'*, *v.i.* to grow together or unite into one body: to combine in an association.—*n.* **coales'cence**, growing into each other: fusion.—*adj.* **coales'cent.**—*ns.* **coali'tion**, a combination or alliance short of union, esp. of states or political parties; **coali'tionist.** [L. *coalescĕre—co-*, together, *alescĕre*, to grow up.]

coarse, *kōrs, körs, adj.* common, base, or inferior: rough: rude: gross.—*adv.* **coarse'ly.**—*n.* **coarse'ness.**—*v.t.* **coars'en**, to make coarse.—*adj.* **coarse'-grained**, large in grain, as wood; (*fig.*) lacking in fine feelings.—**coarse fish**, freshwater fish other than those of the salmon family; **coarse fishing**. [From phrase 'in course', hence *ordinary*.]

coast, *kōst, n.* (*obs.*) side: border of land next the sea: the seashore: (*obs.*) limit or border of a country.—*v.i.* to sail along or near a coast: to travel downhill in a vehicle without mechanical propulsion: to succeed without effort.—*v.t.* to sail by or near to.—*adj.* **coast'al**, pertaining to the coast.—*ns.* **coast'er**, a vessel that sails along the coast: a small mat to protect the surface of a table, &c. from the imprint of glasses; **coast'-guard**, a man, or body of men who watch the coast for prevention of smuggling, &c.—*adj.* **coast'ing**, trading between ports in the same country.—*adv.* **coast'wise**, along the coast.—*adj.* carried on along the coast. [O.Fr. *coste* (Fr. *côte*)—L. *costa*, a rib, side.]

coat, *kōt, n.* a kind of outer garment with sleeves: the hair or wool of a beast: vesture or habit: any covering: a membrane or layer, as of paint, &c.—*v.t.* to cover with a coat or layer.—*ns.* **coatee'**, a short close-fitting coat;

coat-frock, a dress for use without coat or jacket: a tailored dress with fastening from neckline to hem (also **coat'-dress**); **coat'ing**, a covering: cloth for coats.—**coat of arms**, the heraldic bearings or family insignia embroidered on the surcoat worn over the coat of mail: the coat itself: such bearings wherever displayed; **coat of mail**, a piece of armour for the upper part of the body, made of metal scales or rings linked one with another. [O.Fr. *cote* (Fr. *cotte*)—Low L. *cottus, cotta*, a tunic.]

coati, *kō-ä'ti*, or *kō'ä-ti, n.* an American plantigrade carnivorous mammal allied to the raccoons. [South American Indian.]

coax, *kōks*, *v.t.* to persuade by fondling or flattery: to humour or soothe.—*adv.* **coax'ingly.** [M.E. *cokes*, a simpleton.]

coaxial, *kō-ak'si-äl, adj.* having the same axis.

cob, *kob, n.* a lump: a corn-cob (q.v.): a short-legged strong horse: a male swan—also **cob'-swan.**—*n.* **cob'nut**, a large hazel-nut.

cobalt, *kō'bölt, n.* metallic element (symbol Co; at no. 27): blue pigment prepared from it—**cō'balt-blue.**—*adj.* of this deep-blue colour.—**cobalt-60**, a radioactive isotope of cobalt used in the gamma-ray treatment of cancer. [Ger. *kobalt*, from *kobold*, a demon, so called by the German miners, who supposed it to be mischievous and hurtful.]

cobble, cobble-stone, *kob'l-stōn, ns.* a rounded stone used in paving.—*v.s.t.* to pave with such. [Ety. uncertain.]

cobble, *kob'l*, *v.t.* to patch up or mend coarsely as shoes.—*n.* **cobb'ler**, one who cobbles or mends shoes. [Ety. unknown.]

co-belligerent, *kō-be-lij'e-rént, adj.* co-operating in warfare.—Also *n.* [**co-**, and **belligerent**.]

coble, cobble, *kōb'l, kob'l, n.* a small flat-bottomed fishing-boat. [Cf. W. *ceubal*, a hollow trunk, a boat.]

cobra, cobra de capello, *kō'bra, kob'ra, di ka-pel'ō, n.* a poisonous snake, found in India and Africa, which dilates its neck so as to resemble a hood. [Port., 'snake of the hood'.]

cobweb, *kob'web, n.* the spider's web or net: any snare or trap: anything flimsy. [Prob. O.E. *attercop-web—ātor*, poison, *coppa*, a head, tuft. See also **web**.]

coca, *kō'ka, n.* a shrub of Peru and Bolivia, whose leaves yield cocaine.—*n.* **cocaine** (*kō'kä-in, ko-kān*), an alkaloid obtained from coca-leaves, used as a local anaesthetic and as an intoxicant. [Sp.—Peruvian.]

coccus, *kok'us, n.* a spherical bacterium:—*pl.* **cocci** (*kok'sī*). [L.,—Gr. *kokkos*, a grain.]

coccyx, *kok'siks, n.* the small triangular bone at the end of the spinal column. [Gr. *kokkyx*, cuckoo, as resembling its bill.]

cochineal, *koch'i-nēl, n.* a scarlet dye-stuff consisting of the dried bodies of an insect gathered from a cactus in Mexico, the West Indies, &c.: the insect itself. [Sp. *cochinilla*.]

cochlea, *kok'le-a, n.* anything spiral-shaped, esp. a snail-shell: (*anat.*) the spiral cavity of the ear. [L.,—Gr. *kochlias*, a snail.]

cock, *kok, n.* the male of birds (esp. domestic fowl), and of fish: a weathercock: a strutting chief or leader: anything set erect: a tap for liquor: the hammer in the lock of a gun: its position, as **at half cock**, drawn back half-way and held by a catch.—*v.t.* to set erect or upright: to set up, as the brim of the hat: to draw back the cock of a gun: to tilt up.—*v.i.* to strut, to swagger.—*adjs.* **cockahoop′**, exultant; **cock-and-bull′**, incoherent and incredible.—*ns.* **cock′chafer**, a large greyish-brown beetle; **cock′-crow**, **-ing**, early morning; **cock′er**, a small spaniel; **cock′erel**, a young cock: a young man; **cock′-eye**, a squinting eye.—*adj.* **cock′-eyed**.—*ns.* **cock′-fight**, **-fighting**, a fight or contest between gamecocks: **cock′-horse**, a child's imaginary or toy horse; **cock′loft**, the room in a house next the roof; **cock′pit**, a pit or enclosed space where gamecocks fought: a frequent battle-ground: part of a ship-of-war used for the wounded in action: a compartment in the fuselage of an aircraft for pilot or passenger: the driver's seat in a racing car; **cocks′-comb**, the comb or crest on a cock's head: a cox-comb: the name of various plants: **cock′-shot**, **-shy**, a throw at a thing, as for amusement.—*adj.* **cock′sure**, very sure: over-confident.—*ns.* **cock′swain** (see **coxswain**); **cock′tail**, a mixture of spirituous or other liquors, used as an appetiser.—*adj.* **cock′y**, impudent.—*ns.* **cock′y-leek′y**, soup made of a fowl boiled with leeks; **cocked hat**, an old-fashioned three-cornered hat; **cock of the walk**, chief of a set; **cock's-foot grass**, a coarse strong grass, whose flowers branch from the stem like the talons of a cock.—**knock into a cocked hat**, to overwhelm and utterly discomfit. [O.E. *coc*; O.N. *kokkr*.]

cock, *kok*, *n.* a small pile of hay. [Swed. *koka*, a lump of earth; Ger. *kugel*, a ball.]

cockade, *kok-ād′*, *n.* a rosette worn on the hat as a badge. [Fr. *cocarde*—*coq*, cock.]

cockaigne, cockayne, *kok-ān′*, *n.* an imaginary country of luxury and delight. [Ety. uncertain; Fr. *cocagne*, acc. to some from L. *coquĕre*, to cook.]

cockatoo, *kok-a-tōō′*, *n.* the name given to a number of parrots with large crests, of the Australian region. [Malay, *kakatúa*.]

cockatrice, *kok′a-trīs*, *-tris*, *n.* a fabulous monster, often confounded with the *basilisk* (q.v.): (*her.*) a cock-like monster with a dragon's tail. [O.Fr. *cocatris*.]

cock-boat, *kok′bōt*, *n.* a small frail boat. [M.E. *cogge*, ship, and **boat**.]

cocker, *kok′er*, *v.t.* to pamper, fondle, indulge. [Ety. uncertain: cf. Du. *kokelen*, O.Fr. *coqueliner*, to dandle.]

cockle, *kok′l*, *n.* a cornfield weed. [O.E. *coccel*.]

cockle, *kok′l*, *n.* a large genus of bivalve mollusc with a heart-shaped shell.—*n.* **cock′leshell**, the shell of a cockle: a frail boat.—**warm the cockles of the heart**, to cheer up or gladden. [Fr. *coquille*—Gr. *konchylion*—*konchē*, a cockle.]

cockney, *kok′ni*, *n.* (often *cap.*) one born in London, strictly, within hearing of Bow Bells—*ns.* **cock′neydom**, the domain of Cockneys; **cock′neyism**, dialect or manners of a Cockney.

cockroach, *kok′rōch*, *n.* the so-called black beetle, any of a family of insects often included in the same order as the grasshopper. [Sp. *cucaracha*.]

coco, *kō′kō*, *n.* a tropical palm-tree producing the coconut.—*ns.* **co′conut**, a large edible nut

yielding **co′conut-butt′er** or **co′conut-oil′**, and **co′conut-milk**; **co′conut-matt′ing**, matting made from the husk of the coconut. [Port. and Sp. *coco*.]

cocoa, *kō′kō*, *n.* the seed of the cacao or chocolate tree: a powder made from the seeds: a drink made from the powder. [A corr. of **cacao**.]

cocoon, *ko-kōōn′*, *n.* the silken sheath spun by many insect larvae in passing into the pupa stage, and by spiders for their eggs. [Fr. *cocon*, from *coque*, a shell—L. *concha*, a shell.]

cod, *kod*, **codfish**, *kod′fish*, *ns.* a food fish of northern seas.—*n.* **cod′ling**, a small cod.—**cod′liver oil**, a medicinal oil extracted from the fresh liver of the common cod.

cod, *kod*, *n.* a husk or shell containing seeds. [O.E. *codd*, a small bag.]

coda, *kō′da*, *n.* (*mus.*) a passage forming the conclusion of a piece and rounding it off in a satisfactory manner. [It.,—L. *cauda*, a tail.]

coddle, *kod′l*, *v.t.* to pamper, treat as an invalid.

code, *kōd*, *n.* a collection or digest of laws, rules, or regulations: a standard of behaviour: a system of words, letters, or symbols, to ensure economy or secrecy in transmission of messages.—*v.t.* to codify.—*v.t.* **cod′ify** (*kod′-, kōd′-*), to put into the form of a code: to digest, to systematise:—*pr.p.* cod′ifying; *pa.p.* cod′ified.—*n.* **codifica′tion**. [Fr. *code*—L. *cōdex*, book.]

codex, *kō′deks*, *n.* a manuscript volume of classical or other ancient texts:—*pl.* **codices** (*kōd′i-sēz*). [L. *cōdex* or *caudex*, a book.]

codicil, *kod′i-sil*, *n.* a short addition to a will or treaty. [L. *cōdicillus*, dim. of *cōdex*, book.]

codling, *kod′ling*, **codlin**, *kod′lin*, *n.* an elongated variety of apple. [Ety. uncertain.]

codon, *kō′don*, *n.* a triplet of bases in the DNA of the chromosomes which determines the genetic code. [**code**.]

co-education, *kō-ed-ū-kā′sh(ò)n*, *n.* education of pupils or students of each sex in the same school or college. [**co-**, and **education**.]

coefficient, *kō-ef-ish′ent*, *n.* that which acts together with another thing: (*math.*) the numerical or literal factor prefixed to an unknown quantity in any algebraic term: (*phys.*) a numerical *constant* used as a multiplier of a *variable* quantity in calculating the magnitude of a particular physical property (e.g. expansion when heated) of a particular substance. [**co-**, and **efficient**.]

coenobite, cenobite, *sēn′o-bīt*, *n.* a monk who lives along with others, as opposed to a hermit.—*adjs.* **coenobit′ic**, **-al**; **cenobit′ic**, **-al**. [Gr. *koinobion*—*koinos*, common, *bios*, life.]

coenzyme, *kō-en′zīm*, *n.* the non-protein part of an enzyme system, which is unaffected by heat.

coerce, *kō-ûrs′*, *v.t.* to restrain by force: to compel (a person) to (with *into*): to enforce.—*adj.* **coer′cible**.—*n.* **coer′cion** (*-sh(ò)n*), restraint: government by force.—*adj.* **coer′cive**, having power to coerce: compelling.—*adv.* **coer′cively**. [L. *coercēre*—*co-*, together, *arcēre*, to shut in.]

coeval, *kō-ē′val*, *adj.* of the same age.—*n.* one of the same age, a contemporary. [L. *coaevus*—*co-*, together, and *aevum*, age.]

co-exist, *kō-egz-ist′*, *v.i.* to exist at the same

Neutral vowels in unaccented syllables: *em′pér-òr*; for certain sounds in foreign words see p. ix.

time.—*n.* **co-exist′ence.**—*adj.* **co-exist′ent.**— **peaceful co-existence,** the living peacefully side by side of countries whose political ways and beliefs are different. [L. *co-*, together, and **exist.**]

co-extensive, *kō-eks-ten′siv, adj.* equally extensive. [L. *co-*, together, and **extensive.**]

coffee, *kof′i, n.* a drink made from the seeds or beans of various species of **coffee-tree**: the powder made by roasting and grinding the seeds.—*ns.* **coff′ee-house, coff′ee-room, coff′ee-stall,** a house, room, movable street stall, where coffee and other refreshments are served.—**white, black, coffee,** coffee respectively with and without milk. [Turk. *qahveh*—Ar. *qahwah,* orig. meaning wine.]

coffer, *kof′ėr, n.* a chest for holding money or treasure.—*n.* **coff′er-dam,** a water-tight structure used for building the foundations of bridges, &c., under water. [O.Fr. *cofre,* a chest—L. *cophinus,* a basket—Gr. *kophinos.*]

coffin, *kof′in, n.* a coffer or chest for a dead body: a thick-walled container, usu. of lead, for transporting radioactive materials.—*v.t.* to place within a coffin. [O.Fr. *cofin*—L. *cophinus*—Gr. *kophinos,* a basket.]

cog, *kog, v.t.* in the phrase **cog dice,** to manipulate them so that they may fall in a given way. [Thieves′ slang.]

cog, *kog, n.* a catch or tooth on a wheel.—*v.t.* to fix teeth in the rim of a wheel:—*pr.p.* **cogg′ing;** *pa.p.* **cogged.**—*n.* **cog′-wheel,** a toothed wheel. [M.E. *cogge;* ety. uncertain.]

cogent, *kō′jėnt, adj.* powerful, convincing.—*n.* **cō′gency,** convincing power.—*adv.* **cō′gently.** [L. *cogēre*—*co-,* together, *agēre,* to drive.]

cogitate, *koj′i-tāt, v.i.* to turn a thing over in one′s mind, meditate, ponder.—*n.* **cogita′tion,** meditation.—*adj.* **cog′itative,** meditative, reflective. [L. *cōgitāre, -ātum,* to think deeply—*co-,* together, and *agitāre.* See **agitate.**]

cognac, *kon′yak, n.* a French brandy, so called because much of it is made near the town of *Cognac.*

cognate, *kog′nāt, adj.* related, esp. on the mother′s side: allied to (with *with*): of the same kind, nature, or origin: (of words) developed from the same original word but having undergone a different series of sound changes in separate languages (e.g. Eng. *father,* L. *pater,* &c.—see deriv. of **father**).—*n.* one related by blood, a kinsman (often, any kinsman other than an *agnate*).—**cognate object,** a word akin in origin or meaning to a normally intransitive verb and used as its object (e.g. *to live a life*). [L. *cognātus*—*co-,* together, *(g)nasci, (g)nātus,* to be born.]

cognition, *kog-nish′(ŏ)n, n.* knowledge: the mental processes (sensation, perception, &c.) by which knowledge is apprehended.—*adj.* **cog′nisable,** that may be known or understood: that may be judicially investigated.—*n.* **cog′nisance, cog′nizance,** knowledge or. notice, judicial or private: observation: jurisdiction: a badge.—*adj.* **cog′nisant,** having cognisance or knowledge (of).—*adj.* **cog′nitive,** capable of, or pertaining to, cognition. [L., from *cognoscēre, cognitum*—*co-,* together, and *(g)noscēre,* to know.]

cognomen, *kog-nō′men, n.* a surname: a nickname: a name: the last of the three names usually borne by a Roman, as Marcus Tullius *Cicero.* [L.,—*co-,* together, *(g)nomen,* a name—*(g)noscēre,* to know.]

cohabit, *kō-hab′it, v.i.* to dwell together as, or as if, husband or wife.—*n.* **cohabita′tion.** [L. *cohabitāre*—*co-,* together, *habitāre,* to dwell.]

cohere, *kō-hēr′, v.i.* to stick together: to be consistent.—*ns.* **cohēr′ence,** a sticking together: *(fig.)* a consistent connection between several parts; **cohēr′ency,** the quality of being coherent.—*adj.* **cohēr′ent,** sticking together: *(fig.)* connected: *(fig.)* consistent.—*adv.* **cohēr′ently.**—*n.* **cohē′sion,** the act of sticking together: a form of attraction by which particles of bodies stick together: logical connection.—*adj.* **cohē′sive,** tending to unite into a mass.—*adv.* **cohē′sively.**—*n.* **cohē′siveness.** [L. *cohaerēre, cohaesum*—*co-,* together, *haerēre,* to stick.]

cohort, *kō′hört, n.* a tenth part of a Roman legion: any band of warriors: *(bot.)* (esp. formerly) a division of plants between a class and an order: in the classification of higher animals, one of the divisions between subclass and order: a group of individuals: a companion or follower. [Fr.,—L. *cohors, -tis,* an enclosed place, a multitude enclosed, a company of soldiers.]

coif, *koif, n.* a covering for the head: a close-fitting cap of lawn or silk formerly worn by lawyers: a woman′s head-dress.—*ns.* **coiff′eur** *(kwäf-œr′),* a hairdressing: a head-dress. [Fr. *coiffe*—L.L. *cofia,* a cap.]

coign, *koin, n.* another spelling of **quoin** (q.v.). —**coign of vantage,** a commanding position.

coil, *koil, v.t.* to wind (flexible material) in concentric rings.—*v.i.* to wind in rings.—*n.* a length (of flexible material) coiled in rings: one of these rings: an arrangement of one or more turns of bare or insulated wire in an electrical circuit. [O.Fr. *coillir*—L. *colligēre*—*col-,* together, *legēre,* to gather.]

coil, *koil, n.* tumult: fuss.—**mortal coil,** the turmoil and vexation of human life.

coin, *koin, n.* a piece of metal legally stamped and current as money.—*v.t.* to convert a piece of metal into money: to stamp: to invent (a word, phrase).—*ns.* **coin′age,** the act of coining money: the currency: the pieces of metal coined: invention, fabrication: what is invented; **coin′er,** one who coins money: a maker of counterfeit coins: an inventor. [Fr. *coin,* a wedge, also the die to stamp money—L. *cuneus,* a wedge.]

coincide, *kō-in-sīd′, v.i.* to occupy the same space or time: to be identical: to agree, correspond (often with *with*).—*ns.* **coin′cidence,** act or condition of coinciding: the occurrence of one event at the same time as, or following, another without any causal connection; **coin′cidency.**—*adj.* **coin′cident.**—*adv.* **coin′cidently.** [L. *co-,* together, *incidēre*—*in,* in, *cadēre,* to fall.]

Cointreau, *kwē-trō, n.* an orange-flavoured liqueur. [Trademark.]

coir, *koir, n.* the strong fibre of the coconut. [Dravidian (q.v.) *kāyar,* cord—*kāyaru,* to be twisted.]

coke, *kōk, n.* a fuel obtained by distilling coal, driving off its more volatile constituents:

residue when any substance (e.g. petrol) is carbonised.

col, *kol, n.* (*geog.*) a depression or pass in a mountain range. [Fr.,—L. *collum,* a neck.]

cola, kola, *kō'la, n.* a genus of West African trees producing nuts used in drugs and for flavouring soft drinks: a soft drink so flavoured. [African name.]

colander, cullender, *kul'end-ér,* or *kol'-, n.* a vessel having small holes in the bottom, used as a strainer. [L. *cōlāre,* to strain—*cōlum,* a strainer.]

cold, *kōld, adj.* the opposite of hot: chilly, without passion or zeal: indifferent: unfriendly: reserved: without application of heat.—*n.* lack of heat: the feeling or sensation caused by the absence of heat: cold weather: a disease caused by cold: catarrh: chillness.—*adv.* **cold'ly.**—*n.* **cold'ness.**—*adj.* **cold'-blood'ed,** having cold blood (e.g. as a fish): unfeeling, cruel: frigid, unemotional.—*n.* **cold'-cream,** a cream-like ointment, used to cool the skin.— **cold feet,** lack of courage; **cold front** (see **front**); **cold storage,** storage and preservation of goods in refrigerating chambers: (*fig.*) abeyance; **cold turkey,** the plain truth: sudden withdrawal of narcotics: narcotics hangover; **cold war** (see **war**).—(**give the**) **cold shoulder,** to show studied indifference to, give a rebuff; **in cold blood,** with deliberate intent; **throw cold water on,** to discourage. [O.E. *cald, ceald*; Ger. *kalt*; cog. also with Eng. **cool.**]

cole, *kōl, n.* a general name for all sorts of cabbage.—*ns.* **cole'-slaw,** cabbage salad; **cole'-wort,** cole—esp. heartless kinds. [O.E. *cāwel*; Ger. *kohl,* Scot. *kail*; L. *colis, caulis,* a stem, esp. of cabbage.]

Coleoptera, *kol-e-op'tér-a, n.pl.* an order of insects having two pairs of wings, the outer pair being hard or horny, serving as wing-cases for the true wings—the beetles. [Gr. *koleos,* a sheath, and *pteron,* a wing.]

colic, *kol'ik, n.* severe pain in the abdomen. [Fr., through L.—Gr. *kolikos—kolon,* the large intestine.]

coliseum. See **colosseum.**

colitis. See **colon** (2).

collaborate, *kol-ab'ór-āt, v.i.* to work in association: to work with, help, an enemy of one's country, &c.—*ns.* **collabora'tion; collab'orator.** [L. *collaborāre, -atum—col-,* with, *laborāre,* to work.]

collage, *kol-äzh, n.* a picture made up from scraps of paper and other odds and ends pasted out: any work made from assembled fragments. [Fr., pasting.]

collapse, *kol-aps', n.* a falling away or breaking down: any sudden or complete breakdown or prostration.—*v.i.* to fall or break down: to go to ruin.—*adj.* **collaps'ible, -able,** capable of collapsing or being reduced to a more compact form. [L. *collapsus—col-,* together, and *lābī, lapsus,* to slide or fall.]

collar, *kol'àr, n.* something worn round the neck: the part of a garment at the neck: a band.—*v.t.* to seize by the collar: to put a collar on: (*slang*) to seize.—*ns.* **coll'ar-beam,** a beam connecting or bracing two opposite rafters; **coll'ar-bone,** the clavicle. [O.Fr. *colier*—L. *collāre—collum,* neck.]

collate, *kol-āt', v.t.* to examine and compare, as books, and esp. old manuscripts: to place in, appoint to, a benefice: to place in order, as the sheets of a book for binding.—*ns.* **colla'tion,** act of collating: a bringing together for examination and comparison: presentation to a benefice: a repast between meals; **colla'tor,** one who collates or compares: one who bestows or presents. [L. *collātum,* used as supine of *conferre—col-,* together, and *lātum* (*ferre,* to bring).]

collateral, *kol-at'àr-àl, adj.* side by side: running parallel or together: descended from the same ancestor, but not in direct line: related (to a subject, &c.) but not forming an essential part.—*n.* a collateral kinsman: a collateral security.—*adv.* **collat'erally.**—**collateral security,** an additional and separate security for the performance of an obligation. [L. *col-,* together, and *latus, lateris,* a side.]

colleague, *kol'ēg, n.* one associated with another in a profession or occupation. [Fr. *collègue*—L. *collēga—col-,* together, and *legēre,* to choose.]

collect, *kol-ekt', v.t.* to assemble or bring together: to call for and remove: to gather (payments or contributions): to infer: to put (one's thoughts) in order.—*v.i.* to run together, to accumulate.—*n.* **coll'ect,** a short prayer, consisting of one sentence, conveying one main petition.—*adj.* **collect'ed,** composed, cool.—*adv.* **collect'edly.**—*ns.* **collect'edness,** self-possession, coolness; **collec'tion,** act of collecting: gathering of contribution, esp. money: the money collected: an assemblage: a book of selections: range of new fashion clothes by a couturier: regular uplifting of mail by a postal official.—*adj.* **collect'ive,** pertaining to a group of individuals, common (e.g. interests, action, responsibility): derived from a number of flowers, as the fruit of the mulberry: (*gram.*) expressing a number of individuals as a single group (with sing. verb).— *adv.* **collect'ively.**—*ns.* **collect'ivism,** the economic theory that industry should be carried on with a collective capital (i.e. under common or government ownership); **collect'ivist.**—Also *adj.*—*n.* **collect'or,** one who collects, as tickets, money specimens, &c.—**collective agreement,** one reached by collective bargaining; **collective bargaining,** negotiation on conditions of service between an organised body of workers on one side and an employer or association of employers on the other; **collective farm,** state-controlled farm consisting of a number of small-holdings operated on a co-operative basis. [L. *colligĕre, -lectum —col-,* together, *legĕre,* to gather.]

colleen, *kol'ēn, n.* a girl. [Irish *cailín.*]

college, *kol'ij, n.* a society of persons joined together, generally for literary or scientific purpose and often possessing peculiar or exclusive privileges: a body or society that is a member of a university or is coextensive with a university: a seminary of learning: the premises of a college.—*adj.* **colle'gial,** pertaining to a college.—*n.* **colle'gian,** a member or inhabitant of a college.—*adj.* **colle'giate,** pertaining to or resembling a college.—**college of cardinals,** sacred (q.v.); **college of education,** one for training teachers. [Fr. *col-*

Neutral vowels in unaccented syllables: *em'pér-òr*; for certain sounds in foreign words see p. ix.

lège—L. *collegium*, from *col-*, together, and *legĕre*, to gather.]

collet, *kol'ét, n.* a ring or collar: the part of a ring that contains the stone. [Fr.,—L. *collum*; cf. **collar.**]

collide, *kol-īd', v.i.* to dash together: to clash.—*p.adjs.* **collid'ed, collid'ing.**—*n.* **colli'sion**, state of being struck together: a violent impact, a crash: conflict, opposition. [L. *collīdĕre*, *collīsum—co-*, together, *laedĕre*, to strike.]

collie, colly, *kol'i, n.* a breed of sheepdog originating in Scotland. [Ety. uncertain.]

collier, *kol'yér, n.* one who works in a coal-mine: a ship that carries coal: a sailor in such a ship.—*n.* **coll'iery**, a coal-mine. [**coal.**]

collinear, *ko-lin'e-ár, adj.* in the same straight line. [L. *col-*, together, *līnea*, a line.]

collocate, *kol'ō-kāt, v.t.* to place together: to arrange.—*n.* **colloca'tion.** [L. *collocāre, -ātum*—*col-*, together, *locāre*, to place.]

collodion, *kol-ō'di-on, n.* a gluey solution of cellulose nitrates in alcohol and ether, used in surgery and photography. [Gr. *kollōdēs*—*kolla*, glue, *eidos*, form, appearance.]

collogue, *ko-lōg', v.i.* to converse confidentially. [Prob.—L. *colloquī*, to speak together.]

colloid, *kol'oid, n.* a substance in a state in which it can be suspended in a liquid, but (unlike a substance in true solution) is not able to pass through a parchment membrane.—*adj.* **colloid'al.** [Gr. *kolla*, glue, *eidos*, form.]

collop, *kol'op, n.* a slice of meat. [Ety. dub.]

colloquy, *kol'ō-kwi, n.* a speaking together, mutual discourse, conversation.—*adj.* **collō'-quial**, pertaining to, or used in, common conversation.—*n.* **collō'quialism**, a form of expression used in familiar talk.—*adv.* **collō'-quially.** [L. *colloquium—col-*, together, *loquī*, to speak.]

collotype, *kol'ō-tīp, n.* a form of gelatine process in book illustration and advertising. [Gr. *kolla*, glue, and **type.**]

collude, *kol-(y)ōōd', v.i.* to act in concert, esp. in a fraud.—*n.* **collu'sion**, act of colluding: a secret agreement to deceive.—*adj.* **collu'sive**, fraudulently concerted: acting in collusion.—*adv.* **collu'sively.** [L. *collūdĕre, collūsum*, from *col-*, together, *ludĕre*, to play.]

coion, *kō'lon, n.* a punctuation mark (:) used especially to indicate a distinct member or clause of a sentence. [Gr. *kōlon*, a limb.]

colon, *kō'lon, n.* the greater portion of the large intestine.—*ns.* **coli'tis**, inflammation of the colon; **colic** (see separate article); **colos'tomy**, making of an artificial anus by surgical means; **colot'omy**, cutting of or incision into the colon. [L.—Gr. *kolon*, the large intestine.]

colonel, *kûr'nél, n.* an officer who has command of a regiment.—*n.* **col'onelcy**, his office or rank, or one of equivalent rank. [Fr. and Sp. *coronel*; a corr. of It. *colonello*, the leader of a *colonna*, or column—L. *columna*.] .

colonnade, *kol-én-ād', n.* a range of columns placed at regular intervals: a similar row, as of trees. [Fr.,—L. *columna*.]

colony, *kol'ón-i, n.* a body of persons who form a fixed settlement in another country: the settlement so formed: (*zool.*) a collection of individuals living together (strictly, connected organically with one another).—*adj.* **colon'ial.**—*n.* an inhabitant of a colony, esp. of the British Empire.—*ns.* **colon'ialism**, a trait of colonial life or speech: the theory that colonies should be exploited for the benefit of the mother country: the practice of treating them this way; **colon'ialist.** —*v.t.* **col'onise**, to plant or establish a colony in: to form into a colony.—*ns.* **colonisa'tion; col'onist**, an inhabitant of a colony. [L. *colōnia—colĕre*, to till.]

colophon, *kol'ō-fon, n.* an inscription at the end of a book or literary composition with name, date, &c.: a publisher's imprint or device. [L. *colophōn*—Gr. *kolophōn*, end.]

colophony, *kol-of'o-ni*, or *kol'-*, *n.* rosin—the residue of distillation of crude turpentine. [Gr., from *Colophon*, in Asia Minor.]

Colorado beetle, *kol-ór-ä'dō bē'tl*, an American beetle with black stripes, a potato pest.

coloratura, *kol-or-ä-tōō'rä, n.* (*mus.*) florid ornaments, or florid passages, in vocal music.— Also *adj.*—**coloratura soprano**, a high and flexible soprano voice, capable of singing coloratura passages: a singer with such a voice. [It., lit. colouring.]

colossus, *kol-os'us, n.* a gigantic statue, esp. that of Apollo which stood at (but not astride of) the entrance to the harbour of Rhodes.—*adj.* **coloss'al**, like a colossus: gigantic.—*n.* **colossē'um, colisē'um**, a large place of entertainment, from Vespasian's amphitheatre at Rome, which was the largest in the world. [L.,—Gr. *kolossos*.]

colour, *kul'ór, n.* a sensation induced in the eye by light of certain wavelengths—the particular colour being determined by the wavelength: a property whereby bodies present different appearances to the eye through their differing ability to absorb or reflect light of different wavelengths: hue: appearance of blood in the face: paint: race or race-mixture other than European: false show: pretext: kind: (*pl.*) a flag, ensign, or standard.—*v.t.* to put colour on, to stain, to paint: to set in a fair light: to exaggerate: to misrepresent: to give a certain quality to (e.g. *fear of loss coloured his attitude to the problem*).—*v.i.* to show colour: to blush.—*adjs.* **colorif'ic** (*kol-*), producing colours; **col'ourable** (*kul-*), apparently genuine, plausible: designed to conceal.—*adv.* **col'-ourably.**—*ns.* **colo(u)rā'tion; col'our-bar'**, social discrimination between white and other races.—*adj.* **col'our-blind**, unable to distinguish certain colours.—*n.* **col'our-blind'-ness.**—*adjs.* **col'oured**, having colour: belonging to a dark-complexioned race; **col'ourful**, full of colour: vivid.—*ns.* **col'ouring**, any substance used to give colour: manner of applying colours: specious appearance; **col'ourist**, one who colours or paints: one who excels in colouring.—*adj.* **col'ourless**, without colour: without distinctive quality, not vivid: impartial, neutral.—*n.* **col'our-ser'geant**, the sergeant who guards the colours of a regiment.—**change colour**, to turn pale: to blush; **come off with flying colours**, to win triumphantly; **come out in one's true colours**, to appear in one's real character; **give colour to**, to give plausibility to; **high colour**, pronounced redness of complexion; **off-colour**, faded: not at one's best: slightly indecent; **paint in bright colours**, to embellish: to exaggerate; **primary colours** (see **primary**). [O.Fr. *color*—L. *color*; akin to *celāre*, to cover.]

colporteur, *kol-pŏr-tûr'*, *-pör*, or *kol'pŏrt-ér*, *n.* a peddler, esp. one selling tracts and religious books.—*n.* **col'portage** (or *kol-pŏr-täzh'*), the distribution of books by colporteurs. [Fr. *colporteur*, from *col* (L. *collum*), the neck, and *porter* (L. *portāre*), to carry.]

colt, *kōlt, n.* a young horse: an inexperienced youth: (*B.*) a young camel or ass.—*adj.* **colt'ish**, like a colt: frisky: wanton.—*n.* **colts'foot**, a composite (q.v.) plant with large soft leaves. [O.E. *colt*; Swed. *kult*, a young boar, a stout boy.]

colter. Same as **coulter**.

columbine, *kol'um-bīn, adj.* of or like a dove: dove-coloured.—*n.* a genus of flowers of the buttercup family having five spurred petals suggestive of a group of pigeons (*cap.*) in pantomime, the sweetheart of Harlequin (q.v.).—*ns.* **columbā'rium**, a dovecot: a niche for a sepulchral urn; **col'umbary**, a dovecot. [L. *columba*, a dove.]

columbium, *kō-lum'bi-ùm, n.* a metallic element (symbol Cb; at. no. 41), now officially *niobium* (q.v.). [*Columbia*, U.S.A.]

column, *kol'um, n.* a long, round body, used to support or adorn a building: any upright body or mass suggestive of a column: a body of troops with narrow front: a perpendicular row of figures &c.: a perpendicular section of a page of print, &c.—*adj.* **colum'nar**, like a column: formed in columns. [L. *columen*, *columna*, akin to *celsus*, high; Gr. *kolōnē*, a hill.]

colza, *kol'za, n.* cole-seed, yielding oil. [Du. *koolzaad*, cabbage-seed.]

coma, *kō'ma, n.* deep sleep: stupor.—*adj.* **com'atose**, in a stupor: drowsy. [Gr. *kōma*.]

comb, *kōm, n.* a toothed instrument for separating and cleaning hair, wool, flax, &c.: the fleshy crest of some birds: the top or crest of a wave, of a roof, or of a hill: an aggregation of cells for honey.—*v.t.* to separate, arrange, or clean by means of a comb: (*fig.*) to search thoroughly (with *for*).—*n.* **comb'er**, one who, or that which, combs wool, &c.: a long foaming wave.—*n.pl.* **comb'ings**, hairs combed off.—**comb'-out'**, the process of searching for and removing men for military service, &c. [O.E. *camb.*]

combat, *kum'bat,* or *kom'bat, v.i.* to contend or struggle.—*v.t.* to contend against, oppose.—*n.* a struggle: a fight.—*adj.* **com'batant**, fighting.—*n.* one who is fighting.—*adj.* **com'bative**, contentious.—*n.* **com'bativeness.**—**combat fatigue**, mental disturbance in a fighting soldier, formerly called shell-shock. [Fr. *combattre*, to fight—L. *com-*, together, *bātuëre*, to strike.]

combe. See **coomb.**

combine, *kom-bīn', v.t.* to join together in one whole: to unite closely: (*fig.*) to possess together (diverse qualities): to follow (various pursuits), hold (various offices).—*v.i.* to come into close union: to co-operate towards (an end or result—with *to*): (*chem.*) to unite and form a compound.—*n.* (*kom'bīn*), an association of trading companies: a combine har-

vester.—*n.* **combinā'tion**, the act of combining: union: persons united for a purpose: a motor-bicycle with sidecar: (*math.*) a possible set of a given number of things selected from a given number, irrespective of arrangement within the set: the series of letters or numbers that must be dialled to move the mechanism of a combination lock and so open it.—*n.pl.* **combinā'tions**, an undergarment comprising vest and drawers.—*adj.* **com'binative.**—**combination lock**, a lock used on safes, &c. with numbered dials which must be turned in a special order a certain number of times to open it; **combine harvester**, a combined harvesting and threshing machine. [L. *combināre*, to join—*com-*, together, and *bīnī*, two and two.]

combustible, *kom-bust'ibl, adj.* liable to take fire and burn: (*fig.*) excitable.—*n.* anything that will take fire and burn.—*ns.* **combust'ibleness**, **combustibil'ity**; **combustion** (*kom-bust'yón*, or *-bus'ch(ò)n*), burning: oxidation or analogous process with evolution of heat. [L. *combūrëre*, *combustum*, to consume—*com-*, inten., *ūrëre*, to burn.]

come, *kum, v.i.* to move towards this place (*lit.* and *fig.*—opp. of *go*): to draw near: to extend (*to*): to issue: to arrive at (a certain state or condition—with *to*): to amount (*to*): to become (e.g. *to come loose*): to chance, to happen: to occur, be found:—*pr.p.* com'ing; *pa.t.* came; *pa.p.* come.—*interj.* (or *imper.*) as in **come**, **come** or **come now**, implying remonstrance or encouragement.—(With sense of *prep.*) by, on, or before, as in 'come Monday' = 'let Monday come', i.e. 'when (or before) Monday comes'.—*n.* **com'er**, one who comes (usu. qualified, as *new-comer*, *late-comer*, *all comers*).—**come about**, to happen; **come across**, to meet; **come back**, to return to popularity, office, &c. (*n.* a return); **come by**, to obtain; **come down**, to descend: to be reduced (*n.* a descent: loss of prestige); **come home to**, to touch (one) closely (i.e. one's interests, feelings); **come in**, to enter a room, &c.: to reply to a radio signal or call: (*fig.*) to find a place: to become fashionable: to take a (specified) place in a race or contest: to assume power or office; **come in for**, to obtain: to receive (e.g. abuse); **come into**, to fall heir to; **come of**, to be the result of; **come of age**, to reach full legal age; **come out**, to become known: to show itself, to develop: to be published: to enter society: to go on strike; **come out with**, to utter; **come round**, to recover from a faint, ill-humour, &c.; **come short of**, to fail to reach; **come to**, to recover consciousness or sanity; **come to pass**, to happen; **come true**, to be fulfilled; **come up with**, to overtake.—**to come** (predicative *adj.*), future. [O.E. *cuman*; Ger. *kommen.*]

comedy, *kom'e-di, n.* a dramatic piece of a pleasant or humorous character.—*n.* **comē'dian**, one who writes comedies: an actor of comic parts:—*fem.* (Fr.) **comédienne** (*kom-ā-dē-en'*). [Through Fr. and L.,—Gr. *kōm-ōīdia*—*kōmos*, revel, *ōidē*, song.]

comely, *kum'li, adj.* pleasing, graceful, handsome.—*n.* **come'liness**. [O.E. *cȳmlic*—*cȳme*, suitable, *lic*, like.]

Neutral vowels in unaccented syllables: *em'pér-òr*; for certain sounds in foreign words see p. ix.

comestible, *kom-est'ibl, adj.* eatable.—Also *n.*
[Fr.,—L. *comedĕre,* to eat up.]

comet, *kom'ét, n.* a heavenly body with a very
eccentric orbit, having a definite nucleus and
commonly a luminous tail.—*adj.* **com'etary.**
[Gr. *komētēs,* long-haired—*komē,* the hair.]

comfit, *kum'fit, n.* a sweetmeat. [Fr. *confit.*]

comfort, *kum'fort, v.t.* to relieve from pain or
distress: to cheer, revive.—*n.* relief: encouragement: ease: quiet enjoyment: freedom
from annoyance: any source of ease, enjoyment, &c.—*adj.* **com'fortable,** imparting, or
enjoying, comfort.—*adv.* **com'fortably.**—*n.*
com'forter, one who comforts: (*cap.*) the Holy
Spirit: a scarf or other device for increasing
bodily comfort: a nipple-like object, usu. of
rubber, for a baby to suck.—*adj.* **com'fortless,**
without comfort. [O.Fr. *conforter*—L. *con-,*
inten., *fortis,* strong.]

comic, *kom'ik, adj.* pertaining to comedy: raising mirth: droll.—*n.* (*coll.*) an amusing person:
an actor of droll parts, a comedian: (*coll.*)
a comic paper.—*adj.* **com'ical,** funny.—*ns.*
comical'ity, com'icalness.—*adv.* **com'ically.**—
comic opera, a light opera, with a comic or
farcical plot and much spoken dialogue; **comic
paper,** one containing comic stories told
mainly in pictures like those of a comic strip;
comic relief, comic scene in a tragedy affording, or supposed to afford, relief to the har-
rowed feelings; **comic strip,** a strip of small
pictures showing consecutive stages in an
adventure, normally one of a series of adventures befalling a stock character or stock
characters. [L. *cōmicus*—Gr. *kōmikos.*]

Cominform, *kom'in-förm, n.* the *Com*munist *Inform*ation Bureau (1947-56) which succeeded
the Comintern.

Comintern, *kom'in-tûrn, n.* the *Com*munist *Intern*ational (1919-43) or Third International.
[See **international.**]

comity, *kom'i-ti, n.* courteousness, civility. [L.
cōmitās—*cōmis,* courteous.]

comma, *kom'a, n.* in punctuation, the point (,)
which marks the smallest division of a sentence.—**inverted commas,** marks of quotation
("—", '—'). [L.,—Gr. *komma,* a section of a
sentence, from *koptein,* to cut off.]

command, *kom-änd', v.t.* to order: to bid: to
exercise supreme authority over: to have
within sight, influence, or control.—*v.i.* to have
chief authority, to govern.—*n.* an order:
authority: control: the thing commanded: in a
remote-control guidance system, a signal activating a mechanism or setting in motion a
sequence of operations by instruments.—*n.*
commandant', an officer who has the command of a place or of a body of troops.—*v.t.*
commandeer' (*Afrikaans*), to compel to military service, or seize for military use.—*ns.*
command'er, one who commands: an officer
in the navy next in rank under a captain;
command'er-in-chief, the officer in supreme
command of an army, or of the entire forces of
the state; **command'ership.**—*adj.* **command'-
ing,** fitted to impress, or to control: dominating.—*adv.* **command'ingly.**—*ns.* **command'-
ment,** a command: a precept: one of the ten
Mosaic laws; **command'o,** (*Port.*) in South
Africa, a military party: a unit of specially

trained troops for hit-and-run raids and other
tasks demanding special courage, skill, and
initiative: (*loosely*) one serving in such a unit.
[Fr. *commander*—L. *commendāre*—*com-,*
inten., *mandāre,* to entrust.]

commemorate, *ko-mem'o-rāt, v.t.* to call to remembrance, esp. by a solemn or public act: to
celebrate: to serve as a memorial of.—*n.* **com-
memorā'tion,** preserving the memory (of
some person or thing) by a solemn ceremony,
&c.—*adj.* **commem'orative,** [L. *commemorāre,*
-ātum, to remember—*com-,* inten., and
memor, mindful.]

commence, *kom-ens', v.i.* and *v.t.* to begin: to
originate.—*n.* **commence'ment.** [O.Fr. *com-
(m)encer*—L. *com-,* inten., *initiāre,* to begin.]

commend, *kom-end', v.t.* to commit as a charge
(to): to recommend as worthy: to praise.—*adj.*
commend'able, praiseworthy.—*n.* **commend'-
ableness.**—*adv.* **commend'ably.**—*n.* **com-
mendā'tion,** the act of commending: praise:
declaration of esteem.—*adj.* **commend'atory,**
commending, containing praise or commendation.—**commend me to,** give me for preference. [L. *commendāre*—*com-,* inten., *mandāre,*
to trust.]

commensalism, *ko-men'sál-izm, n.* the living
together for mutual benefit of two organisms
of different kinds. [L. *com-,* together, *mensa,* a
table.]

commensurable, *ko-men'sū-ra-bl, adj.* having a
common standard of measurement: in due
proportion.—*adv.* **commen'surably.**—*adj.*
commen'surate (*-āt*), equal in measure or
extent: in due proportion (with, to).—*adv.*
commen'surately. [L. *com-,* with, *mensūra,* a
measure—*mētīrī, mensus,* to measure.]

comment, *kom'ent, n.* a note conveying an
illustration or explanation: a remark, observation, criticism.—*v.i.* (or *kom-ent'*) to make
critical or explanatory notes.—*ns.* **comm'en-
tary,** a book in which the text of another book
is closely examined and explained: (*pl.*) a
memoir, history: a series of comments, esp. by
a spectator at a ceremony, game, &c.;
comm'entator. [Fr.,—L. *commentārī*—*com-,*
and *mens,* the mind.]

commerce, *kom'érs, n.* interchange of merchandise on a large scale between nations or individuals: social intercourse: communion: sexual intercourse (esp. in bad sense).—*adj.* **commer'cial,** pertaining to commerce, mercantile.—*n.* commercial traveller: radio or television programme sponsored by a business
firm or organisation: an advertisement in
such a programme.—*n.* **commer'cialism,** the
commercial spirit: an expression characteristic of commercial language.—*adv.* **commer'cially.**—**commercial traveller,** the
accredited travelling representative of a
business firm. [Fr.,—L. *commercium*—*com-,*
with, *merx, mercis,* merchandise.]

commère, *kom-mer', n. fem.* corresponding to
compère. [Fr.]

comminate, *kom'in-āt, v.t.* to threaten.—*n.* **com-
minā'tion,** threatening, denunciation: a recital
of God's threatenings in a church service.—
adj. **comm'inatory,** threatening punishment.
[L. *comminārī, -ātum*—*com-,* inten., and
minārī, to threaten.]

commingle, *ko-ming'gl, v.t.* and *v.i.* to mingle: to mix (with). [L. *com-*, together, **mingle.**]

comminute, *kom'in-ūt, v.t.* to break in minute pieces, to pulverise.—*n.* **comminū'tion.**—**comminuted fracture** (see **fracture**). [L. *comminuĕre, -ūtum—com-, minus,* less.]

commiserate, *kom-iz'ér-āt, v.t.* to feel or express compassion for, to pity.—*n.* **commiserā'tion.** [L. *com-*, with, *miserārī,* to deplore—*miser,* wretched.]

commissary, *kom'is-ár-i, n.* one to whom any charge is committed: a deputy: an officer who furnishes provisions, &c., to an army: (*Scots law*) a judge in a **commissary court,** one which appoints executors of estates, &c.—*ns.* **commissar** (-är), a commissary: in U.S.S.R. the head of a government department; **commissā'riat,** the department charged with the furnishing of provisions, as for an army: the supply of provisions: the office of a commissary. [Low L. *commissārius*—L. *committĕre, commissum,* to entrust.]

commission, *kom-ish'(ó)n, n.* act of committing: that which is committed: a document conferring authority, or the authority itself: something to be done by one person on behalf of another: an order for a work of art, &c.: (of a warship, &c.) a state of being manned, equipped, and ready for service: the fee paid to an agent for transacting business: a body of persons appointed to perform certain duties.—*v.t.* to give a commission to or for: to empower.—*ns.* **commiss'ion-ag'ent,** one who sells goods for another and receives a certain percentage of the proceeds: a book-maker; **commissionaire',** a messenger or door-keeper in uniform; **commiss'ioner,** one who holds a commission to perform some business, as to exercise authority on behalf of the Government: member of a commission; **commiss'ionership.**—**commissioned officer,** one appointed by commission—in the army and navy, an officer of or above the rank of lieutenant; in the air force, of or above rank of pilot officer; **High Commissioner,** the chief representative in a British Commonwealth country of another country that is also a member of the Commonwealth. [From **commit.**]

commit, *kom-it', v.t.* to give in charge or trust: to consign: to become guilty of, perpetrate: to compromise, involve: to pledge (oneself):—*pr.p.* **committ'ing;** *pa.p.* **committ'ed.**—*ns.* **commit'ment,** act of committing: an order for sending to prison: imprisonment: an obligation, promise, engagement: declared attachment to a doctrine or a cause; **committ'al,** commitment: a pledge, actual or implied.—*adj.* **committ'ed,** having entered into a commitment: (of literature) written from, (of author) writing from, a fixed standpoint or with a fixed purpose, religious, political, or other.—*n.* **committ'ee,** a number of persons, selected from a more numerous body, to whom some special business is committed.—**commit to memory,** to learn by heart; **commit to writing,** to set down in writing. [L. *committĕre—com-,* with, *mittĕre, missum,* to send.]

commix, *kom-iks', v.t.* to mix together.—*v.i.* to mix.—*n.* **commix'ture,** act of mixing together:

the state of being mixed: the compound so formed. [L. *com-*, with, **mix.**]

commodious, *kom-ō'di-ús, adj.* convenient: spacious: comfortable.—*n.* **commode',** a small sideboard: a box for holding a chamber utensil.—*adv.* **commō'diously.**—*ns.* **commō'diousness; commōd'ity,** convenience: an article of traffic: (*pl.*) goods, produce. [L. *commodus—com-*, with, *modus,* measure.]

commodore, *kom'o-dōr, n.* an officer intermediate between an admiral and a captain: the senior captain in a fleet of merchantmen: the president of a yacht-club. [Perh. from Du. *kommandeur.*]

common, *kom'ón, adj.* belonging equally to more than one: public (e.g. *common crier, nuisance*): general: usual: frequent: easy to be had: of little value: vulgar: without rank.—*n.* a tract of open land, used in common by the inhabitants of a town, parish, &c.—*ns.* **comm'onalty,** the general body of the people without any distinction of rank or authority; **comm'oner,** one who is not a noble: a member of the House of Commons: at Oxford, a student who is not on the foundation of a college and pays for his *commons* or share of provisions.—*adv.* **comm'only.**—*ns.* **comm'onness; comm'onplace,** a common topic: a platitude: a memorandum.—*adj.* lacking distinction: hackneyed.—*ns.* **comm'onplace-book,** a note or memorandum book; **Common Prayer (Book of),** the liturgy of the Church of England; **comm'on-riding,** the Scottish equivalent of beating the bounds (see **beat**); **comm'on-room,** in schools, colleges, &c., a room to which the members have common access.—*n.pl.* **comm'ons,** the common people: (*cap.*) their representatives, the lower House of Parliament or House of Commons.—*n.* **comm'on sense,** good sense or practical sagacity: the opinion of a community.—**Common Bench, Common Pleas,** one of the divisions of the High Court of Justice; **common chord,** a tone with its third (major or minor) and perfect fifth; **common gender,** the gender of a noun having only one form to denote male or female (e.g. L. *bōs,* bull, cow, or Eng. *teacher, pupil*); **common law,** in England, the ancient customary law of the land; **common market,** an association of countries as a single economic unit with internal free trade and common external tariffs: (*caps.*) the European Economic Community formed in 1957 by the Treaty of Rome by France, West Germany, Italy, Belgium, the Netherlands and Luxembourg, later (1973) joined by Britain, Denmark and Eire; **common noun,** a name that can be applied to all the members of a class; **common time,** (*mus.*) four beats to the bar.— **House of Commons,** the lower House of Parliament in Britain and in Canada; **in common,** shared; equally (with others); **make common cause with,** to side with; **short commons,** scant fare; **the common,** that which is common or usual; **the common good,** the interest of the community at large: the corporate property of a burgh in Scotland. [Fr. *commun*—L. *commūnis,* prob. from *com-*, together, and *mūnis,* serving, obliging.]

commonwealth, *kom'ón-welth, n.* the common

Neutral vowels in unaccented syllables: *em'pér-ór*; for certain sounds in foreign words see p. ix.

136

or public good (also **comm'onweal**, -*wēl*): the whole body of the people: a form of government in which the power rests with the people: an association of states so governed, as the Commonwealth of Australia, the (British) Commonwealth of Nations: (*cap.*) the government of England from 1649 to 1660.

commotion, *kom-ō'sh(ó)n*, *n.* a violent motion or moving: excited or tumultuous action, physical or mental: agitation: tumult. [L. *com-*, inten., and *movēre*, *mōtum*, to move.]

commune, *kom'ūn*, *n.* a corporation: in France, &c., a small territorial divison: (*cap.*) the government of Paris 1792-94: a group of people living together and sharing possessions.—*adj.* **commū'nal** (or *kom'-*), pertaining to a commune or a community. owned in common. [Fr. *commune*- L. *commūnis*. See **common**.]

commune, *kom-ūn'*, *v.i.* to converse together spiritually or confidentially. [O.Fr. *comuner*, to share.]

communicate, *kom-ū'ni-kāt*, *v.t.* to make known: to give.—*v.i.* to have mutual access: to exchange information by letter, etc.; to partake of Holy Communion: to succeed in conveying one's meaning to others.—*adj.* **commū'nicable**, that may be communicated.—*ns.* **commū'nicant**, one who communicates; **communica'tion**, act, or means, of communicating: information given: a letter, message: (in *pl.*) routes and means of transport: (in *pl.*) means of giving information, as the press, cinema, radio, and television.—*adj.* **commū'nicative**, inclined to give information, unreserved.—*n.* **commū'nicativeness.**—*adj.* **commū'nicatory**, imparting knowledge.—*n.* **communiqué** (*kom-ū'ni-kā*), official announcement. [L. *commūnicāre*, -*ātum*—*commūnis*, common.]

communion, *kom-ūn'yón*, *n.* act of communing: spiritual intercourse: fellowship: common possession: union in religious service: the body of people who so unite.—**the Communion, Holy Communion**, the celebration of the Lord's Supper. [L. *commūniō*, -*ōnis*—*commūnis*, common.]

communism, *kom'ū-nizm*, *n.* a social order under which private property is abolished, and all things held in common: (loosely) the form of socialism (q.v.) developed in the U.S.S.R.—*n.* **comm'unist**, one who believes in or supports communism.—*adj.* **communist'ic.** [Fr. *communisme*—L. *commūnis*; cf. **common.**]

community, *kom-ūn'i-ti*, *n.* common possession or enjoyment: agreement: a society of people having common rights, &c.: the public in general.—**community centre**, a place where members of a community may meet for social, recreational, educational, and other activities; **community singing**, organised singing by a large company. [O.Fr.,—L. *commūnitās*—*commūnis*, common.]

commute, *kom-ūt'*, *v.t.* to exchange: to exchange (a punishment) for one less severe: to compound for (a sum due—by a single payment, &c.): to change (electric current) from direct to alternating, or vice versa.—*v.i.* to travel regularly between two places, esp. between suburban home and place of work in town.—*adj.* **commut'able**, that may be commuted or exchanged.—*ns.* **commutabil'ity;**

commuta'tion.—*adj.* **commu'tative** (*math.*), such that x*y = y*x—where * denotes a binary operation.—*ns.* **comm'utātor**, an apparatus for reversing electric currents; **commut'er**, one who commutes.—*adj.* **commut'ual**, mutual. [L. *commūtāre*—*com-*, with, *mūtāre*, to change.]

compact, *kom-pakt'*, *adj.* closely placed or fitted together: firm: brief.—*v.t.* to press closely together: to consolidate.—*adv.* **compact'ly.**—*n.* **compact'ness.**—**powder compact**, a small case containing compacted face-powder. [Fr.,—L. *compactus*, pa.p. of *compingĕre*—*com-*, together, *pangĕre*, to fix.]

compact, *kom'pakt*, *n.* a mutual bargain or agreement: a league, treaty, or union. [L. *compactum*—*compaciscī*, from *com-*, together, and *pacisci*, to make a bargain.]

companion, *kom-pan'yón*, *n.* one who keeps company or frequently associates with another, including one who is paid for doing so: an associate or partner.—*adj.* of the nature of a companion: accompanying.—*adj.* **companionable**, fit to be a companion: agreeable.—*adv.* **compan'ionably**.—*adj.* **companionless**.—*n.* **compan'ionship**. [Fr. *compagnon*, from Low L. *compānium*, a messmate—L. *com-*, with, and *pānis*, bread.]

companion, *kom-pan'yón*, *n.* (*naut.*) a skylight or window-frame through which light passes to a lower deck or cabin.—*ns.* **compan'ionladd'er**, **compan'ion-way**, the ladder or stair from an upper to a lower deck or to a cabin. [Du. *kompanje*, store room.]

company, *kum'pa-ni*, *n.* any assembly of persons. a number of persons associated together for trade, &c.: a society: a subdivision of a regiment: the crew of a ship: fellowship: society. [Fr. *compagnie*, conn. with *compagnon*. See **companion** (1).]

compare, *kom-pār'*, *v.t.* to set (things) together to ascertain how far they agree or disagree: to set (one thing) beside another for such a purpose (with *with*): to liken or represent as similar (*to*): (*gram.*) to give the degrees of comparison of.—*v.t.* to stand in comparison.—*adj.* **com'parable**, that may be compared (*with*): worthy to be compared (*to*).—*n.* **com'parableness.**—*adv.* **com'parably.**—*adj.* **compār'ative**, pertaining to comparison: estimated by comparing with something else: not positive or absolute: (*gram.*) expressing more.—*adv.* **compār'atively.**—*n.* **compār'ison**, the act of comparing: comparative estimate: a simile or figure by which two things are compared: (*gram.*) the inflection of an adjective or adverb to express different relative degrees of its quality.—**beyond compare**, unrivalled. [Fr.,—L. *comparāre*, to match, from *com-*, together, *parāre*, to make or esteem equal—*par*, equal.]

compartment, *kom-pärt'mént*, *n.* a separate part or division of any enclosed space: a division of a railway carriage.—**compartment'alise**, to divide into categories or into units. [Fr., from *compartir*—L. *com-*, with, *partīre*, to part.]

compass, *kum'pás*, *n.* a circuit or circle: space: limit, bounds: range of pitch of a voice or instrument: an instrument consisting of a magnetised needle, used to find directions:

(*pl.*) an instrument consisting of two movable legs, for describing circles, &c.—*v.t.* to pass or go round: to surround or enclose: to besiege: to bring about or obtain: to contrive or plot.—**box the compass** (see **box**); **fetch a compass** (*arch.*), to go round in a circuit. [Fr. *compas*, a circle, prob. from Low L. *compassus*—L. *com-*, together, *passus*, a step.]

compassion, *kom-pash'(ò)n*, *n.* fellow-feeling, or sorrow for the sufferings of another—usually a warmer feeling than pity.—*adj.* **compassionate** (*-sh(ó)n-àt*), inclined to pity or mercy.—*adv.* **compass'ionately.**—*n.* **compass'ionateness.—compassionate leave**, leave granted in exceptional circumstances for personal reasons. [Fr.,—L. *compassiō*—*com-*, with, *patī*, *passus*, to suffer.]

compatible, *kom-pat'ibl*, *adj.* consistent: consistent (with): able to coexist.—*n.* **compatibil'ity**, ability to coexist: ability of a television set not made for colour to receive colour signals in black and white.—*adv.* **compat'ibly.** [Fr.,—L. *com-*, with, *patī*, to suffer.]

compatriot, *kom-pā'tri-ót*, or *-pat'-*, *n.* a fellow countryman.—Also *adj.* [Fr.,—L. *com-*, with, and **patriot.**]

compeer, *kom-pēr'*, *n.* one who is equal (to another—e.g. in age, rank, achievements): a companion. [L. *compar*—*com-*, with, *par*, equal.]

compel, *kom-pel'*, *v.t.* to drive or urge on forcibly: to oblige (e.g. *to compel to go*): to force (e.g. *obedience*):—*pr.p.* **compell'ing**: *pa.p.* **compelled'.**—*adjs.* **compell'able**; **compell'ing**, forcing attention. [L. *com-*, inten., *pellĕre*, *pulsum*, to drive.]

compendium, *kom-pen'di-ùm*, *n.* a shortening or abridgment: a summary: an abstract:—*pl.* **compendiums**, **-dia.**—*adj.* **compen'dious**, short: comprehensive.—*adv.* **compen'diously.** —*n.* **compen'diousness.** [L. *compendium*, what is weighed together, hung up together, stored, or saved—*com-*, together, *pendĕre*, to weigh.]

compensate, *kom'pen-sāt*, *v.t.* to recompense (make up for loss, or remunerate for trouble): to counterbalance.—*v.i.* to make up (for).—*n.* **compensā'tion**, act of compensating: that which counterbalances: reward for service: amends for loss sustained: process of compensating for sense of failure or inadequacy by concentrating on some other achievement or superiority, real or fancied.—*adj.* **compen'satory**, giving compensation. [L. *com-*, inten., and *pensāre*, freq. of *pendĕre*, to weigh.]

compère, *kɔ̄-*, *kom-per*, *n.* one who introduces items of an entertainment.—*v.t.* to act as compère to. [Fr., *gódfather.*]

compete, *kom-pēt'*, *v.i.* to seek or strive for something in opposition to others: to contend (for a prize).—*n.* **competition** (*-pet-i'-*), act of competing: rivalry.—*adj.* **compet'itive**, pertaining to, or characterised by, competition: (of e.g. price) such as to give a chance of successful result in conditions of rivalry.—*n.* **compet'itor**, one who competes: a rival or opponent. [L. *competĕre*—*com-*, together, *petĕre*, to seek.]

competent, *kom'pe-tént*, *adj.* suitable: sufficient: capable: legally qualified: permissible (e.g. *it is competent to you to do so*).—*ns.* **com'**

petence, **com'petency**, fitness: sufficiency: enough to live on with comfort: capacity: legal power or capacity.—*adv.* **com'petently.** [Fr.,—L. *competĕre*—*com-*, with, *petĕre*, to seek, to strive after.]

compile, *kom-pīl'*, *v.t.* to write or compose by collecting the materials from other books: to draw up or collect.—*ns.* **compīlā'tion**, the act of compiling: the thing compiled, a literary work made by gathering the material from various authors; **compīl'er.** [Fr. *compiler*, prob. from L. *compilāre*—*com-*, together, *pilāre*, to plunder.]

complacent, *kom-plā'sént*, *adj.* showing satisfaction: self-satisfied.—*ns.* **complā'cence**, **complā'cency**, contentment: self-satisfaction.—*adv.* **complā'cently.** [L. *complacēre*—*com-*, inten., *placēre*, to please.]

complain, *kom-plān'*, *v.i.* to express grief, pain, sense of injury (*abs.* or with *of* or *about*): to state a grievance or make a charge (against someone—with *of* and *to*): to make a mournful sound: to be sick.—*ns.* **complain'ant**, one who complains: (*law*) a plaintiff; **complain'er**, a murmurer: complainant; **complaint'**, a complaining: an expression of grief, distress, or dissatisfaction: the thing complained of: an ailment. [Fr. *complaindre*—Low L. *complangĕre*—L. *com-*, inten., *plangĕre*, bewail.]

complaisant, *kom'ple-zánt*, *kom-ple-zant'*, *kom-plā'zànt*, *adj.* desirous of pleasing, obliging: lenient.—*n.* **com'plaisance** (or *komplāz'-àns*), care or desire to please: an obliging civility.—*adv.* **com'plaisantly** (or *-zant'-*, or *-plā'-*). [Fr.,—*complaire*—L. *complacēre.*]

complement, *kom'pli-mént*, *n.* that which completes or fills up: full number or quantity: that by which an angle or arc falls short of a right angle or quadrant: a colour which, combined with another, gives white: (*math.*) all members of a set not included in a given subset.—*adjs.* **complement'al**, of the nature of a complement; **complement'ary**, supplying a mutual deficiency: together making up a whole, or a right angle. [L. *complēmentum*—*com-*, inten., *plēre*, to fill.]

complete, *kom-plēt'*, *adj.* free from deficiency: perfect: entire: finished.—*v.t.* to finish: to make perfect or entire.—*adv.* **complete'ly.**—*ns.* **complete'ness**, the state of being complete; **complē'tion**, the act of completing: the state of being complete: fulfilment. [L. *complēre*, *-ētum*, to fill up; *com-*, inten.]

complex, *kom'pleks*, *adj.* composed of more than one, or of many, parts: not simple, intricate, difficult.—*n.* a complex whole: (*psychology*) a group of ideas or impressions, regarded as the causes of an abnormal mental condition: (loosely) the mental condition itself.—*n.* **complex'ity**, state of being complex: complication.—*adv.* **com'plexly.**—**complex number; complex sentence**, a sentence containing one or more subordinate clauses. [L. *complex*—*com-*, *plicāre*; see **complicate.**]

complexion, *kom-plek'sh(ò)n*, *n.* colour or look of the skin, esp. of the face: (*fig.*) general appearance: temperament.—*adj.* **complex'ioned**, having a specified complexion, or temperament. [Fr.,—L. *complexiō*, *-ōnis*, a

Neutral vowels in unaccented syllables: *em'pér-ór*; for certain sounds in foreign words see p. ix.

138

combination, physical structure of body—com-, and *plectĕre*, to plait.]

compliance, *kom-plī′áns*, *n.* action in obedience to another's wish, request, &c.—the act of complying.—*adj.* **complī′ant**, yielding, submissive.—*adv.* **complī′antly.** [comply, and suffx. -*ance*.]

complicate, *kom′pli-kāt*, *v.t.* to twist or plait together: to entangle: to render complex, intricate, difficult.—*ns.* **com′plicacy**, the quality or state of being complicated; **complicā′tion**, an intricate blending or entanglement: an involved state of affairs: an additional circumstance making (e.g. situation) more difficult: a condition or additional disease making recovery from the primary disease more difficult; **complicity** (*kom-plis′i-ti*), state or condition of being an accomplice.—**complicated fracture** (see **fracture**). [L. *com*-, together, and *plicāre*, -*ātum*, to fold.]

compliment, *kom′pli-mént*, *n.* an expression of regard or praise, or of respect or civility: delicate flattery.—*v.t.* **compliment′**, to pay a compliment to: to congratulate (on).—*adj.* **compliment′ary**, conveying, or expressive of, civility or praise: using compliments: given free.—**left-handed compliment**, a compliment so worded that it admits of an uncomplimentary interpretation: a veiled censure. [Fr. *compliment*—L. *complēmentum*.]

complin, compline, *kom′plin*, *n.* the concluding church service of the day. [O.Fr. *complie*—L. *complēta* (*hora*).]

comply, *kom-plī′*, *v.i.* to act in accordance (with the wishes or command of another, or with conditions laid down, &c.)—or *abs.*:—*pr.p.* comply′ing; *pa.t.* and *pa.p.* complied′. [It. *complire*, to fulfil, to suit, to offer courtesies—L. *complēre*, to fill full, to fulfil.]

compo, *kom′po*, *n.* a mortar of cement: stucco: any composite material. [Abbrev. of **composition**.]

component, *kom-pō′nént*, *adj.* making up: forming one of the elements of a compound whole.—*n.* one of the elements of a compound: one of the parts of which anything is made up. [L. *compōnĕre*, to make up.]

comport, *kom-pōrt′*, *-pört′*, *v.i.* to agree, suit (with).—*v.t.* to bear, behave (oneself). [L. *comportāre*—*com*-, together,*portāre*, to carry.]

compose, *kom-pōz′*, *v.t.* to form by putting together or being together: to set in order or at rest: to settle (e.g. dispute): to set up for printing: to create (esp. in literature or music).—*v.i.* to create: to set type.—*p.adj.* **composed′**, settled, quiet, calm.—*adv.* **compos′edly.**—*ns.* **compos′edness; compos′er**, a writer, an author, esp. of a piece of music.—*adj.* **com′posite**, made up of two or more distinct parts: (*cap.*—*archit.*) a blending of the Ionic and the Corinthian orders: (*bot.*) belonging to the family or order **Compositae**, a very large group of plants having small flowers or florets arranged in heads resembling single flowers (e.g. the daisy).—*n.* a composite thing: a plant of the Compositae.—*adv.* **com′positely.**—*n.* **com′positeness; compos′ing-stick**, an instrument, usu. of metal, used for holding assembled printing-types when setting by hand; **composi′tion**, the act of putting together, or

that which is put together: the nature and proportion of the ingredients (of anything): a work in literature, music, or painting: an artificial mixture, esp. one used as a substitute: a coming together or agreement, an arrangement or compromise: a percentage accepted by a bankrupt's creditors in lieu of the full payment: a picture, photograph, formed from several images; **compos′itor**, one who puts together, or sets up, types for printing; **com′post**, a mixture, esp. for manure; **com-pō′sure**, calmness, self-possession, tranquility. [Fr. *composer*, from L. *com*-, together, *pōnĕre*, to place, influenced in some meanings by confusion with *pausāre*, to cease, to rest.]

compos mentis,*kom′pos ment′is*, of sound mind, sane. [L.]

compot, compote, *kom′pot*, or *kom′pōt*, *n.* fruit stewed in syrup. [Fr. *compote*.]

compound, *kom-pownd′*, *v.t.* to mix or combine: to settle or adjust by agreement: to agree for a consideration not to prosecute (a felony).—*v.i.* to agree, or come to terms (*with* a person, or *for* a thing).—*adj.* **com′pound**, mixed or composed of a number of parts: not simple.—*n.* a mass made up of a number of parts: a word made up of two or more words: (*chem.*) a new and distinct substance formed from two or more elements in definite proportions by weight.—*n.* **compound′er.**—**compound fracture** (see **fracture**); **compound interest** (see **interest**); **compound sentence**, a sentence containing more than one principal clause. [O.Fr. from L. *compōnĕre*—*com*-, together, *pōnĕre*, to place.]

compound, *kom′pownd*, *n.* an enclosure round a house or factory (in India, &c.), or for confining native labourers (S. Africa). [Malay *kampong*, enclosure.]

comprehend,*kom-pré-hend′*, *v.t.* to seize or take up with the mind, to understand: to comprise or include.—*adj.* **comprehen′sible**, capable of being understood.—*adv.* **comprehen′sibly.**—*ns.* **comprehensibil′ity, comprehen′sibleness.**—*n.* **comprehen′sion**, power of the mind to understand: act of understanding, or of including: comprehensiveness.—*adj.* **comprehen′sive**, having the quality or power of comprehending much: inclusive: including much.—*adv.* **comprehen′sively.**—*n.* **comprehen′siveness**, fullness, completeness.—**comprehensive school**, a school that combines the various types of secondary school in one institution. [L. *comprehendĕre*—*com*-, together, *prehendĕre*, -*hensum*, to seize.]

compress, *kom-pres′*, *v.t.* to press together: to force into a narrower space: to condense.—*n.* **com′press**, a pad used in surgery to apply pressure to any part: a folded cloth applied to the skin.—*adj.* **compress′ible**, that may be compressed.—*ns.* **compress′ibleness**, the property of being reduced in volume by pressure; **compressibil′ity, compressibleness:** (*aero.*) a shock-wave phenomenon causing increased drag (q.v.), which asserts itself when an aircraft in flight approaches the speed of sound, the hypothesis of the air as an incompressible fluid being no longer valid; **compress′ion**, act of compressing: state of being compressed: the stroke that compresses

fāte, *fär*; *mē*, *hûr* (her); *mīne*; *mōte*, *för*; *mūte*; *mōōn*, *fŏŏt*; ᴛʜen (then) the gases in an internal-combustion engine.—*adj.* **compress'ive,** able to compress.—*n.* **compress'or,** anything that compresses, thereby raising pressure, as a device that compresses air or gas.—**compress'ion-igni'tion,** ignition by means of the heat of compressed air. [L. *compressāre—com-,* together, and *pressāre,* to press—*premēre, pressum,* to press.]

comprise, *kom-prīz', v.t.* to contain, include: to consist of.—*adj.* **compris'able.**—*n.* **comprisal,** the act of comprising. [Fr. *compris,* pa.p. of *comprendre*—L. *comprehendēre.* See **comprehend.**]

compromise, *kom'prō-mīz, n.* a settlement of differences by mutual concession: partial waiving of one's theories or principles for the sake of settlement: anything of intermediate or mixed kind:—*v.t.* to settle by mutual concession: to involve in risk of injury, suspicion, &c.—*v.i.* to make a compromise.—*p.adj.* **com'-promised,** exposed to danger or discredit. [Fr. *compromis*—L, *comprōmittēre, -missum—com-,* together, *prōmittēre,* to promise.]

comptroll, comptroller. See under **control.**

compulsion, *kom-pul'sh(ó)n, n.* the act of compelling: force, constraint, coercion.—*adj.* **compul'sive,** coercive: with power to compel.—*adv.* **compul'sively.**—*adj.* **compul'sory,** obligatory: enforced: compelling.—*adv.* **compul'sorily.** [Fr.,—L.L. *compulsiō, -ōnis*—L. *compellēre.* See **compel.**]

compunction, *kom-pungk'sh(ó)n, n.* uneasiness of conscience: remorse tinged with pity.—*adj.* **compunc'tious,** repentant: remorseful.—*adv.* **compunc'tiously.** [O.Fr.,—L. *compunctiō, -ōnis—com-,* inten., and *pungēre, punctum,* to prick.]

compurgation, *kom-pûr-gā'sh(ó)n, n.* in old English and other Germanic law, the clearing of the accused by **compurgators,** witnesses testifying to his innocence or veracity: evidence in favour of the accused: vindication. [L. *compurgāre,* to purify wholly—*com-,* inten. See **purge.**]

compute, *kom-pūt', v.t.* to calculate: to number: to estimate.—*adj.* **comput'able** (or *kom'-*), calculable.—*ns.* **computā'tion,** act of computing: reckoning: estimate; **comput'er,** a calculator: a mechanical, electric or electronic device that stores numerical or other information and provides logical answers at high speed to questions bearing on that information.—**analogue computer** (see **analogue**); **digital computer** (see **digit**).—*v.t.* **comput'erise,** to bring computer(s) into use to control (an operation): to process (data) by computer. [L. *computāre—com-,* together, *putāre,* to reckon.]

comrade, *kom'rād, kum'rād, n.* a close companion, intimate associate: in some socialist and communist circles used as a term of address or prefixed to a name.—*n.* **com'rade-ship.** [Sp. *camarada,* a roomful, a room-mate—L. *camera,* a room.]

con, *kon,* a contraction of L. *contrā,* against, as in **pro and con,** for and against.

con, *kon, v.t.* to study carefully: to commit to memory:—*pr.p.* **conn'ing;** *pa.p.* **conned.** [O.E. *cunnian,* to try to know—*cunnan,* to know.]

con, conn. *kun, kon, v.t.* to direct the steering of.—*n.* **conn'ing-tow'er,** the pilot-house of a warship or submarine. [Older form *cond,* apparently—Fr. *conduire*—L. *condūcere;* see **conduct.**]

con, *kon, adj.* abbrev. for **confidence** as in **con game,** a swindle, **con man,** a swindler, esp. one with a persuasive way of talking.—*v.t.* to swindle, trick.

concatenate, *kon-kat'e-nāt, v.t.* (*fig.*) to link together, to connect in a series.—*n.* **concatenā'tion,** act of concatenating: state of being linked or mutually dependent: a series of things (e.g. events) linked to each other. [L. *con-,* together, and *catēna,* a chain.]

concave, *kon'kāv, adj.* curved inwards (opposed to *convex*).—*n.* a hollow: an arch or vault.—*n.* **concāv'ity,** the quality of being concave: the inner surface of a concave or hollow body. [L. *concavus,* from *con-,* inten., and *cavus,* hollow. See **cave.**]

conceal, *kon'sēl, v.t.* to hide completely: to hide intentionally: to keep secret.—*n.* **conceal'-ment,** act of concealing: secrecy: disguise: hiding-place. [O.Fr. *conceler*—L. *concēlāre—con-,* inten., and *cēlāre,* to hide.]

concede, *kon-sēd', v.t.* to admit (e.g. a claim, a point in argument): to grant (e.g. a right).—*v.i.* to admit or grant (that). [L. *concēdēre, cessum—con-,* wholly, and *cēdēre,* to yield.]

conceit, *kon-sēt', n.* overweening self-esteem: opinion: favourable opinion: fancy: a witty thought, esp. far-fetched, affected, or over-ingenious.—*adj.* **conceit'ed,** clever, witty (*obs. uses*): having a high opinion of oneself, egotistical.—*adv.* **conceit'edly.**—*n.* **conceit'ed-ness.**—**out of conceit with,** no longer satisfied, pleased, with. [From **conceive,** on the analogy of *deceive, deceit.*]

conceive, *kon-sēv', v.t.* to become pregnant with, form in the womb; to form in the mind: to imagine or think: to understand.—*v.i.* to become pregnant: to think.—*adj.* **conceiv'-able.**—*adv.* **conceiv'ably.**—*ns.* **conceivabil'ity, conceiv'ableness.** [O.Fr. *concever*—L. *concipēre, conceptum,* from *con-,* and *capēre,* to take.]

concentrate, *kon'sen-trāt,* or *kon-sen'-, v.t.* to bring towards a common centre: to focus: to direct with a single purpose or intention: to condense, to render more intense the properties of.—*v.i.* to draw towards a common centre: to direct one's energies to a single aim.—*n.* a product of concentration: concentrated animal feed.—*n.* **concentrā'tion,** act of concentrating: condensation.—*adj.* **concen'trative,** tending to concentrate.—**concentration camp,** a settlement in which persons obnoxious to the governing power are segregated for reasons of state. [A lengthened form of *con-centre,* to bring, or come, together to a focus or centre.]

concentric, -al, *kon-sent'rik, -ál, adj.* having a common centre. [Fr. *concentrique*—L. *con-,* with, *centrum*—Gr. *kentron,* a point.]

concept, *kon'sept, n.* a thing conceived, a general notion.—*n.* **concep'tion,** the act of conceiving: the thing conceived: the formation in the mind of an image or idea: a concept: a

Neutral vowels in unaccented syllables: *em'pér-ór;* for certain sounds in foreign words see p. ix.

140

notion.—*adj.* **concep'tual,** pertaining to conception or to concepts.—*n.* **concep'tualism,** the doctrine in philosophy that universals (q.v.) exist in the mind but in the mind only—cf. *nominalism, realism.* [L. *concipĕre, -ceptum,* to conceive.]

concern, *kon-sûrn', v.t.* to relate or belong to: to affect or interest: to make uneasy: to interest, trouble (oneself—with *with, in, about*).—*n.* that which concerns or belongs to one: interest: regard: anxiety: a business, or those connected with it.—*adj.* **concerned',** having connection with: interested: anxious.—*adv.* **concern'edly.**—*n.* **concern'edness.**—*prep.* **concern'ing,** regarding: pertaining to.—*n.* **concern'ment,** (*arch.*) affair: importance: anxiety: participation in (with *with*). [Fr.,—L. *concernĕre*—*con-,* together, *cernĕre,* to distinguish, perceive.]

concert, *kon'sėrt, n.* union or agreement in any undertaking: harmony: musical harmony: a musical entertainment.—*v.t.* **concert',** to frame or devise together: to arrange, plan.—*ns.* **concertina** (*kon-sėr-tē'na*), a musical instrument the sounds of which are produced by free vibrating reeds of metal, as in the accordion; **concerto** (*kon-chèr'to*), a composition for solo instrument(s), with orchestral accompaniments;—*pl.* **concer'tos.—concert pitch,** the (higher) pitch at which instruments for concert use are tuned: preparedness. [It. *concertare,* to sing in concert.]

concession, *kon-sesh'(ô)n, n.* the act of conceding: the thing conceded: a grant, esp. of land, &c., for a specified purpose.—*n.* **concessionaire',** one who has obtained a concession.—*adj.* **concess'ive,** implying concession: expressing concession. [**concede.**]

conch, *kongk, n.* a marine shell: the outer ear or its cavity.—*adjs.* **conchif'erous,** having a shell; **conch'iform,** conch-shaped.—*adj.* **conchoid'al,** shell-like, applied to the fracture of a mineral.—*ns.* **conchol'ogy,** that branch of natural history which deals with the shells of mollusks, **conchol'ogist.** [L. *concha*—Gr. *konchē,* a cockle.]

concierge, *kɔ̃-si-erzh', n.* a door-keeper, esp. in a block of flats. [Fr.; ety. unknown.]

conciliate, *kon-sil'i-āt, v.t.* to gain or win over: to appease.—*ns.* **concilia'tion,** act of conciliating; **concil'iator.**—*adj.* **concil'iatory.** [L. *conciliāre, -ātum*—*concilium,* council.]

concise, *kon-sīs', adj.* cut short: brief, using, or expressed in, few words.—*adv.* **concise'ly.**—*ns.* **concise'ness;** **concision** (*-sizh'-*), conciseness; (*B.*) circumcision. [Fr.,—L. *concīdĕre, concīsum,* from *con-,* and *caedĕre,* to cut.]

conclave, *kon'klāv, n.* the room in which cardinals meet to elect a pope: the body of cardinals: any secret assembly. [L. *conclāve,* from *con-,* together, *clāvis,* a key.]

conclude, *kon-klōōd', v.t.* (*arch.*) to enclose, shut up: to end: to decide: to infer.—*v.i.* to end: to form a final judgment.—*n.* **conclusion** (*-clōō'zh(ô)n*), act of concluding: the end, close, or last part: inference: judgment.—*adj.* **conclusive** (*-clōō'siv*), final: convincing.—*adv.* **conclus'ively.**—*n.* **conclus'iveness.—in conclusion,** finally; **to try conclusions,** to engage in a contest. [L. *conclūdĕre, conclūsum*—*con-,* together, *claudĕre,* to shut.]

concoct, *kon-kokt', v.t.* to make up (as a dish in cookery): to fabricate (e.g. a story).—*n.* **concoc'tion,** act of concocting: preparation of a mixture: the mixture so prepared: a made-up story. [L. *concoquĕre, concoctum*—*con-,* together, and *coquĕre,* to cook, to boil.]

concomitant, *kon-kom'i-tánt, adj.* connected with some thing, action, or state, and accompanying it (e.g. *concomitant pleasures, circumstances*).—Also *n.*—*ns.* **concom'itance, concom'itancy,** co-existence. [L. *con-,* with, and *comitans,* pr.p. of *comitārī,* to accompany—*comes,* a companion.]

concord, *kon'kórd,* or *kong'-, n.* state of being of the same heart or mind: agreement: a treaty: a combination of sounds satisfying to the ear.—*n.* **concord'ance,** agreement: an index or dictionary of the words or passages of a book or author.—*adj.* **concord'ant,** harmonious: (*fig.*) in harmony (with).—*n.* **concord'at,** an agreement, esp. a treaty between the pope and a secular government. [Fr. *concorde*—L. *concordia*—*concors,* of the same heart, from *con-,* together, *cor, cordis,* the heart.]

concourse, *kon'-, kong'kórs, -kôrs, n.* a moving or flowing together of persons, animals, or things: a crowd of persons running together: a throng. [Fr.,—L. *concursus*—*con-,* together, *currĕre,* to run.]

concrescence, *kon-kres'ėns, n.* a growing together. [L. *concrescentia*—*con-,* together, *crescĕre,* to grow.]

concrete, *kon'krēt,* or *-krēt', adj.* formed into one mass: (the opposite of *abstract*) denoting a thing, not a quality or state: particular, not general: made of (building) concrete.—*n.* a mass formed by parts growing or sticking together: a mixture of lime, sand, pebbles, &c., used in building.—*v.t.* **concrete',** to form into a solid mass.—*v.i.* to harden.—*adv.* **concrete'ly.**—*ns.* **concrete'ness; concre'tion,** a mass concreted: a growth forming in certain parts of the body, as calculi, &c.—**concrete poetry,** an art form which makes use of visual effects such as the arrangement of letters on the printed page. [L. *concretus*—*con-,* together, *crescĕre, crētum,* to grow.]

concubine, *kong'kū-bīn, n.* a woman who cohabits or lives with a man without being married to him.—*n.* **concu'binage,** state of living together as man and wife without being married: (*hist.*) an inferior form of marriage. [Fr.,—L. *concubina*—*con-,* together, *cubāre,* to lie down.]

concupiscence, *kon-kū'pis-ėns, n.* violent desire: sexual appetite, lust.—*adj.* **concu'piscent.** [Fr.,—L. *concupiscentia*—*concupiscĕre*—*con-,* inten., *cupĕre,* to desire.]

concur, *kon-kûr', v.i.* (*obs.*) to run together: to meet in one point: to coincide: to act together: to agree in opinion (with):—*pr.p.* **concurr'ing;** *pa.p.* **concurred'.**—*n.* **concurr'ence,** the meeting of lines in one point: coincidence: joint action: assent.—*adj.* **concurr'ent,** meeting in the same point: coming, acting, or existing together: coinciding: accompanying.—*adv.* **concurr'ently.** [L. *concurrĕre*—*con-,* together, *currĕre,* to run.]

concuss, *kon-kus', v.t.* to shake violently: to

coerce.—*n.* **concussion** (-*kush'*-), state of being shaken: a violent shock caused by sudden impact: a condition produced by a heavy blow, esp. on the head.—*adj.* **cuss'ive,** having the power or quality of concussion. [L. *concussus,* pa.p. of *concutĕre—con-,* together, *quatĕre,* to shake.]

concyclic, *kon-sī'klik, adj.* (*geom.*) lying on the circumference of the same circle. [L. *con-,* together, Gr. *kyklos,* a circle.]

condemn, *kon-dem', v.t.* to pronounce guilty: to censure or blame: to sentence to punishment or to an unpleasant fate: to pronounce unfit for use.—*adj.* **condem'nable** (-*dem'nà-bl*).—*n.* **condemnā'tion,** state of being condemned: blame: cause of being condemned.—*adj.* **condem'natory,** expressing or implying condemnation.—**condemned cell,** a cell occupied by a prisoner under sentence of death. [L. *condemnāre,* from *con-,* inten., and *damnāre,* to condemn.]

condense, *kon-dens', v.t.* to render more dense: to reduce to smaller compass.—*v.i.* to become condensed: of vapour, to turn to liquid form.—*adj.* **condens'able.**—*ns.* **condensabil'ity; condensā'tion,** act, or process, of condensing: what is produced by condensing; **condens'er,** an apparatus for reducing vapours to a liquid form: formerly more common name for a capacitor.—**condensation trail** (see **contrail**); **condensed milk,** milk reduced by evaporation, and (usually) sugared. [L. *condensāre—con-,* inten., and *densus,* dense.]

condescend, *kon-di-send', v.i.* to act graciously or patronisingly to inferiors: to deign: to stoop (to what is unworthy).—*adj.* **condescend'ing,** gracious to inferiors: patronising.—*adv.* **condescend'ingly.**—*n.* **condescen'sion**—**condescend upon,** (*Scot.*) to specify, mention. [L. *con-,* inten., and *descendĕre,* to descend.]

condign, *kon-dīn', adj.* well merited: adequate (of punishment).—*adv.* **condign'ly.**—*n.* **dign'ness.** [L. *condignus—con-,* wholly, *dignus,* worthy.]

condiment, *kon'di-mènt, n.* a seasoning used at table to give flavour to food. [L. *condīmentum—condīre,* to preserve, to pickle.]

condition, *kon-dish'(ò)n, n.* (usu. *pl.*) state, circumstances, in which a person or thing exists: a particular state of being (e.g. *in a liquid condition*): rank, standing: a prerequisite (e.g. *air to breathe is a condition of survival*): a stipulation: a term of a contract.—*v.i.* to make terms.—*v.t.* to agree upon: to limit, determine, control: to put into the required state, e.g. to clean, warm, and render humid (the air admitted to a building): to prepare, train (person, animal) for a certain activity or for certain conditions of living: to secure by training (a certain behavioural response to a stimulus).—*adj.* **condi'tional,** expressing condition: depending on conditions: not absolute.—*adv.* **condi'tionally.**—*adj.* **condi'tioned,** having a (specified) condition, state, or quality: circumstanced: subject to condition.—*ns.* **condi'tioner,** a person, substance, or apparatus that brings into good or required condition; **condi'tioning.**—**conditioned reflex,** a reflex response to a stimulus which depends on the

former experience of the individual. [L. *condīciō, -ōnis,* a compact (later false spelling *conditio*)—*condīcĕre—con-,* together, *dīcĕre,* to say.]

condole, *kon-dōl', v.i.* to grieve (with another): to express sympathy in sorrow.—*ns.* **condole'ment, condol'ence,** expression of sympathy with another's sorrow. [L. *con-,* with, *dolēre,* to grieve.]

condominium, *kon-dō-min'i-um, n.* joint sovereignty: a government administered by two or more powers: a region under such a government. [L. *con-,* together, *dominium,* lordship.]

condone, *kon-dōn', v.t.* to pass over without blame, to excuse.—*n.* **condonā'tion,** forgiveness (expressed or implied). [L. *con-,* inten., *donāre,* to give. See **donation.**]

condor, *kon'dór, n.* a large vulture found among the Andes of S. America. [Sp.,—Peruvian *cuntur.*]

condottiere, *kon-dot-tyā'rā, n.* a leader of a band of mercenary soldiers in 14th and 15th centuries:—*pl.* **condottieri** (-*rē*). [It.,—*conditto,* way—L. *con-, ducĕre,* to lead.]

conduce, *kon-dūs', v.i.* to tend, to contribute (to some end).—*adj.* **conduc'ive,** leading or tending (to), having power to promote.—*n.* **conduc'iveness.** [L. *condūcĕre—con-,* together, *dūcĕre,* to lead.]

conduct, *kon-dukt', v.t.* to lead or guide: to convey (water, &c.): to direct (e.g. an orchestra): to manage (e.g. a business): to behave (oneself): (*elect., heat*) to transmit.—*ns.* **con'duct,** act or method of leading or managing: guidance: management: behaviour; **conduct'ance,** power of conducting electricity.—*adj.* **conduct'ible,** capable of conducting heat, &c.: capable of being conducted or transmitted.—*ns.* **conductibil'ity; conduc'tion,** act or property of conducting or transmitting: transmission (e.g. of heat) by a conductor.—*adj.* **conduct'ive,** having the quality or power of conducting or transmitting.—*ns.* **conductiv'ity,** a power that bodies have of transmitting heat and electricity; **conduct'or,** the person or thing that conducts: a leader: a manager: a director of an orchestra or choir: one in charge of a bus, &c. (*fem.* **conduct'ress**): that which has the property of transmitting electricity, heat, &c. [L. *conductus—condūcĕre.* See **conduce.**]

conduit, *kun'dit,* or *kon'-, n.* a channel or pipe to convey water, &c. [Fr. *conduit*—L. *conductus—condūcĕre,* to lead.]

cone, *kōn, n.* a solid figure with a vertex and a circular or elliptical base, esp. that generated by the revolution of a right-angled triangle about a shorter side (*right circular cone*): fruit, more or less conical, as that of the pine, fir, &c.: anything shaped like a cone.—*adjs.* **cō'nic, -al,** having the form of or pertaining to a cone.—*n.* **con'ics,** that part of geometry which deals with the cone and its sections.—*adj.* **cō'niform,** in the form of a cone.—**conic section,** a figure made by the section of a cone by a plane. [Gr. *kōnos.*]

coney. See **cony.**

confabulate, *kon-fab'ū-lāt, v.i.* to chat.—*n.* **confabulā'tion** (*coll.* **confab'**—or *kon'fab*). [L. *con-,* together, *fābulārī,* to talk.]

Neutral vowels in unaccented syllables: *em'pér-ór*; for certain sounds in foreign words see p. ix.

142

confection, *kon-fek'sh(ò)n, n.* mixing, preparation: a preserve: a sweetmeat: a ready-made article of women's dress.—*ns.* **confec'tionary** (*B.*) a confectioner: confectionery; **confec'tioner,** one who makes or sells sweets; **confec'tionery,** the shop or business of a confectioner: sweetmeats in general. [L. *conficĕre, confectum,* to make up together—*con-,* together, *facĕre,* to make.]

confederate, *kon-fed'ér-át, adj.* leagued together, allied.—*n.* one united in a league, an ally: accomplice.—*v.i.* and *v.t.* (*-at*) to league together or join in a league.—*ns.* **confed'eracy,** a league, alliance: conspiracy: persons or states united by a league; **confederā'tion,** the forming of an alliance (of): a league, esp. of princes, states, &c. [L. *confoederāre, -ātum—con-,* together, and *foedus, foedĕris,* a league.]

confer, *kon-fûr', v.t.* to give or bestow: to compare, to collate, now only used in the imperative (*abbrev.* **cf.**).—*v.i.* to talk or consult together:—*pr.p.* **confer'ring;** *pa.p.* **conferred'.**—*n.* **con'ference,** the act of conferring: an appointed meeting for consultation or discussion: a combine [Fr.—L. *conferre—con-,* together, *ferre,* to bring.]

confess, *kon-fes', v.t.* to acknowledge fully, esp. something wrong: to own or admit: to make known, as sins to a priest: to hear confession from, as a priest.—*v.i.* to make confession.—*ns.* **confess'ion,** acknowledgment of a crime or fault: a thing confessed: a statement of religious belief: acknowledgment of sin to a priest; **confess'ional,** the seat or recess where a priest hears confessions.—*adj.* pertaining to confession or to a creed.—*n.* **confess'or,** a priest who hears confessions and grants absolution: one who makes avowal, esp. of religious faith and particularly of belief in Christ.—*adj.* **confessed'**, admitted, avowed.—*adv.* **confessedly** (*kon-fes'id-li*)—**confession of faith,** the creed of a church or sect.—**stand confessed,** to be revealed. [Fr. *confesser*—L. *confitēri, confessus—con-,* signifying completeness, and *fatēri,* to confess.]

confetti, *kon-fet'tē, n.pl.* sweetmeats: plaster or paper imitations of them flung in carnival: (*kon-fet'*) bits of coloured paper thrown at bride and bridegroom. [It. (sing. *confetto*); cf. **comfit, confection.**]

confide, *kon-fīd', v.i.* to trust wholly or have faith (with *in*): to impart secrets with trust.—*v.t.* to entrust (to one's care): to impart with reliance upon secrecy.—*ns.* **confidant'**, one to whom secrets are confided: a bosom friend:—*fem.* **confidante'; con'fidence,** firm trust, belief, or expectation: admission to knowledge of private affairs, &c.: a confidential communication: self-reliance: boldness, impudence.—*adj.* **con'fident,** trusting firmly: positive: bold.—*adv.* **con'fidently.**—*adj.* **confiden'tial,** confided (e.g. information): entrusted with secrets (e.g. *confidential secretary*): secret-service (*confidential agent*).—*adv.* **confiden'tially.**—**confidence trick,** a swindler's trick, whereby a person is induced to hand over money as a mark of confidence in the swindler. [L. *confidĕre—con-,* inten., *fidĕre,* to trust.]

configuration, *kon-fig-ū-rā'sh(ò)n, n.* external figure or shape, outline: relative position or aspect, as of planets: the spatial arrangement of atoms in a molecule. [L. *configūrātiō—con-,* together, and *figurāre,* to form—*figūra,* shape. Cf. **figure.**]

confine, *kon'fīn, n.* border, boundary, or limit—generally in *pl.*—*v.t.* (*kon-fīn'*) to limit: to imprison.—*adj.* **confīn'able.**—*n.* **confine'ment,** state of being shut up: restraint: imprisonment: restraint from going out by sickness, and esp. of women in childbirth.—**be confined,** to be limited: to be in childbed. [Fr. *confiner*—L. *confīnis,* bordering—*con-,* together, *fīnis,* the end.]

confirm, *kon-fûrm', v.t.* to strengthen, to establish more firmly: to make (a person) more firm (e.g. in belief, habit): to ratify: to corroborate: to verify: to admit to full communion.—*n.* **confirmā'tion,** a making firm or sure: convincing proof: the rite by which persons are admitted to full communion by a bishop in episcopal churches.—*adjs.* **confirm'ative,** tending to confirm; **confirm'atory,** giving further proof, confirmative, corroborative; **confirmed',** settled, inveterate. [O.Fr. *confermer*—L. *confirmāre—con-,* inten., and *firmāre—firmus,* firm.]

confiscate, *kon'fis-kāt,* or *-fis'-, v.t.* to appropriate to the state as a penalty: to seize by authority.—*adj.* forfeited to the state.—*adjs.* **confis'cable; confis'catory** (or *kon'-*), effecting, of the nature of, characterised by, confiscation.—*ns.* **confiscā'tion,** act of confiscating: state of being confiscated; **con'fiscator.** [L. *confiscāre, -ātum—con-,* together, *fiscus,* the state treasury.]

conflagration, *kon-fla-grāsh'(ò)n, n.* a great burning or fire. [L. *conflagrāre—con-,* inten., and *flagrāre,* to burn.]

conflict, *kon'flikt, n.* violent collision: a struggle or contest: a mental struggle.—*v.i.* (*kon-flikt'*) to fight, contend: to be in opposition: to clash.—*adj.* **conflict'ing,** clashing: contradictory. [L. *conflīgĕre—con-,* together, and *flīgĕre,* to strike.]

confluence, *kon'flōō-éns, n.* a flowing together: the place of meeting, as of rivers: a concourse.—*adj.* **con'fluent,** flowing together: uniting.—*n.* a stream uniting and flowing with another.—*adv.* **con'fluently.**—*n.* **con'flux,** a flowing together. [L. *confluĕre, confluxum,* from *con-,* together, *fluĕre,* to flow.]

conform, *kon-förm', v.i.* to be or become of the same form: to comply with (with *to*).—*v.t.* to make (something) like (to): to adapt.—*adj.* **conform'able,** corresponding in form: suitable: compliant.—*adv.* **conform'ably.**—*ns.* **conformā'tion,** particular form, shape, or structure: adaptation; **conform'er, conform'ist,** one who conforms, esp. with the worship of the established church; **conform'ity,** likeness: compliance: consistency.—**conformation theory,** the theory of the structure of molecules, particularly of the arrangement of atoms in very complex molecules. [L. *conformāre—con-,* with, *formāre—forma,* form.]

confound, *kon-fownd', v.t.* to mingle so as to make the parts indistinguishable: to confuse, fail to distinguish between: to throw into disorder: to defeat: to discomfit: to perplex: to astonish.—*p.adj.* **confound'ed,** confused: astonished; (*coll.*) abominable, horrible.—*adv.* **confound'edly.—confound you,** a mild execration. [O.Fr. *confondre*—L. *confundĕre,* -*fūsum*—*con*-, together, *fundĕre,* to pour.]

confraternity, *kon-fra-tûr'ni-ti, n.* a brotherhood. [L. *con*-, intensive, and **fraternity.**]

confrère, *kō-frer, n.* a colleague: a fellow-member or associate. [Fr.,—L. *con*-, together, *frāter,* a brother.]

confront, *kon-frunt', v.t.* to stand in front of: to face in a hostile manner: to oppose: to bring face to face: to compare.—*n.* **confrontā'tion.** [Fr. *confronter,* through Low L.—L. *con*-, together, *frons, frontis,* forehead.]

Confucian, *kon-fū'shyän, adj.* of or belonging to *Confucius,* the Chinese philosopher (551-479 B.C.).

confuse, *kon-fūz', v.t.* to pour or mix together so that things cannot be distinguished: to throw into disorder: to perplex: to fail to distinguish.—*adj.* **confused',** perplexed: abashed: disordered.—*adv.* **confus'edly.—n. confū'sion,** disorder: a mixing up in thought or in statement: overthrow: perplexity: embarrassment. [A doublet of **confound.**]

confute, *kon-fūt', v.t.* to prove to be false (e.g. an argument), to refute: to prove (a person) to be wrong.—*adj.* **confūt'able.—n. confutā'tion.** [L. *confutāre.*]

conga, *kong'ga, n.* a dance of Cuban origin in which dancers follow a leader, usu. in single file: music for it. [Amer. Sp., Congo.]

congé, *kō'zhā,* **congee,** *kon'ji, n.* a bow: dismissal: leave to depart. [Fr. *congé*—L. *commeātus,* leave of absence—*com*-, together, *meāre,* to go.]

congeal, *kon-jēl', v.t.* to freeze: to change from fluid to solid by cold: to solidify, as by cold.—*v.i.* to freeze: to stiffen: to coagulate.—*adj.* **congeal'able.—ns. congeal'ment, congelā'tion,** act or process of congealing. [L. *congelāre,* from *con*-, and *gelu,* frost.]

congener, *kon'je-ner, n.* a person or thing of the same kind or nature. [L.,—*con*-, with, and *genus, generis,* kind.]

congenial, *kon-jē'ni-äl, adj.* of the same nature or tastes, kindred, sympathetic: in accordance with one's tastes: agreeable (to).—*n.* **congēnial'ity.—adv. congē'nially.** [L. *con*-, with, *geniālis,* genial. See **genial.**]

congenital, *kon-jen'i-täl, adj.* begotten or born with a person, said of diseases or deformities dating from birth.—*adv.* **congen'itally.** [L. *congenitus,* from *con*-, together, *gignĕre, genitum,* to beget.]

conger, *kong'gér, n.* a large sea fish of the eel family. [L.,—Gr. *gongros.*]

congeries, *kon-jûrí-ēz, n.* an aggregation, a mass. [L.,—*con*-, together, *gerĕre, gestum,* to bring.]

congest, *kon-jest', v.t.* to pack closely: to cause congestion in.—*v.i.* to accumulate excessively.—*adj.* **congest'ed,** affected with an unnatural accumulation of blood: overcrowded.—*n.* **congest'ion,** an accumulation of blood in any part of the body: an overcrowded condition: an accumulation caus ng obstruction.—*adj.* **congest'ive,** indicating or tending

to congestion. [L. *congerĕre, congestum*—*con*-, together, and *gerĕre, gestum,* to bring.]

conglob'ate, *kon-glōb'āt, adj.* formed into a globe or ball.—*v.t.* to form into a globe or ball.—*n.* **conglobā'tion.—v.i. conglob'ūlate,** to gather into a globule or small globe. [L. *con*-, together, and *globāre,* -*ātum*—*globus,* a ball, globe.]

conglomerate, *kom-glom'ér-āt, adj.* gathered into a rounded mass.—*v.t.* and *v.i.* to gather into a ball.—*n.* (*geol.*) gravel cemented into a compact and coherent mass.—*n.* **conglomerā'tion,** state of being conglomerated: a collection (of things of mixed kind or origin). [L. *conglomerāre,* -*ātum*—*con*-, together, and *glomus, glomeris,* a ball of yarn.]

conglutinate, *kon-glōō'tin-āt, v.t.* to stick together with glue or with a glutinous substance.—*v.i.* to unite or grow together.—*adj.* **conglu'tinant.—n. conglutinā'tion.—adj. conglu'tinātive.** [L. *conglūtināre,* -*ātum*—*con*-, together, and *glūten,* glue.]

Congoese, *kong'gō-ēz,* **Congolese,** *kong'gō-lēz, ns.* (*sing.* and *pl.*) a native, or natives, of the Congo.

congratulate, *kon-grat'ū-lāt, v.t.* to express pleasure in sympathy with, to felicitate: to deem happy (esp. *reflex.*).—*n.* **congratulā'tion,** act of congratulating: an expression of joyful sympathy.—*adj.* **congrat'ulatory,** expressing congratulations. [L. *congrātulāri,* -*ātus*—*con*-, inten., *grātulāri*—*grātus,* pleasing.]

congregate, *kong'grē-gāt, v.t.* to gather together, to assemble.—*v.i.* to flock together.—*n.* **congregā'tion,** an assemblage of persons or things: a body of people united to worship in a particular church.—*adj.* **congregā'tional,** pertaining to a congregation.—*ns.* **Congregā'tionalism,** a form of church government in which each congregation is independent in the management of its own affairs—also called *Independency:* **Congregā'tionalist,** an adherent of Congregationalism, an *Independent.* [L. *congregāre,* -*ātum*—*con*-, together, and *grex, gregis,* a flock.]

congress, *kong'gres, n.* the act of meeting together: an assembly of diplomats or delegates: (*cap.*) the federal legislature of the United States and of some other American republics.—*adj.* **congressional** (*kon-gresh'-ōn-äl*).—*n.* **Con'gressman,** a member of U.S. Congress, esp. of the House of Representatives (q.v.) [L. *con*-, together, and *gradī, gressus,* to step, to go.]

congruence, *kong'grōō-ens,* **congruency,** *kong'-grōō-en-si, ns.* agreement: suitableness.—*adj.* **cong'ruent,** agreeing: suitable: of two geometrical figures, coincident at all points when one is superimposed on the other.—*n.* **congru'ity,** agreement, harmony, consistency: fitness.—*adj.* **cong'ruous,** suitable: consistent (with).—*adv.* **cong'ruously.—n. cong'ruousness.** [L. *congruĕre,* to run together.]

conic, -al; conics. See **cone.**

Coniferae, *kon-if'ér-ē, n.pl.* a group of plants, including pines, firs, &c., which bear cones in which the seed is contained.—*n.* **con'ifer,** one of the Coniferae.—*adj.* **conif'erous,** cone-bearing, as the fir, &c. [**cone,** and L. *ferre,* to bear.]

Neutral vowels in unaccented syllables: *em'pér-ór*; for certain sounds in foreign words see p. ix.

coniform. See **cone.**

conjecture, *kon-jek'tyúr, n.* an opinion formed on slight or defective evidence: the act of forming such: a guess.—*v.t.* to infer on slight evidence: to guess.—*adj.* **conjec'tural.**—*adv.* **conjec'turally.** [L. *conjicĕre, conjectum,* to throw together—*con-,* together, and *jacĕre,* to throw.]

conjoin, *kon-join', v.t.* to join together.—*adj.* **conjoint',** united (e.g. *conjoint efforts*).—*adv.* **conjoint'ly.** [Fr. *conjoindre*—L. *conjungĕre*—*con-,* together, and *jungĕre, junctum,* to join.]

conjugal, *kon'jōō-gál, adj.* pertaining to marriage.—*adv.* **con'jugally.** [L. *conjugālis*—*con-ju(n)x,* a spouse—*con-,* and *jugum,* a yoke.]

conjugate, *kon'jōō gāt, v.t.* (*gram.*) to give the various inflections or parts of a verb: to couple, unite.—*adj.* (*-át*) joined, connected.—*n.* a word agreeing in derivation with another word.—*n.* **conjugā'tion,** the act of joining: union: (*gram.*) the inflection of the verb: a class of verbs inflected in the same manner. [L. *conjugāre, -ātum*—*con-,* together, and *jugāre*—*jugum,* a yoke.]

conjunct, *kon-junkt', adj.* conjoined.—*ns.* **conjunc'tion,** connection, union: (*gram.*) a word that connects sentences, clauses, and words: one of the aspects of the sun, moon, or planets when two of these bodies have the same celestial longitude (cf. *opposition*); **conjuncti'va,** the modified epedermis of the front of the eye; **conjunctivītis,** inflammation of the conjunctiva.—*adj.* **conjunc'tive,** serving to unite: (*gram.*) introduced by, or of the nature of, a conjunction.—*adv.* **conjunc'tively.**—*n.* **conjunc'ture,** combination of circumstances: important occasion, crisis. [L. *conjunctus*—*conjungĕre.* See **conjoin.**]

conjure, *kun'jér* and *kon'jōōr* (*kun'jér,* generally of the art of legerdemain, &c.; *kon'jōōr,* of actions treated as religious or solemn), *v.i.* to practise magical arts.—*v.t.* (*obs.*) to invoke by a sacred name or in a solemn manner: to compel (a spirit) by incantation: to implore earnestly: to call before the imagination: to effect by magic or jugglery:—*pr.p.* con'juring; *pa.p.* con'jured.—*ns.* **conjura'tion,** act of summoning by a sacred name or solemnly: enchantment; **con'jurer, -or,** one who practises magic: a juggler; **conju'ror,** one bound by oath with others. [Fr.—L. *con-,* together, and *jurāre,* to swear.]

conn. See **con** (3).

connate, *kon'āt, adj.* inborn, innate.—**connate water,** water which has been trapped in sediments since their deposition. [L. *con-,* with, and *nascī, nātus,* to be born.]

connect, *kon-ekt', v.t.* to tie or fasten together: to establish a relation between: to associate in the mind.—Also *v.i.*—*adj.* **connect'ed,** linked: related: coherent.—*adv.* **connect'edly,** in a connected manner.—*n.* **connec'tion, connex'ion,** act of connecting: that which connects: a body or society held together by a bond: coherence: opportunity of change of trains, buses, &c.: intercourse: context: a relative.—*adj.* **connect'ive,** binding together.—*n.* a word that connects sentences and words.— **connecting-rod,** in a reciprocating-engine or pump, the rod connecting the piston or cross-

head to the crank; **connective tissue,** a group of animal tissues supporting and holding together—as bone, cartilage, ligaments. [L. *con-,* and *nectĕre, nexum,* to tie.]

conning-tower. See **con** (3).

connive, *kon-īv', v.i.* to wink (at a fault): to give tacit consent, to be an accomplice.—*n.* **conniv'ance.** [Fr.,—L. *connīvēre,* to wink.]

connoisseur, *kon-es-ûr', or kon-is-ûr', n.* one who has knowledge, an expert critic of art, music, &c.—*n.* **connoisseur'ship,** the skill of a connoisseur. [Fr. (now *connaisseur*)—*con-noître* (*connaître*)—L. *cognoscĕre,* to know.]

connote, *kon-ōt', v.t.* to signify secondarily: to imply as inherent attributes: to include.—*v.t.* **conn'otate,** to connote.—*n.* **connotā'tion,** the sum of attributes implied by a term: what is implied in a word or suggested by it beyond its recognised simple meaning.—*adj.* **conn'otative** (or *-nōt'a-tiv*). [L. *con-,* with, *notāre,* to mark.]

connubial, *kon-ū'bi-ál, adj.* pertaining to marriage.—*adv.* **connu'bially.** [L. *con-,* with, and *nubĕre,* to marry.]

conoid, *kōn'oid, n.* anything like a cone in form.—*adjs.* **con'oid, conoid'al.** [Gr. *kōnos,* a cone, *eidos,* form.]

conquer, *kong'kér, v.t.* to gain by force: to overcome or vanquish.—*v.i.* to be victor.—*adj.* **con'querable,** that may be conquered.—*ns.* **con'queror,** a victor: **conquest** (*kong'-kwest*), the act of conquering: that which is conquered or acquired by physical or moral force. [O.Fr. *conquerre*—L. *conquīrĕre*—*con-,* inten., *quaerĕre,* to seek.]

conquistador, *kong-kēs'ta-dōr, dōr, or kon-kwis'-, n.* one of the Spanish conquerors of Mexico and Peru:—*pl.* **-dors, -dores** (*-dōr'es*). [Sp.,—L. *conquīrĕre;* see **conquer.**]

consanguine, *kon-sang'gwin, adj.* related by blood, of the same family or descent—also **consanguin'eous.**—*n.* **consanguin'ity,** relationship by blood, opposed to affinity or relationship by marriage. [L. *consanguineus*—*con-,* with, *sanguis,* blood.]

conscience, *kon'shéns, n.* the knowledge, or the consciousness, of our own acts and feelings as right or wrong: scrupulousness, conscientiousness: scruple, compunction.—*adj.* **conscientious** (*-shi-ensh'-*), regulated by a regard to conscience: scrupulous.—*adv.* **conscien'tiously.**—*n.* **conscien'tiousness.**— **conscience clause,** a clause in a law relieving from its application those whose conscience forbids them to obey it; **conscience money,** money given to relieve the conscience, by discharging a claim previously evaded; **conscientious objector,** one who objects on grounds of conscience, esp. to military service.—**good,** or **bad, conscience,** an approving or reproving conscience; **in all conscience,** certainly. [Fr.,—L. *conscientia,* knowledge—*conscīre,* to know well.]

conscious, *kon'shús, adj.* having awareness or knowledge (of): aware (that): unduly aware: awake mentally: deliberate, intentional.—*adv.* **con'sciously.**—*n.* **con'sciousness,** the totality of mental states and processes (perceptions, feelings, thoughts), mind in its widest sense: awareness: the waking state of the mind. [L.

conscius—conscīre, to know well, be conscious of (wrong).]

conscript, *kon'skript*, *adj.* enrolled, registered.—*n.* one enrolled and liable to serve in the armed forces or otherwise, as directed by the state.—*v.t.* (*kon-script'*) to enlist compulsorily.—*n.* **conscrip'tion**, a compulsory enrolment for service of the state.—*adj.* **conscrip'tional** (*-sh(ó)n-ál*).—**conscript fathers** (L. *patres conscripti*), the senators of ancient Rome. [L. *conscrībĕre, conscriptum,* to enrol.]

consecrate, *kon'se-krāt*, *v.t.* to set apart for a holy use: to devote: to render holy or venerable.—*n.* **consecrā'tion**. [L. *consecrāre, -ātum,* to make wholly sacred.]

consecution, *kon-se-kū'sh(ó)n*, *n.* a train of consequence or deductions: a series of things that follow one another.—*adj.* **consec'utive**, following in regular order: (*gram.*) expressing consequence.—*adv.* **consec'utively**.—*n.* **consec'utiveness**. [L. *consequī—con-*, and *sequī, secūtus*, to follow.]

consensus, *kon-sen'sus*, *n.* co-operation (of different bodily organs): unanimity: (loosely) trend (of opinion). [L. *consentīre.* See **consent**.]

consent, *kon-sent'*, *v.i.* (*arch.*) to be of the same mind: to agree to give assent (to).—*n.* agreement, concurrence.—*adjs.* **consentā'neous**, agreeable (to), consistent (with): unanimous; **consen'tient** (*-shént*), agreeing in opinion.—**age of consent**, the age at which a person is legally competent to give consent to certain acts, esp. marriage, sexual intercourse; **with one consent**, unanimously. [L. *consentire—con-*, with, *sentīre*, to feel, to think.]

consequence, *kon'si-kwéns*, *n.* that which follows or comes after as a result, or as an inference: importance: social standing.—*adj.* **con'sequent**, following, esp. as a natural effect or deduction.—*n.* the natural effect of a cause: the second number in a ratio.—*adv.* **con'sequently**.—*adj.* **consequen'tial** (*-shál*), following as a result: self-important.—*adv.* **consequen'tially**. [Fr.,—L. *consequī—con-*, together, and *sequī*, to follow.]

conserve, *kon-sûrv'*, *v.t.* to keep entire: to keep from damage or loss: (*obs.*) to preserve in sugar.—*n.* something preserved, as fruits in sugar.—*adj.* **conser'vable**.—*ns.* **conser'vancy**, a board having authority to preserve the fisheries, &c., on a river: the act of preserving, esp. official care of a river, forest, &c.; **conservā'tion**, act of conserving (as old buildings, flora and fauna, environment); **conservā'tionist**, one interested in conservation; **conser'vatism**, the opinions and principles of a Conservative: dislike of innovation.—*adj.* **conser'vative**, tending or having power to conserve: (loosely) moderately estimated, understated. —*n.* (*politics—cap.*) one of the party that desires to preserve the institutions of the country against innovation (official name since 1830—see *Tory*): one averse to change.—*ns.* **conser'vativeness; conservatoire** (*kon-sér-vä-twär'*), **conservatō'rium**, a school in which the best traditions of musical training are preserved; **con'servātor** (or *kon-sûr'va-tór*), one who preserves from injury, a custodian; **conser'vatory**, a storehouse: a

greenhouse or place in which exotic plants are kept: a conservatoire; **conser'ver.—conservation of energy**, the law that in any isolated system the total amount of energy is constant. [L. *conservāre—con-*, together, and *servāre*, to keep.]

consider, *kon-sid'ér*, *v.t.* (*arch.*) to look at carefully: to think or deliberate on: to weigh advantages and disadvantages, with a view to action (e.g. *to consider going abroad*): to take into account: to show regard or consideration for: to believe, think.—*v.i.* to think seriously or carefully, to deliberate.—*adj.* **consid'erable**, worthy of being considered: important: more than a little.—*n.* **consid'erableness**.—*adv.* **consid'erably**.—*adj.* **consid'erāte**, serious: prudent: mindful of the feelings or claims of others.—*adv.* **consid'erately**.—*ns.* **consid'erateness**, thoughtfulness for others; **considerā'tion**, deliberation: motive, reason, inducement, argument for or against: a taking into account: importance: compensation or reward: considerateness.—*prep.* **consid'ering**, in view of.—*conj.* seeing that.—**in consideration of**, in return for. [Fr.,—L. *consīderāre*, supposed to have been orig. a term of augury—*con-*, and *sīdus, sīderis*, a star.]

consign, *kon-sīn'*, *v.t.* (*obs.*) to sign or seal: to entrust: to commit (to): to transmit, send by rail, &c.—*ns.* **consignee'**, one to whom anything is consigned or sent; **consign'er; consign'ment**, the act of consigning: the thing consigned: a set of things consigned together. [Fr.,—L. *consignāre*, to attest.]

consist, *kon-sist'*, *v.i.* (*arch.*) to exist: (*arch.*) to co-exist: to be composed (of): to be comprised (in), or to be essentially: to agree, be consistent (with).—*ns.* **consist'ence, consist'ency**, degree of density: coherence: agreement.—*adj.* **consist'ent**, (*obs.*) fixed: not fluid: agreeing together, compatible: true to one's principles.—*adv.* **consist'ently**, uniformly, invariably: in accordance (with).—*n.* **con'sistory** (or *kon-sist'-*), an assembly or council: a spiritual or ecclesiastical court.—*adj.* **consistō'rial**. [L. *consistĕre—con-*, together, *sistĕre*, to stand.]

consociate, *kon-sō'shi-āt*, *v.t.* and *v.i.* to associate together.—*n.* **consociation** (*kon-sō-shi-ā'sh(ó)n*). [L. *consociāre, -ātum—con-*, with, *sociāre*. See **sociable**.]

console, *kon-sōl'*, *v.t.* to give solace or comfort to.—*adj.* **consol'able**, that may be comforted.—*ns.* **consolā'tion**, solace: alleviation of misery; **consolā'tion-match, -prize, -race**, &c., a match, prize, race, &c., in or for which only those who have been previously unsuccessful may compete.—*adj.* **consol'atory**, offering, or giving, consolation.—*n.* **consol'er**. [L. *con-*, inten., and *sōlārī*, to comfort.]

console, *kon'sōl*, *n.* a bracket to support cornices: the key-desk of an organ: a large radio or television set standing on the floor: a panel or cabinet with dials, switches, &c., control unit of an electrical, electronic, or mechanical system. [Fr. *console*; prob. conn. with **consolidate**.]

consolidate, *kon-sol'i-dāt*, *v.t.* to make solid: to strengthen: to merge, combine.—*v.i.* to grow solid or firm: to unite.—*n.* **consolidā'tion**, act of consolidating: strengthening. [L. *consoli-*

dāre, *-ātum*—*con-*, inten., and *solidus*, solid.]

consols, *kon'solz*, or *kon-solz'*, *n.pl.* (short for **consolidated annuities**) that part of the British national debt which consists of several stocks consolidated into one fund.

consommé, *kǒ-som-ā'*, *n.* a kind of clear meat soup. [Fr.,—L. *consummāre*, to consummate.]

consonant, *kon'son-ànt*, *adj.* consistent (with, to): harmonious (opposite of *dissonant*).—*n.* an articulation that can be sounded only with a vowel: a letter of the alphabet representing such a sound.—*ns.* **con'sonance**, a state of agreement: agreement or unison of sounds; **con'sonancy**, harmony.—*adj.* **consonant'al**, pertaining to a consonant—*adv.* **con'sonantly**, consistently, harmoniously. [L. *consonans*, *-antis*, pr.p. of *consonāre*, to harmonise—*con-*, with, and *sonāre*, to sound.]

consort, *kon'sórt*, *n.* a partner, companion, esp. a wife or husband: an accompanying ship.—*v.i.* **consort'**, to associate or keep company: to agree.—*n.* **consortium** (*kon-sör'ti-um*, or *-shi-um*), an international banking or financial combination.—**in consort**, in company: in harmony. [L. *consors*, *consortis*, from *con-*, with, *sors*, a lot.]

conspectus, *kon-spek'tus*, *n.* a comprehensive survey: a synopsis. [L. *conspectus*—*conspicĕre*, to look at.]

conspicuous, *kon-spik'ū-us*, *adj.* catching the eye (*lit.* and *fig.*), noticeable.—*n.* **conspic'uousness**.—*adv.* **conspic'uously**. [L. *conspicuus*—*conspicĕre*—*con-*, inten., *specĕre*, to look.]

conspire, *kon-spīr'*, *v.i.* to plot or scheme together: to co-operate (towards one end).—*v.t.* to plot.—*ns.* **conspir'acy**, a secret union for an evil purpose: a plot: joint action, concurrence; **conspir'ator**, one who conspires.—*adj.* **conspirato'rial**, like a conspirator. [L. *conspīrāre*—*con-*, together, *spīrāre*, to breathe.]

constable, *kun'sta-bl*, or *kon'sta-bl*, *n.* formerly a state-officer of the highest rank: a policeman.—*n.* **constab'ulary**, an organised body of constables *adj.* of or pertaining to constables.—**outrun the constable**, to go too fast: to get into debt; **special constable**, a citizen enrolled to act as a police-constable on special occasions. [O.Fr. *conestable*—L. *comes stabulī*, count of the stable.]

constant, *kon'stànt*, *adj.* fixed: unchangeable: faithful: continual.—*n.* (*math.*) a quantity that remains fixed in value—opp. to a *variable*.—*n.* **con'stancy**, fixedness: unchangeableness: faithfulness.—*adv.* **con'stantly**, firmly: continually. [L. *constans*, *-antis*, from *constāre*, to stand firm—*con-*, inten., *stāre*, to stand.]

constellation, *kon-stel-ā'sh(ó)n*, *n.* a group of stars: an assemblage of brilliant persons: (*astrol.*) a particular disposition of the planets. [L. *constellātus*, studded with stars—*con-*, with, *stellāre*—*stella*, a star.]

consternation, *kon-stér-nā'sh(ó)n*, *n.* astonishment, dismay, panic. [L. *consternāre*, *-ātum*, from *con-*, wholly, *sternĕre*, to strew.]

constipate, *kon'stip-āt*, *v.t.* to stop up, to make costive.—*n.* **constipa'tion**, costiveness. [L. *con-*, together, *stīpāre*, *-ātum*, to pack.]

constitute, *kon'stit-ūt*, *v.t.* to set up, to establish: to appoint: to form, make up, be equivalent to.—*n.* **constit'uency**, the electors, or the community, represented by a member of parliament or other elected representative.—*adj.* **constit'uent**, constituting or forming: essential, elemental: electing: constitution-making. —*n.* an essential or elemental part: one of those who elect a representative, esp. in parliament.—*n.* **constitu'tion**, the natural condition of body or mind: disposition: structure: the rules adopted by a society for the conduct of its affairs: the established form of government: a particular law or usage: (*chem.*) molecular structure, taking into account not only the kind and numbers of atoms but the way in which they are linked.—*adj.* **constitu'tional**, inherent in the natural frame, natural: agreeable to the constitution or frame of government, legal: reigning subject to fixed laws.—*n.* a walk for the sake of one's health.—*n.* **constitu'tion(al)ist**, a student of political constitutions: a supporter of constitutional government or of a particular constitution.—*adv.* **constitu'tionally**.—*adj.* **con'stitutive**, that constitutes or establishes: having power to constitute: component. [L. *constituĕre*, *constitūtum*, from *con-*, together, and *statuĕre*, to make to stand, to place.]

constrain, *kon-strān'*, *v.t.* to force, compel: to confine, imprison (*lit.* and *fig.*).—*p.adj.* **constrained'**, forced, not natural, embarrassed.—*n.* **constraint'**, compulsion: confinement: a reserved or embarrassed manner. [O.Fr. *constraindre*—L. *constringĕre*—*con-*, together, *stringĕre*, to press.]

constrict, *kon-strikt'*, *v.t.* to press together, to cramp: to cause to contract.—*n.* **constric'tion**, a pressing together: tightness.—*adj.* **constrict'ive**.—*n.* **constrict'or**, that which constricts or draws together: the boa-constrictor (q.v.). [L. *constringĕre*, *constrictum*.]

constringe, *kon-strinj'*, *v.t.* to draw together: to cause to contract.—*adj.* **constrin'gent**, having the quality of contracting. [L. *constringĕre*.]

construct, *kon-strukt'*, *v.t.* to build up: to put together the parts of: (*fig.*) to compose: to draw.—*ns.* **construct'or**; **construc'tion**, the act of constructing: anything piled together, building: manner of forming: (*gram.*) the syntactic relations of words in a sentence: meaning, interpretation (e.g. of conduct).—*adjs.* **construc'tional**, pertaining to construction; **construct'ive**, capable of, or tending towards, constructing—opposite of *destructive*: not direct or expressed, but inferred (e.g. *constructive permission*).—*adv.* **construct'ively**.—*n.* **construct'iveness**, the faculty of constructing; **construct'ivism**, a non-representational style of art, using man-made industrial materials and processes such as welding.—**bear a construction**, to allow of a particular interpretation; **put a construction on**, to explain, interpret in a particular way. [L. *construĕre*, *-structum*—*con-*, together, *struĕre*, to build.]

construe, *kon'strōō*, or *kon-strōō'*, *v.t.* to elucidate grammatically: to translate literally: to interpret.—*v.i.* to admit of grammatical analysis. [L. *construĕre*, *constructum*, to build.]

consubstantial, *kon-sub-stan'shàl*, *adj.* of the same substance, nature, or essence, esp. of the

---

fāte, *fär*; *mē*, *hûr* (her); *mīne*, *mōte*, *för*; *mūte*; *mōōn*, *fŏŏt*; *ᴛʜen* (then)

Trinity.—*n.* **consubstantiā′tion** (*theol.*), the Lutheran doctrine of the actual, substantial presence of the body and blood of Christ co-existing in and with the bread and wine used at the Lord's Supper. [L. *con-*, with, and **substantial**.]

consuetude, *kon′swe-tūd*, *n.* custom: social intercourse.—*adj.* **consuetū′dinary**, customary.—*adj.* a ritual of customary devotions. [L. *consuetūdō*, custom.]

consul, *kon′sul*, *n.* one of the two chief magistrates in the Roman republic: an agent for a foreign government, appointed to attend to the interests of its citizens and to commerce.—*adj.* **con′sular**, pertaining to a consul.—*n.* a man of consular rank.—*ns.* **con′sulate**, the office, residence, or jurisdiction of a consul; **con′sulship**. [L.]

consult, *kon-sult′*, *v.t.* to ask advice or information of: to act in accordance with (e.g. wishes).—*v.i.* to consider in company: to take counsel: to give professional advice.—*n.* **consult′ant**, one who asks advice: one who gives professional advice; **consultā′tion**, deliberation, or a meeting for such, esp. of physicians or lawyers.—*adjs.* **consult′ative**, of or pertaining to consultation, esp. of persons who are entitled to speak at a consultation but not to vote; **consult′ing**, (of a physician or lawyer) who gives advice.—**consult′ing-room**, room in which a doctor sees a patient. [L. *consultāre*, inten. of *consulěre*, to consult.]

consume, *kon-sūm′*, *v.t.* to destroy by wasting, fire, &c.: to devour: to waste or spend.—*v.i.* to waste away.—*adj.* **consum′able**.—*n.* **consum′er**, (as opposed to *producer*) one who uses an article made by another.—**consumer(s′) goods**, goods to be used, without further manufacturing process, to satisfy human needs. [L. *consūměre*, to destroy—*con-*, signifying completeness, *sūměre*, sumptum, to take.]

consummate, *kon′sum-āt*, *v.t.* to complete or finish, esp. to complete (a marriage) by sexual inte.rcourse.—*adj.* **consumm′ate** (*-āt*), complete, supreme, perfect.—*adv.* **consumm′ately**.—*n.* **consummā′tion**, act of completing: perfection: the final issue or result. [L. *consummāre*, to perfect—*con-*, with, and *summa*, the sum.]

consumption, *kon-sum′sh(ō)n*, *n.* the act or process of consuming: the amount consumed: tuberculosis of the lungs.—*n.* **consumpt** (*kon′sum(p)t*, *kon-sum(p)t′*), quantity consumed.—*adj.* **consump′tive**, wasting away: inclined to tubercular disease.—*n.* one affected by consumption.—*adv.* **consump′tively**.—*n.* **consump′tiveness**, a tendency to consumption. [See **consume**.]

contact, *kon′takt*, *n.* touch (*lit.* and *fig.*): meeting: association: close proximity allowing passage of electric current or communication of disease: a place where electric current may be allowed to pass: a person who has been exposed to contagion: a person through whom one can get in touch (esp. secretly) with an individual or group, esp. with disreputable or criminal person(s): an influential acquaintance.—*v.t.* and *v.i.* to bring or come into touch, connection, with (esp. *fig.*).—*adj.* **con-**

tact′ual, pertaining to contact.—**contact flight**, navigation of an aircraft by observation of land or sea over which it is flying; **contact lens**, a lens, usu. of plastic material, worn in contact with the eyeball instead of spectacles; **contact man**, an intermediary in transactions, esp. shady ones. [L. *contingěre*, *contactum*, to touch—*con-*, wholly, *tangěre*, to touch.]

contadina, *kon-ta-dē′na*, *n.* an Italian peasant woman:—*pl.* **contadi′ne** (*-nā*), **-nas.** [It.]

contagion, *kon-tā′jon*, *n.* (transmission of a disease by) direct contact with an infected person or object: a contagious disease: a hurtful influence.—*adj.* **contā′gious**, communicable by contact.—*adv.* **contā′giously**.—*n.* **contā′giousness**. [L. *contagiō*, *-ōnis*—*con-*, together, *tangěre*, to touch.]

contain, *kon-tān′*, *v.t.* to have within, enclose: to comprise, include: to restrain: to keep (an enemy force) from moving.—*adj.* **contain′able**.—*n.* **contain′er**, a receptacle.—*v.t.* **contain′erise**, to put (freight) into standard sealed containers: to use such containers.—*n.* **contain′ment**, the act or policy of building up power against an enemy while hoping that differences may be settled without war. [Through Fr. from L. *continěre*, *contentum*—*con-*, together, *tenēre*, to hold.]

contaminate, *kon-tam′i-nāt*, *v.t.* to defile by touching or mixing (with): to pollute, corrupt, infect.—*n.* **contaminā′tion**, pollution. [L. *contāmināre*, *-ātum*—*contāmen* (for *contagmen*), pollution—root of *tangěre*. See **contact**.]

contango, *kon-tang′gō*, *n.* a percentage paid by the buyer to the seller of stock for keeping back its delivery to the next settling-day. [Formed from **continue**.]

conte, *kõt*, *n.* a short story (as a literary genre). [Fr.]

contemn, *kon-tem′*, *v.t.* to despise: to neglect.—*n.* **contem′ner**. [Fr.,—L. *contemněre*, *-temptum*, to value little—*con-*, inten., *temněre*, to slight.]

contemplate, *kon′tem-plāt*, *kon-tem′plāt*, *v.t.* to consider or look at attentively: to meditate on or study: to intend.—*v.i.* to think seriously, to meditate.—*n.* **contemplā′tion**, attentive study or observation.—*adj.* **con′templātive** (or *-tem′-plā-*), given to, concerned with, marked by, contemplation.—*adv.* **con′templatively**. [L. *contemplārī*, *-ātus*, to mark out a *templum* or place for auguries.]

contemporaneous, *kon-tem-po-rā′ne-us*, *adj.* living, happening, or being at the same time.—*adv.* **contemporā′neously**.—*n.* **contemporā′neousness**.—*adj.* **contem′porary**, contemporaneous: of the same age: present day (an inaccurate use), esp. up to date, fashionable.—*n.* one who lives at the same time: a newspaper or magazine of the same time. [L. *con-*, together, and *temporāneus*—*tempus*, time.]

contempt, *kon-tempt′*, *n.* scorn: disgrace: (*law*) disregard of the dignity (of a court).—*adj.* **contempt′ible**, despicable: mean.—*adv.* **contempt′ibly**.—*adj.* **contempt′uous**, haughty, scornful.—*adv.* **contempt′uously**.—*n.* **contempt′uousness**. [L. *contemptus*—*contemněre*. See **contemn**.]

contend, *kon-tend′*, *v.i.* to strive: to struggle in emulation or in position: to dispute or de-

Neutral vowels in unaccented syllables: *em′pėr-ȯr*; for certain sounds in foreign words see p. ix.

148

bate.—*v.t.* to maintain (that).—*n.* **conten'tion** (*-sh(ô)n*), a struggle to attain an object: strife: debate: an opinion maintained in debate.—*adj.* **conten'tious** (*-shŭs*), quarrelsome: involving dispute.—*adv.* **conten'tiously.**—*n.* **conten'tiousness.** [L. *contendēre, -tentum*—*con-*, with, *tendēre*, to stretch.]

content, *kon'tent,* or *kon-tent',* n. capacity or extent: (*pl.*) things contained: (*pl.*) the list of subjects treated of in a book. [O.Fr.—L. *contentus*, pa.p. of *continēre.* See **contain.**]

content, *kon-tent',* adj. satisfied: quietly happy.—*n.* satisfaction—often 'heart's content'.—*v.t.* to make content: to satisfy the mind: to quiet.—*adj.* **content'ed,** content.—*adv.* **content'edly.**—*ns.* **content'edness, content'ment.** [Fr.,—L. *contentus*, contained, hence satisfied—*con-*, *tenēre*, hold.]

conterminous, *kon-tér'min-us,* adj. having a common boundary: co-extensive (with).—Also **conter'minal.** [L. *conterminus*, neighbouring—*con-*, together, *terminus*, boundary.]

contest, *kon-test',* v.t. to call in question or make the subject of dispute: to contend for.—*n.* **con'test,** a struggle for superiority: strife: debate.—*adj.* **contest'able.**—*n.* **contest'ant,** one who contests. [Fr.,—L. *contestārī*, to call to witness—*con-*, and *testārī*, to be a witness.]

context, *kon'tekst,* n. the parts of a discourse or treatise that precede and follow a passage under consideration and may fix its meaning: associated surroundings, setting.—*n.* **contex'ture,** the interweaving of parts into a whole: the structure or system so made.—**in this context,** in these surroundings, in this particular connection. [L. *contextus*—*con-*, together, *texĕre*, *textum*, to weave.]

contiguous, *kon-tig'ū-us,* adj. touching, adjoining: near.—*ns.* **contigu'ity, contig'uousness.**—*adv.* **contig'uously.** [L. *contiguus*—*contingĕre*, to touch on all sides.]

continent, *kon'ti-nént,* n. a large extent of land not broken up by seas: one of the great divisions of the land surface of the globe: the mainland of Europe.—*adj.* restraining the indulgence of pleasure, esp. sexual, temperate.—*ns.* **con'tinence, con'tinency,** the restraint imposed by a person upon his desires and passions: chastity.—*adj.* **continent'al,** characteristic of a continent.—**continental shelf,** a gently sloping zone, under relatively shallow seas, offshore from a continent or island. [L. *continens, -entis*—*continēre*, to contain.]

contingent, *kon-tin'jént,* adj. dependent (on something else): liable but not certain to happen: accidental.—*n.* a quota or group, esp. of soldiers.—*ns.* **contin'gence, contin'gency,** quality of being contingent: an uncertain event.—*adv.* **contin'gently.** [L. *contingens, -entis*—*con-*, *tangĕre*, to touch.]

continue, *kon-tin'ū,* v.t. to draw out or prolong: to extend: to go on with: to resume.—*v.i.* to remain in the same place or state: to last or endure: to preserve.—*adj.* **contin'ual,** unceasing: very frequent.—*adv.* **contin'ually.**—*ns.* **contin'uance,** duration: uninterrupted succession: stay; **continuā'tion,** going on: constant succession: extension: resumption: a further instalment.—*adj.* **contin'uative,** continuing.—*n.* **contin'uātor,** one who continues (esp. a book begun by another).—*adj.* **contin'ued,** uninterrupted: unceasing: resumed: in instalments: extended.—*adv.* **contin'uedly.**—*ns.* **continū'ity,** state of being continuous: uninterrupted connection: a complete scenario of a motion picture; **continu'ity-wri'ter.**—*adj.* **contin'uous,** joined together without interruption.—*adv.* **contin'uously.**—*n.* **contin'uum,** that which must be regarded as continuous and the same and which can be described only relatively.—**space-time continuum,** physical space or reality, regarded as having four dimensions (length, breadth, height, and time), in which an event can be represented as a point fixed by four co-ordinates. [Fr.,—L. *continuāre*—*continuus*, joined, connected, from *continēre*.]

continuo, *kon-tēn'uō,* *kon-tin'ū-ō,* (in full, **bass continuo**), *n.* a modern term for a thoroughbass (q.v.). [It.]

contort, *kon-tört',* v.t. to twist or turn violently, distort.—*ns.* **contor'tion,** a violent twisting; **contor'tionist,** a gymnast who practises contorted postures. [L. *con*, inten., and *torquēre, tortum*, to twist.]

contour, *kon'tōōr,* or *kon-tōōr',* n. the outline: one of the lines bounding the figure of any object: artistic quality of outline.—**contour cultivation, farming, ploughing,** ploughing (and planting) of sloping land along the contour lines in an effort to prevent erosion; **contour line,** a line drawn on a map through all points at the same height above sea-level; **contour map,** a map in which the configuration of land is shown by contour lines. [Fr. *con,* and *tour,* a turning—L. *tornus,* a lathe.]

contra, *kon'tra,* prep. against.—*n.* an argument against (usu. **con**): the other side (of an account). [L. *contrā*.]

contraband, *kon'tra-band,* adj. excluded by law, prohibited.—*n.* illegal traffic: smuggled or prohibited goods.—**contraband of war,** goods which a belligerent may lawfully seize on the way to his enemy's country. [Sp. *contrabanda*—It. *contrabbando*—L. *contrā,* against, L.L. *bandum,* ban.]

contrabass, *kon'tra-bās,* n. the double-bass.—Also **contrabass'o** and **count'erbase.**

contraception, *kon-tra-sep'sh(ô)n,* n. prevention of conception.—*n.* **contracep'tive,** a means of contraception.—Also *adj.* [L. *contrā*, against, and Eng. **(con)ception.**]

contract, *kon-trakt',* v.t. to draw together: to lessen: to undertake by agreement: to incur (e.g. a debt): to form (e.g. a habit): to betroth.—*v.i.* to shrink, to become less: to bargain (for).—*n.* **con'tract,** an agreement on fixed terms: a bond: the writing containing an agreement: a betrothal.—*adjs.* **contract'ed,** drawn together: narrow: mean; capable of being contracted.—*ns.* **contractibil'ity, contract'ibleness.**—*adj.* **contract'ile** (or *-īl*), tending or having power to contract.—*ns.* **contractil'ity; contrac'tion,** act of contracting: a word shortened in speech or spelling.—*adj.* **contract'ive,** tending to contract.—*n.* **contract'or,** one of the parties to a bargain or agreement: one who engages to execute work or furnish supplies at a fixed rate.—**contract bridge**, a development of auction bridge in which tricks beyond the contracted number count only like honours; **contract out**, to make a bargain for exemption from an obligation. [L. *contractus*—*con*-, together, *trahĕre*, *tractum*, to draw.]

contra-dance. See **country-dance**.

contradict, *kon-tra-dikt'*, *v.t.* to assert the contrary of, to deny: to accuse (a person) of a misstatement: to be contrary to, inconsistent with.—*n.* **contradic'tion**, act of contradicting: denial: inconsistency.—*adjs.* **contradic'tive**, **contradict'ory**, affirming the contrary: inconsistent.—*n.* **contradict'oriness.**—*adj.* **contradic'tious** (*shŭs*), prone to contradict.—**contradiction in terms**, a group of words containing a contradiction. [L. *contrādīcĕre*, *-dictum.*]

contradistinction, *kon-tra-dis-tingk'sh(ŏ)n*, *n.* distinction by contrast.—*adj.* **contradistinct'ive.**—*v.t.* **contradistin'guish**, to contrast and mark the difference by opposite qualities. [L. *contrā*, against, and **distinction**.]

contrail, *kon'trāl*, *n.* a trail of condensed vapours left by a high-flying aircraft. [**con(densation)** and **trail**.]

contralto, *kon-tral'tō*, *n.* the lowest musical voice in women. [It. *contra*, against, *alto*, alto (q.v.).]

contraption, *kon-trap'sh(ŏ)n*, *n.* a contrivance. [Perh. arbitrarily from **contrive**.]

contrapuntal. See **counterpoint**.

contrary, *kon'tra-ri*, *adj.* opposite: contradictory: (*kon-trā'ri*), perverse.—*n.* a thing that is contrary or of opposite qualities.—*n.* **contrarī'ety**, opposition: inconsistency.—*adv.* **contrarily** (*kon'*- or *-trā'*-).—*n.* **contrariness** (*kon'*- or *-trā'*-).—*adv.* **con'trariwise**, on the other hand: vice versa; in the opposite way: perversely. [L. *contrārius*—*contrā*, against.]

contrast, *kon-träst'*, *v.i.* (with *with*) to stand in opposition to, show marked difference from.—*v.t.* to set in opposition, to compare.—*n.* (*kon'träst*) opposition or unlikeness in things compared: exhibition of differences: thing showing marked unlikeness (to another). [Fr. *contraster*—L. *contrā*, opposite to, *stāre*, to stand.]

contravallation, *kon-trä-val-ā'sh(ŏ)n*, *n.* a fortification built by besiegers against the place invested. [L. *contrā*, opposite, *vallāre*, *-ātum*, to fortify.]

contravene, *kon-tra-vēn'*, *v.t.* to oppose in argument: to infringe (a law).—*n.* **contraven'tion**. [L. *contrā*, against, *venīre*, to come.]

contretemps, *kõ-tr'-tä*, *n.* an untimely occurrence: a hitch. [Fr. *contre* (L. *contrā*), against, and *temps* (L. *tempus*), time.]

contribute, *kon-trib'ūt*, *v.t.* to give, along with others, for a common purpose: to furnish for publication.—*v.i.* to give a share: to furnish an item: to help to bring about (with *to*).—*n.* **contribū'tion**, the act of contributing: anything contributed.—*adjs.* **contrib'utive**, **contrib'utory**, giving a share: helping towards a result.—*n.* **contrib'utor**. [L. *con*-, with *tribuĕre*, *-ūtum*, to give, pay.]

contrite, *kon'trīt*, *adj.* broken-hearted for sin: showing penitence.—*adv.* **con'tritely.**—*ns.* **con'triteness**, **contri'tion**, state of being contrite: remorse. [L. *contrītus*—*conterĕre*—*con*-, wholly, *terĕre*, to rub, bruise.]

contrive, *kon-trīv'*, *v.t.* to plan: to invent: to manage: to effect (sometimes with difficulty or by artifice).—*n.* **contriv'ance**, act of contriving: the thing contrived: invention: artifice.—*adj.* **contrived**, having been contrived: artificial, over-elaborated.—*n.* **contriv'er.** [O.Fr. *controver*—*con*-, and *trover*, to find.]

control, *kon-trōl'*, *n.* restraint: authority, command: a lever or wheel for controlling movements: a means of controlling or testing: a place for doing so: an experiment performed to afford a standard of comparison for other experiments (aslo **control experiment**).—*v.t.* to check, verify: to restrain: to govern:—*pr.p.* **controll'ing**: *pa.p.* **controlled'.**—Formerly **comptroll'.**—*adj.* **controll'able.**—*ns.* **controll'er**, one who, or that which, controls, esp. one who checks the accounts of others (often **comptroll'er** in this sense); **control'ment**, act or power of controlling: state of being controlled: control.—**control room**, a room in which control instruments are placed, e.g. in a broadcasting station; **control tower**, a building at an aerodrome from which take-off and landing instructions are given. [Fr. *contrôle*, from *contre-rôle*, a duplicate register—L. *contrā*, against, *rotulus*, a roll.]

controvert, *kon'tro-vûrt* (or *-vûrt'*), *v.t.* to dispute about: to argue against, deny.—*adj.* **controvert'ible**, disputable.—*adv.* **controvert'ibly.**—*n.* **con'troversy** (or *-trov'*), a discussion of opposing views, esp. in print: contention, strife in words.—*adj.* **controver'sial** (*-shäl*), relating to controversy: open to dispute (e.g. a statement).—*n.* **controver'sialist**, one given to controversy.—*adv.* **controver'sially.** [L. *contrā*, against, and *vertĕre*, to turn.]

contumacious, *kon-tū-mā'shŭs*, *adj.* opposing lawful authority with contempt, obstinate, rebellious.—*adv.* **contumā'ciously.**—*ns.* **contumā'ciousness**, **con'tumacy**, obstinate disobedience or resistance. [L. *contumax*, *-ācis*, insolent—*con*-, and *tumēre*, to swell, or *temnēre*, to despise.]

contumely, *kon'tūm-li*, *n.* rudeness, scornful insolence, or reproach: disgrace.—*adj.* **contumē'lious**, haughtily reproachful: insolent.—*adv.* **contumē'liously.**—*n.* **contumē'liousness.** [L. *contumēlia*, prob. from the same source as *contumax*; see **contumacious**.]

contuse, *kon-tūz'*, *v.t.* to beat or bruise, to crush.—*n.* **contū'sion**, act of bruising: state of being bruised: a bruise. [L. *contundĕre*, *con*-, and *tundĕre*, to bruise.]

conundrum, *kon-un'drum*, *n.* a riddle turning on a play on words: any puzzling question.

conurbation, *kon-ûr-bā'sh(ŏ)n*, *n.* a group of towns, forming a single built-up area. [L. *con*-, together, *urbs*, a city.]

convalesce, *kon-val-es'*, *v.i.* to regain health.—*adj.* **convales'cent**, gradually recovering health.—*n.* one recovering health.—*n.* **convales'cence.** [L. *con*-, and *valescĕre*—*valēre*, to be strong.]

convection, *kon-vek'sh(ŏ)n*, *n.* transmission, esp. that of heat through fluids by means of currents due to the greater density of the colder parts: (*meteor.*) vertical movement, esp. upwards, of air or atmospheric conditions. [L. *convectiō*, *-ōnis*, a bringing

Neutral vowels in unaccented syllables: *em'pér-òr*; for certain sounds in foreign words see p. ix.

150

together—*con-*, and *vehĕre*, to carry.]
convenance, *kō'vé-näs*, *n.* propriety: (*pl.*)
etiquette, correct behaviour. [Fr.]
convene, *kon-vēn'*, *v.i.* to assemble.—*v.t.* to call
together.—*n.* **convēn'er**, one who convenes a
meeting: the chairman of a committee. [Fr.
convenir—L. *convenīre*, from *con-*, together,
and *venīre*, to come.]
convenient, *kon-vēn'yént*, *adj.* suitable: handy:
commodious: occasioning little or no trouble
(as, *it is convenient for me to go today*). -ns.
conven'ience, **conven'iency**, suitableness: an
advantage: material advantage (as, *marriage
of convenience*): any means or device for promoting ease or comfort.- *adv.* **conven'iently**.
—**convenience food**, food (partly) prepared
before sale so as to be ready, or almost ready,
for the table. [L. *conveniens, -entis-
convenīre*, to come together, to fit.]
convent, *kon'vent*, *n.* an association of persons
secluded from the world and devoted to a
religious life: the house in which they live, a
monastery or nunnery.—*adj.* **convent'ual**, he
longing to a convent.—*n.* a monk or nun.
[Through Fr. from L. *conventus*—*conventre,
conventum*, to come together.]
conventicle, *kon-vent'i-kl*, *n.* an illegal gathering, esp. the religious meetings held by non-
conformists and covenanters in the 17th century: any irregular meeting. [L. *conventi-
culum*, a secret meeting of monks, dim. of
conventus; see **convene**.]
convention, *kon-ven'sh(ó)n*, *n.* the act of con-
vening: an assembly, esp. of representatives
for some common object: a temporary treaty:
an agreement: established usage.—*adj.* **conven'tional**, formed by convention: customary:
bound or influenced by convention or tradition: not natural, spontaneous, or original.—
ns. **conven'tionalism**, that which is established by tacit agreement, as a mode of speech
&c.; **conventional'ity**, state of being conventional: that which is established by use or
custom.—*adv.* **conven'tionally**.—**conventional
arms**, weapons, without using nuclear
energy. [Fr.,—L. *conventiō, -ōnis-convenīre.
See **convene**.]
converge, *kon-vûrj'*, *v.i.* to tend towards, or meet
in, one point or value.—*ns.* **conver'gence**, **conver'gency**.—*adj.* **conver'gent**. [L. *con-*,
together, *vergēre*, to bend, incline.]
conversazione, *kon-vér-sat-se-ō'ne*, *n.* a meeting for conversation, particularly on literary
subjects:—*pl.* **conversaziō'nes**, or **conversaziō'ni** (*-nē*). [It.]
converse, *kon-vûrs'*, *v.i.* to talk familiarly.—*n.*
con'verse, familiar intercourse: conversation.—*adjs.* **convers'able**, disposed to converse: sociable; **con'versant**, acquainted by
study, familiar (with a subject, &c.).—*n.* **conversa'tion**, intercourse: talk, familiar discourse: (*B.*) behaviour or deportment.—*adj.*
conversa'tional.—*n.* **conversa'tionalist**, one
who excels in conversation.—**conversation
piece**, a painting of a number of persons,
grouped indoors or outside: a play, &c., in
which the dialogue is as important as, or more
important than, the action: an object that
arouses comment by its novelty. [Fr.,—L. *con-
versārī*, to live with.]

convert, *kon-vûrt'*, *v.t.* to change or turn from
one thing, condition, or religion to another: to
change from a sinful to a holy life: to alter
(into): to apply (to a particular purpose): to
exchange for an equivalent, as paper money
for specie.—*n.* **con'vert**, a converted person,
esp. one whose religious convictions have
been changed.—*adj.* **con'verse**, reversed in
order or relation.—*n.* that which is the opposite of another: a proposition in which the
subject and predicate have changed places.—
adv. **converse'ly**.—*ns.* **conver'sion** (*-sh(ó)n*),
change from one state, opinion, or religion to
another: the conscious change of heart in a
repentant sinner: appropriation to a special
purpose: (*logic*) act of interchanging the
terms of a proposition; **convert'er**, one who
converts: a vessel in which materials are
changed from one condition to another: an
apparatus for making a change in an electric
current (also **convertor**).-*adj.* **convert'ible**,
that may be converted: exchangeable at a
fixed price for gold or other currency.—*n.*
anything convertible: a car with a folding
top.—*adv.* **convert'ibly**.—*n.* **convertibil'ity**. [L.
convertĕre, conversum-con-, and *vertĕre*, to
turn.]
convex, *kon'veks*, also *kon-veks'*, *adj.* rising into
a round form on the outside, the reverse of
concave.—*n.* **convex'ity**, roundness of form on
the outside.—*adv.* **con'vexly** (or *-veks'-*). [L.
convexus-convehĕre, to carry together.]
convey, *kon-vā'*, *v.t.* to carry: to transmit: to
impart, communicate: to make over in
law—*ns.* **convey'er, -or** (also *adj.*); **convey'al:
convey'ance**, act of conveying: a vehicle of
any kind: (*law*) the act of transferring
property: the writing which transfers it; **convey'ancer**, a lawyer who effects transference
of property; **convey'ancing**.—**conveyor-belt**,
an endless belt of rubber, metal, &c., moving
continuously and thus transporting articles,
e.g. from one part of a building to another
(also *fig.*) [O.Fr. *conveier* (Fr. *convoyer*)—L.
con-, and *via*, a way.]
convict, *kon-vikt'*, *v.t.* to prove guilty: to pro
nounce guilty.—*n.* (*kon'vikt*) one convicted or
found guilty of crime, esp. one who has been
condemned to penal servitude.—*n.* **convic'-
tion**, act of convincing or convicting: strong
belief: consciousness (of sin).—**carry conviction**, to bear irresistibly the stamp of truth.
[Same root as **convince**.]
convince, *kon-vins'*, *v.t.* to overcome the doubts
of: to satisfy (as to truth or error): (*B.*) to
convict.—*adj.* **convinc'ible**.—*adv.* **convincingly**.—*n.* **conviction** (see **convict**). [L. *con-
vincĕre-con-*, signifying completeness, and
vincĕre, victum, to conquer.]
convivial, *kon-viv'i-ál*, *adj.* pertaining to a feast:
social, jovial.—*n.* **convivial'ity**.—*adv.* **con-
viv'ially**. [From L.—*convīvium*, a living
together, a feast—*con-*, together, *vīvĕre*, to
live.]
convoke, *kon-vōk'*, *v.t.* to call together, to assemble—also **con'vocāte**.—*n.* **convocā'tion**, act
of convoking: an ecclesiastical or academic
assembly, esp. a provincial synod of clergy in
the Church of England. [L. *convocāre-con-*,
together, *vocāre, -ātum*, to call.]

fāte, fär; mē, hûr (her); mīne; mōte, för; mūte; mōōn, fŏŏt; тнen (then)

convolve, *kon-volv'*, *v.t.* to roll together, or one part on another.—*adjs.* **con'volute, -d,** convolved.—*n.* **convolū'tion,** a twisting: a fold. [L. *convolvĕre*—*con-*, together, *volvĕre, volūtum*, to roll.]

convolvulus, *kon-vol'vū-lus, n.* a genus of twining or trailing plants, called also *bindweed.* [L.,—*convolvĕre.* See **convolve.**]

convoy, *kon-voi', v.t.* to accompany for protection.—*n.* (*kon'voi*) the act of convoying: protection: that which convoys or is convoyed, esp. a fleet of merchantmen escorted by ships of war: a column of military supplies. [Fr. *convoyer.* See **convey.**]

convulse, *kon-vuls', v.t.* (*lit.* and *fig.*) to agitate violently: to affect with immoderate laughter, &c.—*n.* **convul'sion,** any involuntary contraction of the muscles by which the body is thrown into violent spasms: any violent disturbance.—adj. **convuls'ive,** attended with convulsions: spasmodic.—*adv.* **convuls'ively.**—*n.* **convuls'iveness.** [L. *con-*, inten., and *vellĕre, vulsum*, to pluck, to pull.]

cony, coney, *kō'ni,* or *kun'i, n.* a rabbit: (*B.*) a small pachyderm. [Prob. through O.Fr. *connil*, from L. *cunīculus,* a rabbit.]

coo, *kōō, v.i.* to make a sound as a dove: to talk caressingly:—*pr.p.* **cōō'ing;** *pa.p.* **cōōed.**—*n.* the sound emitted by doves. [Imit.]

cooee, *kōō'ē,* **cooey,** *koo'i n.* the signal-call of the native Australians in the bush.—*v.i.* to make such a call.—*interj.* a call to attract attention.

cook, *kŏŏk, v.t.* to prepare food: to manipulate for any purpose, or falsify, as accounts, &c.: to concoct (often **cook up**).—*n.* one who cooks: one whose business is to cook.—*ns.* **cook'ery,** the art or practise of cooking; **cook'ery-book,** a book of recipes for cooking dishes; **cook'shop,** an eating-house.—**to cook one's goose** (*slang*), to ruin or spoil one's plans. [O.E. *cōc*, a cook—L. *coquus.*]

cookie, *kŏŏk'i, n.* a kind of bun: (*U.S.*) a biscuit. [Du. *koekje,* a cake.]

cool, *kōōl, adj.* slightly cold: free from excitement, calm: not zealous, ardent, or cordial—indifferent: impudent: of jazz, in an intellectual style, restrained in expression of feeling and using techniques of classical music: (*slang*) very good (a term of approval applicable to many things).—*v.t.* to make cool: (*fig.*) to allay or moderate.—*v.i.* to grow cool: to lose radioactivity.—*n.* that which is cool: coolness: (*slang*) self-possession.—*n.* **cool'er,** anything that cools: a vessel in which something is cooled.—*adjs.* **cool'-head'ed,** not easily excited, capable of acting with composure; **cool'ish,** somewhat cool.—*adv.* **cool'ly,** in a cool manner: indifferently: impudently.—*n.* **cool'ness,** moderate cold: indifference: want of zeal: lack of agitation: self-possession.—**cool off,** to become less angry and more amenable to reason: to grow less passionate. [O.E. *cōl*; Ger. *kühl.* Cog. with **cold** and **chill.**]

coolie, cooly, *kōōl'i, n.* an Indian or Chinese hired labourer. [Prob. *Kulī,* a tribe of Bombay; or orig. Tamil (q.v.); cf. *kūli,* hire.]

coom, *kōōm, n.* soot: coal-dust. [App. Northern form of **culm** (2).]

coomb, combe, *kōōm, n.* a deep little wooded valley: a hollow in a hillside. [O.E. *cumb.*]

coon, *kōōn, n.* the raccoon: a sly fellow: a Negro. [Abbreviated form of **raccoon.**]

coop, *kōōp, n.* a wicker basket: a box or cage for fowls or small animals: a confined, narrow place.—*v.t.* to confine in a coop or elsewhere.—Also **coop up.** [M.E. *cupe, coupe,* basket.]

cooper, *kōōp'ér, n.* one who makes tubs, casks, &c.—*n.* **coop'erage,** the work or workshop of a cooper: the sum paid for a cooper's work. [App. Low German—L.L. *cūpārius*—*cūpa,* cask.]

co-operate, *kō-op'ér-āt, v.i.* to work together (towards some end).—*n.* **co-opera'tion.**—*adjs.* **co-op'erative, co-op'erant,** working together. —*n.* **co-op'erātor.**—**co-operative society,** a profit-sharing association of consumers for the cheaper purchase of goods or for other trading purposes. [**co-**, and **operate.**]

co-opt, *kō-opt', v.t.* to elect any body by the votes of its members.—*ns.* **co-optā'tion, co-op'tion.**—*adj.* **co-op'tative.** [L. *cooptāre, -ātum*—*co-*, together, *optāre,* to choose.]

co-ordinate, *kō-ōr'di-nāt, adj.* holding the same order or rank (e.g. *co-ordinate clauses*).—*v.t.* (*-āt*) to make co-ordinate: to adjust the relations or movements of, to harmonise.—*n.* an equal thing or person: one of two or more measures that determine the position of a point, &c., with reference to a fixed system of axes, &c. (see **polar co-ordinates**).—*adv.* **co-or'dinately.**—*n.* **co-ordinā'tion,** state of being co-ordinate: act of co-ordinating: harmonious functioning of parts or agents towards the production of a normal or a desired result.— **co-ordinate geometry,** analytical geometry. [L. *co-*, and *ordināre, -ātum.* See **ordain.**]

coot, *kōōt, n.* a genus of water-fowl with a characteristic white spot—an extension of the bill—on the forehead: (*coll.*) a foolish person. [M.E. *cote;* Du. *koet.*]

cop, *kop, v.t.* (*slang*) to catch.—*ns.* **cop, copp'er,** policeman. [Ety. uncertain.]

copacetic, copesettic, *kō-pä-set'ik, adj.* sound: excellent.—*interj.* all clear. [U.S. slang.]

copal, *kō'pal, n.* a hard resin got from many tropical trees, and also fossil. [Sp.,—Mexican *copalli,* resin.]

copartner, *kō-pärt'nér, n.* a partner, sharer.—*ns.* **copart'nership,** **copart'nery,** a company of copartners: the state, or right, of a copartner or copartners: (**copartnership**) specifically, a system of profit-sharing by employees. [L. *co-*, together, and **partner.**]

cope, *kōp, n.* an ecclesiastical vestment consisting of a long semicircular cloak, originally with a hood: a covering.—*v.t.* to cover with a cope, or with coping.—*ns.* **cope'-, cop'ing-stone,** the stone that tops a wall: (*fig.*) the finishing touch; **cop'ing,** the covering course of masonry of a wall. [From root of **cap.**]

cope, *kōp, v.i.* to contend (with) esp. on equal terms or successfully: to deal with successfully. [Fr. *couper*—L. *colaphus*—Gr. *kolaphos,* a buffet.]

copeck. Same as **kopeck.**

Copernican, *ko-pûr'ni-kán, adj.* relating to *Copernicus,* the famous astronomer (1473-1543), or to his discovery that the earth revolves about the sun.

Neutral vowels in unaccented syllables: *em'pér-ór*; for certain sounds in foreign words see p. ix.

coping. See **cope**(1).

copious, *kō′pi-us, adj. (lit.* and *fig.)* plentiful, overflowing: not concise.—*adv.* **cō′piously.**—*n.* **cō′piousness.** [L. *cōpiōsus—cōpia,* plenty.]

copper, *kop′ėr, n.* a reddish metallic element (symbol Cu—see derivation; at. no. 29): money made of copper: a vessel made of copper, as a clothes-boiler.—*adj.* made of copper: copper-coloured.—*v.t.* to cover with copper.—*adj.* **copp′er-bott′omed,** having the bottom covered with copper.—*ns.* **copp′er-head,** a poisonous United States snake; **copp′erplate,** a plate of polished copper on which something has been engraved: an impression taken from the plate: faultless handwriting; **copp′er-smith,** a smith who works in copper.—*adj.* **copp′ery,** like copper. See also **cupri-, cupro-.** [Low L. *cuper*—L. *cuprum,* a contr. of *cyprium aes,* 'Cyprian brass', because found in *Cyprus.*]

copperas, *kop′ėr-as, n.* sulphate of iron, used in dyeing black, or making ink. [Fr. *couperose.*]

coppice, *kop′is,* **copse,** *kops, n.* a wood of small growth for periodical cutting.—*n.* **copse′wood,** underwood of a coppice, [(1) Fr. *copeis,* wood newly cut—Low L. *colpare,* to cut.]

copra, *kop′ra, n.* the dried kernel of the coconut, yielding coconut oil. [Port., from Malay.]

coprolite, *kop′ro-līt, n.* fossilised excrement of animals. [Gr. *kopros,* dung, *lithos,* a stone.]

copse, copsewood. See **coppice.**

Copt, *kopt, n.* a Christian descendant of the ancient Egyptians.—*adj.* **Copt′ic.**—*n.* the language of the Copts. [A corr. of Gr. *Aigyptios,* Egyptian.]

copula, *kop′ū-la, n.* that which joins together, a bond or tie.—*v.t.* and *v.i.* **cop′ulāte,** to unite in sexual intercourse.—*n.* **copulā′tion.**—*adj.* **cop′ulātive,** uniting.—*n. (gram.)* a conjunction that merely joins or adds (e.g. and) and does not indicate an alternative or a contrary idea (cf. **disjunctive).** [L.]

copy, *kop′i, n.* an imitation: a reproduction: a transcript: an individual specimen of a book: a model for imitation: matter for printing: material for a newspaper writer: something newsworthy.—*v.t.* to write, paint, &c., after an original: to imitate: to transcribe: to reproduce or duplicate by copying-press or otherwise:—*pa.p.* cop′ied.—*ns.* **cop′y-book,** a writing or drawing book with models for imitation; **cop′yhold** (*Eng. law),* a species of tenure or right of holding land, part of a manor, the owner's title being evidenced by a copy of the lord's court; **cop′yholder; cop′ying-ink,** ink suitable for copying by impression; **copy′right,** the sole right to reproduce a literary, dramatic, musical, or artistic work—also to perform, translate, film, or record such a work. —*adj.* protected by copyright.—*n.* **copy-writer,** a writer of copy (esp. advertisements) for the press. [Fr. *copie*—Low L. *cōpia,* a transcript— L. *cōpia,* plenty.]

coquet, coquette, *ko-ket′, v.i.* to flirt: to dally (e.g. with a suggestion):—*pr.p.* coquett′ing; *pa.p.* coquett′ed.—*ns.* **cō′quetry,** act of coquetting; attempt to attract admiration without genuine affection: fickleness in love; **cŏquette′,** a woman addicted to coquetry.— *adj.* **cŏquett′ish,** [Fr. *coqueter—coquet,* dim. of *coq,* a cock.]

coracle, *kor′a-kl, n.* a small oval rowboat used in Wales made of skins or oilcloth stretched on wickerwork. [W. *corwgl.*]

coral, *kor′ál, n.* a hard substance of various colours deposited on the bottom of the sea, skeletons, mostly calcareous, of zoophytes (q.v.): the animal or colony producing this substance: a toy of coral: eggs of a lobster, coral red when cooked: shade of red or pink.—*adj.* made of or like coral.—*adjs.* **coral-lif′erous,** containing coral: having the form of coral; **cor′alline,** of, like, or containing coral.—*n.* a seaweed with a limy encrustation resembling coral.—*n.* **cor′al-reef,** a reef formed by the growth and deposit of coral. [O.Fr.—L. *coralium*—Gr. *korallion.*]

cor anglais, *kör ä-glä′, n.* English horn (q.v.). [Fr.]

corban, *kör′ban, n.* anything devoted to God in fulfilment of a vow. [Heb. *qorbān.*]

corbel, *kör′bel, n.* (*archit.*) a projection from the face of a wall, supporting a superincumbent weight. [O.Fr. *corbel*—Low L. *corvellus,* dim. of *corvus,* a raven.]

corbie (crow), *kör′bi (krō), n.* a raven: a carrion crow. [O.Fr. *corbin*—L. *corvus,* crow.]

cord, *körd, n.* a small rope or thick string: something resembling a cord: anything that binds or restrains: a measure of cut wood (128 cubic feet).—*v.t.* to supply with a cord: to bind with a cord.—*ns.* **cord′age,** a quantity of cords or ropes; **cord′ite,** a smokeless explosive, so called from its cord-like appearance. [Fr. *corde*—L. *chorda.* See **chord.**]

cordelier, *kör-dé-lēr′, n.* a Franciscan friar, so named from the knotted cord worn as a girdle. [O.Fr. *cordele,* dim. of *corde,* a rope.]

cordial, *kör′di-ál, adj.* hearty, sincere: affectionate: reviving the heart or spirits.—*n.* anything which revives or comforts the heart: an invigorating medicine or drink.—*n.* **cor′dial′ity.**—*adv.* **cor′dially.** [Low L. *cordiālis*—L. *cor, cordis,* the heart.]

cordillera, *kör-dil-yä′rä* (or *-dil′ér-á), n.* a chain of mountains. [Sp.,—Old Sp. *cordilla*-L. *chorda,* cord.]

cordon, *kör′don, -dón, n.* a cord or ribbon be stowed as a badge of honour: a line of sentries or policemen to prevent access to an area.— *v.t.* to enclose with a cordon. [Fr.]

cordon bleu, *kör-dŏ′blø,* blue ribbon: a cook of the highest excellence. [Fr.]

corduroy, *kor-du-roi′, n.* a thick cotton fabric, corded or ribbed: (*pl.*) trousers made of corduroy.—**corduroy road,** a track laid transversely with tree-trunks. [Perh. Fr. *corde du roi,* king's cord.]

cordwain, *körd′wān, n.* (*arch.*) fine leather, originally from *Cordova* in Spain.—*n.* **cord′-wainer,** a shoemaker.

core, *kör, kör, n.* the heart: the inner part of anything, esp. of fruit.—*v.t.* to take out the core of. [Perh. conn. with L. *cor,* heart.]

co-relation, co-relative. Same as **correlation, correlative.**

co-respondent, *kö-ré-spond′ént, n.* (*law*) a person charged with adultery, and proceeded against along with the petitioner's wife or husband, who is the *respondent.*

corgi, *kör'gē, n.* a small Welsh dog. [Welsh *corr,* dwarf, *ci,* dog.]

coriaceous, *kōr-i-ā'shus, adj.* leathery, of or like leather. [L. *corium,* skin, leather.]

coriander, *kor-i-an'dér, n.* an umbelliferous plant, whose seeds are used as spice, &c. [Fr.,—L. *coriandrum*—Gr. *koriannon.*]

Corinthian, *kor-inth'i-án, adj.* of Corinth, Greece, or an ornate style of Greek architecture: profligate.—*n.* man of fashion.—**Corinthian brass,** alloy of gold, silver, and copper.

cork, *körk, n.* (*bot.*) a layer of dead cells on the outside of a stem or root, formed by a special cambium, **cork cambium,** and protecting the living cells inside: this layer in the **cork-tree,** an oak of S. Europe, N. Africa, &c.: a stopper made of cork: any stopper.—*adj.* made of cork.—*v.t.* to stop with a cork: to plug.—*n.* **cork'screw,** a screw for drawing corks from bottles.—*adj.* like a corkscrew in shape. [Sp. *corcho*—L. *cortex,* bark, rind.]

corm, *körm, n.* the short, bulb-like subterranean stem of the crocus, &c.—sometimes called a *solid bulb.* [Gr. *kormos,* the lopped trunk of a tree.]

cormorant, *kör'mó-ránt, n.* a genus of web-footed sea-birds, of great voracity: a glutton. [Fr. *cormoran,* from L. *corvus marīnus,* sea crow.]

corn, *körn, n.* a grain, hard particle: a kernel: (collectively) seeds of cereal plants or the plants themselves: (in England) wheat, (in Scotland and Ireland) oats, (in North America) maize: (*slang*) something old-fashioned or hackneyed.—*v.t.* to form into grains: to sprinkle with grains of salt.—*ns.* **corn'-cob,** the elongated, woody centre of the ear of maize; **corn'crake,** the landrail, named from its cry, frequenting cornfields.—*adj.* **corned,** granulated: salted—e.g. **corned beef, corn'-beef.**—*ns.* **corn'-exchange',** a mart where grain is sold; **corn'-flour,** the finely ground flour of maize, or of rice or other grain; **corn'-flower,** a composite (q.v.) weed of cornfields, having a beautiful deep azure flower; **corn'-law,** a law for regulation of the trade in corn: esp. in *pl.* (in England), laws restricting the importation of corn, repealed in 1846; **corn'-maid'en,** or **kir'n-maiden**—same as **harvest-queen** (q.v.). [O.E. *corn*; akin to L. *grānum.*]

corn, *körn, n.* a small hard growth chiefly on the foot.—**tread on one's corns,** to injure one's feelings. [L. *cornū,* a horn.]

cornea, *kör'ne-a, n.* the transparent horny membrane that forms the front covering of the eye.—*adj.* **cor'neal.**—**corneal lens,** a contact lens covering the transparent part of the eye only. [L. *cornea* (*tela*), horny (*tissue*).]

cornel, *kör'nél, n.* the so-called cornelian cherry, a small tree of middle and southern Europe, with oblong, shining, generally red, fruit. [Low L. *cornolium*—L. *cornus,* cornel.]

cornelian, *kör-nē'li-án, n.* a fine chalcedony, generally translucent and red.—Also **carnē'lian.** [Fr. *cornaline*—L. *cornū,* a horn; or *cornum* (*cornus*), see previous word.]

corner, *kör'nér, n.* the point where two lines meet: a secret or confined place: an awkward position, difficulty: in association football, a free kick from the corner flag: an operation by which a few speculators gain control of the whole available supply of a commodity.—*v.t.* to put in a corner: (*fig.*) to drive into an embarrassing position from which escape is difficult: to gain control of the supplies of (a commodity).—*v.i.* to turn a corner.—*n.* **cor'ner-stone,** the stone that unites the two walls of a building at a corner: the principal stone, esp. the corner of the foundation of a building—hence (*fig.*) something of very great importance.—**cut corners,** to do a piece of work skimpily or with the minimum of effort; **turn the corner,** to go round the corner: to get past a difficulty or danger; **within the four corners of,** contained in (a document, &c.). [O.Fr. *corniere*—L. *cornū,* a horn.]

cornet, *kör'net, n.* a treble valve-instrument of brass, more tapering than the trumpet: any funnel-shaped object. [Fr. *cornet,* dim. of *corne,* a horn, trumpet—L. *cornū,* a horn.]

cornet, *kör'net, n.* till 1871 a cavalry officer—later sublieutenant: a standard-bearer at a common-riding.—*n.* **cor'netcy.** [Fr. *cornette*—L. *cornū,* a horn.]

cornice, *kör'nis, n.* (*classical archit.*) the highest moulded projection of a wall or column: plaster moulding round a ceiling. [Fr.,—It., perh. Gr. *korōnis,* a curved line; cf. L. *corōna.*]

corniculate, *kör-nik'ū-lát, adj.* horned: shaped like a horn. [L. *corniculātus*—*cornū,* a horn.]

Cornish, *körn'ish, adj.* pertaining to Cornwall.—*n.* the people or dialect of Cornwall.

cornucopia, *kör-nū-kō'pi-a, n.* the horn of plenty: according to the fable, the horn of the goat that suckled Jupiter, placed among the stars as an emblem of plenty. [L. *cornū,* horn, and *cōpia,* plenty.]

corny, *kör'ni, adj.* (*U.S. slang*) old-fashioned, out-of-date, uninteresting from frequent use, dull, foolish.

corolla, *kor-ol'a, n.* the inner covering of a flower composed of one or more leaves called petals. [L. *corolla,* dim. of *corōna,* a crown.]

corollary, *kor-ol'á-ri,* or *kor'ol-á-ri, n.* an obvious inference: a consequence or result. [L. *corollārium,* a garland—*corolla;* see above.]

corona, *ko-rō'na, n.* a coloured ring round the sun or moon, distinguished from a halo by having the red outermost: the circle of florets in flowers like the daisy.—*n.* **cor'onal,** a crown or garland: the frontal bone of the skull.—*adjs.* **corōn'al; cor'onary,** pertaining to a crown, or to the top of the head: resembling a circlet and surrounding a part (**coronary arteries,** arteries that supply blood to the muscle of the heart-wall; **coronary thrombosis,** the formation of a clot in one of these arteries).—*n.* **coronā'tion,** the act of crowning a sovereign. [L. *corōna,* a crown.]

coronach, *kor'o-näн, n.* a funeral dirge or lamentation. [Ir. *coranach,* Gael, *corranach.*]

coroner, *kor'o-nér, n.* an officer of the Crown who holds inquest into the causes of accidental or suspicious deaths. [O.Fr.—L. *corōna.*]

coronet, *kor'o-net, n.* a small crown worn by the nobility: an ornamental head-dress.—*adj.* **cor'oneted.** [O.Fr., dim. of *corone,* crown—L. *corōna,* a crown.]

corporal, *kör'po-rál, n.* the grade of non-commissioned officer below a sergeant: in the

Neutral vowels in unaccented syllables: *em'pér-ôr*; for certain sounds in foreign words see p. ix.

154

navy, —*n.* **cor′poralship.** [Fr. *caporal*—It. *caporale*—*capo,* the head—L. *caput,* the head.]

corporal, *kör′po-rál, adj.* belonging or relating to the body: having a body: not spiritual.—*n.* the cloth used in Catholic churches for covering the elements of the Eucharist.—*adv.* **cor′porally.**—*adj.* **cor′porate,** legally united into a body so as to act as an individual: belonging to a corporation: united.—*adv.* **cor′porately.**—*ns.* **cor′porateness; corporā′tion,** a body or society, such as a Town Council, authorised by law to act as one individual: (*coll.*) the paunch, esp. when prominent.—*adj.* **corpō′real,** having a body or substance, material.— **corporal punishment,** punishment inflicted on the body, as flogging, &c. [L. *corporālis*—*corpus, corpŏris,* the body.]

corps, *kör, n.* a division of an army forming a tactical unit: an organised group:—*pl.* **corps** (*körz*). [Fr., from L. *corpus,* the body.]

corps de ballet, *kör dé ba-le,* the company of ballet dancers at a theatre. [Fr.]

corpse, *körps,* or *kors, n.* a dead body, esp. of a human being. [M.E. *corps,* earlier *cors*—O.Fr. *cors,* the body—L. *corpus.*]

corpus, *kör′pus, n.* a body, a body of literature:—*pl.* **cor′pora.**—*ns.* **cor′pulence, cor′pulency,** fleshiness of body, excessive fatness.— *adj.* **cor′pulent,** fleshy or fat.—*adv.* **cor′pulently.**—*n.* **cor′puscle** (or *-pusl*), a minute particle: a cell not in continuous contact with others (e.g. lying in a fluid such as the blood plasma)—also **corpus′cule** (*-kūl*).—*adj.* **corpus′cular** (*-kū-*).—**Corpus Christi,** the festival in honour of the Eucharist, held on the Thursday after Trinity Sunday. [L. *corpus,* the body.]

corral, *kor-al′, n.* an enclosure for cattle, &c.: a defensive enclosure in an encampment made by placing wagons in a circle.—*v.t.* to form, or put in, a corral. [Sp.]

correct, *kor-ekt′, v.t.* to remove faults from: to mark faults in: to set right (a person): to punish: to counteract, neutralise (e.g. a tendency).—*adj.* free from faults: true: in accordance with the accepted standard (of conduct, taste, &c.).—*adv.* **correct′ly.**—*n.* **correc′tion,** amendment: punishment.—*adjs.* **correc′tional, correct′ive,** tending, or having the power, to correct.—*ns.* **correct′ive,** that which corrects; **correct′ness; correct′or.**—**corrective training,** reformative imprisonment for persistent offenders of 21 or over for periods of from 2 to 4 years. [L. *corrigĕre, correctum*—*con-,* inten., *regĕre,* to rule.]

correlate, *kor′e-lāt, v.i.* to be related to one another, esp. by close or necessary connection.—*v.t.* to bring into relation with each other, to connect systematically.—*n.* **correlā′tion.**—*adj.* **correl′ative,** mutually or reciprocally related: corresponding and used together (e.g. the words *either*—*or*)—Also *n.*—*adv.* **correl′atively.** [Coined from L. *con-,* with, and **relate.**]

correspond, *kor-e-spond′, v.i.* to suit, to agree (with *to,* *with*): to be analogous (to) in function, position, or other respect: to hold intercourse, esp. by letter.—*n.* **correspond′ence,** harmony, relation of agreement part to part (also **correspond′ency**): friendly intercourse:

communication by letters: letters sent or received.—*adj.* **correspond′ent,** answering: analogous.—*n.* one with whom intercourse is kept up by letters: one who contributes letters or news to a journal: person or firm that regularly does business for another elsewhere.—*advs.* **correspond′ently, correspond′ingly.** [Coined from L. *con-,* with, and *respondēre,* to promise, answer.]

corridor, *kor′i-dör, n.* a passage-way or gallery communicating with separate rooms, &c.—*ns.* **corr′idor-carr′iage, -train,** a carriage, train, with a corridor along which one can pass from one compartment to another.—**corridors of power** (*fig.*), higher reaches of government administration. [Fr.,—It. *corridore*—It. *correre,* to run—L. *currĕre.*]

corrie, *kor′i, n.* a semicircular recess in a mountain. [Gael. *coire,* a cauldron.]

corrigendum, *kor-i-jen′dum, n.* that which requires correction: *-pl.* **corrigen′da.** [L., gerundive of *corrigĕre,* to correct.]

corrigible, *kor′ij-ibl, adj.* that may be corrected: open to correction.—*n.* **corrigibil′ity.** [Fr.,—L. *corrigĕre.* See **correct.**]

corroborate, *kor-ob′o-rāt, v.t* to confirm, esp. by evidence. *adj.* **corrob′orative,** tending to confirm.—*n.* that which corroborates.—*n.* **corroborā′tion,** confirmation. [L. *cor-,* intensive, *rōborāre, -ātum,* to make strong—*rōbur,* oak, strength.]

corroboree, *ko-rob′ō-rē, n.* a dance of Australian aborigines: a song for such a dance: a festive gathering. [Native word.]

corrode, *kor-ōd′, v.t.* to eat away by degrees (*obs.* in literal sense), as rust, chemicals, &c.—*v.i.* to be eaten away—*adj.* **corrod′ent,** having the power of corroding.—*n.* that which corrodes.—*n.* **corro′sion,** act or process of wasting away. *adj.* **corros′ive,** having the quality of eating away.—*n.* that which has the power of corroding.—*adv.* **corros′ively.**—*n.* **corros′iveness.**—**corrosive sublimate,** a highly poisonous compound of mercury and chlorine. [L. *cor-,* inten., *rōdĕre, rōsum,* to gnaw.]

corrugate, *kor′(y)ŏŏ-gāt, v.t.* to wrinkle or draw into folds.—*n.* **corrugā′tion.**—**corrugated iron,** sheet iron rolled into a wavy surface for the sake of strength. [L. *cor-,* inten., *rūgāre, -ātum,* to wrinkle—*rūga,* a wrinkle.]

corrupt, *kor-upt′, v.t.* to make putrid: to defile: to debase: to bribe.—*v.i.* to rot: to lose purity.— *adj.* putrid: depraved: defiled: not genuine: full of errors: venal.—*adv.* **corrupt′ly.**—*ns.* **corrupt′ness; corrupt′er; corrup′tion,** decomposition: impurity: bribery: perversion (e.g. of language).—*adjs.* **corrupt′ive,** having the quality of corrupting; **corrupt′ible,** liable to corruption: capable of being bribed.—*ns.* **corruptibil′ity, corrupt′ibleness.** [L. *cor-,* inten., and *rumpĕre, ruptum,* to break.]

corsage, *kör′sij, kör-säzh′, n.* the bodice or waist of a woman's dress: a bouquet to be worn. [O.Fr.,—*cors*—L. *corpus,* the body.]

corsair, *kör′sār, n.* a privateer (man or ship) esp. of the Barbary coast (North Africa): a pirate. [Fr. *corsaire,* one who courses or ranges—L. *cursus,* a running—*currĕre,* to run.]

corse, *körs, n.* a poetic form of **corpse.**

corselet. Same as **corslet.**

corset, *kör'set, n.* a close-fitting stiff inner bodice, stays. [Dim. of O.Fr. *cors*—L. *corpus,* the body.]

corslet, corselet, *körs'let, n.* (*hist.*) a defensive covering for the body, chiefly of leather: a form of corset. [Fr. *corselet,* dim. of O.Fr. *cors*—L. *corpus,* the body.]

cortège, *kör-tezh', n.* a train of courtiers: a procession, esp. a funeral procession. [Fr.,—It. *corte,* court.]

Cortes, *kör'tes, n.* the parliament of Spain and of Portugal. [Sp., pl. of *corte,* a court.]

cortex, *kör'teks, n.* a cylinder of cells between the epidermis of a plant and the vascular bundles: a covering: (*zool.*) the outer layer of an organ, esp. the brain:—*pl.* **cortices** (*kör'ti-sēz*).—*adjs.* **cor'ticate, -d** furnished with bark.—*n.* **cortisone,** *kör'ti-sōn,* a substance present in the cortex of a gland lying close to the kidney in higher animals—used in medicine. [L. *cortex, corticis,* bark.]

corundum, *ko-run'dum, n.* a mineral consisting of alumina, second in hardness only to the diamond: forms include sapphire, ruby, emery. [Tamil (q.v.) *kurundam,* ruby.]

coruscate, *kor'us-kāt, v.i.* to sparkle, throw off flashes of light (*lit.* and *fig.*).—*adj.* **corus'cant,** flashing.—*n.* **corusca'tion,** a glittering: sudden flashes of light. [L. *coruscāre, -ātum,* to vibrate, glitter.]

corvée, *kör-vā', n.* the obligation to perform unpaid labour for the sovereign or feudal lord. [Fr.,—Low L. *corrogāta*—L. *corrogāre*—*cor-,* together, *rogāre,* to ask.]

corvette, *kör-vet', n.* formerly a vessel with flush-deck and one tier of guns: now an escort vessel, specially designed for protecting convoys against submarine attack. [Fr.,—Sp. *corbeta*—L. *corbīta,* a slow-sailing ship, from *corbis,* a basket.]

corvine, *kör'vīn, adj.* pertaining to the crow. [L. *corvinus*—*corvus,* a crow.]

Corybant, *kor'i-bant, n.* a priest of the goddess Cybele, whose rites included frantic music and dances:—Eng. *pl.* **Cor'ybants;** L. *pl.* **Corybantes** (*kor-i-ban'tēz*).—*adj.* **coryban'tic,** wildly excited. [Gr. *Korybās,* gen. *Korybantos.*]

coryphaeus, *kor-i-fē'us, n.* the chief or leader, esp. the leader of a chorus:—*pl.* **coryphaei** (*-fē'ī*). [L.,—Gr. *koryphaios*—*koryphē,* the head, top.]

cos, *kos, n.* long-leafed type of lettuce. [Introduced from the Aegean island of *Cos,* Gr. *Kōs.*]

cos. See **cosine.**

cosecant, *kō-sē'kant, -sek'-, n.* one of the six trigonometrical functions of an angle, the reciprocal of the sine (q.v.)—identical with the secant (q.v.) of the complementary angle.—*abbrev.* **cosec** (*cō'sek*).

cosh, *kosh, n.* (*slang*) a piece of flexible tubing filled with metal, a lead-pipe, or the like, used as a weapon.—Also *v.t.*

co-signatory, *kō-sig'na-tō-ri* (or *-tō-*), *adj.* uniting with others in signing.—*n.* one who does so. [**co-,** and **signatory.**]

cosine, *kō'sīn, n.* one of the six trigonometrical functions of an angle, the ratio of the base to the hypotenuse—identical with sine of complementary angle.—*abbrev.* **cos** (*kos*).

cosmetic, *koz-met'ik, adj.* purporting to enhance beauty, esp. that of the complexion: correcting defects of the face, &c., (as *cosmetic surgery*) or supplying deficiencies (as *cosmetic hands*).—*n.* a preparation to enhance beauty.—*adj.* **cosmet'ical.**—*adv.* **cosmet'ically.** [Gr. *kosmētikos*—*kosmeein*—*kosmos,* order.]

cosmic. See **cosmos.**

cosmogony, *koz-mog'o-ni, n.* a theory, or a myth, of the origin of the universe: the science of the origins of stars, planets, and satellites.—*n.* **cosmog'onist.** [Gr. *kosmogonia*—*kosmos,* order, and root of *gignesthai,* to be born.]

cosmography, *koz-mog'rä-fi, n.* a description of the world: the science of the constitution of the universe.—*n.* **cosmog'rapher.**—*adjs.* **cosmograph'ic, -al.** [Gr. *kosmographia*—*kosmos,* order, the universe, *graphein,* to write.]

cosmology, *koz-mol'o-ji, n.* the science of the universe as a whole: a treatise on the structure and parts of the system of creation.—*adj.* **cosmolog'ical.**—*n.* **cosmol'ogist,** one versed in cosmology. [Gr. *kosmos,* order, the universe, *logos,* discourse.]

cosmonaut, *koz'mō-nöt, n.* one who has travelled round the world in space. [From Russian—Gr. *kosmos,* the universe, *nautes,* sailor.]

cosmopolitan, *koz-mo-pol'i-tán, n.* a citizen of the world: one free from local or national prejudices.—*adj.* belonging to all parts of the world: having international tastes: unprejudiced.—*n.* **cosmopol'itanism.** [Gr. *kosmopolītēs*—*kosmos,* the world, *polītēs,* a citizen—*polis,* a city.]

cosmos, *koz'mos, n.* the universe as an orderly or systematic whole—opp. to *chaos:* a complex but orderly system.—*adjs.* **cos'mic,** of, or relating to, the cosmos: orderly; **cos'mical,** cosmic: (*astron.*) happening at sunrise.—*adv.* **cos'mically.**—**cosmic radiation, rays,** a very complex radiation of subatomic particles, thought to come from interstellar space. [Gr.]

cossack, *kos'ak, n.* one of a people in southeastern Russia, famous as light cavalry. [Turk.]

cosset, *kos'et, n.* a lamb reared by hand.—*v.t.* to pamper. [Ety. uncertain.]

cost, *kost, v.t.* to bring, or be valued at (a specified price): to require, involve (in suffering, or loss): to estimate the cost of production of:—*pa.t.* and *pa.p.* cost.—*n.* what is paid or suffered to obtain anything: (*pl.*) expenses of a lawsuit.—*adj.* **cost'ly,** of great cost: valuable.—*n.* **cost'liness.—cost price,** the price the merchant pays for goods bought.—**cost of living,** the total cost of goods ordinarily required in order to live up to one's usual standard; **cost of living index,** an official number indicating the cost of living at a certain date compared with that at another date taken as a standard. [O.Fr. *couster* (Fr. *coûter*)—L. *constāre,* to stand at.]

costal, *kos'tál, adj.* relating to the ribs, or to the side of the body. [L. *costa,* a rib.]

costard, *kos'tárd, n.* a large kind of apple with rib-like markings.—*ns.* **cos'tardmonger, cos'termonger, cos'ter,** a seller of apples and other fruit, or of other wares, from a barrow. [Perh. from L. *costa,* a rib.]

Neutral vowels in unaccented syllables: *em'pér-ôr;* for certain sounds in foreign words see p. ix.

156

costive, *kos'tiv, adj.* having the motion of the bowels too slow, constipated.—*adv.* **cos'tively.**—*n.* **cos'tiveness.** [O.Fr. *costivé*—L. *constīpātus*—*constīpāre.* See **constipate.**]

costume, *kos'tūm, kos-tūm', n.* a manner of dressing: dress: a woman's outer dress.—*p.adj.* **costumed'.**—*ns.* **costum'er, costum'ier,** one who makes or deals in costumes.—**costume jewellery,** jewellery worn as an adornment only, without pretence of value. [Fr.,—L. *consuētūdō,* custom.]

cosy, cozy, *kō'zi, adj.* (*Scot.*) snug: comfortable.—*n.* a covering for a teapot, to keep the tea warm (also **tea'-cos'y**).—*adv.* **cō'sily.**

cot, *kot, n.* a small dwelling, a cottage. [O.E. *cot(e)*; cf. O.N. and Du. *kot*; Low L. *cota* is from Gmc.]

cot, *kot, n.* a small bed or crib with high sides: (*naut.*) a swinging bed of canvas. [Anglo-Ind.,—Hindustani *khāt.*]

cotangent, *kō-tan'jént, n.* one of the six trigonometrical functions of an angle, the reciprocal of the tangent (q.v.)—identical with the tangent of the complementary angle. —*abbrev.* **cot** (*kot*).

cote, *kōt, n.* a cot: a place for animals, as *dove-cote* (or *dove-cot*), *sheep-cote.* [O.E. *cote*; cf. **cot** (1).]

cotemporaneous, -temporary. Same as **contemporaneous, -temporary.**

coterie, *kō'te-rē, n.* a social, literary, or other exclusive circle. [Fr.; orig. a number of peasants obtaining a joint tenure of land from a lord—Low L. *cota,* a hut—Gmc.]

cothurnus, *kō-thûr'nus, n.* a buskin (q.v.):—*pl.* **cothur'nī.** [L. *cothurnus*—Gr. *kothornos.*]

cotillion, *ko-til'yón,* **cotillon,** *ko-tē'yō, n.* a sort of country dance. [Fr., *petticoat*—*cotte,* a coat—Low L. *cotta,* a tunic; cf. **coat.**]

cottage, *kot'ij, n.* a small dwelling-house: a country residence.—*n.* **cott'ager,** one who dwells in a cottage, esp. of labourers.—**cottage cheese,** a soft white cheese made from skim milk curds; **cottage piano,** a small upright piano. [L.L. *cottagium*—O.E. *cot*; see **cot** (1).]

cottar, cotter, *kot'ėr, n.* (*Scot.*) a peasant occupying a cot or cottage for which he has to give service in lieu of rent. [From root of **cot** (1), partly through Low L.]

cotton, *kot'n, n.* a soft substance like fine wool, the hairs covering the seeds of cotton-plants: any of four species of plants from which cotton is obtained: yarn or cloth made of cotton.—*adj.* made of cotton.—*v.i.* to agree (with): to become attached (to).—*ns.* **cott'on-gin,** a machine for separating the seeds from the fibre of cotton; **cott'on-grass,** a genus of sedges with long, silky, or cotton-like hairs; **cott'on-tail,** the ordinary United States rabbit; **cott'on-tree, cott'on-wood,** any one of several American species of poplar; **cott'on-wool,** cotton in its raw or woolly state: loose cotton pressed in a sheet as an absorbent or protective agent.—**cotton on to** (*slang*), to take to: to understand. [Fr. *coton*—Ar. *qutun.*].

cotyledon, *kot-i-lē'don, n.* (*bot.*) a seed-leaf or seed-lobe, one of the leaves of the embryo in a flowering plant.—*adj.* **cotyle'donous,** pertaining to, or having, cotyledons. [L.,—Gr. *kotyledōn*—*kotylē,* a cup.]

couch, *kowch, v.t.* to lay down on a bed, &c.: to express (in words): to depress or remove a cataract in the eye.—*v.i.* to lie down for the purpose of sleep, concealment, &c.—*n.* any place for rest or sleep: a bed.—*adj.* **couch'ant,** couching or lying down with the head raised.—**couch a spear,** to fix it in its rest at the side of the armour. [Fr. *coucher,* to lay down—L. *collocāre.* See **collocate.**]

couch (-grass), *kowch', kōōch'(-gräs), n.* grass akin to wheat, a troublesome weed. [A variant of *quitch*—Q.E. *cwice,* prob. akin to *cwic,* living.]

couchette, *kōō-shet', n.* a sleeping berth on a continental train. [Fr.]

cougar, *kōō'gär, n.* a puma. [Fr. *couguar,* adapted from a South American name.]

cough, *kof, v.i.* to expel air with a sudden opening of the glottis and a harsh sound.—*v.t.* **cough out, up,** to expel by coughing.—*n.* the act or sound of coughing [M.E. *coughen,* cf. Du *kuchen* Ger. *keuchen, keichen,* to gasp.]

could, *kōōd, pa.t.* of **can.** [M.E. *coude, couth*—O.E. *cūthe* for *cunthe,* was able; *l* is inserted from the influence of *would* and *should.*]

coulée, *kōō-lā', kōō'li, n.* a ravine. [Fr.,—*couler,* to flow.]

coulisse, *kōō-lēs', n.* a slide in which a side-scene of a theatre runs—hence, a side-scene or wing. [Fr.,—*couler,* to glide, to flow—L. *cōlāre,* to strain, purify.]

coulomb, *kōō-lom', n.* the unit of quantity in measuring electric charge—the quantity furnished by a current of one ampere in one second. [From the French physicist, C. A. de *Coulomb.*]

coulter, colter, *kōl'tér, n.* the iron cutter in front of a ploughshare. [O.E. *culter*—L. *culter,* knife.]

council, *kown'sil, n.* a deliberative or legislative assembly: the members of such an assembly.—*n.* **coun'cillor,** a member of a council.—**council estate,** an area set apart for council houses; **council house,** one subsidised by government money and built by a local authority; **council of war,** a conference of military or naval officers summoned by the commander. [Fr. *concile*—L. *concilium.*]

counsel, *kown'sel, n.* consultation: deliberation: advice: plan, purpose: one who gives counsel, a barrister or advocate.—*v.t.* to advise: to recommend:—*pr.p.* **coun'selling;** *pa.p.* **coun'selled.**—*ns.* **coun'sellor,** one who counsels: a barrister; **coun'sellorship.**—**counsel of perfection,** an injunction regarded as not applying to the ordinary person because the course it commends is too hard (see Matthew xix. 21).—**keep counsel,** to keep intentions, &c., secret. [Fr. *conseil*—L. *consilium,* advice—*consulere,* to consult.]

count, *kownt, n.* on the Continent, a noble equal in rank to an English earl:—*fem.* **count'ess,** the wife of a count or earl.—*n.* **coun'ty,** the domain of a count: one of the territorial units into which a state is divided, a shire.—Also *adj.* (*esp.,* of a county family)—**county-borough** (see **borough**); **county council,** a council for managing the affairs of a county; **county family,** a family of the nobility or gentry with estates in the county; **county**

town, the town in which the public business of a county is transacted. [O.Fr. *conte* — L. *comes, comitis,* a companion.]

count, *kownt, v.t.* to number, sum up: to ascribe: to esteem, consider.—*v.i.* to have a (specified) value: to be of account: to be reckoned: to depend, reckon (with *on, upon*).—*n.* act of numbering: the number counted: a particular charge in an indictment.—*ns.* count′-down, a descending count to zero which marks the moment of action, as e.g. the moment of firing a rocket; count′er, he who, or that which, counts: that which indicates a number: a token used in reckoning: a table on which money is counted or goods laid; count′ing-house, the premises in which a merchant keeps his accounts and transacts business.— *adj.* count′less, innumerable.— count out, of a meeting (esp. of the House of Commons), to bring to an end by pointing out that a quorum is not present. — Geiger counter (see Geiger); out for the count, unconscious, or completely exhausted (derived from boxing); under the counter, hidden from customer's sight (*adj.* under-the-counter, reserved for favoured customers: secret, furtive). [O.Fr. *cunter* (Fr. *compter*) — L. *computāre.*]

countenance, *kown′ten-áns, n.* the face: the expression of the face: appearance: good will, support.—*v.t.* to favour or approve.— in countenance, confident, unabashed (because of support); out of countenance, disconcerted, abashed. [O.Fr. *contenance* — L. *continentia,* restraint, demeanour—L. *continēre,* to contain.]

counter. See count (2).

counter, *kown′tér, adv.* in the opposite direction: in opposition.—*adj.* contrary: opposite.—*n.* that which is counter or opposite: the part of a horse's breast between the shoulders and under the neck: (*naut.*) the curved part of a ship's hull over the sternpost and rudder.—*v.t.* (see next article).—*v.t.* counteract′, to act in opposition to, to hinder or defeat: to neutralise.—*n.* counterac′tion.—*adj.* counterac′tive, tending to counteract.—*n.* one who or that which counteracts.—*adv.* counterac′tively.— *ns.* coun′ter-attack′, an attack in reply to an attack; coun′ter-attrac′tion, a rival attraction.—*v.t.* counterbal′ance, to balance by weight on the opposite side: to act against with equal weight, power, or influence.—*ns.* coun′terbalance, an equal weight, power, or agency working in opposition; coun′terblast, a vigorous retort; coun′tercharge, an accusation made in opposition to another; coun′ter-claim, a claim brought forward as a partial or complete set-off against another claim.—*adv.* coun′ter-clock′wise, in a direction contrary to that of the hands of a clock.—*ns.* coun′ter-curr′ent, a current flowing in the opposite direction; coun′ter-esp′ionage, spying directed against an enemy's spy system; coun′-ter-ev′idence, evidence in opposition to other evidence; coun′terfoil, a coupon detached from a bank cheque, &c., and kept as a voucher by the giver; coun′ter-intell′igence, activities aimed at preventing an enemy from obtaining correct information—including use of codes, camouflage, &c.; coun′ter-irr′itant,

an irritant used to relieve another irritation.—*v.i.* coun′ter-march, to march back or in a contrary direction.—*n.* a marching backward or in a different direction: (*mil.*) an evolution by which a body of men change front, and still retain the same men in the front rank: change of measures.—*ns.* coun′-ter-meas′ure, an action taken to prevent or counteract the effect of another action; coun′termine, (*mil.*) a mine excavated by the besieged to counteract the mines made by the besiegers: (*fig.*) any means of counteraction.—*v.t.* countermine′, to make a mine in opposition to: (*fig.*) to frustrate by secret working:—*pr.p.* countermin′ing; *pa.p.* countermined′.—*ns.* coun′ter-mŏ′tion, a proposal in opposition to a motion already made; coun′-terpart, part that answers to another part: that which fits into or completes another: a duplicate, double; coun′terplot, plot or stratagem intended to frustrate another plot.—*v.t.* coun′terpoise, to poise or weigh against or on the opposite side: to act in opposition to with equal effect—*n.* an equally heavy weight in the other scale.—*ns.* Count′er Reformation (*hist.*), a reform movement within the Roman Catholic Church, following and counteracting the Reformation; coun′ter-revolū′tion, a revolution undoing a previous revolution; coun′terscarp (*fort.*), the side of the ditch nearest to the besiegers and opposite to the scarp.—*v.t.* countersign′, to sign on the opposite side of a writing: to sign in addition to another, to attest the authenticity of a writing.—*ns.* coun′tersign, a military private sign or word, which must be given in order to pass a sentry: (also coun′ter-sig′nature) a name countersigned to a writing.—*v.t.* countervail′, to be of avail against: to compensate for (counter and avail). [Fr.,—L. *contrā,* against.]

counter, *kown′tér, v.t.* to contradict, combat: to meet or answer by a stroke or move (also *v.i.*).—*v.t.* to deliver a blow while parrying one. [Partly from encounter, partly directly from L. *contrā,* against.]

counterfeit, *kown′tér-fit, -fēt, v.t.* to imitate: to copy without authority, to forge.—*n.* something false or copied that pretends to be genuine—Also *adj.* [O.Fr. *contrefet,* from *con-trefaire,* to imitate—L. *contrā,* against, *facĕre,* to do.]

countermand, *kown-tér-mänd′, v.t.* to recall or to stop by a command in opposition to one already given (e.g. reinforcements): to revoke, cancel (a command, an order).—*n.* a revocation of a former order.—*adj.* countermand′-able. [O.Fr. *contremander* — L. *contrā,* against, and *mandāre,* to order.]

counterpane, *kown′tér-pān, n.* a coverlet for a bed. [O.Fr. *contrepointe,* a corr. of *coulte-pointe* — L. *culcita puncta,* a stitched pillow or cover; cf. quilt.]

counterpoint, *kown′tér-point, n.* (*mus.*) the art of combining melodies: a melody added as accompaniment to another.—*adj.* contra-punt′al, according to the rules of counterpoint. [Fr.,—*contre,* against, *point,* a point, from the pricks, points, or notes placed against those of the original melody.]

counter-tenor, *kown′tér-ten′ór, n.* a male voice

Neutral vowels in unaccented syllables: *em′pér-ór*; for certain sounds in foreign words see p. ix.

158

higher than a tenor, alto (q.v.). [Fr. *contre-teneur*.]

country, *kun'tri*, *n.* a rural, as distinct from an urban, region: a tract of land: the land in which one was born, or in which one resides: the territory of a nation: a nation.—*adj.* belonging to the country: rustic, rude. —*adj.* **coun'trified**, **coun'tryfied**, rustic.—*ns.* **coun'try-dance**, **con'tradance**, dance in which partners are arranged in opposite lines. —*n.pl.* **coun'try-folk**, the inhabitants of the country.—*ns.* **coun'try-house**, **-seat**, a landed proprietor's residence in the country; **coun'tryman**, one who lives in the country: a farmer: one born in the same country with another.—*fem.* **coun'try-woman**; **coun'tryside**, a district or part of the country.—**country cousin**, a relative from the country, unaccustomed to town sights or manners.—**go to the country**, in parliamentary usage, to hold a general election. [O.Fr. *contrée*—L. *contrā*, opposite.]

county. See **count** (1).

coup, *kōō*, *n.* a blow, stroke: a successful stroke or stratagem.—**coup de grâce** (*dé gräs*), a finishing blow; **coup d'état** (*dā-tä*), a sudden and violent change in government; **coup de poing** (*dé pwē*), a typical Old Stone Age axe consisting of a roughly pointed piece of stone held in the hand (*lit.* blow of the fist); **coup de théâtre** (*dé tä ä-tr'*), a sudden dramatic happening or action. [Fr., through L.—Gr. *kolaphos*, a blow.]

coupé, *kōō-pā*, *n.* a covered motor-car seated for two: an end compartment of a railway carriage with a seat on one side only. [Fr. *couper*, to cut.]

couple, *kup'l*, *n.* that which joins two things together: two of a kind joined together, or connected: two: a pair.—*v.t.* to join together.—*ns.* **coup'let**, two consecutive lines of verse that rhyme with each other; **coup'ling**, that which connects, as a contrivance for joining railway carriages: an appliance for transmitting motion in machinery. [O.Fr. *cople*—L. *copula*.]

coupon, *kōō'pon(g)*, *n.* a billet, check, or other slip of paper cut off from its counterpart: a voucher that payment will be made, goods sold, &c.: a piece cut from an advertisement entitling one to some privilege: a small subdivision of a page of a ration book entitling the holder to a specified amount of a foodstuff or other commodity: a party leader's recommendation of an electoral candidate: a printed betting form on which to enter forecasts of sports results. [Fr., *-couper*, to cut off.]

courage, *kur'ij*, *n.* the quality that enables men to meet dangers without giving way to fear, bravery: spirit.—*interj.* take courage!—*adj.* **coura'geous**, full of courage, brave.—*adv.* **coura'geously.**—*n.* **coura'geousness.**—**Dutch courage**, boldness induced by drinking; **the courage of one's convictions**, courage to put one's opinions into practice. [O.Fr. *corage* (Fr. *courage*)—L. *cor*, heart.]

courier, *kōō'ri-ér*, *n.* a messenger: a state messenger: a travelling attendant: an official guide who travels with tourists. [Fr.,—L. *currĕre*, to run.]

course, *kōrs*, *körs*, *n.* act of running: path in which anything moves: a channel for water: the direction pursued: the ground over which a race is run, golf is played, &c.: a race: regular progress: method of procedure: conduct: a prescribed series, as of lectures, &c.: each of the successive divisions of a meal: a range of bricks or stones on the same level in building.—*v.t.* to run, chase, or hunt after.—*v.i.* to move with speed, as in a race or hunt.—*ns.* **cours'er**, a runner: a swift horse: one who courses or hunts; **cours'ing**, hunting with greyhounds.—**of course**, naturally, needless to say. [Fr. *cours*—L. *cursus*, from *currĕre*, *cursum*, to run.]

court, *kōrt*, *kört*, *n.* a space enclosed: a space surrounded by houses: the palace of a sovereign: the body of persons who form his suite or council: attention designed to procure favour, affection, &c., as 'to pay court': (*law*) the hall of justice: the judges and officials who preside there, and body of persons assembled to decide causes.—*v.t.* to pay attentions to: to woo: to solicit, to seek.—*ns.* **court'-dress**, the special costume worn on state or ceremonious occasions; **court'-house**, a building where the law-courts are held; **court'ier**, one who frequents courts or palaces: one who courts or flatters.—*adj.* **court'ly**, having stately manners like those of a court.—*ns.* **court'liness**; **court'martial** (*-shäl*), a court held by officers of the armed forces to try offences against service discipline:—*pl.* **courts'-mar'tial**; **court'-plas'ter**, sticking-plaster made of silk, originally applied as patches on the face by ladies at court; **court'ship**, the act of wooing; **court shoe**, a light high-heeled dress shoe; **court'yard**, a court or enclosed ground before a house. [O.Fr. *cort*—Low L. *cortis*, a courtyard—L. *cors*, *cohors*, an enclosure.]

courtesan, **-zan**, *kōrt'-* or *kürt'i-zan*, *n.* a fashionable prostitute, mistress. [Fr. *courtisane*—It. *cortigiana*.]

courteous, *kürt'yus*, *kōrt'yus*, *adj.* polite, considerate and respectful in manner and action.—*adv.* **court'eously.**—*ns.* **court'eousness**; **courtesy** (*kûrt'-* or *kōrt'e-si*), courteous behaviour: an act of civility or respect: a curtsy.—*n.pl.* **court'esy-ti'tles**, titles allowed, by courtesy of society and not by legal right, to near relations of peers and to some others. [O.Fr. *corteis*, *cortois*—*cort*; see **court.**]

cousin, *kuz'n*, *n.* formerly a kinsman generally: now, the son or daughter of an uncle or aunt: a term used by a sovereign in addressing another, or to one of his own noblemen.—*n.* **cous'in-ger'man**, a first cousin.—**first cousins**, children of brothers and sisters—also called *cousins-german, full cousins*; **second cousins**, the children of first cousins: (loosely) one of two first cousins and the other's child—(*sing.*) sometimes called **first cousin once removed.** [Fr.,—L. *consōbrīnus—con-*, signifying connection, *sōbrīnus*, applied to the children of sisters—from the root of *soror*, a sister.]

couture, *kōō-tür'*, *n.* dressmaking or dress designing.—*n.* **couturier** (*kōō-tür-yā*), fem. **couturière** (*-yer*), a dressmaker or dress designer. [Fr.]

cove, *kōv*, *n.* a small inlet of the sea, a bay: a

fāte, *fär*; *mē*, *hûr* (her); *mīne*; *mōte*, *för*; *mūte*; *mōōn*, *fŏŏt*; *ᴛнen* (then) cavern or rocky recess. [O.E. *cofa*, a room; O.N. *kofi*, Ger. *koben*.]

cove, *kōv*, *n*. (*slang*) a fellow, a person.

covenant, *kuv´ė-nånt*, *n*. a mutual agreement: the writing containing the agreement: an engagement entered into between God and a person or a people.—*v.i.* to enter into an agreement: to contract or bargain.—*adj.* **cov´enanted**, agreed to by covenant: bound by covenant.—*n.* **cov´enanter** (usually in Scot. *kuv-ėn-ant´ėr*), one who signed or adhered to the *Scottish National Covenant* of 1638. [O.Fr.,—L. *con-*, together, *venīre*, to come.]

Coventry, *kov´-*, *kuv´ėnt-ri*, *n*. in **to send to Coventry**, to exclude from social intercourse.

cover, *kuv´ėr*, *v.t.* to put or spread something on, over, or about: to overspread: to clothe, be a covering to: to hide: to screen, protect: to extend over: to comprise: to be sufficient for: to traverse: to command with a weapon: to report (an occurrence) for a newspaper.—*n.* that which covers or protects: undergrowth, thicket, concealing game, &c.—*ns.* **cov´erage**, area, or aggregate of items, or (*insurance*) aggregate of risks, covered: part of the community reached by (a particular advertising medium); **cov´ering**; **cov´er-point** (*cricket*), the fielder who supports point and stands to his right.—*adj.* **cov´ert**, covered: secret, concealed.—*n.* a place that covers or affords protection.—*adv.* **cov´ertly.**—*n.* **cov´erture**, covering, shelter: (*law*) the condition of a married woman as legally under the protection of her husband.—**cover charge**, a charge per person, additional to the price of food and service, made by some restaurants; **covering letter**, a letter to explain documents enclosed with it; **cover up**, to cover completely: (*coll.*) to conceal, withhold information. [Fr. *couvrir*—L. *co-operīre*.]

coverlet, *kuv´ėr-let*, *n*. a bedcover. [Fr. *couvrir*, to cover, *lit*, a bed—L. *lectum*.]

covet, *kuv´et*, *v.t.* to desire or wish for eagerly: to wish for (what is unlawful):—*pr.p.* **cov´eting**; *pa.p.* **cov´eted.**—*adjs.* **cov´etable**; **cov´etous**, inordinately desirous: avaricious.—*adv.* **cov´etously.**—*n.* **cov´etousness.** [O.Fr. *coveiter*—L. *cupiditās, -ātis—cupĕre*, to desire.]

covey, *kuv´i*, *n*. a brood or hatch (of partridges): a small flock of game-birds. [O.Fr. *covée*—L. *cubāre*, to lie down.]

cow, *kow*, *n*. the female of bovine and certain other animals, as the elk, elephant, whale, &c.: (*slang*) an ugly or slovenly woman:—*pl.* **cows**, older **kine** (*kīn*), **kye** (*kī*).—*ns.* **cow´boy** (*U.S.*), a man who has charge of cattle on a ranch; **cow´-catch´er** (*U.S.*), an apparatus on the front of railway engines to throw off obstacles; **cow´herd**, one who herds cows; **cow´hide**, the hide of a cow made into leather: a whip made of cowhide; **cow´house**, **cow´shed**; **cow´-pars´ley**, an umbelliferous European plant of the hedges and woods; **cow´pox**, a disease which appears in pimples on the teats of the cow, the matter from the pimples being used for vaccination; **cow´-tree**, S. Amer. tree yielding nourishing fluid like milk. [O.E. *cū*, pl. *cȳ*; Ger. *kuh*; Sans. *go*.]

cow, *kow*, *v.t.* to subdue, intimidate. [Perh. from O.N. *kūga*; Dan. *kue*, to subdue.]

coward, *kow´ård*, *n*. one who turns tail, one without courage: often applied to one who brutally takes advantage of the weak.—*adjs.* **cow´ard**, **cow´ardly**, afraid of danger, timid: befitting a coward.—*ns.* **cow´ardice**, **cow´ardliness**, want of courage, timidity. [O.Fr. *couard*—L. *cauda*, a tail.]

cower, *kow´ėr*, *v.i.* to sink down through fear, &c.: to crouch timidly. [Cf. O.N. *kūra*, Dan. *kure*, to lie quiet.]

cowl, *kowl*, *n*. a cap or hood: a monk's hood: a cover for a chimney, &c.: an engine bonnet: a cowling.—*adj.* **cowled**, wearing a cowl.—*n.* **cowl´ing**, the casing of an aeroplane engine. [O.E. *cugele*; O.N. *kofl*; L. *cucullus*, hood.]

cowrie, **cowry**, *kow´ri*, *n*. a large genus of sea-shells used among primitive peoples as money and magical objects. [Hindi (*q.v.*) *kaurī*.]

cowslip, *kow´slip*, *n*. a beautiful species of primrose, common in English pastures. [O.E. *cū*, cow, *slyppe*, slime.]

coxcomb, *koks´kōm*, *n*. a strip of red cloth notched like a cock's comb, which professional fools used to wear: a fool: a fop. [**cockscomb**.]

coxswain, **cockswain**, *kok´swān*, or *kok´sn*. *n*. one who steers a boat: a petty officer in charge of a boat and crew.—Often contr. **cox**. [**cock** (cf. **cock-boat**) and **swain**.]

coy, *koy*, *adj.* modest: coquettishly bashful.—*adv.* **coy´ly.**—*n.* **coy´ness**. [Fr. *coi*—L. *quiētus*, quiet.]

coyote, *kō-yō´tā*, (*Amer.*) *kī-ōt´ē*, *kī´ōt*, *n*. a prairie-wolf of N. America. [Mexican *coyotl*.]

coypu, *koi´poo*, or *-pōo´*, *n*. a large South American water rodent yielding fur, now found wild in East Anglia—Also called **nutria**. [Native name.]

coz, *kuz*, *n*. a contraction of **cousin**.

cozen, *kuz´n*, *v.t.* to cheat.—*ns.* **coz´enage**, deceit; **coz´ener**. [Perh. *cousiner*, to claim kindred.]

cozy. See **cosy**.

crab, *krab*, *n*. any of the short-tailed decapod crustaceans: (*cap.*) *Cancer* (*q.v.*).—**catch a crab**, in rowing, to fail to dip the oar correctly and thus lose balance. [O.E. *crabba*; Ger. *krebs*.]

crab, *krab*, *n*. any of several wild bitter apples: a sour-tempered person.—*ns.* **crab´-apple**; **crab´-tree**. [Ety. doubtful.]

crabbed, *krab´id*, *adj.* ill-natured, morose: (of writings) intricate, difficult to understand: (of handwriting) ill-formed, cramped.—*adv.* **crabb´edly.**—*n.* **crabb´edness**. [**crab** (1), intermixed in meaning with **crab** (2).]

crack, *krak*, *v.t.* and *v.i.* to make, or cause to make, a sharp sudden sound: to break into chinks: to split: to break partially or suddenly and sharply: in distilling petroleum, to break down hydro-carbons into simpler ones.—*v.t.* to break open (as a safe): to solve the mystery of (a code).—*v.i.* (*Scot.*) to chat.—*n.* a sudden sharp splitting sound: a chink: a flaw: a blow: friendly chat: (*U.S.*) a biting comment: an expert.—*adj.* (*coll.*) excellent.—*n.* **crack´-brain**, a crazy person.—*adjs.* **crack´-brained**; **cracked**, rent: damaged: crazy.—*ns.* **crack´er**, one who or that which cracks: a thin crisp biscuit: a small firework, exploding when

Neutral vowels in unaccented syllables: *em´pėr-ór*; for certain sounds in foreign words see p. ix.

160

pulled asunder; **cracks'man**, a burglar.—**crack a joke**, to utter a joke with some effect; **crack down on**, to take firm action against; **crack up**, to extol: to fail suddenly, to go to pieces. [O.E. *cracian*, to crack; cf. Du. *kraken*, Gael. *crac*.]

crackle, *krak'l*, *v.i.* to give out slight but frequent cracks.—*n.* the sound of such cracks.—*n.* **crack'ling**, the rind of roast pork.—*adj.* **crack'ly**, brittle.—*n.* **crack'nel**, a light, brittle biscuit. [Freq. of **crack**.]

cradle, *krā'dl*, *n.* a bed or crib in which a child is rocked: (*fig.*) infancy: a place where anything (e.g. a race) is nurtured in the earliest period of its existence: a supporting framework, a frame in which anything is enclosed or partly enclosed: a frame to keep bedclothes from pressing on a patient: a frame under a ship for launching it.—*v.t.* to lay or rock in a cradle: to nurture. [O.E. *cradol*; ety. obscure.]

craft, *krāft*, *n.* cunning: dexterity: an art, skilled trade: one or more ships (originally small): aircraft spacecraft.—*ns.* **crafts'man**, one engaged in a craft, **crafts'manship**, skill in a craft.—*adj.* **craft'y**, having skill: cunning, wily.—*adv.* **craft'ily**.—*n.* **craft'iness**. [O.E. *cræft*; Ger. *kraft*, power.]

crag, *krag*, *n.* a rough steep rock or point: (*geol.*) a type of shelly and sandy deposit.—*adjs.* **cragg'ed**, **cragg'y**, full of crags or broken rocks: rough, rugged.—*ns.* **cragg'edness**, **cragg'iness**; **crags'man**, one skilled in climbing rocks. [W. *craig*, a rock; Gael. *creag*, *carraig*.]

crake, *krāk*, *v.i.* to utter a cry like a crow, &c.

cram, *kram*, *v.t.* to press close: to stuff, to fill to superfluity: to stuff the memory with (information required for a special examination).—*v.i.* to eat greedily: to learn by cram ming:—*pr.p.* cramm'ing; *pa.p.* crammed.—*n.* a crush.—*adj.* **cram'-full**.—*n.* **cramm'er**, one who crams a pupil, or a subject, for an examination. [O.E. *crammian*; O.N. *kremja*, to squeeze.]

crambo, *kram'bo*, *n.* a game in which one gives a word to which another finds a rhyme: rhyme. [Prob. from L. *crambē repetita*, cabbage served up again.]

cramp, *kramp*, *n.* a spasmodic contraction of the muscles: restraint: a cramp-iron: a contrivance with a movable part which can be screwed tight so as to press things together.—*v.t.* to affect with spasms: to confine narrowly: to restrict, restrain unduly (e.g. efforts): to fasten with a cramp-iron.—*ns.* **cramp'-i'ron** a piece of metal bent at both ends for binding things together; **cramp'on**, a grappling-iron: an iron plate with spikes, for the foot, for hill-climbing, walking on ice, &c.—**writer's cramp** (see **writer**). [O.Fr. *crampe*; cf. Du. *kramp*, Ger. *krampf*.]

cran, *kran*, *n.* a measure of capacity for herrings just landed, comprising about 1000 on an average. [Prob. Gael. *crann*.]

cranberry, *kran'ber-i*, *n.* the red acid berry of a genus of small evergreen shrubs growing in marshy ground: any of the shrubs themselves. [For *craneberry*; origin obscure; cf. Ger. *kranbeere*, *kranich-beere*, crane berry.]

crane, *krān*, *n.* any of several large wading birds, with long legs, neck, and bill: a bent

pipe for drawing liquor out of a cask, or a machine for raising heavy weights—both named from their likeness to the bird.—*v.t.* to raise with a crane.—*v.t.* or *v.i.* to stretch out (the neck).—*ns.* **crane'-fly**, one of several flies with very long legs, the daddy-long-legs; **cranes'bill**, **crane's'-bill**, any species of wild geranium (q.v.), so called from shape of car pels. [O.E. *cran*; Ger. *kranich*, W. *garan*.]

cranium, *krā'ni-um*, *n.* the skull: the bones enclosing the brain:—*pl.* **crā'nia**.—*adj.* **crā'nial**, pertaining to the cranium.—*n.* **craniol'ogy**, the study of skulls: phrenology.—*adj.* **craniolog'ical**.—*n.* **craniol'ogist**, one skilled in craniology. [Low L. *crānium*—Gr. *krānion*.]

crank, *krangk*, *n.* a crook or bend: a conceit in speech: a whim: an eccentric person: (*mach.*) an arm on a shaft for communicating motion to or from the shaft.—*v.t.* to move or seek to move by turning a crank (also **crank up**)—*adj.* **crank'y**, crooked: in bad condition, shaky: full of whims: cross.—*n.* **crank'iness**.—*ns.* **crank'case**, a box-like casing for the crankshaft and connecting-rods of some types of reciprocating-engine; **crank'shaft**, the main shaft of an engine or other machine, which carries a crank or cranks for the attachment of connecting-rods. [O.E. *cranc*; cf. Ger. *krank*.]

crank, *krangk*, **crank-sided**, *krangk-sī'ded*, *adj.* (*naut.*) liable to be upset.—*n.* **crank'ness**.

crankle, *krangk'l*, *n.* a turn, winding, bend.—*v.t.* to bend: to twist. [Freq. of **crank** (1).]

crannog, *kran'og*, *n.* in Scotland and Ireland, a fortified island (partly natural and partly artificial) in a lake: a lake-dwelling. [Gael. *crann*, a tree.]

cranny, *kran'i*, *n.* a fissure, chink: a secret place.—*adj.* **crann'ied**, having crannies or fissures. [Fr. *cran*, a notch.]

crape, *krāp*, *n.* a thin silk fabric with wrinkled surface, usually dyed black, used for mournings.—*adj.* made of crape. [O.Fr. *crespe* (Fr. *crêpe*)—L. *crispus*, crisp.]

crapulence, *krap'ū-lens*, *n.* sickness caused by intemperance.—*adjs.* **crap'ulous**, **crap'ulent**. [Fr. *crapule*—L. *crāpula*, intoxication.]

crash, *krash*, *n.* a noise as of things breaking or being crushed by falling: a collision: a disastrous fall or failure.—*adj.* involving suddenness or speed or great effort: planned to deal with an emergency speedily: intended to lessen effects of a crash.—*v.i.* to fall to pieces with a loud noise: to be violently impelled (against, into): to land in such a way as to be seriously damaged, or destroyed.—Also *v.t.*—*ns.* **crash'-dive'**, a sudden dive of a submarine; **crash'-hel'met**, a cushioned safety headdress worn by racing-motorists, motor cyclists, &c.—*v.i.* and *v.t.* **crash'-land**, to land (an aircraft) in an emergency without lowering the undercarriage.—*n.* **crash'-land'ing**. [From the sound.]

crash, *krash*, *n.* a coarse strong linen. [Perh. from Russ.]

crasis, *krā'sis*, *n.* (*gram.*) the mingling or contraction of two vowels into one long vowel, or into a diphthong:—*pl.* **crā'sēs**. [Gr. *krāsis*—*kerannȳnai*, to mix.]

crass, *kras*, *adj.* thick: coarse: stupid.—*ns.*

crass′itude; crass′ness. [O.Fr. *cras*—L. *crassus*.]

cratch, *krach, n.* a crib to hold hay for cattle, a manger. [Fr. *crèche,* a manger; from a Gmc. root, whence also **crib.**]

crate, *krāt, n.* an openwork container, now usu. of wood slats, for packing crockery or for carrying fruit, &c: (*slang*) a dilapidated aeroplane or car. [L. *crātis,* a hurdle.]

crater, *krāt′ér, n.* the bowl-shaped mouth of a volcano: a hole made in the ground by the explosion of a shell, mine, bomb, &c. [L. *crātēr*—Gr. *krātēr,* a large bowl for mixing wine, from *kerannȳnai,* to mix.]

cravat, *kra-vat′, n.* a kind of neckcloth worn chiefly by men. [Fr. *cravate*—introduced in 17th cent. from the *Cravates* or Croatians.]

crave, *krāv, v.t.* to beg earnestly, to beseech: to long for: to require.—*n.* **crav′ing,** desire, longing. [O.E. *crafian*; O.N. *krefja.*]

craven, *krāv′n, n.* a coward, a spiritless fellow.—*adj.* cowardly, spiritless.—*adv.* **crav′enly.**—*n.* **crav′enness.** [Origin obscure.]

craw, *krö, n.* the crop or first stomach of fowls, a pouchlike enlargement of the gullet. [M.E. *crawe*; cf. Du. *kraag,* neck.]

crawfish. See **crayfish.**

crawl, *kröl, v.i.* to move as a worm: to behave abjectly: to move slowly or stealthily: to be covered with crawling things.—*n.* the act of crawling: a slow pace: an alternate overhand swimming stroke.—*n.* **crawl′er.** [Scand.,—Ger. *krabbeln,* to creep.]

crayfish, *krā′fish,* **crawfish,** *krö′fish, n.* a family of fresh-water crustaceans: the small spiny lobster. [M.E. *crevice*—O.Fr. *crevice*—Old High Ger. *krebiz,* a crab.]

crayon, *krā′on, n.* a pencil made of chalk or pipeclay, variously coloured, used for drawing: a drawing in crayons. [Fr. *crayon*—*craie,* chalk, from L. *crēta,* chalk.]

craze, *krāz, v.t.* to weaken: to derange (of the intellect).—*n.* a foolish enthusiasm, fashion, hobby.—*adj.* **craz′y,** frail: demented: fantastically composed of irregular pieces (as a quilt or pavement).—*n.* **craz′iness.** [Scand.; Swed. *krasa,* Dan. *krase,* to crackle; whence also Fr. *écraser,* to crush.] ·

creak, *krēk, v.i.* to make a sharp, grating sound, as of a hinge, &c.—*n.* a noise of this kind.—*adj.* **creak′y.** [From sound, cf. *crake, croak.*]

cream, *krēm, n.* the oily substance that forms on milk: the best part of anything: any creamlike preparation or refreshment.—*v.t.* to take off the cream.—*v.i.* to gather or form cream.—*adj.* **cream′-col′oured,** of the colour of cream, light yellow.—*n.* **cream′ery,** an establishment where butter and cheese are made.—*adjs.* **cream′-faced,** pale-faced; **cream′y,** full of or like cream: gathering like cream.—*n.* **cream′iness.**—**cream of tartar,** purified tartar (q.v.), an ingredient in baking powders. [O.Fr. *cresme, creme*—L. *chrisma.*]

crease, *krēs, n.* a mark made by folding or doubling anything: (*cricket*) a line defining the position of the batsman or of the bowler.—*v.t.* to make creases in anything.—*v.i.* to become creased.—*adjs.* **crease′-resist′ant, -resist′ing,** of a fabric, not becoming creased in the course of normal wear.

create, *krē-āt′, v.t.* to bring into being: to invest with (a new form, character, rank, or office): to produce, as any work of imagination: to act for the first time (a character in a new play): to make (e.g. an impression).—*v.i.* (*slang*) to make a fuss.—*n.* **crea′tion,** the act of creating, esp. the universe: that which is created: the universe.—*adj.* **crea′tive,** having power to create: that creates: showing imagination or orginality.—*adv.* **crea′tively.**—*ns.* **crea′tiveness; creativ′ity; crea′tor,** he who creates, a maker; **creature** (*krē′tyŭr, -chŭr*), what has been created, esp. an animated being, an animal, a man: a term of contempt or of endearment: a dependent or puppet.—**the Creator,** the Supreme Being, God. [L. *creāre, -ātum.*]

creatine, *krē′a-tin, n.* a constant and characteristic constituent of the striped muscle of vertebrates. [Gr. *kreas,* gen. *kreatos,* flesh.]

crèche, *kresh, n.* a public nursery for children. [Fr.]

credence, *krē′déns, n.* belief: (*obs.*) trust: small table beside the altar on which the bread and wine are placed before being consecrated.—*adjs.* **crē′dent,** apt to believe; **crēden′tial,** giving a title to belief or credit.—*n.* that which entitles to credit or confidence: (*pl.*) written evidence of trustworthiness or authority.—*adj.* **credible** (*kred′-*), that may be believed.—*ns.* **credibil′ity, cred′ibleness.**—*adv.* **cred′ibly.**—*n.* **cred′it,** belief: honour: reputation: influence derived from good reputation: a source of honour: sale on trust: time allowed for payment: the side of an account on which payments received are entered: a sum placed at a person's disposal in a bank: a credit title.—*v.t.* to believe: (*lit., fig.*) to enter on the credit side of an account: to attribute to (foll. by *with*).—*adj.* **cred′itable,** trustworthy: bringing credit or honour.—*n.* **cred′itableness.**—*adv.* **cred′itably.**—*n.* **cred′itor,** one to whom a debt is due.—*adj.* **cred′ulous,** apt to believe without sufficient evidence: unsuspecting.—*adv.* **cred′ulously.**—*ns.* **cred′ulousness, credū′lity,** disposition to believe on insufficient evidence.—**credibility gap,** gap between what is claimed and what seems likely; **credit card,** a card issued by a credit card company which enables the holder to have purchases debited to an account kept by the company: a similar card issued by other concerns, e.g. banks; **credit squeeze,** restriction placed by a government on the amount of credit an individual or firm may obtain; **credit titles,** acknowledgments of the work of participants other than actors, projected on the screen at the showing of a cinematograph film.—**letter of credence,** letter of introduction, credential. [L. *crēdere,* to believe.]

creed, *krēd, n.* a summary of articles of religious belief. [O.E. *crēda*—L. *credo,* I believe.]

creek, *krēk, n.* a small inlet or bay, or the tidal estuary of a river: in America and Australia, a small river. [Prob. Scand., O.N. *kriki,* a nook; cf. Du. *kreek,* a bay.]

creel, *krēl, n.* a basket, esp. a fish basket. [Prob. Celt.; cf. Old Ir. *criol,* a chest.]

creep, *krēp, v.i.* to move on or near the ground: to move slowly or stealthily (*lit.* and *fig.*): to

Neutral vowels in unaccented syllables: *em′pér-ór*; for certain sounds in foreign words see p. ix.

grow along the ground or on supports, as a vine: to fawn or cringe: to shudder:—*pa.t.* and *pa.p.* crept.—*n.* a crawl: a narrow passage: (*slang*) an unpleasant person: (*pl.*) horrible shrinking.—*n.* creep′er, a creeping plant: a genus of small climbing birds.—*adj.* creep′y, creeping: causing creeps, weird. [O.E. *crēopan*; Du. *kruipen.*]

creese, crease. See kris.

cremation, *krem-ā′sh(ó)n, n.* act of burning, esp. of the dead.—*v.t.* cremate′.—*n.* cremā-tōr′ium, a place where cremation is done. [L. *crematiō, -ōnis—cremāre,* to burn.]

crème, (properly crème), *krem, n.* French for cream, applied to various creamy substances.—crème de la crème (*de la krem*), (*Fr.*) *lit.* cream of the cream, the very best; crème (crème) de menthe (*dé māt*), a peppermint-flavoured liqueur.

cremona, *krem-ō′na, n.* a superior kind of violin made at *Cremona* in Italy.

crenate, -d, *krēn′āt, krēn′ät, krēn ät′, -id, adjs.* (*bot.*) having rounded teeth between sharp notches.—*n.* crenā′tion, a formation of this type. [Low L. *crēna,* a notch.]

crenellated, *kre′nel-āt-id, adj.* furnished with battlements: indented. [Fr.,—Low L. *crēna,* a notch.]

Creole, *krē′ōl, adj.* and *n.* strictly applied in former Spanish, French, and Portugese colonies to persons born in the colony of pure European blood: (loosely) anyone born in these countries of a race not native to them, even if of mixed blood.—Also creole. [Fr *créole*—Sp. *criollo—criadillo,* a nursling.]

creosote, *krē′ō-sōt,* creasote, *krē′a-sōt, n.* an oily liquid obtained by the destructive distillation of wood-tar.—*v.t.* to treat with creosote as preservative. [Gr. *kreas,* flesh, *sōtēr,* saviour—*sōzein,* to save.]

crêpe, *krāp, n.* a crape like fabric: rubber rolled in thin crinkly sheets: a thin pancake.—*v.t.* to frizz, as hair.—*n.* crêpe-de-chine (*dé shēn*), a crape-like fabric, originally of silk. [Fr., see crape.]

crepitate, *krep′i-tāt, v.i.* to crackle, snap.—*n.* crepitā′tion, the sound detected in the lungs by auscultation in certain diseases. [L. *crepi-tāre, -ātum,* freq. of *crepāre,* to crack, rattle.]

crept, *krept, pa.t.* and *pa.p.* of creep.

crepuscular, *kre-pus′kū-lår, adj.* of or pertaining to twilight. [L. *crepusculum—creper,* dusky, obscure.]

crescendo, *kresh-en′dō, adv.* (*mus.*) gradually increasing in force or loudness.—*n.* a passage so marked: (*lit.* and *fig.*) increasing loudness or intensity.—Often *cres., cresc.,* or <. [It.]

crescent, *kres′ent, adj.* increasing: shaped like the new or old moon.—*n.* the moon as she increases towards half-moon: a figure like the crescent moon: the Turkish standard or emblem: (the symbol of) the Moslem faith: a range of buildings in curved form.—*adjs.* cres′cented, crescent′ic. [L. *crescens, -entis,* pr.p. of *crescēre,* to grow.]

cress, *kres, n.* a name of many pungent-leaved plants. [O.E. *cresse, cerse;* cf. Du. *kers,* Ger. *kresse.*]

cresset, *kres′et, n.* an iron basket, or the like, for combustibles, placed on a beacon, lighthouse,

wharf, &c.: a torch generally. [O.Fr. *cresset, crasset*—Old Du. *kruysel,* a hanging lamp.]

crest, *krest, n.* the comb or tuft on the head of a cock or other bird: the summit of anything: a plume of feathers or other ornament on the top of a helmet: a badge or emblem.—*v.t.* to furnish with, or serve for, a crest: to surmount.—*adjs.* crest′fallen, dejected, dispirited; crest′less, without a crest: not of high birth. [O.Fr. *creste*—L. *crista.*]

cretaceous, *krē-tā′shus, adj.* composed of or like chalk.—*n.* (*cap.*) the latest period of the Secondary geological era.—Cretaceous System, the rocks formed during this period. [L. *crētāceus—crēta,* chalk.]

cretin, *krē′tin* (or *kre′-*), *n.* one affected with cretinism.—*n.* crē′tinism (or *kre′-*), a state of mental defect, associated with bodily deformity or arrested growth.—*adj.* cre′tinous. [Fr. *crétin*—Swiss *crestin*—L. *christianus*—cf. the frequent use of *innocent* for *idiot.*]

cretonne, *kret on′* or *kret′on, n.* a strong printed cotton fabric used for curtains or for covering furniture. [Fr.; *Creton* in Normandy.]

crevasse, *krév-as′, n.* a crack or split, esp. applied to a cleft in a glacier.—*n.* crevice (*krev′is*), a crack, fissure: a narrow opening. [O.Fr. *crevace*—L. *crepāre,* to creak.]

crew, *krōō, n.* a company (often contemptuous): ship's company: those in charge of travelling bus, train, aeroplane.—*v.i.* to act as a member of the crew of a ship, &c.—crew cut, a short, cropped hair style. [O.Fr. *creue,* increase *croistre,* to grow.]

crew, *krōō, pa.t.* of crow.

crewel, *krōō′el, n.* a fine worsted yarn used for embroidery and tapestry. [Orig. a mono syllable, *crule, crewle*; ety. uncertain.]

crib, *krib, n.* a manger or fodder-receptacle: a stall for oxen: a child's bed: a small cottage or hovel: a confined place: (*coll.*) a key or baldly literal translation used by schoolboys.—*v.t.* to put in a crib, confine: to pilfer: to plagiarise:—*pr.p.* cribb′ing; *pa.p.* cribbed.—*n.* crib′bage (*krib′ij*), a card game in which each player discards a certain number of cards for the crib, and scores by holding certain combinations, &c. [O.E. *crib*; Ger. *krippe.*]

crick, *krik, n.* a spasm or cramp of the muscles, especially of the neck. [Prob. onomatopoeic.]

cricket, *krik′et, n.* a family of insects of the same order as the grasshoppers, the males of which make a chirping noise with their wing-covers. [O.Fr. *criquet*; cf. Du. *krekel,* Ger. *kreckel.*]

cricket, *krik′et, n.* an outdoor game played with bats, a ball, and wickets, between two sides of eleven each: (*coll.*) fair play.—*n.* crick′eter. [Fr. *criquet*; ety. uncertain.]

cried, *krīd, pa.t.* and *pa.p.* of cry.—*n.* crī′er, one who cries or proclaims, esp. an officer who makes public announcements.

crime, *krīm, n.* an act punishable by law: such acts collectively: an offence, sin.—*adj.* criminal (*krim′-*), relating to crime: guilty of crime: of the nature of crime.—*n.* one guilty of crime.—*n.* criminal′ity, guiltiness.—*adv.* crim′inally.—*v.t.* crim′ināte, to accuse.—*n.* criminā′tion.—*adj.* crim′inatory.—*ns.* criminol′ogy, that branch of anthropology which treats of crime and criminals; **criminol'ogist.** [Fr.,—L. *crīmen, -inis.*]

crime passionel, *krēm pa-syo-nel,* a crime motivated by (sexual) passion. [Fr.]

crimp, *krimp, adj.* made crisp or brittle.—*v.t.* to press into folds or pleats: to give a corrugated appearance to: to make crisp: to seize or decoy.—*n.* a pleat: one who presses or decoys sailors, &c. [O.E.*gecrympan,* to curl; same root as **cramp.**]

crimson, *krim'zn, n.* a deep red colour, tinged with blue.—*adj.* deep red.—*v.t.* to dye crimson.—*v.i.* to become crimson: to blush. [M.E. *crimosin* —O.Fr. *cramoisin* —Ar. word—*qirmiz,* kermes, the insect from which the dye was first made.]

cringe, *krinj, v.i.* to bend or crouch with servility or fear: to behave obsequiously.—*n.* **cringe'-ling,** one who cringes. [Related to O.E. *crincan, cringan,* to shrink.]

cringle, *kring'gl, n.* an eyelet of rope or metal in the edges of a sail. [Gmc.; cf. Ger. *kringel.*]

crinkle, *kring'kl, v.t.* to twist, wrinkle, crimp.—*v.i.* to wrinkle up, curl.—*n.* a wrinkle.—*adj.* **crink'ly,** wrinkly. [Frequentative of O.E. *crincan;* same root as **cringe.**]

crinoline, *krin'o-lin, n.* a stiff fabric of horsehair and flax, employed to distend women's attire: a petticoat or skirt distended by hoops of steel-wire. [Fr., *crin* (L. *crīnis*), hair, and *lin* (L. *līnum*), flax.]

cripple, *krip'l, n.* a lame person.—*adj.* lame.—*v.t.* to lame: to disable, deprive of power. [O.E. *crypel;* conn. with **creep.**]

crisis, *krī'sis, n.* point or time for deciding anything: the decisive moment or turning-point:—*pl.* **crises** (*krī'sēz*). [Gr. *krīsis,* from *krīnein,* to decide.]

crisp, *krisp, adj.* curling closely: having a wavy surface: dry and brittle: fresh and bracing: firm, decided (e.g. style).—*v.t.* to curl or twist: to make crisp or wavy.—*adv.* **crisp'ly.**—*n.* **crisp'ness.**—*adj.* **crisp'y.** [O.E.,—L. *crispus.*]

criss-cross, *kris'-kros, n.* a mark formed by two lines in the form of a cross: (*hist.*) the cross at the beginning of the alphabet on a hornbook (also *Christ-cross*): a network of crossing lines.—*adj.* and *adv.* crosswise.—*v.t.* and *v.i.* to cross repeatedly. [**Christ('s) cross.**]

cristate, *kris'tāt, adj.* crested. [L. *cristātus*—*crista,* a crest.]

criterion, *krī-tē'ri-on, n.* a means or standard of judging:—*pl.* **crite'ria.** [Gr. *kritērion*—*kritēs,* a judge.]

critic, *krit'ik, n.* one who appraises literary or artistic work: a fault-finder.—*adj.* **crit'ical,** relating to criticism: discriminating: captious: at or relating to a turning-point, transition, or crisis: decisive.—*adv.* **crit'ically.**—*n.* **crit'ical-ness.**—*v.t.* **crit'icise,** to pass judgment on: to censure.—*ns.* **crit'icism,** the art of judging, esp. in literature or the fine arts: a critical judgment or observation; **critique** (*kri-tēk'*), a critical examination of any production, a review.—**higher criticism,** as distinguished from *textual* or *verbal criticism,* the enquiry into the composition, date, and authenticity of the books of Scripture, from historical and literary considerations. [Gr. *krītikos*—*krīnein,* to judge.]

croak, *krōk, v.i.* to utter a low hoarse sound, as a frog or raven: to grumble: to forebode evil: (*slang*) to die.—*n.* the sound of a frog or raven.—*n.* **croak'er.**—*adj.* **croak'y.** [From the sound. Cf. **crake, crow.**]

crochet, *krō'shā, n.* fancy knitting done by means of a small hook.—*v.i.* and *v.t.* to do, or to make in, such work. [Fr. *crochet*—*croche, croc,* a hook.]

crock, *krok, n.* a pot or jar.—*n.* **crock'ery,** earthenware, vessels of baked clay: all types of domestic pottery. [O.E. *croc;* Ger. *krug;* perh. of Celt. origin.]

crock, *krok, n.* an old horse: a decrepit person. [Cf. Norw. and Swed. *krake,* a poor beast.]

crocodile, *krok'o-dīl, n.* a genus of large amphibious reptiles found in the rivers of Asia, Africa, South America, and northern Australia: a family including alligators, &c.: the order to which these belong: a double file of schoolgirls.—**crocodile tears,** affected tears, hypocritical grief—from the legend that crocodiles shed tears over killing animals. [O.Fr. *cocodrille* —L. *crocodīlus* —Gr. *krokodeilos,* a lizard.]

crocus, *krō'kus, n.* a bulbous plant with brilliant yellow, purple, or white flowers, growing from a corm. [L. *crocus*—Gr. *krokos;* prob. of Eastern origin.]

croft, *kroft, n.* a small piece of arable land adjoining a dwelling: a kind of small farm.—*n.* **croft'er.** [O.E. *croft;* perh. cog. with Du. *kroft.*]

cromlech, *krom'lek, n.* a stone circle: formerly applied to a dolmen (q.v.). [W. *cromlech*—*crom,* curved, circular, and *llech,* a stone.]

crone, *krōn, n.* an old woman, usually in contempt. [Perh. O.Fr.*carogne,* a crabbed woman; or Celt.]

crony, *krōn'i, n.* a close companion.

crook, *krook, n.* a bend: anything bent: a staff bent at the end, as a shepherd's or bishop's: a trick: a swindler.—*v.t.* to bend or form into a hook.—*v.i.* to bend or be bent.—*adj.* **crook'ed** (*-id*), not straight: dishonest: (in this sense *krookt*) bent like a crook.—*adv.* **crook'edly.**—*n.* **crook'edness.** [Prob. Scand.; cf. O.N. *krōkr,* Dan. *krog.*]

croon, *krōōn, v.t.* and *v.i.* to sing or hum in an undertone: to sing quietly in an extravagantly sentimental manner.—Also *n.*—*n.* **croon'er.** [Cf. Du. *kreunen,* to groan.]

crop, *krop, n.* the top of anything: a sprout: a hunting whip: mode of cutting or wearing short hair: the total quantity cut or harvested: total growth or produce: the craw of a bird.—*v.t.* to cut off the top or ends: to cut short: to raise crops on: to cut the hair of:—*pr.p.* **cropp'ing;** *pa.p.* **cropped.**—*adj.* **crop'-eared,** having ears cropped, or hair cropped to show the ears.—**crop out,** to appear above the surface; **crop up** (*lit.* and *fig.*), to come up unexpectedly.—**neck and crop,** headlong: completely. [O.E. *crop,* the top shoot of a plant, the crop of a bird.]

cropper, *krop'ér, n.* a fall: a failure.—**come a cropper,** to have a fall, to fail, perhaps from phrase *neck and crop* (see **crop**).

croquet, *krō'kā, n.* a game in which wooden balls are driven by long-handled mallets through a series of arches set in the ground. [Fr. *croquet,*

Neutral vowels in unaccented syllables: em'pér-òr; *for certain sounds in foreign words see p. ix.*

a dial. form of *crochet*, dim. of *croc*, *croche*, a crook.]

croquette, *krok-et′*, *n.* a fried ball or cake of minced meat or fish. [Fr. *croquer*, to crunch.]

crosier, **crozier**, *krō′zhyér*, *n.* the pastoral staff or crook of a bishop or abbot. [M.E. *crose* or *croce*—Late L. *crocia*, a crook.]

cross, *kros*, *n.* a gibbet on which the Romans exposed malefactors, consisting of two beams, one placed transversely to the other: the gibbet on which Christ suffered: (the symbol of) the Christian religion: the sufferings of Christ: anything that crosses or thwarts: adversity or affliction in general: a hybrid: a monument, often in the form of a cross, where proclamations are made, &c.: a cross-shaped decoration.—*v.t.* to mark with a cross, or to make the sign of the cross over: to set something across: to draw a line across: to place crosswise: to pass, or cause to pass, from one side to the other of: to thwart: to interbreed.—*v.i.* to lie or pass across: to meet and pass.—*adj.* lying across, transverse: oblique: adverse: ill-tempered: reciprocal: hybrid.—*adv.* **cross′ly**, peevishly.—**Geneva cross** (see **Geneva**); **Greek cross**, an upright cross with limbs of equal length; **Latin cross**, an upright cross having the lower limb longer than the others; **Maltese cross**, the badge of the knights of Malta, converging towards a point in the centre with two points to each limb; **St Andrew's cross**, a cross of two shafts of equal length crossed diagonally; **Southern Cross**, the chief constellation of the southern hemisphere, the stars of which form a cross.—*n.* **cross′-bench**, a bench laid crosswise: a bench on which independent members of parliament sit.—*adj.* independent.—*n.* **cross′-bill**, a genus of finches with the mandibles of the bill crossing each other near the points.—*n.pl.* **cross′-bones**, two thigh-bones laid across each other—forming, with the skull, a conventional emblem of death or piracy.—*ns.* **cross′bow**, a weapon for shooting arrows, formed of a bow placed crosswise on a *stock* or wooden bar; **cross′-breed**, a breed produced by the crossing or intermixing of different races.—*adj.* **cross′-bred**.—*n.* **cross′-bun**, a bun marked with a cross, customarily eaten on Good Friday.—*v.t.* **cross′-check**, to test the accuracy of a statement, &c. by consulting various sources of information.—Also *v.i.* and *n.*—*adjs.* **cross′-coun′try**, across the fields; **cross′-cut**, cut transversely: made or used for cutting transversely.—*v.t.* **cross′-exam′ine**, to test the evidence of a witness by subjecting him to an examination by the opposite party: to question searchingly (often impertinently).—*n.* **cross′-examina′tion**.—*adj.* **cross′-eyed**, having a squint.—*ns.* **cross′-fertilisa′tion**, the fertilisation of a plant by pollen from another; **cross′-fire** (*mil.*), the crossing of lines of fire from two or more points.—*adj.* **cross′-grained**, having the grain or fibres crossed or intertwined: perverse, contrary, intractable.—*ns.* **cross′ing**, act of going across: the place where a roadway, &c., may be crossed: thwarting: cross-breeding.—*adj.* **cross′-legged**, having the legs crossed.—*ns.* **cross′-over**, a road passing over the top of another; **cross′-patch**, an

ill-natured person; **cross′-ply tyre**, a tyre in which the layers of fabric forming the carcass are wrapped so that they cross each other diagonally; **cross′-pur′pose**, a contrary purpose (e.g. *at cross-purposes*).—*v.t.* **cross′-ques′tion**, to question minutely, to cross-examine.—*ns.* **cross′-ref′erence**, a reference in a book to another title or passage; **cross′road**, a road crossing the principal road: (*pl.*) the place of crossing of two roads: (*fig.*) a point where a critical choice of action has to be made; **cross′-sec′tion**, a transverse section: a comprehensive representation (e.g. of the people of a locality, of their opinions): effective target area of a nucleus for a particular reaction under specified conditions.—*n.pl.* **cross′trees**, pieces of timber placed across the upper end of the lower masts and topmasts of a ship.—*n.* **cross′-wind′**, a wind blowing across the path of, e.g. an aeroplane.—*adv.* **cross′wise**, in the form of a cross, across.—*ns.* **cross′word** (**puzzle**), a puzzle in which a square with blank spaces is to be filled with letters which, read across or down, will make words corresponding to given clues; **crossed cheque**, a cheque with two lines drawn across it to indicate that it is payable only to a bank account.—**on the cross**, diagonally. [O.E. *cros*—O.N. *kross*—L. *crux*, *crucis*.]

crotal, **crottle**, *krot′l*, *n.* a lichen (of various kinds) used for dyeing. [Gael. *crotal*.]

crotchet, *kroch′et*, *n.* a hook: a note in music, equal to half a minim, 𝄾: a crooked or perverse fancy, a whim.—*adj.* **crotch′ety**, having crotchets or peculiarities, whimsical. [Fr. *crochet*, dim. of *croche*, a hook.]

croton, *krō′ton*, *n.* a genus of tropical plants, producing a brownish-yellow oil, a violent purgative, having a hot, biting taste [Gr. *krotōn* a tick or mite, which the seed of the plant resembles.]

crouch, *krowch*, *v.i.* to squat or lie close to the ground: to cringe, to fawn. [M.E. *cruchen*, *crouchen*; possibly connected with **crook**.]

croup, *krōōp*, *n.* inflammation of the larynx and trachea in children, associated with a peculiar ringing cough, present especially in diphtheria. [Imitative.]

croup, *krōōp*, *n.* the rump of a horse: the place behind the saddle. [Fr. *croupe*, protuberance.]

croupier, *krōō′pi-ér*, *n.* one who sits at the lower end of the table as assistant chairman at a public dinner: a vice-president: he who watches the cards and collects the money at the gaming-table. [Fr. 'one who rides on the *croup*'; see **croup** (2).]

crow, *krō*, *n.* a genus of moderately large birds, generally black, uttering a cawing cry, the British species of which are the raven, the rook, the hooded crow, and the carrion crow: the cry of a cock: a child's inarticulate cry of joy.—*v.i.* to croak: to cry as a cock: to boast, swagger:—*pa.t.* crew (*krōō*) or crowed; *pa.p.* crowed.—*ns.* **crow′-bar**, a large iron lever bent at the end like the beak of a crow; **crowfoot**, a buttercup: sometimes extended to other plants; **crow's′-bill**, **crow′-bill**, a kind of forceps for extracting bullets, &c., from wounds; **crow's′-foot**, one of the wrinkles produced by age, spreading out from the corners of the

fāte, *fär*; *mē*, *hûr* (her); *mīne*; *mōte*, *för*; *mūte*; *mōōn*, *fŏŏt*; *then* (then)

eyes; **crow's-nest,** a shelter at the mast-head of whalers, &c., for the man on the lookout.— **as the crow flies,** in a straight line; **have a crow to pluck with,** to have a dispute to settle with. [O.E. *crāwe,* a crow, *crāwan,* to cry like a cock; imit.]

crowd, *krowd, n.* a number of persons or things closely pressed together, without order: the rabble, multitude: (*coll.*) a set of people.—*v.t.* to fill by pressing or driving together: to fill excessively full: to compress (with *into*).—*v.i.* to press on: to press together in numbers, to swarm.—*p.adj.* **crowd'ed.—crowd sail,** to hoist every available sail. [O.E. *crūdan,* to press.]

crown, *krown, n.* a circular head-ornament, esp. as a mark of honour: (*fig.*) reward: completion or consummation: the diadem or state-cap of royalty: kingship: the sovereign: governing power in a monarchy: the top of anything, as a head, hat, tree, hill: a coin stamped with a crown, esp. a silver 5s. piece.—*v.t.* to cover or invest with a crown: to invest with royal dignuty: to adorn: to dignify: to complete happily: (*slang*), to hit on the head.—*ns.* **crown'col'ony,** a colony whose administration is directly under the home government; **crown'glass,** a kind of window-glass formed in circular plates or discs.—*n.pl.* **crown'-jew'els,** jewels pertaining to the crown or sovereign.—*ns.* **crown'-land,** land belonging to the crown or sovereign; **crown'-liv'ing,** a church living in the gift of the crown; **crown'-prince,** the prince who is heir to the crown.— **crown of the causeway,** the middle of the street. [O.Fr. *corone* — L. *corōna* ; cf. Gr. *korōnos,* curved.]

crozier. See crosier.

crucial, *krōō'shǎl, adj.* cross-like: testing or decisive; cf. **crux.** [Fr. *crucial,* from L. *crux, crucis,* a cross.]

crucible, *krōō'si-bl, n.* an earthen pot for melting ores, metals, &c.: (*fig.*) severe trial. [Low L. *crucibulum.*]

Cruciferae, *krōō-sif'ér-ē, n.pl.* a family of plants with a corolla of four petals arranged in the form of a cross (e.g. cabbage, cress, wallflower).—*adj.* **crucif'erous.** [L. *crux, crucis,* a cross, *ferre,* to bear.]

cruciform, *krōō'si-förm, adj.* in the form of a cross. [L. *crux, crucis,* a cross, and **form.**]

crucify, *krōō'si-fī, v.t.* to put to death on a cross: (*fig.*) to subject to comparable torment: to subdue completely, to mortify (e.g. the flesh):—*pa.p.* cru'cified.—*ns.* **cru'cifix,** a figure or picture of Christ fixed to the cross; **crucifix'ion,** death on the cross, esp. that of Christ. [O.Fr. *crucifier* — L. *crucifīgěre, crucifixum— crus,* cross, and *fīgěre,* to fix.]

crude, *krōōd, adj.* raw, unprepared: not reduced to order or form, unfinished, undigested: immature: unrefined.—*adv.* **crude'ly.—ns.** **crude'ness; crud'ity,** rawness: unripeness: that which is crude. [L. *crūdus,* raw.]

cruel, *krōō'el, adj.* disposed to inflict pain, or pleased at suffering: void of pity, merciless, savage.—*adv.* **cru'elly.—n.** **cru'elty.** [Fr. *cruel*— L. *crūdēlis.*]

cruet, *krōō'et, n.* a small jar or phial for sauces and condiments.—*n.* **cru'et-stand,** a stand or frame for holding cruets. [Anglo-Fr., dim. of O.Fr. *cruye,* a jar.]

cruise, *krōōz, v.i.* to sail, fly, drive, or wander to and fro.—*n.* a voyage from place to place for pleasure or on a naval commission.—*ns.* **cruis'er,** one who cruises: a speedy warship, specially intended for cruising; **cruiserweight,** (*boxing*) a light heavy-weight, weighing 161 to 175 pounds. [Du. *kruisen,* to cross.]

crumb, *krum, n.* a small bit or morsel of bread: any small particle: the soft part of bread.—*n.* **crumb'-cloth,** a cloth laid under a table to keep crumbs from the carpet.—*adjs.* **crumb'y, crumm'y,** in crumbs: soft. [O.E. *cruma* ; Du. *kruim* ; Ger. *krume.*]

crumble, *krum'bl, v.t.* to break into crumbs.—*v.i.* to fall into small pieces: to decay.—*adj.* **crum'bly,** apt to crumble, brittle. [Orig. dim. of **crumb.**]

crumpet, *krump'et, n.* a kind of crumby or soft cake or muffin: (*slang*) (attractive) young woman. [M.E. *crompid,* cake.]

crumple, *krump'l, v.t.* to twist or crush into folds or wrinkles: to crease.—*v.i.* to become wrinkled: (usu. **crumple up**) to collapse. [Formed from *crump* (obs.), to curve, curl up.]

crunch, *krunch* (or *-sh*), *v.t.* to crush with the teeth or underfoot: to chew (anything) hard, and so make a noise.—*n.* the act or sound of crunching: (with **the**) crucial, testing moment. [From the sound; cf. Fr. *grincer.*]

crupper, *krup'ér, n.* a strap of leather fastened to the saddle and passing under the horse's tail to keep the saddle in its place: the hind part of a horse. [O.Fr. *cropiere— crope,* the croup.]

crural, *krōō'rǎl, adj.* belonging to or shaped like a leg. [L. *crūrālis,* from *crūs, crūris,* the leg.]

crusade, *krōō-sād', n.* (*hist.*) a military expedition under the banner of the cross to recover the Holy Land from the Turks: any daring or romantic undertaking: concerted action to further a cause.—*v.i.* to go on a crusade.—*n.* **crusad'er.** [Fr. *croisade*— L. *crux,* a cross.]

cruse, *krōōz, n.* a small earthen pot, cup, or bottle. [Cf. O.N. *krūs* ; Dan. *kruus* ; Ger. *krause.*]

crush, *krush, v.t.* to break, bruise, or crumple: to squeeze together: to beat down or overwhelm, to subdue.—*n.* a violent squeezing: a throng: (*slang*) an infatuation (often, *on* a person) or the object of it: a drink made of juice crushed from fruit.—*ns.* **crush'-barr'ier,** a barrier erected to restrain the crowd e.g. at a football match; **crush'-hat,** a collapsible hat, opera-hat. [O.Fr. *croissir.*]

crust, *krust, n.* the hard rind or outside coating of anything: the outer part of bread: covering of a pie, &c.: the solid exterior of the earth.— *v.t.* to cover with a crust or hard case.—*v.i.* to gather into a hard crust.—*adj.* **crustāt'ed,** covered with a crust.—*n.* **crustā'tion,** an adherent crust.—*adj.* **crust'y,** of the nature of or having a crust: having a hard or harsh exterior: surly.—*adv.* **crust'ily.—n.** **crust'iness.** [L. *crusta,* rind.]

Crustacea, *krus-tā's(h)i-a, n.pl.* a large class of animals, including crabs, lobsters, shrimps, whose bodies are in most cases covered with a crust-like shell.—*n.* **crustā'cean,** one of the Crustacea.—*adjs.* **crustā'ceous, crustā'cean,** pertaining to the Crustacea: crust-like. [crust, and suffx. *-acea,* neut. pl. of *-aceous.*]

Neutral vowels in unaccented syllables: *em'pér-ör*; for certain sounds in foreign words see p. ix.

crutch, *kruch, n.* a staff with a cross-piece at the head to place under the arm of a lame person: any support like a crutch (also *fig.*). [O.E. *crycc.*]

crux, *kruks, n.* a cross: something difficult to explain: (the) essential difficulty:—*pl.* **crux′es, cruces** (*krōō′sēz*); cf. **crucial.** [L. *crux,* cross.]

cry, *krī, v.i.* to utter a shrill loud sound, esp. one of pain or grief: to shed tears, weep.—*v.t.* to utter loudly, to exclaim: to proclaim or make public: to offer for sale by crying:—*pa.t* and *pa.p.* **cried.**—*n.* any loud sound, esp. of grief or pain: a call or shout: a watchword or slogan: a prayer: a fit of weeping: lamentation: particular sound uttered by an animal:—*pl.* **cries.**—*adj.* **cry′ing,** calling loudly: claiming notice, notorious.—**cry down,** to disparage, decry; **cry off,** to cancel, as an agreement; **cry quits,** to end a contest on even terms; **cry up,** to praise.—**a far cry,** a great distance; **in full cry,** in full pursuit, used of dogs in hunt. [Fr. *crier*—*quaritare,* to scream—*quĕri,* to lament.]

cryogen, *krī′ō-jen, n.* a substance used to obtain low temperatures. *adj.* cryogen′ic, pertaining to the science of cryogenics or to work done, apparatus used, or substances kept, at low temperatures.—*n.* **cryogen′ics,** the branch of physics concerned with phenomena at very low temperatures. [Gr. *kryos,* frost, and root of *gignesthai,* to become.]

cryolite, *krī′ō-līt, n.* ice-stone or Greenland spar, earliest source of aluminium. [Gr. *kryos,* frost, and *lithos,* a stone.]

cryosurgery, *krī′ō-sûr′jér-i, n.* surgery using instruments at very low temperatures. [Gr. *kryos,* frost, and **surgery.**]

crypt, *kript, n.* an underground cell or chapel.—*adjs.* **cryp′tic, -al,** hidden, secret: enigmatic (e.g. a *cryptic* saying). [L. *crypta*—Gr. *kryptē*—*kryptein,* to conceal.]

crypt-, crypto-, *kript′(o)-,* in composition, hidden—*n.* **crypto,** *krip′to,* a secret member of a party, sect, organisation, &c.—*ns.* **crypto-Christian; crypto-communist.** [Gr. *kryptos,* hidden.]

cryptogam, *krip′tō-gam, n.* a plant without flowers—and often without distinct stem, leaves, and root.—*adjs.* **cryptogam′ic, cryptog′amous.** [Gr. *kryptos,* concealed, and *gamos,* marriage.]

cryptogram, *krip′tō-gram,* **cryptograph,** *krip′tō-gräf, ns.* anything written in cipher. [Gr. *kryptos,* secret, and *graphein,* to write.]

crystal, *krist′l, n.* rock-crystal, a clear quartz: a body, generally solid, whose atoms are arranged in a definite pattern, expressed outwardly by geometrical form with plane faces: anything bright or clear: a superior glass of various kinds: cut glass: a vessel of this material: glassware: a globe of rock-crystal or the like in which one may see visions.—*adjs.* **crys′tal, crys′talline,** of or like crystal.—*v.t.* and *v.i.* **crys′tallīse,** to form into crystals: to cover with sugar crystals: to make or become definite or concrete.—*ns.* **crystallisā′tion, crystallog′raphy,** the science of crystallisation.—**crystal set,** a simple wireless receiving apparatus in which the incoming high-frequency currents are rectified by a crystal rectifier. [O.Fr. *cristol*—L. *crystallum*—Gr. *krystallos,* ice—*kryos,* frost.]

cub, *kub, n.* the young of certain animals, as foxes, &c.: a young boy or girl (in contempt or playfully): (cap.) a member of the **Cub Scouts** (orig. **Wolf Cubs,** q.v.): a young or inexperienced reporter.—*v.i.* to bring forth young:—*pr.p.* **cubb′ing;** *pa.p.* **cubbed.**—*n.* **cubb′ing,** hunting young foxes. [Ety. dub.]

cube, *kūb, n.* a solid body having six equal square faces, a solid square: the third power of a quantity.—*v.t.* to raise to the third power: to cut into cubes.—*adjs.* **cū′bic, -al,** pertaining to a cube: of the third power or degree: solid.—*adv.* **cū′bically.**—*adj.* **cū′biform.**—*ns.* **cū′bism,** a movement in painting which seeks to represent several aspects of an object seen from different standpoints arbitrarily grouped in one composition; **cū′boid,** a rectangular parallelepiped, esp. one whose faces are not all equal.—*adjs.* **cū′boid, cuboid′al,** resembling a cube in shape.—**cube root,** the number or quantity that produces a given cube by being raised to the third power—thus 2 is the cube root of 8. [Fr.—L. *cubus*—Gr. *kybos,* a die.]

cubicle, *kū′bi-kl, n.* a small place (esp. for sleeping) partitioned off from a larger room. [L. *cubiculum*—*cubāre,* to lie down.]

cubit, *kū′bit, n.* a measure employed by the ancients, equal to the length of the arm from the elbow to the tip of the middle-finger, from 18 to 22 inches. [L. *cubitum,* the elbow; cf. L. *cubāre,* to lie down.]

cucking-stool, *kuk′ing-stōōl, n.* a stool in which scolds and other culprits were placed to be pelted by the mob.

cuckold, *kuk′old, n.* a man whose wife has proved unfaithful.—*v.t.* to wrong (a husband) by unchastity. [O.Fr. *cucuault*—*cucu,* cuckoo.]

cuckoo, *kŏŏk′ōō, n.* a bird that cries cuckoo, remarkable for depositing its eggs in the nests of other birds.—*ns.* **cuck′oo-clock,** a clock in which the hours are told by a cuckoo-call; **cuck′oo-flow′er,** a name given to various wild flowers including lady's smock and ragged robin; **cuck′oo-pint** (*-pīnt*), wild arum (q.v.); **cuck′oo-spit, -spitt′le,** a froth secreted on plants by certain insects. [Imitative.]

cucumber, *kū′kum-bér, n.* a creeping plant, with large elongated fruit used as a salad and pickle. [L. *cucumis, -eris.*]

cud, *kud, n.* the food brought from the first stomach of a ruminating animal back into the mouth and chewed again.—*n.* **cud′weed,** a popular name for many species of plants covered with a cottony down.—**chew the cud,** (*fig.*) to meditate. [O.E. *cwidu.*]

cuddle, *kud′l, v.t.* to hug, to embrace, to fondle.—*v.i.* to lie close and snug together.—*n.* a close embrace. [Origin unknown.]

cuddy, *kud′i, n.* a small cabin or cookroom, in the fore-part of a boat or lighter: in large vessels, officers' cabin under the poopdeck.

cuddy, cuddie, *kud′i, n.* a donkey: (*coll.*) a horse. [Perh. *Cuthbert.*]

cudgel, *kuj′l, n.* a heavy staff, a club.—*v.t.* to beat with a cudgel:—*pr.p.* **cudg′elling;** *pa.p.* **cudg′elled.**—**take up the cudgels,** to engage in a contest. [O.E. *cycgel.*]

fāte, fär; mē, hûr (her); *mīne; mōte, för; mūte; mōōn, fŏŏt;* ᴛнen (then)

cue, *kū, n.* the last word of an actor's speech serving as a hint to the next speaker: any hint: the part one has to play.—**on cue**, just at the right moment. [According to some from Fr. *queue* (see next word); in 17th century written Q, and derived from L. *quando,* 'when' i.e. when to begin.]

cue,*;kū, n.* a twist of hair at the back of the head: a rod used in playing billiards. [Fr. *queue*—L. *cauda,* a tail.]

cuff, *kuf, n.* a stroke with the open hand.—*v.t.* to strike with the open hand. [Origin obscure; cf. Swed. *kuffa,* to knock.]

cuff, *kuf, n.* the end of the sleeve near the wrist: a covering for the wrist: (*U.S.*) a turned-up fold at the bottom of a trouser leg.—**off the cuff,** unofficially and extempore. [Prob. cog. with **coif.**]

cuirass, *kwi-ras´,* or *kū-, n.* a defensive covering for the breast and back, esp. one of leather or iron fastened with straps and buckles.—*n.* **cuirassier** (*-ēr´*), a horse-soldier so armed. [Fr. *cuirasse—cuir,* leather—L. *corium,* skin, leather.]

cuisine, *kwi-zēn´, n.* a kitchen department: style of cookery. [Fr. (It. *cucina*)—L. *coquīna—conquĕre,* to cook.]

Culdee, *kul´dē, n.* one of a fraternity of monks living in Scotland and Ireland from the 8th century. [Latinised from Old Ir. *céle dé,* servants or companions of God.]

cul-de-sac, *kü(l)-dé-sak, n.* a street, &c., closed at one end, a blind alley. [Fr. *cul,* bottom, *de,* of, *sac,* sack.]

culinary, *kū´lin-ár-i, adj.* pertaining to the kitchen or to cookery: used in the kitchen. [L. *culīnārius—culīna,* a kitchen.]

cull, *kul, v.t.* to select: to pick, gather: to pick out and destroy members of a group, e.g. of seals, deer. [Fr. *cueillir,* to gather—L. *colligĕre—col-,* together, *legĕre,* to gather. Doublet of **collect.**]

cullender. See **colander.**

culm, *kulm, n.* a grass or sedge stem.—*adj.* **cul´miferous,** bearing a culm. [L. *culmus,* a stalk.]

culm, *kulm, n.* anthracite dust.

culminate, *kul´min-āt, v.i.* (*astron.*) to be at, or come to, the meridian and thus the highest point of altitude: to reach the highest point (with *in*).—*n.* **culminā´tion,** act of culminating: the highest point: (*astron.*) transit of a body across the meridian. [Low L. *culmināre, -ātum*—L. *culmen,* properly *columen,* a summit.]

culpable, *kul´pa-bl, adj.* (*rare*) criminal: deserving of blame.—*ns.* **culpabil´ity, cul´pableness,** liability to blame.—*adv.* **cul´pably.** [O.Fr. *coupable*—L. *culpābilis—culpa,* a fault.]

culprit, *kul´prit, n.* one in fault: a criminal: (*Eng. law*) a prisoner accused but not yet tried. [From the fusion in legal phraseology of *cul* (Anglo-Fr. *culpable,* or L. *culpābilis*) and *prit, prist* (O.Fr. *prest*), ready.]

cult, *kult, n.* a system of religious belief: (with *of*) worship of, devotion to: enthusiastic, often excessive, admiration.—Also **cult´us.** [L. *cultus—colĕre,* to worship.]

cultivate, *kul´ti-vāt, v.t.* to till or prepare for crops: to produce by tillage: to devote attention to: to civilise or refine.—*ns.* **cultivā´tion,** the art or practice of cultivating: cultivated

ground: cultivated state: refinement; **cul´tivator,** an agricultural implement for breaking up the surface of the ground among crops. [Low L. *cultivāre, -ātum*—L. *colĕre,* to till, to worship.]

culture, *kul´tyúr, -chúr, n.* cultivation: the state of being cultivated: educated refinement: a type of civilisation (e.g. *Bronze Age culture*): a crop of experimentally grown bacteria or the like.—*v.t.* to cultivate: to improve.—*adj.* **cul´tural.**—*p.adj.* **cul´tured,** cultivated: well educated, refined.—**culture vulture,** derogatory term for one who has an excessive interest in the arts. [L. *cultūra—colĕre.*]

cultus. See **cult.**

culverin, *kul´vér-in, n.* an early form of cannon of great length. [Fr. *coulevrine,* from *couleuvre,* a snake—L. *coluber,* a snake.]

culvert, *kul´vért, n.* an arched water-course under a road, &c. [Perh. from Fr. *couler,* to flow—L. *colāre.*]

cumber, *kum´bér, v.t.* to impede, to get in the way of: to burden uselessly.—*adjs.* **cum´bersome,** unwieldy: burdensome: **cum´brous,** hindering, obstructing: heavy.—*adv.* **cum´brously.**—*n.* **cum´brousness.** [O.Fr. *combrer,* to hinder—Low L. *cumbrus,* a heap; corr. of L. *cumulus,* a heap.]

cummerbund, *kum´ér-bund, n.* a waist-belt, a sash. [Anglo-Ind.—Pers. *kamarband,* a loinband.]

cummin, cumin, *kum´in, n.* an umbelliferous plant, the seeds of which are valuable as a carminative.—**black cummin,** fitch. [L. *cumīnum*—Gr. *kymīnon.*]

cumulate, *kūm´ū-lāt, v.t.* to heap together: to accumulate.—*adj.* **cum´ulative,** becoming greater by successive additions (e.g. force, effect, evidence, sentence).—*adv.* **cum´ulatively.**—**cumulative vote,** a method of election by which each voter has as many votes as there are vacancies and may give more than one vote to the same candidate. [L. *cumulāre, -ātum—cumulus,* a heap.]

cumulus, *kū´mū-lus, n.* a heap: a cloud consisting of rounded heaps with a darker horizontal base:—*pl.* **cumuli.** [L.]

cuneal, *kū´ni-ál,* **cuneate,** *kū´ni-āt, adjs.* of the form of a wedge.—*adj.* **cuneiform** (*kū-nē´i-förm, kūni-(i-)förm*), wedge-shaped—specially applied to the old Babylonian, Assyrian, &c., writing, in which the characters, impressed by a stylus, were wedge-shaped. [L. *cuneus,* a wedge.]

cunning, *kun´ing, adj.* (*arch.*) knowing: skilful: ingenious: crafty: (*U.S.*) dainty, quaintly pleasing.—*n.* knowledge: skill: faculty of using artifice to gain an end.—*adv.* **cunn´ingly.** [O.E. *cunnan,* to know.]

cup, *kup, n.* a drinking-vessel: the liquid contained in a cup: an ornamental vessel used as a prize: that which we must receive or undergo—blessings, afflictions.—*v.t.* to take or place as in a cup: to extract blood from the body by using cupping-glasses:—*pr.p.* **cupp´ing;** *pa.p.* **cupped.**—*ns.* **cup´bear´er,** an attendant at a feast to pour out and hand the wine; **cupboard** (*kub´órd*), a place for keeping victuals, dishes, &c.—*v.t.* to store.—*ns.* **cup´board-love,** love inspired by hope of gain;

Neutral vowels in unaccented syllables: *em´pér-ór*; for certain sounds in foreign words see p. ix.

168

cup′ful, as much as fills a cup:—*pl.* **cup′fuls; cupp′ing-glass**, a glass from which the air has been exhausted, used in the operation of cupping or drawing blood; **cup′-tie**, one of a series of games in a competition in which the prize is a cup.—**in his cups**, tipsy. [O.E. *cuppe*—L. *cūpa*, a tub.]

Cupid, *kū′pid*, *n.* the Roman god of love, son of Venus, represented as a mischievous boy with a bow and arrows.—*n.* **cūpid′ity**, covetousness. [L. *Cupīdō*, *-inis*—*cupĕre*, to desire.]

cupola, *kū′po-la*, *n.* a spherical vault on the top of a building: a dome, esp. a small one. [It.—L. *cūpola*, dim. of *cūpa*, a cask.]

cupri-, cupro-, *kū′pri*, *-ō*, (in composition) of or containing copper. [L. *cuprum*, copper]:—e.g. **cup′reous**, of, containing, copper; **cupri′- ferous** (*-ferous* from L. *ferre*, to bear), of rocks, yielding copper; **cup′ro(-)nick′el**, composed of copper and nickel (also *n.*). Adjs. **cupric, cuprous** are used for compounds in which copper has respectively its higher and its lower combining power (the former a valency of 2, the latter a valency of 1):—e.g. **cupric oxide** (CuO), black copper oxide; **cuprous oxide** (CU_2O), red copper oxide.

cur, *kûr*, *n.* a worthless dog, of low breed: a churlish fellow.—*adj.* **curr′ish**.—*adv.* **curr′- ishly**.—*n.* **curr′ishness**. [M.E. *curre;* cf. O.N. *kurra*, to grumble.]

curaçoa, curaçao, *kū′ra-sō, kōō-ra-sō′, kōō′rä- sä-ō*, *n.* a liqueur, named from the island of *Curaçoa* in the West Indies, where it was first made.

curare, *ku-ra′ri*, *n.* orig. an arrow poison prepared by South American Indians from an extract obtained from woody vines of the same genus as that which yields strychnine, now a source of valuable drugs: e.g. **curarine** (*ku-ra′rēn*; used to relax muscles) [Port., from South American Indian.]

curate, *kūr′āt*, *n.* one who has the cure of souls: a clergyman in the Church of England, assisting a rector or vicar.—*ns.* **cur′acy, cur′ateship**. [L.L. *cūrātus*—L. *cura*, care.]

curator, *kūr-a′tor*, *n.* one who has the charge of anything: a superintendent, esp. formerly, of a museum: one appointed by law as guardian.—*n.* **cura′torship**, the office of a curator. [L. *cūrātor*.]

curb, *kûrb*, *n.* a chain or strap attached to the bit for restraining a horse: (*fig.*) a check or restraint: a hearth fender: the edge of a pavement (also **kerb**). —*v.t.* to furnish with, or guide by, a curb: to restrain or check.—*ns.* **curb′-, kerb′-crawling**, driving along slowly with the intention of enticing people into one's car; **curb′stone, kerb′stone**, a stone placed as an edging to a path or pavement. [Fr. *courbe*—L. *curvus*, bent.]

curd, *kûrd*, *n.* milk thickened or coagulated by acid: the cheese part of milk, as distinguished from the whey: any similar substance.—*v.t.* and *v.i.* **curd′le**, to turn into curd: (*lit.* and *fig.*) to congeal (e.g. blood, with horror). [Prob. Celt.; Gael. *gruth*, Ir. *cruth*.]

cure, *kūr*, *n.* care of souls or spiritual charge: care of the sick: act of healing: that which heals: remedial treatment.—*v.t.* to heal: to rid (one) of (e.g. a bad habit): to preserve, as by

drying, salting, &c.:—*pr.p.* cur′ing; *pa.p.* cured.—*adj.* **cur′able**, that may be cured.—*n.* **cūrabil′ity**.—*adjs.* **cur′ative**, tending to cure; **cure′less**, that cannot be cured. [O.Fr. *cure*—L. *cūra*, care; not the same as **care**.]

curé, *kū′rā*, *n.* a parish priest in France. [Fr.,—L.L. *cūrātus*; see **curate**.]

curfew, *kûr′fū*, *n.* in feudal times the ringing of a bell as a signal to put out all fires and lights: a prohibition against being abroad in the streets after a specified hour. [O.Fr. *covrefeu* (Fr. *couvre-feu—couvrir*, to cover, *feu*, fire).]

curia, *kū′ri-a*, *n.* court of the Pope. [L.]

curio, *kū′ri-o*, *n.* any rare and curious article:— *pl.* **cu′rios**. [For **curiosity**.]

curious, *kū′ri-ùs*, *adj.* anxious to learn: inquisitive: showing great care or nicety, skilfully made: singular, rare: (*coll.*) odd.—*n.* **curi- os′ity**, state or quality of being curious: inquisitiveness: anything rare or unusual.—*adv.* **cū′riously**. *n.* **cū′riousness**. **curious arts** (*B.*), magical practices. [Fr. *curieux*—L. *curiōsus—cūra*.]

curium, *kū′ri-ùm*, *n.* a transuranium element (atomic number 96; symbol Cm), named after Marie and Pierre Curie, discoverers of radium.

curl, *kûrl*, *v.t.* to twist into ringlets, to coil.—*v.i.* to shrink into coils: to move in curves: to play at the game of curling.—*n.* a ringlet of hair, or anything like it: a wave, bending, or twist.—*ns.* **curl′er**, one who, or that which, curls: a player at the game of curling, **curl′ing**, a game, common in Scotland, akin to bowls, played by hurling heavy smooth stones over ice towards a mark.—*ns.pl.* **curl′ing-ī′ron(s), curl′ing-tongs**, an iron instrument used for curling the hair.—*n.* **curl′ing-stone**, a heavy stone with a handle, used in the game of curling.—*adj.* **curl′y**, having curls: full of curls. *n.* **curl′iness**. [M.E. *crull*, Du. *krullen*, Dan. *krolle*, to curl.]

curlew, *kûrl(y)ōō*, *n.* any of a number of moorland birds of the woodcock family, having long curved bill and long legs, and a plaintive cry. [O.Fr. *corlieu*; prob. from its cry.]

curmudgeon, *kûr-muj′ôn*, *n.* a churlish, ill-natured fellow: a miser.—*adj.* **curmudge′only**. [Origin unknown.]

currant, *kur′ànt*, *n.* a small kind of black raisin or dried seedless grape (imported from the Levant): the fruit of several garden shrubs. [From *Corinth*.]

current, *kur′ént*, *adj.* running or flowing: passing from person to person: generally received: now passing: present.—*n.* a running stream: a body of water or air moving in a certain direction: a flow of electricity: course (e.g. of events).—*n.* **curr′ency**, circulation: that which circulates, as the money of a country: prevalence: general acceptance.—*adv.* **curr′ently**. [L. *currens, -entis—currĕre*, to run.]

curricle, *kur′i-kl*, *n.* a two-wheeled open carriage, drawn by two horses abreast.—*n.* **curric′ulum**, a course, esp. the course of study at a school or university.—**curriculum vitae**, *kū rik′ū-lum vī′tē, kōōr-ik′ōō-lōōm vē′tī (wē′tī),* (biographical sketch of) the course of one's life. [L. *curriculum*, from *currĕre*, to run; *vita*, life.]

curry, *kur′i*, *n.* a condiment much used in India,

compounded of turmeric and mixed spices: a stew flavoured with curry.—*v.t.* to cook with curry. [Tamil (q.v.) *kari*, sauce.]

curry, *kur'i*, *v.t.* to dress (leather): to rub down and dress (a horse): to drub:—*pr.p.* curr'ying; *pa.p.* curr'ied.—*ns.* **curr'ier**, one who curries or dresses tanned leather; **curr'y-comb**, an iron instrument or comb used for grooming horses.—**curry favour** (corruption of **curry favell**, to curry the chestnut horse), to seek favour by flattery. [O.Fr. *correier*—*conrei*, outfit.]

curse, *kûrs*, *v.t.* to invoke or wish evil upon: to consign to perdition: to vex or torment.—*v.i.* to utter imprecations: to swear.—*n.* invocation or wishing of evil or harm: evil invoked on another: any great evil.—*adj.* **curs'ed** (also *kûrst*), under, blasted by, a curse: hateful.—*adv.* **curs'edly.**—*n.* **curs'er.** [O.E. *cursian*—*curs*, a curse; ety. doubtful; not conn. with **cross.**]

cursive, *kûr'siv*, *adj.* written with a running hand (of handwriting): flowing.—*adv.* **cur'sively.** [Low L. *cursīvus*—L. *currĕre*, to run.]

cursory, *kûr'sŏr-i*, *adj.* running quickly over, hasty, superficial.—*adv.* **cur'sorily.** [L. *currĕre*, *cursum*, to run.]

curt, *kûrt*, *adj.* (*lit.*) short: concise: discourteously brief.—*adv.* **curt'ly.**—*n.* **curt'ness.** [L. *curtus*, shortened.]

curtail, *kûr-tāl'*, *v.t.* to cut short: to deprive of a part (of): to abridge:—*pr.p.* curtail'ing; *pa.p.* curtailed'.—*n.* **curtail'ment.** [Old spelling *curtal*—O.Fr. *courtault*—L. *curtus.*]

curtain, *kûr't(i)n*, *n.* the hanging drapery at a window, around a bed, &c.: the part of a rampart between two bastions.—*v.t.* to enclose, or to furnish, with curtains.—*ns.* **cur'tain-lec'ture**, a reproof given in bed by a wife to her husband; **cur'tain-rais'er**, a short play preceding the main performance in a theatre; **curtain wall**, a wall that is not load-bearing, e.g. does not support a roof.—**curtains**, death: the end. [O.Fr. *cortine*—Low L. *cortina*; prob. L. *cors, cortis*, a court.]

curtal, *kûr'tàl*, *adj.* (*obs.*) having a docked tail: wearing a short frock. [See **curtail.**]

curtsy, curtsey, *kûrt'si*, *n.* an obeisance, made by bending the knees, proper to women and children.—*v.i.* to make a curtsy. [A variant of **courtesy.**]'

curule, *kū'rōōl*, *adj.* applied to the official chair of the higher Roman magistrates. [L. *curūlis*—*currus*, a chariot.]

curve, *kûrv*, *n.* a bend in a direction continuously deviating from a straight line: anything so bent: a line (including a straight line) answering to an equation.—*v.t.* and *v.i.* to bend, or to be bent, in a curve: to move in a curve.—*adj.* **curvaceous, curvacious** (*kûr-vā'shus*), (*slang*) having shapely curves.—*n.* **cur'vature**, a curving or bending: the continual bending or the amount of bending from a straight line. [L. *curvus*, crooked.]

curvet, *kûr'vet*, *kûr-vet'*, *n.* a light leap of a horse in which he curves his body: a leap, frolic.—*v.i.* to leap in curvets: to frisk:—*pr.p.* cur'veting, curvett'ing; *pa.p.* cur'veted, curvett'ed. [It. *corvetta*, dim. of *corvo*—L. *curvus*, crooked.]

curvilinear, *kûr-vi-lin'i-àr*, **curvilineal**, *kûr-vi-*

lin'i-àl, *adjs.* bounded by curved lines. [L. *curvus*, and *līneāris*—*līnea*, a line.]

cushat, *kush'at*, *n.* the ringdove or wood-pigeon. [O.E. *cūscute*, perh. from its note and *scēotan*, to shoot.]

cushion, *kōōsh'on*, *n.* a case filled with some soft, elastic stuff, for resting on: a pillow: any elastic pad or lining: anything that serves to deaden a blow.—*v.t.* to seat on, or furnish with, a cushion: to serve as a cushion for or against: to suppress (complaints) by ignoring. [O.Fr. *coissin*—L. *coxīnum*—*coxa*, hip.]

cushy, *kōōsh'i*, *adj.* easy and comfortable. [Perh. Hindustani *khushī*, pleasure.]

cusp, *kusp*, *n.* an apex: a prominence on a tooth: the point or horn of the moon, &c.—*adjs.* **cus'pidāte, -d** (*bot.*), having a rigid point. [L. *cuspis, -idis*, a point.]

cuspidor, *kus'pi-dōr, -dör*, *n.* (*U.S.*) a spittoon. [Port.—L. *conspuĕre*, to spit upon.]

cuss, *kus*, *n.* (*slang*) a curse: a fellow.—*adj.* **cuss'ed**, cursed: obstinate: perverse.—*n.* **cuss'edness.** [Obviously **curse**; in the personal sense, prob. with a supposed reference to **customer** (q.v.).]

custard, *kus'tàrd*, *n.* a composition of milk, eggs, &c., sweetened and flavoured.—*n.* **cus'tard-app'le**, the fruit of a West Indian tree, having an eatable pulp, like a custard. [Earlier *custade*, a corr. of *crustade*, a pie with **crust** (q.v.).]

custody, *kus'to-di*, *n.* a watching or guarding: care: imprisonment.—*adj.* **custō'dial.**—*n.* **custō'dian**, a keeper: a guardian: a caretaker. [L. *custōdia*, from *custōs, -ōdis*, a keeper.]

custom, *kus'tom*, *n.* what one is wont to do: usage: frequent repetition of the same act: regular trade or business: a tax on goods: (*pl.*) duties imposed on imports and exports.—*adj.* **cus'tomary**, usual: habitual: holding, or held, by custom.—*adv.* **cus'tomarily.**—*adjs.* **cus'tom-built, cus'tom-made**, built or made to a customer's order.—*ns.* **cus'tomer**, one who buys from one: (*slang*) a person; **cus'tom-house**, the place where customs or duties on exports and imports are collected.—**customs union**, two or more states united as a single area for purposes of customs duties; **go through the customs**, to have one's luggage passed by the customs authorities; **the customs**, the customs authorities. [O.Fr. *custume, costume*—L. *consuētūdō, -inis*—*consuescĕre*, to accustom.]

cut, *kut*, *v.t.* to make an incision in: to cleave or pass through: to sever a piece, pieces of, from a larger portion: to fell, hew, mow, trim: to carve, hew, or fashion by cutting: to strike sharply: to wound or hurt: to shorten (e.g. a writing): to divide (a pack of cards) into two portions, or to draw (a card) from the pack: to refuse ostentatiously to recognise (an acquaintance): to reduce or lessen (e.g. a price): to intersect (a line): to absent oneself from: to execute (as *to cut a caper*): to strike (a ball) obliquely to the off side by a sharp movement: to impart spin to (a ball).—*v.i.* to make an incision: to intersect: to move quickly (through): (*slang*) to run away, be off: to twiddle the feet rapidly in dancing: (in motion pictures) to cease photographing:—*pr.p.*

Neutral vowels in unaccented syllables: *em'pėr-ôr*; for certain sounds in foreign words see p. ix.

cutt'ing; *pa.t.* and *pa.p.* cut.—*n.* a cleaving or dividing: a stroke or blow: an excavation for a road, railway, &c.: an incision or wound: a piece cut off: a varying unit of length for cloth and yarn: an engraved block, or the picture from it: manner of cutting, or fashion: type, kind: a degree, grade: a stroke that cuts a ball: spin imparted by such a stroke: (*pl.*) sticks drawn as lots: (*slang*) a rake-off.—*ns.* cut'back, a going back in a plot to earlier happenings: a reduction; cut'-glass (see glass).—*adj.* cut'-price, at a reduced rate.—*ns.* cut'purse, a pickpocket; cutt'er, the person or thing that cuts: a small swift vessel with one mast and sharp prow, fore-and-aft rigged; cut'-throat, an assassin; cutt'ing, a dividing or lopping off: an incision: a piece cut out or off: a piece of plant cut off for propagation: a passage cut from a newspaper: a piece of road or railway excavated: editing of film or recording.—cut a dash, to have a striking appearance: (*erroneously*) to move off quickly; cut-and-dry, or cut-and-dried, ready made, fixed exactly beforehand—from the state of herbs in the shop as opp. to the field; cut a poor, sorry, figure, to make an unimpressive or humiliating appearance; cut dead, to ignore the presence of; cut down, to take from the gallows by cutting the rope: to reduce, curtail; cut in, to interpose: to intrude: (*coll.*) having left a line of traffic, to break into it again farther forward: to give a share; cut off, to destroy: intercept: stop; cut off with a shilling, to disinherit; cut out, to shape: prepare: to eliminate: to get between a ship and the shore: to supplant: to disconnect from the source of power: (*v.i.* of an engine) to fail, stop: (*adj.*) innately suited to be (with *for*, *to be*—e.g. *he was not cut out for a parson*); cut short, to abridge: check; cut the teeth, to have the teeth grow through the gums—of an infant; cut up, to carve: to criticise severely: (to be) distressed; cut up rough, to become very resentful.—a cut above (*coll.*), a degree above; short cut, or near cut, a short way. [Origin unknown.]

cutaneous. See cutis.

cute, *kūt, adj.* acute, shrewd: (*U.S.*) quaintly pleasing. [acute.]

cutis, *kū'tis, n.* the skin: the true skin, as distinguished from the cuticle.—*adj.* cutān'eous, belonging to the skin.—*n.* cu'ticle, the outermost or thin skin. [L.]

cutlass, *kut'las, n.* a short, broad sword, with one cutting edge, used in the navy. [Fr. *coutelas*—L. *cultellus*, dim. of *culter*, a ploughshare, a knife.]

cutler, *kut'lėr, n.* one who makes or sells knives.—*n.* cut'lery, the business of a cutler: edged or cutting instruments in general: implements for eating food. [Fr. *coutelier*—L. *culter*, knife.]

cutlet, *kut'let, n.* a slice of meat cut off for cooking, esp. of mutton or veal—generally the rib and the meat belonging to it. [Fr. *côtelette*, dim. of *côte*, from L. *costa*, a rib.]

cuttle, *kut'l, n.* a cephalopod, one of the *Decapoda*, belonging to the same family as the squid, (*loosely*) any cephalopod.—Also cutt'le-(-)fish.—*n.* cutt'lebone, the internal shell of a

cuttlefish. [O.E. *cudele*.]

cutty, *kut'i, adj.* (*Scot.*) short, curtailed.—*n.* a short clay pipe: a short, dumpy girl. [cut.]

cyanogen, *sī-an'o-jen, n.* a gas, compound of carbon and nitrogen—an essential ingredient of Prussian blue.—*adj.* cyan'ic, of or belonging to cyanogen.—*ns.* cy'anide, a direct compound of cyanogen with a metal; cy'aniding, extraction of gold or silver from ore by means of potassium cyanide; cy'anine, any of a group of dyes used as sensitisers in photography; cyanō'sis, morbid blueness of the skin. [Gr. *kyanos*, blue.]

cybernetics, *sī-bėr-net'iks, n.* (*pl.* treated as *sing.*) the comparative study of automatic communication and control in functions of living bodies and in mechanical and electronic systems (such as in computers). [Gr. *Kybernētēs*, a steersman.]

cyclamate, *sik'la-māt, sīk'-, n.* any of a number of very sweet substances derived from petrochemicals.

cyclamen, *sik'la-men, n.* a genus of the same family as the primrose, with nodding flowers and petals bent back. [Gr. *kyklaminos*.]

cycle, *sī'kl, n.* a period of time in which events happen in a certain order, and which constantly repeats itself: an age: a recurring series of changes: a measure of the frequency (vibrations per sec.) of an alternating current (*so many cycles per sec.*; see hertz): a series of poems, prose romances, &c., centring round a figure or event: an abbreviation for bicycle and tricycle: sequence of computer operations which continues until a criterion for stoppage is reached, or the time of this.—*v.i.* to move in cycles: to ride a bicycle or tricycle.—*v.t.* to cause to pass through a cycle of operations or events.—*adjs.* cy'clic, -al, pertaining to or containing a cycle: recurring in cycles: arranged in a ring or rings: contained in a circle.—*ns.* cy'clist, one who rides a bicycle or tricycle; cy'cloid, a curve made by a point in a circle, when the circle is rolled along a straight line.—*adj.* cycloid'al. [Gr. *kyklos*, a circle.]

cyclone, *sī'klōn, n.* a system of winds blowing spirally inwards towards a centre of low barometric pressure: (*loosely*) a wind-storm.—*adj.* cyclon'ic. [Gr. *kyklōn*, pr.p. of *kykloein*, to whirl round—*kyklos*, a circle.]

cyclopaedia, cyclopedia, *sī-klō-pē'di-a.* Same as encyclopaedia.

cyclorama, *sī-klō-rä'mä, n.* a circular panorama: a curved background in stage and cinematograph sets, used to give impression of sky distance, and for lighting effects. [Gr. *kyklos*, circle, *horāma*, view.]

cyclostyle, *sī'klō-stīl, n.* an apparatus for multiplying copies of a writing. [Gr. *kyklos*, circle, and style.]

cyclotron. See accelerator (under accelerate).

cyesis, *sī-ēs'is, n.* pregnancy. [Gr. *kyēsis*.]

cygnet, *sig'net, n.* a young swan. [Dim. of L. *cygnus*, a swan, directly or through Fr. *cygne*.]

cylinder, *sil'in-dėr, n.* a figure generated by a straight line remaining parallel to a fixed axis and moving round a closed curve (ordinarily a circle perpendicular to the axis): a roller-shaped object: applied to many parts of machinery of cylindrical shape, solid or hol-

fāte, fär; mē, hûr (her); *mīne; mōte, för; mūte; mōōn, fŏŏt; ŧħen* (then)

low.—*adjs.* **cylin'dric, -al,** having the form or properties of a cylinder.—**cylinder head,** the closed end of the cylinder of an internal-combustion engine. [Gr. *kylindros—kylindein,* to roll.]

cymbal, *sim'bál, n.* a hollow brass, basin-like, musical instrument, beaten together in pairs. [L. *cymbalum*—Gr. *kymbalon—kymbē,* the hollow of a vessel.]

cyme, *sīm, n.* an inflorescence the main shoot of which ends in a flower, subsequent flowers growing on lateral branches.—*adj.* **cym'ose.** [L. *cȳma, cīma,* a sprout—Gr. *kȳma.*]

Cymric, *kim'rik, adj.* Welsh. [W. *Cymru,* Wales.]

cynic, -al, *sin'ik, -ál, adj.* surly, snarling: misanthropic, disinclined to recognise goodness or selflessness.—*ns.* **cyn'ic,** one of a sect of ancient philosophers so called from their morose manners: a morose man, a snarler: one who takes a low view of human character and conduct; **cynicism** (*sin'-i-sizm*), surliness: contempt for human nature: a saying characterised by such contempt.—*adv.* **cyn'ically.** [Gr. *kynikos,* dog-like—*kyōn,* gen. *kynos,* a dog; cf. L. *canis.*]

cynosure, *sin'ō-shōōr,* or *sī'-, n.* (*cap.*) the Dog's Tail, or Little Bear, a constellation containing the pole star: hence anything that strongly attracts attention or admiration. [Gr. *kyōn,* gen. *kynos,* a dog, *oura,* a tail.]

cypress, *sī'pres, n.* an evergreen tree whose branches used to be carried at funerals: hence a symbol of death. [O.Fr. *ciprès*—L. *cupressus*—Gr. *kyparissos.*]

cyst, *sist, n.* (*biol.*) a bladder or bag-like structure, whether normal or containing morbid matter.—*adjs.* **cyst'ic, cyst'iform.** [Gr. *kystis,* a bladder.]

cytology, *sī-tol'ō-ji, n.* the branch of biology that deals with cells. [Gr. *kytos,* vessel.]

cytoplasm, *sīt'ō-plazm, n.* the protoplasm of a cell apart from that of the nucleus. [Gr. *kytos,* vessel, *plasma,* form, body.]

cytosine, *sī'to-sēn, n.* one of the four bases in deoxyribo-nucleic acids, in close association with guanine. [Gr. *kytos,* vessel.]

czar, czari'na. See tsar, tsarina.

Czech, *chek, n.* a member of a westerly branch of the Slavs—Bohemians and Moravians: the language of the Czechs, closely allied to Polish.—*n.* **Czecho-Slovak,** a native or citizen of Czechoslovakia.—Also *adj.* [Polish.]

Neutral vowels in unaccented syllables: *em'pér-ór*; for certain sounds in foreign words see p. ix.

D

D-day, *dē'dā,* (D for unnamed *d*ay), the opening day (6th June 1944) of the Allied invasion of Europe in World War II: any critical day of action; **D-notice,** *dē'-nōt'is,* (D for *d*enial), a notice officially sent to newspapers, &c., asking them not to publish certain information.

dab, *dab, v.t.* to strike gently with something soft or moist: to peck:—*pr.p.* **dabb'ing;** *pa.p.* **dabbed.**—*n.* a gentle blow: a small lump of anything soft or moist: a species of flounder of light-brown colour: (usu. in *pl.*; slang) fingerprint.—*n.* **dab'chick,** the little grebe. [First appears about 1300; cf. Ger. *tappe,* a pat. Confused with **daub** and **tap.**]

dab, *dab, n.* an expert person—also **dab-hand.** [Prob. a corr. of **adept.**]

dabble, *dab'l, v.i.* to play in wager with hands or feet: to do anything in a trifling way.—*n.* **dabb'ler,** one who does things superficially. [Freq. of **dab.**]

da capo, *dä kä'pō,* a term in music, indicating 'return to the beginning'—usually written *D.C.* [It., 'from the beginning'—L. *da,* from, *caput,* head.]

dace, *dās,* **dare,** *dār,* **dart,** *därt, n.* a small river fish of the carp family. [M.E. *darce*—Low L. *dardus,* a dart or javelin. So called from its quickness.]

dachshund, *däks'hŏŏnt, n.* a badger-dog. [Ger. *dachs,* a badger, *hund,* dog.]

dacoit, dakoit *da-koit', n.* in India and Burma, one of a gang of robbers or brigands.—*n.* **da-coit'y,** brigandage. [Hindustani.]

dactyl, *dak'til, n.* in poetry, a foot of three syllables, one long (or accented) followed by two short (or unaccented), like the joints of a finger.—*adj.* **dactyl'ic.**—*ns.* **dactylog'raphy,** the study of finger-prints as a means of identification; **dactylol'ogy,** the art of talking with the fingers. [Gr. *daktylos,* a finger.]

dad, *dad,* **daddy,** *dad'i, n.* father, a word used by children—*n.* **dadd'y long legs,** the crane-fly (q.v.). [Ety. uncertain.]

dad, *dad, v.t.* (*dial.*) to throw against something: to dash.—*n.* a lump: a thump.

dado, *dä'do, n.* the cubic block forming the body of a pedestal: a skirting of wood, wall-paper, or paint-work, along the lower part of the walls of a room. [It.]

daffodil, *daf'o-dil,* **daffodilly,** *daf'o-dil-i,* **daffodowndilly,** *daf'o-down-dil'i, n.* a yellow-flowered narcissus. [M.E. *affodille*—Gr. *asphodelos;* the *d* is unexplained.]

daft, *däft, adj.* (*Scot.*) silly: insane: unreasonably merry.—*adv.* **daft'ly.**—*n.* **daft'ness.** [From same root as **deft.**]

dagger, *dag'er, n.* a short sword for stabbing: a mark of reference (†).—**at daggers drawn,** in a state of hostility. [M.E.]

dago, *dä'go, n.* (*U.S.*) a man of Spanish, Portuguese, or Italian origin. [Prob. Sp. *Diego*—L.

Jacobus, James.]

dagoba, *dä'gō-ba, n.* in Ceylon, a tope (q.v.). [Native word.]

daguerreotype, *dä-ger'-ō-tīp, n.* an early method of photography on a copper plate: a photograph so taken. [Fr., from Louis *Daguerre.*]

dahlia, *däl'yä,* (*U.S.*) *däl'yä, n.* a genus of garden composites (q.v.) with large flowers. [From *Dahl,* a Swedish botanist.]

Dail, *doil, n.* the lower house of the legislature of Eire. [Irish, assembly.]

daily, *dā'li, adj.* and *adv.* every day.—*n.* a daily paper: a non-resident servant. [**day.**]

daimio, *dī'myō, n.* a Japanese noble under the old feudal system. [Jap.]

dainty, *dān'ti, adj.* pleasant to the palate: delicate: tasteful: fastidious.—*n.* a delicacy.—*adv.* **dain'tily.**—*n.* **dain'tiness.** [M.E. *deintee*—L. *dignitās, -ātis*—*dignus,* worthy.]

dairy, *dā'ri, n.* the place where milk is kept, and butter and cheese made: an establishment for the supply of milk.—*ns.* **dai'ry-farm; dai'ry-maid; dai'ryman.**—**dairy cattle,** cattle reared mainly for the production of milk, as distinct from *beef cattle;* **dairy products,** milk and its derivatives, butter, cheese, &c. [O.E. *dæge,* a dairymaid.]

dais, *dās, n.* a raised floor at the end of a hall: a raised floor with a seat and canopy. [O.Fr. *deis*—Gr. *diskos,* a disk.]

daisy, *dā'zi, n.* a low composite (q.v.) plant having heads with white or pink rays and a yellow disk: a term of admiration, often ironical.—*ns.* **dai'sy-chain,** a row of daisies linked together; **dai'sy-cutt'er,** a ball skimmed along the ground. [O.E. *dæges ēage,* day's eye.]

dâk, *dök, n.* in India, transport on a relay system: the mail-post.—**dâk bungalow,** a resthouse for travellers in India. [Hindustani, *dâk,* relay (of men).]

dakoit. See **dacoit.**

Dalai Lama, *däl'ī läm'a,* or *däl-ī', n.* the head of the Buddhist hierarchy in Tibet. [Tibetan.]

dale, *dāl, n.* the low ground between hills: the valley through which a river flows.—*n.* **dales'man,** specifically, a man of the dales of the Lake District. [O.E. *dæl.*]

dally, *dal'i, v.i.* to lose time by idleness or trifling: to play (with): to exchange caresses:—*pr.p.* **dally'ing;** *pa.p.* **dall'ied.**—*n.* **dall'iance,** trifling: interchange of embraces: delay. [O.Fr. *dalier,* to chat.]

Dalmatian, *dal-mā'sh(ä)n, n.* a spotted dog, resembling the pointer in shape. [Conn., prob. erroneously, with *Dalmatia,* on the N.E. Adriatic.]

dalmatic, *dal-mat'ik, n.* a loose-fitting, wide-sleeved ecclesiastical vestment: a similar garment worn by a king on state occasions. [Low L. *dalmatica,* a robe on the pattern of a dress worn in *Dalmatia.*]

fāte, fär; mē, hûr (her); *mīne; mōte, för; mūte; mōŏn, fŏŏt; th*en (then)

Daltonism, *döl′ton-izm, n.* a school method by which a pupil does individual work, assigned to him in monthly 'contracts' or instalments, at his own speed.—Also **Dalton plan.** [First tried in 1920 at *Dalton,* Massachusetts.]

dam, *dam, n.* an embankment to restrain water: the water thus confined.—*v.t.* to keep back by a bank or similar obstruction (also *fig.*):—*pr.p* damm′ing; *pa.p.* dammed. [M.E., of Germanic origin.]

dam, *dam, n.* a mother, usu. of animals, or contemptuously. [A form of *dame.*]

damage, *dam′ij, n.* injury: loss: the value of what is lost: (*coll.*) cost: (*pl.*) payment due for loss or injury sustained by one person through the fault of another.—*v.t.* to harm.—*v.i.* to take injury. [O.Fr. *damage*—L. *damnum,* loss.]

damask, *dam′åsk, n.* figured stuff, originally of silk, now usu. of linen, the figure being woven, not printed: Damascus steel or its surface pattern.—*adj.* of a red colour, like that of a damask rose.—*n.* **damascene** (*dam′a-sēn*), (*cap.*) a native of Damascus: a Damascus sword: inlay of metal (esp. gold) on steel.—*v.t.* to decorate metal (esp. steel) by inlaying or encrusting: to ornament with the wavy appearance of Damascus steel—also **damasceene, damaskeen.**—*ns.* **dam′ask-plum,** the damson; **dam′ask-rose,** a species of pink rose. [From *Damascus,* in Syria, where damask was orig. made.]

dame, *dām, n.* the mistress of a house, a matron (now usu. jocular or patronising): (*slang*) a woman: the comic, vulgar old woman of the pantomime (often played by a man): a noble lady: a lady of the same rank as a knight.—*n.* **dame′-school** (chiefly *hist.*), a school for children kept by a woman. [Fr. *dame*—L. *dòmina,* a mistress.]

damn, *dam, v.t.* to censure or condemn: to sentence to eternal punishment: to doom.—*n.* an oath, a curse.—*adj.* **dam′nable,** deserving damnation: hateful, pernicious: (*coll.*) very annoying.—*adv.* **dam′nably.**—*n.* **damna′tion,** condemnation: eternal punishment.—*adj.* **dam′natory,** consigning to damnation.—*p.adj.* **damned,** sentenced to everlasting punishment: hateful, deserving of condemnation (in this sense often **damn**).—*adv.* very, exceedingly (often **damn**).—*adj.* **damning** (*dam′ing*), exposing (a person) to conviction of fault or crime, or to condemnation. [Fr. *damner*—L. *damnāre,* to condemn—*damnum,* loss.]

Damoclean, *dam-ō-clē′án, adj.* like *Damocles,* flatterer of the tyrant Dionysius, taught the insecurity of happiness by being made to sit through a feast with a sword suspended over his head by a single hair.

damosel, damozel, *dam′ō-zel, n.* Same as **damsel.**

damp, *damp, n.* vapour, mist: moist air: in mines, any gas other than air.—*v.t.* to wet slightly: to chill: to discourage.—*adj.* moist, foggy.—*v.t.* and *v.i.* **damp′en,** to make or become damp or moist.—*n.* **damp′er,** one who, or that which, damps: a depressive influence: shutter for shutting off or regulating a draught: (*Australia*) a kind of unfermented bread.—*n.* **damp′ness.**—**damp-proof course,** a layer of material impervious to water—built

into the wall of a building to prevent moisture from rising from the foundations. [M.E. *dampen*; akin to Ger. *dampf,* vapour.]

damsel, *dam′zel, n.* a young unmarried woman: a girl. [O.Fr. *dameisele*—Low L. *domicella,* dim. of L. *domina,* lady.]

damson, *dam′z(ó)n, -són, n.* a rather small oval-fruited variety of plum. [Shortened from *Damascene*—*Damascus.*]

dance, *däns, v.i.* to move with measured steps, esp. to music: to move lightly and gaily: (*fig.*) to seem to move in such a way (e.g. of eyes).—*v.t.* to make to dance or to move up and down: to perform (a dance).—*n.* rhythmic movement with measured steps: a social function at which dancing is the chief entertainment: a tune to which dancing is performed.—*ns.* **danc′er,** one who dances, esp. as a profession; **danc′ing-girl,** a professional dancer in the East.—**dance attendance,** to wait obsequiously; **Dance of Death,** Death, sometimes represented as a skeleton, leading all men to the grave—a theme popular in mediaeval drama, painting, sculpture, &c.—Also **Dance Macabre.**—**lead one a dance,** to keep one involved in a series of wearying perplexities; **merry dancers,** the aurora. [O.Fr. *danser.*]

dandelion, *dan′di-lī-ón, n.* a common composite (q.v.) with jagged-tooth leaves and yellow flower. [Fr. *dent de lion,* lion tooth.]

dander, daunder, *dön′dér, v.i.* (*Scot.*) to walk idly.—*n.* an easy, aimless walk.

dander, *dan′dér, n.* anger, passion. [A form of **dandruff.**]

Dandie Dinmont, *dan′di din′mónt, n.* a short-legged, rough-haired Scottish Border terrier of pepper and mustard colour. [Called after *Dandie Dinmont* in Scott's *Guy Mannering,* who owned such dogs.]

dandle, *dan′dl, v.t.* to fondle or toss in the arms, as a baby. [Origin unknown.]

dandruff, dandriff, *dand′rúf, n.* a scaly scurf on the skin under the hair. [Origin unknown.]

dandy, *dan′di, n.* a foppish person, one who pays much attention to dress.—*adj.* (*coll.*) smart, fine.—*v.t.* **dan′dify,** to dress up.—*adj.* **dandī′acal.** [Origin unknown.]

Dane, *dān, n.* a native of *Denmark:* **a Great Dane,** a large, short-haired breed of dog.—*adj.* **Dan′ish,** belonging to Denmark.—*n.* the language of the Danes.—*n.* **Dane′geld,** a tax imposed in the 10th century, to buy off the Danes or to defend the country against them. [Dan. *Daner* (pl.); O.E. *Dene.*]

danger, *dān′jér, n.* a state or circumstances involving peril or risk: a source of peril or risk.—*adj.* **dan′gerous,** very unsafe: (of persons) not to be trusted.—*adv.* **dan′gerously.**—*ns.* **dan′gerousness; dan′ger-money,** extra money paid for doing a more than usually perilous job; **dan′ger-sig′nal.** [O.Fr. *dangier,* absolute power, hence power to hurt—L. *dominus,* a lord.]

dangle, *dang′gl, v.i.* to hang loosely: to follow (after someone), to hang (about, around someone).—*v.t.* to make to dangle. [Scand.; cf. O.N. *dingla,* to swing.]

dank, *dangk, adj.* moist, wet.

Neutral vowels in unaccented syllables: *em′pér-ór*; for certain sounds in foreign words see p. ix.

174

danseuse, *dä-soez'*, *n.* a female dancer, esp. a ballet dancer. [Fr.]

dap, *dap*, *v.i.* to drop (bait) gently into the water.

dapper, *dap'ér*, *adj.* quick: little and active: spruce. [Du. *dapper*, brave.]

dapple, *dap'l*, *adj.* marked with spots.—*v.t.* to variegate with spots.—*adj.* **dapp'le-bay**, of bay colour variegated with spots of a different shade; **dapp'le-grey**. [Origin unknown.]

Darby and Joan, *där'bi änd jōn'*, a devoted elderly married couple. [Poss. from characters in an 18th-cent. song.]

dare, *dār*, *v.i.* and *v.t.* to be bold enough: to venture:—*3rd pers. sing.* dare(s); *pa.t.* durst, dared.—*v.t.* to challenge: to defy:—*pa.t.* dared.—*n.* a challenge.—*n.* **dare'-dev'il**, a rash, venturesome fellow.—*adj.* reckless.—*adj.* **dar'ing**, bold: courageous.—*n.* boldness.—*n.* **dar'ing-do** (see **derring-do**).—*adv.* **dar'ingly.—I dare say**, I suppose. [O.E. *dearr*, present sing. (orig. preterite) of *durran*.]

darg, *därg*, *n.* a day's work (*Scot.*) a task.—*n.* **love'-darg**, work done for a charitable cause. [Contr. from *day-wark*, day-work.]

dark, *därk*, *adj.* without light: gloomy: blackish: difficult to understand: secret: sinister: unenlightened.—*n.* absence of light: obscurity: a state of ignorance.—*v.t.* **dark'en**, to make dark or darker (*lit.* and *fig.*): to sully.—*v.i.* to grow dark or darker.—*adj.* **dark'ish**, somewhat dark: dusky.—*adv.* and *adj.* **dark'ling**, in the dark: dark.—*adv.* **dark'ly.**—*n.* **dark'ness.**—*n.* **dark'y**, **dark'ey** (*coll.*; *old-fashioned*), a Negro.—**dark ages**, the period of intellectual darkness in Europe, from the 5th to the 15th century; **a dark horse**, in racing, a horse whose capabilities are not known: a person whose character is not easily read; **dark room**, a room free from such light as would affect photographic films, &c.—**be in the dark about**, be ignorant of; **darken one's door**, (often with negative, often implying unwelcomeness) to appear as a visitor; **keep dark**, be silent or secret about, conceal; **Prince of Darkness**, Satan. [O.E. *deorc*.]

darling, *där'ling*, *n.* one dearly beloved: a favourite. [O.E. *dēorling*—*adj. dēore*, dear, and noun-ending *-ling*.]

darn, *därn*, *v.t.* to mend by interwoven stitches.—*n.* the place darned.—*n.* **darn'ing-need'le**.

darn, *därn*, *v.i.*, *v.t.*, *n.* and *adj.* a weakened form of **damn**.

dart. See **dace**.

dart, *därt*, *n.* a pointed weapon or toy for throwing with the hand: anything that pierces: a tapering fold sown on the reverse of material in order to shape it: (in *pl.*) a game in which darts are thrown at a board.—*v.t.* to send or shoot forth.—*v.i.* to start or shoot forth rapidly.—*ns.* **dart'-board**, the target in the game of darts; **dar'ter**, a genus of fresh-water diving birds allied to cormorants. [O.Fr. *dart*.]

Darwinism, *där'win-izm*, *n.* the theory of the origin of species (of the manner in which the different types of living things have developed) propounded by Charles *Darwin* (1809-82).—*adj.* and *n.* **Darwin'ian**. See **natural selection**.

dash, *dash*, *v.t.* to throw, thrust, or drive violently: to break by throwing together: to

bespatter: to frustrate (hopes): to depress, confound (e.g. one's spirits): to modify by dilution (with).—*v.i.* to rush violently.—*n.* a violent striking: a rush: a violent onset: a blow: a mark (—) at a break in a sentence: verve: ostentation: a slight admixture.—*n.* **dash'-board**, a board or screen in front of a driver in a horse-vehicle to keep off splashes of mud, in a motor-car or aeroplane to carry instruments.—*adj.* **dash'ing**, spirited: showy: ostentatiously fashionable—**dash off** (*coll.*), to throw off or produce hastily: to hurry away; **dash out**, to knock out by striking against something. [M.E. *daschen*, *dassen*, to rush, or strike with violence—Scand.]

dastard, *das'tárd*, *n.* a cowardly fellow: (*loosely*) one who does a cowardly act without giving his victim a chance.—*adj.* cowardly.—*adj.* and *adv.* **das'tardly.**—*ns.* **das'tardliness**, **das'tardy**. [From a Scand. stem *dast* = Eng. *dazed*, and Fr. suffix, *-ard*.]

data, *dā'ta*, *n.pl.* facts given, from which others may be deduced:—*sing.* **dā'tum** (q.v.).—**data processing** (see **process**). [L., pa.p. neut. pl. of *dāre*, to give.]

date, *dāt*, *n.* a statement of time (or time and place) of writing, sending, executing, as on a letter, book, document: the time of an event: (*coll.*) an appointment or engagement: (*coll.*) the person with whom an appointment is made.—*v.t.* to affix a date to: to ascertain or suggest the date of: (*coll.*) to make an appointment with: (*coll.*) to go out with (a member of the opposite sex) esp. regularly.—*v.i.* to take beginning (e.g. *this practice dates from the first century* A.D.): to reflect strongly the taste of the time at which it was produced: hence to become old-fashioned.—*adj.* **dat'able.—*n.* date'-cod'ing**, marking in code on the container a date after which food should not be used.—*adj.* **date'less**, without date: without fixed limit: immemorial.—*n.* **date'-line**, the line east and west of which the date differs by one day—the 180th meridian with certain deviations: a line giving the date, as in a newspaper.—**out of date**, antiquated; **up to date**, abreast of the times: modern: adapted or corrected so as to reflect the attitude of the present time or to indicate the facts or knowledge now available. [L. *datum*, as in *datum Romae* = given (or written) at Rome.]

date, *dāt*, *n.* the fruit of the date-palm.—*ns.* **date'-palm**, **date'-tree**, a tree, a native of North Africa and south-west Asia. [Fr. *datte*—Gr. *daktylos*, a finger.]

dative, *dāt'iv*, *adj.* (*gram.*) expressing an indirect object.—*n.* the dative case: a word in the dative. [L. *dativus*—*dāre*, to give.]

datum, *dā'tum* (see **data**).—*n.* **dā'tum-line**, the horizontal base-line from which heights and depths are measured. [L. *dātum*, given—*dāre*, to give.]

daub, *döb*, *v.t.* to smear: to paint coarsely.—*n.* a coarse painting.—*n.* **daub'er**.—*adj.* **daub'y**, sticky. [O.Fr. *dauber*, to plaster—L. *dē*, down, and *albus*, white.]

daughter, *dö'tér*, *n.* a female child: a female descendant: a woman (generally).—*n.* **daugh'ter-in-law**, a son's wife: formerly a step-daughter:—*pl.* **daughters-in-law.** [O.E. *dohtor.*]

daunt, *dönt* or *dänt, v.t.* (*obs.*) to subdue: to frighten: to discourage.—*adj.* **daunt′less,** not to be daunted.—*adv.* **daunt′lessly.**—*n.* **daunt′lessness.** [O.Fr. *danter*—L. *domitāre—domāre,* to tame.]

dauphin, *dö′fin, n.* the name given to the eldest son of the king of France, from 1349 down to 1830.—*n.* **dau′phiness,** his wife. [O.Fr. *daulphin.* From *Delphinus,* family name of lords of part of south-east France (province of Dauphiné) ceded to the king in 1349.]

davenport, *dav′én-pört, -pört, n.* a small ornamental writing-desk—also **dev′onport.** [From the maker.]

davit, *dav′it, n.* one of a pair of pieces of timber or iron to raise a boat over a ship's side or stern. [Cf. Fr. *davier,* a forceps.]

Davy, *dä′vi,* **Davy-lamp,** *dä′vi-lamp, n.* the safety-lamp used in coalmines invented by Sir Humphry *Davy* (1778-1829).

Davy Jones, *dä′vi jönz, n.* a sailor's familiar name for the (malignant) spirit of the sea, the devil; hence **Davy Jones's locker,** the sea, as the grave of men drowned at sea.

daw, *döw, n.* a jackdaw. [M.E. *dawe.*]

dawdle, *dö′dl, v.i.* to waste time by trifling: to act or move slowly.—*n.* **daw′dler.** [Perh. connected with (dial.) *daddle,* to totter.]

dawn, *dön, v.i.* to become day: to begin to grow light: to begin to appear.—*n.* daybreak: beginning.—Also **dawn′ing.**—**dawn (up)on,** to become suddenly clear to. [O.E. *dagian,* to dawn, *dæg,* day.]

day, *dā, n.* the time of light, from sunrise to sunset: twenty-four hours, the time the earth takes to make a revolution on her axis: from midnight to midnight (*civil day*): the hours spent at work (*working day*): a day set apart for a purpose, as for receiving visitors: lifetime: time of existence, vogue, or influence: ground surface over a mine.—*ns.* **day′break,** dawn; **day′-coal,** the upper stratum of coal; **day′-dream,** a dreaming or musing while awake (also *v.i.*); **day′-lā̄bour,** labour paid by the day; **day′-lā̄bourer; day′light,** light of day: clear space.—*adj.* **day′long,** during the whole day.—*n.* **daylight-saving,** reduction of loss of daylight, for work or play, by advancing the clock, as in summer time (q.v.).—*adj.* **day′-release′,** freed from employment during the day so as to attend an educational course.—*ns.* **day′-schol′ar,** a pupil who attends a boarding-school during the school-hours, but boards at home; **day′-school,** a school held during the day, as opposed both to a nightschool and to a boarding-school; **day′star,** the morning star; **day′time.**—**day about,** on alternate days; **day by day,** daily; **day in, day out,** for an indefinite succession of days; **day off,** a day's holiday; **day out,** a servant's free day; **days of grace,** three days allowed for payment of bills, &c., beyond the day named.—**carry or win, lose, the day,** (*lit.* and *fig.*) to gain the victory, lose the battle; **the other day,** not long ago; **the time of day,** the hour of the clock; **pass the time of day with,** to exchange greetings or polite small-talk with. [O.E. *dæg.*]

daze, *dāz, v.t.* to stun, to stupefy.—*n.* bewilderment.—*adj.* **dazed** (*dāzd*).—*adv.* **dazedly**

(*dāz′id-li*). [O.N. *dasask,* to be breathless.]

dazzle, *daz′l, v.t.* to daze or overpower with a strong light: to confound by brilliancy, beauty, or cleverness.—*n.* the act of dazzling: that which dazzles.—*n.* **dazz′ler.** [Freq. of *daze.*]

D.D.T. (in full, *dichloro-diphenyl-trichloro-ethane*), a white, practically odourless powder used to kill lice and thus prevent the spread of typhus—effective also against other insects, but having long-term disadvantages.

de-, *dē-, di-, pfx.* down: away from: completely. [L. *dē,* from, down from, away from]:—e.g. **depose, derail, denude** (see these words). Also used (as a living prefix) to form words reversing or undoing an action:—e.g. **decentralise** (q.v.), **de-Nazification.**

deacon, *dē′kón, n.* in episcopal churches, a member of the clergy under priests: a church officer: in Scotland, the master of an incorporated company:—*fem.* **dea′coness,** in some Protestant churches a woman whose duties are pastoral, educational, social and evangelical.—*ns.* **dea′conhood, dea′conry, dea′conship.** [L. *diāconus*—Gr. *diākonos,* a servant.]

dead, *ded, adj.* without life: death-like: without vegetation: extinguished (e.g. of fire): numb (e.g. of a limb): spiritually or emotionally insensitive: dull (of colour, sound, &c.): without motion: out of play (of a ball): obsolete: unsaleable: complete: absolutely accurate: unerring: of a golfball, lying very near the hole.—*adv.* in a dead manner: absolutely: utterly.—*n.* one who is dead: the time of greatest stillness, as 'the dead of night'.—*adjs.* **dead′-alive′, dead′-and-alive′,** dull, inactive; **dead′-beat′,** quite overcome, exhausted; **dead′-born,** still-born.—*v.t.* **dead′en,** to make dead: to deprive partly of vigour or sensibility: to lessen (a sensation, as pain): to deprive of force or brightness (e.g. a sound).—*ns.* **dead-end,** a pipe, passage, &c., closed at one end: (*lit.* and *fig.*) a cul-de-sac; **dead′-eye** (*naut.*), a round, flattish wooden block with a rope or iron band passing round it, and pierced with three holes for a lanyard; **dead′(-)fire,** an appearance of fire taken as a death omen; **dead′-ground** (*mil.*), ground which cannot be covered by fire; **dead′-heat,** a race in which two or more competitors are equal at the end; **dead′-lett′er,** one undelivered and unclaimed at the post-office: a law or rule which has been made but is not enforced; **dead′-lev′el,** a stretch of land without any rising ground: sameness; **dead′(-)line,** a line drawn in a military prison, by going beyond which a prisoner makes himself liable to be shot instantly: also *fig.:* the closing date; **dead′lock,** a standstill, state of inaction, resulting from the opposing aims of different people, an impasse; **dead loss,** a loss without any compensation.—*adj.* **dead′ly,** causing death: fatal: death-like: implacable (e.g. *deadly hatred*): bringing damnation (e.g. *deadly sin*): intense (e.g. *deadly earnestness*).—*ns.* **dead′liness; dead′ly-night′shade,** the plant belladonna (q.v.); **dead′(-)march,** a piece of solemn music played at funerals; **dead′-meat,** the flesh of animals ready for the market.—*n.p.* **dead′-men,** empty bottles after a carouse.—*ns.* **dead′ness; dead′-nett′le,** a genus of plants

---

Neutral vowels in unaccented syllables: *em′pér-ór*; for certain sounds in foreign words see p. ix.

deaf
debenture

superficially like nettles but without stings; **dead'-pan,** an expressionless face: one having such.—*adj.* of manner, expressionless, emotionless, esp. when the situation implies feeling of some kind, e.g. amusement.—*ns.* **dead'reck'oning,** an estimation of a ship's place simply by the logbook; **dead'-set,** a determined and prolonged attempt; **dead'-wa'ter,** the eddy water closing in behind a ship's stern as she sails; **dead'(-)weight,** unrelieved weight; a heavy or oppressive burden; **dead'-wind,** a calm (in the vortex of a storm); **dead'-wood,** pieces of timber laid on the upper side of the keel at either end: useless material.—**dead language,** one no longer spoken; **dead-men's bells,** the foxglove; **dead-men's shoes,** succession to one who dies.—**be dead set against,** to be utterly opposed to; **dead to the world,** very soundly asleep: unconscious. [O.E. *dēad.*]

deaf, *def, adj.* dull of hearing: unable to hear: not willing to hear.—*v.t.* **deaf'en,** to make deaf: to stun, to render impervious to sound.—*n.* **deaf'ening,** stuffing put into floors, partition-walls, &c., to prevent sounds from passing through.—*adj.* making deaf: very loud.—*ns.* **deaf'-mute,** one who is both deaf and dumb; **deaf'ness.** [O.E. *dēaf.*]

deal, *dēl, n.* a portion, amount (**a great, good, deal**) with other *adjs.*, *arch.* or *dial.*): (*coll.*) a large amount: the act of dividing cards: a business transaction, esp. a favourable one.—*v.t.* to divide, to distribute: to deliver (e.g. a blow),—*v.i.* to transact business (with): to trade (in): (with *with*) to act towards: to distribute cards:—*pa.t.* and *pa.p.* dealt (*delt*).—*ns.* **deal'er,** a trader: in cards, one whose turn it is to deal or who has dealt the hand in play; **deal'ing,** manner of acting towards others (**double dealing,** see **double**): intercourse of trade, &c. (usu.*pl.*).—**deal with,** to tackle and dispose of (any problem or task). [O.E. *dǣlan—dǣl,* a part; Ger *teilen—teil,* a part or division. A doublet of **dole.**]

deal, *dēl, n.* a fir or pine board of a standard size: softwood.—*adj.* of deal. [Middle Low Ger. *dele;* cf. O.E. *thille.*]

dean, *dēn, n.* a small valley.—Also **dene.** [O.E. *denu,* a valley. Cf. **den.**]

dean, *dēn, n.* a dignitary in cathedral and collegiate churches who presides over the canons: the president of a faculty in a university, &c.: a resident fellow of a college who has administrative and disciplinary functions.—*ns.* **dean'ery,** group of parishes presided over by a dean: a dean's house; **dean'ship,** the office of a dean.—**Dean of Guild,** a municipal official in Scotland, who has authority over building and altering of houses; **rural dean,** one who, under the bishop, has the special care and inspection of the clergy. [O.Fr. *deien*—Low L. *decānus,* a chief of ten—L. *decem,* ten.]

dear, *dēr, adj.* high in price, costly: highly valued: beloved: a conventional form of address used in letter-writing.—*n.* one who is beloved.—*adv.* at a high price.—*interj.* indicating surprise, pity, or other emotion, as in 'Oh dear!' 'Dear me!'—*adv.* **dear'ly.**—*ns.* **dear'ness;** **dearth** (*dûrth*), (*obs.*) high price: scarcity:

famine. [O.E. *dēore.*]

dearticulate, *dē-är-tik'ū-lāt, v.t.* to disjoint. [Pfx. **de-,** and **articulate.**]

death, *deth, n.* state of being dead: cessation of life: manner or cause of dying: a deadly plague.—*ns.* **death'-ag'ony,** the struggle often preceding death; **death'-bed,** the bed on which one dies: the last illness; **death'-blow,** a blow that causes death: a mortal blow; (*pl.*) **death'-dū'ties,** duties paid to government on the inheritance of property after the death of the owner.—*adj.* **death'less,** never dying: everlasting.—*n.* **death'lessness.**—*adj.* **deathly,** deadly: deathlike.—*ns.* **death'-mask,** a plaster-cast taken from the face after death; **death'-rate,** the proportion of deaths to the population; **death'-rat'le,** a rattling in the throat which sometimes precedes death; **death'-roll,** a list of the dead; **death's-door,** the point of death; **death's'-head,** the skull of a human skeleton, or a figure of it; **death'-stroke,** a death-blow, **death'-trap,** an unsafe structure or place that exposes one to great danger of death; **death'-warr'ant,** an order for the execution of a criminal; **death'-watch,** a watch by a dying person: a popular name for several insects that produce a ticking noise; **death'-wish,** conscious or unconscious wish for death for oneself or for another; **death's'-head moth,** a hawk-moth having skull-like markings on the back of the thorax.—**be in at the death,** in hunting, to be up on the animal before the dogs have killed it (also *fig.*); **be the death of,** to annoy beyond endurance; **do, put, to death,** to kill. [O.E. *dēath.*]

débâcle, debacle, *dā-bäk'l, di-bak'l, n.* a breaking up of ice on a river: a complete break-up or collapse: a stampede. [Fr. *débâcle; dé-* (—*des-*), and *bâcler,* to bar—L. *baculus,* a stick.]

debar, *di bär', v.t.* to bar out (from): to exclude:—*pr.p.* debar'ring; *pa.p.* debarred',—*n.* **debar'ment.** [Fr. *débarrer*—L.L. *dēbarrāre,* which meant 'to unbar'.]

debark, *di-bärk', v.t.* or *v.i.* to disembark.—*ns.* **dēbarkā'tion, dēbarcā'tion.** [Fr. *débarquer—des-* (L. *dis-*), away, and *barque,* a ship.]

debase, *di-bās', v.t.* to lower: to make mean or of less value, to degrade: to adulterate, as the coinage.—*adj.* **debased',** degraded.—*n.* **debase'ment.** [Pfx. **de-,** and obs. *base*—**abase.**]

debate, *di-bāt', n.* a contention in words: argument: a (parliamentary) discussion.—*v.t.* to argue about.—*v.i.* to deliberate: to join in debate.—*adj.* **debat'able, debāte'able,** liable to be disputed.—*n.* **debāt'er.** [O.Fr. *debatre*—L. *dē,* and *bātuěre,* to beat.]

debauch, *di-böch', v.t.* to lead away from duty or allegiance: to corrupt: to seduce.—*v.i.* to overindulge.—*n.* a fit of intemperance or debauchery.—*p.adj.* **debauched',** corrupt: profligate.—*n.* **debauch'ery,** excessive intemperance: habitual lewdness. [O.Fr. *desbaucher,* to corrupt; origin uncertain.]

debenture, *di-ben'tyūr, -chúr, n.* a written acknowledgment of a debt: a security issued by a company for borrowed money: a certificate authorising a repayment of import duty. [L. *dēbentur,* there are due, 3rd pers. pl. pass. of *dēbēre,* to owe—the first word of the receipt.]

fāte, fär; mē, hûr (her); *mīne; mōte, för; mūte; mōōn, fŏŏt;* THen (then)

debilitate, *di-bil'i-tāt*, *v.t.* to make weak, to impair, the strength of.—*ns.* **debilitā'tion**; **debil'ity**, bodily weakness and languor. [L. *dēbilitāre*, *-ātum*—*dēbilis*, weak.]

debit, *deb'it*, *n.* something due: an entry on the debtor side of an account.—*v.t.* to charge (a person, with a debt): to enter on the debtor side of an account. [L. *dēbitum*, what is due, from *dēbēre*, to owe.]

debonair, debonnaire, *deb-o-nār'*, *adj.* of good appearance and manners: gay and gracious. [O.Fr. *de*, of, *bon*, good, *aire*, manner.]

debouch, *di-bowch'*, *di-bōōsh'*, *v.i.* to issue forth from a narrow pass or confined place.—*n.* **debouchure'**, the mouth of a river or strait. [Fr. *déboucher*—*de*, from, *bouche*, the mouth.]

debrief, *dē-brēf'*, *v.t.* to gather information from a soldier, astronaut, &c. on his return from a mission. [Pfx. **de-**, and **brief**.]

débris, dȧb'rē, debris, *deb'rē*, *déb-rē'*, *n.* wreckage, ruins, rubbish: a mass of rocky fragments. [Fr., from *briser*, to break; akin to **bruise**.]

debt, *det*, *n.* what one owes to another: what one becomes liable to do: a state of obligation or of indebtedness.—*n.* **debt'or**, one who owes a debt.—**debt of honour**, a debt not recognised by law, but binding in honour—esp. a gambling or betting debt.—**bad debt**, a debt of which there is no prospect of payment; **in one's debt**, under an obligation, not necessarily pecuniary, to one. [O.Fr. *dette*—L. *dēbitum*, *dēbēre*, to owe.]

debug, *dē-bug'*, *v.t.* to remove concealed listening devices from: to find faults or errors in and remove them from (something mechanical). [Pfx. **de-**, and **bug** (2).]

debunk, *dē-bungk'*, *v.t.* (*slang*) to clear of humbug: to strip (a person) of an unmerited reputation: to show up (e.g. a theory) as false. [Pfx. **de-**, and **bunk** (see **bunkum**).]

début, *dā-bū'*, *n.* a beginning or first attempt: a first appearance before the public or in society.—*n.* **débutant** *dā-bü-tä*, *deb'ü-tant*), one who makes his first appearance:—*fem.* **débutante** (*-tät*, *deb'ü-tänt*; U.S. dim. **deb.**). [Fr. *début*, a first stroke—*débuter*—*de*, from, *but*, aim, mark.]

deca-, deka-, *dek'a*. Pfx. used, esp. in the metric system, to indicate quantities or magnitudes in multiples of ten. [Gr. *deka*, ten.]

decade, decad, *dek'ād, -ād', dek'ad*, *n.* a group of ten, esp. a series of ten years. [Fr. *décade*—Gr. *dekas*, *-ados*—*deka*, ten.]

decadence, *dek'a-déns*, or *de-kā'-*, **dec'adency** (or *de-kā'-*), *n.* state of decay: deterioration—used esp. in speaking of the art or literature, or the general moral character, of a period.—*adj.* **dec'adent** (or *de-kā'-*), decaying: lacking in vigour, moral and physical.—*n.* one who is degenerate: one belonging to a school in later 19th century French literature, also known as the symbolists. [Fr.,—L. *dē*, down, *cadēre*, to fall.]

decagon, *dek'a-gon*, *n.* a plane figure of ten angles and sides.—*adj.* **decag'onal**. [Gr. *deka*, and *gōnia*, an angle.]

decahedron, *dek-a-hē'dron*, *n.* a solid figure having ten faces.—*adj.* **decahē'dral**. [Gr. *deka*, ten, and *hedra*, a seat.]

decalogue, *dek'a-log*, *n.* the ten commandments. [Gr. *deka*, ten, *logos*, a discourse.]

decamp, *di-kamp'*, *v.i.* to make off, esp. secretly.—*n.* **decamp'ment**. [Fr. *décamper*.]

decant, *di-kant'*, *v.t.* to pour off, leaving sediment: to pour from one vessel to another.—*ns.* **decantā'tion; decant'er**, an ornamental bottle for holding decanted liquor. [Fr. *décanter*—L. *dē*, from, *canthus*, beak of a vessel—Gr. *kanthos*, corner of the eye.]

decapitate, *di-kap'i-tāt*, *v.t.* to behead.—*n.* **decapitā'tion**. [L. *dē*, from, *caput*, *capitis*, head.]

Decapoda, *di-kap'o-da*, *n.pl.* an order of Crustaceans with ten feet—crabs, lobsters, shrimps, prawns: cephalopods with ten arms, as cuttlefishes (cf. *Octopoda*).—*n.* **dec'apod**, a member of either of these orders.—Also *adj.* [Gr. *deka*, ten, *pous*, gen. *podos*, a foot.]

decarbonise, *dē-kär'bon-īz*, *v.t.* to remove carbon or carbon dioxide from.—*n.* **decarbonisā'tion**. [Pfx. **de-**, and **carbonise**.]

decastich, *dek'a-stik*, *n.* a poem of ten lines. [Gr. *deka*, *stichos*, row, verse.]

decastyle, *dek'a-stīl*, *n.* a portico with ten columns in front.—Also *adj.* [Gr. *deka*, ten, *stylos*, a column.]

decasyllable, *dek-a-sil'a-bl*, *n.* a verse line, or a word, with ten syllables.—*adj.* **decasyllab'ic**. [Gr. *deka*, ten, *syllabē*, a syllable.]

decathlon, *dek-ath'lon*, *n.* a two-day contest of ten events held at the modern Olympic Games since 1912. [Gr. *deka*, ten, *athlon*, a contest.]

decay, *di-kā'*, *v.i.* to fall away from a state of health or excellence: to waste away: to rot.—*v.t.* to cause to waste away: to impair.—*n.* a falling into a worse state: a wearing away: loss of fortune: disintegration of a radioactive substance.—*p.adj.* **decayed'**, (*fig.*) reduced in circumstances.—*n.* **decayed'ness**. [L. *dē*, from, *cadēre*, to fall.]

Decca, *dek'a*, *n.* a radio aid to navigation used by ships and aircraft.

decease, *di-sēs'*, *n.* death.—*v.i.* to die.—*p.adj.* **deceased'**, dead.—*n.* the dead person previously referred to. [L. *dē*, away, *cēdēre*, *cessum*, to go.]

deceit, *di-sēt'*, *n.* act of deceiving: anything intended to mislead: fraud: falseness.—*adj.* **deceit'ful**, disposed or tending to deceive: insincere.—*adv.* **deceit'fully**.—*n.* **deceit'fulness**.—*v.t.* **deceive** (*di-sēv'*), to mislead: to cheat: to disappoint.—*n.* **deceiv'er**. [L. *dēcipēre*, *dēceptum*—*dē*, from, *capēre*, to take.]

decelerate, *dē-sel'ér-āt*, *v.t.* and *v.i.* to slow down. [L. *dē*, down, *celer*, swift.]

December, *di-sem'bér*, *n.* the tenth month among the Romans: with us, the twelfth month of the year. [L. *decem*, ten.]

decent, *dē'sént*, *adj.* becoming, seemly, proper: moderate: fairly good, passable: (*coll.*) showing tolerant or kindly moderation.—*n.* **dē'cency**, seemliness, propriety, modesty: (*coll.*) considerateness, sense of what may be fitly expected of one.—*adv.* **dē'cently**. [L. *decens*, *-entis*, pr.p. of *decēre*, to be becoming.]

decentralise, *dē-sen'trál-īz*, *v.t.* to withdraw from the centre: to transfer functions from central government, organisation or head to local centres.—*n.* **decentralisā'tion**. [Pfx. **de-**, and **centralise**.]

Neutral vowels in unaccented syllables: *em'pér-ór*; for certain sounds in foreign words see p. ix.

deception, di-sep'sh(ó)n, n. act of deceiving: state of being deceived: means of deceiving or misleading: trick: illusion.—adj. **decep'tive,** tending to deceive: misleading.—adv. **deceptively.**—n. **decep'tiveness.** [Low L. dēceptiō, -ōnis—dēcipĕre, to deceive.]

deci-, des'ī. Pfx. used, esp. in the metric system, to indicate a quantity or magnitude of one-tenth unit. [L. decimus, tenth—decem, ten.]

decibel, des'i-bel, n. the tenth part of a bel—unit more commonly used than bel (q.v.). [Pfx. **deci-,** and **bel.**]

decide, di-sīd', v.t. to determine, to end, to settle: to resolve.—v.i. to make up one's mind.—adj. **decid'ed,** determined, settled: clear, unmistakable: resolute.—adv. **decid'edly.** [O.Fr. decider—L. dēcīdĕre—dē, away, caedĕre, to cut.]

deciduous, di-sid'ū-us, adj. liable to be shed at a certain period: shedding (leaves, antlers, &c.): (fig.). transitory, not permanent [L. dēciduus—dēcidĕre—dē, from, and cadĕre, to fall.]

decimal, des'i-m(á)l, adj. numbered or proceeding by tens.—n. decimal fraction.—v.t. **dec'imalise,** to reduce to a decimal system.—adv. **dec'imally.**—**decimal currency,** one in which the basic unit is divided into ten, or a multiple of ten, parts; **decimal notation,** a system of writing numbers as ten and powers of ten, our ordinary system; **decimal system,** a system of weights or measures (e.g. the metric system) in which each unit is ten times the next below it; **decimal fraction,** a fraction expressed by continuing ordinary decimal notation to negative powers of ten (a point being used to mark off the fraction from the whole number, as $0.1 = {}^1/_{10}$; $1.273 = 1^{273}/_{1000}$; $1.875 = 1^7/_8$). [Low L. decimālis—decem, ten.]

decimate, des'i-māt, v.t to punish by killing every tenth man: to reduce greatly in number, as by slaughter or disease.—n. **decimā'tion.** [L. decimāre, -ātum—decem, ten.]

decipher, di-sī'fér, v.t. to read or transliterate from secret writing: to make out what is unknown or difficult.—adj. **deci'pherable.** [Pfx. **de-,** and **cipher.**]

decision, di-sizh'(ó)n, n. the act of deciding: a settlement: a judgment: firmness (e.g. to act with decision): the quality of being decided in character.—adj. **deci'sive,** having the power of deciding: showing decision: final: positive.—adv. **deci'sively.**—n. **deci'siveness.** [L. dēcīsiō, -ōnis—dēcīdĕre. See **decide.**]

deck, dek, v.t. to cover: to adorn.—n. a platform extending from one side of a vessel to the other, thereby joining them together and forming both a floor and a covering: a floor, platform, or tier elsewhere, as in a bus, bridge, mine-cage: a pack of cards, or part of a pack.—ns. **deck'-chair,** a light collapsible chair of spars and canvas; **deck'er,** a vessel or vehicle which has a deck or decks (used only in composition, as a three-decker, double-decker); **deck'-hand,** a person employed on deck.—**clear the decks,** to tidy up, remove encumbrances, esp. in preparation for action (orig. naval action, now often fig.). [Du. dekken, to cover.]

deckle, dek'l, n. in paper-making a contrivance for fixing the width of a sheet.—n. **deck'le-edge,** the raw or ragged edge of hand-made paper, or imitation of it. [Ger. deckel, lid.]

declaim, di-klām', v.i. and v.t. to make a rhetorical speech: to recite.—n. **declamation,** de-kla-māsh'(ó)n, act of declaiming: a set speech.—adj. **declăm'atory,** appealing to the passions: noisy and rhetorical merely. [L. dēclāmāre—dē, inten., clāmāre, to cry out.]

declare, di-klār', v.t. to make known: to assert: to make a full statement of, as of goods at a custom-house: (bridge) to announce as one's choice (trump suit or no trumps).—v.i. (law) to make a statement: (with for, against) to announce one's decision or sympathies: (cricket) to end an innings before ten wickets have fallen.—adj. **declăr'able,** capable of being declared, or proved.—n. **declaration** (dek-la-rā'sh(ó)n), act of declaring: that which is declared: a written affirmation.—adj. **declared',** avowed.—**declaratory act** (di-klar'a-tòr-i), an act intended to explain an obscure or disputed law. [Fr. déclarer, from L. dēclārāre, -ātum—pfx. dē-, clārus, clear.]

declass, dē-kläs', v.t. to remove or degrade from one's class.—adj. **déclassé** (dā-klä-sā), having lost caste or social standing. [Fr. déclasser.]

declassify, dē-klas'i-fī, v.t. to take off the secret list. [Pfx. de-, and **classify.**]

declension, di-klen'sh(ó)n, n. a decline: (gram.) system of cases and case endings: a class of words similarly declined. [From. L. dēclīnātiō, -ōnis, a bending aside—dēclīnāre; perh. through Fr. déclinaison. See **decline.**]

decline, di-klīn', v.i. to deviate: to bend, or slope, down: to deteriorate: to fail: to draw to an end: to refuse.—v.t. to turn away from, to refuse: (gram.) to give the various cases of.—n. a falling off: a down-slope: decay: a gradual sinking of the bodily faculties, consumption.—n. **declinā'tion,** (U.S.) act of declining: a sloping downward: (astron.) angular distance from the celestial equator.—**declination of the compass,** deviation of the compass needle from the true north. [Fr. décliner—L. dē clīnāre—dē, down, away from, clīnāre, to bend.]

declivity, di-kliv'i-ti, n. a place that slopes downward: a gradual descent.—adj. **decliv'itous.** [Fr.,—L. dēclīvitās—dē, downward, clīvus, sloping, akin to clīnāre, to bend.]

declutch, dē-kluch', v.i. to release the clutch. [Pfx. de-, and **clutch.**]

decoct, di-kokt', v.t. to prepare or extract by boiling.—n. **decoc'tion,** an extract of anything got by boiling. [L. dēcoquĕre, dēcoctum—dē, down, coquĕre, to cook.]

decode, dē-kōd', v.t. to translate from a code. [Pfx. de-, and **code.**]

decoke, v.t. (coll.) to decarbonise (an internal combustion engine). [Pfx. de-, and **coke.**]

décolleté, dā-kol-tā, adj. cut low at the neck: wearing a frock that leaves neck and shoulders bare. [Fr.; ultimately from L. collum, neck.]

decolour, decolo(u)rise, dē-kul'ór, dē-kul'ór-īz, v.t. to deprive of colour. [Fr. décolorer—L. dē, from, color, colour.]

decompose, dē-kom-pōz', v.t. to separate the component parts of: to resolve into elements.—*v.i.* to decay.—*adj.* **decompos′able.**—*n.* **decomposi′tion,** act or state of decomposing: decay.—*v.t.* **decompound′,** to decompose. [Fr. *décomposer*—pfx. *dé,* apart, and *composer.* See **compose.**]

decompress, *dē-kom-pres′, v.t.* to decrease the pressure on, esp. gradually.—*n.* **decompression** (*presh′(ō)n*). [Pfx. *de-,* and **compress.**]

decontaminate, *dē-kon-tam′in-āt, v.t.* to free from contamination.—*n.* **decontaminā′tion.**—**decontamination squad,** a party equipped to cleanse from poison gas. [L. pfx, *dē,* and **contaminate.**]

decontrol, *dē-kon-trōl′, v.t.* to remove (esp.) official control.—*n.* removal of control. [Pfx. **de-,** and **control.**]

décor, *dā-kör, n.* scenery and stage embellishments: disposition of ornament: general decorative effect, e.g. of a room. [Fr.]

decorate, *dek′o-rāt, v.t.* to ornament: to honour with a badge or medal.—*adj.* **dec′orated.**—*n.* **decorā′tion,** ornament: badge of an order.—*adj.* **dec′orative,** ornamental.—*n.* **dec′orātor,** one who decorates, esp. houses.—**decorated style** (*archit.*), a style of Gothic architecture elaborated and richly decorated. [L. *decorāre,* -*ātum—decus,* what is becoming—*decēre,* to be becoming.]

decorous, *dek′o-rus,* or *de-kō′rus, adj.* becoming, proper, decent: showing propriety and dignity.—*adv.* **decō′rously** (or *dek′o-rus-li*).—*ns.* **decō′rousness** (or *dek′o-*); **decō′rum,** what is becoming in outward appearance, propriety of conduct, decency. [L. *decōrus,* becoming.]

decorticate, *dē-kör′ti-kāt, v.t.* to deprive of the bark, husk, or peel.—*n.* **decorticā′tion.** [L. *decorticāre,* -*ātum—de,* from, and *cortex,* bark.]

decoy, *di-koy′, v.t.* to lure into a trap.—*n.* anything intended to allure into a snare: a trap for wild-ducks. [Perh. Du. *kooi*—L. *cavea,* a cage.]

decrease, *di-krēs′, v.i.* to become less.—*v.t.* to make less.—*n.* (*dē′krēs*) a growing less: the amount of diminution.—*adv.* **decreas′ingly.** [L. *dēcrescēre—dē,* from, *crescēre,* to grow.]

decree, *di-krē′, n.* an order, edict or law: a judicial decision; a predetermined purpose (of God).—*v.t.* to decide by sentence in law: to appoint.—*v.i.* to make a decree:—*pr.p.* decree′ing; *pa.p.* decreed′.—*adj.* **decrē′tive,** having the force of a decree.—**decree nisi** (*nī′sī*—L. *nisi,* unless), a decree that becomes absolute unless cause be shown to the contrary—granted esp. in divorce cases. [L. *dēcrētum—dēcernēre,* to decide.]

decrement, *dek′re-mént, n.* the act or state of decreasing: the quantity lost by decrease. [L. *dēcrēmentum.*]

decrepit, *di-krep′it, adj.* worn out by the infirmities of old age: in the last stage of decay.—*ns.* **decrep′itness, decrep′itude.** [L. *dēcrepitus,* noiseless, very old—*crepitus,* a noise.]

decrepitate, *di-krep′i-tāt, v.i.* to crackle, as salts when heated.—*n.* **decrepitā′tion.** [L. *dē-,* inten., *crepitāre,* to rattle much.]

decrescent, *di-kres′ént, adj.* becoming gradually less.—*n.* (*mus.*) **decrescen′do** (*dā-kre-shen′-dō*), diminuendo (q.v.). [L. pfx, *dē-,* and *crescēre,* to increase.]

decretal, *di-krē′tál, n.* a decree, esp. of the Pope: a book containing decrees. [L. *dēcrētālis—dēcrētum;* see **decree.**]

decry, *di-krī′, v.t.* to cry down, to censure as worthless:—*pa.p.* decried′.—*ns.* **decrī′al, decrī′er.** [Fr. *dé-, des-* (L. *dis*), and *crier,* to cry. See **cry.**]

decuman, *dek′ū-man, n.* a great wave, as every tenth wave was supposed to be. [L. *decumānus—decem,* ten.]

decumbent, *di-kum′bént, adj.* reclining on the ground. [L. *dēcumbens—dē,* down, *cumbēre* for *cubāre,* to lie.]

decussate, *di-kus′āt, v.t.* to divide in the form of an X.—*v.i.* to cross in such a form. Also *adj.* [From L. *decussis,* a Roman coin of ten asses (*decem asses*) marked with X, i.e. 10.]

dedicate, *ded′i-kāt, v.t.* to consecrate (to some sacred purpose): to devote wholly or chiefly: to inscribe (to someone).—*ns.* **dedicā′tion,** the act of dedicating: an address to a patron; or a similar inscription, prefixed to a book; **ded′icātor.**—*adj.* **ded′icātory.** [L. *dēdicāre,* -*ātum—dē,* down, *dicāre,* to declare.]

deduce, *di-dūs′, v.t.* to derive: to infer from what precedes or from premises.—*adj.* **deduc′ible** (*-dūs′-*).—*v.t.* **deduct′,** to take (from): to subtract.—*adj.* **deduct′ible.**—*n.* **deduc′tion,** (1) the act of deducing: that which is deduced: the drawing of a particular truth from a general, as distinguished from *induction,* rising from particular truths to a general; (2) the act of deducting: that which is deducted, abatement.—*adj.* **deduct′ive,** concerned with deduction from premises.—*adv.* **deduct′ively.** [L. *dēdūcēre, dēductum—dē,* from, *dūcēre,* to lead.]

deed, *dēd, n.* an act: an exploit: a legal document recording a transaction.—*n.* **deed′-pōll** (see **poll,** head). [O.E. *dǣd—dōn,* to do.]

deem, *dēm, v.t.* or *v.i.* to judge: to think, to believe.—*ns.* **deem′ster, demp′ster,** a judge, esp. in the Isle of Man. [O.E. *dēman,* to form a judgment—*dōm,* judgment.]

deep, *dēp, adj.* extending or placed far down or far from the outside: far involved (in, e.g. difficulties): engrossed (in, e.g. study): profound, intense (e.g. learning, sleep, distress, sin), heartfelt (e.g. thankfulness), penetrating (e.g. understanding): difficult to understand: secret: cunning: sunk low: low in pitch: (of a colour) of high saturation and low brilliance: (*cricket*) in the outfield, not close to the wicket.—*adv.* in a deep manner: far in, into (e.g. *deep in the forest, in the night*).—*n.* that which is deep: the sea.—*adj.* **deep′-dyed,** thorough-going, extreme—in a bad sense.—*v.t.* **deep′en,** to make deeper in any sense: to increase.—*v.i.* to become deeper.—*n.* **deep′-freeze′,** storage of foodstuffs, or other perishable substances, at very low temperature: the container in which the material is stored—Also *v.t.*—*adv.* **deep′ly.**—*n.* **deep′ness.**—*adj.* **deep′seat′ed** (*fig.*), firmly rooted.—**deep litter,** a method of keeping hens with a peat material on the floor of the hen-house; **Deep South,** the region of the South-east United States, esp. with reference to its clinging to the ways of the past; **in deep water,** in difficulties; **go off the deep end,** to express strong feelings freely; **two deep, three deep,** &c., in two,

Neutral vowels in unaccented syllables: *em′pér-ór*; for certain sounds in foreign words see p. ix.

180

three, layers or rows. [O.E. *dēop.*]

deer, *dēr, n.* any animal of the *Cervidae*, a family characterised by the possession of antlers, by the males at least, including stag, reindeer, &c.:—*pl.* **deer.**—*ns.* **deer′-for′est,** wild tract (not necessarily woodland) reserved for deer; **deer′-stalk′er,** one who stalks deer: a sportsman's cap peaked at back and front. [O.E. *dēor.*]

de-escalate, *de-es′ka lāt, v.t.* to reverse or slow down escalation—*n.* **de-escalation.**

deface, *di-fās′, v.t.* to disfigure: to obliterate.—*n.* **deface′ment.** [O.Fr. *desfacer*—L. *dis-*, away, *faciēs,* face.]

de facto, *dē fak′tō, adv.* and *adj.* in fact (e.g. *the ruler de facto of the country*): actual, real (e.g. *the de facto ruler*). See **de jure.** [L.]

defaecate. Same as **defecate.**

defalcate, *dē′-* or *de′fal-kāt,* or *di-fal′kāt, v.i.* to embezzle.—*ns.* **defalca′tion, defʹalcātor.** [Low L. *dēfalcāre, -ātum,* to cut away—L. *dis-,* away, *falx, falcis,* a sickle.]

defame, *di fām′, v.t.* to destroy the good reputation of: to speak evil of.—*n.* **defama′tion,** slander.—*adv.* **defam′atorily.**—*adj.* **defam′atory,** injurious to reputation. [O.Fr.—L. *diffāmāre*—*dis,* away, *fāma,* report.]

default, *di-fölt′, n.* a fault or failure: neglect to do what duty or law requires: failure to fulfil a financial obligation.—*v.i.* to fail in one's duty (as honouring a financial obligation, or appearing in court).—*n.* **default′er,** one who defaults.—**in default of,** in the absence of: for lack of; **judgment by default,** judgment given against a person because he fails to plead. [O.Fr.—L. pfx. *dē-,* and *fallĕre.* See **fault.**]

defeasible, *di-fēz′ibl, adj.* that may be defeated or annulled. [From O.Fr. *defaire,* to undo.]

defeat, *di-fēt′, v.t.* to frustrate: to win a victory over—*n.* a frustration of plans: overthrow, as of an army in battle: loss of a game, race, &c.—*ns.* **defeat′ism,** disposition to accept defeat; **defeat′ist**—also *adj.* [O Fr. *defeit, de(s)fait, pa.p.* of *desfaire,* to undo—L. *dis-,* neg. *facĕre,* to do.]

defecate, *def′e-kāt, def′- v.t.* to clear from impurities or extraneous matter (also *fig.*).—*v.i.* to void excrement.—*n.* **defeca′tion.** [L. *dēfaecāre, -ātum,* to cleanse—*dē,* from, *faex, faecis,* dregs.]

defect, *di-fekt′, dē′fekt, n.* a deficiency: a blemish, fault.—*v.i.* (*di-fekt′*), to desert one's country or a cause, transferring one's allegiance (to another).—*ns.* **defec′tion,** failure: a falling away from duty or allegiance; **defec′tionist.**—*adj.* **defec′tive,** having a defect: faulty: incomplete: (*gram.*) not having all the inflections.—*n.* a person defective in physical or mental powers.—*adv.* **defect′ively.**—*ns.* **defect′iveness; defect′or.—the defects of one's qualities,** virtues carried to excess, the faults apt to accompany or flow from good qualities. [L. *dēficĕre, dēfectum,* to fail—*dē,* down, and *facĕre,* to do.]

defence, *di-fens′, n.* a defending: capability or means of resisting an attack: protection: vindication: (*law*) a defendant's plea: the defending party in legal proceedings.—*pa.p.* **defenc′ed** (*B.*), fortified.—*adj.* **defence′less.**—*adv.* **defence′lessly.**—*n.* **defence′lessness.**

[O.Fr. *defens(e)*—L. *dēfendĕre.* See **defend.**]

defend, *di-fend′, v.t.* to prohibit: to guard or protect: to maintain against attack: (*law*) to resist, as a claim: to contest (a suit).—*adj.* **defend′able,** that may be defended.—*ns.* **defend′ant,** a defender: (*law*) a person accused or sued; **defend′er; defense,** American spelling of **defence.**—*adj.* **defens′ible,** that may be defended.—*n.* **defensibil′ity.**—*adj.* **defens′ive,** serving to defend: in a state or posture of defence.—*n.* that which defends: posture of defence.—*adv.* **defens′ively.—Defender of the Faith,** a title borne by the sovereigns of England since Henry VIII., on whom it was conferred by the Pope. [L. *dēfendĕre, dēfensum,* to ward off—*dē,* off, and *fendĕre,* to strike (found in compounds).]

defer, *di-fûr′, v.t.* to put off to another time: to delay:—*pr.p.* **defer′ring;** *pa.p.* **deferred′.**—*n.* **defer′ment.—deferred annuity,** an annuity, payment of which does not begin till after a certain number of years; **deferred payment,** payment by instalments; **deferred shares,** shares not entitling the holder to a full share of profits, and sometimes to none at all, until the expiration of a specified time or the occurrence of some event. [L. *differre*—*dis-,* asunder, *ferre,* to bear, carry.]

defer, *di-fûr′, v.i.* to yield (to wishes or opinions of another, or to authority):—*pr.p.* **defer′ring;** *pa.p.* **deferred′.**—*n.* **deference** (*def′ér-ēns*), a deferring or yielding in judgment or opinion: respectful or courteous willingness to defer.—*adj.* **deferen′tial,** expressing deference or respect.—*adv.* **deferen′tially.** [L. *dēferre*—*dē,* down, and *ferre,* to bear.]

defiance, *di-fī′áns, n.* the act of defying: a challenge to combat: contempt of opposition.—*adj.* **defi′ant,** full of defiance, insolently bold.—*adv.* **defi′antly.** [O.Fr.—*defier;* see **defy.**]

deficient, *di-fish′ént, adj.* wanting, lacking.—*ns.* **defic′iency,** defect: lack; **def′icit,** deficiency, esp. of revenue, as compared with expenditure.—**deficiency disease,** one due to the lack of an essential element (as a vitamin or vitamins) in the diet—e.g. rickets, scurvy. [L. *dēficĕre;* see **defect.**]

defile, *di-fil′, v.i.* to march off in file or line, or file by file.—*n.* (*dē′fīl, di-fīl′*) a long narrow pass or way, in which troops can march only in file or with a narrow front.—*n.* **defile′ment.** [Fr. *défiler*—L. *dis-,* and *fīlum,* a thread.]

defile, *di-fil′, v.t.* (*lit.* and *fig.*) to pollute or corrupt: (*arch.*) to ravish.—*ns.* **defile′ment,** act of defiling: foulness; **defil′er.** [L. *dē,* and O.E. *fȳlan*—*fūl,* foul; confused with O.Fr. *defouler,* to trample, violate.]

define, *di-fin′, v.t.* to fix the bounds or limits of: to mark the limits or outline of clearly: to describe accurately: to fix the meaning of.—*adjs.* **defin′able,** that may be defined; **def′inite,** defined: having distinct limits: fixed: exact: clear—*adv.* **def′initely.**—*ns.* **def′initeness; defini′tion,** a defining: a description of a thing by its properties: an explanation of the exact meaning of a word, term, or phrase: sharpness of outline.—*adj.* **defin′itive,** defining or limiting: decisive, final—*n.* (*gram.*) an adjective used to limit the signification of a noun.—*adv.* **defin′itively.** [Fr.—L. *dēfīnīre, -ītum,* to set bounds to—*dē*, and *fīnis*, a limit.]

deflagrate, *def'la-grāt*, or *dē'-*, *v.i.* or *v.t.* to burn suddenly, generally with flame and crackling noise.—*n.* **deflagrā'tion.** [L. *dēflagrāre*—*dē*, down, *flagrāre*, to burn.]

deflate, *dē-flāt'*, *v.t.* to undo or reverse the process of inflation.—*n.* **deflā'tion.** [L. *dē*, down, *flāre*, *flātum*, to blow.]

deflect, *di-flekt'*, *v.t.* or *v.i.* to turn aside: to swerve or deviate from a right line or proper course.—*ns.* **deflex'ion, deflec'tion,** deviation; **deflec'tor,** a device for deflecting a flame, electric arc, &c. [L. *dē*, from, and *flectĕre*, *flexum*, to bend, turn.]

deflorate, *dē-flō'rāt*, *-flō'*, *adj.* past flowering: of an anther, having shed its pollen.—*n.* **deflorā'tion,** the act of deflowering. [See **deflower**.]

deflower, *di-flow'(é)r*, *v.t.* to deprive of flowers: to deprive of grace and beauty: to ravish. [O.Fr. *deflorer*—Low L. *dēflōrāre*, to strip flowers off—L. *dē*, from, *flōs*, *flōris*, a flower.]

defoliation, *di-fo-li-ā'sh(ó)n*, *n.* the falling off of leaves: the time of shedding leaves. [Low L. *dēfoliāre*, *-ātum*—*dē*, off, *folium*, a leaf.]

deforce, *di-fōrs'*, *-fōrs'*, *v.t.* (*law*) to keep out of possession by force.—*n.* **deforce'ment.** [Anglo-Fr. *deforcer*—*de*- (L. *dis-*). See **force**.]

deforest, *dē-for'est*, *v.t.* to deprive of forests.—*n.* **deforestā'tion.** [O.Fr. *desforester*—*des*- (L. *dis-*). See **forest**.]

deform, *di-förm'*, *v.t.* to alter or injure the form of: to disfigure.—*ns.* **deformā'tion; deform'ity,** ugliness: disfigurement: an ugly feature or characteristic. [L. *dēformis*, ugly—*dē*, from, *forma*, beauty.]

defraud, *di-fröd'*, *v.t.* to deprive by fraud (of): to cheat or deceive. [L. *dēfraudāre*—*dē*, from, *fraus*, *fraudis*, fraud.]

defray, *di-frā'*, *v.t.* to pay:—*pr.p.* defray'ing; *pa.p.* defrayed'.—*ns.* **defray'ment, defray'al.** [O.Fr. *desfrayer*—*des*- (L.*dis-*), and *frais*, expenses.]

defrost, *dē-frost'*, *v.t.* to remove frost or ice from: to thaw out.—Also *v.i.* [Pfx. **de-**, and **frost**.]

deft, *deft*, *adj.* adroit, skilful, quick and neat in action.—*adv.* **deft'ly.**—*n.* **deft'ness.** [M.E. *defte*, *dafte*, simple, meek; O.E. *gedæfte*, meek—*dæftan*, *gedæftan*, prepare, make fit.]

defunct, *di-fungkt'*, *adj.* having finished the course of life, dead.—*n.* a dead person. [L. *dēfungī*, *dēfunctus*, to finish—*dē*, *fungī*, to perform.]

defuze, defuse, *dē'fūz'*, *v.t.* to remove the fuze from (a bomb or mine). [Pfx. **de-**, and **fuze, fuse.**]

defy, *di-fī'*, *v.t.* to challenge: to brave: to flout, or to resist (e.g. convention, order, person):—*pr.p.* defy'ing; *pa.p.* defied'.—*n.* **defi'er.** [O.Fr. *defier*—Low. L. *diffīdāre*, renounce allegiance.]

degauss, *dē-gows'*, *v.t.* equip with means of neutralising the earth's magnetic field. [Pfx. **de-**, **gauss,** unit of intensity of magnetic field—K. F. *Gauss*, physicist.]

degenerate, *di-jen'ér-át*, *adj.* having departed from the high qualities of race or kind.—Also *n.*—*v.i.* to fall from nobler state, be or grow worse.—*n.* **degen'eracy, degenerā'tion,** the act or process of becoming degenerate: the state of being degenerate.—*adv.* **degen'erately.**—*n.* **degen'erateness.**—*adj.* **degen'era-**

tive, tending or causing to degenerate. [L. *dēgenerāre*, *-ātum*, to depart from its kind—*dē*, from, *genus*, *genéris*, kind.]

deglutition, *dē-gloō-tish'(ó)n*, *n.* the act or power of swallowing. [Fr.,—L. *dē*, down, and *glūtīre*, to swallow.]

degrade, *di-grād'*, *v.t.* to lower in grade or rank: to deprive of office or dignity: to debase: to disgrace.—*n.* **degradation** (*deg-ra-dā'sh(ó)n*), disgrace: abasement: degeneration. [Fr.*dégrader*—L. *dē*, down, and *gradus*, a step.]

degree, *di-grē'*, *n.* a grade or step: (*fig.*) one of a series of steps in a process (e.g. *by degrees*): rank: a relative quantity or stage in intensity (e.g. *in a minor degree, a high degree; with some degree of certainty*): one of the three stages (*positive, comparative, superlative*) in the comparison of an adjective or an adverb: a title conferred by universities: the 360th part of a revolution: 60 geographical miles: a unit of temperature.—**forbidden degrees,** the degrees of consanguinity and affinity within which it is not permitted to marry; **third degree,** an American police method of extorting a confession by bullying or torture: any ruthless interrogation; **to a degree,** to a great degree, to an extreme. [Fr.*degré*—L. *dē*, down, *gradus*, a step.]

dehisce, *dē-his'*, *v.i.* to gape, to open as the fruits of some plants.—*n.* **dehis'cence.**—*adj.* **dehis'cent.** [L. *dehiscēns*, pr.p. of *dehiscĕre*—*dē*, inten., and *hiscĕre*, to gape.]

dehumanise, *dē-hū'man-īz*, *v.t.* to deprive of human qualities, to brutalise. [Pfx. **de-**, and **humanise.**]

dehydrate, *dē-hī-drāt'*, *v.t.* to deprive of water chemically: to dry (foodstuffs): (*fig.*) to deprive of strength, interest, &c.—*n.* **dehydrā'tion,** loss of moisture: (*med.*) excessive loss of water from the tissues of the body. [L. *dē*, from, Gr. *hydōr*, water.]

deicide, *dē'i-sīd*, *n.* the killing of a god: the putting to death of Jesus Christ. [From a supposed Low L. form *deicidium*—*deus*, a god, and *caedĕre*, to kill.]

deify, *dē'i-fī*, *v.t.* to exalt to the rank of a god: to worship as a deity:—*pr.p.* de'ifying; *pa.p.* de'ified.—*n.* **deifica'tion,** the act of deifying.—*adj.* **dē'iform,** god-like in form. [Fr. *déifier*—L. *deificāre*—*deus*, a god, and *facĕre*, to make.]

deign, *dān*, *v.i.* to condescend.—*v.t.* to condescend to give. [Fr. *daigner*—L. *dignārī*, to think worthy—*dignus*, worthy.]

deist, *dē'ist*, *n.* one who believes in the existence of God, but not in revealed religion.—*n.* **dē'ism,** the creed of a deist.—*adjs.* **deist'ic, -al.** [Fr. *déiste*, *déisme*—L. *deus*, a god.]

deity, *dē'i-ti*, *n.* divinity: godhead: a god or goddess: (*cap.*) the Supreme Being. [Fr.,—Low L. *deitās*—L. *deus*, god.]

déjà vu, *dā-zhä vü*, *n.* in any of the arts, unoriginal material: an illusion of having experienced before something that is really being experienced for the first time. [Fr., already seen.]

deject, *di-jekt'*, *v.t.* to cast down the spirits of.—*adj.* **deject'ed,** cast down, dispirited.—*adv.* **deject'edly.**—*ns.* **deject'edness; dejec'tion,** lowness of spirits. [L. *dējicĕre*, *-jectum*—*dē*, down, *jacĕre*, to cast.]

Neutral vowels in unaccented syllables: *em'pér-ör*; for certain sounds in foreign words see p. ix.

de jure, *dē jōō're*, *adv.* and *adj.* by right and lawful title (e.g. *the ruler de jure of the country*): rightful, lawful (e.g. *the de jure ruler*). See **de facto**. [L.]

deka-, see **deca-**.

delaine, *di-lān'*, *n.* a light dress material [Fr. *mousseline de laine*, wool muslin.]

delate, *di-lāt'*, *v.t.* to charge with a crime.—*n.* **delā'tion**. [L. *dēferre*, *dēlātum*, to bring a report against, to inform—*dē*, inten., *ferre*, to bear.]

delay, *di-lā'*, *v.t.* to put off to another time, to defer: to hinder or retard.—*v.i.* to pause, linger, or put off time:—*pr.p.* delay'ing; *pa.p.* delayed'.—*n.* a putting off or deferring: a lingering: hindrance. [O.Fr. *delaier*.]

delectable, *di-lekt'a-bl*, *adj.* delightful, pleasing.—*n.* **delect'ableness**.—*adv.* **delect'ably**.—*n.* **delectā'tion**, delight. [Fr.,—L. *dēlectābilis*—*dēlectāre*, to delight.]

delegate, *del'e-gāt*, *v.t.* to send as a legate or representative: to entrust or commit (e.g. power *to* a person or assembly).—*n.* (-*gát*) a deputy or an elected representative.—*adj.* delegated, deputed.—*n.* **delegā'tion**, a delegating: a body of delegates. [L. *dē*, away and *lēgāre*, *-ātum*, to send as ambassador.]

delete, *di-lēt'*, *v.t.* to blot out, to erase.—*n.* **delē'tion**. [L. *delere*, *dēlētum*, to blot out.]

deleterious, *del-e-tē'ri-us*, *adj.* tending to destroy life: hurtful or destructive.—*adv.* **deletē'riously**.—*n.* **deletē'riousness**. [Gr. *dēlētērios*, hurtful—*dēleesthai*, to hurt.]

delf, **delft**, *delf(t)*, *n.* a contraction for **delft'ware**, a kind of earthenware originally made at *Delft*, Holland.

deliberate, *di-lib'er-āt*, *v.t.* to weigh well in one's mind. *v.i.* to consider the reasons for and against: to reflect, to consider.—*adj.* (-*át*) well considered: intentional: considering carefully: cautious: quiet, unflurried.—*adv.* **delib'erately**.—*ns.* **delib'erateness**; **deliberā'tion**, the act of deliberating: mature reflection: calmness, coolness.—*adj.* **delib'erative**, proceeding or acting by deliberation. [L. *dēlīberāre*, *-ātum*—*dē*, inten., and *lībrāre*, to weigh—*lībra*, a balance.]

delicate, *del'i-kát*, *adj.* pleasing to the senses, esp. the taste: dainty: of a fine, slight texture or constitution: frail, not robust: pale: requiring nice handling (e.g. a problem): deft: nicely discriminating, fastidious: refined in manners: polite, considerate: luxurious.—*n.* **del'icacy**, state of quality of being delicate: anything delicate or dainty.—*adv.* **del'icately**, in a delicate manner: (*B.*) luxuriously.—*n.* **del'icateness**.—*n.pl.* **del'icates** (*B.*), delicacies. [L. *dēlicātus*—*dēliciae*, allurements, luxury—*dēlicěre* *dē*-, inten., and earlier *lacěre*, to entice.]

delicatessen, *del-i-ká-tes'n*, *n.* prepared foods, esp. meat: a shop selling these. [Ger. pl. of Fr. *délicatesse*, delicacy.]

delicious, *di-lish'us*, *adj.* highly pleasing to the senses, esp. taste: affording exquisite pleasure.—*adv.* **deli'ciously**, delightfully: (*B.*) luxuriously.—*n.* **deli'ciousness**. [L. *dēliciōsus*—*dēliciae*. See **delicate**.]

delight, *di-līt'*, *v.t.* to please highly.—*v.i.* to have or take great pleasure.—*n.* a high degree of pleasure: that which gives great pleasure.—*adjs.* **delight'ful**, **delight'some**, affording delight.—*adv.* **delight'fully**.—*n.* **delight'fulness**. [O.Fr. *deliter*—L. *dēlectāre*, inten. of *dēlicěre*; spelling influenced by confusion with *light*.]

delimit, *di-lim'it*, *v.t.* to fix or mark the limit of.—*n.* **delimitā'tion**. [L. *dēlīmitāre*—*dē*-, inten., and *līmitāre*. See **limit**.]

delineate, *di-lin'e-āt*, *v.t.* to mark out with lines: to represent by a sketch or picture: to describe accurately in words.—*ns.* **delineā'tion**, the act of delineating: a sketch, representation, or description; **delin'eator**. [L. *dēlīneāre*, *-ātum*—*dē*, down, and *līnea*, a line.]

delinquent, *di-ling'kwént*, *adj.* failing in duty.—*n.* one who fails in or leaves his duty: a transgressor: a criminal.—*n.* **delin'quency**, failure in or omission of duty: a fault: a crime.—*adv.* **delin'quently**. [L. *dēlinquens*, *-entis*, pr.p. of *dēlinquěre*—*dē*-, inten., and *linquěre*, to leave.]

deliquesce, *del-i-kwes'*, *v.i.* to melt and become liquid by absorbing moisture, as certain salts, &c.—Also *fig.*—*n.* **deliques'cence**.—*adj.* **deliques'cent**, liquefying in the air. [L. *dēliquescěre*—*dē*, inten., *liquescěre*, to become fluid—*liquēre*, to be fluid.]

delirious, *di-lir'i-us*, *adj.* wandering in mind, light-headed: ecstatic.—*adv.* **delir'iously**.—*ns.* **delir'iousness**; **delir'ium**, state of being delirious: strong excitement: wild enthusiasm.—**delirium tremens**, a delirious disorder of the brain produced by excessive drinking and often marked by convulsive or trembling symptoms. [L. *dēlīrus*, crazy—*dēlīrāre*, lit. to turn aside—*dē*, from, and *līra*, a furrow; *tremens*, the pr.p. of *tremēre*, to tremble.]

delitescent, *del-i-tes'ént*, *adj.* lying hid: latent.—*n.* **delites'cence** [L. *dēlitescens*, pr.p. of *dēlitescěre*—*dē*, from, and *latescěre*—*latēre*, to lie hid.]

deliver, *de-liv'ér*, *v.t.* to liberate or set free (*from*): to rescue: to give up or part with: to give forth: to deal, as a blow: to bring: to distribute: to pronounce (e.g. a judgment): to disburden of a child in childbirth.—*adj.* **deliv'erable**.—*ns.* **deliv'erance**, act of delivering or freeing: act of transferring from one to another: parturition: the utterance of a judgment or authoritative opinion; **deliv'erer**; **deliv'ery**, the act of delivering: a giving up: the manner of delivering anything: the act of giving birth. [Fr. *délivrer*—L. *dē*, from, *līberāre*, to set free—*līber*, free.]

dell, *del*, *n.* a little hollow, usu. with trees. [Same root as **dale**.]

Delphic, *del'fik*, *adj.* relating to Delphi, celebrated for its oracle: oracular.—Also **Del'phian**.

delphinium, *del-fin'i-um*, *n.* a genus of garden flowers including the common larkspur. [Gr. *delphinion*, larkspur.]

delta, *del'ta*, *n.* the fourth letter of the Greek alphabet, the capital form of which is △: a tract of land of like shape formed at the mouth of a river.—*adj.* **del'toid**, of the form of the Greek △, triangular.—**del'ta-wing** (**aero plane**), a jet aeroplane with triangular wings. [Gr.,—Heb. *daleth*, a tent-door.]

delude, *di-l(y)ōōd'*, *v.t.* to deceive, to cause to accept what is false as true. [L. *dēlūděre*, to play false—*dē*, down, *lūdĕre, lūsum*, to play.]

deluge, *del'ūj, n.* a great overflow of water: a flood, esp. that in the days of Noah: (*fig.*) ăn overwhelming flow.—*v.t.* to overwhelm as with water, to inundate (*lit.* and *fig.*). [Fr.,—L. *dīluvium*—*dīluĕre*—*dis-*, away, *luĕre*, to wash.]

delusion, *di-l(y)ōō'zh(ŏ)n, n.* the act of deluding: the state of being deluded: a false belief: a false belief due to mental derangement.—*adjs.* **delu'sive, delu'sory,** apt or tending to delude, deceptive.—*adv.* **delu'sively.**—*n.* **delu'siveness.** [L. *dēlūsiō, -ōnis*—*dēlūdĕre*; see **delude.**]

de luxe, *dé lüks', di lōōks', luks', adj.* sumptuous, luxurious. [Fr.]

delve, *delv, v.t.* and *v.i.* to dig with a spade.—*n.* **delv'er.** [O.E. *delfan,* to dig.]

demagnetise, *dē-mag'net-īz, v.t.* to deprive of magnetic power.—*n.* **demagnetisā'tion.** [Pfx. de-, and **magnetise.**]

demagogue, *dem'a-gog, n.* a leader of the people: a political orator who appeals to the passions and prejudices of the people.—*adjs.* **demagogic, -al** (*-gog'-* or *-goj'-*).—*n.* **demagogy** (*-goj'-*). [Fr.,—Gr. *dēmagōgos*—*dēmos*, people, *agōgos*, leading—*agein*, to lead.]

demain. See **demesne.**

demand, *di-mänd', v.t.* to require, call for: to ask peremptorily or authoritatively.—*n.* the asking for what is due: an asking for with authority: a claim: desire shown by consumers (for specified goods): inquiry.—*n.* **demand'ant,** one who demands: a plaintiff. [Fr. *demander*—Low L. *dēmandāre*—L. *dē-*, inten., and *mandāre,* to put into one's charge.]

demarcation, demarkation, *dē-märk-ā'sh(ŏ)n, n.* the act of marking off or setting bounds to: division: a fixed limit: the strict marking off of work to be done by one kind of craftsmen from that to be done by craftsmen of other trades.—*v.t.* **dē'marcate,** to mark off or limit. [Sp. *demarcación*—*de,* from, *marcar,* to mark.]

demean, *di-mēn', v.t.* (*arch.*) to conduct (with *self*), to behave.—*n.* **demeanour,** conduct: bearing. [O.Fr. *demener*—*de-*, inten., *mener,* to lead—Low L. *mināre,* to drive cattle—L. *minārī,* to threaten.]

demean, *di-mēn', v.t.* to make mean: to lower in dignity. [Prob. on the analogy of *debase,* from pfx. de-, and **mean** (1).]

dement, *di-ment', v.t.* to render insane.—*p.adj.* **dement'ed,** out of one's mind: insane.—*n.* **dementia** (*de-men'shi-a*), any form of insanity characterised by the failure or loss of mental powers. [L. *dēmēns, dēmentis,* out of one's mind—*dē,* from, and *mēns,* the mind.]

démenti, *dā-mä-tē, n.* a contradiction. [Fr.—*dé-mentir,* to give the lie to.]

demerara, *dem-é-rā'ra, n.* brown sugar in large crystals. [*Demerara* (*-rä'-*) in Guyana.]

demerit, *dē-mer'it, n.* ill desert, the opposite of merit: want of merit: a fault. [L. *dēmererī, dēmeritum,* to deserve fully, later understood as 'tc deserve ill'—*dē-*, fully, *merērī,* to deserve.]

demesne, *di-mān', -mēn', n.* a manor-house, with lands adjacent to it out leⴹ out to tenants: any estate in land. [Forms of **domain.**]

demi-, *dem'ī,* in composition, half. [Fr See

demy.]

demigod, *dem'i-god, n.* one whose nature is partly divine—a hero fabled to be the offspring of a god and a mortal, or a man regarded with worshipful admiration. [Fr. *demi,* half, and **god.**]

demi-john, *dem'i-jon, n.* a glass bottle with a full body and narrow neck, enclosed in wickerwork. [Fr. *dame-jeanne,* Dame Jane.]

demise, *di-mīz', n.* a transferring: a transfer of the crown or of an estate to a successor: death, esp. of a sovereign or a distinguished person.—*v.t.* to send down to a successor: to bequeath by will. [O.Fr. *demise,* pa.p. of *desmettre,* to lay down—L. *dis-*, aside, *mittĕre, missum,* to send.]

demi-semiquaver, *dem'i-sem'i-kwā-vér,* 𝄇 *n.* (*mus.*) a note equal in time to the half of a semiquaver. [Fr. *demi,* half, and **semiquaver.**]

demission, *di-mish'(ŏ)n, n.* relinquishment (of). [Same root as **demise.**]

demit, *di-mit', v.t.* to relinquish, to resign. [Same root as **demise.**]

demobilise, *dē-* or *di-mōb'il-īz,* or *-mob'-, v.t.* to take out of mobilisation, to disband: (*coll.*) to discharge from the army.—*n.* **demobilisā'tion.** [Pfx. de-, and **mobilise.**]

democracy, *di-mok'ra-si, n.* a form of government in which the supreme power is vested in the people collectively: the people, esp. the common people: a state or society characterised by recognition of equality of rights and privileges: political, social or legal equality: in the United States, the democratic party.—*n.* **dem'ocrat,** one who adheres to or promotes democracy as a principle: a member of the **Democratic party** (one of the two great political parties in the United States).—*adjs.* **democrat'ic, -al,** relating to democracy: insisting on equal rights and privileges for all.—*adv.* **democrat'ically.**—*v.t.* **democratise'**, to render democratic. [Fr. *démocratie*—Gr. *dēmokratiā*—*dēmos,* the people, and *krateein,* to rule—*kratos,* strength.]

demoded, *dē-mōd'id, adj.* no longer in fashion. [Pfx. de-, and **mode.**]

demography, *di-mog'ra-fi, n.* the scientific study of vital and social statistics with reference to nations and to regional groups. [From Gr. *dēmos,* people, *graphein,* to write.]

demolish, *di-mol'ish, v.t.* to lay in ruins: to destroy, put an end to.—*n.* **demoli'tion** (*dem-*), act of pulling down: overthrow, destruction. [Fr. *démolir*—L. *dēmōlīrī,* to throw down—*dē,* down, and *mōlīrī,* to build—*mōles,* a heap.]

demon, *dē'mon, n.* a spirit or genius: an evil spirit, a devil.—*adjs.* **demoniac** (*di-mōn'i-ak*), **demoniacal** (*dē-mo-nī'a-kl*), pertaining to or like demons or evil spirits: influenced by demons.—*n.* **demon'iac,** one possessed by a demon or evil spirit.—*adv.* **demonī'acally.**—*ns.* **demonol'atry,** the worship of demons; **demonology,** an account of, or the study of, demons and their agency; **demonol'ogist,** a writer on demonology. [L. *daemon*—Gr. *daimōn,* a spirit, genius; in N.T. and Late Greek, a devil.]

demonetise, *dē-mon'i-tīz, v.t.* to divest, of value as money. [Fr. *démonétiser*—L. *monēta.* See **money.**]

demonstrate, *dem'on-strāt,* or *di-mon'strāt, v.t.*

Neutral vowels in unaccented syllables: *em'pér-ór*; for certain sounds in foreign words see p. ix.

184

to show or point out clearly: to prove with certainty.—*v.i.* to exhibit one's feelings or sentiments.—*adj.* **demon′strable** (or *dem′-*), that may be demonstrated.—*n.* **demon′strability.**—*adv.* **demon′strably** (or *dem′-*).—*n.* **demonstrā′tion,** a pointing out: proof beyond doubt: a practical display or exhibition: a display of emotion: a public manifestation of opinion, as by a mass-meeting, a procession, &c. (*coll.* abbrev. **demo**): a movement to exhibit military intention, or to deceive the enemy.—*adj.* **demon′strative,** pointing out (as a *demonstrative adj.*): making evident: proving with certainty: of the nature of proof: given, addicted, to showing one's feelings.—*adv.* **demon′stratively.**—*ns.* **demon′strativeness; dem′onstrator,** one who proves beyond doubt: a teacher or assistant who helps students with practical work: one who takes part in a public manifestation of opinion. [L. *dēmonstrāre, -ātum—dē,* inten., and *monstrāre,* to show.]

demoralise, (*h̄-mor′āl-īz,* v.t. to corrupt in morals: to lower the *morale* of—that is, to deprive of spirit and confidence or to throw into confusion.—*n.* **demoralisā′tion.** [Fr. *démoraliser—dé-* (L. *dis-*), un-, and *moraliser.*]

demos, *dē′mos, n.* the people (esp. contemptuously).—*adj.* **demot′ic,** pertaining to the people: popular: of a simplified kind of ancient Egyptian writing distinguished from the hieratic (q.v.), and from hieroglyphics (q.v.). [Gr.]

demote, *dē-mōt′, v.t.* to reduce in rank. [On the analogy of *promote*—L. *de,* down.]

demulcent, *di-mul′sent, adj.* soothing. [L. *dēmulcēns, -entis—dē,* down, *mulcēre,* to stroke, to soothe.]

demur, *di-mûr′, v.i.* to hesitate from uncertainty or before difficulty: to object:—*pr.p.* **demurr′ing;** *pa.p.* **demurred′.**—*n.* a hesitation: an objection.—*ns.* **demurr′age,** undue delay or detention of a vessel or railway wagon, &c.: compensation for such detention, **demurr′er,** one who demurs: (*law*) a plea in law that, even if the opponent's facts are as he says, they yet do not support his case. [Fr. *demeurer*—L. *dēmorārī,* to loiter, linger—*dē-,* inten., and *morārī,* to delay—*mora,* delay.]

demure, *di-mūr′, adj.* sober, staid, modest: affectedly modest: making a show of gravity.—*adv.* **demure′ly.**—*n.* **demure′ness.** [O.Fr. *meur* (Fr. *mûr*)—L. *maturus,* ripe; pfx. unexplained.]

demy, *di-mī′, n.* a size of paper 22½ by 17½ in. for printing—for writing, 20 by 15½ in.: a holder of certain scholarships in Magdalen College, Oxford:—*pl.* **demies′.**—*n.* **demy′ship.** [Fr. *demi*—L. *dimidium,* half—*di-,* apart, *medius,* the middle.]

den, *den, n.* the hollow lair of a wild beast: a cave: a haunt of vice or misery: private retreat: (*dial.*) a narrow valley. [O.E. *denn,* a cave, akin to *denu,* a valley.]

denary, *dēn′ar-i, adj.* containing ten.—*n.* the number ten. [L. *dēnārius—dēnī—decem,* ten.]

denationalise, *dē-nash′ón-ál-īz, v.t.* to deprive of national rights: to return from state to private ownership. [Pfx. **de-,** and **nationalise.**]

denaturalise, *dē-nat′ūr-ál-īz, v.t.* to make un-

natural: to deprive of acquired citizenship in a foreign country. [Pfx. **de-,** and **naturalise.**]

denature, *dē-nā′tyùr, -chùr, v.t.* to render (alcohol, &c.) unfit for consumption.—*n.* **denā′turant,** a substance used for this purpose. [Pfx. *de-,* and **nature.**]

dendroid, *den′droid, adj.* having the form of a tree. [Gr. *dendron,* a tree, and *eidos,* form.]

dendrology, *den-drol′o-ji, n.* a treatise on trees: the natural history of trees. [Gr. *dendron,* a tree, and *logos,* a discourse.]

dene. See **dean** (1).

denial, *di-nī′al, n.* act of denying or saying no: contradiction: refusal (of request, claim, &c.): disavowal, rejection.—*adj.* **deni′able,** that may be denied. [**deny.**]

denier, *dé-nēr′,* an old small French silver coin: (usu. *den′i-ér*) a unit of silk, rayon, and nylon yarn weight. [Fr.—L. *dēnārius,* a Roman silver coin.]

denigrate, *den′i-grāt, v.t.* to blacken (esp. a reputation).—*n.* **denigrā′tion.** [L. *dē-,* inten., *nigrāre,* to blacken—*niger,* black.]

denim, *den′im, n.* a durable coarse cotton cloth: (*pl.*) garments made of denim. [Fr. *de,* of, and *Nîmes,* a town in France.]

denizen, *den′i-zn, n.* an inhabitant (human or animal): one admitted to the rights of a citizen.—*n.* **den′izenship.** [O.Fr. *deinzein—deinz, dens* (Fr. *dans*), within—L. *dē intus,* from within.]

denominate, *di-nom′in-āt, v.t.* to give a name to: to name, call.—*n.* **denominā′tion,** the act of naming: a name or title: a collection of individuals called by the same name, a sect: a class of units in weights, measures, &c.—*adj.* **denominā′tional,** belonging to a denomination or sect.—*n.* **denominā′tionalism,** devotion to the interests of a sect: a policy governed by such devotion.—*adj.* **denom′inative,** giving or having a name.—*adv.* **denom′inatively.**—*n.* **denom′inator,** he who, or that which, gives a name: (*arith.*) the number which denominates a vulgar fraction by specifying the number of parts into which a whole has been divided. [L. *dē-,* inten., and *nōmināre,* to name—*nōmen,* a name.]

denote, *di-nōt′, v.t.* to note, mark: to indicate, be the sign of: to mean: (*logic*) to indicate the objects comprehended in a class.—*n.* **denotā′tion.** [Fr.—L. *dēnotāre, -ātum—dē-,* inten., and *notāre,* to mark—*nota,* a mark or sign.]

dénouement, *dā-nōō′mä, n.* the unravelling of a plot or story: the issue, event, or outcome. [Fr. *dénouement* or *dénoûment; dénouer,* to untie—L. *dis-,* apart, *nodāre,* to tie—*nodus,* a knot.]

denounce, *di-nowns′, v.t.* to inform against or accuse publicly: to inveigh against (a person, practice): to notify formally termination of (treaties, &c.).—*n.* **denounce′ment** (same as **denunciation**). [Fr. *dénoncer*—L. *dēnuntiāre—dē-,* inten., and *nuntiāre,* to announce.]

dense, *dens, adj.* thick, close, compact: impenetrably stupid.—*adv.* **dense′ly.**—*ns.* **dense′ness; dens′ity,** the quality of being dense: the mass of unit volume of a substance. [L. *densus,* thick.]

dent, *dent, n.* a small hollow made by the pressure or blow of a harder body on a softer.—*v.t.*

---

fāte, fär; mē, hûr (her); *mīne, mōte, för; mūte; mōōn, fŏŏt;* тнen (then)

to make a mark by means of a blow. [A variant of **dint**.]

dental, *den'tăl, adj.* of, or for, the teeth: produced by the aid of the teeth.—*n.* a sound produced by applying the tongue to the teeth. [L. *dens, dentis,* a tooth. See **tooth**.]

dentate, -d, *den'tāt, -id, adj.* toothed: notched: set as with teeth. [L. *dentātus,* toothed—*dens,* a tooth.]

denticle, *den'ti-kl, n.* a small tooth.—*adjs.* **den'ticŭlate, -d,** having notches.—*n.* **denticulā'tion.** [L. *denticulus,* dim. of *dens,* a tooth.]

dentiform, *den'ti-förm, adj.* having the form of a tooth or of teeth. [L. *dens, dentis,* tooth, and *forma,* form.]

dentifrice, *den'ti-fris, n.* a substance used in rubbing or cleaning the teeth. [Fr.,—L. *dentifricium—dens,* a tooth, *fricāre,* to rub.]

dentine, dentin, *den'tin, n.* the substance of which teeth are mainly composed. [L. *dens, dentis,* a tooth.]

dentist, *den'tist, n.* one who extracts teeth, remedies diseases of the teeth, or inserts artificial teeth.—*n.* **den'tistry,** the business of a dentist. [Fr. *dentiste*—L. *dens, dentis,* a tooth.]

dentition, *den-tish'(ŏ)n, n.* the cutting or growing of teeth: the conformation, number, and arrangement of the teeth: a set of teeth (e.g. the milk dentition). [L. *dentītiō, -ōnis—dentīre—dens, dentis,* a tooth.]

denture, *den'tyur, -chur, n.* a set of teeth, esp. artificial. [L. *dens, dentis,* a tooth.]

denude, *di-nūd', v.t.* to make nude, to lay bare: to divest, strip (of).—*n.* **dēnudā'tion,** a making nude or bare: (*geol.*) the wearing away of rocks by water and atmospheric action, whereby the underlying rocks are laid bare. [L. *dēnūdāre—dē-,* inten., and *nūdāre, -ātum,* to make naked—*nūdus,* naked.]

denunciate, *di-nun's(h)i-āt, v.t.* same as **denounce.**—*ns.* **denunciation** (*-shi-ā'-,* or *-si-ā'-*), act of denouncing: an arraignment (of); **denun'ciator,** one who denounces.—*adj.* **denun'ciatory,** containing, or of the nature of, a denunciation. [L. *dēnuntiātus,* pa.p. of *dēnuntiāre.* See **denounce.**]

deny, *di-nī', v.t.* to gainsay or declare not to be true: to reject: to refuse: to disown:—*pr.p.* **deny'ing;** *pa.p.* **denied'.**—**deny oneself,** to refuse to yield to natural desires and impulses. [Fr. *dénier*—L. *dēnegāre—dē-,* inten., and *negāre,* to say no. See **negation.**]

deodar, *dē-o-där', n.* an Indian cedar. [Sans. *deva-dāru,* divine tree.]

deodorise, *dē-ō'dor-īz, v.t.* to take the odour or smell from.—*ns.* **deō'dorant, deō'doriser,** a substance that destroys or conceals unpleasant smells. [L. *dē,* from, *odor,* smell.]

Deo volente (abbrev. **D.V.**), *dā'ō, dē'ō, vo-len'tā, vo-len'tē,* God willing.

deoxidate, *dē-oks'i-dāt, v.t.* to take oxygen from, or reduce from the state of an oxide—also **deox'idise.**—*n.* **deoxidā'tion.** [L. *dē,* from, and **oxide.**]

deoxyribonucleic acids, *dē-oks-i-rī'bō-nū-klē'ik as'ids,* nucleic acids containing deoxyribose (sugar), which function in the transfer of hereditary characteristics, present in cell nuclei and obtainable from the thymus gland.—abbrev. **DNA.** [Pfx. **de-.**]

depart, *di-pärt', v.i.* to go away: to leave, start: to die: to deviate, diverge (from).—*n.* **depart'ure,** act of departing: a going away from a place: deviation: death.—**a new departure,** a change of purpose or procedure. [Fr. *départir*—L. *dis-,* apart, and *partīrī,* to part, to divide.]

department, *di-pärt'mént, n.* a part: a special sphere of activity or duty: a section of an administration, university, office, &c.: a division of a country, esp. of France.—*adj.* **departmental** (*dē-pärt-ment'ál*).—*adv.* **department'ally.** [Fr. *département—départir.* See **depart.**]

depend, *di-pend', v.i.* to hang down: to be sustained by or connected with anything: to be contingent (on): to be pending: to rely (on).—*adj.* **depend'able,** that may be depended on.—*n.* **depend'ant** (also **-ent**), one who depends on, or is sustained by, another.—*adj.* **depend'ent** (also **-ant**), depending, relying on, contingent: subordinate.—*ns.* **depend'ence** (rarely **-ance**), state of being dependent: reliance, trust: that on which one depends; **depend'ency,** that which depends: a foreign territory dependent on a country, a kind of subordinate colony without selfgovernment. [Fr. *dépendre*—L. *dēpendēre* —*dē,* from, and *pendēre,* to hang.]

depict, *di-pikt', v.t.* to paint carefully: to make a likeness of: to describe minutely. [L. *dēpingĕre, dēpictum—dē-,* inten., *pingĕre,* to paint.]

depilatory, *di-pil'a-tór-i, adj.* taking hair off.—*n.* an application for removing superfluous hairs. [L. *dēpilāre, -ātum—dē,* from, *pilus,* hair.]

deplete, *di-plēt', v.t.* to empty, reduce, exhaust.—*n.* **deplē'tion,** the act of emptying or exhausting: (*med.*) the act of relieving congestion or plethora. [L. *dēplēre, dēplētum,* to empty—*dē-,* neg., *plēre,* to fill.]

deplore, *di-plōr', -plör', v.t.* to feel or express deep grief for loss of (a person): to express disapproval and regret about (a circumstance).—*adj.* **deplor'able,** lamentable, sad: hopelessly bad.—*n.* **deplor'ableness.**—*advs.* **deplor'ably, deplor'ingly.** [Fr.,—L. *dēplōrāre—dē-,* inten., *plōrāre,* to weep.]

deploy, *di-ploi', v.t.* to unfold: to open out or extend: to spread out and place strategically (any forces).—*v.i.* to open: to extend from column into line, as a body of troops.—*n.* **deploy'ment.** [Fr. *déployer*—L. *dis-,* apart, and *plicāre,* to fold. Doublet of **display.**]

deplume, *di-plōōm', v.t.* to take the plumes or feathers from.—*n.* **deplumā'tion.** [Fr. *déplumer*—L. *dē,* from, *plūma,* a feather.]

depolarise, *dē-pō'lär-īz, v.t.* to deprive of polarity.—*n.* **depōlarisā'tion.** [Pfx. **de-,** and **polarise.**]

depone, *di-pōn', v.t.* to testify upon oath.—*adj.* **depōn'ent,** (*gram.*) applied to verbs with a passive (orig. middle or reflexive) form but an active meaning (so called from the idea that they had *laid aside* the passive sense).—*n.* one who makes a deposition, or whose written testimony is used as evidence in a court of justice. [L. *dēpōnĕre;* pr.p. *dēpōnēns, -entis—dē,* down, *pōnĕre,* to place.]

depopulate, *di-pop'ū-lāt* (or *dē-*), *v.t.* to deprive of population, to dispeople.—*v.i.* to become dispeopled.—*ns.* **depopulā'tion,** act of depopulating: (*obs.*) havoc, destruction; **de-**

Neutral vowels in unaccented syllables: *em'pér-ór*; for certain sounds in foreign words see p. ix.

pop′ulator. [L. *dēpopulārī*, *-ātus—dē-*, inten.,
and *populārī*, to spread over a country, said of
a hostile people (L. *populus*)—hence to
ravage, to destroy.]

deport, *di-*, *dē-pōrt′*, *-pört′*, *v.t.* to transport, to
exile.—*n.* **deportā′tion**, transportation, exile.
[Fr. *déporter*—L. *dēportāre—dē-*, away, and
portāre, *-ātum*, to carry.]

deport, *di-pōrt′*, *-pört′*, *v.t.* to behave (*refl.*).—*n.*
deport′ment, bearing, manners: behaviour.
[O.Fr. *deporter*—L. *dē-*, inten., *portāre*, to
carry.]

depose, *di-pōz′*, *v.t.* to remove from a high
station: to degrade: to attest.—*adj.* **depos′-
able.**—*n.* **depos′al.** [Fr. *déposer*—L. *dē*, from,
pausāre, to pause, (late) to place.]

deposit, *di-poz′it*, *v.t.* to put or set down: to let
fall, leave (*a river deposits soil; a liquid deposits sediment*): to entrust for safe keeping:
to lodge as a pledge.—*n.* that which is deposited or put down: an accumulation of
sedimentary matter: precipitation from a fluid
medium, by settling from a solution in water:
something entrusted to another's care, esp.
money put in a bank: a pledge.—*ns.* **depos′i-
tary,** a person with whom anything is left for
safe keeping: a guardian—sometimes **depos′i-
tory; depos′itor; depos′itory,** a place where
anything is deposited—sometimes **depos′i-
tary.** [L. *dēpŏsitum*, placed—*dēpōnĕre—dē*,
down, *pōnĕre*, to place.]

deposition, *dep-o-zish′(ó)n*, *n.* act of deposing:
act of deponing: declaration, testimony used
as a substitute for the evidence of the witness
in open court: removal (from office): act of
depositing: what is deposited, sediment. [**deposit;** blended with root of **depose.**]

depot, *dep′ō*, *dē′pō*, *n.* a place of deposit, a
storehouse: a military station where stores
are kept and recruits trained: the headquarters of a regiment (*U.S.*) a railway station.
[Fr. *dépôt*—L. *dēpōnĕre*, *-pōsitum.*]

deprave, *di-prāv′*, *v.t.* to make bad or worse: to
corrupt.—*n.* **deprāvā′tion**, act of depraving:
state of being depraved, depravity.—*adj.* **de-
prāved′**, corrupt.—*adv.* **deprāv′edly.**—*ns.* **de-
prāv′edness; deprāv′ity,** a vitiated or corrupt
state of moral character: extreme wickedness:
corruption. [L. *dēprāvāre—dē-*, inten., *prāvus*,
bad.]

deprecate, *dep′ri-kāt*, *v.t.* to try to ward off by
prayer: to desire earnestly the prevention or
removal of: to express disapproval of.—*n.* **de-
precā′tion**, act of deprecating: earnest prayer,
esp., in litanies, a petition against a particular
evil.—*adv.* **dep′recatingly.**—*adjs.* **dep′recative,
dep′recatory,** tending to avert evil by prayer:
intended to ward off possible disapproval,
apologetic. [L. *dēprecārī*, *-ātus—dē*, away, and
precārī, to pray.]

depreciate, *di-prē′shi-āt*, *v t* to lower the worth
of: to undervalue: to disparage.—*v.i.* to fall in
value.—*n.* **depreciā′tion**, the falling of
value: disparagement.—*adjs.* **deprē′ciative,
deprē′ciatory,** tending to depreciate: disparaging. [L. *dēpretiāre*, *-ātum—dē*, down, and
pretium, price.]

depredate, *dep′ri-dāt*, *v.t.* to plunder or prey
upon, to lay waste.—*ns.* **depredā′tion**, act of
plundering: state of being depredated: (*pl.*)

ravages; **dep′redator.** [L. *dēpraedārī*, *-ātus—
dē-*, inten., and *praedārī—praeda*, plunder.]

depress, *di-pres′*, *v.t.* to press down: to lower: to
humble: to lessen activity of: to dispirit, cast a
gloom over.—*p.adj.* **depressed′**, pressed down:
dejected, dispirited.—*adj.* **depress′ing,** able or
tending to depress.—*adv.* **depress′ingly.**—*n.*
depress′ion, a falling in or sinking: a region of
low barometric pressure: a hollow: abasement: dejection: a reduced condition of trade
and prosperity.—**depressed area,** a region of
particularly heavy unemployment. [L. *dēpri-
mĕre*, *-pressum—dē*, down, *premĕre*, to press.]

deprive, *di-prīv′*, *v.t.* to dispossess (of): to debar
from possession: to degrade (esp. a clergy-
man) from office.—*n.* **deprivā′tion**, act of depriving: state of being deprived: loss.—*adj.*
deprived′, underprivileged: suffering from
hardship. [Low L. *dēprīvāre*, to degrade—L.
dē, from, and *prīvāre*, to deprive—*prīvus*,
one's own.]

depth, *depth*, *n.* deepness: the measure of deep
ness down or inwards: a deep place: intensity:
the intensest stage: abstruseness: extent of
sagacity and penetration.—*n.* **depth′ charge,** a
powerful bomb that explodes under water.—
in depth, extending far inwards: (*fig.*) exten-
sive(ly) and thorough(ly); **out of one's depth,**
in water where one cannot touch bottom:
(*fig.*) in a situation with which one cannot
cope. [Not in O.E.: possibly O.N. *dýpth*; or
formed from *deep* on the analogy of *length*.]

depute, *di-pūt′*, *v.t.* to appoint or send as a substitute or agent: to send with a special commission: to make over (one's powers, authority, to a person as deputy).—*n.* **depūtā′tion,**
act of deputing: the person or persons deputed
or appointed to transact business for
another.—*v.i.* **dep′utise,** to act as deputy.—*n.*
dep′uty, one deputed or appointed to act
for another: a delegate or representative, or
substitute. [Fr.—L. *deputāre*, to prune,
(late) to select.]

derail, *dē-rāl′*, *v.t.* to cause to leave the rails.
[Pfx. **de-**, and **rail.**]

derange, *di-rānj′*, *v.t.* to put out of place or order:
to put out of normal working order: to make
insane.—*p.adj.* **deranged′**, disordered: insane.—*n.* **derange′ment**, disorder: insanity.
[Fr. *déranger dé-* (L. *dis-*), asunder, and
ranger, to rank.]

derate, *dē-rāt′*, *v.t.* to relieve, wholly or partially,
from local rates.—*n.* and *adj.* **derāt′ing.** [Pfx.
de-, and **rate** (1).]

Derby, *där′bi*, *n.* an annual horse-race held on
Epsom Downs for the Derby Stakes, instituted
by the Earl of *Derby* in 1780.

derelict, *der′e-likt*, *adj.* forsaken, abandoned:
falling in ruins.—*n.* anything forsaken or
abandoned.—*n.* **derelic′tion,** act of forsaking:
neglect (of duty), remissness: state of being
abandoned. [L. *dērelinquĕre*, *-lictum—dē-*,
inten., *re-*, behind, and *linquĕre*, to leave.]

deride, *di-rīd′*, *v.t.* to laugh at, to mock.—*n.* **de-
rid′er.**—*adv.* **derid′ingly.** [L. *dēridēre*,
-rīsum—dē-, inten., and *rīdēre*, to laugh.]

derision, *di-rizh′(ó)n*, *n.* act of deriding: mockery: a laughing-stock.—*adjs.* **deri′sive, de-
ris′ory,** mocking. [L. *dērīsiō—dērīdēre.* See
deride.]

derive, *di-rīv′, v.t.* to draw, take or receive (from a source or origin): to infer, deduce (from): to trace (a word) to its root.—*v.i.* to descend or issue (from).—*adj.* **derīv′able.**—*n.* **derivation** (*dĕr-iv-ā′sh(ŏ)n*), act of deriving: the tracing of a word to its root: that which is derived: source: descent.—*adj.* **deriv′ative,** derived or taken from something else: not radical or original.—*n.* that which is derived: a word formed from another word.—*adv.* **deriv′atively.** [O.Fr. *deriver*—L. *dērīvāre*—*dē*, down, from, *rīvus*, a river.]

derm, *dûrm, n.* the skin—also **der′ma, der′mis.**—*adj.* **der′mal,** pertaining to the skin: consisting of skin.—*n.* **dermatol′ogy,** the branch of science that treats of the skin. [Gr. *derma, -atos,* the skin—*derein,* to flay.]

dernier cri, *der-ne-ā krē,* the last word (*lit.* cry): the latest fashion. [Fr.]

derogate, *der′o-gāt, v.i.* (with *from*) to lessen by taking away, to detract.—*n.* **deroga′tion,** a taking from, detraction, depreciation.—*adj.* **derog′atory,** detracting from, impairing (with *to*): disparaging, depreciating.—*adv.* **derog′atorily.**—*n.* **derog′atoriness.** [L. *dērogāre, -ātum,* to repeal part of a law—*dē,* down, from, and *rogāre,* to propose a law.]

derrick, *der′ik, n.* an apparatus for lifting weights, resembling a crane. [From *Derrick,* the name of a hangman in the 17th century.]

derring-do, *der′ing-dōō, n.* (false archaic) daring action. [Spenser mistook for a noun *derrynge do,* misprinted in Lydgate (*c.* 1370-*c.* 1450) in place of *dorrying do,* i.e. daring (to) do.]

derris, *der′is, n.* any of a genus of tropical vines: a powder (**derris dust**) or a liquid prepared from the roots and stems of some species of these, used as an arrow poison, a fish poison, and an insecticide. [Formed from Gr. *derris,* a leather covering.]

derv, *dûrv, n.* diesel engine fuel oil. [From *d*iesel *e*ngine *r*oad *v*ehicle.]

dervish, *dûr′vish, n.* a member of one of numerous Mahommedan fraternities professing poverty and leading an austere life. [Pers. *darvīsh,* a poor man.]

descant, *des′kant, n.* an accompaniment above and harmonising with the air: a discourse under several heads.—*v.i.* **descant′,** to discourse at length: to comment. [O.Fr. *descant*—L. *dis-,* apart, and *cantus,* a song.]

descend, *di-send′, v.i.* to climb down: to pass from a higher to a lower place or condition: to incline downward: to make an invasion (with *on, upon*): to be derived.—*v.t.* to go down.—*n.* **descend′ant,** one who descends, as offspring from an ancestor.—*adjs.* **descend′ent,** going down: proceeding from an ancestor; **descend′ible** (also **-able**), that may descend or be descended: heritable.—*n.* **descent′,** act of descending: motion or progress downward: slope: a raid or invasion: transmission by succession: derivation from an ancestor. [Fr. *descendre*—L. *dēscendĕre*—*dē,* down, *scandĕre,* to climb.]

describe, *di-skrīb′, v.t.* to trace out or delineate: to give an account of.—*adj.* **descrīb′able.** [L. *dēscrībĕre*—*dē,* down, and *scrībĕre, scriptum,* to write.]

description, *di-skrip′sh(ŏ)n, n.* act of describing: an account of anything in words: (*loosely*) sort, class, or kind.—*adj.* **descrip′tive,** serving to describe: containing description.—*adv.* **descrip′tively.**—*n.* **descrip′tiveness.** [O.Fr.,—L. *descriptiō, -ōnis*—*descrībĕre.* See **describe.**]

descry, *di-skrī′, v.t.* to discover by the eye, to espy:—*pr.p.* descry′ing; *pa.p.* descried′. [Apparently two words: (1) O.Fr. *descrire* for *descrivre*—L. *dēscrībĕre*: a doublet of **describe**: (2) O.Fr. *descrier,* announce—*des-, de-,* and *crier,* to cry: a doublet of **decry.**]

desecrate, *des′i-krāt, v.t.* to divert from a sacred purpose: to profane.—*n.* **desecrā′tion,** act of desecrating: profanation. [Coined on the analogy of **consecrate**—L. *dē,* from. L. *dēsecrāre* meant 'consecrate'.]

desegregate, *dē-seg′ri-gāt, v.t.* to abolish racial segregation in (e.g. a university).—*n.* **desegregā′tion.** [Pfx. **de-,** and **segregate.**]

desert, *di-zûrt′, n.* that which is deserved: claim to reward: merit. [O.Fr., pa.p. of *deservir.* See **deserve.**]

desert, *di-zûrt′, v.t.* to leave: to forsake.—*v.i.* to run away: to quit a service, as the army, without permission.—*ns.* **desert′er; deser′tion,** act of deserting: state of being deserted. [L. *dēserēre, dēsertum*—*dē-,* neg., and *serēre,* to join together.]

desert, *dez′ért, adj.* (*arch.*) deserted: desolate: uninhabited: uncultivated: barren.—*n.* a barren place: a waste: a solitude.—**desert rat** (from the divisional sign, a jerboa), a soldier of the British 7th Armoured Division with service in North Africa in 1941-42. [O.Fr. *desert*—L. *dēsertum*—*dēserēre,* to desert, disjoin.]

deserve, *di-zûrv′, v.t.* to earn by service: to merit.—*v.i.* to be worthy of reward.—*adj.* **deserv′ing,** worthy.—*advs.* **deserv′ingly, deserv′edly** (*-id-*), according to desert, justly. [O.Fr. *deservir*—L. *dēservīre*—*dē-,* inten., *servīre,* to serve.]

deshabille. Same as **dishabille.**

desiccate, *des′i-kāt, v.t.* to dry up: to preserve by drying: (*fig.*) to dry up spiritually or emotionally, to exhaust of vitality and responsiveness.—*v.i.* to grow dry.—*adjs.* **des′iccant, desicc′ative,** drying: having the power of drying.—*n.* a drying agent.—*ns.* **desiccā′tion; des′iccātor,** apparatus for drying. [L. *dēsiccāre, -ātum,* to dry up—*dē,* and *siccus,* dry.]

desiderate, *di-sid′ér-āt, v.t.* to long for or earnestly desire: to miss, feel to be missing.—*adj.* **desid′erative,** implying desire (as in *desiderative verb*).—*n.* **desiderā′tum,** something desired or much wanted:—*pl.* **desiderā′ta.** [L. *dēsīderāre, -ātuṁ,* to long for. A doublet of **desire.**]

design, *di-zīn′, v.t.* (*obs.*) to draw: to form a plan of: to contrive: to intend, destine.—*n.* a preliminary sketch, plan in outline: a plan or scheme formed in the mind: intention: relation of parts to the whole, disposition of forms and colours: pattern.—*adj.* **design′able.**—*adv.* **design′edly** (*-id-li*), intentionally.—*n.* **design′er,** one who furnishes designs or patterns: a plotter.—*adj.* **design′ing,** artful, scheming.—*n.* the art of making designs or patterns.—*v.t.* **des′ignate** (*-ig-nāt*), to mark

Neutral vowels in unaccented syllables: *em′pér-ór*; for certain sounds in foreign words see p. ix.

out, specify, make known: to name: to be a name for: to appoint or nominate.—*adj.* (*-ăt*) appointed to office but not yet installed (placed after noun).—*n.* **designā'tion,** a pointing out: name: title. [Fr.,—L. *dēsignāre, -ātum—dē,* off, *signum,* a mark.]

desire, *di-zīr', v.t.* to long for, wish for: request, ask.—*n.* an earnest longing or wish: a prayer or request: the object desired: lust.—*adj.* **desir'able,** worthy of desire: pleasing, agreeable.—*ns.* **desir'ableness, desirabil'ity.**—*adv.* **desir'ably.**—*adj.* **desir'ous,** full of desire: wishful: (*obs.*) desirable. [Fr. *désirer*—L. *dēsīderāre.* See **desiderate.**]

desist, *di-zist', -sist', v.i.* to stop, forbear (from). [L. *dēsistĕre—dē-,* away, and *sistĕre,* to cause to stand.]

desk, *desk, n.* a table for writing or reading: a shut-up writing-box: a pulpit or lectern. [M.E. *deske*—L. *discus*—Gr. *diskos.*]

desolate, *des'o-lāt, v.t.* to make solitary: to make joyless, wretched: to deprive of inhabitants: to lay waste.—*adj.* (*des'o-lăt*) solitary: joyless: destitute of inhabitants: laid waste.—*adv.* **des'olately.**—*ns.* **des'olateness; desolā'tion,** waste, destruction: a place desolated: sorrow without hope. [L. *dēsōlāre, -ātum—dē-,* inten., and *sōlāre,* to make alone—*sōlus,* alone.]

desorption, *dē-sörp'shón, n.* release from an adsorbed state.—*v.t.* **desorb'.** [Pfx. **de-.**]

despair, *di-spār', v.i.* to be without, lose hope (of): to despond.—*n.* hopelessness: that which causes despair.—*adv.* **despair'ingly.** [O.Fr. *desperer*—L. *dēspērāre, -ātum—dē-,* neg., and *spērāre,* to hope.]

despatch. Same as **dispatch.**

desperado, *des-pér-ä'dō, -ä'dō, n.* a desperate or reckless fellow: a ruffian:—*pl.* **despera'do(e)s.** [O.Sp. (mod. *desesperado*)—L. *dēsperātus.*]

desperate, *des'pér-ăt, adj.* in a state of despair: hopeless: despairingly reckless. (*loosely*) frantic: extremely bad.—*adv.* **des'perately.**—*ns.* **des'perateness, desperā'tion,** state of despair: disregard of danger, recklessness. [L. *dēsperāre.* See **despair.**]

despicable, *des'pi-ka-bl, -pik', adj.* deserving to be despised, contemptible, worthless.—*n.* **des'picableness.**—*adv.* **des'picably.** [L. *dēspicēre.* See **despise.**]

despise, *di-spīz', v.t.* to look down upon with contempt: to scorn. [O.Fr. *despire*—L. *dēspicĕre—dē,* down, *specĕre,* to look.]

despite, *di-spīt', n.* a looking down upon with contempt: violent malice or hatred.—*prep.* in spite of, notwithstanding.—*adj.* **despite'ful.**—*adv.* **despite'fully.**—*n.* **despite'fulness.** [O.Fr. *despit*—L. *dēspectus—dēspicēre.* See **despise.**]

despoil, *di-spoil', v.t.* to spoil or strip completely (e.g. of possessions): to rob.—*ns.* **despoil'er; despoliā'tion.** [O.Fr. *despoiller* (mod. *dépouiller*)—L. *dēspoliāre—dē-,* inten., and *spolium,* spoil.]

despond, *di-spond', v.i.* to be wanting in hope, to be dejected.—*ns.* **despond'ence, despond'ency,** dejection.—*adj.* **despond'ent,** desponding.—*advs.* **despond'ently; despond'ingly.** [L. *dēspondēre—dē,* away, and *spondēre,* to promise.]

despot, *des'pot, n.* one invested with absolute power: a tyrant.—*adjs.* **despot'ic, -al,** pertain-

ing to or like a despot: having absolute power: tyrannical.—*adv.* **despot'ically.**—*n.* **des'potism,** absolute power: a state governed by a despot. [O.Fr. *despot*—Gr. *despotēs,* a master.]

despumate, *di-spū'māt,* or *des'pū-māt, v.i.* to throw off in foam or scum. [L. *dēspūmāre, -ātum—dē,* off, and *spūma,* foam.]

desquamate, *des'kwa-māt, v.i.* to scale off.—*n.* **desquamā'tion,** a scaling off: the separation of the cuticle or skin in scales. [L. *dēsquāmāre, -ātum—dē-,* off, and *squāma,* a scale.]

dessert, *diz-ûrt', n.* fruits, confections, &c., served at the close of an entertainment after the rest has been taken away.—*n.* **dessert'spoon, dessert'spoon,** a spoon smaller than a table-spoon and larger than a tea-spoon. [O.Fr. *dessert*—*desservir,* to clear the table—*des-* (L. *dis-*), away, and *servir* (L. *servīre*), to serve.]

destemper. See **distemper** (1).

destine, *des'tin, v.t.* to ordain or appoint to a certain use, state, &c. (e.g. *money destined to pay his debts; destined for the Church*): (in passive) to be bound (for), on its, one's, way to: to doom (to good or evil).—*ns.* **destinā'tion,** the place to which one, anything, is going; **des'tiny,** the purpose or end to which any person or thing is appointed: unavoidable fate. [Fr.,—L. *dēstināre—dē-,* inten., and root *sta-,* in *stāre,* to stand.]

destitute, *des'ti-tūt, adj.* (*arch.*) forsaken: in utter want: (with *of*) entirely lacking in.—*n.* **destitū'tion,** the state of being destitute: poverty. [L. *dēstituĕre, -ūtum—dē,* away, and *statuĕre,* to place.]

destroy, *di-stroi', v.t.* to pull down, demolish, to ruin, to put an end to, to do away with, to kill:—*pr.p.* **destroy'ing;** *pa.p.* **destroyed'.**—*n.* **destroy'er,** a person or thing that destroys: a torpedo-boat destroyer, a swift war vessel orig. for attacking ordinary torpedo-boats (q.v.). [O.Fr. *destruire*—L. *dēstruĕre, dēstructum dē-,* down, and *struĕre,* to build.]

destruction, *di-struk'sh(ó)n, n.* act, or means, of destroying: ruin.—*v.t.* **destruct',** to destroy a rocket or missile in flight.—*adj.* **destruc'tible,** able, or liable, to be destroyed.—*n.* **destructibil'ity.**—*adj.* **destruc'tive,** causing destruction: mischievous: (with *of* or *to*) ruinous, deadly: opp. to *constructive,* merely negative (e.g. *destructive criticism*).—*adv.* **destruc'tively.**—*ns.* **destruc'tiveness; destruc'tor,** a furnace for burning up refuse. [L. *dēstructiō, -ōnis—dēstruĕre.* See **destroy.**]

desuetude, *des'wi-tūd, n.* disuse, discontinuance (of custom, habit, or practice). [L. *dēsuētūdō—dē-,* neg., and *suēscĕre,* to become used.]

desultory, *des'ul-tór-i, adj.* jumping from one thing to another, unmethodical (e.g. *desultory reading*): without logical connection, rambling (e.g. *desultory remarks*).—*adv.* **des'ultorily.**—*n.* **des'ultoriness.** [L. *dēsultōrius—dēsultor,* a vaulter—*dēsilīre, -sultum,* to leap—*dē,* from, and *salīre,* to jump.]

detach, *di-tach', v.t.* to unfasten: to separate, disunite (from): to send off on special service.—*v.i.* to separate.—*adj.* **detach'able.**—*p.adj.* **detached',** unconnected: separate: aloof: free from emotion.—*n.* **detach'ment,** state of being detached: that which is detached, as a body of troops. [Fr. *détacher*—O.Fr. *des-* (L.

dis-), apart, neg., and root of **attach**.]

detail, *di-tāl′, v.t.* to relate minutely: to enumerate: to set apart for a particular service.—*n.* (*dē′tāl,* or *di-tāl′*) a small part: an item: an account that goes into particulars.—*adj.* **detailed′,** giving full particulars: exhaustive. [Fr. *détailler*—*dē-,* inten., and *tailler,* to cut; cf. **tailor.**]

detain, *di-tān′, v.t.* (*arch.*) to hold from, back: to delay, stop: to keep in custody.—*ns.* **detainee** (*di-tān′ē*), one who is held in custody; **detain′er,** one who detains: (*law*) the holding of what belongs to another: a warrant to retain in custody; **detain′ment** (same as **detention**). [O.Fr. *detenir*—L. *dētinēre*—*dē,* from, and *tenēre,* to hold.]

detect, *di-tekt′, v.t.* (*lit.*) to uncover—hence to discover: to find out: to discern.—*adj.* **detect′able, detect′ible.**—*n.* **detec′tion,** discovery (of something hidden): state of being found out.—*adj.* **detect′ive,** employed in detecting.—*n.* a person, usually a police-officer not in uniform, employed to detect criminals and to watch the behaviour of suspected persons.—*n.* **detec′tor,** one who detects: an apparatus for detecting presence of electric currents, &c. [L. *dētegēre, -tectum*—*dē-,* neg., *tegēre,* to cover.]

détente, *dā-tät′, n.* relaxation of strained relations (esp. between countries). [Fr.]

detention, *di-ten′sh(ó)n, n.* act of detaining: state of being detained: confinement: keeping in school as a punishment. [L. *dētentiō, -ōnis*—*dētinēre.* See **detain.**]

deter, *di-tûr′, v.t.* to frighten, hinder, or prevent (from):—*pr.p.* deter′ring; *pa.p.* deterred′.—*adj.* **deterrent** (*di-ter′ént*), serving to deter.—*n.* anything that deters: specifically a nuclear weapon. [L. *dēterrēre*—*dē,* from, *terrēre,* to frighten.]

deterge, *di-tûrj′, v.t.* to wipe off: to cleanse (as a wound).—*adj.* **deterg′ent,** cleansing: purging.—*n.* a cleansing agent. [L. *dētergēre, dētersum*—*dē,* off, and *tergēre,* to wipe.]

deteriorate, *di-tē′ri-ō-rāt, v.t.* to make worse.—*v.i.* to grow worse.—*n.* **detēriorā′tion.** [L. *dēteriōrāre, -ātum,* to make worse—*dēterior,* worse—*dē,* down.]

determine, *di-tûr′min, v.t.* to put terms or bounds to, to limit: to fix or settle (e.g. the form, character, direction, or course of): to cause (a person) to resolve: to put an end to.—*v.i.* to come to a decision: to come to an end.—*adj.* **deter′minable,** capable of being determined, decided, or finished.—*adj.* **deter′minant,** serving to determine.—*n.* that which serves to determine: (*math.*) a square array of numbers conventionally representing the algebraic sum of the products of the numbers, one from each row and column (the sign of each product being determined by the number of interchanges required to restore the product to its proper order).—*adj.* **deter′minate,** determined or limited: fixed: decisive.—*adv.* **deter′minately.**—*n.* **determinā′tion,** that which is determined or resolved on: direction to a certain end: resolution: fixed purpose: decision of character.—*adjs.* **deter′minative,** that determines, limits, or defines; **deter′mined,** firm in purpose, resolute: fixed.—*adv.* **deter′minedly.**—*n.* **deter′minism,**

the doctrine that all things, including the will, are determined by causes. [Fr.,—L. *dētermināre, -ātum*—*dē-,* inten., and *terminus,* a boundary.]

detersion, *di-tûr′sh(ó)n, n.* act of cleansing.—*adj.* and *n.* **detersive,** detergent. [See **deterge.**]

detest, *di-test′, v.t.* to hate intensely.—*adj.* **detest′able,** worthy of being detested, extremely hateful, abominable.—*n.* **detest′ableness.**—*adv.* **detest′ably.**—*n.* **dētestā′tion,** extreme hatred, [Fr. *détester*—L. *dētestārī*—*dē-,* inten., and *testārī,* to call to witness, execrate—*testis,* a witness.]

dethrone, *di-thrōn′, v.t.* to remove from a throne: depose.—*n.* **dethrone′ment.** [Pfx. **de-,** and **throne.**]

detonate, *det′o-nāt, dē′to-nāt, v.i.* to explode rapidly and violently.—*v.t.* to cause so to explode.—*ns.* **detonā′tion,** the act of detonating: a violent explosion: in a petrol engine, the spontaneous combustion of part of the compressed charge after the passage of the spark: the accompanying noise or knock; **det′onātor,** a substance or contrivance that initiates an explosion. [L. *dētonāre, -ātum*—*dē,* down, and *tonāre,* to thunder.]

detour, *dē′tōōr, di-tōōr′, n.* a winding (e.g. of a river): a circuitous way, esp. one temporarily replacing a more direct route.—**make a detour,** to go by a roundabout way. [Fr. *dé-* (L. *dis-*), asunder, and *tour,* turning.]

detract, *di-trakt′, v.t.* to take away.—*v.i.* to take away (from), lessen, esp. reputation or worth.—*ns.* **detrac′ter, detrac′tor; detrac′tion,** depreciation, slander. [L. *dē,* from and *trahēre, tractum,* to draw.]

detrain, *dē-trān′, v.t.* to set down out of a railway train, as troops.—*v.i.* to come out of a train. [Pfx. **de-,** and **train** (n).]

detriment, *det′ri-mént, n.* diminution: damage, injury.—*adj.* and *n.* **detrimental.** [L. *dētrīmentum*—*dē,* off, and *terēre, trītum,* to rub.]

detritus, *di-trī′tus, n.* a mass of substance gradually worn off solid bodies: an aggregate of loosened fragments, esp. of rock.—*n.* **detri′tion,** a wearing away. [L.,—*dē,* off, and *terēre, trītum,* to rub.]

de trop, *di trō, adj.* (of a person; used predicatively) in the way, unwelcome at the particular time and place. [Fr.]

detumescence, *dē-tū-mes′éns, n.* diminution of swelling—opp. to *intumescence.* [L. *dētumescēre*—*de-,* neg., and *tumescēre,* to swell.]

deuce, *dūs, n.* a card or die with two spots: (*lawn tennis*) a situation in which one side must gain *two* successive points to win the game, or two successive games to win the set. [Fr. *deux,* two—L. *duos,* acc. of *duo,* two.]

deuce, *dūs, n.* the devil—in exclamatory phrases.—*adj.* **deuced** (*dū′sid,* or *dūst*), devilish: excessive.—*adv.* confoundedly. [Prob. from *deuce*—see **deuce** (1)—the lowest throw at dice.]

deus ex machina, *dē′ús eks mak′in-a, n.* the god from the machine who came to clear up difficulties in a classical play (see **machine**): any person, thing, event, that solves a difficulty in an unpredictable or an unnatural manner. [L.]

deuterium, *dū-tēr′i-úm, n.* heavy hydrogen (q.v.).—*n.* **deuteron** (*dū′tér-on*), the nucleus of

Neutral vowels in unaccented syllables: em′pér-ór; *for certain sounds in foreign words see p. ix.*

a heavy hydrogen atom, consisting of one proton and one neutron. [Gr. *deuteros*, second.]

deuterogamy, *dū-tér-og'a-mi*, *n.* second marriage. [Gr. *deuteros*, second, *gamos*, marriage.]

Deuteronomy, *dū-tér-on'o-mi*, or *dū'tér-on-o-mi*, *n.* the fifth book of the Pentateuch, containing a repetition of the decalogue and laws given in Exodus. [Gr. *deuteros*, second, *nomos*, law.]

devalue, *dē-val'ū*, *v.t.* to reduce the value of.—*vs.t.* **deval'uate**, **deval'orise**.—*ns.* **devalua'tion**, **devalorisa'tion**. [Pfx **de-**, and **value**.]

devastate, *dev'as-tāt*, *v.t.* to lay waste: to plunder.—*p.adj.* **dev'astating**, overwhelming.—*adv.* **dev'astatingly**.—*n.* **devastā'tion**, act of devastating: state of being devastated: havoc. [L. *dēvastāre*, *-ātum—dē*, inten., *vastāre*, to lay waste.]

develop, **-e**, *di-vel'op*, *v.t.* to unroll: to lay open by degrees: to bring out what is latent in: to bring to a more advanced or more highly organised state: to show, reveal the symptoms of (e.g. a habit, a disease): to elaborate (e.g. a plan): to open (an attack): (*chess*) to bring into a position of usefulness in attack: (*math.*) to express in expanded form: to make (a photograph) visible by treating the film or plate with chemicals: to treat (a film or plate) for this purpose.—*v.i.* to grow (into): to open out: to evolve: to become apparent:—*pr.p.* devel'oping; *pa.p.* devel'oped.—*ns.* devel'oper, one who or that which develops: a reagent for developing photographs: an apparatus for developing muscles; **devel'opment**, a gradual unfolding or growth, evolution: the act of developing: (*math.*) the expression of a function in the form of a series: (*mus.*) the elaboration of a theme, or that part of a movement in which this occurs: a new situation that emerges,—**development area**, a region of particularly heavy unemployment where the government offers inducement to establish new industries. [Fr. *développer*, opposite of *envelopper*; of obscure origin.]

deviate, *dē'vi-āt*, *v.i.* to go from the way: to turn aside (from a course, topic, principle, &c.): to diverge, differ, from a standard, norm, &c.: to vary from type.—*ns.* **dev'iant**, that which deviates (from an accepted norm).—also *adj.*; **deviā'tion.—deviation of the compass**, deflection of the magnetic needle due to the ship's magnetism. [L. *dēviāre*, *-ātum—dē*, from, *via*, the way.]

device, *di-vīs'*, *n.* that which is devised or designed: a contrivance: power of devising: (*her.*) an emblem: a motto: (*pl.*) inclinations. [O.Fr. *devise*. See **devise**.]

devil, *dev'l*, *n.* (*cap.*) supreme spirit of evil, Satan: any evil spirit: a very wicked person: a reckless, lively person: someone or something difficult to deal with: an expletive, in 'What the devil?' &c.: a drudge: a grilled and highly seasoned dish.—*v.t.* to season highly and broil.—*v.i.* to drudge for another:—*pr.p.* dev'illing; *pa.p.* dev'illed.—*adj.* **dev'ilish**, fiendish, malignant.—*adv.* (*coll.*) very, exceedingly.—*adv.* **dev'ilishly**,—*adj.* **dev'il-may-care**, reckless, audacious.—*n.* **dev'ilry**, conduct worthy of the devil.—**devil a bit**, not at all; **devil's**

advocate, an advocate at the papal court whose duty it is to propose all reasonable objection against a person's claims to canonisation: an adverse or captious critic; **the devil to pay**, serious trouble ahead.—**printer's devil**, the youngest apprentice in a printing-office: a printer's errand-boy; **Tasmanian devil**, a fierce carnivorous marsupial of Tasmania.—**play the devil with**, to ruin. [O.E. *dēofol*, *dēoful*—L. *diabolus*—Gr. *diabolos*, from *diaballein*, to slander, from *dia*, across, and *ballein*, to throw.]

devious, *dē'vi-us*, *adj.* out of the way, remote: roundabout: erring: tricky: rather dishonest (e.g. *devious methods*).—*adv.* **dē'viously**.—*n.* **dē'viousness**. [L. *dēvius*. See **deviate**.]

devise, *di-vīz'*, *v.t.* to invent, contrive: to scheme: to leave by will (real estate; cf. bequeath).—*n.* act of leaving property by will: a will: property bequeathed by will.—*ns.* **devīs'er**, one who contrives; **devīs'or**, one who bequeaths. [O.Fr. *deviser*, *devise*—Low L. *dīvīsa*, a division of goods, a mark.]

devitalise, *dē-vī'ta-līz*, *v.t.* to deprive of vitality or life-giving qualities.—*n.* **devitalisā'tion**. [Pfx. **de-**, and **vitalise**.]

devoid, *di-void'*, *adj.* (with *of*) destitute of: free from. [O. Fr. *desvoidier—des-* (L. *dis-*), away, *voidier*—l. *viduāre—viduus*, deprived.]

devolution, *dev-* or *dev-ol-ū'sh(ó)n*, *n.* a transference from one person to another: delegation of power or responsibility, as to regional governments by central governments. [Low L. *dēvolūtiō*—L. *dēvolvēre*. See **devolve**.]

devolve, *di-volv'*, *v.t.* to roll down: to hand down: to deliver over.—*v.i.* to roll down: (*fig.*; with *upon*) to fall or be transferred to. [L. *dēvolvēre*, *-volūtum—dē*, down, *volvēre*, *-ūtum*, to roll.]

Devonian, *di-vō'ni-án*, *adj.* belonging to Devonshire.—*n.* a period of the Primary geological era between the Silurian and the Carboniferous: the system of strata formed during this period, which abound in Devonshire.

devote, *di-vōt'*, *v.t.* to set apart or dedicate by solemn act: to give up wholly: to consign (to destruction), to doom.—*adj.* **devōt'ed**, given up, as by a vow: zealous: strongly attached: doomed.—*adv.* **devōt'edly**.—*ns.* **devotee** (*-tē'* or *dev'-*), one wholly or superstitiously devoted (with *of* or *to*): a fanatic; **devō'tion**, consecration: giving up of the mind to the worship of God: piety: strong affection, or attachment (*tō*): ardour: (*pl.*) prayers.—*adj.* **devō'tional**.—*adv.* **devō'tionally**. [L. *dēvovēre*, *dēvōtum—dē-*, away, and *vovēre*, to vow.]

devour, *di-vowr'*, *v.t.* to swallow greedily: to eat up: to consume or waste: to take in eagerly by the senses or mind.—*n.* **devour'er**. [O.Fr. *devorer*—L. *dēvorāre—dē-*, inten., and *vorāre*, to swallow.]

devout, *di-vowt'*, *adj.* given up to religious thoughts and exercises, pious: solemn, earnest.—*adv.* **devout'ly**.—*n.* **devout'ness**. [O.Fr. *devot*—L. *dēvōtus—dēvovēre*. See **devote**.]

dew, *dū*, *n.* moisture deposited from the air on cooling, esp. at night, in minute specks upon the surface of objects—or similar deposit or exudation.—*v.t.* to wet with dew: to moisten.—*ns.* **dew'drop**; **dew'point**, the tem-

fāte, *fär*; *mē*, *hûr* (her); *mīne*; *mōte*, *för*; *mūte*; *mōōn*, *fōŏt*; *then* (then) perature at which dew begins to form; **dew′-pond**, a hollow supplied with water by mist—*adj.* **dew′y.** [O.E. *dēaw*; cf. O.N. *dögg*, Ger. *thau*, dew.]

dewlap, *dū′lap, n.* the pendulous skin under the throat of oxen, dogs. &c.—*adj.* **dew′lapped.** [Prob. **dew** and O.E. *læppa*, a loose hanging piece.]

dexter, *deks′tėr, adj.* on the right-hand side: right.—*n.* **dexter′ity,** right-handedness: readiness and skill, adroitness.—*adjs.* **dex′terous, dex′trous,** right-handed: adroit, clever.—*adv.* **dex′terously.**—*n.* **dex′terousness.**—*adj.* **dex′tral,** right, as opposed to left. [L. *dexter*; Gr. *dexios,* Sans. *dakṣina*, on the right, on the south.]

dextrin, *deks′trin, n.* British gum, a gummy mixture got from starch.—Also **dextrine.**—*n.* **dex′trose,** the form of glucose (q.v.) that occurs in nature. [Fr.]

dey, *dā, n.* the pasha or governor of Algiers before the French conquest. [Turk. *dāi,* orig. a maternal uncle, a familiar title of the chief of the Janizaries (q.v.).]

dhooly. See **doo′lie.**

dhow, dow, *dow, n.* a lateen-sailed Arab vessel of the Indian Ocean. [Origin unknown.]

di-, *dī, pfx.* two, twice, double. [Gr. *dis,* twice.]

dia-, *dī′a, pfx.* through. [Gr.]

diabetes, *dī-a-bē′tēz, n.* a disease marked by a morbid and excessive discharge of urine, a disorder of metabolism in which excess of sugar appears in the blood and the urine.—*adjs.* **diabet′ic, -al.**—*n.* **diabet′ic,** a person who suffers from diabetes. [Gr. *diabetes,* a siphon—*dia,* through, and *bainein,* to go.]

diablerie, diablery, *dē-äb′lé-rē, n.* magic, the black art, sorcery: the mythology of devils: wickedness: mischievousness. [Fr.,—*diable*—L. *diabolus.* See **devil.**]

diabolic, -al, *dī-ä-Lol′ik, -al, adjs.* devilish.—*adv.* **diabol′ically.** [L.,—Gr. *diabolikos—diabolos,* the devil. See **devil.**]

diaconate, *dī-ak′o-nát, n.* the office of a deacon.—*adj.* **diac′onal,** pertaining to a deacon. [L.L. *diaconātus*—L. *diāconus.* See **deacon.**]

diacritic, -al, *dī-a-krit′ik, -äl, adjs.* distinguishing between—used of marks or points attached to letters to indicate differences of sound. [Gr. *diakritikos, diakrinein—dia,* between, and *krinein,* to distinguish.]

diadem, *dī′a-dem, n.* a band or fillet worn round the head as a badge of royalty: a crown: royalty.—*adj.* **dī′ademed,** wearing a diadem. [O.Fr. *diademe*—L. *diadēma*—Gr. *diadēma—dia,* round, and *deein,* to bind.]

diaeresis, dieresis, *dī-ēr′é-sis, n.* a mark (¨) placed over the second of two vowels to show that each is to be pronounced separately, as *naïve:*—*pl.* **diaer′eses, dier′eses.** [Gr.,—*dia,* apart, *haireein,* to take.]

diagnosis, *dī-ag-nō′sis, n.* the identification of a disease by means of its symptoms: an estimate based on observed facts:—*pl.* **diagnō′ses.**—*v.t.* **diagnose** (*-nōz′, -nōs′*), to ascertain, or to recognise, from symptoms.—*adj.* **diagnōs′tic,** distinguishing: differentiating.—*n.* that by which anything is known: a symptom. [Gr., *dia,* between, *gnōsis—gnōnai,* to know.]

diagonal, *dī-ag′o-nál, adj.* stretching from one corner to an opposite corner of a figure with four or more sides: slantwise.—*n.* a straight line so drawn.—*adv.* **diag′onally.** [Fr.,—L. *diagōnālis,* from Gr. *diagōnios—dia,* through, and *gōnia,* a corner.]

diagram, *dī′a-gram, n.* a figure or plan drawn in outline to illustrate any statement.—*adj.* **diagrammat′ic.**—*n.* **dī′agraph,** an instrument for copying, enlarging, or projecting drawings. [Through L.,—Gr. *diagramma—dia,* round *graphein,* to write.]

dial, *dī′ål, n.* an instrument for showing the time of day by the sun's shadow: the face of a watch or clock: a circular plate with a movable index used for various purposes.—*v.t.* to measure or indicate by dial: to manipulate a telephone or other dial in a specified way, so as e.g. to connect with (a specified number). [M.E. *dial*—Low L. *diālis,* daily—L. *diēs,* a day.]

dialect, *dī′a-lekt, n.* a variety or form of a language peculiar to a district or class. [Through Fr. and L. from Gr. *dialektos,* speech, peculiarity of speech—*dia,* between, *legein,* to speak.]

dialectic, -al *dī-a-lek′tik, -ál, adjs.* pertaining to dialect, or to discourse, or to dialectics: logical.—*ns.* **dialec′tic, dialec′tics,** art of discussing: that branch of logic which teaches the rules and modes of reasoning.—*adv.* **dialec′tically.**—*n.* **dialecti′cian** (*-shán*), one skilled in dialectics, a logician.—**dialectical materialism,** a form of materialism (q.v.) expounded by Karl Marx (see **Marxian**) which considers human history as an evolutionary process in which development is the result of conflict between opposites, the present world conditions being due to a class struggle between the capitalists, whose aim is private profit, and the workers, who resist exploitation. [Gr. *dialektikos—dialegesthai,* to argue.]

dialogue, *dī′a-log, n.* conversation between two or more persons, esp. of a formal or imaginary nature: an exchange of views in the hope of ultimately reaching agreement.—*adjs.* **dialog′ic** (*-loj′-*), **dialogist′ic** (*-loj-*), **-al,** in the form of a dialogue.—*n.* **dial′ogist** (*-oj-*), a speaker in, or writer of, a dialogue. [Fr.,—L. *dialogus*—Gr. *dialogos,* a conversation—*dialegesthai,* to discourse.]

dialysis, *dī-al′i-sis, n.* (*chem.*) the separation of a colloid from a substance in true solution by allowing the latter to diffuse through a parchment membrane: dissolution:—*pl.* **dial′yses** (*-sēz*).—*v.t.* **dialyse** (*dī′á-līz*), to separate by dialysis.—*n.* **dialyser.**—*adj.* **dialy′tic.** [Gr. *dialysis—dia,* asunder, *lyein,* to loose.]

diamagnetic, *dī-a-mag-net′ik, adj.* cross-magnetic—applied to any substance which, when suspended between the poles of a magnet, arranges itself across the line joining the poles (a rod that arranges itself parallel to the line joining the poles is said to be *paramagnetic*). [Gr. *dia,* through, and **magnetic.**]

diamanté, *dē-a-mä-tā, n.* a decoration, e.g. on a dress, consisting of glittering particles: a fabric so decorated. [Fr. *diamant,* diamond.]

diameter, *dī-am′é-tér, n.* the measure through or across: a straight line passing through the centre of a circle or other figure, terminated at both ends by the circumference.—*adjs.* **dia-**

Neutral vowels in unaccented syllables: *em′pėr-ŏr*; for certain sounds in foreign words see p. ix.

met′ric, -al, in the direction of a diameter: pertaining to the diameter: like the opposite ends of the diameter (as in *diametrical opposition*).—*adv.* **diamet′rically.** [Through Fr. and L. from Gr. *diametros*—*dia*, through, *metron*, a measure.]

diamond, *dī′a-mŏnd, n.* a crystallised form of pure carbon, the most valuable of all gems, and the hardest of all minerals: a rhombus: one of a suit of playing cards marked with diamond pips: one of the smallest kinds of English printing type.—*adj.* resembling diamonds: made of diamonds: marked with diamonds: lozenge-shaped.—*ns.* **di′amond-drill,** a boring tool whose head is set with rough diamonds; **di′amond-field,** a region that yields diamonds; **di′amond-ju′bilee,** a sixtieth anniversary (of marriage, **di′amond-wed′ding**). —**diamond cut diamond,** an encounter between two very sharp persons; **black diamonds,** (*fig.*) coal.—**rough diamond,** an uncut diamond: a worthy but unpolished person. [M.E. *adamaunt*—O.Fr. *adamant.* See **adamant.**]

diapason, *dī-a-pā′zŏn, n.* (*obs.*) an interval of an octave, hence, concord: a full volume of various sounds in concord: the compass of a voice or instrument: a standard of pitch: one of two organ stops (*open* and *stopped diapason*). [Gr. *dia*, through, and *pasōn*, gen. pl. fem of *pas*, all part of the Gr. phrase, *dia pasōn chordōn symphōnia*, concord through all the notes.]

diaper, *dī′a-pėr, n.* linen or cotton cloth woven in slightly defined figures, used for table linen, &c.: a floral or geometric pattern in low relief in architecture, often repeated over a considerable surface: a baby's napkin.—*v.t.* to variegate with figures, as diaper. [O.Fr. *diaspre, diapre*—Gr. *dia*, through, *aspros*, white.]

diaphanous, *dī-af′a-nus, adj.* allowing to shine or appear through, transparent, clear; light delicate.—*adv.* **diaph′anously.** [Gr. *diaphanēs*—*dia*, through, *phainein*, to show, shine.]

diaphoretic, *dī-a-fo-ret′ik, adj.* promoting perspiration. n. a medicine that increases perspiration. [Gr. *diaphoreein*, to carry off sweat.—*dia*, through, *pherein*, to bear.]

diaphragm, *dī′a-fram, n.* a thin partition or dividing membrane: the midriff, a structure separating the chest from the abdomen.—*adj.* **diaphragmat′ic** (*-frag-mat′ik*). [Gr. *diaphragma*—*dia*, across, *phragma*, a fence.]

diarchy, *dī′ar-ki, n.* a form of government in which two persons, states, or bodies are jointly vested with supreme power—less correctly **dy′archy.** [Formed from Gr. *di-*, twice, *archein*, to rule.]

diarrhoea, diarrhea, *dī-a-rē′a, n.* a persistent purging or looseness of the bowels.—*adj.* **diarrhoet′ic.** [Gr. *diarroia*—*dia*, through, *rheein*, to flow.]

diary, *dī′a-ri, n.* a daily record.—*n.* **di′arist,** one who keeps a diary. [L. *diārium*—*diēs*, a day.]

diastase, *dī′as-tās, n.* an enzyme (q.v.), or group of enzymes, having the power of converting starch into sugar. [Gr. *diastasis*, division—*dia*, apart, *stasis*, setting.]

diathermy, *dī-a-thûr′mi, n.* the generation of heat in body tissues by the passage of an electric current through them. [Gr. *dia*, through, *thermē*, heat.]

diatom, *dī′a-tom, n.* any of a group of unicellular algae having a heavily silicified cell wall (consisting of two halves, one fitting into the other like a box and its lid) of which there are many hundreds of species inhabiting fresh and salt water, and (less frequently) the soil.—*n.* **dī-a′tomite** (see **kieselguhr**). [Gr. *diatomos*—*diatemnein*, to cut in two.]

diatonic, *dī-a-ton′ik, adj.* proceeding by the tones and intervals of the natural scale in music.—*adv.* **diaton′ically.** [Gr. *dia*, through, *tonos*, tone.]

diatribe, *dī′a-trīb, n.* a continued discourse or disputation: an invective harangue. [Gr. *diatribē*, a spending of time—*dia*, through, *tribein*, to rub, wear away.]

dibble, *dib′l, n.* a pointed tool used for making holes to put seed or plants in—also **dibb′er.**— *v.t.* **dibb′le,** to plant with a dibble.—*v.i.* to make holes: to dip, as in angling. [Porb. conn. with **dab.**]

dice. See **die** (2).

dicephalous, *dī-sef′a-lus, adj.* two-headed. [Gr. *dikephalos*—*di-*, double, *kephalē*, a head.]

dichlor(o)-, *dī-klōr(-ō)-, -klōr-,* in composition, having two atoms of chlorine esp. replacing hydrogen.

dichotomy, *dī-kot′o-mi, n.* a division into two parts: strongly contrasted groups or classes.—*adj.* **dichot′omous.** [Gr. *dicha*, in two, and *temnein*, to cut.]

dick, *dik, n.* (*slang*) man: (*slang*) detective. [*Dick* for Richard.]

dickens, *dik′enz, n.* the deuce, the devil, as in 'play the dickens with'. [App. from *Dickon*—Richard, used as a substitute for *devil.*]

dicker, *dik′ėr, n.* (*U.S.*) haggling, bargaining: petty trade by barter, &c.—*v.i.* to haggle. [Prob. the obs. *dicker*, the number ten, esp. of hides or skins.]

dickey, dicky, *dik′i, n.* a leathern apron for a gig, &c.: the driver's seat in a carriage: a seat at the back of a carriage or motor-car: a false shirt-front. [Perh. from *dick*, a dial. Eng. word for a leathern apron: prob. Du. *dek*, a cover.]

dicky, dickey, *dik′i, adj.* (*coll.*) shaky.

dicky-bird, *dik′i-bûrd, n.* a small bird. [From *Dick*, familiar of Richard—like *Jack*, in jackass.]

dicotyledon, *dī-kot-i-lē′dŏn, n.* a plant having two seed-lobes.—*adj.* **dicotyle′donous.** [Gr. *di-*, twice, and *cotyledon.*]

dictaphone, *dik′ta-fōn, n.* (properly *cap.*) a recording apparatus for dictating letters, &c. [Trade mark: L. *dictāre*, to dictate, Gr. *phōnē*, sound.]

dictate, *dik-tāt′, v.t.* to say or read for another to write: to lay down with authority: to command, require.—*v.i.* to give orders (to).—*n.* (*dik′tāt*) an order, rule, direction, impulse.— *ns.* **dicta′tion,** act of dictating: overbearing command: something dictated; **dicta′tor,** one invested with absolute authority—originally an extraordinary Roman magistrate.—*adj.* **dictātō′rial,** like a dictator: absolute: overbearing.—*adv.* dictătō′rially.—*n.* dictă′torship. [L. *dictāre, -ātum—dīcĕre,* to say.]

diction, *dik′sh(ó)n, n.* manner of speaking, enunciation: choice of words, style. [Fr., or L. *dictiō, -ōnis—dīcĕre, dictum,* to say.]

dictionary, *dik′sh(ó)n-à-ri, n.* a book containing the words of a language alphabetically arranged, with their meanings, &c., a lexicon: a work containing information on any department of knowledge, alphabetically arranged. [Low L. *dictiōnārium—dīcĕre.* See **diction.**]

dictograph, *dik′tō-gräf, n.* (properly *cap.*) a telephone for transmitting speech from room to room, with or without the speaker's knowledge. [Trade-mark: L. *dictum,* thing said, and Gr. *graphein,* to write.]

dictum, *dik′tum, n.* a saying: an authoritative saying: a judicial opinion:—*pl.* **dic′ta.** [L.]

did, *did, didst, didst, pa.t.* of **do.**

didactic, -al, *di-dak′tik, -ál* (or *dī-*), *adjs.* fitted, or intended, to teach, instructive.—*adv.* **didac′tically.** [Gr. *didaktikos—didaskein,* to teach; akin to L. *docēre, discēre.*]

diddle, *did′l, v.t.* to cajole, swindle. [Origin uncertain.]

die, *dī, v.i.* to lose life, to perish, to wither, to languish:—*pr.p.* dy′ing; *pa.t.* and *pa.p.* died (dīd).—*n.* **die-hard,** one who prolongs vain resistance: often applied to an extreme conservative.—**die away,** to fade from sight or hearing; **die hard** (see **hard**); **die off,** to die quickly or in′large numbers; **die out,** to become extinct; **die the death** (*theat. slang*), to arouse no response from one's audience. [Prob. from a lost O.E. *dēgan;* but commonly referred to a Scand. root seen in O.N. *deyja.* The O.E. word is *steorfan,* whence our *starve.*]

die, *dī, n.* a small cube with numbered faces thrown from a box in gaming: a small cubical piece: hazard: a stamp for impressing coin, &c.:—*pl.* (gaming and the like) **dice** (dīs); (stamping) **dies** (dīz).—*v.i.* **dice,** to play with dice.—*v.t.* to mark with squares:—*pr.p.* **dic′ing;** *pa.p.* **diced** (dīst).—*adj.* **dīc′ey** (*coll.*), risky: tricky: uncertain in result.—*n.* **die-sinking,** the engraving of dies.—**no dice,** no answer, or negative answer: no success; **the die is cast,** an irrevocable step has been taken. [O.Fr. *de,* pl. *dez,* from Low L. *dadus—L. datus,* given or cast (*talus,* a piece of bone used in play, being understood).]

dielectric, *dī-e-lek′trik, adj.* non-conducting: transmitting electric effects without conducting.—*n.* a substance, solid, liquid or gas, capable of supporting an electric stress, hence an insulator. [Gr. *dia,* through, and **electric.**]

diesel, *(dēz′l)* **engine,** an internal-combustion engine in which heavy oil is ignited by heat generated by compression—*adj.* **dies′el-elec′tric,** using power obtained from a diesel-operated electric generator. [Rudolf *Diesel* (1858-1913), the inventor.]

dies non, *dī′ēz non,* a day on which the business of the law courts cannot be carried on: a day that cannot be used for some other business or purpose. [L.; for *dies non jūridicus,* a day not for the administration of justice.]

diet, *dī′et, n.* mode of living, now only with especial reference to food: food planned or prescribed: (*obs.*) allowance of provisions.—*v.t.* to furnish with food: to put on a diet.—*v.i.* to take food according to rule.—*adj.* **dī′etary,** pertaining to diet or the rules of diet.—*n.* course of diet: allowance of food, esp. in large institutions.—*adjs.* **dīetĕt′ic, -al,** pertaining to diet.—*ns.* **dīetet′ics,** rules for regulating diet; **dietitian, -cian** (-*ish′án*), an authority on diet. [Fr. *diète—*L.L. *diaeta—*Gr. *diaita,* mode of living, diet.]

diet, *dī′et, n.* a national, federal, or provincial assembly, council, or parliament: a conference. [O.Fr. *diete—*Low L. *diēta—*Gr. *diaita,* way of life; or from L. *diēs,* a (set) day, with which usage cf. Ger. *tag* (a day) and *reichstag* (q.v.).]

differ, *dif′ér, v.i.* to be unlike, distinct, or various (used by itself, or followed by *from*): to disagree with (with *with, from*): to quarrel, be at variance (with):—*pr.p.* diff′ering; *pa.p.* diff′ered.—*n.* **diff′erence,** that which distinguishes one thing from another: a contention or quarrel: the point in dispute: the excess of one quantity or number over another.—*adj.* **diff′erent,** distinct, separate: unlike, not the same (with *from, to,* not now *than*): novel.—*n.* **differen′tia** (-*shi-ä:* L.), in logic, that property which distinguishes a species from others:—*pl.* **differen′tiae** (-*shi-ē*).—*adj.* **differen′tial,** constituting, or pertaining to, a difference, discriminating: (*math.*) pertaining to a quantity or difference infinitely small.—*n.* (*math.*) an infinitesimal difference, an arbitrary constant increment of a variable: differential gear: a price or wage difference.—*v.t.* **differen′tiāte,** to constitute a difference between (*this differentiates A and B,* or *A from B*): to classify or distinguish as different: (*math.*) to find the value of the differential coefficient of.—*v.i.* to constitute, or to recognise, a difference (between): to become different by specialisation.—*n.* **differentiā′tion.**—*adv.* **diff′erently.**—**differential calculus** (see **calculus**); **differential coefficient,** the ratio of the differential of a function to that of its independent variable; **differential gear,** a gear permitting relative rotation of two shafts driven by a third. [L. *differre—dif-* (=*dis-*), apart, *ferre,* to bear.]

difficult, *dif′i-kult, adj.* not easy: hard to be done: requiring labour and pains: hard to please: not easily persuaded.—*adv.* **diff′icultly** (mainly *chem.*; as difficultly soluble, soluble, but not easy to dissolve).—*n.* **diff′iculty,** laboriousness: obstacle: objection: that which cannot be easily understood or believed: embarrassment of affairs. [The adj. was formed from *difficulty,* Fr. *difficulté—*L. *difficultās—difficilis—dif-* (=*dis-*), neg., and *facilis,* easy.]

diffident, *dif′i-dént, adj.* (*arch.*) distrustful (of): wanting in self-confidence.—*n.* **diff′idence.**—*adv.* **diff′idently.** [L. *diffīdens, -entis,* pr.p. of *diffīdere,* to distrust—*dif-* (=*dis-*), neg., *fīdĕre,* to trust.]

diffraction, *di-frak′sh(ó)n, n.* the spreading of light and other rays passing through a narrow opening, or by the edge of an opaque body, &c. [L. *diffringĕre, diffractum—dis-,* asunder, *frangĕre,* to break.]

diffuse, *di-fūz′, v.t.* to pour out all round: to spread in all directions.—*v.i.* to spread.—*v.t.*

Neutral vowels in unaccented syllables: *em′pér-ór*; for certain sounds in foreign words see p. ix.

194

and *v.i.* in the case of gases or liquids in contact, to intermingle.—*pa.p.* and *adj.* **diffūsed'**, spread widely, not concentrated.—*ns.* **diffūs'edness, diffūs'er.**—*adj.* **diffūs'ible**, that may be diffused.—*ns.* **diffūsibil'ity, diffū'sion.**—*adj.* **diffūs'ive**, extending: spreading widely.—*adv.* **diffūs'ively.**—*n.* **diffūs'iveness.**—**diffused lighting**, lighting that is transmitted or reflected in all directions and being evenly distributed, produces no glare. [L. *diffundēre, diffūsum*—*dif-* (=*dis-*), asunder, *fundēre*, to pour out.]

diffuse, *di-fūs'*, *adj.* diffused, widely spread: wordy, not concise.—*adv.* **diffuse'ly.**—*n.* **diffuse'ness.** [See **diffuse**, vb.]

dig, *dig*, *v.t.* to turn up with a spade or otherwise: to poke or thrust: to taunt: (*slang*) to understand, approve: (*slang*) to take note of.—*v.i.* to use a spade: to mine: to seek (for) by digging (*lit.* and *fig.*): (*slang*) to lodge: —*pr.p.* digg'ing; *pa.t.* and *pa.p.* dug, (*B.*) digged.—*n.* a thrust, a poke (*lit.* and *fig.*—*fig.* often with **at**): an archaeological excavating expedition: an excavation made by archaeologists.—*n.* **digg'er,** one who, or that which, digs: a gold-miner: a machine for digging, as a *steam digger.*—*n.pl.* **digg'ings,** places where mining is carried on, esp. for gold: (*slang*) lodgings.—**dig in,** to cover by digging (*lit.* or *fig.*) to entrench; **dig up,** to excavate: (*coll.*) to obtain by seeking: (*coll.*) to produce, esp. reluctantly. [Prob. O.Fr. *diguer*, to dig; of Gmc. origin.]

digamma, *dī-gam'a*, *n.* an obsolete letter of the Greek alphabet, having the force of our *w*. [So called from its form (F), like one capital gamma (Γ) placed over another.]

digest, *di-jest'*, *v.t.* to dissolve (of a plant or animal body) to prepare food material for assimilation, by breaking it down into simpler chemical compounds through the action of enzymes contained in secretions such as the saliva: to endure patiently (e.g. an insult): to prepare or classify in the mind: to think over, to take in gradually the meaning and implications of.—*v.i.* to undergo digestion.—*adj.* **digest'ible**, that may be digested (*lit.* or *fig.*).—*ns.* **digesti-bil'ity; digestion** (*di-jes'ch(ó)n, di-jest'y(ó)n,* or *dī*), the act or process of digesting: the ability to digest: orderly arrangement.—*adj.* **digest'ive**, pertaining to or promoting digestion.—*adv.* **digest'ively.** [L. *dīgerēre, dīgestum*, to carry asunder or dissolve—*dī* (=*dis-*), asunder, and *gerēre*, to bear.]

digest, *dī'jest*, *n.* a body of laws collected and arranged, esp. the Justinian code of civil laws: an orderly summary of any written matter: a magazine consisting of extracts from other sources. [L. *dīgesta*, neut. pl. of *dīgestus*, pa.p. of *dīgerēre*, to carry apart, to arrange.]

dight, *dīt*, *adj.* equipped, adorned. [O.E. *dihtan*, to arrange, prescribe, from L. *dictāre*, to dictate.]

digit, *dij'it*, *n.* a finger's breadth or $^3/_4$ inch: from the habit of counting on the fingers, a figure representing one of the first nine cardinal numbers: the twelfth part of the diameter of the sun or moon.—*adj.* **dig'ital**, pertaining to the fingers or to arithmetical digits.—*n.* a key of an organ, &c.—*n.* **digitā'lis,** a genus of

plants including the foxglove: a powerful heart stimulant obtained from dried leaves of the common or purple foxglove.—*adjs.* **dig'i-tate, -d,** consisting of several finger-like sections.—*n.* **digitā'tion.**—*adj.* **dig'itigrade,** walking on the toes.—*n.* an animal that walks on its toes, as the lion (cf. *plantigrade*).—*v.t.* **dig'itise,** to put (data) into digital form for use in a digital computer.—**digital computer,** an electronic calculating machine using arithmetical digits. [L. *digitus*, a finger or a toe.]

dignify, *dig'ni-fī*, *v.t.* to invest with honour: to exalt:—*pr.p.* dig'nifying; *pa.p.* dig'nified.—*adj.* **dig'nified,** marked with dignity: exalted: noble: grave. [Low L. *dignificāre*—*dignus*, worthy, *facēre*, to make.]

dignity, *dig'ni-ti*, *n.* the state of being dignified: elevation of mind or character: grandeur of mien: elevation in rank, place, &c.—*n.* **dig'ni-tary,** one in a dignified position or rank, esp. in the church.—**be on one's dignity,** to be very punctilious or the respect due to one and ready to take offence at any slight. [Fr. *dignité*—L. *dignitās*—*dignus*, worthy.]

digraph, *dī'gräf*, *n.* two letters expressing one sound, as *ph* in *digraph*, *ea* in *dead, eo* in *people.* [Gr. *di-*, twice, *graphē*, a mark, a character—*graphein*, to write.]

digress, *di-gres', dī-gres',* *v.i.* to turn aside from the main theme: to introduce irrelevant matter.—*n.* **digress'ion.**—*adjs.* **digress'ional, digress'ive,** of the nature of a digression.—*adv.* **digress'ively.** [L. *dīgredī, digressus*—*di-* (*dis-*), aside, *gradī*, to step.]

dihedral, *dī-hē'drāl*, *adj.* bounded by two plane faces (as *dihedral angle*). [Gr. *di-*, twice, *hedrā*, seat.]

dike, dyke, *dīk*, *n.* a trench, or the earth dug out and thrown up: a ditch: a mound raised to prevent inundation: in Scotland, a wall: (*geol.*) a wall-like mass of igneous rock. [O.E. *dīc*; Du. *dijk*, Ger. *teich*, a pond.]

dilapidate, *di lap'i-dāt*, *v.t.* to pull down stone from stone: to suffer to go to ruin.—Also *v.i.*—*adj.* **dilap'idated,** in structural disrepair.—*ns.* **dilapidā'tion,** state of damage or disrepair: impairing of property during a tenancy; **dilap'idator.** [L. *dīlapidāre*—*dī*, asunder, *lapis, lapidis*, a stone.]

dilate, *di-lāt', dī-lāt',* *v.t.* to spread out in all directions: to enlarge: the opposite of *contract.*—*v.i.* to widen: to swell out: to speak at length.—*adj.* **dīlāt'able,** that may be dilated or expanded.—*ns.* **dilātabil'ity; dilātā'tion, dilā'-tion,** expansion: (*math.*) a transformation which produces a figure similar to, but not congruent with the original; **dilāt'or, dilāt'er.** [L. *dīlātus* (used as pa.p. of *differre*) from *dī-* (=*dis-*), apart, and *lātus*, wide.]

dilatory, *dil'a-tòr-i*, *adj.* given to procrastination: tardy: tending to delay.—*adv.* **dil'atorily.**—*n.* **dil'atoriness.** [L. *dīlātōrius*, extending or putting off (time)—*dīlatus*. See **dilate**.]

dilemma, *di-lem'a, dī-lem'a*, *n.* a form of argument (the 'horned syllogism') in which a disputant is obliged to accept one or other of two conclusions (sometimes called the **horns of a dilemma**) each of which contradicts his original proposition: a position where each of two alternative courses (or of all the feasible courses) is eminently undesirable. [L.,—Gr. *dilēmma—di-*, twice, double, *lēmma*, an assumption—*lambanein*, to take.]

dilettante, *dil-et-an'ti*, *n.* one animated by a superficial enthusiasm for art, science, or literature:—*pl.* **dilettan'ti** (*-tē*).—*ns.* **dilettan'tism, dilettan'teism.** [It., pr.p. of *dilettare*, to take delight in—L. *dēlectāre*, to delight.]

diligent, *dil'i-jént*, *adj.* steady and earnest in application, industrious.—*n.* **dil'igence**, steady application, industry: a continental stage-coach (also pronounced *dē-lē-zhэ̄s*).—*adv.* **dil'igently.** [Fr.,—*dīligēns, -entis*, pr.p. of L. *dīligĕre*, to choose.]

dill, *dil*, *n.* a plant, akin to parsnip: the fruits used as a condiment or carminative. [O.E. *dile*; Ger. and Swed. *dill.*]

dilly-dally, *dil'i-dal'i*, *v.i.* to loiter, trifle. [A kind of reduplication of **dally.**]

dilute, *di-l(y)o͞ot'*, *dī-l(y)o͞ot'*, *v.t.* to make thinner or more liquid: to diminish the strength, &c., of, by mixing, esp. with water: of labour, to increase the proportion of unskilled to skilled.—*adj.* (also *dī'l(y)o͞ot*), diminished in strength by mixing.—*adj.* **dīl'uent**, diluting.—*n.* that which dilutes.—*n.* **dilu'tion.** [L. *dīluĕre, dīlūtum—dī-*, away, *luĕre*, to wash.]

diluvium, *dil-(y)o͞o'vi-um*, *n.*, an inundation or flood.—*adjs.* **dilū'vial, dilū'vian**, pertaining to a flood, esp. that in the time of Noah: caused by a deluge. [L. *dīluvium—dīluĕre.* See **dilute.**]

dim, *dim*, *adj.* not bright or distinct: obscure: not seeing, hearing, understanding, &c., clearly.—*v.t.* to make dark: to obscure.—*v.i.* to become dim:—*pr.p.* **dimm'ing**; *pa.p.* **dimmed.**—*adv.* **dim'ly.**—*ns.* **dimm'er**, an arrangement for regulating the supply of light; **dim'ness.—take a dim view** (*coll.*), to take an unfavourable view. [O.E. *dimm*; akin to O.N. *dimmr*, dark, and Ger. *dämmerung*, twilight.]

dime, *dīm*, *n.* the tenth part of an American dollar, 10 cents. [Fr. orig. *disme*, from L. *decima* (*pars*), a tenth (part).]

dimension, *di-, dī-men'sh(ó)n*, *n.* measure in length, breadth, and thickness (the three dimensions of space as understood in Euclidean geometry): extent: size.—*adj.* **dimen'sional**, concerning dimension (one, two, three-dimensional space = space of one, two, three dimensions).—*adj.* **three-dimen'sional**, having, or seeming to have, three dimensions: of picture or sound, giving the effect of being seen or heard in three dimensions—usu. 3D: of, e.g. a literary work, developed in detail and thus realistic. [Fr.,—L. *dīmensiō—dīmetīrī, dīmensus—dī-* (=*dis-*), apart, *mētīrī*, to measure.]

dimeter, *dim'e-tér*, *adj.* containing two measures, i.e. two or four metrical feet.—*n.* a verse of two measures. [L.,—Gr. *dimetros—di-*, twice, *metron*, a measure.]

diminish, *di-min'ish*, *v.t.* to make less: to take a part from: to degrade.—*v.i.* to grow or appear less: to subside.—*p.adj.* **dimin'ished** (*mus.*), of an interval, less by a semitone than the perfect or the minor of the same name.—*adj.* **dimin'ishable.**—*adv.* **dimin'ishingly.—diminished responsibility**, limitation in law of criminal responsibility on ground of mental weakness or abnormality, not merely of actual

insanity. [Coined from **minish** in imitation of L. *dīminuĕre—dī-* (*dis-*), apart, *minuĕre*, to make less.]

diminuendo, *di-min-ū-en'dō*, *adj.* and *adv.* (*mus.*) a direction to let the sound die away, marked thus ≻.—Also *n.* [It.,—L. *dēminuĕre*, to lessen.]

diminution, *dim-in-ū'sh(ó)n*, *n.* a lessening: degradation.—*adj.* **dimin'utive**, very small: expressing diminution (e.g. of a suffix).—*n.* (*gram.*) a word formed from another to express a little one of the kind.—*adv.* **dimin'utively.**—*n.* **dimin'utiveness.** [L. *dīminūtiō, -ōnis—dīminuĕre, dīminūtum*, to lessen.]

dimissory, *dim'is-ór-i*, or *-is'-*, *adj.* sending away or giving leave to depart to another jurisdiction. [L. *dīmissōrius—dīmittĕre, dīmissum.*]

dimity, *dim'i-ti*, *n.* a kind of stout white cotton cloth, striped or figured in the loom by weaving with two threads. [Gr. *dimitos—di-*, twice, *mitos*, a thread.]

dimorphism, *dī-mör'fizm*, *n.* (*biol.*) occurrence of two forms in the same species: the property of crystallising in two forms.—*adj.* **dimor'phic, dimor'phous.** [Gr. *di-*, twice, *morphē*, form.]

dimple, *dim'pl*, *n.* a small hollow, esp. on the surface of the body.—*v.i.* to form dimples.—*v.t.* to mark with dimples. [Apparently cog. with Ger. *tümpel*, pool.]

din, *din*, *n.* a loud continued noise.—*v.t.* to urge, repeat, loudly and persistently:—*pr.p.* **dinn'ing**; *pa.p.* **dinned.** [O.E. *dynn, dyne*; cf. O.N. *dynr*, Dan. *dön*, noise.]

dine, *dīn*, *v.i.* to take dinner.—*v.t.* to furnish with a dinner.—*ns.* **din'er**, one who dines: a restaurant car on a train; **dinette'**, an alcove or other part of a room set apart for meals; **din'ing(-)room**, a room used for meals.—**dine out**, to dine elsewhere than at home. [Perh. O.Fr. *disner* (Fr. *dîner*)—Low L. *disjūnāre*, for *disjējūnāre*, to break one's fast. See **dinner.**]

ding, *ding*, *v.t.* to dash or hurl. [M.E. *dingen*; cf. O.N. *dengja*, Swed. *dänga*, to bang.]

ding, *ding*, *v.i.* to ring, keep sounding.—*n.* **ding'-dong**, the monotonous sound of bells: an argument or fight.—*adj.* stubbornly contested with alternate success and failure.—Also *adv.* [Imit.]

dinghy, dingy, dingey, *ding'gi*, *n.* a small rowing-boat or ship's tender. [Hindi (q.v.) *dīngī*, a small boat.]

dingle, *ding'gl*, *n.* a dell. [Origin unknown.]

dingle-dangle, *ding'gl-dang'gl*, *adv.* hanging loose: swinging to and fro. [A kind of reduplication of **dangle.**]

dingo, *ding'gō*, *n.* the native dog of Australia:—*pl.* **ding'oes** (*-ōz*). [Native name.]

dingy, *din'ji*, *adj.* of a dim or dark colour: dull: soiled.—*n.* **din'giness.** [Origin obscure.]

dinkum, *ding'kum*, *adj.* (*Austr. slang*) real, genuine, honest, square.—Also *adv.*

dinner, *din'ér*, *n.* the chief meal of the day: a feast.—*n.* **dinn'er-wag'on**, (orig.) a movable piece of furniture with shelves, for a dining-room: now a tiered sideboard. [O.Fr. *disner*, properly breakfast. See **dine.**]

dinosaur, *dī'no-sör*, *n.* any of an order of extinct (Mesozoic) reptiles from two to eighty feet long. [Gr. *deinos*, terrible, and *sauros*, lizard.]

dinotherium, *dī-no-thē'ri-um*, *n.* an extinct

Neutral vowels in unaccented syllables: *em'pér-ór*; for certain sounds in foreign words see p. ix.

animal of huge size, with elephant-like tusks and trunk. [Gr. *deinos*, terrible, *thērion*, a beast.]

dint, *dint*, *n.* a blow or stroke: the mark of a blow: force (as in *by dint of*).—*v.t.* to make a dint in. [O.E. *dynt*, a blow; Scot. *dunt*, a blow with a dull sound, O.N. *dyntr*.]

diocese, *dī'o-sēs*, *-sis*, *n.* the circuit or extent of a bishop's jurisdiction.—*adj.* **diocesan** (*dī-os'ésn*, *-ēzn*), pertaining to a diocese. *n.* a bishop as regards his diocese. [Through Fr. and L. from Gr. *dioikēsis*—*dioikeein*, to keep house—*oikos*, a house.]

diode, *dī'ōd*, *n.* the simplest electron tube with heated cathode and anode: a two-electrode semi-conductor device evolved from primitive crystal rectifiers. [Gr. *di-*, twice, *hodos*, way.]

dioecious, *dī-ē'shús*, *adj.* having the sexes separate: having male and female flowers on different plants. [Gr. *di-*, twice, *oikos*, a house.]

diorama, *dī-o-rä'ma*, *n.* an exhibition of pictures, illuminated, and viewed through an opening.—*adj.* **dioram'ic**. [Gr. *dia*, through, *horama*, a sight.]

dip, *dip*, *v.t.* to plunge into any liquid for a moment: to lower and raise again (as a flag).—*v.i.* to sink: (with *into*) to take a casual glance at or interest in: to incline downwards.—*prp.* dipp'ing; *pa.p.* dipped.—*n.* the action of dipping: angular inclination downwards: (*geol.*) the angle a stratum of rock makes with a horizontal plane: a bath: a short swim: a candle made by dipping a wick in tallow: liquid or creamy mixture into which bread, biscuits, &c. are dipped.—*n.* **sheep-dip** (*see* **sheep**). [O.E. *dyppan*, causal of *dypan*, to plunge in—*dēop*, deep.]

dipetalous, *dī-pet'a-lus*, *adj.* having two petals. [Gr. *di-*, twice, and *petalon*, a leaf.]

diphtheria, *dif-thē'ri-a*, *n.* an infectious throat disease in which the air-passages become covered with a leathery membrane.—*adjs.* **diphther'ic**, **diphtherit'ic**. [Gr. *diphthera*, leather.]

diphthong, *dif'thong*, *n.* two vowel-sounds (represented by one letter or by two) pronounced as one syllable, as in *my* (*ma'i*), *roam* (*rō'um*) and other so-called 'long vowels': (*loosely*) a diagraph: the ligature æ or œ.—*adj.* **diphthongal** (*dif-thong'gal*), relating to, of the nature of, a diphthong.—*v.t.* **diphthongise** (*dif'thong-gīz*, or *-īz*). [Gr. *diphthongos*, with two sounds—*di-*, twice, *phthongos*, sound.]

diploma, *di-plō'ma*, *n.* a writing conferring some honour or privilege: a certificate. [L.,—Gr. *diplōma*, a letter folded double—*diploos*, double.]

diplomacy, *di-plō'ma-si*, *n.* the art of negotiation, esp. of treaties between states: political skill: tact.—*adjs.* **diplomat'ic**, **-al**, pertaining to diplomacy: skilful in negotiation.—*adv.* **diplomat'ically**.—*ns.* **diplo'matist**, **dip'lomat**, one skilled in diplomacy.—**diplomatic corps**, the whole body of foreign diplomatists resident in any capital. [From **diploma**.]

dipole, *dī'pōl*, *n.* two equal and opposite electric charges or magnetic poles of opposite sign a small distance apart: a body or system having such: a type of aerial.—*adj.* **dipol'ar**, having

two poles. [Pfx. **di-**, and **pole**.]

dipper, *dip'ér*, *n.* one that dips: a ladle: a bird that dips or dives for food, as the water-ouzel, the dabchick: (*cap.*) the Plough (q.v.). [**dip**.]

dipsomania, *dip-sō-mā'ni-a*, *n.* a morbid craving for alcoholic stimulants.—*n.* **dipsomā'niac**. [Gr. *dipsa*, thirst, and *mania*, madness.]

Diptera, *dip'tér-a*, *n.pl.* an order of two-winged insects.—*adjs.* **dip'terous**, **dip'teral**. [Gr. *dipteros*, two-winged—*di-*, twice, *pteron*, a wing.]

diptych, *dip'tik*, *n.* a double-folding writing-tablet: a pair of pictures as folding-tablets. [Gr. *diptychos*—*di-*, twice, *ptyssein*, to fold.]

dire, *dīr*, *adj.* dreadful: calamitous in a high degree.—*adj.* **dire'ful**.—*adv.* **dire'fully.**—*n.* **dire'fulness**. [L. *dīrus*; cf. Gr. *deinos*, frightful.]

direct, *di-rekt'*, *dī'rekt*, *adj.* straight: straightforward: immediate: lineal, not collateral: outspoken, frank.—*v.t.* (*lit.* and *fig.*) to turn in a particular direction (e.g. *to direct one's steps towards, one's attention or energies towards, one's remarks to a person*): (*fig.*) to aim (at) in hostile spirit: to instruct, order: to tell, point out, the way (to): to guide: to instruct, send (unemployed persons, labour) to work at a particular place or in a particular occupation: to control, to regulate: to mark with the name and residence of a person: to guide, control the production of (a motion picture).—*n.* **direc'tion**, aim at a certain point: the line or course in which anything moves: guidance: command: the body of persons who guide or manage a matter: the written name and residence of a person: (*pl.*) instructions (for the use of something).—*adjs.* **direc'tional**, relating to direction in space; **direct'ive**, having power or tendency to direct.—*n.* a general instruction as to procedure or tactics, issued by a higher authority.—*adv.* **direct'ly**, in a direct manner: without intermediary: immediately (in time and otherwise).—*ns.* **direct'ness**; **direct'or**, one who directs: a manager or governor: a counsellor: a spiritual guide: part of a machine or instrument that guides its motion.—*fem.* **direct'ress**, **direct'rix**,—*ns.* **direct'orate**, **direct'orship**, the office of director: a body of directors.—*adjs.* **directō'rial**; **direct'ory**, containing directions: guiding.—*n.* a body of directions: a guide: a book with the names and residences of the inhabitants of a place: a body of directors.—**direct current**, an electric current flowing in one direction only; **direct speech**, speech reported as spoken, in the very words of the speaker (L. *oratio recta*); **direct tax**, one levied directly on the person who bears the burden of it, e.g. an income tax or property tax—cf. *indirect tax*; **direction-find'er**, a wireless receiver that determines the direction of arrival of incoming waves. [L. *dīrigēre*, *dīrectum*—*di-*, apart, and *regere*, to rule, to make straight.]

dirge, *dûrj*, *n.* a funeral song or hymn. [Contracted from *dīrige* (imper. of *dīrigēre*, to direct) the first word of Psalm v. 8 in the Vulgate, sung in the office for the dead.]

dirigible, *dir'i-ji-bl*, *adj.* that can be directed.—*n.* a navigable balloon or airship. [From root of **direct**.]

dirk, *dûrk*, *n.* a Highland dagger.—*v.t.* to stab with a dirk. [Ety. unknown.]

dirt, *dûrt*, *n.* any filthy substance, such as dung, mud, &c.: foreign matter adhering to anything: loose earth: (*fig.*) obscenity: spiteful gossip.—*adj.* **dirt'-cheap**, very cheap.—*n.* **dirt'-track**, a motor-cycle racing track with earthy or cindery surface.—*adj.* **dirt'y**, foul, filthy: unclean: despicable: mean.—*v.t.* to soil with dirt: to sully.—*pr.p.* **dirt'ying**; *pa.p.* **dirt'ied.**—*adv.* **dirt'ily.**—*n.* **dirt'iness.** [M.E. *drit*, prob.—O.N. *drit*, excrement.]

dis-, di-, *dis-*, *di-*, *pfx.* in two, asunder: negative: privative: intensive. [L. *dis-*, *di-*]

disable, *dis-ā'bl*, *v.t.* to deprive of power (with *for*, *from*): to cripple: to disqualify.—*ns.* **dis-ā'blement; disabil'ity**, want of power: want of legal qualification: disqualification. [L. *dis-*, priv., and **able.**]

disabuse, *dis-a-būz'*, *v.t.* to undeceive or set right. [L. *dis-*, priv., and **abuse.**]

disadvantage, *dis-ad-vänt'ij*, *n.* unfavourable circumstance or condition: loss, detriment.—*adj.* **disadvantā'geous**, attended with disadvantage: unfavourable.—*adv.* **disadvantā'geously.** [L. *dis-*, priv., and **advantage.**]

disaffect, *dis-a-fekt'*, *v.t.* to make discontented or unfriendly.—*pa.p.* and *adj.* **disaffect'ed**, ill-disposed, disloyal.—*adv.* **disaffect'edly.**—*ns.* **disaffect'edness, disaffec'tion**, state of being disaffected: want of affection or friendliness: alienation: disloyalty. [L. *dis-*, priv., **affect.**]

disaffirm, *dis-a-fûrm'*, *v.t.* to deny (what has been affirmed), to contradict. [L. *dis-*, neg., and **affirm.**]

disafforest, *dis-a-for'est*, *v.t.* to deprive of the privilege of forest laws: to clear of forest. [L. *dis-*, neg., and Low L. *afforestāre*, to make into a forest. See **forest.**]

disagree, *dis-a-grē'*, *v.i.* to differ or be at variance: to dissent: to prove unsuitable, as of food.—*adj.* **disagree'able**, not agreeable, unpleasant, offensive.—*n.* **disagree'ableness**;—*adv.* **disagree'ably.**—*n.* **disagree'ment**, want of agreement: incongruity: a dispute. [L. *dis-*, neg., and **agree.**]

disallow, *dis-a-low'*, *v.t.* not to allow, to refuse to sanction: to deny the authority, validity, or truth of, to reject. [O.Fr. *desalouer*—*des-* (L. *dis-*), neg., *alouer.* See **allow.**]

disannul, *dis-a-nul'*, *v.t.* to annul completely.—*n.* **disannul'ment.** [L. *dis-*, inten., and **annul.**]

disappear, *dis-a-pēr'*, *v.i.* to vanish from sight: to fade out of existence.—*n.* **disappear'ance**, a ceasing to be in sight or existence: removal from sight, secret withdrawal. [L. *dis-*, neg., and **appear.**]

disappoint, *dis-a-point'*, *v.t.* to frustrate, fall short of, the hopes of (a person): to defeat the fulfilment of (e.g. hopes).—*n.* **disappoint'ment**, the defeat of one's hopes: frustration: vexation due to failure. [O.Fr. *desapointer*—*des-* (L. *dis-*), away, and *apointer*, to appoint. See **appoint.**]

disapprobation, *dis-ap-ro-bā'sh(ó)n*, *n.* disapproval. [L. *dis-*, neg., and **approbation.**]

disapprove, *dis-a-prōōv'*, *v.t.* and *v.i.* to give or have an unfavourable opinion (*v.i.* with *of*).—*n.* **disapprov'al**—*adv.* **disapprov'ingly.** [L. *dis-*, neg., and **approve.**]

disarm, *dis-ärm'*, *v.t.* to deprive of weapons: to render defenceless or harmless: (*fig.*) to conciliate.—*v.i.* to reduce national armaments.—*n.* **disarm'ament.**—*adj.* **disarm'ing**, (*fig.*) conciliating, instantly gaining good will or favour (e.g. of a manner, a smile). [L. *dis-*, priv., and **arm.**]

disarrange, *dis-a-rānj'*, *v.t.* to undo the arrangement of, to disorder, to derange.—*n.* **disarrange'ment.** [L. *dis-*, priv., and **arrange.**]

disarray, *dis-a-rā'*, *v.t.* to throw into disorder: to strip of array or dress.—*n.* want of array or order: undress. [L. *dis-*, priv., and **array.**]

disassociate, *dis-a-sō'shi-āt*, *v.t.* to disconnect: to dissociate. [L. *dis-*, priv., and **associate.**]

disaster, *diz-äs'tér*, *n.* an adverse or unfortunate event: great and sudden misfortune, calamity.—*adj.* **disas'trous**, calamitous, ruinous: gloomy, foreboding disaster.—*adv.* **disas'trously.** [O.Fr. *desastre*—*des-* (L. *dis-*), with evil sense, *astre*, a star, destiny—L. *astrum*, Gr. *astron*, star.]

disavow, *dis-a-vow'*, *v.t.* to disclaim, to disown, to deny.—*n.* **disavow'al.** [O.Fr. *desavouer*—*des-* (L. *dis-*), away, *avouer*, to avow. See **avow.**]

disband, *dis-band'*, *v.t.* to disperse, break up (esp. an army).—*v.i.* to break up.—*n.* **disband'ment.** [O.Fr. *desbander*, to unbind—*des-* (L. *dis-*), neg. *bander.*]

disbar, *dis-bär'*, *v.t.* to expel a barrister from the bar. [L. *dis-*, priv., and **bar.**]

disbelieve, *dis-bi-lēv'*, *v.t.* to believe to be false: to refuse belief or credit to.—*v.i.* to have no faith (in).—*ns.* **disbelief', disbeliev'er.** [L. *dis-*, neg., and **believe.**]

disburden, *dis-bûr'dn*, **disburthen**, *disbûr'тнn*, *v.t.* to rid of a burden, unload (e.g. a ship): (*fig.*) to free (of something oppressive). [L. *dis-*, priv., and **burden.**]

disburse, *dis-bûrs'*, *v.t.* to pay out.—*ns.* **disburs'al, disburse'ment.** [O.Fr. *desbourser*—*des-* (L. *dis-*), apart, and *bourse*, a purse.]

disc. Same as **disk.**

discard, *dis-kärd'*, *v.t.* and *v.i.* to throw away (a card) as useless: to cast off, get rid of. [L. *dis-*, away, and **card.**]

discern, *di-sûrn'*, *di-zûrn'*, *v.t.* to distinguish clearly by the eye or understanding: to detect: (*arch.*) to discriminate.—*n.* **discern'er.**—*adj.* **discern'ible**—*adv.* **discern'ibly.**—*p.adj.* **discern'ing**, discriminating, acute: having insight and understanding.—*n.* **discern'ment**, power or faculty of discriminating: acuteness, insight. [L. *discernĕre*—*dis-*, thoroughly, *cernĕre*, to perceive.]

discharge, *dis-chärj'*, *v.t.* to free from a charge in any sense: to unload, as a cargo: to set free: to acquit: to dismiss: to fire, as a gun: to let out, emit: to perform, as duties: to pay, as a debt.—*v.i.* to unload: to be released from a charged state.—*n.* act or process of discharging: that which is discharged: release: dismissal: acquittal: payment.—*n.* **discharg'er.**—**discharge tube**, a tube in which an electric discharge takes place in a vacuum or in a gas at low pressure. [O.Fr. *descharger*—*des-*, apart, and *charger.* See **charge.**]

disciple, *dis-ī'pl*, *n.* one who follows or believes in the doctrine of another: one of the twelve

---

Neutral vowels in unaccented syllables: *em'pér-òr*; for certain sounds in foreign words see p. ix.

198

apostles of Christ.—n. disci′pleship. [Fr.,—L. discipulus—discēre, to learn.]

discipline, dis′i-plin, n. instruction: a branch of learning, or field of study: training, or mode of life in accordance with rules: subjection to control: order maintained by control: penance.—v.t. to subject to discipline: to train: to bring under control: to chastise.—adj. **dis′ciplinable.**—n. **disciplinā′rian**, one who enforces strict discipline.—adj. **dis′ciplinary**, of the nature of discipline. [L. disciplīna, from discipulus. See **disciple**.]

disclaim, dis-klām′, v.t. to renounce all claim to: to refuse to acknowledge, to repudiate.—n. **disclaim′er**, a denial, disavowal, or renunciation. [O.Fr. disclaimer—L. dis-, apart, clāmāre, to cry out.]

disclose, dis-klōz′, v.t. (obs.) to unclose, open: to lay open, bring to light: to reveal.—n. **disclō′sure**, act of disclosing: a revelation: that which is disclosed. [O.Fr. desclos—L. dis-, apart, claudĕre, clausum, to shut.]

discobolus, dis-kob′o-lus, n. a quoit-thrower: the name of a famous ancient Greek statue. [L.,—Gr. diskos, a quoit, ballein, to throw.]

discoid, -al, dis′koid, -ál, adj. having the form of a disk. [Gr. diskos, a quoit, eidos, form.]

discolour, dis-kul′ór, v.t. to take away colour from: to change or to spoil the natural colour of: to stain.—Also v.i.—n. **discolo(u)rā′tion**, act of discolouring: state of being discoloured: stain. [O.Fr. descolorer—L. dis-, apart, and colōrāre—color, colour.]

discomfit, dis-kum′fit, v.t. to disconcert, abash: to balk: to defeat, rout:—pr.p. **discom′fiting**; pa.p. **discom′fited.**—n. **discom′fiture**. [O.Fr. desconfit, pa.p. of desconfire—L. dis-, neg. conficĕre, to prepare—con-, inten., facĕre, to make.]

discomfort, dis-kum′fôrt, n. want of comfort, uneasiness.—v.t. to deprive of comfort, to make uneasy. [O.Fr. desconforter—des-, apart, conforter, to comfort. See **comfort**.]

discommode, dis-kom-ōd′, v.t. to inconvenience. [L. dis-, priv., and obs. commode—L. commodāre—commodus. See **commodious**.]

discompose, dis-kom-pōz′, v.t. to deprive of composure, agitate: to disarrange, disorder.—n. **discompō′sure**. [L. dis-, priv., and **compose**.]

disconcert, dis-kon-sûrt′, v.t. to throw into confusion, frustrate (e.g. plans): to abash, embarrass, fluster, take aback. [O.Fr. disconcerter—des- (L. dis-), apart, and concerter, to concert.]

disconnect, dis-kon-ekt′, v.t. to separate or disjoin.—p.adj. **disconnect′ed**, separated: incoherent.—n. **disconnexion, disconnec′tion**. [L. dis-, priv., and **connect**.]

disconsolate, dis-kon′so-lát, adj. without consolation or comfort, forlorn, dejected.—adv. **discon′solately.** [L. dis-, neg., and consolārī, consōlātus, to console.]

discontent, dis-kon-tent′, adj. not content, dissatisfied (with).—n. want of contentment: dissatisfaction: ill-humour.—v.t. to deprive of content.—p.adj. **discontent′ed**, dissatisfied: fretful.—adv. **discontent′edly.**—ns. **discontent′edness; discontent′ment**, discontent. [L. dis-, priv., and **content**.]

discontinue, dis-kon-tin′ū, v.t. to leave off, to stop: to put an end to.—v.i. to cease.—ns. **discontin′uance, discontinuā′tion**, a breaking off or ceasing; **discontinu′ity**, want of continuity or of coherence.—adj. **discontin′uous**, not continuous, interrupted, intermittent. [O.Fr. discontinuer—L. dis-, neg., and continuāre, to continue.]

discord, dis′kord, n. opposite of concord: disagreement, strife: a combination of inharmonious sounds, esp. unintentional (cf. **dissonance**): uproarious noise.—ns. **discord′ance, discord′ancy.**—adj. **discord′ant**, without concord or agreement: harsh, jarring: inconsistent, contradictory.—adv. **discord′antly.** [O.Fr. descord—L. discordia—dis-, priv., and cor, cordis, the heart.]

discothèque, -theque, dis′ko-tek, dēs-kō-tek, n. a place where music for dancing is provided by records. [Fr.]

discount, dis′kownt, n. a sum taken from the reckoning: a sum returned to the payer of an account: a deduction made for interest in advancing money on a bill.—v.t. **discount′**, to allow discount on: to pay beforehand the present value of: (fig.) to put a reduced value on (e.g. a story, by allowing for exaggeration): to leave out of account, ignore.—v.i. to practise discounting—adj. **discount′able.**—n. **discount′er.**—**at a discount**, below par: not in demand. [O.Fr. descompter—des- (L. dis-), away, compter, to count.]

discountenance, dis-kown′ten-áns, v.t. to refuse countenance or support to, to discourage: to abash. [O.Fr. descontenancer—des-, neg., contenance, countenance.]

discourage, dis-kur′ij, v.t. to take away the courage of, to dishearten: to oppose by showing disfavour.—n. **discour′agement**, act of discouraging: that which discourages: dejection. [O.Fr. descourager (—descoragier)—L. dis-, neg See **courage**.]

discourse, dis-kōrs′, -kôrs′, or dis′-, n. (obs.) the reasoning faculty: (arch.) conversation: a treatise, a speech, a sermon.—v.i. to talk or converse: to hold forth (with of, upon).—v.t. to give forth, as music. [Fr. discours—L. discursus—dis-, away, currĕre, to run.]

discourteous, dis-kûrt′yus, adj. wanting in courtesy, uncivil.—adv. **discourt′eously.**—ns. **discourt′eousness, discourt′esy.** [L. dis-, neg., and **courtesy**.]

discover, dis-kuv′er, v.t. to uncover: to lay open or expose, to make known: to manifest, exhibit: to espy: to find out.—adj. **discover′able.**—ns. **discov′erer; discov′ery**, the act of finding out: the thing discovered: ascertainment by investigation: exploration: (arch.) unravelling of plot. [O.Fr. descouvrir—des (L. dis-), away, couvrir, to cover.]

discredit, dis-kred′it, n. want of credit, doubt: ill-repute: source of disgrace.—v.t. to refuse credit to, or belief in: to deprive of credibility: to disgrace, bring into disrepute.—adj. **discred′itable**, not creditable, disgraceful.—adv. **discred′itably.** [L. dis-, **credit**.]

discreet, dis-krēt′, adj. having discernment: wary, circumspect, prudent.—adv. **discreet′ly.**—n. **discreet′ness.** [O.Fr. discret—L. discrētus—discernĕre, to separate, to perceive. See **discern, discrete**.]

discrepancy · disfranchise

discrepancy, *dis-krep'ǎn-si*, or *dis'-*, *n.* disagreement, variance (of facts or sentiments).—*adj.* **discrep'ant**, contrary, disagreeing. [Fr.,—L. *discrepāns*, *-antis*, different—*dis-*, asunder, and *crepāns*, pr.p. of *crepāre*, to sound.]

discrete, *dis'krēt*, *dis-krēt'*, *adj.* separate: consisting of distinct parts: abstract—opposite of *concrete.—adv.* **discrete'ly.—***n.* **discrete'ness.** [A doublet of **discreet**.]

discretion, *dis-kresh'(ö)n*, *n.* quality · of being discreet: prudence: one's own judgment (e.g. *they left it to his discretion what to do then*).—*adjs.* **discre'tional**, **discre'tionary**, left to discretion: unrestricted.—**at the discretion of**, left to the judgment or will of; **surrender at discretion**, to surrender unconditionally. [O.Fr. *discrecion*—L. *discrētiō*, *-ōnis*—*discernĕre*, *-crētum*. See **discern**.]

discriminant, *dis-krim'i-nǎnt*, *n.* (*math.*) the discriminant of an equation is a special function of the roots of the equation, expressible in terms of the coefficients; if it equals zero, at least two of the roots are equal. [L. *discrīminans*, *-antis*, pr.p. of *discrīmināre*. See **discriminate**.]

discriminate, *dis-krim'i-nāt*, *v.t.* to constitute the difference between: to note the difference between, to distinguish (from).—*v.i.* to make a difference or distinction: (with *in favour of*, *against*) to treat favourably or unfavourably in comparsion with others.—*p.adj.* **discrim'inating**, making distinctions: gifted with judgment and penetration.—*n.* **discrimina'tion**, act or quality of discriminating: discernment, judgment.—*adj.* **discrim'inative**, that marks a difference: characteristic: observing distinctions.—*adv.* **discrim'inatively.—***adj.* **discrim'inatory**, discriminative. [L. *discrīmināre*, *-ātum*—*discrīmen*, that which separates—root of *discernĕre*. See **discern**.]

discrown, *dis-krown'*, *v.t.* to deprive of a crown. [L. *dis-*, priv., and **crown**.]

discursive, *dis-kûr'siv*, *adj.* (*lit.*) running to and fro: (*fig.*) apt to stray from the main theme: (*logic*) proceeding regularly from premises to conclusion.—*adv.* **discur'sively.—***n.* **discur'siveness.** [L. *dīs-*, *currĕre*, run.]

discus, *dis'kus*, *n.* a disk, circular plate: a heavy disk thrown for distance in competition in ancient and modern Olympic games and other athletic contests. [L.,—Gr. *diskos.*]

discuss, *dis-kus'*, *v.t.* to examine in detail, or by argument: to debate: (*coll.*) to consume, as food.—*n.* **discuss'ion**, debate. [L. *discutĕre*, *discussum*—*dis-*, asunder, *quatĕre*, to shake.]

disdain, *dis-dān'*, *v.t.* to think unworthy or unfit: to scorn, reject.—*n.* scornful aversion: haughtiness.—*adj.* **disdain'ful.—***adv.* **disdain'fully.—***n.* **disdain'fulness.** [O.Fr. *desdaigner* with substitution of *des-* (L. *dis-*) for L. *dē* in L. *dēdignārī*—*dignus*, worthy.]

disease, *diz-ēz'*, *n.* want of ease (in this sense pron. *dis-ēz'*): want of health in mind or body: ailment.—*p.adj.* **diseased'**, affected with disease.—*n.* **diseas'edness.** [O.Fr. *desaise*—*des-* (L. *dis-*), neg., *aise*, ease.]

disembark, *dis-ĕm-bärk'*, *v.t.* to set ashore.—*v.i.* to quit a ship, to land.—*ns.* **disembarkā'tion**, **disembark'ment.** [O.Fr. *desembarquer*—*des-* (L. *dis-*), neg., *embarquer*. See **embark**.]

disembarrass, *dis-ĕm-bar'as*, *v.t.* to free from embarrassment or perplexity: rid (of).—*n.* **disembarr'assment.** [L. *dis-*, priv., and **embarrass**.]

disembody, *dis-ĕm-bod'i*, *v.t.* to take away from or out of the body (esp. of the spirit): to discharge from military service or array. [L. *dis-*, priv., and **embody**.]

disembogue, *dis-ĕm-bōg'*, *v.t.* and *v.i.* to discharge at the mouth, as a stream.—*n.* **disembogue'ment.** [Sp. *desembocar*—*des-* (L. *dis-*), asunder, *embocar*, to enter the mouth—*em* (L. *in*), into, *boca* (L. *bucca*), cheek, mouth.]

disembowel, *dis-ĕm-bow'ĕl*, *v.t.* to take out the bowels or inside of. [L. *dis-*, priv., and **embowel**.]

disenchant, *dis-ĕn-chänt'*, *v.t.* to free from enchantment or illusion.—*n.* **disenchant'ment.** [L. *dis-*, priv., and **enchant**.]

disencumber, *dis-ĕn-kum'bĕr*, *v.t.* to free from encumbrance, to disburden.—*n.* **disencum'brance.** [L. *dis-*, priv., and **encumber**.]

disendow, *dis-ĕn-dow'*, *v.t.* to take away the endowments of (esp. of an established church).—*n.* **disendow'ment.** [L. *dis-*, priv., and **endow**.]

disengage, *dis-ĕn-gāj'*, *v.t.* to separate or free from being engaged: to separate: to release.—*n.* **disengage'ment**, a separating, releasing: a mutual withdrawal of potential combatants from a position.—*p.adj.* **disengaged'**, at leisure, not engaged. [O.Fr. *desengager*—*des-* (L. *dis-*), neg., *engager*, to engage.]

disentail, *dis-ĕn-tāl'*, *v.t.* to break the entail of (an estate). [L. *dis-*, priv., and **entail**.]

disentangle, *dis-ĕn-tang'gl*, *v.t.* to free from entanglement or disorder: to unravel: to disengage or set free.—*n.* **disentang'lement.** [L. *dis-*, priv., and **entangle**.]

disenthral, disenthrall, *dis-ĕn-thröl'*, *v.t.* to free from enthralment. [L. *dis-*, priv., and **enthral**.]

disentitle, *dis-ĕn-tī'tl*, *v.t.* to deprive of title. [L. *dis-*, priv., and **entitle**.]

disentomb, *dis-ĕn-tōōm'*, *v.t.* to take out from a tomb. [L. *dis-*, priv., and **entomb**.]

disentrance, *dis-ĕn-träns'*, *v.t.* to awaken from a trance, enchantment, or reverie. [L. *dis-*, priv., and **entrance**, vb.]

disestablish, *dis-es-tab'lish*, *v.t.* to deprive (a church) of state support hitherto legally afforded to it.—*n.* **disestab'lishment.** [L. *dis-*, priv., and **establish**.]

disesteem, *dis-es-tēm'*, *n.* want of esteem, disfavour.—*v.t.* to disapprove, to dislike. [L. *dis-*, priv., and **esteem**.]

diseuse, *dē-zœz*, *n.* a woman who, as a profession, gives solo dramatic turns. [Fr., fem. of *diseur*, one who recites.]

disfavour, *dis-fā'vôr*, *n.* want of favour, displeasure, dislike: condition of being out of favour.—*v.t.* to withhold favour from, to disapprove. [L. *dis-*, priv., and **favour**.]

disfigure, *dis-fig'ŭr*, *v.t.* to spoil the beauty or excellence of, to deface.—*ns.* **disfig'urement**, **disfigūrā'tion.** [O.Fr. *desfigurer*—L. *dis-*, neg., *figūrāre*, to figure.]

disfranchise, *dis-fran'chīz*, *-shīz*, *v.t.* to deprive of a franchise, or of rights and privileges, esp. that of voting for an M.P.—*n.* **disfran'chisement.** [L. *dis-*, priv., and **franchise**.]

Neutral vowels in unaccented syllables: *em'pér-ôr*; for certain sounds in foreign words see p. ix.

disfrock, dis-frok', v.t. to unfrock (q.v.). [L. dis-, priv., and **frock**.]

disgorge, dis-görj', v.t. to discharge from the throat, to vomit: to throw out with violence: to give up (what one has wrongfully seized). [O.Fr. desgorger—des- (L. dis-), away, gorge, throat. See **gorge**.]

disgrace, dis-grās', n. state of being out of grace or favour: cause of shame: dishonour.—v.t. to put out of favour: to bring disgrace or shame upon.—adj. **disgrace'ful**, bringing disgrace: causing shame: dishonourable.—adv. **disgrace'fully**—n **disgrace'fulness**. [Fr. disgrâce—L. dis-, neg., and gratia, favour, grace.]

disgruntle, dis-grun'tl, v.t. to disappoint, make dissatisfied and morose. [L. dis-, inten., and gruntle, freq. of **grunt**.]

disguise, dis-gīz', v.t. to conceal by a dress intended to deceive, or by a counterfeit manner: to conceal by misrepresenting (as): to hide, cloak (e.g. intentions).—n. a dress intended to conceal the identity of the wearer: a false appearance. [O.Fr. desguiser—des- (L. dis-), neg., guise, manner. See **guise**.]

disgust, dis-gust', n. loathing, strong distaste, nausea.—v.t. to excite disgust in.—adv. **disgust'edly**.—adjs. **disgust'ing**, **disgust'ful**.—adv. **disgust'ingly**. [O.Fr. desgouster—des- (L. dis-), and gouster (L. gustāre), to taste.]

dish, dish, n. a vessel in which food is served: the food in a dish: a particular kind of food: a concave reflector used for directive radiation and reception, esp. for radar or radio telescopes.—v.t. to put in a dish, for table: (coll.) to circumvent, outwit. (coll.) to ruin.—ns. **dish'-clout**, **dish'-cloth**, a cloth for wiping dishes. **dish out**, to serve out: (fig.; coll.; usu. disparagingly) to give out; **dish up**, to serve up, esp. (fig.) of old materials cooked up anew. [O.E. disc, a plate, a dish, a table—L. discus—Gr. diskos.]

dishabille, dis-a-bēl', n. a careless toilet: undress.—Also **deshabille**. [Fr. deshabillé, pa.p. of deshabiller, to undress—des (L. dis), apart, habiller, to dress.]

disharmony, dis-här'mo-ni, n. lack of harmony: discord: incongruity. [L. dis-, priv., and **harmony**.]

dishearten, dis-härt'n, v.t. to deprive of heart, courage, or spirits, to discourage, to depress. [L. dis-, priv., and **hearten**.]

dishevel, di-shev'el, v.t. to disorder, as hair:—pr.p. dishev'elling; pa.p. and adj. **dishev'elled**, untidy, unkempt. [O.Fr. discheveler—Low L. discapillāre, to tear out or disorder the hair—L. dis-, in different directions, capillus, the hair.]

dishonest, dis-on'est, adj. not honest: wanting integrity: disposed to cheat: insincere.—adv. **dishon'estly**.—n. **dishon'esty**. [O.Fr. deshoneste—des- (L. dis), neg., honeste (L. honestus), honest.]

dishonour, dis-on'ör, n. want of honour: disgrace: shame, reproach.—v.t. to deprive of honour: to treat with indignity: to disgrace: to seduce: to refuse the payment of, as a cheque.—adj. **dishon'ourable**, having no sense of honour: disgraceful.—n. **dishon'ourableness**.—adv. **dishon'ourably**. [O.Fr. deshonneur—des- (L. dis-), neg., honneur (L. honor),

honour.]

disillusion, dis-i-l(y)ōō'zh(ô)n, n. act of setting free from illusion: state of being freed from illusion.—v.t. to set free from illusion: to undeceive.—p.adj. freed from illusions, esp. taking a cynical view of human nature and human affairs.—n. **disillu'sionment**. [L. dis-, priv., and **illusion**.]

disincentive, dis-in-sen'tiv, n. a discouragement to effort.—Also adj. [L. dis-, and **incentive**.]

disinclination, dis-in-kli-nā'sh(ô)n, n. want of inclination, unwillingness.—v.t. **disincline'**, to make unwilling (to, for).—adj. **disinclined'**, not inclined: averse (to). [L. dis-, priv., and **incline**.]

disincorporate, dis-in-kör'po-rāt, v.t. to deprive of corporate rights. [L. dis-, priv., and **incorporate**.]

disinfect, dis-in-fekt', v.t. to cleanse from infection.—n. **disinfect'ant**, anything that destroys the causes of infection.—Also adj.—ns. **disinfec'tion**, **disinfect'or**. [L. dis-, priv., and **infect**.]

disingenuous, dis-in-jen'ū-us, adj. not ingenuous, not frank or open, crafty.—adv. **disingen'uously**.—n. **disingen'uousness**. [L. dis-, neg., and **ingenuous**.]

disinherit, dis-in-her'it, v.t. to cut off from hereditary rights, to deprive of an inheritance.—n. **disinher'itance**. [L. dis-, priv., and **inherit**.]

disintegrate, dis-in'ti-grāt, v.t. and v.i. to separate into parts: to crumble.—ns. **disintegra'tion**; **disin'tegrator**, a machine for crushing oil-cake, mineral ores, &c. [L. dis-, neg., and **integrate**.]

disinter, dis-in-tûr', v.t. to take out of a grave or from obscurity.—n. **disinter'ment**. [L. dis-, neg., and **inter**.]

disinterested, dis-in'tér-est-ed, adj. not inspired or influenced by private feelings or considerations: impartial: (wrongly) uninterested—adv. **disin'terestedly**.—n. **disin'terestedness**. [L. dis-, neg., and **interested**.]

disjoin, dis-join', v.t. to separate what has been joined.—v.i. **disjoint'**, to put out of joint: to separate united parts: to break the natural order or relations of things.—p.adj. **disjoint'ed**, incoherent, esp. of discourse.—adv. **disjoint'edly**.—n. **disjoint'edness**. [O.Fr. desjoindre—L. disjungĕre—dis-, apart, jungĕre, to join.]

disjunct, dis-jungkt', adj. disjoined.—n. **disjunc'tion**, the act of disjoining: disunion: separation.—adj. **disjunc'tive**, disjoining: tending to separate: (gram.) uniting sentences but marking a contrast in sense (e.g. of conjunctions such as either, or).—n. a word which disjoins.—adv. **disjunc'tively**. [O.Fr. desjoinct—desjoindre. See **disjoin**.]

disk, **disc**, disk, n. a quoit thrown by athletes: any flat thin circular body: the circular figure presented by a spherical body, as the sun: a layer of fibrocartilage (cartilage with embedded fibres) between vertebrae, which sometimes slips out of position and causes pain: a gramophone record.—**disk brake**, one in which the friction is obtained by pads hydraulically forced against a disk on the wheel; **disk'-jockey** (slang), one who announces and provides a commentary on a programme of popular recorded music; **disk'-park'ing**, a system according to which the motorist is responsible for affixing to his car special disk(s) showing his time of arrival and the time when permitted parking ends, there being no charge during the permitted period. [Gr. *diskos*.]

dislike, *dis-līk'*, *v.t.* to be displeased with, to disapprove of, to have an aversion to.—*n.* disinclination: aversion, distaste, disapproval. [L. *dis-*, neg., and **like**; the genuine Eng. word is *mislike*.]

dislocate, *dis'lo-kāt*, *v.t.* (*lit.* and *fig.*) to put out of joint: to displace.—*n.* **disloca'tion**, a dislocated joint: displacement: (*geol.*) a fault. [Low L. *dislocāre, -ātum*—L. *dis-*, apart, *locāre*, to place.]

dislodge, *dis-loj'*, *v.t.* to drive from a place of rest, or of hiding, or of defence: to force, or to knock accidentally, out from its place.—*n.* **dislodg(e)'ment**. [O.Fr. *desloger, des-* (L. *dis-*), apart, *loger*, to lodge.]

disloyal, *dis-loi'ál*, *adj.* not loyal, false, faithless.—*adv.* **disloy'ally.**—*n.* **disloy'alty**. [O.Fr. *desloyal—des-* (L. *dis-*), neg., *loyal, leial*—L. *lēgālis*, legal.]

dismal, *diz'mál*, *adj.* gloomy, dreary, cheerless.—*adv.* **dis'mally.** [O.Fr. *dismal*—L. *dies malī*, evil, unlucky days.]

dismantle, *dis-man'tl*, *v.t.* to strip, deprive of furniture, fittings, &c., so as to render useless: to raze the fortifications of. [O.Fr. *desmanteller—des-* (L. *dis-*), away, *manteler—mantel*, a mantle.]

dismast, *dis-mäst'*, *v.t.* to deprive of a mast or masts. [L. *dis-*, priv., and **mast**.]

dismay, *dis-mā'*, *v.t.* to appal: to discourage.—*n.* loss of strength and courage through fear: consternation. [Apparently through O.Fr.—L. *dis-*, and O.H.G. *magan* (O.E. *magan*), to have might or power. See **may**.]

dismember, *dis-mem'bér*, *v.t.* (*obs.*) to separate a limb from the body: to tear limb from limb: to tear to pieces.—*n.* **dismem'berment**. [O.Fr. *desmembrer—des-* (L. *dis-*), neg., *membre* (L. *membrum*), a member.]

dismiss, *dis-mis'*, *v.t.* to send away, disperse: to put away (from one's thoughts), refuse to consider: to remove from office or employment: (*law*) to reject, to put out of court, to discharge: (*cricket*) to put out (batsman, -men).—*ns.* **dismiss'al, dismiss'ion**. [L. *dis-*, away, *mittēre, missum*, to send.]

dismount, *dis-mownt'*, *v.i.* to come down: to come off a horse.—*v.t.* to cast down or remove from any elevated place as a stand, framework: to unhorse. [O.Fr. *desmonter—des-* (L. *dis-*), neg., *monter*, to mount.]

disobedient, *dis-o-bēd'yént*, *adj.* neglecting, or refusing, to obey.—*n.* **disobe'dience.**—*adv.* **disobe'diently.** [L. *dis-*, neg., and **obedient**.]

disobey, *dis-o-bā'*, *v.t.* to neglect, or refuse, to obey or do what is commanded. [O.Fr. *desobeir—des-* (L. *dis-*), and *obeir*, to obey.]

disoblige, *dis-o-blīj'*, *v.t.* to relieve from an obligation: to show disregard of claims or wishes of (a person).—*adj.* **disoblig'ing**, not obliging: not careful to attend to the wishes of others, unaccommodating: unkind.—*adv.* **disoblig'ingly.** [L. *dis-*, neg., and **oblige**.]

disorder, *dis-ör'dér*, *n.* want of order, confusion: disturbance, breach of the peace: a disease.—*v.t.* to throw out of order, disarrange: to upset the health of.—*adj.* **disor'dered**, confused, deranged.—*adj.* **disor'derly**, out of order, in confusion: irregular, lawless.—*n.* **disor'derliness.**—**disorderly house**, a gaming house, &c.: often a brothel. [O.Fr. *desordre—des-* (L. *dis-*), neg., *ordre*, order.]

disorganise, *dis-ör'gan-īz*, *v.t.* to destroy the organic structure of: to throw into disorder.—*n.* **disorganisā'tion.** [L. *dis-*, neg., and **organise**.]

disown, *dis-ōn'*, *v.t.* to refuse to acknowledge as belonging to oneself, to disclaim: to repudiate, cast off. [L. *dis-*, neg., and **own**.]

disparage, *dis-par'ij*, *v.t.* to bring discredit on (e.g. *to disparage glorious arms*): to talk slightingly of.—*ns.* **dispar'agement, dispar'ager.**—*adv.* **dispar'agingly.** [O.Fr. *desparager—des-* (L. *dis-*), neg., and *parage*, equality of birth—L. *par*, equal.]

disparate, *dis'pár-át*, *adj.* unequal, incapable of being compared. [L. *disparātus—dis-*, neg., and *parāre*, make ready; influenced by *dispar*, unequal.]

disparity, *dis-par'i-ti*, *n.* inequality, difference in age, amount, &c. (sometimes implying incongruity): the quality of being unlike. [L. *dispar*, unequal—*dis-*, neg., *par*, equal.]

dispark, *dis-pärk'*, *v.t.* to throw open enclosed ground. [L. *dis-*, neg., and **park**.]

dispart, *dis-pärt'*, *v.t.* to part asunder: to divide, to separate.—*v.i.* to separate. [L. *dis-*, asunder, and **part**.]

dispassion, *dis-pash'(ó)n*, *n.* freedom from passion: calm state of mind.—*adj.* **dispass'ionate** (-*át*), free from passion, cool, impartial.—*adv.* **dispass'ionately.** [L. *dis-*, neg., and **passion**.]

dispatch, despatch, *dis-pach'* *v.t* to send away (to some place, e.g. a messenger): to put to death: to dispose of: to perform speedily.—*n.* a sending away (e.g. of mails): rapid performance: haste: that which is despatched, as a message, esp. telegraphic: (*pl.*) state-papers (military, diplomatic, &c.).—*ns.* **dispatch'-box**, a box for holding dispatches or valuable papers; **dispatch-rider**, a carrier of dispatches on motor-bicycle, &c. [It. *dispacciare*, or Sp. *despachar*—L. *dis-*, apart, and root of *pangēre, pactum*, to fasten; not conn. with Fr. *dépêcher*.]

dispeace, *dis-pēs'*, *n.* lack of peace, dissension. [L. *dis-*, neg., and **peace**.]

dispel, *dis-pel'*, *v.t.* to drive away, make disappear (e.g. fears, darkness):—*pr.p.* dispell'ing; *pa.p.* dispelled'. [L. *dispellēre—dis-*, away, *pellēre*, to drive.]

dispensable, *dis-pens'á-bl*, *adj.* that may be dispensed, or dispensed with. [Low L. *dispensābilis*—L. *dispensāre*. See **dispensation**.]

dispensary, *dis-pens'ár-i*, *n.* a place where medicines are dispensed. [Root of **dispensation**.]

dispensation, *dis-pen-sā'sh(ó)n*, *n.* the act of dispensing or dealing out: an act or operation of divine Providence: licence or permission to neglect a rule.—*adjs.* **dispens'ative, dispens'atory**, granting dispensation.—*v.t.* **dispense**, to deal out in portions: to distribute: to administer.—*n.* **dispens'er**, one who dispenses: a container or machine that gives out a product in

Neutral vowels in unaccented syllables: *em'pér-ór*; for certain sounds in foreign words see p. ix.

202

prearranged quantities.—**dispense with,** to permit the want of, to do without (e.g. *to dispense with ceremony*); **dispense with one's services,** to dismiss one from employment. [O.Fr.,—L. *dispensātiō, -ōnis—dispensāre—dis-,* asunder, *pensāre,* inten. of *pendēre,* to weigh.]

dispeople, *dis-pē'pl, v.t.* to empty of inhabitants. [L. *dis-,* priv., and **people.**]

disperse, *dis-pûrs', v.t.* to scatter in all directions: to send in different directions: to spread (as news): to cause to vanish.—*v.i.* to separate: to spread: to vanish.—*ns.* **dispers'al,** dispersion; **dispers'ant,** a substance causing dispersion; **dispers'er,** dispers'ive, tending to disperse. [L. *dīspergĕre, dīspersum—dī-(dis-),* asunder, apart, *spargĕre,* to scatter.]

dispersion, *dis-pûr'sh(ŏ)n, n.* a scattering, or state of being scattered: (*med.*) the removal of inflammation: the separation of light into its different rays. [**disperse.**]

dispirit, *dis-pir'it, v.t.* to dishearten, discourage.—*p.adj.* **dispir'ited,** dejected.—*adv.* **dis-pir'itedly.**—*n.* priv., and **spirit.**]

displace, *dis-plās', v.t.* to put out of place, disarrange: to remove from a state, office, or dignity: to take the place of, or put something else in the place of.—*adj.* **displace'able.**—*n.* **displace'ment,** a putting or being out of place: the difference between the position of a body at a given time and that occupied at first: the quantity of water displaced by a floating body.—**displaced person,** one removed from his country as a prisoner or as slave labour: a refugee or stateless person. [O.Fr. *desplacer—des-* (L. *dis-*), neg., and *place,* place.]

displant, *dis-plänt', v.t.* to remove from its native soil, to uproot. [Fr. *desplanter*—L. *dis-,* neg., and *plantāre,* to plant.]

display, *dis-plā', v.t.* to unfold or spread out: to exhibit: to set out ostentatiously.—*n.* a displaying or unfolding: exhibition: ostentatious show: the 'picture' on a cathode-ray tube screen making the information visible.—*n.* **display'er.** [O.Fr. *despleier—des-* (L. *dis-*), neg., and *plier, ploier* (L. *plicāre*), to fold; doublet of **deploy. See ply.**]

displease, *dis-plēz', v.t.* to offend, anger slightly: to be disagreeable to. *v.i.* to raise aversion.—*p.adj.* **displeased',** vexed, annoyed.—*n.* **displeasure** (*dis-plezh'ûr*), the feeling of one who is offended: anger: cause of irritation. [O.Fr. *desplaisir—des-* (L. *dis-*), neg. *plaisir,* to please.]

displenish, *dis-plen'ish, v.t.* to deprive of plenishing or furniture, implements, &c. [L. *dis-,* priv., and **plenish.**]

displume, *dis-plōōm', v.t.* to deprive of plumes or feathers. [L. *dis-,* priv., and **plume.**]

dispone, *dis-pōn', v.t.* (*Scots law*) to make over to another, to convey legally. [L. *dispōnĕre,* to arrange.]

disport, *dis-pōrt', -pört', v.t.* (usu. reflexive) and *v.i.* to divert, amuse: to frolic, gambol. [O.Fr. *desporter* (with *se*), to carry (oneself) away from one's work, to amuse (oneself)—*des-* (L. *dis-*), and *porter* (L. *portāre*), to carry. See **sport.**]

dispose, *dis-pōz', v.t.* to arrange: to distribute: to incline, give a tendency (to).—*v.i.* to arrange

what is to happen.—*adj.* **dispos'able,** able to be disposed of: intended to be thrown away or destroyed after use.—*n.* **dispos'al,** the act of disposing: order, arrangement: the getting rid (of): right of bestowing, disposing of, or using.—*p.adj.* **disposed',** inclined: of a certain disposition (with *well, ill,* &c.).—*n.* **dispos'er.—dispose of,** to settle what is to be done with: to make an end of: to sell. [Fr. *disposer—dis-* (L. *dis*), asunder, *poser,* to place—L. *pausāre.*]

disposition, *dis-po-zish'(ŏ)n, n.* arrangement: plan for disposing one's property, &c.: natural tendency, temper: (*N.T.*) ministration: (*Scots law*) conveyance or assignment.—*adj.* **disposi'tioned,** having a (specified) temperament. [Fr.,—L., from *dis-,* apart, *pōnĕre,* to place.]

dispossess, *dis-poz-es', v.t.* to put out of possession (of)—*adj.* **dispossessed',** deprived of possessions: deprived of one's country, rights, &c.—*n.* **dispossess'or.** [L. *dis-,* priv., and **possess.**]

dispraise, *dis-prāz', n.* expression of an unfavourable opinion: blame, reproach.—*v.t.* to censure. [O.Fr. *despreisier—des-* (L. *dis*), neg., *preisier,* to praise.]

disproof, *dis-prōōf', n.* a disproving: refutation. [L. *dis-,* priv., and **proof.**]

disproportion, *dis-pro-pōr'sh(ŏ)n, n.* want of suitable proportion.—*v.t.* to make unsuitable in form or size, &c.—*adj.* **dispropor'tional.**—*adv.* **dispropor'tionally.**—*adj.* **dispropor'tionate,** ill-proportioned: too large or too small in relation to something else.—*adv.* **dispropor'tionately.**—*n.* **dispropor'tionateness.** [L. *dis* , priv., and **proportion.**]

disprove, *dis-prōōv', v.t.* to prove to be false or wrong. [O.Fr. *desprover—des-* (L. *dis-*), and *prover.* See **prove.**]

dispute, *dis-pūt', v.t.* to make a subject of argument: to oppose by argument: to call in question: to resist: to contend for.—*v.i.* to argue: to debate.—*n.* a contest with words: a debate: a quarrel.—*adj.* **disput'able** (also *dis'-*), that may be disputed: of doubtful certainty.—*n.* **disputableness.**—*adv.* **dis'putably.**—*ns.* **dis'putant, disput'er; disputā'tion,** a contest in argument: an exercise in debate.—*adjs.* **disputā'tious, disput'ative,** inclined to dispute, cavil, or controvert.—*adv.* **disputā'tiously.**—*n.* **disputā'tiousness.** [O.Fr. *desputer*—L. *dis-putāre—dis-,* apart, and *putāre,* to think.]

disqualify, *dis-kwol'i-fī, v.t.* to deprive of qualification: to declare unqualified: to make unfit, to disable.—*n.* **disqualificā'tion,** state of being disqualified: anything that disqualifies or incapacitates. [L. *dis-,* priv., and **qualify.**]

disquiet, *dis-kwī'et, n.* want of quiet: uneasiness, restlessness: anxiety.—*v.t.* to render unquiet: to make uneasy, to worry.—*n.* **disqui'etude,** state of disquiet. [L. *dis-,* priv., and **quiet.**]

disquisition, *dis-kwi-zish'(ŏ)n, n.* a careful inquiry into any matter by arguments, &c.: an essay.—*adj.* **disquisi'tional.** [L. *disquīsītiō, -ōnis—disquīrĕre—dis-,* inten., *quaerĕre, quaesītum,* to seek.]

disregard, *dis-ri-gärd', v.t.* to pay no attention to.—*n.* want of attention: neglect (of—also with *for*). [L. *dis-,* neg., and **regard.**]

disrelish, *dis-rel'ish, v.t.* not to relish, to dislike the taste of, to dislike.—*n.* distaste, dislike, mild disgust. [L. *dis-,* neg., and **relish.**]

disrepair, *dis-ri-pār', n.* state of being out of repair. [L. *dis-,* neg., and **repair.**]

disrepute, *dis-ri-pūt', n.* bad repute: discredit.— Also **disreputā'tion.**—*adj.* **disrep'utable,** disgraceful, discreditable: of low character: not respectable in appearance.—*adv.* **disrep'utably.** [L. *dis-,* neg., and **repute.**]

disrespect, *dis-ri-spekt', n.* want of respect: discourtesy, incivility.—*adj.* **disrespect'ful,** showing disrespect: irreverent: uncivil.—*adv.* **disrespect'fully.** [L. *dis-,* neg., and **respect.**]

disrobe, *dis-rōb', v.t.* to undress: to uncover. [L. *dis-,* priv., and **robe.**]

disroot, *dis-rōōt', v.t.* to root up. [L. *dis-,* priv., and **root.**]

disrupt, *dis-rupt', v.t.* and *v.i.* to burst asunder: *(fig.)* to break up.—*n.* **disrup'tion,** the act of breaking asunder: the act of bursting and rending: breach.—*adj.* **disrup'tive,** causing, or accompanied by, disruption. [L. *disruptus, dīruptus—dīrumpĕre—dis-,* asunder, *rumpĕre,* to break.]

dissatisfy, *dis-sat'is-fī, v.t.* to fail to satisfy or come up to the requirements or expectations of: to make discontented.—*n.* **dissatisfac'tion,** state of being dissatisfied. [L. *dis-,* neg., and **satisfy.**]

dissect, *di-sekt', v.t.* to cut asunder: to cut into parts for the purpose of minute examination: to analyse and criticise (often hostilely, as a man's character or motives).—*adj.* **dissect'-ible.**—*ns.* **dissec'tion,** the act or the art of cutting in pieces a plant or animal to ascertain the structure of its parts—also *fig.;* **dissec'tor.** [L. *dissecāre, dissectum—dis-,* asunder, *secāre,* to cut.]

dissemble, *di-sem'bl, v.t.* to disguise: to mask: *(obs.)* to feign.—*v.i.* to assume a false appearance: to play the hypocrite.—*n.* **dissem'bler.** [L. *dissimulāre—dissimilis,* unlike—*dis-,* neg., and *similis,* like.]

disseminate, *di-sem'i-nāt, v.t.* to sow or scatter abroad (usually *fig.*), to propagate.—*n.* **dissemina'tion.**—*n.* **dissem'inator.**—**disseminated sclerosis,** a chronic progressive disease in which patches of thickening appear throughout the central nervous system, resulting in various forms of paralysis. [L. *disseminare, -ātum—dis-,* asunder, *sēmināre,* to sow—*sēmen, sēminis,* seed.]

dissent, *di-sent', v.i.* to refuse assent: to disagree in opinion, to differ (with *from*).—*n.* the act of dissenting: difference of opinion: a protest by a minority: a differing or separation from an established church.—*ns.* **dissen'sion,** disagreement in opinion: discord, strife; **dissent'er,** member of sect which has seceded from an established church, a nonconformist.—*adj.* **dissen'tient** (*-shént*), declaring dissent: disagreeing.—*n.* one who disagrees: one who declares his dissent. [Fr.,—L. *dissentīre, dissensum—dis-,* apart, *sentīre,* to think.]

dissertate, *dis'ėr-tāt, v.i.* to discourse.—*n.* **dissertā'tion,** a formal discourse: a treatise.—*adj.* **dissertā'tional.**—*n.* **dissertātor.** [L. *dissertāre,* inten. of *disserĕre,* to discuss—*dis-, serĕre,* to put together.]

disserve, *dis-sûrv', v.t.* to do an ill turn to.—*n.* **disserv'ice,** injury, an ill turn.—*adj.* **disserv'iceable.** [O.Fr. *desservir*—L. *dis-,* neg., *servīre,* to serve.]

dissever, *di-sev'ėr, v.t.* to sever: to separate, disunite.—*n.* **dissev'erance.** [O.Fr. *dessevrer*—L. *dis-,* apart, *sēparāre,* to separate.]

dissident, *dis'i-dént, adj.* dissenting.—*n.* a dissenter.—*n.* **diss'idence,** disagreement. [L. *dissidens, -entis,* pr.p. of *dissidēre—dis-,* apart, *sedēre,* to sit.]

dissimilar, *di-sim'i-lár, adj.* unlike.—*ns.* **dissimilar'ity, dissimil'itude.** [L. *dissimilis—dis-,* neg., and *similis,* like.]

dissimulate, *di-sim'ū-lāt, v.t.* to pretend the contrary of: to conceal or disguise, dissemble.—*v.i.* to practise dissimulation, play the hypocrite.—*n.* **dissimulā'tion,** the act of dissembling: a hiding under a false appearance: hypocrisy. [L. *dissimulāre, -ātum,* to dissimulate—*dis-,* neg., *similis,* like.]

dissipate, *dis'i-pāt, v.t.* to scatter: to dispel (e.g. a fog, fears): to squander, to waste.—*v.i.* to separate and disappear: to waste away: to indulge in trivial amusements.—*p.adj.* **diss'ipated,** dissolute, esp. addicted to drinking.—*n.* **dissipā'tion,** dispersion: state of being dispersed: lack of concentration: wasteful expenditure (e.g. of energy, funds): a dissolute course of life: a course of frivolous amusement. [L. *dissipāre, -ātum—dis-,* asunder, and archaic *supāre,* to throw.]

dissociate, *di-sō'shi-āt, v.t.* to think of apart (from), separate in thought: *(reflex.)* to repudiate connection with, refuse to give support to: to disconnect, separate (also *v.i.*).—*n.* **dissociā'tion** (*-sō-si*). [L. *dissociāre, -ātum—dis-,* asunder, *sociāre,* to associate.]

dissolve, *di-zolv', v.t.* to loose (bonds; *fig.*): to break up: to put an end to (as a parliament): to melt.—*v.i.* to break up: to waste away: to melt.—*adj.* **dissol'vent,** having power to dissolve or melt.—*n.* that which can dissolve or melt.—*adj.* **dissoluble** (*dis'ol-(y)ōō-bl,* or *dis-ol'ū-bl*), capable of being dissolved.—*n.* **dissolubil'ity.**—*adj.* **diss'olute,** loose, esp. in morals, lewd, licentious.—*adv.* **diss'olutely.**—*ns.* **diss'oluteness; dissolū'tion,** undoing: breaking up of an assembly: change from a solid to a liquid state: separation of a body into its original elements, decompositon: death. [L. *dissolvĕre, -solūtum—dis-,* asunder, *solvĕre, solūtum,* to loose.]

dissonant, *dis'-o-nánt, adj.* not agreeing or harmonising in sound, &c.: discordant: incongruous.—*n.* **diss'onance,** a discord, esp. one deliberately used in music and subsequently resolved (q.v.): discord, disagreement. [Fr.,—L. *dissonans, -antis—dis-,* apart, *sonāre,* to sound.]

dissuade, *di-swād', v.t.* to prevent or deter by advice or persuasion.—*n.* **dissuā'sion.**—*adj.* **dissuā'sive,** tending to dissuade.—*n.* that which tends to dissuade.—*adv.* **dissuā'sively.** [L. *dissuādēre—dis-,* apart, *suādēre, suāsum,* to advise.]

dissyllable. Form of **disyllable,** etymologically less correct.

distaff, *dis'täf, n.* the stick that holds the bunch of flax, tow, or wool in spinning.—**distaff side,**

Neutral vowels in unaccented syllables: *em'pėr-ör;* for certain sounds in foreign words see p. ix.

204

the female part of a family. [O.E. *distæf*, from Low Ger. *diesse*, the bunch of flax on the staff, and *stæf*, staff.]

distal, *dis'tal*, *adj.* (*biol.*) far apart, widely spaced: pertaining to or situated at the outer end: farthest from the point of attachment. [Formed from **distance**.]

distance, *dis'tans*, *n.* a space or interval (between): a distant place or point (e.g. *in the distance*): remoteness: reserve of manner.— *v.t.* to place at a distance: to leave at a distance behind.— **keep one's distance** (*lit.* and *fig.*), to keep aloof. [O.Fr. *distance* — L. *distantia* — *distans*. See **distant**.]

distant, *dis'tant*, *adj.* remote, in time, place, or connection: at a great distance: not obvious: reserved or aloof in manner.—*adv.* **dis'tantly.** [Fr.,—L. *distans*, *-antis* — *dis-*, apart, *stans*, *stantis*, pr.p. of *stāre*, to stand.]

distaste, *dis-tāst'*, *n.* disrelish: dislike.—*adj.* **distaste'ful**, unpleasant to the taste: disagreeable.—*adv.* **distaste'fully.**—*n.* **distastefulness.** [L. *dis-*, neg. and *taste*.]

distemper, *dis-tem'per*, *n.* a mode of painting in size or other watery vehicle giving body to the pigment — instead of in oil: paint of this kind for indoor walls, &c.—*v.t.* to paint in distemper.—Also **destem'per.** [L. *dis-*, neg., *temperāre*, to regulate, mix in proportion. See next, word.]

distemper, *dis-tem'pèr*, *n.* a morbid or disorderly state of body or mind: disease, esp. of animals, specifically a serious ailment of young dogs: ill-humour.—*v.t.* to derange the temper: to disorder [O.Fr. *destemprer*, to derange.—L. *dis-*, apart, *temperāre*, to govern, regulate.]

distend, *dis-tend'*, *v.t.* to stretch in three dimensions: to swell.—*v.i.* to swell.—*adjs.* **disten'sible**, that may be stretched; **disten'sive**, capable of stretching or of being stretched.— *n.* **disten'sion**, sometimes **disten'tion**, act of distending or stretching: state of being stretched. [L. *distendēre* — *dis-*, asunder, *tendēre*, *tensum* or *tentum*, to stretch.]

distich, *dis'tik*, *n.* a couple of lines or verses making complete sense, a couplet. [Gr. *distichos* — *dis*, twice, *stichos*, a line.]

distil, *dis-til'*, *v.i.* to fall in drops: to flow gently: to use a still.—*v.t.* to let or cause to fall in drops: to convert a liquid into vapour by heat, and then to condense it again: to extract the spirit or essential oil from anything by evaporation and condensation:—*pr.p.* **distill'ing**; *pa.p.* **distilled'.**—*ns.* **distilla'tion**, the act of distilling; **dis'tillate**, the product of distillation.—*adj.* **distill'atory**, of or for distilling.—*ns.* **distill'er**; **distill'ery**, a place where distilling is carried on. [O.Fr. *distiller*, with change of prefix—L. *dēstillāre*, *-ātum* — *dē*, down, *stillāre*, to drop—*stilla*, a drop.]

distinct, *dis-tingkt'*, *adj.* separate: different: well-defined: clear.—*adj.* **distinct'ive**, marking or expressing difference: characteristic.—*adv.* **distinct'ly.**—*n.* **distinct'ness.** [O.Fr.,—L. *distinctus*. See **distinguish**.]

distinction, *dis-tingk'sh(ò)n*, *n.* separation or division: difference: that which distinguishes: discrimination: singular merit or reputation: a mark of honour. [Fr.,—L. *distinctiō*, *-ōnis* —

distinguère. See **distinguish**.]

distingué, *dis-tang'gā*, *dēs-tē-gā*, *adj.* (with appearance, air, manner) suggesting birth and breeding or illustrious character. [Fr.]

distinguish, *dis-ting'gwish*, *v.t.* to mark off, set apart (often with *from*): to characterise: to make out, discern, recognise: to confer distinction on, to make eminent or known.—*v.i.* to recognise a difference (often with *between*).—*adj.* **disting'uishable**, capable of being distinguished.—*adv.* **disting'uishably.**—*p.adjs.* **disting'uished**, illustrious: suggesting illustriousness, distingué; **disting'uishing**, characteristic. [L. *distinguère*, *distinctum* — *dī-*, asunder, *stinguère*, orig. to prick.]

distort, *dis-tört'*, *v.t.* to twist out of shape: to pervert: to misrepresent.—*n.* **distor'tion**, a twisting out of regular shape: crookedness: perversion: any departure from the initial wave-form during electrical transmission of signals. [L. *dis*, asunder, *torquère*, *tortum*, to twist.]

distract, *dis-trakt'*, *v.t.* to draw astray, esp. of the mind or attention: hence, to confuse: hence also, to provide relaxation for: to harass: to render crazy.—*adj.* **distract'ed.**—*adv.* **distract'edly.**—*n.* **distrac'tion**, state of being distracted: perplexity: agitation: madness. that which distracts or diverts attention. [L. *distrahēre*, *-tractum* — *dis-*, apart, *trahēre*, to draw]

distrain, *dis-trān'*, *v.t.* to seize, esp. goods for debt.—*v.i.* to seize the goods of a debtor.—*ns.* **distrain'or**, **distrain'er**; **distraint'**, seizure of goods. [O.Fr. *destraindre* — L. *dī-*, asunder, *stringĕre*, to draw tight.]

distrait, *dis-trā'*, *adj.* absent-minded: inattentive because worried or harassed. [Fr.]

distraught, *dis-tröt'*, *adj.* distracted, wildly perplexed: crazy. [distract, modified by association with words like **caught**, **taught**.]

distress, *dis-tres'*, *n.* extreme pain: that which causes suffering: calamity: misfortune: act of distraining goods: in a structure, a sign of weakness arising from stress.—*v.t.* to afflict with pain or suffering: to harass: to grieve: to distrain.—*adj.* **distress'ful.**—*adv.* **distress'fully.**—*p.adj.* **distress'ing.**—*adv.* **distressingly.**—**distressed area**, a region of unusually severe unemployment. [O.Fr. *destresse* — L. *distringĕre*; see **distrain**.]

distribute, *dis-trib'ūt*, *v.t.* to divide among several: to deal out or allot: to disperse (about a space): to classify: (*print*) to separate (type) and put back in compartments: (*logic*) to use (a term) so as to include every individual to which the term is applicable (e.g. *the statement 'all chairs have legs' distributes the term 'chair'*).—*adjs.* **distrib'utable**, that may be allotted; **distrib'utary**, distributing—*n.* a branch of a distributing system: an off-flow from a river that does not return to it—*ns.* **distrib'uter**, **-or**; **distribū'tion**, allotment: dispersal: the manner of allotment or dispersal: the manner in which the products of industry are shared among the people: classification.—*adj.* **distrib'utive**, that distributes or divides: concerned with distribution: (*math.*) such that $a(x + y + z + \ldots) = ax + ay + az + \ldots$ —*n.* a word like *each* or *every* that indicates the several individuals of a number.—*adv.* **dis-trib′utively**. [L. *distribuĕre*—*dis-*, asunder, *tri-buĕre*, *tribūtum*, to allot.]

district, *dis′trikt, n.* a portion of territory defined for political, judicial, educational, or other purposes: a region.—*v.t.* to divide into districts.—**district attorney** (see **attorney**). [Fr.,—L.L. *dīstrictus*—*dīstringĕre*, to draw tight.]

distrust, *dis-trust′, n.* want of trust, want of faith or confidence, doubt.—*v.t.* to have no trust in: to disbelieve: to doubt.—*adj.* **distrust′ful**, full of distrust: apt to distrust: suspicious.—*adv.* **distrust′fully.**—*n.* **distrust′fulness**. [L. *dis-*, priv., and **trust**.]

disturb, *dis-tûrb′, v.t.* to throw into confusion: to agitate, to disquiet: to interrupt.—*ns.* **disturb′ance**, tumult: agitation: interruption or confusion (of procedure, arrangement, &c.); **disturb′er**. [O.Fr. *destourber*—L. *disturbāre*—*dis-*, asunder, *turbāre*, to agitate—*turba*, a crowd.]

disunion, *dis-ūn′y(ô)n, n.* want of union or concord: breaking up of union: separation. [L. *dis-*, priv., and **union**.]

disunite, *dis-ū-nīt′, v.t.* to undo the union of, to sever or sunder.—*v.i.* to fall asunder, to part.—*n.* **disū′nity.** [L. *dis-*, priv., and **unite**.]

disuse, *dis-ūs′,* or *dis′ūs, n.* cessation or giving up of use (of): state of not being used, desuetude.—*v.t.* (*dis-ūz′*) to cease to use or practise. [L. *dis-*, priv., and **use**.]

disyllable, *dis-il′ä-bl, n.* a word of two syllables.—*adj.* **disyllab′ic**. [Through Fr. and L. from Gr. *di-*, twice, *syllabē*, a syllable.]

ditch, *dich, n.* a trench dug in the ground: any long narrow depression carrying water.—*v.i.* to make a ditch or ditches.—*v.t.* to dig a ditch in or around: to drain by ditches: to drive into a ditch: (*slang*) to bring down in the sea: (*slang*) to get rid of, abandon, leave in the lurch.—*n.* **ditch′er**, a man or machine that makes, cleans, or repairs ditches. [O.E. *dīc*, whence also **dike**.]

ditheism, *dī′thē-izm, n.* the doctrine of the existence of two supreme gods. [Gr. *di-*, twice, and *theos*, a god.]

dither, *dith′er, v.i.* to tremble, quake: to waver.—*n.* a trembling: agitation: perturbation. [Prob. imit.]

dithyramb, *dith′i-ram(b), n.* an ancient Greek hymn sung in honour of Bacchus: a short poem of a like character.—*adj.* **dithyram′bic**, of or like a dithyramb: wildly enthusiastic. [L.,—Gr. *dithyrambos*.]

dittany, *dit′ä-ni, n.* a genus of aromatic perennial plants, formerly much used medicinally as a tonic. [O.Fr. *dictame*—L. *dictamnus*—Gr. *diktamnos*; prob. from Mt. *Diktē* in Crete.]

ditto, *dit′ō,* contracted **do.,** *n.* that which has been said: the same thing.—*adv.* as before, or aforesaid: in like manner. [It. *ditto*—L. *dictum*, said, pa.p. of *dīcĕre*, to say.]

ditty, *dit′i, n.* a song: a little poem to be sung. [O.Fr. *ditie*—L. *dictātum*, neut. of *dictātus*, perf. part. of *dictāre*, to dictate.]

ditty-bag, *dit′i-bag, n.* a sailor's bag for needles, thread, &c.—Also **ditt′y-box.**

diuretic, *dī-ū-ret′ik, adj.* promoting the dis-

charge of urine.—*n.* a medicine causing this discharge. [Fr.,—Gr. *diourētikos*—*dia,* through, *ouron,* urine.]

diurnal, *dī-ûr′näl, adj.* daily: relating to, or performed in, or lasting, a day.—*n.* a book containing the services for day hours: a diary, journal.—*adv.* **diur′nally.** [L. *diurnālis*—*dies*, a day. See **journal**.]

diva, *dē′va, n.* a popular female singer: a primadonna. [It.,—L. *dīva,* fem. of *dīvus,* divine.]

divagate, *dī′va-gāt, v.i.* to wander about: to digress.—*n.* **dīvagā′tion.** [L. *dīvagārī,* to wander.]

divalent, *div′äl-ént,* or *dī-vā′lént, adj.* of a chemical atom or radical, capable of uniting with two atoms of hydrogen or their equivalent. [Gr. *di-*, twice, and L. *valens, -entis,* pr.p. of *valēre*, to have power.]

divan, *di-van′, n.* an Oriental council of state: a court of justice: used poetically of any council or assembly: a council-chamber with cushioned seats: an Eastern couch: a couch of similar type (without back or sides) often used as couch and bed (**divan-bed**): a smoking-room: a collection of poems. [Ar. and Pers. *dīwān,* a long seat.]

divaricate, *dī-var′i-kāt, v.i.* to part into two branches, to fork: to diverge.—*v.t.* to divide into two branches.—*adj.* widely divergent, spreading apart.—*n.* **divarica′tion.** [L. *dīvaricāre, -ātum*—*dī-,* asunder, *varicāre,* to spread the legs—*vārus,* bent apart.]

dive, *dīv, v.i.* to plunge into water or down through the air: to go headlong into a recess, forest, &c.: (*lit.* or *fig.*) to plunge deeply.—*n.* a plunge: a swoop.—*n.* **dive′-bomb′er**, an aeroplane that discharges a bomb while in a steep dive.—*v.t.* and *v.i.* **dive′-bomb**, to attack with, or as if with, a dive-bomber: to discharge bombs while diving.—*ns.* **div′er**, one who dives: one who works from a diving bell or in a diving-dress: a bird expert at diving, esp. any one of several species of loon; **diving-bell**, a hollow chamber, originally bell-shaped, open at the bottom and supplied with air for respiration, in which one may work under water; **diving-dress**, a diver's water-tight costume with equipment for respiration under water. [O.E. *dȳfan, dūfan*; O.N. *dȳfa.*]

diverge, *di-* or *dī-vûrj′, v.i.* to tend from a common point in different directions: to differ, deviate (from a standard).—*ns.* **diverg′ence, diverg′ency.**—*adj.* **diverg′ent.** [L. *dis-*, asunder, *vergĕre,* to incline.]

divers, *dī′vérz, adj.* sundry, several, more than one: (*B.*) same as **diverse**. [See **divert**.]

diverse, *dī′vérs,* or *dī-vûrs′, adj.* different, unlike: multiform, various.—*adv.* **dī′versely** (or *dī-verse′ly*).—*n.* **diver′sity,** state of being diverse: difference, unlikeness: variety. [See **divert**.]

diversify, *di-vûr′si-fī, v.t.* to make diverse or different: to give variety to: to make (investments) in securities of different types so as to lessen risk of loss: to engage in production of a variety of (manufactures, crops).—Also *v.i.*—*pr.p.* diver′sifying; *pa.p.* diver′sified.—*n.* **diversifica′tion.** [Fr.,—Low L. *dīversificāre*—*dīversus,* diverse, *facĕre,* to make.]

diversion, *di-vûr′sh(ô)n, n.* act of diverting or turning aside: that which diverts: amusement,

---

Neutral vowels in unaccented syllables: *em′pér-ór*; for certain sounds in foreign words see p. ix.

recreation: a tactical move to take an enemy's attention off a more important operation: a detour round a part of a road that is temporarily closed.—*adj.* **diver'sionary**, of the nature of a diversion. [See **divert.**]

divert, *di-vûrt'*, *v.t.* to turn aside: to change the direction of: to distract (the attention): to turn from business or study: to amuse.—*adj.* **divert'ing.**—*adv.* **divert'ingly.** [Fr.,—L. *dīvertĕre*, *dīversum*—*dī-*, aside, *vertĕre*, to turn.]

divertimento, *di-vêr-ti-men'tō*, *n.* (*mus.*) a divertissement. [It.]

divertissement, *dē-ver-tēs'mз*, *n.* a diversion, amusement: a short ballet, primarily for presentation between longer ballets: a short light-hearted piece of music: a musical pot-pourri. [Fr.]

Dives, *dī'vēz*, *n.* a very wealthy man (Luke xvi. 19). [L. *dīves*, rich (man).]

divest, *di-* or *dī-vest'*, *v.t.* to strip or deprive (of anything). [O.Fr. *desvestir*, with change of prefix (*dis-* for *dē-*) from L. *dēvestīre*—*dē*, away from, *vestīre*, to clothe *vestis*, a raiment.]

divide, *di-vīd'*, *v.t.* to break up, or mark off, into parts, actually or in imagination: to part among, to allot, &c.: to keep apart: to cause to vote for and against a motion: (*math.*) to ascertain how many times one quantity contains another.—*v.i.* to separate: to fall apart: to vote for and against.—*n.* (*coll.*, esp. in *U.S.*) a watershed.—*adv.* **divid'edly.**—*n.* **divid'er**, he who or that which divides: (*pl.*) a kind of compasses for dividing lines, &c.—*adj.* **divid'ing**, separating. [L. *dīvidĕre*, *dīvīsum*—*dis-*, asunder, root *vid*, to separate.]

dividend, *div'i-dend*, *n.* that which is to be divided: the share of a sum divided that falls to each individual, e.g. by way of interest on shares. [L. *dīvidendum*—*dīvidĕre*. See **divide.**]

divine, *di-vīn'*, *adj.* belonging to or proceeding from a god: holy: excellent in the highest degree. *n.* one skilled in divine things: a minister of the gospel: a theologian.—*v.t.* to foresee or foretell as if divinely inspired: to guess or make out.—*v.i.* to profess or practise divination: to have forebodings.—*ns.* **divinā'tion**, the act or practice of foretelling the future or of finding a hidden thing by supernatural means: instinctive foresight: insight: an intuitive perception; **divin'er**, one who divines or professes divination.—*adv.* **divine'ly.**—*n.* **divin'ing-rod**, a rod, usu. of hazel, used by those professing to discover water or metals under ground. [O.Fr. *devin*, soothsayer—L. *dīvīnus*, from *dīvus*, *deus*, a god.]

divinity, *di-vin'i-ti*, *n.* godhead, the nature or essence of God: (*cap.*) God: any god: theology: a person whom one adores. [O.Fr. *devinite*—L. *dīvīnitās*, *-ātis*. See **divine.**]

division, *di-vizh'(ö)n*, *n.* act of dividing: state of being divided: that which divides, a partition, a barrier: a portion or section: an army unit (usually half an army corps): separation: difference in opinion, &c.: disunion: (*arith.*) the rule or process of finding how many times one number is contained in another.—*adj.* **divis'ible**, capable of being divided or separated: capable of being divided without remainder.—*n.* **divisibil'ity.**—*adv.* **divis'ibly.**—*adjs.*

divi'sional (*-vizh'-*), pertaining to or marking a division or separation; **divīs'ive**, forming division or separation: creating discord.—*n.* **divīs'or** (*math.*), the number that divides the dividend. [O.Fr.,—L. *dīvīsiō*, *-ōnis*—*dīvidĕre.* See **divide.**]

divorce, *di-vōrs'*, *-vörs'*, *n.* the legal dissolution of marriage: in widest sense (*loosely*) including judicial separation and decree of nullity: severance.—*v.t.* to dissolve the marriage of: to put away by divorce: to separate.—*ns.* **divorcee'**, a divorced person; **divorce'ment** (*B.*), divorce. [Fr.,—L. *dīvortium*—*dīvortĕre*, another form of *dīvertĕre.* See **divert.**]

divot, *div'ŏt*, *n.* (*Scot.*) a piece of turf, sod.

divulge, *di-vulj'*, *v.t.* (*rare*) to make public: to let out (a secret): to reveal (that). [Fr.,—L. *dīvulgāre*—*dī-*, abroad, *vulgāre*, to publish—*vulgus*, the common people.]

dizen, *dī'zn*, or *diz'n*, *v.t.* to dress gaudily. [From a root seen in **distaff.**]

dizzy, *diz'i*, *adj.* giddy: confused: causing giddiness (*adv.*) silly: (*coll.*) extreme.—*v.t.* to make dizzy: to confuse.—*adv.* **dizz'ily.**—*n.* **dizz'iness**, giddiness. [O.E. *dysig*, foolish; cf. Dan. *dösig*, drowsy.]

djinn. See **jinn.**

DNA, *dē-en-ā*, *n.* deoxyribo-nucleic acid (q.v.).

do, *dōō*, *v.t.* to perform: to bring about or effect: to accomplish or finish: to make, prepare: to put or bring into any form or state: to swindle: to treat: to make the round of, as sights.—*v.i.* to act or behave: to fare: to suffice:—*2nd sing.* do'est, dost (*dust*), *3rd* does (*duz*), also do'eth, doth (*duth*); *pa.t.* did; *pr.p.* do'ing; *pa.p.* done (*dun*). Do serves as substitute for other verbs to save repeating them (as in *I didn't mean to speak, but if I do*, &c.). It is used as an auxiliary verb with an infinitive in negative, interrogative, emphatic and rhetorically inverted sentences.—*p.adj.* **dō'ing**, active.—*n.* (*coll.*) a scolding, severe treatment: (in *pl.*) things done, events, behaviour: (*slang*; in *pl.*) the food or other things necessary.—*n.* **do'-good'er**, a slighting name for one who tries to benefit others by social reforms, &c., implying that his, her, efforts are unwelcome or ineffectual.—*adj.* **do-it-yourself**, designed to be built, constructed, &c., by an amateur, rather than one specially trained.—Also *n.* —**do away with**, to abolish: to destroy; **do down**, to cheat, get the better of; **do for**, to suit: to provide for, esp. to keep house or do housework for: to ruin: (*vulg.*) to kill; **do in**, (*coll.*) to get the better of: (*coll.*) to murder; **do one proud**, (*coll.*) to make one feel flattered: (*coll.*) to treat one lavishly; **do time** (see **time**); **do up**, put up, make tidy, tie up, dress (linen): redecorate: apply cosmetics: to fatigue utterly. —**have done**, to desist: to have no more dealings (with); **have to do with**, to have a connection with; **nothing doing** (*slang*), no; **what's to do?** what is the matter? [O.E. *dōn*, *dyde*, *gedōn*; Du. *doen*, Ger. *tun*; conn. with Gr. *tithenai*, to put.]

do, **doh**, *dō*, *n.* (*mus.*) the first tone or keynote of the scale. See **sol-fa.**

doat. Same as **dote.**

dobbin, *dob'in*, *n.* a workhorse. [An altered dim. of *Robert.*]

doch-an-doris, do*n'n*-*dō'ris*, *n.* a stirrup-cup, a parting-cup. [Gael., *deoch,* drink, *an,* the, *doruis,* gen. of *dorus,* door.]

docile, *dō'sīl,* or *dos'īl, adj.* teachable: easily managed.—*n.* **docil'ity.** [Fr.,—L. *docilis—docēre,* to teach.]

dock, *dok, n.* a genus of weeds with large leaves and a long root. [O.E. *doice.*]

dock, *dok, v.t.* to cut short: to curtail: to clip.—*n.* the part of a tail left after clipping. [M.E. *dok,* prob.—O.N. *dokkr,* a stumpy tail.]

dock, *dok, n.* an artificial basin for the reception of ships: the box in court where the accused stand: any similar enclosure.—*v.t.* to place in a dock: to join (spacecraft) together in space.—Also *v.i.—v.i.* to enter a dock.—*ns.* **dock'age,** accommodation in docks for ships: dock-dues; **dock'er,** one who works at the docks; **dock'yard,** a naval establishment with docks, building-slips, stores, &c.; **dry'-dock, graving dock,** a dock that can be emptied of water so as to expose the hull of a ship for cleaning and repairs; **float'ing-dock,** a dock that can, by emptying tanks in its sides, be raised high in the water with any ship that has been floated into it; **wet'-dock,** a dock maintaining a level nearly equal to that of high water. [Old Du. *dokke.*]

docket, *dok'ét, n.* a summary of a larger writing: a ticket affixed to anything indicating its contents: a label: a list or register of cases in court: an official permit to buy.—*v.t.* to make a summary of the heads of a writing: to enter such in a book: to mark the contents of papers on the back:—*pr.p.* dock'eting; *pa.p.* dock'eted. [Perh. a dim. of **dock** (2).]

doctor, *dok'tor, n.* (*arch.*) a teacher: a cleric especially skilled in theology or ecclesiastical law: one who has received from a university the highest degree in a faculty: a physician.—*v.t.* to treat as a doctor does: to patch up: to tamper with.—*n.* **doc'torate,** the degree of doctor.—**Doctors' Commons,** a law-court superseded by the Divorce Court and Probate Court in 1857.—**what the doctor ordered** (*slang*), the very thing that's needed. [L., a teacher—*docēre,* to teach.]

doctrinaire, *dok-tri-nār', n.* one whose opinions are formed by theory rather than by experience.—*adj.* unduly influenced by theory. [Fr.,—Late L. *doctrīnārius.*]

doctrine, *dok'trin, n.* (*arch.*) teaching: a thing taught: a principle of belief.—*adj.* **doc'trinal** (or *-trī'nál*), relating to, or containing, doctrine: relating to the act of teaching.—*adv.* **doc'trinally.** [Fr.,—L. *doctrīna—docēre,* to teach.]

document, *dok'ū-mént, n.* a paper containing information, or proof or evidence of anything.—*v.t.* (*dok'ū-mént,* or *-ment'*) to furnish with documents: to support or prove by documents.—*adj.* **document'ary,** relating to, or found in, documents: aiming at presentation of reality.—*ns.* **documentary,** a motion-picture portraying a particular human activity without fictional colouring and without professional actors; **documentā'tion.** [Fr.,—L. *documentum—docēre,* to teach.]

dodder, *dod'ér, n.* a genus of leafless, twining, pale-coloured parasitic plants of the same order as the convolvulus genus. [M.E. *doder*; cf. Ger. *dotter.*]

dodder, *dod'ér, v.i.* to shake, to totter, to be decrepit: to maunder in speech. [Poss. conn. with Norw. *dudra,* to tremble.]

dodeca-, *dō-deka-,* in composition, having twelve (Gr. *dōdeka,* twelve).—*ns.* **dodec'agon,** a plane figure having twelve angles and sides (Gr. *gonia,* an angle); **dodecasyll'able,** &c.

dodge, *doj, v.i.* to start aside or shift about: to evade an obligation: to use mean tricks: to quibble.—*v.t.* to avoid by a sudden movement or shift of place: to evade (e.g. a question): to trick.—*n.* an evasion: a trick: a quibble.—*n.* **dodg'er.**—*adj.* **dodg'y,** tricky, artful: difficult to do or carry out: risky. [Origin obscure.]

dodo, *dō'dō, n.* a large clumsy bird, now completely extinct, about the size of a turkey, and without the power of flight:—*pl.* **do'do(e)s.** [Port. *doudo,* silly.]

doe, *dō, n.* the female of the fallow-deer or buck: female of antelope, rabbit, and hare.—*n.* **doe'skin,** the skin of a doe: a smooth, close-woven, woollen cloth. [O.E. *dā*; Dan. *daa,* a deer.]

doer, *dōō'er, n.* one who does, or habitually does, anything: an agent. [**do.**]

does, *duz,* 3rd pers. sing. pres. indic. of **do.**

doff, *dof, v.t.* to take off, remove. [**do, off.**]

dog, *dog, n.* a wild or domestic quadruped of the same genus as the wolf: a male of the species: a mean scoundrel: a term of familiarity or contempt for a man (often with adj., as *gay, sly, lazy dog*): (*cap.*) either of two constellations, the Greater and the Lesser Dog: an andiron: a grappling iron or the like.—*adj.* male, as in dog-fox, dog-wolf.—*v.t.* to follow as a dog: to track and watch persistently:—*pr.p.* dogg'ing; *pa.p.* dogged.—*ns.* **dog'-belt,** a broad leather belt round the waist for drawing sledges, &c., in the low workings of coal-mines; **dog'cart,** a two-wheeled carriage with seats back to back, so called from sporting-dogs being originally carried inside the box; **dog'-coll'ar,** a collar for dogs: a close-fitting clerical collar; **dog'-days,** the period when the Dogstar rises with the sun (generally reckoned July 3rd to August 11th)—erroneously supposed to be the time when dogs are specially liable to hydrophobia—*adj.* **dog'-eared,** of the pages of a book, turned down like the ears of a dog: hence, shabby, scruffy. —*ns.* **dog'-end** (*slang*), a cigarette-end; **dog'fan'cier** (see **fancier**); **dog'-fight,** a fight between dogs: a single combat (esp. of aeroplanes) at close quarters; **dog'fish,** a small shark of various kinds.—*adj.* **dogg'ed,** doglike: sullen: pertinacious.—*adv.* **dogg'edly.**—*n.* **dogg'edness.**—*adj.* **dogg'ish,** like a dog: churlish, snarling.—*adv.* **dogg'ishly.**—*ns.* **dogg'ishness; dog-Latin,** bad Latin: jargon: in imitation of Latin; **dog-French, -Greek; dog'rose,** a species of wild rose; **dog's'body,** a general drudge; **dog('s)'-ear,** the corner of a leaf of a book turned down like a dog's ear.—*v.t.* to turn down the corners of pages.—*ns.* **dog'-sleep,** a light sleep broken by the slightest noise; **Dog'star,** Sirius, a star in the Greater Dog, brightest star in the heavens, whose rising with the sun gave name to the dog-days.—*adjs.* **dog's-**

Neutral vowels in unaccented syllables: *em'pér-ór*; for certain sounds in foreign words see p. ix.

208

tooth, of a broken-check pattern used extensively in the weaving of tweeds; **dog'-tired**, utterly exhausted.—*ns.* **dog-tooth** (*arch.*), a moulding consisting of a series of ornamented square pyramids; **dog'-trot**, a gentle trot like that of a dog.—*n.pl.* **dog'-watches**, on shipboard, the watch 4-6 p.m. or 6-8 p.m., consisting of two hours only instead of four.—*n.* **dog-wood**, the wild cornel.—**dog's chance**, a bare chance; **dog's life**, a wretched, miserable life.—**go to the dogs**, to ruin oneself; **in the doghouse**, in disgrace, in disfavour; **like a dog's dinner**, very smart (often ironic): flamboyantly dressed; **not to lead the life of a dog**, to lead a life more wretched than that of a dog; **throw, give**, or **send to the dogs**, to throw away or abandon; **the dogs**, greyhound racing. [Late O.E. *docga*; cf. Du. *dog*, a mastiff; Ger. *dogge*.]

doge, *dōj*, or *dō'jā*, *n.* the chief magistrate in republican Venice and Genoa. [It. (Venetian dial.), for *duce* (=Eng. *duke*)—L. *dux*, a leader.]

doggerel, *dog'ér-él*, *n.* irregular measures in burlesque poetry, so named in contempt: worthless verses.—*adj.* irregular in rhythm: mean, trivial. [Origin unknown.]

dogma, *dog'ma*, *n.* a settled opinion, a principle or tenet: a doctrine laid down with authority.—*adjs.* **dogmat'ic, -al**, pertaining to a dogma: asserting a thing as if it were a dogma: asserting positively: overbearing.—*adv.* **dogmat'ically**.—*n.* **dogmat'ics**, science or statement of Christian doctrines, systematic theology.—*v.i.* **dog'matise**, to state one's opinion dogmatically or arrogantly.—*ns.* **dog'matiser**; **dog'matism**, dogmatic or positive assertion of opinion; **dog'matist**, one who makes positive assertions. [Gr. an opinion, from *dokeein*, to think, seem.]

dog-shores, *dog'-shōrz*, *n.pl.* props or shores used in launching a ship. [**shore** (3).]

doh. See do (*n.*).

doily, *doi'li*, *n.* a small ornamented mat, often laid on or under dishes. [From *Doily* or *Doyley*, a famous haberdasher.]

doings, *dōō'ingz*, *n. pl.* See do (*vb.*).

doit, *doit*, *n.* a small Dutch coin worth about half a farthing: a thing of little or no value. [Du. *duit*.]

dolce, *dol'chā*, *adj.* (*mus.*) sweet.—*n.* a soft-toned organ-stop. [It.]

doldrums, *dol'drumz*, *n.pl.* those parts of the ocean about the equator where calms and light baffling winds prevail: low spirits. [Prob. conn. with obs. *dold*, stupid, or *dol*, dull.]

dole, *dōl*, *n.* a share: something given in charity: (*coll.*) state pay to unemployed: a small portion.—*v.t.* to deal (out) in small portions. [O.E. *dāl*; cf. **deal**.]

dole, *dōl*, *n.* pain: grief: (*arch.* and *poet.*) heaviness at heart.—*adj.* **dole'ful**, full of dole or grief, melancholy.—*adv.* **dole'fully**.—*n.* **dole'fulness**. [O.Fr. *doel* (Fr. *deuil*), grief—L. *dolēre*, to feel pain.]

dolicho-, *dol-i-kō-*, in composition, long.—*adj.* **dolichocephalic**, *dol-i-ko-sef-al'ik*, long-headed, applied to skulls whose breadth is less than four-fifths of their length (opp. to *brachycephalic*)—also **dolichoceph'alous**. [Gr.

dolichos, long, *kephalē*, the head.]

doll, *dol*, *n.* a toy in human form: a pretty woman without personality: a woman.—*n.* **doll'y**, a little doll: instrument for turning or pounding, used in washing clothes, mining, &c: a trolley, truck or platform on wheels or roller: an attractive young girl (also **dolly girl**, **dolly bird**): (*cricket*) a slow, easy catch.—*v.t.* to turn or pound with a dolly.—*ns.* **dolly camera**, a camera moving on a dolly; **dolly girl**, **dolly-bird** (see **dolly**); **doll'y-shop**, a marine store or pawnshop—often having a black doll as sign. [Prob. from *Dolly*, familiar dim. of *Dorothy*.]

dollar, *dol'ár*, *n.* a silver coin (=100 cents) of the United States, Canada and other countries (there are between two and three United States dollars to £1): a thaler: (*slang*) five shillings (now twenty-five pence).—**dollar area**, the group of countries whose currencies are linked to the U.S. dollar; **dollar gap**, the excess of imports from a dollar country over exports to it, necessitating settlement by dollar exchange or in gold. [Ger. *t(h)aler* (Low Ger. *daler*), short for *Joachimsthaler*, because first coined at the silver-mines in Joachimsthal (Joachim's dale) in Bohemia.]

dolly. See **doll**.

dolman, *dol'mán*, *n.* a Turkish robe with slight sleeves: a mantle worn by women in the 19th century. [Fr.,—Turk. *dōlāmān*.]

dolmen, *dol'mén*, *n.* a prehistoric structure of two or more erect unhewn stones, supporting a large flattish stone. [Fr. *dolmen*; usually explained as Breton *dolmen*—*dol*, *taol*, table, *men*, a stone. But *tolmēn* in Cornish meant 'hole of stone'.]

dolomite, *dol'o-mīt*, *n.* a limestone consisting of calcium magnesium carbonate. [Named in honour of the French geologist *Dolomieu* (1750-1801).]

dolour, *dol'ór, dōl'ór*, *n.* pain, grief, anguish.—*adj.* **dol'orous**, full of pain or grief: doleful.—*adv.* **dol'orously**.—*n.* **dol'orousness**. [O.Fr.,—L. *dolēre*, to grieve.]

dolphin, *dol'fin*, *n.* any of several animals of the whale order, about 8 or 10 feet long, resembling the porpoises and in certain cases popularly confused with them: a coryphaena, either of two species of fish about 5 feet in length, noted for the brilliancy of their colours when dying. [O.Fr. *daulphin*—L. *delphīnus*—Gr. *delphis*, *-phinos*.]

dolt, *dōlt*, *n.* a dull or stupid fellow.—*adj.* **dolt'ish**, dull, stupid.—*adv.* **dolt'ishly**.—*n.* **dolt'ishness**. [Dolt=*dulled* (see **dull**) or blunted.]

Dom, *dom*, *n.* a title given to certain R.C. dignitaries. [Port. *Dom*—L. *dominus*, lord.]

domain, *do-mān'*, *n.* what one has dominion over (*lit.* and *fig.*): an estate: territory: ownership of land: (*math.*) an aggregate to which a variable belongs. [Fr.,—L. *dominium*—*dominus*, a master.]

dome, *dōm*, *n.* a structure raised above a large building, usually hemispherical: a large cupola: a cathedral: (*poet.*) a building: anything resembling a hemispherical vault in shape.—*adj.* **domed**, having a dome. [L. *domus*, a house; Fr. *dôme*, It. *duomo*, Ger. *dom*.]

Domesday (Doomsday) Book, *dōōmz'dā bŏŏk*,

n. a book compiled by order of William the Conqueror, containing a survey of all the lands in England, their value, owners, &c.—so called from its authority in judgment (O.E. *dōm*) on the matters contained in it.

domestic, *do-mes'tik, adj.* belonging to the house: remaining much at home: private: tame: not foreign.—*n.* a servant in the house.—*adv.* **domes'tically.**—*v.t.* **domes'ticāte,** to make domestic: to tame: to naturalise.—*ns.* **domesticā'tion; domestic'ity** (-*tis'-*), domestic or domesticated state: home life.—**domestic architecture,** the architecture of mansions, dwelling-houses, cottages, &c.; **domestic economy,** the principles of thrifty housekeeping; **domestic science,** household arts, such as catering, cookery, laundry-work, studied in the light of physiological, chemical, &c., knowledge; **domestic system,** the system of industry, earlier than the factory system, under which workers made goods in their own homes. [L. *domesticus—domus,* a house.]

domicile, *dom'i-sil, -sīl, n.* a house, an abode: a man's legal place of residence.—*v.t.* to establish in a fixed residence.—*adj.* **domicil'iary,** pertaining to the domicile. [Fr.—L. *domicilium—domus,* a house.]

dominant, *dom'in-ánt, adj.* prevailing, predominant: overtopping others.—*n.* (*mus.*) the fifth note above the tonic.—*n.* **dom'inance,** ascendancy.—*adv.* **dom'inantly.** [L. *dominans, -antis,* pr.p. of *domināri,* to be master.]

dominate, *dom'in-āt, v.t.* to be lord over: to tower over (*lit.* and *fig.*), have a commanding influence over: to occupy a conspicuous position in.—Also *v.i.* (with *over*).—*n.* **dominā'tion,** government: absolute authority: tyranny. [L. *domināri, -ātus,* to be master—*dominus,* master—*domāre* (from the same Indo-Gmc. root as Eng. *tame*).]

domineer, *dom-in-ēr', v.i.* to exercise arrogant mastery: to be overbearing. [Prob. through Du.—O.Fr. *dominer*—L. *domināri,* see above.]

dominical, *do-min'ik-ál, adj.* belonging to the Lord, as the Lord's Prayer, the Lord's Day. [Low L. *dominicālis*—L. *dominicus—dominus,* lord, master.]

Dominican, *do-min'i-kán, adj.* belonging to St *Dominic* or to the monastic order founded by him in 1215.—*n.* a friar or monk of that order.

dominie, *dom'i-ni, n.* (*Scot.*) a schoolmaster, a tutor. [L. *domine,* voc. of *dominus,* master.]

dominion, *do-min'yón, n.* lordship, sovereignty: a domain or territory with one ruler, owner, or government: a completely self-governing colony, not subordinate to, but freely associating with, the mother-country: control: (*pl., B.*) one of the orders of angels (Col. i. 16).—**Dominion Day,** a Canadian festival on the anniversary of the union of the provinces, July 1, 1867. [Low. L. *dominiō, -ōnis—dominus,* master.]

domino, *dom'i-nō, n.* hooded cape worn by a master or by a priest: a long hooded cloak used at masked balls: one of the oblong pieces, with two compartments each blank or marked with from one to six spots, with which the game of **dom'inoes** (-*nōz*) is played. [Sp. *domino*—L. *dominus.*]

don, *don, n.* a Spanish title, corresponding to English Sir, Mr, formerly applied only to noblemen, now to all classes: a fellow of a college: (*coll.*) an expert. [Sp.,—L. *dominus.*]

don, *don, v.t.* to put on, to assume:—*pr.p.* don'ning; *pa.p.* donned. [A contr. of **do, on.**]

donation, *do-nā'sh(ó)n, n.* act of giving: that which is given, a gift of money or goods: (*law*) the act by which a person freely transfers his title to anything to another—*v.t.* **donāte',** to give as a gift: to contribute, esp. to a charity.—*n.* **dōn'ative,** a gift: a gratuity: a benefice presented by the founder or patron without reference to the bishop.—*adj.* vested or vesting by donation.—*ns.* **dōnee',** the person to whom a gift is made; **dō'nor,** a giver. [Fr.,—L. *dōnāre, -ātum—dōnum,* a gift—*dāre,* to give.]

done, *dun, pa.p.* of **do,** often implying utter exhaustion.—Used elliptically for 'Agreed!'

donga, *dong'gä, n.* (*S. Africa*) a water-worn ravine. [Zulu, bank, side of a gully.]

donjon, *dun'jón, n.* a strong central tower in ancient castles, to which the garrison retreated when hard pressed. [A doublet of **dungeon.**]

Don Juan, *don jōō'án,* a libertine of Spanish legend who has been the subject of plays, poems, and operas in several European countries—Mozart's operatic version of the story (*Don Giovanni*) did much to popularise it: any attractive libertine. [**don** (1), Sp. *Juan,* John.]

donkey, *dong'ki, n.* an ass.—*ns.* **don'key-en'gine,** a small auxiliary engine; **don'key-jacket,** a strong jacket, with shoulders of leather or (usu.) of simulated leather, and patch pockets; **don'key-work,** drudgery. [Still regarded as slang in 1823. Perh.—*dun-ik-ie,* a double dim. of *dun,* from its colour; or from *Duncan.*]

donnée, *do'nā, n.* datum: basic assumption(s). [Fr.]

Don Quixote. See **quixotic.**

don't, *dōnt.* For **do not.**

doodle, *dōōd'l, v.i.* to scrawl, scribble meaninglessly.

doolie, *dōōli, n.* a litter or palanquin. [Hindi (q.v.) *dōlī.*]

doom, *dōōm, n.* judgment: condemnation: destiny: ruin: final judgment.—*v.t.* to pronounce judgment on: to condemn, destine (often in *pass.,* e.g. *it was doomed to failure*):—*pr.p.* dōōm'ing; *pa.p.* dōōmed.—*ns.* **dooms'day,** the day of doom, the day when the world will be judged; **Dooms'day Book** (see **Domesday**). [O.E. *dōm,* judgment.]

door, *dōr, dör, n.* usual entrance into an enclosed space: the movable frame by which the entrance can be closed: a means of approach or access.—*adj.* in composition, belonging to a door, as **door'-bell, door'step.**—*ns.* **door'-plate,** a plate on or at a door with the householder's name on it; **door'post,** the jamb or side-piece of a door.—**darken one's door,** to cross one's threshold; **next door to,** in the house next to: near to, bordering upon, very nearly; **out of doors,** in the open air. [O.E. *duru*; Ger. *tor, tür*; Gr. *thyra,* L. *fores* (pl.), a door.]

dope, *dōp, n.* a thick pasty material: lubricating grease: aeroplane varnish: opium: a drug, narcotic or stimulative: anything calculated to dull mental and moral energy: (*slang*) infor-

Neutral vowels in unaccented syllables: *em'pér-ór*; for certain sounds in foreign words see p. ix.

mation.—*v.t.* (*coll.*) to drug (*lit.* and *fig.*).—*n.*
dop'ing (*electronics*), addition of known impurities to a semiconductor to achieve the
desired properties in diodes and transistors.
[Du. *doop*, a dipping, sauce; *doopen*, to dip.]
dor, dorr, *dör, n.* a kind of dung-beetle, named
from its droning flight: a cockchafer. [O.E.
dora, a humble-bee.]
Dorcas society, *dör'kas sō-sī'e-ti*, a group of
charitable women who make clothes for the
poor, as *Dorcas* (Acts ix.) did.
doree. See **dory.**
Doric, *dor'ik, adj.* belonging to *Doris* in Greece,
denoting one of the Greek orders of architecture.—*n.* a broad dialect of ancient Greek: any
corresponding modern dialect, as Scottish. [Fr.
dorique—L. *Dōricus*—Gr. *Dōrikos*—*Dōris.*]
dorking, *dörk'ing, n.* a breed of poultry, named
from *Dorking* in Surrey.
dormant, *dör'mänt, adj.* sleeping: with suspended animation of development (*lit.* or *fig.*):
in abeyance (as a title): (*her.*) in a sleeping
posture.—*n.* **dor'mancy.** [Fr. *dormir*—L. *dormīre*, to sleep.]
dormer, *dör'mér, n.* (*obs.*) a bedroom.—*n.*
dor'mer-win'dow, a small window with a gable
or triangular top, projecting from a sloping
roof (orig. a dormitory window). [L. *dormī-
torium*—*dormīre*, to sleep.]
dormitory, *dör'mi-tór-i, n.* a large sleeping
chamber with many beds. [L. *dormitōrium*—
dormīre, to sleep.]
dormouse, *dör'mows, n.* any member of a family
of rodents akin to mice but somewhat
squirrel-like in form and habit:—*pl.* **dor'mice.**
[Perh. conn. with L. *dormīre*, to sleep (from
their hibernation), and prob. **mouse.**]
dormy, dormie, *dör'mi, adj.* (*golf*) said of a
player when he is as many holes 'up' or ahead
as there are holes still to play. [Poss. conn.
with L. *dormīre*, to sleep.]
dorsal, *dor'sàl, adj.* pertaining or belonging to
the back. [Fr.,—L. *dorsum*, the back.]
dory, *dō'ri, n.* a golden-yellow fish of the mackerel family.—Also **John Dory** and **doree.** [Fr.
dorée, from *dorer,* to gild—L. *deaurāre,* to
gild—*dē-, aurum,* gold and **John,** the name.]
dose, *dōs, n.* the quantity of medicine, X-rays,
&c., administered at one time: a graduated
amount: an ample portion: anything disagreeable forced on one.—*v.t.* to give medicine in
doses to: to give anything nauseous to.—*ns.*
dos'age, a method or rate of dosing: **dosi-
m'eter,** an instrument for measuring radiation
(also called **dose'-met'er).** [Fr.,—Gr. *dosis,* a
giving—*didonai,* to give.]
doss, *dos, n.* (*slang*) a bed.—*v.i.* to sleep.—*ns.*
doss'-house, a very cheap lodging-house;
doss'er, a lodger in a doss-house. [Perh. from
doss, a dial. Eng. name for a hassock, or perh.
from L. *dorsum,* back.]
dossier, *dos'i-ér, do-syā, n.* a bundle of documents: a brief. [Fr.]
dost, *dust,* 2nd pers. sing. pres. indic. of **do.**
dot, *dot, n.* a very small spot: a short element in
the Morse code.—*v.t.* to mark with dots: to
diversify (with objects).—*v.i.* to form
dots:—*pr.p.* **dott'ing;** *pa.p.* **dott'ed.**—*adj.* **dott'y,**
composed of dots: feeble: crazy. [Du. *dot,* knot,
tuft.]

dot, *dot, n.* a marriage portion.—*adj.* **dō'tal,** pertaining to dowry or to dower. [Fr.,—L. *dōs,
dōtis*—*dōtāre,* to endow.]
dote, doat, *dōt, v.i.* (*arch.*) to be stupid or foolish:
to show weak or excessive affection (with
on).—*ns.* **dōt'age,** a doting: childishness of old
age: excessive fondness; **dōt'ard,** one who
dotes: one showing the weakness of old age,
or excessive fondness. [Cf. Old Du. *doten,* to be
silly and Fr. *radoter,* to rave.]
doth, *duth,* 3rd pers. sing. pres. indic. of **do.**
dotterel, *dot'ér-el, n.* a kind of plover easily
duped and caught: a stupid fellow. [**dote.**]
douane, *dōō-an', n.* a custom-house. [Fr.]
double, *dub'l, adj.* twofold: consisting of two of a
sort together (e.g. *a double cherry*): having
two similar parts (e.g. *a double eagle*—i.e. one
with two heads): having two dissimilar qualities, &c. (e.g. *a double meaning, double use*):
twice as large: twice as great in quantity:
twice as strong, valuable, &c.; (*bot.*) having
more than the normal number of petals:
folded over once: sounding an octave lower:
acting two parts, insincere: often in composition, e.g. **doubl'e-barr'elled,** having two barrels; **doub'le-deck'er,** a ship or vehicle with
two decks.—*adv.* to twice the extent: twice
over: two together: deceitfully.—*v.t.* to increase twofold: to multiply by two: to increase
the points value of (an opponent's bid) in the
expectation that he will lose: to fold in two: to
pass (esp. to sail) round or by: to play (two
rôles in the same play),—*v.i.* to increase to
twice the quantity: to turn sharply back in
running.—*n.* twice as much: a duplicate: an
actor's substitute: the spectre of a living person: an exact counterpart: a quick pace (short
for **double-quick**): a combined bet on two
races, stake and winnings from the first being
bet on the second.—*adv.* **doub'ly,** twice: twofold: falsely.—*ns.* **doub'le-a'gent,** one secretly
acting simultaneously for two opposing
powers; **doub'le-bass,** a stringed instrument,
the largest and deepest of the violin kind—
contra-bass or *violone*; **doub'le-cross,** double
trick in which a swindler (1) persuades
another to take part in a fraud, and (2) fails
to keep faith with him.—Also *v.t.*—*ns.*
doub'le-deal'er, deceitful person; **doub'le-
deal'ing,** duplicity; **doub'le-Dutch** (see
Dutch).—*adjs.* **doub'le-dyed,** deeply stained;
doub'le-edged, having two edges: (*fig.*) capable of being used to thwart the purpose it is
intended to serve.—*n.* **doub'le-en'try,** (*book-
keeping*) method in which two entries are
made of each transaction.—*adj.* **doub'le-faced,**
two-faced, false.—*n.* **doub'le-glāz'ing,** a double
layer of glass in a window with an air-space
between the layers to act as insulation.—*adj.*
doub'le-jointed, having joints admitting some
degree of movement backwards.—*n.* **doub'leness,** the state of being double: duplicity.—
adj., adv. **doub'le-quick,** at a pace approaching a run.—*n.* the double-quick pace.—*ns.*
doub'le-stout, extra strong stout or porter;
doub'le-take, a quick second look in admiration or surprise: (*fig.*) a delayed reaction;
doub'le-talk, talk that sounds to the purpose
but amounts to nothing: ambiguous, deceptive
talk; **doub'le-think,** the power of simul-

taneously accepting and holding two completely conflicting beliefs—coined by George Orwell in his *Nineteen Eighty-Four* (1949).—*adj.* **doub'le-tongued,** deceitful in speech.—**double star** (see **binary**).—**at the double,** running. [O.Fr. *doble*—L. *duplus,* double—*duo,* two.]

double entendre, *dōō-blä-tä-dr',* n. a word or phrase with two meanings, one usually absurd or indelicate. [Fr. of 17th century, superseded now by (*mot*) *à double entente.*]

doublet, *dub'lét,* n. a close-fitting garment for the upper part of the body: one of a pair, esp. one of two words orig. the same but varying in spelling and meaning, e.g. *balm, balsam.* [O.Fr., dim. of *double.*]

doubloon, *dub-lōōn',* n. an obs. Spanish gold coin, so called because it was *double* the value of a pistole. [Sp. *doblón.*]

doubt, *dowt,* v.i. to be undecided in opinion.—*v.t.* to hold in doubt: to distrust: to suspect: to incline to think (esp.*Scot.*).—n. uncertainty of mind: suspicion: fear.—n. **doubt'er.**—*adj.* **doubt'ful,** full of doubt: not confident: suspicious: undetermined, uncertain: not clear.—*adv.* **doubt'fully.**—n. **doubt'fulness.**—*advs.* **doubt'less,** without doubt, certainly; **doubt'lessly.** [O.Fr. *douter*—L. *dubitāre,* akin to *dubius,* doubtful, moving in two (*duo*) directions.]

douce, *dōōs,* adj. (*obs.*) sweet: (*Scot.*) sedate.—n. **douceur** (*dōō-sûr'*), gratuity to ensure good will. [Fr., *doux, douce,* mild—L. *dulcis,* sweet.]

douche, *dōōsh,* n. a jet of water directed upon the body, externally or internally, from a pipe: an apparatus for throwing the jet. [Fr.,—It. *doccia,* a water-pipe—L. *dūcěre,* to lead.]

dough, *dō,* n. a mass of flour or meal moistened and kneaded, but not baked: (*slang*) money.—n. **dough'nut,** sweetened dough fried in fat: (*nucleonics*) an accelerating tube in the form of a toroid: (*nucleonics*) a toroidal assembly of enriched fissile material for increasing locally the nuetron intensity in a reactor.—*adj.* **dough'y,** like dough: soft: (*coll.*) pallid, pasty. [O.E. *dāh;* Ger. *teig,* O.N. *deig.*]

doughty, *dow'ti,* adj. able, strong: brave.—*adv.* **dough'tily.** [O.E. *dyhtig,* valiant—*dugan,* to be strong.]

dour, *dōōr,* adj. (*Scot.*) obstinate: sullen: grim. [Apparently L. *dūrus,* hard.]

douse, dowse, *dows,* v.t. to plunge into water: to strike or lower, as a sail: to put out, quench. [Cf. Old. Du. *dossen,* to beat.]

dove, *duv,* n. a bird of several varieties of the pigeon kind: a word of endearment: an emblem of innocence, gentleness: a member of the conciliatory party in a conflict, political administration, &c.—ns. **dove'-col'our,** grey tinged with pink or purple; **dove'cot, -cote,** a box or building in which pigeons breed; **dove'-tail,** a mode of fastening boards together by fitting pieces shaped like a wedge or a dove's tail spread out (*tenons*) into like cavities (*mortises*).—*v.t.* (*lit.* and *fig.*) to fit (one thing exactly into another).—Also *v.i.* —**flutter the dovecots,** to alarm timid conventional people (see *Coriolanus* V. vi. 115). [O.E. *dūfe,* as in *dūfedoppe,* diving bird.]

dowager, *dow'ä-jér,* n. a widow with a dower or jointure: a title given to a widow to distinguish her from the wife of her husband's heir: an elderly and formidable woman. [O.Fr. *douagere*—Low L. *dōtārium*—L. *dōtāre,* to endow.]

dowdy, *dow'di,* n. a woman whose dress is drab and unbecoming.—*adj.* slovenly: not smart.

dowel, *dow'el,* n. a pin of wood or iron inserted in the edges of two adjacent boards for the purpose of fastening them together. [Prob. related to Ger. *döbel,* a plug.]

dower, *dow'ér,* n. a jointure, that part of the husband's property which his widow enjoys during her life: sometimes used for *dowry:* gifts of nature.—*adj.* **dow'ered,** furnished with dower: endowed by nature.—n. **dow'er-house,** the house set apart for the widow.—*adj.* **dow'erless.** [O.Fr. *douaire*—Low L. *dōtārium*—L. *dōtāre,* to endow.]

dowie, *dow'i,* adj. (*Scot.*) dull, low-spirited, sad. [Prob. O.E. *dol,* dull.]

dowlas, *dow'lás,* n. a coarse linen cloth. [From *Daoulas* or *Doulas,* near Brest, in Brittany.]

down, *down,* n. soft feathers: a soft covering of fluffy hairs.—*adj.* **down'y,** covered with, or made of, down or the like: soft. [O.N. *dūnn;* Ger. *daune, dune.*]

down, *down,* n. a bank of sand thrown up by the sea (same as **dune**): (*pl.*) an undulating upland tract of pasture-land.—**The Downs,** an anchorage between the coast of Kent and the Goodwin Sands. [O.E. *dūn,* a hill—Celt. *dun.*]

down, *down,* adv. (passing into adj. in predicative use) to or in a lower position or state: away from a centre (capital, university, &c.): under the surface, below the horizon: from earlier to later times: from greater to less: to a final state of impotence: in a fallen state: in writing, type, &c.: on the spot, in cash.—Also elliptically, passing into an interjection or verb by omission of *go, come, put,* &c., often followed by *with.*—*adj.* moving, or destined to move, in the direction indicated by *adv.* **down** (e.g. *the* down *train*): descending (e.g. *on the* down *grade*).—*prep.* in a descent along, through, or by: to or in a lower position on: in the direction of the current of.—*v.t.* to knock or lay down.—*adjs.* **down'-and-out,** at the end of one's resources; **down'-at-heel,** having the back of the shoe trodden down: shabby; **down'-cast,** dejected.—ns. **down'come, down'fall,** fall, failure, humiliation, ruin: a falling down, as of rain; **down'grade,** downward slope or course.—*adj., adv.* downhill.—*v.t.* to reduce in status: to belittle.—*adjs.* **down'-heart'ed,** dejected; **down'hill,** descending, sloping.—n. **down'pour,** a heavy fall of rain, &c.—*adv.* **down'right,** in plain terms: utterly.—*adj.* plain spoken: brusque: absolute.—*advs.* **down'stage',** towards the footlights; **down'stairs,** in, or to, a lower floor or storey.—*adj.* **down'trodden,** trampled on, oppressed.—*advs.* **down'ward, down'wards,** from higher to lower: from source to outlet: from more ancient to modern: in the lower part.—*adj.* **down'ward.—down in the mouth,** in low spirits; **down on one's luck** (see **luck**); **down tools,** to cease work; **go downhill** (*fig.*) to deteriorate. [M.E. *a-down, adun*—O.E. *of dūne,* from the hill.]

Neutral vowels in unaccented syllables: *em'pér-ór;* for certain sounds in foreign words see p. ix.

212

dowry, *dow'ri, n.* the property which a woman brings to her husband at marriage: sometimes used for *dower.* [Same root as **dower.**]

dowse, *dowz, v.i.* to use a divining-rod.—*n.* **dows'er.** [Orig. uncertain.]

doxology, *doks-ol'o-ji, n.* a hymn or liturgical formula ascribing glory to God. [Gr. *doxologia—doxa,* praise, and *legein,* to speak.]

doyen, *doi'én, dwä-yā, n.* dean, senior member (of an academy, &c.). [Fr.,—L. *decānus.*]

doze, *dōz, v.i.* to sleep lightly: to be half-asleep or in a stupefied state.—*v.t.* to spend in drowsiness (with*away*).—*n.* a short light sleep. [Cf. O.N. *dūsa,* Dan. *dōse,* to dose.]

dozen, *duz'n, n.* a set of twelve.—**baker's dozen,** thirteen; **daily dozen** (*coll.*), physical exercises done regularly, *usu.* daily. [O.Fr. *dozeine*—L. *duodecim—duo,* two, and *decem,* ten.]

drab, *drab, n.* thick, strong, grey cloth: a grey or dull-brown colour, perh. from the muddy colour of undyed wool.—*adj.* dull, monotonous, uninteresting.—*n.* **drab'ness.** [Fr. *drap,* cloth—Low L. *drappus.*]

drachm, *dram, n.* a drachma: a dram.—*n.* **drachma** (*drak'ma*), an ancient Greek weight and silver coin: a modern Greek franc. [Gr. *drachmē—drassesthai,* to grasp.]

Draconian, *dra-kō'nyän, adj.* severe. Also **Dracōn'ic.** [After *Draco,* author of a severe code of laws at Athens (621 B.C.).]

droff, *dräf, n.* dregs: the refuse of malt after brewing. [Prob. related to Du. *draf.*]

draft, *dräft, n.* anything drawn: a smaller body (of men, animals, things) selected from a larger: (esp. *U.S.*) conscription: an order for the payment of money: a demand (upon resources, credulity, &c.): a plan: a preliminary sketch: sometimes (esp. *U.S.*) spelling for **draught** in other senses.—*v.t.* to draw an outline of: to draw up in preliminary form: to draw off (for a special purpose).—*n.* **drafts'man,** one who draws up documents, plans, designs, &c. [Same word as **draught.**]

drafts, *dräfts, n. pl.* Same word as **draughts.**

drag, *drag, v.t.* to draw by force: to draw slowly: to pull roughly and violently: to explore (a river-bed) with a drag net or hook.—*v.i.* to hang so as to trail on the ground: to move slowly and heavily:—*pr.p.* **dragg'ing,** *pa.p.* **dragged**—*n.* a net (**drag-net**) or hook for dragging along to catch things under water: a heavy harrow: a long open carriage, with transverse or side seats: a contrivance for retarding a wheel: any obstacle to progress: (*aero.*) the component of the aerodynamic force on an aircraft which lies along the longitudinal axis of the machine: (*slang*) something boring or tedious: (*U.S.*) influence: (*slang*) women's clothing worn by a man.— **drag one's feet,** to hang back deliberately in doing something. [O.E. *dragan* or O.N. *draga*; Ger. *tragen*; cf. **draw.**]

dragée, *drä-zhā, n.* a sugar-coated almond, &c.: a small silver ball for cake decoration: a sugar-coated pill: a chocolate drop. [Fr.]

draggle, *drag'l, v.t.* or *v.i.* to make or become wet and dirty as by dragging along the ground.—*n.* **dragg'le-tail,** a slut. [Freq. of **drag,** and a doublet of **drawl.**]

dragoman, *drag'o-mán, n.* an interpreter or guide in Eastern countries:—*pl.* **drag'omans.** [Fr., from Ar. *tarjumān—tarjama,* to interpret.]

dragon, *drag'ón, n.* a fabulous winged reptile: (*cap.*) the constellation Draco: a fierce person: a genus of lizards of the E. Indies.—*ns.* **drag'onet,** a little dragon: a fish of the goby family; **drag'on(-)fly,** any of an order (or a family) of insects with a long body and brilliant colours; **drag'on's-blood,** the red resinous exudation of several kinds of trees, used for colouring varnishes, &c. [Fr.,—L. *drakō, -ōnis*—Gr. *drakōn, -ontos.*]

dragonnade, *drag-on-ād', n.* the persecution of French Protestants under Louis XIV by means of dragoons: any persecution by military means (esp. in *pl.*). [Fr., from *dragon,* dragoon.]

dragoon, *dra-gōōn', n.* an old fire-spitting musket: a mounted infantryman thus armed (*obs.*): a heavy cavalryman, opp. to a hussar or lancer—surviving in the names of certain regiments.—*v.t.* to harass or compel by bullying commands. [Fr. *dragon,* dragon, dragoon.]

drain, *drān, v.t.* to draw (off or away) by degrees: to clear of water by drains: to make dry: to exhaust.—*v.i.* to flow off gradually: to lose moisture by its flowing or trickling away.—*n.* watercourse: ditch: sewer: exhausting expenditure.—*ns.* **drain'age,** act, process, method, or means of draining: a system of drains; **drain'age-bas'in,** the area of land which drains into one river; **drain'er,** a utensil on which articles are placed to drain; **drain'-pipe,** a pipe to carry away waste water or rainwater: (in *pl., coll.*) very narrow trousers.—**down the drain** (*slang*), gone for good: wasted. [O.E. *dreahnian.*]

drake, *drāk, n.* the male of the duck. [Ety. obscure; cf. dial. Ger. *draak.*]

dram, *dram, n.* a contraction of **drachm:** 1/16th of an oz. avoirdupois: formerly, with apothecaries, 1/8th of an oz.: a small drink, esp. of alcoholic liquor. [Through Fr. and L., from Gr. *drachmē.* See **drachma.**]

drama, *dräm'ä, n.* a story of life and action for representation by actors: a composition intended to be represented on the stage: dramatic literature: a dramatic situation or a series of deeply interesting events.—*adjs.* **dramatic** (*drà matʹik*), **-al,** belonging to, or in the form of, a drama: vivid, striking, often with an element of unexpectedness.—*adv.* **dramat'ically.**—*n.* **dramat'ics** (*pl.* treated as *sing.*), the acting, production, study of plays: (*coll.*) show of excessive, exaggerated emotion.—*v.t.* **dram'atise,** to compose in, or turn into, the form of a drama or play: to exaggerate the importance or emotional nature of.—*n.* **dram'atist,** a writer of plays.—**dramatic ūn'ities** (see **unity**); **dram'atis persōnae** (*ē*), the characters of a drama or play. [L.,—Gr. *drāma, -atos—drāein,* to do.]

dramaturgy, *dram'a-tûr-ji, n.* the principles of dramatic composition: theatrical art. [Gr. *drāmatourgia—drāma* and *ergon,* work.]

drank, *drangk, pa.t.* of **drink.**

drape, *drāp, v.t.* to cover as with cloth: to hang

cloth in folds about: (*refl.*) to assume a casual, graceful pose.—*n.* a hanging or curtain.—*ns.* **drāp′er,** a dealer in cloth and cloth goods; **drāp′ery,** cloth goods: hangings: the draper's business. [O.Fr. *draper,* to weave, drape—*drap,* cloth, prob. of Gmc. origin.]

drastic, *dras′tik, adj.* active, powerful in action (e.g. of a purgative): violent, radical (e.g. of measures). [Gr. *drastikos—drāein,* to act, to do.]

drat, *drat, v.t.* a minced oath used to express vexation, as 'Drat the boy!' [Shortened from **God rot!**]

draught, *dräft, n.* act of drawing or pulling: the thing or quantity drawn: the act of drinking: the quantity drunk in one breath: that which is taken in a net by drawing: a current of air: the depth of water a ship requires to float freely: a thick disk used in the game of draughts: (*pl.*) a game played by two persons moving draughtsmen alternately on a chequered board: an outline, preliminary sketch (usu. **draft** in this sense): a chosen detachment of men (usu. **draft**).—*v.t.* to sketch out (also **draft**).—*ns.* **draught-animal,** one used for drawing heavy loads; **draught′-screen,** a screen for warding off a current of air; **draughts′man,** a piece used in playing draughts: one skilled in drawing, a draftsman.—*adj.* **draught′y,** full of currents of air.— **on draught,** of liquor, sold from the cask. [O.E. *draht—dragan,* to draw. Cf. **drag** and **draw.**]

drave, *drāv,* old *pa.t.* of **drive.**

Dravidian, *dra-vid′i-àn, n.* an individual of a non-Aryan race of Southern India.—**Dravidian languages,** a family of languages spoken by the Dravidian peoples. [Sans. *Drāviḍa,* an ancient province of S. India.]

draw, *drö, v.t.* to pull (along): to pull (towards one): to pull or take out: to eviscerate: to deduce (*draw conclusions*): to receive (money, benefit): to make a picture of, to sketch: to write out (a cheque): to describe: (*naut.*) to require (a depth of water) for float‐ ing: (*sport*) to play (a game) with indecisive result.—*v.i.* to move, either towards or away from (*draw near, back*): to allow a free cur‐ rent (as of air) to pass through: to play a game with indecisive result: practise sketch‐ ing: to cast lots:—*pa.t.* drew (*drōō*); *pa.p.* drawn.—*n.* the act of drawing: an attraction: a drawn or undecided game: the selection of winning tickets in a lottery.—*ns.* **draw′back,** a disadvantage: a repayment of some part of the duty on goods on their exportation; **draw′-bridge,** a bridge that can be drawn up or let down at pleasure; **draw′er,** he or that which draws: a thing drawn out, like the sliding boxes in a **chest of drawers:** (*pl.*) a close undergarment for the lower limbs; **draw′ing,** the art of representing objects by lines drawn, shading, &c.: a picture so made.—*n.* **draw′ing-pin,** one with large flat head, for fastening paper on a board.—*adj.* **drawn,** pulled to‐ gether: closed: neither won nor lost: un‐ sheathed: eviscerated: strained, tense.—**draw a blank,** to get a lottery ticket that wins no prize: to obtain no result; **draw a cover, covert,** to send the hounds into a cover to frighten out a fox; **draw in,** to retract: to become shorter;

draw it mild, (*coll.*) to state a thing without exaggeration; **draw on,** to approach: to pull on (e.g. gloves); **draw on, upon,** to make a demand upon (one's credulity, resources, &c.); **draw out,** to prolong: to elicit: to induce to speak freely: to depart; **draw rein,** to slacken speed; **draw the line,** to fix a limit; **draw up,** to form in regular order: to draft (a document): to stop (as in driving a motor-car): to move closer; **out of the top drawer,** of top grade, esp. socially. [O.E. *dragan;* cf. **drag.**]

drawing(-)room, *drö′ing-rōōm, n.* a room to which the company withdraws after dinner: a reception of company at court. [Orig. *withdrawing-room.*]

drawl, *dröl, v.t.* and *v.i.* to speak or utter in a slow, lengthened tone.—*n.* a slow, lengthened utterance. [Connected with **draw.**]

dray, *drā, n.* a low strong cart for heavy goods. [Cf. O.E. *dræge,* drag-net—*dragan,* to draw.]

dread, *dred, n.* great fear: awe: an object of fear or awe.—*adj.* dreaded, inspiring great fear or awe.—*v.t.* to fear greatly: to reverence.—*adj.* **dread′ful,** (*orig.*) full of dread: producing great fear or awe: terrible: (*coll.*) very bad, annoying, boring, &c.—*adv.* **dread′fully.**—*n.* **dread′fulness.**—*n.* **dread′nought, dread′-naught,** a thick, strong cloth: a type of war‐ ship, both swift and heavily armoured, esp. of the early 20th century. [M.E. *dreden*—O.E. *ondrǣdan,* to fear.]

dream, *drēm, n.* a sequence of thoughts and fancies, or a vision during sleep: a state of abstraction, a reverie: an unrealised ambition: something only imaginary.—*v.i.* to fancy things during sleep: to think idly.—*v.t.* to see in, or as in, a dream:—*pa.t.* and *pa.p.* dreamed or dreamt (*dremt*).—*n.* **dream′er.**—*adj.* **dream′y,** full of dreams, languid: addicted to dreaming, abstracted, unpractical: (*coll.*) lovely.—*adv.* **dream′ily.**—*n.* **dream′iness.**—*ns.* **dream′land,** the land of dreams, reverie, or imagination; **dream′world,** a world of illu‐ sions.—**dream up,** to plan in the mind, often unrealistically. [M.E. *dream, drēm;* not re‐ corded in O.E.; cf. O.H.G. *troum,* O.N. *draumr.*]

dreary, *drēr′i, adj.* gloomy: cheerless.—*adv.* **drear′ily.**—*n.* **drear′iness.** [O.E. *drēorig,* mournful, bloody—*drēor,* gore.]

dredge, *drej, n.* a bag-net for dragging along the ocean or river bottom to take specimens of plants and animals, mud, &c.: apparatus for deepening a harbour or channel by removing mud from the bottom, or for raising alluvial deposits containing minerals.—*v.t.* to gather with a dredge: to deepen.—*n.* **dredg′er,** a ves‐ sel fitted with dredging apparatus. [Conn. with **drag, draw.**]

dredge, *drej, v.t.* to sprinkle.—*ns.* **dredg′er, dredge′-box, dredg′ing-box,** a vessel with pre‐ forated lid for sprinkling. [O.Fr. *dragie,* sugar-plum—Gr. *tragēmata,* dessert.]

dree, *drē, v.t.* (*Scot.*) to endure, esp. in **dree one's weird,** to undergo one's destiny. [O.E. *drēogan,* suffer, accomplish.]

dregs, *dregz, n.pl.* impurities in liquor that fall to the bottom, the grounds: dross: the vilest part of anything. [Prob. O.N. *dreggjar.*]

drench, *drench* or *-sh, v.t.* to administer medi‐ cine by force: to wet thoroughly, to soak: (*lit.*

Neutral vowels in unaccented syllables: *em′pėr-ôr;* for certain sounds in foreign words see p. ix.

and *fig.*) to saturate.—*n.* a dose of medicine forced down the throat.—*n.* **drench′ing**, a soaking, as by rain. [O.E. *drencan*, to cause to drink, from *drincan*, to drink.]

dress, *dres*, *v.t.* to straighten: to set in order: to prepare: to draw (fowl): to trim: to treat, bandage: to tend: to clothe: to adorn.—*v.i.* to come into line: to put on clothes:—*pa.t.* and *pa.p.* dressed (rarely, drest).—*n.* the covering or ornament of the body: a lady's gown: manner of clothing.—*adj.* **dress′y**, showy: too fond of dress or adornment.—*ns.* **dress′-cir′cle**, part of a theatre (usually the first gallery) intended for people in evening dress; **dress′-coat**, a fine black coat with narrow or cutaway skirts, worn in full dress; **dress′er**, one who dresses: a person who assists an actor to dress: a kind of kitchen sideboard; **dress′ing**, dress or clothes: any application used in a preparation process (as manure applied to land, sauce or stuffing added to food): the bandage, &c., applied to a wound; **dress′ing-case**, a case of toilet requisites; **dress′ing-gown**, a loose garment used in dressing, or in deshabille; **dress′ing-sta′tion**, a place where wounded are collected and tended by members of a field ambulance.—**dress down**, to scold severely; **dress up**, to dress elaborately: to dress for a part or in masquerade: to treat so as to make appear better, more interesting &c., than it really is; **dress rehearsal** (see **rehearsal**).—**evening dress**, **full dress**, style or manner of dress proper for a formal occasion; **fancy dress**, clothes worn in masquerade (as at a *fancy-dress ball*). [O.Fr. *dresser*, to prepare, through Low L.—L. *dīrigĕre*, to direct.]

dressage, *dres-äzh*, *n.* training of a horse in deportment and response to controls. [Fr.]

drew, *drōō*, *pa.t.* of **draw**.

drey, *drā*, *n.* a squirrel's nest. [Unknown.]

dribble, *drib′l*, *v.i.* to fall in small drops: to allow saliva to trickle from the mouth.—*v.t.* to spend in small amounts: (*football*) to kick (the ball) along little by little.—*n.* **drib′let**, **dribb′let**, a drop, trickle, small quantity. [Freq. of obs. vb. *drib*, akin to **drip**.]

dried, *drīd*, *pa.t.* and *pa.p.* of **dry**.

drier, **dryer**, *drī′ér*, *adj.* comp. degree of **dry**.—*n.* a person, machine, apparatus, or substance, that dries or hastens drying. [**dry**.]

drift, *drift*, *n.* a heap of matter driven together, as snow: the direction in which a thing is driven: natural course, tendency: the general sense or intention (of what is said): (*geol.*) one of the superficial, as distinct from the solid, formations of the earth's crust: (*S. Africa*) a ford.—*v.t.* to carry by drift.—*v.i.* to be floated or blown along: to be driven into heaps: to wander around without any definite aim.—*ns.* **drift′er**, that which drifts: a fisherman or a fishing-boat that uses a drift-net; **drift′-net**, a net which is allowed to drift with the tide; **drift′-wood**, wood drifted by water. [**drive**.]

drill, *dril*, *n.* a West African baboon, smaller than the mandrill. [Obs. Fr. *drill*, a man.]

drill, *dril*, *v.t.* to bore, pierce, as with a drill: to exercise (soldiers, pupils, &c.): to sow in rows.—*n.* an instrument that bores: the exercising of soldiers, &c.: exercise, practice: (*coll.*) correct procedure or routine: a furrow with seed or growing plants in it. [Prob. borrowed from Du. *drillen*, to bore; *dril*, *drille*, a borer; cf. **thrill**.]

drilling, *dril′ing*, *n.* stout twilled linen or cotton cloth.—Also **drill**. [Ger. *drillich*, ticking—L. *trilīx*, three-threaded—*trēs*, *tria*, three, *līcium*, thread.]

drily. See under **dry**.

drink, *dringk*, *v.t.* to swallow, as a liquid: to take in through the senses.—*v.i.* to swallow a liquid: to take intoxicating liquors to excess:—*pr.p.* drink′ing; *pa.t.* drank; *pa.p.* drunk.—*n.* something to be drunk: intoxicating liquor.—*n.* **drink′er**, a tippler.—**drink in**, to absorb: to take in, understand, with appreciation; **drink to** (**a person's health**), to drink wine or other beverage with good wishes for a person's health.—**strong drink**, alcoholic liquor. [O.E. *drincan*; Ger. *trinken*.]

drip, *drip*, *v.i.* to fall in drops: to let fall drops:—*pr.p.* drip′ping; *pa.p.* dripped.—*n.* a falling in drops: that which falls in drops: the edge of a roof: a device for passing a fluid slowly and continuously, esp. into a vein of the body: the material so passed: (*slang*) a forceless person.—*adj.* **drip′-dry′**, of a material or garment, requiring little or no ironing when allowed to dry by dripping.—Also *v.i.*, *v.t.*—*ns.* **drip′ping**, that which falls in drops, as fat from meat in roasting; **drip′-stone**, a projecting moulding over doorways, &c., serving to throw off the rain.—**dripping roast**, a source of easy and continuous profit. [O.E. *dryppan—drēopan.*]

drive, *drīv*, *v.t.* to urge along: to hurry on: to control or guide the movements or operations of: to hit with force, as a ball (esp. a golf ball from a tee), a nail, &c.: (*fig.*) to impel (to): to carry on (e.g. a brisk trade): to conclude (e.g. a hard bargain).—*v.i.* to press (forward) with violence: to be forced along: to go in a carriage: to work, strive hard (at):—*pa.t.* drove; *pa.p.* driv′en.—*n.* an excursion in a carriage: a road for driving on, esp. a private one to a house: driving mechanism: energy, push: an organised campaign to attain any end: any driving shot in sport.—*ns.* **driv′er**, one who or that which drives, in all senses; **drive′-in**, a refreshment halt, store, cinema, &c., where patrons are catered for whilst still remaining in their motor-cars.—Also *adj.*—*n.* **driv′ing-wheel**, a main wheel that communicates motion to other wheels.—**drive at**, to tend towards in argument, to mean. [O.E. *drīfan*, to drive; Ger. *treiben*, to push.]

drivel, *driv′l*, *v.i.* to slaver: to speak like an idiot:—*pr.p.* driv′elling; *pa.p.* driv′elled.—*n.* slaver: nonsense.—*n.* **driv′eller**. [M.E. *drevelen*, *dravelen*—O.E. *dreflian*.]

drizzle, *driz′l*, *v.i.* to rain in small drops.—*n.* a small, light rain.—*adj.* **drizz′ly**. [Freq. of M.E. *dresen*—O.E. *drēosan*, to fall.]

droll, *drōl*, *adj.* odd: amusing.—*n.* a jester.—*n.* **droll′ery**. [Fr. *drôle*, prob. from Du. *drollig*, odd—*trold*, a hobgoblin.]

dromedary, *drom′i-där-i*, or *drum′-*, *n.* a swift camel: a one-humped Arabian camel. [Fr.,—Low L. *dromedārius*—Gr. *dromas*,

---

fāte, *fär*; *mē*, *hûr* (her); *mīne*; *mōte*, *för*; *mūte*; *mōōn*, *fŏŏt*; *THen* (then)

-ados, running—*dromos*, a course, run.]

drone, *drōn*, *n.* the male of the honey-bee: one who lives on the labour of others, like the drone-bee—a lazy, idle fellow: a deep humming sound: a bass-pipe of a bagpipe: a monotonous tiresome speaker or speech: an aircraft piloted by remote control.—*v.i.* to emit a monotonous humming sound. [O.E. *drān*, bee.]

drool, *drōōl*, *v.i.* to slaver—a form of **drivel**.

droop, *drōōp*, *v.i.* to sink or hang down: to grow weak or faint: to decline. [O.N. *drūpa*, to droop; from the same root as **drop**.]

drop, *drop*, *n.* a small rounded blob of liquid that hangs or falls at one time: a small quantity: anything hanging like a drop: anything arranged to drop: a fall: a lessening in amount of value: a descent, esp. a steep one: an unpleasant surprise.—*v.i.* to fall in drops: to fall suddenly, steeply, or sheer: to diminish.—*v.t.* to let fall: to let go, relinquish, abandon: to omit (a letter): to utter, write in a casual manner (as *drop a remark, note*): (of animals) to give birth to: to cause to fall: to cease to associate with—*pr.p.* dropp'ing; *pa.p.* dropped.—*ns.* drop'-kick (see **kick**); dropp'ing, dung; drop'-scene (or drop'-curtain), a painted curtain lowered to conceal all or part of the stage in a theatre.—**drop in**, to come in casually; **drop off**, to fall asleep; **drop on**, to single out for rebuke or for an unpleasant task; **drop out**, to disappear from one's place: withdraw, esp. from an academic course or from conventional life in society (*n.* drop'-out).—**at the drop of a hat**, immediately: on the smallest provocation. [O.E. *dropa*, drop—*dropian, droppian*, to drop; Du. *drop*, Ger. *tropfe*.]

dropsy, *drop'si*, *n.* an unnatural collection of water in any part of the body.—*adj.* drop'sical. [Through Fr. from L. *hydrōpisis*—Gr. *hydrōps, -ōpos*—*hydōr*, water.]

droshky, *drosh'ki*, **drosky**, *dros'ki*, *n.* a low four-wheeled open carriage used in Russia. [Russ. *drozhki*.]

dross, *dros*, *n.* the scum of melting metals: very small or waste coal: waste matter: refuse. [O.E. *drōs*.]

drought, *drowt*, **drouth**, *drowth* (*Scot. drōōth*), *n.* dryness: want of rain or of water: (in following senses esp. **drouth**) thirst: an insatiable tippler: atmosphere good for drying.—*adjs.* drought'y, drouth'y. [O.E. *drūgath*, dryness—*drūgian*, to dry.]

drove, *drōv*, *pa.t.* of **drive**.—*n.* a number of cattle, or other animals, driven.—*n.* drov'er, one whose occupation is to drive cattle. [O.E. *drāf*—*drīfan*, to drive.]

drown, *drown*, *v.i.* to die of suffocation in liquid.—*v.t.* to kill by suffocation in liquid: to submerge: to flood: to overwhelm. [M.E. *drounen*; origin obscure.]

drowse, *drowz*, *v.i.* to be heavy with sleep.—*v.t.* to make heavy with sleep: to stupefy.—*adj.* drows'y, sleepy.—*adv.* drows'ily.—*n.* drows'iness. [Apparently O.E. *drūsian*, to be sluggish.]

drub, *drub*, *v.t.* to beat or thrash:—*pr.p.* drub'b'ing; *pa.p.* drubbed.—*n.* drubb'ing, a cudgelling. [Possibly Ar. *daraba*, to beat.]

drudge, *druj*, *v.i.* to do dull, laborious, or very

mean work.—*n.* one who does such work—a hack, or a menial servant.—*n.* drudg'ery, the work of a drudge, hard or humble labour. [Ety. unknown; perh. from root of O.E. *drēogan*, to perform, undergo.]

drug, *drug*, *n.* any substance used in the composition of medicine: a substance used to stupefy or poison or for self-indulgence: an article that cannot be sold, generally owing to overproduction.—*v.t.* to mix or season with drugs: to dose to excess, poison, or stupefy, with, or as with, drugs.—*v.i.* (*coll.*) to be addicted to taking drugs:—*pr.p.* drugg'ing; *pa.p.* drugged.—*ns.* drug'-add'ict, drug'-fiend, a habitual taker of drugs; drugg'ist, one who deals in drugs. [O.Fr. *drogue*, of uncertain origin.]

drugget, *drug'ét*, *n.* a woven and felted coarse woollen fabric. [O.Fr. *droguet.*]

druid, *drōō'id*, *n.* (also *cap.*) a priest among the ancient Celts of Britain, Gaul, and Germany: an Eisteddfod official:—*fem.* dru'idess.—*adjs.* druid'ic, -al.—*n.* dru'idism, the doctrines and ceremonies of the druids. [L. pl. *druidae*, from a Celtic stem *druid-*, whence Gael. *draoi*, magician.]

drum, *drum*, *n.* an instrument of percussion, stretched on a frame (usu. cylindrical or hemispherical in shape): anything shaped like a drum, as a container for liquids: the tympanum of the ear: (*archit.*) the upright part of a cupola.—*v.i.* to beat a drum: to beat or tap rhythmically: to thump continuously. —*v.t.* to expel with beat of drum (with *out, down*): to summon as by drum (with *up*): to impress by continued repetition (with *into*):—*pr.p.* drumm'ing; *pa.p.* drummed.—*ns.* drum'head court-martial, a court-martial (q.v.) improvised in time of war round an upturned drum for summary judgment; drum'-ma'jor, the marching leader of a military band, in command of the drummers; drumm'er, one who plays upon the drum; drum'stick, the knobbed stick with which a drum is beaten: the lower joint (tibia) of the leg of a cooked fowl. [From a Gmc. root; cf. Ger. *trommel*, drum; prob. imit.]

drunk, *drungk*, *pa.p.* of **drink**.—*p.adj.* intoxicated.—*n.* a drunk person.—*n.* drunk'ard, one who frequently drinks to excess.—*p.adj.* drunk'en, given to excessive drinking: resulting from, showing the effects of (or as if of), intoxication.—*n.* drunk'enness, intoxication: habitual intoxication.

drupe, *drōōp*, *n.* a fleshy fruit containing a stone, as the plum, &c.—*adj.* drupa'ceous. [L. *drūpa*—Gr. *dryppā*, an over-ripe olive.]

dry, *drī*, *adj.* free from, deficient in, moisture, sap, rain: not green: not giving milk: thirsty: uninteresting: quiet, restrained (e.g. of humour): frigid and precise (of manner): not sweet (of wine): legally forbidding trade in intoxicating liquor:—*comp.* drī'er; *sup.* drī'est.—*v.t.* to free from water or moisture: to exhaust of moisture.—*v.i.* to become dry: to evaporate entirely (also **dry up**):—*pr.p.* dry'ing; *pa.p.* dried.—*ns.* drī'er (separate article); dry'ness.—*adv.* dry'ly, drī'ly.—*ns.* dry-battery, -cell (*elect.*), one in which the electrolyte is in the form of paste, not

---

Neutral vowels in unaccented syllables: *em'pér-ór*; for certain sounds in foreign words see p. ix.

liquid.—*v.t.* **dry'-clean**, to clean with chemicals, without water.—*ns.* **dry'-dock** (see **dock**); **dry'er**, a spelling of **dri'er; dry'-fly** (*angling*), a fly that is not sunk in the water; (*pl.*) **dry'-goods**, drapery, &c., as opp. to hardware, groceries; **dry'-ice**, solid carbon dioxide; **dry'-nurse**, a nurse who feeds a child without milk from the breast; **dry'-point**, a needle by which fine lines are drawn without acid in copper-plate engraving: an engraving so produced; **dry'-rot**, a decay of timber caused by fungi which reduce it to a dry, brittle mass; **dry'-salter**, a dealer in gums, dyes, &c., **dry'-saltery.**—*adj.* **dry'-shod**, without wetting the shoes or feet.—**dry steam**, steam unmixed with liquid drops.—*adj.* **dry'-stone**, built of stone without mortar, as some walls.—**dry up** to cease to produce liquid (water, milk, &c.): (*slang*) to stop talking: to forget one's lines or part (as an actor, &c).—**go dry**, to adopt liquor prohibition. [O.E. *drŷge*; cf. Du. *droog* Ger. *trocken*.]

dryad, *drī'ad*, *n.* a wood nymph: *pla.* **dry'ads, -ades.** [Gr. *dryas*, *-ados*, from *drys*, oak tree.]

dual, *dū'ál*, *adj.* twofold: consisting of two.—*n.* (also **dual number**—*gram.*) an inflected form of noun, verb, or pronoun indicating that *two* persons or things are spoken of.—*adj.* **du'al-control**, able to be operated by either or both of two persons (as an aeroplane).—*ns.* **dū'al-ism** (*philos.*), the doctrine of the entire separation of spirit and matter, of two distinct principles of good and of evil, or of two distinct supernatural beings of these characters; **dū'alist**, a believer in dualism; **dual'ity**, doubleness, state of being double.—*adj.* **du'al-pur'pose**, serving or intended to serve two purposes.—**dual carriageway**, a road consisting of two separated parts, each for use of traffic in one direction only; **dual personality**, a condition in which the same individual shows at different times two very different characters. [L. *duālis*—*duo*, two.]

dub, *dub*, *v.t.* to confer knighthood upon by touching each shoulder with a sword: to confer any dignity upon: to nickname, style:—*pr.p.* dubb'ing; *pa.p.* dubbed.—*n.* **dub'b'ing**, the accolade: (or **dubb'in**) a preparation of grease for softening leather. [O.E. *dubbian.*]

dub, *dub*, *v.t.* to give (a film) a new sound-track, e.g. one in a different language: to add sound effects or music to (a film, &c.): to transfer (recorded music, &c.) to a new disk or tape: to combine so as to make one record (music, &c., from more than one source, e.g. a live performance and a recording).—*n.* **dubb'ing**. [Abbrev. of **double**.]

dubious, *dū'bi-us*, *adj.* doubtful (about, of): uncertain as to the result (e.g. *a dubious contest*): equivocal (e.g. *dubious reply*): of questionable nature (e.g. *dubious dealings*; *a dubious compliment*).—*adv.* **dū'biously.**—*ns.* **dū'biousness, dūbī'ety.** [L. *dubius.*]

ducal, *dū'kál*, *adj.* pertaining to a duke.

ducat, *duk'át*, *n.* a gold coin, formerly much used on the Continent, its commonest value being about 47p; there were also silver ducats in Italy worth 17p [O.Fr. *ducat* It. *ducato*—Low L. *ducātus*, a duchy.]

duchy, *duch'i*, *n.* the territory of a duke, a

dukedom.—*ns.* **duch'ess**, the consort or widow of a duke: a woman of the same rank as a duke in her own right; **duchesse** (*duch'es, dü-shes'*), a table-cover or centre-piece.—Also **duchesse cov'er.**—**duchesse set**, a set of covers for a dressing-table. [O.Fr. *duché*—Low L. *ducātus.*]

duck, *duk*, *n.* coarse cloth for small sails, sacking, &c.: (*pl.*) garments made of duck. [Du. *doeck*, linen cloth; Ger. *tuch.*]

duck, *duk*, *v.t.* to dip for a moment in water: (*coll.*) to avoid.—*v.i.* to dip or dive: to lower the head suddenly.—*n.* a quick lowering of the head or body.—*n.* **duck'ing-stool**, a stool or chair in which scolds, &c., were formerly tied and ducked in the water. [M.E. *douken*; Ger. *tauchen*, Du. *duiken.*]

duck, *duk*, *n.* any of a family of water-birds, the prominent marks of which are webbed feet, a small hind-toe not reaching the ground, netted scales in front of the lower leg, and a long bill: the female duck as distinguished from the male *drake*: in cricket (originally *duck's egg*), the zero (0), which records that a player has made no runs: (*coll.*) a darling, sweetheart.—*ns.* **duck'(-)bill** (see **platypus**); **duck'-board**, planking or other wooden pathway for swampy ground, trenches, &c.; **duck'ling**, a young duck.—**break one's duck** (*cricket*), open one's score; **lame duck**, a defaulter, bankrupt: any disabled or inefficient person or thing; **make ducks and drakes of, play ducks and drakes with**, to squander, waste. [O.E. *duce*, a duck; from the same root as **duck** (2).]

duck, *duk*, *n.* a kind of amphibious military transport vehicle or landing craft. [From manufacturers' code initials, DUKW.]

duct, *dukt*, *n.* a tube or pipe for fluids, electric cable, &c.—**ductless glands**, masses of glandular tissue that lack ducts and discharge their products directly into the blood, e.g. the lymph glands. [L. *ductus*—*dūcĕre*, to lead.]

ductile, *duk'til*, *-til*, *adj.* easily led: yielding: capable of being drawn out into threads.—*n.* **ductil'ity.** [Fr.,—L. *ductilis*—*dūcĕre*, to lead.]

dud, *dud*, *n.* (*slang*) anything worthless, useless, or bogus.—Also *adj.* [Origin unknown.]

dude, *dūd*, *n.* fop, dandy. [Origin unknown.]

dudgeon, *duj'ón*, *n.* resentment: angry feeling.

dudgeon, *duj'ón*, *n.* the haft of a dagger: a small dagger. [Anglo-Fr. *digeon*, knife-handle.]

duds, *dudz*, *n.pl.* poor or ragged clothes: (*coll.*) clothes. [Perh. M.E. *dudde*, cloak.]

due, *dū*, *adj.* owed: that ought to be paid or done to another: proper: expected to arrive, be ready, be paid, &c.—*adv.* directly (e.g. *due east*).—*n.* what is owed: what one has a right to: perquisite: fee or tribute.—**due to**, caused by: (wrongly) owing to, because of. [O.Fr. *deü*, pa.p. of *devoir*—L. *dēbēre*, to owe.]

duel, *dū'él*, *n.* a combat, under fixed conditions, between two persons over a matter of honour, &c.: (*fig.*) single combat of any kind (e.g. *a verbal duel*).—*v.i.* to fight in a duel:—*pr.p.* du'elling; *pa.p.* du'elled.—*ns.* **dū'eller, dū'ellist.** [It. *duello*—L. *duellum*, the original form of *bellum*, war—*duo*, two.]

duenna, *dū-en'a*, *n.* an elderly lady who acts as guardian to a younger. [Sp. *dueña*, a form of *doña,* mistress—L. *domina,* fem. of *dominus,* lord.]

duet, duett, *dū-et′,* **duetto,** *dū-et′tō, n.* a composition in music for two performers: the performance or performers of such.—*n.* **duett′ist.** [It. *duetto*—*duo,* two—L. *duo,* two.]

duffel, *duf′l, n.* a thick, coarse woollen cloth, with a thick nap.—**duffel coat,** a coat, usu. hooded, made of duffel. [Du., from *Duffel,* a town near Antwerp.]

duffer, *duf′ér, n.* an unskilful person: an unproductive mine. [Origin unknown.]

dug, *dug, n.* a nipple or udder of a cow or other beast. [Cf. Sw. *dægga,* Dan. *dægge,* to suckle.]

dug, *dug, pa.t.* and *pa.p.* of **dig.**—*n.* **dug′out,** a boat made by hollowing out the trunk of a tree: a rough dwelling or shelter, *dug out* of a slope or bank or in a trench.

dugong, *dōō′gong, n.* a herbivorous marine mammal—the supposed original of the mermaid. [Malayan *dūyong.*]

duiker, duyker, *dī′kér, n.* a genus of small South African antelopes. [Du.]

duke, *dūk, n.* the highest order of nobility: on the Continent, frequently a sovereign prince.—*n.* **duke′dom,** the title, rank, or territories of a duke. [O.Fr. *duc*—L. *dux, ducis,* a leader—*dūcĕre,* to lead.]

D(o)ukhobor, *dōō′hō-bór,* or *-kō-, n.* a member of a Russian religious sect, holding certain unorthodox beliefs and refusing military service, many of whom live in Canada. [Russ. *Dukhoborets*—*dukhu,* spirit, *boroti,* to fight.]

dulcet, *duls′et, adj.* sweet to the taste, or to the ear: melodious, harmonious. [L. *dulcis,* sweet.]

dulcimer, *dul′si-mér, n.* a musical instrument played by striking the wires with small pieces of wood or cork-headed hammers: a Jewish musical instrument, probably a bagpipe. [Sp. *dulcemele*—L. *dulce melos,* a sweet song—*dulcis,* sweet, *melos* (Gr. *melos*), a song.]

dulcitone, *dul′si-tōn, n.* a piano-like instrument having tuning-forks in place of wires. [L. *dulcis,* sweet, Gr. *tonos,* tone.]

dull, *dul, adj.* slow of hearing, of learning, or of understanding: without life or spirit: drowsy, sleepy: sad: not bright or clear: cloudy: blunt: muffled.—*v.t.* to make dull or stupid: to blunt: to dim, to cloud.—*v.i.* to become dull.—*adv.* **dul′ly**—*ns.* **dull′ness, dull′ness; dull′ard,** a dull and stupid person.—*adjs.* **dull′sight′ed; dull′witt′ed.** [Related to O.E. *dol,* foolish, and *dwellan,* to err; Ger. *toll,* mad.]

dulse, *duls, n.* an edible red seaweed. [Gael. *duileasg,* perh. *duille,* leaf, *uisge,* water.]

duly, *dū′li, adv.* properly: fitly: at the proper time. [See **due.**]

Duma, *dōō′ma, n.* the Russian parliament of 1905-17. [Russ.]

dumb, *dum, adj.* without the power of speech: silent, soundless: stupid.—*n.* **dumb′ness.**—*ns.* **dumb′-bell,** a double-headed weight swung in the hands to develop the muscles; **dumb′-show′,** gesture without words: pantomime; **dumb′-wait′er,** a movable table for conveying food, dishes, &c., at meals.—*v.t.* **dumb(b)-found′, -er,** to strike dumb: to confuse greatly: to astonish.—*n.* **dumm′y,** one who is dumb: a sham article in a shop: a block or lay-figure: an exposed hand of cards: (*rugby*) a feint of

passing.—**dummy run,** an experimental run: a try-out or testing. [O.E. *dumb*; Ger. *dumm,* stupid.]

dumb, *dum, adj.* (*orig. U.S.*) very stupid. [Ger. *dumm,* or Du. *dom*; cf. **dumb** (1).]

dumdum, *dum′dum, n.* a soft-nosed expanding bullet, first made at *Dum Dum* near Calcutta.

dummy. See **dumb** (1).

dump, *dump, v.t.* to set (down) heavily: to unload: to discard, as on a rubbish heap: to sell quantities of goods at a very low price, esp. in another country where cost of production is higher than in the exporting country.—*n.* a thud or dull blow: a place for the discharge of goods or rubbish: a dirty, dilapidated place. [Cf. Dan. *dumpe,* Norw. *dumpa,* to fall plump.]

dump, *dump, n.* gloominess, low spirits—now only used in *pl.* [Cf. Ger. *dumpf,* gloomy.]

dumpling, *dump′ling, n.* a kind of thick pudding or mass of soft paste. [Origin obscure.]

dumpy, *dump′i, adj.* short and thick.—*ns.* **dump′iness; dump′y-lev′el,** a spirit-level used in surveying, having a short telescope rigidly connected to the vertical spindle.

dun, *dun, adj.* greyish-brown in colour: dark. [O.E. *dun,* prob. Celt.]

dun, *dun, v.t.* to importune for payment:—*pr.p.* **dunn′ing;** *pa.p.* **dunned.** [Perh. allied to **din.**]

dunce, *duns, n.* one slow at learning: a stupid person. [*Duns* Scotus (died 1308), the leader of a group of schoolmen (from him called *Dunses*) who at a later period, on the revival of learning, opposed classical studies—hence an opposer of learning, a blockhead.]

dunderhead, *dun′dér-hed, n.* a stupid person—also **dun′derpate.** [Origin unknown.]

dune, *dūn, n.* a low hill of sand, esp. on the seashore. [Fr.—O.Du. *dūna*; cf. **down.**]

dung, *dung, n.* excrement: manure.—*v.t.* to manure with dung.—*n.* **dung′hill,** a heap of dung. [O.E.]

dungaree, *dung-gá-rē′,* or *dung′-, n.* a coarse Indian calico: (*pl.*) overalls, esp. ones including trousers, made of it. [Hindustani *dungrī.*]

dungeon, *dun′jón, n.* (*orig.*) the principal tower of a castle: a close, dark prison, esp. a cell under ground. [O.Fr. *donjon*—Low L. *domniō, -ōnis*—L. *dominus,* a lord.]

dunk, *dungk, v.t.* and *v.i.* to dip cake, &c., that one is eating in one's coffee or other beverage. [Ger. *tunken,* to dip.]

dunlin, *dun′lin, n.* the red-backed sandpiper. [Dim. of **dun.**]

dunnock, *dun′ok, n.* the hedge-sparrow. [Dim. of **dun** (1).]

duo, *dū′ō, n.* a duet: two persons associated in some way. [It.—L. *duo,* two.]

duodecennial, *dū-ō-di-sen′yál, adj.* occurring every twelve years. [L. *duodecim,* twelve, *annus,* year.]

duodecimal, *dū-ō-des′i-ml, adj.* computed by twelves: twelfth.—**duodecimal system,** a system of numbers (used by builders, &c.) in which each denomination is twelve times the next, instead of ten times, as in ordinary (decimal) arithmetic. [L. *duodecim,* twelve—*duo,* two, and *decem,* ten.]

duodenum, *dū-ō-dē′num, n.* the first portion of the small intestine, so called because about twelve fingers′-breadth in length.—*adj.* **duo-**

Neutral vowels in unaccented syllables: *em′pér-ór*; for certain sounds in foreign words see p. ix.

218

dĕ'nal. Formed from L. *duodēnī*, twelve each.]

duologue, *dū'ō-log, n.* a piece spoken between two. [Irregularly formed from L. *duo* (or Gr. *dyo*), two, Gr. *logos*, discourse.]

dupe, *dūp, n.* one who is cheated.—*v.t.* to deceive: to trick.—*n.* **dū'pery,** the art of deceiving others. [Fr. *dupe*; of uncertain origin.]

duple, *dū'pl, adj.* double, twofold: (*mus.*) having two beats to the bar. [L. *duplus*; cf. **double.**]

duplex, *dū'pleks, adj.* twofold, double.—*n.* **duplicity** (*dū-plis'i-ti*), doubleness, esp. in conduct and intention, deceitfulness. [L. *duplex, -icis.*]

duplicate, *dū'pli-kåt, adj.* double: twofold: exactly like.—*n.* another thing of the same kind: a copy or transcript.—*v.t.* (*dū'pli-kāt*) to double: to make an exact copy or copies of: to repeat.—*ns.* **duplica'tion; dū'plicātor,** a copying apparatus.—**duplicate ratio,** ratio of the squares of the quantities.—**in duplicate,** in two copies. [L. *duplicāre, -ātum—duo,* two, *plicāre,* to fold.]

durable, *dūr'ā-bl, adj.* able to last or endure, resisting wear, &c.—*ns.* **dur'ableness, durabil'ity.**—*ns.* **dur'ance,** continuance: durability: imprisonment; **durā'tion,** continuance in time: time indefinitely: power of continuance. [L. *dūrāre,* to harden, endure, last.]

duraluminium, *dūr-al-ūm-in'i-um, n.* an aluminium-base alloy.—Also **dural'umin; dural.** [L. *dūrus,* hard, and **aluminium.**]

durbar, *dûr'bär, n.* an audience-chamber: a reception or levee, esp. of Indian princes: a court: the body of officials at an Indian court. [Pers. *dar-bār,* a prince's court, lit. a 'door of admittance'.]

duress, duresse, *dūr'es* or *dūr-es', n.* constraint: imprisonment: constraint illegally exercised to force a person to perform some act. [O.Fr. *duresse*—L. *dūritia—dūrus,* hard.]

during, *dū'ring, prep.* throughout the time of: in the course of. [Orig. pr.p. of obs. *dure,* to last.]

durra, *door'ä, n.* Indian millet, a sorghum, a grass akin to sugar-cane, much cultivated for grain in Asia and Africa.—Also **doura, dhurra.** [Ar. *dhurah.*]

durst, *dûrst, pa.t.* of **dare,** to venture. [O.E. *dorste,* pa.t. of *durran,* to dare.]

dusk, *dusk, adj.* darkish: of a dark colour.—*n.* twilight: partial darkness: shade of colour—*adj.* **dusk'y,** partially dark or obscure: dark-coloured: gloomy.—*ns.* **dusk'iness, dusk'ness.** [Apparently connected with O.E. *dox,* dark.]

dust, *dust, n.* fine particles of solid matter: powdery matter, whether lying as a deposit or carried in the air: earth: (*fig.*) the grave, where the body becomes dust.—*v.t.* to free from dust: to sprinkle with dust, or the like.—*adj.* **dust'y,** covered with, containing, or characterised by, dust: like dust.—*ns.* **dust'-bin,** receptacle for household rubbish; **dust'-bowl,** a drought area subject to dust-storms; **dust'-cover,** paper cover of a book; **dust'er,** cloth for removing dust; **Red Duster,** the Red Ensign (see **Ensign**); **dust'-man,** one who clears away household refuse; **dust'-sheet,** a sheet used for covering furniture; **dust'-storm,** a storm in which a column of dust whirls across a dry country; **dust'-up,** a quarrel, a commotion;

dus'ty-mill'er, the auricula.—**bite the dust,** to be knocked to the ground: to be defeated; **not so dusty,** not so bad; **raise a dust,** to cause a commotion, esp. in complaint; **throw dust in the eyes of,** to deceive. [O.E. *dūst*; cf. Ger. *dunst,* vapour.]

Dutch, *duch, adj.* pertaining to Holland, its people, or language: (*obs.*) German: heavy, clumsy, as in *Dutch-built*—**double Dutch,** any unknown or unintelligible language. For **Dutch auction, courage, treat,** see **auction, courage, treat.**—**pay Dutch** (*coll.*), to pay each for himself. [Ger. *deutsch, (lit.)* belonging to the people—O.H.G. *diutis,* of which *-is* = the Eng. suffx. *-ish,* and *diut* = O.E. *thēod,* a nation.]

duty, *dū'ti, n.* that which one is bound by any obligation to do: one's business, occupation, functions, &c. (e.g. *on duty,* the *duties of this post*): service: respect: tax on goods, &c.—*adjs.* **dū'teous,** devoted to duty: obedient; **dū'tiable,** liable to be taxed; **dū'tiful,** attentive to duty: respectful; **dū'ty-free,** free from tax or duty. [Anglo-Fr. *dueté*; cf. **due.**]

duumvirate, *dū-um'vi-rāt, n.* the union of two men (**dūum'virs**) in the same office—a form of government in ancient Rome. [L.—*duo,* two, and *vir,* a man.]

dux, *duks, n.* a leader: (*Scot.*) the head boy or girl in a school or class:—*pl.* **dux'es.** [L., a leader.]

dwarf, *dwörf, n.* an animal or plant much below the ordinary height: a diminutive person.—*v.t.* to hinder from growing: to make to appear small.—*adj.* **dwarf'ish,** like a dwarf: very small. [O.E. *dweorg*; Ger. *zwerg.*]

dwell, *dwel, v.i.* to abide (in a place): to remain, to continue long: (with *on*) to rest the attention on, to talk at length about:—*pr.p.* **dwell'ing;** *pa.t.* and *pa.p.* **dwelt** (or **dwelled**).—*ns.* **dwell'er; dwell'ing,** the place where one dwells, habitation. [O.E. *dwellan,* to cause to wander, lead astray, delay.]

dwindle, *dwin'dl, v.i.* to grow less: to grow feeble: to become degenerate. [Dim. of *dwine* (Scot.), to waste away—O.E. *dwīnan,* to fade.]

dye, *dī, v.t.* to stain: to give a new colour to:—*pr.p.* **dye'ing;** *pa.p.* **dyed.**—*n.* colour: tinge: a colouring material, esp. in solution.—*ns.* **dy'er,** one whose trade is to dye cloth, &c.; **dye'(-)stuff,** material used in dyeing; **dye'(-)wood,** any wood from which colouring matter is obtained for dyeing; **dye'-work(s),** an establishment for dyeing.—**dyed in the wool,** dyed in the raw state: of firmly fixed convictions. [O.E. *dēagian,* to dye, from *dēag* or *dēah,* colour.]

dying, *dī'ing, pr.p.* of **die.**—*adj.* occuring immediately before death, as *dying words*: pertaining to death: declining, becoming extinct.—*n.* death. [See **die** (1).]

dyke. Same as **dike.**

dynam-, dynamo-, *din'am(-ō)* or *dī'-,* combining form of Gr. *dynamis,* power—*dynasthai,* to be able.—*adjs.* **dynam'ic, -al,** relating to force: causal: forceful, very energetic.—*adv.* **dynam'ically.**—*ns.* **dynam'ic,** a moving or driving force; **dynamics** (*pl.* as *sing.*), the science which treats of matter and motion, or mechanics, sometimes restricted to kinetics;

dyn′amite, a powerful explosive agent (nitro-glycerine and kieselguhr); **dyn′amītard, dyn′amīter,** user of dynamite, esp. for political purposes; **dynamo,** contr. for **dynamo-electric machine,** a machine which generates electric currents by means of the relative movement of conductors and magnets:—*pl.* **dyn′amos; dynamom′eter,** an instrument for measuring force or power (Gr. *metron,* a measure).

dynast, *din′ast,* or *dīn′-, n.* a ruler.—*n.* **dyn′asty,** a succession of monarchs of the same family or of members of any powerful family or connected group.—*adj.* **dynas′tic.** [Gr. *dynastēs,* a lord.]

dyne, *dīn, n.* the unit of force in the centimetre-gram-second system—that which, acting on a mass of 1 g imparts to it an acceleration of 1 cm per s per s.—Equals 10^{-5} newtons. [Fr., formed from Gr. *dynamis,* power.]

dys-, *dis-, pfx.* ill, bad, abnormal. [Gr.]

dysentery, *dis′en-tri, n.* a term formerly applied to inflammation of the colon, associated with frequent discharges from the bowels mixed with blood: now confined to such conditions resulting from infection with certain micro-organisms.—*adj.* **dysenter′ic.** [Gr. *dysenteria—dys-,* ill, *enteron,* intestine.]

dysfunction, *dis-fung(k)′sh(ȯ)n, n.* imperfect functioning of an organ of the body.[Pfx. **dys-,** and **function.**]

dyslexia, *dis-leks′i-ȧ, n.* word-blindness: great difficulty in learning to read or spell.—*adjs.* **dyslec′tic, dyslex′ic.** [Pfx. **dys-** and Gr. *lexis,* word.]

dysmenorrhoea, -rhea, *dis-men-ō-rē′ȧ, n.* difficult or painful menstruation. [Pfx. **dys-,** and Gr. *mēn,* month, *rhoiā,* flow.]

dyspepsia, *dis-pep′si-a, n.* indigestion—also **dyspep′sy.**—*n.* **dyspep′tic,** a person afflicted with dyspepsia.—*adjs.* **dyspep′tic, -al** pertaining to, or suffering from, dyspepsia: (*fig.*) gloomy, bad-tempered.—*adv.* **dyspep′tically.** [Gr. *dys-,* ill, *pessein, peptein,* to digest.]

dysprosium, *dis-prō′si-ŭm, n.* a metallic element (symbol Dy; atomic no. 66) of the rare-earth group. [Gr. *dysprositos,* hard to get at.]

dystrophy, *dis′trō-fi, n.* imperfect nutrition: any of several disorders in which there is wasting of muscle tissue, &c. [Pfx. **dys-** and Gr. *trophē,* nourishment.]

Neutral vowels in unaccented syllables: *em′pér-ór*; for certain sounds in foreign words see p. ix.

E

E-boat, ē′bot, (E for enemy), n. a fast German motor torpedo-boat.

each, ēch, adj. every one, separately considered, in any number. [O.E. ǣlc—ā, ever, gelīc, alike.]

eager, ē′gér, adj. excited by desire (to do, or for): earnest, keen, enthusiastic.—adv. ea′gerly.—n. ea′gerness.—**eager beaver,** an enthusiast: a zealous person. [O.Fr. aigre—L. ācer, sharp.]

eagle, ē′gl, n. a large bird of prey noted for its keen sight, any one of various genera of the same family as the hawks: a military standard carrying the figure of an eagle: a gold coin of the United States, worth ten dollars.—adj. ea′gle-eyed.—n. ea′glet, a young or small eagle. [O.Fr. aigle—L. aquila.]

eagre, ē′gér, n. a bore or sudden rise of the tide in a river. [Ety. uncertain.]

ear, ēr, n. a spike, as of corn.—v.i. to put forth ears. [O.E. ēar; Ger. ähre.]

ear, ēr, n. the organ of hearing, or the external part merely: the sense or power of hearing: the faculty of distinguishing sounds, esp. of different pitch: attention: anything shaped like an ear.—ns. ear′ache, an ache or pain in the ear; ear′-drum, the tympanum (q.v.), ear′mark, an owner's mark set on the ears of sheep: a distinctive mark.—v.t. to put an ear-mark on: to set aside (for a particular purpose).—adj. ear′-pierc′ing, shrill, screaming.—ns. ear′-ring, an ornament attached to the lobe of the ear: ear′shot, (the distance at which a sound can be heard, ear′-trum′pet, a tube to aid in hearing; ear′wig, any of a family of insects once supposed to creep into the ear: a flatterer (O.E. ēarwicga—ēare, ear, wicga, insect, beetle).—**give ear,** to attend; **over head and ears,** overwhelmed, deeply engrossed or involved (in); **set by the ears,** to set at strife; **turn a deaf ear,** to refuse to listen; **walls have ears,** a proverbial phrase implying that there may be listeners behind the wall. [O.E. ēare; cf. Ger. ohr, L. auris.]

earl, ûrl, n. a British nobleman ranking between a marquis and a viscount:—fem. count′ess.—ns. earl′dom, the dominion or dignity of an earl; **Earl Mar′shal,** an English officer of state, president of the Heralds' College—the Scottish form Earl Marischal. [O.E. eorl, a warrior, hero; cf. O.N. jarl.]

early, ûr′li, adj. belonging to or happening in the first part (of a time, period, series): happening in the remote past or near future.—adv. near the beginning: soon: in good time: before the appointed time.—n. ear′liness.—**early bird,** an early riser: one who gains by acting more promptly than his competitors; **Early English** (archit.), the form of Gothic that succeeded the Norman towards the end of the 12th century: (philology, see **English**) [O.E. ǣrlīce—ǣr, before.]

earn, ûrn, v.t. to gain by labour: to acquire: to deserve.—n.pl. **earn′ings,** what one has earned: wages. [O.E. earnian, to earn; cf. O.H.G. aran, harvest; Ger. ernte.]

earnest, ûr′nest, adj. intent: sincere: serious.—n. seriousness (**in earnest,** serious, not jesting: intent on one's purpose, not trifling: seriously: purposefully).—adv. ear′nestly.—n. ear′nestness. [O.E. eornost, seriousness; Ger. ernst.]

earnest, ûr′nest, n. money given in token of a bargain made: a pledge. [Ety. obscure.]

earth, ûrth, n. the third planet in order from the sun: the world: the inhabitants of the world: the matter on the surface of the globe: soil: dry land, as opposed to sea: dirt: dead matter: the human body: a burrow: an electrical connection with the earth, usually by a wire soldered to a metal plate sunk in moist earth: an old name for certain oxides of metals.—v.t. to hide or cause to hide in the earth or in a hole: to connect to earth electrically.—adj. earth′en, made of earth or of baked clay.—ns. earth′enware, crockery; earth′-house, an ancient underground dwelling, also called Picts' house; earth′-hung′er, the passion for acquiring land.—adj. earth′ly, belonging to the earth: passed on earth: worldly, not spiritual.—ns. earth′liness; earth′(-)nut, the edible root-tuber of an umbelliferous plant: name extended to other roots, tubers, pods, e.g. the pods of the pea-nut or ground-nut; earth′-pillar, column of soft material protected from erosion by an overlying stone; earth′quake, a shaking of the earth's crust, caused, perhaps in most cases, by movement along a fault (q.v.); earth′ trem′or, a slight earthquake; earth′work, a fortification of earth; earth′worm, any of numerous invertebrate animals of several genera living in damp earth: a mean person, a poor creature.—adj. earth′y, consisting of, relating to, or resembling earth or soil: gross: unrefined.—n. earth′iness.—**go to earth,** to seek a hole or hiding place (also fig.). [O.E. eorthe; cf. Du. aarde, Ger. erde.]

ease, ēz, n. freedom from pain or disturbance: rest from work: quiet: freedom from difficulty: naturalness.—v.t. to free from pain, trouble, or anxiety: to relieve (e.g. the mind): to relax, slacken, release (e.g. pressure, tension): to moderate, make less intense: to facilitate: to manoeuvre very gradually.—v.i. to become less intense (also **ease off**): to become less in demand.—n. ease′ment, relief: (law) the right to use land, &c., not one's own, or to prevent its owner from making an inconvenient use of it.—adj. eas′y, at ease: free from pain, trouble, anxiety, difficulty: unconstrained (e.g. of manner): not tight: not strict: (coll.) equally pleased with either alternative: in cards, equally divided between the opposing sides: of market, not showing unusually great activity.—adv. eas′ily.—n. eas′iness.—interj. easy! a command to go gently.—*n.* **eas′y-chair,** an arm-chair for ease or rest.—*adjs.* **eas′y-gō′ing, -ō′sy,** indolent: placid.—**ease off,** to slacken gradually, to make, or become, less intense; **easy money,** money made without trouble or exertion; **easy street** (*slang*), a situation of comfort or affluence.—**easy on the eye** (*slang*), good to look at. [O.Fr. *aise*; cog. with It. *agio*; Provençal *ais*, Port. *azo.*]

easel, *ēz′l, n.* the frame on which painters support their pictures while painting. [Du. *ezel,* or Ger. *esel,* an ass.]

east, *ēst, n.* that part of the heavens where the sun rises at the equinox: one of the four cardinal points of the compass: the east part of a region.—*adj.* toward the rising of the sun.—*adjs.* **east′ern,** toward the east: connected with, or dwelling in, the east; **east′erly,** coming from the eastward: looking toward the east—also *adv.*; **east′ernmost, east′-most,** situated farthest east.—*n.* **east′ing,** the course gained to the eastward: distance eastward from a given meridian.—*adv.* **east′ward,** toward the east.—**the East,** the countries to the east of Europe (*Near East,* Turkey, Balkans, &c.; *Middle East,* Iran, India, &c.; *Far East,* China, Japan, &c.). [O.E. *ēast*; Ger. *ost*; akin to Gr. *ēōs,* the dawn.]

Easter, *ēst′ér, n.* a Christian festival commemorating the resurrection of Christ, held on the Sunday after Good Friday.—*ns.* **East′er-day,** Easter Sunday; **East′ertide,** the time at which Easter is celebrated. [O.E. *ēastre*; Ger. *ostern.* Perh. from *Eostre,* a goddess whose festival was held at the spring equinox.]

eat, *ēt, v.t.* to chew and swallow, or to swallow: to consume: (also with *into*) to waste away, to corrode.—*v.i.* to take food:—*pr.p.* eat′ing; *pa.t.* ate (*et* or *āt*); *pa.p.* eaten (*ētn*).—*adj.* **eat′able,** fit to be eaten.—*n.* anything used as food (chiefly *pl.*).—*n.* **eat′ing-house,** a place where meals are sold, a restaurant.—**eat its head off,** used of an animal that costs more for food that it is worth; **eat one's words,** to take back what one has said, to recant. [O.E. *etan*; cf. Ger. *essen,* L. *edĕre,* Gr. *edein.*]

Eau de Cologne, *ō dé kó-lōn′, n.* a perfumed spirit first made at Cologne in 1709 (often **eau** without *cap.*).—**eau de vie** (*ō dé vē*), brandy. [Fr. *eau,* water, *de,* of, *vie,* life.]

eaves, *ēvz, n.pl.* the projecting edge of the roof: anything similarly projecting.—*n.* **eaves′drop,** the water that falls from the eaves of a house: the place where the drops fall.—*v.i.* to listen in order to overhear private conversation.—*n.* **eaves′dropper,** one who tries to overhear private conversation. [O.E. *efes,* the clipped edge of thatch.]

ebb, *eb, n.* the going back or receding of the tide: a decline.—*v.i.* to flow back: to sink, to decline.—*n.* **ebb′-tide,** the ebbing tide. [O.E. *ebba.*]

ebony, *eb′ón-i,* **ebon,** *eb′ón, n.* a kind of wood almost as heavy and hard as stone, usually black, admitting of a fine polish.—*adj.* made of ebony: black as ebony.—*n.* **eb′onite,** vulcanised rubber. [L. (*h*)*ebenus*—Gr. *ebenos*; cf. Heb. *hobnīm,* pl. of *hobni, obni*—*eben,* a stone.]

ebriated, *ē′bri-āt-id, adj.* intoxicated.—*n.*

ebrī′ety, drunkenness. [L. *ēbriāre, -ātum,* to make drunk.]

ebullient, *e-bul′yént, adj.* boiling up or over: exuberant, enthusiastic.—*n.* **ebulli′tion,** act of boiling: exuberance (also **ebull′ience**): an outbreak. [L. *ēbulliēns, -entis*—*ē,* out, *bullīre,* boil.]

écarté, *ā-kär′tā, n.* a card game for two, one feature of which is the discarding or exchanging of certain cards for others. [L. *ē,* out, Fr. *carte,* card.]

eccentric, -al, *ek-sen′trik, -ál, adj.* with the axis or support not placed centrally: (of circles) not having the same centre: (of an orbit) not circular: not conforming to common rules (e.g. of conduct): (of a person, character) odd, whimsical.—*n.* **eccen′tric,** (*mech.*) a wheel having its axis out of the centre: an eccentric person.—*adv.* **eccen′trically.**—*n.* **eccentric′ity** (-*tris′*-), condition of being eccentric: singularity of conduct: oddness. [Gr. *ek,* out of, *kentron,* centre.]

ecclesia, *e-klē′zi-a, n.* a popular assembly, esp. of Athens, where the people exercised full sovereignty, and every male citizen above twenty years could vote.—*n.* **ecclēsias′tic,** a priest, a clergyman.—*adjs.* **ecclēsias′tic, -al,** of, belonging to, the church or clergy.—*ns.* **ecclesiol′ogy,** science of building and decorating churches; **ecclesiol′ogist.** [Gr. *ekklēsia,* assembly summoned by crier: (later) the Church—*ek,* out of, *kalein,* to call.]

ECG. Abbrev. of **electrocardiogram.**

echelon, *esh′e-lon, āsh′e-lō, n.* a stepwise arrangement of troops, ships, or aeroplanes, each line being a little to the right or left of that in front of it: a group of persons of one grade in an organisation. [Fr. *échelon,* from *échelle,* a ladder or stair—L. *scala.*]

echidna, *ek-id′nä, n.* a genus of Australian toothless, spiny, egg-laying, burrowing mammals, outwardly resembling hedgehogs—sometimes called *porcupine ant-eater.* [Gr., viper.]

echo, *ek′ō, n.* the repetition of sound caused by a sound-wave coming against some opposing surface, and being reflected: imitation: an imitator:—*pl.* **echoes** (*ek′ōz*).—*v.i.* to reflect sound: to be sounded back: to resound.—*v.t.* to send back the sound of: to repeat: to imitate: to flatter slavishly:—*pr.p.* ech′oing; *pa.p.* ech′ōed.—*ns.* **ech′o-loca′tion,** determining the position of unseen objects by means of sound echoes, as bats do (the sounds they make are too high to be heard by man); **ech′o-sound′er,** the apparatus used in echo-sounding; **ech′o-sound′ing,** a method of measuring depth of water, locating shoals of fish, &c., by noting time for return of echo from the bottom, or bottom and shoal, &c. [L.—Gr. *ēchō,* a sound.]

éclair, *ā-klār′, n.* a cake long in shape but short in duration, with cream filling and chocolate or other icing. [Fr., lightning.]

éclat, *ā-klä′, n.* (*obs.*) a striking effect: social distinction or notoriety: striking success: applause. [Fr. from O.Fr. *esclater,* to break, to shine.]

eclectic, *ek-lek′tik, adj.* selecting or borrowing: choosing the best out of everything.—*n.* one who selects opinions from different systems.

Neutral vowels in unaccented syllables: *em′pér-ór*; for certain sounds in foreign words see p. ix.

eclipse   edit

[Gr. *eklektikos—ek*, from, *legein*, to choose.]

eclipse, *e-klips'*, *n.* the total or partial disappearance of a heavenly body by the interposition of another between it and the spectator (as when the moon's disk is interposed between the sun and the earth), or by its passing into the shadow of another (as when the moon enters the earth's shadow): (*fig.*) obscuration, loss of brilliancy: darkness.—*v.t.* to hide wholly or in part: to darken: to throw into the shade, surpass.—*n.* **eclip'tic**, the line in which eclipses take place, i.e. a great circle (*celestial ecliptic*), the apparent path of the sun's annual motion among the fixed stars: a great circle on the globe corresponding to the celestial ecliptic.—*adj.* pertaining to an eclipse or the ecliptic. [O.Fr.,—L. *eclīpsis*—Gr. *ekleipsis—ek*, out of, *leipein*, to leave.]

eclogue, *ek'log*, *n.* a short pastoral poem. [L. *ecloga*—Gr. *eklogē*, a selection, esp. of poems—*ek*, out of, *legein*, to choose.]

eco-, *ek'ō-*, in composition, concerned with habitat and environment in relation to living organisms. [Gr. *oikos*, a house.]

ecology, *ē-kol'o-ji*, *n.* the study of organisms in relation to environment. [Gr. *oikos*, house, *logos*, discourse.]

economy, *ek-* or *ēk-on'o-mi*, *n.* the management of a household or of money matters: a frugal and judicious use of money or goods: a system of management characteristic of a particular body or group, as 'socialist economy', 'national economy': regular operations, as of nature: the efficient use of something, e.g. speed, effort.—*adjs.* **econom'ic, -al**, pertaining to economy: (usu. **economic**) considered from the point of view of supplying man's needs (e.g. *economic botany*): capable of yielding a profit: (usu. **economical**) frugal, careful.—*adv.* **econom'ically**.—*n.* **econom'ics**, the science of wealth generally, comprising its production, consumption, and distribution: political economy (q.v.).—*v.i.* **econ'omise**, to spend money or goods carefully: to save.—*v.t.* to use prudently, to spend with frugality.—*n.* **econ'omist**, one who studies economics: one who manages money, &c., esp. thriftily. [L. *oeconomia*—Gr. *oikonomia—oikos*, a house, *nomos*, a law.]

écru, *ā'krōō*, *adj.* having the appearance of unbleached linen or other unbleached material. [Fr.]

ecstasy, *ek'stà-si*, *n.* a state of being beside oneself: excessive joy: poetic frenzy: any exalted feeling.—*adj.* **ecstat'ic**, causing ecstasy: rapturous.—*adv.* **ecstat'ically**. [Gr. *ekstasis—ek*, from, *histanai*, to make to stand.]

ecto-, *ek-to-*, in composition, outside—often opposed to *endo-*, *ento-*. [Gr. *ektos*, outside.]:—e.g. *ns.* **ectopar'asite**, an external parasite; **ectoplasm**, the outer layer of the cytoplasm of a cell: an emanation of bodily appearance believed by some spiritualists to come from a medium.

ecumenic, -al, *ēk-* or *ek-ū-men'ik, -àl, adj.* general, universal, belonging to the entire Christian Church. [L. *oecumenicus*—Gr. *oikoumenē* (*gē*), inhabited (world).]

eczema, *ek'si-ma*, *n.* an eruptive disease of the skin, occurring as a reaction to irritants, e.g.

poisons of some plants, materials used in trades, &c. [Gr. *ek*, out of, *zeein*, to boil.]

edacious, *e-dā'shús*, *adj.* of eating: gluttonous.—*n.* **edac'ity**. [L. *edax*, *edācis—edĕre*, to eat.]

Edda, *ed'a*, *n.* the name of two Scandinavian books, the one a collection of ancient mythological and heroic songs, the other a prose composition of the same kind. [O.N., apparently akin to *ōdr*, mad, *ōthr*, spirit, mind, poetry.]

eddy, *ed'i*, *n.* a current of water or air running back, contrary to the main stream, thus causing a circular motion—a small whirlpool or whirlwind.—*v.i.* to move round and round:—*pr.p.* edd'ying; *pa.p.* edd'ied. [Prob. conn. with O.E. pfx. *ed-*, back.]

edelweiss, *ā'del-vīs*, *n.* a small white flower, with woolly heads, found in damp places on the Alps. [Ger. *edel*, noble, *weiss*, white.]

edema. Same as **oedema**.

Eden, *e'dn*, *n.* the garden where Adam and Eve lived: a paradise. [Heb. *ēden*, delight, pleasure.]

edentate, *e-den'tāt*, *adj.* without teeth: lacking front teeth.—*n.* **Edenta'ta**, an order of mammals, having no front teeth or none at all: in later classification, a group of such belonging to several orders. [L. *ēdentātus*, toothless—*ē*, out of, *dens*, *dentis*, a tooth.]

edge, *ej*, *n.* the border of anything: the brink: the cutting side of an instrument: something that wounds or cuts: sharpness (e.g. of mind, appetite), keenness.—*v.t.* to put an edge on: to border: to move by little and little: to insinuate.—*v.i.* to move sideways.—*adjs.* **edged**; **edge'less**.—*advs.* **edge'ways**, **edge'wise**, in the direction of the edge: sideways.—*adj.* **edg'y**, with edges, sharp, hard in outline: irritable.—*ns.* **edg'iness**, angularity, over sharpness of outline: irritability; **edg'ing**, any border or fringe round a garment, &c.: a border of box, &c., round a flower-bed.—*n.* **edge'(-)bone**, erroneous form of aitchbone.—**on edge**, in a state of excitement, apprehension, irritability; **set the teeth on edge**, to cause a grating feeling in the teeth: to give a feeling of abhorrent discomfort.—**have the edge on**, to have the advantage over. [O.E. *ecg*; cf. Ger. *ecke*, L. *acies*.]

edible, *ed'i-bl*, *adj.* fit to be eaten.—*n.* something for food.—*ns.* **edibil'ity**, **ed'ibleness**. [L. *edibilis—edĕre*, to eat.]

edict, *e'dikt*, *n.* something proclaimed by authority: an order issued by a king or lawgiver. [L. *ēdictum—ē*, out of, *dīcĕre*, *dictum*, to say.]

edifice, *ed'i-fis*, *n.* a large building or house: also *fig. édifice*—L. *aedificium—aedificāre*; see **edify**.]

edify, *ed'i-fī*, *v.t.* (*arch.*) to build: to build up the faith of: to comfort: to improve the mind of:—*pr.p.* ed'ifying; *pa.p.* ed'ified.—*n.* **edifica'tion**, instruction: progress in knowledge or in goodness.—*adjs.* **ed'ificatory**; **ed'ifying**, instructive: improving. [Fr. *édifier*—L. *aedificāre—aedes*, a house, *facĕre*, to make.]

edile. See **aedile**.

edit, *ed'it*, *v.t.* to prepare for publication, broadcasting, &c.: to superintend the publication of: to make up the final version of a motion

fāte, *fär*; *mē*, *hûr* (her); *mīne*; *mōte*, *för*; *mūte*, *mōōn*, *fŏŏt*; *ʈнen* (then)

picture by selection, rearrangement, &c., of material photographed previously.—*ns.* **edi'tion,** number of copies of a book, &c., printed at a time; **ed'itor,** one who edits books, &c.: one who conducts a newspaper, periodical, &c.:—*fem.* **ed'itress.**—*adj.* **edito'rial,** of or belonging to an editor.—*n.* an article in a newspaper, written by an editor or leader writer.—*n.* **ed'itorship.** [L. *ēdĕre, ēdĭtum—ē,* from, *dăre,* to give.]

educate, *ed'ū-kāt, v.t.* to bring up, train and instruct, according to an accepted standard.—*adj.* **ed'ucable.**—*ns.* **educabil'ity educa'tion,** the bringing up or training, as of a child: the development (of one or all of a person's powers of body and mind): instruction as given in schools or universities: a course or type of instruction (e.g. *a college, a classical education*): the principles and practice of teaching or educating.—*adj.* **educā'tional.**—*adv.* **educā'tionally.**—*n.* **educā'tion(al)ist,** one skilled in methods of educating or teaching: one who promotes education.—*adj.* **ed'ucative,** tending to teach.—*n.* **ed'ucator.** [L. *ēducāre, -ātum,* to rear.]

educe, *e-dūs', v.t.* to extract: (*fig.*) to draw out, to cause to appear: to infer.—*adj.* **educ'ible.** [L. *ēdūcĕre—ē,* from, and *dūcĕre,* to lead.]

Edwardian, *ed-wörd'i-án, adj.* characteristic of the time of Edward VII.—Also *n.*

EEC. Abbrev. for **European Economic Community.**

EEG. Abbrev. for **electroencephalogram.**

eel, *ēl, n.* one of an order of fishes with long smooth cylindrical or ribbon-shaped bodies. [O.E. *æl;* Ger.; Du. *aal.*]

e'en, *ēn,* a contraction of **even.**

e'er, *ār,* a contraction of **ever.**

eerie, eery, *ē'ri, adj.* exciting fear, weird: affected with fear, timorous.—*adv.* **ee'rily.**—*n.* **ee'riness.** [M.E. *arh, eri*—O.E. *ærg* (*earg*), timid.]

efface, *e-fās', v.t.* to destroy the surface of a thing: to rub out: (*fig.*) to obliterate, wear away: to eclipse: to treat (oneself) as insignificant, to shun notice.—*adj.* **efface'able,** that can be rubbed out.—*n.* **efface'ment.** [Fr. *effacer*—L. *ex,* out, *faciēs,* face.]

effect, *e-fekt', n.* the result, consequence, outcome: impression produced: purport (e.g. *what he said was to this effect*): reality (*in effect*): efficacy: (*pl.*) goods, property: (*pl.*) in the theatre, cinema, sound and lighting devices contributing to the illusion of the place and circumstances in which the action is carried on.—*v.t.* to produce: to accomplish.—*n.* **effec'ter.**—*adjs.* **effec'tible,** that may be effected; **effec'tive,** having power to produce a specified effect: powerful: serviceable (e.g. fighting force): not merely nominal: striking (e.g. illustration, speech).—*n.* one capable of service.—*adv.* **effec'tively.**—*n.* **effec'tiveness.**—*adjs.* **effect'less,** without effect, useless; **effec'tual,** successful in producing the desired effect (e.g. of measures).—*n.* **effectual'ity.**—*adv.* **effec'tually.**—**give effect to,** make operative; **in effect,** in truth, really: substantially; **take effect,** to come into force. [O.Fr.,—L. *effectus—ex,* out, *facĕre,* to make.]

effeminate, *e-fem'in-āt, adj.* womanish: unmanly: weak, soft: voluptuous.—*n.* an effeminate person.—*n.* **effem'inacy.**—*adv.* **effem'i-**nately.—*n.* **effem'inateness.** [L. *effēmināre, -ātum,* to make womanish—*ex,* out, and *fēmina,* a woman.]

effendi, *e-fen'di, n.* a title for civil officials and educated persons generally (abolished in Turkey in 1934). [Turk.; from Gr. *authentēs,* an absolute master.]

efferent, *ef'é-rént, adj.* conveying outward or away, as **efferent nerve,** one carrying impulses away from the central nervous system. [L. *ē,* from, *ferens, -entis,* pr.p. of *ferre,* to carry.]

effervesce, *ef-ér-ves', v.i.* to froth up, emit bubbles of gas: also *fig.*—*n.* **efferves'cence.**—*adj.* **efferves'cent.** [L. *effervescĕre—ex,* inten., and *fervēre,* to boil.]

effete, *e-fēt', adj.* exhausted: degenerate. [L. *effētus,* weakened by having brought forth young—*ex,* out, *fētus,* a bringing forth, young.]

efficacious, *ef-i-kā'shús, adj.* producing the result intended (of an impersonal agent, e.g. a medicine).—*adv.* **effica'ciously.**—*n.* **eff'icacy.** [L. *efficax, -ācis—efficĕre;* see **efficient.**]

efficient, *e-fish'ént, adj.* capable of doing what may be required (of a person or other agent or of an action).—*n.* **efficiency** (*e-fish'n-si*), power to produce the result intended: the ratio of the energy output of a machine, &c., to the energy input: capability, competence.—*adv.* **effi'ciently.** [Fr.,—L. *efficiens, -entis,* pr.p. of *efficĕre—ex,* out, *facĕre,* to make.]

effigy, *ef'i-ji, n.* a likeness or figure of a person: the head or impression on a coin. [Fr.,—L. *effigiēs—effingĕre—ex,* inten., *fingĕre,* to form.]

effloresce, *ef-lo-res', v.i.* to blossom forth: (*chem.*) to become covered with a powdery crust, esp. as a result of giving up water of crystallisation to the atmosphere.—*n.* **efflores'cence.**—*adj.* **efflores'cent.** [L. *efflōrescĕre—ex,* out, *flōrescĕre,* to blossom—*flōs, flōris,* a flower.]

effluent, *ef'lōō-ént, adj.* flowing out.—*n.* a stream that flows out of another stream or a lake.—*n.* **eff'luence,** a flowing out: that which flows out (e.g. electricity, influence). [L. *effluens, -entis,* pr.p. of *effluĕre—ex,* out, *fluĕre,* to flow.]

effluvium, *e-flōō'vi-um, n.* minute particles that flow out from bodies: disagreeable vapours, e.g. rising from decaying matter:—*pl.* **efflu'via.**—*adj.* **efflu'vial.** [Low L.,—L. *effluĕre.*]

efflux, *ef'luks, n.* act of flowing out: that which flows out.—Also **effluxion** (*e-fluk'sh(ó)n*). [L. *effluĕre, effluxum.*]

effort, *ef'órt, n.* a putting forth of strength: attempt: struggle.—*adj.* **eff'ortless,** without effort, or apparently so. [Fr.,—L. *ex,* out, *fortis,* strong.]

effrontery, *e-frunt'ér-i, n.* shamelessness, impudence, insolence. [Fr. *effronterie*—L. *effrōns, effrontis—ex,* out, *frons, frontis,* the forehead.]

effulgence, *e-fulj'éns, n.* great lustre or brightness: a flood of light.—*adj.* **effulg'ent,** shining forth: extremely bright: splendid. [L. *effulgēre,* to shine out, pr.p. *effulgens, -entis—ex,* out, *fulgēre,* to shine.]

effuse, *e-fūz', v.t.* to pour out: to pour forth (as words): to shed.—*n.* **effū'sion,** act of pouring out: that which is poured out or forth: a wordy epistle or other composition.—*adj.* **effū'sive,**

Neutral vowels in unaccented syllables: *em'pér-ór*; for certain sounds in foreign words see p. ix.

224

pouring forth abundantly: gushing, expressing one's emotions freely.—*adv.* **effū′sively.** —*n.* **effū′siveness.** [L. *effundēre, effūsum*—*ex*, out, *fundĕre*, to pour.]

eft, *eft, n.* (*obs.*) a lizard: now a newt. [O.E. *efeta*. Origin obscure. See **newt**.]

egalitarian, *ē-gal-i-tā′ri-ǎn, adj.* and *n.* equalitarian.—*n.* **egalitā′rianism.** [O.Fr. *egal*—L. *aequālis*—*aequus*, equal.]

egest, *c-jest′, v.t.* to throw out, expel: to excrete. [L. *ēgerĕre, ēgestum—e*, out of, *gerĕre*, to carry.]

egg, *eg, n.* an oval body laid by birds and certain other animals, from which the young is hatched: an ovum: anything shaped like an egg.—*adj.* **egg′-box,** used of type of building appearing as if made of numbers of unadorned rectangular sections.—*n.* **egg′-flip,** a drink made of ale, wines, spirits, or milk, with eggs, sugar, spice, &c.; **egg′head,** an intellectual; **egg′mass′,** intellectuals as a group. *adj.* **egg′shell,** thin and delicate: of paint, having a slight gloss. [O.N. *egg*; cf. O.E. *æg*, Ger. *ei*, perh. L. *ōvum*, Gr. *ōon.*]

egg, *eg, v.t.* (followed by *on*) to incite (a person, to do something). [O.N. *eggja—egg*, an edge; cog. with O.E. *ecg*, edge.]

eglantine, *eg′lan-tīn, n.* the sweet-brier [Fr.,—O.Fr. *aiglent*, as if from a L. *aculentus*, prickly—*acus*, a needle, and suffx. *-lentus.*]

ego, *c′gō, ē′gō, n.* the 'I', or self—that which is conscious and thinks.—*adj.* **egocen′tric,** self-centred.—*ns.* **e′gōism** (*phil.*), the doctrine that we have proof of nothing but our own existence: the theory that self-interest is the basis of morality: self-interest: selfishness: egotism; **e′goist,** one who holds the doctrine of egoism; one who thinks and speaks too much of himself.—*adjs.* **egoist′ic, -al.**—*n.* **e′gotism,** a frequent use of the pronoun I, speaking much of oneself, self-exaltation.—*v.i.* **e′gotise,** to talk much of oneself.—*n.* **e′gotist.**—*adjs.* **egotist′ic, -al.** [L. *ego*, I.]

egregious, *e-grē′jyus, adj.* (*arch.*) prominent, distinguished: outrageous: notorious.—*adv.* **egrē′giously.**—*n.* **egrē′giousness.** [L. *ēgregius*, chosen out of the flock—*ē*, out of, *grex, gregis*, a flock.]

egress, *ē′gres, n.* act of going out: the power or right to depart: the way out.—*n.* **egress′ion** (*-gresh′(ó)n*). [L. *ēgredī, ēgressus—ē*, out of, *gradī*, to go.]

egret, *ē′gret* Same as **nigrette.**

Egyptian, *ē-jip′sh(à)n, adj.* belonging to Egypt.—*n.* a native of Egypt: a gypsy.—*n.* **Egypt′ology,** the science of Egyptian antiquities.—*adj.* **Egyptolog′ical.**—*n.* **Egypt′ologist.**

eider, *ī′dĕr, n.* the *eider-duck,* any of several northern sea-ducks, sought after for their fine down.—*n.* **ei′der-down,** the soft down of the eider-duck, used for stuffing quilts: a quilt made with eider-down. [Prob. from O.N. *æthr*, an eider-duck.]

eidograph, *ī′do-gräf, n.* an instrument for reducing and enlarging plans. [Gr. *eidos*, form, *graphein*, to write.]

eigen-, *i-gén-*, in composition, proper, as in *n.* **eigenval′ue,** any of the possible values for a parameter of an equation for which the solutions will be compatible with the boundary conditions. [Ger.]

eight, *āt, adj.* and *n.* the cardinal number next above seven.—*n.* the figure 8 or viii denoting this: the crew (comprising eight oarsmen) of a racing boat.—*adj.* **eighth** (*āt′th*), last of eight: being one of eight equal parts.—Also *n.*—*adv.* **eighth′ly,** in the eighth place.—**one over the eight,** one drink too many; **piece of eight,** a Spanish coin. [O.E. *eahta, ahta*; Ger. *acht*, L. *octō*, Gt. *oktō.*]

eighteen, *āt′ēn* (when used absolutely, *ā-tēn′*), *adj.* and *n.* eight and ten.—*adj.* **eighteenth,** the last of eighteen: being one of eighteen equal parts.—Also *n.* [O.E. *eahtatēne.*]

eighty, *ā′ti, adj.* and *n.* eight times ten.—*adj.* **eigh′tieth,** the last of eighty: being one of eighty equal parts.—Also *n.* [O.E. *eahtatig—eahta*, eight, *tig*, ten (related to *tien, tēn*).]

eikon. Same as **icon.**

einsteinium, *īn-stīn′i-ùm, n.* a transuranium element (atomic number 99; symbol Es) named after Albert Einstein (1879–1955).

Eisteddfod, *ī-steth′vod, n.* a congress of Welsh bards and musicians to promote the arts of national poetry and music. [W. *eistedd*, to sit.]

either, *ī′thĕr*, or *ē′thĕr, adj.* or *pron.* the one or the other: one of two: each of two.—*conj.* correlative to *or*: (*B.*) or. [O.E. *ǣghter*, a contr. of *ǣghwæther = ā*, aye, the pfx. *ge-*, and *hwæther*, mod. Eng. *whether.*]

ejaculate, *e-jak′ū-lāt, v.t.* to utter with suddenness.—Also *v.i.*—*n.* **ejaculā′tion.**—*adj.* **ejac′ulatory,** [L. *ē*, from, and *jaculāri, ātus jacēre*, to throw.]

eject, *e-jekt′, v.t.* to cast out: to emit: to turn out, to expel.—*v.i.* to cause oneself to be ejected from an aircraft or spacecraft.—*ns.pl.* **eject′a, ejectament′a,** matter thrown out, esp. by volcanoes.—*n.* **ejec′tion,** act of ejecting: that which is ejected.—*adj.* **ejec′tive.**—*ns.* **eject′ment,** expulsion: (*law*) an action for recovery of the possession of land, &c.; **eject′or,** one who ejects: any mechanical apparatus for ejecting.—*n.* **eject′or-seat,** seat that can be shot clear with its occupant in an emergency. [L. *ējectāre*, freq. of *ējicĕre, ējectum—ē*, from, *jacĕre*, to throw.]

eke, *ēk, v.t.* to add to, to lengthen.—**eke out,** to supplement (with): to use sparingly so as to make suffice: to manage to make (a scanty living), or to support (existence). [O.E. *ēcan*—L. *augēre*, to increase.]

eke, *ēk, adv.* in addition to: likewise. [O.E. *ēac*; Ger. *auch*; perh. from root of **eke** (1).]

elaborate, *e-lab′ór-āt, v.t.* to work out in detail: to improve by successive operations: to fashion, develop (usu. a natural product) from elements.—Also *v.i.* (often with *on, upon*).—*adj.* (*-āt*) worked out with fullness and exactness: highly detailed.—*adv.* **elab′orately.**—*ns.* **elab′orateness; elaborā′tion,** act of elaborating: refinement: the process by which substances are built up in the bodies of animals or plants.—*adj.* **elab′orative.**—*n.* **elab′orator.** [L. *ēlabōrāre, -ātum—ē*, from, *labōrāre—labor*, labour.]

élan, *ā-la′, n.* impetuosity, dash. [Fr.]

eland, *ē′land, n.* the South African antelope, resembling the elk in having a protuberance on the larynx. [Du.—Ger. *elend*, elk.]

elapse, *e-laps', v.i.* to slip or glide away: to pass silently, as time.—*n.* passing. [L. *ē*, from, *lābī, lapsus,* to slide.]

elastic, *e-las'tik, adj.* having a tendency to recover the original form, completely or partially, when forces that changed that form are removed: springy: (*fig.*) able to recover quickly a former state or condition after a shock: (*fig.*) flexible (e.g. *elastic conscience*). —*n.* a string or ribbon with rubber strands.— *adv.* **elas'tically.**—*v.t.* **elas'ticate,** to make elastic.—*ns.* **elasticity** (-*tis'-*), tendency of a body to return to its original size or shape, after having been stretched, compressed, or deformed: springiness: power to recover from depression; **elas'tin,** a protein, chief constituent of elastic tissue.—**elastic collision** (*nucleonics*), one in which the bombarding particle does not excite or break up the struck nucleus and is simply scattered. [Late Gr. *elastikos—elaunein,* to drive.]

elate, *e-lāt', v.t.* (*obs.*) to raise, exalt: to make exultant or proud.—*adv.* **elat'edly.**—*n.* **ela'tion,** pride resulting from success: elevation of spirits. [L. *ēlātus,* used as pa.p. of *efferre—ē,* from, *lātus,* carried.]

elbow, *el'bō, n.* the joint where the arm bows or bends: any sharp turn or bend.—*v.t.* to push with the elbow: to jostle.—*ns.* **el'bow-grease,** humorously applied to vigorous rubbing: hard work; **el'bow-room,** room to extend the elbows: space enough for moving or acting: freedom.—**at one's elbow,** close at hand; **be out at elbow,** to wear a coat ragged at the elbows, be very shabby; **up to the elbows,** completely engrossed (in). [O.E. *elnboga.* See **ell; bow,** *n. v.t.*]

eld, *eld, n.* old age, senility: former times, antiquity. [O.E. *eldo.*]

elder, *eld'ér, n.* a genus of shrubs or trees, with pinnate leaves, small flowers, and three-seeded fruits.—*n.* **eld'er-wine,** wine made from elder-berries. [O.E. *ellærn.*]

elder, *eld'ér, adj.* older: having lived a longer time: prior in origin.—*n.* one who is older: an ancestor: one advanced to office on account of age: one of a class of office-bearers in presbyterian churches: the pastor of an early Christian church.—*adj.* **eld'erly,** somewhat old: bordering on old age.—*n.* **eld'ership,** state of being older: the office of an elder.—*adj.* **eld'est,** oldest. [O.E. *eldra,* comp, of *eald,* old.]

El Dorado, *el dō-rä'dō,* the golden land of imagination of the Spanish conquerors of America: any place where wealth is easily to be made. [Sp. *el,* the, *dorado,* gilded.]

eldritch, *el'drich, adj.* (*Scot.*) weird, hideous. [Ety. obscure; perh. conn. with **elf.**]

elect, *e-lekt', v.t.* to choose (in preference): to select for any office or purpose: to select by vote.—*adj.* chosen: chosen for an office but not yet in it (as *the president, bride, elect*): chosen by God for salvation.—*n.* the chosen of God: any group of persons set apart by excellence.—*n.* **elec'tion,** the act of electing or choosing: the public choice of a person for office: free choice.—*v.i.* **electioneer',** to labour to secure the election of a candidate.—*adj.* **elec'tive,** pertaining to, dependent on, or exerting the power of, choice.—*n.* **elect'or,** one who elects: one who has a vote at an election: formerly, any of those princes and archbishops of the German Empire who had the right to elect the Emperor (*fem.* **elect'ress**).—*adj.* **elect'oral,** pertaining to elections or to electors.—*n.* **elect'orate,** the dignity or the territory of an elector: the body of electors. [L. *ēligĕre, ēlectum—ē,* from, *legĕre,* to choose.]

electrical, -al, *e-lek'trik, -äl, adj.* pertaining to, produced by, or operated by, electricity: (*fig.*—e.g. of atmosphere) charged with excitement: (*fig.*) electrifying.—*adv.* **elec'trically.**—*ns.* **electrician** (*e-lek-trish'án*), one who studies electricity: an engineer specialising in electrical appliances and installations; **electricity** (*tris'-*), manifestation of a form of energy due to the separation of movement of certain constituent parts of an atom, electrons or protons: the attractive power of amber and other substances when rubbed: a feeling of excitement.—*v.t.* **elec'trify,** to communicate electricity to: to adapt to electricity as the motive power: to excite suddenly: to astonish:—*pa.p.* elec'trified.—*n.* **electrifica'tion.**— **electric chair,** a chair used in electrocuting condemned criminals; **electric eye,** a photoelectric cell: a miniature cathode ray tube; **electric field,** the region in the neighbourhood of an electrically charged body in which the forces due to the charge are acting; **electric guitar,** one with a built-in amplifying device; **electric motor,** any device for converting electrical energy into mechanical energy; **electric organ** (*mus.*), an organ in which the sound is produced by means of electrical devices instead of wind. [L. *ēlectrum*—Gr. *ēlektron,* amber, in which electricity was first observed.]

electro-, *e-lek'trō-, prefix,* pertaining to, associated with, accomplished by, electricity.—*ns.* **elec'trocar'diogram,** a photographic record of the electrical variations that occur during contraction of the muscle of the heart; **elec'-trocar'diograph,** an instrument for making such a record.—*v.t.* **elec'trocute,** to inflict a death penalty by means of electricity: to kill by electricity.—*ns.* **electrocū'tion; elec'trode** (see next article); **elec'troenceph'alogram** (-*sef', -kef'*), a graph showing variations in the electric currents that originate in the brain; **elec'troenceph'alograph,** an instrument for continuously recording these currents.—*v.t.* **elec'trolyse** (-*īz*), to subject to electrolysis.— *ns.* **electrol'ysis** (-*isis*), the decomposition of a chemical compound by electricity; **elec'trolyte** (-*līt*), a substance that admits of electrolysis.—*adj.* **electrolytic** (-*lit'ik*), pertaining to, associated with, or deposited or made by, electrolysis.—*n.* **electrolytic cell,** a vessel in which electrolysis is carried out.—*ns.* **elec'tro(-)mag'net,** a piece of soft iron rendered magnetic by a current of electricity passing through a coil of wire wound round it; **elec'tro(-)mag'netism,** a branch of science which treats of the relation of electricity to magnetism: magnetism developed by a current of electricity.—*adj.* **elec'tro(-)magnet'ic,** pertaining to, or produced by, electromagnetism.—**electromagnetic waves,** a travelling disturbance in space, of which light,

Neutral vowels in unaccented syllables: *em'pér-ór*; for certain sounds in foreign words see p. ix.

226

radio, TV and radar waves are examples.—
ns. **elec′tro-met′allurgy** (*-ji*), industrial working of metals by means of electricity; **electro-
m′eter**, an instrument for measuring difference of electric potential; **electromo′tive-
force** (*abbrev.* **e.m.f.**), the force which
tends to cause a movement of electricity
round an electric circuit; **electromo′tor**, an
apparatus for applying electricity as a motive-
power.—*v.t.* **elec′troplate**, to plate or cover
with metal by electrolysis.—*n.* articles covered
with silver in this way,—*ns.* **elec′troplating;**
elec′trotype, a printing plate made by elec-
trolytically coating a mould with copper.

electrode, *el-ek′trōd*, *n.* a conductor through
which a current of electricity enters or leaves
an electrolytic cell, gas discharge tube, or
thermionic valve. [**electro-**, and Gr. *hodos*,
way.]

electron, *el-ek′tron*, *n.* an alloy of gold and silver
(also, Latinised, **electrum**): a particle, with
negative charge, revolving round the nucleus
of an atom, or (**free electron**) detached from
its atom, e.g. as cathode rays.—*adj.* **electron′-
ic.**—*n.* **electron′ics**, the science of conduction
of electricity in vacuum, gas, or semiconductor: art of making electronic devices.— **electronic brain**, any electronic computer; **electronic music**, music made by arranging
sounds previously generated electrically in
the laboratory and recorded on tape; **electron
microscope** (see **microscope**); **electron pair,**
an electron and a positron; **electron shell**, one
of several groups of electrons arranged con-
centrically round the nucleus of an atom;
electron tube, an electronic device in which
the electron conduction is in a vacuum or gas
inside a gas-tight enclosure—including thermionic valve; **electron(-)volt**, unit of energy
associated with an electron which has freely
changed its potential by one volt (*abbrev.*
eV.). [Gr.]

electuary, *e-lek′tū-ár-i*, *n.* a medicine mixed with
honey or the like. [Low L. *ēlectuārium*—perhaps Gr. *ekleikton—ekleichein*, to lick up.]

eleemosynary, *el-i-ē-moz′i-nàr-i*, or *-mos′-, adj.*
relating to charity or almsgiving: given in
charity. [Gr. *eleēmosynē*, alms—*eleos*, pity.]

elegant, *el′e-gànt*, *adj.* expensive and in good
taste (e.g. of clothes): graceful (e.g. of manner): refined (e.g. of literary style).—*n.* **elegance.**—*adv.* **el′egantly.** [Fr.,—L. *ēlegāns,
-antis—ē*, from, and root of *legěre*, to choose.]

elegy, *el′e-ji*, *n.* a song of mourning: a funeral-
song.—*adj.* **elegi′ac**, belonging to elegy:
mournful: (*poet.*) consisting of alternate
hexameter and pentameter lines (**elegiac
couplet**).—*n.* an elegiac verse: (in *pl.*) a poem
in elegiac metre.—*adj.* **elegi′acal**, elegiac.—*n.*
el′egist, a writer of elegies —*v.i.* **el′egise**, to
write an elegy. [Through Fr. and L.—Gr.
elegos, a lament.]

element, *el′e-mént*, *n.* a first principle: one of
the essential parts of anything: an ingredient:
the proper state or sphere of any thing or
being: any one of the four substances supposed by the ancients to be the foundation of
everything—namely, fire, air, water, and
earth: (*chem.*) a substance that cannot be
resolved by chemical means into simpler sub-

stances (the number of these was for long
stated to be 92, but is now known to be larger:
some of the transuranium (*q.v.*) elements
have been produced or identified in the
laboratory—obtained as the result of nuclear
disintegration either artificially produced
or spontaneous: a resistance wire in an electric heater: an electrode: a determining fact or
condition in a problem: (*pl.*) the rudiments of
learning: (*pl.*) the bread and wine used in the
Eucharist: (*pl.*) the weather: (*pl.*) the powers
of nature.—*adjs.* **element′al**, pertaining to elements, or produced by elements; **element′ary**,
primary: uncompounded: pertaining to the
elements: treating of first principles.— **elementary particle**, a particle, esp. electron, proton, neutron, or pion—so-called because supposed indivisible; term is going out of use. [L.
elementum, pl. *elementa*, first principles.]

elephant, *el′e-fànt*, *n.* any of a family of quadrupeds having a very thick skin, a trunk, and
two ivory tusks—esp. two existing species (or
genera), the Asiatic and the African.—*n.* **ele-
phantī′asis**, a disease in which the legs become thick like an elephant's.—*adj.* **elephan-
t′ine**, pertaining to an elephant: like an elephant: very large or ungainly.—**a white elephant**, an albino of the Asiatic species: a possession that occasions the owner more trouble
than it is worth—a white elephant being a
common gift of the kings of Siam to a courtier
they wished to ruin. [Fr.— L. *elephās, -antis*—
Gr. *elephas*; or possibly from O.E. *olfend,*
camel.]

elevate, *el′e-vāt*, *v.t.* to raise to a higher position:
to raise in mind or morals: to cheer: to exhilarate, esp. by liquor or drugs.—*ns.* **eleva′tion,**
the act of elevating or raising, or the state of
being raised: exaltation: an elevated place,
rising ground: height: angular height above
the horizon: (*urchit.*) a representation of the
flat side of a building; **el′evator**, person or
thing that lifts up: a lift or machine for raising
persons, goods, grain, &c., to a higher floor: a
high storehouse for grain: a muscle raising a
part of the body: a hinged section of the tail-
plane of an aircraft by use of which it is made
to climb or dive. [L. *ēlevāre, -ātum—ē*, from,
levāre, to raise—*levis*, light.]

eleven, *e-lev′n*, *adj.* and *n.* the cardinal number
next above ten.—*n.* the figures 11 or xi denoting this: a team of eleven (cricket, association football, &c).—*adj.* **elev′enth**, the last of
eleven: being one of eleven equal parts.—Also
n.—**at the eleventh hour**, at the last moment,
in the nick of time. [O.E. *en(d)le(o)fan*; perh.
(ten and) *one left.*]

elevon, *el′e-vón*, *n.* a wing flap on delta-wing or
tailless aircraft acting both as *elev*ator and as
an aile*v*on.

elf, *elf*, *n.* in European folklore, a supernatural
being, generally of human form but diminu-
tive size, more malignant than a fairy: a fairy:
a dwarf:—*pl.* **elves.**—*adjs.* **elf′in**, of, like, or
relating to elves; **elf′ish**, **elv′an**, **elv′ish**, elf-
like: mischievous, tricky. [O.E. *ælf*; cf. O.N.
ālfr, Swed. *elf.*]

elicit, *e-lis′it*, *v.t.* to draw forth, esp. *fig.* (e.g. a
truth, information, an admission).—*n.* **elicitā′-
tion.** [L. *ēlicěre, ēlicitum.*]

fāte, *fär*; *mē*, *hûr* (her); *mīne*; *mōte*, *för*; *mūte*; *mōōn*, *fŏŏt*; *тнеn* (then)

elide   embalm

elide, *e-līd'*, *v.t.* to omit, pass over: to omit in pronunciation, as a vowel or syllable.—*n.* **eli'sion**, the suppression of a vowel or syllable: an omission. [L. *ēlīdĕre*, *ēlīsum*—*ē*, from, *laedĕre*, to strike.]

eligible, *el'i-ji-bl*, *adj.* fit or worthy to be chosen: legally qualified: desirable.—*ns.* **el'igibleness**, **eligibil'ity**. [Fr.,—L. *ēligĕre*. See **elect**.]

eliminate, *e-lim'in-āt*, *v.t.* to thrust out, expel: to remove, to exclude (e.g. *to eliminate errors*): to ignore, leave out of consideration: to get rid of (e.g. an unknown from an equation).—*adj.* **elim'inable**.—*n.* **elimina'tion**. [L. *ēlīmināre*, *-ātum*—*ē*, from, *līmen*, *-inis*, a treshold.]

elision. See **elide**.

élite, *ā-lēt'*, *n.* a chosen or select part: the pick or flower of anything. [Fr. *élite*—L. *electa* (*pars*), a chosen (part).]

elixir, *e-liks'ėr*, *n.* a liquor once supposed to have the power of indefinitely prolonging life or of transmuting metals: the quintessence of anything: a panacea. [Low L.,—Ar. *al-iksīr*, the philosopher's stone.]

Elizabethan, *e-liz-a-bēth'an*, *adj.* pertaining to Queen Elizabeth or her time (reigned 1558-1603)—also to Elizabeth II; used of dress, manners, literature, &c.—*n.* a poet, dramatist, or other person of that age.

elk, *elk*, *n.* the largest of all living deer, found in the north of Europe and Asia, identical with or close akin to the moose of North America. [O.N. *elgr*, Swed. *elg*, L. *alcēs*, Gr. *alkē*.]

ell, *el*, *n.* a measure of length originally taken from the arm: a cloth measure equal to 1¼ yd. [O.E. *eln*; Du. *el*, Ger. *elle*, L. *ulna*, Gr. *ōlenē*, elbow.]

ellipse, *el-ips'*, *n.* an oval: (*geom.*) a curve, one of the conic sections, being the intersection of a cone and a plane passing obliquely through the opposite sides.—*n.* **ellip'sis** (*gram.*), a figure of syntax in which a word or words are left out but implied:—*pl.* **ellip'sēs**.—*n.* **ellip'soid** (*math.*), a surface (or the enclosed solid) of which every plane section is an ellipse (or a circle.)—*adjs.* **ellipsoi'dal**; **ellip'tic**, **-al**, pertaining to an ellipse or ellipsis: oval: having a part understood.—*adv.* **ellip'tically.**— **ellipsoid of revolution**, one generated by the revolution of an ellipse about one of its axes, the major axis giving the *prolate* form, the minor axis the *oblate*. [L.,—Gr. *elleipsis*—*elleipein*, to fall short—*en*, in, *leipein*, to leave.]

elm, *elm*, *n.* a genus of tall deciduous trees, with tough wood, luxuriant foliage, wind-borne fruits (*samara*), and corrugated bark. [O.E. *elm*; Ger. *ulme*, L. *ulmus*.]

elocution, *el-o-kū'sh(ô)n*, *n.* the art of effective speaking, from the point of view of utterance or delivery.—*adj.* **elocu'tionary.**—*n.* **elocu'tionist**. [Fr.,—L. *ēlocūtiō*, *-ōnis*—*ēloquī*, *ēlocutus*—*ē*, from, *loquī*, to speak.]

éloge, *ā-lōzh'*, **elogium**, *e-lō'ji-um*, **elogy**, *el'o-ji*, *n.* a funeral oration: a panegyric.—*n.* **el'ogist**. [Fr. *éloge*—L. *ēlogium*, a short statement, an inscription on a tomb.]

elongate, *ē'long-gāt*, *v.t.* to make longer, to extend.—*p.adj.* **e'longated**, long and (usually) narrow.—*n.* **elonga'tion**, act of lengthening out: the part thus added to the length: the angular distance of a planet from the sun.

[Low L. *ēlongāre*, *-ātum*—*ē*, from, *longus*, long.]

elope, *e-lōp'*, *v.i.* to escape privately, esp. with a lover: to run away, bolt.—*ns.* **elope'ment**; **elop'er**. [Cf. Old Du. *ontlōpen*, Ger. *entlaufen*, to run away.]

eloquence, *el'o-kwėns*, *n.* the power of uttering strong emotion in appropriate, expressive, and fluent language: the art of fine speaking: persuasive speech.—*adj.* **el'oquent**, having eloquence: persuasive.—*adv.* **el'oquently**. [L. *ēloquens*, *-entis*, pr.p. of *ēloquī*.]

else, *els*, *adv.* otherwise: besides, except that mentioned.—*adv.* **else'where**, in or to another place. [O.E. *elles*, otherwise—orig. gen. of *el*, other; cf. O.H.G. *alles* or *elles*.]

elucidate, *e-l(y)ōō'si-dāt*, *v.t.* to make lucid or clear, to throw light on.—*n.* **elucida'tion**—*adjs.* **elu'cidative**, **elu'cidatory.**—*n.* **elu'cidator**. [Low L. *ēlūcidāre*, *-ātum*—*ē*, inten., *lūcidus*, clear.]

elude, *e-l(y)ōōd'*, *v.t.* to escape or avoid by stratagem or nimbleness: to baffle (e.g. the memory, understanding).—*adjs.* **elu'sive**, **elu'sory.** —*adv.* **elu'sively.**—*ns.* **elu'siveness**, **elu'soriness**. [L. *ēlūdĕre*, *ēlūsum*—*ē*, from, *lūdĕre*, to play.]

elvan, **elves**, **elvish**. See under **elf**.

elver, *el'vėr*, *n.* a young eel. [Variant of *eelfare*, the passage of young eels up a river (O.E. *fær*, a journey), hence a brood of eels.]

Elysium, *e-liz(h)'i-um*, *n.* in Gr. mythology, the abode of the blessed after death: any delightful place.—*adj.* **Elys'ian**, pertaining to Elysium: exceedingly delightful. [L.,—Gr. *ēly'sion* (*pedion*), the Elysian (plain).]

em, *em*, *n.* (*print.*) the unit of measurement (a pica or 12 point m) for lines of type, &c.

em-, *em-*, *pfx.* See **en-**.

emaciate, *e-mā'sh-āt*, *'si-āt*, *v.t.* to make meagre or lean, to waste.—*v.i.* to become lean, to waste away.—*p.adjs.* **emā'ciate** (*-āt*), **-d**.—*n.* **emacia'tion**. [L. *ēmaciāre*, *-ātum*—*maciēs*, leanness.]

emanate, *em'a-nāt*, *v.i.* to issue (from): (*fig.*) to proceed (from some source).—*n.* **emana'tion**, that which issues or proceeds (from some source), as a scent, rays, or (*fig.*) moral qualities or powers: radioactive, chemically inert, gas resulting from the disintegration of radium, &c. [L. *ē*, out from, *mānāre*, to flow.]

emancipate, *e-man'si-pāt*, *v.t.* to set free from restraint or bondage or disability of any kind.—*ns.* **emancipa'tion**; **emancipa'tionist**, an advocate of the emancipation of slaves; **eman'cipātor**. [L. *ē*, away from, *mancipāre*, *-ātum*, to transfer property—*manus*, the hand, *capĕre*, to take.]

emasculate, *e-mas'kū-lāt*, *v.t.* to castrate: to deprive of strength (*lit.* and *fig.*): to make effeminate.—*adj.* (*-lāt*), deprived of vigour or strength: effeminate.—*n.* **emascula'tion**.—*adj.* **emas'culatory**, tending to deprive of vigour. [Low L. *ēmasculāre*, *-ātum*—*ē*, from, *masculus*, dim. of *mas*, a male.]

embalm, *em-bäm'*, *v.t.* to preserve from decay by treatment with aromatic drugs, as a dead body: to perfume: to preserve with care and affection.—*ns.* **embalm'er**; **embalm'ing**; **embalm'ment**. [Fr. *embaumer*, from *em-*, in, and *baume*; see **balm**.]

Neutral vowels in unaccented syllables: *em'pėr-ór*; for certain sounds in foreign words see p. ix.

embank, em-bangk', v.t. to enclose or defend with a bank or dike.—n. **embank′ment,** the act of embanking: a bank, mound, or ridge, made for a definite purpose (e.g. to carry a railway). [Pfx. em-, in, and **bank.**]

embarcation. Same as **embarkation.**

embargo, em-bär′gō, n. a temporary order from the Admiralty to prevent the arrival or departure of ships: a stoppage of trade for a short time by authority: a prohibition, ban:—pl. **embar′goes.**—v.t. to lay an embargo on: to seize (ships, goods):—pr.p. embar′gōing; pa.p. embar′gōed. [Sp.,—embargar, to impede, to restrain—Sp. pfx. em-, in, Low L. (and Sp.) barra, a bar.]

embark, em-bärk', v.t. to put on board ship.—v.i. to go on board ship: to engage (in, on, upon any affair).—n. **embarka′tion,** a putting or going on board: that which is embarked. [Fr. embarquer, from em-, in, barque, ship.]

embarrass, em-bar′as, v.t. to encumber, impede: to involve in difficulty, esp. in money matters: to perplex: to put out of countenance, disconcert.—p.adj. **embarr′assed.**—n. **embarr′assment,** perplexity; money difficulties: a perplexing amount (as of choice, riches). [Fr. embarrasser—em-, in barre, bar.]

embassy, em′bas-i, n. the charge or function of an ambassador: the person or persons sent on an undertaking: an ambassador's official residence. [O.Fr. ambassée, from same root as **ambassador.**]

embattle, em-bat′l, v.t. to furnish with battlements.—p.adj. **embatt′led** —n. **embatt′lement** (same as **battlement.**) [Pfx. em-, and O.Fr. bataillier, to embattle. See **battlement.**]

embattle, em-bat′l, v.t. to range in order of battle.—p.adj. **embatt′led** [O.Fr. embataillier—pfx. em-, in, bataille, battle.]

embay, em-bā', v.t. to lay or force (a ship within a bay: (lit. and fig.) to enclose, as in a bay.—n. **embay′ment,** a bay. [Pfx. em-, in, and **bay.**]

embed, em-bed', v.t. to fix in a mass of matter: to lay, as in a bed.—Also **imbed.** [Pfx. em-, and **bed.**]

embellish, em-bel′ish, v.t. to make beautiful with ornaments: to illustrate pictorially: to increase the interest of (a narrative) by addition of fictitious details.—ns. **embell′isher; embell′ishment,** act of adorning: decoration. [Fr. embellir, embellissant—em-, in, bel (beau), beautiful.]

ember, em′bér, n. a piece of live coal or wood: (pl.) smouldering remains of a fire (lit. and fig.). [O.E. æmerge; O.N. eimyrja.]

Ember(-)days, em′bér-dāz, n. pl. in R.C. and English Church the three fast-days in each quarter.—n. **Em′ber(-)week,** the week in which the Ember-days occur. [O.E. ymbryne, a circuit—ymb, round, and ryne, a running, from rinnan, to run.]

embezzle, em-bez′l, v.t. to appropriate fraudulently (now only what has been entrusted).—ns. **embezz′lement,** fraudulent appropriation of property entrusted; **embezz′ler.** [Anglo-Fr. enbesiler, to make away with.]

embitter, em-bit′er, v.t. to make bitter or more bitter; to make bitterly hostile (with against).—p.adj. **embitt′ered,** soured.—Also **imbitter.**

[Pfx. em-, and **bitter.**]

emblazon, em-blā′zón, v.t. to adorn with heraldic devices, &c.: to depict or show conspicuously: to celebrate, extol.—ns. **emblā′zoner; emblā′zonment; emblā′zonry,** the art of emblazoning or adorning: devices on shields. [Pfx. em-, and **blazon.**]

emblem, em′blem, n. an object or a picture suggesting and representing an idea, or an object different from itself (see **symbol**): a heraldic device, a badge.—adjs. **emblemat′ic, -al,** pertaining to or containing emblems: symbolical.—adv. **emblemat′ically.** [Through L.—Gr. emblēma—Gr. en, in, ballein, to throw.]

embody, em-bod′i, v.t. to form into a body: to give a body to (spirit): to incorporate(in): to include, comprise: to express in words, in tangible form, &c.—p.adj. **embod′ied.**—n. **embod′iment,** act of embodying: state of being embodied: the representation (of a quality) in living form.—Also **imbody.** [Em-, in, and **body.**]

embolden, em-bōld′n, v.t. to make bold or courageous: to give (one) courage (to do). [Pfx. em-, **bold,** and suffx. -en.]

embolism, em′bo-lizm, n. the insertion of days in the calendar to correct error: (med.) the presence of obstructing clots in the bloodvessels.—adjs. **embolis′mal, embolis′mic.** [Late Gr. embolismos—emballein, to throw in.]

embonpoint, ä-bō-pwē, n. plumpness, stoutness. [Fr.,—en bon point, in good form.]

embosom, em-bōōz′óm, v.t. to take into the bosom: to receive into the affections: to enclose or surround.—Also **imbosom.** [Pfx em-, and **bosom.**]

emboss, em-bos', v.t. to raise bosses on, to ornament with raised work: to mould or carve in relief.—p.adj. **embossed′.**—n. **emboss′ment,** raised work. [Pfx. em-, and **boss.**]

embouchure, ä-bōō-shü', n. the mouth of a river: the mouthpiece of a wind instrument: the disposition of the mouth in playing a wind instrument. [Fr.,—emboucher, to put to the mouth—en, in, bouche, a mouth.]

embowel, em-bow′él, v.t. (obs.) to enclose: to disembowel, to remove the entrails from.—pr.p. embow′elling; pa.p. embow′elled.—n. **embow′elment.** [Pfx. em-, in, and **bowel.**]

embower, em-bow′ér, v.t. to place in a bower: to shelter, as with trees. Also **imbower.** [Pfx. em-, and **bower.**]

embrace, em-brās', v.t. to take in the arms: to press to the bosom with affection: to take eagerly (e.g. an opportunity): to adopt or receive (e.g. Christianity): to comprise.—v.i. to join in an embrace.—Also n. [O.Fr. embracer (Fr. embrasser)—L. in, in, into, brā(c)chium, an arm.]

embrasure, em-brā′zhúr, n. an opening in a wall for cannon, widening from within: a splayed (q.v.) recess of a door or window. [Fr.,—O.Fr. embraser, to slope the sides of a window—em- (L. in), braser, to skew.]

embrocate, em′brō-kāt, v.t. to moisten and rub, as with a lotion.—n. **embrocā′tion,** act of embrocating: the lotion used. [Low L. embrocāre, -ātum, from Gr. embrochē, a lotion.]

embroider   empire

embroider, em-broid′ér, *v.t.* to ornament with designs in needlework: to add ornament or fictitious detail to.—*ns.* **embroid′erer; embroid′ery,** the art of producing ornamental designs in needlework on textile fabrics, &c.: ornamental needlework: embellishment: exaggerated or invented detail. [M.E. *embrouderie*—O.Fr. *embroder*.]

embroil, em-broil′, *v.t.* to involve (a person) in hostility (with another or others): to bring (persons) into a state of discord: to throw into confusion.—*n.* **embroil′ment.** [Fr. *embrouiller*—pfx. *em-*, and *brouiller*; see **broil** (1).]

embryo, em′bri-ō, *n.* a young animal or plant in its earliest stages of development, contained in seed, protective tissue, egg, or womb: anything in a rudimentary state:—*pl.* **em′bryos.**—Also *adj.*—*ns.* **embryol′ogy,** the science of the formation and development of the embryo; **embryol′ogist.**—*adjs.* **embryon′ic, embryot′ic,** of or relating to anything in an imperfect state: rudimentary. [Low L.,—Gr. *embryon*—*en,* in, *bryein,* to swell.]

emend, ē-mend′, e-mend′, *v.t.* to correct errors or apparent errors in (a literary text).—Also **em′endate.**—*ns.* **emenda′tion,** improvement, correction: a word, phrase, &c., substituted in a text because considered to be that intended by the author; **e′mendātor.**—*adj.* **emen′datory.** [L. *ēmendāre, -ātum*—ē, from, *menda,* a fault.]

emerald, em′ér-áld, *n.* a very highly esteemed gem-stone, a beautiful velvety green variety of beryl.—**Emerald Isle,** Ireland, from its greenness. [O.Fr. *esmeralde*—L. *smaragdus*—Gr. *smaragdos.*]

emerge, e-mûrj′, *v.i.* to rise out of (orig. a liquid—with *from*): to come forth, come into view: (*fig.*) to come out as a result of enquiry: to crop up (e.g. a difficulty).—*ns.* **emer′gence,** act of emerging or coming out (*lit.* and *fig.*); **emer′gency,** an unexpected occurrence or situation demanding immediate action: a substitute in reserve.—*adj.* **emer′gent,** emerging: coming into being in the course of evolution: urgent.—*n.* **emer′sion,** act of emerging: (*astron.*) the reappearance of a heavenly body after eclipse or occultation.—**emergency exit,** one to be used only in an emergency, e.g. fire. [L. *ēmergĕre, ēmersum*—ē, out of, *mergĕre,* to plunge.]

emeritus, e-mer′i-tus, *adj.* and *n.* honourably discharged from public duties (e.g. *emeritus professor, professor emeritus*). [L. *ēmeritus,* having served one's time.]

emerods, em′é-rodz, *n.pl.* (*B.*) now **haemorrhoids.**

emery, em′ér-i, *n.* a very hard mineral, used as powder for polishing, &c. [O.Fr. *esmeril, emeril*—Low L. *smericulum*—Gr. *smēris, smỹris.*]

emetic, e-met′ik, *adj.* causing vomiting.—*n.* a medicine that causes vomiting. [Gr. *emetikos*—*emeein,* to vomit.]

emigrate, em′i-grāt, *v.i.* and *v.t.* to leave one's country in order to settle in another.—*adj.* **em′igrant,** emigrating or having emigrated.—Also *n.*—*ns.* **emigrā′tion; émigré** (ā-mē-grā′), a royalist who quitted France during the Revolution. [L. *ēmigrāre, -ātum*—ē, from, *migrāre,* to remove.]

éminence grise, ā-mē-näs grēz, one exercising

power in the background, as Cardinal Richelieu's private secretary, Père Joseph, nicknamed *l'Éminence Grise* ('the Grey Eminence'). [Fr.]

eminent, em′i-nént, *adj.* rising above others: conspicuous: distinguished: exalted in rank or office.—*adv.* **em′inently,** in a distinguished manner: in a conspicuous degree.—*ns.* **em′inence, em′inency,** a rising ground, hill: (*lit.* and *fig.*) height: distinction: a title of honour. [L. *ēminens, -entis,* pr.p. of *ēminēre*—ē, from, *minēre,* to project.]

emir, ā́m-ēr′, or ē′mir, *n.* a title given in the East and in North Africa to all independent chieftains, and also to all the supposed descendants of Mohammed.—*n.* **emir′ate,** the office, jurisdiction, or state of an emir.—Also **ameer, emer.** [Ar. *amīr,* ruler.]

emit, e-mit′, *v.t.* to give out (e.g. light, heat, sound, water): to issue (paper currency, bills):—*pr.p.* emitt′ing; *pa.p.* emitt′ed.—*ns.* **em′issary,** one sent out on a secret mission (often used rather contemptuously); **emiss′ion,** the act of emitting: that which is issued at one time.—*adj.* **emiss′ive.** [L. *ēmittĕre, ēmissum*—ē, out of, *mittĕre,* to send.]

emmet, em′et, *n.* (*arch.* and *dial.*) the ant. [O.E. *ǣmete.*]

emollient, e-mol′yént, *adj.* softening: making supple.—*n.* (*med.*) a softening application, as poultices, fomentations, &c. [L. *ēmollīre, ēmollītum*—ē-, inten., *mollīre,* to soften—*mollis,* soft.]

emolument, e-mol′ū-mént, *n.* (*obs.*) advantage: (often in *pl.*) profit arising from employment, as salary or fees. [L. *ēmolimentum*—prob. from *ēmŏlĕre,* to grind out.]

emotion, e-mō′sh(ó)n, *n.* a moving of the feelings: agitation of mind.—*v.i.* **emote′,** to show or express exaggerated emotion.—*adj.* **emō′tional,** of the emotions: liable to emotion.—*adv.* **emō′tionally.**—*adj.* **emō′tive,** tending to arouse emotion. [L. *ēmōtiō, -ōnis*—*ēmovēre, -mōtum,* to stir up—ē-, and *movēre,* to move.]

emp-, for words not found under this, see **imp-.**

empanel, em-pan′él, *v.t.* to enter (the names of a jury) on a panel or list.—*n.* **empan′elment.**—Also **impanel.** [Anglo-Fr. *empaneller*—pfx. *em-*, and O.Fr. *panel;* see **panel.**]

empathy, em′pa-thi, *n.* power of entering into another's personality and imaginatively experiencing his experiences: ability to participate in another's feelings: power of entering into the feeling or spirit of something (says a work of art).—*v.i.* **em′pathise.** [Gr. *en,* in, *pathos,* feeling.]

emperor, em′pér-ór, *n.* the head of an empire: the highest title of sovereignty:—*fem.* **em′press.** [O.Fr. *emperere*—L. *imperātor* (fem. *imperātrix*)—*imperāre,* to command.]

emphasis, em′fa-sis, *n.* forcible or impressive expression: insistent or vigorous way of attributing importance, or of thrusting upon attention: stress:—*pl.* **em′phases** (*-sēz*).—*v.t.* **em′phasise,** to lay stress on.—*adjs.* **emphat′ic, -al,** expressed, or expressing, with emphasis: forcible (of an action).—*adv.* **emphat′ically.** [Gr. *emphasis,* image, significance—*en,* in, *phainein,* to show.]

empire, em′pīr, *n.* (*loosely*) a widespreading

Neutral vowels in unaccented syllables: em′pér-ór; for certain sounds in foreign words see p. ix.

dominion, or group of states, &c., under the same sovereign power, not always an emperor: supreme control or dominion. [Fr.,—L. *imperium*.]

empiric, -al, em-pir′ik, -ál, *adj.* resting on trial or experiment: known by experience only.—*n.* **empir′ic**, one who makes trials or experiments: one whose knowledge is got from experience only: a quack. *adv.* **empir′ically.**—*ns.* **empir′icism** (*phil*.), the system which regards experience as the only source of knowledge: dependence of a professed physician on his experience alone without a regular medical education; **empir′icist.**—**empirical formula** (*chem*.), a formula expressing the simplest numerical relationship between the atoms of the elements present in a compound—e.g. the empirical formula of benzene is CH, though its molecular formula is C_6H_6. [Fr.,—L. *empīricus*—Gr.*empeirikos*—*en*, in,*peira*, a trial.]

emplacement, em-plās′mént, *n.* the act of placing: (*mil*.) a gun platform. [Fr.]

emplane, em-plān′, *v.t.* to put or take on an aeroplane.—*v.i.* to mount an aeroplane. [Pfx. *em-*, and **plane** (1).]

employ, em-ploi′, *v.t.* to occupy the time or attention of: to use as a means or agent: to give work, to.—*n.* employment.—*adj.* **employ′-able.**—*p.adj.* **employed′**, having employment.—*ns.* **employ′ee**, a person employed; **employ′er; employ′ment**, act of employing: state of being employed: occupation, esp. regular trade, business, or profession. [Fr. *employer* L. *implicāre*, to entold.—*in*, in and *plicāre*, to fold.]

emporium, em-pō′ri-um, -pō′, *n.* a place to which goods are brought from various parts for sale, a mart: (*vulg*.) a big shop:—*pl.* **empō′ria, emporiums**. [L.,—Gr. *empōrion*—*empōros*, a trader, *en*, in, *poros*, a way.]

empower, em-pow′ér, *v t* to authorise. [Pfx. *em-*, and **power**.]

empty, emp′ti, *adj.* having nothing within: unoccupied: destitute (of): having no contact with reality, no practical effect (e.g. dreams, words, threats, boasts): vain, worthless (e.g. pleasures).—*v.t.* to make empty: to transfer by emptying.—*v.i.* to become empty: to discharge:—*pa.p.* emp′tied.—*n.* an empty vessel, box, sack, &c.:—*pl.* emp′ties. —*n.* emp′tiness, state of being empty.—*adj.* emp′ty-hand′ed, bringing nothing, esp. no gift. [O.E. *æmetig*—*æmetta*, leisure, rest. The *p* is excrescent.]

empurple, em-pûr′pl, *v.t.* to dye or tinge purple. [Pfx. *em-*, and **purple**.]

empyema, em-pī-ē′ma, or -pi-, *n.* a collection of pus in any cavity, esp. the pleura. [Gr.,—*en*, in, *pyon*, pus.]

empyreal, em-pir-ē′ál, em-pir′i-ál, *adj.* formed of pure fire or light: pertaining to the highest and purest region of heaven: sublime.—*adj.* **empyrē′an**, (or -*pir′*-), empyreal.—*n.* the highest heaven, where the pure element of fire was supposed by the ancients to subsist: the visible heavens. [Gr. *empyros*, fiery—*en*, in, and *pyr*, fire.]

emu, ē′mū, *n.* either of two species of Australian running bird, related to the ostrich. [Port. *ema*, an ostrich.]

emulate, em′ū-lāt, *v.t.* to strive to equal or excel:

to rival: (*loosely*) to imitate.—*n.* **emulā′tion**, act of emulating or attempting to equal or excel: rivalry, competition.—*adj.* **em′ulative**, inclined to emulation, rivalry, or competition.—*n.* **em′ulator.**—*adj.* **em′ulatory.**—*adj.* **em′ulous**, eager to emulate: engaged in competition or rivalry.—*adv.* **em′ulously.** [L. *aemulārī, aemulātus*—*aemulus*, emulous.]

emulsion, e-mul′sh(ó)n, *n.* a milky liquid prepared by mixing oil and water (or other substances), one being held in suspension in the other by the agency of a third substance: a light-sensitive coating on photographic plates.—*v.t.* emul′sify.—*adj.* emul′sive.—**emulsion paint**, a water-thinnable paint made from a pigmented emulsion of a resin in water. [Fr.,—L. *ēmulgēre, ēmulsum*, to milk out—*ē*, from, and *mulgēre*, to milk.]

en-, en-, *pfx.,* used to form verbs, meaning:—(1) to put into, e.g. **encage**; (2) to bring into the condition of e.g **enslave**; (3) to make, e.g. **endear**. Before *b, p*, and sometimes *m*, en-becomes *em-*, e.g. **embed, emplane, emmesh** for **enmesh**. [Fr.,—L. *in*.]

enable, en-ā′bl, *v.t.* to make able, by supplying the means: to give power or authority to. [Pfx. *en-*, and **able**.]

enact, en-akt′, *v.t.* to act the part of: to establish by law, to decree (that).—*adjs.* **enact′ing, enact′ive**, that enacts.—*n.* **enact′ment**, the passing of a bill into law: that which is enacted: a law. [Pfx. *en-*, and **act**.]

enamel, en-am′él, *n.* a variety of glass applied as coating to a metal or other surface and fired: any glossy enamel-like surface or coating, esp. that of the teeth: a glossy paint: a complexion cosmetic: a work of art in enamel.—*v.t.* to coat with or paint in enamel: to form a glossy surface upon, like enamel: to enamel—*pr.p.* enam′elling; *pa.p.* enam′elled. [O.Fr. *enameler*—*en*, in, *esmail*, enamel.]

enamour, en-am′ór, *v.t.* to inflame with love: to charm.—Usually in phrase **be enamoured of, with**. [O.Fr. *enamourer*—pfx. *en-, amour*—L. *amor*, love.]

en bloc, ã blok, as one unit, wholesale. [Fr.]

encage, en-kāj′, *v.t.* to shut up as in a cage. Also **incage**. [Pfx. *en*, and **cage**.]

encamp, en-kamp′, *v.t.* to settle in a camp.—*v.i.* to pitch tents: to make a stay in a camp.—*n.* **encamp′ment**, the act of encamping: the place where a camper or company is encamped: a camp. [Pfx. *en-*, and **camp**.]

encase, en-kās′, *v.t.* to enclose in a case: to surround, cover.—*n.* **encase′ment**.—Also **incase**. [Pfx. *en-*, and **case** (1).]

encaustic, en-kös′tik, *adj.* having the colours burned in.—*n.* an ancient method of painting in melted wax,—**encaustic tile**, a glazed tile, having patterns of different coloured clays inlaid in it and burnt with it. [Gr. *enkaustikos*—*en*, in, *kaiein*, to burn.]

enceinte, ã-sẽt′, *n.* (*fort*.) an enclosure, generally the whole area of a fortified place. [Fr.,—*enceindre*, to surround—L. *in*, in, *cingĕre, cinctum*, to gird.]

enceinte, ã-sẽt′, *adj.* pregnant, with child. [Fr., prob. through L.L.—L. *in*, in, *cingĕre, cinctum*, to gird.]

encephal(o)-, **en-sef′al(-ó)-, -kef′, in composition, pertaining to the brain.—*ns.* **encepha-li'tis, inflammation of the brain; **encephal'o-gram,** an X-ray photograph of the brain. [Gr. *enkephalos,* the brain—*en,* in, *kephate,* head.]

enchain, *en-chān',* *v.t.* to put in chains: to hold fast, fetter.—*n.* **enchain'ment.** [Fr. *enchaîner* —*en,* and *chaîne,* a chain—L. *catēna.*]

enchant, *en-chänt',* *v.t.* to act on by songs or rhymed formulas of sorcery: to charm, delight in a high degree.—*p.adj.* **enchant'ed,** under the power of enchantment: delighted.—*n.* **enchant'er:**—*fem.* **enchant'ress.**—*adv.* **enchant'-ingly.**—*n.* **enchant'ment,** act of enchanting: enchanted state: that which enchants. [Fr. *enchanter* —L. *incantāre,* to sing a magic formula over—*in,* on, *cantāre,* to sing.]

enchase, *en-chās',* *v.t.* to fix in a border or setting: to set with jewels: to engrave: to adorn with raised or embossed work, or with inlaid work. [Fr. *enchâsser*—*en,* in, *châsse,* a shrine, setting—L. *capsa,* a case.]

encircle, *en-sûrk'l,* *v.t.* to surround (with): to go or pass round. [Pfx. *en-,* and **circle.**]

enclave, *en'klāv,* also *en-klāv',* or *ä-kläv',* *n.* a piece of territory entirely enclosed within foreign territory. [Fr.,—Late L. *inclāvāre*—L. *in,* and *clāvis,* a key.]

enclitic, *en-klit'ik,* *n.* (*gram.*) a word or particle without accent which always follows another word and usually modifies the accentuation of the word it follows (e.g. Gr. *te,* L. *-que, -ne*).— Also *adj.* [Gr. *enklitikos*—*en,* in, *klīnein,* to lean.]

enclose, *en-klōz',* *v.t.* to close or shut in: to confine: to surround: to put within, esp. of something sent within a letter or its envelope: to fence, esp. used of waste land.—*n.* **enclos'ure,** the act of enclosing: state of being enclosed: that which is enclosed: that which encloses.—Also **inclose.** [Fr.,—L. *inclūdĕre, in-clūsum*—*in,* in, *claudĕre,* to shut.]

encomium, *en-kō'mi-um,* also **encōm'ion,** *n.* high commendation: a formal expression of praise:—*pl.* **encōm'iums, encō'mia.**—*n.* **en-cō'miast,** one who utters or writes an encomium.—*adjs.* **encomias'tic, -al.**—*adv.* **en-comias'tically.** [L.,—Gr. *enkōmion,* a song of praise—*en,* in, *kōmos,* festivity.]

encompass, *en-kum'pàs,* *v.t.* to surround or enclose: (*obs.*) to go round. [Pfx. *en-,* and **compass.**]

encore, *ong-kōr',* *interj.* again!—*n.* (also *ong'-*) a call for the repetition of a performance: repetition (or a further performance) in response to a call.—*v.t.* to call for a repetition of (a performance), or a further performance by (a person). [Fr. (It. *ancora*)—perh. from L. (*in*) *hanc horam,* till this hour, hence = still.]

encounter, *en-kown'tér,* *v.t.* to meet, esp. hostilely or unexpectedly.—*n.* a meeting: a fight, passage of arms (*lit.* and *fig.*). [O.Fr. *encon-trer*—L. *in,* in, *contra,* against.]

encourage, *en-kur'ij,* *v.t.* to put courage in: to inspire with spirit or hope: to incite.—*n.* **en-cour'agement,** act of encouraging: that which encourages.—*p.adj.* **encour'aging.**—*adv.* **en-cour'agingly.** [O.Fr. *encoragier* (Fr. *encour-ager*)—pfx. *en-, corage,* courage.]

encroach, *en-krōch',* *v.i.* to extend into (terri-

tory, sphere, &c., of others—with *on*), to seize on the rights of others.—*n.* **encroach'er.**—*adv.* **encroach'ingly.**—*n.* **encroach'ment,** act of encroaching: that which is taken by encroaching. [O.Fr. *encrochier,* to seize—*en-,* and *croc,* a hook.]

encrust, *en-krust',* **incrust',** *in-,* *v.t.* to cover with a crust or hard coating e.g. of precious materials: to form a crust on the surface of. —*v.i.* to form a crust.—*n.* **encrustā'tion** (usu. **incrusta'tion**) act of encrusting: a crust or layer of anything: an inlaying of marble, mosaic, &c. [Fr.,—L.*incrustāre, -ātum*—*in,* on, *crusta,* crust.]

encumber, *en-kum'bér,* *v.t.* to impede the motion of, to burden: to load with debts (e.g. an estate).—*n.* **encum'brance,** that which encumbers or hinders: a legal claim on an estate. [O.Fr. *encombrer,* from *en-,* and *combrer.* See **cumber.**]

encyclical, *en-sīk'lik-àl,* or *-sik'-,* *adj.* sent round to many persons or places.—*n.* a letter addressed by the pope to all his bishops. [Gr. *enkyklios*—*en,* in, *kyklos,* a circle.]

encyclopaedia, -pedia, *en-sī-klo-pē'di-a,* *n.* a work containing information on every department, or on a particular department, of knowledge: (*cap.*) the great French work on the sciences and the arts (including practical arts), prepared in the third quarter of the 18th century.—*adjs.* **encyclopae'dian,** encyclo-paedic; **encyclopae'dic, -al,** of the nature of, or pertaining to, an encyclopaedia: embracing a large amount and great variety of information.—*n.* **encyclopae'dist,** the compiler, or one who assists in the compilation, of an encyclopaedia: esp. (*cap.*) a writer for the 18th century French Encyclopaedia. [Gr.*enkyklios,* circular, *paideia,* instruction.]

end, *end,* *n.* the last point or portion: termination or close: death: consequence: object aimed at: a fragment, an odd piece.—*v.t.* to bring to an end: to destroy.—*v.i.* to come to an end: to result (in).—*adj.* **end'ed,** brought to an end: having ends.—*n.* **end'ing,** termination: (*gram.*) the terminating syllable or portion of a word.—*adj.* **end'less,** without end: returning upon itself: everlasting: objectless.—*adv.* **end'-lessly.**—*n.* **end'lessness.**—*advs.* **end'ways, end'wise,** on end: with the end forward.—*n.* **end'-product,** the final product of a series of operations.—*adj.* **end'-stopped,** (of verse) having a pause at the end of each line.—**at a loose end,** with nothing to do; **at one's wits' end,** at the end of one's ability to decide or act; **come to the end of one's tether,** to reach the limit of one's power or resources; **get hold of the wrong end of the stick,** to misunderstand, take up wrongly (e.g. a situation, an idea, a theory); **have at one's finger-ends,** to be thoroughly acquainted with: to have in perfect readiness; **keep one's end up,** to maintain one's part; **loose ends,** unsettled matters; **make both ends (of the year) meet,** to live within one's income; **the end,** the last straw, the limit. [O.E. *ende;* cf. Ger. and Dan. *ende;* Sans. *anta.*]

endanger, *en-dān'jér,* *v.t.* to place in danger. [Pfx. *en-,* and **danger.**]

endear, *en-dēr',* *v.t.* to make dear or more

Neutral vowels in unaccented syllables: *em'pér-ór*; for certain sounds in foreign words see p. ix.

232

dear.—*adjs.* **endeared'; endear'ing.**—*adv.* **endear'ingly.**—*n.* **endear'ment,** act of endearing: a caress or utterance of love. [Pfx. *en-,* and **dear.**]

endeavour, en-dev'ór, *v.i.* to strive or attempt (to).—Also (*arch.*) *v.t.*—*n.* a strenuous attempt. [From Fr. *se mettre en devoir,* to make it one's duty, to do what one can; Fr. *en,* in, *devoir,* duty.]

endemic, -al, en-dem'ik, -ál (also **ende͞'mial),** *adjs.* regularly found in a people or a district.—*n.* **endem'ic,** a disease constantly or generally present in a place owing to local conditions.—*adv.* **endem'ically.** [Gr. *endēmios*—*en,* in, and *dēmos,* a people, a district.]

endive, en'div, -div', *n.* a salad plant of the same genus as chicory. [Fr.,—L. *intibus.*]

endo-, in composition, within [Gr. *endon,* within], e.g.:—**endopar'asite,** an internal parasite; **end'oplasm,** the inner portion of the cytoplasm of a cell; **endoskel'eton,** the internal skeleton or framework of the body, **en'doscope** (Gr. *skopein,* to view), an instrument for viewing the inside of hollow organs of the body. See **ento-.**

endocardium, en-dō-kär'dı-um, *n.* the lining membrane of the heart.—*n.* **endocardi'tis,** disease of this membrane. [Gr. *endon,* within, *kardia,* heart.]

endocrine, en'do-krīn, *adj.* secreting internally—applied esp. to glands (e.g. the thyroid) which pour their secretions into the blood. [Gr. *endon,* within, *krinein,* to separate.]

endorse, en-dörs', *v.t.* to write (e.g. one's signature, a note of contents) on the back of: to assign by writing on the back of: to give one's sanction to: to confirm (e.g. a statement): to express approbation of (an action, &c.).—*ns.* **endors'ee,** the person to whom a bill, &c., is assigned by endorsement; **endorse'ment,** act of endorsing: that which is written on the back: sanction; **endors'er.**—Also **indorse.** [Changed from M.E. *endosse* under the influence of Low L. *indorsāre*—*in,* on, *dorsum,* the back.]

endosperm, en'dō-spûrm, *n.* (*bot.*) the nutritive material enclosed with the embryo in a seed. [**endo-,** and **sperm.**]

endow, en-dow', *v.t.* to give a dowry or marriage portion to: to settle a permanent provision on: to enrich (with any gift or faculty).—*ns.* **endow'er; endow'ment,** act of endowing: that which is settled on any person or institution: a quality or faculty bestowed on anyone by nature. [Fr. *en* (=L. *in*), *douer,* to endow—L. *dōtāre*—*dōs, dōtis,* a dowry.]

endue, en-dū', *v.t.* to put on, as clothes (also *fig.*): to clothe (with): to invest, supply (with—e.g. a quality). [O.Fr. *enduire*—L. *indūcĕre*—*in, into, dūcĕre,* to lead, with meaning influenced by *induĕre,* to put on.]

endure, en-dūr', *v.t.* to remain firm under, to bear with patience: to undergo: to tolerate.—*v.i.* to remain firm: to last.—*adj.* **endur'able,** that can be endured or borne.—*n.* **endur'ableness.**—*adv.* **endur'ably.**—*n.* **endur'ance,** state, or the power, of enduring or bearing: continuance [O.Fr. *endurer*—L. *indūrāre*—*in,* in, *dūrus,* hard.]

enema, en'e-ma, or e-nē'ma, *n.* a liquid medicine

injected into the rectum: the process of injecting such a fluid. [Gr.,—*enienai,* to send in—*en,* in, and *hienai,* to send.]

enemy, en'e-mi, *n.* one who hates or dislikes and wishes to injure another, a foe: a hostile force or a hostile ship: an opponent (*of, to,* a policy, a way of life, &c.). [O.Fr. *enemi*—L. *inimīcus*—*in-,* neg., *amīcus,* a friend.]

energy, en'ėr-ji, *n.* (*phys.*) capacity of a material body or of radiation to do work: power exerted: vigorous activity: capacity to do work: vigour: forcefulness: (*pl.*) powers of acting.—*adjs.* **energet'ic, -al,** strenuously active: operating with force, vigour and effect.—*adv.* **energet'ically.**—*v.t.* **en'ergise,** to give strength or active force to: to stimulate to activity.—*v.i.* to act with force.—**conservation of energy, kinetic energy, potential energy** (see **conservation, kinetic, potential**). [Gr. *energeia*—*en,* in, *ergon,* work.]

enervate, en'ér-vāt, sometimes -nûr'-, *v.t.* to deprive of nerve and strength: to weaken the moral, or the literary or artistic, vigour of.—*adj.* (-vāt) weakened: spiritless.—*adj.* **en'ervating.** [L. *ēnervāre, -ātum   ē,* out of, *nervus,* a nerve.]

enfant terrible, ä fä te-rē-bl', precocious child whose sayings embarrass his elders. [Fr.]

enfeeble, en-fē'bl, *v.t.* to make feeble: to weaken.—*n.* **enfee'blement,** weakening: weakness. [O.Fr. *enfe(i)blir*—*en* (L. *in*), and *feible, foible.* See **feeble.**]

enfeoff, en-fef', en-fēf', *v.t.* (*hist.*) to give a fief (q.v.) to: (*fig.*) to hand over completely.—*n.* **enfeoff'ment.** [O.Fr. *en-,* and *fief.* See **fief.**]

enfilade, en-fi-lād', *n.* a vista, as between rows of trees: a fire that rakes a line of troops, or a position, from end to end.—*v.t.* to rake with shot through the whole length of a line. [Fr.,—*enfiler*—*en* (=L. *in*), and *fil,* a thread. Cf. **file,** a line or wire.]

enfold, en-fōld', *v.t.* to wrap up (in, with): to embrace.—Also **infold.** [Pfx. *en-,* and **fold** (1).]

enforce, en-fōrs', -förs', *v.t.* (*arch.*) to force, compel: to impose (e.g. obedience): to compel the observance or carrying out of (e.g. the law, a demand): to press home, urge (e.g. an argument).—*n.* **enforce'ment,** act of enforcing. [O.Fr. *enforcer*—*en* (=L. *in*), and *force.* See **force.**]

enfranchise, en-fran'chīz, -shīz, -chiz, *v.t.* to set free: to give a franchise or political privileges to.—*n.* **enfran'chisement,** act of enfranchising: admission to civil or political privileges. [O.Fr. *enfranchir*—*en,* and *franc,* free.]

engage, en-gāj', *v.t.* to bind by a gage or pledge, promise, or obligation: to secure for service: to bespeak, reserve: to enlist (e.g. one's sympathies): to hold, engross (e.g. attention): to employ (in *pass.,* e.g. *to be engaged in*): to enter into contest with: to bring (troops) into conflict (with): to interlock (parts of a machine): to entangle, involve.—*v.i.* to promise (to): to become bound: to take a part (in): to enter into conflict (*mach.*): to interlock.—*p.adj.* **engaged'.**—*n.* **engage'ment,** act of engaging: state of being engaged: betrothal: promise: appointment: employment: a fight or battle: commitment.—*p.adj.* **engag'ing,** winning, attractive (e.g. of manner).—*adv.*

engag'ingly. [Fr. *engager—en gage*, in pledge—O.Fr. *guage*.]

engender, *en-jen'dér, v.t.* to beget (now only *fig.*), to produce, cause to develop (e.g. hatred, strife, heat). [Fr. *engendrer*—L. *ingenerāre*—*in*, and *generāre*, to generate.]

engine, *en'jin, n.* a mechanical contrivance, esp. a complex and powerful machine in which power is applied to work: a locomotive: a military machine: anything used to effect a purpose.—*n.* **engineer'**, one who designs or makes engines or machinery: one who designs, constructs, or manages, public works such as roads, railways, bridges, sewers, &c. (**civil engineer**—orig. opposed to a **military engineer**): an officer who manages a ship's engines: (esp. *U.S.*) an engine-driver: a soldier of a division of an army called Engineers, concerned with road- and bridge-making, &c.—*v.t.* to arrange, contrive.—*n.* **engin-eer'ing,** the art or profession of an engineer. [O.Fr. *engin*—L. *ingenium*, skill.]

engird, *en-gûrd', v.t.* to gird round:—*pa.t.* and *pa.p.* engirt. [Pfx. *en-*, and **gird** (2).]

English, *ing'glish, adj.* belonging to *England* or its inhabitants or language.—*n.* the language of the people of England, now of Britain, a great part of the British Commonwealth, U.S.A., &c.—**Basic English** (see **basic**); **Old English,** English language as spoken down to about 1100 (popularly known as *Anglo-Saxon*); **Middle English,** from then till about 1500; **Modern English,** from about 1500 onwards.—**Early English,** often means **Early Middle English.** [O.E. *Englisc, Engle,* Angles.]

engraft, *en-gräft', v.t.* to graft: to insert, incorporate (into): to join on to something already existing (with *upon*): to implant in the mind. [Pfx. *en-*, and **graft** (1).]

engrain, *en-grān', ingrain, in-, v.t.* to dye a fast or lasting colour: to infix deeply (*lit.* and *fig.*, e.g. a stain, a habit), esp. in the *p.adj.* **en-grained',** more often **ingrained'** (or *in'-*). [Orig. 'to dye in grain' (meaning *with grain*) —i.e. kermes insects. See **grain.**]

engrave, *en-grāv', v.t.* to cut with a graver (on wood, steel, &c.): to ornament thus (with): to impress deeply (upon, e.g. the memory).—*ns.* **engrav'er; engrav'ing,** act or art of cutting designs on metal, wood, &c.: an impression taken from an engraved plate, a print. [Pfx. *en-*, and **grave,** vb.]

engross, *en-grōs', v.t.* to absorb wholly (e.g. a person, his attention, powers): to copy in a large hand or in distinct characters: to write in legal form.—*ns.* **engross'er; engross'ment,** act of engrossing: that which has been en-grossed: a fair copy. [From Fr. *en gros,* in large. See **gross.**]

engulf, *en-gulf',* **ingulf,** *in-, v.t.* to swallow up wholly, as in a gulf: to cause to be swallowed in a gulf.—*n.* **engulf'ment.** [Pfx. *en-*, and **gulf.**]

enhance, *en-häns', v.t.* to heighten or intensify: to raise in value or in importance: to add to, increase.—*n.* **enhance'ment.** [Prob. from O.Fr. *enhaucer*—L. *in*, and *altus,* high.]

enharmonic, *en-här-mon'ik, adj.* (*mus.*) pertaining to an interval, smaller than a semitone, that can be distinguished in writing but is not provided for on normal keyed instruments, e.g. A♯ to B♭. [L.L. *enharmonicus*—Gr. *enarmonikos—en,* in, *harmonia,* harmony.]

enigma, *en-ig'ma, n.* a statement with a hidden meaning to be guessed, a riddle: a puzzling person or thing.—*adjs.* **enigmat'ic, -al.**—*adv.* **enigmat'ically.** [L. *aenigma*—Gr. *ainigma*—*ainissesthai,* to speak in riddles—*ainos,* a fable.]

enjambment, enjambement, *en-jamb'mént, ä-zhäb'mä, n.* the continuation of the sense without a pause beyond the end of a line of verse. [Fr. *enjambement—enjamber,* to stride, encroach—*en,* in, *jambe,* leg.]

enjoin, *en-join', v.t.* to order or direct with authority or urgency: to impose (on a person, e.g. a line of conduct). [Fr. *enjoindre*—L. *in-jungĕre—in,* and, *jungĕre,* to join.]

enjoy, *en-joi', v.t.* (with *oneself*) to experience pleasure: to take pleasure or delight in: to possess or use (with satisfaction or delight): to experience.—*adj.* **enjoy'able.**—*n.* **enjoy'-ment.** [O.Fr. *enjoier,* to give joy to—*en* (= L. *in*), and *joie,* joy; or O.Fr. *enjoir,* to enjoy—*en,* and *joir*—L. *gaudēre,* to rejoice.]

enkindle, *en-kin'dl, v.t.* to kindle or set on fire (*obs.* except *fig.*): to inflame (e.g. the passions).—*p.adj.* **enkin'dled.** [Pfx. *en-*, and **kindle.**]

enlarge, *en-lärj', v.t.* to increase in size or quantity: to reproduce on a larger scale (e.g. a photograph): to expand or increase the capacity of (e.g. ideas, heart, mind): to exaggerate.—*v.i.* to grow large or larger: to be diffuse in speaking or writing: to expatiate (upon).—*adj.* **enlarged'.**—*ns.* **enlarge'ment; enlar'ger,** or **enlarging machine,** the apparatus for projecting a negative on to a sensitive surface for making an enlarged print. [O.Fr. *enlarger—en* (= L. *in*), *larᵦ .,* broad.]

enlighten, *en-līt'n, v.t.* to shed light on: to make clear to the mind: to impart knowledge or information to: to elevate by knowledge or religion.—*p.ad.* **enlight'ened,** free from prejudice or superstition: informed.—*n.* **enlight'-enment,** act of enlightening: information: state of being enlightened: the spirit of the French philosophers of the 18th century. [O.E. *inlīhtan—in,* in, and *līhtan,* to light.]

enlist, *en-list', v.t.* to engage as a soldier, &c.: to employ in advancing a project.—*v.i.* to register for service, esp. as a soldier: to enter heartily into a cause.—*n.* **enlist'ment.** [Pfx. *en-*, and **list** (2).]

enliven, *en-līv'n, v.t.* to excite or make active: to make sprightly or cheerful. [Pfx. *en-*, **life,** and suffx. *-en.*]

en masse, *ä mas,* in a body, all together. [Fr.]

enmesh, *en-mesh', v.t.* to catch, entangle, as in a mesh or net.—Also **emmesh', immesh'.** [Pfx. *en-*, and **mesh.**]

enmity, *en'mi-ti, n.* unfriendliness, ill-will: state of hostility. [O.Fr. *enemistié*—L. *inimīcus.* See **enemy.**]

ennoble, *e-nō'bl, v.t.* to make noble, to elevate (in character, quality): to raise to the nobility.—*n.* **ennō'blement.** [Fr. *ennoblir*—Fr. *en* (= L. *in*), and **noble.**]

ennui, *ä-nwē, on'wē, on-wē', n.* a feeling of weariness or languor: boredom.—*adj.* **ennuyé** (*-yā*). [Fr.,—O.Fr. *anoi.* See **annoy.**]

Neutral vowels in unaccented syllables: *em'pér-ôr*; for certain sounds in foreign words see p. ix.

234

enormous, e-nör′mus, adj. very large: (arch.) atrocious.—n. **enor′mity,** a great crime: great wickedness (often loosely, for e.g. heartlessness, inappropriateness).—adv. **enor′mously.** [L. ēnormis—ē, out of, norma, rule.]

enough, e-nuf′, adj. sufficient, giving content, satisfying want.—adv. sufficiently: (foll. another adv.) rather (e.g. funnily enough).—n. a sufficiency.—**have enough of,** to be tired of; **well, good, enough,** quite well, quite good. [O.E. genōh, genōg; Ger. genug; O.N. gnōgr.]

enow, e-now′, adj. and adv. (arch.) = **enough.**

en passant, ã pa-sã, in passing, incidentally. [Fr.]

en pension, ã pã-syõ, at a fixed rate covering board and lodging. [Fr.]

enquire. See **enquire.**

enrage, en-rāj′, v.t. to make angry.—p.adj. **enraged′.** [O.Fr. enrager—en (= L. in), and rage, rage.]

enrapture, en-rap′tyùr, -chùr, v.t. to transport with pleasure or delight. [Pfx. en-, and rapture.]

enrich, en-rich′, v.t. to make rich (lit. and fig.): to fertilise: to adorn (with costly ornaments): to increase the proportion of some valuable substance to: to increase the proportion of a particular isotope in a mixture of the isotopes of an element.—n. **enrich′ment.** [Fr. enrichir—en- (L. in), and riche, rich.]

enrol, enroll, en-rōl′, v.t. to insert in a roll, list, or register: to enter in a list as pupil, member, &c.: to enter in the records of a court of law.—v.i. to register:—pr.p. enrōll′ing; pa.p. enrōlled.—n. **enrol′ment.** [O.Fr. enroller—en, and rolle, roll.]

en route, ã rōōt, on the way (for, to): while on the way. [Fr.]

ensample, en-säm′pl, n. a corr. of **example.**

ensanguined, en-sang′gwind, adj. bloodstained. [Pfx. en-, L. sanguis, -inis, blood, and suffx. -ed.]

ensconce, en-skons′, v.t. to hide (oneself, &c.) safely, to settle comfortably. [Fr. en (- L. in), and Eng. **sconce** (1).]

ensemble, ã-sã-bl′, n. all the parts of a thing taken together: (mus.) union of performers in a concerted number: a group of supporting dancers, corps de ballet: the group of musicians so combining: the general or combined effect: a woman's costume considered from the point of view of the combined effect of the different garments.—Also **tout** (tōōt) **ensemble.** [Fr. ensemble, together—L. in, in, simul, at the same time.]

enshrine, en-shrīn′, v.t. to enclose in or as in a shrine (lit. and fig.). [Fr. en (= L. in), and Eng. **shrine.**]

enshroud, en-shrowd′, v.t. to cover with a shroud: to cover completely. [Pfx. en-, and **shroud.**]

ensiform, en′si-förm, adj. sword-shaped. [L. ensis, sword, and suffx. -form.]

ensign, en′sīn, en′sin, n. a mark or badge: the sign or flag distinguishing a nation or a regiment: one who carries the colours: formerly, the officer of lowest commisioned rank in the British infantry. **Blue, Red, White Ensign,** flags respectively of the naval reserve, the merchant navy, and the Royal Navy. [O.Fr.

enseigne—L. insignia, pl. of insigne, a distinctive mark—in, and signum, a mark.]

ensilage, en′sil-ij, n. the storing of green vegetable matter in pits or silos: the fodder thus prepared. [Fr.,—Sp. en, in, and silo—L. sīrus—Gr. sīros, &c., pit for corn.]

enslave, en-slāv′, v.t. to reduce to slavery: to subject to a dominating influence.—n. **enslave′ment.** [Pfx. en-, and **slave.**]

ensnare, en-snār′, v.t. to catch in a snare (lit. and fig.). [Pfx. en-, and **snare.**]

ensue, en-sū′, v.i. to follow, to come after: to result (from, on).—v.t. (B., arch.) to seek after:—pr.p. ensū′ing; pa.p. ensūed′. [O.Fr. ensuir—L. in, after, sequī, to follow.]

en suite, ã swēt, in succession or connected series: forming a unit, or a set. [Fr.]

ensure, en-shōōr′, v.t. to make sure, certain, or safe. See **insure.**

entablature, en-tab′la-tyùr, n. in classic architecture, the part (consisting of architrave, frieze, and cornice) that surmounts the columns, resting on the capitals. [It. intavolatura—in, in, tavola, a table—L. tabula.]

entail, en-tāl′, v.t. to settle on a series of heirs, so that the immediate possessor may not dispose of the estate: to bring on as an inevitable consequence: to necessitate.—n. an estate entailed: the rule of descent of an estate. [Pfx. en-, and **tail** (2).]

entangle, en-tang′gl, v.t. to twist into a tangle: to make (things) intricate: to involve in complications or difficulties: to ensnare.—n. **entang′lement,** act of entangling: state of being entangled: a tangled obstacle or snare: conditions causing perplexity, embarrassment, or anxiety. [Pfx. en-, and **tangle.**]

entente, ã-tãt, n. an understanding: a friendly agreement or relationship between states. [Fr.]

enter, en′tér, v.i. to go or come in: to become a party or participator: to put down one's name (with for).—v.t. to come or go into: to penetrate: to join or engage in: to begin: to put into: to enrol or record.—**enter a protest,** to write it in the books: thence simply, to protest; **enter into,** to become a party to: to participate actively or heartily in: to understand sympathetically (another's feelings): to take up the discussion of: to be part of; **enter on,** to begin: to engage in. [Fr. entrer—L. intrāre, to go into, related to inter, between.]

enter-, en′tér-, pfx. between, among. [Fr. entre —L. inter.]

enteric, en-ter′ik, adj. pertaining to the intestines: typhoid.—n. typhoid fever.—n. **enterī′tis,** inflammation of the intestines. [Gr. enteron, intestine.]

enterprise, en′tér-prīz, n. that which is attempted: a bold or dangerous undertaking: willingness to engage in undertakings of risk.—v.t. (arch.) to undertake.—p.adj. **en′terprising,** forward in undertaking projects: adventurous.—adv. **en′terprisingly.** [O.Fr. entreprise, pa.p. of entreprendre—entre, between (L. inter), and prendre (L. prehendēre), to seize.]

entertain, en-tér-tān′, v.t. to receive and treat hospitably: to hold the attention or thoughts of: to amuse: to harbour (e.g. an idea, a feeling): to admit to consideration.—*n.* **enter-tain′er.**—*p.adj.* **entertain′ing.**—*adv.* **enter-tain′ingly.**—*n.* **entertain′ment**, act of enter-taining: that which entertains: (*arch.*) hospi-tality: the provisions of the table: performance or show intended to give pleasure: amuse-ment. [Fr. *entretenir*—L. *inter*, among, *tenēre*, to hold.]

enthrall, enthral, *en-thröl′, v.t.* to bring into thraldom or bondage: to hold spell-bound:—*pr.p.* enthrall′ing; *pa.p.* enthralled′.—*n.* **enthral′ment**, act of enthralling: slavery.— Also **inthrall(l)′.** [Pfx. *en-*, and **thrall.**]

enthrone, *en-thrōn′, v.t.* to place on a throne (*lit.* and *fig.*): to install as a king or bishop.—*n.* **enthrone′ment.** [**en-**, throne; cf. Fr. *enthroner*, from *en*, and *trône*—Gr. *thronos*, a throne.]

enthusiasm, *en-thū′zi-azm, n.* intense interest: passionate zeal.—*n.* **enthū′siast**, one filled with enthusiasm.—*adjs.* **enthūsias′tic, -al,** zealous: ardent.—*adv.* **enthūsias′tically.**—*v.t.* and *v.i.* **enthūse′** (back-formation), to make, be, become, or appear enthusiastic. [Gr. *en-thousiasmos*, a god-inspired zeal—*enthousiazein*, to be inspired by a god—*en*, in, *theos*, a god.]

entice, *en-tīs′, v.t.* to induce by exciting hope or desire: to lead astray.—*adj.* **entice′able.**—*ns.* **entice′ment**, act of enticing: that which en-tices or tempts: allurement; **entic′er.**—*p.adj.* **entic′ing.**—*adv.* **entic′ingly.** [O.Fr. *enticier*, provoke; prob. related to L. *titiō*, a firebrand.]

entire, *en-tīr′, adj.* whole: complete: unimpaired, unbroken, unmingled: not castrated (esp. of a horse).—*adv.* **entire′ly.**—*ns.* **entire′ness,** **en-tire′ty**, completeness: the whole. [O.Fr. *en-tier*—L.*integer*, whole, from *in-*, not, and root of *tangĕre*, to touch.]

entitle, *en-tī′tl, v.t.* to give the title of, to style: to give a claim (to). [O.Fr. *entiteler*—Low L. *in-titulāre*—*in*, in, *titulus*, title.]

entity, *en′ti-ti, n.* (*rare*) being, existence: a real substance: a thing that exists. [Low L. *entitās, -ātis*—*ens, entis*, being—*esse*, to be.]

ento-, in composition, inside [Gr. *entos*, within]. It often interchanges with **endo-** (q.v.):—e.g. **entopar′asite, endopar′asite.**

entomb, *en-tōōm′, v.t.* (*lit.* and *fig.*) to place in a tomb: to serve as a tomb for.—*n.* **entomb′-ment**, burial. [O.Fr. *entoumber*—*en*, in, *tombe*, a tomb.]

entomology, *en-to-mol′o-ji, n.* the science of insects.—*adj.* **entomolog′ical.**—*n.* **entomo-l′ogist**, one learned in entomology. [Fr. *ento-mologie*—Gr. *entoma*, insects, *logos*, dis-course.]

entourage, *ä-tōō-räzh′, n.* surroundings: fol-lowers. [Fr.—*entourer*, to surround—*en*, in, *tour*, a circuit.]

entozoon, *en-tō-zō′on, n.* an animal living parasitically within the body of its host (q.v.):— (*pl.*) **entozō′a.** [Gr. *entos*, within, *zōon*, an animal.]

entr′acte, *ä-trakt′, n.* the interval between acts in a play: a piece of music or other performance between acts. [Fr. *entre*, between, *acte*, an act.]

entrails, *en′trālz, n.pl.* the internal parts of an animal's body, the bowels. [O.Fr. *entraille*— Low L. *intrālia*—*inter*, within.]

entrain, *en-trān′, v.t.* to put into a railway train

(esp. troops).—*v.i.* to go into a train. [Pfx. *en-*, and **train.**]

entrain, *in-trān′, v.t.* (*arch.*) to draw after: to transport one substance, e.g. small liquid par-ticles, in another, e.g. a vapour: to suspend bubbles or particles in a moving fluid.—*n.* **entrain′ment.** [Fr.]

entrance, *en′trans, n.* act of entering: power or right to enter: a place of entering: a door: the beginning.—*n.* **en′trant**, one who, or that which, enters (esp. a competition, a pro-fession, &c.). [Fr. *entrer*—L. *intrāre*, to enter.]

entrance, *en-träns′, v.t.* to put into a trance: to fill with rapturous delight.—*n.* **entrance′ment.** [Pfx. *en-*, and **trance.**]

entrap, *en-trap′, v.t.* to catch, as in a trap: to ensnare: to entangle. [O.Fr. *entraper*—*en*, in, *trappe*, a trap.]

entreat, *en-trēt′, v.t.* to ask earnestly: to beg for: (*orig.*) to treat, act towards.—*n.* **entreat′y**, act of entreating: earnest prayer. [O.Fr. *en-traiter*—*en*, and *traiter*, to treat.]

entrechat, *ä-tré-shä, n.* in ballet dancing, a leap during which the heels are struck together several times. [Fr.]

entrée, *ä′trā, n.* the right or privilege of ad-mission: a made dish served at dinner be-tween the chief courses or as a substitute. [Fr.]

entremets, *ä-tré-mä, n.* any dainty served at table between the chief courses. [Fr.]

entrench, *en-trench′, -sh, v.t.* to dig a trench around: to fortify with a ditch and parapet: to establish in a strong position.—*v.i.* to encroach (upon).—*n.* **entrench′ment**, defensive earth-work of trenches and parapets: an encroach-ment.—Also **intrench′.** [Pfx. *en-*, and **trench.**]

entre nous, *ä-tr′ nōō,* between ourselves. [Fr.]

entrepôt, *ä′tré-pō, n.* a storehouse: a seaport, or other centre where goods are collected and distributed. [Fr.]

entrepreneur, *ä-tré-pré-nœr′, n.* one who undertakes a business enterprise, esp. one involving risk. [Fr.]

entresol, *en′tér-sol, ä′tré-sol, n.* a low storey between the ground floor and the first floor. [Fr.,—*entre*, between, *sol*, the ground.]

entropy, *en′trō-pi, n.* in thermodynamics, a measure of energy that is not available for doing work, or of heat content: a measure of the degree of disorder in the molecules of a substance; at absolute zero, all substances are in state of complete order and have zero en-tropy. [Gr. *en*, in, *tropē*, turning, intended to represent 'transformation content'.]

entrust, *en-trust′, v.t.* to give in trust (to): to commit as a trust (to): to charge trustingly (with).—Also **intrust.** [Pfx. *en-*, and **trust.**]

entry, *en′tri, n.* act of entering (in any sense): entrance: act of committing to writing in a record: the thing so written: (*law*) taking possession. [Fr. *entrée.* See **enter.**]

entwine, *en-twīn′, v.t.* to interlace: to twine (with, about, round). [Pfx. *en-*, and **twine.**]

entwist, *en-twist′, v.t.* to twist together: to twist (with). [Pfx. *en-*, and **twist.**]

enumerate, *e-nū′mer-āt, v.t.* to count the num-ber of: to name over.—*n.* **enumerā′tion**, act of numbering: a detailed account. [L. *ē*, from, *numerāre, -ātum*, to number.]

enunciate, *e-nun′s(h)i-āt, v.t.* to state formally:

Neutral vowels in unaccented syllables: *em′pér-ŏr*; for certain sounds in foreign words see p. ix.

to pronounce distinctly.—*n.* **enunciation** (*e-nun-s(h)i-ā'sh(ó)n*), act of enunciating: manner of uttering or pronouncing: a distinct statement or declaration.—*adj.* **enun'ciative** (*-si-ā-* or *-sh(y)ā-*).—*n.* **enun'ciātor.** [L. *ēnuntiāre, -ātum—ē,* from, *nuntiāre,* to tell—*nuntius,* a messenger.]

enure, *en-ūr'.* Same as **inure.**

envelop, *en-vel'óp, v.t.* to cover by wrapping: to surround entirely: to hide.—*ns.* **envelope** (*en'vel-ōp, on'-*), that which envelops, wraps, or covers: a cover for a letter: (*electronics*) the outer containing vessel of a discharge tube; **envel'opment,** a wrapping or covering on all sides. [O.Fr. *enveloper;* origin obscure.]

envenom, *en-ven'óm, v.t.* to put venom on, into: to poison: to taint with bitterness or malice. [O.Fr. *envenimer—en,* and *venim,* venom.]

environ, *en-vī'rón, v.t.* to surround: to encircle: to surround with hostile intention.—*n.* **envī'ronment,** a surrounding: conditions influencing development or growth.—*n.pl.* **environs** (*en-vī'rónz or en'vi-*), the outskirts of a place: neighbourhood. [Fr. *environner—environ,* around—*virer,* to turn round; cf. **veer.**]

envisage, *en-viz'ij, v.t.* to face, confront (e.g. danger): to picture, set before one's mind and consider. [Fr. *envisager—en,* and *visage,* the face.]

envoy, *en'voi, n.* a messenger, esp. one sent to transact business with a foreign government: a diplomatic minister of the second order.—*n.* **en'voyship.** [For Fr. *envoyé—*pa.p. of *envoyer,* to send.]

envoy, envoi, *en'voi, n.* the concluding part of a poem or a book: the author's final words, esp. now the short stanza concluding a poem written in certain archaic metrical forms. [O.Fr. *envoye—envoier,* to send—*en voie,* on the way.]

envy, *en'vi, n.* (*obs.*) ill-will: a feeling of mortification at another's well-being or success: a good thing looked upon with grudging or with emulous feeling.—*v.t.* to feel envy towards: to feel envy on account of, to grudge—*pr.p.* **en'vying;** *pa.p.* **en'vied.**—*adjs.* **en'viable,** that is to be envied; **en'vious,** feeling envy: directed by envy.—*adv.* **en'viously.** *ns.* **en'viousness; en'vying** (*B.*), jealousy, ill-will. [Fr. *envie—*L. *invidia—in,* on, *vidēre,* to look.]

enwrap, *en-rap', v.t.* to cover by wrapping: to wrap (in): to engross.—Also **inwrap'.** [Pfx. *en-,* and **wrap.**]

enzyme, enzym, *en'zīm, en'zim, n.* a substance produced by living cells, which accelerates or retards chemical changes without itself undergoing any alteration, e.g. an enzyme produced by the micro-organisms in yeasts brings about alcoholic fermentation. Cf. *catalyst.* [Gr. *en,* in, *zȳmē,* leaven.]

Eocene, *ē'ō-sēn, adj.* (*geol.*) belonging to the oldest period of the Tertiary (q.v.) era. [Gr. *ēōs,* daybreak, *kainos,* new.]

Eolian. Same as **Aeolian.**

eolith, *ē'ō-lith, n.* a very early roughly-shaped stone implement, or one naturally formed, assumed to have been used by man.—*adj.* **eolith'ic.** [Gr. *ēōs,* dawn, *lithos,* stone.]

epact, *ē'pakt, n.* the moon's age at the beginning of the year: the excess of the calendar month

or solar year over the lunar. [Fr. *épacte—*Gr. *epaktos,* brought on—*epi,* on, *agein,* to bring.]

epaulet, epaulette, *ep'ól-et, n.* a shoulder-piece or ornament, esp. one worn by a military or naval officer (now disused in the British army). [Fr. *épaulette—épaule,* the shoulder.]

epergne, *e-pûrn', n.* a branched ornamental centrepiece for the table. [Perh. from Fr. *épargne,* saving—*épargner,* to save.]

ephemera, *ef-em'ér-a,* or *ēm'-, n.* a genus of short-lived insects, the mayflies: that which lasts a short time.—*adj.* **ephem'eral,** existing only for a day: short-lived.—*n.* **ephem'eris,** an account of daily transactions: an astronomical almanac tabulating the daily positions of the sun, moon, planets, and certain stars, &c.:—*pl.* **ephemerides** (*ef-e-mer'i-dēz*). [Gr. *ephēmeros,* living a day—*epi,* for, during, *hēmera,* day.]

ephod, *ef'od, n.* a kind of linen surplice worn by the Jewish priests. [Heb. *āphad,* to put on.]

epi-, In composition, above, outside [Gr. *epi,* upon], e.g.:—*n.* **ep'iblast,** the outer germinal layer of an embryo.—*adj.* **epicer'ebral,** above or upon the brain.

epic, *ep'ik, adj.* applied to a long narrative poem that recounts heroic events in an elevated style: showing a quality or qualities characteristic of an epic poem: impressive, large-scale.—*n.* an epic poem: a story comparable to that of an epic poem, esp. a long adventure novel or film.—**beast epic,** a long narrative relating in mock-elevated style the actions and adventures of animal characters. [Gr. *epikos—epos,* a word.]

epicene, *ep'i-sēn, adj.* common to both sexes: having characteristics of both sexes: (of a noun) of common gender: sometimes restricted to nouns that have only one grammatical gender (i.e. are qualified by adjs. of one gender only) though used for both sexes (e.g. L. *mus,* a mouse (*masc.*), *avis,* a bird (*fem.*). [Gr. *epi,* upon, *koinos,* common.]

epicentre, *ep'i-sen-tér, n.* that point on the earth's surface directly over the point of origin of an earthquake. [Gr. *epi,* upon, *kentron,* a point.]

epicure, *ep'i-kyur, n.* a person of refined and fastidious taste, esp. in the luxuries of the table.—*adj.* **epicure'an,** pertaining to Epicurus, the Greek philosopher who taught that pleasure was the chief good: given to luxury.—*n.* a follower of Epicurus: one given to the luxuries of the table.—*ns.* **epicure'anism,** the doctrines of Epicurus: attachment to these doctrines; **ep'icurism,** pursuit of pleasure: fastidiousness in luxury. [Through L.—Gr. *Epikouros.*]

epicycle, *ep'i-sī-kl, n.* a circle having its centre on the circumference of a greater circle on which it moves. [Gr. *epi,* upon, *kyklos,* a circle.]

epidemic, -al, *ep-i-dem'ik, -ál, adj.* affecting a community at a certain time.—*n.* **epidem'ic,** a disease that attacks great numbers in one place at one time: an outbreak (of). [Gr. *epi,* among, *dēmos,* the people.]

epidermis, *ep-i-dûr'mis, n.* scarf-skin or cuticle, forming an external covering for the true skin: a sheath of closely united cells forming a layer over the surface of the leaves and young stems of a plant.—*adjs.* **epider'mal, epider'mic.** [Gr. *epidermis*—*epi*, upon, *derma*, the skin.]

epidiascope, *ep-i-dī'a-skōp, n.* a lantern for projecting images of objects whether opaque or not. Cf. *episcope.* [Gr. *epi*, upon, *dia*, through, *skopeein*, to look at.]

epiglottis, *ep-i-glot'is, n.* a cartilaginous flap over the glottis (q.v.). [Gr. *epi*, over, *glōttis*, glottis.]

epigram, *ep'i-gram, n.* a concise and pointed, often sarcastic, saying: a short poem expressing an ingenious thought with point, usually satirical.—*adjs.* **epigrammat'ic, -al,** relating to or dealing in epigrams: like an epigram: concise and pointed.—*adv.* **epigrammat'ically.**—*v.t.* **epigramm'atise,** to make an epigram on.—*n.* **epigramm'atist.** [Through Fr. and L. from Gr. *epigramma*—*epi*, upon, *gramma*, a writing—*graphein*, to write.]

epigraph, *ep'i-gräf, n.* an inscription, esp. on a building: a citation or motto at the beginning of a book or of one its parts. [Gr. *epigraphē*—*epi*, upon, *graphein*, to write.]

epilepsy, *ep'i-lep-si, n.* a chronic functional disease of the nervous system, manifested by recurring attacks of sudden insensibility or impairment of consciousness, commonly accompanied by peculiar convulsive seizures.—*adj.* and *n.* **epilep'tic.** [Gr. *epilēpsia*—*epi*, upon, and root of *lambanein*, to seize.]

epilogue, *ep'i-log, n.* a speech or short poem at the end of a play: the concluding section of a book, &c. [Fr., through L.—Gr. *epilogos*, conclusion—*epi*, upon, *legein*, to speak.]

epiphany, *e-pif'an-i, n.* a church festival celebrated on January 6, in commemoration of the manifestation of Christ to the wise men of the East. [Gr. *epiphaneia*, appearance—*epi*, to, *phainein*, to show.]

episcopacy, *e-pis'ko-pás-i, n.* the government of the church by bishops: the office of a bishop: a bishop's period of office: the bishops, as a class.—*adj.* **epis'copal,** governed by bishops: belonging to or vested in bishops.—*adj.* **episcopā'lian,** pertaining to bishops, or to government by bishops.—*n.* one who belongs to an episcopal (esp. Anglican) church: (*cap.*) a member of the Scottish Episcopal Church.—*ns.* **episcopā'lianism,** episcopalian government and doctrine; **epis'copate,** a bishopric: the office of a bishop: the order of bishops. [L. *episcopātus*—Gr. *episkopos*, an overseer.]

episcope, *ep'i-skōp, n.* a lantern for projecting images of opaque objects. [Gr. *epi*, on, over, *skopeein*, to look.]

episode, *ep'i-sōd, n.* a story introduced into a narrative or poem, or a passage introduced into a piece of music, to give variety: an incident, or a distinct series of events, occurring in a longer story, play, &c.: a part of a radio or television serial which is broadcast at one time.—*adj.* **episŏd'ic(al),** pertaining to or contained in an episode: brought in as a digression: consisting largely of episodes. [Gr. *epeisodion*—*epi*, upon, *eisodos*, a coming in—*eis*, into, *hodos*, a way.]

epistemology, *ep-is-te-mol'oj-i, n.* the theory of

knowledge. [Gr. *epistēmē*, knowledge, *logos*, discourse.]

epistle, *e-pis'l, n.* a letter, esp. one to an individual or church from an apostle: a verse composition in letter form.—*adj.* **epis'tolary,** of, pertaining to, consisting of, suitable to, or contained in, letters. [O.Fr.,—L. *epistola*—Gr. *epistolē*—*epi*, on the occasion of, *stellein*, to send.]

epitaph, *ep'i-täf, n.* a tombstone inscription: a composition in the form of a tombstone inscription. [Gr. *epitaphion*—*epi*, upon, *taphos*, a tomb.]

epithalamium, *ep-i-tha-lā'mi-um, n.* a song or poem in celebration of a marriage. [Gr. *epithalamion*—*epi*, upon, *thalamos*, a bride-chamber.]

epithelium, *ep-i-thē'li-um, n.* the cell-tissue that covers the outer surface, and lines the closed cavities, of the body. [Mod. L.—Gr. *epi*, upon, *thēlē*, nipple.]

epithet, *ep'i-thet, n.* an adjective expressing a quality or attribute considered characteristic of the noun (e.g. the *blue* sky, *dutiful* Aeneas): an appellation or descriptive term (e.g. Charles *the Bold*, Edmund *Ironside*).—*adj.* **epithet'ic(al),** pertaining to an epithet: abounding with epithets. [Gr. *epitheton*, neut. of *epithetos*, added—*epi*, on, *tithenai*, to place.]

epitome, *e-pit'o-mē, n.* an abridgment or short summary of anything, as of a book: something that represents or typifies another on a small scale.—*v.t.* **epit'omise,** to condense: to represent on a small scale.—*ns.* **epit'omiser, epit'omist.** [Gr.,—*epi*, *tomē*, a cut.]

epizoon, *ep-i-zō'on, n.* an animal that lives on the surface of another animal: *pl.* **epizō'a.** [Gr. *epi*, upon, *zōion*, an animal.]

epoch, *ēp'ok, ep'ok, n.* a point of time fixed or made remarkable by some great event from which dates are reckoned: an age in history: (*geol.*) a division of time constituting part of a *period* (q.v.).—*adjs.* **ep'ochal; ep'och-mā'king,** great enough to affect the course of history and begin a new epoch. [Gr. *epochē*—*epechein*, to stop—*epi*, upon, *echein*, to hold.]

epode, *ep'ōd, n.* a kind of lyric poem in which a longer verse is followed by a shorter one: the last part of a lyric ode, sung after the strophe and antistrophe. [Gr. *epōidos*—*epi*, on, *ōidē*, an ode.]

eponym, *ep'o-nim, n.* one who gives his name to something: a hero invented to account for the name of a place or people.—*adj.* **epon'ymous.** [Gr. *epōnymos*—*epi*, upon, to, *onoma*, a name.]

epopee, *ep'o-pē,* **epopoeia,** *ep-o-pē'ya, n.* epic poetry: an epic poem. [Gr. *epopoiia*—*epos*, a word, an epic poem, *poieein*, to make.]

epoxy, *e-pok'sē, adj.* containing oxygen bound to two other atoms, often carbon, which are already attached in some way.—**epoxy** (or **epoxide**) **resins,** synthetic polymers used as structural plastics, surface coatings, adhesives, &c.

equable, *ek'wà-bl,* or *ēk'-, adj.* uniform: free from extremes (e.g. of climate): of even temper, not easily annoyed or agitated.—*n.* **equabil'ity.**—*adv.* **e'quably.** [L. *aequābilis*—*aequāre*—*aequus,* equal.]

Neutral vowels in unaccented syllables: *em'pėr-ŏr*; for certain sounds in foreign words see p. ix.

equal, *ē′kwál, adj.* identical in quantity: of the same value: evenly balanced: equitable (e.g. laws): (*arch.*) just (e.g. a judge): having sufficent courage, presence of mind, &c. for (e.g. *equal to doing this*).—*n.* one of the same age, rank, &c.—*v.t.* to be, or to make, equal to:—*pr.p.* e′qualling; *pa.p.* e′qualled.—*v.t.* **e′qualise**, to make equal.—*n.* **equalisa′tion**, the act of making equal: state of being equalised—*adj.* **equalitār′ian** (-*kwol-*) of or pertaining to the equality of mankind.—*n.* one who believes that all men are equal, and should be treated as equal.—*n.* **equality** (*ē-kwol′iti*), the condition of being equal: sameness: evenness.—*adv.* **e′qually.**—*v.t.* **equāte′**, to state as equal (to): to regard as equal or equivalent.—*n.* **equā′tion**, the act of making equal or equivalent: a statement of the equality of two quantities: a formula expressing a chemical action and the proportions of the substances involved: correction to compensate for an error, &c.—**equal to (the occasion)**, fit or able for (the emergency).—**personal equation**, the correction to be applied to the reading of an instrument on account of the tendency of the individual observer to read too high or too low: generally, the bias in any judgment due to individual temperament or limitations. [L. *aequālis*—*aequāre*, to make equal—*aequus*, equal.]

equanimity, *ē-kwa-nim′i-ti, e-, n.* evenness of mind or temper, calmness, composure. [L. *aequanimitās*—*aequus*, equal, *animus*, the mind.]

equator, *e-kwā′tòr, n.* (*geog.*) an imaginary circle passing round the globe, equidistant from N. and S. poles: (*astron.*) the celestial (q.v.).—*adj.* **equatō′rial.**—*n.* a telescope, mounted on an axis parallel to the plane of the equator and revolving round an axis parallel to the earth's axis, which, when set on a star, will keep that star in the field of view continuously. [L.L. *aequator*—L. *aequus*, equal.]

equerry, *ek′wé-ri, n.* one who has the charge of horses: an official in attendance upon a prince or personage. [Fr. *écurie*—Low L. *scūria*, a stable.]

equestrian, *e-kwes′tri-án, adj.* pertaining to horsemanship: on horseback—*n.* one who rides on horseback:—*fem.* (sham Fr.) **equestrienne′.** [L. *equester, equestris*—*eques*, a horseman—*equus*, a horse.]

equi-, *ē′kwi-, pfx.* equal [L. *aequus*, equal], e.g.:—*adjs.* **equian′gular**, having equal angles; **equidis′tant**, equally distant (from); **equilat′eral**, having all sides equal.

equilibrium, *ēk-wi-lib′ri-um, n.* balance: a state of even balance: a state in which opposing forces or tendencies neutralise each other.—*v.t.* and *v.i.* **equilibrate** (*ēk-wi-lib′rāt*, (or *-lib′rāt*, or *-kwil′-*), to balance: to counterpoise.—*n.* **equilibrā′tion**; **equil′ibrātor** (or *-lib′-*), a balancing or stabilising device, esp. an aeroplane fin; **equil′ibrist** (or *-lib′-*, or *-līb′-*), one who does balancing tricks. [L. *aequilībrium*—*aequus*, equal, *lībra*, balance.]

equine, *e′kwīn, adj.* **equinal**, *e kwīn′ál, adj.* pertaining to or of the nature of a horse. [L. *equīnus*—*equus*, a horse.]

equinox, *ek′wi-noks, ēk′wi-noks, n.* the time when the sun crosses the equator, making the night equal in length to the day, about March 21 and September 23.—*adj.* **equinoc′tial** (-*shál*), pertaining to the equinoxes, to the time of these, or to the regions about the equator.—*n.* the celestial equator or equinoctial line—the great circle in which the plane of the earth's equator intersects the celestial sphere—so called because day and night are equal when the sun reaches it.—**equinoctial gales**, high gales popularly supposed to prevail about the times of the equinoxes—the belief is unsupported by observation. [L. *aequus*, equal, *nox, noctis*, night.]

equip, *e-kwip′, v.t.* to fit out, to furnish with everything needed:—*pr.p.* equipp′ing; *pa.p.* equipped′.—*ns.* **e′quipage**, that with which one is equipped: articles required for any operation, e.g. making and serving tea: a carriage and attendants; **equip′ment**, the act of equipping, things used in equipping or furnishing (in *pl.* **equip′ments**, when the articles are thought of individually), outfit: the machines, tools, &c., necessary (for a particular kind of work). [Fr. *équiper*, prob.—O.N. *skipa*, to set in order—*skip*, a ship.]

équipe, *ā-kēp, n.* in motor-racing and other sport, a team. [Fr.]

equipoise, *ek′wi-poiz, n.* a state of balance: a counterpoise.—Also *v.t.* [L. *aequus*, equal, and **poise.**]

equipollent, *ē-kwi-pol′ént, adj.* having equal power or force: equivalent. *n.* **equipoll′ence.** [L. *aequus*, equal, *pollens, pollentis*, pr.p. of *pollēre*, to be able.]

equiponderate, *ē-kwi-pon′dèr-āt, v.i.* to be equal in weight: to balance.—*n.* **equipon′derance.**—*adjs.* **equipon′derant.** [L. *aequus*, equal, *pondus, ponderis*, weight.]

equitation, *ek-wi-tā′sh(ò)n, n.* the art of riding on horseback. [L. *equitāre*, to ride—*equus*, a horse.]

equity, *ek′wi-ti, n.* fairness: appeal to general principles of justice in cases not covered by the law or where the law would apply unfairly: (in England, Ireland, U.S.) a system of law that grew up alongside statute law and common law and has now generally been incorporated with them: (in *pl.; coll.*) ordinary shares, as opp. to *debenture* and *preference shares.*—*adjs.* **e′quitable**, fair: pertaining to equity in the legal sense.—*n.* **eq′uitableness.**—*adv.* **eq′uitably.** [O.Fr. *equité*—L. *aequitās, -ātis*—*aequus*, equal.]

equivalent, *e-kwiv′á-lént, adj.* equal in value, power, meaning, &c.: (*chem.*) of like combining value.—*n.* a thing equivalent: (*chem.*) an equivalent weight.—*n.* **equiv′alence.**—*adv.* **equiv′alently.**—**equivalent weight** (*chem.*), that weight which displaces or combines with or otherwise represents a standard unit—atomic weight divided by valence; superseded by **mole** (q.v.). [Fr.,—L. *aequus*, equal, *valens, valentis*, pr.p. of *valēre*, to be worth.]

equivocal, *e-kwiv′o-kál, adj.* capable of meaning two or more things: capable of a double explanation: suspicious, questionable.—*adv.* **equiv′ocally.**—*n.* **equiv′ocalness.**—*v.i.* **equiv′ocāte**, to use equivocal words in order to mislead.—*ns.* **equivoca′tion; equiv′ocātor.** [L. *aequus,* equal, *vox, vōcis,* the voice, a word.]

era, *ē′ra, n.* a series of years reckoned from a particular point, or that point itself: a main division of geological time, subdivided into *periods.* [Late L. *aera,* a number, orig. counters, pieces of copper used in counting, pl. of *aes,* copper.]

eradicate, *e-rad′i-kāt,* or *ē-, v.t.* to pull up by the roots: to extirpate.—*adj.* **erad′icable,** that can be eradicated.—*n.* **eradicā′tion,** the act of eradicating: state of being eradicated. [L. *ērādicāre, -ātum,* to root out—*ē,* from *rādix, -īcis,* a root.]

erase, *e-rāz′, e-rās′, v.t.* to rub or scrape out: to efface (e.g. from the memory): to destroy.—*ns.* **erā′ser,** one who, or that which, erases, as *ink-eraser*; **erā′sure** (*-zhŭr, -zhūr*), the act of erasing: a rubbing out: the place where something written has been rubbed out. [L. *ērādĕre—ē,* from, *rādĕre, rāsum,* to scrape.]

Erastian, *e-rast′yán, n.* a follower of Thomas *Erastus,* a Swiss physician, who denied the church the right to inflict disciplinary penalties: one who would subordinate the jurisdiction of the church to that of the state.—Also *adj.—n.* **Erast′ianism,** control of church by state.

erbium, *ŭr′bi-ùm, n.* a metallic element (symbol Er; at. no. 68), member of rare-earth group. [Name formed from *Ytterby* in Sweden.]

ere, *ār, prep.* and *conj.,* before. [O.E. *ǣr*; cf. Du. *eer.*]

erect, *e-rekt′, adj.* upright: directed upward.—*v.t.* to set upright: to build: to construct on a given base.—*n.* **erec′tion,** act of erecting: state of being erected: a building or structure of any kind.—*adv.* **erect′ly.—*n.*** **erect′ness.—erect into,** to form into, to set up as. [L. *ērectus, ērigĕre,* to set upright—*ē,* from, *regĕre,* to direct.]

eremite, *er′e-mīt, n.* now **hermit.**

erg, *ŭrg, n.* the unit of work in the centimetre-gram-second system. See **joule.** [Gr. *ergon,* work.]

ergo, *ŭr′gō, adv. (logic)* therefore, used to mark the conclusion of a syllogism. [L. *ergō.*]

ergonomics, *ér-go-nom′iks, n.* the study of man or of individual men in relation to working environment: adaptation of machines and general conditions to fit the individual so that he may work at maximum efficiency.—*n.* **ergono′mist.** [Gr. *ergon,* work, *nomos,* law.]

ergot, *ŭr′got, n.* a disease of grasses (esp. rye) and sedges due to a parasitical fungus.—*n.* **er′gotism,** poisoning caused by eating bread made of rye diseased with ergot. [Fr.]

ermine, *ŭr′min, n.* the stoat: a white fur, the stoat's winter coat in northern lands, used—with the black tail-tip attached—for the robes of judges, magistrates, &c.—*adj.* **er′mined,** adorned with ermine. [O.Fr. *ermine,* perh. from L. (*mus*) *Armēnius,* lit. mouse of Armenia, whence it was brought to Rome.]

erne, *ŭrn, n.* the eagle. [O.E. *earn*; cf. O.N. *örn.*]

Ernie, *ŭr′ni, n.* the electronic machine which picks, by methods that allow full scope for chance, numbers to be used as winning numbers on premium bonds. [Abbrev. of *e*lectronic *r*andom *n*umber *i*ndicator *e*quipment.]

erode, *e-rōd′, v.t.* (of acids, &c.) to eat away.—*n.* **erō′sion** (*e-rō′zh(ó)n*), eating away: (*geol.*) the denuding action of weathering by water, ice, wind, &c.—*adj.* **erō′sive.** [L. *ē,* from, *rōdĕre, rōsum,* to gnaw.]

erotic, *e-rot′ik, adj.* pertaining to love: amatory.—*n.* **erotomā′nia,** morbid sexual passion. [Gr. *Erōs, -rōtos,* Greek god corresponding to Cupid.]

err, *ŭr, v.i.* (*arch.*) to wander: to go astray: to make a mistake, be wrong: to sin.—*adjs.* **errat′ic, -al,** wandering: having no certain course: irregular, not dependable (in conduct, &c.).—*adv.* **errat′ically.—*ns.*** **errat′ic** (also **errat′ic block, boulder**), a stone or boulder transported by ice, and deposited far from its original source; **errā′tum,** an error in writing or printing:—*pl.* **errā′ta.—*adj.*** **errō′neous,** wrong: mistaken.—*adv.* **errō′neously.—*ns.*** **errō′neousness; err′or,** (*arch.*) wandering: a blunder or mistake: wrong-doing. [Fr. *errer*—L. *errāre,* to stray; cog. with Ger. *irren,* and *irre,* astray.]

errand, *er′ánd, n.* a short journey on which one is sent to say or do something on behalf of another: the object of a journey.—**a fool's errand,** a useless mission. [O.E. *ǣrende*; O.N. *eyrindi.*]

errant, *er′ánt, adj.* wandering in search of adventure (as in *knight-errant*): itinerant: straying: erring, or liable to err.—*n.* **err′antry,** a wandering state: the occupation, conduct, or characteristics of a knight-errant. [Fr.,—L. *errans, errantis,* pr.p. of *errāre.*]

ersatz, *er-zäts′, adj.* substitute (e.g. *ersatz coffee*). [From a Ger. noun meaning compensation, replacement.]

Erse, *ers, ŭrs, n.* corr. of *Irish,* the name formerly given by Lowland Scots to the language of the West Highlands, as being of Irish origin: now sometimes used for Irish Gaelic.

erst, *ŭrst, adv.* at first: formerly.—*adv.* **erst′-while,** formerly.—*adj.* former. [O.E. *ǣrest,* superl. of *ǣr.* See **ere.**]

erubescent, *er-(y)ŏŏ-bes′ént, adj.* growing red: blushing.—*n.* **erubes′cence.** [L. *ērubescĕre,* to grow red—*ē-,* intent., and *rubescĕre—rubēre,* to be red.]

eruct, *e-rukt′,* or *ē-rukt′,* **eructate,** *-āt, v.t.* to belch out, as wind from the stomach.—*n.* **eructā′tion** (*ē-*). [L. *ēructāre, -ātum—ē,* from, *ructāre,* to belch forth.]

erudite, *er′(y)ŏŏ-dīt, adj.* learned.—*adv.* **er′uditely.—*n.*** **erudi′tion,** state of being learned: knowledge gained by study. [L. *ērudīre, ērudītum,* to free from roughness—*ē,* from, *rudis,* unformed.]

erupt, *e-rupt′, v.i.* to break out or through, as a volcano.—*n.* **erup′tion,** a breaking or bursting forth (e.g. of lava from a volcano: of strong feeling): that which bursts forth: a breaking out of spots on the skin, a rash.—*adj.* **erupt′ive,** breaking forth: attended by or producing eruption: produced by eruption. [L. *ērumpĕre, ēruptum—ē,* from, *rumpĕre,* to break.]

erysipelas, *er-i-sip′e-läs, n.* an inflammatory disease, generally in the face, marked by a bright redness of the skin. [Gr.; prob. from the root of *erythros,* red, *pella,* skin.]

erythema, *er-i-thē′má, n.* redness of the skin.—

Neutral vowels in unaccented syllables: *em′pér-ór*; for certain sounds in foreign words see p. ix.

adjs. **erythematic, erythem'atous.** [Gr. *ery-thēma*—*erythainein*, to redden—*erythros*, red.]

escalade,*es-ka-lād', n.* the scaling of the walls of a fortress by means of ladders.—*v.t.* to scale: to mount and enter by means of ladders.—*v.i.* **es'calate,** to ascend, descend on an escalator: to increase rapidly in scale or intensity.—Also *v.t.*—*ns.* **escalā'tion; es'calātor,** a moving stair. [Fr.,—Sp. *escalada*—*escala,* a ladder—L.*scāla.*]

escallop, *es-kal'op, n.* a variant of **scallop.**

escape, *es-kāp', v.t.* to get clear away from (e.g. custody): to evade (e.g. punishment): to go unnoticed (by eye or ear, &c.): to elude the memory: of words or sounds, to issue inadvertently from (a person, lips).—*v.i.* to emerge into or gain freedom: to flee: to leak (e.g. of gas).—*n.* act of escaping: a means of escaping: flight: a garden plant now growing wild: a leakage: flight from reality.—*adj.* **es-cāp'able,** that can be avoided, evaded.—*ns.* **escapāde',** a mischievous adventure; **escāpe'-ment,** part of a timepiece connecting the wheelwork with the pendulum or balance, and allowing a tooth to escape at each vibration; **escāp'ism,** desire or tendency to escape from reality into fantasy; **escāp'ist,** one who seeks escape, esp. from reality (also *adj.*).—**escape mechanism** (*psych.*) a mental process by which one evades the unpleasant; **escape valve,** a valve to let steam, &c., escape when desired. [O.Fr. *escaper* (Fr. *échapper*)—L. *cappā,* (lit.) 'out of one's cape or cloak'.]

escarp,*es-kärp', n.* a steep slope or *scarp* (*fort.*) the side of the ditch next the rampart.—*v.t.* to make into an escarp.—*n.* **escarp'ment,** the precipitous side of a hill or rock, an escarp. [Fr. *escarper,* to cut down steep.]

eschatology, *es-ka-tol'o-ji, n.* the doctrine of the last or final things, as death, judgment, the state after death. [Gr. *eschatos,* last, *logos,* a discourse.]

escheat, *es-chēt', n.* property that falls to the state for want of an heir, or by forfeiture.—*v.i.* to fall to the lord of the manor or the state. [O.Fr. *eschete*—*escheoir* (Fr. *échoir*)—L. *ex,* from, *cadēre,* to fall.]

eschew, *es-chōō', v.t.* to shun, to abstain from. [O.Fr. *eschever*; cog. with Ger. *scheuen,* to shun.]

escort, *es'kört, n.* a person or persons, ship or ships, &c. accompanying for protection, guidance, custody, or merely courtesy.—*v.t.* **es-cort',** to attend as escort. [Fr. *escorte*—It. *scorta*—*scorgere,* to guide—L. *ex,* out, *corri-gère,* to set right.]

escritoire, *es-kri-twär', n.* a writing-desk. [Fr. *escritoire*—Low L. *scrīptōrium*—L. *scrībĕre, scrīptum,* to write.]

Esculapian. Same as **Aesculapian.**

esculent, *es'kū-lênt, adj.* fit to be used for food by man.—*n.* something that is eatable. [L. *esculentus,* eatable—*esca,* food—*edĕre,* to eat.]

escutcheon, *es-kuch'ŏn, n.* a shield on which a coat of arms is represented: a family shield: the part of a vessel's stern bearing her name: a plate round an opening, e.g. a key-hole plate.—**a blot on the escutcheon,** a stain on one's good name. [O.Fr. *escuchon*—L. *scūtum,* a shield.]

Eskimo, *es'ki-mō, n.* and *adj.* one of the aboriginal inhabitants of extreme northern latitudes.—*n.* **Eskimo dog,** one of a breed of powerful dogs with a double coat of hair, found in the Arctic regions, used for drawing sledges. [Said to be from an Indian word meaning 'eaters of raw flesh'—in reference to an Eskimo practice.]

esophagus. See **oesophagus.**

esoteric, *es-o-ter'ik, adj.* (*phil.*) taught to a select few: secret, mysterious: initiated. Opp. to *exoteric.* [Gr. *esōterikos*—*esōtcrō,* comp. of *esō, eisō,* within.]

ESP. See **extra-sensory.**

espalier, *es-pal'yér, n.* a lattice-work of wood to train fruit-trees on: a fruit-tree trained on stakes or lattice-work. [Fr.,—It. *spalliera,* a support for the shoulders—*spalla,* a shoulder.]

esparto, *es-pär'tō, n.* a strong grass grown in Spain. N. Africa, &c., and used for making paper, &c. [Sp.,—L. *spartum*—Gr. *sparton,* a kind of rope.]

especial, *es-pesh'(ä)l, adj.* beyond or out of the ordinary (e.g. *with especial care*): particular, chiefly to one person, &c. (e.g. *his especial merit*). More formal, and more restricted in use, than *special* (q.v.).—*adv.* **espec'ially.** [O.Fr.,—L. *speciālis*—*speciēs,* species.]

Esperanto, *es-per-an'tō, n.* an auxiliary international language. [From the pseudonym of the inventor.]

espionage,*es'pyon-äzh, es'pi-ó-nij, es-pī'ó-nij, n.* spying: use of spies. [Fr. *espionnage*—*espionner cspion,* a spy.]

esplanade, *es-pla-nād', n.* a level space between a citadel and the first houses of the town: any level space for walking or driving, esp. at the seaside. [Fr.,—Sp. *esplanada*—L. *explānāre*—*ex,* out, *plānus,* flat.]

espouse, *es-powz', v.t.* to give or take in marriage or betrothal: to support or embrace, as a cause.—*n.* **espous'al,** the act of espousing or betrothing: adoption, support (of a cause): (*pl.*) a contract or mutual promise of marriage. [O.Fr. *espouser* (Fr. *épouser*)—L. *spon-sāre*—*spondēre, sponsum,* to vow.]

espresso, *es-pres'ō, n.* a type of coffee-making machine in which pressure of steam is used to get as much flavour as possible out of the coffee beans: coffee so made. [It., *pressed.*]

esprit, *es-prē, n.* wit: liveliness.—**esprit de corps** (*es-prē dé kor*), regard for the honour and well-being of the body or society to which one belongs. [Fr. *esprit,* spirit, *corps,* body.]

espy, *es-pī', v.t.* to catch sight of: to observe by chance or suddenly. [O.Fr. *espier.*]

Esquimau, *es'ki-mō* (*pl.* **Esquimaux,***es'ki-mōz*). Same as **Eskimo.**

esquire, *es-kwīr', n.* (*orig.*) a squire or shield-bearer, an attendant on a knight: a title of dignity next below a knight: a general title of respect in addressing letters. [O.Fr. *esquier*—L. *scūtārius*—*scūtum,* a shield.]

essay, *es'ā, n.* a trial: an attempt: a written composition less elaborate than a treatise.—*v.t.* **essay',** to test (e.g. one's powers): to attempt:—*pr.p.* essay'ing; *pa.p.* essayed'.—*n.* **ess'ayist,** a writer of essays. [O.Fr. *essai*—L.L. *exagium,* a weighing.]

fāte, fär; mē, hûr (her); *mīne; mōte, för; mūte; mōōn, fŏŏt; ᴛʜen* (then)

essence, *es'éns, n.* the inner distinctive nature of anything: (*logic*) the qualities, properties, that make an object what it is: (*loosely*) the most important, most characteristic, quality (hence, **in essence,** when reduced to its most important, characteristic, quality): a being: extracted virtues of a plant, drug, &c.: alcoholic solution of a volatile (essential) oil: a perfume.—*adj.* **essen'tial** (*-shál*), relating to, constituting, or containing the essence: indispensable, important in the highest degree.—*n.* something necessary: a leading principle.—*n.* **essential'ity,** the quality of being essential: an essential quality or element.—*adv.* **essen'tially,** in essence, characteristically (e.g. *she is an essentially selfish person*).—**essential oils,** oils contained in many plants and flowers giving them their characteristic odour—also called *ethereal oils, volatile oils.* [Fr.,— L. *essentia—essens, -entis,* assumed pr.p. of *esse,* to be.]

establish, *es-tab'lish, v.t.* to settle or fix firmly in a position: to place in possession or in power (in): to settle in business: to found: to prove and secure acceptance of (e.g. a point): to secure permanence for (e.g. a custom): to institute by law as the recognised state church.—*n.* **estab'lishment,** act of establishing: fixed state: that which is established: a permanent civil or military force or commercial staff: one's residence, household, and style of living: the church established by law.—**the Establishment,** the class of persons in a community, or in a field of activity, who hold power, who are usually linked socially and who are considered to have conservative opinions and conventional values.—**on the establishment,** on the permanent staff. [O.Fr. *establir,* pr.p. *establissant*— L. *stabilīre—stabilis,* firm—*stāre,* to stand.]

estancia, *es-tän'sya, n.* a Spanish-American cattle-estate.—*n.* **estanciero** (*es-tan-sē-ā'rō*), a farmer. [Sp. = station—L. *stāre,* to stand.]

estate, *es-tāt', n.* condition or rank: total possessions: property, esp. landed property: an order or class of men in the body politic.— **estate agent,** manager of landed property: intermediary in the sale of landed property; **estate car,** a car of large enough interior for both passengers and goods.—**the estates of the realm** are three—Lords Spiritual, Lords Temporal, and Commons—often misused for the !egislature (King, Lords, and Commons); **fourth estate, real estate** (see **fourth, real**). [O.Fr. *estat* (Fr. *état*)—L. *status.* See **status.**]

esteem, *es-tēm', v.t.* to set a high value on: to regard with respect or friendship: to consider or think.—*n.* high estimation, favourable opinion.—*adj.* **es'timable,** that can be estimated, valued: deserving our good opinion.— *adv.* **es'timably.**—*v.t.* **es'timāte,** to judge the worth of: to calculate.—*n.* judgment or opinion of the worth or size (of anything): a preliminary calculation of value or cost.—*n.* **estimā'tion,** a reckoning: judgment: esteem, honour.—**the estimates,** accounts laid before parliament, &c., showing the probable expenditure for the year. [Fr. *estimer*—L. *aestimāre.*]

ester, *es'tér, n.* one of a class of derivatives of acids obtained by the exchange of the re-

placeable hydrogen for hydrocarbon radicals—used in artificial fruit essences and as solvents. [Name coined by German chemist.]

esthetic, *esthetics.* See **aesthetic, aesthetics.**

estimate. See **esteem.**

estrange, *es-trānj', v.t.* to alienate, esp. from friendship: to divert from original use or possessor.—*p.adj.* **estranged'.**—*n.* **estrange'ment.** [O.Fr. *estranger*—L. *extrāneus.*]

estuary, *es'tū-ār-i, n.* the wide lower tidal part of a river.—*adj.* **es'tūarine.** [L. *aestuārium— aestus,* burning, commotion, tide.]

et cetera, *et set'ér-a,* usually written **etc.** or **&c.,** a Latin phrase meaning 'and so on'.—*n.* **etcet'era,** something in addition, whose nature can be understood from the context: —*pl.* **etcet'eras,** sundries, usual additional articles. [L. *et,* and, *cētera,* the rest.]

etch, *ech, v.t.* or *v.i.* to make designs on metal, glass, &c., by eating out the lines with an acid.—*n.* **etch'ing,** the act or art of etching or engraving: the impression from an etched plate. [From Ger. *ätzen,* to corrode by acid; from same root as Ger. *essen,* to eat.]

eternal, *e-* or *ē-tûr'nál, adj.* without beginning or end of existence, everlasting: unchangeable: (*coll.*) incessant.—*v.t.* **eter'nise** (or *ē'tér-nīz*), to make eternal: to immortalise with fame.— *adv.* **eter'nally.**—*n.* **eter'nity,** eternal duration: the state or time after death.—**eternity ring,** a ring set all round with stones, symbolic of faithfulness without end.—**the Eternal,** an appellation of God. [Fr. *éternel*—L. *aeternus— aevum,* a period of time, an age.]

etesian, *e-tē'zh(y)án, -zyán, adj.* periodical: blowing at stated seasons, as certain winds. [L. *etēsius*—Gr. *etēsios,* annual—*etos,* a year.]

ethanol. See **ethyl alcohol.**

ether, *ē'thér, n.* the clear, upper air: the nonmaterial medium formerly supposed to fill all space and transmit electromagnetic waves: a colourless, transparent, volatile liquid used as a solvent of fats, &c., and as an anaesthetic: any similar compound derived from two molecules of an alcohol by the elimination of one molecule of water.—*adj.* **ethē'real, ethē'rial,** consisting of ether: heavenly: airy: spiritlike.—*vs.t.* **ethē'realise,** to convert into ether, or the fluid ether: to render spirit-like; **e'therise,** to convert into ether: to stupefy with ether.—**ethereal oils** (see **essential oils**). [L.,— Gr. *aithēr—aithein,* to burn, light up.]

ethic, *eth'ik, adj.* (*rare*) relating to morals.—*n.* (more commonly **eth'ics**) the science of morals: a treatise on morals: moral principles, rules of behaviour.—*adj.* **eth'ical.**—*adv.* **eth'ically.**—**ethic(al) dative,** a dative implying an indirect interest in the fact stated—e.g. 'He plucked *me* ope his doublet.' [Gr. *ēthikos— ēthos,* custom, character.]

Ethiopian, *ē-thi-ō'pi-án, adj.* pertaining to *Ethiopia* or its natives: pertaining to the countries south of Egypt inhabited by Negro races.—*n.* a native of Ethiopia. [Gr. *Aithiops—aithein,* to burn, *ōps,* face.]

ethnic, -al, *eth'nik, -ál, adj.* concerning nations or races: pertaining to the Gentiles or the heathen.—*n.* **ethnog'raphy,** the scientific description of the races of the earth.—*adj.* **ethnograph'ic.**—*ns.* **ethnog'rapher; ethnol'ogy,** the

---

Neutral vowels in unaccented syllables: *em'pér-ór*; for certain sounds in foreign words see p. ix.

science that treats of the varieties of the human race.—*adj.* **ethnolog′ical.**—*adv.* **ethnolog′ically.**—*n.* **ethnol′ogist.** [Gr. *ethnos,* a nation, *graphē,* writing, *logos,* discourse.]

ethos, *ē′thos, n.* habitual character and disposition of individual, group, race, &c.: moral significance. [Gr. *ēthos,* custom, character.]

ethyl, *ēth′il, eth′il, n.* the base (C_2H_5) of common alcohol, ether, &c.—**ethyl alcohol,** ordinary alcohol—also **ethanol, ǀether,** and Gr. *hȳle,* matter.]

etiolate, *ē′-ti-o-lāt, v.t.* (*bot.*) to cause to grow pale from want of light, to blanch.—*v.i.* to become pale.—*n.* **etiolā′tion.** [Fr. *étioler,* to become pale, to grow into stubble—*éteule,* stubble—L. *stipula,* a stalk.]

etiology, *ē-ti-ol′o-ji, n.* Same as **aetiology.**

etiquette, *et′i-ket,* or *-ket′, n.* forms of ceremony or decorum in society or at court: the unwritten or conventional laws observed in the common interest by members of a particular profession (e.g. *medical, legal etiquette*). [Fr. *étiquette.* See **ticket.**]

Etonian, *ē-tōn′i-än, n.* one educated at *Eton* College.—Also *adj.*—**Eton collar,** a boy′s broad starched turned-down collar: a like-shaped collar on a woman′s jumper, &c.; **Eton crop,** a fashion of cutting woman′s hair short and sleeking it; **Eton jacket,** a boy′s black dresscoat, waist-length, untailed.

Etruscan, *e-trus′kán,* of or pertaining to Etruria, a region of ancient Italy west of the Tiber and the Apennines, or to its people or their language or civilisation. [L. *Etruscus.*]

etude, *ā-tūd′, n.* (*mus.*) a composition intended either to train or to test the player′s technical skill. [Fr., study.]

etymology, *et-i-mol′o-ĭ, n.* the science or investigation of the derivation and original meaning of words: the source and history (of a word).—*adj.* **etymolog′ical** (*-loj′-*).—*adv.* **etymolog′ically.**—*n.* **etymol′ogist** (*jist*). [Through O.Fr. and L. from Gr. *etymologia—etymos,* true, *logos,* a discourse.]

eucalyptus, *ū-ka-lip′tus, n.* a large characteristically Australian genus of evergreen trees, yielding timber, oils, and gum:—*pl.* **eucalyp′tuses, eucalyp′tī.** [Latinised from Gr. *eu,* well, *kalyptos,* covered.]

eucharist, *ū′ka-rist, n.* the sacrament of the Lord′s Supper: the elements of the sacrament.—*adjs.* **eucharist′ic, -al.** [Gr. *eucharistia,* thanksgiving—*eu,* well, and *charizesthai,* to show favour—*charis,* grace, thanks.]

euchre, *ū′kér, n.* an American card game.

Euclidean, *ū-klid′e-an, ū-kli-dē′an, adj.* pertaining to *Euclid,* a geometrician of Alexandria *c.* 300 B.C.—**Euclidean geometry,** the geometry of space according to Euclid′s assumptions.

eugenic, *ū-jen′ik, adj.* pertaining to race improvement by judicious mating, &c.—*n.pl.* **eugen′ics,** the science of such. [Gr. *eugenēs,* of good stock.]

eulogium, *ū-lō′ji-um,′ n.* high praise: a speech or writing in warm praise of (someone, occasionally something—with *on*).—*v.t.* **eu′logīse,** to praise.—*n.* **eu′logist,** one who praises or extols another.—*adj.* **eulogist′ic,** full of praise.—*adv.* **eulogist′ically.** [Late L. *eulogium*—Gr. *eulogion* (classical

eulogia)—*eu,* well, *logos,* a speaking.]

eunuch, *ū′nuk, n.* a castrated man, esp. one in charge of a harem, or a high-voiced singer.—*n.* **eu′nuchism.** [Gr. *eunouchos—eunē,* a bed, *echein,* to have (charge of).]

euphemism, *ū′fem-izm, n.* a mild or inoffensive term employed to express what is disagreeable: the use of such a term.—*adj.* **euphemist′ic.** [Gr. *euphēmismos cuphēmizein,* to speak words of good omen—*eu,* well, *phanai,* to speak.]

euphony, *ū′fo-ni, n.* agreeableness of sound: pleasing, easy pronunciation.—*adjs.* **euphon′ic, -al, euphō′nious.**—*adv.* **euphō′niously.** [Gr. *euphōnia—eu,* well, *phonē,* sound.]

euphoria, *ū-fō′ri-ā, -fō′, n.* a feeling of well-being.—*adj.* **euphoric** (*-for′*). [Gr. *euphōriā.*]

euphuism, *ū′fū-izm, n.* the affected and bombastic literary style brought into vogue by John Lyly′s romance *Euphues* (1579-80): a high-flown expression.—*n.* **eu′phuist.**—*adj.* **euphuist′ic.** [Gr. *euphyēs,* graceful.]

Eurasian, *ūr-ā-zh(y)án, -shan, adj.* of mixed European and Asiatic descent: of, or pertaining to, Europe and Asia (Eurasia) taken as one continent.—Also *n.*

eurhythmy, eurythmy, *ūr-rith′mi, n.* rhythmical movement or order: harmony of proportion.—*adj.* **eurhyth′mic.**—*n.pl.* **eurhyth′mics,** the art or system of rhythmic movement expounded by E. Jaques-Dalcroze (1865-1950). [Gr. *eu,* well, *rhythmos,* rhythm.]

European, *ū-ro-pē′an, adj.* belonging to *Europe.*—*n.* a native of Europe: a member of the white race of man characteristic of Europe.—**European Economic Community** (EEC). See **Common Market.**

europium, *ū-rō′pi-úm, n.* a metallic element (symbol Eu; at. no. 63), a member of the rare earth group. [*Europe.*]

eutectic, *ū-tek′tik, n.* a mixture in such proportions that the melting-point (or freezing-point) is a minimum, the constituents melting (or freezing) simultaneously. [Gr. *eutēktos,* easily, melted—*eu,* well, *tēkein,* to melt.]

euthanasia, *u-than-ā′zi-a, n.* an easy mode of death: the act or practice of putting to death painlessly, esp. in order to release from incurable suffering. [Gr. *euthanasia—eu,* well, *thanatos,* death.]

evacuate, *e-vak′ū-āt, v.t.* to throw out the contents of: to withdraw from or leave (a town, fortified place, &c.); to clear out (troops, inhabitants, &c.) from a town, &c.—*ns.* **evacuā′tion,** act of evacuating: that which is discharged; **evac′uātor; evac′uee,** a person removed in an evacuation. [L. *ē,* from, *vacuāre, -ātum,* to empty—*vacuus,* empty.]

evade, *e-vād′, ē-vād′, v.t.* to escape or avoid artfully: (of things) to baffle. [Fr. *évader*—L. *ēvādēre*—*ē,* from, *vādēre,* to go.]

evaluate, *ē-,* or *e-val′ū-āt, v.t.* to determine the value of.—*n.* **evaluā′tion.** [Fr. *évaluer.*]

evanescent, *ev-än-es′ent, adj.* fleeting: vanishing.—*n.* **evanes′cence.**—*adv.* **evanes′cently.** [L. *ēvānescens, -entis—ē,* from, *vānescēre,* to vanish—*vānus,* empty.]

evangel, *e-van′jél, n.* (*poet.*) good news: gospel: a doctrine or principle (in morals or politics) regarded as certain to produce good results.—*adjs.* **evangelic(al)** (*e-, ē-van-jel'ik-äl*), of, according to, the doctrine of the gospel: of the Protestant school that insists on the natural depravity of human nature and the saving of the sinner by faith, not by works.—*adv.* **evangel'ically.**—*ns.* **evangel'icism** (*-sizm*), **evangel'icalism**, evangelical principles.—*v.t.* **evan'gelīse**, to make acquainted with the gospel.—*v.i.* to preach the gospel from place to place.—*n.* **evan'gelist**, one who evangelises: one of the four writers of the gospels.—*adj.* **evangelis'tic**. [L.L. *ēvangelium*—Gr. *euangelion*—*eu*, well, *angellein*, to bring news.]

evaporate, *e-vap'ór-āt, v.i.* to become gaseous at a temperature below boiling point, to fly off in vapour: to pass into an invisible state: to depart, vanish: of a metal, to sublimate in order to deposit as a film.—*v.t.* to convert into vapour.—*adj.* **evap'orable.**—*n.* **evapora'tion.** [L. *ē*, from, *vapōrāre, -ātum*—*vapor*, vapour.]

evasion, *e-vā'zh(ó)n, n.* act of evading or eluding: an attempt to escape the force of an argument or accusation, a subterfuge.—*adj.* **evā'sive**, that evades or seeks to evade: not straightforward.—*adv.* **evā'sively.**—*n.* **evā'siveness.**—**take evasive action**, to move or act in such a way as to avoid an object or consequence. [Fr. *évasion*—L.L. *ēvāsiō, -ōnis*—L. *ēvādēre*. See **evade.**]

eve. See **even** (2).

even, *ēv'n, adj.* level: smooth: uniform in quality: equal in number or amount: balanced: exact: divisible by 2 without a remainder: equable (of temper).—*v.t.* to make even or smooth: to treat as equal (to).—*adv.* exactly (so): so much as: still (e.g. *even better*). Used also to emphasise the extreme or unexpected nature of an action, &c. (e.g. *he suspects even his friends*).—*adv.* **ev'enly**, equally, impartially: uniformly: smoothly: equable, without sign of annoyance.—*adjs.* **ev'en-hand'ed**, fair, impartial; **ev'en-mind'ed**, equable, calm.—*n.* **ev'enness.**—**even money**, an equal sum bet on each side: (*loosely*) an equal chance.—**be even with**, to be revenged on: to be quits with; **even date**, the same date. [O.E. *efen*; Du, *even*, Ger. *eben*.]

even, *ēv'n, n.* (*poet.*) evening: (*obs.* or *dial.*) eve.—Also **e'en** (*ēn*).—*ns.* **eve** (*ēv*), the night, or the whole day, before a festival: the time just preceding an event: (*poet.*) evening; **evening** (*ēv'ning*), the close of the daytime: the decline or end of life; **eve'ning star**, a planet, esp. Venus, seen in the west at or soon after sunset; **ev'ensong**, evening prayer, the Anglican form appointed to be said or sung at evening; **ev'entide**, the time of evening, evening: declining years. [O.E. *æfen, æfnung.*]

event, *e-vent', n.* that which happens: the result: any incident or occurrence: an item in a programme of sports.—*adjs.* **event'ful**, full of events: momentous; **event'ual**, happening as a consequence: final.—*n.* **eventual'ity**, a contingency.—*adv.* **event'ually**, finally, at length.—*v.i.* **event'ūate**, to turn out.—**at all events**, in any case. [L. *ēventus*—*ēvenīre*—*ē*, from, *venīre*, to come.]

ever, *ev'ér, adv.* (*arch.* except in *for ever*) always, at all times: at any time. Used also idiomatically to give emphasis (e.g. *as politely as ever I can*; *ever so quietly*; *what ever did she say?*).—*adj.* **ev'ergreen**, always green.—*n.* a plant that remains green all the year.—*adj.* **everlast'ing**, endless: eternal.—*n.* eternity: a flower that may be kept for years without much change of appearance.—*adv.* **everlast'ingly.**—*n.* **everlast'ingness.**—*adv.* **evermore'**, unceasingly: eternally.—**ever and anon**, now and then. [O.E. *æfre*, always.]

every, *ev'ér-i, ev'ri, adj.* each of a number without exception.—*prons.* **ev'erybody, ev'eryone**, every person.—*adj.* **ev'eryday**, daily: common, usual: pertaining to weekdays, not Sunday.—*pron.* **ev'erything**, all things: all.—*n.* **Ev'eryman**, the hero of an old morality play, representing mankind.—*adv.* **ev'erywhere**, in every place.—**every other**, every second (e.g. *every other day,* every alternate day). [O.E. *æfre*, ever, and *ælc*, each.]

evict, *ē-, or e-vikt', v.t.* to dispossess by law: to expel.—*n.* **evic'tion**, the act of expelling from house or lands: the dispossession of one person by another having a better title of property in land. [L. *ēvictus*, pa.p. of *ēvincēre*, to overcome.]

evident, *ev'i-dént, adj.* that can be seen: clear to the mind: obvious.—*adv.* **ev'idently.**—*n.* **ev'idence**, indication, sign: proof: clearness: information in a law case: testimony: a witness (chiefly in the phrase *King's evidence*).—*v.t.* to indicate: to prove.—*adj.* **eviden'tial** (*-shál*), furnishing evidence: tending to prove.—**turn King's (Queen's) evidence**, (of an accomplice in a crime) to give evidence against his partners. [L. *ēvidens, -entis*—*ē*, from, *vidēre*, to see.]

evil, *ē'vl, ē'vil, adj.* bad: wicked: slanderous.—*adv.* (also **ē'villy**) in an evil manner: badly.—*n.* harm: wickedness: sin.—*ns.* **e'vil-do'er**, one who does evil; **e'vil-eye**, a supposed power to cause harm by a look; **e'vil-fa'vouredness** (*B.*), ugliness: deformity.—*adj.* **e'vil-mind'ed**, inclined to evil thoughts: malicious.—*n.* **e'vil-speak'ing**, the speaking of evil: slander.—**the evil one**, the devil. [O.E. *yfel*; Du. *euvel*; Ger. *übel*. **ill** is a doublet.]

evince, *e-vins', v.t.* to show (e.g. a quality).—*adj.* **evinc'ible.**—*adv.* **evinc'ibly.**—*adj.* **evinc'ive**, showing, tending to show. [L. *ēvincēre*—*ē-*, inten., *vincēre*, to overcome.]

eviscerate, *ē-, or e-vis'ér-āt, v.t.* to tear out the viscera or bowels of.—*n.* **eviscera'tion.** [L. *ē*, from, *viscera*, the bowels.]

evocative. See **evoke.**

evoke, *e-vōk', v.t.* to draw out or bring forth: to call up or awaken in the mind.—*adj.* **evoc'ative** (*-vok'*), having power to evoke: serving to awaken (e.g. feelings, memories). [L. *ēvocāre*—*ē*, from, and *vocāre*, to call.]

evolution, *ev-, ēv-ol-(y)ōō'sh(ó)n, n.* the act of unrolling or unfolding: gradual working out or development: a series of things unfolded: the doctrine according to which higher forms of life have gradually arisen out of lower: the giving off (e.g. of gas, heat): (*math.*) the extraction of roots: (usu.*pl.*) orderly movements as of a body of troops, flock of birds, &c.—*adj.* **evolu'tionary**, of or pertaining to evolution.—*n.* **evolu'tionist**, one who believes in evolution

Neutral vowels in unaccented syllables: *em'pér-ór*; for certain sounds in foreign words see p. ix.

244

as a principle in science. [L. *ēvolūtiō, -ōnis—ēvolvĕre*; see **evolve**.]

evolve, *ē-*, or *e-volv'*, *v.t.* to unroll, open out (*fig.*); to disclose: to develop (*lit.*; also *fig.* of a theory): to give off (e.g. gas).—*v.i.* to disclose itself. [L. *ēvolvĕre—ē*, from, *volvĕre, volūtum*, to roll.]

ewe, *ū*, *n.* a female sheep.—*n.* **ewe'-lamb**, a female lamb: a poor man's one possession (2 Sam. xii.). [O.E. *ēowu*; cf. L. *ovis*, Gr. *oïs*, Sans. *avi*, a sheep.]

ewer, *ū'ér*, *n.* a large water jug with a wide spout. [Through Fr. from L. *aquārium—aqua*, water, whence also Fr. *eau*.]

ex-, *eks-*, *pfx.* indicating that the term following has been, but is no longer, applicable [L. *ex*, out of, from], e.g.:—**ex-pres'ident**, one who has been, but is no longer, president.

exacerbate, *eks-*, or *egz-as'ér-bāt*, *v.t.* to embitter: to provoke: to render more violent or severe, as a disease.—*n.* **exacerbā'tion**, embitterment: increase in violence of a disease, &c. [L. *exacerbāre*, *-ātum—ex*, inten., *acerbāre*, from *acerbus*, bitter.]

exact, *egz-akt'*, *v.t.* to compel payment of: to extort, to demand and obtain (with *from, of*): to require as indispensable.—*adj.* rigorous (e.g. laws): precise (e.g. a scientific instrument): accurate (e.g. a person): absolutely correct.—*p.adj.* **exact'ing**, unreasonable in making demands: demanding much.—*ns.* **exac'tion**, act of demanding strictly: an oppressive demand: that which is exacted, as excessive work or tribute; **exact'itude**, exactness: correctness.—*adv.* **exact'ly.**—*n.* **exact'ness.—exact sciences**, the mathematical sciences whose results are precise or quantitative. [L. *exigĕre, exactum*, to drive out, to exact—*ex*, from, *agĕre*, to drive.]

exaggerate, *egz-aj'ér-āt*, *v.t.* to magnify unduly: to represent too strongly.—*ns.* **exaggerā'tion**, extravagant representation: a statement in excess of the truth; **exagg'erātor.**—*adjs.* **exagg'erative**, **exagg'eratory.** [L. *exaggerāre*, *-ātum—ex-, aggerāre*, to heap up—*agger*, a heap.]

exalt, *egz-olt'*, *v.t.* to set aloft: to elevate in rank, &c.: to extol: to elate or fill with the joy of success.—*n.* **exaltā'tion**, elevation in rank or dignity: high estate: elation.—*p.adj.* **exalt'ed**, elevated: lofty: dignified.—*n.* **exalt'edness.** [L. *exaltāre—ex-*, inten., *altus*, high.]

examine, *egz-am'in*, *v.t.* to test: to question: to look closely into: to enquire into.—*ns.* **examinā'tion**, close inspection: test of knowledge (familiarly contracted to **exam'**): formal questioning; **examinee'**, one under examination; **exam'iner**, one who examines. [Fr.,—L. *exāmināre—exāmen*, the tongue of a balance.]

example, *egz-äm'pl*, *n.* a specimen: an illustration: a copy of a book: a person or thing to be imitated or not to be imitated—a pattern, a warning: a problem or exercise in mathematics.—**make an example of**, to punish as a warning to others. [O.Fr.,—L. *exemplum—eximĕre*, to take out—*ex*, out of, *emĕre, emptum*, to take, buy.]

exasperate, *egz-as'pér-āt*, *v.t.* (*obs.*) to make very rough: to irritate in a high degree: to make worse.—*n.* **exasperā'tion.** [L. *ex-*, inten.,

asperāre, to make rough—*asper*, rough.]

excavate, *eks'ka-vāt*, *v.t.* to hollow or scoop out (e.g. a hole): to dig out (soil): to lay bare by digging (as buried ruins).—*n.* **excavā'tion**, act of excavating: a hollow or cavity made by excavating; **ex'cavātor**, one who excavates: a machine used for excavating. [L. *excavāre—ex-*, out, *cavus*, hollow.]

exceed, *ek-sēd'*, *v.t.* to go beyond (the limit set or required): to be greater than: to surpass or excel.—*v.i.* to go beyond a given or proper limit.—*p.adj.* **exceed'ing**, surpassing: excessive.—*adv.* **exceed'ingly.** [L. *ex-*, beyond, *cēdĕre, cessum*, to go.]

excel, *ek-sel'*, *v.t.* to be superior to, to surpass.—*v.i.* to show good qualities in a high degree (with, *in, at*):—*pr.p.* excell'ing; *pa.p.* excelled'.—*ns.* **exc'ellence**, **exc'ellency**, great merit: any excellent quality: (usually *cap.*) a title of honour given to persons high in rank or office.—*adj.* **exc'ellent**, surpassing others in some good quality: of great virtue, worth, &c.—*adv.* **exc'ellently.** [L. *excellĕre—ex-*, out, up, *celsus*, high.]

excentric. Same as **eccentric.**

except, *ek-sept'*, *v.t.* to leave out, exclude.—*v.i.* to object (with *against, to*).—*prep.* (also **except'ing**, chiefly after *not*) excluding: but.—*n.* **excep'tion**, that which is excepted: exclusion: objection.—*adjs.* **excep'tionable**, liable to objection, open to criticism; **excep'tional**, unusual, uncommon: more than ordinary, very great; **except'ive**, including, making, or being an exception.—**take exception to, against, at**, to object to: to take offence at; **the exception proves the rule**, the making of an exception proves that the rule holds in cases not excepted. [L. *excipĕre, exceptum—ex*, from, *capĕre*, to take.]

excerpt, *ek'sérpt*, or *ek sérpt'*, *n.* a passage selected from a book, opera, &c., an extract. [L. *excerptum*, pa.p. of *excerpĕre—ex*, from, *carpĕre*, to pick.]

excess, *ek-ses'*, *n.* a going beyond what is usual or proper: intemperance: that which exceeds: the degree or amount by which one thing exceeds another.—*adj.* **excess'ive**, beyond what is right and proper, immoderate.—*adv.* **excess'ively.—excess fare**, payment for distance travelled beyond, or in class superior to, that allowed by the ticket; **excess luggage**, luggage above that allowed free.—**carry to excess**, to do too much. [L. *excessus—ex-cēdĕre, excessum*, to go beyond.]

exchange, *eks-chānj'*, *v.t.* to give or give up in return for something else: to give and take mutually.—*n.* the giving and taking of one thing for another: the thing exchanged: process by which accounts between distant parties are settled by bills instead of money: the difference between the value of money in different places: the building where merchants, &c., meet for business: a central office where telephone lines are connected.—*adj.* **exchange'able.**—*n.* **exchangeabil'ity.** [O.Fr. *eschangier* (Fr. *échanger*)—Low L. *excambiāre—L. ex*, from, *cambīre*, to barter.]

exchequer, *eks-chek'ér*, *n.* (*cap.*) a department of state having charge of revenue, so named from the chequered cloth which covered the

fāte, fär; mē, hûr (her); *mīne, mōte, för; mūte, mōōn, fōōt; then* (then) table: (*cap.*) the Court of Exchequer: a national treasury: one's funds, finances.— **Chancellor of the Exchequer,** (see **Chancellor**); **Court of Exchequer,** in England, originally a revenue court, now merged in the King's (Queen's) Bench Division. [O.Fr. *eschequier,* a chessboard. See **check.**].

excise, *ek-sīz',* *n.* a tax on certain home commodities and on licences for certain trades: the department in the civil administration, that is concerned with this tax.—*adj.* **excīs'able,** liable to excise duty.—*n.* **excise'man,** an officer charged with collecting the excise. [Old Du. *excijs*—O.Fr. *acceis,* tax—Low L. *accēnsāre,* to tax—*ad,* to, *cēnsus,* tax.]

excise, *ek-sīz',* *v.t.* to cut out or off, esp. surgically: to remove, delete (a part of a book or writing).—*n.* **excision** (*ek-sizh'(ó)n*), a cutting out or off of any kind: extirpation: excommunication. [L. *excīdĕre,* to cut out—*ex,* from, *caedĕre,* to cut.]

excite, *ek-sīt',* *v.t.* to rouse (e.g. feelings): to arouse strong emotion in, to agitate: to stir up (e.g. insurrection): to stimulate the activity of: to produce electric or magnetic activity in: to raise (an electron, atom, &c.) to an excited state.—*adj.* **excīt'able,** capable of being excited: easily excited.—*ns.* **excītabil'ity; excitant** (*ek'si-tánt,* or *ek-sī'tánt*), that which excites or rouses the vital activity of the body, a stimulant; **excitā'tion,** act of exciting.—*adjs.* **excīt'ative, excīt'atory,** tending to excite.—*adj.* **excīt'ed,** agitated: roused emotionally: in a state of great activity: having energy higher than that of the ground, or normal, state.—*n.* **excīte'ment,** agitation: stimulation: that which excites. [Fr.,—L. *excitāre,* *-ātum*—*exciēre*—*ex-,* out, *ciēre,* to set in motion.]

exclaim, *eks-klām',* *v.i.* to cry out.—*v.t.* to utter or speak vehemently.—*n.* **exclāmā'tion,** vehement protest, &c.: an uttered expression of surprise, and the like: the mark expressing this (!).—*adj.* **exclam'atory,** containing or expressing exclamation. [Fr. *exclamer*—L. *exclāmāre,* *-ātum*—*ex-,* out, *clāmāre,* to shout.]

exclude, *eks-klōōd',* *v.t.* to shut out: to thrust out: to except.—*n.* **exclu'sion,** a shutting or putting out: exception.—*adj.* **exclu'sive,** able or tending to exclude: sole: desirous of excluding others: (used adverbially) not taking into account (followed by *of*).—*adv.* **exclu'sively.**—*n.* **exclu'siveness.** [L. *exclūdĕre*—*ex-,* out, *claudĕre,* to shut.]

excogitate, *eks-koj'i-tāt,* *v.t.* to discover by thinking: to think out earnestly or laboriously.—*n.* **excogitā'tion.** [L. *excōgitāre,* *-ātum*—*ex-,* out, *cōgitāre,* to think.]

excommunicate, *eks-kom-ūn'i-kāt,* *v.t.* to expel from the communion of the church, to deprive of church privileges.—*n.* **excommunicā'tion.** [From Late L. *excommūnicāre*—L. *ex,* from, *commūnis,* common.]

excoriate, *eks-kō'ri-āt,* *-kō',* *v.t.* to strip the skin from: (*fig.*) to criticise severely. [L. *excoriāre,* *-ātum*—*ex,* from, *corium,* the skin.]

excrement, *eks'krē-mént,* *n.* useless matter discharged from the animal system, dung.—*adjs.* **excrement'al, excrementi'tious,** pertaining to or containing excrement. [L. *excrēmentum*—*excernĕre*—*ex-,* out, *cernĕre,* to sift.]

excrescence, *eks-kres'éns,* *n.* an outgrowth or projection, esp. abnormal, grotesque, or offensive: an outbreak.—*adj.* **excres'cent,** growing out: superfluous. [Fr.,—L.,—*excrēscĕre*—*ex-,* out, *crēscĕre,* to grow.]

excrete, *eks-krēt',* *v.t.* to separate and discharge (waste matter).—*n.pl.* **excrē'ta,** poisonous or waste substances eliminated from a cell, a tissue, or an organism.—*n.* **excrē'tion,** the excreting of matter from an organism: that which is excreted.—*adjs.* **excrē'tive,** able to excrete; **excrē'tory,** having the quality of excreting.—*n.* a duct that helps to receive and excrete matter. [L. *ex,* from, *cernĕre,* *crētum,* to separate.]

excruciate, *eks-krōō'shi-āt,* *v.t.* to torture (*lit.* or *fig.*).—*p.adj.* **excru'ciāting,** extremely painful, agonising.—*adv.* **excru'ciātingly.**—*n.* **excruciā'tion.** [L. *ex-,* out, *cruciāre,* *-ātum,* to crucify—*crux, crucis,* a cross.]

exculpate, *eks'kul-pāt,* or *-kul'-,* *v.t.* to clear from the charge of a fault or crime.—*n.* **exculpā'tion.**—*adj.* **excul'patory,** tending to free from the charge of fault or crime. [L. *ex,* from, *culpa,* a fault.]

excursion, *eks-kûr'sh(ó)n,* *n.* (*arch.*) a going forth: a pleasure trip: a deviation (from): a digression.—*n.* **excur'sionist,** one who goes on a pleasure trip.—*adj.* **excur'sive,** rambling: deviating.—*adv.* **excur'sively.**—*ns.* **excur'siveness; excur'sus,** a dissertation on some particular point appended to a book or chapter. [L. *ex-,* out, *currĕre, cursum,* to run.]

excuse, *eks-kūz',* *v.t.* to free (a person) from blame or guilt: to overlook (an offence): to free from an obligation: to serve as exculpation for (a person): to make an apology or ask pardon for.—*n.* (*eks-kūs'*) a plea offered in extenuation of a fault: the reason or pretext offered.—*adj.* **excusable** (*eks-kūz'á-bl*).—*adv.* **excus'ably.**—*adj.* **excūs'atory,** making or containing excuse. [L. *excūsāre*—*ex,* from, *causa,* a cause, accusation.]

execrate, *eks'e-krāt,* *v.t.* to curse: to detest utterly.—*adj.* **ex'ecrable,** deserving to be execrated, abominable.—*adv.* **ex'ecrably.**—*n.* **execrā'tion,** act of execrating: a curse pronounced. [L. *exsecrārī,* *-ātus,* to curse—*ex,* from, *sacer,* sacred.]

execute, *eks'e-kūt,* *v.t.* to perform: to carry into effect: to put to death by law.—*adj.* **executable** (*eg-zek'ūt-á-bl,* or *ek-sek'-*), that can be performed.—*ns.* **exec'ūtant,** one who executes or performs: a technically accomplished performer of music; **ex'ecūter; execū'tion,** act of executing or performing: carrying into effect the sentence of a court of law: the warrant for so doing; **execū'tioner,** one who executes, esp. one who inflicts capital punishment.—*adj.* **exec'ūtive,** designed or fitted to execute: concerned with performance, administration, or management: qualifying for or pertaining to the execution of the law.—*n.* the power or authority in government that carries the laws into effect: the persons who administer the government or an organisation: one concerned with administration or management.—*adv.* **exec'ūtively.**—*n.* **exec'ūtor,** one who executes or performs: the person appointed to see a will carried into effect:—

Neutral vowels in unaccented syllables: *em'pėr-ór*; for certain sounds in foreign words see p. ix.

*fem.*exec′utrix.—*n.* exec′utorship.—*adj.* exec′ū-tory, executing official duties: designed to be carried into effect. [Fr. *exécuter*—L. *exsequī, exsecūtus*—*ex*, out, *sequī*, to follow.]

exegesis, eks-e-jē′sis, *n.* interpretation, esp. Biblical.—*adjs.* exegēt′ic, -al, pertaining to exegesis, explanatory.—*adv.* exegēt′ically.—*n.pl.* exegēt′ics, the science of exegesis. [Gr. *exēgēsis*—*exēgeesthai*, to explain—*ex*-, out, *hēgeesthai*, to guide.]

exemplar, eg-zem′plär, *,*-plär, *n.* a person or thing to be imitated: an ideal model: a type, specimen, example. a copy of a book.—*adj.* exemplary (eg-zem′plär-i, or 1g-), worthy of imitation or notice: serving as a model, illustration, or warning.—*adv.* exem′plarily. [L. *exemplar*, a copy; also O.Fr. *exemplaire*—Low L. *exemplārium*—*exemplum*, example.]

exemplify, egz-em′pli-fī, *v.t.* to illustrate by example: to be an example of: to make an attested copy of: to prove by an attested copy—*p.r.p.* exem′plifying; *pa.p.* exem′pli-fied.—*n.* exemplifica′tion, act of exemplifying: that which exemplifies: a copy or transcript. [L. *exemplum*, example, *facĕre*, to make.]

exempt, egz-emt′, *v.t.* to free, or grant immunity (with *from*).—*adj.* not liable.—*n.* exemp′tion, act of exempting: freedom from any service, duty, burden, &c. [Fr.,—L. *eximĕre, exemp-tum*—*ex*, from, *emĕre*, to buy.]

exequies, eks′e-kwiz, *n.pl.* (rare) a funeral pro-cession: funeral rites. [L. *ex(s)equiae*—*ex*, from, *sequī*, to follow.]

exercise, eks′ér-sīz, *n.* a putting in practice: exertion of the body for health or amusement or acquisition of skill: a similar exertion of the mind: a lesson or task: a written school task: (pl.) military drill: an act of worship.—*v.t.* to train by use: to give exercise to: to trouble, worry (e.g. *he was exercised about the mat-ter*): to put in practice, to use (e.g. discretion, authority). [O.Fr. *exercice*—L. *exercitium*—L. *exercēre, -citum*—*ex*-, inten., *arcēre*, to shut up, restrain.]

exert, egz-ûrt′, *v.t.* to bring into active operation (e.g. strength, influence).—*n.* exer′tion, a bringing into active operation: striving: ac-tivity. [L. *exserēre, exsertum*, to put, thrust, forth or out—*ex*, from, *serĕre*, to put together.]

exfoliate, eks-fō′li-āt, *v.t.* to shed or remove in flakes.—*v.i.* to come off in flakes or layers.—*n.* exfoliā′tion. [L. *exfoliāre, -ātum*—*ex*, from, *folium*, a leaf.]

exhale, eks-hāl′, egz′ āl′, *v.t.* to breathe forth: to emit or send out as vapour, smell, &c.—*v.i.* to breathe out: to rise or come off as vapour.—*n.* exhalation (eks-, egz-a-lā′sh(ó)n, or eks′ha-), act or process of exhaling: evaporation: that which is exhaled, vapour, effluvium. [Fr. *ex-haler*—L. *exhālāre*—*ex*, from *hālāre, -ātum*, to breathe.]

exhaust, egz-öst′, *v.t.* to draw out the whole of: to empty: to use the whole strength of: to wear or tire out: to treat of or develop completely (a subject).—*n.* the exit for used working fluid from the cylinder of an engine: the fluid so escaping (exhaust′-gas′, -steam′).—*p.adj.* ex-haust′ed, drawn out: emptied: consumed: tired out.—*adj.* exhaust′ible.—*n.* exhaust′ion, act of exhausting or consuming: state of being

exhausted: extreme fatigue.—*adj.* exhaust′ive, tending to exhaust: comprehensive, thorough.—*adv.* exhaust′ively, very thorough-ly. [L. *exhaurīre, exhaustum*—*ex*, from, *haurīre*, to draw.]

exhibit, egz-ib′it, *v.t.* to present to view: to manifest: to present formally or publicly.—*n.* (*law*) a document or an article produced in court to be used as evidence: an article at an exhibition.—*ns.* exhib′itor. *adj.* exhib′itory, exhibiting.—*ns.* exhibi′tion, presentation to view: display: a public show, esp of works of art, manufactures, &c.: an allowance towards support, esp. to scholars in a university; ex-hibi′tioner, one who enjoys an exhibition at a university; exhibi′tionism, morbid inclination towards self display: extravagant behaviour aimed at drawing attention to oneself; exhi-bi′tionist. [L. *exhibēre, -itum*—*ex*, out, *habēre, -itum*, to have.]

exhilarate, egz-il′a-rāt, *v.t.* to make hilarious or merry: to enliven. *adj.* exhil′arant, exhilar-ating.—*n.* exhilara′tion, state of being exhilar-ated: joyousness. [L. *exhilarāre, -ātum*—*ex*-, inten., *hilaris*, cheerful.]

exhort, eg-zört′, *v.t.* to urge strongly and earn-estly (a course of action, a person to do): to admonish strongly.—*n.* exhortā′tion, act of exhorting: speech, or formal discourse, in-tended to exhort: counsel.—*adjs.* exhort′ative, exhort′atory, tending to exhort or advise. [L. *exhortārī, -ātus*—*ex*-, inten., *hortārī*, to urge.]

exhume, eks-hūm′, *v.t.* to take out of the ground or place of burial: (*fig.*) to bring to light.—*n.* exhuma′tion. [L. *ex*, out of, *humus*, the ground.]

exigent, eks′i-jent, *adj.* pressing, urgent: exact-ing.—*adj.* exigeant (eks-ē-zhä′; Fr.), exact-ing:—*fem.* exigeante (-zhät).—*ns.* ex′igence, ex′igency, pressing necessity: emergency. [L. *exigens, -entis*, pr.p. of *exigĕre*—*ex*, from, *agĕre*, to drive.]

exigible, eks′i-jibl, *adj.* liable to be exacted. [From L. *exigĕre*. See exact.]

exiguous, egz-, eks-ig′ū-us, *adj.* scanty: diminu-tive. [L. *exiguus*—*exigĕre*. See exact.]

exile, eks′īl, or egz′īl, *n.* enforced or regretted absence from one's country or home: banish-ment: one who is in exile, a banished per-son.—*v.t.* to expel from one's country, to ban-ish. [O.Fr. *exil*—L. *exsilium*, banishment—*ex*, out of, and root of *salīre*, to leap; affected by L. *exsul*, an exile.]

exility, egz-, eks-il′i-ti, *n.* slenderness: subtlety. [L. *exīlis*, slender.]

exist, egz-ist′, *v.i.* to have an actual being.—*n.* exist′ence, state of existing or being: liveli-hood: life: anything that exists.—*adj.* exist′ent, having being: at present existing.—*n.* existen′tialism, a doctrine, more recent than surrealism, popularly understood to be that life is purposeless and man petty and miserable. [L. *existĕre, exsistĕre*, to stand forth—*ex*, out, *sistĕre*, to stand.]

exit, eks′it, egz′-, *n.* departure of a player from the stage: any departure: death: a way of departure: a passage out—*pl.* ex′its.—*v.i.* to make an exit. [L. *exit*, he goes out, *exīre*, to go out—*ex*, out, and *īre, itum*, to go.]

exo-, in composition, outside [Gr. *exō*, without],

e.g.:—**exoskel′eton,** a hard supporting or protective structure on the outside of the body, e.g. a shell: applied also to scales, hoofs, &c.

exodus, *eks′o-dus,* n. a going out, esp. (*cap.*) that of the Israelites from Egypt: (*cap.*) the second book of the Old Testament. [L.,—Gr. *exodos—ex,* out, *hodos,* a way.]

ex officio, *eks o-fish′i-ō,* by virtue of the office one holds. [L.]

exogamy, *eks-og′a-mi,* n. the practice of marrying only outside of one's own group. [Gr. *exō,* out, *gamos,* marriage.]

exonerate, *egz-on′ér-āt,* v.t. to free from the burden of blame or obligation: to acquit.—n. **exonerā′tion.**—adj. **exon′erative,** freeing from blame or obligation. [L. *exonerāre, -ātum—ex,* from, *onus, oneris,* burden.]

exorbitant, *egz-ör′bi-tànt,* adj. going beyond the usual limits, excessive.—n. **exor′bitance,** great excess.—adv. **exor′bitantly.** [L. *exorbitans, -antis,* pr.p. of *exorbitāre—ex,* out of, *orbita,* a track—*orbis,* a circle.]

exorcise, *eks′ór-sīz,* v.t. to adjure by some holy name: to call forth or drive away, as a spirit: to deliver from the influence of an evil spirit.—ns. **ex′orcism,** act of exorcising; **ex′orcist** (also **exorcis′er**). [Late L., from Gr. *exorkizein—ex,* out, *horkos,* an oath.]

exordium, *egz-ör′di-ùm,* n. the introductory part of a discourse or composition.—adj. **exor′dial,** pertaining to the exordium. [L.—*exordīrī—ex,* out of, *ordīrī,* to begin.]

exoteric, -al, *eks-o-ter′ik, -ăl,* adj. external: suitable for communication to the public or multitude: not included among the initiated. Opp. to *esoteric.* [Gr. *exōterikos—exōterō,* comp. of *exō,* outside.]

exotic, *egz-ot′ik,* adj. introduced from a foreign country—the opposite of *indigenous*: alien: romantically strange, or rich and showy or glamorous.—n. something not native to a country, as a plant, a word, a custom. [L.,—Gr. *exōtikos—exō,* outside.]

expand, *eks-pand′,* v.t. to spread out: to enlarge in bulk or surface: to develop in fuller detail, to express at length.—v.i. to become opened: to increase in size: (*fig.*) to become communicative.—n. **expanse′,** a wide extent: amount of spread or stretch.—adj. **expans′ible,** capable of being expanded.—ns. **expansibil′ity, expan′sion,** act of expanding: state of being expanded: enlargement: extension.—adj. **expans′ive,** widely extended: having a capacity to expand: causing expansion: worked by expansion: comprehensive: talkative, communicative.—adv. **expans′ively.**—n. **expans′iveness.**—**expanded plastic,** foam plastic. [L.*expandĕre—ex,* out, *pandĕre, pansum,* to spread.]

ex parte, *eks pär′tē,* (*adverbially*) on one side, in the interests of one side, only: (*adjectivally*) from the point of view of, in the interests of, one side (e.g. *an ex parte statement*). [L.]

expatiate, *eks-pā′shi-āt,* v.i. to range at large (usu. *fig.*): to enlarge in discourse, argument, writing, (on).—n. **expatiā′tion.**—adj. **expā′tiatory,** expansive. [L. *exspatiārī, -ātus—ex,* out of, *spatiārī,* to roam—*spatium,* space.]

expatriate, *eks-pā′tri-āt,* v.t. to banish or exile (oneself, another).—Also v.i.—n. and adj. (person) expatriated, exiled by self or other(s).—n. **expatriā′tion,** act of expatriating: exile, voluntary or compulsory. [Low L. *expatriāre, -ātum—ex,* out of, *patria,* fatherland.]

expect, *eks-pekt′,* v.t. to look forward to as likely to come or happen, or as due: (*coll.*) to suppose.—ns. **expect′ance, expect′ancy,** act or state of expecting: that which is expected: hope.—adj. **expect′ant,** looking or waiting for something.—Also n.—adv. **expect′antly.**—n. **expectā′tion,** act or state of expecting: that which is, or may fairly be, expected: (*pl.*) prospect of fortune or profit by a will. [L. *exspectāre, -ātum—ex,* out, *spectāre,* to look, freq. of *specĕre,* to see.]

expectorate, *eks-pek′to-rāt,* v.t. and v.i. to expel (phlegm) from the breast or lungs by coughing, &c.: (*coll.*) to spit.—ns. **expectorā′tion,** act of expectorating: that which is expectorated; **expec′torant,** a medicine that promotes expectoration.—Also adj. [L. *expectorāre, -ātum—ex,* out of, from, *pectus, pectoris,* the breast.]

expedient, *eks-pē′di-ént,* adj. suitable, advisable: politic.—n. means suitable to an end: contrivance, shift, emergency measure.—ns. **expē′dience, expē′diency,** fitness, prudence, advisability: that which is opportune or politic: self-interest.—adv. **expē′diently.** [L.*expediens, -entis,* pr.p. of *expedīre.* See **expedite.**]

expedite, *eks′pe-dīt,* v.t. to hasten, accelerate: to dispatch (business).—n. **expedi′tion,** speed, promptness: an organised journey to attain some object, as exploration, &c.: the party undertaking such a journey.—adj. **expedi′tionary,** belonging to an expedition; **expedi′tious,** speedy, characterised by speed and efficiency. [L. *expedīre, -ītum—ex,* from, *pēs, pedis,* foot.]

expel, *eks-pel′,* v.t. to drive out, to eject: to banish:—pr.p. expell′ing; p.a.p. expelled′. [L. *expellēre, expulsum—ex,* from, *pellēre,* to drive.]

expend, *eks-pend′,* v.t. to spend (often with *on, upon*): to employ or consume in any way.—adj. **expend′able,** that may be sacrificed to achieve some end.—ns. **expend′iture** (*-tyùr, -chúr*), act of expending: that which is expended: money spent: **expense′,** outlay: cost: (in *pl*; *Scots law*) costs in a lawsuit.—adj. **expens′ive,** causing or requiring much expense, costly.—n. **expens′iveness.**—**expense(s) account,** statement of outlay incurred in carrying out a business commission. [L. *expendĕre—ex,* out, *pendĕre, pensum,* to weigh.]

experience, *eks-pē′ri-éns,* n. practical acquaintance with any matter gained by trial: long and varied observation, personal or general: wisdom derived from the changes and trials of life: any event or course of events by which one is affected.—v.t. to meet with, undergo: to prove or know by use.—p.adj. **expē′rienced,** taught by experience—skilful, wise.—adj. **expērien′tial** (*-shál*), pertaining to or derived from experience. [Fr.,—L. *experientia,* from *experīrī—ex-,* inten., and old verb *perīrī,* to try.]

experiment, *eks-per′i-mént,* n. (*obs.*) experience: anything done to test a theory, or to discover something unknown.—v.i. to make experiment or trial: to search by trial.—adj.

Neutral vowels in unaccented syllables: *em′pér-ór*; for certain sounds in foreign words see p. ix.

experiment'al, pertaining to experiment: based on or proceeding by experiment: based on experience: tentative.—*ns.* **experiment'alist, experiment'er,** one who makes experiments. [L. *experīmentum—experīrī*; see **experience.**]

expert, *eks-pûrt', adj.* taught by practice: skilful (at, in): based on, showing, special knowledge or skill.—*ns.* **ex'pert,** one who is specially skilled in any art or science: a scientific or professional witness: **expert'ness,** skill, adroitness. [Fr.—L. *expertus—experīrī*; see **experience.**]

expertise, *eks-pûrt-ēz', n.* expert knowledge: expertness, skill: expert appraisal, valuation. [Fr.]

expiate, *eks'pi-āt, v.t.* to suffer the penalty of: to make complete reparation for.—*adj.* **ex'piable,** capable of being expiated.—*ns.* **expia'tion,** act of expiating: the means by which atonement is made; **ex'piator,** one who expiates.—*adj.* **ex'piatory,** [L. *expiāre -ātum—ex-,* intens., *piāre,* to appease, atone for.]

expire, *eks-pīr', v.t.* to breathe out: to emit.—*v.i.* to breathe out: to die: to come to an end: to lapse or become void.—*n.* **expira'tion,** the act of breathing out: end, termination.—*adj.* **expī'ratory,** pertaining to expiration, or the emission of the breath.—*p.adjs.* **expīred',** lapsed, invalid; **expī'ring,** dying: pertaining to, or uttered at the time of, dying.—*n.* **expi'ry,** the end or termination, esp. by lapse of time: (*arch.*) death. [Fr. *expirer*—L. *ex,* from *spīrāre, -ātum,* to breathe.]

explain, *eks-plān', v.t.* to make plain or intelligible: to expound: to account for.—*adj.* **explain'able.** *n.* **explāna'tion,** act of explaining or clearing from obscurity: that which explains or clears up: the meaning or sense given: a mutual clearing up of misunderstanding. *adj.* **explan'atory,** serving to explain or clear up.—**explain away,** to modify, lessen the force of, by explanation (e.g. *he tried to explain away his previous statement*). —**explain oneself,** to make one's meaning, or the reason of one's actions, clear. [O.Fr. *explaner*—L. *explānāre—ex,* out, *plānāre—plānus,* plain.]

expletive, *eks'ple-tiv, eks-plē'tiv, adj.* filling out: added merely to fill up.—*n.* a word inserted to fill up a gap: a meaningless oath. [L. *explētīvus—ex,* out, *plēre,* to fill.]

explicate, *eks'pli-kāt, v.t.* to develop, show what is involved or implied in (e.g. a statement, principle): (*arch.*) to explain.—*adj.* **explic'able,** capable of being explained.—*n.* **explica'tion,** act of explicating or explaining: explanation.—*adjs.* **ex'plicative, ex'plicatory,** serving to explicate or explain. [L. *explicāre, explicātum* or *explicitum—ex,* out, *plicāre,* to fold.]

explicit, *eks-plis'it, adj.* not implied merely, but distinctly stated—opp. of *implicit*: plain in language: outspoken.—*adv.* **explic'itly.**—*n.* **explic'itness.** [See **explicate.**]

explode, *eks-plōd', v.t.* (*obs.*) to cry down, as an actor: to bring into disrepute', and reject: to cause to blow up.—*v.i.* to burst with a loud report: to burst into (e.g. into laughter).—*p.adj.* **explō'ded,** blown up: rejected, discarded.—*n.*

explō'sion (-*zh(ó)n*), act of exploding: a sudden violent burst with a loud report: an outburst of feelings, &c.: a great and rapid increase or expansion, as *population explosion.*—*adj.* **explō'sive** (-*siv, -ziv*), worked by an explosion: liable to or causing explosion: bursting out with violence and noise.—*n.* something that will explode: a stop consonant (*p, b,* &c.). **explosion welding,** welding metals with very different melting points by means of pressure produced by an explosion.—**high explosive,** a material having a violent explosive effect. [L. *explōdere, explōsum—ex,* from, *plaudĕre,* to clap hands.]

exploit, *eks-ploit',* or *eks'ploit, n.* a deed or achievement, esp. an heroic one.—*v.t.* (*eks-ploit'*) to work, make available (e.g. natural resources): to make gain out of, or at the expense of (e.g. a person).—*n.* **exploitā'tion,** the act of successfully applying industry to any object, as the working of mines, &c.: the act of using for selfish purpose: the operations involved in obtaining ore from a mine. [O.Fr. *exploit*—L. *explicitum,* unfolded.]

explore, *eks-plōr', -plōr', v.t.* to search or travel through for the purpose of discovery: to examine thoroughly.—Also *v.i.*—*n.* **explorā'tion,** act of searching thoroughly: travel for the sake of discovery.—*adjs.* **explor'ative, explor'atory,** serving, or intended, to explore or investigate (e.g. *an exploratory operation*): for exploration (e.g. *exploratory zeal*).—*n.* **explor'er.** [Fr. *explorer*—L. *explōrāre, -ātum,* to search out—prob. from *ex,* from, *plōrāre,* to call out.]

exponent, *eks-pō'nént, n.* an expounder: (*mus.*) an interpreter by performance: (*math.*) a symbol showing what power a quantity is raised to, an index.—*adj.* interpreting, expounding. *adj.* **exponen'tial** (*eks-pon-en'shal*), pertaining to or involving exponents.—**exponential function,** a quantity with a variable exponent, esp. e^x, where *e* is the base of natural (q.v.) logarithms. [L. *expōnens—ex,* out, *pōnĕre,* to place.]

export, *eks-pōrt', -pōrt', v.t.* to carry or send out of a country, as goods in commerce.—*n.* **ex'port,** act of exporting: that which is exported: a commodity that is, or may be, sent from one country to another.—*adj.* **export'able.**—*ns.* **exportā'tion; export'er,** the person who ships goods to a foreign or distant country for sale—opp. to *importer.* [L. *exportāre, -ātum—ex,* out of, *portāre,* to carry.]

expose, *eks-pōz', v.t.* to lay forth to view: to lay bare: to deprive of cover, protection, or shelter: to subject to an influence (as light, weather): to make liable (to—e.g. to danger): to disclose (a secret): to show up.—*ns.* **exposé** (*eks pō-zā*), an exposing: a shameful showing up: a formal statement or exposition; **expō'sure** (-*zhùr*), act of laying bare: subjection to an influence: (*photography*) act of allowing access of light: duration of such access: act of showing up an evil: state of being laid bare: openness to danger: shelterless state: position with regard to the sun, influence of climate, &c. [Fr. *exposer*—L. *ex,* out, and Fr. *poser,* to place, from L.L. *pausāre,* to rest, not from L. *pōnĕre, positum,* to place.]

fāte, fär; mē, hûr (her); *mīne; mōte, fōr; mūte; mōōn, fōōt;* *τhen* (then)

exposition, *eks-po-zish'(ò)n, n.* act of exposing: a public exhibition: act of expounding: an explanatory discourse: enunciation of themes in a musical composition.—*n.* **expos'itor**, one who, or that which expounds: an interpreter.—*adj.* **expos'itory**, serving to explain, explanatory. [L. *expositiō, -ōnis,* exposition—*expōnēre, expositum,* to expose, set forth; see **exponent.**]

ex post facto, *eks pōst fak'tō,* retrospective (e.g. *an ex post facto law is applicable to crimes committed before its passing*): retrospectively. [L.]

expostulate, *eks-post'ū-lāt, v.i.* to remonstrate.—*n.* **expostūlā'tion.**—*adj.* **expost'ūlatory,** containing expostulation. [L. *expostulāre, -ātum*—*ex-,* inten., *postulāre,* to demand.]

expound, *eks-pownd', v.t.* to present in detail (e.g. a doctrine): to explain, interpret (e.g. the Scriptures). [O.Fr. *espondre*—L. *expōnēre*—*ex-,* out, *pōnēre,* to place.]

express, *eks-pres', v.t.* to press or force out: to represent or make known by a likeness, signs, symbols, &c.: to put into words: (*reflex.*) to put one's thought, feeling into words: to reveal (e.g. an emotion, a quality).—*adj.* exact (e.g. *his express image*): directly stated, explicit: intended or sent for a particular purpose (e.g. *an express messenger*): expeditious (e.g. method): travelling at high speed over long distances.—*adv.* with haste: specially: by express train or messenger.—*n.* a messenger sent on a special errand: a regular and quick conveyance: express train.—*adv.* **express'ly,** definitely, explicitly: of set purpose: (*arch.*) directly and quickly.—*adjs.* **express'ible; express'ive,** serving to express (with *of*): conveying vividly or forcibly meaning or feeling, full of expression.—*adv.* **express'ively.**—*ns.* **express'iveness; express'ion,** act of forcing out by pressure: act of representing or giving utterance: representation or revelation by language, art, the features, &c.: look: intonation: due indication of feeling in performance of music: word, phrase; **express'ionism,** in literature and painting, a revolt against impressionism (q.v.) in which the artist sought to express his emotions and thoughts through non-realistic or stylised forms: see *post-impressionism.*—*adj.* **express'ionless.**—*ns.* **express letter, express parcel,** a letter or parcel to be delivered by special messenger; **express rifle,** a rifle for large game at short range, with heavy charge of powder and light bullet; **express train,** a railway train running at high speed and with few stops. [O.Fr. *expresser*—L. *ex,* from, *pressāre,* frequentative of *premēre, pressum,* to press.]

expropriate, *eks-prō'pri-āt, v.t.* to dispossess: to take (property) from its owner.—*n.* **expropriā'tion.** [L. *expropriāre, -ātum*—*ex,* from, *proprium,* property.]

expulsion, *eks-pul'sh(ò)n, n.* the act of expelling: banishment.—*adj.* **expul'sive,** able or serving to expel. [L. *expulsāre,* frequentative of *expellēre.* See **expel.**]

expunge, *eks-punj', v.t.* to cancel by a mark, to efface, erase. [L. *ex,* out, *pungěre,* to prick.]

expurgate, *eks'pûr-gāt, v.t.* to purify (esp. a book) from anything supposed to be noxious or erroneous.—*ns.* **expurgā'tion; expurgator** (*eks'pûr-gā-tŏr,* or *eks-pûr'gā-tŏr*).—*adj.* **expur'gatory,** tending to expurgate or purify. [L. *expurgāre, -ātum*—*ex,* out, *purgāre,* to purge.]

exquisite, *eks'kwi-zit,* also *-kwiz', adj.* of consummate excellence (e.g. of workmanship): very beautiful: showing delicate perception or close discrimination: fastidious: extreme, as pain or pleasure.—*n.* one extremely fastidious in dress, a fop.—*adv.* **ex'quisitely.**—*n.* **ex'quisiteness.** [L. *exquīsītus*—*ex,* out, *quaerěre, quaesītum,* to seek.]

exscind, *ek-sind', v.t.* to cut off or out. [L. *ex,* from, *scinděre,* to cut.]

ex-serviceman, *eks-sûr'vis-man, n.* a man formerly in one of the fighting services. [Pfx. **ex-,** **service** (1), and **man.**]

exsiccate, *ek'si-kāt, v.t.* to dry up.—*n.* **exsicca'tion.** [L. *exsiccāre*—*ex,* out, *siccus,* dry.]

extant, *eks'tănt', adj.* (*rare*) standing out, or above the rest: still existing. [L. *ex(s)tans, -antis*—*ex,* out, *stāre,* to stand.]

extasy, extatic. Same as **ecstasy, ecstatic.**

extempore, *eks-tem'po-re, adv.* on the spur of the moment: without preparation.—*adj.* composed and delivered or performed impromptu—also **extemporā'neous, extem'porary.**—*v.i.* **extem'porise,** to speak, or compose and play, extempore.—*n.* **extemporīsā'tion.** [L. *ex,* out of, and *tempore,* abl. of. *tempus, temporis,* time.]

extend, *eks-tend', v.t.* to stretch out: to prolong in any direction: to enlarge (e.g. power, meaning): to hold out (e.g. the hand): to offer, accord (e.g. sympathy).—*v.i.* to stretch, reach.—*adjs.* **extens'ible, extens'ile** (or *-il*), that may be extended.—*ns.* **extensibil'ity; exten'sion,** act of extending: condition of being extended: an added part: the property of occupying space: (*gram.*) a word or words added to the subject, predicate, or object: an additional telephone using the same line as the main one.—*adj.* **extens'ive,** large: comprehensive.—*adv.* **extens'ively.**—*ns.* **extens'iveness; extent',** the space or degree to which a thing is extended: scope: degree or amount (as, *to some extent*); **exten'sor,** a muscle which, by its contraction, straightens a limb or a part of the body.—**extended play,** of a gramophone record, giving longer playing than an ordinary record of the same size because of a closer groove and the use of a larger part of its surface area.—**university extension,** the enlargement of the aim of a university by providing instruction for those unable to become regular students. [L. *extendēre, extentum,* or *extensum*—*ex,* out, *tendēre,* to stretch.]

extenuate, *eks-ten'ū-āt, v.t.* to lessen the magnitude of (a crime, &c.), to palliate.—*p.adj.* **exten'ūāting,** palliating.—*n.* **extenūā'tion,** act of representing anything as less wrong or criminal than it is, palliation, mitigation.—*adj.* **exten'ūātory,** tending to extenuate. [L. *extenuāre, -ātum,* to make thin, weaken—*ex,* inten., *tenuis,* thin.]

exterior, *eks-tē'ri-ŏr, adj.* outer: outward, external: on or from the outside.—*n.* the outside, outer surface: outward form or deportment: a representation of an outdoor scene. [L. *exterior,* comp. of *exter,* outward—*ex,* from.]

Neutral vowels in unaccented syllables: *em'pér-ór*; for certain sounds in foreign words see p. ix.

250

exterminate, *eks-tûr'mi-nāt*, *v.t.* to destroy utterly.—*n.* **extermina'tion**, complete destruction or extirpation.—*adj.* **exter'minatory**, serving or tending to exterminate.—*n.* **exter'minātor.** [L. *extermināre, -ātum—ex*, out of, *terminus*, boundary.]

external, *eks-tûr'nál*, *adj.* exterior: outward: belonging to the world of outward things: not innate or intrinsic: foreign (e.g. trade).—*n.* (in *pl.*) the outward parts: outward forms and ceremonies: outward circumstances or appearances.—*adv.* **exter'nally.**—*v.t.* **exter'nalise**, to give external expression to: to ascribe to causes outside oneself: to regard as consisting of externals only.—**external student**, one examined by a university from whose normal regulations as to residence, or attendance at classes, &c. he has been exempt. [L. *externus*, outward—*exter*, outside.]

extinct, *eks-tingkt'*, *adj.* put out, extinguished (as fire, life): (of a volcano) no longer erupting: no longer existing.—*n.* **extinc'tion**, extinguishing, quenching, or wiping out: becoming extinct. [See **extinguish.**]

extinguish, *eks-ting'gwish*, *v.t.* to quench: to destroy: to obscure by superior splendour.—*adj.* **exting'uishable.**—*n.* **exting'uisher**, a small hollow conical instrument for putting out a candle: a device for putting out fire. [L. *ex-(s)tinguĕre, ex(s)tinctum—ex*, out, *stinguĕre*, to quench.]

extirpate, *eks'tėr-pāt*, *v.t.* to root out: to destroy totally.—*ns.* **extirpā'tion**, extermination, total destruction; **ex'tirpātor.** [L. *ex(s)tirpāre, -atum—ex*, out, and *stirps*, a root.]

extol, *eks-tol'*, *v.t.* to praise highly:—*pr.p.* extol'ling; *pa.p.* extolled' [L. *extollĕre—ex*, up, *tollĕre*, to lift or raise.]

extort, *eks-tört'*, *v.t.* to obtain extract (from) by compulsion or violence (usu. *fig.*; e.g. a promise, confession, money).—*n.* **extor'tion**, illegal or oppressive exaction, esp. of money: that which is extorted.—*adjs.* **extor'tionary**, pertaining to or implying extortion; **extor'tionate**, oppressive, exorbitant.—*n.* **extor'tioner**, one who practises extortion. [L. *extorquĕre, extortum—ex*, out, *torquĕre*, to twist.]

extra, *eks'tra*, *adj.* beyond or more than the usual or the necessary: additional.—*adv.* unusually.—*n.* what is extra or additional: an actor temporarily engaged for a minor part, as to be one of a crowd. [L. *extrā*, outside.]

extra-, *eks'tra-*, *pfx.* used to form adjectives, meaning beyond, beyond the scope of, e.g.:—*adjs.* **ex'tra-curric'ular**, of a subject or activity, outside, and additional to, the regular academic course; **ex'tra-galac'tic**, outside, beyond our Galaxy; **ex'tra-judi'cial**, not made in court, beyond the usual course of legal proceeding; **ex'tra-mar'ital**, of relations, &c., outside marriage, though properly confined to marriage, **ex'tra-mun'dāne**, beyond the material world; **ex'tra-mū'ral**, without or beyond the walls: (of teachers, teaching) connected with a university but not under its direct control; **ex'tra-sens'ory**, beyond the powers of the ordinary five senses (**extra-sensory perception**, an awareness of objects or of facts which seems to have been given by means other than

through the senses, as in telepathy and clairvoyance—abbrev. **ESP**; **ex'tra-terres'trial**, outside, or from outside, the earth. [L.]

extract, *eks-trakt'*, *v.t.* to draw out by force (*lit.* and *fig.*—e.g. a tooth, money, a confession): to take, derive (from—e.g. good from evil): to select, quote (passages from a book, &c.): to take or withdraw by chemical or physical means (a substance forming part of a mixture or of a compound): (*math.*) to find (the root of a number).—*n.* **ex'tract**, anything drawn from a substance by heat, solvents, distillation, &c. as an essence: a passage taken from a book or writing.—*adj.* **extract'able** (also **extract'ible**).—*n.* **extrac'tion**, act of extracting: lineage: that which is extracted.—*adj.* **extract'ive**, tending or serving to extract.—*n.* an extract.—*n.* **extract'or**, he who, or that which, extracts. [L. *extrahĕre, extractum—ex*, from, *trahĕre*, to draw.]

extradition, *eks-tra-dish'(ó)n*, *n.* a delivering up by one government to another of fugitives from justice.—*v.t.* **ex'tradīte.** [L. *ex*, from, *trā-ditiō—trādĕre, trāditum*, to deliver up.]

extraneous, *eks-trān'yús*, *adj.* coming from without: foreign (e.g. to other substances with which it is found, as *extraneous matter*): not belonging (to e.g. the subject under consideration): not essential.—*adv.* **extrān'eously.** [L. *extrāneus*, external—*extrā*, outside.]

extraordinary, *eks-trör'di nár-i*, or *eks-tra-ör'-*, *adj.* beyond ordinary, not usual or regular: wonderful, surprising: additional (e.g. *envoy extraordinary*). *adv.* **extraor'dinarily.** [L. *extrā*, outside, *ordō, -inis*, order.]

extrapolate, *eks trap'ō-lāt*, *v.t.* to estimate from observed tendencies the value of (any variable) outside the limits between which values are known: to infer, conjecture from what is known: to project into a new area of experience or activity.—Also *v.i.*—*n.* **extrapolā'tion.** [L. *extrā*, outside, and **interpolate.**]

extraterritorial, *eks-trá-ter-i-tō'ri-ál, -tö'-*, *adj.* outside a territory or territorial jurisdiction—also **exterritō'rial.**—*n.* **extraterritorial'ity** (or **exterritorial'ity**), the privilege (accorded, e.g. to diplomatic agents) of being outside the jurisdiction of the country in which one is.—**extraterritorial rights**, extraterritoriality. [L. *extrā*, outside, and *territōriālis* (*−territōrium*, territory).]

extravagant, *eks-trav'a-gánt*, *adj.* (*obs.*) wandering beyond bounds: unrestrained, excessive (e.g. grief, praise): lavish in spending: wasteful: exorbitant (price).—*n.* **extrav'agance**, excess: lavish expenditure. [L. *extrā*, beyond, *vagans, -antis*, pr.p. of *vagāri*, to wander.]

extravaganza, *eks-trav-a-gan'za*, *n.* an extravagant or eccentric musical, dramatic, or literary production. [It *(e)stravaganza*.]

extravasate, *eks-trav'a-sāt*, *v.t.* to force out of vessels or arteries, as blood: to pour out from a vent in the earth, as lava or water.—*v.i.* to escape from its proper vessels. [L. *extrā*, out of, *vas*, a vessel.]

extravert, extrovert, *eks'tra-vûrt*, or *-trō-*, *n.* one whose interests are in objects and matters outside of himself:—opp. to *introvert* (q.v.). [L. *extrā*, outside, *vertĕre*, to turn: *extro-*, by analogy with *intro-*.]

---

fāte, fär; mē, hûr (her); *mīne; mōte, för; mūte; mōōn, fŏŏt;* 'ᴛнen (then)

extreme **eyry**

extreme, *eks-trēm', adj.* outermost: most remote: last (e.g. *extreme unction*): highest in degree, greatest (e.g. *extreme penalty*): very violent (e.g. pain): stringent (e.g. measures): (of opinions) thoroughgoing, marked by excess—opp. to *moderate.—n.* the utmost point or verge, the end: utmost or highest limit or degree.—*adv.* **extreme′ly.—*ns.* extrē′mist,** one ready to use extreme measures; **extremity** (*-trem′i-ti*), the utmost limit: the highest degree: greatest necessity or distress: (*pl.*) extreme measures: (*pl.*) hands or feet.—**extreme unction** (see **unction**); **go to extremes,** to go too far: to use extreme measures; **in the extreme,** in the last, highest degree: extremely. [O.Fr. *extreme*—L. *extrēmus,* superl. of *exter,* outside.]

extricate, *eks′tri-kāt, v.t.* to free (from difficulties or perplexities): to set free, to disentangle.—*adj.* **ex′tricable.—*n.* extricā′tion,** disentanglement: act of setting free. [L. *extrīcāre, -ātum—ex,* from, *trīcae,* hindrances.]

extrinsic, -al, *eks-trin′sik, -ǎl, adj.* not contained in or belonging to a body: operating from without: not essential—opp. to *intrinsic.* [Fr.,—L. *extrinsecus—exter,* outside, suffx. *-in, secus,* beside.]

extrude, *eks-trŏŏd', v.t.* to force or thrust out.—*v.i.* to protrude.—*n.* **extrusion** (*-trŏŏ′zh(ȯ)n*), act of extruding, thrusting, or throwing out.—*adj.* **extru′sive,** forcing out: (of rocks) consolidated on the surface of the ground. [L. *extrūdĕre, extrūsum—ex,* out, *trūdĕre,* to thrust.]

exuberant, *egz-, eks-(y)ŏŏ′bér-ǎnt, adj.* luxuriant: lavish: effusive: in high spirits.—*ns.* **exū′berance, exū′berancy,** luxuriance: cŏpiousness: superabundance: high spirits.—*adv.* **exū′berantly.** [L. *exūberans,* pr.p. of *exūberāre—ex-,* inten. *über,* rich.]

exude, *egz-, eks-ūd', v.t.* to discharge by sweating: to discharge through pores or incisions (*lit.* and *fig.*).—*v.i.* to ooze out of a body as through pores.—*n.* **exudā′tion** (*eks-*), act of exuding or discharging through pores: that which is exuded. [L. *ex,* from, *sūdāre,* to sweat.]

exult, *egz-ult', v.i.* to rejoice exceedingly (at): to triumph (over).—*adj.* **exult′ant,** exulting: triumphant.—*n.* **exultā′tion,** triumphant delight.—*adv.* **exult′ingly.** [L. *ex(s)ultāre, -ātum,* from *ex(s)ilīre—ex,* out or up, *salīre,* to leap.]

exuviae, *egz-, eks-(y)ŏŏ′vi-ē, n.pl.* cast-off skins, shells, or other coverings of animals: (*geol.*) fossil remains of animals.—*v.t.* and *v.i.* **exū′viāte,** to shed (an old covering).—Also *fig.* [L., from *exuĕre,* to draw off.]

eyas, *ī′as, n.* an unfledged hawk. [*eyas,* a corr. of *nyas*—Fr. *niais*—L. *nīdus,* nest.]

eye, *ī, n.* the organ of sight or vision, more correctly the globe or movable part of it: the power of seeing: sight: regard: keenness of perception: anything resembling an eye, as the hole of a needle, loop or ring for a hook, &c.: the seed-bud of a potato.—*v.t.* to look on: to observe narrowly:—*pr.p.* ey′ing, or eye′ing; *pa.p.* eyed (*īd*).—*ns.* **eye′-ball,** the ball or globe of the eye; **eye′bright,** a little plant formerly used as a remedy for eye diseases; **eye′brow,** the hairy arch above the eye.—*adj.* **eye′-cat′ching,** striking.—*n.* **eye′lash,** hair, line of hairs that edges the eyelid.—*adj.* **eye′less,** without eyes or without sight.—*ns.* **eyelet** (*ī′let*), **eye′let-hole,** a small eye or hole to receive a lace or cord, as in garments, sails, &c.; **eye′lid,** the lid or cover of the eye; **eye′-ō′pener,** something astonishing that opens the eyes literally or figuratively; **eye′-piece,** the lens or combination of lenses at the eye-end of a telescope or microscope (also known as *ocular*); **eye′-serv′ice,** service performed only under the eye or inspection of authority; **eye′-shadow,** a cosmetic applied to the eyelids; **eye′-shot,** the reach or range of sight of the eye; **eye′sight,** power of seeing; **eye′sore,** anything that is offensive to look at; **eye′tooth,** a canine tooth, esp. in the upper jaw, below the eye; **eye′-wash,** a lotion for the eye: humbug, deception; **eye′-wit′ness,** one who sees a thing done.—**an eye for an eye** (Exod. xxi. 24), the law of retaliation: exaction of penalty identical with injury suffered; **eye of day,** the sun; **eyeball to eyeball,** (of discussion, confrontation, diplomacy) at close quarters, dealing with matters very frankly and firmly.—**clap, lay, set, eyes on** (*coll.*), to see; **have an eye to,** to have regard to: to give one's particular attention to; **in one's mind's eye,** in imagination; **in the eyes of,** in the estimation, opinion, of; **keep one's eye on,** to observe closely: to watch; **make eyes at,** to look at in an amorous way, to ogle; **one in the eye,** a rebuff; **see eye to eye,** from Is. lii. 8, but used in the sense of 'to think alike'; **up to the eyes,** deeply engaged or involved; **with an eye to,** (*fig.*) with (the end specified) in view (e.g. *with an eye to his subsequent promotion*). [O.E. *ēage*; Ger. *auge,* Du. *oog,* O.N. *auga.*]

eyre, *ār, n.* a journey or circuit: a court of itinerant justices.—**justices in eyre,** judges who went on circuit. [O.Fr. *eire,* journey, from L. *iter,* a way, a journey—*īre, itum,* to go.]

eyry, eyrie. See **aerie.**

Neutral vowels in unaccented syllables: *em′pér-ȯr*; for certain sounds in foreign words see p. ix.

252

F

Fabian, *fā'bi-án, adj.* delaying, avoiding battle, cautious: favouring the gradual introduction and spread of Socialism—as in *Fabian Society.—n.* a supporter of the Fabian Society. [From Q. *Fabius* Maximus, who baffled Hannibal by evading conflict.]

fable, *fā'bl, n.* a short story, often with animal characters, intended to teach a moral lesson: any tale in literary form intended to instruct or amuse: the plot or series of events in an epic or dramatic poem: fiction: a falsehood.—*v.t.* and *v.i.* to invent (fables), tell (stories without basis in fact).—*p.adj.* **fā'bled,** mentioned or celebrated in fable: fictitious.—*n.* **fab'ulist** (*fab'-*), one who invents fables.—*adj.* **fab'ulous,** feigned, false: related in fable: immense, amazing: (*coll.*) excellent. [Fr. *fable* — L. *fābula*—*fārī,* to speak.]

fabliau, *fab'li-ō, n.* a metrical tale after the type of those, usually satirical in quality, produced in France in the 12th and 13th centuries:—*pl.* **fabliaux** (*fab'li-ōz,* or *-ō*). [Fr. dim. of *fable,* fable.]

fabric, *fab'rik, n.* anything framed by art and labour: a building: manufactured cloth—now used only of a textile: frame, structure (*lit.* and *fig.*): texture, workmanship. [Fr. *fabrique*—L. *fabrica*—*faber,* a worker in hard materials.]

fabricate, *fab'ri kāt, v.t.* (*rare*) to put together by art and labour, to manufacture: to devise falsely (e.g. a lie).—*ns.* **fabrica'tion,** construction: manufacture: that which is fabricated or invented: a story: a falsehood; **fab'ricator.** [L. *fabricāri*—*fabrica,* fabric.]

fabulist, fabulous. See **fable.**

facade, *fa-sād', n.* the exterior front or face of a building: (*fig.*) the appearance presented to the world, esp. if showy and with little behind it. [Fr.,—*face,* after It. *facciata,* the front of a building—*faccia,* the face.]

face, *fās, n.* the front part of the head, including forehead, eyes, nose, mouth, cheeks, and chin: a front or surface of anything (e.g. of a solid geometrical figure): a coal-seam actually being mined: outward show or appearance: cast of features: special appearance or expression of the countenance, as a grimace: boldness, effrontery: (*arch.*) presence: (*B.*) anger or favour.—*v.t.* to meet in the face or in front: to stand opposite to: to confront: to resist: to put an additional face or surface on.—*v.i.* to turn the face: to take or have a direction.—*n.* **face'-cloth,** a cloth laid over the face of a corpse or living person: a cloth for washing the face.—*adj.* **face'less,** without a face: (of person(s) concerned in some action) with identity concealed.—*ns.* **face'-lift,** an operation to smooth and firm the face: a renovating process, esp. one applied to the outside of a building: (*fig.*) a renewing, renovating process; **fac'er** (*slang*), a blow on the face: (*slang*) anything that nonplusses one: (*slang*) a problem—*n* and *adj.* **face'-saving,** avoiding the appearance of climbing down or humiliation.—*n.* **fac'ing,** a covering in front for ornament or protection.—**face out,** to carry off by bold looks; **face up to,** to meet boldly (*lit.* and *fig.*); **face value,** the value as stated on the face of a coin, &c.: nominal worth: apparent worth.—**be two-faced,** to be disingenuous, given to double-dealing; **fly in the face of,** to defy: to disobey; **in the face of,** in defiance of, despite; **on the face of it,** judging by appearance; **put a good face on,** to assume a bold or contented bearing as regards; **save one's face,** to evade open discomfiture; **lose face,** to suffer open loss of dignity or prestige; **set one's face against,** to oppose strenuously; **show one's face,** to appear. [Fr. *face* — L. *faciēs,* form, face; perh. from *facĕre,* to make]

facet, *fas'et, n.* a side of a many-sided object, as a crystal: an aspect or view (of a subject).—*adj.* **fac'eted,** having facets. [Fr. *facette,* dim. of *face,* face.]

facetious, *fa-sē'shús, adj.* jocose: addicted to, or containing, witticisms that are ill-timed, or otherwise inappropiate.—*n.pl.* **facetiae** (*fa-sē'shi-ē*), witty or humorous sayings or writings.—*adv.* **face'tiously.—*n.* **face'tiousness.** [Fr., from L. *facētia*—*facetus,* merry, witty.]

facia, fascia, *fash'i a, n.* the part of a shop-front bearing the owner's name: a facia-board.—*n.* **facia-board,** in a motor-car, the dash board. [L. *fascia,* a band.]

facial, *fā'shál, adj.* of or relating to the face.—*n.* beauty treatment to the face.—*adv.* **fa'cially.** [Fr.—L. *faciēs,* face.]

facile, *fas'īl,* or *-il, adj.* easy of accomplishment: easily persuaded, yielding: ready, fluent.—*v.t.* **facil'itāte,** to make easy.—*n.* **facil'ity,** ease: dexterity: easiness to be persuaded, pliancy: opportunity:—*pl.* **facil'ities,** means that render anything easily done: means provided (as *transport facilities*). [Fr.,—L. *facilis,* easy—*facĕre,* to do.]

facsimile, *fak-sim'i-le, n.* an exact copy.—**facsimile radio,** the transmission of a still picture by means of radio; **facsimile telegraphy,** the transmission of a still picture over a telegraph circuit, and its reproduction. [L. *fac,* imper. of *facĕre,* to make, *simile,* neut. of *similis,* like.]

fact, *fakt, n.* (*arch.*) a deed or anything done: anything known to have happened or to be true: (*loosely*) anything alleged to be true and used as basis of argument: reality.—*adj.* **fac'tual,** of, or containing, facts: actual.—*adj.* **fact'-finding,** appointed to ascertain, directed towards ascertaining, all the facts of a situation.—**as a matter of fact,** in reality; **facts of life,** the details of reproduction, esp. human reproduction: (*fig.*) the realities of a situation; **the fact of the matter,** the plain truth. [L. *factum*—*facĕre,* to make.]

faction, *fak'sh(ŏ)n, n.* a company of persons associated or acting together, mostly used in a bad sense: a contentious party in a state or society: dissension.—*adj.* **fac′tious,** turbulent: disloyal.—*adv.* **fac′tiously.**—*n.* **fac′tiousness.** [L. *factiō, -ōnis*—*facĕre,* to do.]

factitious, *fak-tish′ús, adj.* (*obs.*) made by art, in opposition to what is natural (e.g. *a factitious mound*): produced or induced artificially (e.g. *factitious value, taste*).—*adv.* **facti′tiously.** [L. *factitius*—*facĕre,* to make.]

factor, *fak′tór, n.* a doer or transactor of business for another, an agent: one who buys and sells goods for others, on commission: (*math.*) one of two or more quantities, which, when multiplied together, produce a given quantity: any circumstance that influences the course of events.—*n.* **fac′torage,** the fees or commission of a factor.—*adj.* **facto′rial,** of or pertaining to a factor.—*n.* the product of all whole numbers from a given number down to 1.—*v.t.* **fac′torise,** to resolve into factors.—*ns.* **fac′torship; fac′tory,** a manufactory: a trading settlement in a distant country.—**factory-farming,** farming by methods of feeding and housing animals in which everything is subordinated to achieving maximum production. rapid growth.—**judicial factor,** a person appointed by the court to manage the estate of a person under some incapacity. [L.,—*facĕre.*]

factotum, *fak-tō′tum, n.* a person employed to do all kinds of work. [Low L.,—L. *fac,* imper. of *facĕre,* to do, *tōtum,* all.]

faculty, *fak′úl-ti, n.* an original power of the mind (e.g. reason): a physical capability or function (e.g. hearing): natural aptitude: right, authority, or privilege to act: a department of study in a university, or the professors constituting it: the members of a profession. [Fr.,—L. *facultās, -ātis*—*facilis,* easy.]

fad, *fad, n.* a whim, craze.—*adjs.* **fadd′ish, fadd′y.**—*ns.* **fadd′ishness; fadd′ism; fadd′ist.** [Ety. uncertain.]

fade, *fād, v.i.* to lose freshness or colour gradually: to grow faint, to die away.—*v.t.* to cause (an image or a sound) to become gradually less distinct or loud.—*adj.* **fade′less,** not liable to fade. [O.Fr. *fader*—*fade*—L. *vapidum.*]

faeces, feces, *fē′sēz, n.pl.* sediment after infusion or distillation, dregs: solid excrement.—*adj.* **faecal** (*fē′kál*) of or pertaining to faeces. [L., pl. of *faex, faecis,* grounds.]

faerie, faery, *fā′ér-i, n.* (*arch.*) the world of fairies, fairyland: (*obs.*) a fairy. [A variant of **fairy.**]

fag, *fag, v.i.* to become weary or tired out: to work hard: to be a fag.—*v.t.* to weary: to use as a fag:—*pr.p.* fagg′ing; *pa.p.* fagged.—*n.* a schoolboy forced to do menial offices for an older boy: drudgery: (*slang*) a cigarette.—*n.* **fag′-end,** the end of a web of cloth that hangs loose: the untwisted end of a rope: the refuse or last part of a thing: the stump of a cigar or cigarette. [Ety. uncertain; perh. a corr. of **flag,** to droop.]

faggot, fagot, *fag′ót, n.* a bundle of sticks for fuel: a stick: anything like a faggot: a bundle of

iron or steel rods: a voter who acquired his votes expressly for party purposes, on a sham qualification: a derogatory term for an old woman.—*adj.* got up for a purpose, as in 'faggot vote'. [Fr. *fagot,* a bundle of sticks, perh. from L. *fax,* a torch.]

Fahrenheit, *fä′ren-hīt,* or *far′en-īt, adj.* (of a thermometer . or thermometer scale) having the freezing-point of water marked at 32 degrees, and the boiling-point at 212 degrees. [Named from the inventor, Gabriel D. *Fahrenheit* (1686-1736).]

faience, *fä-yäs, n.* glazed and coloured earthenware. [Fr.; prob. from *Faenza* in Italy.]

fail, *fāl, v.i.* to fall short or be wanting (with *in*): to be or become insufficient in quantity or quality (e.g. a crop, a stream): to cease from a required action (e.g. *the engine failed*): to decay or lose vigour: to prove deficient under a test: to be disappointed or baffled (in an attempt—with *in, to*): to become bankrupt.—*v.t.* to be wanting to (e.g. *words fail me*): to disappoint or desert (a person): to reject (a candidate) as unsatisfactory in an examination:—*pr.p.* fail′ing; *pa.p.* failed.—*n.* **fail′ing,** a fault, weakness: a foible.—*prep.* in default of.—*n.* **fail′ure,** lack of success: cessation: omission: decay: bankruptcy: an unsuccessful person.—*adj.* **fail′-safe,** pertaining to a mechanism incorporated in a system to ensure that there will be no accident if the system does not operate properly.—**without fail,** assuredly. [O.Fr. *faillir*—L. *fallĕre,* to deceive; cf. Du. *feilen,* Ger. *fehlen.*]

fain, *fān, adj.* glad or joyful: content for want of better (to): compelled (to).—*adv.* gladly. [O.E. *fægen,* joyful.]

fainéant, *fen′ā-ā, n.* a do-nothing, a nonentity. —Also *adj.* [Fr. as if from *faire,* to do, *néant,* nothing; really—O.Fr. *faignant,* pr.p. of *faindre,* to skulk.]

faint, *fānt, adj.* wanting in strength: dim: lacking distinctness: weak in spirit: done in a feeble way.—*v.i.* to lose strength, colour, &c.: to swoon: to lose courage or spirit.—*n.* a swoon.—*adv.* **faint′ly.**—*adjs.* **faint′-heart, faint′heart′ed,** spiritless, timorous; **faint′ish,** slightly faint.—*n.* **faint′ness,** want of strength: feebleness of colour, light, &c. [O.Fr. *feint* (Fr. *feindre*), feigned—L. *fingĕre,* to feign.]

fair, *fār, adj.* bright: clear: free from blemish: pure: pleasing to the eye: of a light hue: free from clouds or rain: unobstructed: favourable: prosperous: equitable, impartial, just: plausible: specious: reasonable: hopeful: pretty good.—*n.* (*arch.*) a woman.—*v.i.* to become clear, as the weather from rain.—*adv.* **fair′ly.**—*n.* **fair′ness.**—*adj.* **fair′-and-square,** honest.—*adv.* **fair and square,** honestly: squarely, cleanly (e.g. *hit him fair and square*).—*ns.* **fair′-cop′y,** a clean copy after correction; **fair′-field (and no favour),** just conditions; **fair game,** an object for justifiable attack or ridicule; **fair′ing,** adjustment or testing of curves in ship-building: means of reducing head-resistance in an aeroplane; **fair′-play,** honest dealing: justice.—*adj.* **fair-spok′en,** bland and civil.—*n.* **fair′-way,** the channel by which vessels enter or leave a harbour: any clear course: (*golf*) the smooth turf between

Neutral vowels in unaccented syllables: *em′pér-òr*; for certain sounds in foreign words see p. ix.

254

the tee and putting-green.—*adj.* **fair′-weath′er**, suitable only in favourable conditions: loyal only in prosperous times.—**be in a fair way to (succeed in)**, to be likely to succeed in; **keep fair with**, to keep on amiable terms with; **stand fair with**, to be in the good graces of; **the fair, the fair sex**, the female sex. [O.E. *fæger*.]

fair, *fār, n.* a periodical market of considerable importance, often the occasion for a local holiday: a bazaar with amusements, &c.—*n.* **fair′ing**, a present given at a fair, any complimentary gift.—**a day after the fair**, too late. [O.Fr. *feire*—L. *fēria*, holiday.]

fairy, *fār′i, n.* an imaginary being, generally of diminutive and graceful human form, capable of kindly or unkindly acts towards man: an enchantress.—*adj.* like a fairy, fanciful, delicate.—*n.* **fair′yland**, the country of the fairies.—*ns.pl.* **fair′y-rings**, **-cir′cles**, spots or circles in pastures, due to the outwardly spreading growth of fungi.—*n.* **fair′y-tale**, a story about fairies: an incredible tale, a fib, beautiful, fortunate, as in a fairy-tale. [O.Fr. *faerie*, enchantment—*fae* (Fr. *fée*). See **fay**.]

fait accompli, *fet a-kȯ-plō, n.* an accomplished fact, a thing already done and irrevocable, hence not worth protesting against. [Fr.]

faith, *fāth, n.* trust or confidence: belief in the statement of another: a belief in the truth of revealed religion: confidence and trust in God: that which is believed: any system of religious belief: fidelity to promises: honesty of intention: word or honour pledged.—*adj.* **faith′ful**, full of faith, believing: firm in adherence to promises, duty, allegiance, &c.: loyal: true, true to an original, accurate.—*adv.* **faith′-fully.**—*ns.* **faith′fulness**; **faith′-healing**, **-cure**, a system of belief based on James v. 15, that sickness may be cured through prayer and without medical aid—*adj.* **faith′less**, without faith or belief: not believing, esp. in God or Christianity: false: disloyal.—*adv.* **faith′less-ly.**—*n.* **faith′lessness**.—**bad faith**, treachery; **father of the faithful**, the caliph; **in good faith**, with sincerity; **the faithful**, believers. [M.E. *feith, feyth*—O.Fr. *feid*—L. *fidēs fidēre*, to trust.]

fake, *fāk, v.t.* to falsify or counterfeit: to produce an illusion of by trick (q.v.) photography.—*n.* a swindle, dodge, sham: a faked article. [Cf. Ger. *fegen*, to furbish up.]

fakir, *fa-kēr′,* or *fā′kir, n.* a (esp. Mohammedan) religious mendicant in India, &c. [Ar. *faqīr*, a poor man, *fakr, fagr*, poverty.]

falcate, **-d**, *fal′kāt, -id, adj.* bent like a sickle. [L. *falx, falcis*, a sickle.]

falchion, *föl′ch(ȯ)n, n.* a short, broad sword, bent somewhat like a sickle. [O.Fr. *fauchon*, through Low L., from L. *falx*, a sickle.]

falcon, *föl′kȯn,* or *fö′kn, n.* any of various hawks (by falconers, usu. restricted to the females) formerly trained to the pursuit of game: now a genus or subfamily of long-winged hawks that usu. strike their prey from above.—*ns.* **fal′coner**, one who sports with, or who breeds and trains, falcons or hawks for taking wild-fowl; **fal′conry**, the art of training or hunting with falcons. [O.Fr. *faucon*—Low L. *falcō, -ōnis*.]

falderal, *fal′de-ral, n.* a meaningless refrain in songs: any kind of flimsy trifle.—Also **fol′-derol**.

faldstool, *föld′stōol, n.* a folding or camp stool: a kind of stool for the king at his coronation: a bishop's armless seat: a small desk in churches in England, at which the litany should be sung or said. [Low L. *faldistolium*—O.H.G. *faldan* (Ger. *falten*), to fold, *stuol* (Ger. *stuhl*), stool.]

fall, *föl, v.i.* to descend, esp. by force of gravity: to drop prostrate: to collapse: to drop dead, or as if dead, esp. in fight: to be overthrown: to be taken or captured: to become a victim: to sink or decline, literally or figuratively: to subside, to abate (e.g. the wind): (of the face) to relax into an expression of disappointment: (of the eyes) to droop: to flow, or slope, downwards: to hang down: to yield to temptation: to pass into any state or action: to come to be: to begin (e.g. *to fall a-weeping*): to occur: to come on (e.g. *night falls*): to come as one's share but that they fall, falling said, fell, *pa.p.* fallen (*fō′l(ė)n*).—*n.* the act of falling, in any of its senses: that which falls: as much as comes down at one time (as, *a fall of snow*): overthrow: descent from a better to a worse position: slope or declivity: a descent of water (usu. in *pl.*; e.g. *Niagara Falls*): length of a fall: decrease in value: a sinking: the time when the leaves fall, autumn: a bout at wrestling: a lapse into sin, esp. (*cap.*) that of Adam and Eve.—*adj.* **fall′en**, killed in war: in a degraded state, ruined.—*ns.* **fall′ing-off**, decline; **fall′ing sick′ness**, epilepsy; **tall′ing-star**, a meteor; **fall′-out**, a deposit of radioactive dust from a nuclear explosion or plant: (*coll.*) by-product, side benefit.—**fall away**, to decline gradually: to revolt or apostatise; **fall back**, to retreat, give way; **fall back upon**, to have recourse to (an expedient or resource in reserve); **fall behind**, to slacken, to be outstripped: to get in arrears (with); **fall down on**, to fail in; **fall flat**, to be unsuccessful; **fall for** (*U.S.*), to be captivated by; **fall foul of** (see **foul**); **fall in** (*mil.*), to take places in ranks; **fall in with**, to meet, or find, casually: to concur, agree with, comply with; **fall off**, to deteriorate: to die away: to revolt (from), desert (from e.g. an allegiance); **fall on**, to begin eagerly: to begin to eat: to make an attack on: to meet, find, **fall on one's feet**, to succeed where failure was to be feared: to land fortunately, be lucky; **fall out**, to quarrel: to happen or befall: (*mil.*) quit ranks; **fall over oneself** (*coll.*), to put oneself about (to do something); **fall short of**, to fail to reach; **fall through**, to fail, come to nothing; **fall to**, to begin hastily and eagerly: to apply oneself to. [O.E. *fallan* (W.S. *feallan*); Ger. *fallen*; prob. conn. with L. *fallĕre*, to deceive.]

fall, *föl, n.* a trap.—*n.* **fall′-guy**, a dupe, easy victim: a scapegoat. [O.E. *fealle*—*feallan*, to fall.]

fallacy, *fal′a-si, n.* an apparently genuine but really illogical argument: unsoundness (of argument): delusion (e.g. *pathetic fallacy*, q.v.).—*adj.* **fallacious** (*fa-lā′shús*), calculated to deceive or mislead: not well founded.—*adv.* **falla′ciously.**—*n.* **falla′ciousness**. [O. Fr. *fallace*, deceit—L. *fallācia*—*fallax*, deceptive—*fallĕre*, to deceive.]

fallal, *fal-al'*, *n.* a trifling ornament.—*adj.* foppish. [Ety. uncertain.]

fallible, *fal'i-bl*, *adj.* liable to error or mistake.—*n.* **fallibil'ity,** liability to err.—*adv.* **fall'ibly.** [Fr.,—Low L. *fallibilis*, from *fallĕre*, to deceive.]

Fallopian, *fäl-lō'pi-än*, *adj.* relating to the Italian anatomist *Fallopio*.—**Fallopian tubes,** two tubes or ducts through which the ova pass from the ovary to the uterus.

fallow, *fal'ō*, *adj.* left untilled or unsowed for a time.—*n.* land that has lain a year or more untilled or unsown after having been ploughed.—*v.t.* to plough land without seeding it.—*n.* **fall'owness,** state of being fallow or untilled. [O.E. *fealgian*, to fallow; *fealh*, fallow land.]

fallow, *fal'ō*, *adj.* of a brownish-yellow colour.—*n.* **fall'ow-deer,** a yellowish-brown deer smaller than the red-deer, with broad flat antlers. [O.E. *falu*; cf. O.N. *folr*, Ger. *fahl*.]

false, *föls*, *adj.* wrong, erroneous: incorrect, not according to rule or standard: purposely untrue (as *false witness*): deceptive or deceiving: untruthful: unfaithful: not genuine or real, counterfeit: artificial, as opposed to natural (of teeth, &c.).—*adv.* **false'ly.**—*ns.* **false'hood,** state or quality of being false: want of truth: want of honesty, deceitfulness: an untrue statement; **false'ness; fals'ity,** quality of being false: a false assertion.—**play one false,** to cheat, to betray one; **put in a false position,** to bring anyone into a position in which he is liable to be misunderstood. [O.Fr. *fals* (Fr. *faux*)—L. *falsus*, pa.p. of *fallĕre*, to deceive.]

falsetto, *föl-set'ō*, *n.* a forced voice of a range or register above the natural, the head voice—esp. in a man.—Also *adj.* [It. *falsetto*, dim. of *falso*, false.]

falsify, *föls'i-fī*, *v.t.* to make false or incorrect: to tamper with (a document): to misrepresent: to prove false or incorrect:—*pr.p.* **fals'ifying;** *pa.p.* **fals'ified.**—*ns.* **falsifica'tion,** the act of making false: the giving to a thing the appearance of something which it is not; **fals'ifier,** one who falsifies. [Fr.,—Low L. *falsificāre*—L. *falsus*, false, *facĕre*, to make.]

falter, *föl'tér*, *v.i.* to stumble: to fall or stammer in speech: to flinch: to waver, hesitate in action.—*adv.* **fal'teringly,** in a faltering or hesitating manner. [Prob. a freq. of M.E. *falden*, to fold.]

fame, *fām*, *n.* public report or rumour: renown or celebrity, chiefly in good sense.—*adj.* **famed,** renowned. [Fr.,—L. *fāma*, from *fārī*, to speak.]

familiar, *fa-mil'yár*, *adj.* well acquainted or intimate: showing the manner of an intimate, unceremonious: having a thorough knowledge of (with *with*): well known: common.—*n.* one well or long acquainted: a spirit or demon supposed to attend a person at call.—*v.t.* **famil'iarise,** to make thoroughly acquainted: to accustom: to make easy by practice or study.—*n.* **familiar'ity,** intimate acquaintanceship: freedom from constraint: undue freedom in speech or behaviour.—*adv.* **famil'iarly.** [O.Fr. *familier*—L. *familiāris*, from *familia*, a family.]

family, *fam'i-li*, *n.* the household, or all those who live in one house (as parents, children, servants): parents and their children: the children alone: the descendants of one common progenitor: honourable or noble descent: a group of animals, plants, languages, &c., consisting of several allied genera (see **genus**): (*math.*) a collection of curves in the equations of which different values are given to constants or parameters.—**family circle,** the members of a family taken collectively; **family planning,** regulating size and spacing of family, e.g. by using contraceptives; **family tree,** a genealogical (q.v.) tree. [L. *familia*—*famulus*, a servant.]

famine, *fam'in*, *n.* general scarcity of food: extreme scarcity of anything: hunger, starvation. [Fr.,—L. *famēs*, hunger.]

famish, *fam'ish*, *v.t.* to starve.—*v.i.* to die of or suffer extreme hunger or thirst.—*n.* **fam'ishment,** starvation. [Obs. *fame*, to starve—L. *famēs*, hunger.]

famous, *fā'mus*, *adj.* renowned, noted.—*adv.* **fā'mously,** (*coll.*) very well. [O.Fr.,—L. *fāmōsus*—*fāma*. See **fame.**]

fan, *fan*, *n.* an instrument for winnowing grain or causing a current of air: a broad, flat instrument used by ladies to cool themselves, typically in or spreading into the shape of a sector of a circle: a small sail to keep a windmill to the wind: a rotating ventilating or blowing apparatus: anything spread in a fan shape.—*v.t.* to cool, or to kindle, as with a fan: to winnow: to ventilate:—*pr.p.* **fann'ing;** *pa.p.* **fanned.**—*ns.* **fan'light,** a window resembling in form an open fan; **fann'er,** a machine with revolving fans, used for winnowing grain, &c.; **fan'tail,** a variety of domestic pigeon with tail feathers spread out like a fan; **fan-tracery, -vaulting** (*archit.*), tracery spread like the folds of a fan over the surface of a vault. [O.E. *fann*, from L. *vannus*, a fan.]

fan, *fan*, *n.* a fanatic: now (from U.S. use) an enthusiastic follower of some sport, or hobby, or public favourite.—**fan club,** group united by devotion to a celebrity. [From **fanatic.**]

fanatic, *fa-nat'ik*, *adj.* extravagantly or unreasonably zealous, esp. in religion: excessively enthusiastic.—Also *n.*—*adj.* **fanat'ical,** fanatic.—*adv.* **fanat'ically.**—*n.* **fanat'icism,** wild and excessive enthusiasm, esp. in religious matters. [Fr.,—L. *fānāticus*, belonging to a temple, inspired by a god, *fānum*, a temple.]

fancy, *fan'si*, *n.* that faculty of the mind by which it recalls, represents, or makes to appear past images or impressions—imagination, esp. of a more trivial or more capricious kind: an image or representation thus formed: a delusion: an unreasonable or capricious opinion, a whim: capricious inclination or liking, taste: (*Shak.*) love.—*adj.* pleasing to, or guided by, fancy or caprice: elegant or ornamental.—*v.t.* to portray in the mind: to imagine: to have a fancy or liking for: to be pleased with:—*pr.p.* **fan'cying;** *pa.p.* **fan'cied.**—*n.* **fan'cier,** one who takes pains to acquire a stock of an article, or more usu. an animal, for which he has a special liking, as a *bird-fancier*, a *dog-fancier*.—*adj.* **fan'ciful,** guided or created by fancy: imaginative: whimsical.—*adv.* **fan'cifully.**—*n.* **fan'cifulness.**—*ns.* **fan'cy-**

Neutral vowels in unaccented syllables: *em'pér-ór*; for certain sounds in foreign words see p. ix.

256

(dress-)ball, a ball at which fancy-dresses are worn; **fan′cy-dress,** dress arranged according to the wearer's fancy, e.g. to represent a character in history or fiction; **fan′cy-fair,** a special sale of fancy articles for a charitable purpose.—*adj.* **fan′cy-free** (*Shak.*), free from the power of love.—*n.pl.* **fan′cy-goods,** articles of show and ornament.—**fancy oneself,** to be conceited. [Contracted from **fantasy.**]

fandango, *fan dang′go, n.* an old Spanish dance, proceeding gradually from a slow and uniform step to the liveliest motion. [Sp.]

fane, *fān, n.* a temple. [L. *fānum.*]

fanfare, *fan′fār, fȫfär, n.* a flourish of trumpets or bugles—also **fanfarāde′.**—*ns.* **fan′faron,** one who uses bravado: a braggart; **fanfaronāde′,** vain boasting: bluster. [Fr., perh. from the sound.]

fang, *fang, n.* the tooth of a ravenous beast: a claw or talon: the venom-tooth of a serpent.—*adjs.* **fanged,** having fangs, clutches, or anything resembling them; **fang′less,** having no fangs in tusks numbuned. [O.E. *fang,* from the same root as *fon,* to seize.]

fantasia, *fan-tä′zi-a, n.* a musical composition not governed by the ordinary rules of form. [It.—Gr. *phantasiā.* See **phantasia.**]

fantasy, phantasy, *fan′ta-zi, -si, n.* fancy: imagination: mental image: love: whim, caprice: fantasia: a story, film, &c., not based on realistic characters or setting.—*adjs.* **fantas′tic, -al,** fanciful: not real: capricious: whimsical.—*adv.* **fantas′tically.** [O.Fr., through Low L. from Gr. *phantasiā*—*phantazein,* to make visible. **fancy** is a doublet.]

far, *fär, adj.* remote: more distant of two.—*adv.* to, at, or over a great distance (*lit.* and *fig.*): to or at an advanced stage: in a great degree: very much.—*adjs.* **far′-away′,** distant: abstracted, absent-minded, dreamy (e.g. *a far-away look, expression*), *adv.* **far away,** to or in a distant place); **far′-fetched′,** fetched or brought from a remote place: forced, unnatural (e.g. of a comparison), **far′-off,** distant: (*fig.*) remote: abstracted, far-away (*adv.* **far off,** to or at a considerable distance); **far(-)out,** of jazz or its addicts, more up to date than 'cool': a general term of approval: up to date: eccentric, way-out; **far′-sight′ed,** able to see to a great distance: having defective eyesight for near objects: foreseeing what is likely to happen and preparing for it; **far′-spent,** almost at an end.—**far and away,** by a great deal; **far be it from me to,** God forbid that I should, I would on no account; **far between,** at wide intervals: rare; **far cry,** a long distance, **far from it,** on the contrary.—**by far,** in a very great degree; **in so far as,** to the extent that. See also **farther.** [O.E. *feor(r)*; Du. *ver*; O.N. *fiarre.*]

farad, *far′ad, n.* SI derived unit of electrical capacitance, the capacitance of a capacitor between the plates of which appears a difference of potential of one volt when it is charged by one coulomb of electricity. [From Michael Faraday (1791-1867).]

farce, *färs, n.* a comedy, or style of comedy, marked by broad humour and extravagant wit: ridiculous or empty show.—*adj.* **far′cical,** ludicrous.—*adv.* **far′cically.** [Fr. *farce,* stuffing,

---

from L. *farcīre,* to stuff, apparently applied orig. to a gag introduced into a religious play.]

fardel, *fär′del, n.* a pack: anything burdensome. [O.Fr. *fardel,* dim. of *farde,* a burden—possibly Ar. *fardah,* a package.]

fare, *fār, v.i.* to travel: to get on (well, ill): (*impers.*) to happen (well or ill—with *with*): to be fed.—*n.* the price of passage—(*orig.*) a course or passage: a passenger in a public conveyance: food or provisions for the table.—*interj.* **farewell′,** may you fare well! a wish for safety or success —*n.* well wishing at parting: the act of departure.—*adj.* parting: final. [O.E. *faran*; Ger. *fahren.*]

farina, *fa-rī′na,* or *fa-rē′na, n.* ground corn: meal: starch: pollen of plants.—*adj.* **farina′ceous,** mealy. [L., —*far,* grain.]

farm, *färm, n.* (*obs.*) a fixed payment: land (originally let or rented) for cultivation or pasturage, with the necessary buildings: a piece of land or water used for breeding animals (as *tox-farm, oyster farm*)—*v.t.* to grant, or receive, the revenues of, for a fixed payment: to rent or lease to or from another: to cultivate, as land.—*ns.* **farm′er,** one who farms or cultivates land: the tenant of a farm: one who collects taxes, &c., for a certain rate per cent.; **farm′-house,** a house attached to a farm in which the farmer lives; **farm′ing,** the business of cultivating land; **farm′stead,** a farm with the buildings belonging to it; **farm′-yard,** the yard or enclosure surrounded by the farm buildings.—**farm out,** to board out for fixed payment: to give, e.g. work for which one has made oneself responsible, to others to carry out. [O.E. *feorm,* goods, entertainment, from Low L. *firma,* a fixed payment—L. *firmus,* firm.]

faro, *fār′o, n.* a game of chance played with cards. [Perh. from Pharaoh: reason unknown.]

farrago, *fa-rä′gō,* or *-rä′, n.* a confused mass. [L. *farrago,* mixed fodder—*far,* grain.]

farrier, *far′i-ér, n.* one who shoes horses: one who treats horses's diseases.—*n.* **farr′iery,** the farrier's art: veterinary surgery. [O.Fr. *ferrier*—L. *ferrum,* iron.]

farrow, *far′ō, n.* a litter of pigs.—*v.i.* or *v.t.* to bring forth (pigs). [O.E. *fearh,* a pig.]

farther, *fär′THér*; **far′thermost, far′thest.** Same as **further,** &c. (sometimes preferred when the notion of distance is more prominent). [A variant (M.E. *ferther*) of **further,** that came to be thought a comp of **far.**]

farthing, *fär′THing, n.* coin, the fourth of a pre-1971 penny, withdrawn 1961: anything very small: (*B.*) the name used for two coins, one = 2 farthings, and the other = ¼ of our farthing. [O.E. *fēorthing,* a fourth part—*fēortha,* fourth, and *ing.*]

farthingale, *fär′THing-gāl, n.* a kind of crinoline of whalebone for distending women's dress. [O.Fr. *verdugale*—Sp. *verdugado,* hooped.]

fasces, *fas′ēz, n.pl.* a bundle of rods, with or without an axe, borne before ancient Roman magistrates. [L. pl. of *fascis,* a bundle.]

fascia. See **facia.**

fascicle, *fas′i-kl, n.* a bundle or bunch, esp. a bunched tuft of branches, roots, fibres, &c.: a part of a book issued in parts.—Also **fascicule** (*fas′i-kūl*).—*adjs.* **fascic′ular** (*fas-ik′-*), **fasci-**

c'ulate, -d, united as in a bundle. [L. *fasciculus,* dim. of *fascis,* a bundle.]

fascinate, *fas'i-nāt, v.t.* (*obs.*) to bewitch, enchant: to cast the evil eye upon: to control by the eye like a snake: to hold spellbound: to charm, attract irresistibly.—*adj.* **fas'cinating.**—*n.* **fascinā'tion,** the act of charming: power to harm or influence by looks or spells: mysterious attractive power: state of being fascinated. [L. *fascināre, -ātum,* perh. allied to Gr. *baskainein,* to bewitch.]

Fascism, *fash'izm, n.* the principles and practice of those who believe in a strong centralised government similar to that in Italy from 1922-1944, with suppression of all criticism or opposition.—*n.* and *adj.* **Fasc'ist.** [It. *fascismo—fascio,* a political group, a bundle— L. *fascis.* Cf. **fasces.**]

fash, *fāsh, v.t.* (*Scot.*) to annoy.—*v.i.* to worry.—*n.* trouble. [O.Fr. *fascher* (Fr. *fâcher*)—L. *fastīdium,* disgust.]

fashion, *fash'(ò)n, n.* the make or cut of a thing: form or pattern: prevailing mode or shape of dress: a prevailing custom: manner: genteel society: appearance.—*v.t.* to make: to mould according to a pattern: to suit or adapt.—*n.* **fash'ioner.**—*adj.* **fash'ionable,** according to prevailing fashion: prevailing or in use at any period: observant of the fashion in dress or living: moving in high society.—*n.* **fash'ionableness.**—*adv.* **fash'ionably.**—*ns.* **fash'ionhouse,** an establishment in which fashionable clothes are designed, made and sold; **fash'ion-plate,** a pictorial representation of the latest style of dress: (*fig.*) a very smartly dressed person.—**after, in, a fashion,** in a way: to a certain extent; **in the fashion,** in accordance with the prevailing style of dress, &c.—opp. to *out of fashion.* [O.Fr. *fachon*—L. *factiō, -ōnis—facĕre,* to make.]

fast, *fāst, adj.* firm: fixed: steadfast (e.g. *a fast friend*): unfading (of a colour).—*adv.* firmly, unflinchingly: soundly or sound (asleep): (*poet.*) close, near, hard (by).—*ns.* **fast-andloose,** a cheating game practised at fairs; **fast'ness,** fixedness: a stronghold, fortress, castle.—**make fast,** to lock, bar: to fortify (against); **play fast and loose,** to act unscrupulously; **hard-and-fast,** rigid. [O.E. *fæst*; Ger. *fest.*]

fast, *fāst, adj.* quick: rapid: before time (as a clock): dissipated.—*adv.* swiftly: in rapid succession: in a dissipated manner.—**fast worker,** one who gains his ends quickly and easily by unscrupulous means.—**pull a fast one,** to gain an advantage by trickery. [A special use of *fast,* firm, derived from the Scand., in the sense of urgent.]

fast, *fāst, v.i.* to go hungry: to abstain from food in whole or part, esp. as a religious duty.—*n.* abstinence from food, esp, that enjoined by the church: the day or time of fasting.—*ns.* **fast'ing; fast'-day,** a day of religious fasting. [O.E. *fæstan,* to fast; Ger. *fasten,* to keep.]

fasten, *fäs'n, v.t.* to make fast or firm: to fix securely: to attach.—Also *v.i.—ns.* **fast'ener** (*fäsn'ér*), a clip, catch, or other means of fastening; **fas'tening,** that which fastens.— **fasten (up)on,** to direct (e.g. one's eyes) on: to seize on (e.g. a fact, a statement): to fix

(something disagreeable—e.g. blame) on; **fasten a quarrel on,** to pick a quarrel with. [O.E. *fæstnian.*]

fastidious, *fas-tid'i-us, adj.* affecting superior taste: over-nice: difficult to please.—*adv.* **fastid'iously.**—*n.* **fastid'iousness.** [L. *fastīdiōsus—fastīdium,* loathing.]

fat, *fat, adj.* plump: corpulent: fruitful, profitable.—*n.* an oily substance under the skin: solid animal oil: the richest part of anything.—*v.t.* to make fat.—*v.i.* to grow fat:—*pr.p.* **fatt'ing;** *pa.p.* **fatt'ed.**—*ns.* **fat'head,** a dullard; **fat'ling,** a young animal fattened for slaughter; **fat'ness,** quality or state of being fat: fullness of flesh: richness: fertility.—*v.t.* **fat'en,** to make fat or fleshy: to make fertile.— *v.i.* to grow fat.—*n.* **fatt'ening,** the process of making fat: state of growing fat.—*adjs.* **fat'witt'ed,** dull, stupid; **fatt'y,** containing fat or having the qualities of fat.—*n.* **fatt'iness.—fat stock,** livestock fattened for market; **fatty acids,** acids which with glycerine form fats.— **the fat is in the fire,** something has been imprudently said or done and trouble has begun. [O.E. *fǣtt,* fatted.]

fata morgana, *fä'ta mor-gä'na,* a mirage oftenest seen in the Strait of Messina. [Said to be caused by the fairy (*fata*) *Morgana* of Arthurian romance.]

fate, *fāt, n.* inevitable destiny or necessity: appointed lot: ill-fortune: doom: ultimate lot: (*cap.—pl.*) the three goddesses who determined the birth, life and death of man.—the **fatal sisters.**—*adj.* **fāt'al,** belonging to, or appointed by, fate: causing ruin or death: mortal: disastrous (to): ill-advised.—*ns.* **fāt'alism,** the doctrine that all events happen by unavoidable necessity: acceptance of this doctrine: lack of effort in the face of threatened difficulty or disaster; **fāt'alist,** one who believes in fatalism.—*adj.* **fāt'alistic,** belonging to or partaking of fatalism.—*n.* **fatal'ity,** the state of being fatal or unavoidable: the decree of fate: fixed tendency to disaster or death: an occurrence resulting in death: a death caused by accident.—*adv.* **fāt'ally.**—*adjs.* **fāt'ed,** doomed: destined (to); **fate'ful,** charged with fate. [L. *fātum,* a prediction—*fātus,* spoken— *fārī,* to speak.]

father, *fä'тнér, n.* a male parent: an ancestor or forefather: a fatherly protector: a contriver or originator: a title of respect applied to monks, priests, &c.: the oldest member of any company: one of a group of ecclesiastical writers of the early centuries: (*cap.*) the first person of the Trinity.—*v.t.* to beget: to act as a father towards: to pass as, acknowledge oneself as, the author or originator of: to ascribe to one as his offspring or production (with *on, upon*).—*ns.* **fa'ther-fig'ure,** a senior person of experience and authority looked on as a trusted leader; **fa'therhood,** state of being a father: fatherly authority; **fa'ther-in-law,** the father of one's husband or wife; **fa'therland,** the land of one's fathers.—*adjs.* **fa'therless,** destitute of a living father: without a known author; **fa'therly,** like a father in affection and care: paternal.—*n.* **fa'therliness.—Holy Father,** the Pope. [O.E. *fæder*; Ger. *vater*; L. *pater,* Gr. *patēr,* Sans. *pitṛ.*]

Neutral vowels in unaccented syllables: *em'pėr-ór*; for certain sounds in foreign words see p. ix.

fathom   feather

fathom, *fa·ᴛʜ'ŏm, n.* a nautical measure = 6 feet.—*v.t.* to measure the depth of: to comprehend or get to the bottom of.—*adjs.* **fath'omable; fath'omless.**—*n.* **fath'om-line,** a sailor's line and lead for taking soundings. [O.E. *fæthm*; Du. *vadem,* Ger. *faden.*]

fatigue, *fa-tēg', n.* weariness from labour of body or of mind: toil: military work, distinct from the use of arms, esp. when allotted as a punishment: lessened power of response to a stimulus resulting from excessive activity.—*v.i.* to reduce to weariness: to exhaust the strength or power of recovery of.—*v.i.* to tire:—*pr.p.* fatigu'ing; *pa.p.* fatigued'. [Fr. *fatigue*—L. *fatigāre,* to weary.]

fatuous, *fat'ū-us, adj.* silly, idiotic.—*ns.* **fat'ūousness; fatū'ity,** silliness, inanity: an instance of this. [L. *fatuus.*]

fauces, *fö'sēz, n.pl.* the upper part of the throat, from the root of the tongue to the entrance of the gullet. [L.]

faucet, *fö'set, n.* a pipe inserted in a barrel to draw liquid (U.S.): a water tap. [Fr. *fausset.*]

faugh, *fö, fö, interj.* an exclamation of contempt or disgust. [Prob. from the sound.]

fault, *fölt, n.* failing: error: blemish: a slight offence: (*geol.*) a fracture in the earth's crust causing displacement of strata or veins.—*v.t.* to find fault with: to find flaw(ε) in: (*geol.*) to cause a fault in.—*adj.* **fault'y,** imperfect: (*obs.*) guilty of a fault.—*adv.* **fault'ily.**—*n.* **fault'iness.**—*adj.* **fault'less,** without fault or defect.—*adv.* **fault'lessly.**—*n.* **fault'lessness.—at fault,** (of dogs) unable to find the scent: at a loss: in error; **in fault,** to blame; **find fault** (with), to censure—whence *ns.* **fault'finder, fault'finding.** [O.Fr. *faute, falte*—L. *fallĕre,* to deceive.]

fauna, *fön'a, n.* the animals (collectively) of a region or a period: a list or account of them:—*pl.* **faun'as, faun'ae** (-ē).—*n.* **faun,** a Roman rural deity with horns and tail. [L. *Fauna, Faunus,* tutelary deities of shepherds *favĕre, fautum,* to favour.]

faute de mieux, *fōt dĕ myø,* for want of better. [Fr.]

fauteuil, *fō-tœ-y', also fō'til, n.* an arm-chair: a theatre-stall. [Fr.]

faux pas, *fō' pä', n.* a mistake, esp. one injurious to reputation: a social blunder:—*pl.* **faux pas** (usu. *päz*). [Fr., lit. false step.]

favour, *fā'vŏr, n.* good-will: approval: a kind deed: an act of grace or lenity: partiality: a knot of ribbons worn at a wedding or an election, or anything worn as a token of a lady's favour: (*arch.*) appearance: (*commercial jargon*) a letter.—*v.t.* to regard with good-will: to be on the side of: to treat indulgently: to afford advantage to: to oblige (with): (*coll.*) to resemble.—*adj.* **fā'vourable,** friendly: propitious: conducive (to): expressing approval.—*n.* **fā'vourableness.**—*adv.* **fā'vourably.**—*p.adj.* **fā'voured,** preferred: enjoying advantages: having a certain appearance, featured (as in *ill-favoured, well-favoured*).—*ns.* **fā'vourer; fā'vourite,** a person or thing regarded with favour or preference: one unduly preferred: one expected to win.—*adj.* esteemed, preferred.—*n.* **fā'vouritism,** the showing of undue favour.—**in favour of,** ap-

proving of, in support of: for the benefit of (*withdraw in favour of*): for the account of (a *cheque in favour of*); **in (out of) favour,** (not) approved of. [O.Fr.,—L. *favor—favēre,* to favour, befriend.]

fawn, *fön, n.* a young deer—esp. a fallow deer: its colour—light yellowish-brown.—*adj.* resembling a fawn in colour.—*v.t.* and *v.i.* to bring forth (a fawn). [O.Fr. *faon,* through L.L. from L. *fētus,* offspring.]

fawn, *fön, v.i.* to make demonstrations of affection as a dog does: to flatter in a servile way (with *upon*).—*n.* **fawn'er.**—*adv.* **fawn'ingly.** [A variant of obs. *fain,* to rejoice—O.E. *fægen,* glad.]

fay, *fā, n.* a fairy. [O.Fr. *fae*—L.L. *fāta* (sing.)—L. *fāta* (pl.), the Fates. See **fate.**]

fealty, *fē'al-ti,* or *fēl'ti, n.* the vassal's obligation of fidelity to his feudal lord: loyalty. [O.Fr. *fealte*—L. *fidēlitās, -atis—fidēlis,* faithful—*fidĕre,* to trust.]

fear, *fēr, n.* a painful emotion excited by danger, alarm: apprehension of danger or pain: the object of fear: risk: (*B.*) deep reverence, piety towards God.—*v.t.* to regard with fear: to expect with alarm: to be regretfully inclined to think: (*B.*) to stand in awe of, to venerate: (*obs.*) to make afraid.—*v.i.* to be afraid: to be in doubt.—*adj.* **fear'ful,** timorous: apprehensive (of): exciting intense fear, terrible: (*coll.*) very bad, excessive.—*adv.* **fear'fully.**—*n.* **fear'fulness.**—*adj.* **fear'less,** without fear: daring, brave.—*adv.* **fear'lessly.**—*n.* **fear'lessness.** *adj.* **fear'some,** causing fear, frightful.—**for fear lest, that,** in order that (something may) not (happen); **for fear of,** in order not to (e.g. *for fear of losing it*); **no fear,** it is not likely (that). (*interj.*; *coll.*) not if I can help it! [O.E. *fǣr,* fear, *fǣran,* to terrify.]

feasible, *fēz'i-bl, adj.* practicable, possible.—*ns.* **feas'ibleness, feasibil'ity,**—*adv.* **feas'ibly.** [Fr. *faisable,* that can be done—*faire, faisant*—L. *facēre,* to do.]

feast, *fēst, n.* a day of unusual solemnity or joy: a festival in commemoration of some event: a rich and abundant repast: rich enjoyment for the mind or heart.—*v.i.* to hold a feast: to eat sumptuously: to receive intense delight.—*v.t.* to entertain sumptuously: to delight.—*ns.* **feast'-day; feast'er.** [O.Fr. *feste* (Fr. *fête*)—L. *festum,* a holiday, *festus,* solemn, festal.]

feat, *fēt, n.* a deed manifesting extraordinary strength, skill, or courage. [Fr. *fait*—L. *factum*—L. *facēre,* to do.]

feather, *feᴛʜ'ér, n.* one of the growths that form the covering of a bird: plumage: a feather-like ornament or appearance: anything light or trifling.—*v.t.* to furnish or adorn with feathers: to turn edgewise (as an oar) to lessen air resistance, or to make (a propellor-blade, &c.) rotate in such a way as to lessen resistance.—*ns.* **feath'er-bed,** a mattress filled with feathers (*v.t.* to pamper); **feath'er-brain,** a frivolous person; **feath'er-stitch,** one of a series of stitches making a zigzag feather-like line; **feath'er(-)weight,** the lightest weight that may be carried by a racehorse: a boxer of not less than 8 st. 6 lb. (amateur 8 st. 7 lb.) and not more than 9 st.: a person of small importance or ability.—*adj.*

fāte, fär; mē, hûr (her); *mīne; mōte, för; mūte, mōōn, fŏŏt;* ᴛʜen (then)

259

feath′ery, pertaining to, resembling, or covered with, feathers.—**feather one's nest,** to accumulate wealth for oneself while serving others in a position of trust.—**a feather in one's cap,** striking mark of distinction; **birds of a feather,** persons of like character; **be in high feather,** to be in high spirits; **show the white feather,** to show signs of cowardice—a white feather in a gamecock's tail being considered as a sign of degeneracy. [O.E. *fether*; Ger. *feder*; L. *penna,* Gr. *pteron.*]

feature, *fē′tyùr, -chùr, n.* a prominent trait: a characteristic: a part of the body, esp. of the face: anything offered as a special attraction: a non-news article in a newspaper: (*pl.*) the countenance.—*v.t.* (*coll.*) to have features resembling: to give special prominence to.—*adj.* **fea′tureless,** destitute of distinct features.—**feature programme,** radio, &c. programme that presents dramatically the life of a prominent person, an event, or an activity. [O.Fr *faiture* — L. *factūra* — *facĕre,* to make.]

febrifuge, *feb′ri-fūj, n.* a medicine for reducing fever. [L. *febris,* fever, *fugāre,* to put to flight.]

febrile, *fēb′ril,* or *feb′ril, adj.* pertaining to fever: feverish.—*n.* **febril′ity.** [Fr.,—L. *febris,* fever.]

February, *feb′rōō-àr-i, n.* the second month of the year. [L. *Februārius* (*mensis*), the month of expiation, *februa,* the feast of expiation.]

feces, fecal. See **faeces, faecal.**

feckless, *fek′les, adj.* shiftless, worthless, inefficient. [Scot. *feck,* perh. from **effect,** and suffx. *-less.*]

feculent, *fek′ū-lént, adj.* containing faeces or sediment: foul: turbid.—*ns.* **fec′ulence, fec′ulency.** [L. *faecula,* dim. of *faex,* dregs.]

fecund, *fek′und, adj.* fruitful, fertile, prolific.—*v.t.* **fec′undāte** (or *fek-und′āt*), to make fruitful: to impregnate.—*ns.* **fecundā′tion,** the act of impregnating: the state of being impregnated; **fecund′ity,** fruitfulness, prolificness. [Fr.,—L. *fēcundus,* fruitful.]

fed, *pa.t.* and *pa.p.* of **feed.**

federal, *fed′ér-ál, adj.* pertaining to or consisting of a treaty or covenant: confederated, founded upon mutual agreement: of a union or government in which several states, while independent in home affairs, combine for national or general purposes, as in the United States—(in the American Civil War, *Federal* was the name applied to the states of the North which defended the Union against the *Confederate* separatists of the South).—*n.* a supporter of federation.—*v.t.* **fed′eralise.**—*ns.* **fed′eralism,** the principles or cause maintained by federalists; **fed′eralist,** a supporter of a federal constitution or union.—*v.t.* and *v.i.* **fed′erāte,** to join in a league or federation.—*adj.* (*-àt*) united by league: confederated.—*n.* **federā′tion,** the act of uniting in league: a federal union.—*adj.* **fed′erātive,** of, of the nature of, forming part of, inclined to or tending to form, a federation or league.—**Federal Bureau of Investigation,** in the United States, a bureau or subdivision of the Department of Justice which investigates crimes, such as smuggling and espionage, that are the concern of the federal government; **Federal Parliament,** the parliament of the Commonwealth of Australia. [Fr. *fédéral* — L. *foedus, -eris,* a treaty, akin to *fīdĕre,* to trust.]

fee, *fē, n.* price paid for professional services: wages: the sum exacted for any special privilege.—*v.t.* to pay a, fee to: to hire:—*pr.p.* fee′ing; *pa.p.* feed. [O.E. *feoh,* cattle, property: a special kind of property, property in land; Ger. *vieh,* O.N. *fē*; allied to L. *pecus,* cattle, *pecūnia,* money.]

fee, *fē, n.* a grant of land for feudal service: fee-simple: possession, ownership.—*n.* **fee′-sim′ple,** unconditional inheritance. [Anglo-Fr. *fee,* O.Fr. *fi(e)u, fief* —Gmc., prob. allied to **fee** (1).]

feeble, *fē′bl, adj.* very weak: lacking force, ability, or effectiveness: faint—*adj.* **fee′ble-mind′ed,** weak-minded, mentally deficient: irresolute.—*n.* **fee′bleness.**—*adv.* **fee′bly.** [O.Fr. *feble, foible,* for *floible* — L. *flēbilis,* lamentable, from *flēre,* to weep.]

feed, *fēd, v.t.* to give food to: to nourish: to furnish with necessary material: to furnish (an actor) with cues or opportunities for achieving an effect: in football, to pass the ball to: to foster.—*v.i.* to take food: to nourish oneself by eating:—*pr.p.* feed′ing; *pa.t.* and *pa.p.* fed.—*n.* an allowance of provender, esp. to cattle.—*n.* **feed′er,** one who feeds, or that which supplies: a feeding-bottle: a bib.—*adj.* secondary, subsidiary, tributary.—*ns.* **feed′-back,** return of part of the output of a system to the input as a means towards improved quality or self-correction of error; used also of biological, &c., self-adjusting systems; **feed′ing-bott′le,** a bottle for supplying liquid food to an infant; **feed′-pipe,** a pipe for supplying a boiler or cistern with water; **feed′-water,** water supplied to a boiler, &c.—**fed up** (*slang*), sated and wearied (with; also with *of*). [O.E. *fēdan,* to feed.]

feel, *fēl, v.t.* to perceive by the touch: to try by touch: to grope (one's way): to be conscious of: to have an inward persuasion of: to experience.—*v.i.* to know by the touch: to have the emotions excited: to produce a certain sensation when touched (as *to feel hard* or *hot*):—*pr.p.* feel′ing; *pa.t.* and *pa.p.* felt.—*n.* the sense of touch: a quality as revealed to the touch (e.g. *it has a soapy feel*): a quality of atmosphere of which one is conscious (e.g. *an eerie feel*).—*ns.* **feel′er,** a remark or an action intended to sound the opinions of others: a tentacle: an antenna; **feel′ing,** the sense of touch: perception of objects by touch: consciousness of pleasure or pain: tenderness: emotion: emotional responsiveness: opinion as resulting from emotion: (*pl.*) the affections or passions: (*pl.*) sensibilities.—*adj.* expressive of great sensibility or tenderness: easily affected.—*adv.* **feel′ingly.**—**bad feeling,** animosity: ill-feeling; **good feeling,** kindly feeling: amicable relations. [O.E. *fēlan,* to feel; Ger. *fūhlen*; prob. akin to L. *palpāre,* to stroke.]

feet, *fēt, pl.* of **foot.**

feign, *fān, v.t.* to invent: (*arch.*), to imagine: to make pretence of, simulate.—*adj.* **feigned,** pretended.—*adv.* **feign′edly.**—*n.* **feign′edness.** [Fr. *feindre,* pr.p. *feignant,* to feign—L. *fingĕre, fictum,* to form.]

feint, *fānt, n.* a false appearance, a pretence: a

Neutral vowels in unaccented syllables: *em′pér-ór*; for certain sounds in foreign words see p. ix.

260

mock-assault: a deceptive movement in fencing, &c.—*v.i.* to make a feint. [Fr. *feinte*—*feindre*. See **feign**.]

feint, *fānt*, *adj.* a printers' and stationers' spelling of **faint**.

feldspar, *fel(d)'spär*, **felspar**, *fel'spär*, *n.* any member of the most important group of rock-forming minerals, compounds of aluminium and silicon, containing also potassium, calcium or sodium.—*adj.* **fel(d)spathic**, pertaining to or consisting of feldspar. [Swed. *feldtspat*—*feld*, field, *spat*, spar.]

felicity, *fe-lis'i-ti*, *n.* happiness: a blessing: a happy event: an appropriateness or happiness (of expression).—*v.t.* **felic'itāte**, to express joy or pleasure to: to congratulate.—*n.* **felicitā'tion**, the act of congratulating.—*adj.* **felic'itous**, happy: prosperous: delightful: appropriate.—*adv.* **felic'itously**. [Fr.,—L. *fēlicitās*, *-ātis*—*fēlix*, *-īcis*, happy.]

feline, *fē'līn*, *adj.* pertaining to the cat or the cat kind: like a cat. [L. *fēlīnus*—*fēles*, a cat.]

fell, *fel*, *n.* a hill, an upland tract of waste, pasture, or moorland. [O.N. *fjall*; Dan. *fjeld*.]

fell, *fel*, *pa.t.* of **fall**.

fell, *fel*, *v.t.* to cause to fall: to strike to the ground: to cut down.—*n.* **fell'er**. [O.E. *fellan*, causal form of *fallan*, to fall.]

fell, *fel*, *n.* a skin. [O.E. *fel*; cf. L. *pellis*, Gr. *pella*, Ger. *fell*.]

fell, *fel*, *adj.* cruel, fierce, bloody, deadly.—*adv.* (*Scot.*) very, very much. [O.Fr. *fel*, cruel—Low L. *fellō*, *-ōnis*. See **felon**.]

fellah, *fel'ä*, *n.* a peasant, esp. in Egypt: *pl.* **fell'ahs**, **fell'ahīn**. [Ar. *fellāh*, tiller of the soil.]

felloe. See **felly**.

fellow, *fel'ō*, *n.* an associate: a companion and equal: one of a pair, a mate: a member of a university who holds a fellowship: a member of a scientific or other society: a man generally: a worthless person.—*adj.* belonging to the same group or class, as **fell'ow-cit'izen**, **fell'ow-man**, &c.—*ns.* **fell'ow-feel'ing**, feeling between fellows or equals, sympathy; **fell'owship**, the state of being a fellow or partner: friendly intercourse: communion: an association: an endowment in a college for the support of graduates called fellows: the position and income of a fellow.—**fellow traveller**, one who travels in the same railway carriage, bus, &c., or along the same route: (*fig.*, used derogatorily) one who takes the same political road, a sympathiser. [M.E. *felawe*—O.N. *fēlagi*, a partner in goods, from *fē* (Ger. *vieh*), cattle, property, and root *lag-*, a laying together, a law.]

felly, *fel'i*, **felloe**, *fel'i*, or *-ō*, *n.* one of the curved pieces in the circumference of a wheel: the whole circular rim of the wheel. [O.E. *felg*; Ger. *felge*.]

felo de se, *fel'ō di sē'*, *n.* one who kills himself: self-murder. [Anglo-L., a felon towards himself.]

felon, *fel'ón*, *n.* one guilty of felony: a convict: a wicked person: an inflamed sore.—*adj.* wicked or cruel.—*adj.* **felō'nious**, wicked: depraved: done with the deliberate intention to commit crime.—*adv.* **felō'niously**.—*n.* **fel'ony**, (*orig.*) a crime punished by total forfeiture of lands, &c.: a crime punishable by penal servitude or

death. [O.Fr.,—Low L. *fellō*, *-ōnis*, a traitor.]

felspar. See **feldspar**.

felt, *felt*, *pa.t.* and *pa.p.* of **feel**.

felt, *felt*, *n.* a woollen fabric formed without weaving.—*v.i.* to become like felt.—*v.t.* to make into felt: to cover with felt.—*n.* **felt'ing**, the art or process of making felt: the felt itself. [O.E. *felt*; cf. Du. *vilt*, Ger. *filz*.]

felucca, *fe-luk'a*, *n.* a small merchant-vessel used in the Mediterranean. [It. *feluca*—Ar. *fulk*, a ship.]

female, *fē'māl*, *adj.* of the sex that produces young: pertaining to females: (*bot.*) having a pistil or fruit-bearing organ.—*n.* one of the female sex: a woman (sometimes used derogatorily). [Fr. *femelle*—L. *femella*, dim. of *fēmina*, a woman.]

feminine, *fem'i-nin*, *adj.* pertaining to women: womanly: womanish: (*gram.*) of that gender to which words denoting females belong.—*adv.* **fem'ininely**.—*ns.* **fem'inism**, advocacy of women's rights: feminist: support of femininism; **femininity**, the quality of being feminine.—**fem'inine end'ing**, (Fr. prosody) ending of a line in mute 'e' (because this is a feminine suffix): (English) ending in an unstressed, following a stressed, syllable; **feminine rhyme**, a rhyme on a feminine ending. [L. *fēmina*, woman.]

femme fatale, *fam fä-täl*, a woman of irresistible charm, esp. one who brings unhappiness to herself and others. [Fr., fatal woman.]

femur, *fē'mùr*, *n.* the thigh-bone.—*adj.* **fēm'oral**, belonging to the thigh. [L. *fēmur*, *-ŏris*, thigh.]

fen, *fen*, *n.* a kind of low marshy land wholly or partially covered with water, or often inundated:—*adjs.* **fenn'y**, **fenn'ish**. [O.E. *fenn*; O.N. *fen*.]

fence, *fens*, *n.* a barrier for enclosing, bounding, or protecting land: the art of fencing with a sword: defence: (*slang*) a receiver of stolen goods.—*v.t.* to enclose with a fence: to fortify—*v.i.* to practise fencing: to make evasive answers: (*slang*) to be a receiver or purchaser of stolen goods.—*ns.* **fenc'er**, a maker of fences: one who practises fencing with a sword; **fenc'ible**, (*hist.*) a militiaman or enlisted volunteer for local defence in a crisis; **fencing**, the act of erecting a fence: material for doing so: the art of attack and defence with a sword or other hand-weapon: parrying argument.—**sunk fence**, a ditch or watercourse. [Abbrev. of **defence**.]

fend, *fend*, *v.t.* to ward (off): to shut out: (*arch.*) to defend.—*v.i.* to offer resistance: to provide (for). [Abbrev. of **defend**.]

fender, *fend'ér*, *n.* a guard before a hearth to confine the ashes: a bundle of rope, &c., to protect a ship's side against piers, &c.: any structure serving as a guard against contact or impact. [**fend**.]

fenestra, *fe-nes'tra*, *n.* a window.—*adj.* **fenes'tral**, belonging to, or like, a window: perforated—also **fenes'trāte(d)**.—*n.* **fenestrā'tion**, the arrangement of windows in a building. [L.]

Fenian, *fē'ni-án*, *n.* a member of an association of Irishmen founded in 1857 for the overthrow of the English government in Ireland.—*n.* **Fē'nianism**. [Old Ir. *Féne*, one of the names of the ancient population of Ireland.]

---

fāte, *fär*; *mē*, *hûr* (her); *mīne*, *mōte*, *för*; *mūte*, *mōōn*, *fŏŏt*; THen (then)

fennel, *fen'él, n.* a genus of fragrant umbelliferous plants with yellow flowers. [O.E. *finul*— L. *fēniculum,* fennel—*fēnum,* hay.]

feoff, *fef, n.* a fief.—*n.* **feoff'ment,** the gift of a fief. [O.Fr. *feoffer* or *fiefer*—O.Fr. *fief.* See **fee** (2).]

feral, *fē'rál, adj.* wild: untamed: pertaining to or like a wild beast.—Also **fēr'ine** (*-rīn, -rin*). [L. *fera,* a wild beast.]

ferial, *fē'ri-ál, adj.* pertaining to holidays: (*eccles.*) belonging to any day of the week that is neither a fast nor a festival. [Fr.,—L. *fēria,* a holiday.]

ferment, *fûr'mént, n.* a substance that excites fermentation—formerly divided into *organised ferments* (i.e. living organisms) and *chemical ferments* (enzymes); but it is now known that the organised ferments produce enzymes, and these cause the fermentátion: internal motion among the parts of a fluid: (*fig.*) agitation, tumult.—*v.t.* **ferment',** to excite fermentation in: to inflame.—*v.i.* to rise and swell by the action of fermentation: to work, used of wine, &c.: to be in excited action: to be stirred with anger.—*adj.* **ferment'able,** capable of fermentation.—*ns.* **fermentabil'ity, fermentā'tion,** a slow decomposition of organic substances, usually accompanied by evolution of heat and gas, e.g. alcoholic fermentation of sugar and starch: restless action of the mind or feelings.—*adj.* **ferment'ative,** causing, or consisting in, fermentation. [Fr.,—L. *fermentum,* for *fervi mentum*—*fervēre,* to boil.]

fermi, *fûr'mi, n.* obsolescent unit of distance $= 10^{-15}$m.—*ns.* **fer'mion,** one of a group of subatomic particles; **fer'mium,** a transuranium element, atomic number 100, symbol Fm. [Italian physicist Enrico *Fermi* (1901-54).]

fern, *fûrn, n.* an order of plants with no flowers and beautiful feather-like leaves, some of which, in the tropics, attain the dimensions of a tree.—*adj.* **fern'y.** [O.E. *fearn;* Ger. *farn.*]

ferocious, *fe-rō'shús, adj.* savage, fierce: cruel.—*adv.* **ferō'ciously.**—*ns.* **ferō'ciousness;** **feroc'ity,** savage cruelty of disposition: untamed fierceness: an act showing this. [L. *ferŏx, ferŏcis,* wild—*ferus,* wild.]

ferrara, *fer-ä'ra, n.* a famous make of swordblade said to have been named after an Italian family of sword-makers. [Perh. a native of *Ferrara,* or prob. merely the It. *ferrajo,* a cutler—L. *ferrārius,* a smith.]

ferret, *fer'et, n.* a half-tamed albino variety of the polecat, employed in unearthing rabbits.—*v.t.* to drive out of a hiding-place: to search (out) cunningly and persistently:—*pr.p.* ferr'eting; *pa.p.* ferr'eted. [O.Fr. *furet,* a ferret—Low L. *fūrō, -ōnis,* ferret—L. *fūr,* a thief.]

ferri-, ferro-, (ferr-), in composition, of, containing iron [L. *ferrum,* iron]:—e.g. **ferr'eous,** of, containing, iron; **ferr'ite,** a form of pure iron: any of a type of new magnetic materials, mixed oxides of iron, manganese, aluminium, &c., which are also electric insulators; **ferrug'inous** (*-ōōj*- or *-ūj*-; L. *ferrūgŏ, -īnis,* iron rust), containing iron rust or iron: rust-coloured; **ferri'ferous,** (*-ferous* from L. *ferre,* to bear), of rocks, iron-yielding; **ferr'o-all'oy,**

an alloy of iron and some other metal; **ferr'o-con'crete,** reinforced concrete; **ferr'o-type,** a photograph taken on a thin iron plate.—**ferri-, ferro-,** and similarly the *adjs.* **ferric** and **ferrous,** are used for compounds in which iron has respectively its higher and its lower combining power (the former almost always a valency of 3, the latter a valency of 2), e.g. *ferric oxide* (Fe_2O_3) hematite; *ferrous oxide* (FeO).—*adj.* **ferromagnet'ic,** highly magnetic.

ferrule, *fer'úl, fer'(y)ŏŏl, n.* a metal ring or cap on a staff, &c., to keep it from splitting. [O.Fr. *virole*—L. *viriola,* a bracelet.]

ferry, *fer'i, v.t.* to carry or convey over water (or land), esp. along a regular route, in a boat, ship, or aircraft: to deliver (an aircraft coming from a factory) under its own power:—*pr.p.* ferr'ying; *pa.p.* ferr'ied.—*n.* a place or route of carriage across water: the right of ferrying: a ferryboat. [O.E. *ferian,* to convey, *faran,* to go; Ger. *fähre,* a ferry—*fahren,* to go, to carry.]

fertile, *fûr'tīl, -til, adj.* able to bear or produce abundantly: rich in resources: inventive.—*adv.* **fer'tilely.**—*v.t.* **fer'tilīse,** to make fertile or fruitful: to enrich: to impregnate: to pollinate.—*ns.* **fertilisā'tion; fer'tiliser; fertil'ity,** fruitfulness, richness: abundance. [Fr.,—L. *fertilis*—*ferre,* to bear.]

ferule, *fer'(y)ŏŏl, n.* a rod used for punishment. [L. *ferula,* a cane—*ferīre,* to strike.]

fervent, *fûr'vént, adj.* hot: ardent, zealous, warm in feeling.—*n.* **fer'vency,** eagerness: emotional warmth.—*adv.* **fer'vently.**—*adj.* **fer'vid,** very hot: having burning desire or emotion: zealous.—*adv.* **fer'vidly.**—*ns.* **fer'vidness; fer'vour,** heat: heat of mind, zeal. [Fr.,—L. *fervēre,* to boil.]

fess, fesse, *fes, n.* (*her.*) a band drawn horizontally across the middle of an escutcheon. [Fr. *fasce*—L. *fascia,* a band.]

festal, *fes'tál, adj.* pertaining to a feast or holiday: joyous: gay.—*adv.* **fes'tally.** [Fr.,—O.Fr. *feste.* See **feast.**]

fester, *fes'tér, v.i.* to become corrupt: to suppurate: (*fig.*) to rankle.—*v.t.* to cause to fester or rankle.—*n.* a wound discharging corrupt matter. [O.Fr. *festre*—L. *fistula,* an ulcer.]

festive, *fes'tiv, adj.* festal: mirthful.—*n.* **fes'tival,** a joyful celebration: a feast: a season of performances of music, plays, or the like.—*adv.* **fes'tively.**—*n.* **festiv'ity,** social mirth: a festive celebration: gaiety. [L. *fēstīvus*—*fēstus.*]

festoon, *fes-tōōn', n.* a garland suspended between two points: (*archit.*) an ornament like a wreath of flowers, &c.—*v.t.* to adorn as with festoons. [Fr. *feston,* app. conn. with L. *fēstum.* See **feast.**]

fetal. See **foetus.**

fetch, *fech, v.t.* to bring: to go and get: to obtain as its price: to cause to come: (*coll.*) to interest, delight: to heave (a sigh): to utter (a groan): to draw (a breath).—*n.* range, sweep (e.g. of imagination): a stratagem, trick.—*adj.* **fetch'ing,** fascinating.—**fetch up,** to recover: to stop suddenly. [O.E. *feccan,* app. an altered form of *fetian,* to fetch; cf. Ger. *fassen,* to seize.]

fetch, *fech, n.* the apparition of a living person.—*n.* **fetch'-can'dle,** a nocturnal light, supposed to portend a death. [Ety. unknown.]

Neutral vowels in unaccented syllables: *em'pér-ór;* for certain sounds in foreign words see p. ix.

fête, *fet, fāt, n.* a festival: a holiday.—*v.t.* to entertain at a feast: to honour with festivities. [Fr.]

fetich, fetish, *fet'ish, fē'tish, n.* an object believed to procure for its owner the services of a spirit lodged within it: something regarded with irrational reverence.—*ns.* **fet'ichism, fet'ishism**, the worship of a fetish: a belief in charms. [Fr. *fétiche*—Port. *feitico*, magic: a name given by the Portuguese to the gods of West Africa—Port. *feitiço*, artificial—L. *factītius—facĕre*, to make.]

feticide. See **foetus.**

fetid, *fē'tid, or fet'id, adj.* stinking, having a strong offensive smell. [L.*foetidus—foetēre*, to stink.]

fetlock, *fet'lok, n.* a tuft of hair that grows above a horse's hoof: the part where this hair grows. [History obscure; compounded of *foot* and *lock* (of hair); cf. Ger. *fissloch.*]

fetter, *fet'ér, n.* (used chiefly in *pl.*) a chain or shackle for the feet: anything that restrains.—*v.t.* to put fetters on: to restrain.—*adj.* **fett'ered.** [O.E. *feter—fōt*, foot.]

fettle, *fet'l, n.* trim, form, condition, as *in fine fettle.* [Prob. O.E. *fetel*, a belt.]

fetus. See **foetus.**

feu, *fū, n.* a tenure by which the vassal, in place of military services, made a return in grain or in money: (*Scot.*) a right to the use of land in perpetuity for a stipulated annual payment (**feu'-dū'ty**).—*v.t.* to vest in one who undertakes to pay the feu-duty.—*n.* **feu'ar**, one who holds real estate in consideration of payment of feu-duty.—*adj.* **feud'al**, pertaining to a feu.—**ground to feu**, ground for feuing, to be feued. [O.Fr. *fi(e)u.* See the variant **fee** (2).]

feud, *fūd, n.* a deadly quarrel between families or clans: a persistent state of enmity. [O.Fr. *faide, feide*—Low L. *faida*—O.H.G. *fēhida.* Akin to **foe.**]

feud, *fūd, n.* a fief or land held on condition of service.—*adj.* **feud'al**, pertaining to feuds or fiefs: belonging to feudalism.—*n.* **feud'alism**, the feudal system or its principles: a class-conscious social or political system resembling the mediaeval feudal system.—*adj.* **feud'atory**, holding lands or power by a feudal tenure. Also *n.*—**feudal system**, the system, during the Middle Ages, by which vassals held lands from lords-superior on condition of military service. [Low L. *feudum*—Gmc.; connected with **fee** (2).]

feuilleton, *fœy-tō, n.* in French and other newspapers, a part ruled off at the bottom of the page for a serial story, critical article, &c.: a contribution of such a kind. [Fr. double dim. of *feuille*, a leaf—L. *folium.*]

fever, *fē'vér, n.* disease, esp. infectious, marked by great bodily heat and quickening of pulse: extreme excitement of the passions, agitation: a painful degree of anxiety.—*v.t.* to put into a fever.—*v.i.* to become fevered.—*adj.* **fē'vered**, affected with fever: excited.—*ns.* **fē'ver-few**, a herb allied to camomile, formerly used as a febrifuge; **fē'ver-heat**, the heat of fever: an excessive degree of excitement.—*adj.* **fē'verish**, slightly fevered: indicating fever: restlessly excited.—*adv.* **fē'verishly.**—*n.* **fē'verishness.** [O.E. *fēfor*—L. *febris.*]

few, *fū, adj.* small in number, not many.—*n.*

few'ness.—**a few**, a small number (of)—used as a noun, or virtually a compound adjective; **a good few** (*dial.*), a considerable number. [O.E. *fēa*, pl. *fēawe*; Fr. *peu*; L. *paucus*, small.]

fey, fay, *fā, adj.* (*Scot.*) doomed, fated soon to die—a condition said to be marked often by extravagantly high spirits: (*Scot.*) foreseeing the future, esp. calamity: eccentric, slightly mad: supernatural: fairy-like: elfin. [M.E. *fay, fey*—O.E. *fǣge*, doomed; cf. Du. *veeg*, about to die.]

fez, *fez, n.* a red brimless cap with black tassel worn in Egypt, and formerly in Turkey, a variety of *tarboosh*:—*pl.* **fezz'es.** [From *Fez* in Morocco.]

fiancé, *fem.* **fiancée**, *fē-ä'sā, n.* a person engaged to be married (with possessive case of noun or pronoun—e.g. *her fiancé was there*). [Fr.]

fiasco, *fi-as'kō, n.* a failure in a musical performance: an utter failure of any kind. [It. *fiasco*, bottle, perh.—L. *vasculum.* See **flask.**]

fiat, *fī'at, n.* a formal or solemn command: a decree. [L. 'let it be done', 3rd pers. sing. pres. subj. of *fiĕrī*, passive of *facĕre*, to do.]

fib, *fib, n.* something untrue (a mild expression for a lie).—*v.i.* to tell a fib or lie:—*pr.p.* **fib'bing;** *pa.p.* **fibbed.** [Perh. **fable.**]

fibre, *fī'bér, n.* any fine thread-like object of animal, vegetable or mineral origin, natural or synthetic: a structure or material composed of fibres: texture.—*n.* **fi'breboard**, a building-board made from compressed fibrous materials.—*adj.* **fi'bred**, having fibres—*n.* **fi'breglass**, a synthetic fibre made of extremely fine filaments of molten glass, used in textile manufacture, in heat and sound insulation and in reinforced plastics.—*adj.* **fi'breless**, without fibre, strength, or nerve.—*n.* **fi'bril**, a small fibre: one of the extremely minute threads composing muscle fibre, &c.—*adj.* **fi'brillous**, formed of small fibres.—*ns.* **fi'brin**, an insoluble protein precipitated as a network of fibres when blood coagulates; **fibrosit'is**, inflammation (esp. rheumatic) of fibrous tissues.—*adj.* **fi'brous**, composed of fibres.—*n.* **fi'brousness.** [Fr.,—L. *fibra*, a thread.]

fibula, *fib'u-la, n.* a brooch: the outer of the two bones from the knee to the ankle. [L.]

fichu, *fē'shū, n.* a woman's three-cornered cape for the neck and shoulders. [Fr.]

fickle, *fik'l, adj.* inconstant: changeable.—*n.* **fick'leness.** [O.E. *ficol; gefic*, fraud.]

fictile, *fik'tīl, -til, adj.* used, or fashioned, by the potter: of pottery: (*rare*) plastic. [L. *fictilis—fingĕre*, to fashion.]

fiction, *fik'sh(ō)n, n.* a feigned or false story: a falsehood: a pretence: the novel as a branch of literature.—*adjs.* **fic'tional**, imaginative, not restricted to fact: pertaining to fiction; **fic'titious** (*-tish'ŭs*), imaginary, not real, feigned.—*adv.* **ficti'tiously.** [Fr.,—L. *fictiō, -ōnis—fictus*, pa.p. of *fingĕre.*]

fiddle, *fid'l, n.* a violin: extended to similar instruments, as *bass fiddle*: a device to keep dishes from sliding off a table at sea: (*slang*) a swindle, esp. petty.—*v.t.* or *v.i.* to play on a fiddle.—*v.t.* to swindle: to falsify.—*v.i.* to be busy over trifles, to trifle.—*interjs.* **fidd'le-dedee, fidd'lestick** (often *pl.*), nonsense!—*n.* **fidd'ler**, one who fiddles: a kind of small crab.— **play first,** or **second, fiddle,** to take a leading, or a subordinate, part in anything. [O.E. *fithele*; Ger. *fiedel*. From same root as **viol, violin.**]

fidelity, *fi-del′i-ti, n.* faithful performance of duty: loyalty: faithfulness to a husband or wife: exactitude in reproducing. [L. *fidēlitās, -ātis—fidēlis,* faithful—*fīdĕre,* to trust.]

fidget, *fij′et, v.i.* to be unable to rest: to move uneasily:—*pr.p.* fidg′eting; *pa.p.* fidg′eted.—*n.* one who fidgets: restlessness: (*pl.*) general nervous restlessness.—*adj.* **fidg′ety,** restless: uneasy.—*n.* **fidg′etiness.** [Perh. related to O.N. *fīkja.*]

fiducial, *fi-dū′shi-ăl, adj.* showing confidence or reliance: of the nature of trust: serving as a standard of reference (in surveying, &c., *fiducial line, point*).—*adv.* **fidū′cially.**—*adj.* **fidū′ciary,** of the nature of a trust: depending upon public confidence: held in trust.—*n.* one who holds anything in trust. [L. *fīdūcia,* confidence, from *fīdĕre,* to trust.]

fief, *fēf, n.* (*hist.*) land held of a feudal superior in return for service: land held in *fee.* [O.Fr. See **fee** (2).]

field, *fēld, n.* country or open country in general: a piece of ground enclosed for tillage, pasture, or sport: the locality of a battle (*lit.* and *fig.*): the battle itself: an expanse (e.g. *icefield*): a tract yielding a natural product (e.g. gold, coal): an area affected in a particular way (e.g. *magnetic field*): the area visible at one time (as in microscopy): (*fig.*) sphere of activity, knowledge, &c.: (*her.*) the surface of a shield: the background on which figures are drawn: those taking part in a hunt or a horse-race: players or competitors collectively: (*math.*) a system or collection of elements upon which binary operations of addition, subtraction, multiplication, and division can be performed except that division by 0 is excluded.—*v.t.* at cricket and baseball, to catch or stop and return to the fixed place: to put (e.g. a team) into the field to play.—*v.i.* to stand ready to stop the ball in cricket or baseball.—*ns.* **field′-artill′ery,** ordnance (light, medium, or heavy) suited for active operations in the field; **field′-batt′ery,** a battery of field-artillery; **field′-book,** a book used in surveying fields, &c.; **field′-day,** a day when troops are drawn out for instruction in field exercises: any day of unusual bustle or success; **field′er,** one who fields; **field′-event,** an athletic event other than a race; **field′fare,** a species of thrush, having a reddish-yellow throat and breast spotted with black; **field′-glass,** a telescope (usu. binocular) for use in the field; **field′-gun,** a light cannon mounted on a carriage; **field′-hos′pital,** a temporary hospital near the scene of battle; **field′-ice,** ice formed in the polar seas in large surfaces, distinguished from icebergs; **field′-mar′shal,** an officer of the highest rank in the army; **field′-off′icer,** a military officer above the rank of captain, and below that of general; **field′piece,** a field-gun; **fields′man,** a fielder; **field′-sport,** a sport of the field, as hunting, racing; **field trial,** a test in practice, as distinct from one under laboratory conditions; **field′work,** (*hist.*; often in *pl.*) a temporary

fortification thrown up by troops in the field: farm work in the fields: scientific work, e.g. collecting facts, carried on outside the laboratory or office.—*ns.* **field mouse, field vole** (see **mouse, vole**).—**keep the field,** to hold one's ground. [O.E. *feld*; cf. Du. *veld,* the open country, Ger. *feld.*]

fiend, *fēnd, n.* (*cap.*) Satan: a devil: one actuated by the most intense wickedness or hate: (*coll.*) an enthusiast.—*adj.* **fiend′ish,** like a fiend: devilishly cruel.—*n.* **fiend′ishness.** [O.E. *fēond,* enemy; Ger. *feind,* Du. *vijand.*]

fierce, *fērs, adj.* ferocious, angry: violent.—*adv.* **fierce′ly.**—*n.* **fierce′ness.** [O.Fr. *fers* (Fr. *fier*) —L. *ferus,* wild, savage.]

fiery, *fīr′i, adj.* like, or consisting of, fire: ardent, impetuous: irritable.—*adv.* **fier′ily.**—*ns.* **fier′iness; fier′y-cross,** a cross of two sticks, charred and dipped in blood, sent round a district to summon clansmen to arms. [**fire.**]

fiesta, *fē-es′ta, n.* a saint's day: holiday: festivity. [Sp.]

fife, *fīf, n.* a small variety of the flute.—*v.i.* to play on the fife.—*n.* **fif′er,** one who plays on a fife. [Ger. *pfeife,* pipe, or Fr. *fifre,* fife, fifer; both from L. *pīpāre,* to cheep.]

fifteen, *fif′tēn* (when used absolutely, *fif-tēn′*), *adj.* and *n.* five and ten: a rugby team.—*adj.* **fifteenth,** the last of fifteen: being one of fifteen equal parts.—*n.*—**the Fifteen,** the Jacobite rising of 1715. [O.E. *fīftēne.*]

fifth, *fifth, adj.* last of five: being one of five equal parts.—Also *n.*—*adv.* **fifth′ly,** in the fifth place.—**fifth column,** traitors among the population of a town, or of a country, who give help to an enemy attacking from outside—as certain Spaniards did in Madrid in 1936-9, during the Spanish Civil War. [O.E. *fīfta*; affected in M.E. by the *-th* in *fourth.*]

fifty, *fif′ti, adj.* and *n.* five times ten.—*adj.* **fif′tieth,** the last of fifty: being one of fifty equal parts.—Also *n.*—**fif′ty-fif′ty,** half-and-half: (of chances) equal. [O.E. *fīftig—fīf,* five, *tig,* ten, related to *tiēn, tēn.*]

fig, *fig, n.* any of a very large genus of trees, growing in warm climates, with pear-shaped, pulpy fruit: the fruit itself: a thing of little consequence.—*n.* **fig′-leaf,** the leaf of the fig-tree: any scanty clothing (from Gen. iii. 7): symbol of affected modesty: something intended to conceal the reality of actions or motives, esp. political or international. [Fr. *figue*—L. *ficus,* a fig-tree.]

fight, *fīt, v.i.* to strive (for): to contend in war or in single combat.—*v.t.* to engage in conflict with: to win (one's way) by conflict:—*pr.p.* fight′ing; *pa.t.* and *pa.p.* fought (*föt*).—*n.* a struggle: a combat: a battle or engagement: strong disagreement: the will, or strength, to contend.—*n.* **fight′er,** one who fights: one who does not give in easily: an aeroplane for fighting, as opposed to bombing.—*adj.* **fight′ing,** engaged in, or fit for, combat.—*n.* the act of fighting or contending.—**fighting chance,** a chance of success given supreme effort.—*adj.* **fight′ing-fit,** in good condition.—**fight it out,** to fight on to a decisive end; **fight shy of,** to avoid. [O.E. *fehtan*; Ger. *fechten.*]

figment, *fig′ment, n.* a fabrication or invention. [L. *figmentum—fingĕre,* to form.]

Neutral vowels in unaccented syllables: *em′pér-ór*; for certain sounds in foreign words see p. ix.

figure, *fig'ûr*, *n.* the form of anything in outline: a geometrical form: a representation in drawing, &c.: a design: a statue: appearance: a personage: a character denoting a number: a number: value or price: a deviation from the ordinary mode of expression, in which words are changed from their literal signification or usage: (*logic*) the form of a syllogism with respect to the position of the middle term: a set of steps in a dance or a series of movements in skating: a type or emblem.—*v.t.* to form or shape: to make an image of: to mark with figures or designs: to imagine: to symbolise: to foreshow: to note, or to calculate, by figures.—*v.i.* to make figures: to play a part (in), be conspicuous (in): (*coll.*) to follow as a logical consequence, to be expected.—*adj.* **fig'urative** (*rhet.*), representing by, containing, or abounding in figures: metaphorical: typical.—*adv.* **fig'uratively.**—*adj.* **fig'ured,** marked or adorned with figures.—*ns.* **fig'urehead,** the figure or bust under the bowsprit of a ship: a nominal head or leader; **fig'urine,** a small carved or sculptured figure.—**cut a figure,** to make a conspicuous appearance. [Fr.,—L. *figūra,* cognate with *fingĕre,* to form.]

filament, *fil'a-mént, n.* a slender or thread-like object: a fibre: a thread of high resistance in electric lamps and radio valves· (*bot.*) the stalk of a stamen: a chain of cells.—*adj.* **filament'ous,** thread-like. [L. *fīlum,* a thread.]

filbert, *fil'bért, n.* the nut of the cultivated hazel. [Prob. from St *Philibert,* whose day fell in the nutting season.]

filch, *filch, v.t.* to steal, to pilfer.—*n.* **filch'er,** thief. [Ety. unknown.]

file, *fīl, n.* a line or wire on which papers are strung: any contrivance for keeping papers in order: the papers so kept: a roll or list: a line of soldiers ranged behind one another.—*v.t.* to put upon file: to arrange in order: to put among the records of a court: to bring (a suit) before a court.—*v.i.* to march in a file.—**(in) single file, Indian file,** (moving forward) singly, one behind another. [L. *fīlum,* a thread.]

file, *fīl, n.* a steel instrument with sharp-edged furrows for smoothing or rasping metals, &c.: a cunning fellow.—*v.t.* to cut or smooth with, or as with, a file: to polish, improve.—*n.* **fil'ing,** a particle rubbed off with a file. [O.E. *fȳl;* Ger. *feile;* Du. *vijl.*]

filial, *fil'yál, adj.* pertaining to, or becoming in, a son or daughter: bearing the relation of a child.—*adv.* **fil'ially.** [Fr.,—Low L. *fīliālis*—L. *fīlius,* a son.]

filiate, filiation. Same as **affiliate, affiliation.**

filibeg, philibeg, *fil'i-beg, n.* (*Scot.*) a kilt. [Gael. *feileadhbeag.*]

filibuster, fillibuster, *fil'i-bus-tér, n.* a military or piratical adventurer: a buccaneer: one who makes an excessively long speech to obstruct legislation.—*v.i.* to act as a filibuster. [Sp. *filibustero,* through Fr. from Du. *vrijbueter, vrijbuiter.* See **freebooter.**]

filiform, *fil'i-förm, adj.* having the form of a filament: long and slender [L. *fīlum,* thread, *forma,* form.]

filigree, *fil'i-grē, n.* a kind of ornamental work in which threads of precious metal are inter-

laced (formerly made with beads of metal): anything delicate and fragile like such metal work.—Also *adj.* [Fr. *filigrane*—It. *filigrana*—L. *fīlum,* thread, *granum,* a grain.]

Filipino, *fil-i-pē'no, n.* a native of the *Philippine Islands:—fem.* **Filipi'na.**

fill, *fil, v.t.* to make full: to put into until all the space is occupied: to supply abundantly: to satisfy: to glut: to perform the duties of: to supply a vacant office: to occupy (time).—*v.i.* to become full.—*n.* as much as fills or satisfies· a full supply.—*ns.* **fill'er; fill'ing,** anything used to fill up a cavity, &c.—**filling station,** a roadside installation where petrol and oil are sold to motorists.—**fill in,** to occupy (time): to add what is necessary to complete (e.g. a form): (*coll.*) to act as a temporary substitute; **fill one in** (*slang*), to give one detailed information about a situation; **fill the bill,** to be adequate. [O.E. *fyllan*—*full,* full.]

fillet, *fil'ét, n.* a little string or band, esp. to tie round the head: a piece of meat composed of muscle, esp. the fleshy part of the thigh: a boneless slice of fish· (*archit.*) a small space or band used along with mouldings.—*v.t.* to bind with a fillet: to make into fillets, to bone:—*pr.p.* **fill'eting;** *pa.p.* **fill'eted.** [Fr. *filet,* dim. of *fil,* from L. *fīlum,* a thread.]

fillip, *fil'ip, v.t.* to strike with the nail of the finger, forced from the thumb with a sudden jerk:—*pr.p.* **fill'iping;** *pa.p.* **fill'iped.**—*n.* a jerk of the finger from the thumb: a stimulus. [A form of **flip.**]

filly, *fil'i, n.* a young mare: an irresponsible young girl. [Dim. of *foal.*]

film, *film, n.* a thin skin or membrane: a very slender thread: the sensitive coating of a photographic plate: a ribbon of transparent plastic material with such a coating, used in taking still or cinematographic photographs: (*pl.*) the cinema: a motion picture: a slight haziness.—*v.t.* to cover with a film; to make a motion picture of.—*adj.* **film'y,** composed of film or membranes: very light and thin: misty.—*ns.* **film'iness; film'-star,** a favourite cinematograph performer. [O.E. *filmen,* conn. with *fell,* a skin.]

filter, *fil'tér, n.* an apparatus for purifying a liquid or solid matter by passing it through a porous substance: (*elect.*) a device used in electrical communication circuits to discriminate between currents of different frequencies and keep transmitted signals in their proper channels, &c.: in photography, a plate through which light is passed to alter the relative intensity of the different component wavelengths: at a road junction, an auxiliary traffic light in the form of a green arrow which allows one lane of traffic to move while the main stream is held up.—*v.t.* to purify liquid by a filter: to separate by a filter (esp. with *out*).—*v.i.* to pass through a filter, to percolate: to pass gradually, a little at a time, through obstacles: to join gradually a stream of traffic: of a lane of traffic, to move in the direction specified by the filter: (*fig.*) to become known gradually.—*ns.* **fil'ter-bed,** a bed of sand, gravel, &c., used for filtering water or sewage; **fil'ter-pā'per,** porous paper for use in filtering; **fil'ter-pass'er,** a filter-passing virus,

fāte, fär; mē, hûr (her); *mīne; mōte, för; mūte; mōōn, fŏŏt;* тнen (then)

or **filterable virus** (see **virus**). [O.Fr. *filtre* — Low L. *filtrum*, felt.]

filth, *filth, n.* foul matter: anything that defiles, physically or morally.—*adj.* **filth′y**, foul, unclean: obscene.—*n.* **filth′iness.**—*adv.* **filth′ily.** [O.E. *fȳlth* — *fūl*, foul.]

filtrate, *fil′trāt, v.t.* to filter or percolate.—*n.* a liquid that has been filtered.—*n.* **filtrā′tion,** act or process of filtering. [**filter.**]

fimbriate, -d, *fim′bri-āt, -ed, adj.* fringed. [L. *fimbriātus* — *fimbriae*, fibres.]

fin, *fin, n.* an organ by which a fish balances itself and swims: a portion of a mechanism like a fish's fin in shape or purpose.—*adjs.* **finned, finn′y,** furnished with fins. [O.E. *finn*; L. *pinna.*]

final, *fī′nál, adj.* last: decisive, conclusive: relating to the end or motive.—*n.* the last contest in a knock-out competition: (*pl.*) the concluding examination for a university degree.—*v.t.* **fī′nalise,** to put the finishing touches to: put an end to completely.—*n.* **final′ity,** state of being final: completeness or conclusiveness.—*adv.* **fī′nally.**—**final cause** (see **cause**). [Fr.,—L. *fīnālis* — *fīnis,* an end.]

finale, *fi-nä′lā, n.* the end: the last movement in a musical composition: the concluding piece in a concert. [It. *finale,* final—L. *fīnālis.*]

finance, *fi-nans′, fī-, n.* money affairs or revenue, esp. of a ruler or state: public money: the art of managing or administering money (esp. public): (*pl.*) money resources.—*v.t.* to manage financially: to furnish with money. —*adj.* **finan′cial** (*-shál*), pertaining to finance.—*adv.* **finan′cially.**—*n.* **finan′cier,** one skilled in finance: an officer who administers the public revenue. [Fr.,—Low L. *financia* —Low L. *fināre,* to pay a fine—*fīnis.* See **fine** (2).]

finch, *finch, -sh, n.* a name applied to many sparrow-like birds, many of them excellent singers. [O.E. *finc*; Ger. *fink.*]

find, *fīnd, v.t.* to come upon or meet with: to experience: to discover by search: to discover by trial: to succeed in obtaining, to obtain (e.g. time, money, reward, courage): to supply: to determine after judicial inquiry:—*pr.p.* find′ing; *pa.t.* and *pa.p.* found.—*n.* something found, esp. of value or interest.—*ns.* find′er; **find′ing,** act of one who finds: a judicial verdict.—**find one in** (something), to supply one with (something); **find one's feet,** to become able to stand, able to cope readily with new conditions; **find oneself,** to feel (as regards health, happiness, &c.): to provide for oneself: to come to full consciousness of, and mastery of, one's natural powers; **find out,** to discover by investigation or calculation: to detect (in crime or delinquency): to discover the true character or conduct of.—**well-found,** well provided. [O.E. *findan*; Ger. *finden.*]

fin de siècle, *fẽ de sye-kl′,* the end of the (19th) century or of an era: characteristic of the ideas, &c., of that time: decadent. [Fr.]

fine, *fīn, adj.* excellent: beautiful: not coarse or heavy: thin: slender: delicate: subtle: affecting refinement: showy: splendid (often *ironically*): refined: containing a specified proportion of the precious metal (e.g. *gold* 18 *parts fine*): of high quality: sharp, keen.—*adj., adv.*

(*cricket*) at a more acute angle with the line of flight of the ball (as, *fine leg*).—*v.t.* to make fine: to refine, to purify.—*adv.* narrowly, with little to spare: in a manner intended to impress (*to talk fine*).—*adv.* **fine′ly.**—*ns.* **fine′ness; fin′ery,** splendour, fine or showy things: a place where anything is fined or refined: a furnace for making iron malleable.—*adjs.* **fine′-drawn,** drawn out too finely: of an athlete, much reduced in weight by training: thin: subtle (e.g. a *fine-drawn argument*); **fine′-spun,** finely spun out: artfully contrived.—**fine arts,** as painting, sculpture, music, those chiefly concerned with the beautiful—opp. to the *useful* or *industrial arts*; **fine feathers,** costly clothing. [Fr.,—L. *fīnītus*, finished, from *fīnīre,* to finish, *fīnis,* an end.]

fine, *fīn, n.* (*obs.*) end: a sum of money paid by way of settlement: a sum of money imposed as a punishment.—*v.t.* to impose a fine on.—**in fine,** in conclusion. [Low L. *fīnis,* a fine—L. *fīnis,* an end.]

finesse, *fi-nes′, n.* subtlety of contrivance: a cunning strategy.—*v.i.* to use artifice. [Fr.]

finger, *fing′gėr, n.* one of the five terminal parts of the hand, or of the four other than the thumb: anything shaped like a finger: a finger-breadth.—*v.t.* to control with the fingers: (*coll.*) to pilfer: to toy or meddle with: (*mus.*) to make or indicate choice of fingers in performing.—*ns.* **fing′er-board,** the part of a musical instrument on which the fingers are placed; **fing′er-bowl, -glass,** a small table bowl for water used to cleanse the fingers after a meal.—*adj.* **fing′ered,** having fingers, or anything like fingers: having indication of fingering.—*ns.* **fing′ering,** act or manner of touching: the choice of fingers as in playing a musical instrument: the indication of this; **fing′er-mark,** a mark, esp. a stain, made by the finger; **fing′er-plate,** a plate on a door near the handle, to prevent finger-marks; **fing′er-post,** a post with a finger pointing the way; **fing′er-print,** an ink or other impression of the ridges of the finger-tip used as a means of identification.—*v.t.* to take the finger-prints of.—*n.* **fing′er-stall,** a stall or sheath for a finger.— **finger-and-toe,** a disease of turnips in which the taproot branches.—**a finger in (the pie),** a share in (an action); **having at one's fingerends,** to be perfect master of (a subject); **have one's fingers all thumbs,** to have awkward fingers; **point the finger at,** to call attention to in reproof; **put one's finger on,** (*fig.*) to identify, diagnose, define exactly. [O.E. *finger.*]

fingering, *fing′gėr-ing, n.* a thick woollen yarn for stockings. [Perh.—Fr. *fin grain,* fine grain.]

finial, *fin′i-ál, n.* (*archit.*) the bunch of foliage, &c., at the top of a pinnacle, spire, &c. [From L. *fīnis,* end.]

finical, *fin′i-kál, adj.* affectedly fine or precise in trifles: foppish.—*adv.* **fin′ically.**—*adj.* **fin′icking,** fussy and fastidious. [Prob. conn. with **fine** (1).]

fining, *fīn′ing, n.* process of refining or purifying [**fine** (1).]

finis, *fī′nis, n.* the end, conclusion. [L.]

finish, *fin′ish, v.t.* to end: to complete the making of: to perfect: to put an end to: to consume, -read, the whole of, or the remainder of: to

Neutral vowels in unaccented syllables: *em′pėr-ór*; for certain sounds in foreign words see p. ix.

complete the education of before introduction to society.—*v.i.* to leave off: to end (in, by): to complete the course of a race.—*n.* that which finishes or completes: the end: last touch, polish.—*p.adj.* **fin′ished**, incapable of further effort: debarred from further success: polished, excellent.—*n.* **fin′isher**, one who completes or perfects. [Fr. *finir, finissant*—L. *finīre*—*finīs*, an end.]

finite, *fī′nīt, adj.* having an end or limit—opp. to *infinite*: (*gram.*) of a part of a verb, limited by number and person, forming a predicate (e.g. *he speaks*)—not an infinitive, participle, or gerund (e.g. *to speak, speaking*).—*adv.* **fi′nitely.**—*n.* **fi′niteness.** [L. *finītus*, pa.p. of *finīre.*]

Finn, *fin, n.* of the people dwelling in Finland or of a kindred race. [O.E. *Finnas*, Finns.]

finnan-haddock, *fin′an-had′ok, n.* a kind of smoked haddock, originally prepared at Findon, Kincardineshire, Scotland.

fiord, fjord, *fyōrd, n.* a long, narrow, rockbound inlet. [Nor w.]

fir, *fûr, n.* a genus of cone-bearing, resinous trees, valuable for their timber: any of several related species, e.g. **Scotch fir**. [O.E. *fyrh*; cf. Ger. *föhre.*]

fire, *fīr, n.* the heat and light caused by burning: flame: anything burning, as fuel in a grate, &c.: a conflagration: severe trial: anything inflaming or provoking: ardour of passion: vigour: brightness of fancy: enthusiasm: discharge of firearms.—*v.t.* to set on fire: to subject to heat so as to bake, dry, &c.: to inflame: to irritate: to animate: to cause the explosion of: to discharge (*lit.* and *fig.*): (*coll.*) to dismiss from a post.—*v.i.* to take fire: to be, or become, irritated or inflamed: to discharge fire arms.—*ns.* **fire′-alarm′**, an alarm of fire: an apparatus for giving such; **fire′arm**, (usu. in *pl.*) a weapon discharged by an explosion; **fire′ball**, (*hist.*) a ball filled with combustibles to be thrown among enemies: a meteor; **fire′-box**, the box or chamber of a steam-engine in which the fire is placed; **fire′brand**, a brand or piece of wood on fire: one who foments strife; **fire′-break**, a strip of land cleared to stop the spread of a fire; **fire′brick**, a brick so made as to resist the action of fire; **fire′-brigade′**, a brigade or company of men for extinguishing fires or conflagrations; **fire′-buck′et**, a bucket for carrying water to extinguish a fire; **fire′-clay**, a kind of clay, capable of resisting fire, used in making firebricks; **fire′-damp**, a combustible gas in coal-mines—chiefly *methane* (a compound of hydrogen and carbon); **fire′-dog** (same as **andiron**), **fire′-eat′er**, a juggler who pretends to eat fire: one given to needless quarrelling; **fire′-en′gine**, an engine or forcing-pump used to extinguish fires with water; **fire′-escape′**, an iron stairway or other special means of exit from a building for use in case of fire; **fire′-fly**, an insect, usually a beetle, that emits light by night; **fire′-guard**, a protective framework placed in front of a fire; **fire′-insur′ance**, insurance against loss by fire; **fire′-i′ron**, a fireside implement—e.g. a poker—not necessarily of iron; **fire′-light′er**, a composition of pitch and sawdust, or the like, for kindling fires; **fire′lock**, an antiquated gun

discharged by a lock (q.v.) with steel and flint; **fire′man**, a man whose business it is to assist in extinguishing fires: a man who tends the fires, as of a steam-engine; **fire′place**, the place in a room appropriated to the fire: a hearth; **fire′plug**, a plug placed in a pipe which supplies water in case of fire.—*adj.* **fire′proof**, proof against fire.—*ns.* **fire′-rais′ing**, the crime of arson; **fire′-screen**, a screen for intercepting the heat of the fire; **fire′-ship**, a ship filled with combustibles, to set an enemy's vessels on fire; **fire′side**, the side of the fireplace: the hearth: home.—*adj.* homely, intimate.—*ns.* **fire′stone**, a rock, esp. a kind of sandstone, that stands much heat without injury; **fire′-wa′ter**, ardent spirits; **fire′wood**, wood for burning; **fire′work**, a contrivance for producing sparks, jets, flares, or flowing pictorial designs in fire for amusement: (in *pl.*) a display of fire as an entertainment: (in *pl.*) the materials for such a display: (in *pl.*) display of wit, temper, &c.—*ns.* **fire′-wor′ship**, homage to fire (e.g. by Parsees—q.v.) as a symbol of deity; **fir′ing**, application of fire or heat to: discharge of guns: fuel; **fir′ing-par′ty**, a detachment told off to fire over the grave of one buried with military honours, or to shoot one sentenced to death; **fir′ing-point**, the temperature at which an inflammable oil takes fire spontaneously; **firing squad**, a detachment told off to shoot a condemned prisoner.—**fire off**, to discharge (e.g. a shot, a gun, or—*fig.*—questions); **fire up**, to start a fire: to fly into a passion.—**catch** or **take fire**, to begin to burn; **on fire**, burning; **set on fire, set fire to**, ignite; **under fire**, exposed to the enemy's fire: (*fig.*) exposed to criticism. [O.E. *fȳr*; Ger. *feuer*; Gr. *pyr.*]

firkin, *fûr′kin, n.* a measure equal to the fourth part of a barrel, 9 gallons of liquid, 56 lb. of butter. [With dim. suffx. *-kin*, from Old Du. *vierde*, fourth.]

firm, *fûrm, adj.* fixed: compact: strong: not easily moved or disturbed: unshaken: resolute: decided.—*adv.* **firm′ly.**—*n.* **firm′ness.** [O.Fr. *ferme*—L. *firmus.*]

firm, *fûrm, n.* the title under which a company transacts business: a business house or partnership. [It. *firma*, from L. *firmus*. See **farm.**]

firmament, *fûr′má-ment, n.* the sphere or vault in which the stars were once thought to be fixed: the sky.—*adj.* **firmament′al**, celestial. [Fr.,—L. *firmāmentum*—*firmus, firm.*]

first, *fûrst, adj.* foremost: preceding all others in place, time, or degree: most eminent: chief.—*adv.* before anything else, in time, space, rank, &c.—*n.* **first′-aid**, treatment of a wounded or sick person before the doctor's arrival.—*adj.* **first′-born**, born first.—*n.* the first in the order of birth: the eldest child.—*adj.* **first′-class**, of best quality.—*ns.* **first cousin** (see **cousin**); **first′-foot** (*Scot.*), the first person to enter a house on New Year's Day (also *v.t.* to visit—a household with the intention of being their first-foot); **first′-fruit, first′-fruits**, the fruits first gathered in a season: the first profits or effects of anything. *adj.* **first′-hand**, obtained directly, without an intermediary.—Also *adv.*—*n.* **first′ling**, the first produce or offspring, esp. of animals.—*adv.* **first′ly**, in the first place.—*adj.* **first'-rate,** of the highest class, excellence: very well.—**first wa'ter,** (of) the first or highest quality, purest lustre—of diamonds and pearls.—**not to know the first thing about,** to know nothing about. [O.E. *fyrst,* superl. before.]

firth, *fûrth, n.* an arm of the sea, esp. a river-mouth.—Also **frith.** [O.N. *fiörthr;* Norw. *fjord.*]

fisc, fisk, *fisk, n.* the public treasury of ancient Rome: the imperial purse: (*rare*) the public revenue.—*adj.* **fisc'al,** pertaining to the public treasury or revenue.—*n.* a treasure: a public prosecutor: (*Scot.*) an officer who prosecutes in criminal cases in local and inferior courts—fully, *procurator-fiscal.* [O.Fr.—L. *fiscus,* a purse.]

fish, *fish, n.* a vertebrate that lives in water, and breathes through gills: the flesh of fish: loosely, any exclusively aquatic animal:—*pl.* **fish,** or **fish'es.**—*v.i.* to catch, or try to catch, fish, &c.: to search (for) under water: to seek to obtain by artifice (with *for*).—*v.t.* to catch or bring out of water: to draw (out or up): to try to catch fish in (a stream).—*ns.* **fish'er, fish'erman,** one who fishes, or whose occupation is to catch fish; **fish'ery,** the business of catching fish: a place for catching fish; **fish'-farming,** rearing fish in ponds or tanks; **fish'-glue,** glue made from the swimming bladders of fish.—*adj.* **fish'ing,** used in fishery.—*n.* the art or practice, or the right, of catching fish.—*ns.* **fish'-kettle,** an oval pan for boiling fish; **fish'-ladd'er, fish'-way,** an arrangement for enabling a fish to ascend a fall, &c.; **fish'-monger,** a dealer in fish.—*adj.* **fish'-net,** woven as a fine net.—*n.* **fish'-slice,** a carving-knife for flat cooking utensil for lifting fish.—*adj.* **fish'-tail,** shaped like the tail of a fish.—*ns.* **fish'-wife, fish'-wom'an,** a woman who carries fish about for sale.—*adj.* **fish'y,** consisting of fish: like a fish: abounding in fish: (*coll.*) dubious, suspicious, or improbable.—*n.* **fish'iness.**—**fish-eye lens,** an ultra-wide-angle lens covering up to 180°.—**fish out of water,** a person ill at ease in an unaccustomed situation; **a queer fish,** a person of odd habits, or of a nature with which one is not in sympathy; **be neither fish nor flesh,** to be neither one thing nor another; **have other fish to fry,** to be otherwise engaged. [O.E. *fisc;* Ger. *fisch;* O.N. *fiskr;* L. *piscis;* Gael. *iasg.*]

fish, *fish, n.* (*naut.*) a piece of wood placed alongside another to strengthen it.—*n.* **fish'-plate,** an iron plate, one of a pair used to join railway rails. [Prob. Fr. *fiche,* peg.]

fissile, *fis'il, -īl, adj.* that may be cleft or split in the direction of the grain: fissionable—used of isotopes capable of maintaining a chain reaction in a nuclear reactor.—*n.* **fission** (*fish'ön*), a split or cleavage—used e.g. of the splitting in half of the nucleus of an atom, accompanied by great release of energy, and of the division of an organism into two or more parts each of which becomes a new organism.—*adj.* **fiss'ionable.—fission bomb** (see **bomb**). [L. *fissilis,* from *findĕre, fissum,* to cleave.]

fissiparous, *fi-sip'a-rus, adj.* propagated by fission or self-division. [L. *fissus,* pa.p. of *findĕre,* to cleave, *parĕre,* to bring forth.]

fissure, *fish'ûr, n.* a narrow opening or chasm.

[Fr.,—L. *fissūra,* from *findĕre, fissum,* to cleave.]

fist, *fist, n.* the closed or clenched hand.—*v.t.* to strike or grip with the fist.—*n.* **fist'icuff,** a blow with the fist: (*pl.*) boxing, blows. [O.E. *fȳst;* Ger. *faust.*]

fistula, *fist'ū-la, n.* a narrow passage or duct: a long narrow pipe-like ulcer.—*adjs.* **fist'ular,** hollow like a pipe; **fist'ulous,** of the form of a fistula. [L. *fistula,* a pipe.]

fit, *fit, adj.* suitable in condition or ability (for): qualified: convenient: proper: well trained and ready: hence, in good health.—*n.* adjustment and correspondence in shape and size: anything that fits.—*v.t.* to make fit or suitable (for): to adjust (one thing to another): to be adapted to: to qualify.—*v.i.* to be suitable, accurately adjusted, or becoming:—*pr.p.* **fitt'ing;** *pa.p.* **fitt'ed.**—*adv.* **fit'ly.**—*n.* **fit'ness.**—*adj.* **fitt'ing,** that fits: appropriate.—*n.* (usu. *pl.*) a small auxiliary part of an engine or machine: a boiler accessory, as a valve, a gauge: a fixture.—*n.* **fit'ment,** a piece of furniture, esp. if built in: (*pl.*) fittings.—*adv.* **fitt'ingly.**—*n.* **fitt'ing-shop,** the department of an engineering workshop where finished parts are assembled.—**fit out,** to equip; **fit up,** to fix in position: to provide (with). [Origin obscure.]

fit, *fit, n.* an attack of illness, esp. epilepsy: a convulsion or paroxysm: a temporary attack of anything, as laughter, &c.: a sudden and transitory state: a passing humour.—*adj.* **fit'ful,** marked by sudden impulses: spasmodic.—*adv.* **fit'fully.**—*n.* **fit'fulness.**—**fits and starts,** spasmodic and irregular bursts of activity. [O.E. *fitt,* a struggle.]

fit, *fit, n.* (*arch.*) a division of a poem, a canto: a strain.—Also **fitt, fitte, fytte.** [O.E. *fitt,* a song.]

fitch, *fich, n.* Isa. xxviii. 25, black cummin or black caraway, a plant with aromatic seeds: in Ezek. iv. 9, spelt. [Variant of **vetch.**]

fitch, *fich, n.* a polecat; the fur of the polecat.—Also **fitch'et, fitch'ew** (*fich'ōō*). [O.Fr. *fissel,* from root of Du. *visse,* nasty.]

fitz, *fits, n.* (as prefix) son of—used in England esp. of the illegitimate sons of kings and princes, as *Fitzclarence,* &c. [Anglo-Fr. *fiz* (Fr. *fils*)—L. *fīlius.*]

five, *fīv, adj.* and *n.* the cardinal number next above four.—*n.* the figure 5 or v denoting this.—*adj.* **fifth** (see separate article).—*n.* **fiv'er,** (*coll.*) a five-pound note.—*n.* **fivepins, five-pins** (also known as **five-back**), a game resembling ninepins in which balls are bowled at five 'pins'.—**five-day week,** a working week of five days only, usu. Monday to Friday. [M.E. inflected form *five*—O.E. *fīf;* Ger. *fünf.*]

fives, *fīvz, n.pl.* a game of handball played in a roomy court against a wall. [Origin obscure.]

fix, *fiks, v.t.* to make firm or fast: to drive in: to establish: to determine: to give a permanent form to: to make (a photograph) permanent by means of chemicals: to prepare (an organism, tissues) for microscopic study by means of chemicals: to cause (e.g. nitrogen) to form a compound: to direct steadily (e.g. *to fix the eyes on an object*): (*coll.*) to put to rights, repair: (*coll.*) to deal with a person in such a way (e.g. by bribery) that he will not, or can-

Neutral vowels in unaccented syllables: *em'pêr-ôr*; for certain sounds in foreign words see p. ix.

268

not, protest or interfere: (*coll.*) to arrange things so that (a difficult situation) will not bring legal or other unpleasant consequences: (*U.S.*) to prepare (a meal): to cook food.—*v.i.* to settle or remain permanently: to become firm or stable.—*n.* (*coll.*) a difficulty, a dilemma: (*aero.*) the position of an aircraft as ascertained by any means: (*slang*) a shot of heroin or other drug.—*ns.* **fixa′tion**, act of fixing, or state of being fixed: steadiness, firmness: state in which a body does not evaporate: the conversion (of nitrogen from the air) into nitrogen compounds: an arrested emotional development: loosely, an abnormal attachment, or an obsession; **fix′ative**, that which fixes or sets colours.—*adj.* **fixed**, settled: not apt to evaporate: steadily directed: fast, lasting.—*adv.* **fix′edly** (*-id-li*).—*ns.* **fix′edness**, **fix′ity**; **fix′er**; **fix′ture**, what is fixed to anything, as to land or to a house: a fixed article of furniture: a fixed or appointed time or event.—**fixed stars**, stars which appear always to occupy the same position in the heavens—opp. to *planets*. [L. *fixus*, *figĕre*, to fix, prob. through Low L. *fixāre*.]

fizz, *fiz*, *v.i.* to make a hissing or sputtering sound.—*n.* any frothy drink.—*adj.* **fizz′y**, effervescent.—*v.i.* **fizz′le**, to hiss or sputter: (also **fizzle out**) to splutter and go out, to come to nothing. [Formed from the sound.]

flabbergast, *flab′ér-gäst*, *v.t.* (*coll.*) to stun, confound. [Prob. conn. with **flabby** and **aghast**.]

flabby, *flab′i*, *adj.* soft, yielding: hanging loose.—*n.* **flabb′iness**. [From **flap**.]

flaccid, *flak′sid*, *adj.* flabby: easily yielding to pressure.—*adv.* **flac′cidly**.—*ns.* **flac′cidness**, **flaccid′ity**, want of firmness. [Fr.,—L. *flaccidus*—*flaccus*, flabby.]

flag, *flag*, *v.i.* to grow languid or spiritless.—*pr.p.* **flag′ging**; *pa.p.* **flagged**. [Perh., O.Fr. *flac*—L. *flaccus*; prob. influenced by imit. forms as *flap*.]

flag, *flag*, *n.* a plant with sword-shaped leaves—an iris, or a reed.—*adj.* **flagg′y**, abounding in flags. [Ety. obscure; cf. Du. *flag*.]

flag, *flag*, *n.* a piece of bunting, usu. with a design, used to show nationality, party, a particular branch of the armed forces, &c., or to mark a position, or to convey information.—*v.t.* to decorate with flags: to inform by flag-signals.—*ns.* **flag′-captain**, in the navy, the captain of a flag-ship; **flag′-day**, a day on which small flags are sold, and worn as a badge, in aid of a good cause; **flag′-off′icer**, a naval officer privileged to carry a flag denoting his rank—admiral, vice-admiral, rear-admiral, or commodore; **flag′-ship**, the ship in which an admiral sails, and which carries his flag; **flag′-staff**, a staff or pole on which a flag is displayed.—**flag down**, to signal (e.g. a car) to stop.—**red, yellow flag** (see **red, yellow**); **show the flag**, to put in an appearance to ensure that one, or the nation, firm, &c., one represents is not overlooked. [Origin unknown; cf. Dan. *flag*; Du. *vlag*, Ger. *flagge*.]

flag, *flag*, *n.* a stone that separates in flakes or layers: a flat stone used for paving. [O.N. *flaga*, a slab.]

flagellate, *flaj′ĕl-āt*, *v.t.* to whip or scourge.—*ns.* **flagellā′tion**; **flagell′ant** (also *flaj′-*), one who

scourges himself in religious discipline. [L. *flagellāre*, *-ātum*—*flagellum*, dim. of *flagrum*, a whip.]

flagellum, *flā-jel′um*, *n.* (*zool.*) a thread-like extension of the protoplasm of a cell, or of a protozoan, which is capable of carrying out lashing movements. [L. See **flagellate**.]

flageolet, *flaj-o-let′*, or *flaj′-*, *n.* the modern form of the straight flute—not used in orchestral music. [Fr. dim. of O.Fr. *flageol*, *flajol*, a pipe.]

flagitious, *fla-jish′us*, *adj.* grossly wicked, guilty of enormous crimes.—*adv.* **flagi′tiously**.—*n.* **flagi′tiousness**. [L. *flāgitiōsus*—*flāgitium*, a disgraceful act—*flagrāre*, to burn.]

flagon, *flag′ón*, *n.* a vessel with a narrow neck for holding liquids. [Fr. *flacon* for *flascon*—Low L. *flascō*, *-ōnis*. See **flask**.]

flagrant, *flā′grant*, *adj.* glaring, notorious.—*n.* **flā′grancy**.—*adv.* **flā′grantly**. [L. *flagrāns*, *-antis*, pr.p. of *flagrāre*, to burn.]

flail, *flāl*, *n.* an implement for threshing corn. [O.E. *flĭgel*, prob. from L. *flagellum*, a scourge.]

flair, *flār*, *n.* intuitive discernment: aptitude, bent. [Fr. 'scent'.]

flak, *flak*, *n.* an anti-aircraft gun: the missiles of such a gun. [Ger., abbrev. of *flieger-abwehr-kanone*, anti-aircraft gun.]

flake, *flāk*, *n.* a small layer or film: a very small loose mass, as of snow or wool.—*v.t.* to form into flakes.—*adj.* **flak′y**.—**flake out** (*coll.*), to collapse from weariness or illness. [Prob. Scand.; O.N. *floke*, flock of wool; O.H.G. *floccho*.]

flambeau, *flam′bō*, *n.* a flaming torch:—*pl.* **flam′beaux** (*-bōz*). [Fr., *flambe*—L. *flamma*.]

flamboyant, *flam-boi′ánt*, *adj.* (*arch.*) with waving or flame-like tracery: gorgeously coloured: too ornate, conspicuous, ostentatious: also *fig.* [Fr. *flamboyer*, to blaze.]

flame, *flām*, *n.* the gleam or blaze of a fire: rage: ardour of temper: vigour of thought: warmth of affection: love: (*coll.*) the object of love.—*v.i.* to burn as flame: to break out in passion.—*adjs.* **flame′less**; **flām′ing**, red: gaudy: violent.—*adv.* **flām′ingly**.—*adjs.* **flam′mable**, inflammable; **flammif′erous**, producing flame. [O.Fr. *flambe*—L. *flamma*—*flagrāre*, to burn.]

flamingo, *fla-ming′gō*, *n.* any of several tropical or subtropical birds of a pink or bright-red colour, with long legs and neck:—*pl.* **flaming′o(e)s**. [Sp. *flamenco*—L. *flamma*, a flame.]

flan, *flan*, *n.* an open tart with custard, or fruit, or other filling. [Fr.]

flâneur, *flä-nœr′*, *n.* an idler. [Fr.,—*flâner*, to stroll, idle.]

flange, *flanj*, *n.* a projecting or raised edge, as of a wheel or of a rail.—*adj.* **flanged**. [Prob. related to **flank**.]

flank, *flangk*, *n.* the side of an animal from the ribs to the thigh: the side or wing of anything, esp. of an army or fleet.—*v.t.* to attack the side of: to pass round the side of: to be situated at the side of. [Fr. *flanc*.]

flannel, *flan′ĕl*, *n.* a soft woollen cloth of loose texture: (*pl.*) garments of such cloth: (*fig.*) flattery, soft-soap.—*n.* **flannelette′**, a cotton fabric, made in imitation of flannel.—*adj.* **flann′elled**. [Perh. O.Fr. *flaine*, blanket, or Welsh *gwlan*, wool.]

flap, *flap, n.* the blow, or motion, of a broad loose object: anything broad and flexible hanging loose, as material covering an opening: (*coll.*) fluster, panic.—*v.t.* to beat or move with a flap: (*coll.*) to fluster.—*v.i.* to move, as wings: to hang like a flap: (*coll.*) to get into a panic or fluster.—*pr.p.* flapp'ing; *pa.p.* flapped.—*ns.* **flap'doodle,** nonsense: gross flattery; **flap'-jack,** a flat face-powdering outfit: a pancake; **flapp'er,** young wild duck or partridge: (*slang*) a flighty young girl. [Prob. imit.]

flare, *flār, v.i.* to burn with a glaring, unsteady light: to flash suddenly: to blaze (up—*lit.* or *fig.*): to widen out bell-wise.—*n.* an unsteady glare: a flash: a bright light used as a signal or illumination: a widening, or a part that widens, bell-wise.—*n.* **flare'-path,** a path lit up to enable an aircraft to land or take off when natural visibility is insufficient. [Perh. conn. with Norw. *flara,* to blaze.]

flash, *flash, n.* a momentary gleam of light: a sudden burst, as of merriment: an instant of time: a sudden rush of water: a bright garter worn with knickerbockers or kilt: a distinctive mark on a uniform: thieves' slang: a brief news dispatch by telegraph: in a film, a scene shown momentarily by way of explanation or comment, esp. (**flash-back**) a scene of the past: (*coll.*) vulgar ostentation.—*v.i.* to break forth, as a sudden light: to break out into intellectual brilliancy: to burst out into violence.—*v.t.* to cause to flash.—*adj.* **flash'y,** dazzling for a moment: showy but empty: tawdry.—*adv.* **flash'ily.**—*ns.* **flash'iness; flash'-board,** one of a set of boards set up at the sides of a water-channel to deepen it; **flash'-light,** a light that flashes periodically: a sudden light used to take photographs: an electric torch; **flash'-point,** the temperature at which the vapour of an inflammable liquid takes fire: a point in the development of a tense situation when violent action takes place.—*n.* **news'-flash,** brief preliminary dispatch about news just becoming known.— **flash in the pan** (see **pan**). [Prob. imit.; cf Swed. prov. *flash,* to blaze.]

flask, *fläsk, n.* a narrow-necked vessel for holding liquids: a bottle: a vessel for holding gunpowder. [O.E. *flasce;* Ger. *flasche;* prob. from Low. L. *flascō*—L. *vasculum,* a small vessel—*vas,* a vessel.]

flat, *flat, adj.* smooth: level: wanting points of prominence or interest: monotonous: uniform: no longer sparkling: insipid: dejected: downright, sheer.—*n.* a level part: a plain: a tract covered by shallow water: something broad: (*theat.*) a flat piece of scenery pushed or lowered on to the stage: a storey or floor of a house, esp. one, or part of one, as a separate residence: (*mus.*) a character (♭) which lowers a note a semitone: a fool, a bore.—*adv.* **flat'ly.**—*ns.* **flat'ness; flat'-fish,** a fish with a flat body—flounder, turbot, &c.; **flat'-foot,** condition in which the arch of the instep is flattened.—*adj.* **flat'-footed,** having flat feet: (*fig.*) ponderous, unimaginative.—*n.* **flat'-ī'ron,** an iron for smoothing cloth; **flat-race,** a race over level ground; **flat-spin** (*fig.*), confused excitement.—*v.t.* **flatt'en,** make flat.—*v.i.* to become flat.— **flatten out,** to bring an aeroplane into a

horizontal course after a climb or dive: (of an aeroplane) to assume such a position.—*adj.* **flatt'ish,** somewhat flat.—*adj.* or *adv.* **flat'ways, flat'wise,** with the flat side.—*n.* **flat'-worm,** a tapeworm. [O.N. *flatr,* flat.]

flatter, *flat'ér, v.t.* to treat with insincere praise and servile attentions: to represent over-favourably: to please (with false hopes).—*n.* **flatt'erer.**—*adj.* **flatt'ering,** uttering false praise: pleasing to pride or vanity.—*adv.* **flatt'eringly.**—*n.* **flatt'ery,** false praise. [O.Fr. *flater* (Fr *flatter*)—Gmc.]

flatulent, *flat'ū-lént, adj.* affected with air in the stomach: apt to generate such: pretentious, vain.—*ns.* **flat'ulence, flat'ulency,** air generated in the stomach: windiness, emptiness. —*adv.* **flat'ulently.**—*n.* **flatus** (*flā'tus*), a puff of wind: air generated in the stomach or intestines. [Fr.,—Low L. *flātulentus*—L. *flāre, flātum,* to blow.]

flaunt, *flönt, v.i.* to wave in the wind: to move or behave ostentatiously.—*v.t.* to display.—Also *n.* [Prob. Scand.]

flautist, *flöt'ist, n.* a flute player. [It. *flautista.*]

flavour, *flā'vór, n.* that quality of anything which affects the smell or the taste: a relish: (*fig.*) savour: characteristic quality.—*v.t.* to impart flavour to.—*adj.* **flā'vorous.**—*n.* **flā'vouring,** any substance used to give a flavour.—*adj.* **flā'vourless.** [O.Fr. *flaur;* prob. influenced by **savour.**]

flaw, *flö, n.* a gust of wind. [Cf. Du. *vlaag,* Swed. *flaga.*]

flaw, *flö, n.* a break, a crack: a defect.—*v.t.* to crack or break.—*adjs.* **flaw'less; flaw'y.** [O.N. *flaga,* a slab.]

flax, *flaks, n.* the fibres of a plant, which are woven into linen cloth: this plant, or any other of the same genus.—*adj.* **flax'en,** made of or resembling flax: light yellow. [O.E. *flæx;* Ger. *flachs.*]

flay, *flā, v.t.* to strip off the skin:—*pr.p.* flay'ing; *pa.p.* flayed.—*n.* **flay'er.** [O.E. *flēan;* O.N. *flā,* to skin.]

flea, *flē, n.* an order of parasitic insects of great agility.—*ns.* **flea'-bane,** a genus of plants whose smell is said to drive away fleas; **flea'-bite,** the bite of a flea: (*fig.*) a trifle.—**a flea in one's ear,** a stinging rebuff. [O.E. *flēah;* cf. Du. *floh,* Du. *vloo.*]

flèche, *flesh, n.* a slender spire. [Fr., arrow.]

fleck, *flek, n.* a spot or speckle: a little bit of a thing.—*vs.t.* **fleck, fleck'er,** to spot: to streak. [O.N. *flekkr,* a spot; Ger. *fleck,* Du. *vlek.*]

flection. Same as **flexion.**

fled, *fled, pa.t.* and *pa.p.* of **flee.**

fledge, *flej, v.t.* to bring up a bird until it is ready to fly: to furnish with feathers, as an arrow.— *v.i.* to acquire feathers for flying.—*n.* **fledg(e)-ling,** a little bird just fledged. [M.E. *fligge, flegge*—O.E. *flycge,* fledged—*flēogan,* to fly (Ger. *fliegen*).]

flee, *flē, v.i.* to run away, as from danger: to disappear.—*v.t.* to keep at a distance from:—*pr.p.* flee'ing; *pa.t.* and *pa.p.* fled. [O.E. *flēon* (Ger. *fliehen*). Not akin to *fly,* but influenced by it.]

fleece, *flēs, n.* a sheep's coat of wool.—*v.t.* to clip wool from: to plunder: to cover, as with wool.—*adjs.* **fleeced,** having a fleece; **fleece'-**

Neutral vowels in unaccented syllables: *em'pér-ór;* for certain sounds in foreign words see p. ix.

270

less; **fleec′y,** woolly. [O.E. *flēos*; Du. *vlies,* Ger. *fliess.*]

fleer, *flēr, v.i.* to make wry faces in contempt.— *v.t.* to mock.—*n.* mockery. [Cf. Norw. *flira,* Swed. *flissa,* to titter.]

fleet, *flēt, n.* a number of ships, birds, aircraft, motor-cars, &c., in company or otherwise associated: a division of the navy, commanded by an admiral: the navy. [O.E. *flēot,* a ship— *flēotan,* to float.]

fleet, *flēt, adj.* swift: nimble: transient.—*adv.* **fleet′ly.**—*n.* **fleet′ness.** [Prob. O.N. *fliōtr,* swift; but ult. cog. with succeeding word.]

fleet, *flēt, v.i.* to move, pass swiftly, hasten.—*v.t.* to while away:—*pr.p.* fleet′ing; *pa.p.* fleet′ed. [O.E. *flēotan,* to float.]

fleet, *flēt, n.* a shallow creek or brook, as in North-*fleet, Fleet*-ditch, &c.—**the Fleet,** or **Fleet Prison,** a London gaol; **Fleet Street,** journalism or its ways and traditions, from the street near the Fleet with many newspaper offices. [O.E. *flēot,* an inlet.]

Flemish, *flem′ish, adj.* of or belonging to the *Flemings* or people of Flanders, or their language. [Du. *Vlaamsch.*]

flench, *flench, -sh, v.t.* to cut out the blubber of, as a whale. Also **flense, flinch.** [Dan. *flense.*]

flesh, *flesh, n.* muscular tissue, the soft substance that covers the bones of animals: animal food: the bodies of beasts and birds, not fish: the body, not the soul: mankind: kindred: bodily appetites: the present life: the soft substance of fruit.—*v.t.* to train to an appetite for flesh, as dogs for hunting: to inure: to glut: to use upon flesh, as a sword, esp. for the first time.—*adj.* **fleshed** (*flesht*), having flesh: fat.—*n.* **flesh′-fly,** a fly that deposits its eggs in and foods on flesh. *n.pl.* **flesh′ings,** flesh-coloured tights.—*adj.* **flesh′less,** without flesh: lean—*adj* **flesh′ly,** corporeal: carnal: not spiritual.—*ns.* **flesh′liness; flesh′-pot,** a pot in which flesh is cooked: (*pl.—fig.*) abundance, luxury; **flesh′-wound,** a wound not reaching beyond the flesh.—*adj.* **flesh′y,** fat: pulpy: plump.—*n.* **flesh′iness.—an arm of flesh,** human strength; **in the flesh,** alive; **flesh and blood,** human nature: kindred. [O.E. *flǣsc*; cog. forms in all Gmc. languages.]

fleur-de-lis, *flœr′-de-lē′,* or *-lēs′, n.* the flower of the lily: an ornament and heraldic bearing borne by the kings of France:—*pl.* **fleurs′-de-lis′.** [Fr., *lis*—L. *lilium,* a lily.]

flew, *flōō, pa.t.* of **fly.**

flex, *fleks, v.t.* and *v.i.* to bend.—*n.* a bending: a flexible cord or line, esp. of insulated wire.— *adjs.* **flexible** (*fleks′i-bl*), **flexile** (*fleks′īl*), easily bent, pliant: docile.—*ns.* **flex′ibleness, flexibil′ity,** pliancy: easiness to be persuaded.—*adv.* **flex′ibly.**—*ns.* **flex′ion,** a bend: a fold; **flex′or,** a muscle that bends a joint.— *adjs.* **flex′uous, flex′uose,** full of windings and turnings: variable.—*n.* **flex′ure,** a bend or turning: (*math.*) the curving of a line or surface: the bending of loaded beams. [L. *flectĕre, flexum,* to bend.]

flick, *flik, v.t.* to strike lightly.—*n.* a flip. [Imit.]

flicker, *flik′er, v.i.* to flutter and move the wings, as a bird: to burn unsteadily, as a flame. [O.E. *flicorian;* imit.]

flier, flyer, *flī′er, n.* one who flies or flees: a part

of a machine with rapid motion. [**fly.**]

flight, *flīt, n.* act, or manner of passing through the air: distance flown: a sally (e.g. of wit, ambition): a series of steps: a flock of birds flying together: the birds produced in the same season: a volley (e.g. of arrows): a unit in the Air Force answering to a platoon in the army.—*adjs.* **flight′less,** without power of flight; **flight′y,** fanciful: changeable: giddy.— *adv.* **flight′ily.**—*ns.* **flight′iness; flight′-deck,** the deck of an aircraft-carrier where the planes take off or land; **flight′-lieuten′ant,** an Air Force officer of rank answering to naval lieutenant or army captain; **flight′-recorder,** a device which records information about the functioning of an aircraft and its systems.—**in the first flight,** in the highest class. [O.E. *flyht*—*flēogan,* to fly.]

flight, *flīt, n.* an act of fleeing. [Assumed O.E. *flyht*—*flēon,* to flee.]

flimsy, *flim′zi, adj.* thin: without solidity, strength, or reason: weak.—*n.* thin paper: reporters' copy written on thin paper.—*adv.* **flim′sily.**—*n.* **flim′siness.** [First in 18th century. Prob. suggested by **film.**]

flinch, *flinch, -sh, v.i.* to shrink back: to wince.—*n.* **flinch′er.**—*adv.* **flinch′ingly.** [Prob. conn. with M.E. *fleechen,* O.Fr. *flechir,* L. *flectĕre,* to bend.]

fling, *fling, v.t.* to cast, toss, throw: to dart: to scatter.—*v.i.* to kick out: to dash or rush: to throw oneself impetuously:—*pr.p.* fling′ing; *pa.t.* and *pa.p.* flung.—*n.* a cast or throw: a taunt: a season of freedom to indulge impulses: a bout of pleasure: a lively dance. [O.N. *flengja*; Swed. *flänga.*]

flint, *flint, n.* a hard mineral, a variety of quartz, from which fire is readily struck with steel: anything proverbially hard.—*adj.* made of flint, hard. *ns.* **flint′ glass,** a very fine and pure glass, originally made of calcined flints; **flint′-lock,** an antiquated gun-lock having a flint fixed in the hammer for striking fire.— *adj.* **flint′y,** consisting of or like flint: hard, cruel.—*n.* **flint′iness.** [O.E. *flint*; Dan. *flint*; Gr. *plinthos,* a brick.]

flip, *flip, n.* a hot drink of beer (or egg and milk) and spirits sweetened. [Prob.—**flip** (2).]

flip, *flip, v.t.* and *v.i.* to flick: to flap.—*n.* a flick: a short flight.—*adv.* **flip′-flap,** with repeated flapping.—*ns.* **flip′-flop,** orig. and still in U.S., a bistable pair of valves or transistors, two stable states being switched by pulses: in Britain, a similar circuit with one stable state temporarily achieved by pulse; **flip′er,** a limb adapted for swimming: a rubber foot-covering imitating an animal's flipper, worn by frogmen; **flip′-side,** the side of a gramophone record carrying the song, &c., of lesser importance. [Cf. **fillip, flap.**]

flippant, *flip′ant, adj.* quick and pert of speech: frivolous.—*ns.* **flipp′ancy, flipp′antness,** pert fluency of speech: levity.—*adv.* **flipp′antly.** [Cf. **flip** (2) and O.N. *fleipa,* to prattle.]

flirt, *flûrt, v.i.* to trifle with love: to play at courtship.—*v.t.* to move (a light article) jerkily.—*n.* a sudden jerk: a trifler with the opposite sex (used esp. of a woman).—*n.* **flirta′tion,** the act of flirting—*adj.* **flirta′tious,** given to flirting. [Onomatopoeic.]

fāte, fär; mē, hûr (her); *mīne; mōte, för; mūte; mōōn, fŏŏt;* ᴛʜen (then)

flit, *flit, v.i.* to flutter on the wing: to fly silently or quickly: to migrate: to depart: (*Scot.*) to change one's abode:—*pr.p.* flitt'ing; *pa.p.* flitt'ed.—Also *v.t.*—*n.* **flitt'ing.** [O.N. *flytja*; Swed. *flytta.*]

flitch, *flich, n.* the side of a hog salted and cured. [O.E. *flicce*; O.N. *flikki.*]

flitter, *flit'ér, v.i.* to flutter.—*n.* **flitt'er-mouse,** a bat. [**flit.**]

float, *flōt, v.i.* to be supported or suspended in a liquid: to be buoyed up: to move lightly: to drift about aimlessly.—*v.t.* to cause to float: to cover with liquid: to set agoing, or give support to (e.g. a scheme, a company).—*n.* anything that floats: a raft: the cork on a fishing-line: a low cart for carrying cattle, &c.: a tool for smoothing: money in hand, e.g. to give change to customers—*adj.* **float'able.**—*ns.* **float'age, float'age,** buoyancy: anything that floats; **floata'tion,** more usually **flota'tion** (q.v.); **float'er.**—*adj.* **float'ing,** that floats, in any sense: not fixed: circulating.—*ns.* **float'ing-batt'ery,** a vessel heavily armed, used in coast defence or in attacks on marine fortresses; **float'ing-bridge,** a bridge supported on pontoons; **float'ing crane,** a large crane carried on a pontoon, used in docks; **float'ing-dock** (see **dock**); **float'ing-light,** a light on a ship.—**floating kidney,** an abnormally mobile kidney, associated with general displacement downwards of other abdominal organs; **floating ribs,** ribs not connecting with the breast-bone; **floating vote,** the votes of electors who are not permanently attached to any one political party. [O.E. *flotian,* to float; O.N. *flota.*]

flock, *flok, n.* a company of animals: a company generally: a Christian congregation.—*v.i.* to gather, come together, in crowds.—*n.* **flock'-mas'ter,** an owner or overseer of a flock. [O.E. *flocc,* a flock, a company; O.N. *flokkr.*]

flock, *flok, n.* a lock of wool: woollen or cotton refuse.—*adj.* **flocc'ulent,** woolly, flaky.—*ns.* **flocc'ūlence; flock'-bed,** a bed stuffed with wool refuse. [O.Fr. *floc*—L. *floccus,* a lock of wool.]

floe, *flō, n.* a field of floating ice. [Prob. Norw. *flo,* layer.]

flog, *flog, v.t.* to beat, or strike, to lash, to chastise with blows: (*slang*) to sell, or try to sell, sometimes not through the usual trade channels.—*pr.p.* flogg'ing: *pa.p.* flogged. [Late; prob. an abbrev. of *flagellate.*]

flood, *flud, n.* a great flow of water: an inundation, a deluge: (*poet.*) a river or other water: the rise of the tide: any great quantity.—*v.t.* to overflow, to inundate:—*pr.p.* flood'ing; *pa.p.* flood'ed.—*ns.* **flood'-gate,** a gate for allowing or stopping the flow of water, a sluice; **flood'-light, flood'-lighting,** strong illumination from many points to eliminate shadows.—*v.t.* **flood'light.**—*ns.* **flood'mark,** the mark or line to which the tide rises; **flood'-tide,** the rising or inflowing tide.—**the Flood,** Noah's deluge. [O.E. *flōd;* Du. *vloed,* Ger. *flut*; cog. with **flow.**]

floor, *flōr, flôr, n.* the part of a room on which we stand: a platform: the rooms in a house on the same level, a storey: any levelled area: the part of a legislative assembly where members sit and speak: a lower limit of prices, &c.—*v.t.*

to furnish with a floor: to throw or place on the floor: (*coll.*) to defeat: to stump.—*ns.* **floor'cloth,** a covering for floors made of canvas oil-painted on both sides; **floor'ing,** material for floors: a platform; **floor'-walker,** a supervisor of a section of a large store, who attends to customers' complaints, &c.; **first'-floor,** the floor in a house above the ground-floor, the second storey: (*U.S.*) usually the **ground-floor,** i.e. the floor on a level with the ground.—**hold the floor,** to dominate a meeting by talking a great deal: to speak at length and boringly. [O.E. *flōr;* Du. *vloer,* a flat surface, Ger. *flur,* flat land.]

flop, *flop, v.i.* to fall down suddenly.—*n.* a fall plump on the ground: a collapse: (*slang*) a failure, fiasco: (U.S.) a doss house. [A form of **flap.**]

flora, *flō'ra, flō', n.* the plants (collectively) of a region or of a period: a list of these:—*pl.* usu. **flō'ras,** sometimes **flō'rae** (-ē).—*adj.* **flō'ral,** pertaining to the goddess Flora or to flowers: (*bot.*) containing the flower.—*adv.* **flō'rally.**—*n.* **flōres'cence,** a bursting into flower: (*bot.*) the time when plants flower.—*adj.* **flōres'cent,** bursting into flowers.—*n.* **flō'ret** (*bot.*), a small flower in a close-packed inflorescence (q.v.).—*adj.* **flō'riated,** decorated with floral ornaments.—*n.* **flō'riculture,** the culture of flowers or plants.—*adj.* **floricul'tural.**—*n.* **flōricul'turist,** a florist.—*adj.* **flōr'id,** flowery: too bright in colour: flushed with red: containing flowers of rhetoric: too richly ornamental.—*adv.* **flor'idly.**—*n.* **flor'idness.**—*adjs.* **flōrif'erous,** bearing or producing flowers; **flō'riform,** flower-shaped.—*n.* **flōr'ist,** a cultivator, seller, or student of flowers or of floras. [L. *Flōra,* goddess of flowers—*flōs, flōris,* a flower.]

Florentine, *flor'én-tīn, adj.* pertaining to the Italian city of *Florence.*

florin, *flor'in, n.* an English silver coin worth one-tenth of a pound, first minted in 1849: in Holland the silver monetary unit: (*orig.*) a Florentine gold coin with a lily stamped on one side, first struck in the 11th century. [Fr., from It. *fiorino*—*fiore,* a lily—L. *flōs, flōris.*]

floruit, *flō'rōō-it,* or *flor-, v.* he (she) flourished.—*n.* the period during which a person lived. [L. 3rd pers. sing. perf. of *flōrēre,* to flourish.]

floscule, *flos'kūl, n.* a floret.—*adjs.* **flos'cular, flos'culous.** [L. *flōsculus,* dim. of *flōs,* a flower.]

floss, *flos, n.* the rough outside of the silkworm's cocoon and other waste of silk manufacture: fine silk used in embroidery: any loose downy plant substance.—*n.* **floss'-silk.**—*adj.* **floss'y.** [Prob. O.Fr. *flosche,* down: or from some Gmc. word cog. with *fleece;* cf. O.N. *flos,* nap.]

floss, *flos, n.* (*rare*) a stream. [Ger.; perhaps influenced by George Eliot's The Mill on the Floss (1860), where Floss is a proper name.]

flotage. See **floatage.**

flotation, *flo-tā'sh(ó)n, n.* the act of floating: the science of floating bodies: act of starting a business, esp. a limited liability company. [See **float.**]

flotilla, *flō-til'a, n.* a fleet of small ships. [Sp., dim. of *flota,* a fleet.]

flotsam, *flot'säm, n.* goods lost by shipwreck, and found floating on the sea (cf. **jetsam**).

Neutral vowels in unaccented syllables: *em'pér-ör;* for certain sounds in foreign words see p. ix.

[Anglo-Fr. *floteson* (Fr. *flottaison*)—O.F. *floter*, to float.]

flounce, *flowns*, *v.i.* to move abruptly or impatiently.—*n.* an impatient fling, flop, or movement. [Prob. cog. with Norw. *flunsa*, to hurry, Swed. dial. *flunsa*, to plunge.]

flounce, *flowns*, *n.* a hanging strip sewed to the skirt of a dress.—*v.t.* to furnish with flounces.—*n.* **floun'cing**, material for flounces. [Earlier form *frounce*—O.Fr. *froncir*, to wrinkle.]

flounder, *flown'dér*, *v.i.* to struggle with violent and awkward motion: to stumble helplessly in thinking or speaking. [Prob. an onomatopoeic blending of the sound and sense of earlier words like *founder*, *blunder*.]

flounder, *flown'dér*, *n.* a small flat-fish, generally found in the sea near the mouth of rivers. [Anglo-Fr. *floundre*—O.Fr.; most prob. of Scand. origin.]

flour, *flowr*, *n.* the finely ground meal of wheat or other grain: the fine soft powder of any substance.—*v.t.* to reduce into, or to sprinkle with, flour.—*adj.* **flour'y**. [Same word as **flower**.]

flourish, *flur'ish*, *v.i.* to grow luxuriantly: to thrive, be prosperous: to live and work (in, at about, a specified time): to use copious and flowery language: to make ornamental strokes with the pen: to show off.—*v.t.* to adorn with flourishes or ornaments: to brandish in show or triumph.—*n.* decoration: showy splendour: a figure made by a bold stroke of the pen: the waving of a weapon or other thing: a parade of words: a showy, fantastic, or highly ornamental passage of music.—*adj.* **flour'ishing**, thriving: prosperous: making a show.—*adv.* **flour'ishingly.—flourish of trumpets**, a trumpet call heralding great persons. [O.Fr. *florir*—L. *flōs*, *flōris*, flower.]

flout, *flowt*, *v.t.* to jeer at, to mock: to treat with contempt.—Also *v.i.*—*n.* a jeer. [Prob. a specialised use of *floute*, M.E. form of *flute*, to play on the flute.]

flow, *flō*, *v.i.* to run, as water: to rise, as the tide: to move in a stream: to glide smoothly: to circulate, as the blood: to abound: to hang loose and waving (*B.*) to melt.—*n.* a stream or current: the rise of the tide: a smooth, gradual movement (*lit.* and *fig.*): abundance, copiousness.—*adj.* **flow'ing**, moving, as a fluid: fluent or smooth: falling in folds or in waves.—*adv.* **flow'ingly.—flow chart**, a chart pictorially representing the logical nature and sequence of operations to be carried out in e.g. a computer program. [O.E. *flōwan*.]

flow, *flō*, *n.* a morass. [O.N. *floi*, a marsh—*flōa*, to flood.]

flower, *flow'ér*, *flowr*, *n.* a growth comprising the reproductive organs of seed-plants: the blossom of a plant: the best of anything: the prime of life: the person or thing most distinguished: a figure of speech: an embellishment: (*pl.*) menstrual discharge (*B.*): (*pl.*) a sublimate (as *flowers of sulphur*).—*v.t.* to adorn with figures of flowers.—*v.i.* to blossom: to flourish.—*n.* **flow'eret**, a little flower: a floret.—*adj.* **flow'ery**, full of, or adorned with, flowers: highly embellished.—*n.* **flow'eriness**. [O.Fr. *flour* (Fr. *fleur*)—L. *flōs*, *flōris*, a flower.]

flown, *flōn*, *pa.p.* of **fly**.

flu, **flue**, *flōō*, *n.* (coll.) abbrev. of **influenza**.

fluctuate, *fluk'tū-āt*, *v.i.* to move like a wave: to go up and down or to and fro: to vary.—*n.* **fluctua'tion**, a rise and fall: motion to and fro: alternate variations. [L. *fluctuāre*, *-ātum*—*fluctus*, a wave—*fluēre*, to flow.]

flue, *flōō*, *n.* a pipe for conveying hot air, smoke, &c.: small chimney.—*n.* **flue(-)pipe**, (*mus.*) a pipe, esp. in an organ, in which the sound is produced by air impinging on an edge (cf. **reed pipe**). [Origin doubtful.]

fluent, *flōō'ént*, *adj.* ready in the use of words: voluble.—*n.* **flu'ency**, readiness or rapidity of utterance: volubility.—*adv.* **flu'ently.** [L. *fluēns*, *fluentis*, pr.p. of *fluēre*, to flow.]

fluff, *fluf*, *n.* a soft down from cotton, &c. [Origin doubtful.]

fluid, *flōō'id*, *adj.* that flows, as water: unsolidified: unstable.—*n.* a substance whose particles can move about with freedom—a liquid or gas.—*ns.* **fluid'ics**, the science and technology of using a flow of liquid or gas for certain operations in place of a flow of electrons; **fluid'ity**, **flu'idness**, liquid or gaseous state: state or quality of instability.—**fluid drive**, a system of transmitting power smoothly through the medium of the change in momentum of a fluid, usu. oil; **fluid ounce**, a former measure for liquid medicines—in Britain, 1/20 of an imperial (q.v.) pint, or 28·4 cubic centimetres. [Fr.,—L. *fluidus*, fluid—*fluēre*, to flow.]

fluke, *flōōk*, *n.* a flounder: a worm which causes the liver-rot in sheep, so called because like a miniature flounder. [O.E. *flōc*, a plaice; cf. O.N. *flōke*.]

fluke, *flōōk*, *n.* the part of an anchor which fastens in the ground. [Prob. a transferred use of **fluke** (1).]

fluke, *flōōk*, *n.* an accidental success.

flume, *flōōm*, *n.* an artificial channel for water, used to drive a mill-wheel, &c. [O.Fr. *flum*—L. *flūmen*, a river—*fluēre*, to flow.]

flummery, *flum'ér-i*, *n.* an acid jelly made from the husks of oats: anything insipid: empty compliments. [W. *llymru*—*llymrig*, harsh, raw—*llym*, sharp, severe.]

flung, *flung*, *pa.t.* and *pa.p.* of **fling**.

flunkey, *flung'ki*, *n.* a livery servant: a footman: a mean, cringing fellow.—*n.* **flun'keyism**. [Perh. orig. *flanker*, one who runs alongside.]

fluor, *flōō'ór*, *n.* a mineral in which fluorine is combined with calcium—also **flu'orite**, **flu'orspar**.—*n.* **fluores'cence**, the absorption of radiation of a particular wavelength by a substance and its re-emission as light of greater wavelength e.g. absorption of ultraviolet radiations and emission of visible light by varieties of fluor (cf. **phosphorescence**).—*adjs.* **fluores'cent**; **fluor'ic**.—*n.* **flu'oride**, a compound of fluorine with another element or radical.—*v.t.* **flu'oridise**, **-idate**, to treat (drinking water) with a fluoride.—*ns.* **fluoridīsā'tion**, **-idā'tion**.—*v.t.* **flu'orinate**, to treat with fluorine.—*n.* **flu'orine**, an element (symbol F; atomic no. 9); a very active pale greenish-yellow gas.—**fluorescent lighting**, brighter lighting obtained, for the same consumption of electricity, by using fluorescent material to convert ultraviolet radiation in the electric lamp into visible light. [L. *fluor,* flow, from its use as a flux.]

flurry, *flur'i, n.* a sudden blast or gust: agitation: bustle.—*v.t.* to agitate, to confuse:—*pr.p.* flurr'ying; *pa.p.* flurr'ied. [Prob. onomatopoeic, suggested by **flaw** (1), **hurry,** &c.]

flush, *flush, n.* a sudden flow: a flow of blood to the skin causing redness: sudden impulse: freshness, vigour: abundance.—*v.i.* to become red in the face: to flow swiftly.—*v.t.* to make red in the face: to cleanse by a copious flow of water: to excite with joy—mostly in the *pa.p.* (e.g. *flushed with victory*).—*adj.* abounding: well supplied, as with money. [Prob. onomatopoeic, but meaning influenced by **flash, blush.**]

flush, *flush, adj.* having the surface in one plane with the adjacent surface.—*n.* **flush'-deck,** a deck continuous from bow to stern at the same level. [Prob. related to **flush** (1).]

flush, *flush, v.i.* (of birds) to start up suddenly and fly away.—*v.t.* to rouse (game birds) suddenly.—*n.* a number of birds roused at the same time. [M.E. *fluschen.* Perh. imitative.]

flush, *flush, n.* a run of cards all of the same suit. [O.Fr. *flux.* See **flux.**]

fluster, *flus'tér, n.* hurrying: flurry: heat.—*v.t.* to make hot and confused.—*v.i.* to bustle: to be agitated. [O.N. *flaustr,* hurry.]

flute, *flōōt, n.* a very old musical wind instrument, of which there were several varieties: now usu. confined to a pipe, with finger-holes and keys, blown through a lateral hole: one of a series of curved vertical furrows, as on a pillar, called also **flut'ing.**—*v.i.* to play the flute.—*v.t.* to form flutes or grooves in.—*ns.* **flut'er,** one who makes flutings: a flautist (q.v.); **flut'ist,** flautist. [O.Fr. *fleüte.*]

flutter, *flut'ér, v.i.* to flap the wings: to move about with bustle: to vibrate: to be in agitation or in uncertainty.—*v.t.* to throw into disorder.—*n.* quick, irregular motion: agitation: confusion: a gambling transaction. [O.E. *flotorian,* to float about, from *flot,* the sea, stem of *flēotan,* to float.]

fluvial, *flōō'vi-ál, adj.* of or belonging to rivers.—*adj.* **fluviat'ic,** belonging to or formed by rivers. [L. *fluviālis*—*fluvius,* a river, *fluĕre,* to flow.]

flux, *fluks, n.* act of flowing: a flow of matter: (a state of) flow or continuous change: matter discharged: a purifying agent used in soldering, welding, &c.: the rate of flow of mass, volume or energy.—*v.t.* to melt.—*v.i.* to flow.—*n.* **fluxion** (*fluk'sh(ó)n*), a flowing or discharged: a substance added to another to make it more fusible: the rate of flow of mass,

fly, *flī, v.i.* to move through the air, esp. on wings or in aircraft: to move swiftly: to pass away: to flee: to burst quickly or suddenly (e.g. *the glass flew into pieces*): to flutter.—*v.t.* to avoid, flee from: to cause to fly, as a kite: to cross by flying:—*pr.p.* fly'ing; *pa.p.* flew (*flōō*); *pa.p.* flown (*flōn*).—*n.* a family of insects with two transparent wings, esp. the common house-fly: a fish-hook dressed with silk, &c., in imitation of a fly: a flap of material with buttonholes: a flap over the entrance to a tent: a light double-seated carriage: (*mech.*) a fly-wheel: (*pl.*) in a theatre, the part above the

stage from which the scenes are controlled.—*adj.* (*slang*) wide-awake, knowing.—*n.* **fly'-blow,** the egg of a fly.—*adj.* **fly'blown,** tainted with the eggs which produce maggots.—*ns.* **fly'boat,** a long, narrow, swift boat used on canals; **fly'-catch'er,** a bird that catches flies on the wing; **fly'-fish'er,** one who uses artificial flies as bait; **fly'-half,** stand-off (half); **fly'ing bomb,** a long-range projectile consisting of a warhead, planes, directional apparatus, and a jet-propulsion (q.v.) unit; **fly'ing-butt'ress,** a prop for a roof, vault, or wall in the form of a half arch thrown from a detached pier or buttress.—*n.pl.* **fly'ing-col'ours,** flags unfurled: triumphant success.—*ns.* **Fly'ing-Corps,** the precursor (1912-18) of the Royal Air Force; **fly'ing doctor,** a doctor, esp. orig. in the remote parts of Australia, who can be called by radio and who flies to visit patients; **Fly'ing-Dutch'man,** a Dutch black spectral ship, whose captain is condemned to sweep the seas around the Cape of Storms for ever; **fly'ing-fish,** a fish that can leap from the water and sustain itself in the air for a short time, by its long pectoral fins, as if flying; **fly'ing-fox,** a large bat; **fly'ing-machine,** a dirigible contrivance to convey human beings into and through the air: an aircraft; **fly'ing-off'icer,** an officer in the Air Force of rank answering to sub-lieutenant in the navy or lieutenant in the army; **fly'ing-shot,** a shot fired at something in motion; **flying saucer,** a disk-like flying object in the sky reported to have been seen by a number of people; **fly'ing-squirr'el,** a name for several kinds of squirrels that have a fold of skin between the fore and hind leg, by means of which they can take great leaps in the air; **fly'ing-start,** in a race, a start in which the signal is given after the competitors are in motion: a favourable beginning leading to an advantage over others or to initial rapid progress; **flying wing,** an arrow-head-shaped aircraft designed to minimise drag at very high speeds; **fly'leaf,** a blank leaf at the beginning or end of a book; **fly'man,** one who works the ropes in theatre flies, or who drives a fly; **fly'-over,** a processional flight of aircraft: a road or railway-line carried over the top of another one at an intersection; **fly'-pā'per,** a sticky or poisonous paper for destroying flies; **fly'-past,** a ceremonial flight involving more aircraft than a fly-over; **fly'-under,** a road or railway-line carried under another one at an intersection; **fly'(-)weight,** a boxer not heavier than 8 st.; **fly'wheel,** a wheel, usu. relatively massive, which stores energy by inertia, used e.g. to equalise effect of driving effort.—**fly at, upon,** to attack suddenly; **fly in the face of,** to oppose, defy; **fly open,** to open suddenly or violently; **fly out,** to break out in a rage. [O.E. *flēogan,* to fly, *flēoge,* fly; Ger. *fliegen.*]

foal, *fōl, n.* the young of the horse family.—*v.i.* and *v.t.* to bring forth (a foal). [O.E. *fola*; Ger. *fohlen,* Gr. *pōlos*; L. *pullus.*]

foam, *fōm, n.* froth: bubbles on the surface of liquor: (*poet.*) the sea.—*v.i.* to gather foam: to run foaming (over, &c.): to be in a rage.—*v.t.* (*B.*) to throw out with rage or violence (with *out*).—*adv.* **foam'ingly.**—*adjs.* **foam'less,** with-

Neutral vowels in unaccented syllables: *em'pér-ór*; for certain sounds in foreign words see p. ix.

out foam; **foam′y**, frothy.—**foam**, or **foamed, plastics**, very light plastics, soft and flexible like sponges, or rigid, with excellent heat-insulation properties; **foam rubber**, rubber in the form of a foam-like substance, used chiefly in upholstery. [O.E. *fām*; Ger. *feim*, prob. akin to L. *spuma*.]

fob, *fob*, *v.t.* (*arch.*) to cheat: to foist (off upon): to put (off with). [Cf. Ger. *foppen*, to jeer.]

fob, *fob*, *n.* a small pocket for a watch: the watch chain or ribbon hanging from such a pocket. [Perh. conn. with Low Ger. *fobke*, High Ger. dial. *fuppe*, pocket.]

fo′c′sle. Contr. form of **forecastle**.

focus, *fō′kus*, *n.* (*optics*) a point in which rays converge after reflection or refraction: any central point:—*pl.* **fō′cuses, foci** (*fō′sī*).—*v.t.* to bring to a focus: to concentrate:—*pa.p.* fō′cus(s)ed.—*adj.* **fō′cal**, of or belonging to a focus.—*v.t.* **fō′calise**, to bring to a focus: to concentrate.—**in focus**, placed or adjusted so as to secure distinct vision, or a sharp, definite image. [L. *focus*, a hearth.]

fodder, *fod′er*, *n.* food for cattle.—*v.t.* to supply with fodder. [O.E. *fōdor*; allied to **food**, **feed**.]

foe, *fō*, *n.* an enemy.—*n.* **foe′man**, an enemy in war:—*pl.* **foe′men.** [M.E. *foo*—O.E. *fāh, fā* (adj.) and *gefá* (noun).]

foetid, *fē′tid*, *adj.* Same as **fetid**.

foetus, fetus, *fē′tus*, *n.* the young animal in the egg or in the womb, after its parts are distinctly formed, until its birth.—*adjs.* **foe′tal, fē′tal.**—*ns.* **foe′ticide, fē′ticide** (-*sīd*), destruction of the foetus. [L. *fētus*, offspring.]

fog, *fog*, *n.* a thick mist: watery vapour condensed about dust particles: obscurity.—*v.t.* to shroud in fog: to obscure.—*v.i.* to become coated, clouded.—*n.* **fog′-bank**, a dense mass of fog like a bank of land.—*adjs.* **fog′-bound**, impeded by fog; **fogg′y**, misty: clouded in mind: confused, indistinct.—*adv.* **fogg′ily.**—*ns.* **fogg′iness, fog′horn**, a horn sounded as a warning signal in foggy weather; **fog′-signal**, a detonating cap or other audible warning in fog. [Perh. conn. with Dan. *fog*, as in *snee-fog*, thick falling snow.]

fog, *fog*, **foggage**, *fog′ij*, *n.* grass that grows after the hay is cut: (*Scot.*) moss.—*adj.* **fogg′y.**

fogy, fogey, *fō′gi*, *n.* a dull old fellow: a person with antiquated notions [Prob. from **foggy** in sense of 'moss-grown'.]

föhn, foehn, *fœn*, *n.* a hot dry wind blowing down a mountain valley. [Ger. L. *Favōnius*, the west wind.]

foible, *foi′bl*, *n.* a weakness, a failing: a penchant. [O.Fr. *foible*, weak; cf. **feeble**.]

foil, *foil*, *v.t.* to defeat: to baffle: to frustrate:—*pr.p.* foil′ing; *pa.p.* foiled.—*n.* a check, repulse, frustration: a light, blunt-edged sword with a button at the point, used in fencing. [O.Fr. *fuler*, to stamp or crush—L. *fullō*, a fuller of cloth.]

foil, *foil*, *n.* a leaf or thin plate, usu. of metal, as tin-foil: a thin leaf of metal put under a precious stone to show it to advantage: anything that serves as contrast for something else, as a minor character in a play: a small arc in the tracery of a window. [O.Fr. *foil* (Fr. *feuille*)—L. *folium*, a leaf.]

foist, *foist*, *v.t.* to bring in by stealth: to palm off

(upon): to pass off as genuine. [Prob. Du. prov. *vuisten*, to take in the hand; *vuist*, fist.]

fold, *fōld*, *n.* a doubling of anything upon itself: a crease: a part laid over on another: (*geol.*) a bend produced in layers of rock.—*v.t.* to lay in folds: to wrap up, envelop: to interlace (one's arms): clasp (one's hands): to embrace.—*v.i.* to become folded: to cease to function (also **fold up**).—*n.* fold, in composition with numerals = times, e.g. **ten′fold**.—*n.* **fold′er**, a person or thing that folds: a folding case for loose papers.—*adj.* **fold′ing**, that folds, or that can be folded, as *folding-bed, -net, -table*, &c.—*n.* **fold′ing**, a fold or plait: (*geol.*) the bending of strata usu. as the result of compression.—**folded mountains**, mountains produced in the course of millions of years by folding processes.—**fold in** (*cookery*), to mix in carefully and gradually. [O.E. *fealdan*, to fold; Ger. *falten*.]

fold, *fōld*, *n.* an enclosure for domestic animals, esp. sheep: a flock of sheep in a fold: (*fig.*) the Church.—*v.t.* to confine in a fold.—*n.* **fold′ing.** [O.E. *falod, fald*, a fold, stall.]

foliaceous, *fō-li-ā′shŭs*, *adj.* pertaining to or consisting of leaves or laminae. [L. *foliāceus*—*folium*, a leaf.]

foliage, *fō′li-ij*, *n.* leaves collectively: a cluster of leaves: plant forms in art.—*adj.* **fō′liaged**, having natural foliage: ornamented with foliage.—*v.t.* **fō′liate**, (*orig.*) to beat into a leaf: to cover with leaf-metal.—*adj.* **fō′liated**, beaten into a thin leaf: decorated with leaf ornaments: consisting of layers or laminae.—*n.* **fō′liation**, the leafing, esp. of plants: the act of beating a metal into a thin plate. [Fr. *feuillage*—L. *folium*, a leaf.]

folio, *fō′li-ō*, *n.* a leaf (two pages) of a book: a sheet of paper once folded: a book of such sheets: (*book-k.*) a page in an account-book, or two opposite pages numbered as one.—*adj.* pertaining to or containing paper only once folded [Abl. of L. *folium*, a leaf, a sheet of paper.]

foliole, *fō′li-ōl*, *n.* (*bot.*) a leaflet of a compound leaf. [Fr., dim. of L. *folium*, a leaf.]

folk, *fōk*, *n.* people: people of a specified class (e.g. *country folk, menfolk*): a nation or people (esp. at a lower stage of political organisation—*pl.* always *folks*): those of one's own family or acquaintance (*coll.*):—the word is collective *sing.*, or *pl.*—*pl.* also **folks** (*fōks*).—*adj.* handed down by tradition of the people.—*ns.* **folk′land**, in old English times public land as distinguished from *bocland* (bookland)—i.e. land granted to private persons by a written charter; **folk′lore**, the ancient customs, traditions, beliefs, superstitions, &c. of the common people: the study of these; **folk′moot**, an assembly of the people among the old English; **folk′-song, -dance**, a song or dance originating among the people and traditionally handed down by them; **folk′-tale**, a popular story handed down by oral tradition from a more or less remote antiquity. [O.E. *folc*; O.N. *folk*; Ger. *volk*.]

follicle, *fol′i-kl*, *n.* (*bot.*) a fruit formed from a single carpel and containing several seeds—resembling a pod, but splitting along one suture only: (*zool.*) any small sac-like struc-

fāte, fär; mē, hûr (her); *mīne; mōte, för; mūte; mōōn, fŏŏt;* THen (then)

ture, as the pit surrounding a hair root. [Fr.,—L. *folliculus*, dim. of *follis*, a windbag.]

follow, *fol'ō*, *v.t.* to go or come after or behind: to pursue: to proceed along (a road): to practise (a profession): to imitate: to obey: to adopt, as an opinion: to keep the eye or mind fixed on: to grasp or understand the whole course of: to come after in time: to result from: (*B.*) to strive to obtain.—*v.i.* to come after another: to result: to be the logical conclusion.—*ns.* **fol'lower**, one who comes after: a disciple or adherent: a servant-girl's sweetheart; **foll'owing**, the whole body of supporters.—*adj.* coming next after: to be next after: to be next mentioned.—**follow out**, to follow to the end; **follow suit**, in card-playing, to play a card of the same suit as the one that was led: to do what another has done; **follow up**, to pursue (an advantage) closely: to pursue a question, inquiry, &c., that has been started (*n.* **foll'ow-up**).—**follow the sea**, to be a sailor (or sailors). [O.E. *folgian*, *fylgan*; Ger. *folgen*.]

folly, *fol'i*, *n.* silliness or weakness of mind: a foolish thing: (*B.*) sin. [O.Fr. *folie*—*fol*, foolish.]

foment, *fo-ment'*, *v.t.* to apply a warm lotion to: to cherish with heat: to foster (usually evil). —*ns.* **fomenta'tion**, a bathing or lotion with warm water (sometimes extended to a cold or a dry application): instigation; **foment'er**. [Fr. *fomenter*—L. *fōmentāre*—*fōmentum* for *fovimentum*—*fovēre*, to warm.]

fond, *fond*, *adj.* (*arch.*) foolish: foolishly tender and loving: weakly indulgent: prizing highly (with *of*): very affectionate.—*v.t.* **fond'le**, to treat with fondness: to caress.—*n.* **fond'ling**, treating fondly: a pet.—*adv.* **fond'ly**.—*n.* **fond'ness**. [For *fonned*, pa.p. of M.E. *fonnen*, to act foolishly—*fon*, a fool.]

fondant, *fon'dänt*, *n.* a soft sweetmeat that melts in the mouth. [Fr.*fondre*, to melt—L.*fundēre*.]

font, *font*, *n.* the repository of baptismal water. [O.E. *font*—L. *fons*, *fontis*, a fountain.]

font. See **fount** (1).

food, *fōōd*, *n.* what one feeds on: that which, being digested, nourishes the body: whatever sustains or promotes growth or activity (*lit.* and *fig.*).—*n.* **food-stuff**, a commodity used as food.—**food chain**, a series of organisms connected by the fact that each forms food for the next higher organism in the series; **food values**, the relative nourishing powers of foods. [O.E. *fōdal*; Swed. *föda*.]

fool, *fōōl*, *n.* a person showing lack of wisdom, or of common sense: a person of weak mind: a jester.—*v.t.* to deceive: to treat as a fool.—*v.i.* to play the fool: to trifle.—*n.* **fool'ery**, an act of folly, instance of foolishness or absurdity: habitual folly: fooling.—*adj.* **fool'hardy**, foolishly bold: rash, incautious.—*n.* **fool'-hard'i-ness**.—*adj.* **fool'ish**, weak in intellect: wanting discretion: ridiculous: marked with folly.—*adv.* **fool'ishly**.—*n.* **fool'ishness**.—*adj.* **fool'-proof**, not liable to sustain or inflict injury as a result of wrong usage: such that even a fool could not misunderstand or upset (e.g. *fool-proof instructions*, *arrangements*).—*ns.* **fool's'-err'and**, a silly or fruitless enterprise: search for what cannot be found; **fool's para-**

dise, a state of happiness based on fictitious hopes or expectations. [O.Fr. *fol* (Fr. *fou*), It. *folle*—L. *follis*, a wind-bag.]

fool, *fōōl*, *n.* crushed fruit scalded or stewed, mixed with cream and sugar (e.g. *gooseberry fool*). [Prob. **fool** (1), suggested by *trifle*.]

foolscap, *fōōlz'kap*, *n.* a long folio writing or printing paper, 17 x 13½ in., originally bearing the water-mark of a fool's cap and bells.

foot, *fōōt*, *n.* that part of its body on which an animal stands or walks: the lower part or base: a measure = 12 in., orig. the length of a man's foot: foot-soldiers: a division of a line of poetry:—*pl.* **feet** (**foot** in phrases such as *a ten-foot wall*, *five foot six*—sometimes also *five feet six*).—*v.i.* to dance: to walk.—*v.t.* to put new feet to: to add up (an account): to pay (a bill):—*pr.p.* **foot'ing**; *pa.p.* **foot'ed**.—*ns.* **foot'ball**, a large ball for kicking about in sport: play with this ball; **foot'boy**, an attendant in livery; **foot'bridge**, a bridge for foot-passengers.—*p.adj.* **foot'ed**, provided with a foot or feet, esp. of a specified kind (e.g.*light-footed*).—*ns.* **foot'er**, football; **foot'fall**, the sound of setting the foot down; **foot'-gear**, shoes and stockings.—*n.pl.* **foot'-guards**, guards that serve on foot.—*ns.* **foot'hill**, a minor elevation below a high mountain (usu. in *pl.*); **foot'hold**, space on which to plant the feet: (*fig.*) a grip, position secured, esp. if difficult to maintain; **foot'ing**, place for the foot to rest on: placing of the feet: foundation: position, status, conditions (e.g. *on a friendly footing*, *on this footing*): settlement; **foot'light**, one of a row of lights in front of and on a level with the stage in a theatre, &c.; **foot'man**, a servant or attendant in livery:—*pl.* **foot'men**; **foot'mark**, **foot'print**, the mark or print of a foot; **foot'note**, a note of reference or comment, esp. at foot of page (also *fig.*); **foot'pad**, a highwayman on foot; **foot'-pass'enger**, one who travels on foot; **foot'path**, a way for foot-passengers only; **foot'plate**, the platform for footplate-men, train driver and assistant (on steam train, stoker); **foot'pound (force)**, the energy needed to raise a mass of one pound the height of one foot; **foot'-race**, a race on foot; **foot'rule**, a rule or measure in feet and inches.—*v.i.* **foot'slog**, (*slang*) to march, tramp.—*n.* **foot'-sol'dier**, a soldier serving on foot.—*adj.* **foot'-sore**, having sore feet, as by much walking.—*ns.* **foot'-stalk** (*bot.*), the stalk or petiole of a leaf; **foot'step**, the step or impression, or the sound, of the foot: (*pl.*) trace of a course pursued: (*pl.*—*fig.*) course, example.—*ns.* **foot'stool**, a stool to support the feet; **foot'-warm'er**, a contrivance for keeping the feet warm; **foot'-wear**, boots and shoes.—**foot-and-mouth disease** (see **murrain**).—**foot the bill**, to pay up (*lit.* and *fig.*); **foot it**, to walk: to dance.—**have one's feet on the ground**, to act habitually with practical good sense; **put one's best foot foremost** (see **best**); **put one's foot down**, (*fig.*) to take a firm stand, to announce one's views and insist on their being put into effect; **put one's foot in it**, to commit an indiscretion; **set on foot**, to originate: to set in motion (*fig.*). [O.E. *fōt*, pl. *fēt*; Ger. *fuss*, L. *pēs*, *pedis*, Gr. *pous*, *podos*, Sans. *pād*.]

Neutral vowels in unaccented syllables: *em'pér-òr*; for certain sounds in foreign words see p. ix.

footle   foreclose

footle, *foot'l, v.i. (slang)* to trifle, potter.—*adj.*
foot'ling, *(slang)* trivial, ineffectual, purposeless. [Ety. obscure.]

foozle, *fōoz'l, n. (coll.)* a tedious fellow:. a
bungled stroke at golf, &c.—*v.i.* to fool away
one's time.—*v.i.* and *v.t.* to bungle. [Cf. Ger.
dial. *fuseln,* to work badly.]

fop, *fop, n.* an affected dandy.—*ns.* **fop'ling,** a
vain affected person; **fopp'ery,** vanity in dress
or manners: affectation.—*adj.* **fop'pish.**—*adv.*
fopp'ishly.—*n.* **fopp'ishness.** [Cf. Ger. *foppen,*
to hoax.]

for, *för, fôr, prep.* generally used in phrases
indicating a relation of cause or purpose:—
because of, in consequence of (e.g. *he wept for
shame*): in payment of, or recompense of: in
order to be, to serve as, with the object of (e.g.
*enlisted for a soldier, use this for a plate, a
case for holding books*): appropriate to, or
adapted to: in quest of: in the direction of: on
behalf of: in place of: in favour of: with respect to: notwithstanding, in spite of: to the
extent of: through the space of: during.—*conj.*
because.—**as for,** as far as concerns; **for all
(that),** notwithstanding; **for that** *(obs.),* because; **for to** (now *vulg.*), in order to; **for why**
(obs.), why: because. [O.E. *for.*]

forage, *for'ij, n.* fodder, or food for horses and
cattle: provisions: the act of foraging.—*v.i.* to
go about and forcibly carry off food for horses
and cattle, as soldiers: to rummage about (for
what one wants).—*v.t.* to plunder.—*n.*
for'age-cap, the undress cap worn by land and
air forces. [Fr. *fourrage,* O.Fr. *feurre,* fodder, of
Gmc. origin.]

foramen, *fo-rā'men, n.* a small opening:—*pl.*
foram'ina.—*adjs.* **foram'inated, foram'inous,**
pierced with small holes: porous. [L.,—*forare,*
to pierce.]

forasmuch as, *for-az-much' az, conj.* because,
since.

foray, *för'ā, n.* a raid. [Ety. obscure, but cf.
identical with **forage**.]

forbade, *för-bad', pa.t.* of **forbid.**

forbear, *för-bār', v.i.* to be patient: to abstain
(with *to*).—*v.t.* to abstain from: to avoid voluntarily:—*pa.t.* **forbore'**; *pa.p.* **forborne'.**—*n.* **forbear'ance,** exercise of patience, command of
temper: clemency.—*adj.* **forbear'ing,** long-
suffering, patient.—*adv.* **forbear'ingly.** [O.E.
forberan, pa.t. *forbær,* pa.p. *forboren.* Pfx. *for-,*
signifying abstention, and **bear.**]

forbid, *för-bid', v.t.* to prohibit: to command not
(to do): to prevent:—*pa.t.* **forbade** *(för-bad'),*
or **forbad'**; *pa.p.* **forbidd'en.**—*adjs.* **forbidd'en,**
prohibited: unlawful; **forbidd'ing,** repulsive,
raising dislike, unpleasant.—*adv.* **forbidd'-
ingly.** [O.E. *forbēodan,* pa.t. *forbēad,* pa.p. *for-
boden.* Pfx. *for-,* signifying prohibition, and
bid; cf. Ger. *verbieten.*]

force, *förs, förs, n.* strength, power, energy: efficacy: validity (of an argument): significance:
influence: vehemence: violence: coercion or
compulsion: a body of men prepared for action (e.g. *police force, armed forces*): *(mech.)*
any cause which changes the direction or
speed of the motion of a portion of matter.—
v.t. to draw, push, by exertion of strength: to
thrust: to compel, to constrain: to ravish: to
take by violence: to achieve by force: to pro-

duce with effort: to cause (a plant) to grow or
ripen rapidly.—*p.* and *adj.* **forced,** accomplished by great effort (e.g. *a forced march*):
strained, excessive, unnatural: caused to grow
or develop unnaturally fast.—*adj.* **force'ful,**
full of force, vigorous.—*adv.* **force'fully.**—*adj.*
force'less, weak.—*n.* **force'-pump, forc'ing-
pump,** a pump that delivers under pressure
greater than its suction pressure.—*adj.* **forc'-
ible,** having force: done by force.—*n.* **forc'-
ibleness.**—*adv.* **forc'ing.**—*n.* **forc'ing—forced
landing** *(aero.),* a landing at a place where no
landing was orig. planned, necessary because
of some mishap; **forced loan,** a loan extorted
by force; **force the pace,** to increase speed by
special effort. [Fr.,—Low L. *fortia*—L. *fortis,*
strong.]

force, *förs, förs,* **foss,** *fos, n.* a waterfall. [O.N.
fors.]

force, *förs, förs, v.t. (cook.)* to stuff, as a fowl.—*n.*
force'meat, meat chopped fine and highly
seasoned, used as a stuffing or alone. [For
farce—Fr. *farcir,* to stuff.]

forceps, *för'seps, n.* a pincer-like instrument or
organ for holding, lifting, or removing:—*pl.*
for'ceps (also **for'cepses, for'cipēs**).—*adj.*
for'cipated, formed and opening like a forceps. [L., from *formus,* hot, and *capĕre,* to
hold.]

ford, *förd, förd, n.* a place where water may be
crossed on foot.—*v.t.* to cross water on foot.—
adj. **ford'able.** [O.E. *ford*—*faran,* to go; Ger.
furt—*fahren,* to go on foot.]

fore, *för, fôr, adj.* front.—*n.* the front.—*adv.* at or
towards the front (of a ship).—*interj. (golf)* a
warning cry to anybody in the way of the
ball.—**fore and aft,** lengthwise of a ship; **fore-
and-aft sail** (see **sail**); **fore-and-aft rigged,**
with fore-and-aft sails.—**at the fore,** displayed
on the foremast (of a flag), to the **fore,** at
hand: *(Scot.)* in being, alive: *(loosely)* prominent. [O.E. *fore,* radically the same as **for,**
prep.; to be distinguished from pfx. *for-* .]

forearm, *för'ärm, n.* the part of the arm between
the elbow and the wrist. [Pfx. *fore-,* front part
of, and **arm** (1).]

forearm, *för-ärm', v.t.* to arm or prepare beforehand. [Pfx. *fore-,* before, and **arm** (2).]

forebear, *för'bār, n. (Scot.)* an ancestor. [Pfx.
fore , before, **be,** and suffix. *ar, er.*]

forebode, *för-bōd', v.t. (rare)* to foretell: to portend: to have a premonition (esp. of evil).—*n.*
forebod'ing, apprehension of coming evil. [Pfx.
fore-, before, and O.E. *bodian,* to announce—
bod, a message.]

forecabin, *för-kab'in, n.* a cabin in a ship's forepart. [**fore, cabin.**]

forecast, *för'käst, v.t. (arch.)* to plan ahead: to
reckon beforehand: to predict: to fore-
shadow.—*v.i.* to estimate beforehand:—*pa.t.*
and *pa.p.* **fore'cast** (sometimes **forecast'ed**).—
n. **fore'cast** *(obs.),* a plan made beforehand:
(rare) foresight: a prediction. [Pfx. *fore-,* before, and **cast,** to reckon.]

forecastle, fo'c's'le, *fōk's'l,* sometimes *för'käs-l, n.*
a short raised deck at the fore-end of a vessel:
the forepart of the ship under the maindeck,
the quarters of the crew. [**fore, castle.**]

foreclose, *för-klōz', v.t.* to preclude: to prevent:
to take away the right of redeeming (a mort-

fāte, fär; mē, hûr (her); *mīne, mōte, för; mūte; mōōn, fŏŏt;* THen (then)

gage).—*n.* **foreclos′ure**, a foreclosing: (*law*) the process by which a mortgager failing to repay the loan is deprived of his right to redeem the estate.—[O.Fr. *forclos*, pa.p. of *forclore*, to exclude—L. *forīs*, outside, and *claudĕre*, *clausum*, to shut.]

foredate, *fōr-dāt′, v.t.* to date before the true time. [Pfx. *fore-*, before, and **date** (1).]

foredeck, *fōr′dek, n.* the forepart of a deck or ship. [**fore, deck.**]

foredoom, *fōr-dōōm′, v.t.* to doom beforehand. [Pfx. *fore-*, before, and **doom.**]

forefather, *fōr′fä-ᴛʜér, n.* an ancestor. [Pfx. *fore-*, before, and **father.**]

forefinger, *fōr′fing-gér, n.* the finger next the thumb. [**fore, finger.**]

forefoot, *fōr′fŏŏt, n.* one of the anterior feet of a quadruped. [**fore, foot.**]

forefront, *fōr′frunt, n.* the very front or foremost part. [**fore, front.**]

forego, *fōr-gō′, v.t.* to go before, precede—chiefly used in its *pr.p.* foregō′ing and *pa.p.* foregone′.—*n.* **foregō′er.**—**foregone conclusion,** a conclusion come to before examination of the evidence: an inevitable result. [Pfx. *fore-*, before, and **go.**]

forego, better **forgo** (q.v.).

foreground, *fōr′grownd, n.* the part of a picture or field of view nearest the observer's eye, as opposed to the *background* or *distance.* [**fore, ground** (2).]

forehand, *fōr′hand, n.* the part of a horse that is in front of its rider.—*adj.* done beforehand: with the palm in front.—*adj.* **fore′handed,** forehand, as of payment for goods before delivery, or for services before rendered. [**fore, hand.**]

forehead, *for′id, -ed,* or *-hed, n.* the forepart of the head above the eyes, the brow. [Pfx. *fore-*, front part of, and **head.**]

foreign, *for′in, adj.* belonging to another country: from abroad: alien (to), not belonging (to), not appropriate: introduced from outside (as *foreign body*): dealing with, or intended for dealing with, countries other than one's own (as *Foreign Office, foreign bill*).—*n.* **for′eigner,** a native of another country. [O.Fr. *forain*—Low L. *forāneus*—L. *forās, forīs,* out of doors.]

forejudge, *fōr-juj′, v.t.* to judge before hearing the facts and proof. [Pfx. *fore-*, before, and **judge.**]

foreknow, *fōr-nō′, v.t.* to know beforehand: to foresee.—*n.* **foreknowl′edge,** knowledge of a thing before it happens. [Pfx. *fore-*, before, and **know.**]

foreland, *fōr′land, n.* a point of land running forward into the sea, a headland. [**fore, land.**]

foreleg, *fōr′leg, n.* a front leg. [**fore, leg.**]

forelock, *fōr′lok, n.* the lock of hair on the forehead.—**take time by the forelock,** to seize the occasion promptly. [**fore, lock** (2).]

foreman, *fōr′man, n.* the first or chief man: an overseer:—*pl.* **fore′men.** [**fore, man.**]

foremast, *fōr′mäst, -mást, n.* the mast that is forward, or next the bow of a ship. [**fore, mast.**]

foremost, *fōr′mōst, adj.* first in place: most advanced: first in rank or dignity. [O.E. *forma,* first, superl. of *fore,* and superl. suffx. *-st*; it is

therefore a double superl. The O.E. form *formest* was wrongly divided *for-mest* instead of *form-est,* and *-mest* mistaken for *-most.*]

forenoon, *fōr′nōōn, fōr-nōōn′, n. the* the part of the day before midday. [Pfx. *fore-*, before, and **noon.**]

forensic, *fo-ren′sik, adj.* belonging to courts of law, held by the Romans in the forum: used in law pleading.—**forensic medicine,** medical jurisprudence, the application of medical knowledge to the elucidation of doubtful questions in a court of justice. [L. *forēnsis—forum,* market-place.]

fore-ordain, *fōr-or-dān′, v.t.* to arrange beforehand: to predestinate.—*n.* **fore-ordinā′tion.** [Pfx. *fore-*, before, and **ordain.**]

forepart, *fōr′pärt, n.* the front: the early part. [**fore, part.**]

forepeak, *fōr′pēk, n.* the contracted part of a ship's hold, close to the bow. [**fore, peak.**]

foreran, *fōr-ran′, pa.t.* of **forerun.**

forerun, *fōr-run′, v.t.* to run or come before: to precede.—*n.* **forerunn′er,** a runner or messenger sent before: a precursor: an omen. [Pfx. *fore-*, in front of, and **run.**]

foresail, *fōr′s(ā)l, n.* the chief and lowest square sail on the foremast: a triangular sail on the forestay. [**fore, sail.**]

foresee, *fōr-sē′, v.t.* or *v.i.* to see or known beforehand:—*pa.t.* foresaw′; *pa.p.* foreseen′. [Pfx. *fore-*, before, and **see** (2).]

foreshadow, *fōr-shad′ō, v.t.* to shadow or indicate beforehand.—*n.* **foreshad′owing.** [Pfx. *fore-*, before, and **shadow.**]

foreshore, *fōr′shōr, n.* the space between the high and low water marks. [Pfx. *fore-*, the front part of, and **shore** (2).]

foreshorten, *for-shört′n, v.t.* (of the effect of perspective) to cause (an object that projects towards the spectator) to appear as if shortened in the direction of the line of sight, or in any direction making an acute angle with the line of sight: to draw, &c. (an object) so as to show this apparent shortening: also *fig.*—*n.* **foreshort′ening.** [**fore, shorten.**]

foreshow, *fōr-shō′, v.t.* to show or represent beforehand: to predict. [Pfx. *fore-*, before, and **show.**]

foresight, *fōr′sīt, n.* act of foreseeing: wise forethought, prudence: the sight on the muzzle of a gun. [Pfx. *fore-*, before, and **sight.**]

foreskin, *fōr′skin, n.* the skin that covers the glans penis. [**fore, skin.**]

forest, *for′est, n.* a large uncultivated tract of land covered with trees and underwood: woody ground and rough pasture: a preserve for large game (see *deer forest*).—*ns.* **for′ester,** one who has charge of a forest: an inhabitant of a forest; **for′estry,** the art of cultivating forests; **for′est-tree,** a timber-tree. [O.Fr. *forest* (Fr. *forêt*)—Low L. *forestis (silva),* the outside wood, as opposed to the *parcus* (park) or walled-in wood—L. *forīs,* out of doors.]

forestall, *fōr-stöl′, v.t.* (*hist.*) to buy up before reaching the market, so as to sell again at higher prices: to anticipate, to be beforehand in action.—*n.* **forestall′er.** [O.E. *foresteall,* an ambush—*fore-*, before, *steall,* stall.]

forestay, *fōr′stā, n.* a rope reaching from the

Neutral vowels in unaccented syllables: *em′pér-ór*; for certain sounds in foreign words see p. ix.

foremast-head to the bowsprit end to support the mast. [**fore, stay** (2).]

foretaste, *fōr-tāst'*, *v.t.* to taste before possession: to anticipate: to taste before another.—*n.* **fore'taste,** a taste beforehand: a partial experience beforehand of something pleasant or unpleasant. [Pfx. *fore-*, before, and **taste**.]

foretell, *fōr-tel'*, *v.t.* to tell before, to predict.—*v.i.* to utter prophecy.—*n.* **foretell'er.** [Pfx. *fore-*, before, and **tell**.]

forethought, *fōr'thöt*, *n.* thought or care for the future, provident care. [Pfx. *fore-*, before, and **thought**.]

foretoken, *fōr'tō-kn*, *n.* a token or sign beforehand.—*v.t.* **foretō'ken,** to portend. [Pfx. *fore-*, before, and **token**.]

foretop, *fōr'top*, *n.* (*naut.*) the platform at the head of the foremast.—*n.* **foretop'mast,** in a ship, the mast erected at the head of the foremast; at the top of the foretopmast is the **fore'top-gall'ant-mast.** [**fore, top** (1).]

forever, *for ev'ér*, more usually **for ever,** *ev'r* for all time to come: incessantly.—*adv.* **forever'more',** for ever (emphatic).

forewarn, *fōr-wörn'*, *v.t.* to warn beforehand: to give previous notice.—*n.* **forewarn'ing.** [Pfx. *fore-*, before, and **warn**.]

forewing, *fōr'wing*, *n.* one of an insect's front pair of wings. [**fore, wing**.]

forewoman, *fōr'wŏŏm-án*, *n.* a female overseer: *pl.* **fore'women** (*fōr'wim én*). [**fore, woman**.]

foreword, *fōr'würd*, *n.* a preface. [**fore, word**—a 19th century coinage, on analogy of Ger. *vorwort*.]

forfeit, *fōr'fit*, *v.t.* to lose the right to by some fault or crime: (*arch.*) to confiscate: to penalise by forfeiture. (*loosely*) to give up voluntarily (a right).—*n.* that which is forfeited: a penalty for a fault: a fine: something deposited and redeemable.—*adj.* **for'feitable.**—*n.* **for'feiture,** act of forfeiting: state of being forfeited: the thing forfeited. [O.Fr. *forfait*—Low L. *forisfactum*—*forisfacĕre,* to transgress.]

forfend, *fōr-fend'*, *v.t.* (*arch.*) to ward off, avert. [Pfx. *for-*, signifying prohibition, and **fend**.]

forgat, *fōr-gat'*, old *pa.t.* of **forget.**

forgather, *fōr-ga·rнér*, *v.i.* (*Scot.*) to meet. [Pfx. *for-*, inten., and **gather**.]

forgave, *fōr-gāv*, *pa.t.* of **forgive.**

forge, *fōrj*, *fōrj*, *n.* the workshop of a workman in iron, &c.: a furnace, esp. one in which iron is heated: a smithy: a place where anything is shaped or made.—*v.t.* to form by heating and hammering: to form: to fabricate (e.g. a story): to counterfeit (e.g. a signature): to form by great pressure, electricity, or explosion.—*v.i.* to commit forgery.—*ns.* **forg'er,** one who forges or makes: one guilty of forgery; **forg'ery,** fraudulently making or altering any writing: that which is forged or counterfeited. [O.Fr. *forge*—L. *fabrica*—*faber,* a workman.]

forge, *fōrj*, *fōrj*, *v.t.* to move steadily on (usu. with *ahead*). [Origin obscure.]

forget, *fōr-get'*, *v.t.* to put away from the memory: to fail to remember, neglect, omit: to leave behind accidentally:—*pr.p.* forgett'ing; *pa.t.* forgot'; *pa.p.* forgot', forgott'en.—*adj.* **forget'ful,** apt to forget, inattentive.—*adv.* **for-**

get'fully.—*ns.* **forget'fulness; forget'-me-not,** a small herb with beautiful blue flowers, regarded as the emblem of remembrance: a keepsake: a blue colour.—**forget oneself,** to lose one's self-control or dignity. [O.E. *forgietan*—pfx. *for-,* away, *gietan,* to get.]

forgive, *fōr-giv'*, *v.t.* to pardon, or cease to feel resentment against (a person): to pardon, overlook (a debt or trespass).—*v.i.* to be merciful or forgiving:—*pa.t.* forgave'; *pa.p.* forgiv'en.—*n.* **forgive'ness,** pardon, remission: disposition to pardon.—*adj.* **forgiv'ing,** ready to pardon, merciful. [O.E. *forgiefan*—pfx. *for-,* away, *giefan,* to give; cf. Ger. *vergeben*.]

forgo, *fōr-gō'*, less correctly **forego,** *fōr-gō'*, *v.t.* to give up: to forbear the use of. [Pfx. *for-,* signifying abstention, and **go**.]

forgot, forgotten. See **forget.**

fork, *fōrk*, *n.* a pronged instrument: anything that divides into prongs or branches: the space or angle between two branches: one of the branches into which a road or river divides, also the point of separation.—*v.i.* to divide into two branches: to shoot into blades, as corn.—*v.t.* to form as a fork: to move with a fork.—*adjs.* **forked, fork'y,** shaped like a fork.—**fork-lift truck,** a power-driven truck with an arrangement of steel prongs which can lift, raise up high, and carry heavy packages and stack them where required (often used with a pallet). [O.E. *forca*—L. *furca*.]

forlorn, *fōr-lörn'*, *adj.* (*obs.*) quite lost: forsaken: wretched.—*adv.* **forlorn'ly.** [O.E. *forloren,* pa.p. of *forlēosan,* to lose—pfx. *for-,* away, and *lēosan,* to lose.]

forlorn-hope, *fōr-lörn'-hōp*, *n.* a body of soldiers selected for some service of uncommon danger: a desperate enterprise. (from association with hope = expectation) a vain or faint hope. [From the Du. *verloren hoop,* the lost troop.]

form, *förm*, *n.* shape: mode of arrangement: system (e.g. of government): style and arrangement of a musical or literary composition: a prescribed set of words: an established course of procedure, a formality: ceremony: social behaviour : condition of fitness or efficiency: a blank schedule to be filled with details: a mould: (*print.*) the type from which an impression is to be taken arranged and secured in a chase (often **forme**): a long seat, a bench: a class in school: the bed of a hare, shaped by its body: (*slang*) criminal record.—*v.t.* to give form or shape to: to make: to conceive in the mind, as an opinion: to develop (e.g. a habit): to go to make up: (*gram.*) to make by derivation.—*v.i.* to assume a form.—*adj.* **form'al,** according to form or established mode: ceremonial: punctilious: stiff: having the form only, not the spirit: confined to theory.—*ns.* **form'alism,** excessive observance of form or conventional usage, esp. in religion; **form'alist,** one having exaggerated regard to rules or established usages; **formal'ity,** the precise observance of forms or ceremonies: a ceremonial act: a conventional method of procedure: mere convention: stiffness, conventionality, lack of emotional expression.—*adv.* **form'ally.**—*n.* **forma'tion,** act of making or producing: that which is formed: structure: regular array or prearranged order (e.g. *to fly in formation*): (*geol.*) a group of strata with a common characteristic, constituting part of a series.— *adj.* **form'ative,** giving form, determining, fashioning, moulding: (*gram.* —of suffixes, &c.) used in forming words.—*n.* a derivative. —*adj.* **form'less,** shapeless.—**good,** or **bad, form,** according to approved social usage, or the opposite. [O.Fr. *forme* —L. *forma,* shape.]

formalin, *förm'á-lin, n.* name (orig. trade name) for a gas in solution used as an antiseptic, germicide, or preservative.

format, *för'mat, n.* of books, &c., the size, form, shape in which they are issued. [Fr.]

former, *förm'ér, adj.* (*comp.* of **fore**) before in time: past: first mentioned (of two).—*adv.* **form'erly,** in former times, heretofore. [Formed late on analogy of M.E. *formest,* foremost, by adding comp. suffx. *-er* to base of O.E. *forma,* first, itself superlative.]

formic, *för'mik, adj.* pertaining to ants, as formic acid, originally obtained from ants.—*n.* **for'micary,** an ant-hill.—*adj.* **for'micate,** resembling an ant.—*n.* **formica'tion,** a sensation like that of ants creeping on the skin. [L. *formīca,* an ant.]

formidable, *för'mi-dá-bl, adj.* causing fear: redoubtable, difficult to deal with.—*n.* **for'midableness.**—*adv.* **for'midably.** [Fr.,—L. *formīdābilis* —*formīdō,* fear.]

formula, *förm'ū-la, n.* a prescribed form: a formal statement of doctrines: a list of ingredients (of a patent medicine): (*math.*) a general expression for solving problems: (*chem.*) a set of symbols expressing the composition of a substance: a fixed method according to which something is to be done: a statement of joint aims or principles worked out for practical purposes by diplomats of divergent interests: technical specification governing cars entered for certain motor-racing events:—*pl.* **formulae** (*form'ū-lē*), **form'ūlas.**—*ns.* **formularisā'tion, formūlā'tion; form'ūlary,** a formula: a book of formulae or precedents.—*adj.* prescribed: ritual.—*vs.t.* **form'ūlāte, form'ūlīse,** to reduce to or express in a formula: to state or express in a clear or definite form. [L., dim. of *forma.*]

fornicate, *för'ni-kát, adj.* arched: (*bot.*) arching over.—*n.* **fornicā'tion.** [L. *fornicātus* —*fornix,* an arch.]

fornicate, *för'ni-kāt, v.i.* to commit fornication.—*ns.* **fornicā'tion,** sexual intercourse of the unmarried: (*B.*) adultery, and applied frequently by a figure of speech to idolatry; **for'nicātor:**—*fem.* **for'nicātress.** [L. *fornicārī, -ātus* —*fornix,* a brothel.]

forsake, *för-sāk', v.t.* to desert: to give up:—*pr.p.* forsāk'ing; *pa.t.* forsook'; *pa.p.* forsāk'en. [O.E. *forsacan* —*for-,* away, *sacan,* to strive.]

forsooth, *för-sōōth', adv.* in truth, certainly (now only ironically). [**for, sooth.**]

forswear, *för-swār', v.t.* to renounce, esp. upon oath.—*v.i.* to swear falsely:—*pa.t.* forswore'; *pa.p.* forswōrn'.—**forswear oneself,** to swear falsely. [Pfx. *for-,* signifying abstention, and **swear.**]

fort, *fört, fört, n.* a small fortress: an outlying trading-station.—**hold the fort,** to take temporary charge. [Fr.,—L. *fortis,* strong.]

fortalice, *fört'al-is, n.* a small outwork of a fortification. [O.Fr. *fortelesce* —Low L. *fortalitia* —L. *fortis,* strong.]

forte, *fört, n.* that in which one excels. [Fr. *fort,* strong.]

forte, *för'te, adj.* and *adv.* (*mus.*) loud:—*superl.* **fortis'simo,** very loud. [It.]

forth, *förth, förth, adv.* forward: onward: out: into the open: progressively, in continuation: abroad.—*adj.* **forth'coming,** about to appear: approaching: ready to be produced, available at need.—*adv.* **forth'right,** straightforward.— *adj.* straightforward: honest: downright.—*adv.* **forthwith',** immediately. [O.E. *forth* —*fore,* before.]

fortify, *för'ti-fī, v.t.* to strengthen against attack: to impart vigour or endurance to: to confirm (a statement): to add alcohol to (a wine): to add vitamins, &c., to (a food):—*pa.p.* for'tified.—*ns.* **fortificā'tion,** the art of strengthening a military position by means of defensive works: the act of doing so: the work so constructed: that which fortifies; **for'tifier.** [Fr. *fortifier* —Low L. *fortificāre* —*fortis,* strong, *facĕre,* to make.]

fortissimo. See **forte.**

fortitude, *för'ti-tūd, n.* courage in endurance. [L. *fortitūdō* —*fortis,* strong.]

fortnight, *fört'nīt, n.* two weeks or fourteen days.—*adj.* and *adv.* **fort'nightly,** once a fortnight. [Contr. of O.E. *fēowertēne niht,* fourteen nights.]

fortress, *för'tres, n.* a fortified place: a defence. [O.Fr. *forteresse,* another form of *fortelesce.* See **fortalice.**]

fortuitous, *för-tū'i-tus, adj.* happening by chance.—*adv.* **fortū'itously.**—*ns.* **fortū'itousness, fortū'ity.** [L. *fortuitus* —*forte,* by chance.]

fortune, *för'tūn, -chùn, n.* whatever comes by lot or chance, luck: the arbitrary ordering of events: prosperity, success: a large sum of money, wealth.—*adj.* **for'tunāte,** happening by good fortune: lucky: felicitous.—*adv.* **for'tunātely.**—*n.* **for'tune-hunt'er,** one who hunts for wealth, esp. by marriage.—*adj.* **for'tuneless,** without fortune: luckless.—*ns.* **for'tunetell'er,** one who pretends to foretell one's fortune; **for'tune-tell'ing.** [Fr.,—L. *fortūna.*]

forty, *för'ti, adj.* and *n.* four times ten.—*adj.* **for'tieth** (*för'ti-éth*), the last of forty: being one of forty equal parts.—Also *n.* —**forties,** a sea area off the south-west coast of Norway, so called because its depth is forty fathoms; **for'ty-five,** a microgrooved disk record played at a speed of 45 revolutions per minute: (*cap.,* with *the*) the Jacobite rebellion of 1745; **forty winks,** a short nap, esp. after dinner; **the Forty,** the French Academy; **roaring forties** (see **roaring**). [O.E. *fēowertig* —*fēower,* four, *tig,* ten, related to *tien, tēn.*]

forum, *fō'-, fō'rum, n.* a market-place, esp. the market-place in Rome, where public business was transacted and justice dispensed: the courts of law as opposed to the Parliament: a meeting to discuss topics of public concern. [L. *fŏrum,* akin to *forīs,* out of doors.]

forward, *för'wárd, adj.* near or at the forepart: in advance: (*fig.*) advanced (e.g. opinions, party): well-advanced (e.g. a crop): ready: too ready: presumptuous.—*v.t.* to help on: to send

Neutral vowels in unaccented syllables: *em'pér-ór*; for certain sounds in foreign words see p. ix.

on: (*loosely*) to dispatch.—*advs.* **for'ward, for'wards,** towards what is in front, on-ward.—*n.* **for'ward,** in football, &c., a player in the front line.—*adv.* **for'wardly.**—*n.* **for'ward-ness.** [O.E. *foreweard*—*fore*, and -*weard*, sig-nifying direction. *Forwards* (M.E. *forwardes*) was orig. the gen. form (cf. Ger. *vorwärts*).]

foss, fosse, *fos, n.* (*fort.*) a ditch or moat in front of a fortified place. [Fr. *fosse*—L. *fossa*—*fodēre, fossum,* to dig.]

foss. See **force** (2).

fossick, *fos'ik, v.i.* to be troublesome: to under mine another's diggings, or work over waste-heaps for gold: to search about for any kind of profit. [Australian.]

fossil, *fos'il, n.* the petrified remains of an ani-mal or vegetable found embedded in the strata of the earth's crust: anything antiquated.—*adj.* in the condition of a fossil: antiquated.—*adj.* **fossilif'erous,** bearing or containing fos-sils.—*v.t.* **foss'ilise,** to convert into a fossil—*v.i.* to be changed into a stony or fossil state.—*ns.* **fossilisa'tion,** a changing into a fossil; **foss'ilist,** one skilled in fossils. [Fr. *fos-sile*—L. *fossilis*—*fodēre,* to dig.]

foster, *fos'tér, v.t.* to bring up or nurse, esp. a child not one's own: to encourage.—*ns.* **fos'ter-broth'er,** a male child, fostered or brought up with a family of different parent age; **fos'ter-child; fos'ter-daugh'ter; fos'terer; fos'ter-fa'ther,** one who brings up a child in place of its father; **fos'terling,** a foster-child; **fos'ter-moth'er,** one who brings up a child not her own; **fos'ter-par'ent; fos'ter-sis'ter; fos'ter-son.** [O.E. *fōstrian,* to nourish, *fōstor,* food.]

fought, *föt, pa.t.* and *pa.p.* of **fight.**

foul, *fowl, adj.* filthy: loathsome: impure: ob-scene: unfavourable, stormy: unfair, against the rules (e.g. a *foul stroke*). (*arch.*) ugly. choked up: entangled (e.g. a rope).—*v.t.* to make foul: to collide with: to become en-tangled with.—*v.i.* to become foul: to collide: to become entangled.—*n.* act of fouling: any breach of the rules in games or contests.—*adv.* **foul'ly.**—*ns.* **foul'ness; foul'-brood,** a bacterial disease of bee larvae.—*adj.* **foul'-mouthed,** ad-dicted to the use of foul or profane lan-guage.—*n.* **foul'-play,** unfair action in any game or contest: dishonesty: violence or mur-der.—**fall foul of,** to come against: to quarrel with: to assault. [O.E. *fūl;* Ger. *faul.*]

foulard, *fōō'ärd, n.* soft untwilled silk fabric. [Fr.]

foumart, *fōō'märt, n.* an old name for the pole-cat, from its offensive smell. [M.E. *fulmard*—O.E. *fūl,* foul, *mærth,* a marten.]

found, *pa.t.* and *pa.p.* of **find.**—*n.* **found'ling,** a little child found deserted.

found, *fownd, v.t.* to lay the bottom of or founda-tion of: to originate: to endow: to base on some ground, principle, &c. (e.g. on fact, on justice).—*v.i.* to rely.—*ns.* **founda'tion,** the act of founding: the base of a building: the groundwork or basis: a permanent fund for a benevolent purpose or for some special object; **founda'tioner,** one supported from the funds or foundation of an institution; **founda'tion-stone,** one of the stones forming the founda-tion of a building, esp. a stone laid with public ceremony; **found'er,** one who founds, estab-

lishes, or originates: an endower:—*fem.* **found'ress.**—**well founded,** reasonable, justi-fied. [Fr. *fonder*—L. *fundāre, -ātum,* to found—*fundus,* the bottom.]

found, *fownd, v.i.* to form by melting and pour-ing into a mould, to cast.—*ns.* **found'er,** one who melts and casts metal, as a *brassfounder*; **found'ing,** metal-casting; **found'ry,** the art of founding or casting: the place where founding is carried on. [Fr. *fondre*—L. *fundēre, fusum,* to pour.]

founder, *fownd'er, v.i.* to subside, to collapse: to fill with water and sink: to go lame (of a horse).—*v.t.* to cause to founder. [O.Fr. *fon-drer,* to fall in—*fond,* bottom—L. *fundus,* bot-tom.]

fount, *fownt, font, font, n.* a complete assortment of type of one sort, with all that is necessary for printing in that kind of letter. [Fr. *fonte*—*fondre*—L. *fundēre,* to cast.]

fount, *fownt, n.* a spring of water: a source. [L. *fons, fontis.*]

fountain, *fownt'in, -en, n.* a spring of water, natural or artificial: the structure for produc-ing a jet or jets, &c., of water: the source of anything: a reservoir for holding oil, &c., in a lamp.—*ns.* **fount'ain-head,** the head or source, the beginning; **fount'ain-pen,** a pen having a reservoir for holding ink. [Fr. *fontaine*—Low L. *fontāna*—L. *fons, fontis,* a spring.]

four, *fōr, fōr, adj.* and *n.* the cardinal number next above three.—*n.* the figure 4 or iv de-noting this.—*adjs.* **fourth** (see below); **four'-foot'ed,** having four feet; **four'-hand'ed,** of a game, played by four people.—*ns.* **four'-in-hand,** a coach drawn by four horses; **four'-post'er,** a large bed with four posts on which to hang curtains.—*adjs.* **four'score,** four times a score—80; **four'some,** by fours: in which four act together (also *n.*), **four'-square,** square: presenting a firm, bold front to all.—**four-letter word,** any of a number of vulgar short words, esp. of four letters, referring to sex or excrement, formerly taboo.—**on all fours,** on hands and knees: analogous, strictly comparable. [O.E. *fēower;* Ger. *vier.*]

fourteen, *fōr'tēn* (when used absolutely), *fōr-tēn'), adj.* and *n.* four and ten.—*adj.* **four-teenth,** the last of fourteen: being one of four-teen equal parts.—Also *n.* [O.E. *fēowertēne.*]

fourth, *fōrth, adj.* last of four: being one of four equal parts.—Also *n.*—*adv.* **fourth'ly,** in the fourth place.—**fourth dimension,** time, re garded as the fourth measurable extent in the *space time continuum* (q.v.) in which events take place; **fourth estate,** a group of people other than the lords, commons and clergy, who influence a country's politics: the news-papers. [O.E. *fēowertha, fēortha.*]

fowl, *fowl, n.* a bird: a bird of the poultry kind, a cock or hen: the flesh of a fowl:—*pl.* **fowls, fowl.**—*v.i.* to kill, or try to kill, wildfowl.—*ns.,* **fowl'er,** one who takes wildfowl; **fowl'ing-piece,** a light gun for small-shot, used in fowling. [O.E. *fugol;* Ger. *vogel.*]

fox, *foks, n.* any of several animals akin to the dog (*fem.* **vix'en**): anyone notorious for cun-ning.—*v.t.* (*coll.*) to baffle, deceive, cheat.—*v.i.* (*coll.*) to sham, cheat.—*ns.* **fox'-brush,** the tail of a fox; **fox'-earth,** a fox's burrow; **fox'glove,**

a plant (genus *Digitalis*) with flowers like glove-fingers; **fox′hound,** a hound for hunting foxes; **fox′-hunt; fox′-hunt′er; fox′-terr′ier,** a kind of terrier trained to unearth foxes; **fox′-trot,** a horse's pace with short steps, as in changing from trotting to walking: a dance to syncopated music.—*adj.* **fox′y,** of foxes: cunning: reddish-brown. [O.E. *fox*; Ger. *fuchs.*]

foyer, *fwä′yā, n.* in theatres, a lobby, an anteroom for waiting, &c. [Fr.,—L. *focus,* hearth.]

fracas, *frak′ä, frä-kä′, n.* uproar: a noisy quarrel. [Fr.,—It. *fracasso*—*fracassare,* to make an uproar.]

fraction, *frak′sh(ó)n, n.* a fragment or very small piece: (*arith.*) any part of a unit: any one of several portions collected separately in e.g. fractional distillation.—*adj.* **frac′tional,** belonging to, or containing, a fraction or fractions.—*v.t.* **frac′tionalise,** to break up into parts.—*ns.* **frac′tionalist,** a breaker up of political unity; **frac′tionalism,** state of consisting of discrete units: action of forming a fraction within the Communist party.—**fractional distillation,** a distillation process for the separation of the various constituents of liquid mixtures by means of their different boiling points. [O.Fr. *fraccion*—L. *fractiō, -ōnis*—*frangēre, fractum,* to break.]

fractious, *frak′shús, adj.* ready to quarrel: peevish.—*adv.* **frac′tiously.**—*n.* **frac′tiousness.** [From *fraction* in obs. sense of quarrelling, dissension.]

fracture, *frak′tyùr, -chùr, n.* the breaking of any hard body: the breach or part broken: the breaking of a bone.—*v.t.* and *v.i.* to break.—**simple fracture,** one in which the bone is broken at one place and there is no wound of the skin communicating with the fracture; **comminuted fracture,** one in which the bone is broken in several places; **greenstick fracture,** one in which the bone is partly broken, partly bent; **impacted fracture** (see **impacted**); **compound fracture,** one in which there is a wound of the skin communicating with the fracture; **complicated fracture,** one in which there is some other injury, e.g. rupture of a large blood-vessel. [L. *fractūra*—*frangēre, fractum,* to break.]

fragile, *fraj′īl, fraj′il, adj.* easily broken: frail: delicate.—*n.* **fragil′ity,** the state of being fragile. [Fr.,—L. *fragilis*—*frangēre,* to break.]

fragment, *frag′mént, n.* a piece broken off: an unfinished portion: an extant portion of something of which the rest has been destroyed or lost.—*adjs.* **fragment′al** (also *frag′-; geol.*), composed of fragments of older rocks; **frag′mentary,** consisting of fragments or pieces: existing or operating in separate parts; **fragmentā′tion,** division into fragments. [Fr.,—L. *fragmentum*—*frangēre,* to break.]

fragrant, *frāg′ránt, adj.* sweet-scented.—*ns.* **frā′grance, frā′grancy,** pleasantness of smell: sweet or grateful influence.—*adv.* **frā′grantly.** [Fr.,—L. *frāgrans, -antis,* pr.p. of *frāgrāre,* to smell.]

frail, *frāl, adj.* very easily shattered: of weak health or physique: morally weak.—*ns.* **frail′ness, frail′ty,** weakness: infirmity. [O.Fr. *fraile*—L. *fragilis,* fragile.]

fraise, *frāz, n.* (*fort.*) a horizontal or nearly horizontal palisade of pointed stakes. [Fr.]

frame, *frām, v.t.* to form: to put together: to plan: to adapt (with *to, into*): to articulate (e.g. *he could not frame the words*): to enclose in a frame or border: to serve as a frame for.—*v.i.* (*B.*) to contrive (to).—*n.* form, system: a putting together of parts: a structure made to enclose or support anything: the skeleton: state (of mind): a unit picture in a cinema film: (*TV*) one of the two interlaced sets of scanning lines, or (now usu.) both together, giving a complete image: in certain games, or a definite number of games.—**frame of reference** (*lit.*), a set of axes with reference to which the position of a point, &c., is described: (*fig.*) the structure of standards, arising from the individual's experience, and continually developing, to which he refers, in all cases from the simplest to the most complicated, when judging or evaluating.—*ns.* **frame′-house,** a house consisting of a skeleton of timber covered with boards, &c.; **fram′er,** he who forms or constructs: one who makes frames for pictures, &c.; **frame′-up,** a fraudulent scheme: a plot to incriminate a person on false evidence (*v.t.*—also **frame**—to incriminate a person thus); **frame′work,** work that forms the frame: the skeleton or outline of anything; **fram′ing,** the act of constructing: a frame or setting. [O.E. *framian,* to be helpful, *fram,* forward.]

franc, *frangk, n.* a coin, forming since 1795 the unit of the French monetary system (**new,** or **heavy, franc** introduced 1960): the unit also in Belgium and Switzerland. [O.Fr. *franc,* from the words *Francorum rex* (King of the Franks) on the first coins.]

franchise, *fran′chīz, -shīz, -chiz, n.* a privilege or right granted: the right of voting for a member of Parliament. [O.Fr.,—*franc,* free.]

Franciscan, *fran-sis′kán, adj.* belonging to the order of St *Francis* in the R.C. Church.—*n.* a monk of this order. [L. *Franciscus,* Francis.]

Franco-, *frangk′ō,* French, in combinations as *Franco-German, Franco-Russian,* &c.—*ns.* **Franc′ophil(e)** (*-fīl*), a lover of things French (Gr. *philos,* dear); **Franc′ophobe** (*-fōb*), a hater of things French (Gr. *phobos,* fear).

franc-tireur, *frä-tē-rœr′, n.* a French sharpshooter. [Fr. *franc,* free, *tireur,* a shooter.]

frangible, *fran′ji-bl, adj.* easily broken.—*n.* **frangibil′ity.** [O.Fr. Same root as **fraction.**]

frangipane, *fran′ji-pān, n.* a rich kind of pastry-cake: a perfume. [Fr.]

frank, *frangk, adj.* (*obs.*) free: open, candid: avowed.—*v.t.* (*hist.*) to sign so as to ensure free carriage, as a letter: to mark by means of a **franking machine** to show that postage has been paid.—*n.* the signature of a person who had the right to frank a letter.—*adv.* **frank′ly,** candidly.—*n.* **frank′ness.** [O.Fr. *franc*—Low L. *francus*—O.H.G. *Franko,* Frank, hence a free man.]

Frank, *frangk, n.* a German of a confederation in *Franconia,* of which a branch conquered Gaul in the 5th century, and founded France: the name given in the East to a native of Western Europe.—*adj.* **Frank′ish.**

Frankenstein, *frangk′en-stīn, n.* the hero of

Neutral vowels in unaccented syllables: *em′pér-ór*; for certain sounds in foreign words see p. ix.

282

Mary Shelley's romance so named, who by his skill forms an animate creature like a man, only to his own torment: (*erroneously*) the monster: any creation that brings disaster to its author.

Frankfurter, *frangk'fŏŏr-tér, n.* a small smoked sausage. [Ger.]

frankincense, *frangk'in-sens, n.* sweet-smelling resin from Arabia. [O.Fr. *franc encens,* pure incense.]

franklin, *frangk'lin, n.* an old English freeholder. [Low L. *francus.* See **frank.**]

frantic, *fran'tik, adj.* mad: furious, wild.—*adv.* **fran'tically.** [O.Fr. *frenetique*—L. *phreneticus*—Gr. *phrenētikos,* mad—*phrēn,* the mind. Cf. **frenzy.**]

fraternal, *fra-tûr'nål, adj.* belonging to a brother or brethren: brotherly.—*adv.* **frater'nally.**—*v.i.* **frat'ernise,** to associate as brothers: to seek brotherly fellowship.—*ns.* **fraternisā'tion; frat'erniser; frater'nity,** the state of being brethren: a society formed on a principle of brotherhood. [L. *fráter,* a brother, Gr. *phrátēr,* a clansman.]

fratricide, *frat'ri sīd, n.* one who kills his brother: the murder of a brother.—*adj.* **frat'-ricīdal.** [Fr.,—L. *fráter, frátris,* brother, *caedĕre,* to kill.]

frau, *frow, n.* Ger. for a woman, or (*cap.*) Mrs. See **hausfrau.**

fraud, *frŏd, n.* deceit: imposture: a deceptive trick: (*coll.*) a cheat, impostor: a fraudulent production.—*adj.* **fraud'ulent,** using fraud: dishonest. *adv.* **fraud'ulently.**—*ns.* **fraud'ulence, fraud'ulency**—**pious fraud,** a deception carried out from pious motives and supposed to benefit the deceived. [O.Fr.,—L. *fraus, fraudis,* fraud.]

fraught, *frŏt, adj.* freighted, laden: filled. [Prob. Old Du. *vracht.* Cf. **freight.**]

fray, *frā, n.* a conflict: a brawl.—*v.t.* (*B.*) to frighten. [Abbrev. of **affray.**]

fray, *frā, v.t.* to wear off by rubbing: to ravel out the edge of.—*v.i.* to become frayed. [Fr. *frayer*—L. *fricāre,* to rub.]

freak, *frēk, n.* a sudden caprice or fancy: a prank: an abnormal production of nature, a monstrosity: an eccentric.—*adj.* abnormal (e.g. *a freak storm, result*).—*adj.* **freak'ish,** apt to change the mind suddenly, capricious: suggestive of a freak: unusual, odd.—*adv.* **freak'ishly.**—*n.* **freak'ishness.** [A late word; cf. O.E. *frician,* to dance.]

freak, *frēk, v.t.* to spot or streak, to variegate.—*n.* a streak of colour. [Perh. same as **freak** (1).]

freckle, *frek'l, v.t.* to spot: to colour with spots.—*n.* brownish-yellow spot on the skin: any small spot.—*adjs.* **freck'ly, freck'led,** full of freckles. [O.N. *freknur* (pl.), Dan. *fregne.*]

free, *frē, adj.* not bound: at liberty: not under arbitrary government: unrestrained: unconstrained: frank: ready (e.g. *free to confess*): lavish: not attached: exempt (from): having a franchise (with *of*): without payment: not literal (e.g. *a translation*).—*v.t.* to set at liberty: to deliver from what confines: to rid (with *from, of*):—*pr.p.* free'ing; *pa.p.* freed—*adv.* **free'ly.**—*ns.* **free'-ag'ency,** state or power of acting freely and independently; **free'-ag'ent; free'-board,** the space between water-line and deck.—*adj.* **free'born,** born of free parents.—*ns.* **freed'man,** a man who has been a slave, and has been set free:—*pl.* **freed'men; free'dom,** liberty: frankness: boldness: exemption, immunity: privileges connected with a city: improper familiarity: licence; **free enterprise,** the conduct of business without interference from the state; **free'-fall,** the motion of an unpropelled body in a gravitational field, as that of a spacecraft in orbit: the part of a parachute jump before the parachute opens; **free fight,** an indiscriminate, riotous fight, a mêlée; **free-for-all,** a race or contest open to anyone, or a free fight.—*adjs.* **free'-hand,** (of drawing) done by the unguided hand; **free'-hand'ed,** open-handed, liberal; **free'-heart'ed,** open-hearted: liberal.—*ns.* **free'hold,** a property held free of duty except to the king; **free'holder,** one who possesses a freehold; **free house,** a public-house that is not tied to a particular supplier; **free kick,** a kick allowed without interference; **free'labour,** a mercenary knight or soldier: one who works for himself without an employer: an unattached journalist, politician, &c.; **free'man,** a man who is free or enjoys liberty: one who holds a particular franchise or privilege:—*pl.* **free'men; free'mason,** in the Middle Ages, a stone-mason of a superior grade: a member of a secret fraternity united in lodges for social enjoyment and mutual assistance; **free-ma'sonry,** the institutions, practices, &c. of freemasons: sense of fellowship, instinctive sympathy; **free'ness.**—*adj.* **free'-range',** (of poultry) allowed some freedom to move about: (of eggs) laid by free-range hens.—*ns.* **free'stone,** any easily wrought building stone; **free'thinker,** one who rejects authority in religion: a rationalist; **free'-thinking** (also *adj.*), **free'-thought, free trade,** free or unrestricted trade: free interchange of commodities without protective duties; **free'way,** (*U.S.*), a toll-free road for high speed traffic; **free' wheel',** the mechanism of a bicycle by which the hind-wheel may be temporarily disconnected and set free from the driving-gear.—*v.i.* (of motor vehicle or its driver) to coast: (*fig.*) to move, act, live, without restraint or concern.—*n.* **free'-will,** liberty of choice: power of acting freely, not under the compulsion of fate or of fixed laws governing human actions (opp. to *determinism* and to *necessity*).—*adj.* spontaneous, voluntary. **free love,** freedom in sexual relations, **free on board** (F.O.B.), delivered on the vessel or other conveyance without charge; **free verse,** verse disregarding usual metrical laws.—**a free hand,** liberty to choose for oneself, or to act as one thinks best; **make free with,** to take liberties with. [O.E. *frēo;* Ger. *frei,* O.N. *frī.*]

freebooter, *frē'bŏŏt-ér, n.* one who roves about freely in search of booty: a plunderer. [Du. *vrijbuiter*—*vrij,* free, *buit,* booty.]

freeze, *frēz, v.i.* to become ice: to become solid by fall of temperature: to be very cold: to become motionless, stiff, &c.: as if with cold (e.g. *to freeze with terror*): to become fixed, attached (to) by cold.—*v.t.* to cause to freeze: to prevent the use of, or dealings in, (credits, assets): to fix at a specific amount (prices, wages, &c.):—*pr.p.* freez'ing; *pa.t.* froze; *pa.p.* froz'en.—*ns.* **freeze'-dry'ing,** freezing (a solution) rapidly, and then drying by evaporation, under high vacuum, of moisture from the ice; **freez'er.** a freezing apparatus; **freez'ing-down,** lowering of the body temperature, in preparation of heart and other operations; **freez'ing-mix'ture,** a mixture, as of pounded ice and salt, producing cold sufficient to freeze a liquid; **freez'ing-point,** temperature at which a liquid solidifies—that of water being 32° Fahrenheit, 0° centigrade (Celsius).—**freeze on to,** to cling to; **freeze out** (*coll.*), to drive (a person) away from one's society by an unfriendly attitude: to exclude, as a firm from business dealings. [O.E. *frēosan,* pa.p. *froren*; Du. *vriezen,* Ger. *frieren,* to freeze.]

freight, *frāt, n.* the lading or cargo, esp. of a ship: the charge for transporting goods by water or land.—*v.t.* to load a ship.—*ns.* **freight'age,** money paid for freight; **freight'-car** (*U.S.*), a goods wagon; **freight'er,** one who freights a vessel: a cargo-boat: a cargo aircraft. [Prob. Old Du. *vrecht,* a form of *vracht.* See **fraught.**]

French, (in names of commodities sometimes spelt without *cap.*), *french, -sh, adj.* belonging to *France* or its people: originating in France.—*n.* the people or language of France.—*ns.* **French bean,** a kidney bean, the green pods and seeds of which are eaten; **French'-chalk,** a soft mineral (soapstone) ground fine, used in dry-cleaning, &c.; **French'man,** a native or naturalised inhabitant of France:—*fem.* **French'woman;** **French'-pol'ish,** a varnish for furniture, consisting chiefly of shellac dissolved in some spirit; **French window,** a long window opening like a door.—**take French leave,** to depart hastily or secretly without warning.

frenetic. See **phrenetic.**

frenzy, *fren'zi, n.* a violent excitement: a paroxysm of madness.—*adj.* **fren'zied.** [O.Fr. *frenesie* — Gr. *phrenītis,* inflammation of the brain—*phrēn,* the mind.]

frequent, *frē'kwént, adj.* coming or occurring often.—*v.i.* (*fré-kwent'*) to visit often: to resort to.—*ns.* **frē'quency,** repeated occurrence: commonness of occurrence: the number per second of vibrations, cycles, or other recurrences; **frēquentā'tion,** the act of visiting often.—*adj.* **frequent'ative** (*gram.*), denoting the frequent repetition of an action.—*n.* (*gram.*) a verb expressing such repetition.—*n.* **frequent'er.**—*adv.* **frē'quently.**—*n.* **frē'quentness.** —**frequency modulation** (see **modulation**). [L. *frequēns, frequentis*; conn. with *farcīre,* to stuff.]

fresco, *fres'kō, n.* a painting executed on walls covered with damp freshly-laid plaster.—*v.t.* to paint in fresco. [It. *fresco,* fresh.]

fresh, *fresh, adj.* in a state of activity: untired: blooming, healthy-looking: in new condition, not stale, faded, or soiled: another (e.g. *a fresh chapter, venture, start*): invigorating: (of wind) strong: (*slang*) making obnoxious advances: without salt: (of food) not preserved in any way: (*Scot.*) not frosty.—*adv.* newly. —*n.* the fresh part (e.g. of the day).—*v.t.* **fresh'en,** to make fresh: to take the saltness from.—*v.i.* to grow fresh: to grow brisk

or strong.—*n.* **fresh'et,** a pool or stream of fresh water: the sudden overflow of a river from rain or melted snow.—*adv.* **fresh'ly.** —*ns.* **fresh'man,** a university student in his first year—also **fresh'er;** **fresh'ness.**—*adj.* **fresh'(-)water,** living in water not salt: accustomed to sail only in fresh water—hence unskilled, raw. [O.E. *fersc*; *cf.* Du. *versch,* Ger. *frisch.*]

fret, *fret, v.t.* to eat into: to wear away (e.g. a passage) by rubbing: to roughen by rubbing: to ripple (water): to vex.—*v.i.* to wear, fray: to vex oneself: to be peevish:—*pr.p.* fret'ting; *pa.p.* fret'ed; (*B.*) fret.—*n.* irritation: a worn or eroded place.—*adj.* **fret'ful,** peevish.—*adv.* **fret'fully.**—*n.* **fret'fulness.** [O.E. *fretan,* to gnaw—pfx. *for-,* inten., and *etan,* to eat; Ger. *fressen.*]

fret, *fret, v.t.* to ornament with interlaced work: to variegate:—*pr.p.* fret'ting; *pa.p.* fret'ed.—*n.* ornamental network: (*archit.*) an ornament consisting of small fillets (straight bands) meeting usually at right angles.—*n.* **fret'-saw,** a saw with a narrow blade and fine teeth, used for fret-work, &c.—*adj.* **frett'ed,** ornamented with frets.—*n.* **fret'-work,** ornamental work consisting of a combination of frets: perforated woodwork. [O.Fr. *frete,* trellis-work.]

fret, *fret, n.* a wooden or metal ridge on the finger-board of a guitar or other instrument.—*v.t.* to furnish with frets. [Prob. same as **fret** (2).]

Freudian, *froid'i-án, adj.* pertaining to' Sigmund Freud (1856-1939) and his psychology of the unconscious.

friable, *frī'á-bl, adj.* apt to crumble: easily reduced to powder.—*ns.* **frī'ableness, friabil'ity.** [Fr.—L. *friābilis*—*friāre, friātum,* to crumble.]

friar, *frī'ár, n.* a member of one of the mendicant monastic orders in the R.C. Church.—*n.* **frī'ary,** a monastery.—**friar's balsam,** compound tincture of benzoin; **friar's lantern,** the will o' the wisp. [O.Fr. *frere*—L. *frāter,* a brother.]

fribble, *frib'l, v.i.* to trifle.—*n.* a trifler. [Onomatopoeic; prob. influenced by **frivol.**]

fricassee, *frik-a-sē', n.* a dish made of fowl, rabbit, &c. cut into pieces and cooked in sauce.—*v.t.* to dress as a fricassee:—*pr.p.* fricassee'ing; *pa.p.* fricasseed'. [Fr. *fricassée.*]

fricative. See **friction.**

friction, *frik'sh(ò)n, n.* rubbing: (*statics*) when two bodies are in contact, the resistance to motion (of one or both) caused by the surfaces of the bodies: disagreement.—*n.* **fric'a-tive,** a consonant produced by the breath being forced through a narrow opening (as *f, th*), an open consonant, a spirant.—Also *adj.* [L. *fricāre, frictum,* to rub.]

Friday, *frī'dā, n.* the sixth day of the week. [O.E. *Frīgedæg,* day of (the goddess) *Frīgg.*]

fried, *frīd, pa.t.* and *pa.p.* of **fry.**

friend, *frend, n.* an intimate acquaintance: a well-wisher.—*adj.* **friend'less,** without friends.—*n.* **friend'lessness.**—*adj.* **friend'ly,** like a friend: having the disposition of a friend: favourable.—*ns.* **friend'liness; friend'ship,** attachment from mutual esteem: friendly assistance.—**Friendly Society,** a benefit society, an association for relief dur-

Neutral vowels in unaccented syllables: *em'pér-òr*; for certain sounds in foreign words see p. ix.

284

ing sickness, old age, widowhood; **Society of Friends**, the sect of Christians better known as Quakers. [O.E. *frēond*, orig. a pr.p.; cf. *frēon*, to love; Ger. *freund*.]

frieze, *frēz*, *n.* a rough, heavy woollen cloth. [Fr. *frise*.]

frieze, *frēz*, *n.* (*archit.*) the part of the entablature (q.v.) between the architrave and cornice: a decorative band along the top of the wall of a room. [O.Fr. *frize*; It. *fregio*; perh. L. *Phrygium*, Phrygian.]

frig, **fri(d)ge**, *frij*, *n.* refrigerator.

frigate, *frig'ăt*, *n.* orig. a light vessel driven by oars or by sails: later a vessel in the class next to ships of the line—not now denoting a distinct class.—*n.* **frig'ate-bird**, a large tropical sea-bird, with very long wings. [O.Fr. *fregate*—It. *fregata*; ety. uncertain.]

fright, *frīt*, *n.* sudden fear: terror: (*coll.*) a figure of grotesque or ridiculous appearance.—*v.t.* **fright**, **fright'en**, to make afraid: to alarm.—*adj.* **fright'ful**, terrible, shocking: (*coll.*) exessive, very bad.—*adv.* **fright'fully**.—*n.* **fright'fulness**, quality of being terrifying or shocking: a policy of intimidating by means of brutality. [O.E. *fyrhto*; cf. Ger. *furcht*, fear.]

frigid, *frij'id*, *adj.* frozen or stiffened with cold: cold: without spirit or feeling: unanimated: sexually unresponsive.—*n.* **frigid'ity**.—*adv.* **frig'idly**.—*n.* **frig'idness**.—*adj.* **frigorif'ic** (*frig*-), causing cold.—**frigid zones**, the parts of the earth's surface within the polar circles. [L. *frīgidus*—*frīgēre*, to be cold—*frīgus*, cold.]

frill, *fril*, *v.t.* to furnish with a frill or frills.—*n.* a ruffle: a ruffled or crimped edging: (*pl.*) superfluous ornament or elaboration.

fringe, *frinj*, *n.* a border of loose threads: hair cut falling over the brow: a border: a margin: anything bordering on or additional to an activity (also *adj.*)—*v.t.* to adorn with fringe: to border.—*adj.* **fringe'less**. [O.Fr. *frenge*—L. *fimbriae*, threads, fibres, akin to *fibra*, a fibre.]

frippery, *frip'ėr-i*, *n.* (*obs.*) cast-off clothes: (*obs.*) an old-clothes shop: tawdry finery: useless trifles. [O.Fr. *freperie*, *frepe*, a rag.]

Frisian, *frizh'ăn*, *friz'i-ăn*, *n.* one of an ancient Germanic tribe of northern Holland, the *Frisii*: the language of the Frisii, akin to Old English: a native or inhabitant of modern Friesland: the province of Holland.—Also *adj.*

frisk, *frisk*, *v.i.* to gambol: to leap playfully.—*v.t.* (*slang*) to search the pockets, &c., of (a person): to search for radioactive emission by e.g. contamination meter.—*n.* a frolicsome movement.—*adj.* **frisk'y**, lively, jumping with gaiety, frolicsome.—*adv.* **frisk'ily**.—*n.* **frisk'iness**. [O.Fr. *frisque*.]

frisson, *frē-sɔ̄*, *n.* shiver: shudder: thrill.

frit, *frit*, *n.* the mixed materials for making glass, pottery, &c. [L. *frīgĕre*, *frīctum*, to roast.]

frith, *frith*. Same as **firth**.

fritter, *frit'ėr*, *n.* a piece of fruit, &c. fried in batter. [O.Fr. *friture*—L. *frīgĕre*, to fry.]

fritter, *frit'ėr*, *n.* a fragment.—*v.t.* to break into fragments: to squander piecemeal (with *away*). [Obs. n.pl. *fitters*, rags, fragments.]

frivolous, *friv'ŏ-lŭs*, *adj.* trifling: silly.—*v.t.* and *v.i.* **frivol**, to trifle.—*n.* **frivol'ity**, trifling habit or nature: levity: an act, or a thing, that is frivolous.—*adv.* **friv'olously**.—*n.* **friv'olous-**

ness. [L. *frīvolus*, perh.—*fricāre*, to rub.]

frizz, friz, *friz*, *v.t.* and *v.i.* to form into, or to be or become, small short crisp curls.—*n.* a curl: a mass of curls. [O.Fr. *friser*, to curl; perh. conn. with *frieze*, cloth.]

frizzle, *friz'l*, *v.t.* and *v.i.* to frizz.—*n.* a curl. [Related to **frizz**.]

frizzle, *friz'l*, *v.t.* and *v.i.* to fry: to scorch. [Perh. onomatopoeic adaptation of **fry**.]

fro, *frō*, *adv.* away: back or backward. [O.N. *frā*.]

frock, *frok*, *n.* a monk's wide-sleeved garment: a long coat: a woman's or child's gown.—*n.* **frock'-coat**, a double-breasted full-skirted coat for men.—*adj.* **frocked**, clothed in a frock. [O.Fr. *froc*, a monk's frock—Low L. *frocus*—L. *floccus*, a flock of wool; or from Low L. *hrocus*—O.H.G. *hroch*, a coat.]

frog, *frog*, *n.* any of numerous tailless web-footed amphibians, more agile than toads, though some species are called by either name: (*coll.*) a Frenchman (more commonly **frogg'y**).—*ns.* **frog'man**, an under water swimmer with devices like a frog's webbed feet attached to his own feet to assist him in swimming under water; **frog('s)'march**, a method of carrying a refractory or drunken prisoner face downwards between four men, each holding a limb.—**frog in the throat**, hoarseness. [O.E. *frogga*; also *trox*; cog. with O.N. *froskr*; Ger. *frosch*.]

frog, *frog*, *n.* a V-shaped band of horn on the underside of a horse's hoof. [Perh. **frog** (1).]

frog, *frog*, *n.* on a railway or a tramway, a structure in the rails allowing passage across, or to, another line. [Perh. **frog** (1).]

frog, *frog*, *n.* an ornamental fastening or tasselled button.—*adj.* **frogged**, having such frogs.

frolic, *frol'ik*, *adj.* (*arch.*) merry, full of pranks.—*n.* gaiety: a prank: a merry-making.—*v.i.* to play wild pranks or merry tricks: to gambol:—*pr.p.* frol'icking; *pa.p.* frol'icked.—*adj.* **frol'icsome**, gay: sportive.—*n.* **frol'icsomeness**. [Du. *vrolijk*, merry: cf. Ger. *fröhlich*, joyful, gay.]

from, *from*, *prep.* indicating departure, origin, subtraction, exclusion, difference; meanings include:—out of: springing out of: beginning at: at a distance with reference to (a particular place—e.g. *he is from home*). [O.E. *fram*, *from*; akin to O.N. *frā*.]

frond, *frond*, *n.* (*bot.*) a leaf, esp. of a palm or fern.—*adj.* **frond'ed**, having fronds. [L. *frons*, *frondis*, a leaf.]

front, *frunt*, *n.* the forehead: the face: the forepart of anything: the foremost line: the scene of hostilities: the diverse forces contending for a political or ideological object: a dickey: a wig for the forehead: the most conspicuous part: demeanour (*a bold front*): land along the edge of the sea, a river, &c.: a promenade there: the bounding surface between two masses of air of different density and temperature, (**cold front**, one in which colder air is following warmer air; **warm front**, one in which warmer air is following cooler): something acting as a cover or disguise for secret or disreputable activities.—*adj.* of, relating to, or in, front.—*v.t.* to stand in front of or opposite: to oppose face to face: to add a front to.—*v.i.* to face.—*n.* **front'age**, the front part of a building: the ground in front.—*adj.* **front′al,** of or belonging to the front or forehead.—*n.* something worn on the forehead or face: a covering for the front of an altar: a facade.—*n.* **front′let,** a band worn on the forehead.—*adj.* **front′-page,** of special interest or importance.—**front man,** a figurehead: the nominal head of an organisation or leader of a gang.—**in front (of),** before. [O.Fr.,—L. *frōns, frontis,* the forehead.]

frontier, *frunt′yėr, front′yėr,* or *-ēr′, n.* the boundary of a country: (chiefly *U.S.*) the border of settled country: (in *pl.*) the extreme limit of knowledge and attainment in a particular field.—*adj.* belonging to a frontier: bordering.—*n.* **front′iersman,** a dweller on a frontier. [O.Fr. *frontier*—L. *frōns, frontis.*]

frontispiece, *frunt′i-spēs* (or *front′-*), *n.* (*archit.*) the principal face of a building: a picture in front of a book before the textual matter. [Fr.,—Low L. *frontispicium*—*frōns, frontis,* forehead, *specĕre,* to see; not conn. with **piece.**]

frost, *frost, n.* a state of freezing: temperature at or below the freezing point of water: frozen dew, also called *hoar-frost:* (*coll.*) a failure, a disappointment, a fraud.—*v.t.* to cover with anything resembling hoar-frost: to sharpen (the points of a horse's shoe) that it may not slip on ice.—*n.* **frost′bite,** injury, sometimes ending in mortification, to a part of the body by exposure to cold.—*adjs.* **frost′-bitt′en,** bitten or affected by frost; **frost′-bound,** bound, or confined, by frost; **frost′ed,** covered by frost: having a frostlike appearance (as glass by roughening): injured by frost.—*n.* **frost′ing,** material or treatment to give appearance of hoar-frost.—*adj.* **frost′y,** producing or containing frost: chill: frost-like.—*adv.* **frost′ily.**—*n.* **frost′iness.** [O.E. *frost, forst*—*frēosan*; cf. Ger. *frost.*]

froth, *froth, n.* foam: (*fig.*) chatter: something frivolous.—*v.t.* to cause froth on.—*v.i.* to throw up froth.—*adj.* **froth′y,** full of froth or foam: empty, unsubstantial (e.g. talk).—*adv.* **froth′ily.**—*n.* **froth′iness.** [O.N. *frotha,* Dan. *fraade.*]

froward, *frō′wård, adj.* (*arch.*) self-willed: perverse.—*adv.* **frō′wardly.**—*n.* **frō′wardness.** [fro and suffx. *-ward.*]

frown, *frown, v.i.* to wrinkle the brow as in anger or concentration: to regard with displeasure or disapproval (with *upon*).—*v.t.* to force by a frown.—*n.* a wrinkling or contraction of the brow in displeasure, &c.: a stern look.—*adj.* **frown′ing,** gloomy.—*adv.* **frown′ingly.** [From O.Fr. *froignier* (mod. *refrogner*), to knit the brow; origin unknown.]

frowsty, *frow′sti, adj.* fusty, smelling unpleasantly. [Conn. with **frowzy.**]

frowzy, frowsy, *frow′zi, adj.* fusty: dingy: unkempt. [Origin unknown.]

frozen, *frōz′n, pa.p.* of **freeze.—the frozen mitt,** (*slang*) a rebuff, a chilly reception.

fructify, *fruk′ti-fī, v.t.* to make fruitful, to fertilise.—*v.i.* to bear fruit.—*n.* **fructes′cence,** the time for the ripening of fruit.—*adj.* **fructi′ferous,** bearing fruit.—*ns.* **fructificā′tion,** fruit-production: (*bot.*) a structure that contains spores or seeds; **fruc′tōse,** a sugar, existing in a number of forms, found along with

glucose in sweet fruit juices. [L. *frūctus,* fruit.]

frugal, *frōō′gál, adj.* economical in the use of resources: spare, scanty (e.g. *frugal fare*).—*n.* **frugal′ity,** economy: thrift.—*adv.* **fru′gally.** [L. *frūgālis*—*frux, frūgis,* fruit.]

frugiferous, *frōō-jif′ėr-us, adj.* fruit-bearing.— *adj.* **frugiv′orous,** feeding on fruits or seeds. [L. *frux, frūgis*—*ferre,* to bear, *vorāre,* to eat.]

fruit, *frōōt, n.* the produce of the earth, which supplies the wants of men and animals: an edible part of a plant, esp. that which contains the seed: (*bot.*) a fructification, esp. the structure that develops from the ovary and its contents after fertilisation, sometimes including also structures formed from other parts of the flower: (*arch.*) the offspring of animals: product, consequence.—*v.i.* to produce fruit.—*ns.* **fruit′age,** fruit collectively: fruits; **fruitā′rian,** one who lives on fruit; **fruit′erer,** one who deals in fruit.—*adj.* **fruit′ful,** producing fruit abundantly: productive.—*adv.* **fruit′fully.**—*n.* **fruit′fulness.**—*adj.* **fruit′less,** barren: without profit: useless.—*adv.* **fruit′lessly.**—*n.* **fruit′lessness.**—*adj.* **fruit′y,** like, or tasting like, fruit.—**fruit-machine,** a coin-operated gaming machine in which chance must bring fruits together in a certain combination to give a win.—**first-fruits** (see **first**). [O.Fr. *fruit, fruict*—L. *frūctus*—*fruī, frūctus,* to enjoy.]

fruition, *frōō-ish′(ò)n, n.* use or possession, esp. accompanied with pleasure: (by confusion) the state of bearing fruit (*fig.*)—realisation (e.g. of hopes). [O.Fr. *fruition*—L. *fruī,* to enjoy.]

frumenty, *frōō′men-ti, n.* food made of hulled wheat boiled in milk.—Also **fur′mety.** [O.Fr. *frumentee*—*frument*—L. *frumentum.*]

frump, *frump, n.* a plain and dowdy woman.

frustrate, *frus-trāt′, v.t.* to make vain or of no effect, to thwart, to defeat (e.g. an attempt): to thwart, balk (a person).—*p.adj.* vain, ineffectual, defeated.—*adj.* **frustrat′ed,** having sense of discouragement and dissatisfaction.—*n.* **frustrā′tion,** act of frustrating: state of being frustrated: thwarting, defeat.—**frustration dream,** dream, induced by frustration in waking life, in which the dreamer keeps on trying ineffectually e.g. to get ready for something. [L. *frustrāre*—*frustrā,* in vain.]

frustum, *frus′tum, n.* a slice of a solid body: the part of a cone or pyramid between the base and a plane parallel to it, or between two planes. [L. *frustum,* a bit.]

frutescent, *frōō-tes′ént, adj.* becoming shrubby. —*adj.* **fru′ticōse,** shrub-like: shrubby. [L. *frutex, fruticis,* a shrub.]

fry, *frī, v.t.* to cook with oil or fat in a pan.—*v.i.* to undergo the action of frying: to burn or scorch:—*pr.p.* fry′ing; *pa.p.* fried.—*n.* a dish of anything fried. [Fr. *frire*—L. *frīgĕre*; cf. Gr. *phrygein.*]

fry, *frī, n.* young, collectively: a swarm of fishes just spawned: young of salmon in their second year.—**small fry,** persons or things of little importance: children. [O.N. *frió*; Dan. and Swed. *frö.*]

fuchsia, *fū′shi-a, n.* a shrub with long pendulous flowers, native to South America. [Leonard *Fuchs,* a German botanist, 1501-66.]

Neutral vowels in unaccented syllables: *em′pér-ór*; for certain sounds in foreign words see p. ix.

fuddle, *fud'l, v.t.* to stupefy with drink.—*v.i.* to drink to excess or habitually. [Cf. Du. *vod,* soft, Ger. dial, *fuddeln,* to swindle.]

fuddy-duddy, *fud'i-dud'i, n.* an old fogy, stick-in-the-mud: a carper.—*adj.* old-fogyish: stuffy: prim: censorious.

fudge, *fuj, n.* nonsense: a soft sweetmeat.—*v.t.* to patch up: to fake.—*interj.* nonsense!

fuel, *fū'el, n.* anything that feeds a fire, supplies energy, &c. (also *fig.*).—*v.t.* to furnish with fuel. [O.Fr. *fowaille* — Low L. *focāle* — L. *focus,* a fireplace.]

fug, *fug, n.* a hot, stuffy atmosphere.

fugacious, *fū-gā'shus, adj.* fugitive: fleeting.—*ns.* **fugā'ciousness, fugac'ity** (*-gas'i-ti*). [L *fugax, fugācis,* from *fugĕre,* to flee.]

fugitive, *fūj'i-tiv, adj.* apt to flee away: fleeting: evanescent: written for some passing occasion.—*n.* one who flees or has fled: a refugee.—*adv.* **fūg'itively.**—*n.* **fūg'itiveness.** [L. *fugitīvus*—*fugĕre,* to flee.]

fugue, *fūg, n.* (*mus.*) a form of composition in which the subject is given out by one part and immediately taken up by a second, its *answer,* during which the first part supplies an accompaniment or counter-subject, and so on. [Fr.,—It. *fuga* — L. *fuga,* flight.]

Führer, Fuehrer, *fü'rer, n.* leader: Hitler's title as leader of Nazi Germany. [Ger.]

fulcrum, *ful'krum, n.* (*mech.*) the prop or fixed point on which a lever moves: a prop: (*fig.*) a means to an end.—*pl.* **ful'crums, ful'cra.** [L. *fulcrum,* a prop—*fulcīre,* to prop.]

fulfil, *fool-fil', v.t.* to complete (e.g. a work): to carry into effect: to observe (conditions laid down): to realise completely (e.g. hopes):—*pr.p.* **fulfill'ing;** *pa.p.* **fulfilled'.**—*ns.* **fulfill'er; fulfil'ment,** full performance: completion: accomplishment. [O.E. *fullfyllan*—*full,* full, *fyllan,* to fill.]

fulgent, *ful'jent, adj.* shining: bright.—*n.* **ful'gency.**—*adv.* **ful'gently.** [L. *fulgēns, -entis,* pr.p. of *fulgēre,* to shine.]

fulgurate, *ful'gū-rāt, v.i.* to flash as lightning. [L. *fulgur,* lightning.]

fuliginous, *fū-lij'i-nus, adj.* sooty: dusky. [L., *fūlīgō, -inis,* soot.]

full, *fool, adj.* having all that can be contained: having no empty space: abundantly supplied or furnished: abounding: containing the whole matter: complete (e.g. *a full year*): strong (e.g. of a voice): eager to talk about (something—with *of*).—*n.* completest extent, as of the moon: highest degree: the whole: time of full moon. *adv.* quite: thoroughly: veritably: directly.—*adv.* **full'y,** completely: entirely.—*adjs.* **full'-blood'ed,** vigorous: of pure blood; **full'-blown,** fully expanded, as a flower; **full'-bott'omed,** of wig, long behind.—*n.* **full'-dress,** the dress worn on occasions of ceremony (*adj.* important).—*adjs.* **full'-face,** showing the front of the face completely (also *adv.* and *n.*); **full'-faced,** having a plump face; **full'-fash'ioned** (or **full'y-**), of knitted garments, made in flat-shaped pieces and sewn together at the edges, so as to fit the curves of the body exactly, **full'-fed,** fed to plumpness; **full'-grown,** grown to maturity; **full'-length,** extending, or showing, the whole length (*n.* a portrait showing such).—*ns.* **full'-moon,** the

moon with its whole disk illuminated; **full'-ness, ful'ness,** the state of being filled: completeness: satiety: force and volume, as of sound.—*adjs.* **full'-orbed,** having the orb or disk fully illuminated, as the full-moon: round; **full'-out,** at full power: total; **full'-scale,** of the same size as the original: involving full power or maximum effort.—**full of years,** at a good old age; **full stop,** a point marking the end of a sentence.—**in the fullness of time,** at the proper or destined time. [O.E. *full;* O.N. *fullr,* Ger. *voll.*]

full, *fool, v.t.* to scour and thicken (cloth).—*ns.* **full'er,** a bleacher or cleanser of cloth; **fuller's-earth,** a soft earth or clay, capable of absorbing grease, used in fulling cloth, refining oils, &c. [O.Fr. *fuler*—Low L. *fullāre*—L. *fullō,* a cloth-fuller.]

fulmar, *fool'mär, -mär, n.* a gull-like bird of the petrel family. [Perh. O.N. *fūll,* foul, *mār,* gull.]

fulminate, *ful'min-āt, v.i.* to thunder or make a loud noise: to issue decrees with violence or threats: to inveigh (against).—*v.t.* to cause to explode: to send forth, as a denunciation.—*n.* a salt of fulminic acid (often dangerously detonating).—*n.* **fulminā'tion,** an act of fulminating or detonating: a denunciation.—*adj.* **fulmin'ic,** pertaining to an acid used in preparing explosive compounds. [L. *fulmināre, -ātum*—*fulmen,* lightning—*fulgēre,* to shine.]

fulsome, *fool'sum, ful'sum, adj.* cloying through excess: gross: offensive to smell or other sense: disgustingly fawning.—*adv.* **ful'somely.**—*n.* **ful'someness.** [**full** (1) and suffx. *-some.*]

fulvous, *ful'vus, adj.* deep or dull yellow, tawny.—Also **ful'vid.** [L. *fulvus,* tawny.]

fumarole, *fūm'a-rōl, n.* a hole emitting gases in a volcano or volcanic region. [Fr. *fumerole*—L. *fumus,* smoke.]

fumble, *fum'bl, v.i.* to grope about awkwardly: to use the hands awkwardly.—*v.t.* to handle or manage awkwardly: (*cricket*) to drop (the ball), thus missing a catch.—*n.* **fum'bler.** [Du. *fommelen,* to fumble.]

fume, *fūm, n.* smoke or vapour (often in *pl.*): any volatile matter, esp. if pungent (often in *pl.*): heat of mind, rage: anything unsubstantial, vain conceit.—*v.i.* to smoke: to throw off vapour: to be in a rage.—*adjs.* **fūmif'erous, fūm'ous, fūm'y,** producing fumes.—**fumed oak,** oak darkened by ammonia fumes. [O.Fr. *fum*—L. *fūmus,* smoke.]

fumigate, *fūm'i-gāt, v.t.* to expose to fumes, esp. for purposes of disinfecting: to perfume.—*ns.* **fūmigā'tion; fūm'igător,** a fumigating apparatus. [L. *fūmigāre, -ātum.*]

fumitory, *fūm'i-tór-i, n.* a herb formerly used in medicine. [O.Fr. *fume-terre,* earth-smoke—L. *fūmus,* smoke, *terra,* earth.]

fun, *fun, n.* merriment: sport.—**fun and games,** (*slang*) exciting events. [Prob. a form of obs. *fon,* to befool; cf. Ir. *fonn,* delight.]

funambulate, *fū-nam'bū-lāt, v.i.* to walk on a rope.—*ns.* **funambulā'tion; funam'bulist,** a rope-walker. [L. *fūnis,* a rope, *ambulāre,* to walk.]

function, *fungk'sh(ó)n, n.* (*obs.*) the doing of a thing: activity proper to anything: duty peculiar to any office: a ceremony or formal entertainment: (*math.*) a quantity so connected with another that any change in the one produces a corresponding change in the other.—*v.i.* to perform a function: to act, operate.—*adj.* func'tional, pertaining to, or performed by, functions—opp. to *organic* or *structural* (e.g. of a disease, affecting the *functions* of an organ): designed with special, or exclusive, regard to the purpose which it is to serve (as a building).—*n.* func'tionalism, the theory or practice of adapting method, form, materials, &c., primarily with regard to the purpose in hand.—*adv.* func'tionally.—*n.* func'tionary, one who discharges a duty or holds an office. [O.Fr.,—L. *functiō, -ōnis—fungī, functus,* to perform.]

fund, *fund, n.* a sum of money on which some enterprise is founded or expense supported: a supply or source of money: a store laid up, supply (e.g. of stories, common sense): (*pl.*) permanent debts due by a government and paying interest.—*v.t.* to form into a stock charged with interest: to place in a fund.—*p.adj.* fund'ed, invested in public funds: existing in the form of bonds. [Fr. *fond*—L. *fundus,* the bottom.]

fundamental, *fun-dá-ment'ál, adj.* basal, essential, primary: important.—*n.* that which serves as a groundwork: an essential.—*ns.* funda'ment, the buttocks or seat of the body; fundament'alism, belief in the literal truth of the Bible; fundament'alist, one who holds this belief.—*adv.* fundament'ally.—fundamental particle (same as elementary particle). [Fr.,—L. *fundāmentum—fundāre,* to found.]

funeral, *fū'nér-ál, n.* burial or cremation: the ceremony, &c., connected with burial or cremation.—*adj.* pertaining to or used at a funeral.—*adj.* fūnēr'eal (*-é-ál*), pertaining to or suiting a funeral: dismal, mournful.—funeral director, an undertaker. [O.Fr.,—Low L. *fūnerālis*—L. *fūnus, fūnéris,* a funeral procession.]

fungus, *fung'gus, n.* a plant of one of the lowest groups, without chlorophyll, and therefore living as saprophytes or parasites—e.g. mushrooms, toadstools, moulds:—*pl.* fungi (*fun'jī*), or funguses (*fung'gus-ez*).—*n.* fungicide (*fun'ji-sīd*), any substance that kills fungi.—*adjs.* fungici'dal, pertaining to a fungicide; fung'oid, fungus-like; fung'ous, of or like fungus: soft: spongy: growing suddenly: ephemeral. [L. *fungus,* a mushroom—Gr. *sphongos, spongos,* a sponge.]

funicle, *fū'ni-kl, n.* a small cord or ligature: a fibre.—*adj.* fūnic'ular—funicular railway, a cable-railway, esp. one ascending a hill. [L. *fūniculus,* dim. of *fūnis,* a rope.]

funk, *fungk, n.* (*coll.*) panic: one who funks.—*v.i.* and *v.t.* to shrink through fear: to shirk.—*adj.* funk'y.—*n.* funk-hole, a dug-out: any place to which one flees for safety. [Ety. uncertain.]

funnel, *fun'l, n.* a passage for the escape of smoke, &c.: a vessel, usually a cone ending in a tube, for pouring fluids into bottles, &c.—*adj.* funn'elled, provided with a funnel. [Prob. through Fr. from L. *infundibulum—fundēre,* to pour.]

funny, *fun'i, adj.* full of fun, droll: perplexing, odd.—*adv.* funn'ily.—funny bone, a popular name for the ulnar nerve, because of the tingling sensation produced by a blow on the elbow. [fun.]

fur, *fūr, n.* the thick, soft, fine hair of certain animals: their skins with the hair attached: a garment, esp. a shoulder-wrap, of fur: furred animals: a fur-like coating on the tongue: a crust in boilers, &c.—*v.t.* to line with fur: to coat.—*v.i.* to become coated:—*pr.p.* furr'ing; *pa.p.* furred.—*ns.* furr'ier, a dealer in furs: a dresser of furs; furr'iery, furs in general: trade in furs.—*adj.* furr'y, consisting of, like, covered with, or dressed in, fur. [O.Fr. *forre, fuerre,* sheath.]

furbelow, *fûr'bé-lō, n.* a plaited border or flounce: a superfluous ornament. [Fr., It., and Sp. *falbala* ; of unknown origin.]

furbish, *fûr'bish, v.t.* to rub up until bright: to renovate (often with *up*). [O.Fr. *fourbir, fourbissant,* from O.H.G. *furban,* to purify.]

furcate, *fûr'kāt, adj.* forked, branching like the prongs of a fork.—Also fur'cated. [L. *furca,* a fork.]

furfur, *fûr'fúr, n.* dandruff, scurf.—*adj.* furfūrā'ceous (*-shús*), branny: scaly. [L. *furfur,* bran.]

furious, *fū'ri-ús, adj.* full of fury: violent.—*adv.* fū'riously.—*n.* fū'riousness. [O.Fr. *furieus*—L. *furiōsius—furia,* rage.]

furl, *fûrl, v.t.* to roll up. [Perh. conn. with fardel.]

furlong, *fûr'long, n.* 220 yards, one-eighth of a mile. [O.E. *furlang—furh,* furrow, *lang,* long.]

furlough, *fûr'lō, n.* leave of absence.—*v.t.* to grant furlough to. [Du. *verlof.*]

furnace, *fûr'nis, n.* an enclosed structure in which great heat is produced: a time or place of grievous affliction or torment. [O.Fr. *fornais*—L. *fornāx, -ācis—fornus,* an oven.]

furnish, *fûr'nish, v.t.* to fit up or supply completely, or with what is necessary: to supply (a person with): to provide (e.g. food, reasons). —*n.* fur'nisher.—*n.pl.* fur'nishings, fittings of any kind, esp. articles of furniture, &c., within a house. [O.Fr. *furnir, furnissant*—O.H.G. *frummen,* to accomplish.]

furniture, *fûr'ni-tyûr, -chúr, n.* movables, either for use or ornament, with which a house is equipped: (*arch.*) equipment: decorations. [Fr. *fourniture.*]

furor, *fū'rör, n.* fury: enthusiasm (of poets and prophets): a craze. [L.]

furore, *fōō-rō'ā, fū'rör, n.* a craze: wild enthusiasm: wild excitement. [It.]

furrow, *fur'ō, n.* the trench made by a plough: a groove: a wrinkle.—*v.t.* and *v.i.* to form furrows in: to wrinkle. [O.E. *furh;* cf. Ger. *furche,* L. *porca,* a ridge.]

further, *fûr'тнér, adv.* at or to a greater distance or degree: in addition.—*adj.* more distant: additional.—*adv.* fur'thermore, in addition to what has been said, moreover, besides.—*adj.* fur'thermost, most remote.—*adv.* fur'thest, at or to the greatest distance.—*adj.* most distant. —further education, post-school education other than university education. [O.E. *furthor* (adv.) *furthra* (adj.)—*fore* or *forth* with comp. suffix.]

further, *fûr'тнér, v.t.* to help forward, promote.—*n.* fur'therance, a helping forward. [O.E. *fythran.*]

Neutral vowels in unaccented syllables: *em'pér-ór*; for certain sounds in foreign words see p. ix.

furtive, *fûr′tiv, adj.* stealthy: secret.—*adv.* **fur′tively.**—*n.* **fur′tiveness.** [Fr. *furtif, -ive*—L. *furtīvus*—*fūr,* a thief.]

fury, *fū′ri, n.* rage: violent passion: madness: (*cap.*) one of the three goddesses of vengeance: hence, a passionate, violent woman. [Fr. *furie*—L. *furia*—*furĕre,* to be angry.]

furze, *fûrz, n.* whin or gorse.—*adj.* **furz′y,** overgrown with furze. [O.E. *fyrs.*]

fuscous, *fus′kūs, adj.* brown: dingy. [L. *fuscus,* akin to *furvus.*]

fuse, *fūz, v.t.* to melt, to liquefy by heat: (*elect.*) to cause to fail by melting of a fuse: to join by, or as if by, melting together (*lit.* and *fig.*).—*v.i.* to be melted: to be reduced to a liquid: to blend: (of an electrical appliance) to fail by melting of a fuse.—*n.* a bit of fusible metal inserted as a safeguard in an electric circuit.—*adj.* **fu′sible,** that may be fused or melted.—*ns.* **fūsibil′ity; fūsing-point,** temperature at which any solid substance becomes liquid: **fū′sion,** act of melting: the state of fluidity from heat: a close union of things, as if melted together. [L. *fundĕre, fūsum,* to melt.]

fuse, *fūz, n.* a train of combustible material in waterproof covering, used with a detonator to initiate an explosion: (*usu.* **fuze**) a device to cause a bomb, shell, mine, &c. to detonate. [It. *tuso*—L. *fūsus,* a spindle.]

fusee, fuzee, *fū-zē′, n.* the spindle in a watch or clock on which the chain is wound: a match with long, oval head for outdoor use: a fuse: a fusil. [O.Fr. *fusée,* a spindleful—L. *fūsus,* a spindle.]

fuselage, *fūz′él-ij,* or *-äzh, n.* the body of an aeroplane. [Fr.,—L. *fūsus,* a spindle.]

fusel-oil, *fū′zl-oil, n.* a nauseous oil in spirits distilled from potatoes, grain, &c. [Ger. *fusel,* bad spirits.]

fusil, *fū′zil, n.* a flint lock musket.—*ns.* **fusilier′, fusileer′,** formerly a soldier armed with a fusil, now simply a historical title borne by a few regiments; **fusillade** (*-ād′*), simultaneous or continuous discharge of firearms.—*v.t.* to shoot down by a simultaneous discharge of firearms. [O.Fr. *fusil,* a flint-musket, same as It. *focile*—Low L. *focile,* steel (to strike fire

with), dim. of L. *focus,* a fireplace.]

fuss, *fus, n.* a bustle or tumult: haste, flurry.—*v.i.* to be in a bustle.—*v.t.* to agitate.—*adj.* **fuss′y,** making a fuss: given to making a fuss: over-particular: over-elaborate: troublesome to do or to make.—*n.* **fuss′iness.**—*adv.* **fuss′ily.**

fust, *fust, n.* a mouldy or musty smell.—*v.i.* to grow mouldy.—*adj.* **fust′y.** [O.Fr. *fust,* cask—L. *fustis,* cudgel.]

fustanella, *fus-ta-nel′ä, n.* a white kilt worn by Greek men. [Mod. Gr. *phoustanella.*]

fustet, *fus′tet, n.* Venetian sumach, source of the dye called *young fustic,* or its wood. [Fr.,—Port.—Ar. *fustuq.*]

fustian, *fust′yán, n.* kinds of coarse, twilled cotton fabric, including moleskin, velveteen, corduroy, &c.: a pompous and unnatural style of writing or speaking, bombast.—*adj.* made of fustian: bombastic. [O.Fr. *fustaigne*—It.—Low L.—prob. from *El-Fustat* (Old Cairo) where it may have been made.]

fustic, *fus′tik, n.* the wood of a tropical American tree, yielding a yellow dye (*old fustic*). Cf. **fustet.** [Fr. *fustoc,* yellow—L. *fustis.*]

fustigate, *fus′ti-gāt, v.t.* to cudgel.—*n.* **fustigā′tion.** [L. *fustīgāre, -ātum*—*fustis,* a stick.]

fusty. See **fust.**

futile, *fū′tīl, fū′til, adj.* ineffectual: frivolous, trifling.—*adv.* **fū′tilely.**—*n.* **futil′ity,** uselessness. [Fr.,—L. *fūtilis*—*fundĕre,* to pour.]

futtock, *fut′ók, n.* one of the crooked timbers of a wooden ship. [Perh. for *foot-hook.*]

future, *fūt′yūr, -chūr, adj.* about to be: that is to come. (*gram.*) expressive of time to come.—*n.* time to come.—*ns.* **fūt′ūrism** (*art*), an ultra modern movement claiming to point the way for the future, esp. a 20th-century revolt against tradition; **fūt′ūrist; futur′ity,** time to come: the state of being yet to come: an event yet to come. [Fr.,—L. *futūrus,* used as fut.p. of *esse,* to be.]

fuze. See **fuse** (2).

fuzz, *fuz, n.* fine light particles: fluff: (*slang*) police.—*v.i.* to fly off in minute particles.—*v.t.* to cover with fine particles.—*adj.* **fuzz′y,** fluffy: blurred.—*n.* **fuzz′ball,** a puff-ball.

fāte, fär; mē, hûr (her); mīne; mōte, för; mūte; mōōn, fōōt; ᴛʜen (then)

G

G-man *jē'man,* (G for government), an agent of the United States Federal Bureau of Investigation; **G-string,** *jē'string,* (origin obscure), a string or strip worn round the waist and between the legs; **g-suit,** *jē-sūt,* (g symbol for acceleration due to gravity), a close-fitting suit with cells that inflate to prevent flow of blood away from the head, worn by airmen against blackout during high accelaration.

gab, *gab, n.* (*coll.*) idle chatter.—**gift of the gab,** ability to talk fluently. [Ety. uncertain.]

gabble, *gab'l, v.i.* to talk quickly and inarticulately: to cackle like geese.—Also *n.*—*ns.* **gabb'ler; gabb'ling.** [Perh. freq. of **gab.**]

gaberdine, *gab'ėr-dēn,* **gabardine,** *n.* a loose cloak, esp. a Jew's: a twill fabric, esp. of cotton and wool: a coat of this material. [O.Fr. *gauvardine*; perh. Mid. High Ger. *wallevart,* pilgrimage.]

gabion, *gā'bi-ón, n.* (*fort.*) a bottomless basket of wicker-work, &c., filled with earth, used in fortification and engineering.—*n.* **gā'bionāde,** a work formed of gabions. [Fr.,—It. *gabbione,* a large cage—*gabbia*—L. *cavea,* a cage.]

gable, *gā'bl, n.* (*archit.*) the triangular part of an exterior wall of a building between the top of the side-walls and the slopes on the roof. [Prob. through O.Fr. *gable,* from O.N. *gafl.*]

gaby, *gā'bi, n.* a simpleton. [Origin unknown.]

gad, *gad, v.i.* to rove restlessly or idly (often with *about*): (*arch.*—of plants) to straggle:—*pr.p.* gadd'ing; *pa.p.* gadd'ed.—*n.* **gad'about,** one who rushes from place to place. [Prob. conn. with *gad* in **gadfly;** or obsolete *gadling,* vagabond.]

gadfly, *gad'flī, n.* a blood-sucking fly that distresses cattle: a mischievous gadabout. [M.E. *gad* (O.N. *gaddr*), a spike, or O.E. *gād* (see **goad**), and **fly.**]

gadget, *gaj'ét, n.* any small ingenious device. [Ety. uncertain.]

Gadhel, *gad'el, n.* a Gael, a Celt of the branch to which the Irish, the Scottish Highlanders, and the Manx belong.—*adj.* **Gadhelic** (*gad-el'ik*). [Ir. *Gaedheal* (pl. *Gaedhil*), a Gael.]

gadolinium, *gad-ō-lin'i-úm, n.* a metallic element (symbol Gd; at. no. 64), a member of the rare-earth group. [Named from *Gadolin,* a Finnish chemist.]

Gael, *gāl, n.* one whose language is Gadhelic, esp. a Scottish Highlander.—*adj.* **Gaelic** (*gāl'-ik,* also *gal'ik*), pertaining to the Gaels.—*n.* the language of Ireland and (now *esp.*) that of the Scottish Highlands. [Gael. *Gaidheal.*]

gaff, *gaf, n.* a hook, esp. one for landing large fish: (*naut.*) the spar to which the head of a fore-and-aft sail is bent. [Fr. *gaffe.*]

gaff, *gaf, n.* (*slang*) humbug, nonsense.—**blow the gaff,** to disclose a secret, blab. [Prob. conn. with **gab** and **gaffe.**]

gaffe, *gaf, n.* an indiscreet remark. [Fr.]

gaffer, *gaf'ér, n.* originally a word of respect applied to an old man, now familiar (*fem.* **gammer**): the foreman of a squad of workmen. [**grandfather** or **godfather.**]

gag, *gag, v.t.* to stop the mouth of forcibly: to compel to keep silence.—*v.i.* to introduce *gag* into a play:—*pr.p.* gagg'ing; *pa.p.* gagged.—*n.* something thrust into the mouth or put over it to enforce silence (also *fig.*): the closure applied in a debate: (*slang*) an actor's interpolation: amusing remark: piece of comic business. [Prob. imit. of sound of choking.]

gaga, *gag'a, adj.* (*slang*) fatuous: doddering. [Fr.]

gage, *gāj, n.* a pledge: something thrown down as a challenge, as a glove.—*v.t.* to bind by pledge or security: offer as a guarantee: to stake, wager. [O.Fr. *guage, gage,* from Gmc.; vb. from Fr. *gager.* See **wage.**]

gage. See **gauge.**

gage, *gāj, n.* the greengage (q.v.).

gaggle, *gag'l, n.* a flock of geese. [Prob. imit.]

gaiety, gaily. See **gay.**

gain, *gān, v.t.* to obtain to one's advantage: to earn: to win: to draw to one's own party: to reach: to increase (speed, weight).—*v.i.* to profit: to become or appear better: (of clock, &c.) to go fast by so much in a given time.—*n.* that which is gained: profit: (*elect.*) ratio of an output quantity to an input quantity, e.g. the output power to input power of an amplifier.—*n.* **gain'er.**—*adj.* **gain'ful,** lucrative: profitable.—*adv.* **gain'fully.**—*n.pl.* **gain'ings,** what has been gained or acquired by labour or enterprise.—**gain ground** (see **ground** (2)); **gain (up)on,** to overtake by degrees: to increase one's advantage against: to encroach on. [O.Fr. *gain, gaain, gaigner, gaaignier,* from Gmc.]

gainsay, *gān-sā', gān'sā, v.t.* to contradict: to deny: to dispute:—*pa.t.* and *pa.p.* **gainsaid** (*-sād', -sed'*).—*n.* **gain'sayer** (*B.*), an opposer. [O.E. *gegn,* against, and **say.**]

gait, *gāt, n.* way or manner of walking. [O.N. *gata,* a way.]

gaiter, *gāt'ér, n.* a covering for the ankle, fitting down upon the shoe. [Fr. *guêtre, guietre.*]

gala, *gā'la, gä'la, n.* a festivity, fête.—*n.* **ga'la-dress,** gay costume for a gala-day. [Fr. *gala,* show—It. *gala,* finery.]

galantine, *gal'án-tēn, -tin, n.* a dish of poultry, veal, &c., served cold in jelly. [Fr.,—Low L. *galatina* for *gelatina,* jelly. See **gelatine.**]

galaxy, *gal'ak-si, n.* (usu. *cap.*) the Milky Way, a luminous band of stars stretching across the heavens: any similar system of stars: any splendid assemblage.—*adj.* **galactic,** of a galaxy or galaxies. [Through Fr. and L., from Gr. *galaxias*—*gala, -aktos,* milk.]

gale, *gāl, n.* a strong wind, between a stiff breeze and a hurricane. [Origin obscure.]

gale, *gāl, n.* bog-myrtle, usually called *sweet-*

Neutral vowels in unaccented syllables: *em'pér-ór*; for certain sounds in foreign words see p. ix.

290

gale. [Prob. O.E. *gagel*; cf. Ger. *gagel*.]

galena, *ga-lē'na, n.* native sulphide of lead. [L. *galēna,* lead-ore.]

Galilean, *gal-i-lē'an, adj.* of or pertaining to Galileo, a great Italian mathematician (1564-1642).

Galilean, *gal-i-lē'an, adj.* of or pertaining to Galilee, one of the Roman divisions of Palestine.—*n.* a native or inhabitant of Galilee, esp. (with *the*) Jesus Christ.

gall, *göl, n.* bile, the greenish-yellow fluid secreted. from the liver: bitterness: malignity.—*ns.* **gall'-bladder,** a reservoir for bile; **gall'-duct,** a tube for conveying bile; **gall'-stone,** a concretion in the gall-bladder or bile ducts. [O.E. *galla, gealla,* gall; cf. Ger. *galle,* Gr. *cholē,* L. *fel.*]

gall, *göl, n.* an abnormal growth produced by an insect or other parasite on oaks and other plants.—*n.* **gall'-nut,** a nut-like gall produced on oaks by an insect known as a gall-wasp or gall-fly, used for making ink [Fr. *galle*—L. *galla,* oak-apple (one type of oak-gall).]

gall, *göl, n.* a sore due to chafing.—*v.t.* to fret or hurt by rubbing: to irritate. [O.E. *galla, gealla,* a sore place.]

gallant, *gal'ant, adj.* brave: noble: stately, splendid (e.g. *a gallant ship*): attentive to ladies (esp. formally or obsequiously): sometimes *gal-ant'*).—*n.* a man of fashion: suitor, seducer (also *gal-ant'* in this sense).—*adv.* **gall'antly.**—*ns.* **gall'antness;** **gall'antry,** bravery, intrepidity: attention or devotion to ladies, often in a bad sense. [Fr. *galant*—O.Fr. *gale,* a merrymaking; prob. Gmc.; cf. **gala.**]

galleon, *gal'i-on, n.* a large Spanish vessel with lofty stem and stern. [Sp. *galeón*—Low L. *galea.* Cf. **galley.**]

gallery, *gal'ér-i, n.* a covered walk: a long balcony: a long passage: an upper floor of seats, esp. (in a theatre) the highest: the occupants of the gallery: a body of spectators: a room or building for the exhibition of works of art: a horizontal underground passage.—**play to the gallery,** to play for the applause of the least cultured. [O.Fr. *galerie* (It. *galleria*).]

galley, *gal'i, n.* a long, low-built ship with one deck, propelled by oars: a state barge: the captain's boat on a warship: the cooking place on board ship (*print.*) a flat oblong tray in which type that has been set up is assembled.—*ns.* **gall'ey-proof,** an impression taken from type on a galley, a slip-proof; **gall'ey-slave,** one condemned to work as a slave at the oar of a galley. [O.Fr. *galie*—Low L. *galea.*]

galliard, *gal'yård, n.* a spirited dance: a gay fellow. [O.Fr. *gaillard.*]

Gallic, *gal'ik, adj.* pertaining to Gaul or France.—*n.* **gall'icism** (*-is-izm*), the use in another language of an expression or idiom peculiar to French.—**Gallo-** (*gal'o-*), in composition, French:—as, **Gall'ophil, Gall'ophile,** one who is friendly to the French; **Gall'ophobe,** one who dislikes or fears the French or what is French. (Same as **Francophil,** -phile, -phobe.) [L. *Gallus,* a Gaul; *Gallicus,* Gaulish.]

galligaskins, *gal-i-gas'kinz, n.pl.* wide hose or breeches. [A corr. of O.Fr. *garguesque*—It. *gre-*

chesco, Greek—L. *Graecus,* Greek.]

gallinaceous, *gal-in-ā'shús, adj.* applied to a group of birds (e.g. turkeys, grouse, &c.) akin to the domestic fowl. [L. *gallīna,* a hen—*gallus,* a cock.]

gallipot, *gal'i-pot, n.* a small glazed pot, esp. for medicine. [Prob. a pot brought in a *galley.*]

gallium, *gal'i-ùm, n.* a metallic element (symbol Ga; at. no. 31), resembling aluminium, with low melting point. [Name formed from *Gallia,* Gaul, France.]

gallivant, *gal-i-vant', v.i.* to spend time frivolously, esp. in flirting: to gad about. [Perh. **gallant.**]

galloglass, *gal'ō-glas, n.* a soldier or armed retainer of a chief in ancient Ireland and other Celtic countries.—Also **gall'owglass.** [Ir. *gallóglách*—Ir. *gall,* foreign, *óglách,* youth.]

gallon, *gal'ón, n.* a unit of capacity equal to 277.4 cubic inches, in U.S. 231 cubic inches. [O. Norm. Fr. *galun, galon* (O.Fr. *jalon*).]

gallop, *gal'óp, v.i.* to go at a gallop: to ride a galloping horse: to move in impetuous haste: to go fast.—*v.t.* to cause to gallop.—*n.* a horse's or other animal's swiftest pace, in which all feet are off the ground together at a point in each stride.—*pr.p.* and *adj.* **gall'oping,** proceeding at a gallop: (*fig.*) advancing rapidly. [O.Fr. *galoper, galop;* prob. Gmc.]

Gallovidian, *gal-ō-vid'i-án, adj.* belonging to Galloway.—*n.* a native thereof. [*Gallovidia,* Latinised from Welsh *Gallwyddel.*]

galloway, *gal'ō-wā, n.* a small strong horse: a breed of large black hornless cattle. [Orig. from *Galloway* in Scotland.]

gallows, *gal'ōz,* or (old-fashioned) *gal'us, n.* a wooden frame on which criminals are hanged.—*ns.* **gall'ows-bird,** one who deserves hanging; **gall'ows-tree,** a gallows.—**cheat the gallows,** to deserve, but escape, hanging. [M.E. *galwes* (pl.)—O.E. *galga,* Ger. *galgen.*]

Gallup poll, *gal'úp pōl,* a method of ascertaining public feeling on any subject used by George Gallup, who founded the American Institute of Public Opinion (1935).

galop, *ga-lop', gal'óp, n.* a lively dance: music for such a dance. [Fr.; cf. **gallop.**]

galore, *ga-lōr', -lör', adv.* in abundance. [Ir. *go,* a particle used in forming advs., *leór,* sufficient.]

galosh, galoche, *gá-losh', golosh, n.* an overshoe, usu. of rubber. [Fr. *galoche*—Gr. *kălopodion,* dim. of *kălopous,* a shoemaker's last—*kălon,* wood, *pous,* foot.]

galumph, *ga-lumf', v.i.* to prance along boundingly and exultingly. [A coinage of Lewis Carroll (C. L. Dodgson; 1832-1898)—prob. *gallop* and *triumph.*]

galvanism, *gal'ván-izm, n.* current electricity: medical treatment by electric currents.—*adj.* **galvanic** (*-van'-*).—*v.t.* **gal'vanīse,** to subject to the action of an electric current: to stimulate to spasmodic action by, or as if by, an electric shock: to confer a false vitality upon.—*ns.* **galvanom'eter,** an instrument for measuring electric currents; **galvan'oscope,** an instrument for detecting electric currents.—**galvanic battery, cell,** an electric battery, cell; **galvanised iron,** iron coated with zinc. [From *Galvani,* of Bologna, the discoverer (1737-98).]

Galwegian, *gal-wē'ji-án, adj.* belonging to

fāte, fär; mē, hûr (her); *mīne; mōte, för; mūte; mōōn, fŏŏt;* THen (then)

Galloway.—n. a native thereof.—Also **Gallowe′gian.**

gambit, *gam′bit, n.* a chess opening in which a sacrifice is offered for the sake of an advantage: an opening move of this type in conversation, in a transaction, &c. [It. *gambetto,* a tripping up—*gamba,* leg.]

gamble, *gam′bl, v.i.* to play for money, esp. for high stakes: to speculate wildly: (with *on*) to take risks on (the supposition that such-and-such will happen).—*v.t.* to squander (away). —*n.* an undertaking in which success is dependent on chance.—*n.* **gam′bler.** [For *gamm-le* or *gam-le,* a freq. which has ousted M.E. *gamenen*—O.E. *gamenian,* to play at games—*gamen,* a game.]

gamboge, *gam-boozh′, -bōj′, -booj′, n.* a yellow gum-resin used as a pigment and in medicine. [From *Cambodia,* whence brought about 1600.]

gambol, *gam′bl, -bol, v.i.* to leap, skip: to frisk in sport:—*pr.p.* **gam′bolling**; *pa.p.* **gam′bolled.**—*n.* a frisk: playfulness. [Formerly *gambold*—O.Fr. *gambade*—It. *gambata,* a kick—Low L. *gamba,* a leg.]

game, *gām, n.* sport of any kind: (in *pl.*) athletic sports: a contest for recreation: the stake in a game: the manner of playing a game: form in playing: the requisite number of points to be gained to win a game: jest, sport, trick: any object of pursuit: wild animals hunted by sportsmen.—*adj.* of or belonging to animals hunted as game: plucky (as a fighting cock is).—*v.t., v.i.* to gamble.—*ns.* **game′cock,** a cock trained to fight; **game′keeper,** one who has the care of game.—*n.pl.* **game′-laws,** laws for protection of game.—*ns.* **game′-preserve′,** a tract of land where wild animals are protected (wholly, or for regulated hunting); **games′-manship,** the art of winning games by talk or conduct aimed at putting one's opponent off (invented by Stephen Potter, b.1900).—*adj.* **game′some,** playful.—*ns.* **game′ster,** a gambler; **gam′ing,** gambling.—*adj.* **gam′y,** having the flavour of game, esp. that kept till tainted.—**die game,** to keep up courage to the last; **make game of,** to make sport of, to ridicule; **play the game,** (see **play**); **round game,** (see **round**); **the game is not worth the candle** (see **candle**); **the game is up,** the scheme has failed. [M.E. *gamen,* a game; O.N. *gaman,* Dan. *gammen.*]

game, *gām, adj.* (*slang*) lame. [Most prob. not the Celt *cam,* crooked.]

gamete, *gam′ēt, gam-ēt′, n.* a sexual reproductive cell—an egg-cell or sperm-cell. [Gr. *gametēs,* husband, *gametē,* wife—*gameein,* to marry.]

gamin, *gam′in, n.* a street Arab: *fem.* **gamine,** *-mēn,* a girl of a pert, boyish, impish appearance and disposition.—Also *adj.* [Fr.]

gamma, *gam′a, n.* the third letter of the Greek alphabet.—**gamm′a rays,** a penetrating radiation given off by radium and other radioactive substances. [Gr.]

gammer, *gam′ér, n.* an old woman:—*masc.* **gaf′fer.** [grandmother or godmother.]

gammon, *gam′ón, n.* (mostly *coll.*) a hoax: nonsense.—*v.t.* to hoax, impose upon. [Prob. O.E. *gamen,* a game.]

gammon, *gam′ón, n.* the cured thigh of a hog. [O. Norm. Fr. *gambon*—*gambe,* a leg.]

gamp, *gamp, n.* (*slang*) a large, clumsy umbrella. [From Mrs Sarah *Gamp,* in Dickens's *Martin Chuzzlewit.*]

gamut, *gam′ut, n.* (*hist. mus.*) the lowest note of Guido of Arezzo's 'great scale' (now G the first note of the bass stave): Guido's scale of six overlapping hexachords (the forerunners of octaves) reaching from that note to what is now E the fourth space of the treble: the whole compass of a voice or instrument: the full extent of anything. [From *gamma,* the Greek letter G, and *ut,* the syllable later superseded by *doh.*]

gander, *gan′dér, n.* the male of the goose.—**take a gander at** (*slang*), to take a look at. [O.E. *ganra, gandra;* Du. and Low Ger. *gander.*]

gang, *gang, n.* a number of persons or animals associating together, often in a bad sense: a number of labourers working together.—*ns.* **gang′er,** the foreman of a gang; **gang′ster** (*U.S.*), a member of a gang of roughs or criminals.—**gang up on,** to make a concerted attack on; **gang up with,** to join in the (doubtful) activities of anything. [O.E. *gang* (Dan. *gang,* Ger. *gang*), *gangan,* to go.]

gangboard, *gang′bōrd, börd, n.* a board or plank on which passengers may enter or leave a ship.—Also **gang′plank.** [O.E. *gangan,* to go.]

gangling, *gang′gling, adj.* loosely-built, lanky.— Also **gangly,** *gang′gli.* [Orig. Scot. and Eng. dialect.]

ganglion, *gang′gli-ón, n.* a tumour in a tendon sheath: a nerve-centre—used also *fig.*:—*pl.* **gang′lia, gang′lions.** [Gr.]

gangrene, *gang′grēn, n.* mortification, death of a part of the body: sometimes used for the first stage in mortification.—*v.t.* to cause gangrene in.—*v.i.* to become gangrenous.—*adj.* **gang′rēnous,** mortified. [L. *gangraena*—Gr. *gangraina, grainein,* to gnaw.]

gangway, *gang′wā, n.* a passage (often movable) into, out of, or through any place, esp. a ship: a way between rows of seats, esp. the cross-passage in the House of Commons.—*interj.* make way! [O.E. *gangweg;* cf. **gang** and **way.**]

gannet, *gan′et, n.* any of several large web-footed birds found in the northern seas, of which the solan goose is the best known: (*slang*) a greedy person. [O.E. *ganot,* a sea-fowl; Du. *gent.*]

ganoid, *gan′oid, adj.* belonging to an order of fishes having hard glistening scales, as the sturgeon. [Gr. *ganos,* brightness, *eidos,* appearance.]

gantlet. Same as **gauntlet** (1 and 2).

gantlope, *gant′lōp.* Same as **gauntlet** (2).

gantry, *gan′tri, n.* a stand for barrels: a working platform for a travelling-crane, &c.: a structure to which are attached railway signals for a number of tracks.—Also (in first sense) **gauntry** (*gön′tri*), **gaun′tree.** [Perh. O.Fr. *gantier*—L. *cantērius,* a trellis.]

gaol, gaoler, old spellings of **jail, jailer.**

gap, *gap, n.* an opening or breach: a passage: a notch or pass in a mountain-ridge: any breach of continuity.—*adj.* **gap′-toothed,** lacking some of the teeth. [O.N. *gap.*]

gape, *gāp, v.i.* to open the mouth wide: to yawn: to stare with open mouth: to be wide open, like a gap.—*n.* act of gaping: the extent to

Neutral vowels in unaccented syllables: *em′pér-ór*; for certain sounds in foreign words see p. ix.

which the mouth can be opened.—**the gapes**, a yawning fit: a disease of poultry, of which gaping is a symptom, caused by a thread-worm in the windpipe and bronchial tubes. [O.N. *gapa*, to open the mouth; Ger. *gaffen*, to stare.]

gar. Shortened from **garfish**.

garage, *gar'ij, gar'äzh, gä-räzh', n.* a building where motor-vehicles are housed or tended. [Fr.—*garer*, to secure—Gmc.; related to **wary**.]

garb, *gärb, n.* fashion of dress, esp. distinctive: dress (*lit.* and *fig.*).—*v.t.* to clothe, array. [It. *garbo*, grace; of Gmc. origin.]

garbage, *gär'bij, n.* refuse, as animal offal: any worthless matter. [Of doubtful origin.]

garble, *gär'bl, v.t.* to select from book, writing, &c., what may serve one's own purpose, esp. in a bad sense: to misrepresent or falsify by suppression and selection: to mangle. [It. *gar-bellare*—Ar. *ghirbāl*, a sieve.]

garcon, *gär-sõ, n.* boy: a waiter in a restaurant. [Fr.]

garden, *gär'dn, n.* a piece of ground on which flowers, &c., are cultivated: a pleasant spot: a fertile region.—*v.i.* to cultivate, or work in, a garden.—*ns.* **gar'den-cit'y**, a model town, with much garden ground between the houses; **gar'dener; gar'dening**, the laying out and cul-tivation of gardens; **gar'den-par'ty**, a social gathering held on the lawn or in the garden of a house.—**hanging garden**, a garden formed in terraces rising one above another; **market garden**, a garden in which vegetables, fruits, &c., are raised for sale. [O.Fr. *gardin* (Fr. *jar-din*); from Gmc.; allied to **yard**.]

gardenia, *gär-dē'ni a, n.* any of a genus of tropi-cal shrubs, with beautiful and fragrant flowers. [Named from the American botanist, Dr Alex. *Garden* (died 1791).]

gardyloo, *gär'di lōō, interj.* the old warning cry before throwing slops from windows of high houses in Edinburgh. [Fr. *gare l'eau*.]

garefowl, *gär'fowl, n.* the great auk. [O.N. *geir-fugl*.]

garfish, *gär'fish, n.* a pike-like fish with long slender beaked head. [O.E. *gār*, spear.]

gargantuan, *gär-gan'tū-án, adj.* like, or worthy of, *Gargantua*, Rabelais's hero, a giant of vast appetite: enormous, prodigious.

gargle, *gär'gl, v.t.* and *v.i.* to wash (the throat), preventing the liquid from going down by expelling air against it.—*n.* a liquid for wash-ing the throat. [O.Fr. *gargouiller*—*gargouille*, the throat.]

gargoyle, *gar'goil, n.* a projecting spout, usually grotesquely carved, from a roof-gutter: a per-son suggestive of a figure carved on such a spout. [O.Fr. *gargouille*—L. *gurgulio*, throat.]

garish, *gär'ish, adj.* showy, gaudy: glaring (e.g. of light).—*adv.* **gar'ishly**.—*n.* **gar'ishness**. [Earlier *gaurish, gawrish*—*gaure*, to stare.]

garland, *gär'land, n.* a wreath of flowers or leaves: a book of selections in prose or poetry.—*v.t.* to deck with a garland. [O.Fr. *garlande*.]

garlic, *gär'lik, n.* a bulbous-rooted plant having a pungent taste and very strong smell.—*adj.* **gar'licky**, like garlic. [O.E. *garleac*—*gār*, a spear, *leac*, a leek.]

garment, *gär'mént, n.* any article of clothing.

[O.Fr. *garniment*—*garnir*, to furnish.]

garner, *gär'nér, n.* (*poet.*) a granary: a store of anything.—*v.t.* to store: to collect. [O.Fr. *ger-nier* (Fr. *grenier*)—L. *grānārium* (usu. in pl.), a granary.]

garnet, *gär'net, n.* a precious stone resembling the seeds of the pomegranate. [O.Fr. *grenat*—Low L. *grānātum*, pomegranate: or Low L. *grānum*, grain, kermes, red dye.]

garnish, *gär'nish, v.t.* to adorn: to surround with extras, as a dish of food.—*n.* something placed round a principal dish at table, whether for embellishment or relish.—*ns.* **gar'nishing**, **gar'nishment**, **gar'niture**, that which gar-nishes or embellishes: ornament. [O.Fr.*garnir, garnissant*, to furnish, from a Gmc. root seen in O.E. *warnian*, to warn.]

garret, *gar'et, n.* a room just under the roof of a house.—*n.* **garreteer'**, one who lives in a gar-ret: a poor author. [O.Fr. *garite*, a place of safety, *guarir, warir*, to defend (Fr. *guérir*)—from the Gmc. root seen in **wary**.]

garrison, *gar'i-s(ó)n, n.* a supply of soldiers for guarding a fortress: a fortified place.—*v.t.* to furnish with troops: to defend by fortresses manned with troops. [O.Fr. *garison—garir, guarir*, to defend, furnish; Gmc., see **garret**.]

garrotte, garotte, *ga-rot', n.* a Spanish mode of putting criminals to death: apparatus for the purpose—originally a string round the throat tightened by twisting a stick, later a brass collar tightened by a screw, whose point en-tered the spinal marrow.—*v.t.* to execute by the garrotte: suddenly to render insensible by semi-strangulation, in order to rob:—*pr.p.* gar-(r)ott'ing; *pa.p.* gar(r)ott'ed.—*ns.* **garrott'er**, **garott'er**, one who garrottes. [Sp. *garrote*; cf. Fr. *garrot*, a stick.]

garrulous, *gar'ū-lus, -oo-lus, adj.* talkative.—*ns.* **garrullty** (*gar-(y)ōō'li ti*), **gar'ulousness**, talkativeness, loquacity. [L. *garrulus—garrire*, to chatter.]

garter, *gar'tér, n.* a band used to support a stock-ing: (*cap.*) badge of the highest order of knighthood in Great Britain.—*v.t.* to support, bind, decorate, or surround. [O.Fr. *gartier*—*garet* (Fr. *jarret*), the ham of the leg, prob. Celt.]

garth, *gärth, n.* (*arch.* and *dial.*) an enclosure or yard, a garden: a cloister-garth, an open space between cloisters: a weir in a river for catching fish. [O.N. *garthr*, court; cf. O.E. *geard*, Ger. *garten, yard*.]

gas, *gas, n.* one of the three states of matter—it has no definite boundaries but will fill any space: a substance or mixture which is in this state in ordinary terrestrial conditions: coal-gas, or other gas for lighting and heating: any gas, liquid, or solid used in war to make the atmosphere poisonous or otherwise harmful: gaslight: (*U.S.*) short for gasoline: laughing gas (see **laughing**): (*coll.*) empty, boastful, garrulous, or pert talk:—*pl.* **gas'es**.—*v.t.* to supply, attack, poison, light, inflate, or treat with gas.—*v.i.* to talk gas:—*pr.p.* gass'ing; *pa.p.* gassed.—*v.t.* and *v.i.* **gas'ify**, to turn into gas—as in the **gasificā'tion** of coal, effected by setting it alight underground and collecting the gas and by-products through pipes.—*adj.* **gaseous** (*gāz'-, gās'-*, or *gas'i-us*).—*ns.* **gasa-**

lier', gaselier', a hanging frame with branches for gas-jets; **gas'-bag**, a bag for holding gas: a talkative person; **gas'-brack'et**, a gas pipe, with a burner, projecting from the wall of a room; **gas'-burn'er**, a piece of metal at the end of a gaspipe, usually with holes to spread the flame; **gas chamber, oven**, an enclosed place designed for killing by means of gas; **gas'-coal**, any coal suitable for making gas: anthracite; **gas-discharge tube**, any tube in which an electric discharge takes place through a gas; **gas'-en'gine**, an engine worked by the explosion of gas.—*adj.* **gas'-fired'**, fuelled, or heated, by gases.—*ns.* **gas'-fitter**, one who fits up gas appliances for heating, &c.; **gas'holder**, a large metal container for storing gas; **gas'-jet**, a gas flame, or burner; **gas'-mantle**, a gauze covering, chemically prepared, enclosing a gas-jet, and becoming incandescent when heated; **gas'-mask**, a respiratory device (covering nose, mouth, and eyes) as a protection against poisonous gases; **gas'-mē'ter**, an instrument for measuring gas consumed; **gas'ogene** (see gazogene); **gas'olene, -oline**, rectified petroleum; **gasom'eter**, a storage tank for gas; **gas'-pok'er**, a gas-jet that can be inserted among fuel to kindle a fire; **gas'-retort'**, a closed heated chamber in which gas is made; **gas'-stove**, an apparatus in which coal-gas is used for heating or cooking; **gas'-trap**, a trap in a drain to prevent the escape of foul gas; **gas turbine**, a machine consisting of a combustion chamber, to which air is supplied by a compressor and in which the air is heated at constant pressure, and a turbine driven by the hot expanding gases; **gas'works**, a factory where gas is made.—**gas and gaiters**, nonsense; **natural gas** (see **natural**); **step on the gas** (i.e. gasoline), to press the accelerator pedal of a motor-car: to speed up. [A word invented by J. B. Van Helmont (1577–1644)—suggested by Gr. *chaos.*]

Gascon, *gas'kŏn, n.* a native of Gascony: a boaster.—*n.* **gasconāde'**, boasting talk.—Also *v.i.* [Fr.]

gash, *gash, v.t.* to cut deeply into.—*n.* a deep, open cut. [Formerly *garse*—O.Fr. *garser*, to scarify—Low L. *garsa*, scarification, possibly —Gr. *charassein*, to scratch.]

gasket, *gas'kit, n.* (*naut.*) a canvas band used to bind the sails to the yards when furled: a strip of tow, &c., for packing a piston, &c.: a layer of packing material, esp. a flat sheet of asbestos compound, sometimes between thin copper sheets, used for making gas-tight joints between engine cylinders and heads, &c.

gasp, *gäsp, v.i.* to gape for breath: to catch the breath: (with *for*) to desire eagerly.—*v.t.* to utter with gasps.—*n.* the act of gasping.—*n.* **gasp'er**, (*slang*) a cheap cigarette.—**the last gasp**, the point of death: the utmost extremity. [O.N. *geispa*, to yawn; cf. *geip*, idle talk.]

gasteropod, *gas'tėr-ō-pod*, **gastropod**, *gas'trō-, n.* one of a class of molluscs (**Gasterop'oda, Gastrop'oda**) embracing whelks, limpets, snails, &c., having a muscular disk under the belly, which serves them as feet. [Gr. *gastēr*, belly, *pous*, gen. *podos*, a foot.]

gastric, *gas'trik, adj.* belonging to the stomach—also **gas'tral.**—*ns.* **gastrec'tomy,**

surgical removal of the stomach, or part of it; **gastrī'tis**, inflammation of the stomach; **gastrol'ogy**, science of cookery, of good eating; **gas'troenterī'tis**, inflammation of the mucous membrane of the stomach and the intestines; **gas'troenterol'ogy**, the study of the stomach and the intestines. [Gr. *gastēr*, the belly.]

gastronomy, *gas-tron'o-mi, n.* the art or science of good eating.—*ns.* **gas'tronome, gastron'omer**, an epicure. [Gr. *gastēr*, belly, *nomos*, law.]

gat, *gat* (*B.*), pa.t. of **get**.

gat, *gat, n.* (*slang*) a gun, revolver. [**gatling-gun.**]

gate, *gāt, n.* a passage into a city, enclosure, or any large building: a frame for closing an entrance: an entrance, passage, or channel: the number of people who pay to get in to a football field or other ground to witness a game: the total amount of money paid for entrance (also **gate'-money**): electronic circuit which passes impressed signals when permitted by another independent source of similar signals: the location of a film in a projector, printer or camera when it is being acted on or scanned: an H-shaped series of slots for controlling the movement of a gear-lever in a gear-box.—*v.t.* to supply with a gate: to punish (students or school-children) by imposing a curfew on or by confining to school precincts for a time.—*ns.* **gate'-crash'er**, an intruder; **gate'-house** (*archit.*), a building over or near the gate giving entrance to a city, abbey, college, &c.; **gate'way**, the way through a gate: a structure at a gate: any entrance.—**gate'-legged table**, a table with gate-like legs that can be swung inwards so as to let down the leaves. [O.E. *geat*, a way; Du. *gat*, O.N. *gat.*]

gâteau, *gat'ō, n.* a fancy cake: *pl.* **gâteaux**. [Fr.]

gather, *ga·𝘵𝘩'ér, v.t.* to collect, to amass: to assemble: to cull: to draw together: in sewing, to draw in puckers by passing a thread through: to deduce, learn by inference.—*v.i.* to assemble or muster: to increase: to suppurate.—*n.* a plait or fold in cloth, made by drawing the thread through.—*ns.* **gath'erer**, one who collects, amasses, assembles, or culls; **gath'ering**, the action of one who gathers: a crowd or assembly: a suppurating swelling; **gath'ering ground**, a catchment area.—**gather oneself together**, to collect all one's powers, like one about to leap; **gather way**, (of a ship) to begin to move: to move with increasing speed. [O.E. *gaderian, gæderian*; same root as **together.**]

gatling-gun, *gat'ling-gun, n.* a machine-gun invented by R. J. *Gatling* about 1861.

gauche, *gōsh, adj.* clumsy: tactless.—*n.* **gaucherie** (*gōsh'é-rē, -rē'*), clumsiness: social awkwardness. [Fr.,—*gauche*, left.]

gaucho, *gow'chō, n.* a cowboy of the pampas of South America. [Sp.]

gaud, *göd, n.* an ornament, a piece of finery: showy ceremony (usu. in *pl.*).—*ns.* **gaudeā'mus** (in Scotland *gow-di-ā'moos*; L. 'let us rejoice'), a students' merrymaking; **gaud'y**, an English college or other festival.—*adj.* **gaud'y**, showy: vulgarly bright.—*adv.* **gaud'ily.**—*n.* **gaud'iness**, showiness. [In part app.—O.Fr. *gaudir*—L. *gaudēre*, to be glad, *gaudium*,

Neutral vowels in unaccented syllables: *em'pér-ór*; for certain sounds in foreign words see p. ix.

gauge

joy; in part directly from L.]
gauge (also **gage**), *gāj, n.* a measuring apparatus: a standard of measure: a means of limitation or adjustment to a standard: an instrument for recording the varying force or quantity of wind, rain, &c.—*v.t.* to measure: to estimate.—*ns.* **gaug′er**, one who gauges: an exciseman; **gauge′-glass**, a tube to show height of water; **gaug′ing**, the measuring of casks holding excisable liquors; **gaug′ing-rod**, an instrument for measuring the contents of casks.—*adjs.* **broad-**, **narr′ow-gauge**, in railroad construction, a distance between the rails greater or less than **standard-gauge**, 56$\frac{1}{2}$ inches. [O.Fr. *gauge* (Fr. *jauge*).]
Gaul, *göl, n.* a name of ancient France: an inhabitant of Gaul.—*adj.* **Gaul′ish.** [Fr. *Gaule*—L. *Gallia, Gallus*; perh. conn. with O.E. *wealh*, foreign.]
gauleiter, *gow′lī-tér, n.* head of a district organisation of the Nazi Party in Germany (see **Nazi**). [Ger.]
gaunt, *gönt, adj.* thin: of a pinched appearance: grim.—*adv.* **gaunt′ly.**—*n.* **gaunt′ness.** [Perh. allied to Norw. *gand*, pointed stick, and Swed. dial. *gank*, a lean horse.]
gauntlet, *gönt′let, n.* the iron glove of armour, formerly thrown down in challenge and taken up in acceptance: a long glove covering the wrist.—*n.* **gaunt′let-guard**, a protection for the hand on a sword or dagger.—**throw down, take up, the gauntlet** (*fig.*), to give, to accept, a challenge. [Fr. *gantelet*, dim. of *gant*, glove, of Gmc. origin.]
gauntlet, *gönt′let,* **gantlope**, *gant′lōp, ns.* the military punishment of having to run through a lane of soldiers who strike as one passes.—**run the gauntlet**, to undergo the punishment of the gauntlet: to be exposed to unpleasant remarks or treatment. [Swed. *gatlopp gata*, lane, *lopp*, course.]
gauntry. See **gantry**.
gauze, *göz, n.* a thin, transparent fabric: material slight and open like gauze.—*adj.* **gauz′y.** [Fr. *gaze*; origin uncertain.]
gave, *gāv, pa.t.* of **give**.
gavel, *gav′l, n.* a mallet: a chairman's hammer.
gavelkind, *gav′l-kīnd, n.* a tenure by which lands descend from the father to all sons in equal portions. [O.E. *gafol*, tribute; conn. with *giefan*, to give.]
gavotte, *ga-vot′, n.* a dance, somewhat like a country-dance, originally a dance of the *Gavots*, people of the French Upper Alps: the music for such a dance.
gawk, *gök, n.* an awkward or ungainly person, esp. from tallness, shyness, or simplicity: one who stares and gapes.—*adj.* **gawk′y**, awkward, ungainly.—Also *n.* [Ety. obscure; most prob. not related to Fr. *gauche*, left.]
gay, *gā, adj.* lively: sportive, merry: of loose life: bright, showy: (*slang*) homosexual.—*n.* **gai′ety.**—*adv.* **gai′ly.** [O.Fr. *gai*—perh. O.H.G. *wâhi*, pretty.]
gaze, *gāz, v.i.* to look fixedly.—*n.* a fixed look: (*arch.*) the object gazed at. [Prob. cog. with obs. *gaw*, to stare, O.N. *gā*, to heed.]
gazebo, *gä-zē′bō, n.* a belvedere. [Ety. dub.]
gazelle, *gazel*, *ga-zel′, n.* a small antelope with beautiful dark eyes, found in North Africa and

gelatine

S.W. Asia, or kindred species. [Fr.,—Ar. *ghazāl*, a wild-goat.]
gazette, *ga-zet′, n.* a newspaper: an official newspaper with lists of government appointments (civil, military), legal notices (e.g. of bankruptcies), despatches, &c.—*v.t.* to publish or mention in a gazette:—*pr.p.* gazett′ing; *pa.p.* gazett′ed.—*n.* **gazetteer′** (*gaz-*), a geographical dictionary: (*orig.*) a writer for a gazette. [Fr.,—It. *gazzetta*, a small coin; or from It. *gazzetta*, dim, of *gazza*, magpie.]
gazogene, *gaz′o-jēn*, **gasogene**, *gas′-, n.* an apparatus for making aerated waters. [Fr. *gazogène—gaz*, gas. Gr. suffx. *-genēs*—root of *gignesthai*, to become.]
gean, *gēn, n.* the wild cherry. [O.Fr. *guigne*.]
gear, *gēr, n.* equipment: clothes: harness: tackle: (*Scot.* and *dial.*) possessions: any moving part or system of parts for transmitting motion: working connection: the actual gear-ratio in use, or the gear-wheels involved in transmitting that ratio, in an automobile gear box, e.g. first gear (low gear), fourth gear (high gear).—*v.t.* to put in gear, as machinery.—*n.* **gear′ing**, harness: (*mech.*) means of transmission of motion, esp. a train of toothed wheels and pinions. *ns.* **gear′-box**, the box containing the apparatus for changing gear; **gear′-lever, -shift, -stick**, a device for selecting or engaging and disengaging gears; **gear′-ratio**, the ratio of the driving to the driven members of a gear mechanism; **gear′-wheel**, a wheel with teeth or cogs which impart or transmit motion by acting on a similar wheel or a chain.—*adjs.* **high′-gear, low′-gear**, geared to give a high or a low number of revolutions of the driven part relatively to the driving part—**out of gear**, not connected with the motor: (*fig.*) out of running order, unprepared: **to be geared to** (*fig.*), of an operation, to be subsidiary to, dependent on the progress of (another operation). [M.E. *gere*, prob. O.N. *gervi*, cf O.E. *gearwe.*]
gecko, *gek′ō, n.* any of a family of small dull-coloured lizards. [Malay *gēkoq.*]
gee, *jē, n.* an air-navigation radar (q.v.) system in which three ground stations, A (*master*), B and C (*slave*), give for AB and AC two sets of intersecting hyperbolae which, charted, give an equipped aircraft its geographical position over a few hundred miles' range from A.
geese, *pl.* of **goose**.
Gehenna, *ge-hen′a, n.* the valley of Hinnom, near Jerusalem, in which the Israelites sacrificed their children to Moloch, and to which, at a later time, the refuse of the city was conveyed to be slowly burned: hence (*N.T.*) hell: a place of torment. [L.,—Heb. *Ge-hinnōm*, valley of Hinnom.]
Geiger (-Müller) counter, *gī′gér (mül′ér) kown′tér*, an instrument for detecting radioactivity by means of the ionising effect of the charged particles (alpha particles, protons, electrons, or photons) and counting the particles mechanically.
geisha, *gā′sha, n.* a Japanese dancing-girl. [Jap.]
gelatine, **gelatin**, *jel′a-tin, n.* a colourless, odourless, and tasteless glue, prepared from albuminous substances, e.g. bones and hides, used for foodstuffs, photographic films, &c.—*vs.t.*

fāte, fär; mē, hûr (her); *mīne; mōte, för; mūte; mōōn, fŏŏt;* ᴛʜen (then)

gelat′inate (*jel-at′-*), **gelat′inīse**, to make into gelatine or jelly.—*vs.i.* to be converted into gelatine or jelly.—*n.* **gelatinā′tion.**—*adj.* **gel-at′inous**, resembling, or formed into, jelly. [Fr.,—It. *gelatina, gelata*, jelly—L. *gelāre*, to freeze.]

geld, *geld*, *v.t.* to emasculate, castrate: to deprive of anything essential, to enfeeble: (*obs.*) to expurgate.—*ns.* **geld′er**; **geld′ing**, act of castrating: a castrated animal, esp. a horse. [O.N. *gelda*; Dan. *gilde*.]

gelder-rose. Same as **guelder-rose.**

gelid, *jel′id, adj.* icy cold: cold.—*adv.* **gel′idly.—***ns.* **gel′idness, gelid′ity.** [L. *gelidus—gelū*, frost.]

gelignite, *jel′ig-nīt, n.* a powerful explosive used in mining. [Perh. from **gelatine** and L. *ignis*, fire.]

gem, *jem, n.* any precious stone, esp. when cut: anything extremely admirable, or flawless.—*v.t.* to adorn with gems:—*pr.p.* **gemm′ing**; *pa.p.* **gemmed.**—*ns.* **gem′-cutt′ing,** the art of cutting and polishing precious stones; **gem′-engrāv′ing,** the art of engraving figures on gems. [O.E. *gim*; O.H.G. *gimma*—L. *gemma*, a bud.]

geminate, *jem′in-āt, adj.* (*bot.*) in pairs.—*n.* **geminā′tion.** [L. *gemināre, -ātum—geminus*, twin.]

Gemini, *jem′i-nī, n.pl.* the twins, a constellation and sign of the zodiac containing the two bright stars Castor and Pollux.—*adj.* **gem′in-ous,** (*bot.*) double, in pairs. [L. *geminus*, twin.]

gemmation, *jem-ā′sh(ò)n, n.* (*bot.*) act or time of budding: arrangement of buds on the stalk.—*adjs.* **gemm′āte,** having buds; **gem-mif′erous,** producing buds; **gemmip′arous** (*zool.*), reproducing by buds growing on the body. [L. *gemma*, a bud.]

gen, *jen, n.* (*slang*) general information: inside information, the low-down.

gendarme, *zhä-därm′, n.* originally a man-at-arms, horseman in full armour: in France since the Revolution, one of a corps of military police: a similar policeman elsewhere:—*pl.* **gendarmes′, gensdarmes′.**—*n.* **gendar′me-rie** (*-é-rē*), an armed police force. [Fr. *gendarme*, sing. from pl. *gens d'armes*, men-at-arms—*gens*, people, *de*, of, *armes*, arms.]

gender, *jen′dér, n.* (*gram.*) a distinction of words, roughly corresponding to sex. [Fr. *genre*—L. *genus, generis*, a kind, kin.]

gender, *jen′dér, v.t.* (*arch.*) to beget.—*v.i.* (*arch.*) to copulate. [Fr. *gendrer*—L. *generāre.*]

gene, *jēn, n.* in chromosome theory, one of a set of hypothetical units supposed to be arranged in linear fashion on the chromosomes, each having a specific effect on the observable characteristics of the new organism. [Gr. *genos*, race.]

genealogy, *jēn-i-al′o-ji*, or *jen-, n.* history of the descent of families: the pedigree of a particular person or family.—*adj.* **genealog′ical.**—*n.* **geneal′ogist,** one who studies or traces genealogies or descents.—**genealogical tree,** a table of descent in the form of a tree with branches. [Gr. *geneālogia—genea*, race, *logos*, discourse.]

genera. See **genus.**

general, *jen′ér-ál, adj.* relating to a *genus* or whole class: not special: not restricted: relating to the whole, or to all or most: universal, nearly universal, common, prevalent, wide-spread: vague: not entering into details: roughly corresponding: (after an official title, &c.) chief, of highest rank.—*n.* an officer who is head over a whole department: a general officer: the chief commander of an army in service: one skilled in leadership, tactics, management: a general servant: (*R.C. Church*) the head of a religious order, responsible only to the Pope: (*Shak.*) the public, the vulgar.—*v.t.* **gen′eralīse,** to include under a general term: to reduce to a general form: to infer (the nature of a class) from instances: to extend the application of and make vague: to give only the general features of (a picture).—*v.i.* to reason inductively.—*ns.* **generalīsā′tion; generaliss′imo** (It. *superl.*), supreme commander of a great or combined force; **gener-al′ity,** state or quality of being general: indefiniteness, vagueness: a general principle, statement, &c.: the bulk, the majority.—*adv.* **gen′erally,** in a general or collective manner or sense: in most cases: upon the whole.—*n.* **gen′eralship,** the position of a military commander: military skill.—**General Assembly** (see **assembly**); **general confession,** a confession to be made by the whole congregation; **general election,** an election of all the members of a body at once; **general epistle** (see **catholic**); **general officer,** an officer above the rank of colonel; **general post-office,** the head post-office of a town or district; **general practitioner,** a physician who devotes himself to general practice rather than to special diseases; **general principle,** a principle to which there are few exceptions within its range of application.—*adj.* **gen′eral-pur′pose,** generally useful, not restricted to a particular function.—*n.* **general servant,** a servant whose duties embrace domestic work of every kind.—**General Certificate of Education,** in secondary education in England and Wales, a certificate obtainable at ordinary, advanced and scholarship levels for proficiency in one or more subjects. [O.Fr.,—L. *generālis—genus*, birth, kind.]

generate, *jen′ér-āt, v.t.* to produce: to bring into life or being: to originate: (*geom.*) to trace out.—*n.* **generā′tion,** production or formation: a single stage in natural descent: the people of the same age or period: offspring, progeny, race: (*pl.*) genealogy, history (*B.*).—*adj.* **gen′erātive,** having the power of generating or producing.—*ns.* **gen′erātor,** begetter or producer: apparatus for producing gases, &c.: any machine for turning mechanical energy into electrical energy, a dynamo; **generating-station,** a building where electricity is made on a large scale for distribution; **generation gap,** a lack of communication and understanding between one generation and the next. [L. *generāre, -ātum—genus*, a kind.]

generic, -al, generically. See **genus.**

generous, *jen′ér-us, adj.* (*arch.*) of noble birth: of a noble nature: courageous: free in giving: rich, invigorating (of food, drink, &c.).—*adv.* **gen′erously.—***ns.* **gen′erousness, generos′ity,** nobleness or liberality of nature: magna-

Neutral vowels in unaccented syllables: *em′pér-ór*; for certain sounds in foreign words see p. ix.

nimity or munificence in an act or acts. [Fr. *généreux*—L. *generōsus*, of noble birth—*genus*, birth.]

genesis, *jen'es-is, n.* origin, mode of formation or production: (*cap.*) the first book of the Bible. [Gr.]

genet, gennet. Same as **jennet.**

genet, genette, *jen'et, n.* a genus, mostly African, of carnivorous animals allied to the civet: their fur. [Fr. *genette*—Sp. *gineta*—Ar. *jarnait.*]

genetic, -al, jen-et'ik, -ål, *adjs.* pertaining to origin.—*n.* **genetics,** the branch of biology that deals with descent, variation, and heredity. [Improperly formed from **genesis.**]

Genevan, *je-nē'van, adj.* pertaining to *Geneva.*—**Geneva Convention,** an international agreement of 1865 providing for the neutrality of hospitals in war, and for the security of those whose business it was to tend the wounded and of chaplains; **Geneva Cross** (see **Red Cross**).

genial, *jē'ni-ål, adj.* cheering: kindly, sympathetic: healthful.—*ns.* **gēnial'ity, gē'nialness.**—*adv.* **gē'nially.** [L. *geniālis*—*genius,* a guardian spirit. See **genius.**]

geniculate, -d, *je-nik'ū-låt, -id, adjs.* bent like a knee. jointed: knotted.—*n.* **genicula'tion.** [L. *geniculātus*—*geniculum,* a little knee—*genū,* the knee.]

genital, *jen'i-tål, adj.* belonging to generation or the act of producing.—*n.pl.* **gen'itals,** the organs of generation, esp. external. [L. *geni tālis*—*gignĕre, genitum,* to beget.]

genitive, *jen'i-tiv, adj.* (*gram.*) of or belonging to the case expressing origin, possession, or similar relation.—*n.* the genitive case—*subjective* (e.g. God's mercy), or *objective* (e.g. God's praise); a word in the genitive case. **partitive genitive,** a genitive denoting that a part is taken of a divisible whole, e.g. in Latin *stulorum quisquam,* any foolish person, *lit.* any of the foolish. [L. *genitīvus* (*gignĕre, genitum,* to beget), for Gr. *genikos*—*genos,* a class.]

genius, *jēn'yus, or jē'ni-us, n.* the special inborn faculty of any individual: special taste or natural disposition: consummate intellectual, creative, or other power, more exalted than talent: one so endowed: a good or evil spirit, supposed to preside over each person, place, and thing, and esp. to preside over a man's destiny from his birth: prevailing spirit or tendency: a person who exerts a power, influence (whether good or bad) over another:—*pl.* **geniuses** (*jēn'yus-ez*); in sense of spirits, **genii** (*jē'ni-ī*). [L. *genius*—*gignĕre, genitum,* to beget.]

gennet. Same as **jennet.**

genocide, *jen'ō-sīd, n.* deliberate extermination of a race or other group: one who exterminates, or approves extermination of, a race, &c.—*adj.* **genocīd'al.** [Gr. *genos,* race, L. *caedĕre,* to kill.]

genre, *zhä-r', n.* kind: a literary species: a style of painting scenes from familiar or rustic life. [Fr.—L. *genus.*]

gent, *jent, n.* vulg. abbrev. of *gentleman:* one who apes the gentleman.

genteel, *jen-tēl', adj.* well-bred: graceful in manners or in form: now used only with mocking reference to a standard of obsolete snobbery or false refinement.—*n.* **genteel'ism,** a would-be refined substitute for the right word or phrase.—*adv.* **genteel'ly.**—*n.* **genteel'ness.** [Due to a second borrowing of Fr. *gentil,* later than that which gave **gentle.**]

gentian, *jen'shån, n.* any of a number of plants of alpine regions, usually blue-flowered: the roots and rhizome of the yellow gentian used in medicine.—**gentian violet,** a mixture of three dyes which is antiseptic and germicidal. [L. *gentiāna,* according to Pliny from *Gentius,* king of Illyria, who introduced it in medicine (2nd cent. B.C.).]

gentile, *jen'tīl, n.* (*B.*) anyone not a Jew.—*adj.* belonging to the Gentiles: (*gram.*) denoting a race or country. [L. *gentīlis*—*gens,* a nation.]

gentle, *jen'tl, adj.* well-born: mild and refined in manners: mild in disposition or action: amiable: soothing: moderate: gradual (e.g. a slope).—*n.pl.* **gen'tles,** (*arch., vulg*) gentlefolk.—*n.* **gentil'ity,** good birth or extraction: good breeding: politeness of manners.—*n.pl.* **gen'tlefolk,** people of good family.—*n.* **gen'tleness.**—*adv.* **gent'ly.**—**gentle craft,** shoe-making: angling. [Fr. *gentil*—L. *gentilis,* belonging to the same *gens* or clan, later, well-bred. See **genteel.**]

gentleman, *jen'tl-mån, n.* (*hist.*) one who without a title wears a coat of arms: more generally every man above the rank of yeoman, including the nobility: a man of good social position: a well-to-do man of no occupation: a man of refined manners: a man of good feeling and instincts, courteous and honourable: a polite term used for men in general:—*pl.* **gen'tlemen**—also a word of address:—*fem.* **gen'tlewoman**:—*pl.* **gen'tlewomen.**—*n.* **gen'tleman-at-arms,** a member of the royal bodyguard. *adjs.* **gen'tlemanlike, gen'tlemanly,** well-bred, refined, generous.—*n.* **gen'tlemanliness.**—**gentleman's (-men's) agreement,** one resting upon honour, not law; **gentleman's gentleman,** a valet. [**gentle** and **man.**]

gentry, *jen'tri, n.* the class of people next below the rank of nobility: (*coll.*) people of a particular, often an inferior, stamp. [O.Fr. *genterise, gentelise,* formed from adj. *gentil,* gentle.]

genuflect, *jen-ū-flekt', v.i.* to bend the knee in worship or respect.—*n.* **genūflex'ion** (also **genūflec'tion**). [L. *genū,* the knee, *flectĕre, flexum,* to bend.]

genuine, *jen'ū-in, adj.* pure-bred: authentic, not spurious: real, not counterfeit: properly so called: pure: sincere.—*adv.* **gen'uinely.**—*n.* **gen'uineness.** [L. *genuīnus*—*gignĕre,* to beget.]

genus, *jē'nus, n.* (*biol.*) a classified group of lower rank than a family, consisting of closely related species, in extreme cases of one species only: (*logic*) a class of objects comprehending several subordinate species:—*pl.* **genera** (*jen'ér-a*).—*adjs.* **generic, -al** (*jen-er'ik, -ål*), characteristic of a genus: denoting a genus (e.g. *a generic name*): general, of wide application.—*adv.* **gener'ically.** [L. *gĕnus, generis,* birth; cog. with Gr. *genos.*]

geo-, *jē'ō-, pfx.* earth, world, forming words such as: *ns.* **geochem'istry,** study of the chemical composition of the earth's crust; **geochron-**

ol'ogy, study of dating, by various methods, events in the earth's history before the time of written history; **geomag'netism,** study of magnetic forces at the surface of the earth at different places and times; **geomorphol'ogy,** study of present-day landscapes and explanations of the changes by which their features (hills, valleys, &c.) have been formed; **geophys'ics,** study of the physical characteristics of the earth, esp. those below the surface, making use of data supplied by the study of earthquakes, earth magnetism, tidal phenomena, &c. (See also separate articles following.) [Gr. *gē,* the earth.]

geocentric, *jē-ō-sen'trik, adj.* having the earth for centre: (*astron.*) as viewed or reckoned from the centre of the earth: taking life on earth as the basis for evaluation.—Also **geocen'trical.**—*adv.* **geocen'trically.** [Gr. *gē,* the earth, *kentron,* centre.]

geode, *jē'ōd, n.* (*min.*) a rounded nodule of ironstone having a cavity lined with crystals. [Fr.,—Gr. *geōdēs,* earthy—*gē,* earth, *eidos,* form.]

geodesy, *jē-od'e-si, n.* earth-measurement on a large scale: surveying with allowance for the earth's curvature. [Fr. *géodésie*—Gr. *geōdaisia*—*gē,* the earth, *daiein,* to divide.]

geogony, *jē-og'o-ni, n.* the science or theory of the formation of the earth. [Gr. *gē,* the earth, *gonē,* generation.]

geography, *jē-og'ra-fi, n.* the science that describes the surface of the earth and its inhabitants: a book containing a description of the earth.—*n.* **geog'rapher.**—*adjs.* **geograph'ic** (*-graf'-*), **-al.**—*adv.* **geograph'ically.**—**geographical mile** (see **mile**). [Fr.,—L.,—Gr. *geōgraphia*—*gē,* earth, *graphē,* a description—*graphein,* to write.]

geoid, *jē'oid, n.* the figure of the earth's mean sea-level surface assumed to be continued across the land, approximately an oblate ellipsoid of revolution. [Gr. *gē,* earth, *eidos,* form.]

geology, *jē-ol'o-ji, n.* the science relating to the history and development of the earth's crust, with its successive floras, faunas.—*n.* **geol'ogist.**—*adjs.* **geolog'ic, -al.**—*adv.* **geolog'ically.** —*v.i.* **geol'ogise,** to work at geology in the field.—**geological time,** time before written history, divided into epochs each of which saw the formation of one of the great rock systems. [Fr. *géologie*—Gr. *gē,* earth, *logos,* a discourse.]

geometry, *jē-om'e-tri, n.* that part of mathematics which treats of the properties of points, lines, surfaces, and solids, either under classical Euclidean assumptions or (in the case of *elliptic, hyperbolic,* &c. *geometry*) involving postulates not all of which are identical with Euclid's: any study of a mathematical system in which figures undergo transformations, concerned with discussion of those properties of the figures which remain constant: a textbook of geometry.—*ns.* **geom'eter, geometri'cian** (*-shān*), one skilled in geometry.—*adjs.* **geomet'ric, -al.**—*adv.* **geomet'rically.**—**geometrical progression,** a series of numbers such that the ratio of successive terms is constant, e.g. 2, 4, 8, 16. [Fr. *géométrie*—L., Gr.

geōmetria—*gē,* earth, *metron,* a measure.]

geophagy, *jē-of'á-ji, n.* the practice of eating earth. [Gr. *gē,* earth, *phagein,* to eat.]

geopolitics, *jē-o-pol'i-tiks, n.* the science or study of the effect of geographical factors, such as position or natural products, on the policy of a state or people, and of the ways in which inventions and discoveries alter the values of the geographical factors.—*adj.* **geopolit'ical.** [Gr. *gē,* earth, and **politics.**]

George, *jörj, n.* the automatic pilot of an aircraft.—**George Cross (G.C.), George Medal (G.M.),** decorations, primarily for civilian gallantry, instituted in World War II in the reign of George VI.

georgette, *jör-jet', n.* a thin silk stuff. [Named after a milliner.]

Georgian, *jörj'i-án, adj.* relating to or contemporary with any of the various *Georges,* kings of Great Britain: belonging to *Georgia* in the Caucasus: pertaining to the American state of *Georgia.*

georgic, *jörj'ik, adj.* relating to agriculture or rustic affairs.—*n.* a poem on husbandry. [L. *geōrgicus*—Gr. *geōrgikos*—*geōrgia,* agriculture—*gē,* earth, *ergon,* a work.]

geotropism, *jē-ot'ro-pizm, n.* (*bot.*) tendency to growth downward under the influence of gravity.—*adj.* **geotrop'ic.** [Gr. *gē,* the earth, *tropos,* a turning.]

geranium, *je-rān'i-um, n.* a genus of plants with seed-vessels similar in shape to a crane's bill: most commonly used of a garden plant or flower of the allied genus *Pelargonium.* [L.,—Gr. *geranion*—*geranos,* a crane.]

gerbil, *jûr'bil, n.* a small desert-dwelling rodent which can be kept as a pet.—Also (esp. formerly) **gerbille.** [Fr. *gerbille.*]

gerfalcon, gyrfalcon, jerfalcon, *jûr'fö(l)-kòn, n.* a large northern falcon of various kinds. [O.Fr. *gerfaucon*—Low L. *gyrofalcō,* most prob. O.H.G. *gîr,* a vulture (Ger. *geier*). See **falcon.**]

geriatry, *jer-i'á-tri, n.* care of the old, old people's welfare.—*adj.* **geriatric** (*jer-i-at'rik*). —*n.* **geriat'rics,** the branch of medicine concerned with the diseases of old age. [Gr. *gēras,* old age.]

germ, *jûrm, n.* a rudimentary form of a living thing, whether plant or animal: a shoot: that from which anything springs, the origin: a first principle: that from which a disease springs: a micro-organism, esp. a malign one.—*n.* **germ'icide,** that which destroys disease germs.—*adjs.* **germ'inal,** pertaining to a germ or rudiment: in the germ; **germ'inant,** sprouting, budding, capable of development.—*v.i.* **germ'ināte,** to begin to grow (esp. of a seed or spore).—*v.t.* to cause to sprout.—*n.* **germinā'tion.**—*adj.* **germ'inātive.**—**germ warfare,** warfare in which bacteria are used as weapons. [Partly through Fr. *germe,* from L. *germen, -inis,* a sprout, bud, germ—*germināre, -ātum,* to sprout.]

german, *jûr'mán,* **germane,** *-mān, adj.* of the first degree: full (see **brother, cousin**): closely allied: (**germane**) relevant (to). [O.Fr. *germain*—L. *germānus.*]

German, *jûr'mán, n.* a native or citizen of *Germany:* the German language:—*pl.* **Ger'mans.**—*adj.* of or from Germany, or of

Neutral vowels in unaccented syllables: *em'pėr-ôr*; for certain sounds in foreign words see p. ix.

298

the same linguistic or ethnological stock.—*adj.*
German'ic, pertaining to Germany, the Germans (see **Teutonic**), or the German language, or to a branch of Indo-Germanic (see below).—*n.* an extinct Indo-Germanic tongue differentiated into *East Germanic* (Gothic and other extinct languages), *North Germanic* or Scandinavian (Norwegian, Danish, Swedish, Icelandic), and *West Germanic* (English, Frisian, Dutch, Low German, High German). —*ns.* **German flute,** the ordinary modern flute; **German silver** (see **nickel silver**). —**High German,** the speech originally of High or Southern Germany, now the literary language throughout Germany; **Low German,** the language of Low or Northern Germany: formerly applied to all the West Germanic dialects except High German.—*ns.* **German'ophil (-phobe),** one who admires (hates) Germans and things German. [L. *Germāni,* Germans; origin unknown.]

germanium, *jer-mā'ni-um, n.* a metallic element (symbol Ge; at. no. 32), important in the electronics industry. [Formed from *Germany.*]

gerontology, *jer-ont-ol'o-ji, n.* the scientific study of the processes of growing old. [Gr. *gerōn, -ontos,* an old man, *logos,* a discourse.]

gerrymander, *ger-, jer-i-man'dér, v.t.* (*U.S.*) to rearrange (voting districts) in the interests of a particular party or candidate: to manipulate (facts, arguments, &c.) so as to reach undue conclusions.—Also *n.* [Formed from the name of Governor Elbridge *Gerry* (1744-1814) and sala*mander,* from the likeness to that animal of the gerrymandered map of Massachusetts in 1811.]

gerund, *jer'und, n.* a part of the Latin or other verb with the value of a verbal noun (e.g. in Latin, *operandum* working, *modus operandi,* way of working, operating; in English, *he resented my correcting him*).—*adj.* **gerund'ial.**—*n.* **gerund'ive,** a Latin verbal adjective, as *amandus, -a, -um,* deserving or requiring to be loved. [L. *gerundium—gerēre,* to bear.]

gest, geste, *jest, n.* an exploit: a tale of adventure, a romance.—**chanson de geste,** (*shä'sõ de zhest*), any Old French epic poem. [O.Fr. *geste*—L. *gesta*; see **jest.**]

gestalt, *ge-shtält, n.* form, structure, pattern: an organised whole (e.g. a living organism, a picture, a melody, the solar system) in which each individual part affects every other, the whole being more than the sum of its parts.— **gestalt psychology,** the psychology of a school which demonstrated the tendency of the mind to perceive situations as a whole, rather than as a number of isolated elements or sensations. [Ger.]

gestapo, *ge-stä'põ, n.* the secret police in Germany under the Nazis. [From Ger. *ge*heime *sta*ats *po*lizei, secret state police.]

gestate, *jes-tāt', v.t.* to carry in the womb during the period from conception to birth: (*fig.*) to conceive and develop slowly in the mind.—*v.i.* to be in the process of gestating.—*n.* **gesta'tion,** (*jes-tā'sh(ó)n; arch.*) being carried in a vehicle, &c.: the act of gestating (*biol.* and *fig.*). [Fr.,—L. *gestātiō, -ōnis—gestāre, -ātum,* to carry—*gerēre,* to bear.]

gesticulate, *jes-tik'ū-lāt, v.i.* to make vigorous

gestures, esp. when speaking.—*n.* **gesticulā'tion,** act of making gestures in speaking: a gesture.—*adj.* **gestic'ulatory.** [L. *gesticulārī, -ātus—gesticulus,* dim. of *gestus,* gesture—*gerēre,* to carry.]

gesture, *jes'tyûr, -chûr, n.* (*obs.*) posture, or carriage of the body: a movement of the body expressive of feeling, or emphasising something said: the use of such movements: an action dictated by courtesy or by diplomacy (e.g. *he made this gesture of friendship towards him*). [Low L. *gestūra*—L. *gestus,* from L. *gerēre,* to carry.]

get, *get, v.t.* to obtain, gain: to procure: to receive: to have (*coll.* and inelegantly, in *perf.*; e.g. *I have got two brothers*): to beget (offspring): to cause to be in any state, condition, or position (e.g. *to get the fire lit, to get oneself untidy, to get the nails out of the box*): to persuade (to do): (*B.*) to betake (oneself): to contract (a disease): to capture: (*slang*) to *murder* (a person), or to kill (him) purposely: to achieve a likeness of (e.g. *the painter hadn't quite got his expression, you haven't quite got the tune*): to succeed in coming into touch with (e.g. a wireless station): in idiomatic phrases (chiefly *coll.*)—to baffle, to irritate, to grip emotionally, &c.—*v.i.* to arrive at, or put oneself in, any place or condition (with *to*): to become (e.g. *to get old, thirsty*): (*coll.*) to manage, or to be allowed (e.g. *did he get to go?*):—*pr.p.* get'ting; *pa.t.* got; *pa.p.* got, (*arch., Scot.,* and *U.S.*) got'en.—*adj.* **get-at-able,** accessible.—*ns.* **get'-away,** (*slang*) an escape; **get'ter,** one who gets: that which evacuates: a material used, when evaporated by high-frequency induction currents, for absorption of gas left in vacuum valves after sealing during manufacture: (style of) outfit, make-up, equipment. **get across** (*coll.*), to communicate successfully; **get along,** to proceed, move on: (*coll.*) to manage: to agree, get on (with); **get at,** to reach: to ascertain, find out: to hint at: to tamper with: to bribe: (*coll.*) to poke fun at; **get away,** to start: to set out, esp. with difficulty: to escape: (*interj.*; also **get away with you!**) used as an expression of protest or incredulity; **get away with,** to make off successfully with: (*coll.*) to do, carry out (something more or less reprehensible) without being punished; **get a move on,** (*slang*) to bestir oneself, to begin an action or operation energetically, or to accelerate one already begun, **get by,** to succeed in passing: to elude notice and come off with impunity: to manage satisfactorily, be sufficiently good; **get by heart,** to learn word for word or exactly; **get cracking,** (*slang*) to get a move on; **get down to,** to set to work on, tackle seriously; **get going,** (*coll.*) to begin, esp. energetically, get on the move; **get in,** to enter a vehicle: to reach a station or port: to succeed in entering or gaining admission (e.g. *the door was closed and I could not get in*): to be elected: to include: to succeed in including: to land (a blow): to succeed in delivering (e.g. a jibe); **get in with,** to become intimate, friendly with; **get it,** (*coll.*) to receive a scolding or punishment; **get off,** to escape, to be let off: to start: to dismount; **get on,** to put on (clothes): to mount: to advance: to proceed: to prosper: to agree, be friendly (with); **get out,** to take, or to succeed in taking, out: to elicit: to utter: to publish: to go out or away; **get over,** to sur- mount: to cover: to become accustomed to: to recover from; **get round,** to circumvent: to persuade, talk over; **get round to,** to bring oneself to do (something); **get there,** (*slang*) to achieve one's object, succeed; **get through,** to finish: to pass an examination: to survive; **get up,** to arise: to ascend: to arrange, prepare; **get weaving** (see **weaving**). [O.N. *geta*; cog. with O.E. *gietan* (occurring in compounds).]

geum, *jē'um, n.* any one of a genus of plants (also known as *avens*) of the rose family, one species of which is the herb-bennet. [L., herb- bennet.]

gewgaw, *gū'gö, n.* a toy: a bauble.—*adj.* showy, without value. [Origin unknown.]

geyser, *gā'-, gē'-, gī'zér, n.* a volcano in miniature from which hot water and steam are erupted periodically instead of lava and ashes: a heater for bath-water: (*slang*) a fellow (usu. depreciatingly). [*Geysir,* a geyser in Ice- land—O.N. *geysa,* to gush.]

Ghanaian, *gä-nä'yán, -nä', adj.* of or pertaining to Ghana.—Also *n.*

ghastly, *gäst'li, adj.* death-like: hideous: (*coll.*) deplorable.—*n.* **ghast'liness.** [M.E. *gastlich,* terrible—O.E. *gæstan.* See **aghast.**]

ghat, ghaut, *göt, n.* in India, a mountain-pass: a riverside landing-stair: a place of cremation (*burning ghat*). [Hindustani *ghāt,* descent.]

ghee, *gē, n.* an Indian clarified butter, generally prepared from water-buffaloes' milk. [Hindu- stani *ghī.*]

gherkin, *gûr'kin, n.* a small cucumber used for pickling. [From an earlier form of Du. *augurkje,* a gherkin; app. from Slavonic.]

ghetto, *get'ō, n.* the Jews' quarter in an Italian or other city, where they used to be strictly con- fined: a quarter, esp. poor, inhabited by any racial or religious group. [It.]

ghost, *gōst, n.* a spirit: the soul of man: a spirit appearing after death, an apparition, spectre: a faint semblance (e.g. *a ghost of an idea, of a chance*): (*slang*) one who does another's work for him, as writing speeches and the like: (*TV*) a duplicated image.—*adjs.* **ghost'-like; ghost'ly,** spiritual: religious: pertaining to ap- paritions.—*n.* **ghost'liness.—ghost town,** one which once flourished due to some natural resource in the vicinity but which is now deserted, the natural resource having been exhausted.—**give up the ghost** (*B.*), to die. [O.E. *gäst,* Ger. *geist.*]

ghoul, *gōōl,* now often *gowl, n.* an Eastern de- mon that preys on the dead: a human being whose tastes or pursuits are equally grim or revolting.—*adj.* **ghoul'ish.** [Ar. *ghūl.*]

ghyll. Same as **gill** (3).

giant, *jī'ánt, n.* a huge mythical being of more or less human form: a person of abnormally great stature: anything much above the usual size of its kind: a person of extraordinary powers:—*fem.* **gī'antess.**—*adj.* gigantic.—*n.* **gi'antism,** gigantism (q.v.). [O.Fr. *geant* (Fr. *géant*), through L. from Gr. *gigās,* gen. *gigantos.*]

giaour, *jowr, n* infidel, a term applied by the Turks to all who are not of their own religion. [Through Turk.—Pers. *gaur.*]

gibber, *jib'ér, v.i.* to utter senseless or inarticu- late sounds.—*n.* **gibberish** (*gib'ér-ish, jib'-*), rapid, gabbling talk: unmeaning words.—*adj.* unmeaning. [Imit.]

gibbet, *jib'et, n.* a gallows: the projecting beam of a crane.—*v.t.* to expose on, or as on, a gibbet. [O.Fr. *gibet,* a stick; origin unknown.]

gibbon, *gib'ón, n.* any of several East Indian anthropoid apes with very long arms.

gibbous, *gib'us, adj.* hump-backed: humped: un- equally convex on two sides, as the moon between half and full.—Also **gibb'ōse.** [L. *gib- bōsus—gibbus,* a hump.]

gibe, jibe, *jīb, v.i.* to scoff, jeer (at).—Also *v.t.*—*n.* a jeer, a taunt.—*adv.* **gib'ingly** (*jīb'-*).

giblets, *jib'lets, n.pl.* the internal eatable parts of a fowl, &c.: entrails. [O.Fr. *gibelet;* origin un- known; not a dim. of *gibier,* game.]

gibus, *jī'bus, n.* a crush-hat, opera-hat. [Fr.]

giddy, *gid'i, adj.* unsteady: dizzy: that causes giddiness: whirling: light-headed: flighty.— *adv.* **gidd'ily.—*n.*** **gidd'iness.** [O.E. *gidig* (for *gydig*), possessed by a god, insane.]

gier-eagle, *jēr-ē'gl, n.* (*B.*) a vulture. [*gier* (see **gerfalcon**), and **eagle.**]

gift, *gift, n.* a thing given: a bribe: a quality bestowed by nature: the act of giving: (*coll.*) something easily obtained, understood, &c.—*v.t.* to endow (with any power or fac- ulty): to present.—*adj.* **gift'ed,** highly endowed by nature.—**look a gift horse in the mouth,** to criticise a gift (orig. looking at the horse's teeth to tell its age). [Root of **give.**]

gig, *gig, n.* a light, two-wheeled carriage: a long, light boat. [M.E. *gigge,* a whirling thing (cf. **whirligig**); origin obscure.]

giga-, *jī-gä-, pfx.* meaning ten to the ninth power, i.e. one thousand million.

gigantic, *jī-gan'tik, adj.* of, like, or characteristic of, a giant: huge.—*adv.* **gigan'tically.—*n.*** **gigan'tism,** hugeness: uniformly excessive growth of the lobe, due to overactivity of the anterior lobe of the pituitary gland. [L. *gigās, gigantis,* Gr. *gigās, -antos,* a giant.]

giggle, *gig'l, v.i.* to laugh with short catches of the breath, or in a silly manner.—*n.* a laugh of this kind.—*ns.* **gigg'ler; gigg'ling.** [Imit.]

gigolo, *jig'ō-lō, n.* a male professional dancing partner: a young man living at the expense of older women. [Fr.]

Gilbertian, *gil-bûrt'i-án, adj.* whimsically or paradoxically humorous. [Sir. W. S. *Gilbert,* librettist, &c. (1836-1911).]

gild, *gild, v.t.* to cover or overlay with gold: to cover with any gold-like substance: to give a specious appearance to:—*pr.p.* **gild'ing;** *pa.t.* and *pa.p.* **gild'ed** or **gilt.—*ns.*** **gild'er,** one who coats articles with gold; **gild'ing,** act or trade of a gilder: gold laid on any surface for or- nament.—**gilded chamber,** the House of Lords; **gilded youth,** rich young people of fashion; **gild the lily,** to embellish to an un- necessary extent; **gild the pill,** to make a disagreeable thing seem less so. [O.E. *gyldan—gold.* See **gold.**]

gill, *gil, n.* an organ for breathing in water: the flap below the bill of a fowl. [Cf. Dan. *giælle;* Swed. *gäl.*]

Neutral vowels in unaccented syllables: *em'pér-ôr;* for certain sounds in foreign words see p. ix.

gill, *jil, n.* a measure, now = ¼ pint. [O.Fr. *gelle*.]

gill, *gil, n.* a small ravine, a wooded glen: a brook.—Also **ghyll**. [O.N. *gil*.]

gillie, *gil′i, n.* an attendant, esp. on a sportsman. [Gael. *gille*, a lad, Ir. *giolla*.]

gillyflower, *jil′i-flow-(ė)r, n.* a name for various flowers that smell like cloves. [O.Fr. *girofle*— Gr. *karyophyllon*, the clove-tree—*karyon*, a nut, *phyllon*, a leaf.]

gilt, *gilt, pa.t.* and *pa.p.* of **gild**.—*n.* gilding.—*adj.* **gilt′ edged**, having the edges gilt: of the highest quality, as 'gilt-edged securities' (those stocks whose interest is considered perfectly safe).

gimbals, *jim′bălz, n.pl.* a two-ring contrivance for supporting an object, such as a ship's chronometer, so that it remains horizontal.— A sing. form occurs in composition, e.g. **gim′bal-ring**. [L. *gemelli*, twins.]

gimcrack, **jimcrack**, *jim′krak, n.* a paltry ill-made frail article: a trivial mechanism.—*adj.* trumpery. [Origin obscure.]

gimlet, *gim′let, n.* a small tool for boring holes, with a screw point and a wooden crosspiece as handle.—*v.t.* to pierce as with a gimlet.—*adj.* **gim′let-eyed**, very sharp-sighted and observant. [O.Fr. *guimbelet*, from Gmc.]

gimmer, *gim′er, n.* a young ewe. [O.N. *gymbr*; cf. Swed. *gimmer*, Dan. *gimmer*.]

gimmick, *gim′ik, n.* a secret device for performing a trick: an ingenious mechanical device: a device to attract notice, peculiar to the person adopting it: an addition or accessory, not necessarily useful, intended to make an article for sale seem more attractive.— **gimm′ickry**, gimmicks in quantity: use of gimmicks.—*adj.* **gimm′icky**. [Orig. unknown.]

gimp, *gimp, n.* a yarn with a hard core: a trimming thereof. [Fr. *guimpe*, app. from O.H.G. *wimpal*, a light robe; Eng. **wimple**.]

gin, *jin, n.* a shortened form of *geneva*, a spirit distilled from grain and flavoured with juniper berries or other aromatic substances—*ns.* **gin′-pal′ace**, **gin′-shop**, a shop where gin is sold. [Du. *genever*, *jenever*, O.Fr. *genevre*—L. *juniperus*, the juniper; confused with the town of Geneva.]

gin, *jin, n.* a snare or trap: a machine, esp. one for hoisting: a cotton (q.v.) gin:—*v.t.* to trap or snare: to clear of seeds by a cotton gin:—*pr.p.* **ginn′ing**; *pa.p.* **ginned**.—*ns.* **gin′-horse**, a millhorse, **gin′-house**, **ginn′ery**, a place where cotton is ginned. [Abbreviated form of O.Fr. *engin*. See **engine**.]

ginger, *jin′jer, n.* the root-stock or rhizome of a plant in the E. and W. Indies, with a hot taste, used as a condiment or stomachic: *(fig.)* energy: stimulation.—*v.t.* to put ginger into: *(fig.)* to make spirited—*ns.* **gingerāde′**, **ginger-ale′**, an aerated drink flavoured with ginger; **ginger-beer′**, an effervescent drink made with fermenting ginger; **gin′ger-group′**, a group within e.g. a political party seeking to inspire the rest with its own enthusiasm; **gingersnap′**, a biscuit spiced with ginger; **ginger-wine′**, a liquor made by the fermentation of sugar and water, and flavoured with various spices, chiefly ginger. [M.E. *gingivere*—O.Fr. *gengibre*—L. *zingiber*—Gr. *zingiberis*.]

gingerbread, *jin′jer-bred, n.* a cake flavoured with treacle and usually ginger.—**take the gilt off the gingerbread**, to destroy the illusion. [O.Fr. *gingimbrat*—L. *zingiber* (see **ginger**); confused with **bread**.]

gingerly, *jin′jer-li, adv.* with soft steps: with extreme wariness and delicate gentleness.— Also *adj.*—*n.* **gin′gerliness**. [Perh. O.Fr. *gensor*, comp. of *gent*—L. *gentīlis*, gentle.]

gingham, *ging′am, n.* a kind of cotton cloth, woven from coloured yarns with stripes or checks. [Fr. *guingan*, orig. from Malay *ginggang*, striped.]

ginseng, *jin′seng, n.* a Chinese plant: its root, said to be a remedy for exhaustion of body or mind. [Chin. *jên-shên*.]

Giorgi system, *jör′je sis′tim*, the **metre-kilogram(me)-second system**. [After Giovanni *Giorgi*, Italian physicist, died 1950.]

gipsy. See **gypsy**.

giraffe, *ji-räf′, n.* the camelopard, an African quadruped with remarkably long neck and fore-legs. [Fr.,—Sp. *girafa*—Ar. *zarāfah*.]

gird, *gûrd, v.i.* to gibe, jeer (with *at*).—Also *n.* [From obs. *gird*, to strike; same as **gird** (2).]

gird, *gûrd, v.t.* to bind round: to make fast by means of a belt or girdle: to equip (with sword in belt): to encompass (e.g. with strength), to encircle, surround:—*pa.t.* and *pa.p.* **gird′ed** or **girt**. *n.* **gird′er**, a great beam (simple or built-up, of wood, iron, or steel) to take a lateral stress, e.g. to support a floor, wall, roadway of a bridge. [O.E. *gyrdan*; cf. Ger. *gürten*.]

girdle, *gûrd′l, n.* a waist-belt: a cord worn about the waist by a monk, &c.: anything that encloses like a belt: a ring-shaped cut around a tree.—Also *v.t.* [O.E. *gyrdel*—*gyrdan*, to gird.]

girdle. See **griddle**.

girl, *gûrl, n.* a female child: a young woman. *n.* **girl′hood**, the state or time of being a girl.— *adj.* **girl′ish**, of or like a girl.—*adv.* **girl′ishly**.—*n.* **girl′ishness**.—**Girl Friday**, a young woman acting as secretary or personal assistant in a business office; **Girl Guide**, a member of an organisation for girls, analogous to the (Boy) Scouts' Association. [Origin obscure.]

Giro, *jī′rō, n.* a banking system by which money can be transferred direct from the account of one holder to that of another. [Ger., transfer—Gr. *gyros*, ring.]

Girondist, *ji-rond′ist, n.* a member of the moderate republican party during the French Revolution: its earliest leaders came from the *Gironde* department.—Also **Giron′din**.

girt, *gûrt, v.t.* to gird: to put a girth on. [**gird**.]

girth, *gûrth, n.* a belly-band of a saddle: a measure round about.—Also **girt**. [O.N. *gjörth*.]

gist, *jist, n.* the main point or pith of a matter. [O.Fr. *gist* (Fr. *gît*)—O.Fr. *gesir* (Fr. *gésir*), to lie—L. *jacēre*.]

give, *giv, v.t.* to bestow: to hand over: to pay: to impart: to yield as product or result: to do suddenly (an action, as a cry, a jump): to afford, to furnish: to render (e.g. thanks): to pronounce (e.g. a decision): to show (e.g. a result): to apply (oneself): to allow or admit.—*v.i.* to yield to pressure: to begin to melt: to open, or give an opening or view, or lead, into (with *upon, on, into*):—*pr.p.* **giv′ing**; *pa.t.*

gave; *pa.p.* given (*giv'n*).—*p.adj.* **giv'en**, bestowed: specified: stated as hypothesis: admitted: addicted, disposed (to).—*ns.* **give'away'**, a betrayal, revelation, esp. if unintentional: something given free; **giv'er**, one who gives. —**give chase**, to pursue; **give ear**, to listen; **give forth**, to emit: to publish; **give ground**, **place**, (see **ground**, **place**); **give in to**, to yield to; **give me**, I would choose if I had the choice; **give one his due**, to admit any merits he may have; **give oneself away**, to betray one's secret unawares; **give out**, to report: to announce: to emit: to run short: (of an engine) to fail; **give over**, to cease; **give tongue**, to bark, as hounds on picking up the scent; **give up**, to abandon; **give way**, to yield, to withdraw: to collapse under strain: to begin rowing: to allow traffic in a direction crossing one's path to proceed first. [O.E. *gefan* (W.S. *giefan*); Ger. *geben*.]

gizzard, *giz'ärd*, *n.* a muscular stomach, esp. the second stomach of a bird.—**to stick in one's gizzard**, to be more than one can stomach or tolerate. [M.E. *giser*—O.Fr. *guiser*.]

glacé, *glä'sā*, *adj.* iced: glossy, lustrous. [Fr.]

glacial, *glä'shi-ál*, *adj.* icy: frozen: pertaining to ice or its action.—*v.t.* **glaciate** (*glāsh'-*, *glās'-*, or *glas'-*), to subject to the action of land-ice.—*n.* **glacia'tion.**—**glacial epoch**, an Ice Age (q.v.); **glacial period**, the period containing the glacial epochs. [L. *glaciālis*, icy, *glaciāre*, -*ātum*, to freeze—*glaciēs*, ice.]

glacier, *glas'i-ėr*, -*yėr* (also *glāsh'-*), *n.* a mass of ice, fed by snow on a mountain, slowly creeping downhill to where it melts or breaks up. [Fr.,—*glace*, ice—L. *glaciēs*, ice.]

glacis, *glās'is*, *n.* an inclined bank. [Fr.,—O.Fr. *glacier*, to slip.]

glad, *glad*, *adj.* pleased: cheerful, bright: giving pleasure.—*v.t.* to make glad:—*pr.p.* **gladd'ing**; *pa.p.* **gladd'ed.**—*v.t.* **gladd'en**, to make glad: to cheer: to animate.—*adv.* **glad'ly.**—*n.* **glad'ness.**—*adj.* **glad'some**. [O.E. *glæd*; Ger. *glatt*, smooth, O.N. *glathr*, bright, Dan. *glad*.]

glade, *glād*, *n.* an open space in a wood. [Origin obscure; poss. conn. with **glad**.]

gladiator, *glad'i-ā-tór*, *n.* in ancient Rome, a professional combatant with men or beasts in the arena.—*adj.* **gladiätō'rial**, **glad'iatory**. [L. *glädiätor*—*glädius*, a sword.]

gladiolus, *glad'yō-lus*, *gla-dī'ō-lus*, very commonly *glad-i-ō'lus*, *n.* any one of a genus of plants known also as sword-lily:—*pl.* **gladiolī**, **gladioluses**. [L. *glädiŏlus*, dim. of *glädius*, a sword.]

gladstone-bag, *glad'stón-bag*, *n.* a travelling hand-bag, named in honour of the statesman, W. E. *Gladstone* (1809-98).

glair, *glār*, *n.* the clear part of an egg used as varnish: any viscous, transparent substance.—*v.t.* to varnish with white of eggs.—*adjs.* **glair'y**, **glaireous** (*glār'i-us*). [Fr. *glaire*—Low L. *clāra* (*ōvī*), white (of egg)—L. *clārus*, clear.]

glaive, *glāv*, *n.* (*arch.*) a sword, esp. a broadsword: (*hist.*) a long-shafted weapon like a halberd.—Also **glāve**. [O.Fr. *glaive*, perh.—L. *gladius*, a sword.]

glamour, *glam'ór*, *n.* the supposed influence of a charm on the eyes, making them see things as fairer than they are: deceptive fascination,

charm enhanced by means of illusion: groomed beauty and studied charm.—*adj.* **glam'orous**. [A corruption of **gramary**.]

glance, *gläns*, *v.i.* to fly obliquely (off, from, aside): to make a passing allusion to (with *at*): to dart a reflected ray: to flash: to snatch a momentary look (at).—Also *v.t.*—*n.* an oblique impact or movement: a passing allusion (esp. satirical): a sudden shoot of reflected light: a darting of the eye: a momentary look.—*adv.* **glanc'ingly**.

gland, *gland*, *n.* a structure for secreting substances to be used in, or eliminated from, the body.—*adjs.* **glandif'erous**, bearing acorns or nuts; **gland'iform**, resembling a gland: acorn-shaped; **gland'ūlar**, **gland'ūlous**, containing, consisting of, or pertaining to, glands. [L. *glans*, *glandis*, an acorn.]

glanders, *gland'érz*, *n.* a malignant, contagious, and fatal disease of the horse and ass, showing itself esp. on the mucous membrane of the nose, upon the lungs, and on the lymphatic system.—*adj.* **gland'ered**, affected with glanders. [O.Fr. *glandre*, a gland.]

glare, *glār*, *n.* an oppressive or unrelieved dazzling light: overpowering lustre: a fierce stare.—*v.i.* to emit a hard, fierce, dazzling light: to be obtrusively noticeable: to stare fiercely.—*adj.* **glar'ing**, bright and dazzling: flagrant.—*adv.* **glar'ingly**.—*n.* **glar'ingness**. [M.E. *glären*, to shine; akin to **glass**, O.E. *glær*, amber, L. Ger. *glaren*, to glow.]

glass, *gläs*, *n.* a hard, brittle substance, usually transparent, generally made by fusing together a silica (as sand) with an alkali (q.v.) and another base (q.v.): an article made of or with glass, esp. a drinking-vessel, a mirror, a weather glass, a telescope, &c.: the quantity of liquid a glass holds: (*pl.*) spectacles.—*adj.* made of glass.—*v.t.* to case in glass: to furnish with glass: to polish highly.—*ns.* **glass'-blow'ing**, one process of making glassware; **glass'-blow'er**; **glass'-cloth**, a cloth for drying glasses: a material woven from glass-thread; **glass'-cutting**, the act or process of cutting, shaping, and ornamenting the surface of glass; **glass'-cutter**; **glass'-house**, a building made of glass or largely of glass, esp. a greenhouse: (*slang*) military detention barracks.—*adjs.* **glass'y**; **glass'-like**.—*adv.* **glass'ily**.—*ns.* **glass'iness**; **glass'-ware**, articles made of glass.—**cut'-glass**, flint-glass shaped or ornamented by cutting or grinding; **flint-glass** (see **flint**); **ground'-glass**, glass dulled by sandblast, grinding, or etching, so as to destroy its transparency; **plate'-glass**, glass in large thick plates made by casting, rolling, grinding, and polishing; **vita-glass** (see **vita**). [O.E. *glæs*.]

Glaswegian, *glas-wēj'i-àn*, *n.* a native or citizen of *Glasgow*. —Also *adj.*

glaucous, *glö'kus*, *adj.* sea-green: greyish-blue: (*bot.*) covered with a fine greenish or bluish bloom. [L. *glaucus*—Gr. *glaukos*, bluish-green or grey (orig. gleaming).]

glave. See **glaive**.

glaze, *glāz*, *v.t.* to furnish or set with glass: to cover with a thin surface of glass or something glassy: to give a glassy surface to.—*v.i.* to become glassy.—*n.* the glassy coating put upon pottery: any shining appearance.—*ns.*

Neutral vowels in unaccented syllables: *em'pér-ór*; for certain sounds in foreign words see p. ix.

glāz′er, a workman who glazes pottery, paper, &c.; **glā′zier** (-zyėr), one who sets glass in window-frames, &c.; **glāz′ing**, the act or art of setting glass: the art of covering with a vitreous substance: (*paint.*) semi-transparent colours put thinly over others to modify the effect. [M.E. *glasen—glas*, glass.]

gleam, *glēm, v.i.* to glow or shine, transiently or not very brightly.—*n.* a faint or moderate glow (of light): a transient show of some emotion, quality, &c. (e.g. of joy, humour): (*arch.*) brightness.—*n.* **gleam′ing**. [O.E. *glǣm*, gleam, brightness.]

glean, *glēn, v.t.* to gather in handfuls after the reapers: to collect (what is thinly scattered, e.g. news, facts).—*v.i.* to gather the corn left by a reaper or anything that has been left by others. [O.Fr. *glener* (Fr. *glaner*).]

glebe, *glēb, n.* (*obs.*) a clod: a field: the land attached to a parish church [L. *glēba*, a clod.]

glee, *glē, n.* mirth and gaiety delight: (*mus.*) a song or catch in parts.—*adj.* **glee′ful**, merry.—*n.* **glee′man**, a minstrel. [O.E. *glēo, glīw*, mirth; O.N. *glȳ*.]

gleet, *glēt, n.* a viscous, transparent discharge from a mucous surface.—*adj.* **gleet′y**. [O.Fr. *glettc, glecte*, a flux.]

glen, *glen, n.* a narrow valley with a stream, often with trees: a depression, usu. of some extent, between hills. [Gael. *gleann*; cf. W. *glyn*.]

glengarry, *glen-gar′i, n.* a Highlander's woollen cap, generally rising to a point in front, with ribbons hanging down behind. [*Glengarry*, in Inverness-shire.]

glib, *glib, adj.* (*rare*—e.g. of a surface) smooth, slippery, easy: fluent and plausible.—*adv.* **glib′ly**.—*n.* **glib′ness**. [Cf. Du. *glibberig*, slippery.]

glide, *glīd, v.i.* to slide smoothly and easily: to flow gently: to pass smoothly or stealthily: to travel by glider.—*n.* act of gliding.—*n.* **glīd′er**, one who, or that which, glides: an aircraft like an aeroplane without engine (a *powered glider* has a small engine).—*adv.* **glīd′ingly**. [O.E. *glīdan*, to slip; Ger. *gleiten*.]

glimmer, *glim′ėr, v.i.* to burn or appear faintly.—*n.* a faint light: feeble rays of light, hope, &c.: an inkling.—*n.* **glimm′ering**, a glimmer: an inkling. [M.E. *glemern*, freq. from root of **gleam**.]

glimpse, *glimps, n.* a short gleam: a passing appearance: a momentary view.—*v.i.* to glimmer: (*arch.*) to appear by glimpses.—*v.t.* to get a glimpse of. [M.E. *glymsen*, to glimpse.]

glint, *glint, v.i.* to shine, gleam, sparkle.—*v.t.* reflect.—*n.* a gleam. [Earlier *glent*; prob. Scand.]

glissade, *glēs-äd′, v.i.* to slide or glide down.—*n.* act of sliding down a slope: a gliding movement in dancing. [Fr. from *glisser*, to slip.]

glisten, *glis′n, v.i.* to shine as light reflected from a wet or oily surface: to sparkle, scintillate. [M.E. *glistnen*—O.E. *glisnian*, to shine.]

glister, *glis′tėr, v.i.* (*arch.*) to sparkle, glitter. [M.E. *glistren*; cf. **glisten**, and Du. *glisteren*.]

glitter, *glit′ėr, v.i.* to sparkle with light: to be splendid: to be showy.—*n.* sparkle: showiness.—*adj.* **glitt′ering**.—*adv.* **glitt′eringly**. [M.E. *gliteren*; cf. O.N. *glitra*, Ger. *glitzern*.]

gloaming, *glōm′ing, n.* twilight, dusk. [O.E. *glōmung—glōm*, twilight.]

gloat, *glōt, v.i.* to gaze exultingly, esp. with a wicked or a malicious joy. [Perh. O.N. *glotta*, to grin.]

globe, *glōb, n.* a ball: a sphere: the earth: a sphere representing the earth (terrestrial globe) or the heavens (celestial globe): a lamp-glass.—*adjs.* **glōb′al**, spherical: affecting the whole world; **glōb′ate, -d**, globe-shaped; **glōb′ous; globular** (*glob′ū-lar*); **glōb′ūlous; glōb′ūlose.**—*n.* **glōbūlar′ity**. *adv.* **glōb′ūlarly**, —*ns.* **glōb′ūle**, a little globe or round particle: a drop; **globe′-flow′er**, a small genus of plants with yellow globe-shaped flowers, of the same family as buttercups; **globe′-trott′er**, one who goes sight-seeing about the world. [L. *globus.*]

globigerina, *glob-i-jé-rī′na, n.* a genus of tiny marine creatures, whose shells, consisting of globular chambers in a spiral, form a large part of the ocean bottom [L. *globus*, globe, *gerĕrē*, to carry.]

glomerate, *glom′ėr-āt, v.t.* to gather into a ball.—*adj.* clustered in heads.—*n.* **glomerā′-tion.** [L. *glomerāre, -ātum—glomus, glomeris*, a ball of yarn.]

gloom, *glōōm, n.* partial darkness: heaviness of mind: sullenness.—*v.i.* to be or look sullen or dejected: to be cloudy or obscure.—*adj.* **gloom′y**, dim or obscure: depressed in spirits: depressing, disheartening.—*adv.* **gloom′ily**. —*n.* **gloom′iness**. [M.E. *gloumbe*. See **glum**.]

glorify, *glō′-, glō′ri-fī, v.t.* to make glorious, invest with glory: to advance the glory of (God): to extol, to honour: to transform (an ordinary thing) into something more splendid—to regard it, or to speak of it, in such a way:—*pa.p.* glo′rified.—*n.* **glorificā′tion**. [L. *gloria*, glory, *facĕre*, to make.]

glory, *glō′-, glō′ri, n.* renown: exalted or triumphant honour: an object of supreme pride: splendour: brightness: circle of rays surrounding the head of a saint: (*B*) the presence of God: the manifestation of God to the blessed in heaven: heaven.—*v.i.* to boast, to exult proudly (in):—*pr.p.* glor′ying; *pa.p.* glō′-ried.—*n.* **glō′riōle**, a halo or glory.—*adj.* **glō′rious**, noble, splendid: conferring renown: (*coll.*) very delightful.—*adv.* **glō′riously**.—*n.* **glō′riousness.—Old Glory**, the Stars and Stripes, the flag of the United States. [O.Fr. *glorie* and L. *glōria*.]

gloss, *glos, n.* brightness or lustre, as from a polished surface: external show.—*v.t.* to give a superficial lustre to: (often with *over*) to give a superficially good appearance to (e.g. a transaction), to make light of (e.g. faults, hardships).—*adj.* **gloss′y**, smooth and shining: highly polished.—*n.* (*coll.*), glossy magazine.—*adv.* **gloss′ily**.—*n.* **gloss′iness. glossy magazine**, a woman's magazine, usually printed on glossy paper, abounding in illustrations and advertisements. [Cf. O.N. *glossi*, blaze, *glōa*, to glow; akin to **glass**.]

gloss, *glos, n.* a marginal or interlinear explanation of an unusual word: an explanation: a collection of explanations of words.—*v.t.* to comment or make explanatory remarks: to read a different sense into.—*n.* **gloss′ary**, a collection of glosses.—*adj.* **glossā′rial**, relating

to a glossary: containing explanation.—*n.*
gloss'arist, a writer of a glossary. [Gr. *glōssa,*
glōtta, tongue, a word requiring explanation.]
glottis, *glot'is, n.* the opening from the pharynx
into the trachea or windpipe.—*adj.* **glott'al.—**
glottal stop, a consonant sound produced by
shutting the glottis, recognised in Hebrew and
Arabic, and often substituted for *t* by careless
speakers in Scotland and England. [Gr. *glōt-*
tis—*glōtta,* the tongue.]
glove, *gluv, n.* a covering for the hand, esp. with
a sheath for each finger.—*v.t.* to cover with, or
as with, a glove.—*ns.* **glov'er,** one who makes
or sells gloves; **glove'-maker; glove'-**
stretch'er, a scissors-shaped instrument for
stretching the fingers of gloves. [O.E. *glōf.*]
glow, *glō, v.i.* to shine with an intense heat: to
burn without flame: to emit a steady light: to
flush: to tingle with bodily warmth or with
emotion: to be ardent.—*n.* shining due to heat:
a feeling of warmth: brightness of colour:
warmth of feeling.—*ns.* **glow'-lamp,** an incandescent lamp, usually electric; **glow'-worm,** a
beetle whose larvae and wingless females are
luminous. [O.E. *glōwan,* to glow; Ger. *glühen,*
O.N. *glōa,* to glow.]
glower, *glow'èr, v.i.* to stare frowningly: to
scowl.—*n.* a fierce or threatening stare.
gloze, *glōz, v.i.* to flatter: (*arch.*) to comment.—
v.t. to palliate by specious explanation: to flatter. [O.Fr. *glose*—L. *glōssa*—Gr. *glōssa.* See
gloss (2).]
glucinum, *glu-sī'nùm.* See **beryllium.**
glucose, *glōō'kōs, n.* a kind of sugar obtained
from plants, e.g. from sweet fruit juices—occurring in several forms, one of which is
known as grape-sugar or dextrose. [Gr.*glykys,*
sweet.]
glue, *glōō', n.* an impure gelatine got by boiling
animal refuse, used as an adhesive substance.—*v.t.* to join as with glue:—*pr.p.* glu'ing;
pa.p. glued.—*adj.* **glu'ey,** containing glue:
sticky, viscous. [Fr. *glu*—Low L. *glus, glūtis.*]
glum, *glum, adj.* sullen: gloomy.—*adv.* **glum'ly.**
[M.E. *glombe, glome,* to frown.]
glume, *glōōm, n.* an outer chaff-like bract which,
along with others, encloses the spikelet in
grasses and sedges.—*adj.* **gluma'ceous**
(*-shùs*). [L. *glūma,* husk—*glūbĕre,* to peel.]
glut, *glut, v.t.* to gorge: to feed to satiety: to
saturate: to overstock (the market):—*pr.p.*
glutt'ing; *pa.p.* glutt'ed.—*n.* a surfeit: an over-
supply. [L. *gluttīre,* to swallow.]
gluten, *glōō'tén, n.* the nitrogenous part of the
flour of wheat and other grains.—*adj.* **glu'ti-**
nous, gluey: tenacious: sticky. [L.*glūten, -inis,*
glue; akin to **glue.**]
glutton, *glut'(ò)n, n.* one who eats to excess: a
northern carnivore of the weasel family, reputed a great eater: one who has a great
appetite (as for work).—*v.i.* **glutt'onise,** to
eat to excess.—*adjs.* **glutt'onous, glutt'onish,**
given to, or consisting in gluttony.—*n.*
glutt'ony, excess in eating. [Fr. *glouton*—L.
glūtō, -ōnis—*glūtīre, gluttīre,* to devour.]
g lycerine, glycerin, *glis'ér-ēn, -in, n.* a colourless, viscid fluid, of a sweet taste. [Gr. *gly-*
keros, sweet—*glykys,* sweet.]
glycogen, *glik'ō-jén,* or *glīk'-, n.* animal starch, a
starch found in the liver, yielding glucose on

hydrolysis. [Gr.*glykys,* sweet, and the root of
gennaein, to produce.]
glyph,*glif, n.* (*archit.*) an ornamental channel or
fluting, usually vertical. [Gr. *glyphē*—*gly-*
phein, to carve.]
glyptic, *glip'tik, adj.* pertaining to carving, esp.
gem-carving.—*n.pl.* **glyp'tics,** the art of gem-
engraving.—*n.* **glyptog'raphy,** the art of engraving on precious stones.—*adj.* **glypto-**
graph'ic. [Gr. *glyptos,* carved.]
gnar, när, *v.i.* to snarl or growl.—Also **gnarr,**
knar, gnarl. [Onomatopoeic; cf. Ger. *knurren,*
Dan. *knurre,* to growl.]
gnarl, knarl, *närl, n.* a lump or knot in a tree.—
adj. **gnarled,** knotty: rugged, weatherbeaten.
[Cf. O.N. *gnerr,* Ger. *knurren,* Dan. *knort,* a
knot, gnarl.]
gnash, *nash, v.t.* and *v.i.* to grind (the teeth) in
rage or pain: (of teeth) to strike together.—*n.*
a grinding of the teeth. [M.E. *gnasten*; prob.
from O.N., ultimately onomatopoeic.]
gnat, *nat, n.* any small fly of which the females
are commonly blood-suckers—a mosquito: extended to other small insects. [O.E. *gnæt.*]
gnaw, *naw, v.t.* and *v.i.* to bite with a scraping or
mumbling movement: to wear away: to bite in
agony or rage: (*fig.*) to distress persistently.
[O.E. *gnagan*; cf. Du. *knagen,* mod. Icel. *naga.*]
gneiss, *nīs, n.* laminated (q.v.) rock, usually
composed of quartz, feldspar, and mica.—*adj.*
gneiss'oid, like gneiss. [Ger. *gneis.*]
gnome, *nōm, n.* a pithy and sententious saying,
generally in verse, embodying some moral
sentiment or precept.—*adj.* **gnōm'ic.** [Gr.
gnōmē, an opinion, maxim.]
gnome,*nōm, n.* a sprite guarding the inner parts
of the earth and its treasures: a dwarf or
goblin.—**the gnomes of Zürich, Europe,** &c.,
the big bankers. [*gnomus,* Mediaeval Latin
word used by Paracelsus (see **sylph**).]
gnomon, *nō'mon, n.* the pin, rod, &c., of a sun-
dial, whose shadow points to the hour:
(*geom.*) that which remains of a parallelogram when a similar parallelogram within
one of its angles is taken away. [Gr. *gnōmōn,*
a gnomon, a carpenter's square—*gnōnai* (aorist), to know.]
gnostic, *nos'tik, n.* (*theology*; *cap.*) one of a sect,
esp. in early Christian times, who maintained
that knowledge, not faith, was the way of
salvation, claiming themselves to have superior knowledge of spiritual things.—*adj.*
having knowledge: pertaining to the Gnostics.—*n.* **gnos'ticism** (*-ti-sizm*), the doctrines
of the Gnostics. [Gr. *gnōstikos,* good at
knowing—*gignōskein,* to know.]
gnotobiology, *nō-tō-bī-ol'ó-ji, n.* study of life
under germ-free conditions. [Gr. *gnōtos,*
known, *bios,* life, *logos,* discourse.]
gnu,*nōō, nū, n.* any of a genus of large antelopes
in S. and E. Africa. [From Hottentot.]
go,*gō, v.i.* to move, be in motion: (*obs.*) to walk:
(of mechanism) to act, work: to be habitually
in a specified condition (e.g. *to go barefoot,*
hungry): to be guided (by): various *fig.*
senses, e.g. to circulate, to be current, to follow
the metre of a tune: to depart: to get away
(*free,* &c.): to be spent, to be given up, to be
lost: to give way, to break, to fail: to pass, be
conveyed (to): in phrases, to adopt a profes-

Neutral vowels in unaccented syllables: *em'pér-òr*; for certain sounds in foreign words see p. ix.

304

sion, course of action indicated (e.g. *go to the bar, go to sea, go on the stage, go to law, war*): to extend: to be allotted (to): to be applied (to): to contribute (to): to turn out: to happen (in a particular way, e.g. *to go well, hard*): (usu. in participle) to be about (to), to intend (to):—*pr.p.* gō'ing; *pa.t.* went; *pa.p.* gone (*gon.*).—*n.* (all meanings *coll.*) an attempt, turn (at): a bargain: an incident: (with *the*) the fashion: energy, spirit.—*adj* go'-**ahead**', dashing, energetic.—*n.* permission to proceed.—**go-as-you-please,** not limited by rule: informal.—*ns.* go'-**between**', an intermediary; go'-**by** (*to give someone the go-by,* to outstrip him, to elude him, to pass him without notice); go'-**cart**', a wheeled apparatus for teaching children to walk: a form of child's carriage; go'er; go'-**gett'er,** (*coll.*) forceful aggressive person who sets about getting what he wants; go'-**kart,** a low racing vehicle consisting of a frame with wheels, engine and steering gear.—**go about,** to be current: to set to work at: to tack; **go about one's business,** to attend to one's duties: to be off; **go back on,** to retrace (one's steps): to fail to act up to (one's word, a promise); **go black, native,** to adopt ways of black people, natives; **go down,** to sink: to decline: to be believed or accepted: to leave university; **go far,** to last long: to come to importance; **go halves,** to share equally, **go hard with,** to turn out ill for; **go in for,** to make a practice of: to devote oneself to; **go in with,** to enter into partnership with; **go off,** to leave: to die: to deteriorate: to explode; **go on,** to proceed: (*coll.*) to talk at length: (*coll.*) to conduct oneself; **go one better,** to take a bet and add another higher to it (also *fig.*); **go out,** to be extinguished, **go over to,** to transfer allegiance to; **go places,** to travel widely: (*fig.*) to go far in personal advancement; **go slow,** of workers, deliberately to restrict output or effort in order to obtain concessions from employers.—*adj.* and *n.* go'-**slow**'.—**go through,** to perform: to examine in order: to undergo; **go to!** come now! (a kind of interjection); **go to pieces,** to break up entirely (*lit.* and *fig.*); **go under,** to be overwhelmed or ruined, to die: to be called by (the name of); **go up,** to ascend: to be created: to increase (as prices); **go with,** to be associated with: to be a concomitant of: to harmonise with: to agree with, think the same as; **go without,** to suffer the want of.—**that goes for,** that applies to. [O.E. *gan,* to go; cf. Ger. *gehen,* Du. *gaan.*]

goad, gōd, *n.* a sharp-pointed stick, often shod with iron, for driving oxen: a stimulus.—*v.t.* to drive with a goad: to urge forward: to irritate, annoy excessively. [O.E. *gād,* a goad.]

goal, gōl, *n.* a mark set up to bound a race: the winning-post: the two upright posts between which the ball is kicked or driven in some games: aim. [Origin obscure.]

goat, gōt, *n.* any of several agile, hairy, ruminant quadrupeds, allied to sheep: (*cap.*) the sign of the zodiac or the constellation Capricorn.—*ns.* **goatee**', a beard on the chin only; **goat'-herd,** one who tends goats; **goat'-moth,** a large moth whose larva gives forth a goat-like smell; **goats'-beard, goats'-rue, goats'-thorn,** names of plants; **goat'sucker,** the nightjar, any of

several birds akin to the swift, falsely thought to suck the milk of goats. [O.E. *gāt*; Ger. *geiss,* Du. *geit.*]

gobbet, gob'et, *n.* a mouthful: a lump to be swallowed. [O.Fr. *gobet,* dim. of *gobe,* mouthful, lump; cf. Gael. *gob,* mouth.]

gobble, gob'l, *v.t.* to swallow in lumps: to swallow hastily.—*v.i.* to make a noise in the throat, as a turkey. [O.Fr. *gober,* to devour.]

gobelin, gob'e-lin, *-lē, n.* a rich French tapestry (also *cap.*). [From the *Gobelins,* famous French dyers settled in Paris in the 15th century.]

goblet, gob'let, *n.* a large drinking-cup without a handle. [O.Fr. *gobelet,* dim. of *gobel.*]

goblin, gob'lin, *n.* a frightful sprite, a bogy or bogle. [O.Fr. *gobelin*—Low. L. *gobelīnus,* perh.—*cobālus*—Gr. *kobālos,* a mischievous spirit.]

goby, gō'bi, *n.* a genus of small sea-fishes, with ventral fins forming a sucker. [L. *gōbius*—Gr. *kōbios.*]

god, god, *n.* a superhuman being, an object of worship: (*cap.*—as proper name) the Supreme Being of monotheist religions, the Creator: an idol: an object of excessive devotion or reverence: (*pl.*) (the occupants of) the gallery of a theatre—*fem* **godd'ess.**—*ns.* **god'father, god'mother,** one who, at baptism, guarantees a child's religious education—whence **god'child, god'daughter, god'son.**—*adjs.* **God'-fearing,** reverencing God; **god'-forsaken,** remote, miserable, behind the times.—*n.* **god'head,** state of being a god: deity, divine nature.—*adj.* **god'less,** living without God: impious or atheistical.—*n.* **god'lessness.**—*adjs.* **god'like,** like a god: divine; **god'ly,** like God in character: pious: according to God's law.—Also *adv.*—*ns.* **god'liness; god'send,** a very welcome piece of good fortune; **god'speed,** an expressed wish that God may speed one.—*adv.* **god'ward,** toward God.—**God's acre,** a burial ground. [O.E. *god;* Ger. *gott;* from a Gmc. root *guth-,* god, and quite distinct from *good.*]

godown, gō-down', *n.* a warehouse in the East. [Malay *godong.*]

godwit, god'wit, *n.* a genus of birds with a long slightly up-curved bill and long slender legs, that frequents marshes. [Origin obscure.]

goffer, gof'er, *v.t.* to plait or crimp.—*n.* **goff'ering.** [O.Fr. *gauffrer*—*goffre,* a wafer.]

goggle, gog'l, *v.i.* to strain, or roll, the eyes.—*adj.* rolling: staring: prominent.—*n.* a stare or affected rolling of the eye: (*pl.*) spectacles with projecting eye-tubes: protective spectacles.—**gogg'le-box** (*slang*), a television-set. [Possibly related to Ir. and Gael. *gog,* to nod.]

Goidel, goid'él, *n.* Same as **Gadhel.**

going, gō'ing, *n.* the act of moving: departure: (*B.*) course of life: conditions of travel: condition of the ground for, e.g. walking, racing.—**going concern,** a business in actual activity (esp. successfully); **going forth** (*B.*), an outlet; **goings on,** behaviour, esp. reprehensible behaviour. [**go.**]

goitre, goi'tér, *n.* morbid enlargement of the thyroid gland in the throat.—*adjs.* **goi'tred, goi'trous.** [Fr. *goître*—L. *guttur,* the throat.]

gold, gōld, *n.* a precious metal (symbol Au; L.

aurum; at. no. 79), for coin: money: riches: anything very precious: yellow, gold colour: the centre of an archery target.—*ns.* **gold'-beat'er**, one whose trade is to beat gold into gold-leaf; **gold'-beat'ing**; **gold'-digg'er**, one who digs for or mines gold, esp. a placer-miner: (*slang*) a woman who attaches herself to a man for the sake of the presents he gives her; **gold'-dust**, gold in fine particles, as found in some rivers.—*adj.* **gold'en**, of gold: of the colour of gold: bright: most valuable: happy: highly favourable.—*ns.* **gold'-field**, a region where gold is found; **gold'finch**, a finch, the adult male of which has plumage in which black, red, yellow, and white are exquisitely mingled; **gold'fish**, a Chinese and Japanese fresh-water fish, golden-yellow in its domesticated state, brownish when wild; **gold'foil**, gold beaten into thin sheets; **gold'ylocks**, a species of buttercup; **gold'-leaf**, gold beaten extremely thin; **gold'-mine**, a mine from which gold is dug: a source of great profit; **gold'-plate**, vessels and utensils of gold collectively; **gold'-rush**, a rush to a new gold-field; **gold'smith**, a worker in gold and silver.—**golden age**, an imaginary past time of innocence and happiness: any time of highest achievement; **golden eagle**, the common eagle, so called because of a slight golden gleam about the head and neck; **golden fleece**, in Greek mythology, the fleece sought by the Argonauts: the name of an order of knighthood in Spain, &c.; **golden handshake**, a large sum given to an employee or member forced to leave a firm, &c.; **Golden Legend**, a celebrated mediaeval collection of saints' lives; **golden mean**, the middle way between extremes, moderation; **golden rectangle**, one in which the ratio of width to length is the same as that of length to the sum of width and length; **golden rule**, doing as one would be done by; **golden wedding** (see **wedding**); **gold standard**, a standard consisting of gold (or of a weight in gold) in relation to which money values are assessed (**on, off, the gold standard**, using, or not using, gold as standard). [O.E. *gold*; O.N. *gull*, Ger. *gold*.]

golf, *golf, gof, n.* a game with a ball and a set of clubs, in which the ball is played along a course and into a series of small holes set in the ground at considerable intervals.—*ns.* **golf'-course**, **golf'-links**, the ground on which golf is played; **golf'er**; **golf'ing**. [Origin obscure: perh. Du. *kolf*, a club.]

Goliath, *gō-lī'ath, n.* a giant. [See 1 Sam. xvii.]

gollywog, golliwog, *gol'i-wog, n.* a fantastical doll, with black face, staring eyes, and bristling hair. [A recent coinage.]

golosh, *gō-losh', n.* Same as **galosh**.

gonad, *gon'ad, n.* (*biol.*) an organ that produces sex-cells.—*n.* **gonadotrop(h)'in**, a substance which stimulates the gonads and which is used as a drug to promote fertility. [Gr. *gonē*, generation.]

gondola, *gon'do-la, n.* a long, narrow boat used chiefly on the canals of Venice.—*n.* **gondolier** (-*lēr'*), one who propels a gondola. [It.]

gone, *gon, pa.p.* of **go**, lost, passed beyond help: departed: dead: insane, or acting so: (*slang*) in an exalted state: (*slang*) enamoured of (with *on*).

gonfalon, *gon'fa-lon, n.* an ensign or standard with streamers.—*n.* **gonfalonier** (-*ēr'*), one who bears a gonfalon: the chief magistrate in some mediaeval Italian republics. [It. *gonfalone* and O.Fr. *gonfanon*—O.H.G. *gundfano—gund*, battle, *fano*, a flag.]

gong, *gong, n.* a metal disk, usu. rimmed, that sounds when struck or rubbed with a drumstick: an instrument of call, esp. to meals. [Malay.]

gonorrhoea, *gon-o-rē'a, n.* a contagious infection of the mucous membrane of the genital tract. [Gr. *gonorroia—gonos*, seed, *rheein*, to flow, from a mistaken notion of its nature.]

goo, *gōō, n.* (*slang*) sticky substance: sentimentality.—*adj.* **goo'ey**. [Origin unknown.]

good, *gŏŏd, adj.* having desirable or suitable qualities: promoting health, welfare or happiness: virtuous, pious: kind, benevolent: worthy: competent: sufficient: valid: sound: serviceable: beneficial: genuine: pleasing: considerable, as in 'good deal': to be counted on.—*comp.* **bett'er**; *superl.* **best**.—*n.* that which promotes happiness, success, &c.—opp. to *evil*: welfare: advantage, temporal or spiritual: virtue: (*pl.*) movable property, chattels: (*pl.*) merchandise: (*pl.*) freight.—*interj.* right!—*n.* **good'-breed'ing**, polite manners formed by a good bringing up.—*ns.* or *interjs.* **goodbye'**, **good-bye'**, contr. of 'God be with you': farewell, a form of address at parting; **good'-)day'**, a common salutation, contraction of 'I wish you a good day.'—*ns.* **good'-fell'ow**, a jolly or boon companion; **good'-fell'owship**, merry or pleasant company: conviviality.—*n.pl.* **good'-folk**, a euphemism for the fairies, of whom it is best to speak respectfully.—*adj.* **good'-for-nothing**, worthless, useless.—*n.* an idle or worthless person.—*ns.* **Good Fri'day**, the Friday of Passion Week; **good-hŭ'mour**, a cheerful, tolerant mood.—*adjs.* **good-hŭ'moured**; **good'-look'ing**, handsome; **good'ly**, good-looking: fine: excellent:—*comp.* **good'lier**; *superl.* **good'liest**.—*ns.* **good'liness**; **goodman'**, (esp. *Scot.*) a householder or husband:—*fem.* **goodwife'**.—*n.* and *interj.* **good morn'ing**, a salutation at meeting early in the day.—*n.* **good-nä'ture**, natural goodness and mildness of disposition.—*adj.* **good-nä'tured**.—*n.* **good'ness**, virtue: excellence: benevolence: substituted for God in certain expressions, and as *interj.*—*n.* and *interj.* **good night'**, a common salutation, a contraction of 'I wish you a good night'.—*ns.* **good'-sense'**, sound judgment; **good-speed'**, a contraction of 'I wish you good speed' (i.e. success); **goods'-train**, a train of goods wagons; **goodwill'**, benevolence: well-wishing: the established custom or popularity of any business or trade—often appearing as one of its assets, with a marketable money value.—*adj.* **good'y**, mawkishly good: weakly benevolent or pious—also **good'y-good'y**.—**goodman's croft**, a patch once left untilled in Scotland, to avert the malice of the devil from the crop; **good-neighbour policy**, a U.S. policy from 1931 for co-operation in all fields between all the countries of North, South and Central America; **good offices**, mediation; **good templar**, a member of a temperance society.—**as good as**,

Neutral vowels in unaccented syllables: *em'pėr-ȯr*; for certain sounds in foreign words see p. ix.

the same as, no less than: virtually; **be as good as one's word**, to fulfil one's promise; **for good (and all)**, permanently: irrevocably; **make good**, to fulfil, perform (a promise, a boast): to supply, make up for (a loss): to prove (an accusation): to get on in the world: to do well, redeeming a false start; **no good**, useless: unavailing: worthless; **not good enough**, not sufficiently good: mean, unfair, very different from what was expected or promised; **to the good**, for the best: on the credit side. [O.E. *gōd*; Du. *goed*, Ger. *gut*, O.N. *gothr*.]

googly, *gōōg'li*, n. (*cricket*) an off-breaking ball with an apparent leg-break action on the part of the bowler, or conversely. [Origin obscure.]

Goorkha. See **Gurkha.**

goose, *gōōs*, n. a subfamily of web-footed animals like ducks, but larger: a stupid, silly person:—*pl.* **geese** (*gēs*).—*ns.* **goose'-flesh**, a puckered condition of the skin through cold, horror, &c.; **goose'-grass**, cleavers, any of several plants with curved prickles on the stem; **goose'-quill**, one of the wing-feathers of a goose, esp. used as a pen; **goos'ery**, a place for keeping geese; **goose'-step** (*mil.*), method of marching (resembling a goose's walk) with knees stiff and soles brought flat on the ground. [O.E. *gōs* (pl. *gēs*); O.N. *gās*, Ger. *gans*, L. *anser* (for *hanser*), Gr. *chēn*.]

gooseberry, *gōōz'ber-i* (also *gōōs'*), n. the fruit of several species of prickly shrubs of the same name: an unwanted third person.—*n.* **gooseberry-fool** (see **fool** (2). [Perh. **goose** and **berry**; or **goose** may be from M.H.G. *krus*, crisp, curled; cf. O.Fr. *groisele, grosele*, gooseberry, Scot. *grossart*.]

gopher, *gō'fėr*, n. a name in America applied to various burrowing animals. [Perh. Fr. *gaufre*, honeycomb.]

gopher, *gō'fėr*, n. (*B.*) a kind of wood, prob. cypress. [Heb.]

Gordian, *gōrd'yán*, adj. intricate: difficult.—**cut the Gordian knot**, to overcome a difficulty by violent measures—Alexander, unable to untie the knot tied by *Gordius*, king of Phrygia, cut it through with his sword.

gore, *gōr, gör*, n. clotted blood: blood.—*adj.* **gōr'y**, covered with gore, bloody. [O.E. *gor*, filth, dung; O.N. *gor*, cud, slime.]

gore, *gōr, gör*, n. a triangular piece of land: a triangular piece let into a garment to widen it.—*v.t.* to shape like, or furnish with, gores: to pierce with anything pointed, as a spear or horns. [O.E. *gāra*, a pointed triangular piece of land; cf. *gār*, a spear.]

gorge, *görj*, n. the throat: a ravine: (*fort.*) the entrance to an outwork.—*v.t.* to swallow greedily: to glut.—*v.i.* to feed gluttonously.—*n.* **gorg'et**, a piece of armour for the throat: a neck ornament. [O.Fr.]

gorgeous, *gör'jus*, adj. showy, splendid, magnificent (often used loosely).—*n.* **gor'geousness**. [O.Fr. *gorgias*, gaudy.]

gorgon, *gör'gon*, n. one of three fabled female monsters of horrible and petrifying aspect: anyone very ugly or formidable.—*adjs.* **gor'gon, gorgō'nian**. [Gr. *Gorgō*, pl. *-ónes—gorgos*, grim.]

gorgonzola, *gör-gón-zō'la*, n. a kind of Italian cheese. [From *Gorgonzola*, near Milan.]

gorilla, *gor-il'a*, n. a great African ape, the largest anthropoid: (*slang*) a thug. [Gr. *gorillai* (pl.), reported by Hanno the Carthaginian as a tribe of hairy women; supposed to be an African word.]

gormand, *gör'mánd*, n. older form or **gourmand**.—*v.i.* **gor'mandīse**, to eat hastily or voraciously.—*ns.* **gor'mandīser; gor'mandīsing**. [See **gourmand**.]

gorse, *gors*, n. furze or whin, a prickly shrub with yellow flowers. [O.E. *gorst*.]

goshawk, *gos'hawk*, n. a short-winged hawk, once used for hunting wild-geese and other fowl. [O.E. *gōshafoc—gōs*, goose, *hafoc*, hawk.]

gosling, *goz'ling*, n. a young goose. [O.E. *gōs*, goose, and double dim. *-l-ing*.]

gospel, *gos'pėl*, n. the teaching of Christ: a narrative of the life of Christ, esp. one of those included in the New Testament: any strongly advocated principle or system: absolute truth. [O.E. *godspel—gōd*, good (with shortened vowel being understood as *god*, God), and *spell*, story; a translation of L.L. *evangelium* (see **evangel**). The other Germanic languages, receiving the word from English, assimilate it to their forms of *god*, not *good*.]

gossamer, *gos'ä-mėr*, n. very fine spider-threads which float in the air or form webs on bushes in fine weather: any very thin material. [M.E. *gossomer*; perh. goose-summer, a St. Martin's summer, when geese are in season and gossamer abounds.]

gossip, *gos'ip*, n. (*arch.*) a woman friend who came at a birth: a familiar friend: one who goes about telling and hearing news, or idle, malicious, scandalous tales.—*v.i.* to run about telling idle tales: to talk much: to chat.—*ns.* **goss'iping; goss'ipry.** [O.E. *godsibb*, godfather, one who is *sib* (i.e. related) in God, spiritually related.]

gossoon, *go-sōōn'*, n. a boy or boy-servant. [Anglo-Irish—Fr. *garçon*, boy.]

got, gotten. See under **get.**

Goth, *goth*, n. one of an ancient Germanic nation who invaded the Roman Empire and later founded kingdoms in Italy, southern France, and Spain: a rude or uncivilised person, a barbarian.—*adj.* **Goth'ic**, belonging to the Goths or their language: barbarous: denoting style of architecture with high-pointed arches, clustered columns, &c. (applied in reproach at the time of the Renaissance): of literature, orig. applied to 18th-cent. novels of mystery with gloomy, sinister backgrounds, now denoting psychological horror-tales.—*n.* Gothic architecture: the language of the Goths, particularly that of the Eastern Goths in which fragments of a 4th century translation of the Bible have been preserved—the earliest considerable record of a Gmc. language: a bold-faced printing type.—*v.t.* **Goth'icise** (*-sīz*), to make Gothic.—*n.* **Goth'icism** (*-sizm*), a Gothic idiom or style of building: rudeness of manners. [The native names *Gutans* (sing. *Guta*) and *Gutôs* (sing. *Guts*), *Gutthiuda*, 'people of the Goths'; Latinised as *Gothī, Gotthī*.]

gothamite, *got'ám-īt, goth'-*, **gothamist**, *-ist*, n. a simpleton: a wiseacre. [Orig. 'man of *Gotham*', a village of Nottinghamshire, with which are connected many of the simpleton stories of immemorial antiquity.]

gouache, *gwash, gōō-ash'*, *n.* opaque colours mixed with water, honey, and gum, applied in impasto (q.v.) style. [Fr., through It., from L. *aquātiō*, a watering-place, pool.]

gouge, *gowj*, also *gōōj*, *n.* a chisel with a hollow blade, for cutting grooves or holes.—*v.t.* to scoop out, as with a gouge: to force out, as the eye with the thumb. [O.Fr.,—Low L. *gubia*, a kind of chisel.]

goulash, *gōō'lash*, *n.* a stew of beef, vegetables esp. onions, and paprika. [Hung. *gulyás (hús)*, herdsman (meat).]

gourd, *gōrd, görd*, or *gōōrd*, *n.* a large fleshy fruit: rind of one used as a bottle, cup, &c.: a gourd-bearing plant. [O.Fr. *gourde*, contr. from *cougourde*—L. *cucurbita*, a gourd.]

gourmand, *gōōr'mánd, -mä*, *n.* one who eats greedily: a glutton.—*adj.* voracious: gluttonous. [Fr.; cf. **gormand**.]

gourmet, *gōōr-mä*, *n.* an epicure, originally one with a delicate taste in wines. [Fr., a wine-merchant's assistant.]

gout, *gowt*, *n.* an acute inflammation of the smaller joints, and esp. of the great toe.—*adj.* **gout'y**, relating to gout: diseased with or subject to gout.—*n.* **gout'iness.** [O.Fr. *goutte*—L. *gutta*, a drop, the disease supposed to be caused by a humour (q.v.) settling on the joints in drops.]

gout, *gōō*, *n.* taste: relish. [Fr.,—L. *gustus*, taste.]

govern, *guv'érn*, *v.t.* to direct: to control: to rule with authority: (*gram.*) to determine the case of.—*v.i.* to exercise authority: to administer the laws.—*adj.* **gov'ernable.**—*ns.* **gov'ernance** (*arch.*) government: control: direction; **gov'ernante**, a female ruler: a governess; **gov'erness**, a lady who has charge of the instruction of the young; **gov'erness-car, -cart**, a light, low, two-wheeled vehicle with face-to-face seats at the sides; **government** (*guv'ér-(n)- mént*), a ruling or managing: control: system of governing: the persons authorised to administer the laws: the territory over which sovereign power extends: (*gram.*) the power of one word in determining the case of another.—*adj.* of or pursued by government.—*adj.* **governmental** (*guv-ér(n)-ment'-ál*), pertaining to government.—*ns.* **gov'ernor**, a ruler: one invested with supreme authority: a tutor: (*mach.*) a regulator, or contrivance for maintaining uniform velocity with a varying resistance: (*B.*) a pilot; **gov'ernor-gen'eral**, orig. the supreme governor in a country, &c.: the representative of the British crown in Commonwealth countries which recognise the monarch as head of state:—*pl.* **gov'ernors-gen'eral; gov'ernorship.** [O.Fr. *governer*—L. *gubernāre*—Gr. *kybernaein*, to steer.]

gowan, *gow'án*, *n.* (*Scot.*) the wild daisy: the ox-eye daisy. [Apparently a form of *gollan(d)*, a northern name for various yellow flowers.]

gowk, gouk, *gowk*, *n.* (*Scot.*) a cuckoo: a fool. [O.N. *gaukr*; O.E. *gēac*.]

gown, *gown*, *n.* a loose flowing outer garment: a woman's dress: an academic, clerical, or official robe.—*adj.* **gowned**, dressed in a gown.—*ns.* **gown'man, gowns'man**, one who

wears a gown, as a divine or lawyer, and esp. a member of an English university. [O.Fr. *goune*—Low L. *gunna*.]

goy, *goi*, *n.* a non-Jew, Gentile:—*pl.* **goy'im.** [Heb., nation.]

grab, *grab*, *v.t.* (*coll.*) to seize or grasp suddenly: to appropriate unscrupulously:—*pr.p.* **grabb'-ing**; *pa.p.* **grabbed.**—*n.* a sudden grasp or clutch [Cf. Swed. *grabba*, to rasp.]

grabble, *grab'l*, *v.i.* to grope. [Freq. of **grab.**]

grace, *grās*, *n.* easy elegance in form or manner: what adorns and commends to favour: becomingness: sense of what is fitting: the undeserved mercy of God: divine influence: mercy, clemency: a short prayer at meat: a ceremonious title in addressing a duke or an archbishop: (*pl.*) favour, friendship (with *good*): (*myth.*, cap.) the three sister goddesses in whom beauty was deified.—*v.t.* to mark with favour: to adorn.—*adj.* **grace'ful**, elegant and easy: marked by propriety or fitness.—*adv.* **grace'fully.**—*n.* **grace'fulness.**—*adj.* **grace'less**, lacking grace or excellence: depraved: without sense of decency.—*n.* **grace'lessness.**—*n.* **grace'-note** (*mus.*), a note introduced as an embellishment, not being essential to the harmony or melody.—*adj.* **gracious** (*grā'shús*), abounding in grace or kindness: proceeding from divine favour: condescending.—*adv.* **grā'ciously.**—*n.* **grā'ciousness.**—**days of grace**, (three) days allowed for the payment of a note or bill of exchange, after it falls due; **fall from grace**, to backslide, to lapse; **with good (bad) grace**, in amiable (ungracious) fashion; **year of grace**, year of Christian era, A.D. [Fr. *grâce*—L. *grātia*, favour—*grātus*, agreeable.]

grade, *grād*, *n.* a degree or step in quality, rank, or dignity: gradient or slope.—*v.t.* to arrange acc. to grade.—*v.i.* to shade off.—*n.* **grādā'tion**, a scale or series of degrees: (*pl.*) degrees of rank, quality, &c.: state of being arranged in ranks or degrees: action of arranging in such a way: insensible shading off or passing from one colour to another: (*mus.*) a diatonic (q.v.) succession of chords: ablaut (q.v.).—*adj.* **grādā'tional.**—*n.* **gradient** (*grā'di-ént*), the degree of slope as compared with the horizontal: rate of change in any quantity with distance or elevation (e.g. in barometer readings): an incline.—*adj.* **grad'ual**, advancing by grades or degrees: gentle and slow.—*n.* in the Roman Church, the portion of the mass between the epistle and the gospel, formerly always sung from the steps of the altar: the book containing such anthems.—Also **grail.**—*n.* **grādual'ity.**—*adv.* **grad'ually.**—*n.* **grad'uand**, one about to receive a university degree.—*v.t.* **grad'uāte**, to divide into regular intervals: to mark with degrees: to proportion.—*v.i.* to pass by grades: to receive a university degree: to qualify or perfect oneself (as): to change gradually (into).—*n.* one admitted to a degree in a university, &c.—*ns.* **grādūā'tion; grad'ūator**, an instrument for dividing lines at regular intervals; **grā'dus**, a dictionary of Greek or Latin prosody.—**down**, and **up, grade**, (*lit.* and *fig.*) a descending or ascending part, as of a road. [L. *gradus*, a step—*gradī*, to step, walk, go.]

Neutral vowels in unaccented syllables: *em'pér-ór*; for certain sounds in foreign words see p. ix.

graecise, *grē'sīz, v.t.* to make Greek, to hellenise.—*v.i.* to conform to Greek ways or idioms.—*n.* **grae'cism**, a Greek idiom: the Greek spirit. [L. *Graecus*—Gr. *Graikos*, Greek; *graikizein*, to speak Greek.]

graffiti, *gräf-fē'tē, n. pl.* scribblings or drawings, often indecent, found on public buildings. [It.,—Gr. *graphein*, to write.]

graft, *gräft, n.* a small piece of a plant or animal inserted in another individual or another part so as to come into organic union.—*v.t.* to insert a graft in: to insert as a graft: (*fig.*) to insert (*in* or *upon*) so as to produce complete union.—*v.i.* to insert grafts.—Older form **graff.**—*ns.* **graft'er; graft'ing.** [O.Fr. *graffe*—L. *graphium*—Gr. *graphion, grapheion*, a style, pencil.]

graft, *gräft, n.* (*U.S. slang*) illicit profit by corrupt means, esp. in public life: corruption in official life.—Also *v.i.* [Origin uncertain.]

grail, *grāl, n.* in mediaeval legend, the platter (sometimes supposed to be a cup) used by Christ at the Last Supper, in which Joseph of Arimathaea caught his blood, said to have been brought by Joseph to Glastonbury, and the object of quests by King Arthur's knights. [O.Fr. *graal* or *grael*, a flat dish—Low L. *gradālis*, ultimately from Gr. *krātēr*, a bowl.]

grain, *grān, n.* a single small hard seed: corn in general: a hard particle: a very small quantity: the smallest British weight: the arrangement and size of the particles or fibres of anything, as stone or wood: texture: the crimson dye made from the dried bodies of kermes or cochineal insects, once thought to be seeds: any fast dye—to *dye in grain* (i.e. *with grain*) is to dye deeply, also to dye in the wool: innate quality or character.—*v.t.* to paint (wood) in imitation of grain.—*adj.* **grained,** rough: furrowed. *n.* **grain'ing,** painting so as to imitate the grain of wood.—**against the grain,** against the fibre of the wood—hence against the natural temper or inclination: **with a grain of salt,** with reservation, as of a story that cannot be believed. [Fr. *grain,* collective *graine*—L. *grānum,* seed, akin to **corn.**]

graip, *grāp, n.* (*Scot.* and *North*) a three- or four-pronged fork used for lifting dung or digging potatoes. [A form of **grope.**]

gralloch, *gral'oн, n.* a deer's entrails.—*v.t.* to disembowel (deer). [Gael. *grealach.*]

gram, gramme, *gram, n.* formerly the mass of a cubic centimetre of water at maximum density point, 4° C.; now 1/1000 part of International Prototype Kilogram (me).—**gram'equiv'alent,** the quantity of a substance whose mass in grams is equal to its equivalent weight.[Fr.,—L.,—Gr.*gramma,* a letter, a small weight.]

-gram, *-gram,* in composition, something written or drawn to form a record. [Gr.*gramma,* a letter.]

gramary, *gram'a-ri, n.* magic: enchantment.—Also **gram'arye.** [M.E. *gramery,* skill in grammar, hence magic—O.Fr.*gramaire,* grammar.]

Gramineae, *gra-min'e-ē,* or *grā-, n.pl.* the grass family—*adjs.* **graminā'ceous, gramin'eous,** like or pertaining to grass: grassy; **gramin'ivorous,** grass-eating. [L. *grāmen, grāminis,* grass.]

grammalogue, *gram'ä-log, n.* a word represented by a single sign: a sign for a word in shorthand. [Gr. *gramma,* a letter, *logos,* a word.]

grammar, *gram'är, n.* the science of language, from the point of view of pronunciation, inflexion, syntax, and historical development: now often from the point of view of inflexion and syntax only: one's manner of speaking or writing as regards inflexion and syntax (*e.g. his grammar is very bad*): a book that teaches grammar: the rudiments of a subject.—*ns.* **grammā'rian,** one versed in grammar: a teacher of, or writer on, grammar; **gramm'ar-school,** (*orig.*) a school in which Latin grammar was taught: a higher school, in which academic subjects, esp. Latin and Greek, predominate.—*adjs.* **grammat'ic, -al,** belonging to, or according to, the rules of grammar.—*adv.* **grammat'ically.** [O.Fr. *gramaire*; from Low L.*gramma,* a letter (with the termination *ārius*)—Gr. *gramma,* a letter—*graphein,* to write.]

gramophone, *gram'o-fōn, n.* an instrument for reproducing sounds by means of a needle on a revolving grooved disk. [Ill-formed from Gr. *gramma,* letter, record, *phone,* sound.]

gram-positive, -negative (or with *cap.*), *adjs.* (applied to bacteria) which stain, or do not stain, when treated with gentian violet followed by certain other substances. [Hans C. J. *Gram,* Danish physician.]

grampus, *gram'pus, n.* a popular name for many whales, esp. the killer: one who puffs. [16th century *graundepose*—L. *crassus,* fat, *piscis,* fish, confused with Fr. *grand,* big.]

granary, *gran'är-i, n.* a storehouse for grain or threshed corn. [L. *grānārium grānum,* seed.]

grand, *grand, adj.* of highest rank: chief: main: exalted: magnificent: dignified: sublime: imposing: on a great scale: in complete form: would-be imposing: (*coll.*) very good, very fine: of the second degree of parentage or descent, as **grand'father,** a father's or mother's father, **grand'child,** a son's or daughter's child; so **grand'mother, grand'son, grand'daughter,** &c.—*n.* (*U.S. slang*) 1000 dollars: a grand-piano.—*adv.* **grand'ly.**—*ns.* **grand'ness; grand'(d)ad,** an old man: a grandfather; **gran'dam,** an old dame or woman: a grandmother; **grandee',** a Spanish nobleman of the first rank: a man of high rank or station; **grandeur** (*grand'yūr*), vastness: splendour of appearance: loftiness of thought or deportment; **grand'father('s)-clock,** an old-fashioned clock with a long case standing on the ground; **grand'mother-clock,** a clock of the same kind as a *grandfather-,* but smaller.—*adj.* **grandil'oquent,** speaking grandly or bombastically: pompous.—*n.* **grandil'oquence.**—*adv.* **grandil'oquently.**—*adj.* **gran'diose,** grand or imposing: bombastic.—*ns.* **grand'-mas'ter,** the head of a religious order of knighthood (Hospitallers, Templars, and Teutonic Knights), or of the Freemasons, &c.; **grand'-piano,** a large harp-shaped piano, with horizontal strings; **grand'sire,** a grandfather: any ancestor; **grand'stand,** an elevated erection on a racecourse, &c., affording a good view (**grandstand finish,** a close and rousing finish to a sporting contest: a supreme effort to win at the close of a sporting contest (also *fig.*)).—**grand jury**, in England, a special jury which decides whether there is sufficient evidence to put an accused person on trial (abolished, except in a few cases, 1933); **grand opera**, opera without spoken dialogue; **grand slam**, the winning of all the tricks at bridge, &c.; **grand style**, a style adapted to lofty or sublime subjects. [Fr. *grand*—L. *grandis*, great.]

grange, *grānj*, *n.* (*arch.*) a granary: a country house with farm buildings attached. [O.Fr. *grange*, barn—Low L. *grānea*—L. *grānum*, grain.]

granite, *gran'it*, *n.* a coarse-grained igneous crystalline rock, composed of quartz, feldspar, and mica.—*adjs.* **granit'ic**, pertaining to, consisting of, or like granite; **granit'iform**, **gran'itoid**, of the form of or resembling granite; **granolith'ic**, composed of cement and granite chips. [It. *granito*, granite, lit. grained—L. *grānum*, grain.]

granivorous, *gran-iv'ŏr-us*, *adj.* eating grain: feeding on seeds. [L. *grānum*, grain, *vorāre*, to devour.]

grant, *gränt*, *v.t.* to bestow: to admit as true: to concede.—*n.* à bestowing: something bestowed, an allowance: (*Eng. law*) conveyance of property by deed.—*ns.* **grantee'** (*law*), the person to whom a grant, gift, or conveyance is made; **grant'er**, **grant'or** (*law*), the person by whom a grant, or conveyance is made.—**grant-in-aid**, an official money grant for a particular purpose.—**take for granted**, to presuppose, assume, esp. tacitly or unconsciously. [O.Fr. *graanter*, *craanter*, *creanter*, to promise—L. *crēdĕre*, to believe.]

granule, *gran'ūl*, *n.* a little grain: a fine particle.—*adjs.* **gran'ular**, **gran'ulate**, **gran'ulous**, consisting of or like grains or granules.—*v.t.* **gran'ūlāte**, to form or break into grains or small masses: to make rough on the surface.—*v.i.* to be formed into grains.—*n.* **granūlā'tion**, the act or process of forming into grains: (*pl.*) the materials of new texture as first formed in a wound or on an ulcerated surface. [L. *grānulum*, dim. of *grānum*, grain.]

grape, *grāp*, *n.* the fruit of any grape-vine (see **vine**): a tumour on the legs of horses: grapeshot.—*ns.* **grape'-fruit**, a fine variety of the shaddock, with slightly grape-like taste; **grape'-hy'acinth**, a genus of bulbous-rooted plants, nearly allied to the hyacinths; **grap'ery**, a place where grapes are grown; **grape'shot**, shot which scatter on being fired; **grape'-su'gar**, dextrose—so called because obtained from ripe grapes; **grape'-vine** (see **vine**): (*fig.*) rumour (from its far-stretching branches): (*fig.*) the bush telegraph.—*adj.* **grap'y**, made of or like grapes.—**sour grapes**, things decried because they cannot be attained (from Aesop's fable of the fox and the grapes). [O.Fr. *grape*, *grappe*, a cluster of grapes—*grape*, a hook; orig. Gmc.]

graph, *graf*, *gräf*, *n.* a symbolic diagram, a curve representing the variation of a quantity.—*adjs.* **graph'ic, -al**, pertaining to writing, describing, or delineating: picturesquely described or describing.—*adv.* **graph'ically.**—*ns.*

graph'īte, a mineral, commonly called blacklead or plumbago (though a form of carbon); **graphol'ogy**, the art of estimating character, &c., from handwriting.—**graphic arts**, painting, drawing, engraving, as opposed to music, sculpture, &c.; **graphic formula**, (*chem.*) a *constitutional* or *structural formula*, one that shows the relation of the atoms within the molecule, e.g. H—O—H for water. [Gr. *graphē*, a writing—*graphein*, to write.]

grapnel, *grap'nél*, *n.* a small anchor with several claws or arms: a grappling-iron. [Dim. of O.Fr. *grapin*—*grape*, a hook; of Gmc. origin.]

grapple, *grap'l*, *n.* an instrument for hooking or holding.—*v.t.* to seize: to lay fast hold of: to grip.—*v.i.* to contend in close fight: to try to deal (with, e.g. a problem).—*n.* **grapp'ling-i'ron**, an instrument for grappling: a large grapnel formerly used for seizing hostile ships in naval engagements. [Cf. O.Fr. *grappil*—*grape*, a hook.]

grasp, *gräsp*, *v.t.* to seize and hold: to hold firmly: to comprehend.—*v.i.* to endeavour to seize: (with *at*) to accept eagerly.—*n.* grip: power of seizing: mental power of apprehension.—*p.adj.* **grasp'ing**, seizing: avaricious. [M.E. *graspen*, *grapsen*, from the root of *grāpian*, to grope.]

grass, *gräs*, *n.* common herbage: an order of plants with long, narrow leaves and tubular stem, including wheat and other cereals, &c.: (*slang*) an informer: (*slang*) hashish.—*v.t.* to cover with grass: (*slang*) to inform on.—*adj.* **grass'y**, covered with, or resembling, grass.—*ns.* **grass'iness**; **grass'-cloth**, a name for various coarse cloths made of fibres, esp. cloth made from ramie.—*adj.* **grass'-grown**, grown over with grass.—*ns.* **grass'hopper**, a name for various hopping insects that feed on plants, belonging to two families, of the same order as the crickets; **grass'-land**, permanent pasture; **grass'-roots'**, (orig. *U.S.*) the rural areas of a country: the dwellers there, regarded as representing the true character of a people: foundation, basis, primary aim or meaning.—Also *adj.*; **grass sickness**, a disease of horses: (*coll.*) an ailment of sheep and lambs; **grass'-snake**, the harmless common ringed snake; **grass'-wid'ow**, a wife temporarily separated from or deserted by her husband.—**let the grass grow under one's feet**, to loiter, delay. [O.E. *gærs*, *græs*; O.N., Ger., Du., *gras*; prob. allied to **green** and **grow**.]

grate, *grāt*, *n.* a framework of bars with interstices, esp. one of iron bars for holding a fire.—*adj.* **grat'ed**, having a grating.—*n.* **grat'ing**, the bars of a grate: a partition or frame of bars.—**interior grate**, an open grate with boiler built in for heating water. [Low L. *grāta*, a grate—L. *crātis*, a hurdle; cf. **crate**.]

grate, *grāt*, *v.t.* to rub hard, or wear away, with or on anything rough: to irritate, jar on.—*v.i.* to make a harsh sound: to jar.—*n.* **grat'er**, an instrument with a rough surface for grating down a substance.—*adj.* **grat'ing**, jarring on the feelings, harsh, irritating.—*adv.* **grat'ingly**. [O.Fr. *grater*, through Low L., from O.H.G. *chrazzōn* (Ger. *kratzen*), to scratch, akin to Swed. *kratta*.]

grateful, *grāt'fŏōl*, *-fl*, *adj.* causing pleasure:

Neutral vowels in unaccented syllables: *em'pėr-ór*; for certain sounds in foreign words see p. ix.

310

acceptable: thankful: having a due sense of benefits.—*adv.* **grate′fully.**—*n.* **grate′fulness.**—*v.t.* **grăt′ify,** to do what is agreeable to: to please: to indulge:—*pa.p.* grat′ified.—*p.adj.* **grat′ifying.**—*ns.* **gratifica′tion,** a pleasing or indulging: that which gratifies: delight; **grat′ifier** (-*fī-ér*). [O.Fr. *grat*—L. *grātus,* pleasing, thankful, and suffx. -*ful.*]

gratis, *grā′tis, grä′-, adv.* for nothing: without payment or recompense. [L. *grātis,* contr. of *grātīs,* abl. pl. of *grātia,* favour—*grātus* pleasing.]

gratitude, *grat′i-tūd, n.* warm and friendly feeling towards a benefactor: thankfulness. [Fr.,—Low L. *grātitūdō*—L. *grātus,* pleasing.]

gratuity, *gra-tū′i-ti, n.* an acknowledgment of service, generally pecuniary, a tip: a bounty.—*adj.* **gratū′itous,** done or given for nothing: voluntary: unwarranted, uncalled-for.—*adv.* **gratū′itously.** [Fr.,—Low L. *grātuitās,* -*ātis*—L. *grātus,* pleasing.]

gratulatory, *grat′ū-lá-tŏr-i,* or -*lā′-, adj.* congratulatory (q.v.).

gravamen, *grav-ā′men, n.* a grievance: the essence or most important part of a complaint or accusation. [L. *gravāmen*—*gravis,* heavy.]

grave, *grāv, v.t.* (*obs.*) to dig: (*obs.*) to carve, sculpture: to engrave.—*v.i.* to engrave:—*pa.p.* graved or grav′en.—*n.* a pit or hole dug out, esp. one to bury the dead in: any place of burial: (*fig.*) death, destruction.—*n.pl.* **grave′clothes,** the clothes in which the dead are buried.—*ns.* **grav′er,** an engraver's tool, e.g. a burin; **grave′-stone,** a stone placed as a memorial at a grave; **grave′yard,** a burial-ground.—**with one foot in the grave,** on the brink of death. [O.E. *grafan,* to dig, *græf,* a cave, grave, trench; Du. *graven,* Ger. *graben.*]

grave, *grāv, v.t.* to clean (by burning, &c.) and smear with tar (a wooden ship's bottom).—*n.* **graving-dock,** a dry-dock for cleaning and repair of ships. [Perh. O.Fr. *grave,* beach.]

grave, *grāv, adj.* of importance, weighty: threatening, serious: not gay or showy, sober, solemn: low in pitch.—*adv.* **grave′ly.**—*n.* **grave′ness.** [Fr.,—L. *gravis.*]

grave accent, *grāv ak′sént,* a mark (`) over a vowel indicating:—(1) a falling inflexion of voice; (2) that -*ed* forms a separate syllable (e.g. *belovèd*); (3) in French, a distinction between two words otherwise spelt alike, as *là,* there, *la,* the (*fem.*); (4) the French vowel sound in *mère,* mother, &c. [Fr. *grave* (see **grave** (3), and **accent.**]

gravel, *grav′l, n.* an assemblage of small rounded stones: small collections of gravelly matter in the kidneys or bladder.—*v.t.* to cover with gravel: to puzzle, nonplus:—*pr.p.* grav′elling; *pa.p.* grav′elled.—*adj.* **grav′elly.** [O.Fr. *gravele*; prob. Celt.]

graves. See greaves.

gravity, *grav′i-ti, n.* importance: seriousness: solemnity: lowness of pitch: gravitation, esp. the force by which bodies are attracted towards the earth.—*v.i.* **grav′itāte,** to be acted on by gravity: to tend towards the earth: to be strongly attracted, hence to move (towards). —*n.* **gravita′tion,** act of gravitating: the tendency of matter to attract and be attracted, the force of attraction between bodies.—*adjs.* **gravita′tional, grav′itātive.—acceleration due**

to gravity, (symbol *g*), the acceleration of a body falling freely under the action of gravity in a vacuum, about 32.174 feet or 9.8 metres per second per second; **specific gravity** (see **specific**). [L. *gravitās,* -*ātis*—*gravis,* heavy.]

gravy, *grāv′i, n.* the juices from meat that is cooking: (*slang*) money, profit.—*n.* **grav′y-boat,** a vessel for gravy. [Perh. *gravé,* a copyist's mistake for O.Fr. *grané*—*grain,* a cookery ingredient.]

gray. Same as **grey.**—*n.* **gray′ling,** a genus of silvery-grey fishes of the salmon family, with a smaller mouth and teeth, and larger scales.

graze, *grāz, v.t.* to eat or feed on (growing grass or pasture): to put to feed on growing grass: (of land) to supply food for (animals).—*v.i.* to eat grass: to supply grass.—*ns.* **grazier** (*grā′zi-ér,* -*zyér, zhyér*), one who grazes or pastures cattle and rears them for the market; **graz′ing,** the act of feeding on grass: the feeding or raising of cattle: pasture. [O.E. *grasian—græs,* grass.]

graze, *grāz, v.t.* to pass lightly along the surface of: to scrape.—*n.* a passing touch: scratch, abrasion. [Ety. uncertain.]

grease, *grēs, n.* soft thick animal fat: oily matter of any kind.—*v.t.* (sometimes pron. *grēz*) to smear with grease, to lubricate: (*slang*) to bribe: to facilitate.—*adj.* **greas′y** (sometimes *grēz′i*), of or like grease or oil: smeared with grease: shiny: unctuous.—*ns.* **greas′iness; grease-paint,** a tallowy composition used by actors in making up. [O.Fr. *gresse,* fatness, *gras,* fat—L. *crassus.*]

great, *grāt, adj.* large: of a high degree of magnitude of any kind: elevated in power, rank, &c.: highly gifted: sublime: chief: weighty: (*arch.*) pregnant: indicating one degree more remote in the direct line of descent, as **great′-grandfather, great′-grandson,** and similarly **great′-great′-grandfather,** &c.—*adv.* **great′ly.** —*ns.* **great′ness; great′coat,** an overcoat.— *adjs.* **great′er,** *comp.* of great: (with geographical names) in an extended sense (as *Greater Britain,* Britain and the Dominions; *Greater London*); **great′-heart′ed,** having a great or noble heart, high-spirited, noble.—*n.pl.* **Greats,** the final honour school of Literae Humaniores (Classical Greats) or of Modern Philosophy (Modern Greats) at Oxford.— **Great Bear,** *Ursa Major,* a northern constellation in which the seven brightest stars are known as the Plough; **great circle** (see **circle**); **great Dane** (see **Dane**); **great unwashed,** a contemptuous term for the populace. [O.E. *grēat*; Du. *groot,* Ger. *gross.*]

greave, *grēv, n.* armour for the leg below the knee. [O.Fr. *grève,* shin, greave.]

greaves, *grēvz,* **graves,** *grāvz, n.pl.* dregs of melted tallow. [Low Ger. *greven*; cf. Ger. *griebe.*]

grebe, *grēb, n.* a genus of short-winged almost tailless fresh-water diving birds, including the dabchick or little grebe. [Fr. *grèbe.*]

Grecian, *grēsh′(y)án,* Greek.—*n.* a Greek: one well versed in the Greek language and literature: (*B.*) a Jew who spoke Greek. [L. *Graecia,* Greece—Gr. *Graikos,* Greek.]

grecise. Same as **graecise.**

greedy, *grēd′i, adj.* having a voracious appetite: covetous: eagerly desirous (of).—*n.* **greed,** an eager desire or longing (with *of*): covetousness.—*adv.* **greed'ily.**—*n.* **greed'iness.** [O.E. *grǣdig*; Du. *gretig.*]

Greek, *grēk, adj.* of Greece, its people, or its language.—*n.* a native or citizen of Greece: the language of Greece: (*B.*) a Hellenising Jew; any language of which one is ignorant, jargon, anything unintelligible.—**Greek Church, Greek Orthodox Church (Eastern Church),** the form of Christianity prevailing in Greece, Russia, Turkey, &c.: the Church holding this form of Christianity and acknowledging the Patriarch of Constantinople, not the Pope, as its head; **Greek cross** (see **cross**); **Greek fire,** a composition that took fire when wetted, used in war, long a secret of the Byzantine Greeks; **Greek gift,** a treacherous gift (from Virgil's *Aeneid*, ii, 49).—**at the Greek calends,** never, the Greeks having no calends. [O.E. *Grēcas, Crēcas,* Greeks, or L. *Graecus*—Gr. *Graikos,* Greek.]

green, *grēn, adj.* of the colour of growing plants: growing: vigorous: young: new: unripe: inexperienced: easily imposed on: unseasoned: not dried: jealous.—*n.* the colour of growing plants: a small grassy plot or patch of ground: (*pl.*) green vegetables for food, esp. the cabbage kind.—*adj.* **green'ish,** somewhat green.—*adv.* **green'ly,** immaturely, unskilfully.—*ns.* **green'ness; green belt,** a strip of open land surrounding town; **green'-cloth,** a gaming-table: a department of the royal household, chiefly concerned with the commissariat—from the green cloth on the table round which its officials sat; **green'-crop,** a crop of green vegetables, as grasses, turnips, &c.; **green'ery,** green plants: verdure; **green-eyed monster,** jealousy; **green fingers,** a knack of making plants grow well; **green'-fly,** an aphis or plant louse; **green'grocer,** a dealer in fresh vegetables; **green'-hand,** an inexperienced sailor: a novice; **green'-horn,** a raw, inexperienced youth, easily imposed on; **green'house,** a glass-house for plants, esp. one with little or no artificial heating: (*airman's slang*) the cockpit of an aircraft—from the transparent sides; **green light,** permission to go ahead; **green'room,** a retiring-room for actors in a theatre, which originally had the walls coloured green; **green'sand,** a sandstone in which green specks of iron occur; **green'sick'ness,** chlorosis, a peculiar form of anaemia or bloodlessness, affecting young women; **green'sward,** sward or turf green with grass; **green'-tea** (see **tea**); **green'-vit'riol,** sulphate of iron; **green'-wood,** a leafy wood or forest: wood newly cut.—Also used as an *adj.,* as in 'the greenwood shade'.—**greenstick fracture** (see **fracture**). [O.E. *grēne*; Ger. *grün,* Du. *groen,* green, O.N. *grœnn.*]

greengage, *grēn'gāj', n.* a greenish yellow, very sweet variety of plum. [Said to be named from Sir W. *Gage,* before 1725.]

Greenwich (mean) time, *grin'ij (mēn) tīm,* time found from the sun's passage over the meridian (0°) at Greenwich, on which the former Royal Observatory stands.

greet, *grēt, v.t.* to accost with salutation or kind wishes: to send kind wishes to: to hail: to meet, become evident to (the senses).—*v.i.* to

meet and salute:—*pr.p.* greet'ing; *pa.p.* greet'ed.—*n.* greet'ing, expression of kindness or joy: salutation. [O.E. *grētan,* to greet, to meet; Du. *groeten,* Ger. *grüssen,* to salute.]

greet, *grēt, v.i.* (*Scot.*) to weep, wail, mourn. [O.E. *grēotan.*]

gregarious, *gre-gā'ri-us, adj.* associating in flocks and herds: fond of company.—*adv.* **grega'riously.**—*n.* **grega'riousness.** [L. *gregārius*—*grex, gregis,* a flock.]

Gregorian, *gre-gō', -gō', ri-an, adj.* belonging to or established by *Gregory,* e.g. the **Gregorian chants** (ritual plain-song melodies) or the **Gregorian tones** (nine tunes with variants to which the psalms were sung), named after Pope Gregory I (6th century), who made a collection of them.—**Gregorian calendar,** the calendar as reformed by Gregory XIII (1582; adopted in England 1752); it omitted certain leap years included in the *Julian calendar* (q.v.)—centesimal years (1600, 1700, &c.) were to be regarded as leap years only if exactly divisible by 400.

gremlin, *grem'lin, n.* (*orig.*) a goblin accused of vexing airmen, causing mechanical trouble to aircraft: an imaginary mischievous agency.

grenade, *gre-nād', n.* a small bomb thrown by the hand or shot from a rifle: a glass projectile containing chemicals for putting out fires, testing drains, &c.—*n.* **grenadier** (*gren-a-dēr'*), (*orig.*) a soldier who threw grenades: now used as the title of the first regiment of footguards. [Fr.,—Sp. *granada,* promegranate—L. *grānātus,* full of seeds (*grāna*).]

grew, *grōō, pa.t.* of **grow.**

grey, gray, *grā, adj.* of mixture of black and white: ash-coloured: between light and dark: (*fig.*) dull, dismal: (*fig.*) aged.—*n.* a grey colour: a grey or greyish animal, esp. a horse.—*ns.* **grey'beard,** one whose beard is grey: an old man: a stoneware jar for liquor; **grey eminence** (see **éminence grise**); **grey'-goose', grey'lag,** the common wild goose.—*adj.* **grey'ish,** somewhat grey.—*ns.* **grey matter,** the ashen-grey active part of the brain and spinal cord: (*coll.*) brains, intellect; **grey'ness.** [O.E. *grǣg*; cf. Ger. *grau.*]

greyhound, *grā'hownd, n.* a tall and slender dog, with great speed and keen sight. [O.E. *grīghund*; cf. O.N. *greyhundr*—O.N. *grey,* a dog, *hundr,* a hound.]

grid. See **gridiron.**

griddle, *grid'l, n.* a flat iron plate for baking cakes.—Also (*Scot.,* &c.) **girdle** (*gûrd'l*). [Anglo-Fr. *gridil,* from a dim. of L. *crātis,* a hurdle.]

gridiron, *grid'ī-ėrn, n.* a frame of iron bars for broiling flesh or fish over the fire.—*n.* **grid,** a grating: a gridiron: a network of power-transmission lines. [M.E. *gredire,* a griddle. From the same source as **griddle**; but the term. *-ire* became confused with M.E. *ire,* iron.]

grief, *grēf, n.* deep sorrow: distress.—*adj.* **grief'-strick'en,** bowed down with sorrow.—**come to grief,** meet with reverse, mishap, disaster. [O.Fr.,—L. *gravis,* heavy.]

grieve, *grēv, v.t.* to cause grief or pain of mind to: to vex.—*v.i.* to feel grief: to mourn.—*n.* **griev'ance,** a hardship, injury, real or fancied

Neutral vowels in unaccented syllables: *em'pėr-ór*; for certain sounds in foreign words see p. ix.

ground of complaint.—*adj.* **griev'ous,** causing grief: burdensome, painful, severe.—*adv.* **griev'ously.**—*n.* **griev'ousness.** [O.Fr. *grever*—L. *gravāre—gravis,* heavy.]

griffin, *grif'in,* **griffon, gryphon, -ón,** *n.* an imaginary animal, with lion's body and eagle's beak and wings: a duenna. [Fr.—*griffon*—L. *grȳphus*—Gr. *gryps,* a bird, probably the great bearded vulture—*grȳpos,* hook-nosed.]

griffon, *grif'ón,* *n.* a French dog like a coarsehaired terrier. [Prob. from **griffin.**]

grig, *grig,* *n.* a cricket, grasshopper: a small lively eel, the sand-eel. [Origin obscure.]

grill, *gril,* *v.t.* to broil on a gridiron: to torment: to cross-examine harassingly.—*n.* a grating: a gridiron: a grill-room.—*n.* **grill'-room,** part of a restaurant, where beefsteaks, &c., are grilled to order. [Fr. *griller—gril,* a gridiron—from a dim. of L. *crātis,* a hurdle.]

grille, *gril,* *n.* a lattice, or grating, often protecting a window, shrine, &c.: a grating in a convent or jail door. [Fr. Same root as **grill.**]

grilse, *grils,* *n.* a young salmon on its first return from salt water. [Origin unknown.]

grim, *grim,* *adj.* of forbidding aspect: fierce, cruel: ghastly, unmirthful: stern, unyielding.—*adv.* **grim'ly.**—*n.* **grim'ness.** [O.E. *grim(m)*; Ger. *grimmig—grimm,* fury, Du. *grimmig,* O.N. *grimmr.*]

grimace, *gri-mās',* *n.* a distortion of the face, in jest, &c.: a smirk.—Also *v.i.* [Fr.]

grimalkin, *gri-mal'kin,* or *-mawl'kin,* *n.* an old cat, a cat generally, esp. female. [grey and *malkin,* a dim. of Maud, Matilda.]

grime, *grīm,* *n.* sooty or coaly dirt: ingrained dirt.—*v.t.* to soil deeply.—*adj.* **grim'y,** foul, dirty. [Cf. Flem. *grijm.*]

Grimm's law, the law formulating certain changes undergone by Indo-Germanic stopped consonants in Germanic, stated by Jacob *Grimm* (1785-1863).

grin, *grin,* *v.i.* to set the teeth together and withdraw the lips: to smile with some accompanying distortion of the features, expressive of pain, derision, clownish admiration, glee. —*v.t.* to express by grinning:—*pr.p.* grinn'ing; *pa.t.* and *pa.p.* grinned.—*n.* act of grinning. [O.E. *grennian*; O.N. *grenja,* Ger. *greinen,* Du. *grijnen,* to grumble, Scot. *girn.*]

grind, *grīnd,* *v.t.* to reduce to powder by friction or crushing: to wear down, sharpen, smooth, or roughen by friction: to rub together: to oppress or harass (often with *down*): to work by a crank: to produce by great effort (with *out*).—*v.i.* to be moved or rubbed together: to jar or grate: to drudge at any tedious task: to study hard:—*pr.p.* grīnd'ing; *pa.t.* and *pa.p.* ground (*grownd*).—*n.* the act, sound, or jar of grinding: drudgery.—*ns.* **grind'er,** he who, or that which, grinds: a tooth that grinds food; **grind'stone,** a circular revolving stone for grinding or sharpening tools.—**keep one's nose to the grindstone,** to subject one to severe continuous toil or punishment. [O.E. *grindan.*]

grip, *grip,* *n.* grasp or firm hold with the hand or mind: the handle or part by which anything is grasped: a mode of grasping: power, control: (*coll.*) an article of hand-luggage, a bag.—*v.t.* to take or maintain fast hold of: to hold fast

the attention or interest of: to command the emotions of.—**come to grips** (*lit.* and *fig.*), to get into close combat (with). [O.E. *gripe,* grasp, *gripa,* handful, *grippan,* to seize.]

gripe, *grīp,* *v.t.* to grasp: to seize and hold fast: to squeeze: to give pain to the bowels.—*v.i.* to clutch: (*coll.*) to keep on complaining.—*n.* (esp. in *pl.*) severe spasmodic pain in the intestines: (*coll.*) a grumble.—*p.adj.* **grīp'ing,** avaricious: of a pain, seizing acutely. [O.E. *gripan* (*grāp, gripen*); O.N. *grīpa,* Ger. *greifen,* Du. *grijpen.*]

grippe, *grēp,* *n.* influenza. [Fr.,—*gripper,* to seize.]

grisette, *gri-zet', grē'-,* *n.* a gay young workingclass Frenchwoman. [Fr. *grisette,* a grey gown, which used to be worn by that class—*gris,* grey.]

grisled, *griz'ld.* Same as **grizzled.**

grisly, *griz'li, adj.* frightful: hideous. [O.E. *grislic.*]

grist, *grist,* *n.* corn for grinding, or that has been ground, at one time: (*fig.*) profit.—**bring grist to the mill,** to be a source of profit. [O.E. *grist,* same root as **grind.**]

gristle, *gris'l, n.* a soft elastic substance in animal bodies, cartilage.—*adj.* **grist'ly.**—*n.* **grist'liness.** [O.E. *gristle.*]

grit, *grit, n.* small hard particles of sand, stone, &c.: a coarse sandstone: firmness of character, spirit.—*adj.* **gritt'y,** having hard particles: sandy: determined, plucky.—*n.* **gritt'iness.** [O.E. *grēot*; Ger. *griess,* gravel.]

grizzle, *griz'l, n.* a grey colour.—*adjs.* **grizz'led,** grey, or mixed with grey; **grizz'ly,** of a grey colour.—*n.* the grizzly bear. [M.E. *griscl*—Fr. *gris,* grey.]

grizzie, *griz'l, v.i.* to grumble, to whimper, to fret.—*n.* a bout of grizzling.—*n.* **grizz'ler.**

groan, *grōn, v.i.* to utter a deep rumbling or voiced sound as in distress or disapprobation: (*fig.*) to be afflicted by (with *under*): (of a table, &c.) to be, as it were, oppressed with an overload e.g. of food—*n.* a deep moan.—*n.* **groan'ing.** [O.E. *grānian.*]

groat, *grōt, n.* an English silver coin, worth fourpence (1.66p) after 1662 coined only as Maundy (q.v.) money: a very small sum, proverbially. [Old Low Ger. *grote,* or Du. *groot,* lit. great, i.e. thick.]

groats, *grōts, n.pl.* the grain of oats deprived of the husks [O.E. *grotan* (pl.).]

grocer, *grōs'ér, n.* a dealer in staple foods, general household supplies.—*n.* **groc'ery** (gen. *pl.* **groc'eries**), articles sold by grocers. [Earlier *grosser,* wholesale dealer; O.Fr. *grossier*—Low L. *grossārius—grossus.* See **gross.**]

grog, *grog, n.* a mixture of spirits and cold water, without sugar: strong drink.—*adj.* **grogg'y,** affected by grog, partially intoxicated: weak and staggering, e.g. from blows or from illness. [From 'Old Grog', the nickname (apparently from his grogram cloak) of Admiral Vernon, who in 1740 ordered that rum (until 1970 officially issued to sailors) should be mixed with water.]

grogram, *grog'rám, n.* a kind of coarse cloth of silk and mohair. [O.Fr. *gros grain,* coarse grain.]

groin, *groin, n.* the fold between the belly and the thigh: (*archit.*) the angular curve formed by the crossing of two arches.—*adj.* **groined,** having angular curves made by the intersection of two arches.—*n.* **groin'ing.** [Early forms *grind, grine,* perh.—O.E. *grynde,* abyss.]

groom, grōōm, grōōm, *n.* one who has the charge of horses: a title of several officers of the royal household: a bridegroom.—*v.t.* to tend, esp. a horse: to make smart and neat (used esp. in *pa.p.,* as, *well groomed*): to prepare (for political office, or for stardom) by publicity and other means.—*n.* **grooms'man,** the attendant on a bridegroom at his marriage. [Origin obscure; influenced by O.E. *guma* (as in bride-*groom*), a man.]

groove, grōōv, *n.* a furrow, or long hollow, such as is cut with a tool: the track cut into the surface of a gramophone record along which the gramophone needle moves: (*jazz slang*) an exalted mood, one's highest form: (*fig.*) unvarying course, fixed routine, rut.—*v.t.* to grave or cut a groove or furrow in.—*adj.* **groovy** (also **in the groove**), (*jazz slang*) in the top form or in perfected condition: up to date in style: a general term of approval: following a set routine. [Prob. Du. *groef, groeve,* a furrow; cog. with O.N. *grōf,* Eng. **grave.**]

grope, grōp, *v.i.* (*lit.* and *fig.*) to search (for something) as if blind or in the dark.—*v.t.* to search by feeling (*to grope one's way*).—*adv.* **grop'ingly.** [O.E. *grāpian*; allied to **grab, gripe.**]

grosbeak, grōs'bēk, *n.* the hawfinch, or other finch of the same subfamily, with a thick, heavy, seed-crushing bill. [Fr. *grosbec*—*gros,* thick, *bec,* beak.]

gross, grōs, *adj.* coarse: dense: palpable, flagrant, glaring: overfed, unpleasantly fat: coarse in mind or manners: sensual: obscene: total, including everything.—*n.* the main bulk: the whole taken together: twelve dozen.—*adv.* **gross'ly.**—*n.* **gross'ness.**—**great gross,** a dozen gross; **in gross,** in bulk, wholesale. [Fr. *gros*—L. *grossus,* thick.]

grotesque, grō-tesk', *adj.* extravagantly formed: fantastic.—*n.* (*art*) extravagant ornament, containing animals, plants, &c., not really existing.—*adv.* **grotesque'ly.**—*n.* **grotesque'ness.** [Fr. *grotesque*—It. *grottesca*—*grotta,* a grotto.]

grotto, grot'ō, *n.* a cave: an imitation cave, usu. fantastic.—Also **grot**—*pl.* **grott'oes, grott'os.** [It. *grotta* (Fr. *grotte*)—L. *crypta*—Gr. *kryptē,* a crypt, vault.]

grotty, grot'i, *adj.* (*slang*) ugly, in bad condition, or useless. [**grotesque.**]

grouch. See **grouse** (2).

ground, grownd, *pa.t.* and *pa.p.* of **grind.**

ground, grownd, *n.* the solid surface of the earth: a portion of the earth's surface: (*pl.*) enclosed land attached to a house: field or place of action: position: soil: (*arch.*) bottom, esp. sea-bottom: (*pl.*) dregs or sediment: that on which something is raised, foundation: (often *pl.*) sufficient reason: (*pl.*) basis of justification: (*art*) the surface on which the figures are represented.—*v.t.* to cause to run aground: to bring to the ground: to prohibit (aircraft, airman) from flying: to fix (on a foundation or principle): to instruct in first principles.—*v.i.* to come to the ground: to strike the bottom and remain fixed: to have a

basis, be founded, in (with *in, upon*).—*adjs.* **grounded,** (of an aircraft) unable to fly; **ground'less,** without ground, foundation, or reason.—*adv.* **ground'lessly.**—*ns.* **ground'lessness; ground'age,** a charge on a ship in port; **ground'-bait,** bait dropped to the bottom to bring fish to the neighbourhood; **ground'-control',** control, by information radioed from a ground installation, of aircraft observed by radar; **ground'-floor, -storey,** the floor on or near a level with the ground; **ground'-game,** hares, rabbits, as opposed to winged game; **ground'-ice,** the ice formed at the bottom; **ground'-i'vy,** a common British creeping-plant whose leaves when the edges curl become ivy-like; **ground'ling,** a fish that keeps near the bottom: (*arch.*) a spectator in the pit of a theatre—hence one of the common herd; **ground'-nut,** the peanut, a plant, grown in warm countries, with pods that push down into the earth and ripen there: any of several plants with tuberous roots; **ground'-plan,** plan of the horizontal section of the lowest or ground storey of a building; **ground'-plot,** the plot of ground on which a building stands; **ground'-rent,** rent paid to a landlord for the use of the ground; **ground'-sheet,** a waterproof sheet spread on the ground by campers, &c.; **grounds'man, ground'man,** a man charged with the care of a sports-field: an aerodrome mechanic; **ground'-speed,** (*aero.*) speed of an aircraft relative to the ground; **ground'-staff,** aircraft mechanics, &c., whose work is on the ground; **ground'-state,** state of nuclear system, atoms, &c., when at their lowest (or normal) energy; **ground'-swell,** a broad, deep undulation of the ocean due to past storm, &c.; **ground'work,** that which forms the ground or foundation of anything, the basis.—**break ground,** to take the first step in any project; **fall to the ground,** to come to nothing; **gain ground,** to advance: to become more widely influential: to spread; **give ground, lose ground,** to fall back, to lose advantage; **off the ground,** started, under way; **shift one's ground,** to change one's standpoint in a situation or argument; **stand,** or **hold, one's ground,** to stand firm. [O.E. *grund*; cog. with Ger. *grund,* O.N. *grunnr.*]

groundsel, grown(d)'sél, *n.* a very common yellow-flowered weed of waste ground. [O.E. *gundæswelgiæ,* appar. from *gund,* pus, *swelgan,* to swallow, from its use in poultices, influenced by *grund,* ground.]

group, grōōp, *n.* a number of persons or things together: a clique, school, section, or party: (*art*) a combination of figures forming a harmonious whole: (*geol.*) the rocks formed during an era: (*math.*) a system of elements having a binary operation that is associative, an identity element for the operation, and an inverse for every element: (*coll.*) a pop group.—*v.t.* and *v.i.* to form into a group or groups.—*ns.* **group'-cap'tain,** an Air Force officer corresponding to a colonel or a naval captain; **group'ing** (*art*), the act of disposing and arranging, or the disposition of, figures or objects in a group.—**group therapy,** therapy in which a small group of people with the same psychological or physical problems discuss

---

Neutral vowels in unaccented syllables: *em'pér-ór*; for certain sounds in foreign words see p. ix.

their difficulties under the chairmanship of e.g. a doctor. [Fr. *groupe* – It. *groppo*, a bunch, knot; from Gmc.]

grouse, *grows*, *n.* a family or subfamily consisting chiefly of game birds, including the ptarmigans: the red grouse, a ptarmigan, a plump bird with a short curved bill, short legs, and feathered feet, which frequents moors and hills in Scotland, north England, and north Ireland:–*pl.* **grouse**. [Origin unknown.]

grouse, *grows* (also **grouch**, *growch*), *v.i.* to grumble.–*n.* a grumble.–*n.* **grous'er**, one given to grumbling. [O.Fr. *groucher*, *grocher*, *gruchier*, to grumble.]

grout, *growt*, *n.* coarse meal: the sediment of liquor: a fluid mortar.–*v.t.* to fill in with grout. [O.E. *grūt*, coarse meal; or perh. in part Fr. *grouter*, to finish with grout.]

grove, *grōv*, *n.* a wood of small size, generally of a pleasant or ornamental character: an avenue of trees. [O.E. *grāf*.]

grovelling, *gruv'- grov'(e)-ling, adv.* (*arch.*) and *adj.* prone: face-down: *orig. adv.* but later felt to be the *pr.p.* of a new *v.i.* **grov'el** (a backformation), to crawl on the earth, esp. in abject fear, &c.: to be base, abject:–*pa.p.* **grov'elled.**–*n.* **grov'eller.** [M.E. *groveling*, *grofling*, prone–O.N. *grūfa*, and adverbial suffx. *-ling.*]

grow, *grō*, *v.i.* to have life: to have a habitat: to become enlarged by a natural process: to advance towards maturity: to develop: to become greater in any way: to become.–*v.t.* to cause to grow: to cultivate:–*pa.t.* grew (*grōō*); *pa.p.* grown (*grōn*).–*ns.* **grow'er; growth**, a growing: gradual increase: development: that which has grown: a morbid formation: product.–**grow on, upon,** to gain a greater hold on (e.g. of a habit, esp. bad): to gain in the estimation of; **grow out of,** to result from: to pass beyond in development; **grow up,** to advance in growth: to become adult: to spring up: become common (e.g. a custom). [O.E. *grōwan*; O.N. *grōa*.]

growl, *growl*, *v.i.* to utter a deep, rough, murmuring sound like a dog: to grumble surlily.–*v.t.* to express by growling.–*n.* a murmuring, snarling sound, as of an angry dog: a surly grumble.–*n.* **growl'er**, one who, or that which, growls: a small iceberg: an old-fashioned four-wheeler horse cab. [Cf. Du. *grollen*, to grumble; allied to Gr. *gryllizein*, to grunt.]

groyne, *groin*, *n.* a breakwater, usu. wooden, to check erosion and sand-drifting [Prob. **groin**.]

grub, *grub*, *v.i.* to dig in the dirt: to be occupied meanly: (*slang*) to eat.–*v.t.* to dig or root out of the ground (generally followed by *up*):–*pr.p.* grubb'ing; *pa.p.* grubbed.–*n.* the larva of a beetle, moth, &c.: (*slang*) food.–*adj.* **grubb'y**, dirty.–*ns.* **grubb'er; grubb'iness.**–*n.* **Grub'-street**, a former name of Milton Street, London, once inhabited by booksellers' hacks and shabby writers generally.–*adj.* applied to any mean literary production. [M.E. *grobe.*]

grudge, *gruj*, *v.t.* to give or allow unwillingly: to be unwilling (to).–*n.* a feeling of resentment (with *against*) due to some specific cause.–*adj.* **grudg'ing**, unwilling, reluctant.–*adv.* **grudg'ingly.** [O.Fr. *groucher*, *grocher*, *gruchier*, to grumble.]

gruel, *grōō'el*, *n.* a thin food made by boiling oatmeal in water: (*coll.*) punishment, severe treatment.–*v.t.* to subject to a severe or exhausting experience.–*adj.* **gru'elling**, exhausting. [O.Fr. *gruel*, groats–Low L. *grūtellum*, of Gmc. origin.]

gruesome, *grōō'sum*, *adj.* horrible, grisly.–*vs.i.* **grue**, **grew** (*dial.*), to shudder. [Cf. Du. *gruwzaam*, Ger. *grausam.*]

gruff, *gruf*, *adj.* rough or abrupt in manner or sound.–*adv.* **gruff'ly.**–*n.* **gruff'ness.** [Du. *grof*; cog. with Swed. *grof*, Ger. *grob*, coarse.]

grumble, *grum'bl*, *v.i.* to murmur with discontent: to growl: to rumble.–*n.* the act of or an instance of grumbling.–*n.* **grum'bler.**–*adj.* **grum'bly**, inclined to grumble. [Cf. Du. *grommelen*, freq. of *grommen*, to mutter; Ger. *grummeln.*]

grume, *grōōm*, *n.* a thick fluid: a clot.–*adj.* **grum'ous**, composed of grains. [O.Fr *grume*, a bunch–L. *grūmus*, a little heap.]

grumpy, *grum'pi*, *adj.* surly.–*adv.* **grum'pily**,–*n.* **grum'piness.** [Obs. *grump*, a snub, sulkiness.]

Grundyism, *grun'di-izm*, *n.* conventional prudery, from the question 'But what will Mrs Grundy say?' in Thomas Morton's *Speed the Plough* (1798).–**Mrs Grundy**, the personification of conventional prudery.

grunt, *grunt*, *v.i.* to make a sound like a pig.–*n.* sound made by a pig.–*n.* **grunt'er.** [O.E. *grunnettan*, freq. of *grunian*.]

guanaco, *gwä nä'ko*, *n.* a S. American wild animal related to the llama–perh. the form from which the llama and alpaca were developed. [American Sp.]

guano, *gwä'no*, *n.* the long-accumulated dung of sea fowl, used for manure.–*n.* **gua'nin(e)**, a yellowish-white amorphous substance, found in guano, liver, pancreas, and other organs of animals, and germ cells of plants–a constituent of nucleic acids. [Sp. *guano*, or *huano*, from Peruvian *huanu*, dung.]

guarantee, *gar-an-tē*, **guaranty** (*law*), *gar'än-ti*, *n.* a warrant or surety: a contract to see performed what another has undertaken: the person who makes such a contract: (**guarantee**) the person to whom it is made.–*v.t.* to undertake as surety for another: to be responsible for (the truth of a statement): to answer for (the genuineness or good qualities of an article): to promise, engage (that): to secure (a person *against*):–*pr.p.* guarantee'ing; *pa.p.* guaranteed'.–*n.* **guar'antor.**–**guarantee association, company, society**, a joint-stock company on the insurance principle, which becomes security to an employer for the integrity of his cashiers, &c. [Anglo-Fr. *garantie–garant*, warrant. Cf. **warrant**.]

guard, *gärd*, *v.t.* to protect from danger or attack: to prevent from escaping (*lit.* and *fig.*): to keep under restraint (*fig.*).–*v.i.* to take precautions (against): to be wary.–*n.* that which guards from danger: a man or body of men stationed to watch and prevent from escaping, &c., or to protect: one who has charge of a coach (*hist.*) or railway-train: state of caution: posture of defence: part of the hilt of a sword: a cricketer's pad: a watchchain: (*pl.*; *cap.*) household troops (Foot, Horse, Life Guards).–*adjs.* **guard'ant, gardant** (*her.*), having the face turned towards the beholder; **guard'ed**, wary, cautious: uttered with caution.—*adv.* **guard'edly.**—*ns.* **guard'house, guard'room**, a house or room for the accommodation of guards; **guard'ian**, one who guards or takes care: (*law*) one who has the care of the person, property, and rights of another, as a minor, a lunatic.—*adj.* protecting.—*ns.* **guard'ianship; guard'-ring**, a keeper, or finger-ring that serves to keep another from slipping off; **guards'man**, a soldier of the guards.—**guardian angel**, an angel supposed to watch over a particular person: a person specially devoted to the interests of another.—**mount guard**, to go on guard duty; **on**, or **off, one's guard**, on the watch, prepared, or the opposite. [O.Fr. *garder*—O.H.G. *warten*; O.E. *weardian*; cf. **ward**.]

guava, *gwä'vä, n.* a tropical American genus of trees and shrubs, with yellow, pear-shaped fruit used for jelly. [Sp. *guayaba*, guava fruit; of South American origin.]

guayule, *gwä-ū'lä, n.* a Mexican plant: the rubber yielded by it. [Sp.]

gubernatorial, *gū-bér-nä-tō'ri-äl, adj.* pertaining to a governor or government. [L. *gubernātor*, steersman, governor.]

gudgeon, *guj'ón, n.* a pivot or journal. [O.Fr. *goujon.*]

gudgeon, *guj'ón, n.* an easily caught small carp-like fresh-water fish: a person easily cheated. [O.Fr. *goujon*—L. *gōbiō*, *-ōnis*, a kind of fish—Gr. *kōbios.*]

guelder-rose, *gel'dér-rōz, n.* the snowball-tree, a tree with large white balls of flowers. [From *Geldern* (Prussia) or from *Gelderland* (Holland).]

guerdon, *gûr'dón, n.* a reward or recompense. [O.Fr. *guerdon, gueredon*—Low L. *widerdonum.*]

guernsey, *gûrn'zi, n.* a close-fitting knitted garment, worn by sailors: (*cap.*) one of a breed of dairy cattle from *Guernsey* in the Channel Islands.

guerrilla, guerilla, *gér-il'a, n.* the harassing of an army by small bands acting independently, as in the Peninsular war: a member of such a band.—Also *adj.*, e.g. in **guer(r)illa warfare.**—**guerrilla strike**, a sudden and brief industrial strike. [Sp. *guerrilla*, dim. of *guerra*, war—O.H.G. *werra*; cf. **war**; Fr. *guerre.*]

guess, *ges, v.t.* (*arch.* and *U.S.*) to think, believe, suppose: to judge upon inadequate knowledge or none at all: to conjecture: to hit on, or solve, by conjecture.—Also *v.i.* and *n.*—*n.* **guess'work**, process or result of guessing.—**anybody's guess**, purely a matter of individual conjecture. [M.E. *gessen*; cog. with mod. Icel. *giska, gizka*, for *gitska*—*geta*, to get, think.]

guest, *gest, n.* a visitor received and entertained gratuitously or for payment.—*adj.* and *n.* (an artist, conductor, &c.) not a regular member of a company, &c., or not regularly appearing on a programme, but taking part on a special occasion.—*ns.* **guest'-cham'ber** (*B.*), **guest'-room**, a room for the accommodation of a guest; **guest'-house**, a boarding-house; **guest'-night**, a night when non-members of a society are entertained. [O.E. (Anglian) *gest* (W.S. *giest*); allied to L. *hostis*, stranger, enemy.]

guff, *guf, n.* (*slang*) empty talk, humbug. [Perh. imit.]

guffaw, *guf-ö', v.i.* to laugh loudly.—*n.* a loud laugh. [From the sound.]

guide, *gīd, v.t.* to lead, conduct, or direct: to regulate: to influence.—*n.* he who, or that which, guides: one who conducts travellers, tourists, &c.: one who directs another in his course of life: a device to secure that movement takes place along a particular line: a book of instructions: a guide-book: a Girl Guide.—*ns.* **guid'ance**, direction: leadership; **guide'-book**, a book of information for tourists; **guide'-dog**, a dog trained to lead a blind person; **guide'line**, a line drawn, or a rope, &c., fixed, to act as a guide: (*fig.*) an indication of the course that should be followed, or of what future policy will be; **guide'post**, a post to guide the traveller; **guider**, a senior Girl Guide.—**guided missile** (see **missile**). [O.Fr. *guider*; prob. from a Gmc. root, as in O.E. *witan*, to know, &c.]

guild, (*orig.*) **gild**, *gild, n.* an association for mutual aid: (*hist.*) a mediaeval association of merchants, or of craftsmen of a particular trade, whose purpose was to provide for masses for the dead, maintenance of common interests, mutual support and protection.—*ns.* **guild'hall**, the hall of a guild: a town-hall; **guild'ry** (*Scot.*), the corporation of a royal burgh: membership thereof. [O.E. *gield*, influenced by O.N. *gildi*.]

guilder, gilder, *gild'ér, n.* an old Dutch and German gold coin: a modern Dutch silver coin, the florin. [Du. *gulden.*]

guile, *gīl, n.* cunning, deceit.—*adj.* **guile'ful**, crafty, deceitful.—*n.* **guile'fulness.**—*adj.* **guile'less**, without deceit: artless.—*adv.* **guile'lessly.**—*n.* **guile'lessness.** [Norm. Fr. *guile*, deceit; prob. Gmc.; cf. **wile**.]

guillemot, *gil'i-mot, n.* a genus of diving birds with a pointed bill and very short tail. [Fr., dim. of *Guillaume*, William, perh. suggested by Breton *gwelan*, gull.]

guillotine, *gil'o-tēn, -tēn', n.* an instrument for beheading by descent of a heavy oblique blade—adopted during the French Revolution, and named after *Guillotin* (1738-1814), a physician, who first proposed its adoption: a machine for cutting paper, straw, &c.: a surgical instrument for cutting the tonsils: a drastic rule for shortening discussion.—*v.t.* to behead, crop, or cut short by guillotine.

guilt, *gilt, n.* the state of having done wrong: the state of having broken a law.—*adj.* **guilt'y**, justly chargeable, culpable: wicked: pertaining to, or evincing, or conscious of, guilt.—*adv.* **guilt'ily.**—*n.* **guilt'iness.**—*adj.* **guilt'less**, free from crime: innocent.—*adv.* **guilt'lessly.**—*n.* **guilt'lessness.**—**guilty of** (sometimes in *B.*), deserving. [Orig. a payment or fine for an offence; O.E. *gylt.*]

guinea, *gin'i, n.* an obsolete English gold coin, first made of gold brought from *Guinea*, in Africa: its value finally 21s. (£1.05).—*ns.* **guin'ea-fowl**, an African bird of the pheasant family, dark grey with white spots; **guin'ea-pig**, a small South American rodent, a species of cavy: (*fig.*) a human being used as the subject of an experiment.

Neutral vowels in unaccented syllables: *em'pér-ór*; for certain sounds in foreign words see p. ix.

guise, *gīz, n.* external appearance: assumed appearance (e.g. *in the guise of*): (*arch.*) manner, behaviour: (*arch.*) dress.—*n.* **guis'er** (*Scot.*), a person in disguise or fancy dress. [O.Fr. *guise;* cf. O.H.G. *wisa,* a way, guise, O.E. *wise,* way.]

guitar, *gi-tär', n.* a fretted musical instrument, now six-stringed, like the lute, but flat-backed. [Fr. *guitare*—L. *cithara.* See **cithara.**]

gulch, *gulch, gulsh, n.* (*U.S.*) a ravine or narrow rocky valley, a gully. [Origin doubtful.]

gules, *gūlz, n.* (*her.*) a red colour, marked in engraved figures by perpendicular lines. [O.Fr. *gueules;* perh.—L. *gula,* the throat.]

gulf, *gulf, n.* an indentation in the coast: a deep place, an abyss: (*lit.* and *fig.*) a whirlpool: (*fig.*) a deep, usu. impassable, division.—**gulf stream,** a great current of warm water flowing out of the Gulf of Mexico along the eastern coast of the United States, then deflected near the banks of Newfoundland diagonally across the Atlantic; **gulf-weed,** sargasso. [O.Fr. *golfe*—Gr. *kolpos,* bosom.]

gull, *gul, n.* one of several kinds of web-footed sea-fowl with long wings. [Perh. W. *gwylan,* to weep, wail.]

gull, *gul, n.* a dupe: an easily duped person: (*slang*) a cheat: (*arch.*) a trick.—*v.t.* to beguile, hoax.—*adj.* **gull'ible,** easily deceived.—*n.* **gullibil'ity.** [Origin uncertain.]

gullet, *gul'et, n.* the oesophagus (q.v.): the throat. [O.Fr. *goulet,* dim. of *goule*—L. *gula,* the throat.]

gully, *gul'i, n.* a channel worn by running water, as on a mountain side: a deep artificial channel: (*cricket*) position between slips and point.—*v.t.* to wear a gully or channel in. [Prob. **gullet**.]

gully, *gul'i, n.* (*Scot.* and *North*) a large knife.

gulp, *gulp, v.t.* to swallow spasmodically or in large draughts.—*n.* a spasmodic or copious swallow: a movement as if of swallowing: a quantity swallowed at once. [Cf. Du. *gulpen, gulp.*]

gum, *gum, n.* the firm fleshy tissue that surrounds the bases of the teeth.—*n.* **gum'-boil,** a small abscess on the gum. [O.E. *gōma,* palate; O.N. *gōmr.*]

gum, *gum, n.* a substance that exudes from certain plants, and hardens on the surface: a plant gum or similar substance used as an adhesive, a stiffener, &c.: a transparent sweet-meat: chewing-gum (q.v.).—*v.t.* to coat or to unite with gum:—*pr.p.* gumm'ing; *pa.p.* gummed.—*adjs.* **gumm'ous, gumm'y,** consisting of or resembling gum: producing or covered with gum; **gummif'erous,** producing gum.—*ns.* **gumm'iness; gum'-ar'abic,** a gum obtained from various acacias; **gum'-boot,** a rubber boot; **gum'-elas'tic,** rubber; **gum'-tree,** a tree that exudes gum, &c., e.g. a eucalyptus tree, or any one of several unrelated American trees. [O.Fr. *gomme*—L. *gummi*—Gr. *kommi;* prob. of Egyptian origin.]

gumption, *gum(p)'sh(ó)n, n.* shrewdness: common sense. [Perh. conn. with O.N. *gaumr,* heed.]

gun, *gun, n.* a tubular weapon, from which projectiles are discharged, usually by explosion: a cannon, rifle, revolver, &c.: a starting pistol:

(*U.S.*) the accelerator of a car: the throttle of an aircraft.—*v.t.* to shoot: to provide with guns: to open the throttle of an aircraft.—*ns.* **gun'-barrel,** the tube of a gun; **gun'boat,** a small vessel of light draught, fitted to carry one or more guns (**gunboat diplomacy,** show or threat of (orig. naval) force in international negotiation); **gun'-carriage,** the support on which an artillery weapon is mounted; **gun'-cotton,** an explosive, cotton saturated with nitric and sulphuric acid; **gun dog,** a dog trained to assist sportsmen shooting game; **gun'fire,** the firing of guns: the hour at which a morning or evening gun is fired; **gun'-maker,** a man who carries a gun, esp. a ruffian with a revolver; **gun'-met'al,** an alloy of copper and tin: the colour of this alloy; **gunn'age,** the number of guns carried by a ship of war; **gunn'er,** one who works a gun: a private in the artillery: (*naut.*) branch-officer in charge of naval ordnance; **gunn'ery,** the art of managing guns, or the science of artillery; **gun'-powder,** an explosive mixture of saltpetre, sulphur, and charcoal; **gun'-room,** the apartment on board ship occupied by the gunner, or by the lieutenants as a mess-room: a room in a house for sporting guns, &c.; **gun'-running,** smuggling guns into a country; **gun'shot,** the range of a gun.—*adj.* caused by the shot of a gun.—*adj.* **gun'-shy,** frightened by guns.—*ns.* **gun'smith,** a smith or workman who makes or repairs guns or small-arms; **gun'stock,** the piece on which the barrel of a gun is fixed. **beat the gun,** jump the gun (see **jump**); **blow great guns,** to blow tempestuously (of wind); **great gun** (*coll.*), a person of great importance; **gun for,** to seek, try to obtain: to seek to ruin or to wreak revenge on; **stand, stick, to one's guns,** maintain one's position staunchly. [M.E. *gonne,* poss. from the woman's name *Gunhild.*]

gunny, *gun'i, n.* a strong coarse jute fabric. [Hindustani *gōn, gōnī,* sacking.]

gunter, *gun'tér,* or **Gunter's chain,** *n.* a chain of 100 links, 66 feet long, used for land measurement. [Edmund *Gunter,* astronomer (1581–1626).]

gunwale, gunnel, *gun'l, n.* (*orig.*) the wale or upper edge of a ship's side next to the bulwarks, so called because the upper guns were pointed from it: now usu. applied to the upper edge of the hull of a small boat.

gurgitation, *gûr-ji-tā'sh(ó)n, n.* surging. [L. *gurges, -itis,* whirlpool.]

gurgle, *gûr'gl, v.i.* to flow in an irregular noisy current: to make a bubbling sound. [Cf. It. *gorgogliare.*]

Gurkha, Goorkha, *gōōr'ka, gûr'-, n.* one of the dominant people of Nepal, a broad-chested fighting race.

gurnard, *gûr'nárd,* **gurnet,** *-net, ns.* a genus of fishes with large angular head. [O.Fr. *gornard,* related to Fr. *grogner,* to grunt—L. *grunnīre,* to grunt; from the sound they emit when taken.]

guru, gooroo, *gōō'rōō, n.* a spiritual teacher: a venerable person. [Hind. *gurū*—Sans. *guru,* venerable.]

gush, *gush, v.i.* to flow out with violence or copiously: to be effusive, or highly sentimental.—*n.* that which flows out: a violent issue of a fluid: (*fig.*) an uprush (of emotion): a spate of demonstrative phrases, usu. insincere.—*n.* **gush′er,** one who gushes: an oil-well that does not need to be pumped.—*adj.* **gush′ing.** [M.E. *gosche, gusche.*]

gusset, *gus′et, n.* the piece of chain mail covering a joint in armour, as at the armpit: an angular piece inserted in a garment to strengthen or enlarge some part of it. [O.Fr. *gousset—gousse,* a pod, husk.]

gust, *gust, n.* a sudden blast of wind: a violent burst (e.g. of passion).—*v.i.* to blow in gusts.—*adj.* **gust′y,** stormy, characterised by gusts of wind, subject to, characterised by, fits or bursts (e.g. of anger).—*n.* **gust′iness.** [O.N. *gustr,* blast.]

gust, *gust, n.* (*arch.*) relish.—*n.* **gustā′tion,** the act of tasting: the sense of taste.—*adj.* **gust′ā-tory,** of or pertaining to the sense of taste.—*n.* **gust′o** (*It.*), taste: zest. [L. *gustus,* taste; cf. Gr. *geuein,* to cause to taste.]

gut, *gut, n.* the alimentary canal: intestines or glands prepared for violin-strings, &c.: (*pl.*) entrails: a narrow passage, channel, lane: (*pl. coll.*) toughness of character.—*v.t.* to take out the guts of: to reduce to a shell (by burning, plundering, &c.):—*pr.p.* **gutt′ing;** *pa.p.* **gutt′ed.**—*adj.* **guts′y,** (*slang*) greedy: (*slang*) plucky: (*slang*) lusty, passionate.—*ns.* **gutt′er,** one who guts fish, &c.; **gut′-scrap′er,** a fiddler. [O.E. *guttas* (pl.); cf. *gēotan,* to pour.]

gutta-percha, *gut′a-pûr′cha,* or *-ka, n.* solidified juice of various Malayan trees. [Malay *getah,* gum, *percha,* a tree producing it.]

gutter, *gut′ėr, n.* a channel for conveying away water, esp. at a roadside or at the eaves of a roof: (*fig.*) slum life, social degradation.—*adj.* low, disreputable.—*v.t.* to cut or form into small hollows.—*v.i.* to become hollowed: to run down in drops, as a candle.—*ns.* **gutter press, journalism,** sensational journalism; **gutt′er-snipe,** a neglected child, a street Arab. [O.Fr. *goutiere—goute*—L. *gutta,* a drop.]

gutter. See **gut.**

guttural, *gut′ûr-ål, adj.* pertaining to the throat: formed in the throat.—*n.* (*phonet.*) a sound pronounced in the throat or (*loosely*) by the back part of the tongue.—*adv.* **gutt′urally.** [Fr.,—L. *guttur,* the throat.]

guy, *gī, n.* a rope, rod, &c., to steady anything.— *v.t.* to keep in position by a guy. [O.Fr. *guis, guie*; Sp. *guia,* a guide.]

guy, *gī, n.* an effigy of *Guy* Fawkes, dressed up grotesquely on the anniversary of the Gunpowder Plot (5th November): a person of odd appearance: (*slang*) a person.—*v.t.* (*coll.*) to turn to ridicule, make fun of.

guzzle, *guz′l, v.t.* and *v.i.* to swallow greedily.—*n.* **guzz′ler.** [Perh. conn. with Fr. *gosier,* throat.]

gymkhana, *jim-kä′na, n.* a place of public resort for athletic games, &c.: a meeting for such sports. [Hindustani *gend-khāna* ('ball-house'), racket-court, remodelled on *gymnastics.*]

gymnasium, *jim-nā′zi-um, n.* a place, hall, building, or school for gymnastics: (*orig.*) a place where athletic exercises were practised

naked: (usu. *gim-nä′zi-ŏŏm*) a secondary school (esp. on the Continent):—*pl.* **gym-na′siums, -ia.**—*ns.* **gym′nast** (*-nast*), one skilled in gymnastics; **gymnas′tic,** a system of training by exercise: (usu. in *pl.* **gymnas′tics,** used as *sing.*) exercises devised to strengthen the body: feats or tricks of agility.—*adjs.* **gymnas′tic, -al.** [Latinised from Gr. *gymnasion— gymnos,* naked.]

gymn(o)-, *gim′n(ō)-, jim′n(ō)-, gimn(o)′-, jimn(o)′-,* in composition, esp. of biol. terms, naked.—*ns.* **gym′nosoph, gymnos′ophist** (Gr. *sophos,* wise), an ancient Hindu philosopher who wore little or no clothing, and lived solitarily in mystical contemplation; **gymnosperm** (Gr. *sperma,* seed), any of the lower or primitive group of seed-plants whose seeds are not enclosed in an ovary. [Gr. *gymnos,* naked.]

gynaeceum, *jin-e-sē′um, n.* (Greek and Roman *hist.*) women's apartments: (*bot.*) the carpel, or carpels collectively, of a flower (cf. **pistil**). In the latter sense sometimes pronounced in the same way as **gynoecium** (q.v.). [Gr. *gynaikeion,* women's quarters.]

gynaecocracy, *gīn-, jīn-, jin-ē-kok′ra-si, n.* government by women or a woman—also **gynoc′racy.** [Gr. *gynē, -aikos,* a woman, *krateein,* to rule.]

gynaecology, *gīn-, jīn-, jin-ē-kol′o-ji, n.* that branch of medicine which treats of the diseases of women.—*adj.* **gynaecolog′ical.**—*n.* **gynaecol′ogist.** [Gr. *gynē,* a woman, *logos,* discourse.]

gynoecium, gynecium, *jin-, jīn-ē′si-um, n.* (*bot.*) gynaeceum. [Mod. L.,—Gr. *gynē,* woman, *oikos,* house.]

gyp, *jip, n.* a college servant at Cambridge. [Perh. **gypsy**; or perh. obs. *gippo,* a short jacket, a varlet—obs. Fr. *jupeau.*]

gypsum, *jip′sum, n.* hydrous calcium sulphate (hydrated sulphate of lime). See **plaster of Paris.** [L.,—Gr. *gypsos,* chalk.]

gypsy, gipsy, *jip′si, n.* a Romany a member of a wandering people of Indian origin: a dark-skinned person: a sly, tricking woman. [**Egyp-tian,** because once thought to have come from Egypt.]

gyre, *jīr, n.* a circular motion.—*v.i.* **gyr′āte** (or *-āt′*), to spin, whirl.—*n.* **gyra′tion,** whirling motion.—*adjs.* **gyr′ātory,** spinning round; **gyromagnet′ic,** pertaining to magnetic properties of rotating electric charges.—*ns.* **gyro-mag′netism; gyr′omancy,** divination by walking in a circle; **gyr′oscōpe,** an apparatus in which a heavy fly-wheel or top rotates at high speed, the turning movement resisting change of direction of axis, used as a toy, a compass, a stabiliser of ships, &c (also **gyrostat,** *jī′rō-stat*).—*adj.* **gyroscop′ic.**—*n.* **gyrostab′iliser,** a gyroscopic device for countering the roll of a ship, &c. [L. *gȳrus*—Gr. *gȳros,* a ring.]

gyrfalcon. See **gerfalcon.**

gyrus, *jīr′ús, n.* a convoluted ridge between two grooves: a convolution of the brain. [See **gyre.**]

gyve, *jīv, v.t.* to fetter.—*n.* shackle, fetter. [M.E. *gives, gyves.*]

Neutral vowels in unaccented syllables: *em′pėr-ŏr*; for certain sounds in foreign words see p. ix.

H

H'-bomb, *āch'bom,* (II for *h*ydrogen), hydrogen bomb. (See **bomb.**)

ha', *ha, ha̐,* a shortened form of **have.**

habanera, *(h)ä-bä-nā'rä, n.* a Cuban negro dance or dance-tune in 2-4 time: a piece of instrumental music inspired by this. [*Habana* or Havana, in Cuba.]

habeas-corpus, *hā'be-as-kör'pus, n.* a writ to a jailer to produce a prisoner in person, and to state the reasons of detention. [L., lit. 'have the body', from L. *habēre,* to have, and *corpus,* the body.]

haberdasher, *hab'ér-dash-ér, n.* a seller of small-wares, as ribbons, tape, &c.—*n.* **hab'er-dashery,** goods sold by a haberdasher. [O.Fr. *hapertas,* ety. uncertain.]

habergeon, *hab'ér-jón, ha-bûr'ji-ón, n.* a sleeveless coat of mail. [O.Fr. *haubergeon,* dim. of *hauberc.*]

habiliment, *ha-bil'i-mént, n.* attire (esp. in *pl.*). [Fr. *habillement*—*habiller,* to dress—L. *habilis,* fit, ready—*habēre.*]

habit, *hab'it, n.* ordinary course of behaviour, practice, custom: an aptitude for, or tendency to perform, certain actions, due to frequent repetition: bodily or mental constitution: characteristic mode of growth: outward appearance: dress, esp. any official or customary costume: a garment, esp. a riding-habit.—*v.t.* to dress:—*pr.p.* hab'iting; *pa.p.* hab'ited.—*adj.* **habit-form'ing,** (of a drug) such as a taker will find it difficult or impossible to give up using.—*n.* **hab'it-mak'er,** one who makes women's riding-habits.—*adj.* **habit'ual,** constant: customary: confirmed in a practice by frequent repetition (e.g. a habitual drunkard).—*adv.* **habit'ually.**—*v.t.* **habit'ūate,** to accustom.—*ns.* **hab'itūde,** characteristic condition: custom; **habitué** (*hab-it'ū-ā*), a habitual frequenter (of any place). [Fr.,—L. *habitus,* state, dress—*habēre,* to have.]

habitable, *hab'it-a-bl, adj.* that may be dwelt in.—*ns.* **habitabil'ity, hab'itableness.**—*adv.* **hab'itably.**—*ns.* **hab'itat,** the normal abode or locality of an animal or plant: place of abode generally; **habitā'tion,** act of inhabiting: a dwelling or residence. [Fr.,—L. *habitābilis*—*habitāre, -ātum,* to inhabit, frequentative of *habēre,* to have.]

habitant, *ab-ē-tä, n.* a native of Canada or of Louisiana of French descent. [Fr., inhabitant.]

hacienda, *(h)as-i-en'da, n.* (*Sp. Amer.*) an estate or ranch. [Sp.,—L. *facienda,* things to be done.]

hack, *hak, v.t.* to cut with rough blows: to chop or mangle: to notch: to kick.—*n.* a gash: a chap in the skin: a kick on the shin.—*n.* **hack'saw,** a saw for cutting metal.—*n.* **hacking cough,** a rough, troublesome cough. [Assumed O.E. *haccian,* found in composition *tō-haccian* ; cf. Du. *hakken,* Ger. *hacken.*]

hack, *hak, n.* a horse kept for hire, esp. a poor one: any person overworked on hire: a literary drudge.—*adj.* hired: hackneyed.—*v.t.* and *v.i.* to use, let out, or act, as a hack.—*ns.* **hack'ing-jack'et, -coat,** a waisted jacket with slits in the skirt and flapped pockets on a slant; **hack'-work,** literary drudgery. [Contr. of **hackney.**]

hackle, *hak'l, n.* a comb for hemp or flax: a cock's neck-feather: the hair of a dog's neck: an angler's artificial fly made of a cock's hackle.—*v.t.* to dress with a hackle, as flax: to tear rudely asunder.—*adj.* **hack'ly,** rough and broken, as if hacked or chopped: (*min.*) jagged and rough.—**with hackles up,** roused, ready for combat. [Allied to **heckle.**]

hackney, *hak'ni, n.* a horse for general use, esp. for hire.—*v.t.* to use too much: to make commonplace.—*adjs.* **hack'ney, hack'neyed,** let out for hire: too much used, trite.—*n.* **hack'ney-carriage,** a vehicle let out for hire. [O.Fr. *haquenée,* an ambling nag.]

had, *pa.t.* and *pa.p.* of **have.**

haddock, *had'ók, n.* a sea-fish of the cod family. [M.E. *haddok* ; ety. unknown.]

Hades, *ha'dez, n.* the under-world: the abode of the dead: hell. [Gr. *Aides, Haides.*]

hadji, hajji, *häj'i, n.* one who has performed a Mohammedan pilgrimage to Mecca or Medina. [Ar., 'a pilgrimage'.]

haemal, hemal, *hē'mal, adj.* relating to the blood or blood-vessels.—*adj.* **hae'matoid,** resembling blood. [Gr. *haima, -atos,* blood.]

haematite, hematite, *hem'a-tīt, hē'-ma-tīt, n.* a valuable ore of iron, in some varieties blood red. [Gr. *haima, -atos,* blood.]

haematology, hem-, *hēm-a-tol'ó-ji, n.* the study of blood.—*n.* **haematol'ogist.** [Gr. *haima,* blood, *logos,* discourse.]

haemoglobin, hem-, *hē-mō-glō'bin, n.* the red oxygen-carrying pigment in the red blood-corpuscles. [Gr. *haima,* blood, L. *globus,* a ball.]

haemophilia, hem-, *hēm-,* or *hem-ō-fil'i-a, n.* a constitutional tendency to excessive bleeding when any blood-vessel is even slightly injured.—*n.* **haemophil'iac, hem-,** a person afflicted with haemophilia. [Gr. *haima,* blood, *philia,* love.]

haemorrhage, hem-, *hem'ór-ij, n.* a discharge of blood from the blood-vessels.—*adj.* **haemorrhag'ic** (*-raj'ik*). [Gr. *haimorrhagia*—*haima,* blood, *rhēgnynai,* to burst.]

haemorrhoids, hem-, *hem'ór-oidz, n. pl.* dilated veins about the anus, liable to discharge blood, piles.—*adj.* **haemorrhoid'al.** [Gr. *haimorrhoides*—*haima,* blood, *rheein,* to flow.]

hafnium, *haf'ni-úm, n.* a metallic element (symbol Hf; at. no. 72) akin to zirconium, found in 1922 by two professors at Copenhagen. [L. *Hafnia,* Copenhagen.]

haft, *häft, n.* a handle (e.g. of a knife). [O.E. *hæft* ; Ger. *heft.*]

fāte, fär; mē, hûr (her); *mīne; mōte, för; mūte; mōōn, fōōt;* THEN (then)

hag, *hag*, *n.* an ugly old woman—originally a witch.—*adj.* **hagg′ish**, hag-like.—*adv.* **hagg′ishly.**—*adj.* **hag′-ridd′en**, ridden by witches, as a horse: troubled by nightmare: obsessed: tormented. [O.E. *hægtesse*, a witch; Ger. *hexe*.]

haggard, *hag′ärd*, *n.* an untamed hawk.—*adj.* untamed: lean: hollow-eyed.—*adv.* **hagg′ardly.** [O.Fr. *hagard*.]

haggis, *hag′is*, *n.* a Scottish dish made of the heart, lungs, and liver of a sheep, calf, &c., chopped up with suet, onions, oatmeal, &c., seasoned and boiled in a sheep's stomach-bag.

haggle, *hag′l*, *v.t.* to cut unskilfully.—*v.i.* to bargain contentiously: to stick at trifles, to cavil.—*n.* **hagg′ler.** [A variant of **hackle**.]

Hagiographa, *hag-i-og′ra-fa*, or *hāj-*, *n.pl.* certain books (Psalms, Proverbs, Job, &c.) constituting a division of the Old Testament—the other major divisions being the Law and the Prophets.—*n.* **hagiog′rapher**, one of the writers of the Hagiographa: a sacred writer: a writer of saints' lives. [Gr. *hagiographa* (*biblia*)—*hagios*, holy, *graphein*, to write.]

hagiology, *hag-i-ol′o-ji*, or *hāj-*, *n.* history and legends of saints. [Gr. *hagios*, holy, *logos*, discourse.]

hagioscope, *hag′i-ō-skōp*, or *hāj′-*, *n.* a squint, an opening through an interior wall of a church to allow people in the transepts to see the altar. [Gr. *hagios*, holy, *skopeein*, to look at.]

ha-ha, *hä′-hä*, **haw-haw**, *hö′-hö*, *n.* a sunk fence. [Fr. *haha*.]

hail, *hāl*, *n.* (*obs.*) health: a call from a distance: greeting: earshot.—*v.t.* to call to, from a distance: to greet, welcome (as).—(*lit.*) may you be in health.—*adj.* **hail′-fell′ow** (**-well-met′**), readily friendly and familiar.—also *n.* and *adv.*—**hail from**, to come from, belong to (a place). [O.N. *heill*, health.]

hail, *hāl*, *n.* frozen rain or particles of ice falling from the clouds.—*v.i.* to shower hail.—*v.t.* to pour down in rapid succession.—*n.* **hail′stone**, a single stone or ball of hail. [O.E. *hægl* (*hagol*); Ger. *hagel*.]

hair, *hār*, *n.* a filament growing from the skin of an animal: a mass of hairs, esp. that covering the human head: an outgrowth of the epidermis of a plant: a fibre: anything very small and fine.—*ns.* **hair′breadth**, **hair′s-breadth**, a minute distance.—*adj.* very close or narrow.—*ns.* **hair′cloth**, cloth made partly or entirely of hair; **hair′dresser**, one whose occupation is the cutting, dressing, &c., of hair.—*adj.* **haired**, having hair—as *black*-haired, *fair*-haired, &c.—*ns.* **hair′iness**; **hair′-pen′cil**, a fine paint-brush; **hair′-piece**, a length of false hair or a wig covering only part of the head; **hair′-pin**, a bent wire, or the like, used for fastening the hair.—*adj.* narrowly U-shaped (of a bend on a road).—*n.* **hair′-pow′der**, (*hist.*) white powder for dusting hair.—*adj.* **hair′-rais′ing**, terrifying.—*ns.* **hair′-shirt**, a penitent's shirt of haircloth; **hair′-slide**, a clip to keep hair in place; **hair′-spring**, a very fine hair-like spring coiled up within the balance-wheel of a watch; **hair′-stroke**, in writing, a fine stroke with the pen; **hair′-trigg′er**, a trigger which discharges a gun or pistol by hair-like spring; **hair′-worm**, a worm, like a horse-hair, which when young lives in the bodies of insects.—*adj.* **hair′y**, of or resembling hair: covered with hair.—**by the short hairs**, in a powerless position, at one's mercy; **get in one's hair**, to become a source of irritation; **keep one's hair on** (*slang*), to keep cool; **let one's hair down**, to forget reserve and speak or behave freely; **make the hair stand on end**, to terrify; **not to turn a hair**, to remain perfectly calm; **split hairs**, to make subtle distinctions; **to a hair**, **to the turn of a hair**, accurately. [O.E. *hær*; Ger., Du., and Dan. *haar*.]

Haitian, *hā′ti-án*, *adj.* of, or pertaining to, *Haiti*, in the W. Indies.—*n.* a native or citizen of Haiti: the language of Haiti (a debased form of French).

hake, *hāk*, *n.* a genus of fishes allied to the cod. [Prob. Scand.; cf. Norw. *hake-fisk*, lit. 'hook-fish'.]

hakeem, hakim, *hä-kēm′*, *n.* a physician. [Ar.]

hakim, *hä′kim*, *n.* a judge or governor in Mohammedan India. [Ar.]

halberd, *hal′bérd*, *n.* a weapon consisting of an axe-like blade with a hook or pick on its back, at the end of a long shaft.—*n.* **halberdier′** (*-dēr′*), one armed with a halberd. [O.Fr. *halebard*—Mid. High Ger. *helmbarde*—*halm*, handle, or *helm*, helmet; O.H.G. *barta*, an axe.]

halcyon, *hal′si-ón*, *n.* the kingfisher, once believed to make a floating nest on the sea, which remained calm while the bird was hatching.—*adj.* calm, peaceful, happy. [L. *alcyon*—Gr. *alkyōn*; as if *hals*, sea, *kyōn*, conceiving.]

hale, *hāl*, *adj.* healthy, robust. [North. form, from O.E. *hāl*; the S. and Midl. development gives **whole**; parallel form **hail** (1)—O.N.]

hale, *hāl*, *v.t.* to drag. [O.Fr. *haler*]

half, *häf*, *n.* one of two equal parts of a whole:—*pl.* **halves** (*hävz*).—*adj.* consisting of, forming, one of two equal parts: incomplete (e.g. *half measures*).—*adv.* to the extent of one-half: in part: imperfectly.—*adj.* and *adv.* **half-and-half**, in the proportion of one to one.—*ns.* **half′-back**, in football, a position directly behind the forwards: a player occupying this position; **half′-bind′ing**, a style of bookbinding in which the backs and corners are of leather, and the sides of paper or cloth; **half′-blood**, relation between those who have only one parent in common: a half-breed; **half′-blue**, a distinction less important than a blue (q.v.) and usu. a step towards one; **half′-boot**, a boot reaching halfway to the knee; **half′-breed**, a person born of or descended from different races.—*adj.* **half′-bred**, poorly bred or trained: mongrel.—*ns.* **half′-broth′er**, **half′-sis′ter**, a brother or sister by one parent only; **half′-caste**, a half-breed; **half′-cock** (see **cock**); **half′(-)crown**, a coin, orig. silver, later cupronickel, worth 2s. 6d. (12½p) (withdrawn 1970); **half′-doz′en**, six.—*adj.* **half′-heart′ed**, lacking in zeal.—*ns.* **half′-hitch**, a simple knot tied round an object; **half′-life**, the period of time in which the activity of a radioactive substance falls to half its original value; **half′-mast**, the position of a flag partly lowered in respect for the dead or in signal of distress; **half′-moon**, the moon when only half of it is illuminated: anything semicircular; **half′-pay**,

Neutral vowels in unaccented syllables: *em′pér-ór*; for certain sounds in foreign words see p. ix.

320

reduced pay, as of naval or military officers when not in active service; **halfpenny** (*hā'-pen-i*), a coin worth ½ d. (withdrawn 1969), or half a new penny.—*pl.* **halfpence** (*hā'pēns*), **half'pennies; half'pennyworth, ha'p'orth** (*hā'-pórth*), the value of a halfpenny: a very small quantity; **half'-sov'ereign**, a gold coin, no longer in circulation: **half'-time'**, half of full or whole time: in industry, half the time usually worked: (*sport*) a short break halfway through a game; **half'-tim'er**, one, who works only half the full time.—*adj.* **half-tone**, representing light and shade photographically by dots of different sizes.—*ns.* **half'-track**, a motor vehicle with wheels in front and caterpillar tracks behind; **half'-truth**, a statement conveying part, but not the whole, of the truth.—*adv.* **half'-way**, at half the way or distance: imperfectly.—*adj.* equally distant from two points.—*n.* **half'-wit**, an idiot.—*adjs.* **half'-witt'ed; half'-year'ly,** occurring at every half-year or twice in a year.—*adv.* twice in a year.—**by half**, by a long way, **by halves,** incompletely; **go halves**, to share equally with another. [O.E. *half, healf,* side, half; cf. Ger. *halb,* Dan. *halv.*]

halibut, *hal'i-but, n.* the largest of the flat fishes. [M.E. *hali,* holy, and *butte,* a flounder, plaice, the fish being much eaten on holy days; cf. Du. *heilbot,* Ger. *heilbutt.*]

halidom, *hal'i-dóm, n.* a holy place or thing—esp. in an oath. [O.E. *hāligdōm*—*hālig,* holy.]

halitosis, *hal-i-tō'sis, n.* foul breath. [L. *hālitus,* breath.]

hall, *höl, n.* the main room in a great house: a space just inside an entrance door: a large chamber for public gatherings: an edifice in which courts of justice are held: a manor house: the main building of a college: the great room in which the students dine together: a place for special professional education.—*n.* **hall'-mark,** the authorised stamp impressed on gold or silver articles at Goldsmiths Hall: any mark of authenticity, or of sterling quality.—*v.t.* to stamp with a hall-mark. [O.E. *hall* (*heall*); Du. *hal,* O.N. *höll,* &c.]

hallelujah, halleluiah, *hal-é-lōō'ya, interj.* and *n.* the exclamation 'Praise Jehovah': a song of praise to God. [Heb. *hallelū,* praise ye, and *Jāh,* Jehovah.]

halliard. See **halyard.**

halloo, *ha-lōō', n.* a cry to urge a chase or to draw attention.—*v.i.* to cry dogs on: to raise an outcry.—*v.t.* to encourage or chase with shouts. [Perh. variant of **hollo.**]

hallow, *hal'o, v.t.* to make holy, to consecrate: to reverence.—*n.* (*obs.*) a saint.—*ns.* **hall'owe'en,** the evening before All-hallows or All Saints' Day; **hall'owmas,** the Feast of All Saints, 1st November. [O.E. *hālgian,* to hallow—*hālig,* holy.]

hallucination, *hal-(y)ōō-sin-ā'sh(ó)n, n.* a vision without objective reality or a sensation with no external cause—a delusion.—*adjs.* **hallū'cinative, hallū'cinatory,** productive of, or partaking of, hallucination.—*n.* **hallū'cinogen,** a drug producing hallucinatory sensations.—*adj.* **hallūcinogen'ic.** [L. *(h)a(l)lūcinārī, -ātus,* to wander in mind.]

halm. See **haulm.'**

halo, *hā'lō, n.* a ring of light or colours, esp. one round the sun or moon caused by refraction by ice-crystals, or round the head of a saint in a painting: any ideal or sentimental glory:—*pl.* **halo(e)s** (*hā'lōz*). [L. *halōs*—Gr. *halōs,* a round threshing-floor.]

halogen, *hal'ō-jén, n.* any member of a group of elements (astatine, chlorine, bromine, iodine, fluorine) that form with metals compounds like common salt (sodium *chloride*). [Gr. *hals,* salt, *gennaein,* to produce.]

halser, *höz'ér, n.* Same as **hawser.**

halt, *hölt, v.i.* to come to a standstill: to make a temporary stop.—*v.t.* to cause to stop.—*n.* a standstill: a stopping-place. [Ger. *halt,* stoppage.]

halt, *hölt, v.i.* to be lame, to limp: to hesitate.—*adj.* lame—*n.* a limp. [O.E. *halt* (*healt*); Dan. *halt.*]

halter, *hölt'ér, n.* a head-rope for holding and leading a horse: a rope for hanging criminals: a strong strap or cord. *v.t.* to catch or bind with a rope. [O.E. *hœlftre;* Ger. *halfter.*]

halve, *häv, v.t.* to divide into halves: in golf, to draw. [**half.**]

halyard, halliard, *hal'yárd, n.* (*naut.*) a rope for hoisting or lowering a sail, yard, or flag. [From *halier, hallyer*—**hale** (2); altered through association with **sail-yard.**]

ham, *ham, n.* the back of the thigh: the thigh of an animal, esp. of a hog salted and dried; an amateur or inexperienced actor or performer: an amateur radio operator: (*U.S.*) a nitwit.—*v.i.* to overact. *adjs.* **ham' fist'ed, ham'-hand'ed,** clumsy. [O.E. *hamm;* cf. dial. Ger. *hamme.*]

hamadryad, *ha-ma-drī'ad, n.* (*myth.*) a wood nymph who lived and died with the tree in which she dwelt: a large poisonous Indian snake: a baboon of Abyssinia:—*pl.* **hamadry'ads, hamadry'ades** (*-ēz*). [Gr. *hamadryas*—*hama,* together, *drys,* a tree.]

hamartia, *ha-mär'tē-a, n.* in a literary work, the flaw or defect in the character of the hero which leads to his downfall, according to Aristotle. [Gr. *hamartiā,* failure, error of judgment, sin.]

hamburger, *ham'bûrg-ér, n.* Hamburg steak, chopped meat seasoned and cooked: this shaped into a round, flat cake, fried, and put into a bread roll. [*Hamburg,* Germany.]

hame, *hām, n.* either of two curved bars to which the traces are attached in the harness of a draught-horse. [Cf. Du. *haam,* Low Ger. *ham.*]

Hamitic, *ham-it'ik, adj.* pertaining to *Ham,* a son of Noah, or to his supposed descendants in N.E. Africa—a dark-brown, long-headed race: (of a language) belonging to a N. African family distantly related to Semitic.

hamlet, *ham'let, n.* a cluster of houses in the country, a small village. [O.Fr. *hamelet,* dim. of *hamel*—from Gmc.; O.E. *hām.*]

hammer, *ham'ér, n.* a tool for beating or breaking hard substances, driving nails, or the like: a striking-piece in the mechanism of a clock, piano, &c.: the apparatus that causes explosion of the charge in a firearm: the mallet with which an auctioneer announces that an article is sold.—*v.t.* to drive, beat, shape, or fashion with a hammer: to produce or create by intellectual labour (with *out*); to beat severely.—*v.i.* to use a hammer: to make a loud knocking.—*ns.* **hamm'erhead,** any of various sharks with hammer-shaped head; **hamm'erman,** a man who hammers, as a blacksmith, goldsmith, &c.; **hamm'er-toe,** a condition in which a toe is permanently bent upwards at the base and doubled down upon itself.—**hammer home,** to impress (a fact) strongly (on someone); **hammer and sickle,** the emblem (adopted 1923) on the flag of the U.S.S.R., symbolising the worker in industry and on the farm; **hammer-and-tongs,** with great noise and vigour, violently.—**bring to the hammer,** to sell by auction; **under the hammer,** up for sale by auction. [O.E. *hamor*; Ger. *hammer*; O.N. *hamarr.*]

hammock, *ham'ŏk, n.* a piece of strong cloth or netting suspended by the ends, and used as a bed or couch. [Sp. *hamaca,* of Carib (q.v.) origin.]

hamper, *ham'pėr, v.t.* to impede the free movement of: (*lit.* and *fig.*) to obstruct: to derange (e.g. a lock).—*n.* an impediment. [Cf. O.N. and Mod. Icel. *hemja,* to restrain; Ger. *hemmen.*]

hamper, *ham'pėr, n.* a large basket with a lid, a basket-work case. [Obs. *hanaper*—O.Fr. *hanapier,* a case for a *hanap* or drinking-cup.]

hamster, *ham'stėr, n.* a rodent with large cheek pouches, native of Europe east of Rhine and of part of western Asia. [Ger.]

hamstring, *ham'string, n.* in man, one of the tendons behind the knee: in quadrupeds, the great tendon at the back of the hock of the hind-leg.—*v.t.* to lame by cutting the hamstring. [**ham** and **string.**]

hand, *hand, n.* the extremity of the arm below the wrist: a similar part of any of the four limbs of a monkey: the fore-foot of a quadruped: a pointer or index: a measure of four inches: a workman, esp. in a factory: share (in performance): control, authority: assistance: agency (e.g. *by the hands of*): manner of performing: skill (e.g. *a hand for pastry, at carpentry*): pledge: style of handwriting: signature: the set of cards held by a player at one deal: side: direction: round of applause.—*v.t.* to pass with the hand: to lead or conduct: to transfer or deliver (with *over, in*): (*fig.*) to pass on (e.g. *to hand down to one's successors*).—**hand-,** in composition, by hand or direct bodily operation (as **hand'-made'**); operated by hand (as **hand-or'gan**); for the hand (as **hand'-rail**); held in the hand (as **hand'-bask'et**).—*ns.* **hand'-bag,** a bag for small articles, carried in the hand; **hand'-ball,** a game between goals in which the ball is struck with the palm of the hand: (**hand'ball**) a game similar to fives in which a ball is struck with the gloved hand against a wall or walls (usu. four); **hand'-barr'ow,** a barrow without a wheel, carried by handles: a two-wheeled barrow with handles; **hand'bill,** a pruning-hook used in the hand: a bill or loose sheet bearing an announcement; **hand'-book,** a manual or guide-book; **hand'-breadth,** the breadth of a hand: a palm (measure of length); **hand'-cart,** a small cart drawn by hand; **hand'cuff** (esp. in *pl.*), a shackle for the

wrists, a pair of metal rings joined by a chain.—*v.t.* to put handcuffs on.—*n.* **hand'fast,** a contract, betrothal.—*v.t.* to betroth.—*ns.* **hand'ful,** enough to fill the hand: a small number or quantity: a charge that taxes one's powers:—*pl.* **hand'fuls; hand'gall'op,** an easy gallop, in which the speed of the horse is restrained by the bridle-hand; **hand'-glass,** a glass or small glazed frame used to protect plants: a small mirror; **hand'-grenade',** a grenade to be thrown by the hand.—*adj.* **hand'less,** without hands: unskilful with the hands, awkward.—*ns.* **hand'maid, hand'maiden,** (*arch.* or *fig.*) a female servant; **hand'-out,** something given out, as food or clothing: an official news item given to the press for publication; **hand'-post,** a finger-post, guidepost; **hand'-spike,** a bar used as a hand-lever; **hand'spring,** a cartwheel or similar somersault; **hand's'-turn,** a single small act of work; **hand'writing,** written, script: style of writing.—**hand and** (or **in**) **glove (with),** on very intimate terms: in close co-operation; **hand in hand,** with hands mutually clasped: in close association; **hand it to one,** (*slang*) to acknowledge one's skill, success in the matter; **hand out,** to distribute: to give, bestow; **hands down,** with great ease; **hands off!** keep off! **hands up!** a call to surrender; **hand to hand,** at close quarters; **hand to mouth,** without thought for the future, precariously.—**at first hand,** directly from the source; **at hand,** near in place or time; **be no hand at,** to be unable to do skilfully; **bear a hand,** to help; **change hands,** to pass to a new owner; **get one's hand in,** get into the way or knack; **have a hand in,** to take part in; **in good hands,** in the care of those who may be trusted to treat one well: of an affair, in the care of those who will carry it through efficiently; **in hand,** as present payment: in preparation: under control; **lend a hand,** to assist; **old hand,** a veteran; **on one's hands,** under one's care or responsibility; **out of hand,** at once: out of control; **throw in one's hand,** give up a venture; **tie one's hands,** (*fig.*) to render powerless; **try one's hand at,** to attempt: to test one's prowess at; **under one's hand,** with one's proper signature attached; **wash one's hands (of),** to disclaim responsibility (for; Matt. xxvii. 24). [O.E. *hand.*]

handicap, *hand'i-kap, v.t.* to impose special disadvantages or impediments upon, in order to offset advantages and make a better contest: (*fig.*) to place at a disadvantage.—*n.* any contest so adjusted, or the condition imposed: (*fig.*) a disadvantage.—*adj.* **handicapped,** suffering from some disability or disadvantage. [Prob. *hand i' cap,* from the drawing from a cap in an old lottery game.]

handicraft, *hand'i-kräft, n.* a manual craft or trade.—*n.* **hand'icraftsman,** a man skilled in a manual art. [O.E. *handcræft*—*hand* and *cræft,* craft, assimilated to **handiwork.**]

handiwork, handywork, *hand'i-wûrk, n.* work done by the hands: work done personally: work of skill or wisdom. [O.E. *handgewerc*—*hand,* and *gewerc,* work.]

handkerchief, *hang'kėr-chif, n.* a piece of material for wiping the nose, &c.: a neckerchief. [**hand** and **kerchief.**]

Neutral vowels in unaccented syllables: *em'pėr-ôr*; for certain sounds in foreign words see p. ix.

handle, *hand'l, v.t.* to touch, hold, or feel with the hand: to wield, use: to manage (a person, affair): to deal with: to deal in (goods).—*n.* that part of anything held in the hand: (*fig.*) that of which use is made—a tool, an opportunity.—*ns.* **hand'ler,** one who handles: one who trains and uses a dog which works for the police or an armed service: one who holds, controls, or shows off an animal at a show, &c.; **hand'ling.—a handle to one's name,** a title; **fly off the handle,** to lose one's temper. [O.E. *handlian*—*hand,* a hand.]

handsel, hansel, *hand'sel, han'sel, n.* a gift at New Year: an inaugural gift: earnest-money: the first use of anything.—*v.t.* to give a handsel: to use or do anything the first time. [O.E. *handselen,* hand-gift; or O.N. *handsal.*]

handsome, *han'som, adj.* good-looking: dignified: generous: ample.—*adv.* **hand'somely.**—*n.* **hand'someness.** [**hand** and suffx. *-some*; cf. Du. *handzaam.*]

handy, *han'di, adj.* dexterous: ready to the hand, near: convenient.—*n.* **hand'y-man,** a man for doing odd jobs. [**hand.**]

hang, *hang, v.t.* to support from above against gravity, to suspend: to decorate with pictures, &c., as a wall: to put to death by suspending by the neck: to exhibit (works of art): to prevent (a jury) from coming to a decision.—*v.i.* to be suspended, so as to allow of free lateral motion: to droop: to hover or impend: to be in suspense:—*pa.t.* and *pa.p.* hanged (by the neck) or hung.—*n.* action of hanging: mode in which anything hangs or is disposed.—*n.* **hang'-dog,** a low fellow.—*adj.* like such a fellow, esp. in his sneaking look.—*ns.* **hang'er,** that on which anything is hung: a short sword, curved near the point; **hang'er-on,** an importunate acquaintance: a dependent.—*adj.* **hang'ing,** deserving death by hanging.—*n.* death by the halter: (esp. in *pl.*) that which is hung, as drapery, &c.—*ns.* **hang'-man,** a public executioner; **hang'over,** a survival: after-effects esp. of drinking; **hang' up** (*slang*), a problem, &c., about which one is obsessed.—**hanging garden** (see **garden**); **hanging matter,** a crime leading to capital punishment: (*coll.*) a serious matter; **hung jury,** a jury that fails to agree.—**hang about,** to loiter; **hang back,** to hesitate; **hang by a thread,** to be in a very precarious position or condition; **hang, draw, and quarter,** to hang, cut down while still alive, disembowel, and cut in pieces for exposure at different places; **hang fire,** to be long in exploding or discharging, as a gun: (also *fig.*); **hang on,** to cling (to): to give close admiring attention (to): to linger: to depend upon: to weigh down or oppress; **hang out** (*slang*), to lodge or reside; **hang out for,** to insist on; **hang together,** to keep united: to be consistent; **hung up** (*slang*), obsessed. [O.E. *hangian* and O.N. *hanga* and *hengja*; Du., Ger. *hangen.*]

hangar, *hang'ar, hang'gär, n.* a shed for carriages, aircraft, &c. [Fr.]

hank, *hangk, n.* a coil or skein (esp. 840 yds. of cotton, 560 of worsted): a loop. [O.N. *hanki,* a hasp.]

hanker, *hangk'er, v.i.* to yearn (with *after, for*). [Perh. conn. with **hang**; cf. Du. *hunkeren.*]

Hanoverian, *han-ō-vē'ri-án, adj.* pertaining to *Hanover,* as of the dynasty that came to the British throne in 1714.—*n.* a native of Hanover: a supporter of the house of Hanover, opp. to a Jacobite.

Hansard, *han'särd, n.* the printed reports of the debates in parliament, first published by Luke *Hansard* (1752-1828).

Hanse, *hans, n.* a league, esp. the league of German commercial cities in the Middle Ages.—*adj.* **Hanseatic** (*han-si-at'ik*). [O.Fr. *hanse*—O.H.G. *hansa,* a band of men.]

hansel, See **handsel.**

hansom, *han'som, n.* a light two-wheeled cab with driver's seat raised behind. [Invented by Joseph A. *Hansom,* 1803-82.]

hap, *hap, n.* chance, fortune, accident.—*adj.* **hap'less,** unlucky, unhappy.—*adv.* **hap'lessly.** —*n.* **hap'lessness.**—*adv.* **hap'ly,** by hap, chance, or accident: perhaps, it may be. [O.N. *happ,* good luck.]

haphazard, *hap-haz'ard, n.* chance, accident.— *adj.* random, accidental.—*adv.* at random. [**hap, hazard.**]

happen, *hap'én, v.i.* to befall, to take place, to occur.—*adv.* (*dial.*) perhaps, maybe.—*n.* **happ'ening,** event: (*theat.*) a performance consisting of discrete events, in which elements from everyday life are put together in a non-realistic way, usu. demanding audience participation: a weird event.—**happen on, upon,** to come on by chance. [**hap.**]

happy, *hap'i, adj.* lucky: possessing or enjoying pleasure or good: pleased: furnishing or expressing enjoyment: apt, felicitous (e.g. a phrase): in composition, delighted by the possession of or use of, as *power-happy, bomb-happy* usu. implying irresponsibility or dazed as a result of.—*adv.* **happ'ily.**—*n.* **happ'iness**—*adj.* **happ'y-go-luck'y,** easy going, irresponsible.—**happy medium,** a prudent or sensible middle course. [**hap.**]

hara-kiri, *hä'ra-kē'rē, n.* ceremonious suicide formerly common in Japan. [Jap. *hara,* belly, *kiri,* cut.]

harangue, *ha-rang', n.* a loud speech addressed to a multitude: a pompous or wordy address.—*v.i.* to deliver a harangue.—*v.t.* to address by a harangue:—*pr.p.* haranguing (*-rang'ing*); pa.p. harangued (*-rangd'*).—*n.* **harang'uer.** [O.Fr. *arenge, harangue,* from O.H.G. *hring,* a ring of auditors.]

harass, *har'as, v.t.* to distress, wear out: to annoy, to pester:—*pr.p.* har'assing, *pa.p.* and *pa.t.* har'assed.—*ns.* **har'asser; har'assment.** [O.Fr. *harasser*; prob. from *harer,* to incite a dog.]

harbinger, *här'bin-jér, n.* a forerunner, a pioneer: originally, one who goes forward to provide lodging. [M.E. *herbergeour,* allied to **harbour.**]

harbour, (in *U.S.,* **harbor**) *här'bor, n.* any refuge or shelter: a port for ships—obs. form *har'borough.*—*v.t.* to lodge or entertain: to protect: to possess or indulge, as thoughts—in all senses, the object is usu. bad or evil.—*v.i.* to take shelter.—*ns.* **har'bourage,** place of shelter: entertainment; **har'bourer,** one who harbours or entertains.—*adj.* **har'bourless.**—*n.* **har'bourmas'ter,** the public officer who has charge of a harbour. [M.E. *herberwe*—an assumed O.E. *herebeorg*—*here,* army, *beorg,* protection.]

hard, *härd, adj.* not easily penetrated, firm, solid: stiff: difficult to understand: difficult to do: difficult to bear, painful: severe, strenuous, rigorous: unfeeling: niggardly, ungenerous: intractable: of sound, harsh: of colour, brillant and glaring: (of drug) habit-forming: (of news) definite, substantiated: (of drink) very alcoholic: (*phonet.*) of *c, g,* pron. as stop consonants (e.g. *c* in *cat, g* in *good*; cf. **soft**).—*adv.* with urgency, vigour, &c.: earnestly, forcibly, with difficulty, as in **hard-earned,** &c.: close, near, as in **hard by.**—*adv.* **hard-a-lee,** close to the lee-side, &c.—*adj.* **hard'-and-fast',** rigid.—*ns.* **hard'board,** fibreboard that has been compressed in drying; **hard'-cash,** ready money; **hard coal,** anthracite (cf.*soft coal*); **hard core** (*fig.*), something very resistant to change, as e.g. the most loyal or the most die-hard members of a group; **hard currency,** metallic money: the currency of any foreign country with which one has an adverse balance of payments; **hard'-drink'er,** a heavy and constant drinker.—*v.t.* **hard'en,** to make hard or harder: make firm: strengthen: to confirm in wickedness: to make insensible.—*v.i.* to become hard or harder, either *lit.* or *fig.*—*adj.* **hard'ened,** made hard, unfeeling.—*n.* **hard'ener.**—*adjs.* **hard'-fav'oured,** having coarse features; **hard'feat'ured,** of hard, coarse, or forbidding features; **hard'-fist'ed,** having hard or strong fists or hands: close-fisted, niggardly; **hard'-fought,** stubbornly contested; **hard'-grained,** having a close firm grain: forbidding; **hard'-hand'ed,** having hard hands: rough, severe; **hard'-headed,** shrewd, intelligent; **hard'-heart'ed,** pitiless, cruel; **hard'ish,** somewhat hard.—*n.* **hard'-la'bour,** severe work, esp. that compulsorily performed by prisoners.—*adj.* **hard'line,** of an attitude or policy (**hard line**), definite and unyielding: having such an attitude or policy.—*n.* **hard'liner.**—*adv.* **hard'ly,** with difficulty: scarcely, not quite: severely, harshly.—*adj.* **hard'-mouthed,** having a mouth hard or insensible to the bit: not easily managed.—*ns.* **hard'ness** (*min.*), power of, and resistance to, scratching; **hard'-pan,** a hard layer often underlying the superficial soil (*lit.* and *fig.*); **hard'ship,** a hard state, or that which is hard to bear, as toil, injury, &c.; **hard'tack,** ship's biscuit—hard and saltless.—*adj.* **hard'-vis'aged,** of a hard, coarse, or forbidding visage.—*ns.* **hard'ware,** goods made of the baser metals, such as iron or copper: mechanical equipment: in computing, equipment used in processing information; **hard'-wood,** timber of deciduous trees, whose comparatively slow growth produces compact hard wood, as oak, ash, elm, walnut, &c.—**hard facts,** inescapable, undeniable facts; **hard hit,** seriously hurt, as by a loss of money; **hard lines,** bad luck; **hard of hearing,** pretty deaf; **hard sell,** aggressive and insistent method of advertising or selling; **hard swearing,** swearing (as a witness) persistently to what is false, perjury; **hard up,** short of money; **hard water,** water containing a relatively large proportion of dissolved salts, esp. of calcium and magnesium salts.—be

hard put to it, to be in, have, great difficulty; **die hard,** to make a vain and desperate struggle for life: to be unwilling to die, or to be slow in dying; **go hard with,** turn out ill for. [O.E. *heard,* Du. *hard,* Ger. *hart*; allied to Gr. *kratys,* strong.]

hards, *härdz, n. pl.* coarse or refuse flax.

hardy, *härd'i, adj.* daring, brave, resolute: impudent: able to bear cold, exposure, or fatigue: (of plants) able to grow in the open air throughout the year.—*ns.* **hard'ihood, hard'iness.**—*adv.* **hard'ily.**—**hardy annual,** an annual plant which can survive frosts: (*fig.*) a story, topic, &c., which crops up regularly; **half hardy** (of plants), able to grow in the open air except in winter. [O.Fr. *hardi*—O.H.G. *hartjan,* to make hard.]

hare, *här, n.* any of various timid and very swift rodents with divided upper lip and long hind-legs.—*v.i.* (*coll.*) to run with great speed, as if pursued.—*ns.* **hare-and-hounds,** a paper-chase; **hare'bell,** a plant with blue bell-shaped flowers.—*adj.* **hare'-brained,** giddy, very rash.—*n.* **hare'-lip,** a fissure in the upper human lip like that of a hare.—*adj.* **hare'-lipped.**—**jugged hare,** hare cut into pieces and stewed with wine and other seasoning. [O.E. *hara*; Du. *haas,* Dan. *hare,* Ger. *hase.*]

harem, *hä'rem, hä-rēm', n.* the portion of a Mohammedan house allotted to females: the wives and concubines of a Mohammedan. [Ar. *harīm, haram,* anything forbidden—*harama,* to forbid.]

haricot, *har'i-kō, -kot, n.* a stew of mutton and beans or other vegetables: the kidney-bean or French bean. [Fr. *haricot.*]

hari-kari, *härē-kär'ē,* an incorrect form of **hara-kiri.**

hark, *härk, v.i.* to listen (usu. with *to*).—**hark away, back, forward,** cries to urge hounds and hunters; **hark back,** to revert to a previous topic, esp. to a sore subject, as a grievance). [Same root as **hearken.**]

harl, *härl, n.* fibre of flax, feathers, &c [L. Ger.]

harl, *härl, v.t.* (*Scot.*) to roughcast. [M.E. *harlen,* to drag; ety. uncertain.]

Harlequin, *här'lē-kwin,* or *-kin, n.* a figure in old Italian comedy and old French pantomime, in a parti-coloured dress with a visor and magic sword, prone to play tricks: a buffoon.—*adj.* parti-coloured.—*n.* **harlequināde',** the portion of a pantomime in which the harlequin plays a chief part. [Fr. *harlequin, arlequin,* prob. the same as O.Fr. *Hellequin,* a devil in mediaeval legend.]

harlot, *här'lot, n.* a prostitute.—Also *adj.*—*n.* **har'lotry,** prostitution: unchastity. [O.Fr. *herlot, arlot,* a base fellow; origin unknown.]

harm, *härm, n.* injury: moral wrong.—*v.t.* to injure.—*adj.* **harm'ful,** hurtful.—*adv.* **harm'fully.**—*n.* **harm'fulness.**—*adj.* **harm'less,** not injurious: (*arch.*) innocent: unharmed.—*adv.* **harm'lessly.**—*n.* **harm'lessness.** [O.E. *hearm*; Ger. *harm.*]

harmattan, *här-mä-tan', här-mät'an, n.* a dry dusty N.E. wind from the desert in W. Africa. [African word.]

harmonic, -al, *här-mon'ik, -äl, adjs.* (*arch.*) musical: pertaining to harmony: concordant.—*n.* (**harmonic**) an overtone (*q.v.*): a

---

Neutral vowels in unaccented syllables: *em'pėr-ör*; for certain sounds in foreign words see p. ix.

flutelike sound produced on a violin, &c., by lightly touching a string at a node: (in *pl.* form as *sing.*) musical acoustics.—*n.* **harmon'ica,** the musical glasses invented by Benjamin Franklin, consisting of a series of bell-shaped glasses placed on a framework that revolved about its centre while the rims were touched by the performer's moistened finger: a musical instrument in which strips of glass or metal are struck by a hammer: a mouthorgan.—*adv.* **harmon'ically.**—*n.* **harmon'icon,** a harmonica: a large barrel-organ.—*adj.* **harmō'nious,** having harmony: concordant: congruous: free from dissension: justly proportioned.—*adv.* **harmō'niously.**—*n.* **harmō'niousness.**—*v.i.* **har'monīse,** to be in harmony: to agree.—*v.t.* to bring into harmony: to cause to agree: (*mus.*) to provide parts to.—*ns.* **harmonisā'tion; harmonīs'er; har'monist,** one skilled in harmony: a musical composer; **harmōn'ium,** a reed-organ, esp. one in which the air is forced (not drawn) through the reeds; **har'mony,** a fitting together of parts so as to form a connected whole: in art, a normal state of completeness and order in the relations of things to each other: (*mus.*) a simultaneous combination of accordant sounds: concord: a collation of parallel passages intended to demonstrate agreement—as of the Gospels.— **harmonic minor scale,** a form of minor scale which has the semitones between the 2nd and 3rd and 5th and 6th, with an interval of three semitones between the 6th and 7th; **harmonic progression,** a series of numbers whose reciprocals form an arithmetical progression (q.v.); (**simple**) **harmonic motion,** a type of vibration which may be represented by projecting on to a diameter the uniform motion of a point round a circle—the motion of a pendulum bob is approximately this. [Gr. *harmonia,* music *harmos,* a joint, fitting.]

harness, *här'nes, n.* arrangement of straps, bands, &c., forming the equipment of a horse: similar equipment for attaching something: formerly, armour of man or horse: apparatus in a loom for moving warp threads.—*v.t.* to put harness on: to attach by harness.—**in harness,** working, not on holiday or retired. [O.Fr. *harneis,* armour.]

harp, *härp, n.* a musical instrument played by plucking strings stretched from a curved neck to an inclined sound-board.—*v.i.* to play on the harp: to dwell tediously (on anything).—*ns.* **harp'er, harp'ist,** a player on the harp.—**harp on one string,** to dwell tediously and continually on one subject.—**Jew's-harp** (see **Jew**). [O.E. *hearpe;* Ger. *harfe.*]

harpoon, *här-pōōn', n.* a barbed dart, esp. one for striking and killing whales.—*v.t.* to strike with the harpoon.—*ns.* **harpoon'er, harpooneer',** one who uses a harpoon. [Fr. *harpon—harpe,* a clamp, perh.—L. *harpa,* Gr. *harpē,* sickle.]

harpsichord, *härp'si-körd, n.* a keyed musical instrument, where the sound is produced by a quill or a piece of hard leather in the mechanism which twitches the strings. [O.Fr. *harpechorde*—Low. L. *harpa,* of Gmc. origin. See **harp, chord** (2).]

harpy, *här'pi, n.* (*myth.*) a rapacious and filthy monster, part woman and part bird of prey: a South American eagle: a rapacious person. [L. *harpȳia*—Gr., pl. *harpyiai,* lit. snatchers, symbols of the storm-wind—*harpazein,* to seize.]

harquebus, harquebuse, harquebuss, *här'kwibus, n.* Same as **arquebus.**

harridan, *harī-dän, n.* a vixenish old woman. [Prob. O.Fr. *haridelle,* a lean horse, a jade.]

harrier, *harī-ér, n.* a small kind of dog with a keen smell, for hunting hares: a cross-country runner. [hare or harry.]

harrier. See **harry.**

Harrovian, *har-ō'vi-án, adj.* pertaining to *Harrow.*—*n.* one educated at the public school there.

harrow, *har'ō, n.* a spiked frame for smoothing and pulverising ploughed land, and for covering seeds.—*v.t.* to draw a harrow over: to tear: to distress deeply.—*adj.* **harr'owing,** acutely distressing to the mind.—*adv.* **harr'owingly.** [M.E. *harwe.*]

harry, *har'i, v.t.* to plunder, ravage: to harass: —*pr.p.* harr'ying; *pa.p.* harr'ied.—*n.* **harr'ier,** one who, or that which, harries: a genus of hawks that harry small animals.—**harrying,** or **harrowing, of hell,** the spoiling of hell, Christ's delivery of the souls of patriarchs and prophets—a favourite subject of mediaeval painters and dramatists. [O.E. *hergian—here,* an army; Ger. *heer.*]

harsh, *härsh, adj.* rough: jarring on the senses or feelings: rigorous: cruel.—*adv.* **harsh'ly.**—*n.* **harsh'ness.** [M.E. *harsk,* a northern word; cf. Swed. *härsk* and Dan. *harsk,* rancid, Ger. *harsch,* hard.]

hart, *härt, n.* a stag or male deer (esp. red deer) esp. over five years old:—*fem.* **hind.**—*ns.* **harts'horn,** a solution of ammonia in water, orig. a decoction of the shavings of a hart's horn; **harts'tongue,** a fern with strap shaped leaves. [O.E. *heort;* Du. *hert,* Ger. *hirsch.*]

hartal, *här'tal, n.* a stoppage of work in protest or boycott. [Hindustani.]

hartebeest, *här'té-best, n.* a South African antelope.—Also **hart'beest.** [S. Afr. Du., 'hart-beast'.]

harum-scarum, *hā'rum-skā'rum, adj.* flighty: rash.—*n.* a giddy, rash person. [Prob. from obs. *hare,* to harass, and **scare.**]

harvest, *här'vest, n.* the time of gathering in the ripened crops: the crops gathered in: fruits: the product of any labour or action.—*v.t.* to reap and gather in.—*ns.* **har'vest-bug, -louse, -mite, -tick,** a minute larval form of mite abundant in late summer, a very troublesome biter; **har'vester,** a reaper in harvests: a reaping machine: any of several insects superficially resembling spiders with very long legs; **har'vest-home,** the feast held at the bringing home of the harvest; **har'vest-man,** a labourer in harvest: a harvester or harvest spider; **har'vest-moon',** the full moon nearest the autumnal equinox, rising nearly at the same hour for several days; **har'vest mouse,** a species of mouse, a very small rodent animal that builds its nest in the stalks of growing corn; **har'vest-queen,** an image of the goddess Ceres (or of other spirit believed to be responsible for the growth of vegetation) in earlier times carried about on the last day of harvest.

---

fāte, fär; mē, hûr (her); *mīne; mōte, för; mūte, mōōn, fŏŏt;* THen (then)

[O.E. *hærfest*; Ger. *herbst*, Du. *herfst*.]

has, *haz,* 3rd pers. sing. pres. ind. of **have.**

hash, *hash, v.t.* to hack: to mince, to chop small.—*n.* that which is hashed: a mixed dish of meat and vegetables in small pieces: a mixture and preparation of old matter.—**make a hash of,** to spoil or ruin completely: **settle one's hash,** to silence or subdue one. [Fr. *hacher—hache,* hatchet.]

hash, slang abbrev. for **hashish.**

hashish, *hash'ish, -ēsh, n.* the leaves, shoots, or resin of hemp, smoked or swallowed in various forms as an intoxicant. [Ar.]

hasp, *häsp, n.* a clasp: the clasp of a padlock.— *v.t.* to fasten with a hasp. [O.E. *hæpse*; Dan. and Ger. *haspe.*]

hassock, *has'ók, n.* a tuft of grass: a stuffed stool for feet or knees. [O.E. *hassuc.*]

hast, *hast,* 2nd pers. sing. pres. ind. of **have.**

hastate, -d, *hast'āt, -id, adjs.* (*bot.*) spear-shaped. [L. *hastātus—hasta,* spear.]

haste, *hāst, n.* hurry, precipitancy, rashness.—*vs.t.* **haste, hasten** (*hās'n*), to accelerate: to hurry on.—*vs.i.* to move with speed: to do without delay (e.g. *he hastened to add*): to be in a hurry:—*pr.p.* hast'ing, hastening (*hās'ning*); *pa.p.* hast'ed, hastened (*hās'nd*).—*adj.* hast'y, speedy: hurried: rash: passionate.—*adv.* hast'ily.—*ns.* hast'iness; **hast'y-pudd'ing,** pudding made from flour or oatmeal and milk or water.—**make haste,** to hasten. [O.Fr. *haste* (Fr. *hâte*), from Gmc.; cf. O.E. *hæst,* Du. *haast,* Ger. *hast.*]

hat, *hat, n.* a covering for the head, generally with crown and brim: the dignity of a cardinal, from his red hat.—*v.t.* to provide with, or cover with, a hat: to salute by raising the hat.—*adj.* hatt'ed, covered with a hat.—*ns.* hatt'er, one who makes or sells hats; **hat'-trick,** in cricket, the feat of a bowler who takes three wickets by three successive balls—deserving a new hat: a corresponding feat (as three goals) in other games.—**keep under one's hat,** to keep secret; **pass, send, round the hat,** to take up a collection; **take off one's hat to** (*fig.*), to acknowledge in admiration: to praise. [O.E. *hæt*; Dan. *hat.*]

hatch, *hach, n.* a half-door with an opening above it, a wicket or door made of cross-bars: the covering of an opening in a floor, wall, &c.: the opening itself.—*n.* hatch'way, the opening in a ship's deck into the hold, or from one deck to another. [O.E. *hæcc, hæc,* a grating: Du. *hek,* a gate.]

hatch, *hach, v.t.* to produce from the egg: to develop or concoct (e.g. a plot).—*v.i.* to produce young from the egg: to come from the egg.—*n.* act of hatching: brood hatched.—*n.* hatch'ery, a place for artificial hatching of eggs, esp. those of fish. [Early M.E. *hacchen,* from an assumed O.E. *hæccean.*]

hatch, *hach, v.t.* to shade by fine lines, incisions, &c., in drawing and engraving.—*n.* hatch'ing, the mode of so shading. [O.Fr. *hacher,* to chop.]

hatchet, *hach'et, n.* a small axe used by one hand.—*adj.* hatch'et-faced, having a narrow, sharp-featured face.—*n.* hatch'et-man, a gun-man: a militant journalist: one who does shady jobs for a politician or political party. [Fr. *hachette—hacher,* to chop.]

hatchment, *hach'mént, n.* the escutcheon of a deceased person formerly placed on the front of his house. [Corruption of **achievement.**]

hate, *hāt, v.t.* to dislike intensely.—*n.* (chiefly poetical) hatred.—*adjs.* hat'able, hate'able, deserving to be hated; hate'ful, exciting hate, odious, detestable; feeling or manifesting hate.—*adv.* hate'fully.—*ns.* hate'fulness; hat'er; hat'red, extreme dislike: enmity, malignity. [O.E. *hete,* hate, *hatian,* to hate; Ger. *hasz.*]

hath, *hath* (*arch.*), 3rd pers. sing. pres. ind. of **have.**

hauberk, *hö'bérk, n.* a long coat of chain-mail. [O.Fr. *hauberc*—O.H.G. *halsberg—hals,* neck, *bergan,* to protect.]

haughty, *hö'ti, adj.* proud, arrogant: (*arch.*) exalted in character, rank, &c.—*adv.* haught'ily.—*n.* haught'iness. [O.Fr. *halt, haut,* high—L. *altus,* high.]

haul, *höl, v.t.* to drag: to pull with violence.—*v.i.* to tug: to alter a ship's course.—*n.* a pulling: a draught, as of fishes: an acquisition made at one time of stolen goods, loot, or profits.—*ns.* haul'age, act of hauling: charge for hauling: transport, esp. heavy road transport; haul'er, haulier (*höl'yér*; the latter form is used esp. for a man who conveys coal from the workings to the foot of the shaft, or for one who engages in road haulage business).—**haul up,** (*coll.; fig.*) to call to account (for.) [A variant of **hale** (2).]

haulm, halm, *höm, n.* the stalk of beans, peas, &c.: straw consisting of such stalks. [O.E. *healm*; Du., Ger. *halm.*]

haunch, *hönch, -sh, n.* expansion of the body at and near the pelvis: the hip with buttock: the leg and loin of venison, &c. [O.Fr. *hanche*: prob. of Gmc. origin.]

haunt, *hönt, v.t.* to frequent: to intrude upon continually: to inhabit or visit as a ghost: to keep recurring to the memory of.—*v.i.* to be much about (with *in, about*).—*n.* a place much resorted to.—*p.adj.* haunt'ed, frequented, esp. by ghosts or apparitions. [O.Fr. *hanter*; perh. a corr. of L. *habitāre.*]

hausfrau, *hows'frow, n.* a housewife, esp. one whose interests are bounded by the household. [Ger.]

haut, *ō,* high—**haut monde** (*mȯd*), high society. [Fr.]

hautboy, *hö'boi, ö'boi, n.* an older form of the name **oboe**: a large kind of strawberry. [Fr. *hautbois*—*haut,* high, *bois,* wood.]

haute, *ōt,* fem. of **haut.**—**haute couture** (*kōō-tür'*), very high-class dressmaking; **haute cuisine** (*kwē-zēn'*), high-class cookery; **haute école** (*ā-kol'*), horsemanship of the most difficult kind. [Fr.]

hauteur, *ō-tûr', hō-tœr', n.* haughtiness. [Fr.]

Havana, *ha-vän'a, `n.* a fine quality of cigar, named from *Havana,* the capital of Cuba.

have, *hav, v.t.* to hold: to keep: to possess: to own: to entertain in the mind: to enjoy: to suffer: to give birth to: to allow, or to cause to be (e.g. *I will not have it*; *you should have the picture framed*): to be obliged: as an auxiliary, used with the pa.p. to form the perfect tenses (e.g. *they have gone*):—*pr.p.* hav'ing: *pa.t.* and *pa.p.* had.—*n.* **have-not',** one who lacks pos-

Neutral vowels in unaccented syllables: *em'pér-ór*; for certain sounds in foreign words see p. ix.

326

sessions.—**had better, best,** would do best to; **had rather,** would prefer; **have at,** (let me) attack; **have done, have to do with** (see do); **have it,** to prevail (e.g. *the ayes have it*): to get punishment, unpleasant consequences; **have it in for someone,** to have a grudge against someone; **have it out,** to discuss exhaustively a subject of difference or dispute; **have up,** to call to account before a court of justice, &c.; **have what it takes,** to have the necessary qualities or capabilities to do something.—**you have had it,** (*slang*) you are not going to get it: you are done for, it's all up with you. [O.E. *habban,* pa.t. *hæfde,* pa.p. *gehæfd*; Ger. *haben,* Dan. *have.*]

haven, *hā′vn, n.* an inlet of the sea, or mouth of a river, where ships can get good and safe anchorage: any place of safety, an asylum. [O.E. *hæfen*; Du. *haven,* Ger. *hafen.*]

haver, *hā′vér, v.i.* (*Scot.*) to talk nonsense, or to talk pointlessly and at length: (Eng.; prob. through confused association with *waver,* &c.) to hesitate, vacillate.

haversack, *hav′ér-sak, n.* a bag worn over one shoulder, in which a soldier or traveller carries food, &c., orig. his horse's oats. [Fr. *havresac*—Ger. *habersack,* oat-sack—*haber, hafer,* oats.]

havildar, *hav′il-där, n.* an Indian sergeant [Pers *hawāl dār.*]

havoc, *hav′ok, n.* general destruction, devastation.—*interj.* an ancient war signal for plunder. [O.Fr. *havot,* plunder.]

haw, *hö, n.* (*obs.*) a hedge: an enclosure: a message: the fruit of the hawthorn.—*ns.* **haw′finch,** the common grosbeak; **haw′thorn,** a small tree of the rose family, bearing white or pink blossom known as may-blossom. [O.E. *haga,* a yard or enclosure; Du. *haag,* a hedge, Ger. *hag,* a hedge, O.N. *hagi,* a field.]

haw, *hö, v.i.* to speak with hesitation or a drawling manner.—*n.* **haw-haw,** a hesitation in speech: affected speech: loud vulgar laughter. Also *adj. v.i.* to guffaw. [Imit.]

Hawaiian, *hä-wī′(y)än, adj.* of Hawaii in the Pacific.—Also *n.*

haw-haw. See ha-ha, haw (2.)

hawk, *hök, n.* the name of several birds of prey of the same family as eagles and vultures: a member of the aggressive party in a conflict, political administration, &c.—*v.i.* to hunt birds with hawks trained for the purpose: to attack on the wing.—*adj.* **hawk′-eyed,** having keen sight.—*n.* **hawk′-moth,** any of a family of very large moths, so called from their hovering motion. [O.E. *hafoc*; Du. *havik,* Ger. *habicht,* O.N. *haukr.*]

hawk, *hök, v.i.* to force up matter from the throat.—*n.* the effort to do this. [Imit.]

hawker, *hok′er, n.* one who goes about offering goods for sale—now confined to one who has a beast of burden or a vehicle.—*v.t.* **hawk,** to convey about for sale: to cry for sale. [Cf. Low Ger. and Ger. *höker,* Du. *heuker.*]

hawse, *höz, n.* part of a vessel's bow in which the hawse-holes are cut.—*n.pl.* **hawse′-holes,** holes through which a ship's cables pass. [O.N. *hāls,* the neck.]

hawser, *hö′zér, n.* a small cable: a large rope for towing, &c. [O.Fr. *haucier, haulser,* to raise—

Low L. *altiāre*—L. *altus,* high.]

hawthorn. See haw (1).

hay, *hā, n.* grass cut down and dried for fodder.—*ns.* **hay′-box,** an air-tight box of hay used to continue the cooking of dishes already begun; **hay′cock,** a conical pile of hay in the field; **hay′-fē′ver,** irritation of the nose, throat, &c., by pollen, with sneezing and headache—also called **hay′-asth′ma; hay′-loft,** a loft in which hay is kept; **hay′mak′er,** one employed in cutting and drying grass for hay: (*pl.*) a kind of country-dance: (*slang; boxing*) a wild swinging blow; **hay′-mow,** a rick of hay: a mass of hay stored in a barn; **hay′rick, hay′-stack,** a pile of hay methodically stacked; **hay′tedd′er,** a machine for scattering hay and exposing it to the sun and air; **hay′wire,** wire used to bind hay, &c.: a tangled mass of such wire: (*slang*; as predicative *adj.* or *adv.*) used of anything wildly complicated, disordered, disarranged, or crazy. [O.E. *hīeg, hīg, hēg*; Ger. *heu,* Du. *hooi,* O.N. *hey.*]

hazard, *haz′ärd, n.* a game played with dice: chance, accident: risk: a difficulty on a golf-course—e.g. a bunker, a stream.—*v.t.* to expose to chance: to risk, to venture.—*adj.* **haz′ardous,** dangerous, perilous: uncertain.—*adv.* **haz′ardously.** [O.Fr. *hasard*; prob. through the Sp. from Arab. *al zār,* the die; perh. from *Hasart,* a castle in Syria, where the game was invented during the Crusades.]

haze, *hāz, n.* vapour or mist obscuring vision.—*adj.* **hāz′y,** thick with haze: dim: confused (of the mind).—*adv.* **haz′ily.**—*n.* **hāz′iness.**

hazel, *hā′zl, n.* a genus of small trees yielding an edible nut enclosed in a leafy cup.—*adj.* pertaining to the hazel: of a light brown colour, like a hazel-nut.—Also **hā′zelly.**—*n.* **hā′zelnut,** the nut of the hazel-tree. [O.E. *hæsel*; Ger. *hasel,* O.N. *hasl,* L. *corylus.*]

he, *hē, nom. masc. pron.* of *3rd pers.,* the male (or thing spoken of as male) named before.—*adj.* male (esp. in composition), e.g. **hē′-goat.—hē′-man,** a man of extreme virility. [O.E. *hē, he.*]

head, *hed, n.* the uppermost or foremost part of an animal's body: the brain: the understanding: a chief or leader: the place of honour or command: the front or top of anything: a promontory: a froth on beer, &c.: point of suppuration: an individual animal or person as one of a group: a topic or chief point of a discourse: the source or spring: the culmination: a body of water: strength (as *gather head*): (*coll.*) a headache: (*slang*) one who takes hallucinogenic drugs.—*v.t.* to lead: to be at the head of: to get ahead of and turn (e.g. cattle; often with *off,* sometimes with *back*): **head off** also means to divert, or to avert): to strike with the head.—*v.i.* to grow to a head: to sail or make straight (for).—*adj.* pertaining to the head: chief or most important (often in composition, as **head′master, head′-mas′ter, head′-mis′tress, head′mis′tress,** &c.): at, or coming from, the front.—*n.* **head′ache,** pain, or a pain, in the head: a troublesome problem: a source of worry.—*adj.* **head′achy.**—*ns.* **head′-dress,** a covering for the head, esp. an ornamental one; **head′er,** a dive head foremost; **head′-gear,** gear, covering, or ornament

fāte, fär; mē, hûr (her); *mīne; mōte, för; mūte; mōōn, fōōt;* THen (then)

of the head; **head′-hunt′ing**, the practice of collecting human heads as trophies; **head′ing**, that which stands at the head: a title: striking a ball with the head: **head′land**, a point of land running out into the sea, a cape.—*adj.* **head′less**, without a head.—*ns.* **head′light**, **head′-light**, a light in front of a ship or vehicle; **head′line**, **head′-line**, line at the top of a page, or at the beginning of a newspaper article, containing title, caption, &c.: (*radio, TV*) a news item given very briefly.—*v.t.* to give as a headline: to publicise.—*adv.* **head′long**, with the head foremost or first: without thought, rashly: precipitately.—*adj.* rash: precipitate: steep.—*n.* **head′-mon′ey**, a tax counted per head: a reward for an outlaw's head.—*adjs.* **head′most**, most advanced or forward; **head′-on′**, head to head: with head pointing directly forward: directly opposed (also *adv.*).—*ns.* **head′-phones**, telephone receivers that fix on the head, one on each ear, for listening to wireless messages, &c.; **head′-piece**, a helmet: a hat: head, intelligence: the top part, as the lintel of a door, &c.—*n. pl.* **headquar′ters**, the quarters or residence of a commander-in-chief or general: a central or chief office, &c.—*ns.* **head′-race**, the race (current or channel) leading to an hydraulically operated machine; **head′ship**, the office of head or chief authority; **heads′man**, an executioner; **head′stall**, the part of a bridle round the head; **head′-stā′tion**, the dwelling-house, &c., on an Australian sheep or cattle station; **head′stone**, the principal stone of a building (also *fig.*): corner-stone: grave-stone.—*adj.* **head′-strong**, self-willed, obstinate.—*ns.* **head voice**, head register (see *register*); **head′way**, motion ahead, esp. of a ship; **head′-wind**, a directly opposing wind; **head′-word**, a word serving as a heading: a word under which others are grouped, as in a dictionary.—*adj.* **head′y**, affecting the head or the brain, intoxicating: rash, violent, wilful.—*adv.* **head′ily**.—*n.* **head′iness.—heads or tails**, a phrase used when tossing a coin to see whether the side with the sovereign's head will fall uppermost or the reverse; **head over heels**, in a somersault: deeply, thoroughly.—**above one′s head**, beyond one's comprehension; **come to a head**, to reach a climax; **have a head on one′s shoulders**, to have ability or balance; **hit the headlines**, to get prominent notice in the press (also *fig.*); **keep, lose, one′s head**, to keep, lose, one's presence of mind; **make head against**, to advance against, make progress against; **make neither head nor tail of**, to be unable to understand, take any definite meaning from; **off one′s head**, demented, crazy; **over one′s head**, beyond, too difficult for, one's powers of understanding. [O.E. *hēafod*, Du. *hoofd*, Ger. *haupt*.]

heal, *hēl*, *v.t.* to make whole and healthy: to cure: to remedy, repair.—*v.i.* to grow sound:—*pr.p.* heal′ing; *pa.p.* healed.—*ns.* **heal′er; heal′ing**, the act or process by which anything is healed or cured: the power to heal.—*adj.* tending to cure or heal. [O.E. *hǣlan*—*hāl*, whole; cf. Ger. *heil*, Du. *heel*, O.N. *heill*; cf. **hail** (1), **hale** (1), **whole**.]

health, *helth*, *n.* wholeness or soundness, esp. of

the body: general state of the body: a toast, as 'to drink one's health'.—*adj.* **health′ful**, full of or enjoying health: indicating health: wholesome: salutary.—*adv.* **health′fully.**—*n.* **health′-fulness.**—*adv.* **health′y** (*lit.* and *fig.*), in a state of good health: conducive to health: vigorous.—*adv.* **health′ily.**—*ns.* **health′iness; health′-centre**, a general medical centre run by general practitioners working as a group; **health′-resort**, a place to which people go for health's sake. [O.E. *hǣlth*—*hāl*, whole.]

heap, *hēp*, *n.* a mass of things resting one above another: a mound: a great quantity (often in *pl.*).—*v.t.* to throw in a heap: to amass: to pile high:—*pr.p.* heap′ing: *pa.p.* heaped. [O.E. *hēap*; O.N. *hōpr*, Ger. *haufe*, Du. *hoop*.]

hear, *hēr*, *v.t.* to perceive by the ear: to listen to: to try judicially: to grant or (*arch.*) to obey: (*arch.*) to answer favourably: to be informed.—*v.i.* to have the sense of hearing: to listen.—*pr.p.* hear′ing; *pa.t.* and *pa.p.* heard (*hûrd*).—*ns.* **hear′er; hear′ing**, act of perceiving by the ear: the sense of perceiving sound: opportunity to be heard: earshot: news; **hear′say**, common talk, rumour, report.—**hear, hear!** an exclamation of approval; **hear tell of**, to hear someone speak of; **will not hear of**, will not allow, tolerate. [O.E. *hȳran*; Du. *hooren*, O.N. *heyra*, Ger. *hören*.]

hearken, *härk′n*, *v.i.* to listen (to, unto), esp. attentively. [O.E. *he(o)rcnian*; *cf.* **hark, hear**; Ger. *horchen.*]

hearse, *hûrs*, *n.* (*orig.*) a framework for holding candles at a church service, and esp. at a funeral service: a carriage in which a corpse is conveyed to the grave. [O.Fr. *herse* (It. *erpice*)—L. *hirpex*, a harrow.]

heart, *härt*, *n.* the organ that circulates the blood: the core: the chief or vital part: the seat of the affections, &c., esp. love: desire or liking: courage, spirit: vigour: (*pl.*) one of the four suits in a pack of cards, bearing heart-shaped pips.—*adj.* **heart′y**, full of, proceeding from, the heart: warm, genuine: strong, healthy: abundant.—*adv.* **heart′ily**, cordially, eagerly.—*n.* **heart′iness**, the state or quality of being hearty.—*adj.* **heart′less**, pitiless, merciless.—*adv.* **heart′lessly.**—*ns.* **heart′lessness; heart′ache**, sorrow, mental anguish; **heart′-('s)-blood**, life-blood: life, essence; **heart′-break**, a deep, shattering sorrow.—*adjs.* **heart′-break′ing**, crushing with grief or sorrow; **heart′-brok′en**, intensely afflicted or grieved.—*ns.* **heart′-burn**, an affection of the stomach causing a burning acrid feeling near the heart; **heart′-burning**, discontent, secret enmity.—*adj.* **heart′ed**, having a heart of a specified kind (*hard-hearted, &c*).—*v.t.* **heart′en**, to encourage.—*n.* **heart′-fail′ure**, stoppage or inadequate functioning of the heart.—*adj.* **heart′-felt**, felt deeply, sincere.—*n.* **heart′land**, an area of a country that is centrally situated or vitally important.—*adj.* **heart-rend′ing**, agonising.—*n.* **hearts′-ease, heart′s′-ease**, the wild pansy, an infusion of which was once thought to ease the love-sick heart.—*adj.* **heart′-sick**, pained in mind: depressed.—*ns.* **heart′-sick′ness; heart′-string**, a nerve or tendon imagined to brace and sustain the heart: (*pl.*) affections;

Neutral vowels in unaccented syllables: *em′pér-òr*; for certain sounds in foreign words see ρ. ix.

heart'-throb (*slang*), a sentimental emotion for one of the opposite sex: the source of it.—*adj.* **heart'-whole,** sincere: out-and-out: unmoved in the affections or spirits.—*n.* **heart'-wood,** the hard inner wood of the trunk of a tree.—**heart-and-soul,** with complete devotion; **heart of hearts,** the inmost heart: deepest affections.—**after one's own heart,** exactly to one's liking; **at heart,** in real character: substantially; **break one's heart,** to give way to grief or disappointment: to cause one deep grief; **by heart,** by rote, from memory; **have a change of heart,** to alter one's former opinion or viewpoint; **heart to heart,** with candour and absence of reserve; **lay to heart,** to consider seriously, draw a lesson from; **take to heart,** to be affected or upset by. [O.E. *heorte*; Du. *hart*; Ger. *herz*.]

hearth, *härth, n.* the part of the floor on which the fire is made: the fireside: the house itself.—*n.* **hearth'-rug,** a rug laid before the hearth. [O.E. *heorth*; Du. *haard,* Ger. *herd.*]

heat, *hēt, n.* that which excites the sensation of warmth: sensation of warmth, esp. in a high degree: a high temperature: the hottest period (e.g. *the heat of the day*): redness of the skin: vehemence, passion: violent or excited stage (e.g. *in the heat of the debate, the moment*): period of sexual desire in animals: (*coll.*) pressure intended to coerce: (*coll.*) period of intensive search: a single course in a race, esp. a preliminary one to eliminate some of the competitors.—*v.t.* to make hot: to agitate.—*v.i.* to become hot:—*pr.p.* **heat'ing;** *pa.p.* **heat'ed.**—*ns.* **heat barrier,** a thin envelope of hot air developing round aircraft at high speeds and occasioning structural and other problems: the structural and other difficulties; **heat'er,** one whose work it is to heat: that which heats, esp. a stove or other device for heating a room, &c.; **heat'-pump,** a device (on the refrigerator principle) for drawing heat from water, air, or the earth, and giving it out again, e.g. to warm a room; **heat sink,** something into which unwanted heat can be transferred; **heat'-ū'nit,** amount of heat required to raise a pound of water one degree Fahrenheit in temperature (*British Thermal Unit*) or one gram one degree centigrade (*calorie*); **heat'-wave,** (*coll.*) a spell of very hot weather.—**(specific) latent heat,** the heat required to change solid to liquid or liquid to gas without change of temperature; **specific heat (capacity),** the amount of energy required to raise the unit of mass of a given substance one degree in temperature.—**turn on the heat,** (U.S. *slang*) to use some form of torture or intimidation, esp. in order to extract a confession. [O.E. *hǣto,* heat; *hāt,* hot; Ger. *hitze.*]

heath, *hēth, n.* barren open country, esp. covered with low shrubs: any of a genus of hardy evergreen under-shrubs.—*n.* **heath'-cock,** the male black grouse. [O.E. *hǣth.*]

heathen, *hē'rn, n.* one who belongs to a people of some lower form of religion, esp. polytheistic, a pagan: an irreligious person: (*coll.*) an uncivilised person:—*pl.* **heathen** (collectively).—*adj.* pagan, irreligious.—*v.t.* **hea'-thenise,** to make heathen or heathenish.—*adj.* **hea'thenish,** relating to the heathen:

uncivilised: cruel.—*adv.* **hea'thenishly.**—*ns.* **hea'thenishness; hea'thenism,** the religious system of the heathens, paganism: barbarism; **hea'thendom,** those regions of the world where heathenism prevails. [O.E. *hǣthen*; Du. *heiden.*]

heather, *heTH'ér, n.* ling, a common low shrub of the heath family.—*adj.* of the colour of heather.—*adj.* **heath'ery.** [Older Scots *hadder.*]

Heath(-)Robinson, *hēth'-rob'in-són,* used adjectively to describe an over-ingenious mechanical contrivance (usually destined not to work). [*Heath Robinson* (1872-1944), an artist who drew such contraptions.]

heave, *hēv, v.t.* to lift up, esp. with great effort: to throw: to haul: to cause to swell: to force (a sigh) from the breast.—*v.i.* to rise like waves, to rise and fall: to retch:—*pr.p.* **heav'ing;** *pa.t.* and *pa.p.* heaved or (*naut.*) hōve.—*n.* an effort upward: a throw: a swelling: an effort to vomit: in space flight, motion perpendicular to the surge.—*ns.* **heave'-off'ering,** a Jewish offering lifted up by the priest; **heav'er,** one who, or that which, heaves.—**heave ho!** an exclamation used by sailors in putting forth exertion, as in raising the anchor; **heave in sight,** to come into view; **heave to,** to bring a vessel to a standstill, to make her lie to. [O.E. *hebban,* pa.t. *hóf,* pa.p. *hafen*; Ger. *heben.*]

heaven, *hev'n, n.* the vault of sky overhanging the earth: (commonly in *pl.*) the upper regions of the air: the dwelling-place of the Deity and the blessed: the Deity: supreme happiness.—**heaven-,** (in composition) by or from heaven—e.g. **heav'en-sent'.**—*adj.* **heav'enly,** of or inhabiting heaven: celestial, pure: of very high excellence: (*coll.*) very good.—*n.* **heav'enliness.**—*adj.* **heav'enly-mind'ed,** having the mind placed upon heavenly things, pure.—*n.* **heav'enly-mind'edness.**—*advs.* **heav'enward, heav'enwards,** toward heaven.—**heaven of heavens** (*B.*), the highest of the seven heavens believed in by the Jews, the abode of God; **good heavens!** exclamation of surprise; **in the seventh heaven,** in state of bliss. [O.E. *heofon.*]

Heaviside layer. Same as **Kennelly-Heaviside layer.**

heavy, *hev'i, adj.* weighty: not easy to bear: oppressive: laden: dull, lacking brightness and interest: drowsy: violent: deep-toned: not easily digested, as food: miry, as soil: strong, as liquor: dark with clouds: gloomy: sad.—*adv.* **heav'ily.**—*n.* **heav'iness; heavy chemicals,** those produced on a large scale for use in industry.—*adjs.* **heav'y-dut'y,** made to withstand very hard wear or use; **heav'y-hand'ed,** clumsy, awkward: oppressive; **heav'y-head'ed,** dull, stupid, drowsy; **heav'y-heart'ed,** sorrowful. **heavy hydrogen,** nitrogen, oxygen, &c., any isotope (q.v.) of these whose atomic mass or weight is greater than that of the most abundant isotope—e.g. the isotope of hydrogen known as *deuterium,* which has atomic weight 2, or *tritium,* isotope having atomic weight 3, as compared with ordinary hydrogen which has atomic weight 1.—*adj.* **heav'y-lād'en,** bearing a heavy burden.—**heavy water,** any kind of water denser than ordinary water, esp. water with deuterium in its com-

fāte, fär; mē, hûr (her); *mīne; mōte, för; mūte; mōōn, fŏŏt;* THen (then)

position; **heavy metal,** alloy of tungsten: guns or shot of large size: great influence or power: a person to be reckoned with; **heavy-weight,** a boxer beyond the average weight—not less than 12$\frac{1}{2}$ stone, amateur not less than 12 st. 10 lb: (*coll.*) a very influential person. [O.E. *hefig—hebban,* to heave; O.H.G. *hebig.*]

hebdomadal, *heb-dom′a-dál, adj.* occurring every seven days, weekly—also **hebdom′adary.**—*n.* **hebdom′adary,** a member of a chapter or convent who is officiating in the choir, &c., during the week in question. [L. *hebdomadālis*—Gr. *hebdomas,* a period of seven days—*hepta,* seven.]

Hebrew, *hē′brōō, n.* a Jew: the language of the Hebrews.—*adj.* relating to the Hebrews.—*adjs.* **Hebrā′ic, -al,** relating to the Hebrews or to their language.—*adv.* **Hebrā′ically,** after the manner of the Hebrew language: from right to left.—*v.t.* **hē′brāise,** to make Hebrew.—*v.i.* to use a Hebrew idiom.—*ns.* **Hē′brāism,** a Hebrew idiom; **Hē′brāist,** one skilled in Hebrew.—*adjs.* **hebrāist′ic, -al,** of or like Hebrew.—*adv.* **hebrāist′ically.** [O.Fr. *Ebreu*—L. *Hebraeus*—Gr. *Hebraios*—Heb. *'ibrī,* lit. 'one from the other side (of the river)'.]

hecatomb, *hek′a-tom, n.* a great public sacrifice: any large number of victims. [Gr. *hekatombē—hekaton,* a hundred, *bous,* an ox.]

heckle, *hek′l, v.t.* to comb: to ply with embarrassing questions (as at an election).—*n.* same as **hackle.**—*n.* **heck′ler.** [M.E. *hekelen.*]

hectare, *hek′tar, n.* 100 ares—2·47 acres.

hectic, -al, *hek′tik, -ál, adj.* pertaining to the constitution or habit of body: affected with hectic fever: (*coll.*) intense, feverish, rushed.—*n.* **hec′tic,** a habitual or remittent fever, usually associated with consumption. [Fr. — Gr. *hektikos,* habitual — *hexis,* habit.]

hecto-, *hek′to-,* **hect-,** in composition, 100 times, as in **hectogram,** 100 grams.

hectograph, *hek′to-gräf, n.* a gelatine pad for printing copies of a writing or drawing. [Gr. *hakaton,* hundred, *graphein,* to write.]

hector, *hek′tór, n.* a bully, a braggart.—*v.t.* to treat insolently: to annoy.—*v.i.* to play the bully. [Gr. *Hector,* the Trojan hero.]

heddle, *hed′l, n.* an arrangement on a loom for moving the threads of the warp so as to allow the shuttle to pass bearing the weft.

hedge, *hej, n.* a close row of bushes or small trees serving as a fence: (*fig.*) a barrier.—*v.t.* to enclose with a hedge: to surround: to hem in: to guard.—*v.i.* to make hedges: to place secondary bets as a precaution: to shuffle, as in argument, avoid committing oneself.—*ns.* **hedge′bill, hedg′ing-bill,** a bill or hatchet for dressing hedges; **hedge′hog,** a genus of prickly-backed insectivorous animals that live in hedges and bushes, and have a snout like a hog: a fortified stronghold, with mine-fields, pill-boxes, artillery, &c.—*v.i.* and *v.t.* **hedge′-hop,** to fly (an aeroplane) very close to the ground.—*ns.* **hedge′-par′son, hedge′-priest,** a vagrant disreputable parson or priest; **hedg′er,** one who hedges or trims hedges; **hedge′row,** a line of hedge, often with trees; **hedge′-school,** a school kept by the side of a hedge, common in Ireland in 17th and 18th centuries during the ban on Catholic education: a mean school; **hedge′-sparr′ow, hedge′-war′bler,** a warbler, superficially like a sparrow, that frequents hedges. [O.E. *hecg, hegg*; Du. *hegge,* Ger. *hecke.*]

hedonism, *hē′dón-izm, n.* in ethics, the doctrine that pleasure is the highest good.—*n.* **hē′donist,** one who holds, or puts into practice, the doctrine of hedonism. [Gr. *hēdonē,* pleasure.]

heed, *hēd, v.t.* to attend to, to concern oneself about.—*n.* notice, careful attention.—*adj.* **heed′ful,** attentive, cautious.—*adv.* **heed′fully.** —*n.* **heed′fulness.**—*adj.* **heed′less,** inattentive: careless.—*adv.* **heed′lessly.**—*n.* **heed′lessness.** [O.E. *hēdan*; Du. *hoeden.*]

heehaw, *hē′hô, v.i.* to bray, like an ass. [Imit.]

heel, *hēl, n.* hind part of the foot below the ankle: the whole foot (esp. of beasts): the covering or support of the heel in footwear: a thing like a heel in shape, or in a corresponding position: (*slang*) a cad.—*v.t.* to strike, or pass back, with the heel: to furnish with heels.—*ns.* **heel′-ball,** a black waxy composition for blacking the heels and soles of boots, for taking impressions of coins, &c: by rubbing; **heel′piece,** a piece or cover for the heel; **heel′-tap,** a small quantity of liquor left in the glass after drinking.—**at, on, upon, a person's heels,** close behind; **back on one's heel,** driven back by an opponent: on the defensive; **come to heel,** to obey or follow like a dog: to submit to authority; **cool** or **kick one's heels,** to be kept waiting for some time; **down at heel,** having the heels of one's shoes trodden down: slovenly: in poor circumstances; **lay, set, clap, by the heels,** to fetter: to put in confinement; **take to one's heels,** to flee; **turn on (upon) one's heel,** to turn sharply round. [O.E. *hēla*; Du. *hiel.*]

heel, *hēl, v.i.* to incline: to lean on one side, as a ship.—*v.t.* to tilt. [Earlier *heeld, hield*—O.E. *hieldan,* to slope; cf. Du. *hellen.*]

heft, *heft, v.t.* to lift: to estimate a weight by hand. [Same root as **heave.**]

hefty, *heft′i, adj.* rather heavy: muscular: vigorous. [Same root as **heave.**]

hegemony, *hē-, he-gem′ón-i,* or *-jem′-,* or *hē′-, he′-, n.* leadership: preponderant influence, esp. of one state over others. [Gr. *hēgemonia—hēgemōn,* leader.]

hegira, hejira, *hej′i-ra, n.* the flight of Mohammed from Mecca, 622 A.D., from which is dated the Mohammedan era: any flight. [Ar. *hijrah,* flight, *hajara,* to leave.]

heifer, *hef′ér, n.* a young cow. [O.E. *hēahfore, hēahfru, -fre*; prob. 'high-goer'—*hēah,* high, *faran,* to go.]

heigh-ho, *hā′-,* or *hī′-hō, interj.* an exclamation expressive of weariness. [Imit.]

height, *hīt, n.* the condition of being high: distance upwards: that which is elevated, a hill: elevation in rank or excellence: utmost degree.—*v.t.* **height′en,** to make higher, to advance or improve: to make brighter or more prominent, or (*fig.*) stronger or more intense. [For *highth*—O.E. *hīehtho, hēahthu—hēah,* high.]

heinous, *hā′nús, adj.* wicked in a high degree: atrocious.—*adv.* **hei′nously.**—*n.* **hei′nousness.** [O.Fr. *hainos—haïr,* to hate.]

Neutral vowels in unaccented syllables: *em′pér-ór*; for certain sounds in foreign words see p. ix.

heir, *ār*, *n.* one who inherits anything after the death of the owner: one entitled to anything after the present possessor: a child, esp. a first-born son: a successor to a position: inheritor of qualities or of social conditions, or the past generally:—*fem.* **heiress** (*ār'es*).—*ns.* **heir'-appā'rent**, the one by law acknowledged to be heir; **heir'-at-law**, an heir by legal right; **heir'dom**, **heir'ship.**—*adj.* **heir'less**, without an heir.—*ns.* **heir'loom**, any piece of furniture or personal property which descends to the heir-at-law by special custom (O.E. *gelōma*; see **loom** (1)): a valued inherited possession; **heir'-presump'tive**, one who will be heir if no nearer relative should be born. [O.Fr. *heir*—L. *hērēs*, an heir.]

hejira. See **hegira.**

held, *pa.t.* and *pa.p.* of **hold.**

heli-, *hel'i-*, in composition, helicopter, as in *ns.* **hel'ibus**; **hel'idrome**; **hel'ipilot**; **hel'iport**; **hel'iscoop**, a net let down from a helicopter to rescue persons in difficulty.

helical. See **helix.**

helicopter, *hel'i-kop-tėr*, *n.* an aircraft sustained by a power-driven screw or screws revolving on a vertical axis. [Gr. *helix*, screw, *pteron*, wing.]

helio-, *hē-li-ō-*, in composition, sun [Gr. *hēlios*, sun]:—e.g. **heliocentric**, *he-li-o-sen'trik*, *adj.* referred to the sun as centre.

heliograph, *hē'li-o-graf*, *n.* an apparatus for signalling by flashing the sun's rays: an engraving obtained photographically: an apparatus for photographing the sun.—*v.t.* to signal to by means of the sun's rays—*n.* **heliog'rapher.**—*adjs.* **heliograph'ic**, **-al.** *n.* **heliog'raphy.** [Gr. *hēlios*, sun, *graphē*, a drawing—*graphein*, to write.]

heliolatry, *hē-li-ol'a-tri*, *n.* sun-worship.—*n.* **heliol'ater**, a sun-worshipper. [Gr. *hēlios*, sun, *latreia*, worship.]

heliometer, *hē-li-om'e-tėr*, *n.* an instrument originally for measuring the sun's diameter, now for measuring the angular distance between two celestial objects in close proximity. [Gr. *hēlios*, sun, *metron*, a measure.]

helioscope, *hē'li-ō-skōp*, *n.* an apparatus for observing the sun without injury to the eyes.—*adj.* **helioscŏp'ic.** [Fr. *hélioscope*—Gr. *hēlios*, sun, *skopeein*, to look, to spy.]

heliostat, *hē'li-ō-stat*, *n.* an instrument by means of which a beam of sunlight is reflected in an invariable direction. [Gr. *hēlios*, sun, *statos*, fixed—*histanai*, to stand.]

heliotrope, *hē'li-ō-trōp*, *n.* a genus of plants whose flowers were fabled always to turn towards the sun: a shade of purple: (*min.*) a bloodstone: a surveyor's heliograph.—*n.* **heliot'ropism**, the tendency that the stem and leaves of a plant have to bend towards, and the roots from, the light. [Gr. *hēliotropion*—*hēlios*, the sun, *tropos*, a turn.]

helium, *hē'li-ùm*, *n.* a gaseous element (symbol He; at. no. 2), first discovered in the sun's atmosphere—very light and non-inflammable. [Gr. *hēlios*, sun.]

helix, *hē'liks*, *n.* a line, thread, or wire curved into a shape such as it would assume if wound in a single layer round a cylinder: (*zool.*) a genus of molluscs including the best known land-snails: (*anat.*) the rim of the ear:—*pl.* **hē'lixes** or **helices** (*hel'i-sēz*).—*adj.* **helical** (*hel'i-kál*). [L. *helix*, *-icis*—Gr. *helix*, a spiral —*helissein*, to turn round.]

hell, *hel*, *n.* the place of the dead: the place or state of punishment of the wicked after death: the abode of evil spirits: the powers of hell: any place of vice or misery: (a state of) supreme misery or discomfort: severe censure or chastisement: gambling-house.—*ns.* **hell'er**, an obstreperous person: **hell'hound**, a hound of hell: an agent of hell; **hellion** (*hel'yón*), a troublesome child: one given to diabolical conduct.—*adj.* **hell'ish**, pertaining to or like hell: very wicked.—*adv.* **hell'ishly.**—*n.* **hell'ishness.** [O.E. *hel*; O.N. *hel*, Ger. *hölle*.]

he'll, contraction for **he will.**

hellebore, *hel'é-bōr*, *-bôr*, *n.* a genus of plants of the buttercup family used in medicine, one of them anciently prescribed as a cure for insanity: a winter aconite: a small genus of herbs with poisonous rhizomes used in medicine. [Gr. *helleboros*.]

Hellene, *hel'ēn*, *n.* a Greek.—*adj.* **Hellēn'ic** (or -*en*-), Greek.—*v.i.* **hell'enīse**, to conform to Greek usages.—*v.t.* to make Greek.—*ns.* **Hell'enism**, a Greek idiom: the Greek spirit; **Hell'enist**, one skilled in the Greek language: a Jew who spoke Greek and adopted Greek usages.—*adjs.* **Hellenist'ic**, **-al**, pertaining to the Hellenists: pertaining to Greek language and culture affected by foreign influences after the time of Alexander. [Gr. *Hellēn*, a Greek.]

hello, **hullo**, **hallo**, **halloa**, *hul-ō'*, *he-lō'*, *interj.* expressing surprise, &c.: used also in calling attention: a form of greeting.—*n.* a call of hello. *v.i.* to call hello. [Imit.]

helm, *helm*, *n.* the apparatus by which a ship is steered.—*n.* **helm'man**, one who steers. [O.E. *helma*; O.N. *hjālm*, a rudder, Ger. *helm*, a handle.]

helm, *helm*, **helmet**, *hel'met*, *n.* a covering of armour for the head: the hooded upper lip of certain flowers.—*adjs.* **helmed**, **hel'meted**, furnished with a helmet. [O.E. *helm*; Ger. *helm*.]

helminth, *hel'minth*, *n.* a worm, esp. an intestinal one.—*adjs.* **helmin'thic**; **helmin'thoid**, worm-shaped.—*ns.* **helminthol'ogy**, the study of worms; **helminthol'ogist.** [Gr. *helmins*, *-inthos*, a worm.]

helot, *hel'ot*, *n.* (often *cap.*) one of a class of serfs among the ancient Spartans.—*ns.* **hel'otism**, the condition of the Helots: slavery; **hel'otry**, the whole body of the Helots: any class of slaves. [Gr. *Heilōtēs*, also *Heilōs*.]

help, *help*, *v.t.* to aid, to assist: to relieve the wants of: to serve (food) at table: to contribute towards the success of: to remedy: to refrain from.—*v.i.* to give assistance: to contribute:—*pa.p.* helped, (*B.*) hōlp'en.—*n.* means or strength given to another for a purpose: assistance: relief: one who assists: (*U.S.*) a hired servant, esp. a domestic: an employee.—*n.* **help'er.**—*adj.* **help'ful**, giving help: useful.—*adv.* **help'fully.**—*ns.* **help'fulness**; **help'ing**, a portion served at a meal.—*adj.* **help'less**, unable to help oneself: lacking assistance.—*adv.* **help'lessly.**—*ns.* **help'less-**

ness; **help′mate,** modification of **help′meet,** from the phrase in Gen. ii. 18, 'an help meet for him', a wife.—**help oneself,** to pilfer (often with *to*); **help out,** to eke out, to supplement: to assist. [O.E. *helpan,* pa.t. *healp,* pa.p. *holpen*; O.N. *hjälpa,* Ger. *helfen.*]

helter-skelter, *hel′tér-skel′tér, adv.* in haste and confusion.—*adj.* disorderly.—*n.* a spiral slide, an amusement in a fair-ground. [Imit.]

helve, *helv, n.* the handle of an axe or similar tool.—*v.t.* to furnish with a helve. [O.E. *helfe,* a handle.]

Helvetic, *hel-vet′ik, adj.* pertaining to Switzerland. [L.—*Helvētia,* Switzerland.]

hem, *hem, n.* the border of a garment doubled down and sewed.—*v.t.* to form a hem on: to edge: to sew with the stitch usu. used in making a hem:—*pr.p.* hemm′ing; *pa.p.* hemmed.—*n.* **hem′-stitch,** an ornamental finishing of the inner side of a hem, made by pulling out several threads adjoining it and drawing together the cross-threads in groups.—*v.t.* to embroider thus.—**hem in,** to surround, confine. [O.E. *hemm,* a border.]

hem, *hem, hm, n.* and *interj.* a sort of half-cough to draw attention.—*v.i.* to utter the sound *hem!*—*pr.p.* hemm′ing; *pa.p.* hemmed. [Imit.]

hematite. See **haematite.**

hemi-, *hem′i-,* in composition, half. [Gr. **hēmi-,** half.]

Hemiptera, *hem-ip′tér-a, n.pl.* an order of insects, variously defined, with wings (when present) often half leathery, half membranous—the bugs, cicadas, green fly, &c. [Gr. *hēmi-,* half, *pteron,* a wing.]

hemisphere, *hem′i-sfēr, n.* a half-sphere: half of the globe or a map of it: one of the two divisions of the cerebrum.—*adjs.* **hemispher′ic, -al.** [Gr. *hēmisphairion*—*hēmi-,* half, *sphaira,* a sphere.]

hemistich, *hem′i-stik, n.* half a line, an incomplete line of poetry.—*adj.* **hem′istichal** (or *-is′-*). [L. *hēmistichium*—Gr. *hēmistichion*—*hēmi-,* half, *stichos,* a line.]

hemlock, *hem′lok, n.* a poisonous spotted umbelliferous plant: a deadly potion: any of a genus of N. American trees (*hemlock spruces*). [O.E. *hymlīce.*]

hemorrhage, hemorrhoid. See **haemorrhage, haemorrhoid.**

hemp, *hemp, n.* a plant of the mulberry order, yielding a coarse fibre, a narcotic drug, and an oil: the fibre: the drug: a similar fibre (as *Manila, sisal* hemp).—*adj.* **hemp′en,** made of hemp. [O.E. *henep, hænep*; cf. Gr. *kannabis.*]

hen, *hen, n,* the female of any bird, esp. the domestic fowl.—*adj.* female.—*ns.* **hen′bane,** a poisonous plant of the nightshade family; **hen′coop,** a coop or large cage for domestic fowls; **hen′-harr′ier,** a species of hawk, the common harrier (see **harry**).—*adjs.* **hen′-pecked,** weakly subject to his wife; **hen′-toed,** with toes turned in. [O.E. *henn,* fem. of *hana,* a cock; Ger. *henne* (*hahn,* cock).]

hence, *hens, adv.* from this place: from this time onward: in the future: from this cause or reason: from this origin.—*interj.* away! be-gone!—*advs.* **hence′forth, hencefor′ward,** from this time forth or forward. [M.E. *hennes,*

formed with genitive ending from *henne*—O.E. *heonan,* from base of **he.**]

henchman, *hench′man, -sh′-, n.* a servant: a page: an active supporter. [O.E. *hengest,* a horse, and **man.**]

hendecagon, *hen-dek′a-gon, n.* a plane figure of eleven angles and eleven sides. [Gr. *hendeka,* eleven, *gōnia,* an angle.]

hendecasyllable, *hen′dek-å-sil′å-bl, n.* a metrical line of eleven syllables.—*adj.* **hendecasyllab′ic.** [Gr. *hendeka,* eleven, *syllabē,* a syllable.]

hendiadys, *hen-dī′a-dis, n.* a rhetorical figure in which one complex idea (such as that normally contained in a noun and an adjective) is expressed by means of two words connected by 'and', as 'with might and main', meaning 'by main strength'. [Gr. *hen dia dyoin,* lit. 'one by two'.]

henequen, *hen′ē-ken, n.* a tropical American agave: its leaf-fibre, used for cordage. Cf. **sisal.** [Sp. *jeniquén.*]

henna, *hen′a, n.* a small Oriental shrub: a pigment made from its leaves for dyeing the nails and hair and for skin decoration. [Ar. *hennā′.*]

henry, *hen′ri, n.* (*elect.*) the unit of inductance such that an electromotive force of one volt is induced in a circuit by rate of change of current of one ampere per second. [Joseph *Henry,* American physicist (1797-1878).]

hep, *hep, n.* See **hip** (2).

hep, *hep, adj.* (*obsolescent slang*) knowing, informed: well abreast of fashionable knowledge and taste, esp. in the field of jazz.—*ns.* **hep′cat, hep′ster,** one who is hep: a hipster (q.v.). [Perh. *hep,* left (common in drilling)—with ideas of being in step.]

hepatic, *hep-at′ik, adj.* belonging to the liver.—*ns.* **hepatī′tis,** inflammation of the liver; **hepatos′copy,** divination by inspection of the livers of animals. [Gr. *hēpar, hēpatos,* the liver.]

hept(a)-, in composition, seven [Gr. *hepta,* seven]:—e.g. **heptangular,** *hept-ang′gū-lår, adj.* having seven angles.

heptad, *hep′tad, n.* a group of seven. [Gr. *heptas, -ados*—*hepta,* seven.]

heptagon, *hep′ta-gon, n.* a plane figure with seven angles and seven sides.—*adj.* **heptag′-onal.** [Gr. *heptagōnos,* seven-cornered—*hepta,* seven, *gōnia,* an angle.]

heptarchy, *hep′tär-ki, n.* a government by seven persons: the country governed by seven: a misleading term for a once supposed system of seven English kingdoms.—*adj.* **heptar′chic.** [Gr. *hepta,* seven, *archē,* sovereignty.]

her, *hûr, pron.* the objective case (*dat.* or *acc.*) of the *pron.* **she:** also the possessive case (*gen.*)—in this use described also as *possessive adjective.* [M.E. *here*—O.E. *hire,* gen. and dat. sing. of *hēo,* she.]

herald, *her′åld, n.* in ancient times, an officer who made public proclamations and arranged ceremonies: in mediaeval times, an officer who had charge of all the etiquette of chivalry, keeping a register of the genealogies and armorial bearings of the nobles: an officer whose duty is to read proclamations, to blazon the arms of the nobility, &c.: a proclaimer: a forerunner.—*v.t.* to usher in: to proclaim.—*adj.*

Neutral vowels in unaccented syllables: *em′pér-ór*; for certain sounds in foreign words see p. ix.

heral′dic, of or relating to heralds or heraldry.—*adv.* **heral′dically.**—*n.* **her′aldry**, the art or office of a herald: the science of recording genealogies and blazoning coats of arms.—**Heralds′ College**, an official body first set up in 1483 to regulate all matters of chivalry; now concerned with armorial bearings only. [O.Fr. *herault*; of Gmc. origin.]

herb, *hûrb, n.* a plant with no woody stem above ground, as distinguished from a tree or shrub: a plant used in medicine: an aromatic plant used in cookery.—*adj.* **herbā′ceous**, pertaining to, of the nature of, or containing, herbs.—*n.* **herb′age**, herbs collectively: (*law*) right of pasture.—*adj.* **herb′al**, pertaining to herbs.—*n.* a book containing descriptions of plants with medicinal properties, orig. of all plants.—*ns.* **herb′alist**, one who sells or prescribes herbs: an early botanical writer; **herbā′rium**, a classified collection of preserved plants:—*pl.* **herbā′riums**, **herbā′ria**; **herb′ary**, a garden of herbs; **herb′ bonn′et**, a species of *ccum* (q.v.)—from L. *herba benedicta*, blessed herb; **herb′icide** (*-i-sīd*), a substance for killing weeds, &c., esp. selective weedkiller; **herb′ivore** (*-vŏr, -vör*), a grass-eating animal.—*adj.* **herbiv′orous**, eating or living on herbaceous plants.—*n.* **herb′-Rob′ert**, a common kind of geranium. [Fr. *herbe*—L. *herba.*]

Herculean, *hûr-kū′li-án,* also *-lē′án, adj.* of or pertaining to *Hercules*, son of Zeus, noted for the twelve difficult tasks imposed on him: extremely difficult or dangerous, as the twelve labours of Hercules: of extraordinary strength and size.—**Pillars of Hercules**, two rocks flanking the Strait of Gibraltar.

herd, *hûrd, n.* a company of animals of one kind, esp. large animals, that habitually keep together: a group of domestic animals: a stock of cattle: a company of inferior people, the rabble.—*v.i.* to go in herds.—*v.t.* to tend, as a herdsman.—*ns.* **herd**, **herds′man**, **herd′man** (*B.*), one who tends a herd: **herd′-book**, a pedigree book of cattle and pigs; **herd′-instinct**, gregariousness: the instinct that urges men or animals to obey a common impulse, thus acting alike and simultaneously. [O.E. *hæord, hirde, hierde*; Ger. *heerde, hirte.*]

here, *her, adv.* in this place: hither: in the present life or state: at this point.—*advs.* **here′-about**, also **-abouts**, near this place; **hereaf′ter**, after this, in some future time or state.—*n.* a future state.—*advs.* **hereby′**, not far off: by this; **herein′**, in this; **hereof′**, of this; **hereon′**, on or upon this; **hereto′**, till this time: for this object; **heretofore′**, before this time, formerly; **hereunto′** (also *-un′-*), to this point or time; **hereupon′**, on this, immediately after this; **herewith′**, with this—**here and there**, in this place, and then in that: thinly: irregularly; **neither here nor there**, unimportant. [O.E. *hēr*, from base of *hē*, he; Du. and Ger. *hier*, Swed. *här.*]

heredity, *he-red′i-ti, n.* the transmission of physical and psychical characteristics from ancestors to their descendants.—*adj.* **hered′itable**, that may be inherited.—*n.* **heredit′ament**, any property that may pass to an heir.—*adj.* **hered′itary**, descending by inheritance: transmitted to offspring. [L. *hērēditās, -ātis—hērēs, -ēdis,* an heir.]

heresy, *her′i-si, n.* an opinion or belief (esp. in theology) adopted in opposition to that accepted or usual in the community to which one belongs: heterodoxy.—*ns.* **heresiarch** (*her′e-si-ärk,* or *he-rē′zi-ärk*), a leader in heresy; **her′etic**, the upholder of a heresy.—*adj.* **heret′ical.**—*adv.* **heret′ically.** [O.Fr. *heresie*—L. *hacresis*—Gr. *hairesis—haireein,* to take.]

heriot, *her′i-ót, n.* (*Eng. law*) a fine due to the lord of a manor on the death of a tenant originally his best beast or chattel. [O.E. *heregeatu,* a military preparation—*here*, an army, *geatwe*, equipment.]

heritable, *her′i-ta-bl, adj.* that may be inherited.—*n.* **her′itor**, in Scotland, a landholder in a parish.—**heritable property** (*Scots law*), real property, as opposed to movable property or chattels; **heritable security**, same as English mortgage. [Fr. *héritable, héréditable* Low L. *hērēditābilia—hērēs,* heir.]

heritage, *her′it-ij, n.* that which is inherited: inherited lot, condition to which one is born: (*B.*) the children (of God). [O.Fr. *heritage, heriter*—Late L. *hērēditāre,* to inherit.]

hermaphrodite, *hûr-maf′rod-īt, n.* an animal or a plant with the organs of both sexes: a compound of opposite qualities.—*adj.* uniting the distinctions of both sexes.—*adjs.* **hermaphrodit′ic, -al.** [Gr. *Hermaphrodītos,* the son of *Hermēs* and *Aphroditē,* who grew together with the nymph Salmacis into one person.]

hermeneutic, -al, *hûr-mē-nū′tik, -ál, adj.* interpreting, explanatory.—*adv.* **hermeneu′tically.**—*n.sing.* **hermeneu′tics**, the science of interpretation, esp. of the Scriptures. [Gr. *hermēneutikos—hermēneus,* an interpreter, from *Hermēs,* the herald of the gods.]

hermetic, -al, *hûr-met′ik, -ál, adj.* belonging in any way to the beliefs current in the Middle Ages which were attributed to *Hermes Trismegistos:* belonging to magic or alchemy, magical: perfectly close.—*adv.* **hermet′ically.**—**hermetically sealed**, closed completely. [From *Hermēs Trismegistos,* Hermes 'the thrice-greatest', the Greek name for the Egyptian Thoth, god of science, esp. alchemy.]

hermit, *hûr′mit, n.* a solitary religious ascetic: a recluse.—*n.* **her′mitage** (*-ij*), the dwelling of a hermit: a retired abode. [M.E. *eremite,* through Fr. and L. from Gr. *erēmītēs—erēmos,* solitary.]

hern. Same as **heron.**

hernia, *hûr′ni-a, n.* the protrusion of a viscus, or part of a viscus, through an opening or weak spot or defective area in the cavity containing it—esp. an abdominal viscus.—*adj.* **her′nial.** [L.]

hero, *hē′rō, n.* a man of distinguished bravery: any illustrious person: a person reverenced and idealised: the principal male figure in a history or work of fiction: (*orig.*) a man of superhuman powers, a demigod:—*pl.* **hē′roes:**—*fem.* **heroine** (*her′ō-in*).—*adj.* **heroic** (*hē-rō′ik*), befitting a hero: of heroes (e.g. *the heroic age*): concerned with heroes, epic: courageous.—*n.pl.* **herō′ics,** extravagant phrases, bombast.—*adj.* **herō′ical.**—*adv.* **herō′ically.**—*adjs.* **herō′i-com′ic, -al,** consisting of a mixture of heroic and comic, high burlesque.—*ns.* **heroism** (*her'ō-izm*), the qualities of a hero: high courage; **hē'ro-wor'ship**, the worship of heroes: excessive admiration.—**heroic age**, any semi-mythical period when, it was represented, heroes or demigods lived among men; **heroic verse**, the form of verse in which the exploits of heroes are celebrated (in classical poetry, the hexameter; in English, the iambic pentameter; in French, the alexandrine); **hero'ic coup'let**, a pair of rhyming lines of heroic verse. [Through O.Fr. and L. from Gr. *hērōs*; akin to L. *vir*, O.E. *wer*, a man, Sans. *vīra*, a hero.]

Herodians, *he-rō'di-ănz, n.pl.* a party among the Jews, adherents of the family of *Herod*.

heroin, *her'ō-in, n.* a derivative of morphine used in medicine and by drug-addicts. [Said to be from Gr. *hērōs*, a hero, from its effect.]

heron, *her'ón, n.* a genus of large screaming wading birds, with long legs and neck.—*n.* **her'onry**, a place where herons breed. [O.Fr. *hairon*—O.H.G. *heigir*.]

heronshaw, *her'ón-shō, n.* a young heron. [Properly *heronsewe* (O.Fr. *herounçel*), confounded with *hernshaw*, a heronry, from *heron*, and *shaw*, a wood.]

herpes, *hûr'pēz, n.* a spreading disease of the skin, esp. shingles. [Gr. *herpēs*—*herpein*, to creep.]

Herr, *her*, a German title equivalent to English Mr. [Ger.]

herrenvolk, *her'en-fōlk, n.* master-race, fitted and entitled by their superior qualities to rule the world. [Ger.]

herring, *her'ing, n.* a common small sea-fish of great commercial value, found moving in great shoals or multitudes.—*adj.* **herr'ingbone**, like the spine of a herring, applied to a kind of masonry in which the stones slope in different directions in alternate rows, to a similar stitch, &c.: in skiing, of a method of climbing a slope, the skis being placed at an angle and leaving a herring-bone-like pattern in the snow.—*n.* **herr'ing-pond**, the N. Atlantic Ocean.—**red herring**, herring cured and dried: a subject introduced to divert a discussion. [O.E. *hǣring, hēring*; cf. Ger. *häring, heer*.]

hers, *hérz, pron.* the possessive (*gen.*) case of **she**. See **theirs**.

herself, *hér-self', pron.* the emphatic form of **she** (nominative), **her** (objective—accusative or dative): in her real character: having the command of her faculties: sane: in good form: the reflexive form of **her** (objective).

hertz, *hûrts, n.* SI unit of frequency, that of a periodic phenomenon of which the periodic time is one second—sometimes called cycle per second in U.K.—**Hertzian waves**, electromagnetic waves used in communicating information through space. [Heinrich *Hertz* (1857–94), German physicist.]

hesitate, *hez'i-tāt, v.i.* to pause irresolutely: to be in doubt: to be reluctant (to): to stammer.—*ns.* **hes'itancy**, **hesitā'tion**, wavering: doubt: stammering.—*adj.* **hes'itant**, hesitating.—*adv.* **hes'itātingly**. [L. *haesitāre, -ātum*, freq. of *haerēre, haesum*, to stick.]

Hesper, *hes'pér*, **Hesperus**, *hes'pér-us, n.* Venus

as the evening-star.—*adj.* **Hespē'rian**, in the west. [Gr. *hesperos*, evening.]

Hessian, *hes'i-ăn*, sometimes *hesh'-, adj.* of or pertaining to *Hesse*.—*n.* a native of Hesse: (without *cap.*) a coarse cloth made of jute, used for sacks, &c.: (*pl.*) short for **Hessian boots**, a kind of long boots first worn by Hessian troops.—**Hessian fly**, a midge whose larva attacks wheat stems. [From *Hesse*, Ger. *Hessen*, in Germany.]

hest, *hest, n.* a command. [O.E. *hǣs.*]

hetero-, *het'ér-o-, -ō'-*, **heter-**, in composition, different, other—often opposed to *homo-*, *auto-* [Gr. *heteros*]:—e.g. **heterocarpous**, *het-ér-ō-kär'pùs, adj.* bearing fruit of more than one kind (Gr. *karpos*, fruit); **heterosexual** (*het-ér-ō-seks'ū-ál*), having or pertaining to sexual attraction towards the opposite sex.

heteroclite, *het'ér-ō-klīt, adj.* (*gram.*) irregularly inflected—also **heteroclit'ic -al.**—*n.* **het'eroclīte**, a word irregularly inflected. [Gr. *heteroklitos*—*heteros*, other, *klitos*, inflected—*klinein*, to inflect.]

heterodox, *het'ér-ō-doks, adj.* holding an opinion other than, different from, the one generally received, esp. in theology—heretical.—*n.* **het'erodoxy**, heresy. [Gr. *heterodoxos*—*heteros*, other, *doxa*, an opinion—*dokeein*, to think.]

heterodyne, *het'ér-ō-dīn, n.* (in (radio) communication, applied to a method of imposing on a carrier wave another of different frequency to produce audible beats. [Gr. *heteros*, other, *dynamis*, strength.]

heterogeneous, *het-ér-ō-jē'ni-ùs, adj.* differing in kind: composed of parts or elements of different kinds—opposed to *homogeneous.*—*ns.* **heterogene'ity**, **heterogēn'eousness**.—*adv.* **heterogēn'eously**. [Gr. *heterogenēs*—*heteros*, other, *genos*, a kind.]

heterogenesis, *het-ér-ō-jen'e-sis, n.* (*biol.*) spontaneous generation: alternate generation (see *generation*).—*adj.* **heterogenet'ic**. [Gr. *heteros*, other, *genesis*, generation.]

hetman, *het'man, n.* (*hist.*) a Polish officer: the head or general of the Cossacks. [Russ.]

heuristic, *hū-ris'tik, adj.* serving, or leading one, to find out: pertaining to the method of education by which the pupil is set to find out things for himself: (of method, argument) depending on assumptions based on past experience: consisting of guided trial and error.—Also *n.* [Gr. *heuriskein*, to find.]

hew, *hū, v.t.* to cut (away, down, in pieces, &c.) with blows: to shape: to cut (a path; e.g. to *hew one's way*):—*pa.p.* hewed, or hewn.—*n.* **hew'er**, one who hews. [O.E. *hēawan*; Ger. *hauen*.]

hexa-, **hex-**, in composition, six [Gr. *hex*]:—e.g. **hexad**, *hek'sad, n.* a group of six (Gr. *hexas*, -*ados*); **hex'ose**, a sugar (of various kinds) with six carbon atoms to the molecule.

hexachord, *hek'sa-körd, n.* a series of six notes having a semitone between the third and fourth notes and a tone between each of the other pairs of consecutive notes—the forerunner of the octave. [**hexa-** and Gr. *chordē*, a string.]

hexagon, *heks'a-gon, n.* a figure with six sides and six angles.—*adj.* **hexag'onal.**—*adv.* **hex-**

Neutral vowels in unaccented syllables: *em'pér-ór*; for certain sounds in foreign words see p. ix.

ag'onally. [Gr. *hexagōnon*—*hex*, six, *gōnia*, an angle.]

hexahedron, *heks-a-hē'dron*, *n.* a solid with six sides or faces, especially a cube.—*adj.* **hexahē'dral.** [Gr. *hex*, six, *hĕdra*, a base.]

hexameter, *hek-sam'et-ér*, *n.* a verse of six measures or feet.—*adj.* having six metrical feet. [L.,—Gr. *hex*, six, *metron*, a measure.]

hexapla, *heks'a-pla*, *n.* an edition, esp. of the Bible, consisting of six versions in parallel columns.—*adj.* **hex'aplar.** [Gr. *hexapla*, pl. neut. *hexaplous*, sixfold.]

hexapod, *heks'a-pod*, *n.* an animal with six feet. [Gr. *hexapous, -podos*—*hex*, six, *pous*, a foot.]

hexastich, *heks'a-stik*, *n.* a poem or stanza of six lines. [Gr. *hexastichos*—*hex*, six, *stichos*, a line.]

hexastyle, *heks'a-stīl*, *adj.* having six columns.—*n.* a building or portico having six columns in front. [Gr. *hexastylos*—*hex*, six, *stylos*, a pillar.]

hey, hā. *interj.* expressive of joy or interrogation or calling attention.—*n.* **hey'day,** exuberance: period of fullest vigour. [Imit.]

hiatus, *hī-ā'tus*, *n.* (*rare*) a gap, a chasm: a break in continuity: a place in a manuscript, &c., where something is missing: (*gram.*) a slight pause between two vowels coming together in successive words or syllables:—*pl.* **hiā'tuses.**—**hiatus hernia,** one in which a part of a viscus protrudes through a natural opening, esp. through that in the diaphragm intended for the oesophagus. [L., —*hiāre, hiātum*, to gape.]

hibernate, *hī'bér nāt*, *v.i.* to winter: to pass the winter in torpor: (*fig.*) to remain in a state of inactivity.—*n.* **hibernā'tion.**—**hibernation anaesthesia,** freezing-down. [L. *hibernāre, -ātum*—*hibernus*, wintry—*hiems*, winter.]

Hibernian, *hī bûr'ni-an*, *adj.* relating to *Hibernia* or Ireland.—*n.* an Irishman.—*ns.* **Hiber'nianism, Hiber'nicism,** an Irish idiom or peculiarity: a bull in speech. [L. *Hibernia*, Ireland.]

Hibiscus, *hib-is'kus*, *n.* a genus of malvaceous plants, mostly tropical. [L.,—Gr. *ibiskos*, marshmallow.]

hiccup, *hik'up*, *n.* a sudden spasm of the diaphragm followed immediately by closure of the glottis: the sound caused by this.—*v.i.* to be affected with hiccup.—*v.t.* to say with a hiccup:—*pr.p.* **hicc'uping;** *pa.p.* **hicc'uped.** [Imit.; cf. Du. *hik*, Dan. *hik*, Breton *hik* The spelling *hiccough* is due to a confusion with cough.]

hick, *hik*, *n.* a lout: a booby.—*adj.* pertaining to a hick: rural and uncultured. [A familiar form of *Richard*.]

hickory, *hik'ór-i*, *n.* a genus of North American trees of the walnut family, some yielding edible nuts, some strong tenacious wood. [Earlier *pohickery*; of Amer. Indian origin.]

hid, hidden. See hide.

hidalgo, *hi-dal'gō*, *n.* a Spanish nobleman of the lowest class:—*pl.* **hidalgōs.** [Sp. *hijo de algo*, 'the son of something'.]

hide, *hīd*, *v.t.* to conceal: to put out of sight: to keep secret: to screen.—*v.i.* to go into, or stay in, concealment:—*pa.t.* hid; *pa.p.* hidd'en, hid.—*adj.* hidd'en, concealed: unknown.—*n.*

hid'ing, the act or state of concealing: a place of concealment. [O.E. *hȳdan*, to hide.]

hide, *hīd*, *n.* the skin of an animal: (in contempt) human skin.—*v.t.* to flog or whip.—*adj.* **hide'-bound** (of an animal), having the hide clinging too closely to the body: (of trees) having the bark so close that it impedes the growth: bigoted, obstinate.—*n.* **hid'ing,** a thrashing. [O.E. *hȳd*; Ger. *haut*, L. *cutis*.]

hide, *hīd*, *n.* in old English law, a variable unit of area of land, enough for a household. [O.E. *hīd*, contracted from *hīgid*; cf. *hīwan, hīgan*, household.]

hideous, *hid'i-ús*, *adj.* frightful, horrible, ghastly: extremely ugly.—*n.* **hid'eousness.**—*adv.* **hid'eously.** [O.Fr. *hideus, hisdos*—*hide, hisde*, dread; perh. from L. *hispidus*, rough, rude.]

hie, *hī*, *v.i.* to hasten:—*pr.p.* hie'ing; *pa.p.* hied. [O.E. *hīgian.*]

hiemal, *hē'mal*, *hī'e-mál*, *adj.* belonging to winter. [L. *hiems*, winter.]

hierarch, *hī'ér-ärk*, *n.* a ruler in sacred matters, as a chief priest.—*adjs.* **hi'erarchal, -arch'ic(al).**—*ns.* **hi'erarchism; hi'erarchy,** the collective body of angels, grouped in three divisions and nine orders of different power and glory: a series of successive officers of different rank: a body classified in successively subordinate grades: a government by priests [Gr. *hierarchēs*—*hieros*, sacred, *archein*, to rule.]

hieratic, *hī-ér-at'ik*, *adj.* priestly: applying to a kind of ancient Egyptian writing consisting of abridged forms of hieroglyphics. [L. *hieraticus*—Gr. *hieratikos*—*hieros*, sacred.]

hieroglyph, *hī'ér-o-glif*, *n.* a sacred character used in ancient Egyptian picture-writing, or in picture-writing in general.—*n.* **hieroglyph'ic,** a hieroglyph: any written character difficult to read.—*adjs.* **hieroglyph'ic, -al.**—*adv.* **hieroglyph'ically.**—*n.* **hierog'lyphist,** one skilled in hieroglyphics. [Gr. *hierogly-philon hieros*, sacred, *glyphein*, to carve.]

hierograph, *hī'ér-ō-gräf*, *n.* a sacred symbol.—*adjs.* **hierograph'ic, -al,** pertaining to sacred writing. [Gr. *hieros*, sacred, *graphein*, to write.]

hierology, *hī-ér-ol'o-ji*, *n.* sacred literature, esp. Egyptian, Greek, Jewish, &c. [Gr. *hieros*, sacred, *legein*, to speak.]

hierophant, *hī'ér-ō-fant*, *n.* one who officially reveals sacred things: a priest: an expounder. [Gr. *hierophantēs*—*hieros*, sacred, *phainein*, to show.]

hi-fi, *hī-fī*. See high.

higgle, *hig'l*, *v.i.* to make difficulty in bargaining: to chaffer.—*n.* **higg'ler.** [Prob. a form of **haggle.**]

higgledy-piggledy, *hig'l-di-pig'l-di*, *adv.* and *adj.* haphazard: in confusion.

high, *hī*, *adj.* elevated, lofty, tall: far up from a base, as the ground, sea-level, low-tide, the zero of a scale: advanced in a scale, esp. the scale of nature: expressible by means of a large number: of an advanced degree of intensity, extreme: advanced in time (e.g. *high summer*): acute in pitch: exalted in quality (e.g. *high aims*): powerful, eminent: chief: noble: haughty, arrogant: angry (e.g. words): loud: tempestuous: dear (of price): for heavy stakes: slightly tainted (of game, &c.): over-excited, nervy: drunk: (*slang*) under the influence of a drug.—*adv.* aloft: arrogantly: eminently: powerfully.—'*adv.* **high′ly,** in a high degree: very: very favourably.—*ns.* **high′-al′tar,** the principal altar in a church; **high′-ball** (*U.S.*), whisky and soda or the like with ice in a tall glass.—*adjs.* **high′-born,** of noble birth; **high′-bred,** of noble breed, training, or family.—*n.* **high-brow,** one who makes undue intellectual pretensions (also *adj.*).—*adj.* **High′-Church,** of a party within the Church of England that exalts the authority of the episcopate and the priesthood, the saving grace of sacraments, &c.—*ns.* **High′-Church′ism; High′-Church′man.**—*adjs.* **high′-col′oured,** having a strong colour: having a ruddy complexion; **high′ly-col′oured,** (*fig.*) exaggerated.—*ns.* **High′-Court,** a supreme court; **high′-day,** a holiday or festival: (*hī-dā′*) broad daylight.—*n. pl.* **High′ers** (*coll.*), school examinations leading to the Scottish Certificate of Education at higher level: passes in these.— *adjs.* **high′-falut′in(g)** (*-lōōt′-*), bombastic: pompous (also *n.*); **high′-fed,** fed luxuriously, pampered; **high-fidel′ity,** good in reproduction of sound (abbrev. **hi-fi**).—*n.* **high′-flier,** a bird that flies high: one who runs into extravagance of action, an ambitious person.—*adjs.* **high′-flown** (of style), extravagant, turgid; **high′-fly′ing; high′-hand′ed,** overbearing, violent, arbitrary.—*v.t.* **high′-hat′,** to adopt a superior attitude towards (someone) or to ignore (someone) socially.—*adj.* **high′-heart′ed,** full of courage.—*n.* **high-jinks,** boisterous play or jollity.—*n.* and *adj.* **high′land,** a mountainous district, esp. (in *pl.*) the north-west of Scotland (bordered geologically by the great fault running from Dumbarton to Stonehaven), or the narrower area in which Gaelic is, or was recently, spoken.—*ns.* **high′lander, high′landman,** an inhabitant of a mountainous region.—*n.pl.* **high′-lights,** the most brightly lighted spots in a picture or photograph: the most striking or memorable parts of an entertainment or other experience.—*v.t.* **high′-light,** to throw into relief by a strong light (*lit.* and *fig.*).—*n.* **high′-mass** (see **mass**).—*adj.* **high′-mind′ed,** having a high, proud, or arrogant mind: having honourable pride: magnanimous.—*ns.* **high′-mind′edness; high′ness,** the state of being high: dignity of rank: a title of honour given to princes.—*adj.* **high′-oc′tane** (of petrol) of high octane number and so of high efficiency.—*n.* **high′-place** (*B.*), an eminence on which idolatrous rites were performed by the Jews—hence the idols, &c., themselves.—*adjs.* **high′-pow′ered,** very forceful and efficient; **high′-press′ure,** making or allowing use of steam or other fluid at pressure much above that of the atmosphere: involving intense activity.—*n.* **high priest,** the chief priest.—*adjs.* **high′-prin′cipled,** of high, noble, or strict principle; **high′-proof,** proved to contain much alcohol: highly rectified; **high′-rank′ing,** of high rank in the armed forces: senior: eminent; **high′-rise,** (of flats, office blocks, &c.) containing a large number of storeys.—*n.* **high′-road,** a highway: an easy way.—*adjs.* **high′-sea′soned,** made rich or piquant with spices or other seasoning;

high′-souled, having a lofty soul or spirit; **high′-sound′ing,** pompous, ostentatious; **high′-spirited,** high-souled: having natural fire: bold, daring.—*n.* **high′-stepp′er,** a horse that lifts its feet high from the ground: (*coll.*) a person of imposing bearing or fashionable pretensions.—*adj.* **high′-,** or **high′ly-strung,** nervously sensitive.—*n.* **hight, highth,** obsolete forms of *height.*—*adj.* **high′-test** (of petrol), boiling at comparatively low temperature and so of high performance.—*ns.* **high′-trea′son,** treason against the sovereign or state; **high′-up,** one in a position of authority (also *adj.*); **high′(-)wa′ter,** the time at which the tide is highest: the greatest elevation of the tide; **high′(-)water mark,** the line on the shore of a sea, lake, &c., reached by the tide at high water: (*fig.*) the highest point or degree; **high′way,** a public road, esp. a main road: the main or usual way or course; **high′wayman,** a robber who attacks people on the public way.—*adj.* **high′-wrought,** wrought with exquisite skill, highly finished: worked-up, agitated.—**high latitudes,** latitudes far from the equator; **high life,** the life of fashionable society; **high living,** luxurious feeding; **high noon,** exactly noon: (*fig.*) the peak; **high polymer,** polymer of high molecular weight; **high seas,** the open sea beyond territorial waters; **high table,** the dons' table in a college dining-hall; **high tea,** a tea with meat, &c., as opposed to a plain tea.—**a high hand,** or **arm,** power: audacity; **a high (old) time,** a time of special jollity; **high time,** quite time (that something was done): on **high,** aloft: in heaven. [O.E. *hēah*; O.N. *hār,* Ger. *hoch.*]

hight, *hīt, v.t.* (*obs.*) to be named:—*arch. pa.t.* and *pa.p.* **hight.** [O.E. *hātte,* is or was called. Cf. Ger. *ich heisse,* I am named, from *heissen,* to call.]

hijacker, highjacker, *hī′jak-ér, n.* (*hist.*) a highwayman: a robber: one who hijacks.—*v.t.* **hi′jack, high′jack,** to stop and rob (a vehicle): to steal in transit: to force a pilot to fly (an aeroplane) to an unscheduled destination.— Also *v.i.* [Origin obscure.]

hike, *hīk, v.t.* (*coll.*) to raise up with a jerk: to increase (e.g. prices) sharply and suddenly.— *v.i.* to travel on foot with equipment on back: (of skirts, &c.) to move up out of place.—*ns.* **hike,** a walking tour; **hiker.** [Perh. **hitch.**]

hilarious, *hi-lā′ri-ús, adj.* gay, very merry.—*adv.* **hilā′riously.**—*n.* **hilarity** (*hi-lar′-*), gaiety. [L. *hilaris*—Gr. *hilaros,* cheerful.]

Hilary, *hil′ár-i, adj.* a term or session of the High Court of Justice in England, beginning at or near St *Hilary's* Day, Jan. 13.

hill, *hil, n.* a high mass of land, less than a mountain: a mound: an incline on a road.—*n.* **hill′ock,** a small hill.—*adj.* **hill′y,** full of hills.—**over the hill,** past one's highest point of efficiency: on the downgrade: past the greatest difficulty. [O.E. *hyll*; allied to L. *collis,* a hill, *celsus,* high.]

hilt, *hilt, n.* the handle, esp. of a sword.—**up to the hilt,** completely. [O.E. *hilt*; M.Du. *hilte,* O.H.G. *helza*; not conn. with **hold.**]

hilum, *hī′lum, n.* the scar on a seed where it joined its stalk:—*pl.* **hī′la.** [L. *hīlum,* a trifle, 'that which adheres to a bean'.]

Neutral vowels in unaccented syllables: *em′pér-ór*; for certain sounds in foreign words see p. ix.

him, *him, pron.* the objective case (*dat.* or *acc.*) of the *pron.* **he.** [O.E. *him,* dat. sing. of *hē, he, he, hit,* it.]

himself, *him-self′, pron.* the emphatic form of **he, him:** in his real character: having command of his faculties: sane: in good form: the reflexive form of **him** (objective).

hind, *hīnd, n.* a female deer, esp. the female of the stag or red-deer. [O.E. *hind*; Du. and Ger. *hinde.*]

hind, *hīnd, n.* a farm-servant, a ploughman, a peasant. [O.E. *hīna* = *hīwna,* gen. pl. of *hīwan,* domestics.]

hind, *hīnd, adj.* placed in the rear: pertaining to the part behind: back:—opposed to *fore.*— Also **hind′er.**—*adjs.* **hind′ermost, hind′-most,** superlative of **hind,** farthest behind.—*n.pl.* **hind′quarters,** the rear parts of a quadruped.—*n.* **hind′sight,** wisdom after the event. [O.E. *hinder,* backwards; Ger. *hinter,* behind; cf. O.E. *hindan* (adv.), back.]

hinder, *hin′dėr, v.t.* to keep back: to stop, or prevent progress of.—*v.i.* to be an obstacle.— *ns.* **hin′drance, hin′derance,** act of hindering: that which hinders, an obstacle. [O.E. *hindrian*; Ger. *hindern.*]

Hindi, *hin′dē, n.* and *adj.* an Indo-Germanic language of N. India, of which *Hindustani* is a dialect: a recent literary form of it, with terms from Sanskrit. [From *Hind,* India.]

Hindu, Hindoo, *hin-dōō′,* or *hin′-, n.* (*arch.*) a member of any of the races of Hindustan or all India: now a believer in a form of Brahmanism —*n.* **Hin′duism, Hin′dooism,** the religion and customs of the Hindus. [Pers. *Hindu*— *Hind,* India.]

Hindustani, Hindoostanee, *hin-dōō-stä′ne, n.* a form of *Hindi* containing elements from other languages.—Also *adj.*

hinge, *hinj, n.* the hook or joint on which a door or lid turns: the principle or fact on which anything depends or turns.—*v.t.* to furnish with hinges: to bend.—*v.i.* to hang or turn as on a hinge: to depend (on):—*pr.p.* hing′ing; *pa.p.* hinged.—*n.* **hinge′-joint** (*anat.*), a joint that allows movement in one plane only. [Re lated to **hang.**]

hinny, *hin′i, n.* the offspring of a stallion and a she-ass: (*coll.*) a term of endearment. [L. *hinnus*—Gr. *ginnos,* later *hinnos,* a mule.]

hint, *hint, n.* a distant or indirect indication or allusion: slight mention: a helpful suggestion.—*v.t.* to intimate or indicate indirectly.— *v.i.* to give hints. [O.E. *hentan,* to seize.]

hinterland, *hint′ér-land, n.* a region lying inland from a port or centre of influence. [Ger.]

hip, *hip, n.* the projection of the pelvis and the upper part of the thigh bone.—*n. pl.* **hip′sters,** trousers slung from the hips, not the waist.— **hip and thigh,** utterly. [O.E. *hype*; Ger. *hüfte.*]

hip, *hip,* **hep,** *hep, n.* the fruit of the dog-rose or other rose. [O.E. *hēope.*]

hip, *hip, n.* hypochondria.—*adjs.* **hipped,** melancholy: obsessed: peevish, annoyed; **hipp′ish.** [A corr. of **hypochondria.**]

hip, *hip, adj.* a later form of **hep.**—*ns.* **hipp′y,** one of the hippies, successors of the beatniks as rebels against society, who stress the importance of love, peace, and experiences under hallucinogenic drugs; **hipster,** modern

form of hepster: a member of the beat generation (1950s and early 1960s).

hippocampus, *hip-ō-kam′pus, n.* a genus of small fishes with horse-like head and neck, the sea-horse. [Gr. *hippokampos*—*hippos,* a horse, *kampos,* a sea-monster.]

Hippocratic oath, an oath taken by a doctor binding him to observe the code of medical ethics contained in it—first drawn up (perhaps by Hippocrates, Greek physician) in the 4th or 5th century B.C.

hippodrome, *hip′o-drōm, n.* a racecourse for horses and chariots: an equestrian circus: by extension, a theatre. [Fr.,—Gr. *hippodromos*—*hippos,* a horse, *dromos,* a course.]

hippogriff, hippogryph, *hip′ō-grif, n.* a fabulous animal, a winged horse with the head of a griffin. [Fr. *hippogriffe*—Gr. *hippos,* a horse, *gryps,* a griffin.]

hippopotamus, *hip-ō-pot′a-mus, n.* any of several large African quadrupeds, of aquatic habits, with very thick skin, short legs, and a large head and muzzle:—*pl.* **-muses** or **-mī.** [L.,—Gr. *hippopotamos*—*hippos,* a horse, *potamos,* a river.]

hircine, *hûr′sīn, adj.* goat-like: having a strong goatish smell. [Fr.,—L. *hircīnus*—*hircus,* a he-goat.]

hire, *hīr, n.* wages for service: the price paid for the use of anything: an arrangement by which use or service is granted for payment.—*v.t.* to procure the use or service of, at a price: to engage for wages: to grant temporary use of (esp. a vehicle) for compensation (also **hire out**): to bribe.—*ns.* **hire′ling,** a hired servant—used contemptuously (also *adj.*); **hir′er,** one who hires, esp. one who makes a business of hiring out vehicles; **hire′-pur′chase,** a system by which a hired article becomes the property of the hirer after a stipulated number of payments.—**on hire,** for hiring; **be worthy of his, one's, hire,** to deserve to be recompensed for the services he, one, has done (Luke x. 7). [O.E. *hȳr,* wages, *hȳrian,* to hire.]

hirsute, *hér-sūt′, adj.* hairy: rough, shaggy: (*bot.*) having long, stiffish hairs. [L. *hirsūtus*—*hirsus, hirtus,* shaggy.]

hirundine, *hi-run′din, -din, adj.* of or pertaining to the swallow. [L. *hirundō,* a swallow.]

his, *hiz, pron.* possessive (*gen.*) form of **he**— described also as a *possessive adjective:* (*B.* and *Shak.*) its. [O.E. *his,* gen. of *hē, he,* he, and of *hit,* it.]

hispid, *his′pid, adj.* (*bot.*) rough with, or having, strong hairs or bristles. [L. *hispidus.*]

hiss, *his, v.i.* to make a sibilant sound like that usually represented by the letter *s,* as the goose, serpent, &c.: to express contempt, &c., by hissing. *v.t.* to condemn by hissing.—*n.* the sound of the letter *s,* an expression of disapprobation, contempt, &c.—*n.* **hiss′ing.** [Imit.]

hist, *hist, interj.* demanding silence and attention: hush! silence! [Imit.]

hist(o)-, *hist(ō)-, -o′-,* in composition, tissue, as in *ns.* **histamine,** (*hist′a-mēn*), a chemical released by the body tissue in cases of injury (e.g. causing redness or swelling when the skin is cut or burned) or of allergy; **histology,**

his-tol'o-ji, the study of the minute structure of the tissues of organisms. [Gr. *histos,* web, and *logos,* discourse.]

history, *hist'ór-i, n.* an account of an event or events: an account of the origin and progress of a nation, institution, &c.: the knowledge of past events: a past of more than common interest.—*n.* **historian** (*hist'-ōr'i-án*), a writer of history: one who is learned in history.— *adjs.* **histŏr'ical,** pertaining to history: containing history: derived from history—real (not legendary), accurate, without fictitious elements; **histŏr'ic,** famous in history: memorable.—*adv.* **histŏr'ically.**—*ns.* **historic'ity** (*-is'-*), historical truth, actuality; **historiog'rapher,** a writer of history, esp. an official historian; **historiog'raphy,** the art or employment of writing history.—**historic present,** the present tense used for the past, to add life and reality to the narrative. [L. *historia*—Gr. *historia*—*histōr,* knowing.]

histrionic, -al, *his-tri-on'ik, -ál, adj.* relating to the stage or actors: stagy: feigned: melodramatic: hypocritical.—*adv.* **histrion'ically.** —*n.pl.* **histrion'ics,** play-acting. [L. *histriōnicus*—*histrio,* an actor.]

hit, *hit, v.t.* to strike: to reach with a blow or missile: to affect painfully: to find or attain by chance.—*v.i.* to come in contact: to strike (with *out*):—*pr.p.* **hitt'ing;** *pa.t.* and *pa.p.* **hit.**—*n.* a lucky chance: a quick success: a stroke: a happy turn of thought or expression.—*n.* **hitt'er.**—*adj.* **hit-and-run** (see **tip-and-run**): (of a driver) causing injury or death and then driving away without reporting the incident: (of an accident) caused by a hit-and-run driver.—*n.* **hit'-parade',** a list of currently popular songs.—**hit below the belt,** to deal an unfair blow (*lit.* and *fig.*); **hit it off,** to agree: to be compatible and friendly; **hit off,** to imitate or describe exactly; **hit upon,** to come upon, discover; **make a hit with,** to make a good impression on: to become popular with. [O.E. *hyttan,* app. O.N. *hitta,* to light on, to find.]

hitch, *hich, v.i.* to move jerkily: to catch on an obstacle.—*v.t.* to jerk: to hook: to fasten.—*n.* a jerk: a catch or anything that holds: a stoppage owing to a small or passing difficulty: (*naut.*) a knot or noose, usually temporary.— *v.i.* **hitch-hike,** to hike with the help of lifts in vehicles.

hither, *hiᴠᴠ'ér, adv.* to this place.—*adj.* toward the speaker: nearer.—*adj.* **hith'ermost,** nearest on this side.—*advs.* **hith'erto,** up to this time; **hith'erward(s),** towards this place.— **hither and thither,** in various directions. [O.E. *hider;* O.N. *hethra.*]

Hitlerism, *hit'lér-izm, n.* militant anti-Jewish nationalism, subordinating everything to the state.—*adj.* (used derogatorily) **Hit'lerite.** [From Adolf *Hitler,* German Nazi dictator, 1933-1945.]

hive, *hīv, n.* a box or basket in which bees live and store up honey: a colony of bees: a scene of great industry.—*v.t.* to collect into a hive: to lay up in store.—*v.i.* to take shelter (together), as if bees.—**hive off,** to withdraw, as if in a swarm: to assign (work) to a subsidiary company: to divert (assets or sections of an industrial concern) to other concerns. [O.E. *hȳf.*]

hoar, *hōr, hör, adj.* white or greyish-white, esp. with age or frost.—*adj.* **hoar'y,** white or grey with age: (*bot.*) covered with short, dense, whitish hairs.—*ns.* **hoar, hoar'iness.**—*n.* **hoar'-frost,** rime or white frost, the white particles formed by the freezing of dew. [O.E. *hār,* hoary, gray; O.N. *hārr.*]

hoard, *hōrd, hörd, n.* a store: a hidden stock.—*v.t.* to store, esp. in excess: to amass and deposit in secret.—Also *v.i.*—*n.* **hoard'er.** [O.E. *hord;* O.N. *hodd,* Ger. *hort.*]

hoard, *hōrd, hörd, hoarding, hōrd'ing, hörd-, n.* a screen of boards, esp. for enclosing a place where builders are at work or for display of bills. [O.Fr. *hurdis*—*hurt, hourt, hourd,* a palisade.]

hoarhound. Same as **horehound.**

hoarse, *hōrs, hörs, adj.* having a rough, husky voice, as from a cold: harsh: discordant.—*adv.* **hoarse'ly.**—*n.* **hoarse'ness.** [M.E. *hōrs, hoors*—O.E. recorded from *hās,* inferred *hārs.*]

hoast, *hōst, n.* (*dial.*) a cough.—*v.i.* to cough. [O.N. *hōste;* cf. O.E. *hwōsta,* Du. *hoest.*]

hoax, *hōks, n.* a deceptive trick: a practical joke.—*v.t.* to trick, by a practical joke or fabricated tale, for sport, or without malice.— *n.* **hoax'er.** [Prob. *hocus.*]

hob, *hob, n.* a hub: a surface beside a fireplace, on which anything may be laid to keep hot.—*n.* **hob'nail,** a nail with a thick, strong head, used in horseshoes, &c.: a clownish fellow.—*adj.* **hob'nailed.** [Ety. uncertain.]

hob, *hob, n.* a clownish fellow: a rustic: a fairy.—*n.* **hob'goblin,** a mischievous fairy: a frightful apparition. [A form of *Rob* for *Robin, Robert.*]

hobble, *hob'l, v.i.* to walk with short unsteady steps, to walk awkwardly: (*fig.*) to move irregularly.—*v.t.* to fasten the legs of (horses, &c.) loosely together.—*n.* an awkward hobbling gait: a difficulty. [Cf. Du. *hobbelen, hobben,* to toss.]

hobbledehoy, *hob'l-di-hoi', n.* a stripling, neither man nor boy. [Origin obscure.]

hobby, *hob'i, n.* a smallish strong, active horse: a pacing horse: a subject on which one is constantly 'mounting': a favourite pursuit.—*n.* **hobb'y-horse,** a stick or figure of a horse on which children ride: one of the chief parts played in the ancient morris dance: the wooden horse of a merry-go-round. [M.E. *hobyn, hoby,* prob. *Hob,* a by-form of *Rob.*]

hobgoblin. See **hob** (2).

hobnail. See **hob** (1).

hobnob, *hob'nob, adv.* with alternate or mutual drinking of healths.—*v.i.* to associate familiarly. [Prob. *hab, nab,* have, have not (*ne-have*).]

hobo, *hō'bō, n.* (*U.S.*) a vagrant workman: a tramp. [Origin unknown.]

Hobson's choice, *hob'sónz chois,* a choice of one or none. [*Hobson,* a Cambridge horse hirer, gave his customers no choice but to take the horse nearest the door.]

hock, *hok, n.* and *v.* See **hough.**

hock, *hok, n.* properly, the wine made at *Hochheim,* on the Main, in Germany; now applied to all white Rhine wines.

hockey, *hok'i, n.* a game played with a ball and

Neutral vowels in unaccented syllables: *em'pér-ór;* for certain sounds in foreign words see p. ix.

stick curved at one end; a similar game on ice with a puck instead of a ball. [Prob. O.Fr. *hoquet*, a crook.]

hocus-pocus, *hō′kus-pō′kus, n.* a juggler's trick or formula: deception.—*v.t.* **hō′cus**, to cheat: to drug:—*pr.p.* hō′cusing; *pa.p.* hō′cused. [Sham Latin.]

hod, *hod, n.* a V-shaped stemmed trough for carrying bricks or mortar on the shoulder.—*n.* **hod′man**, a man who carries a hod: a mason's labourer. [Cf. prov. *hot, hott,* Ger. *hotte,* obs. Du. *hodde,* Fr. *hotte,* a basket.]

hodden, *hod′n, n.* coarse undyed homespun woollen cloth.—*adj.* of or clad in hodden: rustic.—*n.* **hodd′engrey,** hodden made of mixed black and white wool.

hodgepodge, *hoj′poj, n.* See **hotchpotch.**

hodometer, *hod-om′é-tér, n.* an instrument for measuring distance travelled. [Gr. *hodos,* a way, *metron,* a measure.]

hoe, *hō, n.* an instrument for scraping or digging up weeds and loosening the earth.—*v.t.* to scrape or clean with a hoe: to weed.—*v.i.* to use a hoe:—*pr.p.* hoe′ing; *pa.p.* hoed.—*n.* **hō′er.—a hard,** or **long, row to hoe,** a hard or wearisome task to perform. [O.Fr. *houe*—O.H.G. *houwâ,* a hoe.]

hog, *hog, n.* a general name for swine: a castrated boar: a yearling sheep not yet shorn (also **hogg**): a greedy person: a person of coarse manners.—*v.t.* and *v.i.* to eat or seize hoggishly.—*v.i.* to cut like a hog's mane: to take or use selfishly:—*pr.p.* hogg′ing; *pa.p.* hogged.—*n.* **hog-back,** a hill ridge, or other object, shaped like a hog's back.—*adj.* **hogg′ish,** resembling a hog: brutish: filthy: selfish.—*adv.* **hogg′ishly.**—*ns.* **hogg′ishness; hog′-mane,** a mane clipped short, or naturally short and upright; **hog′skin,** leather made of the skin of swine; **hog′-wash,** the refuse of a kitchen, brewery, &c., given to pigs.—**go the whole hog,** to do a thing thoroughly or completely; **road hog,** a selfish motorist who, by speeding and by cutting in, forces others to give way to him. [O.E. *hogg.*]

hogmanay,*hog-mā-nā′, n.* (*Scot.*) the last day of the year. [Origin unknown.]

hogshead, *hogz′hed, n.* a measure of capacity = 52½ imperial gallons (see *imperial measure*). [Apparently **hog's** and **head;** reason unknown.]

hoi polloi, *hoi po-loi′,* (*lit.*) the many—the populace, the masses. [Gr., pl. of definite article and *adj.*]

hoise, *hoiz, v.t.* (*arch.*) to hoist:—*pa.t.* and *pa.p.* hoised, hoist.—**hoist with one's own petard,** beaten with one's own weapons, caught in one's own trap. [Perh. Old Du. *hijssen,* Du. *hijschen,* to hoist.]

hoist, *hoist, v.t.* to raise with tackle: to heave up: to raise on high (as a flag).—*n.* act of lifting: the height of a sail: a lift for heavy goods. [**hoise.**]

hoity-toity, *hoi′ti-toi′ti, interj.* an exclamation of surprise or disapprobation.—*adj.* giddy: huffy: haughty. [From obs. *hoit,* to romp.]

hokum, *hō′kum, n.* (*slang*) orig. applied to any device of proved efficacy used by a showman to produce applause: any commonplace artifice used by a writer or speaker to stimulate

emotion in an audience or to induce a particular opinion. [Conn. with **hocus-pocus.**]

hold, *hōld, v.t.* to keep: to possess: to contain: to grasp: to keep back, to keep in check (e.g. the enemy): to restrain: to defend (successfully): to occupy: to bind (e.g. to a promise): to have as an opinion (that): to consider, regard as (e.g. a fool, guiltless): to persist in: to give or have (e.g. a dance, a public meeting).—*v.i.* to remain fixed: to be true or unfailing: to remain valid: to continue unbroken or unsubdued: to adhere (to):—*pr.p.* hōlding;*pa.t.* held; *pa.p.* held (*obs.* hōld′en).—*n.* act or manner of holding: grip: tenacity: a thing held: influence: a place of confinement: a stronghold.—*ns.* **hold′-all,** an accommodating receptacle for clothes &c., esp. a canvas bag; **hold′er; hold′fast,** that which holds fast: a long nail: a catch; **hold′ing,** anything held: a farm held of a superior: hold: influence; **hold′-up,** an attack with a view to robbery; a stoppage (*v.t.* **hold up**).—**hold down,** to restrain: to keep (a job) by carrying out its duties efficiently, esp. in spite of difficulties; **hold forth,** to harangue; **hold good,** to remain the case; **hold hard!** stop! **hold one's hand,** to cease, or to refrain from, action; **hold one's own,** to maintain one's position; **hold one's peace, hold one's tongue,** to keep silence; **hold out on,** (*coll.*) to keep information from; **hold over,** to postpone; **hold with,** to take sides with, to approve of; **no holds barred,** not observing any rule of fair play. [O.E. *haldan* (W.S. *healdan*); O.H.G. *haltan.*]

hold, *hōld, n* the interior cavity of a ship used for the cargo. [**hole,** with excrescent *d.*]

hole, *hōl, n.* a hollow place: a cavity: a pit: an animal's burrow: an aperture: a perforation: a means of escape: a difficult situation: a scrape: a mean lodging. (*slang*) a dull and unattractive place: (*electronics*) a vacancy in an energy band, caused by removal of an electron, which moves and is equivalent to a positive charge.—*v.t.* to form holes in: to send into a hole.—*v.i.* to go into a hole.—*adj.* **hole′-and-cor′ner,** secret, underhand.—**hole in the heart,** imperfect formation of the partition which should separate entirely the right side of the heart from the left side—often used as *adj.* [O.E. *hol,* a hole, cavern; Du. *hol,* Dan. *hul,* Ger. *hohl,* hollow.]

holiday, *hol′i-dā, n.* (*orig.*) a religious festival: a day or season of idleness and recreation. [**holy, day.**]

holla, *hol′ä, interj.* ho, there! attend!: (*naut.*) the usual response to 'Ahoy!'—*n.* a loud shout. [Fr. *holà—ho* and *là—*L. *illāc,* there.]

holland, *hol′änd, n.* a coarse linen fabric, unbleached or dyed brown: (*orig.*) a fine kind of linen first made in *Holland.—n.* **holl′ands,** gin made in Holland.

hollo, *hol′ō,* **holloa,** *hol-ō′, n.* and *interj.* a shout of encouragement or to call attention.—*v.i.* and *v.i.* to shout. [Cf. **holla, hello.**]

hollow, *hol′ō, n.* a hole: a cavity: a depression: a groove, channel.—*adj.* having an empty space within or below: sunken: empty: insincere (e.g. protestations, promises).—*v.t.* to make a depression in: to make hollow: to excavate.—*adjs.* **holl′ow-eyed′,** having sunken eyes;

holl'ow-heart'ed, faithless: treacherous.—*ns.* **holl'owness**, the state of being hollow: a cavity: insincerity; **holl'ow-ware**, trade name for hollow articles of iron, as pots and kettles.— **beat hollow**, to beat wholly. [O.E. *holh,* a hollow place—*hol.* See **hole**.]

holly, *hol'i, n.* a genus of evergreen shrubs having prickly leaves and scarlet or yellow berries. [O.E. *hole(g)n*; cf. W. *celyn,* Ir. *cuileann.*]

hollyhock, *hol'i-hok, n.* a plant of the mallow family, with spikes of large flowers, brought into Europe from the Holy Land. [M.E. *holihoc*—*holi,* holy, and O.E. *hoc,* mallow.]

holm, *hōm, n.* an islet, esp. in a river: rich flat land beside a river. [O.E. *holm.*]

holmium, *hōl'mi-úm, n.* metallic element (symbol Ho; at. no. 67), of the rare-earth group. [*Holmia,* Latinised form of Stockholm.]

holm-oak, *hōm'-ōk', n.* the evergreen oak, not unlike holly. [M.E. *holin*—O.E. *hole(g)n,* holly.]

holo-, *hol'ō-,* **hol-**, *hol-,* in composition, whole: wholly. [Gr. *holos,* hole.]

holocaust, *hol'ō-köst, n.* a sacrifice in which the whole of the victim was burnt: a huge slaughter or destruction of life. [Gr. *holokauston*— *holos,* whole, *kaustos,* burnt.]

holograph, *hol'ō-gräf, n.* a document (e.g. a will) wholly in the handwriting of the person from whom it proceeds.—Also *adj.*—*adj.* **holographic** (-*graf'ik*). [Gr. *holos,* whole, *graphein,* to write.]

holp, *hōlp,* **holpen**, *hōlp'n,* old *pa.t.* and *pa.p.* of **help**.

holster, *hōl'stér, r* a pistol-case, on saddle or belt.—*adj.* **hol'stered**. [Perh. Du. *holster,* pistol-case; cf. O.E. *heolster,* hiding-place.]

holt, *hōlt, n.* a wood or woody hill. [O.E. *holt,* a wood; O.N. *holt,* a copse, Ger. *holz.*]

holus-bolus, *hōl'us-bōl'us, adv.* all at a gulp: altogether. [Sham L.; perh.—Eng. *whole bolus* or Gr. *holos* and *bōlos,* lump, bolus.]

holy, *hō'li, adj.* perfect in a moral sense: pure in heart: religious: set apart to a sacred use: (*coll.*) awe-inspiring, formidable.—*ns.* **hō'liness**, state of being holy: religious goodness: sanctity: (*cap.*) a title of the pope; **hō'ly-day**, a religious festival; **hō'ly-off'ice**, the Inquisition; **hō'ly-rood**, Christ's cross: a cross, esp. in R.C. churches over the entrance to the chancel; **hō'lystone**, a sandstone used by seamen for cleansing the decks.—*v.t.* to scrub with a holystone.—*ns.* **Hō'ly-Thurs'day**, Thursday in Holy-Week: Ascension Day, ten days before Whitsuntide; **hō'ly-wa'ter**, water blessed for religious uses; **Hō'ly(-)Week**, the week before Easter; **hō'ly-writ**, the holy writings, the Scriptures.—**Holy City**, Jerusalem, Rome, Mecca, Benares, Allahabad, &c.; **Holy Family**, the infant Christ with Joseph, Mary, &c.; **Holy Ghost, Spirit**, the third person of the Trinity; **Holy Land**, Palestine; **holy of holies**, the inner chamber of the Jewish tabernacle: (*fig.*) the innermost shrine; **Holy One**, God: Christ: one set apart for the service of God; **holy orders** (see **order**); **holy war**, a war for the extirpation of heresy, a crusade. [O.E. *hālig,* lit. whole, perfect, healthy—*hāl,* sound, whole; conn. with **hail, heal, whole**.]

homage, *hom'ij, n.* a vassal's acknowledgment that he is the man of his feudal superior: anything done or rendered as such an acknowledgment: reverence, esp. shown by outward action. [O.Fr. *homage*—Low L. *hominā̆ticum*—L. *homō,* a man.]

homburg hat, *hom'bûrg hat,* a man's hat, of felt, with narrow brim, and crown dinted in at the top. [First worn at *Homburg,* north-west of Frankfurt-am-Main.]

home, *hōm, n.* habitual abode: residence of one's family: the scene of domestic life: one's own country: habitat: an institution affording refuge or residence for the poor, the afflicted, &c.: a private hospital: in some games, destination, result aimed at.—*adj.* pertaining to one's dwelling or country: near the dwelling or headquarters: coming or reaching home: domestic.—*v.i.* to go home: to find the way home: to be guided to a target or destination.—*adv.* to home: to the place where it belongs: to the point aimed at (*lit.* and *fig.*).—*adj.* **home'-bred**, bred at home: native: domestic: plain: unpolished.—*ns.* **home'-farm**, the farm attached to and near a great house; **home'-grown**, produced at home or in one's own country; **home'-guard**, a member of a volunteer force for home defence: a force of the kind (in the war of 1939-45, **Home Guards, Guard**); **home'-help'**, a woman hired part-time to help with housework; **home'-land**, native land.—*adj.* **home'less**, without a home.—*n.* **home'lessness**.—*adj.* **home'ly**, having the characteristics of a home: familiar: simple, unpretentious, plain: (*U.S.*) ugly.— **home'liness**.—*adjs.* **home'-made**, made at home, or in one's own country: amateurish; **home'-produced**, produced within the country, not imported; **home'sick**, pining for home.—*n.* **home'sickness**.—*adj.* **home'spun**, spun or wrought at home: plain, inelegant.—*n.* cloth made at home.—*ns.* **home'-stead**, a dwelling-house with outhouses and enclosures immediately connected with it; **home'-truth**, a statement that strikes home to the feelings because unanswerable or unkindly frank.—*advs.* **home'ward, home'wards**.—*adjs.* **home'ward**, in the direction of home; **home'ward-bound**, bound homeward or to one's native land; **home'ing**, having a tendency to return home: trained to return home: guiding to target or destination.—**Home counties**, the counties over and into which London has extended; **Home Department**, that part of government which is concerned with the maintenance of the internal peace of England—its headquarters the **Home Office**, its official head the **Home Secretary; home rule**, self-government such as was claimed by Irish Nationalists before 1922; **home thrust**, a pointed remark that goes home.—**at-home**, a reception; **at home**, receiving visitors; **at home with**, familiar and at ease with (person or—also **on, in**—subject); **bring home to**, to prove to in such a way that the conclusion cannot be escaped: to make to feel or understand (through personal experience). [O.E. *hām;* Du. and Ger. *heim.*]

homeopathy, Same as **homoeopathy**.

homer, *hō'mér, n.* a pigeon trained to fly home from a distance. [**home**.]

Homeric, *hō-mer'ik, adj.* pertaining to *Homer,*

Neutral vowels in unaccented syllables: *em'pér-ór*; for certain sounds in foreign words see p. ix.

the great poet of Greece: pertaining to or resembling his poetry: worthy of Homer: heroic. [Gr. *hŏmērikos*—*Hŏmēros*, Homer.]

homicide, *hom'i-sīd, n.* manslaughter: one who kills another.—*adj.* **homici'dal,** pertaining to homicide: murderous. [Fr.,—L. *homicīdium*—*homō,* a man, *caedĕre,* to kill.]

homily, *hom'i-li, n.* a sermon explaining a passage from Scripture and offering practical guidance rather than discussing religious doctrine: a moral discourse, esp. one that is tedious and unwanted.—*adjs.* **homilet'ic, -al.**—*ns.* **homilet'ics,** the art of preaching; **hom'ilist.** [Gr. *homilia,* an assembly, a sermon—*homos,* the same, *īlē,* a crowd.]

hominy, *hom'i-ni, n.* maize hulled, or hulled and crushed, boiled with water—a kind of Indian-corn porridge. [American Indian.]

homo, *hŏ'mō, n.* (*zool.*) the human genus.— **ho'mo sapiens,** the only existing species of man. [L. *hŏmō,* man, *sapiens,* wise, (here) intelligent, able to reason.]

homo-, *hom'ō, hŏ'mo-, hom-, hom-,* in composition, same [Gr. *homos*].—*e.g.* **hŏmograph,** *hom'o-gräf, n.* a word of the same spelling as another but of different meaning and origin (Gr. *graphein,* to write).

homocentric, *hom o-sen'trik, adj.* concentric: proceeding from the same point. [Gr. *homo-kentros*—*homos,* the same, *kentron,* centre, point.]

homoeopathy, homeopathy, *hŏm-i-op'a-thi,* or *hom-, n.* the system of treating diseases by small quantities of drugs that excite symptoms similar to those of the disease. *ns.* **ho'moeopath,** **homoeop'athist,** one who believes in or practises homoeopathy.—*adj.* **homoeopath'ic.**—*adv.* **homoeopath'ically.** [Gr. *homoios,* similar, *pathos,* feeling.]

homogeneous, *hom-ō-jēn'i-ùs, adj.* of the same kind or nature: having all the constituent parts or elements similar: (*math.*) of the same degree or dimensions in every term.—*ns.* **homoge'neousness, homogene'ity,** sameness or uniformity of nature or kind.—*v.t.* **homog'enise,** (or *hom'o-jėn-īz*), to make homogeneous: to make (milk) more digestible by breaking up fat globules, &c.: to produce (milk, &c.) from its constituent materials. [Gr. *homogenēs*—*homos,* one, same, *genos,* kind.]

homologate, *hom ol'o-gāt, v.t.* to confirm: to approve, to consent to, to ratify.—*n.* **homologa'-tion.** [Low L. *homologāre, -ātum*—Gr. *homologeein,* to agree—*homos,* same, *logos,* speech.]

homologous, *hom-ol'o-gùs, adj.* agreeing: corresponding in relative position, general structure and descent.—*ns.* **hom'ologue** (*-log*), that which is homologous to something else, as a man's arm to a whale's flipper and a bird's wing; **homol'ogy,** the quality of being homologous: affinity of structure and origin, apart from form or use.—*adj.* **homological** (*-loj'-*). [Gr. *homologos;* cf. **homologate.**]

homonym, *hom'o-nim, n.* a word having the same sound as another, but a different meaning and origin.—*adj.* **homon'ymous,** having the same name: having different significations but origins but the same sound. [Gr. *homōnymos*—*homos,* the same, *onyma,* *onoma,* name.]

homophone, *hom'o-fōn, n.* a character representing the same sound as another: a word pronounced exactly as another but differing from it in meaning.—*adj.* **homophonous** (*-of'-*).—*n.* **homoph'ony.** [Gr. *homos,* the same, *phōnē,* sound.]

homosexual, *hom-ō-seks'ū-ál, adj.* having, or pertaining to, sexual desire directed towards one of the same sex.—Also *n.*—*n.* **homosexual'ity.** [**homo-,** and **sexual.**]

homotype, *hom'ō-tīp, n.* that which has the same fundamental type of structure with something else. [Gr. *homos,* same, *typos,* type.]

homonculus, *hŏ-mung'kū-lus, n.* a dwarf, manikin.—Also **homunc'ule.** [L., dim. of *homō,* man.]

hone, *hōn, n.* a smooth stone used for sharpening instruments.—*v.t.* to sharpen as on a hone. [O.E. *hān;* O.N. *hein;* allied to Gr. *kōnos,* a cone.]

honest, *on'ėst, adj.* (*obs.*) holding an honourable position: (now only patronisingly) respectable: fair-dealing: upright: the opposite of thievish or fraudulent: gained by fair means: sincere, candid, truthful, ingenuous: (*arch.*) chaste.—*adv.* **hon'estly.**—*n.* **hon'esty,** the state of being honest: integrity: candour: a garden plant, so called from its transparent seed pouch. [Fr.,—L. *honestus honor.*]

honey, *hun'i, n.* a sweet thick fluid developed in the honey-sac of the bee from the nectar of flowers: anything sweet like honey.—*v.t.* to sweeten: to make agreeable:—*pr.p.* **hon'eying;** *pa.p.* **honeyed** (*hun'id*).—*ns.* **hon'ey-bag, hon'ey-sac,** an enlargement of the alimentary canal of the bee in which it carries its load of honey; **hon'eybear,** a South American carnivorous mammal about the size of a cat, with a long protrusive tongue, which it uses to rob the nests of wild bees, **hon'ey buzz'ard,** a species of hawk that feeds on the larvae of wasps and bumble-bees, &c.; **hon'eycomb,** a comb or mass of waxy cells formed by bees, in which they store their honey: anything like a honeycomb.—*v.t.* to make like a honeycomb.—*adj.* **hon'eycombed** (*-kōmd*).—*n.* **hon'eydew,** a sugary secretion from aphides (plant lice) or plants: tobacco moistened with molasses (**honeydew melon,** sweet-flavoured melon with smooth green rind).—*adjs.* **hon'eyed, hon'ied,** covered with honey: sweet: flattering.—*n.* **hon'eymoon,** the first weeks after marriage: a holiday spent together during that time.—*adj.* **hon'ey-mouthed,** soft or smooth in speech.—*n.* **hon'eysuckle,** genus of climbing shrubs with cream-coloured flowers, so named because honey is readily sucked from the flower.—*adj.* **hon'ey-tongued,** soft, pleasing, persuasive, or seductive in speech: eloquent.— **wild honey,** honey made by wild bees. [O.E. *hunig;* Ger. *honig,* O.N. *hunang.*]

honk, *hongk, n.* the cry of the wild goose: the noise of a motor horn.—Also *v.t.* and *v.i.* [Imit.]

honorarium, *hon-or-ā'ri-um, on-, n.* a voluntary fee paid, esp. to a professional man for his services. [L. *honōrārium* (*dōnum*), honorary (gift).]

honorary, *on'ór-är i, adj.* conferring honour: holding a title or office without performing

fāte, fär; mē, hûr (her); *mīne; mōte, för; mūte; mōōn, fŏŏt;* тнen (then)

services, or without reward. [L. *honorārius*— *honor*.]

honorific, *on-ôr-if'ik, adj.* (of a word or phrase) conferring or doing honour, used in the East ``in ceremonial address.—Also *n.* [L. *honōrificus*—*honor,* honour, and suffx. -*ficus*—*facĕre,* to make.]

honour, (in U.S. **honor**),*on'ôr, n.* the esteem due or paid to worth: high estimation: exalted rank: any mark of respect or esteem: a title or decoration: that which confers distinction or does credit: self-respecting integrity: a fine and scrupulous sense of what is due: chastity: (*pl.*) civilities paid: (*pl.*) highest cards in cardplaying: (*pl.*) academic prizes or distinctions.—*v.t.* to hold in high esteem: to do honour to: to confer honour upon: to grace: to accept (a bill, &c.) and pay when due.—*adj.* **hon'ourable,** worthy of honour: illustrious: actuated by principles of honour: conferring honour: becoming men of exalted station: prefixed to names of various persons as a title of distinction.—*n.* **hon'ourableness,** eminence: conformity to the principles of honour: fairness.—*adv.* **hon'ourably.**—*n.* **hon'ours-man,** one who has taken a university degree with honours.—**honours of war,** the privilege granted to a capitulating force of marching out with their arms, flags, &c.:—**affair of honour** (see **affair**); **Companions of Honour,** an order instituted in 1917 for those who have rendered conspicuous service of national importance; **debt of honour** (see **debt**); **maid of honour,** a lady in the service of a queen or princess: a kind of cheese-cake; **point of honour,** any scruple caused by a sense of duty: the obligation to demand and to receive satisfaction for an insult, esp. by a duel. [Anglo-Fr. (*h)onour*—L. *honor, honōs, -ōris.*]

hooch. See **hootch.**

hood, *hŏŏd, n.* a flexible covering for the head and back of the neck: a collapsible cover for a motor-car, &c.: an ornamental fold worn on the back over an academic gown.—*v.t.* to cover with a hood: to blind.—*adj.* **hood'ed.**—*n.* **hood'ie-crow,** the hooded crow. [O.E. *hōd*; Du. *hoed,* Ger. *hut.*]

-hood, *-hŏŏd, n. suffx.* indicating state, nature, as *hardihood, manhood.*—Also **-head,** (*-hed*), as *Godhead.* [O.E. *hād,* Ger. *-heit,* state.]

hoodlum, *hŏŏd'lŭm, n.* a rowdy, street bully: a small-time criminal or gangster.

hoodoo, *hŏŏ'dŏŏ, n.* voodoo: a person or thing that brings bad luck: bad luck. [App. **voodoo.**]

hoodwink, *hŏŏd'wingk, v.t.* to blindfold: to deceive, impose on. [**hood, wink.**]

hooey, *hŏŏ'i, n.* (*slang*) nonsense.

hoof, *hŏŏf, n.* horny substance on the feet of certain animals, as horses, &c.: a hoofed animal:—*pl.* **hoofs, hooves.**—*adj.* **hoofed.** [O.E. *hōf*; Ger. *huf,* O.N. *hōfr.*]

hoo-ha, *hŏŏ'hä, n.* (*slang*) noisy fuss. [Imit.]

hook, *hŏŏk, n.* an object of bent form, such as would catch or hold anything: (*fig.*) a snare: a curved instrument for cutting grain: a boxer's blow with bent elbow.—*v.t.* to catch, fasten, hold, as with a hook: to form into or with a hook: to ensnare: (*golf* and *cricket*) to pull sharply: (*Rugby*) to obtain possession of the ball in the scrum (*n.* **hook'er,** one whose part

it is to do so).—*v.i.* to bend, be curved.—*p.p.* or *adj.* **hooked** (*hŏŏkt*), physically dependent on drugs: addicted to some activity or indulgence (with *on, by*).—*adj.* **hook'-nosed.**—*ns.* **hook'up,** (*coll.*; *fig.*) the establishment of a connection: an alliance: a temporary linking up of separate broadcasting stations; **hookworm,** a parasitic worm with hooks in the mouth: the disease it causes.—**by hook or by crook,** one way if not another; **off the hook,** ready-made: out of difficulty or trouble; **on one's own hook,** on one's responsibility, initiative, or account. [O.E. *hōc*; Du. *hoek.*]

hookah, hooka, *hŏŏk'a, n.* the tobacco-pipe of Arabs, Turks, &c., in which the smoke is passed through water. [Ar. *huqqah,* bowl, casket.]

hooker, *hŏŏk'ér, n.* a two-masted Dutch vessel, a small fishing smack. [Du. *hoeker.*]

hooligan, *hŏŏl'i-gàn, n.* a street rough.—*n.* **hoo'liganism.** [Said to be the name of a leader of a gang.]

hoop, *hŏŏp, n.* a ring or band for holding together the staves of casks, &c.: a large ring for a child to trundle, for expanding a skirt, or other purpose: a ring.—*v.t.* to bind with hoops: to encircle.—**go through the hoop,** to suffer ordeal or punishment. [O.E. *hōp*; Du. *hoep.*]

hoop, hooping-cough. See under **whoop.**

hoopoe, *hŏŏp'ŏŏ, n.* a genus of crested birds, one of which is an occasional visitor to Britain. [Earlier *hoop*—O.Fr. *huppe,* partly remodelled on L. *ūpūpa*; cf. Gr. *epops.*]

hoot, *hŏŏt, v.i.* to shout in contempt: to cry like an owl: to sound a motor-horn, siren, &c.—*v.t.* to greet, or to drive, with such sounds.—*n.* the sound of hooting: the note of an owl, motor-horn, &c.—*n.* **hoot'er,** a siren or steam-whistle. [Imit., prob. immediately Scand.; cf. Swed. *hut.* begone.]

hoo(t)ch, *hŏŏch, n.* a drink made by Indians of N.W. Canada and Alaska from fermented dough and sugar: whisky, esp. when illegally made or obtained. [*Hoo(t)chino,* name of an Indian tribe.]

hop, *hop, v.i.* to leap on one leg: to move in jumps, like a bird: to walk lame: to fly (in aircraft):—*pr.p.* **hopp'ing**; *pa.t.* and *pa.p.* **hopped.**—*n.* a leap on one leg: a jump: (*coll.*) a dance: a stage in a journey by air.—*ns.* **hopp'er,** one who hops: a shaking or conveying trough in which something is placed to be passed or fed, as to a mill: a barge with an opening in its bottom for discharging refuse: a receptable in which seed-corn is carried for sowing; **hop'-scotch,** a game in which children, while kicking a puck, hop over lines scotched or traced on the ground.—**hop it,** (*slang*), be off with speed! [O.E. *hoppian,* to dance; Ger. *hopfen, hüpfen.*]

hop, *hop, n.* a plant with a long twining stalk: (in *pl.*) its bitter fruit-clusters used for flavouring beer and in medicine: opium or other narcotic.—*v.t.* to flavour with hops.—*v.i.* to gather hops:—*pr.p.* **hopp'ing**; *pa.t.* and *pa.p.* **hopped.**—*ns.* **hop'bind, hop'bine,** the stalk of the hop; **hop'-bitt'ers,** a drink like ginger-beer, flavoured with hops; **hop'-oast,** a kiln for drying hops.—*adj.* **hopped'-up** (*slang*), drugged: excited: artificially stimulated.—*n.*

Neutral vowels in unaccented syllables: *em'pér-ôr*; for certain sounds in foreign words see p. ix.

hop'-vine, the hop-plant: its stock or stem. [Du. *hop*; Ger. *hopfen.*]

hope, *hōp, v.i.* to cherish a desire (*for* something) with some expectation of obtaining it: to look forward to good with a measure of confidence: to have confidence (in).—*v.t.* to desire with expectation with belief in the prospect of obtaining.—*n.* a desire of some good, with expectation of obtaining it: confidence: anticipation: that on which hopes are grounded: that which is hoped for.—*adj.* **hope'ful,** full of hope: having qualities that promise good or success.—*n.* a promising young person.—*adv.* **hope'fully.**—*n.* **hope'fulness.**—*adj.* **hope'less,** without hope: giving no ground to expect good or success: incurable.—*adv.* **hope'lessly.**—*n.* **hope'lessness.**—**hope against hope,** to cherish hope in spite of every discouragement. [O.E. *hopian*—*hopa,* hope; Du. *hopen,* Ger. *hoffen.*]

hope. See **forlorn hope.**

horal, *hōr'ál, adj.* relating to hours.—*adj.* **hor'ary,** pertaining to an hour: noting the hours: hourly. [L. *hōra,* an hour.]

Horatian, *hor-ā'shán, adj.* pertaining to Horace (Quintus *Horatius* Flaccus; 65 B.C.-8 B.C.), the Latin poet, or to his manner or verse.

horde, *hōrd, hôrd, n.* a migratory or wandering tribe or clan: a multitude. [Fr.,—Turk. *ordū,* camp.]

horehound, hoarhound, *hōr'-, hôr'hownd, n.* a hoary labiate plant once popular as a remedy for coughs. [O.E. *hār,* hoar, *hūne,* horehound.]

horizon, *hor-ī'zón, n.* the circle in which earth and sky seem to meet: (*fig.*) the boundary or limit of one's experience, interests, &c.—*adj.* **horizontal** (*hor-i-zont'ál*), pertaining to the horizon: near the horizon: parallel to the horizon: level.—*adv.* **horizon'tally.**—*n.* **horizon,** from Gr. *horizōn* (*kyklos*), bounding (circle), pr.p. of *horizein,* to bound—*horos,* a limit.]

hormone, *hôr'mōn, n.* any of a number of very complicated internal secretions produced by the endocrine or ductless glands of the body, each stimulating in a specific way organs to which it is carried by the blood: similar secretions carried by the sap in plants. [Gr. *hormōn,* pr.p. of *hormaein,* to set in motion, stir up.]

horn, *hôrn, n.* a hard outgrowth on the head of an animal: the material of which this is made: a snail's tentacle: any projection resembling a horn: a crescent tip: something made of, or curved like, a horn: a wind instrument orig. made from a horn, now of brass, &c.: a hooter, siren.—*v.t.* to furnish with horns: to remove horns from.—*ns.* **horn'beam,** any of several trees resembling a beech with hard tough wood; **horn'bill,** any of a large number of birds with a horny excrescence on their bills; **horn'book** (*hist.*), a first book for children, which consisted of a single leaf set in a frame, with a thin plate of transparent horn in front to preserve it.—*adj.* **horned.**—*n.* **horned'-owl, horn'owl,** an owl with horn-like tufts of feathers on its head.—*adj.* **horn'-foot'ed,** hoofed.—*ns.* **horn'ing,** appearance of the moon when in its crescent form; **horn'-sil'ver,** silver chloride; **horn'stone,** a flinty chalcedony.—*adj.* **horn'y,** like horn: hard: callous.—

n. **horn'iness,** hardness, callousness.—*adj.* **horn'y-hand'ed,** with hands hardened by toil.—**horn in,** butt in; **horn of plenty** (see **cornucopia**); **horns of a dilemma** (see **dilemma**); **horns of the altar,** the projections at the four corners of the Hebrew altar, to which the victim was bound when about to be sacrified; **pull, or draw, in one's horns,** to abate one's ardour or one's pretensions: to curtail or restrict one's activities, spending, &c.—**English horn,** a *cor anglais,* a wood-wind instrument similar to the oboe but lower in pitch; **French horn,** a brass-wind instrument developed from a hunting-horn; **hunting-horn,** a wind instrument used in the chase, similar in shape to the trumpet (*q.v.*). [O.E. *horn*; Scand. and Ger. *horn,* Gael. and W. *corn,* L. *cornu,* Gr. *keras.*]

hornblende, *hôrn'blend, n.* a rock-forming mineral, generally green to black, found in many rocks both igneous (e.g. granite) and metamorphic. [Ger. *horn,* horn, and *-blende*—*blenden,* to dazzle.]

hornet, *hôrn'et, n.* a large kind of wasp. [O.E. *hyrnet.*]

hornpipe, *hôrn'pīp, n.* an old Welsh musical instrument like a clarinet: a lively English dance, usually by one person, associated with sailors: a tune for such a dance: a piece of instrumental music in the style of this. [**horn, pipe.**]

horography, *hor-og'ra-fi, n.* the art of constructing sundials, clocks, &c.—*n.* **horog'rapher.** [Gr. *hōra,* an hour, *graphein,* to write, describe.]

horologe, *hor'o-loj, n.* any instrument for telling the hours.—*ns.* **horol'oger, horol'ogist,** a maker of clocks, &c.—*adjs.* **horolog'ic, -al.**—*n.* **horol'ogy,** the science of time-measurement: the art of clock-making. [O.Fr. *orloge*—L. *hōrologium*—Gr. *hōrologion*—*hōra,* an hour, *legein,* to tell.]

horoscope, *hor'o-skōp, n.* an observation of the heavens at the hour of a person's birth, by which the astrologer predicted the events of his life: a representation of the heavens for this purpose: any similar prediction about a person's future.—*adj.* **horoscopic** (*skop'-*).—*ns.* **horos'copist,** an astrologer; **horos'copy,** the art of predicting the events of a person's life from his horoscope: aspect of the stars at the time of birth. [Gr. *hōroskopos*—*hōra,* an hour, *skopeein,* to observe.]

horrent, *hor'ent, adj.* bristling. [L. *horrens, -entis,* pr.p. of *horrēre,* to bristle.]

horrible, *hor'i-bl, adj.* exciting horror: dreadful: (*coll.*) unpleasant, detestable.—*n.* **horr'ibleness.**—*adv.* **horr'ibly.** [L. *horribilis*—*horrēre,* to shudder, bristle.]

horrid, *hor'id, adj.* (*arch.*) shaggy, bristling: horrible, shocking, offensive.—*adv.* **horr'idly.**—*n.* **horr'idness.** [L. *horridus*—*horrēre,* to bristle.]

horrify, *hor'i-fī, v.t.* to strike with horror:—*pr.p.* **horr'ifying;** *pa.p.* **horr'ified.**—*adj.* **horrif'ic,** exciting horror: frightful. [L. *horrificus*—root of *horrēre,* and *facēre,* to make.]

horror, *hor'ôr, n.* shuddering: excessive fear or loathing: a source of such feeling: (*coll.*) a disagreeable person or thing.—*adj.* of a comic paper, film, novel, &c., having gruesome, violent, horrifying or bloodcurdling themes.

[L.,—*horror, horrēre,* to bristle, shudder.]

hors de combat, *ör dē kō-ba,* out of the struggle, no longer in a condition to fight or to take part. [Fr.]

hors-d'œuvre, *ör-dœ-vr',* n. a whet for the appetite (olives, sardines, or the like) served before a meal or after soup. [Fr.]

horse, *hörs,* n. a solid-hoofed quadruped with flowing tail and mane: cavalry: a horse-like piece of apparatus for gymnastics: a support on which clothes are dried.—*v.t.* to provide with a horse.—*ns.* **horse'-artill'ery,** field artillery with the gunners mounted; **horse'back,** the back of a horse; **horse'-block,** a block for mounting or dismounting by; **horse'-boat,** a boat for carrying horses, or one towed by a horse; **horse'-bot,** a botfly; **horse'-box,** a van for carrying horses: a stall; **horse brass,** a brass ornament orig. for hanging on the harness of a horse; **horse'-break'er, -tām'er,** one who breaks or tames horses, or teaches them to draw or carry; **horse'-chest'nut,** a smooth, brown, bitter seed or nut, perhaps so called from its coarseness contrasted with the edible chestnut (see **chestnut**): the tree that produces it; **horse'-cōp'er, horse'-deal'er,** one who deals or trades in horses; **horse'-flesh,** the flesh of a horse: horses collectively; **horse'-fly,** any fly that stings horses.—*n.pl.* **horse'-guards,** horse-soldiers employed as guards: (*cap.*) cavalry brigade of British household troops: their headquarters in London.—*ns.* **horse'-knacker,** one who buys and slaughters worn-out horses; **horse'-lat'itudes,** two zones of the Atlantic Ocean (about 30° N. and 30° S., esp. the former) noted for long calms; **horse'-laugh,** a harsh, boisterous laugh; **horse'-leech,** a large species of leech, so named from its fastening on horses: (*arch.*) a horse doctor: an insatiable person; **horse'-litt'er,** a litter borne between two horses; **horse'man,** a rider on horseback: one skilled in managing a horse: a mounted soldier; **horse'manship,** the art of riding and of training and managing horses; **horse'-marine',** a person quite out of his element: a member of an imaginary corps proverbially credulous (see **marine**); **horse opera,** (*slang*) a Western (q.v.) film; **horse'-pis'tol,** a large pistol carried in a holster; **horse'-play,** rough, boisterous play; **horse'-pow'er,** the power a horse can exert, or its conventional equivalent (taken as 746 watt); **horse'-rad'ish,** a plant with a pungent root, used as a condiment; **horse'-sense,** plain robust sense; **horse'-shoe,** a shoe for horses, consisting of a curved piece of iron: anything shaped like a horse-shoe; **horse'-tail,** any one of a group of flowerless plants with hollow rush-like stems, so called from their likeness to a horse's tail; **horse'-train'er,** one who trains horses for racing, &c.; **horse'-whip,** a whip for driving horses.—*v.t.* to strike with a horse-whip: to lash.—*n.* **hors'ing,** birching a schoolboy mounted on another's back.—*adj.* **hors'y,** of or pertaining to horses: horse-like: devoted to horse racing or breeding.—**get on, mount, the high horse,** to put on arrogant airs, or to be very much on one's dignity; **(straight) from the horse's mouth,** from a very trustworthy source; **take horse,** to

mount on horseback; **willing horse,** a willing, obliging, worker. [O.E. *hors;* O.N. *hross;* O.H.G. *hross, hros.*]

hortative, *hört'a-tiv,* adj. inciting: encouraging: giving advice.—Also **hort'atory.** [L. *hortārī, -ātus,* to incite.]

horticulture, *hör'ti-kul-tyůr, -chůr,* n. the art of cultivating gardens.—adj. **horticul'tural.—n. horticul'turist,** one versed in horticulture. [L. *hortus,* a garden, *cultūra—colēre,* to cultivate.]

hosanna, *hō-zan'a,* n. an exclamation of praise to God, or a prayer for blessings. [Gr. *hōsanna*—Heb. *hōshī'āhnnā—hōshīā',* save, *nā,* pray.]

hose, *hōz,* n. a close-fitting covering for the legs: stockings: socks (*half-hose*):—*pl.* **hose;** (*arch.*) **hosen.**—*n.* a flexible pipe for conveying water, so called from its shape:—*pl.* **hoses.**—*ns.* **hose'pipe; hōsier** (*hōzh'(y)ér, hōz'yér*), a dealer in hō'siery, i.e. hose collectively, knitted goods. [O.E. *hosa,* pl. *hosan;* Du. *hoos,* Ger. *hose.*]

hospice, *hos'pis, -pēs,* n. a guest-house for travellers, esp. one kept by monks on Alpine passes. [Fr.,—L. *hospitium—hospes,* a stranger treated as a guest.]

hospitable, *hos'pit-à-bl,* adj. kind to strangers: giving a generous welcome to guests.—*n.* **hos'pitableness.**—*adv.* **hos'pitably.**—*n.* **hos'pitality,** welcome and entertainment of guests. [L. *hospes, -itis,* stranger, guest.]

hospital, *hos'pit-ál,* n. (*obs.*) a hostel for travellers: formerly a charitable institution for the old or destitute and for reception (and education) of the needy young: an institution for the treatment of the sick or injured: a building for any of these purposes.—*v.t.* **hos'pitalise,** to send to hospital.—*ns.* **hos'pitaller** one of a charitable brotherhood for the care of the sick in hospitals: one of the Knights of St John, an order which built a hospital for pilgrims at Jerusalem; **hos'pital-ship,** a ship fitted out for the treatment and transport of the sick and wounded. [O.Fr. *hospital*—Low L. *hospitāle—hospes,* a guest.]

host, *hōst,* n. one who lodges or entertains a stranger or guest at his house: an innkeeper:—*fem.* **host'ess.**—*n.* an animal or plant on which another lives as a parasite.—**reckon, count, without one's host,** to count one's bill without reference to the landlord, i.e. to fail to take account of some important possibility, as the action of another. [O.Fr. *hoste*—L. *hospes, hospitis,* guest, also host.]

host, *hōst,* n. an army, a large multitude.—**Lord of hosts,** a favourite Hebrew term for Jehovah. [O.Fr. *host*—L. *hostis,* an enemy.]

host, *hōst,* n. in the R.C. Church, the consecrated wafer of the Eucharist—a thin circular wafer of unleavened bread. [L. *hostia,* a victim.]

hostage, *hos'tij,* n. one in the custody of the enemy as a pledge for the fulfilment of the conditions of a treaty. [O.Fr. *hostage*—L. *obses, obsidis,* a hostage.]

hostel, *hos'tél,* n. an inn: a communal residence for students or others: simple temporary accommodation for hikers, &c.—*n.* **hos'telry,** an inn. [O.Fr. *hostel, hostellerie*—L. *hospitāle;* cf. **hospital.**]

hostile, *hos'tīl, -til,* adj. belonging to an enemy:

Neutral vowels in unaccented syllables: *em'pér-ör;* for certain sounds in foreign words see p. ix.

showing enmity: warlike: adverse: resistant (to; esp. to new ideas, change).—*n.* hostil′ity, enmity:—*pl.* hostil′ities, acts of warfare. [L. *hostīlis*—*hostis*, enemy.]

hostler, ostler, *hos′lĕr,* or *os′-, n.* he who has the care of horses at an inn. [**hostel.**]

hot, *hot, adj.* having a high temperature: very warm: fiery: pungent: animated: vehement: passionate: lustful: (*slang*—of swing music) played with interpolations suggestive of excitement, which do not, however, alter the original melody or rhythm: (*slang*) good enough to excite: (*slang* of news) fresh, exciting: (*slang*) recently obtained in a dishonest manner: (*coll.*) highly radioactive.—*adv.* hot′ly.—*ns.* hot′ness; hot′bed, a bed (sometimes glass-covered) heated, e.g. by rotting manure, for bringing forward plants rapidly: any place favourable to rapid growth or development, esp. of disease, or of subversive doctrines; hot blast, a blast of heated air.—*adjs.* hot′-blood′ed, having hot blood: high-spirited: ardent: irritable; hot′-brained, hot-headed, rash and violent.—*n.* hot dog, a hot sausage sandwich.—*adv.* hot′foot, in hot haste.—*n.* hot′head, an impetuous headstrong person.—*adj.* hot′-headed.—*ns.* hot′-house, a house kept hot for the rearing of tender plants; hot line, any line of speedy communication ready for an emergency; hot′-plate, the flat top surface of a stove for cooking: a similar plate, independently heated, for keeping things hot; hot-rod (*U.S. slang*), a motor car converted for speed by stripping off non-essentials and increasing power; hot seat, (*slang*), the electric chair: (*fig.*) an uncomfortable or potentially dangerous situation; hot′spur, a violent, rash man.—*adj.* hot′-tempered, prone to anger.—hot water (*fig.*), trouble. [O.E. *hāt*; Ger. *heiss,* Swed. *het.*]

hotchpotch, *hoch′poch,* **hotchpot,** *hoch′pot,* **hodge-podge,** *hoj′poj, n.* a confused mass of ingredients shaken or mixed together as in the same pot (*lit* and *fig.*). [Fr. *hochepot—hocher,* to shake, and *pot,* a pot; cf. Du. *hutspot.*]

hotel, *hō-tel′, n.* a superior house for the accommodation of strangers: an inn: in France, also a public office, or a palace. [M.E. *hostel*—O.Fr. *hostel* (Fr. *hôtel*)—L. *hospitālia,* guest-chambers—*hospes,* guest.]

hotelier, *hō-tel′i-er,* a hotel-keeper. [Fr. *hôtelier.*]

Hottentot, *hot′n-tot, n.* one of a dwindling, nomad, pastoral race of south-west Africa: a barbarian. [Du. imit.; from their staccato manner of speech.]

hough, *hok* (*Scot. hoи*), **hock,** *n.* the joint on the hind-leg of a quadruped, between the knee and fetlock, corresponding to the ankle-joint in man: in man, the back part of the knee-joint: the ham.—*v.t.* to hamstring:— *pr.p.* hough′ing;*pa.p.* houghed (*hokt*). [O.E. *hōh,* the heel.]

hound, *hownd, n.* (*arch.*) a dog: a dog used in hunting: a mean scoundrel.—*v.t.* to set on, incite: to pursue, drive by harassing.—**master of hounds,** master of a pack of foxhounds. [O.E. *hund*; Ger. *kyōn,* gen. *kynos,* L. *canis.*]

hour, *owr, n.* 60 min., or the 24th part of a day:

the time as indicated by a clock, &c.: a time or occasion: (*pl.*; *cap.*) the goddesses of the seasons and the hours: set times of prayer, the *canonical hours*: the services prescribed for these: (*pl.*) the prescribed times for doing business.—*ns.* hour′-glass, an instrument for measuring the hours by the running of sand through a narrow neck; hour′-hand, the hand that shows the hour on a clock, &c.—*adj.* hour′ly, happening or done every hour: frequent.—*adv.* every hour: frequently.—*n.* hour′plate, the plate of a timepiece on which the hours are marked, the dial.—at the eleventh hour, at the last moment (Matt. xx. 6, 9); in a good (or evil) hour, under a fortunate (or unfortunate) impulse—from the old belief in astrological influences. [O.Fr. *hore*—L. *hōra*—Gr. *hōra.*]

houri, *hōō′ri, how′ri, n.* a nymph of the Mohammedan paradise. [Pers. *huri*—Ar. *hūriya,* a black-eyed girl.]

house, *hows n* a building for dwelling in: a dwelling-place: an inn: a household: a family: kindred: a trading establishment: a legislative body, or its meeting-place: a theatre, &c.: an audience. a section of a school: one of the twelve divisions of the heavens in astrology:—*pl.* houses (*howz′iz*).—*v.t.* house (*howz*), to shelter: to store: to provide houses for.—*v.i.* to take shelter: to reside.—*ns.* house′-a′gent, one who arranges the sale or letting of houses; house′-arrest′, confinement under guard to one's house, instead of imprisonment; house′-boat, a barge furnished and used as a dwelling-place; house′-break′er, one who breaks open and enters a house for the purpose of stealing, esp. by day: one who demolishes old houses; house′-break′ing; house′coat, a woman's frock-like garment with a long skirt, for wearing indoors; house′-craft, skill in domestic work; house′hold, those who are living together in the same house, and compose a family—*adj.* pertaining to the house and family.—*ns.* house′holder, the occupier, tenant of a house; house′keeper, a domestic who has the chief care of a house; house′keeping, the management of a house or of domestic affairs.—*adj.* domestic.—*adj.* house′less, without a house or home: having no shelter.—*ns.* house′maid, a maid employed to keep a house clean, &c.; house′man, a recent graduate in medicine holding a junior resident post in a hospital; house martin, the common European martin; house′-master, the head of a boarding-house at a public school.—*adj.* house′-proud, taking (too much) pride in the condition of one's house.—*ns.* house′-stew′ard, a steward who manages the household affairs of an establishment; house′-sur′geon, a resident surgeon in a hospital.—*adj.* house′-trained, of animals, taught to be cleanly indoors: (*coll.*) of human beings, well-mannered.—*ns.* house′-warm′ing, an entertainment given after moving into a new house; housewife (*hows′wīf,* or *huz′if*), the mistress of a house: a female domestic manager: a pocket sewing outfit (*huz′if*).—*adj.* house′wifely.—*ns.* housewifery (*huz′if-ri, hows′wīf-ri, -wif-ri*); house′work, the work—or any part of it—of keeping a house tidy and

fāte, *fär*; *mē,* *hûr* (her); *mīne*; *mōte, för*; *mūte; mōōn, fŏŏt*; ᴛʜen (then) clean; **housing** (*howz'ing*), houses, accommodation, or shelter, or the provision thereof—also *adj.*; **housing estate,** a planned residential area, whether built by a local authority or not; **household gods,** one's favourite domestic things—a playful use of the Roman *penātes* (q.v.); **household suffrage,** or **franchise,** the right of householders to vote for members of parliament; **household troops,** Guards regiments whose peculiar duty is to attend the sovereign and defend the metropolis; **household word,** a familiar saying or name; **housemaid's knee,** an inflammation of the knee, to which housemaids are specially liable through kneeling on damp floors.— **House of Assembly, Commons, Keys, Representatives** (see **assemble, common, Keys, represent**).—**keep house,** to maintain or manage an establishment; **keep the house,** to be confined to the house; **on the house,** of drinks, at the publican's expense; **the household,** the royal domestic establishment. [O.E. *hūs*; Ger. *haus.*]

housel, *howz'él, n.* the Eucharist. [O.E. *hūsel,* sacrifice.]

housey-housey, *hows'i-hows'i, n.* a gambling game in which each player has a board with numbers which he covers as the corresponding numbers are drawn and announced.

housing, *howz'ing, n.* an ornamental covering for a horse: a saddle-cloth: (*pl.*) the trappings of a horse. [O.Fr. *houce,* a mantle.]

hove, *pa.t.* and *pa.p.* of **heave.**

hovel, *hov'él, huv'él, n.* a small or wretched dwelling: a shed.—*v.t.* to put in a hovel: to shelter:—*pr.p.* hov'elling; *pa.p.* hov'elled.

hover, *huv'ér, hov'ér, v.i.* to remain aloft flapping the wings: to remain suspended: to linger.—*n.* **hov'ercraft,** an aircraft flying a short distance above sea or land supported by a down-driven blast of air.

how, *how, adv.* in what manner: to what extent: by what means: in what condition. [O.E. *hū,* prob. an adverbial form from *hwā,* who.]

howbeit, *how-bē'it, conj.* be it how it may: notwithstanding, yet, however. [**how, be, it.**]

howdah, houdah, *how'da, n.* a pavilion or seat fixed on an elephant's back. [Ar. *houdaj.*]

however, *how-ev'ér, adv.* and *conj.* in whatever manner or degree: nevertheless: at all events. [**how, ever.**]

howitzer, *how'its-ér, n.* a short gun, used for shelling at a steep angle. [Ger. *haubitze*— Czech *houfnice,* a sling.]

howl, *howl, v.i.* to yell or cry, as a wolf or dog: to make or utter a long, loud, whining sound.— *v.t.* to utter (words) with outcry:—*pr.p.* howl'ing; *pa.p.* howled.—*n.* a loud, prolonged cry of distress: a yell: a loud sound like a yell made by the wind, &c.—*n.* **howl'er** (*slang*), a ridiculous mistake. [O.Fr. *huller*—L. *ululāre,* to shriek or howl—*ulula,* an owl.]

howlet, *how'lit, n.* an owlet: an owl. [**owlet.**]

howso, *how'sō, adv.* (*obs.*) howsoever.

howsoever, *how-so-ev'ér, adv.* in what way soever. [**how, so, ever.**]

hoy, *hoi, n.* a large one-decked boat, commonly rigged as a sloop. [Du. *heu,* Flem. *hui.*]

hoyden, hoiden, *hoi'dén, n.* a bold, frolicsome girl. [Perh. Du. *heyden,* a heathen, a gipsy—

heyde, heath.]

hub, hub, *n.* the nave of a wheel: the centre: a mark at which quoits, &c., are cast. [Prob. a form of **hob** (1).]

hubble-bubble, *hub'l-bub'l, n.* a bubbling sound: confusion: a crude kind of hookah. [**bubble.**]

hubbub, *hub'ub, n.* a confused sound of many voices, riot, uproar. [App. of Irish origin.]

hubris, *hū'bris,* **hybris,** *hī'bris, n.* insolent pride, such as invites disaster.—*adj.* **hūbris'tic.** [Gr., wanton violence arising from passion or pride.]

huckaback, *huk'a-bak, n.* a coarse linen or cotton with raised surface used for towels, &c.

huckle, *huk'l, n.* a hunch: the hip:—*adjs.* **huck'le-backed, -shoul'dered,** having the back or shoulders round.—*n.* **huck'le-bone,** the hip-bone, or ankle-bone.

huckleberry, *huk'l-bér-i, n.* a genus of North American shrubs with dark-blue berries: (improperly) the whortleberry or other plant of its genus. [App. for *hurtleberry.* See derivation of **whortleberry.**]

huckster, *huk'stér, n.* a retailer of smallwares, a hawker or pedlar: a mean, higgling fellow.— *v.i.* to deal in small articles: (*U.S. slang*) an advertising man.

huddle, *hud'l, v.t.* to throw or crowd together in disorder: to put (on) hastily: to perform perfunctorily or hastily: to crouch, to draw (oneself) together (usu. with *up*).—*v.i.* to crowd in confusion.—*n.* a confused mass: a jumble: a secret conference. [Poss. conn. with **hide.**]

hue, *hū, n.* (*obs.*) appearance: colour: tint: the attribute of colour which differentiates it from grey of equal brilliance. [O.E. *hīow, heow*; Swed. *hy,* complexion.]

hue, *hū, n.* a shouting.—**hue and cry,** a loud summons to join in pursuit of an escaping criminal: an outcry. [Fr. *huer,* imit.]

huff, *huf, n.* a fit of anger, sulks, or offended dignity.—*v.t.* to swell: to bully: (in draughts) to remove a piece from the board for omitting to take 'a man'.—*v.i.* to swell: to bluster.—*adjs.* **huff'ish, huff'y,** given to huff, touchy.—*adv.* **huff'ishly.**—*ns.* **huff'ishness, huff'iness.** [Imit.]

hug, *hug, v.t.* to clasp close with the arms: to cherish: to keep close to (e.g. *to hug the shore*):—*pr.p.* hugg'ing; *pa.p.* hugged.—*n.* a close embrace: a particular grip in wrestling.—**hug oneself,** to congratulate oneself.

huge, *hūj, adj.* enormous: very great.—*adv.* **huge'ly.**—*n.* **huge'ness.** [O.Fr. *ahuge.*]

hugger-mugger, *hug'ér-mug'ér, n.* secrecy: confusion. [Origin obscure.]

Huguenot, *hū'gé-not,* or *-nō, n.* (*hist.*) a French Protestant. [Fr.,—earlier *eiguenot*—Ger. *eidgenoss,* confederate, assimilated to the name *Hugues,* Hugh.]

hulk, *hulk, n.* an unwieldy ship: a dismantled ship: anything unwieldy:—*pl.* **the hulks,** old ships formerly used as prisons.—*adjs.* **hulk'ing, hulk'y,** clumsy. [O.E. *hulc,* perh.—Gr. *holkas*—*helkein,* to draw.]

hula-hula, *hōō'la-hōō'la, n.* a Hawaiian women's dance. [Hawaiian.]

hull, *hul, n.* a husk or outer covering.—*v.t.* to separate from the hull, to husk. [O.E. *hulu,* a husk, as of corn—*helan,* to cover; Ger. *hülle,* a covering—*hehlen,* to cover.]

Neutral vowels in unaccented syllables: *em'pér-ór*; for certain sounds in foreign words see p. ix.

hull, *hul, n.* the frame or body of a ship.—*v.t.* to pierce the hull of. [Perh. same word as above, modified in meaning by confusion with Du. *hol,* a ship's hold, or with **hulk.**]

hullabaloo, *hul′a-ba-lōō′, n.* an uproar. [Perh. from **hullo** (**hello**).]

hum, *hum, v.i.* to make a sound like bees: to sing with closed lips: to pause in speaking and utter an inarticulate sound: to be busily active: (*slang*) to have a strong unpleasant smell.—*v.t.* to render by humming:—*pr.p.* humm′ing; *pa.p.* hummed.—*n.* the noise of bees: a murmur.—*n.* **humm′er,** a person or thing that hums: (*slang*) an unpleasant smell.—**make things hum,** to cause brisk activity. [Imit.; cf. Ger. *hummen, humsen.*]

human, *hū′man, adj.* belonging or pertaining to man or mankind: having the qualities of a man.—*n.* **hū′mankind,** the human species.—*adv.* **hū′manly,** according to, in keeping with, human standards, qualities, or abilities.—**human nature,** the nature of man: the qualities of character common to all men that differentiate them from other species: (often *facet.*) irrational, or less than saintly, behaviour. [Fr. *humain*—L. *hūmānus*—*homō,* a human being.]

humane, *hū-mān′, adj.* having the feelings proper to man: kind, tender, merciful: benevolent: humanising (classical, elegant, polite), as *humane letters.—adv.* **humane′ly.** [**human.**]

humanise, *hū′man-īz, v.t.* to render *human* or *humane*: to soften.—*v.i.* to become humane or civilised.

humanist, *hū′man-ist, n.* a student of polite literature: at the Renaissance, a student of Greek and Roman literature: a student of human nature: advocate of humanism.—*adj.* **humanist′ic.**—*n.* **hu′manism,** literary culture: any system which puts human interests and the mind of man paramount, rejecting the supernatural. [L. (*literae, litterae*) *hūmaniores,* polite literature.]

humanitarian, *hū-man-i-tā′ri-än, n.* one who denies Christ's divinity, and holds Him to be a mere man: a philanthropist.—*adj.* of or belonging to humanity, benevolent.—*n.* **humanitā′rianism.** [**humanity.**]

humanity, *hū-man′it-i, n.* the nature peculiar to a human being: the kind feelings of man, benevolence: mankind collectively:—*pl.* **human′ities,** in Scotland, grammar, rhetoric, Latin, Greek, and poetry, so called from their humanising effects.—**professor of Humanity,** in Scottish universities, the professor of Latin. [Fr.,—L. *hūmānitās*—*hūmānus*—*homō,* a man.]

humble, *hum′bl* (old-fashioned *um′bl*), *adj.* low: lowly: unpretentious, modest.—*v.t.* to bring down to the ground: to degrade: to mortify: to abase (oneself).—*n.* **hum′bleness.**—*adv.* **hum′bly.** [Fr.,—L. *humilis,* low—*humus,* the ground.]

humble-bee, *hum′bl-bē, n.* the bumble-bee. [Perh. from *humble,* freq. of **hum.**]

humble-pie, *hum′bl-pī, n.* a pie made of the umbles or numbles (liver, heart, &c.) of a deer.—**eat humble-pie,** to undergo humiliation. [O.Fr. *nombles,* for *lomble*—*le omble*—*le,* the, *omble,* navel—L. *umbilīcus.*]

humbug, *hum′bug, n.* an imposition, trick: one who imposes or tricks: fair pretences: a peppermint sweetmeat.—*v.t.* to deceive: to hoax:—*pr.p.* hum′bugging; *pa.p.* hum′bugged.

humdinger, *hum-ding′ér, n.* (*slang*) an exceptionally excellent person or thing: a swift vehicle or aircraft: a smooth-running engine. [Prob. **hum,** and **ding** (1).]

humdrum, *hum′drum, adj.* dull, monotonous: commonplace.—*n.* a stupid fellow: monotony. [**hum** and perh. **drum.**]

humerus, *hū′mér-us, n* the bone of the upper arm:—*pl.* **hūm′erī.**—*adj.* **hū′meral,** belonging to the shoulder. [L. (*h*)*umerus,* the shoulder.]

humid, *hū′mid, adj.* moist, damp, rather wet.—*adv.* **hū′midly.**—*ns.* **humid′ifier,** a device for increasing or maintaining humidity; **hū′midness, hūmid′ity,** moisture: degree of moistness.—**relative humidity,** the ratio of the amount of water vapour present in the air to the amount that would saturate the air at the same temperature. [L. *hūmidus*—*hūmere,* to be moist.]

humiliate, *hū-mil′i-āt, v.t.* to humble: to wound the self respect of, or mortify.—*n.* **humiliā′tion.** [L. *humiliāre, -ātum*—*humilis,* low.]

humility, *hū-mil′i-ti, n.* the state of being humble: lowliness of mind, modesty. [O.Fr. *humilite*—L. *humilitās*—*humilis,* low.]

humming, *hum′ing, n.* a low, murmuring sound.—*ns.* **humm′ing-bird,** a family of tropical birds, of brilliant plumage and rapid flight, so called from the humming sound of their wings; **humm′ing-top,** a top which when spun gives a humming sound. [**hum.**]

hummock, *hum′ok, n.* a small hillock: a pile or ridge on an icefield. [Origin unknown.]

humour, in U.S. **humor,** *hū′mör,* or *u′mor, n.* (*arch.*) moisture: a fluid of the animal body, esp. one of the four that were formerly believed to determine temperament: temperament, disposition: state of mind (e.g. *good humour, ill humour*): inclination: caprice: a mental quality that apprehends and delights in ludicrous and mirthful ideas: that which causes mirth and amusement.—*v.t.* to indulge: to gratify by compliance.—*adj.* **hū′moral,** pertaining to or proceeding from the humours.—*ns.* **humoresque′,** a musical caprice; **hū′morist,** (*arch.*) one whose behaviour is regulated by humour or caprice: one who studies or portrays the ludicrous and mirthful in human life and character: a maker of jokes.—*adj.* **hu′morous,** (*arch.*) governed by humour, capricious: having and indulging a sense of the ludicrous and mirthful: funny, exciting laughter.—*adv.* **hū′morously.**—*n.* **hū′morousness.**—**comedy of humours,** the comedy of Ben Jonson and his school in which the characters are little more than personifications of single qualities; **out of humour,** displeased. [O.Fr. *humor*—L. (*h*)*ūmor*—(*h*)*ūmēre,* to be moist.]

hump, *hump, n.* a lump or hunch upon the back: a knoll: (*coll.*—**the hump**) a fit of depression.—*v.t.* (*Austr.*) to shoulder, to carry on the back.—*n.* **hump′back,** a back with a hump or hunch: a person with a humpback.—*adj.* **hump′backed,** having a humpback.—**over the hump,** past the crisis or difficulty.

humus, *hūm′us, n.* decomposed organic matter

in the soil. [L. *humus*; cf. Gr. *chamai*, on the ground.]

Hun, *hun, n.* one of a savage nomad race of Asia, which overran Europe in 5th century A.D.: a ruthless savage: (*war slang*) a German. [O.E. (pl.) *Hūne, Hūnas*; L. *Hunni.*]

hunch, *hunch, -sh, n.* a hump: a lump: a premonition.—*v.t.* to hump, bend.—*n.* **hunch'-back,** one with a hunch or lump on his back.—*adj.* **hunch'backed,** having a humpback. [Origin obscure.]

hundred, *hun'drĕd, n.* the number of ten times ten: a set of a hundred things: a division of a county in England, orig. supposed to contain a hundred families:—*pl.* **hundreds** or (preceded by a numeral) **hundred** (e.g. *seven hundred of them*).—*adj.* to the number of a hundred.—*adj., adv.* **hun'dredfold,** a hundred times as much.—*adj.* **hun'dredth,** last of a hundred.—*n.* one of a hundred equal parts.—*n.* **hun'dredweight,** the twentieth part of a ton, or 112 lb. avoirdupois; orig. a hundred lb., abbreviated *cwt.* (*c.* standing for L. *centum, wt.* for weight).—**Chiltern Hundreds** (see **Chiltern**); **one, two,** &c., **hundred hours,** one, two, &c., o'clock, from the method of writing hours and minutes 1.00, 2.00, &c. [O.E. *hundred*—old form *hund,* a hundred, with the suffix. *-red,* a reckoning.]

hung, *pa.t.* and *pa.p.* of **hang.**

hunger, *hung'gĕr, n.* craving for food: need, or lack, of food: any strong desire.—*v.i.* to crave food: to long (for).—*adjs.* **hung'er-bitt'en,** bitten, pained, or weakened by hunger; **hung'ry,** having, showing, eager desire, esp. for food: greedy: lean, barren, poor.—*adv.* **hung'rily.**—*n.* **hung'er-strike,** prolonged refusal of all food by a prisoner, as a form of protest. [O.E. *hungor* (n.), *hyngran* (vb.); cf. Ger. *hunger,* Du. *honger.*]

hunks, *hungks, n.sing.* a miser.

hunt, *hunt, v.t.* to chase for prey or sport: to search for: to hound, drive.—*v.i.* to go out in pursuit of game: to search.—*n.* a chase of wild animals: a search: an association of huntsmen.—*ns.* **hunt'er,** one who hunts (*fem.* **hunt'ress**): a horse used in the chase: a watch whose face is protected by a metal case; **hunter's-moon,** full moon following harvestmoon; **hunt'ing-box, -lodge, -seat,** a temporary residence for hunting; **hunt'ing-crop, -whip,** a short whip with a crooked handle and a loop of leather at the end; **hunting-ground,** any field of activity; **hunts'man,** one who hunts: a man who manages the hounds during the chase; **hunts'manship,** the qualifications of a huntsman.—**hunt down,** to search for relentlessly until found: to persecute out of existence; **hunt out,** or **up,** to search out.—**happy hunting grounds,** the paradise of the Red Indian. [O.E. *huntian*; prob. conn. with *hentan,* to seize.]

hurdle, *hûr'dl, n.* a frame of twigs or sticks interlaced: (*agriculture*) a movable frame of timber or iron for gates, &c.: in certain races, a portable barrier over which runners jump: a rude sledge on which criminals were drawn to the gallows.—*v.t.* to enclose with hurdles.—*v.i.* to leap, as over a hurdle: to run a hurdlerace.—*n.* **hur'dle-race,** a race in which the

runners have to leap over a succession of hurdles. [O.E. *hyrdel*; Ger. *hürde.*]

hurdy-gurdy, *hûr'di-gûr'di, n.* (*obs.*) a musical stringed instrument, like a rude violin, whose strings are sounded by the turning of a wheel: a hand-organ. [Imit.]

hurl, *hûrl, v.t.* to fling with violence (*lit.* and *fig.*).—*v.i.* to dash.—*n.* act of hurling. [Cf. Low Ger. *hurreln,* to hurl; influenced by **hurtle** and **whirl.**]

hurly-burly, *hûr'li-bûr'li, n.* tumult: confusion. [Perh. from **hurl.**]

hurrah, hurra, *hur-ä', hŏŏr-ä', interj.* an exclamation of enthusiasm or joy. [Cf. Scand. *hurra,* Ger. *hurrah,* Du. *hoera.*]

hurricane, *hur'i-kin, -kăn, n.* a West Indian cyclone, i.e. storm of great violence: a wind of extreme violence (over 75 miles per hour).—*ns.* **hurr'icane-deck,** a deck above the main deck in steamships; **hurr'icane-lamp,** a lamp designed to defy strong wind. [Sp. *huracán,* from Carib (q.v.).]

hurry, *hur'i, v.t.* to urge forward: to hasten.—*v.i.* to move or act with haste:—*pa.p.* **hurr'ied.**—*n.* a driving forward: haste: flurried haste: necessity for haste.—*adv.* **hurr'iedly.**—*n.* **hurr'y-skurr'y,** confusion and bustle.—*adv.* confusedly. [Prob. imit. Cf. Old Swed. *hurra,* to whirl round.]

hurst, *hûrst, n.* a wood, a grove. [O.E. *hyrst.*]

hurt, *hûrt, v.t.* to cause bodily pain to: to damage: to wound, as the feelings.—*v.i.* to give pain:—*pa.t.* and *pa.p.* hurt.—*n.* a wound: injury.—*adj.* **hurt'ful,** causing hurt or loss: injurious.—*adv.* **hurt'fully.**—*n.* **hurt'fulness.**—*adj.* **hurt'less,** harmless: without hurt or injury.—*adv.* **hurt'lessly.**—*n.* **hurt'lessness.** [O.Fr. *hurter,* to knock, to run against.]

hurtle, *hûrt'l, v.t.* to dash, to hurl.—*v.i.* to move rapidly with a whirl or clatter. [Freq. of **hurt** in its original sense (see ety.).]

husband, *huz'bănd, n.* a man to whom a woman is married: a thrifty manager.—*v.t.* to supply with a husband: to conserve: to manage thriftily, to economise.—*ns.* **hus'bandman,** a working farmer: one who labours in tillage; **hus'bandry,** the business of a farmer: tillage: economical management, thrift.—**ship's husband,** owners' agent who manages the affairs of a ship in port. [O.E. *hūsbonda,* O.N. *hūsbōndi*—*hūs,* a house, *būandi,* inhabiting, pr.p. of O.N. *būa,* to dwell.]

hush, *hush, interj.* or *imper.* silence! be still!—*v.t.* and *v.i.* to quieten.—*n.* a silence, esp. after noise.—*n.* **hush'aby,** a lullaby.—*adj.* **hush'-hush',** secret.—*n.* **hush'-mon'ey,** a bribe for silence.—**hush up,** to keep secret or little known by suppressing talk concerning (an affair). [Imit. Cf. **hist** and **whist.**]

husk, *husk, n.* the dry, thin covering of certain fruits and seeds: a case, shell or covering: (*pl.*) refuse.—*v.t.* to remove the husk from.—*adj.* **husked,** covered with a husk: stripped of husks.—*n.* **husk'ing,** the stripping of husks. [M.E. *huske,* perh. connected with **house.**]

husky, *husk'i, adj.* hoarse (of the voice): rough in sound: sturdy, strong.—*adv.* **husk'ily.**—*n.* **husk'iness.** [From **husk,** a dry covering.]

husky, *hus'ki, n.* an Eskimo sledge-dog: an Eskimo: the Eskimo language. [App.—*Eskimo.*]

Neutral vowels in unaccented syllables: *em'pĕr-ŏr*; for certain sounds in foreign words see p. ix.

hussar, *hŏŏ-zär′, n.* a soldier of a light cavalry regiment: (*orig.*) a soldier of the national cavalry of Hungary. [Hungarian *huszar*, through Old Serbian—It. *corsaro*, a freebooter.]

hussy, *hus′i, huz′i, n.* a pert girl: a wench. [Abbreviation of **housewife** (q.v.).]

hustings, *hus′tingz, n.sing.* the principal court of the city of London: formerly the booths where the votes were taken at an election of an M.P., or the platform from which the candidates gave their addresses: electioneering: speeches given by parliamentary candidates. [O.E. *hústing,* a council—O.N. *hústhing—hús,* a house, *thing,* an assembly.]

hustle, *hus′l, v.t.* to shake or push together: to push roughly or unceremoniously (into—*lit.* and *fig.*): to jostle.—*vi.* to act strenuously.—*n.* frenzied activity.—*n.* **hus′tler,** an energetic fellow. [Du. *hutsen, hutselen,* to shake to and fro; cf. **hotchpotch.**]

hut, *hut, n.* a small or mean house: a small temporary building.—*v.t.* to quarter in huts: *pr.p.* **hutt′ing,** *pa.p.* **hutt′ed—***n.* **hutt′ment,** an encampment of huts: lodging in huts. [Fr. *hutte—*O.H.G. *hutta.*]

hutch, *huch, n.* a box, a chest: a coop for rabbits: a low wagon in which coal is drawn up out of the pit. [Fr. *huche,* a chest—Low L. *hútica,* a box; prob. Gmc.]

huzza, *hooz-ä′, huz-ä′, interj.* and *n.* hurrah! a shout of joy or approbation.—*v.t.* to attend with shouts of joy.—*v.i.* to utter shouts of joy or acclamation:—*pr.p.* huzza′ing;*pa.p.* huzzaed (*-zäd′*). [Perh. Ger. *hussa.*]

hyacinth, *hī′a-sinth, n.* a bulbous genus of the lily family: a blue stone of the ancients: a precious stone, red, brown, or orange, sometimes regarded as identical with the jacinth, sometimes distinguished from it: a purple colour of various hues.—*adj.* **hyacin′thine** consisting of or resembling hyacinth: as beautiful as Hyacinthus, a beautiful youth (beloved by Apollo) from whose blood is said to have sprung the hyacinth flower: of a colour variously understood as golden, purpleblack, or blue. [Through L. from Gr. *Hyakinthos.*]

hyaline, *hī′a-lin, adj.* glassy: of or like glass. [Gr. *hyalos,* glass, prob. Egyptian.]

hybrid, *hī′brid, n.* an organism which is the offspring of a union between two different races, species, genera or varieties: a mongrel: a word formed of elements from different languages.—*adjs.* **hy′brid, hyb′ridous.** [Fr.,—L. *hibrida,* a mongrel.]

hybris. See **hubris.**

hydra, *hī′dra, n.* (*myth.*) a water-monster with many heads, which when cut off were succeeded by others: any manifold evil: a genus of fresh-water polyps remarkable for their power of multiplication on being cut or divided.—*adj.* **hy′dra-head′ed,** difficult to root out, springing up vigorously again and again. [Gr. *hydra—hydōr,* water.]

hydrangea, *hī-drān′j(y)a, n.* a genus of shrubby plants with large heads of showy flowers, natives of China and Japan. [Gr. *hydōr,* water, *angeion,* vessel.]

hydrant, *hī′drant, n.* a connection for attaching a hose to a water-main, a fire-plug. [Gr. *hydōr,* water.]

hydrate, *hī′drāt, n.* a compound containing water chemically combined, e.g. copper sulphate crystals, which contain 5 molecules of water of crystallisation for every molecule of copper sulphate ($CuSO_4 \cdot 5H_2O$): an old word for a hydroxide.—*v.t.* to combine with water.—*adj.* **hy′drated,** containing water chemically combined.—*n.* **hydra′tion.** [Gr. *hydōr,* water.]

hydraulic, *hī-drōl′ik, adj.* relating to hydraulics: conveying water worked by water or other liquid in pipes.—*adv.* **hydraul′ically.**—*n.pl.* **hydraul′ics,** used as *sing.,* the science of hydrodynamics in general, or its practical application to water-pipes, &c.—**hydraulic jack,** a jack or lifting apparatus, in which oil, &c., is pumped against a piston to supply pressure; **hydraulic press,** a press operated by forcing water into a cylinder in which a ram or plunger works; **hydraulic ram,** a device whereby the pressure head produced when a moving column of water is brought to rest is caused to deliver some of the water under pressure. [From Gr. *hydōr,* water, *aulos,* a pipe.]

hydro-, hydr-, in composition, water. [Gr.*hydōr.*]

hydrocarbon, *hī-drō-kär′bon, n.* a chemical compound containing only hydrogen and carbon.

hydrocephalus, *hī-drō-sef′a-lus, n.* water in the head, dropsy of the brain. [Gr. *hydōr,* water, *kephalē,* the head.]

hydrochloric, *hī-drō-klōr′ik, -klor′ik, adj.* applied to an acid composed of hydrogen and chlorine.

hydrodynamics, *hī-drō di nam′iks,* or *-dī-, n.pl.* used as *sing.,* the science that treats of the motions and equilibrium of a material system partly or wholly fluid, called **hydrostatics** when the system is in equilibrium, **hydrokinetics** when it is not.—*adjs.* **hydrodynam′ic, -al.** [Gr. *hydōr,* water, and *dynamics.*]

hydroelectricity, *hī-drō-el-ek-tris′i-ti, n.* electricity produced by means of water.—*adj.* **hydroelec′tric.** [Gr. *hydōr,* water, and **electricity.**]

hydrogen, *hī′drō jen, -jen, n.* a gas which combined with oxygen produces water, an element (symbol H; at. no. 1), the lightest of all known substances, and very inflammable.—*n.* **hydrogena′tion,** addition of hydrogen in gaseous form to substances in the presence of a catalyst—process used in obtaining liquid products from coal, hardening oils, &c.—*v.t.* **hy′drogenate** (*-droj′*).—*adj.* **hydrog′enous.**—**hydrogen bomb** (see **bomb**).—**heavy hydrogen** (see **heavy**). [A word coined by the scientist Cavendish from Gr. *hydōr,* water, and *gennaein,* to produce.]

hydrography, *hī-drog′ra-fi, n.* the investigation of seas and other bodies of water, including charting, sounding, study of tides, currents, &c.—*n.* **hydrog′rapher.**—*adjs.* **hydrographic** (*-graf′ik*), **-al.** [Gr. *hydōr,* water, *graphein,* to write.]

hydrokinetics, *hī-drō-ki-net′iks, n.pl.* used as *sing.,* a branch of **hydrodynamics** (q.v.).

hydrology, *hī-drol′o-ji, n.* the science of water, esp. underground waters, or of medical treatment by baths. [Gr. *hydōr,* water, *logos,* discourse.]

hydrolysis, *hī-drol'i-sis*, *n.* the formation of an acid and a base from a salt by interaction with water: the decomposition of organic compounds by interaction with water.—*adj.* **hydrolyt'ic.** [Gr. *hydōr*, water, *lysis*, loosing—*lyein*, to loose.]

hydrometer, *hī-drom'ét-ér*, *n.* a float for measuring specific gravity.—*adjs.* **hydrometric** (-*met'-*), **-et'ry.** [Gr. *hydōr*, water, *metron*, a measure.]

hydropathy, *hī-drop'a-thi*, *n.* the treatment of disease by water.—*adjs.* **hydropathic** (*hī-drō-path'ik*), **-al.**—**hydropathic establishment,** or simply **hydropath'ic,** or (*coll.*) **hy'dro,** a hotel (with special baths, &c.) where the guests can have hydropathic treatment if desired. [Gr. *hydōr*, water, *pathos*, suffering—*pathein*, to suffer.]

hydrophobia, *hī-drō-fō'bi-a*, *n.* horror of water: inability to swallow water owing to a contraction in the throat, a symptom of rabies: rabies itself.—*adj.* **hydrophobic** (-*fob'ik*). [Gr. *hydōr*, water, *phobos*, fear.]

hydroplane, *hī'drō-plān*, *n.* a light, flat-bottomed fast motor-boat: (erroneously) a *hydro-aeroplane* i.e. a seaplane. [Gr. *hydōr*, water, L. *planus*, plane.]

hydroponics, *hī-drō-pon'iks*, *n.* the art or practice of growing plants in a chemical solution without soil. [Gr. *hydōr*, water, *ponos*, toil.]

hydrosphere, *hī'drō-sfēr*, *n.* the water-envelope of the earth—the seas and oceans. [Gr. *hydōr*, water, *sphaira*, sphere.]

hydrostatics, *hī-drō-stat'iks*, *n.pl.* used as *sing.,* a branch of **hydrodynamics** (q.v.).—*n.* **hy'drostat,** a contrivance for indicating or regulating height of water.—*adjs.* **hydrostat'ic, -al.**—**hydrostatic balance,** a balance for weighing bodies in water to determine their specific gravity; **hydrostatic drive, transmission,** in vehicle, drive consisting of system transmitting power through oil, under pressure. [Gr. *hydōr*, water, *statikē* (*epistēme*), statics.]

hydrotropism, *hī-drot'rop-izm*, *n.* turning of an organ (e.g. a plant root) towards water. [Gr. *hydōr*, water, *tropos*, turn.]

hydrous, *hī'drŭs*, *adj.* (*chem., min.*) containing water. [Gr. *hydōr*, water.]

hydroxide, *hī-droks'īd*, *n.* a chemical compound containing one or more **hydroxyl** group (i.e. the group OH), as calcium hydroxide $Ca(OH)_2$. [**hydrogen, oxygen.**]

Hydrozoa, *hī-drō-zō'a*, *n.pl.* (*sing.* **hydrozō'on**) a class of chiefly marine organisms, in which alternation (q.v.) of generations typically occurs (cf. **zoophytes**).

hyena, hyaena, *hī-ē'na*, *n.* a genus of bristly-maned quadrupeds, feeding on carrion, emitting at times a sound somewhat like hysterical laughter. [L.,—Gr. *hyaina*—*hŷs*, a pig.]

hygeian, *hī-jē'án*, *adj.* relating to *Hygieia,* goddess of Health, or to health and its preservation. [Gr. *Hygieia,* later *Hygeia.*]

hygiene, *hī'ji-ēn*, also *-jēn*, *n.* the science or art of preserving health: sanitary principles.—*adj.* **hygienic** (*hī-ji-en'ik*, also *-jēn'-*).—*adv.* **hygien'ically.**—*n.pl.* (as *sing.*) **hygien'ics,** principles of hygiene. [Fr. *hygiène*—Gr. *hygieinē* (*technē*), hygienic (art) —*hygieia*, health, *hygiēs*, healthy.]

hygrometer, *hī-grom'ét-ér*, *n.* an instrument for measuring the relative humidity of the atmosphere or of other gases.—*adjs.* **hygrometric** (-*met'rik*), **-al.**—*n.* **hygrom'etry.** [Gr. *hygros*, wet, *metron*, a measure.]

hygroscope, *hī'grō-skōp*, *n.* an instrument that shows, without measuring, changes in the humidity of the atmosphere.—*adjs.* **hygroscopic** *·*(-*skop'ik*), **-al,** relating to the hygroscope: readily absorbing moisture from the atmosphere. [Gr. *hygros*, wet, *skopeein*, to view.]

Hymen, *hī'men*, *n.* (*myth.*) the god of marriage: marriage.—*adjs.* **hymenē'al, hymenē'an.** [Gr. wedding-cry, perh. also a god.]

hymen, *hī'men*, *n.* a membrane: a thin membrane partially closing the virginal vagina.—*n.pl.* **Hymenop'tera,** an order of insects with four transparent wings—ants, bees, wasps. &c. [Gr. *hymen*, membrane.]

hymn, *him*, *n.* a song of praise.—*v.t.* to celebrate in song: to worship in hymns.—*v.i.* to sing in adoration.—*ns.* **hym'nal, hym'nary,** a hymn book.—*adj.* **hym'nic.**—*ns.* **hymnol'ogy,** the study or composition of hymns; **hymnol'ogist.** [Gr. *hymnos.*]

hyoscine, *hī'ō-sēn*, *n.* a form of scopolamine (q.v.). [Gr. *hyoskyanos*, henbane.]

hyper-, *hī'pér-*, *pfx.* beyond: over, in excess [Gr. *hyper*]:—e.g. **hyperphys'ical,** beyond physical laws, supernatural; **hypersen'sitive,** oversensitive; **hypersen'sitiveness.**

hyperbaric, *hī-pér-bar'ik*, *adj.* pertaining to conditions of high atmospheric pressure with a greater concentration of oxygen than normal, as in a **hyperbaric chamber,** a chamber containing oxygen at high pressure: having specific gravity greater than that of cerebrospinal fluid. [Gr. *hyper*, beyond, *barys*, heavy.]

hyperbaton, *hī-pûr'ba-tón*, *n.* a figure of speech in which words are transposed from their natural order (e.g. *in the evening home came the jackdaw*). [Gr.,—*hyperbainein*—*hyper*, beyond, *bainein*, to go.]

hyperbola, *hī-pûr'bo-la*, *n.* (*geom.*) a curve, one of the conic sections, being the intersection of a (double) cone and a plane making a greater angle with the base than the side of the cone makes.—*adjs.* **hyperbol'ic, -al.**—**hyperbolic logarithms,** natural (q.v.) logarithms. [L.,—Gr. *hyperbolē,* overshooting—*hyperballein*—*hyper*, beyond, *ballein*, to throw.]

hyperbole, *hī-pûr'bo-lē*, *n.* a figure of speech that produces a vivid impression by extravagant and obvious exaggeration.—*adjs.* **hyperbol'ic, -al.**—*adv.* **hyperbol'ically.**—*v.t.* **hyper'bolise,** to represent hyperbolically.—*v.i.* to speak hyperbolically or with exaggeration.—*n.* **hyper'bolism.** [A doublet of the above.]

hyperborean, *hī-pér-bō'ri-án*, *adj.* belonging to the extreme north.—*n.* an inhabitant of the extreme north. [Gr. *hyperboreos*—*hyper*, beyond, *Boreas*, the north wind.]

hypercritic, *hī-pér-krit'ik*, *n.* one who is over-critical.—*adjs.* **hypercrit'ic, -al,** overcritical.—*adv.* **hypercrit'ically.**—*n.* **hypercrit'icism.** [Gr. *hyper*, over, and **critic.**]

hyperglycaemia, *hī-pér-glī-sēm'i-á*, *n.* abnormal rise in the sugar content of the blood. [Gr. *hyper*, beyond, *glykys*, sweet.]

Neutral vowels in unaccented syllables: *em'pér-ór*; for certain sounds in foreign words see p. ix.

hypermarket, *hī-pér-mär′kit*, *n.* a self-service multiple store on a larger scale than a super-market. [Gr. *hyper*, beyond, and **market**.]

hypermetrical, *hī-pér-met′rik-ál*, *adj.* beyond or exceeding the ordinary metre of a line: having an additional syllable. [Gr. *hyper*, beyond, and **metrical**.]

hypermetropia, *hī-pér-me-trō′pi-a*, *n.* long-sightedness. [Gr. *hyper*, beyond, *metron*, measure, *ōps*, eye.]

hyperon, *hī′pér-ón*, *n.* any of six particles (and six antiparticles) found in cosmic rays; they are heavier than protons or neutrons. [Gr. *hyper*, beyond, exceeding.]

hypersonic, *hī-pér-son′ik*, *adj.* of speeds, above Mach 5 (or 5 times the speed of sound). [Gr. *hyper*, beyond, and **sonic**.]

hypertension, *hī-pér-ten′sh(ó)n*, *n.* blood pressure higher than normal. [Gr. *hyper*, beyond, and **tension**.]

hypertrophy, *hī-pûr′tro-fi*, *n.* over-nourishment: abnormal enlargement.—*v.i.* to increase in size beyond the normal.—*adj.* **hypertrophied**. [Gr. *hyper*, over, *trophē*, nourishment.]

hypha, *hī′fa*, *n.* one of the threadlike elements of the thallus (q.v.) of a fungus:—*pl.* **hyph′ae** (*-ē*) (See **mycelium**). [Gr. *hyphō*, web.]

hyphen, *hī′fén*, *n.* a short stroke (-) joining two syllables or words.—*v.t.* to join by a hyphen.—*v.t.* **hy′phenate**, to hyphen.—*p.adj.* **hy′phenated**, hyphened: of nationality expressed by a hyphened word, as German-American (often implying divided loyalties). [Gr.,—*hypo*, under, *hen*, one.]

hypnosis, *hip-nō′sis*, *n.* a sleeplike state in which the mind responds to external suggestion and can recover forgotten memories.—*n.* **hypnother′apy**, treatment of illness by hypnosis.—*adj.* **hypnot′ic**, of or relating to hypnosis: soporific.—*n.* a narcotic: one who is subject to hypnosis.—*v.t.* **hyp′notise**, to put in a state of hypnosis: (*fig.*) to fascinate.—*n.* **hyp′notism**, the science of hypnosis: the art or practice of inducing hypnosis: hypnosis. [Gr. *hypnos*, sleep.]

hypo-, *hī′pō-*, **hyp-**, in composition, under, below [Gr. *hypo*]:—e.g. **hypoglycaem′ia**, abnormal reduction of sugar content of the blood; **hypostom′atous**, having the mouth placed on the lower side of the head, as sharks (Gr. *stoma*, *-atos*, mouth); **hypoten′sion**, blood-pressure lower than normal; **hypotympan′ic**, below the tympanum.

hypocaust, *hip′-*, *hīp′ō-köst*, *n.* a space under a floor for heating by hot air or furnace gases. [Gr. *hypokauston—hypo*, under, *kaiein*, to burn.]

hypochondria, *hip-*, *hīp-ō-kon′dri-a*, *n.* a nervous malady, often arising from indigestion, and tormenting the patient with imaginary fears: morbid anxiety about health.—*adj.* **hypochon′driac**, relating to or affected with hypochondria: melancholy.—*n.* one suffering from hypochondria. [Gr. *hypochondria* (neut. pl.)—*hypo*, under, *chondros*, a cartilage.]

hypocrisy, *hi-pok′ri-si*, *n.* a feigning to be what one is not, as good or virtuous: simulating feeling one does not experience. [Gr. *hypokrisis—hypokrinesthai*, to play on the stage, from *hypo*, under, *krinesthai*, to dispute.]

hypocrite, *hip′o-krit*, *n.* one who practises hypocrisy.—*adj.* **hypocrit′ical**, practising hypocrisy.—*adv.* **hypocrit′ically**. [Fr.,—Gr. *hypokritēs*, actor; see preceding.]

hypodermic, *hip-*, or *hīp-ō-dûr′mik*, *adj.* under the skin, subcutaneous, esp. of a method of injecting a drug in solution under the skin by means of a fine hollow needle to which a small syringe is attached.—*n.* a hypodermic needle or syringe. [Gr. *hypo*, under, *derma*, skin.]

hypostasis, *hip-*, *hīp-os′ta-sis*, *n.* essential substance: the essence or real personal substance of each of the three divisions of the Trinity: (*med.*) sediment: (*med.*) excessive blood in a part of the body as a result of faulty circulation.—*adjs.* **hypostatic** (*-stat′ik*), **-al**.—*adv.* **hypostat′ically**. [Gr. *hypostasis—hypo*, under, *stasis*, setting.]

hypotenuse, *hīp-*, *hip-ot′én-ūs*, or *-ūz*, *n.* the side of a right-angled triangle opposite to the right angle (*hīr.,—Gr. hypoteinousa (grammē)*, (a line) subtending or stretching under—*hypo*, under, *teinein*, to stretch.]

hypothec, *hip-*, *hīp-oth′ek*, *n.* in Roman law, Scots law, &c., a security over goods, given to a creditor, in respect of a debt due by the owner of the goods.—*v.t.* **hypoth′ecate**, to place or assign as security under an arrangement: to mortgage.—*n.* **hypotheca′tion**. [L. *hypotheca*—Gr. *hypothēkē*, a pledge.]

hypothermia, *hī-pō-thûr′mi-á*, *n.* subnormal body temperature, esp. that induced for purposes of heart and other surgery (freezing-down). [Gr. *hypo*, under, *thermē*, heat.]

hypothesis, *hī-poth′e-sis*, *n.* a supposition, as a proposition assumed for the sake of argument, a theory to be proved or disproved by reference to facts, a provisional explanation of anything:—*pl.* **hypoth′eses** (*-sēs*), *adjs.* **hypothet′ic, -al**.—*adv.* **hypothet′ically**. [Gr. *hypothesis—hypo*, under, *thesis*, placing.]

hyson, *hī′son*, *n.* a very fine sort of green tea. [From Chinese.]

hyssop, *his′óp*, *n.* an aromatic plant: (*B.*) an unknown wall-plant used as a ceremonial sprinkler. [L. *hyssopum*—Gr. *hyssōpos*, or *-on*; cf. Heb. *ēzōb*.]

hysterectomy, *his-tér-ek′tóm-i*, *n.* surgical removal of the womb. [Gr. *hystera*, the womb, *ectomē*, a cutting out.]

hysteria, *his-tē′ri-a*, *n.* a mental disorder giving rise to loss of memory, sleep-walking, &c., and manifested by various physical symptoms: an outbreak of wild emotionalism in an individual or in a community.—*n.pl.* **hyster′ics**, fits of hysteria: popularly, alternate paroxysms of laughing and crying, often with a choking sensation in the throat.—*adjs.* **hysteric** (*-ter′ik*), **-al**, pertaining to, of the nature of, or affected with hysterics or hysteria: like hysterics: fitfully and violently emotional.—*adv.* **hyster′ically**. [Gr. *hystera*, the womb, with which hysteria was formerly thought to be connected.]

hysteron-proteron, *his′tér-on-prot′ér-on*, *n.* a figure of speech in which what should follow comes first: an inversion of the natural or rational. [Gr., lit. latter-former.]

I

I, *ī, pron.* the nominative case singular of the first personal pronoun: the word used by a speaker or writer in mentioning himself. [M.E. *ich* – O.E. *ic*; Ger. *ich*, O.N. *ek*, L. *ego*, Gr. *egō*.]

iambus, *ī-am'bus, n.* a metrical foot of two syllables, the first short and the second long, as in L. *fīdēs*; or the first unaccented and the second accented, as in *deduce.* – Also **i'amb.** – *adj.* **iam'bic,** consisting of iambuses. [L. *īambus* – Gr. *iambos*, from *iaptein*, to assail, this metre being first used by writers of satire.]

Iberian, *ī-bē'ri-án, adj.* of Spain and Portugal: of ancient Iberia (now Georgia) in the Caucasus. [L. and Gr. *Ibēria*, Spain and Portugal, Georgia.]

ibex, *ī'beks, n.* any of several large-horned mountain wild goats. [L. *ibex.*]

ibis, *ī'bis, n.* a genus of wading birds with curved bill, akin to the spoonbills, one species worshipped by the ancient Egyptians. [L. and Gr. *.ibis*, prob. an Egyptian word.]

Icarian, *ī-kā'ri-án, adj.* belonging to, or like, *Icārus*, who was provided with wings by his father, Daedalus, but soared too near the sun which melted the wings.

ice, *īs, n.* water congealed by freezing: concreted sugar on a cake, &c.: ice-cream: (*fig.*) coldness of manner. – *v.t.* to cover with, or as with, ice: to freeze: to cool with ice: to cover with concreted sugar. – *v.i.* (sometimes with *up*) to freeze: to become covered with ice: – *pr.p.* ic'ing; *pa.p.* iced. – *ns.* **ice age** (*geol.*), any epoch when a great part of the earth's surface has been covered with ice, esp. the Pleistocene (q.v.) epoch, when the northern parts of the Northern Hemisphere were affected; **ice'blink,** the peculiar appearance in the air reflected from distant masses of ice; **ice'boat,** a boat used for forcing a passage through, or sailing or being dragged over, ice. – *adj.* **ice'-bound,** bound, surrounded, or fixed in, with ice. – *ns.* **ice'-box,** the freezing compartment of a refrigerator: (*U.S.*) a refrigerator; **ice'-break'er,** a ship for breaking a channel through ice; **ice'-cream, iced'-cream,** cream, or a substitute, sweetened or flavoured, and artificially frozen. – *adj.* **iced,** covered with ice: encrusted with sugar. – *ns.* **ice'-field,** a large area covered with ice, esp. floating ice; **ice'float, ice'floe,** a mass of floating ice smaller than an icefield; **ice'-house,** a house for preserving ice; **ice'pack,** drifting ice packed together; **ice'-pail, -buck'et,** a pail with ice for cooling wine; **ice'-plant,** a plant whose leaves glisten in the sun as if covered with ice; **ice'-plough,** an instrument for cutting grooves in ice to facilitate its removal; **ic'ing,** a covering of ice or of concreted sugar. – *adj.* **ic'y,** composed of, abounding in, or like ice: very cold: without friendliness or warmth of affection. – *adv.* **ic'ily.** – *n.* **ic'iness.** – **break the ice** (see **break**); **cut no ice,** count for nothing; **on ice** (*fig.*), kept, or waiting, in readiness; **on thin ice** (*fig.*), in a situation requiring great care or tact. [O.E. *īs*; O.N. *īss*; Ger. *eis,* Dan. *is.*]

iceberg, *īs'bėrg, n.* a huge mass of floating ice. [From Scand. or Du., the latter part, *berg,* meaning 'mountain'.]

Icelandic, *īs-land'ik, adj.* of *Iceland.* – *n.* the language of the Icelanders: sometimes used for **Old Icelandic** or Old Norse (closely resembling modern Icelandic) in which the sagas were written between the 11th and 13th centuries.

Iceland-moss, *īs'land-mos, n.* a lichen of northern regions, used as a medicine and for food.

Iceland-poppy, *īs'land-pop'i, n.* a dwarf poppy with grey-green pinnate leaves and flowers varying from white to orange-scarlet.

Iceland-spar, *īs'land-spär, n.* a transparent variety of calcite (carbonate of lime) with strong double refraction.

Ichabod, *ik'a-bod, interj.* the glory is departed. [From Heb.; see 1 Sam. iv. 21.]

ichneumon, *ik-nū'mòn, n.* any of a genus of small carnivorous animals, esp. a species in Egypt once believed to destroy crocodiles' eggs: any of a large group of insects whose larvae are parasitic in or on other insects. [Gr. *ichneumōn,* lit. tracker – *ichneuein,* to hunt after – *ichnos,* a track.]

ichnography, *ik-nog'raf-i, n.* (*archit.*) a ground-plan of a work or building: the art of drawing ground-plans. – *adjs.* **ichnograph'ic, -al.** [Gr. *ichnographia* – *ichnos,* a track, *graphein,* to draw.]

ichnology, *ik-nol'o-ji, n.* footprint lore: the science of fossil footprints. [Gr. *ichnos,* a track, *logos,* discourse.]

ichor, *ī'kór, n.* (*myth.*) the ethereal juice in the veins of the gods: watery, colourless matter from an ulcer, &c. – *adj.* **i'chorous.** [Gr. *īchōr.*]

ichthyography, *ik-thi-og'ra-fi, n.* a description of fishes. [Gr. *ichthÿs,* a fish, *graphein,* to write.]

ichthyolite, *ik'thi-o-līt, n.* a fossil fish or part of one. [Gr. *ichthÿs,* a fish, *lithos,* a stone.]

ichthyology, *ik-thi-ol'o-ji, n.* the branch of natural history that treats of fishes. – *adj.* **ichthyolog'ical.** – *n.* **ichthyol'ogist.** [Gr. *ichthÿs,* a fish, *logos,* discourse.]

ichthyophagy, *ik-thi-of'a-ji, n.* the practice of eating fish. – *adj.* **ichthyoph'agous** (-*gùs*). [Gr. *ichthÿs,* a fish, *phagein,* to eat.]

ichthyosaurus, *ik'thi-ō-sör-us, n.* a genus of gigantic fossil fishlike marine reptiles of the Mesozoic era. [Gr. *ichthÿs,* a fish, *sauros,* a lizard.]

icicle, *īs'i-kl, n.* a hanging, tapering piece of ice formed by the freezing of dropping water.

Neutral vowels in unaccented syllables: *em'pėr-ór*; for certain sounds in foreign words see p. ix.

[O.E. *īsesgicel*; *īses* being the gen. of *īs*, ice, and *gicel*, an icicle.]

icon, *ī′kon, n.* an image: in the Greek Church, a figure in painting, mosaic, &c. (not sculpture), representing Christ, or a saint. [L. *īcōn*—Gr. *eikōn*, an image.]

iconoclast, *ī-kon′ō-klast, n.* a breaker of images: one opposed to image-worship: one who assails old cherished errors and superstitions.—*adj.* **iconoclast′ic,**—*n.* **icon′oclasm,** act of breaking images (*lit.* and *fig.*). [Gr. *eikōn*, an image, *klaein*. to break.]

iconoscope, *ī-kon′ō-skōp. n.* a form of electron camera. [Gr. *eikon*, an image, *skopeein*, to look at.]

ictus, *ik′tus, n.* rhythmical accentuation. [L., a blow.]

id, *id, n.* the sum total of the instinctive forces in an individual. [L. *id*, it.]

idea, *ī-dē′a, n.* an image of an external object formed by the mind: a notion, thought, any product of intellectual action—of memory and imagination: an archetype, a pattern or model belonging to the supersensible world, of which existent things in any class are imperfect imitations. *adj.* **idē′al,** existing in idea: existing in imagination only: highest and best conceivable, perfect, as opposed to the real, the imperfect.—*n.* the highest conception of anything.—*v.i.* **idē′alise,** to regard as, or to represent as, ideal.—Also *v.i.*—*ns.* **idealisā′tion; idē′alism,** a name given to several philosophical doctrines stressing the part played in our knowledge of the external world by ideas in the mind, the extreme theories asserting that objects of perception have no independent reality: love for or search after the best and highest: the imaginative treatment of subjects: the habit or practice of idealising: impracticality, **idē′alist,** one who holds one of the doctrines of idealism. one who strives after the ideal: an unpractical person.—*adj.* **idealist′ic,** pertaining to idealists or to idealism,—*n.* **ideal′ity,** ideal state: ability and disposition to form ideals of beauty and perfection.—*adv.* **idē′ally.** [L. *īdĕa*—Gr. *idĕā*; cf. *idein* (aor.), to see.]

idée fixe, *ē-dā fēks,* a fixed idea, a monomania: a recurring theme in music. [Fr.]

identify, *ī-den′ti-fī, v.t.* to make, reckon, ascertain, or prove to be, the same: to ascertain the identity of: to assign to a species: to regard, or wish to regard, (oneself) as sharing (with a person or group) interests, experiences, attitudes, behaviour, &c.:—*pa.p.* iden′tified.—*n.* **identificā′tion.—identify oneself with,** associate oneself inseparably with (party, policy, &c.). [L.L. *identificāre*—*idem*, the same, *facĕre*, to make.]

identity, *ī-den′ti ti, n.* state of being the same: sameness: individuality: personality: who or what a person is: (*math.*) an equation true for all values of the symbols involved.—*adj.* **iden′tical,** the very same: agreeing in every detail.—*adv.* **iden′tically.**—*n.* **iden′ticalness.—identical twins,** twins developing from one zygote; **identity card,** a card, issued by the State, containing name, address, and registration number; **identity disk,** a small disk worn in wartime by a soldier or other, whose name,

&c., it bears. [Fr. *identité*—Low L. *identitās, -ātis*—L. *idem,* the same.]

identikit, *ī-den′ti-kit,* (orig. *U.S.* **Identi-Kit**) *n.* a device for building up a composite portrait from a large number of different features on transparent slips (also *fig.*).

ideogram, *id′i-ō-gram,* or *īd′-,* **ideograph,** *-gräf, ns.* a written character or symbol that stands not for a word or sound but for the thing itself directly.—*adjs.* **ideograph′ic, -al.** [Gr. *idea, gramma,* a drawing—*graphein,* to write.]

ideology, *id-,* or *īd-i-ol′o-ji, n.* the science of ideas, metaphysics: a system of ideas belonging to, or way of thinking characterising, a party, class, or culture.—*adjs.* **ideolog′ic, -al.** [Gr. *idea,* idea, *logos,* discourse.]

ides, *īdz, n.pl.* in ancient Rome, the 15th day of March, May, July, October, and the 13th of the other months. [Fr. *ides*—L. *īdūs* (pl.).]

idiocy. See **idiot.**

idiom, *id′i-ōm, n.* a mode of expression peculiar to a language or dialect: an expression characteristic of a language not logically or grammatically explicable: a characteristic mode of expression.—*adjs.* **idiomat′ic, -al,**—*adv.* **idiomat′ically.** [Gr. *idiōma,* peculiarity—*idios,* one's own.]

idiosyncrasy, *id-i-ō-sing′kra-si, n.* peculiarity of temperament or mental constitution: any characteristic of a person.—*adj.* **idiosyncratic** (*-krat′ik*). [Gr. *idios,* own, *synkrāsis,* a mixing together—*syn,* together, *krāsis,* a mixing.]

idiot, *id′i-ōt,* or *id′yōt, n.* one afflicted with the severest grade of feeble-mindedness: a foolish or unwise person.—Also *adj.*—*n.* **id′io(t)cy** (*-si*), state of being an idiot: imbecility: folly.—*adjs.* **idiotic** (*-ot′ik*), **-al.**—*adv.* **idiot′ically.**—*n.* **id′iotism,** the state of being an idiot [Fr.,—L. *idiōta*—Gr. *idiōtēs,* a private person, one who holds no public office or has no professional knowledge—*idios,* own, private.]

idle, *ī′dl, adj.* unemployed: averse to labour: not occupied or in use: useless, vain: baseless.—*v.t.* to spend in idleness.—*v.i.* to be idle or unoccupied.—*ns.* **i′dleness; i′dler; i′dle-wheel,** a wheel placed between two others for transferring the motion from one to the other without changing the direction.—*adv.* **i′dly.** [O.E. *īdel*; Du. *ijdel,* Ger. *eitel.*]

idol, *ī′dol, n.* an image of some object of worship: a person or thing too much loved, admired, or honoured.—*v.t.* **i′dolise,** to make an idol of, for worship: to love to excess. [O.Fr. *idole*—L. *īdōlum*—Gr. *eidōlon eidōs,* what is seen—*idein* (aor.), to see.]

idolater, *ī-dol′a-tēr, n.* a worshipper of idols: a great admirer:—*fem.* **idol′atress.**—*adj.* **idol′atrise.**—*adj.* **idol′atrous.**—*adv.* **idol′atrously.**—*n.* **idol′atry,** the worship of idols: excessive love. [Fr. *idolâtre*—Gr. *eidōlolatrēs*—*eidōlon,* idol, *latreia,* worship.]

idyll, *id′il, īd′il, n.* a short pictorial poem, chiefly on pastoral subjects: a story, episode, or scene of happy innocence or rusticity: a work of art of like character, in music, &c.—*adj.* **idyll′ic.** [L. *īdyllium*—Gr. *eidyllion,* dim. of *eidos,* image.]

if, *if, conj.* on condition that: in case that: supposing that: whether. [O.E. *gif*; cf. Du. *of,* O.N. *ef.*]

fāte, fär; mē, hûr (her); *mīne; mōte, fōr; mūte; mōōn, fōŏt;* THen (then)

igloo, *ig'lōō*, *n.* a snow-hut. [Eskimo.]

igneous, *ig'nē-us*, *adj.* pertaining to, consisting of, or like, fire: (*geol.*) produced by the action of heat. [L. *ignis*, fire.]

ignis-fatuus, *ig'nis-fat'ū-us*, *n.* will-o'-the-wisp—the light of combustion of marsh-gas, apt to lead travellers into danger: any delusive ideal that leads one astray:—*pl.* **ignes-fatui** (*ig'nēz-fat'ū-ī*). [L. *ignis*, fire, *fatuus*, foolish.]

ignite, *ig-nīt'*, *v.t.* to set on fire: to heat to the point at which combustion occurs: to render luminous by heat.—*v.i.* to take fire.—*adj.* **ignīt'able** (also **ignīt'ible**).—*n.* **igni'tion**, act of igniting: the firing of an explosive mixture of gases, vapours, or other substances, e.g. by means of an electric spark: the means of igniting: state of being ignited. [L. *ignīre*, *ignītum*, to set on fire, make red-hot—*ignis*, fire.]

ignoble, *ig-nō'bl*, *adj.* of low birth: mean or worthless: dishonourable.—*n.* **ignō'bleness**.—*adv.* **ignō'bly**. [Fr.,—L. *ignōbilis—in-*, not, *gnōbilis* (*nōbilis*), noble.]

ignominy, *ig'nō-min-i*, *n.* the loss of one's good name, public disgrace: infamy.—*adj.* **ignomin'ious**, dishonourable: humiliating, degrading: contemptible, mean.—*adv.* **ignomin'iously**.—*n.* **ignomin'iousness**. [Fr.,—L. *ignōminia—in-*, not, *(g)nōmen*, *-inis*, name.]

ignoramus, *ig-nō-rā'mus*, *n.* an ignorant person, esp. one making a pretence to knowledge:—*pl.* **ignorā'muses**. [L. *ignōrāmus*, we are ignorant, 1st pers. pl. pres. indic. of *ignōrāre*.]

ignorant, *ig'nŏr-ǎnt*, *adj.* without knowledge: uninformed: resulting from want of knowledge.—*n.* **ig'norance**, state of being ignorant: want of knowledge: (*pl.*) sins committed through ignorance.—*adv.* **ig'norantly**. [Fr.,—L. *ignōrans*, *-antis*, pr.p. of *ignōrāre*. See **ignore**.]

ignore, *ig-nōr'*, *-nŏr'*, *v.t.* to disregard wilfully: (*law*) to set aside. [L. *ignōrāre*, not to know—*in-*, not, and the root of *(g)nōscĕre*, to know.]

iguana, *i-gwä'na*, *n.* a genus of large thick-tongued arboreal lizards in tropical America. [Sp. from Carib (q.v.).]

ikebana, *ē'ke-bä'nä*, *n.* Japanese art of flower arrangement.

il- *il-*, *pfx.* a form of **in-** used before *l*.

ilex, *ī'leks*, *n.* the holly genus: the evergreen or holm oak. [L. *īlex*, holm-oak.]

Iliad, *il'i-ad*, *n.* a Greek epic, ascribed to Homer, on the siege of Troy: a long story or series of woes. [Gr. *Ilias*, *-ados—Ilios* or *Ilion*, Ilium, Troy.]

ilk, *ilk*, *adj.* same.—**of that ilk**, of that same, that is, of the estate of the same name as the family: (through misunderstanding) of that family, class, or kind. [O.E. *ilca*, prob.—*līk*, like.]

ill, *il*, *adj.* (*comp.* **worse**; *superl.* **worst**) morally evil: implying moral evil (e.g. *an ill name*): malevolent, cruel: bad, in senses other than moral: producing evil: hurtful: unfavourable, unlucky: unskilful: difficult: sick: diseased.—*adv.* badly, not well: not rightly: with difficulty.—*n.* evil: wickedness: misfortune.—*adjs.* **ill'-advised'**, imprudent; **ill'-affect'ed**, not well disposed.—**ill at ease**, uncomfortable: embarrassed.—*ns.* **ill'-blood'**, **ill'-feel'ing**, resent-

ment, enmity.—*adj.* **ill'-bred**, badly bred or educated: uncivil.—*n.* **ill'-breed'ing**.—*adjs.* **ill'-condi'tioned**, in bad condition: churlish; **ill'-disposed**, unfriendly: inclined to evil; **ill'-fāt'ed**, unlucky; **ill'-fā'voured**, ill-looking, ugly: unpleasant; **ill'-got'**, **-gott'en**, procured by bad means; **ill'-hum'oured**, bad-tempered; **ill'-mann'ered**, rude: ill-bred; **ill'-nā'tured**, of a bad temper: cross, peevish.—*adv.* **ill'-nā'turedly**.—*n.* **ill'ness**, sickness: disease.—*adjs.* **ill'-off**, in poor or bad circumstances; **ill'-starred**, born under the influence of an unlucky star: unlucky; **ill'-tem'pered**, having a bad temper: morose; **ill'-timed'**, inopportune: at an unsuitable time; **ill'-used'**, badly used or treated (*v.t.* **ill'-use**, to treat ill: to abuse).—*n.* **ill'-will'**, unkind feeling: enmity.—**take it ill**, to be offended. [O.N. *illr*; not connected with O.E. *yfel*, evil, but formerly confused with it.]

illation, *il-ā'sh(ô)n*, *n.* act of inferring from premises: inference: conclusion.—*adj.* **illative** (*il'a-tiv*), pertaining to, of the nature of, expressing, or introducing, an inference. [L. *illātiō*, *-ōnis—illātus*, used as pa.p. of *inferre*, to infer—*il-* (*in-*), in, *lātus*, carried.]

illegal, *il-ē-gál*, *adj.* contrary to law.—*v.t.* **illē'galise**, to render unlawful.—*n.* **illegal'ity**, the quality or condition of being illegal, or an instance of it.—*adv.* **illē'gally**. [L. *il-* (*in-*), not, and **legal**.]

illegible, *il-ej'i-bl*, *adj.* that cannot be read: indistinct.—*ns.* **illeg'ibleness**, **illegibil'ity**.—*adv.* **illeg'ibly**. [L. *il-* (*in-*), not, and **legible**.]

illegitimate, *il-ē-jit'i-mát*, *adj.* not according to law: not in the legal position of those born in wedlock: not properly inferred or reasoned: not recognised by authority or good usage.—*n.* a bastard.—*n.* **illegit'imacy**.—*adv.* **illegit'imātely**. [L. *il-* (*in-*), not, and **legitimate**.]

illiberal, *il-ib'ér-ál*, *adj.* niggardly, mean: narrow in opinion or culture.—*n.* **illiberal'ity**. [Fr. *il-libéral*—L. *illīberālis—il-* (*in-*), not, *libērālis*, liberal.]

illicit, *il-is'it*, *adj.* not allowable: unlawful: unlicensed.—*adv.* **illic'itly**.—*n.* **illic'itness**. [L. *il-licitus—il-* (*in-*), not, *licitus*, pa.p. of *licēre*, to be allowed.]

illimitable, *il-im'it-à-bl*, *adj.* that cannot be bounded: infinite.—*n.* **illim'itableness**.—*adv.* **illim'itably**. [L. *il-* (*in-*), not, and **limitable**.]

illiterate, *il-it'ér-át*, *adj.* without book-learning: uneducated: unable to read.—*n.* an illiterate person: one who cannot read.—*ns.* **illit'erateness**, **illit'eracy** (*-si*), state of being illiterate: want of learning. [L. *illīterātus* (or *-litt-*)—*il-* (*in-*), not, *līterātus* (or *litt-*), learned.]

illogical, *il-oj'i-kál*, *adj.* contrary to the rules of logic: regardless of, or incapable of, logic.—*adv.* **illog'ically**.—*n.* **illog'icalness**. [L. *il-* (*in-*), not, and **logical**.]

illume. See **illuminate**.

illuminate, *il-(y)ōō'min-āt*, *v.t.* to light up: to enlighten: to throw light on (a subject): to adorn with ornamental lettering or illustrations.—*adj.* enlightened.—*adj.* **illu'minant**, enlightening.—*n.* a means of lighting.—*n.pl.* **Illuminā'tī**, the enlightened, a name given to various sects, and especially to a society of German Freethinkers at the end of the 18th century.—*n.* **illuminā'tion**, lighting up: en-

Neutral vowels in unaccented syllables: *em'pér-ôr*; for certain sounds in foreign words see p. ix.

lightenment: brightness: a decorative display of lights: adorning of books with coloured lettering or illustrations.—*adj.* **illu′minative,** tending to give light: illustrative or explanatory.—*n.* **illu′minator.**—*vs.t.* **illu′mine, illume′,** to make luminous or bright: to enlighten: to adorn. [L. *illūmināre, -ātum*—*in,* in, upon, *lūmināre,* to cast light.]

illusion, *il-(y)oo̅′zh(ŏ)n, n.* deceptive appearance: (*arch.*) an apparition: false conception or delusion: (*psych.*) a false sense impression of something actually present.—*n.* **illu′sionist,** one who produces illusions, a conjurer. *adjs.* **illu′sive, illu′sory,** deceiving by false appearances.—*adv.* **illu′sively.**—*n.* **illu′siveness.** [Fr.,—L. *illūsiō, -ōnis*—*illūdēre*—*in,* on, *lūdēre,* to play.]

illustrate, *il′us-trāt, il-us′trāt, v.t.* to make clear to the mind: to exemplify: to explain, or to adorn, by pictures.—*n.* **illustrā′tion,** act of making clear, explaining: exemplification: an example: a picture or diagram accompanying letterpress, *adjs.* ill′ustrated (in ous̅′), having pictorial illustrations; **illustrative** (*il′us-trā-tiv* or *il-us′tra-tiv*), **illus′tratory,** having the quality of making clear or explaining.—*n.* **ill′ustrātor.**—*adj.* **illus′trious,** highly distinguished: noble.—*adv.* **illus′triously.**—*n.* **illus′triousness.** [L. *illūstris*—*illūstrāre, -ātum*—*lūstrāre,* to light up, prob.—*lūx,* light.]

im-, *im-,* pfx. a form of **in-** used before *b, m* and *p.*

image, *im′ij, n.* a likeness: a statue: an idol: a representation in the mind, esp. of a visible object: a reproduction in the memory of a sensation of sight, hearing, smell, &c.: (*optics*) the figure of any object formed by rays of light, through the use of a mirror, lens, &c.: that which very closely resembles anything: a type: (*rhet.*) a metaphor or simile: public image (see **public**). *vs.t.* to form an image of: to form a likeness of in the mind.—*ns.* **imagery** (*im′ij-ri,* or *im′ij-ēr-i*), the work of the imagination: mental pictures: figures of speech: images in general or collectively; **im′agist,** one of a 20th-century school of poetry aiming at concentration, exact and simple language, and freedom of form and subject; **im′agism,** the theory or practice of this school. [O.Fr.,—L. *imāgō,* image; cf. *imitārī,* to imitate.]

imagine, *im-aj′in, v.t.* to form an image of in the mind: to conceive: to think vainly or falsely: to suppose, conjecture: (*arch.*) to contrive or devise.—*v.i.* to form mental images.—*adj.* **imag′inable.**—*n.* **imag′inableness.**—*adv.* **imag′inably.**—*adj.* **imag′inary,** existing only in the imagination, not real, non-existent.—*n.* **imaginātion,** act of imagining: the faculty of forming images in the mind: the artist's creative power: that which is imagined. (*arch.*) a scheme, plot.—*adj.* **imag′inative,** full of imagination.—*ns.* **imag′inativeness; imag′iner; imag′ining,** that which is imagined. [O.Fr. *imaginer*—L. *imāgināri*—*imāgō,* an image.]

imago, *i-mā′gō, n.* the last or perfect state of insect life: an image or optical counterpart of a thing:—*pl.* **imagines** (*i-mā′jin-ēz*), **ima′gōs.** [L.]

imâm, *i-mäm′,* **imaum,** *i-mŏm′, n.* the officer who leads the devotions in a mosque: a title among Mohammedans. [Ar. *imām,* chief.]

imbalance, *im-bal′áns, n.* lack of balance in the adjustment of parts in the body, e.g. the muscles of the eyes: lack of balance among the elements of a diet: temporary lack of balance in a self-adjusting system: lack of balance in a sphere of a nation's economy. [L. *in-,* not, and **balance.**]

imbark. Same as **embark.**

imbecile, *im′be-sil, -sēl, adj.* feeble (now generally in mind). fatuous.—*n.* one whose defective mental state (from birth or an early age) does not amount to idiocy, but who is incapable of managing his own affairs.—*n.* **imbecil′ity.** [Fr. *imbécille* (now *imbécile*)—L. *imbēcillus;* origin unknown.]

imbed, *im-bed′, v.t.* See **embed.**

imbibe, *im-bīb′, v.t.* to drink, drink in: to absorb (moisture): to receive into the mind.—Also *v i — n* **imbib′er.** [L. *imbibēre*—*in,* in, into, *bibēre,* to drink.]

imbitter, imbody, &c. See **embitter, embody,** &c.

imbricate, *im′bri-kāt, v.t.* (*bot.* and *zool.*) to lay one over another, as tiles on a roof.—*v.i.* to be so placed.—*adj.* (*-āt*) overlapping like roof-tiles.—Also **im′bricāted.**—*n.* **imbricā′tion.** [L. *imbricāre, -ātum,* to tile—*imbrex,* a tile *imber,* a shower.]

imbroglio, *im-brōl′yō, n.* (*rare*) a confused mass, a tangle: an embroilment: (*mus.*) an ordered confusion. [It., confusion—*imbrogliare,* to confuse, embroil.]

imbrue, *im-broo̅′, v.t.* (*obs.*) to wet, moisten, soak: to stain or dye (with blood). [O.Fr. *embreuver*—*bevrer* (Fr. *boire*)—L. *bibēre,* to drink.]

imbue, *im-bū′, v.t.* to saturate (with): to tinge deeply: (*fig.*) to permeate (with feeling, opinion). [O.Fr. *imbuer*—L. *imbuēre*—*in,* and root of *bibēre,* to drink.]

imitate, *im′i-tāt, v.t.* to strive to produce something like, or to be like: to mimic.—*adj.* **im′itable,** that may be imitated or copied.—*ns.* **imitabil′ity; imitā′tion,** act of imitating: that which is produced as a copy or counterfeit: a performance in mimicry.—*adj.* sham, counterfeit.—*adj.* **im′itātive,** inclined to imitate: formed after a model: mimicking.—*ns.* **im′itātiveness; im′itātor.** [L. *imitāri, imitātus.*]

immaculate, *im-ak′ū-lāt, adj.* spotless: unstained: pure.—*adv.* **immac′ulately.**—*n.* **immac′ulateness.—immaculate conception,** the R.C. dogma that the Virgin Mary was conceived without original sin. [L. *immaculātus*—*in-,* not, *maculāre,* to spot.]

immanent, *im′a-nént, adj.* indwelling, inherent (in): pervading.—*ns.* **imm′anence, imm′anency,** the pervasion of the universe by the intelligent and creative principle, a fundamental conception of Pantheism. [L. *in,* in, *manēre,* to remain.]

immaterial, *im-a-tē′ri-ál, adj.* not consisting of matter, incorporeal: unimportant.—*v.t.* **immatē′rialise,** to separate from matter.—*ns.* **immatē′rialism,** the doctrine that there is no material substance; **immatē′rialist,** one who believes in this; **immaterial′ity,** the quality of being immaterial or of not consisting of mat-

---

fāte, fär; mē, hûr (her); *mīne; mōte, för; mūte; mōo̅n, foo̅t;* THen (then) ter. [Low L. *immāteriālis*—*im*- (*in*-), not, *māteriālis*. See **material**.]

immature, *im-à-tūr'*, **immatured**, *im-à-tūrd'*, *adjs.* not ripe: not perfect: not come to full development: showing marks of incomplete development.—*ns.* **immature'ness, immatur'ity**. [L. *immātūrus*—*im*- (*in*-), not, *mātūrus*. See **mature**.]

immeasurable, *im-ezh'ūr-à-bl*, *adj.* that cannot be measured: very great.—*n.* **immeas'urableness**.—*adv.* **immeas'urably**. [L. *im*- (*in*-), not, and **measurable**.]

immediate, *im-ē'di-àt*, *adj.* with nothing between: not acting by second causes: direct: next, nearest: without delay.—*adv.* **imme'diately**.—*ns.* **imme'diacy** (-*si*), state of being immediate: direct appeal to intuitive understanding; **imme'diateness**. [Low L. *immediātus*—*im*- (*in*-), not, *mediātus*—*mediāre*. See **mediate**.]

immemorial, *im-e-mōr', mör', i-àl*, *adj.* beyond the reach of memory: very old. [Low L. *immemoriālis*—L. *im*- (*in*-), not, *memoriālis*—*memor*, memory.]

immense, *i-mens'*, *adj.* that cannot be measured: vast in extent: very large: (*slang*) very good, or vastly amusing.—*adv.* **immense'ly**.—*ns.* **immense'ness; immens'ity**, an extent not to be measured: infinity: greatness. [Fr.,—L. *immensus*—*in*-, not, *mensus*, pa.p. of *metīrī*, to measure.]

immerge, *im-(m)ûrj'*, *v.t.* and *v.i.* to plunge in. [L. *in*, into, *mergĕre, mersum*, to plunge.]

immerse, *im-(m)ûrs'*, *v.t.* to dip under the surface of a liquid: to baptise by dipping the whole body: to engage or involve deeply (e.g. of thought, of difficulties).—*adj.* **immers'ible**, capable of being immersed, or of working under water.—*n.* **immer'sion**, act of immersing: state of being immersed: deep absorption or involvement: baptism by immersing.—*n.* **immersion-heater**, an electrical apparatus designed for heating water, &c., by direct immersion of an element in the liquid. [Same root as **immerge**.]

immigrate, *im'i-grāt*, *v.i.* to migrate or remove into a country.—*ns.* **imm'igrant**, one who immigrates; **immigrā'tion**. [L. *immigrāre*—*in*, into, *migrāre, -ātum*, to remove.]

imminent, *im'i-nént*, *adj.* near at hand: impending: threatening.—*ns.* **imm'inence, imm'inency**.—*adv.* **imm'inently**. [L. *imminens, -entis*—*in*, upon, *minēre*, to project.]

immiscible, *im-is'i-bl*, *adj.* not capable of being mixed. [L. *im*- (*in*-), not, and **miscible**.]

immitigable, *im-it'i-gà-bl*, *adj.* incapable of being mitigated.—*adv.* **immit'igably**. [L. *immītigābilis*—*im*- (*in*-), not, *mītigābilis*—*mītigāre*, to soften.]

immobile, *im-(m)ō'bil, -bīl, -bēl*, *adj.* immovable: not readily moved: motionless: stationary.—*n.* **immobilīsā'tion**.—*v.t.* **immob'ilise**, to render immobile: to keep out of action or circulation.—*n.* **immobil'ity**. [Fr.,—L. *immōbilis*—*im*- (*in*-), not, *mōbilis*. See **mobile**.]

immoderate, *im-od'ér-àt*, *adj.* exceeding due bounds, extravagant, unrestrained.—*n.* **immoderā'tion**, want of moderation, excess. [L. *immoderātus*—*im*- (*in*-), not, *moderātus*. See **moderate**.]

immodest, *im-od'est*, *adj.* wanting restraint: impudent, exceedingly self-assertive: wanting shame or delicacy: indecent.—*adv.* **immod'estly**.—*n.* **immod'esty**. [L. *immodestus*—*im*- (*in*-), not, *modestus*. See **modest**.]

immolate, *im'ō-lāt*, *v.t.* (*lit.* and *fig.*) to offer in sacrifice.—*ns.* **immolā'tion**, sacrifice: that which is offered in sacrifice; **imm'olātor**. [L. *immolāre, -ātum*, to sprinkle meal (on a victim), hence to sacrifice—*in*, upon, *mola*, meal.]

immoral, *im-(m)or'ál*, *adj.* inconsistent with what is right: wicked: licentious.—*n.* **immorality** (*im-or-al'i-ti*), quality of being immoral, esp. unchaste: an immoral act or practice. [L. *im*- (*in*-), not, and **moral**.]

immortal, *im-ör'tál*, *adj.* exempt from death: imperishable: never to be forgotten (as a name, poem, &c.).—*n.* one who will never cease to exist, or to be remembered.—*v.t.* **immortalise** (*im-ör'tál-iz*), to make immortal: to confer enduring fame on: to perpetuate.—*n.* **immortality**. [L. *immortālis*—*im*- (*in*-), not, *mortālis*. See **mortal**.]

immortelle, *im-ör-tel'*, *n.* an everlasting flower. [Fr. (*fleur*) *immortelle*, immortal (flower).]

immovable, *im-ōōv'á-bl*, *adj.* impossible to move: motionless: unalterable: steadfast, unyielding.—*ns.* **immov'ableness, immovabil'ity**.—*adv.* **immov'ably**. [L. *im*- (*in*-), not, and **movable**.]

immune, *im-ūn'*, *adj.* (*obs.*) free from obligation, exempt: not liable to danger, esp. infection.—*v.t.* **imm'unise**, to render immune, esp. to make immune to a disease by injecting its poison, or dead disease germs, or antibodies (q.v.).—*ns.* **immunīsā'tion; immun'ity**, state of being immune: exemption.'—**immuno-**, in composition, immune, immunity. [L. *immūnis*—*in*-, not, *mūnus*, service.]

immure, *i-mūr'*, *v.t.* to shut (oneself) up: to imprison: to entomb in a wall. [L. *in*, in *mūrus*, a wall.]

immutable, *im-ūt'á-bl*, *adj.* unchangeable: invariable.—*ns.* **immutabil'ity, immūt'ableness**.—*adv.* **immūt'ably**. [L. *immūtābilis*—*im*- (*in*-), not, *mūtābilis*. See **mutable**.]

imp, *imp*, *n.* (*obs.*) a shoot, scion, graft: a teasing or mischievous child: a little devil or wicked spirit.—*v.t.* to graft, engraft: (*falconry*) to engraft feathers in (to mend a wing).—*adj.* **imp'ish**, like or characteristic of an imp, teasingly mischievous. [O.E. *impa*—Low L. *impotus*, a graft—Gr. *emphytos*, engrafted.]

impact, *im-pakt'*, *v.t.* to press firmly (in, into). —*n.* **im'pact**, the blow of a body in motion impinging on another body: collision: (*fig.*) effect, influence.—*p.adj.* **impact'ed**, as in **impacted fracture**, a fracture in which the broken bones are firmly wedged together, **impacted tooth**, a tooth wedged between the jawbone and another tooth and thus unable to come through the gum. [L. *impactus*, pa.p. of *impingĕre*. See **impinge**.]

impair, *im-pār'*, *v.t.* to diminish in quantity, value, or strength: to injure: to weaken. [O.Fr. *empeirer* [Fr. *empirer*, from L. *im*- (*in*-), intensive, *pējōrāre*, to make worse—L. *pējor*, worse.]

impale, *im-pāl'*, *v.t.* (*rare*) to fence in with stakes: to put to death by spitting on a stake:

Neutral vowels in unaccented syllables: *em'pér-ór*; for certain sounds in foreign words see p. ix.

to transfix.—*n.* **impale′ment**. [Fr. *empaler*—L. *in*, in, *pālus*, a stake.]

impalpable, *im-pal′pá-bl, adj.* not perceivable by touch: extremely fine-grained: eluding apprehension.—*n.* **impalpabil′ity**. [Low L. *impalpābilis*—*im-* (*in-*), not, *palpābilis*. See **palpable**.]

impart, *im-pärt′, v.t.* to bestow a part of: to give: to communicate, to make known. [O.Fr. *empartir*—L. *impartīre*—*in*, on, *pars, partis*, a part.]

impartial, *im-pär′sh(à)l, adj.* not favouring one more than another: just.—*n.* **impartiality** (-shi-al′i-tl), quality of being impartial, freedom from bias.—*adv.* **impar′tially**. [L. *im-* (*in-*), not, and **partial**.]

impartible, *im-pärt′i-bl, adj.* not partible (e.g. an estate).—*n.* **impartibil′ity**. [L.L. *impartibilis*—*im-* (*in-*), not, *partibilis*. See **partible**.]

impassable, *im-päs′á-bl, adj.* not capable of being passed or traversed.—*ns.* **impassabil′ity**, **impass′ableness**.—*adj.* **impass′ably**.—*n.* **impasse** (ē päs′, im-päs′), a place from which there is no outlet: a deadlock. [L. *im-* (*in*), not, and **passable**.]

impassion, *im-pash′(ò)n, v.t.* to move with passion.—*adj.* **impassioned** (*im-pash′ònd*), moved by strong passion, animated, inflamed with passion. [It. *impassionāre*—L. *in*, in, *passiō, -ōnis*, passion.]

impassive, *im-pas′iv, adj.* not susceptible of feeling: imperturbable.—*adv.* **impass′ively**.—*ns.* **impass′iveness**, **impassiv′ity**. [L. *im-* (*in-*), not, and **passive**.]

impasto, *im-pas′tō, n.* pigment applied thickly, or thickened pigment applied, to a canvas or other surface: this method of applying colour. [It.]

impatient, *im-pā′shént, adj.* lacking patience: showing want of patience: not able to endure or tolerate (with *of*); restlessly eager (for, to do).—*n.* **impa′tience**. *adv.* **impa′tiently**. [L. *im-* (*in-*), not, and **patient**.]

impavid, *im-pav′id, adj.* without fear. [L. *impavidus*—*im-* (*in-*), not, *pavor*, fear.]

impeach, *im-pēch′, v.t.* (*obs.*) to hinder: to find fault with: to call in question: to arraign (esp. when the lower legislative house charges a high officer with grave offences before the upper house as judges).—*adj.* **impeach′able**, liable to impeachment: chargeable with a crime.—*ns.* **impeach′er**, one who impeaches; **impeach′ment**. [O.Fr. *empescher*, to hinder—L. *impedicāre*, to fetter.]

impeccable, *im-pek′á-bl, adj.* not liable to sin: faultless.—*n.* **impeccabil′ity**. [L. *im-* (*in-*), not, and *peccāre*, to sin.]

impecunious, *im-pi-kū′ni-us, adj.* habitually without money, poor.—*n.* **impecunios′ity**. [L. *im-* (*in-*), not, *pecūnia*, money.]

impedance, *im-pēd′áns, n.* the apparent resistance in an electric circuit to an alternating current flowing in the circuit. [**impede**, and suffx. *-ance*.]

impede, *im-pēd′, v.t.* to hinder or obstruct.—*n.* **imped′iment**, that which impedes: hindrance: a defect preventing fluency (in speech).—*n.pl.* **impediment′a**, military baggage, baggage generally.—*adj.* **imped′itive**, causing hindrance. [L. *impedīre*—*in*, in, *pēs, pedis*, a foot.]

impel, *im-pel′, v.t.* to urge forward, to propel: to excite to action: to instigate:—*pr.p.* **impell′ing**; *pa.p.* **impelled′**.—*adj.* **impell′ent**, impelling or driving on.—*n.* a force that impels.—*n.* **impel′ler**. [L. *impellēre, impulsum*—*in* on *pellēre*, to drive.]

impend, *im-pend′, v.i.* to hang over: to threaten: to be about to happen.—*adj.* **impend′ent**, imminent: ready to act or happen. [L. *impendēre*—*in*, on, *pendēre*, to hang.]

impenetrable, *im-pen′e-trà-bl, adj.* (*lit.* and *fig.*) incapable of being pierced (with *to* or *by*): (*phys.*) having impenetrability, the quality which prevents another body from occupying the same space at the same time: not to be impressed (in mind or heart), inaccessible to reason or to an emotional appeal: inscrutable.—*n.* **impenetrabil′ity**.—*adv.* **impen′etrably**. [Fr.*impénétrable*—L.*impĕnĕtrābilis*—*im-* (*in-*), not, *penetrābilis*—*penetrāre*. See **penetrate**.]

impenitent, *im-pen′i-tént, adj.* not repenting of sin or transgression: one who does not repent: a hardened sinner.—*n.* **impen′itence**.—*adv.* **impen′itently**. [L. *im-* (*in-*), not, and **penitent**.]

imperative, *im-per′á-tiv, adj.* expressive of command: authoritative: obligatory: urgently necessary.—*adv.* **imper′atively**.—**imperative mood**, the form of a verb expressing command or advice. [L. *imperātīvus*—*imperāre*, to command—*in*, in, *parāre*, to prepare.]

imperceptible, *im-per-sep′ti-bl, adj.* not discernible, insensible: minute: gradual.—*ns.* **impercep′tibleness**, **imperceptibil′ity**.—*adv.* **impercep′tibly**. [L. *im-* (*in-*), not, and **perceptible**.]

imperfect, *im-pûr′fekt, adj.* falling short of perfection: incomplete: defective: (*gram.*) of a tense, denoting an action that is still going on, or is thought of as not completed (e.g. they *are, were, talking the matter over*).—*n.* an imperfect tense, esp. the past imperfect.—*adv.* **imper′fectly**.—*ns.* **imper′fectness**, **imperfec′tion**. [L. *im-* (*in-*), not, and **perfect**.]

imperforate, **-d**, *im-pûr′fo-rāt, -id, adjs.* not pierced through: having no opening.—*adj.* **imper′forable**, that cannot be perforated.—*n.* **imperforā′tion**. [L. *im-* (*in-*), not, and **perforate**.]

imperial, *im-pē′ri-ál, adj.* pertaining to, or of the nature of, an empire or an emperor: sovereign, supreme: commanding, august.—*n.* a tuft of hair on the lower lip.—*adv.* **impē′rially**.—*ns.* **impē′rialism**, the power or authority of an emperor: the spirit of empire: belief in the policy of extending an empire, or otherwise increasing its strength; **impē′rialist**, a soldier or partisan of an emperor: a believer in the policy of developing and utilising the spirit of empire.—*adj.* **impērialist′ic**.—**imperial federation**, a scheme to federate the self-governing parts of the British Empire; **imperial measure, weight**, the standard of measure, weight, fixed by parliament for the United Kingdom (e.g. *imperial gallon*); **imperial parliament**, the parliament of the United Kingdom; **imperial preference**, the favouring of trade within the Empire by discriminating tariffs. [Fr.,-L. *impĕriālis*—*impĕrium*, sovereignty.]

---

fāte, *fär*; *mē*, *hûr* (her); *mīne*; *mōte*, *för*; *mūte*; *mōōn*, *fŏŏt*; ᴛʜen (then)

imperil, im-per'il, *v.t.* to put in peril, to endanger. [L. *in*, in, and **peril.**]

imperious, im-pē'ri-us, *adj.* haughty, tyrannical:
authoritative, imperative.—*adv.* **impē'riously.**
—*n.* **impē'riousness.** [L. *imperiōsus*—*imperium*, command, rule.]

imperishable, im-per'ish-ȧ-bl, *adj.* indestructible: everlasting.—*ns.* **imper'ishableness, im-
perishabil'ity.**—*adv.* **imper'ishably.** [L. *im-
(in-)*, not, and **perishable.**]

impermanent, im-pûr'mȧn-ėnt, *adj.* not permanent, not lasting.—*n.* **imper'manence.** [L.
im- (in-), not, and **permanent.**]

impermeable, im-pûr'mē-ȧ-bl, *adj.* not permitting passage, esp. to fluids: impervious.—*ns.*
impermeabil'ity, imper'meableness.—*adv.*
imper'meably. [L. *im- (in-)*, not and **permeable.**]

impersonal, im-pûr'sȯn-ȧl, *adj.* not having personality: *(gram.)* not used in the first and
second persons: without reference to any particular person.—*n.* **impersonal'ity.**—*adv.* **imper'sonally.** [L. *im- (in-)*, not, and **personal.**]

impersonate, im-pûr'sȯn-āt, *v.t.* to ascribe the
qualities of a person to, to personify: to assume the person or character of, esp. on the
stage.—*ns.* **impersonā'tion; imper'sonātor.** [L.
in, in, and **personate.**]

impertinent, im-pûr'ti-nėnt, *adj.* not pertaining
to the matter in hand: trivial: intrusive, saucy,
impudent.—*n.* **imper'tinence.**—*adv.* **imper'tinently.** [L. *im- (in-)*, not, and **pertinent.**]

imperturbable, im-pėr-tûr'bȧ-bl, *adj.* that cannot be disturbed or agitated, permanently
calm.—*n.* **imperturbabil'ity.**—*adv.* **impertur'b-
ably.**—*n.* **imperturbā'tion.** [L. *imperturb-
ābilis—in-*, not, *perturbāre*, to disturb.]

imperviable, im-pûr'vi-ȧ-bl (with *by* or *to*), **impervious,** impêr'vi-ús, (often with *to*), *adjs.*
(lit. and *fig.)* not to be penetrated: *(fig.)* not
easily influenced by ideas, arguments,
&c.—*ns.* **imper'viableness, imperviabil'ity,
imper'viousness.**—*adv.* **imper'viously.** [L. *im-
pervīus*; cf. **pervious.**]

impetigo, im-pe-tī'go, *n.* a skin disease characterised by thickly set clusters of pustules.
[L.,—*impetĕre*, to rush upon, attack.]

impetuous, im-pet'ū-us, *adj.* rushing with impetus or violence: acting with headlong energy: impulsive.—*adv.* **impet'uously.**—*ns.* **im-
pet'uousness, impetuos'ity.** [L. *impetus*, an
attack; cf. **impetus.**]

impetus, im'pė-tus, *n.* momentum (in popular
sense): impulse, incentive:—*pl.* **im'petuses.**
[L.,—*in*, into, on, *petĕre*, to seek.]

impiety, im-pī'ė-ti, *n.* want of piety or veneration. [L. *impietās*, -*ātis*; cf. **piety.**]

impinge, im-pinj', *v.i.* (with *on, upon, against*) to
strike or fall: to touch: to encroach. [L. *impingĕre—in*, against, *pangĕre*, to fix, drive in.]

impious, im'pi-us, *adj.* irreverent, wanting
in veneration for God, profane.—*adv.* **im'-
piously.**—*n.* **im'piousness.** [L. *impius*; cf.
piety.]

implacable, im-plak'ȧ-bl, or -plāk'-, *adj.* not to
be appeased, inexorable.—*ns.* **implāc'ableness, implācab'l'ity.**—*adv.* **implac'ably.** [L. *im-
plācābilis*; cf. **placable.**]

implant, im-plänt', *v.t.* to fix into: to insert: to
inculcate (e.g. an idea).—*n.* something im-

planted in body tissue, as a graft, a pellet
containing a hormone, a tube containing a
radioactive substance.—*n.* **implantā'tion,** the
act of infixing. [L. *in*, in, and **plant.**]

implead, im-plēd', *v.t.* to prosecute a suit at
law.—*n.* **implead'er.** [L. *in*, in, and **plead.**]

implement, im'plė-mėnt, *n.* a tool or instrument
of labour.—*v.t.* (*im-ple-ment'*) to fulfil or perform.—*n.* **implē'tion,** a filling: the state of
being full. [Low L. *implementum*—L. *implēre*,
to fill.]

implicate, im'pli-kāt, *v.t.* to enfold: to entangle:
to involve (in a crime or fault), to incriminate:
to involve as a consequence, imply.—*n.* **im-
plicā'tion,** the act of implicating: entanglement: that which is implied.—*adjs.* **im'plicative,** tending to implicate; **implic'it** (-*plis'it*),
implied—opp. of *explicit*: unquestioning (e.g.
trust).—*adv.* **implic'itly.**—*n.* **implic'itness.** [L.
implicāre, -*ātum—in*, in, *plicāre*, to fold.]

implore, im-plōr', -plör', *v.t.* to ask earnestly
(for): to entreat (to do).—*adv.* **implor'ingly,**
beseechingly. [Fr.,—L. *implōrāre—in*, in,
plōrāre, to weep.]

impluvium, im-plōō'vi-um, *n.* a basin in the
atrium or hall of Roman houses to receive
rain-water. [L.—*impluĕre—in*, in, *pluĕre*, to
rain.]

imply, im-plī', *v.t.* (*Spens.*) to enfold: to involve
(a fact not expressly stated): to mean, signify:
to express indirectly, to insinuate:—*pr.p.* imply'ing; *pa.p.* implied'. [O.Fr. *emplier*—L. *implicāre*. See **implicate.**]

impolite, im-po-līt', *adj.* of unpolished manners:
uncivil.—*adv.* **impolite'ly.**—*n.* **impolite'ness.**
[L. *impŏlītus*; cf. **polite.**]

impolitic, im-pol'i-tik, *adj.* not politic, inexpedient.—*n.* **impol'icy,** imprudence. [L. *im-
(in-)*, not, and **politic.**]

imponderable, im-pon'dér-ȧ-bl, *adj.* not able to
be weighed or estimated: without sensible
weight.—*ns.* **impon'derableness, imponder-
abil'ity, impon'derable,** any of the once-
supposed fluids without sensible weight, as
heat, light, electricity, and magnetism, considered as material: (usu. in *pl.*) factor in a
situation whose influence cannot be assessed.
[L. *im- (in-)*, not, and **ponderable.**]

import, im-pōrt', -pört', *v.t.* to bring in: to bring
from abroad: to imply, signify: *(arch.)* to
make known: to be of consequence to.—*n.*
im'port, that which is brought from abroad:
meaning: tendency: importance.—*adj.* **import'able,** that may be imported or brought
into a country.—*adj.* **import'ant,** of great
weight, significance, or consequence: pompous.—*n.* **import'ance.** **import'antly.**—
ns. **importā'tion,** the act of importing: the
goods imported; **import'er,** one who brings in
goods from abroad. [Fr.,—L. *importāre*,
-*ātum—in*, in, *portāre*, to carry.]

importune, im-pȯr-tūn', *v.t.* to urge with
troublesome persistence: to press urgently
(for): to solicit for immoral purposes, make
improper advances to.—*ns.* **impor'tunacy, import'unāteness.**—*adj.* **import'unāte,** trouble-
somely urgent.—*adv.* **import'unātely.**—*ns.* **importun'er; importun'ity,** urgency in demand.
[Fr.,—L. *importūnus*, inconvenient—*im- (in-)*,
not, *portus*, a harbour; cf. **opportune.**]

Neutral vowels in unaccented syllables: *em'pér-ȯr*; for certain sounds in foreign words see p. ix.

impose, im-pōz′, v.t. to place upon something: to lay on: to enjoin, to put over by authority or force: to pass off unfairly.—v.i. (with upon) to mislead or deceive, esp. by false pretences.—adjs. **impos′able**, capable of being imposed or laid on: **impos′ing**, commanding, impressive.—adv. **impos′ingly**. [Fr. imposer—im (in), on, poser. See **compose**.]

imposition, im-poz-ish′(ō)n, n. a laying on: laying on of hands in ordination: a tax, a burden: a deception: a punishment task. [L. impositiō, -ōnis—in, on, pōnĕre, pŏsitum, to place.]

impossible, im pos′i-bl, adj. that cannot exist: that cannot be true: that cannot be done or dealt with: hopelessly unsuitable.—n. **impossibil′ity**. [L. im- (in-), not, and **possible**.]

impost, im′pōst, n. a tax, esp. on imports. [O.Fr. impost—L. impōnĕre, impŏsitum, to lay on.]

impost, im′pōst, n. (archit.) the upper part of a pillar supporting a vault or arch. [Fr. imposte—It. imposta—L. impōnĕre, impŏsitum.]

impostor, im-pos′tŏr, n. one who assumes a false character or personates another.—n. **impos′ture**, fraud. [L.L.—impōnĕre, impŏsitum, to impose.]

impotent, im′po-tént, adj. powerless: helpless: wanting in sexual power.—n. **im′potence**.—adv. **im′potently**. [L. impŏtens, -entis; cf. **potent**.]

impound, im-pownd′, v.t. to confine, as in a pound: to restrain within limits: to take legal possession of. [**In** and **pound**, enclosure.]

impoverish, im-pov′ér-ish, v.t. to make poor: to make poor in quality.—n. **impov′erishment**. [From O.Fr. empovrir—L. in, in, pauper, poor.]

impracticable, im-prak′tik-a-bl, adj. not able to be done or used: unmanageable.—ns. **impracticabil′ity**, **imprac′ticableness**.—adv. im **prac′ticably**. [L. im- (in-), not, and **practicable**.]

imprecate, im′pre-kāt, v.t. to call down by prayer (esp. something evil): to curse.—n. **impreca′tion**, the act of imprecating: a curse.—adj. **im′precatory**. [L. imprecārī—in, upon, precārī, -ātus, to pray.]

impregnable, im-preg′na-bl, adj. that cannot be taken, proof against attack.—Also fig.—n. **impregnabil′ity**.—adv. **impreg′nably**. [Fr. imprenable—L. in-, not, prendĕre, prehendĕre, to take; g, a freak of spelling, has come to be pronounced.]

impregnate, im-preg′nāt, v.t. to make pregnant: to impart the particles or qualities of one thing to another, to saturate (with): to imbue (with—e.g. feelings, principles).—n. **impregna′tion**, the act of impregnating: that with which anything is impregnated. [Low L. impraegnāre, -ātum—in, in, praegnans, pregnant.]

impresario, im-pre-zä′ri-ō, or -sä′-, n. the manager of a theatrical company, &c. [It.—impresa, enterprise.]

impress, im-pres′, v.t. to press (something on): to mark by pressure: to fix deeply in the mind: to produce a profound effect on, or on the mind of.—n. **im′press**, that which is made by pressure: stamp: distinctive mark.—adj. **impress′ible**, susceptible.—n. **impression** (-presh′(ō)n), act or result of impressing: a single printing of a book: the idea or emotion left in the mind by any experience: a vague, uncertain memory.—adj. **impress′ionable**, able to receive an impression: very susceptible to impressions.—ns. **impressionabil′ity**; **impress′ionism**, a 19th-century movement in art and literature, employing general effects and vigorous touches, and dealing in masses of form and colour; **impress′ionist**.—adj. **impress′ive**, capable of making a deep impression on the mind: solemn.—adv. **impress′ively**.—n. **impress′iveness**.—be under the **impression** (that), to think (that), to have a vague idea (that). [L. imprimĕre, impressum—im- (in-), in, premĕre. See **press** (1).]

impress, im-pres′, v.t. to force into service, esp. the public service.—n. **impress′ment**, the act of impressing or seizing for service, esp. in the navy. [L. im- (in-), in, and prest. See **press** (2).]

imprimatur, im-pri-mā′tŭr, n. a licence to print a book, &c. (fig.) sanction. [Lit. 'let it be printed': from L. imprimĕre—in, on, premĕre, to press.]

imprimis, im-prī′mis, adv. in the first place. [L.—in prīmis (abl. pl.).]

imprint, im-print′, v.t. to print: to stamp: to impress: to fix in the mind.—n. **im′print**, that which is imprinted: the name of the publisher, time and place of publication of a book, &c., usually printed on the title-page: the printer's name on the back of the title-page or at the end of the book. [L. im- (in-), on, and **print**.]

imprison, im-priz′n, v.t. to put in prison: to shut up: to confine or restrain.—n. **impris′onment**. [L. im- (in-), into, and **prison**.]

improbable, im-prob′a-bl, adj. unlikely.—n. **improbabil′ity**.—adv. **improb′ably**. [L. im- (in-), not, and **probable**.]

improbity, im-prŏb′i-ti, n. want of probity, dishonesty. [L. improbitas; cf. **probity**.]

impromptu, im-promp′tū, adj. improvised: unprepared.—adv. without preparation, on the spur of the moment.—n. an extempore witticism or speech: an improvised composition: a musical composition with the character of an extemporisation. [L. in promptū (abl.) —promptus, readiness.]

improper, im-prop′ér, adj. not suitable, unfit, unbecoming: incorrect, wrong: not properly so called (improper fraction, a fraction not less than unity, e.g. 22/7: indecent.—adv. im **prop′erly**.—n. **impropri′ety**. [L. im- (in-), not, proprius, own.]

impropriate, im-prō′pri-āt, v.t. to appropriate to private use: to place (ecclesiastical property) in the hands of a layman.—n. **impropria′tion**, act of impropriating: property impropriated. —**impropriated benefice**, one in which the tithes belong to a layman or lay corporation [Low L. impropriātus—L. in, in, proprius, one's own.]

improve, im-prōōv′, v.t. (obs.) to raise in value or in price: to make better: (rare) to employ to good purpose.—v.i. to grow better: to make progress: to increase in worth.—adj. **improv′able**.—ns. **improvabil′ity**, **improv′ableness**.— adv **improv′ably**.—ns. **Improve′ment**, the act of improving: progress: a change for the better; **improv′er**, a worker who is in part a learner:—*pr.p.* and *adj.* improv′ing, tending to cause improvement: edifying.—*adv.* improv′ingly.—improve the occasion, to draw a moral from what has happened. [Anglo-Fr. *emprower*—O.Fr. *en preu*, into profit.]

improvident, *im-prov′i-dént, adj.* not provident or thrifty: wanting foresight, thoughtless.—*n.* improv′idence.—*adv.* improv′idently. [L. *improvidus*, improvident; cf. provide.]

improvise, *im-pro-vīz′, v.t.* to compose and recite, or perform, without preparation: to contrive a substitute for, from materials available (e.g. *to improvise a bed, a knife*): to arrange without previous preparation.—Also *v.i.*—*ns.* improvisā′tion, the act of improvising: that which is improvised; improvisā′tor, improvisātō′re (-*rā*), one who improvises: one who composes and recites verses without preparation:—*pl.* improvisatō′ri (-*rē*).—*n.* improvīs′er. [Fr. *improviser*—L. *in-*, not, *prōvīsus*, foreseen—*prōvidēre*.]

imprudent, *im-prōō′dént, adj.* wanting foresight or discretion, incautious.—*n.* impru′dence.—*adv.* impru′dently. [L. *imprūdens, -entis*, rash; cf. prudent.]

impudent, *im′pū-dént, adj.* wanting shame or modesty, shamelessly bold: insolent.—*n.* im′pudence.—*adv.* im′pudently. [L. *im-* (*in-*), not, *pudens, -entis*—*pudēre*, to be ashamed.]

impugn, *im-pūn′, v.t.* to attack by words or arguments, to call in question.—*adj.* impugn′able.—*n.* impugn′er. [L. *impugnāre*—*in*, against, *pugnāre*, to fight.]

impulse, *im′puls, n.* the act of impelling: effect of an impelling force: force suddenly and momentarily communicated: a disturbance travelling along a nerve or a muscle: influence on the mind: a sudden inclination (to act).—*n.* impul′sion, impelling force: instigation.—*adj.* impuls′ive, having the power of impelling: acting or actuated by impulse: prone to act on impulse: not continuous.—*adv.* impuls′ively.—*n.* impuls′iveness. [L. *impulsus*, pressure—*impellēre*. See impel.]

impunity, *im-pūn′i-ti, n.* freedom or safety from punishment: exemption from injury or loss. [L. *impūnitās, -ātis*—*in*-, not, *poena*, punishment.]

impure, *im-pūr′, adj.* mixed with something else: unholy: unchaste: unclean.—*adv.* im-pure′ly.—*ns.* impur′ity, impure′ness. [L. *impūrus*—*in*-, not, *pūrus*, clean.]

impurple, *im-pûr′pl.* Same as empurple.

impute, *im-pūt′, v.t.* to ascribe (usu. of evil—with *to*): to charge: (*theology*) to attribute vicariously.—*adj.* imput′able, capable of being imputed or charged, attributable.—*ns.* imput′ableness, imputabil′ity.—*adv.* imput′ably.—*n.* imputā′tion, act of imputing or charging, censure: suggestion of fault.—*adj.* imput′ative, imputed.—*adv.* imput′atively. [Fr. *imputer*—L. *imputāre, -ātum*—*in*, in, *putāre*, to reckon.]

in, *in, prep.* expressing the relation of a thing to that which surrounds, encloses, or includes it (referring to place, time, or circumstances): e.g. at: among: into: within: during: wearing: belonging to: being a member of.—*adv.* with-in: not out: inside: inwards: (*cricket*) at the bat: short for various phrases, e.g. *in office, in*

favour, *in fashion.*—*adj.* inward: proceeding inwards: that is fashionable, much in use, as in-word, in-thing: within a small group.—*ns.* in′-fighting, (more or less secret) fighting or rivalry between individuals or within a group. in′-joke, joke appreciated only by the members of a particular and limited group; in′-pā′tient, a patient lodged and fed as well as treated in a hospital.—*adjs.* in′-ser′vice, carried out while continuing with one's ordinary mployment, as *in-service training*; in′shore, close to the shore: moving towards the shore.—*n.* in′-tray, a shallow container for letters, &c., still to be dealt with.—in as far as, to the extent that; in as much as, inasmuch as, considering that; in that, for the reason that.—ins and outs, nooks and corners: the whole details of any matter.—be in for, destined to receive (esp. unpleasant consequences); be in on (*coll.*), to participate in; be in with, to be friends with, to enjoy the favour of. [O.E. *in*; Du., Ger. *in*, O.N. *ī*, W. *yn*, L. *in*, Gr. *en*.]

in-, *in-, pfx.* not [L.]:—e.g. insincere, insincerity. It appears also as i-, il-, im-, ir-:—e.g. ignoble, illegal, immortal, irregular (see these words). It is allied to O.E. *un-* and is sometimes interchangeable with it:—e.g. *inexpressive, unexpressive.*

in-, *in-, pfx.* in, into [L.]:—e.g. include, infuse, ingredient (see these words). It appears also as il-, im-, ir-:—e.g. illuminate, immerse, irrigate (see these words). There is also an Old English prefix of the same form and meaning seen in words of Gmc. origin:—e.g. income, inland, insight.

inability, *in-ā-bil′i-ti, n.* want of sufficient power: incapacity. [L. *in-*, not, and ability.]

in absentia, *in ab-sensh′yā, ab-sen′ti-ā, in* absence. [L.]

inaccessible, *in-ak-ses′i-bl, adj.* not to be reached, obtained, or approached.—*ns.* inaccess′ibility, inaccess′ibleness.—*adv.* inaccess′ibly. [L. *inaccessībilis*, unapproachable—*in*-, not, *accessībilis*; cf. accede.]

inaccurate, *in-ak′ūr-āt, adj.* not exact or correct: erroneous.—*n.* inacc′uracy, want of exactness: a mistake.—*adv.* inacc′urately. [L. *in-*, not, and accurate.]

inactive, *in-akt′iv, adj.* inert: not active: not operating:. lazy: (*chem.*) not showing any action.—*n.* inac′tion, idleness: rest.—*adv.* inact′ively.—*n.* inactiv′ity, idleness: lack of action. [L. *in-*, not, and active.]

inadequate, *in-ad′e-kwát, adj.* insufficient: not adequate (to.)—*ns.* inad′equacy, inad′equateness.—*adv.* inad′equately. [L. *in-*, not, and adequate.]

inadmissible, *in-ad-mis′i-bl, adj.* not allowable.—*n.* inadmissibil′ity.—*adv.* inadmiss′ibly. [L. *in-*, not, and admissible.]

inadvertent, *in-ad-vûrt′ént, adj.* inattentive: (of actions) resulting from inattentiveness, unintentional.—*ns.* inadvert′ence, inadvert′ency, negligence: oversight.—*adv.* inadvert′ently. [L. *in-*, not, and *advertens, -entis*—*advertĕre*. See advert.]

inadvisable, *in-ad-vīz′á-bl, adj.* unadvisable, inexpedient.—*n.* inadvisabil′ity. [L. *in-*, not, and advisable.]

Neutral vowels in unaccented syllables: *em′pér-ór*; for certain sounds in foreign words see p. ix.

inalienable, *in-āl'yen-ā-bl, adj.* not capable of being taken away or transferred.—*n.* **inal'ienableness.** [L. *in-*, not, and **alienable.**]

inamorata, *in-am-o-rä'ta, n.fem.* a woman beloved, or in love:—*masc.* **inamora'to.** [It. *innamorata, -to*—Low L. *inamorāre,* to cause to love—L. *in,* in, *amor,* love.]

inane, *in-ān', adj.* empty, void: vacuous: silly.—*ns.* **inanition** (*in-a-nish'(ò)n*), exhaustion from want of food; **inan'ity,** senselessness: an insipid empty-headed utterance. [L. *inānis.*]

inanimate, -d, *in-an'im-āt, -id, adj.* not having animal life. lifeless, dead: spiritless: dull.—*n.* **inanimā'tion.** [L. *inanimātus,* lifeless; cf. **animate.**]

inapplicable, *in-ap'lik-ā-bl, adj.* not applicable or suitable.—*n.* **inapplicabil'ity.** [L. *in-*, not, and **applicable.**]

inapposite, *in-ap'oz-it, adj.* not apposite or suitable.—*adv.* **inapp'ositely.** [L. *in-*, not, and **apposite.**]

inappreciable, *in-a-prē'sh(y)ā-bl, adj.* not appreciable or able to be valued, negligible. [L. *in-*, not, and **appreciable.**]

inappropriate, *in-a-prō'pri-āt, adj.* not suitable.—*adv.* **inapprō'priately.**—*n.* **inapprō'priateness.** [L. *in-*, not, and **appropriate.**]

inapt, *in-apt', adj.* not apt: unfit, inappropriate: unskilful.—*n.* **Inapt'itude, inapt'ness,** unfitness: awkwardness.—*adv.* **inapt'ly.** [L. *in-*, not, and **apt.**]

inarticulate, *in-är-tik'ūl-āt, adj.* not jointed or hinged: indistinctly uttered: incapable of clear and fluent expression.—*adv.* **inartic'ulately.** —*ns.* **inartic'ulateness, inarticulā'tion,** indistinctness of sounds in speaking. [L. *inarticulātus;* cf. **articulate.**]

inartistic, -al, *in-är-tis'tik, -ål, adj.* not artistic: deficient in appreciation of works of art.—*adv.* **inartis'tically.** [L. *in-*, not, and **artistic.**]

inasmuch, *in-az-much'.* See **in.**

inattentive, *in-a-tent'iv, adj.* not fixing the mind to attention: careless: neglectful.—*ns.* **inattention** (*-ten'sh(ò)n*), **inatten'iveness.**—*adv.* **inatten'tively.** [L. *in-*, not, and **attentive.**]

inaudible, *in-öd'i-bl, adj.* not able to be heard.—*ns.* **inaudibil'ity, inaud'ibleness.**—*adv.* **inaud'ibly.** [L. *inaudībilis;* cf. **audible.**]

inaugurate, *in-ö'gūr-āt, v.t.* to induct formally into an office: to cause to begin: to open formally to the public.—*n.* **inaugurā'tion.**—*adj.* **inau'gural**, pertaining to, or done at, an inauguration.—*n.* **inau'gurātor,** one who inaugurates.—*adj.* **inau'guratory.** [L. *inaugurāre, -ātum,* to inaugurate with taking of the auspices—*in,* in, *augurāre—augur.* See **augur.**]

inauspicious, *in-ö-spish'us, adj.* not auspicious, ill-omened: unlucky.—*adv.* **inauspic'iously.**—*n.* **inauspic'iousness.** [L. *inauspicātus,* without auspices, ill-omened—*in-,* not, *auspicātus—auspicāre.*]

inborn, *in'börn, adj.* born in or with one, innate. [L. *in,* in, and **born.**]

inbreathe, *in-brē̆TH', in'brē̆TH, v.t.* to breathe in (*lit.* and *fig.*). [L. *in,* in, and **breathe.**]

inbreed, *in'brēd, in'brēd', v.t.* to breed or generate within: to breed from animals closely related.—*pa.p.* **in'bred,** innate: bred in-and-in, i.e. from parents that are closely akin.—*n.* **in'breeding.** [L. *in,* in, and **breed.**]

Inca, *ing'ka, n.* an Indian of Peru: a member of the old royal family of Peru: a Peruvian king or emperor. [Sp.—South American Indian, prince.]

incalculable, *in-kal'kū-lā-bl, adj.* not calculable or able to be reckoned: too great to calculate: unpredictable.—*adv.* **incal'culably.** [L. *in-*, not, and **calculable.**]

in camera. See **camera.**

incandescent, *in-kan-des'ent, adj.* glowing or white with heat.—*n.* **incandescence** (*-es'ens*), white heat.—**incandescent lamp,** one whose light is produced by heating something to white or red heat, e.g. by heating a filament by the passage of an electric current, or a mantle by a flame. [L. *in,* in, *candēscĕre—candēre,* to glow.]

incantation, *in-kan-tā'sh(ò)n, n.* a formula of words said or sung for purposes of enchantment. [L. *incantātiō, -ōnis—incantāre,* to sing a magical formula over.]

incapable, *in-kāp'ā-bl, adj.* not capable (with *of*): incompetent: lacking legal qualification or power.—*n.* **incapabil'ity.**—*adv.* **incap'ably.** [L. *in-*, not, and **capable.**]

incapacious, *in-kap-ā'shùs, adj.* not large, narrow.—*v.t.* **incapacitate** (*-as'it-at*), to make incapable or unfit for: to disqualify.—*n.* **incapac'ity,** want of capacity: inability: legal disqualification. [L. *incapax, -ācis.*]

incarcerate, *in-kär'ser-āt, v.t.* to imprison, to confine.—*n.* **incarcerā'tion,** imprisonment. [L. *in,* in, *carcer,* a prison.]

incarnadine, *in-kär'na-din, -dīn, v.t.* to dye a red colour.—*adj.* flesh-coloured: blood-red. [Fr. *incarnadin(e)*—Low L. *incarnātus—incarnāre.* See **incarnate.**]

incarnate, *in-kär'nāt,* or *in'-, v.t.* to embody in flesh: to give concrete form to (e.g. an idea). —*adj.* (*-kär'nāt*) invested with flesh, personified.—*n.* **incarnā'tion,** act of embodying in flesh, esp. of Christ: manifestation, visible embodiment: living type: (*surgery*) the process of healing, or forming new flesh. [Low L. *incarnāre, -ātum*—L. *in,* in, *carō, carnis,* flesh.]

incautious, *in-kö'shùs, adj.* not cautious or careful.—*n.* **incau'tiously.** [L. *incautus—in-,* not, *cautus—cautiō.* See **cautious.**]

incendiary, *in-sen'di-ār-i, n.* one that sets fire to a building, &c., maliciously: one who promotes strife.—*adj.* relating to incendiarism: adapted or used for setting buildings, &c., on fire: tending to excite strife.—*n.* **incen'diarism,** the act or practice of setting on fire maliciously or of stirring up strife.—**incendiary bomb,** a bomb containing a highly inflammable substance and designed to burst into flames on striking its objective. [L. *incendiārius—incendium—incendēre, incensum,* to kindle.]

incense, *in-sens', v.t.* to inflame with anger. [O.Fr. *incenser*—L. *incendēre, incensum,* to set on fire.]

incense, *in'sèns, n.* material burned or volatilised to give fragrant fumes, esp. in religious rites: the fumes so obtained: any pleasant smell: (*fig.*) homage, adulation.—*adj.* **incense'-breathing,** exhaling fragrance. [O.Fr. *encens*—L. *incensum—incendēre,* to set on fire.]

incentive, *in-sent'iv, adj.* inciting, encouraging.—*n.* that which incites to action or moves the mind: a motive for (with *to*). [L. *incentīvus*, striking up a tune—*incinēre*—*in*, in, *canĕre*, to sing.]

inception, in-sep'sh(ŏ)n, *n.* a beginning.—*adj.* **incep'tive**, beginning, or marking the beginning. [L. *inceptiō*, *-ōnis*—*incipĕre*, *inceptum*, to begin—*in*, on, *capĕre*, to take.]

incertitude, in-sûr'ti-tūd, *n.* want of certainty: indecision: insecurity. [Fr.,—Low L. *incertitūdō*—L. *incertus*, uncertain.]

incessant, in-ses'ánt, *adj.* uninterrupted: continual.—*adv.* **incess'antly**, unceasingly. [L. *incessans*, *-antis*—*in*-, not, *cessāre*, to cease.]

incest, in'sest, *n.* sexual intercourse within the forbidden degrees of kindred.—*adj.* **incest'uous**, guilty of incest.—*adv.* **incest'uously**. [L. *incestum*—*in*-, not, *castus*, chaste.]

inch, inch, *-sh*, *n.* the twelfth part of a foot, equal to 2.54 cm.: proverbially, a small distance or degree: (in *pl.*) stature.—**inch by inch**, **by inches**, by small degrees; **every inch**, entirely, thoroughly. [O.E. *ynce*, an inch—L. *uncia*, the twelfth part of anything; cf. **ounce**.]

inch, insh, *n.* (*Scot.*) an island: a low-lying meadow beside a river. [Gael. *innis*, island.]

inchoate, in'kō-āt, in-kō'āt, *adj.* only begun: rudimentary.—*adv.* **inchoately** (*in'-*, or *-ko'-*).—*n.* **inchoa'tion**, beginning.—*adj.* **inchō'ative**, incipient: (*gram.*) denoting the beginning of an action. [L. *inchoāre* (for *incohāre*), *-ātum*, to begin.]

incident, in'si-dént, *adj.* falling or striking (upon something): liable to occur (with *to*): naturally belonging or consequent (to).—*n.* an event of subordinate kind: an episode: an occurrence involving hostility.—*n.* **in'cidence**, the frequency or range of occurrence: fact or manner of falling: burden, as of tax that falls unequally: falling of ray of heat, light, &c., or of a line, on a surface.—*adj.* **incident'al**, striking or impinging: liable to occur in the circumstances specified (with *to*): casual: (of music) accompanying action of play, &c.—*adv.* **incident'ally**, by chance: in passing, as an aside.—*n.* **incident'alness**. [L. *incĭdens*, *-entis*—*in*, on, *cadĕre*, to fall.]

incinerate, in-sin'ér-āt, *v.t.* to reduce to ashes.—*ns.* **incinera'tion**; **incin'erātor**, a furnace for burning up anything. [L. *incinerāre*, *-ātum*—*in*, in, *cinis*, *cineris*, ashes.]

incipient, in-sip'í-ént, *adj.* beginning: nascent.—*ns.* **incip'ience**, **incip'iency**.—*adv.* **cip'iently**. [L. *incipiens*, *-entis*, pr.p. of *incipĕre*, to begin.]

incise, in-sīz', *v.t.* to cut into: to engrave.—*n.* **incision** (in-sizh'(ŏ)n), the act of cutting into a substance: a cut, a gash.—*adj.* **incisive** (*-sīs'-*), having the quality of cutting in (*lit.* and *fig.*): acute in mind: (of style) trenchant, sarcastic.—*adv.* **incisively**.—*ns.* **incisiveness**; **incisor** (*-sīz'ór*), a cutting or fore tooth.—*adj.* **inci'sory**. [Fr. *inciser*—L. *incīdĕre*, *incīsum*—*in*, into, *caedĕre*, to cut.]

incite, in-sīt', *v.t.* to move to action: to goad (to).—*ns.* **incitant** (in'sit-ánt, in-sīt'ánt), that which incites: a stimulant; **incita'tion** (*-sit-*, *sīt-*), the act of inciting or rousing: an incentive; **incite'ment**; **incit'er**.—*adv.* **incit'ingly**. [Fr.,—L. *incitāre*—*in*, in, *citāre*, to rouse—

ciēre, to put in motion.]

incivility, in-si-vil'í-ti, *n.* want of civility or courtesy, impoliteness: an act of discourtesy (in this sense, *pl.* **incivil'ities**). [Fr.,—L. *incīvīlis*—*in*-, not; cf. **civil.**]

inclement, in-klem'ént, *adj.* unmerciful: stormy: very cold.—*n.* **inclem'ency**.—*adv.* **inclem'ently**. [L. *inclēmens*, unmerciful—*in*-, not; cf. **clement.**]

incline, in-klīn', *v.i.* to lean (towards): to bow or bend: to deviate, slant, slope: to be disposed: to have some slight desire.—*v.t.* to cause to bend downwards: to cause to deviate: to dispose.—*n.* (in'klīn, in-klīn') a slope.—*adj.* **inclīn'able**, capable of being tilted or sloped: somewhat disposed.—*n.* **inclīna'tion**, a bend or bow: a slope or tilt: angle with the horizon or with any plane or line: tendency: disposition of mind, natural aptness: favourable disposition, affection.—*p.adj.* **inclined'**, bent: sloping: disposed.—**inclined plane**, a slope or plane up which one may raise a weight one could not lift. [Fr.,—L. *inclīnāre*, to bend towards—*in*, into, *clīnāre*, to lean.]

inclose, **inclosure**. Same as **enclose**, **enclosure**.

include, in-klōōd', *v.t.* to enclose: to comprise as a part: to take in.—*n.* **inclusion** (*-klōō'zh(ŏ)n*), act of including: that which is included.—*adj.* **inclu'sive**, enclosing: comprehensive, including everything: taking in (with *of*): reckoning in the stated extremes (e.g. 2*nd to* 5*th Jan.* inclusive, i.e. four days).—*adv.* **inclu'sively.—include (one) out** (*coll.*), to exclude (one). [L. *inclūdĕre*, *inclūsum*—*in*, in, *claudĕre*, to shut.]

incog, in-kog', *adv.* an abbreviation of **incognito**.

incognito, in-kog'ni-tō, *adj.* unknown, unidentified: disguised.—*adv.* under an assumed name: with concealment, real or feigned, of identity.—*n.* a man unknown (*fem.* **incog'nita**). [It.,—L. *incognitus*—*in*-, not, *cognitus*, known—*cognoscĕre*, to know.]

incoherent, in-kō-hēr'ént, *adj.* not coherent: loose, rambling.—*ns.* **incoher'ence**, **-ency**.—*adv.* **incoher'ently**. [L. *in*-, not, and **coherent.**]

incombustible, in-kom-bust'i-bl, *adj.* incapable of combustion.—*ns.* **incombustibil'ity**, **incombust'ibleness**.—*adv.* **incombust'ibly**. [L. *in*-, not, and **combustible.**]

income, in'-kùm, *n.* the gain, profit, or interest resulting from anything: revenue: (*loosely*) salary.—*ns.* **in'comer**, one who comes in: one who comes to live in a place, not having been born there; **in'come-tax**, a tax directly levied on income or on income over a certain amount.—*adj.* **in'coming**, coming in. [**in**, **come.**]

incommensurable, in-kom-en'sū-rá-bl, *adj.* having no common measure (with another): having no basis of comparison.—*ns.* **incommensurabil'ity**, **incommen'surableness**.—*adv.* **incommen'surably**.—*adj.* **incommen'surāte**, (with *with*, *to*) disproportionate: not adequate: incommensurable.—*adv.* **incommen'surātely**. [L. *in*-, not, and **commensurable.**]

incommode, in-kom-ōd', *v.t.* to cause trouble or inconvenience to.—*adj.* **incommō'dious**, inconvenient, uncomfortable, not roomy.—*adv.* **incommō'diously**.—*n.* **incommō'diousness**. [Fr.,—L. *incommodāre*—*in*-, not, *commodus*,

Neutral vowels in unaccented syllables: em'pér-ór; for certain sounds in foreign words see p. ix.

commodious.]

incommunicable, *in-kom-ūn'i-kà-bl*, *adj.* that cannot be communicated or imparted to others.—*ns.* **incommunicabil'ity, incommun'i-cableness.**—*adv.* **incommun'icably.**—*adj.* **incommun'icative,** uncommunicative. [L. *in-*, not, and **communicable.**]

incommunicado, *in-kóm-ūn-i-kä'dō,* *adj.* and *adv.* without means of communication: in solitary cônfinement. [Sp. *incomunicado.*]

incomparable, *in-kom'pár-à-bl,* *adj.* not admitting comparison (with): matchless.—*n.* **incom'parableness,**—*adv* **incom'parably.**.[Fr., —L. *incompărābĭlis*; cf. **comparable.**]

incompatible, *in-kom-pat'i-bl,* *adj.* not consistent, contradictory: incapable of existing together in harmony, or at all: (as *n.pl.*) things which cannot coexist.—*n.* **incompatibil'ity.**—*adv.* **incompat'ibly.** [Low L. *incompatābĭlis*; cf. **compatible.**]

incompetent, *in-kom'pè-tènt,* *adj.* lacking adequate powers: lacking the proper legal qualifications: grossly deficient in ability for such work.—*ns.* **incom'petence, incom'petency.**—*adv.* **incom'petently.** [Fr. *incompétent*—Low L.; cf. **competent.**]

incomplete, *in-kom-plēt',* *adj.* imperfect: unfinished.—*adv.* **incomplete'ly.**—*n.* **incomplete'ness.** [Low L. *incomplētus*; cf. **complete.**]

incompliance, *in-kom-plī'áns,* *n.* refusal to comply: an unaccommodating disposition.—*adj.* **incompli'ant.** [L. *in-*, not, and **compliance.**]

incomprehensible, *in-kom-pre-hen'si-bl,* *adj.* not capable of being understood: not to be contained within limits.—*ns.* **incomprehensibil'ity, incomprehen'sibleness, incomprehen'sion,** failure, or inability, to understand.—*adv.* **incomprehen'sibly.**—*adj.* **incomprehen'sive,** limited.—*n.* **incomprehen'siveness.** [L. *incomprehensĭbĭlis*; cf. **comprehensible.**]

incompressible, *in-kom-pres'i-bl,* *adj.* that cannot be compressed into smaller bulk.—*n.* **incompressibil'ity.** [L. *in-*, not, and **compressible.**]

inconceivable, *in-kon-sēv'à-bl,* *adj.* that cannot be conceived by the mind: (*coll.*) taxing belief or imagination.—*n.* **inconceiv'ableness.**—*adv.* **inconceiv'ably.** [L. *in-*, not, and **conceivable.**]

inconclusive, *in-kon-klōōs'iv,* *adj.* not settling a point in debate, indecisive.—*adv.* **inconclus'ively.**—*n.* **inconclus'iveness.** [L. *in-*, not, and **conclusive.**]

incongruous, *in-kong'grōō-us,* *adj.* not in harmony, out of keeping, out of place: inconsistent.—*n.* **incongru'ity** (*-grōō'-*).—*adv.* **incong'ruously.** [L. *incongrŭus*; cf. **congruous.**]

inconnu, *fem.* **inconnue,** *ē-ko-nü,* *n.* an unknown person. [Fr.]

inconsequent, *in-kon'si-kwènt,* *adj.* not following from the premises, illogical: irrelevant: disconnected.—*n.* **incon'sequence.**—*adj.* **inconsequential** (*-kwen'shál*), not following from the premises: of no consequence or value.—*advs.* **inconsequen'tially, incon'sequently.** [L. *inconsĕquens, -entis*; cf. **consequent.**]

Inconsiderable, *in-kon-sid'èr-à-bl,* *adj.* not worthy of notice: unimportant: of no great size.—*adv.* **inconsid'erably.** [Fr. *inconsidérable*; cf. **considerable.**]

inconsiderate, *in-kon-sid'ér-àt, adj.* not mindful of the claims of others: thoughtless, ill-advised: rash, imprudent.—*adv.* **inconsid'erately.**—*n.* **inconsid'erateness.** [L. *inconsīdĕrātus*; cf. **considerate.**]

inconsistent, *in-kon-sist'ént, adj.* not consistent: not suitable or agreeing (with): intrinsically incompatible: self-contradictory: changeable, fickle.—*ns.* **inconsist'ence, inconsist'ency.**—*adv.* **inconsist'ently.** [L. *in-*, not, and **consistent.**]

inconsolable,*in-kon-sōl'à-bl, adj.* not to be comforted.—*adv.* **inconsol'ably.** [L. *inconsōlābĭlis*; cf. **consolable.**]

inconsonant, *in-kon'són-ànt, adj.* not harmonising (with). [L. *in-*, not, and **consonant.**]

inconspicuous, *in-kon-spik'ū-us, adj.* not conspicuous.—*adv.* **inconspic'uously.**—*n.* **inconspic'uousness.** [L. *inconspĭcŭus*; cf. **conspicuous.**]

inconstant, *in-kon'stànt, adj.* subject to change: fickle.—*n.* **incon'stancy.**—*adv.* **incon'stantly.** [L. *inconstans, -antis*; cf. **constant.**]

incontestable, *in-kon-test'à-bl, adj.* too clear to be called in question, undeniable.—*adv.* **incontest'ably.** [Fr.; cf. **contestable.**]

incontinent, *in-kon'ti-nént, adj.* not restraining the passions or appetites: unchaste: (*med.*) unable to restrain the natural discharges or evacuations from the body.—*ns.* **incon'tinence, incon'tinency.**—*adv.* **incon'tinently.** [L. *incontinens, -entis in-*, not, *continens.* See **continent.**]

incontinent,*in-kon'ti-nént, adv.* (*arch.*) straightway.—Also **incon'tinently.** [Fr.—L.L. *in continenti (tempore)*, in unbroken time.]

incontrovertible, *in-kon-tro-vûrt'i-bl, adj.* too clear to be called in question.—*n.* **incontrovertibil'ity.**—*adv.* **incontrovert'ibly.** [L.*in-*, not, and **controvertible.**]

inconvenient, *in-kon-vēn'yént, adj.* causing trouble or difficulty: incommodious.—*v.t.* **inconven'ience,** to trouble or incommode.—*ns.* **inconven'ience, inconven'iency.**—*adv.* **inconven'iently.** [Fr. *inconvénient*; cf. **convenient.**]

inconvertible, *in-kon-vûrt'i-bl, adj.* that cannot be changed or exchanged.—*n.* **inconvertibil'ity.** [Low L. *inconvertĭbĭlis*; cf. **convertible.**]

inconvincible, *in-kon-vin'si-bl, adj.* not capable of being convinced. [L. *in-*, not, and **convincible.**]

incorporate, *in-kör'pó-rāt, v.t.* to form into one mass: (*lit.* and *fig.*) to combine with other ingredients already in a mass (*incorporate into* a specified whole): to merge, blend (with): to include, contain as a part: to form into a corporation.—*v.i.* to unite into one mass: to form a corporation.—*adj.* united in one body.—*p.adj.* **incor'porated,** formed into a corporation (abbreviated in names of U.S. firms such as *Edwards Publishing Company, Inc.*).—*n.* **incorporā'tion,** act of incorporating: state of being incorporated: formation of a legal or political body: an association. [L. *incorporāre, -ātum—in,* in, into, *corpus, -oris,* body.]

incorporate, *in-kör'pó-rát, adj.* without a body: unembodied.—*adj.* **incorporeal** (*-pō', -pō'ri-ál*), not having a body: spiritual.—*adv.* **incorpō'really.** [L. *incorporātus, incorporālis,* bodiless—*in-,* not, *corpus, -oris,* body.]

incorrect, *in-kor-ekt',* adj. containing faults: not accurate, wrong: not correct in manner or character.—*adv.* **incorrect'ly.**—*n.* **incorrect'ness.** [L. *incorrectus;* cf. **correct.**]

incorrigible, *in-kor'i-ji-bl, adj.* beyond correction or reform.—Also *n.*—*ns.* **incorr'igibleness, incorrigibil'ity.**—*adv.* **incorr'igibly.** [Fr.; see **correct.**]

incorrupt, *in-kor-upt', adj.* sound: pure: not depraved: not to be tempted by bribes.—*adj.* **incorrupt'ible,** not capable of decay: that cannot be bribed: inflexibly just.—*ns.* **incorrupt'ibleness**∕ **incorruptibil'ity.**—*adv.* **incorrupt'ibly.**—*ns.* **incorrup'tion, incorrupt'ness.**—*adv.* **incorrupt'ly.** [L. *incorruptus;* cf. **corrupt.**]

increase, *in-krēs', v.i.* to grow in size, numbers, or (*arch.*) wealth.—*v.t.* to make greater in size, numbers, or (*arch.*) wealth.—*n.* **in'crease,** growth: addition to original stock, as profit, produce, progeny.—*adv.* **increas'ingly.** [M.E. *encressen*—Anglo-Fr. *encresser*—L. *increscĕre*—*in,* in, *crescĕre,* to grow.]

incredible, *in-kred'i-bl, adj.* surpassing belief: (*coll.*) unusual, unusually good.—*ns.* **incredibil'ity, incred'ibleness.**—*adv.* **incred'ibly.** [L. *incrēdibĭlis;* cf. **credible.**]

incredulous, *in-kred'ū-lus, adj.* unbelieving: showing disbelief.—*ns.* **incredū'lity, incred'ūlousness.**—*adv.* **incred'ūlously.** [L. *incrēdulus;* cf. **credulous.**]

increment, *ing'-* or *in'kri-mént, n.* increase: amount of increase: an amount or thing added: (*math.*) the finite increase of a variable quantity.—**unearned increment,** any exceptional increase in the value of land, houses, &c., not due to the owner's labour or outlay. [L. *incrēmentum*—*increscĕre,* to increase.]

incriminate, *in-krim'in-āt, v.t.* to charge with a crime or fault, to criminate: to implicate: to involve in a charge.—*adj.* **incrim'inatory** (or *-ā-*). [Low L. *incrīmĭnāre, incrīmĭnātum;* cf. **criminate** (see **crime**).]

incrust, incrustation. See **encrust, encrustation.**

incubate, *in'kū-bāt,* or *ing'-, v.i.* to sit on eggs: to hatch.—*v.t.* to hatch: to keep (bacteria) at a temperature suitable for (their) development: (*fig.*) to brood or ponder over.—*ns.* **incubā'tion,** the act of sitting on eggs to hatch them: (*med.*) the period between infection and appearance of symptoms; **in'cubator,** an apparatus for hatching eggs by artificial heat, for rearing prematurely born children, or for developing bacteria. [L. *incubāre, -ātum* (usu. *-ĭtum*)—*in,* on, *cubāre,* to lie, recline.]

incubus, *in'kū-bus, n.* the nightmare (q.v.): any oppressive influence:—*pl.* **in'cubuses, incubi** (*in'kū-bī*). [L. *incŭbus,* nightmare—*in,* on, *cubāre,* to lie.]

inculcate, *in'kul-kāt* (or *-kul'-*), *v.t.* to teach by frequent admonitions or repetitions.—*ns.* **inculcā'tion; in'culcātor.** [L. *inculcāre, -ātum*—*in,* into, *calcāre,* to tread—*calx,* the heel.]

inculpate, *in'kul-pāt* (or *-kul'-*), *v.t.* to involve in a charge or blame: to charge.—*n.* **inculpā'tion.**—*adj.* **incul'patory.** [Low L. *inculpāre, -ātum*—L. *in,* in, *culpa,* a fault.]

incumbent, *in-kum'bént, adj.* lying or resting (on): imposed or resting as a duty (with impersonal construction, e.g. *it is incumbent on you to be present*).—*n.* one who holds an ecclesiastical benefice.—*n.* **incum'bency,** a lying or resting on: the holding of an office: an ecclesiastical benefice.—*adv.* **incum'bently.** [L. *incumbens, -entis,* pr.p. of *incumbĕre,* to lie upon.]

incunabula, *in-kū-nab'ū-la, n.pl.* books printed in the early period of the art, before the year 1500: the origin, early stages of anything. [L. *incūnābŭla,* swaddling-clothes, infancy, earliest stage—*in,* in, *cūnābula,* dim. of *cūnae,* a cradle.]

incur, *in-kûr', v.t.* to become liable to: to bring upon oneself:—*pr.p.* incurr'ing; *pa.p.* incurred'. [L. *incurrĕre, incursum*—*in,* into, *currĕre,* to run.]

incurable, *in-kūr'á-bl, adj.* not admitting of cure or correction.—*n.* one beyond cure.—*ns.* **incur'ableness, incurabil'ity.**—*adv.* **incur'ably.** [O.Fr.,—L. *incūrābilis*—*in-,* not, *cūrābilis,* curable.]

incurious, *in-kū'ri-us, adj.* without curiosity: indifferent (about): careless: uninteresting (e.g. *a not incurious circumstance*):· [L. *incūriōsus*—*in-,* not, *cūriōsus,* attentive, inquisitive.]

incursion, *in-kûr'sh(ö)n, n.* a hostile inroad.—*adj.* **incur'sive,** making inroads: aggressive. [L. *incursiō, -ōnis*—*incurrĕre.*]

incurve, *in-kûrv', v.t.* and *v.i.* to curve: to curve inward.—*v.t.* and *v.i.* **incur'vate** (or *in'-*), to bend, esp. inwards.—*adj.* curved inward.—*n.* **incurvā'tion.** [L. *incurvāre,·* to bend in—*incurvus,* bent.]

indebted, *in-det'id, adj.* being in debt (to): obliged by something received.—*n.* **indebt'edness.** [O.Fr. *endetté,* pa.p. of *endetter*—*en,* in, *dette,* debt.]

indecent, *in-dē'sént, adj.* offensive to common modesty or propriety.—*n.* **indē'cency.**—*adv.* **indē'cently.** [L. *indēcens;* cf. **decent.**]

indecipherable, *in-di-sī'fér-á-bl, adj.* incapable of being deciphered. [L. *in-,* not, and **decipherable.** See **decipher.**]

indecision, *in-di-sizh'(ö)n, n.* want of decision or resolution: hesitation.—*adj.* **indecisive** (*-sīz'iv*), inconclusive: irresolute.—*adv.* **indecī'sively.**—*n.* **indecī'siveness.** [L. *in-,* not, and **decisive.**]

indeclinable, *in-di-klīn'á-bl, adj.* (*gram.*) not varied by inflection.—*adv.* **indeclin'ably.** [Fr. *indéclinable*—L. *indēclīnābĭlis.*]

indecorous, *in-dek'ö-rūs,* sometimes *-di-kō'-,* or *-kō'-, adj.* unseemly: violating good manners.—*adv.* **indec'örously.**—*n.* **indecō'rum,** want of propriety of conduct. [L. *indēcōrus.*]

indeed, *in-dēd', adv.* in fact: in truth: in reality. The word is also used to increase emphasis.—*interj.* expresses surprise, interrogation, disbelief, or mere acknowledgment. [**in, deed.**]

indefatigable, *in-di-fat'i-gá-bl, adj.* not to be wearied out: unremitting in effort.—*n.* **indefat'igableness.**—*adv.* **indefat'igably.** [Fr.,—L. *indēfatīgābilis*—*in,* not, *dē,* from, *fatīgāre,* to tire.]

indefeasible, *in-di-fēz'i-bl, adj.* not to be made void (e.g. a right or title).—*n.* **indefeasibil'-**

Neutral vowels in unaccented syllables: *em'pér-ór;* for certain sounds in foreign words see p. ix.

364

ity.—*adv.* **indefeas'ibly.** [L. *in-*, not, and **defeasible.**]

indefensible, *in-di-fens'i-bl, adj. (lit.* and *fig.)* that cannot be defended, maintained, or justified.—*adv.* **indefens'ibly.** [L. *in-*, not, and **defensible.** See **defend.**]

indefinable, *in-di-fīn'ā-bl, adj.* that cannot be defined.—*adv.* **indefin'ably.** [L. *in-*, not, and **definable.** See **define.**]

indefinite, *in-def'i-nit, adj.* without clearly marked outlines or limits: not precise: *(gram.)* not referring to a particular person or thing (see **article).**—*adv.* **indef'initely.**—*n.* **indef'initeness.** [L. *indēfīnītus*; cf. **definite** (see **define).**]

indehiscent, *in-dē-his'ént, adj. (bot.)* not opening naturally when ripe. [L. *in-*, not, and **dehiscent.**]

indelible, *in-del'i-bl, adj.* that cannot be blotted out or effaced: making a mark that is not erased by rubbing.—*ns.* **indelibil'ity, indel'ibleness,**—*adv.* **indel'ibly.** [L. *indēlēbilis—in-*, not, *dēlēre* to destroy.]

indelicate, *in-del'i-kàt, adj.* offensive to purity of mind: wanting in fineness of feeling or tact: coarse.—*n.* **indel'icacy** (*-kà-si*).—*adv.* **indel'icately.** [L. *in-*, not, and **delicate.**]

indemnify, *in-dem'ni-fī, v.t.* to secure (with *against*): to compensate: to free, exempt (with *from*):—*pa.p.* indem'nified.—*n.* **Indemnification** (*-fi-kā'sh(ò)n*). [L. *indemnis,* unhurt (*in-*, not, *damnum,* loss), and suffx. *-fy.*]

indemnity, *in-dem'ni-ti, n.* security from damage, loss, or punishment: compensation for loss or injury. [Fr. *indemnité*—L. *indemnis,* unharmed—*damnum,* loss.]

indemonstrable, *in-dem'ón-strà-bl,* or *in-di-mon'-, adj.* that cannot be demonstrated or proved. [L. *in-*, not, and **demonstrable.** See **demonstrate.**]

indent, *in dent', v.t.* to cut into zigzags: to divide (a document) along a zigzag line (*i* notch): to begin farther in from the margin than the rest of a paragraph. *v.i.* to make out a written order with counterfoil (for).—*n.* (*in'dent,* also *in-dent'*) a cut or notch: a recess like a notch: an order for goods (from abroad or from store).—*ns.* **indenta'tion,** act of indenting or notching: a notch: a recess, e.g. in a coastline; **inden'ture,** a written agreement between two or more parties: a contract.—*v.t.* to bind by indentures: to indent. [Two different words fused together: (1)—Low L. *indentāre*—L. *in,* in, *dens, dentis,* a tooth; (2)—English **in** and **dint, dent.**]

independent, *in-di-pend'ént, adj.* (with *of*) not dependent or relying on (others): thinking or acting for oneself: too self-respecting to accept help: completely self-governing: not dependent on something else (of a proof, investigation, &c.): not subject to or showing the influence of others (e.g. *independent judgment*): having or affording a comfortable livelihood without necessity of working or of help from others: belonging to the Independents.—*n.* (*cap.*) a Congregationalist (q.v.): one who commits himself to no party.—*ns.* **independ'ence, independ'ency.**—*adv.* **independ'ently.**—**Independence Day,** the 4th of July, a holiday in U.S., the anniversary of the

Declaration of Independence, 1776; **independent school,** a public school. [L. *in-*, not, and **dependent.** See **depend.**]

indescribable, *in-di-skrīb'á-bl, adj.* that cannot be described: vague, difficult to define: possessing its characteristic quality in a high degree. [L. *in-*, not, and **describable.** See **describe.**]

indestructible, *in-di-struk'ti-bl, adj.* that cannot be destroyed.—*n.* **indestructibil'ity.**—*adv.* **indestruc'tibly.** [L. *in-*, not, and **destructible.** See **destruction.**]

indeterminable, *in-di-tûr'min-á-bl, adj.* not to be ascertained or fixed.—*adv.* **indeter'minably.**—*adj.* **indeter'minate** (*-àt*), not determinate: uncertain: having no defined or fixed value.—*adv.* **indeter'minately.**—*n.* **indetermina'tion,** want of determination: want of fixed direction.—*adj.* **indeter'mined,** not determined: unsettled. [L. *indēterminābilis*; cf. **determinable.**]

index, *in'deks, n.* the fore finger (also **index'ing'er**); a pointer or hand on a dial or scale, &c.: anything that gives an indication: an alphabetical register of subjects dealt with, usu. at the end of a book: *(math.)* a symbol denoting a power:—*pl.* (of a book) usu. **in'dexes,** (other senses) **indices** (*in'di-sēz*).—*v.t.* to provide with, or place in, an index.—**in'dex num'ber,** a number indicating the general cost of living, taking the prices of various commodities into account.—**the Index,** a list of books forbidden to Roman Catholics, or allowed only in expurgated editions. [L. *index, indicis—indicāre,* to show.]

Indian, *in'di-an, adj.* belonging to India, to the Indies, East or West, or to the aborigines of America.—*n.* a member of one of the races of India: (formerly) a European long resident in India: an aboriginal of America.—*ns.* **In'diaman,** a large ship employed in trade with India, **In'dia-rubb'er,** an elastic gummy substance, the inspissated (q.v.) juice of various tropical plants—also known as *rubber, caoutchouc, gum-elastic:* a piece of this, esp. for rubbing out pencil-marks.—**Indian club,** a bottle-shaped block of wood, swung in various motions by the arms to develop the muscles; **Indian corn,** maize, so called because brought from the West Indies; **Indian cress,** a garden plant from Peru (see **nasturtium**); **Indian fig,** the banian (q.v.): prickly pear; **Indian file** (see **file**); **Indian gift,** a gift that is asked back or for which a return gift is expected; **Indian hemp,** hemp, esp. the variety grown in India; **Indian, India ink** (see **ink**); **Indian meal,** ground Indian corn or maize; **Indian summer** (originally in America), a period of warm, dry, calm weather in late autumn; **India paper,** a thin soft absorbent paper, of Chinese or Japanese origin, used in taking proofs from engraved plates, &c.: a thin, strong, opaque, rag paper, used for Bibles, &c.—**East India Company,** a chartered company formed (1600) for trading with India and the East Indies; **Red Indian** (see **red**). [L. *India—Indus* (Gr. *Indos*), the Indus (Pers. *Hind*)—Sans. *sindhu,* a river.]

indicate, *in'di-kāt, v.t.* to point out: to show: to give some notion of: *(med.)* suggest or point to (as suitable treatment): also (*pass.*) used loosely of any desirable course of action.—*n.* **indica′tion**, act of indicating: mark: token: symptom.—*adj.* **indic′ative**, showing the existence, presence, or nature (of), giving intimation (of): (*gram.*) applied to the mood of the verb that affirms or denies.—*adv.* **indic′atively.**—*n.* **in′dicātor**, one who, or that which, indicates: a measuring contrivance with a pointer or the like: any device for exhibiting condition for the time being.—*adj.* **in′dicatory** (or -*dĭk′-*). [L. *indicāre, -ātum—in,* in, *dicāre,* to proclaim.]

indict, *in-dīt′, v.t.* to charge with a crime formally or in writing.—*adj.* **indict′able,** liable: making one liable to be indicted (e.g. *an indictable offence*).—*n.* **indict′ment,** the written accusation against one who is to be tried by jury: formal accusation. [With Latinised spelling (but not pronunciation) from Anglo-Fr. *enditer,* to indict—L. *in,* in, *dictāre,* to declare.]

indifferent, *in-dif′ėr-ėnt, adj.* of a middle quality: rather poor or bad: neutral: without importance (to): unconcerned.—*ns.* **indiff′erence, indiff′erency; indiff′erentism,** spirit of indifference: the doctrine that religious differences are of no moment.—*adv.* **indiff′erently,** in an indifferent manner: tolerably, passably: without distinction, impartially. [L. *indifferens, -entis;* cf. **different.**]

indigenous, *in-dij′ėn-us, adj.* produced naturally in a country or soil (often with *to*)—opp. to *exotic*: native born: (*fig.*) originating in (with *to*): inborn. [L. *indigena,* a native—*indu,* old form of *in,* in, and *gen-,* root of *gignĕre,* to produce.]

indigent, *in′di-jėnt, adj.* in need, esp. of means of subsistence.—*n.* **in′digence.**—*adv.* **in′digently.** [Fr.,—L. *indigens, -entis,* pr.p. of *indigēre*—from the old word *indu,* in, *egēre,* to need.]

indigested, *in-di-jest′id, adj.* not digested: not thought out: not methodised.—*n.* **indigestion** (*in-di-jes′ch(ŏ)n*), want of digestion: painful effects of imperfect digestion.—*adj.* **indigest′ible,** not digestible: not easily digested: not to be patiently accepted or endured.—*n.* **indigestibil′ity.**—*adv.* **indigest′ibly.** [L. *indīgestus,* unarranged—*in-,* not, *dīgerĕre,* to arrange, digest.]

indignant, *in-dig′nánt, adj.* affected with anger mixed with disdain or sense of injustice.—*adv.* **indig′nantly.**—*ns.* **indignā′tion,** the feeling caused by what is unworthy or base or by an unjustified slight: anger mixed with contempt; **indig′nity,** unmerited contemptuous treatment: incivility with contempt or insult. [L. *indignus,* unworthy—*in-,* not, *dignus,* worthy.]

indigo, *in′di-gō, n.* a violet-blue dye obtained from the leaves of plants of the indigo genus, from woad, or synthetically. [Sp. *índico, índigo*—L. *indicum*—Gr. *Indikon,* Indian (neut. adj.).]

indirect, *in-di-rekt′,* or *-dī-, adj.* not direct or in a straight line (*lit.* and *fig.,* e.g. *indirect approach, reference, result*): not straightforward or honest.—*adv.* **indirect′ly.**—*n.* **indirect′ness.—indirect evidence,** or **testimony,** circumstantial or inferential evidence; **indirect object** (*gram.*), a noun or pronoun (L. dative

case) less immediately dependent on the verb than the noun or pronoun forming the *direct object* (L. accusative case), e.g. 'she gave *me* the money,' where *me* is the indirect object; **indirect speech,** speech reported, with the necessary adjustment of the speaker's actual words; **indirect tax,** one paid by the consumer in the form of increased prices for goods that are subject to customs and excise duties, &c. [L. *indīrectus;* cf. **direct.**]

indiscernible, *in-di-sûrn′i-bl,* or *-zûrn′-, adj.* not discernible.—*adv.* **indiscern′ibly.** [L. *in-,* not, and **discernible. See discern.**]

indiscreet, *in-dis-krēt′, adj.* not discreet, imprudent, injudicious.—*adv.* **indiscreet′ly.**—*ns.* **indiscreet′ness, indiscretion** (-*kresh′(ŏ)n*), want of discretion: rashness: an indiscreet act. [L. *in-,* not, and **discreet.**]

indiscriminate, *in-dis-krim′i-nát, adj.* not distinguishing relative merits (e.g. *indiscriminate praise, blame, generosity*).—Also **indiscrim′inating, indiscrim′inative.**—*adv.* **indiscrim′inately.** [L. *in-,* not, and **discriminate.**]

indispensable, *in-dis-pens′á-bl, adj.* that cannot be dispensed with: absolutely necessary.—*ns.* **indispensabil′ity, indispens′ableness.**—*adv.* **indispens′ably.** [Low L. *indispensābilis.*]

indispose, *in-dis-pōz′, v.t.* to render indisposed, averse, or unfit.—*pa.p.* and *adj.* **indisposed′,** averse (with *to*): slightly disordered in health.—*ns.* **indispos′edness, indisposition** (-*poz-ish′(ŏ)n*), state of being indisposed: disinclination: slight illness. [L. *in-,* not, and **dispose.**]

indisputable, *in-dis-pū′tá-bl,* also *-dis′,* *adj.* certainly true, certain.—*n.* **indisputableness.**—*adv.* **indisputably.** [Low L. *indisputābilis;* cf. **disputable.**]

indissoluble, *in-dis′ol-(y)ōō-bl,* or *-di-sol′-, adj.* that cannot be broken or violated: inseparable: binding for ever.—*ns.* **indiss′olubleness, indissolubil′ity** (-*ū-bil′-*).—*adv.* **indiss′olubly.** [L. *indissōlūbilis;* cf. **dissoluble.**]

indistinct, *in-dis-tingkt′, adj.* not plainly marked: confused: dim: not clear to the mind.—*adv.* **indistinct′ly.**—*n.* **indistinct′ness.**—*adj.* **indistinctive,** not distinctive. [L. *indistinctus;* cf. **distinct.**]

indistinguishable, *in-dis-ting′gwish-á-bl, adj.* that cannot be distin′guished.—*adv.* **indisting′uishably.** [L. *in-,* not, and **distinguishable.**]

indite, *in-dīt′, v.t.* to compose or write.—*v.i.* to compose.—*ns.* **indite′ment; indit′er.** [O.Fr. *enditer,* to make known; cf. **indict.**]

indium, *in′di-um, n.* a metallic element (symbol In; atomic no. 49) found in small quantities in ores of certain other metals. [L. *indicum,* indigo (from two indigo-coloured lines in the spectrum), and *-ium.*]

individual, *in-di-vid′ū-ál, adj.* pertaining to one only, or to each one separately, of a group: special, particular—opp. to *general*: single, separate: of marked individuality.—*n.* a single person, animal, plant, or thing.—*v.t.* **individ′ualise,** to stamp with individual character: to particularise.—*n.* **individualīsā′tion.**—*ns.* **individ′ualism,** individual character: egoism: independent action as opp. to co-operation: theory that the rights of individuals are of

Neutral vowels in unaccented syllables: *em′pėr-ŏr*; for certain sounds in foreign words see p. ix.

366

higher importance than advantage of e.g. the state; **individ'ualist**, one who thinks and acts with great independence: one who advocates individualism; **individual'ity** (-al'i-ti), separate, distinct existence: distinctive character or personality.—*adv.* **individ'ually.**—*v.t.* **individ'uate**, to individualise: to give individuality to.—*n.* **individua'tion.** [L. *individuus*—*in*-, not, *dīviduus*, divisible—*dīvidēre*, to divide.]

indivisible, *in-di-viz'i-bl, adj.* not divisible.—*n.* (*math.*) an indefinitely small quantity.—*ns.* **indivisibil'ity**, **indivis'ibleness.**—*adv.* **indivis'ibly.** [L. *indīvīsibilis*; cf. **divisible** (see **division**).]

indocile, *in-dō'sīl*, or *in-dos'il, adj.* not docile: not disposed to be instructed.—*n.* **indocil'ity.** [L. *indŏcilis*; cf. **docile.**]

indoctrinate, *in-dok'trin-āt, v.t.* to instruct in any doctrine: to imbue (with any opinion).—*n.* **indoctrina'tion.** [Low L. *in*, in, *doctrināre*, to teach; cf. **doctrine.**]

Indo-European, *in'dō ū-rō-pē'an, adj.* a term applied to the family of peoples and languages also called **Indo-Germanic** and sometimes called **Aryan** (q.v.), whose great branches are Aryan proper or Indian, Iranian, Armenian, Greek or Hellenic, Italic, Celtic, Tocharian, Balto-Slavonic, Albanian and Germanic. [Indo = Indian—L. *Indus*—Gr. *Indos*.]

indolent, *in'dŏl-ént, adj.* indisposed to activity, lazy.—*n.* **in'dolence.**—*adv.* **in'dolently** [L. *in*-, not, *dolens*, *-entis*, pr.p. of *dolēre*, to suffer pain.]

indomitable, *in-dom'it-à-bl, adj.* (in a flattering sense) not to be overcome (e.g. courage).—*adv.* **indom'itably.** [Low L. *indŏmitābilis*—*dŏmitāre*, to tame.]

indoor, *in'dōr, -dŏr, adj.* practised, used, or being, within a building.—*adv.* **indoors'**, within doors.—**indoor relief**, support given to paupers in the workhouse. [**in, door.**]

indorse. See **endorse.**

indubitable, *in-dū'bit-à-bl, adj.* that cannot be doubted, certain.—*n.* **indu'bitableness.**—*adv.* **indu'bitably.** [L. *indūbitābilis*—*in*, not, *dūbitāre*, to doubt.]

induce, *in-dūs', v.t.* to prevail on: to bring on or about: (*physics*) to cause, as an electric state by mere proximity: to infer by the method of *induction* (q.v.).—*n.* **induce'ment**, that which induces, incentive, motive. [L. *indūcēre, inductum*—*in*, into, *dūcēre*, to lead.]

induct, *in-dukt', v.t.* to introduce (to, into): to put in possession, as of a benefice.—*ns.* **inductance**, the property of inducing an electromotive force by variation of current in a circuit; **induc'tion**, installation in office, benefice, &c.: magnetising by proximity without contact: the production by one body of an opposite electric state in another by proximity: (*logic*) reasoning from particular cases to general conclusions—opp. to *deduction*.—*adjs.* **induc'tional**, **induc'tive.**—*adv.* **induc'tively.**—*n.* **induc'tor**. [Same root as **induce.**]

inductile, *in-duk'tīl, adj.* not ductile.—*n.* **inductibility** (-bil'i-ti).—[L. *in*-, not, and **ductile.**]

indulge, *in-dulj', v.t.* to yield to the wishes of: to favour or gratify: not to restrain.—*v.i.* (with *in*) to gratify (one's appetites) freely: (*coll.*) to partake, esp. of alcohol.—*n.* **indul'gence**, the

act or practice of gratifying: self-gratification, esp. excessive: excessive leniency: a grant of religious liberty: a privilege granted: in the R.C. Church, a remission, to a repentant sinner, of the temporal punishment which remains due after the sin and its eternal punishment have been remitted.—*adj.* **indul'gent**, ready to gratify the wishes of others: compliant: weakly lenient.—*adv.* **indul'gently.** [L. *indulgēre*, to be kind to, indulge—*in*, in, and prob. L. *dulcis*, sweet.]

indurate, *in'dū-rāt, v.t.* and *v.i.* to harden (as skin, the feelings).—*n.* **Indura'tion.** [L. *indūrāre*, *-ātum*—*in*, in, *dūrāre*, to harden.]

indusium, *in-dū'zi-um, n.* a protective membrane or scale, esp. that covering a cluster of the receptacles containing the spores of ferns: an insect larva-case:—*pl.* **indu'sia.**—*adj.* **indu'sial**, containing fossil insect indusia. [L. *indūsium*, an under-garment—*induĕre*, to put on.]

industry, *in'dus-tri n* quality of being diligent: steady application to labour: systematic economic activity: any branch of manufacture or trade.—*adj.* **indus'trial**, relating to or consisting in industry.—*v.t.* **indus'trialise**, to give an industrial character to.—*ns.* **indus'trialism**, that system or condition of society in which industrial labour is the chief and most characteristic feature; **indus'trialist**, a manufacturer: an industrial worker.—*adj.* **indus'trious**, diligent or active in one's labour: diligent in a particular pursuit.—*adv.* **indus'triously.**—**industrial action**, a strike, go-slow or work-to-rule; **industrial estate**, a planned industrial area, with factories organised to provide varied employment; **industrial relations**, relations between workers and management in industry; **industrial school**, a school in which some industrial art is taught: a school where neglected or delinquent children are taught mechanical arts.—**heavy, light industry**, industry producing respectively very large products e.g. ships (usually involving heavy equipment) and relatively small products e.g. knitwear. [L. *industria*, perh. from the old word *indu*, in, within, and *struĕre*, to build up.]

indwelling, *in'dwel-ing, adj.* dwelling within, abiding permanently in the mind or soul.—*n.* residence within, or in the heart or soul. [in, **dwell.**]

inebriate, *in-ē'bri-āt, v.t.* to make drunk, to intoxicate.—*n.* a drunk person: a drunkard.—*ns.* **inebria'tion**, **inebriety** (*in-ē-brī'i-ti*), drunkenness. [L. *inēbriāre*, *-ātum*—*in*-, inten., *ēbriāre*, to make drunk—*ēbrius*, drunk.]

inedible, *in-ed'i-bl, adj.* unfit to be eaten. [L. *in*-, not, and **edible.**]

ineducable, *in-ed'ū-kà-bl, adj.* incapable of education.—*n.* **ineducabil'ity.** [L. *in*-, not, and **educable.** See **educate.**]

ineffable, *in-ef'à-bl, adj.* that cannot be described, inexpressible.—*n.* **ineff'ableness.**—*adv.* **ineff'ably.** [L. *ineffābilis*—*in*-, not, *effābilis*, that can be uttered—*fārī*, to speak.]

ineffaceable, *in-e-fās'à-bl, adj.* that cannot be rubbed out.—*adv.* **inefface'ably.** [L. *in*-, not, and **effaceable.** See **efface.**]

ineffective, *in-e-fek'tiv, adj.* not effective, useless.—*adv.* **ineffec'tively.**—*adj.* **ineffec'tual**, fruitless (e.g. attempt).—*n.* **ineffec′tualness.**—*adv.* **ineffec′tually.**—*adj.* **ineffica′cious** (*-shús*), not having power to produce an effect.—*adv.* **ineffica′ciously.**—*n.* **ineff′icacy** (*-kä-si*), want of efficacy.—*adj.* **ineffic′ient** (*-fish′ént*), not efficient.—*n.* **ineffic′iency.**—*adv.* **ineffic′iently.** [L. *in-*, not. See **effective** and **effectual** (under **effect**), **efficacious, efficient.**]

inelastic, *in-ē-las′tik, adj.* not elastic: unyielding. [L. *in-*, not, and **elastic.**]

inelegance, *in-el′i-gáns, n.* want of gracefulness or refinement—also **inel′egancy.**—*adj.* **inel′egant.**—*adv.* **inel′egantly.** [Fr. *inélégance*; cf. **elegance** (see **elegant**).]

ineligible, *in-el′i-ji-bl, adj.* not qualified for election: not suitable for choice.—*n.* **ineligibil′ity.**—*adv.* **inel′igibly.** [L. *in-*, not, and **eligible.**]

ineluctable, *in-e-luk′ta-bl, adj.* not to be escaped from. [L. *inēluctābilis*—*in-*, not, *ē,* from, *luctārī,* to struggle.]

inept, *in-ept′, adj.* irrelevant and futile: fatuous: unfit.—*n.* **inept′itūde.**—*adv.* **inept′ly.** [L. *ineptus*—*in-*, not, *aptus,* apt.]

inequality, *in-e-kwol′i-ti, n.* want of equality: unevenness: variableness. [O.Fr. *inequalité*—Low L.; cf. **equality** (see **equal**).]

inequitable, *in-ek′wi-tä-bl, adj.* unfair, unjust.—*adv.* **ineq′uitably.** [L. *in-*, not, and **equitable.**]

ineradicable, *in-e-rad′i-kä-bl, adj.* not able to be eradicated or rooted out.—*adv.* **inerad′icably.** [L. *in-*, not, and **eradicable.**]

inert, *in-úrt′, adj.* without inherent power of moving, or of active resistance to motion: passive: chemically inactive: disinclined to move or act.—*ns.* **inert′ness; inertia** (*in-úr′shi-a*), inertness: the inherent property of matter by which it tends to remain at rest when still, and in motion when moving.—*adj.* **iner′tial,** of, or pertaining to, inertia.—*adv.* **inert′ly.**—**inert gas,** one of several elements whose outer electron orbits are complete, rendering them inert to all the usual chemical reactions; **inertia selling,** sending unrequested goods to householders and attempting to charge for them if they are not returned. [L. *iners, inertis,* unskilled, idle—*in-*, not, *ars, artis,* art.]

inescapable, *in-es-kā′pá-bl, adj.* not to be escaped: inevitable. [L. *in-*, not, and **escapable.**]

inessential, *in-es-en′sh(á)l, adj.* not essential or necessary. [L. *in-*, not, and **essential.**]

inestimable, *in-es′tim-á-bl, adj.* not able to be estimated or valued: priceless.—*adv.* **ines′timably.** [O.Fr.,—L. *inaestimābilis*; cf. **estimable** (see **esteem**).]

inevitable, *in-ev′it-á-bl, adj.* not to be evaded or avoided: certain to happen: giving the feeling that it could not have been other than it is.—*ns.* **inev′itableness, inevitabil′ity.**—*adv.* **inev′itably.** [L. *inēvītābilis*—*in-*, not, *ē,* from, *vītāre,* to avoid.]

inexact, *in-egz-akt′, adj.* not precisely correct or true.—*ns.* **inexact′itude, inexact′ness.** [L. *in-*, not, and **exact.**]

inexcusable, *in-eks-kūz′á-bl, adj.* not justifiable: unpardonable.—*n.* **inexcus′ableness.**—*adv.* **inexcus′ably.** [L. *inexcūsābilis*; cf. **excusable**

(see **excuse**).]

inexhausted, *in-egs-ös′tid, adj.* not exhausted or spent.—*adj.* **inexhaust′ible,** not able to be exhausted or spent: unfailing.—*n.* **inexhaustibil′ity**—*adv.* **inexhaust′ibly.** [L. *in-*, not, and **exhaustible.**]

inexorable, *in-eks′ór-á-bl, adj.* not to be moved by entreaty, unrelenting: unyielding.—*ns.* **inex′orableness, inexorabil′ity.**—*adv.* **inex′orably.** [L. *inexōrābilis*—*in-*, not, *exōrāre*—*ex,* out of, *ōrāre,* to entreat.]

inexpedient, *in-eks-pē′di-ént, adj.* contrary to expediency, impolitic.—*ns.* **inexpē′dience, inexpē′diency.**—*adv.* **inexpē′diently.** [L. *in-*, not, and **expedient.**]

inexpensive, *in-eks-pens′iv, adj.* not costly. [L. *in-*, not, and **expensive.**]

inexperience, *in-eks-pē′ri-éns, n.* want of experience.—*adj.* **inexpē′rienced,** not having experience: (with *in*) unskilled or unpractised. [Fr. *inexpérience*; cf. **experience.**]

inexpert, *in-eks′púrt* or *in-eks-púrt′, adj.* unskilled.—*n.* **inexpert′ness.** [O.Fr.,—L. *inexpertus*; cf. **expert.**]

inexpiable, *in-eks′pi-á-bl, adj.* not able to be expiated or atoned for.—*n.* **inex′piableness.**—*adv.* **inex′piably.** [L. *inexpīābĭlis*; cf. **expiable** (see **expiate**).]

inexplicable, *in-eks′pli-kä-bl, adj.* (*obs.*) that cannot be disentangled: incapable of being explained or accounted for.—*ns.* **inexplicabil′ity, inex′plicableness.**—*adv.* **inex′plicably.** [L. *inexplicābĭlis*; cf. **explicable** (see **explicate**).]

inexplicit, *in-eks-plis′it, adj.* not clear and exact. [L. *inexplĭcitus*—*in-*, not; cf. **explicit.**]

inexpressible, *in-eks-pres′i-bl, adj.* that cannot be expressed, unutterable, indescribable.—*adv.* **inexpress′ibly.**—*adj.* **inexpress′ive,** without expression: not expressive.—*n.* **inexpress′iveness.** [L. *in-*, not, and **expressible.**]

inextensible, *in-eks-ten′si-bl, adj.* not able to be extended. [L. *in-*, not, and **extensible.**]

inextinguishable, *in-eks-ting′gwish-á-bl, adj.* (*lit.* and *fig.*) that cannot be extinguished, quenched, or destroyed.—*adv.* **inexting′uishably.** [L. *in-*, not, and **extinguishable.**]

inextricable, *in-eks′tri-kä-bl, adj.* not able to be extricated or disentangled.—*adv.* **inex′tricably.** [L. *inextrīcābĭlis*; cf. **extricable** (see **extricate**).]

infallible, *in-fal′i-bl, adj.* incapable of error: certain to succeed: unfailing.—*n.* **infallibil′ity.**—*adv.* **infall′ibly.** [Low L. *infallibilis*; cf. **fallible.**]

infamous, *in′fa-mus, adj.* having a reputation of the worst kind: notoriously vile: disgraceful.—*adv.* **in′famously.**—*n.* **in′famy,** ill fame or repute: an infamous act: public disgrace: extreme vileness. [L.L. *infāmōsus*—*in-*, not, *fāma,* fame.]

infant, *in′fánt, n.* a babe: (*Eng. law*) a person under the age of legal maturity.—*adj.* of or belonging to infants or infancy.—*n.* **in′fancy,** the state or time of being an infant: childhood: the beginning of anything.—*adjs.* **infantile** (*in′fánt-īl,* also *-fant′-*), pertaining to infancy or to an infant: having characteristics of infancy: undeveloped.—Also **infantine** (*-īn*). —**infantile paralysis,** poliomyelitis. [L. *infāns, -antis*—*in-*, not, *fāns,* pr.p. of *fārī,* to speak.]

Neutral vowels in unaccented syllables: *em′pér-ór*; for certain sounds in foreign words see p. ix.

infante, *in-fan'tā, n.* (*hist.*) a prince of the blood royal of Spain or Portugal, esp. a son of the king other than the heir-apparent:—*fem.* **infant'a**, a princess likewise defined: the wife of an infante. [Sp. and Port. from the root of **infant**.]

infanticide, *in-fant'i-sīd, n.* child murder: the murderer of an infant.—*adj.* **infant'icidal.** [L.L. *infanticīdium*, child-killing, *infanticīda*, child-killer—*infāns*, an infant, *caedĕre*, to kill.]

infantry, *in'fant-ri, n.* foot-soldiers: a part of an army composed of such soldiers. [Fr. *infanterie*—It. *infanteria*—*infante*, youth, servant, foot-soldier—L. *infāns, -antis.*]

infarct, *in-färkt', n.* a portion of body tissue that is dying because blood supply to it has been cut off.—*n.* **infarc'tion.** [Mediaeval L. *īnfarctus*—in, in, *far(c)tus*—*farcīre*, to cram, stuff.]

infatuate, *in-fat'ū-āt, v.t.* to turn to folly: to deprive of judgment: to inspire with foolish passion.—*adj.* **infat'uated.**—*n.* **infatuā'tion.** [L. *infatuāre, -ātum*—in, in, *fatuus*, foolish.]

infect, *in-fekt', v.t.* to taint with micro-organisms that cause disease: to impart disease to: (*lit.* and *fig.*) to corrupt: (*fig.*) to impart some quality to (e.g. *to infect with enthusiasm*).—*n.* **infection** (*in-fek'sh(ó)n*), act of infecting: that which infects or taints.—*adjs.* **infec'tious**, **infec'tive**, having the quality of infecting: corrupting: apt to spread.—*adv.* **infec'tiously.** —*n.* **infec'tiousness.** [L. *inficĕre*—in, into, *facĕre*, to make.]

infelicitous, *in-fe-lis'i-tus, adj.* not happy or fortunate: inappropriate, inapt.—*n.* **infelic'ity.** [L. *in-*, not, and **felicitous.**]

infer, *in-fûr', v.t.* to derive, as a consequence: to conclude: (popularly) to imply:—*pr.p.* **infer'ring**; *pa.p.* **inferred'.**—*adjs.* **in'fer(r)able** (also **-ible**), that may be inferred or deduced.—*n.* **in'ference**, that which is inferred or deduced, conclusion: the act of drawing a conclusion from premises. *adj.* **inferential** (*-en'sh(d)l*), deducible or deduced by inference.—*adv.* **inferen'tially.** [L. *inferre*—in, into, *ferre*, to bring.]

inferior, *in-fē'ri-or, adj.* lower in any respect: subordinate: poor or poorer in quality.—*n.* one lower in rank or station.—*n.* **inferior'ity**, **inferior'ity com'plex** (*psych.*), a mental state involving a suppressed sense of personal inferiority: popularly, a sense of inferiority. [L. *inferior*, comp. of *inferus*, low.]

infernal, *in-fûr'nal, adj.* belonging to the lower regions: resembling or suitable to hell, devilish: (*coll.*) detestable or highly annoying.—*adv.* **infer'nally.**—**infernal machine**, a contrivance made to resemble some ordinary harmless object, but charged with a dangerous explosive. [L. *infernus*—*inferus*, low.]

inferno, *in-fûr'nō, n.* hell: the pit in which the damned suffer, as described in the *Divina Commedia* of Dante (1265-1321): any place literally or figuratively comparable with hell: a conflagration. [It.]

infertile, *in-fûr'til, -tīl, adj.* not productive: barren.—*n.* **infertility** (*til'-*). [Low L. *infertīlis*; cf. **fertile.**]

infest, *in-fest', v.t.* to harass: to swarm in or

about. [L. *infestāre*, from *infestus*, hostile.]

infidel, *in'fi-del, adj.* disbelieving Christianity or whatever may be the religion of the user of the word: unbelieving, sceptical.—*n.* one who rejects Christianity, &c.: loosely, one who disbelieves any theory, &c.—*n.* **infidel'ity**, want of faith or belief: disbelief in Christianity, &c.: unfaithfulness, esp. of husband to wife or wife to husband. [O.Fr. *infidèle*—L. *infidēlis*—in-, not, *fidēlis*, faithful—*fidēs*, faith.]

infield, *in'fēld, n.* land under crop, esp. near the farm buildings: (*cricket*) the field near the wicket, or the fielders there. [**in**, and **field.**]

infiltrate, *in'fil-trāt, v.t.* to cause to percolate (with *into, through*): to permeate.—*v.i.* to sift or filter in.—*v.t., v.i.* of troops, agents, to enter (hostile area) secretly and for subversive purposes.—*ns.* **infiltrā'tion**, the process of infiltrating: gradual permeation or interpenetration: a deposit or substance infiltrated; **in'filtrator**, one who gets himself accepted as a member of a group towards which he has hostile or subversive intentions. [L. *in*, into, and **filtrate.**]

infinite, *in'fin-it, adj.* without end or limit: (*math.*) greater than any quantity that can be assigned: extending to infinity: *n.* that which is infinite: (*cap.*) the Infinite Being or God.—*adv.* **in'finitely.** *ns.* **infin'itūde**, **infin'lty**, immensity: a countless number: an infinite quantity.—*adj.* **infinites'imal**, infinitely small: (*loosely*) extremely small.—*n.* an infinitely small quantity.—*adv.* **infinites'imally.**—**infinite set** (*math.*), one that can be put into a one-to-one correspondence with part of itself. [L. *infīnītus*; cf. **finite.**]

infinitive, *in-fin'it-iv, adj.* (*gram.*) in the mood that expresses the idea without person or number.—*n.* a verb in the infinitive mood. [L. *infīnītīvus*—in-, not, *fīnīre*, to limit.]

infirm, *in-tûrm', adj.* feeble, sickly: weak (in purpose or character).—*ns.* **infirm'ity**; **infirmary** (*in-fûrm'ār-i*), a hospital or place for the treatment of the sick. [L. *infirmus*—in-, not, *firmus*, strong.]

infix, *in-fiks', v.t.* to fix in: to set in by piercing: to inculcate. [L. *infixus*—in, in, *fīgĕre*, *fixum*, to fix.]

inflame, *in-flām', v.t.* to cause to flame or burn: to make hot, red, or inflamed: to arouse passions in, to excite: to exacerbate.—*v.i.* to become hot, painful, red, or excited. [O.Fr. *enflammer*—L. *inflammāre*—in, into, *flamma*, a flame.]

inflammable, *in-flam'ä-bl, adj.* easily set on fire: easily angered, or very emotional.—*ns.* **inflammabil'ity**, **inflamm'ableness.**—*adv.* **inflamm'ably.**—*n.* **inflammā'tion**, state of being in flame: morbid heat of a part of the body, with pain, redness, and swelling: kindling of the passions.—*adj.* **inflamm'atory**, tending to inflame, esp. the passions, irritating, exciting: accompanied by inflammation. [L. *inflammāre*—in, into, *flamma*, a flame.]

inflate, *in-flāt', v.t.* to swell with air or gas: (*fig.*) to puff up (e.g. with pride): to increase artifically or unduly (e.g. prices, the amount of money in circulation, a reputation).—*adj.* **inflat'ed**, swollen or blown out: (*lit.* and *fig.*) turgid.—*adv.* **inflat'ingly.**—*n.* **inflation** (*in-*

flā'sh(ŏ)n), the condition of being inflated: sudden and undue increase in currency in proportion to buying power.—*adj.* **infla'tionary**, pertaining to inflation: tending to produce inflation.—*ns.* **inflat'or**, a pump for a tyre or bladder: **inflā'tus** (L.), inspiration. [L. *inflāre, -ātum—in*, into, *flāre*, to blow.]

inflect, *in-flekt'*, *v.t.* to bend.in: to turn from a direct line or course: to modulate, as the voice: (*gram.*) to vary in the terminations.—*ns.* **inflex'ion, inflec'tion**, a bending or deviation: modulation of the voice: (*gram.*) the varying in termination to express the relations of case, number, gender, person, tense, &c.—*adjs.* **inflex'ional, inflec'tional; inflec'tive**, subject to inflection.—*n.* **inflexure** (*in-flek'shŭr*), an inward bend or fold. [L. *inflectĕre—in*, in, *flectĕre, flexum*, to bend, *flexiō, -ōnis*, a bend.]

inflexible, *in-flek'si-bl*, *adj.* that cannot be bent: (*fig.*) unyielding, unbending.—*ns.* **inflexibil'ity, inflex'ibleness.**—*adv.* **inflex'ibly.** [L. *in-*, not, and **flexible**.]

inflict, *in-flikt'*, *v.t.* to give (e.g. a wound): to impose (as punishment, pain).—*n.* **inflic'tion**, act of inflicting or imposing: that which is inflicted.—*adj.* **inflictive**, tending or able to inflict. [L. *inflīgĕre, inflictum—in*, against, *flīgĕre*, to strike.]

inflorescence, *in-flor-es'ens*, *n.* mode of branching of a flower-bearing axis: aggregate of flowers on an axis. [L. *inflōrēscĕre*, to begin to blossom.]

influence, *in'flŏŏ-ens*, *n.* (*astrol.*) the power or virtue supposed to flow from planets upon men and things: power of producing an effect, esp. unobtrusively: a person or thing exercising such power: ascendancy, often of a secret or undue kind: exertions of friends in important positions.—*v.t.* to have or exert influence upon, to affect.—*adj.* **influential** (*-en'shàl*), having much influence: effectively active (in).—*adv.* **influen'tially.** [O.Fr.,—Low L. *influentia*—L. *in*, into, *fluĕre*, to flow.]

influenza, *in-flŏŏ-en'za*, *n.* a severe epidemic virus disease attacking esp. the upper respiratory tract. [It. Allied to **influence**.]

influx, *in'fluks*, *n.* a flowing in: a coming in to a place in considerable numbers or quantity (e.g. of people, commodities). [L. *influxus—influĕre*.]

infold. See **enfold.**

inform, *in-förm'*, *v.t.* (*obs.*) to give form to: to animate or give life to: to impart (a quality) to (with *with*): to impart knowledge to: to tell.—*v.i.* to carry tales to persons in authority (often with *against a person*).—*ns.* **inform'ant**, one who informs or gives intelligence; **informā'tion**, intelligence given: knowledge: an accusation given to a magistrate or court.—*adjs.* **inform'ative**, having power to form: instructive; **inform'atory**, instructive.—*n.* **inform'er**, one who gives information: one who informs against another. [O.Fr. *enformer*—L. *informāre—in*, into, *formāre*, to form, *forma*, form.]

informal, *in-förm'àl*, *adj.* not in proper form, irregular: unceremonious.—*n.* **informál'ity.**—*adv.* **inform'ally.** [L. *in-*, not, *forma*, form; *in-formis*, formless, misshapen.]

infraction, *in-frak'sh(ŏ)n*, *n.* violation, esp. of

law: breach. [L.,—*in*, in, *frangĕre, fractum*, to break.]

infra dig, *in'frä dig*, coll. abbrev. form of **infra dignitatem**, (*dig-ni-tä'tém, -tä'tém*), below one's dignity. [L.]

infrangible, *in-fran'ji-bl*, *adj.* that cannot be broken: not to be violated.—*ns.* **infrangibil'ity, infran'gibleness.** [L. *in-*, not, *frangĕre*, to break.]

infra-red, *in'fra-red'*, *adj.* beyond the red end of the visible spectrum.—**infra-red rays**, invisible radiations of wavelength greater than visible light, heat rays that may be detected by thermal effect. [L. *infra*, below, **red**.]

infrastructure, *in'frä-struk-tyŭr*, or *-chŭr*, *n.* inner structure, structure of component parts: a system of communications and services as backing for military operations. [L. *infra*, below, and **structure**.]

infrequent, *in-frē'kwènt*, *adj.* seldom occurring.—*n.* **infrē'quency.**—*adv.* **infrē'quently.** [L. *infrĕquens, -entis*; cf. **frequent**.]

infringe, *in-frinj'*, *v.t.* to violate, esp. law: to trespass on (a right or privilege): to neglect to fulfil.—*n.* **infringe'ment.** [L. *infringĕre—in*, in, *frangĕre*, to break.]

infuriate, *in-fū'ri-āt*, *v.t.* to enrage: to madden. [L. *in*, in, *furiāre, -ātum*, to madden—*furĕre*, to rave.]

infuse, *in-fūz'*, *v.t.* to pour (something—into): to instil: to animate (with): to extract properties by steeping.—*n.* **infusion** (*in-fū'zh(ŏ)n*), pouring in: the pouring of water over any substance, in order to extract its active qualities: a solution in water of an organic, esp. a vegetable, substance: admixture: instilling. [L. *infundĕre, infūsum—in*, into, *fundĕre, fūsum*, to pour.]

infusible, *in-fūz'i-bl*, *adj.* that cannot be dissolved or melted. [L. *in-*, not, and **fusible**.]

infusoria, *in-fū-zō'ri-a, -sō'-*, *n.pl.* (*orig.*) minute organisms found in stagnant infusions of animal or vegetable material: a lowly class of animal life with cilia.—*adjs.* **infūsō'rial, infū'sory**, composed of or containing infusoria. [Neut. pl. of modern L. *infūsōrius—infundĕre*. See **infuse.**]

ingathering, *in'gaτṛ-ér-ing*, *n.* collection: harvest. [**in**, and **gathering**.]

ingenious, *in-jē'ni-ús*, *adj.* skilful in invention: skilfully contrived.—*adv.* **ingē'niously.**—*n.* **ingē'niousness**, power of ready invention: facility in combining ideas: curiousness in design. [L. *ingenium*, natural ability, skill—root, of *gignĕre*, to beget, produce.]

ingenuity, *in-jen-ū'i-ti*, *n.* (*orig.*) ingenuousness: (by confusion with foregoing) ingeniousness. [L. *ingenuitās, -ātis—ingenuus*; see next word.]

ingenuous, *in-jen'ū-us*, *adj.* frank, artless; free from deception: (*arch.*) honourable or of honourable birth.—*adv.* **ingen'uously.**—*ns.* **ingen'uousness** (see previous word); **ingénue** (*ē-zhā-nü*), a naïve young woman. [L. *ingenuus*, free-born, ingenuous.]

ingle, *ing'gl*, *n.* (*Scot.*) a fire, a fireplace.—*n.* **ing'le-nook**, a fireside corner. [Possibly Gael. *aingeal*; or L. *igniculus*, dim. of *ignis*, fire.]

inglorious, *in-glō'ri-us, -glö'-*, *adj.* not glorious, unhonoured, shameful.—*adv.* **inglō'riously.**—

Neutral vowels in unaccented syllables: *em'pĕr-òr*; for certain sounds in foreign words see p. ix.

n. **inglō′riousness.** [L. *in-*, not, and *glōriōsus* —*gloria*, glory.]

ingot, *ing′got, n.* a mass of unwrought metal, esp. gold or silver, cast in a mould. [Perh. O.E. *in*, in, and the root *got*, as in *goten,* pa.p. of *gēotan,* to pour; Ger. *giessen.*]

ingraft. Same as **engraft.**

ingrain, *in-grān′, v.t.* the same as **engrain.**—*adj.* (before noun, *in-grān′*) dyed in the yarn or thread before manufacture: (*fig.*) deeply fixed, through and through.—*n.padj.* **ingrained′** (before noun, *in′-*). [**in, grain.**]

ingrate, *in-grāt′, in′grāt, n.* one who is ungrateful. [L. *ingrātus*—*in-*, not, *grātus*, pleasing, grateful.]

ingratiate, *in-grā′shi-āt, v.t.* to commend to grace or favour (used reflexively, and followed by *with*). [L. *in*, into, *grātia*, favour.]

ingratitude, *in-grat′i-tūd, n.* unthankfulness. [Low L. *ingrātitūdō*—L. *ingrātus*, unthankful.]

ingredient, *in-grē′di-ėnt, n.* that which enters into a mixture, a component. [L. *ingrediens, -entis,* pr.p. of *ingredī*—*in*, into,*gradī*, to walk.]

ingress, *in′gres, n.* entrance: power, right, or means of entrance. [L.*ingressus*—*ingredī*—*in*, into, *gradī*, to walk.]

ingrowing, *in′grō-ing, adj.* growing inward: growing into the flesh. [**in, growing.**]

inguinal, *ing′gwin-ål, adj.* relating to the groin. [L. *inguinālis*—*inguen, inguinis*, the groin.]

ingulf. See **engulf.**

ingurgitate, *in-gûr′ji-tāt, v.t.* (*lit.* and *fig.*) to swallow up greedily, as in a whirlpool. [L. *ingurgitāre, -ātum*—*in*, into, *gurges, -itis*, a whirlpool.]

inhabit, *in-hab′it, v.t.* to dwell in: to occupy.—*adj.* **inhab′itable,** that may be inhabited.—*ns.* **inhab′itant,** one who inhabits: a resident; **inhabitā′tion,** the act of inhabiting: dwellingplace; **inhab′iter** (*B.*), an inhabitant.[L.*inhabitāre*—*in*, in, *habitāre*, to dwell.]

inhale, *in-hāl′, v.t.* and *v.i.* to breathe in.—*ns.* **inhā′lant,** a drug to be inhaled; **inhalation** (*in-hä-lā′sh(ȯ)n*), the act of drawing into the lungs: something to be inhaled. [L. *in*, in *hālāre*, to breathe.]

inharmonious, *in-här-mō′ni-us, adj.* discordant, unmusical: inartistic: characterised by dissension.—*adv.* **inharmō′niously.**—*n.* **inharmō′niousness.** [L. *in-*, not, and **harmonious.**]

inhere, *in-hēr′, v.i.* (*rare*) to stick, remain firm (in): to belong to (with *in*) as a right: to be a permanent quality of.—*adj.* **inher′ent,** sticking fast: existing in and inseparable from something else, inher′ence, inher′ency. —*adv.* **inher′ently.** [L. *inhaerēre, inhaesum in*, in, *haerēre*, to stick.]

inherit, *in-her′it, v.t.* to get as heir: to possess by transmission from past generations.—Also *v.i.*—*adj.* **inher′itable,** same as **heritable.**—*n.* **inher′itance,** that which is or may be inherited: act or fact of inheriting; **inher′itor,** one who inherits or may inherit: an heir:—*fem.* **inher′itress, inher′itrix.** [O.Fr. *enhériter*, to put in possession as heir—Low L. *inhērēditāre*, to inherit—L. *in*, in, *hērēs, hērēdis*, an heir.]

inhesion, *in-hē′zh(ȯ)n, n.* Same as **inherence.**

inhibit, *in-hib′it, v.t.* to hold in or back, to check: to forbid.—*n.* **inhibi′tion,** the act of inhibiting

or restraining: the state of being inhibited: prohibition: a writ from a higher court to an inferior judge to stay proceedings: a restraining action of the unconscious will: stoppage, complete or partial, of a physical process by some nervous influence.—*p.adj.* **inhib′ited,** suffering from inhibitions or unnatural restraints imposed by the unconscious will.—*n.* **inhib′itor,** that which inhibits: a substance that interferes with a chemical or biological process.—*adj.* **inhib′itory,** prohibitory: restraining, hindering. [L. *inhibēre, -hibitum*—*in*, in, *habēre*, to have.]

inhospitable, *in-hos′pit-ä-bl, adj.* unwilling to show hospitality: (of a region) barren.—*ns.* **inhos′pitableness, inhospital′ity.**—*n.* **inhos′pitably.** [O.Fr.,—Low L. *inhospitābilis*; cf. **hospitable.**]

inhuman, *in-hū′mán, adj.* barbarous, cruel, unfeeling.—*n.* **inhumanity** (*in-hū-man′i-ti*), the state of being inhuman: barbarity, cruelty.—*adv.* **inhū′manly.** [L. *inhūmānus*; cf. **human.**]

inhumane, *in-hū-mān′, adj.* not humane, cruel. [L. *in-*, not, and **humane.**]

inhume, *in-hūm′, v.t.* to inter.—*n.* **inhumā′tion,** burial. [L. *inhumāre*—*in*, in, *humus*, the ground.]

inimical, *in-im′i-kål, adj.* unfriendly, hostile: unfavourable (to): opposed (to).—*adv.* **inim′ically.** [L. *inimīcālis*—*inimīcus*, enemy—*in-*, not, *amīcus*, friend.]

inimitable, *in-im′it-ä-bl, adj.* that cannot be imitated: surpassingly excellent.—*adv.* **inim′itably.** [L. *inimītābilis*; cf. **imitable.**]

iniquity, *in-ik′wi-ti, n.* want of equity or fairness: injustice: wickedness: a sin.—*adj.* **iniq′uitous,** unjust: scandalously unreasonable: wicked.—*adv.* **iniq′uitously.** [Fr.,—L. *iniquitās, -ātis*—*inīquus,* unequal—*in-*, not, *aequus*, equal.]

initial, *in-ish′ál, adj.* commencing: of, at, or serving as, the beginning.—*n.* the letter beginning a word, esp. a name.—*v.t.* to put the initials of one's name to:—*pr.p.* ini′tialling; *pa.p.* ini′tialled.—*adv.* **ini′tially.**—*v.t.* **ini′tiate,** to start, originate: to introduce (e.g. to knowledge): to admit, esp. with rites (as to a secret society, mystery).—*v.i.* to perform the first act or rite.—*n.* one who is initiated.—*adj.* begun: initiated.—*n.* **initiā′tion,** act or process of initiating: act of admitting to a society.—*adj.* **ini′tiative,** serving to initiate: introductory.—*n.* the lead, first step, considered as determining the conditions for others: right or power of beginning.—*adj.* **ini′tiatory,** introductory.—*n.* introductory rite.—**Initial Teaching Alphabet,** teaching alphabet of 44 characters. [L.*initium,* beginning.]

inject, *in-jekt′, v.t.* to force in: to inspire or instil.—*n.* **injec′tion,** act of injecting or forcing in, esp. a liquid: the process of spraying oilfuel into the cylinder of a compression-ignition engine by means of an injection pump: a liquid injected into the body: (*space*) see **insertion.** [L. *injicēre, injectum*—*in*, into, *jacēre*, to throw.]

injudicious, *in-jōō-dish′us, adj.* wanting in judgment: ill-judged.—*adj.* **injudic′ial,** not according to law forms.—*adv.* **injudic′iously.**—*n.* **injudic′iousness.** [L. *in-*, not, and **judicious.**]

injunction, *in-jung(k)'sh(ò)n*, *n.* act of enjoining or commanding: an order, command: an inhibitory writ by which a superior court stops or prevents some inequitable or illegal act being done. [Low L. *injunctiō, -ōnis—in*, in, *jungēre, junctum*, to join.]

injure, *in'júr*, *v.t.* to wrong: to harm, damage, hurt.—*adj.* **injurious** (*in-jōō'ri-us*), tending to injure, hurtful: damaging to reputation.—*adv.* **inju'riously.**—*ns.* **inju'riousness**; **injury** (*in'jùr-i*), that which injures: wrong: damage.—**injury time**, in ball games, extra time allowed for play to compensate for time lost due to injury during the game. [L. *injūria*, injury—*in*-, not, *jūs, jūris*, law.]

injustice, *in-jus'tis*, *n.* violation of, or withholding of, another's rights or dues: a wrong: an unjust act. [Fr.—L. *injūstitia—in-*, not. See **justice**.]

ink, *ingk*, *n.* black or coloured liquid, or sticky material, used in writing, printing, &c.: dark liquid ejected by cuttlefishes, &c.—*v.t.* to daub or cover with ink.—*adj.* **ink'y**, consisting of or resembling ink: blackened with ink.—*n.* **ink'iness.**—*ns.* **ink'bottle**; **ink'pot**; **ink'stand**, a stand or tray for ink-bottles and (usually) pens; **ink'well**, a reservoir for ink let into a desk.—**China ink**, **Indian ink**, a mixture of lampblack and size or glue, kept in solid form and rubbed down in water for use. [O.Fr. *enque* (Fr. *encre*)—Low L. *encaustum*, purple-red ink used by later Roman emperors.]

inkling, *ingk'ling*, *n.* a hint or intimation: a suspicion (with *of*). [M.E. *inclen*, to hint.]

in-kneed, *in'-nēd*, *adj.* bent inward at the knees: knock-kneed. [Adv. **in**, and **knee**.]

inlaid, *in-lād'*, or *in'-*, *adj.* inserted by inlaying: having a pattern set into the surface. [Pa.p. of **inlay**.]

inland, *in'land*, *in'lànd*, *n.* the interior part of a country.—*adj.* remote from the sea: carried on or produced within a country.—*adv.* in, to the interior.—*n.* **in'lander**, one who lives inland.—**inland navigation**, passage of boats or vessels on rivers, lakes, or· canals within a country; **inland revenue**, internal revenue, derived from excise, stamps, income-tax, &c. [O.E. *inland*, a domain—**in**, and **land**.]

in-law, *in-lö'*, *n.* (*coll.*) a relative by marriage:—*pl.* **in-laws'.**

inlay, *in-lā'*, *v.t.* to insert: to ornament by inserting pieces of metal, ivory, &c.:—*pa.p.* inlaid.—*n.* (*in'-*) inlaying: inlaid work: material inlaid.—*ns.* **inlayer** (*in'lā-ér*, *in-lā'ér*); **inlay'ing.** [Adv. **in**, and **lay** (2).]

inlet, *in'let*, *n.* an entrance: a small bay: a piece inserted. [Adv. **in**, and **let** (1).]

in loco parentis, *in lō'kō pá-ren'tis*, in place of a parent. [L.]

inly, *in'li*, *adv.* inwardly: in the heart: thoroughly, entirely. [O.E. *inlīc—in*, and *līc*, like.]

inmate, *in'māt*, *n.* one of those who live in a house, esp. an institution. [**in** or **inn, mate**.]

inmost. See **innermost**.

inn, *in*, *n.* a house open to the public for the lodging and entertainment of travellers—commonly used for a hotel of a smaller type.—*n.* **inn'keeper**, one who keeps an inn.—**Inns of Court**, the four voluntary societies that have the exclusive right of calling persons to the English bar. [O.E. *inn*, an inn, house—*in*, **inn**, within (adv.), from the prep. *in*, **in**.]

innards, *in'árdz*, *n. pl.* (*coll.*) entrails: internal parts of a mechanism: interior. [**inwards**.]

innate, *in-āt'*, or *in'āt*, *adj.* inborn: inherent.—*adv.* **inn'ately** (or *-nāt'-*).—*n.* **inn'ateness** (or *-nāt'-*). [L. *innātus—in*, in, *nāscī, nātus*, to be born.]

inner, *in'ér*, *adj.* (*comp.* of *in*) farther in: interior.—*n.* (a hit on) that part of a target next the bull's eye.—*adjs.* **inn'ermost**, **in'most** (*superl.* of *in*), farthest in: most remote from outside.—**inner space**, the undersea region regarded as an environment. [O.E. *in*, comp. *innera*, superl. *innemest = inne-m-est*—thus a double superlative.]

inning, *in'ing*, *n.* ingathering, esp. of crops: (*pl.* for *sing.*) a team's turn for batting in cricket: hence, a spell or turn of possession or power: (*pl.*) lands recovered from the sea. [**in** or **inn.**]

innocent, *in'o-sènt*, *adj.* not hurtful: harmless: inoffensive: blameless: guileless: ignorant of evil: simple, imbecile: not guilty: (*coll.*) lacking, without (*innocent of*).—*n.* one free from fault: an idiot.—*ns.* **inn'ocence**, harmlessness: blamelessness: guilelessness: ignorance of evil: simplicity: freedom from legal guilt; **inn'ocency**, the quality of being innocent.—*adv.* **inn'ocently.**—**Innocents' Day** (see **Childermas**). [O.Fr.,—L. *innocens, -entis—in-*, not, *nocēre*, to hurt.]

innocuous, *in-ok'ū-us*, *adj.* harmless.—*adv.* **innoc'uously.**—*n.* **innoc'uousness**. [L. *innocuus—in-*, not, *nocuus*, hurtful—*nocēre*, to hurt.]

innominate, *i-nom'i-nāt*, *adj.* having no name.—**innominate artery**, the first large branch given off from the arch of the aorta (q.v.); **innominate bone**, the haunch-bone, hip-bone. [L. *in-*, not, *nōmināre, -ātum*, to name.]

innovate, *in'o-vāt*, *v.i.* to introduce novelties: to make changes.—*ns.* **innova'tion**, act of innovating: a thing introduced as a novelty; **inn'ovātor**. [L. *innovāre, -ātum,—in*, in, *novus*, new.]

innoxious, *in-(n)ok'shùs*, *adj.* not harmful.—*adv.* **innox'iously.**—*n.* **innox'iousness**. [L. *in-*, not, and **noxious**.]

innuendo, *in-ū-en'dō*, *n.* insinuation: an indirect reference or intimation:—*pl.* **innuen'do(e)s**. [L. *innuendō*, by nodding at, ablative gerund of *innuēre*, to nod to, indicate—*in*, to, *nuēre*, to nod.]

innumerable, *in-(n)ū'mér-á-bl*, *adj.* that cannot be numbered: countless.—*ns.* **innūmerabil'ity**, **innū'merableness.**—*adv.* **innū'merably**. [L. *in-numerābilis*—L. *in-*, not, *numerābilis*, that can be counted.]

innumerate, *in-nūm'ér-át*, *adj.* having no understanding of mathematics or science.—Also *n.*—*n.* **innum'eracy**. [Coined 1959, by Sir Geoffrey Crowther (on analogy of *illiterate*)—L. *numerus*, number.]

innutrition, *in-(n)ū-trish'ón*, *n.* want of nutrition: failure of nourishment.—*adj.* **innutrit'ious**, not nutritious. [L. *in-*, not, and **nutrition**.]

inobservant, *in-ob-zér'vànt*, *adj.* unobservant:

Neutral vowels in unaccented syllables: *em'pér-ór*; for certain sounds in foreign words see p. ix.

372

heedless.—*n.* **inobser'vance**. [L.L. *inobservans* (L. *inobservantia*, carelessness)—*in-*, not, *observans*—*observāre*. See **observe**.]

inoculate, *in-ok'ū-lāt*, *v.t.* to insert as a bud or graft: to graft: to imbue: to introduce (e.g. a disease) into the body: to make an inoculation upon, esp. for the purpose of safeguarding against subsequent infection.—*adj.* **inoc'ulable**.—*n.* **inocula'tion**, act or practice of inoculating: insertion of the buds of one plant into another: the introduction into an experimental animal of infected material or of pathogenic bacteria: the injection of a vaccine into a person for protection against subsequent infection with the organisms contained in the vaccine. [L. *inoculāre*, *-ātum—in*, into, *oculus*, an eye, a bud.]

inodorous, *in-ō'dòr-us*, *adj.* without smell. [L. *in-*, not, and **odorous**. See **odour**.]

inoffensive, *in-o-fen'siv*, *adj.* giving no offence: harmless.—*adv.* **inoffen'sively**.—*n.* **inoffen'siveness**. [L. *in-*, not, and **offensive**.]

inoperable, *in-op'ér-à-bl*, *adj.* that cannot be operated on successfully, or without undue risk. [L. *in-*, not, **operate**, suffx. *-able*.]

inoperative, *in-op'ér-à-tīv*, *adj.* not in action: producing no effect.[L. *in-*, not, and **operative**. See **operate**.]

inopportune, *in-op'òr-tūn*, *-tūn'*, *adj.* unseasonable, ill-timed.—*adv.* **inopp'ortunely** (or *-tūn'-*). [L. *inopportūnus—in-*, not, *oppor tūnus*, suitable.]

inordinate, *in-ör'di-nát*, *adj.* unrestrained: excessive, immoderate.—*n.* **inor'dinateness.**—*adv.* **inor'dinately**. [L. *inordinātus—in-*, not, *ordināre*, *-ātum*, to arrange, regulate.]

inorganic, *in-ör-gan'ik*, *adj.* not organic: not organised: not belonging to an organism: of accidental origin, not normally developed.—*adv.* **inorgan'ically.—inorganic chemistry**, the chemistry of all substances but carbon compounds (including, however, the oxides and the sulphide of carbon). [L. *in-*, not, and **organic**. See **organ**.]

inosculate, *in-os'kū-lāt*, *v.t.* and *v.i.* to unite by mouths or ducts, as two vessels in an animal body: to unite closely.—*n.* **inoscula'tion**. [L. *in*, in, and *ōsculāri*, *-atus*, to kiss.]

in-patient. See **in**.

input, *in'pŏŏt*, *n.* amount, material, or energy, that is put in: power, or energy, or coded information, stored or for storage: information available in a computer for dealing with a problem: process of feeding in data.—*adj.* relating to computer input.—*v.t.* to feed into a computer. [**in**, and **put**.]

inquest, *in'kwest*, *n.* (*rare*) enquiry (into): judicial inquiry before a jury into any matter, esp. any case of violent or sudden death (also *fig.*): the body of men appointed to hold such an inquiry: the decision reached. [O.Fr. *enqueste*—L.L. *inquesta*—L. *inquīsīta* (*rēs*)—*inquīrēre*, to inquire.]

inquietude, *in-kwī'et-ūd*, *n.* disturbance: uneasiness. [Fr. *inquiétude*—L.L. *inquietūdō*—L. *inquiētus*, restless—*in-*, not. See **quiet**.]

inquire, enquire, *in-*, *en-kwīr'*, *v.i.* to ask a question: to seek information: to make an investigation (into): to ask (for, after).—*v.t.* to ask for (a piece of information).—*n.* **inquir'er**,

enquir'er.—*adj.* **inquir'ing**, given to inquiry. —*adv.* **inquir'ingly**.—*n.* **inquir'y, enquir'y**, act of inquiring: search for knowledge: investigation: a question. In legal senses *inquire, inquiry* are usual. [Fr.,—L. *inquīrēre—in*, in, *quaerēre, quaesītum*, to seek.]

Inquisition, *in-kwi-zish'(ò)n*, *n.* searching examination: investigation: judicial inquiry: (*cap.*) a tribunal in the R.C. Church for examining and punishing heretics, &c.—*adjs.* **inquisit'ional**, searching or vexatious in making inquiry: relating to inquisition or the Inquisition; **inquis'itive**, eager to know: apt to ask questions, esp. about other people's affairs, curious.—*adv.* **inquis'itively**. —*ns.* **inquis'itiveness; inquis'itor**, one who inquires, esp. with undue pertinacity: an official inquirer: a member of the Court of Inquisition.—*adj.* **inquisitō'rial**.—*adv.* **inquisitō'rially**. [L. *inquīsītiō*, *-ōnis—inquīrēre*. See **inquire**.]

inroad, *in'rōd*, *n.* an incursion into an enemy's country, a raid: (*fig.*) encroachment. [**in**, and **road**; cf. **raid**.]

insalubrious, *in-sa-l(y)ōō'bri-us*, *adj.* unhealthy.—*n.* **insalū'brity**. [L. *insalūbris—in-*, not, and *salūbris*. See **salubrious**.]

insane, *in-sān'*, *adj.* not sane or of sound mind, mad: utterly unwise: for the insane.—*adv.* **insane'ly**.—*n.* **insanity** (*in-san'i-ti*), want of sanity: mental disorder, madness. [L. *in-*, not, and **sane**.]

insanitary, *in-san'i-tàr-i*, *adj.* not sanitary. [L. *in-*, not, and **sanitary**.]

insatiable, *in-sā'sh(y)à-bl*, *adj.* that cannot be satiated or satisfied.—*ns.* **insā'tiableness, insātiabil'ity**.—*adv.* **insā'tiably**.—*adj.* **insā'tiate**, not sated: insatiable.[Fr.,—L.*insatiābilis—in-*, not. See **satiate**.]

inscribe, *in-skrīb'*, *v.t.* to engrave or otherwise mark: to engrave or mark on: to enter in a book or roll: to dedicate: (*geom.*) to draw (one figure) within another.—*ns.* **inscrib'er; inscription** (*in-skrip'sh(ò)n*), the act of inscribing: that which is inscribed: dedication: a record inscribed on stone, metal, &c.—*adj.* **inscrip'tive**. [L. *inscrībēre, inscriptum—in*, upon, *scrībēre*, to write.]

inscrutable, *in-skrōōt'à-bl*, *adj.* that cannot be searched into and understood, inexplicable: enigmatic (e.g. of a person, a smile).—*ns.* **inscrutabil'ity, inscrut'ableness**.—*adv.* **inscrut'ably**. [L. *inscrūtābilis—in-*, not, *scrūtāri*, to search into.]

insect, *in'sekt*, *n.* a word loosely used for a small invertebrate creature, esp. one with a body as if cut into or divided into sections: (*zool.*) a member of the Insecta.—*adj.* like an insect: small: mean.—*n.pl.* **Insec'ta**, a subphylum of Arthropoda (q.v.) having the body sharply divided into head, thorax, and abdomen, and having three pairs of legs attached to the thorax.—*ns.* **insec'ticide**, killing of insects: an insect-killer; **insec'tion**, an incision: a notch: division into segments; **in'sect-pow'der**, a powder for stupefying and killing insects, an insecticide. [L. *insectum*, pa.p. of *insecāre—in*, into, *secāre*, to cut.]

Insectivora, *in-sek-tiv'òr-a*, *n.pl.* an order of mammals, mostly terrestrial, insect-eating,

fāte, fär; mē, hûr (her); *mīne; mōte, fòr; mūte; mōōn, fŏŏt;* THen (then) nocturnal in habit, and small in size (e.g. moles, hedgehogs).—*n.* **insect′ivore,** one of the Insectivora.—*adj.* **insectiv′orous,** living on insects. [Modern L. *insectum,* an insect, *vorāre,* to devour.]

insecure, *in-se-kūr′, adj.* apprehensive of danger or loss: uncertain: exposed to danger or loss: unsafe: in anxious state because not well-adjusted to life: not firm or firmly fixed.—*adv.* **insecure′ly.**—*n.* **insecur′ity.** [L. *in-,* not, and **secure.**]

inseminate, *in-sem′in-āt, v.t.* to sow: (*fig.*) to implant: to impregnate.—*n.* **inseminā′tion,** (*zool.*) the approach and entry of the spermatozoon to the ovum, followed by the fusion of male and female pronuclei. [L. *insēmināre—in,* in, *sēmen, -inis,* seed.]

insensate, *in-sen′sāt, adj.* callous: dull: unconscious, or good sense, or sensibility. [L. *insensātus—in-,* not, *sensātus,* intelligent—*sensus,* feeling.]

insensible, *in-sen′si-bl, adj.* callous: dull: unconscious: unaware (of—also with *to*): imperceptible by the senses.—*n.* **insensibil′ity.**—*adv.* **insen′sibly.** [L. *in-,* not, and **sensible.**]

insensitive, *in-sen′si-tiv, adj.* not sensitive. [L. *in-,* not, and **sensitive.**]

insentient, *in-sen′sh(y)ent, adj.* not having perception: inanimate. [L. *in-,* not, and **sentient.**]

inseparable, *in-sep′ar-a-bl, adj.* that cannot be separated: always associated with (with *from*).—*n.* an inseparable companion (usu. in *pl.*).—*ns.* **insep′arableness, inseparabil′ity.**—*adv.* **insep′arably.** [L. *in-,* not, and **separable.**]

insert, *in-sûrt′, v.t.* to put in.—*n.* (*in′sert*) something additional inserted: an extra leaf or leaves placed within a magazine, &c.—*n.* **inser′tion,** act of inserting: condition of being inserted: that which is inserted: the putting of man-made craft or satellite into orbit (also **injection**). [L. *inserĕre, insertum—in,* in, *serĕre,* to join.]

insessorial, *in-se-sō′ri-ál, adj.* of perching birds: adapted for perching. [L. *insessor,* pl. *-ōrēs,* besetters (of the roads), highwaymen, adopted with the meaning 'perchers'—*insidēre—in,* on, *sedēre,* to sit.]

inset, *in′set, n.* something set in, an insertion or insert, e.g. a small picture within a larger one: a leaf or leaves inserted between the folds of others.—*v.t.* (*in-set′*) to set in, to infix or implant. [**in,** and **set.**]

inshore, *in′shōr′, in-shōr′, adv.* near or towards the shore.—*adj.* (*in′shōr* or *in-shōr′*) situated near the shore, as fishings. [**in,** and **shore.**]

inshrine, *in-shrīn′.* Same as **enshrine.**

inside, *in-sīd′, in′sīd, n.* side, space, or part within: entrails: inner nature: passenger in the interior part of a vehicle.—*adj.* being within: interior: indoor: within, or coming from within, an organisation or an industrial plant (e.g. of a spy, information).—*adv.* in or to the interior: indoors: (*slang*) in or into prison.—*prep.* within.—*n.* **insï′der,** one who is inside: one possessing some particular advantage. [**in,** and **side.**]

insidious, *in-sid′i-us, adj.* watching an opportunity to ensnare: intended to entrap: advancing imperceptibly or secretly.—*adv.* **insid′iously.**—*n.* **insid′iousness.** [L. *insidiōsus—*

insidiae, an ambush—*insidēre—in,* in, *sedēre,* to sit.]

insight, *in′sīt, n.* power of seeing into and understanding things: awareness, often of one's own mental condition: an imaginative view (into any condition or experience). [**in,** and **sight.**]

insignia, *in-sig′ni-a, n.pl.* signs or badges of office or honour, authority, &c.: marks by which anything is known. [L., neut. pl. of *insignis,* remarkable, distinguished—*in-,* in, *signum,* a mark.]

insignificant, *in-sig-nif′i-kánt, adj.* destitute of meaning: unimportant: petty.—*ns.* **insignif′icance, insignif′icancy.**—*adv.* **insignif′icantly.** [L. *in-,* not, and **significant.**]

insincere, *in-sin-sēr′, adj.* deceitful: dissembling: not frank.—*adv.* **insincere′ly.**—*n.* **insincerity** (*-ser′i-ti*). [L. *insincērus—in-,* not. See **sincere.**]

insinuate, *in-sin′ū-āt, v.t.* to introduce gently or artfully: to hint, esp. a fault: to hint (that): to work (into favour), obtain access for (oneself, another) by flattery or stealth—esp. in *p.adj.* **insin′uating.**—*adv.* **insin′uatingly.**—*n.* **insinuā′tion,** the act or process of introducing gently or artfully, or of hinting a fault, or of working into favour: an instance of any of these, esp. an indirect hint.—*adj.* **insin′uative.**—*n.* **insin′uātor.** [L. *insinuāre, -ātum—in,* in, *sinus,* a curve.]

insipid, *in-sip′id, adj.* tasteless: without definite flavour: wanting spirit or interest, dull.—*adv.* **insip′idly.**—*ns.* **insip′idness, insipid′ity.** [L.L. *insipidus—*L. *in-,* not, *sapidus,* well-tasted—*sapĕre,* to taste.]

insist, *in-sist′, v.i.* to dwell (on) emphatically in discourse: to hold firmly to (an intention—with *on*): to persist in demanding (with *on*).—*adj.* **insist′ent,** urgent: persistent.—*n.* **insist′ence.** [L. *insistĕre—in,* upon, *sistĕre,* to stand.]

in situ, *in sī′tū, (geol.)* in its original place or position. [L. *in,* in, *sitū,* abl. of *situs,* position, site.]

insnare. Same as **ensnare.**

insobriety, *in-so-brī′e-ti, n.* want of sobriety. [L. *in-,* not, and **sobriety.** See **sober.**]

insolate, *in′so-lāt, v.t.* to expose to the sun's rays.—*n.* **insolā′tion,** exposure to the sun's rays: radiation received from the sun: injury caused by the sun. [L. *insōlāre, -ātum—in,* in, *sōl,* the sun.]

insolent, *in′sol-ént, adj.* overbearing, insulting: rude.—*n.* **in′solence.**—*adv.* **in′solently.** [L. *insolens, -entis—in-,* not, *solens,* pa.p. of *solēre,* to be wont.]

insoluble, *in-sol′ū-bl, adj.* not capable of being dissolved: not capable of being solved or explained.—*ns.* **insolubil′ity, insol′ubleness.** [L. *insolūbilis—in-,* not, and **soluble.**]

insolvent, *in-solv′ént, adj.* not able to pay one's debts: bankrupt: pertaining to insolvent persons.—*n.* one unable to pay his debts.—*n.* **insolv′ency.** [L. *in-,* not, and **solvent.** See **solve.**]

insomnia, *in-som′ni-a, n.* sleeplessness—*n.* **insom′niac,** (a person) suffering from insomnia.—*adj.* suffering from, causing, or caused by, insomnia. [L. *insomnis,* sleepless.]

insomuch, *in-sō-much′, adv.* to such a degree

Neutral vowels in unaccented syllables: *em′pér-ór*; for certain sounds in foreign words see p. ix.

(that, as): inasmuch (as). [**in**, **so**, **much**.]

insouciant, *in-sōō'si-ánt, ē-sōō-sē-ā̇*, *adj.* indifferent, unconcerned.—*n.* **insouciance** (*in-sōō'si-áns, ē-sōō-sē-äs*). [Fr.—*in-*, not, *souciant*, pr.p. of *soucier*—L. *sollicitāre*, to disturb.]

inspan, *in-span'*, *v.t.* to yoke to a vehicle. [Du. *inspannen*, to yoke—*in*, in, *spannen*, to tie.]

inspect, *in-spekt'*, *v.t.* to look into, to examine: to look at narrowly, officially, or ceremonially.—*ns.* **inspec'tion**, the act of inspecting or looking into: careful or official examination; **inspec'tor**, one who inspects: an examining officer: a police officer ranking below a superintendent; **inspec'torāte**, a district under charge of an inspector: the office of inspector: a body of inspectors.—*adj.* **inspecto'rial**.—*ns.* **inspec'torship**, the office of inspector; **inspec'tress**, a female inspector. [L. *inspectāre*, freq. of *inspicĕre, inspectum*—*in*, into, *specĕre*, to look.]

inspire, *in-spīr'*, *v.t.* to breathe or blow (into): to draw or inhale into the lungs: to infuse into (the mind) esp. with an encouraging or exalting influence: to instruct by divine influence: to instruct or affect with a particular emotion: to bring about, cause to occur: to animate (a person *with* feelings, thoughts).—*v.i.* to draw in the breath.—*adj.* **inspīr'able**, able to be inhaled.—*n.* **inspirā'tion** (*in-spir-, -spīr-*), the act of inspiring or breathing in: a breath: instruction or stimulation by a divinity: an inspired condition: an inspired thought.—*adjs.* **inspiratory** (*in-spīr'a-tór-i, in-spīr'a-tór-i*, or *in'spir*), belonging to or aiding inspiration or inhalation; **inspīred'**, breathed in: moved or directed by, or as if by, divine influence: secretly prompted by someone with superior knowledge or authority.—*n.* **inspīr'er**. [L. *in-spīrāre*—*in*, in, into, *spīrāre*, to breathe.]

inspirit, *in-spir'it*, *v.t.* to infuse spirit or energy into: to encourage. [**in**, and **spirit**.]

inspissate, *in-spis'āt*, or *in'-*, *v.t.* and *v.i.* to thicken, as by evaporation.—*n.* **inspissā'tion**. [L. *in*, in, *spissāre*—*spissus*, thick.]

instability, *in-sta-bil'i-ti*, *n.* want of steadiness. [Fr. *instabilité* L. *instabilitās*—*in-*, not. See **stable** (1).]

install, *in-stöl'*, *v.t.* to place in a seat: to place in an office or order: to invest with any charge or office with the customary ceremonies: to set up and put in use.—*ns.* **installā'tion**, the act of installing or placing in an office with ceremonies: a placing in position for use: apparatus placed in position for use: complete apparatus e.g. for electric lighting; **instal'ment**, (*arch.*) installation. [L.L. *in, stallum*, stall—O.H.G. *stal*.]

instalment, *in-stöl'mént*, *n.* one of series of partial payments: portion supplied at one time, e.g. of serial story. [A.F. *estaler*, to fix, set, probably influenced by **install**.]

instance, *in'stáns*, *n.* quality of being urgent: instigation, suggestion (*at the instance of*): occasion: example: (*law*) process, suit.—*v.t.* to mention as an example.—**in the first instance**, in the first place. [O.Fr.,—L. *instantia*—*instans* See **instant**.]

instant, *in'stánt*, *adj.* pressing, urgent: immediate: present, current, as the passing month: (of food, drink) pre-prepared so that little has

to be done to it before use.—*n.* the present moment of time: any moment or point of time.—*adj.* **instantān'eous**, done in an instant: occurring or acting at once or very quickly.—*advs.* **instantān'eously**; **instanter** (*in-stan'tér*; L.), immediately; **in'stantly**, on the instant or moment, immediately: (*B.*) importunately, zealously. [L. *instans, -antis*, pr.p. of *instāre*, to be near, press upon, urge—*in*, upon, *stāre*, to stand.]

instead, *in-sted'*, *adv.* in the stead, place, or room (of): as an alternative course, substitute person or thing, &c. [Prep. **in**, and **stead**.]

instep, *in'step*, *n.* the prominent upper part of the human foot near its junction with the leg: in horses, the hind-leg from the ham to the pastern joint. [Origin obscure.]

instigate, *in'sti-gāt*, *v.t.* to urge on, incite: to foment.—*ns.* **instigā'tion**, the act of inciting, esp. to evil; **in'stigātor**, an inciter, generally in a bad sense. [L. *instigāre, -ātum*.]

instil, *in-stil'*, *v.t.* to drop in: to infuse slowly (into the mind):—*pr.p.* instil'ling; *pa.p.* instilled'.—Also **instill'**.—*ns.* **instillā'tion**, **instil'ment**. [L. *instillāre*—*in*, in, *stillāre*, to drop.]

instinct, *in'stingkt*, *n.* the natural impulse apparently independent of reason or experience by which animals are guided: intuition: natural aptitude.—*adj.* (*in-stingkt'*) instigated or incited: imbued (with a quality).—*adj.* **instinc'tive**, prompted by instinct: involuntary.—*adv.* **instinc'tively**. [L. *instinctus*—*instinguĕre*, to instigate.]

institute, *in'sti-tūt*, *v.t.* to set up, establish: to set on foot (e.g. an enquiry): to appoint (a person).—*n.* established law, precept or principle: an institution: a literary and philosophical society or organisation for education, &c.: a foundation for further education: (*pl.*) a book of precepts, principles, or rules.—*n.* **institū'tion**, the act of instituting or establishing: that which is instituted or established: enactment: a society established for some object, esp. cultural or charitable: the building housing it: a custom or usage: a system of principles or rules.—*adjs.* **institū'tional**, pertaining to institution, institutions, or institutes: of the nature of an institution; **institū'tionary**, institutional.—*n.* **in'stitutor**. [L. *instituĕre, -ūtum*—*in*, in, *statuĕre*, to cause to stand—*stāre*, to stand.]

instruct, *in-strukt'*, *v.t.* to inform: to teach: to direct, to order or command: (of a judge) to give (a jury) guidance concerning the legal issues of a case.—*adj.* **instruct'ible**, able to be instructed.—*n.* **instruc'tion**, the act of instructing or teaching: information: direction, command.—*adjs.* **instruc'tional**, relating to instruction: educational; **instruc'tive**, affording instruction: conveying knowledge.—*adv.* **instruc'tively**.—*ns.* **instruc'tiveness**; **instruc'tor**:—*fem.* **instruc'tress**. [L. *instruĕre, instructum*—*in*, in, *struĕre*, to pile up.]

instrument, *in'strōō-mént*, *n.* a tool or utensil: a contrivance for producing musical sounds: a writing containing a contract: one who, or that which, is made a means or agency: a term generally employed to denote an indicating device but also other pieces of small electrical apparatus.—*v.t.* (*-ment'*) to score for instruments: to equip with indicating, measuring, or control, &c. apparatus—*adj.* for instruments: by means of instruments (as *instrument flight*).—*adj.* **instrumental** (*-mént'ál*), acting as an instrument or means, serving to promote an object (e.g. *he was instrumental in securing this*): performed by, or for performance by, musical instruments: due to the instrument (e.g. *an instrumental error*): (*gram.*) of the case of the means or agent (a separate case in Sanskrit, Gr. dative, L. ablative; see **the** (2)).—*ns.* **instrument'alist**, one who plays on a musical instrument; **instrumentality** (*-mént-al'i-ti*), agency.—*adv.* **instrument'ally**. —*n.* **instrumentā'tion**, use or provision of instruments: (*mus.*) the arrangement of a composition for performance by different instruments.—*adj.* **instrumen'ted**, equipped with instruments. [L. *instrūmentum*—*instruĕre*, to instruct.]

insubordinate, *in-sub-ör'din-át, adj.* not subordinate or submissive, rebellious.—*n.* **insubordinā'tion**. [L. *in-*, not, and **subordinate**.]

insufferable, *in-suf'ér-á-bl, adj.* that cannot be endured: detestable.—*adv.* **insuff'erably**. [L. *in-*, not, and **sufferable**.]

insufficient, *in-suf-ish'ént, adj.* not enough: not of sufficient power or ability: inadequate.—*n.* **insuffic'iency**.—*adv.* **insuffic'iently**. [O.Fr., —L.L. *insufficiens*—*in-*, not, *sufficĕre*. See **suffice**.]

insular, *in'sū-lár, adj.* belonging to an island: surrounded by water: narrow, prejudiced.—*n.* **insularity** (*-ar'i-ti*), the state of being insular.—*adv.* **in'sularly**.—*v.t.* **in'sulate**, to place in a detached situation: to cut off from connection or communication: (*electricity*) to separate by a non-conductor.—*ns.* **insulā'tion**; **in'sulator**, one who, or that which, insulates: a non-conductor of electricity; **in'sulin**, an extract got from the islands or islets in the pancreas of animals, used for treating diabetes, &c. [L. *insulāris*—*insula*, an island.]

insult, *in-sult', v.t.* to treat with indignity or contempt, to affront.—*n.* (*in'sult*) affront, contumely.—*adj.* **insult'ing**.—*adv.* **insult'ingly**. [L. *insultāre*—*insilīre*, to spring at—*in*, upon, *salīre*, to leap.]

insuperable, *in-sū'pér-á-bl, adj.* that cannot be overcome or surmounted.—*n.* **insuperabil'ity**. —*adv.* **insu'perably**. [L. *insuperābilis*—*in-*, not, *superābilis*—*superāre*, to pass over—*super*, above.]

insupportable, *in-sup-ört'á-bl, -ört', adj.* unbearable, insufferable: that cannot be justified—*n.* **insupport'ableness**.—*adv.* **insupport'ably**. [Fr. —L.L. *insupportābilis*—*in-*, not. See **support**.]

insure, *in-shōōr', v.t.* to make an arrangement for the payment of a sum of money in the event of loss of or injury to: (better **ensure**) to make sure (e.g. *success*).—*v.i.* to effect or undertake insurance: to secure (against).— *adj.* **insur'able**, that may be insured.—*ns.* **insur'ance**, the act or system of insuring: a contract of insurance, a policy: the premium paid for insuring: the sum to be received; **insur'er**, either party to a contract of insurance (now, strictly the insurance company). [O.Fr. *enseurer*—*en*, and *seur*, sure. See **sure**.]

insurgent, *in-sûr'jént, adj.* rising: rising in revolt.—*n.* one who rises in opposition to estab-

lished authority, a rebel.—*ns.* **insur'gence**, **insur'gency**, insurrection, rebellion. [L. *insurgens, -entis*—*in*, upon, *surgĕre*, to rise.]

insurmountable, *in-sûr-mownt'á-bl, adj.* not surmountable: that cannot be overcome.—*adv.* **insurmount'ably**. [L. *in-*, not, and **surmountable**.]

insurrection, *in-sur-ek'sh(ó)n, n.* a rising or revolt.—*adjs.* **insurrec'tional**, **insurrec'tionary**.—*n.* **insurrec'tionist**. [L. *insurrectiō, -ōnis*—*insurgĕre*. See **insurgent**.]

insusceptible, *in-sus-ep'ti-bl, adj.* not susceptible.—*n.* **insusceptibil'ity**. [L. *in-*, not, and **susceptible**.]

intact, *in-takt', adj.* untouched: unimpaired: undiminished: whole. [L. *intactus*—*in-*, not, *tangĕre*, *tactum*, to touch.]

intaglio, *in-täl'yō, n.* a figure cut into any substance: a stone or gem in which the design is hollowed out—opp. to *cameo*: a printing process in which the ink-carrying areas of the printing surface are hollows below the surface, not designs in relief.—*adj.* **intagl'iated** (*-tal'yāt-id*), incised, engraved. [It.,—*in*, into, *tagliare*, to cut—L. *tālea*, a cutting, layer.]

intake, *in'tāk, n.* that which is taken in: place where e.g. water is taken in: an airway in a mine: the decrease in width in a stocking-leg by knitting two stitches together: a piece of reclaimed land: a body of people taken into an organisation, as new recruits, or new pupils at a school: the point at which fuel mixture enters the cylinder of an internal-combustion engine. [Adv. **in**, and **take**.]

intangible, *in-tan'ji-bl, adj.* not tangible or perceptible to touch: eluding the grasp of the mind.—*n.* something intangible.—*ns.* **intan'gibleness**, **intangibil'ity**.—*adv.* **intan'gibly**. [Low L. *intangibilis*; cf. **tangible**.]

integer, *in'té-jér, n.* a whole: (*arith.*) a whole number, as opposed to a fraction.—*adj.* **in'tegral** (*-grál*), entire or whole: not fractional: intrinsic, belonging as a part to the whole.—*n.* a whole: the whole as made up of its parts: (*math.*) the value of a function of a variable whose differential coefficient is known.—*adv.* **in'tegrally**.—*adj.* **in'tegrant**, making part of a whole, necessary to form an integer or an entire thing.—*v.t.* **in'tegrāte**, to make up as a whole: to make entire: to unite the parts of so that they become whole: to find the integral of.—Also *v.i.*—*ns.* **integrā'tion**, act or process of integrating: unification into a whole, e.g. of diverse elements in a society, as white and coloured: (*psych.*) formation of a unified personality; **integrity** (*in-teg'ri-ti*), entireness, wholeness: the unimpaired state of anything: uprightness, honesty, purity.—**integral calculus** (see **calculus**). [L. *integer*—*in-*, not, root of *tangĕre*, to touch.]

integument, *in-teg'ū-mént, n.* an external covering, as the skin or a seed-coat.—*adj.* **integumentary** (*-mént'ár-i*). [L. *integumentum*—*in*, upon, *tegĕre*, to cover.]

intellect, *int'é-lekt, n.* the mind, in reference to its rational powers: the thinking principle.—*n.* **intellec'tion**, the act of understanding: the exercise of the intellect.—*adjs.* **intellect'ive**, able to understand: produced or perceived by the understanding; **intellectual** (*-ek'tū-ál*), of

Neutral vowels in unaccented syllables: *em'pér-ór*; for certain sounds in foreign words see p. ix.

or relating to the intellect: perceived or performed by the intellect: having the power of understanding: well endowed with intellect.—*n.* a person of superior intellect (often implying doubt as to practical sagacity).—*ns.* **intellect′ualism,** the doctrine which derives all knowledge from pure reason: the culture (esp. exclusive or unbalanced) of the intellect; **intellect′ualist; intellectuality** (-*al′i-ti*), intellectual power.—*adv.* **intellect′ually.** [L. *intellectus*—*intelligĕre, intellectum,* to understand—*inter,* between, *legĕre,* to choose.]

intelligent, *in-tel′i-jent, adj.* endowed with the faculty of reason: alert, bright, quick of mind: showing intelligence (e.g. *an intelligent question*).—*n.* **intell′igence,** the faculty of understanding: mental brightness: information communicated, news: a mutual understanding: intelligence department: a spiritual being.—*adj.* **intelligential** (-*jen′shál*), pertaining to the intelligence: consisting of spiritual being.—*adv.* **intell′igently.**—*adj.* **intell′igible,** that may be understood: clear.—*ns.* **intell′igibleness, intelligibil′ity.**—*adv.* **intell′igibly.** —**intelligence (department, service),** a department of a state or armed service for securing information, openly or secretly, and collating it; **intelligence quotient,** ratio, commonly expressed as a percentage, of a person's mental age to his actual age; **intelligence test,** a test by questions and tasks to determine a person's relative mental capacity. [L. *intelligens, -entis,* pr.p. of *intelligĕre.*]

intelligentsia, intelligentzia, *in-tel-i-jent′si-a, n.* the intellectual or cultured classes. [Russ.—L. *intelligentia.*]

intemperance, *in-tem′pér-áns, n.* want of due restraint: excess of any kind: habitual overindulgence in intoxicating liquor.—*adj.* **intem′perate,** indulging to excess any appetite or passion: given to an immoderate use of intoxicating liquors: exceeding the usual degree.—*adv.* **intem′perately.**—*n.* **intem′perateness.** [Fr. *intempérance*—L. *intemperantia*—*in-,* not. See **temperance.**]

intend, *in-tend′, v.t.* (*arch.*) to fix the mind upon: to design, to purpose: to mean.—*v.i.* to purpose.—*ns.* **intend′ant,** an officer who super intends some public business; **intend′ancy,** the office of an intendant: a body of intendants.—*adj.* **intend′ed,** purposed.—*n.* (*coll.*) betrothed. [O.Fr. *entendre*—L. *intendĕre, intentum* and *intensum*—*in,* towards, *tendĕre,* to stretch.]

intense, *in-tens′, adj.* concentrated: extreme in degree: deeply emotional, or earnestly purposeful, in manner.—*adv.* **intense′ly.**—*ns.* **tense′ness, inten′sity.**—*v.t.* **inten′sify,** to make more intense.—*v.i.* to become more intense:—*pr.p.* intens′ifying; *pa.p.* intens′ified.—*ns.* **Intensificā′tion; inten′sion,** intentness: intensity: intensification: (*logic*) the sum of the qualities implied by a general name.—*adj.* **inten′sive,** concentrated, intense: unremitting: serving to intensify: (*gram.*) giving force or emphasis.—*n.* an intensive word.—*adv.* **inten′sively.**—*n.* **inten′siveness.**—**intensive culture,** getting the very most out of the soil of a limited area.—**intensive care unit,** an area in a hospital where a patient's condition is care-

fully monitored. [See **intend.**]

intent, *in-tent′, adj.* having the mind bent (on): fixed with close attention: diligent, earnest.— *n.* the thing aimed at or intended: purpose, design.—*n.* **intention** (*in-ten′sh(ó)n*), design, purpose.—*adjs.* **inten′tional, inten′tioned,** with intention: intended, designed.—*advs.* **inten′tionally,** with intention: on purpose; **inten′tly.**—*n.* **intent′ness.**—**to all intents and purposes,** in every important respect: virtually; **well- (or ill-) intentioned,** having good (or ill) designs.—**first intention,** the healing of a wound by direct union of the parts without granulation. [See **intend.**]

inter, *in-tûr′, v.t.* to bury:—*pr.p.* interr′ing; *pa.p.* interred′.—*n.* **inter′ment.** [Fr. *enterrer*—Low L. *interrāre*—L. *in,* into, *terra,* the earth.]

inter-, *in′tér-, pfx.* [L.] expressing reciprocal relation, as *interconnect, interconnection, interlink, interloop*: between, or among, as *intercity, interracial* (between races of people), *internode* (*bot.,* the part of the stem between two nodes).

interact, *in-tér-akt′, v.i.* to act on one another.— *n.* **interaction** (*in-tér-ak′sh(ó)n*), mutual action. [L. *inter,* between, and **act.**]

inter alia, *in′ter a′li a, ā′li á,* among other things. [L.]

interallied, *in-tér-al′īd,* or *-īd′, adj.* between or among allies. [L. *inter,* between, and **allied.** See **ally.**]

intercalate, *in-tér′kál-āt, v.t.* to insert between others, as a day in a calendar: to interpolate.—*adjs.* **inter′calary, inter′calar,** inserted between others.—*n.* **intercalā′tion.** [L. *intercalāre, -ātum*—*inter,* between, *calāre,* to proclaim. See **calends.**]

intercede, *in-tér-sēd′, v.i.* to act as peacemaker between two: to plead on behalf of (usu. with *with* and *for*).—*adj.* **interced′ent.**—*n.* **interced′er.** [L. *intercēdĕre, -cessum*—*inter,* between, *cēdĕre,* to go.]

intercellular, *in-tér-sel′ū-lár, adj.* placed among cells. [L. *inter,* between, and **cellular.**]

intercept, *in-tér-sept′, v.t.* to stop or seize on the way from place to place: to cut off: (*math.*) to take or include (space).—*n.* (*in′tér-sept*) a part of a line intercepted.—*ns.* **intercep′ter, intercep′tor,** one who or that which intercepts: a light, swift aeroplane for pursuit; **intercep′tion.**—*adj.* **intercep′tive.** [L. *intercipĕre, -ceptum*—*inter,* between, *capĕre,* to seize.]

intercession, *in-tér-sesh′(ó)n, n.* act of interceding or pleading for another.—*adj.* **intercess′ional.**—*n.* **intercessor** (-*ses′ór*), one who intercedes: a bishop who acts during a vacancy in a see.—*adjs.* **intercessō′rial, intercess′ory,** interceding. [Fr. *intercession*—L. *intercessiō, -ōnis*—*intercēdĕre.* See **intercede.**]

interchange, *in-ter-chānj′, v.t.* to give and take mutually: to exchange, put (each of two) in the other's place.—*v.t.* and *v.i.* to alternate.—*n.* **in′terchange,** mutual exchange: alternate succession.—*adj.* **interchange′able,** that may be interchanged.—*ns.* **interchange′ableness, interchangeabil′ity.**—*adv.* **interchange′ably.** [L. *inter,* between, and **change.**]

intercollegiate, *in-tér-ko-lē′ji-át, adj.* between colleges. [L. *inter,* between, and **collegiate.**]

intercolonial, *in-tér-kol-ō'ni-ál, adj.* between colonies. [L. *inter,* between, and **colonial.**]

intercom, *in-tér-kom', n.* a telephone system within a building, aeroplane, tank, &c. [*Inter*nal *com*munication.]

intercommune, *in-tér-kom-ūn', v.i.* to commune mutually or together.—*v.t.* and *v.i.* **intercommun'icate,** to communicate mutually or together.—*ns.* **intercommunica'tion; intercommun'ion,** mutual communion; **intercommun'ity,** state of being or having in common. [L. *inter,* between, and **commune,** vb.]

intercostal, *in-tér-kost'ál, adj.* (*anat.*) between the ribs. [L. *inter,* between, *costa,* a rib.]

intercourse, *in'tér-kōrs, -körs, n.* a connection by dealings: communication: commerce: sexual union. [O.Fr. *entrecours*—L. *intercursus,* a running between—*inter,* between, *currĕre, cursum,* to run.]

intercurrent, *in-tér-kur'ént, adj.* running between: intervening.—*n.* **intercurr'ence.** [L. *inter,* between, *currĕre,* to run.]

interdependence, *in-tér-di-pend'éns, n.* mutual dependence: dependence (of parts) one on another.—*adj.* **interdepend'ent.** [L. *inter,* between, and **dependence.**]

interdict, *in-tér-dikt', v.t.* to prohibit by decree (e.g. to *interdict trade with a country*): to forbid (a person) the use of (e.g. *interdicted him fire and water, i.e. banished him*): to forbid (a thing to a person): to restrain (a person from): to lay (a community or person) under an interdict.—*n.* (*in'tér-dikt*) prohibition: a prohibitory decree: a prohibition of the Pope restraining the clergy from performing divine service.—*n.* **interdic'tion.**—*adjs.* **interdic'tive, interdic'tory,** containing interdiction: prohibitory. [L. *interdīcĕre, -dictum*—*inter,* between, *dīcĕre,* to say.]

interest, *int'(é-)rest, -rist, n.* advantage: premium paid for the use of money: any increase: concern: claim to participate: share: personal influence: the body of persons whose advantage is bound up in anything (e.g. *the landed interest*): inclination to give one's attention to, liking for, a subject: a state of engaged attention and curiosity: power or quality of exciting such a state: that in which one has a concern or stake or which engages one's attention.—*v.t.* to concern deeply: to engage the attention of: to cause to take a share (in), or to regard as a personal concern.—*adj.* **in'terested,** having an interest or concern: affected or biased by personal considerations, &c.—*adv.* **in'terestedly.**—*adj.* **in'teresting,** engaging or apt to engage the attention or regard: exciting emotion or passion.—*adv.* **in'terestingly.**—**compound interest,** interest added to the principal at the end of each period (usually a year) to form a new principal for next period; **in the interest(s) of,** with a view to furthering or to helping. [From obs. *interess,* influenced by O.Fr. *interest*—L. *interest,* it concerns, 3rd pers. sing. pres. ind. of *interesse*—*inter,* between, among, *esse,* to be.]

interfere, *in-tér-fēr', v.i.* to come in the way of (with *with*): to meddle (with, in): to act reciprocally—said of waves, rays of light, &c.—*ns.* **interfēr'ence,** the act of interfering: the effect of combining similar rays of light,

&c.: the spoiling of a wireless signal, &c. by others or by natural disturbances; **interfēr'er.** [O.Fr. *enterférir*—L. *inter,* between, *ferīre,* to strike.]

interferon, *in-tér-fer'on, n.* a protein produced naturally in the body, active against many viruses. [**interfere.**]

interfused, *in-tér-fūzd', adj.* poured between or through: fused together: associated.—*n.* **interfusion** (*-fū'zh(ó)n*). [L. *interfūsus*—*inter,* between, *fundĕre, fūsum,* to pour.]

intergalactic, *in-tér-gal-ak'tik, adj.* between or among galaxies. [L. *inter,* between, **galactic.**]

interglacial, *in-tér-glā'shi-ál, adj.* (*geol.*) occurring between two epochs of glacial action. [L. *inter,* between, and **glacial.**]

interim, *in'tér-im, n.* time between or intervening: the meantime.—*adj.* temporary.—*adv.* meanwhile. [L.]

interior, *in-tē'ri-ór, adj.* inner: remote from the frontier or coast, inland.—*n.* the inside of anything: the inland part of a country: a picture of a scene within a house: (*cap.*) a department dealing with the domestic affairs of a country.—*adv.* **inte'riorly.**—**interior decoration, design,** the construction and furnishing of the interior of a building. [L., comp. of assumed *interus,* inward.]

interjacent, *in-tér-jā'sént, adj.* lying between: intervening.—*n.* **interja'cency.** [L. *interjacens, -entis,* pr.p. of *interjacēre*—*inter,* between, *jacēre,* to lie.]

interjaculate, *in-tér-jak'ū-lāt, v.i.* to interrupt conversation with an exclamation.—*adj.* **interjac'ulatory** (*-ū-lā-tór-i*). [L. *inter,* between, *jaculārī,* to throw.]

interject, *in-tér-jekt', v.t.* to throw between: to interpose, to exclaim in interruption or parenthesis.—*n.* **interjec'tion,** (*gram.*) a word thrown in to express emotion.—*adj.* **interjec'tional.** [L. *inter(j)icere, interjectus*—*inter,* between, *jacĕre,* to throw.]

interlace, *in-tér-lās', v.t.* and *v.i.* to lace, weave, or entangle together.—*n.* **interlace'ment.** [O.Fr. *entrelacier*—*entre,* between. See **lace.**]

interlard, *in-tér-lärd', v.t.* to mix in, as fat with lean: to diversify by mixture. [Fr. *entrelarder*—*entre,* between. See **lard.**]

interleave, *in-tér-lēv', v.t.* to put a leaf between: to insert blank leaves in. [L. *inter,* between. See **leaf.**]

interline, *in-tér-līn', v.t.* to insert between lines: to write between the lines of.—*adj.* **interlinear** (*-lin'i-ár*), written between lines.—*ns.* **interlinea'tion, interlīn'ing.** [L. *inter,* between, and **line**—or perh. from Low L. *interlineāre.*]

interlink, *in-tér-lingk', v.t.* and *v.i.* to link together. [L. *inter,* between, and **link** (1).]

interlock, *in-tér-lok', v.t.* to lock or clasp together: to connect so as to work together.—*v.i.* to be locked together. [L. *inter,* between, and **lock** (1).]

interlocution, *in-tér-lo-kū'sh(ó)n, n.* conference.—*n.* **interloc'utor,** one who speaks in dialogue: (*Scots law*) an intermediate decree before final decisions.—*adj.* **interloc'utory.** [L. *interlocūtiō, -ōnis*—*inter,* between, *loquī, locūtus,* to speak.]

interloper, *in'tér-lōp-ér, n.* (*orig.*) one who trades without licence: an intruder.—*v.i.*

Neutral vowels in unaccented syllables: *em'pér-ór*; for certain sounds in foreign words see p. ix.

interlope', to intrude into any matter in which one has no fair concern. [Prob. L. *inter*, between, and **lope**.]

interlude, *in'tėr-l(y)ōōd, n.* a short light play introduced between the acts of the mysteries and moralities, &c. and unconnected with them: any episode in contrast to what precedes and follows: an early form of modern drama: a short piece of music played between the parts of a drama, opera, song, &c.: an interval, or what happens in it. [L. *inter*, between, *lūdus*, play.]

interlunar, *in-tėr-l(y)ōō'når, adj.* belonging to the moon's monthly period of invisibility.— Also **interlu'nary**. [L. *inter*, between, *lūna*, the moon.]

intermarry, *in-tėr-mar'ī, v.i.* to marry, esp. of different races or groups, or of near kin.—*n.* **intermarr'iage**. [L. *inter*, between, and **marry**.]

intermeddle, *in-tėr-med'l, v.i.* to meddle, to interfere improperly.—*n.* **intermedd'ler**. [O.Fr. *entremedler, entremesler—entre*, between. See **meddle**.]

intermediate, *in-tėr-mē'di-åt, adj.* placed, occurring, or classified between others, or between extremes or stages: intervening: of igneous rocks, between acid and basic in composition.—*adj.* **interme'diary**, acting between others: intermediate.—*n.* an intermediate agent.—*adv.* **interme'diately**.—*n.* **interme'dium**, an intervening agent or instrument. [Low L. *intermediātus*—L. *intermedius*—*inter*, between, *medius*, middle.]

interment, *in tėr'mėnt, n.* burial. [**inter**.]

intermezzo, *in-tėr-med'zō* (or *-met'sō*), *n.* a short dramatic or musical entertainment between parts of a play, &c.: a movement in a larger instrumental work: a similar independent work. [It.,—L. *intermedius*.]

interminable, *in-tûr'min-å-bl, adj.* without termination, boundless, endless: wearisomely long. *n.* **inter'minableness.** *adv.* **inter'minably**. [L.L. *interminābilis—in-*, not, *terminus*, a boundary.]

intermingle, *in-tėr-ming'gl, v.t.* and *v.i.* to mingle or mix together. [L. *inter*, among, and **mingle**.]

intermit, *in-tėr-mit', v.t.* and *v.i.* to stop for a time.—*n.* **intermission** (-*mish'ŏn*), act of intermitting: interval: music played during a theatre, &c., interval: pause.—*adj.* **intermissive** (-*mis'iv*), coming and going: intermittent.—*adj.* **intermitt'ent**, intermitting or ceasing at intervals.—*n.* **intermitt'ence**.—*adv.* **intermitt'ently**. [L. *intermittēre*, *-missum—inter*, between, *mittēre*, to cause to go.]

intermix, *in-tėr-miks', v.t.* and *v.i.* to mix together.—*n.* **intermix'ture**, a mixing together: a mass formed by mixture: something added and intermixed. [L. *intermiscēre*, *mixtum inter*, among, *miscēre*, to mix.]

intern, *in-tûrn', v.t.* to send into the interior of a country: to confine within fixed bounds, as within a district, camp, port.—*n.* an inmate: (*U.S.*) a resident assistant surgeon or physician in a hospital.—*ns.* **internee'**, one confined within fixed bounds; **intern'ment**, confinement of this kind. [Fr., *interne*—L. *internus*, inward.]

internal, *in-tûr'nål, adj.* in the interior: domestic, as opposed to foreign: intrinsic: pertaining to the inner nature or feelings:—opp. to *external.*—*adv.* **inter'nally.**—**inter'nal combust'ion en'gine**, an engine in which the fuel, such as petrol vapour, is burned within the working cylinder; **internal evidence**, evidence afforded by the thing itself. [L. *internus—inter*, within.]

international, *in-tėr-nash'ŏn-ål, adj.* pertaining to the relations between nations.—*n.* (*coll.*) a game or contest between players chosen to represent different nations: a player who takes (or has taken) part in such a game: (*cap.*) an association to unite the working classes of all countries in efforts for their economic emancipation—First International formed in London, 1864; Second (Fr. **Internationale**) in Paris, 1889; Third in Moscow, 1919.—*ns.* **Internationale** (*ė-tėr-na-syŏ-näl'*), an international communist song, composed in France in 1871; **interna'tionalist**, one who seeks to promote the common interests, and to encourage the joint action of all nations: one who favours the principles of the International; **interna'tionalism**.—*adv.* **interna'tionally.**—**interna'tional law** (see **law**).—**international system of units** (see **SI units**). [L. *inter*, between, and **national**.]

internecine, *in-tėr-nē'sīn, adj.* deadly, murderous: (*loosely*) mutually destructive: involving conflict within a group. [L. *internecīnus*, *-īvus—internecāre—inter*, between (used intensively), *necāre*, to kill, *nex, necis*, murder.]

internuncio, *in-tėr-nun'shi-ō, n.* a messenger between two parties: the Pope's representative at minor courts.—*adj.* **internun'cial**. [It. *internunzio*, Sp. *internuncio*, and L. *internuntius—inter*, between, *nuntius*, a messenger.]

interpellation, *in tėr pel ā'sh(ŏ)n, n.* a question raised during a debate: formal questioning: interruption—*v.t.* **inter'pellate** (or *-pel'-*), to question formally. [Fr.,—L. *interpellāre*, *ātum*, to disturb by speaking *inter*, between, *pellēre*, to drive.]

interpenetrate, *in-tėr-pen'e-trāt, v.t.* to penetrate thoroughly: to penetrate reciprocally—*n.* **interpenetra'tion**. [L. *inter*, between, and **penetrate**.]

interphone, *in'tėr-fōn.* Same as **intercom**.

interplanetary, *in-tėr-plan'ėt-år-i, adj.* between or among planets. [L. *inter*, between, and **planetary**.]

interplay, *in'tėr-plā, n.* mutual action: interchange of action and reaction. [L. *inter*, between, and **play**.]

Interpol, *in'tėr-pol, n.* the *Inter*national Criminal *Pol*ice Commission, directed to international co-operation in the suppression of crime.

interpolate, *in tėr'po lāt, v.t.* to insert unfairly, as a spurious word or passage in a book or manuscript: to insert, interject: (*math.*) to fill in as an intermediate term of a series.—*ns.* **interpola'tion; inter'polator**. [L. *interpolāre*, *-ātum—inter*, between, *polīre*, to polish.]

interpose, *in-tėr-pōz', v.t.* to place between: to thrust in: to put in by way of interruption.—*v.i.* to come between: to mediate: to interfere.—*ns.* **interpos'al; interpos'er; interposition** (*in-tėr-poz-ish'(ŏ)n*), act of interposing: intervention: anything interposed. [Fr. *inter-*

poser — L. *inter*, between, Fr. *poser*, to place. See **pose**.]

interpret, *in-tûr'pret, v.t.* to explain the meaning of: to translate into intelligible terms, or into a familiar language: to take the purport or meaning of to be (with *as* — e.g. *Doddridge interpreted the remark, action, gesture, as a threat*): to show the significance of by some artistic means, as acting, playing, painting: to act as an interpreter. — *adj.* **inter'pretable,** capable of being explained. — *n.* **interpretā'tion,** act of interpreting: the sense, meaning, taken from words, or an action, or an event (e.g. a dream): the representation (of a dramatic part, &c.) according to one's conception of ṭt. — *adj.* **inter'pretātive,** containing interpretation. — *adv.* **inter'pretatively.** — *n.* **inter'preter,** one who translates orally for persons conversing or discussing who speak different languages: an expounder: a translator. [L. *interpretārī*, *-ātus* — *interpres, -etis*.]

interregnum, *in-tèr-reg'num, n.* the time between two reigns: the time between the cessation of one and the establishment of another government. [L. *inter*, between, *regnum*, rule.]

interrelation, *in-tèr-ri-lā'sh(ó)n, n.* reciprocal relation. — *n.* **interrelā'tionship.** [L. *inter*, between, and **relation**.]

interrogate, *in-ter'ō-gāt, v.t.* to question: to examine by asking questions. — *v.i.* to ask questions: to inquire. — *n.* **interrogā'tion,** act of interrogating: a question put: the mark placed after a question (?). — *adj.* **interrogative** (*in-tèr-og'á-tiv*), denoting a question: expressed as a question. — *n.* a word used in asking a question. — *adv.* **interrog'atively.** — *ns.* **inter'rogātor; interrog'atory,** a question or inquiry. — *adj.* expressing a question. [L. *interrogāre* — *inter*, between, *rogāre*, to ask.]

interrupt, *in-tèr-upt', v.t.* to break in upon: to obstruct (e.g. a view): to break continuity in. — *adj.* **interrupt'ed,** broken in continuity. — *adv.* **interrup'tedly.** — *ns.* **interrup'ter, interrup'tor; interrup'tion,** act of interrupting: break, temporary cessation: cessation. — *adj.* **interrup'tive,** tending to interrupt. [L. *interrumpĕre, -ruptum* — *inter*, between, *rumpĕre*, to break.]

intersect, *in-tèr-sekt', v.t.* to cut across: to cut or cross mutually: to divide by cutting or crossing. — Also *v.i.* — *n.* **intersec'tion,** intersecting: (*geom.*) the point or line in which two lines or two surfaces cut each other: (*math.*) the set of elements which two or more sets have in common: a crossroads. [L. *inter*, between, *secāre, sectum*, to cut.]

intersperse, *in-tèr-spûrs', v.t.* to scatter or set here and there (between, among, in): to diversify (something — with things scattered here and there). — *n.* **interspersion** (*-spér'sh(ó)n*). [L. *interspergĕre, -spersum* — *inter*, among, *spargĕre*, to scatter.]

interstate, *in-tèr-stāt, adj.* pertaining to relations, esp. political and commercial, between states. [L. *inter*, between, and **state**.]

interstellar, *in-tèr-stel'ár, adj.* situated beyond the solar system and among the stars: in the intervals between the stars. — Also **interstell'ary.** [L. *inter*, between, *stella*, a star.]

interstice, *in-tûr'stis, n.* a small space between

things closely set or between the parts which compose a body: a space between atoms in a lattice where other atoms can be located. — *adj.* **interstitial** (*-stish'ál*), occurring in interstices. — *n.* an extra atom in a crystal lattice, causing a defect. [L. *interstitium* — *inter*, between, *sistĕre, stătum*, to stand, set.]

intertidal, *in-tèr-tī'dál, adj.* (living) between low-water and high-water mark. [L. *inter*, between. See **tide**.]

intertribal, *in-tèr-trī'bal, adj.* between tribes. [L. *inter*, between. See **tribe**.]

intertwine, *in-tèr-twīn', v.t.* and *v.i.* to twine or twist together. [L. *inter*, together, and **twine**.]

interval, *in'tèr-vál, n.* time or space between: a break, or free spell between lessons, or acts of play, &c.: (*mus.*) the difference of pitch between any two musical notes. [L. *intervallum* — *inter*, between, *vallum*, a rampart.]

intervene, *in-tèr-vēn', v.i.* to come, or to be, between: to occur between points of time: to happen so as to interrupt: to interpose. — *n.* **intervention** (*-ven'sh(ó)n*), intervening: interference: mediation. [L. *inter*, between, *venīre*, to come.]

interview, *in'tèr-vū, n.* a personal meeting for conference: a meeting between a candidate for a post and a representative of those who are seeking to fill it: a conference with an interesting person aimed at publishing or broadcasting his opinions. — *v.t.* to visit for this purpose. — *n.* **in'terviewer,** a journalist or other who interviews. [O.Fr. *entrevue* — *entre*, between, *voir*, to see.]

interweave, *in-tèr-wēv', v.t.* and *v.i.* to weave together: to intermingle. [L. *inter*, together, and **weave**.]

intestate, *in-tes'tát, adj.* (dying) without having made a valid will: not disposed of by will. — *n.* a person who dies without making a valid will. — *n.* **intes'tacy** (*-tá-si*), the state of one dying without having made a valid will. [L. *intestātus* — *in-*, not, *testārī, -ātus*, to make a will.]

intestine, *in-tes'tin, adj.* (*obs.*) internal: contained in the animal body: domestic, not foreign (e.g. *intestine strife*). — *n.pl.* a part of the digestive system, divided into the smaller and the greater intestine. — *adj.* **intes'tinal** (also *-tīn'-*), pertaining to the intestines of an animal body. [L. *intestīnus* — *intus*, within.]

intimate, *in'ti-mát, adj.* pertaining to the essential nature of a thing: close (e.g. *intimate connection*): closely acquainted, familiar: private, personal: encouraging informality and closer personal relations through smallness. — *n.* a familiar friend: an associate. — *v.t.* (*-māt*) to hint: to announce. — *n.* **in'timacy** (*-má-si*), state of being intimate: close familiarity. — *adv.* **in'timately.** — *ns.* **intimā'tion,** indication, hint: announcement; **in'timism,** a genre of French impressionist painting of the early 20th cent. based on subject-matter from everyday life. [L. *intimāre, -ātum* — *intimus*, innermost — *intus*, within.]

intimidate, *in-tim'i-dāt, v.t.* to strike fear into: to influence by threats or violence. — *n.* **intimidā'tion,** act of intimidating: use of violence or threats to influence the conduct or compel the consent of another: state of being intimidated.

Neutral vowels in unaccented syllables: *em'pér-ór*; for certain sounds in foreign words see p. ix.

intituled

intrude

[L. *in*, into, *timidus*, fearful.]

intituled, *in-tit'ūld*. Same as **entitled**.

into, *in'tŏō*, *in'tōō*, prep. noting passage inwards (*lit.* and *fig.*): noting the passage of a thing from one state to another: noting parts made by dividing (e.g. *folded into four, broken into fragments*, 6 *into* 42 *gives* 7): by (*multiplied into*). [**in, to.**]

intoed, *in-tōd'*. adj. having the toes more or less turned inwards. [Adv. **in**, and **toed**. See **toe**.]

intolerable, *in-tol'ér-ä-bl*. adj. that cannot be endured —*n*. **intol'erableness.**—*adv.* **intol'erably.**—*adj.* **intol'erant**, not able or willing to endure (with *of*): not enduring difference of opinion.—*n.* one opposed to toleration.—*n.* **intol'erance.**—*adv.* **intol'erantly.** [L. *intolerābilis*—*in-*, not. See **tolerable**.]

intonate, *in'ton-āt*, v.t. and v.i. to intone.—*n.* **intonā'tion**, the opening phrase of any plainsong melody, sung usually either by the officiating priest alone, or by one or more selected choristers: pitching of musical notes: modulation or rise and fall in pitch of the voice in speech: intoning.—*v.t.* and v.i. **intone** (*in-tōn'*), to chant, utter, or read in musical tones, singsong, or monotone: to begin by singing the opening phrase: to utter with a particular intonation.—*n.* **intōn'ing.** [Low L. *intonāre*, *-ātum* —L. *in tonum*, according to tone.]

in toto, *in tō'tō*, entirely. [L.]

intoxicate, *in-toks'i-kāt*, v.t. to make drunk: to excite to enthusiasm or madness.—*ns.* **intox'icant**, an intoxicating agent; **intoxic'ātion**, state of being drunk: high excitement or elation. [Low L. *intoxicāre*, *ātum toxicum* —Gr. *toxikon*, arrow-poison—*toxon*, a bow.]

intra-, *in'tra-*, pfx. within, as in **in'tramū'ral**, within walls, **intramus'cūlar**, within a muscle; **in'tra ur'bnus**, within a city; **intravē'nous**, within, or introduced into, a vein. [L. *intrā*, within.]

intractable, *in-trakt'ä-bl*. adj. unmanageable: obstinate.—*ns.* **intractabil'ity, intract'ableness.**—*adv.* **intract'ably.** [L. *intractābilis*—*in-*, not, and **tractable**.]

intransigent, *in-tran'si-jént* (or *-zi-*), adj. refusing to come to any understanding, irreconcilable.—*ns.* **intran'sigence, intran'sigency**; **tran'sigentist**, one who practises such a method of opposition in politics; **intran'sigentism.** [Fr. *intransigeant*—Sp. *intransigente*—L. *in-*, not, *transigens*, *-entis*, pr.p. of *transigĕre*, to transact. See **transact**.]

intransitive, *in-tran'si-tiv*, adj. (*gram.*) representing action confined to the agent (i.e. having no object).—*adv.* **intran'sitively.** [L.L. *intransitīvus*—*in-*, not. See **transitive**.]

intrant, *in'tränt*, n. one who enters, esp. on membership, office, or possession [L. *intrans*, *-antis*—*intrāre*, to enter.]

intrench, intrenchment. Same as **entrench, entrenchment.**

intrepid, *in-trep'id*, adj. without trepidation or fear, undaunted, brave.—*n.* **intrepid'ity**, firm, unshaken courage.—*adv.* **intrep'idly.** [L. *intrepidus*—*in-*, not, *trepidus*, alarmed.]

intricate, *in'tri-kāt*, adj. involved: complicated.—*ns.* **in'tricacy** (*-ä-si*), **in'tricateness.**—*adv.* **in'tricately.** [L. *intrīcātus*—*in*, in, *trīcāre*,

to make difficulties—*trīcae*, hindrances.]

intrigue, *in-trēg'*, n. indirect or underhand scheming or plot: a private or party scheme: a secret illicit love affair.—*v.i.* to engage in intrigue.—*v.t.* to puzzle, to fascinate (a Gallicism).—*n.* **intriguer** (*-trēg'ér*).—*adj.* **intrigu'ing.**—*adv.* **intrigu'ingly.** [Fr.,—L. *intrīcāre*. See **intricate**.]

intrinsic, -al, *in-trin'sik*, *-äl*, p.adj. inward: inherent, essential—opp. to *extrinsic*.—*n.* **intrinsicality** (*-al'i-ti*).—*adv.* **intrin'sically.** [Fr. *intrinsèque*—Low L. *intrinsecus*—*intra*, within, suffix. *-in*, *secus*, following.]

intro-, *in'trō-*, *in-trō'-*, pfx. within, into. [L. *intrō*, inwards.]

intro, *in'tro*, n. contraction of **introduction**, used esp. of the opening passage of a popular music piece.

introduce, *in-trō-dūs'*, v.t. to lead or bring in: to put (into a place): formally to make known or acquainted: to make acquainted with (with *to*; *lit.* and *fig.*): to bring into notice, or into practice: to preface.—*n.* **introduction** (*-duk'-sh(ô)n*), act of introducing, or of being introduced (e.g. *introduction to a person, to society, to a subject*): first acquaintance with (with *to*): preliminary matter to a book: a treatise introductory to a science or course of study.—*adjs.* **introduc'tory, introduc'tive**, serving to introduce: preliminary: prefatory. [L. *introdūcĕre*, *-ductum*—*intrō*, inwards, *dūcĕre*, to lead.]

introit, *in-trō'it*, n. (in the R.C. Church) an anthem sung at the beginning of the mass, when the priest has ascended to the altar: (in other Churches) an introductory hymn, psalm, or anthem. [L. *introitus*—*introīre*—*intrō*, inwards, *īre*, *itum*, to go.]

intromit, *in-trō-mit'*, v.t. (*arch.*) to permit to enter: to insert:—*pr.p.* **intromitt'ing;** *pa.p.* **intromitt'ed.**—*n.* **intromission** (*-mish'(ô)n*), sending within: insertion: (*Scots law*) the assumption of authority to deal with another's property. [L. *intrō*, inward, *mittĕre*, *missum*, to send.]

introspect, *in-tro-spekt'*, v.t. to look into (anything).—*v.i.* to practise introspection.—*n.* **introspection** (*-spek'sh(ô)n*), a viewing of the inside or interior: the act of directly observing the processes of one's own mind, self-examination.—*adj.* **introspec'tive.** [L. *intro*, within, *specĕre*, to see.]

introvert, *in-tro-vûrt'*, v.t. to turn inward: to turn outside in: to draw part within the rest of.—*ns.* **in'trovert**, anything introverted: (*psych.*) a person interested mainly in his own mental processes, given to introspection and fantasy (cf. **extravert**); **introver'sion.** [L. *intrō*, inwards, *vertĕre*, *versum*, to turn.]

intrude, *in-trōōd'*, v.i. to thrust oneself in: to enter uninvited or unwelcome.—*v.t.* to force in.—*ns.* **intrud'er; intrusion** (*-trōō'zh(ô)n*), act of intruding: encroachment: an injection of rock in a molten state among and through existing rocks.—*adj.* **intru'sive**, tending or apt to intrude: entering without welcome or right: inserted where it does not belong etymologically (e.g. the *d* in *admiral* and the *n* in *passenger* are intrusive; an intrusive *r* is sometimes pronounced, though not written, be-

fāte, *fär*; *mē*, *hûr* (her); *mīne*; *mōte*, *för*; *mūte*; *mōōn*, *fŏŏt*; THen (then)

381

tween vowels—a habit many people deplore—as in *no idea(r) of time*).—*adv.* **intru′sively**.—*n.* **intru′siveness**. [L. *in*, in, *trūdĕre, trūsum*, to thrust.]

intrust. A variant of **entrust**.

intuition, *in-tū-ish′(ò)n*, *n.* the power of the mind by which it immediately perceives the truth of things without reasoning or analysis: a truth so perceived.—*adj.* **intūit′ional**.—*n.* **intūit′ionalism**, the doctrine that the perception of truth is by intuition.—*adj.* **intū′itive**, perceived, or perceiving, by intuition: received or known by simple inspection.—*adv.* **intu′itively**. [L. *in*, into or upon, *tuērī, tuitus*, to look.]

intumesce, *in-tū-mes′*, *v.i.* to swell up.—*n.* **intumes′cence**, swelling. [L. *in*, in, *tumēscĕre*, to swell.]

intwine, *in-twīn′*. Same as **entwine**.

intwist, *in-twist′*. Same as **entwist**.

inundate, *in′un-dāt*, *v.t.* to flow upon or over in waves (said of water): to flood: (*fig.*) to overwhelm: to fill with an overflowing abundance.—*n.* **inundā′tion**. [L. *inundāre, -ātum—in*, in,*undāre*, to rise in waves—*unda*, a wave.]

inure, *in-ūr′*, *v.t.* to accustom, habituate: to harden.—*v.i.* (*law*) to come into use or effect.—Also **enure′**.—*n.* **inure′ment**, act of inuring: state of being inured. [Pfx. *in-, en-*, in, and obsolete word *ure*, practice, operation.]

inutility, *in-ū-til′i-ti*, *n.* want of utility, uselessness, unprofitableness. [Fr. *inutilité*—L. *inūtilitās—in-*, not. See **utility**.]

in vacuo, *in vak′ū-ō, -ŏŏ-ō, wak′-*, in a vacuum. [L.]

invade, *in-vād′*, *v.t.* to enter as an enemy (*lit.* and *fig.*): to encroach upon, to violate (e.g. rights).—*ns.* **invad′er; invasion** (*vā′zh(ò)n*), the act of invading: an incursion: an attack on the rights of another, an encroachment.—*adj.* **invasive** (*-vā′ziv*), making invasion: agressive: infringing another's rights. [L. *invādĕre, invāsum—in*, in, *vādĕre*, to go.]

invalid, *in-val′id*, *adj.* not valid, not sound (e.g. of an argument): without legal force, void, null.—*adj.* **invalid** (*in′val-ēd, -id*), sick, weak.—*n.* an ailing person: one disabled for active work, e.g. in the services.—*v.t.* to make invalid or affect with disease: to enrol or discharge as an invalid.—*v.t.* **inval′idate**, to render invalid: to make of no effect.—*ns.* **invalidā′tion; invalid′ity, inval′idness**, want of cogency or force. [Fr. *invalide*—L. *invalidus—in-*, not, *validus*, strong—*valēre*, to be strong.]

invaluable, *in-val′ū-ȧ-bl*, *adj.* that cannot be valued too highly, priceless.—*adv.* **inval′uably**. [L. *in-*, not, and **valuable**.]

Invar, *in′vär, in-vär′*, *n.* an alloy of iron, nickel and carbon, which is only very slightly expanded by heat, much used in the making of scientific instruments. [Trade-mark, from **invariable**.]

invariable, *in-vā′ri-ȧ-bl*, *adj.* without variation or change: unalterable: constantly in the same state.—*n.* **inva′riableness**.—*adv.* **invā′riably**—*n.* **invā′riant**, that which does not alter. [L. *in-*, not, and **variable**.]

invasion, invasive. See **invade**.

invective, *in-vek′tiv*, *n.* an attack with words: a violent abusive attack in speech or writing: the utterance of censure.—*adj.* railing, ab-

usive. [Fr.,—L.L. *invectiva* (*orātiō*), abusive (speech)—*invehĕre, invectum*. See **inveigh**.]

inveigh, *in-vā′*, *v.i.* to make an attack with words, to rail (against). [L. *invehĕre, invectum—in*, in, *vehĕre*, to carry.]

inveigle, *in-vē′gl*, also *in-vā′gl*, *v.t.* to entice, to wheedle (into): to ensnare by cajolery.—*n.* **invei′glement**. [Prob. altered from Anglo-Fr. *enveogler* (Fr. *aveugler*), to blind to—L. *ab*, from, *oculus*, the eye.]

invent, *in-vent′*, *v.t.* to devise or contrive, to originate: to frame by imagination, to fabricate.—*n.* **inven′tion**, that which is invented: contrivance: a deceit: power or faculty of inventing: ability displayed by any invention or effort of the imagination.—*adj.* **inven′tive**, able to invent: ready in contrivance.—*adv.* **inven′tively**.—*ns.* **inven′tiveness; inven′tor**. [L. *invenīre, inventum—in*, upon, *venīre*, to come.]

inventory, *in′ven-tór-i*, *n.* a list or schedule of articles comprised in an estate, &c.: a catalogue (listed) stock of goods: the total quantity of material in a nuclear reactor.—*v.t.* to make an inventory of. [L.L. *inventōrium*, for L. *inventārium*, a list of things found—*invenīre*, to find.]

inverse, *in′vėrs, in-vûrs′*, *adj.* in the reverse or contrary order or relation: opposite in nature and effect.—*n.* a thing, process, condition, that is the direct opposite (of another).—*adv.* **inverse′ly**.—*n.* **inver′sion**, the act of inverting: the state of being inverted: a change of order or position.—**in inverse ratio, proportion**, said of two quantities when the increase in one is proportioned to the decrease in the other. [L. *inversus*, pa.p. of *invertĕre*. See **invert**.]

invert, *in-vûrt′*, *v.t.* to turn upside down: to reverse the customary order or position of.—*adj.* **inver′ted**, turned inwards: turned upside down: reversed.—**inverted commas** (see **comma**). [L. *invertĕre, inversum—in*, in, *vertĕre*, to turn.]

invertebrate, *in-vûrt′e-brȧt*, *adj.* without a vertebral column or backbone: weak, irresolute.—*n.* an animal destitute of a skull and vertebral column: a weak, irresolute person. [L. *in-*, not, and **vertebrate**.]

invest, *in-vest′*, *v.t.* to put vesture on, to clothe: to place in office or authority: to adorn: to envelop or to endue (with): to lay siege to: to lay out for profit, as by buying property, shares. &c.—*ns.* **inves′titure**, investing: ceremony of investing: in feudal and ecclesiastical history, the formal act of giving possession of a manor, office, or benefice; **invest′ment**, the act of investing: the act of surrounding or besieging: a blockade: any placing of money to secure income or profit: that in which money is invested; **inves′tor**, one who invests, esp. money—**investment trust** (see **trust**). [L. *investīre, -ītum—in*, on, *vestīre*, to clothe.]

investigate, *in-vest′i-gāt*, *v.t.* to search or inquire into with care and accuracy.—*adj.* **invest′igable**, able to be investigated.—*n.* **investigā′tion**, act of examining: research.—*adjs.* **invest′igative, invest′igatory**.—*n.* **invest′igātor**. [L. *investīgāre, -ātum—in*, in, *vestīgāre*, to track.]

inveterate, *in-vet′ér-ȧt*, *adj.* firmly established

Neutral vowels in unaccented syllables: *em′pėr-ór*; for certain sounds in foreign words see p. ix.

382

by long continuance, deep-rooted: confirmed in any habit.—*adv.* **invet′erately.**—*ns.* **invet′erateness, invet′eracy** (-*ă-si*), firmness produced by long use or continuance. [L. *inveterātus*, stored up, long continued—*in*, in, *vetus, veteris*, old.]

invidious, *in-vid′i-us, adj.* likely to provoke ill-will: offensively discriminating (e.g. *an invidious distinction*).—*adv.* **invid′iously.**—*n.* **invid′iousness.** [L. *invidiōsus—invidia,* envy.]

invigilate, *in-vij′i-lāt, v.t.* and *v.i.* to supervise (at examinations).—*ns.* **invigilā′tion; invig′ilātor.** [L. *in,* on, *vigilāre, -ātum,* to watch.]

invigorate, *in-vig′ór-āt, v.t.* to give vigour to, strengthen, animate.—*n.* **invigorā′tion.** [L. *in,* in, *vigor.* See **vigour.**]

invincible, *in-vin′si-bl, adj.* that cannot be overcome: insuperable.—*ns.* **invin′cibleness, invincibil′ity.**—*adv.* **invin′cibly.** [Fr.,—L. *invincibilis—in-,* not, *vincĕre,* to overcome.]

inviolable, *in-vī′ól-a-bl, adj.* that must not be profaned: that cannot be broken (e.g. an oath, a law), or infringed (e.g. rights).—*ns.* **inviolabil′ity, invī′olableness,** the quality of being inviolable.—*adv.* **invī′olably.**—*adjs.* **invī′olāte, -d,** not violated: unprofaned: not broken. [Fr.,—L. *inviolābilis—in-,* not, *violābilis violāre,* to injure, profane.]

invisible, *in-viz′i-bl, adj.* incapable of being seen: unseen.—*ns.* **invisibil′ity, invis′ibleness.**—*adv.* **invis′ibly.** [Fr.,—L. *invīsibilis—in-,* not. See **visible.**]

invite, *in-vīt′, v.t.* to ask hospitably or graciously to come: to express willingness to receive, or to solicit (e.g. suggestions): to be of such a kind as to encourage (e.g. criticism).—*ns.* **invitation** (*in-vi-tā′sh(ó)n*), the act of inviting: the written or verbal form with which a person is invited; **invit′er.**—*p.adj.* **invīt′ing,** alluring, attractive.—*adv.* **invit′ingly,** in an inviting manner. [L. *invītāre, -ātum.*]

in vitro, *in vit′rō, vīt′ō, wit′ō,* in glass: in the test tube—opp. to *in vivo.*

in vivo, *in vīv′ō, vē′vō, wē′wō,* in the living organism. [L.]

invocation, *in-vō-kā′sh(ó)n, n.* the act, or the form, of addressing in prayer: any formal invoking of the blessing or help of a god, a muse, &c.—*adj.* **invocatory** (*in-vok′a-tór-i*), making invocation. [O.,Fr.,—L. *invocātiō, -ōnis—invocāre.* See **invoke.**]

invoice, *in′vois, n.* a letter of advice of the despatch of goods, with particulars of their price and quantity.—*v.t.* to make an invoice of. [Prob. pl. of Fr. *envoi.*]

invoke, *in-vōk′, v.t.* to address (God, &c.) in prayer: to call upon earnestly or solemnly: to implore assistance of: to cite as supporting evidence: to summon by charm or incantation. [Fr. *invoquer*—L. *invocāre, -ātum—in,* on, *vocāre,* to call.]

involucre, *in′vol-(y)ōō-kér, n.* (*anat.*) an envelope: (*bot.*) a ring or crowd of bracts around an expanded flower, &c. [L. *involūcrum—involvēre,* to involve.]

involuntary, *in-vol′un-tàr-i, adj.* not under the control of the will: not done voluntarily: unwilling: unintentional.—*adv.* **invol′untarily.**—*n.* **invol′untariness.** [L.L. *involuntārius—in-,* not. See **voluntary.**]

involute, *in′vol-(y)ōōt, adj.* involved: (*bot.*) rolled inward at the margins: turned inward.—*n.* that which is involved or rolled inward: a curve traced by the end of a string unwinding itself from another curve.—*n.* **involu′tion,** the action of involving: state of being involved or entangled: a complication (*lit.* and *fig.*): raising to a power. [L. *involūtus—involvēre.* See **involve.**]

involve, *in-volv′, v.t.* to coil, wind: to wrap up, envelop: to comprise: to implicate: to entail or imply, bring as a consequence: to complicate: (*math.*) to raise to a power: to make (oneself) emotionally concerned (in, with): to engage the emotional interest of.—*n.* **involve′ment.** [L. *involvēre — in,* in, *volvēre, volūtum,* to roll.]

invulnerable, *in-vul′nér-ă-bl, adj.* that cannot be wounded.—*ns.* **invulnerabil′ity, invul′nerableness.**—*adv.* **invul′nerably.** [L. *invulnerābilis—in-,* not. See **vulnerable.**]

inward, *in′wàrd, adj.* placed or being within, internal: seated in the mind or soul: not perceptible to the senses: (in *pl.*) entrails (also **innards**).—*adv.* toward the interior: into the mind or thoughts.—*adv.* **in′wardly,** within: in the heart: privately: toward the centre.—*adv.* **in′wards,** inward. [O.E. *inneweard* (adv.).]

inwrought, *in-röt′, adj.* wrought in or among other things: adorned with figures. [Adv. **in,** and **wrought.**]

inwrap. Same as **enwrap.**

inwreathe, *in-rēTH′, v.t.* to wreathe: to encircle with a wreath. [**in,** and **wreath**]

iodine, *ī′o-dēn, -dīn, -din, n.* a non-metallic element (symbol I; atomic no. 53) giving a violet-coloured vapour.—*v.t.* **i′odīse,** to treat with iodine.—*n.* **iōd′oform,** a lemon-yellow crystalline compound of iodine, with a saffron-like odour, used as an antiseptic.—**iodine-131,** a radioactive isotope of iodine, present in nuclear fall-out but short lived. [Gr. *iōdēs,* violet-coloured—*ion,* a violet, *eidos,* form.]

ion, *ī′on, n.* an electrically charged particle formed by loss or gain by an atom of electrons.—*v.t.* and *v.i.* **i′onise,** to convert, or to be converted, into ions, or into an ion.—*n.* **ion′osphere,** the region of the upper atmosphere that includes the highly ionised Appleton and Kennelly-Heaviside layers.—**ion-exchange,** transfer of ions from a solution to a solid or another liquid, used in water-softening and many industrial processes. [Gr. *iōn,* neut. pr.p. of *ienai,* to go.]

Ionic, *ī-on′ik, adj.* relating to the *Ionians,* one of the main divisions of the ancient Greeks, or to Ionia, the coast district of Asia Minor settled by them: denoting an order in architecture distinguished by the ram's-horn volute of its capital.—**Ionic dialect,** the main dialect of ancient Greek, marked by softness and smoothness; its later form was Attic. [Gr. *Iōnikos, Iōnios.*]

ionium, *ī-ōn′i-ùm, n.* a radioactive isotope of thorium [**ion.**]

iota, *ī-ō′ta, n.* a jot, very small quantity. [Gr. *iōta,* the smallest letter in the alphabet, I, ι; Heb. *yōd.*]

I O U, *ī ō ū,* standing for *I owe you,* used as noun

for a signed acknowledgment (bearing these letters) of a debt.

ipecacuanha, *ip-e-kak-ū-an'a,* or **ipecac,** *ip'e-kak, n.* a Brazilian plant whose root affords a useful emetic: the emetic, obtained from this and other plants. [Port. from Amer. Indian.]

ipse dixit, *ip'sē dik'sit, ip-se dēk'sit,* he himself said it: his mere word: a dogmatic pronouncement.

ipso facto, *ip'so fak'tō,* by that very fact or act (e.g. in helping A he was, *ipso facto,* cutting himself off from the possible support of B). [L.]

ir-, *ir-,* pfx. a form of **in-** used before *r.*

Iranian, *ī-rān'i-ân, adj.* and *n.* Persian. [Pers. *Irān,* Persia.]

Iraqi, *i-rä'kē, n.* a native of Iraq: the form of Arabic spoken in Iraq.—Also *adj.* [Ar. *'Irāqī.*]

irascible, *ir-as'i-bl,* or *īr-, adj.* prone to ire or anger, irritable.—*n.* **irascibil'ity.**—*adv.* **iras'cibly.** [Fr.—L. *īrāscibilis*—*īrāscī,* to be angry—*īra,* anger.]

ire, *īr, n.* anger: keen resentment.—*adjs.* **irate** (*ī-rāt'* or *īr'āt*), enraged, angry; **ire'ful,** full of wrath: resentful.—*adv.* **ire'fully.** [L. *īra,* anger.]

iris, *ī'ris, n.* the rainbow: an appearance resembling the rainbow: the contractile curtain perforated by the pupil, and forming the coloured part of the eye: a genus of flowers having the three outer perianth leaves reflexed, the three inner arched inwards, and three petal-like stigmas covering the stamens:—*pl.* **i'rises.**—**iridescence** (*ir-i-des'ēns*), play of rainbow colours, caused by interference (as on bubbles, mother-of-pearl).—*adjs.* **irides'cent, irisated** (*ī'-*), showing iridescence.—*ns.* **irid'-ium** (*īr-* or *ir-*), a very heavy steel-grey metallic element (Ir; at. no. 77) with very high melting-point (some of its solutions are iridescent); **iridosmine** (*ir-id-oz'min,* or *īr-,* or *-os'-*), a native alloy of iridium and osmium used for pen-points—also called *osmiridium;* **irī'tis,** inflammation of the iris of the eye. [Gr. *Iris, -idos,* the messenger of the gods, the rainbow.]

Irish, *ī-rish, adj.* relating to, or produced in, *Ireland.*—*n.* the Celtic language of Ireland: (*pl.*—**Irish**) the natives or inhabitants of Ireland.—**Irish Guards,** a regiment formed in 1900 to represent Ireland in the Foot Guards; **Irish stew,** mutton, onions, and potatoes, stewed with thick gravy.

irk, *ûrk, v.t.* to weary, trouble, distress (often used impers.).—*adj.* **irk'some,** tedious: burdensome.—*adv.* **irk'somely.**—*n.* **irk'someness.** [M.E. *irken.*]

iron, *ī'ern, n.* the most widely used metallic element (at. no. 26; symbol Fe): weapon or instrument made of iron, as a hand-harpoon, branding instrument, flat-iron: a golf-club with an iron head: (*slang*) a pistol or revolver: strength, firmness (as, *man of iron*): (*pl.*) fetters, chains.—*adj.* formed of iron: resembling iron: rude, stern, harsh: fast-binding: not to be broken (e.g. *iron grip*): inflexible (iron will): robust.—*v.t.* to smooth with a flat-iron: to arm with iron: to fetter.—*adjs.* **i'ron-bound,** bound with iron: (of a coast) rugged; **i'ron-clad,** clad in iron: covered or protected with iron.—*n.* a ship defended by iron plates.—*ns.*

i'ron-found'er, one who makes castings in iron; **i'ron-found'ry.**—*adj.* **i'ron-gray', -grey',** of a grey colour, like that of iron freshly cut or broken.—*n.* this colour.—*adjs.* **i'ron-hand'ed,** rigorous: despotic; **i'ron-heart'ed,** having a heart hard as iron, unfeeling.—*ns.* **i'ron-master,** proprietor of ironworks; **i'ronmonger,** dealer in iron or hardware; **i'ronmongery,** articles made of iron, hardware; **i'ronmould,** a stain on cloth caused by rusty iron or by ink; **i'ronside, ironsides,** a nickname for a man of iron resolution: (*cap.*—*pl.*) a name given to Cromwell's irresistible cavalry: (*cap.*—*sing.*) a Puritan; **i'ron-stone,** any iron ore; **i'ronware,** wares or goods of iron; **i'ronwood,** timber of great hardness, and many kinds of trees producing it; **i'ronwork,** the parts of a building, &c., made of iron: anything of iron, esp. artistic work: (often in *pl.*) an establishment where iron is smelted, or made into heavy goods.—*adj.* **i'rony,** made, consisting, or partaking, of iron: like iron: hard.—**Iron Age,** an archaeological term indicating the stage of culture of a people using iron as the material for their cutting tools and weapons: a period of cruel tyranny; **iron curtain,** the safety curtain in front of the stage in a theatre (also **the iron**): (*fig.*) an impenetrable barrier to observation or communication, esp. between communist Russia with its satellites and the West; **iron lung,** an apparatus consisting of a chamber that encloses a patient's chest, the air pressure within the chamber being varied rhythmically so that air is forced into and out of the patient's lungs; **iron ration,** an emergency ration, esp. of concentrated food.—**iron out** (*fig.*), to smooth out, to clear up.—**rule with a rod of iron,** to rule with stern severity; **too many irons in the fire,** too many things on hand at once. [O.E. *īren,* (*īsern, īsen*); Ger. *eisen.*]

irony, *ī'roni, n.* conveyance of meaning (generally satirical) by words whose literal meaning is the opposite: a condition in which one seems to be mocked by fate or the facts: an utterance (as in a tragedy) that has a significance unperceived by the speaker.—*adjs.* **ironic** (*ī-ron'ik*), **iron'ical.**—*adv.* **iron'ically.** [L. *īrōnīa*—Gr. *eirōneiā,* dissimulation—*eirōn,* a dissembler, perh. *eirein,* to talk.]

irradiate, *ir-ā'di-āt, v.t.* to shed light upon or into: to treat by exposure to rays: to light up, brighten (esp. one's face, with joy).—*n.* **ir-rā'diance.**—*adj.* **irrā'diant.**—*n.* **irradiā'tion,** act of irradiating: exposure to rays: a ray of light, &c.: brightness: intellectual light. [L. *irradiāre, -ātum*—*in,* on; cf. **radiate.**]

irrational, *ir-ash'ón-âl, adj.* not reasonable, absurd: not logical: not endowed with reasons: (*math.*) not expressible accurately by a finite number of figures.—*n.* **irrational'ity.**—*adv.* **irra'tionally.** [L. *irratiōnālis*—*in-,* not. See **rational.**]

irreclaimable, *ir-i-klām'á-bl, adj.* that cannot be reclaimed: that cannot be reformed.—*adv.* **irreclaim'ably.** [L. *in-,* not, and **reclaimable.**]

irreconcilable, *ir-ek-ón-sīl'á-bl, adj.* incapable of being brought back to a state of friendship or agreement: inconsistent.—*n.* **irreconcil'ableness.**—*adv.* **irreconcil'ably.** [L. *in-,* not,

Neutral vowels in unaccented syllables: *em'pér-ór;* for certain sounds in foreign words see p. ix.

and **reconcilable**.]

irrecoverable, *ir-i-kuv'ér-à-bl, adj.* irretrievable, beyond recovery.—*adv.* **irrecov'erably**. [L. *in-*, not, and **recoverable**.]

irredeemable, *ir-i-dēm'á-bl, adj.* not redeemable: (of paper money) that cannot be converted into specie: not terminable by repayment of principal: hopeless.—*ns.* **irredeem'ableness, irredeemabil'ity**.—*adv.* **irredeem'ably**. [L. *in-*, not, and **redeemable**.]

irredentism, *ir-i-dent'izm, n.* the doctrine of 'redeeming' territory from foreign rule—i.e. reincorporating in one's country territory formerly belonging to it. [Through It.—L. *in-*, not, *redemptus*, redeemed.]

irreducible, *ir-i-dūs'i-bl, adj.* that cannot be reduced or brought from one degree, form, or state to another: not to be lessened.—*adv.* **irreduc'ibly**. [L. *in*, not, and **reducible**.]

irrefragable, *ir-ef'rä-gá-bl, adj.* that cannot be refuted, unanswerable.—*ns.* **irretragabil'ity, irref'ragableness**.—*adv.* **irref'ragably**. [L. *irrefrāgābilis—in-*, not, *re-*, backwards, *frangére*, to break.]

irrefutable, *ir-ef'ūt-à-bl*, also -*ut'-, adj.* that cannot be refuted.—*adv.* **irref'utably** (also *ut'*). [L.L. *irrefūtābilis—in-*, not. See **refutable**.]

irregular, *ir-eg'u-lár, adj.* not regular: not conforming to rule: variable: disorderly: uneven: unsymmetrical: (of troops) not trained under authority of a government.—*n.* an irregular soldier.—*n.* **irregularity** (-*larï-ti*).—*adv.* **irreg'ularly**. [O.Fr. *irregular* Low L. *irrēgulāris—in-*, not See **regular**.]

irrelative, *ir-el'a-tiv, adj.* not relative: irrelevant.—*adv.* **irrel'atively**. [L. *in-*, not, and **relative**.]

irrelevant, *ir-el'é-vánt, adj.* not relevant. *ns.* **irrel'evance, irrel'evancy**—*adv.* **irrel'evantly**. [L. *in-*, not, and **relevant**.]

irreligious, *ir-i-lij'us, adj.* destitute of religion: ungodly.—*adv.* **irrelig'iously**.—*ns.* **irrelig'iousness, irrelig'ion**, want of religion. [L. *irreligiōsus—in-*, not. See **religious**.]

irremediable, *ir-i-mē'di-à-bl, adj.* beyond remedy or redress.—*n.* **irreme'diableness**.—*adv.* **irreme'diably**. [L. *irremediābilis—in-*, not. See **remediable**.]

irremissible, *ir-i-mis'i-bl, adj.* not to be remitted or forgiven: obligatory. [Fr. *irrémissible*—L.L. *irremissibilis—in-*, not. See **remissible**.]

irremovable, *ir-i-mōōv'á-bl, adj.* not removable: not liable to be displaced.—*ns.* **irremovabil'ity, irremov'ableness**.—*adv.* **irremov'ably**. [L. *in-*, not, and **removable**.]

irreparable, *ir-ep'ár-à-bl, adj.* that cannot be made good or rectified: beyond repairing.—*ns.* **irreparabil'ity, irrep'arableness**. *adv.* **irrep'arably**. [Fr. *irréparable*—L. *irreparābilis—in-*, not. See **reparable**.]

irreplaceable, *ir-i-plās'á-bl, adj.* whose loss cannot be made good. [L. *in-*, not, and **replaceable**.]

irrepressible, *ir-i-pres'i-bl, adj.* not to be put down or kept under.—*adv.* **irrepress'ibly**. [L. *in-*, not, and **repressible**.]

irreproachable, *ir-i-prōch'á-bl, adj.* free from blame: faultless.—*adv.* **irreproach'ably**. [L. *in-*, not, and **reproachable**.]

irresistible, *ir-i-zist'ibl, adj.* not to be opposed

with success: overmastering: extremely charming.—*ns.* **irresist'ibleness, irresistibil'ity**.—*adv.* **irresist'ibly**. [L. *in-*, not, and **resistible**.]

irresolute, *ir-ez'ól-(y)ōōt, adj.* not firm in purpose: hesitating.—*adv.* **irres'olutely**.—*ns.* **irres'oluteness, irresolution** (-ōō'sh(o)n, -ū'sh(ò)n), want of resolution. [L. *irresolūtus—in-*, not, and **resolute**.]

irrespective, *ir-i-spek'tiv, adj.* not having regard to (with *of*).—*adv.* **irrespec'tively**. [L. *in-*, not, and **respective**.]

irresponsible, *ir-i-spons'i-bl, adj.* (of a person, or of conduct or an action) showing a lack of sense of responsibility.—*n.* **irresponsibil'ity**. —*adv.* **irrespons'ibly**.—*adj.* **irrespons'ive**, not responding: not inclined to respond.—*n.* **irrespons'iveness**. [L. *in-*, not, and **responsible**.]

irretentive, *ir-i-ten'tiv, adj.* lacking the power to retain. [L. *in-*, not, and **retentive**.]

irretrievable, *ir-i-trev'à-bl, adj.* not to be recovered: not to be made good.—*n.* **irretriev'ableness**.—*adv.* **irretriev'ably**. [L. *in-*, not, and **retrievable**.]

irreverent, *ir-ev'ér-ént, adj.* not reverent: proceeding from irreverence.—*n.* **irrev'erence**, want of reverence or veneration, esp. for God.—*adv.* **irrev'erently**. [L. *irreverens in-*, not. See **reverent**.]

irreversible, *ir-i-vûrs'i-bl, adj.* not reversible: incapable of changing back: that cannot be recalled or annulled.—*ns.* **irreversibil'ity, irrevers'ibleness**.—*adv.* **irrevers'ibly**. [L. *in-*, not, and **reversible**.]

irrevocable, *ir-ev'ok-à-bl, adj.* that cannot be recalled or revoked: unalterable. *n.* **irrev'ocableness**.—*adv.* **irrev'ocably**. [Fr. *irrévocable*—L. *irrevocābilis—in-*, not, **revocable**. See **revoke**.]

irrigate, *ir'i-gāt, v.t.* (of rivers) to supply (land) with water: to water by means of canals or water-courses: to cause a stream of liquid to flow upon.—*adj.* **irr'igable**.—*n.* **irriga'tion**. [L. *irrigāre, -ātum*, to water—*in*, upon, *rigāre*, to wet.]

irritate, *ir'i-tāt, v.t.* to excite or stimulate: to provoke: to make angry or fretful: to excite heat and redness in.—*adj.* **irr'itable**, that may be irritated: easily annoyed: capable of being excited by stimuli.—*ns.* **irr'itableness, irritabil'ity**, the quality of being easily irritated: the peculiar susceptibility to stimuli possessed by living matter.—*adv.* **irr'itably**.—*adj.* **irr'itant**, irritating.—*n.* that which causes irritation.—*n.* **irrita'tion**, act of irritating or exciting: excitement: anger, annoyance: (*med.*) any morbid excitement of a bodily organ not amounting to inflammation.—*adj.* **irr'itative**, tending to irritate or excite: accompanied with or caused by irritation. [L. *irritāre, -ātum*.]

irruption, *ir-up'sh(ò)n, n.* a breaking or bursting in: a sudden invasion or incursion.—*adj.* **irrup'tive**, rushing suddenly in.—*adv.* **irrup'tively**. [L. *irrumpēre, irruptum—in*, in, *rumpēre*, to break.]

is, *iz*, third pers. sing. pres. indic. of **be**. [O.E. *is*; Ger. *ist*, L. *est*, Gr. *esti*, Sans. *asti*.]

isch(a)emia, *is-kē'mi-à, n.* deficiency of blood in a part of the body. [Gr. *ischein*, to restrain, *haima*, blood.]

-ise, -ize, *suffx.* forming verbs from adjs. (meaning to make), as equal*ise,* or from nouns, as satir*ise.* [L. *-izāre,* from Gr. *-izein*; Fr. *-iser.*]

-ish, *adj. suffx,* signifying somewhat, as old*ish*: sometimes implying deprecation as child*ish.* [O.E. *-isc.*]

Ishmael, *ish'mā-él, n.* one like Ishmael (Gen. xvi. 12), at war with society.—*n.* **Ish'maelite,** a descendant of Ishmael.

isinglass, *ī'zing-gläs, n.* a material, mainly gelatin, got from sturgeons' air-bladders and other sources. [App. from obs. Du. *huizenblas—huizen,* a kind of sturgeon, *blas,* a bladder.]

Islam, *iz'läm,* or *is'-,* or *-läm',* **Is'lamism,** *ns.* the Mohammedan religion: the whole Mohammedan world.—*adjs.* **Islam'ic, Islamit'ic.** [Ar. *islām,* surrender (to God).]

island, *ī'land, n.* land surrounded with water: anything detached and differing from its surroundings: a raised traffic-free area in a street for pedestrians or for traffic control.—*n.* **islander** (*ī'land-ér*), an inhabitant of an island. [M.E. *iland*—O.E. *īegland, īgland, ēgland—īeg, īg, ēg,* island (from a root which appears in Angles*ea,* Alder*n*ey, &c., O.E. *ēa,* L. *aqua,* water), and *land.* The *s* is due to confusion with *isle.*]

isle, *īl, n.* an island.—*ns.* **isles'man,** an islander, esp. an inhabitant of the Hebrides—also **isle'man; islet** (*ī'let*), a little isle. [M.E. *ile, yle*—O.Fr. *isle*—L. *insula.*]

-ism, -asm or (with **-ic**) **-icism,** *suffx.* forming abstract nouns signifying condition, system, as ego*ism,* Calvin*ism,* Anglic*ism.* [L. *-ismus, -asmus*—Gr. *-ismos, -asmos.*]

ism, *izm, n.* any distinctive doctrine, theory, or practice—usually in disparagement. [From the suffx. *-ism.*]

iso-, *ī-sō-,* in composition, equal. [Gr. *isos,* equal]:—e.g. **isochromatic** (*ī-sō-krō-mat'ik*), *adj.* having the same colour (Gr. *chrōma, -ātos,* colour); **isochronal** (*ī-sok'ron-ál*), **isoch'ronous** (*-us*), *adjs.* of equal time: performed in equal times (Gr. *chronos,* time).

isobar, *ī'sō-bär, n.* a line on a map passing through places of equal barometric pressure. [Gr. *isos,* equal, *baros,* weight.]

isobare, *ī'sō-bär, n.* either of two atoms of different chemical elements but of identical atomic mass; e.g. both titanium and chromium have an isotope (q.v.) of atomic mass 50, and each of these is spoken of as an *isobare* of the other.—Also **i'sobar.** [Same as **isobar** above.]

isohyet, *ī-sō-hī'et, n.* a contour line of equal rainfall. [Gr. *isos,* equal, *hyetos,* rain—*hyein,* to rain.]

isolate, *ī'sō-lāt, v.t.* to place in a detached situation, like an island: to insulate: to separate (esp. from those who might be infected): to obtain in an uncompounded state.—*ns.* **isolā'tion; isolā'tionism,** the policy of avoiding political entanglements with other countries; **isolātionist.** [It. *isolare—isola*—L. *insula,* an island.]

isomeric, *ī-sō-mer'ik, adj.* (*chem.*) applied to compounds which are made up of the same elements in the same proportions and have the same molecular weight, but differ in constitution or the mode in which the atoms are arranged.—*ns.* **i'somer,** a substance isomeric

with another; **isom'erism.** [Gr. *isos,* equal, *meros,* part.]

isometric, -al, *ī-sō-met'rik, -ál, adj.* having equality of measure: pertaining to isometrics.—*ns.* **isometr'ics,** system of strengthening the muscles and toning up the body by opposing one muscle to another or to a resistant object; **isom'etry,** equality of pressure. [Gr. *isos,* equal, *metron,* measure.]

isomorphism, *ī-sō-mörf'izm, n.* (*biol.*) similarity in unrelated forms: in the case of two or more minerals, close similarity in crystalline form combined with similar chemical constitution.—*adj.* **isomorph'ous.** [Gr. *isos,* equal, *morphē,* form.]

isopod, *ī'sō-pod, n.* a member of the Isopoda.—*n.pl.* **Isopoda** (*ī-sop'o-da*), an order of Crustaceans with no shell, unstalked eyes, and seven pairs of nearly equal legs—woodlice, fishlice, &c.—*adj.* **isop'odous.** [Gr. *isos,* equal, *pous, podos,* a foot.]

isosceles, *ī-sos'e-lēz, adj.* (*geom.*) having two equal sides, as a triangle. [Gr. *isoskelēs—isos,* equal, *skelos,* a leg.]

isotherm, *ī'so-thérm, n.* a contour line of equal temperature.—*adj.* **isotherm'al.** [Gr. *isos,* equal, *thermē,* heat—*thermos,* hot.]

isotope, *ī'sō-tōp, n.* one of a set of chemically identical species of atom which have the same atomic number but different mass numbers; a natural element is made up of isotopes, always present in the same proportions.—*adj.* **isotopic** (*-top'ik*).—**radio-isotope** (or **radio-element**), a radioactive isotope of a stable element; **stable isotope,** a non-radioactive isotope found in nature. [Gr. *isos,* equal, *topos,* place.]

isotron, *ī'sō-tron, n.* a device for separating isotopes by accelerating ions by means of an electric field. [isotope, and suffx. **-tron.**]

Israelite, *iz'ri-él-īt, n.* a descendant of Israel or Jacob, a Jew.—*adjs.* **Israelīt'ic, Israelīt'ish.**—*adj.* **Israeli** (*iz-rā'li*), pertaining to the modern state of Israel.—*n.* a citizen of the modern state of Israel. [Gr. *Isrāēlītēs—Isrāēl,* Heb. *Yisrāēl,* perh. contender with God—*sara,* to fight, *El,* God.]

issue, *ish'(y)ōō, is'ū, n.* a going or flowing out: act of sending out: that which flows or passes out: fruit of the body, children: produce, profits: a putting into circulation, as of banknotes: publication, as of a book: a giving out for use: ultimate result, outcome: point in dispute: a question awaiting, or ripe for, decision: (*med.*) a discharge: an ulcer produced artificially.—*v.i.* to go, flow, or come out: to proceed, as from a source, to spring: to be produced: (*law*) to come to a point in fact or law: to result, terminate.—*v.t.* to send out: to put into circulation: to give out for use.—*adj.* **iss'ueless,** without issue: childless.—*n.* **iss'uer.**—**at issue,** in quarrel or controversy: in dispute; **join,** or **take, issue,** to take an opposite position, or opposite positions, in dispute; **side-issue,** (see **side**). [O.Fr. *issue—issir,* to go or flow out—L. *exīre—ex,* out, *īre,* to go.]

-ist, -ist, *suffx.* denoting the person who holds a doctrine or practises an art, as Calvin*ist,* novel*ist.* [L. *-ista*—Gr. *-istēs.*]

Neutral vowels in unaccented syllables: *em'pér-ór*; for certain sounds in foreign words see p. ix.

isthmus, *is(th)'mus, n.* a narrow neck of land connecting two larger portions.—*adj.* **isth'mian,** pertaining to an isthmus, esp. the Isthmus of Corinth. The **Isthmian games** were held here by the ancient Greeks every two years. [L.,—Gr. *isthmos,* from root of *ienai,* to go.]

It, it, *it,* abbrev. for Italian vermouth.

it, *it, pron.* the thing spoken of: (*coll.*) that which answers exactly to what one is looking for: (*coll.*) extreme perfection: (*slang*) personal magnetism, sex appeal. [O.E. *hit,* neut. of *he*; Du. *het*; akin to Ger. *es,* L. *id,* Sans. *i,* pronominal root = here. The *t* is an old neuter suffix, as in *that, what,* and cognate with *d* in L. *illud, istud, quod.*]

Italian, *i-tal'yán, adj.* of or relating to Italy or its people.—*n.* a native or citizen of Italy: the language of Italy.—*v.t.* **Ital'ianīse,** to make Italian.—*adjs.* **Italianate, Italianised; Ital'ic,** pertaining to ancient Italy: (usu. without *cap.*) of a sloping type used esp. for emphasis or other distinctive purpose.—*n.* (*pl.*; usu. without *cap.*) italic letters, e.g. *italic letters.*—*v.t.* **ital'icise** (-*is-īz*), to put in italics.—**Italian iron,** a smoothing iron for fluting; **Italian warehouseman,** a dealer in such groceries as macaroni, dried fruits, &c. [L. *Italiānus* and Gr. *Italikos*—*Italia,* Italy.]

itch, *ich, n.* an uneasy irritating sensation in the skin: an eruptive disease in the skin, caused by a parasitic mite: a constant teasing desire.—*v.i.* to have an uneasy, irritating sensation in the skin: to have a constant, teasing desire.—*adj.* **itch'y,** pertaining to or affected with itch.—*n.* **itch'iness.** [O.E. *giccan,* to itch; Ger. *jucken,* to itch.]

item, *ī'tem, adv.* likewise, also.—*n.* a separate article or particular: a piece of news, &c., in a newspaper. [L. *item,* likewise.]

iterate, *it'ér-āt, v.t.* to do again: to say again, repeat.—*n.* **iterā'tion,** repetition.—*adj.* **it'erāt-**

ive, repeating. [L. *iterāre, -ātum*—*iterum,* again.]

itinerant, *it-in'ér-ánt,* also *īt-, adj.* making journeys from place to place: travelling.—*n.* one who travels from place to place, esp. a judge, a Methodist preacher, a strolling musician, or a pedlar.—*ns.* **itin'eracy, itin'erancy.**—*adj.* **itin'erary,** travelling: relating to roads or journeys.—*n.* a plan or record of a journey: a route: a road-book.—*v.i.* **itin'erāte,** to travel from place to place, esp. for the purpose of judging, preaching, or lecturing. [L. *iter, itineris,* a journey.]

-itis, *-ītis, n. suffix.* indicating a disease (now inflammation), as bronch*itis*: also jocularly indicating an imaginary disease, as jazz*itis.*

its, *its, poss. pron.* the possessive of **it.** [The old form was **his, its** not being older than the end of the 16th century. *Its* does not occur in the English Bible of 1611, or in Spenser, occurs rarely in Shakespeare, and is not common until the time of Dryden.]

itself, *it-self', pron.* the emphatic and reflexive form of **it.**—**by itself,** alone, apart; **in itself,** by its own nature.

ivory, *ī'vō-ri, n.* dentine, esp. the hard, white substance composing the tusks of elephants, walruses, &c.—*adj.* made of, or resembling, ivory. *ns.* **i'vory-black,** a black powder, originally made from burnt ivory, but now from bone; **i'vory-nut,** the nut of a species of palm, yielding **vegetable ivory,** a substance like ivory. [O.Fr. *ivurie*—L. *ebur, eboris,* ivory; Sans. *ibhās,* an elephant.]

ivy, *ī'vi, n.* a creeping evergreen plant on trees and walls.—*adjs.* **i'vied, i'vyed; i'vy-man'tled,** overgrown or mantled with ivy. [O.E. *īfig,* O.H.G. *ebah.*]

iwis, ywis, *i-wis', adv.* (*arch.*) certainly, surely: sometimes treated as if it stood for *I wis* (see **wis.**) [O.E. p.adj. *gewis,* certain.]

-ize. See **-ise.**

---

fāte, fär; mē, hûr (her); *mīne; mōte, för; mūte; mōōn, fŏŏt;* ᴛʜᴇn (then)

J

jab, *jab, v.t.* and *v.i.* to poke, stab.—*n.* a sudden thrust or stab. [App. imitative.]

jabber, *jab'ér, v.i.* to gabble or talk rapidly.—*v.t.* to utter indistinctly.—*n.* rapid indistinct speaking.—*n.* **jabb'erer.**—*adv.* **jabb'eringly.** [Imit.]

jabot, *zha'bō, n.* a frill of lace, &c., worn in front of a woman's dress or on a man's shirt-front, esp. (now) as part of full Highland dress. [Fr.]

jacinth, *jas'inth, n.* (*orig.*) a blue gem-stone, perh. sapphire: a red variety of zircon, a hyacinth: (*jewellery*) a variety of garnet, topaz, &c.: a reddish-orange colour. [O.Fr. *iacinte*—L. *hyacinthus.* See **hyacinth.**]

jack, *jak, n.* used as a familiar name or diminutive of John: a saucy or paltry fellow: a sailor: any instrument serving to supply the place of a boy or helper, as a bootjack for taking off boots, a contrivance for turning a spit (**smoke-jack, roasting-jack**), an apparatus for raising heavy weights, a figure that strikes the bell in clocks: the male of some animals: a young pike: a flag displayed from the bowsprit of a ship: a knave in cards: the small white ball that forms the mark in bowls.—*ns.* **jack'-a-dan'dy,** a dandy or fop; **jack'-a-lan'tern, jack'-o-lan'tern,** will-o'-the-wisp.—*n.* **jack'boot,** a large boot reaching above the knee, to protect the leg, orig. covered with plates of iron and worn by cavalry: (*fig.*) military rule, esp. when brutal.—*ns.* **jack'-in-office,** a vexatiously self-important petty official; **jack'-in-the-box,** a box with a figure in it that springs up when the lid is released; **jack'-knife,** a large clasp-knife: a dive in which the performer doubles up in the air and straightens out again.—*v.i.* and *v.t.* to double up as a jack-knife does: (of connected vehicles) through faulty control to form, or cause to form, an angle of 90° or less.—*n.* **jack'-of-all'-trades,** one who can turn his hand to anything; **jack'-plane,** a large, strong plane used by joiners; **jack'pot,** a money pool in card games, competitions, &c., that can be won only on the fulfilment of certain conditions and accumulates till such time as they are fulfilled: a prize-money fund; **jack'-rabb'it,** a long-eared American hare; **jack'-screw,** a jack in which a screw is used for raising heavy weights; **jack'-staff,** a short staff at the bowsprit for the jack-flag.—*n.pl.* **jack'-stays,** ropes or strips of wood or iron stretched along the yards of a ship to bind the sails to.—*ns.* **jack'-straw,** a straw effigy: a man of straw, of no real significance; **jack'-tar',** a sailor; **jack'-tow'el,** long endless towel passing over a roller.—**Jack Frost,** frost personified; **Jack Ketch,** a public hangman—from one so named under James II; **Jack Sprat,** a diminutive fellow.—**jack up,** to raise with, or as if with, a jack: (*slang*) to throw up or

abandon promptly (also **jack in**): increase (as prices).—**cheap jack** (see **cheap**); **every man jack,** one and all; **yellow jack** (*slang*), yellow fever; **hit the jackpot,** to win a jackpot: to have a big success. [Apparently Fr. *Jacques,* the most common name in France, hence used as a substitute for *John,* the most common name in England; really, *James* or *Jacob*—L. *Jacōbus*; but possibly partly from *Jackin, Jankin,* dim. of John.]

jack, *jak, n.* a mediaeval foot-soldier's coat of leather, &c.: a leather pitcher or bottle. [Fr. *jaque,* a coat of mail; through Sp. from Ar.]

jack, *jak, jak, n.* a tree of the East Indies of the bread-fruit genus. [Port. *jaca*—Malay *chakka.*]

jackal, *jak'öl, n.* any of several wild, gregarious animals of the same genus as dogs and wolves: formerly supposed to act as the lion's 'provider' or hunting scout, hence one who does another's dirty work, known to eat the remains of animals slain by others, hence one who claims part of the spoil without facing the danger of obtaining it. [Pers. *shaghāl.*]

jackanapes, *jak'a-nāps, n.* an impudent fellow: a coxcomb: a forward child.

jackaroo, *jak-a-rōō', n.* (*Austr.*) a newcomer, from England or elsewhere, gaining experience in the bush. [**Jack** with affix on the analogy of kang*aroo.*]

jackass, *jak'as, n.* a he-ass: a blockhead.—**laughing jackass,** an Australian kingfisher that laughs, the kookaburra. [**jack, ass.**]

jackdaw, *jak'dö, n.* a species of crow, a daw. [**jack, daw.**]

jacket, *jak'et, n.* a short coat: a loose paper cover: outer casing of a boiler, pipe, &c.: the aluminium or zirconium alloy covering of the fissile elements in a reactor.—*adj.* **jack'eted,** wearing a jacket. [O.Fr. *jaquet,* dim. of *jaque.* See **jack** (2).]

Jacobean, *jak-o-bē'an, adj.* of, or characteristic of, the period of James I of England (1603-1625). [L. *Jacōbus,* James.]

Jacobin, *jack'o-bin, n.* a French Dominican monk, so named because their first convent in Paris was near to, and associated with, the church of St. *Jacques*: one of a society of revolutionists in France, so called from their meeting in a Jacobin convent: a demagogue: an extremist or radical, esp. in politics: a hooded pigeon.—*adjs.* **Jacobin'ic, -al.**—*n.* **Jac'obinism,** the principles of the Jacobins (French revolutionists). [Fr.,—L. *Jacōbus,* James.]

Jacobite, *jak'o-bīt, n.* an adherent of James II and his descendants.—*adjs.* **Jac'obite, Jacobit'ic, -al.**—*n.* **Jac'obītism.** [L. *Jacōbus,* James.]

Jacob's-ladder, *jā'kobz-lad'ér, n.* (*naut.*) a ladder of ropes with wooden steps: a wild and garden plant with ladder-like leaves. [From the *ladder Jacob* saw in his dream, Gen. xxviii. 12.]

Neutral vowels in unaccented syllables: *em'pér-ór*; for certain sounds in foreign words see p. ix.

388

jaconet, *jak'ŏ-net, n.* a plain, thin cotton cloth with smooth finish: a thin material of rubber and linen used for medical dressings. [The town of *Jagannath* (Puri), India, where the famous idol, Jagannath (see **juggernaut**) is kept.]

jacquard loom, *jak'ärd, jak-ärd', n.* one for weaving figured goods. [J. M. *Jacquard,* who invented it, 1801.]

jade, *jād, n.* a worthless nag: a woman (in contempt or irony).—*v.t.* to tire: to harass (esp. in *pa.p.* jad'ed). [Origin unknown; cf. O.N. *jalda,* a mare; Scot. *yaud.*]

jade, *jād, n.* various mineral substances of tough texture and green colour (*jadeite, nephrite,* and others)—once held to cure side pains.— Also *adj.* [Fr.,—Sp. *ijada,* the flank—L. *ilia.*]

jag, *jag, n.* a notch: a sharp or rugged point of rock, &c.: (*bot.*) a cleft or division: (*Scot.*) a prick: an inoculation, injection: a thrill: a bout of indulgence, e.g. in liquor or narcotics.—*v.t.* to cut into notches: to prick.—*pr.p.* jagg'ing; *pa.p.* jagged.—*adj.* jagged (*jag'id*), notched, rough-edged.—*adv.* **jaggedly** (*jag'id-li*).—*n.* **jaggedness** (*jag'id-nes*). [Origin unknown.]

jaguar, *jag'wär,* or *jag'ū-är, n.* a powerful beast of prey, one of the cat family, found in South America resembling the leopard of Asia and Africa. [South American Indian *jaguára.*]

Jah, *jä, n.* Jehovah. [Heb. *Yah.*]

jail, gaol, *jāl, n.* a prison.—*ns.* **jail'-bird, gaol'-bird,** one who is or has been in jail; **jail'er, gaol'er,** one who has charge of a jail or of prisoners, a turnkey; **jail'-deliv'ery, gaol'-deliv'ery,** the clearing of a jail by sending all prisoners to trial; **jail'-fē'ver, gaol'-fē'ver,** typhus fever, once common in jails. [Norm. Fr. *gaiole*—Low L. *gabiola,* a cage—L. *cavea,* a cage—*cavus,* hollow.]

jalap, *jal'ap, n.* the purgative root of a plant first brought from *Jalapa* or Xalapa, in Mexico.

jalop(p)y, *jă-lop'i, n.* an old motor-car or aero-plane.

jalousie, *zhal-ŏŏ-zē',* or *zhal'-, n.* an outside shutter with slats. [Fr. *jalousie,* jealousy.]

jam, *jam, n.* a conserve of fruit boiled with sugar: (*slang*) good luck.—*adj.* **jamm'y.** [Perh. from **jam** (2).]

jam, *jam, v.t.* to press or squeeze tight: to crowd full: to block by crowding: to wedge: to bring (machinery) to a standstill by wedging or disarranging the parts: to interfere with a wireless signal by sending out other signals on a similar wavelength.—*v.i.* to become stuck, wedged, &c.: in jazz, to play enthusiastically, interpolating and improvising freely (**jam session,** a gathering of jazz musicians (orig. an informal one) at which jazz is played in this way).—*pr.p.* jamm'ing; *pa.p.* jammed.—*n.* a crush: a block: a difficulty: a difficult or embarrassing situation. [Perh. allied to **champ.**]

Jamaica pepper, *ja-mā'ka pep'ér,* allspice (q.v.). [*Jamaica,* **pepper.**]

jamb, *jam, n.* the sidepiece or post of a door, fireplace, &c. [Fr. *jambe,* perh. Celt. *cam,* bent.]

jambok. See **sjambok.**

jamboree, *jam-bō-rē', n.* in euchre, a hand holding the five highest trump cards: (*slang*) a boisterous frolic, a spree: a great Scout rally.

jangle, *jang'gl, v.t.* and *v.i.* to sound harshly or discordantly, as bells: to render, or be, disordered, as nerves—*v.i.* to wrangle or quarrel.—*n.* dissonant clanging: contention.—*ns.* **jang'ler; jang'ling.** [O.Fr. *jangler.*]

janitor, *jan'i-tór, n.* a doorkeeper: an attendant or caretaker:—*fem.* **jan'itrix, jan'itress.** [L. *jānitor*—*jānua,* a door.]

janizary, *jan'i-zär-i, n.* a soldier of the old Turkish infantry forming the Sultan's guard and the main part of the Turkish army, consisting originally of children taken as tribute from Christian subjects—also **jan'issary** (-*zär-i*).— *adj.* **janizā'rian.** [Fr. *Janissaire*—Turk, *yeñi,* new, *tsheri,* soldiery.]

Jansenism, *jan'sen-izm, n.* the doctrines of Cornelius *Jansen* (1585-1638), Roman Catholic Bishop of Ypres.—*n.* **Jan'senist,** a believer in Jansenism.

janty. See **jaunty.**

January, *jan'ū-ár-i, n.* the first month of the year (the eleventh month in the Julian calendar), dedicated by the Romans to *Janus,* the god of opening, who had two faces, one at the front of his head and the other at the back. [L. *Jānuārius.*]

japan, *ja-pan', v.t.* to varnish after the manner or in imitation of Japanese lacquered ware: to make black and glossy: *pr.p.* japann'ing; *pa.p.* japanned'.—*n.* Japanese ware, varnish, or lacquer for japanning: japanned work.—*adj.* **Japanese',** of Japan, of its people, or of its language.—Also *n.*

jar, *jär, v.i.* to make a harsh discordant sound or an unpleasant vibration: to clash (e.g. of interests): to quarrel: to be inharmonious.—*v.t.* to cause to vibrate unpleasantly: to grate (on):—*pr.p.* jarr'ing; *pa.p.* jarred.—*n.* a harsh sudden vibration: clash of interests or opinions: displeasure: a shock to body, nerves, or sensibilities.—*adv.* **jarr'ingly.** [Imit.]

jar, *jär, n.* an earthen or glass bottle with a wide mouth: the amount this will contain. [Fr. *jarre,* or Sp. *jarra*—Ar. *jarrah.*]

jargon, *jär'gón, n.* confused talk, gibberish: artificial or barbarous language: the special or technical vocabulary of a science, art, profession, &c. [Fr. *jargon.*]

jargonelle, *jär-go-nel', n.* a kind of pear. [Fr.]

jarrah, *jar'ä, n.* a Western Australian timber tree. [From native name.]

jasmine, *jas'min,* **jessamine,** *jes'a-min, n.* a genus of shrubs, many with very fragrant flowers. [Fr. *jasmin, jasemin*—Ar. *yāsmīn, yāsamīn*—Pers. *yāsmīn.*]

jasper, *jas'pér, n.* a precious stone, an opaque quartz of various colours: a fine hard porcelain (also **jasper-ware**). [O.Fr. *jaspe, jaspre*—L. *iaspis, -idis*—and Gr. *iaspis, -idos;* of Eastern origin.]

jaundice, *jön'dis,* or *jän'dis, n.* a disease, characterised by a yellowing of the eyes, skin, &c., by bile pigment: state of taking an unfavourable prejudiced view.—*adj.* **jaun'diced,** affected with jaundice: (of person, judgment) biassed by envy, disillusionment, &c. [Fr. *jaunisse*—*jaune,* yellow—L. *galbīnus,* yellowish, *galbus,* yellow.]

jaunt, *jönt,* also *jänt, v.i.* to go from place to place: to make an excursion.—*n.* an excursion:

a ramble.—*adj.* **jaunt′ing.**—*n.* **jaunt′ing-car,** a low-set, two-wheeled, open vehicle used in Ireland, with side-seats usually back to back.

jaunty, janty, *jönt′i,* or *jänt′i, adj.* having an airy or sprightly manner approaching swagger.—*adv.* **jaunt′ily.**—*n.* **jaunt′iness.** [Fr. *gentil.*]

javelin, *jav′(é-)lin, n.* a light spear thrown by the hand. [Fr. *javeline*; prob. Celt.]

jaw, *jö, n.* a mouth-structure for biting or chewing: one of a pair of parts for gripping, crushing, &c.: the bone of a jaw: (*pl.*) a narrow entrance.—*ns.* **jaw′ing** (*slang*), talk, esp. unrestrained or reproving; **jaw′bone.** [Perh. **chaw** (a chew), modified by Fr. *joue,* cheek.]

jay, *jā, n.* a noisy bird of the crow family with bright plumage: an impertinent chatterer.—*n.* **jay′walker** (*coll.*), a careless pedestrian whom motorists are expected to avoid running down. [O.Fr. *jay.*]

jazz, *jaz, n.* a type of American music, esp. for dancing, developed from ragtime (q.v.), characterised by improvisation, syncopation and feverish or subtle rhythm: garish colouring: a quality, impulse, or manner analogous to the spirit of jazz: (*slang*) insincere, lying talk.—*adj.* **jazz′y.**

jealous, *jel′us, adj.* suspicious of or incensed at rivalry: envious (of): anxiously heedful.—*adv.* **jeal′ously.**—*n.* **jeal′ousy.** [O.Fr. *jalous*—L. *zēlus*—Gr. *zēlos,* emulation.]

jean, *jēn, jān, n.* a twilled-cotton cloth: (*pl.*) trousers or overalls of jean: (*pl.*) close-fitting, sometimes three-quarter length, casual trousers of jean or similar material. [O.Fr. *Janne*—L. *Genua,* Genoa.]

jeep, *jēp, n.* a light military vehicle with heavy duty tyres and good ground clearance for use on rough terrain. [G.P. = general purpose.]

jeer, *jēr, v.t.* to treat with derision.—*v.i.* to scoff (at).—*n.* a railing remark.—*adv.* **jeer′ingly.**

jehad. See **jihad.**

Jehovah, *ji-hō′vä, n.* Yahweh, the Hebrew God, a name used by Christians since the 16th century. [The most sacred name of God in the Hebrew scriptures (never uttered) is represented by four consonants, variously written (JHVH, &c.). Later Jewish scholars indicated three vowels, probably intended as those of *Adōnāi,* Lord—the word actually to be read—but taken as being those of the sacred name.]

jehu, *jē′hū, n.* (*coll.*) a driver, esp. a furious whip. [A reference to 2 Kings, ix. 20.]

jejune, *ji-jōōn′, adj.* empty: barren: void of interest (e.g. a narrative): naïve, immature: showing lack of information or experience.—*adv.* **jejune′ly.**—*n.* **jejune′ness.** [L. *jējūnus,* fasting, empty.]

Jekyll and Hyde, *jēk′il* (or *jek′il*) and *hīd,* the good and the bad side of a human being—from R. L. Stevenson's *The Strange Case of Dr Jekyll and Mr Hyde* (1886).

jelly, *jel′i, n.* anything gelatinous: the juice of fruit boiled with sugar.—*v.t.* and *v.i.* **jell,** to set as a jelly: to take distinct shape.—*adj.* **jell′ied,** in the state of jelly: in or with jelly.—*n.* **jell′y(-)fish,** any of several invertebrate animals, almost exclusively marine, of two classes, with jelly-like body:—*pl.* **jelly(-)fish(es).** [Fr. *gelée,* from *geler*—L. *gelāre,* to freeze.]

jemmy, *jem′i, n.* a burglar's short crowbar. [A form of the name James.]

je ne sais quoi, *zhë né se kwa,* an indefinable something. [Fr., I don't know what.]

jennet, *jen′et, n.* a small Spanish horse.—Also **genn′et, gen′et.** [O.Fr. *genet*—Sp. *jinete,* a light horseman; perh. of Arab origin.]

jenny, *jen′i, n.* a country lass: a womanish man: a wren or owl regarded as female: a she-ass: a spinning-jenny. [From the name *Jenny.*]

jeopardy, *jep′ärd-i, n.* hazard, danger.—*v.t.* **jeop′-ardise,** to put in jeopardy.—*adj.* **jeop′ardous.** [Fr. *jeu parti,* a divided or even game—Low L. *jocus partītus*—L. *jocus,* a game, *partītus,* divided—*partīrī,* to divide.]

jerboa, *jér-bō′ä, n.* any of several Old World desert rodents that jump like a kangaroo (esp. the African type). [Ar. *yarbū′.*]

jeremiad, *jer-e-mī′ad, n.* a lamentation: a doleful story. [From *Jeremiah,* reputed author of the Book of Lamentations.]

jerfalcon. Same as **gerfalcon.**

Jericho, *jer′i-kō, n.* a remote place, to which one is humorously consigned—from *Jericho* in Palestine and the story in 2 Sam. x. 4, 5.

jerk, *jûrk, n.* a short movement begun and ended suddenly: an involuntary spasmodic contraction of a muscle: (*slang*) a useless or despicable person.—*v.t.* to throw or move with a jerk.—Also *v.i.*—*adj.* **jerk′y.**—*n.* **jerki′ness.** [An imitative word.]

jerked-meat, *jûrkt′-mēt, n.* meat cut into thin pieces and dried in the sun. Also called *charqui,* of which 'jerked' is a corrupted form. [Amer. Sp., *charqui*—Amer. Indian.]

jerkin, *jûr′kin, n.* a close-fitting jacket, a short coat or close waistcoat. [Origin unknown.]

jerry, *jer′i, n.* (*slang*) a German soldier: a German aeroplane: (*cap.*) the Germans.—Also *adj.* [Corr. of *German.*]

jerry-builder, *jer′i-bild′ér, n.* one who builds flimsy houses cheaply and hastily, a speculative builder.—*adj.* **jerr′y-built.** [Prob. the personal name.]

jerrymander, a mistaken form of **gerrymander.**

jersey, *jûr′zi, n.* the finest part of wool: combed wool: a close-fitting woollen upper garment: a cow of Jersey breed. [From the island *Jersey.*]

jerusalem artichoke, *jer-ōōs′ä-lem är′ti-chōk.* See **artichoke.**

jess, *jes, n.* a short strap round the leg of a hawk.—*adj.* **jessed,** having jesses on. [O.Fr. *ges*—L. *jactus,* a cast—*jacêre,* to throw.]

jessamine, *jes′a-min.* See **jasmine.**

jest, *jest, n.* something ludicrous, an object of laughter: a joke: fun: something uttered in sport.—*v.i.* to make a jest.—*ns.* **jest′-book,** a collection of funny stories; **jest′er,** one who jests: a professional buffoon, esp. one kept in a king's or nobleman's household.—*adv.* **jest′ingly.** [Orig. 'a deed, a story', M.E. *geste*—O.Fr. *geste*—L. *gesta,* things done, doings—*gerēre,* to do.]

Jesuit, *jez′ū-it, n.* one of the Society of Jesus, founded in 1534 by Ignatius Loyola: (*opprobriously*) a crafty or insidious person, an intriguer, a prevaricator.—*adjs.* **Jesuit′ic, -al.**—*adv.* **Jesuit′ically.**—*n.* **Jes′uitism,** the principles and practices of the Jesuits.

Jesus, *jē′zus, n.* the founder of Christianity:—

Neutral vowels in unaccented syllables: *em′pér-ór*; for certain sounds in foreign words see p. ix.

390

also (esp. in vocative) **Jesu** (*jē'zū*). [Gr. *Iēsous*—Heb. *Yēshūa'*, contr. of *Yehōshūa'*, Joshua.]

jet, *jet*, *n.* a black mineral, very hard and compact, used for ornaments.—*adj.* **jet'-black'**. [O.Fr. *jaiet*—L. and Gr. *gagatēs*—*Gagas* or *Gangai*, a town and river in Lycia, in Asia Minor, where it was obtained.]

jet, *jet*, *n.* a fluid stream issuing from an orifice or nozzle: a small nozzle: a jet-propelled aeroplane.—*v.t.* and *v.i.* to spout.—**jet propulsion**, propulsion by means of the reaction of a jet of fluid (in the case of aircraft, air) expelled backwards from the machine—in narrower sense not including rocket propulsion (see **rocket**). Types of jet-propelled aeroplane are named after the types of compression-ignition engine used, which include the following, **ramjet**, the simplest type, in which the air is compressed solely as the result of forward speed; **turbojet**, an engine comprising compressor(s) and turbine(s); **turboprop**, an engine differing from the turbojet in the fact that the turbine develops extra power to drive a propeller.—**the jet set**, moneyed social set able to spend much of their time travelling to fashionable resorts all over the world. [O.Fr. *jetter*—L. *jactāre*, to fling, freq. of *jacĕre*, to throw.]

jetsam, *jet'săm*, *n.* (*obs.*) jettison: goods thrown overboard and washed up on the shore: goods from a wreck that remain under water (cf. **flotsam**)—also **jet'som**, **jet'son.**—*n.* **jett'ison**, the act of throwing goods overboard to lighten a vessel.—*v.t.* to throw overboard, as goods, in time of danger: (*fig.*) to abandon, reject.—**flotsam and jetsam**, (often) unclaimed odds and ends: waifs and strays. [A.F. *jetteson* —L. *jactātiō, -ōnis,* a casting—*jactāre, freq.* of *jacĕre,* to cast.]

jetty, *jet'i, n.* a projection: a pier. [O.Fr. *jettee,* thrown out—*jetter.* See **jet** (2).]

jeu d'esprit, *zhø des-prē', * a witticism: a witty literary trifle:—*pl.* **jeux** (*zhø*) **d'esprit.** [Fr.]

Jew, *jōō, n.* a person of Semitic race, of Hebrew descent or religion—an Israelite: (offensively) used for a usurer, miser, &c.:—*fem.* **Jew'ess.**—*n.* **Jew'-bait'ing**, the persecuting of Jews.—*adj.* **Jewish.**—*ns.* **Jew'ishness**; **Jew's'-harp**, a small lyre-shaped musical instrument played against the teeth by twitching a metal tongue. [O.Fr. *Jueu*—L. *Jūdaeus*—Gr. *Ioudaios*—Heb. *Yehudah,* Judah.]

jewel, *jōō'él, n.* a precious stone: a personal ornament of precious stones: anything or anyone highly valued.—*v.t.* to adorn with jewels: to fit with a jewel:—*pr.p.* **jew'elling**; *pa.p.* **jew'elled.**—*ns.* **Jew'el-house**, a room in the Tower of London where the crown-jewels are kept; **jew'eller**, one who makes or deals in jewels; **jewellery** (*jōō'él-ri*), **jew'elry**, jewels in general. [O.Fr. *jouel* (Fr. *joyau*): either a dim. of Fr. *joie*, joy, from L. *gaudium,* or derived through Low L. *jocāle,* from L. *jocārī,* to jest.]

Jewry, *jōō'ri, n.* Judea: a district inhabited by Jews.

Jezebel, *jez'é-b(é)l, n.* a bold, vicious woman. [1 Kings, xvi. 31; 2 Kings, ix. 30-37.]

jib, *jib, n.* a triangular sail borne in front of the foremast in a ship: the boom of a crane or derrick.—*v.i.* (of a sail) to gybe or swing from one side to the other: to move restively: (of a horse) to balk or shy: (*fig.*) to refuse, show objection (with *at*).—*v.t.* to cause to gybe.—*n.* **jib'-boom'**, a boom or extension of the bowsprit, on which the jib is spread.

jibe. Same as **gibe.**

jig, *jig, n.* a lively dance usually in 6-8 time: a dance tune of like kind—a gigue: a pattern or guide used in a machine shop.—*v.t.* and *v.i.* to dance a jig: to move up and down rapidly and jerkily.—*n.* **jigg'er**, anything that jigs: one of many kinds of subsidiary appliances, esp. one that works with a jerky or a reciprocating motion, as an apparatus for separating ores by jolting in sieves in water, a simple potter's wheel or a template (q.v.) used with the wheel: a warehouse crane: the bridge or rest for the cue in billiards: a form of iron-headed golf-club: an old-fashioned sloop-rigged boat: a contemptuous term for a vehicle of various kinds: a contraption: an odd-looking person, esp. one attired in an unbecoming fashion, a fright: a measure for drinks, about 1½ ounces.—*ns.* **jig'saw**, a narrow saw used for cutting curved or irregular lines or ornamental patterns; **jigsaw puzzle**, a picture cut up into pieces, as by a jigsaw, to be fitted together:—*pr.p.* **jigg'ing**; *pa.p.* **jigged.**

jigger. See **chigoe.**

jihad, **jehad**, *ji häd', n.* a war by Mohammedans against unbelievers or heretics: a war for or against a doctrine or principle. [Ar. *jihād.*]

jilt, *jilt, n.* one, esp. a woman, who encourages and then rejects a lover.—*v.t.* to discard a lover after encouragement. [Possibly *jillet* or *gillet*, dim. of the name Jill.]

Jim Crow, *jim krō, n.* a generic name for the Negro (*derog.*).—**Jim Crow car, school,** &c., one for Negroes only. [From the refrain of a song popularised by a famous Negro minstrel.]

jingle, *jing'gl, n.* a sound like that of small bells, coins shaken together, &c.: phrases or sentences, often in metre, in which the same or similar sounds recur: verse without poetic quality.—Also *v.t.* and *v.i.* [Imit.]

jingo, *jing'gō, n.* a name used in mild oaths. From its occurrence in a music-hall song of 1878 that conveyed a threat against Russia, a jingo has come to mean one who is aggressively or bellicosely patriotic.—*adjs.* **jing'o, jing'oish.**—*n.* **jing'oism** (cf. **chauvinism**). [Used first as a conjurer's summoning call; possibly from Basque *Jinkoa, Jainko,* God.]

jinn, *jin, n.pl.* (*sing.* **jinnee, jinni, djinni, genie,** *jin-ē', jēn'i*) a class of spirits in Mohammedan mythology, assuming various shapes, sometimes as men of enormous size and portentous hideousness, The *jinn* are often called *genii* by a confusion. A plural **jinns** is sometimes erroneously used. [Ar. *jinn.*]

jinricksha, *jin-rik'shă, -shō.* See **rickshaw.**

jinx, *jingks, n.* a bringer of bad luck.

jitter, *jit'ér, v.i.* (*slang*) to be nervous, to show nervousness.—*adj.* **jitt'ery.**—*ns.* **jitt'ers**, jumps, nervous alarm; **jitt'erbug**, an enthusiast for a violent and spasmodic type of dancing to jazz music: an alarmist.

jive, *jīv, n.* a style of jazz music: dancing to this:

fāte, fär; mē, hûr (her); *mīne; mōte, för; mūte; mōōn, fŏŏt;* THen (then)

jargon.—v.i. to play or dance jive: to talk·jargon.

job, *job, n.* a sudden thrust with anything pointed, as a beak.—*v.t.* and *v.i.* to prod or peck suddenly:—*pr.p.* jobb'ing; *pa.p.* jobbed. [App. imitative.]

job, *job, n.* any definite piece of work: a piece of work of a trifling or temporary nature: any undertaking or employment with a view to profit: a mean transaction in which private gain is sought under pretence of public service: anything one has to do: a state of affairs (as, *a bad job*).—*v.i.* to work at jobs: to make dishonest arrangements.—*v.t.* to buy and sell, as a broker: to hire or let out, esp. horses: to sublet (work): to carry out dishonestly.—*ns.* **jobb'er,** one who jobs: one who buys and sells, as a broker: one who turns official actions to private advantage: one who engages in a mean lucrative affair; **jobb'ery,** jobbing: unfair means employed to procure some private end; **job'-lot,** a collection of odds and ends.—**just the job** (*coll.*), exactly what is wanted; **have a job to** (*coll.*), to have difficulty in.

Job's comforter, *jōbz kum'fŭrt-ér,* one who aggravates the distress of an unfortunate man he has come to comfort. [*Job* called his three friends 'miserable comforters'—Job xvi. 2.]

jockey, *jok'i, n.* a man (orig. a boy) who rides in a horse-race: a horse-dealer: one who takes undue advantage in business.—*v.t.* to jostle by riding against: to cheat: to manoeuvre (into). —*v.i.* to cheat: to manoeuvre for position.—*ns.* **jock'eyism, jock'eyship.—Jockey Club,** an association for the promotion and ordering of horse-racing. [Dim. of *Jock,* northern Eng. for **Jack.**]

jockstrap, *jok'strap, n.* genital support worn by men participating in athletics.

jocose, *jo-kōs', adj.* full of jokes: facetious.—*adv.* **jocose'ly.**—*n.* **jocose'ness.** [L. *jocōsus—jocus,* a joke.]

jocular, *jok'ū-lár, adj.* given to jokes: humorous (e.g. a remark).—*n.* **jocularity** (-ar'i-ti).—*adv.* **joc'ularly.** [L. *joculāris—jocus,* joke.]

jocund, *jōk'ŭnd, jok'ŭnd, adj.* mirthful, merry, cheerful, pleasant.—*n.* **jocundity** (-kund'i-ti). —*adv.* **joc'undly.** [Fr.,—L.L. *jocundus* for L. *jūcundus,* pleasant, modified by association with *jocus.*]

jodhpurs, *jod'pûrz, n.pl.* riding breeches fitting tightly from knee to ankle. [*Jodhpur,* in India.]

jog, *jog, v.t.* to shake: to push with the elbow or hand: to stimulate, stir up, as the memory.— *v.i.* to move up and down with unsteady motion: (*lit.* and *fig.*) to trudge (with *on, along*):—*pr.p.* jogg'ing; *pa.p.* jogged.—*n.* a slight shake: a push.—*ns.* **jogg'ing,** exercising by running in a slow bouncing manner; **jog'-trot,** a slow jogging trot.

joggle, *jog'l, v.t.* to jog or shake slightly: to jostle.—*v.i.* to shake:—*pr.p.* jogg'ling; *pa.p.* jogg'led. [App. dim. or freq. of **jog.**]

John, *jon, n.* a proper name, one of whose diminutives, **Johnn'y, Johnn'ie,** is sometimes used in slang for a simpleton, a fashionable idler, or a fellow generally.—**John Bull,** a generic name for an Englishman from Arbuthnott's *History of John Bull,* 1712; **John Company,** a

familiar name for the East India Company; **John Dory** (see **dory**).

Johnsonian, *jon-sō'ni-án, adj.* pertaining to Dr Samuel *Johnson,* man of letters and lexicographer (1709-84).—*n.* **John'sonese,** the Johnsonian style, or an imitation of it—ponderous English, full of antitheses, balanced sets of clauses, and words of classical origin.

joie de vivre, *zhwa dé vē-vr',* joy in living: high spirits, zest. [Fr.]

join, *join, v.t.* to connect, fasten (one thing to another): to connect by a line: to add or annex: to unite in any association (e.g. in marriage): to come into association with or the company of: to become a member of: to go to and remain with, in, or on (e.g. *he joined the group at the fire, his ship*).—*v.i.* to come together so as to be united: to unite (with): to take part (with).—*ns.* **join'er,** one who joins or unites: a worker in wood, esp. one who makes smaller structures than a carpenter (e.g. finishings of a building); **join'ery,** the art of the joiner; **joint,** the place where, or mode in which, two or more things join: a place where two things, esp. bones, meet with power of movement as of a hinge: a node, or place where a stem bears leaves: (*cookery*) part of the limb of an animal cut off at the joint: (*slang*) place for meeting, a resort, often a mean establishment: a reefer.—*adj.* united or combined: shared by two or more.—*v.t.* to unite by joints: to provide with joints: to cut into joints, as an animal.—*adj.* **joint'ed.**—*adv.* **joint'ly,** in a joint manner: unitedly or in combination: together.—*ns.* **joint'-stock,** stock held jointly or in company; **joint'ure,** property settled on a woman at marriage to be enjoyed after her husband's death; **join'tress,** a woman on whom a jointure is settled.—**join battle,** to begin a fight or contest; **join hands,** (*fig.*) to combine (to do, in doing); **join issue** (see **issue**); **join up,** to enlist.—**out of joint,** dislocated: (*fig.*) disordered; **put one's nose out of joint,** to supplant in another's love or confidence; **universal joint,** a contrivance by which one part of a machine is able to move freely in all directions, as in the ball-and-socket joint. [O.Fr. *joindre*—L. *jungĕre, junctum,* to join.]

joist, *joist, n.* beam supporting the boards of a floor or the laths of a ceiling.—*v.t.* to fit with joists. [O.Fr. *giste—gesir—* L. *jacēre,* to lie.]

joke, *jōk, n.* a jest, a witticism, anything said or done to excite a laugh: an absurdity.—*v.t.* to banter.—*v.i.* to jest: to make sport.—*n.* **jok'er,** one who jokes or jests: a fifty-third card in the pack, used at euchre, poker, &c.—*adv.* **jok'ingly.** [L. *jocus.*]

jolie laide, *zho-lē led,* a woman whose very ugliness is part of her charm. [Fr.]

jolly, *jol'i, adj.* merry: expressing or exciting mirth: comely, robust: (*coll.*) used as an indefinite expression of approval, sometimes ironical.—*n.* **jollifica'tion,** noisy festivity and merriment.—*ns.* **joll'iness, joll'ity.** [O.Fr. *jolif, joli.*]

jollyboat, *jol'i-bōt, n.* a ship's boat.

jolt, *jōlt, v.i.* to shake: to proceed with sudden jerks.—*v.t.* to shake with a sudden shock.—*n.* a sudden jerk. [Etymology obscure.]

Neutral vowels in unaccented syllables: *em'pér-ór;* for certain sounds in foreign words see p. ix.

Jonah, *jō'na, n.* a bringer of ill-luck, on shipboard, or elsewhere. [From the prophet *Jonah*—Jonah i. 3-15.]

Jonathan, *jon-a-thån, n.* the people of the United States, collectively, or a typical specimen, **Brother Jonathan**: an American variety of apple. [Perh. from the sagacious Governor *Jonathan* Trumbull, 1710-85.]

jongleur, *zhɔ-glœr', n.* a wandering minstrel. [Fr.,—O.Fr.*jogleor*—L.*joculātor.* Same root as **juggler.**]

jonquil, *jon'kwil, n.* a name given to certain species of narcissus with rush-like leaves. [Fr. *jonquille*—L. *juncus*, a rush.]

jordan, *jör'dan, n.* (*Shak.*) a chamber-pot. [According to some from *Jordan*-bottle, a pilgrim's bottle containing *Jordan* water.]

Jordanian, *jör-dān'-i-ån, adj.* belonging to *Jordan,* a country in S.W. Asia.—*n.* a native of Jordan.

jorum, *jōr', jör'úm, joram, n.* a large drinking bowl: a great drink. [Ety. unknown; perh. from *Joram* in 2 Sam viii. 10.]

joss, *jos, n.* a Chinese idol.—*n.* **joss-stick**, a stick of gum burned by Chinese as incense to their gods. [Port. *deos*, god—L. *deus.*]

jostle, *jos'l, v.t.* and *v.i.* to shake or jar by collision: to hustle: to elbow.—Also *n.* [Freq. of **joust, just.**]

jot, *jot, n.* an iota, a whit, a tittle.—*v.t.* to set (down) briefly, to make a memorandum of:—*pr.p.* jott'ing; *pa.p.* jott'ed.—*ns.* **jott'er**, one who jots: a book for rough notes or exercises not intended for preservation; **jott'ing**, a memorandum [L. *iōta* (read as *jōta*)—Gr.*iōta*, the smallest letter in the alphabet equivalent to *i*; Heb. *yōd.*]

jougs, *jōōgz, jugz, n.pl.* an iron neck-ring—the old Scottish pillory. [Prob. O.Fr. *joug,* a yoke—L. *jugum.*]

joule, *jōōl, jowl, n.* the SI unit of work, energy, heat, the work done when the point of application of a force of one newton is displaced through a distance of one metre in the direction of the force (= 10^{7} ergs). [J. P. Joule, physicist.]

journal, *jûr'n(å)l, n.* a diary: in bookkeeping, a book containing an account of each day's transactions: a newspaper published daily (or otherwise): a magazine: the transactions of any society: that part of a shaft or axle which rests in the bearings (reason for name unknown).—*n.* **journalese'**, the jargon of bad journalism.—*v.i.* **jour'nalise**, to keep a diary or journal.—*v.t.* to enter in a journal.—*ns.* **jour'nalism**, the profession of conducting, or writing for, public journals; **jour'nalist**, one who writes for or conducts a newspaper.—*adj.* **journalist'ic**. [Fr.,—L. *diurnālis*. See **diurnal.**]

journey, *jûr'ni, n.* (*obs.*) a day's work or travel: any travel: a tour.—*v.i.* to travel:—*pr.p.* jour'neying; *pa.p.* jour'neyed (-*nid*).—*n.* **jour'neyman**, one who works by the day: any hired workman: one whose apprenticeship is completed. [Fr. *journée*—*jour*, a day—L. *diurnus.*]

joust, just, *just* (*jōōst* and *jowst* are recent pronunciations due to the spelling), *n.* the encounter of two knights on horseback at a tournament.—*v.i.* to tilt. [O.Fr. *juste, jouste, joste*—L. *juxtā*, near.]

Jove. See **Jupiter.**

jovial, *jō'vi-ål, adj.* joyous: full of jollity and geniality.—*ns.* **joviality** (-*al'i-ti*), **jo'vialness.**—*adv.* **jo'vially.** [L. *joviālis*—*Jovis*, the god Jove or Jupiter (q.v.), or the planet Jupiter, an auspicious star.]

jowl, *jōl, jowl, n.* the jaw: the cheek. [Probably several different words. M.E. forms are *chaul, chol*; O.E. *ceafl*, jaw.]

joy, *joi, n.* intense gladness: a cause of this.—*v.i.* to rejoice:—*pr.p.* joy'ing; *pa.p.* joyed.—*adj.* **joy'ful**, feeling, expressing, or giving joy.—*adv.* **joy'fully.**—*n.* **joy'fulness.**—*adj.* **joy'less**, without joy: not giving joy.—*adv.* **joy'lessly.**—*n.* **joy'lessness.**—*adj.* **joy'ous**, joyful (often poetical).—*adv.* **joy'ously.**—*n.* **joy'ousness.**—**no joy** (*slang*), no news, reply, information, luck. [Fr. *joie* (cf. It. *gioja*)—L. *gaudium.*]

jubilant, *jōō'bi-lånt, adj.* uttering songs of triumph: rejoicing.—*ns.* **ju'bilance, -ancy.**—*v.i.* **ju'bilate**, to exult, rejoice.—*ns.* **jubilate** (*yōō-bi-lä'tå, jōō-bi-lā'tē*), the 100th Psalm, which in the English Prayer Book is a canticle, used as an alternative for the Benedictus: (R.C. Church) the third Sunday after Easter, so called because the service begins on that day with the 66th Psalm, 'Jubilate Deo', &c.; **jubilā'tion**, a shout for joy.] [L. *jūbilāre*, to shout for joy.]

jubilee, *jōō'bi-lē, n.* among the Jews, every fiftieth year, a year of release of slaves, cancelling of debts, &c., proclaimed by the sound of a trumpet: the celebration of a fiftieth anniversary: any season or condition of great joy and festivity. [Fr. *jubilé*—L. *jūbilaeus*—Heb. *yōbēl*, a ram, ram's horn (trumpet).]

Judaean, Judean, *jōō-dē'án, adj.* belonging to Judaea or the Jews.—*n.* a native of Judaea [L. *Judaea.*]

Judaic, -al, *jōō dā'ik, ål, adj.* pertaining to the Jews.—*v.t.* **Judaise** (*jōō'dā-īz*), to conform to or practise Judaism.—*n.* **Judaism** (*jōō'dā-izm*), the doctrines and rites of the Jews: conformity to the Jewish rites. [L. *Jūdaicus*—*Jūda*, Judah, a son of Israel.]

judas, *jōō'das, n.* (*cap.*) a traitor: a spy-hole in a jail door, &c.—*n.* **Ju'das-kiss**, any act of treachery under the guise of kindness (Matt. xxvi. 48, 49).

judder, *jud'ér, n.* a vibratory effect in singing produced by alternations of greater and less intensity of sound: aircraft or other vibration.—Also *v.i.*

judge, *juj, v.i.* to try and decide questions of law or of guilt: to pass sentence: to compare facts to determine the truth: to estimate: to conclude.—*v.t.* to hear and determine authoritatively: to sentence: to decide the merits of: to be censorious towards: (*B.*) to condemn.—*n.* one who judges: one appointed to hear and settle causes, and to try accused persons: one who can decide upon the merit of anything: in Jewish history, a supreme magistrate having civil and military powers: (*pl.*) title of 7th book of the O.T.—*ns.* **judge'-ad'vocate**, the crown-prosecutor at a court-martial; **judge'ship**, the office of a judge; **judg'ment, judge'ment**, act of judging: the comparing of ideas to elicit truth: faculty by which this is done, the reason: opinion formed: taste: sentence: condemnation: doom; **judg'ment-day**, a day of final judgment on mankind; **judg'ment-seat,**

seat or bench in a court from which judgment is pronounced. [Anglo-Fr. *juger*—L. *jūdicāre*—*jūs*, law, *dīcěre*, to declare.]

judicature, *jōō'di-ka-tyùr*, *n.* power of dispensing justice by legal trial: the office of judge: the body of judges: a court: a system of courts. [L. *jūdicāre*, -*ātum*, to judge.]

judicial, *jōō-dish'ál*, *adj.* pertaining to a judge or court of justice: established by statute: of the nature of judgment: critical.—*adv.* **judic'ially.**—**judicial separation**, legal separation of husband and wife which does not, however, leave either free to marry again. [L. *jūdiciālis*—*jūdicium*.]

judiciary, *jōō-dish'(y)ár-i*, *adj.* pertaining to judgment, judges, or courts of law.—*n.* a body of judges: a system of courts. [L. *jūdiciārius*.]

judicious, *jōō-dish'ús*, *adj.* according to sound judgment: possessing sound judgment: discreet.—*adv.* **judic'iously.**—*n.* **judic'iousness.** [Fr. *judicieux*—L. *jūdicium*.]

judo, *jōō'dō*, *n.* ju-jitsu. [Jap.]

jug, *jug*, *n.* a vessel with a handle, and a spout or lip for pouring liquids: (*slang*) prison.—*v.t.* to boil or stew as in a closed jar:—*pr.p.* jug'ging; *pa.p.* jugged. [Origin unknown.]

jug, *jug*, *n.* a note of the nightingale.—*v.i.* to utter the sound.—Also **jug'-jug'.** [Imit.]

juggernaut, *jug'ér-nöt*, **jagannath**, *jug'ä-nät*, *n.* an incarnation of Vishnu, beneath whose car devotees were supposed by Europeans to immolate themselves; hence the 'car of Juggernaut' stands metaphorically for any relentless destroying force or object of devotion and sacrifice: a large, heavy lorry. [Sans. *Jagannātha*, lord of the world. See **jaconet.**]

juggle, *jug'l*, *v.i.* to manipulate balls, &c. dexterously: to practise artifice or imposture.—*v.t.* to move, get, change, &c., by artifice: (usu. **juggle with**) to misrepresent (facts).—*n.* a trick by sleight-of-hand: an imposture.—*ns.* **jugg'ler**, one who performs tricks by sleight-of-hand: a trickish fellow; **jugg'lery**, art or tricks of a juggler, legerdemain: trickery. [O.Fr. *jogler*—L. *joculārī*, to jest—*jocus*, a jest.]

jugular, *jug'ū-lär*, *adj.* pertaining to the neck.—*n.* one of the large veins on each side of the neck. [L. *jugulum*, the collar-bone—*jungěre*, to join.]

juice, *jōōs*, *n.* the fluid part of fruits, vegetables, or of animal bodies: (*coll.*) electricity: (*coll.*) petrol.—*adj.* **juice'less.**—*adj.* **juic'y**, (*fig.*) highly interesting because of suggestiveness or obscenity.—*n.* **juic'iness.** [Fr. *jus*—L. *jūs*, broth, lit. mixture.]

ju-jitsu, **jiu-jitsu**, *jōō-jit'sōō*, *n.* a system of wrestling and athletic exercises originating in Japan. [Jap. *jū-jutsu*.]

ju-ju, *jōō'-jōō*, *n.* an object of superstitious worship in West Africa: a fetish or charm. [App. Fr. *joujou*, a toy.]

jujube, *jōō'jōōb*, *n.* the fruit, which is dried as a sweetmeat, of any of several spiny shrubs or small trees of the buckthorn family: the trees themselves: a lozenge made of sugar and gum. [Fr. *jujube*, or Low L. *jujuba*—Gr. *zizyphon*.]

juke box, *jōōk boks*, an instrument that plays gramophone records automatically—one record for each coin inserted in a slot in the mechanism. [Southern U.S. *juke*, joint, place,

e.g. a roadhouse, for dancing and drinking.]

julep, *jōō'lep*, *n.* a sweet drink, often medicated: an American drink of spirits, sugar, ice, and mint (also **mint'-julep**). [Fr.,—Sp. *julepe*—Ar. *julāb*—Pers. *gulāb*—*gul*, rose. *āb*, water.]

Julian, *jōōl'yán*, *adj.* pertaining to C.*Julius* Caesar (100-44 B.C.).—**Julian calendar**, the system of reckoning years and months for civil purposes, based on a solar year of 365¼ days, instituted by Julius Caesar 45 B.C., and still the basis of our calendar, although modified in 1752. (See **Gregorian.**)

julienne, *zhü-li-en'*, *n.* a clear soup, with shredded herbs: any foodstuff which has been shredded. [French name.]

July, *jōō-lī'*, *n.* the seventh month of the year. [L. *Jūlius* from Caius (or Gaius) Julius Caesar, who was born in it.]

jumble, *jum'bl*, *v.t.* (often with *up*) to mix confusedly: to throw together without order.—*v.i.* to become mixed together confusedly.—*n.* a confused mixture.—*n.* **jum'ble-sale**, a sale of odds and ends, often for charity.

jumbo, *jum'bō*, *n.* anything very big of its kind: an elephant (after a famous large one so named).—*adj.* huge: colossal.—*v.t.* **jum'boise** (-*bō-īz*), to enlarge (a ship) by adding a prefabricated section, e.g. amidships. [Prob. mumbo-*jumbo*: earlier than Jumbo the elephant.]

jump, *jump*, *v.i.* to spring or bound: to move suddenly: to start: to rise suddenly (e.g. of prices): to throb.—*v.t.* to cause or help to leap: to leap over: (*U.S.*) to leap aboard, or to leap from:—*pr.p.* jump'ing; *pa.p.* jumped.—*n.* act of jumping: a sudden movement: a sudden rise: a gap in a series, &c.: (in *pl.*) often **the jumps**), nervous agitation.—*adj.* **jump'y**, nervy, inclined to start.—*adj.* **jumped'-up** (*coll.*), upstart.—*ns.* **jump'-jet**, a fighter plane able to fly straight up or down; **jump'-off** (*U.S.*) the start: starting-place; **jump'-seat**, a movable carriage-seat: a carriage with a movable seat: a folding seat; **jump suit**, a one-piece, trouser and jacket or blouse, garment for either sex.—**jump at**, to accept with eagerness; **jumping-off place**, the terminus of a route: the point where one sets forth into the wilds, unknown, &c.; **jump on** (*coll.*), to censure promptly and vigorously; **jump one's bail**, to abscond, forfeiting one's bail; **jump the gun** (i.e. the starting-gun in a race), to get off one's mark too soon, start before time, act prematurely, take an unfair advantage; **jump the queue**, to take a position in a queue to which one is not entitled: to get ahead of one's turn; **jump to conclusions**, to arrive at a conclusion hastily without giving proper consideration to the evidence. [Prob. onomatopoeic.]

jumper, *jump'é⁻*, *n.* an overall slipped over the head: a woman's knitted garment like a blouse, orig. one loose at the waist.

junction, *jungk'sh(ò)n*, *n.* joining, a union or combination: place or point of union: a railway station where lines from different parts of the country meet. [L. *junctiō*, -*ōnis*—*jungěre*. See **join.**]

juncture, *jungk'tyùr*, -*chùr*, *n.* a joining, a union: a critical or important point of time. [L. *junctūra*—*jungěre*. See **join.**]

Neutral vowels in unaccented syllables: *em'pér-ór*; for certain sounds in foreign words see p. ix.

June, _jōōn, n._ the sixth month. [L. _Jūnius._]

jungle, _jung′gl, n._ a dense tropical growth of thickets, brushwood, &c.: any wild tangled mass (_lit._ or _fig._): a place or situation where there is ruthless competition, or cruel struggle for survival,—_n._ **jung′le-fē′ver,** a severe malarial fever; **jung′le-fowl,** the wild parent of the barn-door fowl. [Sans. _jāngala,_ desert.]

junior, _jōōn′yȯr, adj._ younger: less advanced.—_n._ one younger or less advanced.—_n._ **juniority** (_-or′i-ti_).—**junior service,** the army. [L. _jūnior,_ compar. of _jŭvenis,_ young.]

juniper, _jōō′ni-pẽr, n._ a genus of evergreen shrubs, one species of which yields berries used to flavour gin. [L. _jūniperus._]

junk, _jungk, n._ a Chinese vessel, with high fore-castle and poop, sometimes large and three-masted. [Port. _junco,_ app.—Javanese _djong._]

junk, _jungk, n._ pieces of old cordage: rubbish generally: (_fig._) nonsense: a thick piece, chunk: salt meat, perhaps because it becomes as hard as old rope: a narcotic. _n._ **junk′er,** **junk′ic,** a narcotics addict. [Origin doubtful.]

junker, _yŏŏng′kẽr, n._ a young German noble or squire: an overbearing, narrow-minded, reactionary aristocrat. [Ger.,—_jung,_ young, _herr,_ lord.]

junket, _jung′ket, n._ (_dial._) a rush basket: any sweetmeat: curds mixed with cream, sweetened and flavoured: a feast or merry-making.—_v.i._ to feast, banquet.—_v.t_ to feast, entertain:—_pr.p._ junk′eting; _pa.p._ junk′eted.—_n._ **junk′eting,** a merry feast or entertainment, banqueting. [Anglo Fr. _jonquette,_ rush basket—L. _juncus,_ a rush.]

junta, _jun′ta, n._ a meeting, council: a Spanish grand council of state: (in the following meanings also **jun′to,** _pl._ **jun′tos**) a body of men joined or united for some purpose, usu. political—a confederacy, cabal, or faction: a government formed by a group following a coup d'état. [Sp.—L. _jungĕre, junctum,_ to join.]

Jupiter, _jōō′pi-tẽr, n._ the chief god among the Romans—also **Jove:** the largest and, next to Venus, the brightest of the planets. [L. _Jūpiter, Juppiter_ (_Jovis pater_), Father Jove, the usual nom., the oblique cases being formed from _Jovis_ alone.]

jurassic, _jōō-ras′ik, adj._ (_geol._) one of the three divisions of the Secondary or Mesozoic rocks, so called from its well-developed strata in the _Jura_ Mountains.

juridical, _jōō-rid′ik-ȧl, adj._ relating to the distribution of justice: pertaining to a judge: used in courts of law.—_adv._ **jurid′ically.** [L. _jūridicus—jūs, jūris,_ law, _dīcere,_ to declare.]

jurisconsult, _jōō-ris-kon-sult′, n._ one who is consulted on the law, a jurist. [L. _jūs, jūris,_ law, _consulĕre, consultum,_ to consult.]

jurisdiction, _jōō-ris-dik′sh(ȯ)n, n._ the distribution of justice: legal authority: extent of power: district over which any authority extends.—_adj._ **jurisdic′tional.** [L. _jūrisdictio, -ōnis._]

jurisprudence, _jōō-ris-prōō′dẽns, n._ the science of law.—**medical jurisprudence,** forensic medicine (see **forensic**). [L. _jūrisprūdentia—jūs, jūris,_ law, _prūdentia,_ knowledge.]

jurist, _jōō′rist, n._ one who is versed in the science of law, esp. Roman or civil law.—_adjs._

jurist′ic, -al. [Fr. _juriste._]

jury, _jōō′ri, n._ a body of persons sworn to give a verdict on evidence before them: a committee of adjudicators or examiners.—_ns._ **ju′ror,** one who serves on a jury—also **ju′ryman, ju′ry-woman; ju′ry-pro′cess,** a writ summoning a jury.—**grand jury** (see **grand**); **special jury,** a body of jurors chosen, at the request of either party in a civil case, from a special list comprising names of persons possessing a higher qualification than is required for members of an ordinary or _common_ jury. [Anglo-Fr. _juree—jurer_—L. _jūrāre,_ to swear.]

jurymast, _jōō′ri-mäst, n._ a temporary mast raised in place of one lost.—_n._ **ju′ry-rudd′er,** a temporary rudder for one lost. [Not _injury-mast,_ but perh. O.Fr. _ajurie,_ aid—L. _adjūtāre,_ to aid.]

jussive, _jus′iv, adj._ expressing command. [L. _jubēre,_ perf. _jussī,_ to command.]

just. Same as **joust.**

just, _just, adj._ righteous (esp. in the Bible): fair, impartial: deserved, due: in accordance with facts: exact.—_adv._ precisely: very lately: only: merely: barely: (_coll._) quite.—_adv._ **just′ly,** equitably: uprightly: accurately: by right.—_n._ **just′ness,** equity: fittingness: exactness. [Fr. _juste,_ or L. _jūstus—jūs,_ law.]

justice, _jus′tis, n._ quality of being just: integrity: impartiality: rightness: the awarding of what is due: a judge: a magistrate.—_ns._ **jus′ticeship,** office or dignity of a justice or judge; **justiciar** (_-tish′i-är; hist._), an administrator of justice: a chief-justice; **justiciary** (_tish′i är i_), a judge: a chief-justice.—**Justice of the Peace** (_J.P._), a local minor magistrate commissioned to keep the peace.—**High Court of Justice,** a section of the English Supreme Court, comprising Chancery and King's Bench Divisions; **High Court of Justiciary,** the supreme criminal court of justice in Scotland. [Fr.,—L. _justitia._]

justify, _jus′ti fī, v.t_ to prove or show to be just or right, to vindicate: (of circumstances) to furnish adequate grounds for: to corroborate: to absolve:—_pr.p._ jus′tifying; _pa.p._ jus′tified.—_adj._ **just′ifiable** (_or fī′-_), that may be justified or defended.—_n._ **justifi′ableness.**—_adv._ **justifi′ably.**—_n._ **justifica′tion,** vindication: sufficient grounds or reason (for): absolution.—_adjs._ **jus′tificātive, jus′tifica′tory,** having power to justify.—_n._ **jus′tifier,** one who defends, or vindicates: he who pardons and absolves from guilt and punishment.—**justifi′able hom′icide,** the killing of a person in self-defence, or to prevent an atrocious crime; **justification by faith,** the doctrine that men are justified (saved, or rendered worthy of salvation) by faith in Christ. [Fr. _justifier_ and L. _jūstificāre—jūstus,_ just, _facĕre,_ to make.]

justle. Same as **jostle.**

jut, _jut, v.i._ to project:—_pr.p._ jutt′ing; _pa.p._ jutt′ed. [A form of **jet** (2).]

jute, _jōōt, n._ the fibre of two Indian plants of the lime family, used for making coarse bags, mats, &c. [Bengali _jhuto_—Sans. _jūṭa,_ matted hair.]

juvenescent, _jōō-vẽn-es′ẽnt, adj._ becoming youthful.—_n._ **juvenes′cence.** [L. _juvenēscĕre,_ to grow young.]

juvenile, $j\overline{oo}'vé$-*nīl*, *adj.* young: pertaining, or suited, to youth: childish.— Also *n.*— *n.pl.* **juvenilia** (-*il'ya*), writings or works of one's childhood or youth.—*n.* **juvenility** (-*il'i-ti*). —**juvenile delinquent**, a young law-breaker, in Britain under the age of seventeen. [L. *juvenīlis*—*juvenis*, young.]

juxtaposition, *juks-tá-poz-ish'(ó)n*, *n.* a placing or being placed close together.—*v.t.* **juxtapose'**. [L. *juxtā*, near, and **position**.]

Neutral vowels in unaccented syllables: *em'pér-ór*; for certain sounds in foreign words see p. ix.

K

Kaaba, *kä´bä, n.* the holy building at Mecca into which the Black Stone, believed by Mohammedans to have been given to Abraham by Gabriel, is built. [Ar. *ka´bah—ka´b,* cube.]

Kaffir, *kaf´ér, n.* a name applied to certain indigenous peoples of S. Africa (*hist.*) or to their languages: now often used derogatorily: (*pl.*) S. African mining shares. [Ar. *Kāfir,* unbeliever.]

kaftan. Same as **caftan.**

kaiser, *kī´zér, n,* an emperor, esp. a German Emperor.—*n.* **kai´sership.** [Ger.,—L. *Caesar.*]

kaka, *kä´ka, n.* a New Zealand parrot. *n.* **ka´kapo,** the New Zealand owl-parrot, large-winged but almost flightless. [Maori *kaka,* parrot, *po,* night.]

kale, kail, *kāl, n.* a cabbage with open curled leaves: (*Scot.*) cabbage generally: (*Scot.*) broth in which kail is the chief ingredient.— **kailyard-school,** a group of writers (*c.* 1890) of stories of humble Scots country life—S. R. Crockett, Ian Maclaren, &c. [Northern form of **cole.**]

kaleidoscope, *ka-lī´dō-skōp, n.* an optical toy in which we see an endless variety of beautiful colours and forms.—*adj.* **kaleidoscop´ic** (*-skop´ik*; usu. *fig.*), exhibiting constantly changing brightly coloured patterns: full of change and variety (e.g. a career). [Gr. *kalos,* beautiful, *eidos,* form, *skopeein,* to look at.]

kalends. Same as **calends.**

kalif, *kā´lif, n.* Same as **caliph.**

kalium, *kā´li-um n.* a modern Latin name for potassium formed from *obs. kali* (Ar. *qili*), potash—whence the *chem.* symbol K for potassium.

kamikaze, *kä-mi-kä´zē, n.* (a Japanese airman, or plane, making) a suicidical attack. [Jap., divine wind.]

Kanaka, *kan´ä-ka,* in Australia *kan-ak´a, n.* a South Sea Islander, esp. an indentured or forced labourer. [Hawaiian, 'a man'.]

kangaroo, *kang-gár-ōō´, n.* a family of marsupials (q.v.) of Australia, New Guinea, &c., with very long hind-legs and great power of leaping—esp. the largest species of these.—*n.* **kangaroo´-grass,** valuable Australian fodder grass.—**kangaroo closure,** the method (employed in the House of Commons) of allowing the chairman to decide which clauses shall be discussed and which passed or leaped over; **kangaroo court,** a court operated by a mob, by prisoners in a jail, by any improperly constituted body: a tribunal before which a fair trial is impossible; **kangaroo justice,** the kind of justice dispensed by a kangaroo court. [Supposed to be a native name.]

Kantian, *kant´i-án, adj.* pertaining to the great German philosopher, Immanuel *Kant* (1724-1804), or his philosophy.

Kanuck, *ka-nuk´.* Same as **Canuck.**

kaolin, *kā´ō-lin, n.* China clay (q.v.). [From the mountain *Kao-ling* ('high ridge') in China.]

kapellmeister, *ka-pel´mīs-tér, n.* the director of an orchestra or choir, esp. formerly of the band of a ruling prince in Germany. [Ger. *kapelle,* chapel, orchestra, *meister,* master.]

kapok, *käp´ok,* or *käp´-, n.* a very light, waterproof, oily fibre, covering the seeds of a species of silk-cotton tree, used for stuffing pillows, life-belts, &c. [Malay *kāpoq.*]

kaputt, *kä-pŏŏt´, adj.* ruined: broken. [Ger. slang.]

karate, *ka-rä´tä, n.* a Japanese combative sport using blows and kicks.—**karate chop,** a sharp downward blow with the side of the hand.

karma, *kär´mä, n.* the Buddhist conception of the quality of a person's actions, including both merit and demerit—the whole determining his fate in his next existence: the theory of inevitable consequences generally. [Sans. *karma,* act.]

karoo, karroo, *kä-rōō´, n.* (*S. Africa*) a high inland pastoral tableland. [Believed to be of Hottentot origin.]

kari, *kar´i, n.* a Western Australian gum tree: its red timber. [Native name.]

kart, *kärt, n.* go-kart (q.v.).

kasba(h), casbah, *kaz´ba, n.* a castle or fortress in a N. African town or the area round it, esp. in Algiers.

katabolism, *kat-ab´ol-izm, n.* (*biol.*) the disruptive processes of chemical change in organisms—destructive metabolism (q.v.), opposed to **anabolism.** [Gr. *katabolē—kataballein,* to throw down—*kata,* down, *ballein,* to throw.]

katydid, *kā´ti did, n.* any of a number of American insects akin to the grasshopper. [Imit. of its note.]

kauri, *kow´ri,* or **kauri-pine,** *n.* a coniferous forest-tree of New Zealand, source of **kau´ri-gum,** a resin used in making varnish: extended to others of the same genus. [Maori.]

kayak, *kī´ak, n.* an Eskimo seal-skin canoe. [Eskimo.]

kea, *kā´ä, kē´a, n.* a New Zealand parrot that sometimes kills sheep. [Maori.]

kebab, *ké-bab´, n.* small cubes of meat cooked with vegetables, seasoning and usu. served on skewers.

kedge, *kej, n.* a small anchor for keeping a ship steady, and for warping (q.v.) the ship.—*v.t.* to move by means of a kedge, to warp.—*n.* **kedg´er,** a kedge. [Origin doubtful.]

kedgeree, *kej´é-rē, n.* a mess of rice, cooked with butter and dal (a kind of pea), flavoured with spice, &c., common on Anglo-Indian breakfast-tables: a similar European dish made with fish, rice, &c. [Hindustani *khichrī.*]

keel, *kēl, n.* the part of a ship extending along the bottom from stem to stern, and supporting the whole frame: (*bot.*) the lowest petals of a papilionaceous (q.v.) flower, arranged like a

---

fāte, fär; mē, hûr (her); *mīne; mōte, för; mūte; mōōn, fŏŏt;* THen (then)

keel   ketchup

ship's keel.—*v.t.* or *v.i.* (*rare*) to navigate: to turn keel upwards.—*n.* **keel′age,** dues for a keel or ship in port.—*adj.* **keeled** (*bot.*), keel-shaped: having a ridge on the back.—*v.t.* **keel′haul,** to punish by hauling under the keel of a ship, from the one side to the other, by means of ropes: to treat in a galling manner. [O.N. *kjölr.*]

keel, *kēl, n.* a low flat-bottomed boat: a coal-lighter: a ship. [Du. *kiel,* ship, prob.—O.E. *cēol,* ship.]

keel, *kēl, v.t.* (*Shak.*) to cool. [O.E. *cēlan,* to chill.]

keen, *kēn, adj.* having a sharp point or a fine edge: affecting one's senses somewhat as a sharp instrument might—vivid (of light), intense (of cold), piercing (of wind), acute (of pain), &c.: piercing, acute of mind: (of eyes, sight, and other sense-organs and senses) sharp, acute, sensitive: (of person, interest, &c.) eager, ardent.—*adv.* **keen′ly.**—*n.* **keen′ness.**—**keen on** (*coll.*), fond of: much interested in. [O.E. *cēne,* bold, fierce, keen; Ger. *kühn,* bold; O.N. *kœnn,* expert.]

keen, *kēn, n.* a lamentation over the dead.—*v.i.* to wail over the dead.—*n.* **keen′er,** a professional mourner. [Ir. *caoine.*]

keep, *kēp, v.t.* to guard: to have in one's care: to support, supply with necessaries: to attend to (e.g. sheep, a garden): to have in one's service: to cause to remain in a certain place, condition, &c. (as, *to keep under lock and key*): to retain in one's power or possession: to have habitually in stock for sale: in *fig.* senses, to maintain, observe, not fall away from or neglect:—to preserve (e.g. silence), to remain true to (e.g. the faith), to solemnise, celebrate (e.g. a fast, Christmas): to conduct or manage (e.g. a school, house): to make a continuous record in (e.g. an account book, a diary).—*v.i.* to remain: to remain in good condition: to continue: to refrain:—*pr.p.* keep′ing; *pa.t.* and *pa.p.* kept.—*n.* subsistence, food: the innermost and strongest part of a castle, the donjon (q.v.): a stronghold.—*ns.* **keep′er,** an attendant: a custodian: a gamekeeper; **keep′ing,** care: custody; **keep′sake,** something given to be kept for the sake of the giver.—**keep at it,** to persist in, work persistently at anything; **keep from,** to abstain from: to restrain from; **keep in with,** to maintain the confidence or friendship of (someone); **keep one's countenance,** to preserve a calm appearance, hiding one's emotions; **keep one's hand in,** to retain one's skill by means of constant practice; **keep up,** to retain one's strength or spirit: to keep from falling (e.g. prices): to keep in a proper state—of repair, &c.: to carry on (e.g. a conversation): to continue to be in touch (with): to proceed at an equal pace (with), or abreast of (a person or thing—e.g. the times); **keep up with the Joneses,** to keep on social equality with one's neighbours, e.g. by having possessions of like quality in like quantity.—**in (out of) keeping,** in (or not in) just proportion, harmonious (or inharmonious), consistent (or inconsistent). [O.E. *cēpan.*]

keg, *keg, n.* a small cask. [Earlier *cag*—O.N. *kaggi.*]

kelp, *kelp, n.* any large brown seaweed, wrack: the calcined ashes of seaweed, a source of

soda, iodine, &c. [M.E. *culp*; origin unknown.]

kelpie, kelpy, *kel′pi, n.* (*Scot.*) a water-sprite in the form of a horse. [Origin uncertain.]

kelt, *kelt, n.* a salmon that has just spawned.

Kelt, Keltic. Same as **Celt, Celtic.**

kelvin, *kel′vin, n.* the SI unit of temperature—with absolute zero as zero and centigrade degrees (abbrev. K). [Lord *Kelvin* (1824-1907), physicist.]

ken, *ken, v.t.* (mainly *Scot.*) to know: (*arch.*) to see and recognise at a distance.—*n.* range of sight or knowledge.—*n.* **kenn′ing,** a periphrastic formula in Old Norse or other old Germanic poetry (e.g. *the pathway of the whale,* for 'the sea'). [O.E. *cennan,* causative of *cunnan*; O.N. *kenna*; cf. **can, con.**]

Kendal-green, *ken′dál-grēn, n.* green cloth for foresters made at *Kendal* in Westmorland.

kennel, *ken′él, n.* a house for dogs: a pack of hounds: the hole of a fox, &c.: a haunt.—*v.t.* to keep in a kennel.—*v.i.* to live in a kennel:—*pr.p.* kenn′elling; *pa.p.* kenn′elled. [Norm. Fr. *kenil* (Fr. *chenil*)—L. *canīle*—*canis,* a dog.]

kennel, *ken′él, n.* the water-course of a street, a gutter. [Same root as **canal** and **channel.**]

Kennelly-Heaviside layer, *ken′é-li-hev′i-sīd lā′ér,* a region of the upper atmosphere, 60 or more miles up in the daytime, strongly ionised, which reflects long radio waves. [A.E. *Kennelly* and O. *Heaviside,* who inferred its existence.]

kenning. See **ken.**

kepi, *kāp′ē, n.* a flat-topped forage-cap with a straight peak. [Fr. *képi.*]

kept, *pa.t.* and *pa.p.* of **keep.**

kerb, *kûrb, n.* the edging of a pavement: a domestic fender.—*n.* **kerb′stone.**—See **curb.** [Variant of **curb.**]

kerchief, *kûr′chif, n.* a square piece of cloth worn originally to cover the head, now often the neck, &c.: a handkerchief. [O.Fr. *cuevrechief* (Fr. *couvrechef*)—*covrir,* to cover, *chief,* the head.]

kermes, *kûr′mēz, n.* the bodies of the females of an insect found on a dwarf evergreen oak (**kermes,** or **kermes oak**), used as a red dyestuff. The kermes insect was used to make dye at an earlier date than the cochineal insect (to which it is allied). [Pers. and Ar. *qirmiz.*]

kermis, *kûr′mis, n.* a wake or fair in the Low Countries: in America, an indoor fair.—Also **ker′mess, kir′mess.** [Du. *kermis*—*kerk,* church, *mis,* mass.]

kern, kerne, *kûrn, n.* an Irish foot-soldier. [Ir. *ceatharnach.*]

kernel, *kûr′nél, n.* a seed within a hard shell: the edible part of a nut: the important part of anything. [O.E. *cyrnel*—*corn,* grain, and dim. suffx. *-el*; Ger. *kern,* a grain.]

kerosene, *ker′o-sēn, n.* a paraffin-oil obtained from shale or by distillation of petroleum. [Gr. *kēros,* wax.]

kersey, *kûr′zi, n.* a coarse woollen cloth. [Perh. from *Kersey* in Suffolk.]

kerseymere, *kûr′zi-mēr.* See **cassimere.**

kestrel, *kes′trél, n.* a small species of falcon. [O.Fr. *quercerelle.*]

ketch, *kech, n.* a small two-masted vessel. [Earlier *catch,* perh. from the vb. **catch.**]

ketchup, *kech′up, n.* a sauce made from tom-

Neutral vowels in unaccented syllables: *em′pér-ór*; for certain sounds in foreign words see p. ix.

atoes, mushrooms, &c.—Also **catch'up**, **cat'sup**. [Malay *kēchap*, perh. from Chinese.]

kettle, *ket'l, n.* a vessel, now usu. one with a spout, lid, and handle, for heating or boiling liquids.—*n.* **kett'le-drum**, a musical instrument consisting of a hollow metal hemisphere with a parchment head, tuned by screws.—**a pretty kettle of fish**, a task of great difficulty, an awkward state of affairs. [O.E. *cetel*; Ger. *kessel*; perh. from L. *catillus*, dim. of *catīnus*, a deep cooking-vessel.]

key, *kē, n.* an instrument for locking or unlocking, winding up, turning, tightening or loosening: that which gives command of anything or upon which success turns: that which leads to the solution of a problem: a set of answers to problems: a crib translation: the middle stone of an arch: a piece of wood let into another piece crosswise to prevent warping: in musical instruments, a lever or piston-end pressed to produce the sound required: a similar part in other instruments for other purposes, e.g. in a typewriter, type-setting machine: the lowest note or tone of a musical scale or sequence of notes arranged in order of pitch: the system on which the notes of a scale are built up, each bearing a definite relation to the lowest note or tonic: general tone of voice, emotion, morals, &c.—*v.t.* to attune (with *to*): to stimulate (to a state of excitement or tension): raise (in pitch or standard), increase (with *up*): to set (type) by machine.—*adj.* vital: essential: controlling—as in **key talks**, **key industries**, **key position**.—*ns.* **key'board**, the keys or levers in a piano, organ, typewriter, or other instrument, arranged along a flat board; **key'hole**, the hole in which a key of a lock is inserted; **key industry**, an industry indispensable to others and essential to national economic welfare and independence; **key'-man**, an indispensable worker, essential to the continued conduct of a business, &c.; **key'-note**, the fundamental note of a piece of music: any central principle or controlling thought; **key'-stone**, the stone at the apex of an arch.—**power of the keys**, the power to loose and bind, to administer ecclesiastical discipline, conferred by Christ on Peter (Matt. xvi. 19), and claimed by the Popes. [O.E. *cǣg.*]

key, *kē, n.* a low island or reef. [Sp. *cayo*.]

Keys, *kēz, n.pl.* in full, **House of Keys**, the lower branch of the legislature (Court of Tynwald) of the Isle of Man.

khaki, *kā'ki, adj.* dust-coloured, dull brownish or greenish yellow.—*n.* a light drab cloth used for military uniforms. [Hindustani and Pers. *khākī*, dusty.]

khamsin, *kam'sin, -sēn, n.* a hot S. or S.E. wind in Egypt, blowing for about fifty days from mid-March. [Ar. *khamsīn—khamsūn*, fifty.]

khan, *kän, n.* in N. Asia, a prince or chief: in Persia, a governor.—*n.* **khan'ate**, a khan's dominion or jurisdiction. [Turki (q.v.), and thence Pers., *khān*, lord or prince.]

Khedive, *ked-ēv', n.* the title (1867-1914) of the viceroy of Egypt, granted by the Sultan of Turkey. [Fr. *Khédive*—Turk. *Khidīv*—Pers. *khidīw*, prince.]

kibbutz, *kē-bōōts', n.* a Jewish communal agricultural settlement in Israel:—*pl.* **kibbutzim**

(*kē-bōōts-ēm*). [Heb.]

kibe, *kīb, n.* a chilblain. [Cf. W. *cibwst.*]

kiblah, *kib'lä, n.* the point toward which Mohammedans turn in prayer.—Also **keb'lah**. [Ar. *qiblah.*]

kick, *kik, v.t.* to hit with the foot: to put or drive by a blow with the foot: to free oneself from (e.g. a habit).—*v.i.* to thrust out the foot with violence: to show resistance: to recoil violently.—*n.* a blow with the foot: the recoil of a gun: (*slang*) spirit, energy: (*slang*) a pleasant thrill: (*slang*) an enthusiastic but short-lived interest. *ns.* **kick' off**, the first kick in a game of football; **kick'-up'**, a disturbance.—**kick against the pricks**, to resist when one can only hurt oneself by doing so (Acts ix. 5; see also **prick**); **kick over the traces**, (*fig.*) to throw off control; **kick upstairs**, to promote (usu. to a less active or less powerful position).—**drop kick** (*Rugby*), a kick made as the ball, dropped from the hand, rebounds from the ground; **for kicks**, for thrills; **place kick**, a kick made when the ball is laid on the ground. [M.E. *kiken*; origin unknown. W. *cicio*, to kick, comes from Eng.]

kickshaws, *kik'shöz*, **kickshaw**, *-shö, n.* something fantastical: (*cookery*) a fantastical dish. [Fr. *quelque chose*, something.]

kid, *kid, n.* a young goat, extended to a young antelope, &c.: (*slang*) a child: leather of kid skin, or a substitute.—*v.t.* and *v.i.* to bring forth (of a goat): to deceive, hoax (esp. for amusement): to tease:—*pr.p.* **kid'ding**; *pa.p.* **kid'ded.**—*n.* **kid'-glove'**, a glove of kid.—*adj.* as if done by one wearing kid-gloves, overdainty, fastidious. [O.N. *kith*, cf. Dan. *kid.*]

kidnap, *kid'nap*, also *-nap', v.t.* to steal, as a human being:—*pr.p.* **kid'napping**; *pa.t.* and *pa.p.* **kid'napped.**—*n.* **kid'napper**. [*kid*, a child, *nap*, to seize, steal.]

kidney, *kid'ni, n.* one of two flattened glands that secrete urine: temperament, humour, disposition—hence, sort or kind (e.g. *persons of the same kidney*), &c. *n.* **kid'ney bean'**, a French bean or haricot bean. [M.E. *kidenei* (pl. *kideneiren*), the second element perh. being *ei* (pl. *eiren*), egg, confused sometimes with *nere*, kidney.]

kieselguhr, *kē'z(ė)l-gōōr, n.* a whitish powder, consisting chiefly of the remains of diatoms (q.v.), used as an absorbent of nitroglycerine in the manufacture of explosives, and for other purposes. Also called *diatomite*. [Ger. *kiesel*, flint, *guhr*, fermentation.]

kill, *kil, v.t.* to put to death, to slay: to cause the death of: put an end to: to defeat or veto (a bill): to neutralise by contrast (e.g. a colour): to stop (e.g. an engine, a ball in play): to exhaust: to cause severe pain to: (*coll.*) to consume completely.—*n.* the act of killing: prey or game killed.—*n.* **kill'er**.—*p.adj.* **kill'ing**, fatal: exhausting: (*coll.*) fascinating: (*coll.*) very amusing.—**kill off**, to exterminate; **kill time**, to occupy oneself with amusements, &c., in order to pass spare time or to relieve boredom.—**killer (whale)**, any of several rapacious whales gregarious in habit; **killing time**, the days of the persecution of the Covenanters. [M.E. *killen*, or *cullen.*]

kiln, *kil, kiln, n.* a large oven in which corn,

fāte, fär; mē, hûr (her); mīne; mōte, för; mūte; mōōn, fŏŏt; ᴛʜen (then)

kilo
kinsfolk

bricks, &c., are dried: bricks placed for burning.—*v.t.* **kiln'-dry**, to dry in a kiln. [O.E. *cyln*, *cylen*—L. *culīna*, a kitchen.]

kilo,*kil'ō, n.* a shortened form of **kilogram**, or of other words with the prefix **kilo-**, used in the metric system to indicate multiplication by a thousand.—*ns.* **kil'ocycle**, 1000 cycles (q.v.), used in measuring frequency; **kil'ogram**, 1000 grams, the mass of a platinum iridium cylinder kept at the International Bureau of Weights and Measures near Paris—1 lb.= 0·45359237 kg; **kil'olitre**, 1000 litres; **kil'ometre**, 1000 metres, or nearly ⁵/₈ of a mile.— *adj.* **kil'oton**, of a bomb, having the explosive force of a thousand tons of TNT (trinitrotoluene).—*n.* **kil'owatt**, 1000 watts. [Gr. *chīlioi*, a thousand.]

kilt,*kilt, n.* a kind of short pleated skirt, forming part of the Highland dress.—*v.t.* to tuck up (skirts): to pleat vertically. [Scand.; cf. Dan. *kilte*, to tuck up; O.N. *kilting*, a skirt.]

kimono, *ki-mō'nō, n.* a loose robe with wide sleeves, fastening with a sash, the principal outer garment in typically Japanese dress. [Jap.]

kin, *kin, n.* relatives: ancestral stock.—*adj.* related.—*n.* **kin'ship**, blood-relationship: similarity in character.—**next of kin**, the relatives (lineal or collateral) of a deceased person, among whom his personal property is distributed if he dies intestate. [O.E. *cynn*; O.N. *kyn*, family, race; cog. with L. *genus*, Gr. *genos*.] **-kin**, *noun suffix* denoting a diminutive as in lamb*kin*. [Prob. Du. or L.G.]

kind, *kīnd, n.* (*obs.*) those of kin: a natural group of animals, plants, &c. (e.g. human kind): sort, species, variety, class (natural or conventional): (*arch.*) nature: character, natural fashion: produce, as distinguished from money.—*adj.* having, or springing from, the feelings natural for those of the same family: disposed to do good to others.—*adjs.* **kind'heart'ed.**—*n.* **kind'ness.**—**a kind of** (with noun), something resembling the thing, quality, &c., mentioned; **in kind**, in quality: (of repayment, generally *fig.*) in something of the same kind as that received: in goods instead of money; **of a kind**, of the same character, quality, species, &c.: scarcely deserving the name (e.g. *hospitality of a kind*). [O.E. (*ge*)*cynde*—*cynn*, kin.]

kindergarten, *kin'dér-gär-t(é)n, n.* an infant school on Froebel's principle (1826), in which object-lessons and games figure largely. [Ger.—*kinder*, children, *garten*, garden.]

kindle, *kin'dl, v.t.* to set fire to: to light: to inflame, as the passions: to provoke: to incite.— *v.i.* to take fire: to begin to be excited: to be roused.—*n.* **kin'dling**, the act of causing to burn: the materials for starting a fire. [Cf. O.N. *kyndill*, a torch—L. *candēla*, candle.]

kindly, *kīnd'li, adj.* (*orig.*) belonging to the kind or race: (*arch.*) natural: kind-hearted, disposed to kind acts: genial: comfortable, pleasant, mild, clement.—*adv.* in a kind or kindly manner.—*n.* **kind'liness.** [O.E. *gecyndelic*; cf. **kind.**]

kindred, *kin'dred, n.* relationship by blood (less properly, by marriage): relatives.—*adj.* akin: cognate: congenial. [M.E. *kinrede*—O.E. *cynn*,

kin, and the suffx. *-rǣden*, expressing mode or state.]

kine, *kīn, n.pl.* (*B.*) cows. [M.E. *kyen*, a doubled plural of O.E. *cū*, a cow, the plural of which is *cȳ*; cf. Scots *kye*, cows.]

kinema, kinematograph. See **cinematograph.**

kinematics,*kin-ē-mat'iks, or kīn-, n.* the science of motion without reference to force.—*adjs.* **kinemat'ic, -al.** [Gr. *kīnēma*, motion—*kīneein*, to move.]

kinesis, *ki-nē'sis, kī-, n.* movement, change of position. [Gr. *kīnēsis*, movement.]

kinetics, *ki-net'iks, or kī-, n.* the science of the action of force in producing or changing motion.—*adjs.* **kinet'ic, -al.—kinetic art, sculpture,** art, sculpture, in which movement (produced by air currents, electricity, &c.) plays an essential part; **kinetic energy,** energy or power of doing work possessed by a body in virtue of its motion. [Gr. *kīnētikos*—*kīneein*, to move.]

king, *king, n.* a hereditary chief ruler or titular head of a nation: one who is pre-eminent among his fellows: (*obs.*) a queen bee: a playing-card having the picture of a king: the most important piece in chess:—*fem.* **queen.**—*v.t.* to make king: to play the king (usu. *to king it*).—*ns.* **king crab,** several species of large marine arthropods (i.e. animals of the phylum Arthropoda), last survivors of their class; **king'craft,** the art of governing, mostly in a bad sense; **king'cup,** a buttercup: a marsh marigold; **king'dom,** the state or attributes of a king: a state having a king (or queen) as its constitutional ruler: territory subject to a king (or queen): one of the three grand divisions of the natural world—the animal, vegetable, or mineral; **king'fisher,** a family of birds with very brilliant plumage, feeding on fish.—*adj.* **king'less.**—*n.* **king'let,** a little or petty king: the golden-crested wren.—*adjs.* **king'-like; king'ly,** of royal rank: suitable for a king, royal: dignified, regal, noble.—*ns.* **king'liness; King'-of-Arms'** (sometimes, **-at-Arms'**), a principal herald; **king'pin,** a tall, prominent, or central pin: the most important person of a group engaged in an undertaking; **king's-é'vil,** a scrofulous disease or evil formerly supposed to be healed by the touch of the king.—*adj.* **king-size,** big, esp. very long.—**King Charles spaniel** (see **spaniel**); **King's Bench** (*Queen's Bench* in a queen's reign), formerly a court in which the king sat: now a division of the High Court of Justice; **King's Counsel** (or *Queen's Counsel*), an honorary rank of barristers and advocates; **king's English,** correct standard speech; **King's (Queen's) Speech,** the sovereign's address to parliament at its opening and closing.—**turn king's evidence,** to become a witness against an accomplice. [O.E. *cyning*—*cynn*, a tribe, with suffx. *-ing*; cog. with **kin.**]

kink, *kingk, n.* a twisted loop in a string, rope, &c.: a mental twist: a whim: an imperfection.—*adj.* **kink'y,** twisted: curly: (*coll.*) eccentric, mad: (*coll.*) out of the ordinary in an attractive way: (*slang*) sexually perverted or homosexual. [Prob. Du. *kink*; but cf. Ger., Swed., and Norw., *kink.*]

kinsfolk, *kinz'fōk, n.* folk or people kindred or

Neutral vowels in unaccented syllables: *em'pér-ór*; for certain sounds in foreign words see p. ix.

related to one another.—*n.* **kins'man,** a man of the same kin or family with another:—*fem.* **kins'woman.** [**kin,** and **folk.**]

kiosk, *ki-osk',* *n.* an Eastern garden pavilion: a small roofed stall for sale of papers, sweets, &c., either out-of-doors or inside a public building: a public telephone box: a bandstand. [Turk. *kiöshk*—Pers. *kūshk.*]

kipper, *kip'ér, n.* a male salmon after the spawning season: a salmon or (esp.) herring split open, seasoned, and dried.—*v.t.* to cure or preserve, as a salmon or herring. [Perh. O.E. *cypera,* a spawning salmon.]

kirk, *kirk, kûrk, n.* (*Scot.*) church, in any sense.—*n.* **kirk-session,** the lowest court (consisting of minister and elders) in a Presbyterian church. [A Northern Eng. form of **church.**]

kirtle, *kûr'tl, n.* (*arch.*) a sort of gown or outer petticoat, a tunic, &c. [O.E. *cyrtel*; Dan. *kjortel*; O.N. *kyrtill*; app.—L. *curtus,* short.]

kismet *kis'met* *n.* fate, destiny. [Turk. *qismet.*]

kiss, *kis, v.t.* to caress or salute with the lips: to touch gently.—*v.i.* to salute with the lips: to touch lightly (as two balls in motion).—*n.* a caress or salute with the lips.—**kiss hands,** to kiss the sovereign's hands on acceptance of office; **kiss of life,** a mouth-to-mouth method of restoring breathing: (*fig.*) a means of restoring vitality or vigour; **kiss the book,** in England, to kiss a copy of the New Testament after taking a legal oath; **kiss the dust,** to be felled to the ground, to be slain or vanquished; **kiss the rod,** to submit to punishment. [O.E. *cyssan,* to kiss—*coss,* a kiss; Ger. *küssen,* Dan. *kys.*]

kit, *kit, n.* a small wooden tub: an outfit: equipment: a container and/or the tools, instructions, &c. assembled in it for some specific purpose.—*n.* **kit'-bag,** a strong bag for holding one's kit or outfit. [Prob. Middle Du. *kitte,* a hooped beer-can.]

kit, *kit, n.* (*rare*) a small pocket violin.

kitcat, *kit'kat, n.* (*cap.*) name of a Whig London literary club in the reign of Queen Anne, which met at the pie-shop of Christopher *Cat*: a portrait 36 by 28 inches in size, so called from the portraits of the *Kitcat* Club painted by Sir G. Kneller (1646–1723).

kitchen, *kich'ón, n.* a place where food is cooked: cooking department or equipment.—*ns.* **kitchenette',** a tiny kitchen: a compact combined kitchen and pantry; **kitch'en-gar'den,** a garden where vegetables are cultivated for the kitchen; **kitch'en-maid,** a maid or servant whose work is in the kitchen; **kitch'en-midd'en** (Dan. *kjökken-mödding*), prehistoric rubbish-heap.—*adj.* **kitch'en-sink',** of plays, &c., dealing with life under sordid conditions.—**kitchen unit,** a modern kitchen fitment. [O.E. *cycene*—L. *coquīna*—*coquĕre,* to cook.]

kite, *kīt, n.* any of several rapacious birds of the hawk family, feeding partly on offal: a rapacious person: a light frame covered with paper or cloth for flying in the air: a more complicated structure built up of boxes (**box kite**) for carrying recording instruments or a man in the air.—**to fly a kite,** to give a hint of intended political or other action in order to test public opinion (as a kite serves to show the direction and force of the wind)—whence, *n.* **kite'-fly'ing.** [O.E. *cȳta*; cf. W. *cud,* Breton *kidel,* a hawk.]

kith and kin, *kith, kin,* friends (originally home-country) and relatives. [O.E. *cȳth*—*cun-nan,* to know.]

kitsch, *kich, n.* trash: work in any of the arts that is pretentious and inferior or in bad taste. [Ger.]

kitten, *kit'n, n.* a young cat.—*v.t.* and *v.i.* (of a cat) to bring forth.—*adj.* **kitt'enish,** playful (usu. disparaging). [M.E. *kitoun,* dim. of **cat.**]

kittiwake, *kit'i-wāk, n.* any of several gulls with long wings and rudimentary hind-toe. [Imit.]

kittle, *kit'l, adj.* (*Scot.*) ticklish: difficult to manage or deal with: difficult to understand: perilous.—**kittle cattle,** people difficult to manage or understand. [Ety. obscure.]

kitty, *kit'i, n.* a jail: money pooled for a special purpose or the receptacle containing it.

kiwi, *kē'wi, n.* the apteryx (*q.v.*): (*slang*) a New Zealander: (*slang*) a non-flying member of an airfield staff. [Maori, from its cry.]

klaxon, *klaks'ón, n.* an electric motor-horn. [Registered trade-mark; hence properly spelt with *cap.*]

kleptomania, *klep-to-mā'ni-a, n.* mania for stealing, a morbid impulse to secrete things.—*n.* **kleptomā'niac.** [Gr. *kleptein,* to steal, *maniā,* madness.]

kloof, *klōōf, n.* a mountain ravine. [Du., 'a cleft'.]

knack, *nak, n.* (*arch.*) an ingenious device or crafty trick: the faculty of doing a particular thing adroitly, dexterously: a habit or trick of action, &c.: a clever contrivance, a toy, a trinket. [Orig. imit.; cf. Du. *knak,* a crack, Gr. *knacken,* to crack.]

knacker, *nak'ér, n.* a horse-slaughterer: a worn-out horse: one who buys and breaks up old houses, ships, &c. [Origin obscure.]

knag, *nag, n.* a knot in wood: a peg.—*adj.* **knagg'y,** knotty: rugged. [Cf. Dan. *knag,* Ger. *knagge.*]

knap, *nap, v.t.* to snap, or break with a snapping noise: to break stones with a hammer:—*pr.p.* **knapp'ing;** *pa.p.* **knapped.** [Du. *knappen,* to crack or crush.]

knapsack, *nap'sak, n.* a case for necessaries borne on the back, a rucksack. [Du. *knappen,* to crack, eat.]

knarl. Same as **gnarl.**

knave, *nāv, n.* (*orig.*) a boy: a serving boy: a false, deceitful fellow: a playing-card bearing the picture of a servant or soldier.—*n.* **knav'ery,** dishonesty.—*adj.* **knav'ish,** fraudulent: rascally.—*adv.* **knav'ishly.** [O.E. *cnafa, cnapa,* a boy, a youth; Ger. *knabe, knappe.*]

knead, *nēd, v.t.* to work and press together into a mass, as flour into dough: to operate upon in massage. [O.E. *cnedan*; O.N. *knotha,* Ger. *kneten,* to knead.]

knee, *nē, n.* in man, the joint between the thigh and shin bones: a joint in an animal (e.g. a horse) regarded as corresponding to the human knee: part of a garment covering the knee: a piece of timber or metal like a bent knee.—*n.pl.* **knee'-breech'es,** breeches extending to just below the knee, as in court-dress.—*n.* **knee'-cap,** the knee-pan or patella, a flat, round bone on the front of the knee-joint: a cap or strong covering for the knee, used chiefly for horses, to save their knees in case of a fall.—*adj.* **kneed, knee'd,** having knees or angular joints: baggy at the knees.—*n.* **knee'-pan,** the knee-cap. [O.E. *cnēow, cnēo*; Ger. *knie,* L. *genu,* Gr. *gony.*]

kneel, *nēl, v.i.* to rest or fall on the bended knee:—*pa.t.* and *pa.p.* kneeled, knelt. [O.E. *cnēowlian.*]

knell, *nel, n.* the stroke of a bell: the sound of a bell at a death or funeral: (*fig.*) a warning of the passing of anything.—*v.i.* (*arch.*) to sound as a bell: to toll (also *v.t.*): to sound ominously. [O.E. *cnyllan,* to beat noisily; Du. and Ger. *knallen.*]

knew, *nū, pa.t.* of **know.**

knickerbockers, *nik'ér-bok-érz, n.pl.* loose breeches gathered in at the knee.—Also **knick'ers,** knickerbockers: a woman's undergarment of similar form, covering the whole or part of the thigh and not always gathered in. [From the widebreeched Dutchmen in 'Knickerbocker's' (Washington Irving's) humorous *History of New York* (1809).]

knick-knack, *nik'-nak, n.* a small trifling ornamental article. [A double of **knack.**]

knife, *nīf, n.* an instrument for cutting:—*pl.* **knives** (*nīvz*).—*v.t.* to stab with a knife.—*ns.* **knife'-edge,** a sharp-edged ridge: a piece of steel, &c., like a knife's edge serving as the axis of a balance, for a pendulum, &c. (also *fig.*); **knife'-grinder,** one who grinds or sharpens knives.—**under the knife,** undergoing a surgical operation; **war to the knife,** mortal combat (*lit.* and *fig.*). [M.E. *knif.*—O.E. *cnīf.*]

knight, *nīt, n.* (*orig.*) a lad, a servant: one of gentle birth and bred to arms, admitted in feudal times to a certain honourable military rank: one devoted to the service of a lady: one of the rank, with the title 'Sir', next below a baronet: a piece used in the game of chess.—*v.t.* to create a knight.—*ns.* **knight'-bach'elor,** a knight not a member of any order; **knight'-err'ant,** a knight who travelled in search of adventures: a man of chivalrous or quixotic spirit; **knight'-err'antry; knight'hood,** the rank, title, or status of knight: the order or fraternity of knights.—*adj., adv.* **knight'ly.** —*n.* **knight'-mar'shal,** formerly an officer of the royal household.—**knight of industry,** a footpad, thief, or sharper; **knight of the shire,** a member of parliament for a county; **knights templars** (see **templar**). [O.E. *cniht,* youth, servant, warrior; Ger. and Du. *knecht,* servant.]

knit, *nit, v.t.* (*arch.*) to form into a knot: to form (material, or a garment) by interlooping yarn by means of needles: to unite closely, to interlock (e.g. timbers): to cause to grow together (e.g. broken bones): (*fig.* of common interests, &c.) to draw (persons) close together: to contract, wrinkle (the brows).— *v.i.* to make material from yarn by means of needles: to grow together:—*pr.p.* knitt'ing; *pa.t.* and *pa.p.* knitt'ed or knit.—*ns.* **knitt'er; knitt'ing,** the work of a knitter: union, junction: the material formed by knitting; **knitt'ing-need'le,** a thin rod of steel, bone, or other substance used in knitting. [O.E. *cnyttan — cnotta,* a knot.]

knives, *pl.* of **knife.**

knob, *nob, n.* a hard protuberance: a hard swelling: a round ornament or handle.—*adjs.* **knobbed,** containing or set with knobs; **knobb'y,** full of knobs: knotty.—*ns.* **knobb'iness; knob'stick,** a stick with knobbed head: (*slang*) a synonym for a *blackleg,* a workman who works during a strike. [Cf. Low Ger. *knobbe*; **knop.**]

knock, *nok, v.i.* to strike a blow or blows with something hard or heavy: to drive or be driven (against): to rap for admittance: (of machinery) to rattle.—*v.t.* to strike: to drive against: to stun, daze: (*slang*) to arrest: (*coll.*) to criticise harshly.—*n.* a sudden stroke: a rap: noise of detonation (q.v.) in an internal-combustion engine.—*n.* **knock'er,** the hammer suspended to a door for making a knock.—*adj.* **knock'-kneed,** having knees that knock or touch in walking.—**knock down,** to fell with a blow: assign to a bidder with a tap of the auctioneer's hammer; **knock off,** to desist, cease: to accomplish hastily: (*slang*) to steal; **knock on the head,** to bring to a sudden stop; **knock out,** to strike insensible in boxing: to overcome (**knock-out,** *adj.* depriving one temporarily or permanently of power to fight); **knock together,** to get together or construct hastily; **knock under,** to give in, yield; **knock up,** to rouse by knocking: wear out, or be worn out: to construct hastily: to score (a specified number of runs) in cricket. [O.E. *cnocian*; perh. imit.]

knoll, *nōl, n.* a round hillock. [O.E. *cnol*; Ger. *knollen,* a knob, lump.]

knoll, *nōl.* Same as **knell.**

knop, *nop, n.* a knob: a bud: a loop: a tuft. [Cf. O.N. *knappr*; Du. *knop,* Ger. *knopf.*]

knot, *not, n.* an interlacement of parts of a cord or cords, &c., by twisting the ends about each other, and then drawing tight the loops thus formed: a piece of ribbon, lace, &c., folded or tied upon itself in some particular form, as *shoulder-knot,* &c.: anything like a knot in form: a bond of union: a tangle: a difficulty: a cluster: the base of a branch buried in a later growth of wood: a node or joint in a stem, esp. of a grass: a division of the knot-marked log-line (q.v.): a nautical mile per hour.—*v.t.* to tie in a knot: to unite closely.—*v.i.* to form a knot or knots: to knit knots for a fringe:—*pr.p.* knott'ing; *pa.t.* and *pa.p.* knott'ed.—*n.* **knot'-grass,** a much jointed common weed or grass.—*adj.* **knott'y,** containing knots: hard, rugged: difficult, intricate.—*n.* **knott'iness.** [O.E. *cnotta*; Ger. *knoten,* Dan. *knude,* L. *nōdus.*]

knout, *knoot,* also *nowt, n.* a whip formerly used as an instrument of punishment in Russia: punishment inflicted by the knout. [French spelling of Russ. *knut.*]

know, *nō, v.t.* to be informed of: to be assured of: to have personal experience of: to be acquainted with: to recognise: to be versed in: (*B.*) to approve: (*B.*) to have sexual intercourse with:—*pr.p.* know'ing; *pa.t.* knew (*nū*); *pa.p.* known (*nōn*).—*adj.* **know'ing,** intelligent: skilful: cunning.—*adv.* **know'ingly,** in a

---

Neutral vowels in unaccented syllables: *em'pér-ór*; for certain sounds in foreign words see p. ix.

knowing manner: consciously, intentionally.—**in the know,** in possession of the facts, esp. facts not generally known; **I wouldn't know,** I am not in a position to know; **know all the answers,** to be completely informed on everything, or to think one is; **know better,** to know not to do this or that; **know better than,** to be too wise (to do this or that); **know on which side one's bread is buttered,** to be fully alive to one's own interest; **know the ropes,** to understand the detail or procedure, as a sailor does his rigging; **what do you know?,** a greeting or an expression of incredulity. [O.E. *cnāwan*; O.N. *knā*, L. *noscĕre*, for *gnoscere*, Gr. *gignōskein*.]

knowledge, *nol'ij, n.* assured belief: information: familiarity gained by experience: the sum of what is known: enlightenment, learning: practical skill.—*adj.* **knowl'edgeable** (*coll.*), possessing knowledge: intelligent. [M.E. *knowleche*, where -*leche* is unexplained; see **know.**]

knuckle, *nuk'l, n.* projecting joint of a finger: (*cookery*) knee-joint of a calf or pig.—*v.i.* (usu. with *down* or *under*) to bend the knuckles or knee: to yield.—*n.* **knuck'ledust'er,** a metal covering for the knuckles, for attack or defence. [M.E. *knokel.*]

knurl, *nûrl, n.* a small knob or ridge, esp. one of a number.—*adj.* **knurl'ed.** [O.E. *knur.*]

koala, *kō-ä'la, n.* an Australian marsupial, like a small bear, and so called also 'native bear'. [Australian native name *kūlā.*]

kobold, *kō'bold, n.* in German folklore, a spirit of the mines. [Ger.]

kohl, *kōl, n.* a fine powder of antimony used in the East for staining the eyelids. [Ar. *koh'l.*]

kohlrabi, *kol'ra-bi, n.* a cabbage with a turnip-shaped stem. [Ger.,—It. *cavolo rapa,* cole-turnip.]

kola, *kō'lä, n.* either of two tropical trees whose seeds (called **ko'la-nuts**) have stimulant properties: an aerated non-alcoholic beverage. [West African name.]

kolinsky, *ko-lin'ski, n.* the fur of the Siberian polecat or mink. [Russ. *kolinski*—*Kola,* a peninsula in the north west of European Russia.]

Kominform, Komintern. Same as **Cominform, Comintern.**

Komsomol, *kom'sō-mol, n.* the Communist youth organisation of Russia

kookaburra, *kook'ä-bur-a,* or -*bur'-, n.* the laughing jackass. [Austr. native name.]

kookie, kooky, *kook'i, adj.* eccentric, crazy: (of clothes) smart and eccentric.

kopeck, copeck, *kō-pek', n.* a Russian coin, the hundredth part of a rouble. [Russ. *kopeika.*]

kopje, *kop'i, n.* a low hill. [Afrikaans (q.v.),—*kop,* head.]

Koran, *kō-rän',* sometimes *kō-rán', n.* the Mohammedan Scriptures. [Ar. *qurān,* reading.]

kosher, *kō'shér, adj.* pure, clean, according to the Jewish ordinances—as of meat killed and prepared by Jews. [Heb. *kāshēr,* right.]

kosmos. Same as **cosmos.**

kotow, *kō-tow', n.* the Chinese ceremony of prostration.—*v.i.* to perform that ceremony: to abase oneself before someone (*to kotow to*).—More often spelt **kowtow'.** [Chinese *k'o,* knock, *t'ou,* head.]

koumiss. Same as **kumiss.**

kraal, *kräl, n.* a S. African native village: a corral: also, a native hut with bush stockade round it. [Du. *kraal*—Port. *curral*—L. *currĕre.*]

kraken, *krä'kén, n.* a fabled sea-monster. [Norw.]

kreatine. Same as **creatine.**

kremlin, *krem'lin, n.* a citadel, esp. that of Moscow: (cap.) Soviet government. [Russ. *kreml'.*]

kreosote, *krē'o-sōt, n.* Same as **creosote.**

kreutzer, *kroit'zér, n.* an obs. copper coin of Austria, &c. [Ger. *kreuzer*—*kreuz,* cross, because at one time stamped with a cross.]

krill, *kril, n.* a species of phosphorescent shrimps.

kris, *krēs, n.* a Malay dagger with wavy blade.—Also **creese, crease, kreese.** [Malay.]

Krishna, *krish'na, n.* a deity in later Hinduism.

krone, *krōn'é, n.* a silver coin of Denmark and Norway equal to 100 øre:—*pl.* **kron'er:** (in Sweden **kron'a,** *pl.* **kronor**): in Germany, a former gold coin of ten marks:—*pl.* **kron'en.**

Kroo, Kru, *krōō, adj.* pertaining to certain Negro tribes of Liberia, noted as seamen.—*n.* **Kroo'-boy.** [W. African.]

krypton, crypton, *krip'ton, n.* an element (symbol Kr; atomic no. 36), one of the rare gases, discovered in the air by Sir W. Ramsay in 1898. [Gr. *krypten,* to hide.]

kudos, *kū'dos, n.* fame, renown. [Gr. *kȳdos,* glory.]

Ku-klux Klan, *kū'kluks klan,* or **Ku-klux,** (*U.S.*), a secret organisation in several Southern states after the Civil War of 1861-65, to oppose Northern influence, and prevent Negroes from enjoying their rights as freemen—revived in 1916 to deal drastically with Jews, Catholics, Negroes, &c., and again after the Second World War. [Gr. *kyklos,* a circle, and **clan.**]

kukri, *kook'ri, n.* a sharp, curved Gurkha knife. [Hindustani.]

kulak, *koo-lak', n.* a rich peasant: an exploiter. [Russ., fist.]

kultur, *kool-toor', n.* culture: civilisation: a type of civilisation (sometimes used ironically). [Ger.]

kumiss, *koo'mis, n.* fermented mare's milk: [Russ. *kumis.*]

kümmel, *küm'-, kim'él, n.* a German liqueur flavoured with caraway seeds and cumin. [Ger.]

kumquat, *kum'kwot, n.* a small fruit of the citrus genus: the tree that bears it. [From Chinese; lit. 'golden orange'.]

Kuomintang, *kwō'min-täng', n.* the nationalist people's party in China, organised chiefly by Sun Yat-Sen (1866-1925). [Chinese.]

kurchatovium, *kûr-chä-tō'vi-ùm, n.* element 104 named by Russians, who claimed its discovery in 1966, after a Russian physicist.—Also (U.S.) **rutherfordium.**

Kurd, *koord, kûrd, n.* one of the people of *Kurdistan,* often blonde in colouring (Xenophon's *Kardouchoi*), speaking a language of the same group as Persian.

kwashiorkor, *kwä-shi-ör'kör, n.* a widespread nutritional disease of children in tropical and subtropical regions due to deficiency of protein. [Ghanaian name.]

kyle, *kīl, n.* a narrow strait. [Gael. *caol.*]

kyloe, *kī'lō, n.* one of the cattle of the Hebrides.

Kyrie eleison, *kēr'i-e el-ā'i-son,* abbrev. **Kyrie,** *n.* a form of prayer in all the ancient Greek liturgies, retained in the R.C. mass, following immediately after the introit (including both words and music). [L.L. from Gr. *kȳrie, eleēson,* Lord, have pity.]

Neutral vowels in unaccented syllables: *em′pér-ór*; for certain sounds in foreign words see p. ix.

L

laager, lager, *lä′gėr,* Afrik. form **laer** not used in S. Afr. Eng., *n.* in South Africa, a camp made by a ring of ox-wagons set close together for defence: an encampment. [Cape Du. *lager*—Ger. *lager,* a camp.]

labarum, *lab′a-rum, n.* a Roman military standard adopted as the imperial standard after Constantine's conversion, with the Greek letters XP (Chr), joined in a monogram, to signify the name of Christ. [L.,—Late Gr. *labaron.*]

labdanum. See **ladanum.**

label, *lā′b(ė)l, n.* a small slip placed on or near anything to denote its nature, contents, ownership, &c.: (*law*) a paper annexed to a will, as a codicil: (*her.*) a little bar with pendants.—*v.t.* (*lit.* and *fig.*) to affix a label to: to designate (as):—*pr.p.* lā′belling; *pa.t.* and *pa.p.* lā′belled.—**labelled atom,** a tagged atom. [O.Fr. *label* (Fr. *lambeau*), perh.—O.H.G. *lappa* (Ger. *lappen*).]

labellum, *la-bel′um, n.* the lower petal of a flower, esp. an orchid. [L., dim. of *labrum, labium,* a lip.]

labial, *lā′bi-ál, adj.* pertaining to the lips: formed by the lips.—*n.* a sound formed by the lips.—*adv.* **lā′bially.**—*adj.* **lā′biate,** lipped: having a lipped corolla.—*adj.* and *n.* **lābiodent′al,** of a sound, pronounced by lips and teeth. [L. *labium,* a lip.]

laboratory, *lā-bor′ā-tō-ri lab′ó-rā-tō-ri n.* a chemist's workroom: a place where scientific experiments are systematically carried on: a place where drugs, &c., are prepared for use. [L. *labōrāre*—*labor,* work.]

labour, *lā′bôr, n.* toil or exertion, esp. when fatiguing: work: persevering effort: a task requiring hard work: labourers, artisans, &c., collectively: the pangs of childbirth.—*v.i.* to work: to take pains: to be oppressed: to move slowly: to be in travail: (*naut.*) to pitch and roll heavily.—*adj.* **labō′rious,** full of labour: wearisome: given up to, devoted to, labour: industrious.—*adv.* **labō′riously.**—*n.* **labō′riousness.**—*adj.* **la′boured,** bearing marks of effort in the execution.—*n.* **lā′bourer,** one who labours: one who does heavy work requiring little skill.—*adj.* **lā′bour-sav′ing,** intended to supersede or lessen labour.—**Labour Bureau, Exchange,** formerly, a public office which found work for the unemployed, now **employment exchange; labour market,** the supply of labour in relation to the demand for it; **Labour Party,** a party aiming at securing for workers by hand or brain the fruits of their industry and equitable distribution thereof: its representatives in parliament.—**hard labour,** compulsory work imposed in addition to imprisonment, abolished in U.K. in 1948. [O.Fr. *labour, labeur*—L. *labor.*]

Labrador (retriever), *lab′rä-dör* (*ri-trēv′ér*), *n.*

either of two varieties of sporting dog—**black,** or **yellow** or **golden.** [*Labrador.*]

laburnum, *la-bûr′num, n.* a small tree of the pea family with beautiful hanging yellow flowers, a native of the Alps. [L.]

labyrinth, *lab′i-rinth, n.* a place full of tangled windings: (*orig.*) a building consisting of halls connected by intricate passages: a maze: a perplexity: (*anat.*) the cavities of the internal ear.—*adjs.* **labyrinth′al, labyrinth′ian, labyrinth′ine.** [Gr. *labyrinthos,* perh. conn. with *labrys,* the double axe.]

lac, Same as **lakh.**

lac, *lak, n.* a dark-red transparent resin produced on the twigs of trees in the East by the lac insect, used in dyeing.—*adj.* **laccic** (*lak′sik*).—*ns.* **laccine** (*lak′sin*), a brittle, translucent, yellow substance, obtained from shell-lac; **lac′-dye, lac′-lake,** scarlet colouring matters obtained from **stick′-lac,** the twigs, with attached resin, enclosed insects, and ova; **seed′-lac,** granular substance formed by crushing and washing stick-lac; **shellac, shell-lac** (*she-lak′, shel′ak*), purified lac resin prepared by melting and straining seed-lac and allowing it to solidify in thin sheets or flakes.—*v.t.* to coat with shellac.—*pr.p.* shellacking; *pa.t.* and *pa.p.* shellacked. [Hindustani, *lākh*—Sans. *lākgā,* 100000, hence the (teeming) lac insect.]

lace, *lās* n. a string for fastening: an ornamental fabric of fine thread delicately woven.—*v.t.* to fasten with a lace: to adorn with lace: to add a dash of spirits to.—*v.i.* to have lacing as means of fastening. [O.Fr. *las,* a noose—L. *laqueus,* a noose.]

lacerate, *las′ér-āt, v.t.* to tear, to rend, to wound: to afflict.—*adj.* **lac′erable,** that may be lacerated.—*n.* **lacerā′tion,** tearing: having power to tear. [L. *lacerāre, -ātum,* to tear—*lacer,* torn.]

lachrymal, *lak′ri-mál, adj.* of or pertaining to tears.—*n.* a bone near the tear-gland.—*adjs.* **lach′rymary, lach′rymatory,** lachrymal: containing tears: causing tears to flow, blinding; **lach′rymose,** shedding tears: given to weeping.—*adv.* **lach′rymosely.** [*lachryma,* mediaeval spelling of L. *lacrima,* a tear; Gr. *dakry,* Eng. **tear.**]

lacing, *lās′ing, n.* the act of fastening with a lace or cord through eyelet-holes: a cord used in fastening. [**lace.**]

lack, *lak, n.* want, deficiency.—*v.t.* to want: to be deficient in: to be destitute of.—*v.i.* to be missing, deficient (now used chiefly in tenses formed with *pr.p.,* e.g. *is lacking*).—*adj.* **lack′-lus′tre,** wanting brightness. [M.E. *lak,* defect; cf. Middle Low Ger. and Du. *lak,* blemish.]

lackadaisical, *lak-a-dā′zi-kál, adj.* affectedly pensive, sentimental: listless. [From archaic interj. *lackadaisy!*]

lacker   lake

lacker. See **lacquer.**

lackey, lacquey, *lak'i, n.* a menial attendant: a
footman or footboy: a servile, obsequious person.—*v.t.* and *v.i.* to serve or attend as or like
a footman. [O.Fr. *laquay* (Fr. *laquais*)—Sp.
lacayo, a lackey; perh. Ar. *luka',* servile.]

laconic, -al, *la-kon'ik, -ál, adj.* expressing in few
words after the manner of the *Laconians* or
Spartans: concise, sententiously brief.—*adv.*
lacon'ically.—*ns.* **laconism** (*lak'-*), **lacon'icism** (*-is-izm*), a concise style: a short, pithy
phrase. [Gr. *Lakōnikos.*]

lacquer, lacker, *lak'ér, n.* a varnish made of lac
and alcohol: a substance sprayed on the hair
to keep it in place.—*v.t.* to cover with lacquer,
to varnish.—*n.* **lac'querer.** [Fr. *lacre*—Port.
lacre, laca—Hindustani. See **lac** (2).]

lacrosse, *la-kros', n.* a game (orig. N. American)
played by two sets of twelve, the ball being
driven through the opponents' goal by means
of a *crosse,* a long stick with a shallow net at
one end. [Fr.]

lacteal, *lak'ti-ál, adj.* pertaining to or resembling
milk: conveying chyle, lymph with a milky
appearance due to minute fat globules in suspension.—*n.* one of the absorbent vessels of
the intestines which convey the chyle to the
thoracic duct.—*n.* **lacta'tion,** the act of giving
milk: the period of suckling.—*adjs.* **lac-
tes'cent,** turning to milk: producing milky
juice; **lac'tic,** pertaining to milk; **lactif'erous,**
conveying or producing milk or milky
juice.—*n.* **lac'tose,** milk-sugar.—**lactic acid,**
an acid obtained from milk. [L. *lacteus,* milky
—*lac,* gen. *lactis,* milk; Gr. *gala,* gen. *galak-
tos,* milk.]

lacuna, *la-kū'na, n.* a gap or hiatus:—*pl.* **lacū'nae**
(*-nē*). [L. *lacūna,* hollow, gap.]

lacustrine, *la-kus'trīn, adj.* pertaining to lakes:
dwelling in or on lakes. [L. *lacus,* a lake.]

lad, *lad, n.* a boy: a youth: a dashing fellow:—
fem. **lass.** [M.E. *ladde,* youth, servant.]

ladanum, *lad'a-num, n.* a resin exuded from
shrubs growing in Mediterranean countries.—Also **lab'danum.** [L. *lādanum*—Gr.
lādanon—prob. Pers. *lādan.*]

ladder, *lad'ér, n.* a contrivance, generally portable, with rungs between two supports, for
going up and down: anything by which one
ascends (also *fig.*): a fault in knitwear extending from broken stitch(es).—*v.t.* to cause
a ladder in (e.g. a stocking).—*v.i.* of a stocking,
to develop a ladder. [O.E. *hlǣder*; Ger. *leiter.*]

lade, *lād, v.t.* to load: to throw in or out, as a
fluid, with a ladle or dipper.—*adj.* **lad'en,** lad-
ed or loaded: burdened.—*n.* **lad'ing,** the act of
loading: that which is loaded: cargo: freight.
[O.E. *hladan,* pa.t. *hlōd,* to load, to draw out
water.]

ladle, *lād'l, n.* a large spoon for lifting out liquid,
&c., from a vessel: a vessel used for conveying
molten metal from the furnace to the mould
or from one furnace to another. [O.E. *hlǣ-
del*—*hladan,* to lade.]

lady, *lā'di, n.* the mistress of a house: used as the
feminine of *lord* (common noun and—*cap.*—
title): (*cap.*) title given to the wife of a knight
or a baronet: feminine of *gentleman*: woman
of refinement of manners and instincts:—*pl.*
ladies (*lā-diz*).—*ns.* **lā'dybird,** a family of little
round beetles, often brightly spotted, most of
which feed on insects—also **lā'dybug; lā'dy-
chap'el,** a chapel dedicated to 'Our Lady', the
Virgin Mary; **Lā'dy Day,** March 25, the day of
the Annunciation of the Virgin; **lā'dy-fern,** a
pretty British fern, common in moist woods;
lā'dy-help, one paid to assist in housework,
but treated more or less as one of the family;
la'dy-in-wait'ing, an attendant to a lady of
royal status.—*adj.* **lā'dylike,** like a lady in
manners: refined: effeminate.—*ns.* **lā'dylove,**
a lady or woman loved, a sweetheart; **lā'dy-
ship,** the title of a lady.—**Ladies' Gallery,** a
gallery in the House of Commons, once
screened off by a grille; **ladies' man,** one fond
of women's society. [O.E. *hlǣfdige,* lit. app. the
bread-kneader—*hlāf,* loaf, and a lost word
from the root of **dough.**]

laevo-, levo-, *lē-vō-,* in composition, on, or to,
the left. [L. *laevus,* left.]

laevulose, levulose, *lev'ū-lōs, n.* one of the forms
of fructose (q.v.). [L. *laevus,* left.]

lag, *lag, n.* he who, or that which, comes behind:
the fag-end: (of one phenomenon, or condition, in relation to another or others) retardation, act of falling behind or amount of that
fall.—*v.i.* to move or walk slowly: to loit-
er:—*pr.p.* **lagg'ing;** *pa.p.* **lagged.**—*adj.* **lagg'ard,**
lagging: slow: backward.—*ns.* **lagg'ard, lagg'-
er,** one who lags behind: a loiterer: an
idler.—*adv.* **lagg'ingly.** [Origin unknown.]

lag, *lag, n.* a stave, a lath, boarding: a non-conducting covering.—*v.t.* to case with lags.—*n.*
lagg'ing, boarding: non-conducting covering.
[Prob. O.N. *lögg,* barrel-rim; cf. Swed. *lagg,*
stave.]

lag, *lag, n.* a convict, jail-bird. [Ety. uncertain.]

lager, *lä'ger,* in full **lager-beer,** *n.* a kind of light
beer. [Ger. *lager-bier*—*lager,* a store-house,
bier, beer.]

lagoon, *la-gōōn', n.* a shallow pond into which
the sea flows. [It. *laguna*—L. *lacūna.*]

laic, laical. See **lay** (4).

laid, *lād, pa.t.* and *pa.p.* of **lay** (2).—Used of
paper, meaning marked in manufacture by
wires in parallel lines (cf. **wove**).—**laid up,** ill
in bed.

lain, *pa.p.* of **lie** (2).

lair, *lār, n.* a lying-place, esp. the den or retreat
of a wild beast. [O.E. *leger,* a couch—*liegan,* to
lie down; Du. *leger,* Ger. *lager.*]

laird, *lārd, n.* (*Scot.*) a landed proprietor.—*n.*
laird'ship, an estate. [N. form of **lord.**]

laissez-faire, *les'ā-fer', n.* a general principle of
non-interference with the free action of the
individual: the let-alone principle in government, business, &c.—Also **laiss'er-faire'.** [Fr.
laisser (imper. *laissez*), to allow (L. *laxāre,* to
relax), *faire* (L. *facĕre*), to do.]

laity. See **lay** (4).

lake, *lāk, n.* a reddish pigment originally got
from lac: carmine. [Fr. *laque*—Hindustani. See
lac (2).]

lake, *lāk, n.* a large body of water within
land.—*ns.* **lake'-dwell'ing,** a settlement, esp.
prehistoric, built on piles in a lake; **lake'let,** a
little lake.—*adj.* **lā'ky,** pertaining to a lake or
lakes.—**Lake District,** picturesque mountainous region in Cumberland, Westmorland,
and Lancashire. (now Cumbria) with many

Neutral vowels in unaccented syllables: *em'pér-ór*; for certain sounds in foreign words see p. ix.

406

lakes/, **Lake poets, Lake school,** Wordsworth, Coleridge, and Southey, dwellers in the Lake District. [M.E. *lac* — L. *lacus*.]

lakh, lac, *lak, n.* the number 100000: 100000 rupees. [Hindustani *lākh* — Sans. *lāksā,* 100000.]

Lallan, *lal'an,* **Lallans,** *n.* Lowland Scottish dialect, broad Scots. [Scot. variant of Lowland.]

lam, *lam, v.t.* to beat. [Cf. O.E. *lemian,* to subdue, to lame.]

lama, *lä'mä, n.* a Buddhist priest in Tibet. — *ns.* **Lamaism** (*lä'mä-izm*), the religion prevailing in Tibet and Mongolia, being Buddhism with elements borrowed from other Eastern religions; **la'masery** (or *lä-mä'sér-i*), **lamaserai** (*-ī*), a Tibetan monastery. [Tibetan *blama,* the *b* silent.]

lamb, *lam, n.* the young of a sheep: the flesh of the young sheep: one simple, innocent, or gentle as a lamb. — *v.i.* to bring forth, as sheep. — *n.* **lamb'kin,** a little lamb. — *adj.* **lamb' like,** like a lamb, gentle. [O.E. *lamb;* Ger. *lamm,* Du. *lam.*]

lambent, *lam'bént, adj.* licking: moving about as if touching lightly: gliding over: flickering. [L. *lambēre,* to lick.]

lame, *lām, adj.* disabled, esp. in the use of a leg: hobbling: unsatisfactory: imperfect. — *v.t.* to make lame: to cripple: to render imperfect. — *adv.* **lame'ly.** — *n.* **lame'ness** — **lame duck** (see **duck**). [O.E. *lama,* lame; Du. *lam,* Ger. *lahm*.]

lamella, *la-mel'a, n.* (*zool.*) a structure resembling a thin plate. — *n.* **lamell'ibranch** (*-brangk*), one of the **Lamellibranchiata,** a class of molluscs, including oysters, &c., having a shell consisting of two valves alike externally — Also *adj.* [L., dim. of *lamina,* a thin plate.]

lament, *la-ment', v.i.* to wail: to mourn. — *v.t.* to mourn for: to deplore. — *n.* sorrow expressed in cries: an elegy or dirge. — *adj.* **lamentable** (*lam'ént-ā-bl*), (*arch.*) expressing sorrow, doleful: sad: regrettable: (*coll.*) worthless.— *adv.* **lam'entably.** — *n.* **lamenta'tion,** act of lamenting: audible expression of grief: wailing: (*pl., cap.*) a book of the Old Testament, traditionally ascribed to Jeremiah. — *p.adj.* **lament'ed,** bewailed: mourned. — *adv.* **lament'ingly,** with lamentation. [Fr. *lamenter* — L. *lāmentāri.*]

lamina, *lam'i-na, n.* a thin plate or layer: a leaf-blade. — *pl.* **lam'inae** (*-nē*). — *adjs.* **lam'inable; lam'inar, lam'inary,** consisting of or like thin plates or layers: of or relating to a fluid, streamlined flow. — *n.* **Lamina'ria,** a genus of brown seaweeds with large leathery fronds. — *v.t.* **lam'inate,** to make into a thin plate: to separate into layers: to make by putting layers together. — *n.* a laminated plastic or other material similarly made. — *adjs.* **lam'inate, -d,** in laminae or thin plates: consisting of scales or layers, over one another. — *n.* **lamina'tion,** the arrangement in thin layers: a thin layer. — *adj.* **laminif'erous,** consisting of laminae or layers. — **laminated plastics,** sheets of paper, canvas, linen or silk, impregnated with a resin, dried, and pressed together. [L. *lamina,* a thin plate.]

Lammas, *lam'as, n.* the feast of first-fruits on August 1. — *n.* **Lamm'as-tide,** the season of

Lammas. [O.E. *hlāf-mæsse* and *hlāmmæsse* — *hlāf,* loaf, *mæsse,* feast.]

lamp, *lamp, n.* a vessel for burning oil with a wick, and so giving light: a gas or electric light, &c. — *n.* **lamp'black,** soot from a lamp, or from the burning of substances rich in carbon (mineral oil, tar, &c.) in a limited supply of air: a pigment made from this. [Fr. *lampe* and Gr. *lampas, -ados* — *lampein,* to shine.]

lampoon, *lam-pōōn', n.* a personal satire in writing: low censure. — *v.t.* to assail with personal satire: to satirise: — *pr.p.* lampōōn'ing; *pa.p.* lampōōned'. — *ns.* **lampoon'er, lampoon'ery.** [O.Fr. *lampon,* orig. a drinking-song, with the refrain *lampons* — let us drink — *lamper,* to drink (*lapper,* to lap).]

lamprey, *lam'pri, n.* a genus of water creatures resembling the eels that fix themselves to stones or to their prey by their mouths. [O.Fr. *lamproie* — Low L. *lamprēda, lampetra* — explained as from L. *lambēre,* to lick, *petra,* rock.]

lance, *lans, n.* a weapon with a long shaft, a spearhead, and often a small flag: a surgeon's lancet: the bearer of a lance. — *v.t.* to pierce, as with a lance: to open with a lancet. — *ns.* **lance'-cor'poral,** an acting corporal; **lan'cer,** a light cavalry soldier armed with a lance, or of a regiment formerly so armed: (*pl.*) a set of quadrilles of a certain arrangement. [Fr., — L. *lancea;* Gr. *lonchē,* a lance.]

lanceolate, d, *län'si-ō-lāt, -id, adjs.* shaped like a lance-head: lancet-shaped: (*bot.*) tapering towards both ends and two or three times as long as broad [L. *lanceolātus* — *lanceola,* dim. of *lancea,* a lance.]

lancet, *län'set, n.* a surgical instrument used for opening veins, abscesses, &c.: a lancet window: a lancet arch. — **lancet arch,** a high and narrow pointed arch; **lancet window,** a window terminating in an arch acutely pointed, often double or triple. [O.Fr. *lancette,* dim. of *lance.* See **lance.**]

lanch. Same as **launch.**

land, *land, n.* earth, the solid portion of the surface of the globe: a country: a district: a constituent part of an empire or federation: real estate: ground: soil: a nation. — *v.t.* to set on land or on shore: to bring onto land (e.g. a fish — also *fig.*): (*coll.*) to deal (a person e.g. a blow). — *v.i.* to come on land or on shore: to alight or to fall. — *ns.* **Land Army,** a body of women organised in wartime for farm work; **land-breeze,** a breeze setting from the land towards the sea; **land'-crab,** any crab that lives much or chiefly on land. — *adj.* **land'ed,** possessing land or estates. — *ns.* **land'fall,** an approach to land after a journey by sea or air: the land so approached; **land'-force,** a military force serving on land; **land'-hold'er,** a tenant or proprietor of land; **land'-hung'er,** desire to possess land; **land'ing,** disembarkation: a coming to ground: a place for getting on shore or upon the ground: the level part of a staircase between the flights of steps. — *adj.* relating to the unloading of a vessel's cargo. — *ns.* **land'ing-beam,** a radio beam by which an aircraft is guided in to land; **landing-field,** field of size and nature to permit aircraft to land and take off safely; **land'ing-gear,** the parts of an aircraft that carry the load when it alights; **land'ing-net,** a kind of scoop-net for landing a fish that has been caught; **land'ing-strip,** a narrow, hard-surfaced runway; **land'lady,** a woman who has tenants or lodgers: the mistress of an inn; **land'-line,** overland line of communication or transport.—*v.t.* **land'lock,** to enclose by land.—*adj.* **land'locked.**—*ns.* **land'lord,** one who has tenants or lodgers: the master of an inn; **land'-lubb'er,** a landsman (a sailor's term of contempt); **land'mark,** anything serving to mark the boundaries of land: any object on land that serves as a guide to seamen or others: any event, &c., that marks a turning-point or a stage; **land'-mine,** a mine laid on or near the surface of the ground, to explode when an enemy is over it; **land'rail,** a rail (*q.v.*) frequenting fields, also called the corncrake; **land'-shark,** a land-grabber; one who plunders sailors on shore; **land'skip** (same as **landscape**); **land'slide,** a portion of land that falls down from a cliff or the side of a hill (also **land'slip**): in an election, a great majority of votes for one side, a great transference of votes; **lands'man, land'man,** one who lives or serves on land: one inexperienced in seafaring; **land'-steward,** a person who manages a landed estate; **land'-tax,** a tax upon land; **land'wait'er,** a custom-house officer who attends on the landing of goods from ships.—*adv.* **land'ward, -s,** toward the land.—*adj.* **land'ward,** lying toward the land, away from the sea-coast.—**landed interest,** the land-holding class in a community; **land with,** to encumber with (a problem, difficult situation, &c.); **see how the land lies,** to find out in advance how matters stand. [O.E. *land*; Du., Ger. *land.*]

landau, *lan'dö, n.* a carriage with a top that may be opened centrally and thrown back.—*n.* **landaulet', -ette',** a covered motor-car, the back portion of which can be uncovered by lowering part of the roof and sides: a small landau. [*Landau* in Germany, where it is said to have been first made.]

lande, *lād, n.* a heathy plain or sandy tract·(now forested) along the coast in S.W. France. [Fr.]

landgrave, *land'grāv, n.* a German count:—*fem.* **landgravine** (*land'gra-vēn*).—*n.* **landgrā'viäte,** the territory of a landgrave. [Ger. *landgraf—land,* land, *graf,* count.]

landscape, *land'skāp, n.* portion of land that the eye can comprehend in a single view: inland scenery: the aspect of a country, or a picture representing it.—*v.t.* to improve by landscape gardening.—**land'scape-gar'dening,** the art of laying out grounds to produce the effect of a picturesque landscape. [Du. *landschap,* from *land* and *-schap,* a suffix equivalent to Eng. *-ship.*]

lane, *lān, n.* a narrow road or (*fig.*) passage: a narrow street: a prescribed course for ships: a division of a road for one line of traffic. [O.E. *lane, lone.*]

language, *lang'gwij, n.* human speech: a variety of speech or body of words and idioms, esp. that of a people: mode of expression: any manner of expressing thought (e.g. *sign language*).—**language laboratory,** a room in which pupils in separate cubicles are taught a language by means of material recorded on tapes.—**bad language,** profane oaths, &c.; **dead language,** one no longer spoken, as opp. to **living language; speak the same language,** of two or more people, to have the same tastes, feelings, background knowledge or habit of mind and thus be capable of mutual understanding. [Fr. *langage—langue*—L. *lingua,* the tongue.]

Langue d'oc, *läg dok, n.* a collective name for the Romance dialects spoken in the Middle Ages from the Alps to the Pyrenees—the tongue of the troubadours, often used as synonymous with Provençal, one of its chief branches.—**langue d'oui** (*läg dwē*), **langue d'oïl** (*dö-ēl*), the Romance dialect of northern France, the language of the trouvères, the dominant factor in the formation of modern French. [O.Fr. *langue* (L. *lingua*), tongue; *de,* of; Provençal *oc,* yes (L. *hoc,* this); *oui, oïl,* yes (L. *hoc illud,* this (is) that, yes).]

languid, *lang'gwid, adj.* feeble, flagging, exhausted, sluggish, spiritless.—*adv.* **lang'uidly.** —*n.* **lang'uidness.** [L. *languidus—languēre,* to be weak.]

languish, *lang'gwish, v.i.* to become languid: to lose strength and animation: to pine: to become dull, as of trade.—*adj.* **lang'uishing,** expressive of languor, or merely of sentimental emotion.—*adv.* **lang'uishingly.**—*n.* **lang'uishment,** the act or state of languishing: tenderness of look. [Fr. *languiss-* (serving as pr.p. stem of *languir*)—L. *languescĕre—languēre,* to be faint.]

languor, *lang'g(w)òr, n.* state of being languid, faint: dullness: listlessness: soft or tender mood or emotion.—*adj.* **lang'uorous.** [L. *languor, -ōris.*]

laniferous, *lan-if'ėr-us, adj.* wool-bearing.—Also **lanigerous** (*-ij'-*). [L. *lānifer, lāniger—lāna,* wool, *ferre, gerĕre,* to bear.]

lank, *langk, adj.* thin: shrunken: tall and lean: long and limp: straight and limp.—*adv.* **lank'ly.**—*n.* **lank'ness.**—*adj.* **lank'y,** lean, tall, and ungainly: long and limp.—*n.* **lank'iness.** [O.E. *hlanc.*]

lanolin, lanoline, *lan'ō-lin, -lēn, n.* a fat extracted from wool, used as a basis for ointments. [L. *lāna,* wool, *oleum,* oil.]

lansquenet, *läns'ké-net, n.* a German foot-soldier: a card-game. [Fr.,—Ger. *landsknecht.*]

lantern, *lant'ėrn, n.* a case for holding or carrying a light: an ornamental structure surmounting a building to give light and air and to crown the fabric.—*adj.* **lant'ern-jawed,** with long thin jaws, hollow-faced.—**Chinese lantern,** a collapsible paper lantern; **dark lantern,** a lantern having an opaque slide; **magic lantern,** an instrument by means of which magnified images of small pictures are thrown upon a screen. [Fr. *lanterne*—L. *lanterna*—Gr. *lamptēr—lampein,* to give light.]

lanthanum, *lan'thán-ùm, n.* a metallic element (symbol La; atomic no. 57), one of the rare-earths.—*n. pl.* **lan'thanides,** the rare-earth elements. [From Gr. *lanthanein,* to be unseen.]

lanthorn, *lant'ėrn, n.* an obsolete spelling of **lantern,** from the use of horn for the sides of lanterns.

Neutral vowels in unaccented syllables: *em'pėr-ór;* for certain sounds in foreign words see p. ix.

lanyard   lash

lanyard, laniard, *lan'yàrd, n.* a short rope used on board ship for fastening or stretching: a cord for hanging a knife, whistle, or the like about the neck. [Fr. *lanière*, perh. from L. *lānārius*, made of wool—*lāna*, wool.]

Laodicean, *lā-od-i-sē'an, adj.* lukewarm in religion, like the Christians of *Laodicea* (Rev. iii. 14-16).

lap, *lap, v.t.* to lick up with the tongue: to wash or flow against: (*lit.* and *fig.*) to drink (up) greedily.—*v.i.* to drink by licking up a liquid: to wash (against), making a sound of such a kind:—*pr.p.* lapp'ing; *pa.t.* and *pa.p.* lapped. [O.E. *lapian*; Low Ger. *lappen*; L. *lambĕre*; Gr. *laptein.*]

lap, *lap, n.* a flap: a fold: part of a garment folded to hold anything: the part from waist to knees of the clothes and body of a person sitting: place where one is nurtured (*fig.*; in phrases): a round of a race-course.—*v.t.* to wrap, enfold, surround: to get or be a lap ahead of.—*v.i.* to lie with an overlap, project (over)—*ns.* **lap'-ding,** a small dog functinof in the lap: a pet dog; **lap'ful,** as much as fills a lap.—**lap of honour,** a round of the field run by a person or a team that has just had a notable victory. [O.E. *læppa,* a loosely hanging part; Ger. *lappen,* a rag.]

lapel, lappel, *la-pel', n.* part of a coat folded back, continuing the collar.—*adj.* **lapelled'.** [Dim. of **lap.**]

lapidary, *lap'i-dàr-i, n.* a cutter of stones, esp. gem-stones—also **lapidā'rian, lap'idārist.**—*adj.* pertaining to stones and the cutting of stones: inscribed on stone.—*adj.* **lapides'cent,** becoming stone: petrifying.—*n.* **lapides'cence.**—*v.t.* and *v.i.* **lapid'ify,** to turn into stone:—*pr.p.* lapid'ifying; *pa.p.* lapid'ified.—*n.* **lapidificā'tion.**—*n.pl.* **lapilli** (*la-pil'ī*), small fragments of lava ejected from a volcano.—**lap'is laz'uli,** a stone of azure-blue colour. [L. *lapidārius—lapis, -idis,* a stone.]

Lapp, Laplander, *ns.* a native or inhabitant of *Lapland.—adj.* **Lap'landish, Lapp'ish.**

lappet, *lap'et, n.* a little lap or flap.—*adj.* **lapp'-eted.** [Dim. of **lap.**]

lapse, *laps, v.i.* to slip or glide: to pass by degrees: to fall away by cessation or relaxation of effort or cause: to fall from the faith: to fail in duty: to pass into disuse: to become void.—*n.* a slip: passage (of time): a failure (in virtue, memory, &c.).—*adj.* **lapsed,** having fallen into disuse or become void: fallen into sin or from the faith. [L. *lapsāre,* to slip, *lapsus,* a slip—*lābī, lapsus,* to slip.]

lapwing, *lap'wing, n.* a crested species of plover, the peewit. [M.E. *lappewinke*—O.E. *læpewince, hlæpewince, hléapewince*; modified by confusion with **wing.**]

larboard, *lär'bord, labord, n.* and *adj.* (*obs.*) port or left. [M.E. *laddeborde,* influenced by **starboard**; origin unknown.]

larceny, *lär'sen-i, n.* the legal term in England and Ireland for stealing: theft.—*n.* **lar'cenist.**—**petty larceny, grand larceny,** before 1827, distinguished as theft of property valued at under or over 12d. [O.Fr. *larrecin* (Fr. *larcin*)—L. *latrōcinium—latrō,* a robber.]

larch, *lärch, n.* a genus of cone-bearing trees related to the pines and firs. [Gr. *larix.*]

lard, *lärd, n.* the melted fat of the hog.—*v.t.* to smear or enrich with lard: to stuff with bacon or pork: to fatten: to mix (with anything).—*adjs.* **lardā'ceous; lard'y.** [O.Fr.,—L. *lāridum, lārdum*; cf. Gr. *lārīnos,* fat, *lāros,* pleasant to taste.]

larder, *lärd'ér, n.* a room or place where food is kept. [O.Fr. *lardier,* a bacon-tub—*lard.* See **lard.**]

lares, *lā'rēz, n.pl.* deities worshipped orig. as protectors of a particular locality, later as protectors of the home.—**lares and penates,** one's home or one's household effects. [L. (sing. *lar*).]

large, *lärj, adj.* great in size, extensive, bulky: broad: copious, abundant: (*fig.*) wide (e.g. powers), generous, unprejudiced (e.g. *large charity, large-minded*).—*adj.* **large'-heart'ed,** sympathetic, kindly, generous.—*adv.* **large'ly.**—*n.* **large'ness.—at large,** at liberty: at random: in general. [Fr.,—L. *largus,* copious.]

largess, largesse, *lärj'es, n.* a present or donation: money, presents, bestowed. [Fr. *largesse* and L. *largītiō, -ōnis—largus,* copious.]

largo, *lär'gō, adj.* (*mus.*) slow and dignified.—*n.* a movement to be so performed. [It.,—L. *largus,* copious.]

lariat, *lar'i-at, n.* a rope for picketing animals: a lasso. [Sp. *la,* the, *reata,* a rope for tying animals together.]

lark, *lärk, n.* a family of singing-birds which includes the skylark.—*n.* **lark'spur,** a genus of plants with spurred flowers. [M.E. *laverock*—O.E. *lǽwerce, lāwerce*; Ger. *lerche.*]

lark, *lärk, n.* a frolic: a piece of mischief.—*v.i.* to frolic.—*adj.* **lark'y.** [Perh. from the preceding: some connect it with O.E. *lāc,* play.]

larrikin, *lar'i-kin, n.* (*Austr.*) a street rough or hooligan—also *adj.* [Origin doubtful.]

larva, *lär'va, n.* an animal in an immature but active state markedly different from the adult, e.g. a caterpillar:—*pl.* **larvae** (*lär'vē*). *adj.* **lar'val.** [L. *lārva, lārua,* a spectre, a mask.]

larynx, *lar'ingks, n.* the vocal organ in all land vertebrates except birds, at the upper end of the windpipe.—*adj.* **laryngeal** (*lar-in'ji-ál*).—*n.* **laryngitis** (*-jī'tis*), inflammation of the larynx.—*n.* **laryng'oscope** (*-ing'gō-*), a mirror for examining the larynx. [L.,—Gr. *larynx, -yngos.*]

lascar, *las'kär, -kär,* or *las-kär', n.* an Oriental (originally Indian) sailor or camp-follower. [Hindustani and Pers. *lashkar,* army, or *lashkarī,* a soldier.]

lascivious, *la-siv'i-us, adj.* lustful: tending to produce lustful emotions.—*adv.* **lasciv'iously.**—*n.* **lasciv'iousness.** [L.L. *lascīviōsus—lascīvus,* playful.]

laser, *lāz'ér, n.* a device which amplifies an input of light, producing an extremely narrow and intense monochromatic beam.—*v.i.* **lase,** of a crystal, &c., to be, or become, suitable for use as a laser. [*L*ight *a*mplification by *s*timulated *e*mission of *r*adiation.]

lash, *lash, n.* a thong or cord: the flexible part of a whip: an eyelash: a stroke with a whip or anything pliant: a stroke of satire.—*v.t.* to strike with or as if with a lash: to dash against: to fasten or secure with a rope or cord: to scourge with censure or satire.—*v.i.* to

fāte, fär; mē, hûr (her); *mīne; mōte, för; mūte; mōōn, fŏŏt;* THen (then)

strike hard (at): to make a sudden or restless movement (with e.g. a tail).—*n.* **lash'ing,** act of whipping: a rope for making things fast.— **lash out,** to kick out, as a horse: to break out recklessly. [Origin obscure; perh. several different words, with possible connections with **latch** and **lace.**]

lass, *las, n.* a girl, esp. a country girl: a sweetheart. [Origin obscure; the association with **lad** may be accidental.]

lassitude, *las'i-tūd, n.* faintness, weakness, weariness, languor. [L. *lassitūdō—lassus,* faint.]

lasso, *las'ō,* also *la-sōō', n.* a long rope with a running noose for catching wild horses, &c.:—*pl.* **lasso(e)s.**—*v.t.* to catch with the lasso:—*pr.p.* lass'ōing (or -ōō'-); *pa.p.* lass'oed (*las'ōd* or -ōō̄d'). [S. Amer. pronunciation of Sp. *lazo*—L. *laqueus,* a noose.]

last, *läst, n.* a shoemaker's model of the foot on which boots and shoes are made or repaired. [O.E. *läst,* footprint.]

last, *läst, v.i.* to continue, endure.—*adj.* **last'ing,** enduring: durable.—*adv.* **last'ingly.**—*n.* **last'-ingness.** [O.E. *læstan,* to follow a track, keep on. See foregoing word.]

last, *läst, n.* a load, cargo: a weight generally estimated at 4000 lb., but varying in different articles. [O.E. *hlæst—hladan,* to lade; Ger. *last,* O.N. *hlass.*]

last, *läst, adj.* latest: coming or remaining after all the others: final: next before the present: utmost (importance): lowest in rank or merit.—*advs.* **last, last'ly.**—**be the last person to do a thing,** to be the least likely, suitable, willing, &c., to do it; **breathe one's last,** to die; **die in the last ditch,** to fight to the bitter end; **on one's last legs,** on the verge of utter failure or exhaustion; **the last day,** the Day of Judgment; **the last post,** (*mil.*) the second of two bugle-calls denoting the hour of retiring for the night: a farewell bugle-call at military funerals; **the last straw,** that beyond which there can be no endurance. [O.E. *latost,* superl. of *læt,* slow, late.]

latakia, *lat-a-kē'a, n.* a fine kind of tobacco produced at *Latakia* in Syria.

latch, *lach, n.* a small catch of wood or iron to fasten a door.—*v.t.* to fasten with a latch.—*n.* **latch'key,** a key to raise or withdraw the latch of a door: (loosely) a small front-door key.— **latch-key child,** one who regularly returns home to an empty house; **latch on to** (*coll.*), to attach oneself to: gain comprehension of.—**on the latch,** not locked, but to be opened by a latch. [O.E. *læccan,* to catch.]

latchet, *lach'et, n.* a thong or lace, as for a shoe. [O.Fr. *lachet,* dim. of *laz, las.* See **lace.**]

late, *lāt, adj.* (*comp.* **lat'er;** *superl.* **lat'est**) slow, tardy: behindhand: coming after the expected time: long delayed: far advanced towards the close: last in any place or character: deceased: departed: out of office: not long past.—*advs.* **late; late'ly,** recently.—*n.* **late'ness.**—*adj.* **lat'ish,** somewhat late. [O.E. *læt,* slow; Du. *laat,* O.N. *latr,* Ger. *lass,* weary; L. *lassus,* tired.]

lateen, *la-tēn', adj.* applied to a triangular sail, common in the Mediterranean, &c. [Fr. (*voile*) *latine*—L. *Latīnus,* Latin.]

latent, *lā'tént, adj.* hidden: not visible or apparent: dormant: undeveloped, but capable of development.—*n.* **lā'tency.**—*adv.* **lā'tently.**— **latent heat** (see **heat**). [L. *latens, -entis,* pr.p. of *latēre,* to lie hid, Gr. *lanthanein,* to be unseen.]

lateral, *lat'ér-àl, adj.* belonging to the side.—*adv.* **lat'erally.**—*n.* **lateral'ity,** state of belonging to the side: physical one-sidedness, either right or left. [L. *laterālis—latus, latĕris,* a side.]

latex, *lā'teks, n.* the milky juice of plants. [L.]

lath, *läth, n.* a thin slip of wood used in slating, plastering, &c.:—*pl.* **laths** (*lä'ϝɦz*).—*v.t.* to cover with laths. [O.E. *lætt.*]

lathe, *lā'ϝɦ, n.* a machine for turning and shaping articles of wood, metal, &c.

lather, *lä'ϝɦér, n.* a foam made with water and soap: froth from sweat: (*coll.*) state of agitation.—*v.t.* to spread over with lather.—*v.i.* to form a lather, to become frothy. [O.E. *lēathor*; O.N. *lauthr.*]

Latin, *lat'in, adj.* pertaining to ancient Latium (esp. Rome) or its inhabitants, or its language, or to languages descended from Latin or to the peoples speaking them: written or spoken in Latin.—*n.* an inhabitant of ancient Latium: the language of ancient Latium: a speaker of a language derived from Latin.—*v.t.* **lat'inīse,** to give Latin forms to: to render into Latin.— *ns.* **Lat'inism,** a Latin idiom; **Lat'inist,** one skilled in Latin; **Latin'ity,** the quality of one's Latin.—**Latin Church,** the church that uses Latin and recognises the primacy of Rome— the Roman Catholic Church.—**Classical Latin,** the Latin of the writers who flourished from about 75 B.C. to A.D. 200; **Late Latin,** the Latin written by authors between A.D. 200 and (*circa*) 600; **Mediaeval Latin,** the Latin of the Middle Ages, between A.D. 600 and A.D. 1500, containing many words not of Latin origin—also called **Low Latin.** [L. *Latīnus,* belonging to *Latium,* the district round Rome.]

Latin-American, *lat'in-am-er'i-kàn, adj.* belonging to Latin America, i.e. to those countries of Central and South America where a language derived from Latin (Spanish, Portuguese, French) is the official language.

latitude, *lat'i-tūd, n.* breadth in interpretation: freedom from restraint: (*geog.*) angular distance from the equator: (*astron.*) angular distance from the ecliptic (*celestial latitude*): (*pl.*) regions (with reference to climate).— *adjs.* **latitūd'inal,** pertaining to latitude: in the direction of latitude; **latitūdinā'rian,** broad or liberal, esp. in religious belief: lax.—*n.* one who regards specific creeds, methods of church government, &c., with indifference.— *n.* **latitūdinā'rianism.**—*adj.* **latitūd'inous,** broad, wide, esp. in interpretation. [Fr.,—L. *lātitūdō, -inis—lātus,* broad.]

latrine, *la-trēn', n.* a privy, esp. in barracks, factories, hospitals, &c. [L. *lātrīna—lavā-trīnā—lavāre,* to wash.]

latter, *lat'ér, adj.* coming or existing after: second-mentioned of two: belonging to the end of a period of time: modern: recent.—*adv.* **latt'erly,** of late.—**Latter-day Saint,** a Mormon. [O.E. *lætra,* comp. of *læt,* slow, late.]

lattice, *lat'is, n.* a network of crossed laths or bars, called also **latt'ice-work:** anything of lattice-work, as a window: the geometrically

Neutral vowels in unaccented syllables: *em'pér-òr*; for certain sounds in foreign words see p. ix.

regular three-dimensional arrangement of fissionable and non-fissionable material in an atomic pile: the regular arrangement of atoms in crystalline material.—*v.t.* to form into open work: to furnish with a lattice. [Fr. *lattis—latte*, a lath.]

laud, *löd*, *v.t.* to praise: to celebrate.—*adj.* **laud′able**, praiseworthy.—*n.* **laud′ableness.**—*adv.* **laud′ably.**—*adj.* **laud′atory**, containing praise: expressing praise. [L. *laudāre—laus*, *laudis*, praise.]

laudanum, *löd′(a)-num*, *n.* tincture of opium. [Coined by Paracelsus (1493-1541) for a different drug; later transferred to opium preparations.]

laugh, *läf*, *v.i.* to emit explosive inarticulate sounds of the voice under the influence of amusement, joy, scorn, or other emotion.—*v.t.* to render, put, or drive with laughter.—*n.* an act of laughing: a sound of laughing.—*adj.* **laugh′able**, ludicrous.—*n.* **laugh′ableness.**—*adv.* **laugh′ably.**—*n.s.* **laugh′ing-gas**, nitrous oxide, which may excite laughter when breathed; **laugh′ing-jack′ass** (see **jack′ass**). —*adv.* **laugh′ingly**, with a laugh: jestingly.—*ns.* **laugh′ing-stock**, an object of ridicule; **laugh′ter**, the act or sound of laughing.—**laugh at**, to ridicule; **laugh in, up, one's sleeve** (see **sleeve**). [O.E. (Anglian) *hlæhhan* (W.S. *hliehhan*); Ger. *lachen.*]

launch, **lanch**, *lönch*, *länch*, or *-sh*, *v.t.* to throw or hurl: to send forth: to start on a course (person, enterprise): to cause to slide into the water or to take off from land.—*v.i.* to throw oneself freely or venturesomely into some activity.—*n.* the act or occasion of launching.—**launch′ing-pad**, a platform from which a rocket can be launched. [O.Fr. *lanchier*, *lancier* (Fr. *lancer*)—*lance*. See **lance**.]

launch, *lönch*, *länch*, *-sh*, *n.* the largest boat carried by a man-of-war: a large power driven boat for pleasure or short runs. [Sp. *lancha*, perh. from Malay *lanchār*, swift.]

launder, *lön′dér*, *län′-*, *n.* a trough for conveying water.—*v.t.* and *v.i.* to wash and iron, as clothes.—*ns.* **laun′dress**, a woman who washes and irons clothes; **laun′dry**, a place where clothes are washed: clothes sent to be washed. [M.E. *lavander*—O.Fr. *lavandier*—L. *lavandāria*, neut. pl. from gerundive of *lavāre*, to wash.]

launderette, *lön-dér-et′*, *n.* a shop where customers wash clothes in washing machines. [Orig. trademark.]

laureate, *lö′ri-āt*, *adj.* consisting of laurel: crowned with laurel (as a mark of honour).—*n.* one crowned with laurel: a poet-laureate.—Also *v.t.*—*n.* **lau′reateship**, office of a laureate.—*n.* **po′et-lau′reate**, an official poet attached to the royal household, who writes odes, &c., for court and national occasions. [L. *laureātus*, laurelled—*laurus*, laurel.]

laurel, *lö′rél*, *n.* the bay-tree (*laurus nobilis*), used by the ancients for making honorary wreaths: any other tree of the same genus: honours gained (usu. in *pl.*).—*adj.* **lau′relled**, crowned with laurel. [Fr. *laurier*—L. *laurus.*]

lava, *lä′va*, *n.* matter discharged in a molten stream from a volcano or fissure. [It.,—L. *lavāre*, to wash.]

lave, *lāv*, *v.t.* and *v.i.* to wash: to bathe.—*ns.* **lav′atory**, a place for washing: popularly, a water-closet; **lā′ver**, a large vessel for washing, esp. ritual washing. [L. *lavāre*, *-ātum*; Gr. *louein*, to wash.]

lavender, *lav′én-dér*, *n.* a labiate plant, with fragrant pale-lilac flowers, yielding a volatile oil.—*n.* **lav′ender-wa′ter**, a perfume composed of spirits of wine, essential oil of lavender, and ambergris. [Anglo-Fr. *lavendre* (Fr. *lavande*), perh. conn. with *līvidus*, livid.]

laverock, *lav′ér-ók*, (*Scot.*) *lāv′-*, *n.* an archaic and dialectal form of **lark.**

lavish, *lav′ish*, *v.t.* to expend profusely: to waste.—*adj.* bestowing profusely, prodigal: extravagant, unrestrained.—*adv.* **lav′ishly.**—*ns.* **lav′ishment**, **lav′ishness.** [Perh. O.Fr. *lavasse*, *lavache*, deluge of rain—*laver*—L. *lavāre*, to wash.]

law, *lö*, *n.* a rule of action established by authority: a statute: the rules of a community or state: the science of law: the legal profession: established usage: a rule or code in any department of action: (*cap.*) the Mosaic code or the books containing it: observed regularity: a statement or formula expressing the order or relation constantly observed in the case of certain phenomena (as, *the law of gravity*, *laws of thermodynamics*, *Grimm's law*).—*adj.* **law′-abid′ing**, obedient to the law.—*n.* **law′break′er**, one who violates a law —*adj.* **law′ful**, allowed by law: rightful.—*adv.* **law′fully.**—*ns.* **law′fulness; law′giver**, one who enacts laws: a legislator —*adj.* **law′less.**—*adv.* **law′lessly.**—*ns.* **law′lessness; law′-lord**, a peer in parliament who holds or has held high legal office: in Scotland, a judge of the Court of Session; **law′mong′er**, a low pettifogging lawyer; **law′suit**, a suit or process in law; **law′yer**, a practitioner in the law, esp. a solicitor: (*N.T.*) an interpreter of the Mosaic Law.—**case law**, law established by judicial decision in particular cases, in contradistinction to *statute law*; **common law**, the unwritten law (esp. of England) which receives its binding force, not from statutes, but from ancient usage; **international law**, the body of rules accepted by civilised nations as governing their conduct towards each other; **martial law, salic law** (see **martial, salic**); **statute law**, law depending on statutes expressly enacted by the legislature, e.g. on Acts of Parliament (as opposed to *common law*).—**lay down the law**, to speak authoritatively or dictatorially. [M.E. *lawe*—late O.E., of O.N. origin, from the same root as **lie, lay.**]

lawn, *lön*, *n.* a sort of fine linen or cambric.—*adj.* made of lawn. [Prob. from *Laon*, near Rheims.]

lawn, *lön*, *n.* (*arch.*) an open space between woods: a space of ground covered with grass, generally in front of or around a house or mansion.—*n.* **lawn tennis**, a ball and racket game, a variety of tennis played on an open lawn or other unenclosed space (see **tennis**). [Earlier *laund*—O.Fr. *launde*, *lande*; prob. Celt.]

lawrencium, *lö-ren′si-úm*, *n.* transuranic element (symbol Lr; at. no. 103), named after the scientist, Ernest O. *Lawrence.*

lax, *laks*, *adj.* slack, loose: flabby: not strict in

discipline or morals: loose in the bowels.—*adj.*
lax′ative, having the power of loosening the
bowels.—*n.* a purgative or aperient medicine.—*ns.* **lax′ity, lax′ness,** state or quality of
being lax.—*adv.* **lax′ly.** [L. *laxus,* loose.]
lay, *lā, pa.t.* of **lie** (2).
lay, *lā, v.t.* to cause to lie: to place or set down:
to beat down: (*lit.* and *fig.*) to exorcise (a
ghost), cause it to cease haunting a place or
person: to spread on a surface: to cause to
subside: to wager: to put forward (e.g. a
claim): to impose (e.g. a tax, a command): to
attribute (e.g. blame).—*v.i.* to produce eggs: to
wager, bet:—*pr.p.* lay′ing; *pa.t.* and *pa.p.*
laid.—*ns.* **lay′about,** a lounger, a loafer;
lay′-by, an expansion of a roadway to allow
vehicles to draw up out of the stream of
traffic; **lay′er,** one who or that which lays—e.g.
a hen, a bricklayer: a course, bed, or stratum:
a shoot bent down to earth in order to take
root: **lay′ering,** the propagation of plants by
layers; **lay′out,** that which is laid out: display:
arrangement, plan, esp. of buildings or
ground.—**lay about one,** to deal blows vigorously and on all sides; **lay a plot, scheme,**
plan(s), to plot, scheme, to arrange the details
of a plot, scheme, or plan (often in passive);
lay in, to get in a supply of; **lay off,** to take off:
to harangue: to discontinue work or activity:
to dismiss (employees) temporarily: (*coll.*) to
cease to; **lay on,** to install a supply of: to deal
blows vigorously; **lay oneself out to,** to put
forth one's best efforts in order to; **lay out,** to
display: to expend: to dress in graveclothes: to
fell; **lay to,** to apply with vigour: to bring a
ship to rest; **lay up,** to put away, to store, for
future use: to prepare future (trouble) for
oneself: to cease for a time to use, run (a boat,
a car): (see also **laid**); **lay wait,** to lie in wait
(for); **lay waste,** to devastate, to destroy. [O.E.
lecgan, to lay, causative of *licgan,* to lie; cf.
O.N. *leggja,* Ger. *legen.*]
lay, *lā, n.* a short narrative poem: a lyric: a song.
[O.Fr. *lai;* origin obscure.]
lay, *lā,* **laic, -al,** *lā′ik, -ǎl, adjs.* pertaining to the
people: not clerical: non-professional.—*ns.*
lā′ity, the people as distinct from the clergy;
lay′-broth′er, -sister, one under vows of celibacy and obedience, who serves a religious
house, but is exempt from the studies and
religious services required of the monks or
nuns; **lay′man,** one of the laity: a non-professional man; **lay′-read′er,** in the Anglican
Church, a layman authorised to read part of
the service. [O.Fr. *lai*—L. *lāicus*—Gr. *lāikos*—
lāos, the people.]
layette, *lā-yet′, n.* a complete outfit for a new-
born child. [Fr.]
lay-figure, *lā′-fig′ūr, n.* a jointed figure used by
painters in imitation of the human body, as a
support for drapery: a living person, or a
fictitious character, lacking in individuality.
[Earlier *lay-man*—Du. *leemǎn*—*led* (now *lid*),
joint, *man,* man.]
lazar, *laz′ǎr, n.* one afflicted with a loathsome
and pestilential disease like *Lazarus,* the beggar (Luke xvi. 20).—*n.* **la′zar-house,** a lazaretto.—*adj.* **la′zar-like,** full of sores: leprous.
lazaretto, *laz-a-ret′ō, n.* a hospital for infectious
diseases, esp. leprosy.—Also **laz′aret.** [It.
lazzeretto.]
lazy, *lā′zi, adj.* disinclined to exertion, averse to
labour: sluggish: arising from, or inducing,
disinclination to exertion.—*adv.* **lā′zily.**—*n.*
lā′ziness. [Origin unknown.]
lea, *lē, n.* open country—meadow, pasture or
arable.—Also **lay** (*lā*). [O.E. *lēah.*]
leach, *lēch, v.t.* to moisten: to percolate (a
liquid) through something, e.g. ashes: to extract (a soluble metallic compound) from an
ore by treating the ore with a solvent and
later precipitating the compound from the
solution—to lixiviate. [O.E.*leccan,* to moisten.]
lead, *lēd, v.t.* to show the way by going first: to
precede: to guide by the hand: to direct by
example (e.g. an orchestra): to convey (e.g.
water): to guide by persuasion or argument:
to live (life, existence).—*v.i.* to be first or
among the first: to be guide: to afford a
passage (to):—*pa.t.* and *pa.p.* led.—*n.* first
place: precedence: direction: guidance: a leash
for a dog, &c.: a first card played: a chief part
in a play (e.g.*juvenile lead*): a main conductor
in electrical distribution.—*ns.* **lead′er,** one
who leads or goes first: a chief: the leading
editorial article in a newspaper (also **leading**
article): principal wheel in any machinery;
lead′ership, office of leader or conductor: the
quality of a leader, ability to lead; **lead′-in′,**
the part of the groove on a disk before the
start of the recording (opp. to *lead-out*): the
cable connecting the transmitter or receiver
to the elevated part of an aerial; **leading edge,**
(*aero.*) the edge of a streamlined body or
aerofoil which is forward in normal motion
(cf. **trailing edge**); **leading question,** a
question so put as to suggest the desired
answer.—*n.pl.* **lead′ing-strings,** strings used to
lead children beginning to walk.—**lead by the**
nose, to make (one) follow submissively; **lead**
on, to persuade to go on: to persuade to a
foolish course: to hoax; **lead up to,** to bring
about by degrees, to prepare for by steps or
stages. [O.E. *lædan,* to lead, *lād,* a way; Ger.
leiten, to lead.]
lead, *led, n.* a soft bluish-grey metal (sym. Pb [L.
plumbum]; at. no. 82): a plummet for sounding:
thin lead plate separating lines of type: (*pl.*)
a flat roof covered with sheets of lead.—*v.t.*
to cover or fit with lead: (*print.*) to separate
the lines of (type) with leads.—*adj.* **lead′en,**
made of lead: heavy: dull.—*ns.* **lead′-line,** a
sounding-line; **lead′-pen′cil,** a blacklead (i.e.
graphite—q.v.) pencil for writing or drawing;
lead′-poi′soning, poisoning by the absorption
of lead into the system. [O.E. *lēad;* Ger. *lot.*]
leaf, *lēf, n.* one of the lateral organs developed
from the stem or axis of the plant below its
growing-point: anything beaten thin like a
leaf: two pages of a book on front and back of
the same paper: a part or division, as of
folding doors, table-tops, &c.:—*pl.* **leaves**
(*lēvz*).—*v.t.* to turn the pages (of a book,
&c.).—*v.i.* to produce leaves:—*pr.p.* leaf′ing;
pa.p. leafed.—*n.* **leaf′age,** foliage.—*adj.* **leaf′-**
less, destitute of leaves.—*ns.* **leaf′let,** a little
leaf: a tract or other short printed exhortation,
instruction, or appeal; **leaf′-mould,** earth
which is formed from decayed leaves, used as
a soil for plants.—*adj.* **leaf′y.**—*n.* **leaf′iness.**

Neutral vowels in unaccented syllables: *em′pér-ŏr*; for certain sounds in foreign words see p. ix.

[O.E. *lēaf*; Ger. *laub*, Du. *loof*, a leaf.]

league, *lēg, n.* a nautical measure, 1/20th of a degree, 3 international nautical miles, 3·456 statute miles: an old measure of length, varying in different countries, but usu. about 3 miles. [L.L. *leuga, leuca,* a Gallic mile of 1500 Roman paces.]

league, *lēg, n.* a bond or alliance: union for mutual advantage: an association (*oi* clubs for games, &c.): a class or group.—*v.t.* and *v.i.* to join in league.—*pr.p.* leag'uing; *pa.t.* and *pa.p.* leagued. [Fr. *ligue*—Low L. *liga*—L. *ligāre,* to bind.]

leaguer, *lēg'ér, n.* (*hist.*) a camp, esp. of a besieging army: siege. [Du. *leger,* a lair, bed, camp.]

leak, *lēk, n.* a crack or hole in a vessel through which liquid may pass: passage through such an opening.—*v.i.* to have a leak: to pass through a leak.—*n.* **leak'age,** a leaking: that which enters or escapes by leaking: an allowance for leaking —*adj.* **leak'y.** *n.* **leak'i ness,—leak out** to come to be known in spite of efforts at concealment; **spring a leak,** to become leaky. [O.E. *hlec,* leaky; or perh. reintroduced from Du. or Low Ger. *lek,* leak; or O.N. *leka,* to leak.]

leal, *lēl, adj.* true-hearted, faithful.—**Land o' the Leal,** the home of the blessed after death—heaven. [O.Fr. *leel, leiel;* doublet of **loyal.**]

lean, *lēn, v.i.* to incline: to be or become inclined to the vertical: to rest (against): to bend (over): to rely (on).—*v.t.* to cause to lean: to support, rest:—*pa.t.* and *pa.p.* leaned or leant (*lent*).—*ns.* **lean'ing,** inclination; **lean'-to,** a shed or penthouse whose supports lean upon another building or wall. [O.E. *hleonian, hlinian,* and causative *hlǣne*; Du. *leunen.*]

lean, *lēn, adj.* thin, wanting flesh: not fat: lacking richness, deficient in quality or contents (*e.g.* harvest, discourse, purse).—*n.* flesh without fat.—*adv.* **lean'ly.**—*n.* **lean'ness.** [O.E. *hlǣne;* Low Ger. *leen.*]

leap, *lēp. v.i.* to jump: to rush with vehemence.—*v.t.* to bound over:—*pr.p.* leap'ing; *pa.t.* and *pa.p.* leaped or leapt (*lept*).—*n.* act of leaping: bound: space passed by leaping: an abrupt transition.—*ns.* **leap'-frog,** a sport in which one places his hands on the back of another stooping in front of him, and vaults over his head; **leap'-year,** every fourth year (excluding centesimal years not exactly divisible by 400, e.g. excluding 1900), consisting of 366 days, adding one day in February. —**leap in the dark,** an act of which we cannot foresee the consequences. [O.E. *hlēapan;* Ger. *laufen,* to run.]

learn, *lûrn, v.t.* to be informed, to get to know: to gain knowledge, skill, or ability in: to commit to memory.—*v.i.* to gain knowledge: to improve by example:—*pa.t.* and *pa.p.* learned (*lérnd*) or learnt.—*adj.* **learned** (*lérn'id*), having learning: versed in literature, &c.: used by learned men, not in ordinary popular use.—*adv.* **learn'edly.**—*ns.* **learn'edness; learn'er,** one who learns: one who is yet in the rudiments of any subject; **learn'ing,** knowledge: scholarship: skill in languages or science. [O.E. *leornian;* Ger. *lernen;* cf. *lǣran* (Ger. *lehren*), to teach.]

lease, *lēs, n.* a contract letting a house, farm, &c., for a term: the period of time for which the contract is made.—*v.t.* to grant or take under lease:—*pr.p.* leas'ing; *pa.t.* and *pa.p.* leased.—*adj.* **lease'hold,** held by lease or contract.—*n.* a tenure by lease or the land so held. [Fr. *laisser,* to leave—L. *laxāre,* to loose, *laxus,* loose.]

leash, *lēsh, n.* a lash or line by which a hawk or hound is held: a set of three, esp. animals.— *v.t.* to hold by a leash: to bind. [O.Fr. *lesse* (Fr. *laisse*), a thong to hold a dog by—L. *laxus,* loose.]

leasing, *lēz'ing, n.* falsehood, lies: lying. [O.E. *lēasung—lēasian,* to lie—*lēas,* false, loose.]

least, *lēst, adj.* (serves as *superl.* of **little**) little beyond all others: smallest.—*adv.* in the smallest or lowest degree. [O.E. *lǣst* (adj. and adv.); comp. *lǣssa* (adj.), *lǣs* (adv.); no positive.]

leat, **leet**, *lēt, n.* (*dial.*) a trench for bringing water to a mill-wheel, &c. [O.E. *gelǣt.*]

leather, *le'thér, n.* the prepared skin of an animal.—*adj.* consisting of leather.—*v.t.* to thrash.—*n.* **leath'er-jack'et,** one of various fishes: a grub of any of several crane-flies.— *adjs.* **leath'ern,** consisting of leather; **leath'ery,** resembling leather: tough.—*n.* **leath'eriness.**—**patent leather,** leather with a finely varnished surface. [O.E. *lether,* leather; Du. and Ger. *leder.*]

leave, *lēv, n.* permission: permission to be absent: period covered by this: formal parting: farewell.—**take leave of,** to bid farewell to. [O.E. *lēaf,* permission, cog. with *lēof,* dear. See **lief.**]

leave, *lēv, v.t.* to allow to remain: to abandon: to depart from: to have remaining at death, to bequeath: to refer for decision (to): to allow (a person to do) without supervision —*v.i.* to depart:—*pr.p.* leav'ing; *pa.t.* and *pa.p.* left,—*n.pl.* **leav'ings,** things left: relics. refuse.—**leave alone,** not to interfere with; **leave in the dark,** to withhold information from. [O.E. *lǣfan.*]

leaved, *lēvd, adj.* furnished with leaves: made with folds. [**leaf.**]

leaven, *lev'n, n.* the ferment which makes dough rise in a spongy form: anything that makes a general change, whether good or bad.—*v.t.* to raise with leaven: to permeate with an influence. [Fr. *levain*—L. *levāmen*—*levāre,* to raise—*levis,* light.]

leaves, *lēvz, pl.* of **leaf.**

lebensraum, *lā'béns-rowm, n.* space inhabited by living things: room to live (and, if necessary, expand). [Ger.]

lecher, *lech'ér, n.* a man addicted to lewdness.— *adj.* **lech'erous,** lustful: provoking lust.—*adv.* **lech'erously.**—*ns.* **lech'erousness, lech'ery** [O.Fr. *lecheor—lechier,* to lick; O.H.G. *leccôn,* Ger. *lecken,* Eng. **lick.**]

lectern, *lek'térn, n.* a church reading-desk from which the lessons are read. [Low L. *lectrīnum—lectrum,* a pulpit—Gr. *lektron,* a couch.]

lection, *lek'sh(ó)n, n.* a reading: a lesson read in church.—*n.* **lec'tionary,** a book of church lessons for each day. [L. *lectiō, -ōnis—legĕre,* *lectum,* to read.]

lector, *lek'tôr, -tór, n.* a reader, esp. in a college:

---

fāte, fär; mē, hûr (her); *mīne; mōte, för; mūte; mōōn, fŏŏt;* THen (then)

an ecclesiastic in one of the minor orders. [L. *lector, -ōris—legĕre, lectum,* to read.]

lecture, *lek'tyur, -chur, n.* a discourse on any subject, to a class or other audience, esp. with the aim of instructing: a formal reproof.—*v.t.* to instruct by discourses: to reprove.—*v.i.* to give a lecture or lectures.—*ns.* **lec'turer,** one who lectures: a college or university instructor of lower rank than a professor: one of a class of preachers in the Church of England, supported by voluntary contributions; **lec'tureship,** the office of a lecturer. [L. *lectūra—legĕre, lectum,* to read.]

led, *led, pa.t.* and *pa.p.* of **lead,** to show the way.

ledge, *lej, n.* a shelf or shelf-like projection: a ridge or shelf of rocks: a lode. [M.E. *legge,* prob. from the root of **lay** (2).]

ledger, *lej'ér, n.* the principal book of accounts among merchants, in which entries from all the other books are recorded.—*n.* **ledger-line,** *(angling)* a line fixed in one place: *(mus.)* a short line added above or below the stave when required (often **leger-line**). [App. from O.E. *licgan,* to lie, *lecgan,* to lay.]

lee, *lē, n.* the sheltered side: the quarter toward which the wind blows.—*adj.* (opp. to *windward* or *weather*) sheltered: on or toward the sheltered side.—*ns.* **lee'-shore,** a shore on or facing the lee-side of a ship; **lee'-side,** the sheltered side.—*adj.* **lee'ward** *(naut. lū'árd, lōō'árd),* pertaining to, or in, the direction toward which the wind blows.—*adv.* toward the lee.—*n.* **lee'way,** the distance a ship, aircraft, &c., is driven to leeward of her true course.—**make up leeway,** to make up for lost time, ground, &c. [O.E. *hlēo(w),* gen. *hlēowes,* shelter; O.N. *hlē,* Low Ger. *lee.*]

leech, *lēch, n.* any of a class of blood-sucking worms: *(fig.)* a human being who ruthlessly sucks profit out of another or others: a physician.—*v.t.* to apply leeches to. [O.E. *læce,* perh. orig. two different words.]

leek, *lēk, n.* a vegetable of the same genus as the onion—national emblem of Wales.—**eat the leek,** to be compelled to take back one's words or put up with insulting treatment—*Henry V,* v. 1. [O.E. *lēac,* a leek plant.]

leer, *lēr, n.* a sly, sidelong, or lecherous look.—*v.i.* to look slyly, obliquely, or lecherously.—*adv.* **leer'ingly.**—*adj.* **leer'y,** cunning: wary (with *of*). [O.E. *hlēor,* face, cheek.]

lees, *lēz, n.pl.* sediment or dregs of liquor. [Fr. *lie*—Low L. *lia.*]

leet, *lēt, n.* (Scot.) a selected list of candidates for an office. [Perh. **élite;** but cf. O.E. *hlēt,* lot.]

left, *left, pa.t.* and *pa.p.* of **leave.**—*adj.* **left'-off,** laid aside, discarded.

left, *left, adj.* on, for, or belonging to the side which has normally the weaker or less skilful hand (opp. to *right*): *(cap.)* belonging to the political Left.—*n.* the left side: the left hand: *(with cap.)* those members of certain of the legislative assemblies in Europe who have seats to the left of the presiding officer—traditionally the most progressive party: advanced or innovating section of philosophical school, &c.—*adjs.* **left-hand; left'-hand'ed,** having the left hand stronger and readier than the right: awkward: unlucky: ambiguous (compliment): morganatic.—**left-hand drive,**

a driving mechanism on the left side of a vehicle which is intended to be driven on the right-hand side of the road. [M.E. *lift, left*—O.E. *left* for *lyft,* weak.]

leg, *leg, n.* a walking limb: the human hindlimb: a long, slender support of anything, as of a table: a distinct part or stage of any course or journey: one event or part won in a contest consisting of two or more parts or events: *(cricket)* the quarter of the field behind and to the right of the batsman when he is in position.—*adj.* **legged,** having legs.—*n.* **legg'ing,** an outer gaiter-like covering for the lower leg.—*adjs.* **legg'y,** having disproportionately long and lank legs; **leg'less,** without legs.—**leg before wicket** (abbrev. l.b.w.), having the leg in front of the wicket so that a ball hits the leg and is thereby prevented from striking the wicket.—**a leg up,** assistance. [O.N. *leggr,* a leg; Dan. *læg,* Swed. *lägg.*]

legacy, *leg'a-si, n.* that which is left to one by will: anything material or immaterial handed down by a predecessor.—*ns.* **leg'acy-hunt'er,** one who hunts after legacies by courting those likely to leave them; **legatee',** one to whom a legacy is bequeathed. [L. *lēgāre, -ātum,* to leave by will.]

legal, *lē'gál, adj.* pertaining to, or according to, law: lawful.—*v.t.* **lē'galise,** to make legal or lawful.—*n.* **lēgal'ity.**—*adv.* **lē'gally.**—**legal aid,** aid granted to individuals by the State towards the payment of legal fees, &c., in certain cases; **legal tender,** money which a creditor cannot refuse in payment of debt. [L. *lēgālis—lex, lēgis,* law.]

legate, *leg'át, n.* an ambassador, esp. from the Pope.—*n.* **leg'ateship.**—*adj.* **leg'atine** (*-īn, -in*), of or relating to a legate.—*n.* **lega'tion,** the person or persons sent as legates or ambassadors: the official abode of a legation. [Through Fr. *légat,* It. *legato,* or directly, from L. *lēgātus—lēgāre,* to send with a commission.]

legato, *lā-gä'tō, adj.* and *adv. (mus.)* smooth, smoothly, the notes running into each other without a break. [It., bound, tied—L. *ligāre, -ātum,* to tie.]

legend, *lej'énd,* sometimes *lēj'-, n.* a traditional story: a myth: words accompanying an illustration or picture.—*n.* **leg'endary,** a book of legends: a writer of legends.—*adj.* pertaining to, or consisting of legend: fabulous. [Fr. *légende*—Low L. *legenda,* to be read, a book of chronicles of the saints read at matins—*legĕre,* to read.]

legerdemain, *lej-ér-dē-mān', n.* sleight-of-hand: jugglery. [Lit. light of hand—Fr. *léger,* light, *de,* of, *main,* hand.]

leger-line—better **ledger-line.** See **ledger.**

leghorn, *leg'hórn, leg-örn', n.* fine straw plait made in Tuscany: a hat made of it: a small breed of domestic fowl. [*Leghorn,* in Italy.]

legible, *lej'i-bl, adj.* clear enough to be read.—*ns.* **leg'ibleness, legibil'ity.**—*adv.* **leg'ibly.** [L. *legibilis—legĕre,* to read.]

legion, *lē'jón, n.* in ancient Rome, a body of soldiers of from three to six thousand: a military force: a great number: a national association of those who have served in war.—*adj.* **lē'gionary.**—*n.* a soldier of a legion.

Neutral vowels in unaccented syllables: *em'pér-ór*; for certain sounds in foreign words see p. ix.

[L. *legiō*, *-ōnis—legĕre*, to levy.]

legislate, *lej′is-lāt*, *v.i.* to make laws.—*n.* **legislā′tion.**—*adj.* **leg′islātive,** law-making: pertaining to legislation.—*ns.* **leg′islātor,** a lawgiver: a member of a legislative body; **leg′islāture,** the body of those in a state who have the power of making laws.—**Legislative Council,** the upper house of the General Assembly or parliament of New Zealand (abolished Jan. 1951). [L. *lex, lēgis,* law, *lātum,* serving as supine to *ferre,* to bear.]

legitimate, *le-jit′i-māt*, *adj.*·lawful: born in wedlock: fairly deduced (conclusion): conforming to accepted rules (e.g. argument): reasonable (result).—*v.t.* to make lawful: to give the rights of a legitimate child to.—*n.* **legit′imacy,** state of being legitimate: lawfulness of birth: regular deduction.—*adv.* **legit′imately.**—*ns.* **legitimā′tion,** act of rendering legitimate, esp. of conferring the privileges of lawful birth; **legit′imist,** one who believes in the right of royal succession according to the principle of heredity and primogeniture.—**legitimate drama,** (*orig.*) drama of permanent value: drama of typical form, distinguished from opera, play with music, &c. and from cinema and television. [Low L. *legitimāre, -ātum*—L. *legitimus,* lawful—*lex,* law.]

legume, *leg′ūm*, *n.* a pod splitting along both sutures (as in pea, bean, &c): a leguminous plant: such a plant used as food.—*adj.* **legū′minous,** pertaining to peas, beans, &c. bearing legumes. [Fr. *légume,* a vegetable—L. *legūmen,* pulse, prob.—*legĕre,* to gather.]

lei, *lā′ē*, *n.* a garland, wreath. [Hawaiian.]

leisure, *lezh′ŭr*, or (old-fashioned) *lēzh′ŭr, -ŭr, n.* time free from employment and at one's own disposal: freedom from occupation.—*adj.* free from necessary business.—*adj.* **lei′sured,** having leisure.—*adj.* and *adv.* **lei′surely,** not hasty or hastily. [O.Fr. *leisir*—L. *licēre,* to be permitted.]

leitmotiv, leitmotif, *līt′mō-tēf, n.* (*mus.*) a theme associated with a person or a thought, recurring when the person appears on the stage or the thought becomes prominent in the action: (*fig.*) a recurring theme. [Ger.,—*leiten,* to lead, and *motiv,* a motif.]

leman, *lem′an,* or *lēm′-, n.* a sweetheart: now chiefly *fem.* and in a bad sense. [O.E. *lēof,* lief, *mann,* man]

lemma, *lem′a, n.* (*math.*) a preliminary proposition used in the main argument or proof: argument or subject of literary composition, &c., prefixed as heading:—*pl.* **lemm′as, lemm′ata.** [Gr. *lēmma,* from the root of *lambanein,* to take.]

lemming, *lem′ing, n.* any of several small northern rodents, nearly allied to the voles. [Norw. *lemming.*]

lemon, *lem′on, n.* an oval fruit of the *Citrus* genus with an acid pulp: the tree that bears it: (*slang*) something disappointing, worthless, unattractive, unpleasant.—*ns.* **lemonade′,** a drink (still or aerated) made with lemon juice; **lemon sole,** a small species of sole. [Fr. *limon* (now the lime); cf. Pers. *līmūn;* cf. **lime** (2)]

lemur, *lē′mŭr, n.* a group of mammals (chiefly in Madagascar) akin to monkeys, mainly nocturnal:—*pl.* **lē′murs.** [L. *lĕmūrēs,* ghosts.]

lend, *lend, v.t.* to give the use of for a time: to afford, grant, or furnish, in general: to let for hire:—*pr.p.* lend′ing; *pa.t.* and *pa.p.* lent.—*n.* **lend′er.** [O.E. *lǣnan*—*lǣn, lān,* a loan.]

length, *length, n.* quality of being long: extent from end to end: the longest measure of anything: long continuance: prolixity (e.g. of discourse): a piece (e.g. of cloth).—*v.t.* and *v.i.* **length′en,** to increase in length.—*advs.* **length′ways, length′wise,** in the direction of the length.—*adj.* **length′y,** of great or tedious length.—*adv.* **length′ily.**—*n.* **length′lness.—at length,** in detail or without curtailment: at last; **go to all, any, lengths,** to do everything possible to achieve a purpose. [O.E. *lengthu—lang,* long.]

lenient, *lē′ni-ent, lē′nyent, adj.* softening: mild: merciful.—*n.* (*med.*) that which softens, an emollient.—*ns.* **lē′nience, lē′niency.**—*adv.* **lē′niently.**—*adj.* **lenitive** (*len′-*), soothing: mitigating: laxative.—*n.* (*med.*) an application for easing pain: a mild purgative.—*n.* **lenity** (*len′-*), mildness: clemency. [L. *lēniens, -entis,* pr.p. of *lēnīre,* to soften—*lēnis,* soft.]

lens, *lenz, n.* (*optics*) a piece of transparent substance with one or both sides convex or concave, the purpose of which is to make a beam of light more, or less, convergent: any device performing a similar function: the refracting structure (*crystalline lens*) between the crystalline and vitreous humours of the eye:—*pl.* **lens′es.** [So called from its lentil-like shape; L. *lens, lentis,* lentil.]

Lent, *lent, n.* an annual fast of forty days in commemoration of Christ's fast in the wilderness (Matt. iv. 2), from Ash-Wednesday to Easter.—*adj.* **lent′en,** relating to, or used in, Lent: sparing. [O.E. *lencten,* the spring; Du. *lente,* Ger. *lenz.*]

lenticular, *len-tik′ū-lar, adj.* shaped like a lens or lentil seed: double convex.—*adv.* **lentic′ularly.** [L. *lens, lentis,* a lentil.]

lentil, *len′til, n.* an annual plant, common near the Mediterranean: its seed used for food. [O.Fr. *lentille*—L. *lens, lentis,* the lentil.]

lentisk, *len′tisk, n.* the mastic-tree. [L. *lentiscus.*]

lento, *len′tō, adj.* (*mus.*) slow. *adv.* slowly.—*n.* a slow passage or movement. [It.,—L. *lentus.*]

Leo, *lē′ō, n.* the Lion, a constellation: the fifth sign of the zodiac.—*adj.* **lē′onine,** lion-like: of a kind of Latin verse, generally alternate hexameter and pentameter, rhyming at the middle and end. [L. *leō, -ōnis,* lion.]

leopard, *lep′ärd, n.* a large spotted animal of the cat genus. [O.Fr.,—L. *leopardus*—Gr. *leopardos* (for *leontopardos*)—*leōn,* lion, *pardos,* pard.]

leotard, *lē′ō-tärd, n.* a skin-tight garment (sleeveless or long-sleeved), legs varying from none at all to ankle-length, worn by dancers and acrobats. [Julius *Leotard,* 19th-cent. Fr. trapeze artist.]

leper, *le′pér, n.* one affected with leprosy: (*fig.*) an outcast. [O.Fr. *lepre*—L. and Gr. *lepra*—Gr. *lepros,* scaly—*lepos* or *lepis,* a scale.]

Lepidoptera, *lep-i-dop′tér-a, n.pl.* an order of insects with four wings covered with fine scales—butterflies and moths.—*adjs.* **lepidop′teral, lepidop′terous.** [Gr. *lepis, -idos,* a scale, *pteron,* a wing.]

fāte, fär; mē, hûr (her); *mīne; mōte, för; mūte; mōōn, fōōt;* тнen (then)

leprechaun, *lep-ré-ı ı ön´, n.* a small-sized Irish brownie. [Perh. Old Irish *luchorpan—lu,* small, *corp(an),* a body.]

leprosy, *lep´ro-si, n.* a name formerly applied to several contagious skin diseases: now to one caused by a bacillus.—*adj.* **lep´rous,** affected with leprosy. [Through O.Fr.—L.L. *leprōsus—lepra.* See **leper.**]

lepton, *lep´ton, n.* any of a group of subatomic particles with weak interactions, electrons, negative muons and neutrinos. [Gr. *leptos,* small, light.]

Lesbian, *lez´bi-ăn, adj.* of the island of Lesbos: (of women) homosexual.—*n.* a woman homosexual.—*n.* **Les´bianism.**

lese-majestie, leze-majesty, *lēz´-maj´es-ti, n.* an offence against the sovereign power in a state, treason. [Fr. *lèse majesté—*L. *laesa mājestās,* injured majesty—*laedĕre,* to hurt.]

lesion, *lē´zh(ò)n, n.* an injury: *(med.)* any wound or morbid change anywhere in the body. [Fr. *lésion—*L. *laesiō, -ōnis—laedĕre, laesum,* to hurt.]

less, *les, adj.* (used as *comp.* of **little**) diminished: smaller.—*adv.* not so much: in a lower degree.—*n.* a smaller portion: the inferior or younger. [O.E.*lǣssa,* less, *lǣs* (adv.); not conn. with **little.**]

-less, *-les, adj. suffx.* free from, wanting, as guilt*less,* god*less.* [O.E. *-lēas,* Ger. *-los,* Goth. *-laus.*]

lessee, *les-ē´, n.* one to whom a lease is granted. [O.Fr. *lessé;* root of **lease.**]

lessen, *les´n, v.t.* to make less, in any sense.—*v.i.* to become less. [**less.**]

lesser, *les´ér, adj.* less: smaller: inferior. [Double comp. formed from **less.**]

lesson, *les´(ò)n, n.* a portion of Scripture appointed to be read in divine service: that which a pupil learns at a time: a precept or doctrine inculcated: instruction derived from experience. [Fr. *leçon—*L. *lectiō, -ōnis—legĕre,* to read.]

lessor, *les´ór, n.* one who grants a lease. [Anglo-Fr.; root of **lease.**]

lest, *lest, conj.* that not: for fear that. [From O.E. *thў lǣs the,* for the reason less that, which became in M.E. *les te.*]

let, *let, v.t.* to allow, permit, suffer: to grant to a tenant or hirer: to cause (with infinitive without *to—arch.* except in *let know,* e.g. *he will let you know*): in the imper. with acc. and infin. without *to,* often used virtually as an auxiliary with imperative or optative effect (e.g. *let the people sing, let us pray*):—*pr.p.* let´ting; *pa.t.* and *pa.p.* let.—**let alone,** to refrain from interfering with: to leave out, not to mention; **let blood,** to open a vein; **let down,** to lower: to disappoint the expectations of, desert; **let go,** to cease holding; **let in,** to allow to enter, admit (*lit.* and *fig.*); **let in for,** to involve in; **let into,** to admit to the knowledge of; **let off,** to discharge, as a gun: to excuse; **let on,** to pretend; **let out,** to release: to hire: to divulge.—**to let,** for letting, to be let (e.g. *house to let*). [O.E. *lǣtan,* to permit, pa.t. *lēt,* pa.p. *lǣten;* Ger. *lassen.*]

let, *let, v.t.* (*arch.*) to prevent.—*n.* hindrance, obstruction (as in tennis): delay. [O.E. *lettan,* to hinder—*lǣt,* slow.]

-let, *-let, n. suffx.* used to form diminutives as leaf*let.*

lethal, *lē´thál, adj.* death-dealing, designed to cause death.—*adj.* **lēthif´erous,** carrying death. [L. *lēt(h)ālis—lēt(h)um,* death.]

lethargy, *leth´ár-ji, n.* heavy unnatural slumber: torpor.—*adjs.* **lethar´gic, -al** (*-är´-*), pertaining to lethargy: unnaturally sleepy: torpid.—*adv.* **lethar´gically.** [L. and Gr. *lēthargia,* drowsy forgetfulness—*lēthē,* forgetfulness.]

Lethe, *lē´thē, n.* one of the rivers of hell causing forgetfulness of the past to all who drank of it: oblivion.—*adj.* **Lethē´an,** of Lethe, causing oblivion. [Gr.,—*lēthein,* old form of *lanthanein,* to be hidden.]

Lett, *let, n.* one of a people inhabiting Lettland or Latvia.—*adjs.* **Lett´ic, Lett´ish,** pertaining to the Letts or to their language. [Ger. *Lette—*Lettish *Latvi.*]

letter, *let´ér, n.* a conventional mark to express a sound: a written or printed message: literal meaning: a printing-type: (*pl.*) learning, literary culture.—*v.t.* to mark letters upon.—*ns.* **lett´er-book,** a book in which letters or copies of letters are kept; **lett´er-box,** a box for receiving letters; **lett´er-card,** a card folded and gummed like a letter, with perforated margin to facilitate opening.—*adj.* **lett´ered,** marked with letters: educated: versed in literature: belonging to learning.—*ns.* **lett´er-file,** appliance for holding letters for reference; **lett´-ering,** the act of forming letters: the letters formed; **lett´er of cred´ence** (see **credence**); **lett´er-of-cred´it,** a letter authorising cash to a certain sum to be paid to the bearer; **lett´er-of-marque** (*märk*), a commission authorising a private ship to attack or seize vessels of another state; **lett´erpress,** printed matter, especially printed matter relating to illustrations in a book: a copying-press.—*n.pl.* **lett´ers-pat´ent** (see **patent**).—**the letter,** the strict verbal interpretation (e.g. of the law)—often opp. to *the spirit,* the (usu. more liberal) intention of the framer. [Fr. *lettre—*L. *lītera, littera.*]

lettuce, *let´is, n.* a plant containing a milky juice, its leaves used as a salad. [Fr. *laitue—*L. *lactūca—lac,* milk.]

leuco-, *lū-kō-,* in composition, white [Gr. *leukos*]:—e.g. **leucocyte,** *lū´kō-sīt, n.* a white corpuscle of the blood or lymph (Gr. *kytos,* a hollow vessel); **leucot´omy,** lobotomy (Gr. *tomē,* a cutting).

leukaemia, *lū-kē´mi-á, n.* a disease in which there is an increase in the number of white corpuscles. [Gr. *leukos,* white, *haima,* blood.]

Levant, *le-vant´, n.* originally, the point where the sun rises, the East: the Eastern Mediterranean and its shores.—*n.* **Levant´er,** a strong easterly wind in the Levant.—*adj.* **Levant´ine,** belonging to the Levant. [Fr. *levant,* rising—L. *levāre,* to raise.]

levant, *le-vant´, v.i.* to decamp, to abscond.—*n.* **levant´er.** [Sp. *levantar,* to move—L. *levāre,* to raise.]

levee, *lev´ā, lev´ē, le-vē´, n.* a morning assembly of visitors: an assembly received by a sovereign or other great personage. [Fr. *levée—lever—*L. *levāre,* to raise.]

levee, *lev´e, le-vē´, n.* an embankment, esp. on

Neutral vowels in unaccented syllables: *em´pér-ór;* for certain sounds in foreign words see p. ix.

the lower Mississippi: a quay. [Fr. *levée*, raised.]

level, *lev'l, n.* an instrument for testing horizontality: a horizontal line or surface: a surface without inequalities: the horizontal plane, literal or figurative, that anything occupies or reaches up to: height: appropriate position or rank.—*adj.* horizontal: even, smooth: uniform: well-balanced: in the same line or plane: equal in position or dignity.—*v.t.* to make horizontal: to make flat or smooth: to raze (e.g. *to level to, with, the ground*): to make equal: to aim (at):—*pr.p.* lev'elling; *pa.t.* and *pa.p.* lev'elled.—*n.* **lev'el-cross'ing,** a place at which a road crosses a railway at the same level.—*adj.* **lev'el-head'ed,** having sound common sense.—*ns.* **lev'eller,** one who levels: one who would remove all social or political inequalities; **lev'elling,** the act of making uneven surfaces level: the process of finding the differences in level between different points on the surface of the earth; **lev'elness,** state of being level, even, or equal.—**(find) one's level,** (to find) the place or rank to which one naturally belongs, **level off,** to make flat or even: to reach and maintain equilibrium; **on the level,** (*slang*) honest(ly), playing fair (as predicative *adj.* or *adv.*). [O.Fr. *livel*, *liveau*—L. *lībella*, a plummet, dim. of *lībra*, a balance.]

lever, *lē'vér, n.* one of the simplest machines—a bar, turning on a support called the prop or fulcrum, for imparting force or effort to a load: (*fig.*) anything that exerts influence.— *v.t.* to move, as with a lever.—*ns.* **lē'verage,** the mechanical power gained by the use of the lever: power, advantage that can be used to achieve a purpose; **lē'ver-watch,** a watch having a vibrating lever in the mechanism of the escapement. [Fr. *levier*—*lever*—L. *levāre*, to raise.]

leveret, *lev'ér-et, n.* a hare in its first year. [O.Fr. *levrette*—L. *lepus*, *lepŏris*, a hare.]

leviable, *levi-à-bl, adj.* able to be levied or assessed. [From **levy**.]

leviathan, *le-vī'a-thán, n.* (*B.*) a huge aquatic animal: anything of huge size. [Heb. *livyāthān.*]

levis, (properly *cap.*), *lē'vīz, n.* heavy, close-fitting trousers, with low waist, made of denim, &c. [Trademark.]

levitation, *lev-i-tā'sh(ó)n, n.* the act of rising by virtue of lightness: the (illusion of) raising a heavy body in the air without support: raising and floating on a cushion of air.—*v.t.* **lev'itate,** to cause to float. [L. *levis*, light.]

Levite, *lē'vīt, n.* a descendant of *Levi*: an inferior priest of the ancient Jewish Church.—*adjs.* **levit'ic, -al.**—*adv.* **levit'ically.**—*n.* **Levit'icus,** third book of Old Testament, containing the laws relating to the priests.

levity, *lev'iti, n.* lightness of weight: lightness of temper shown, as in thoughtlessness, untimely frivolity, disposition to trifle: lightness of conduct, fickleness. [L. *levitās,-ātis*—*levis*, light.]

levy, *lev'i, v.t.* to raise, collect, esp. by authority, as an army or a tax: to make (war):—*pr.p.* lev'ying; *pa.t.* and *pa.p.* lev'ied.—*n.* the act of collecting by authority: the troops or money so collected. [L. *levāre*, to raise.]

lewd, *l(y)ōōd, adj.* lustful, unchaste, debauched: (*obs.*) ignorant, rude, vulgar: (*obs.*) vicious or bad.—*adv.* **lewd'ly.**—*n.* **lewd'ness.** [O.E. *lǣwede*, ignorant, belonging to the laity.]

Lewis gun, *lōō'is gun, n.* a light machine gun invented by Isaac Newton *Lewis*.

lexicon, *leks'i-kon, n.* a word-book or dictionary.—*adj.* **lex'ical,** belonging to a lexicon: pertaining to the words of a language as distinct from its grammar.—*n.* **lexicog'raphy,** the art of compiling a dictionary, **lexicog'rapher,** one skilled in lexicography—*adjs.* **lexicograph'ic, -al.**—*n.* **lexicol'ogy,** that branch of philology which treats of the proper signification and use of words. [Gr. *lexicon*, a dictionary—*lexis*, a word, *legein*, to speak.]

Leyden jar, *lī'dén jär, n.* a capacitor for storing electricity, a glass jar coated inside and outside with tinfoil or other conducting material. [*Leyden* in Holland, where it was invented.]

liable, *lī-à-bl, adj.* subject (to an obligation, legal demand, or penalty—with *for, to*): exposed (to a risk): apt (to happen).—*n.* **liabil'ity,** state of being liable: that for which one is liable, an obligation, debt, &c. [Fr. *lier*—L. *ligāre*, to bind.]

liaison, *lē-ā-zō, li-āz'(ó)n, n.* union, or bond of union: (orig. *mil.*) intercommunication: illicit union between a man and a woman: in French, the linking in pronunciation of a final (and otherwise silent) consonant to the succeeding word when that begins with a vowel or *h* mute.—*v.i.* **liaise** (*lē-āz'*; back-formation), to form a link: to be or get in touch. [Fr.,—L. *ligātiō, -ōnis*—*ligāre*, to bind.]

liana, *li-an'a, n.* a general name for climbing plants in tropical forests. [Fr. *liane*—*lier*—L. *ligāre*, to bind.]

liar, *lī'ár, n.* one who utters a lie or lies (esp habitually). [From **lie** (1).]

Lias, *lī'as, n.* (*geol.*) the lowest division of the Jurassic system in Europe—of argillaceous limestone, &c.—*adj.* **Liass'ic,** pertaining to the lias formation. [A Somerset quarryman's word, app.—O.Fr. *liois*.]

libation, *lī-bā'sh(ó)n, n.* the pouring forth of wine or other liquid in honour of a deity: the liquid poured. [L. *lībātiō, -ōnis*—*lībāre*, *-ātum*—Gr. *leibein*, to pour.]

libel, *lī'bél, n.* any defamatory publication or (loosely) statement: anything that misrepresents or depreciates, as an unskilful portrait: (*law*) the statement of a plaintiff's grounds of complaint.—*v.t.* to defame by a libel: to satirise unfairly: (*law*) to proceed against by producing a written complaint:—*pr.p.* li'belling; *pa.t.* and *pa.p.* li'belled.—*n.* **li'beller.**—*adj.* **li'bellous,** containing a libel: defamatory.—*adv.* **li'bellously.** [L. *libellus*, dim. of *liber*, a book.]

liberal, *lib'ér-ál, adj.* (*rare*) suitable to a gentleman (e.g. *liberal education*): generous: broadminded, unprejudiced: candid: ample (e.g. of a quantity).—*n.* one who advocates greater freedom, esp. in political institutions: (*cap.*) a member of the Liberal Party.—*v.t.* **lib'eralise,** to make liberal, or enlightened: to enlarge.—*ns.* **lib'eralism,** the principles of a liberal, or of a Liberal; **liberal'ity,** the quality

liberate   lief

of being liberal: generosity: impartiality, breadth of mind.—*adv.* **lib′erally.**—**Liberal Party,** the name adopted by the Whigs (1830) to denote the body formed by their union with the Radicals. [Fr.,—L. *līberālis,* befitting a freeman—*līber,* free.]

liberate, *lib′ér-āt, v.t.* to set free, to release from restraint, confinement, or bondage.—*ns.* **liberā′tion; lib′erator.** [L. *līberāre, -ātum—līber,* free.]

liberty, *lib′ér-ti, n.* freedom from constraint or tyranny: freedom to do as one pleases: power of free choice: (*pl.*) privileges, rights, immunities: licence (e.g. *take the liberty of saying, doing*): unseemly freedom of speech or action.—*adj.* (*naut.*) having, pertaining to, liberty or shore-leave (e.g. *liberty man, liberty boat*).—*ns.* **lib′ertinage,** debauchery; **lib′ertine,** formerly one who professed free opinions, esp. in religion: one who leads a licentious life, a rake or debauchee.—*adj.* belonging to a freedman: unrestrained: licentious.—*n.* **lib′ertinism,** licentiousness of opinion or practice: lewdness or debauchery. [Fr. *liberté*—L. *lībertās, -ātis*—L. *lībertīnus,* a freedman—*līber,* free.]

libido, *li-bē′do, n.* (*psych.*) the emotional desire (sex, or urge to live) which prompts all human activities: sexual desire.—*adj.* **libīd′inous,** pertaining to the libido: lustful, lascivious, lewd.—*n.* **libid′inousness.**—*adv.* **libid′inously,** [L. *libīdō, -inis,* desire.]

Libra, *lī′bra, lē′- li′- n.* the balance, the seventh sign of the zodiac. [L.]

library, *lī′brär-i, n.* a building or room containing a collection of books: a collection of books: a collection of gramophone records, computer programs, &c.—*ns.* **librā′rian,** the keeper of a library; **librā′rianship.** [L. *librārium—liber,* a book.]

librate, *lī′brāt, v.i.* to balance, to be poised.—*n.* **librā′tion,** balancing: a state of equipoise: a slight swinging motion.—*adj.* **lī′bratory.** [L. *lībrāre, -ātum—lībra,* balance.]

libretto, *li-bret′ō, n.* a book of the words of an opera, oratorio, ballet, &c.: the text itself:—*pl.* **librett′i, librett′os.** [It., dim. of *libro*—L. *liber,* a book.]

lice, *līs, pl.* of **louse.**

licence, *lī′séns, n.* grant of permission, as for manufacturing a patented article, driving a vehicle, using a television set, owning a gun: the document by which authority is conferred: legal permission to sell alcoholic liquors, for consumption on the premises (**on-licence**), or for taking away (**off-licence**): abuse of freedom.—Also **license.**—*v.t.* **lī′cense,** to grant licence to, to authorise or permit.—Also **licence.**—*adj.* **lī′censable.**—*ns.* **licensee′,** one to whom licence is granted; **lī′censer,** one who grants licence; **licen′tiate,** among Presbyterians, a person authorised by a Presbytery to preach: the holder of an academic diploma of various kinds.—*adj.* **licen′tious,** showing excessive freedom from rules: given to the indulgence of the animal passions, dissolute.—*adv.* **licen′tiously.**—*n.* **licen′tiousness.**—**licensed victualler,** a victualler who holds a licence to sell intoxicating liquors. [Fr. *licence*—L. *licentia—licēre,* to be allowed.]

lichee, *lē-chē, n.* (also various other spellings) a fruit originating in China, oval with a reddish brown hard outer covering, growing in bunches on a tall tree. [From Chinese.]

lichen, *lī′kén,* rarely *lich′én, n.* any of a large group of plants consisting of an alga and a fungus in close association, growing on stones, trees, &c.: an eruption on the skin. [L. *līchēn*—Gr. *leichēn—leichein,* to lick.]

lichgate, *lich′gāt, n.* a churchyard gate with a porch under which to rest the bier.—*n.* **lich′wake,** the wake or watch held over a dead body.—Also **lykewake.** [M.E. *lich*—O.E. *līc* (Ger. *leiche*), a corpse.]

licit, *lis′it, adj.* lawful, allowable. [L. *licitus.*]

lick, *lik, v.t.* to pass the tongue over: to lap: to beat: (*coll.*) to overcome.—*n.* a passing the tongue over: a slight smear: a blow.—*ns.* **lick′er; lick′ing,** a thrashing; **lick′spittle,** a mean, servile dependent.—**lick into shape,** to put into more perfect form; **lick the dust,** to be utterly abased. [O.E. *liccian*; Ger. *lecken,* L. *lingĕre,* Gr. *leichein.*]

lickerish, *lik′ér-ish, adj.* eager to taste or enjoy. [M.E. *likerous,* a variant of **lecherous.**]

licorice. Same as **liquorice.**

lictor, *lik′tór, n.* an officer who attended a Roman magistrate, bearing the fasces. [L.]

lid, *lid, n.* a cover: that which shuts a receptacle: the cover of the eye. [O.E. *hlid* (Du. *lid*)—*hlīdan,* to cover.]

lie, *lī, n.* a false statement made to deceive, an intentional violation of truth: anything that misleads.—*v.i.* to utter falsehood with an intention to deceive: to give a false impression:—*pr.p.* ly′ing; *pa.t.* and *pa.p.* lied.—**lie detector,** an instrument said to be able to detect abnormal involuntary bodily reactions in a person not telling the truth.—**lie in one's throat,** to lie shamelessly; **give the lie to,** to charge with falsehood: to show (e.g. a statement) to be false; **white lie,** an excusable lie, one told from good motives. [O.E. *lēogan* (*lyge,* a falsehood); Du. *liegen,* Ger. *lügen,* to lie.]

lie, *lī, v.i.* to be in, or assume, a recumbent posture: to lean: to be situated: to extend, stretch: to remain in a specified position (e.g. on the table) or state (e.g. hidden, idle): of a ship, to direct its course: to consist (in): to be comprised, comprehended (in): (*law*) to be sustainable: to lodge, pass the night:—*pr.p.* ly′ing; *pa.t.* lay; *pa.p.* lain; (*B.*) lī′en.—*n.* manner of lying: relative position: slope and disposition.—*ns.* **lī′er, lie′-abed′,** one who rises late—also *adj.*—**lie at one's door,** to be directly imputable to one; **lie in,** to be in childbed; **lie in wait,** to lie in ambush; **lie low,** to keep quiet or hidden; **lie over,** to be postponed; **lie to,** of a ship, to lie almost at a stop with head to windward; **lie up,** to rest in bed: of a ship, to be in dock or beached for the winter; **lie with,** to lodge or sleep with: to have sexual intercourse with: to rest with, to belong to as a privilege or as an obligation.—**take it lying down,** to endure tamely. [O.E. *licgan*; Ger. *liegen.*]

lied, *lēt, n.* a German song of lyric type:—*pl.* **lieder** (*lē′der*). [Ger.]

lief, *lēf, adj.* (*arch.*) loved, dear.—*adv.* willingly —now chiefly in the phrases, 'I had as lief' 'to

Neutral vowels in unaccented syllables: *em′pér-ór*; for certain sounds in foreign words see p. ix.

418

have liefer'. [O.E. *lēof*; Ger. *lieb*, loved.]

liege, *lēj, adj.* entitled to receive allegiance from a vassal: obliged to give allegiance and service to an overlord: under a feudal tenure.—*n.* a vassal: a loyal vassal, a subject: a lord or another's (also **liege'-lord**). [O.Fr. *lige*, prob. from O.H.G. *ledic*, free, *līdan*, to depart.]

lien, *lē'én, lēn, n.* (*law*) a right to retain possession of another's property until the owner pays a debt due to the holder. [Fr.,—L. *ligāmen*, tie, band.]

lien, *lī'én* (*B.*), *pa.p.* of **lie** (2).

lieu, *l(y)ōō, n.* place.—**in lieu of,** in place of, instead of. [Fr.,—L. *locus,* place.]

lieutenant, *léf-ten'ánt, n.* one representing, or performing the work of, a superior: an officer holding the place of another in his absence: a commissioned officer in the army next below a captain, or in the navy (pronounced *lĕ-* or *lōō-ten'ánt*) next below a lieutenant-commander and ranking with captain in the army: one holding a place next in rank to a superior, as in the compounds **lieuten'ant-col'onel, lieuten'ant-command'er,** &c.—*ns.* **lieuten'ancy, lieuten'antship,** office or commission of a lieutenant: the body of lieutenants; **lord'-lieuten'ant,** title of the viceroy of Ireland (till 1922): a magistrate appointed by the sovereign as the chief executive authority of a British county. [Fr.—*lieu,* place, *tenant,* pr.p. of *tenir,* to hold.]

life, *līf, n.* state of living: the sum of the activities of plants and animals: conscious existence: the period between birth and death: a series of experiences: manner of living: moral conduct: animation: a quickening principle: a living being: living things: human affairs: narrative of a life:—*pl.* **lives** (*līvz*),—*adj.* (often in composition) lasting for life: pertaining to life: (*art*) from a living model.—*ns.* **life assurance, insurance,** any form of insurance based upon the life of a person and payable at his death or at a specified age; **life'-belt,** a belt either inflated with air, or with cork attached, for sustaining a person in the water; **life'-blood,** the blood necessary to life: any influence that gives strength and energy; **life'-boat,** a boat for saving shipwrecked persons; **life'-buoy,** a buoy intended to support a person in the water till he can be rescued; **life'-guard,** a guard of the life or person: a guard of a prince or other dignitary; **life'-his'tory, life'-cy'cle,** the various stages through which an organism passes from the ovum to full development; **life'-jacket,** a sleeveless buoyant jacket for sustaining a person in the water.—*adj.* **life'less,** dead: without vigour, insipid, sluggish.—*adv.* **life'lessly.**—*n.* **life'lessness.**—*adj.* **life'-like,** like a living person: vivid.—*n.* **life'line,** a rope for support of sailors in dangerous operations: a line thrown to rescue a drowning person: (*fig.*) a vital line of communication.—*adj.* **life'long,** during the length of a life.—*ns.* **life'manship,** the art of making the other fellow feel inferior (invented by Stephen Potter, 1900-69); **life'-preserv'er,** invention for the preservation of life in cases of shipwreck: a cane with a loaded head used as a bludgeon; **life'-sav'er,** one who saves from death, esp. from drowning: one employed to

rescue bathers in difficulty: (*fig.*) that which aids one at a critical moment; **life sentence,** a sentence of imprisonment for life (in practice twenty years, or less in cases of good conduct): also *fig.*; **life'-tā'ble,** a table of statistics as to the probability of life at different ages; **life'time,** continuation or duration of life; **life'-work,** the work to which one's life is or is to be devoted.—**life-and-death struggle,** a desperate struggle.—**high life,** life or the manner of living in fashionable society; **to the life,** exactly like the original. [O.E. *līf*; O.N. *līf,* Swed. *līf;* Ger. *leib,* body.]

lift, *lift, v.t.* to bring to a higher position, to elevate (*lit.* and *fig.*): to hold on high: to take and carry away.—*v.i.* to rise: to disperse, as a fog.—*n.* act of lifting: upward movement: that which is to be raised: distance through which a thing rises or is lifted: lifting power: that which assists to lift: an elevator: (*aero.*) the component of the aerodynamic force on an aircraft acting upwards at right angles to the *drag* (q.v.).—*n.* **lift'-off,** the take-off of an aircraft or rocket: the moment when this occurs.—**lift the face,** to perform an operation for smoothing out wrinkles. [O.N. *lypta—lopt,* the air.]

ligament, *lig'a-mént, n.* anything that binds: (*anat.*) the bundle of fibrous tissue joining the movable bones: (*arch.*) a bond of union.—*adjs.* **ligament'al, ligament'ous.**—*ns.* **liga'tion,** act of binding: state of being bound; **lig'ature,** anything that binds: a bandage: (*mus.*) a line connecting notes: (*print.*) a type of two or more letters (e.g. ff, ffi): (*med.*) a cord for tying the blood-vessels, &c. [L. *ligāre,* to bind.]

light, *līt, n.* the agency by which objects are rendered visible, electromagnetic radiation capable of inducing visual sensation through the eye: (*poet.*) the power of vision: a source of light, as the sun or a lamp: an aperture for admitting light: the illuminated part of a picture: means of kindling or illuminating: (*fig.*) mental or spiritual illumination, enlightenment, knowledge: open view: aspect: a conspicuous person.—*adj.* not dark: bright: whitish.—*v.t.* to give light to: to set fire to: to attend with a light.—*v.i.* to become light or bright:—*pr.p.* **light'ing;** *pa.t.* and *pa.p.* **light'ed** or **lit.**—*n.* **light'ness.**—*n.pl.* **light'-dues,** tolls taken from ships in certain waters, for the maintenance of lighthouses.—*ns.* **light'er,** one who lights: a device for producing a light, e.g. by means of a spark from a flint and petrol vapour: (see also **light** (2)): **light'house,** a building with a light to guide or warn ships or aircraft; **light'-ship,** a stationary ship carrying a light and serving the purpose of a lighthouse; **light'-wave,** an electromagnetic (q.v.) wave on which visual sensation depends; **light'-year,** the distance light travels in a year ($5 \cdot 880 \times 10^{12}$ miles)—a unit used to express distances in the stellar universe.—**light up,** to put on the lights (**lighting-up time,** the time when street lights, motor-car lights, &c., must, in accordance with regulations, be put on): to illumine, or (*fig.*) to animate (**light up well,** to look well by artificial light).—**according to one's lights,** in accordance with one's degree of enlightenment, measured by one's own natural or acquired standards; **see the light,** to be born: to grasp an idea, to come to an understanding of a situation, explanation, problem: to be converted; **shed light on,** to make (e.g. a reason, motive, situation) more clear. [M.E. *liht*—O.E. *leht, lēoht*; Ger. *licht.*]

light, *līt, adj.* not heavy: of short weight: not massive in appearance: acting delicately: easily endured: easily performed: easily digested: not heavily armed: not heavily burdened: nimble: not dense or copious or intense ʼ(e.g. of mist, rain, frost): gay, lively: idle, worthless: unchaste: loose, sandy.—*adv.* **lightʼly,** in a light manner: slightly.—*adj.* **lightʼ-armed,** armed in a manner suitable for active service.—*ns.* **lightʼer,** a large open boat used in unloading and loading ships; **lightʼerage,** price paid for unloading ships by lighters: the act of thus unloading.—*adjs.* **lightʼ-fingʼered,** light or active with oneʼs fingers: thievish; **lightʼ-foot, -ed,** nimble, active; **lightʼ-handʼed,** with light or dexterous touch; **lightʼ-headʼed,** giddy, delirious: thoughtless, unsteady; **lightʼ-heartʼed,** light or merry of heart: free from anxiety, cheerful.—*ns.* **lightʼ-horse,** light-armed cavalry; **lightʼ-horseʼman; lightʼ-inʼfantry,** infantry lightly armed.—*adj.* **lightʼ-mindʼed,** having a light or unsteady mind, frivolous.—*n.* **lightʼ-oʼ-love,** a wanton woman.—*n.pl.* **lights,** the lungs of an animal.—*adj.* **lightʼsome,** light, gay, cheering.—*ns.* **lightʼsomeness; lightʼweight,** (*boxing*) a man intermediate between middle-weight and feather-weight (not more than 9 st. 9 lb., amateur 9 st. 7 lb., or less than 9 st.): a person of little importance.—**light engine,** one without coaches or trucks attached; **light industry** (see **industry**); **light literature, music,** &c., such as requires little mental effort.—**make light of,** to treat as unimportant. [O.E. *līht, lēoht*; Ger. *leicht,* O.N. *lēttr*; L. *lĕvis.*]

light, *līt, v.i.* to dismount, to alight: to come by chance (upon):—*pr.p.* lightʼing; *pa.t.* and *pa.p.* lightʼed or lit.—Also (*Pr. Bk.*) **lighten.** [O.E. *līhtan,* to dismount.]

lighten, *lītʼ(é)n, v.t.* to make brighter: to illuminate.—*v.i.* to become brighter: to flash.—*n.* **lightʼning,** the flash or very large spark that marks the discharge of an electrified cloud either to earth or to another cloud.—*adj.* characterised by speed and suddenness.—*n.* **lightʼning-conducʼtor, lightʼning-rod,** a metallic rod for protecting buildings from lightning. [**light** (1).]

lighten, *lītʼ(é)n, v.t.* to make less heavy: to alleviate: to cheer. [**light** (2).]

lignum, *ligʼnum, n.* (*obs.*) wood.—*adjs.* **ligʼneous,** woody: wooden; **lignifʼerous,** producing wood.—*v.t.* **ligʼnify,** to turn into wood.—*v.i.* to become wood or woody:—*pr.p.* ligʼnifying; *pa.p.* ligʼnified.—*ns.* **lignificaʼtion; ligʼnin,** a complicated mixture of substances found particularly in woody tissue; **ligʼnīte,** brown coal, coal retaining the texture of wood.—*adj.* **lignitʼic,** containing, of the nature of, lignite. —*n.* **ligʼnum-viʼtae,** popular name of a South American tree with very hard wood. [L. *lignum,* wood.]

ligule, *ligʼūl, n.* (*bot.*) a scale at the top of a leaf-sheath in grasses: strap-shaped corolla in composite flowers. [L. *ligula,* dim. of *lingua,* a tongue.]

ligure, *ligʼūr, n.* (*B.*) an unknown precious stone. [Gr. *ligŷrion.*]

like, *līk, adj.* identical, equal, or nearly equal in any respect: similar: characteristic of (sometimes in compound *adjs.*): likely (with *infin.*). —*n.* one of the same kind: the same thing (e.g. *to do the like*): an exact counterpart. —*adv.* (*arch.*) in the same manner: probably: (*coll.*) nearly.—*prep.* in the same manner as: to the same extent as.—*ns.* **likeʼliness, -lihood.**—*adj.* **likeʼly,** like the thing required: credible: probable: promising.—*adv.* probably.—*adj.* **likeʼ-mindʼed,** having a similar disposition or purpose.—*v.t.* **likʼen,** to represent as like or similar: to compare.—*n.* **likeʼness,** resemblance: one who or that which has a resemblance: a portrait, picture, or effigy.—*adv.* **likeʼwise,** in like manner: also, moreover.—**feel like,** to be disposed to, inclined for (any action or thing); **look like,** to suggest the effects, symptoms, or portents of, or the likelihood of: to appear similar to. [O.E. *līc,* seen in *gelīc*; O.N. *līkr,* Du. *gelijk.*]

like, *līk, v.t.* to be pleased with: to approve: to enjoy: (*obs.*) to please.—*n.* a liking, chiefly in phrase ʼlikes and dislikesʼ.—*adj.* **lik(e)ʼable,** loveable, amiable.—*n.* **likʼing,** attraction, inclination towards (with *for*), taste (for): satisfaction or taste (e.g. *to my liking*). [Orig. impersonal—O.E. *līcian—līc,* like.]

lilac, *līʼlák, n.* a tree (*Syringa vulgaris*) with a flower commonly of a light-purple colour: any other species of the same genus.—*adj.* having the colour of the lilac flower. [Sp.,—Pers. *līlak,* bluish.]

Lilliputian, *lil-i-pūʼsh(y)án, n.* one of the tiny inhabitants of *Lilliput,* an island described by Swift in his *Gulliverʼs Travels*: a pygmy.—*adj.* diminutive.

lilt, *lilt, v.i.* to sing or play merrily.—*v.t.* to sing easily or gaily.—*n.* a cheerful song or air: a rhythmical swing, melodious modulation: a springy movement. [M.E. *lulte.*]

lily, *lilʼi. n.* a bulbous plant belonging to the genus Lilium, of which the white madonna lily and the tiger lily are species: extended to include other flowers of the same family, as those of the genus *Narcissus:* (*her.*) fleur-de-lis.—*adj.* resembling a lily: white: pure.—*adjs.* **liliāʼceous,** pertaining to, or resembling, lilies; **lilʼied,** adorned with lilies; **lilʼy-livʼered,** white-livered, cowardly (see **liver**).—**lily of the valley,** a small perennial plant with a raceme of white bell-shaped flowers, sometimes considered as belonging to the same family as the lilies. [O.E. *lilie*—L. *lilium*—Gr. *leirion,* lily.]

limb, *lim, n.* a member or organ of the body, now only an arm, leg, or wing: a projecting part: a branch.—*v.t.* to tear or cut off the limbs of.—**out on a limb,** in danger or difficulty and on oneʼs own. [O.E. *lim*; O.N. *limr.*]

limb, *lim, n.* an edge or border, as of the sun, &c.: the edge of a sextant, &c. [Fr. *limbe*—L. *limbus,* a border.]

limber, *limʼbér, n.* the detachable fore-part of a gun-carriage.—*v.t.* to attach to the limber. [Perh. Fr. *limonière.*]

Neutral vowels in unaccented syllables: *emʼpér-ór*; for certain sounds in foreign words see p. ix.

limber, *lim'bėr, adj.* pliant, flexible: lithe.

limbo, *lim'bō, n.* the borderland of Hell, assigned to the unbaptised: a place of confinement: a place of oblivion. [From the Latin phrase *in limbo—in,* in, and abl. of *limbus,* border.]

limbo, *lim'bō, n.* a West Indian dance in which the dancer bends backwards and passes under a bar which is progressively lowered. [Perh. **limber** (1).]

lime, *līm, n.* any slimy or gluey material: birdlime: quicklime, the white caustic substance (calcium oxide when pure) obtained by calcining limestone, &c., used for cement.—*v.t.* to cover with lime: to cement: to manure with lime: to ensnare.—*ns.* **lime'kiln,** a kiln or furnace in which limestone is burned to lime; **lime'light,** light produced by a blowpipe-flame directed against a block of quicklime: the glare of publicity; **lime'stone,** a sedimentary rock composed essentially of calcium carbonate; **lime'twig,** a twig smeared with bird-lime: a snare.—*adjs.* **lim'ous,** gluey: slimy: muddy; **lim'y,** glutinous: sticky: containing, resembling, or having the qualities of lime. [O.E. *līm*; Ger. *leim,* glue, L. *līmus,* slime.]

lime, *līm, n.* a tree of the same genus as the lemon, or its small greenish-yellow fruit.—*n.* **lime'-juice,** the acid juice of the lime, used at sea as a specific against scurvy. [Fr.—Sp. *lima*; cf. **lemon.**]

lime, *līm, n.* the linden-tree. [Variant of obs. *lind,* **linden.**]

limerick, *lim'er-ik, n.* a form of humorous verse in a five-line jingle. [Said to be from a refrain referring to *Limerick* in Ireland.]

limicoline, *li-mik'o-līn, -lin, adj.* inhabiting the seashore.—*adj.* **limic'olous,** living in mud. [L. *līmus,* mud, *colěre,* to live in.]

limit, *lim'it, n.* boundary: utmost (largest or smallest) extent: (*restriction.—v.t.* to confine within bounds: to restrict.—*adjs.* **lim'itable; lim'itary,** placed at the boundary as a guard, &c.: confined within limits.—*n.* **limitā'tion,** the act of limiting: the state of being limited: restriction: a falling short of the highest excellence in character or talent.—*adj.* **lim'itless,** having no limits: boundless, immense, infinite.—**limited liability,** a principle of modern statute law which limits the responsibilities of members of a joint-stock company by the extent of their personal interest therein; **limited (liability) company; limited monarchy,** one in which the monarch shares supreme power with others. [L. *līmes, -itis,* boundary.]

limn, *lim, v.t.* to draw or paint, esp. in watercolours: (*orig.*) to illuminate with ornamental letters, &c.—*n.* **lim'ner,** one who paints on paper or parchment: a portrait-painter. [O.Fr. *enluminer*—L. *illumināre.*]

limousine, *lim'ōō-zēn, n.* a large closed motor-car with a separate compartment for the chauffeur: loosely, any large motor-car (sometimes used ironically). [Fr.]

limp, *limp, adj.* wanting stiffness, flexible: weak, flaccid. [Origin obscure.]

limp, *limp, v.i.* to walk lamely, to halt: of ship or aircraft, after suffering damage, to move with difficulty.—*n.* act of limping: a halt. [O.E. *lemp-healt,* halting.]

limpet, *lim'pet, n.* any of a number of molluscs with conical shell, that cling to rocks: a person difficult to dislodge. [O.E. *lempedu,* lamprey.]

limpid, *lim'pid, adj.* clear (of a stream, the air, eyes, style, &c.): transparent.—*ns.* **limpid'ity, lim'pidness.**—*adv.* **lim'pidly.** [L. *limpidus,* liquid.]

linchpin, *linch'pin,* or *linsh'-, n.* a pin used to keep a wheel on its axle-tree. [O.E. *lynis,* axle, and **pin.**]

Lincoln-green, *lingk'ŏn-grēn, n.* a bright green cloth once made at Lincoln.

linden, *lin'den, n.* any tree of the genus *Tilia,* having deciduous, heart-shaped, serrated leaves. [O.E. *lind*; cf. O.N. *lind,* Ger. *linde.*]

line, *līn, v.t.* to cover on the inside: to pad.—*n.* **lin'ing,** material thus applied to a surface. [O.E. *līn,* flax.]

line, *līn, n.* a thread, string, cord, rope: (*math.*) that which has length without breadth or thickness: a long narrow mark: a row: a queue: a route, system: a railroad: a service of ships: a telegraph or telephone wire or section of wires: a system (of pipes) for conveying a fluid, as oil: a trench: a series or succession: lineage: direction (e.g. *in the line of fire*): outline, contour: limit, mark of division (as in *draw the line*): method, plan, course of conduct (e.g. *on the lines of, take the line of least resistance*): sphere of activity or interest (e.g. *in his own line*): class of goods: the equator: a verse: a note or short letter: the twelfth part of an inch: the regular army: (*coll.*) relevant information: (*slang*) glib talk: in TV, the path traversed by the electron beam or scanning spot in moving once from side to side (horizontal scanning) or from top to bottom (vertical scanning) of the picture: (*pl.*) a marriage certificate: (*pl.*) a certificate of church membership: (*pl.*) military field-works.—*v.t.* to mark out with lines: to cover with lines: to put in line.—*v.i.* to take a place in a line.—*n.* **lineage** (*lin'i-ij*), ancestry, race, family.—*adj.* **lineal** (*lin'i-ál*), linear: descended in a direct line from an ancestor (opp. to *collateral*).—*adv.* **lin'eally.**—*n.* **lin'eament,** feature: distinguishing mark in the form, esp. of the face.—*adj.* **lin'ear,** of or belonging to a line: consisting of, or having the form of, lines: involving measurement in one dimension only: capable of being represented on a graph by a straight line: of a system, in which doubling the cause doubles the effect.—*adv.* **lin'early.**—*adjs.* **lineate, -d,** marked longitudinally with lines or stripes.—*ns.* **lineā'tion,** marking with lines: arrangement of, or in, lines; **line'-engrav'ing,** the process of engraving in lines, steel or copperplate engraving; **lin'er,** a vessel or aircraft of a regular line or company; **line'-fish,** fish caught with the line; **line'-shoot'er,** one who shoots a line; **line(s)'man,** one who attends to lines of railway, telegraph, telephone, &c.; **lines'man,** a soldier in a regiment of the line: in football, one who marks the spot at which the ball goes into touch, and indicates which side is responsible for some infringements of rules: in tennis, one who decides on which side of a line the ball falls.—**linear programming,** that which enables a computer to give an optimum result when fed with a number of unrelated variables.—**bring into line**, to cause to conform; **hard lines**, bad luck; **line of country**, field of study or interest; **line up**, to arrange, get ready (for a person or occasion); **shoot a line**, to brag, exaggerate. [Partly from O.E. *līne*, cord (from or cognate with L. *līnum*, flax); partly through Fr. *ligne*, and partly directly, from L. *līnea*, thread.]

linen, *lin′én*, *n.* cloth made of flax: underclothing, particularly that made of linen: household coverings as sheets and tablecloths.—*adj.* made of flax: resembling linen cloth.—*n.* **lin′en-drap′er**, a merchant who deals in linens. [O.E. *līnen* (adj.)—*līn*, flax.]

ling, *ling*, *n.* a fish resembling the cod. [Prob. conn. with **long**.]

ling, *ling*, *n.* heather. [O.N. *lyng*.]

-ling, *-ling*, *n. suffx.* denoting a diminutive, as duck*ling*.

linger, *ling′gér*, *v.i.* to remain long: to loiter: to delay.—*n.* **ling′erer**.—*adj.* **ling′ering**, remaining long: protracted. [O.E. *lengan*, to protract—*lang*, long.]

lingerie, *lēzh-(é-)rē*, *n.* linen goods, esp. women's underclothing: underwear of any material. [Fr.,—*linge*, linen—L. *līnum*.]

lingo, *ling′gō*, *n.* (*derogatory*) language. [L. *lingua*, language.]

lingua franca, *ling′gwa frangk′a*, *n.* a mixed Italian trade jargon used in the Levant: any international jargon. [Ital., Frankish language.]

lingual, *ling′gwál*, *adj.* pertaining to the tongue or to utterance.—*n.* a letter pronounced mainly by the tongue.—*adv.* **ling′ually**.—*n.* **ling′uist**, one skilled in languages.—*adjs.* **linguist′ic, -al**, pertaining to languages and the affinities of languages.—*adv.* **linguist′ically**.—*n.pl.* **linguist′ics**, the general or comparative science, or study, of languages.—*adjs.* **lingulate** (*ling′gū-lāt*), **linguiform** (*-gw-*), tongue-shaped. [L. *lingua*, the tongue.]

liniment, *lin′i-mént*, *n.* a thin ointment: an embrocation. [L. *linīmentum*—*linēre*, to besmear.]

link, *lingk*, *n.* a ring of a chain: anything connecting (also *fig.*): a single part of a series: the 1/100th part of the surveyor's chain, 7·92 inches.—*v.t.* to connect as by a link.—*v.i.* to be connected.—*ns.* **link′age** (*-ij*), act of linking or state of being linked: the tendency of certain genetical characters to be inherited together; **link′-up**, a connection, union.—**missing link**, a point or fact needed to complete a series or a chain of argument: a hypothetical intermediate form in the evolution of man from his ape-like ancestors. [O.E. *hlence*; O.N. *hlekkr*, Ger. *gelenk*, a joint.]

link, *lingk*, *n.* (*hist.*) a torch of pitch and tow.—*ns.* **link′boy**, **link′man**, an attendant carrying a link in dark streets.

links, *lingks*, *n.pl.* a stretch of flat or gently undulating ground along a sea-shore, suitable for a golf-course: a golf-course. [O.E. *hlinc*, a ridge of land, a bank.]

linn, *lin*, *in*, *n.* a waterfall: a cascade pool. [O.E. *hlynn*, a torrent; Gael. *linne*, pool.]

Linnaean, Linnean, *lin-ē′án*, *adj.* pertaining to *Linnaeus* or von *Linné*, Swedish botanist (1707-78), or to his system of classification of plants.

linnet, *lin′et*, *n.* a common finch (so called because it likes to feed on flax-seed). [O.Fr. *linot*—*lin*, flax—L. *līnum*.]

linoleum, *lin-ō′li-um*, *n.* a preparation used as a floorcloth, in the making of which linseed-oil is much used. [L. *līnum*, flax, *oleum*, oil.]

linocut, *lī′nō-kut*, *n.* a linoleum block cut in relief, or a print from it. [*lino*leum and **cut**.]

Linotype, *līn′ō-tīp*, *n.* a machine for producing castings of complete lines of words, &c. Cf. *Monotype*. [**line**, **o′ type**. Trademark.]

linseed, *lin′sēd*, *n.* flax seed—also **lint′seed**.—*ns.* **lin′seed-cake**, the cake remaining when the oil is pressed out of flax seed, used as a food for sheep and cattle; **lin′seed-oil**, oil from flax seed. [O.E. *līn*, flax, *sǣd*, seed.]

linsey, linsey-woolsey, *lin′zi*, *-wōōl′zi*, *ns.* a thin coarse stuff of linen or cotton and wool mixed: inferior stuffs of doubtful composition. [**line** (1), and **wool**.]

linstock, *lin′stok*, *n.* (*hist.*) a staff to hold a lighted match for firing cannon.—Also **lint′stock**. [Du. *lontstok*—*lont*, a match, *stok*, a stick.]

lint, *lint*, *n.* linen scraped into a soft woolly substance for dressing wounds. [M.E. *lynt*, perh.—L. *linteus*, of linen—*līnum*, flax.]

lintel, *lint′(é)l*, *n.* a timber or stone over a doorway or window, a headpiece. [O.Fr. *lintel*, dim. of L. *līmes, -itis*, border.]

linters, cotton linters, *lin′térz*, short stiff fibres remaining on cotton seeds after removal of the longer fibres—used in the manufacture of rayon, gun-cotton, &c. [*linter*, a machine for removing short cotton fibres—*lint*, cotton fibre, same as **lint**.]

lion, *lī′ón*, *n.* a large, tawny, carnivorous animal of the cat family (*fem.* **lī′oness**): (*fig.*) a man of unusual courage: (*cap.*) Leo, a sign of the zodiac: any object of interest, esp. a celebrated person.—*n.* **lī′on-heart**, a man of great courage.—*adj.* **lī′on-heart′ed**.—*n.* **lī′on-hunt′er**, a hunter of lions: one who seeks the company of celebrities.—*v.t.* **lī′onise**, to treat as a lion or object of interest.—*adj.* **lī′on-like.—lion's share**, the largest share. [Anglo-Fr. *liun*—L. *leō, -ōnis*—Gr. *leōn*.]

lip, *lip*, *n.* either of the muscular flaps in front of the teeth by which things are taken into the mouth: the edge of anything.—*v.t.* to touch the edge of:—*pr.p.* lipp′ing; *pa.p.* lipped.—*adj.* of the lip: (in composition) from the lips only, insincere, as *lip-homage*.—*adj.* **lipped**, having lips, or edges like lips, labiate.—*ns.* **lip′-read′ing**, reading what a person says by watching the movement of his lips; **lip′-service**, insincere devotion or worship; **lip′-stick**, rouge in stick form for the lips. [O.E. *lippa*; Du. *lip*, Ger. *lippe*, L. *labium*.]

lip-, lipo-, *lip-, līp-(ō-)*, in composition, fat, as in **lip′ase**, an enzyme that breaks up fats. [Gr. *lipos*, fat.]

liquate, *lik′wāt*, *v.t.* to melt: to separate by melting (mixed metals that solidify or fuse at different temperatures).—*n.* **liqua′tion**. [L. *liquāre, -ātum*, to liquefy.]

liquefy, *lik′we-fī*, *v.t.* to make liquid, to dissolve.—*v.i.* to become liquid:—*pa.t.* and *pa.p.* liq′uefied.—*n.* **liquefac′tion**, the act or process

Neutral vowels in unaccented syllables: *em′pér-ór*; for certain sounds in foreign words see p. ix.

422

of making liquid: the state of being liquid.—
adj. **liq'uefiable.**—*n.* **liq'uefier.**—*adj.* **liques'c-
ent,** melting.—*n.* **liques'cency.** [L. *liquefacĕre*
—*liquēre,* to be liquid, *facĕre,* to make.]

liqueur, *lik-ūr',* or *lē-kœr',* *n.* an alcoholic
beverage flavoured or perfumed and sweetened. [Fr.—L. *liquor.*]

liquid, *lik'wid, adj.* flowing: fluid, but not
gaseous: resembling clear liquid in appearance: clear in sound: (of assets) in cash, or
convertible into it.—*n.* a liquid substance: a
flowing consonant sounds, as *l, r*—*ns.* **liquid'-
ity, liq'uidness.**—*vt.* **liq'uidate,** to clear or pay
off (a debt): to arrange or wind up (the affairs
of a bankrupt estate): to clear up and dispose
of (any thing or condition): (*coll.*) to kill or
eradicate ruthlessly.—*ns.* **liquidā'tion; liqui-
dāt'or.**—**liquid helium, oxygen,** &c., these elements in the liquid state, obtained by subjecting them to very low temperatures. [L. *liquid-
us,* liquid, clear—*liquēre,* to be clear.]

liquor, *lik'òr, n.* anything liquid: strong drink: a
strong solution of a particular substance.—*n.*
liq'uor-gauge, a rod used by excisemen for
measuring the depth of liquid in a cask.—
liquor laws, laws restricting the sale of intoxicating drink.—**In liquor,** drunk. [O.Fr.
licour, licour—L. *liquor, ōris.*]

liquorice, *lik'òr-is, n.* a plant with a sweet root,
used for medicinal purposes. [Low L. *liquirītia,*
a corr. of Gr. *glykyrrhiza*—*glykys,* sweet, *rhiza,*
root.]

lira, *lē'ra, n.* the Italian monetary unit (coins of
50, 10, etc. lire being in circulation).—*pl.* **lire**
(*lē'rā*), **lir'as.** [It.—L. *libra,* a pound.]

lisle thread, *līl' thred, n.* a fine hard-twisted
thread, originally of linen, now often of cotton,
first made at *Lille* in France.

lisp, *lisp, v.i.* to speak with the tongue against
the upper teeth or gums, as in pronouncing *th*
for *s* or TH for *z*: to articulate as a child: to
utter imperfectly.—*v.t.* to utter with a lisp.—*n.*
the act or habit of lisping—*adv.* **lisp'ingly**
[O.E. *wlisp,* stammering; Du. *lispen,* Ger. *lis-
peln.*]

lissome, lissom, *lis'òm, adj.* lithesome, nimble,
flexible. [Shortened form of **lithesome** (see
lithe).]

list, *list, n.* a strip: a selvage: a boundary: (in *pl.*)
the boundary of a tilting-ground, hence the
ground itself, combat.—**enter the lists,** to en-
gage in contest. [O.E. *līste* | *līste* | *leiste* | affect-
ed in some senses by O.Fr. *lisse,* barrier.]

list, *list, n.* a catalogue, roll, or enumeration: a
book, &c., containing a series of names of
persons or things.—*v.t.* to place in a list or
catalogue: to engage for the public service, as
soldiers.—*v.i.* to enlist.—**active list,** the roll of
soldiers on active service, **civil list** (see **civil**).
[O.Fr. *liste* of Gmc. origin, ultimately same
word as above.]

list, *list, v.i.* (*arch.*) to desire, choose: (*impers.*)
to please: (*naut.*) to incline or heel over to one
side.—*v.t.* to cause to heel over.—*n.* such a
heeling over.—*adj.* **list'less,** having no desire
or wish, uninterested, weary, indolent.—*adv.*
list'lessly.—*n.* **list'lessness.** [O.E. *lystan,*
impers., please—*lust,* pleasure.]

list, *list, v.i.* (*arch.* or *poet.*) to listen.—*v.t.* to
listen to. [O.E. *hlystan.*]

listen, *lis'n, v.i.* to give ear or hearken: to follow
advice.—*n.* **list'ener,** one who listens or
hearkens.—*v.i.* **list'en-in,** to listen to a wireless broadcast. [O.E. *hlysnan.*]

lit, *pa.t.* and *pa.p.* of **light** (vb. 1 and 3).—**lit up,**
(*coll.*) drunk.

litany, *lit'a-ni, n.* an appointed form of prayer
with responses, in public worship. [O.Fr.,—
Low L. *litanīa*—Gr. *litaneia*—*litesthai,* to
pray.]

litchi. Same as **lichee.**

literal, *lit'ér-àl, adj.* according to the letter: not
figurative or metaphorical: following the exact
meaning, word for word.—*adv.* **lit'erally.**—*n.*
lit'eralness. [L. *līterālis, litterālis*—*lītera,
littera,* a letter.]

literary, *lit'ér-ar-i, adj.* belonging to letters or
learning: versed in, or concerned with, the
writing of books.—*n.* **lit'eracy,** state of being
literate.—*adj.* **lit'erate** (-*àt*), able to read and
write: learned.—Also *n.*—*n.pl.* **litera'ti,** men of
letters, the learned.—*adv.* **litera'tim,** letter for
letter. [L. *līterārius, litterārius, līterātus,
litterātus*—*lītera, littera,* a letter.]

literature, *lit'ér-a-tūr, -chùr, n.* compositions in
verse or prose, esp. those distinguishable by
beauty of style: the whole body of literary
compositions in any language: the whole body
of writings on a given subject: (*arch.*) literary
culture: the writer's profession. [L. *līterātūra,
litterātūra*—*lītera, littera,* a letter.]

litharge, *lith'ärj, n.* an oxide of lead separated
from silver in refining. [Fr.,—Gr. *lithar-
gyros*—*lithos,* a stone, *argyros,* silver.]

lithe, *līTH, adj.* flexible, pliant. *adv.* **lithe'ly.**—*n.*
lithe'ness.—*adj.* **lithe'some.**—*n.* **lithe'someness.** [O.E. *līthe,* soft, mild; Ger. *lind* and
gelinde.]

lithium, *lith'i-ùm, n.* the lightest metallic element (symbol Li, at. no. 3). [Gr. *lithos,* stone.]

lithograph, *lith'ō-gräf, v.t.* to print from stone, or
a substitute, as zinc or aluminium, with
greasy ink—*n.* a print so made (abbrev.
lī'tho).—*n.* **lithog'rapher.**—*adjs.* **lithograph'ic,
-al.**—*adv.* **lithograph'ically.**—*n.* **lithog'raphy.**
[Gr. *lithos,* a stone, *graphein,* to write.]

lithology, *lith-ol'o-ji, n.* the science of rocks as
mineral masses.—*adjs.* **litholog'ic, litholog'ical.**—*n.* **lithol'ogist.** [Gr. *lithos,* a stone,
logos, discourse.]

lithophyte, *lith'ō-fīt, n.* a plant growing on rocks
or stones. [Gr. *lithos,* stone, *phyton,* plant.]

lithosphere, *lith'ō-sfēr, n.* the rocky crust of the
earth. [Gr. *lithos,* stone, *sphaira,* sphere.]

lithotomy, *lith-ot'o-mi, n.* cutting for stone in the
bladder.—*n.* **lithot'omist.** [Gr. *lithos,* a stone,
tomē, a cutting—*temnein,* to cut.]

litigate, *lit'i-gāt, v.t.* and *v.i.* to dispute, esp. by a
lawsuit.—*adjs.* **lit'igable,** that may be
contested in law; **lit'igant,** contending at law,
engaged in a lawsuit.—*n.* person engaged in a
lawsuit.—*n.* **litigā'tion.**—*adj.* **litigious** (*li-tij'-
us*), inclined to engage in lawsuits: conten-
tious.—*n.* **litig'iousness.**—*adv.* **litig'iously.** [L.
lītigāre, -ātum—*līs, lītis,* a dispute, lawsuit,
agĕre, to do.]

litmus, *lit'mus, n.* a substance obtained from
certain lichens, turned red by acids, blue by
bases. [O.N. *litr,* colour, *mosi,* moss.]

litotes, *līt'-* or *lit'ō-tēz, n.* meiosis or understatement, esp. affirmation by negation of the contrary. [Gr. *lītotēs,* simplicity—*lītos,* plain.]

litre, *lē'tér, n.* the metric unit of capacity, 1 cubic decimetre, about 1¾ pt. [Fr.]

litter, *lit'ér, n.* a heap of straw for animals to lie upon: materials for a bed: objects, esp. of little value, lying scattered about: a couch carried by men or beasts: a brood of animals.—*v.t.* to cover or supply with litter: to scatter carelessly about: to give birth to (said of animals). —*v.i.* to produce a litter or brood.—*ns.* **litter-bug, litter lout,** one who throws rubbish about in streets, &c. [O.Fr. *litiere*—Low L. *lectāria*—L. *lectus,* a bed.]

littérateur, *lē-tā-ra-tœr, n.* a literary man. [Fr.]

little, *lit'l, adj.* (*comp.* **less**; *superl.* **least**) small in amount or importance: not much: petty.—*n.* that which is small in quantity or extent: a small amount.—*adv.* in a small quantity or degree: not much.—*ns.* **litt'le-go,** the first examination for the B.A. at Cambridge University; **litt'leness.**—**Little Bear,** *Ursa Minor,* the northern constellation that contains the pole-star; **Little Englander,** an opponent of British imperialism and empire-building; **little magazine,** a small high-brow magazine; **little man,** a man of no importance, an underdog; **little theatre,** a small theatre in which experimental plays, and other plays unlikely to achieve commercial success, are produced.—**make little of,** to treat as easy, or as unimportant: to understand very imperfectly; **think little of** (see **think**). [O.E. *lўtel.*]

littoral, *lit'ór-ál, adj.* belonging to the seashore.—*n.* the strip of land along it. [L.,—*lītus, littus, lītoris, littoris,* shore.]

liturgy, *lit'úr-ji, n.* the form of service or regular ritual of a church.—*adjs.* **litur'gic, -al.**—*adv.* **litur'gically.** [Gr. *leitourgiā.*]

live, *liv, v.i.* to have life, be alive: to continue to be in life: to dwell: to subsist (on): to be supported by or nourished by (with *on*): to get a livelihood (by): to pass one's life in a specified manner or specified circumstances (e.g. frugally, in affluence): to enjoy life: to direct one's course of life: to be life-like or vivid: to survive in human memory.—*v.t.* to spend (e.g. *to live a life of ease*): to act in conformity to (e.g. *to live a lie*)—*pr.p.* liv'ing; *pa.t.* and *pa.p.* lived.—*adj.* **liv'able,** capable of being lived: habitable.—*n.* **liv'er.—live down,** to undo the effect of by good conduct; **live in** (or **out**), to reside in (or away from) a shop, house, &c., where one is employed; **live it up,** to go on the spree: to live strenuously, in pursuit of maximum enjoyment. [O.E. *lifian.*]

live, *līv, adj.* (used attributively) having life, not dead: active: charged with energy: burning: vivid: of a performance, in the actual theatre or concert hall: of a broadcast or telecast, heard, seen as the events occur, not a recording.—**lived** (*līvd;* sometimes *livd* in composition), having life (*long-lived,* &c.).—*ns.* **live'-rail,** a rail carrying an electric current; **live'-wire,** a wire carrying an electric current: a person of energy and forcefulness; **live'-stock,** domestic animals, esp. horses, cattle, sheep, and pigs.—**live shell,** a shell still capable of exploding.—**the live theatre,** performances to an audience actually present in the place of

performance. [From **alive,** which is the form used predicatively.]

livelihood, *līv'li-hood, n.* means of living, support. [O.E. *līflād*—*līf,* life, *lād,* course; confused with *livelihood,* liveliness.]

livelong, *liv'long, adj.* very long: whole. [**lief,** used intensively, and **long.**]

lively, *līv'li, adj.* showing life: vigorous, active: sprightly.—*n.* **live'liness.** [O.E. *līflic*—*līf,* life.]

liver, *liv'ér, n.* a large gland that secretes bile, formerly regarded as the seat of courage.—*n.* **liv'erwort,** any plant of the Hepaticae, a class belonging to the same division as the mosses.—*adjs.* **liv'erish, liv'ery,** suffering from disordered liver: irritable. [O.E. *lifer*; Ger. *leber,* O.N. *lifr.*]

livery, *liv'ér-i, n.* (*orig.*) the distinctive dress worn by the household of a king or nobleman, so called because delivered or given at regular periods: uniform worn by men-servants: a dress peculiar to certain persons or things, as in the trade-guilds of London: any characteristic dress: maintenance at a certain rate, as horses *at livery.*—*adj.* **liv'eried,** clothed in livery.—*ns.* **liv'eryman,** a man who wears a livery: a freeman of the city of London; **liv'ery-stā'ble,** a stable where horses and vehicles are kept at livery and for hire. [Fr. *liverée*—*livrer,* to deliver—L. *līberāre,* to free.]

lives, *līvz, pl.* of **life.**

livid, *liv'id, adj.* discoloured: black and blue: of a lead colour: pale with emotion: (*coll.*) extremely angry.—*n.* **liv'idness.** [L. *līvidus*—*līvēre,* to be of a lead colour.]

living, *liv'ing, adj.* having life: active, lively: vital: flowing, not stagnant: exact (of a likeness).—*n.* means of subsistence: manner of life: a property: the benefice of a clergyman.—*n.* **living-wage,** a wage on which it is possible for a workman and his family to live decently.—**living language,** one still spoken as a mother-tongue; **living prefix,** one that can still be used freely to form new compound words (e.g. *re-,* again, afresh, *sub-,* under—in contrast to such prefixes as *ad-* and *con-*); **living rock, stone,** rock unquarried, in its natural location or its natural state.—**the living,** those alive; **the living theatre,** the live theatre. [**live,** vb.]

livre, *lē'vr, n.* an old French coin, superseded by the franc in 1795: an old French weight, about 1 lb. avoirdupois. [Fr.,—L. *lībra,* a pound.]

lixiviate, *liks-iv'i-āt, v.t.* to leach.—*n.* **lixiviā'tion.** [L. *lixīv(i)us,* made into lye—*lix,* ashes.]

lizard, *liz'árd, n.* an order of four-footed scaly reptiles. [Fr. *lézard*—L. *lacerta.*]

llama, *lä'mä, n.* a S. American ruminant of the camel family. [Sp., from native name.]

llano, *lyä'no* or *lä'no, n.* one of the vast steppes or plains in the northern part of South America:—*pl.* **lla'nos.** [Sp.,—L. *plānus,* plain.]

Lloyd's, *loidz, n.* a corporation whose individual members (underwriters) undertake, through brokers, shipping and other insurance.—**Lloyd's Register,** a list of ships classified according to type, size, seaworthiness, &c. (as A1, &c.). [From *Lloyd's* coffee-house, 17th-century meeting-place of merchants, to exchange shipping news, &c.]

Neutral vowels in unaccented syllables: *em'pér-ór;* for certain sounds in foreign words see p. ix.

loach, loche, *lōch, n.* any of several small river-fishes. [Fr. *loche,* Sp. *loja.*]

load, *lōd, n.* that which is carried: as much as can be carried at once: a freight or cargo: a burden: a weight or task sustained with difficulty: the output of an electrical machine, generating station, &c.: the power carried by a particular circuit.—*v.t.* to put a load on, in: to burden: to confer or give in great abundance: to weigh down, to oppress: to weight (as, *to load dice,* for the purpose of cheating): to charge, as a gun: to put film in (a camera): to add charges to (insurance): to adulterate (a drink) to increase strength.—*adj.* **loaded,** (*coll.*) rich, wealthy: (*coll.*) under the influence of drink or drugs: weighted in discussion in a certain direction: (*lit.* and *fig.*) containing elements that may become dangerous, as in **loaded question,** a question designed to make the unwilling answerer commit himself to some opinion, action or course.—*ns.* **load'ing,** the act of loading: a charge: a load: a cargo, lading; **load'ing-gauge,** a suspended bar that marks how high a railway truck may be loaded; **load'-line,** a line along the ship's side to mark the depth to which her proper cargo causes her to sink (see **Plimsoll('s) line, mark**).—**get a load of (this)** (*slang*), listen to, look at, pay attention to (this). [O.E. *lād, course,* journey, conveyance: meaning affected by the unrelated **lade.**]

loadstar, loadstone. See **lodestar, lodestone.**

loaf, *lōf, n.* a regularly shaped mass of bread: a conical mass of sugar: any lump:—*pl.* **loaves** (*lōvz*).—*n.* **loaf'-sug'ar,** refined sugar in the form of a cone, often formed into cubes. [O.E. *hlāf,* bread.]

loaf, *lōf, v.i.* to loiter, pass time idly.—*n.* **loaf'er.**

loam, *lōm, n.* earth for brick-making, &c., composed of clay and sand: a fertile soil, of clay, sand, and animal and vegetable matter.—*v.t.* to cover with loam.—*adj.* **loam'y.** [O.E. *lām;* Ger. *lehm;* allied to **lime** (1).]

loan, *lōn, n.* anything lent, esp. money at interest: the act of lending: permission to use.—*v.t.* (chiefly *U.S.*) to lend.—*n.* **loan'-office,** a public office at which loans are negotiated, a pawnbroker's shop. [O.N. *lān;* related to O.E. *lǣnan;* cf. **lend.**]

loath, loth, *lōth, adj.* reluctant, unwilling (to).—**nothing lo(a)th,** willing, willingly. [O.E. *lāth,* hateful.]

loathe, *lōTH, v.t.* to dislike greatly, to feel disgust at.—*n.* **loath'ing,** extreme hate or disgust, abhorrence.—*adjs.* **loath'ly** (*arch.*), **loath'some** (*th* or *TH*), exciting loathing or abhorrence, detestable.—*adv.* **loath'somely.**—*n.* **loath'someness.** [O.E. *lāthian—lāth.* See **loath.**]

loaves. See **loaf** (1).

lob, *lob, n.* something thick or heavy: in cricket, a slow high underhand ball: in tennis, a ball high overhead dropping near the back of the court.—*v.t.* to bowl or strike as a lob. [Allied to Du. *lob.*]

lobby, *lob'i, n.* a small hall or waiting-room: a passage serving as a common entrance to several apartments: a group of people who campaign to persuade legislators to make laws favouring their particular interests.—*v.i.* to frequent the lobby of a legislative chamber in order to influence members' votes or to gather political information.—*n.* **lobby'ist.** [Low L. *lobia*—Middle High Ger. *loube,* portico, arbour—*laub,* leaf.]

lobe, *lōb, n.* the soft lower part of the ear: a division of the lungs, brain, &c.: a division of a leaf.—*adjs.* **lob'ate, lobed,** having or consisting of lobes; **lob'ular,** shaped like a lobe. [Gr. *lobos,* lobe.]

lobelia, *lob-ē'li-a, n.* a large genus of garden plants, usually with blue flowers. [*Lobel,* a Flemish botanist.]

lobotomy, *lob-ot'ō-mi, n.* cutting off of certain fibres of the brain in order to relieve certain mental disorders, e.g. severe schizophrenia. [Gr. *lobos,* lobe, *tomē,* cut.]

lobscouse, *lob'skows, n.* a stew or hash with vegetables. [Origin uncertain.]

lobster, *lob'stér, n.* a shellfish with large claws, used for food—belonging to any of several genera. [O.E. *loppestre*—L. *locusta,* a lobster.]

lobworm, *lob'wûrm, n.* a lugworm. [**lob,** worm.]

local, *lō'kál, adj.* of or belonging to a place: confined to a spot or district.—*n.* (*coll.*) the local inn or public-house.—*n.* **locale** (-*kāl'*), the scene (of some event).—*v.t.* **lō'calise,** to assign to a place: to confine or restrict to a place or area.—*n.* **localisā'tion.**—*n.* **local'ity,** existence in a place: position: a district.—*adv.* **lō'cally.**—*v.t.* **locāte',** to place, to set in a particular position: to designate, or find, the place of.—*n.* **locā'tion,** act of locating: a claim or place marked off: situation: (*law*) a leasing on rent: (*cinema*) a site for filming outside the studio.—*adj.* **loc'ative,** pertaining to location.—*n.* (*gram.*) a case denoting 'place where'—**local authorities,** elected bodies for local government, e.g. county, district councils; **local colour,** details characteristic of time or place added to give verisimilitude; **local government,** self-administration (in local affairs) by counties (*Scot.* regions), &c., opp. to national or central govt.; **local option,** the right of a town or district to regulate liquor licences within its bounds; **local time,** the time of a place as shown by the sun.—**on location,** (*cinema*) on the exact place, in natural surroundings outside the studio. [L. *locālis—locus,* a place.]

loch, *loch, n.* a lake: an arm of the sea. [Gael. *loch.*]

Lochaber-axe, *loṇ-ā'ber-aks, n.* a long-handled Highland variety of halberd. [*Lochaber* district of Inverness-shire.]

lock, *lok, n.* a device to fasten doors, &c.: an enclosure in a canal for raising or lowering boats: an air-lock (q.v.): the part of a firearm by which the charge is exploded: a grapple in wrestling: a state of being immovable: a block, jam.—*v.t.* to fasten with a lock: to fasten so as to impede motion: to jam: to close fast: to embrace closely: to furnish with locks.—*v.i.* to become locked: to unite closely: the full extent of the turning arc of the front wheels of a motor vehicle.—*ns.* **lock'age,** the locks of a canal: the difference in their levels, the materials used for them, or the tolls paid for passing through them; **lock'er,** a small cupboard, for sports gear &c.; **lock'et,** a little ornamental case, usually containing a miniature, and hung from the neck.—*adj.* **lock′fast**, firmly fastened by locks.—*ns.* **lock′jaw**, a form of tetanus (q.v.) affecting the muscles of the jaw; **lock′-keep′er**, one who keeps or attends the locks of a canal; **lock′-out**, the act of locking out, esp. used of the closing of works by employers during a trade dispute; **lock′smith**, a smith who makes and mends locks; **lock′-stitch**, a stitch formed by the locking of two threads together; **lock′up**, a place for locking up prisoners, motor-cars, &c.—**lock, stock, and barrel**, completely. [O.E. *loc.*]

lock, *lok*, *n.* a tuft or ringlet of hair. [O.E. *locc*; O.N. *lokkr*, Ger. *locke*, a lock.]

locomotive, *lō-ko-mōt′iv*, *adj.* moving from place to place: capable of, or assisting in, locomotion.—*n.* a locomotive machine: a railway engine.—*ns.* **locomō′tion; locomotiv′ity.—locomotor ataxy**, a chronic degenerative disease of the nervous system, marked by lack of power to co-ordinate the muscles. [L. *locus*, a place, *movēre, mōtum*, to move.]

loculus, *lok′ū-lus*, *n.* (*bot., anat., zool.*) a small compartment or cell:—*pl.* **loc′ulī.**—*adj.* **loc′ulous.** [Dim. of L. *locus*, a place.]

locum (tenens), *lō′kum* (*tēn′-, ten′enz*), *n.* a deputy or substitute, esp. for a doctor or clergyman. [L. *locus*, a place, *tenēre*, to hold.]

locus, *lō′kus*, *n.* a place, locality: (*math.*) the line or surface constituted by all positions of a point or line satisfying a given condition:—*pl.* **loci** (*lō′sī*).—**locus classicus** (*klas′i-kus*), the passage in literature regarded as most authoritative (or most often quoted) in establishing the meaning of a word or the facts of a subject. [L. *locus*, place.]

locust, *lō′kust*, *n.* a family of insects akin to the grasshoppers, esp. certain migratory species very destructive to crops: the carob tree (because the beans of the tree resemble insects): any of several other trees of different genera.—*n.* **lō′cust-bean**, the sweet pod of the carob tree. [L. *locusta*, lobster, locust.]

locution, *lō-kū′sh(ō)n*, *n.* act or mode of speaking: word or phrase. [L. *locūtiō, -ōnis—loquī, locūtus*, to speak.]

lode, *lōd*, *n.* a vein containing metallic ore.—*ns.* **lode′star**, the star that guides, the polestar—often used figuratively; **lode′stone**, magnetic iron ore in the form in which it not only is attracted but also attracts. [O.E. *lād*, a course.]

lodge, *loj*, *n.* an abode, esp. if secluded, humble, small, or temporary: the meeting-place of a branch of some societies: the branch itself.—*v.t.* to furnish with a temporary dwelling: to deposit: to infix, to settle: to drive to covert: to lay flat, as grain: to deposit in the appropriate quarter a formal statement of (e.g. a complaint).—*v.i.* to reside: to rest: to dwell for a time: to become fixed (in).—*ns.* **lodg′er**, one who lodges or lives at board or in a hired room; **lodg′ing**, temporary habitation: a room or rooms hired in the house of another (often in *pl.*): harbour; **lodg(e)′ment**, act of lodging, or state of being lodged: accumulation of something that remains at rest: (*mil.*) the occupation of a position by a besieging party, and the works thrown up to maintain it. [O.Fr. *loge*—O.H.G. *lauba*, shelter.]

loess, *lœs, lō′es*, *n.* a loamy deposit in certain

river valleys—Rhine, Rhone, Mississippi, &c. [Ger. *löss.*]

loft, *loft*, *n.* a room or space immediately under a roof: a gallery in a hall or church: slope on a golf-club face.—*v.t.* to cause to rise into the air.—*adj.* **loft′y**, very high in position, character, sentiment, or diction: stately, haughty.—*adv.* **loft′ily.**—*n.* **loft′iness.** [Late O.E. *loft*—O.N. *lopt*, the sky, an upper room; O.E. *lyft*, Ger. *luft*, the air.]

log, *log*, *n.* a thick piece of unshaped wood, esp. a tree trunk or part of one: (*fig.*) an inert or insensitive person: an apparatus, originally a block of wood, for ascertaining a ship's speed: a log-book.—*v.t.* to cut or haul in the form of logs: to record in a log-book.—*ns.* **log′-book** or **log**, an official record of a ship's or aircraft's progress and proceedings on board: similar record kept by headmaster of a school: a traveller's diary of his journey; **log′-cab′in, -house, -hut**, a cabin or hut built of logs; **log-canoe**, a boat made by hollowing out the trunk of a tree; **logg′erhead**, a blockhead, a dunce: (*naut.*) a round piece of timber, in a whaleboat, over which the line is passed: a species of sea-turtle; **log′-line**, the line fastened to the log and marked for finding the speed of a vessel; **log′-roll′ing**, act or process of rolling logs: (used opprobriously) mutual aid among politicians or others; **log′wood**, a tropical American tree whose dark-red wood is much used in dyeing.—**at loggerheads**, at variance.

log, *log*, abbrev. for **logarithm**.

loganberry, *lō′gan-ber-i*, *n.* a fruit usually considered to be a hybrid between raspberry and blackberry, obtained by Judge *Logan*.

logarithm, *log′a-rithm, -ri*ᴛʜᴍ, *n.* the power to which a base (10 in *common logarithms, e* in *natural*, or *hyperbolic, logarithms*) must be raised to produce a given number; e.g. the common logarithm of 50 to the base 10 (written $\log_{10}50$, or more usually log 50) is 1.69897 because $50 = (10)^{1.69897}$; the natural logarithm of 50 is 3.91202 because $50 = e(= 2.71828)^{3.91202}$.—*adjs.* **logarith′mic, -al**, pertaining to, or consisting of, logarithms: based on a system of logarithms.—*adv.* **logarith′mically.** [Gr. *logos*, ratio, *arithmos*, number.]

loggia, *lōj′a, lōj′ya*, *n.* an open arcade, gallery, or balcony, common in Italy. [It.]

logia, *log′i-a, n.pl.* sayings, esp. early collections of those attributed to Jesus:—*sing.* **logion.** [Gr.]

logic, *loj′ik*, *n.* the science and art of reasoning correctly: a treatise on this: train of reasoning: soundness, correctness of reasoning: basis of operation as designed and effected in a computer, comprising **logical elements**, which perform specified elementary arithmetical functions.—*adj.* **log′ical**, according to the rules of logic: skilled in logic: discriminating.—*adv.* **log′ically.**—*n.* **logic′ian**, one skilled in logic. [Gr. *logikē* (*technē*), logical (art)—*logos*, word, reason.]

logistic, -al, *loj-is′tik, -ál, adj.* pertaining to reasoning or logic: pertaining to reckoning or calculation. [Gr. *logistikos—logizesthai*, to compute.]

Neutral vowels in unaccented syllables: *em′pér-ôr*; for certain sounds in foreign words see p. ix.

logistics, *loj-is′tiks, n.* the branch of military art concerned with transport, housing, and supply of troops. [Fr. *logistique*—*loger,* to quarter.]

logogram, *log′o-gram, n.* a single sign for a word: a riddle. [Gr. *logos,* word, *gramma,* letter.]

logography, *log-og′ra-fi, n.* a method of printing with whole words cast in a single type. [Gr. *logos,* word, *graphein,* to write.]

logomachy, *lo-gom′a-ki, n.* contention about words or in words merely. [Gr. *logomachia*—*logos,* word, *machē,* fight.]

logos, *log′os, n.* the Word of God incarnate. [Gr.]

-logy, *-lo-ji, suffix.* indicating science, theory: discourse, treatise. [Gr. *logos,* word, reason.]

loin, *loin, n.* the back of a beast cut for food: (*pl.*) the reins, or the lower part of the back.—*n.* **loin′cloth,** a piece of cloth worn round the loins, esp. in India and south-east Asia.—**gird up the loins,** to prepare for energetic action. [O.Fr. *loigne*—L. *lumbus,* loin.]

loiter, *loi′tér, v.i.* to proceed slowly: to dawdle.—*n.* **loi′terer.** [Du. *leuteren,* to dawdle; Ger. dial. *lottern,* to waver.]

loll, *lol, v.i.* to lie lazily about, to lounge: to hang down or out (now mainly of the tongue).—*v.t.* let hang out. [Perh. imit.; cf. Du. *lollen,* to sit over the fire.]

Lollard, *lol′ärd, n.* a follower of Wycliffe, a religious reformer in the 14th century. [Middle Du. *lollaerd,* droner—*lollen,* to mumble; but influenced by **loll.**]

lollipop, *lol′i-pop, n.* a large sweetmeat impaled on a stick: any sweetmeat.—**lollipop man, woman,** a person appointed to conduct children across a busy street (so called because of the pole with a disk on the end carried by him). [Perh. Northern dial. *lolly,* tongue.]

lolly, *lol′i, n.* coll. abbrev. for lollipop. (*slang*) money.

Lombard Street, *lom′bärd strēt,* the chief centre of the banking interest in London, so called because Italian traders from *Lombardy* established the business of money-lending here in the 13th century. [O.Fr.,—Low L. *Langobardus;* ety. uncertain.]

Londoner, *lun′dón-ér, n.* a native or citizen of *London.*—**London clay,** a formation in the lowest division of the Eocene in south-eastern England; **London pride,** a hardy perennial—also *none-so-pretty* (usu. in the corrupted form *Nancy Pretty*) and *St. Patrick's cabbage.*

lone, *lōn, adj.* isolated: solitary: unfrequented, uninhabited: unmarried or widowed.—*n.* **loner,** a lone wolf.—*adj.* **lone′some,** solitary: dismal, or depressed, because of solitariness.—*adv.* **lone′somely.**—*n.* **lone′someness.**—**lone wolf,** one who prefers to act on his own and does not have close friends. [**alone,** the form used predicatively.]

lonely, *lōn′li, adj.* unaccompanied: isolated: uninhabited, unfrequented: uncomfortably conscious of being alone. [**alone.**]

long, *long, adj.* (*comp.* **longer** [*long′gér*]: *superl.* **longest** [*long′gest*]) extended in space or time: not short: (radio waves) of wavelength over 1000 metres: slow (in coming): tedious: far-reaching: (*pros.,* of accentual verse, *loosely*)

accented.—*adv.* to a great extent of time: through the whole time (as, *all day long*).—*v.i.* to desire earnestly.—*adv.* **long′-agō′,** in the far past.—*ns.* **long′boat,** the largest and strongest boat of a ship; **long′bow,** a great bow drawn by hand (cf. **crossbow**).—*n.pl. pl.* **long′-clothes,** a baby's first dress.—*adjs.* **long′-drawn (out),** prolonged (in time); **longevous** (*-jē′-*), of great age, long-lived.—*ns.* **longevity** (*-jev′-*); **long-hair,** a highbrow (also *adj.*).—*adj.* **long′-haired** (*fig.*), highbrow.—*n.* **long′hand,** writing of the ordinary kind, as opposed to shorthand.—*adj.* **long′-head′ed,** far-seeing, shrewd: dolichocephalic.—*n.* **long′ing,** an eager desire, craving.—*adj.* yearning.—*adv.* **long′ingly.**—*ns.* **long′-leg** (*cricket*), a position in leg (q.v.) distant from the wicket; **long′-meas′ure,** lineal measure.—*adjs.* **long′-playing,** of a gramophone record, giving length in reproduction because of the extremely fine groove; **long′-range,** able to reach or hit from a considerable distance: covering a long future time.—*n.* **long′shoreman,** a stevedore: a man employed along the shore.—*adj.* **long′-sight′ed,** able to see far but not close at hand: having foresight.—*n.* **long′-sight (cdness).**—*adj.* **long′-sta′ple,** having a long fibre.—*n.* **long′-stop** (*cricket*), one who stands behind the wicket-keeper and tries to stop balls missed by him.—*adj.* **long′-suff′ering,** enduring much and patiently.—*n.* long endurance or patience.—*adjs.* **long′-term,** extending over a long time: of a policy, concerned with time ahead as distinct from the immediate present; **long′-tongued,** talkative; **long′-wave** (*radio*), of, or using wavelengths over 1000 metres; **long′-wind′ed,** long-breathed, having ability to run far without rest: of speaker or of speech, tediously long.—**long home,** the grave; **long odds,** in betting, unfavourable odds; **long shot,** (a bet, venture, &c., with) a remote chance of success.—**before long, ere long,** soon; **draw the longbow, long bow,** to exaggerate, make extravagant statements; **in the long run,** ultimately, in the end; **the long and the short,** the sum and substance. [O.E. *lang;* Ger. *lang,* O.N. *langr.*]

longitude, *lon′ji-tūd, n.* length: arc of the equator between the meridian of a place and a standard meridian (usually that of Greenwich) expressed in degrees E. or W.: (*astron.*) the arc of the ecliptic between a star's circle of latitude and the vernal equinox.—*adj.* **longitud′inal.**—*adv.* **longitud′inally.** [L. *longitūdō, -inis,* length—*longus,* long.]

longueur, *l3̄-gœr, n.* a wearisome passage in a play, novel, &c. [Fr., length, slowness.]

loo, *lōō, n.* a card game.—*v.t.* to beat at loo:—*pr.p.* lōō′ing; *pa.p.* lōōed. [Formerly *lan-terloo*—Du. *lanterlu.*]

loo, *lōō, n.* (*slang*) a lavatory.

loofa, loofah. See **luffa.**

look, *lōōk, v.i.* to direct the sight with attention: to gaze: to seem: to face, as a house.—*v.t.* to express by a look: to give (a look): (*fig.*—often with *at, into* &c.) to pay attention to, to consider: (with *neg.*) to reject (e.g. *he would not look at the proposal*): to take care (that).—*n.* the act of looking or seeing: sight: air (e.g. *look of scorn*): appearance.—*imp.* or *interj.*

loom

see, behold.—*ns.* **look′er,** one who looks; **look′er-on,** a mere spectator; **look′ing-for** (*B.*), expectation; **look′ing-glass,** a glass mirror; **look′out,** a careful watch: a place from which to observe: one engaged in watching: prospect: concern (e.g. *that's your lookout*). —**look after,** to attend to or take care of; **look down on,** to despise; **look for,** to search for: to expect: **look forward,** to anticipate with pleasure; **look in** (*coll.*), to make a short call: to watch television; **look into,** to inspect closely; **look on,** to be a spectator: to regard, view (as): **look out,** to watch: to search for or select: (*imper.,* an *interj.* of warning), beware! **look over,** to examine cursorily: to overlook or pass over; **look sharp** (see **sharp**); **look to,** to take care of: to turn to with expectation: to expect; **look up,** to improve: to pay a visit to (a person): to search for in a book of reference; **look up to,** to venerate. [O.N. *lōcian,* to look.]

loom, *lōōm, n.* a machine in which yarn or thread is woven into a fabric: the handle of an oar, or the part within the rowlock. [O.E. *gelōma,* a tool.]

loom, *lōōm, v.i.* to appear indistinctly or as in a mirage, often with a suggestion of exaggerated size or of menacing quality (*lit.* and *fig.*): to take shape, as an impending event.

loon, *lōōn, n.* a low fellow: a rascal: (*Scot.*) a lad.

loon, *lōōn,* **loom,** *lōōm, ns.* the diver, any of several species of a genus of fish-eating diving-birds. [O.N. *lomr.*]

loop, *lōōp, n.* a doubling of a cord, chain, &c., through which another cord, &c., may pass: a U-shaped bend (e.g. in a river): an ornamental doubling in fringes.—*v.t.* to fasten, encircle, or ornament with loops: to form into a loop or loops.—*n.pl.* **loop′ers,** the caterpillars of certain moths, which move by drawing up the hindpart of their body to the head.—*n.* **loop′line,** a branch of a railway that returns to the main line.—*adj.* **loop′y,** having loops: (*slang*) slightly crazy.—**loop the loop,** to move in a complete vertical loop or circle.

loop, *lōōp,* **loophole,** *lōōp′hōl, ns.* a slit in a wall &c.: a means of escape or evasion.—*adj.* **loop′holed.** [Perh. Middle Du. *lûpen,* to peer.]

loose, *lōōs, adj.* slack: unbound: not confined: free: not compact: indefinite, vague: not strict in form or logic: unrestrained: licentious.—*v.t.* to unfasten: to untie: to release: to relax.—*v.i.* (*B.*) to set sail.—*adv.* **loose′ly.**—*v.t.* **loos′en,** to make loose: to relax: to open, as the bowels.—*v.i.* to become loose: to become less tight.—*n.* **loose′ness.**—**loose box,** a part of a stable where horses are kept untied.—**break loose,** to escape from confinement; **let loose,** to set at liberty; **on the loose,** going about without definite purpose: on a bout of dissipation. [O.N. *lauss;* O.E. *lēas.*]

loot, *lōōt, n.* plunder: (*slang*) money.—*v.t.* or *v.i.* to plunder, ransack. [Hindi (q.v.) *lūt.*]

lop, *lop, v.i.* to hang down loosely.—*adjs.* **lop′-eared,** having drooping ears; **lop′-sīd′ed,** ill-balanced. [Perh. conn. with **lob.**]

lop, *lop, v.t.* to cut off the top or ends of, esp. of a tree: to curtail by cutting away superfluous parts:—*pr.p.* **lopp′ing;** *pa.t.* and *pa.p.* **lopped.**—*n.* twigs of trees cut off. [O.E. *loppian.*]

lope, *lōp, v.i.* to run with a long stride. [O.N.

lose

hlaupa; allied to **leap.**]

loquacious, *lo-kwā′shus, adj.* talkative.—*adv.* **loquā′ciously.**—*ns.* **loquā′ciousness, loquac′ity** (*-kwas′-*), talkativeness. [L. *loquax, -ācis—loquī,* to speak.]

loran, *lō′-, lō′ran, n.* long-range aid to navigation (a form of radar). [From the initial letters.]

lorcha, *lör′cha, n.* a light vessel of European build, but rigged like a Chinese junk. [Port.]

lord, *lörd, n.* a master: a superior: a husband: a ruler: the proprietor of a manor: a baron: a peer of the realm: the son of a duke or marquis, or the eldest son of an earl: a bishop, esp. if a member of the House of Lords: (*cap.*) used as part of various official titles, as **Lord Mayor, Lord Provost:** (*cap.*) God, Christ.—*v.i.* to act the lord: to tyrannise.—*n.* a little lord: a would-be lord.—*adj.* **lord′ly,** like, becoming, or pertaining to a lord: dignified: haughty: tyrannical: grand.—Also *adv.*—*ns.* **lord′liness; Lord's′-day** the first day of the week; **lord′ship,** state or condition of being a lord: the territory belonging to a lord: dominion, authority.—**Lords of Session,** the judges of the Scottish Court of Session; **lords spiritual,** the archbishops and bishops in the House of Lords—opp. to **lords temporal,** the peers proper; **Lord's Supper,** (sacrament in commemoration of) the last supper of Jesus with his disciples.—**House of Lords,** the upper house in the British parliament. [M.E. *loverd, laverd*—O.E. *hlāford*—*hlāf,* bread, *weard,* guardian.]

lore, *lōr, lör, n.* that which is learned: knowledge: the whole body of knowledge on a subject (esp. traditional, and therefore often containing elements not based on scientific fact). [O.E. *lār.*]

lorgnette, *lörn-yet′, n.* eye-glasses with a handle: an opera-glass. [Fr. *lorgner,* to look sidelong at, to ogle.]

lorica, *lō-rī′ka, n.* a leather corslet: the case of a protozoan:—*pl.* **loricae** (*-sē*).—*v.t.* **lor′icāte,** to furnish with a protective covering.—*adj.* covered with armour: of the nature of a lorica.—*n.* **loricā′tion.** [L. *lōrīca*—*lōrum,* a thong.]

lorn, *lörn, adj.* (*arch.*) lost: forsaken. [O.E. *loren,* pa.p. of *lēosan,* to lose.]

lorry, *lor′i, n.* a road wagon without sides, or with low sides: any large haulage vehicle.

lory, *lō′ri, n.* any of a number of parrots, natives of New Guinea, Australia, &c. [Malay, *luri.*]

lose, *lōōz, v.t.* to be deprived of (e.g. by death or accident): to cease to have: to cease to hear, see or understand: to mislay: to waste, as time: to miss (e.g. *to lose one's way*): to cause to perish (now usu. in passive): to fail to gain—opp. of *win* (a game, prize).—*v.i.* to be unsuccessful: to suffer deprivation, decrease, depreciation, &c.: of a clock or watch, to go too slowly:—*pr.p.* **los′ing;** *pa.t.* and *pa.p.* **lost.**—*adj.* **los′able.**—*n.* **los′er.**—*adj.* and *n.* **los′ing.**—*n.* **loss** (*los*), the act of losing: injury: destruction: defeat: that which is lost: waste.—*adj.* **lost** (*lost*), parted with: no longer possessed: missing: thrown away: squandered: ruined: (*lit.* and *fig.*) unable to find the way.—**lose oneself,** to lose one's way: to become engrossed (in); **lose out** (*coll.*), to suffer loss or

Neutral vowels in unaccented syllables: *em′pér-ŏr;* for certain sounds in foreign words see p. ix.

428

disadvantage; **lost to,** insensible to.—**a losing fight, game,** &c., one in which defeat is certain; **at a loss,** in uncertainty. [O.E. *losian,* usually impersonal, to be a loss.]

lot, *lot, n.* an object drawn from among a number to reach a decision by chance: that which falls to anyone as his fortune: a separate portion: a large quantity or number (*coll.* usually in *pl.* e.g. *lots of people*).—*v.t.* to allot: to separate into lots:—*pr.p.* lott'ing; *pa.p.* lott'ed. [O.E. *hlot,* a lot—*hlēotan,* to cast lots.]

loth, *lōth, adj.* Same as **loath.**

Lothario, *lō-thā'ri-ō, n.* a libertine, rake. [From *Lothario,* in Rowe's play, *The Fair Penitent* (1703).]

lotion, *lō'sh(ó)n, n.* a liquid preparation, medicinal or cosmetic. [L. *lōtiō, -ōnis—lavāre, lōtum,* to wash.]

lottery, *lot'ér-i, n.* a distribution of prizes by lot: a game of chance (also *fig.*). [It. *lotteria,* of Gmc. origin; allied to **lot.**]

lotus, *lō'tus, n.* either of two African water-lilies; an ornament in Egyptian art probably suggested by these: a genus of plants of the pea family, popularly known as *bird's-foot trefoil,* used as fodder: in Greek legend, a tree of North Africa whose fruit induced in the eater a state of blissful indolence and forgetfulness. Also **lote, lō'tos.**—*n.* **lō'tus-eat'er,** an eater of the lotus: one given up to sloth. [L.—Gr. *lōtos.*]

louche, *lōōsh, adj.* squinting: ambiguous: shady, suspicious. [Fr.]

loud, *lowd, adj.* making a great sound: noisy: showy, untastefully conspicuous.—*advs.* **loud, loud'ly.**—*ns.* **loud'ness; loud'-speak'er,** an electro-acoustic device which produces sound from an electrical signal. [O.E. *hlūd;* Ger *laut;* L. *inclytus,* renowned, Gr. *klytos,* heard.]

lough, *loh, n.* the Irish form of **loch.**

louis d'or, *lōō'i dör, n.* a French gold coin superseded in 1795 by the 20-franc piece. [Fr.]

lounge, *lownj, v.i.* to loll: to move about listlessly.—*n.* the act or state of lounging: an idle stroll: a room in a public building for sitting or waiting, often providing refreshment facilities: a sitting-room in a private house: a kind of sofa.—*n.* **loung'er,** one who habitually lounges, an idler.—**lounge suit,** an ordinary informal suit for a man.

lour, lower, *lowr, low'ér, v.i.* to look sullen or threatening: to scowl.—*adj.* **lour'ing, low'ering.**—*adv.* **lour'ingly, low'eringly.** [M.E. *louren;* cf. Du. *loeren.*]

louse, *lows, n.* an order of wingless insects parasitic on men and animals: any of various other small parasites on animals and plants:—*pl.* **lice** (*līs*).—*adj.* **lousy** (*low'zi*), swarming with lice: (*slang*) of very poor quality, arousing contempt or strong disapproval.—*n.* **lous'iness.** [O.E. *lūs,* pl. *lȳs;* Ger. *laus.*]

lout, *lowt, n.* a clown: an awkward fellow.—*adj.* **lout'ish,** clownish: awkward and clumsy.—*adv.* **lout'ishly.**—*n.* **lout'ishness.** [O.E. *lūtan,* to stoop.]

louver, louvre, *lōō'vér, n.* a turret-like structure on a roof for escape of smoke or for ventilation: a ventilator in a car bonnet, &c.—*n.* **lou'vre-win'dow,** an open window crossed by a series of sloping boards. [O.Fr. *lover, lovier;*

origin obscure.]

love, *luv, n.* fondness: an affection of the mind caused by that which delights: pre-eminent kindness: benevolence: reverential regard: devoted attachment to one of the opposite sex: the object of affection: (*cap.*) the god of love, Cupid: a score of nothing, in billiards, tennis, and some other games.—*v.t.* to be fond of: to regard with affection: to delight in with exclusive affection: to regard with benevolence.—*v.i.* to have the feeling of love.—*adj.* **lov'able,** worthy of love.—*ns.* **love'-affair,** love and love-making not typically ending in marriage (including an *amour*); **love'-app'le,** the fruit of the tomato; **love'-bird,** any of a large number of small parrots, strongly attached to their mates; **love'-feast,** the agape (q.v.) of the early Christians, or a religious feast held periodically in imitation of it; **love'-in-ī'dleness,** the heartsease; **love'-knot,** an intricate knot, used as a token of love.—*adj.* **love'less,** without love.—*ns.* **love'-lett'er,** a letter of courtship, **love'lessness, love'lock,** a lock of hair hanging at the ear, worn by men of fashion in the reigns of Elizabeth and James I.—*adjs.* **love'lorn,** forsaken by one's love; **love'ly,** exciting love or admiration: beautiful: (*coll.*) delightful in any way, including 'amusing'.—*ns.* **love'liness; love'match,** a marriage for love; **lov'er,** one who loves, esp. one in love with a person of the opposite sex (in the singular, usually of the man)—sometimes used in a bad sense: one who is fond (of anything): (*B.*) a friend.—*adj.* **love'-sick,** languishing with amorous desire.—*n.* **love'to'ken,** a gift in evidence of love.—*adj.* **lov'ing,** affectionate, fond: expressing love.—*ns.* **lov'ing-cup,** a cup passed round at the end of a feast for all to drink from; **lov'ing-kind'ness,** kindness full of love, mercy, favour.—*adv.* **lov'ingly.**—*n.* **lov'ingness.—for love or money,** in any way whatever; **in love,** enamoured; **make love to,** to try to gain the affections of, to court: to caress amorously: to have sexual intercourse with. [O.E. *lufu,* love; Ger. *liebe;* cf. L. *libet, lubet,* it pleases.]

low, *lō, v.i.* to make the noise of oxen.—*n.* the sound made by oxen. [O.E. *hlōwan,* Du. *loeien.*]

low, *lō, adj.* (*comp.* **low'er;** *superl.* **low'est**) lying in an inferior place or position: not high: grave in pitch: not loud: small: moderate: cheap: dejected: mean (e.g. of a dwelling): plain (of diet): vulgar, coarse, indecent: (*arch.*) meek, humble: (of latitude) near the equator.—*adv.* in or to a low position, state, or manner: not loudly.—*ns.* **low'-brow,** one whose tastes are not intellectual (also *adj.*)—opp. of *high-brow;* **Low Church,** a party within the Church of England setting little value on sacerdotal claims, ecclesiastical constitutions, ordinances, and forms, holding evangelical views of theology—opp. to *High Church;* **low comedy,** comedy approaching farce: comedy with characters or incidents from low life.—*v.t.* **low'er,** to make lower: to let down: to lessen.—*v.i.* to become lower or less.—*adj.* **low'er-case** (*print.*), kept in a lower case, denoting small letters as distinguished from capitals; **low'ermost, lowest.**—*ns.* **low'-gear** (see **gear**); **low'land,** land low with respect to

higher land; **low′lander**, a native of low-
lands.—*adj.* **low′ly**, humble in rank: modest in
character, demeanour.—*ns.* **low′liness**; **low′-
ness.**—*adjs.* **low′-paid′**, (of worker) receiving,
(of job) rewarded by, low wages; **low′-
press′ure**, employing or exerting a low degree
of pressure (e.g. less than 50 lbf per sq. in.,
of steam and steam-engines): at low atmospheric pressure (e.g. an area); **low′-spir′ited**,
in low spirits, not lively, sad.—*ns.* **low
tide, water** (*adjs.* **low′-tide, -wat′er**), the lowest point of the tide at ebb: also *fig.*; **low′-
wat′er mark**, a mark showing this: (*fig.*) the
lowest point reached with regard to quantity,
number, condition, &c.—**Low German** (see
German); **Low Latin** (see **Latin**); **low mass**
(see **mass**); **Low Sunday**, the first Sunday
after Easter; **lower deck**, the (quarters of)
petty officers and men; **Lower House**, the
larger and more representative branch of a
legislature having two chambers; **lower mast**
(see **mast**).—**low temperature physics**, study
of physical phenomena at temperatures approaching absolute zero—also **cryogenics.—the low-down on**, (*U.S. slang*) inside
information, esp. damaging revelations, about
(a person, organisation, activity). [O.N. *lāgr*,
Du. *laag*, low; allied to O.E. *licgan*, to lie.]

lower. See **lour.**

lower, *lō′ér, v.t.* See **low** (2).

loyal, *loi′ál, adj.* faithful: firm in allegiance, esp.
to a sovereign.—*n.* **loy′alist**, a loyal adherent
of his sovereign, esp. in English history, a
partisan of the Stuarts: in the American War
of Independence, one who sided with the
British.—*adv.* **loy′ally.**—*n.* **loy′alty.** [Fr.,—L.
lēgālis—lex, lēgis, law.]

lox, *loks, n. l*iquid *ox*ygen, one component of
rocket propellant.

lozenge, *loz′énj, n.* a diamond-shaped parallelogram or rhombus: a small sweetmeat, originally diamond-shaped: (*her.*) the diamond-
shaped figure in which the arms of maids,
widows, and deceased persons are borne. [Fr.
losange; of unknown origin.]

LSD. See under **lysis.**

lubber, *lub′ér,* **lubbard,** *lub′árd, n.* an awkward,
clumsy fellow: a lazy, sturdy fellow.—*adj.* and
adv. **lubb′erly.** [Origin doubtful.]

lubricate, *l(y)ōō′bri-kāt, v.t.* to make smooth or
slippery: to oil.—*ns.* **lu′bricant; lubrica′tion;
lū′bricator; lubricity** (*lū-bris′i-ti*), slipperi-
ness: smoothness: instability: lewdness. [L.
lūbricāre, -ātum—lūbricus, slippery.]

luce, *l(y)ōōs, n.* a fresh-water fish, the pike.
[O.Fr. *lus*—Low L. *lūcius.*]

lucent, *l(y)ōō′sént, adj.* shining: bright.—*n.*
lū′cency, brightness.—*adj.* **lucer′nal,** pertaining to a lamp. [L. *lūcens, -entis,* pr.p. of *lūcēre,*
to shine—*lux, lūcis,* light.]

lucerne, *l(y)ōō′sérn, n.* a valuable forage-plant,
alfalfa. [Fr. *luzerne.*]

lucid, *l(y)ōō′sid, adj.* shining: transparent: easily understood: intellectually bright: not
darkened with madness.—*ns.* **lucid′ity, lu′cid-
ness.**—*adv.* **lu′cidly.—lucid intervals,** times of
sanity in madness, of quietness in fever, politics, &c. [L. *lūcidus—lux, lūcis,* light.]

Lucifer, *l(y)ōō′si-fér, n.* the planet Venus as
morning-star: Satan: a match of wood tipped

with a combustible substance ignited by friction. [L. *lūcifer,* light-bringer—*lux, lūcis,* light,
ferre, to bring.]

luck, *luk, n.* fortune, good or bad: chance: good
fortune.—*adj.* **luck′less,** without good luck,
unfortunate.—*adv.* **luck′lessly.**—*n.* **luck′less-
ness.**—*adj.* **luck′y,** having good luck: auspicious.—*adv.* **luck′ily.**—*n.* **luck′iness.—be
down on one's luck,** to be undergoing a period
of misfortune: to be depressed by misfortune;
push one's luck (*coll.*), to try to make too
much of an advantage, risking total failure.
[Low Ger. or Du. *luk*; cf. Ger. *glück,* prosperity.]

lucre, *l(y)ōō′kér, n.* gain (esp. sordid), riches.
—*adj.* **lu′crative,** bringing gain, profitable.
—*adv.* **lu′cratively.** [L. *lucrum,* gain.]

lucubrate, *lōō′kū-brāt,* or *lū′-, v.i.* to study by
lamplight or at night.—*n.* **lucubra′tion,** a product of protracted study or thought (usu. derogatory).—*adj.* **lu′cubratory.** [L. *lūcubrāre,
-ātum—lux,* light.]

luculent, *lōō′kū-lent,* or *lū′-, adj.* bright, clear,
transparent: evident.—*adv.* **lu′culently.** [L.
lūculentus—lux, light.]

ludicrous, *l(y)ōō′dik-rús, adj.* absurd, laugh-
able.—*adv.* **lu′dicrously.**—*n.* **lu′dicrousness.** [L.
lūdicrus—lūdĕre, to play.]

ludo, *lōō′dō, n.* a parlour game played with counters on a board marked with squares. [L., I
play.]

luff, *luf, n.* the windward side of a ship: the act
of sailing a ship close to the wind.—*v.t.* to turn
a ship towards the wind. [Origin obscure.]

luffa, *luf′a, n.* a genus of the gourd and melon
family: the fibrous network of its fruit, used
as a flesh-brush.—Also **loof′a, loof′ah.** [Ar.]

luftwaffe, *lōōft′vaf-e, n.* the German air force.
[Ger.—*luft,* air, *waffe,* weapon.]

lug, *lug, v.t.* to pull along, to drag heavily:—*pr.p.*
lugg′ing; *pa.t.* and *pa.p.* **lugged.**—*n.* **lugg′age,**
the trunks and other baggage of a traveller.
[Swed. *lugga,* to pull by the hair—*lugg,* the
forelock.]

lug, lug, lugsail, *lug′sāl, lug′sl, ns.* a square sail
bent upon a yard that hangs obliquely to the
mast.—*n.* **lugg′er,** a small vessel with lugsails.

lug, *lug, n.* (chiefly *Scot.*) the ear: an earlike
projection or appendage: a handle. [Perh.
conn. with **lug** (1).]

lugubrious, *l(y)ōō-gū′bri-us, adj.* mournful, dismal, esp. when the melancholy expressed is
excessive or insincere.—*adv.* **lugu′briously.** [L.
lūgubris—lūgēre, to mourn.]

lugworm, *lug′wûrm, n.* any of several worms
found in the sand on the seashore, used for
bait by fishermen.—Also **lob′worm.**

lukewarm, *lōōk′wórm, adj.* partially or moderately warm: indifferent, not ardent (e.g. of
interest, supporters).—*adv.* **luke′warmly.**—*n.*
luke′warmness. [M.E. *leuk, luke*; cf. Du. *leuk.*]

lull, *lul, v.t.* to soothe, to quiet.—*v.i.* to become
calm, to subside.—*n.* a season, interval, of
calm.—*n.* **lull′aby** (*-bī*), a song to lull children
to sleep. [Swed. *lulla.*]

lumbago, *lum-bā′gō, n.* a rheumatic pain in the
loins and small of the back.—*adj.* **lum′bar,**
pertaining to, or near, the loins.—*n.* a lumbar
vertebra, nerve, &c. [L.,—*lumbus,* loin.]

lumber, *lum′bér, n.* anything cumbersome or

Neutral vowels in unaccented syllables: *em′pér-ór*; for certain sounds see in foreign words see p. ix.

useless: timber sawed or split for use.—*v.t.* to fill with lumber: to heap together in confusion.—*ns.* **lum′berer, lum′ber-jack, lum′berman,** one employed in **lum′bering,** the felling, sawing, and removal of timber. [Perh. from **lumber** (2).]

lumber, *lum′bér, v.i.* to move heavily and clumsily. [M.E. *lomeren*; cf. dial. Swed. *lomra,* to resound.]

lumen, *l(y)ōō′mén, n.* SI unit of luminous flux, one candela per steradian. [L. *lumen, -inis,* light.]

luminary, *l(y)ōō′min-ar-i, n.* a source of light, esp. one of the heavenly bodies: one who illuminates any subject or instructs mankind.—*n.* **lumines′cence** (*-es′éns*), the emission of light as a result of causes other than high temperature.—*adj.* **lumines′cent.**—*adjs.* **luminif′erous,** transmitting light; **lū′minous,** giving light: shining: illuminated: clear, lucid.—*adv.* **lū′minously.**—*ns.* **lū′minousness, luminos′ity.** [L. *lūmen, -inis,* light—*lucēre,* to shine.]

lump, *lump, n.* a small shapeless mass: a protuberance, swelling: the whole together, the gross.—*v.t.* to throw into a confused mass: to treat as all alike (with *together*): (*coll.*) to put up with (e.g. *to lump it*).—*v.i.* to form into lumps.—*ns.* **lump′er,** a labourer employed in the loading or unloading of ships; **lump′fish,** a clumsy sea-fish with a short, deep, thick body and head.—Also called **lump′sucker,** from the power of its sucker.—*adjs.* **lump′ing,** in a lump: heavy: bulky; **lump′ish,** like a lump: heavy: gross: dull.—*adv.* **lump′ishly.**—*ns.* **lump′ishness; lump′-sug′ar,** loaf-sugar in small pieces.—*adj.* **lump′y,** full of lumps. [Origin doubtful: found in various Gmc. languages.]

lunar, *lū′når, lōō′når, adj.* belonging to or referring to the moon: measured by the moon's revolutions: caused by the moon: like the moon.—Also **lu′nary.**—*ns.* **lu′nacy,** a kind of madness, once believed to come with changes of the moon: insanity.—*adjs.* **lū′nāte, -d,** crescent-shaped; **lū′natic,** affected with lunacy.—*n.* a person so affected, a madman.—*n.* **lunā′tion,** the period between one new moon and the next, a lunar month.—**lunar caustic,** fused crystals of nitrate of silver, applied to ulcers, &c.; **lunar cycle,** metonic (q.v.) cycle; **lunatic fringe,** the more extreme or eccentric in belief or action among the members of a community, party, &c.—**Lunar Excursion Module,** module for use in the last stage of the journey to land on the moon. [L. *lunaris—luna,* the moon—*lūcēre,* to shine.]

lunatic. See **lunar.**

lunch, *lunch,* or *-sh, n,* a repast, usu. slight, between breakfast and dinner: mid-day meal.—*v.i.* to take lunch.—*n.* **luncheon** (*lunch′ón, lunsh′ón*), lunch.—**luncheon voucher,** a ticket or voucher given by employer to employee to be used to pay for the latter's lunch. [Perh. altered from **lump;** or from Sp. *lonja,* a slice of ham.]

lune, *l(y)ōōn, n.* anything in the shape of a half-moon.—*n.* **lunette′,** a little moon: (*fort.*) a detached bastion: a hole in a concave ceiling to admit light: a watch-glass flattened more

than usual in the centre. [Fr. *lune*—L. *lūna.*]

lung, *lung, n.* one of the organs of breathing, either of two vascular sacs filled with constantly renewed air.—*adj.* **lunged.** [O.E. *lungen.*]

lunge, *lunj, n.* a sudden thrust, as in fencing.—*v.i.* to make such a thrust. [Fr. *allonger,* to lengthen—L. *ad,* to, *longus,* long.]

lupin, lupine, *lōō′pin, n,* a genus of plants of the pea family, with flowers on long spikes: their seed. [L. *lupīnus.*]

lupine, *lū′pīn, adj.* like a wolf, wolfish. [L. *lupīnus—lupus,* a wolf.]

lupus, *lōō′pus, n.* a chronic tuberculosis of the skin, often affecting the nose. [L. *lupus,* a wolf.]

lurch, *lûrch, n.* in cribbage, &c., a state of the score when the winner is far ahead of the loser.—**leave in the lurch,** to desert in adversity. [O.Fr. *lourche.*]

lurch, *lûrch, v.i.* to roll or pitch suddenly to one side, or forward.—*n.* a sudden roll or pitch. [Perh. from **lurch.**]

lurcher, *lûr′chér, n.* a pilferer: a spy: a cross-bred dog with distinct greyhound characteristics. [From *lurch,* obs. variant of **lurk.**]

lure, *l(y)ōōr, n.* any enticement, bait, decoy.—*v.t.* to entice, decoy. [O.Fr. *loerre*—Middle High Ger. *luoder,* bait.]

lurid, *l(y)ōō′rid, adj.* ghastly pale, wan: gloomily threatening: sensational.—*adv.* **lū′ridly.** [L. *lūridus.*]

lurk, *lûrk, v.i.* to lie in wait: to skulk: to be concealed. [Perh. freq. from **lour.**]

luscious, *lush′us, adj.* sweet in a great degree: delightful: (*fig.*) over-rich, cloying, fulsome.—*adv.* **lusc′iously.**—*n.* **lusc′iousness.**

lush, *lush, adj.* rich and juicy: luxuriant. [Obs. *lash*—M.E. *lasche,* slack.]

lust, *lust, n.* longing desire (for), eagerness to possess: sensual appetite: (*B.*) any violent or depraved desire.—*v.i.* to desire eagerly (with *after, for*): to have carnal or depraved desires.—*adj.* **lust′ful,** having lust: inciting to lust: sensual.—*adv.* **lust′fully.**—*n.* **lust′fulness.**—*adj.* **lust′y,** vigorous: healthy: stout.—*n.* **lust′iness.**—*adv.* **lust′ily.** [O.E. *lust,* pleasure.]

lustre, *lus′tér, n.* gloss, brightness, splendour: (*fig.*) renown: a chandelier ornamented with pendants of cut-glass: a dress material having a highly finished surface.—*adj.* **lus′trous,** bright, shining, luminous.—*adv.* **lus′trously.** [Fr.,—L. *lustrāre,* to shine.]

lustre, *lus′tér,* **lustrum,** *lus′trum, n.* a period of five years: (*orig.*) the purification of the Roman people made every five years at the conclusion of the census.—*n.* **lustrā′tion,** a purification by sacrifice: act of purifying.—*adj.* **lus′tral,** relating to or used in lustration: of or pertaining to a lustre. [L. *lustrum,* perh. *luēre,* to wash, to purify.]

lustring, *lus′tring, n.* a glossy silk cloth.—Also **lus′trine, lute′string.** [Fr. *lustrine*—It. *lustrino.*]

lusty. See **lust.**

lute, *lōōt, lūt, n.* an old stringed instrument shaped like half a pear.—*ns.* **lut′anist, lut′er, lut′ist,** a player on a lute; **lute′-string,** the string of a lute.—**rift in the lute** (see **rift**). [O.Fr. *lut;* like Ger. *laute,* from Ar. *al,* the, *'lūd,* wood, lute.]

lute, *lōōt, lūt, n.* clay, cement, &c., used as a protective covering, air-tight stoppings, &c.—*v.t.* to close or coat with lute.—*n.* **lutā′tion**. [L. *lutum*, mud—*luĕre*, to wash.]

lutetium, (formerly **lutecium**), *lū-tē′shi-úm, n.* a metallic element (symbol Lu; at. no. 71) a member of the rare-earth group. [L. *Lutetium*, Paris.]

Lutheran, *lōō′thér-án, adj.* pertaining to *Luther*, the great German Protestant reformer (1483-1546), or to his doctrines.—*n.* a follower of Luther.—*n.* **Lū′theranism**.

lux, *luks, n.* SI unit of illumination, one lumen per square metre.

luxate, *luks′āt, v.t.* to put out of joint, dislocate.—*n.* **luxā′tion**, a dislocation. [L. *luxāre*, *-ātum—luxus—*Gr. *loxos*, slanting.]

luxury, *luk′shû-ri, lug′zhû-ri, n.* free indulgence in costly pleasures: anything rare and delightful (often expressive): something beyond what is essential or what one is accustomed to (opp. to *necessity*)—*adj.* relating to or providing luxury.—*adj.* **luxū′riant**, (*lug-zhōō′ri-ánt, luk-*) exuberant in growth: overabundant.—*ns.* **luxū′riance, luxū′riancy**.—*adv.* **luxū′riantly**.—*v.i.* **luxū′riate**, to be luxuriant: to live luxuriously: to revel (in).—*adj.* **luxū′rious**, given to, indulging in, luxury: contributing to luxury: furnished, supplied, with luxuries: softening by pleasure.—*adv.* **luxū′riously**.—*n.* **luxū′riousness**. [O.Fr. *luxurie—*L. *luxuria*, luxury—*luxus*, excess.]

lyceum, *lī-sē′um, n.* a gymnasium and grove beside the temple of Apollo in Athens, in whose walks Aristotle taught: a college: a place or building devoted to literary studies or lectures. [L. *Lycēūm—*Gr. *Lykeion—Lykeios*, an epithet of Apollo.]

lychgate. Same as **lichgate**.

lyddite, *lid′īt, n.* a powerful explosive used in shells. [Tested at *Lydd* in Kent.]

lye, *lī, n.* a strong alkaline solution obtained by leaching (q.v.): wood ashes: a solution got by leaching: a liquid used for washing. [O.E. *lēah, lēag*; Ger. *lauge*; allied to L. *lavāre*, to wash.]

lying, *lī′ing, adj.* addicted to telling lies.—*n.* the habit of telling lies.—*adv.* **ly′ingly**. [From **lie** (1).]

lykewake, *līk′wāk, n.* Scot. and N. Engl. variant of **lichwake** (q.v.).

lymph, *limf, n.* water: a colourless or faintly yellowish fluid in animal bodies, closely resembling blood plasma in composition: a vaccine.—*adj.* **lymphat′ic**, pertaining to lymph: sluggish.—*n.* a vessel which conveys the lymph.—*adj.* **lymph′oid**, like, or pertaining to, lymph, or the tissue of lymph glands. [L. *lympha*, water.]

lynch, *linch, -sh, v.t.* to condemn and put to death, without the usual forms of law.—*n.* **lynch′-law**. [Captain William *Lynch* of Virginia, 18th century planter and justice of the peace, who employed such methods.]

lynx, *lingks, n.* a genus of the cat family noted for its sharp sight.—*adj.* **lynx′-eyed**, sharpsighted. [L.,—Gr. *lynx.*]

Lyon Court, *lī′ón kōrt, n.* the Heralds' College of Scotland, presided over by the **Lyon King-of-arms, Lyon King-at-arms**. [From the heraldic lion of Scotland.]

lyre, *līr, n.* a musical instrument like the harp, anciently used as accompaniment to poetry. —*adjs.* **ly′rate, -d** (*bot.*), lyre-shaped.—*n.* **lyre′-bird**, any of three species of Australian birds having the tail-feathers of the male arranged in a form like that of a lyre.—*adjs.* **lyric, -al** (*lir′-*), pertaining to the lyre: fitted to be sung to the lyre: of poetry, expressing individual emotions of the poet: that composes lyrics: enthusiastically eloquent.—*n.* **lyric** (*lir′-*), a lyric poem: a song: (*pl.*) the words of a popular song. [Fr.,—L. *lyra—*Gr.]

lysis, *lī′sis, n.* the gradual abatement of a disease: (*biol.*) breaking down as of a cell.—*n.* **ly′sin**, a substance that causes breakdown of cells.—**lysergic acid** (*lī-sûr′jik*), a substance, $C_{16}H_{16}O_2N_2$, causing (in the form of lysergic acid diethylamide—LSD) a schizophrenic condition, with hallucinations and thought processes outside the normal range. [Gr. *lysis*, dissolution, *lyein*, to loose.]

Neutral vowels in unaccented syllables: *em′pér-ôr*; for certain sounds in foreign words see p. ix.

M

Mab, *mab, n.* the queen of the fairies.

macabre, *ma-kä'br', -bér, adj.* gruesome: like the Dance of Death. [Fr.; formerly *macabré.*]

macadamise, *mäk-ad'am-īz, v.t.* to cover with small broken stones, so as to form a smooth, hard surface.—*n.* **macadamisā'tion.** [From John *McAdam* (1756-1836), road-surveyor.]

macaroni, *mak-a-rō'ni, n.* a paste of hard wheat flour, pressed out through a perforated vessel into long tubes, and dried: in the 18th century, a dandy.—*adj.* **macaronic** (*-on'ik*), of a kind of burlesque verse, intermixing modern words Latinised, or Latin words modernised, with genuine Latin.—*n.* (often in *pl.*) macaronic verse. [It. *maccaroni* (now *maccheroni*), pl. of *maccarone,* prob.—*maccare,* to crush.]

macaroon, *mak-a-rōon', n.* a sweet biscuit made of almonds. [Fr. *macaron*— It. *maccarone*; (see above).]

Macassar oil, *ma-kas'ar oil,* an oil once much used for the hair. [From *Macassar* in Celebes.]

macaw, *ma kö', n.* any of numerous large long-tailed, showy tropical American parrots. [Port. *macao.*]

McCarthyism, *má-kär'thi-izm, n.* the hunting down and removal from public employment of all suspected of communism. [From Joseph *McCarthy* (1909-1957), U.S. politician.]

mace, *mās, n.* a metal or metal-headed war club, often spiked: a somewhat similar staff used as a mark of authority: a mace-bearer: a light, flat-headed stick sometimes used in bagatelle.—*n.* **mac'er,** a mace-bearer: in Scotland, an usher in a law court. [O.Fr. *mace* (Fr. *masse*)—hypothetical L. *mat(t)ea,* whence L. dim. *mat(t)eola,* a kind of tool.]

mace, *mās, n.* the inner coat of the nutmeg. [O.Fr. *macis,* possibly—L. *maccis, -idis,* a word supposed to have been invented by Plautus, Roman comic poet (250-184 B.C.), for an imaginary spice.]

macerate, *mas'ér-āt, v.t.* and *v.i.* to soften by steeping: to waste away by fasting, &c.—*ns.* **macerā'tion; mac'erator,** one who macerates: a paper-pulping apparatus. [L. *māccrāre, -ātum,* to steep.]

Machiavellian, *mak-i-a-vel'yán, adj.* ruled by expediency only: cunning and unscrupulous in statecraft: crafty: perfidious.—*n.* any cunning and unprincipled statesman—also **Machiavel.**—*n.* **Machiavell'ianism.** [From *Machiavelli,* a statesman and political writer of Florence (1469-1527).]

machicolation, *ma-chik-ō-lā'sh(ó)n, n.* (archit.) a projecting parapet, &c., with openings for dropping solids or liquids down on assailants: an opening for this purpose.—*adj.* **machic'olated.** [Fr. *mâchicoulis.*]

machinate, *mak'i-nāt, v.i.* to form a plot or scheme, esp. for doing harm.—*ns.* **machinā'tion,** act of machinating: an intrigue or plot;

mach'inator, one who machinates. [L. *māchinārī, ātus*—*māchina*—Gr. *mēchanē,* contrivance.]

machine, *ma-shēn', n.* any artificial means or contrivance: any instrument for the conversion of motion: an engine: one who can do only what he is told: an apparatus, especially in the ancient Greek theatre, for producing stage effects—in particular, the contrivance for enabling gods to descend from, or ascend to, heaven (see **deus ex machina**): a supernatural agency or personage employed in carrying on the action of a poem: an organised system.—*ns.* **machine'-gun,** an automatic quick-firing gun on a stable mounting; **machine'-rul'er,** an instrument for ruling lines on paper; **machin'ery,** machines in general: the working parts of a machine: means for keeping in action: supernatural agents in a poem, **machine'-shop,** workshop where metal, &c., is shaped by machine-tools; **machine'-tool,** a power-driven machine for shaping, planing, &c.; **machin'ist,** one who works a machine, esp. a machine-tool: one who makes or repairs machinery. [Fr.—L. *māchina*—Gr. *mēchanē,* akin to *mēchos,* contrivance.]

Mach number, *mäh num'bér,* the ratio of the air speed (i.e. speed with relation to the air) of an object to the velocity of sound under the given conditions—Mach 1 indicating that the aircraft is flying at the speed of sound. *n.* **mach'meter,** instrument for measuring Mach number. [Ernst *Mach,* Austrian physicist, and number.]

Machtpolitik, *mäht'pō-le-tēk', n.* power politics, esp. the doctrine that a state should use force to attain its ends. [Ger.]

mackerel, *mak'er-el, n.* a food-fish, bluish green, with wavy cross-streaks above, and silvery below: other fish of the same family, e.g. the **horse mackerel.**—*n.* **mack'erel-sky,** a sky with clouds broken into long, thin, white, parallel masses. [O.Fr. *makerel* (Fr. *maquereau*).]

mackintosh, *mak'in-tosh, n.* a waterproof overcoat. [From *Macintosh* (1766-1843), the patentee.]

macro-, *mak-rō-,* in composition, large, long [Gr. *makros,* large]:—e.g. **macroscosm** (*mak'rō-kozm*), the great world: the whole universe—opp. to *microcosm* (Gr. *kosmos,* world).

macroscopic, *mak-rō-skop'ik, adj.* visible to the naked eye—opp. to *microscopic.* [Gr. *makros,* large, *skopeein,* to look at.]

macula, *mak'ū-la, n.* a spot, as on the skin, the sun, a mineral, &c.:—*pl.* **maculae** (*-lē*).—*v.t.* **mac'ulāte,** to spot.—*n.* **maculā'tion,** act of spotting: a spot (see **immaculate**). [L. *macula,* a spot]

mad, *mad, adj.* (*comp.* **madd'er;** *superl.* **madd'est**) insane: proceeding from madness:

infatuated: frantic (with pain, violent passion, &c.): (*coll.*) very angry: rash, foolish.—*n.* **mad'cap,** a wild, rash, hot-headed person: an exuberantly frolicsome person.—*v.t.* **madd'en,** to make mad: to enrage.—*v.i.* to become mad: to act as one mad (whence *adj.* **madd'ing,** acting madly).—*adv.* **mad'ly.**—*ns.* **Mad Hatter,** (one who is) like the Mad Hatter or his tea-party in *Alice in Wonderland*— harmlessly crazy; **mad'house,** a lunatic asylum: a place where there is noise and confusion; **mad'man,** a maniac: a foolish man; **mad'ness.** [O.E. *gemǣd(e)d*; Old Saxon *gimēd*, foolish.]

madam, *mad'ăm, n.* a courteous form of address to a lady:—*pl.* **mad'ams,** or (in letters) **mes-dames** (*mā-dam'*).—Also **madame':**—*pl.* **mes-dames.** [Fr. *madame*, i.e. *ma*, my, *dame*, lady—L. *mea domina.*]

madder, *mad'ér, n.* a plant whose root affords a red dye. [O.E. *mǣd(d)re*; O.N. *mathra.*]

made, *mād, pa.t.* and *pa.p.* of **make.**—**be a made man,** to be assured of success; **made up,** fully manufactured (e.g. a garment): artificial (e.g. a complexion): fabricated (e.g. a story).

Madeira, *ma-dē'ra, ma-dā'ra, n.* a rich wine of the sherry class produced in *Madeira*.

mademoiselle, *mad-mwä-zel', mad-é-mō-zel', n.* a form of address to a young lady: Miss.—*pl.* **mesdemoiselles** (*mād-mwä-zel*). [Fr. *ma*, my, *demoiselle*, young lady. See **damsel.**]

Madonna, *ma-don'a, n.* the Virgin Mary, esp. as seen in works of art. [It., lit. 'my lady'—L. *mea domina.*]

madrepore, *mad're-pör, n.* any coral of the common reef-building type. [It. *madrepora*— *madre*, mother—L. *māter*, and Gr. *pōros*, a soft stone, stalactite, &c., or L. *porus*, a pore.]

madrigal, *mad'ri-gál, n.* (*mus.*) an unaccompanied song in several parts: a lyrical poem suitable for such treatment. [It. *madrigale*, perh. from *mandr(i)a*, a cattle-shed—L. *man-dra*—Gr. *mandrā.*]

Maecenas, *me-sē'nàs, n.* any rich patron of art or literature. [Name of the patron of the Latin poets Virgil and Horace.]

maelstrom, *māl'strom, n.* a celebrated whirlpool, or more correctly current, off the coast of Norway: any whirlpool (*lit.* and *fig.*). [Du. (now *maalstroom*), a whirlpool.]

maenad, *mē'nad, n.* female follower of Bacchus, a woman beside herself with frenzy. [Gr. *mainas, -ados*, raving—*mainesthai*, to be mad.]

maestro, *mä-es'trō, mī'strō, n.* a master, esp. an eminent musical composer or conductor. [It.]

Mae West, *mā west, n.* (R.A.F. *slang*) an inflatable, life-saving jacket. [Name of a large-bosomed film actress.]

mafia, maffia, *mä'fē-ä, n.* a spirit of opposition to the law in Sicily, favouring private rather than legal justice: a secret criminal society originating in Sicily, controlling many illegal activities, e.g. gambling, narcotics, &c., in many parts of the world, esp. active in the U.S.—Also called *Cosa Nostra*. [Sicilian Italian.]

mafficking, *maf'ik-ing, n.* noisy patriotic rejoicings. [From the celebrations in London on the relief of *Mafeking*, May 17, 1900.]

magazine, *mag-à-zēn', n.* a place for military stores: the gunpowder-room in a ship: a compartment in a rifle for holding extra cartridges: a periodical publication or broadcast containing articles, stories, &c., by various writers.—*n.* **magazine'-gun,** one from which a succession of shots can be fired without reloading. [Fr. *magasin*—It. *magazzino*— Ar. *makhāzin*, pl. of *makhzan*, a storehouse.]

Magdalen, Magdalene, *mag'dà-lén, n.* a repentant prostitute. [From Mary *Magdalene* (i.e. of *Magdala*—Luke viii. 2); see **maudlin.**]

magenta, *ma-jen'ta, n.* a reddish-purple colour. [From its discovery about the time of the battle of *Magenta* in North Italy, 1859.]

maggot, *mag'ót, n.* a legless grub, esp. of a fly: a fad.—*adj.* **magg'oty,** full of maggots. [Perh. modification of M.E. *maddok, mathek*, dim.; same root as **mawkish.**]

Magi, Magian. See **magus.**

magic, *maj'ik, n.* the pretended art of producing marvellous results by compelling the aid of spirits, or by using the secret forces of nature: any inexplicable influence producing surprising results: the art of producing illusions by legerdemain.—*adjs.* **mag'ic,** pertaining to, used in, magic: possessing marvellous qualities, or causing wonderful or startling results; **mag'ical,** produced, or as if produced, by magic.—*adv.* **mag'ically.**—*ns.* **magician** (*má-jish'án*), one skilled in magic; **mag'ic-lan'tern** (see **lantern**).—**magic eye,** a miniature cathode ray tube resembling an eye, used as a tuning device in certain electronic systems, e.g. in a radio receiver.—**black magic,** magic by means of union with evil spirits. [Gr. *ma-gikē* (*technē*), magic, (art)—Pers. See **magus.**]

magisterial, *maj-is-tē'ri-ál, adj.* pertaining or suitable to, or in the manner of, a teacher, master artist, or magistrate: dictatorial: authoritative.—*adv.* **magistē'rially.**—*ns.* **magistē'rialness; mag'istracy,** the office or dignity of a magistrate: body of magistrates; **mag'istrāte,** one who has the power of putting the laws in force, esp. a justice of the peace, or one who sits in a police court. [L. *magister.*]

magma, *mag'ma, n.* the molten material existing within the earth from which igneous rocks are considered to have been derived by cooling and crystallisation. [Gr.]

Magna Carta (Charta), *mag'na kär'ta, n.* the Great Charter obtained from King John, 1215: (*fig.*) any charter of liberty. [L.]

magnalium, *mag-nā'li-ùm, n.* a light, strong, easily-worked and rust-resisting alloy of *magn*esium and *al*uminium used in aircraft construction, &c.

magnanimity, *mag-na-nim'i-ti, n.* greatness of soul: that quality of mind which raises a person above all that is mean or unjust: generosity.—*adj.* **magnan'imous.**—*adv.* **magnan'imously.** [L. *magnanimitās*—*magnus*, great, *animus*, the mind.]

magnate, *mag'nāt, n.* a noble: a man of rank or wealth, or of power. [L. *magnās, -ātis*— *magnus*, great.]

magnesium, *mag-nē'z(h)i-um, -z(h)yum, -shi-um, -shyum, n.* metallic element (symbol Mg; at. no. 12) of a bright, silver-white colour, burning with a dazzling white light.—*n.* **mag-nē'sia,** a light white powder, oxide of mag-

Neutral vowels in unaccented syllables: *em'pér-ór*; for certain sounds in foreign words see p. ix.

434

nesium: basic magnesium carbonate, used as a medicine. [Prob. *Magnēsia*. See **magnet**.]

magnet, *mag'net*, *n.* a mass of iron or other material that possesses the property of attracting or repelling other masses of iron, and which also exerts a force on a current-carrying conductor placed in its vicinity: (*fig.*) any thing or person exercising a strong attraction.—*adjs.* **magnet'ic**, **-al**, having, or capable of acquiring, the properties of the magnet: attractive.—*adv.* **magnet'ically.**—*v.t.* **mag'netise**, to render magnetic: to attract as if by a magnet: to hypnotise. *ns.* **mag'netiser; mag'netism**, the cause of the attractive power of the magnet: the phenomena connected with magnets: the science which treats of the properties of the magnet: attraction; **mag'netite**, an oxide of iron, attracted by a magnet, but having no power of attracting particles of iron to itself, except in the form known as lodestone; **magneto** (*mag-nē'tō*), a small permanent-magnet electric generator, esp. for providing the ignition in an internal-combustion engine.—**magneto-**, in composition, magnetic: pertaining to magnetism.—**magnetic field**, the space over which magnetic force is felt; **magnetic flux**, the surface integral of the product of the permeability of the medium and the magnetic field intensity perpendicular to the surface; **magnetic mine**, a mine sunk to the sea-bottom, detonated by a pivoted magnetic needle when a ship approaches; **magnetic needle**, any light slender bar of magnetised steel, esp. that in the mariner's compass which, because it is magnetised, points always to the north; **magnetic north**, direction indicated by the magnetic needle—usually either east or west of the geographical pole or true north (see **declination, variation**); **magnetic storm**, a disturbance in the magnetism of the earth; **magnetic tape**, flexible plastic tape, coated on one side with magnetic material, used to register for later reproduction television images, or sound, or computer data [Through O.Fr. or L. from Gr. *magnētis* (*lithos*), magnesian (stone), from *Magnēsia* in Lydia or *Magnēsia*, eastern part of Thessaly.]

magnetron, *mag'nē-tron*, *n.* a thermionic tube in which the inter-electrode space is traversed by a magnetic field acting transversely to the cathode to anode path, causing deflection of the electrons in their flight.

magnific, *mag-nif'ik*, **magnifical**, **-al**, *adjs.* (*arch.*) magnificent: exalted: pompous. [L. *magnificus*; cf. **magnify**.]

Magnificat, *mag-nif'i-kat*, *n.* the song of the Virgin Mary, Luke i. 46-55, beginning in the Vulgate with this word. [L. '(my soul) doth magnify', 3rd pers. sing. pres. ind. of *magnificāre*.]

magnificence, *mag-nif'i-séns*, *n.* the quality of being magnificent.—*adj.* **magnif'icent**, great in deeds or in show: grand: noble: pompous: displaying greatness of size or extent: (*coll.*) very fine.—*adv.* **magnif'icently.** [L. *magnificens, -entis.*]

magnify, *mag'ni-fī*, *v.t.* to cause to appear greater: to exaggerate: (*arch.*) to praise highly:—*pa.p.* mag'nified.—*n.* **magnifica'tion**, act

of magnifying, or state of being magnified: (also **mag'nifying power**) the ratio of the apparent size of the image of an object formed by an optical instrument to that of the object as seen by the naked eye. [L. *magnificāre—magnus*, great, *facĕre*, to make.]

magniloquent, *mag-nil'o-kwént*, *adj.* speaking in a grand or pompous style.—*n.* **magnil'oquence.**—*adv.* **magnil'oquently.** [L. *magnus*, great, *loquens, -entis*, pr.p. of *loquī*, to speak.]

magnitude, *mag'ni-tūd*, *n.* greatness: size: importance. [L. *magnitūdō—magnus*, great.]

magnolia, *mag-nōl'i-a*, or *-ya*, *n.* an American and Asiatic genus of trees with beautiful foliage, and large solitary flowers. [From Pierre *Magnol* (1638-1715), a botanist.]

magnum, *mag'num*, *n.* a two-quart bottle or vessel. [L. *magnum* (neut), big.]

magnum opus, *mag'num ōp'us, mag'nŏŏm ōp'ŏŏs*, a great work, esp. of literature or learning, esp. a person's greatest achievement [L.]

magpie, *mag'pī*, *n.* the pie, any of a large number of black and white chattering birds of the crow family: a chattering person. [*Mag*, for *Margaret*, and **pie** (1).]

magus, *mā'gus*, *n.* an ancient Persian priest: (*cap.*) a Wise Man of the East:—*pl.* **Ma'gi** (*-jī*).—*adj.* **Ma'gian**, pertaining to the Magi or (without *cap.*) to a sorcerer.—*n.* a magus: a sorcerer. [L.,—Gr. *magos*—O.Pers. *magus*. See **magic**.]

Magyar, *mag'yär* or *mod'yor*, *n.* a Hungarian: the Hungarian language. [Hungarian.]

Maharaja, Maharajah, *mä-hä-rä'jä*, *n.* the title given to a great Indian prince.—*fem.* **Maharani, Maharanee** (*-rä'nē*). [Hindustani—Sans. *mahāt*, great, *rājan*, king, *rānī*, queen.]

mahatma, *ma-hat'ma*, *n.* one skilled in mysteries or religious secrets. [Sans. *mahātman*, 'high-souled'.]

mah-jong(g), *mä jong'*, *n.* an old Chinese table game for four, played with small painted bricks or 'tiles'. [Chinese.]

mahogany, *ma-hog'a-ni*, *n.* a tropical American tree: its wood, valued for furniture-making: the colour of the timber, a dark reddish-brown. [Origin unknown.]

Mahommedan, Mahometan. See **Mohammedan.**

mahout, *mä-howt'*, *n.* the keeper and driver of an elephant. [Hindustani *mahāut, mahāwat*.]

maid, *mād*, *n.* an unmarried woman, esp. a young one: a virgin: a female servant. [Shortened from **maiden.**]

maiden, *mād'n*, *n.* a maid: (*hist.*) a Scottish beheading machine.—*adj.* pertaining to a virgin or young woman: consisting of maidens: (*fig.*) unpolluted: fresh: unused: first.—*ns.* **maid'enhair**, a fern with fine hair-like stalks; **maid'enhead**, virginity; **maidenhood**, the state or time of being a maiden.—*adj.* **maid'enly**, of, or becoming to, a maiden.—*n.* **maid'enliness.**—**maiden assize**, an assize at which there are no criminal cases; **maiden castle**, a castle never taken; **maiden name**, the family name of a married woman before her marriage; **maiden over**, in cricket, an over in which no runs are made; **maiden speech**, one's first speech, esp. in Parliament; **maiden stakes**, in horse-racing, the prize in a race between horses that, at the date of entry, have not won in any race; **maiden voyage,** a first voyage. [O.E. *mægden.*]

mail, *māl, n.* defensive armour for the body formed of steel rings or network: armour generally.—*v.t.* to clothe in mail.—**mailed fist,** physical force. [Fr. *maille*—L. *macula,* a spot or a mesh.]

mail, *māl, n.* a bag for the conveyance of letters, parcels, &c.: letters, parcels, &c., by post: postal delivery or dispatch: a person (*hist.*) or vehicle by which the mail is conveyed.—*v.t.* (esp. *U.S.*) to post, send by post, (e.g. a letter). —*ns.* **mail′-cart,** a kind of perambulator for children; **mail′-catch′er,** an apparatus attached to a mail-carriage to catch up mailbags while the train is in motion.—**mail order** (when used adjectivally, **mail-order**), an order by post, a purchase effected by post. [O.Fr. *male,* a trunk, a mail—O.H.G. *malha, malaha,* a sack.]

maim, *mām, v.t.* to disable: to mutilate: to render defective. [O.Fr. *mahaing.*]

main, *mān, n.* physical force (*might and main*): the principal part: the high sea: the mainland: a principal pipe or conductor in a branching system.—*adj.* chief, principal: first in importance or extent: sheer (e.g. strength): leading.—*ns.* **main′deck,** the principal deck of a ship—so in other compounds, **main′mast, main′sail, main′spring, main′stay, main′top, main′yard** (see **mast, sail, spring,** &c.).—*adj.* **main′door** (*Scot.*; of a house or flat), on the ground-floor in a tenement building and entered from the street by a door of its own.—*ns.* **main′land** (-*lánd,* -*land*), the principal or larger land, as opposed to neighbouring islands; **main line,** a railway line between important centres: (*slang*) an important vein.—*v.i.* (*slang*) to take narcotics intravenously.—*n.* **main′liner.**—*adv.* **main′ly,** chiefly, principally.—**main stream,** a river with tributaries (*fig.*) the chief direction or trend. —*adj.* (*jazz*) of swing, coming between early and modern.—**Spanish Main** (see **Spanish**). [Partly O.E. *mægen,* strength, partly O.N. *meginn,* strong; influence of O.Fr. *maine, magne* (L. *magnus*) great, is questioned.]

maintain, *mān -tān′, mén-, men-, v.t.* to keep in a particular condition (e.g. a road, health, reputation): to preserve, continue in (e.g. integrity, reserve): to keep up (e.g. an attack): to carry on (e.g. a correspondence): to support, to bear the expenses of (e.g. a family): to give support to (e.g. the law): to back up (e.g. a cause, a party): to give support by argument: to affirm.—*adj.* **maintain′able.**—*n.* **maintenance** (*mān′tén-áns*), the act of maintaining: the means of support: the upkeep (e.g. of property).—**maintenance man,** one keeping machines, &c., in working order [Fr. *maintenir*—L. *manū* (abl.) *tenēre,* to hold in the hand.]

maisonnette, *mez-on-et′, n.* a small house or flat. [Fr.]

maize, *māz, n.* a staple cereal in America, &c., with large ears—called also **Indian corn,** or **mealies.** [Sp. *maíz*—Haitian.]

majesty, *maj′es-ti, n.* greatness and glory of God: impressive dignity or stateliness of manner, language, &c.: a title of monarchs.—*adjs.* **majes′tic, -al,** having or exhibiting majesty: stately: sublime. [Fr. *majesté*—L. *mājestās, -ātis*—*mājor, mājus,* comp. of *magnus,* great.]

majolica, *ma-jol′i-ka,* or -*yol′-, n.* glazed or enamelled earthenware. [Perh. from *Majorca.*]

major, *mā′jór, adj.* greater in number, quantity, size, value, importance.—*n.* a person of full legal age (in U.K. before 1970, 21 years; from 1970, 18 years): an officer in rank between a captain and lieutenant-colonel.—*ns.* **mā′jordō̆′mō** (Sp. *mayordomo,* L. *mājor domūs*), an official who has the general management in a princely household: (loosely) a butler or a steward; **mā′jor-gen′eral,** an officer in the army below a lieutenant-general; **majority** (*ma-jor′i-ti*), the greater number: the difference between the greater and the less number: full legal age: the office or rank of major; **mā′jorship; major interval,** the second, third, sixth, or seventh (as opp. to **perfect;** cf. also **minor**); **major key, scale,** one with its third a major third above the tonic; **major premise,** in a syllogism, the more general of the two propositions from which the conclusion is drawn; **major term,** the term in a syllogism that forms the predicate of the conclusion; **major third,** an interval of four semitones (e.g. C to E). [L. *mājor,* comp. of *magnus.*]

make, *māk, v.t.* to fashion, frame, or form: to bring about (a change): to perform (e.g. a journey): to carry out (e.g. an attempt): to compel: to render, to bring into any state or condition (e.g. safe, fast, known, homeless): to represent as doing or being (e.g. a person a liar): to occasion (e.g. trouble): to prepare (e.g. tea): to obtain, gain, earn (e.g. a living): to arrive in sight of, to reach (e.g. the shore): to amount to.—*v.i.* to behave in a specified way (with *adjs.,* e.g. bold, merry):—*pa.t.* and *pap.* made.—*n.* form or shape: structure, texture.—*v.i.* **make believe,** to pretend, feign (*n.* **make′-believe**).—*ns.* **maker,** one who makes: the Creator: (*arch.*) a poet; **make′shift,** a temporary expedient or substitute.—Also *adj.*—*ns.* **make′-up,** the way anything is arranged, composed, or constituted: character, temperament: an actor's cosmetics, wigs, &c.: a woman's cosmetics; **make′-weight,** that which is thrown into a scale to make up the weight: something of little value added to supply a deficiency.—**be the making of,** ensure success or favourable development of; **have the makings of,** have the essential qualities of; **make account of** (see **account**); **make a figure,** to be conspicuous; **make as if,** to act as if, to pretend that: to make a movement as if (to); **make a face,** to contort the features; **make away with** (see **away**); **make for,** to set out for, seek to reach: to conduce to (e.g. happiness); **make good, make head against, make light of, little of** (see **good, head, light, little**); **make it,** to reach a goal: to succeed in a purpose; **make much of,** to treat with fondness: to treat as if of importance; **make nothing of** (see **nothing**); **make of,** to construct from (material): to understand by; **make off,** to run away; **make off with,** to run away with, steal; **make out,** to discern: to

Neutral vowels in unaccented syllables: *em′pér-ór*; for certain sounds in foreign words see p. ix.

mal-   malpractice

comprehend: to (try to) prove: to draw up: to succeed; **make over**, to transfer: to remake; **make up for**, to compensate for; **make up to**, to make friendly approaches to; **on the make**, bent on self-advancement and profit. [O.E. *macian*; Ger. *machen*.]

mal-, *mal-*, *pfx.* bad, badly. [Fr.—L. *male*, badly.]

Malacca cane, *mal-ak′a kān*, *n.* a brown walking-cane made from the stem of one of the rattan palms. [*Malacca*, in the Malay Peninsula.]

malachite, *mal′a-kīt*, *n.* a green mineral—basic copper carbonate. [Gr. *malache*, mallow, as of the colour of a mallow leaf.]

maladdress, *mal-a-dres′*, *n.* awkwardness: clumsiness, tactlessness. [Fr. *maladresse*.]

maladjusted, *mal-a-just′ed*, *adj.* poorly or inadequately adjusted, esp. to one's environment or circumstances.—*n.* **maladjust′ment**. [Fr. *mal*, ill, and **adjusted**.]

maladministration, *mal-ad-min-is-trā′sh(ó)n*, *n.* bad management, esp. of public affairs. [Fr. *mal*, ill, and **administration**.]

maladroit, *mal′a-droit* (or *-droit′*) *adj.* not dexterous, clumsy, bungling [Fr.]

malady, *mal′a-di*, *n.* an illness, disease, either of the body or of the mind. [Fr. *maladie—malade*, sick—L. *male habitus*, in ill condition—*male*, badly, *habitus*, pa.p. of *habēre*, have, hold.]

Malagasy, *mal-a-gas′i*, *adj.* of or pertaining to Madagascar (Malagasy Republic). *n.* the people and the language of Madagascar.

malaise, *mal′āz*, *ma-lcz′*, *n.* a feeling of discomfort or of sickness. [Fr. *malaise*.]

malapert, *mal′a-pért*, *adj.* (arch.) saucy, impudent.—*adv.* **mal′apertly.**—*n.* **mal′apertness.** [O.Fr., unskilful—*mal*—L. *malus*, bad, *appert* for *espert*—L. *expertus*, but understood in English as if—Fr. *apert*, open, outspoken—L. *apertus*, open.]

malapropism, *mal′a-prop-izm*, *n.* misapplication of words (without mispronunciation), from Mrs *Malaprop* in Sheridan's play, *The Rivals*, who uses words *malapropos*.

malapropos, *mal′-a-pro-pō′*, *adj.* out of place. unsuitable.—Also *adv.* [Fr. *mal*, ill, and **apropos**.]

malaria, *ma-lā′ri-a*, *n.* poisonous air arising from marshes: the fever once attributed thereto, actually due to any of several species of protozoan parasites transmitted by the bite of the females of certain species of mosquito.—*adjs.* **malā′rious, malā′rial.** [It. *mal′ aria*—L. *malus*, bad, *āēr*, *āēris*, air.]

malcontent, *mal′kon-tent*, *adj.* discontented, dissatisfied, esp. in political matters.—*n.* a person who is discontented, esp. one inclined to active rebellion against conditions.—*adj.* **malcontent′ed**. [O.Fr. *malcontent*.]

maldistribution, *mal-dis-tri-bū′-shón*, *n.* uneven, unfair, or inefficient distribution. [Fr. *mal*, ill, and **distribution**.]

male, *māl*, *adj.* characteristic of or pertaining to the sex that begets (not bears) young: (*bot.*) bearing stamens.—*n.* one of the male sex. [O.Fr. *male*—L. *maculus*, male—*mās*, a male.]

malediction, *mal-é-dik′sh(ó)n*, *n.* a curse: reviling, slander.—*adj.* **maledict′ory**. [L. *maledīcĕre*, *-dictum—male*, ill, *dīcĕrc*, to speak.]

malefactor, *mal′ē-fak-tór*, *n.* an evil-doer: a

criminal. [L. *male*, ill, *facĕre*, to do.]

malevolent, *mal-ev′o-lént*, *adj.* wishing evil, ill-disposed towards others, rejoicing in another's misfortune.—*adv.* **malev′olently.** [L. *male*, ill, *volens, -entis*, pr.p. of *velle*, to wish.]

malformation, *mal-för-mā′sh(ó)n*, *n.* faulty structure: a deformity. [Fr. *mal*, ill, and **formation**.]

malic, *mā′lik*, *mal′ik*, *adj.* obtained from apple juice—applied to an acid found in unripe fruits.—**maleic acid** (*má-lē′ik*), an acid got from malic acid. [L. *mālum*, an apple; Gr. *mēlon*.]

malice, *mal′is*, *n.* ill-will, spite: disposition or intention to harm another or others: a playfully mischievous attitude of mind.—*adj.* **malicious** (*má-lish′ús*), bearing ill-will or spite: proceeding from hatred or ill-will: mischievous.—*adv.* **malic′iously.**—*n.* **malic′iousness.**—**with malice aforethought**, with deliberate intention to commit the evil act in question. [Fr.—L. *malitia malus*, bad.]

malign, *ma-līn′*, *adj.* injurious: malignant.—*v.t.* to speak evil of: to slander, misrepresent in so doing.—*ns.* **malign′er; malignity** (*ma-lig′ni-ti*), great hatred, virulence: deadly quality.—*adv.* **malign′ly.** [Fr. *malin*, *fem. maligne*—L. *malignus* for *maligenus*, of evil disposition—*malus*, bad, and *gen-*, root of *genus*, race.]

malignant, *ma-lig′nánt*, *adj.* disposed to do harm or to cause suffering: actuated by great hatred: (of disease) tending to cause death or to go from bad to worse: cancerous.—*n.* (*hist.*) a Royalist or Cavalier.—*ns.* **malig′nance, malig′nancy.**—*adv.* **malig′nantly.** [L. *malignans, -antis*, pr.p. of *malignāre*, to act maliciously.]

malinger, *ma-ling′gér*, *v.i.* to feign sickness in order to avoid duty. *n.* **maling′erer.** [Fr. *malingre*, sickly.]

malison, *mal′i-zn -sn*, *n.* (*arch.*) a curse—opp. to *benison*. [O.Fr. *maleīson*; a doublet of **malediction**.]

mall, *möl*, or *mal*, *n.* a mallet for the old game of pall-mall: the game itself: a level shaded walk: a public walk. [Same root as **maul**; see **pall-mall.**]

mallard, *mal′árd*, *n.* the male of the common wild-duck. [O.Fr. *mallart, malart*.]

malleable, *mal′é-āt*, *v.t.* to hammer: to beat thin.—*adj.* **mall′eable**, capable of being beaten, rolled, &c., into a new shape.—*ns.* **mall′eableness, malleabil′ity; malea′tion**, hammering: a hammer mark. [L. *malleus*, a hammer.]

mallet, *mal′et*, *n.* a small wooden hammer: a long-handled hammer for playing croquet or polo. [Fr. *maillet*, dim. of *mail*, a mall.]

mallow, *mal′ō*, *n.* a genus of plants having downy leaves and emollient properties. [O.E. *m(e)alwe*—L. *malva*; Gr *malachō malassein*, to soften.]

malmsey, *mäm′zi*, *n.* a sort of grape: a strong and sweet wine. [L.L. *malmasia*; cf. O.Fr. *malvesie*, Fr. *malvoisie*.]

malnutrition, *mal-nū-trish′(ó)n*, *n.* imperfect or faulty nutrition. [Fr. *mal*, ill, and **nutrition**.]

malodorous, *mal-ō′dór-us*, *adj* evil-smelling. [Fr. *mal*, ill, and **odour**.]

malpractice, *mal-prak′tis*, *n.* evil practice or

fāte, fär; mē, hûr (her); *mīne; mōte, för; mūte, mōōn, fŏŏt; *THen* (then)

437

conduct: professional misconduct. [Fr. *mal*, ill, and **practice**.]

malt, *mölt, n.* barley or other grain steeped in water, allowed to sprout, and dried in a kiln.—*v.t.* to make into malt: to treat or combine with malt.—Also *v.i.* and *adj.*—*ns.* **malt′-ex′tract,** a fluid medicinal food made from malt; **malt′-house, malt′ing,** a building where malt is made; **malt′ster,** one whose occupation it is to make malt.—*adj.* **malt′y.—malt liquor,** a liquor, as ale or porter, formed from malt; **malt whisky,** unblended whisky distilled from fermented malt. [O.E. *m(e)alt*; cf. Ger. *malz.*]

Malthusian, *mal-thū̄z′i-án, adj.* relating to *Malthus* or his teaching regarding the necessity of preventing population from increasing faster than the means of living—which he said it naturally tended to do. [Rev. T. R. *Malthus* (1766-1834).]

maltreat, *mal-trēt′, v.t.* to use roughly or unkindly.—*n.* **maltreat′ment.** [Fr. *maltraiter*—L. *male,* ill, *tractāre,* to treat.]

malvaceous, *mal-vā′shŭs, adj.* (*bot.*) pertaining to plants of the family to which the mallows belong. [See **mallow.**]

malversation, *mal-vér-sā′sh(ó)n, n.* misbehaviour, corruption, or extortion, in office or in a position of trust: corrupt use (of public money). [Fr.,—L. *male,* badly, *versārī, -ātus,* to occupy oneself.]

mamba, *mam′ba, n.* any of several venomous snakes allied to the cobras, esp. a large, deadly, black or green snake of S. Africa, very quick in movement. [Kaffir *im mamba,* large snake.]

mambo, *mam′bō, n.* a voodoo priestess: a dance, or dance-tune, like the rumba, with syncopation, originating in Haiti.

Mameluke, *mam′e-lōōk, n.* one of a military force originally of Circassian slaves, afterwards the ruling class and (1250-1517) sultans of Egypt. [Ar. *mamlūk,* a purchased slave—*malaka,* to possess.]

mamillary, *mam′il-ár-i, adj.* pertaining to the breast: nipple-shaped. [L. *mam(m)illa,* dim. of *mamma.*]

mamma, mama, *mä-mä′, n.* (*arch.*) mother.—*n.* **mamm′y** (*U.S.*), coloured nurse. [Repetition of *ma,* one of the first syllables a child naturally utters.]

mamma, *mam′á, n.* the milk gland: the breast:—*pl.* **mammae** (-ē).—*adj.* **mamm′ary,** of the nature of, relating to the mammae or breasts.—*n.* **mammog′raphy,** radiological examination of the breast. [L. *mamma.*]

mammal, *mam′ál, n.* a member of the **Mammalia** (*ma-mā′li-a*), the whole class of animals that suckle their young.—*adj.* **mā′lian.**—*n.* **mammal′ogy,** the scientific knowledge of mammals. [L. *mammālis,* of the breast—*mamma,* the breast.]

mammon, *mam′ón, n.* riches; the god of riches.—*ns.* **mamm′onist, mamm′onite,** a person devoted to riches: a worldling. [Low L. *mam-(m)ōna*—Gr. *mam(m)onās*—Aramaic (q.v.) *māmōn,* riches.]

mammoth, *mam′óth, n.* any of several extinct elephants.—*adj.* resembling a mammoth in size: very large. [Former Russ. *mammot,* (now *mamont*).]

man, *man, n.* a human being, a member of the genus Homo: mankind: a grown-up human male: a male attendant: a member of a team: one possessing a distinctively manly character: a husband: a piece used in playing chess or draughts:—*pl.* **men.**—*v.t.* to furnish with men for service or defence (e.g. a ship, a gun):—*pr.p.* **mann′ing**; *pa.t.* and *pa.p.* **manned.**—*ns.* **man′-at-arms,** a soldier; **man′child,** a male child; **man′-eater,** a cannibal: a tiger.—*adj.* **man′ful,** showing manliness: courageous—*adv.* **man′fully.**—*n.* **man′fulness.**—*v.t.* **man′handle,** to move by man-power: to handle roughly.—*ns.* **man′-hole,** a hole large enough to admit a man, esp. to a sewer, or the like; **man′hood,** state of being a man: manly quality; **man′-hour,** an hour's work of one man:—*pl.* **man-hours; man-kind** (*man′kind* or *man′ kind′*), the human race.—*adj.* **man′ly,** befitting a man: brave, dignified: not childish or womanish.—*n.* **man′liness.**—*adj.* **mann′ish,** (of a woman) masculine in manner.—*ns.* **man′-of-war,** a warship: (*B.*) a soldier; **man′power,** power supplied by the physical effort of man: the rate at which a man can work (cf. **horse-power**): available resources in population or in able-bodied men.—*adj.* **man′size(d),** suitable for, or requiring, a man.—*n.s.* **man′slaughter,** the slaying of a man: (*law*) criminal or culpable homicide—without malice aforethought; **man′trap,** a trap for catching trespassers: (*fig.*) any source of potential danger.—**man about town,** a fashionable, sophisticated man; **Man Friday,** a servile attendant, factotum—from Robinson Crusoe's man; **man in the street,** the ordinary, everyday man—Tom, Dick, or Harry; **man of letters,** a scholar and writer; **man of straw,** a person of no substance or means: one nominally responsible but of no real character or influence: an imaginary opponent in an argument; **man of the moment,** the man (most capable of) dealing with the situation in hand; **man of the world,** one accustomed to the ways and dealings of men.—**to a man,** every one, without exception. [O.E. *mann*; Ger. *mann,* Du. *man.*]

manacle, *man′á-kl, n.* a handcuff.—*v.t.* to handcuff. [O.Fr. *manicle*—L. *manicula,* dim. of *manica,* sleeve, glove, handcuff—*manus,* hand.]

manage, *man′ij, v.t.* to train by exercise, as a horse: to handle, to wield (e.g. a tool): to conduct (e.g. an undertaking): to control (e.g. a household): to domineer: to deal tactfully with: to contrive (to do something): to bring about.—*v.i.* to conduct affairs.—*adj.* **man′ageable,** that can be managed: submitting to control.—*n.* **man′ageableness.**—*ns.* **man′agement,** art or act of managing: manner of directing or of using anything: a body of managers; **man′ager.**—*adjs.* **managerial,** of, pertaining to, management, a manager; **man′-aging,** controlling: administering: domineering. [It. *maneggio*—L. *manus,* the hand.]

manatee, manati, *man-a-tē′, n.* a genus of aquatic mammals inhabiting the warm parts of the Atlantic Ocean. [Sp. *manaté*—Carib (q.v.) *mantoui.*]

Manchester school, *n.* the followers of Cobden

Neutral vowels in unaccented syllables: *em′pér-ór*; for certain sounds in foreign words see p. ix.

and Bright, advocates of free-trade.

Manchu, Manchoo, *man-chōō′, n.* one of the race from which Manchuria took its name, and which governed China in the 17th century.—Also *adj.*

manciple, *man′si-pl. n.* a steward, a purveyor, particularly of a college or an inn of court. [O.Fr.,—L. *manceps, -cipis,* a purchaser—*manus,* hand, *capĕre,* take.]

Mancunian, *man-kūn′i-àn, adj.* belonging to Manchester.—*n.* a Manchester man. [Doubtful L. *Mancunium,* a Roman station in Manchester, *Mamucium* is probably right.]

mandamus, *man-dā′mus, n.* writ issued by higher court to lower. [L., 'we command'.]

mandarin, *man′da-rin, -rēn, n.* a member of any of nine ranks of officials under the Chinese Empire: (*cap.*) the most important Chinese language: a man in office, bureaucrat: a person of standing in the literary world, often reactionary or pedantic: a small kind of orange prob. of Chinese origin.—**mandarin collar,** a high, narrow, stand-up collar, the front ends of which do not quite meet. [Port. *mandarim*—Malayan *mantrī,* counsellor—Sans. *mantra,* counsel.]

mandate, *man′dāt, n.* a command from a superior authority (judicial or legal): a papal rescript: political instructions held to be given by electors to a legislative body or to one of its members: power to govern territory taken from a defeated state granted to another state, e.g. by the League of Nations in 1919.—*n.* **man′datary, man′datory,** the holder of a mandate.—*adj.* **man′datory,** containing a command: obligatory because of a command. [L. *mandātum, mandāre*—*munus,* hand, *dăre,*give.]

mandible, *man′di-bl, n.* a jaw or jawbone, esp. the lower: part of the beak of a bird, esp. the lower: one of the first pair of mouth appendages in insects or crustaceans. *adj.* **mandib′ular,** relating to the jaw. [L. *mandibula*—*mandĕre,* to chew.]

mandoline, mandolin, *man′do-lin, n.* a round-backed instrument like a guitar. [It. *mandola, mandora,* a lute, dim. *mandolino.*]

mandragora. See **mandrake.**

mandrake, *man′drāk, n.* a poisonous, narcotic plant, of the potato family, the subject of many strange fancies—also **mandrag′ora.** [L. *mandragora*—Gr. *mandragorās.*]

mandrel, *man′drel, n.* blunted steel cone fitted to a turning-lathe by which articles are secured while they are being turned. [Fr. *mandrin.*]

mandrill, *man′dril, n.* a large West African baboon. [Prob. **man,** and **drill** (baboon).]

mane, *mān, n.* long hair on the back of the neck and neighbouring parts, as in the horse and the lion. [O.E. *manu*; O.N. *mön*; Ger. *mähne.*]

manège, *man-ezh′, n.* the art of horsemanship or of training horses: a riding-school. [Fr.; cf. **manage.**]

manes, *mā′nēz, n. pl.* the spirits of departed persons, benevolent or tutelary: the spirit of an individual. [L.]

manganese, *mang′ga-nēz,* or *-nēz′, n.* a hard brittle greyish-white metallic element (symbol Mn; at. no. 25).—*adj.* **mangane′sian.** [Fr. *manganèse*—It. *manganese*—L. *magnesia.*]

mange. See **mangy.**

mangel-wurzel, mangold-wurzel, *mang′gl-wûr′zl, n.* a variety of beet cultivated as cattle food. [Ger. *mangold,* beet, *wurzel,* root.]

manger, *mānj′ér, n.* a trough in which food is laid for horses and cattle.—**dog in the manger,** one who will neither enjoy something himself nor let others do so—also used adjectively. [O.Fr. *mangeoire*—L. *mandūcāre,* to chew, eat.]

mangle, *mang′gl. v.t.* to hack to raggedness: to mutilate: to distort: to spoil by gross blunders (e.g. a quotation, a piece of music).—*n.* **mang′ler.** [Anglo-Fr. *ma(ha)ngler,* . prob. a freq. of O.Fr.*mahaigner,* to maim—*mahaing,* a hurt.]

mangle, *mang′gl, n.* a rolling-press for smoothing linen.—*v.t.* to smooth with a mangle: to calender.—*n.* **mang′ler.** [Du. *mangel*—Gr. *manganon.*]

mango, *mang′gō, n.* an East Indian tree: its fleshy fruit: a green musk-melon pickled:—*pl.* **mang′oes.** [Port. *manga*—Malay *mangga* Tamil (q.v.) *mān-kāy,* mango-fruit.]

mangold, mangold-wurzel. Same as mangel-wurzel.

mangrove, *mang′grōv, n.* a genus of trees that grow in swamps covered at high tide, or on tropical coasts and estuary shores.

mangy, *mānj′i, adj.* scabby: affected with mange: shabby, seedy: mean.—*ns.* **mange** (*mānj*), inflammation of the skin of animals caused by various mites; **mang′iness.** [Fr. *mangé,* eaten, pa.p. of *manger*—L.*mandūcāre,* to chew.]

manhandle. See **man.**

mania, *mā′ni-a, n.* violent madness: excessive or unreasonable desire, excitement, or enthusiasm.—*adj.* **ma′nic.**—*n.* **ma′niac,** a person affected with mania: a madman.—*adj.* **maniacal** (*má nī′á kl*).—*n.* **man′ic-depress′ive,** a person suffering from a type of mental illness, characterised by periods of elation and periods of depression. [L.,—Gr. *maniā.*]

manicure, *man′i-kūr, n.* the care of hands and nails: professional treatment for the hands and nails. one who practises this.—*v.t.* to apply manicure to.—*n.* **man′icurist.** [L. *manus,* hand, *cūra,* care.]

manifest, *man′i-fest, adj.* that may be easily seen by the eye or perceived by the mind.—*v.t.* to show plainly: to be evidence of: to display (e.g. a quality, a feeling): to reveal (itself) as existing: to reveal its presence (e.g. a ghost).—*n.* a list or invoice of the cargo of a ship or aeroplane to be exhibited at the custom-house: a list of passengers carried by an aeroplane.—*adj.* **manifest′able, manifest′ible,** that can be clearly shown.—*n.* **manifestā′tion,** act of disclosing: display: revelation: a public demonstration by a government or a political party.—*adv.* **man′ifestly.**—*n.* **man′ifestness.** [L. *manifestus,* prob.—*manus,* the hand, *festus,* pa.p. of obs. *fendĕre,* to dash against (as in *offendĕre*).]

manifesto, *man-i-fest′ō, n.* a public written declaration of the intentions of a sovereign or of a party. [It., L. See **manifest.**]

manifold, *man′i-fōld, adj.* showing number and variety: having various forms, applications.

&c.—*v.t.* to make manifold: to make several copies of.—*n.* that which is manifold: a carbon copy: a pipe with several outlets on the side: (**induction** or **inlet manifold**) in a multi-cylinder petrol-engine, the branched pipe that leads the mixture from the carburettor to each of the cylinders.—*adv.* **man'ifoldly.** [**many**, and suffx. -*fold.*]

manikin, mannikin, *man'i-kin, n.* a dwarf: an anatomical model: a mannequin. [Du. *manne-ken,* double dim. of *man*; Eng. **man.**]

Manila, Manilla, *ma-nil'a, n.* Manila hemp or abaca (q.v.) cheroot made in *Manila* : strong paper once made from hemp.

manioc, *man'i-ok, n.* cassava, a tropical plant from which tapioca is obtained. [S. Amer. Indian *mandioca.*]

maniple, *man'i-pl, n.* a company of foot-soldiers in the Roman army: in the Western Church, a eucharistic vestment, a narrow strip worn on the left arm.—*adj.* and *n.* **manipular** (*ma-nip'ū-lár*). [L. *manipulus,* (lit.) a handful—*manus,* the hand, *plēre,* to fill.]

manipulate, *ma-nip'ū-lāt, v.t.* to operate with the hands or by mechanical means: to handle with skill (e.g. a concrete object, a question): to manage by unfair means (a person, committee): to give a false appearance to (accounts).—*v.i.* to use the hands, esp. in scientific experiments.—*n.* **manipulā'tion.**—*adjs.* **manip'ular, manip'ulative, manip'ulatory.**—*n.* **manip'ulator.** [Low L. *manipulāre,* -*ātum*—L. *manipulus.* See **maniple.**]

manito, *man'i-tō, n.* a spirit or object of reverence among American Indians.—Also **manitou** (*-tōō̄*). [Amer. Indian.]

manna, *man'a, n.* the food of the Israelites in the wilderness: delicious food for body or mind: a sugary exudation from the **manna-ash** of Sicily and other trees. [Heb. *mān hū,* what is it? or from *man,* a gift.]

mannequin, *man'i-kin, n.* a dummy figure: a person, usu. a woman, employed to wear and display clothes. [Fr.—Du.; see **manikin.**]

manner, *man'er, n.* the way in which anything is done: personal style of acting or deportment: distinguished deportment: style of writing, painting, thought, &c.: habit: (*pl.*) morals, social customs: (*pl.*) breeding, social conduct esp. good: (*arch.*) kind, kinds (*sing.* as *pl.*—e.g. *all manner of excuses*).—*adj.* **mann'ered,** having manners (esp. in compounds, as *well-* or *ill-mannered*): affected with mannerism.—*n.* **mann'erism,** a marked peculiarity of style or manner, esp. in literary composition, carried to excess and hence tending to become wearisome.—*adj.* **mann'erly,** showing good manners.—*n.* **mann'erliness.—in a manner,** to a certain degree; **to the manner born,** (*Shak.* 'Hamlet', i. 4, 15) accustomed to the practice from birth: fitted by nature to perform an action, play a part, fill a position. [Fr. *manière*—*main*—L. *manus,* the hand.]

manoeuvre, *ma-nōō'vér,* or *-nū'-, n.* a piece of dexterous management: a stratagem: a planned movement of military or naval forces.—*v.i.* and *v.t.* to manage with art: to change the position of (troops, ships).—*adj.* **manoeu'vrable.**—*n.* **manoeuvrabil'ity.** [Fr.,—Low L. *manuopera*—L. *manū* (abl.), the

hand, *opera,* work. Cf. **manure.**]

manor, *man'ór, n.* the land belonging to a nobleman, or so much as he formerly kept for his own use: the district over which the court of the lord of the manor had authority: (*slang*) a police district.—*ns.* **man'or-house, -seat,** the house or seat belonging to a manor.—*adj.* **manorial** (*ma-nō'ri-ál*), pertaining to a manor. [O.Fr. *manoir*—L. *manēre, mansum,* to stay.]

manqué, *mā-kā, adj.* (placed after the noun) who, that, has not reached hoped-for, or possible, achiévement or fulfilment: lost or missed (e.g. *he is a poet manqué*). [Fr.]

mansard, *man'särd, n.* a roof having the lower part steeper than the upper.—Usually **mansard-roof.** [Designed by François *Mansard* or *Mansart* (1598-1666).]

manse, *mans, n.* the residence of a clergyman (*Scot.*). [Low L. *mansus, mansa,* a dwelling—*manēre, mānsum,* to remain.]

mansion, *man'sh(ó)n, n.* a house, esp. a large one: a manor-house: (*obs.*) a separate apartment or lodging in a large house.—*n.* **man'sion-house,** a mansion: (*cap.*) the official residence of the Lord Mayor of London. [O.Fr.,—L. *mansiō, -ōnis*—*manēre, mansum,* to remain.]

manteau, *man'tō, n.* (17th and 18th cents.) a woman's loose outer gown. [Fr.]

mantel, *man'tl, n.* the ornamental shelf over a fireplace.—Also **man'telpiece, man'telshelf.** [Same word as **mantle.**]

mantilla, *man-til'a, n.* a small mantle: a kind of veil covering the head and falling down upon the shoulders. [Sp.; dim. of *manta.*]

mantis, *man'tis, n.* a genus of orthopterous insects somewhat like locusts, carrying their large spinous forelegs in the attitude of prayer. [Gr. *mantis.*]

mantissa, *man-tis'a, n.* the fractional part of a logarithm. [L., make-weight.]

mantle, *man'tl, n.* a cloak or loose outer garment: a covering: a fold of the integument of a mollusc, secreting the shell: a scum on a liquid: an incandescent covering for a flame: the part of the earth immediately beneath the crust.—*v.t.* to cover: to suffuse (the cheeks). —*v.i.* to spread like a mantle: to develop a scum: to froth: to be suffused with blood.—*ns.* **man'tlet, man'telet,** a small cloak for women: (*fort.*) a movable shield or screen; **man'tling** (*her.*), the drapery of a coat-of-arms. [Partly through O.E. *mentel,* partly through O.Fr. *mantel* (Fr. *manteau*)—L. *mantellum.*]

mantua, *man'tū-a, n.* same as **manteau.**—*n.* **man'tua-mak'er,** a dressmaker. [*manteau,* confused with *Mantua* in Italy.]

manual, *man'ū-ál, adj.* of the hand: done, worked, or used by the hand.—*n.* a handbook or handy compendium of a large subject or treatise: a key-board (for the fingers) of an organ, &c.: an old office-book like the modern R.C. *Rituale.*—*adv.* **man'ually.—manual alphabet,** the signs for letters made by the deaf and dumb; **manual exercise,** drill in handling arms; **manual worker,** one who works with his hands. [L. *manuālis*—*manus,* the hand.]

manufacture, *man-ū-fakt'yur, -chúr, v.t.* to make, orig. by hand, now usu. by machinery

Neutral vowels in unaccented syllables: *em'pér-ór*; for certain sounds in foreign words see p. ix.

440

and on a large scale: to fabricate, concoct.—*n.* the process of manufacturing: anything manufactured.—*n.* **manufact′ory**, a factory a place where goods are manufactured.—*adj.* **manufact′ural.**—*n.* **manufact′urer**, one who manufactures: one who owns a factory (in whole or in part). [Fr.,—L. *manū* (abl.) by hand, *factūra*, a making, from *facĕre*, *factum*, to make.]

manumit, *man-ū-mit′*, *v.t.* to release from slavery: to set free:—*pr.p.* manūmitt′ing; *pa.t.* and *pa.p.* manūmitt′ed.—*n.* **manumission** (*-mish′(ŏ)n*) [L. manūmittĕre—*manū*, from the hand, *mittĕre*, *missum*, to send, release.]

manure, *man-ūr′*, *v.t.* to enrich with any fertilising substance.—*n.* any substance applied to land to make it more fruitful.—*n.* **manūr′er.** [Anglo-Fr. *maynoverer* (Fr. *manœuvrer*). See **manoeuvre.**]

manuscript, *man′ū-skript*, *adj.* written by hand.—*n.* a book or document written by hand: an author's copy of a work whether in writing or in typescript: writing in former times as opp. to print. [L. *manu* (abl.), by hand, *scrībĕre*, *scrīptum*, to write.]

Manx, *mangks*, *n.* the language of the Isle of Man, a Celtic language of the same group as Gaelic.—*adj.* pertaining to the Isle of Man or to its inhabitants.—**Manx cat**, a breed of cat with only a rudimentary tail.

many, *men′i*, *adj.* amounting to a great number: numerous:—*comp.* **more** (*mōr*, *mör*) *superl.* **most** (*mōst*).—*n.* many persons: a great number.—*adj.* **man′y-sid′ed**, having many qualities or aspects: having wide interests or varied abilities.—*n.* **man′y-sid′edness.—many a** (with *sing.* noun), a large number of (individual persons, things, occasions, &c.).—**one too many,** one more than is necessary or desired: hence, in the way; **one too many for one,** beyond one's powers to cope with, to circumvent, or to forestall; **the many,** the crowd. [O.E. *manig.*]

manyplies, *men′i-plīz*, *n. sing.* and *pl.* the third stomach of a ruminant. [**many**, **ply** (1).]

Maori, *mow′ri*, *mä′ō-ri*, *n.* a member of the brown race of New Zealand: the language of this race:—*pl.* **Mao′ris.** [Maori.]

map, *map*, *n.* a representation in outline of the surface features of the earth, the moon, &c., or of part of it, usu. on a plane surface: a similar plan of the stars in the sky: a representation or scheme of the disposition or state of anything.—*v.t.* to make a map of: (*math.*) to place (the elements of a set) in one-to-one correspondence with the elements of another set:—*pr.p.* mapp′ing; *pa.t.* and *pa.p.* mapped. —**map out**, (*lit.* and *fig.*) to plan in detail (a route, a course of action). [L. *mappa*, a napkin, a painted cloth, orig. Punic (q.v.).]

maple, *mā′pl*, *n.* a tree of several species, from the sap of some of which sugar can be made. [O.E. *mapul*, maple.]

maqui, *mä′kē*, *n.* (*bot.*) a thicket formation of shrubs, esp. along the Mediterranean coast. The *dial.* form **maquis** (*mä′kē*) was applied to members of the French underground anti-German movement in the Second World War. [Fr.,—It. *macchia*—L. *macula*, mesh.]

mar, *mär*, *v.t.* to spoil, to impair, to injure, to

damage, to disfigure:—*pr.p.* marr′ing; *pa.t.* and *pa.p.* marred. [O.E. *merran.*]

marabou(t), *mar′a-bōō*, *n.* a species of W. African stork, the feathers of which are used as trimming, &c. [Fr.—prob. from the following.]

marabout, *mar′a-bōōt*, *n.* a Mohammedan hermit, esp. in N. Africa: a Moslem shrine. [Ar.]

marah, *mä′ra*, *n.* bitterness: something bitter. [Heb.]

maraschino, *mar as kē′nō*, *n.* a liqueur distilled from a cherry grown in Dalmatia. [It.—*marasca*, *amarasca*, a sour cherry—L. *amārus*, bitter.]

Marathi, *ma-rä′-ti*, or *-rat′i*, *n.* a Sanskritic language, spoken by the *Mahrattas* of southwestern and central India.

marathon, *mar′a-thon*, *n.* (also **marathon race**) a long-distance foot-race (now usu. 26 miles 385 yards): a long-distance race in other sports, e.g. swimming: any contest in endurance. [*Marathon*, town and plain 22 miles from Athens. A soldier ran this distance without stopping bringing news of a Greek victory over the Persians, 490 B.C.]

maraud, *ma-röd′*, *v.i.* to rove in quest of plunder.—*n.* **maraud′er.** [Fr. *maraud*, rogue.]

marble, *mär′bl*, *n.* any species of limestone taking a high polish: a slab, work of art, or other object made of marble; a little hard ball (originally of marble) used by boys in play.— *adj.* composed of marble: hard: insensible.— *v.t.* to stain or vein like marble.—*n.* **mar′bler.**—*adj.* **mar′bly**, like marble.—**Elgin marbles,** a collection of marbles obtained chiefly from the Parthenon by Lord *Elgin* in 1811, now in the British Museum. [O.F. *marbre.*—L. *marmor*; cf. Gr. *marmaros*—*marmairein*, to sparkle.]

marcel, *mär-sel′*, *n.* (in full **marcel wave**) an artificial wave imparted to hair by a hot iron, a comb, and manipulation. [*Marcel*, a French hairdresser, the inventor (1872).]

March, *märch*, *n.* the third month of the year (in England until 1752 the year began on March 25th). [L. *Martius* (*mēnsis*), (the month) of Mars.]

march, *märch*, *n.* a boundary: border: a border district:—used chiefly in *pl.* **march′es.**—*v.i.* to have a common frontier (with).—**riding the marches,** a ceremony in which the magistrates and others ride round the bounds of a municipality, so as to mark plainly what are its limits. [Fr. *marche*; of Gmc. origin; cf. **mark** (1).]

march, *märch*, *v.i.* to walk in a markedly rhythmical military manner, or in a grave, stately, or resolute manner.—*v.t.* to cause to march.—*n.* a marching movement: distance traversed at a stretch by marching: regular forward movement (e.g. of events): a piece of music fitted for marching to.—**forced march,** a march in which the men are vigorously pressed forward for combative or strategic purposes; **steal a march on,** to gain an advantage over, esp. in a sly or secret manner. [Fr. *marcher*, to walk, prob.—L. *marcus*, a hammer.]

marchioness, *mär′shon-es*, *n. fem.* of **marquis.** [L.L. *marchionissa*, fem. of *marchiō*, *-ōnis*, a lord of the marches.]

marconigram, *mär-kŏ'ni-gram, n.* a message transmitted by wireless telegraphy. [*Marconi* (1874-1937), the inventor, and Gr. *gramma,* a letter.]

mare, *mār, n.* the female of the horse.—*ns.* **mare's'-nest,** a supposed discovery that turns out to be an illusion or a hoax; **mare's'-tail,** a tall, erect marsh plant. [O.E. *mere,* fem. of *mearh,* a horse; cog. with Ger. *mähre,* O.N. *merr,* W. *march,* a horse.]

mare, *mā'rē, mä'rā, n.* any of various darkish level areas in (*a*) the moon, (*b*) Mars:—*pl.* **maria** (*mā'ri-a, mä'-*). [L., sea.]

mareschal, *mär'shäl.* Same as **marshal.**

margarine, *mär'gár-ēn* (sometimes *märj'ár-ēn*), *n.* a butterlike substance made from vegetable oils and fats, &c. [Gr. *margarītēs,* a pearl.]

marge, *märj, n.* (*poet.*) margin, brink. [Fr.,—L. *margō, -inis.*]

margin, *mär'jin, n.* an edge, border (e.g. of a lake): the blank edge on the page of a book: something (e.g. money, time, space) allowed more than is needed, as provision against unforeseen happenings: condition near the limit below, or beyond, which a thing ceases to be possible or desirable.—*adj.* **mar'ginal,** pertaining to a margin: placed in the margin: close to the limit: barely sufficient.—*n.* **marginā'lia,** notes written on the margin.—*adv.* **mar'ginally.**—*adjs.* **mar'ginate, -d,** having a margin.—**marginal constituency, seat,** a constituency that does not provide a safe seat for any of the political parties; **marginal land,** less fertile land which will be cultivated only if economic conditions justify this. [L. *margō, -inis*; cf. **mark, march** (2).]

margrave, *mär'grāv, n.* a German nobleman of rank equivalent to an English marquis:—*fem.* **margravine** (*mär'grä-vēn*). [Middle Du. *markgrave* (Du. *markgraaf*; Ger. *markgraf*)—*mark,* a border, *grave* (mod. *graaf*), a count.]

marguerite, *mär'gē-rēt, n.* the oxeye daisy or other single chrysanthemum. [Fr. *marguerite,* daisy—Gr. *margarītēs,* pearl.]

marigold, *mar'i-gōld, n.* a yellow-flowered composite, or its flower. [From the Virgin *Mary* and **gold.**]

marijuana, marihuana, *mä-ri-*(H)*wä'nä, n.* dried flowers and leaves of hemp smoked for their intoxicating effect. [Amer. Sp.]

marina, *mä-rē'nä, n.* a yacht station equipped with every kind of facility for a yachting holiday. [Formed from **marine.**]

marine, *ma-ren', adj.* of, in, near, or belonging to, the sea: done or used at sea: inhabiting, found in, or got from the sea.—*n.* a soldier serving on shipboard: shipping, naval and mercantile: naval affairs.—*n.* **mar'iner,** a sailor.—**tell that to the marines,** a phrase expressive of disbelief and ridicule, from the sailor's contempt for the marine's ignorance of seamanship. [Fr.,—L. *marīnus—mare,* sea.]

Mariolatry, *mä-ri-ol'a-tri, n.* worship of the Virgin *Mary* (usu. expressing disapprobation). [Gr. *Maria,* Mary, *latreiā,* worship.]

marionette, *mar-i-o-net', n.* a puppet moved by strings. [Fr., dim. of the name *Marion.*]

marish, *mar'ish, n.* and *adj.* Same as **marsh.**

marital, *mar'i-tál, ma-rī'tál, adj.* pertaining to a husband: pertaining to marriage. [L. *marī-*

tālis—marītus, a husband.]

maritime, *mar'i-tīm, adj.* pertaining to the sea: relating to sea-going or sea-trade: having a sea-coast: situated near the sea: having navy and sea-trade. [L. *maritimus—mare,* sea.]

marjoram, *mär'jo-räm, n.* an aromatic plant used as a seasoning: various other plants of the same family. [O.Fr. *majorane.*]

mark, *märk, n.* a boundary: a border territory: a boundary stone, post, or the like: an object serving as a guide: an object aimed at: a visible sign: an impressed stamp or other distinctive device (see **earmark, hall-mark, trade-mark**): a substitute for a signature: a distinguishing characteristic: distinction: a stain, scar, &c.: a point awarded for merit: a written symbol (as, *a question mark*): the impression of a rugby footballer's heel on the ground, made on obtaining a fair catch.—*v.t.* to make a mark on: to impress with a sign: to note: to indicate: to destine: to record (points gained in a game): to keep close (to an opponent) so as to hamper him if he receives the ball (in football, &c.): to be a feature of.—*adj.* **marked,** having marks: indicated: noticeable: prominent: emphatic: watched and suspected: doomed.—*adv.* **mark'edly** (*-id-*), noticeably. —*ns.* **mark'er,** one who marks the score at games, as at billiards: a counter or other device for scoring: something that marks a position, as a stationary light, a flare; **mark'ing-ink,** indelible ink, used for marking clothes; **marks'man,** one good at hitting a mark; one who shoots well.—**mark time,** to move the feet alternately in the same manner as in marching, but without changing ground: to keep things going without progressing.—**make one's mark,** to leave a lasting impression: to gain great influence; **up to the mark,** perfect, measured by a certain standard: in good health. [O.E. (Mercian) *merc* (W.S. *mearc*), a boundary.]

mark, *märk, n.* an obsolete English coin= 13s. 4d. (66.6p): a coin of Germany (1924 reichsmark, 1948 deutsche mark), of Finland, and formerly of various other European countries. [O.E. *marc,* of doubtful origin.]

market, *mär'ket, n.* a periodic concourse of people for the purpose of buying and selling: public place used for such meetings: sale: rate of sale: demand (for), or region in which that demand is felt (e.g. *there is no market for these goods; India was once a profitable market for Lancashire cotton*).—*v.i.* to deal at a market: to buy and sell.—*v.t.* to put on the market.—*adj.* **mar'ketable,** fit for the market: saleable.—*ns.* **mar'ket-cross,** a cross anciently set up where a market was held; **mar'ket-gar'den** (see **garden**); **mar'ket-price,** the current price; **mar'ket-research',** research into consumers' preferences and spending power; **mar'ket-town,** a town having the privilege of holding a public market.—**Common Market,** see **common.** [Late O.E. *market*—Norman-Fr. *market*—L. *mercātus,* trade,—a market—*merx,* merchandise.]

marl, *märl, n.* a limy clay often used as manure.—*v.t.* to cover with marl.—*adj.* **mar'ly,** like marl: abounding in marl. [O.Fr. *marle* (Fr. *marne*)—Low L. *margila,* a dim. of L. *marga.*]

Neutral vowels in unaccented syllables: *em'pér-ór*; for certain sounds in foreign words see p. ix.

marline, *mär′lin*, *n.* a small rope for winding round a larger one to keep it from wearing.— *n.* **mar′linespike**, a spike for separating the strands of a rope in splicing. [Du. *marling— marren*, to bind, and *lijn*, rope.]

marmalade, *mär′má-lād*, *n.* a jam or preserve generally made of the pulp of oranges, originally of quinces. [Fr. *marmelade*, through Port. and L.—Gr. *melimēlon*, a sweet apple—*meli*, honey, *mēlon*, an apple.]

marmoreal,*mär-mōr′e-ál*, *-mōr′-*, *adj.* of, or like, marble. [L. *marmor*, marble.]

marmoset, *mär′mō* ȥet, *n.* a group of very small American monkeys. [Fr. *marmouset*, grotesque figure.]

marmot,*mär′mot*, *n.* a genus of stout burrowing rodents, in America called woodchucks. [It. *marmotto*—L.*mūs*, *mūris*, mouse,*mons*, *montis*, mountain.]

marocain, *mar′ō-kān*, *n.* a dress material finished with a grain surface like morocco leather [Fr.—*maroquin*, morocco leather.]

maroon, mar-rōōn′, n. a brownish-red: a loud warning firework. [Fr. *marron*, a chestnut.]

maroon, *ma-rōōn′*, *n.* a fugitive slave: a marooned person.—*v.t.* to put on shore on a desolate island: to isolate uncomfortably. [Fr. *marron*—Sp. *cimarrón*, wild.]

marque, *märk*, *n.* See **letter-of-marque**. [Fr.]

marquee, *mär-kē′*, *n.* a large tent. [From **mar-quise**, as if that word were pl.]

marquetry, marqueterie,*märk′et-ri*, *n.* work inlaid with pieces of various-coloured wood. [Fr. *marqueterie—marqueter*, to inlay—*marque*, a mark.]

marquis, marquess, *mär′kwis*, *n.* a title of nobility next below that of a duke:—*fem.* **mar′chioness**. *ns.* **mar′quisāte**, **-quessāte**, the lordship of a marquis; **marquise** (*mär-kēz′*), in France, a marchioness: a marquee: a finger-ring set with a cluster of gems, the cluster being oval in shape but with pointed ends. [From O.Fr. *marchis* (but assimilated later to Fr. *marquis*.)—Low L. *marchensis*, a prefect of the marches.]

marriage, *mar′ij*, *n.* the ceremony, act, or contract by which a man and woman become husband and wife: the union of a man and woman as husband and wife: (*fig.*) union, joining together.—*adj.* **marr′iageable**, suitable, or at a proper age, for marriage.—*ns.* **marr′iage(-)li′cence**, a licence to marry without proclamation of banns in a church; **mar-r′iage(-)portion**, a dowry, **marr′iage(-)sett′le-ment**, an arrangement of property, &c., before marriage, by which something is secured to the wife or her children if the husband dies.—**marriage of convenience**, a marriage entered into because of the ensuing political, economic, &c. advantages. [O.Fr. *mariage— marier*. See **marry**.]

marron glacé, *mar-ō gla-sā*, a sweet chestnut preserved in syrup or iced with sugar. [Fr.]

marrow, *mar′ō*, *n.* the soft tissue in the hollow parts of the bones: a vegetable marrow (see under **vegetable**): the essence or best part of anything.—*n.* **marr′ow-bone**, a bone containing marrow.—*adj.* **marr′owy**, full of marrow: pithy. [O.E. (Anglian) *merg*, *mærh* (W.S. *mearg*), Ger. *mark*.]

marry, *mar′i*, *v.t.* to take for husband or wife: to give in marriage: to unite in matrimony: to unite, join, put together.—*v.i.* to enter into the married state:—*pr.p.* marr′ying;*pa.t.* and *pa.p.* marr′ied. [Fr. *marier*—L. *marītāre*, to marry, *marītus*, a husband—*mās*, *maris*, a male.]

Mars,*märz*, *n.* the Roman god of war: the planet next after the earth in the order of distance from the sun. [L. *Mars*, *Mārtis*.]

Marsala, *mär-sä′lä*, *n.* a light wine resembling sherry, from *Marsala* in Sicily.

Marseillaise, *mär-sě-lāz′*, *n.* the French national anthȯm, orig. a revolutionary hymn, first sung by men of *Marseilles* as they entered Paris in 1792 to aid in the Revolution.

marsh, *märsh*, *n.* a tract of low wet land: a morass, swamp, or fen.—*adj.* inhabiting or found in marshes.—*ns.* **marsh′-fē′ver**, malaria; **marsh′-gas**, fire-damp (q.v.); **marsh′-mall′ow**, a marsh-growing plant: a gelatinous sweetmeat, originally made from its root.—*adj.* **marsh′y**, of the nature of marsh: abounding in marshes.—*n.* **marsh′iness**.[O.Fr. *marer*, *marish*, orig. adj.—*mere*. See **mere**(1).]

marshal, *mär′shál*, *n.* an officer charged with the care of military arrangements, regulation of ceremonies, preservation of order, &c.: the chief officer who regulated combats in the lists: in France, &c., an officer of the highest military rank: (*U.S.*) a civil officer appointed to execute the process of the courts.—*v.t.* to arrange in order (e.g. troops, or *fig.* facts, arguments): to usher:—*pr.p.* mar′shalling; *pa.t.* and *pa.p.* mar′shalled.—*ns.* **mar′shaller**; **mar′shalship**.—**air′-mar′shal** (see **air**); **field′-mar′shal** (see **field**); **marshal of the Royal Air Force**, an officer of supreme rank in the Royal Air Force, ranking with an admiral of the fleet or a field-marshal. [O.Fr.*mareschal* (Fr.*maréchal*); from O.H.G. *marah*, a horse, *schalh* (Ger. *schalk*), a servant.]

marsupial, *mär-sū′pi-ál*, *adj.* carrying young in a pouch.—*n.* a marsupial animal. [L. *mar-sūpium*—Gr. *marsipion*, *marsypion*, a pouch.]

mart,*märt*, *n.* a place of trade. [Du.*markt*, *mart*; cf. **market**.]

martello, *mär-tel′ō*, *n.* a circular fort for coast defence. [From *Mortella* Point in Corsica, where one resisted for some time a British cannonade in 1794.]

marten, *mär′tēn*, *n.* any of several carnivorous mammals allied to the weasel, valued for their fur. [Fr. *martre*, from the Gmc. root seen in Ger. *marder*, and O.E. *mearth*, marten.]

martial, *mär′shál*, *adj.* belonging to Mars, the god of war: of or belonging to war: warlike.— *adv.* **mar′tially**.—**martial law**, the law administered by the military power in times of war and in great national emergencies, ordinary administration ceasing to be operative. [Fr. *martial*—L. *mārtiālis*—*Mārs*.]

Martian, *mär′shán*, *-shi-án*, *adj.* of Mars (god or planet): of battle.—*n.* an imagined inhabitant of Mars. [L. *Mārtius—Mārs*.]

martin, *mär′tin*, *n.* any of several species of swallow. [The name *Martin*; cf. **robin**, &c.]

martinet, *mär-ti-net′*, or *mär′-*, *n.* a strict disciplinarian. [From *Martinet*, a very strict officer in the army of Louis XIV of France.]

martingal(e), *mär′tin-gāl*, *-gal*, *n.* a strap

fastened to a horse's girth, passing between his forelegs, and attached to the bit or reins, so as to keep his head down: a short spar under the bowsprit. [Fr., perh. from a kind of breeches worn at *Martigues* in Provence.]

Martinmas, *mär'tin-màs, n.* the mass or feast of St *Martin,* Nov. 11.

martlet, *märt'let, n.* a martin: (*her.*) a footless bird. [From Fr. *martinet,* dim. of *martin.*]

martyr, *mär'tér, n.* one who by his death bears witness to his belief: one who suffers for his belief: a chronic sufferer from a disease (with *to*).—*v.t.* to put to death for his belief: to inflict suffering on.—*ns.* **mar'tyrdom,** the sufferings or death of a martyr; **martyrol'ogy,** a history of martyrs: a discourse on martyrdom; **martyrol'ogist.** [O.E.,—L.,—Gr., a witness.]

marvel, *mär'vél, n.* anything astonishing or wonderful.—*v.i.* to wonder (how, why): to feel astonishment (at):—*pr.p.* **mar'velling;** *pa.t.* and *pa.p.* **mar'velled.**—*adj.* **mar'vellous,** astonishing: beyond belief, improbable: (*coll.*) very good, extremely pleasing.—*adv.* **mar'vellously.** —*n.* **mar'vellousness.** [Fr. *merveille*—L. *mīrābilis,* wonderful—*mīrārī,* to wonder.]

Marxian, *märks'i-àn, n.* a follower of the socialist Karl *Marx* (1818-83).—*adj.* pertaining to Marx or to his theories (see **dialectical materialism**).—*adj.* **Marxist.**

marybud, *mā'ri-bud, n.* a marigold bud. [**Mary, bud.**]

marzipan, *mär-zi-pan', n.* a sweetmeat of crushed almonds and sugar. [Through Low L. from Ar.; older form *marchpane;* marzipan is Ger. form.]

Masai, *mä'sī, n.* an African people of the highlands of Kenya and Tanzania.—Also *adj.*

mascara, *mas-kä'rä, n.* colouring for the eyelashes. [Sp. *máscara.* See **mask.**]

mascon, *mas'kon, n.* any of several mass concentrations of dense material lying beneath the moon's surface. [*mass con*centration.]

mascot, *mas'kot, n.* a person, creature, or thing supposed to bring good luck. [Fr. *mascotte.*]

masculine, *mas'kū-lin, adj.* characteristic of, peculiar to, or appropriate to, a man or the male sex: mannish: (*gram.*) of that gender to which belong words denoting males.—*adv.* **mas'culinely.**—*ns.* **mas'culineness, masculin'ity.** [Fr.,—L. *masculīnus*—*masculus,* male—*mās,* a male.]

maser, *māz'ér, n.* a device used to amplify long range radar, television, radio astronomy, &c. signals (very small when not amplified) while generating little unwanted noise within itself. [*M*icrowave *a*mplification by *s*timulated *e*mission of *r*adiation.]

mash, *mash, n.* in brewing, a mixture of crushed malt and hot water: a mixture, as of bran with meal or turnips, beaten and stirred as a food for animals.—*v.t.* to make into a mash: to pound down or crush. [O.E. *masc(-wyrt), mash(-wort).*]

mashie, mashy, *mash'i, n.* an iron golf club for lofting. [Perh. Fr. *massue,* club.]

mask, masque, *mäsk, n.* anything disguising or concealing the face: anything that disguises or conceals: a pretence: a masquerade: a dramatic spectacle in which the actors sometimes appear masked: a drama for such: a pageant: a likeness of a face in any material, as in clay: a protective covering for the face: a fox's head.—*v.t.* to cover the face of with a mask: to hide: to disguise.—*v.i.* to masquerade: to be disguised in any way. [Fr. *masque.*—Sp. *máscara* or It. *maschera,* of doubtful origin.]

masochism, *maz'o-kizm, n.* (*psych.*) abnormal pleasure obtained from the suffering of physical or mental pain, esp. as inflicted by a member of the other sex. [From the novelist Sacher-*Masoch* who described it.]

mason, *mā'sn, n.* one who cuts, prepares, and lays stones, a builder in stone: a freemason.—*adj.* **masonic** (*ma-son'ik*), relating to freemasonry.—*n.* **mā'sonry,** work executed by a mason, stonework: the art of building in stone: freemasonry. [O.Fr. *masson* (Fr. *maçon*)—Low L. *maciō, -ōnis,* prob. Gmc.]

masque. See **mask.**

masquerade, *mäsk-ér-ād', n.* an assembly of persons wearing masks, generally at a ball: acting or living under false pretences.—*v.i.* to join in a masquerade: to assume a false appearance: to pretend to be (*to masquerade as*).—*n.* **masquerad'er.** [Fr. *mascarade,* from Sp. cf. **mask.**]

mass, *mas, n.* a lump of matter: a large quantity: a dense aggregate of objects: a body of persons regarded as an aggregate in which individuality is lost: the principal part or main body (e.g. of exports): quantity of matter in any body, weight being proportional to mass: (*pl.*) the lower classes of the people.—*adj.* pertaining to a mass or to large numbers or quantities, or to ordinary people as a whole.—*v.t.* to bring together in masses: to concentrate (troops).—Also *v.i.*—*adj.* **massive** (*mas'iv*), bulky: weighty: large and bold (of the features): without crystalline form, geologically homogeneous: (*fig.*) on a very large scale, of great size or power.—*adv.* **mass'ively.** —*ns.* **mass'iveness; mass medium,** any medium of communication (e.g. newspapers, television) reaching large numbers of people: —*pl.* **mass media; mass'-meet'ing,** a large meeting for a public discussion; **mass number,** the sum of the protons and neutrons present in the nucleus of a particular isotope; **mass'-produc'tion,** production on a huge scale by a standardised process (*v.t.* **mass'-produce'**).—*adj.* **mass'y,** having bulk and weight. [Fr. *masse*—L. *massa,* a lump, prob.— Gr. *māza,* a barley cake—*massein,* to knead.]

mass, *mass, mäss, n.* the celebration of the Lord's Supper in R.C. churches: also the office for it: a musical setting of certain parts of the R.C. liturgy: a church festival or feast-day, as in *Candlemas, Christmas, Martinmas,* &c.—**High Mass,** a mass celebrated with music, ritual, ceremonies, and incense; **Low Mass,** the ordinary mass celebrated without music and incense; **Solemn Mass,** a mass resembling a High Mass, but without some of its special ceremonies. [O.E. *mæsse*—Low L. *missa*—L. *mittére,* to send away, perh. from the phrase at the close of the service, *Ite, missa est* (*ecclesia*), 'Go, (the congregation) is dismissed'.]

massacre, *mas'ak-ér, n.* an indiscriminate slaughter, esp. with cruelty: carnage.—*v.t.* to

Neutral vowels in unaccented syllables: *em'pér-ór*; for certain sounds in foreign words see p. ix.

444

kill with violence and cruelty. [Fr.]

massage, *ma-säzh′*, *n.* a system of remedial treatment by stroking, pressing, tapping, friction, &c.—*v.t.* to subject to massage.—*n.* **masseur** (*-œr′*):—*fem.* **masseuse** (*-œz′*). [Fr., from Gr. *massein*, to knead.]

massif, *ma-sēf′*, *mas′if*, *n.* a central mountain-mass. [Fr.]

mast, *mäst*, *n.* a long upright pole, esp. one for carrying the sails of a ship.—*v.t.* to supply with a mast or masts.—*adj.* **mast′ed.**—*n.* **mast′-head**, the head or top of the mast of a ship: the name of a newspaper or magazine in the typographical form in which it normally appears, or a similar block of information regularly used as a heading.—**lower mast, topmast, topgallant mast, royal mast,** names of the lengths (reckoning from the deck upwards) of which a built-up mast on a large sailing vessel is formed. [O.E. *mæst*; Ger. *mast.*]

mast, *mäst*, *n.* the fruit of the oak, beech, chestnut, and other forest trees, on which swine feed. [O.E. *mæst*; Ger. *mast.*]

mastectomy, *mas-tek′to mi*, *n.* surgical removal of a breast. [Gr. *mastos*, breast, *ektomē*, cutting out.]

master, *mäs′tẽr*, *n.* one who commands or controls: an owner (e.g. of a slave, a dog): a teacher (of pupils, disciples): an employer: the commander of a merchant ship: formerly the navigator or sailing-master of a ship-of-war: one eminently skilled in anything: a painting by a great artist: a title of dignity or office, as *Master of the Rolls* (a high judicial officer): a degree conferred by universities, as *Master of Arts.*—*adj.* chief: predominant: of the rank of a master: showing the ability of a master.—*v.t.* to become master of: to overcome: to become skilful in.—*ns.* **mas′ter-build′er**, **mās′on**, &c., a chief builder, mason, &c., one who directs or employs others; **mas′ter(-)card**, the card that commands a suit.—*adj.* **mas′terful**, exercising the authority or power of a master: imperious.—*adv.* **mas′terfully.**—*ns.* **mas′ter hand**, the hand of a master: a person highly skilled; **mas′ter(-)key**, a key that opens many locks.—*adjs.* **mas′terless**, without a master or owner: unsubdued; **mas′terly**, like, with the skill of, a master.—*ns.* **mas′ter-mar′iner**, the captain of a merchant vessel or fishing vessel; **mas′termind**, one who exhibits superior mental power: the controlling spirit in any project (*v.t.* to originate, think out, and direct); **mas′terpiece**, piece of work worthy of a master: one's greatest achievement; **mas′tership**, the office of master; **mas′ter stroke**, a stroke or performance worthy of a master, a skilful move; **master switch**, a switch for controlling the effect of a number of other switches or contactors; **mas′tery**, the power or authority of a master: upper hand: control: masterly skill or knowledge.—*past(-)master*, one who has occupied the office of master, esp. among freemasons—hence a thorough master in or of a subject. [Partly O.E. *mægester*, partly O.Fr. *maistre* (Fr. *maître*), both from L. *magister*, from root of *magnus*, great.]

mastic, mastich, *mas′tik*, *n.* a pale yellow gum-resin from the lentisk and other trees, used for fine varnish: a tree exuding mastic: a bituminous or oily cement of various kinds. [Fr. *mastic*—L.L. *mastichum*—Gr. *mastichē.*]

masticate, *mas′ti-kāt*, *v.t.* to chew: to knead mechanically, as in rubber manufacture.—*adj.* **mas′ticable**, that may be chewed.—*n.* **masticā′tion.**—*adj.* **mas′ticatory**, chewing: adapted for chewing.—*n.* a substance chewed to increase the saliva. [L. *masticāre, -ātum*; cf Gr. *mastax*, jaw.]

mastiff, *mas′tif*, *n.* a thick-set and powerful variety of dog, formerly used in hunting. [O.Fr. *mastin*, app. L. *mansuētus*, tame; perh. confused with O.Fr. *mestif*, mongrel.]

mastodon, *mas′to-don*, *n.* a genus of extinct elephants, so named from the teat-like prominences on the molar teeth. [Gr. *mastos*, breast, *odous, -ontos*, a tooth.]

mastoid, *mas′toid*, *adj.* breast-like.—*n.* the **mastoid process**, a bone projection behind the ear: loosely, inflammation of the air cells of the mastoid process [Gr. *mastos*, a breast, *eidos*, form.]

masturbation, *mas-tūr-bā′shŏn*, *n.* stimulation by oneself of the sexual organs.—*v.i.* **mas′turbate.** [L. *masturbārī.*]

mat, *mat*, *n.* a piece of fabric of plaited rushes, straw, coarse fibre, &c., or of rubber, wire, or other material, for wiping shoes, for covering a floor, for standing, sleeping, &c., on, or for other purposes.—*v.t.* to cover with mats: to interweave: to tangle closely.—Also *v.i.* to become thickly tangled:—*pr.p.* **matt′ing**; *pa.t.* and *pa.p.* **matt′ed.**—*n.* **matt′ing**, process of becoming matted: material used as mats. [O.E. *matt(e), meatte*—L. *matta*, a mat.]

mat(t), *mat*, *adj.* having a dull surface, without lustre. [Fr. *mat*; Ger. *matt*, dull.]

matador, matadore, *mat′a-dör*, *n.* the man who is appointed to kill the bull in bull-fights. [Sp. *matador*—*matar*, to kill—L. *mactāre*, to kill, to honour by sacrifice.]

match, *mach*, *n.* short stick of wood or other material tipped with an easily ignited material: a prepared cord for firing a gun, &c.—*ns.* **match′lock**, (*hist.*) the lock of a musket containing a match for firing it: a musket so fired; **match′wood**, wood suitable for matches: splinters. [O.Fr. *mesche* (Fr. *mèche*).]

match, *mach*, *n.* that which tallies or exactly agrees with another thing: an equal: a person able to cope with another (e.g. *Jack is a match for Jim*): a contest or game: a marriage: a person considered from the point of view of his or her eligibility in marriage.—*v.i.* to be exactly or nearly alike: to fit in (with), be suitable (to).—*v.t.* to be equal or similar to in size, figure, colour, &c.: to find an equal to, in size, &c.: to be fit to compete with: to encounter successfully: to set against as equal: to join in marriage.—*adj.* **match′less**, having no equal: peerless.—*adv.* **match′lessly.**—*n.* **match′lessness.** [O.E. *gemæcca.*]

mate, *māt*, *n.* a companion: a fellow workman: a friendly or ironic form of address: an equal: a husband or wife: an animal with which another is paired: one of a pair: a ship's officer under the captain or master: an assistant to some functionary (e.g. surgeon's mate).—*v.t.*

and *v.i.* to marry: to pair.—*adj.* **mate′less,** without a mate or companion. [Prob. Middle Low Ger. *mate,* or Du. *maet* (now *maat*); cf. O.E. *gemetta,* a messmate, and **meat.**]

mate, *māt, v.t.* to checkmate: to baffle.—*n.* and *interj.* checkmate. [O.Fr. *mat,* checkmated. See **checkmate.**]

mate, maté, *mä′tā, n.* a South American species of holly: an infusion of its leaves and green shoots, Paraguay tea. See **yerba mate.** [Sp. *mate,* orig. the vessel in which it was infused for drinking.]

mater, *mā′tér, mä′ter, n.* a mother.—**māterfamil′ias,** a mother and head of a household. [L. *māter,* mother, *familiās,* old gen. of *familia,* household.]

material, *ma-tē′ri-ál, adj.* relating to, or consisting of, matter: corporeal, not spiritual: lacking spirituality in conduct or point of view: essential (e.g. to happiness, to one's advantage): important, esp. of legal importance.—*n.* that out of which anything is or may be made.—*v.t.* **matē′rialise,** to render material: to reduce to or regard as matter: to render materialistic.— *v.i.* to take bodily form: (*coll.*) to become actual.—*ns.* **materialisā′tion; matē′rialism,** any doctrine that denies the independent existence of spirit, and maintains that there is but one substance—matter: the theory that all phenomena, all developments, connected with human life on this earth are traceable to physical or material causes, not due to the operation of spiritual forces: tendency to attach too great importance to one's material interests; **matē′rialist.**—Also *adj.*—*adjs.* **materialist′ic, -al.**—*adv.* **matē′rially.**—*ns.* **matē′rialness, materiality** (*-al′i-ti*).—**material evidence,** evidence tending to prove or to disprove the matter under judgment.—**dialectical materialism** (see **dialectical**); **raw material,** material suitable for manufacture, development, training, &c., but still in, or nearly in, the natural state. [L. *māteriālis*—*māteria,* matter.]

materia medica, *mä-tē′ri-a med′i-ka,* (the science of) the substances used as remedies in medicine. [Mediaeval L.]

maternal, *ma-tûr′nál, adj.* belonging or pertaining to a mother: becoming to a mother, motherly.—*adv.* **mater′nally.**—*n.* **mater′nity,** the state, character, or relation of a mother.—*adj.* intended for women during pregnancy or confinement. [Fr. *maternel* (It. *maternale*) and *maternité.*—L. *māternus*—*māter,* mother.]

mathematic, -al, *math-ē-mat′ik, -ál, adj.* pertaining to, or done by, mathematics: very accurate.—*adv.* **mathemat′ically.**—*ns.* **mathematician** (*-ish′án*), one versed in mathematics; **mathemat′ics** (treated as *sing.*), the science of magnitude and number, the relations of figures and forms, and of quantities expressed as symbols. [Gr. *mathēmatikē* (*epistēmē*), mathematical (knowledge, science)— *mathēma*—*manthanein,* to learn.]

matin, *mat′in, n.* (*pl.*) the daily morning service of the Church of England: (*pl.*) one of the seven canonical hours of the R.C. Church usually sung between midnight and daybreak: morning song of birds.—*adjs.* **matin; mat′inal.**—*n.* **matinée** (*mat′i-nā*; Fr.), a public entertainment or reception held in the daytime,

usually in the afternoon. [Fr. *matines* (fem.pl.)—L. *mātūtīnus,* belonging to the morning.]

matriarchy, *mā′tri-är-ki, n.* government by a mother or by mothers: an order of society in which descent is reckoned in the female line.—*n.* **mā′triarch,** a woman who is head and ruler of her family and descendants: an elderly woman who dominates her family or associates: an old woman of great dignity.— *adj.* **matria′rchal.** [From L. *māter,* mother, on analogy of **patriarch(y).**]

matricide, *mat′ri-sīd, n.* one who murders his (her) own mother: the murder of one's own mother.—*adj.* **matrici′dal.** [L. *mātricīda, mātricīdium*—*māter,* mother, *caedēre,* to kill.]

matriculate, *ma-trik′ū-lāt, v.t.* to admit (student, &c.) to membership of a college, &c., by entering his or her name in a register.—*v.i.* to become a member of a college, university, &c., by being enrolled.—*n.* **matriculā′tion,** act of matriculating: state of being matriculated: an entrance examination (familiarly **matric′**). [Late L. *mātrīcula,* a register, dim. of *mātrīx*; see **matrix.**]

matrimony, *mat′ri-món-i, n.* a state of being married: rite of marriage: a card game.—*adj.* **matrimonial** (*-mō′ni-ál*).—*adv.* **matrimō′nially** [O.Fr. *matrimoine*—L. *mātrimōnium*— *māter, mātris,* mother.]

matrix, *mā′triks,* or *mat′riks, n.* (*anat.*) the womb: the cavity in which anything is formed: that in which anything is embedded: a mould: (*math.*) a rectangular array of quantities or symbols:—*pl.* **matrices** (*māt-,* or *mat′-ris-ēz*) or **matrixes.** [L. *mātrīx, -īcis,* a breeding animal, later, the womb—*māter,* mother.]

matron, *mā′trón, n.* a married woman: an elderly lady of staid and sober habits: a woman in charge of nursing and domestic arrangements in a hospital, school, or other institution.—*adj.* **mā′tronly,** like, becoming, or belonging to a matron: elderly: sedate. [Fr. *matrone*—L. *mātrōna*—*māter,* mother.]

matt. See **mat** (2).

matter, *mat′ér, n.* that which occupies space, and with which we become acquainted by our bodily senses: physical substance as opposed to spirit, mind: that out of which anything is made, material: subject or material of thought, speech, writing, &c.: thing, affair, concern, business (*also pl.*): something that is amiss: pus, or the fluid in boils, tumours, and festering sores.—*v.i.* to be of importance: to signify: to form or discharge pus:—*pr.p.* **mat′tering;** *pa.p.* **mat′tered.**—**a matter of** (with quantity), approximately; **matter for, of,** occasion for, of; **matt′er-of-fact,** adhering to literal or actual fact: not fanciful: prosaic; **matter of course,** a thing occurring in natural time and order, a thing to be expected: **no matter,** it makes no difference. [O.Fr. *matiere*—L. *māteria,* matter.]

mattins. Same as **matins,** *pl.* of **matin.**

mattock, *mat′ók, n.* a kind of pickaxe for loosening the soil, having one or both of the iron ends broad instead of pointed. [O.E. *mattuc.*]

mattress, *mat′res, n.* a bed made of a stuffed bag, or a substitute or supplementary structure of wire, hair, &c. [O.Fr. *materas* (Fr.

Neutral vowels in unaccented syllables: *em′pér-ór*; for certain sounds in foreign words see p. ix.

matelas)—Ar.*matrah*, a place where anything is thrown.]

mature, *ma-tūr'*, *adj.* fully developed: ripe: completely worked out (of a plan): ripe (of a bill).—*v.t.* to bring to ripeness, full development, or perfection: to bring to a head.—*v.i.* to become ripe: to become due (of a bill).—*adj.* **matūr'able.**—*adv.* **mature'ly.**—*ns.* **mature'ness; matūr'ity**, ripeness: full development: the time when a bill becomes due.—*v.t.* **mat'ūrate**, to make mature: to promote the suppuration of.—*v.i.* to ripen, mature: to suppurate perfectly.—*n.* **matūrā'tion**, the formation of pus: (*bot., zool.*) the final stage in the development of a germ cell.—*adj.* **matūr'ative**, promoting ripening: promoting suppuration. [L. *mātūrus*, ripe.]

matutinal, *ma-tūt'i-nál*, *adj.* pertaining to the morning: early.—Also **matutine** (*mat'ū-tīn*). [L. *mātūtīnālis, mātūtīnus*. See **matin**.]

maudlin, *möd'lin*, *adj.* silly: sickly sentimental: fuddled, half-drunk. [M.E. *Maudelein*, through O.Fr. and L. from Gr. *Magdalēnē*, (woman) of Magdala, from the assumption that Mary Magdalene was the penitent woman of Luke vii. 37 ff.; see **Magdalen**.]

maugre, maulgre, *mö'ger*, also *-gri*, *mö(l)-grē'*, *prep.* (*arch.*) in spite of.—Also *adv.* [O.Fr. *maugré*, ill-will.]

maul, *möl*, *n.* a heavy wooden hammer or beetle: a mall.—*v.t.* to beat with a maul or heavy stick: to handle roughly. [O.Fr. *mail*—L. *malleus*.]

maulstick, *möl'stik*, *n.* a stick used by painters as a rest for the hand.—Also **mahl'stick**. [Du. *maalstok malen*, to paint, *stok*, stick, assimilated to **stick**.]

maunder, *mön'dér*, *v.i.* to speak indistinctly or disconnectedly: to move, act listlessly.

Maundy Thursday, *mön'di thûrz'dā*, the day before Good Friday, when royal charity is distributed to the poor at Whitehall. [Fr. *mandó*—L. *mandātum*, command (John xiii. 34).]

mausoleum, *mö-sö-lē'um*, *n.* a magnificent tomb or monument.—*adj.* **mausolē'an**. [L. *mausōlēum*—Gr. *Mausōleion*, the magnificent tomb of a certain *Mausōlus* (d. 353 B.C.).]

mauve, *möv*, *möv*, *n.* a purple aniline dye: its colour, that of mallow flowers. [Fr.,—L. *malva*, mallow.]

mavis, *mā'vis*, *n.* the song-thrush. [Fr. *mauvis*.]

mavourneen, *ma-vōōr'nēn*, *n.* and *interj.* (Ir.) my dear one. [Ir. *mo mhurnín*.]

maw, *mö*, *n.* the stomach, esp. in the lower animals: the craw, in birds: a wide chasm.—*n.* **maw'worm**, a worm infesting the stomach or intestines. [O.E. *maga*; Ger. *magen*.]

mawkish, *mök'ish*, *adj.* (*obs.*) squeamish: insipid: sickly sentimental, maudlin.—*adv.* **mawk'ishly**.—*n.* **mawk'ishness**. [O.N. *mathkr*, maggot.]

maxi, *maks'i*, *adj.* of a skirt or dress, having the hemline at ankle length.—Also *n.* Cf. **mini, mini-skirt**.

maxilla, *maks-il'a*, *n.* the upper jaw: a bone of the upper jaw: in Arthropoda, an appendage behind the mouth modified in connection with feeding.—*adj.* **maxillary** (*maks-il'ár-i*, or *maks'-*). [L. *maxilla*, jawbone.]

maxim, *maks'im*, *n.* a general principle, serving as a rule or guide: a proverb. [Fr. *maxime*—L.

maxima (*sententia*, or some other word), greatest (opinion, &c.), fem. superl. of *magnus*, great.]

Maxim, *maks'im*, *n.* often put for **Max'im-gun**, an automatic machine-gun invented by Hiram *Maxim* (1840-1916).

maximum, *maks'i-mum*, *adj.* greatest.—*n.* the greatest number, quality, or degree: (*math.*) the value of a variable when it ceases to increase and begins to decrease:—*pl.* **max'ima**. [L., superl. neut. of *magnus*, great.]

maxwell, *maks'wél*, *n.* the CGS unit of magnetic flux, equal to 10^{-8} *weber* (the SI unit). [James Clerk-*Maxwell* (1831-79), Scottish physicist.]

may, *mā*, *v.i.* now generally used as an auxiliary expressing ability, permission, possibility, wish, or softening a blunt question. Infin. and participles are obs.:—*pa.t.* might (*mīt*).—*adv.* **maybe**, perhaps, possibly. [O.E. *mæg*, pr.t. (old pa.t.) of *magan*, to be able, pa.t. *mihte*; cog. with Ger. *mögen*.]

May, *mā*, *n.* the fifth month of the year: the early or gay part of life: *may-blossom*—*v.i.* to gather may on May Day: to participate in May sports:—*pr.p.* may'ing.—*ns.* **may'-bee'tle, may'-bug**, the cockchafer; **may'-bloss'om**, the hawthorn flower; **May Day**, the first day of May; **may'fly**, any of a genus (*Ephemera*), or family, of fragile short-lived flies which appear in May; **may'-lil'y**, the lily of the valley; **may'pole**, a pole erected for dancing round on May Day; **May'-queen**, a young woman crowned with flowers as queen on May Day. [O.Fr. *Mai*—L. *Māius* (*mēnsis*, month), sacred to *Māia*, mother of Mercury.]

mayday, *mā'dā*, *n.* the international radio-telephonic distress signal for ships and aircraft. [Fr. *m'aidez* (pron. *mā'dā*), help me.]

Mayfair, *mā'fār*, *n.* the aristocratic West End of London. [From a *fair* formerly held in that district in *May*.]

mayonnaise, *mā-ôn-āz'*, or *mā'-*, *n.* a sauce composed of the yolk of eggs, olive-oil, and vinegar or lemon-juice, seasoned: any cold dish of which it is an ingredient. [Fr.]

mayor, *mā'ór, mâr, n.* the chief magistrate of a city or borough in England, Ireland, &c., whether man or woman.—*ns.* **may'oralty**, **may'orship**, the office of a mayor; **mayoress**, a mayor's wife, or other lady who performs her social and ceremonial functions; **Lord May'or**, the chief magistrate of certain English, Welsh, Irish, and Australian cities and boroughs. [Fr. *maire*—L. *major*, comp. of *magnus*, great.]

maze, *māz*, *n.* a place full of intricate windings: confusion of thought: perplexity.—*v.t.* to bewilder: to confuse.—*adj.* **maz'y**, full of mazes or windings: intricate.—*adv.* **maz'ily**.—*n.* **maz'iness**, bewilderment. [Prob. from lost O.E. word; compound *āmasod*, amazed, occurs.]

mazurka, *ma-zōōr'ka*, or *-zûr'-*, *n.* a lively Polish dance: a piece of music for it in triple time. [Pol., Masurian woman—i.e. a woman of the province of Mazovia.]

me, *mē*, *personal pron.* the objective (acc. or dat.) case of **I**. [O.E. *mē*.]

mea culpa, *mē'a kul'pa, mā'a kŏŏl'pa*, by my own fault. [L.]

mead, *mēd*, *n.* honey and water fermented and

fāte, fär; mē, hûr (her); *mīne; mōte, för; mūte; mōōn, fŏŏt;* ᴛʜen (then)

447

flavoured. [O.E. *meodu*; Ger. *met*, W. *medd*.]

mead, *mēd* (*poet.*) and **meadow**, *med'ō, ns.* a level tract producing grass to be mown down: a rich pasture-ground, esp. beside a stream. —*adj.* **mead'owy.**—*n.* **meadow-sweet**, a wild flower of the spiraea genus with a heavy scent. [O.E. *mǣd*, in oblique cases *mǣdwe*—*māwan*, to mow; Ger. *matte*.]

meagre, *mē'gér, adj.* lean: poor in quality: scanty, deficient in quantity.—*adv.* **mea'grely.**—*n.* **mea'greness.** [Fr. *maigre*—L. *macer*, lean; cf. Ger. *mager*.]

meal, *mēl, n.* the food taken at one time: the act or occasion of taking food.—**meals-on-wheels**, a welfare service taking cooked, usu. hot, meals to old people in need of such help; **meal ticket**, one that can be exchanged for a meal: someone or something that is the source of one's income.—**square meal**, a full meal. [O.E. *mǣl*, time, portion of time; Du. *maal*, Ger. *mahl*.]

meal, *mēl, n.* grain ground to powder.—*adj.* **meal'y**, resembling meal: covered with meal or with something like meal.—*n.* **meal'iness.**—*adj.* **meal'y-mouthed**, smooth-tongued: over-squeamish in choice of words. [O.E. *melu, melo*; Ger. *mehl*, Du. *meel*, meal.]

mealie, *mēl'i*, (S. Africa) an ear of maize: esp. in *pl.* maize. [Afrikaans *milie*, millet.]

mean, *mēn, adj.* low in rank or birth: low in worth or estimation: humble or sordid (e.g. dwelling): inferior (e.g. understanding): ignoble (e.g. motive): small minded: stingy.— *adv.* **mean'ly.**—*n.* **mean'ness.**—*adj.* **mean'-spir'ited.**—**no mean**, good, admirable, important (e.g. *he is no mean orator*; *no mean city*). [O.E. *gemǣne*; Ger. *gemein*; L. *commūnis*, common.]

mean, *mēn, adj.* intermediate: average.—*n.* quality, condition, course, &c., equally removed from two opposite extremes.—*n.* **means**, (*pl.* in form) that by instrumentality of which anything is caused or brought to pass: the way to an end (treated as *sing.* or *pl.*): pecuniary resources, what is required for comfortable living (treated as *pl.*).—*ns.* and *advs.* **mean'time**, **mean'while**, the intervening time, in the intervening time.—**mean sun**, a fictitious point imagined as moving along the celestial equator at the same average rate as the average rate of the true sun in the ecliptic, but uniformly; **mean time**, time as given by the position of the mean sun.—**golden mean**, the middle course between two extremes: a wise moderation; **means test**, the test of private resources, determining or limiting claim to a concession or allowance. [O.Fr. *meien* (Fr. *moyen*)—L. *mediānus*—*medius*, middle.]

mean, *mēn, v.t.* to intend, to purpose (to do something—also, mischief, business, &c.): to design or destine (a person or thing for a specified object, &c.): to signify: to intend to indicate (a certain object), or to convey (a certain sense).—*v.i.* (with *well, ill*) to have good, bad, intentions or dispositions: (with *much, little*, &c.) to be of much, little, importance (to):—*pr.p.* **meaning**; *pa.t.* and *pa.p.* meant (*ment*).—*n.* **mean'ing**, signification: the sense intended: purpose.—*adj.* significant.—**mean well**, to have good intentions;

mean well by, be kindly disposed towards. [O.E. *mǣnan*; Ger. *meinen*, to think.]

meander, *mē-an'dér, n.* (usu. *pl.*) a winding course: a winding, loop, of a river: a circuitous journey.—*v.i.* (of a river) to wind about: to wander aimlessly or listlessly: to be intricate.—*adj.* **mean'dering.** [L. *Maeander*—Gr. *Maiandros*, a winding river in Asia Minor.]

meant, *ment, pa.t.* and *pa.p.* of **mean** (3).

measles, *mē'zlz, n.* (*pl.* in form, treated as *sing.*) an infectious fever accompanied with eruptions of small red spots upon the skin: a disease affecting pigs and cattle due to infection by larval tapeworms.—*adjs.* **mea'sled**, infected with measles: spotty; **mea'sly**, measled: infected with tapeworm larvae: paltry.—**German measles**, a name somewhat loosely used of a disease resembling measles, but mostly less prolonged and severe. [M.E. *maseles*; cf. Du. *mazelen*, Ger. *masern*.]

measure, *mezh'úr, n.* the dimensions, capacity, or quantity of anything, ascertained or ascertainable by measurement: an instrument for measuring: a unit of measurement: a system of measuring: a quantity by which another can be divided without a remainder (e.g. in the phrase *Greatest Common Measure*): proportion, moderation: prescribed extent or limit: metre: a metrical unit: musical time: a dance, esp. a slow and stately one: (usu. *pl.*) steps towards an end: an enactment or bill: (*pl.*) a series of beds or strata (e.g. of coal).— *v.t.* to ascertain or show the dimensions or amount of: to bring into comparison (with *with* or *against*).—*v.i.* to be of (a stated size): to take measurements.—*adj.* **meas'urable**, that may be measured or computed: moderate.—*adv.* **meas'urably.**—*adjs.* **meas'ured**, determined by measure: rhythmical: considered: restrained; **measureless**, boundless.—*n.* **meas'urement**, the act of measuring: quantity found by measuring.—**measure one's length**, to fall at full length.—**above**, or **beyond**, **measure**, to an exceedingly great degree; **dry measure**, any system of measures of volume for dry substances, esp. that in which the denominations are pint, quart, peck, bushel; **in a measure**, **in some measure**, to some degree; **measure up to**, to be adequate for; **take measures**, to adopt means (to gain an end); **take one's measure**, to gauge one's character, &c.; **without measure**, immoderately. [O.Fr. *mesure*—L. *mensūra*, a measure—*mētīrī, mensus*, to measure.]

meat, *mēt, n.* anything eaten as food: the flesh of animals used as food.—*ns.* **meat'-off'ering**, a Jewish sacrificial offering consisting of food; **meat'-safe**, a receptacle for storing meat, walled with perforated zinc or gauze; **meat'-tea**, a high tea, at which meat is served.—*adj.* **meat'y**, full of meat: (*fig.*) full of substance. [O.E. *mete*.]

Mecca, *mek'a, n.* the birthplace of Mohammed and goal of Mohammedan pilgrims: (*fig.*; also without *cap.*) any place holding a similar position in the esteem of the supporters of any creed, enthusiasm, or policy.

mechanic, *me-kan'ik, adj.* mechanical.—*n.* a handicraftsman: a skilled worker, esp. one who makes or maintains machinery.—*adj.*

Neutral vowels in unaccented syllables: *em'pér-ór*; for certain sounds in foreign words see p. ix.

mechan′ical, pertaining to machines: worked or done by machinery or by mechanism: machine-like: performed simply by force of habit: performed without enthusiasm, ability: engaged on manual labour: having a bent or talent for machinery.—*n.* (*Shak.*) a mechanic.—*adv.* **mechan′ically.**—*ns.* **mechanician** (*mek-an-ish′an*), a machine-maker: one skilled in the structure of machines; **mechan′ics** (*sing.*), the science of the action of forces on bodies (including both kinetics and statics): the art or science of machine construction: the details of manufacturing or creating something: system on which something works.—*v.t.* **mech′anise,** to make mechanical, to adapt to mechanical working: to transfer (a manufacturing process) to machinery, esp. replacing manual labour: to equip (forces) with armed and armoured motor vehicles.—*ns.* **mech′anism,** the parts of a machine taken collectively: arrangement and action by which a given result is produced, including a natural process considered as machine-like: mechanical operation: a combination of mental processes: artistic technique: theory that all the processes of life are machine-like and can be explained entirely by the laws of chemistry and physics: (*psych.*) the means adopted unconsciously towards a subconscious end, **mech′anist,** a mechanician: a believer in mechanism.—*adj.* **mechanist′ic.**—**defence mechanism,** (*psych.*) the combination of mental processes which automatically produce a defensive reaction to a situation unconsciously regarded as unpleasant. [Gr. *mēchanikos—mēchanē,* a contrivance.]

Mechlin, *mek′-,* or *meн′lin, n.* lace, such as that made at *Mechlin* or Malines, in Belgium.

medal, *med′al, n.* a piece of metal in the form of a coin bearing some device or inscription: a reward of merit.—*adj.* **medallic** (*mē-dal′ik*).—*ns.* **medallion** (*mē-dal′yon*), a large medal: a bas-relief of a round form: a round ornament, panel, tablet, or design of similar form; **med′allist,** one skilled in medals: an engraver of medals: one who has gained a medal. [Fr. *médaille*—It. *medaglia*; through a Low L. form from L. *metallum,* metal.]

meddle, *med′l, v.i.* to interfere unnecessarily, rashly, or without being entitled (with *with* or *in*).—*n.* **medd′ler.**—*adj.* **medd′lesome,** given to meddling.—*n.* **medd′lesomeness.**—*adj.* **medd′ling,** interfering in the concerns of others. officious.—Also *n.* [O.Fr. *medler,* a variant of *mesler* (Fr. *mêler*)—Low L. *miscŭlāre*—L. *miscēre,* to mix.]

mediū. See **medium.**

mediaeval, medieval, *med-i-ē′val, adj.* of the Middle Ages.—*n.* **mediae′valist, mediē′valist,** one versed in history, art, &c., of the Middle Ages. [L. *medius,* middle, *aevum,* age.]

medial, *mē′di-al, adj.* of or pertaining to a mean or average.—*adj.* **mē′dian,** being in the middle.—*n.* a straight line joining an angular point of a triangle with the middle point of the opposite side.—*n.* **mē′diant** (It. *mediante*), the third note of a scale. [L.L. *mediālis,* L. *mediānus,* L.L. *medians, -antis*—L. *medius,* middle.]

mediate, *mē′di-āt, adj.* related, or acting,

through a person or thing intervening, not directly.—*v.i.* (*-āt*) to interpose between parties as a friend of each: to intercede.—*v.t.* to bring about by mediation.—*adv.* **mē′diately.** —*ns.* **mē′diateness; mēdiā′tion,** the act of mediating or coming between: entreaty for another.—*v.t.* **mē′diatīse,** to annex, or to subordinate, as a smaller state to a larger neighbouring one.—*n.* **mē′diator,** one who mediates between parties at strife: an intercessor.—*adj.* **mēdiatō′rial.**—*adv.* **mediatō′rially.** [Low L. *mēdiāre,* to be in the middle—L. *mēdius.*]

medical, *med′i-kal, adj.* relating to the art of healing: relating to the art of the physician, distinguished from surgery.—*n.* (*coll.*) a medical examination to ascertain the state of one's physical health.—*adv.* **med′ically.** [Low.L. *medicālis*—L. *medicus,* pertaining to healing, a physician—*medērī,* to heal.]

medicament, *med-ik′a-ment, n.* any substance used in curative treatment, esp. externally. [L. *medicāmentum—medicāre.*]

medicate, *med′i-kāt, v.t.* to treat with medicine: to impregnate with anything medicinal.—*adj.* **med′icable,** that may be healed.—*adj.* **med′icated,** mixed with medicine: treated with medicine.—*n.* **medicā′tion.**—*adj.* **med′icative,** healing: tending to heal. [L. *medicāre, -ātum,* to heal.]

medicine, *med′sin, -sn, n.* any substance used (esp. internally) for the treatment or prevention of disease: the science or art of preventing, alleviating, or curing disease, esp. the branch dealt with by the physician as opposed to surgery or obstetrics.—*adj.* **medicinal** (*med-is′in-al*), used in medicine: curative: relating to medicine.—*adv.* **medic′inally.**—*n.* **med′icine-man,** among savages, a witch-doctor or magician. [O.Fr. *medecine*—L. *medicīna.*]

medick, *med′ik, n.* a genus of plants distinguished from clover by their spiral or sickle-shaped pods and short racemes—including lucerne. [L. *medica*—Gr. *Mēdikē* (*poa*), Median (herb) i.e. lucerne.]

medieval. Same as **mediaeval.**

mediu-, *mē′di-ō-,* in composition, middle. [L. *medius,* middle.]

mediocre, *mē-di-ō′kér,* or *mē′-, adj.* of middling goodness, ability, &c, (usu. disparagingly): moderate.—*n.* **mediocrity** (*-ok′-*), a middling degree of merit or eminence in any sphere: a mediocre person. [Fr. *médiocre*—L. *mediocris—medius,* middle.]

meditate, *med′i-tāt, v.i.* to consider thoughtfully (with *on, upon*): to engage in contemplation, esp. religious.—*v.t.* to consider deeply: to intend.—*adj.* **med′itated.**—*n.* **meditā′tion,** deep thought: serious continuous contemplation esp. on a religious or spiritual theme: a meditative treatment of a literary or a musical theme.—*adj.* **med′itative,** marked by deep or serious contemplation.—*adv.* **med′itatively.**—*n.* **med′itativeness.** [L. *meditārī,* prob. cog. with L. *medērī,* to heal.]

mediterranean, *med-i-tér-ā′nē-an, adj.* situated in the middle of earth or land: land-locked: of the **Mediterranean Sea** (so called from being in the middle of the land of the Old World) or its shores.—**Mediterranean climate**, the type of climate experienced in the Mediterranean region—mild, moderately wet winters and warm, dry summers; **Mediterranean race**, a division of the white race, long-headed, dark-complexioned men, of medium stature, belonging to the region round the Mediterranean Sea. [L. *mediterrānus—medius*, middle, *terra*, earth.]

medium, *mē′di-um, n.* the middle condition or degree: any intervening means, instrument, or agency: a substance through which any effect is transmitted: a channel (as newspapers, radio, television) through which information is transmitted: in spiritualism, the person through whom spirits are said to communicate with the material world:—*pl.* **mē′dia**, or **mē′diums.**—*adj.* **mē′dium**, intermediate in amount, quality, position, &c.—*adj.* **medium-wave** (*radio*), of, or using, wavelengths between 200 and 1000 metres. [L. *mē-dium.*]

medlar, *med′lår, n.* a small tree akin to the apple: its fruit. [O.Fr. *medler, mesler*—L. *mespilum*—Gr. *mespilon.*]

medley, *med′li, n.* a mingled and confused mass: a miscellany. [O.Fr. *medler, mesler*, to mix.]

medullar, *me-dul′år*, **medullary**, *me-dul′år-i, adjs.* consisting of, or resembling, marrow or pith. [L. *medulla*, marrow.]

medusa, *me-dū′za, n.* (*cap.*) one of the Gorgons whose head, which had snakes for hair, and turned beholders into stone, was cut off by Perseus: a jelly-fish, prob. from the likeness of its tentacles to the snakes on Medusa's head:—*pl.* **medū′sae** (*-zē, -sē*). [L. *Medūsa*—Gr. *Medousa.*]

meed, *mēd, n.* wages, reward: what is bestowed for merit. [O.E. *mēd*; Ger. *miete.*]

meek, *mēk, adj.* mild and gentle of temper: submissive.—*adv.* **meek′ly.**—*n.* **meek′ness.** [O.N. *mjūkr*; early modern Du. *muik.*]

meerschaum, *mēr′shám, n.* a fine light whitish clay—once supposed to be a petrified seafoam: a tobacco-pipe made of it. [Ger.,—*meer*, sea, *schaum*, foam.]

meet, *mēt, adj.* (*arch.*) fitting, proper (*meet for, meet to do, meet that*).—*adv.* **meet′ly.**—*n.* **meet′ness.** [Prob. from an O.E. (Anglian) form answering to W.S. *gemǣte—metan*, to measure.]

meet, *mēt, v.t.* to come face to face with: to come into the company of: to be introduced to: to encounter in conflict: to experience (with *with*): to receive (e.g. a welcome): to come up to (e.g. expectations): to satisfy (e.g. requirements): to answer (e.g. objections): to cause to meet, bring into contact: to keep an appointment with.—*v.i.* to come together: to assemble: to have an encounter:—*pa.t.* and *pa.p.* met.—*n.* a meeting, as of huntsmen.—*ns.* **meet′ing**, an interview: an assembly: a junction (e.g. of rivers); **meet′ing-house**, a house or building where people, esp. Dissenters, meet for public worship.—**meet the ear, or eye**, to be readily apparent. [O.E. *mētan*, to meet—*mōt, gemōt*, a meeting.]

mega-, *meg′a-*, **meg-**, *meg′-*, in composition, great, powerful, or (metric system) a million of.—*ns.* **meg′adeath**, death of a million people,

unit used in estimating casualties in nuclear war; **meg′ahertz**, a million cycles per second, used in measuring frequency; **meg′awatt**, a million watts: **meg′ohm**, a million ohms.—**megaton bomb**, a bomb having the explosive force of a million tons of TNT (trinitrotoluene). [Gr. *megas*, great.]

megalith, *meg′a-lith, n.* a huge stone.—*adj.* **megalith′ic**, [Gr. *megas*, great, *lithos*, a stone.]

megalomania, *meg-a-lō-mā′ni-a, n.* the delusion that one is great or powerful: a mania, or passion, for big things. [Gr. *megas*, great, *mania*, madness.]

megalosaurus, *meg-a-lō-sö′rus, n.* a genus of gigantic extinct reptiles of carnivorous habits. [Gr. *megas*, fem. *megalē*, great, *sauros*, a lizard.]

megaphone, *meg′a-fōn, n.* a form of speaking-trumpet for causing sounds to be heard better and at a greater distance. [Gr. *megas*, great, *phōnē*, voice.]

megatherium, *meg-a-thē′rium, n.* a genus of gigantic extinct South American ground-sloths. [Gr. *megas*, great, *thērion*, wild beast.]

megrim, *mē′grim, n.* a pain affecting the head or face, usually on one side only: a whim or fancy: (*pl.*) low spirits. [Fr. *migraine*—Gr. *hēmikrānia—hēmi*, half, *krānion*, skull.]

meiosis, *mī-ō′sis, n.* understatement, as a figure of speech—litotes: division of cell nuclei with reduction of the number of chromosomes in the resulting potential cell nuclei.—*adj.* **meiot′ic.**—Cf. **mitosis.** [Gr. *meiōsis*, diminution.]

meistersinger, *mīs′ter-zing-ér, -sing-ér, n.* one of the burgher poets and musicians of Germany in the 14th-16th centuries, the successors of the minnesinger:—*pl.* **meis′tersinger.** [Ger.]

melancholy, *mel′án-kol-i, -kól-i, n.* continued depression of spirits, dejection: indulgence in thoughts of pleasing sadness, pensiveness.—*adj.* depressed: depressing.—*n.* **melanchō′lia**, a mental state characterised by dejection and misery.—*adj.* **melancholic** (*-kol′ik*). [O.Fr. *melancholic*—L. *melancholia*—Gr. *melancholiā—melās, -ānos*, black, *cholē*, bile.]

Melanesian, *mel-án-ēz′i-án, adj.* pertaining to *Melanesia*, a group of islands in the W. Pacific, lying N.E. of Australia, in which the dominant race is dark-skinned.—*n.* a native, or a language, of these islands. [Gr. *melās, -ānos*, black, *nēsos*, island.]

mélange, *mā-lāzh′ n.* a mixture: a medley. [Fr.]

melanism, *mel′án-izm, n.* more than normal development of dark colouring matter in the skin. [Gr. *melās, -ānos*, black.]

mêlée, *mel′ā, n.* a confused conflict between opposing parties. [Fr.—*mêler*, to mix.]

meliorate, *mē′li-ó-rāt, v.t.* to make better.—*v.i.* to grow better.—*n.* **meliorā′tion.**—*adj.* **mē′liorātive**, tending towards improvement. [L. *melior*, better.]

mellay, *mel′ā, n.* another form of **mêlée.**

melliferous, *mel-if′ér-us, adj.* honey-producing.—*n.* **mellif′luence**, a flow of sweetness: a smooth, sweet flow.—*adjs.* **mellif′luent, mellif′luous**, flowing with honey or sweetness: sweet as honey (e.g. of voice, words).—*advs.* **mellif′luently, mellif′luously.** [L. *mel*, honey.]

Neutral vowels in unaccented syllables: *em′pér-òr*; for certain sounds in foreign words see p. ix.

mellow, *mel'ō, adj.* soft and ripe (of fruit): well matured (of wine): soft, not harsh (of sound, colour, light): softened by age or experience (of character).—*v.t.* to soften by ripeness or (also *fig.*) by age: to mature.—*v.i.* to become soft: to be matured: (*fig.*) to become gentler and more tolerant.—*n.* **mell'owness.**—*adj.* **mell'owy,** soft. [Prob. O.E. *melu,* meal, influenced by *mearu,* soft, tender.]

melodrama, *mel'ō-drä-ma, n.* a kind of romantic and (now especially) sensational drama, formerly largely intermixed with song.—*adj.* **melodramatic** (-*at'ik*), of the nature of melodrama: overstrained· sensational.—*n.* **melodramatist** (-*dram'a-tist*), a writer of melodramas. [Gr. *melos,* a song, *dráma,* action.]

melody, *mel'o-di, n.* an air or tune: sweet music: tunefulness: an agreeable succession of single musical sounds, as distinguished from *harmony* or the concord of a succession of simultaneous sounds: the air in harmonised music.—*n.* **melō'deon,** a small reed organ: a kind of accordion.—*adjs.* **melōd'ic,** of the nature of, or pertaining to, melody; **melō'dious,** full of melody: agreeable to the ear.—*adv.* **melō'diously.**—*ns.* **melō'diousness; mel'odist**—**melodic minor scale,** a form of minor scale with the semitones between the 2nd and 3rd and the 7th and 8th notes ascending, and between the 5th and 6th and 2nd and 3rd descending. [Fr.,—Late L.—Gr. *melōidiā*—*melos,* a song, *ōidē,* a lay.]

melon, *mel'ŏn, n.* a large sweet juicy gourd or the plant bearing it, the musk-melon: the water-melon (q.v.) [Fr.,—L. *mēlō, -ōnis*—Gr. *mēlon,* an apple.]

melt, *melt, v.i.* to become liquid: to dissolve: to dwindle away: to shade off or pass imperceptibly into something else: to be softened emotionally.—*v.t.* to cause to melt in any sense.—*n.* and *adj.* **melt'ing.**—*adv.* **melt'ingly.**—*ns.* **melt'ing-pot,** a vessel for melting things in; **melt-water,** water running off melting ice or snow.—*p.adj.* **mōlt'en,** melted: made of melted metal. [O.E. *meltan* (intr. strong vb.), and *mæltan, meltan* (causative weak vb.; W.S. *mieltan*).]

member, *mem'bĕr, n.* a limb of an animal: a clause (of a sentence): one of a society: a representative in a legislative body: any essential part of a structure.—*adj.* **membered,** having limbs.—*n.* **mem'bership,** the state of being a member or one of a society: the members of a body regarded as a whole.—**member of parliament,** a member of the House of Commons. [Fr. *membre*—*membrum.*]

membrane, *mem'brān, -brin, n.* a thin flexible solid sheet or film, esp. of animal or vegetable origin: a skin of parchment.—*adjs.* **membranā'ceous, mem'branous,** like, or of the nature of, a membrane.—**mucous membrane,** the membrane lining the various channels of the body that communicate with the outside. [Fr.,—L. *membrāna*—*membrum.*]

memento, *me-men'tō, n.* something as a reminder:—*pl.* **memen'tos** or **-toes.** [L., imper. of *meminisse,* to remember.]

memo, *mem'ō, n.* note sent between employees about company business. [**memorandum.**]

memoir, *mem'wär, -wŏr, n.* (*pl.*) record of events

set down from personal knowledge and intended as material for history or biography: a biographical sketch: a record of researches on any subject. [Fr. *mémoire*—L. *memoria,* memory—*memor,* mindful.]

memorable, memorial, &c. See **memory.**

memorandum, *mem-ŏr-an'dum, n.* something to be remembered: a note to assist the memory: (*law*) a brief note of a transaction (e.g. terms of contract): (*diplomacy*) a summary of the state of a question:—*pl.* **memoran'dums, memoran'da.** [L. a thing to be remembered, neut. gerundive of *memorāre,* to remember.]

memory, *mem'ŏ-ri, n.* the power of retaining and reproducing mental or sensory impressions: an impression so reproduced: a having or keeping in the mind: time within which past things can be remembered: commemoration: remembrance: of computers, a store.—*adj.* **mem'orable,** deserving to be remembered: remarkable.—*adv.* **mem'orably.**—*adj.* **memō'rial,** serving, or intended, to preserve the memory of anything: pertaining to memory.—*n.* that which serves to keep in remembrance: a monument: (*pl.*) memoirs: a memorandum: a written statement of facts.—*v.t.* **memō'rialise,** to present a memorial to: to petition by a memorial.—*n.* **memō'rialist,** one who writes, signs, or presents a memorial.—*v.t.* **mem'orise,** to commit to memory. [L. *memoria,* memory.]

men, *pl.* of **man.**

menace, *men'ās, n.* a threat: a threatening danger.—*v.t.* to threaten.—*adj.* **men'acing.** —*adv.* **men'acingly.** [Fr.,—L. *minaciae,* threats —*minae,* overhanging parts, threats.]

ménage, *mā-näzh', n.* a household: the management of a house.—**ménage à trois** (*a trwa*), a household composed of a husband and wife and the lover of one of them. [Fr. through Late L.,—L. *mānsiō -ōnis,* a dwelling.]

menagerie, *men-aj'ĕr-i, n.* a place for keeping wild animals for exhibition: a collection of such animals, esp. travelling. [Fr. *ménagerie*—*ménage;* see above.]

mend, *mend, v.t.* to repair: to correct, improve (one's ways, manners).—*v.i.* to grow better.— *ns.* **mend'er; mend'ing,** the act of repairing: things requiring to be mended.—**on the mend,** improving, recovering. [Shortened form of **amend.**]

mendacious, *men-dā'shŭs, adj.* lying, untruthful.—*adv.* **mendā'ciously.**—*n.* **mendacity** (-*das'i-ti*), lying, untruthfulness. [L. *mendāx, -ācis,* conn. with *mentīrī,* to lie.]

mendelevium, *men-de-lē'(-lā'-)vi-um, n.* a transuranium element (atomic number 101; symbol Mv), named after the Russian scientist *Mendeleev* (1834-1907) who developed the periodic table, a classification of the chemical elements.

Mendelism, *mend'ĕl-izm, n.* doctrines of the Austrian-German Gregor *Mendel* (1882-84) regarding some characteristic features of heredity.—*adj.* **Mendēl'ian.**

mendicant, *men'di-kânt, adj.* begging.—*n.* a beggar: a begging friar.—*ns.* **men'dicancy, mendicity** (-*dis'i-ti*), the condition of a beggar: begging. [L. *mendīcans, -antis,* pr.p. of *mendīcāre,* to beg—*mendīcus,* a beggar.]

fāte, fär; mē, hûr (her); *mīne; mōte, för; mūte; mōōn, fŏŏt;* ᴛʜen (then)

menhir, *men'hēr, n.* a tall, often massive, stone, set up on end as a monument in ancient times, either singly or in circles, &c. [W. *maen,* a stone, *hir,* long.]

menial, *mē'ni-ál, adj.* servile, humiliating.—*n.* a domestic servant: one performing servile work: a person of servile disposition. [Anglo-Fr. *menial;* cf. O.Fr. *mesnie*—L. *mansiō, -ōnis,* a dwelling.]

meningitis, *men-in-jī'tis, n.* inflammation of the membranes investing the brain or spinal cord. [Gr. *mēninx, -ingos,* a membrane.]

meniscus, *men-is'kus, n.* a crescent-shaped figure: a crescentic fibrous cartilage in a joint: a lens convex on the one side and concave on the other: the curved surface of a liquid.—*adj.* **menis'coid,** watchglass-shaped. [Gr. *mēniskos,* dim. of *mēnē,* the moon (*iskos,* small).]

menopause, *men-ō-pöz, n.* permanent end of menstruation. [Gr. *mēn,* month, *pausis,* end.]

menses, *men'sēz, n. pl.* the monthly discharge from the uterus. [L. *mēnsēs,* pl. of *mēnsis.* month.]

menstruum, *men'strŏŏ-um, n.* a solvent (from a fancy of the alchemists):—*pl.* **men'strua,** the menses.—*adj.* **men'strual,** monthly: pertaining to the menses.—*v.i.* **men'struāte,** to discharge the menses.—*n.* **menstruā'tion.**—*adj.* **men'-struous.** [L. neut. of *mēnstruus,* monthly.]

mensurable, *men'sh(y)ùr-á-bl,* or *-sūr-, -shūr-, adj.* measurable.—*n.* **mensurabil'ity.**—*adj.* **mens'ural,** pertaining to measure.—*n.* **mensurā'tion,** the act or art of finding by measurement and calculation the length, area, volume, &c., of bodies. [L. *mēnsūrāre,* to measure.]

mental, *men'tál, adj.* pertaining to the mind: done in the mind (e.g. *mental or head work*): done, made, happening, in the mind alone without outward expression (e.g. *mental arithmetic; mental reservation; mental picture*): of abnormal or unbalanced mind (*slang* when used predicatively): for the mentally abnormal (e.g. *a mental home*): suffering from or involved in the care of disease or disturbance of the mind.—*n.* **mentality** (*-tal'-i-ti*), mind: mental endowment: way of thinking.—*adv.* **men'tally.**—**mental age,** the age in years at which the average individual reaches the same stage of mental development as the person under consideration; **mental deficiency, retardation,** retarded development of learning ability. [Fr.,—L. *mēns, mentis,* the mind.]

menthol, *men'thol, n.* a camphor obtained from oil of peppermint by cooling, which gives relief in colds, &c. [L. *mentha,* mint.]

mention, *men'sh(ó)n, n.* a brief notice: a casual introduction into speech or writing.—*v.t.* to notice briefly: to remark: to name.—*adj.* **men'tionable,** fit to be mentioned. [L. *mentiō.*]

mentor, *men'tór, n.* a wise counsellor.—*adj.* **mentōr'ial.** [Gr. *Mentōr,* the tutor by whom Telemachus was guided.]

menu, *men'ū, mē'nü, n.* a bill of fare. [Fr.,—L. *minūtus,* small.]

mepacrine, *mep'á-krēn, n.* a synthetic substitute for quinine, found in 1942, formerly taken to suppress the symptoms of malaria.

Mephistopheles, *mef-is-tof'i-lēz, n.* a mediaeval devil found in Marlowe's *Dr. Faustus* and Goethe's *Faust.*—*adj.* **Mephistophelē'an, Mephistophē'lian,** cynical, scoffing, fiendish. [Ety unknown; prob. influenced by Gr. *mē,* not, *phōs,* gen. *phōtos,* light, *philos,* loving.]

mephitis, *me-fī'tis, n.* a poisonous exhalation: a foul stink.—*adjs.* **mephitic** (*-fit'-*), **-al.** [L. *mephītis.*]

mercantile, *mûr'kàn-tīl, adj.* pertaining to merchants: commercial.—**mercantile marine,** the ships and crews of any country that are employed in commerce; **mercantile system** (*economics*), the system of encouraging exportation and restricting importation so that more money may be received than is paid away. [Fr.,—It. *mercantile*—L. *mercārī,* to trade.]

Mercator's projection, *mér-kā'tórz pro-jék'-sh(ó)n,* a representation of the surface of the globe in which the meridians are parallel straight lines, and the parallels of latitude straight lines at right angles to these, the distance between the parallels of latitude increasing towards the poles. [*Mercator* (merchant), a Latin translation of the name of the cartographer Gerhard Kremer (lit. shopkeeper): 1512-94.]

mercenary, *mûr'sén-àr-i, adj.* hired for money: too strongly influenced by desire of gain: sold or done for money.—*n.* one who is hired: a soldier hired into foreign service. [L. *mercēnārius*—*mercēs,* hire.]

mercer, *mûr'sér, n.* a dealer in textiles: a dealer in small wares.—*n.* **mer'cery,** the trade of a mercer: the goods of a mercer. [Fr. *mercier.*]

mercerise, *mûr'sér-īz, v.t.* to treat cotton so as to make it appear like silk. [From John *Mercer* (1791-1866), the inventor of the process.]

merchant, *mûr'chànt, n.* a trader, esp. wholesale: (*Scot.* and *U.S.*) a shopkeeper.—*adj* commercial.—*ns.* **mer'chandise** (*-dīz*), goods bought and sold for gain; **mer'chantman,** a trading-ship: (*B*) a merchant:—*pl.* **mer'chantmen; merchant service,** the mercantile marine (q.v.).—**speed merchant,** one whose chief interest in driving is in moving fast. [O.Fr. *march(e)ant*—L. *mercārī,* to trade.]

Mercian. See **Anglian.**

mercury, *mûr'kū-ri, n.* (*cap.*) the Roman god of merchandise, &c., the messenger of the gods: (*cap.*) planet nearest the sun: a silvery, liquid metallic element, quicksilver (atomic no. 80; symbol Hg, for *hydrargyrum*—L. *hydrargyrus*—Gr. *hydrargyros*—*hydōr,* water, *argyros,* silver): a messenger.—*adj.* **mercū'rial,** having the qualities of the god Mercury or of quicksilver: active, volatile in temperament: containing mercury.—*v.t.* **mercū'rialise** (*med.*), to treat with mercury.—*adjs.* **mercu'ric, mercu'rous,** used respectively of compounds in which mercury has a valency of 2 and a valency of 1, e.g. *mercuric chloride* ($HgCl_2$), corrosive sublimate, *mercurous chloride* ($HgCl$), calomel; **mercury,** as *adj.* is used for any compound containing mercury. [Fr.,—L. *Mercûrius,* prob. *merx, mercis,* merchandise.]

mercy, *mûr'si, n.* forbearance towards one who is in one's power: a forgiving disposition: clemency: compassion for the unfortunate.—*adj.* **mer'ciful,** full of, or exercising, mercy.—

Neutral vowels in unaccented syllables: *em'pér-ór*; for certain sounds in foreign words see p. ix.

452

adv. **mer'cifully.**—*n.* **mer'cifulness.**—*adj.* **mer'ciless,** without mercy: unfeeling: cruel.— *adv.* **mer'cilessly.**—*ns.* **mer'cilessness; mer'cy-seat,** the seat or place of mercy: the covering of the Jewish Ark of the Covenant, the propitiatory, on which the blood of animals being sacrificed was sprinkled: the throne of God.—**mercy killing,** killing to prevent incurable suffering.—**at the mercy of,** wholly in the power of. [Fr. *merci,* grace—L. *mercēs, -ēdis,* pay, later favour.]

mere, *mēr, n.* a pool or lake. [O.E. *mere,* sea, lake, pool; Ger. *meer,* L. *mare,* the sea.]

mere, *mēr, adj.* only what the noun indicates and nothing else.—*adv.* **mere'ly,** simply: solely. [L. *merus,* unmixed.]

mere, *mēr, n.* a boundary.—*n.* **mere'stone,** a boundary stone. [O.E. *gemǣre.*]

meretricious, *mer-ē-trish'us, adj.* characteristic of or worthy of a harlot: flashy: gaudy or showily attractive (of dress, literary style, &c.).—*adv.* **meretric'iously.**—*n.* **meretric'iousness.** [L. *meretrix, -īcis,* a harlot—*merēre,* to earn.]

merganser, *mer-gan'sėr, n.* any of several diving birds, sea-duck. [L. *mergus,* a diving bird, *ānser,* a goose.]

merge, *mûrj, v.t.* to cause to be swallowed up, or absorbed, in something greater or superior.— *v.i.* to be swallowed up, or lost.—*n.* **mer'ger** *(law),* a sinking of an estate, business corporation, &c., in one of larger extent or of higher value: a combine. [L. *mergēre, mersum.*]

meridian, *me-rid'i-àn, adj.* of or at midday: on the meridian: at culmination or highest point.—*n.* midday: the highest point (of a star's course, of success): an imaginary circle on the earth's surface passing through the poles and any given place (also used of the half-circle from pole to pole): *(astron.)* an imaginary circle, passing through the poles of the heavens, and the zenith of the spectator.—*adj.* **merid'ional,** pertaining to the meridian: southern.—*adj* a southerner, esp. in France.—*n.* **meridional'ity.**—*adv.* **merid'ionally.**—**prime** (or **first**) **meridian,** the meridian from which longitudes are measured east or west, specifically that through Greenwich. [L. *merīdiānus, merīdiōnālis—merīdiēs* (for *mediīdiēs*), midday—*medius,* middle, *diēs,* day.]

meringue, *mė-rang', n.* a crisp cake or covering made of a mixture of sugar and white of eggs, [Fr.; origin unknown.]

merino, *mė-rē'nō, n.* a sheep of a fine-woolled Spanish breed: a fine dress fabric, originally of merino wool.—*adj.* belonging to the merino sheep or its wool. [Sp., a merino sheep, also a governor.—L. *mājōrīnus,* greater, also (L.L.) *mājōrīnus,* a headman—L. *mājor,* greater.]

merit, *mer'it, n.* excellence that deserves honour or reward: that which one deserves: worth, value: *(pl.)* rights and wrongs (of a case).—*v.t.* to deserve as reward or punishment.—*n.* **meritoc'racy,** (government by) the class of persons who are in leading positions because of their ability, real or apparent.—*adj.* **meritō'rious,** deserving (in a moderate degree) of reward, honour, or praise.—*adv.* **meritō'riously.**—*n.* **meritō'riousness.**—**make a merit of,** represent (some action of one's own) as meritorious. [O.Fr. *merite*—L. *meritum—merēre, -ītum,* to obtain as a lot, to deserve.]

merk, *merk, n.* the old Scots mark or 13s. 4d. Scots, $13\frac{1}{3}$d. sterling, about $5\frac{1}{2}$p. [**mark** (2).]

merle, *mûrl, n.* the blackbird. [Fr.,—L. *merula.*]

merlin, *mûr'lin, n.* a species of small falcon. [Anglo-Fr. *merilun*—O.Fr. *esmerillon.*]

merlon, *mûr'lòn, n. (fort.)* the part of a parapet between embrasures. [Fr. *merlon*—It. *merlone—merlo,* battlement.]

mermaid, *mûr'mād, n.* a sea-woman—a woman to the waist with fish's tail:—*masc.* **mer'man.** [O.E. *mere,* lake, sea, *mǣgden,* maid.]

merry, *mer'i, adj.* pleasant: cheerful, noisily gay: causing laughter: lively.—*adv.* **merrily.**—*ns.* **merr'iment,** gaiety with laughter and noise, mirth, hilarity; **merr'iness; merr'y-an'drew,** a mountebank's or quack doctor's zany: a buffoon: one who makes sport for others—also **merr'yman; merr'y-go-round,** a revolving ring of hobbyhorses, &c.; **merr'y(-)mak'ing,** a merry entertainment: a festival; **merr'ythought,** a wish-bone, a forked bone between the neck and breast of a bird; **Merry England,** originally, pleasant England. [O.E. *myr(i)ge.*]

mersion, *mûr'sh(ò)n, n.* dipping. [L. *mersiō, -ōnis*; cf. **merge.**]

mesdames. See **madam.**

meseems, *me-sēmz, v.impers.* it seems to me *(poet.).* [**me** (dat.), and **seem.**]

mesembryanthemum, -bri-, *me-zem-bri-an'-the-mum, n.* genus of succulent plants, mostly South African. [Gr. *mesēmbriā,* midday *(mesos,* middle, *hēmerā,* day), *anthemon,* a flower.]

mesentery, *mes'ėn-tėr-i,* or *mez'-, n.* a membrane in the cavity of the abdomen, attached to the back bone, and serving to keep the intestines in place.—*adj.* **mesenteric** *(-ter'ik).* [Gr. *mesos,* middle, *enteron,* intestine.]

mesh, *mesh, n.* an opening between the threads of a net: *(pl.)* the threads and knots bounding the opening: trap: engagement (e.g. of geared wheels).—*v.t.* to catch in a net, enmesh.—*v.t.* to become engaged or interlocked, as the teeth on geared wheels.—*adj.* **mesh'y,** formed like network. [Perh. Middle Du. *maesche*; cf. O.E. *max,* net; Ger. *masche.*]

mesmerise, *mez'mėr-īz, v.t.* to hypnotise: *(loosely)* to fascinate, dominate the will or fix the attention of.—*adjs.* **mesmeric** *(-mer'ik),* **-al**—*ns.* **mes'meriser, mes'merist; mes'merism,** hypnotism as expounded, with some fanciful notions, from 1775. [From Friedrich Anton or Franz *Mesmer,* a German physician (1734-1815).]

mesne, *mēn, adj. (law)* intermediate.—**mesne lord,** one who held land of a superior, and granted part of it to another person. [Law Fr. *mesne* (O.Fr. *meien*), middle, cf. **mean** (2).]

meson, *mes'on, mēz'on, n.* an extremely short-lived particle (of three types—*eta-, pi-* *(pion),* *kappa-meson* *(kaon))* intermediate in mass between a proton and an electron, positively or negatively charged, or without charge, observed in cosmic rays. [From Gr. *mesos,* neut. *meson,* middle.]

Mesozoic, *mes-o-zō'ik, adj.* of the Secondary geological era, or second of the three main divisions of geological time.—Also *n.* [Gr.

mesos, middle, *zōē*, life.]

mesquite, *mes-kēt', mes'kēt*, *n.* a leguminous tree or shrub of America, with nutritious pods. [Sp.]

mess, *mes*, *n.* a dish of food sufficient for a meal: a number of persons who take their meals together, esp. in the fighting services: a dish of soft, pulpy or liquid stuff: a mixture disagreeable to the sight or taste: disorder, confusion.—*v.t.* to supply with a mess: to make a mess of: to muddle.—*v.i.* to belong to a mess (with), eat one's meals (with): to potter (about).—*n.* **mess'mate**, a member of the same (usu. ship's) mess.—*adj.* **mess'y**, involving or causing dirt or mess: confused, disordered. [O.Fr. *mes* (Fr. *mets*), a dish—L. *mittĕre*, *missum*, to send, in Low L. to place.]

message, *mes'ij*, *n.* any communication, oral or written, from one person to another: an official communication of a president, governor, &c., to a legislature or council: an errand: the teaching of a poet, sage, or prophet.—*n.* **mess'enger**, one who carries messages or a message: a forerunner: (*Scots law*) an officer who executes the summonses of the Court of Session (**mess'enger-at-arms**). [Fr.,—Low L. *missāticum*—L. *mittĕre*, *missum*, to send.]

Messiah, *mé-sī'a*, *n.* the anointed one, the Christ—also **Messī'as**.—*n.* **Messī'ahship**—*adj.* **Messianic** (*mes-i-an'ik*). [Heb. *māshīah*, anointed—*māshah*, to anoint.]

messieurs, *mes-yø*, contracted and anglicised as **messrs** (*mes'érz*), *pl.* of **monsieur**.

messuage, *mes'wij*, *n.* (*law*) a dwelling and offices with the adjoining lands appropriated to the household. [Anglo-Fr.; poss. orig. a misreading of *mesnage* (mod. *ménage*); cf. *ménage*.]

mestizo, *mes-tē'zō* (Sp. *-thō*), *n.* a half-caste, esp. in Spanish America and the Philippines. [Sp. *mestizo*—L. *mixticius*—*miscēre*, to mix.]

met, *pa.t.* and *pa.p.* of **meet** (2).

met(a)-, *met(-ä)-*, in composition, among, with: after, later: often implies change: beyond.

metabolism, *met-ab'ol-izm*, *n.* the sum-total of the chemical changes (constructive and destructive) that take place in a cell or in more complicated living matter.—*adj.* **metabol'ic**, relating to changes of form. [Gr. *metabolē*, change.]

metacarpal, *met-a-kär'pál*, *adj.* pertaining to the part of the hand between the wrist and the fingers. [Gr. *meta*, after, *karpos*, wrist.]

metacentre, *met'a-sen-tér*, *n.* the point of intersection of the vertical line through the centre of buoyancy (also through the centre of gravity) of a body floating in equilibrium and that through the centre of buoyancy when equilibrium is slightly disturbed. (The centre of buoyancy is the centre of gravity of the liquid displaced by the body.)—*adj.* **metacen'tric**. [Gr. *meta*, *kentron*, point.]

metachronism, *met-ak'ron-izm*, *n.* the error of dating an event too late. [Gr. *meta*, beyond, *chronos*, time.]

metage, *mēt'ij*, *n.* official weighing of coal, grain, &c.: charge for such weighing. [Formed from **mete**.]

metal, *met'l*, *n.* an opaque elementary substance, having a peculiar lustre, and possessing fusi-

bility, conductivity for heat and electricity, &c., such as gold, &c.: broken stones used for macadamised roads or as ballast for a railway.—Also *adj.* and *v.t.*—*adjs.* **met'alled; met'allic** (*mé-tal'ik*), consisting of metal: like a metal (e.g. in appearance, hardness, sound); **metallif'erous**, producing or yielding metal; **met'alline**, of, like, consisting of, or mixed with, metal.—*v.t.* **met'allise**, to make metallic.—*ns.* **metallisā'tion; met'allist**, a worker in metals; **met'alloid**, a non-metal: an element resembling a metal in some respects (e.g. arsenic).—*adjs.* **metalloid'(al)**, pertaining to, or of the nature of, the metalloids. [O.Fr.,—L. *metallum*—Gr. *metallon*, a mine.]

metallurgy, *met'al-ûr-ji*, or *-al'-*, ˑ *n.* art and science applied to metals—extraction from ores, refining, &c., and the study of structure, constitution, and properties.—*adjs.* **metallur'gic, -al**, pertaining to metallurgy.—*n.* **met'allurgist**. [Gr. *metallourgeein*, to mine—*metallon*, a mine, *ergon*, work.]

metamorphosis, *met-a-mör'fos-is*, *n.* transformation: change of form, structure, substance, appearance, character, &c., by natural development, or by magic: change of condition (e.g. of affairs): the marked change that some living beings undergo in the course of their growth, as caterpillar to butterfly, tadpole to frog, &c.:—*pl.* **metamor'phoses** (*-sēz*).—*adj.* **metamor'phic**, showing, or relating to, change of form: (*geol.*) formed by alteration of existing rocks by heat, pressure, &c.,—*n.* **metamor'phism**, processes of transformation of rocks in the earth's crust.—*v.t.* **metamor'phose** (*-fōz*), to transform. [Gr. *metamorphōsis*—*meta*, expressing change, *morphē*, form.]

metaphor, *met'a-fór*, *n.* a figure of speech by which a thing is spoken of as being that which it resembles, not fundamentally, but only in a certain marked characteristic, or marked characteristics (e.g. *he is a tiger when roused*, when roused, he shows ferocity suggestive of that of a tiger; cf. *simile*).—*adjs.* **metaphor'ic, -al**.—*adv.* **metaphor'ically**.—**mixed metaphor**, an expression in which two or more metaphors are confused (e.g. *to take arms against a sea of troubles*). [Gr. *metaphorā*—*meta*, over, *pherein*, to carry.]

metaphrase, *met'a-frāz*, *n.* a word for word translation as distinct from a *paraphrase*.—*n.* **met'aphrast**, one who produces a metaphrase.—*adj.* **metaphras'tic**. [Gr. *metaphrasis*—*meta*, over, *phrasis*, a speaking.]

metaphysics, *met-a-fiz'iks*, *n.sing.* the science that investigates ultimate reality—the first principles of nature and of thought: the branch of this science that includes ontology (q.v.): ontology: loosely applied to anything abstruse, abstract, philosophical, subtle or supernatural.—*adj.* **metaphys'ical**, pertaining to metaphysics: abstract: fanciful.—*adv.* **metaphys'ically**.—*n.* **metaphysician** (*-ish'-án*), one versed in metaphysics. [From certain works of Aristotle to be studied after his physics—Gr. *meta*, after, *physika*, physics—*physis*, nature.]

metastable, *met'a-stā-bl*, *adj.* (*chem.*) in a state which is apparently stable (said e.g. of a supersaturated solution).—**metastable state**, an excited state of an atom from which it

Neutral vowels in unaccented syllables: *em'pér-ór*; for certain sounds in foreign words see p. ix.

454

cannot pass directly to the normal state by emitting radiation. [Gr. *meta*, beside, and **stable** (1).]

metatarsal, *met-a-tär'sál, adj.* belonging to the front part of the foot, behind the toes. [Gr. *meta*, beyond, *tarsos*, the flat of the foot.]

metathesis, *met-ath'é-sis, n.* transposition or exchange of places, esp. between the sounds or letters of a word (e.g. O.E. *brid, thridda*, M.E. *drit*, give modern Eng. *bird, third, dirt.*) [Gr.,—*metatithenai*, to transpose—*meta*, in exchange, *tithenai*, to place.]

métayer, *mā-tā'yä, n.* a farmer who pays, instead of money rent, a fixed proportion of the crops.—*n.* **métayage** (-*yäzh'*), this system. [Fr.,—Low L. *medietārius*—L. *medietās*, the half—*medius*, middle.]

metazoa, *met-a-zō'a, n.pl.* many-celled animals possessing cellular differentiation—opp. to single-celled *protozoa*.—*adjs.* **metazō'an** (also *n.*), **metazō'ic**.—*n.sing.* **met'azoon**. [Gr. *meta*, after, *zōion*, animal.]

mete, *mēt, v.t.* to measure: allot (punishment, reward).—*n.* **mete'yard** a measuring rod. [O.E. *metan*; Gr. *messen*.]

metempsychosis, *met-emp-si-kō'sis, n.* the passing of the soul after death into some other body, transmigration of the soul: *pl.* **metempsychō'ses**. [Gr.,—*meta*, expressing change, *empsychōsis*, an animating—*en*, in, *psȳchē*, soul.]

meteor, *mē'tyor, n.* one of numberless small bodies travelling through space, revealed to observation when they enter the earth's atmosphere as aerolites, fire-balls, or shooting-stars: orig., now rarely, any atmospheric phenomenon: anything brilliant or dazzling but short-lived.—*adj.* **meteoric** (*mē-té-or'ik*), of the atmosphere: of or pertaining to meteors: of the nature of a meteor: transiently brilliant.—*n.* **mē'teorite**, a meteor, stony or metallic (chiefly iron alloyed with nickel), that has reached the ground.—Also **met'eorolite**.—*n.* **mēteorol'ogy**, study of weather and climate.—*adjs.* **mēteorolog'ic, al.**—*n.* **mēteorōl'ogist**.—**meteoric showers**, showers of meteors; **meteoric stones**, aerolites. [Gr. *ta meteōra*, things on high—*meta*, beyond, and the root of *aeircin*, to lift.]

meter, *mē'ter, n.* a measurer: an apparatus for measuring, esp. quantity of a fluid, or of elec tricity, used. [**mete**.]

methane, *mēth'ān.* See under **fire-damp**.

methinks, *mi-thingks', methink'eth, v. impers.* it seems to me: I think: *pa.t.* **methought** (*mi-thöt'*). [O.E. *mē thyncth*, it seems to me; *thyncan*, to seem, has been confused with *thencan*, to think.]

method, *meth'ód, n.* the mode or rule of accomplishing an end: orderly procedure: orderly arrangement: system: classification.—*adjs.* **methodic** (*mé-thod'ik*), **-al**, arranged with method: acting with method or order.—*adv.* **method'ically**.—*v.t.* **meth'odise**, to reduce to method: to arrange in an orderly manner.—*ns.* **Meth'odism**, the principles and practice of the Methodists; **Meth'odist**, one of a sect of Christians founded by John Wesley (1703-91), noted for the strictness of its discipline: one who is very strict in religion.—*adjs.* **method-**

ist'ic, -al.—*adv.* **methodist'ically**.—**method acting**, acting by trying to live a part as opposed to giving a mere technical performance. [Gr. *methodos*—*meta*, after, *hodos*, a way.]

methought. See **methinks**.

meths. Abbrev. for **methylated spirit**.

methylated spirit, *meth'il-āt-id spir'it,* methanol or *wood spirit* (q.v.), colourless, but usu. dyed purple for sale to public, used as a solvent. [Gr. *meta*, after, with *hȳlē*, wood.]

meticulous, *me-tik'ū lus, adj.* (*obs.*) timid: over-careful, scrupulously careful about small details.—*adv.* **metic'ulously**. [L. *meticulōsus*, frightened—*metus*, fear.]

métier, *mā-tyā, n.* one's calling or business: that in which one is specially skilled. [Fr.,—L. *ministērium*.]

metonic, *me-ton'ik, adj.* pertaining to the Athenian astronomer *Metōn*, or his lunar cycle of nineteen years, after which the new and full moon happen again on the same dates as at its beginning.

metonymy, *met-on'i-mi, n.* a figure of speech in which the name of one thing is put for that of another related to it (as 'the bottle' for 'drink', &c.—*adjs.* **metonym'ic, -al.**—*adv.* **metonym'ically**. [L.,—Gr. *metōnymiā*—*meta*, expressing change, *onoma*, a name.]

metre, *mē'ter, n.* that regulated succession of certain groups of syllables in which poetry is usually written—the groups (of long and short syllables in classical metres, accented and unaccented in English) being called *feet*: metrical pattern: rhythm: verse, or poetry generally.—*adjs.* **met'ric, -al**, pertaining to metre: consisting of verses.—*adv.* **met'rically**. [O.E. *mēter*, O.Fr. *metre*, both from L. *metrum*—Gr. *metron*, measurement.]

metre, *mē'ter, n.* the fundamental unit of length in the metric system—by British Act of Parliament (1963) one yard equals 0.9144 metre.—*adj.* **met'ric**.—*v.t., v.i.* **met'ricate**, to convert, change, to the metric system.—*n.* **met'rication**—**mētre-kilogram(me) second** (abbrev. MKS) **system**, system of scientific measure having the metre, &c., as units of length, mass, time (with the addition of ampere—MKSA—forming the Giorgi system of units); **metric system**, a decimal system of weights and measures. [Fr. *mètre*—Gr. *metron*.]

metric, *met'rik, adj.* quantitative.—*adj.* **met'rical**, pertaining to measurement.—*n.* **metrol'ogy**, the science of weights and measures. [Gr. *metron*, measure.]

metronome, *met'ro-nōm, n.* an instrument that sets a musical tempo.—*adj.* **metronom'ic**. [Gr. *metron*, measure, *nomos*, law.]

metropolis, *me-trop'o-lis, n.* the capital of a country: the chief cathedral city, as Canterbury of England: a chief centre:—*pl.* **metrop'olises.**—*adj.* **metropol'itan**, belonging to a metropolis: pertaining to the mother-church: (*rare*) consisting of, or pertaining to, the mother-country.—*n.* the bishop of a metropolis, presiding over the other bishops of a province: archbishop. [Gr. *mētropolis*—*mētēr*, mother, *polis*, a city.]

mettle, *met'l, n.* temperament: ardour, spirit, courage.—*adj.* **mett'led, mett'lesome**, high-spirited, ardent.—**put one on his mettle**, to rouse a person to put forth his best efforts. [From the **metal** of a blade.]

meum et tuum, *mē'um et tū'um*, **meum and tuum**, lit. mine and thine—one's own property and that of others. [L. neut. of *meus, tuus*, my, thy; *et*, and.]

MeV, Mev, M.E.V., *mev, n.* a million electron volts, a unit of energy used in nuclear physics.

mew, *mū, n.* a sea-fowl: a gull. [O.E. *mǣw*; Du. *meeuw*, O.N. *mār*, Ger. *möwe*; all imit.]

mew, *mū, v.i.* to cry as a cat.—*n.* the cry of a cat. [Imit.]

mew, *mū, v.t.* to shed or cast (feathers): to confine (as hawks in a cage when moulting). —*v.i.* to cast the feathers, to moult.—*n.* a cage for hawks while mewing: a place for confining.—*n. pl.* **mews**, (now *sing.*—orig. *pl.* of **mew**) a street or yard of stabling, because the royal stables were built where the king's stables were kept. [O.Fr. *muer*—L. *mutāre*, to change.]

mezzo-forte, *met'sō-, med'zō-fôr'tā, adj.* and *adv.* rather loud. [It.]

mezzo-soprano, *met'sō-, med'zō-so-prä'nō, n.* a quality of voice between soprano and alto: low soprano. [It.]

mezzotint, *met'sō-tint,* or *med'zō-tint, n.* a method of copperplate engraving, producing an even gradation of tones.—Also **mezzotint'o**. [It.,—*mezzo*, middle, half, *tinto*, tint—L. *tingēre, tinctum*, to dye.]

miasma, *mī-az'ma, mi-, n.* an unwholesome exhalation:—*pl.* **mias'mata, mias'mas**.—*adjs.* **mias'mal, miasmat'ic**. [Gr. *miasma, -atos*, pollution—*miainein*, to stain.]

mica, *mī'ka, n.* a group of rock-forming minerals, silicates, with flexible and elastic laminae and generally transparent, used as electric insulators and as a substitute for glass.—*adj.* **mica'ceous** (*-shŭs*). [L. *mīca*, a crumb.]

mice, *mīs, pl.* of **mouse**.

Michaelmas, *mik'ál-mas, n.* the festival of St Michael, celebrated Sept. 29: a quarterly rent-day in England: a term or session of the High Court of Justice beginning·soon after Michaelmas.—*n.* **Mich'aelmas-dai'sy**, a wild aster: any of several garden asters.

Mickey (Finn), *mik'i (fin),* (*slang*) a doped drink.

micky, mickey.—**take the micky, mickey, out of**, to tease: to make game of.

micro-, *mī'krō-*, in composition, small:—e.g. **microcephalous** (*mī-krō-sef'ál-us*), *adj.* small-headed (Gr. *kephalē*, head); **microphyte** (*mī'krō-fīt*), *n.* a microscopic plant, esp. one of the bacteria (Gr. *phyton*, a plant): dealing with minute quantities or with a small area: using, or used in, microscopy: reducing, or reduced, to minute size: a millionth part, as in **microampere**, a millionth part of an ampere. [Gr. *mīkros*, small.]

microbe, *mī'krōb, n.* an organism which can be seen by the aid of a microscope, esp. (popularly) a disease-causing bacterium. [Fr.,—Gr. *mīkros*, small, *bios*, life.]

microbiological, *mī-krō-bī-ō-loj'i-kál, adj.* of or pertaining to microscopic living things: used in the study of such living things. [Gr. *mīkros*, small, and **biological**.]

micrococcus, *mī-krō-kok'us, n.* a rounded bacillus. [Gr. *mīkros*, small, *kokkos*, a grain.]

microcosm, *mī'krō-kozm, n.* a little universe or world: (often applied to) man, who was regarded by ancient philosophers as a model or epitome of the universe.—*adjs.* **microcos'mic, -al**, pertaining to the microcosm. [Gr. *mīkros*, little, *kosmos*, world.]

microfilm, *mī'krō-film, n.* a photographic film for preserving a microscopic record of a document, &c., which can be enlarged in projection. [Gr. *mīkros*, small, **film**.]

micrography, *mī-krog'ra-fi, n.* the description of microscopic objects.—*n.* **mī'crograph**, a pictorial reproduction of an object as seen through the microscope. [Gr. *mīkros*, little, *graphein*, to write.]

microgroove, *mī'kro-grōōv, n.* the fine groove of a long-playing gramophone record. [Gr. *mīkros*, small, and **groove**.]

micrometer, *mī-krom'é-tér, n.* an instrument for measuring minute distances or angles.—*adjs.* **micromet'ric, -al**. [Gr. *mīkros*, little, *metron*, measure.]

micrometre. See **micron**.

micromicro-, *mī'krō-mī'krō-*, (better **pico-**) in composition, a millionth of a millionth part. [Gr. *mīkros*, small.]

microminiaturisation, *mī-krō-min'i-(á-)chúr-iz-ā-shòn, n.* reduction to extremely small size of scientific or technical equipment or any part of it. [Gr. *mīkros*, small, and **miniature**.]

micron, *mī'kron, n.* unit of length, 10^{-6} metres now usu. **micrometre** (μm). [Gr. *mīkros*, small.]

micro-organism, *mī'krō-ör'gan-izm, n.* a very small living animal or plant. [Gr. *mīkros*, small, *organon*, instrument.]

microphone, *mī'krō-fōn, n.* an instrument for intensifying sounds: a sensitive instrument for picking up sound waves to be broadcast or amplified and translating them into a fluctuating electric current.—Also (*coll.*) **mike**. [Gr. *mīkros*, small, *phōnē*, voice.]

micropyle, *mī'krō-pīl, n.* (*bot.*) a tiny opening in the integument at the apex of an ovule, through which the pollen tube usually enters: the corresponding opening in the testa of a seed. [Gr. *mīkros*, small, *pylē*, a gate.]

microscope, *mī'krō-skōp, n.* an instrument that magnifies to the eye, by means of a lens or lenses, objects so minute as to be almost or quite indiscernible without its aid. Greater magnifications are possible in radiations of shorter wavelength, and, therefore, some microscopes are now made using a beam of ultraviolet rays (**ultraviolet microscope**), or of electrons (**electron microscope**), or of protons (**proton microscope**), instead of a beam of light, to illumine the object and produce the magnified image. See also **phase-contrast**.—*adjs.* **microscop'ic, -al**, pertaining to a microscope: visible only by the aid of a microscope: minute.—*adv.* **microscop'ically**.—*n.* **mi'croscopy**, use of the microscope.—**reflecting microscope**, a microscope in which reflecting mirrors are used instead of lenses. [Gr. *mīkros*, little, *skopeein*, to look at.]

microwave, *mī'krō-wāv, n.* a very short electromagnetic wave: a wave in the radiation spectrum between normal radio wave and infrared. [Gr. *mīkros*, small, and **wave**.]

mid, *mid, adj.* middle: situated between ex-

Neutral vowels in unaccented syllables: *em'pér-ôr*; for certain sounds in foreign words see p. ix.

tremes.—*prep.* amid.—*n.* **mid'day**, the middle of the day, noon.—Also *adj.*—*adj.* **mid'land**, in the middle of, or surrounded by, land: distant from the coast, inland.—*n.* the interior of a country.—*n.* **mid'night**, the middle of the night, twelve o'clock at night.—*adj.* being at midnight: dark as midnight.—*ns.* **mid-off**, (*cricket*) a fieldsman on the off side nearly in line with the bowler: his position; **mid-on**, a fieldsman on the on side nearly in line with the bowler: his position.—*adj.* **mid'ship**, being in the middle of a ship.—*n.* **mid'shipman**, once title of officer entering navy (orig. quartered *amidships*), later junior ranking below sublieutenant but above naval cadet; since 1957, ranking only during shore-based training.—*adv.* **mid'ships.**—*ns.* **mid'summer**, the middle of summer: the summer solstice about June 21; **mid'way**, the middle of the way or distance.—*adj.* being in the middle of the way or distance.—*adv.* half-way.—*n.* **mid'winter**, the middle of winter: the winter solstice (December 21 or 22), or the time shortly before or after it. [O.F. *midd*, cf. Ger. *mitte*. *medius*. Gr. *mesos*.]

midden, *mid'én, n.* a dunghill: a refuse-heap. [Scand., as Dan. *mödding—mög*, dung.]

middle, *mid'l, adj.* equally distant from the extremes: intermediate: intervening.—*n.* the middle point or part: midst: central portion, waist.—*n.* **midd'leman**, a dealer who intervenes between producer and consumer: a go-between or agent—*adjs.* **midd'lemost**, **mid'most** (*B.*), nearest the middle.—*n.* **midd'leweight**, a professional boxer, wrestler, &c., of over 10 st. 7 lb. but not more than 11 st. 6 lb,—*adj.* **midd'ling**, of middle rate, state, size, or quality: second-rate: moderate.—*adv.* moderately. **Middle Ages**, the time between the downfall of the western Roman empire and the Revival of Learning and the Reformation; **middle class**, that part of the people which comes between the aristocracy and the working class; **Middle East**, the countries of Asia west of India (or China); **middle passage**, the voyage across the Atlantic from Africa to the West Indies on a slave-ship; **middle term** (*logic*), that term of a syllogism which appears in both premises, but not in the conclusion; **middle voice**, voice between active and passive, expressing reflexive action, &c.; **middle watch**, the period from midnight to 4 a.m.; **Middle West**, northern part of Mississippi basin. [O.E. *middel—mid*; Du. *middel*, Ger. *mittel*.]

midge, *mij, n.* any small gnat or fly: a very small person.—*n.* **midg'et**, something very small of its kind. [O.E. *mycg(e)*; Ger. *mücke*.]

midi, *mid'i, adj.* of a skirt or dress, having the hemline at about mid-calf. Cf **maxi**, **mini**.

midriff, *mid'rif, n.* the diaphragm. [O.E. *mid*, middle, *hrif*, the belly.]

midst, *midst, n.* middle.—*prep.* amidst. [M.E. *middes*, with excrescent *t.*]

midwife, *mid'wīf, n.* a woman who assists others in childbirth:—*pl.* **midwives** (*mid'wīvz*).—*n.* **mid'wifery** (-*wif-é-ri, -if-ri, -wīf-ri*), art or practice of a midwife. [O.E. *mid*, with (Ger. *mit*, Gr. *meta*), *wīf*, woman.]

mien, *mēn, n.* the air or look, expression of face,

manner, bearing. [Perh. from obs. n. *demean*—**demean** (2); influenced by Fr. *mine*.]

might, *mīt, pa.t.* of **may** (1).

might, *mīt, n.* power, strength: energy or intensity of purpose or feeling.—*adj.* **might'y**, having great power: very large: (*coll.*) very great: (*B.*) wonderful, miraculous.—*adv.* very.—*adv.* **might'ily.**—*n.* **might'iness**, power: greatness: a title of dignity.—**might and main**, utmost strength. [O.E. *miht, mecht*; Ger. *macht*; cf. **may** (1).]

mignonette, *min-yo-net', n.* a sweet-scented plant with racemes of greyish-green flowers: any other plant of the same genus (*Reseda*). [Fr., fem. dim. of *mignon*, daintily small.]

migraine, *mē-grān', n.* now more usual form of **megrim** (first sense).

migrate, *mī'grāt, v.i.* to pass from one place to another: to do so periodically, as certain birds and animals: to change one's abode to another country: to pass individually (as ions, particles).—*adj.* **mi'gratory**, migrating or accustomed to migrate; wandering.—*n.* **migra'tion**. [L. *migrāre, -ātum*.]

mikado, *mi-kä'dō, n.* a title of the Emperor of Japan. [Jap. 'exalted gate'.]

mike, *mīk, n.* (*coll.*) microphone. [Abbrev. of **microphone**.]

mil, *mil, n.* unit (1/1000 in.) in measuring the diameter of wire, also *thou* (both *coll.*): a proposed coin = £1/1000. [L. *mīlle*, 1000.]

milch, *milch, milsh, adj.* giving milk. [O.E. *milce*; cf. **milk**.]

mild, *mīld, adj.* gentle in temper and disposition: not sharp or bitter: acting gently: gently and pleasantly affecting the senses, temperate, soft.—*adv.* **mild'ly.**—*n.* **mild'ness**. [O.E. *milde*, mild; cf. Ger. *mild*, O.N.*mildr*, gracious.]

mildew, *mil'dū, n.* a disease on organic matter or on living plants, caused by the growth of minute fungi,—*v.t.* to taint with mildew. [O.E. *melēdēaw, mildēaw*, from a lost word for honey, and *dēaw*, dew.]

mile, *mīl, n.* a Roman unit of length, 1000 paces: applied to various later units, now in Britain and U.S. to one of 1760 yards or 1·61 km.—*ns.* **mil(e)'age**, length in miles: expense of travel reckoned by the mile; **mile'stone**, a stone set up to mark the distance of a mile: a stage or reckoning point.—**geographical** or **nautical mile**, one minute of longitude measured along the equator = 6082·66 feet; the approximation adopted by the British Admiralty is 6080 feet. [O.E. *mīl*—L. *mīlia*, thousands.]

miliary, *mil'yár-i, adj.* like a millet-seed: characterised by an eruption of pimples, vesicles, &c., like millet-seeds. [L. *milium*, millet.]

milieu, *mēl-yø, n.* environment, setting, medium, element. [Fr., middle.]

militant, *mil'i-tánt, adj.* fighting, engaged in warfare: combative: using violence: actively contending.—Also *n.*—*n.***mil'itancy**.—*adv.***mil'itantly.**—*v.t.* **mil'itarise**, to convert to a military model: to subject to military domination.—*ns.* **militarisā'tion**; **mil'itarism**, an excess of the military spirit.—*adj.* **mil'itary**, pertaining to soldiers or to warfare: warlike.—*n.* soldiery: the army.—*v.i.* **mil'itate**, to contend: to have weight, tell (esp. with *against*).—**church militant** (see **church**). [L. *mīles, -itis*, a soldier, *mīlitāris*, military, *mīlitāre*, to serve as a soldier.]

militia, *mi-lish′a, n.* a body of men enrolled and drilled as soldiers, but liable only to home service.—*n.* **milit′iaman.** [L. *mīlitia,* military service or force.]

milk, *milk, v.t.* to squeeze or draw milk from: to extract juice, poison, money, &c., from: to exploit.—*n.* a white liquid secreted by female mammals for the nourishment of their young: a milk-like juice or preparation.—*ns.* **milk′-bar,** a shop where milk and milky beverages are sold for drinking on the spot; **milk′er,** one who milks: a machine for milking cows: a cow that gives milk; **milk′-fē′ver,** a fever accompanying the secretion of milk shortly after childbirth.—*adj.* **milk′y,** made of, full of, like, or yielding milk: gentle.—*ns.* **milk′iness; milk′ing,** the act of drawing milk from cows, &c.: the amount of milk drawn at one time; **milk′maid,** a woman who milks: a dairymaid; **milk′man,** a man who sells milk, esp. from door to door; **milk′punch,** a beverage made of milk and rum or whisky; **milk′sop,** a piece of bread sopped or soaked in milk: an effeminate, silly fellow; **milk′-tooth,** one of the first, temporary teeth of a mammal; **milk′-tree,** a tree yielding a milk-like nourishing juice, as the cow-tree of S. America.—*adj.* **milk′-white.**—*n.* **Milk′y Way** (*astron.*), the Galaxy. [O.E. *milc, meolc,* milk; Ger. *milch,* milk; L. *mulgēre,* to milk.]

mill, *mil, n.* a machine for grinding by crushing between hard, rough surfaces: a building where corn is ground: one where manufacture of some kind is carried on.—*v.t.* to grind: to press or stamp in a mill: to put ridges and furrows on the rim of, as coin: to clean, as cloth.—*v.i.* (*slang*) to box, fight: (of cattle or a crowd) to move round and round in a group.—*ns.* **mill′-board,** stout pasteboard, used esp. in binding books; **mill′dam, mill′pond,** a dam or pond to hold water for driving a mill; **mill′er,** one who owns or works a mill; **mill′ing,** the act of passing anything through a mill: the act of fulling cloth: the process of indenting coin on the edge: ridges and furrows on the rim of a coin; **mill′race,** the current of water that turns a mill-wheel, or the channel in which it runs; **mill′stone,** one of the two stones used in a mill for grinding corn: an oppressive burden (of person or thing); **mill′stone-grit,** a hard gritty sandstone, suitable for millstones; **mill′-wheel,** the water-wheel used for driving a mill; **mill′wright,** a wright or mechanic who builds and repairs mills. [O.E. *myln*—L. *mola,* a mill—*molĕre,* to grind.]

millennium, *mil-en′i-um, n.* a thousand years: the thousand years mentioned in *Revelation* xx. between the second coming of Christ, when the righteous are raised from the dead, and the time when the wicked are raised: a coming golden age:—*pl.* **millenn′ia.**—*adj.* **millenā′rian,** pertaining to the millennium. —*n.* one believing in the millennium.—*adj.* **mill′enary,** consisting of a thousand.—*n.* a thousand years: *:* thousandth anniversary.— *adj.* **millenn′ial,** pertaining to a thousand years, or to the millennium. [L. *mīlle,* 1000,

annus, a year.]

milleped. See **millipede.**

miller's-thumb, *mil′erz-thum, n.* a small freshwater fish with a large, broad, and rounded head like a *miller's thumb.*

millesimal, *mil-es′im-ăl, adj.* thousandth: consisting of thousandth parts.—*adv.* **milles′imally.** [L. *millēsimus*—*mille,* a thousand.]

millet, *mil′et, n.* a food-grain. [Fr. *millet*—L. *milium.*]

milliard, *mil′yärd, n.* a thousand millions. [Fr.—L. *mille,* a thousand.]

milli-, *mil′i-,* in composition, in names of units, a thousandth part, as *ns.* **milligram(me), millimetre,** &c., a thousandth part of a gram- (me), metre, &c. [L. *mille,* a thousand.]

millimicro-, nano- (the preferred term). [**milli-, micro-.**]

milliner, *mil′in-ér, n.* one who makes or sells women's headgear, trimmings, &c.—*n.* **mill′inery,** the articles made or sold by milliners: the industry of making them. [Prob. orig. *Milaner,* a trader in Milan wares, esp. silks and ribbons.]

million, *mil′yón, n.* a thousand thousands (1 000 000): a very great number.—*n.* **mill′ionaire** (*-ār*), a man worth a million of money or more or enormously rich.—*adj.* **mill′ionary,** pertaining to, or consisting of, millions.—*adj.* and *n.* **mill′ionth,** the ten hundred thousandth.—**the million,** the great body of the people generally. [Fr.,—Low L. *mīlliō, -ōnis*—L. *mille,* 1000.]

millipede, *mil′i-pēd,* **millepede, milleped,** *mil′é-ped, n.* a myriapod. [L. *mīllĕpeda*—*mīlle,* a thousand, *pēs, pedis,* a foot.]

milt, *milt, n.* (*anat.*) the spleen: the soft roe of male fishes.—*v.t.* (of fishes) to impregnate.— *n.* **milt′er,** a male fish. [O.E. *milte,* spleen.]

mime, *mīm, n.* in Greek and Roman times, a farce in which scenes from actual life were represented by gesture: an actor in such a farce: any dramatic representation consisting of action without words.—*adjs.* **mimet′ic, -al,** apt to imitate: characterised by imitation.—*n.* **mimic** (*mim′ik*), one who imitates, esp. ludicrously.—*adj.* imitative: mock or sham.—*v.t.* to imitate, esp. in ridicule: to ape:—*pr.p.* mim′icking; *pa.p.* mim′icked.—*n.* **mim′icry** (*-kri*), act of mimicking: imitative resemblance. [Gr. *mīmos.*]

mimosa, *mim-ō′za, n.* a genus of leguminous plants, including the common sensitive plant. [Gr. *mīmos,* a mimic.]

mimulus, *mim′ū-lus, n.* a genus of the figwort family with a masklike corolla. [Prob. diminutive of **mime.**]

minar, *mi-när′, n.* a tower.—*n.* **min′aret,** a turret on a mosque, from which the call to prayer is sounded. [Ar. *manār, manārat,* lighthouse— *nār,* fire.]

minatory, *min′a-tór-i* (or *mīn′-*), *adj.* threatening. [L. *minārī, -ātus,* to threaten.]

mince, *mins, v.t.* to cut into small pieces, to chop fine: to diminish or suppress a part of (one's meaning) in speaking: to pronounce affectedly.—*v.i.* to walk with affected nicety: to speak affectedly:—*pr.p.* minc′ing; *pa.p.* minced (*minst*).—*ns.* **mince′meat,** meat chopped small—hence anything thoroughly broken or

Neutral vowels in unaccented syllables: *em′pér-ór*; for certain sounds in foreign words see p. ix.

458

cut to pieces: a mixture of raisins and other fruits with suet, &c.; **mince'-pie**, a pie made with mincemeat; **minc'er**, one who minces: a machine for mincing.—*adj.* **minc'ing**, speaking or walking with affected nicety.—*adv.* **minc'ingly.**—**make mincemeat of**, to destroy utterly (esp. *fig.*); **mince matters, words**, to speak of things with affected delicacy, to soften a statement for politeness' sake. [O.Fr. *mincier*, *minchier*—L. *minūtus*; cf. **minute**, adj.]

mind, *mīnd*, *n.* the faculty by which we think, &c.: the understanding: the whole spiritual nature: memory (e.g. *call to*, *keep in*, *mind*): intention (e.g. *change one's mind*): inclination (e.g. *to have a mind*—with *to*): thoughts or sentiments, candid opinion (e.g. *speak one's mind*): cast of thought and feeling (e.g. *bring to a better mind*): (*B.*) disposition: a thinking or directing person.—*v.t.* to tend: to give heed to: to obey: (*orig.*) to remind: (*Scot.*) to remember.—*v.i.* (*B.*) to intend.—*adjs.* **mind'ed**, having a mind (esp. in compounds—e.g. *small-*, *narrow-minded*): disposed, determined (to); **mind'ful**, bearing in mind (with *of*): attentive: observant.—*adv.* **mind'fully.**—*n.* **mind'fulness.**—*adj.* **mind'less**, without mind: stupid.—**absence of mind**, inattention: inadvertence; **be out of one's mind**, to be insane; **know one's own mind**, to be sure of one's opinions and intentions; **lose one's mind**, to become insane; **make up one's mind**, to decide; **never mind**, do not concern yourself; **of one mind**, agreed; **of, in two minds**, uncertain (what to think or do); **presence of mind**, a state of calmness in which all the powers of the mind are on the alert and ready for action; **speak one's mind**, to say plainly what one thinks; **to one's mind**, in exact accordance with one's wishes. [O.E. *gemynd*—*munan*, to think; L. *mens*, the mind.]

mine, *mīn*, *pron.* the possessive (*gen.*) case of **I** (e.g. *the watch is mine*).—Also *possessive adj.* (now used without noun—e.g. *this is John's watch, that is mine*): (arch.) my, used before a following vowel. [O.E. *mīn.*]

mine, *mīn*, *n.* a place from which metals, &c., are dug: an excavation dug under a fortification to blow it up: an explosive charge for this purpose: a submerged or floating charge of explosives to destroy ships: a rich source.—*v.t.* to excavate, make passages in or under: to obtain by excavation: to beset with, or destroy by, mines.—*v.i.* to dig or work a mine.—*ns.* **mī'ner**, one who works in a mine; **mine'-field**, an area beset with explosive mines; **mine'-layer**, vessel for laying mines; **mine'-sweeper**, a vessel for removing mines. [Fr. *mine.*]

mineral, *min'ér-ál*, *n.* a substance produced by the processes of inorganic nature: often extended to certain substances of organic origin got by mining, as coal, amber: a mineral water.—*adj.* relating to, or having the nature of, minerals.—*v.t.* **min'eralise**, to make into a mineral: to give the properties of a mineral to: to impregnate with mineral matter.—*v.i.* to collect minerals.—*ns.* **mineralisā'tion; mineral'ogy**, the science of minerals.—*adj.* **mineralog'ical**, pertaining to mineralogy.—*adv.* **mineralog'ically.**—*n.* **mineral'ogist**, one

versed in mineralogy.—**mineral water**, spring water impregnated with minerals: an effervescent non-alcoholic beverage. [Fr.,—*miner*, to mine; cf. **mine** (2).]

minestrone, *min-i-strōn'ē*, *n.* a thick vegetable soup with pieces of pasta, &c. [It.]

minever, *min'é-vér*, *n.* Same as **miniver.**

Ming, *ming*, *adj.* of, pertaining to, produced during, the *Ming* dynasty in Chinese history (1368-1643), famous for works of art.

mingle, *ming'gl*, *v.t.* and *v.i.* to mix: to join in mutual intercourse.—*ns.* **ming'ler, ming'ling**, mixture: a mixing or blending together. [O.E. *mengan*; Ger. *mengen.*]

mini-, *min'i-*, in composition, small (abbrev. of **miniature**) as in e.g. the following: **mini-cab**, a small taxi-cab; **mini-car**, a small type of car; **mini-skirt**, a skirt whose hemline is well above the knees.

mini. Abbrev. for **mini-car, mini-skirt.**

miniature, *min'yá-tūr*, *-tyùr*, or *min'i-(a-)*, *n.* a painting on a very small scale: a small or reduced copy of anything.—*adj.* on a small scale, minute.—*v.t.* to represent on a small scale.—*v.t.* **min'iaturise**, much to reduce the size of (electronic equipment).—*n.* **miniaturis'ation**. [It. *miniatura*—L. *minium*, red lead, meaning affected by association with L. *minor*, less, smaller, &c.]

minikin, *min'i-kin*, *n.* a little darling: a small sort of pin.—*adj.* small. [Obs. Du. *minniken*, dim. of *minne*, love.]

minim, *min'im*, *n.* (*mus.*) a note (formerly the shortest) equal to two crotchets: (apothecaries' measure) one-sixtieth of a fluid drachm.—*adj.* **min'imal**, of least, or of least possible, size, amount, or degree.—*v.t.* **min'imise**, to reduce to the smallest possible proportions: to belittle.—*n.* **min'imum**, the least number, quantity, or degree possible under given conditions, or that will satisfy specified requirements: (*math.*) the value of a variable when it ceases to decrease and begins to increase:—*pl.* **min'ima.**—*adj.* **min'imum.** **minimum wage**, the lowest wage permitted by law for certain work: a fixed bottom limit to workers' wages in various industries. [L. *minimus*, the smallest.]

minion, *min'yón*, *n.* a darling, a favourite, esp. of a prince: a servile dependent: (*print.*) a small kind of type. [Fr. *mignon*, a darling.]

minish, *min'ish*, *v.t.* (*B.*) to make little or less. [Fr. *menuiser*—L. *minūtia*, smallness.]

minister, *min'is-tér*, *n.* a servant: one who serves at the altar: a clergyman: one transacting business for another: the responsible head of a department of state affairs: the representative of a government at a foreign court.—*v.i.* to act as a servant: to supply or do things needful: to contribute (to a result).—*v.t.* (*arch.*) to furnish, supply (e.g. *to minister consolation*):—*pr.p* **min'istering**; *pa.p.* **min'istered.**—*adj.* **ministē'rial**, pertaining to a ministry or minister (in any sense).—*adv.* **ministē'rially.**—*adj.* **min'istrant**, administering: attendant.—*n.* **ministrā'tion**, the act of ministering or performing service: office or service of a minister.—*adj.* **min'istrative**, serving to aid or assist: ministering.—*n.* **min'istry**, act of ministering: service: office or duties of a minister: the clerical profession: the body of ministers of state: a department of government. [L.,–*minor*, less.]

miniver, *min'i-vér*, *n.* white fur: the ermine in winter coat. [O.Fr.–*menu*, small (L. *minūtus*), *vair*, fur.]

mink, *mingk*, *n.* either of two small quadrupeds of the weasel genus, valued for their fur. [Perh. from Swed. *mänk*.]

minnesinger, *min'é-sing'ér*, *n.* one of a school of German lyric poets, mostly of knightly birth, in the 12th and 13th centuries:–*pl.* **minne'-singer**. [Ger. *minne*, love, *singer*, singer.]

minnow, *min'ō*, *n.* a very small fresh-water fish akin to the chub: the young of larger fish. [O.E. *myne*.]

minor, *mī'nór*, *adj.* less: inferior in importance, degree, bulk, &c.: inconsiderable: lower: (*mus.*) smaller by a semitone.–*n.* a person under age (18 years):–*n.* **Mī'norite**, a Franciscan friar.–Also *adj.*–*n.* **minor'ity**, the state of being under age: the smaller number: the party of smaller numbers–opp. to *majority.*–**minor interval**, an interval less by a semitone than the major interval of the same scale name; **minor key, scale**, one which has the third note only three semitones above the tonic (see **harmonic minor, melodic minor**). –**minor key** (*fig.*), a doleful tone or mood; **minor premise**, the premise that introduces the minor term; **Minor Prophets**, the twelve from Hosea to Malachi inclusive; **minor term**, the term in a syllogism that forms the subject of the conclusion. [L. *minor*, less.]

minotaur, *min'ō-tör*, *n.* a fabulous bull-headed monster, to whom human sacrifices were made in a labyrinth built for Minos, King of Crete. [Gr. *Mīnōtauros*–*Mīnōs* and *tauros*, a bull.]

minster, *min'stér*, *n.* the church of a monastery: a cathedral church. [O.E. *mynster*–L. *monastērium*, a monastery.]

minstrel, *min'strél*, *n.* a professional entertainer: a musician: a mediaeval harper who sang or recited his own or others' poems.–*n.* **min'strelsy**, the art or occupation of a minstrel: music: a company of minstrels: a collection of songs. [O.Fr. *menestrel*–L. *ministeriālis*–*minister*, attendant.]

mint, *mint*, *n.* the place where money is coined by government: a place where anything is invented or made: a vast sum (of money).–*v.t.* to coin: to invent.–*ns.* **mint'age**, coining: coinage: duty for coining; **mint'er**, one who mints or coins: an inventor; **mint'-mark**, a mark showing where a coin was minted.–**in mint condition**, of coins, books, prints, postage stamps, &c., perfectly clean and unblemished. [O.E. *mynet*, money–L. *monēta*. See **money**.]

mint, *mint*, *n.* any of a large genus of aromatic plants producing highly odoriferous oil. [O.Fr. *minte*–L. *mentha*–Gr. *minthē*.]

minuend, *min'ū-end*, *n.* the number from which another is to be subtracted. [L. *minuendum*–*minuēre*, to lessen.]

minuet, *min-ū-et'*, *n.* a slow, graceful dance with short steps: the music for such a dance. [Fr. *menuet*–*menu*, small–L. *minūtus*, small.]

minus, *mī'nus*, *prep.* (*math.*) diminished by:

(*coll.*) deprived of, without.–*adj.* negative.–*n.* a negative quantity: the sign of subtraction (–).–*n.* **minuscule** (*-us'kūl*), a cursive script originated by the monks in the 7th-9th centuries: any small or lower-case letter. [L., neuter of *minor*, less.]

minute, *mīn-ūt'*, *adj.* extremely small: attentive to small things: exact.–*adv.* **minute'ly**.–*n.* **minute'ness**. [L. *minūtus*, pa.p. of *minuĕre*, to lessen.]

minute, *min'it*, *n.* the sixtieth part of an hour: the sixtieth part of a degree: an indefinitely small space of time: a brief jotting or note: (*pl.*) a brief summary of the proceedings of a meeting.–*v.t.* to make a brief jotting or note of anything.–*ns.* **min'ute-book**, a book containing minutes or short notes; **min'ute-glass**, a sand-glass that measures a minute; **min'ute-gun**, a gun discharged every minute, as a signal of distress or mourning; **min'ute-hand**, the hand that indicates the minutes on a clock or watch.–**up to the minute**, right up to date. [Same word as above.]

minutiae, *mi-nū'shi-ē*, *n.pl.* minute or small things: the smallest particulars or details. [L., pl. of *minūtia*, smallness.]

minx, *mingks*, *n.* a pert young girl. [Poss. from *minikin*.]

Miocene, *mī'o-sēn*, *adj.* of the period of the Tertiary geological system preceding the Pliocene. [Gr. *meiōn*, less, *kainos*, recent.]

miracle, *mir'á-kl*, *n.* a wonder: a prodigy: a supernatural event.–*n.* **mir'acle-play**, a mediaeval form of drama founded on Old or New Testament history or (more exactly) on the legends of the saints.–*adj.* **mirac'ulous** (*-ak'ū-lus*), of the nature of a miracle: done by supernatural power: very wonderful: able to perform miracles.–*adv.* **mirac'ulously**.–*n.* **mirac'ulousness**. [Fr.,–L. *mīrāculum*–*mīrārī*, *-ātus*, to wonder at.]

mirage, *mi-räzh'*, *n.* an optical illusion, esp. that which causes travellers in a desert to imagine they see an expanse of water: (*fig.*) something illusory. [Fr.–*mirer*, to look at–L. *mīrārī*, to wonder at.]

mire, *mīr*, *n.* deep mud.–*v.t.* to plunge and fix in mire: to soil with mud.–*v.i.* to sink in mud.–*adj.* **mī'ry**, consisting of mire: covered with mire.–*n.* **mī'riness**. [O.N. *mýrr*, bog.]

mirror, *mir'ór*, *n.* a looking-glass: a reflecting surface: (*fig.*) a faithful representation: an example, good or bad.–*v.t.* to reflect as in a mirror:–*pr.p.* mirr'oring; *pa.p.* mirr'ored. [O.Fr. *mireor*, *mirour*–L. *mīrārī*, *-ātus*, to wonder at.]

mirth, *mûrth*, *n.* merriness: (*obs.*) pleasure, delight: noisy gaiety: laughter.–*adj.* **mirth'ful**, full of mirth, merry, jovial.–*adv.* **mirth'fully**. –*n.* **mirth'fulness**.–*adj.* **mirth'less**, joyless, cheerless. [O.E. *myrgth*–*myrige*, merry.]

mis-, *pfx.* from (1) O.E. *mis-*, of Gmc. origin, meaning:–wrongly, as **misspell**, badly, as **misbecome**; (*arch.*) with negative force, as **mislike**; with intensive force as, **misdoubt**; (2) O.Fr. *mes-* (L. *minus*, neut. of *minor*, less), with meanings similar to the above.

misadventure, *mis-ad-vent'yŭr*, *-chŭr*, *n.* illluck: mishap: accidental homicide. [**mis-** (2), and **adventure**.]

Neutral vowels in unaccented syllables: *em'pér-ór*; for certain sounds in foreign words see p. ix.

460

misadvise, *mis-ad-vīz'*, *v.t.* to give bad advice to.—*adj.* **misadvised'**, ill-advised, ill-directed. [**mis-** (2), and **advise**.]

misalliance, *mis-a-lī'ans*, *n.* an unsuitable alliance, esp. marriage with one of a lower rank. [After Fr. *mésalliance.*]

misanthrope, *mis'an-thrōp*, *n.* a hater of mankind—also **misan'thropist**.—*adjs.* **misanthrop'ic**, **-al**, hating or distrusting mankind.—*adv.* **misanthrop'ically**.—*n.* **misan'thropy**, hatred or distrust of mankind. [Gr. *misanthrōpos—misein*, to hate, *anthrōpos*, a man.]

misapply, *mis-a-plī'*, *v.t.* to apply wrongly: to use for a wrong purpose.—*n.* **misapplica'tion**. [**mis-** (1), and **apply**.]

misapprehend, *mis-ap-ré-hend'*, *v.t.* to apprehend wrongly, misunderstand.—*n.* **misapprehen'sion**. [**mis-** (1), and **apprehend**.]

misappropriate, *mis-a-prō'pri-āt*, *v.t.* to put to a wrong use, esp. to use (another's money) for oneself.—*n.* **misappropria'tion**. [**mis-** (1), and **appropriate**.]

misbecome, *mis-bi-kum'*, *v.t.* to be unbecoming or unsuitable to. [**mis-** (1), and **become**.]

misbegotten, *mis-bi-got'n*, *adj.* illegitimate: often a vague term of reproach. [**mis-** (1), and pa.p. of **beget**.]

misbehave, *mis-bi-hāv'*, *v.i.* to behave ill or improperly.—*n.* **misbehav'iour**. [**mis-** (1), and **behave**.]

misbelieve, *mis-bi-lēv'*, *v.t.* to believe wrongly or falsely.—*ns.* **misbelief'**, belief in false doctrine; **misbeliev'er**. [**mis-** (1), and **believe**.]

miscalculate, *mis-kal'kū-lāt*, *v.t.* to calculate wrongly.—*n.* **miscalcula'tion**. [**mis-** (1), and **calculate**.]

miscall, *mis-köl'*, *v.t.* to call by a wrong name: to abuse or revile. [**mis-** (1), and **call**.]

miscarriage, *mis-kar'ij*, *n.* an act of miscarrying: failure (e.g. of a plan): failure to attain the appropriate result (*miscarriage of justice*): the act of expelling a foetus prematurely and accidentally.—*v.i.* **miscarr'y**, to be unsuccessful: to fail of the intended effect: to bring forth prematurely. [**mis-** (1), **carriage**, **carry**.]

miscegenation, *mis-é-jén-ā'sh(ô)n*, *n.* interbreeding or intermarriage between different races. [L. *miscēre*, to mix, *genus*, race.]

miscellaneous, *mis-él-ān'i-us*, *adj.* mixed or mingled: consisting of several kinds.—*adv.* **miscellān'eously**,—*ns.* **miscellān'eousness**; **miscell'any**, a mixture of various kinds: a collection of writings on different subjects or by different authors; **miscell'anist**, a writer of miscellanies. [L. *miscellāneus—miscēre*, to mix.]

mischance, *mis-chäns'*, *n.* ill-luck: mishap.—*v.i.* to chance wrongly, come to ill-luck. [O.Fr. *mescheance.*]

mischief, *mis'chif*, *n.* evil, injury, damage: source of harm or annoyance: action or conduct that causes trivial annoyance.—*adj.* **mischievous** (*mis'chi-vus*), injurious: prone to mischief.—*adv.* **mis'chievously**.—*ns.* **mis'chievousness**; **mischief-maker**, one who makes discord or incites quarrels. [O.Fr. *meschef*, from **mis-** (2), and *chef*—L. *caput*, the head.]

mischmetal, *mish'met-l*, *n.* an alloy of cerium

with rare earth metals and iron, used to produce the spark in cigarette lighters, &c. [Ger. *mischen*, to mix, and **metal**.]

miscible, *mis'i-bl*, *adj.* that may be mixed.—*n.* **miscibil'ity**. [Fr.,—L. *miscēre*, to mix.]

misconceive, *mis-kon-sēv'*, *v.t.* and *v.i.* to conceive or apprehend wrongly: to misunderstand, interpret wrongly.—*n.* **misconcep'tion**, an erroneous idea. [**mis-** (1), and **conceive**.]

misconduct, *mis-kon'dukt*, *n.* bad conduct: wrong management.—*v.t.* **misconduct'**. [**mis-** (1), and **conduct**.]

misconstrue, *mis-kon-strōō'* or *-kon'*, *v.t.* to construe, or to interpret, wrongly.—*n.* **misconstruc'tion**. [**mis-** (1), and **construe**.]

miscount, *mis-kownt'*, *v.t.* to count wrongly.—*n.* a wrong counting. [**mis-** (1), and **count** (2).]

miscreant, *mis'kri-ānt*, *n.* orig. a misbeliever, an infidel: a vile wretch, a scoundrel. [O.Fr. *mescreant*—**mis-** (2), and L. *crēdens*, *-entis*, pr.p. of *crēdēre*, to believe.]

misdate, *mis-dāt'*, *v.t.* to date wrongly.—*n.* a wrong date. [**mis-** (1), and **date** (1).]

misdeal, *mis-dēl'*, *n.* a wrong deal, as at cards.—*v.t.* and *v.i.* to deal wrongly: to divide improperly. [**mis-** (1), and **deal**.]

misdeed, *mis-dēd'*, *n.* wrong-doing, an evil deed. [O.E. *misdǣd*—**mis-** (1), and **deed**.]

misdemean, *mis-di-mēn'*, *v.t.* (*refl.*) and *v.i.* to behave badly.—*n.* **misdemean'our**, bad conduct: a petty crime. [**mis-** (1), **demean** (1).]

misdirect, *mis-di-rekt'*, *-dī-*, *v.t.* to direct wrongly.—*n.* **misdirec'tion**. [**mis-** (1), and **direct**.]

misdoubt, *mis-dowt'*, *v.t.* to doubt, suspect: to fear (that). [**mis-** (1), and **doubt**.]

misemploy, *mis-em-ploi'*, *v.t.* to employ wrongly or amiss, to misuse. [**mis-** (1), and **employ**.]

mise en scène, *mēz à sän*, scenery and properties, stage setting: hence (*fig.*) the setting, circumstances of an event. [Fr.]

miser, *mī'zér*, *n.* one who lives miserably in order to hoard wealth: a niggard.—*adj.* **mi'serly**, avaricious: niggardly. [L. *miser*, wretched.]

miserable, *miz'ér-à-bl*, *adj.* wretched, exceedingly unhappy: causing misery: very poor or mean.—*n.* **mis'erableness**.—*adv.* **mis'erably**. [Fr.,—L. *miserābilis—miser.*]

miserere, *miz-e-rē're*, *-rā're*, *n.* in R.C. usage, Psalm 51, from its first words, 'Miserere mei, Domine': a musical composition adapted to this psalm. [L., 2nd pers. sing. imper. of *miserērī*, to have mercy, to pity—*miser*, wretched.]

misery, *miz'ér-i*, *n.* wretchedness: extreme pain or sorrow: (*coll.*) a doleful person. [O.Fr.,—L. *miseria—miser*, wretched.]

misfeasance, *mis-fēz'ans*, *n.* (*law*) wrong done, esp. the doing of a lawful act in a wrongful manner [O.Fr. *mesfaisance—mes-*, wrong, and *faisance* (L. *facēre*, to do).]

misfire, *mis-fīr'*, *v.i.* to fail to explode or ignite: (*fig.*) to produce no effect, achieve no success.—*n.* such a failure. [**mis-** (1), and **fire**.]

misfit, *mis'fit*, *n.* a bad fit: a thing that fits badly: a person not able to live happily or work efficiently in the particular environment in which he finds himself.—Also *v.t.* and *v.i.* [**mis-** (1), and **fit** (1).]

misfortune, *mis-för′tūn, -chūn, n.* ill-fortune, calamity: an evil accident. [**mis-** (1), and **fortune**.]

misgive, *mis-giv′, v.t.* and *v.i.* to give or cause presentiments of evil (usu. said of mind, heart, conscience).—*n.* **misgiv′ing**, lack of confidence: apprehension: mistrust. [**mis-** (1), and **give**.]

misgovern, *mis-guv′ėrn, v.t.* to govern badly or unjustly.—*n.* **misgov′ernment**. [**mis-** (1), and **govern**.]

misguide, *mis-gīd′, v.t.* to guide wrongly: to lead astray.—*n.* **misguid′ance**. [**mis-** (1), and **guide**.]

mishandle, *mis-han′dl, v.t.* to handle unskilfully (*lit.* and *fig.*): to maltreat. [**mis-** (1), and **handle**.]

mishap, *mis′hap, n.* an unlucky accident: misfortune. [**mis-** (1), and **hap**.]

mishear, *mis-hēr′, v.t.* to hear incorrectly. [**mis-** (1), and **hear**.]

misinform, *mis-in-förm′, v.t.* to inform or tell incorrectly.—*ns.* **misinformā′tion**; **misinform′er**. [**mis-** (1), and **inform**.]

misinterpret, *mis-in-tér′pret, v.t.* to interpret, understand, explain, wrongly.—*ns.* **misinterpretā′tion**; **misinter′preter**. [**mis-** (1), and **interpret**.]

misjudge, *mis-juj′, v.t.* and *v.i.* to judge incorrectly: to judge unjustly.—*n.* **misjudg(e)′ment**. [**mis-** (1), and **judge**.]

mislay, *mis-lā′, v.t.* to place badly: to lay in a place not remembered, to lose:—*pa.p.* mislaid′. [**mis-** (1), and **lay** (2).]

mislead, *mis-lēd′, v.t.* to lead astray (*lit.* and *fig.*): to deceive, give wrong notion to:—*pa.t.* and *pa.p.* misled′.—*adj.* **mislead′ing**, deceptive. [**mis-** (1), and **lead**, vb.]

mislike, *mis-līk′, v.t.* (arch.) to displease, or to dislike. [**mis-** (1), and **like**.]

mismanage, *mis-man′ij, v.t.* to conduct, manage, badly, unskilfully.—*n.* **misman′agement**. [**mis-** (1), and **manage**.]

misname, *mis-nām′, v.t.* to call by a wrong name, or by an inappropriate name. [**mis-** (1), and **name**.]

misnomer, *mis-nō′mér, n.* a misnaming: a wrong or unsuitable name. [O.Fr., from **mis-** (2), and *nommer*—L. *nōmināre*, to name.]

misogamist, *mis-og′á-mist, n.* a hater of marriage.—*n.* **misog′amy**. [Gr. *mīseein*, to hate, *gamos*, marriage.]

misogynist, *mis-oj′i-nist, n.* a woman-hater.—*n.* **misog′yny**. [Gr. *mīseein*, to hate, *gynē*, a woman.]

misplace, *mis-plās′, v.t.* to put in a wrong place: to set (e.g. trust, affection) on an unworthy object.—*n.* **misplace′ment**. [**mis-** (1), and **place**.]

misprint, *mis-print′, v.t.* to print wrongly.—*n.* a mistake in printing. [**mis-** (1), and **print**.]

misprise, **misprize**, *mis-prīz′, v.t.* to slight, undervalue. [O.Fr. *mespriser*—**mis-** (2), and Low L. *pretiāre*—L. *pretium*, price.]

misprision, *mis-prizh′(ó)n, n.* mistake: (*law*) criminal oversight or neglect in respect to crime.—**misprision of heresy, treason**, &c., knowledge of and failure to denounce heresy, treason, &c. [O.Fr., **mis-** (2), and Low L. *prēnsiō, -ōnis*—L. *praehendĕre*, to take.]

mispronounce, *mis-pro-nowns′, v.t.* to pronounce wrongly.—*n.* **mispronunciā′tion** (*-nun-*). [**mis-** (1), and **pronounce**.]

misquote, *mis-kwōt′, v.t.* to quote wrongly.—*n.* **misquotā′tion**, an incorrect or inaccurate quotation. [**mis-** (1), and **quotation**.]

misread, *mis-rēd′, v.t.* to read wrongly: to misinterpret.—*n.* **misreading**, an erroneous reading. [**mis-** (1), and **read**.]

misrelated participle, *mis-ri-lāt′id pär′ti-si-pl*, one not properly connected, usu. because its subject is not that of the main verb (e.g. *cycling* to school, a nail punctured my front tyre).

misrepresent, *mis-rep-ré-zent′, v.t.* to represent or interpret incorrectly and unfaithfully.—*n.* **misrepresentā′tion**.—*adj.* **misrepresent′ative**, not representative (of), tending to misrepresent. [**mis-** (1), and **represent**.]

misrule, *mis-rōōl′, n.* unjust rule: disorder: tumult.—**Abbot** or **Lord of Misrule**, or **Unreason**, ancient titles for the leader of the Christmas revels. [**mis-** (1), and **rule**.]

miss, *mis, n.* (*cap.*, with Christian name or surname) a title of address of an unmarried female: also prefixed to a representational title esp. in beauty contests, e.g. *Miss World*: a young woman or girl:—*pl.* **misses**. (*The Misses Smith* is more formal than *the Miss Smiths.*) [Shortened form of **mistress**.]

miss, *mis, v.t.* to fail to hit, reach, attain, find, observe, hear: to fail to take advantage of (an opportunity): to omit, fail to have: to discover the absence of: to feel the want of.—*v.i.* to fail to hit or obtain: to go wrong.—*n.* a failure to hit the mark: loss.—**miss fire** (same as misfire, *vb.*); **miss the boat** (or **bus**) (*fig.*), to lose one's opportunity. [O.E. *missan*; Du. *missen*, to miss.]

missal, *mis′ál, n.* the book that contains the complete service for mass throughout the year. [Low L. *missāle*, from *missa*, mass.]

missel, *mis′l, n.* a large thrush fond of mistletoe berries.—Also **miss′el-bird**, **miss′el-thrush**. [O.E. *mistel, mistil,* mistletoe.]

misshape, *mis-shāp′, v.t.* to shape ill: deform.—*p.adj.* **misshap′en**, ill-shaped. [**mis-** (1).]

missile, *mis′il, -īl, adj.* capable of being thrown or projected: pertaining to a missile.—*n.* a weapon or object for throwing or shooting, esp. a rocket-launched weapon, often nuclear-powered:a projectile.—**guided missile**, a jet- or rocket-propelled missile electronically directed to target. [L. *mittĕre, missum,* to throw.]

missing, *mis′ing, adj.* absent from the place where expected to be found. [**miss** (2).]

mission, *mish′(ó)n, n.* a sending of an agent, delegate, or messenger: a flight with a specific purpose, as a task assigned to an astronaut: the purpose for which one is sent: a vocation: persons sent on a mission: an embassy: the sending out of persons to spread a religion: a station or establishment of missionaries.—*n.* **miss′ionary**, one sent on a mission, esp. religious.—*adj.* pertaining to missions. [L. *missiō, -ōnis*—*mittĕre,* to send.]

missive, *mis′iv, adj.* that may be sent.—*n.* that which is sent, as a letter. [Low L. *missīvus*—L. *mittĕre, missum,* to send.]

Neutral vowels in unaccented syllables: *em′pér-ór*; for certain sounds in foreign words see p. ix.

462

misspell

misspell, *mis-spel', v.t.* to spell wrongly:—*pa.p.* **misspelt'**, **misspelled'**.—*n.* **misspell'ing**, a wrong spelling. [**mis-** (1), and **spell** (2).]

misspend, *mis-spend', v.t.* to spend ill: to waste or squander:—*pa.t.* and *pa.p.* **misspent'**. [**mis-** (1), and **spend.**]

misstate, *mis-stāt', v.t.* to state wrongly or falsely. —*n.* **misstate'ment.** [**mis-** (1), and **state.**]

mist, *mist, n.* watery vapour seen in the atmosphere: rain in very fine drops: anything that dims the sight or the judgement.—*v.t.* and *v.i.* to obscure, or become obscured, as with mist.—*adj.* **mist'y**, full of mist: dim, obscure.—*adv.* **mist'ily.**—*n.* **mist'iness.** [O.E. *mist*, darkness; Du. *mist*.]

mistake, *mis-tāk', v.t.* to understand wrongly: to take for another thing or person.—*v.i.* to err in opinion or judgement:—*pa.t.* **mistook'**; *pa.p.* **mistak'en.**—*n.* a taking or understanding wrongly: a fault in judgement: an error.—*adjs.* **mistak'able**; **mistak'en**, understood wrongly: erroneous: guilty of a mistake.—*adv.* **mistak'enly.** [M.E. *mistaken*—O.N. *mistaka*, to take wrongly—*mis-*, wrongly, *taka*, to take.]

mister, *mis'tér, n.* a title of address to a man, written **Mr.** [**master.**]

misterm, *mis-tûrm', v.t.* to term or name wrongly. [**mis-** (1), and **term.**]

mistime, *mis-tīm', v.t.* to time wrongly: to do or say at an inappropriate time. [**mis-** (1), and **time.**]

mistletoe, *mis'l tō, or miz'l-, n.* a parasitic evergreen plant, with white berries, growing on the apple, apricot, &c. (very rarely on the oak). [O.E. *misteltān—mistel, mistil,* mistletoe, *tān,* twig.]

mistral, *mis'trål, n.* a violent, cold, dry, northwest wind in the south of France. [Fr. *mistral*—L. *magistrālis,* masterful—*magister.*]

mistranslate, *mis-tranz-lāt', or -trans-, v.t.* to translate incorrectly.—*n.* **mistransla'tion.** [**mis-** (1), and **translate.**]

mistreat, *mis-trēt', v.t.* to treat ill.—*n.* **mistreat'ment.** [**mis-** (1), and **treat.**]

mistress, *mis'tres, n.* (fem. of **master**) a woman (*lit.* or personification) having power or ownership: the female head of a household: a woman teacher: a woman well skilled in anything: a woman loved and courted: a concubine: (*fem.* of **mister**) a form of address once applied to any woman or girl, now given to a married woman (usually written **Mrs** and pronounced *mis'iz*). [O.Fr. *maistresse*—L. *magister,* master.]

mistrial, *mis-trī'ål, n.* a trial void because of an error in the proceedings. [**mis-** (1), and **trial.**]

mistrust, *mis-trust', n.* want of trust.—*v.t.* to suspect: to doubt.—*adj.* **mistrust'ful,** full of mistrust.—*adv.* **mistrust'fully.**—*n.* **mistrust'fulness.** [**mis-** (1), and **trust.**]

misunderstand, *mis-un-dėr-stand', v.t.* to take in a wrong sense, misinterpret.—*n.* **misunderstand'ing,** a mistake as to meaning: a slight disagreement.—*adj.* **misunderstood'.** [**mis-** (1), and **understand.**]

misuse, *mis-ūs', n.* wrong or improper use: application to a bad purpose.—*v.t.* **misuse** (*mis-ūz'*), to use wrongly: to treat badly, ill-use. [**mis** (1), and **use.**]

mite, *mīt, n.* any of a large number of very small

mizzen

insects parasitic on other insects or vertebrates or plants, or infesting food such as cheese (the name *Acarus* is applied to a genus including some of the mites, and also, loosely, to any mite).—*adj.* **mīt'y,** infested with mites. [O.E. *mīte.*]

mite, *mīt, n.* an old Flemish coin of small value: (*B.*) a half-farthing: anything very small: a diminutive person. [Middle Du. *mīte* (Du. *mijt*); perh. ult. same as preceding word.]

mitigate, *mit'i-gāt, v.t.* to alleviate (e.g. pain): to appease (e.g. anger): to lessen the severity of (punishment): to temper (e.g. severity): to lessen the gravity of, partially excuse, an offence (e.g. *mitigating circumstances*).—*adj.* **mit'igable.**—*n.* **mitiga'tion.**—*adj.* **mit'igative,** mitigating, tending to mitigate: soothing.—*n.* **mit'igator.** [L. *mītigāre, -ātum*—*mītis,* mild.]

mitosis, *mī-, or mī-tō'sis, n.* the ordinary division of a cell nucleus by which each daughter cell has a set of chromosomes the same as that of the parent cell.—*adj.* **mitotic** (-*tot'ik*). [Gr. *mitos,* fibre.]

mitrailleuse, *mē-trä-yœz', n.* a machine-gun, discharging a stream of small missiles. [Fr.—*mitraille,* grapeshot.]

mitre, *mī'tér, n.* a head-dress worn by archbishops and bishops, and sometimes by abbots: (*fig.*) episcopal dignity.—*adjs.* **mī'tral,** of or like a mitre; **mit'riform,** mitre-shaped. [Fr.—Gr. *mitrā,* a fillet.]

mitre, *mī'tér, n.* a joint between two pieces at an angle to one another, each jointing surface being cut at an angle to the piece on which it is formed.—Also **mī'tre-joint.**—*n.* **mī'tre-wheel,** either of a pair of toothed wheels whose axes are at right angles to one another.

mitten, *mit'n, (contr.)* **mitt,** *n.* a kind of glove, having one cover for all the four fingers: a glove for the hand and wrist, but not the fingers. [O.Fr. *mitaine.*]

mittimus, *mit'i-mus, n.* (*law*) a warrant granted for sending to prison a person charged with a crime. [L., 'we send'—*mittēre,* to send.]

Mitty (Walter), a nobody who lives a life of imaginary roles as a somebody: an intrepid day-dreamer. [*Walter Mitty,* the hero of a short story by James Thurber, 1894-1961.]

mity. See **mite** (1).

mix, *miks, v.t.* to combine as separate units in a composite whole, to mingle: to associate.—*v.i.* to become mixed: to blend: to associate.—*adj.* **mixed,** miscellaneous: confused: including both sexes.—*n.* **mix'er,** one who, or a machine or contrivance which, mixes: (with *good* or *bad*) one who gets on well, or the reverse, with miscellaneous casual acquaintances; **mix'ture** (-*tyûr, -chûr*), act of mixing or state of being mixed: a mass or blend formed by mixing: (*chem.*) a composition in which the ingredients retain their properties.—**mix up,** to confuse (*n.* **mix-up;** *adj.* **mixed-up,** socially confused, bewildered and ill-adjusted). —**mixed marriage,** one between persons of different religions. [O.E. *miscian*; Ger. *mischen*; L. *miscēre, mixtum,* to mix.]

mizzen, mizen, *miz'n, n.* a fore-and-aft sail on the mizzen mast.—*adj.* belonging to the mizzen: nearest the stern.—*n.* **mizz'en-mast,** the mast nearest the stern in a two- or three-masted vessel. [Fr. *misaine* — It. *mezzana* — Low L. *mediānus* — L. *medius*, the middle.]

mizzle, *miz'l*, *v.i.* to rain in small drops. — *n.* fine rain. [Cf. L. Ger. *miseln.*]

mnemonic, -al, *nē-mon'ik, -ál*, *adj.* assisting the memory. — Also *n.* — *n.* **mnemon'ics**, the art or science of assisting the memory. [Gr. *mnēmonikos* — *mnēmōn*, mindful — *mnēmē*, memory.]

moa, *mō'a*, *n.* any of numerous extinct gigantic, flightless birds, confined to New Zealand. [Maori.]

moan, *mōn*, *n.* lamentation: a lament: a low murmur of pain: (*coll.*) a grumble. — *v.t.* to lament. — *v.i.* to utter a moan: (*coll.*) to grumble. [O.E. *mǣnan*, to moan.]

moat, *mōt*, *n.* a deep trench round a castle or fortified place, sometimes filled with water. — *v.t.* to surround with a moat. — *adj.* **moat'ed.** [O.Fr. *mote*, mound.]

mob, *mob*, *n.* the masses regarded as irresponsible, the rabble: a disorderly crowd: a large herd or flock. — *v.t.* to attack in a disorderly crowd: to crowd around: — *pr.p.* mobb'ing; *pa.p.* mobbed. — *n.* **moboc'racy**, rule or ascendancy exercised by the mob. — **mob law**, the will of the mob. [L. *mōbile* (*vulgus*), the fickle (multitude) — *movēre*, to move.]

mob, *mob*, or **mob'-cap**, *n.* a woman's indoor morning cap. [Old Du. *mop.*]

mobile, *mō'bīl, -bēl, -bil*, *adj.* able to move: easily moved: changing rapidly. — *n.* an artistic structure composed of dangling forms which move with any movement of air. — *v.t.* **mō'bilise**, to put in readiness for service: to call into active service, as troops. — *ns.* **mobilisā'tion**; **mobil'ity**, quality of being mobile. — **mobile shop**, one set up in a motor vehicle, driven to customers' homes. [Fr., — L. *mōbilis* — *movēre*, to move.]

moccasin, mocassin, *mok'a-sin*, *n.* a shoe of deerskin or other soft leather, worn by the North American Indians: a bedroom slipper in imitation of this. [Native word.]

mocha, *mō'ka*, *n.* a fine coffee brought from *Mocha* on the Red Sea.

mock, *mok*, *v.t.* to laugh at, to deride: to mimic in ridicule: to disappoint (hopes): to deceive: to defy. — *n.* ridicule: an object of scorn. — *adj.* sham, false. — *ns.* **mock'er**; **mock'ery, mock'ing**, derision, ridicule: subject of ridicule: vain imitation: false show. — *adj.* **mock'-herō'ic**, burlesquing the heroic style, or the actions or characters of heroes. — *n.* **mock'ing-bird**, an American bird of the same family as the thrushes, which imitates the notes of other birds. — *adv.* **mock'ingly.** — **mock orange**, any of several ornamental shrubs with heavily-scented flowers (see **syringa**); **mock turtle soup**, an imitation of turtle soup, made of calf's head or veal. [O.Fr. *mocquer.*]

mod, *mod*, *n.* an assembly, meeting, of a similar nature to the Welsh Eisteddfod. [Gael.]

Mod, *mod*, *n.* a member of a teenage faction in the 1960s, rivals of the Rockers.

mod. con., *mod kon, modern con*venience, any item of up-to-date plumbing.

mode, *mōd*, *n.* manner of acting, doing, or existing: fashion: form: a manifestation or state of being of a thing: (*mus.*) the scheme of

sounds (depending on the position of the tones and semitones) according to which a scale is built up — classed as ancient (Greek), mediaeval, and modern, the last consisting of *major* and *minor*: the value in a series of observed values, or the item in a series of statistical items, that occurs most frequently. — *adj.* **mō'dal**, relating to mode or form: (*mus.*) written in one of the mediaeval modes. — *n.* **modal'ity.** — *adv.* **mō'dally.** [Fr., — L. *modus.*]

model, *mod'l*, *n.* something to be copied: something worthy to be imitated: an imitation, especially on a smaller scale: one who poses for an artist: one who exhibits clothes. — *adj.* serving as a model: fitted by (his, its) perfection to be a model. — *v.t.* to form after a model (with *after, on*): to make a model or copy of: to form in plastic material: to shape. — *v.i.* to practise modelling: — *pr.p.* mod'elling; *pa.p.* mod'elled. — *ns.* **mod'eller**; **mod'elling**, the act or art of making a model, a branch of sculpture. [O.Fr. *modelle* — It. *modello*, dim. of *modo* — L. *modus*, a measure.]

moderate, *mod'ér-āt*, *v.t.* to keep within measure or bounds, reduce in intensity, make temperate or reasonable. — *v.i.* to become less violent or intense: to preside as moderator. — *adj.* (*-át*) kept within measure or bounds, not excessive or extreme: temperate: of middle rate. — *n.* one whose views are far from extreme. — *adv.* **mod'erately.** — *ns.* **mod'erateness**; **moderā'tion**, act of moderating: state of being moderate: freedom from excess: calmness of mind, restraint; **mod'eratism**, moderate opinions in religion or politics. — *adv.* **moderato** (*-ä'to; mus.*), with moderate quickness. — *ns.* **mod'erātor**, one who, or that which, moderates or restrains: a president or chairman, esp. in Presbyterian Church courts: the material in which neutrons are slowed down in an atomic pile; **mod'eratorship.** [L. *moderārī, -ātus* — *modus*, a measure.]

modern, *mod'érn*, *adj.* limited to the present or recent time: not ancient or mediaeval. — *n.* one living in modern times, esp. distinguished from the ancient Greeks and Romans: one whose views or tastes are modern. — *v.t.* **mod'ernise**, to adapt to conditions or taste of the present time. — *ns.* **modernisā'tion**; **mod'erniser**; **mod'ernism**, modern practice or views; **mod'ernist**, an advocate of modern ideas or habits. — *adv.* **mod'ernly.** — *ns.* **modern'ity**, **mod'ernness.** — **modern school**, a school in which courses are less academic than in a grammar or similar school. [L. *modernus* — *modo*, just now, orig. abl. of *modus.*]

modest, *mod'ést*, *adj.* restrained by a sense of propriety: decent: chaste: having a moderate estimate of one's own merits, not vain, boastful, or pushing: unobtrusive: moderate. — *adv.* **mod'estly.** — *n.* **mod'esty**, the fact or quality of being modest. [L. *modestus* — *modus*, a measure.]

modicum, *mod'i-kum*, *n.* a small quantity. [L. neut. of *modicus*, moderate — *modus*, a measure.]

modify, *mod'i-fī*, *v.t.* to moderate: to change the form or quality of: to alter slightly. — *adj.*

Neutral vowels in unaccented syllables: *em'pér-ór*; for certain sounds in foreign words see p. ix.

modifi′able.—*ns.* **modifica′tion**, act of modifying: changed shape or condition: umlaut (q.v.); **mod′ifier.** [Fr. *modifier*—L. *modificāre*, *-ātum*—*modus*, a measure, *facĕre*, to make.]

modish, *mō′dish, adj.* according to the fashion or mode.—*adv.* **mō′dishly.**—*ns.* **mō′dishness; modiste** (*mod-ēst′*), a (fashionable) dressmaker or milliner. [L. *modus*, a measure.]

modulate, *mod′ū-lāt, v.t.* to regulate, to adjust: to vary the pitch, frequency, &c. of.—*v.i.* to pass from one state to another: (*mus.*) to pass from one key into another,—*ns.* **modula′tion**, the act of modulating: the changing from one key to another in music: the inflection or varying of the voice in speech: (*radio*) variation of the frequency (**frequency modulation**), magnitude (**amplitude modulation**), or phase, of a high-frequency electric current (the *carrier*) in accordance with an impressed telephonic, telegraphic, or picture signal—the modulated waves being those that actually transmit the signal; **mod′ulator**, one who, or that which, modulates: a chart in the Tonic Sol-fa nota tion on which modulations are shown; **mod′ule** (*archit.*), a measure, often the semidiameter of a column, for regulating the proportions of other parts: a unit of size used in standardised planning of buildings and design of components: a self-contained unit forming part of a spacecraft—*adj.* **mod′ular**, of or pertaining to mode or modulation, or to a module.—*n.* **mod′ulus** (*math.*), a constant multiplier or coefficient: a quantity used as a divisor to produce classes of quantities, each class distinguished by its members yielding the same remainders:—*pl.* **moduli** (*mod′ū-lī*) [L. *modulārī, -ātus*, to regulate—*modulus*, dim. of *modus*, a measure.]

Mogul, *mō-gul′, n.* a Mongol or Mongolian, esp. one of the followers of Baber, the conqueror of India (1483-1530): (without *cap.*) an influential person, magnate.—**Great Mogul**, the title by which Europeans knew the rulers of the empire founded by him. [Pers., properly 'a *Mongol*'.]

mohair, *mō′hār, n.* the long, white, fine silken hair of the Angora goat: cloth made of it. [Ar. *mukhayyar*, influenced by **hair**.]

Mohammedan, *mō-ham′e-dán,* **Mahommedan,** *mä-hom′e-dán,* **Mahometan,** *mä-hom′ét-án, adj.* pertaining to Mohammed or to his religion.—*n.* a follower of Mohammed: one who professes Mohammedanism.—*ns.* **Mohamm′edanism, Mohamm′edism,** the religion of Mohammed, contained in the Koran.—*v.t.* **Mohammedanise,** to convert to, or make conformable to, Mohammedanism. [Ar. *Muhammad,* the great prophet of Arabia (570-632); lit. 'praised'.]

Mohawk, *mō-hök, n.* one of a tribe of North American Indians. [Native word.]

Mohock, *mō′hok, n.* an aristocratic ruffian of early 18th-century London. [**Mohawk**.]

moidore, *moi′dōr, -dör, n.* a disused gold coin of Portugal. [Port. *moeda d'ouro*—L. *monēta de auro,* money of gold.]

moiety, *moi′e-ti, n.* half: one of two parts. [O.Fr. *moite*—L. *medietās*—*medius,* middle.]

moil, *moil, v.t.* to daub with dirt.—*v.i.* to toil or drudge. [O.Fr. *moillier,* to wet—L. *mollis;* soft.]

moire, *mwär, n.* watered silk, orig. mohair.—Also *adj.* and *n.* **moiré** (*mwär′ā, moi′ri*), (having) a watered appearance: (erroneously) moire. [Fr., from English **mohair**.]

moist, *moist, adj.* damp: humid: rainy.—*v.t.* **moisten** (*mois′n*), to make moist, to wet slightly.—*ns.* **moist′ness; moist′ure,** moistness: that which makes slightly wet: liquid, esp. in small quantity. [O.Fr. *moiste,* perh. —L.—*mustum,* juice of grapes, new wine.]

molar, *mō′lár, adj.* used for grinding.—*n.* a grinding or back tooth. [L. *molāris*—*mola,* a millstone—*molĕre,* to grind.]

molasses, *mo-las′ez, n.sing.* treacle (q.v.). [Port. *melaco* (Fr. *mélasse*)—Low L. *mellāceum,* honey-like—*mel, mellis,* honey.]

mole, *mōl, n.* a small spot on the skin, often coloured and hairy. [O.E. *māl.*]

mole, *mōl, n.* any of numerous small animals, with very small eyes, concealed ears, and soft fur, that burrow in the ground and cast up little heaps of earth. *ns.* **mole′cast, mole′-hill,** a little heap of earth cast up by a mole.—*adj.* **mole′-eyed,** having eyes like those of a mole: seeing imperfectly.—*ns.* **mole′rat,** a name for several burrowing rodents; **mole′-skin,** the skin of a mole: a superior kind of fustian. [M.E. *molle, mulle;* cf. Du. *mol,* L. Ger. *mol, mul;* according to some a shortened form of **mouldwarp.**]

mole, *mōl, n.* a breakwater. [Fr.,—L. *mōles,* mass.]

mole, *mōl, n.* S.I base unit, the amount of substance that contains as many (specified) entities (e.g. atoms, molecules, ions) as there are atoms in 12 grams of carbon-12 (abbrev. **mol,** *mōl*). [Ger.,—*molekül,* molecule.]

molecule, *mol′e-kūl, n.* the smallest particle of any substance that retains the properties of that substance.—*adj.* **molec′ular,** belonging to, or consisting of, molecules.—*n.* **molecular′ity.**—**molecular biology,** study of the molecules of the substances involved in the processes of life; **molecular weight,** the weight of a molecule of a substance referred to that of an atom of carbon-12 taken as 12—also **relative molecular mass.** [Fr. *molécule,* dim. —L. *mōlēs,* a mass.]

molest, *mō-lest′, mó-lest′, v.t.* to meddle with, disturb, annoy.—*ns.* **molesta′tion; molest′er.** [Fr. *molester*—L. *molestāre*—*molestus,* troublesome.]

mollify, *mol′i-fī, v.t.* to soften, to assuage; to appease (a person, anger):—*pa.p.* **molli′fied.**—*ns.* **mollifica′tion; moll′ifier.** [Fr.,—L. *mollificāre*—*mollis,* soft, *facĕre,* to make.]

mollusc, mollusk, *mol′usk, n.* one of the Mollusca, a large division or phylum of invertebrate animals, including shellfish, snails and cuttlefish:—*pl.* **moll′uscs, moll′usks,** or **mollus′ca.**—*n.* **mollus′can,** a mollusc.—*adj.* **mollus′can, mollus′cous,** of or belonging to the Mollusca. [L. *molluscus,* softish—*mollis,* soft.]

molly, *mol′i, n.* a milksop.—*n.* **moll′ycoddle,** an effeminate fellow.—*v.t.* to pamper. [Dim. of Mary.]

Moloch, *mō′lok, n.* a Semitic god to whom children were sacrificed: any cause of dreadful sacrifice or destruction: a spiny Australian lizard. [Heb. *Mōlek.*]

fāte, fär; mē, hûr (her); *mīne; mōte, för; mūte; mōōn, fŏŏt;* ᴛʜᴇn (then)

Molotov cocktail, *mol'ó-tof,* a crude form of hand-grenade consisting of a bottle with inflammable liquid, and a wick to be ignited just before the missile is thrown. [V.M. *Molotov,* Russian statesman.]

molten, *mōlt'n, adj.* melted: made of melted metal. [Old pa.p. of **melt.**]

molybdenum, *mol-ib-dē'num, -ib'den-um, n.* a silvery-white metallic element (symbol Mo; atomic no. 42). [L.,—Gr.,—*molybdos,* lead.]

moment, *mō'mėnt, n.* (*obs.*) moving cause or force: importance in effect, value, consequence: the smallest portion of time in which a movement can be made: an instant: (*mech.*) the *moment of a force* about a point is its turning effect, measured by the product of the force and the perpendicular distance of the point from the line of action of the force.—*adj.* **mō'mentary,** lasting for a moment, short-lived.—*adv.* **mō'mentarily,** for a moment: every moment: at any moment.—*n.* **mō'mentariness.**—*adv.* **mō'mently,** for a moment: in a moment: every moment.—*adj.* **mōment'ous,** of importance, of great consequence.—*adv.* **moment'ously.**—*ns.* **moment'ousness; moment'um,** the quantity of motion in a body, measured by the product of mass and velocity: (popularly—*lit.* and *fig.*) force of motion gained by movement:—*pl.* **moment'a.** [L. *mōmentum,* for *movimentum*—*movēre,* to move.]

monachism, *mon'ák-izm, n.* monasticism.—*adj.* **mon'achal,** monastic. [Gr. *monachos,* solitary—*monos,* alone.]

monad, *mon'ad, n.* the number one: a unit: unit of being, material and psychical: a hypothetical primitive organism: an atom or radical with valency of 1.—*adjs.* **monad'ic, -al.** [Gr. *monas, -ados,* a unit—*monos,* alone.]

monadelphous, *mon-a-delf'us, adj.* (*bot.*) of stamens, united by the filaments in one bundle. [Gr. *monos,* single, *adelphos,* brother.]

monandrous, *mon-an'drus, adj.* (*bot.*) having one stamen. [Gr. *monos,* single, *anēr,* gen. *andros,* a male.]

monarch, *mon'ärk, n.* a sole or supreme ruler: a hereditary sovereign: the chief of its kind.—*adj.* supreme: superior to others.—*adjs.* **monarch'al,** pertaining to a monarch: regal; **monarch'ic, -al,** relating to a monarch or to monarchy: vested in a single ruler.—*n.* **mon'archy,** government by a monarch: a kingdom.—*v.t.* **mon'archise,** to rule over, as a monarch: to convert into a monarchy.—*ns.* **mon'archism,** the principles of monarchy: love of monarchy; **mon'archist,** an advocate of monarchy. [Gr. *monarchēs*—*monos,* alone, *archein,* to rule.]

monastery, *mon'ás-tėr-i, -tri, n.* a house for monks, or (*rarely*) nuns.—*adjs.* **monas'tic, -al,** pertaining to monasteries, monks, and nuns: recluse, solitary.—*n.* **monas'tic,** a monk.—*adv.* **monas'tically.**—*n.* **monas'ticism** (*-sizm*), the corporate monastic life. [Gr. *monastērion, monastikos*—*monastēs,* a monk—*monos,* alone.]

monaural, *mon-ö'rál, adj.* having or using only one ear: pertaining to one ear: of a gramophone record, giving the effect of sound from a single direction—not stereophonic. [Gr.

monos, single, L. *auris,* the ear.]

Monday, *mun'di, -dā, n.* the second day of the week. [O.E. *mōnandæg*—*mōnan,* gen. of *mōna,* moon, *dæg,* day.]

monetary, *mon'-,* or *mun'é-tär-i, adj.* of or relating to money: consisting of money. [L. *monēta.* See **money.**]

money, *mun'i, n.* coin, pieces of stamped metal used in commerce: any currency used in the same way: wealth:—*pl.* **mon'eys.**—*ns.* **mon'eybill,** a bill introduced into parliament or congress for raising revenue or otherwise dealing with money; **mon'ey-brok'er,** one who carries out transactions in money for others; **mon'ey-chang'er,** one who exchanges one currency for another.—*adj.* **mon'eyed,** having money, rich: consisting in money, derived from money.—*ns.* **mon'ey-mar'ket,** the market or field for the investment of money; **mon'eyor'der,** an order for money deposited at one post-office and payable at any other named. [O.Fr. *moneie*—L. *monēta,* a mint, *Monēta* being a surname of Juno, in whose temple at Rome money was coined.]

monger, *mung'gér, n.* a trader: a dealer (chiefly in composition, sometimes depreciatory). [O.E. *mangere*—L. *mangō,* a dealer who polishes up his wares, a slave-dealer.]

Mongol, *mong'gol, n.* and *adj.* one of an Asiatic people mainly inhabiting *Mongolia:* a person affected with **mongolism,** a condition in which mental deficiency is associated with snub nose, Mongol-like eyes, prominent cheek bones, and other characteristics.—**Mongolian race,** one of the great divisions of mankind, having broad heads, yellow skins, straight hair, small noses, and often a fold of skin over the inner junction of the eyelids.

mongoose, *mong'gōōs, n.* a common ichneumon of India, noted as a slayer of snakes:—*pl.* **mong'ooses.** [Marathi (q.v.), *mangūs.*]

mongrel, *mung'grėl, n.* an animal, esp. a dog, of a mixed breed.—*adj.* mixed in breed: of no definite class or type. [Perh. from root of O.E. *mengan,* to mix.]

monism, *mon'izm, n.* a philosophical theory that all being may ultimately be referred to one category. [Gr. *monos,* single.]

monition, *mon-ish'(ó)n, n.* an admonishing: a warning: notice.—*adj.* **mon'itive,** conveying admonition.—*n.* **mon'itor** (*fem.* **mon'itress, mon'itrix**), one who admonishes: an instructor: a senior pupil who assists in school discipline: a low, steady ironclad (so-called from the name of the first of the kind, 1862): an arrangement for tapping on to a communication circuit: a person employed to monitor: a genus of lizards: any of several instruments used to measure radioactivity: apparatus for testing transmission in electrical communication: a screen in a television studio showing the picture being transmitted: an instrument used in a production process to keep a variable quantity within prescribed limits by transmitting a controlling signal.—*v.t.* to check for radioactivity: to track, or to control (an aeroplane, &c.): to check, supervise.—*v.i.* to tap on to a communication circuit, usu. in order to ascertain that the transmission is that desired, without interfering with the

Neutral vowels in unaccented syllables: *em'pér-ór*; for certain sounds in foreign words see p. ix.

transmission: to listen to foreign broadcasts in order to obtain news, code messages, &c.—*adj.* **monito′rial,** relating to a monitor.—*adv.* **monito′rially.**—*adj.* **mon′itory,** giving admonition or warning. [L.,—*monēre, -itum,* to remind.]

monk, *mungk, n.* (*orig.*) a hermit: one of a religious community living in a monastery.—*adj.* **monk′ish,** pertaining to a monk: like a monk: monastic.—*n.* **monks′hood, monk′s′-hood,** an aconite, a poisonous plant with a flower like a monk's hood. [O.E. *munuc*—L. *monachus*—Gr. *monachos*—*monos,* alone.]

monkey, *mungk′i, n.* any mammal of the *Primates* or highest order, except man: any one of the smaller, long-tailed primates, as opp. to apes: name of censure or endearment, esp. for a mischievous child:—*pl.* **monk′eys.**—*v.i.* to meddle (with).—*ns.* **monk′ey-nut,** the pea-nut or ground-nut; **monk′ey-puzz′le,** the Chile pine, a tall evergreen, with stiff sharp-pointed leaves; **monk′ey-wrench,** a screw-key with a movable jaw. [Origin doubtful.]

mono-, mon-, in composition, one, single [Gr. *monos,* alone, single], e.g. **monotint** (*mon′ō-tint*), n. a drawing or painting in a single tint.

mono, *mōn′ō, n.* (*coll.*) a monaural gramophone record or record player.—Also *adj.*

monochord, *mon′ō-körd, n.* a musical instrument with one string. [Gr. *monochordon*—*monos,* single, *chordē,* a string.]

monochromatic, *mon-ō-krō-mat′ik, adj.* of one colour only.—*n.* **mon′ochrome,** a painting, drawing, picture, print, in a single colour: the art or process of making such pictures or prints. [Gr. *monos,* single, *chrōma, -atos,* colour.]

monocle, *mon′o-kl, n.* a single eyeglass. [Fr. *monocle*—Gr. *monos,* single, L. *oculus,* eye.]

monocotyledon, *mon-ō-kot-i-lē′don, n.* a plant with only one cotyledon.—*adj.* **monocoty-lē′donous.** [**mono-,** and **cotyledon.**]

monocular, *mon-ok′ū-lär, adj.* with or for one eye only. [Gr. *monos,* single, L. *oculus,* an eye.]

monody, *mon′o-di, n.* a mournful ode or poem in which a single mourner bewails: a song for one voice.—*adjs.* **monod′ic, -al.**—*n.* **mon′odist,** a writer of monodies. [Gr. *monōidiā*—*monos,* single, *ōidē,* song.]

monoecious, *mon-ē′shüs, adj.* (*bot.*) having separate staminate and pistillate flowers on the same plant: (*zool.*) hermaphrodite. [Gr. *monos,* single, *oikos,* house.]

monogamy, *mon-og′a-mi, n.* marriage to one wife or husband only: the state of such marriage.—*adjs.* **monogam′ic, monog′amous.** —*n.* **monog′amist.** [Gr. *monos,* one, single, *gamos,* marriage.]

monogram, *mon′ō-gram, n.* a figure consisting of several letters interwoven or written into one. [Gr. *monos,* single, *gramma,* a letter.]

monograph, *mon′ō-gräf, n.* a treatise written on one particular subject or any branch of it.—*ns.* **monog′rapher, monog′raphist,** a writer of monographs.—*adjs.* **monograph′ic, -al.** [Gr. *monos,* single, *graphein,* to write.]

monogynian, *mon-o-jin′i-än,* **monogynous,** *mon-oj′i-nus, adjs.* having only one wife: (*bot.*) having only one pistil. [Gr. *monos,* single, *gynē,* a woman.]

monolith, *mon′ō-lith, n.* a pillar or column, of a single stone: anything resembling a pillar in uniformity, massiveness or intractability.—*adj.* **monolith′ic,** pertaining to a monolith: (*fig.*) very large and uniform in character: intractable. [Gr. *monos,* single, *lithos,* a stone.]

monologue, *mon′ō-log, n.* a speech uttered by one person: a soliloquy. [Gr. *monos,* single, *logos,* speech.]

monomania, *mon-ō-mā′ni-a, n.* madness confined to one subject: an unreasonable interest in any particular thing.—*n.* **monomā′niac,** one affected with monomania.—Also *adj.* [Gr. *monos,* single, *maniā,* madness.]

monometalism, *mon-o-met′al-izm, n.* the use of only one metal as a standard of currency. [**mono-,** and **metal.**]

monomial, *mon-ō′mi-ál, n.* an algebraic expression of one term only.—*adj.* **monō′mial.** [Gr. *monos,* single, L. *nōmen,* name.]

monoplane, *mon′ō-plān, n.* an aeroplane with one set of planes or wings. [**mono-, plane.**]

monopoly, *mon-op′ō-li, n.* sole right of dealing in any commodity: exclusive command or possession: that which is thus controlled.—*v.t.* **monop′olise,** to have a monopoly of: to keep exclusive possession, control, &c., of: to engross (e.g. attention).—*ns.* **monop′oliser, monop′olist.**—*adj.* **monopolis′tic.** [L. *monopōlium*—Gr. *monos,* alone, *pōleein,* to sell.]

monorail, *mon′ō-rāl, n.* a railway with carriages suspended from, or running astride of, one rail. [**mono-, rail.**]

monostrophic, *mon-ō-strof′ik, adj.* consisting of strophes or stanzas of the same structure. [Gr. *monos,* single, *strophē,* a strophe.]

monosyllable, *mon-ō-sil′á-bl, n.* a word of one syllable.—*adj.* **monosyllab′ic,** having one syllable: consisting of, or speaking in, monosyllables. [**mono-,** and **syllable.**]

monotheism, *mon′ō-thē-izm, n.* the belief in only one God.—*n.* **mon′otheist.**—*adj.* **monotheist′ic.** [Gr. *monos,* single, *theos,* God.]

monotone, *mon′ō-tōn, n.* a single, unvaried tone: a succession of sounds having the same pitch.—*adj.* **monot′onous,** uttered in one unvaried tone: marked by dull uniformity.—*adv.* **monot′onously.**—*n.* **monot′ony,** dull uniformity of tone or sound: (*fig.*) irksome sameness or want of variety. [Gr. *monos,* single, *tonos,* a tone.]

Monotype, *mon′ō-tīp, n.* a machine that casts and sets type letter by letter. [Gr. *monos,* single, *typos,* type. Registered trade-mark.]

Monroe Doctrine, *mon-rō′ dok′trin,* the principle of the non-intervention of European powers in the affairs of the American continents—President *Monroe's* Message to Congress, December 1823.

monseigneur, *mɔ̃-sen-yœr, n.* my lord: a title in France given to a person of high birth or rank, esp. to bishops, &c. (written *Mgr.*):—*pl.* **messeigneurs** (*me-sen-yœr*).—*n.* **monsieur** (*mės-yø*), sir: (*cap.*) a title of courtesy in France =*Mr* in English (written *M.* or in full; erroneously *Mons.*): (*cap.; hist.*) title of the eldest brother of the King of France:—*pl.* **messieurs** (*mes-yø*; written *MM.*). [Fr. *mon seigneur, sieur,* my lord.]

monsignor, *mon-sē′nyör,* **monsignore,** *mon-sē-*

nyō′rā, n. (usu. *cap.*) a title borne by some prelates (written *Mgr.,* &c.). [It.,—Fr.*monseigneur.*]

monsoon, *mon-sōōn′, n.* a periodical wind of the Indian Ocean, S.W. from April to October, and N.E. the rest of the year: a similar wind elsewhere: the rainy season caused by the S.W. monsoon. [Port. *monção*—Malay *mūsim*—Ar. *mausim,* a time, a season.]

monster, *mon′stėr, n.* anything out of the usual course of nature: a fabulous animal: anything horrible from ugliness or wickedness: an animal or thing very large of its kind.—*adj.* unusually large, huge.—*adj.* **mon′strous,** out of the common course of nature: enormous: wonderful: horrible.—*adv.* **mon′strously.**—*n.* **monstros′ity,** the state or fact of being monstrous: an unnatural production. [Fr.,—L. *mōnstrum,* an omen, a monster—*monēre,* to warn.]

monstrance, *mon′strans, n.* the receptacle in which the consecrated host is exposed for adoration in R.C. churches. [Fr.,—L. *mōnstrāre,* to show, *mōnstrum,* an omen.]

montage, *mɔ̃-täzh′, n.* selection and piecing together of material for a cinematograph film: assemblage, arrangement: a composite photograph: a picture made partly by sticking objects on the canvas. [Fr.—*monter,* to mount.]

Montessori system, *mon-tes-ōr′i sis′tem,* a system of education for children aged 3-6, characterised by free discipline and informal, individual instruction, devised (c. 1900) by Dr. Maria *Montessori.*

month, *munth, n.* the period from new moon to new moon—a *lunar* month (= 29·5306 days): one of the twelve divisions of the year—a calendar month.—*adj.* **month′ly,** performed in a month: happening or published once a month.—*n.* a monthly publication.—*adv.* once a month: in every month. [O.E. *mōnath*—*mōna,* moon.]

monument, *mon′ū-mėnt, n.* anything that preserves the memory of a person or an event: a historic document: a notable or enduring example.—*adj.* **monument′al,** of or relating to or serving as a monument, tomb: memorial: impressive because of size or of lasting qualities.—*adv.* **monument′ally.** [Fr.,—L. *monumentum*—*monēre,* to remind.]

moo, *mōō, v.i.* to low like a cow. [Imit.]

mood, *mōōd, n.* (*gram.*) a form of the verb to express the manner of an action or of a state of being—fact (indicative), possibility, &c. (subjunctive), command (imperative): (*logic*) the form of the syllogism as determined by the quantity and quality of its three constituent propositions. [Partly through Fr. *mode* from L. *modus,* measure.]

mood, *mōōd, n.* temporary state of the mind or emotions: state of gloom or sullenness.—*adj.* **mood′y,** subject to changing moods: out of humour, sullen.—*adv.* **mood′ily.**—*n.* **mood′iness,** sullenness. [O.E. *mōd,* mind; cf. Ger.*mut,* courage.]

moon, *mōōn, n.* the satellite which revolves round the earth: a satellite of any other planet: a month: (*fort.*) a crescent-shaped outwork.—*v.i.* to wander about or gaze vacantly.—*ns.* **moon′beam,** a beam of light from the moon; **moon′light,** the light of the moon.—*adj.* lighted by the moon: occurring in moonlight.—*adj.* **moon′lit,** lit or illumined by the moon.—*ns.* **moon′scape,** the physical appearance of the surface of the moon, or a representation of it; **moon′shine,** the shining of the moon: (*fig.*) show without reality; **moon′shot,** the act or process of launching an object or vehicle, to orbit, or land on, the moon; **moon′stone,** an opalescent felspar; **moon′strike,** the act or process of landing a spacecraft on the surface of the moon.—*adj.* **moon′struck,** affected by the moon, lunatic, crazed.—**moonlight flitting,** a removal by night, with rent unpaid. [O.E. *mōna*; cf. Ger. *mond,* L. *mēnsis,* Gr. *mēn.*]

moonshee. Same as **munshi.**

moor, *mōōr, n.* a large tract of untilled ground, often covered with heath, and having a poor, peaty soil: a heath.—*ns.* **moor′cock, moor′fowl,** the red or black grouse; **moor′hen,** a waterhen: the female moor-fowl.—*adjs.* **moor′ish, moor′y,** resembling a moor: sterile: marshy.—*n.* **moor′land,** a tract of moor. [O.E. *mōr.*]

moor, *mōōr, v.t.* to fasten by cable or anchor.—*v.i.* to be fastened by cables or chains.—*ns.* **moor′age,** a due paid for mooring: a place for mooring; **moor′ing,** act of mooring: that which serves to moor or confine a ship: (in *pl.*) the place or condition of a ship thus moored. [Prob. from an unrecorded O.E. word answering to Middle Du. *mâren.*]

Moor, *mōōr, n.* a member of the dark-skinned race inhabiting Morocco.—*adj.* **Moor′ish.** [Fr. *More, Maure*—L. *Maurus.*]

moose, *mōōs, n.* the largest deer of America, resembling the European elk. [Indian, *mus, moos.*]

moot, *mōōt, n.* (*hist.*) a deliberative or administrative assembly or court: discussion.—*v.t.* to propose for discussion: to discuss, argue for practice.—*adj.* discussed: debatable.—*adj.* **moot′able,** debatable.—**moot point,** an undecided or disputed point. [O.E. *(ge)mōt,* (n.), *mōtian* (vb.), akin to *mētan,* to meet.]

mop, *mop, n.* a bunch of rags or coarse yarn fixed on a handle, for washing floors, windows, &c.: a thick or bushy head of hair.—*v.t.* to rub or wipe with a mop:—*pr.p.* mopp′ing; *pa.t.* and *pa.p.* mopped.—*n.* **mopp′et,** a rag-doll: a dear child.—**mop up,** to clean up with a mop: to dispose of. [O.Fr. *mappe*—L. *mappa,* a napkin.]

mope, *mōp, v.i.* (*obs.*) to go aimlessly and listlessly: to yield to low spirits.—*adv.* **mop′ingly.**—*adj.* **mop′ish,** dull, spiritless.—*n.* **mop′ishness.** [Origin obscure.]

moped, *mō′ped,* n. a *mo*tor-power-assisted *ped*al bicycle.

moraine, *mo-rān′, n.* a continuous line of rocks and gravel borne on, or left by, a glacier. [Fr.]

moral, *mor′ål, adj.* of or relating to character or conduct: conformed to or directed towards right, virtuous: virtuous in matters of sex: capable of knowing right and wrong: subject to the moral law: supported by evidence of reason or probability.—*n.* in *pl.* the doctrine or practice of the duties of life: principles and conduct: manners: in *sing.* the practical lesson

---

Neutral vowels in unaccented syllables: *em′pėr-ȯr*; for certain sounds in foreign words see p. ix.

to be drawn from anything: the condition with respect to discipline, confidence, faith in the cause fought for, &c.: (usu. spelt **morale** to suggest the Fr. pronunciation *mor-äl'*—the French word in this sense is *moral*).—*v.t.* **mor'alise**, to make moral: to apply to a moral purpose: to explain in a moral sense.—*v.i.* to speak or write on moral subjects: to make moral reflections.—*ns.* **mor'aliser**; **mor'alist**, one who teaches morals, or who practises moral duties: one who prides himself on his morality; **moral'ity**, quality of being moral: that which renders an action right or wrong: the practice of moral duties: virtue: the doctrine of actions as right or wrong: a mediaeval allegorical drama in which virtues and vices appear as characters (also **moral'ity-play**).—*adv.* **mor'ally**, in a moral manner: in respect of morals: to all intents and purposes, practically.—**moral certainty**, a likelihood so great as to be safely acted on, although not capable of certain proof; **Moral Rearmament**, a movement succeeding the Oxford Group in 1938, advocating strict private and public morality (abbrev. **M.R.A.**); **moral victory**, a failure more honourable than success. [L. *morālis*—*mōs*, *mōris*, custom, (esp. in *pl.*) morals.]

morale. See **moral**.

morass, *mo-ras'*, *n.* a tract of soft, wet ground: a marsh. [Du. *moeras*.]

moratorium, *mor-a-tō'ri-um*, -*tö'ri-um*, *n.* an emergency measure authorising the suspension of payments of debts for a given time: the period thus declared: a temporary ban on, or enforced cessation of, an activity. [Neut. of L.L. *morātōrius*, *adj.*—*mora*, delay.]

morbid, *mör'bid*, *adj.* diseased, sickly: (of thoughts, feelings) unwholesome: (of mind, temperament) given to unwholesome thoughts or feelings.—*n.* **morbid'ity**.—*adv.* **mor'bidly**.—*n.* **mor'bidness**.—*adj.* **morbif'ic**, causing disease. [L. *morbidus*—*morbus*, disease.]

mordacious, *mor-dā'shus*, *adj.* given to biting: biting (*lit.* or *fig.*).—*adv.* **morda'ciously**—*n.* **mordac'ity** (*das'*).—*adj.* **mor'dant**, (*fig.*) biting: serving to fix colours.—*n.* a corroding substance: any substance that combines with and fixes a dyestuff in material that cannot be dyed direct: a substance used to cause paint or gold-leaf to adhere. [L. *mordēre*, to bite.]

more, *mōr*, *mör*, *adj.* (serves as *comp.* of **many** and **much**) in greater number or quantity: additional: other besides.—*adv.* to a greater degree: again: further:—*superl.* **most** (*mōst*).—**and more**, with an additional number or amount; **the more fool he**, by which action he shows himself a greater fool, very foolish. [O.E. *māra*, greater.]

morel, *mor-el'*, *n.* a genus of edible fungi. [Fr. *morille*; cf. O.H.G. *morhela*, a mushroom.]

moreover, *mōr-ō'vér*, *adv.* more over or beyond what has been said, further, besides, also. [**more**, **over**.]

mores, *mō'*, *mō'rēz*, *n. pl.* social and moral customs, manners. [L.]

moresko, *mor-esk'ō*, *n.* a Moorish dance or morris-dance: a Moor.—*adj.* **Moorish**. [It.]

moresque, *mo-resk'*, *adj.* done after the manner of the Moors. [Fr.,—It. *Moresco*.]

morganatic, *mör-gán-at'ik*, *adj.* noting a marriage of a man with a woman of inferior rank, in which neither the latter nor her children enjoy the rank or inherit the possessions of her husband, though the children are legitimate. [Low L. *morganātica*, a gift from a bridegroom to his bride.]

morgue, *mörg*, *n.* a place where dead bodies are laid out for identification: in a newspaper office, a place where miscellaneous material is kept for reference. [Fr.]

moribund, *mor'i-bund*, *adj.* about to die: in a dying state. [L. *moribundus*—*morī*, to die.]

morion, morrion, *mor'-*, or *mōr'i-ón*, *n.* an open helmet, without visor or beaver. [Fr., prob. from Sp. *morrión*—*morra*, crown of the head.]

Mormon, *mōr'mon*, *n.* one of a religious sect with headquarters since 1847 in Salt Lake City, U.S., polygamous till 1890, calling itself 'The Church of Jesus Christ of Latter-day Saints', founded in 1830 by Joseph Smith, who added to the Bible the *Book of Mormon*.

morn, *morn*, *n.* morning. [M.E. *morwen*—O.E. *mörgen*; Ger. *morgen*.]

morning, *mörn'ing*, *n.* the first part of the day: the early part of anything.—*adj.* of the morning: taking place or being in the morning.—*ns.* **morn'ing(-)star**, a planet, esp. Venus, when it rises before the sun; **morn'ing-watch**, the watch between 4 and 8 A.M. [Contr. of *morwening*; cf. **morn**.]

morocco, *mo-rok'ō*, *n.* a fine leather of goat- or sheep-skin, first brought from *Morocco*.

moron, *mōr'on*, *n.* a somewhat feeble-minded person: (*coll.*) a stupid person.—*adj.* **moron'ic**, pertaining to a moron: (*coll.*) extremely foolish and stupid. [Gr., neut. of *mōros*, stupid.]

morose, *mō-rōs'*, *adj.* of a sour temper: gloomy.—*adv.* **morose'ly**.—*n.* **morose'ness**. [L. *mōrōsus*, peevish—*mōs*, *moris*, manner.]

morphia, *mör'fi-a*, *n.* morphine.—*n.* **mor'phine** (*-fēn*), the chief narcotic principle of opium. [Gr. *Morpheus*, god of dreams.]

morphology, *mör-fol'o-ji*, *n.* the science of form, esp. that of the development of living organisms: also of forms of words, &c. [Gr. *morphē*, form, *logos*, discourse.]

morris, morrice, *mor'is*, **morr'is-dance**, *ns.* a dance, according to some, of Moorish origin, in which bells, rattles, tambours, &c., are introduced.—**nine men's morris**, an old English game in which pieces or stones, nine for each side, are moved alternately as at draughts. [A form of **Moorish**.]

morrow, *mor'ō*, *n.* the day following the present: the next following day: the time immediately after any event. [M.E. *morwe*.]

morse, *mörs*, *n.* the walrus. [Lapp. *morsa*, or Finn. *mursu*.]

Morse, *mörs*, *n.* signalling by a code in which each letter, numeral, &c. is represented by a combination of dashes and dots, invented by Sam. F. B. *Morse* (1791-1872).

morsel, *mör'sél*, *n.* a bite or mouthful: a small piece of food: a small piece of anything. [O.Fr. *morsel*, dim. from L. *morsus*—*mordēre*, *morsum*, to bite.]

mortal, *mör't(á)l*, *adj.* liable to death: causing death, deadly, fatal: punishable with death: implacable (as a foe): human: (*coll.*) ex-

---

fāte, fär; mē, hûr (her); *mīne; mōte, för; mūte; mōōn, fŏŏt; тнen* (then)

469

treme—very great, very long, &c.—*n.* a human being.—*n.* **mortal′ity,** condition of being mortal: frequency or number of deaths, esp. in proportion to population: the human race.—*advs.* **mor′tally** (*coll.*) **mor′tal.**—**mortal sin** (see **sin**). [Fr.,—L. *mortālis*—*morī,* to die.]

mortar, *mör′tár, n.* a vessel in which substances are pounded with a pestle: a short piece of artillery for throwing a heavy shell: a cement of lime, sand, and water, used in building.—*n.* **mor′tar-board,** an academic cap with a square flat top. [O.E. *mortere*—L. *mortārium,* a mortar.]

mortgage, *mör′gij, n.* a conditional conveyance of land or other property as security for the performance of some condition (the conveyance becoming void on the performance of that condition).—*v.t.* to pledge as security for a debt: (*fig.*) to pledge, or to endanger possession of by pledging.—*ns.* **mortgagee′,** one to whom a mortgage is made or given; **mort′-gager, -or,** [O.Fr., *mort,* dead, *gage,* a pledge.]

mortiferous, *mör-tif′ér-us, adj.* death-bringing, fatal. [L. *mors, mortis,* death, *ferre,* to bring.]

mortify, *mör′ti-fī, v.t.* to destroy the vital functions of: to subdue by severities and penance: to humiliate: (*fig.*) to wound.—*v.i.* (of flesh) to gangrene:—*pa.t.* and *pa.p.* mor′tified.—*n.* **mortificā′tion,** act of mortifying or state of being mortified: the death of one part of an animal body: a bringing under of the passions and appetites by severe discipline: humiliation, vexation: that which mortifies or vexes: (*Scots law*) a bequest to a charitable institution. [Fr.,—Low L. *mortificāre,* to cause death to—*mors, mortis,* death, *facĕre,* to make.]

mortise, *mör′tis, n.* a cavity cut into a piece of timber to receive a tenon—also **mor′tice.**—*v.t.* to cut a mortise in: to join by a mortise and tenon.—*ns.* **mor′tise-lock, mor′tice-lock,** a lock whose mechanism is covered by being sunk into the edge of a door, &c. [Fr. *mortaise.*]

mortmain, *mört′mān, n.* the transfer of property to a corporation, which is said to be a dead hand, or one that can never part with it again. [Fr. *mort,* dead, *main* (L. *manus*), hand.]

mortuary, *mört′ū-àr-i, adj.* connected with death or burial.—*n.* a place for the temporary reception of the dead: a payment to the parish priest on the death of a parishioner. [L. *mortuārius*—*mortuus,* dead, *morī,* to die.]

mosaic, *mō-zā′ik, n.* a kind of work in which designs are formed by small pieces of coloured marble, glass, &c.: anything composed by piecing together different items.—*adj.* relating to, or composed of, mosaic.—*adv.* **mosā′ically.** [Fr. *mosaïque*—L.L. *mosaicum*—*mūsa*—Gr. *mousa,* a muse.]

Mosaic, *mō-zā′ik, adj.* pertaining to *Moses,* the great Jewish lawgiver.

moschatel, *mosk-a-tel′, n.* a small plant with pale-green flowers and a musky smell. [Fr. *moscatelle*—It. *moscatella*—*moscato,* musk.]

moselle, *mo-zel′, n.* a light wine from the district of the river *Moselle.*

Moslem, *moz′lem, n.* a Mohammedan.—*adj.* of or belonging to the Mohammedans. [Ar. *muslim,* pl. *muslimīn*—*salama,* to submit (to God).]

mosque, *mosk, n.* a Mohammedan place of worship. [Fr. *mosquée*—It. *moschea*—Ar. *masjid*—*sajada,* to pray.]

mosquito, *mos-kē′tō, n.* any of a family of insects of the order *Diptera,* the females of which suck blood. Diseases such as malaria and yellow fever are spread by certain mosquitoes:—*pl.* **mosqui′to(e)s.**—**mosquito canopy, curtain, net,** an arrangement of netting to keep out mosquitoes. [Sp. dim. of *mosca,* a fly—L. *musca.*]

moss, *mos, n.* a family of flowerless plants with branching stems and narrow, simple leaves: popularly any small cryptogamic plant, esp. a lichen: a piece of ground covered with moss: a bog.—*v.t.* to cover with moss.—*adj.* **moss′-grown,** covered with moss.—*ns.* **moss′-rose,** a variety of rose having a mosslike growth on and below the calyx; **moss′-troop′er,** one of the robbers that used to infest the mosses of the Border.—*adj.* **moss′y,** overgrown, or abounding, with moss.—*n.* **moss′iness.** [O.E. *mōs,* bog; Du. *mos*; Ger. *moos,* moss.]

most, *mōst, adj.* (*superl.* of **more**) greatest: in greatest number or quantity.—*adv.* in the highest degree.—*n.* the greatest number or quantity.—*adv.* **most′ly,** for the most part: mainly. [O.E. *mæst*; cf. Ger. *meist.*]

mot, *mō, n.* a pithy or witty saying. [Fr.]

mote, *mōt, n.* a particle of dust: a speck: anything very small. [O.E. *mot*; Du. *mot.*]

motel, *mō-tel′, n.* a hotel made up of units, each accommodating a car and occupants: a hotel with accommodation and servicing facilities for cars. [**mo**(tor), (**ho**)**tel.**]

motet, *mō-tet′, n.* a choral composition having a biblical or similar prose text. [Fr., dim. of *mot,* word.]

moth, *moth, n.* any of numerous insects of the Lepidoptera (q.v.), seen mostly at night and attracted by light (cf. **butterfly**): the cloth-eating larva of the clothes-moth: (*rare*) that which eats away gradually and silently.—*n.* **moth′-ball,** a ball, orig. of camphor, now of naphthalene, for protecting clothes from moths.—*adj.* **moth′-eat′en,** eaten or cut by moths: (*fig.*) old and worn, hackneyed, or (of a person) old, behind the times, and dull.—*adj.* **moth′y,** full of moths: moth-eaten. [O.E. *moththe, mohthe*; Ger. *motte.*]

mother, *muᴛʜ′ér, n.* a female parent, esp. a human one: the female head of a religious group: that which has produced anything.—*adj.* received by birth, as it were from one's mother: acting the part of a mother: originating.—*v.t.* to adopt or treat as a son or daughter.—*ns.* **moth′er-coun′try, -land,** the country of one's birth: the country from which a colony has gone out; **moth′ercraft,** the knowledge and skill appropriate to, expected of, a mother; **moth′erhood,** state of being a mother; **moth′er-in-law,** the mother of one's husband or wife.—*adjs.* **moth′erless,** without a mother; **moth′erly,** pertaining to, or becoming, a mother: like a mother.—*ns.* **moth′erliness; moth′er-of-pearl′,** the internal layer of the shells of several molluscs, esp. of the pearl-oyster, so called because producing the pearl; **moth′er-tongue,** a person's native language; **moth′er-wit,** native wit, common sense.—

Neutral vowels in unaccented syllables: *em′pér-ór*; for certain sounds in foreign words see p. ix.

Mother Carey's chicken, the storm petrel, or similar bird. [O.E. *mōdor*; Du. *moeder*, O.N. *mōthir*, Ger. *mutter*, L. *māter*, Gr. *mētēr*, &c.]

mother, mu͟TH´ér, *n.* dregs: mother of vinegar, a slimy mass of bacteria that oxidises alcohol into vinegar. [Possibly the same word as **mother** (1); possibly—Du. *modder*, mud.]

motif, mō-tēf´, *n.* an old form of *motive*: a theme or dominant element in a dramatic or musical composition: a design. [Fr.,—Low L. *mōtīvus*. See **motive**.]

motion, mō´sh(ó)n, *n.* act or state of moving: a single movement: change of posture: power of being moved: a mechanism: an evacuation of the bowels: excrement: proposal made, esp. in an assembly.—*v.t.* to direct by a gesture.—*v.i.* to make a movement conveying a direction.—*adj.* **mō´tionless,** without motion.—**motion, moving, picture,** an animated picture: a cinematograph (q.v.) film.—Also *adj.*—**go through the motions (of),** to make a half-hearted attempt (at); to pretend (to). [Fr.,—L. *mōtiō, -ōnis movēre, mōtum,* to move.]

motive, mō´tiv, *adj.* causing motion: having power to cause motion.—*n.* that which moves or excites to action, inducement, reason.—*v.t.* **mō´tivate,** to provide with a motive: to induce.—*ns.* **motivā´tion,** motivating force, incentive; **motiv´ity,** power of moving or producing motion. [Low L. *mōtīvus*—L. *movēre, mōtum,* to move.]

motley, mot´li, *adj.* covered with spots of different colours: variegated: heterogeneous.—*n.* the dress of a jester: any mixture, esp. of colours. [Origin obscure.]

motor, mō´tór, *n.* that which gives motion: a machine (usu. a petrol engine) whereby some source of energy is used to give motion or perform work: a motor-car.—*adj.* giving or transmitting motion: driven by a motor.—*v.t.* and *v.i.* to convey or travel by motor-vehicle.—*ns.* **mō´tor-bi´cycle, -boat, -bus, -car,** &c., one driven by a motor; **motorcade** (mo´tór-kād; after **cavalcade**), a procession of motor-cars.—*v.t.* **motorise,** to furnish with motor vehicles, as troops: to adapt to the use of a motor or motors.—*ns.* **mō´torist,** one who drives a motor-car; **motorway,** a road for motor traffic, esp. one for fast traffic with no crossings on the same level.—*adj.* **mō´tory,** giving motion. [L.,—*movēre, mōtum,* to move.]

mottled, mot´ld, *adj.* marked with spots of various colours or shades. [Prob. from **motley**.]

motto, mot´ō, *n.* a short sentence or phrase adopted as a watchword or maxim: such a phrase attached to a coat-of-arms: a passage prefixed to a book or chapter foreshadowing its matter:—*pl.* **mottoes** (mot´ōz). [It.,—L. *muttum,* a murmur.]

moue, mōō, *n.* a grimace of discontent, a pout. [Fr.]

moujik, mōō´zhik, mōō´zhik. Same as **muzhik.**

mould, mōld, *n.* loose or crumbling earth: earth considered as the material of which the human body is formed and to which it turns: soil rich in decayed matter.—*v.t.* to cover with soil.—*v.i.* **mould´er,** to crumble to mould: to waste away gradually.—*v.t.* to turn to dust.—*adj.* **mould´y,** like or of the nature of mould.—

n. **mould´iness.** [O.E. *molde.*]

mould, mōld, *n.* a woolly or fluffy growth on bread, cheese or other vegetable or animal matter, caused by various small fungi: any fungus producing such a growth.—*v.i.* to become mouldy.—*adj.* **mould´y,** overgrown with mould: like mould: (*slang*) old and stale, or depressing, miserable.—*n.* **mould´iness.** [M.E. *mowle*; cf. O.N. *mygla.*]

mould, mōld, *n.* a hollow form in which anything is cast: a pattern: the form received from a mould: a thing formed in a mould.—*v.t.* to knead: to form in a mould: to form after a particular pattern.—*ns.* **mould´er; mould´ing,** anything formed by or in a mould: an ornamental edging on a picture-frame, a wall, &c. [Fr. *moule*—L. *modulus,* a measure.]

mouldwarp, mōld´wörp, *n.* a mole. [O.E. *molde,* earth, *weorpan,* to throw.]

moult, mōlt, *v.i.* to cast feathers or other covering.—*v.t.* to shed (feathers, &c.). [L. *mūtāre,* to change, with intrusive *l.*]

mound, mownd, *n.* a bank of earth or stone raised as a protection: a hillock: a heap.—*v.t.* to fortify with a mound. [Origin obscure.]

mount, mownt, *n.* (*arch.*) a mountain: a small hill or mound, natural or artificial. [O.E. *munt*—L. *mōns, mōntis,* mountain.]

mount, mownt, *v.i.* to go up: to climb: to extend upward: to rise in level or in amount.—*v.t.* to ascend: to get up upon: to place on horseback or the like: to raise aloft: to put in readiness for use or exhibition.—*n.* a rise: an act of mounting: a riding animal or cycle: that upon which a thing is placed for use or display.—*adj.* **mount´able,** that may be mounted or ascended.—*n.pl.* **Mount´ies,** Canadian mounted police. [Fr. *monter,* to go up—L. *mōns, montis,* mountain.]

mountain, mownt´in, *n.* a high hill: anything very large.—*adj.* of or relating to a mountain: growing or dwelling on a mountain.—*ns.* **mount´ain-ash,** the rowan-tree; **mount´ain-dew,** whisky; **mountaineer´,** an inhabitant of a mountain: a climber of mountains.—*v.i.* to climb mountains.—*adj.* **mount´ainous,** full of mountains: large as a mountain, huge.—*ns.* **mount´ain-rail´way,** a light narrow-gauge railway, usu. with a cogged centre-rail; **mount´ain-sick´ness,** sickness brought on by breathing rarefied air. **mountain limestone,** a series of limestone strata separating the Old Red Sandstone from the coal measures. [O.Fr. *montaigne*—L. *mōns, montis,* mountain.]

mountebank, mown´ti-bangk, *n.* a quack: a boastful pretender: a buffoon. [It. *montambanco*—*montare,* to mount: *in, on, banco,* a bench.]

mourn, mōrn, mörn, *v.i.* to grieve, to be sorrowful: to wear mourning.—*v.t.* to grieve for: to lament.—*n.* **mourn´er,** one who mourns: one who attends a funeral, esp. a relative of the deceased.—*adj.* **mourn´ful,** causing, or expressing, sorrow: feeling grief.—*adv.* **mourn´fully.** —*n.* **mourn´fulness.**—*adj.* **mourn´ing,** grieving, lamenting: for wear as a sign of mourning.—*n.* the act of expressing grief: the dress of mourners.—*ns.* **mourn´ing-border,** a black margin used on notepaper, &c., by mourners; **mourn´ing-coach,** a closed carriage for carrying mourners to a funeral. [O.E. *murnan, meornan*; O.H.G. *mornēn*, to grieve.]

mouse, *mows, n.* any of numerous species of small rodents found in houses and in the fields:—*pl.* **mice** (*mīs*).—*v.i.* (*mowz*), to hunt for mice: to prowl.—*ns.* **mouser** (*mowz′ėr*), a cat, &c., that catches mice: a prying person; **mouse′-hole,** a hole made or used by mice: a small hole or opening.—*adj.* **mousy** (*mows′i*), like a mouse in colour or smell: abounding with mice: of hair, dull, greyish-brown: of person, uninteresting, unassertive.—**field mouse,** any of various wild mice; **short-tailed field mouse,** one of the voles (q.v.). [O.E. *mūs,* pl. *mȳs,* Ger. *maus,* L. *mūs,* Gr. *mȳs.*]

mousse, *mōōs, n.* a sweet dish, frozen or unfrozen, containing eggs and whipped cream.

moustache, mustache, *mus-täsh′, mōōs-täsh′, n.* the hair upon the upper lip—also **mustach′io** (*-tä′shŏ*).—*adjs.* **moustached′, mustach′ioed.** [Fr. *moustache*—It. *mostaccio*—Gr. *mystax, -akos,* the upper lip.]

mouth, *mowth, n.* the opening in the head of an animal by which it eats and utters sound: opening or entrance, as of a bottle, river, &c.: a spokesman: a grimace:—*pl.* **mouths** (*mowтнz*).—*v.t.* (*mowтн*) to utter: to utter affectedly or pompously.—*v.i.* to declaim, rant: to grimace.—*ns.* **mouth′er,** one who mouths; **mouth′ful,** as much as fills the mouth: a small quantity:—*pl.* **mouth′fuls.**—*adj.* **mouth′less,** without a mouth.—*ns.* **mouth′-music,** a tune sung as a substitute for instrumental, usu. dance, music; **mouth′-or′gan,** a small musical instrument played by the mouth; **mouth′piece,** the piece of a musical instrument, or tobacco-pipe, held in the mouth: one who speaks for others.—**down in the mouth,** out of spirits, despondent. [O.E. *mūth*; Ger. *mund,* Du. *mond.*]

move, *mōōv, v.t.* to cause to change place or posture: to set in motion: to excite (to action, or to emotion), to persuade: to arouse: to touch the feelings of: to propose formally in a meeting: to recommend.—*v.i.* to go from one place to another: to change place or posture: to walk, to carry oneself: to change residence: to make a motion as in an assembly.—*n.* the act of moving: a movement, esp. at chess: hence (*fig.*) a step taken to advance an aim.—*adj.* **movable** (*mōōv′á-bl*), that may be moved: not fixed—also (esp. *law*) **move′able.**—*n.* (esp. in *pl.*) a portable piece of furniture or property (opp. to *fixture*).—*ns.* **mov′ableness, movabil′ity; move′ment,** act or manner of moving: change of position: motion of the mind, emotion: activity: process: the moving parts in a mechanism, esp. the wheelwork of a clock or watch: a main division of an extended musical composition: an agitation in favour of, concerted endeavour to further, an object or policy; **mov′er; mov′ie, mov′y** (*coll.*), a moving picture: a cinematograph film: a showing of such: (in *pl.* **movies,** usu. with **the**) motion pictures in general, or the industry that provides them.—*adj.* **mov′ing,** causing motion: changing position: affecting the feelings: pathetic.—*adv.* **mov′ingly.**—**movable feast,** a church feast that depends on the date of Easter for its time of celebration: a meal

taken at no fixed hour. [O.Fr. *movoir*—L. *movēre,* to move.]

mow, *mow, n.* a wry face.—*v.i.* to make grimaces. [Fr. *moue,* a grimace.]

mow, *mow, mō, n.* a pile of hay or corn in sheaves in a barn.—*v.t.* to pile hay or sheaves of grain in a mow:—*pr.p.* mow′ing; *pa.t.* mowed; *pa.p.* mowed or mown. [O.E. *mūga,* heap; O.N. *mūgi,* swath.]

mow, *mō, v.t.* to cut down (grass, &c.), or cut the grass upon: to cut (down) in great numbers:—*pr.p.* mow′ing; *pa.t.* mowed; *pa.p.* mowed or mown.—*adjs.* **mowed, mown,** cut down with a scythe: cleared of grass with a scythe, as land.—*ns.* **mow′er,** one who mows grass, &c.: a machine with revolving blades for mowing grass; **mow′ing,** the act of cutting (grass): land from which grass is cut. [O.E. *māwan*; Ger. *mähen*; L. *metĕre,* to reap.]

much, *much, adj.* (*comp.* **more;** *superl.* **most**) great in quantity.—*adv.* to a great degree: by far: often.—*n.* a great amount.—**much of a muchness,** just about the same value or amount. [M.E. *muche, muchel*—O.E. *micel, mycel.*]

mucid, mucilage. See under **mucus.**

muck, *muk, n.* dung: a mass of decayed vegetable matter: anything low and filthy.—*v.t.* to clear of muck: to manure with muck.—*adj.* **muck′y,** nasty, filthy.—*n.* **muck′iness.** [Prob. Scand.; cf. O.N. *myki,* Dan. *mōg,* dung.]

mucus, *mū′kus, n.* the slimy fluid secreted by the mucous membrane of the nose and other parts.—*adj.* **mū′cid** (*-sid*), mouldy, musty.—*n.* **mucilage** (*mū′sil-ij*), a gluey substance found in some plants: gum.—*adjs.* **mucilaginous** (*-aj′-*), pertaining to, or secreting, mucilage: slimy; **mucous, mucus,** like mucus: slimy: viscous.— **mucous membrane** (see **membrane**). [L., cf. L. *mungēre,* wipe away.]

mud, *mud, n.* wet soft earth.—*v.t.* to dirty: to make turbid.—*adj.* **mudd′y,** foul with mud: containing mud: covered with mud: confused, stupid.—*v.t.* and *v.i.* to make or become muddy:—*pa.t.* and *pa.p.* mudd′ied.—*adv.* **mudd′ily.**—*n.* **mudd′iness.**—*adj.* **mudd′y-head′ed.**—*ns.* **mud′-guard,** a screen to catch mud-splashes from wheels; **mud′-lark,** a name for various birds that frequent mud: one who picks up a living along the banks of tidal rivers: a street Arab.—*v.i.* to work or play in mud. [Old Low Ger. *mudde,* Du. *modder.*]

muddle, *mud′l, v.t.* to render muddy or foul, as water: to bungle.—*v.i.* to blunder.—*n.* confusion, mess: bewilderment.—*n.* **mudd′lehead,** a blockhead.—*adj.* **muddlehead′ed.** [Freq. of **mud.**]

muezzin, *mōō-ez′in, n.* the Mohammedan official who calls to prayer. [Ar.]

muff, *muf, n.* a cylinder of fur or the like for keeping the hands warm. [Prob. from Du. *mof*; cf. Ger. *muff,* a muff.]

muff, *muf, n.* a stupid fellow.—*v.t.* and *v.i.* to bungle. [Origin unknown.]

muffin, *muf′in, n.* a soft cake, eaten hot with butter. [Origin unknown.]

muffle, *muf′l, v.t.* to wrap up for warmth or concealment: to blindfold: to dull or deaden the sound of.—*n.* **muff′ler,** a scarf for the throat: a means of muffling. [App. Fr.

Neutral vowels in unaccented syllables: *em′pėr-ór*; for certain sounds in foreign words see p. ix.

mouffle, mitten.]

mufti, *muf'ti, n.* an expounder of Mohammedan law: the civilian dress of one who wears a uniform when on duty: plain clothes. [Ar.]

mug, *mug, n.* a cup with more or less vertical sides: its contents. [Origin unknown.]

mug, *mug, n.* the face: the mouth. [Perh. from the grotesque face on a drinking mug.]

mug, *mug, n.* (*coll.*) a simpleton.

mug, *mug, v.t.* and *v.i.* (*coll.*) to study hard.

muggy, *mug'i, adj.* foggy: close and damp, as weather: wet or mouldy, as straw.—Also **mugg'ish.** [Perh. O.N. *mugga*, mist.]

mugwump, *mug'wump, n.* an Indian chief: a self-important person: one who dissociates himself from political parties. [Amer. Indian.]

mujik. Same as **muzhik.**

mulatto, *mū-lat'ō, n.* the offspring of a Negro and a person of European stock:—*fem.* **mulatt'ress.** [Sp. *mulato,* dim. of *mulo,* mule.]

mulberry, *mul'ber-i, n.* a genus of trees on the leaves of which silkworms feed: a fruit of any of these. [Poss. O.H.G. *mulberi*—L. *mōrum.*]

mulch, *mulch, mulsh, n.* loose strawy dung, &c., laid down to protect the roots of plants.—Also **mulsh.**—*v.t.* to cover with mulch. [Cf. Ger. dial. *molsch,* soft; O.E. *melsc.*]

mulct, *mulkt, n.* a fine, a penalty.—*v.t.* to fine (*to mulct a person in* £500, *to mulct him* £500): to deprive (*of*) [L. *mulcta,* a fine.]

mule, *mūl, n.* the offspring of the ass and horse (esp. of a male ass and a mare): an instrument for cotton-spinning: an obstinate person.—*n.* **muleteer'**, one who drives mules.—*adj.* **mūl'ish,** like a mule: obstinate.—*adv.* **mūl'ishly.**—*n.* **mūl'ishness.** [O.E. *mūl*—L. *mūlus.*]

mule, *mūl, n.* a heelless slipper. [Fr.]

mull, *mul, n.* a muddle or mess.—*v.t.* to bungle. —**mull over,** (*coll.*) to think, ponder, over.

mull, *mul, v.t.* to warm, spice, and sweeten (wine, ale, &c.).—*adj.* **mulled.**

mull, *mul, n.* (*Scot.*) a cape, promontory. [Gael. *maol*; perh.—Scand.]

mullah, *mul'ä, n.* a Mohammedan versed in theology and law: a Moslem teacher: a fanatical preacher of war on the infidel. [Pers., Turk. and Hindustani *mullā*—Ar. *maulā.*]

mullet, *mul'et, n.* a genus of palatable fishes nearly cylindrical in form. [O.Fr. *mulet,* dim.,—L. *mullus.*]

mulligatawny, *mul-i-ga-tö'ni, n.* an East Indian curry-soup. [Tamil (q.v.) *milagu-tannīr,* pepper-water.]

mullion, *mul'yón, n.* an upright division between the lights of windows, between panels, &c.—*adj.* **mull'ioned.** [Apparently by metathesis from O.Fr. *monial* of unknown origin.]

mullock, *mul'ok, n.* rubbish, esp. mining refuse [mull (1).]

mulsh. Same as **mulch.**

multangular, *mult-an'gūlár, adj.* having many angles or corners. [**mult-, angle.**]

multi-, mult-, in composition, much, many. [L. *multus*]:—e.g. **multiped,** *mul'ti-ped,* an insect having many feet (L. *pēs, pedis,* foot); **multilingual,** *mul-ti-ling'gwäl,* in many languages: speaking many languages (L. *lingua,* tongue); **mul'ti-pur'pose; multiracial,** *mul-ti-rā'shl,* in-

cluding (people of) many races (as, a *multiracial society*).

multifarious, *mul-ti-fā'ri-us, adj.* having great diversity: manifold.—*adv.* **multifā'riously.** [L. *multifārius*—*multus,* many, and perh. *fārī,* to speak.]

multiform, *mul'ti-förm, adj.* having many forms.—*n.* **multiform'ity.** [Fr. *multiforme*—L. *multiformis*—*multus,* many, *forma,* shape.]

multilateral, *mul-ti-lat'ér ál, adj.* many-sided: with several parties or participants.—**multilateral school,** a school providing postprimary courses leading to careers of different types. [**multi-, lateral.**]

multilineal, *mul-ti-lin'i-ál, adj.* having many lines. [**multi-, line.**]

multinomial, *mul-ti-nō'mi-ál, n.* Same as **polynomial.** [**multi-,** L. *nōmen,* a name.]

multiple, *mul'ti-pl, adj.* consisting of many elements, esp. of the same kind: repeated many times.—*n.* a quantity which contains another an exact number of times.—**multiple shop,** a chain store.—**common multiple,** a number or quantity that can be divided by each of several others without a remainder. [Fr.,—L. *multiplus*—L. *multus,* many, and root of *plērē,* to fill.]

multiplex, *mul'ti-pleks, adj.* multiple. [L.,—*multus,* many, *plicāre,* to fold.]

multiply, *mul'ti-plī, v.t.* to increase many times: to make more numerous: (*arith.*) to calculate the sum of a number taken as many times as there are units in another number or **mul'tiplier.**—*v.i.* to increase:—*pr.p.* **mul'tiplying;** *pa.t.* and *pa.p.* **mul'tiplied.**—*adjs.* **multipli'able, mul'tiplicable,** that may be multiplied.—*ns.* **multiplicand'**, a number to be multiplied by another; **multiplica'tion,** the act of multiplying or increasing in number: the rule or operation by which any given number or quantity is multiplied.—*adj.* **mul'tiplicative,** tending to multiply: having the power to multiply.—*n.* **multiplic'ity,** the state of being multiplied or various: a great number. [Fr.,—L. *multiplex*; cf. **multiplex.**]

multitude, *mul-ti-tūd, n.* the state of being many: a great number of individuals: a crowd: the mob.—*adj.* **multitud'inous,** consisting of, or having the appearance of, a multitude. [Fr.,—L. *multitūdō, -inis*—*multus,* many.]

multure, *mul'tūr, n.* the toll paid to a miller for grinding grain. [O.Fr.,—L. *molitūra,* a grinding.]

mum, *mum, adj.* silent.—*n.* silence. *interj.* not a word!—*v.i.* to act in dumb show: to masquerade:—*pr.p.* **mumm'ing;** *pa.p.* **mummed.**—*ns.* **mumm'er,** an actor in folk-play, usu. at Christmas: a masquerader; **mumm'ery,** mumming: foolish ceremonial; **mumm'ing,** the sports of mummers. [An inarticulate sound, closing the lips; partly O.Fr. *momer,* to mum.]

mum, *mum, n.* Abbrev. of **mummy** (2).

mumble, *mum'bl, v.t.* and *v.i.* to utter or speak indistinctly or perfunctorily: to chew, as with toothless gums.—*n.* **mum'bler.**—*adv.* **mum'blingly.** [Freq. of **mum.**]

mumbo-jumbo, *mum'bō-jum'bō, n.* a god worshipped by certain Negro tribes in Africa: any object of foolish worship or fear: hocus-pocus.

mu-(μ-)meson, *mū-, mōō-, mē'zon, n.* a subatomic particle classed formerly as the lightest type of meson, now as the heaviest type of lepton, having unit negative charge.—Abbrev. **mu′on.**

mummy, *mum′i, n.* a human body preserved by the Egyptian art of embalming, in which wax, spices, &c., were employed.—*n.* **mummifica′-tion.**—*v.t.* **mumm′ify,** to make into a mummy: to embalm and dry as a mummy:—*pr.p.* mumm′ifying; *pa.p.* mumm′ified.—*n.* **mumm′y-wheat,** a variety of wheat alleged (incredibly) to descend from grains found in mummy-cases. [O.Fr. *mumie*—Low L. *mumia*—Ar. and Pers. *mūmiyā*.]

mummy, mummie, *mum′i, n.* a childish or affectionate word for mother. [Variant of **mammy.**]

mump, *mump, v.i.* to sulk: to beg.—*n.* **mump′er,** one who mumps: an old cant term for a beggar.—*adj.* **mump′ish,** having mumps: dull, sullen.—*adv.* **mump′ishly.**—*n.* **mump′ishness.**—*n.* (*orig. pl.*) **mumps,** an infectious inflammation of the glands of the neck: gloomy silence. [Cf. **mum** and Du. *mompen,* to cheat.]

munch, *munch, -sh, v.t.* and *v.i.* to chew with marked action of the jaws.—*n.* **munch′er.** [Prob. imit.]

mundane, *mun′dān, adj.* belonging to the world: terrestrial: ordinary, banal.—*adv.* **mun′danely.** [Fr.,—L. *mundānus*—*mundus,* the world.]

mungo, *mung′gō, n.* cloth similar to shoddy made from wool waste. [Origin obscure.]

municipal, *mū-nis′i-pál, adj.* pertaining to a corporation or borough.—*n.* **municipal′ity,** a self-governing town or city: in France, a division of the country.—*adv.* **munic′ipally.** [L. *mūnicipālis*—*mūnicipium,* a free town—*mūnia,* official duties, *capĕre,* to take.]

munificence, *mū-nif′i-séns, n.* magnificent liberality in giving: bountifulness.—*adj.* **munif′-icent.**—*adv.* **munif′icently.** [Fr.,—L. *mūnificentia*—*mūnus,* a present, *facĕre,* to make.]

muniment, *mū′ni-mént, n.* a means of defence: (*pl.*) documents making good a claim (e.g. title-deeds).—*n.* **munition** (*-nish′(ó)n*—commonly in *pl.*), material used in war: military stores: (*fig.*) weapons or equipment necessary for any campaign. [L. *mūnīre, mūnītum,* to fortify; *mūnitiō, -ōnis,* fortification; *mūnīmentum,* fortification, title-deeds—*moenia,* walls.]

munnion, *mun′yón.* Same as **mullion.**

munshi, moonshee, *mōōn′shē, n.* (*India*) a secretary: an interpreter: a language teacher. [Hindustani *munshī*—Ar.]

muon. See **mu-meson.**

mural, *mū′rál, adj.* of, on, attached to, or of the nature of, a wall.—*n.* a painting on a wall. [L. *mūrālis*—*mūrus,* a wall.]

murder, *mûr′dér, n.* the act of putting a person to death, intentionally and unlawfully.—*v.t.* to kill unlawfully and with malice aforethought: to destroy: (*fig.*) to ruin by saying, &c., very badly (e.g. *to murder a poem*).—*n.* **mur′derer:** —*fem.* **mur′deress.**—*adj.* **mur′derous,** of the nature of murder: bloody: cruel.—*adv.* **mur′derously.** [O.E. *morthor*—*morth,* death; Ger. *mord;* cf. L. *mors, mortis.*]

murex, *mū′reks, n.* a shellfish from which the Tyrian purple dye was obtained. [L.]

muriatic, *mū-ri-at′ik, adj.* pertaining to, or obtained from, sea-salt.—**muriatic acid,** a commercial term for hydrochloric acid. [L. *muriāticus*—*muria,* brine.]

murky, *mûrk′i, adj.* dark, obscure, gloomy: of darkness, thick: (*coll.*) of a past, disreputable.—*adv.* **murk′ily.**—*n.* **murk′iness.** [O.E. *mirce;* O.N. *myrkr,* Dan. and Swed. *mörk.*]

murmur, *mûr′mûr, n.* a low, indistinct sound, like that of running water: a subdued grumble or complaint.—*v.i.* to utter a murmur: to grumble:—*pr.p.* mur′muring; *pa.t.* and *pa.p.* mur′mured.—*n.* **mur′murer.**—*adj.* **mur′murous.**—*adv.* **mur′murously.** [Fr.,—L.; imit.]

murrain, *mur′in, -én, n.* (*obs.*) a pestilence: now only a cattle-plague, esp. foot-and-mouth disease. [O.Fr. *morine,* a pestilence, carcass.]

muscadel, *mus-ka-del′,* **mus′ka-del,** **muscatel,** *mus-ka-tel′,* **mus′ka-tel,** *ns.* a rich, spicy wine, or the grape producing it (also **muscat**): a raisin from this grape: a variety of pear. [O.Fr. *muscatel, muscadel*—Provençal, *muscat,* musky.]

muscle, *mus′l, n.* an animal tissue by contraction of which bodily movement is effected. [Fr.,—L. *mūsculus,* dim. of *mūs,* a mouse, a muscle.]

muscoid, *mus′koid, adj.* (*bot.*) moss-like. [L. *muscus,* moss, Gr. *eidos,* form.]

Muscovy, *mus′ko-vi, n.* (*hist.*) the old principality of *Moscow:* extended to Russia in general.—*n.* and *adj.* **Mus′covite,** of Muscovy: Russian: a Russian.

muscular, *mus′kū-lár, adj.* pertaining to a muscle: consisting of muscles: brawny, strong.—*n.* **muscular′ity,** state of being muscular.—*adv.* **mus′cularly.**—**muscular dystrophy** (*dis′trō-fi*), a disease in which muscles progressively deteriorate. [L. *mūsculus.* See **muscle.**]

muse, *mūz, v.i.* to meditate (on, upon): to be absent-minded.—*v.t.* to say musingly.—*n.* deep thought: contemplation: a state or fit of absence of mind.—*n.* **mus′er.**—*adv.* **mus′ingly.** [Fr. *muser,* to loiter, in O.Fr. to muse.]

muse, *mūz, n.* (*cap.*) one of the nine goddesses of poetry, music, and the other liberal arts: poetic inspiration: poetry. [Fr.,—L. *mūsa*—Gr. *mousa.*]

musette, *mū-zet′, n.* a small old French bagpipe: a simple pastoral melody adapted to it. [O.Fr. dim. of *muse,* bagpipe.]

museum, *mū-zē′um, n.* (*orig.*) a temple of the Muses: a repository for the collection, exhibition, and study of objects of artistic, scientific or historic interest:—*pl.* **museums.** [L. *mūsēum*—Gr. *mouseion.*]

mush, *mush, n.* meal boiled in water, esp. Indian meal: anything pulpy. [Prob. **mash.**]

mush, *mush, v.i.* to travel on foot with dogs over snow.—*n.* a journey of this kind. [Prob. Fr. *marcher,* to walk.]

mushroom, *mush′rōōm, n.* the common name of certain fungi, esp. such as are edible: (*fig.*) one who rises suddenly from a low condition, an upstart: anything of rapid growth and decay (also *adj.*—e.g. *a mushroom town, firm*).—*v.i.* to gather mushrooms: to increase, spread with rapidity. [O.Fr. *mousseron,* perh. —*mousse,* moss.]

music, *mū′zik, n.* a connected series of sounds that please the ear: the art of combining

Neutral vowels in unaccented syllables: *em′pér-ór;* for certain sounds in foreign words see p. ix.

sounds so as to do this: an example of this, a musical composition: the score of such: any pleasant sound.—*adj.* **mū′sical,** pertaining to, or producing, music: pleasing to the ear, melodious.—*n.* a musical performance, esp. theatrical or film, in which singing and usu. dancing play an important part.—*adv.* **mū′sically.**—*ns.* **mū′sicalness; mū′sic-hall,** hall or theatre for concerts and variety entertainments: variety entertainment generally (also *adj.*); **musi′cian** (-*shán*), one skilled in the practice or theory of music: a performer of music; **musicol′ogy,** the academic study of music (not including performance or composition as such).—**music(-al) box,** a case containing a mechanism contrived, when the spring is wound up, to reproduce melodies; **musical comedy,** a light dramatic entertainment in which music figures largely; **musical glasses** (see **harmonica**). [Fr. *musique*—L. *mūsica*—Gr. *mousikē (technē*), musical (art) —*mousa,* a muse.]

musique concrète, *mū-zēk kon kret,* music made up of scraps of natural sound recorded and then variously treated. [Fr.]

musk, *musk, n.* a substance with a strong perfume, obtained from a sac under the skin of the abdomen of the male musk-deer: the musk-deer: a name given to a number of plants, esp. to a little yellow-flowered mimulus (whose leaves formerly had a musky scent).—*v.t.* to perfume with musk.—*ns.* **musk-deer,** a small hornless deer, native of the mountains of Central Asia; **musk′-duck,** a duck native to tropical and subtropical America, so called from its musky odour; **musk′-melon,** the common melon (apparently transferred from a musky-scented kind); **musk′-ox,** a ruminant of arctic America, exhaling a strong musky smell; **musk′-rat,** a musky-scented North American rodent, yielding a valuable fur also **mus′quash; musk′-rose,** a fragrant species of rose.—*adj.* **musk′y,** having the odour of musk.—*adv.* **musk′ily.**—*n.* **musk′iness.** [Fr. *musc* L. *muscus,* Gr. *moschos.*]

musket, *mus′ket, n.* (*hist*) a smooth-bore military hand-gun.—*ns.* **musketeer′,** a soldier, armed with a musket; **musketoon′, musquetoon′,** a short musket: one armed with a musketoon; **mus′ketry,** muskets in general: the art of using small-arms.[O.Fr. *mousquet*, a musket, formerly a hawk—It. *moschetto.*]

Muslim, *mus′lim, n.* and *adj.* Same as **Moslem.**

muslin, *muz′lin, n.* a fine soft cotton fabric resembling gauze in appearance.—*adj.* made of muslin. [Fr. *mousseline*—It. *mussolino*, from *Mosul* in Mesopotamia.]

musquash, *mus′kwosh, n.* the musk-rat. [Amer. Indian.]

mussel, *mus′l* (formerly also **muscle, muskle,** *mus′l, mus′kl*), *n.* any of several marine bivalve shellfish, used for food. [O.E. *mūs(c)le*; cf. Ger. *muschal*, Fr. *moule*; all from L. *mūsculus.*]

Mussulman, *mus′ul-man, n.* a Moslem or Mohammedan—*pl.* **Muss′ulmans** (-*manz*). [Pers. *musulmān*—Ar. *muslim, moslim,* Moslem.]

must, *must, v.i.* generally used as an auxiliary, meaning am, is, are, obliged physically or

morally—occurring only in this form (orig. past indic., now present and occasionally past).—*n.* an essential, a necessity: a thing that should not be missed or neglected. [O.E. *mōste,* pa. of *mōt,* may; cf. Ger. *müssen.*]

must, *must, n.* new wine: grape-juice, unfermented or only partially fermented. [O.E. *must*—L. *mustus,* new, fresh.]

mustache. Same as **moustache.**

mustang, *mus′tang, n.* the wild horse of the American prairies. [Sp.]

mustard, *mus′tárd, n.* a pungent condiment made from the powdered seeds of the mustard-plant.—*n.* **mustard-gas,** the vapour from a poisonous blistering liquid.—**wild mustard,** the charlock. [O.Fr. *mostarde*—L. *mustum,* must (because the condiment was prepared with must). See **must** (2).]

muster, *mus′tér, v.t.* to assemble, as troops for duty or inspection: to gather: (*fig.*) to summon up and display (e.g. resolution).—*v.i.* to be gathered together, as troops.—*n.* an assembling of troops for inspection, &c.: a register of troops mustered: an assembly: (*Austr.*) a round-up.—*ns.* **mus′ter-mas′ter,** one who has charge of the muster-roll; **mus′ter-roll,** a register of the officers and men present at the time of muster.—**pass muster,** to escape censure, to bear examination. [O.Fr. *mostre, monstre*—L. *monstrum*—*monēre,* to warn.]

musty, *mus′ti, adj.* mouldy, spoiled by damp, sour, foul.—*adv.* **must′ily.**—*n.* **must′iness.**

mutable, *mū′ta-bl, adj.* that may be changed: subject to change: inconstant.—*ns.* **mutabil′ity, mū′tableness,** state or quality of being mutable.—*adv.* **mū′tably.**—*n.* **muta′tion,** act or process of changing: change: (*biol.*) the inception (esp. the sudden beginning as opp. to the gradual appearance) of a heritable variation: umlaut (q.v.). [L. *mūtabilis*—*mūtāre, -ātum,* to change—*movēre, mōtum,* to move.]

mute, *mūt, adj.* dumb: silent, unpronounced.—*n.* a dumb person: a silent person: a funeral attendant: a stop consonant: *v.t.* to deaden the sound of.—*adj.* **mut′ed** (of e.g. sound, colour) softened, not loud, harsh or bright.—*adv.* **mute′ly.**—*n.* **mute′ness.** [L. *mūtus.*]

mutilate, *mū′ti-lāt, v.t.* to maim: to render defective: to remove a material part of.—*ns.* **mutilā′tion; mū′tilātor.** [L. *mutilāre, -ātum*—*mutilus*—Gr. *mytilos, mitulos,* curtailed.]

mutiny, *mū′ti-ni, v.i.* to rise against authority in army, navy, or air force: to revolt against rightful authority: *pr.p.* **mu′tinying;** *pa.t.* and *pa.p.* **mu′tinied.**—*n.* insurrection, esp. in armed forces: tumult, strife.—*n.* **mutineer′,** one who mutinies.—*adj.* **mū′tinous,** disposed to mutiny, rebellious.—*adv.* **mū′tinously.**—*n.* **mū′tinousness.** [Fr. *mutin,* riotous—L. *movēre, mōtum,* to move.]

muton, *mū′ton, n.* the smallest element of a gene capable of giving rise to a new form by mutation. [See **mutable.**]

mutter, *mut′ér, v.i.* to utter words in a low voice: to murmur: to sound with a low, rumbling noise.—*v.t.* to utter indistinctly.—*n.* **mutt′erer.** [Prob. imit., like dial. Ger. *muttern;* L. *muttīre.*]

mutton, *mut′n, n.* sheep's flesh as food.—*n.* **mutt′on-chop,** a rib of mutton chopped at the small end.—*adj.* suggesting a mutton-chop in shape (of whiskers).—*n.* **mutt′on-head,** a heavy, stupid person. [O.Fr. *moton,* a sheep— Low L. *multō.*]

mutual, *mū′tū-ál, adj.* interchanged, reciprocal (e.g. *mutual suspicion, aid*): (*loosely*) common to two or more, shared (e.g. *mutual friend*).—*n.* **mutual′ity.**—*adv.* **mū′tually.** [Fr. *mutuel*—L. *mūtuus*—*mūtāre,* to change.]

muzhik, moujik, mujik, *mōō-zhik′, mōō′zhik, n.* a Russian peasant. [Russ. *muzhik.*]

muzzle, *muz′l, n.* the projecting jaws and nose of an animal: a fastening for the mouth to prevent biting: the extreme end of a gun, &c.—*v.t.* to put a muzzle on: to keep from hurting: to gag or silence. [O.Fr. *musel* (Fr. *museau*)— L.L. *mūsellum,* dim. of *mūsum* or *mūsus,* beak.]

muzzy, *muz′i, adj.* dazed, tipsy.—*n.* **muzz′iness.**

my, *mī* (sometimes *mi*), *poss. adj.* of or belonging to me. [**mine**—O.E. *mīn* (gen.), of me.]

mycelium, *mī-sē′li-um, n.* the thallus of a fungus when it consists of hyphae (q.v.): mushroom spawn:—*pl.* **myce′lia.** [Gr. *mykēs,* a fungus, *ēlos,* a nail or wart.]

mycology, *mī-kol′o-ji. n.* the study of fungi. [Gr. *mykēs,* fungus, *logos,* discourse.]

myopia, *mī-ō′pi-a, n.* shortness of sight (*lit.* and *fig.*).—*adj.* **myop′ic.**—*n.* **my′ope,** a shortsighted person. [Gr. *myōps,* short-sighted—*ōps,* the eye.]

myosotis, *mī-ō-sō′tis, n.* a genus of herbs which includes the forget-me-not. [Gr. *myosōtis*— *mys,* gen. *myos,* a mouse, *ous,* gen. *ōtos,* an ear.]

myriad, *mir′i-ad, n.* any immense number.—*adj.* numberless. [Gr. *myrias, -ados,* ten thousand.]

myriapod, *mir′i-a-pod,* (more correctly) **myr′iopod,** *n.* a group of animals with many jointed legs. [Gr. *myrios,* numberless, *pous,* gen. *podos,* a foot.]

myrmidon, *mûr′mi-don, n.* (*cap.*) one of a tribe of warriors who accompanied Achilles to Troy: one of a ruffianly band under a daring leader. [L.,—Gr.]

myrrh, *mûr, n.* a bitter, aromatic, transparent gum, exuded from the bark of an Arabian shrub: (*Scot.*) a scented umbelliferous plant, also known as sweet chervil or sweet cicely. [O.E. *myrra*—L. and Gr. *myrrha*; cf. Ar. *murr.*]

myrtle, *mûr′tl, n.* a genus of evergreen shrubs with beautiful and fragrant leaves. [O.Fr. *myrtil,* dim of *myrte*—L. *myrtus*—Gr. *myrtos.*]

myself, *mī-self′,* or *mé-self′, pron.* I, or me, in person—used for emphasis: (reflexively) me. [**me, self.**]

mystery, *mis′tèr-i, n.* a secret doctrine or rite: anything very obscure: that which is beyond human knowledge to explain: anything artfully made difficult: a miracle-play, or, more exactly, one dealing with Scriptural incidents, esp. from the life of Christ (also **mys′tery-play′**): the making a secret of (usu. unimportant) things.—*adj.* **mystē′rious,** containing mystery: obscure: secret: incomprehensible: suggesting, or intended to suggest, mystery.—*adv.* **mystē′riously.**—*n.* **mystē′riousness.**—*n.* **mys′tery-tour,** an excursion to a destination which remains secret until the journey's end. [L. *mystērium*—Gr. *mystērion*—*mystēs,* one initiated—*myein,* to close the eyes.]

mystery, *mis′tèr-i, n.* (*arch.*) a trade, handicraft. [L.L. *misterium*—L. *ministerium*—*minister,* servant. Properly *mistery*; the form *mystery* is due to confusion with **mystery** (1).]

mystic, -al, *mis′tik, -ál, adj.* relating to, or containing, mystery: involving a sacred or a secret meaning revealed only to a spiritually enlightened mind.—*n.* **mys′tic,** one who seeks for direct intercourse with God in elevated religious feeling or ecstasy.—*adv.* **mys′tically.**—*n.* **mys′ticism** (*-sizm*), the doctrine of the mystics: an effort to attain to direct spiritual communion with God.—*v.t.* **mys′tify,** to make mysterious, obscure, or secret: to puzzle, bewilder: to play on the credulity of:—*pr.p.* **mys′tifying;** *pa.t.* and *pa.p.* **mys′tified.**—*n.* **mystifica′tion.** [L. *mysticus*—Gr. *mystikos*; same root as **mystery** (1).]

mystique, *mis-tēk′, mēs-tēk, n.* incommunicable spirit, gift, or quality: secret (of an art) as known to its inspired practitioners: sense of mystery, remoteness from the ordinary, and power surrounding a person, activity, &c. [Fr.]

myth, *mith, n.* an ancient traditional story of gods or heroes, offering an explanation of some fact or phenomenon: a fable: a fictitious person or thing: a commonly-held belief that is untrue or without foundation: myths collectively.—*adjs.* **myth′ic, -al,** relating to myths: fabulous: imaginary.—*adv.* **myth′ically.**—*n.* **mythol′ogy,** a collection of myths: the scientific study of myths.—*adjs.* **mytholog′ic, -al,** relating to mythology, fabulous.—*adv.* **mytholog′ically.**—*n.* **mythol′ogist,** one versed in, or who writes on, mythology. [Gr. *mythos,* story.]

myxomatosis, *miks-ō-má-tō′sis, n.* a contagious disease of rabbits. [Gr. *myxa,* mucus.]

Neutral vowels in unaccented syllables: *em′pér-ór;* for certain sounds in foreign words see p. ix.

N

nabob, *nā'bob, n.* (*obs.*) a nawab: a European who has enriched himself in the East: any man of great wealth or importance. [Hindustani *nawwāb*. See **nawab.**]

nacre, *nā'kêr, n.* mother-of-pearl or a shellfish yielding it. [Fr.; prob. of Eastern origin.]

nadir, *nā'dēr, -dêr, n.* the point of the celestial sphere opposite to the zenith, i.e. that directly under where the observer stands: the lowest point of anything. [Fr.,—Ar. *nadīr* (*nazīr*), opposite to.]

nag, *nag, n.* a horse, esp. a small one. [M.E. *nagge*; origin obscure; cf. Middle Du. *negge, negghe* (mod Du. *nog, negge*).]

nag, *nag, v.t* to find fault with constantly: to worry: to cause pain to continually:—*pr.p.* nagg'ing; *pa.p.* nagged. [Cf. Norw. and Swed. *nagga,* to gnaw.]

naiad, *nī'ad, n.* a nymph, presiding over rivers and springs. [Gr. *nāias, -ados,* pl. *-adēs,* from *naein,* to flow.]

naïf, *nä-ēf', adj., masc.* form, generally replaced by *fem.* **naïve** (q.v.)

nail, *nāl, n.* a horny plate at the end of a finger or toe: the claw of a bird or other animal: a thin pointed piece of metal for fastening wood: a measure of length (2¼ inches).—*v.t.* to fasten as with nails: to pin down, hold fast (e.g. a person to a promise): to waylay and compel the attention of: to expose so as to stop the circulation of (e.g. a lie).—*ns.* **nail'er,** a maker of nails; **nail'ery,** a place where nails are made, **nail'-rod,** a strip of iron to be made into nails: a strong, coarse tobacco.—**hit the nail on the head,** to give the true explanation, or express the exact essential meaning. [O.E. *nægel;* Ger. *nagel.*]

naïve, *nä-ēv', adj.* with natural or unaffected simplicity in thought, speech, or manners: artless, ingenuous.—*n.* **naïveté** (*nä-ēv'tā*). [Fr., fem. of *naïf*—L. *nātīvus,* natural.]

naked, *nāk'id, adj.* without clothes: without the natural or usual covering (e.g. of trees): without a sheath or case (e.g. a sword, a light): unprovided (with clothes and other necessities): defenceless: unconcealed (e.g. dislike): undisguised (e.g. truth).—*n.* **nakedness.**—**naked eye,** the eye unassisted by glasses of any kind. [O.E. *nacod;* Ger. *nackt.*]

namby-pamby, *nam'bi-pam'bi, adj.* sentimentally childish (of talk or writings): insipid: weakly sentimental (of a person). [Nickname for *Ambrose* Philips (1674-1749), whose writings include simple odes to children.]

name, *nām, n.* that by which a person or a thing is known or called: a designation: reputed character (e.g. for honesty; of a miser): reputation: a celebrity: family or clan: authority: behalf: (*gram.*) a noun.—*v.t.* to give a name to: to speak of by name: to nominate: to mention formally (an M.P.) in the House of Commons as guilty of disorderly conduct.—*n.* **name'-dropping,** casual mention of important persons as if they were one's friends, in order to impress.—*v.t.* **name'-drop.**—*adj.* **name'less,** without a name: anonymous: undistinguished: too horrible to be named.—*adv.* **name'ly,** videlicet, that is to say.—*n.* **name'sake,** one bearing the same name as another.—**in name,** nominally: in appearance or seeming, not in reality; **proper name** (see **proper**). [O.E. *nama;* Ger. *name;* L. *nōmen.*]

nancy-pretty, variant of **none-so-pretty.**

nankeen, *nan-kēn', n.* a buff-coloured cotton cloth first made at *Nanking* in China.

nanny, nannie, *nan'i, n.* a children's nurse, esp. one trained to take care of children. [From *Nan—Ann(e).*]

nanny, *nan'i, n.* a female goat.—Also **nann'ygoat.** [Same as **nanny** (1).]

nano-, *nān'ō-, nan'o-,* in composition, one thousand millionth, as in **nan'osecond:** of microscopic size. [Gr. *nanos,* a dwarf.]

nap, *nap, v.i.* to take a short or casual sleep:—*pr.p.* napp'ing; *pa.p.* napped.—Also *n.*—**catch napping,** to take off one's guard: to detect (someone) in an error that might have been avoided. [O.E. *knappian.*]

nap, *nap, n.* a woolly surface on cloth (see **pile**): a cloth with such a surface: a downy covering or surface on anything.—*adj.* **nap'less,** without nap, threadbare. [M.E. *noppe;* app.—Middle Du. or Middle Low Ger. *noppe.*]

nap, *nap, n.* a game of cards. See **napoleon.**

napalm, *nā'pām, na', n.* a petroleum jelly, highly inflammable, used in bombs and flame-throwers. [*na*phthenate *palm*itate.]

nape, *nāp, n.* the back of the neck.

napery, *nā'pêr-i, n.* (*arch.* and *Scot.*) linen, esp. for the table. [O.Fr. *naperie*—Low L. *napāria*—*napa,* a cloth—L. *mappa,* a napkin.]

naphtha, *naf'tha* (sometimes *nap'tha*), *n.* petroleum: a vague name for the inflammable liquids distilled from coal-tar, wood, &c.—*n.* **naph'thalene,** a greyish-white, inflammable substance got by distillation of coal-tar. [Gr.]

Napierian, Naperian, *nā-pēr'i-an, adj.* pertaining to John *Napier* of Merchiston, Edinburgh (1550-1617)—used esp. of the system of natural logarithms (the earliest of all systems) invented by him.

napkin, *nap'kin, n.* a small square of linen, paper, &c., used at table or otherwise. [Dim. of Fr. *nappe*—L. *mappa.*]

napoleon, *na-pōl'yón,* or *-i-ón, n.* a twenty-franc gold coin issued by *Napoleon:* a French modification of the game of euchre, each player receiving five cards and playing for himself (commonly **nap**).—*adj.* **Napoleon'ic,** relating to Napoleon I or III.—**go nap,** in the game of napoleon, to undertake to win all five tricks: to risk all.

---

fāte, fär; mē, hûr (her); *mīne; mōte, för; mūte; mōōn, fŏŏt;* THen (then)

nappy, *nap'i, n.* a baby's napkin.

narcissus, *när-sis'us, n.* the genus, of the family *Amaryllis,* to which daffodils belong:—*pl.* **narciss'uses, -ciss'ī.** [L.,—Gr. *Narkissos,* a youth who fell in love with his own image.]

narcotic, *när-kot'ik, adj.* producing torpor, sleep, or deadness.—*n.* anything producing a narcotic effect, e.g. a drug, an inert gas. [Gr. *narkōtikos—narkē,* numbness, torpor.]

nard, *närd, n.* an aromatic plant usually called *spikenard:* an ointment prepared from it. [L. *nardus—*Gr. *nardos;* apparently an Eastern word.]

narghile, *när'gil-i, n.* a hookah (q.v.). [Pers. *nārgīleh—nārgīl,* a coconut (from which it used to be made).]

narrate, *na-rāt', v.t.* to give a continuous account of (details of an event, or a series of events). —*n.* **narrā'tion,** act of telling: that which is told: an orderly account of a series of events.—*adj.* **narrative** (*nar'a-tiv*), narrating: giving an account of any occurrence: storytelling.—*n.* that which is narrated: a story.—*n.* **narrā'tor,** one who tells a story. [L. *narrāre, -ātum,* prob.—*gnārus,* knowing.]

narrow, *nar'ō, adj.* of little breadth: of small extent: confining: limited (e.g. fortune or circumstances): with little to spare, little margin (e.g. escape, majority): careful (e.g. search, scrutiny): bigoted or illiberal in views: parsimonious.—*n.* a narrow part of place: (usu. in *pl.*) a narrow passage, channel or strait.—*v.t.* to make narrower: to contract.—Also *v.i.—adj.* **narr'ow-gauge,** of a railway, less than 4 ft. 8½ in. in gauge.—*adv.* **narr'owly.**—*adj.* **narr'ow-mind'ed,** of a narrow or illiberal mind.—*ns.* **narr'ow-mind'edness; narr'owness.—narrow seas,** the seas between Great Britain and the Continent and between Great Britain and Ireland. [O.E. *nearu.*]

narwhal, *när'wäl, n.* a kind of whale with one large projecting tusk (occasionally two tusks) in the male. [Dan. *narhval;* O.N. *nāhvalr* is supposed to be from *nār,* corpse, *hvalr,* whale, from the creature's pallid colour.]

nasal, *nā'zál, adj.* belonging to the nose: affected by, or sounded through, the nose.—*n.* a sound uttered through the nose.—*v.i.* **nā'salise,** to render nasal, as a sound.—*adv.* **nā'sally,** by or through the nose. [L. *nāsus,* the nose.]

nascent, *nās'ent, adj.* coming into being. [L. *nāscens, -entis,* pr.p. of *nāscī, nātus,* to be born.]

nasturtium, *nas-tûr'shùm, n.* a genus of plants with a pungent taste, one species of which is the garden flower known as Indian cress. [L. *nāsus,* nose, *torquēre,* to twist (from its pungency).]

nasty, *nas'ti, adj.* disgustingly foul, nauseous: morally filthy: (*lit.* and *fig.*) disagreeable, unpalatable, or annoying: difficult to deal with (e.g. problem): dangerous or serious (e.g. fall, illness).—*adv.* **nas'tily.**—*n.* **nas'tiness.** [Perh. for earlier *nasky* (cf. Swed. dial. *naskug, nasket*); or perh. conn. with Du. *nestig,* dirty.]

natal, *nā'tál, adj.* of or connected with birth: native. [L. *nātālis—nāscī, nātus,* to be born.]

natation, *nat-,* or *nāt-ā'sh(ó)n, n.* swimming.— *adj.* **nā'tatory,** of, pertaining to, used in, swimming. [L. *natāns, -antis,* pr.p. of *natāre,* freq. of *nāre,* to swim.]

nation, *nā'sh(ó)n, n.* a body of people marked off by common descent, language, culture, or historical tradition: the people of a state.—*adj.* **national** (*na'shón-ál*), pertaining to a nation or nations: common to the whole nation: public (e.g. debt): attached to one's own country.—*n.* (usu. in *pl.*) a member or fellow-member of a nation.—*v.t.* **na'tionalise,** to make national: to transfer ownership of from individuals to the state (e.g. *to nationalise the coal-mines*).—*n.* **na'tionalist,** one who favours or strives after the unity, independence, interests, or domination of a nation.—*adj.* **nationalis'tic.**—*ns.* **na'tionalism; nationality** (*-al'i-ti*), membership of a particular nation: fact or state of belonging to a particular nation: nationhood.—*adv.* **na'tionally.**—*adj.* **na'tionwide,** covering the whole nation.—**national anthem,** an official song or hymn of a nation sung or played on ceremonial occasions; **national church,** a church established by law in a country; **national debt,** money borrowed by the government of a country and not yet paid back; **national park,** an area owned by or for the nation; **national school,** in England, a school connected with the National Society, established in 1811 to promote elementary education; **national service,** compulsory service in the armed forces; **national socialism,** the doctrines of the **National Socialist party,** an extreme nationalistic fascist party in Germany, led by Adolf Hitler (d. 1945). [L. *nātiō, -ōnis—nāscī, nātus,* to be born.]

native, *nā'tiv, adj.* natural to a person or thing, innate, inherent: in a natural state, simple, unaffected (as, *native wood-notes*): of, pertaining to, or belonging to the place of one's birth (e.g. language): belonging to the people inhabiting a country originally or at the time of its discovery, esp. when they are coloured or uncivilised (e.g. customs): indigenous, not exotic (of plants): occurring naturally as a mineral, not formed artificially: occurring naturally uncombined (as a metal).—*n.* one born in any place: an original inhabitant: a white born in Australia: (*coll.*) vaguely, a coloured person: an oyster raised in a British (artificial) bed.—*n.* **nativity** (*na-tiv'i-ti*), state of being born: time, place, and manner of birth: state or place of being produced: a horoscope: (*cap.*) the birth of the Saviour, or of the Virgin Mary, or of John the Baptist, or a festival commemorating one of these: (*cap.*) a picture, &c., showing a scene from the early infancy of Christ. [L. *nātīvus—nāscī, nātus,* to be born.]

natron, *nā'trón, n.* an impure carbonate of soda, the nitre of the Bible. In composition **natro(n)-** indicates the presence of sodium. —*n.* **nātrium,** sodium (whence its chemical symbol Na). [Fr. *natrūn—*Gr. *nitron.*]

natter, *nat'er, v.i.* to chatter, sometimes grumblingly: to talk much about little.—Also *n.*

natterjack, *nat'ér-jak, n.* a toad with a yellow stripe down the back. [Origin unknown.]

natty, *nat'i, adj.* dapper, spruce.—*adv.* **natt'ily.** [Possibly connected with **neat.**]

natural, *nat'ūr-ál, na'chûr-ál, adj.* produced by, or according to, nature: not miraculous: not wholly or partly the work of man: having the

---

Neutral vowels in unaccented syllables: *em'pér-ór;* for certain sounds in foreign words see p. ix.

feelings that may be expected to come by nature, kindly: happening in the usual course (e.g. a result): inborn, not acquired (of the qualities of an individual): spontaneous, unaffected, simple (e.g. manner): life-like (e.g. a portrait): pertaining to nature as an object of study or research (e.g. *natural history*): illegitimate: (*mus.*) according to the usual diatonic scale.—*n.* an idiot: one having a natural aptitude (for), or being an obvious choice (for): a thing assured of success by its very nature, a certainty: (*mus.*) a character (♮) cancelling a preceding sharp or flat.—*v.t.* **nat′uralise**, to make natural: to adapt to a different climate (as plants): to adopt (foreign words) into one's language: to grant (people of foreign birth) the privileges of natural-born citizens.—*ns.* **naturalisā′tion; nat′uralism**, practice of, or attachment to, what is natural: in art or literature, a close following of nature without idealisation: in philosophy, a worldview that regards everything as without supernatural or spiritual meaning: in religion, a denial of the miraculous and supernatural; **nat′uralist**, one who studies animals or plants, esp. in the field.—*adj.* **naturalist′ic**, pertaining to, or in accordance with, nature: belonging to the doctrines of naturalism.—*adv.* **nat′urally**. —*n.* **nat′uralness**.—**natural gas**, any gas issuing from the earth, whether from natural fissures or from bored wells; **natural history**, originally the description of all that is in nature, now used of the sciences that deal with the earth and its productions—botany, zoology, and mineralogy, esp. field zoology; **natural logarithm**, a logarithm to the **natural base *e*,**

$$e \text{ being } 1 + \frac{1}{1} + \frac{1}{1.2} + \frac{1}{1.2.3} \ldots, \text{ or } 2 \cdot 71828 \ldots;$$

natural order, in botany, a category now usually called a family; **natural philosophy**, the science of the physical properties of bodies, physics; **natural science**, the science of *nature*, as distinguished from mental and moral science, and from mathematics; **natural selection**, evolution by the *survival of the fittest* (i.e. of those forms of plants and animals best adjusted to the conditions under which they live), with inheritance of their qualities by succeeding generations; **natural theology**, or **natural religion**, religion derived from reason without revelation. [L. *natūrālis* —*nātūra*, nature.]

nature, *nā′chŭr, -tŭr, n.* the power that regulates the world: the established order of things: the external world, esp. as untouched by man: the essential qualities of anything: constitution: kind or order: character, instinct, or disposition: a primitive undomesticated condition before society is organised.—*adj.* **nā′tured**, having a certain temper or disposition (used in compounds, as *good-natured*).—*ns.* **na′ture(-)knowl′edge, nā′ture(-)stud′y**, a branch of school work intended to cultivate the powers of seeing and enjoying nature by the observation of natural objects (e.g. plants, animals, &c.). [Fr.,—L. *nātūra*—*nascī, nātus*, to be born.]

naught, *nöt, n.* nothing.—*adj.* (*arch.*—used predicatively) worthless, bad.—Also **nought**.—

bring to naught, to ruin, frustrate; **come to naught**, to fail completely; **set at naught**, to disregard (e.g. wishes, instructions): to treat (a person) as of no account. [O.E. *nāht, nāwiht*—*nā*, never, *wiht*, whit.]

naughty, *nöt′i, adj.* bad: ill-behaved (now chiefly applied to children).—*adv.* **naught′ily**. —*n.* **naught′iness**. [naught.]

nausea, *nö′si-a, nö′shi-a, n.* sea-sickness: a feeling of inclination to vomit: loathing.—*v.i.* **nau′seate**, to feel nausea or disgust.—*v.t.* to loathe: to strike with disgust.—*adjs.* **nau′seating**, causing nausea or (*fig.*) disgust; **nau′seous** (*-shŭs*), producing nausea: loathsome.—*adv.* **nau′seously**.—*n.* **nau′seousness**. [L.,—Gr. *nautiā*, sea-sickness—*naus*, a ship.]

nautch, *nöch, n.* in India, a performance of professional dancing women known as **nautch′-girls**. [Hindustani *nāch*, dance.]

nautical, *nöt′ik-ál, adj.* of or pertaining to ships, to sailors, or to navigation.—**nautical mile** (see **mile**). [L. *nauticus*—Gr. *nautikos*—*nautēs*, sailor—*naus*, a ship.]

nautilus, *nö′ti-lus, n.* a cephalopod of southern seas, with a chambered external shell (*pearly nautilus*): a Mediterranean cephalopod of a different order, related to the octopus, the female of which has a thin shell (*paper nautilus*):—*pl.* **nau′tiluses**, or **nau′tili**. [L.,—Gr. *nautilos*, a sailor, a paper nautilus *naus*, a ship.]

naval, *nā′vál, adj.* pertaining to warships or to a navy.—**naval brigade**, a body of seamen organised to serve on land. [L. *nāvālis*—*nāvis*, a ship.]

nave, *nāv, n.* the main part of a church, west of the transept and the choir, usu. separated from the aisles by pillars. [L. *nāvis*, a ship.]

nave, *nāv, n.* the hub or central part of a wheel, through which the axle passes. [O.E. *nafu*; cf. Du. *naaf*, Ger. *nabe*.]

navel, *nā′vél, n.* the depression in the centre of the abdomen marking the position of former attachment of the umbilical cord: a central point. [O.E. *nafela*, dim. of *nafu*, nave.]

navicert, *nav′-*, or *nāv′i-sért, n.* a certificate granted by a belligerent to a neutral ship testifying that she carries no contraband of war. [**navigational certificate**.]

navigate, *nav′i-gāt, v.i.* to manage or direct on its course a ship, aircraft, motor vehicle, &c.: to find one's way and keep one's course.—*v.t.* to direct the course of (a ship, an aircraft, motor vehicle): to sail or fly across (a sea) or up and down (a river). *adj.* **nav′igable**, sufficiently deep, wide, &c., to give passage to ships: dirigible.—*ns.* **navigabil′ity, nav′igableness**.—*ns.* **naviga′tion**, the act, science, or art of directing the movement of ships or aircraft; **nav′igator**, one who navigates or sails: one who directs the course of a ship, &c. [L. *nāvigāre, -ātum*—*nāvis*, a ship, *agĕre*, to drive.]

navvy, *nav′i, n.* a labourer—originally a labourer on a canal or other waterway. [**navigator**.]

navy, *nā′vi, n.* a fleet of ships: the whole of a nation's ships-of-war: the officers and men belonging to a nation's warships. [O.Fr. *navie*—L. *nāvis*, a ship.]

nawab, *nā-wäb′, -wöb′, n.* a Mohammedan prince or noble: (*rarely*) a nabob. [Hindustani *nawwāb*—Ar. *nawwāb*, respectful pl. of *nā-ib*, deputy.]

nay, *nā*, *adv.* no: not only so but: and even more than that.—*n.* a denial: a vote against (a motion). [M.E. *nay*, *nai*—O.N. *nei*; Dan. *nei*; cog. with **no**.]

Nazarene, *naz'ár-ēn*, *n.* a follower of Jesus of Nazareth, originally used of Christians in contempt: an early Jewish Christian.

Nazarite, *naz'ár-īt*, *n.* a Jew who vowed to abstain from strong drink, &c.—*n.* **Naz'aritism** (*-īt-izm*). [Heb. *nāzar*, to consecrate.]

naze, *nāz*, *n.* a headland or cape. [O.E. *næs*; cf. **ness**.]

Nazi, *nä'tsē*, *n.* and *adj.* for *Na*tional-*sozi*alist, National Socialist, Hitlerite.—*n.* **Naz'ism**.—*v.t.* **Naz'ify**. [Ger.]

Neanderthal, *ne-an'dér-tal*, *adj.* of, or pertaining to, a Palaeolithic (i.e. Old Stone Age) species of man whose remains were first found in 1857 in a cave in the *Neanderthal*, a valley in the Rhineland.

neap, *nēp*, *adj.* (of a tide) of smallest range (less high and less low than a *spring-tide*—q.v.), occurring when the moon is at the first or third quarter and sun and moon are acting against each other.—*n.* a neap-tide.—*adj.* **neaped**, left aground between spring-tides. [O.E. *nēp*, apparently meaning helpless; *nēp-flod*, neap-tide.]

Neapolitan, *nē-a-pol'i-tán*, *adj.* pertaining to the city of *Naples* or its inhabitants. [L. *Neapolītānus*—Gr. *Neápolis*, Naples—*neos*, new, *polis*, city.]

near, *nēr*, *adv.* to or at a little distance: almost.—*prep.* close to.—*adj.* not far away in place or time: close in kin, friendship, or other relation: close in imitation or resemblance: approximate: narrow, barely missing or avoiding something: stingy: (of horses, vehicles, &c.) left, left-hand.—*v.t.* and *v.i.* to approach: to come nearer.—*adv.* **near'ly**, at or within a short distance: closely: intimately: scrutinisingly: almost: stingily.—*n.* **near'ness.**—*adj.* **near'sight'ed**, short-sighted.—*n.* **near'sight'edness.**—**a near miss**, (*lit.* and *fig.*) a miss that is almost a hit. [O.E. *nēar*, comp. of *nēah*, nigh (adv.), and O.N. *nǣr*, comp. (but also used as positive) of *nā*, nigh; cf. Ger. *näher*.]

neat, *nēt*, *n.* an ox, cow, bull, &c.: cattle of this kind as distinct from horses, sheep, and other flocks and herds.—*n.* **neat'-herd**. [O.E. *nēat*, cattle, a beast—*nēotan*, *niotan*, to use.]

neat, *nēt*, *adj.* trim, tidy, elegant in form: adroit or skilful: skilfully made or done: well and concisely put: ingenious, effective: undiluted (of liquor).—*adv.* **neat'ly.**—*n.* **neat'ness.** [Fr. *net*—L. *nitidus*, shining—*nitēre*, to shine.]

neb, *neb*, *n.* a beak or bill: the nose. [O.E. *nebb*, beak, face; cog. with Du. *neb*, beak.]

nebula, *neb'ū-la*, *n.* a faint, misty appearance in the heavens produced either by a group of stars too distant to be seen singly, or by diffused gaseous matter: a slight opacity of the cornea of the eye—*pl.* **neb'ulae** (*-lē*).—*adjs.* **neb'ular**, pertaining to nebulae; **neb'ulous**, like, of the nature of, or surrounded by, a nebula: misty, vague, formless (used figuratively of a theory or a discourse lacking in

definition, a quality difficult to define, &c.).—*ns.* **nebulos'ity**, **neb'ulousness**. [L. *nebula*, mist; cf. Ger. *nephelē*, cloud, mist.]

necessary, *nes'es-ár-i*, *adj.* indispensable, requisite: requiring to be done: unavoidable or inevitable.—*n.* that which cannot be done without (food, &c.)—used chiefly in *pl.*—*adv.* **nec'essarily**. [L. *necessārius*.]

necessity, *nē-ses'i-ti*, *n.* constraint or compulsion exerted by the laws of the universe or by the nature of things: the constraining power of circumstances: something essential to a projected end: imperative need: poverty.—*n.* **necessitā'rianism**, determinism (q.v.).—*n.* and *adj.* **necessitā'rian**.—*v.t.* **necess'itāte**, to make necessary: to render unavoidable: to compel.—*adj.* **necess'itous**, in necessity, very poor, destitute.—*adv.* **necess'itously**.—*n.* **necess'itousness**. [L. *necessitās*, *-ātis*.]

neck, *nek*, *n.* the part connecting head and trunk: the part connecting the head and body of anything (e.g. of a violin): any narrow connecting part (e.g. an isthmus): anything narrow and throat-like (e.g. the upper part of a bottle).—*v.t.* and *v.i.* (*slang*) to embrace.—*ns.* **neck'cloth**, a piece of folded cloth worn round the neck by men; **neck'erchief**, a kerchief for the neck; **neck'lace** (*-lis*, *-lás*), a lace, chain, or string of beads or precious stones worn on the neck; **neck'tie**, a scarf or band tied round the neck; **neck'-verse**, the verse (generally Ps. li. 1) used as a test of ability to read for those who claimed benefit of clergy (q.v.), success giving the privilege of being branded on the hand instead of being hanged.—**neck and crop** (see **crop**); **neck and neck**, exactly equal: side by side; **neck or nothing**, risking everything; **stick one's neck out**, to put oneself at risk, to invite trouble or contradiction. [O.E. *hnecca*; Ger. *nacken*.]

necro-, *nek'rō-*, *-ro-*, in composition, dead, dead body.—*ns.* **necrol'ogy**, an obituary list; **nec'rō-mancer**, a sorcerer; **nec'rōmancy**, the art of revealing future events by calling up and questioning the spirits of the dead: enchantment.—*adjs.* **necrōman'tic**, **-al**.—*adv.* **necrōman'tically**.—*ns.* **necrop'olis**, a cemetery; **nec'ropsy**, a post-mortem examination; **necrō'sis**, death of part of the living body.—*adj.* **necrot'ic**, affected by necrosis. [Gr. *nekros*, dead body, dead.]

nectar, *nek'tár*, *n.* the beverage of the gods, giving life and beauty: a delicious beverage: a sugary fluid exuded by plants, usually from some part of the flower, which attracts insects.—*adjs.* **nectā'reous**, **nec'tarous**, of or like nectar; **nec'tared**, imbued with nectar: mingled or abounding with nectar; **nec'tarine** (*-in*), sweet as nectar.—*n.* (*-ēn*, *-in*) a variety of peach with a smooth fruit.—*n.* **nec'tary**, the part of a flower that secretes nectar. [Gr. *nektar*; ety. uncertain.]

née, *nā*, *adj.* born (placed before a married woman's maiden-name, to show her own family, as Rebecca Crawley, *née* Sharp). [Fr. fem. of *né*, pa.p. of *naître*, to be born—L. *nascī*, *nātus*, to be born.]

need, *nēd*, *n.* necessity: a time of difficulty or trouble: a state that requires relief; want of the means of living.—*v.t.* to have occasion for:

Neutral vowels in unaccented syllables: *em'pér-ór*; for certain sounds in foreign words see p. ix.

to want.—*v.i.* to be necessary: to be obliged to (used as an auxiliary).—*adjs.* **need′ful**, needy: necessary, requisite; **need′less**, unnecessary: uncalled for.—*adv.* **need′lessly.**—*n.* **need′lessness.**—*adj.* **need′y**, very poor.—*n.* **need′iness**, **needs must**, must needs, must of necessity. [O.E. *nēd*, *nīed*, *nȳd*; Du. *nood*, Ger. *noth.*]

needle, *nēd′l*, *n.* a small, sharp instrument for sewing: any similar slender, pointed instrument for knitting, etching, dissection, playing a gramophone record, &c.: a pointer on a dial: the long, narrow, needle-like leaf of a pine-tree: (*coll.*) a hypodermic injection: irritation.—*v.t.* to pass through: to irritate, to goad: to goad into action: to heckle.—*adj.* (of a contest) intensely keen and critical, sometimes involving animosity.—*ns.* **need′leful**, sufficient thread for one threading of a needle; **need′lewoman**, a woman skilled in sewing: a seamstress; **need′lework**, work done with a needle: the business of a seamstress.—**a needle in a haystack**, anything very difficult or impossible to find. [O.E. *nǣdl*; Ger. *nadel*; cog. with Ger. *nähen*, to sew, L. *nēre*, to spin.]

ne′er, *nār*, *adv.* contr. of **never.**

nefarious, *ni-fā′ri-us*, *adj.* extremely wicked, villainous.—*adv.* **nefā′riously.**—*n.* **nefā′riousness.** [L. *nefārius*—*nefās*, wrong, crime—*ne-*, not, *fas*, divine law, prob. from *fārī*, to speak.]

negate, *ni-gāt′*, *v.t.* to deny: to nullify: to imply the non-existence of.—*n.* **negation** (*ne-gā′sh(ó)n*), act of saying no: denial: the absence or opposite (of something that is actual, positive, or affirmative).—*adj.* **negative** (*neg′ātiv*), expressing denial, refusal, or prohibition—opp. to *affirmative*: lacking distinguishing features, devoid of positive attributes—opp. to *positive*: (*logic*) denying the connection between a subject and a predicate: (*math.*) less than nothing: reckoned or measured in the direction opposite to that chosen as positive: (*elect.*) at relatively lower potential of, having, or producing, negative electricity.—*n.* a proposition by which something is denied: an image in which the lights and shades are the opposite of those in nature: a photographic plate bearing such an image: (*gram.*) a word or grammatical form that expresses denial or negation.—*v.t.* to prove the contrary of: to reject by vote.—*adv.* **neg′atively.**—*n.* **neg′ativeness.**—**negative pole**, that pole of a magnet which turns to the south when the magnet swings freely; **negative proton**, antiproton: a particle of same mass as a proton but with negative charge. [L. *negāre*, *-ātum*, to deny.]

negatron, *neg′ā-tron*, *n.* same as **electron**, a particle having a negative charge—opp. to a positron.

neglect, *ni-glekt′*, *v.t.* to pay little or no respect or attention to: to ignore as of no consequence: to leave uncared for: to omit by carelessness.—*n.* disregard: slight: omission.—*adj.* **neglect′ful**, careless: accustomed to omit or neglect duties, &c.: slighting.—*adv.* **neglect′fully.**—*n.* **neglect′fulness.** [L. *neglegēre*, *neglectum*—*neg-* or *nec-*, not, *legēre*, to gather.]

négligé, *nā′glē-zhā*, *n.* easy undress.—*n.* **négligee** (*neg-li-jē′; hist.*) a loose gown worn by

women in the 18th century: now a women's loose decorative dressing-gown of flimsy material. [Fr. *négligé*, neglected.]

negligence, *neg′li-jéns*, *n.* carelessness or want of attention: an act of carelessness: omission of duty, esp. such care for the interests of others as the law may require: a careless indifference, a disregard of convention in dress or manner, or in literary or artistic style.—*adj.* **neg′ligent**,—*adv.* **neg′ligently.**—*adj.* **neg′ligible**, such as may be ignored or left out of consideration, esp. as being very small. [L. *negligentia* for *neglegentia*—*neglegēre*, to neglect.]

negotiate, *ni-gō′shi-āt*, *v.i.* to bargain (with), to confer (with) for the purpose of coming to an agreement or arrangement.—*v.t.* to arrange for by agreement (e.g. a treaty, a loan): to transfer or exchange for value (e.g. a bill, cheque): to get past (e.g. an obstacle, a difficulty).—*adj.* **nego′tiable** (of bills, drafts, cheques, &c.), capable of being transferred or assigned in the course of business from one person to another. *ns.* **negotiabil′ity**; **negotiā′tion**; **nego′tiator.** [L. *negōtiārī*, *-ātus*—*negōtium*, business—*neg-*, not, *ōtium*, leisure.]

Negrito, *ne-grē′to*, *n.* a member of any of several diminutive Negroid races, esp. in the Malayan region or in Polynesia.

Negro, *nē′grō*, *n.* a member of the black-skinned race of mankind in Africa or originating in Africa, esp. one characterised by woolly hair, protruding lips and a broad, flat nose.—Also *adj.*—*ns.* **Nē′gress**, a Negro woman or girl; **nē′gro-corn** (*W. Indies*), millet; **nē′grohead**, tobacco soaked in molasses and pressed into cakes, named from its colour.—*adj.* **nē′groid.** [Sp. *negro*—L. *niger*, *nigra*, *nigrum*, black.]

negus, *nē′gus*, *n.* a beverage of port or sherry with hot water, sweetened and spiced. [Said to be from Colonel *Negus*, its first maker, in Queen Anne's time.]

Negus, *nē′gus*, *n.* the title of the kings of Abyssinia.

neigh, *nā*, *v.i.* to utter the cry of a horse:—*pr.p.* neigh′ing; *pa.t.* and *pa.p.* neighed (*nād*).—*n.* the cry of a horse [O.E. *hnǣgan.*]

neighbour, *nā′bór*, *n.* a person who dwells near another.—*adj.* (*arch.* and *U.S.*) neighbouring.—*v.t.* and *v.i.* to live or be near.—*n.* **neigh′bourhood**, state of being neighbours: a district, esp. with reference to its inhabitants: a near position, nearness: (*math.*) all the points that surround a given point in a specified degree of closeness.—*adjs.* **neigh′bouring**, adjoining; **neigh′bourly**, friendly, sociable—also *adv.*—*n.* **neigh′bourliness.**—**in the neighbourhood of**, (*fig.*) somewhere about, approximately. [O.E. *nēahgebūr*—*nēah*, near, *gebūr* or *būr*, a farmer.]

neither, *nī′THér*, or *nē′THér*, *adj.* and *pron.* not either.—*conj.* (*arch.*) and not, nor yet.—*adv.* not either. [O.E. *nāther*, *nāwther*, abbrev. of *nāhwæther*—*nā*, never, *hwæther*, whether; the vowel assimilated to **either.**]

Nemesis, *nem′e-sis*, *n.* (*myth.*) the Greek goddess of retribution: (often without *cap.*) retributive justice. [Gr. *nemesis*, retribution—*nemein*, to deal out, dispense.]

nenuphar, *nen′ū-fär*, *n.* a water-lily. [Low L.]

neo-, *nē′ō-,* in composition, new (opp. of *palaeo-*), as in **neoclassic,** belonging to a revival of classicism; **neonāt′al,** newly born. [Gr. *neos.*]

neocolonialism, *nē-ō-kol-ōn′i-al-izm, n.* policy of a strong nation of obtaining control over a weaker through economic pressure, &c.

neodymium, *nē-ō-dim′ium, n.* a metallic element (symbol Nd; at. no. 60), a member of the rare-earth group. [**neo-,** and *didymium,* a mixture of neodymium and praseodymium (q.v.), formerly thought to be an element—Gr. *didymos,* twin.]

neo-Hellenism, *nē-ō-hel′én-izm, n.* the modern Hellenism inspired by the ancient: the devotion to ancient Greek ideals in literature and art, esp. in the Italian Renaissance.—Also **Neohell′enism.**

neolithic, *nē-ō-lith′ik, adj.* of the later or more advanced Stone Age—opp. to *palaeolithic.* [Gr. *neos,* new, *lithos,* a stone.]

neology, *nē-ol′o-ji, n.* the introduction of new words, or of new senses of old words, into a language: a new doctrine or doctrines.—*adj.* **neolog′ic, -al.**—*v.i.* **neol′ogise,** to introduce new words or doctrines.—*n.* **neol′ogism,** a new word, phrase, or doctrine. [Gr. *neos,* new, *logos,* word.]

neon, *nē′on, n.* a rare gaseous element (symbol Ne; at. no. 10) found in the atmosphere by Sir Wm. Ramsay (1852-1916).—**neon lamp,** an electric discharge lamp containing neon and other inert gases, giving a red or other coloured glow, used for advertising signs: loosely, one of a variety of tubular fluorescent lamps giving light of various colours; **neon lighting.** [Neuter of Gr. *neos,* new.]

neophyte, *nē′ō-fīt, n.* a new convert: one newly baptised: a newly ordained priest: a novice, tyro, beginner. [Gr. *neophytos,* newly planted—*phyein,* to produce.]

neoytterbium. See **ytterbium.**

Neozoic, *nē-ō-zō′ik, adj.* denoting all rocks from the end of the Secondary or Mesozoic era down to the most recent formations—opposed to *Palaeozoic.* [Gr. *neos,* new, *zōikos,* of animals.]

nepenthe, *ni-pen′thē, n.* (*poet.*) a sorrow-lulling drink or drug: the plant yielding it.—*n.* **nepen′thes** (*-thēz*), nepenthe: the pitcher-plant genus. [Gr. *nepenthēs, -es*—pfx. *nē-,* not, *penthos,* grief.]

neper, *nā′per, nē′-, n.* a unit for expressing the ratio of two currents, or two voltages, &c., the number of nepers being equal to the natural logarithm of the ratio. [John *Napier;* see **Napierian.**]

nephew, *nev′ū,* or *nef′ū, n.* the son of a brother or sister: (*obs.*) a grandson:—*fem.* **niece** (q.v.). [O.Fr. *neveu*—L. *nepōs, nepōtis,* grandson; cf. O.E. *nefa,* Ger. *neffe,* nephew.]

nephro-, *nef′rō-,* **nephr-,** in composition, kidney [Gr. *nephros,* a kidney]:—e.g. *ns.* **nephralgia** (*nef-ral′ji-a*), **nephral′gy,** pain in the kidneys (Gr. *algos,* pain).—*adj.* **nephrī′tic,** of, or in, the kidneys.—*n.* **nephrī′tis,** inflammation of the kidneys.

ne plus ultra, *nē plus ul′tra, nā plŏŏs ŏŏl′tra,* nothing further: the uttermost point or extreme perfection of anything. [L.]

nepotism, *nep′o-tizm, n.* favouritism shown to relations or (*loosely*) friends in bestowing office or appointing to posts: orig. used of the bestowal of patronage by certain popes on their so-called 'nephews'—really their illegitimate sons.—*n.* **nep′otist.** [L. *nepōs, nepōtis,* a grandson.]

Neptune, *nep′tūn, n.* a remote planet discovered in 1846: chief god of the sea.—*adj.* **Neptū′nian,** pertaining to Neptune or to the sea: (*geol.*) formed by water. [L. *Neptūnus.*]

neptunium, *nep-tūn′i-ūm, n.* a radioactive element (symbol Np; at. no. 93) produced artificially by nuclear reaction between uranium and neutrons (see *plutonium*). [L. *Neptunus.*]

nereid, *nē′rē-id, n.* (*Gr. myth.*) a sea-nymph or daughter of the sea-god *Nereus:* any of a number of marine worms, superficially like long centipedes. [Gr. *nērēis* or *nēreis*—Nēreus.]

nerve, *nûrv, n.* (now chiefly *fig.*) a sinew (as *to strain every nerve*): an animal sinew used as a bowstring: bodily strength: the source of energy in any system: a cord that conveys impulses between the brain or other centre and some part of the body: self-command under strain: cool courage: (*pl.*) the state of sensitiveness or of adjustment between the nervous system and other parts of the body: exaggerated sensitiveness: (*bot.*) a leaf-vein: a vein in the wing of an insect.—*v.t.* to give strength, resolution, or courage to.—*adjs.* **nerve′less,** without strength: inert; **nerv′ine** (*-ēn, -īn*), acting on the nerves: quieting nervous excitement.—Also *n.*—*adj.* **nerv′ous,** having nerve: sinewy: strong, vigorous: (of literary style) vigorous, terse: pertaining to the nerves: having the nerves weak or easily excited: timid.—*adv.* **nerv′ously.**—*n.* **nerv′ousness.**—**nerve centre,** an aggregation of nerve cells from which nerves branch out: (*fig.*) the centre from which control is exercised; **nerve gas,** any of a number of gases, prepared for use in war, having a deadly effect on the nervous system, esp. on nerves controlling respiration; **nervous breakdown,** loose term indicating nervous debility following mental or physical fatigue: euphemism for any mental illness; **nervous system,** the brain, spinal cord, and nerves collectively. [L. *nervus,* sinew; cf. Gr. *neuron.* See **neuro-.**]

nescience, *nesh′(y)éns, n.* want of knowledge.—*adj.* **nes′cient.** [L. *nescientia*—*neseīre,* to be ignorant—*ne,* not, *scīre,* to know.]

ness, *nes, n.* a headland. [O.E. *næs, næss.*]

nest, *nest, n.* a structure prepared for egg-laying, brooding, and nursing, or as a shelter: a comfortable residence: a place where anything teems, prevails, or is fostered: the occupants of a nest, as a brood, a swarm, a gang: a set of things (as boxes) fitting one within another.—*v.i.* to build or occupy a nest.—*n.* **nest′-egg,** an egg left or put in a nest to encourage laying: something laid up as the beginning of an accumulation.—**feather one's nest,** (see **feather**). [O.E. *nest;* Ger. *nest,* L. *nīdus.*]

nestle, *nes′l, v.i.* to lie close or snug as in a nest: to settle comfortably.—*v.t.* to cherish, as a bird does her young.—*n.* **nestling** (*nes′ling*), a

---

Neutral vowels in unaccented syllables: *em′pér-ór;* for certain sounds in foreign words see p. ix.

young bird in the nest.—Also *adj.* [O.E. *nestlian*—*nest.*]

net, *net*, *n.* an open fabric of twine, &c., knotted into meshes for catching birds, fishes, &c.: anything like a net: a snare: a difficulty.—*v.t.* to form into network: to take with a net: to protect with a net.—*v.i.* to form network:—*pr.p.* nett'ing; *pa.t.* and *pa.p.* nett'ed.—*ns.* **net'ball**, a game in which a ball is thrown into a net hung from a pole; **net'-fish**, any fish, like the herring, caught in nets—opp. to *trawl-fish* and *line-fish*; **nett'ing**, act or process of forming network: a piece of network; **net'work**, any structure in the form of a net: a system of lines (e.g. of railways, rivers) resembling a net: a system of units constituting a widely spread organisation and having a common purpose: a system of radio or television stations connected for broadcasting the same programme. [O.E. *net*, *nett*; Du. *net*, Ger. *netz.*]

net, **nett**, *net*, *adj.* clear of all charges or deductions—opp. to *gross*: lowest, subject to no further deductions: of weight, not including that of packaging.—*v.t.* to gain or produce as clear profit:—*pr.p.* nett'ing; *pa.t.* and *pa.p.* nett'ed. [Fr.; same word as **neat** (2.)]

nether, *neTH´ėr*, *adj.* lower.—*n.* **Neth´erlander**, an inhabitant of the *Netherlands* or Low Countries, now Holland, formerly also Belgium.—*adj.* **neth´ermost**, lowest. [O.E. *neothera*, adj.—*nither*, adv., from the root *ni-*, down; Ger. *nieder*, low.]

nettle, *net´l*, *n.* a genus of plants with stinging hairs.—*v.t.* to sting with annoyance, provoke.—*n.* **nett´lerash**, an eruption on the skin resembling the effect of nettle stings. [O.E. *netele*; Ger. *nessel.*]

neur-, *nūr-*, **neuro-**, *nū´rō*, in composition, nerve.—*adj.* **neural** (*nū´ral*), of, or relating to, nerves.—*n.* **neuralgia** (-*ral´ji̇a*; Gr. *algos*, pain), pain in the nerves, usu. of the head or face.—*adj.* **neural´gic**.—*n.* **neurasthenia** (*nu-ras-thē´ni-a*; Gr. *astheneia*, weakness), nervous debility.—*adj.* **neurasthen´ic**.—*n.* one suffering from neurasthenia.—*ns.* **neuritis** (*nū-rī´tis*), inflammation of a nerve; **neurology** (*nū-rol´o-ji*), the study of the nerves.—*adj.* **neurolog´ical**.—*ns.* **neurol´ogist**; **neuron(e)**, a nerve-cell and its processes; **neuro´sis**, functional derangement due to a disordered nervous system, generally not associated with any physical disease or injury: mental disturbance accompanied by anxiety and obsessional fears: loosely, an obsession.—*adj.* **neurotic** (-*rot´ik*), of the nature of, characterised by, or affected by, neurosis: of abnormal sensibility: loosely, obsessive.—*n.* a person with neurosis or disordered nerves: a medicine for nerve diseases. [Gr. *neuron*, a sinew, a nerve. See **nerve**.]

Neuroptera, *nū-rop´tér-a*, *n.pl.* an order of insects that have generally four net-veined wings.—*adj.* **neurop´terous**. [Gr. *neuron*, a sinew, *pteron*, a wing.]

neuter, *nū´tér*, *adj.* neither one thing nor another: (*arch.*) neutral: (*gram.*) neither masculine nor feminine: (*bot.*) without stamens or pistils: (*zool.*) without sex.—*n.* a neutral: a neuter word, plant, or animal, esp. a worker

bee, &c.: castrated cat. &c.—*v.t.* to castrate. [L. *neuter*, neither—*ne*, not, *uter*, either.]

neutral, *nū´tral*, *adj.* indifferent: taking no part on either side: of no decided character: having no decided colour: (*chem.*) neither acid nor alkaline.—*n.* a person or nation that takes no part in a contest: a position or gear in which no power is transmitted.—*n.* **neutrality** (-*tral´i-ti*).—*adv.* **neu´trally.**—*v.t.* **neu´tralise**, to declare neutral: to counterbalance or counteract, to render of no effect.—*ns.* **neu´traliser**; **neutralisa´tion**. [L. *neutrālis*—*neuter*, neither.]

neutron, *nū´tron*, *n.* an uncharged subatomic particle, of about the same mass as a proton.—*n.* **neutrino** (-*trē´nō*), uncharged particle with approx. zero mass. [L. *neuter*, neither.]

never, *nev´ér*, *adv.* not ever, at no time: in no degree: surely not.—*adv.* **nev´ermore**, at no future time.—*n.* **nev´er-nev´er**, an imaginary place, or imaginary conditions too fortunate ever to exist in reality: (*coll.*) the hire-purchase system.—*adv.* and *conj.* **nevertheless´**, notwithstanding: in spite of that. [O.E. *næfre*—*ne*, not *æfre*, ever.]

new, *nū*, *adj.* lately made, invented, discovered: recently heard of, or experienced for the first time: different, changed (e.g. *turn over a new leaf*, *a new man*): unaccustomed: having been in a position, relationship. &c., only a short time (e.g. a member, an assistant): recently commenced: not of an ancient family.—*adv.* recently, in compounds such as **new´born**, **new´-fledged**, **new´-laid.**—*adv.* **new´ly.**—*n.* **new´-com´er**, one who has lately come.—*adj.* **new´-fash´ioned**, made in a new way or fashion: lately come into fashion.—**New England**, a group of six north-eastern states of U.S.A.; **New Englander**; **New Learning**, the new studies (esp Greek) of the Renaissance period; **new look**, a new presentation or form, a radical modification in the existing form of something (first used of the change in women's fashions in 1947); **new style**, the mode of reckoning time after 1752 (see **old** style); **New World** (see **world**); **New Year's Day**, the first day of the year. [O.E. *nīwe*, *nēowe*; Ger. *neu*, Ir. *nuadh*, L. *novus*, Gr. *neos*.]

newel, *nū´él*, *n.* the upright column about which the steps of a circular staircase wind. [O.Fr. *nual* (Fr. *noyau*), fruit-stone—Low L. *nucālis*, nut-like—L. *nux*, *nucis*, a nut.]

newfangled, *nū-fang´gld*, *adj.* (*rare*) unduly fond of new things: newly devised: objectionably novel.—*n.* **newfang´ledness**. [M.E. *newefangel*—*newe* (O.E. *nīwe*), new, *fangel*, ready to catch—*fang-*, the stem of O.E. *fōn*, to take.]

news, *nūz*, *n. sing.* tidings: a report of a recent event: something one had not heard before: matter suitable for newspaper readers.—*ns.* **news´-agent**, one who deals in newspapers; **news´boy**, a boy who delivers or sells newspapers; **news´cast**, a *news* broad*cast* or telecast; **news´caster**, one who gives newscasts: an apparatus which gives a changing display of news headlines, &c.; **news´letter**, a written or printed letter containing news sent by an agent to his subscribers, the predecessor of the newspaper: a sheet of news supplied to members of a particular group; **news´monger**, one who spends much time in hearing and telling news; **news′paper,** a paper published periodically for circulating news, &c.; **news′print,** cheap paper for printing newspapers; **news′-reel,** a short film portraying, or broadcast telling of, very recent events; **news′room,** a reading-room with newspapers; **news′vendor,** a seller of newspapers. [Late M.E. *newes,* an imit. of Fr. *nouvelles.*]

newt, *nūt, n.* a genus of tailed amphibians, of the salamander family. [Formed with initial *n,* borrowed from the article *an,* from *ewt,* a form of *evet* or *eft*—O.E. *efeta, efete.*]

newton, *nū′tón, n.* the MKS(A) and SI unit of force—the force which, acting on a mass of one kilogram, produces an acceleration of one metre per second per second.

next, *nekst, adj.* (*superl.* of **nigh**) nearest in place, time, &c.—*adv.* nearest: immediately after. [O.E. *nēhst* (*nīehst*), superl. of *nēh* (*nēah*), near; Ger. *nächst.*]

nexus, *nek′sus, n.* a bond, link, connection (*fig.*): a linked group. [L. *nexus,* pl. *-ūs—nectĕre,* to bind.]

nib, *nib, n.* something small and pointed: a pen-point: a bird's bill: (*pl.*) crushed fragments of cacao beans.—*adj.* **nibbed,** having a nib. [Variant of **neb.**]

nibble, *nib′l, v.t.* to bite gently or by small bites (as a rabbit or a fish does): to eat by a little at a time.—*v.i.* to make trifling criticisms (with *at*): (*fig.*) to show signs of taking, accepting, yielding to (e.g. *to nibble at an offer, at temptation*). [Origin obscure; cf. L. Ger. *nibbelen,* Du *knibbelen.*]

niblick, *nib′lik, n.* a golf-club with a heavy iron head with wide face, used for lofting: a number eight or nine iron.

nice, *nīs, adj.* hard to please, fastidious (esp. in reference to literary taste): able to make fine distinctions, minutely accurate (e.g. judgment, ear): scrupulous (as to means): requiring great accuracy or care (e.g. an experiment, a problem): displaying fine discrimination (e.g. a distinction): (*coll.*) agreeable, delightful.—*adv.* **nice′ly,** exactness, scrupulousness; **nicety** (*nīs′i-ti*), fastidiousness: fineness of perception: exactness of treatment: intricate or subtle quality: (*pl.*) subtle, trivial, or delicate detail.—**to a nicety,** with great exactness. [O.Fr. *nice,* foolish, simple—L. *nescius,* ignorant—*ne,* not, *scīre,* to know.]

Nicene, *nī′sēn, adj.* pertaining to the town of Nicaea in Asia Minor, where a church council in 325 dealt with the Arian controversy.—**Nicene creed,** a formal statement of Christian belief (in opposition to Arianism) based on that adopted at the first Nicene council.

niche, *nich, n.* a recess in a wall for a statue, &c.: a person's place or condition (suitable or actual) in life or in public estimation. [Fr.,—It. *nicchia,* a niche.]

nick, *nik, n.* a notch: a score for keeping an account: the precise moment (of time): (*slang*) prison.—*v.t.* to notch: to hit with precision.—**in good nick** (*coll.*), in good condition. [Possibly connected with **notch.**]

nick, *nik, n.* the devil, esp. **Old Nick.** [Apparently for *Nicholas.*]

nickel, *nik′él, n.* a white magnetic metallic element (symbol Ni; at. no. 28), very malleable

and ductile: (*U.S.*) 5-cent coin.—*ns.* **nick′el-plat′ing,** the plating of metals with nickel; **nick′el-sil′ver,** German silver, an alloy of copper, zinc, and nickel, like silver in colour, first made in Germany. [Ger. *kupfernickel,* an ore from which nickel is obtained—*kupfer,* copper, *nickel,* a mischievous sprite, because the ore looked like copper ore but yielded no copper.]

nicker, *nik′er, n.* (*slang*) £1.

nicknack. Same as **knick-knack.**

nickname, *nik′nām, n.* a name given in contempt or sportive familiarity.—*vt.* to give a nickname to. [M.E. *neke-name,* for **eke-name,** additional name, surname, with *n* from the indefinite article *an.* See **eke;** cf. **newt.**]

nicotine, *nik′ō-tēn, n.* a poisonous alkaloid got from tobacco leaves. [Jean *Nicot,* who introduced tobacco into France (1560).]

nictate, *nik′tāt, v.i.* to wink—also **nic′titate.**—**nictitating membrane,** the third eyelid developed in birds, &c., a thin movable membrane that passes over the eye. [L. *nictāre, -ātum,* and its L.L. freq. *nictitāre,* to wink.]

nidification, *nid-i-fi-kā′sh(ó)n, n.* the act or art of building a nest. [L. *nīdus,* nest, *facĕre,* to make.]

niece, *nēs, n.* the daughter of a brother or sister: (*obs.*) a granddaughter:—*masc.* **nephew** (q.v.). [O.Fr.,—Low L. *neptia*—L. *nevtia*—L. *neptis,* a granddaughter, niece.]

Nietzschean, *nē′che-án, adj.* pertaining to the philosophy of Friedrich *Nietzsche* (1844-1900), who denounced all religion, declared that moral laws cherished the virtues of the weak, and described as his ideal 'overman' one who ruthlessly sought his own power and pleasure.

nifty, *nif′ti, adj.* (*coll.*) fine: smart: quick: agile.

niggard, *nig′árd, n.* one who grudges to spend or give away.—*adj.* niggardly.—*adj.* **nigg′ardly,** stingy.—*adv.* stingily: grudgingly.—*n.* **nigg′-ardliness,** lack of generosity in bestowing (goods, praise, &c.). [Origin obscure.]

nigger, *nig′er, n.* a Negro (*coll.* and derogatory): loosely, any coloured man.

niggle, *nig′l, v.i.* to trifle, busy oneself with petty matters: to move in a fidgety way: to work with excessive detail: to criticise in a petty way.—*adj.* **nigg′ling,** petty, fussy, unnecessarily minute and careful: (of handwriting) cramped. [Prob. of Scand. origin.]

nigh, *nī, adj.* (*arch.*) near.—*adv.* nearly.—*prep.* near to.—*n.* **nigh′ness.** [O.E. *nēah, nēh* ; Du. *na,* Ger. *nahe.*]

night, *nīt, n.* the time from sunset to sunrise: darkness: (*fig.*) ignorance, affliction, or sorrow: death.—*adj.* and *adv.* **night′long,** (lasting) all night.—*adj.* **night′ly,** done or happening by night or every night.—*adv.* by night: every night.—*ns.* (1) compounds in which *night* means *active by night,* as:—**night′-bird,** a bird that flies or sings at night (e.g. the owl, the nightingale): a person who is active or about at night; **night′-churr,** or **-jar,** a goatsucker, so called from the sound of its cry; **night′-wan′derer;** **night′-watch′man;** (2) compounds in which *night* means *used at night,* as:—**night′-clothes;** **night′-gown;** **night′-rail** (*arch.*), a negligee gown or night-dress;

Neutral vowels in unaccented syllables: *em′pér-ór*; for certain sounds in foreign words see p. ix.

night'-club, a club open between nightfall and morning for amusement or dissipation.—*ns.* **night'fall,** the fall or beginning of the night; **night-life,** activity in the form of entertainment at night; **night'piece,** a picture of literary description of a night scene: **night'-watch,** a watch or guard at night: time of watch in the night. [O.E. *niht*; Ger. *nacht*, L. *nox*; Gr. *nyx*.]

nightingale, *nīt'ing-gāl, n.* a small bird of the thrush family, celebrated for its singing at night. [O.E. *nihtegale—niht*, night, *galan*, to sing; Ger. *nachtigall*.]

nightmare, *nīt'mār, n.* a dreadful dream accompanied with pressure on the breast, and a feeling of powerlessness to move or speak—personified as an incubus or evil spirit: any fantastically horrible dream, impression, or experience. [O.E. *niht*, night, *mara,* a nightmare; cf. O.H.G. *mara*, incubus, O.N. *mara*, nightmare.]

nightshade, *nīt'shād, n.* a name of several plants all having in some degree narcotic properties; see *belladonna* (**deadly nightshade**) and *bittersweet* (**woody nightshade**). [O.E. *nihtscada*, apparently—*niht*, night, *scada*, shade.]

nigrescent, *nī-,* or *nī-gres'ent, adj.* growing black or dark: blackish. [L., *nigrescēre*, to grow black—*niger*, black.]

nigritude, *nig'ri-tūd, n.* blackness. [L. *nigritūdō* —*niger*, black.]

nihilism, *nī'hil-izm, n.* belief in nothing, extreme scepticism: (*hist.*) in tsarist Russia a terrorist movement aiming at the overthrow of all the existing institutions of society in order to build it up anew on different principles.—*n.* **nī'hilist.** [L. *nihil*, nothing.]

nil, *nil, n.* nothing: zero. [L. *nīl*, contracted form of *nihil*, nothing.]

nilgai, *nēl'-,* or *nil'gī,* **nilgau, nylghau,** *gow, -gö, n.* a large Indian antelope, the male slaty-grey, the female tawny. [Pers. and Hindustani *nīl*, blue, Hind. *gāī*, Pers. *gāw*, cow.]

nimble, *nim'bl, adj.* light and quick in motion, active, swift.—*n.* **nim'bleness.**—*adv.* **nim'bly.** [App. O.E. *nǣmel, numōl—niman,* to take; cf. Ger. *nehmen*.]

nimbus, *nim'bus, n.* a raincloud: a luminous cloud or vapour about a god or goddess: (*paint.*) bright disk encircling the head of a saint—aureole, glory, halo. [L.]

niminy-piminy, *nim'i-ni-pim'i-ni, adj.* affectedly fine or delicate.—*n.* affected delicacy. [Imit.]

Nimrod, *nim'rod, n.* any great hunter (see Gen. x. 8, 9).

nincompoop, *nin(g)'kom-pōōp, n.* a simpleton. [Origin unknown; not from L. *non compos* (*mentis*), not in possession of his wits.]

nine, *nīn, n.* the cardinal number next above eight: a symbol representing it (9, ix, &c.): a shoe or other article of a size denoted by 9: a card with nine pips.—*adj.* of the number nine. *adj.* **ninth** (*nīnth*), the last of nine: being one of nine equal parts.—*n.* one of nine equal parts.—*n.* **nine'pins,** game in which ball is bowled at nine 'pins' set up on end.—*n.* and *adj.* **nine'teen** (when used absolutely, *-tēn'*) nine and ten.—*adj.* **nine'teenth** (when used absolutely, *-tēnth'*).—*n.* and *adj.* **nine'ty,** nine times ten. *adj.* **nine'tieth,** the last of ninety.

—*n.* one of ninety equal parts.—**the Nine,** the nine muses (see **muse** (2)); **to the nines,** to perfection, fully, elaborately. [O.E. *nigon*; Du. *negen,* L. *novem,* Gr. *ennea,* Sans. *nava.*]

ninny, *nin'i, n.* a simpleton. [Possibly from **innocent;** poss.—It. *ninno,* child.]

ninon, *nē'nô, n.* a silk voile or other thin fabric. [Fr. *Ninon,* a woman's name.]

niobium, *nī-ō'bi-um, n.* a metallic element (symbol Nb; at. no. 41), steel-grey in colour. [L. *Niobe,* who wept for her children until she was turned to stone.]

nip, *nip, n.* a small quantity, esp. of spirits.

nip, *nip, v.t.* to pinch: to press between two surfaces: to remove or sever by pinching or biting: to check the growth or vigour of: to give a smarting or tingling feeling to: to take, or go (*up, out*) hurriedly or unobserved: —*pr.p.* nipp'ing; *pa.t.* and *pa.p.* nipped.—*n.* a pinch: a bite: a sharp remark: a check to growth of plants due to cold: biting coldness of air.—*n.* nipp'er, one who, or that which, nips (as a crab's claw): (*slang*) a boy: a horse's incisor, esp. one of the middle four: (*pl.*) small pincers.—*adv.* nipp'ingly.—**nip in the bud,** to check, destroy in the earliest stage. [Prob. related to Du. *nippen,* to pinch.]

nipple, *nip'l, n.* the pap of the breast: a teat: a small projection with an orifice. [A dim. of **neb** or **nib.**]

Nippon, *nip-pon', n,* Japan. [Jap.]

nirvana, *nir-vä'nä, n.* the cessation of individual existence—the state to which a Buddhist aspires as the best attainable: loosely, a state of supreme happiness. [Sans. *nirvana,* 'a blowing out'.]

nit, *nit, n.* the egg of a louse or other parasitic insect: the insect itself when young.—*n.* **nit'wit,** (*slang*) a very foolish person. [O.E. *hnitu*; Ger. *niss*.]

nitre. See under **nitrogen.**

nitrogen, *nī'trō-jen, n.* a gas (sym. N; at. no. 7) forming nearly 4/5 of air.—*adj.* **nitrog'enous,** containing, having the nature of, nitrogen.—*adjs.* **nī'tric, nī'trous,** of, pertaining to, or containing nitrogen: of, pertaining to, or derived from nitre (q.v.). In the nitric compounds the nitrogen has a higher valency than in the nitrous:—e.g. **nitric oxide** (NO), a colourless, poisonous gas; **nitrous oxide** (N_2O), laughing gas, a gas used as an anaesthetic; **nitric acid** (HNO_3), a colourless, fuming, corrosive liquid (aqua-fortis); **nitrous acid** (HNO_2), an acid that readily decomposes and is known only in solution.—*ns.* **nī'trate,** **nī'trite,** salts formed from nitric acid and nitrous acid respectively; **nitre** (*nī'tér*), potassium nitrate, saltpetre: (**cubic nitre** is sodium nitrate, known also as Chile saltpetre).—**nī'tro-,** used in the names of certain compounds of nitrogen, e.g. **ni'troglyc'erine,** a powerful explosive, the chief constituent of dynamite.—**nitrogen cycle,** the sum total of the transformations undergone by nitrogen and nitrogenous compounds in nature—from atmospheric nitrogen through soil bacteria, plant-tissues, and animal tissues back to bacteria and atmospheric nitrogen again; **nitrogen fixation** (see **fixation**). [Gr. *nitron,* sodium carbonate (but taken as if meaning nitre).]

fāte, fär; mē, hûr (her); *mīne; mōte, för; mūte; mōōn, fŏŏt;* THen (then)

and the root of *gennaein*, to generate.]

nix, *niks, n.* (*Teutonic myth.*) a water-spirit, usu. malignant:—*fem.* **nix′ie**, **nix′y.** [Ger. *nix*, fem. *nixe.*]

nix, *niks, n.* (*slang*) nothing: short for 'nothing doing, you'll get no support from me'. [Coll. Ger. and Du. for Ger. *nichts*, nothing.]

Nizam, *ni-zäm′, n.* the title of the sovereign of Hyderabad in India. [Hindustani *nizām*, regulator.]

no, *nō, adv.* not so: (with *comp.*) in no degree, as *no sooner than, no less than.—n.* a denial: a refusal: a vote or voter for the negative:—*pl.* **noes.** [O.E. *nā—ne*, not, ā, ever; cf. **nay.**]

no, *nō, adj.* not any: not one: by no means properly called (e.g. *no lady*).—*advs.* **nō′way**, **nō′ways**, **nō′wise**, in no way, manner, or degree.—*n.* **nō′-ball** (*cricket*), a ball bowled in such a way as to be disallowed by the rules. [O.E. *nān*, none. See **none.**]

No., no., abbrev. for L. *numero*, by number.

nob, *nob, n.* (*slang*) the head. [Perh. **knob.**]

nob, *nob, n.* (*slang*) a person of some wealth or social distinction.—*adj.* **nobb′y**, smart.

nobble, *nob′l, v.t.* (*slang*) to get hold of dishonestly: to injure, destroy the chances of, a racer by drugging or laming it.

nobelium, *nō-bēl′i-um, n.* a transuranium element (atomic number 102; symbol No), produced artificially at the *Nobel* Institute, Stockholm.

nobility, *nō-bil′i-ti, n.* high rank: excellence: greatness of mind or character: descent from noble ancestors: the body of nobles. [See next word.]

noble, *nō′bl, adj.* illustrious: high in character or quality: of high birth: magnificent: generous.—*n.* (esp. *hist.*) a person of exalted rank: an obsolete gold coin = 6s. 8d. sterling (33.3p).—*ns.* **nō′bleman**, a man who is noble or of rank, a peer; **nō′bleness;**—*adv.* **nō′bly.**—**noble metal**, one that does not readily tarnish, as gold and silver. [Fr. *noble*—L. (*g*)*nōbilis*—(*g*)*nōscĕre*, to know.]

noblesse oblige, *nō-bles ō-blēzh′*, rank imposes obligations. [Fr.]

nobody, *nō′bod-i, n.* no person, no one: a person of no account. [**no**, **body.**]

nocturnal, *nok-tûr′nál, adj.* belonging to night: happening, done, or active by night.—*n.* an astronomical instrument for finding the hour by night.—*adv.* **noctur′nally.**—*n.* **nocturne** (*nok′tûrn*, or *-tûrn′*), a dreamy or pensive piece, generally for the piano: (*paint.*) a night scene. [L. *nocturnus—nox*, night.]

nocuous, *nok′ū-us, adj.* hurtful, noxious. [L. *nocuus—nocēre*, to hurt.]

nod, *nod, v.i.,* to give a quick forward motion of the head, esp. in assent, salutation, or command: to let the head drop in weariness: to make a slip, esp. through momentary inattention.—*v.t.* to incline: to signify by a nod:—*pr.p.* nodd′ing; *pa.t.* and *pa.p.* nodd′ed.—*n.* a quick bending forward of the head: a slight bow: a command.—*n.* and *adj.* **nodd′ing.**—**nodding acquaintance**, someone with whom one is only slightly acquainted: superficial, incomplete knowledge or understanding. [M.E. *nodde*, not known in O.E.]

noddle, *nod′l, n.* (*obs.*) the back of the head: the head. [Origin obscure.]

noddy, *nod′i, n.* a noodle: an oceanic bird, unaccustomed to man and therefore easily taken and deemed stupid. [Origin obscure.]

node, *nōd, n.* a knot: a knob: (*astron.*) one of the two points in which the orbit of a planet intersects the plane of the ecliptic: a point or line of rest, or of comparative rest, in a vibrating body (such as a stretched string): (*bot.*) the joint of a stem: the point of attachment of a leaf or leaves: a complication in a story.—*adjs.* **nōd′al**, of a node or nodes; **nōdāt′ed**, knotted; **nodose** (*nōd-ōs′, nōd′ōs*), having nodes, knots, or swellings: knotty; **nod′ular**, of or like a nodule.—*n.* **nōd′ūle**, a little rounded lump. [L. *nōdus;* dim. *nōdulus.*]

Noël. See **Nowel.**

noggin, *nog′in, n.* a small mug or wooden cup. [Origin unknown; Ir. *noigin*, Gael. *noigean*, are believed to be from English.]

noise, *noiz, n.* sound of any kind: an unmusical sound: an over-loud or disturbing sound, din: frequent or public talk: interference in a communication channel.—*v.t.* to spread by rumour.—*v.i.* to sound loud.—*adj.* **noise′less**, without noise: silent.—*adv.* **noise′lessly.**—*n.* **noise′lessness.**—*adj.* **nois′y**, making a loud sound: clamorous, turbulent.—*adv.* **nois′ily.**—*n.* **nois′iness.** [Fr. *noise*, quarrel; perh. from L. *nausea*, disgust; but possibly from L. *noxia*, hurt—*nocēre*, to hurt.]

noisome, *noi′súm, adj.* injurious to health: disgusting.—*n.* **noi′someness.** [noy, a form of **annoy.**]

nomad(e), *nōm′ad, nom′-, n.* one of a wandering pastoral community: a rover.—*adj.* **nomadic** (*nōm-ad′ik*).—*n.* **nom′adism.** [Gr. *nomās, -ados—nomos*, pasture—*nemein*, to drive to pasture.]

no-man's-land, *nō′manz-land, n.* a waste region to which no one has a recognised claim: debatable land, esp. between entrenched hostile forces.

nom de plume, *nɔ̃ dé plōōm, n.* a pen-name. [Formed in Eng. from Fr. *nom*, name, *de*, of, *plume*, pen.]

nomenclature, *nō′men-klā-tyùr, -chùr*, or *nō-men′klä-, n.* a system of names: a terminology (e.g. of a science). [L. *nōmen*, a name, *calāre*, to call.]

nominal, *nom′in-ál, adj.* pertaining to a name or to a noun: existing only in name, not real or actual: inconsiderable, hardly more than a matter of form.—*adv.* **nom′inally.**—*ns.* **nom′inalism**, the doctrine that general terms have no corresponding reality either in or out of the mind, being mere words; **nom′inalist.** [L. *nōminālis—nōmen, -inis*, a name.]

nominate, *nom′in-āt, v.t.* to name: to appoint: to propose formally for election.—*n.* **nom′ination**, the act or power of nominating: state of being nominated.—*adj.* **nominative** (*nom′in-á-tiv*), naming: (*gram.*) applied to the case of the subject.—*n.* the case of the subject. [L. *nōmināre,-ātum*, to name—*nōmen, -inis*, name.]

nominee, *nom-in-ē′, n.* one who is nominated by another for an office, duty, or position: one who is named as the recipient in an annuity, a grant, &c. [L. *nōmināre, -ātum*, to name, with *-ee* as if from Fr.]

Neutral vowels in unaccented syllables: *em′pėr-ór;* for certain sounds in foreign words see p. ix.

non, *non*, a Latin word used as a prefix, not (sometimes used of someone or something with pretensions, who, which, is ludicrously unworthy of the name mentioned, e.g. **non-hero, non-event**); the prefix is living and many words using it may be formed.—*ns.* **non-align'ment,** policy of not taking sides in international politics; **non-appear'ance,** failure or neglect to appear, esp. in a court of law; **non-com'batant,** any person connected with an army who is there for some purpose other than that of fighting, as a surgeon, a chaplain: a civilian in time of war.—*adjs.* **non-commiss'ioned,** not having a commission, as an officer in the army below the rank of commissioned officer; **non-committ'al,** not committing one, or refraining from committing oneself, to any particular opinion or course of conduct: implying nothing, one way or the other.—*ns.* **non-commū'nicant,** one who does not take communion on any particular occasion or in general: one who has not yet communicated; **non-compli'ance,** neglect or failure to comply; **non-conduct'or,** a substance or object that does not readily conduct heat or electricity.—*adj.* **nonconform'ing,** not conforming to an established church.—*ns.* **nonconform'ist,** (also *adj.*); **nonconform'ity, non'-content,** one not content: in House of Lords, one giving a negative vote; **non-deliv'ery,** failure or neglect to deliver; **non-exist'ence,** the condition of not being or existing.—*adjs.* **non-exist'ent; non-ferrous,** containing no iron: (relating to metals) other than iron; **non-fict'ion,** of a literary work, without any deliberately fictitious material.—*n.* **non-interven'tion,** a policy of systematic abstention from interference with the affairs of other nations.—*adj.* **nonjur'ing,** not swearing allegiance.—*n.* **nonjur'or,** one of the clergy in England and Scotland who would not swear allegiance to William and Mary in 1689.—*adj.* **non-mor'al,** involving no moral considerations, amoral, unmoral.—*n.* **non'-person,** one previously eminent in politics, &c., now out of favour.—*adjs.* **non-play'ing,** not taking active part in the game(s); **non-res'ident,** not residing within the range of one's responsibilities, absentee (e.g. of clergyman): visiting, not living in, the place in question (also *n.*)—*n.* **non-start'er,** a horse which, though entered for a race, does not run: a person with no chance of success.—*adjs.* **non-stick',** of e.g. a pan, treated so that food or other substance will not stick to it; **non-stop,** uninterrupted, without any stop or halt. [L. *non*, not.]

nonage, *non'ij*, *n.* legal infancy, minority: time of immaturity generally.—*adj.* **non'aged.** [O.Fr. *nonage*—pfx. *non-* (L. *nōn*), and *age*, age.]

nonagenarian, *nōn-*, or *non-a-jé-nā'ri-ān*, *n.* one who is ninety years old or between ninety and a hundred.—*adj.* of that age. [L. *nōnāgēnārius*, relating to ninety—*nōnāgintā*, ninety.]

nonagon, *non'á-gon*, *n.* a polygon with nine angles. [L. *nōnus*, ninth, Gr. *gōniā*, angle.]

nonce, *nons*, *n.* (almost confined to the phrase *for the nonce*) the occasion: the moment, time being.—**nonce-word,** a word specially coined

for use at the moment, like Carlyle's *gigmanity* (people who keep a gig—the smugly respectable and well-to-do). [From 'for the nones', originally *for then ones*, for the once.]

nonchalance, *non'shá-láns*, *n.* unconcern, coolness, indifference.—*adj.* **nonchalant** (*non'-shá-lánt*). [Fr.—*non*, not, *chaloir*, to matter, interest—L. *calēre*, to be warm.]

nondescript, *non'di-skript*, *adj.* not easily classified: not distinctive enough to be described: neither one thing nor another.—Also *n.* [L. *nōn*, not, *dēscrībĕre, -scrīptum*, to describe.]

none, *nun*, *pron.* (*pl.* or *sing*) not one: not any: (*arch.*) no one.—*adj.* (*arch.*) no (before vowel or *h*).—*adv.* not at all (e.g. *none the worse, none the wiser, none too good*).—*n.* **none'-so-pretty,** London pride.—*adv.* **none'-the-less,** nevertheless.—**none of the..., none of your...,** not among the number of or in the class of, not of the kind of (e.g. *his craftsmanship is none of the best*; *he is none of your sticklers for truth*). [O.E. *nān*—*ne*, not, *ān*, one].

nonentity, *non-en'ti-ti*, *n.* the state of not being: a person or thing of no importance. [L. *nōn*, not, and *entitās*. See **entity**.]

nones, *nonz*, *n.pl.* in the Roman calendar, the ninth day before the Ides (both days included)—the 7th of March, May, July, and October, and the 5th day of the other months: a church office orig. for the ninth hour, or three o'clock, afterwards earlier (often *cap.*). [L. *nōnae*—*nōnus* for *novēnus*, ninth—*novem*, nine.]

non(e)such, *non'-, nun'such*, *n.* a unique, unparalleled, or extraordinary thing. [**none, such.**]

nonpareil, *non-pá-rel'*, *n.* a person or thing without equal, or unique: a fine apple: a small printing type. *adj.* without an equal, matchless. [Fr.—*non*, not, *pareil*, from a L.L. dim. of L. *pār*, equal.]

nonplus, *non'plus'*, *n.* a state in which no more can be done or said: a great difficulty.—*v.t.* to perplex completely:—*pr.p.* non'plus(s)ing; *pa.t.* and *pa.p.* non'plussed. [L. *nōn*, not, *plūs*, more.]

nonsense, *non'séns*, *n.* that which has no sense: language without meaning: absurdity: trifling.—*adj.* **nonsensical** (*-sens'-*), without sense: absurd.—*n.* **nonsens'icalness.**—*adv.* **nonsens'ically.**—**nonsense verse,** verse deliberately written to convey an absurd meaning or to convey no obvious meaning at all. [Pfx. *non-*, and **sense.**]

non sequitur, *non sek'wit-úr*, *n.* a statement in which the conclusion does not follow from the premises. [L., it does not follow.]

non-suit, *non'sūt*, *n.* a withdrawal of a suit at law, either voluntarily by the plaintiff, or by the judge when the plaintiff has failed to make out cause of action or to bring sufficient evidence.—*v.t.* to subject to a non-suit. [Anglo-Fr. *no(u)nsute*, dares not pursue.]

non-U. See **U.**

noodle, *nōōd'l*, *n.* a simpleton, a blockhead. [Cf. **noddy.**]

noodle, *nōōd'l*, *n.* a flat macaroni, usually with egg in its composition. [Ger. *nudel*.]

nook, *nōōk*, *n.* a corner: a recess: a secluded

retreat. [M.E. *nok, noke*; prob. Scand.; Gael. and Ir. *niuc* is prob. from the Northern form *neuk*.]

noon, *nōōn, n.* the ninth hour of the day in Roman and ecclesiastical reckoning, three o'clock P.M.: afterwards (when the church service for the ninth hour, called *nones*, was moved to midday) midday: twelve o'clock: middle: highest point.—*adj.* belonging to midday: meridional.—*ns.* **noon′day**, midday: the time of greatest prosperity (also *adj.*); **noon′tide**, the time of noon (also *adj.*). [O.E. *nōn*—L. *nōna* (*hōra*), the ninth (hour).]

noose, *nōōs*, also *nōōz, n.* a loop with a running knot which ties the firmer the closer it is drawn: a snare or bond generally.—*v.t.* to tie or catch in a noose. [Perh. O.Fr. *nous*, pl. of *nou* (Fr. *noeud*)—L. *nōdus*, knot.]

nor, *nôr, conj.* and not: neither—used esp. in introducing the second part of a negative proposition (correlative to *neither*). [App. from *nother*, a form of **neither**.]

Nordic, *nôr′dik, adj.* pertaining to a tall, blond, long-headed type of peoples (generally Germanic) in N.W. Europe: a term used loosely by Nazis.—Also *n.* [Fr. *nord*, north.]

norm, *nôrm, n.* a pattern: an authoritative standard: a type: the most frequent value or state.—*n.* **nor′ma**, a rule, model: a square for measuring right angles.—*adj.* **nor′mal**, according to rule: ordinary: perpendicular.—*n.* a perpendicular.—*ns.* **nor′malcy** (esp. *U.S.*; an illformed word), **normal′ity**, **nor′malness**, quality, state, or fact, of being normal: normal conditions.—*v.t.* **nor′malise**, to make normal.—*v.i.* to become normal, regular.—*adv.* **nor′mally**.—**normal school**, a training-college for teachers. [L. *norma*, a rule.]

Norman, *nôr′mán, n.* a native or inhabitant of Normandy: one of that Scandinavian race which settled in northern France about the beginning of the 10th century.—*adj.* pertaining to the Normans or to Normandy.—**Norman architecture**, a round-arched style, a variety of Romanesque, prevalent in England from the Norman Conquest (1066) till the end of the 12th century; **Norman French**, French as spoken by the Normans. [O.Fr. *Normanz, Normans* (nom. sing. and acc. pl.), Northman, from Scand.]

Norroy, *nor′oi, n.* (*her.*) the third of the three English Kings-of-Arms, or provincial heralds, whose jurisdiction lies north of the Trent. [Fr. *nord*, north, *roy, roi*, king.]

Norse, *nôrs, adj.* Norwegian: ancient Scandinavian.—*n.* the Norwegian language: Old Norse (see **old**). [Prob. Du. *Noorsh*, Norwegian.]

north, *nôrth, n.* the direction to the left of a person facing the rising sun (except at the poles): the region lying in that direction: a part of a country, continent, &c., lying relatively in that direction.—*adj.* situated in, facing towards, the north: blowing from the north: north-seeking (of a pole of a magnet).—Also *adv.*—*v.i.* to turn or move northwards.—*adjs.* **north′erly** (TH) (also *adv.*); **north′ern** (TH); **north′ernmost** (TH); **north′-ward(s)** (also *adv.*); **north′-bound**, travelling northwards.—*ns.* **north′erner** (TH), a native of, or resident in, the north; **northing**, north-

ward progress or deviation in sailing.—Compounds such as:—*ns.* **north-east′** (or **nor′-east**), the direction midway between north and east: the region lying in that direction: (*poet.*) the wind blowing from that direction (also *adj.* and *adv.*); **north-west′** (or **nor′-west**); **north′er** (TH), **north-east′er** (**nor′-east′er**), **north-west′er** (**nor′-west′er**), winds blowing from the directions indicated.—*adjs.* **north-east′ern**; **north-west′ern**.—*advs.* **north-east′ward(s)**; **north-west′ward(s)**.—**north pole**, the end of the earth's axis in the Arctic Ocean: its projection on the celestial sphere: the pole of a magnet which, when free, points to the magnetic north (q.v.); **north star**, the pole star, a star very near the north pole of the heavens; **northern lights**, the aurora borealis. [O.E. *north*; cf. Ger. *nord*.]

Northumbrian, *nôr-thum′bri-án, adj.* of modern *Northumberland*, or of the old kingdom of *Northumbria*, stretching from the Humber to the Forth: the dialect of Old English spoken in Northumbria.—Also *n.* [O.E. *Northhymbre, Northhymbraland*.]

Norwegian, *nôr-wēj(y)án, adj.* of Norway, its people, or its language.—*n.* a native of Norway: the language of Norway. [L.L. *Norvegia*, Norway—O.N. *Norvegr* (O.E. *Northweg*)—O.N. *northr*, north, *vegr*, way.]

nose, *nōz, n.* the organ of smell: the power of smelling: a faculty for tracking out, detecting, or recognising: any projecting part suggestive of a nose: the forward end of an aircraft, a projectile, &c.—*v.t.* to smell: to sound through the nose: to track out, detect, or recognise: to make (one's, its way) by feeling or pushing.—*v.i.* to sniff: to pry: to move nose first.—*ns.* **nose′bag**, a bag for food, hung on a horse's nose; **nose′-dive**, a headlong plunge.—*v.i.* to plunge nose-first.—*adjs.* **nos′ey, nosy**, long-nosed: large-nosed: prying.—*n.* **nos′ing**, the projecting rounded edge of the step of a stair or of a moulding.—**nose to the grindstone** (see **grindstone**); **put one's nose out of joint** (see **joint**); **thrust one's nose into**, to meddle officiously with; **turn up one's nose at**, to refuse, or to receive contemptuously. [O.E. *nosu*; Ger. *nase*, L. *nāsus*.]

nosegay, *nōz′gā, n.* a bunch of fragrant flowers: a posy or bouquet. [**nose gay**.]

noso-, *nos-o-*, in composition, of, or relating to, disease:—e.g. *n.* **nosology** (*nos-ol′o-ji*), the science of diseases: the branch of medicine that treats of the classification of diseases.—*adj.* **nosolog′ical**.—*n.* **nosol′ogist**. [Gr. *nosos*, disease, *logos*, discourse.]

nostalgia, *nos-tal′ji-a, n.* home-sickness: sentimental longing for past times.—*adj.* **nostal′gic**, feeling, showing, or expressing, home-sickness, or, more often, regret for vanished days. [Gr. *nostos*, a return, *algos*, pain.]

nostril, *nos′tril, n.* one of the openings of the nose. [M.E. *nosethirl*—O.E. *nosthyr(e)l*—*nosu*, nose, *thyrel*, opening. Cf. **drill**, to pierce, and **thrill**.]

nostrum, *nos′trum, n.* any secret, quack, or patent medicine: any favourite remedy or scheme for reform. [L. *nostrum* (neut.), our own—*nōs*, we.]

not, *not, adv.* a word expressing denial, nega-

Neutral vowels in unaccented syllables: *em′pér-òr*; for certain sounds in foreign words see p. ix.

tion, or refusal. [Same as **naught, nought.**]

nota bene, *nō'ta ben'i, nō'ta ben'e,* mark well, take notice—often abbrev. **N.B.** [L.]

notable, *nō'tā-bl, adj.* worthy of being known or noted: remarkable: distinguished.—*n.* a person or thing worthy of note.—*ns.* **notabil'ity,** the condition of being notable: a notable person or thing; **no'tableness.**—*adv.* **no'tably.** [L. *notābilis—notāre,* to mark.]

notary, *nō'tā-ri, n.* an officer authorised to certify deeds or other formal writings—generally called a **notary public.**—*adj.* **notā'rial.** [L. *notārius.*]

notation, *nō-tā'sh(ô)n, n.* a system of signs or symbols. [L. *notātiō, -ōnis—notāre, -ātum,* to mark.]

notch, *noch, n.* a nick: an identation: a narrow pass.—*v.t.* to make a nick in. [Supposed to be from Fr. *oche* (now *hoche*) with *n* from the indefinite article.]

note, *nōt, n.* a sign, mark, indication of some quality, condition, or fact: a written or printed symbol other than a letter (as, *a note of interrogation*): a mark representing a musical sound: the sound itself: a key of a piano or other instrument: the song, cry, or utterance of a bird or other animal: a short informal letter: a diplomatic paper: a small size of paper used for writing: a memorandum: (*pl.*) a brief record of topics for speech, sermon, article, &c.: a jotting set down provisionally for use afterwards: a comment (explanatory, illustrative, or critical) attached to a text: a paper acknowledging a debt and promising payment (as, a *banknote,* a *note of hand*).—*v.t.* to make a note of: to notice: to annotate.—*adjs.* **not'ed,** well-known (for): renowned, celebrated, notorious; **note'worthy,** worthy of notice: remarkable.—**note of hand,** a promissory (q.v.) note.—**of note,** distinguished; **take note of,** to notice and make a mental note of as significant or important. [Fr.—L. *nota,* a mark.]

nothing, *nuth'ing, n.* no thing: the non-existent: zero number or quantity: a naught: a thing or person of no significance or value: an empty or trivial utterance: a trifle.—*adv.* in no degree, not at all.—*n.* **noth'ingness,** state of being nothing: worthlessness: a thing of no value.—**come to nothing,** to fail to develop or to show results, to be valueless; **for nothing,** in vain: free of charge; **make nothing of,** to be unable to understand, solve, or accomplish: to consider as of no difficulty or importance. [**no, thing.**]

notice, *nōt'is, n.* intimation: information: warning: a writing, placard, &c., conveying an intimation or warning: observation: announcement by a party to an agreement that it is to terminate at a specified time, esp. such announcement of dismissal from, or of resignation from employment: civility or respectful treatment.—*v.t.* to mark, observe: to mention, make observations upon: to treat with civility.—*adj.* **notice'able,** worthy of notice: likely to be noticed.—*adv.* **notice'ably.** [Fr. *notifier*—L. *nōtitia—nōscĕre, nōtum,* to know.]

notify, *nō'ti-fī, v.t.* to make known, declare: to give notice to (a person—of, that):—*pa.t.* and *pa.p.* **no'tified.**—*adj.* **no'tifiable,** (of diseases)

that must be reported to public-health authorities.—*n.* **notificā'tion,** the act of notifying: the notice given: the paper containing the notice. [Fr.—L. *nōtificāre, -ātum—notus,* known, *facĕre,* to make.]

notion, *nō'sh(ô)n, n.* a conception in the mind of the various marks or qualities (of an object): an idea: an opinion, esp. one not very well founded: a caprice or whim.—*adj.* **nō'tional,** speculative: imaginary: fanciful, addicted to whims or capricious notions.—**no notion of,** no intention of, no inclination to: no faculty of, no idea how to. [Fr.—L. *nōtiō, -ōnis—nōscĕre, nōtum,* to know.]

notorious, *nō-tō'ri-us, -tō', adj.* publicly known (now used in a bad sense): infamous.—*n.* **notorī'ety,** state of being notorious: publicity: public exposure.—*adv.* **notō'riously.**—*n.* **notō'riousness.** [Low L. *nōtōrius—nōtus,* known.]

notwithstanding, *not-with-stand'ing, prep.* in spite of.—*conj.* in spite of the fact that, although—*adv.* nevertheless, however, yet. [Orig. a participial phrase in nominative absolute = L. ablative *non obstante.*]

nougat, *nōō'gä, n.* a confection made of a sweet paste filled with chopped almonds or pistachio-nuts. [Fr. (cf. Sp. *nogado,* an almond-cake)—L. *nux, nucis,* a nut.]

nought, *nöt, n.* not anything: nothing: the figure 0.—*adv.* in no degree.—**set at nought, naught** (see naught). [Same as **naught.**]

noun, *nown, n.* (*gram.*) a word used as a name. [Anglo-Fr. *noun* (O.Fr. *non*: Fr. *nom*)—L. *nōmen,* name.]

nourish, *nur'ish, v.t.* to feed: to furnish with food: to help forward the growth of in any way: to bring up: to cherish (a feeling, &c.).—*adj.* **nour'ishing,** affording nourishment.—*n.* **nour'ishment,** the act of nourishing or the state of being nourished: that which nourishes, nutriment. [O.Fr. *norir, noris sant—* (Fr. *nourrir*)—L. *nūtrīre,* to feed.]

nous, *nōōs, nows, n.* intellect: (*coll.*) common sense. [Gr. *nous,* contracted from *noos.*]

nouveau riche, *nōō-vō' rēsh, n.* a person who has recently become rich, esp. one who has no culture:—*pl.* **nouveaux riches** (pronounced as *sing.*). [Fr.]

nouvelle vague, *nōō-vel' väg,* movement in the French cinema aiming at imaginative quality in films in place of size, expense and box-office appeal. [Fr., new wave.]

novel, *nov'l, nuv'l, adj.* new and strange.—*n.* a fictitious prose narrative or tale, a romance.—*n.* **novelette',** a short novel, esp. one without literary quality: (*mus.*) Schumann's name for a short piano piece in free form.—*adj.* **novelett'ish.**—*ns.* **nov'elist,** a novel-writer; **novella** (*nō-vel'lä*: It.), a tale, short story, such as those, or certain of those, in Boccaccio's *Decameron*: *pl.* **novel'le** (*-lā*); **nov'elty,** newness: anything new or strange: a small, usually cheap, manufactured article of unusual or gimmicky design. [Partly through O.Fr. *novelle* (Fr. *nouvelle*) partly through It. *novella,* partly direct from L. *novellus,* fem. *novella—novus,* new.]

November, *nō-vem'bĕr, n.* the eleventh month, ninth of the Roman year. [L. *November—novem,* nine.]

novennial, *nō-ven'yål, adj.* recurring every ninth year. [L. *novennis*—*novem,* nine, *annus,* a year.]

novice, *nov'is, n.* a beginner: a new convert or church member: an inmate of a religious house who has not yet taken the vow.—*n.* **novi'ciate,** **novi'tiate** (*ish'i-åt*), the state of being a novice: the period of being a novice: a novice. [Fr.,—L. *novīcius*—*novus,* new.]

now, *now, adv.* at the present time, or at the time in question, or a very little before (in *just now*) or after: as things are, in view of the facts: used in taking up a new point in narrative, exposition, &c.—*interj.* used in remonstrance or admonition.—*conj.* at this time, when, because (orig., and still often, **now that**).—*n.* the present time.—**now and then, now and again,** sometimes: from time to time; **now... now,** at one time... at another time. [O.E. *nū*; Ger. *nun,* L. *nunc,* Gr. *nȳn.*]

nowadays, *now'a-dāz, adv.* in these times. [Formerly two words, *adays* being O.E. *dæges,* gen. of *dæg,* day, to which the prep. *a* (O.E. *on*) was later added.]

noway, noways, nowise. See **no.**

Nowel(l), **Noël,** *nō-el', n.* (*obs.* except in Christmas carols) Christmas. [O.Fr. (Fr. *noël*); cf. Sp. *natal,* It. *natale*)—L. *nātālis,* belonging to a birthday.]

nowhere, *nō'hwār, adv.* in or to no place. [**no, where.**]

noxious, *nok'shùs, adj.* hurtful, unwholesome.—*adv.* **nox'iously.**—*n.* **nox'iousness.** [L. *noxius*—*noxa,* hurt—*nocēre,* to hurt.]

nozzle, *noz'l, n.* a little nose: an outlet tube, or spout: an open end fitted to a pipe or tube. [Dim. of **nose.**]

nuance, *nū-ās, nwās, n.* a delicate degree or shade of difference. [Fr.,—L. *nūbēs,* a cloud.]

nub, *nub, n.* the point or gist. [Prob. **knub.**]

nubile, *nū'bil, -bîl, adj.* marriageable (esp. of a woman). [L. *nūbilis*—*nūbĕre,* to veil oneself, to marry.]

nuciferous, *nū-sif'e-rus, adj.* nut-bearing. [L. *nux, nucis,* nut, *ferre,* to bear.]

nucleus, *nū'klē-ùs, n.* a central mass or kernel: the densest part of a comet's head: that around which something may grow, or be collected, or be concentrated: a rounded body in the protoplasm of a cell, the centre of its life: the massive part of an atom distinguished from the outlying electrons: (*organic chem.*) a stable group of atoms to which other atoms may be attached so as to form series of compounds (e.g. the *benzene nucleus, ring,* a ring of six carbon atoms occurring in benzene and other hydrocarbons):—*pl.* **nuclei** (*nū'kli-ī*).—*adjs.* **nū'clēal; nū'clēar,** of a nucleus: pertaining to the nucleus of an atom or to the nuclei of atoms: pertaining to, or derived from, fission or fusion of atomic nuclei; **nū'cleate, -d,** having a nucleus.—*ns.* **nū'cleōle, nuclē'olus,** a body observed within a cell nucleus; **nucleonics,** nuclear physics, esp. its practical applications; **nūc'lide,** species of atom of any element distinguished by number of neutrons and protons in its nucleus, and its energy state.— **nuclear energy,** a more exact name for *atomic energy,* energy released or absorbed during reactions taking place in atomic nuclei; **nu-**

clear fission, spontaneous or induced splitting of atomic nucleus; **nuclear fusion,** creation of new nucleus by merging two lighter ones, with release of energy; **nuclear physics,** the science of forces and transformations within the nucleus of the atom; **nuclear reaction,** a reaction within the nucleus of an atom; **nuclear reactor,** an assembly of uranium or plutonium, with moderator, in which a nuclear chain reaction can develop; **nucleic acid,** any of the complex acids which, combined with proteins, are important constituents of cell nuclei. [L. *nucleus*—*nux, nucis,* a nut.]

nude, *nūd, adj.* naked: bare: undraped.—*n.* an unclothed or undraped figure: the state of being unclothed or undraped.—*ns.* **nū'dist,** one who goes naked or approves of going naked; **nudism;** **nū'dity,** the state of being nude: a nude figure. [L. *nūdus,* naked.]

nudge, *nuj, n.* a gentle poke, as with the elbow.—*v.t.* to poke gently. [Origin obscure; perh. conn. with Norw. dial. *nugga,* to push, or with **knock.**]

nugatory, *nū'ga-tór-i, adj.* trifling, worthless, unavailing: inoperative, invalid. [L. *nūgātōrius*—*nūgae,* trifles, trumpery.]

nugget, *nug'et, n.* a lump, esp. of gold. [Origin unknown; there is a S.W. dialect word *nug,* a lump, block.]

nuisance, *nū'såns, n.* that which annoys or hurts, esp. if there be some legal remedy: that which is offensive to the senses: a person or thing that is troublesome or obtrusive. [Fr.,—L. *nocēre,* to hurt.]

null, *nul, adj.* of no legal force, void, invalid: without character or expression.—*n.* **null'ity,** the state of being null or void: an act, document, &c., that is invalid: a mere nothing: a nonentity.—**decree of nullity,** a decree that a marriage has been void from the beginning, has never been legal. [L. *nūllus,* not any, from *ne,* not, *ūllus,* any.]

nulla(h), *nul'ä, n.* a ravine, a water-course. [Hindustani *nālā.*]

nullify, *nul'i-fī, v.t.* to make null, to annul: to make of no value or efficacy:—*pr. p.* null'i-fying; *pa.t.* and *pa.p.* null'ified.—*n.* **nullificā'-tion.** [Late L. *nūllificāre*—*nūllus,* none, *facĕre,* to make.]

numb, *num, adj.* having diminished power of sensation or of motion: powerless to feel or act: stupefied.—*v.t.* to make numb: to deaden:—*pr.p.* numbing (*num'ing*); *pa.p.* numbed (*numd*).—*n.* **numb'ness.** [O.E. *nymen,* *pa.p.* of *niman,* to take.]

number, *num'bér, n.* that by which single things are counted or reckoned: a particular value or sum of single things or units: a representation in arithmetical symbols of such a value or sum: an arithmetical indication of a thing's or person's place in a series (*number 177*): an issue of a periodical or serial publication: an integral portion of an opera or other composition: a (full) tale or count of a company or class of persons (e.g. *make up their number: in, of, among their number*): (in *pl.*) rhythm, verses, music: (*gram.*) property in words of expressing singular and plural (also dual): (in *pl.*; *cap.*) the fourth book of the Old Testament in which an account of a census is given: a

Neutral vowels in unaccented syllables: *em'pér-ór*; for certain sounds in foreign words see p. ix.

490

single item in a programme, esp. of popular music: (*coll.*) an item of clothing on show.—*v.t.* to count: to assign a number, or numbers, to: to amount to.—*adj.* **num′berless**, without number: more than can be counted. —**number system** (*math.*), any set of elements which has two binary operations called addition and multiplication, each of which is commutative and associative, and which is such that multiplication is distributive with respect to addition; **his days are numbered**, his end is near. [Fr. *nombre*—L. *numerus.*]

numerable, *nū′mér-ábl, adj.* that may be numbered or counted.—*adj.* **nū′meral**, pertaining to, consisting of, or expressing number.—*n.* a figure used to express a number, as 1, 2, 3, &c.—*v.t.* **nū′merāte**, to read off as numbers (from figures): (*orig.*) to enumerate, to number.—*adj.* having some understanding of mathematics and science.—*ns.* **nūmerā′tion**, act of numbering: the art of reading figures and expressing the value in numbers; **nū′merātor**, the upper number of a vulgar fraction, which expresses the number of fractional parts taken.—*adjs.* **nūmeric, -al** (*-mer′ik, -ál*), belonging to, expressed in, or consisting in, number. *adv.* **nūmer′ically.**—*adj.* **nu′merous**, great in number or quantity: many. [L. *numerus*, number.]

numismatic, *nū-miz-mat′ik, adj.* pertaining to money, coins, or medals.—*n.sing.* **nūmismat′ics**, the study of coins and medals.—*ns.* **nūmismatol′ogy**, study of coins and medals in relation to history; **numismatol′ogist.** [L. *numisma*—Gr. *nomisma*, current coin—*nomizein*, to use commonly—*nomos*, custom.]

nummulite, *num′ū-līt, n.* a large coin-shaped fossil shell, forming limestones. [L. *nummus*, a coin, and Gr. *lithos*, a stone.]

numskull, *num′skul, n.* a blockhead. [**numb**, **skull**.]

nun, *nun, n.* a woman who, under a vow, has secluded herself in a religious house, to give her time to devotion: a kind of pigeon with feathers on its head like a nun's hood.—*n.* **nunn′ery**, a house for nuns. [O.E. *nunne*—Low L. *nunna, nonna*, a nun, an old maiden lady, orig. mother.]

nunc dimittis, *nungk di-mit′is, n.* the song of Simeon (Luke ii. 29-32) in the R.C. Breviary and the Anglican evening service [From L. *nunc dimittis*, now lettest thou depart.]

nuncio, *nun′shi-ō, n.* an ambassador from the Pope to an emperor or a king.—*n.* **nun′ciātūre**, a nuncio's office or term of office. [It. (now *nunzio*)—L. *nūntius*, a messenger.]

nuncupative, *nung′kū-pā-tiv, adj.* declaring orally or solemnly: (of a will) oral. [L. *nuncupāre*, to call by name—prob. from *nōmen*, name, *capēre*, to take.]

nuptial, *nup′shál, adj.* pertaining to marriage: (*zool.*) pertaining to mating.—*n.* (usu. in *pl.*) marriage: wedding ceremony. [L. *nuptiālis*—*nubēre, nuptum,* to marry.]

nurse, *nûrs, n.* one who suckles a child: one who tends a child: one who has the care of the sick, feeble, or injured: a shrub or tree that protects a young plant.—*v.t.* to suckle: to tend, as an infant or a sick person: to foster (the arts, a specified feeling—e.g. hatred): to manage

with care and economy (resources).—*ns.* **nurs′ery**, place for nursing: an apartment for children: a place where the growth of anything is promoted: a piece of ground where plants are reared; **nurs′eryman**, one who is employed in cultivating plants, &c., for sale; **nurs′ing-fa′ther** (*B.*), a foster-father; **nurs(e)′-ling**, that which is nursed: an infant.—**nursery school**, a school for very young children (aged two to five); **nursery slopes**, slopes set apart for people learning to ski; **nursing home**, a private hospital. [O.Fr. *norrice* (Fr. *nourrice*)—L. *nutrīx, -īcis*—*nūtrīre*, to nourish.]

nurture, *nûr′tyùr, -chùr, n.* upbringing, rearing, training: food.—*v.t.* to nourish: to bring up: to educate.—*n.* **nurt′urer.** [O.Fr. *noriture* (Fr. *nourriture*)—Low L. *nūtrītūra*—L. *nūtrīre*, to nourish.]

nut, *nut, n.* popularly, any fruit with one seed in a hard shell: (*bot.*) a hard dry fruit that does not dehisce or open at maturity, formed from a gynaeceum consisting of two or more united carpels, and usu. containing one seed: a small block, usu. of metal for screwing on the end of a bolt: (*mus.*) the ridge at the top of the finger-board on a fiddle, &c.: (*mus.*) mechanism for tightening or slackening a bow: a small lump of coal: a small biscuit: (*slang*) a crazy person.—*v.i.* to gather nuts:—*pr.p.* nut′ting; *pa.p.* nutt′ed.—*adj.* **nut′-brown**, brown, like a ripe hazelnut.—*ns.* **nut′cracker**, a bird of the crow family: (usu. in *pl.*) an instrument for cracking nuts; **nut′hatch**, any of several small climbing birds that feed on nuts and insects—also **nut′pecker.**—*adj.* **nutt′y**, containing, abounding in nuts: having the flavour of nuts: (*slang*) smart; (also **nuts**; *slang*) mentally unhinged: (also **nuts**; *slang*) foolishly fond of (with *on*).—**a hard nut to crack**, a difficult problem, person or thing to deal with; **in a nutshell**, in a very small space: expressed very concisely and exactly. [O.E. *hnutu*; O.N. *hnot*, Du. *noot*, Ger. *nuss.*]

nutant, *nū′tánt, adj.* nodding: drooping.—*n.* **nūtā′tion**, a nodding: (*astron.*) a slight oscillation of the earth's axis: the oscillation of a spinning top: movement in the stem of a growing plant. [L. *nūtāre*, to nod.]

nutmeg, *nut′meg, n.* the aromatic kernel of an East Indian tree. [M.E. *notemuge*, a hybrid word formed from **nut**, and O.Fr. *muge*, musk—L. *muscus*, musk.]

nutria, *nū′tri-a, n.* the coypu, a South American aquatic rodent: its fur. [Sp. *nutria*, otter—L. *lūtra.*]

nutrient, *nū′tri-ént, adj.* feeding: nourishing.—*ns.* **nū′triment**, that which nourishes: food; **nutri′tion**, act or process of nourishing: food.—*adjs.* **nutri′tious**, nourishing; **nū′tritive**, nourishing: concerned in nutrition. [L. *nūtrīre*, to nourish.]

nux vomica, *nuks vom′ik-a, n.* a seed that yields strychnine: the East Indian tree that produces it. [L. *nux*, a nut, *vomēre*, to vomit.]

nuzzle, *nuz′l, v.t.* and *v.i.* to poke, press, burrow, root, rub, sniff, caress, or investigate with the nose.—*v.t.* thrust in (the nose or head).—*v.i.* to snuggle: to go with the nose toward the ground. [Freq. vb. from **nose.**]

fāte, fär; mē, hûr (her); *mīne; mōte, för; mūte; mōōn, fōōt;* ᴛʜen (then)

491

nyctalopia, *nik-ta-lō′pi-a, n.* properly, night-blindness, abnormal difficulty in seeing in a faint light: by confusion sometimes, day-blindness. [Gr. *nyktalōps,* night-blind, day-blind—*nyx, nyktos,* night, *alaos,* blind, *ōps.* eye, face.]

nylghau, nilgau. See **nilgai.**

nylon, *nī′lon, n.* name for certain plastics capable of being formed into filaments in which the structural elements are oriented in the direction of the axis: (*pl.—coll.*) stockings made of such material.

nymph, *nimf, n.* (*myth.*) one of the divinities who inhabited mountains, rivers, trees, &c.: a young and beautiful maiden: an immature insect similar to the adult but with wings and sex-organs undeveloped: (*obs.*) an insect pupa.—*n.pl.* **nymphae** (*-ē*).—*n.* **nymph′olepsy,** a species of ecstasy or frenzy said to have seized those who had seen a nymph: a yearning for the unattainable; **nymphomā′nia,** uncontrollable sexual desire in women; **nymphomā′niac.** [L. *nympha*—Gr. *nymphē,* a bride, a nymph.]

Neutral vowels in unaccented syllables: *em′pér-ôr;* for certain sounds in foreign words see p. ix.

O

O-level, *ō'lev'él, n.* G.C.E. examination at end of school course requiring ordinary, i.e. less than A-level, knowledge of a school subject: a pass in an O level

O, oh, *ō, interj.* an exclamation of wonder, pain, desire, fear, &c. The form *oh* is the more usual in prose.

o, usually written **o'**, an abbrev. for **of** and **on**.

oaf, *ōf, n.* a changeling left by the fairies: a dolt: an awkward lout:—*pl.* **oafs.**—*adj.* **oaf'ish.** [O.N. *ālfr,* elf.]

oak, *ōk, n.* a genus of trees of the beech family: their timber valued in shipbuilding, &c. *n.* **oak'-app'le,** a gall caused by an insect on an oak-leaf.—*adj.* **oak'en,** consisting of or made of oak. [O.E. *āc;* O.N. *eik,* Ger. *eiche.*]

oakum, *ōk'úm, n.* tarry ropes untwisted and teased into loose hemp for caulking the seams of ships. [O.E. *ācumba—cemban,* to comb.]

oar, *ōr, ör, n.* a light pole with a flat end (the *blade*) for propelling a boat: an oarsman.—*v.t.* to impel as by rowing.—*v.i.* to row.—*adj.* **oared,** furnished with oars.—*n.* **oars'man,** one who rows with an oar.—**rest, lie on the, one's oars,** to cease rowing without shipping the oars: to rest, take things easily; **put in one's oar,** to interfere. [O.E. *ār.*]

oasis, *ō-ā'sis, ō'ä-sis, n.* a fertile spot or tract in a sandy desert. (*lit.* and *fig.*):—*pl.* **oases** (*ō-ā'sēz*). [Gr. *oasis,* an Egyptian word.]

oast, *ōst, n.* a kiln to dry hops or malt.—*n.* **oast'-house.** [O.E. *āst.*]

oat, *ōt* (oftener in *pl.* **oats,** *ōts*), *n.* a well known genus of grasses, whose seeds are much used as food: the seeds: a musical pipe of oat-straw.—*n.* **oat'-cake',** a thin, hard cake of oatmeal.—*adj.* **oat'en,** consisting of an oat stem or straw: made of oatmeal.—*n.* **oat'meal,** meal made of oats.—**sow one's wild oats,** to indulge in youthful dissipation. [O.E. *āte,* pl. *ātan.*]

oath, *ōth, n.* a solemn appeal to a god or to something holy or reverenced as witness of the truth of a statement or of the inviolability of a promise: an irreverent use of God's name: an ejaculation or imprecation:—*pl.* **oaths** (*ōтнz*). [O.E. *āth;* Ger. *eid,* O.N. *eithr.*]

obbligato, *ob-li-gä'tō, n.* a musical accompaniment that is itself an essential part of the composition, esp. one by a single instrument. [It.—L. *obligātus,* bound, obliged.]

obdurate, *ob'dū-rát* (or *-dū'-*), *adj.* hardened in heart or in feelings: stubborn.—*n.* **ob'duracy,** state of being obdurate: invincible hardness of heart.—*adv.* **ob'durately.**—*n.* **ob'durateness.** [L. *obdūrāre, -ātum—ob-,* against, *dūrāre,* to harden—*dūrus,* hard.]

obeah. See obi (2).

obedience, *ō-bē'dyéns, -di-éns, n.* state of being obedient: compliance with commands, instructions, &c.: dutiful submission to authority.—*adj.* **obe'dient,** obeying: ready to obey.—*adv.* **obe'diently.** [L. *obēdientia—obēdiens,* pr.p. of *obēdīre.* See **obey.**]

obeisance, *ō'bā'sáns, n.* (*obs.*) obedience: a bow or act of reverence. [Fr. *obéissance—obéir.* See **obey.**]

obelus, *ob'é-lus, n.* a dagger-sign (†), used esp. in referring to footnotes:—*pl.* **ob'eli** (*-lī*).—*n.* **ob'elisk,** a tall, four-sided, tapering pillar, usually of one stone, finished at the top like a flat pyramid. [L. *obelus*— Gr. *obelos* (dim. *obeliskos*), a spit.]

obese, *ō'bēs, adj.* fat, fleshy.—*ns.* **obese'ness, obes'ity,** fatness: abnormal fatness. [L. *obēsus—ob-,* completely, *cdēre, ēsum,* to eat.]

obey, *ō-bā', v.i.* to render obedience: to submit.—*v.t.* to do as told by: to comply with: to yield to. [Fr. *obéir*—L. *oboedīre, obēdīre—ob-, towards, audīre,* to hear.]

obfuscate, *ob-fus'kāt, v.t.* to darken: to bewilder.—*n.* **obfusca'tion.** [L. *obfuscāre, -ātum— ob-,* inten., *fuscus,* dark.]

obi, *ō'bi, n.* a broad, gaily embroidered sash worn by Japanese women and children. [Jap.]

obi, *ō'bi,* **obeah,** *ō'bi-ä, n.* witchcraft and poisoning practised by the Negroes of the West Indies. [Of West African origin.]

obit, *ob'it* or *ō'bit, n.* the date of death: funeral ceremonies: an anniversary or other commemoration of a death. *adjs.* **obit'ual,** pertaining to obits; **obit'uary,** relating to the death of a person or persons.—*n.* a register of deaths (*orig.*) in a monastery: an account of a deceased person, or a notice of his death. [L. *obitus—obīre, -itum,* to go to meet, to die—*ob,* in the way of, *īre,* to go.]

object, *ob'jekt, n.* a thing capable of being presented to the senses, a thing observed, a material thing: a sight, a person or thing whose appearance arouses scorn, amusement, or pity: an end or aim: that which is thought of, regarded as exterior to the mind—opposed to *subject:* (*gram.*) part of a sentence denoting that upon which the action of a transitive verb is directed or which is similarly related to a preposition.—*v.t.* **object',** to bring forward in opposition.—*v.i.* to be opposed (to): to feel or express disapproval: to refuse assent.—*ns.* **ob'ject-glass,** in an optical instrument, the lens, or combination of lenses, at the end next the object to be observed or projected; **objec'tion,** act of objecting: feeling or expression of disapproval: an argument against.—*adjs.* **objec'tionable,** that may be objected to: displeasing, distasteful; **object'ive,** relating to an object: exterior to the mind: detached, impartial: as opposed to *subjective,* that which is real or exists in nature in contrast with what is ideal or exists merely in the thought of the individual: also, showing facts without obvious colouring due to the individual tastes and views of the artist (e.g. *objective treat-*

ment): (*gram.*) belonging to the case of the object.—*n.* (*gram.*) the case of the object: the point to which the operations (esp. of an army) are directed: (also **objective-glass**) an object-glass.—*adv.* **object'ively.**—*ns.* **object'-iveness, objectiv'ity; ob'ject-less'on,** a lesson in which a material object is before the class: (*fig.*) an instructive example, esp. a warning example (e.g. *Napoleon's fate is an object-lesson for would-be conquerors*); **objec'tor,** one who objects.—**objective genitive** (see **genitive**).[L.*objectāre,* freq. of *ob(j)icēre—ob,* in the way of, *jacĕre,* to throw.]

objet d'art, *ob-zhā där,* an article with artistic value; **objet trouvé,** *trōō-vā,* something that has been found and is considered to be of artistic value:—*pls.* **objets d'art, trouvés.** [Fr.]

objurgate, *ob'jŭr-gāt, ob-jŭr'gāt v.t.* and *v.i.* to chide.—*n.* **objurgā'tion.**—*adj.* **objur'gatory.** [L. *objurgāre, -ātum,* to rebuke—*ob-,* intensive, *jurgāre,* to chide.]

oblate, *ob-lāt', adj.* (of a spheroid) flattened at opposite poles, shaped like an orange.—*n.* **oblate'ness,** flatness at the poles. [Formed on the analogy of **prolate** with the pfx. *ob-.*]

oblation, *ob-lā'sh(ŏ)n, n.* anything offered in worship: an offering. [L. *oblātiō—oblātus,* pa. p. of *offerre.* See **offer.**]

oblige, *ō-blīj', v.t.* to bind or constrain: to bind by some favour rendered, hence to do a favour to.—*n.* **obligā'tion,** act of obliging: a moral or legal bond: a debt of gratitude: a favour: (*law*) a bond containing a penalty in case of failure.—*adj.* **ob'ligatory** (or *o-blig'-*), binding, constraining: of the nature of an obligation or duty, not subject to discretion or choice.—*adv.* **ob'ligatorily** (or *ob-lig'-*).—*n.* **ob'ligatoriness** (or *ob-lig'-*).—*n.* **obligee** (*ob-li-jē'*), the person to whom another is obliged; **oblīge'ment,** a favour.—*adj.* **oblīg'ing,** disposed to confer favours, ready to do a good turn.—*adv.* **oblīg'ingly.**—*ns.* **oblīg'ingness; obligor** (*ob'lig-ór; law*), person who binds himself to another. [Fr. *obliger*—L. *obligāre, -ātum—ob-,* down, *ligāre,* to bind.]

oblique, *ob-lēk', adj.* slanting: not perpendicular: not parallel: not straightforward, indirect: (*geom.*) not at right angles.—*ns.* **oblique'ness, obliquity** (-*lik'-*), state of being oblique: a slanting direction: error or fault.—*adv.* **oblique'ly.—oblique case** (*gram.*), any case other than the nominative and vocative; **oblique narration** or **speech** (L. *ōrātiō oblīqua*), indirect narration, the words of a speaker reported in the third person. [L. *oblīquus—ob-,* intensive, *līquis,* slanting.]

obliterate, *ob-lit'ér-āt, v.t.* to blot out, to efface, to destroy.—*n.* **obliterā'tion.** [L. *oblīterāre, oblītterāre, -ātum—ob,* over, *lītera, littera,* a letter.]

oblivion, *ob-liv'i-ón, n.* forgetfulness: a state of being forgotten: amnesty.—*adj.* **obliv'ious,** forgetful: unaware (of; also with *to*): causing forgetfulness.—*n.* **obliv'iousness.** [Fr.,—L. *oblīviō, -ōnis—oblīviscī,* to forget.]

oblong, *ob'long, adj.* long in one direction, longer than broad.—*n.* (*geom.*) a rectangle longer than broad: any oblong figure. [L. *oblongus—ob-* (force obscure), *longus,* long.]

obloquy, *ob'lo-kwi, n.* reproachful language, cen-

sure, calumny: disgrace. [L. *obloquium—ob, loquī,* to speak.]

obnoxious, *ob-nok'shŭs, adj.* liable (to hurt or punishment): objectionable, offensive.—*adv.* **obnox'iously.**—*n.* **obnox'iousness.** [L. *obnoxius—ob-,* exposed to, *noxa,* hurt.]

oboe, *ō'bō,* (*arch.*) *ō'boi,* (older form **hautboy,** *hō'-,* or *ō'boi*), *n.* a treble woodwind musical instrument, with a double reed and keys: a treble stop on the organ. [It. *oboe*—Fr. *hautbois—haut,* high, *bois,* wood.]

obol, *ob'ol, n.* in ancient Greece, a small coin, worth about three-halfpence: a weight, the sixth part of a drachma.—Also **ob'olus:**—*pl.* **ob'olī.** [L.,—Gr. *obolos.*]

obscene, *ob-sēn', adj.* foul, digusting: indecent, esp. in a sexual sense: (less strongly) offending against an accepted standard of morals or taste.—*adv.* **obscene'ly.**—*ns.* **obscene'ness, obscen'ity** (-*sen'i-ti*). [L. *obscēnus.*]

obscure, *ob-skūr', adj.* dark, enveloped in darkness: not distinct: not clear or legible: not easily understood, doubtful: hidden: inconspicuous: lowly, unknown to fame.—*v.t.* to darken (*lit* and *fig.*): to hide.—*ns.* **obscū'rant,** one who labours to prevent enlightenment or reform; **obscū'rantism,** opposition to inquiry or reform; **obscū'rantist,** an obscurant; **obscūrā'tion,** the act of obscuring or state of being obscured.—*adv.* **obscūre'ly.**—*n.* **obscū'rity,** state or quality of being obscure: darkness: a humble place or condition: unintelligibleness. [Fr. *obscur*—L. *obscūrus.*]

obsequies, *ob'sé-kwiz, n.pl.* funeral rites and solemnities. [L.L. *obsequiae,* a confusion of *exsequiae,* funeral rites and *obsequium.* See next word.]

obsequious, *ob-sē'kwi-us, adj.* compliant to excess, fawning.—*adv.* **obsē'quiously.**—*n.* **obsē'quiousness.** [L. *obsequiōsus,* compliant, *obsequium,* compliance.]

observe, *ob-zūrv', v.t.* to keep in view: to notice: to regard attentively: to remark in words: to comply with: to keep with ceremony.—*v.i.* to take notice: to attend: to remark (on).—*adj.* **observ'able,** discernible: noteworthy.—*n.* **observ'ableness.**—*adv.* **observ'ably.**—*n.* **observ'ance,** the keeping of, or acting according to, a law, duty, custom, ceremony: the keeping with ceremony or according to custom.—*adj.* **observ'ant,** observing: taking notice: having acute powers of observing and noting: carefully attentive.—*adv.* **observ'antly.**—*n.* **observā'tion,** act of observing: habit, practice, or faculty of observing: the act of recognising and noting phenomena as they occur in nature, as distinguished from *experiment*: that which is observed: fact of being observed: a remark.—*adj.* **observā'tional,** consisting of, or containing, observations or remarks: derived from observation.—*ns.* **observ'atory,** a place for making astronomical, meteorological, &c., observations (also *adj.*); **observ'er,** one who regards attentively: one who complies with or keeps: one engaged in scientifically exact observation: a representative sent to listen to formal discussions but not to take part: formerly, an airman who accompanied a pilot to observe, now **flying officer:** a member of the Royal Observer Corps, a uniformed organisa-

Neutral vowels in unaccented syllables: *em'pér-ŏr*; for certain sounds in foreign words see p. ix.

tion affiliated to the Royal Air Force.—*adj.* **observ'ing,** habitually taking notice. [Fr.,—L. *observāre,* *-ātum*—*ob,* before, *servāre,* to keep.]

obsess, *ob-ses',* *v.t.* to haunt: completely to engage the thoughts of.—*n.* **obsession** (*-sesh'-(ò)n*), morbid persistence of an idea in the mind: a fixed idea. [L. *obsidēre, obsessum,* to besiege.]

obsidian, *ob-sid'i-àn, n.* a vitreous volcanic rock resembling bottle-glass. [From one *Obsidius* (properly *Obsius*), who, according to Pliny, discovered it in Ethiopia.]

obsolescent, *ob-so-les'ént, adj.* going out of use.—*n.* **obsoles'cence.**—*adj.* **ob'solete** (*-lēt*), gone out of use, antiquated: (*biol.*) no longer functional or fully developed.—**planned, built-in, obsolescenece,** the deliberate going out of date of a manufactured article according to a pre-arranged plan—achieved e.g. by change of certain non-essential features of the model. [L. *obsolēscēre, obsolētum,* to decay.]

obstacle, *ob'stà-kl, n.* anything that stands in the way of or hinders progress, an obstruction.—**obstacle race,** a race in which obstacles are laid in the course. [Fr.,—L. *obstāculum*—*ob,* in the way of, *stāre,* to stand.]

obstetric, -al, *ob-stet'rik, -àl, adjs.* pertaining to midwifery.—*ns.* **obstetrician** (*-rish'àn*), one skilled in obstetrics: **obstet'rics,** midwifery. [L *obstetrīcius*—*obstetrix, -īcis,* a midwife.]

obstinate, *ob'sti-nàt, adj.* blindly or excessively firm, stubborn: unyielding: not easily remedied —*ns.* **ob'stinacy, ob'stinateness,** the condition of being obstinate.—*adv.* **ob'stinately.** [L. *obstināre, -ātum, ob,* in the way of, *stāre,* to stand.]

obstreperous, *ob-strep'ér us, adj.* noisy, clamorous: unruly.—*adv.* **obstrep'erously.** [L. *obstreperus*—*ob,* before, against, *strepěre,* to make a noise.]

obstruct, *ob-strukt', v.t.* to block up, make impassable: to hinder from passing: to hamper: to shut off (e.g. light, a view).—*n.* **obstruc'tion,** act of obstructing: state of being obstructed: that which hinders progress or action: an obstacle: opposition by dilatory tactics, as in a legislative assembly.—*adj.* **obstruct'ive,** tending to obstruct: hindering.—*adv.* **obstruct'ively.**—*adj.* **ob'struent,** obstructing, blocking up.—*n.* (*med.*) anything that obstructs, esp. in the passages of the body. [L. *obstruěre, obstructum*—*ob,* in the way of, *struěre, structum,* to build.]

obtain, *ob-tān', v.t.* to get, to procure by effort, to gain.—*v.i.* to be established, prevalent: to hold good: (*arch.*) to prevail.—*adj.* **obtain'able.** [Fr.,—L. *obtinēre,* to occupy—*ob,* against, *tenēre,* to hold.]

obtrude, *ob-trōōd', v.t.* to thrust forward, or upon one, unduly or unwelcomely.—*v.i.* to thrust oneself forward.—*ns.* **obtrud'ing, obtru'sion,** an unwanted thrusting in or forward.—*adj.* **obtrusive** (*ob-trōō'siv*), disposed to thrust oneself forward: unduly prominent or noticeable.—*adv.* **obtrus'ively.** [L. *obtrūděre*—*ob,* before, *trūděre, trūsum,* to thrust.]

obtuse, *ob-tūs', adj.* blunt: not pointed: (*geom.*) greater than a right angle: stupid: insensi-tive.—*adv.* **obtuse'ly.**—*n.* **obtuse'ness.** [L. *obtūsus*—*obtundēre,* to blunt—*ob,* against, *tunděre,* to beat.]

obverse, *ob'vûrs, ob-vûrs', adj.* turned towards one: complemental, constituting the opposite aspect of the same fact: (*bot.*) having the base narrower than the apex.—*n.* **ob'verse,** the side of a coin containing the head or principal symbol: the side of anything normally presented to view.—*adv.* **obverse'ly.** [L. *obversus*—*ob,* towards, *vertěre,* to turn.]

obviate, *ob'vi-āt, v.t.* (*obs.*) to meet on the way: hence to prevent, get round, avert (e.g. a necessity, a difficulty, a danger). [L. *obviāre, -ātum*—*ob,* in the way of, *viāre, viātum,* to go—*via,* a way.]

obvious, *ob'vi-us, adj.* (*arch.*) meeting one in the way: evident.—*adv.* **ob'viously.**—*n.* **ob'viousness.** [L. *obvius*—*ob, via.* See **obviate.**]

obvolute, -d, *ob'vo-lūt, -lōōt, -id, adjs.* (*bot.*) arranged so that each leaf of a pair enfolds one half of the other. [L. *obvolūtus*—*ob,* over, *volvĕre, volūtum,* to roll.]

ocarina, *ok-ä-rē'na, n.* a fluty-toned, bird-shaped, musical toy, orig. of terra-cotta. [It., dim. of *oca,* a goose.]

occasion, *o-kā'zh(ò)n, n.* a special time or season: an event: an opportunity: a reason or excuse: an immediate but subsidiary cause: (usu in *pl.*) business.—*v.t.* to cause: to give occasion to.—*adj.* **occā'sional,** occurring infrequently, irregularly, now and then: produced on or for a special event: subsidiary, secondary (e.g. *occasional cause*) —*adv.* **occā'sionally,** now and then: at infrequent times. [Fr.,—L. *occāsio, -ōnis,* opportunity—*occidēre*—*ob,* in the way of, *cadĕre, cāsum,* to fall.]

occident, *ok'si-dênt, n.* the western quarter of the sky where the heavenly bodies set: (often *cap.*) the West (q.v.; cf. *orient*).—*adj.* **occiden'tal,** setting: western.—*n.* (often *cap.*) a native of the West. [Fr.,—L. *occidēns, -entis,* pr.p. of *occidĕre,* to set.]

occiput, *ok'si-put, n.* the back of the head or skull.—*adj.* **occip'ital,** pertaining to the back of the head. [L.,—*ob,* over against, *caput,* head.]

occlude, *o-klōōd', v.t.* to shut in or out: to stop (as a passage, cavity, or opening): to absorb or retain (as certain metals and other solids do gases).—*n.* **occlu'sion** (*-zh(ò)n*). [L. *occlūděre, -clūsum*—*ob,* in the way of, *claudēre,* to shut.]

occult, *ok-ult', adj.* hidden: beyond the range of sense: mysterious, magical, supernatural.—*ns.* **occultā'tion,** a concealing, esp. of one of the heavenly bodies by another: state of being hid; **occult'ism,** the doctrine or study of things hidden or mysterious—theosophy, &c.—*adv.* **occult'ly.**—*n.* **occult'ness.**—**occult sciences,** alchemy, astrology, magic, &c. [Fr.,—L.*occulĕre, occultum,* to hide.]

occupy, *ok'ū-pī, v.t.* to take or seize: to hold possession of: to take up, as room, &c.: to fill, as an office: to employ, take up (time, a person): (*B.*) to trade with:—*pa.t.* and *pa.p.* occ'ūpied.—*ns.* **occ'upancy,** the act or fact of occupying: possession; **occ'upant,** one who takes or has possession; **occupa'tion,** the act of occupying: possession: state of being occupied:

work that temporarily takes up one's attention: habitual employment, craft, or trade; **occ′upīer**, an occupant.—*adj.* **occupā′tional**, as in **occupational disease**, a disease common among workers engaged in a particular occupation because encouraged by the conditions of that occupation; **occupational therapy**, treatment of a disease (incl. a mental disease) or an injury by a regulated course of suitable work. [Fr.,—L. *occupāre*, *-ātum—ob*, to, on, *capĕre*, to take.]

occur, *o-kûr′*, *v.i.* to come into the mind of a person (e.g. *it occurs to me that*): to happen: to be, to be found:—*pr.p.* occurr′ing; *pa.p.* occurred′.—*n.* **occurr′ence**, act or fact of happening: an event.—*adj.* **occurr′ent**, coming in the way: incidental.—*n.* one who comes to meet another: (*B.*) an occurrence. [L.—*occurrĕre—ob*, in the way of, *currĕre*, to run.]

ocean, *ō′shán*, *n.* the vast expanse of salt water that covers the greater part of the surface of the globe: any one of its five great divisions: any immense expanse or vast quantity.—*adj.* pertaining to the ocean.—*adj.* **oceanic** (*ō-shi-an′ik*), pertaining to the ocean: found or formed in the ocean.—*ns.* **oceanog′raphy**, the scientific description of the ocean; **ocean′og′rapher**, one versed in oceanography.—*adj.* **oceanograph′ic**. [Fr.,—L. *Ŏcĕānus*—Gr. *Ōkĕănos*, the great river supposed to encircle the earth.]

ocelot, *ō′sē-lot*, *n.* an American cat like a small leopard. [Mexican.]

ochlocracy, *ok-lok′ra-si*, *n.* mob-rule. [Gr. *ochlokratiā—ochlos*, a crowd, *kratos*, power.]

ochre, *ō′kér*, *n.* a fine clay, mostly pale yellow.—*adjs.* **o′chreous**, **o′chry**, consisting of, containing, or resembling ochre. [Fr.,—L. *ōchra*—Gr. *ōchrā—ōchros*, pale yellow.]

octachord, *ok′ta-körd*, *n.* a musical instrument with eight strings: a diatonic series of eight tones. [Gr. *oktō*, eight, *chordē*, string.]

octagon, *ok′ta-gon*, *n.* a plane figure of eight sides and eight angles.—*adj.* **octag′onal**. [Gr. *oktō*, eight, *gōniā*, an angle.]

octahedron, *ok-ta-hē′dron*, *n.* a solid bounded by eight plane faces.—*adj.* **octahē′dral**. [Gr. *oktō*, eight, *hedrā*, a base.]

octane, *ok′tān*, *n.* C_8H_{18}, the eighth member of the paraffin series of hydrocarbons. So-called *iso*-octane serves as a standard of petrol comparison, the **octane number** being the percentage by volume of this octane in a mixture which has the same knocking (q.v.) characteristics as the motor fuel under test. [Gr. *oktō*, eight, and *-ane*, a termination used to denote a saturated hydrocarbon.]

octangular, *ok-tang′gū-lár*, *adj.* having eight angles. [L. *octo*, eight, and **angular**.]

octant, *ok′tánt*, *n.* the eighth part of a circle: an instrument for measuring angles. [L. *octāns*, *-antis*, an eighth.]

octave, *ok′tiv*, *-tāv*, *n.* a set of eight: the last day of eight beginning with a church festival: the eight days from a festival to its octave: a note or sound an eighth above (or below) another: the range of notes or keys from any one to its octave: the first eight lines of a sonnet.—*adj.* consisting of eight. [Fr.,—L. *octāvus*, eighth—*octo*, eight.]

octavo, *ok-tā′vō*, *adj.* having eight leaves to the sheet.—*n.* a book printed on sheets folded into eight leaves, contracted 8vo:—*pl.* **octā′vos**. [L. *in octavo*, in the eighth.]

octet, **octette**, *ok-tet′*, *n.* a group of eight (lines, singers, &c.): a composition for eight musicians. [From L. *octo*, on analogy of **duet**.]

October, *ok-tō′bér*, *n.* the eighth month of the Roman year, which began in March: the tenth month in our calendar. [L. *octō*, eight.]

octodecimo, *ok-tō-des′i-mō*, *adj.* having eighteen leaves to the sheet, contracted 18mo. [L. *octōdecim*, eighteen.]

octogenarian, *ok-tō-je-nā′ri-án*, *n.* one who is eighty years old.—Also *adj.*—*adj.* **octog′enary**. [L. *octōgēnārius*, pertaining to eighty.]

octopod, *ok′tō-pod*, *adj.* eight-footed or eight-armed.—*n.* an octopus.—*n.* **Octopoda** (*ok-top′o-da*), cephalopods with eight arms, as octopuses (cf. *Decapoda*). [See **octopus**.]

octopus, *ok′tō-pus*, or *ok-tō′pus*, *n.* a genus of eight-armed cephalopods:—*pl.* **oc′topuses**, **octō′podēs**. [Gr. *okto*, eight, *pous*, gen. *podos*, foot.]

octosyllabic, *ok-tō-sil-ab′ik*, *adj.* consisting of eight syllables.—*n.* **oc′tosyllable**, a word of eight syllables. [L. *octo*, eight, and **syllable**.]

ocular, *ok′ū-lár*, *adj.* pertaining to the eye: formed in, or known by the eye: received by actual sight.—*n.* eye-piece (q.v.).—*adv.* **oc′ularly**.—*n.* **oc′ulist**, a doctor skilled in diseases of the eye. [L. *oculus*, the eye.]

odalisque, **odalisk**, *ō′da-lisk*, *n.* a female slave in a harem. [Fr.,—Turk. *ōdaliq—ōdah*, a chamber.]

odd, *od*, *adj.* not exactly divisible by two: unpaired: not one of a complete set: left over: extra: unusual: queer: eccentric.—*n.* (*golf*) one stroke more than an opponent has played:—in *pl.* **odds** (*odz*), inequalities: difference in favour of one against another: more than an even wager: the amount or proportion by which the bet of one exceeds that of another: chances: dispute, strife: scraps, miscellaneous pieces, as in the phrase **odds and ends**.—*ns.* **odd′fellow**, a member of a secret benevolent society called Oddfellows; **odd′ity**, the state of being odd or singular: strangeness: a singular person or thing.—*adv.* **odd′ly**.—*ns.* **odd′-man-out′**, a man who is left out when numbers are made up: a person set apart, willingly or unwillingly, by difference of interests, &c., from a group in which he finds himself; **odd′ment**, a scrap, remnant; **odd′ness**.—*adj.* **odds′-on′**, of a chance, better than even.—**at odds**, at variance. [O.N. *oddi*, a point, triangle, odd number; cf. O.E. *ord*, point.]

ode, *ōd*, *n.* (*orig.*) a poem intended to be sung: an elaborate lyric, generally addressed to some person or thing. [Fr. *ode*—Gr. *ōidē*, contr. from *aoidē—aeidein*, to sing.]

odium, *ō′di-um*, *n.* general hatred, the bad feeling naturally aroused by a particular action (e.g. *incurred the odium of telling the truth*).—*adj.* **o′dious**, hateful, offensive, repulsive, causing hatred.—*adv.* **o′diously**.—*n.* **o′diousness**. [L. *ōdium.*]

odometer. Same as **hodometer**.

odont-, *od-ont′-*, **od′ont-**, **odonto-**, *-ō*, *-o*, in com-

Neutral vowels in unaccented syllables: *em′pér-ór*; for certain sounds in foreign words see p. ix.

496

position, tooth.—*ns.* **odontalgia** (*-al'ji-a*) toothache; **odontol'ogy**, the science of teeth. [Gr. *odous*, gen. *odontos*, a tooth.]

odour, *ō'dór, n.* smell: (*fig.*) savour: repute.—*adj.* **odorif'erous,** emitting a (usually pleasant) smell, fragant.—*adv.* **odorif'erously.**—*adj.* **o'dorous,** emitting an odour or scent, sweet-smelling, fragant: (*coll.*) bad-smelling.—*adv.* **o'dorously.**—*adj.* **o'dourless,** without odour.— **odour of sanctity** (see **sanctity**),—**in bad odour,** in bad repute [Fr.,—L. *odor.*]

Odyssey, *od'is-i. n.* a Greek epic poem, ascribed to Homer, describing ten years' wanderings of *Odysseus* (Ulysses) on his way home from Troy to Ithaca: (not *cap.*) any adventurous journey:—*pl.* **od'ysseys.**

oecumenical. Same as **ecumenical.**

oedema, *ē-dē'ma, n.* (*med.*) a dropsical swelling of tissues.—Also **edema.** [Gr. *oidēma,* swelling.]

Oedipus complex, *ē'di-pus kom'pleks,* (*psych.*) in a son, a complex involving undue attachment to his mother, hostility to his father, [*Oedipus,* king of Thebes, who unwittingly married his mother, and **complex.**]

o'er, *ōr,* contracted from **over.**

oersted, *ûr'sted, n.* CGS unit of magnetic field strength, about 80 amperes per metre. [Hans Christian *Oersted* (1777-1851), Danish physicist.]

oesophagus, esophagus, *ē-sof'a-gus, n.* in vertebrates, the section of the alimentary canal leading from the pharynx to the stomach, the gullet. [Gr. *oisophagos,* gullet.]

oestrogen, *ēs'trō-jēn, n.* one of the female sex hormones.—Also **estrogen.**

œuvre, *œvr', n.* work (of an artist, writer &c.): *pl.* **œuvres.** [Fr.]

of, *ov, ôv. prep.* orig. meant 'from', 'away from' (see **off**): now has many shades of meaning in idiomatic phrases, including: **from** (*e.g. within a week of, a yard of*; *upwards of*): belonging to: among: proceeding or derived from: owing to (cause or reason, as *to die of, sick of, proud of*): concerning (*e.g. to speak, think of*): (*arch.*) by: indicating material or elements (*e.g. a man of straw, a sum of five hundred pounds*): indicating some form of deprivation (*e.g. rid of, destitute of, take leave of*): showing a possessive relation (*e.g. the son of the owner of the house*): showing an objective relation (*e.g. the care of the sick, loss of appetite*).—**of purpose** (*B.*), intentionally. [O.E. *of*; Du. *af,* Ger. *ab,* L. *ab,* Gr. *apo.*]

off, *of, adv.* away: newly in motion: out of continuity: no longer available: in deterioration or diminution.—*adj.* most distant: on the opposite or farther side: (*cricket*; see **off side**): (*fig.*) remote (*e.g. an off chance*): not devoted to usual business (*e.g. an off day*): not showing the usual activity: not up to the usual standard of quality or efficiency.—*prep.* not on, away from.—*interj.* away! depart!—*n.* (*cricket*) the off side of the wicket.—*adj.* (and *adv.*) **off-and-on',** occasional(ly).—*adj.* **off'-beat,** out of the ordinary (either eccentric or commendably unconventional).—*n.* **off'-break,** (*cricket*) deviation of a ball towards the wicket from the off side.—*n.* **off'-col'our,** out of condition: out of sorts.—*n.* **off'-day,** a

day when one is not at one's best (see also **off,** *adj.* above).—*adv.* **off'hand,** extempore: without hesitating.—*adj.* unceremonious, free and easy: ungraciously lacking in ceremony.—*n.* **off'ing,** visible part of the sea at some distance from the shore: (*fig.*) a place or time a short way off (*e.g. promotion is in the offing*).—*adj.* **off'-key',** (*lit.* and *fig.*) out of tune: not in keeping.—*n.* **off-li'cence,** a licence to sell alcoholic liquors for consumption off the premises only.—*v.t.* **off'-load,** to unload.—*adj.* **off'-peak',** not at (time of) highest demand. *ns.* **off'scouring** (usu. *pl.*), matter scoured off, refuse, anything vile or despised; **off'set,** a thing or value set off against another as an equivalent or compensation: a horizontal ledge on the face of a wall: in surveying, a perpendicular from the main line to an outlying point.—*v.t.* to place (against) as an equivalent: to counterbalance, compensate for.—*n.* **off'shoot,** that which shoots off from the main stem: anything growing out of another: art: something offshore, from the shore: at a distance from the shore.—*ns.* **off side,** the right-hand side in driving: the farther side: (*cricket*) the side of the field opposite to that on which the batsman stands: (*football, &c.*) in a position on the field in which it is not allowable to play the ball (also *adj.*); **off'spring,** a child, or children: issue: production of any kind.—*adj.* **off-white',** not quite white.—**off one's head,** demented.—**be off,** to go away quickly; **finish off,** to finish completely; **ill off,** poor or unfortunate; **well off,** rich, well provided. [Same as **of.**]

offal, *of'al, n.* the part of a carcase that is unfit for human food: entrails (*e.g.* heart, liver) eaten as food (*pl.* **off'als**): refuse: anything worthless. [**off, fall.**]

offend, *of-end', v.t.* to displease, to make angry: to affront. (*B.*) to cause to stumble or sin.—*v.i.* to sin: to transgress (against).—*ns.* **offence',** any cause of anger or displeasure: an affront: an infraction of law: a sin: assault, aggressive action; **offend'er,** one who offends: a trespasser: a criminal; **offense'** (same as **offence**). —*adj.* **offens'ive,** causing offence, displeasure, or injury: disgusting: used in attack: making the first attack.—*n.* the act of the attacking party: the posture of one who attacks: a sustained effort to achieve an end.—*adv.* **offens'ively.**—*n.* **offens'iveness.**—**give offence,** to cause displeasure; **take offence,** to be aggrieved. [L. *offendĕre, offensum—ob,* against, *fendĕre,* to strike.]

offer, *of'ér, v.t.* to present, esp. as an act of devotion: to hold out for acceptance or rejection: to declare a willingness (to do): to lay before one: to present to the mind: to attempt, make a show of attempting (*e.g.* resistance). —*v.i.* to present itself, to be at hand: to declare a willingness.—*n.* act of offering: a bid: (rare) that which is offered: proposal made.—*adj.* **off'erable,** that may be offered.—*ns.* **off'erer; off'ering,** act of making an offer: that which is offered: a gift: (*B.*) that which is offered on an altar: (*pl.*) in Church of England, certain dues payable at Easter; **off'ertory,** act of offering: the thing offered: the verses or the anthem said or sung while the offerings of the congregation are being made and the celebrant is placing the unconsecrated elements on the altar: the money collected at a religious service. [L. *offerre—ob*, towards, *ferre*, to bring.]

office, *of'is*, *n*. an act of kindness or attention, a service: a function or duty: a position of trust or authority, esp. in the government: act of worship: order or form of a religious service: a place where business is carried on: a latrine: (*pl.*) the apartments of a house in which the domestics discharge their duties.—*ns.* **off'ice-bear'er**, one who performs an appointed duty in a company, society, &c.; **off'icer**, a person who performs some public duty: a person holding a commission in the army, navy, or air force.—*v.t.* to furnish with officers: to command as officers.—*adj.* **official** (*of-ish'ál*), pertaining to an office: holding a public position: done by, or issued by, authority.—*n.* one who holds an office: a subordinate public officer: the deputy of a bishop, &c.—*adv.* **offic'ially**.— *n.* **officialese'** (*-ēz'*), stilted, wordy, and stereotyped English alleged to be characteristic of official letters and documents.—*v.i.* **offic'iate**, to perform the duties of an office, esp. on a particular occasion.—**last offices**, rites for the dead. [Fr.,—L. *officium*, a favour, duty, service.]

officinal, *of-is'in-ál*, *adj.* belonging to, or used in, a shop: denoting an approved medicine kept prepared by apothecaries. [Fr.,—L. *officīna*, a workshop—*opus*, work, *facĕre*, to do.]

officious, *of-ish'ús*, *adj.* too forward in offering services: intermeddling.—*adv.* **offic'iously.**—*n.* **offic'iousness**. [Fr.,—L. *officiōsus—officium*; cf. **office**.]

oft, **oft**, **often**, *of'n* (by some educated speakers pronounced *of'ten*), *adv.* frequently: many times.—*adj.* **oft'en** (*B.*), frequent.—*advs.* **oft'-times**, **oft'entimes**, many times: frequently. [O.E. *oft*; Ger. *oft*.]

ogam, *og'ám*, **ogham**, *og'ám*, *o'ám*, *n.* an ancient Celtic alphabet: any one of its twenty characters. [O.Ir. *ogam*, mod. Ir. *ogham*.]

ogee, *ō'jē*, *ō-jē'*, *n.* a moulding S-shaped in section. [Fr. *ogive*.]

ogive, *ō'jīv*, *-jīv'*, *n.* (*archit.*) a pointed arch or window. [Fr.; origin doubtful, perh. Ar. *auj*, summit.]

ogle, *ō'gl*, *v.t.* to look at fondly or impertinently, with side glances, to eye greedily.—*v.i.* to cast amorous glances.—*ns.* **o'gle**; **o'gler**; **o'gling**. [Cf. Low Ger. *oegeln*, Ger. *äugeln*, to leer, *auge*, eye.]

ogre, *ō'gér*, *n.* a man-eating monster or giant of fairy tales: an ugly, cruel, bad-tempered or stern person:—*fem.* **o'gress**.—*adj.* **o'gr(e)ish**. [Fr.]

ohm, *ōm*, *n.* the unit by which electrical resistance is measured in the SI and MKSA systems. [*Ohm*, German physicist (1787-1854).]

oil, *oil*, *n.* any of a large group of greasy liquids immiscible in water. The main classes of oil are (a) fixed (fatty) oils—from animal, vegetable and marine sources; (b) mineral oils—from petroleum, coal, &c.; (c) essential oils—volatile oils with characteristic odours derived from plants.—*v.t.* to smear, lubricate, or anoint with oil.—*ns.* **oil'cake**, a cattle-food made of

oil-seeds when most of the oil has been pressed out; **oil'cloth**, canvas coated with linseed-oil paint; **oil'-col'our**, a colouring substance mixed with oil: a painting in oil-colours **oil'-en'gine**, an internal-combustion engine burning vapour from oil; **oil'er**, one who, or that which, oils: an oil-can; **oil'-field**, a district that produces mineral oil.—*adj.* **oil'-fired**, burning oil as fuel.—*n.* **oil'-length**, the ratio of drying oil to resin in e.g. a varnish (*adjs.* **long-**, **short-oil**, having a high, low proportion of oil).—*ns.* **oil'-painting**, a picture painted in oil-colours: the art of painting in oil-colours; **oil'-palm**, a pinnate-leaved palm, a native of Africa, also widely grown in Brazil (see **palm-kernel oil**, **palm-oil**); **oil'-rig**, see **rig** (*n.*); **oil'skin**, cloth made waterproof by means of oil: a garment made of oilskin; **oil'-well**, a boring made for petroleum.—*adj.* **oil'y**, consisting of, containing, or having the qualities of oil: greasy: (*fig.*) insinuating, unctuous.—*n.* **oil'iness.**—**oil slick**, film of oil on the surface of water. [O.Fr. *oile*—L. *oleum*— Gr. *elaion—elaiā*, the olive.]

ointment, *oint'mént*, *n.* anything used in anointing: (*med.*) any greasy substance applied to diseased or wounded parts, an unguent. [Fr. *oint*, pa.p. of *oindre*—L. *unguēre*, to anoint.]

okapi, *o-kä'pē*, *n.* an animal of Central Africa, related to the giraffe but with a much shorter neck. [African.]

OK, **okay**, *o-kā'*, *adj.* (*coll.*) all correct: all right: satisfactory.—*adv.* yes, certainly.—*n.* approval: sanction: endorsement.—*v.t.* to mark or pass as all right: to sanction. [Origin uncertain.]

old, *ōld*, *adj.* advanced in years: having been long in existence: worn or worn out: out of date, old-fashioned: antique, ancient, early: having the age or duration of: long practised (as *old hand*—see **hand**).—*adjs.* **old'en**, old, ancient; **olde-worlde**, self-consciously imitative of the past; **old-fash'ioned**, of a fashion like that used long ago: out of date: conservative; **old'-hat'**, out of date; **old'ish**, somewhat old.—*n.* **old'-timer**, one who has lived in a place or kept a position for a long time.—*adj.* **old'-world**, belonging to earlier times, antiquated, old-fashioned.—**old age**, the later part of life; **Old Bailey**, the Central Criminal Court in London; **old boy**, a former pupil; **Old English** (see **English**): the form of black-letter used by 16th-century English printers; **old-fashioned look**, a quizzical, critical look; **Old Harry**, **Nick**, **One**, &c., the devil; **Old Hundred**, properly **Old Hundredth**, a famous tune set to the metrical version of the 100th Psalm (used also as a hymn); **Old Icelandic**, the early form of Icelandic (q.v.): sometimes used as equivalent to the wider term **Old Norse** (Old Scandinavian), because it is in Old Icelandic that the chief literary remains of Old Norse were written; **old maid**, a spinster who is unlikely to marry; **old master**, any great painter or painting of a period previous to the 19th cent. (esp. of the Renaissance); **old school**, those whose habits are such as prevailed in the past (also *adj.*); **old school tie**, an emblem of the code and outlook (class loyalty, complacent sense of privilege, conservatism, &c.) popularly attributed to those who have

Neutral vowels in unaccented syllables: *em'pér-ór*; for certain sounds in foreign words see p. ix.

been educated at a public school; **old song,** a mere trifle; **old style** (often written with a date O.S.), the mode of reckoning time before 1752, according to the Julian calendar (q.v.)—the year began on March 25th, and 20th March 1726 O.S. (for instance) is now often written 20th March 1726-7; **Old Testament** (see **testament**); **Old World** (see **world**).—**of old,** long ago. [O.E. *ald, eald*; Du. *oud*; Ger. *alt.*]

oleaginous, *ō-lē-aj'in-us, adj.* oily.—*n.* **oleag'inousness.** [L. *oleāginus—oleum*, oil.]

oleander, *ō-lē-an'dér, n.* an evergreen shrub with lance-shaped leaves and beautiful flowers. [L.L., of doubtful origin.]

oleaster, *ō-lē-as'tér, n.* the wild olive: a very different tree with bitter olive-shaped fruit (also known as 'wild olive'). [L.,—*olea,* an olive-tree—Gr. *elaiā.*]

oleiferous, *ō-lē-if'er-us, adj.* producing oil, as seeds. [L. *oleum,* oil, *ferre,* to bear.]

oleo-, *ō'lē-ō-,* in composition, oil. [L. *oleum,* oil.]

oleograph, *ō'lē-ō-grāf, n.* a print in oil-colours to imitate an oil-painting [L. *oleum,* oil, Gr. *graphein,* to write.]

olfactory, *ol-fak'tór-i, adj.* pertaining to, or used in, smelling. [L. *olfacĕre,* to smell—*olēre,* to smell, *facĕre,* to make.]

oligarchy, *ol'i-gärk-i, n.* government by a small exclusive class: a state governed by such.—*n.* **ol'igarch,** a member of an oligarchy.—*adjs.* **oligarch'al, oligarch'ic, -ical.** [Gr. *oligos,* few, *archē,* rule.]

Oligocene, *ol'i-gō-sēn, adj.* pertaining to a period of the Tertiary geological era—between the Eocene and Miocene. [Gr. *oligos,* little, *kainos,* new.]

olio, *ō'li-ō, n.* a savoury dish of different sorts of meat and vegetables: a mixture, a medley, a miscellany. [Sp. *olla*—L. *ōlla,* a pot.]

olive, *ol'iv, n.* a tree cultivated round the Mediterranean for its oily fruit: its fruit: peace, of which the olive was the emblem: a colour like the unripe olive.—*adj.* of a brownish green colour like the olive.—*adj.* **olivāceous** (*o-li-vā'shus*), olive-coloured.—*n.* **ol'ive-oil,** oil pressed from the fruit of the olive.—**olive branch,** a symbol of peace: (*pl.*) children (Ps. cxxviii. 4, *Pr. Bk.* version). [Fr.,—L. *olīva.*]

olla-podrida, *ol'a-po-drē'da, n.* a Spanish mixed stew or hash of meat and vegetables: any incongruous mixture or miscellaneous collection. [Sp., lit. 'rotten pot'.]

-ology. See **-logy.**

Olympus, *ol-im'pus, n.* a mountain on border of Thessaly and Macedonia, home of the gods.—*n.* **Olym'piad,** in ancient Greece, a period of four years, being the interval from one celebration of the Olympic games to another, used in reckoning time (beginning of first Olympiad is 776 B.C.): a celebration of the modern Olympic games.—*adj.* **Olym'pian,** pertaining to Olympus: godlike.—*n.* a dweller in Olympus, one of the greater gods.—*adj.* **Olym'pic,** of Olympia.—**Olym'pic games,** games celebrated every four years at Olympia, dedicated to Olympian Zeus: quadrennial international athletic contests, held at various centres since 1896. [Gr. *Olympos.*]

ombre, *om'bér, n.* a game of cards played with a pack of forty cards, usually by three persons. [Sp. *hombre*—L. *homō,* a man.]

Ombudsman, *om'bŏŏdz-man, n.* (orig. in Sweden and Denmark), 'a grievance man', an official appointed to investigate complaints against the administration: in Britain officially 'Parliamentary Commissioner for Administration'. [Sw.]

omega, *ō'meg-a, ō-mēg'a, n.* the last letter of the Greek alphabet (Ω, ω): (*B.*) the end. [Gr. *ōmega,* great *O.*]

omelet, omelette, *om'e-let, n.* a pancake made chiefly of eggs. [O.Fr. *amelette,* which through the form *alemette* is traced to O.Fr. *alemelle,* a thin plate—L. *lāmella, lāmina.*]

omen, *ō'mén, n.* a sign of some future event.—*adj.* **o'mened,** affording, or attended by, omens, esp. in composition, as *ill-omened,* inauspicious, hence unlucky.—**of good, ill, omen,** foreshowing good, or ill, fortune. [L. *ōmen, -inis.*]

ominous, *om'in-us, adj.* pertaining to, or containing, an omen: portending evil, inauspicious.—*adv.* **om'inously.**—*n.* **om'inousness.** [L. *ōminōsus—ōmen.* See **omen.**]

omit, *ō-mit', v.t.* to leave out; to fail (to): to fail to use, perform:—*pr.p.* omit'ting; *pa.t.* and *pa.p.* omit'ted.—*adj.* **omiss'ible,** that may be omitted.—*n.* **omiss'ion,** act of omitting: a thing omitted.—*adj.* **omiss'ive,** omitting or leaving out. [L. *omittĕre, omissum—ob,* in front, *mittĕre,* to send.]

omnibus, *om'ni-bus, n.* a large public vehicle (see **bus**) for passengers by road: an omnibus book or edition.—*pl.* **om'nibuses.**—*adj.* widely comprehensive: of miscellaneous contents.—**omnibus book, edition,** a book, edition containing reprints of several works or items, usu. by a single author, or on a single subject, or of the same type. [Dat. pl. of L. *omnis,* all.]

omnifarious, *om-ni-fā'ri-us, adj.* of all varieties or kinds. [L. *omnifarius—omnis,* all; cf. **multifarious.**]

omnipotent, *om-nip'o-tént, adj.* all powerful, possessing unlimited power.—*n.* the **Omnipotent,** God.—*ns.* **omnip'otence, omnipotency,** unlimited power.—*adv.* **omnip'otently.** [L. *omnipotens—omnis,* all, *potens,* powerful.]

omnipresent, *om-ni-prez'ént, adj.* present everywhere.—*n.* **omnipres'ence.** [L. *omnis,* all, *praesens,* present.]

omniscient, *om-nish'ént, adj.* all-knowing.—*adv.* **omnis'ciently.**—*n.* **omnis'cience.** [L. *omnis,* all, *sciens, pr.p.* of *scīre,* to know.]

omnium-gatherum, *om'nium-gaTH'er-um, n.* a miscellaneous collection of things or persons. [L. *omnium,* gen. pl. of *omnis,* all, and **gather.**]

omnivorous, *om-niv'or-us, adj.* all-devouring: (*zool.*) feeding on both animal and vegetable foods. [L. *omnis,* all, *vorāre,* to devour.]

omphalos, *om'fal-os, n.* the navel: a centre.—*adj.* **omphal'ic.** [Gr. *omphalos,* the navel.]

on, *on, prep.* in contact with the upper or presented surface of: indicating position more generally (as, *on the far side, on the Continent*): to and toward the surface of: at or near: acting by contact with: not off: indicating position in time (e.g. *on the last day*): (*fig.*) indicating direction or object (e.g. *money* *spent on provisions, to have pity on*): having for basis, principle, or condition (e.g. *on trust, on loan*): concerning, about (e.g. *to lecture on*): by the agency of, with (e.g. *to tear on barbed wire*): immediately after: (*B.*) off: (*coll.*) at the expense of, to the disadvantage of.—*adv.* in or into a position on something: forward: in continuance: in progress: on the stage: not off.—*interj.* go on! proceed!—*n.* (*cricket*) the on side of the wicket.—*n.* **on'licence,** a licence to sell alcoholic liquors for consumption on the premises.—**on side,** (*cricket*) the side of the field on which the batsman stands; **on to,** to a position on (also **onto**). [O.E. *on*; Du. *aan,* O.N. *ā,* Ger. *an.*]

onager, *on'a-jér, n.* the wild ass of Central Asia. [L.,—Gr. *onagros—onos,* an ass, *agros,* wild.]

once, *ons, n.* Same as **ounce** (2).

once, *wuns, adv.* a single time: at a former time: at some future time.—*n.* **once'-ov'er,** a single, comprehensive survey.—**once in a way, while,** occasionally: rarely.—**at once,** without delay; **for once,** on one occasion only. [O.E. *ānes,* orig. gen. of *ān,* one, used as adv.]

oncoming, *on'kum-ing, n.* approach.—*adj.* advancing, approaching. [**on,** and prp. of **come.**]

oncost, *on'kost, n.* overhead costs. [**on, cost.**]

one, *wun, adj.* a single: of unit number: undivided: the same: a certain.—*n.* the number unity: an individual person or thing.—*pron.* a person (indefinitely), as in 'one may say': any one: some one.—*n.* **one'ness,** singleness, unity.—*pron.* **oneself', one's self,** the emphatic and reflexive form of **one.**—*adj.* **one'sid'ed,** unfair, partial.—*ns.* **one-step,** a ballroom dance of U.S. origin; **one-up'manship** (*facet.*; *Stephen Potter*), the art of being one up.—**one another,** each other; **one-armed bandit,** a fruit-machine; **one day,** at an indefinite time; **one-track mind,** a mind incapable of dealing with more than one idea at a time or a mind obsessed with one idea.—**all one,** just the same, of no consequence; **at one,** agreed; **one up on,** having an advantage over (another). [O.E. *ān*; O.N. *einn,* Ger. *ein,* L. *unus.*]

onerous, *on'ér-us, adj.* burdensome, oppressive.—*adv.* **on'erously.**—*n.* **on'erousness.** [L. *onerōsus—onus, -eris,* a burden.]

ongoing, *on'gō-ing, n.* a going on: course of conduct (esp. if unconventional—often in *pl.*). [**on,** and prp. of **go.**]

onion, *un'yón, n.* an edible bulb of the lily family. [Fr. *oignon*—L. *ūniō, -ōnis,* a large pearl, an onion.]

onlooker, *on'look-ér, n.* a looker on, observer. [**on, look.**]

only, *ōn'li, adj.* single in number: without others of the kind: without others worthy to be counted.—*adv.* not more than: exclusively: alone: merely: barely.—*conj.* but: except that. [O.E. *ānlic* (adj.)—*ān,* one, *-līc,* like.]

onomatopoeia, *on-ō-mat-o-pē'ya, n.* the formation of a word in imitation of the sound of the thing meant: a word so formed, as 'click', 'cuckoo'.—*adjs.* **onomatopoe'ic, onomatopoet'ic.** [Gr. *onoma, -atos,* a name, *poieein,* to make.]

onrush, *on'rush, n.* a rushing onward. [**on, rush.**]

onset, *on'set, n.* violent attack, assault: beginning. [**on, set.**]

onslaught, *on'slöt, n.* an attack, onset, assault. [Prob. Du. *aanslag* or Ger. *anschlag,* refashioned as Eng.]

ontology, *on-tol'o-ji, n.* the science that treats of the principles of pure being, that part of metaphysics which treats of the nature and essence of things.—*adjs.* **ontolog'ic, -al.**—*adv.* **ontolog'ically.**—*n.* **ontol'ogist.** [Gr. *ōn, ontos,* pr.p. of *einai,* to be, *logos,* discourse.]

onus, *ō'nus, n.* (*fig.*) burden: responsibility. [L. *onus,* burden.]

onward, *on'wård, adj.* going forward: advancing.—*adv.* (also **on'wards**) toward a point on or in front: forward. [**on,** and suffx. *-ward.*]

onyx, *on'iks, n.* a variety of silica with parallel layers of different colours (straight, not curved as in *agate*), used for making cameos. [Gr. *onyx,* a finger-nail.]

oölite, *ō'o-līt, n.* (*geol.*) a kind of limestone, composed of grains like the eggs or roe of a fish.—*adj.* **oölit'ic.** [Gr. *ōion,* an egg, *lithos,* stone.]

ooze, *ōōz, n.* slimy mud: a fine-grained, soft, deep-sea deposit, composed of shells and fragments of organisms: gentle flow: the liquor of a tan vat.—*v.i.* to flow gently: to percolate, as a liquid through pores.—*adj.* **ooz'y,** resembling ooze: slimy. [Partly O.E. *wāse,* mud; partly O.E. *wōs,* juice.]

opacity. See under **opaque.**

opah, *ō'pä, n.* a large brilliantly coloured seafish—also called kingfish. [West African.]

opal, *ō'pál, n.* a mineral consisting of silica with some water, usually milky white with fine play of colour, in some varieties precious.—*n.* **opales'cence,** a milky iridescence.—*adj.* **opales'cent.** [Fr. *opale* — L. *opalus.*]

opaque, *ō-pāk', adj.* (*obs.*) dark: impervious to light or other radiation: not transparent: (*fig.*) obscure: obtuse.—*adv.* **opaque'ly.**—*ns.* **opacity** (*ō-pas'i-ti*), **opaque'ness.** [L. *opācus.*]

op art, *op ärt,* art using geometrical forms precisely executed and so arranged that movement of the observer's eye, or inability to focus, produces an illusion of movement in the painting. [*op*tical.]

ope, *ōp, v.t. and v.i.* (*poet.*) short for **open.**

open, *ō'pn, adj.* not shut: allowing passage: uncovered, unprotected: free from trees: not fenced: loose: widely spaced: not frozen up: not frosty: free to be used, &c.: public: without reserve: candid: undisguised: easily understood: liable (to): accessible (to suggestions, &c.): unrestricted: not restricted to any class of persons: of a consonant, made without stopping the breath stream (same as **fricative,** q.v.; see also **spirant**): of a syllable, ending with a vowel.—*v.t.* to make open: to expose to view: to begin.—*v.i.* to become open: to have an opening: to begin to appear: to begin.—*n.* a clear space.—*n.* (also *adj.*) **o'pen-cast,** an excavation for the extraction of ore that is open overhead.—*n.* **o'pener.**—*adjs.* **o'pen-hand'ed,** with an open hand: generous, liberal; **o'pen-heart'ed,** with an open heart, frank, generous.—*n.* **o'pening,** an open place: a breach: an aperture: beginning: opportunity.—*adv.* **o'penly.**—*adjs.* **o'pen-mind'ed,** free to receive and consider new ideas; **o'pen-mouthed,** gaping: expectant: clamorous.—*n.* **o'penness.**—*adj.*

Neutral vowels in unaccented syllables: *em'pér-ór*; for certain sounds in foreign words see p. ix.

500

o'pen-plan', with rooms running from back to front and with windows on both faces.—*ns.* o'pen-ses'ame, a spell or other means of making barriers fly open—from the story of Ali Baba and the Forty Thieves in the *Arabian Nights*; o'pen-work, any work showing openings.—open circuit, electrical circuit broken so that current cannot pass: in television, the customary system in which the showing is for general, not restricted, viewing; open house, hospitality to all comers; open order, in lines some distance apart; open question, a matter undecided, open to further discussion; open secret, a matter known to many but treated as a secret; open shop, a factory not confined to union labour; open town, one without troops or military installations, and hence, according to international law, immune from attack of any kind; open university, a university whose teaching is carried out by correspondence and by radio and television; open verdict, a verdict that a crime has been committed by an unspecified criminal. [O.E. *open*; cf. Du. *open*, O.N. *opinn*, Ger. *offen*; prob. related to up.]

opera, *op'ér-a, n.* musical drama: a musical drama.—*adj.* used in or for an opera.—*ns.* op'era-cloak, an elegant cloak for evening wear, esp. in the auditorium of a theatre; op'era-glass, a small field-glass for use at operas, plays, &c.; op'era-hat, a collapsible tall hat.—*adjs.* operat'ic, -al, pertaining to or resembling opera. [It.,—L. *opera.* Cf. operate.]

opera-bouffe, *op'ér-a-bōōf, n.* a funny or farcical opera. [Fr. *opéra-bouffe* — It. *opera-buffa.* Cf. buffoon.]

operate, *op'ér-āt, v.i.* to work: to exert power or influence. to produce any effect; to carry out military manoeuvres: (*med.*) to take effect upon the human system: (*surg.*) to perform some unusual act upon the body with the hand or an instrument.—*v.t.* to effect: to work (e.g. a machine): to conduct, carry on.—*ns.* op'erand, something on which an operation is performed, e.g. a quantity in mathematics; opera'tion, act, process, or result of operating: agency: influence: method of working: action or movements: surgical performance.—*adjs.* opera'tional, relating to, connected with, operations: ready for action: engaged in, constituting, or forming part of, an operation of war; op'erative, having the power of operating or acting: acting: efficacious.—*n.* a workman in a manufactory, a mill-hand.—*adv.* op'eratively.—*n.* op'erator, one who, or that which, operates or produces an effect.—operative words, the words in a deed legally effecting the transaction (e.g. *devise and bequeath* in a will): (*loosely*) the most significant words. [L. *operārī, -ātus* — *opera,* work, closely conn. with *opus, operis,* work.]

operculum, *ō-pér'kū-lum, n.* (*bot.*) a cover or lid: (*zool.*) the plate over the entrance of a shell: the gill-cover of fishes:—*pl.* oper'cula.—*adjs.* oper'cular, belonging to the operculum; oper'culate, -d, having an operculum. [L.,— *operīre,* to cover.]

operetta, *op-ér-et'a, n.* a short, light musical drama. [It., dim of opera.]

operose, *op'ér-ōs, adj.* laborious: industrious.— *adv.* op'erosely.—*n.* op'eroseness. [L. *operō-*

sus—opus, operis, work.]

ophicleide, *of'i-klīd, n.* a bass or alto key-bugle [Fr. *ophicléide*—Gr. *ophis,* a serpent, *kleis,* gen. *kleidos,* a key.]

ophidian, *o-fid'i-án, adj.* pertaining to serpents: having the nature of a serpent. [Gr. *ophidion,* dim. of *ophis,* a serpent.]

ophthalm-, *of-thalm'-, of'-,* in composition, eye.—*n.* ophthalm'ia, inflammation of the eye.—*adj.* ophthal'mic, pertaining to the eye.—*n.* ophthal'moscope, an instrument for examining the interior of the eye. [Gr.,— *ophthalmos,* eye.]

opiate, *o'pi-át, n.* a drug containing opium to induce sleep: that which dulls sensation, physical or mental.—*adj.* inducing sleep.—*adj.* o'piated, mixed with opiates: drugged. [opium.]

opine, *ō-pīn', v.t.* and *v.i.* to suppose: to form or express as an opinion. [Fr.,—L. *opīnārī,* to think.]

opinion, *ō-pin'yón, n.* what seems to one to be probably true: judgment: view, belief (often in *pl.*): estimation (as, *a high* or *low opinion*).— *adjs.* opin'ionated, opin'ionative, unduly attached to one's own opinions.—*adv.* opin'ionatively.—*n.* opin'ionativeness.—a matter of opinion, a question open to dispute; no opinion of, a very low opinion or estimate of. [L, *opīniō, ōnis.*]

opium, *ō'pi-um, n.* the dried narcotic juice of a Eurasian poppy —*ns.* o'pium-den, a resort of opium-smokers; o'pium-eat'er, one addicted to the use of opium. [L.,—Gr. *opion,* dim. from *opos,* sap.]

opossum, *o-pos'um, n.* any of various small American marsupial mammals, with prehensile tail. [West Indian.]

oppidan, *op'i-dan, n.* at Eton, a student who boards in the town, not in the college. [L. *oppidānus—oppidum,* town.]

opponent, *o-pō'nént, adj.* opposing: placed opposite or in front.—*n.* an adversary: one who opposes a course of action, belief, person, &c. [L. *opponens, -entis,* pr.p. of *opponere—ob,* in the way of, *ponere,* to place.]

opportune, *op-ór-tūn', op',* adj. occurring at a fitting time, timely: convenient.—*adv.* opportune'ly.- ns. opportune'ness; opportun'ist, one (e.g. a politician) who waits for events before declaring his opinions, or shapes his conduct or policy to circumstances of the moment; opportun'ity, an occasion offering a possibility or chance: a combination of favouring circumstances (e.g. *opportunity makes the thief*). [Fr.,—L. *opportūnus—ob,* before, *portus,* a harbour.]

oppose, *o-pōz', v.t.* to place in front of or in the way of (with *to*): to set in contrast (to): to balance against: to place as an obstacle: to resist: to contend with.—*v.i.* to make objection.—*adj.* oppos'able, that may be opposed.—*n.* oppos'er. [Fr.,—L. *ob,* against, Fr. *poser,* to place—L.L. *pausāre,* to rest, stop.]

opposite, *op'o-zit, adj.* placed over against (often with *to*): face to face: (of foliage leaves) in pairs at each node with the stem between: opposed (e.g. *the opposite side in a dispute*): contrary (e.g. *in opposite directions*): diametrically different (with *to*).—*n.* that which

opposition   orb

is opposed or contrary: an opponent.—*adv.*
opp′ositely.—*n.* **opp′ositeness.**—**opposite number,** one who has a corresponding place in another set. [Fr.,—L. *oppositus*—*oppōnĕre*—*ob*, against, *pōnĕre*, *positum*, to place.]

opposition, *op-o-zish′(ó)n, n.* state of being placed over against: position over against: contrast: contradistinction: act of setting opposite: act of opposing: resistance: that which opposes: (*cap.*) political party that opposes the ministry or existing administration: (*astron.*) the situation of heavenly bodies when 180 degrees apart (cf. **conjunction**). [L. *oppositiō, -ōnis*—*oppōnĕre*. See **opposite**.]

oppress, *o-pres′, v.t.* to press against or upon: to lie heavy upon: to overpower: to treat with tyrannical cruelty or injustice.—*n.* **oppress′ion,** act of oppressing: tyranny: state of being oppressed: dullness of spirits.—*adj.* **oppress′ive,** tending to oppress: overburdensome: tyrannical: heavy, overpowering (e.g. of weather).—*adv.* **oppress′ively.**—*ns.* **oppress′iveness; oppress′or.** [Fr.,—L.L. *oppressāre*, freq. of L. *opprimĕre, oppressum*—*ob*, against, *premĕre*, to press.]

opprobrium, *o-prō′bri-um, n.* the disgrace or reproach of shameful conduct: infamy.—*adj.* **oppro′brious,** reproachful, insulting, abusive: disgraceful, infamous.—*adv.* **opprō′briously.** —*n.* **opprō′briousness.** [L.,—*ob*, against, *probrum*, reproach.]

oppugn, *o-pūn′, v.t.* to assail, call in question: (*rare*) to attack or to resist.—*n.* **oppugn′er.** [L. *oppugnāre*, attack—*ob*, *pugna*, fight.]

opt, *opt, v.i.* to choose (with *for, between*).— **optative,** *op′ta-tiv, op-tā′tiv, adj.* expressing desire or wish.—*n.* (*gram.*) a mood of the verb expressing wish.—**opt out** (*of*), to choose to take no part (in). [L. *optāre, -ātum,* to wish.]

optic, -al, *op′tik, -ál, adj.* relating to sight, or to optics: (**optical**) constructed to help the sight: acting by means of light: amplifying radiation: visual.—*adv.* **op′tically.**—*ns.* **optician** (*op-tish′án*), one who makes or sells optical instruments; **op′tics** (*sing.*), the science of light. [Gr. *optikos,* optic—*optos,* seen.]

optimism, *op′ti-mizm, n.* (*phil.*) the doctrine that everything is ordered for the best: a disposition to take a hopeful view of things: (*loosely*) hopefulness.—Opp. to *pessimism.*—*v.t.* **op′timise,** to make the most or best of: to make as efficient as possible: to prepare (a computer programme) that will automatically adjust itself so that the computer works with greatest efficiency.—*n.* **op′timist,** one given to optimism, a sanguine person.—*adj.* **optimist′ic.**—*adv.* **optimist′ically.** [L. *optimus,* best.]

optimum, *op′ti-mum, n.* that point at which any condition is most favourable.—*pl.* **op′tima.**—*adj.* (of conditions) best for the achievement of an aim or result: very best. [L. neut. of *optimus,* best.]

option, *op′sh(ó)n, n.* act of choosing: power of choosing: an alternative for choice.—*adj.* **op′tional,** left to one's choice.—*adv.* **op′tionally.** [L. *optiō, -ōnis*—*optāre,* to choose.]

opulent, *op′ū-lént, adj.* wealthy.—*n.* **op′ulence,** riches.—*adv.* **op′ulently.** [L. *opulentus.*]

opus, *op′us,* or *ō′pus,* a work, a musical com-

position or set of compositions—esp. numbered in order of publication, as *opus 6* (*op. 6*):—*pl.* **opera** (*op′ér-a*). [L., 'work'.]

opuscule, *ō-pus′kūl, n.* a minor work. [L., dim. of *opus.*]

or, *ör, conj.* before (in time).—**or ever,** before ever. [O.E. (Northumbrian) and O.N. *ār,* early, with the sense of O.E. *ǣr,* ere.]

or, *ör, conj.* marking an alternative. [M.E. *other,* either, or.]

or, *ör, n.* (*her.*) gold—indicated in engraving and chiselling by dots. [Fr.,—L. *aurum,* gold.]

oracle, *or′a-kl, n.* a medium or agency of divine revelation: a response by a god: the place where such responses are given: the Jewish sanctuary: the word of God: a person of great wisdom: a wise utterance.—*adj.* **oracular** (*or-ak′ū-lár*), of the nature of an oracle: like an oracle: ambiguous, obscure.—*adv.* **orac′ularly.** [L. *ōrāculum*—*ōrāre,* to speak.]

oral, *ō′rál, ö′rál, adj.* relating to the mouth: uttered by the mouth: spoken, not written: taken through the mouth.—*n.* an oral examination.—*adv.* **o′rally.** [L. *ōs, ōris,* the mouth.]

orang, *ō-rang′, n.* See **orang-utan.**

orange, *or′inj, n.* the gold-coloured fruit of certain trees of the Citrus genus: the trees themselves: a colour between red and yellow.—*adj.* pertaining to an orange: orange-coloured.—*ns.* **orangeäde′,** a drink made with orange juice; **or′angery,** a plantation of orange-trees.—**orange stick,** a thin pointed stick, esp. one of wood from an orange-tree, used in the care of the finger-nails. [Fr., ult. from Ar. *nāranj;* the loss of the *n* due to confusion with the indef. art. and the vowel changes to confusion with L. *aurum,* Fr. *or,* gold.]

Orangeman, *or′inj-man, n.* a member of a society instituted in Ireland in 1795 to uphold Protestantism, or the cause of William of Orange.

orang-utan, *ō-rang-ōō-tan′,* **orang-outang,** *ō-rang′-ōō-tang′, n.* an anthropoid ape, found only in the forests of Sumatra and Borneo, reddish-brown, arboreal in habit.—Also **orang′.** [Malay, 'man of the woods'—said not to be applied by the Malay to the ape.]

oration, *ō-rā′sh(ó)n, n.* a formal speech: a harangue.—*v.i.* **orate′,** to make such a speech. [L. *ōrātiō, -ōnis*—*ōrāre,* to pray.]

orator, *or′a-tór, n.* a public speaker: a man of eloquence:—*fem.* **or′atress, or′atrix.**—*n.* **or′atory,** the art of speaking well, or so as to please and persuade, esp. publicly: the exercise of eloquence: an apartment or building for private worship.—*adj.* **orator′ical,** pertaining to an orator or to oratory.—*adv.* **orator′ically.** [L. *ōrātor, -ōris*—*ōrāre,* to pray.]

oratorio, *or-a-tō′ri-ō, n.* a story, usually Biblical, set to music, without scenery, costumes, or acting:—*pl.* **orato′rios.** [It.,—L. *ōrātōrium,* an oratory, because they developed out of the singing in church oratories.]

orb, *örb, n.* (*rare*) a circle: a sphere: a celestial body: the globe: a wheel: the eye: a part of a monarch's regalia.—*v.t.* (*poet.*) to surround: to form into an orb.—Also *v.i.* (*poet.*).—*adjs.* **orbed,** in the form of an orb, round; **orbic′ular,** spherical: circular.—*adv.* **orbic′ularly.** [L. *orbis,* circle.]

Neutral vowels in unaccented syllables: *em′pér-ór;* for certain sounds in foreign words see p. ix.

orbit, *ör′bit*, *n.* the path in which a heavenly body moves round another, or an electron round the nucleus of an atom, or the like: a path in space round a heavenly body: regular course, sphere of action: the hollow in which the eyeball rests: the skin round a bird's eye.—*v.t.* to put into orbit: to circle round: to go round in orbit.—*adj.* **or′bital**. [L. *orbita*, wheel—*orbis*, a ring.]

orc, *örk*, *n.* a sea-monster: a killer-whale, grampus. [L. *orca*.]

Orcadian, *ör-kā′di-án*, *n.* a native of the Orkney Islands.—Also *adj.* [L. *Orcădes*, the Orkney Islands.]

orchard, *ör′chárd*, *n.* an enclosed garden of fruit-trees. [O.E. *ort-geard*, prob. L. *hortus*, garden, and O.E. *geard*. See **yard**.]

orchestra, *ör′kes-tra*, *n.* in the Greek theatre, the place where the chorus danced: now the part of a theatre in which the musicians are placed: a company of musicians playing together under a conductor.—*adj.* **orches′tral**, of or for an orchestra.—*v.t.* **or′chestrāte**, to arrange for an orchestra: (*fig.*) to organise so as to achieve the best effect. [L.,—Gr. *orchēstra—orcheesthai*, to dance.]

orchid, *ör′kid*, *n.* any of a family of plants with rich, showy, often fragrant flowers.—*adj.* **orchidā′ceous**, pertaining to the orchids.—*n.* **or′chis**, a genus containing several of the British species of orchids; an orchid. [Gr. *orchis*, a testicle.]

ordain, *ör-dān′*, *v.t.* (*obs.*) to arrange in order: (*obs.*) to appoint (to a duty): to invest with the functions of a minister of the Christian Church: to admit to holy orders: to decree, destine: to order.—*v.i.* to enact, command. [O.Fr. *ordener*—L. *ordināre—ordō*, *-inis*, order.]

ordeal, *ör′dēl*, less justifiably *ör-dēl′* or *or-dē′ál*, *n.* an ancient form of referring a disputed question to the judgment of God, by lot, fire, water, &c.: any severe trial or examination. [O.E. *ordēl*, *ordāl*—pfx. *or-*, out, *dæl*, share; cf. Du. *oordeel*, Ger. *urteil*.]

order, *ör′dér*, *n.* arrangement: method: sequence: suitable, normal, or fixed arrangement: regular government: an undisturbed condition: tidiness: a class of society: a body of persons of the same profession, &c.: a religious fraternity: a dignity conferred by a sovereign, &c.: an instruction or authorisation: a rule, regulation: a command: (*archit.*) a style of building: (*biol.*) a group above a family and below a class: (*pl.*) the several degrees or grades of the Christian ministry.—*v.t.* (*arch.*) to arrange: to ordain: to give an order for: to command.—*ns.* **or′der-book**, a book for entering the orders of customers, the special orders of a commanding officer, or the motions to be put to the House of Commons; **or′dering**, arrangement: management.—*adjs.* **or′derless**, without order: disorderly; **or′derly**, in good order: methodical: well regulated: quiet, peaceable, obedient: (*mil.*) charged with passing on, or with carrying out, orders: of military orders.—*n.* a non-commissioned officer who carries official messages for his superior officer: an attendant.—*n.* **or′derliness**. **order-in-council**, an order of the sov-

ereign with advice of the Privy Council; **order-of-the-day**, business set down for the day: a proclamation by a commanding officer; **order-paper**, a paper showing the order of business on a particular day in a legislative assembly, as in the House of Commons.—**holy orders**, the Christian ministry; **standing orders**, rules for procedure adopted by a legislative assembly.—**in order**, and **out of order**, in accordance with regular procedure, or the opposite; **in order to**, for the end that; **take order**, take measures; **take orders**, to be ordained. [Fr. *ordre*—L. *ordō*, *-inis*.]

ordinal, *ör′din-ál*, *adj.* indicating order of sequence.—*n.* an ordinal numeral (as first, second, &c.): a book of forms for ordination. [L.L. *ordinālis*—L. *ordō*, *-inis*, order.]

ordinance, *ör′din-áns*, *n.* that which is ordained by an authority: a law: an established rite.—*n.* **ordinā′tion**, the act of ordaining: admission to the Christian ministry: established order. [L. *ordināre*, *-ātum—ordō*, *-inis*, order.]

ordinary, *ör′di-ná-ri*, *adj.* usual: of common rank: plain, undistinguished.—*n.* something settled or customary: a judge of ecclesiastical or other causes who acts in his own right: a bishop or his deputy: a meal provided at a fixed charge: (*her.*) one of a class of armorial charges, figures of simple and geometrical form.—*adv.* **or′dinarily**. **in ordinary**, in regular and customary attendance. [L. *ordinārius—ordō*, *-inis*, order.]

ordinate, *ör′din-āt*, *adj.* (now *rare*) moderate.—*n.* half of a chord of a conic section bisected by the diameter: for rectilineal axes, the distance of a point from the axis of abscissae (*x*-axis) measured in a direction parallel to the axis of ordinates (*y*-axis).—*adv.* **ord′inately**. [L. *ordinātus*, pa.p. of *ordināre—ordō*, *-inis*, order.]

ordnance, *örd′náns*, *n.* (*orig.*) any arrangement, disposition, or equipment: military supplies: great guns: artillery.—**ordnance survey**, a preparation of official maps of Great Britain and N. Ireland by the Ordnance Survey Department. [Variant of **ordinance**.]

ordure, *ör′dūr*, *n.* dirt: excrement: foul language. [Fr.,—O.Fr. *ord*, foul—L. *horridus*, rough.]

ore, *ör*, *ör*, *n.* a mineral aggregate from which one or more valuable constituents may be obtained: (*poet.*) precious metal. [O.E. *ār*, brass, influenced by *ora*, unwrought metal; cf. L. *aes*, *aeris*, bronze.]

oread, *ö′rē-ad*, *ö′rē-ad*, *n.* (*myth.*) a mountain nymph:—*pl.* **o′reads**, or **orē′ades**. [Gr. *oreias*, gen. *oreiados—oros*, a mountain.]

oregano, *ö-reg-ä′nō*, *ö-reg′á-nō*, *n.* an aromatic culinary herb. [Amer. Sp. *orégano*, wild marjoram.]

organ, *ör′gán*, *n.* an instrument, or means by which anything is done: a part of a body fitted for carrying on a natural or vital operation: a means of communicating information or opinions: a musical wind instrument consisting of pipes made to sound by compressed air, and played upon by means of keys: a musical instrument in some way resembling the pipe-organ, as the barrel-organ, &c.—*ns.* **or′ganist**, one who plays an organ; **or′gan-grind′er**, one who plays a hand-organ by a crank.—*adjs.* **organ′ic, -al**, pertaining to, derived from, of

the nature of, an organ or an organism: organised (e.g. *an organic whole*): structural,
inherent in the constitution: (*med.*) affecting
the structure of an organ—opp. to *functional*:
(*chem.*) containing or combined with carbon:
concerned with carbon compounds.—*adv.*
organ'ically.—*v.t.* **or'ganise,** to supply with
organs: to form into an organised whole: to
prepare for activity: to arrange.—*p.adj.*
or'ganised, (*biol.*) showing the characteristics
of an organism: having the tissues and organs
formed into a unified whole: prepared.—*adj.*
organis'able, that may be organised.—*ns.*
organisa'tion, the act of organising: the state
of being organised: a system or society; **or'-
ganiser; or'ganism,** (*rare*) organic structure: a
living animal or vegetable.—**organic chemistry,** the chemistry of carbon compounds; **organic disease,** a disease accompanied by
changes in the structures involved. [L. *or-
ganum*—Gr. *organon*—*ergon,* work.]
organdie, *ör'gan-di, n.* a fine transparent muslin.
[Fr. *organdi.*]
orgasm, *ör'gazm, n.* immoderate excitement or
action: culmination of sexual excitement: an
instance of it. [Gr. *orgasmos,* swelling.]
orgy, *ör'ji, n.* a riotous or drunken revel: an
excessive indulgence in (with *of*):—*pl.* **or'gies,**
riotous secret rites observed in the worship of
Bacchus. [Fr. *orgies*—L.—Gr. *orgia* (pl.).]
oriel, *ö'ri-él, n.* a recess with a window built out
from a wall.—Also *adj.* [O.Fr. *oriol,* a porch,
recess.]
orient, *ö'ri-ént, adj.* rising, as the sun: eastern:
bright.—*n.* the part where the sun rises: the
East, or the countries of the East.—*v.t.* (*ö'ri-
ént, ör-i-ent'*) to set so as to face the east: to
determine the position of, relative to fixed or
known directions: (*lit.* and *fig.*) to acquaint
with the present position: (*reflex.*) to find
one's bearings.—*adj.* **orien'tal,** eastern: pertaining to, in, or from, the East.—*n.* (often
cap.) a native of the East, Asiatic.—*ns.* **orien'-
talism,** an Eastern expression, custom, &c.;
orien'talist, one versed in Eastern languages:
an oriental.—*adv.* **orien'tally.**—*v.t.* **o'rientäte,**
to orient.—*adj.* **or'ientated,** oriented: directed
towards: often used in composition as second
element of *adj.*—*n.* **orienta'tion,** the process of
determining the east: the act or condition of
facing the east: situation relative to the points
of the compass: (*fig.*) situation with regard to
some person, circumstance, &c.—*n.* **orien-
teer'ing,** the sport of making one's way quickly across difficult country with the help of
map and compass. [L. *oriēns, -entis,* pr.p. of
orīrī, to rise.]
orifice, *or'i-fis, n.* a mouth-like opening. [Fr.,—L.
örificium—*ös, öris,* mouth, *facēre,* to make.]
oriflamme, *or'i-flam, n.* a little banner of red silk
split into many points, borne on a gilt staff—
the ancient royal standard of France.
[Fr.,—Low L. *auriflamma*—L. *aurum,* gold,
flamma, a flame.]
origami, *or-i-gäm'ë, n.* the Japanese art of folding paper so as to make animal forms, &c.
origin, *or'i-jin, n.* the rising or first existence of
anything: that from which anything first proceeds, source: parentage: (*math.*) the fixed
starting-point from which measurement is

made.—*adj.* **orig'inal,** pertaining to the origin
or beginning: existing from or at the beginning: innate: not derived or imitated: novel:
having the power to originate: odd in character.—*n.* origin: the source from which something is derived by imitation or translation.—
n. **original'ity.**—*adv.* **orig'inally.**—*v.t.* **orig'-
inäte,** to give origin or beginning to: to bring
into existence.—*v.i.* to have origin, to begin.—
n. **origina'tion.**—*adj.* **orig'inätive,** having
power to originate or bring into existence.—*n.*
orig'inätor. [Fr. *origine*—L. *orīgō, -inis*—*orīrī,*
to rise.]
oriole, *ör'i-öl, n.* a golden-yellow bird of a family
related to the crows: any other bird of the
same family: various American birds of a
different family. [O.Fr. *oriol*—L. *aureolus,* dim.
of *aureus,* golden—*aurum,* gold.]
Orion, *ö-rī'on, n.* (*astron.*) one of the constellations, containing seven very bright stars,
three of which form Orion's belt. [Gr. *Ōrīon,*
celebrated giant and hunter.]
orison, *or'i-zon, n.* a prayer. [O.Fr. *orison*—L.
ōrātiō, -ōnis—*ōrāre,* to pray.]
Oriya, *ö-rē'yä, n.* the language of Orissa, India,
close akin to Bengali: a member of the people
speaking it.—Also *adj.*
orlop, *ör'lop, n.* the lowest deck in a ship. [Du.
overloop, a covering to the hold—*overloopen,*
to run over.]
ormolu, *ör'mo-lōō, n.* gilt or bronzed metallic
ware: gold-leaf prepared for gilding bronze,
&c. [Fr. *or* (L. *aurum*), gold, *moulu,* pa.p. of
moudre (L. *molĕre*), to grind.]
ornament, *ör'na-mént, n.* anything that adds, or
is meant to add, grace or beauty: additional
beauty: (*pl. Pr. Bk.*) all the articles used in the
services of the church.—*v.t.* (*or-na-ment'*) to
adorn, to furnish with ornaments.—*adj.* **ornament'al,** serving to adorn or beautify: like an
ornament, decorative, beautiful.—*adv.* **ornament'ally.**—*n.* **ornamenta'tion,** act or art
of ornamenting: (*archit.*) ornamental work.
[Fr. *ornement*—L. *ornāmentum*—*ornāre,* to
adorn.]
ornate, *ör-nät', adj.* decorated: much or elaborately ornamented.—*adv.* **ornate'ly.**—*n.* **ornate'ness.** [L. *ornātus,* pa.p. of *ornāre,* to
adorn.]
ornis, *ör'nis, n.* the birds of a region collectively.—*n.* **ornithol'ogy,** the science and study of
birds.—*adj.* **ornitholog'ical,** pertaining to ornithology.—*ns.* **ornithol'ogist,** one versed in
ornithology; **or'nithomancy,** divination by
means of birds, by observing their flight, &c.;
ornithorhynchus (*ör-nith-ō-ring'kus*), the
platypus (q.v.). [Gr. *ornis,* gen. *ornīthos,* a
bird.]
orography, *or-og'ra-fi, n.* the description of
mountains—also **orol'ogy.**—*adjs.* **orographic,
-al.** [Gr. *oros,* a mountain, *graphein,* to write.]
oropesa, *or-o-pē'za, -pä'sa, n.* a fish-shaped float
used in marine mine-sweeping to support the
sweeping wire. [From the name of a trawler.]
orphan, *ör'fán, n.* a child bereft of father or
mother, or (usually) of both.—*adj.* bereft of
parents.—*v.t.* to bereave of parents.—*n.*
or'phanage, the state of being an orphan:
a house for orphans. [Gr. *orphanos,* akin to
L. *orbus,* bereaved.]

Neutral vowels in unaccented syllables: *em'pér-ór*; for certain sounds in foreign words see p. ix.

Orphean, *ŏr-fē'an, adj.* pertaining to *Orpheus,* who tamed wild beasts by the music of his lyre.

orpiment, *ŏr'pi-mėnt, n.* arsenic trisulphide, a yellow mineral used as a pigment. [O.Fr.—L. *auripigmentum—aurum,* gold, *pigmentum,* paint.]

orrery, *or'ėr-i, n.* a clockwork model to illustrate the relative positions, motions, &c., of the heavenly bodies. [From Charles Boyle, Earl of *Orrery* (1676-1731), for whom one was made.]

orris, *or'is, n.* a species of iris of the south of Europe, the dried root of which has the smell of violets, used in perfumery. [Perh **iris.**]

ort, *ŏrt, n.* a fragment, esp. one left from a meal—usually *pl.* [Low Ger. *ort,* refuse of fodder.]

orthodontics, orthodontia, *ŏr-thō-don'tiks, -don'shi-á, ns.* (the art of) rectification of abnormalities of the teeth. [Gr. *orthos,* right, *odous, ondontos,* teeth.]

orthodox, *ŏr'thō-doks, adj.* sound in doctrine: holding the received or established opinions, esp. in religion: according to such opinions—*n. orthodoxy,* soundness of opinion or doctrine: holding of the commonly accepted opinions, esp. in religion. [Through Fr. and Late L. from Gr. *orthodoxos—orthos,* right, *doxa,* opinion—*dokein,* to think.]

orthogonal, *ŏr-thog'on-ál, adj.* right-angled. [Gr. *orthos,* right, *gōniā,* angle.]

orthographer, *ŏr-thog'ra-fėr, n.* one skilled in orthography.—*n* **orthog'raphy** (*gram.*), the art or practice of spelling words correctly.—*adjs.* **orthograph'ic, -al,** pertaining or according to orthography: spelt correctly.—*adv.* **orthograph'ically.** [Gr. *orthographiā,* spelling—*orthos,* right, *graphein,* to write.]

orthopaedia, *ŏr-thō-pē-dī'a, -pē'-, n.* art or process of curing deformities of the body, esp. in childhood—also **orthopaedy, orthopedy.**—*adjs.* **orthopae'dic, -al, orthoped'ic,** *nl. ns.* **orthopae'dics, orthoped'ics,** orthopaedic surgery; **orthopae'dist, orthope'dist,** one skilled in orthopaedic surgery. [Gr. *orthos,* straight, *pais, gen paidos,* a child.]

Orthoptera, *ŏr-thop'tér-a, n. pl.* an order of insects to which grasshoppers belong, usually having firm fore-wings serving as a cover to fan-wise folded hind-wings.—*adj.* **orthop'terous,** pertaining to, or being a member of, the Orthoptera. [Gr. *orthos,* straight, *pteron,* wing.]

ortolan, *ŏr'tō-lán, n.* a kind of bunting, common in Europe, and considered a great table delicacy. [Fr.—It. *ortolano*—L. *hortulānus,* belonging to gardens—*hortulus,* dim. of *hortus,* a garden.]

oscillate, *os'il-lāt, v.i.* to swing to and fro like a pendulum: to vary between certain limits (e.g. between extremes of opinion, action, &c.): to have, or generate, backward and forward urges: to produce electric current which alternates periodically in direction.—*n.* **oscilla'tion.**—*adj.* **os'cillatory,** swinging: vibratory.—*ns.* **oscill'ograph, oscill'oscope,** instruments for recording in visible form oscillatory motion, as electric oscillations or mechanical vibrations. [L. *ōscillāre, -ātum,* to swing.]

osculant, *os'kū'lánt, adj.* kissing: adhering closely.—*v.t.* **os'culate,** to kiss: (*math.*) to have three or more coincident points in common with.—*n.* **oscula'tion.**—*adj.* **os'culatory,** of or pertaining to kissing or osculation. [L. *osculārī, -ātus—osculum,* a little mouth, a kiss, dim. of *os,* mouth.]

osier, *ōzh'(y)ėr, ōz'i-ėr, ōz'yėr, n.* any willow whose twigs are used in making baskets.—*adj.* made of or like osiers.—*adj.* **o'siered,** adorned with willows. [Fr. *osier,* of unknown origin.]

Osmanli, *os-man'li, adj.* of the dynasty of *Osman,* who founded the Turkish Empire in Asia: Turkish. [Cf. **Ottoman.**]

osmiridium. See **iridosmine** at **iris.**

osmium, *os'mi-úm, n.* a grey-coloured metallic element (symbol Os; atomic no. 76), the densest known element, whose oxide has a disagreeable smell. [Gr. *osmē,* smell.]

osmosis, *os-mō'sis,* or *oz-, n.* diffusion of liquids through a porous layer.—Also **os'mose.** [Gr. *ōsmos,* impulse—*ōtheein,* to push.]

osprey, *os'prā, n.* a hawk that feeds on fish: an egret or other plume used in millinery, not from the osprey. [Supposed to be from L. *ossifraga* misapplied. See **ossifrage.**]

osseous, *os'é-us, adj.* bony: composed of, or resembling, bone.—*n.* **oss'icle,** a small bone.—*adj.* **ossif'erous,** producing bone: (*geol.*) containing bones.—*v.t.* **oss'ify,** to make into bone or into a bone-like substance—*v.i.* to become bone:—*pa.p.* ossi'fied.—*n.* **ossifica'tion,** the process or state of being changed into a bony substance.—*adj.* **ossiv'orous,** devouring or feeding on bones. [L. *os, ossis,* bone.]

Ossianic, *os-i-an'ik, adj.* pertaining to *Ossian,* a legendary Gaelic poet whose poems James Macpherson (1736-1796) professed to translate.

ossifrage, *os'i-frāj, n.* the bearded vulture: the osprey: (*U.S.*) the bald eagle. [L. *ossifragus,* breaking bones—*os, bone, frag,* root of *frangere,* to break.]

ossuary, *os'ū-ár-i, n.* a charnel-house or burial chamber: an urn, &c., in which the bones of the dead are deposited. [L. *ossuārium,* a charnel-house—*os,* a bone.]

ostensible, *os-tens'i-bl, adj.* (*obs.*) that may be shown: pretended, professed, apparent (e.g. of a reason).—*n.* **ostensibil'ity.**—*adv.* **ostens'ibly.**—*adj.* **ostens'ive,** showing, exhibiting.—*n.* **ostenta'tion,** act of showing: an ambitious display: boasting.—*adj.* **ostenta'tious,** given to show: fond of self-display: intended for display.—*adv.* **ostenta'tiously**—*n.* **ostenta'tiousness.** [L. *ostendēre* (for *obstendēre*), *ostensum,* to show.]

osteo-, *os'té-ō-, os-té-o'-,* **oste-,** *os'té-,* in composition, bone.—*n.* **osteol'ogy,** the science of bones, part of anatomy.—*adj.* **osteolog'ical,** pertaining to osteology.—*adv.* **osteolog'ically.**—*ns.* **osteomyelitis,** (*-mī-ė-lī'tis*), inflammation of bone and bone-marrow; **osteop'athy,** a therapeutic system which treats disease by manipulation and massage; **os'teopath,** a practitioner of osteopathy. [Gr. *osteon,* bone.]

ostler, *os'lér.* Same as **hostler.**

-ostomy. See **-stomy.**

ostracise, *os'tra-sīz, v.t.* in ancient Greece, to banish by the votes of the citizens recorded on potsherds: to exclude from society.—*n.* **os'tracism** (-*sizm*), banishment by ostracising: expulsion from society. [Gr. *ostrakon,* an earthenware tablet.]

ostrich, *os'trich, n.* a genus of the largest living birds, found in Africa, remarkable for their speed in running, and prized for their feathers. [O.Fr. *ostruche*—L. *avis,* a bird, L.L. *struthiō*—Gr.*strouthiōn,* an ostrich,*strouthos,* a bird.]

other, *uᴛʜ'ér, adj.* (*orig.*) one of two: second: alternate: different from or not the same as: remaining.—*pron.* (or *n.*) other one: another.—*advs.* **oth'erwise,** elsewhere; **oth'erwise,** in another way or manner: by other causes: in other respects: under other conditions.—**every other,** each alternate; **the other day,** quite recently. [O.E. *ōther*; cf. Ger. *ander,* L. *alter.*]

otic, *ō'tik, adj.* of or pertaining to the ear.—*n.* **otī'tis,** inflammation of the internal ear. [Gr. *ous,* gen. *ōtos,* ear.]

otiose, *ō'shi-ōs, adj.* (*rare*) unoccupied, idle: functionless, superfluous. [L. *ōtiōsus*—*ōtium,* leisure.]

ottava rima, *ot-tä'va rēma,* an Italian stanza of eight lines, rhyming *a b a b a b c c.* [It.]

otter, *ot'ér, n.* any of several aquatic fish-eating carnivores of the weasel family: a paravane (q.v.).—*n.* **ott'er-board,** a board to keep open the mouth of a trawl. [O.E.*otor*; akin to **water.**]

otto, *ot'ō* **ottar,** *ot'ár.* Corrs. of **attar.**

Ottoman, *ot'ō-mán, adj.* pertaining to the Turkish Empire, founded by *Othman* or *Osman.*—*n.* a Turk: (without *cap.*) a low, stuffed seat without a back. [Fr.]

oubliette, *ōō-blē-et', n.* a dungeon with no opening except at the top. [Fr.,—*oublier,* to forget—L. *oblīviscī.*]

ouch,*owch, n.* (*arch.*) a brooch, or the socket for a precious stone. [O.Fr. *nouche.*]

ouch, *owch, interj.* expressing pain. [Ger. *autsch.*]

ought, *öt, n.* a variant of **aught.**

ought, *öt, pa.t.* of **owe**: now an auxiliary *v.* (with either present or past sense) to be under obligation: to be proper or necessary.

ouija, *wē'ja, n.* a board with an alphabet, used with a planchette. [Fr. *oui,* Ger. *ja,* yes.]

ounce, *owns, n.* the twelfth part of the (legally obsolete) pound troy: one-sixteenth of a pound avoirdupois.—**fluid ounce** (see **fluid**). [O.Fr. *unce*—L. *uncia,* the twelfth part; cf. **inch.**]

ounce, *owns, n.* a feline carnivorous animal like the leopard. [Fr. *once.*]

our, *owr, possessive adj.* (or *possessive pron.*) pertaining or belonging to us.—**ours,** the possessive (*gen.*) case of **we** (e.g. *the decision is ours*).—Also *possessive adj.* (used without noun—e.g. *that is their share, this is ours*).—**ourself'**, myself (in the regal style):—*pl.* **ourselves** (-*selvz'*), we, not others (emphatic form of **we**): emphatic or reflexive form of **us.** [O.E. *ūre,* gen. of *wē,* we.]

ourang-outang. Same as **orang-utan.**

ousel. See **ouzel.**

oust, *owst, v.t.* to eject, expel, dispossess: —*n.* **oust'er** (*law*), ejection: dispossession. [O.Fr. *oster,* Anglo-Fr. *ouster,* to remove.]

out, *owt, adv.* (shading into *adj.* predicatively) not within: forth: abroad: in or into the open air: in, towards, or at the exterior: to the full stretch or extent: beyond bounds: in a state of exclusion: ruled out, not to be considered: no longer in concealment: no longer in office, in the game, in use, fashion, &c.: on strike: in error: loudly and clearly.—*adj.* external: outlying: outwards: exceeding the usual: in any condition expressed by the adverb *out.*—*interj.* away! begone!—*adj.* **out-of-the-way'**, uncommon.—*ns.* **out-patient** (*owt'pā-shént*), a hospital patient who is not an inmate **out'-tray'**, container for letters, &c. ready for despatch.—**out and away,** by far; **out and out,** thoroughly, completely—also *adj.* (**out-and-out**), thorough, complete; **out at elbow,** threadbare; **out of hand,** instantly: beyond control; **out of joint,** dislocated; **out of one's mind,** mad; **out of temper,** cross, annoyed; **out of the common,** unusual; **out upon,** shame on! [O.E. *ūte, ūt*; Ger. *aus,* Sans. *ud.*]

out, *owt, pfx.* (1) meaning in, or towards, a position external to a position understood (e.g. *outline, outbuilding, outlying, outdoor*; *outgoing, outlook*); also (*fig.*) with suggestion of openness, frankness, completeness (e.g. *outcry, outspoken, outworn*); (2) prefixed to verbs to express the fact that, in some action, the subject goes beyond a standard indicated (e.g. to *outbid, outshine*), and to nouns and adjectives to express the fact of exceeding a standard (e.g. *out-size*). [See above.]

outback, *owt'bak, n.* in Australia, back country or settlements remote from the seaboard towns.—Orig. *adv.*—Also *adj.* [**out, back.**]

outbalance, *owt-bal'áns, v.t.* to outweigh. [**out** (indicating fact of exceeding), **balance.**]

outbid, *owt-bid', v.t.* to offer a higher price than. [**out** (indicating fact of exceeding), **bid.**]

outboard, *owt'bōrd, -bórd, adj.* outside of a ship or boat: having engines outside the boat: towards, or nearer, the ship's side. [**out,** and **board,** ship's side.]

outbreak, *owt'brāk, n.* a breaking out (e.g. of anger, strife, contagious or infectious disease): a disturbance. [**out, break.**]

outbuilding, *owt'bild-ing, n.* a building separate from, but used in connection with, a main building. [**out, build.**]

outburst, *owt'búrst, n.* a bursting out (e.g. a vehement expression of feelings): an explosion. [**out, burst.**]

outcast, *owt'käst, n.* one who is banished from society or home. [**out, cast.**]

outclass, *owt'kläs', v.t.* to surpass so far as to seem in a different class. [**out** (indicating fact of exceeding or excelling), **class.**]

outcome, *owt'kum, n.* the consequence, result. [**out, come.**]

outcrop, *owt'krop, n.* the exposure of a stratum at the surface: the part of a stratum so exposed. [**out** *v.i.* [**out, crop.**]

outcry, *owt'krī, n.* a loud cry of protest, distress, &c.: noise. [**out, cry.**]

outdistance, *owt-dis'táns, v.t.* to leave far behind in any competition. [**out** (indicating fact of exceeding), **distance.**]

outdo, *owt-dōō', v.t.* to surpass, excel. [**out** (indicating fact of exceeding), **do,** vb.]

Neutral vowels in unaccented syllables: *em'pér-ór*; for certain sounds in foreign words see p. ix.

outdoor, *owt'dōr*, *dör*, *adj.* outside the door or the house: in the open air.—*adv.* **out'doors**, out of the house: abroad. [**out, door.**]

outer, *owt'ér*, *adj.* more out or without: external—opp. to *inner.*—*n* the outermost ring of a target: a shot striking here.—*adjs.* **out'ermost, out'most**, most or farthest out: most distant.—**outer bar**, the junior barristers; **outer space**, space beyond solar system, or (*loosely*) at distance from earth reached only by rocket. [O.E. *ūterra, ūtemest,* comp., superl. *adjs.*— *adv. ut(e),* outside.]

outface, *owt-fās'*, *v.t.* to stare down: to bear down by bravery or impudence. [**out** (indicating the fact of exceeding), **face.**]

outfield, *owt'fēld*, *n.* any open field at a distance from the farm-steading: any undefined district or sphere: at cricket and baseball, the outer part of the field: the players who occupy it. [**out, field.**]

outfit, *owt'fit*, *n.* complete equipment: the articles or the expenses for fitting out: any set of persons, a gang. *ns.* **out'fitter**, one who furnishes outfits; **out'fitting**, an outfit: equipment for a voyage. [**out, fit** (1).]

outflank, *owt-flangk'*, *v.t.* to extend beyond or pass round the flank of: to circumvent. [**out** (indicating fact of exceeding), **flank.**]

outgeneral, *owt-jen'ér-ál*, *v.t.* to surpass in generalship. [**out** (indicating fact of exceeding or excelling), **general.**]

outgoing, *owt'gō-ing*, *n.* act or state of going out: extreme limit: expenditure.—*adj.* departing— opp. to *incoming,* as a tenant. [**out, go.**]

outgrow, *owt-grō'*, *v.t.* to surpass in growth: to grow out of.—*n.* **out'growth**, that which grows out from anything: a product. [**out, grow.**]

out-herod Herod, *owt-her'od her'od*, to overact a part: to outdo a person in his characteristic quality. [*Hamlet,* Act iii. Scene 2.]

outhouse, *owt'hows*, *n.* a building separate from, and subsidiary to, the main building. [**out, house.**]

outing, *owt'ing*, *n.* an outdoor excursion. [**out.**]

outlandish, *owt land'ish*, *adj.* foreign: strange: fantastic. [**out, land.**]

outlast, *owt-läst'*, *v.t.* to last longer than. [**out** (indicating fact of exceeding), **last** (2).]

outlaw, *owt'lo*, *n.* one deprived of the protection of the law: (*loosely*) a bandit.—*v.t.* to place beyond the law, to deprive of the benefit of the law: to ban.—*n.* **out'lawry**, the act of putting a man out of the protection of the law: state of being an outlaw. [O.E. *ūtlaga*—O.N. *ūtlāgi—ūt,* out, *lög,* law.]

outlay, *owt'lā*, *n.* that which is laid out: expenditure. [**out, lay** (2).]

outlet, *owt'let*, *n.* the place or means by which anything is let out: the passage outward. [**out, let** (1).]

outline, *owt'līn*, *n.* the line by which any figure is bounded: the line bounding a solid object seen as a plane figure: a sketch without shading: a general indication (e.g. of a plan): a rough draught: a summary: (*pl.*) the main features.—*v.t.* to draw the exterior line of: to delineate or sketch: to summarise, indicate, the main features of. [**out, line** (2).]

outlive, *owt liv'*, *v.t.* to live longer than: to survive: to live through: to live down. [**out**

(indicating fact of exceeding), **live**, vb.]

outlook, *owt'look*, *n.* vigilant watch: a place for looking out from: a view, prospect: a prospect for the future: mental point of view. [**out, look.**]

outlying, *owt'lī-ing*, *adj.* lying out or beyond: remote: on the exterior or frontier. [**out, lie** (2).]

outmanoeuvre, *out-ma-n(y)oo'vér*, *v.t.* to surpass in or by manoeuvring. [**out** (indicating fact of exceeding), **manoeuvre.**]

outmarch, *owt-märch'*, *v.t.* to march faster than. [**out** (indicating fact of exceeding), **march** (3).]

outmoded, *owt-mōd'id*, *adj.* no longer in fashion: no longer accepted. [**out, mode.**]

outmost, *owt'mōst*. Same as **outermost.**

outnumber, *owt-num'bér*, *v.t.* to exceed in number. [**out** (indicating fact of exceeding), **number.**]

outpace, *owt-pās'*, *v.t.* to walk faster than. [**out** (indicating fact of exceeding), **pace.**]

outpost, *owt'pōst*, *n.* a post or station beyond the main body or in the wilds: its occupants. [**out, post** (2).]

outpour, *owt-pōr'*, *-pör'*, *v.t.* to pour out.—*ns.* **out'pour; out'pouring**, a pouring out (*lit.* and *fig.*—e.g. of emotion): an abundant supply. [**out, pour.**]

output, *owt'poot*, *n.* the quantity produced or turned out: data in either printed or coded form after processing by a computer: punched tape or printed page by which processed data leave a computer. [**out, put.**]

outrage, *owt'rij*, *n.* violence beyond measure: gross injury: an atrocious act.—*v.t.* (*rāj'*), to abuse excessively: to injure by violence: to shock.—*adj.* **outrā'geous**, violent: turbulent: atrocious: immoderate.—*adv.* **outrā'geously**. —*n.* **outrā'geousness**. [O.Fr. *oultrage* —L. *ultrā,* beyond]

outrance, *oo̅-trás'*, *n.* the utmost extremity: the bitter end.—**à outrance**, to the bitter end of a combat—erroneously in Eng use, à **l'outrance.** [Fr.]

outré, *oo̅t'rā*, *adj.* eccentric, bizarre. [Fr. pa.p. of *outrer—outrer*—L. *ultrā,* beyond.]

outride, *owt-rīd'*, *v.t.* to ride beyond: to ride faster than.—*n.* **out'rider**, one who rides abroad: a servant on horseback who attends a carriage. [**out, ride.**]

outrigger, *owt'rig-ér*, *n.* a projecting spar for extending sails or any part of the rigging: an apparatus fixed to a boat to increase the leverage of the oar: a boat with this apparatus. [**out, rig** (1).]

outright, *owt'rīt*, *adj.* out-and-out, downright, direct.—*adv.* **outright'**, unreservedly: at once and completely. [**out, right** (adv.).]

outrival, *owt-rī'vál*, *v.t.* to surpass, excel. [**out** (indicating fact of exceeding or excelling), **rival.**]

outrun, *owt-run'*, *v.t.* to go beyond in running: (*fig.*) to exceed: (*fig.*) to elude. [**out** (indicating fact of exceeding), **run.**]

outset, *owt'set*, *n.* a setting out: beginning. [**out, set.**]

outshine, *owt-shīn'*, *v.t.* to surpass in brilliance. [**out** (indicating fact of exceeding or excelling), **shine.**]

outside, *owt'sīd, n.* the outer side: the surface, exterior: the farthest limit.—*adj.* on the outside: exterior: external: remote.—*adv.* on or to the outside: not within.—*prep.* outside of: beyond.—*ns.* **out'side-car,** an Irish car in which the passengers sit back to back; **out'-sider,** one not included in a particular group or set, a stranger, a layman: one not considered fit to associate with: a horse unlikely to win a race. [**out, side.**]

out-size, *owt'sīz, adj.* over normal size.—*n.* an unusually large size. [**out, size** (1).]

outskirt, *owt'skûrt, n.* (usu. in *pl.*) the border. [**out, skirt.**]

out-smart, *owt-smärt', v.t.* (*coll.*; *orig. U.S.*) to show more cleverness or cunning than, to outwit. [**out** (indicating the fact of exceeding), and **smart** (adj.).]

outspan, *owt-span', v.t.* and *v.i.* to unyoke from a vehicle.—*n.* a stopping-place. [Du. *uitspannen.*]

outspoken, *owt-spō'ken, adj.* frank or bold of speech: uttered with boldness. [**out,** and pa.p. of **speak.**]

outspread, *owt-spred', v.t.* to spread out or over.—Also *p.adj.* [**out, spread.**]

outstanding, *owt-stand'ing, adj.* prominent: unpaid: still to be attended to or done. [**out, stand.**]

outstretch, *owt-strech', v.t.* to spread out, extend. [**out, stretch.**]

outstrip, *owt-strip', v.t.* to outrun: to leave behind. [**out** (indicating the fact of exceeding), and late M.E. *strip,* to move swiftly.]

outvie, *owt-vī', v.t.* to compete with and surpass. [**out** (indicating the fact of exceeding), **vie.**]

outvote, *owt-vōt', v.t.* to defeat by votes. [**out** (indicating the fact of exceeding), **vote.**]

outward, *owt'wàrd, adj.* toward the outside: external: exterior.—*adv.* toward the exterior: away from port: to a foreign port.—*adj.* **out'ward-bound,** sailing outwards or to a foreign port: of a system of education, laying great emphasis on outdoor activities.—*adv.* **out'wardly,** in an outward manner: externally: in appearance.—*adv.* **out'wards,** in an outward direction. [**out,** and suffx. *-ward.*]

outweigh, *owt-wā', v.t.* to exceed in weight or importance. [**out** (indicating the fact of exceeding), **weigh.**]

outwit, *owt-wit', v.t.* to surpass in wit or ingenuity: to defeat by superior ingenuity:—*pr.p.* outwitt'ing; *pa.t.* and *pa.p.* outwitt'ed. [**out** (indicating the fact of exceeding or excelling), **wit** (2).]

outwork, *owt'wûrk, n.* a work outside the principal wall or line of fortification. [**out, work.**]

outworn, *owt-wōrn', -wòrn', adj.* worn out: out of date: obsolete. [**out,** and pa.p. of **wear.**]

ouzel, ousel, *ōō'zl, n.* (*arch.*) a blackbird: various kinds of small bird. [O.E. *ōsle*; cog. with Ger. *amsel.*]

ova, *ō'va, pl.* of **ovum.**—*adj.* **o'val,** having the shape of an egg.—*n.* an oval figure or enclosure.—*adv.* **o'vally.** [Fr. *ovale*—L. *ōvum,* an egg.]

ovary, *ō'vàr-i, n.* the female gland producing ova: (*bot.*) the part of the gynaeceum that contains the ovule.—*adjs.* **ova′rian,** pertaining to an ovary; **ovā′rious,** consisting of eggs. [Low L. *ōvāria*—*ōvum,* egg.]

ovate, *ō'vāt, adj.* egg-shaped. [L. *ōvātus*—*ōvum,* egg.]

ovation, *ō-vā'sh(ò)n, n.* in ancient Rome, a lesser triumph: an outburst of popular applause. [L. *ōvātiō, -ōnis*—*ōvāre,* to exult.]

oven, *uv'n, n.* an arched cavity or closed chamber for baking, heating, or drying: a small furnace. [O.E. *ofen*; Ger. *ofen.*]

over, *ō'vér, prep.* higher than—in place, rank, value, &c.: across: above: upon the whole surface of: concerning: on account of: in study of or occupation with: more than.—*adv.* on the top: above: across: from beginning to end, up and down: from one side, person, &c., to another: outward, downward, out of the perpendicular: above in measure: unduly: as surplus, or in an unfinished state (*left over*): again.—*interj.* in telecommunications, indicates that the speaker now expects a reply.—*adj.* upper or superior: surplus: excessive: finished, at an end.—*n.* (*cricket*) the number of balls delivered in succession by the bowler from one end of the pitch.—**over again,** afresh, anew; **over against,** opposite; **over and above,** in addition to: besides; **over and over,** repeatedly; **over head and ears,** deeply: completely; **over seas,** to foreign lands.—**all over,** completely: at an end. [O.E. *ofer*; Ger. *über,* L. *super,* Gr. *hyper.*]

over-, *ō-vér-, pfx.* meaning:—(1) above in position (*lit.* and *fig.*; e.g. *overarch, overlord*), across (e.g. *overleap, overlook*), across the surface (*overrun, overflow, v.t.*), beyond (*lit.* and *fig.*; e.g. *overseas, overtime*), away from the perpendicular (*lit.* and *fig.*; e.g. *overbalance, overthrow*), across the edge or boundary (*overflow, v.t.* and *v.i.*); (2) completely (e.g. *overawe*); (3) beyond the normal or desirable limit, excessively (e.g. *overheat*). Many words with *pfx. over* have more than one meaning (see **overgrow, overprint** (1) and (2)). [See above.]

overact, *ō'vér-akt', v.t.* and *v.i.* to overdo (any part).—*n.* **overact'ing,** acting with exaggeration. [**over** (indicating excess), **act.**]

overactive, *ō-vér-ak'tiv, adj.* acting, working, too rapidly or energetically.—*n.* **overactiv'ity.** [**over** (indicating excess), **active.**]

over(-)all, *ō'vér-ōl, n.* a garment worn over ordinary clothes to keep them clean.—*adj.* including the whole or everything: considering everything. [**over, all.**]

over-anxious, *ō-vér-angk'shùs, adj.* too anxious.—*n.* **over-anxī′ety.**—*adv.* **over-anx′iously.** [**over** (indicating excess), **anxious.**]

overarch, *ō-vér-ärch', v.t.* to arch over. [**over, arch** (1).]

overawe, *ō-vér-ö', v.t.* to dominate by fear or authority. [**over, awe.**]

overbalance, *ō-vér-bal'áns, v.t.* to cause to lose balance: to outweigh.—*v.i.* to lose equilibrium.—*n.* excess of weight or value. [**over, balance.**]

overbear, *ō-vér-bār', v.t.* to bear down or overpower: to overwhelm.—*adj.* **overbear′ing,** haughty and dogmatical: imperious. [**over, bear** (1).]

overboard, *ō-vér-bōrd', adv.* over the board or side of a ship, &c.—**go overboard about** or **for**

Neutral vowels in unaccented syllables: *em'pér-ór*; for certain sounds in foreign words see p. ix.

508

(*slang*), to go to extremes of enthusiasm about or for. [over, and **board**, ship's side.]

overburden, ō-vėr-bûr'dn, *v.t.* to burden too much. [over (indicating excess), **burden**.]

overcapitalise, ō-vėr-kap'it-ȧl-īz, *v.t.* to fix the capital to be invested in, or the capital value of, too high. [over (indicating excess), **capitalise**.]

overcast, ō-vėr-käst', *v.t.* to cloud, cover with gloom: to sew over rough edges of (a piece of cloth).—*adj.* clouded over. [over, **cast**.]

overcharge, ō-vėr-chärj', *v.t.* to load with too great a charge: to charge (a person) too great a price: to charge too great a price for.—Also *v.i.*—*n.* o'vercharge, an excessive load or burden: an undue price. [over (indicating excess), **charge**.]

overcoat, ō'vėr-kōt, *n.* an outdoor coat worn over all the other dress. [over, **coat**.]

overcome, ō-vėr-kum', *v.t.* to get the better of, to conquer or subdue.—*p.adj.* helpless, overpowered by exhaustion or emotion.—*v.i.* to be victorious. [over, **come**.]

over-confident, ō-vėr-kon'fi-dėnt, *adj.* too confident.—*n.* **over-con'fidence.** [over (indicating excess), **confident**.]

overcrowd, ō-vėr-krowd', *v.t.* to fill or crowd to excess. [over (indicating excess), **crowd**.]

overdo, ō-vėr-dōō', *v.t.* to exaggerate, carry to excess: to cook too much.—*p.adj.* **overdone'**, [over (indicating excess), **do**, vb.]

overdose, ō'vėr dōs, *n.* an excessive dose.—*v.t.* **overdose'**, to dose in excess. [over, **dose**.]

overdraw, ō-vėr-drö', *v.t.* to draw beyond one's credit: to exaggerate.—*n.* o'verdraft, the excess of the amount drawn over the sum against which it is drawn. [over (indicating excess), **draw**.]

overdress, ō-vėr-dres', *v.t.* to dress too ostentatiously. [over (indicating excess), **dress**.]

overdrive, ō-vėr-drīv', *v.t.* to drive too hard: to drive beyond.—*n.* a gearing device which transmits to the driving shaft a speed greater than engine crankshaft speed. [over (indicating excess), **drive**.]

overdue, ō-vėr dū', *adj.* unpaid, unperformed, &c., though the time for payment, performance, &c., is past. [over, **due**.]

overestimate, ō-vėr-es'tim-āt, *v.t.* to estimate too highly.—*n.* (-ȧt) an excessive estimate. [over (indicating excess), **estimate**.]

overexert, ō-vėr-eg-zûrt', *v.t.* to exert too much.—*n.* **overexer'tion.** [over (indicating excess), **exert**.]

overexpose, ō-vėr-eks-pōz', *v.t.* to expose too much, esp. to light.—*n.* **overexpos'ure.** [over (indicating excess), **expose**.]

overflow, ō-vėr-flō', *v.t.* to flow over: to flood: (of e.g. people) to fill and then spread beyond (e.g. a room).—*v.i.* to run over: to abound:—*pa.t.* and *pa.p.* overflowed'.—*n.* o'verflow, a flowing over: a pipe or channel for spare water, &c.: an inundation: superabundance.—*adj.* **overflow'ing**, exuberant, very abundant.—**overflow meeting**, a supplementary meeting of those unable to find room in the main meeting. [over, **flow**.]

overgrow, ō-vėr-grō', *v.t.* to grow across: to grow beyond: to grow too great for: (of vegetation) to cover.—*v.i.* to grow beyond the proper

size.—*adj.* **overgrown'**, grown beyond the natural size: covered with overgrowth.—*n.* **o'vergrowth**, excessive growth. [over, **grow**.]

overhand, ō-vėr-hand', or ō'-, *adv.* with hand above the object: palm-downwards: with hand or arm raised above the shoulders or (in swimming) coming out of the water over the head.—*adj.* (ō'verhand) done or performed overhand. [over, **hand**.]

overhang, ō-vėr-hang', *v.t.* to hang over: to project over: to impend over.—Also *v.i.* [over, **hang**.]

overhaul, ō-vėr-höl', *v.t.* to turn over for examination: to examine: (*naut.*) to overtake in a chase.—*n.* **o'verhaul**, examination: repair. [over, **haul**.]

overhead, ō-vėr-hed', *adv.* above one's head: aloft: in the zenith.—**overhead costs, charges**, the general expenses of a business—esp. a manufacturing business—as distinct from the direct cost of producing an article. [over, **head**.]

overhear, ō-vėr-hēr', *v.t.* to hear by stealth or by accident. [over, **hear**.]

overheat, ō-vėr-hēt', *v.t.* to heat to excess.—*n.* **o'verheat**, extreme heat. [over (indicating excess), **heat**.]

overjoy, ō-vėr-joi', *v.t.* to fill with great joy, to transport with delight or gladness. [over (indicating completeness), **joy**.]

overland, ō'vėr-land, *adj.* passing entirely or principally by land.—*adv.* **overland'.**—*v.t.* and *v.i.* to drive (flocks or herds) across country. [over, **land**.]

overlap, ō-vėr-lap', *v.t.* to extend over 'and beyond the edge of. [over, **lap** (2).]

overlay, ō-vėr-lā', *v.t.* to cover by laying or spreading something over: to cover to excess: (by confusion) to overlie:—*pa.t.* and *pa.p.* overlaid'. [over, **lay** (2).]

overleaf, ō-vėr-lēf', *adv.* on the other side of the page. [over, **leaf**.]

overleap, ō-vėr-lēp', *v.t.* to leap over: to leap too far. [over, **leap**.]

overlie, ō vėr lī', *v.t.* to lie above or upon: to smother:—*pr.p.* overly'ing; *pa.t.* overlay'; *pa.p.* overlain. [over, **lie** (2).]

overload, ō-vėr-lōd', *v.t.* to load or fill overmuch. [over (indicating excess), **load**.]

overlook, ō-vėr-lōōk', *v.t.* to look over: to see from a higher position: to view carefully: to fail to notice: to pass by without punishment: to slight. [over, **look**.]

overlord, ō'vėr-lörd, *n.* a feudal superior. [over, **lord**.]

overman, ō'vėr-man, *n.* an overseer: in mining, the person in charge of the work below ground: see also **Nietzschean**. [over, **man**, n.]

overman, ō-vėr-man', *v.t.* to furnish with too many men. [over (indicating excess), **man**, vb.]

overmantel, ō'vėr-man-tl, *n.* an ornamental structure, often with a mirror, set on a mantel-shelf. [over, **mantel**.]

overmuch, ō-vėr-much', *adj.* and *adv.* too much. [over (indicating excess), **much**.]

overnight, ō-vėr-nīt', *adv.* all night: in the course of the night: for the night. [over, **night**.]

overpass, ō'vėr päs, *n.* a road bridging another road, railway, canal, &c. [over, **pass**.]

overpay   overwhelm

overpay, *ō-vėr-pā′, v.t.* to pay too much. [**over** (indicating excess), **pay** (1).]

overplus, *ō′vėr-plus, n.* that which is more than enough: surplus. [**over, plus.**]

overpower, *ō-vėr-pow′ėr, v.t.* to overcome by force, to subdue: to overwhelm. [**over, power.**]

overprint, *ō′vėr-print, v.t.* to print on an already printed surface (e.g. *to overprint a postage stamp*).—*n.* overprinted surface: a word, device, &c., printed across e.g. a stamp. [**over, print.**]

overprint, *ō′vėr-print, v.t.* to print too many copies of. [**over** (in excess), **print.**]

overproduction, *ō-vėr-pro-duk′sh(ó)n, n.* the production of goods in excess of the demand. [**over** (indicating excess), **production.**]

overproof, *ō′vėr-prōōf, adj.* containing more alcohol than proof-spirit. [**over, proof.**]

overrate, *ō-vėr-rāt′, v.t.* to rate or value too highly. [**over** (indicating excess), **rate** (1).]

overreach, *ō-vėr-rēch′, v.t.* to reach or extend beyond: to outwit or get the better of: (*refl.*) to defeat by attempting too much or by being oversubtle. [**over, reach.**]

override, *ō-vėr-rīd′, v.t.* to ride too much: to trample down: to set aside, to be more important than, prevail over. [**over, ride.**]

overrule, *ō-vėr-rōōl′, v.t.* to prevail over: to set aside (e.g. a decision) by greater power: (*law*) to reject or declare invalid. [**over, rule.**]

overrun, *ō-vėr-run′, v.t.* to run or swarm over: to grow over: to spread over and take possession of: to infest. [**over, run.**]

oversea, *ō′vėr-sē, adj.* beyond the sea: abroad.— Also **o′verseas.**—*adv.* **oversea′, overseas′.** [**over, sea.**]

oversee, *ō-vėr-sē′, v.t.* to see or look over, to superintend.—*n.* **o′verseer,** a superintendent: an officer who has the care of the poor, and other duties. [**over, see** (2).]

overset, *ō-vėr-set′, v.t. and v.i.* to turn over: to upset. [**over, set.**]

overshadow, *ō-vėr-shad′ō, v.t.* to throw a shadow over: to cast into the shade by surpassing: to shelter or protect. [**over, shadow.**]

overshoe, *ō′vėr-shōō, n.* a shoe, esp. of waterproof, worn one over another. [**over, shoe.**]

overshoot, *ō-vėr-shōōt′, v.t.* to shoot over or beyond (a mark).—*v.i.* tо shoot or pass beyond the mark.—*n.* (aero.) a going beyond the mark in landing.—*adj.* **o′vershot,** fed from above, as a water-wheel. [**over, shoot.**]

oversight, *ō′vėr-sīt, n.* superintendence: failure to notice: an omission. [**over, sight.**]

oversleep, *ō-vėr-slēp′, v.t. and v.i.* to sleep beyond one's usual time. [**over** (indicating excess), **sleep.**]

overspread, *ō-vėr-spred′, v.t.* to spread over: to scatter over.—*v.i.* to be spread over. [**over, spread.**]

overstate, *ō-vėr-stāt′, v.t.* to state too strongly.— *n.* **overstate′ment.** [**over** (indicating excess), **state.**]

oversteer, *ō-vėr-stēr′, n.* in a motor-car, too quick a response to the steering-wheel. [**over** (indicating excess), **steer.**]

overstep, *ō-vėr-step′, v.t.* to step beyond: to exceed. [**over, step.**]

overstock, *ō-vėr-stok′, v.t.* to stock overmuch: to fill too full.—*n.* **o′verstock,** stock in excess of

need. [**over** (indicating excess), **stock** (1).]

overstrain, *ō-vėr-strān′, v.t. and v.i.* to strain or stretch too far. [**over** (indicating excess), **strain** (1).]

overstretch, *ō-vėr-strech′, v.t. and v.i.* to stretch across: to stretch too far.—*n.* **overstretch′ing.** [**over, stretch.**]

overstrung, *ō-vėr-strung′, adj.* (fig.) too highly strung, overstrained in nerves. [**over** (indicating excess), and pa.p. of **string.**]

overstrung, *ō′vėr-strung, p.adj.* (of a piano) with the lower base strings crossing diagonally over the rest of the strings. [**over,** and pa.p. of **string.**]

overt, *ō′vėrt, ō-vûrt′, adj.* open to view, public, openly done.—*adv.* **o′vertly.** [Fr. *ouvert*, pa.p. of *ouvrir*, to open.]

overtake, *ō-vėr-tāk′, v.t.* to come up with, to catch: to pass from behind: to come upon unexpectedly (e.g. *a storm overtook him*): to get through (a piece of work) in a prescribed time. [**over, take.**]

overtask, *ō-vėr-täsk′, v.t.* to task overmuch: to impose too heavy a task on. [**over** (indicating excess), **task.**]

overtax, *ō-vėr-taks′, v.t.* to tax too highly: to make too great demands on (e.g. one's strength). [**over** (indicating excess), **tax.**]

overthrow, *ō-vėr-thrō′, v.t.* to throw over, overturn: to ruin, to subvert, to defeat utterly: to throw too far.—*n.* **o′verthrow,** act of overthrowing or state of being overthrown: (*cricket*) a ball missed at the wicket and returned from the field: a run scored in consequence. [**over, throw.**]

overtime, *ō′vėr-tīm, n.* time employed in working beyond the regular hours: work done in such time: pay for such work. [**over, time.**]

overtone, *ō′vėr-tōn, n.* a harmonic, i.e. in a complex tone, any of the components above the fundamental frequency: a subtle meaning additional to the main meaning, conveyed by a word or statement: implicit quality. [**over, tone.**]

overtop, *ō-vėr-top′, v.t.* to rise over the top of: to surpass. [**over, top.**]

overtrade, *ō-vėr-trād′, v.i.* to trade beyond capital: to buy in more goods than can be sold or paid for. [**over** (indicating excess), **trade.**]

overture, *ō′vėr-tyúr, -chúr, n.* an opening of negotiations: a proposal: (*mus.*) an instrumental prelude to an opera, oratorio, &c.[O.Fr. *overture,* an opening.]

overturn, *ō-vėr-tûrn′, v.t.* to throw down or over, to upset: to subvert.—*n.* **o′verturn,** state of being overturned. [**over, turn.**]

overvalue, *ō-vėr-val′ū, v.t.* to value too highly. [**over** (indicating excess), **value.**]

overweening, *ō-vėr-wēn′ing, adj.* conceited, arrogant, presumptuous. [From rare verb *overween,* to think too highly (usu. of oneself)—**over** (indicating excess), **ween.**]

overweigh, *ō-vėr-wā′, v.t.* to outweigh.—*n.* **o′verweight,** weight beyond what is required or allowed.—*v.t.* **overweight′,** to overburden.—*adj.* **overweight′ed,** not fairly balanced in presentation. [**over** (indicating excess), **weigh.**]

overwhelm, *ō-vėr-hwelm′, v.t.* to overspread and crush by something heavy or strong: to over-

Neutral vowels in unaccented syllables: *em′pėr-ór*; for certain sounds in foreign words see p. ix.

510

overwork   **ozone**

power: (of emotion) to overcome: (*fig.*) to deluge, oppress (with). [**over, whelm.**]

overwork, ō-vér-wûrk′, *v.t.* and *v.i.* to work too much or too long.—*v.t.* (in *pa.p.*) to decorate all over: to use (e.g. an excuse) too often:—*pa.t.* and *pa.p.* overworked or, in certain senses (see below), overwrought.—*n.* o′verwork, excess of work. [**over** (indicating excess), **work.**]

overwrought, ō-vér-röt′, *pa.p.* of **overwork**, worked too hard: excited, with highly strained nerves: worked or embellished all over.

oviduct, ō′vi-dukt, *n.* (*zool.*) the tube by which the egg passes from the ovary. [L. *ōvum*, egg, *dūcēre*, *ductum*, to convey.]

oviferous, ō-vif′ér-us, *adj.* egg-carrying. [L. *ōvum*, an egg, *ferre*, to bear.]

oviform, ō′vi-färm, *adj.* egg-shaped. [L. *ōvum*, egg, *forma*, form.]

ovine, ō′vīn, *adj.* sheep-like. [L. *ŏvis*, sheep.]

oviparous, ō-vip′a-rus, *adj.* egg-laying. [L. *ōvum*, egg, *parĕre*, to bring forth.]

ovipositor, ō-vi-poz′i-tór, *n.* an egg-laying organ. [L. *ōvum*, egg, *positor—pōnĕre*, to place.]

ovoid, ō′void, *adj.* oval; egg-shaped. *n.* an egg-shaped body. *adj.* **ovoid′al.** [L. *ovum*, egg, Gr. *eidos*, form.]

ovulate, ov′ūl-āte, *v.t.* to produce ova: to discharge ova from the ovary.—*n.* **ovulā′tion.** [From L. *ōvum*, an egg.]

ovule, ō′ūl, *n.* in flowering plants, the body that on fertilisation becomes the seed. [Dim. from L. *ōvum*, an egg.]

ovum, ō′vum, *n.* an egg: (*biol.*) the egg-cell, from which after impregnation the foetus is developed:—*pl.* **o′va.** [L.]

owe, ō, *v.t.* (*obs.* or *dial.*) to own: to be indebted to for (something—to someone or something; e.g. we owe our lives to him, to his skill; also, we owe him (dat., indirect object) our lives, money): to be under an obligation to pay, restore, &c.: to have (a feeling) towards (I owe him a grudge).—*v.i.* to be in debt: *pa.t.* and *pa.p.* owed, (*obs.*) ought. [O.E. *āgan*, pres. indic. *āh*, pa.t. *āhte*, pa.p. *agen*; O.N. *eiga*, O.H.G. *eigan*, to possess.]

owing, ō′ing, *adj.* due, to be paid: imputable, attributable (to).—**owing to,** in consequence of. [**owe.**]

owl, owl, *n.* any of a number of predacious nocturnal birds, noted for their howling or hooting noise.—*n.* **owl′et,** a little or young owl.—*adj.* **owl′ish,** like an owl: solemn: dull-looking. [O.E. *ūle*; Ger. *eule*, L. *ulula*; imit.]

own, ōn, *v.t.* to possess: to acknowledge as one's own: to admit.—*v.i.* to confess (to).—*ns.* **own′er,** possessor; **own′er-occ′upier,** one who owns the house he lives in; **own′ership.** [O.E. *āgnian—āgen*, one's own; cf. **own,** adj.]

own, ōn, *adj.* belonging to oneself: often used with reflexive force, my own, his own.—**get one's own back,** retaliate, get even; **hold one's own** (see **hold**); **on one's own,** on one's own initiative, or by one's own efforts: set up in independence. [O.E. *āgen*, pa.p. of *āgan*, to possess; cf. **owe.**]

ox, oks, *n.* a ruminant quadruped of the bovine genus or a related species: the male of the cow, esp. when castrated:—*pl.* **ox′en,** used for both male and female.—*ns.* **ox′-bot, ox′-war′bler,** a warble-fly or its larva, found under the skin of

cattle; **ox′eye,** a wild chrysanthemum with yellow disk and white (*oxeye daisy*) or yellow (*corn-marigold*) ray.—*adj.* **ox′-eyed,** having large, ox-like eyes. [O.E. *oxa*, pl. *oxan, oxen*; O.N. *uxi*; Ger. *ochs*, Sans. *uksan*.]

oxalis, oks′a-lis, *n.* wood-sorrel (q.v.).—*adj.* **oxal′ic,** applied to an acid obtained from wood-sorrels, &c.—*n.* **ox′alate,** a salt of oxalic acid. [Gr. *oxalis—oxys*, sharp, acid.]

Oxbridge, oks′brij, *n.* Oxford and Cambridge, as opposed to a redbrick university.

Oxford Group, oks′förd grōōp, an evangelical movement originating in America,—**Oxford Movement,** or *Tractarian Movement*, a High Church movement which originated at Oxford in 1833.

oxide, oks′īd, *n.* a compound of oxygen and another element or radical.—*v.t.* **ox′idise,** to combine with oxygen: to add an electropositive atom or group to, or remove an electro-negative atom or group from, a molecule.—Also *v.i.*—*n.* **oxidā′tion.**—*adj.* **oxidis′able.** [Fr. (now *oxyde*) *oxygène*, oxygen.]

oxlip, oks′lip, *n.* orig. cross between primrose and cowslip: species of primula like large pale cowslip. [O.E. *oxanslyppe*; cf. **cowslip.**]

Oxonian, oks-ō′ni-án, *adj.* of Oxford University or Oxford.—*n.* a past or present student, or citizen, of Oxford. [L. *Oxonia*, Oxford.]

oxy-, oks′i-, in composition, sharp: acid: oxygen.—*adj.* **ox′y-acet′ylene,** involving, using, or by means of, a mixture of oxygen and acetylene. [Gr. *oxys*, sharp.]

oxygen, oks′i-jén, *n.* a gaseous element (symbol O; atomic number 8) without taste, colour, or smell, forming part of the air, water, &c., and supporting life and combustion.—*v.t.* **ox′ygenāte,** to impregnate or treat with oxygen.—*n.* **oxygenā′tion,** act of oxygenating.—*v.t.* **ox′ygenise,** to oxygenate,—*adjs.* **oxyg′enous,** pertaining to, or obtained from, oxygen; **oxyhy′drogen,** involving or using a mixture of oxygen and hydrogen.—**oxygen mask,** a mask-like breathing apparatus through which oxygen is supplied in rarefied atmospheres to aviators, mountaineers, &c.; **oxygen tent,** an oxygen-filled tent erected round a patient to aid breathing. [Gr. *oxys*, sharp, *gen-*, the root of *gennaein*, to generate.]

oxymoron, ok-si-mō′, (-mö′)ron, *n.* a figure of speech in which contradictory terms are combined, as *falsely true*, &c. [Gr.,—*oxys*, sharp, *mōros*, foolish.]

oxytone, oks′i-tōn, *adj.* having the acute accent on the last syllable. [Gr. *oxys, tonos*, tone.]

oyer, ō′yér, *n.* a hearing in a law-court, an assize.—**oyer and terminer,** a royal commission conferring power to hear and determine criminal causes. [Anglo-Fr. *oyer* (Fr. *ouïr*)—L. *audīre*, to hear.]

oyez, oyes, ō-yes′, ō′yes, *interj.* the call of a public crier for attention. [O.Fr. *oyez*, imper. of *oïr*, to hear.]

oyster, ois′tér, *n.* a genus of bivalve shellfish, used as food. [O.Fr. *oistre*—L. *ostrea*—Gr. *ostreon*, an oyster—*osteon*, a bone.]

ozone, ō′zōn, *n.* an allotropic form of oxygen, (O_3), with a peculiar smell, a powerful oxydising agent. [Gr. *ozein*, to smell.]

---

fāte, fär; mē, hûr (her); mīne; mōte, för; mūte; mōōn, fŏŏt; тнen (then)

511

P

pabulum, *pab'ū-lum, n.* food: fuel: nourishment for the mind. [L.,—*pāscĕre,* to feed.]

pace, *pās, n.* a stride, step: the space between the feet in walking, 30 inches: rate of motion (of a man or a beast): a mode of stepping in horses in which the legs on the same side are lifted together, amble.—*v.t.* to measure by steps: to train in walking or stepping: to set the pace for in a race by example.—*v.i.* to walk: to walk slowly.—*ns.* **pace′-mak′er,** one who sets the pace, as in a race (also *fig.*): a small mass of muscle cells in the heart which controls the heart-beat electrically: an electronic device (in later models, with radioactive core) used to correct weak or irregular heart rhythms; **pac′er,** one who paces: a horse whose usual gait is a pace; **pace′-setter,** a pace-maker, except in anatomical and electronic senses.—**set the pace,** to fix by example the rate of movement for others (*lit.* and *fig.*); **show one's paces,** to show what one can do. [Fr. *pas*—L. *passus,* a step—*pandĕre, passum,* to stretch.]

pace, *pās′ē, prep.* with all due respect to (so-and-so—accompanying the expression of an opinion contrary to his). [L. abl. of *pāx,* peace.]

pacha, pachalic. See **pasha, pashalik.**

pachyderm, *pak′i-dûrm, n.* one of an order of non-ruminant, hoofed mammals, thick-skinned, as the elephant: an insensitive person.—*adj.* **pachyder′matous,** thick-skinned: of the pachyderms: insensitive. [Gr. *pachys,* thick.]

pacify, *pas′i-fī, v.t.* to appease: to calm: to bring peace to.—*adj.* **pacif′ic,** peace-making: appeasing: peaceful (e.g. of disposition): (*cap.*) of the ocean between Asia and America, because the first European to sail on it, Magellan, happened to cross it under peaceful conditions (also *n.*).—*n.* **pacificā′tion,** peace-making: conciliation: peace treaty.—*adj.* **pacif′icatory.**—*ns.* **pacif′icist** (-*sist*), one who is opposed to war, or believes all war to be wrong; **pacif′icism** (-*sizm*); **pac′ifier; pac′ifist, pac′ifism,** ill-formed but generally preferred forms of **pacificist,** *pacificism.* [Partly through Fr. *pacifier*—L. *pācificus,* pacific—*pācificāre*—*pāx, pācis,* peace, *facĕre,* to make.]

pack, *pak, n.* a bundle (esp. one for carrying on the back, e.g. a pedlar's): a measure of various goods (e.g. wool): a complete set of cards: a number of animals kept together for hunting, or associating together for that and other purposes: the forwards in a rugby football team: a worthless, disreputable, or otherwise objectionable set of persons: a mass of pack-ice: a cosmetic paste: act or method of packing: a compact package, esp. of something for sale.—*v.t.* to make into a bundle or pack: to prepare (food—e.g. meat) and arrange it compactly in boxes, &c., for transport: to put into

a bag or other article of luggage: to press together closely: to crowd, to cram.—*v.i.* to form into a pack: to settle or be driven into a firm mass: to form a scrum: to put one's belongings together in bags or boxes (often with *up*): to take oneself off, to depart in haste.—*n.* **pack′age,** a bundle, packet, or parcel.—*v.t.* to make up into a parcel, esp. to pack in a carton or box.—*ns.* **pack′er; pack′et,** a small package: a ship or vessel employed in carrying letters, passengers, &c.: a vessel plying regularly between one port and another (also **pack′et-boat, pack′et-ship,** &c.).—*v.t.* to parcel up.—*ns.* **pack′-horse,** a horse used to carry goods; **pack′-ice,** collection of large pieces of floating ice; **pack′ing,** the act of putting into packs or of tying up for carriage: material for doing so: anything used to fill an empty space, or to make a joint close; **pack′ing-need′le,** or *sack-needle,* strong needle for sewing up packages; **pack′ing-sheet,** or **pack′sheet,** coarse cloth for packing goods; **pack′man,** a pedlar or a man who carries a pack; **pack′-sadd′le,** a saddle adapted for supporting the load on a pack-animal; **pack′-thread,** a coarse thread used to sew up packages; **pack′-train,** a train of loaded pack-animals.—**package deal,** a bargain or deal which includes a number of clauses and has to be accepted as a whole, the less favourable items along with the favourable; **package holiday, tour,** a package deal holiday, for which most expenses are pre-paid.—**pack it in** (*slang*), to stop doing something; **pack up,** stop: break down; **send one packing,** to dismiss one summarily. [M.E. *packe, pakke,* app.—Middle Flemish *pac,* or Du. or Low Ger. *pak.*]

pack, *pak, n.* (*obs.*) a secret arrangement.—*v.t.* to fill up (a jury, meeting, &c.) with persons of a particular kind for one's own purposes. [Prob. **pact.**]

pact, *pakt, n.* an agreement or compact, esp. one informal and not legally enforceable. [L. *pactum*—*pacīscĕre, pactum,* to contract.]

pad, *pad, n.* a path: a thief on the high-road (usually *footpad*): (abbrev. from *pad-horse*) an easy-paced horse.—*v.i.* to walk on foot, to trudge along: to walk with dull-sounding tread: to rob on foot:—*pr.p.* padd′ing; *pa.t.* and *pa.p.* padd′ed. [Du. *pad,* a path.]

pad, *pad, n.* anything stuffed with a soft material to prevent friction or pressure or injury, or for filling out: a soft saddle: a cushion: a number of sheets of paper or other soft material fastened together in a block: the fleshy, thick-skinned under-surface of the foot of many animals, as, the fox: the paw of a fox, hare, otter, &c.: a rocket-launching platform: (*slang*) a bed, room or home, esp. one's own.—*v.t.* to stuff with anything soft: to fill out to greater length with words or matter that

Neutral vowels in unaccented syllables: *em′pėr-ŏr*; for certain sounds in foreign words see p. ix.

paddle   pair

add nothing to the meaning:—*pr.p.* padd′ing; *pa.t.* and *pa.p.* padd′ed.—*n.* **padd′ing**, stuffing: matter of less value introduced into a book or article to make it of the length desired. [Origin obscure; possibly connected with **pod**.]

paddle, *pad′l, v.i.* to wade about or dabble in water: to walk unsteadily or with short steps, as a young child does: to toy with the fingers (with *in, on, about*). [Cf. **pad** (1), and Low Ger. *paddeln*, to tramp about.]

paddle, *pad′l, n.* a small, long-handled spade: a short, broad, spoon-shaped oar, used for moving canoes: the blade of an oar: one of the boards of a paddle-wheel or waterwheel: a swimming animal's flipper.—*v.i.* to progress by the use of paddles: to row gently: to swim about like a duck.—*v.t.* to propel by paddle.—*ns.* **padd′le-steam′er**, a steamer propelled by paddle-wheels; **padd′le-wheel**, a wheel on a steam-vessel, having boards on its circumference, which by turning in the water causes the vessel to move forward.

paddock, *pad′ok, n.* (*arch.* and *Scot.*) a toad or frog.—*n.* **padd′ock-stool**, a toadstool. [Dim. from late O.E. *pade, padde*, toad; O.N. *padda.*]

paddock, *pad′ok, n.* an enclosed field under pasture, orig. near a house or stable: the saddling enclosure of a race-course. [Apparently from earlier *parrock*—O.E. *pearroc*, park.]

paddy, *pad′i, n.* growing rice: rice in the husk.—*n.* **padd′y-field**. [Malay, *pādi.*]

padishah, *pä′di-shä, n.* great king, a title of the Shah of Persia, the Sultan of Turkey, and the Great Mogul; used also of the (British) Emperor of India (*hist.*) [Pers. *pād*, master, *shāh*, king.]

padlock, *pad′lok, n.* a detachable lock with a link to pass through a staple or other opening.—*v.t.* to fasten with a padlock. [Possibly dial. Eng. *pad*, a basket, and **lock**.]

padre, *pä′drā, n.* father, a title given to priests: (*slang*) an army or navy chaplain.—*n.* **padrō′ne**, the master of a Mediterranean trading vessel: in Italy, an innkeeper: an Italian employer of street musicians, &c. [Port. (also Sp. and It.) *padre*—L. *pater*, a father.]

paduasoy, *pad′ū-a-soi, n.* a corded silk used in the 18th century. [Fr. *pou-de-soie*—*pou, pout, poult* (of unknown origin), *de soie*, of silk; apparently influenced by *Padua.*]

paean, *pē′an, n.* a song of triumph: a hymn to Apollo. [L. *paeān, paeōn*—Gr. *Paiān, -ānos*, name for Apollo.]

paed-, ped-, *pēd-,* in composition, child, boy.—*adj.* **paediat′ric**, (Gr. *iātrikos*, medical), relating to the medical treatment of children.—*ns.* **paediatrics**, the treatment of children's diseases; **paediatric′ian**. [Gr. *pais, paidos*, boy, child.]

paedagogic, paedagogue. See **pedagogue.**

paedobaptism. See **pedobaptism.**

paella, *pī-el′a, n.* a stew containing saffron, chicken, rice, vegetables, &c. [Sp.]

pagan, *pā′gan, n.* a heathen (q.v.), esp. a civilised heathen—originally used of any non-Christian, now not applied to Jews or Mohammedans: often indicating simply a person whose outlook is irreligious.—Also *adj.*—*n.* **pā′ganism**, heathenism. [L. *pāgānus*, rustic, peasant, also civilian (because the Christians reckoned themselves soldiers of Christ)—*pāgus*, a district.]

page, *pāj, n.* a boy attendant: (also **page-boy**) a boy in livery employed to do errands.—*v.t.* to seek (a person) out by sending a page around or by repeatedly calling aloud for him in order to give him a message. [Fr. *page.*]

page, *pāj, n.* one side of a leaf of a book.—*v.t.* to number the pages of: to make up into pages.—*n.* **pagination** (*paj-i-nā′sh(o)n*), the act of paging a book: the figures and marks that indicate the numbers of pages. [Fr.,—L. *pāgīna*]

pageant, *paj′ent*, or *pā′-, n.* (*obs.*) a movable stage or carriage for acting on: a spectacle, esp. one carried around in procession: a series of tableaux or dramatic scenes connected with local history or other topical matter: a fleeting show.—*adj.* of the nature of pageant.—*n.* **page′antry**, splendid display: pompous spectacle.

pagoda, *pa-gō′da, n.* an Eastern temple, esp. in the form of a many-storied, tapering tower: an idol. [Port. *pagode*—Pers. *but-kadah*, idolhouse, or some other Eastern word.]

paid, *pād, pa.t.* and *pa.p.* of **pay.**

paideutics, paedeutics, *pī-, pē-dū′tiks, n.sing.* the science or theory of teaching. [Gr. *pais,* gen. *paidos*, boy, child; *paideutēs*, teacher.]

pail, *pal, n.* an open vessel with a hooped handle, usu. for holding or carrying liquids.—*n.* **pail′ful**, as much as fills a pail. [O.E. *pægel*, a gill measure, apparently combined with or influenced by O.Fr. *paele*, a pan—L. *patella*, a pan.]

paillasse. Same as **palliasse.**

pain, *pān, n.* bodily suffering: anguish: threat of punishment (in *under pain of*): (*pl.*) trouble (taken): (*pl.*) throes of childbirth: punishment (in *pains and penalties*).—*v.t.* to cause suffering to: adj's. **pained**, showing or expressing pain; **pain′ful**, causing pain: toilsome, laborious: distressing.—*adv.* **pain′fully**, —*n.* **pain′fulness.**—*adj.* **pain′less**, without pain.—*adv.* **pains′taking**, taking pains or care: diligent.—**for one's pains**, as reward or result of trouble taken (usu. ironical). [Fr. *peine*—L. *poena*, satisfaction—Gr. *poinē*, penalty.]

paint, *pānt, v.t.* to colour: to represent in colours: to describe.—*v.i.* to practise painting: to lay colours on the face.—*n.* a colouring substance.—*adj.* **paint′able**, suitable for painting.—*ns.* **paint′er**, one who paints: an artist in painting: a house-decorator; **paint′er's-col′ic**, a form of colic produced by chronic lead poisoning; **paint′ing**, the act or employment of laying on colours: a picture: vivid description in words. [O.Fr. *peint, pa.p.* of *peindre*, to paint—L. *pingěre*, to paint.]

painter, *pānt′ér, n.* a rope used to fasten a boat.—**cut the painter**, to sever ties.

pair, *pār, n.* two things equal, or suited to each other, or growing, grouped, or used together: a set of two equal or like things forming one instrument, garment, &c.: a husband and wife: two voters on opposite sides who have an agreement to abstain from voting.—*v.t.* to couple: to sort out in pairs.—*v.i.* to mate: to be a counterpart (with *with*).—**pair off**, to go

fāte, fär; mē, hûr (her); *mīne; mōte, för; mūte; mōōn, fōōt;* THen (then)

513

off in pairs: to make an arrangement with one of an opposite opinion by which the votes of both are withheld. [Fr. *paire*, a couple—L. *paria*, neut. pl. of *pār*, equal, afterwards regarded as a fem. sing.]

Pakistani, *pä-ki-stän′ē*, *adj.* of or pertaining to Pakistan.—*n.* a native or citizen of Pakistan.

pal, *pal*, *n.* (*slang*) a partner, mate: chum. [Gypsy.]

palace, *pal′ās*, *n.* a royal house: a house eminently splendid: a bishop's official residence.—**palace revolution,** a revolution within the government itself. [Fr. *palais*—L. *Palātium*, the Roman emperor's residence on the *Palatine* Hill at Rome.]

paladin, *pal′a-din*, *n.* a knight of Charlemagne's household: a knight-errant. [Fr.,—It. *paladino*—L. *palātīnus*, *adj.* of the palace.]

palae-, palaeo-, paleo-, *pal′i-*, *-ō*, also *pāl′-*, in composition, old: concerned with the distant past. [Gr. *palaios*.]

palaeobotany, *pal-i-ō-bot′ān-i*, *n.* the study of fossil plants. [**palaeo-**, and **botany.**]

palaeography, *pal-i-og′ra-fi*, or *pāl-*, *n.* ancient modes of writing: study of ancient modes of handwriting. [Gr. *palaios*, old, *graphein*, to write.]

palaeolithic, *pal-i-ō-lith′ik*, or *pāl-*, *adj.* of the earlier Stone Age, marked by the use of primitive stone implements. [Gr. *palaios*, old, *lithos*, stone.]

palaeontology, *pal-i-on-tol′o-ji*, or *pāl-*, *n.* the study of fossils.—*adj.* **palaeontolog′ical.**—*n.* **palaeontol′ogist.** [Gr. *palaios*, old, *onta*, neut. pl. of pr.p. of *einai*, to be, *logos*, discourse.]

Palaeozoic, *pal-i-ō-zō′ik*, or *pāl-*, *adj.* and *n.* (of) the *Primary* geological era, the first of the three great divisions of geological time, or (of) the lowest division of the rocks containing fossil remains. [Gr. *palaios*, old, *zōē*, life.]

palaeozoology, *pal-i-ō-zō-ol′o-ji*, or *pāl-*, *n.* the study of fossil animals. [**palaeo-**, and **zoology.**]

palais de danse, *pa-lā dē däs*, *n.* a public dance hall. [Fr. *palais*, palace, *de*, of, *danse*, dance.]

palanquin, palankeen, *pal-an-kēn′*, *n.* a light litter for one, a box borne on poles on men's shoulders. [Port. *palanquim*; cf. Hindustani *palang*, a bed—Sans, *palyaṅka*, a bed.]

palate, *pal′āt*, *n.* the roof of the mouth, consisting of the *hard palate* in front and the *soft palate* behind: taste: relish: mental liking.—*adj.* **palatable** (*pal′āt-à-bl*), pleasant to the taste: (*fig.*) acceptable (e.g. a truth, advice).—*adv.* **pal′atably.**—*adj.* **pal′atal,** pertaining to the palate: uttered by bringing the tongue to or near the hard palate.—*n.* a sound so produced (e.g. *y* as in *yes*). [L. *palātum*.]

palatial, *pa-lā′sh(à)l*, *adj.* of or like a palace. [From L. as **palace.**]

palatine, *pal′a-tīn*, *adj.* of the Palatine hill or the palace of emperors there: of a palace: having royal privileges.—*n.* (*cap.*) one of the hills of Rome: a noble invested with royal privileges and jurisdiction: a subject of a palatinate.—*n.* **pal′atinate** (or *pa-lat′-*), province ruled by a palatine. [L. *palātīnus*—*Palātium*. See **palace.**]

palaver, *pa-läv′er*, *n.* a conference, esp. with African or other natives: idle talk: talk intended to deceive.—Also *v.i.* [Port. *palavra*, word—L. *parabola*, a parable, later a word,

speech—Gr. *parabolē*.]

pale, *pāl*, *n.* a stake of wood driven into the ground for fencing: anything that encloses: an enclosed or limited region or place: a district subject to a particular jurisdiction, as (*hist.*) the *English Pale* in Ireland or in France: (*fig.*) sphere of authority, influence, &c., as *the pale of civilisation*: a broad stripe from top to bottom of a shield in heraldry.—*n.* **pāl′ing,** wood or stakes for fencing: a fence of stakes.—**beyond the pale,** (of a person or his conduct) beyond what is morally or socially tolerable. [Fr. *pal*—L. *pālus*, a stake.]

pale, *pāl*, *adj.* whitish: wan: faint (of colour): dim.—*v.t.* to make pale.—*v.i.* to turn pale: to appear or become pale in comparison with something else. [O.Fr.*palle*, pale (Fr.*pâle*)—L. *pallidus*, pale.]

palette, *pal′ét*, *n.* a little board on which a painter mixes his colours. [Fr.,—It. *paletta*—*pala*, spade—L. *pāla*, a spade.]

palfrey, *pöl′fri*, *n.* (*arch.*) a saddle-horse, esp. for a lady. [O.Fr. *palefrei*—Low L. *paraverēdus.*]

Pali, *pä′lē*, *n.* the sacred language of the Buddhists of India, &c. [Sans. *pāli*, canon.]

palimpsest, *pal′imp-sest*, *n.* a parchment or other piece of writing material on which old writing has been rubbed out to make room for new. [Gr. *palimpsēston*—*palin*, again, *psāein* (contracted *psēn*), to rub, rub smooth.]

palindrome, *pal′in-drōm*, *n.* a word, verse, or sentence that reads the same backward and forward, as *madam*. [Gr. *palindromos*, running back—*palin*, back, *dromos*, a running.]

paling. See under **pale** (1).

palingenesis, *pal-in-jen′e-sis*, *n.* a new birth: regeneration: inheritance of ancestral characters unmodified. [Gr. *palin*, again, *genesis*, birth.]

palinode, *pal′i-nōd*, *n.* a poem retracting something said in a former one: a recantation. [Gr. *palinōidiā*—*palin*, back, *ōidē*, song.]

palisade, *pal-i-sād′*, *n.* a fence of stakes.—*v.t.* to surround or defend with a palisade.—**palisade layer,** a layer of elongated cells (**palisade cells**) set at right-angles to the surface of a leaf, underlying the upper epidermis; **palisade tissue,** one or more layers of palisade cells. [Fr. *palissade*, and Sp. *palizada*—L. *pālus*, a stake.]

pall, *pöl*, *n.* a rich cloth used as covering, esp. for a coffin: a chalice-cover: a mantle: a pallium (q.v.): (*fig.*) a curtain or cloak, as of smoke, darkness.—*n.* **pall′-bear′er,** one of the mourners at a funeral who used to hold up the corners of the pall. [O.E. *pæll*, a rich robe—L. *pallium*. See **pallium.**]

pall, *pöl*, *v.i.* to become insipid, or wearisome to appetite or interest—often, *pall upon* (person, mind, senses, &c.).—*v.t.* to satiate (e.g. the appetite). [Prob. from **appal.**]

palladium, *pa-lā′di-um*, *n.* a statue of *Pallas*, on whose preservation the safety of Troy depended: any safeguard: a metallic element (symbol Pd; at. no. 46) resembling platinum. [L.,—Gr. *palladion*—*Pallas*, *-ados*, Pallas, Greek goddess identified with Roman Minerva.]

pallet, *pal′ét*, *n.* a palette: a flat wooden tool with a handle, as that used for shaping pottery: a

Neutral vowels in unaccented syllables: *em′pér-ór*; for certain sounds in foreign words see p. ix.

board for carrying newly moulded bricks: a platform or tray for lifting and stacking goods. [palette.]

pallet, *pal'ét, n.* a mattress, or couch, properly a mattress of straw: a small or mean bed. [Dial. Fr. *paillet,* dim. of Fr. *paille,* straw—L. *palea,* chaff.]

palliasse, *pal-i-as', pal-yas', n.* a straw mattress: an under-mattress.—Also **paillasse.** [Fr. *paillasse—paille,* straw—L. *palea.*]

palliate, *pal'i-āt, v.t.* (*obs.*) to cover as with a mantle: to extenuate, to soften by favourable representations: to alleviate without curing (a disease).—*n.* **pallia'tion,** extenuation: mitigation.—*adj.* **pall'iative,** serving to extenuate: alleviating.—Also *n.* [L. *palliāre, -ātum,* to cloak—*pallium,* a cloak.]

pallid, *pal'id, adj.* pale, wan. [L. *pallidus,* pale.]

pallium, *pal'i-um, n.* a large, square mantle, worn by learned Romans in imitation of the Greeks: a white woollen vestment, embroidered with crosses, worn by the Pope, and conferred by him upon archbishops. [L. *pallium.*]

pall-mall, *pel'-mel', n.* an old game, in which a ball was driven through an iron ring with a mallet: an alley for the game (hence the street in London now usu. pronounced *pal'-mal'*). [Obs. Fr. *pale-maille*—It. *pallamaglio—palla,* a ball, *maglio,* a mallet (L. *malleus,* a hammer).]

pallor, *pal'or, n.* paleness. [L.,—*pallēre,* to be pale.]

palm, *päm, n.* the inner surface of the hand between wrist and fingers.—*v.t.* to touch or stroke with the palm: to conceal in the palm (in dicing, card-sharping, juggling) ' (esp. with *off,* and *on* or *upon*) to impose, pass off.—*adjs.* **palmar** (*pal'mär*), relating to the palm; **palmate** (*pal'-*), **-d,** hand-shaped: (of leaves) having lobes radiating from one centre. (*zool.*) web-footed.—*n.* **palmiped** (*pal'mi ped*), a web-footed bird.—*adj.* web-footed.—*ns.* **palmist** (*pam'ist*), one who tells fortunes from the lines on the palm; **palm'istry.** [L. *palma;* cf. Gr. *palamē;* O.E. *folm.*]

palm, *päm, n.* a tropical or subtropical tree or shrub of many varieties, bearing at the summit a crown of large fan-shaped leaves: a leaf of this tree borne in token of rejoicing or of victory: (*fig.*) any symbol or token of triumph or pre-eminence.—*ns.* **palm-butt'er,** palm-oil in a solid state; **palmett'o** (*pal-*), a name for several fan-palms, i.e. palms with simple fan-shaped leaves; **palm'house,** a glass house for palms and other tropical plants; **palm'ker'nel,** the kernel of the oil-palm (q.v.), yielding **palm-kernel oil; palm'-oil,** an oil or fat obtained from the pulp of the fruit of palms, esp. of the oil-palm; **palm'-su'gar,** sugar obtained from certain palms, known also as *jaggery;* **Palm'-Sun'day,** the Sunday before Easter, in commemoration of the strewing of palm-branches when Christ entered Jerusalem; **palm'-wine,** fermented palm sap.—*adj.* **palm'y,** bearing palms: palmlike: flourishing. [O.E. *palm, palma, palme*—L. *palma,* palm-tree, from the shape of its leaves. See **palm** (1).]

palmer, *päm'er, n.* a pilgrim from the Holy Land, distinguished by his carrying a palm-

leaf.—*n.* **palm'er-worm,** a hairy caterpillar of various kinds, originally one of wandering habits. [palm (2).]

palmyra, *pal-mī'rä, n.* an African and Asiatic palm yielding palm-wine, palm-sugar, &c. [Port. *palmeira,* palm-tree, confused with *Palmyra* (a city now in ruins) in Syria.]

palpable, *pal'pa-bl, adj.* that can be felt: readily perceived by any of the senses: readily perceived or detected by the mind (e.g. errors, lies).—*ns.* **palpabil'ity, pal'pableness.**—*adv.* **pal'pably.**—*v.t.* **pal'pate,** to examine by touch. [Low L. *palpābilis*—L. *palpāre, -ātum,* to touch softly, stroke, caress, flatter.]

palpitate, *pal'pi-tāt, v.i.* to throb, beat rapidly, pulsate: to tremble.—*n.* **palpita'tion,** act of palpitating: painful awareness of heart-beat: rapid beating of the heart due to disease. [L. *palpitāre, -ātum,* freq. of *palpāre;* cf. **palpable.**]

palsy, *pöl'zi, n.* paralysis.—*v.t.* to affect with palsy: to deprive of action or energy:—*pa.t.* and *pa.p.* pal'sied. [Through O.Fr. from same root as **paralysis.**]

palter, *pöl'ter, v.i.* to trifle (with a subject): to haggle, bargain (with a person about something): to shuffle, equivocate, play false. [Perh. conn. with **paltry.**]

paltry, *pöl'tri, adj.* mean, trashy: not worth considering.—*adv.* **pal'trily.**—*n.* **pal'triness.** [Cf. Dan. *pialter,* rags, Low Ger. *paltrig,* ragged.]

paludal, *pal-(y)ōō'dál,* also *pal'-, adj.* pertaining to marshes: marshy: malarial.—*adjs.* **palūdic'olous, palū'dose,** inhabiting wet places. [L. *palūs, palūdis,* a marsh.]

Paludrine, *pal'(y)ōō-drēn, n.* a synthetic quinine substitute, the most important of a series, for the prevention and treatment of *paludism,* i.e. malaria. [L. *palūs, -ūdis,* a marsh.]

pampas, *pam'pä* (usu. in *pl.*—**pampas**), a vast treeless plain in southern South America.—*n.* **pam'pas grass,** a tall, ornamental, reed-like grass. [Sp.—South Amer. Indian *pampa, bamba,* plain.]

pamper, *pam'per, v.t.* to over-indulge (e.g. a child, oneself, a taste, or an emotion). [A freq. from obs. *pamp, pomp;* cf. Ger. dial. *pampen,* to cram.]

pamphlet, *pam'flet, n.* a small book stitched but not bound: a tract, usu. controversial, on some subject of the day.—*n.* **pamphleteer',** a writer of pamphlets.—Also *v.i.*—*n.* and *p.adj.* **pamphleteer'ing.** [Possibly from a Latin poem *Pamphilus,* very popular in the Middle Ages.]

pan, *pan, n.* a broad, shallow vessel for use in the home or in the arts or manufactures: anything of like shape, as the upper part of the skull (*brain-pan*): the part of the lock of old guns and pistols that holds the priming.—*v.t.* (with *out*) to wash (gold-bearing gravel) in a pan: to criticise, review, harshly.—*v.i.* (with *out*) to yield gold: (with *out, coll.*) to yield a result, turn out.—*n.* **pan'cake,** a thin cake of eggs, flour, sugar, and milk, fried in a pan: a landing of a heavier-than-air craft at a relatively steep angle, with low forward speed.—Also *adj.* and *v.i.*—*n.* **panning,** harsh criticism.—**flash in the pan,** a mere flash in the pan of a flintlock that does not ignite the powder: a momentary promise of achievement that fades before anything is accomplished. [O.E. *panne*; a word common to the West Germanic languages.]

pan-, *pan*, *v.t.* and *v.i.* of a cinema or television camera, to move while taking a picture so as to follow a particular object or to produce a panoramic effect. [**pan**(**orama**).]

Pan-, in composition, all, e.g. **Pan-American**, including all America or Americans, North and South; **Pan-German**; **Pan-Islamism** (*pan-iz'läm-izm*), an inspiration or movement for the union of all Mohammedans. [Gr. *pān*, neut. of *pās*, all.]

panacea, *pan-a-sē'a*, *n.* a universal medicine. [Gr. *panakeia*—*pās*, *pān*, all, *akos*, cure.]

panache, *pä-näsh'*, *n.* a plume, esp. on a helmet: swagger, display, sense of style. [Fr.]

panada, *pa-nä'dä*, *n.* a dish made by boiling bread to a pulp in water, and flavouring: a dish containing soaked breadcrumbs. [Sp.]

panama, *pan-a-mä'*, *n.* a hat made of plaited strips of the leaves of a South American plant: an imitation thereof. [Sp. *Panamá*.]

panchromatic, *pan-krō-mat'ik*, *adj.* equally or suitably sensitive to all colours: rendering all colours in due intensity. [Gr. *pās*, neut. *pān*, all, *chrōma*, *-atos*, colour.]

pancreas, *pan(g)'krē-as*, *n.* the sweetbread, a large gland situated under and behind the stomach, secreting a saliva-like fluid which assists digestion in the intestines.—*adj.* **pancreat'ic.** [Gr. *pās*, *pān*, all, *kreas*, *-atos*, flesh.]

panda, *pan'dä*, *n.* a remarkable raccoon-like animal of the Himalayas.—**giant panda**, a larger animal of Tibet.—**panda car**, a small car used by a policeman on the beat in a residential area. [Orig. uncertain.]

pandect, *pan'dekt*, *n.* a treatise covering the whole of any subject: (in *pl.*) the digest of Roman or civil law made by command of the Emperor Justinian in the 6th century. [L. *pandecta*—Gr. *pandektēs*—*pās*, neut. *pān*, all, *dechesthai*, to receive.]

pandemonium, *pan-dé-mō'ni-um*, *n.* (*cap.*) name of capital of Hell, described in *Paradise Lost*, I. 710 ff.: any very disorderly place or assembly: tumultuous uproar. [Gr. *pās*, *pān*, all, *daimōn*, a spirit.]

pander, *pan'dér*, *n.* one who procures for another the means of gratifying his base passions: a pimp.—*v.t.* to play the pander for: to indulge, gratify (with *to*).—*v.i.* to act as a pander: to minister (to the passions). [*Pandarus*, the pimp in the story of Troilus and Cressida.]

pandit. Same as **pundit.**

pane, *pān*, *n.* (*obs.*) a piece of cloth: a panel: a plate of glass.—*adj.* **paned**, composed of panes or small squares: variegated. [Fr. *pan*—L. *pannus*, a cloth, a rag.]

panegyric, *pan-è-jir'ik*, *n.* (with *upon*) a eulogy, a formal speech or writing in praise of some person, thing, or achievement—often in exaggerated terms.—*adjs.* **panegyr'ic, -al.**—*v.t.* **pan'egyrise**, to write or pronounce a panegyric on: to praise highly.—*n.* **pan'egyrist**. [Gr. *panēgyrikos*, fit for a national festival—*pās*, neut. *pān*, all, *agyris* (form of *agorā*), an assembly.]

panel, *pan'(é)l*, *n.* a bordered rectangular area: a thin flat piece sunk below the general sur-

face of a door, &c.: a flat surface with raised margins, or with a surrounding frame: a slip of parchment containing a list of names, esp. of jurors: a jury or similar body: a group of persons chosen for some purpose, e.g. to be the guessers in radio and television guessing games (**panel games**): (*Scots law*—*sing.*) a prisoner, or prisoners, at the bar.—*v.t.* to furnish with panels:—*pr.p.* pan'elling; *pa.p.* pan'elled.—*n.* **pan'elling**, panel-work.—**panel heating**, indoor heating diffused from floors, walls or ceilings; **panel pin**, a light, narrowheaded nail used chiefly for fixing plywood or hardboard to supports. [O.Fr.,—Low L. *pannellus*—L. *pannus*, a cloth.]

pang, *pang*, *n.* a violent but not long-continued pain: a painful emotion. [Perh. a form of **prong**.]

panga, *pang'ga*, *n.* a broad, heavy, African knife used as a tool and as a weapon.

panic, *pan'ik*, *n.* frantic or sudden fright: contagious fear: general alarm.—Also *adj.*—*v.i.* to be struck by panic.—*adj.* **pan'icky** (*coll.*), inclined to panic, or inspired by panic.—*n.* **pan'ic-mong'er**, one who creates or fosters panics.—*adjs.* **pan'ic-strick'en**, **pan'ic-struck**, struck with a panic or sudden fear. [Gr. *pānikos*, belonging to Pan; *pānikon* (*deima*), panic (fear), fear associated with the god Pan.]

panicle, *pan'i-kl*, *n.* (*bot.*) a raceme (q.v.) whose branches are themselves racemes: (*loosely*) an inflorescence in which the cluster is irregularly branched, as in oats.—*adjs.* **pani'ulāte, -d**, furnished with, arranged in, or like panicles. [L. *pānicum*, Italian millet.]

Panislamism. Same as **Pan-Islamism**. See **Pan-**.

panjandrum, *pan-jan'drum*, *n.* one who assumes grand airs, a burlesque potentate. [From the Grand Panjandrum in a string of nonsense made up by Samuel Foote, the 18th-century actor.]

pannier, *pan'yèr*, or *pan'i-èr*, *n.* one of a pair of baskets slung over a pack-animal's back or over the back of a motor-cycle, &c.: (*archit.*) a sculptured basket: (*hist.*) a contrivance of whalebone, &c., for puffing out a woman's dress at the hips. [Fr. *panier*—L. *pānārium*, a bread-basket—*pānis*, bread.]

panoply, *pan'ō-pli*, *n.* (*lit.* and *fig.*) a full suit of armour: full or brilliant covering or array.—*adj.* **pan'oplied**, in panoply. [Gr. *panopliā*, full armour—*pās*, *pān*, all, *hopla* (pl.), arms.]

panorama, *pan-ō-rä'ma*, *n.* a wide or complete view: (*lit.* and *fig.*) a picture unrolled and made to pass before the spectator.—*adj.* **panoramic** (*-ram'ik*). [Gr. *pās*, neut. *pān*, all, *horāma*, a view—*horaein*, to see.]

panpipe(s), *pan'pīp(s)*, *n.* a musical instrument consisting of a row of parallel pipes of increasing length. [Gr. god *Pan*, and **pipe** (1).]

pansy, *pan'zi*, *n.* a name for various species of violet, esp. the heartsease, and garden kinds derived from it. [Fr. *pensée*—*penser*, to think—L. *pensāre*, to weigh.]

pant, *pant*, *v.i.* to gasp for breath: to run gasping: to throb: to wish ardently (for, after something).—*v.t.* to utter gaspingly. [Apparently related to O.Fr. *pantoisier*, to pant.]

pantagraph. Same as **pantograph**.

Neutral vowels in unaccented syllables: *em'pér-òr*; for certain sounds in foreign words see p. ix.

pantagruelism, *pan-ta-grōō'el-izm, n.* theories and practice of *Pantagruel* as described by Rabelais (*d.* 1553): coarse humour and buffoonery as a cover for serious satire.

pantaloon, *pan-ta-lōōn', n.* a character in Italian comedy, and afterwards in pantomime, a lean old man (originally a Venetian) more or less a dotard: (in *pl.*) a kind of trousers. [Fr. *pantalon*—It. *pantalone,* from St *Pantaleone,* a favourite saint of the Venetians.]

pantechnicon, *pan-tek'ni-kon, n.* a store selling articles of all kinds: furniture-store: furniture-van. [Gr. *pās,* neut. *pān,* all, *technē,* art.]

pantheism, *pan'thē-izm, n.* the doctrine that identifies God with the universe, denying the personality of God: worship of the gods of different creeds and peoples impartially.—*n.* **pan'theist.**—*adjs.* **pantheist'ic, -al.**—*n.* **pantheon** (*pan'thē-on*), a temple of all the gods, esp. the circular one at Rome: a complete mythology. [Gr. *pās,* neut. *pān,* all, *theos,* a god, *pantheion,* a pantheon.]

panther, *pan'thėr, n.* a leopard, esp. a large one. [Gr. *panthēr.*]

pantile, *pan'tīl,* n. a tile whose cross-section is S-shaped, one curve being much larger than the other. [**pan** (1), and **tile.**]

pantograph, *pan'tō-gräf, n.* a jointed framework of rods for copying drawings, plans, &c., on the same, or a different, scale: a current-collecting mechanism on electric trams or trains. [Gr. *pās,* neut. *pān,* all, *graphein,* to write.]

pantomime, *pan'tō-mīm, n.* (*hist.*) a Roman actor in dumb show: a theatrical entertainment, usually about Christmas, in which some nursery story is acted, with showy scenery, topical allusions, songs, and dancing: dumb show.—*adj.* of pantomime: pantomimic.—*adjs.* **pantomimic** (*-mim'ik*), **-al.**—*n.* **pan'tomimist,** an actor in pantomime. [L. *pantomīmus*—Gr. *pantomīmos,* imitator of all—*mīmos,* an imitator.]

pantry, *pan'tri, n.* a room or closet for provisions and table furnishings, or where plate, knives, &c., are cleaned. [Fr. *paneterie*—Low L. *pānitāria*—L. *pānis,* bread.]

pants, *pants, n.* drawers (also **underpants**): (*coll.* and *U.S.*) trousers.—*n.pl.* **panties,** very short drawers for women and children. [**pantaloons.**]

panzer, *pant'sėr, n.* armour: a tank.—*adj.* armoured. [Ger.]

pap, *pap, n.* soft food for infants (often *fig.*): pulp. [Imit.]

pap, *pap, n.* a nipple. [App. Scand.]

papa, *pá-pä', n.* (old-fashioned) father. [Partly through Fr. *papa,* partly directly from L.L. *pāpa,* Gr. *papās, pappās,* father (used as petname).]

papacy, *pā'pa-si, n.* the office of pope: a pope's tenure of office: papal system of government. [L.L. *pāpātia*—*pāpa,* pope, father.]

papal, *pā'pál, adj.* of the pope or the papacy. [L.L. *pāpālis*—*pāpa,* pope.]

papaveraceous, *pā-pav-ėr-ā'shús, adj.* of the poppy family. [L. *papāver,* the poppy.]

papaw, *pa-pö', pö'pö, n.* a tree of the custard-apple family, native to the U.S., or its fruit: the papaya.—Also **paw'paw'.** [Prob. variant of **papaya.**]

papaya, *pa-pä'ya, n.* a small tree, native to South America but common in the tropics, the trunk, leaves, and fruit of which yield *papain,* a substance that encourages the process of digestion.—Also called **papaw.** [Sp. *papayo* (tree), *papaya* (fruit), apparently from Carib.]

paper, *pā'pėr, n.* the material on which we commonly write and print: similar material for wrapping and other purposes: a document: (*pl.*) documents proving identity, authorisation, &c.: a newspaper: an essay or literary contribution, esp. one read before a society: paper-money: paper-hangings for walls: a set of examination questions.—*adj.* consisting, or made, of paper.—*v.t.* to cover with paper.—*ns.* **pa'perback,** a book with a limp paper cover; **pa'per-chase,** the game of hare and hounds, in which some runners (*hares*) set off across-country strewing paper by which others (*hounds*) track them; **paper-clip,** clip of bent wire for holding papers together; **pa'per-hang'er,** one who papers walls—*n.pl.* **pa'per-hang'ings,** paper for covering walls—*n.* **pa'per-ing,** the operation of covering with paper: the paper so used; **pa'per-knife,** a thin, flat blade for cutting open envelopes and other folded papers; **pa'per-mon'ey,** pieces of paper stamped or marked by government or by a bank, as representing a certain value of money, which pass from hand to hand instead of the coin itself; **pa'per-nau'tilus,** or **-sail'or,** see **nautilus;** **pa'per-reed,** the papyrus; **pa'per-stain'er,** one who prepares paperhangings; **pa'per-weight,** a small weight for keeping loose papers from being displaced; **pa'per-work,** clerical work.—**paper tiger,** a person, organisation, that appears to be powerful but is in fact the reverse; **on paper,** theoretically. [A.F. *papir,* O.Fr. (Fr.) *papier*—L. *papyrus*—Gr. *papyros,* papyrus.]

papier collé, *pa'pyā kol'ā,* scraps of paper and odds and ends pasted out as a help to cubist composition. [Fr., glued paper.]

papier-mâché, *pap'yā-mä'shā, n.* a material consisting of paper-pulp or of sheets of paper pasted together, treated so as to resemble varnished or lacquered wood, or plaster. [Would-be French. Fr. *papier* is paper, *mâché,* chewed—L. *masticātus.*]

papilionaceous, *pā-pil-yo-nā'shús, adj.* (*bot.*) having a corolla-shaped somewhat like a butterfly, as the bean, the pea, and other plants of the family **Papiliona'ceae.** [L. *pāpiliō, -ōnis,* butterfly.]

papilla, *pap il'a, n.* a small nipple-like protuberance: a minute elevation on the skin, esp. on the upper surface of the tongue:—*pl.* **papill'ae** (*-ē*).—*adjs.* **papill'ar, papill'ary, pap'illose.** [L., dim. of *papula,* a pimple.]

papist, *pā'pist, n.* an adherent of the pope: a name slightingly given to a Roman Catholic. *adjs.* **pāpist'ic, -al,** pertaining to popery, or to the Church of Rome, its doctrines, &c. (usu. disparaging).—*ns.* **pā'pism, pā'pistry,** popery (in hostile sense). [L.L. *pāpa,* pope.]

papoose, *pap-ōōs', n.* a N. Amer. Indian child. [Amer. Indian, *papoos.*]

pappus, *pap'us, n.* downy appendage growing on the seeds of thistles, dandelions, and other plants.—*adjs.* **papp'ōse** (or *-ōs'*), **papp'ous,**

provided or covered with down. [L. *pappus* — Gr. *pappos*, down.]

papular, *pap'ū-lár*, **papulous**, *pap'ū-lus*, **papulose**, *pap'ū-lōs*, adjs. full of pimples. [L. *papula*, a pimple.]

papyrus, *pa-pī'rus*, n. the paper-reed, a tall sedge, once common in Egypt: its pith prepared as a writing material by the ancients: a manuscript on papyrus:—pl. **papy'rī**. [L. *papȳrus* — Gr. *papȳros*, prob. Egyptian.]

par, *pär*, n. the normal level, the standard or norm: equality in value, condition, or circumstances: (*golf*) the number of strokes for a hole, or a round, that should be taken if play is perfect, two putts being allowed on each green.—**on a par with**, on a level with (*fig.*); **at par**, at exactly the nominal, or face, value (used in speaking of stocks, shares, &c.); **above par**, at a premium, i.e. at more than the face value; **below par**, at a discount, i.e. at less than the face value: (*coll.*) not up to the normal standard (used esp. of health).—**par of exchange**, the value of coin of one country expressed in that of another; **par value**, value at par. [L. *pār*, equal.]

para-, *pa'ra-*, in composition, beside: faulty: irregular, disordered: abnormal: closely resembling, or parallel to (as in *adjs.* **paramed'ical**, helping doctors or supplementing medical work; **paramil'itary**, supplementing the military). [Gr. *para*, beside.]

para-, *pa'ra-*, in composition, parachute, as in *ns.* **par'adoctor**, a doctor who parachutes to patients; **par'aglider**, a glider with inflatable wings. [**para(chute)**.]

parable, *pa'ra-bl*, n. a fable or story told to illustrate some doctrine, or to make some duty clear: (*obs.*) a proverb: (*obs.*) a discourse. [Same as **parabola**.]

parabola, *par-ab'o-la*, n. a curve, one of the conic sections, being the intersection of a cone and a plane parallel to its side or slope:—pl. **parab'olas**.—*adjs.* **parabolic** (*par-a-bol'ik*), **-al**, of or like a parable or a parabola: expressed by a parable: belonging to, or of the form of, a parabola.—*adv.* **parabol'ically**.—*n.* **parab'oloid**, a surface or solid generated by the rotation of a parabola about its axis. [Gr. *parabolē*, a placing alongside, comparison, parabola, &c.—*para*, beside, *ballein*, throw.]

parachute, *par'a-shōōt*, n. an apparatus like an umbrella for descending safely from a height.—*v.i.* to descend by parachute.—*v.t.* to put, send, down by parachute.—*n.* **par'achutist**. [Fr. *parachute* — It. *para*, imper. of *parare*, to ward (L. *parāre*, to prepare), and Fr. *chute*, fall.]

paraclete, *par'a-klēt*, n. an advocate or legal helper, or intercessor—applied to the Holy Ghost (John xiv. 26). [Gr. *paraklētos* — *parakaleein*, to call in, also to comfort—*para*, beside, *kaleein*, to call.]

parade, *pa-rād'*, n. display, ostentation: an assembling in order for exercise, inspection, &c.: a procession: ground for parade of troops: a public promenade.—*v.t.* to show off: to marshal in military order.—*v.i.* to march up and down as if for show: to march in procession: to muster. [Fr.,—Sp. *parada*—*parar*, to halt—L. *parāre*, -*ātum*, to prepare.]

paradigm, *par'a-dīm*, n. an example, exemplar: (*gram.*) a table of the inflections of a word representative of a declension or conjugation.—*adjs.* **paradigmatic** (-*dig-mat'ik*), **-al**.—*adv.* **paradigmat'ically**. [Fr. *paradigme* — Gr. *paradeigma* — *paradeiknynai*, to exhibit side by side—*deiknynai*, to show.]

paradise, *par'a-dīs*, n. a park or pleasure ground, esp. in ancient Persia: the garden of Eden: the abode (intermediate or final) of the blessed dead: a place, or state, of bliss.—*adj.* **paradisiacal** (-*dis-ī'á-kl*).—**bird of paradise**, any of a family of birds, chiefly of New Guinea, with gorgeous plumage; **fool's paradise** (see **fool**). [Fr. *paradis* — L. *paradīsus* — Gr. *paradeisos*, a park—O.Pers. *pairidaēza*, park.]

paradox, *par'a-doks*, n. (*arch.*) that which is contrary to received opinion: a statement that is apparently absurd or self-contradictory, but is or may be really true: a self-contradictory statement that is essentially false: a person whose conduct is puzzlingly inconsistent.—*adj.* **paradox'ical**.—*adv.* **paradox'ically**. [Gr. *paradoxos*, (neut.) -*on*, contrary to opinion—*doxa*, opinion.]

paraffin, *par'a-fin*, n. originally **par'affin wax**, a white, crystalline substance obtained from shale, petroleum, &c., so named because it has little chemical affinity for other substances: now, any of the *paraffin series* of hydrocarbons, which include liquids and gases as well as solids: paraffin oil.—**par'affin oil**, any of various oils obtained in the distillation of shale, petroleum, &c., used for burning, lubricating, and other purposes. [L. *parum*, little, *affīnis*, having affinity.]

paragon, *par'a-gon*, n. a model of perfection or supreme excellence. [O.Fr. *paragon* — It. *paragone*, touchstone; origin obscure.]

paragraph, *par'a-gräf*, n. a distinct part of a discourse or writing, a short passage, or a collection of sentences with unity of purpose: a short separate item of news or comment in a newspaper: a sign (usu. ¶) marking off a section of a book, &c.—*adjs.* **paragraphic** (-*graf'ik*), **-al**. [Gr. *paragraphos*, written alongside—*para*, beside, *graphein*, to write.]

parakeet, parrakeet, *par'a-kēt*, n. a small, long-tailed parrot of various kinds.—Also **paroquet, parroquet, paraquito**. [Sp. *periquito*, It. *parrocchetto*, O.Fr. *paroquet*.]

paraleipsis, paralipsis, *par-a-līp'sis*, -*lip'*-, n. figure of speech by which attention is fixed on a subject by pretending to neglect it, as 'I will not speak of his generosity', &c. [Gr. *paraleipsis* — *paraleipein*, to leave aside—*para*, beside, *leipein*, to leave.]

parallax, *par'a-laks*, n. an apparent change in the position of an object caused by change of position in the observer: (*astron.*) the apparent change (measured angularly) in the position of a heavenly body when viewed from different points.—*adjs.* **parallac'tic**, **-al**. [Gr. *parallaxis*—*para*, beside, *allassein*, to change *allos*, another.]

parallel, *par'a-lel*, adj. extended in the same direction and equidistant in all parts: (*fig.*) like in essential parts, analogous: alongside in time.—n. a parallel line: a line of latitude: a person, thing, &c., exactly analogous to

Neutral vowels in unaccented syllables: *em'pér-ór*; for certain sounds in foreign words see p. ix.

another: a comparison to show resemblance: a besieger's trench parallel to the outline of the place besieged.—*v.t.* to place so as to be parallel: (*fig.*) to represent as similar: to bring forward something as analogous to what is under discussion: to be parallel to:—*pr.p.* par'alleling; *pa.p.* par'alleled.—*n.* **par'allelism**, state or fact of being parallel: resemblance: a balanced construction of a verse or sentence where one part repeats the form or meaning of the other (esp. in Hebrew poetry).—**in parallel**, of electrical apparatus, so arranged that terminals of like polarity are connected together. [Gr. *parallēlos*, as if *par'allēloin*, beside each other.]

parallelepiped, *par-ä-lel-ep'i-ped* (or *-e-pī'ped*), *n.* a solid figure bounded by six parallelograms, opposite pairs being identical and parallel.—Also **parallelepip'edon.** Improperly **parallelopi'ped, parallelopi'pedon.** [L.,—Gr. *parallēlepipedon—parallēlos* and *epipedon*, a plane surface—*epi*, on, *pedon*, ground.]

parallelogram, *par-a-lel'ō-gram*, *n.* a plane four-sided figure, the opposite sides of which are parallel and equal. [Gr. *parallēlogrammon—grammē*, a line.]

paralogism, *pär-al'o-jizm*, *n.* false reasoning. [Gr. *paralogismos—para*, beside, *logismos—logos*, reason.]

paralysis, *pa-ral'i-sis*, *n.* palsy, a loss of power of motion or sensation in any part of the body.—*v.t.* **paralyse** (*par'a-līz*), to afflict with paralysis: to deprive of power of action.—*adj.* **paralytic** (*par-a-lit'ik*), afflicted with or inclined to paralysis.—*n.* one who is affected with paralysis.—**infantile paralysis**, poliomyelitis (q.v.). [Gr. *paralysis*, undoing, *paralysis—para*, beside, *lyein*, to loosen.]

paramagnetic, *par-a-mag-net'ik*, *adj.* less strongly magnetic than a ferromagnetic substance—said of bodies that, when freely suspended between the poles of a magnet, place themselves parallel to the lines of force—opp. to *diamagnetic*. [Gr. *para*, beside, and **magnetic**.]

paramatta, *par-a-mat'ä*, *n.* a fabric like merino made of worsted and cotton. [App. from *Parramatta* in New South Wales.]

parameter, *pa-ram'i-ter*, *n.* a line or quantity which serves to determine a point, line, figure, or quantity in a class of such things: quantity to which an arbitrary value may be given as a convenience in expressing performance or for use in calculations: a variable in terms of which it is convenient to express other interrelated variables which may then be regarded as being dependent upon the parameter. [Gr. *para*, beside, *metron*, measure.]

paramnesia, *par-am-nē'si-a*, *n.* any disorder of memory: the illusion that one remembers things now actually experienced for the first time. [Gr. *para*, and the root of *mimnēskein*, to remind.]

paramount, *par'a-mownt*, *adj.* superior to all others: supreme.—*n.* **par'amount(n)cy.** [O.Fr. *paramont—par* (L. prep. *per*), *à mont* (L. *ad montem*). See **amount**.]

paramour, *par'a-mōōr*, *n.* a lover of either sex, now usually in the illicit sense. [Fr. *par amour*, by or with love—L. *per amōrem*.]

paranoia, *par-a-noi'ä*, *n.* a form of insanity characterised by fixed delusions, esp. of grandeur, persecution.—*adj.* **paranoi'ac.** [Gr. *paranoiä—noos*, mind.]

parapet, *par'a-pet*, *n.* a bank or wall, to protect soldiers from the fire of an enemy in front: a low wall along the side of a bridge, &c.—*adj.* **par'apeted**, having a parapet. [It. *parapetto*, from pfx. *para-* (see **parachute**), and It. *petto*—L. *pectus*, the breast.]

paraph, *par'af*, *n.* a mark or flourish under one's signature.—*v.t.* to sign with initials. [Fr. *paraphe*. Same root as **paragraph**.]

paraphernalia, *par-a-fér-nāl'i-a*, *n.pl.* formerly property that remained under a married woman's own control (esp. articles of jewellery, dress, personal belongings), as distinct from her dowry, which became part of her husband's estate: ornaments of dress of any kind: trappings: equipment: miscellaneous accessories. [Late L. *paraphernālia—parapherna*—Gr., from *para*, beyond, *phernē*, a dowry—*pherein*, to bring.]

paraphrase, *par'a-fräz*, *n.* expression of the same thing in other words: an exercise in such expression: a verse rendering of a biblical passage for church singing.—*v.t.* to express in other words. *v.i.* to make a paraphrase.—*ns.* **par'aphraser, par'aphrast** (*-frast*), one who paraphrases.—*adjs.* **paraphrast'ic, -al.** [Gr. *paraphrasis—para*, beside, *phrasis*, a speaking—*phrazein*, to speak.]

paraquat, *par-a-kwat*, *n.* a weed-killer, very poisonous to human beings.

paraquito, *par-a-kē'tō.* See **parakeet.**

paraselene, *par-a-se-lē'nē*, *n.* a bright spot on a lunar halo (see **halo**), a mock moon. [Gr. *para*, beside, *selēnē*, moon.]

parasite, *par'a-sīt*, *n.* a hanger-on or sycophant who frequents another's table: one who lives at the expense of society or of others and contributes nothing: an organism that lives in or on another organism without rendering it any service in return.—*adjs.* **parasitic** (*-sit'ik*), **-al**, like a parasite: fawning, sycophantic: living on other plants or animals.—*adv.* **parasit'ically.**—*n.* **par'asitism** (*-sīt-izm*). [Gr. *parasītos—para*, beside, *sītos*, corn, bread, food.]

parasol, *par'a-sol*, *n.* a sunshade. [Fr.,—It. *parasole—para*, imper. of *parare*, to ward—L. *parāre*, to prepare, and *sole*—L. *sōl, sōlis*, the sun.]

paratroops, *par'a-trōōps*, *n.pl.* troops carried by air to be dropped by *parachute*.—*n.* **par'atrooper**, a member of a body of troops trained for this purpose.

paratyphoid, *par-a-tī'foid*, *n.* a disease (of various types) resembling typhoid.

paravane, *par'a-vān*, *n.* a fish-shaped rudder-steered device attached by a stout rough wire to a ship's bows for the purpose of cutting sea-mines from their moorings. [Pfx. *para-* (as in **parachute**), and **vane**.]

par avion, *par av-yō*, by airmail. [Fr.]

parboil, *pär'boil*, *v.t.* (*orig.*) to boil thoroughly: (now, by confusion) to boil slightly. [O.Fr. *parboillir*—L.L. *perbullīre*, to boil thoroughly; influenced by confusion with **part**.]

parbuckle, *pär'buk'l*, *n.* an arrangement for raising or lowering a heavy object that will roll

fāte, fär; mē, hûr (her); *mīne; mōte, fôr; mūte; mōōn, fŏŏt;* тнen (then)

(e.g. a barrel), the middle of a rope being made fast to a post and both ends being passed under and over the object. [Earlier *parbunkel, parbuncle*, origin unknown.]

parcel, *pär'sl, n.* an essential part (in *part and parcel*): a portion (e.g. a *parcel of land*, a piece forming part of an estate): a quantity (of a commodity): a set, pack (depreciatively, e.g. of fools): a package, esp. one wrapped in paper and tied with string.—*v.t.* to divide into portions: to make up into a parcel:—*pr.p.* par'celling; *pa.t.* and *pa.p.* par'celled.—*adj.* par'celgilt,* partially gilded.—**parcel(s) post,** the department of the post-office that takes charge of the forwarding and delivery of parcels. [Fr. *parcelle* (It. *particella*)—L. *particula,* dim. of *pars, partis,* a part.]

parch, *pärch, v.t.* to make hot and very dry (of the sun, fever, thirst, cold): to roast slightly.—*v.i.* to become very dry.—*adj.* **parched.** [Origin unknown.]

parchment, *pärch'mént, n.* the skin of a sheep, goat, or other animal prepared for writing on: a document on parchment. [Fr. *parchemin*—L. *pergamēna* (*charta*), Pergamene (paper)—from Gr. *Pergamos,* Bergamo, in Asia Minor.]

pard, *pärd, n.* the leopard. [L. *pardus* (masc.), *pardalis* (fem.)—Gr. *pardos, pardalis*; prob. of Eastern origin.]

pardon, *pär'd(ó)n, v.t.* to forgive (a person, an offence): to remit the penalty of: to make allowance for, excuse.—*n.* forgiveness: remission of a penalty or punishment: a warrant declaring a pardon: a papal indulgence.—*adj.* **par'donable,** that may be pardoned: excusable.—*adv.* **par'donably.**—*n.* **par'doner** (*hist.*), one licensed to sell papal indulgences. [Fr. *pardonner*—Low L. *perdōnāre*—L. *per,* through, away, *dōnāre,* to give.]

pare, *pär, v.t.* to cut or shave off the outer surface or edge of: to diminish by small quantities.—*ns.* **pär'er; pär'ing,** the act of paring: that which is pared off. [Fr. *parer*—L. *parāre,* to prepare.]

paregoric, *par-é-gor'ik, adj.* soothing, lessening pain.—*n.* a medicine that soothes pain.—**paregoric elixir,** an alcoholic solution of opium and other substances. [Gr. *parēgorikos*—*parēgoreein,* to exhort, comfort.]

parent, *pär'ént, n.* a father or a mother: a forefather: a plant or an animal from which others are derived (also *adj.*): (*fig.*) an author, cause, source.—*n.* **pär'entage,** descent from parents: extraction, lineage: hereditary rank or character.—*adj.* **parental** (*pä-rent'ál*).—*adv.* **parent'ally.** [Fr. *parent,* kinsman—L. *parēns, -entis,* old pr.p. of *parĕre,* to bring forth.]

parenthesis, *pä-ren'thé-sis, n.* a word or passage of comment or explanation inserted in a sentence that is grammatically complete without it: a figure of speech consisting of the use of such insertion: a digression: an interval, interlude: (usu. in *pl.*) a round bracket ( ) used to mark off a parenthesis:—*pl.* **paren'theses** (*-sēz*).—*adjs.* **parenthetic** (*par-én-thet'-ik*), **-al.**—*adv.* **parenthet'ically.** [Gr.,—*para,* beside, *en,* in, *thesis,* a placing.]

par excellence, *pär ek-se-läs,* pre-eminently, above all others (e.g. *Lear is the writer par excellence of nonsense verse.*). [Fr.]

parhelion, *pär-hē'li-ón, n.* a bright spot on a solar halo (see **halo**), a mock sun:—*pl.* **parhē'lia.** [Irregularly—Gr. *parēlion*—*para,* beside, *hēlios,* sun.]

pariah, *pär'i-ä, pär'-, pa-rī'ä, n.* in south India, one of low, or no, caste: a social outcast: an ownerless cur of Eastern towns (in full, **pariah dog**). [Tamil (q.v.), *paraiyar.*]

Parian, *pā'ri-án, adj.* of the island of *Paros,* in the Aegean Sea, famed for white marble.

parietal, *pä-rī'é-tál, adj.* of a wall or walls: (*anat.*) forming the sides: (*bot.*) attached to the side of an organ.—*n.* **parietal bone,** one of two bones forming the sides and top of the skull. [L. *parietālis*—*pariēs, parietis,* a wall.]

parish, *par'ish, n.* a district having its own church and clergyman (of the Established Church of the country concerned): a district assigned by a church to a minister or priest: a division of a county for administrative and local government purposes: the people of a parish.—*adj.* belonging or relating to a parish: employed or supported by the parish.—*n.* **parishioner** (*pä-rish'ón-ér*), one who belongs to or is connected with a parish.—**on the parish,** in receipt of poor relief; **parish clerk,** the clerk or recording officer of a parish: the one who leads the responses in the service of the Church of England; **parish council,** a body elected to manage the affairs of a parish; **parish pump,** the symbol of petty local interests; **parish register,** a book in which the births, marriages, and deaths of a parish are registered. [Anglo-Fr. *paroche*—L. *parochia*—Gr. *paroikiā,* an ecclesiastical district.]

Parisian, *pä-riz'yán, -rizh'(y)án, adj.* of or pertaining to *Paris.*—*n.* a native or resident of Paris. [Fr. *parisien*—L. *Parīsiī,* the Gallic tribe of the Paris district.]

parity, *par'i-ti, n.* equality in status: equality in quantity and kind: standard of price in another currency: resemblance, analogy. [Fr. *parité*—L. *paritās*—*pār,* equal.]

park, *pärk, n.* an enclosed piece of land for beasts of the chase: a tract of ground surrounding a mansion: a piece of ground for public recreation: a piece of country kept in its natural condition as a nature-reserve or the like: (*mil.*) a place occupied by artillery, wagons, &c.: a piece of ground where motor-cars or other vehicles may be left untended for a time.—*v.t.* to enclose: to bring together in a body, as artillery: to put in a parking-place: (*coll.*) to deposit and leave.—*ns.* **park'land, -s,** park-like grassland dotted with trees.—**parking meter,** a coin-operated meter that charges for motor-car parking-time. [O.Fr. *parc,* of Gmc. origin; cf. O.E. *pearruc, pearroc.*]

parka, *pär'ka, n.* a fur shirt with a hood: a similar garment made of a wind-proof material. [Aleutian Eskimo word.]

parkin, *pär'kin,* **perkin,** *pér'kin, n.* (*Northern*) a biscuit of oatmeal and treacle. [Ety. unknown.]

Parkinson's disease, *pär'kin-sónz,* a disease characterised by rigidity of muscles, tremor of hands, &c.; studied by James *Parkinson* (1755-1824).—Also called **Parkinsonism.**

Parkinson's law, *pär'kin-sónz,* (*humorous*) any of the laws propounded by C. Northcote *Parkinson,* esp. the law that in officialdom

Neutral vowels in unaccented syllables: *em'pér-ór*; for certain sounds in foreign words see p. ix.

520

work expands so as to fill the time available for its completion.

parky, *pär′ki, adj.* (*coll.*) chilly.

parlance, *pär′lăns, n.* (*arch.*) debate, parley: mode of speech, phraseology (e.g. *legal parlance*).—*v.i.* **par′ley,** to confer: to treat with an enemy.—*n.* a conference, esp. with an enemy. [Fr. *parler*—L. *parabola*—Gr. *parabolē,* a parable, word.]

parliament, *pär′li-mént, n.* a meeting for deliberation: a legislative body: (*usu. cap.*) the legislature of Great Britain, House of Commons and House of Lords: the legislature of various other countries, as Canada, South Africa, Australia (Federal Parliament), &c.—*n.* **parliamentā′rian,** one skilled in the ways of parliament: (*cap.*) adherent of Parliament in opposition to Charles I.—*adj.* **parliament′ary,** pertaining to parliament: enacted or done by parliament: according to the rules and practices of legislative bodies: (of language) civil, decorous. [Fr. *parlement*—*parler,* to speak.]

parlour, *pär′lôr, n.* a room where conversation is allowed in a monastery or nunnery: a family sitting room or living room: a small drawing-room: (*U.S.*) business apartments of a firm providing personal services or amusement (as, *beauty parlour, billiard parlour*).—*ns.* **par′lour-board′er,** a pupil at a boarding-school who enjoys particular privileges; **par′lour-car** (*U.S.*), a luxuriously fitted railway saloon carriage; **par′lour-maid,** a maid-servant who waits at table. [Anglo-Fr. *parlur*—*parler,* to speak.]

parlous, *pär′lus, adj.* full of danger or difficulty, very bad (as *'a parlous state'*): also used loosely as *terrible* is. [Form of **perilous.**]

Parmesan, *pär-mé-zan′,* or *pär′-, adj.* pertaining to *Parma*—*n.* Parmesan cheese, a dry cheese made from skimmed milk.

parochial, *pär-ō′ki-ál, adj.* of or relating to a parish: restricted or confined within narrow limits—of sentiments, tastes, &c.—*n.* **parō′chialism,** a system of local government which makes the parish the unit: provincialism, narrowness of view.—*adv.* **parō′chially.** [L. *parochiālis*—*parochia.* See **parish.**]

parody, *par′o-di, n.* a burlesque imitation.—*v.t.* to make a parody of—*pr.p.* par′odying; *pa.p.* par′odied.—*n.* **par′odist,** one who writes a parody. [Gr. *parōidiā*—*para,* beside, *ōidē,* an ode.]

parole, *pá-rōl′, n.* (*mil.*) word of honour (esp. by a prisoner of war, to fulfil certain conditions): (*obs.*) officers' daily password in a camp or garrison: (*U.S.*) conditional release from prison.—*adj.* (usu. **parol,** *par′ol*) given by word of mouth (as, *parol evidence*). [Fr. *parole,* word—L. *parabola*—Gr. *parabolē.* See **parable.**]

paronomasia, *par-on-o-mā′syä, -zyä, -zh(y)ä, n.* a play upon words, a pun.—*n.* **paronym** (*par′o-nim*), a word from the same root as another: a word having the same sound as another but different spelling and meaning. [Gr. *para,* beside, *onoma, onyma,* name.]

paroquet, parroquet. See **parakeet.**

parotid, *par-ot′id, n.* the parotid gland, a salivary gland in front of the ear. [Gr. *parōtis, idos*—

para, beside, *ous, ōtos,* ear.]

paroxysm, *par′oks-izm, n.* a fit of acute pain: a fit of passion, laughter, coughing, &c.—*adj.* **paroxys′mal.** [Gr. *paroxysmos*—*para,* beyond, *oxys,* sharp.]

parquet, *pär′kā, -két, pär-kā′, -ket′, n.* a floor covering of wooden blocks arranged in a pattern: (*U.S.*) the stalls of a theatre.—*n.* **par′quetry.** [Fr. *parquet,* dim. of *parc,* enclosure.]

parr, pär, *n.* a young salmon in its first two years before it becomes a smolt and descends to the sea. [Orig. uncertain.]

parrakeet. See **parakeet.**

parricide, *par′i-sīd, n.* the murder of a parent or near relative, or of anyone to whom reverence is considered to be due: one who commits such a crime.—*adj.* **parricid′al.** [Fr.,—L. *parricīdium, pāricīdium* (the offence), *parricīda, pāricīda* (the offender)—*caedĕre,* to slay; the connection with *pater,* father, is apparently fanciful.]

parrot, *par′ot, n.* one of a family of tropical and subtropical birds with brilliant plumage, hooked bill, and toes arranged in pairs, two before and two behind, good imitators of human speech: a person who repeats words mechanically and without understanding.—*v.t.* to repeat by rote.—*v.i.* to talk like a parrot.—*n.* **parr′ot-cry,** a catch-phrase senselessly repeated from mouth to mouth. [Possibly Fr. *Perrot,* a dim. of *Pierre,* Peter.]

parry, *par′i, v.t.* to ward or keep off: to turn aside (blow, argument, question, &c.):—*pa.t.* and *pa.p.* parr′ied. [Perh. from Fr. *parez,* imper. of *parer*—L. *parāre,* to prepare, in Low L. to keep off.]

parse, *pärz, v.t.* (*gram.*) to describe (a word) fully by stating the part of speech, inflection and relation to other words in the sentence: to analyse (a sentence).—*n.* **pars′ing.** [L. *pars* (*ōrātiōnis*), a part (of speech).]

parsec, *pär′sec, n.* the chief unit used in measuring stellar distances, approx. equal to 19·2 billion miles (19·2 × 10^{12} miles), [*par*allax, and *sec*ond.]

Parsee, Parsi, *pär′se,* or *-sē′, n.* a descendant of the Zoroastrians (followers of the religious teacher Zoroaster) who emigrated from Persia to India. [Pers. *Pārsī*—*Pārs,* Persia.]

parsimony, *pär′si-món-i, n.* sparingness in the spending of money: economy in the use of means to an end: niggardliness.—*adj.* **parsimonious** (*-mō′ni-us*).—*adv.* **parsimō′niously.**—*n.* **parsimō′niousness.** [L. *parsimōnia*—*parcĕre, parsum,* to spare.]

parsley, *pars′li, n.* a bright-green umbelliferous herb, used in cookery. [O.E. *petersilie,* modified by Fr. *persil;* both—L. *petroselīnum*—Gr. *petroselīnon*—*petros,* a rock, *selīnon,* parsley.]

parsnip, parsnep, *pärs′nip, n.* an umbelliferous plant or its edible carrot-like root. [L. *pastināca*—*pastinum,* a dibble.]

parson, *pär′s(ó)n, n.* the priest or incumbent of a parish, a rector: (*coll.*) any minister of religion.—*n.* **par′sonage,** the residence appropriated to a parson: (*orig.*) the house, lands, tithes, &c., set apart for the support of the minister of a parish. [O.Fr. *persone*—L. *persōna,* a person. See **person.**]

part, *pärt, n.* something less than the whole—a

portion (of a thing), some out of a larger number (of things): a section (of a work in literature or music): an equal division of a whole (e.g. *one part in three*): a (spare) piece of a machine: a member or organ of an animal body: (*pl.*) region: direction, hand, side: an inflected form (of a verb): words and actions of a character in a play: a copy of an actor's words: a voice or an instrument in concerted music: that which is performed by such voice or instrument: a copy of the music for it: (*pl.*) intellectual qualities, talents (e.g. *a man of parts*): share, duty (e.g. *do one's part*): side or party (e.g. *take his part*).—*v.t.* to divide into parts or shares: to separate.—*v.i.* to become separated: to go different ways: to come or burst apart.—*adj.* **part′ible,** separable, divisible.—*n.* **part′ing,** the action of the verb to part: a place of separation or division: leave-taking.—*adv.* **part′ly,** in part: in some degree.—*ns.* **part′-sing′ing; part′-song,** a melody with parts in harmony—*adj.* **part′-time,** for part of working time only.—*n.* **part′-tim′er.— for my part,** as far as concerns me; **for the most part,** commonly; **in good part,** without taking offence; **neither part nor lot (in),** no concern, share (in); **art and part, part and parcel** (see **art, parcel**); **part company,** to separate: to diverge in opinion, purpose, &c.; **parting of the ways,** a point at which a fateful decision must be made; **part of speech,** one of the various grammatical classes of words. [O.E. and Fr. *part*—L. *pars, partis.*]

partake, *pär-tāk′, pär-tāk′, v.i.* to take or have a part or share: to take some (esp. of food or drink—with *of*): (*coll.*) to consume (food or drink—with *of*): to have something of the nature or properties (of): to participate in some condition or action (with *in*):—*pr.p.* parta′king; *pa.t.* partook′; *pa.p.* parta′ken.—*ns.* **partā′ker; partā′king.** [Back-formation from **partaker**—part, taker.]

parterre, *pär-ter′, n.* an arrangement of flower-beds: the pit of a theatre, esp. under the galleries. [Fr.,—L. *per,* along, *terra,* the ground.]

parthenogenesis, *pär-the-nō-jen′e-sis, n.* reproduction (of insects, &c.) by the development of an unfertilised ovum. [Gr. *parthenos,* a virgin, *genesis,* production.]

Parthenon, *pär′the-non, n.* the temple of Athēnē *Parthēnos,* on the Acropolis at Athens. [Gr. *Parthenōn*—*parthenos,* a virgin.]

Parthian, *pär′thi-ȧn, adj.* of Parthia.—*n.* a native of Parthia (a district in what is now Persia or Iran).—**a Parthian shot,** a parting shot, from the Parthian habit of turning round in the saddle to discharge an arrow at a pursuer.

parti, *pär-tē′, n.* a marriageable person considered to be a catch; parti is a French word equivalent to Eng. *party,* in sense of body of persons, side, &c., whence choice, resolution, as in **parti pris** (*prē*; lit. resolution taken), preconceived opinion, prepossession, prejudice.

partial, *pär′shȧl, adj.* not total or complete: inclined to favour one person or party, biased: having a preference or liking for (with *to*): (*bot.*) subordinate.—*n.* **partiality** (*-shi-al′i-ti*). —*adv.* **par′tially.** [Fr.,—Low L. *partiālis*—L. *pars,* a part.]

partible. See **part.**

participate, *pär-tis′i-pāt, v.i.* (in many cases equivalent to **partake,** but not often used of material things) to take a share or part (e.g. in a discussion).—*ns.* **partic′ipant,** a partaker; **participā′tion; partic′ipātor.** [L. *participāre, -ātum*—*pars, partis,* part, *capĕre,* to take.]

participle, *pär′ti-si-pl, n.* a word combining the functions of adjective and verb.—*adj.* **particip′ial.** [Fr.,—L. *participium*—*particeps*—*pars, partis,* a part, *capĕre,* to take.]

particle, *pär′ti-kl, n.* a minute piece of matter: any of the constituents of an atom: a minute quantity of something immaterial (e.g. *a particle of truth*): a short, usually indeclinable word, as a preposition, a conjunction, an interjection: a prefix or suffix: (*R.C. Church*) a crumb of consecrated bread, or a portion used in the communion of the laity.—*adj.* **particular** (*pär-tik′ū-lär*), indicating a single definite person or thing as distinguished from others (e.g. *this particular critic, occasion*): individual (e.g. *my particular views*): special (e.g. *particular care*): concerned with things single or distinct: minutely attentive and careful: fastidious in taste.—*n.* a single point, a detail.—*v.t.* **partic′ularise,** to mention the particulars of: to enumerate in detail.—*ns.* **particularisā′tion; particularity** (*-ari-ti*), quality of being particular, as opp. to general: minuteness of detail.—*adv.* **partic′ularly,** in a particular manner: in a very high degree.—*adj.* **partic′ulate,** of, or relating to, particles: in the form of particles.—**in particular,** especially. [L. *particula,* dim. of *pars, partis,* a part.]

parti-coloured. See **party.**

partim, *pär′tim,* in part. [L.]

partisan, partizan, *pär-ti-zan′, pär′ti-zan, n.* an adherent, esp. a blind or unreasoning adherent, of a party or a faction: a light irregular soldier who scours the country and forays: in the Second World War, a member of Marshal Tito's resistance movement in Yugoslavia.— Also *adj.—n.* **par′tisanship** (or *-zan′-*). [Fr. *partisan,* from a dial. form of It. *partigiano* —*parte* (L. *pars, partis*), part.]

partisan, *pär′ti-zan, n.* a kind of halberd. [Fr. *partizane* (now *pertuisane*)—It. *partesana.*]

partite, *pär′tīt, adj.* divided, cut nearly to the base.—*n.* **partition** (*-tish′(ȯ)n*), act of dividing: state of being divided: separate part: that which divides: a wall between rooms.—*v.t.* to divide into shares: to divide into parts by walls.—*adj.* **par′titive,** dividing: (*gram.*) indicating that a part (of a collective whole) is meant (see **genitive**).—*adv.* **par′titively.** [L. *partītus,* pa.p. of *partīrī* or *partīre,* divide.]

partlet, *pärt′let, n.* a hen: a woman. [Prob. O.Fr. *Pertelote,* a woman's name.]

partner, *pärt′nėr, n.* a sharer: one engaged with another, an associate in business: one who plays on the same side with, and along with, another in a game: one who dances with another: a husband or wife.—*v.t.* to act as partner to: to join as partners.—*n.* **part′nership,** state of being a partner: a contract between persons engaged in any business. —**sleeping partner,** one who has money invested in a business but takes no part in its management. [Prob. a form of *parcener,*

Neutral vowels in unaccented syllables: *em′pėr-ȯr*; for certain sounds in foreign words see p. ix.

a coheir; through Anglo-Fr. and L.L.—L. *pars*, a part.]

partridge, *pär'trij, n.* a genus of game-birds of the pheasant family.—*n.* **par'tridge-wood**, a hard variegated wood, from Brazil and the West Indies, used in cabinet-work. [Fr. *perdrix*—L. *perdīx*—Gr. *perdīx.*]

parturient, *pär-tū'ri-ént, adj.* bringing, or about to bring, forth.—*n.* **parturi'tion**, act of bringing forth. [L. *parturīre*, desiderative from *parĕre*, to bring forth.]

party, *pär'ti, n.* a side in a battle, game, lawsuit, &c.: a body of persons united for political or other action: a meeting or entertainment of guests: one concerned in a contract: a detachment: (*vulg.* or *facetious*) a single individual.—*adj.* pertaining to a party.—*adj.* **par'ti-col'oured**, **par'ty-col'oured**, variegated.—*ns.* **par'ty-line**, a telephone exchange line used by a set of subscribers: a boundary between properties: the policy rigidly laid down by political party leaders; **par'ty-wall**, a joint-wall between two properties. [Fr. *parti(e)*, pa.p. of *partir* L. *partīre*, divide.]

parvenu, *pär've nū, n.* an upstart, one newly risen into notice or power. [Fr., pa.p. of *parvenir*—L. *pervenīre*, to arrive—*per*, through, *venīre*, to come.]

parvis, parvise, *pär'vis, n.* an enclosed space before a church: a room over a church porch. [O.Fr. *parvis.*]

pas, *pä, n.* a step, as in dancing or marching.— **pas de deux** (*pä dé dø*), a dance for two performers; **pas seul** (*sœl*), a dance for one. [Fr.]

pascal, *pas'kal, n.* SI unit of pressure or stress, equal to one newton per square metre. [Blaise *Pascal*, French scientist 1623–62.]

Pasch, *päsk, n* the Passover: (*arch.*) Easter.— *adj.* **pasch'al**, pertaining to the Passover, or to Easter.—**Pasch of the Cross**, Good Friday. [L. *pascha*—Gr.,—Heb. *pesaḥ*, the Passover *pāsaḥ*, to pass over.]

pasha, *pä'shä, pä-shä', n.* a Turkish title (abolished in 1934) given to governors and high military and naval officers.—Also **pacha.**—*n.* **pash'alik, -alic, pach'alic**, the jurisdiction of a pasha. [Turk. *pāshā.*]

pasque-flower, *päsk'-flow'(é)r, n.* a species of anemone. [Fr. *passefleur*, apparently—*passer*, to surpass, modified after *pasque*, Pasch.]

pasquil, *pas'kwil*, **pasquin,** *pas'kwin, ns.* a lampoon or satire.—*v.t.* and *v.i.* to lampoon or satirise.—*n.* **pasquinäde'**, a lampoon. [*Pasquino*, nickname of an ancient statue, dug up in Rome in 1501, to which lampoons were affixed.]

pass, *päs, v.i.* to proceed: to go from one place or state to another: to circulate: to go by: to be regarded as (with *for*): to go unheeded or neglected: to elapse: to go away: to die: to undergo an examination successfully: to be approved: to happen: to thrust, as with a sword: (*cards*) to abstain from making a call.—*v.t.* to go by, over, beyond, through, &c.: to spend (as time): to omit: (*Gr. hist.*) to surpass: to enact: to pronounce (e.g. judgment): to transfer: to emit: to approve: to undergo successfully: to circulate: (*fencing*) to thrust:—*pa.p.* **passed** (*rarely* **past**).—*n.* a

way by which one may pass: a narrow passage or defile: a passport: a ticket for free travel or admission: state or condition: (*fencing*) a thrust: in games, transference of the ball to another member of the team: a movement of the hand: a threatening gesture, or (*slang*) unwelcome amorous approach: success in any test.—*adj.* **pass'able**, that may be passed, travelled over, or navigated: that may bear inspection, tolerable.—*n.* **pass'ableness.**—*adv.* **pass'ably.**—*ns.* **pass'book**, a book that passes between a trader and his customer, in which credit purchases are entered: a bank-book; **pass'-check**, a ticket of admission or of re-admission; **pass'er**; **pass'er-by**, one who passes by or near:—*pl.* **pass'ers-by**; **pass'-key**, a key enabling one to enter a house: a key for opening several locks; **pass'man**, one who gains a degree or passes without honours; **pass'word** (*mil.*), a word by which a friend is recognised and allowed to pass or enter a camp, &c.—**bring to pass**, to cause to happen; **come to pass**, to happen; **pass the buck**, (*fig.; slang*) to shift the responsibility (*to someone else*)—as one passes a marker to the next dealer in forms of poker. [Fr. *pas*, step, and *passer*, to pass—L. *passus*, a step.]

passacaglia, *päs-sä-käl'yä, n,* a slow old Italian or Spanish dance tune or dance.—Also **passacaglio**. [From Sp. *pasacalle*, a certain guitar tune.]

passage, *pas'ij, n.* act of passing: crossing: transition: lapse, course: a journey (now only by water): means of passing to and fro: a sum paid for a voyage: a corridor: a channel: enactment (of a law): right of conveyance: occurrence, episode: a portion of a book, &c., or piece of music.—**passage of arms**, any feat of arms: an encounter.—**bird of passage**, a migratory bird: (*fig.*) a transient visitor. [Fr. *passager*—L. *passus*, step.]

passant, *pas'ánt, adj.* (*her.*) walking. [Fr.]

passé, *pas'ā, pas-ā', adj.* past one's best. [faded: out of date.—*fem.* **passée**. [Fr.]

passenger, *pas'én jér, n.* (*orig.*) one who passes or travels (survives in **foot-passenger**): one who travels in a private or public conveyance (as opposed to one who drives or operates the vehicle, &c.): (*slang*) a member of a crew or team who does not play his part effectively: one carried along by the efforts of others. [O.Fr. *passager*, with inserted *n*, as in *messenger, nightingale.*]

passe-partout, *pas-pär-tōō', n.* the means of passing anywhere, a master key: a kind of simple picture-frame, usually of pasteboard: a method of framing, or a picture framed, with glass front and pasteboard back, the picture being fixed by strips of paper pasted over the edges: strong paper, gummed on one side, used for this and other purposes. [Fr.,—*passer*, to pass, *par*, over, *tout*, all.]

passerine, *pas'er-in, adj.* relating to the order **Passeriformes**, the perching birds, or to the sub-order **Passeres**, the song birds. [L. *passer*, a sparrow.]

passim, *pas'im, adv.* here and there, in many places (used of a word, statement, &c., found repeatedly in a particular author or a particular work). [L.]

fāte, fär; mē, hûr (her); *mīne; mōte, för; mūte; mōōn, fŏŏt;* THen (then)

523

passimeter, *pas-im´i-tér,* n. an automatic ticket-issuing machine. [**pass** and **meter.**]

passing, *pas´ing, adj.* going by: transient: surpassing.—*adv.* exceedingly, very.—*n.* **pass´-ing-bell,** a bell tolled immediately after a death, originally to invite prayers for the soul passing into eternity. [**pass.**]

passion, *pash´(ò)n,* n. the sufferings and death of Christ: a suffering or passive condition, as opposed to action: emotion or agitation of mind, esp. rage: ardent love: eager desire.— *adj.* **pass´ionate,** easily moved to anger, or other strong feeling: intense.—*adv.* **pass´ionately.**—*ns.* **pass´ionateness; pass´ion-flow´er,** a flower so called from a fancied resemblance to a crown of thorns, the emblem of Christ's passion.—*adj.* **pass´ionless,** free from passion, unemotional: calm.—*ns.* **pass´ion-play,** a religious drama representing the sufferings and death of Christ; **Pass´ion Sun´day,** the fifth Sunday in Lent; **Pass´ion Week,** Holy Week: the week before Holy Week. [O.Fr. *passiun* — L. *passiō, -ōnis* — *patī, passus,* to suffer.]

passive, *pas´iv, adj.* (*obs.*) suffering: unresisting: lethargic: not reacting: acted upon: (*gram.*) expressing the suffering of an action by the subject of the verb.—*adv.* **pass´ively.**—*ns.* **pass´iveness, passiv´ity.**—**pass´ive obe´dience,** absolute submission to the ruling power: obedience to the 'divine right of kings'; **pass´ive resis´tance,** deliberate refusal (from scruples of conscience) to comply with the law, and submission to the consequent penalties. [L. *passīvus* — *patī,* suffer.]

passover, *pàs´ō-vér,* n. annual feast of the Jews, to commemorate the destroying angel *passing over* the houses of the Israelites when he slew the first-born of the Egyptians.

passport, *pàs´pōrt, -pört,* n. authorisation to leave a port for a journey by sea or land: a permit for travel: (*fig.*) that which gives privilege of entry. [Fr. *passeport*; cf. **pass, port.**]

past, *pàst, pa.p.* of **pass.**—*adj.* bygone: ended: in time already passed.—*prep.* farther than: beyond: beyond the possibility of.—*adv.* by.—*n.* that which has passed, esp. time.—**past master** (see **master**).

pasta, *pàs´ta,* n. flour dough in fresh, processed (e.g. spaghetti), and/or cooked form. [It.]

paste, *pàst,* n. a soft plastic mass: dough for pies, &c.: a cement made of flour, water, &c.: a fine kind of glass for making artificial gems.—*v.t.* to fasten with paste.—*n.* **paste´board,** a stiff board made of sheets of paper pasted together, &c.—*adj.* made of such: sham. [O.Fr. *paste* — L.L. *pasta* — Gr. *pasta,* porridge — *passein,* to sprinkle.]

pastel, *pas´tél,* n. chalk mixed with other materials and coloured for crayons: a drawing made with such: woad.—**pastel shades,** quiet colours. [Fr. *pastel* — It. *pastello* — L. *pasta,* paste.]

pastern, *pas´térn,* n. the part of a horse's foot from the fetlock to the hoof, where the shackle is fastened. [O.Fr. *pasturon* — O.Fr. *pasture,* pasture, a tether for a horse.]

Pasteurism, *pas´tûr-izm,* n. the method of inoculation with the attenuated virus of certain diseases, esp. hydrophobia, introduced by Louis *Pasteur* (1822-95).—*n.* **pasteurisā´tion,** a method of arresting fermentation in beer, milk, &c., by heating.—*v.t.* **pas´teurise.**

pastiche, *pas-tēsh´,* n. a musical or literary composition made up of parts from other compositions: a work in literature or art in direct imitation of another: a jumble. [Fr.,—L.L. *pasta.* See **paste.**]

pastille, *pas-tēl´,* n. a small cone of charcoal and aromatic substances, burned to perfume: a small confection with gelatinous base: (*art*) the same as **pastel.** [L. *pastillus,* dim. of *panis,* bread.]

pastime, *pàs´tīm,* n. that which serves to pass away the time: recreation. [**pass, time.**]

pastor, *pàs´tór,* n. one who has care of a flock: a shepherd: a clergyman.—*adj.* **pas´toral,** relating to shepherds or to shepherd life: rustic: of or pertaining to the pastor of a church.—*n.* a poem or other composition that professes to depict the life of shepherds: a pastoral letter, esp. one from a bishop.—*adv.* **pas´torally.**—*ns.* **pas´torate, pas´torship,** the office of a pastor: the whole body of pastors.—**pastoral epistles,** those in the New Testament to Timothy and Titus; **pastoral staff,** a bishop's staff or sceptre. [L. *pàstor,* a shepherd—*pàscĕre, pàstum,* to feed.]

pastry, *pàs´tri,* n. articles made of paste or dough: crust of pies, tarts, &c.: act or art of making pastry.—*n.* **pàs´trycook,** a maker or seller of pastry. [**paste.**]

pasture, *pàst´chùr, -yur,* n. growing grass for grazing: grazing land.—*v.i.* and *v.t.* to graze.— *adj.* **past´urable,** fit for pasture.—*n.* **past´ur-age,** the business of feeding or grazing cattle: pasture. [O.Fr. *pasture* — L. *pàstūra* — *pàscĕre, pàstum,* to feed.]

pasty, *pàs´ti, adj.* like *paste.*

pasty, *pàs´ti,* n. a meat-pie baked without a dish. [O.Fr. *pastée* (Fr. *pâté*) — L.L. *pasta.* See **paste.**]

pat, *pat,* n. a gentle tap, as with the palm of the hand: a small lump of butter moulded by an instrument with flat surface: a light sound.— *v.t.* to strike gently: to tap:—*pr.p.* pat´ting; *pa.p.* pat´ed.—*adj.* exactly to the purpose: ready to be given easily or fluently (e.g. *he had his answer, the story, pat*).—*adv.* aptly: promptly.—**pat on the back,** a mark of approbation. [Prob. imit.]

patch, *pach,* n. a piece put on to mend or cover a defect: any similar scrap of material: a plot of ground: a small piece of black silk,·&c., stuck on the face.—*v.t.* to mend with a patch: to join in patchwork: (usu. *patch up*) to mend or fashion clumsily or hastily.—*n.* **patch´work,** work formed of patches or pieces sewed together: work patched up or clumsily executed.—*adj.* **patch´y,** covered with, or consisting of, patches: varying in quality.—*n.* **patch´iness.**—*adv.* **patch´ily.**—**not a patch on,** not fit to be compared with. [M.E.; perh. conn. with **piece.**]

patchouli, *pach´ŏŏ-lē, pä-chōō´lē,* n. a shrub of S.E. Asia: a perfume got from its dried branches. [Tamil (q.v.) *pach,* green, *ilai,* leaf.]

pate, *pàt,* n. the crown of the head: the head.

pâté, *pa-tā,* n. pie: patty: now usu. a paste made of blended meat, herbs, &c.—**pâté de fois gras** (*dè fwa grä*), paste, &c., of fat goose liver. [Fr.]

patella, *pa-tel´a,* n. the knee-cap or knee-pan

Neutral vowels in unaccented syllables: *em´pér-ór*; for certain sounds in foreign words see p. ix.

524

(see **knee**). [L., dim. of *patina*, a pan.]

paten, *pat'én*, *n.* a plate for bread in the Eucharist. [Fr.,—L. *patina*, a plate—Gr. *patanē*.]

patent, *pā'tént*, or *pat'ént*, *adj.* (*pā'tént*) lying open: obvious: (usu. *pat'ént*) open to public perusal: protected by patent: (*bot.*) spreading out from the stem.—*n.* (usu. *pat'ént*) an official document, open, and having the Great Seal of the government attached to it, conferring an exclusive right or privilege, as a title of nobility, or the sole right for a term of years to the proceeds of an invention (also **letters-patent**): something invented and protected by a patent.—*v.t.* to grant or secure by patent.—*adj.* **pa'tentable**.—*n.* **patentee'**, one who holds a patent.—*adv.* **pā'tently**, openly, obviously.— **patent leather**, finely-varnished leather; **patent medicine**, a medicine protected by letters-patent: (*loosely*) any proprietary medicine; **Patent Office**, an office for the granting of patents for inventions. [L. *patēns*, *-entis*, pr.p. of *patēre*, to lie open.]

pater, *pā'tér*, *n.* a father.—*n.* **paterfamilias** (*pa-ter-fa mil'i-as*), the father or head of a family or household. [L. *pāter*, father, *familiās*, old. gen. of *familia*, household.]

paternal, *pa-tûr'nál*, *adj.* fatherly: showing the disposition of a father: derived from a father.—*adv.* **pater'nally**.—*n.* **pater'nity**, fatherhood: the relation of a father to his children: origination or authorship. [L. *pater* (Gr. *patēr*), a father.]

paternoster, *pat-er-nos'tér*, or *pā'tér-nos-tér*, *n.* the Lord's Prayer. [L. *Pater noster*, Our Father, the first words of the Lord's Prayer in Latin.]

path, *päth*, *n.* a way for foot passengers: a track: course of action or conduct:—*pl.* **paths** (*pä'THz*, *paths*).—*n.* **path'finder**, one who explores the route, a pioneer: a radar device used as an aircraft navigational aid: a radar device for guiding missiles into a target area.—*adj.* **path'less**, without a path: untrodden.—*n.* **path'way**, a path. [O.E. *pæth*; Ger. *pfad*.]

pathetic, *pá-thet'ik*, *adj.* affecting the tender emotions, touching.—*adv.* **pathet'ically**.— **pathetic fallacy**, the tendency to impute human emotions to inanimate nature. [Gr. *pathētikos*, subject to suffering.]

pathogenesis, *path-ō-jen'é-sis*, **pathogeny**, *path-oj'é-ni*, *ns.* mode of production or development of disease.—*n.* **path'ogen**, an organism or substance that causes disease.—*adj.* **pathogen'ic**, causing disease. [Gr. *pathos*, suffering, *genesis*, production.]

pathology, *pa-thol'o-ji*, *n.* science of diseases.— *adj.* **patholog'ical**, pertaining to pathology: of the nature of, or arising from, disease.—*adv.* **patholog'ically**.—*n.* **pathol'ogist**, one skilled in pathology: one who performs post-mortems. [Gr. *pathos*, suffering, *logos*, discourse.]

pathos, *pā'thos*, *n.* the quality that excites pity. [Gr.]

patience, *pā'shéns*, *n.* quality of being able calmly to wait or endure: a card-game for one.—*adj.* **pā'tient**, sustaining pain, &c., without repining: not easily provoked, long-suffering: waiting with calmness: persevering, —*n.* a person under medical treatment.—*adv.*

pā'tiently. [Fr.,—L. *patientia*—*patiens*—*patī*, to bear.]

patin, **patine**, *pat'in*, *n.* Same as **paten**.

patina, *pat'in-a*, *n.* the green incrustation on ancient bronzes, &c.: the shine acquired, e.g. by long-polished furniture.—Also *fig.* [L. *patina*, a dish.]

patio, *pat'i-ō*, *n.* a courtyard connected with a house, esp. an inner court open to the sky. [Sp.—L. *spatium*, space.]

patois, *pat'wä*, *n.* a vulgar or provincial dialect. [Fr., origin unknown.]

pâtisserie, *pa-tēs'(é-)rē*, *n.* a pastry shop: a pastry. [Fr.]

patriarch, *pā'tri-ärk*, *n.* one who governs his family by paternal right: (*B.*) one of the early heads of families from Adam downwards to Abraham, Jacob, and his sons: the head of certain Eastern churches (often *cap.*; see **Greek Orthodox Church**): a venerable old man.—*adj.* **pātriarch'al**, pertaining to, or subject to, a patriarch.—*ns.* **pā'triarchate**, the office, jurisdiction, or residence of a church patriarch, **pā'triarchy**, a community of related families under the authority of a patriarch. [Gr. *patriarchēs*—*patriā*, family—*patēr*, father, *archē*, rule.]

patrician, *pā-trish'án*, *n.* a member or descendant of one of the original families of citizens forming the Roman people—opp. to *plebeian*: an aristocrat. Also *adj.* [L. *patrīcius*—*pater*, *patris*, a father.]

patricide, *pat'ri-sīd*, *n.* the murder of one's own father: one who murders his father. [L. *patricīda*—*pater*, *patris*, father, *caedēre*, to kill.]

patrimony, *pat'ri-món-i*, *n.* an inheritance from a father or from ancestors: a church estate or revenue.—*adj.* **patrimō'nial**.—*adv.* **patrimō'nially**. [L. *patrimōnium*, a paternal estate—*pater*, *patris*, a father.]

patriot, *pā'tri-ot*, sometimes *pat'-*, *n.* one who truly loves and serves his country.—*adj.* devoted to one's country.—*adj.* **patriotic** (*pat-ri-ot'ik*, or *pāt-*), like a patriot: actuated by a love of one's country: directed to the public welfare.—*adv.* **patriot'ically**.—*n.* **pa'triotism**. [Gr. *patriōtēs*, fellow-countryman—*patrios*—*patēr*, a father.]

patristic, -al, *pa-tris'tik*, *-ál*, *adj.* pertaining to the fathers of the Christian Church. [Gr. *pater*, a father.]

patrol, *pa-trōl'*, *v.t.* to go the rounds of (e.g. a camp, town), perambulate (streets), in order to watch, protect, inspect.—Also *v.i.*:—*pr.p.* patroll'ing: *pa.t.* and *pa.p.* patrolled'.—*n.* the act or service of going the rounds of a land area, or of similarly watching an area of the sea: a man or body of men who go the rounds: a small reconnoitring party: a small group of Scouts or Girl Guides.—**patrol car**, that used by police to patrol an area. [O.Fr. *patrouille*, a patrol, *patrouiller*, to patrol, orig. to paddle in the mud.]

patron, *pā'trón*, *n.* a protector: one who countenances or encourages: customer: habitual attender: a proprietor of a restaurant, &c.: one who has the right to appoint to any office:— *fem.* **pā'troness**. —*n.* **pat'ronage** (*pat'-*, or *pāt'-*), the support given by a patron: guar-

patronymic

dianship of saints: the right of bestowing offices, privileges, or church benefices.—*v.t.*
pàt′ronise, to act as a patron toward: to assume the air of a patron toward: to treat condescendingly: to countenance, encourage: to give one's custom to, or to frequent habitually.—*adj.* **patronīs′ing,** who or that patronises, esp. with condescension.—*adv.* **pat′ronīsingly.—patron saint,** a saint chosen as a protector. [Fr.,—L. *patrōnus—pater, patris,* a father.]
patronymic, *pat-rō-nim′ik, adj.* derived from the name of a father or an ancestor.—*n.* a name so derived. [Gr. *patrōnymikos—patēr,* a father, *onoma,* a name.]
patten, *pat′n, n.* a wooden sole mounted on an iron ring, to raise the shoe above the mud: the base of a pillar. [O.Fr. *patin,* clog.]
patter, *pat′ér, v.i.* to strike against something with quick successive pats or taps.—*n.* the sound so produced. [Freq. of **pat.**]
patter, *pat′ér, v.i.* to repeat the Lord's Prayer: to mumble: to talk rapidly.—*v.t.* to repeat hurriedly, to gabble.—*n.* glib talk, chatter: the cant of a class: words in a song sung or spoken very rapidly. [**paternoster.**]
pattern, *pat′érn, n.* a person or thing to be copied: a model: a design or guide with the help of which something is to be made: an example of excellence: a sample: a decorative design.—*ns.* **patt′ern-mak′er,** one who makes the patterns for moulders in foundry-work; **patt′ern-shop,** the place in which patterns for a factory are prepared. [Fr. *patron,* patron, pattern; cf. **patron.**]
patty, *pat′i, n.* a little pie: a small flat cake of minced beef, &c.—*pl.* **patt′ies.** [Fr. *pâté;* cf. **pasty,** a pie.]
paucity, *pö′sit-i, n.* fewness: smallness of number or quantity. [L. *paucitās, -ātis—paucus,* few.]
Pauline, *pö′līn, adj.* of or belonging to the Apostle *Paul.*
paunch, *pön(t)sh, n.* the belly: the first and largest stomach of a ruminant. [O.Fr. *panche*—L. *pantex, panticis.*]
pauper, *pö′pér, n.* a destitute person: one supported by charity or by some public provision.—*n.* **pau′perism,** state of being a pauper.—*v.t.* **pau′perise,** to reduce to pauperism.—*n.* **pauperisā′tion.** [L.]
pause, *pöz, n.* a temporary ceasing, stop: cessation caused by doubt, hesitation: a mark for suspending the voice: (*mus.*) continuance of a note or rest.—*v.i.* to make a pause. [Fr.,—L. *pausa*—Gr. *pausis—pauein,* to cause to cease.]
pavan(e), *pav′an,* or *-an′, n.* a slow stately dance: the music for it. [Fr. *pavane,* peacock, from It. or Sp.]
pave, *pāv, v.t.* to cover with flat stones, &c., so as to form a level surface for walking on: (*fig.*) to prepare (a way for, to).—*n.* **pave′ment,** a paved surface: that with which it is paved. [Fr. *paver*—L. *pavīmentum—pavīre,* to beat hard; cog. with Gr. *paiein,* to beat.]
pavilion, *pă-vil′yón, n.* a large and luxurious tent: an ornamental building often turreted or domed: (*mil.*) a tent raised on posts: a clubhouse on a games field.—*v.t.* to furnish with pavilions.—*n.* **pavil′ion-roof,** a roof sloping

equally ·on all sides. [Fr. *pavillon*—L. *pāpiliō, -ōnis,* a butterfly, a tent.]
paw, *pö, n.* a foot with claws: the hand (used in contempt).—*v.i.* to draw the forefoot along the ground: to strike or feel with the paw.—*v.t.* to scrape with the forefoot: to handle with the paws: to touch or caress, esp. offensively. [O.Fr. *poe, powe,* prob. Gmc.; cf. Du. *poot,* Ger. *pfote.*]
pawky, *pök′i, adj.* (*Scot.*) sly, arch, shrewd. [*pawk,* a trick; origin uncertain.]
pawl, *pöl, n.* a catch falling into the notches of a toothed wheel, as on a windlass, &c., to prevent it from running back, &c.—*v.t.* to stop by means of a pawl. [Origin obscure.]
pawn, *pön, n.* something deposited as a pledge for repayment or performance: state of being pledged.—*v.t.* to give in pledge.—*ns.* **pawn′-broker,** a broker who lends money on pawns or pledges; **pawn′er,** one who gives a pawn or pledge as security for money borrowed. [O.Fr. *pan;* cf. Du. *pand.*]
pawn, *pön, n.* a small piece in chess of lowest rank and range: (*fig.;* of a person) a humble tool whose personal fate and rights are not considered. [O.Fr. *paon,* a foot-soldier—L.L. *pedō, -ōnis,* a walker—L. *pēs, pedis,* the foot.]
pax, *paks, n.* the kiss of peace: a tablet used in giving the kiss of peace at celebration of mass. [L., peace.]
paxwax, *paks′waks, n.* (*coll.*) the strong tendon in the neck of animals. [Orig. *fax-wax*—O.E. *fæx, feax,* hair, *weaxan,* to grow.]
pay, *pā, v.t.* (*obs.*) to satisfy: to discharge, as a debt, duty: to requite with what is due or deserved: to reward: to punish: to give, render (e.g. homage, attention).—*v.i.* to hand over money or other equivalent: to yield a profit: be punished (for):—*pa.t.* and *pa.p.* paid.—*n.* money given for service: salary, wages.—*adj.* **pay′able,** that may or should be paid: due.—*ns.* **pay-as-you-earn,** a method of income tax collection in which the tax is deducted from earnings before they are paid over to the worker:—abbrev. **P.A.Y.E.; pay′-bill, -sheet,** a statement of moneys to be paid to workmen, &c.; **pay′-box, -desk,** one at which a customer pays; **payee′,** one to whom money is paid; **pay′er.—***p.adj.* **pay′ing,** remunerative.—*ns.* **pay′(-)load,** the part of an aeroplane's load for which revenue is obtained: the part of a rocket's equipment that is to fulfil the purpose of the rocket, as a warhead; **pay′master,** one who pays workmen, soldiers, &c.; **pay′ment,** the act of paying: that which is paid: recompense, reward; **pay′-off,** payment of what one has earned, or the time of this: the final result, outcome: climax, dénouement; **payōl′a,** a secret payment to secure a favour; **pay-roll,** list of employees to be paid, with amounts due to them: the money for paying wages.—**paying guest,** a boarder in a private house.—**pay off,** to discharge: to take revenge upon: to requite: to yield good results; **pay out,** to cause to run out, as rope: to punish. [Fr. *payer*—L. *pācāre,* to appease; cf. *pax, pācis,* peace.]
pay, *pā, v.t.* to smear with tar, &c. [O.Fr. *peier*—L. *picāre,* to pitch.]
paynim, *pā′nim, n.* (*obs.*) heathendom: (*hist.*) a non-Christian, esp. a Moslem. [O.Fr. *paien-*

Neutral vowels in unaccented syllables: *em′pér-ór;* for certain sounds in foreign words see p. ix.

isme, paganism—L. *pāgānismus—pāgānus,* a pagan.]

pea, *pē, n.* a new singular formed from **pease** (which was mistaken for a plural), with new plural **peas**—the nutritious seed of climbing annual plants of the same family as the bean: the plants themselves: extended to various similar objects.—*n.* **pea'-shoot'er,** a small tube for blowing peas through. [See **pease.**]

peace, *pēs, n.* a state of quiet: freedom from contention, disturbance, or war: a treaty that ends a war: ease (of mind or conscience): silence.—*interj.* silence! be silent!—*adj.* **peace'able,** disposed to peace: peaceful.—*n.* **peace'ableness.**—*adv.* **peace'ably.**—*adj.* **peace'-ful,** full of peace: tranquil: tending towards peace: inclined to peace.—*adv.* **peace'fully.**—*ns.* **peace'fulness; peace'maker,** one who makes or produces peace: one who reconciles enemies; **peace'-off'ering,** among the Jews, a thank-offering to God: a gift offered towards reconciliation; **peace'-pipe,** the calumet (q.v.).—**peace establishment,** the reduced military strength maintained in time of peace.—**hold one's peace,** to be silent. [O.Fr. *pais*—L. *pax, pācis,* peace.]

peach, *pēch, v.i.* to give information against an accomplice. [M.E. *apeche;* cf. **impeach.**]

peach, *pēch, n.* a sweet, juicy, velvety-skinned stone-fruit: the tree bearing it.—*adjs.* **peach'y; peach'-col'oured,** of the colour of a peach-blossom, pale red. [O.Fr. *pesche*—L. *Persicum* (*mālum*), the Persian (apple).]

peacock, *pē'kok, n.* a genus of large birds of the pheasant kind, noted for gay plumage, esp. the tail feathers:—*fem.* **pea'hen.**—*n.* **Pea'cock Throne,** the former throne of the kings of Delhi, now the Persian throne. [O.E. *pēa* (*pawa*)—L. *pāvō,* and **cock** (1).]

pea-jacket, *pē'-jak'et, n.* a coarse thick jacket worn esp. by seamen. [Du. *pie* (now *pij*), a coat of coarse stuff, and **jacket.**]

peak, *pēk, n.* a point: the pointed end of anything: the top of a mountain, a summit: maximum value: the projecting front of a cap (*naut.*) the upper outer corner of a sail extended by a gaff or yard: the upper end of a gaff.—*adj.* **peaked,** pointed.—**peak load,** the maximum load on a generating station or power distribution system. [App. connected with **pike.**]

peak, *pēk, v.i.* to mope: to look thin or sickly.—*adjs.* **peaked, peaky,** having a pinched or sickly look. [Origin unknown.]

peal, *pēl, n.* a loud sound: a set of bells tuned to each other: the changes rung upon a set of bells.—*v.i.* to resound in peals.—*v.t.* to give forth in peals. [Prob. short for **appeal** (perh. through the idea of a summons).]

pea-nut, peanut, *pē'nut, n.* the ground-nut (q.v.) or monkey-nut. [**pea, nut.**]

pear, *pār, n.* a common fruit tapering towards the stalk and bulged at the end: the genus of trees on which it grows, of the same family as the apple. [O.E. *pere, peru*—L. *pirum,* pear.]

pearl, *pûrl, n.* a concretion of nacre found in a pearl-oyster or other shellfish, prized as a gem: anything round and lustrous: a paragon or finest example: cataract of the eye: (*print.*) a size of type immediately above diamond.—

adj. made of, or belonging to, pearls: granulated.—*v.t.* to set or adorn with pearls: to make into small round grains.—*v.i.* to fish or dive for pearls: to form into pearls.—*ns.* **pearl'-bar'ley, pearl'-tapioc'a** (see **barley, tapioca**); **pearl'-div'er, pearl'-fish'er,** one who dives, fishes, for pearls; **pearl'-oys'ter,** the oyster that produces pearls.—*adj.* **pearl'y,** like pearl: rich in pearls.—*n.* **pearl'iness.** [Fr. *perle,* prob. either from L. *pirula,* a dim. of *pirum,* a pear, or from L. *pilula,* dim. of *pila,* a ball.]

peasant, *pez'ant, n.* a small farmer, a countryman, a rustic.—*adj.* of or relating to peasants, rustic, rural.—*n.* **peas'antry,** the body of peasants.—**peasant proprietor,** a peasant who owns and works his own farm. [O.Fr. *paisant* (Fr. *paysan*)—*pays*—L. *pāgus,* a district.]

pease, *pēz, n.* orig. a pea or pea-plant (*pl.* **peas'en**): now almost wholly superseded by the new singular **pea** and plural **peas,** except in a collective sense.—*ns.* **pease'cod, peas'cod, pea'cod,** the pod of the pea; **pease'-meal, pease'-porr'idge, pease'-soup** or **pea'-soup,** meal, porridge, soup, made from pease. [M.E. *pēse,* pl. *pēsen*—O.E. *pise,* pl. *pisan*—L. *pīsum*—Gr. *pison.*]

peat, *pēt, n.* a shaped block dug from a bog and dried for fuel: the decayed vegetable matter from which such blocks are cut.—*ns.* **peat'-bog,** a region covered with peat: a place from which peat is dug—also **peat'-bed, peat'-moor, peat'-moss; peat'-hag,** a ditch whence peat has been dug; **peat'-reek,** the smoke of peat, imagined to add a special flavour to whisky: Highland whisky.—*adj.* **peat'y,** like peat: abounding in, or composed of, peat. [Anglo-Latin *peta,* a peat; possibly of British origin.]

pebble, *peb'l, n.* a small roundish stone, esp. water-worn: transparent and colourless rock-crystal.—*adjs.* **pebb'led, pebb'ly,** full of pebbles.—*ns.* **pebb'le-dash,** a method of coating exterior walls with small pebbles set into the mortar (*v.t.* to coat with pebble-dash); **pebb'le-pow'der,** gunpowder in large cubical grains; **pebb'le-ware,** fine pottery of mixed coloured clays. [O.E. *papol* (-*stān*), a pebble (-stone).]

pecan, *pi-kan', n.* a North American hickory: its nut. [Indian name.]

peccable, *pek'a-bl, adj.* liable to sin.—*ns.* **peccabil'ity; pecc'ancy,** sinfulness: transgression.—*adj.* **pecc'ant,** sinning: offending: (*med.*) morbid.—*adv.* **pecc'antly.** [L. *peccāre,* -*ātum,* to sin.]

peccadillo, *pek-a-dil'ō, n.* a trifling fault:—*pl.* **peccadill'os** (or **peccadill'oes**). [Sp. *pecadillo,* dim. of *pecado*—L. *peccātum,* a sin.]

peccary, *pek'ār-i, n.* either of two species of hog-like South American animals. [Carib (q.v.) *pakira.*]

peck, *pek, n.* formerly a measure of capacity for dry goods = 2 gallons, or one-fourth of a bushel. [M.E. *pekke, pek*—O.Fr. *pek,* generally a horse's feed of oats.]

peck, *pek, v.t.* to strike or pick up with the beak: to eat sparingly: to kiss with a dabbing movement: to strike with anything pointed: to strike with repeated blows.—*n.* **peck'er,** that which pecks: a woodpecker: (*slang*) spirit, as in 'to keep your pecker up'.—*adj.* **peck'ish,**

somewhat hungry.—**pecking order** (*fig.*), order of prestige or power in a human social
group. [App. a form of **pick**.]
Pecksniffian, pek-snif'i-ån, *adj.* hypocritical.
[From Mr *Pecksniff* in Dickens's *Martin
Chuzzlewit.*]
pectin, pek'tin, *n.* any of certain non-crystalline
carbohydrates found as a mixture in the cell
walls of fruits and vegetables; they play an
important part in the setting of jams. [Gr.
pēktos, fixed, congealed.]
pectinal, pek'tin-ål, *adj.* comb-like: having
bones like the teeth of a comb. [L. *pecten,
-inis*, a comb.]
pectoral, pek'to-rál, *adj.* relating to the breast or
chest.—*n.* an ornamental breastplate: a pectoral fin: a medicine for the chest.—*adv.* **pec'-
torally.**—**pectoral fins**, the anterior paired
fins of fishes (corresponding to the fore-limbs
of an animal). [L. *pectorālis*—*pectus, pectoris*,
the breast.]
peculate, pek'ū-lāt, *v.t.* and *v.i.* to appropriate
dishonestly, to pilfer.—*ns.* **pecula'tion**; **pec'u-
lātor.** [L. *pecūlārī, -ātus*—*pecūlium*, private
property, akin to *pecūnia*, money.]
peculiar, pi-kūl'yàr, *adj.* of one's own: belonging
exclusively (to): characteristic: particular,
special: strange.—*n.* **peculiarity** (*pi-kū-li-
ar'i-ti*), that which is found in one and in no
other: a characteristic: oddity.—*adv.* **pecul'iarly.** [L. *pecūlium*, private property.]
pecuniary, pi-kūn'yàr-i, -i-àr-i, *adj.* relating to
money: consisting of money.—*adv.* **pecū'ni-
arily.** [L. *pecūnia*, money, from the root that
appears in L. *pecudes* (pl.), cattle.]
pedagogue, ped'á-gog, *n.* a teacher: a pedant.—
adjs. **pedagogic, -al** (-*gog'-, -goj'-*), relating to
teaching.—*ns.* **pedagogics** (-*goj'iks*), **pedagogy**
(-*goj'i*), the science of teaching. [Gr. *paida-
gōgos*, a slave who led a boy to school—*pais*,
gen. *paidos*, a boy, *agōgos*, leader—*agein*, to
lead.]
pedal, ped'ál, *adj.* pertaining to the foot.—*n.* a
lever pressed by the foot.—*v.i.* to use a pedal.
—*v.t.* to drive by pedals:—*pr.p.* ped'alling; *pa.t.*
and *pa.p.* ped'alled.—*n.* **ped'al-ac'tion**, the apparatus worked by the pedals of a musical
instrument. [L. *pedālis*—*pēs, pedis*, the foot.]
pedant, ped'ánt, *n.* one who makes a vain and
pretentious show of learning: one who
attaches too much importance to minute details or to formal rules in scholarship.—*adjs.*
pedant'ic, -al, of the character, or in the manner, of a pedant.—*n.* **ped'antry**, the behaviour
of a pedant: a pedantic expression: unnecessarily rigorous formality. [It. *pedante* (perh.
through Fr. *pédant*); connection with **pedagogue** not clear.]
peddle, ped'l, *v.i.* to go about as pedlar: to
trifle.—*v.t.* to sell or offer as pedlar.—*n.*
pedd'ler, a pedlar.—*adj.* **pedd'ling**, unimportant.—*n.* the trade of a pedlar. [Perh. **pedlar**.]
pedestal, ped'ės-tál, *n.* the support of a column,
statue, vase, &c. [Fr. *piédestal*—It. *piedi-
stallo*—*piè* (L. *pēs, pedis*), foot, *di* (L. *dē*), of
stallo, stall.]
pedestrian, pi-des'tri-án, *adj.* on foot: of walking
on foot: prosaic, commonplace.—*n.* a foot-
passenger: one who practises feats of walking
or running.—*n.* **pedes'trianism**, walking: the

quality of being pedestrian. [L. *pedester,
-tris*—*pēs, pedis*, foot.]
pedicel, ped'i-sel, *n.* the stalk of a single flower
in a cluster (inflorescence). [Botanists' L.
pedīcellus, dim. of *pēs, pedis*, the foot.]
pediculosis, pi-dik-ū-lō'sis, *n.* infestation with
lice.—*adjs.* **pedic'ular, -ous**, lousy. [L. *pedīcu-
lus*, dim. of *pedis*, louse.]
pedicure, ped'i-kūr, *n.* the treatment of corns,
bunions, or the like: one who treats the feet.
[L. *pēs, pedis*, foot, *cūra*, care.]
pedigree, ped'i-grē, *n.* a line of ancestors: a
scheme or record of ancestry, a genealogy:
lineage: distinguished or ancient lineage: succession, series, set.—*adj.* of known descent,
pure-bred and of good stock.—*adj.* **ped'igreed**,
having a pedigree. [App. Fr. *pied de grue*,
crane's-foot, from the arrow-head figure used
in depicting pedigrees.]
pediment, ped'i-mėnt, *n.* (*archit.*) a triangular
structure crowning the front of a building: a
similar structure, triangular or rounded, over
a portico, &c.—*adj.* **pediment'al.** [Earlier *peri-
ment*, prob. for **pyramid**.]
pedlar, ped'lár, *n.* one who goes about with a
pack of goods for sale.—*n.* **ped'lary**, the wares
or trade of a pedlar. [Ety. uncertain; occurs
earlier than **peddle**.]
pedobaptism, pē-dō-bap'tizm, *n.* infant baptism.—*n.* **pedobap'tist**, one who believes in
infant baptism. [Gr. *pais*, gen. *paidos*, a child,
baptism.]
pedometer, pi-dom'ét-ér, *n.* an instrument for
counting paces and so measuring distance
walked. [L. *pēs, pedis*, a foot, Gr. *metron*, a
measure.]
peduncle, pi-dung'kl, *n.* the stalk of a cluster
or of a solitary flower: the stalk by which
a sedentary animal is attached.—*adjs.*
pedun'cular, pedun'culate, -d. [Low L. *pedun-
culus*—L. *pēs, pedis*, the foot.]
peel, pēl, *v.t.* to strip off the skin or bark from:
to bare.—*v.i.* to come off, as the skin.—*n.* rind,
esp. that of oranges, lemons, &c. [O.E. *pil-
ian*—L. *pīlāre*, to deprive of hair—*pīlus*, a
hair; perh. influenced by Fr. *peler*, to skin.]
peel, pēl, *n.* a palisaded enclosure: a **peel'-house**,
peel'-tower, orig. a fortified dwelling-house,
usu. entered by a ladder to the first floor—
now loosely used for any similar fortalice.
[Anglo-Fr. *pel*—L. *pālus*, stake.]
peel, pēl, *n.* a shovel, esp. a baker's wooden
shovel. [O.Fr. *pele*—L. *pāla*, a spade.]
peeler, pēl'ér, *n.* a policeman, from Sir R. *Peel*,
who reorganised the London Police in 1829.
peep, pēp, *v.i.* to cheep as a chicken. [Imit.]
peep, pēp, *v.i.* to look through a narrow opening:
to look stealthily or cautiously: (to begin) to
appear: to be just showing.—*n.* a sly look: a
glimpse: a first appearance.—*ns.* **peep'er**, one
that peeps: a prying person; **peep'-show**, a
show viewed through a small hole, usually
fitted with a magnifying glass.—**Peeping Tom**,
a prying fellow, esp. one who peeps in at
windows (orig. Peeping Tom figures in the
story of Lady Godiva). [Origin obscure.]
peer, pēr, *n.* an equal: an associate: a nobleman
of the rank of baron upwards: a member of
the House of Lords:—*fem.* **peer'ess.**—*adj.* (of a
group in society) like in age or in some other

Neutral vowels in unaccented syllables: *em'pėr-ór*; for certain sounds in foreign words see p. ix.

528

unifying character: pertaining to a peer group.—*n.* **peer'age**, the rank or dignity of a peer: the body of peers: a book of the genealogy, &c., of the different peers.—*adj.* **peer'less**, unequalled, matchless.—*adv.* **peer'lessly.**—*n.* **peer'lessness.** [O.Fr. (Fr. *pair*)—L. *pār, paris*, equal.]

peer, *pēr, v.i.* to look narrowly or closely: to look with strain: to peep out, appear.

peevish, *pēv'ish, adj.* fretful, querulous.—*adv.* **peev'ishly.**—*n.* **peev'ishness.**

peewit, *pē'wit, pu'it, n.* the lapwing, so named from its cry. [Imit.]

peg, *peg, n.* a pin (esp. of wood) for hanging up or fastening things, or for marking a position: a drink, esp. of brandy and soda: a pin for tuning the string of a musical instrument.—*v.t.* to fasten, mark, score, &c., with a peg.—*v.i.* to work assiduously:—*pr.p.* **pegg'ing;** *pa.t.* and *pa.p.* **pegged.**—*n.* **peg'board,** a board having holes into which pegs are placed, used for playing and scoring in games or for display purposes.—*adj.* **pegged,** fashioned of, or furnished with, pegs.—*ns.* **peg'-leg,** a simple wooden leg; **peg'-top,** a top, with a metal point, spun by winding a string round it.—**off the peg,** ready made; **take down a peg,** to humble, to snub. [Cf. L.Ger. *pigge*; Du. dial. *peg*; Dan. *pig.*]

peignoir, *pen-wär, n.* a loose wrapper worn by women during their toilet: a morning-gown. [Fr., *peigner*—L. *pectināre*, to comb.]

pejorative, *pi-jor'a tiv* (or *pē'jor-*), *adj.* depreciatory, disparaging.—Also *n.* [L. *pejor*, worse.]

Pekin(g)ese, *pē-kin(g)-ēz', n.* a small pugnosed dog of Chinese breed. abbrev. **Peke.** [*Peking*, China.]

pekoe, *pek'ō, pe'kō, n.* a scented black tea. [Chinese.]

pelargonium, *pel-är-gō'ni-um, n.* a vast genus of flowering plants of the geranium family, including the plants grown in greenhouses and gardens and there known as *geraniums*. [Gr. *pelargos*, stork, the beaked capsules resembling a stork's head.]

Pelecypoda, *pel-é-sip'ō-dä, n.* same as Lamellibranchia (q.v.). [Formed from Gr. *pelekys*, hatchet, and *poda*—*pous*, gen. *podos*, foot.]

pelf, *pelf, n.* riches (in a bad sense): money. [O.Fr. *pelfre*, booty; cf. **pilfer.**]

pelican, *pel'i-kán, n.* a large water fowl with an enormous pouched bill. [Low L. *pelicānus*—Gr. *pelekan, -ānos*, pelican; cf. *pelekās, -āntos*, a woodpecker, and *pelekys*, an axe.]

pelisse, *pe-lēs', n.* orig. a furred coat or robe (*hist.*): a lady's long mantle, or a young child's coat. [Fr.,—Low L. *pellicea* (*vestis*)—L. *pellis*, a skin.]

pellagra, *pel-ag'rä* (or *-āg'-*), *n.* a deficiency disease (formerly deadly). [Gr. *pella*, skin, *agrā*, seizure; or It. *pelle agra*, rough skin.]

pellet, *pel'ét, n.* a little ball: a small pill: a ball of shot. [O.Fr. *pelote*—L. *pīla*, a ball.]

pellicle, *pel'i-kl, n.* a thin skin, membrane, or film: a film or scum on liquors.—*adj.* **pellic'ular.** [L. *pellicula*, dim. of *pellis*, skin.]

pell-mell, *pel'-mel', adv.* confusedly, promiscuously: headlong, helter-skelter.—*adj.* disorderly: headlong. [O.Fr. *pesle-mesle, -mesle* being from O.Fr. *mesler*, to mix—Low L. *mis-*

culāre—L. *miscēre*; and *pesle*, a rhyming addition, perh. influenced by Fr. *pelle*, shovel.]

pellucid, *pe-l(y)ōō'sid, adj.* perfectly clear: transparent.—*n.* **pellu'cidness.**—*adv.* **pellu'cidly.** [Fr.,—L. *pellūcidus—per*, through, *lūcidus*, clear—*lūcēre*, to shine.]

pelmet, *pel'mét, n.* a strip of material, or other similar device, placed across the top of a window or door to hide the attachment of a curtain, or for artistic effect. [Perh. Fr. *palmette*, a palm-leaf.]

pelota, *pel-ō'tä, n.* a Spanish ball game like fives. [Sp., a ball.]

pelt, *pelt, n.* a raw hide.—*ns.* **pelt'monger,** a dealer in skins; **pelt'ry,** the skins of animals with the fur on them, furs. [App. a backformation from *peltry*—O.Fr. *pelleterie—pelletier*, a skinner—L. *pellis*, a skin.]

pelt, *pelt, v.t.* to assail with blows, missiles, or words.—*v.i.* to fall heavily, as rain: to speed.—*n.* a blow: a downpour: a rapid pace.

pelvis, *pel'vis, n.* the bony cavity forming the lower part of the abdomen:—*pl.* **pelves** (*pel'vēz*).—*adj.* **pel'vic.** [L. *pelvis*, a basin.]

pemmican, pemican, *pem'i-kán, n.* a North American Indian preparation, consisting of lean flesh-meat, dried, pounded, and mixed with other ingredients. [Indian word.]

pen, *pen, n.* a small enclosure, esp. for animals: a dam or weir.—*v.t.* to put or keep in a pen: to confine within a small space:—*pr.p.* **penn'ing;** *pa.t.* and *pa.p.* **penned** or **pent.**—*n.* **submarine pen,** a dock for a submarine, esp. if protected from attack from above by a deep covering of concrete. [O.E. *penn*, pen.]

pen, *pen, n.* an instrument used for writing, formerly made of the feather of a bird, but now of steel, &c.: the horny internal shell of a squid.—*v.t.* to write:—*pr.p.* **penn'ing;** *pa.t.* and *pa.p.* **penned.**—*ns.* **pen'-friend,** a person, otherwise unknown, assigned to one as a correspondent; **pen'-hold'er,** a rod on which a nib may be fixed; **pen'knife,** a small pocket knife, orig. for making or mending pens; **pen'man,** one skilled in the use of the pen: an author; **pen'manship,** handwriting; **pen'-name,** a name assumed by an author. [O.Fr. *penne*—L. *penna*, a feather.]

penal, *pē'nál, adj.* pertaining to, liable to, imposing, constituting, used for, punishment: constituting a penalty: very severe.—*v.t.* **pē'nalise,** to make punishable: to put under a disadvantage.—*adv.* **pē'nally.—penal laws,** laws imposing penalties; **penal servitude,** hard labour in a prison as a punishment for crime, abolished in 1948. [L. *poenālis—poena*—Gr. *poinē*, punishment.]

penalty, *pen'ál-ti, n.* punishment: suffering or loss imposed for a fault or breach of a law: a fine.—**penalty kick, goal,** a free kick awarded because a player on the opposite side has broken a rule, a goal resulting from such a kick.—**death penalty,** punishment by putting to death. [L.L. *poenālitās, -ātis—poena.* See **penal.**]

penance, *pen'áns, n.* a penalty voluntarily undertaken, or imposed by a priest on a penitent offender.—Also *fig.* [O.Fr. Same root as **penitence.**]

penates, *pe-nā'tēz, n.pl.* the household gods of a

fāte, fär; mē, hûr (her); *mīne; mōte, för; mūte; mōōn, fŏŏt;* THen (then)

Roman family. See **lares**. [L., prob. from root *pen-* in L. *penes*, in the house of, &c.]

pence, *pens, n.* plural of **penny**.

penchant, *pä-shä, n.* inclination, decided taste (for). [Fr., pr.p. of *pencher*, to incline—L.L. *pendicāre*—L. *pendēre*, to hang.]

pencil, *pen'sl, n.* (*arch.*) a fine paint-brush: any pointed instrument for writing or drawing without ink: any small stick of similar shape: a collection of rays of light, or of lines, converging to a point: the art or style of a painter.—*v.t.* to write, sketch, or mark with a pencil: to paint or draw:—*pr.p.* pen'cilling; *pa.t.* and *pa.p.* pen'cilled.—*adj.* pen'cilled, written or marked with a pencil: marked with fine lines, delicately marked.—*n.* pen'cilling. [O.Fr. *pincel*—L. *pēnicillum*, a painter's brush, dim. of *pēnis*, a tail.]

pendant, *pen'dänt,* **pendent**, *n.* anything hanging, esp. for ornament: a pennant: anything attached to another thing of the same kind: an appendix: a companion picture, poem, &c.—*n.* pen'dency, undecided state.—*adj.* pen'dent (sometimes pen'dant), hanging: overhanging: not yet decided.—*adv.* pen'dently. [Fr. *pendant,* pr.p. of *pendre,* to hang—L. *pendens, -entis*—pr.p. of *pendēre,* to hang.]

pending, *pen'ding, adj.* impending: undecided.—*prep.* during: until, awaiting. [Fr. *pendre* or L. *pendēre,* to hang.]

pendragon, *pen-drag'on, n.* an ancient British supreme chief. [W. *pen,* head, *dragon,* a dragon-standard.]

pendulum, *pen'dū-lum, n.* theoretically, a heavy material point suspended by a weightless thread and swinging without friction (**simple pendulum**): any weight so hung from a fixed point as to swing freely (**compound pendulum**): the swinging weight which regulates the movement of a clock: anything that swings or is free to swing to and fro.—*adj.* pen'dulous, hanging loosely: swinging freely.—*adv.* pen'dulously. [L., neut. of *pendulus,* hanging—*pendēre,* to hang.]

penetrate, *pen'é-trāt, v.t.* to thrust or force a way into the inside of: to pierce into or through: to reach the mind or feelings of: to see into, or through, understand.—*v.i.* to make way or pass inwards.—*adj.* pen'etrable.—*n.* penetrabil'ity.—*adj.* pen'etrating, piercing: sharp: discerning.—*n.* penetrā'tion, the act or power of penetrating: acuteness: discernment.—*adj.* pen'etrātive, tending or able to penetrate: piercing: having keen or deep insight: reaching and affecting the mind. [L. *penetrāre, -ātum*—*penes,* in the house, possession, or power of.]

penguin, *peng'gwin,* or *pen'-, n.* any of a family of sea-birds of the Southern Hemisphere, unable to fly. [Ety. uncertain.]

penicillin, *pen-i-sil'in, n.* a group of substances (extracted from certain moulds of the genus *Penicillium,* esp. *Penicillium notatum*) that stop the growth of bacteria. [L. *pēnicillus,* dim. of *pēnis,* a tail.]

peninsula, *pen-in'sū-lä, n.* a piece of land that is almost an island.—*adj.* penin'sular, pertaining to a peninsula: in the form of a peninsula: inhabiting a peninsula.—**Peninsular War,** the war in the Iberian Peninsula (Spain and Portugal) between French and English in 1808-14. [L.,—*paene,* almost, *insula,* an island.]

penis, *pē'nis, n.* the external male organ. [L., orig. a tail.]

penitent, *pen'i-tént, adj.* sorry for sin, contrite, repentant.—*n.* one who sorrows for sin: one under penance.—*n.* pen'itence.—*adv.* pen'itently.—*adj.* penitential (-*ten'shál*), of the nature of, pertaining to, or expressive of, penitence.—*n.* a book of rules relating to penance.—*adv.* peniten'tially.—*adj.* penitentiary (-*ten'shár-i*), relating to penance: penitential.—*n.* a penitent: an office at Rome dealing with cases of penance: a place for penance: a reformatory prison or house of correction.—**penitential psalms,** certain psalms suitable for being sung by penitents, e.g. the 51st. [L. *paenitēns, -entis,* pr.p. of *paenitēre,* to cause to repent.]

penknife, penman. See under **pen.**

pennant, *pen'ánt, n.* a long narrow flag at the mast-heads of warships. [A combination of **pendant** and **pennon**.]

penniform, *pen'i-förm, adj.* feather-shaped. [L. *penna,* feather, (pl.) wing.]

pennon, *pen'on, n.* a mediaeval knight-bachelor's flag or streamer attached to a lance: a long narrow flag. [O.Fr. *penon,* a streamer, prob.—L. *penna,* feather.]

penny, *pen'i, n.* a coin (orig. silver, later copper, then, 1860, bronze) formerly 1/240 of £1 (abbrev. *d.*—L. *denārius*), now (**new penny**) 1/100 of £1 (abbrev. *p*): a small sum: (in *pl.*) money in general: (*N.T.*) a silver coin:—*pl.* pennies (*pen'iz*) as material objects, pence (*pens*) as units of value.—*adj.* sold for a penny.—*adj.* penn'iless, without a penny: without money: poor.—*ns.* penn'y-a-lin'er, a poorly paid and inferior writer; penny-dreadful, a cheap and exciting tale or magazine; penn'yweight, twenty-four grains of troy weight (the weight of a silver penny).—*adj.* penny-wise, intent on petty economies that may entail ultimate loss.—*n.* penn'yworth, a penny's worth: a (good, bad) bargain.—Also **pennorth** (*pen'-ürth*; *coll.*).—**penny gaff** (*slang*), a low-class theatre; **penny wedding,** a wedding at which the guests contribute money as a gift to the bride and bridegroom.—**a pretty penny,** a considerable sum of money; **in penny numbers,** a very few, or a very little, at a time; **pennies from heaven,** money obtained without effort and unexpectedly; **Peter's pence,** (*hist.*) an annual tax of a penny paid to the papal see: now, a voluntary annual contribution paid to it; **two a penny,** in abundant supply and of little value. [O.E. *penig,* oldest form *pending*; cf. Ger. *pfenning* or *pfennig*; Du. *penning*.]

pennyroyal, *pen-i-roi'ál, n.* a species of mint, once esteemed in medicine. [M.E. *puliol real*—Anglo-Fr.,—L. *pūlēium,* pennyroyal, and *rēgālis,* royal.]

pension, *pen'shón, n.* a stated allowance to a person for past services: an allowance to one who has retired or has been disabled or reached old age, or who has been widowed, orphaned, &c.: boarding-school or boarding-house on the Continent (as Fr., *pä-syõ*). —*v.t.* to grant a pension to.—*adjs.* pen'sionable, entitled, or entitling, to a pension;

Neutral vowels in unaccented syllables: *em'pér-ór*; for certain sounds in foreign words see p. ix.

pen′sionary, receiving a pension: of the nature of a pension.—*n.* one who receives a pension.—*n.* **pen′sioner**, one who receives a pension: a dependent, a hireling.—**pension off**, to dismiss, or allow to retire, with a pension. [Fr.,—L. *pēnsiō, -ōnis—pendēre, pensum*, to weigh, pay.]

pensive, *pen′siv, adj.* meditative: expressing thoughtfulness with sadness.—*adv.* **pen′sively.**—*n.* **pen′siveness.** [Fr. *pensif, -ive—penser*, to think—L. *pēnsāre*, to weigh—*pendēre*, to weigh.]

penstock, *pen′stok, n.* a sluice. [**pen** (1), **stock** (1).]

pensum, *pen′sum, n.* a task: (*U.S.*) a school imposition. [L.]

pent, *pa.t.* and *pa.p.* of **pen**, to shut up.

pentagon, *pen′ta-gon, n.* (*geom.*) a rectilineal plane figure having five angles and five sides: (*cap.*) headquarters of the U.S. armed forces at Washington (from the shape of the building).—*adj.* **pentagonal** (*pen-tag′on-ăl*). [Gr. *pentagōnon—pente*, five, *gōniā*, angle.]

pentagram, *pen′tä-gram, n.* a five-pointed star. [Gr. *pente*, five, *gramma*, a letter.]

pentameter, *pen-tam′e-tėr, n.* a verse (line) of five measures or feet.—*adj.* having five metrical feet. [Gr. *pentametros—pente*, five, *metron*, a measure.]

pentasyllabic, *pen-tä-si-lab′ik, adj.* having five syllables. [Gr. *pente*, five, and **syllable.**]

pentateuch, *pen′ta-tūk, n.* the first five books of the Old Testament. *adj.* **pen′tateuchal.** [Gr. *pente*, five, *teuchos*, tool, (later) book.]

pentathlon, *pen-tath′lon, n.* a contest in wrestling, disk-throwing, spear-throwing, leaping, running, held in ancient Greece: a five-event contest at modern Olympic Games, 1906-1924: a five-event Olympic games contest for women· (**modern pentathlon**) an Olympic games contest consisting of swimming, crosscountry riding and running, fencing, and revolver shooting. [Gr. *pente*, five, *athlon*, contest.]

Pentecost, *pent′e-kost, n.* a Jewish festival held on the fiftieth day after the Passover: Whitsuntide.—*adj.* **pentecost′al.** [Gr. *pentēkostē* (*hēmerā*), the fiftieth (day).]

penthouse, *pent′hows, n.* a shed or lean-to projecting from or adjoining a main building: a separate room or dwelling on a roof: a small, select top flat. [M.E. *pentis*—Fr. *appentis*—L. *appendicium*, an appendage.]

pentroof, *pent′rōōf, n.* a roof with a slope on one side only. [**penthouse, roof;** influenced by Fr. *pente*, a slope.]

penult, *pé-nult′, pē′nult*, **penult′ima,** *ns.* the syllable last but one.—*adj.* **penult′imate,** last but one.—*n.* the last but one. [L. *paenultima—paene*, almost, *ultimus*, last.]

penumbra, *pen-um′bra, n.* a partial shadow round the perfect shadow of an eclipse: the part of a picture where the light and shade blend. [L. *paene*, almost, *umbra*, shade.]

penury, *pen′ū-ri, n.* want, great poverty.—*adj.* **penū′rious,** showing penury: scanty, niggardly.—*adv.* **penū′riously.**—*n.* **penū′riousness.** [L. *pēnūria*, want.]

peon, *pē′on, n.* a day-labourer, esp. formerly, in Spanish-speaking America, one working off a debt by bondage: in India (*pūn*), a footsoldier, a policeman (*hist.*), a messenger. [Sp.,—Low L. *pedō*—L. *pēs, pedis,* a foot.]

peony, *pē′o-ni, n.* a genus of plants with large showy flowers. [O.Fr. *pione*—L. *paeōnia*, healing—Gr. *Paiōn* or *Paiān.* See **paean.**]

people, *pē′pl, n.* a nation: a community: a race—in these senses used as *sing.* with a *pl.* **peo′ples:** a body of persons linked by common leadership, &c.: subjects: followers: servants: near kindred: parents: the mass of the nation: persons generally—in these senses used as *pl.*—*v.t.* to stock with people or inhabitants. [O.Fr. *poeple*—L. *populus.*]

pep, *pep, n.* (*coll.*) vigour.—*ns.* **pep′-pill,** a pill containing a stimulant drug; **pep′talk,** a strongly-worded talk designed to arouse enthusiasm for a cause or course of action.—**pep up,** to put pep into. [**pepper.**]

pepper, *pep′ér, n.* a pungent condiment made from the dried berries of the pepper-plants: a genus of plants of which the most important is the common or black pepper: a plant of the genus *Capsicum* or one of its pods.—*v.t.* to sprinkle with pepper: to hit or pelt with shot, &c.—*adj.* **pepp′er-and-salt′,** mingled black and white.— *ns.* **pepp′ercorn,** berry of the pepper-plant: something of little value; **pepp′ermint,** a species of mint, aromatic and pungent like pepper: a liquor distilled from the plant: a lozenge flavoured with it.—*adj.* **pepp′ery,** possessing the qualities of pepper: hot, choleric. **black pepper,** the dried berries of the common pepper, &c.; **white pepper,** these berries when freed from their outer coatings; **green pepper,** a mild sweet Capsicum; **red pepper,** cayenne (q.v.) pepper. [O.E. *pipor*—L. *piper*—Gr. *peperi*—Sans. *pippali.*]

pepsin, *pep′sin, n.* the digestive enzymes (q.v.) of the gastric juice of vertebrates.—*adj.* **pep′tic,** relating to or promoting digestion: of, or relating to, pepsin or the digestive juices.—*n.* **pep′tone,** a product of the action of enzymes on albuminous matter.—*v.t.* **pep′tonise,** to convert into peptones.—**peptic ulcer,** an ulcer of the stomach or duodenum. [Gr. *pepsis*, digestion—*peptein*, to digest.]

per, *pûr, prep.* for each, a (e.g. *sixpence per dozen, £500 per annum*): by (e.g. *per parcel post*).—**per annum** (*an′um*), yearly; **per capita** (*kap′i-ta*), (counting) by heads; **per se** (*sā*), in itself, intrinsically. [L.]

peradventure, *per-ad-vent′yur, -chûr, adv.* by adventure, by chance: perhaps. [L. *per*, by, **adventure.**]

perambulate, *pér-am′bū-lāt, v.t.* to walk through, about, or over: to pass through for the purpose of surveying: to survey the boundaries of.—*ns.* **perambulā′tion,** act of perambulating: encirclement in order to define boundaries: the district within which a person has the right of inspection; **peram′bulātor,** one who perambulates: a light carriage for a child. [L. *perambulāre, -ātum—per*, through, *ambulāre*, to walk.]

perceive, *pér-sēv′, v.t.* to become or be aware of through the senses: to see: to understand: to discern.—*n.* **perceiv′er.** [O.Fr. *perceveir*—L. *percipēre, perceptum—per-,* thoroughly, *capĕre*, to take.]

per cent, *pér sent',* adv. in the hundred, for each hundred.—n. **percent'age,** rate or amount per cent: a proportion: (*slang*) gain, rake-off. [L. *per centum,* per hundred.]

percept, *pûr'sept,* n. an object perceived by the senses: the mental result of perceiving.—adj. **percep'tible,** that can be perceived: discernible.—n. **perceptibil'ity.**—adv. **percep'tibly.**—n. **percep'tion,** act or power of perceiving: discernment: the combining of sensations into recognition of an object.—adj. **percep'tive,** able, or quick to, perceive or discern.—ns. **percep'tiveness, perceptiv'ity.** [From *perceptum.* See **perceive.**]

perch, *pûrch,* n. a genus of spiny-finned fresh-water fishes: (usu. with qualifying word) any of various other spiny-finned fishes, many of them marine. [Fr. *perche*—L. *perca*—Gr. *perkē,* a perch, perh. conn. with *perknos,* dusky.]

perch, *pûrch,* n. a rod on which birds alight, sit, or roost: any high seat or position: a measure = $5^1/_2$ yards: a square measure = $30^1/_4$ square yards.—v.i. to alight, sit, or roost on a perch: to be set on high: to settle.— v.t. to place, as on a perch.—n. **perch'er,** a bird with feet adapted for perching. [Fr. *perche*—L. *pertica,* a rod.]

perchance, *pér-chäns',* adv. by chance: perhaps. [Anglo-Fr. *par chance.*]

percipient, *pér-sip'i-ént,* adj. perceiving: having the faculty of perception.—n. one who perceives or can perceive. [L. *percipiens, -entis,* pr.p. of *percipere*; cf. **perceive.**]

percolate, *pûr'kō-lāt,* v.t. and v.i. to pass through pores: to filter.—ns. **percola'tion,** act of filtering; **per'colator,** an apparatus for percolating, esp. for making coffee. [L. *percōlāre, -ātum— per,* through, *cōlāre,* to strain.]

percussion, *pér-kush'(ó)n,* n. impact: (*med.*) tapping upon the body to find the condition of an organ by the sounds: instruments played by striking—cymbals, &c.—n. **percuss'ion-cap,** a metal case filled with material that explodes when struck, formerly used for firing rifles, &c. [L. *percussiō, -ōnis—percutere, percussum—per-,* thoroughly, *quatere,* to shake.]

perdition, *pér-dish'(ó)n,* n. utter loss or ruin: the utter loss of happiness in a future state, hell. [L. *perditiō, -ōnis—perdere, perditum— per-,* entirely, *dāre,* to give up.]

peregrinate, *per'é-gri-nāt,* v.i. to travel about, journey.—ns. **peregrina'tion,** travel: pilgrimage; **per'egrinator,** one who travels about. —adj. **per'egrine,** foreign: migratory.—n. an immigrant: a kind of falcon. [L. *peregrīnārī, -ātus—peregrīnus,* foreign—*peregre,* abroad —*per,* through, *ager,* field.]

peremptory, *per'ém(p)-tór-i,* or *-em(p)'-,* adj. admitting no refusal: dogmatic: imperious.— adv. **per'emptorily** (or *-em(p)'-*).—n. **per'emptoriness** (or *-em(p)'-*). [Fr.,—L. *peremptōrius—perimēre, peremptum—per-,* entirely, *emēre,* to take, buy.]

perennial, *pér-en'yál,* adj. lasting through the year: perpetual: (*bot.*) lasting more than two years.—adv. **perenn'ially.** [L. *perennis—per,* through, *annus,* a year.]

perfect, *pûr'fekt,* adj. done thoroughly or completely: complete: faultless: having every

moral excellence: completely skilled or versed: (of an insect) in the final adult stage of development: (*bot.*) having both stamens and pistils, hermaphrodite.—v.t. (or *pér-fekt'*) to make perfect: to finish: to make fully skilled in anything.—adv. **per'fectly.**—adj. **perfect'ible,** capable of becoming perfect.—n. **perfectibil'ity; perfec'tion, per'fectness,** state of being perfect: a perfect quality or acquirement: the highest state or degree: consummate excellence; **perfec'tionist,** one who claims to be perfect: one who thinks that moral perfection can be attained in this life; **perfec'tionism.**—adj. **perfect'ive,** tending to make perfect.—adv. **perfect'ively.**—**perfect interval,** the fourth, fifth, or octave; **perfect number,** a number equal to the sum of its aliquot parts, as $6 = 1 + 2 + 3,$ $28 = 1 + 2 + 4 + 7 + 14$; **perfect tense,** tense signifying action completed in the past (e.g. I have come back).—**to perfection,** perfectly. [L. *perfectus,* pa.p. of *perficere—per-,* thoroughly, *facēre,* to do.]

perfervid, *pér-fûr'vid,* adj. very fervid: very eager. [L. *perfervidus,* a misreading for *praefervidus—prae,* before, *fervidus,* fervid.]

perfidious, *pér-fid'i-us,* adj. treacherous, basely violating faith.—adv. **perfid'iously.**—ns. **perfid'iousness, per'fidy,** treachery. [L. *perfidiōsus—perfidia,* faithlessness—pfx. *per-,* implying destruction, *fidēs,* faith.]

perfoliate, *pér-fō'li-āt,* adj. (of a leaf) having the base joined round the stem so as to appear pierced by the stem. [L. *per,* through, *folium,* a leaf.]

perforate, *pûr'fó-rāt,* v.t. to bore through or into, to pierce: to make a hole, or holes, or a row of holes, through.—ns. **perfora'tion,** act of boring through: a hole, or row of holes, made by boring; **per'forator,** one who bores: a boring instrument. [L. *perforāre, -ātum—per,* through, *forāre,* to bore.]

perforce, *pér-fōrs', -fôrs',* adv. by force, of necessity. [O.Fr. *par force.*]

perform, *pér-förm',* v.t. to do: to carry out duly: to carry into effect (e.g. a promise, a command): to act.—v.i. to execute an undertaking: to act a part: to play, as on a musical instrument.—adj. **perform'able,** capable of being performed: practicable.—ns. **perform'ance,** act of performing: a carrying out (of something): a piece of work: an exhibition in a theatre or a place of amusement: an act or action: manner of, or success in, working; **perform'er,** one who performs, esp. one who makes a public exhibition of his skill.—adj. **perform'ing,** (of an animal) trained to perform tricks. [Anglo-Fr. *parfourmer,* app.—O.Fr. *parfournir—par* (L. *per*), through, *fournir,* to furnish.]

perfume, *pûr'fūm,* or *pér-fūm',* n. sweet-smelling smoke: fragrance: fluid containing fragrant essential oil, scent.—v.t. (*pér-fūm'* or *pér'fūm*) to scent.—adj. **perfū'matory,** yielding perfume.—ns. **perfū'mer,** a make or seller of perfumes; **perfū'mery,** perfume in general: the art of preparing perfumes, the place (in a shop) where perfumes are sold. [Fr. *parfum*— L. *per,* through, *fūmus,* smoke.]

perfunctory, *pér-fungk'tó-ri,* adj. done merely as a duty: performed carelessly—hasty or super-

Neutral vowels in unaccented syllables: *em'pér-ór*; for certain sounds in foreign words see p. ix.

ficial: acting without zeal or interest. *adv.*
perfunc′torily.—*n.* **perfunc′toriness.** [L. *per-functōrius—perfunctus,* pa.p. of *perfungī,* to execute—*per-,* thoroughly, *fungī,* to do.]

pergola, *pûr′go-la, n.* a structure with climbing plants along a walk. [It.,—L. *pergula,* a shed.]

perhaps, *pėr-haps′, adv.* it may be, possibly. [From the pl. of **hap,** after the model of **per-chance.**]

peri, *pē′ri, n.* a Persian fairy: a beautiful woman. [Pers. *parī,* a fairy.]

peri-, in composition, around [Gr. *peri,* around], e.g. **periosteum** (*pėr-i-os′tė-um*), *n.* a membrane forming the outer coating of a bone (Gr. *osteon,* bone).

perianth, *per′i-anth, n.* (*bot.*) calyx and corolla together, esp. when not clearly distinguishable. [Gr. *peri,* around, *anthos,* a flower.]

pericardium, *per-i-kär′di-um, n.* (*anat.*) the membrane round the heart.—*adjs.* **pericar′diac, pericar′dial, pericar′dian.** [Latinised from Gr. *perikardion—peri,* around, *kardiā,* heart.]

pericarp, *per′i-kärp, n.* (*bot.*) the wall of a fruit if derived from that of the ovary.—*adj.* **peri-carp′ial.** [Gr. *perikarpion—peri,* around, *karpos,* fruit.]

pericranium, *per-i-krā′ni-um, n.* the membrane that surrounds the cranium: loosely, skull or brain. [Latinised from Gr. *perikrānion—peri,* around, *krānion,* skull.]

perigee, *per′i-jē, n.* (*astron.*) the point of the moon's orbit at which it is nearest the earth—opp. to *apogee.* [Gr. *peri,* near, *gē,* the earth.]

perihelion, *per-i-hē′li-on, n.* the point of the orbit of a planet or a comet at which it is nearest to the sun. [Gr. *peri,* near, *hēlios,* the sun.]

peril, *per′il, n.* danger.—*v.t.* to expose to danger.—*pr.p.* per′illing; *pa.t.* and *pa.p.* per′illed.—*adj.* **per′ilous,** dangerous.—*adv.* **per′ilously.**—*n.* **per′ilousness.** [Fr. *péril*—L. *periculum.*]

perimeter, *pėr-im′e-tėr, n.* (*geom.*) the circuit or boundary of any plane figure, or the sum of all its sides: (*mil.*) the boundary of a fortified position: the outer edge of any area.—*adjs.* **perimet′ric, -al.** [Gr. *perimetros—peri,* around, *metron,* measure.]

period, *pē′ri-od, n.* the time in which anything runs its course: the time in which a heavenly body revolves through its orbit: a division of geological time, itself divided into epochs and forming part of an era: a stated and recurring interval of time: an age, a stage or phase in history: a complete sentence, esp. one of elaborate construction: conclusion: (*gram.*) a mark (.) at the end of a sentence, a full stop, the word is inserted at the end of a sentence to emphasise the finality of the statement: menstrual discharge.—*adjs.* **periodic** (*pėr-i-od′ik*), pertaining to a period: of revolution in an orbit: occurring at regular intervals: loosely, occurring from time to time: pertaining to periodicals; **period′ical,** periodic: published in numbers at stated intervals.—*n.* a magazine or other publication that appears at regular intervals.—*adv.* **period′ically.—***n.* **periodicity** (*-dis′-*), the fact or character of being periodic: rhythmic activity: tendency to recur at regular intervals.—**periodic table,** a table of chemical elements in order of atomic number arranged in horizontal series and vertical groups, showing how similar properties recur at regular intervals; **period piece,** an object belonging to a past age but usu. without charm or value: a person ludicrously behind the times: a play, &c. set in a past time. [Fr. *période*—L. *periodus*—Gr. *periodos—peri,* around, *hodos,* a way.]

peripatetic, *per-i-pa-tet′ik, adj.* walking about: going from place to place on business: of or pertaining to the philosophy of Aristotle, who taught while walking up and down in the Lyceum at Athens.—*n.* a pedestrian, an itinerant: (*cap.*) an adherent of the philosophy of Aristotle.—*n.* **peripatet′icism** (*-is-izm*), the philosophy of Aristotle. [Gr. *peripatētikos—peri,* about, *patieen,* to walk.]

periphery, *pėr-if′ėr-i, n.* the bounding line or surface: the outside of anything.—*adj.* **periph′eral.—peripheral units,** in a computer system, the input, output, and storage devices which are computer-controlled. [Gr. *peri,* around, *pherein,* to carry.]

periphrasis, *pėr-if′ra-sis, n.* a round-about expression: the use of more words than are necessary to express an idea:—*pl.* **periph′rases** (*-sēz*).—*adjs.* **periphrastic** (*per-i-fras′tik*), **-al,** containing or expressed by periphrasis or circumlocution.—*adv.* **periphras′tically.** [L.,—Gr. *periphrasis—peri,* about, *phrasis,* speech.]

periscope, *per′i-skōp, n.* a tube with mirrors by which an observer in a trench, submarine, &c., can see what is going on above. [Gr. *peri,* about, *skopeein,* to look at, look about.]

perish, *per′ish, v.i.* to waste away, to decay: to pass away completely: to lose life: to be very uncomfortable or miserable because of (e.g. *they were perished with cold*)—*adj.* **per′ish-able,** that may perish: subject to speedy decay.—*n.* **per′ishableness.—***adv.* **per′ishably.** [O.Fr. *perir,* pr.p. *perissant*—L. *perīre,* to perish—*per-,* 'to the bad', *īre,* to go.]

peristyle, *per′i-stīl, n.* a range of columns round a building or round a square: a court, square, &c., with columns all round. [L. *peristȳl(i)um*—Gr. *peristȳlon—peri,* around, *stȳlos,* a column.]

peritoneum, *per-i-tōn-ē′um, n.* a membrane that encloses the viscera of the abdomen and pelvis.—*n.* **peritoni′tis,** inflammation of the peritoneum. [Gr. *peritonaion—peri,* around, *teinein,* to stretch.]

periwig, *per′i-wig, n.* a peruke, a wig. [Earlier *perwyke, perwig,* &c.—Fr. *perruque.* See **per-uke, wig.**]

periwinkle, *per′i-wingk-l, n.* a creeping evergreen plant, growing in woods. [M.E. *per-uenke*—O.E. *peruince,* from L. *pervinca.*]

periwinkle, *per′i-wingk-l, n.* a genus of small edible shellfish. [O.E. (pl.) *pinewinclan.*]

perjure, *pûr′jūr, v.t.* to forswear (oneself).—*ns.* **per′jurer; per′jury,** false swearing: the breaking of an oath: (*law*) the crime of wilfully giving false evidence on oath. [O.Fr. *parjurer*—L. *perjūrāre—per-, jūrāre,* to swear.]

perk, *pûrk, v.i.* to bear oneself with self-confidence: to recover spirits or energy (with *up*).—*v.t.* to make smart or trim.—*adj.* brisk.—*adj.* **perk'y,** lively, spry.—*adv.* **perk'-ily.**—*n.* **perk'iness.** [Origin unknown.]

perk, *pûrk, n.* abbrev. for **perquisite.**

perm, *pûrm, n.* (*coll.*) an abbrev. of **permutation** and of **permanent wave.**—*v.t.* to permutate: to impart a permanent wave to.

permafrost, *pûr'ma-frost, n.* permanently frozen subsoil. [*perma*nent *frost.*]

permanent, *pûr'mà-nént, adj.* remaining, or intended to remain, indefinitely.—*ns.* **per'manence,** fact or state of being permanent; **per'manency,** permanence: a thing that is permanent.—*adv.* **per'manently.—permanent teeth,** the adult teeth which come after the milk-teeth lost in childhood; **permanent wave** (*coll.* **perm**), an artificial wave in the hair, normally lasting some months; **permanent way,** the finished road of a railway. [L. *per-manēre—per,* through, *manēre,* to continue.]

permanganate, *pér-mang'ga-nāt, n.* a salt of permanganic acid (HMnO$_4$), as the *manganates* are of manganic acid (H$_2$MnO$_4$; not itself isolated)—an oxidising agent, esp. *potassium permanganate.* [*per-*, indicating excess, and **manganese.**]

permeate, *pûr'mé-āt, v.t.* to pass through the pores, or interstices, of: to pervade.—*v.i.* to diffuse itself (through, among).—*n.* **permeā'tion.**—*adj.* **per'meable.**—*n.* **permeabil'ity.** [L. *permeāre—per,* through, *meāre,* to pass.]

Permian, *pûr'mi-án, n.* the last period of the Palaeozoic geological era: the system of rocks formed during that period.—Also *adj.* [*Perm,* province in Russia.]

permit, *pér-mit', v.t.* to allow: to give opportunity.—Also *v.i.* (often followed by *of*):—*pr.p.* permitt'ing; *pa.t.* and *pa.p.* permitt'ed.—*n.* (*pér'mit*) permission, esp. in writing.—*adj.* **permiss'ible,** that may be permitted: allowable.—*adv.* **permiss'ibly.**—*n.* **permiss'ion,** act of permitting: leave.—*adj.* **permiss'ive,** granting permission or liberty: not prohibited: allowing much freedom in social conduct (as in the **permissive society**—from c. 1960).—*adv.* **permiss'ively.** [L. *permittěre, -missum,* to let pass through—*per,* through, *mittěre,* to send.]

permutable, *pér-mūt'á-bl, adj.* interchangeable.—*v.t.* **per'mutate,** to subject to permutation.—*n.* **permūtā'tion,** act of changing one thing for another: (*math.*) the arrangement of a set of things in every possible order: any one order of a set of things: a forecast of a specified number of results from a larger number of matches based on some defined system of combination or permutation: any such system. [L. *permūtāre—per-, mūtāre,* to change.]

pernicious, *pér-nish'ús, adj.* destructive: highly injurious.—*adv.* **perni'ciously.**—*n.* **perni'ciousness.** [L. *perniciōsus—per-,* completely, *nex, necis,* death by violence.]

pernickety, *pér-nik'é-ti, adj.* fussy, fastidious. [Scots; origin unknown.]

peroration, *per-ō-rā'sh(ó)n, n.* the conclusion of a speech: a rhetorical performance. [L. *per-ōrātiō—perōrāre,* to bring a speech to an end—*per,* through, *ōrāre,* to speak.]

peroxide, *pér-oks'īd, n.* an oxide whose molecules contain two atoms of oxygen linked

together: (*coll.*) hydrogen peroxide.—*v.t.* to treat or bleach with hydrogen peroxide. [*per-,* indicating excess, and **oxygen.**]

perpend, *pér-pend', v.t.* to weigh in the mind, to consider carefully. [L. *perpenděre—per-,* thoroughly, *penděre,* to weigh.]

perpendicular, *pér-pén-dik'ū-lár, adj.* upright: erect: vertical: (*geom.*) at right angles to a given line or surface: (*archit.*) of the latest style of English Gothic (q.v.) remarkable for the use of slender pillars and vertical lines.—*n.* a perpendicular line or plane.—*n.* **perpendicular'ity,** state of being perpendicular.—*adv.* **perpendic'ularly.** [L. *perpendiculāris—perpendiculum,* a plumb-line—*per-,* completely, *penděre,* to hang.]

perpetrate, *pûr'pé-trāt, v.t.* to execute or commit (esp. an offence), or (jocularly) to make (e.g. a poem, a pun).—*ns.* **perpetrā'tion; per'petrātor.** [L. *perpetrāre, -ātum—per-,* thoroughly, *patrāre,* to perform.]

perpetual, *pér-pet'ū-ál, adj.* never ceasing: everlasting: (*coll.*) very frequent.—*adv.* **perpet'ually.—perpetual motion,** the never-ceasing motion (imagined but mechanically impossible) of a machine which, once set a-going, would supply its own motive forces and require no energy from without. [L. *perpetu-ālis—perpetuus,* continuous.]

perpetuate, *pér-pet'ū-āt, v.t.* to preserve from extinction or oblivion, give continued existence to: to pass on, cause to continue to be believed, known, &c.—*ns.* **perpetuā'tion,** continuation or preservation for ever, or for a very long time; **perpetū'ity,** state of being perpetual: endless time: duration for an indefinite period: something lasting for ever: the sum paid for a perpetual annuity. [L. *perpetuāre, -ātum—perpetuus,* perpetual.]

perplex, *pér-pleks', v.t.* to embarrass, puzzle, bewilder: to complicate (e.g. a problem, a situation): (*lit.*) to interweave, to tangle.—*n.* **perplex'ity,** state of being perplexed: confusion of mind, doubt: intricacy. [Fr.,—L. *perplexus,* entangled—*per-,* completely, *plexus,* involved, pa.p. of *plectěre.*]

perquisite, *pûr'kwi-zit, n.* any casual profit from one's employment in addition to salary or wages: anything left over that a servant or other has by custom a right to keep. [L. *perquīsītum,* from *perquīrěre,* to seek diligently—pfx. *per-,* thoroughly, *quaerěre,* to ask.]

perruque. See **peruke.**

perry, *per'i, n.* a drink made from pears. [O.Fr. *peré*—L. *pirum,* a pear.]

persecute, *pûr'sé-kūt, v.t.* to harass, afflict, hunt down, or put to death, esp. for religious or political opinions: to worry continually, to importune.—*ns.* **persecū'tion; per'secutor.** [L. *persequī, persecūtus*—pfx. *per-,* thoroughly, *sequī,* to follow.]

persevere, *pér-sé-vēr', v.i.* to continue steadfastly, esp. in face of discouragement.—*n.* **persevē'rance,** act or state of persevering.—*adj.* **persevē'ring.**—*adv.* **persevē'ringly.** [Fr. *persévérer*—L. *persevērāre—persevērus,* very strict—pfx. *per-,* very, *sevērus,* strict.]

Persian, *pûr'sh(y)án, -zh(y)án, adj.* of, from, or relating to Persia, its inhabitants, or language.—*n.* a native of Persia: the language of

Neutral vowels in unaccented syllables: *em'pér-ór*; for certain sounds in foreign words see p. ix.

Persia.—**Persian blinds** (also **persiennes**—
per-syen; Fr. fem. pl. of adj. *persien*), outside
shutters of thin movable slats in a frame;
Persian carpet, a rich, soft carpet of the kind
woven in Persia; **Persian cat,** a kind of cat
with long silky hair and bushy tail; **Persian
wheel,** a large undershot wheel for raising
water.

persiflage, *per-si-fläzh, n.* banter, flippancy.
[Fr.,—*persifler,* to banter—L. *per,* through, Fr.
siffler—L. *sībilāre,* to whistle, to hiss.]

persimmon, *pèr-sim'on, n.* any of a genus of
trees (known also as *date-plum*) of the ebony
family, or their fruit, esp. the Virginian date-
plum. [From an Amer. Indian word.]

persist, *pèr-sist', v.i.* to continue steadfastly or
obstinately, in spite of opposition or warning:
to persevere: to last, endure.—*ns.* **persis'tence,
persis'tency,** quality of being persistent: persistent methods: doggedness, obstinacy: duration, esp. of an effect after the exciting cause
has been removed.—*adj.* **persis'tent,** persisting: constantly recurring or long-continued
(e.g. efforts): (*zool.* and *bot.*) remaining after
the usual time of falling off, withering, or
disappearing.—*advs.* **persis'tently; persis't-
ingly.** [L. *persistĕre*—*per,* through, *sistĕre,*
to cause to stand, to stand—*stāre,* to stand.]

person, *pûr'son, n.* (*arch.*) assumed character,
as on the stage (*in the person of*): an individual human being: an individual (used
slightingly): (*obs.*) a personage: the outward
appearance, living body (exclusive or inclusive of clothing) of a human being: a living
soul: one of three modes of being of the Godhead (Father, Son, and Holy Spirit): (*law*) a
corporation regarded as having the rights and
duties of an individual human being: (*gram.*)
a form of inflexion or use of a word according
as it or its subject represents the person(s) or
thing(s) speaking (*first person*), spoken to
(*second*), or spoken about (*third*).—*n.* **persona** (*pèr-son'a*), character in fiction, esp. in
drama: social façade or public image.—*adj.*
personable (*pèr'son-a-bl*), of good appearance.—*n.* **per'sonage,** a person: an exalted or
august person: a character in a play or
story.—*adj.* **per'sonal,** of the nature of a person as opposed to a thing or an abstraction: of,
relating to, belonging to, or affecting the individual, the self (e.g. convenience, luggage):
exclusively for a given individual (e.g. letter):
performed, &c., in person (e.g. service, interview): pertaining to or affecting the person or
body (e.g. charm, injury): aimed offensively at
a particular person or persons (e.g. abuse,
remark): making, or given to making, personal remarks: (of telephone call) made to a
particular person (timed only from the moment that the named person is contacted, but
subject to an initial fixed charge): (*law*) of
property or estate, opp. to *real*—denoting all
property except land and those interests in
land that pass on the owner's death to his
heir: (*gram.*) indicating person.—*v.t.* **per'son-
alise,** to personify: to apply to, or take as
referring to, a definite person: to give a mark
or quality to (something) so that it is ident-
ifiable as belonging to a particular person.—
adv. **per'sonally,** in person: as a person: for

(my, his, &c.) own part.—*n.* **personal'ity,** fact
or state of being a person as opposed to a
thing or an abstraction: (*psych.*) the totality
of an individual's characteristics (psychological, intellectual, emotional, and physical), esp.
as they are presented to other people: distinctive or well-marked character: direct reference to, or an utterance aimed at, a particular
person or persons, esp. of a derogatory
nature.—*n.* **per'sonalty** (*law*), same as **personal estate, property** (see *adj.* **personal**
above).—*v.t.* **per'sonate,** to assume the likeness or character of, esp. for fraudulent purposes: to play the part of.—*ns.* **persona'tion;
per'sonātor; personnel'** (Fr.), the persons
employed in any service, as distinguished
from the *matériel* (equipment, supplies, &c.).
—**in person,** by one's own act, not by an agent
or representative; **personal equation** (see
equation); **personal identity,** the continued
sameness of the individual person through
all changes, as testified by consciousness;
personality cult, excessive adulation of a
prominent individual; **personal security,**
pledge given by a person, as distinguished
from the delivery of some object of value
as security; **personal service,** delivery of a
message or an order into a person's hands
directly: attention of the owner of a concern
rather than that of one of his employees. [L.
persōna, a player's mask, player, personage,
person, perh. from Etruscan *phersu,* masked
figures, commonly associated (in spite of
difference of quantity) with *personāre, -ātum*
—*per,* through, *sonāre,* to sound; cf. **parson.**]

persona grata, *pèr-sō'na grä'ta,* an acceptable
person, one welcomed with pleasure—*opp.*
persona non grata. [L.]

personify, *pèr-son'i-fī, v.t.* to represent as a person: to ascribe personality to: to be the embodiment of;—*pa.t* and *pa.p.* person'ified. *n.*
personifica'tion. [L. *persōna,* a person, *facĕre,*
to make. See **personal.**]

personnel. See **person.**

perspective, *pèr-spek'tiv, n.* the art or science of
drawing solid objects on a plane or curved
surface as they appear to the eye: appearance,
or representation of appearance, of objects in
space, with effect of distance, solidity, &c.:
just proportion in all the parts: ability to view
things (*lit.* and *fig.*) in just proportion: a picture in perspective: a vista: a prospect of the
future.—*adj.* pertaining or according to perspective.—**in perspective,** according to the
laws of perspective: (*fig.*) in just relationship,
with the important and the unimportant
things in their proper places. [L. (*ars*) *per-
spectiva,* perspective (art)—*perspicĕre, per-
spectum*—*per,* through, *specĕre,* to look.]

perspicacious, *pèr-spi-kā'shùs, adj.* (*arch.*)
clear-sighted: having clear mental vision or
discernment.—*adv.* **perspica'ciously.**—*n.* **per-
spicacity** (*-kas'i-ti*). [L. *perspicāx, -ācis*—*perspicĕre.* See **perspective.**]

perspicuous, *pèr-spik'ū-us, adj.* clearly expressed, clear: (of a person) lucid, expressing
himself clearly.—*adv.* **perspic'ūously.**—*ns.*
perspic'ūousness, perspicū'ity. [L. *perspi-
cuus*—*perspicĕre.* See **perspective.**]

perspire, *pèr-spīr', v.i.* to sweat: to exude moisture.—*v.t.* to exhale.—*n.* **perspiration** (-*spir-ā'sh(ó)n*), act of perspiring: sweat.—*adj.* **perspīr'atory**. [L. *perspīrāre*, *-ātum*—*per*, through, *spīrāre*, to breathe.]

persuade, *pér-swād'*, *v.t.* to induce by argument, advice, &c. (*to* do, *into* doing something): to convince.—*n.* **persuad'er.**—*adj.* **persuas'ible,** capable of being persuaded.—*ns.* **persuasibility** (*-swāz-i-bil'i-ti*); **persuasion** (*-swā'zh(ó)n*), act of persuading: settled opinion: a creed: a sect adhering to a creed.—*adj.* **persuasive** (*-swāz'-*), having the power to persuade: influencing the mind or passions.—*adv.* **persua'sively.**—*n.* **persua'siveness.**—*adj.* **persuas'ory,** persuasive. [L. *persuādēre, -suāsum* —pfx. *per-*, throughly, *suādēre*, to advise.]

pert, *pûrt, adj.* saucy, presumingly free in speech or conduct: (now *dial.* and *U.S.*) sprightly.—*adv.* **pert'ly.**—*n.* **pert'ness.** [Shortened from *apert*—L. *aperīre, apertum*, to open.]

pertain, *pér-tān', v.i.* to belong as a characteristic quality, function, concern, &c. (with *to*): to be appropriate (to): to relate (to).—*ns.* **per'tinence, per'tinency,** state of being pertinent or to the point.—*adj.* **per'tinent,** pertaining or related to a subject: relevant: apposite.—*n.* (usu. in *pl.*) appurtenances.—*adv.* **per'tinently.** [O.Fr. *partenir*—L. *pertinēre*— pfx. *per-*, thoroughly, *tenēre*, to hold.]

pertinacious, *pér-ti-nā'shús, adj.* (usu. as a bad quality) holding obstinately to an opinion or a purpose, persistent.—*adv.* **pertinā'ciously.**—*ns.* **pertinā'ciousness, pertinacity** (*-nas'i-ti*), quality of being pertinacious: obstinacy. [L. *pertināx, -ācis,* holding fast—pfx. *per-*, thoroughly, *tenāx,* tenacious—*tenēre,* to hold.]

perturb, *pér-tûrb', v.t.* to disturb greatly: to agitate.—*n.* **perturbā'tion,** state of being perturbed: disquiet of mind: (*astron.*) a deviation of a heavenly body from its theoretically regular orbit.—**perturbation theory,** a mathematical method of determining the effect of small local changes on the behaviour of a system. [L. *perturbāre, -ātum*—pfx. *per-*, thoroughly, *turbāre,* to disturb—*turba,* a crowd.]

peruke, perruque, *pér-ōōk', n.* a wig. [Fr. *perruque*—It. *parrucca*; connection with L. *pīlus,* hair, very doubtful.]

peruse, *pér-ōōz', v.t.* to read attentively: (*fig.*) to examine in detail (e.g. a face).—*ns.* **perus'al,** a careful reading; **perus'er.** [L. pfx. *per-*, thoroughly, *ūtī, ūsus,* to use.]

Peruvian, *pér-ōō'vi-án, adj.* of *Peru* in South America.—*n.* a native of Peru.—**Peruvian bark,** cinchona (q.v.) bark.

pervade, *pér-vād', v.t.* (*rare*) to pass through: to diffuse or extend through the whole of (usu. *fig.,* e.g. of an influence).—*adj.* **perva'sive** (*-vā'-ziv*), tending or having power to pervade. [L. *pervādēre*—*per,* through, *vādēre,* to go.]

perverse, *pér-vûrs', adj.* turned aside from right or truth: obstinate in the wrong: capricious and unreasonable in opposition.—*adv.* **perverse'ly.**—*ns.* **perverse'ness; perversion** (*-vér'sh(ó)n*), a turning from truth or propriety: a diversion to a wrong end or use: a perverted or corrupted form of anything (e.g. of the truth): a misdirection of the sex instinct, which finds gratification in abnormal ways, e.g. in sadism; **pervers'ity.**—*v.t.* **pervert',** to turn aside, derange (e.g. the ends of justice, the course of justice): to turn (a person) from truth or virtue: to misinterpret or misapply (e.g. words), esp. on purpose.—*ns.* **per'vert,** one who has abandoned the doctrine assumed to be true—opp. of *convert*: one suffering from derangement of the sex instinct; **pervert'er.** [Partly through Fr.—L. *pervertēre, perversum*—pfx. *per-*, thoroughly, wrongly, *vertēre,* to turn.]

pervious, *pûr'vi-us, adj.* permeable, penetrable. —*adv.* **per'viously.**—*n.* **per'viousness.** [L. *pervius*—*per,* through, *via,* a way.]

peseta, *pe-sā'tä, n.* a Spanish silver coin. [Sp. dim. of *pesa,* weight.]

pesky, *pes'ki, adj.* (*coll.,* esp. *U.S.*) vexatious.

peso, *pā'sō, n.* coin of various values in S. and Central America. [Sp.—L. *pēnsum,* weight.]

pessimism, *pes'i-mizm, n.* (*phil.*) the doctrine that the world is bad rather than good: a temper of mind that looks on the dark side of things: (loosely) despondency, hopelessness—opp. of *optimism.*—*n.* **pess'imist,** one who holds the doctrine of pessimism: one who looks too much on the dark side of things.— *adjs.* **pessimis'tic, -al.** [L. *pessimus,* worst.]

pest, *pest, n.* (now *rare*) any deadly epidemic disease, esp. plague: anything destructive (as, an insect, a fungus, &c., that destroys cultivated plants): a troublesome person.—*ns.* **pest'house,** a hospital for plague, &c; **pesticide** (*pes'ti-sīd*), a pest killer (L. *caedēre,* to kill).—*adjs.* **pesticīd'al; pestif'erous.**—*n.* **pest'ilence,** any deadly epidemic disease.—*adjs.* **pest'ilence-strick'en; pest'ilent,** producing pestilence: hurtful to health and life: injurious to morals, endangering peace, &c.: (*coll.*) annoying, troublesome.—Also **pestilential** (*-len'shäl*).—*ns.* **pestol'ogy,** the study of agricultural pests and of methods of combating them; **pestol'ogist.** [Fr. *peste* and *pestilence*— L. *pestis, pestilentia.*]

pester, *pes'tér, v.t.* (*arch.*) to crowd thickly: to annoy persistently. [App. from O.Fr. *empestrer* (Fr.*empêtrer*), to entangle, from L.*in,* in, Low L. *pāstōrium,* a foot-shackle for a horse—L. *pāstus,* pa.p. of *pāscēre,* to feed; influenced by **pest.**]

pestle, *pes'l,* also *pest'l, n.* an instrument for pounding (e.g. in a mortar).—*v.t.* to pound.— *v.i.* to use a pestle. [O.Fr. *pestel*—L. *pistillum,* a pounder, *pinsēre, pistum,* to pound.]

pet,*pet, n.* a cherished tame animal: an indulged favourite: used as an endearment.—*adj.* kept as a pet: indulged: cherished: favourite.—*v.t.* to treat as a pet: to fondle:—*v.i.* (*coll.*) to indulge in amorous caressing:—*pr.p.* pett'ing; *pa.t.* and *pa.p.* pett'ed.—**pet aversion,** chief object of dislike; **pet name,** a name used in familiar affection. [Origin unknown; not from Gael.]

pet,*pet, n.* a slight or childish fit of aggrieved or resentful sulkiness, huff.—*adj.* **pett'ish,** peevish, sulky.—*adv.* **pett'ishly.**—*n.* **pett'ishness.**

petal, *pet'ál, n.* a corolla leaf.—*adjs.* **petaline** (*pet'ál-īn*), of or like a petal; **pet'alled,** having petals; **pet'aloid,** having the appearance of a petal. [Gr. *petalon,* a leaf.]

Neutral vowels in unaccented syllables: *em'pér-ór*; for certain sounds in foreign words see p. ix.

petard, *pe-tär(d)'*, *n.* a case containing an explosive, used formerly for blowing in doors, &c.—**hoist with one's own petard** (see **hoise**). [O.Fr.—*péter*, to crack or explode—L. *pēdĕre*, to break wind.]

peter, *pē'tér*, *v.i.* (*coll.*) to dwindle away to nothing, be dissipated or exhausted (with *out*). [U.S. mining slang; origin unknown.]

Peter Pan, *pē'tér pan'*, a character in J. M. Barrie's play of that name (1904): the type of person who never grows up.

petersham, *pē'tér-sham*, *n.* a heavy corded ribbon used for belts, hat-bands, &c.: a heavy overcoat or breeches once fashionable: the material used for these. [From Lord *Petersham*.]

Peter's-pence. See **penny**.

petiole, *pet'i-ōl*, *n.* (*bot.*) a leaf-stalk: (*zool.*) a stalk-like structure. [L. *petiolus*, a little foot, a petiole.]

petit, *pĕ-tē*, *adj.* little:—*fem.* **petite** (*pé-tēt*), used esp. to mean 'small and neat in figure'.—**petit bourgeois**, member of the **petite bourgeoisie**, the lower middle class. [Fr.]

petition, *pe-tish'(ŏ)n*, *n.* a formal request to an authority (e.g. to the sovereign, to parliament, or to a court of law): (*obs.*) a parliamentary bill: a written supplication signed by a number of persons: a prayer.—*v.t.* to address a petition to: to ask someone (*for* something, *to* do something).—*adj.* **peti'tionary**.—*ns.* **peti'tioner**; **peti'tioning**. [L. *petītiō*, *-ōnis*—*petĕre*, to ask.]

petre (*coll.*), short for **saltpetre.**

petrel, *pet'rél*, *n.* any of a number of dark-coloured sea-birds akin to the albatrosses and fulmars, esp. the **storm** (popularly **stormy**) **petrel** (see **storm**). [L. *Petrus*, Peter, from its seeming to walk on water; see Matt. xiv. 29.]

petrify, *pet'ri-fī*, *v.t.* to turn into stone: to make hard like a stone: to fix in amazement, horror, &c.—*v.i.* to become stone, or hard like stone:—*pr.p.* **pet'rifying**; *pa.t.* and *pa.p.* **pet'rified**.—*n.* **petrifac'tion**, turning or being turned into stone: a petrified object: a fossil.—*adjs.* **petrifac'tive**, **petrif'ic**, petrifying. [L. *petra*—Gr. *petra*, rock, L. *facĕre*, *factum*, to make.]

petro-, in composition, stone: e.g. **petroglyph** (*pet'rō-glif*; Gr. *glyphein*, to carve), *n.* a rock-carving, esp. prehistoric; **petrography** (*pe-trog'-ra-fi*; Gr. *graphein*, to write), *n.* petrology; **petrology** (*pe-trol'ō-ji*; Gr. *logos*, discourse), *n.* the science of the origin, chemical and mineral composition and structure, and alteration of rocks. [Gr. *petra*, rock.]

petrochemical, *pet-rō-kem'i-kál*, *n.* any chemical obtained from *petro*leum.

petrol, *pet'rol*, *-ról*, *n.* formerly petroleum: now a spirit obtained from petroleum, used for driving motor-cars, aeroplanes, &c.—*n.* **petroleum** (*pē-trō'lé-um*), a mixture of fuel oils got from oil-wells.—**petroleum jelly** (or *soft paraffin*), a mixture of petroleum hydrocarbons used in emollients, as a lubricant, &c.; **petrol pump**, machine for transferring measured amounts of petrol to motor vehicles; **petrol station**, filling station. [L. *petra*, rock, *oleum*, oil.]

petticoat, *pet'i-kōt*, *n.* (*orig.*) a short or small coat: an under-skirt.—*adj.* **pett'icoated.**—**petticoat government**, domination by women.

[petty, coat.]

pettifogger, *pet'i-fog-ér*, *n.* a lawyer who practises only in paltry cases, esp. one whose methods are mean and tricky: a petty practitioner of any kind.—*n.* **pett'ifoggery**, mean tricks: quibbles.—*adj.* **pett'ifogging**. [petty; origin of second part obscure.]

petty, *pet'i*, *adj.* of small importance, trivial: of inferior status, minor: small-minded.—*adv.* **pett'ily.**—*n.* **pett'iness.**—**petty cash**, miscellaneous small sums of money received or paid; **petty larceny** (see **larceny**); **petty officer**, a naval officer ranking with a non-commissioned officer in the army; **petty sessions**, a court in which magistrates try trivial cases, referring others to a higher court. [Fr. *petit*, little, inconsiderable.]

petulant, *pet'ū-lánt*, *adj.* showing peevish impatience, irritation, or caprice: (*rare*) forward, impudent in manner.—*ns.* **pet'ulance**, **pet'ulancy.**—*adv.* **pet'ulantly**. [L. *petulāns*, *-antis*, as from assumed *petulāre*, dim. of *petĕre*, to seek.]

petunia, *pe-tū'ni-a*, *n.* a genus of South American ornamental plants, near akin to tobacco. [South American Indian *petun*, tobacco.]

pew, *pū*, *n.* an enclosed compartment or fixed bench in a church: (*slang*) a seat.—*n.* **pew'-opener**, an attendant who shows strangers to pews. [O.Fr. *puie*, raised place, balcony—L. *podia*, pl. of *podium*—Gr. *podion*, dim. of *pous*, gen. *podos*, foot.]

pewit, *pē'wit*, *pū'it*. Same as **peewit.**

pewter, *pū'tér*, *n.* an alloy of tin and lead: sometimes tin with a little copper and antimony: vessels made of pewter.—Also *adj.*—*n.* **pew'terer**, one who works in pewter. [O.Fr. *peutre*; cf. It. *peltro*, Low Ger. *spialter*, Eng. **spelter.**]

pH. See **pH (value).**

phaeton, *fā'(i-)tn*, *n.* an open four-wheeled carriage for one or two horses, named after *Phaethon*, who was allowed to drive the chariot of the sun for one day. [Gr. *Phaethōn*, *-ontos*, lit. shining, cf. *phaos*, *phōs*, light.]

phage. Short for **bacteriophage.**

phagocyte, *fag'ō-sīt*, *n.* a white blood corpuscle that engulfs harmful bacteria and other particles. [Gr. *phagein*, to eat, *kytos*, a vessel.]

phalanger, *fal-an'jér*, *n.* any one of a group of small arboreal Australasian marsupials. [Gr. *phalangion*, spider's web, from their webbed toes.]

phalanx, *fal'angks* (or *fāl'-*), *n.* a solid formation of ancient Greek heavy-armed infantry: a solid body of men, &c.: a solid body of supporters or partisans:—*pl.* **phal'anxes**; also (*biol.*) **phalanges** (*fal-an'jēz*), the bones of the fingers and toes.—*n.* **Phalan'gist**, a Spanish Fascist. [Gr. *phalanx*, *-angos*, a roller, phalanx, spider.]

phalarope, *fal'a-rōp*, *n.* a genus of wading birds with coot-like feet. [Gr. *phalāris*, a coot, *pous*, a foot.]

phanerogam, *fan'ér-ō-gam*, *n.* a flowering plant, a plant producing seeds—opp. to *cryptogam* (q.v.).—*adjs.* **phanerogam'ic**; **phanerog'amous.** [Gr. *phaneros*, visible, *gamos*, marriage.]

phantasm, *fan'tazm*, *n.* a product of fantasy: a

spectre: a supposed vision of an absent person, living or dead: an illusive likeness (of):—*pl.* **phan'tasms, phantas'mata.**—*adjs.* **phantas'mal; phantas'mic, -al.** See **phantom.** [Gr. *phantasma*—*phantazein,* to make visible—*phainein,* to bring to light—*phaein,* to shine.]

phantasmagoria, *fan-taz-ma-gō'ri-a, -gŏ'-, n.* a fantastic series of images, produced by mechanical means, seen in a dream, or called up by the imagination: something that presents itself to the mind in the form of shifting scenes consisting of many elements.—*adjs.* **phantasmagō'rial, phantasmagŏr'ic, -al.** [Gr. *phantasma,* an appearance, *agorā,* assembly.]

phantasy, phantastic. Same as **fantasy, fantastic.**

phantom, *fan'tóm, n.* an apparition, a spectre: an immaterial form, a vision: a deceitful appearance: a show without reality.—Also *adj.* See **phantasm.** [O.Fr. *fantosme* — Gr. *phantasma.*]

Pharaoh, *fā'rō, n.* a title of the kings of ancient Egypt.

Pharisee, *far'i-sē, n.* one of a religious school among the Jews, marked by their strict observance of the law and of religious ordinances (cf. *Sadducee*): anyone more careful of the outward forms than of the spirit of religion: a very self-righteous or hypocritical person.—*adjs.* **pharisā'ic, -al,** pertaining to, or like, the Pharisees: hypocritical.—*adv.* **pharisā'ically.** —*ns.* **pharisā'icalness; phar'isāism** (also **phar'iseeism**). [O.E. *phariseus* — Late L. *pharisaeus* — Gr. *pharisaios* — Heb. *pārūsh,* separated.]

pharmaceutic, -al, *făr-ma-sū'tik* (or *-kū'tik*),*-ál, adj.* pertaining to the knowledge or art of preparing medicines.—*ns.* **pharmaceutical,** a chemical used in medicine; **pharmaceu'tics,** the science of preparing medicines; **pharmaceū'tist.** [Gr. *pharmakeutikos.*]

pharmacopoeia, *făr-ma-kō-pē'-(y)a, n.* a book or list of drugs with directions for their preparation: a stock of drugs. [Gr. *pharmakopoiiā*—*pharmakon,* a drug, *poieein,* to make.]

pharmacy, *făr'má-si, n.* the art of preparing and mixing medicines: a druggist's shop.—*ns.* **phar'macist,** a druggist, one skilled in pharmacy; **pharmacol'ogy,** the science of pharmacy. [Gr. *pharmakon,* a drug.]

pharos, *fā'ros, n.* a lighthouse or beacon.—Also **phare.** [From the famous lighthouse on the island of *Pharos* in the Bay of Alexandria.]

pharynx, *far'ingks, n.* the portion of the alimentary canal that intervenes between the mouth cavity and the oesophagus.—*adjs.* **pharyngal** (*fa-ring'gál*), **pharyngeal** (*fa-rin'ji-ál*).—*n.* **pharyngitis** (*far-in-jī'tis*), inflammation of the, mucous membrane of the pharynx. [Gr. *pharynx, -yngos.*]

phase, *fāz, n.* the appearance of the moon or a planet at a given time according to the amount of illuminated surface exhibited: any transitory state or stage in a regularly recurring cycle of changes: a separate and homogeneous part of a heterogeneous system (e.g. the solid, the liquid and the gaseous phase of water): a stage in a development (e.g. in a career): an aspect of a thing of varying appearance, or of a problem or situation:—*pl.*

phases.—*v.t.* to do by phases or stages.—*adj.* **phased,** adjusted to be in the same phase at the same time: by stages.—**phase-contrast, -difference, microscope,** a microscope in which clearer detail is obtained by means of a device that alters the speed of some of the rays of light coming from the object.—**phase out,** to cease gradually to use, make, &c. [Gr. *phasis*—*phaein,* to shine.]

pheasant, *fez'(á)nt, n.* a genus of richly coloured, gallinaceous, half-wild game-birds in Britain: the birds as food.—*n.* **pheas'antry,** an enclosure for rearing pheasants. [Anglo-Fr. *fesant* — L. *phāsiānus* — Gr. *Phāsiānos* (*ornis,* bird), from the river Phasis (now Rioni) in Georgia, Asia.]

phenacetin, *fen-as'it-in, n.* a colourless crystalline substance used to decrease fever and to dispel headaches and other pains [*phen(o)-*] (Gr. *phainos,* shining), used of substances derived from benzene, *acetyl,* the radical of acetic acid, and *-in.*]

phenobarbitone, *fē-nō-bär'bi-tōn, n.* a sedative and hypnotic drug.

phenomenon, *fé-nom'é-nón,* or *-non, n.* anything directly apprehended by the senses or by one of them: any fact or event that may be observed in nature or in the realm of a science: (loosely) a remarkable or unusual person, thing, or appearance: something as it is perceived (not necessarily as it really is):—*pl.* **phenom'ena.**—*adj.* **phenom'enal,** known through the senses, perceptible, sensible: dealing with observed data: very unusual or remarkable.—*adv.* **phenom'enally.** [Gr. *phainomenon*—*phainein,* to show.]

phenotype, *fēn'ō-tīp, n.* the observable characteristics of an organism produced by the interaction of genes and environment: a group of individuals having the same characteristics of this kind. [Gr. *phainein,* to show, and **type.**]

phew, *fū, interj.* exclamation of disgust, relief.

phial, *fī'ál, n.* a vessel for liquids, esp. now a small medicine-bottle. [L. *phiala* — Gr. *phialē,* a broad shallow bowl.]

phil-, philo-, *fil-, -ō-,* in composition, loving, friend [Gr. *phileein,* to love, *philos,* loved, loving]:—e.g. **philharmonic** (*fil-här-mon'ik*), *adj.* loving music (Gr. *harmoniā,* harmony); **philomath** (*fil'ō-math*), *n.* a lover of learning: a student, esp. of mathematics (Gr. *math-,* root of *manthanein,* to learn); **philoprogenitive** (*fil-ō-prō-jen'i-tiv*), *adj.* loving one's offspring (L. *progeniēs,* progeny).

philander, *fil-an'dér, v.i.* to make love, esp. in a trifling manner: to be in the habit of so doing.—*n.* **philan'derer.** [Gr. *philandros,* fond of men or of a husband—*phileein,* to love, *anēr,* gen. *andros,* a man, husband; misapplied as if meaning a loving man.]

philanthropy, *fil-an'thró-pi, n.* love of mankind, esp. as shown in services to general welfare.—*n.* **philan'thropist,** one who tries to benefit mankind.—*adjs.* **philanthrop'ic** (*-throp'ik*), **-al,** doing good to others, benevolent.—*adv.* **philanthrop'ically.** [Gr. *philanthrōpiā*—*phileein,* to love, *anthrōpos,* a man.]

philately, *fil-at'é-li, n.* the study and collection of postage and revenue stamps and labels.—*adj.* **philatel'ic.**—*n.* **philat'elist.** [Fr. *philatélie,* in-

Neutral vowels in unaccented syllables: *em'pér-ór*; for certain sounds in foreign words see p. ix.

vented in 1864—Gr. *phileein*, to love, *atelēs*, tax-free—*a-* (privative), *telos*, tax.]

philibeg. See **filibeg.**

Philippian, *fil-ip'i-án, n.* a native of *Philippi* in Macedonia.

philippic, *fil-ip'ik, n.* one of the three orations of Demosthenes against Philip of Macedon: any discourse full of invective. [Gr. *philippikos, philippizein*—*Philippos,* Philip.]

Philistine, *fil'is-tīn, n.* one of the ancient inhabitants of south-west Palestine, enemies of the Israelites: a person indifferent to culture, whose interests are material and whose ideas are ordinary and conventional. *n.* **Phil'istinism.** [*Philistīnos*—Heb. *P'lishtīm.*]

philology, *fil-ol'ō-ji, n.* the science of language, which concerns itself with the sounds of speech, the history of sound changes, etymology, grammar, the history of inflections, &c.: (*orig.*) the study of the classical languages of Greece and Rome.—*n.* **philol'ogist,** one versed in philology.—*adjs.* **philolog'ic, -al.** [Gr. *philologiā*—*philos,* loving, *logos,* word.]

philomel, *fil'ō-mel,* **philomela,** *-mē'la, n.* the nightingale. [Gr. *Philomēla,* who was changed into a nightingale or swallow.]

philosopher, *fil-os'o-fér, n.* a lover of wisdom: one versed in or devoted to philosophy: a metaphysician: one who acts calmly and rationally in the affairs and changes of life.—*adjs.* **philosoph'ic** (*-sof'-, -zof'-*), **-al,** pertaining, or according, to philosophy: skilled in or given to philosophy: befitting a philosopher, rational, temperate, calm (of outlook, behaviour, &c.).—*adv.* **philosoph'ically.** —*v.i.* **philos'ophise,** to reason like a philosopher: to form philosophical theories.—*ns.* **philos'ophiser,** a would-be philosopher; **philos'ophism,** would-be philosophy; **philos'ophist.** *adjs.* **philosophist'ic, -al.**—*n.* **philos'ophy,** orig. all learning excluding only the practical arts: in the Middle Ages, one of the three branches of higher learning, which were *natural philosophy* (knowledge of natural phenomena), *moral philosophy* (study of the principles of human conduct), and *metaphysical philosophy* (metaphysics): now, the moral and metaphysical branches, or, more usually, metaphysics alone (see **metaphysics**): a particular philosophical system (as, *the Platonic philosophy*): the principles underlying any department of knowledge (as, *the philosophy of history*): an individual's view of life or system of conduct: serenity and resignation.—**philosopher's stone,** a substance sought after by alchemists as a means of transforming other metals into gold. [Gr. *phileein,* to love, *sophiā,* wisdom.]

philtre, philter, *fil'tér, n.* a drink or (rarely) a spell to excite love. [Fr. *philtre*—L. *philtrum*—Gr. *philtron*—*phileein,* to love, suffx. *-tron,* denoting the agent.]

phlebitis, *flē-bī'tis, n.* inflammation of a vein.—*n.* **phlebot'omy,** blood-letting. [Gr. *phleps,* gen. *phlebos,* a vein.]

phlegm, *flem, n.* a substance secreted by the mucous membranes, esp. when morbid or excessive, in particular the thick, slimy matter secreted in the throat, and discharged by coughing—regarded in old physiology as one (cold and moist) of the four humours or bodily fluids: the temperament supposed to be due to its predominance, sluggish indifference: calmness.—*adjs.* **phlegmatic** (*fleg-mat'-ik*), **-al.** [By later return to Greek spelling, from M.E. *fleme,* &c., through O.Fr. from L. *phlegma*—Gr. *phlegma, -atos,* flame, inflammation, phlegm (regarded as produced by heat).]

phloem, *flō'em, n.* the conducting tissue present in vascular plants, chiefly concerned with the transport of elaborated food materials about the plant. [Gr. *phloos,* bark.]

phlogiston, *flo-jis'ton, n.* an imaginary element, believed in the 18th century to separate from every combustible body in burning. [Gr. neut. of verbal adj. *phlogistos,* burnt, inflammable—*phlogizein,* to set on fire.]

phlox, *floks, n.* a genus of garden plants with flat-shaped flowers, in some varieties bluish-red. [Gr. *phlox,* flame, wallflower—*phlegein,* to burn.]

phobia, *fō'bi-a,* **phobism,** *fō'bizm, ns.* a fear, aversion, or hatred, esp. morbid or irrational.—Used originally as a suffix in words such as **Anglophobia,** hatred or dread of England and the English.—The suffix **-phobe** forms *adjs.* and *ns.,* as **Anglophobe,** (a person) having a hatred or fear of the English. [Gr. *phobos,* fear.]

phoenix, *fē'niks, n.* a fabulous bird, the only one of its kind, that burned itself every 500 years or so and rose rejuvenated from its ashes—hence, anything that rises from its own or its predecessor's ashes, the emblem of immortality: a paragon. [O.E. *fenix,* later assimilated to L. *phoenix*—Gr. *phoinix.*]

phone, 'phone, *n., v.i.* and *v.t. (coll.)* telephone (q.v.).

phoneme, *fōn'ēm, n.* a group or family of speech sounds felt in any one language to be only variants of one sound. [Gr. *phōnēma,* a sound.]

phonetic, -al, *fō-net'ik, äl, adj.* of, concerning, according to, or representing, the sounds of spoken language.—*adv.* **phonet'ically.**—*n.* **phonetician** (*fō-né-tish'án*), one versed in phonetics.—*n. (pl.* in form, treated as *sing.)* **phonet'ics,** the science that deals with pronunciation and the representation of the sounds of speech. [Gr. *phōnētikos*—*phōnē,* voice.]

phon(e)y, *fōn'i, adj. (slang)* not genuine, counterfeit, of no value. [Ety. unknown.]

phonic, *fōn'ik,* or *fon'ik, adj.* of sound, esp. vocal sound.—**phonic method,** a method of teaching reading through the phonetic value of letters and groups of letters.—*n.* **phon'ics** (or *fon'iks*), the science of sound, or of spoken sounds (phonetics). [Gr. *phōnē,* voice, sound.]

phonogram, *fō'no-gram, n.* a character representing a sound of speech: a phonographic record. [Gr. *phōnē,* voice, *gramma,* that which is written—*graphein,* to write.]

phonograph, *fō'nō-gräf, n.* a character used to represent a sound: Edison's instrument for recording sounds on a cylinder and reproducing them: (*U.S.*) the ordinary word for any gramophone.—*n.* **phonography** (*fō-nog'ra-fi*), the art of representing each spoken sound by a distinct character: Pitman's phonetic short-

fāte, fär; mē, hûr (her); *mīne; mōte, för; mūte; mōōn, fōōt;* ᴛʜᴇn (then) hand. [Gr. *phōnē*, voice, *graphein*, to write.]

phonology, *fō-nol'o-ji*, *n.* phonetics: now generally the study of the system of sounds in a language and of the history of their changes.—*adj.* **phonolog′ical.**—*n.* **phonol′ogist.** [Gr. *phōnē*, voice, *logos*, discourse.]

phormium, *för'mi-um*, *n.* a genus of New Zealand plants of the lily family—New Zealand flax or flax-lily. [Latinised from Gr. *phormion*, a mat, a faggot, a kind of sage.]

phosgene, *fos'jēn*, *n.* a poisonous gas, prepared from carbon monoxide and chlorine in sunlight. [Gr. *phōs*, light, and the root of *gignesthai*, to be produced.]

phosphorus, *fos'för-us*, *n.* the morning star (see morning; also **phos′phor**): a waxy, poisonous, inflammable element (symbol P; atomic no. 15) giving out light in the dark.—*n.* **phos′phor,** a substance characterised by fluorescence or phosphorescence: see also **phosphorus.**—*adjs.* **phosphor′ic, phos′phorous,** of, pertaining to, or resembling phosphorus—used for compounds in which phosphorus has respectively its higher and its lower combining powers (usually a valency of 5 and a valency of 3):—e.g. **phosphoric acid** (H_3PO_4) and **phosphorous acid** (H_3PO_3; a reducing agent). —*ns.* **phosphate** (*fos'fāt*), a salt of phosphoric acid; **phos′phite,** a salt of phosphorous acid; **phos′phide,** a compound of phosphorus and another element.—*adj.* **phos′phuretted** (or *-et'-*), combined with phosphorus, as **phosphuretted** or **phosphoretted hydrogen** (PH_3).—**phosphoro-,** in composition, phosphorus.—*v.i.* **phosphoresce′** (*-es'*), to shine in the dark as phosphorus does, the glow in this, and certain other, cases being due to slow oxidation: (*phys.*) to exhibit a phenomenon which may be regarded as fluorescence (q.v.) persisting after the exciting radiation has ceased.—*n.* **phosphores′cence.**—*adj.* **phosphores′cent.**—*n.* **phossy-jaw,** disease due to phosphorus affecting the jawbone.—**red phosphorus,** known also as *amorphous phosphorus*, a form of phosphorus obtained by raising ordinary phosphorus to a great heat in a closed vessel, used on the boxes of safety matches. [L. *phōsphorus*—Gr. *phōsphoros*, light-bearer—*phōs*, light, *phoros*, bearing, from *pherein*, to bear.]

photo-, *fō'to-,* **phot-,** *fōt-*, in composition, light; as in **photochemistry** (*fō-tō-kem'is-tri*), *n.* the study of the chemical effects of radiation (esp. light) and the production of radiation by chemical change; **photo-electricity,** *n.* electricity, or a change of electric condition, produced by light or other electromagnetic radiation; **photo-electric cell** (or **photo-cell**), any device in which incidence of light of suitable frequency causes an alteration in electrical state, esp. by photo-emission; **photo(-)electron,** *n.* electron ejected from the surface of a body by the action of ultraviolet rays or X-rays upon it; **photo-emiss′ion,** *n.* emission of electrons from the surface of a body on which light falls; **photofobia** (*fō'bi-a*; Gr. *phobos*, fear), *n.* a shrinking from the light.—*adj.* **photofobic; photosens′itive,** *adj.* affected by light, visible or invisible. [Gr. *phōs,* gen. *phōtos*, light.]

photo-, *fō'to-*, in composition, photographic: made by, or by the aid of, photographic means.—**photo,** *n., v.t.* and *adj.,* a *coll.* abbrev. of **photograph(ic); pho′tocopy,** *n.* a photographic reproduction of written matter.—*v.t.* to make a photocopy; **pho′tofinish,** *n.* a finish of a race in which a special type of photography is used to show the winner, &c.: a neck and neck finish of any contest; **photomi′crograph,** photograph taken through a microscope; **pho′tosetting,** *n.* in printing, setting of copy by projecting images of letters successively on a sensitive material (also **pho′tocomposition**). [photograph.]

photochrome, *fō'tō-krōm,* *n.* a photograph in colour. [Gr. *phōs*, gen. *phōtos*, light, *chrōma*, colour.]

photochronograph, *fō-tō-kron'ō-gräf,* *n.* an instrument for taking a rapid series of instantaneous photographs: an instrument for determining the moment of (for example) a star's transit by producing a photographic image.—*n.* **photochronog′raphy** (*-og'ra-fi*). [Gr. *phōs*, *phōtos*, light, *chronos*, time, *graphein*, to write.]

photo-engraving, *fō'tō-en-grā'ving,* *n.* any of several processes of engraving by the aid of photography. [photo, and **engraving.**]

photogenic, *fō-tō-jen'ik,* *adj.* producing light: photographing well, esp. of a person who is a good subject. [Gr. *phōs*, gen. *phōtos*, light, and *gen-*, root of *gignesthai*, to be produced.]

photography, *fō-tog'ra-fi,* *n.* the art or process of producing permanent and visible images by the action of light on chemically prepared surfaces.—*ns.* **phō′tograph** (*-gräf*), an image so produced; **phōtog′rapher.**—*adjs.* **photographic** (*-graf'ik*), **-al.**—*adv.* **photograph′ically.**—*n.* **photogravūre′,** a method of printing using plates, usually copper, on which the design etched is intaglio (i.e. consists of hollows below the surface), not relief: a picture so produced. [Gr. *phōs, phōtos,* light, *graphein*, to draw.]

photo-lithography, *fō'to-li-thog'ra-fi,* *n.* a process of lithographic printing in which the plates have been prepared photographically. —*n.* and *v.t.* **photolith′ograph** (*-o-gräf*). Abbrev. **photoli′tho.** [photo, lithography.]

photometer, *fō-tom'e-têr,* *n.* an instrument for comparing intensity of light. [Gr. *phōs,* gen. *phōtos*, light, *metron*, measure.]

photon, *fō'ton,* *n.* a quantum of electromagnetic radiation. [Gr. *phōs*, gen. *phōtos*, light, and suffx. *-on.*]

photoplay, *fō'tō-plā,* *n.* a drama shown in moving pictures, produced by a cinematograph (q.v.). [photo, and **play.**]

photosphere, *fō'tō-sfēr,* *n.* the luminous envelope of the sun's globe, the source of light. [Gr. *phōs, phōtos,* light, *sphaira,* a sphere.]

Photostat, *fō'tō-stat,* *n.* a photographic apparatus for making facsimiles of MSS., drawings, &c., directly upon prepared paper: a facsimile so made. [Gr. *phōs*, gen. *phōtos*, light, *statos*, set, placed; trade-mark.]

photosynthesis, *fō-tō-sin'the-sis,* *n.* (*bot.*) the building up of complex compounds by the chlorophyll apparatus of plants by means of the energy of light.—*adj.* **photosynthet′ic.** [Gr.

Neutral vowels in unaccented syllables: *em'pêr-ór*; for certain sounds in foreign words see p. ix.

phōs, phōtos, light, *synthesis—syn,* with, together, *thesis,* a placing—*tithenai,* to place.]

phototelegraph, *fō-tō-tel'é-gräf, n.* an instrument for transmitting drawings, photographs, &c., by telegraphy. [**photo,** and **telegraph.**]

phrase, *frāz, n.* manner of expression in language (as, *felicity of phrase*): a group of words (not generally forming a clause) expressing a single idea by themselves: a pithy expression: a catchword: an empty or high-sounding expression: (*mus.*) a short group of notes felt to form a unit.—*v.t.* to express in words: to style: (*mus.*) to mark, or to give effect to, the phrases of.—*ns.* **phrase'-mong'er,** a user or maker of wordy or fine-sounding phrases; **phraseogram** (*frā'zē-ō-gram*), a single sign, written without lifting the pen, for a whole phrase (esp. in shorthand); **phraseol'ogy,** style or manner of expression or arrangement of phrases: peculiarities of diction; **phrā'sing,** the wording of a speech or passage: (*mus.*) the grouping and accentuation of the sounds in a melody. [Gr. *phräsis—phrazein,* to speak.]

phrenetic, frenetic, *fren-et'ik,* formerly *fren'-, adj.* delirious: frenzied: proceeding from madness.—Also *n.*—*n.* **phrenol'ogy,** a would-be science of mental faculties located in various parts of the skull and investigable by feeling the bumps on the outside of the head.—*adjs.* **phrenolog'ic, -al,**—*n.* **phrenol'ogist.** [Gr. *phrēn,* gen. *phrenos,* midriff, supposed seat of passions, mind, will.]

phthisis, *thī'sis,* also *fthī'-, tī'-, n.* wasting disease: consumption of the lungs.—*n.* **phthisic** (*tiz'ik,* sometimes *thī'sik, fthī'sik, tī'sik*), phthisis: vaguely, a lung or throat disease.—*adj.* **phthisical** (*tiz'-*). [Gr. *phthisis—phthi(n)cin,* to waste away.]

phut, *fut, adj.* (*slang*) burst, finished, unserviceable.—**go phut,** to break, become unserviceable: to come to nothing. [Hindustani *phatnā,* to split.]

pH (value), *pē-āch(val'ū), n.* a number used to express degrees of acidity or alkalinity in solutions—values range from 0 (strong acid) to 14 (strong alkali), pH7 represents the neutral condition.

phycology, *fī-kol'ō-ji, n.* the study of seaweeds.—*n.* **phycol'ogist.** [Gr. *phykos,* seaweed, *logos,* discourse.]

phylactery, *fi-lak'tē-ri, n.* among the Jews, a slip of parchment inscribed with certain passages of Scripture, worn in a box on the left arm or forehead. [L.,—Gr. *phylaktērion—phylax,* a guard.]

phylloxera, *fil-ok-sē'ra, n.* a genus of insects very destructive to vines. [Gr. *phyllon,* a leaf, *xēros,* dry.]

phylum, *fī'lum, n.* a category, or group of related forms, a main division of the animal kingdom, larger than a *class.* [Gr. *phylon,* race.]

physic, *fiz'ik, n.* the science, art, or practice of medicine: medicine.—*v.t.* to give medicine to:—*pr.p.* phys'icking; *pa.t.* and *pa.p.* phys'icked.—*adj.* **phys'ical,** pertaining to the world of matter and energy, or its study: material: bodily.—*adv.* **phys'ically.**—*ns.* **physician** (*fi-zish'an*), one skilled in the use of physic or in the art of healing: one who pre-scribes medicine and treatment, distinguished from a surgeon who practises manual operations: (*fig.*) a healer or healing influence; **phys'icist** (*-sist*), a student of nature: one versed in physics, a natural philosopher: one who believes the phenomena of life are purely physical; (*pl.* treated as *sing.*) **phys'ics,** (*orig.*) natural science in general: (now) natural philosophy, the science of the properties (other than chemical) of matter, and energy.—**physical chemistry,** the study of the dependence of physical properties on chemical composition, and of the physical changes accompanying chemical reactions; **physical geography,** the study of the earth's natural features—its mountain chains, ocean currents, &c. [Gr. *physikos,* natural—*physis,* nature.]

physiognomy, *fiz-i-on'o-mi,* or *-og'no-mi, n.* the art of judging character from appearance, esp. from the face: the face as an index of the mind: the general appearance of anything.—*adjs.* **physiognom'ic, -al.**—*n.* **physiog'nomist.** [Gr. *physiognōmiā,* a shortened form of *physiognōmoniā—physis,* nature, *gnōmōn, -onos,* an interpreter.]

physiography, *fiz-i-og'ra-fi, n.* description of nature or natural phenomena, descriptive science: physical geography. [Gr. *physis,* nature, *graphein,* to describe.]

physiology, *fiz-i-ol'o-ji, n.* the science of the processes of life in animals and plants.—*adjs.* **physiologic** (*-ō-loj'ik*)**, -al,**—*adv.* **physiolog'ically.**—*n.* **physiol'ogist.** [Gr. *physis,* nature, *logos,* discourse.]

physiotherapy, *fiz-i-ō-ther'ä-pi, n.* treatment of disease by remedies such as massage, exercise, fresh air, electricity, not drugs.—*n.* **physiother'apist.** [Gr. *physis,* nature, *therapeiā,* treatment.]

physique, *fiz-ēk', n.* bodily type, build, or constitution. [Fr.]

phyto-, *fī-tō-,* in composition, plant:—*e.g. adj.* **phytogenic,** *-jen'ik* (Gr. *genesis,* generation), of vegetable origin.—*n.* **phytology,** *fī-tol'o-ji* (Gr. *logos,* discourse), botany. [Gr. *phyton,* a plant.]

pi, *pī, pe, n.* the sixteenth letter (Π, π) of the Greek alphabet, answering to the Roman P: as a numeral π' stands for 80, ,π for 80,000: (*math.*) a symbol for the ratio of the circumference of a circle to the diameter, approximately 3·14159.—**pi-** (or *π-*) **meson,** particle providing nuclear force holding protons and neutrons together.—Also called **pion.** [Gr. *pī*]

piacular, *pī-ak'ū-lär, adj.* expiatory: requiring expiation: atrociously bad. [L. *piāculum,* sacrifice—*piāre,* expiate—*pius,* pious.]

pianoforte, *pya'nō-fōr-tā,* or *pē-a'-,* generally shortened to **piano** (*pya'nō, pē-a'nō*), *n.* a musical instrument in which wires are struck by hammers moved by keys:—*pl.* **pia'nofortes, pian'os.** *adj.* and *adv.* . **pianissimo** (*pya-nēs'si-mō, pē-ä-nis'i-mō*), very soft(ly).—*n.* **pianist** (*pē'än-ist,* also *pyan'-, pē-an'ist*), one who plays the pianoforte, esp. expertly.—*adj.* and *adv.* **piano** (*pyä'nō, pē-ä'nō*), soft, softly. —*n.* **Pianola** (*pē-ä-nō'lä, pyan-*), an apparatus for playing the piano by means of a perforated roll (trademark). [It.—*piano,* soft (L. *plānus,* level), and *forte,* loud (L. *fortis,* strong).]

fāte, fär; mē, hûr (her); *mīne; mōte, för; mūte; mōōn, fŏŏt;* тнen (then)

piastre, *pi-as'tér, n.* a silver coin of varying value, used in Turkey and elsewhere. [Fr.,—It. *piastra,* a leaf of metal.]

piazza, *pē-ät'sä, n.* a place or square surrounded by buildings: (erroneously) a walk under a roof supported by pillars: (*U.S.*) a veranda. [It.,—L. *platea*—Gr. *plateia,* a street (fem. of *platys,* broad).]

pibroch, *pē'bro* н, *n.* bagpipe music consisting of variations on a theme, often martial. [Gael. *piobaireachd,* pipe-music—*piobair,* a piper—*piob,* from Eng. **pipe.**]

pica, *pī'kä, n.* a printing type, used by printers as a standard unit of measurement. [Possibly used for printing *pies.* See **pie** (2).]

picador, *pik-a-dōr', dōr', n.* a mounted bull-fighter with a lance. [Sp.,—*pica,* a pike.]

picaresque, *pik-a-resk', adj.* resembling the characters or incidents of the *picaresque novels,* tales of Spanish rogue and vagebond life in the 17th century. [Sp. *picaro,* rogue.]

picaroon, *pik-a-rōōn', n.* a rogue: a pirate: a pirate ship. [Sp. *picarón.* See **picaresque.**]

piccalilli, *pik-a-lil'i, n.* chopped vegetables in pickle. [Origin uncertain.]

piccaninny, pickaninny, *pik'a-nin-i, n.* a little child: a Negro child. [Port. *pequenino—pequeno,* little; or Sp. *pequeño.*]

piccolo, *pik'ō-lō, n.* a small flute an octave higher than the ordinary flute. [It., little.]

pice, *pīs, n. sing* and *pl.,* Indian bronze coin formerly worth $1/64$ rupee, now (**new pice**) $1/100$ rupee.

pick, *pik, n.* a tool for breaking ground, rock, &c., with head pointed at one or both ends and handle fitted to the middle: an instrument of various kinds for picking: an act, opportunity, or right of choice: a portion picked: the best or choicest.—*v.t.* to break up, dress, or remove with a pick: to pull apart: to poke or pluck at: to clear (as bones of flesh): to remove (from): to pluck: to peck, bite, or nibble: to select: to open (as a lock) by a sharp instrument: to rifle by stealth.—*v.i.* to use a pick: to eat by morsels: to pilfer.—*ns.* **pick'er; pick'-me-up,** a stimulating drink: a tonic; **pick'-pocket,** one who picks or steals from other people's pockets; **pick'-thank,** one who seeks to ingratiate himself by officious favours, or by tale-bearing; **pick'-up,** an act of picking up: a thing or person picked up: a device for picking up an electric current: accelerating power: a transducer, activated by a sapphire or diamond stylus following the groove on a gramophone record, which transforms the mechanical into electrical impulses: a light motor vehicle with the front part like a private car and the rear in the form of a lorry: a man's chance acquaintanceship with a woman, usu. implying a sexual relationship: the woman in such a relationship.—**pick a quarrel,** to seek and find a pretext for quarrelling (with); **pick at,** to find fault with; **pick faults (in),** to seek occasions of fault-finding or of criticising adversely; **pick oakum,** to make oakum by untwisting tarry ropes; **pick off,** to aim at and kill or wound one by one; **pick on,** to single out, esp. for anything unpleasant: to nag at; **pick one's way,** to choose carefully where to put one's feet; **pick out,** to discern: to select

from a number: **pick to pieces,** to take apart, pull asunder: to criticise adversely in detail; **pick up,** to lift from the ground, &c.: to take into a vehicle with one: to scrape acquaintance informally with: to acquire as occasion offers: to come upon, make out, distinguish (e.g. a signal, a track): to improve gradually: to gain strength bit by bit. [Ety. obscure.]

pickaback, *pik'a-bak, adv.* and *adj.* on the back like a pack.—Also **pick'back, pick'a-pack.**

pickax(e), *pik'aks, n.* a tool used in digging, a pick (q.v.); cf. **mattock.** [M.E. *pikois*—O.Fr. *picois,* a mattock,*piquer,* to pierce,*pic,* a pick.]

picket, *pik'ét, n.* a pointed stake driven into the ground for fortification, tethering, surveying, &c.: a small outpost, patrol, or other body of men set apart for a special duty: a person or group set to watch and dissuade those who go to work during a strike.—*v.t.* to tether to a stake: to strengthen with pickets: to place a picket at or near. [Fr. *picquet,* dim. of *pic,* a pickaxe.]

pickle, *pik'l, n.* a liquid, esp. brine or vinegar, in which food is preserved: anything so preserved: a plight: (*coll.*) a troublesome child.—*v.t.* to preserve with salt, vinegar, &c.—**have a rod in pickle,** to have a punishment ready. [M.E. *pikkyll,* &c.; cf. Du. *pekel*; Ger. *pökel.*]

Pickwickian, *pik-wik'-än, adj.* like, or relating to, Mr *Pickwick,* in Dickens's *Pickwick Papers.*

picnic, *pik'nik, n.* (*orig.*) a fashionable social entertainment towards which each person contributed a share of the food: an open-air repast of a number of persons on a country excursion: an easy or pleasant experience (often ironical or with negative).—Also *adj.*—*v.i.* to have a picnic:—*pr.p.* pic'nicking; *pa.t.* and *pa.p.* pic'nicked. [Fr. *pique-nique.*]

pico-, *pē-kō-, pī-kō-,* in composition, 10^{-12}, one million millionth part.

picric acid, *pik'rik a'sid,* an acid used as a yellow dye-stuff and as the basis of high explosives. [Gr. *pikros,* bitter.]

Pict, *pikt, n.* one of an ancient people of obscure affinities living in Britain, esp. north-eastern Scotland, first mentioned in the 3rd century A.D. [L. *Pictī,* Picts; perh. the same as *pictī,* pa.p. of *pingĕre,* to paint.]

pictograph, *pik'tō-gräf, n.* a picture used as a symbol in picture-writing (q.v.): a record consisting of such symbols. [L.*pictus,* painted, Gr. *graphein,* to write.]

pictorial, *pik-tō', tō', ri-äl, adj.* of or relating to painting or drawing: consisting of, expressed in, or of the nature of, pictures: picturesque: graphic.—*adv.* **picto'rially.** [L. *pictor, -ōris,* painter—*pingĕre, pictum,* to paint.]

picture, *pik'tyùr, -chùr, n.* a representation on a surface, by painting, drawing, &c., of an object or objects, or of a scene, esp. when a work of art: a portrait: a person or a sight worthy of being painted: a person resembling another as closely as his portrait: a symbol or type (as, *a picture of health*): an image formed in the mind: a vivid verbal description: a cinematograph film: (an image on) a television screen: (in *pl.*) a cinematograph show or the building in which it is given.—*v.t.* to depict, represent

Neutral vowels in unaccented syllables: *em'pèr-ór*; for certain sounds see in foreign words see p. ix.

542

in a picture: to form a likeness of in the mind: to describe vividly.—*ns.* **pic′ture-gall′ery,** a gallery where pictures are exhibited; **pic′ture-rod, -mould′ing,** a rod, moulding, from which pictures may be hung; **pic′ture-writ′ing,** the method (used by certain primitive peoples) of recording events or ideas, or of conveying messages, by means of pictures.—**in the picture,** having a share of attention: adequately informed about the situation; **put someone in the picture,** to give someone all the information necessary for understanding the situation. [L. *pictūra—pingĕre, pic tum,* to paint.]

picturesque, *pik-tū-resk′, adj.* such as would make a striking picture, implying some beauty and much quaintness or immediate effectiveness: (of language) vivid and colourful rather than precise.—*adv.* **picturesque′ly.** —*n.* **picturesque′ness.** [It. *pittoresco—pittura,* a picture—L. *pictūra.*]

piddle, *pid′l, v.i.* to deal in trifles: to trifle.

pidgin English, *pij′in ing′glish,* a jargon, mainly English in vocabulary but with Chinese arrangement, used in talking with Chinese: any jargon consisting of English and another language. [Chinese pron. of **business.**]

pie, *pī, n.* a magpie: a chatterer. [Fr.,—L. *pīca.*]

pie, pye, *pī, n.* a book of rules for determining the church office for the day. [L.L. *pīca,* possibly the same as L. *pīca,* magpie (from the black and white appearance of the page).]

pie, pi, *pī, n.* type confusedly mixed: confusion.

pie, *pī, n.* meat or fruit baked within a crust of prepared flour. [Origin unknown.]

piebald, pyebald, *pī′böld, adj.* black and white in patches: *(loosely)* of other colours in patches: motley. [pie (1), **bald.**]

piece, *pēs, n.* a part or portion of anything: a single article: a definite length, as of cloth or paper: a literary, dramatic, musical, or artistic composition: a gun: a coin: a man in chess (sometimes excluding pawns), draughts, &c.: a person (disrespectfully).—*v.t.* to enlarge by adding a piece: to patch: (**piece together**) to form from pieces.—*n.pl.* **piece′-goods,** textile fabrics made in standard lengths.—*adv.* **piece′meal,** in pieces: to pieces: bit by bit.—*adj.* done bit by bit: fragmentary.—*ns.* **piec′er,** a boy or girl employed in a spinning-factory to join broken threads; **piece′work,** work paid for by the piece or quantity, not by time.—**piece of eight,** a Spanish dollar worth *eight* reals.—**a piece,** (of price) each; **a piece of,** an instance, example, of (e.g. *a piece of impertinence*); **a piece of one's mind,** a frank outspoken rebuke or expression of opinion; **go to pieces,** to break into parts: *(fig.)* to break down nervously or physically, losing the power to face and deal with one's circumstances; **of a piece,** of the same kind (e.g. *two of a piece*): of the same kind as (with *with*): in keeping, consistent (with). [O.Fr. *piece*— Low L. *pecia, petium,* a fragment, a piece of land—thought to be of Celtic (Brythonic) origin.]

pièce de résistance, *pyes dĕ rā-zēs-tās,* the main dish of a meal: the most important article in a number of articles. [Fr.]

pied, *pīd, adj.* variegated like a magpie: of various colours. [pie (1).]

pied-à-terre, *pyād a ter,* temporary lodging.

piepowder, *pī′pow-dĕr, n.* (*obs.*) a wayfarer.—**Court of Piepowder,** an ancient court held in fairs and markets to administer justice in a rough-and-ready way to all comers—also *Court of Dusty Foot.* [O.Fr. *piedpoudreux— pied* (L. *pēs, pedis*), foot, *poudre* (L. *pulvis*), dust.]

pier, *pēr, n.* the mass of stone-work between the openings in the wall of a building: the support of an arch, bridge, &c.: a gate pillar: a mass of stone, iron-work, or woodwork projecting into the sea or other water, for landing and other purposes.—*ns.* **pier′-glass,** (*orig.*) a mirror hung between windows: a tall mirror hung between windows: a tall mirror; **pier′-head,** the seaward end of a pier. [M.E. *pēr,* L.L. *pēra.*]

pierce, *pērs, v.t.* to thrust or make a hole through: to enter, or force a way into: to touch or move deeply: to penetrate, see right through (e.g. a mystery).—*v.i.* to penetrate.— *adj.* **pierc′ing,** penetrating: very acute (of cold, pain, &c.)—*adv.* **pierc′ingly.** [O.Fr. *percer.*]

Pierian, *pī-ē′ri-án, adj.* of Pieria, in Thessaly, the country of the Muses: of the Muses.

pierrot, *pē′rō, pyer-ō′, n.* (*cap.*) a figure in old Italian comedy and old French pantomime: a white-faced buffoon: one of a party of entertainers at seaside resorts—often in clown's dress:—*fem.* **Pierrette, pierrette** *(pē-ér-et′).* [Fr., dim. of *Pierre,* Peter.]

pietà, *pyā-tä′, n.* a representation of the Virgin with the dead Christ across her knees. [It.—L. *pietās, -ātis,* dutifulness, piety.]

piety, *pī′e-ti, n.* the quality of being pious: devoutness: sense of duty towards parents, benefactors, &c.: dutiful conduct.—*ns.* **pī′etist,** a person marked by strong devotional feeling: a name first applied to a sect of German religious reformers of deep devotional feeling (end of 17th century); **pī′etism.**—*adjs.* **pietist′ic, -al.** [O.Fr. *piete*—L. *pietās, -ātis.*]

piezo-, *pī-ē′zō-,* in composition, pressure [Gr. *piēzein* to press], e.g. **piezochemistry,** the study of the effect of very high pressures on chemical reactions; **piezoelectricity,** electricity developed in certain crystals by mechanical strains—also, the effect of an electric field in producing in such crystals expansion along one axis and contraction along another; these effects are made use of in types of microphone, &c; **piezomag′netism,** magnetism developed in a similar way to piezoelectricity.

piffle, *pif′l, n.* nonsense, worthless talk.

pig, *pig, n.* a swine: an oblong mass of unforged metal, as first extracted from the ore: the mould into which it is run, esp. one of the branches, the main channel being the *sow.*— *v.i.* to bring forth pigs: to live or feed like pigs:—*pr.p.* **pigg′ing;** *pa.t* and *pa.p.* **pigged**— *adj.* **pig′-eyed,** having small dull eyes with heavy lids.—*n.* **pigg′ery,** a place where pigs are kept.—*adjs.* **pigg′ish,** like a pig: greedy: dirty; **pig′head′ed,** stupidly obstinate.—*ns.* **pig′-iron,** iron in pigs or rough bars; **pig′-sticking,** boar-hunting with spears; **pig′sty,** a pen for keeping pigs; **pig′s′-wash,** swill; **pig′tail,** the tail of a pig: the hair of the head plaited behind in a queue: a roll of twisted tobacco.—**a pig in a poke** (see **poke**); **make a pig of oneself** (*coll.*), to over-indulge in food or drink; **when pigs fly,** never. [M.E. *pigge*; cf. Du. *bigge, big.*]

pigeon, *pij'ón, pij'in, n.* (*orig.*) a young dove: any bird of the dove family (*Columbidae*), esp. a domesticated variety: a simpleton, one who is fleeced.—*adjs.* **pig'eon-breast'ed,** having a narrow chest with breast-bone thrown forward; **pig'eon-heart'ed,** timid.—*n.* **pig'eon-hole,** a niche for a pigeon's nest: a compartment for storing papers, &c.—*v.t.* to classify, arrange systematically: to file for reference: to put aside to be dealt with in an indefinite future, if ever.—*adjs.* **pig'eon-liv'ered,** meek, mild; **pig'eon-toed,** in-toed.—*n.* **clay pigeon,** a clay disk thrown from a trap and shot at as a substitute for a live pigeon. [O.Fr. *pijon*—L. *pīpiō, -ōnis*—*pīpīre,* cheep.]

pigeon. Same as **pidgin** (*q.v.*).—**that's** (**not**) **my pigeon,** (*slang*) that is (not) my business, job, concern.

piggin, *pig'in, n.* a small wooden vessel.

pigment, *pig'mént, n.* paint: any substance used for colouring: that which gives colour to animal and vegetable tissues.—*n.* **pigmenta'tion,** coloration or discoloration by pigments in the tissues. [L. *pīgmentum*—*pingĕre,* to paint.]

pigmy. Same as **pygmy.**

pike, *pīk, n.* a weapon with a long shaft and a sharp head like a spear, formerly used by foot-soldiers: a sharp-pointed hill or summit: a voracious fresh-water fish with pointed snout.—*adj.* **piked** (*pīkt, pīk'ed*), spiked: ending in a point.—*ns.* **pike'man,** a man armed with a pike; **pike'staff,** the staff or shaft of a pike: a staff with a pike at the end. [O.E. *pīc,* pick, spike; similar words occur in Fr., the Scand. languages, &c.]

pilaster, *pi-las'tér, n.* a square column, partly built into, partly projecting from a wall.—*adj.* **pilas'tered.** [Fr. *pilastre*—It. *pilastro*—L. *pīla,* a pillar.]

pilau, pillau, *pi-low', -lō', -lö', n.* a spiced Eastern dish of rice with a fowl, meat or the like, boiled together or separately. [Pers. *pilāw,* Turk. *pilāw, pilāf.*]

pilchard, *pil'chárd, n.* a sea-fish like the herring, but smaller, thicker, and rounder, common off Cornwall. [Origin unknown; poss. Scand.; cf. Norw. *pilk,* artificial bait.]

pile, *pīl, n.* a heap of more or less regular shape: a heap of combustibles, esp. for burning dead bodies: a tall building: (*elect.*) a form of battery: a set of coins placed vertically one upon another: (*slang*) a large amount of money, a fortune.—*v.t.* (usu. with *up* or *on*) to lay in a pile or heap: to heap up.—*v.i.* to become piled up: to accumulate: to get in or out (with *in* or *out*).—*n.* **pile-up,** a collision involving several motor vehicles.—**pile on the agony,** to overdo painful effects by accumulation of details, &c.—**atomic pile,** a device for the controlled release of nuclear energy, e.g. a lattice of small rods of natural uranium embedded in a mass of pure graphite which serves to slow down neutrons. [Fr.,—L. *pīla,* a pillar.]

pile, *pīl, n.* a large stake or cylinder driven into the earth to support foundations.—*v.t.* to drive

piles into.—*ns.* **pile'-driv'er,** an engine for driving in piles: **pile'-dwell'ing,** a house built on piles, esp. a lake-dwelling. [O.E. *pīl*—L. *pīlum,* a javelin.]

pile, *pīl, n.* a covering of hair, esp. soft, fine, or short hair: down: a raised surface on cloth, produced in a different way from *nap* (q.v.). [L. *pĭlus,* a hair.]

pile, *pīl,* (usu, in *pl.*), n. haemorrhoid (q.v.). [L. *pĭla,* a ball.]

pileate, *pī'li-āt,* **-d',** *adjs,* cap-shaped: capped: crested. [L. *pĭleum, pĭleus,* for *pileum, pilleus,* a felt cap; cf. Gr. *pīlos,* felt.]

pilfer, *pil'fér, v.i.* and *v.t.* to steal esp. in small quantities.—*n.* **pil'fering,** petty theft. [Prob. connected with **pelf.**]

pilgrim, *pil'grim, n.* (*arch.* and *poet.*) a wanderer, wayfarer: one who travels to a distance to visit a holy place.—*n.* **pil'grimage,** the journeying of a pilgrim: a journey to a shrine or other holy place: the journey of life.—**Pilgrim Fathers,** the Puritans who sailed in the *Mayflower* and founded the colony of Plymouth (Massachusetts) in 1620. [O.Fr. assumed *pelegrin* (later *pèlerin*)—L. *peregrīnus,* foreigner, stranger.]

pill, *pil, n.* a little ball of medicine: anything nauseous that must be accepted or endured.—*n.* **pillbox** (*mil. slang*), a small concrete blockhouse: a small round brimless hat.—**the Pill, pill,** any of various contraceptive pills. [L. *pĭla,* perh. through O.Fr. *pile,* or from a syncopated form of the dim. *pĭlŭla.*]

pillage, *pil'ij, n.* act of plundering: plunder.—*v.t.* and *v.i.* to plunder.—*n.* **pill'ager.** [O.E. *pylian* and O.Fr. *peler,* both—L. *pīlāre,* to deprive of hair; cf. **peel** (1).]

pillar, *pil'ár, n.* (*archit.*) a detached support, not necessarily cylindrical, or of classical proportions: a structure of like form erected as a monument, &c.: a tall upright rock: one who, or anything that, sustains.—*n.* **pill'ar-box,** a short hollow pillar for posting letters in.—**from pillar to post,** from one state of difficulty to another: hither and thither. [O.Fr. *piler* (Fr. *pilier*)—Low L. *pīlāre*—L. *pīla,* a pillar.]

pillau. See **pilau.**

pillion, *pil'yón, n.* a pad or light saddle for a woman: a cushion behind a horseman for a second rider or for a bag: baggage-carrier of a motor-cycle. [Prob. Ir. *pillín, pilliún,* Gael. *pillean,* a pad, a pack-saddle—*peall,* a skin or mat, L. *pellis,* skin.]

pillory, *pil'ór-i, n.* a wooden frame, supported by an upright pillar or post, and having holes through which the head and hands of a criminal were put as a punishment.—*v.t.* to set in the pillory: to hold up to ridicule:—*pa.t.* and *pa.p.* pill'oried. [O.Fr. *pilori*; perh. through Low L.—L. *speculāria,* window-panes.]

pillow, *pil'ō, n.* a cushion for a sleeper's head: any object used for the purpose: cushion for lace-making: a support for part of a structure.—*v.t.* to lay for support (on): to serve as pillow for.—*ns.* **pill'ow-case, -slip,** a cover for a pillow; **pill'ow-fight,** sport of thumping one another with pillows.—*adj.* **pill'owy,** like a pillow: soft. [O.E. *pyle,* also *pylu*—L. *pulvīnus.*]

pilose, *pī'lōs,* **pilous,** *pī'lus, adj.* hairy.—*n.* **pilos'ity.** [L. *pĭlōsus*—*pĭlus,* hair.]

Neutral vowels in unaccented syllables: *em'pér-ór*; for certain sounds in foreign words see p. ix.

pilot, *pī'lŏt, n.* (*arch.*) a steersman: one who conducts ships in and out of a harbour, along a dangerous coast, &c.: one who actually operates the flying controls of an aircraft: a guide: a mechanical directing device.—*v.t.* to act as pilot to.—*ns.* **pī'lotage,** piloting: pilot's fee; **pī'lot-balloon',** a small balloon sent up to find how the wind blows; **pī'lot-boat,** a boat used by pilots for meeting or leaving ships; **pī'lot-cloth,** a coarse, stout cloth for overcoats; **pī'lot-en'gine,** a locomotive sent before a train to clear its way, as a pilot; **pī'lot-fish,** a fish that accompanies ships and sharks; **pī'lot-flag, -jack,** the flag hoisted at the fore by a vessel requiring a pilot; **pī'lot-jack'et,** a peajacket (q.v.).—*adj.* **pī'lotless,** without a pilot.—*ns.* **pī'lot-light,** a small gas light kept burning to light a larger jet: a small electric light to show when the current is on; **pilot-officer,** an Air Force officer ranking with an army second-lieutenant; **pilot-plant,** prototype machinery set up to begin a new process; **pilot scheme,** a scheme carried out on a small scale to serve as a guide to the working of the scheme when full-scale. [Fr. *pilote,* now *pilote* It. *pilota,* perh.—Gr. *pēdon,* oar, in pl. rudder.]

pimento, *pi-men'tō, n.* allspice or Jamaica pepper: the tree producing it.—Also **pimen'to.** [O.Fr, *piment,* Sp. *pimiento*—L. *pīgmentum,* paint.]

pimp, *pimp, n.* one who procures gratifications for the lust of others, a pander.—Also *v.i.*

pimpernel, *pim'pėr-nel, n.* a genus of plants of the primrose family, with scarlet (or blue, &c.) flowers. [O.Fr. *pimpernelle,* mod. Fr. *pimprenelle*; origin doubtful.]

pimple, *pim'pl, n.* a pustule: a small swelling.—*adjs.* **pim'pled, pim'ply,** having pimples.

pin, *pin, n.* a pointed instrument of wood or metal used for fastening things together: a peg for various purposes: the centre of an archery target: the rod of a golf-flag: a tuning peg in a stringed instrument: anything of little value: (*coll.*) a leg.—*v.t.* to fasten with a pin: (*rare*) to enclose: to transfix with a pin or a sharp weapon: to hold fast, pressed against something: (*fig.*) to fix or fasten (to)—*pr.p.* **pinn'ing;** *pa.t.* and *pa.p.* **pinn'ed.**—*n.* **pin'ball,** a form of bagatelle: a scoring game, played on a slot-machine, in which a ball runs down a sloping board set with pins or other targets.—*adj.* **pin'-eyed',** having the stigma (like a pin head) visible at the throat of the corolla while the stamens are concealed in the tube (esp. of a primula).—*ns.* **pin'-feath'er,** a young unexpanded feather; **pin'-mon'ey,** money allotted to a wife for private expenses, ostensibly to buy pins; **pinn'er,** a pin-maker: a headdress with lappets flying loose; **pin'-point',** the point of a pin: anything very sharp and very minute (*v.t.* **pin'point,** to locate, place, very exactly: to define exactly); **pin'-prick',** (*fig.*) a trifling irritation; **pin'-stripe',** a very narrow stripe in cloth; **pin'-table,** the gaming machine on which pinball is played.—**on pins and needles,** in agitated expectancy; **pin it on to (someone),** to prove, or seem to prove, that he did it; **pin one's faith, hopes,** &c., **on, upon, to,** to put entire trust in:

to rely on absolutely; **pin someone (down) to,** to keep him strictly to (e.g. facts, the truth); **pins and needles,** a tingling feeling in arm, leg, &c. due to impeded circulation. [O.E. *pinn,* prob.—L. *pinna,* a feather, a pinnacle.]

pinafore, *pin'a-fōr, -fōr, n.* a loose covering over a dress, esp. a child's [**pin, afore.**]

pince-nez, *pěs'-nā, n.* pair of eye-glasses with a spring for catching the nose. [Fr., pinch nose.]

pincers, *pin'sėrz, n.* a gripping tool, used for drawing out nails, &c. [O.Fr. *pincer,* to pinch.]

pinch, *pinch* or *-sh, v.t.* to compress a small part of between finger and thumb or between any two surfaces: to nip: to squeeze: to affect painfully or injuriously as cold or hunger: to cause to shrivel up (e.g. a plant): to stint (a person) of food, &c.: (*slang*) to steal: (*slang*) to catch or to arrest, take into custody.—*v.i.* to nip or squeeze: to be painfully tight: to be very economical or niggardly.—*n.* an act or experience of pinching: a quantity that can be taken up between the finger and thumb: a critical time of difficulty or hardship.—*adj.* **pinched,** having the appearance of being tightly squeezed: hard pressed by want or cold.—*adv.* **pinch'ingly.—at a pinch,** in a case of necessity; **know where the shoe pinches,** to know by actual experience what the trouble or difficulty is. [O.Fr. *pincier*; prob. Gmc.; cf. Du. *pitsen,* to pinch.]

pinchbeck, *pinch'bek* or *-sh-, n.* a yellow alloy of copper with much less zinc than ordinary brass, simulating gold, invented by Chris. *Pinchbeck,* a London watchmaker (*d.* 1732): sham: in false taste.

Pindaric, *pin-dar'ik, adj.* after the manner of the Greek lyric poet *Pindar.*—*n.* a Pindaric ode: an irregular ode according to the 17th- and 18th-century conceptions of Pindar's versification. [Gr. *pindarikos*—*Pindaros.*]

pine, *pīn, n.* any tree of the northern temperate coniferous genus *Pinus,* with pairs or bundles of needle-leaves on short shoots and scale leaves only on long shoots, represented in Britain by the Scots pine (often called *Scots fir*): extended to various more or less nearly allied trees and to some plants only superficially like: the timber of the pine.—Also *adj.*—*ns.* **pine'apple,** a tropical plant and its fruit, shaped like a pine-cone; **pine'need'le,** the needle-shaped leaf of the pinetree; **pin'ery,** a hot-house where pineapples are grown.—*adj.* **pī'ny** of, like, or abounding in pine-trees. [O.E. *pīn*—L. *pīnus.*]

pine, *pīn, v.i.* to waste away, esp. under pain or mental distress: to long (with *for, after, to do*). [O.E. *pīnian,* to torment—L. *poena,* punishment.]

pinfold, *pin'fōld, n.* a pound or enclosure for cattle.—*v.t.* to impound. [O.E. *pundfald,* affected by *pyndan,* to shut up, confine. See **pound** (2), **fold** (2).]

ping, *ping, n.* a whistling sound as of a bullet.—*n.* **ping'-pong,** (*properly cap.*) a trade-mark for table tennis. [Imit.]

pinguid, *ping'gwid, adj.* fat.—*n.* **ping'uitude.** [L. *pinguis,* fat.]

pinion, *pin'yŏn, n.* a wing: the last joint of a wing: a flight feather, esp. the outermost.—*v.t.* to cut a pinion of: to confine the wings of: to confine by binding the arms. [O.Fr. *pignon* — L. *pinna* (=*penna*), wing.]

pinion, pin′yón, *n.* a small toothed wheel, meshing with a larger toothed wheel, or with a rack (q.v.). [Fr. *pignon* — O.Fr. *penon*, a battlement — L. *pinna.*]

pink, pingk, *v.t.* to stab or pierce, esp. with a sword or rapier: to decorate by cutting small holes or scallops. [Cf. L. Ger. *pinken*, to peck.]

pink, *pingk, n.* any plant or flower of the genus that includes carnation and Sweet William: extended to some other plants (as **sea′-pink**, thrift): the colour of a wild pink, a light red: a scarlet hunting-coat or its colour: the person wearing it: the most perfect condition: the highest point, the extreme. — *adj.* pale red. [Prob. a different word from the preceding.]

pink, *pingk, v.i.* to wink: to blink: of an internal-combustion engine, to work unevenly with a metallic knock. — *n.* **pink′-eye**, acute contagious conjunctivitis. — *adj.* **pink′-eyed**, having small or half-shut eyes. [Du. *pinken*, to wink.]

pinnace, pin′ás, -is, *n.* a small vessel with oars and sails: a boat with eight oars: a man-of-war's tender or boat. [Fr. *pinasse.*]

pinnacle, pin′ā-kl, *n.* a slender turret: a high pointed rock or mountain like a spire: the highest point. [Fr. *pinacle* — Low L. *pinnāculum*, dim. from L. *pinna*, a feather.]

pinnate, pin′āt, *adj.* shaped like a feather: furnished with wings or fins. — *adv.* **pinn′ately.** [L. *pinna*, a feather.]

pint, pīnt, *n.* measure of capacity = $1/2$ quart or 4 gills — in imperial measure (liquid or dry), about 568 cubic centimetres, in U.S. measure (liquid) 473 cc, (dry) 551 cc. [Fr. *pinte.*]

pintle, pin′tl, *n.* (*arch.*) the penis: a bolt or pin, esp. one on which something turns. [O.E. *pintel.*]

pion, pī′on, *n.* a pi-(π-) meson (see **pi**).

pioneer, pī-ón-ēr′, *n.* a military artisan — in peace-time, employed in such work as repairing barracks, in war, in preparing the way for an army, and minor engineering works as trenching: one who is among the first in new fields of enterprise, exploration, colonisation, research, &c. — Also *v.i.* and *v.t.* [O.Fr. *peonier* — *pion*, a foot-soldier — Low L. *pedō*, *pedōnis* — L. *pēs, pedis,* a foot.]

pious, pī′us, *adj.* (*arch.*) dutiful: showing, having, or proceeding from piety: professing to be religious. — *adv.* **pi′ously. — pious fraud** (see **fraud**). [L. *pius.*]

pip, pip, *n.* a disease of fowls, also called roup. [App. — Middle Du. *pippe* — L.L. *pipīta* — L. *pītuīta*, rheum.]

pip, *pip, n.* a small hard body (seed or fruitlet) in fleshy fruit. [App. from **pippin.**]

pip, *pip, v.t.* (*coll.*) to reject: to fail in an examination: to thwart, get the better of: to kill, wound. — **pipped at the post**, defeated when success seemed certain. [Origin uncertain.]

pip, *pip, n.* a spot on dice, cards, &c.: a star as a mark of rank. [Origin unknown.]

pip, *pip, n.* a short note given on the radio and by telephone as part of a time-signal. [Imit.]

pipe, pīp, *n.* a musical wind instrument, or part of an instrument, consisting of, or including, a tube: any tube: a tube with a bowl at the end

for smoking: a voice, esp. a high voice: the note of a bird: a boatswain's whistle: (often in *pl.*) a bagpipe. — *v.i.* to play upon a pipe: to whistle. — *v.t.* to play on a pipe: to utter shrilly in speech or song: to lead, call, or accompany with a pipe: to supply with pipes: to ornament with piping. — *ns.* **pipe′clay**, fine white nearly pure kaolin used for making tobacco-pipes and fine earthenware, for whitening belts, &c.; **pipe′-dream**, a hope or fancy as futile and unreal as an opium-smoker's dream; **pipe′-line**, **pipe′line**, a long continuous line of pipes to carry water from a reservoir, oil from an oilfield, &c.: a line of piping to carry solid materials: (*fig.*) a line of communication, or supply, or of progress and development; **pipe′-ma′jor**, the chief of a band of bagpipers; **pipe′-organ**, an organ with pipes; **pip′er**, a player on a pipe, esp. a bagpipe. — *adj.* **pip′ing**, playing a pipe: whistling: thin and high pitched. — *n.* pipe-playing: singing (of birds) or similar noise: a system of pipes: small cord used as trimming for clothes: strings of sugar ornamenting a cake. — **piped music, television,** &c., continuous background music, or programme, transmitted from a central room, studio or station to other buildings; **piping hot**, hissing hot. — **in the pipeline**, waiting, ready to be considered or dealt with; **pipe and tabor**, a small recorder fingered by the left hand and a small drum beaten by the right; **pipe down**, to dismiss from muster, as a ship's company: to subside into silence; **pay the piper**, to bear the expense. [O.E. *pīpe* — L. *pīpāre*, to cheep; cf. Du. *pijp*, Ger. *pfeife.*]

pipe, *pīp, n.* a cask or butt of two hogsheads. [O.Fr. *pipe*, cask, tube; cf. **pipe** (1).]

pipette, pip-et′, *n.* a tube for transferring and measuring fluids. [Fr., dim. of *pipe.*]

pipistrelle, pip-is-trel′, *n.* a small reddish-brown bat, the commonest British bat: any other bat of the same genus. [Through It. — L. *vespertīliō*, bat — *vesper*, evening.]

pipit, pip′it, *n.* a lark-like genus of birds, akin to wagtails, including the titlark. [Prob. imit.]

pipkin, pip′kin, *n.* a small pot, now only of earthenware. [Perh. a dim. of **pipe.**]

pippin, pip′in, *n.* a kind of apple. [O.Fr. *pepin.*]

piquant, pē′kánt, *adj.* stinging: pleasantly pungent: appetising: kindling keen interest. — *n.* **piq′uancy.** — *adv.* **piq′uantly.** [Fr., pr.p. of *piquer*, to prick.]

pique, pēk, *n.* animosity or ill-feeling: offence taken. — *v.t.* to wound the pride of: to nettle: to arouse (e.g. curiosity): to pride (*oneself on* or *upon*): — *pr.p.* piquing (pēk′ing); *pa.t.* and *pa.p.* piqued (pēkd). [Fr. *pique*, a pike, pique, *piquer*, to prick.]

piqué, pē-kā, *n.* a stiff corded cotton fabric. — *n.* **piqué-work**, needlework with a design made by stitching. [Fr., pa.p. of *piquer*, to prick.]

piquet, pi-ket′, *n.* a game played with a pack of 32 cards. [Fr.; origin unknown.]

pirate, pī′rát, *n.* a sea-robber: a ship used by one: one who steals or infringes a copyright or encroaches on any other right: a person who runs an unlicensed radio station. — *v.t.* to take, use, and profit from without permission. — *v.i.* to play the pirate. — *n.* **piracy**, (pī′rá-si) robbery on the high seas: infringement

Neutral vowels in unaccented syllables: *em′pér-ór*; for certain sounds in foreign words see p. ix.

copyright.—*adj.* **piratic**, (*pī-rat'ik*), **-al**, pertaining to a pirate: practising piracy.—*adv.* **pirat'ically**. [L. *pīrāta*—Gr. *peirātēs*—*peiraein*, to attempt.]

pirouette, *pir-ōō-et'*, *n.* a spinning about on tip-toe.—*v.i.* to spin round on tiptoe. [Fr.]

Pisces, *pis'ēz*, *n.* the Fishes, the twelfth sign of the zodiac.—*n.* **piscator** (*pis-kā-tór*), an angler.—*adjs.* **piscatorial** (*pis-ka-tō'ri-ál*), **piscatory** (*pis'ka-tór-i*), relating to fishing.—*n.* **pis'ciculture**, the rearing of fish by artificial methods.—*adjs.* **piscine** (*pis'īn*), of fishes; **pisciv'orous**, feeding on fishes. [L. *piscis*, a fish; *piscātor*, fishes.]

piscina, *pis-ē'na*, *-ī'na*, *n.* a fishpond: a basin near the altar. [L. *piscis*, a fish.]

pismire, *pis'mīr*, *n.* an ant or emmet. [**piss**, from the strong smell of the ant-hill, M.E. *mire* (doubtful O.E. *mīre*), ant.]

piss, *pis*, *v.i.* to discharge urine. [Fr. *pisser*.]

pistachio, *pis-ta'(t)shi-ō*, *n.* the almond-flavoured fruit-kernel of a small western Asiatic tree. [Sp. *pistacho* and It. *pistacchio*—forms in L.L., Gr. and Pers.]

piste, *pēst*, *n.* a beaten track esp. a ski trail in the snow. [Fr.]

pistil, *pis'til*, *-til*, *n.* properly the gynaeceum of a flower, but, in cases where the carpels are separate, often used as meaning a single carpel.—*adj.* **pis'tillate**, having a pistil but no functional stamens, female. [L. *pistillum*, a pestle.]

pistol, *pis'tl*, *n.* a small hand-gun.—*v.t.* and *v.i.* to shoot with a pistol.—*ns.* **pistole** (*pis-tōl'*), an old Spanish gold coin = about 85p; **pis'tolet**, a pistol. [O.Fr. *pistole* prob. from *Pistoia* province in Italy.]

piston, *pis'tón*, *n.* a solid piece moving to and fro in a close-fitting hollow container as in engines and pumps.—*n.* **pis'ton-rod**, the rod to which the piston is fixed, and which moves with it. [Fr.,—It. *pistone*—*pestāre*, to pound —L. *pinsēre*, *pistum*.]

pit, *pit*, *n.* a hole in the earth: a mine-shaft: a place whence minerals are dug: the bottomless pit: a grave (esp. for many bodies): a covered heap (of potatoes, &c.): a hole used as a trap for wild beasts: a hole in a garage floor to facilitate repairs to underparts of cars: a place beside the course where cars in a race can be refuelled and repaired: the indentation left by smallpox: ground-floor of theatre behind the stalls: an enclosure for cock-fights or the like: an enclosure in which animals are kept (esp. bears): (*U.S.*) part of a corn exchange floor: a noisy card game mimicking a corn exchange.—*v.t.* to mark with little hollows: to lay in a pit: to set to fight (against another):—*pr.p.* **pit'ting**; *pa.t.* and *pa.p.* **pit'ted**.—*ns.* **pit'fall**, a lightly covered hole as a trap for beasts: (*fig.*) a hidden danger; **pit'-man**, a man who works in a coal-pit or a saw-pit; **pit'prop**, a timber (or sometimes a metal column) used to support the roof in a coal-mine; **pit'-saw**, a saw used in a saw-pit.—**pit of the stomach**, the slight depression in the region of the stomach below the breast-bone.—**arm'-pit**, **arm'pit**, the hollow beneath the junction of the arm and shoulder. [O.E. *pytt*—L. *puteus*, a well.]

pitapat, *pit'a-pat*, *adv.* with palpitation or pattering. [Imit.]

pitch, *pich*, *n.* the black shining residue of distillation of tar, &c.—*v.t.* to smear, cover, or caulk with pitch.—*adj.* **pitch'-black**, black as pitch.—*n.* **pitch'-blende**, a black mineral of resinous lustre, chiefly composed of uranium oxides, important as a source of radium.—*adj.* **pitch'-dark**, utterly dark.—*n.* **pitch'-pine**, a name for several American pines that yield pitch and timber.—*adj.* **pitch'y**, like pitch: smeared with pitch: black. [O.E. *pic*—L. *pix*.]

pitch, *pich*, *v.t.* (*rare*) to thrust or fix in the ground: to fix in position by means of stakes, pegs, &c., driven into the ground, to erect (e.g. a tent): to place or lay out (wares) for sale: to arrange, to set in array: (*mus.*) to set (in a particular key, high, low): (*fig.*) to give this or that emotional tone to: to throw or toss, esp. in such a manner as to cause to fall flat or in a definite position: to let one's choice fall (upon): (*golf*) to lift the ball so that it does not roll much on falling: (*baseball*) to deliver the ball to the batsman.—*v.i.* to plunge or fall, esp. forward: (of a ship) to plunge so that bow and stern alternately rise and fall in the water—opp. to *roll*: to slope down.—*n.* a throw or cast: the place at which one (e.g. a street trader) is stationed: (*cricket*) the ground between the wickets: the distance between two consecutive things or points in a series of corresponding things or points, e.g. between a point on a gear tooth and the corresponding points on the next, or between corresponding points on the thread of a screw: degree of slope: degree, esp. of elevation or depression: any point, degree, or stage, esp. the extreme: the degree of acuteness of sounds.—*n.* **pitch'fork**, a fork for pitching hay, &c.: a tuning-fork.—*v.t.* to lift with a pitchfork. to throw suddenly into (*lit.* and *fig.*),—**pitch and toss**, a game in which coins are thrown at a mark, the player who throws nearest having the right of tossing all and keeping those that come down heads up; **pitch into**, to assail vigorously; **pitch pipe**, a small tuning pipe, used to set the pitch especially for singers; **pitch wickets**, to fix the stumps in the ground and place the bails; **pitched battle**, a deliberate battle on chosen ground between duly arranged sides. [App. conn. with **pick**, **pike**.]

pitcher, *pich'ér*, *n.* a vessel for holding or pouring liquids.—*n.* **pitch'er-plants**, any insectivorous plant with modified leaves in pitcher form. [O.Fr. *picher*—Low L. *picārium*, a goblet—Gr. *bīkos*, a wine-vessel.]

piteous, *pit'é-us*, *adj.* (*arch.*) compassionate: fitted to excite pity.—*adv.* **pit'eously.**—*n.* **pit'eousness**. [O.Fr. *pitos*—root of **pity**.]

pith, *pith*, *n.* the soft substance in the centre of the stems of plants: similar material elsewhere, as the white inner skin of an orange: spinal marrow: importance: condensed substance, essence: vigour.—*adj.* **pith'y**, full of pith: forcible: terse and full of meaning.—*adv.* **pith'ily.**—*n.* **pith'iness.**—*adj.* **pith'less.**—**pith hat**, **helmet**, a sun-helmet made of pith from the *sola*, an Indian tree. [O.E. *pitha*; Du. *pit*, marrow.]

---

fāte, fär; mē, hûr (her); *mīne; mōte, för; mūte; mōōn, fŏŏt;* THen (then)

Pithecanthropus, *pith-ē-kan-thrō′pus, n.* a fossil ape-man, fragments of which were discovered in Java in 1891-92. [Gr. *pithēkos,* ape, *anthrōpos,* man.]

piton, *pē-tõ, n.* a steel peg to be driven into rock or ice, used in climbing. [Fr.]

pittance, *pit′äns, n.* a special additional allowance of food or drink in a religious house, or a bequest to provide it: a dole: a very small portion or quantity, or remuneration. [O.Fr. *pitance*—L. *pietās,* pity.]

pity, *pit′i, n.* a feeling for the sufferings and misfortunes of others: a cause or source of pity or grief: a regrettable fact.—*v.t.* to feel pity for:—*pa.t.* and *pa.p.* pit′ied.—*adj.* **pit′iable.** to be pitied: miserable, contemptible.—*n.* **pit′iableness.**—*adv.* **pit′iably.**—*adj.* **pit′iful,** compassionate: sad: despicable.—*adv.* **pit′ifully.**—*n.* **pit′ifulness.**—*adj.* **pit′iless,** without pity: cruel.—*adv.* **pit′ilessly.**—*n.* **pit′ilessness.**—**it pitieth me, you, them,** &c. (*Pr. Bk.*), it causeth pity in me, you, them, &c. [O.Fr. *pite* (Fr. *pitié,* It. *pietà*)—L. *pietās, pietātis*—*pius,* pious.]

pivot, *piv′ŏt, n.* a pin on which anything turns: a soldier upon whom, or position on which, a body wheels: (*fig.*) that on which anything depends or turns.—*v.i.* to turn on, or as if on, a pivot.—*adj.* **piv′otal.**—*n.* **piv′oting,** the pivotwork in machines. [Fr. *pivot,* perh. related to It. *piva,* a pipe, a peg, a pin.]

pix, *piks, n.* Same as **pyx.**

pixy, pixie, *pik′si, n.* a small fairy.—*n.* **pix′ystool,** a toad-stool or mushroom.

pizza, *pēt′sa, n.* an open pie of bread dough with tomatoes, cheese, &c. [It.]

pizzicato, *pit-si-kä′tõ, adj.* (*mus.*) played by plucking the string, not with the bow.—*adv.* by plucking.—*n.* a tone so produced: a passage so played. [It. twitched.]

placable, *plak′- or plāk′ä-bl, adj.* that may be appeased, willing to forgive.—*ns.* **placabil′ity, plac′ableness.**—*adv.* **plac′ably.**—*v.t.* **placate** (*plak-āt′, plak′-, plāk′āt*), to conciliate. [L. *plācāre,* to appease, akin to *placēre,* to please.]

placard, *plak′ärd, n.* a written or printed paper stuck upon a wall or otherwise displayed as an intimation.—*v.t.* (*pla-kärd′, plak′ärd*) to publish by placard: to display as a placard: to stick placards on. [O.Fr. *plackart, placard,* &c.—*plaquier,* to lay flat, plaster.]

place, *plās, n.* open space in a town, marketplace or square: a locality: a village, town, or city (as, *native place*): a dwelling or home: a mansion-house with its grounds: a building, room, &c., assigned to some purpose (as, *place of business, worship*): a seat or accommodation in a theatre, train, at table &c.: a position in space or on the earth's surface, or in any system, order or arrangement: the position held by anyone: the position of a figure in a series as indicating its value: a position attained in a competition or assigned by criticism: (*racing*) a position in the first three: proper position or dignity: rank: employment, esp. under government or in domestic-service: a step in the progression of an exposition (*in the first place,* &c.): a passage in a book, &c.: a particular place.—*v.t.* to put in any place: to find a place for: to identify: to invest.—*adj.*

placed, set in place or in a place: having a place: among the first three in a race: inducted to a charge.—*ns.* **place′-hunter,** one who covets and strives after a public post; **place′man,** one who has a place or office under a government:—*pl.* **place′men.**—**be one's place,** to be a duty or obligation resulting from one's position; **find place, have place** (*fig.*), to find, have room or opportunity to exist; **give place,** to make room: to be superseded; **in place,** appropriate; **in place of,** instead of; **out of place,** inappropriate, unreasonable; **take someone's place,** to act as substitute for someone. [Partly O.E. (Northumbrian) *plæce,* market-place, but mainly Fr. *place,* both from L. *platĕa*—Gr. *plateia (hodos),* broad (street).]

placebo, *pla-sē′bō, n.* a pharmacologically inactive substance administered as a drug either to humour the patient in the treatment of psychological illness or in the course of drug trials. [L. lit. 'I shall please'.]

placenta, *pla-sen′ta, n.* the structure that unites the unborn mammal to the womb of its mother: (*bot.*) the part of a plant to which the seeds are attached:—*pl.* **placen′tae** (*-tē*).—*adj.* **placen′tal.** [L. *placenta,* a flat cake—Gr. *plakoeis* (contr. *plakous*), from *plax,* gen. *plakos,* anything flat.]

placer, *plas′ér, plās′ér, n.* a surface deposit of sand, gravel, &c., from which gold or other mineral can be washed. [Sp. *placer,* sandbank—*plaza,* place.]

placet, *plā′set, n.* a vote of assent in a governing body. [L. *plăcet,* 'it pleases', 3rd sing. pres. indic. of *placēre,* to please.]

placid, *plas′id, adj.* calm, serene.—*ns.* **placid′ity, plac′idness.**—*adv.* **plac′idly.** [L. *placidus*—*placēre,* to please.]

placket, *plak′ét, n.* a slit or pocket in a skirt. [Perh. a variant of **placard.**]

plagal cadence, *plāg′ál kā′déns,* one in which the subdominant chord precedes the tonic. [Mediaeval L. *plagālis*—Gr. *plagios,* sideways, aslant; and **cadence.**]

plage, *pläzh, n.* a fashionable beach. [Fr.]

plagiary, *plā′ji-àr-i, n.* one who takes the thoughts or writings of others and gives them out as his own.—*v.t.* **pla′giarise,** to steal from the writings or ideas of another.—*ns.* **pla′giarism,** the act or practice of plagiarising; **pla′giarist,** a plagiary. [L. *plăgiārius,* a kidnapper, plagiary—*plăga,* a net.]

plague, *plāg, n.* a deadly epidemic or pestilence esp. a fever caused by a bacillus transmitted by rat fleas from rats to man: any troublesome thing or person: (*coll.*) trouble, nuisance.—*v.t.* to pester or annoy:—*pr.p.* plāg′uing; *pa.t.* and *pa.p.* plāgued.—*n.* **plague′-spot,** a spot on the skin indicating plague: a place where disease is constantly present, a source of pollution (often *fig.*). [O.Fr. *plague*—L. *plāga,* a blow.; cf. Gr. *plēgē.*]

plaice, *plās, n.* a yellow-spotted flat-fish of the flounder genus. [O.Fr. *plaïs* (Fr. *plie*)—Low L. *platessa,* a flat-fish, perh.—Gr. *platys,* flat.]

plaid, *plād, or plad, n.* a long piece of woollen cloth worn over the shoulder, usu. in tartan (as part of Highland dress) or checked (as formerly worn by Lowland shepherds).—*adj.* **plaid′ed,** wearing a plaid. [Perh. Gael. *plaide,* a

Neutral vowels in unaccented syllables: *em′pér-ór;* for certain sounds in foreign words see p. ix.

blanket; but that may be from the Scots word.]

plain, *plān, v.i.* and *v.t.* (*poet.*) to complain: to lament. [O.Fr. *plaigner* (Fr. *plaindre*)—L. *plangĕre,* to beat the breast, lament.]

plain, *plān, adj.* flat, level: unobstructed (e.g. view): open to the mind, manifest, obvious: readily understood: outspoken, candid: without ornament: not intricate or elaborate: not coloured: not rich or highly seasoned (of food): not luxurious (e.g. *plain living*): not highly born, cultivated, or gifted: without beauty.—*n.* an extent of level land.—*adv.* clearly, distinctly.—*adv.* **plain′ly.**—*adj.* **plain′-clothes,** wearing ordinary clothes, not uniform, as a policeman on detective work.—*ns.* **plain cook,** one able to cook simple dishes; **plain′-deal′er,** one who is candid and outspoken.—*n.* and *adj.* **plain′-deal′ing.**—*ns.* **plain sailing** (see **plane sailing**); **plains′man,** a dweller in a plain; **plain′-song,** music in free rhythm sung in unison in ecclesiastical modes (mediaeval scales); **plain′-speak′ing,** straightforwardness or bluntness of speech.—*adj.* **plain′-spoken.** [Fr.,—L. *plānus,* level, flat.]

plaint, *plānt, n.* lamentation: complaint: a mournful song: statement of grievance.—*n.* **plaint′iff** (*Eng. law*), one who commences a suit against another.—*adj.* **plaint′ive,** mournful.—*adv.* **plaint′ively.**—*n.* **plaint′iveness.** [O.Fr. *pleinte* (Fr. *plainte*)—L. *plangĕre, planctum,* to beat the breast, lament.]

plait, *plat, plāt, plēt, n.* a flat fold made by doubling cloth back upon itself (now usu. **pleat**): a fold, crease, or wrinkle: three or more strands of straw, hair, &c., interlaced in a regular pattern: a pigtail, a braid.—Also *v.t.*—*adj.* **plait′ed.** [O.Fr. *pleit, ploit* (Fr. *pli*)—L. *plicāre, -ītum, -ātum,* to fold.]

plan, *plan, n.* a representation of anything projected on a plane or flat surface, esp. that of a building as disposed on the ground: a scheme or project; a way of proceeding.—*v.t.* to make a plan of: to design: to lay plans for: to intend:—*pr.p.* plan′ning: *pa.t.* and *pa.p.* planned.—**plan-position indicator** (*radar*), an apparatus in which the position of reflecting objects is shown on the screen of a cathode-ray tube, as if on a plan:—abbrev. **P.P.I.** [Fr.,—L. *plānus,* flat.]

planchette, *plä-shet′, plan-shet′, n.* a board mounted on two castors and on a vertical pencil point, used as a medium for automatic writing and supposed spirit messages. [Fr., dim. of *planche,* a board.]

plane, *plān, n.* (*geom.*) a surface on which, if any two points be taken, the straight line joining them will lie entirely on the surface: any flat or level surface: one of the thin horizontal structures used as wings and tail to sustain or control aeroplanes in flight: (short for) aeroplane or airplane: any grade of life or of development, or level of thought or existence.—*adj.* perfectly level: pertaining to, lying in, or confined to a plane.—*v.t.* to make smooth.—*adj.* **plane′-pol′arised,** of light, consisting of vibrations in one plane only.—*ns.* **plane′-tā′ble,** an instrument used in field-mapping, and having a sighting-telescope for observing objects, whose angles may be noted on a paper on the table of the instrument;

planisphere (*plan′-*), a sphere projected on a plane.—**plane angle,** an angle contained by two straight lines in a plane; **plane figure,** a figure all of whose points lie in one plane; **plane geometry** the geometry of plane figures; **plane sailing,** the calculation of a ship's place in its course, as if the earth were flat instead of spherical: (also **plain sailing**) sailing on an easy course: hence (*fig.*) easy work, a simple course. [L. *plānum,* a flat surface, neut. of *plānus,* flat; cf. plain (2) and next word.]

plane, *plān, n.* a carpenter's tool for producing a smooth surface.—*v.t.* to make (a surface, as of wood) level by means of a plane. [Fr. *plane*—L.L. *plāna*—*plānāre,* to smooth.]

plane, plane-tree, *plān′trē, n.* any one of the genus *Platanus,* tall trees with large broad leaves (from which they are named). [Fr. *plane*—L. *platanus.* See **platane.**]

planet, *plan′et, n.* a body (other than a comet or meteor) that revolves about the sun or other fixed star, reflecting the latter's light and generating no heat or light of its own.—*n.* **planeta′rium,** a machine showing the motions and orbits of the planets: a building housing such a machine.—*adj.* **plan′etary,** of, or pertaining to, the planets: under the influence of a planet: (*fig.*) wandering, erratic: terrestrial, mundane.—*n.* **plan′etoid,** a minor planet.—*adjs.* **plan′et-strick′en, plan′et-struck** (*astrol.*), affected by the influence of the planets, blasted. [Fr. *planète*—Gr. *planētēs,* wanderer—*planaein,* to make to wander.]

plangent, *plan′jent, adj.* resounding, as breaking waves: clangorous: resounding mournfully. [L. *plangens, -entis,* pr.p. of *plangĕre,* to beat.]

planish, *plan′ish, v.t.* to flatten (e.g. sheet metal) with a smooth-faced hammer: to polish by means of a roller.—*n.* **plan′isher,** a tool for planishing. [Obs. Fr. *planir, -issant*—*plan,* flat.]

plank, *plangk, n.* a long piece of timber thicker than a board: one of the principles or aims that form the 'platform' or programme of a party.—*v.t.* to cover with planks: (*slang*) to pay (money) down.—*n.* **plank′ing,** the act of laying planks: works made up of planks. [L. *planca,* a board.]

plankton, *plangk′ton,* the drifting organisms in oceans, lakes, or rivers. [Neut. of Gr. *planktos, -ē, -on,* wandering.]

plant, *plant, n.* any member of the vegetable kingdom, esp. (popularly) one of the smaller kinds: a vegetable organism, or part of one, ready for planting or lately planted: growth (e.g. *in plant*): equipment, machinery, for an industrial activity: a factory: (*slang*) a swindle, a put-up job.—*v.t.* to put into the ground for growth: to furnish with plants: to set firmly (*in* or *on* the ground): (*fig.*) to implant, to cause to take root (e.g. an idea, a principle): to found, establish (e.g. a colony): to settle (oneself): (*slang*) to conceal (stolen goods): (*slang*) to place (stolen goods, &c.) in another's possession so as to incriminate him: (*slang*) to deliver (a blow in a specified place): (*slang*) to place as evidence.—*ns.* **planta′tion,** a place planted, esp. with trees: a colony: an estate used for growing cotton, rubber, tea, or other product of warm countries: in Southern U.S., a large estate; **plant′er,** one who plants, or introduces: the owner of a plantation; **plant′-house,** a structure in which to grow plants of warmer climates; **plant′ing,** the act of setting in the ground for growth: the art of forming plantations of trees. [O.E. *plante* (n.) – L. *planta,* slip, cutting, and O.E. *plantian* (vb.), and partly from or affected by Fr. *plante.*]

plantain, *plan′tān, n.* a roadside plant that presses its leaves flat on the ground, any plant of the genus *Plantago.* [L. *plantāgō, -inis* – *planta,* the sole of the foot.]

plantain, *plan′tān, n.* a coarse banana.

plantigrade, *plant′i-grād, adj.* walking on the soles of the feet. – *n.* a plantigrade animal, as the bear. [L. *planta,* the sole, *gradī,* to walk.]

plaque, *pläk, n.* a plate, tablet, or slab hung on, applied to, or inserted in a surface as an ornament: a tablet worn as a badge of honour. [Fr.]

plash, *plash, v.t.* to cut partly through, bend down, and interweave, branches or twigs so as to form a hedge. [O.Fr. *plassier* – L. *plectĕre,* to twist; cf. **pleach.**]

plash, *plash, n.* a shallow pool: a puddle. – *adj.* **plash′y.** [O.E. *plæsc.*]

plash, *plash, n.* a dash of water: a splashing sound. – *v.i.* to dabble in water: to splash. – *adj.* **plash′y.** [Cf. Middle Low Ger. *plaschen;* perh. conn. with preceding.]

plasm, *plazm, n.* protoplasm. – *n.* **plas′ma,** plasm: the liquid part of blood, lymph, or milk: a very hot ionised gas. – *adj.* **plas′mic.** [Gr. *plasma, -atos,* a thing moulded – *plassein,* to mould.]

plaster, *pläs′tér, n.* a fabric coated with an adhesive substance for local application as a remedy, or for the protection of a cut, &c.: a pasty composition that sets hard, esp. a mixture of slaked lime, sand, and hair, used for coating walls and ceilings, &c. – *adj.* made of plaster. – *v.t.* to apply plaster, or a plaster, to: to smear: to cover excessively or injudiciously (with something): to damage by a heavy attack. – *p.adj.* **plas′tered,** (*slang*) drunk, intoxicated. – *ns.* **plas′terer,** one who plasters, or one who works in plaster; **plas′tering.** – **plaster cast,** a copy got by pouring a mixture of plaster of Paris and water into a mould formed from the object; **plaster of Paris,** gypsum (originally found near *Paris*) deprived by heat of part of the water in its composition. [O.E. *plaster* (in medical sense), and O.Fr. *plastre* (builder's plaster), both – L.L. *plastrum* – L. *emplastrum* – Gr. *emplastron* – *plassein,* to mould, apply as a plaster.]

plastic, *plas′tik, adj.* giving form to clay, wax, &c.: causing growth of natural forms: (*fig.*) creative (e.g. of imagination): (*lit.* and *fig.*) capable of being easily moulded. – *n.* a name for substances, some natural, most synthetic or semi-synthetic, which, under heat and pressure, become plastic, and can then be shaped or cast in a mould, extruded as rod, tube, &c., or used in the formation of paints, &c. (see **thermoplastic, thermosetting**). – *n.* **plasticity** (*-tis′i-ti*), state or quality of being plastic: quality in a picture of appearing to be

three-dimensional. – **plastic art,** the art of shaping (in three dimensions), as sculpture, modelling: art which is, or appears to be, three-dimensional; **plastic operation,** a surgical operation that restores a lost part to, or repairs a deformed or disfigured part of, the body; **plastic surgery,** the branch of surgery concerned with plastic operations. [Gr. *plastikos* – *plassein,* to mould.]

plastron, *plas′tron, n.* a breastplate: a fencer's wadded breast-shield: the front of a dress-shirt: a separate ornamental front part of a woman's bodice. [Fr. *plastron* – It. *piastrone* – *piastra,* breastplate, plate of metal.]

plat, *plat.* Same as **plait.**

plat, *plat, n.* a plot of ground. [**plot**]

platane, platan, *plat′än, n.* a plane-tree. [L. *platanus* – Gr. *platanos* – *platys,* broad.]

platband, *plat′band, n.* a slightly projecting square moulding: an edging of turf or flowers. [Fr. *platebande,* i.e. flat band.]

plate, *plāt, n.* a flat sheet of metal: the same as part of a mechanism: a broad piece of armour: an engraved piece of metal: an engraved sheet of metal for printing from: an impression printed from it: a whole page, usu. separately printed and inserted, illustration in a book: a mould made from type, or a sheet of metal photographically prepared, for printing from: a sheet, usually of glass, coated with an emulsion sensitive to light for use as a photographic negative: part of a denture fitting the mouth and carrying the teeth: (*hist.*) precious metal, esp. silver (Sp. *plata,* silver): wrought gold or silver: household utensils in gold or silver: plated ware: a shallow dish: contents of a plate, a helping (of food): a vessel used for a church collection. – *v.t.* to overlay with metal: to armour with metal: to cover with a thin film of another metal. – *adj.* **plā′ted,** covered with plates of metal: covered with a coating of another metal, esp. gold or silver. – *ns.* **plā′ting; plate′-arm′our,** armour of metal plates; **plate′-bas′ket,** one for forks, spoons, &c.; **plate′-feet** (*hist.*), ships that carried American silver to Spain; **plate′-glass,** a fine kind of glass, cast in thick plates; **plate′-lay′er,** one who lays, fixes, and attends to the rails of a railway; **plate′-mark,** a hall-mark; **plate′-pow′der,** a polishing powder for silver articles; **plate′-rack,** a frame for holding plates, &c. – **handed to one on a plate** (*fig.*), obtained by one without the least effort; **on one's plate** (*fig.*), in front of one, waiting to be dealt with. [O.Fr. *plate,* fem., and (for the dish) *plat,* masc., flat – Gr. *platys,* broad.]

plateau, *pla′tō, pla-tō′, n.* a tableland: a temporary stable state reached in the course of upward progress: the part of a curve representing this; – *pl.* **plateaux** (*-tōz*), also **plateaus.** [Fr., – O.Fr. *platel,* dim. of *plat,* flat.]

platen, *plat′n, n.* the work table of a machine-tool: the part of a printing-press that presses the paper against the type: the roller of a typewriter. [Fr. *platine* – O.Fr. *plate* – *plat,* flat.]

platform, *plat′förm, n.* a raised level surface: a surface of this kind in a railway station: a raised floor for speakers, musicians, &c.: a position prepared for mounting a gun: a piece

Neutral vowels in unaccented syllables: *em′pér-ôr;* for certain sounds in foreign words see p. ix.

of flooring outside the entrance to a bus, a tramcar, or sometimes a railway carriage: a programme or public declaration of policy, esp. of a political party. [Fr. *plateforme*, lit., flat form.]

platinum, *plat'in-um, n.* a noble metal (symbol Pt; at. no. 78), steel-grey, very valuable, malleable and ductile, very heavy and hard to fuse—older name **plat'ina**.—*adjs.* **platinic** (*pla-tin'ik*), **platinous** (*plat'in-us*), of platinum: containing platinum; **platinif'erous**, platinum-bearing. *v.t.* **plat'inise**, to coat with platinum.—*n.* **plat'inoid**, any of the metals with which platinum is always found associated: an alloy of copper, zinc, nickel, and tungsten resembling platinum.—**platinum blonde**, a woman with metallic silvery hair; **platinum lamp**, an electric lamp with a platinum filament. [Sp. *platina*—*plata*, silver.]

platitude, *plat'i-tūd, n.* commonplaceness: a dull commonplace or truism: an empty remark made as if it were important.—*adj.* **platitud'inous**. [Fr.,—*plat*, flat.]

Platonic, *plä-ton'ik, adj.* pertaining to *Plato* the Greek philosopher, or to his philosophy: (usu. without *cap.*) of love, between soul and soul, without sensual desire (a Renaissance conception): relating to or experiencing platonic love.—*adv.* **platon'ically**.—*ns.* **Plā'tonism**, the philosophy of Plato; **Plā'tonist**, a follower of Plato. [Gr. *platōnikos*—*Platōn, ōnos,* Plato.]

platoon, *pla-tōōn', n.* orig. a small body of soldiers in a hollow square: a subdivision ($^1/_4$) of a company: a squad: a volley. [Fr. *peloton*, ball, knot of men—L. *pila,* ball.]

platter, *plat'ér, n.* a large flat plate or dish. [Anglo Fr. *plater*—*plat,* a plate.]

platypus, *plat'i-pus, -pōōs, n.* the duckbill, a small aquatic mammal of eastern and southern Australia and Tasmania. [Gr. *platys,* flat, *pous,* gen. *podos,* a foot.]

plaudit, *plöd'it, n.* (often *pl.*) a round of applause: praise bestowed emphatically.—*adj.* **plaud'itory**. [Shortened from L. *plaudite,* applaud, an actor's call for applause at the end of a play, pl. imper. of *plaudēre, plausum,* to clap the hands.]

plausible, *plöz'i-bl, adj.* seemingly worthy of approval or praise: specious, apparently reasonable or probable (e.g. of an explanation): ingratiating and fair-spoken.—*ns.* **plausibil'ity, plaus'ibleness**.—*ns.* **plaus'ibly**. [L. *plaudēre,* to clap the hands.]

play, *plā, v.i.* to gambol, to frisk: to perform acts not part of the immediate business of life but in mimicry or rehearsal: to engage in pleasurable activity: to behave without seriousness: to amuse oneself (with), to trifle (with): to take part in a game: (*card-games*) to table a card: to gamble: to act on a stage: to perform on an instrument: to move (*about, round, on, upon* something) irregularly, lightly, or freely, to flicker, to flutter, to shimmer: to discharge or direct a stream or shower (e.g. of water, light): to move or function freely within prescribed limits.—*v.t.* to act a part on the stage or in life (e.g. Hamlet, the woman): to engage in (a game): to contend against in a game: to perform music on: to do or execute for amusement (e.g. a trick): to bring about or work (e.g.

havoc): to direct (*on, over, along,* of a light, a hose, &c.): (*lit.* and *fig.*) to give a limited freedom of action to (e.g. *lit., to play a fish*), hence to manage.—*n.* recreative activity: amusement: the playing of a game: manner of playing: gambling: a drama or dramatic performance: (*fig.*) manner of dealing (as *fair-play*): activity, operation (as, *come into play*): (*lit.* and *fig.*) freedom of movement, scope for activity (e.g. *allow full play to*).—*adj.* **play'able**, capable (by nature or by the rules of the game) of being played or of being played on.—*ns.* **play'-acting**, performance of plays: pretence; **play'-actor; play'back**, act of reproducing a recording of sound or visual material, esp. immediately after it is made: a device for doing this; **play'boy**, a light-hearted irresponsible person, esp. rich and leisured: —*fem.* **play'girl; play'er**, one who plays: an actor.—*adj.* **play'ful**, sportive: humorous.—*adv.* **play'fully**.—*ns.* **play'-bill**, a bill announcing a play; **play'book**, a book of plays; **play'fellow, play'mate**, a companion in play, esp. children's play; **play'-gōer**, one who habitually attends the theatre; **play'-house**, a theatre; **play'ing-card**, one of a pack used in playing games; **play'-pen**, a fencing within which a young child may safely play, **play'thing**, a toy: a person, &c., treated as a mere toy; **play'-wright, play'-writer**, a dramatist.—**hold in play**, to keep occupied, esp. in order to gain time or to detain; **in, out of, play,** in, out of, such a position that the rules allow it to be played (of a ball used in a game); **play ball (with)**, to cooperate (with); **play down**, to treat as less important than is the case; **play ducks and drakes, fast and loose** (see duck (3), fast (1); **play for time,** to delay action or decision in the hope that conditions will become more favourable; **play hard to get,** to make a show of unwillingness to cooperate with a view to strengthening one's position; **play into a person's hands**, to act so as to give him the advantage (deliberately or unintentionally); **play it by ear,** to improvise a plan of action to meet the situation as it develops; **play off,** to oppose (one person against another), esp. for one's own advantage: to pass (a thing) off (as something else): (*golf*) to play from the tee; **play on,** to work upon and make use of (e.g. a person's fears, credulity); **play out,** to play to the end: to finish: to exhaust; **played out,** exhausted: no longer good for anything; **play the game,** to act strictly honourably; **play up,** to redouble one's efforts, to play more vigorously: to show up well in a crisis: to give (esp. undue) prominence to: to boost: to fool; **play upon,** to practise upon, work upon; **play upon words,** a pun or other manipulation of words depending on their sound; **play up to,** to act so as to give opportunities to another actor, &c.; to flatter. [O.E. *pleg(i)an,* vb., *plega,* n.]

plea, *plē, n.* (*Scots law* and *hist.*) a law-suit: a prisoner's or defendant's answer to a charge or claim: an excuse: a pretext: urgent entreaty. [O.Fr. *plai, plaid, plait*—Low L. *placitum,* a decision—L. *placēre, -itum,* to please.]

pleach, *plēch, v.t.* to intertwine the branches of, as a hedge. [Allied to **plash**—from another form of O.Fr. *pless(i)er* — L. *plectĕre,* to plait; Gr. *plekein.*]

plead, *plēd, v.i.* to carry on a plea or law-suit: to argue in support of a cause against another: to put forward an allegation or answer in court: to implore (with *with*).—*v.t.* to maintain by argument: to allege in pleading: to offer in excuse:—*pa.t.* and *pa.p.* plead′ed, or pled.—*n.* **plead′er,** one who pleads: an advocate.—*adj.* **plead′ing,** imploring.—*n.* act of putting forward or conducting a plea: (in *pl.*) the statements of the two parties in a lawsuit.—*adv.* **plead′ingly.—plead guilty,** or **not guilty,** to admit, or refuse to admit, guilt; **special pleading,** unfair argument aiming rather at victory than at truth. [O.Fr. *plaidier*; cf. **plea.**]

please, *plēz, v.t.* to give pleasure to: to delight: to satisfy.—*v.t.* to give pleasure: to seem good: to like, to think fit, to choose.—*n.* **pleasance** (*plez′ăns*), (*arch.*) enjoyment: a pleasure ground.—*adj.* **pleas′ant,** pleasing: agreeable: cheerful: gay: facetious.—*adv.* **pleas′antly.**—*ns.* **pleas′antness; pleas′antry,** jocularity: a facetious utterance or trick.—*adj.* and *n.* **pleas′ing.**—*adv.* **pleas′ingly.**—*adj.* **pleasurable** (*plezh′ŭr-ä-bl*), able to give pleasure, delightful.—*adv.* **pleas′urably.**—*n.* **pleasure** (*plezh′ŭr*), agreeable emotions: gratification of the senses or of the mind: what the will prefers.—*v.t.* (*arch.*) to give pleasure to.—*ns.* **pleas′ure-boat,** a boat used for pleasure or amusement; **pleas′ure-ground,** ground laid out in an ornamental manner for pleasure.—**at pleasure,** when, if, or as one pleases; **if you please,** if you like: a polite formula of request or acceptance (also **please**): (*ironically*) forsooth. [O.Fr. *plaisir* (Fr. *plaire*) — L. *placēre,* to please.]

pleat, *plēt.* Same as **plait.**

plebeian, *plé-bē′ăn, adj.* of the common people: low-born: undistinguished: vulgar.—*n.* one of the common people of ancient Rome: a commoner: a member of a despised social class.—*n.* **pleb** (*coll.*), a person of unpolished manners, usu. of low rank in society. [L. *plēbēius*—*plēbs, plēbis,* the common people.]

plebiscite, *pleb′i-sit,* also *-sīt, n.* a direct vote of the whole nation, or of the people of a district, on a special point: an ascertainment of general opinion on any matter. [Partly through Fr. *plébiscite* — L. *plēbiscītum*—*plēbs,* the people, *scītum,* a decree—*scīscĕre,* to vote for.]

plectrum, *plek′trum, n.* the quill or other form of instrument for plucking the strings of the ancient Greek lyre or other musical instrument. [L. *plēctrum* — Gr. *plēktron*—*plēssein,* to strike.]

pledge, *plej, n.* something given as a security: a token or assuring sign: a solemn promise.—*v.t.* to give as security: to pawn: to bind by solemn promise: to drink to the health of. [O.Fr. *plege* (Fr. *pleige*) — L.L. *plevium, plivium,* prob. of Ger. origin.]

Pleiad, *plī′ad, n.* any one of the seven daughters of Atlas and Pleione, changed into stars (one 'lost' or invisible): a brilliant group of seven persons or things:—*pl.* **Plei′ads, Pleiades** (*plī′ä-dēz*), a group of six (visible) stars on the shoulder of the constellation Taurus. [Gr. *Pleias, Plēias, -ados,* pl. *-adēs.*]

Pleiocene. Same as **Pliocene.**

Pleistocene, *plīs′tō-sēn, adj.* of the earlier period (sometimes also called the *glacial* (q.v.) period), of the *Quaternary* geological era. [Gr. *pleistos,* most, *kainos,* recent.]

plenary, *plē′năr-i, adj.* full, entire, unqualified: fully attended (e.g. of an assembly).—*adv.* **plē′narily.—plenary indulgence,** in the Roman Catholic Church, full remission of temporal penalties to a repentant sinner; **plenary powers,** full powers to carry out some business of negotiations. [Low L. *plēnārius* — L. *plēnus,* full—*plēre,* to fill.]

plenipotentiary, *plen-i-pō-ten′shär-i, adj.* having full powers.—*n.* a person invested with full powers, esp. a special ambassador or envoy. [L. *plēnus,* full, *potentia,* power.]

plenish, *plen′ish, v.t.* to supply, stock: (*Scot.*) to provide, as a house or farm, with necessary furniture, implements, stock.—*n.* **plen′ishing** (*Scot.*), furniture. [O.Fr. *plenir, plenissant,* L. *plēnus,* full.]

plenitude, *plen′i-tūd, n.* fullness, completeness: abundance: repletion. [L. *plēnitūdō, -inis*—*plēnus,* full.]

plenty, *plen′ti, n.* a full supply: abundance.—*adj.* **plenteous** (*plen′tyus*), fully sufficient: abundant.—*adv.* **plen′teously.**—*n.* **plen′teousness.**—*adj.* **plen′tiful,** copious: abundant: yielding abundance.—*adv.* **plen′tifully.**—*n.* **plen′tifulness.—horn of plenty** (see **cornucopia**). [O.Fr. *plente* — L. *plēnitās*—*plēnus,* full.]

plenum, *plē′num, n.* a space completely filled with matter. [L. *plēnum* (*spatium*), full (space).]

pleonasm, *plē′o-nazm, n.* redundancy, esp. of words: a redundant expression.—*adjs.* **pleonas′tic, -al.**—*adv.* **pleonas′tically.** [Gr. *pleonasmos*—*pleōn* (*pleiōn*), more.]

plesiosaur, *ple′si-ō-sör, n.* a gigantic sea-reptile (*Plesiosaurus* or kindred genus) whose fossil remains are found in rocks of the Mesozoic systems. [Gr. *plēsios,* near, *sauros,* lizard.]

plethora, *pleth′or-a, n.* excessive fullness of blood: over-fullness of any kind: a too large quantity (of).—*adjs.* **plethoric** (*-thor′ik;* sometimes *pleth′-*), **plethor′ical.** [Ionic Gr. *plēthōrē,* fullness—*pleos,* full.]

pleura, *plōō′rä, n.* a delicate membrane that covers the lung and lines the cavity of the chest:—*pl.* **pleu′rae** (*-rē*).—*adj.* **pleu′ral.**—*n.* **pleurisy** (*plōō′ri-si*), inflammation of the pleura.—*adjs.* **pleurit′ic, -al,** of; affected with, or causing, pleurisy.—*n.* **pleuro-pneumo′nia,** pleurisy combined with pneumonia. [Gr. *pleurā* and *pleuron,* rib, side.]

plexus, *pleks′us, n.* a number of things, as veins, nerves, &c., woven together: a network. [L. *plexus, -ūs,* a weaving.]

pliable, *plī′ä-bl, adj.* easily bent or folded, flexible: easily persuaded.—*ns.* **pliabil′ity, plī′ableness, plī′ancy, plī′antness.**—*adj.* **plī′ant,** bending easily, flexible: tractable, easily influenced.—*adv.* **plī′antly.** [See **ply.**]

plicate, -d, *plī′kăt, -id, adjs.* folded like a fan: plaited. [L. *plīca,* a fold.]

plied, pliers. See **ply.**

plight, *plīt, n.* pledge: engagement: promise.—*v.t.* to pledge.—*pa.p.* plighted, also plight. [O.E. *pliht,* risk, *plēon,* to risk.]

Neutral vowels in unaccented syllables: *em′pér-ór*; for certain sounds in foreign words see p. ix.

plight, *plīt, n.* condition, state, now usu. bad (e.g. *a hopeless plight*). [Assimilated in spelling to the foregoing, but derived from O.Fr. *plite* — L. *plicāre, -itum, -ātum,* to fold.]

plimsoll, *plim'sŏl, -sol, n.* a rubber-soled canvas shoe. — **Plimsoll('s) line** or **mark**, a ship's load-line (q.v.), or set of load-lines, required by the Merchant Shipping Act (1876), passed at the instance of Samuel *Plimsoll*, M.P.

plinth, *plinth, n.* the square block under the base of a column: a flat-faced projecting band at the bottom of a wall. [L. *plinthus* —Gr. *plinthos*, a brick, squared stone, plinth.]

Pliocene, *plī'ō-sēn, adj.* of the last period of the *Tertiary* (q.v.) geological era. [Gr. *pleiōn* greater, more numerous, *kainos*, recent.]

plod, *plod, v.i.* to walk heavily and laboriously: to study or work steadily and laboriously: — *pr.p.* **plodd'ing**; *pa.t.* and *pa.p.* **plodd'ed**. — *n.* **plodd'er**, one who plods on: one who gets on more by sheer toil than by inspiration or natural aptitude: a dull, heavy, laborious man. — *adj.* and *n.* **plodd'ing**. [Prob. imit.]

plonk, *plongk, n.* wine, esp. cheap.

plop, *plop, n.* the sound of a small object falling into water: the sound of a cork coming out of a bottle. — *v.i.* to make the sound of a plop. [Imit.]

plosive, *plō'siv, -ziv, adj.* and *n.* stop, explosive — used of consonants formed by closing the breath passage completely (e.g. *p, b, t, d*). [From **explosive**.]

plot, *plot, n.* a small piece of ground: a plan of a field, &c.: the story or scheme of connected events running through a play, novel, &c.: a conspiracy, a stratagem or secret contrivance. — *v.t.* to lay out in plots: to make a plan or by means of a graph: to mark (points) on a graph: to conspire or lay plans to achieve. — *v.i.* to lay plots, conspire: — *pr.p.* **plott'ing**, *pa.p.* **plott'ed**. — *n.* **plott'er**. [O.E. *plot*, a patch of ground; influenced by (or partly from) Fr. *complot*, a conspiracy.]

plough, *plow, n.* an instrument for turning up the soil: (*coll.*) failure in an examination — *v.t.* to turn up with the plough: to furrow: to tear, force, or cut a way through, advance laboriously through (*lit.* and *fig.*). — *v.i.* and (*coll.*) to fail in an examination. — *ns.* **plough'ing**; **plough'land**, land suitable for tillage: (*hist.*) as much land as could be tilled with one plough; **plough'man**; a man who ploughs: — *pl.* **plough'men**; **plough'-tree**, a plough-handle; **plough'-wright**, one who makes and mends ploughs. — **plough a lonely furrow**, to be separated from one's former friends and associates and go one's own way: to take one's own course, unsupported by others; **plough back** (*fig.*), to reinvest (profits of a business) in that business; **plough the sands**, to work in vain or to no purpose. — **put one's hand to the plough**, to begin an under taking; **the Plough**, the seven brightest stars in the constellation of the Great Bear. [Late O.E. *plōh, plōg,* a ploughland; cf. O.N. *plógr.*]

ploughshare, *plow'shār, n.* the detachable part of a plough that cuts the under surface of the sod from the ground. [**plough**, and O.E. *scear,* ploughshare — *scieran,* to shear, cut.]

plover, *pluv'ér, n.* a general name for birds of

the family to which the lapwing belongs. [Fr. *pluvier* — L. *pluvia,* rain; possibly from their restlessness before rain; cf. Ger. *regenpfeifer,* lit. rain-piper.]

plow, *plow* (chiefly American). Same as **plough**.

ploy, *ploi, n.* escapade, affair: method or procedure used to achieve a particular result: a manoeuvre in a game, conversation, &c. [Prob. **employ**.]

pluck, *pluk, v.t.* to pull off, out, or away: to snatch: to strip, as a fowl of its feathers: (*coll.*) to reject in an examination. — *n.* a single act of plucking: the heart, liver, and lungs of an animal — hence heart, courage, spirit. — *adj.* **pluck'y**, having courageous spirit and pertinacity. — *adv.* **pluck'ily**. — *n.* **pluck'iness**. — **pluck up**, to pull out by the roots: to summon up, as courage. [O.E. *pluccian*; akin to Du. *plukken,* Ger. *pflücken.*]

plug, *plug, n.* a peg or any piece of wood, metal, or other substance stopping, or for stopping, a hole — a stopper: a fitting for a socket for giving electrical connection: a fire-plug: a non suction in a water main for a fire-hose: a mechanism releasing the flow of water in a water-closet: a compressed cake of tobacco, or a piece of it cut for chewing: (*coll.*) a piece of favourable publicity, esp. one incorporated in other material. — *v.t.* to stop with a plug: (*slang*) to shoot: (*slang*) to punch with the fist: (*coll.*) to advertise or publicise by frequent repetition (as a tune). — *v.i.* to plod: — *pr.p.* **plugg'ing**; *pa.p.* **plugged**. — *n.* **plugg'ing**, the act of stopping with a plug: (*slang*) punching: (*coll.*) publicising: the material of which a plug is made. [App. Du. *plug*, a bung, a peg; cf. Swed. *plugg*, a peg, Ger. *pflock.*]

plum, *plum, n.* a well-known stone-fruit or drupe: the tree producing it, one of various species belonging to the rose family: extended to various fruits or trees more or less similar: a raisin when used in cakes or puddings (*fig.*): a good thing, a choice thing of its kind (e.g. of a position or post). — *n.* and *adj.* **plum'-colour**, dark purple. — *ns.* **plum'-duff**, a flour-pudding boiled with raisins; **plum'-pudd'ing**, a national English dish made of flour and suet, with raisins, currants, and various spices. [O.E. *plūme* — L. *prūnum* — Gr. *prou(m)non.*]

plumage, *plōōm'ij, n.* feathers collectively. [Fr. — *plume* — L. *plūma,* a feather, down.]

plumb, *plum, n.* a mass of lead or other material, hung on a string, to show the vertical line: a sounding lead, plummet. — *adj.* vertical: (of a wicket) level, true: (*coll., fig.*) sheer, out-and-out. — *adv.* vertically: precisely: (*coll.,* esp. *U.S.*) utterly. — *v.t.* to test by a plumb-line: to make vertical: to sound the depth (of water) by a plumb-line: to sound the depth of by eye or understanding (e.g. *to plumb one's motives*): to undergo an unpleasant experience in its extreme form (e.g. *to plumb the depths of misery*). — *ns.* **plumb'-bob**, the weight at the end of a **plumb'-line**, a line to show the vertical, a plummet; **plumb'-rule**, a board with a plumb-line and bob for testing verticality. — *adj.* **plumb'less**, incapable of being sounded. — *n.* **plumbum** (*plum'bum*), lead (whence the chemical symbol Pb). — *adjs.* **plumbeous**

plumbago   ply

(*plum′bĕ-us*), leaden: lead-glazed; **plumbic**
(*plum′bik*), due to lead: combined with lead—
used of chemical compounds in which lead
has a comparatively high valency; **plumbous**,
of lead—used of chemical compounds in
which lead has a low valency.—*ns.* **plumber**
(*plum′ér*), orig. a worker in lead, now one who
instals and mends pipes, cisterns, and other
fittings for conveying water, gas, and sewage;
plumbery (*plum′ér-i*), plumber-work: a plumber's workshop; **plumbing** (*plum′ing*), the
craft of working in lead, esp. the craft of a
plumber: installations fitted by a plumber. [Fr.
plomb—L. *plumbum*, lead.]

plumbago, *plum-bā′gō, n.* graphite, a form of
carbon used for pencils, &c. [L. *plumbāgō,
-inis—plumbum*, lead.]

plumber. See under **plumb.**

plume, *plōōm, n.* a feather, esp. a large showy
one: a bird's crest: something resembling a
feather in structure or lightness (e.g. *a plume
of smoke*): a feather or tuft of feathers, or
anything similar, used as an ornament, e.g. on
a helmet: a token of honour or prowess.—*v.t.*
to preen: to pride, take credit to (with *on*): to
adorn with plumes: to strip of feathers.—*adjs.*
plu′mose, plu′mous, feathery: plume-like.—
borrowed plumes, grandeur or honour that
does not really belong to one (referring to the
fable of the jackdaw in peacock feathers).
[O.Fr.,—L. *plūma*, a small soft feather.]

plummet, *plum′ét, n.* a leaden or other weight,
esp. one on a plumb-line, a sounding-line, or
a fishing-line: a plumb-line: a plumb-rule.—
v.t. to sound.—*v.i.* to plunge headlong. [O.Fr.
plomet, dim. of *plomb*, lead. See **plumb.**]

plump, *plump, v.i.* to fall or drop into liquid, esp.
vertically, passively, resoundingly, without
much disturbance: to give all one's votes to
one candidate (with *for*): to choose, opt, de-
cisively or abruptly (with *for*).—*v.t.* to plunge:
to fling down or let fall flat or heavily.—*n.* the
sound or act of plumping.—*adj.* and *adv.* with
a plump: downright: in plain language: without hesitation, reserve, or qualification.—*n.*
plump′er, an undistributed vote that could
have been divided: one who gives all his votes
to one candidate.—*adv.* **plump′ly.** [L. Ger.
plumpen or Du. *plompen.*]

plump, *plump, adj.* pleasantly fat and rounded,
well filled out.—Also *v.t.* and *v.i.*—*n.* **plump′-
ness.** [App. the same word as Du.*plomp*, blunt,
Low Ger. *plump.*]

plumule,*plōō′mūl, n.* (*bot.*) the embryo shoot in
a seed: a down-feather. [L. *plūmula*, dim. of
plūma, a feather, down-feather.]

plunder, *plun′dér, v.t.* to carry off the goods of
(another) by force: to pillage.—*n.* pillage:
booty.—*n.* **plun′derer.** [Ger. *plündern*, to pillage—*plunder*, household stuff, now trash.]

plunge, *plunj, v.t.* to thrust suddenly (into water,
other fluid, or cavity): to immerse (esp. *fig.*
e.g. *to plunge a person in gloom, plunged in
thought*).—*v.i.* to fling oneself or rush impetuously, esp. into water, downhill, or into
danger, or (*fig.*) into a discussion: to pitch
suddenly forward and throw up the hind-legs,
as a horse: (*coll.*) to gamble or squander recklessly.—*n.* act of plunging.—*n.* **plung′er,** one
who plunges: a solid cylinder used as a forcer

in pumps, &c.—*adj.* and *n.* plung′ing.—**plunge
bath,** a bath large enough to allow the whole
.body to be immersed. [O.Fr. *plonger*—L.*plumbum,* lead.]

pluperfect, *plōō-pér′fĕkt,* or *plōō′-, adj.* (*gram.*)
noting that an action happened before some
other past action referred to. [L. *plūs quam
perfectum* (*tempus*), more than perfect
(tense).]

plural, *plōōr′l, adj.* numbering or expressing
more than one.—*n.* (*gram.*) the form denoting
more than one, or, where dual is recognised,
more than two.—*ns.* **plur′alism,** plurality: the
holding by one person of more than one office
at a time, esp. applied to ecclesiastical livings:
a (condition of) society in which different
ethnic, &c., groups preserve their own customs; **plur′alist,** one who holds more than one
office at one time; **plurality** (-*al′i-ti*), the state
of being plural: a plural number: numer-
ousness: the greater number, more than half:
the holding of more than one benefice at one
time: a living held by a pluralist.—*adv.* **plur′-
ally.** [L. *plūrālis—plūs, plūris,* more.]

plus, *plus, prep.* (*math.* and *coll.*) with the addition of.—*adj.* positive: positively electrified.—
adv. (*coll.*) and a little more.—*n.* the sign (+)
prefixed to positive quantities, or set between
quantities or numbers to be added together—
opp. to *minus*: an addition: a positive quantity
or term. [L. *plūs,* more.]

plus-fours, *plus-fōrz′, -förz′, n.pl.* baggy
knickerbockers or knickerbocker suit. [**plus,
four,** from the four additional inches of
cloth required.]

plush, *plush, n.* a fabric with a longer and more
open pile than velvet.—*adj.* of plush: preten-
tiously luxurious (also **plush′y**). [Fr.*pluche* or
peluche—L. *pīlus,* hair; cf. **pile** (3).]

Pluto, *plōō′tō, n.* the Greek god of the under-
world: a planet beyond Neptune, discovered in
1930.—*adjs.* **Pluto′nian,** of Pluto: of the under-
world; **Plutonic** (-*ton′ik*), of Pluto: (*geol.*) relating to, or formed under conditions of, subterranean heat. [L. *Plūtō, -ōnis*—Gr. *Ploutōn,
-ōnos.*]

plutocracy, *plōō-tok′ra-si, n.* government by the
wealthy: a ruling body or class of rich
men.—*n.* **plutocrat** (*plōō′tō-krat*), one who is
powerful because of his wealth. [Gr. *plouto-
kratia—ploutis,* wealth, and *krateein,* to rule.]

plutonium,*plōō-tō′ni-ùm, n.* an artificial element
(symbol Pu; at. no. 94), product of radioactive decay of *neptunium.* [L. *Plūtō, -ōnis,*
Pluto.]

pluvial,*plōō′vi-ál, adj.* of or by rain: rainy.—*adj.*
plu′vious, rainy. [L. *pluvia,* rain.]

ply, *plī, n.* a fold: a layer or thickness: a bend: a
strand of rope, &c.—*v.t.* and *v.i.* to bend or
fold:—*pr.p.* ply′ing; *pa.p.* plied.—*ns.* **pli′er,** one
who plies: (in *pl.*) small pincers for bending or
cutting wire, &c.; **ply′wood,** boarding made of
thin layers of wood glued together. [O.Fr. *pli,*
a fold, *plier,* to fold—L. *plicāre.*]

ply, *plī, v.t.* to work at steadily: to use or wield
diligently or vigorously: to supply (a person)
persistently (e.g. with food): to assail persistently (e.g. with questions).—*v.i.* to work
steadily: to make regular journeys over a
route: to beat against the wind:—*pr.p.* ply′ing;

Neutral vowels in unaccented syllables: *em′pér-ór*; for certain sounds in foreign words see p. ix.

pa.p. plied. [Shortened from **apply**.]

Plymouth Brethren, *plim′oth* breᴛʜ′ren, *n.pl.* a religious sect, originating at *Plymouth* about 1830; they profess no formal creed and have no regular ministers or clergy.

pneumatic, *nū-mat′ik, adj.* relating to air or gases: containing or inflated with air: worked or driven by air.—*adv.* **pneumat′ically.**—*n.sing.* **pneumat′ics,** the science of the properties of gases: pneumatology.—*ns.* **pneumatol′ogy,** the theory of spiritual beings: psychology: pneumatics; **pneumatol′ogist.**—**pneumatic trough,** a vessel with a perforated shelf, for filling gas-jars over a liquid. [Gr. *pneuma, -atos,* breath—*pneein,* to breathe.]

pneumonia, *nū-mō′ni-a,n.* inflammation of the lung.—*adjs.* **pneumogas′tric,** pertaining to the lungs and stomach; **pneumonic** (*-mon′ik*), pertaining to the lungs. [Gr. *pneumōn, -ŏnos,* lung—*pneein,* to breathe.]

pneumoconiosis, pneumokoniosis, *nū-mō-kō-ni-ōs′is, n.* any of various diseases caused by habitually inhaling mineral or metallic dust, as in coal-mining [Gr. *pneumon, ŏnos,* lung, *konia,* dust.]

poach, *pōch, v.t.* to cook (eggs) by breaking them into boiling water. [App. Fr. *pocher,* to pocket—*poche,* pouch, the white forming a pocket about the yolk.]

poach, *pōch, v.i.* to intrude on another's preserves in order to hunt game or to catch fish: (*lit.* and *fig.*) to encroach.—*v.t.* to seek or take game or fish illegally on (a specified tract of land or water): to take illegally (game or fish).—*ns.* **poach′er; poach′ing.** [A form of **poke** (3), or from O.Fr. *pocher,* to poke.]

pochette, *posh-et′, n.* a small bag carried by women: a pocket note-case or wallet. [Fr.—dim. of *poche,* pocket.]

pock, *pok, n.* a small elevation of the skin containing pus, as in smallpox.—*ns.* **pock′mark, pock′pit,** the mark, pit, or scar left by a pock. See **pox.** [O.E. *pōc,* a pustule; Ger. *pocke,* Du. *pok.*]

pocket, *pok′et, n.* a little pouch or bag, esp. one attached to a garment or a billiard-table: a hollow, a cavity, or (*fig.*) a place of lodgment or concealment containing foreign matter, &c.: (one's) financial resources: a portion of the atmosphere differing in pressure or in other condition from its surroundings: a small isolated area or patch, as of military resistance, unemployment, &c.—*adj.* for the pocket: of small size.—*v.t.* to put in the pocket: to take stealthily:—*pr.p.* **pock′eting;** *pa.t.* and *pa.p.* **pock′eted.**—*ns.* **pock′et-book,** a wallet for papers or money carried in the pocket; **pock′et-hor′ough** (see **borough**); **pock′et-mon′ey,** money carried for occasional expenses: an allowance, esp. to a boy or girl.—**in, out of, pocket,** with, or without, money: the richer or the poorer by a transaction; **pocket an insult, affront,** &c., to submit to or put up with it. [Anglo-Fr. *pokete* (Fr. *pochette,* dim. of *poche,* pouch).]

pod, *pod, n.* the fruit, or its shell, in pease, beans, and other leguminous plants—the legume.—*v.i.* to fill as pods: to form pods:—*pr.p.* **podd′ing;** *pa.t.* and *pa.p.* **podd′ed.**

podgy, *poj′i, adj.* squat: thickset.

poem, *pō′em, -im, n.* a composition in metre: a composition of high beauty of thought or language and artistic form, in verse or prose: a creation, achievement, &c., marked by beauty or artistry. [Fr. *poème*—L. *poēma*—Gr. *poiēma*—*poieein,* to make.]

poesy, *pō′e-si, n.* poetry collectively or in the abstract. [Fr. *poésie*—L. *poēsis*—Gr. *poiēsis*—*poieein,* to make.]

poet, *pō′et, -it, n.* the author of a poem: one skilled in making poetry: one with a poetical imagination:—*fem.* **pō′etess.**—*n.* **pō′etas′ter,** a petty poet.—*adjs.* **poetic, -al** (*pō-et′ik, -ál*), of the nature of, or pertaining to, poetry: expressed in poetry: in the language of poetry: imaginative.—*adv.* **poet′ically.**—*n.sing.* **poet′ics,** the branch of criticism that relates to poetry.—*v.i.* **pō′etise,** to make or compose poetry: to make poetical: to play the poet.—*ns.* **pō′et-lau′reate** (see **laureate**); **pō′etry,** the art of the poet: the essential quality of a poem: poetical compositions or writings collectively (rarely in *pl.*), poetical quality. **poetic justice,** ideal, absolutely just, distribution of rewards and punishments; **poetic licence,** a departing from strict fact or rule by a poet for the sake of effect. [Fr. *poète*—L. *poēta*—Gr. *poiētēs*—*poieein,* to make.]

pogo stick, *pō′gō stik,* a child's toy consisting of a stick with a crossbar on a strong spring on which one stands in order to bounce along the ground. [*Pogo,* a trademark.]

pogrom, *pog-rom′, n.* an organised massacre, orig. (late 19th cent.) esp. of Russian Jews. [Russ., destruction.]

poignant, *poin′ant, adj.* (*obs.*) of weapons, piercing: sharp, pungent, in taste or smell: affecting one's feelings sharply or keenly (e.g. a pathetic scene): painfully sharp (e.g. regret).—*adv.* **poign′antly.** [O.Fr. *poignant, puindre*—L. *pungĕre,* to sting.]

poind, *poind, v.t.* (*Scot.*) to seize, distrain. [O.E. *pyndan,* to impound.]

point, *point, n.* a dot or other small mark used in writing or printing: a mark of punctuation, esp. the full stop: a dot separating the integral from the fractional part of a decimal: (*geom.*) that which has position but no magnitude: a place or station considered in relation to position only: a place in a scale (e.g. *boiling point*), course, or cycle: a moment of time, without duration: a unit in judging, scoring, or measurement: a unit of measurement of printing type: one of thirty-two divisions of the compass: a detail taken into account in judging: a distinctive mark or characteristic: the most important element in an argument, discourse, &c.: that without which a story, joke, &c., is meaningless: a head, clause, or item in a discourse, &c.: a matter in debate, under attention, or to be taken into account: pun gency, sting (e.g. of an epigram): the tapering end of anything: the tip: a dagger or other weapon: a nib: a cape or headland: (in fencing) a thrust or lunge: (in various games) the position of a certain player—e.g. in cricket, that of a fielder on the offside straight out from and near the batsman (as if at the point of the bat), or the player himself: a movable rail for passing vehicles from one track to another: a tagged lace formerly used for fastening clothes.—*v.t.* to give point to: to sharpen: to aim (at): to direct attention to (esp. with *out*): to punctuate, as a sentence: to fill the joints of with mortar, as a wall: to give point, force, or piquancy to (e.g. a remark).—*v.t.* to direct the finger, the eye, or the mind towards an object: to show game by looking, as a dog does.—*p.adj.* **point′ed**, having a sharp point: sharp: (*archit.*) Gothic: epigrammatic: having marked, obvious application.—*adv.* **point′edly.**—*ns.* **point′edness; point′er**, one who points in any sense: a rod for pointing to a blackboard, &c.: a hint, tip, suggestion: an index hand of a balance, &c.: a breed of dogs that point on discovering game: (*cap.*;*pl.*) two stars of the Great Bear nearly in a straight line with the pole-star; **point′ing.**—*adj.* **point′-less.**—*ns.* **point′-duty**, the duty e.g. of a policeman stationed at a particular point to regulate traffic; **point′lace**, lace made with a needle; **points′man**, one on point-duty: one in charge of rail points.—*adj.* **point′-to-point′**, from one fixed point to another: across country.—**point of no return**, that point on a flight after which one can only go on, for want of fuel to return (also *fig.*); **point of order**, a question raised in a deliberative society as to whether proceedings are according to the rules; **point of view**, the position from which one looks at anything, literally or figuratively; **point set** (*math.*), an aggregate; **points of the compass** (see above).—**carry one's point**, to gain what one contends for in controversy; **in point**, apposite; **make a point of**, to attach special importance to; **not to put too fine a point on it**, to speak openly and bluntly. [Partly Fr. *point*, point, dot, stitch, lace, partly Fr. *pointe*, sharp point, pungency—L. *punctum* and L.L. *puncta*, respectively—L. *pungĕre, punctum*, to prick.]

point-blank, *point′-blangk′, adj.* of a shot, fired horizontally, not allowing for any appreciable curve in its trajectory or path: direct, unqualified, blunt (e.g. of a refusal).—Also *adv.* —**point-blank range**, a distance so short that a shot goes practically horizontally to the object aimed at. [App. from **point** (vb.) and **blank** (of the target).]

point-device, -devise, *point′dĕ-vīs′, n.* (*obs.*) the point of perfection (in *at point devise*, to the point arranged, or arranged to the point).—*adj.* (*arch.*) fastidiously neat or exact.—Also *adv.* [O.Fr. *point*, point, *devis*, devised.]

pointillism, *pwan′til-izm*, **pointillisme** (Fr. *pwẽ-tē-yēzm*),*n.* in painting, the use of separate dots of pure colour instead of mixed pigments. [Fr. *pointillisme—pointille*, dim. of *point*, point.]

poise,*poiz, v.t.* (*rare*) to weigh (one thing with another) for comparison (*lit.* and *fig.*): (*arch.*) to counterbalance: to distribute the weight of so as to balance exactly: to carry, support in equilibrium (*lit.* and *fig.*—often reflexive).— *v.i.* to be balanced: to be suspended: to hover.—*n.* (*lit.* and *fig.*) equilibrium: dignity and assurance of manner: carriage (e.g. of head, body): state of indecision or suspense. [O.Fr. *poiser* (Fr. *peser*)—L. *pensāre*, freq. of *pendĕre*, to weigh, and O.Fr.*pois*—L. *pensum*, weight.]

poison, *poi′zn, n.* any substance which, taken into or formed in the body, destroys life or impairs health: any malignant influence.—*v.t.* to injure or to kill with poison: to taint: to make unpalatable: to corrupt (e.g. a person's mind).—*ns.* **poi′soner; poi′son-fang**, one of two large tubular teeth in the upper jaw of venomous snakes, through which poison passes from glands at their roots when the animal bites.—*adj.* **poi′sonous**, having the quality of poison.—*adv.* **poi′sonously.**—*n.* **poi′sonousness.—poison pen**, a writer of malicious anonymous letters. [O.Fr. *puison*, poison—L. *pōtiō, -ōnis*, a draught; cf. **potion**.]

poke, *pōk, n.* a bag: a pouch.—**a pig in a poke**, a blind bargain, as of a pig bought without being seen. [M.E. *poke*; of Gmc. origin.]

poke, *pōk, n.* a projecting brim or front of a bonnet: a poke-bonnet.—*n.* **poke′-bonnet**, a bonnet with a projecting front, as worn by women of the Salvation Army and formerly by women farm-workers. [Perh. from foregoing, or from following word.]

poke, *pōk, v.t.* to thrust or push the end of anything against or into: to thrust forward: to stir up.—*v.i.* to grope or feel (about): to go prying or searching (into): to project (out of): to strike a ball with short strokes: to live in poky quarters.—*n.* an act of poking: a prod, nudge: a look, search.—*ns.* **po′ker**, one who pokes: a rod for poking or stirring the fire; **po′ker-work**, work done by burning a design into wood with a heated point.—*adjs.* **po′king** (*rare*), poky; **pō′ky**, small and cramped: shabby, mean: pottering, petty.—**poke one's nose into**, to pry into (other people's concerns). [M.E. *pōken*; app. of Low Ger. origin.]

poker, *pō′kėr, n.* a gambling game at cards, first played in America about 1835.—*n.* **poker-face**, an inscrutable face, useful to a poker-player.

polar, *pō′lár, adj.* of, or pertaining to, a pole (see **pole** (1)) or poles: belonging to the neighbourhood of a pole: having polarity.—*n.* **polarity** (*pō-lar′i-ti*), the property possessed by certain bodies (a magnetised bar) of turning so that their opposite extremities point towards the magnetic poles of the earth: the possession of two points called poles having contrary tendencies: the tendency to develop differently in different directions along an axis: the electrical condition, positive or negative, of a body: opposedness or doubleness of aspect or tendency.—Also used *fig.*—*v.t.* **polarise** (*pō′lár-īz*), to give polarity to: (*fig.*) to develop new qualities or meanings in.—*v.i.* to acquire polarity.—*n.* **polarisation** (*pō-lár-ī-zā′sh(ö)n*), the act of polarising: the state of being polarised: the restriction of the vibrations in light waves to one plane or direction.—**polar circle**, the Arctic or the Antarctic circle; **pō′lar co-or′dinates**, co-ordinates defining a point by means of a radius vector and the angle which it makes with a fixed line through the origin; **polar lights**, the aurora borealis or the aurora australis. [Low L. *polāris—polus*. See **pole** (1).]

polder, *pōl′dėr, n.* a piece of low-lying reclaimed land, esp. in the Netherlands. [Du.]

pole, *pōl, n.* the end of an axis, esp. of the earth, or any rotating sphere: one of the two points

Neutral vowels in unaccented syllables: *em′pér-ôr*; for certain sounds in foreign words see p. ix.

in the heavens or celestial sphere to which the axis of the earth is directed and round which the stars appear to revolve: either of the two points of a body in which the attractive or repulsive force is concentrated, as in a magnet: an electric terminal: (*geom.*) a fixed point: (*fig.*) an opposite extreme.—*n.* **pole'-star,** a star near the north pole of the heavens: a guide or director. [L. *polus*—Gr. *polos,* pivot, axis, firmament.]

pole, *pōl, n.* a long rounded shaft, rod or post, usu. of wood: a measuring rod of definite length: hence a measure of length, $5\frac{1}{2}$ yards, or of area, $30\frac{1}{4}$ square yards.—*n.* **pole'-vault,** an athletic event in which the competitor uses a pole to achieve great height in jumping over a cross-bar.—Also *v.i.* [O.E. *pāl* (Ger. *pfahl*)—L. *pālus,* a stake.]

Pole, *pōl, n.* a native or citizen of *Poland.*

pole-ax(e), *pōl'-aks, n.* a battle-axe consisting of an axe-head on a long handle: a short-handled axe, formerly used in naval warfare for cutting away rigging, &c. [Orig. *pollax,* from *poll,* head, and *axe* confused later with *pole* (2).]

polecat, *pōl'kat, n.* a large relative of the weasel, which emits a stink—called also *fitch* and *foumart*: (*U.S.*) a skunk. [M.E. *polcat*; perh. Fr. *poule,* hen, and *cat.*]

polemic, *po-lem'ik, adj.* given to disputing: controversial.—*n.* a controversialist: a controversy: (in *pl.,* esp. *theology*) practice or art of controversy.—*adj.* **polem'ical.**—*adv.* **polem'ically.** [Gr. *polemikos—polemos,* war.]

police, *pol-ēs', n.* the system of regulations for the preservation of order and enforcement of law (*arch.*): a body of men employed to keep order, &c.: its members collectively.—*adj.* of the police.—*v.t.* to control (e.g. a country) by means of police: to put or keep in order, to guard.—*ns.* **police-con'stable,** a policeman of ordinary rank; **police court,** a court for trying small offences brought before it by the police; **police'-force',** a separately organised body of police; **police'-inspec'tor,** a superior officer of police who has charge of a department, next in rank to a superintendent; **police'-mag'istrate,** one who presides in a police court; **police'man,** member of a police-force; **police'-off'ice, -sta'tion,** the headquarters of the police of a district, used also as a temporary place of confinement; **police'-off'icer,** an ordinary policeman; **police'woman,** a woman member of a police-force.—**police state,** a country in which secret police are employed to detect and stamp out any opposition to the government in power; **police trap,** a strategic means whereby the police keep motor traffic under scrutiny and detect offenders against the law. [Fr.,—L. *polītīa*—Gr. *polīteiā—polītēs,* a citizen—*polis,* a city.]

policy, *pol'i-si, n.* (*rare*) government, the art of government: a settled course of action adopted and followed (e.g. by the government or by a political party): any course of action followed primarily because it is expedient or advantageous in a material sense: prudence in the management of public or private affairs: in Scotland (in *pl.*) the pleasure-grounds around a mansion. [O.Fr. *policie*—L. *polītīa*

(see **police**); in Scots, perh. influenced by L. *polītus,* embellished.]

policy, *pol'i-si, n.* a writing containing a contract of insurance.—*n.* **pol'icy-hold'er,** one who holds a contract of insurance. [Fr. *police,* a policy, app.—L.L. *apodissa,* a receipt—Gr. *apodeixis,* proof.]

polio, *pōl'i-ō, n.* short for *polio*myelitis: a sufferer therefrom.—Also *adj.*

poliomyelitis, *pōl-i-ō-mī-e-lī'tis, n.* inflammation of the grey matter of the spinal cord, causing paralysis and atrophy of the muscles. [Gr. *polios,* grey, *myelos,* marrow.]

Polish, *pō'lish, adj.* of *Poland,* or its people.—*n.* the language of Poland.

polish, *pol'ish, v.t.* to make smooth and glossy by rubbing: to impart culture and refinement to: to make elegant (e.g. a literary style).—*v.i.* to take a polish.—*n.* an act of polishing: gloss: a substance used to produce a smooth surface: refinement.—*n.* **pol'isher.** [O.Fr. *polir, polissant*—L. *polīre,* to polish.]

Politburo, *-bureau, po-lit'būr-ō, or *pol', n.* in Communist countries, the effectively most powerful organ of the Communist Party's executive (in Russia from 1952 to 1966, name replaced by Presidium). [Russ. *politicheskoe,* political, *byuro,* bureau.]

polite, *po-līt', adj.* refined: of courteous manners.—*adv.* **polite'ly.**—*n.* **polite'ness—polite literature,** belles-lettres (q.v.), as distinguished from scientific treatises and the like. [L. *polītus,* pa.p. of *polīre,* to polish.]

politic, *pol'i-tik, adj.* (of actions) in accordance with good policy, expedient, judicious: (of persons) prudent, discreet, cunning: political (in *body politic*).—*adv.* **pol'iticly.**—*adj.* **polit'ical,** pertaining to polity or government: pertaining to parties differing in their views of government.—*adv.* **polit'ically.**—*n.* **politician** (*-tish'ạn*), one versed in the science of government: one engaged in political life: (usu. disparagingly) one skilled in the ways of party politics (cf. **statesman**). *n. (pl.* in form, treated as *sing.*) **pol'itics,** the art or science of government: the management of a political party: political affairs: political principles.—**political economy,** economics (q.v.; the latter is a newer term); **political geography,** geography which deals with the division of the earth for purposes of government, as states, &c., and the work of man, as towns, canals, &c.; **political science,** the science or study of government, as to its principles, aims, methods, &c.—**body politic** (see **body**). [Gr. *polītikos—polītēs,* a citizen.]

politico, *po-lit'i-kō, n.* a politician, esp. in Spanish-speaking countries—term was applied derogatorily. [It. or Sp.]

polity, *pol'i-ti, n.* the form or constitution of the government of a state, &c.: political organisation: a body of people organised under a system of government. [Gr. *polīteiā.*]

polka, *pōl'ka, n.* a Bohemian dance or its tune, in 2-4 time with accent on the first note of the second beat. [Perh. Czech *pulka,* half, from the half-step prevalent in it; or from Polish *polka,* a Polish woman.]

poll, *pōl, n.* the head: the hair of the head: a head as a unit in numbering, an individual: a register, esp. of voters: a voting: an aggregate of votes: the taking of a vote: a taking of public opinion by means of questioning: a polled animal.—*v.t.* tó cut off the hair, horns, of, or the top of (a tree): to take, register, the votes of: to receive (a specified number of votes): to cast, give (one's vote).—*adj.* **polled**, shorn: pollarded: deprived of horns: hornless.—*ns.* **deed-poll**, a deed executed by one party only, so called because it is *polled* or cut evenly, not *indented*; **poll'ing-booth**, the place where people vote; **poll'ster**, one who carries out, or puts his faith in, polls; **poll'-tax**, a tax of so much a head, i.e. of the same amount on all persons alike. [Cf. obs. Du. and L. Ger. *polle*.]

poll, *pol*, *n.* a parrot. [*Poll*, a common name for a parrot, short for *Polly*.]

pollack, *pol'ák*, *n.* a common fish of the cod family, with long lower jaw.—Also **poll'ock**. [Etymology obscure; connection with Gael. *pollag* doubtful.]

pollard, *pol'árd*, *n.* a tree having the whole crown cut off: a hornless animal of horned kind. [**poll**, the head.]

pollen, *pol'én*, *n.* the fertilising powder formed in the anthers of flowers.—*v.t.* **poll'inate**, to convey pollen to.—*n.* **pollina'tion**, the transferring or supplying of pollen to the stigma of a flower, esp. by aid of insects or other external agents.—**pollen count**, the amount of pollen in the atmosphere. [L. *pollen*, *-inis*, fine flour.]

pollute, *pol-(y)ōōt*, *v.t.* to contaminate, make filthy: to make (any feature of the environment) offensive or harmful to human, animal, or plant life: to make unclean morally: to profane.—*ns.* **pollut'er**; **pollu'tion**, act of polluting: state of being polluted: defilement. [L. *polluĕre*, *pollūtus*—*pol-*, a form of *pro* or *per*, *luĕre*, to wash.]

polo, *pō'lō*, *n.* a game like hockey on horseback—of Oriental origin.—**polo collar, neck**, a high, close-fitting collar with a part turned over at the top. [From a word meaning ball.]

polonaise, *pol-o-nāz'*, *n.* a Polish national dance: music for such a dance. [Fr., 'Polish'.]

polonium, *po-lō'ni-úm*, *n.* a radioactive element (symbol Po; at. no. 84), the last stage element in the radioactive disintegration of radium before the formation of lead. [L. *Polonia*, Poland.]

polony, *po-lō'ni*, *n.* a dry sausage made of meat partly cooked. [Prob. *Bologna sausage*.]

poltergeist, *pol'tér-gīst*, *n.* an alleged spirit said to move heavy furniture, &c., a noisy ghost. [Ger. *poltern*, to make an uproar, *geist*, spirit.]

poltroon, *pol-trōōn'*, *n.* a dastard.—*n.* **poltroon'ery**, cowardice, want of spirit. [Fr. *poltron*—It. *poltro*, lazy.]

poly-, *pol-i-*, in composition, much, many, e.g. **polyphagus**, *pol-if'a-gus*, *adj.* eating many kinds of food (Gr. *phagein* aor., to eat): (*med.*) affecting more than one part: denoting a polymer (q.v.). [Gr. *polys*, *poly*, much.]

polyandrous, *po-li-an'drus*, *adj.* having several husbands or male mates at the same time: (*bot.*) having a large and indefinite number of stamens.—*n.* **polyan'dry**, the social usage by which a woman has more husbands than one

at the same time. [Gr. *polys*, many, *anēr*, gen. *andros*, a man.]

polyanthus, *pol-i-an'thus*, *n.* a primrose with many flowers:—*pl.* **polyan'thuses**. [Gr. *polys*, many, *anthos*, a flower.]

polycarpous, *pol-i-kär'pus*, *adj.* having a gynaeceum consisting of two or more carpels. [Gr. *polys*, many, and **carpel**.]

polychrome, *pol'i-krōm*, *adj.* many-coloured. [Gr. *polys*, many, *chrōma*, colour.]

polycotyledonous, *pol-i-kot-i-lē'dón-us*, *adj.* with more than two cotyledons. [Gr. *polys*, many, and **cotyledon**.]

polyester, *pol-i-es'ter*, *n.* any of a range of polymers, some thermoplastic, some thermosetting. [**poly-**, **ester**.]

polygamy, *pol-ig'a-mi*, *n.* the practice of having more than one spouse at one time: (*bot.*) the occurrence of male, female, and hermaphrodite flowers on the same plant or on different plants.—*n.* **polyg'amist**.—*adj.* **polyg'amous**. [Gr.,—*polys*, many, *gamos*, marriage.]

polyglot, *pol'i-glot*, *adj.* using many languages.—*n.* one who speaks or writes many languages: a collection of versions of the same work in different languages, esp. a Bible of this kind. [Gr. *polys*, many, *glōtta*, tongue, language.]

polygon, *pol'i-gon*, *n.* a plane figure bounded by straight lines, esp. more than four. [L.,—Gr. *polygōnon*—*polys*, many, *gōniā*, a corner.]

polygraph, *pol'i-gräf*, *n.* a copying, multiplying, or tracing apparatus: a copy.—*n.* **polygraphy** (*pol-ig'ra-fi*), voluminous writing. [Gr. *polys*, many, *graphein*, to write.]

polygyny, *pol-ij'i-ni*, or *-ig'-*, *n.* the social usage by which a man has more wives than one at the same time. [Gr. *polys*, many, *gynē*, woman.]

polyhedron, *pol-i-hē'dron*, *n.* a solid figure with many (usu. more than six) faces.—*adjs.* **polyhe'dral**, **polyhe'drous**. [Gr. *polys*, many, *hedra*, a base.]

polymer, *pol'i-mér*, *n.* (*chem.*) one of a series of substances alike in percentage composition, but differing in molecular weight.—*n.* **polymerisa'tion**, the combination of several molecules to form a more complex molecule having the same empirical formula (q.v.) as the simpler ones, but having a greater molecular weight—a process by which many of the plastics (q.v.) are obtained.—*v.t.* **polym'erise**. [Gr.,—*polys*, many, *meros*, part.]

polymorphism, *pol-i-mörf'izm*, *n.* (*min.*, *zool.*) occurrence of the same thing in several different forms.—*n.* **pol'ymorph**, any one of several forms in which the same thing may occur.—*adjs.* **polymorphous**, **-ic**. [Gr. *polymorphos*, many-formed—*polys*, many, *morphē*, form.]

Polynesian, *pol-i-nē'zi-án*, *adj.* pertaining to *Polynesia*, the tropical islands in the Pacific Ocean.—*n.* a native of Polynesia. [Gr. *polys*, many, *nēsos*, an island.]

polynomial, *pol-i-nō'mi-äl*, *n.* an algebraic quantity of many names or terms—same as *multinomial*. [Gr. *polys*, many, L. *nōmen*, a name.]

polyp, polype, *pol'ip*, *n.* orig. (*obs.*) an octopus or cuttlefish: later extended to other animals with many arms or tentacles: an individual of

Neutral vowels in unaccented syllables: *em'pér-ór*; for certain sounds in foreign words see p. ix.

a colonial (q.v.) animal: (*rare*) a polypus:—*pl.*
pol'yps, polypes (*pol'ips*), **polypi** (*pol'i-pī*). [L. *polypus*, -*i* — Gr. *polypous*—*polys*, many, *pous*, foot.]

polypetalous, *pol-i-pet'al-us*, *adj.* with petals separated. [Gr. *polys*, many, *petalon*, a leaf.]

polyphony, *pol-if'on-i*, *n.* composition of music in parts each with an independent melody of its own.—*adj.* **polyphon'ic**. [Gr. *polys*, many, *phōnē*, voice.]

polypod, *pol'i-pod*, *n.* an animal with many feet. [Gr. *polypous*—*polys*, many, *pous*, gen. *podos*, a foot.]

polypus, *pol'i-pus*, *n.* a smooth, soft tumour growing from mucous membrane:—*pl.* **pol'ypi**. [Gr. *polypous*, -*odos*.]

polystyrene, *pol-i-stī'rēn*, *n.* a *polymer* of *styrene* having good mechanical properties, resistant to moisture and to chemicals.

polysyllable, *pol'i-sil-à-bl*, *n.* a word of many, or of more than three, syllables.—*adjs.* **poly-syllab'ic, -al**. [Gr. *polys*, many, and **syllable**.]

polytechnic, -al, *pol-i-tek'nik, -al*, *adj.* of many arts or technical subjects.—*n.* a school in which many such subjects are taught. [Gr. *polys*, many, *technē*, an art.]

polytheism, *pol'i-thē-izm*, *n.* belief in more gods than one.—*n.* **pol'ytheist**, a believer in many gods.—*adjs.* **polytheist'ic, -al**. [Gr. *polys*, many, *theos*, a god.]

polythene, *pol'i-thēn*, or **polyethylene**, *pol-i-eth'i lēn*, *n.* *polymerised ethylene* (ethylene is C₂H₄, an inflammable gas), certain thermoplastic materials widely used for many purposes, including wrappings.

polyurethane, *pol-i-ūr'é-thān*, *n.* any of a range of resins, both thermoplastic and thermosetting, used in production of foamed materials.

Polyzoa, *pol-i-zō'ä*, *n.pl.* a phylum of minute aquatic animals, almost all colonial (q.v.), with a cup-shaped body and a wreath of tentacles about the mouth.—*sing.* **polyzo'on**. [Gr. *polys*, many, *zōion*, an animal.]

pom, *pom*, *n.* (*coll.*) short for *Pomeranian* dog.

pommade, *po-mäd'*, -*mad'*, *n.* ointment for the hair. [Fr. *pommade*—It. *pomada*, *pomata*, lipsalve—L. *pōmum*, an apple.]

pomander, *pom-an'dér*, or *pom'àn-dér*, *n.* a ball of perfumes, or a perforated globe or box in which it was carried. [O.Fr. *pomme d'ambre*, apple of amber.]

pome, *pōm*, *n.* fruit constructed like an apple.—*adj.* **pomaceous** (-*ā'shùs*). [L. *pōmum*.]

pomegranate, *pom'gran-it*, *n.* a fruit with a thick rind and many seeds. [O.Fr. *pome grenate*—L. *pōmum*, apple, *grānātum*, seeded.]

pomelo, *pum'-*, or *pom'el-o*, *n.* the shaddock.

Pomeranian, *pom-é-rā'ni-án*, *adj.* pertaining to *Pomerania* in northern Prussia.—**Pomeranian dog**, a cross from the Eskimo dog, about the size of a spaniel, with a sharp-pointed face and a thick coat.

pommel, *pum'él*, *n.* the knob on a sword-hilt: the high part of a saddle-bow.—*v.t.* (usu. spelt **pummel** (q.v.)). [O.Fr. *pome*—L. *pōmum*, an apple.]

pomp, *pomp*, *n.* a splendid procession: ceremony: grandeur: ostentation: vain show.—*adj.* **pomp'ous**, displaying pomp or grandeur: solemnly consequential: self-important.—*adv.*

pomp'ously.—*ns.* **pomp'ousness, pompos'ity**. [Fr. *pompe*—L. *pompa*—Gr. *pompē*—*pempein*, to send.]

pompadour, *pom'pa-dōōr*, *n.* a fashion of dressing women's hair by rolling it up from the forehead over a cushion: a corsage with low square neck: a pattern for silk, with leaves and flowers pink, blue, and gold. [Marquise de *Pompadour*, 1721-64.]

pom-pom, *pom'-pom*, *n.* (*coll.*) name applied to various types of gun, esp. a multi-barrelled small-shell gun firing a spread of shells. [Imit.]

ponce, *pons*, *n.* a man who lives on the immoral earnings of a woman.

poncho, *pon'chō*, *n.* a South American cloak, a blanket with a hole in the middle for the head: any similar garment. [Sp.—S. Amer. Indian.]

pond, *pond*, *n.* a small, usually artificial, lake. [M.E. *ponde*; variant of **pound** (2).]

ponder, *pon'dér*, *v.t.* to weigh, now only in the mind: to think over, consider.—*v.i.* to think (on, over).—*adj.* **pon'derable**, that may be weighed: having sensible weight.—*n.* **ponderabil'ity**.—*adj.* **pon'derous**, weighty: massive: clumsy, unwieldy: solemnly laboured (e.g. of style).—*adv.* **pon'derously**.—*ns.* **pon'derousness, ponderos'ity**. [L. *ponderāre*, and *pondus*, *ponderis*, a weight.]

pongee, *pon-jē'*, *n.* a soft silk made from the cocoons of a wild silkworm. [Chinese.]

poniard, *pon'yárd*, *n.* a small dagger for stabbing.—*v.t.* to stab with a poniard. [Fr. *poignard*—*poing*—L. *pugnus*, fist.]

pontage, *pont'ij*, *n.* a toll paid on bridges: a tax for repairing bridges. [Low. L. *pontāgium*—L. *pons*, *pontis*, a bridge.]

pontiff, *pon'tif*, *n.* (*R.C.*) a bishop, esp. the pope—orig. an ancient Roman high-priest, the **pon'tifex** (*pl.* **pontif'icēs**).—*adjs.* **pontif'ic, -al**, of or belonging to a pontiff: splendid: authoritative: pompously dogmatic.—*adv.* **pontif'ically**.—*n.pl.* **pontif'icals**, the dress of a priest, bishop, or pope.—*n.* **pontif'icate**, the dignity of a pontiff or high-priest: the office and dignity or reign of a pope.—*v.i.* to perform the duties of a pontiff: to speak in a pompous manner, assuming airs of infallibility. [L. *pontifex*, *pontificis*, (partly through Fr. *pontife*), perh. from *pons*, *pontis*, a bridge, *facĕre*, to make.]

pontoon, *pon-tōōn'*, *n.* a flat-bottomed boat: a float: such a boat or float used to support a bridge: a bridge of boats: the floating gate of a dock. [Fr. *ponton*—L. *pontō*, -*ōnis*, a pontoon—*pons*, a bridge.]

pontoon, *pon-tōōn'*, *n.* Same as **vingt-et-un**—of which name it is a corruption.

pony, *pō'ni*, *n.* a small horse.—*ns.* **pon'y-skin**, the skin of a foal used as a fur; **pony-trekking**, the pastime of riding cross-country in small parties. [From Scots *powny*, prob.—O.Fr. *poulenet*, dim. of *poulain*—L.L. *pullānus*, a foal—L. *pullus*, a young animal.]

poodle, *pōō'dl*, *n.* a curly-haired dog of a very long-established breed (often clipped in places). [Ger. *pudel*; Low Ger. *pudeln*, to splash.]

pooh, *pōō*, *interj.* of disdain.—*v.t.* **pooh-pooh'**, to make light of. [Imit.]

Pooh-Bah, *pōō'bä*, a person who holds many offices simultaneously: one giving himself airs. [Character in Gilbert and Sullivan's *The Mikado.*]

pool, *pōōl, n.* a small body of still water: a deep part of a stream. [O.E. *pōl* (Du. *poel,* Ger. *pfuhl.*)]

pool, *pōōl, n.* the collective stakes in certain games or contests: a game or contest in which the winner takes the pool or part of it: a variety of billiards: a common stock or fund: a combination, e.g. of firms to increase control of the market: a group of people who may be called upon as required, e.g. a pool of typists: (in *pl.*) football pools.—*v.t.* to put into a common fund or stock.—**football pools,** a form of gambling in which participants forecast the results of certain football games, a proportion of the entry money being paid to those who forecast correctly. [Fr. *poule,* a hen, also stakes, associated in English with **pool** (1).]

poop, *pōōp, n.* the after part of a ship: a high deck in the stern of a ship.—*v.t.* to break over the stern of. [Fr. *poupe* —L. *puppis,* the poop.]

poor, *pōōr, adj.* possessing little, without means, needy: deficient: unproductive: inferior, paltry: feeble: humble: unfortunate, to be pitied.—Also as *n.* (collective), those possessing little: those dependent on relief or charity.—*adv.* **poor′ly.**—*adj.* (used predicatively) not in good health.—*ns.* **poor′ness: poor′house,** a house established at the public expense for sheltering the poor.—*n.pl.* **poor′-laws,** laws providing for the support of the poor.—*n.* **poor′-rate,** a rate or tax for the support of the poor.—*adj.* **poor′-spir′ited,** cowardly.—*n.* **poor′-spir′itedness.** [O.Fr. *poure, povre* —L. *pauper,* poor.]

pop, *pop, n.* a sharp, quick sound, as of drawing a cork: a shot: an effervescing drink.—*v.i.* to make a pop: to shoot: to come or go suddenly or quickly (in, out, &c.).—*v.t.* to cause to make a pop: to thrust or put suddenly: (*slang*) to pawn:—*pr.p.* **popp′ing;** *pa.t.* and *pa.p.* **popped;**—*adv.* with a pop: suddenly.—*ns.* **pop′corn,** a kind of maize which when parched pops or bursts open; **pop′-gun,** a tube and rammer for shooting pellets by compressed air; **pop′-shop,** a pawnshop.—**pop off,** to disappear all at once: (*slang*) to die; **pop the question,** to propose marriage; **popping crease,** a batsman's crease (q.v.). [Imit.]

pop, *pop, adj.* (*coll.*) popular.—*n.* currently popular music (also **pop-music**).—*ns.* **pop′-art′,** art drawing deliberately on commonplace material of modern urbanised life; **pop′-concert,** a concert at which pop-music is played; **pop′-group,** a (usu. small) group of musicians who play pop-music.

pope, *pōp, n.* the bishop of Rome, head of the Roman Catholic Church (also, as title or with reference to a particular pope, with *cap.*).—*ns.* **pope′dom,** office, dignity, or jurisdiction of the pope; **pop′ery,** a hostile term for Roman Catholicism.—*adv.* **pop′ish,** relating to the pope or to popery.—*n.* **pope's-eye,** the gland surrounded with fat in the middle of the thigh of an ox or a sheep.—**Pope Joan,** a mythical female pope: an old card game. [O.E. *pāpa* —L. *pāpa* —Gr. *pappas,* a father.]

popinjay, *pop′in-jā, n.* a parrot: a figure of a parrot set up to be shot at: a fop or coxcomb.

[O.Fr. *papegai*; cf. Low L. *papagallus;* Late Gr. *papagas,* a parrot; prob. Eastern.]

poplar, *pop′lär, n.* a genus of trees of the willow family, common in the northern hemisphere. [O.Fr. *poplier* —L. *pōpulus,* poplar-tree.]

poplin, *pop′lin, n.* a corded fabric with a silk warp and worsted weft: an imitation in cotton or other material. [Fr. *popeline* —It. *papalina,* papal, from the papal town of Avignon, where it was made.]

poppet, *pop′ét, n.* a puppet: a darling: a wooden prop used in launching a ship. [**puppet.**]

poppy, *pop′i, n.* a cornfield plant of several species with large showy flowers: any other species of the same genus, as that from which opium is obtained.—*ns.* **popp′y-head,** the capsule of the poppy: a carved ornament in wood, often finishing the end of a pew; **popp′y-oil,** a fixed oil from the seeds of the opium-poppy. [O.E. *popig* —L. *papāver,* poppy.]

populace, *pop′ū-läs, n.* the common people. [Fr.,—It. *popolazzo* —L. *pōpulus,* people.]

popular, *pop′ū-lär, adj.* of the people: pleasing to, enjoying the favour of, prevailing among, the people: liked by one's associates: suited to the understanding or to the means of ordinary people.—*v.t.* **pop′ularise,** to make generally known or widely approved: to present in a manner suited to ordinary people: to extend to the common people (e.g. a privilege).—*n.* **popular′ity,** quality or state of being popular.—*adv.* **pop′ularly.**—*v.t.* **pop′ulāte,** to people: to furnish with inhabitants.—*n.* **populā′tion,** act of populating: the inhabitants of any place or their number: group of persons, objects, &c. considered statistically.—*adj.* **pop′ulous,** thickly inhabited.—*n.* **pop′ulousness.—popular front,** an alliance of the more progressive or extreme political parties in the state. [L. *pōpulus,* the people.]

In the following words, where *pōr-* is given as the pronunciation of **por-** followed by a consonant, *pōr-* is a common alternative pronunciation, e.g. **port** may be *pōrt* or *pōrt*:—

porcelain, *pōrs′lin, n.* a fine earthenware, white, thin, transparent or semi-transparent: china-ware.—Also *adj.*—*ns.* **por′celain-cement,** cement for mending china; **por′celain-clay,** kaolin. [O.Fr. *porcelaine* —It. *porcellana,* cowrie.]

porch, *pōrch, n.* a building forming an enclosure or protection for a doorway: (*obs.*) a portico or colonnade: (*U.S.*) a veranda: (*cap.*) the Stoic philosophy, from the Painted Porch in the forum of Athens where Zeno taught. [O.Fr. *porche* —L. *porticus* —*porta,* a gate.]

porcine, *pōr′sīn, adj.* of pigs: swinish. [L. *porcīnus* —*porcus,* a swine.]

porcupine, *pōr′kū-pīn, n.* a large rodent quadruped of several kinds, bristling with quills. [O.Fr. *porc espin* —L. *porcus,* a pig, *spīna,* a spine.]

pore, *pōr, pör, n.* a minute passage or interstice, esp. the opening of a sweat-gland.—*adjs.* **por′al,** of or pertaining to pores; **porose** (-*ōs′,* or *pōr′-, pör′-*), full of pores.—*n.* **poros′ity.—** *adj.* **por′ous,** having pores: permeable by fluids, &c.—*n.* **por′ousness.—porous plaster,** a plaster for the body, with holes to prevent

Neutral vowels in unaccented syllables: *em′pėr-ör;* for certain sounds in foreign words see p. ix.

wrinkling. [Fr.,—L. *porus*—Gr. *poros*, a passage.]

pore, *pōr*, *pör*, *v.i.* to gaze closely and attentively (with *over*, *upon*): to ponder (on).

Porifera, *por-if'é-rä*, *n.pl.* a phylum of animals, the sponges:—*sing.* **por'ifer.**—*adjs.* **porif'eral, porif'erous.** [L. *porus*, a pore, *ferre*, to bear.]

pork, *pörk*, *pōrk*, *n.* the flesh of swine.—*ns.* **pork'-butch'er**, one who kills pigs or sells pork; **pork'(-)chop**, a slice from a pig's rib; **pork'er**, a young hog: a pig fed for pork; **pork'ling**, a young pig; **pork'(-)pie**, a pie made of minced pork. **pork pie hat**, a soft felt hat with a round flat crown and brim turned up, worn by men and women about 1850. [Fr. *porc*—L. *porcus*, a hog.]

pornography, *pör-nog'ra-fi*, *n.* the discussion of prostitution: obscene writing.—*adj.* **pornograph'ic.**—*n.* **pornog'rapher.** [Gr. *pornē*, a whore, *graphein*, to write.]

porphyry, *pör'fir-i*, *n.* a very hard, variegated rock, of a purple and white colour, used in sculpture.—*adj.* **porphyritic** (-*it'ik*), like, or of the nature of porphyry. [Gr. *porphyrītēs*—*porphyros*, purple.]

porpoise, *pör'pús*, *n.* a short-snouted genus of the dolphin family, 4 to 8 feet long, gregarious, affording oil and leather. [O.Fr. *porpeis*—L. *porcus*, a hog, *piscis*, a fish.]

porridge, *por'ij*, *n.* a food usually made by slowly stirring oatmeal in boiling water. [*pottage*, altered by influence of obs. or dial. *porray*, vegetable soup.]

porringer, *por'in-jér*, *n.* a small dish for soup, porridge, &c. [See **porridge; pottage;** for inserted *n*, cf. **passenger, messenger.**]

port, *pört*, *n.* the left side of a ship, formerly *larboard*.—*v.t.* and *v.i.* to turn left.—**port the helm**, (formerly) turn the tiller to port (or the upper part of the wheel to starboard), and hence the vessel to starboard. Since 1933 **port** means turn the vessel to port. [Ety. doubtful.]

port, *pört*, *n.* bearing, carriage of the body: demeanour.—*v.t.* (*mil.*) to hold in a slanting direction upward across the body.—*adj.* **port'able**, easily or conveniently carried or moved about.—*n.* **port'age**, act of carrying: carriage: price of carriage: a space, track, or journey, over which goods and boats have to be carried or dragged overland.—*ns.* **port(e)-cray'on**, handle for holding a crayon; **porte-monnaie** (-*mon-e'*; Fr.), a purse or pocket-book. [Fr. *port*—L. *portāre*, to carry.]

port, *pört*, *n.* a harbour: a town with a harbour.—*n.* **port'-ad'miral**, the admiral commanding at a naval port.—*n.pl.* **port'-charg'es**, harbour dues.—**port of call**, a port where vessels can call for stores or repairs; **port of entry**, a port where merchandise is allowed by law to enter. [O.E. *port*—L. *portus*, -*ūs*; akin to *porta*, a gate.]

port, *pört*, *n.* (*obs.*) a gate or gateway: (now chiefly *Scot.*) a town gate, or its former position: a porthole or its cover. [Fr. *porte* (perh. also O.E. *port*)—L. *porta*, gate.]

port, *pört*, *n.* a fortified dark-red or tawny wine (sometimes white) of the type shipped from *Oporto*, Portugal.

portal, *pör'tál*, *n.* a gate or doorway, esp. a great or magnificent one: any entrance: (*archit.*)

the arch over a gate: the lesser of two gates.—**portal vein**, vein conveying to the liver the venous blood from the intestines, spleen and stomach. [O.Fr. *portal*—Low L. *portāle*—L. *porta*, a gate.]

portcullis, *pört-kul'is*, *n.* a grating that can be let down to close a gateway. [O.Fr. *porte coleïce*, sliding gate.]

porte, *pört*, *n.* (*hist.*) the Turkish imperial government, so called from the 'Sublime Porte', or 'High Gate', the chief office of the Ottoman government at Constantinople.

portend, *pör-tend'*, *v.t.* to betoken, presage.—*n.* **portent** (*pör'tent*), that which portends or foreshows: an evil omen: ominous character (e.g. *of evil portent*).—*adj.* **portent'ous**, of the nature of, or containing, a portent or warning: (*loosely*; lit. and *fig.*) very great: impressive, solemn (e.g. of a manner). [L. *portendĕre, portentum*—*por*-, equivalent to *prō* or *per, tendĕre*, to stretch.]

porter, *pört'ér*, *n.* a door-keeper or gate-keeper: one who waits at the door to receive messages.—**porter's lodge**, a house or an apartment near a gate for the use of the porter. [O.Fr. *portier*—Low L. *portārius*—L. *porta*, a gate.]

porter, *pört'ér*, *n.* one who carries burdens for hire: a dark malt liquor, prob. because once a favourite drink with London porters.—*ns.* **port'erage**, carriage: charge made by a porter for carrying goods; **port'er-house**, a house where porter is sold. [O.Fr. *porteour*—L. *portātor*, -*ōris*—*portāre*, to carry.]

portfolio, *pört-fō'li-ō*, *n.* a portable case for loose papers, drawings, &c.: a collection of such papers: (*fig.*) the office of minister of state: a list of investments held:—*pl.* **portfo'lios.** [It. *portafogli*—L. *portāre*, to carry, *folium*, a leaf.]

porthole, *pört'hol*, *n.* a hole or opening in a ship's side for light and air, or (formerly) for pointing a gun through. [**port** (4), **hole.**]

portico, *pör'ti-kō*, *n.* (*archit.*) a range of columns with a roof forming a covered walk along the front or side of a building: a colonnade: a porch before the entrance to a building:—*pl.* **por'tico(e)s.**—*adj.* **por'ticoed**, furnished with a portico. [It.,—L. *porticus*, a porch.]

portière, *por-tyer'*, *n.* a curtain hung over the door or doorway of a room. [Fr.]

portion, *pör'sh(ó)n*, *n.* a part: an allotted part—as the part of an estate descending to an heir, or a dowry: destiny.—*v.t.* to divide into portions: to allot as a share: to furnish with a portion.—*adjs.* **por'tioned; por'tionless,** having no portion, dowry, or property. [O.Fr.,—L. *portiō*, -*ōnis*.]

Portland, *pört'länd*, *adj.* belonging to or associated with the Isle of *Portland*, a peninsula of Dorset.—**Portland cement**, a cement made by burning a mixture of clay and chalk, of the colour of Portland stone; **Portland stone**, a kind of limestone for building, quarried in the Isle of Portland.

portly, *pört'li*, *adj.* having a dignified port or mien: corpulent.—*n.* **port'liness.** [**port** (2).]

portmanteau, *pört-man'tō*, *n.* a large travelling bag that folds back flat from the middle.—**portman'teau-word**, Lewis Carroll's term for a word into which are packed the sense (and sound) of two words, e.g. *slithy* for *lithe* and

portrait   post

slimy. See **chortle, galumph.** [Fr.,—*porter,* to carry, *manteau,* a cloak.]

portrait, *pōr′trāt, n.* the likeness of a real person: a vivid description in words.—*ns.* **por′trait-gall′ery; por′trait-paint′er; por′trait-paint′ing; por′traiture,** a likeness: the art or act of making portraits, or describing in words.—*v.t.* **portray** (*pōr-trā′*), to paint or draw the likeness of: to describe in words.—*ns.* **portray′al,** the act of portraying; **portray′er.** [O.Fr. *po(u)rtrait, po(u)rtraire*—L. *prōtrahĕre, -tractum*; see **protract.**]

Portuguese, *pōr-tū-gēz′,* or *pōr′-, adj.* of Portugal, its people, or its language.—*n.* a native or citizen of Portugal: the language of Portugal.

pose, *pōz, n.* a position or attitude: an attitude of body or mind assumed for effect.—*v.t.* to assume or maintain a pose.—*v.t.* to put in a suitable attitude: to propound (a question).—*ns.* **pos′er,** one who poses; **poseur** (*pōz-œr′,* Fr.), an affected person, one who attitudinises;—*fem.* **poseuse** (*-œz′*). [Fr.,—*poser,* to place—Low L. *pausāre,* to cease—L. *pausa,* pause—Gr. *pausis.* Between Fr. *poser* and L. *pōnĕre, positum,* there has been confusion, influencing the derivatives of both words.]

pose, *pōz, v.t.* to puzzle, to perplex by questions.—*ns.* **pos′er,** one who, or that which, poses: a difficult question, a baffling problem; **pos′ing.** [Shortened from **oppose,** or **appose** (to put one thing to or opposite to another).]

posh, *posh, adj.* (*slang*) spruced up: smart: superb. [Pop. supposed to be from *'p*ort *o*utward *s*tarboard *h*ome', the most desirable position of cabins when sailing to and from the East before the days of air-conditioning, but no evidence has been found to support this.]

posit, *poz′it, v.t.* to set in place: to assume as true:—*pr.p.* **pos′iting;** *pa.p.* **pos′ited.** [L. *pōnĕre, positum,* to lay down.]

position, *poz-ish′(ò)n, n.* situation: place occupied: disposition, arrangement (with reference to other things): posture: state of affairs: ground taken in argument or dispute: principle laid down: place in society: official employment.—*v.t.* to set in place: to determine the position of.—*adjs.* **posi′tional; posi′tioned,** placed. [Fr.—L. *positiō, -ōnis*—*pōnĕre, positum,* to place.]

positive, *poz′i-tiv, adj.* definitely, formally, or explicitly laid down: express: downright: (*gram.*) expressing a quality simply without comparison: characterised by the presence of some quality, not merely by the absence of its opposite: dealing with matters of fact (e.g. *positive philosophy*—see below): (*coll.*) out-and-out (often followed by a noun of too-strong meaning, e.g. *the state of the garden was a positive digrace*): (*math.*) greater than zero: in the direction of increase, actual or conventional: having the lights and shades as in the original: (*elect.*) of, having, or producing positive electricity: (of a point of electrode with respect to another point) at more positive electrical potential.—*n.* that which is positive: a reality: a positive quantity: (*gram.*) the positive degree: a photographic plate, or an image, with the lights and shades of the original: (*elect.*) the positive plate of a battery, or pole of a cell, &c.—*adv.* **pos′itively.**—*ns.* **pos′i-**

tiveness, state or quality of being positive: certainty: confidence; **pos′itivism,** certainty: the positive philosophy; **positive philosophy,** the philosophical system originated by Comte (1798-1857)—its foundation the doctrine that man can have no knowledge of anything but phenomena, and that the knowledge of phenomena is relative, not absolute.—**positive electricity,** such as is developed in glass by rubbing with silk, arising from a deficiency of electrons on the glass; **positive electron** (see **positron**); **positive pole,** of a magnet, that end (or pole) which turns to the north when the magnet swings freely; **positive sign,** the sign (+ read *plus*) of addition. [L. *positīvus,* fixed by agreement—*pōnĕre, positum,* to place.]

positron, *poz′i-tron, n.* a particle of same mass as an electron, but with positive charge.

posse, *pos′ē, n.* a force or body (esp. of constables).—**in posse,** in possible existence: in possibility. [L. *posse,* to be able.]

possess, *poz-es′, v.t.* to have or hold as owner: to have (a quality, faculty, &c.): to occupy and dominate the mind of: to maintain (oneself, one's mind, soul, e.g. in patience): various *obs.* or *arch.* meanings, as:—to inhabit: to seize: to put in possession (of): to inform.—*adj.* **possessed′,** dominated by a spirit or other irresistible influence: self-possessed.—*n.* **possession** (*poz-esh′(ò)n*), act, state, or fact of possessing or being possessed: a thing possessed: a subject foreign territory.—*adj.* **possess′ive,** pertaining to or denoting possession: genitive: showing a desire or tendency to treat (a person or thing) as a possession.—*n.* **possess′ive** (*gram.*), a possessive adjective or pronoun: the possessive case.—*adv.* **possess′ively.**—*ns.* **possess′iveness,** extreme attachment to one's possessions: desire to dominate another emotionally; **possess′or.**—*adj.* **possess′ory.** [O.Fr. *possesser*—L. *possidēre, possessum.*]

posset, *pos′et, n.* a drink, milk curdled, as with wine, ale, or vinegar. [M.E. *poschote, possot.*]

possible, *pos′i-bl, adj.* not contrary to the nature of things: that may be or happen: that may be done, practicable: that one may tolerate, accept, or get on with.—*n.* **possibil′ity,** state of being possible: that which is possible: a contingency.—*adv.* **poss′ibly.** [L. *possibilis*—*posse,* to be able.]

post, *pōst, n.* a stout, stiff stake or pillar of timber or other material, usually fixed in an upright position.—*v.t.* to stick up on a post, wall, hoarding, &c.: to announce, advertise, or denounce by placard, or by putting a name on a list intended to read by the public.—*n.* **post′er,** a bill-sticker: a large printed bill or placard for posting. [O.E. *post*—L. *postis,* a doorpost—*pōnĕre,* to place.]

post, *pōst, n.* a fixed place or station, esp. a place where a soldier or body of soldiers is stationed: (*hist.*) a fixed place or stage on a road, for forwarding letters and for change of horses: a public letter-carrier: an established system of conveying letters: a size of writing-paper, double that of common notepaper (orig. with a post-horn as watermark): a trading depot: an office, employment or appointment.—*v.t.* to station: to entrust to the post-office for transmission: (*book-keeping*) to

Neutral vowels in unaccented syllables: *em′pér-ór*; for certain sounds in foreign words see p. ix.

562

transfer (an entry) to the ledger: (*coll.*) to supply with necessary information (often **post up**): to appoint to a post.—*v.i.* to travel with post-horses, or with speed: to move up and down in the saddle, the movements synchronising with those of the horse.—*adv.* with post-horses: with speed.—*ns.* **post′age**, money paid for conveyance by post; **post′age-stamp**, an embossed stamp or an adhesive label to show that the postal charge has been paid.—*adj.* **post′al**, of or pertaining to the mail-service. —*ns.* **post′-bag**, a mail-bag: letters received, collectively; **post′boy**, a boy or man who carries letters: a postilion: **post′(-)card**, a card on which a message may be sent by post; **post′-chaise**, a carriage, usually four-wheeled, for two or four passengers with a postilion, once used in travelling; **Post′code, postal code**, a short series of letters and numbers denoting a very small area, used for sorting mail by machine.—*adj.* **post′-free**, without charge for postage: with postage prepaid.—*n.* **post′-haste**, haste in travelling like that of a post.—*adj.* speedy: immediate.—*adv.* with haste or speed.—*ns.* **post′-horn**, a horn blown by the driver of a mail-coach; **post′-horse**, a horse kept at an inn to supply a change of horse for a postman, messenger, or traveller; **post′-man**, the post impressed upon a letter at a post-office cancelling the stamp or showing the date and place of posting or of arrival; **post′master**, the manager or superintendent of a post-office; **post′master-gen′eral**, formerly, the minister at the head of the post-office department; **post′(-)off′ice**, an office for receiving and transmitting letters by post; **Post Office**, formerly a department of the government which had charge of the reception and conveyance of letters, converted in 1969 into a public corporation, the **Post Office Corporation; post′-town**, a town with a post-office.— **postal order**, an order issued by the postmaster authorising the holder to receive at a post-office payment of the sum printed on it; **Postal Union**, an association of the chief countries of the world for international postal purposes; **postman's knock**, a parlour kissing game; **post-office box**, a box in the post-office into which are put the letters addressed to a particular person or firm; **post-office savings bank**, a branch of the post-office in which money may be deposited at a fixed rate of interest (since 1969, known as the National Savings Bank). [Fr. *poste*—It. *posta* and *posto*—L. *pōnĕre, positum*, to place.]

post-, *pōst-*, *pfx.* after, behind—as *post-classical, post-primary, post-Reformation, post-war,* &c.—*v.t.* **postdate′**, to date after the real time: to mark with a date (as for payment) later than the time of signing.—*adj.* **post′-dilu′vial**, after the Flood.—*n.* and *adj.* **post′-dilu′vian.**— *adj.* **post′-grad′uate**, belonging to study pursued after graduation. Also *n.*—*n.* **post′-impress′ionism**, a movement in painting that came after impressionism (q.v.), aiming at the expression of the spiritual significance of things rather than at mere representation—a form of expressionism (q.v.).—*n.* and *adj.* **post′-impress′ionist.**—*adjs.* **post′-merid′ian,**

coming after the sun has crossed the meridian: in the afternoon; **post′-nup′tial**, after marriage.—*n.* **post-sce′nium**, the part of the stage behind the scenery. [L. *post*, after, behind.]

post-captain, *pōst′-kap′tin, n.* formerly a naval officer *posted* to the rank of captain, a full captain distinguished from a commander (called captain by courtesy). [**post** (2).]

poste restante, *pōst res-tät, n.* a department of a post-office where letters are kept till called for (phrase used in addressing letters). [Fr., remaining post.]

posterior, *pos-tē′ri-ór, adj.* coming after: later: hinder.—*n.* hinder part: (usu. *pl.*) descendants.—*ns.* **posteriority** (*post-tē-ri-or′i-ti*); **posterity** (*-ter′i-ti*), succeeding generations: a race of descendants. [L. *posterior*, comp. of *posterus*, coming after—*post*, after.]

postern, *pōst′ėrn, n.* a back door or gate: a small private door: a sally-port.—*adj.* back: private. [O.Fr. *posterne, posterle*—L. *posterula*, a dim. from *posterus.*]

posthumous, *post′ū-mus, adj.* born after the father's death: published after the author's or composer's death.—*adv.* **post′humously.** [L. *posthumus, postumus,* superl. of *posterus,* coming after—*post,* after; the *h* inserted from false association with *humāre,* to bury.]

postiche, *pos-tēsh′, adj.* superfluously and inappropriately added to a finished work: counterfeit or false.—*n.* a superfluous and inappropriate addition: a false hairpiece, wig. [Fr.,—It. *posticio*—L. *postīcus,* hinder.]

postil, *pos′til, n.* a marginal note, esp. in the Bible: a commentary: a homily.—*v.t.* and *v.i.* to gloss. [O.Fr. *postille* (It. *postilla*)—Low L. *postilla,* possibly—L. *post illa* (*verba*), after those (words).]

postilion, *pos-* or *pōs-til′yón, n.* a postboy: one who guides post-horses, or horses in any carriage, riding on one of them.—Also **postill′ion.** [Fr. *postillon*—It. *postiglione*—*posta,* post.]

post-mortem, *pōst′ mör′tém, adj.* after death.— *n.* a post-mortem examination, autopsy: a discussion after an event. [L. *post mortem* (acc. of *mors, mortis,* death).]

post-obit, *pōst-ob′it, -ōb′it, n.* a borrower's bond securing payment on the death of someone from whom he has expectations. [L. *post obitum* (acc. of *obitus, -ūs*), after the death.]

postpone, *pōs(t)-pōn′, v.t.* to put off to a future time, to defer, to delay.—*n.* **postpone′ment.** [L. *postpōnĕre, -positum*—*post,* after, *pōnĕre,* to put.]

post-prandial, *pōst-pran′di-àl, adj.* after-dinner. [L. *post,* after, *prandium.* See **prandial.**]

postscript, *pōs(t)′skript, n.* a part added to a letter after the signature: an addition to a book after it is finished: a talk following e.g. a news broadcast: additional comment or information. [L. *post,* after, *scrīptum,* written, pa.p. of *scrībĕre,* to write.]

postulate, *pos′tū-lāt, v.t.* to claim: to take for granted, assume.—*n.* a position assumed as self-evident: (*geom.*) an operation whose possibility is assumed.—*ns.* **pos′tulant,** a candidate, esp. for ecclesiastical office, **postulā′tion.**—*adj.* **pos′tulatory,** supplicatory: assuming or assumed as a postulate. [L. *postulāre,*

-ātum, to demand—*poscĕre,* to ask urgently.]

posture, *pos'tūr, n.* the position and carriage of the body as a whole: pose: state of affairs: condition, attitude of mind.—*v.t.* to place in a particular manner.—*v.i.* (*lit.* and *fig.*) to pose. [Fr.,—L. *positūra—pōnĕre, positum,* to place.]

posy, *pō'zi, n.* a motto, as on a ring: a bunch of flowers. [poesy.]

pot, *pot, n.* a deep or deepish vessel for various purposes, esp. cooking: a drinking vessel: an earthen vessel for plants: the quantity in a pot: a hole containing water: a casual shot: a large sum (of money): an important person (usu. *big pot*): (*slang*) cannabis, marijuana. —*v.t.* to put in a pot or pots, esp. in order to preserve: to kill by a pot-shot: to pocket (as a billiard-ball): to epitomise, esp. in travesty.— *v.i.* to shoot (usu. with *at*):—*pr.p.* pott'ing; *pa.p.* pott'ed.—*ns.* **pot'-bar'ley,** barley whose outer husk has been removed by millstones; **pot'-bell'y,** a protuberant belly.—*adj.* **pot'-bell'ied.**—*ns.* **pot'-boiler,** a work in art or literature produced merely to secure the necessaries of life; **pot'-boy,** a boy in a public-house who carries pots of ale to customers; **pot'-companion,** a comrade in drinking; **pot'-hat,** a bowler hat; **pot'-herb,** a vegetable (esp. for flavouring—e.g. parsley); **pot'-hole,** a pot-shaped hole: a hole ground into rock by stones in an eddying current: a deep hole eroded in limestone: a round depression in a road surface; **pot'-holing,** the exploration of limestone pot-holes; **pot'-hook,** a hook for hanging a pot over a fire: a hooked stroke in writing; **pot'-house,** an ale-house; **pot'-hunter,** one who shoots for the sake of a bag or competes for the sake of prizes; **pot'-luck',** what may happen to be in the pot for a meal without special preparation for guests; **pot'-shot,** a shot for the sake of food rather than sport: a shot within easy range: a casual or random shot.— *adjs.* **pott'ed,** condensed: abridged: (of music) recorded for reproduction; **pot'-val'iant,** brave owing to drink.—**go to pot,** (*slang*) to go to ruin, to pieces (orig. in allusion to the cooking-pot); **keep the pot (a-)boiling,** to procure the necessaries of life: to keep going briskly without stop. [Late O.E. *pott*; cf. Ger. *pott*; Fr. *pot*; origin unknown.]

potable, *pō'ta-bl, adj.* fit to drink. [L. *pōtābilis— pōtāre,* to drink.]

potash, *pot'ash, n.* a powerful alkali, potassium carbonate, originally got in a crude state by leaching (q.v.) wood *ash,* and evaporating the residue in *pots*: potassium hydroxide (*caustic potash*), and other salts: potash-water.—*ns.* **pot'ash-wa'ter,** an aerated water containing potassium bicarbonate; **potass'ium,** an alkali metal (symbol **K,** for **kalium,** at. no. 19) discovered in potash.—**potassium-argon dating,** estimating the age of prehistoric organic material from the amount of potassium that has become argon by radioactive decay. Cf. **carbon dating.** [English **pot, ash,** or the corresponding Du. *pot-asschen* (mod. D. *potasch*).]

potation, *pō-tā'sh(ó)n, n.* drinking: a draught. [L. *pōtātiō, -ōnis—pōtāre, -ātum,* to drink.]

potato, *po-* or *pō-tā'tō, n.* a South American plant widely grown for food in temperate regions: its tuber:—*pl.* **pota'toes.**—*ns.* **pota'to-**

app'le, the fruit of the potato; **potā'to-spir'it,** alcohol made from potatoes.—**hot potato** (*slang*), a controversial issue; **sweet'-potā'to** (see **sweet**). [Sp. *patata*—Haitian *batata,* sweet-potato.]

poteen, potheen, *po-tyēn', -chēn', n.* Irish whisky, illicitly distilled. [Ir. *poitín,* dim. of *pota,* pot, from Eng. **pot** or Fr. *pot.*]

potent, *pō'tént, adj.* powerful, mighty, strongly influential: cogent: chemically and medicinally very strong.—*adv.* **pō'tently.**—*ns.* **pō'tency,** power: strength or effectiveness; **pō'tentate,** one who possesses power, a prince.—*adj.* **pōtential** (*-ten'shl*), (*rare*) powerful, efficacious: latent, existing in possibility: (*gram.*) expressing power, possibility, liberty, or obligation.—*n.* anything that may be possible: possibility: powers or resources not yet developed: of a point in a field of force, the work done in bringing a unit (of mass, electricity) from infinity to that point.—*n.* **pōtentiality** (*pō-ten-shi-al'i-ti*).—*adv.* **pōten'tially.—potential difference,** a difference in the electrical states existing at two points which causes a current to tend to flow between them—measured by the work done in transferring a unit of electricity from one point to the other; **potential energy,** the power of doing work possessed by a body in virtue of its position (e.g. a vehicle at the top of a hill, or a body in a state of tension or compression). [L. *potēns, -entis,* pr.p. of *posse,* to be able—*potis,* able, *esse,* to be.]

pother, *puтнér,* now often *poтн'ér,* **pudder,** *pud'ér, n.* a choking smoke or dust: turmoil: fuss, commotion.—*v.t.* to fluster: to perplex.— *v.i.* to make a pother. [Origin unknown.]

potion, *pō'sh(ó)n, n.* a draught: a dose of liquid medicine or poison. [Fr.,—L. *pōtiō, -ōnis— potāre,* to drink.]

pot-pourri, *pō-pōō-rē', n.* a mixture of sweet-scented materials, chiefly dried petals: a selection of tunes strung together: a literary production composed of unconnected parts. [Fr. *pot, pot,pourri,* rotten, pa.p. of *pourrir*—L. *putrēre,* to rot.]

potsherd, *pot'shérd, n.* a piece of broken pottery. [**pot,** and **shard.**]

pottage, *pot'ij, n.* a thick soup of meat and vegetables. [Fr. *potage—pot,* jug, pot.]

potter, *pot'ér, n.* one who makes articles of baked clay, esp. earthenware vessels.—*n.* **pott'ery,** earthenware vessels: a place where such goods are manufactured. [**pot.**]

potter, *pot'ér, v.i.* to be fussily engaged about trifles: to dawdle.—*n.* **pott'erer.** [Obs. *pote,* to push.]

pottle, *pot'l, n.* (*arch.*) half a gallon, or thereby: a chip basket for strawberries. [O.Fr. *potel,* dim. of *pot,* pot.]

potty, *pot'i, adj.* (*coll.*) trifling, petty: crazy.

pouch, *powch, n.* a poke pocket or bag: any pocket-like structure, as a kangaroo's brood-pouch.—*v.t.* to pocket: to enclose like a pouch.—*v.i.* to form a pouch.—*adj.* **pouched,** having a pouch. [O. Norman Fr. *pouche* (O.Fr. *poche*).]

pouf(f), pouffe, *pōōf, n.* a pad worn in the hair by women in the 18th century: in dressmaking, material gathered up into a bunch: a soft

Neutral vowels in unaccented syllables: *em'pér-ór*; for certain sounds in foreign words see p. ix.

564

ottoman or large hassock. [Fr. *pouf.*]

poult, *pōlt, n.* a chicken: the young of a domestic farmyard- or game-bird.—*ns.* **poult′erer,** one who deals in dead fowls and game; **poult′ry,** domestic or farmyard fowls collectively; **poult′ry-farm,** -**farm,** a yard, farm, where poultry are confined and bred. [Fr. *poulet,* dim. of *poule*—L.L. *pulla,* hen, fem. of L. *pullus,* young animal.]

poultice, *pōl′tis, n.* a soft composition applied in a cloth to sores, &c.—*v.t.* to put a poultice on. [L. *pultēs,* pl. of *puls, pultis* (Gr. *poltos*), porridge.]

pounce, *powns, n.* a hawk's (or other) claw: a sudden spring or swoop with intent to seize.—*v.t.* to seize with the claws.—*v.i.* to dart: to fix suddenly or eagerly (on, upon—*lit.* and *fig.*). [Derived in some way from L. *punctiō, -ōnis*—*pungĕre, punctum,* to prick.]

pounce, *powns, n.* fine powder for preparing a writing surface or absorbing ink: coloured powder dusted through perforations to mark a pattern.—*v.t.* to prepare with pounce: to trace, transfer, or mark with pounce.—*n.* **pounce′-box,** a box with a perforated lid for sprinkling pounce. [Fr. *ponce,* pumice—L. *pūmex, pūmicis.*]

pound, *pownd, n.* unit of mass of varying value, long used in western and central Europe, more or less answering to the Roman *libra,* whose symbol *lb.* is used for pound: a mass of 16 oz. avoirdupois or 7000 grains (British pound, by act of parliament, 1963, equal to 0·45359237 kilogram), formerly orig. 12 oz. troy (5760 grains): a unit of money orig. the value of a pound mass of silver: 20 shillings (the pound sterling, written £ for *libra*), later 100 new pence: also represented by a note.—*ns.* **pound′age,** a charge or tax of so much per pound sterling on any transaction in which money passes: a commission, or a share in profits, of so much per pound; **pound′al,** unit of force—that which gives an acceleration of one foot per second per second to a mass of one pound; **pound′-cake,** a sweet cake containing proportionally about a pound of each chief ingredient; **pound′er,** in composition, he who has, or that which weighs, is worth, or carries, a specified number of pounds (e.g. a 12-*pounder*).—*adj.* **pound′-foolish,** neglecting the care of large sums in attending to little ones.—**pound of flesh,** strict, literal fulfilment of a bargain. [O.E. *pund*—L. *(libra) pondō,* (pound) by weight—*pondus,* a weight—*pendēre,* to weigh.]

pound, *pownd, n.* an enclosure in which strayed animals are confined: any confined place.—*v.t.* to put in a pound: to enclose, confine.—*n.* **pound′age,** a charge for pounding stray cattle. [O.E. *pund* (in compounds), enclosure.]

pound, *pownd, n., v.t.* to beat into fine pieces: to bruise: to belabour.—*v.i.* to make one's way heavily.—*n.* **pound′er.** [O.E. *pūnian,* to beat: *d* excrescent.]

pour, *pōr, por, v.t.* to cause or allow to flow in a stream: to send forth or emit in a stream or like a stream.—*v.i.* to stream: to rain heavily. —*n.* **pour′er.** [M.E. *pouren*; origin obscure.]

pourboire, *pōōr-bwär, n.* a tip. [Fr. *pour,* for, *boire,* to drink.]

pourparler, *pōōr-pär′lā, n.* an informal preliminary conference. [Fr.]

pourtray, an old-fashioned spelling of **portray.**

poussin, *poos-ē, n.* a very young chicken. [Fr.]

pout, *powt, v.i.* to push out the lips, in sullen displeasure or otherwise: (of lips) to protrude.—Also *v.t.*—*n.* a protrusion, esp. of the lips.—*n.* **pout′er,** a variety of pigeon, having its breast inflated. [M.E. *powte.*]

poverty, *pov′ėr-ti, n.* the state of being poor: necessity: want: lack, deficiency.—*adj.* **pov′erty-strick′en,** suffering from poverty (*lit.* and *fig.*). [O.Fr. *poverte*—L. *paupertās, -ātis*—*pauper,* poor.]

powder, *pow′dėr, n.* dust: any substance in fine particles: gunpowder: hair-powder: face-powder.—*v.t.* to reduce to powder: to sprinkle, daub, or cover with powder: to salt by sprinkling.—*v.i.* to crumble into powder: to use powder for the hair or face.—*adj.* **pow′dery,** like, of the nature of, or covered with powder: dusty: friable.—*n.* **pow′der-box,** a box for face-powder, hair-powder, &c.—*adj.* **pow′dered,** reduced to powder: sprinkled with powder: salted.—*ns.* **pow′der-flask, pow′der-horn,** (*hist.*) a flask (orig. a horn) for carrying gunpowder; **pow′der-mag′azine,** a place where gunpowder is stored; **pow′der-mill,** a factory where gunpowder is made, **pow′der-monk′ey,** (*hist.*) a boy employed to carry powder to the gunners on a ship-of-war; **pow′der-puff,** a soft pad, &c., for dusting powder on the skin; **pow′der-room,** a ship's powder-magazine: (*hist.*) a room for powdering the hair: ladies' cloak-room.—**powder metallurgy,** preparing metals for use by reducing them, as a stage in the process, to powder form. [O.Fr. *poudre*—L. *pulvis, pulvĕris,* dust.]

power, *pow′ėr, powr, n.* ability to do anything—physical, mental, spiritual, legal, &c.: capacity for producing an effect: strength: one of the mental or bodily faculties: authority: governing office: permission to act: a wielder of authority, strong influence, or rule: a state influential in international affairs: a supernatural agent: an order of angels: (*arch.*) an armed force: (now *dial.* or *coll.*) a great deal or great many: (*physics*) rate of doing work: capacity for exerting mechanical force: (*math.*) the product obtained by multiplying a number by itself a specified number of times: (*optics*) magnifying strength.—*adj.* concerned with power: worked by mechanical power e.g. electricity.—*v.t.* to give power, esp. motive power, to.—*adjs.* **pow′ered; pow′erful,** having great power: forcible: efficacious.—*adv.* **pow′erfully.**—*ns.* **pow′erfulness; pow′er-house,** -**station,** a place where mechanical power (esp. electric) is generated; **pow′er-point,** a point at which an appliance may be connected to the electrical system.—*adj.* **pow′erless,** without power: weak: impotent.—*n.* **pow′erlessness.**—**power plant,** an industrial plant for generating power: the assemblage of parts generating motive power in a motor-car, aeroplane, &c.; **power politics,** international politics in which the course taken by states depends upon their knowledge that they can back their decisions with force or other compulsive action.—**in one's power,** at one's

fāte, fär; mē, hûr (her); mīne; mōte, för; mūte; mōōn, fŏŏt; THen (then)

mercy: within the limits of what one can do; **in power**, in office; **the powers that be**, the existing ruling authorities (from Rom. xiii. 1). [O.Fr. *poer*—Low L. *potēre* (for L. *posse*), to be able.]

powwow, *pow'wow*, **pawaw,** *pä-wŏ́, n.* an American Indian conjurer: a rite, often with feasting: a conference.—*v.i.* **powwow'**, to hold a powwow: to confer. [Amer. Indian *powwaw, powah.*]

pox, *poks, n.* (*pl.* of **pock**) pustules: (as *sing.*) an eruptive disease, esp. smallpox or syphilis.—*v.t.* to infect with pox.—*interj.* plague.

practice, *prak'tis, n.* actual doing: habitual action, custom: repeated performance to acquire skill: a professional man's business: (*arith.*) a method of multiplying quantities involving several units by means of aliquot parts.—*adj.* **prac'ticable**, that may be practised, used, or followed: passable, as a road.—*ns.* **practicabil'ity, practicableness.**—*adj.* **prac'tical**, in, relating to, concerned with or well adapted to actual practice: practising: efficient in action: inclined to action: virtual.—*n.* **practical'ity**, practicalness: a practical matter or feature, aspect, of an affair.—*adv.* **prac'tically**, in a practical way: to all intents and purposes.—*n.* **prac'ticalness.**—*v.t.* **practise** (*prak'tis*), to put into practice: to perform: to do habitually: to exercise, as a profession: to exercise oneself in, or on, or in the performance of, in order to maintain or acquire skill: to train by practice.—*v.i.* to act habitually: to be in practice (esp. medical or legal): to exercise oneself in any art, esp. instrumental music.—*n.* **practitioner** (*-tish'ón-ér*), one who is in practice: one who practises.—**general practitioner**, one who practises medicine and minor surgery without specialising; **practical joke**, a joke that consists in action, not words, usually an annoying trick; **practical politics**, proposals or measures that may be carried out at once or in the near future. [Obs. Fr. *practique*—L. *practicus*—Gr. *prăktikos*, fit for action—*prăssein*, to do.]

prae-. See **pre-.**

praemunire, *prē-mū-nī'ri, n.* a writ issued under a statute of Richard II, summoning a person accused of bringing, in a foreign or papal court, a suit that could be tried by English law. [From the words of the writ, *praemūnīre faciās*, cause to warn, or see that thou warn, the word *praemūnīre*, properly to fortify in front, defend, being confused with *praemonēre*, to forewarn.]

praenomen, *prē-nō'men* (as L., *prī-nō'men*), *n.* the name prefixed to the family name in ancient Rome, as *Caius* in Caius Julius Caesar: the generic name of a plant or animal. [L. *praenōmen.*]

praetor, *prē'tór, n.* a magistrate of ancient Rome, next in rank to the consuls.—*adj.* **praetorian** (*-tō'ri-án*).—*n.* **prae'torship.**—**praetorian gate**, the gate of a Roman camp in front of the general's tent, and nearest to the enemy; **Praetorian Guard**, the bodyguard of the Roman Emperor. [L. *praetor*, for *praeitor*—*prae*, before, *īre, ītum*, to go.]

pragmatic, *prag-mat'ik, adj.* relating to affairs of state: pragmatical.—*adj.* **pragmat'ical**, active:

practical: matter of fact: officious, meddlesome: opinionative.—*ns.* **prag'matism**, pragmatic quality, as officiousness, matter-of-factness: a treatment of history with an eye to cause and effect and practical lessons: a philosophy or philosophical method that makes practical consequences the test of truth; **prag'matist**, a pragmatic person: a believer in pragmatism.—**pragmatic sanction**, a special degree issued by a sovereign, such as that of the Emperor Charles VI, settling his dominions upon Maria Theresa. [Gr. *prăgma, -atos,* deed—*prăssein*, to do.]

prairie, *prā'ri, n.* a treeless plain, flat or rolling, naturally grass-covered.—*ns.* **prai'riechick'-en, -hen,** an American genus of grouse: the sharp-tailed grouse; **prai'rie-dog,** a gregarious burrowing and barking North American marmot; **prai'rie-schoon'er,** an emigrant's long covered wagon; **prai'riewolf,** the coyote. [Fr.,—L. *prātum*, a meadow.]

praise, *prāz, v.t.* to speak highly of, to commend, to extol:. to glorify, as in worship.—*n.* commendation: glorifying: the musical part of worship: (*arch.*) that for which or to whom praise is due (e.g. *God is thy praise*).—*adj.* **praise'worthy**, worthy of praise: commendable.—*n.* **praise'worthiness.** [O.Fr. *preisier*—L.L. *preciāre* for L. *pretiāre*, to prize—L. *pretium*, price.]

Prakrit, *prā'krit, n.* any of the vernacular Indo-Germanic (Aryan) dialects of India as opposed to Sanskrit: also used for these dialects collectively. [Sans. *prākrita*, natural, unrefined.]

praline, *prä'lēn, n.* a confection with nutty centre and a brown coating of sugar. [Fr. *praline*, from Marshal Duplessis-*Praslin*, whose cook invented it.]

pram, praam, *pram, n.* a flat-bottomed Dutch or Baltic lighter: a barge fitted as a floating battery. [Du. *praam.*]

pram, *pram, n.* an abbrev. of **perambulator.**

prance, *präns, v.i.* to bound from the hind legs: to go with a capering or dancing movement: to swagger: to ride a prancing horse.—*adj.* and *n.* **pranc'ing.**—*adv.* **pranc'ingly.** [M.E. *praunce.*]

prandial, *pran'di-ál, adj.* (*facetiously*) relating to dinner. [L. *prandium*, a morning or midday meal.]

prang, *prang, n.* (*R.A.F. slang*) a crash.—*v.t.* to crash or smash.

prank, *prangk, n.* a malicious or mischievous trick: a frolic. [Origin unknown.]

prank, *prangk, v.t.* to dress or adorn showily: to bespangle. [Akin to Du. *pronken*, Ger. *prunken*, to show off.]

praseo-, *prā'zē-ō-*, in composition, green. [Gr. *prasios*, leek-green—*prason*, a leek.]

praseodymium, *prā'zē-ō-dim'i-ùm, n.* a metallic element (symbol Pr; at. no. 59), a member of the rare-earth group, resembling neodymium and occurring in the same minerals. [**praseo-**, and **didymium** (see **neodymium**).]

prate, *prāt, v.i.* to talk foolishly: to tattle: to be loquacious.—*v.t.* to utter pratingly: to blab.—*n.* trifling talk.—*n.* **pra'ter.**—*n.* and *adj.* **pra'ting.**—*adv.* **pra'tingly.** [Cf. Low Ger. *praten*, Dan. *prate*, Du. *praaten.*]

pratique, *prä'tēk, prat'ik, n.* permission for a

Neutral vowels in unaccented syllables: *em'pér-ór*; for certain sounds in foreign words see p. ix.

vessel to communicate with the shore after a clean bill of health. [Fr.]

prattle, *prat'l, v.i.* to talk much and idly: to utter child's talk.—*n.* empty talk.—*n.* **prat'tler**, one who prattles: a child. [Dim. and freq. of **prate**.]

prawn, *prön, n.* any of numerous small edible shrimp-like crustaceans.—*v.i.* to fish for prawns. [M.E. *prayne, prane;* origin unknown.]

praxis, *praks'is, n.* practice: an example or a collection of examples for exercise. [Gr. *prāxis—prāssein,* to do.]

pray, *prā, v.i.* to ask earnestly (with *to, for*): to speak and make known one's desires to God.—*v.t.* to ask earnestly and reverently, as in worship.—*pr.p.* pray'ing; *pa.t.* and *pa.p.* prayed.—*ns.* **pray'er**, the act of praying: entreaty: the words used: solemn giving of thanks and praise to God, and a putting forward of requests: a petition to a public body: *(pl.)* divine services: family worship; **pray'ing**; **pray'er-book**, a book containing prayers or forms of devotion.—*adj.* **pray'erful**, full of, or given to, prayer.—*adv.* **pray'erfully.**—*ns.* **pray'erfulness; pray'er(-)meet'ing**, a shorter and simpler form of public religious service, in which laymen often take part; **pray'er-monger**, one who prays mechanically; **pray'er-rug**, a small carpet on which a Moslem kneels at prayer; **pray'ing machine'**, **-mill, -wheel**, a revolving apparatus used for prayer in Tibet and elsewhere. [O.Fr. *preier*—L. *precāri—prex, precis,* a prayer.]

pre-, *prē-,* (as living prefix), **prae-** (the spelling more common formerly), *prī-, pfx.* before, previous to, in compound words such as *prewar, pre-Christian* (before the Christian era); with *vbs.* and *verbal ns.* denoting that the action is done before some other action, as in **predecease** (*q.v.*): in front of: surpassingly, as pre-eminent. [L. *prae-.*]

preach, *prēch, v.i.* to pronounce a public discourse on sacred subjects: to discourse earnestly: to give advice in an offensive or obtrusive manner.—*v.t.* to teach or publish in religious discourses: to deliver (a sermon): to advocate, inculcate (e.g. a quality, as patience).—*n.* **preach'er.**—*v.i.* **preach'ify**, to preach tediously: to weary with lengthy advice.—*ns.* **preach'ing; preach'ing-cross**, a cross in an open place at which monks, &c., preached.—*n.pl.* **preach'ing fri'ars**, the Dominicans.—*n.* **preach'ment**, (in contempt) a sermon: a discourse affectedly solemn.—*adj.* **preach'y**, given to tedious moralising. [Fr. *prêcher*—L. *praedicāre, -ātum,* to proclaim.]

preamble, *prē-amb'bl, n.* preface: introduction, esp. that of an Act of Parliament.—*adjs.* **pream'bulary, pream'bulatory.** [Fr. *préambule*—L. *prae,* before, *ambulāre,* to go.]

prearrange, *prē-a-rānj', v.t.* to arrange beforehand.—*n.* **prearrange'ment.** [L. *prae,* before, and **arrange.**]

pre-audience, *pre-ö'di-ēns, n.* right to be heard before another: precedence at the bar among lawyers. [L. *prae,* before, and **audience.**]

prebend, *preb'end, n.* the share of the revenues of a cathedral or collegiate church allowed to a clergyman who officiates in it at stated times.—*n.* **preb'endary**, a resident clergyman who enjoys a prebend, a canon. [L.L. *prae-*

benda, an allowance—L. *praebēre,* to grant.]

precarious, *pri-kā'ri-us, adj.* depending on the will of another: depending on chance, uncertain: insecure, perilous.—*adv.* **precā'riously.**—*n.* **precā'riousness.** [L. *precārius—precāri,* to pray.]

precatory, *prek'a-tör-i, adj.* of the nature of, or expressing, a request. [L. *precāri,* to pray.]

precaution, *pri-kö'sh(ö)n, n.* caution or care beforehand: a preventive measure.—*v.t.* to warn or advise beforehand.—*adj.* **precau'tionary**, containing or proceeding from precaution. [Fr.,—L. *prae,* before, *cautio.* See **caution.**]

precede, *prē-sēd', v.t.* to go before in time, rank, or importance.—*v.i.* to be before in time, or place.—*ns.* **precedence** (*pres'i-dēns, prēs'-,* also *pri-sēd'ēns*), the act of going before in time: the state of being before in rank: priority: the foremost place in ceremony—also **precedency** (*pres'i-dēn-si, prēs'-,* also *pri-sē'dēn-si*); **precedent** (*pres'i-dent;* also *prēs'-*), a past instance, that may serve as an example or rule in the future.—*adj.* (*pri-sē'dent*) preceding.—*adjs.* **prec'edented**, having a precedent, warranted by an example; **precē'ding**, going before in time, rank, &c.: antecedent: previous.—**order of precedence**, the rules which fix the places of persons at a ceremony; **take precedence of**, to have a right to a more honourable place than. [Fr. *précéder*—L. *prae-cēdēre—prae,* before, *cēdēre,* go.]

precentor, *pri-* (or *prē-*) *sen'tör, n.* the leader of the singing in a church choir or congregation.—*n.* **precen'torship.** [L. *praecentor*—L. *prae,* before, *canēre,* to sing.]

precept, *prē'sept, n.* rule of action, principle, or maxim: a commandment: (*law*) the written warrant of a magistrate.—*adj.* **precep'tive**, containing or giving precepts.—*n.* **precep'tor**, an instructor: the head of a school: the head of a preceptory.—*fem.* **precep'tress.** *adj.* **precep'tory**, giving precepts.—*n.* a community of Knights Templars. [Fr.,—L. *praeceptum*—*praecipĕre,* to give rules to—*prae,* before, *capĕre,* to take.]

precession, *pri-sesh'(ö)n, n.* the act of going before: a moving forward.—**precession of the equinoxes**, a slow westward motion of the equinoctial points along the ecliptic, caused by the greater attraction of the sun and moon on the excess of matter at the equator, such that the times at which the sun crosses the equator come at shorter intervals than they would otherwise do. [L.L. *praecessio, -onis—praecēdēre.* See **precede.**]

precinct, *prē'singkt, n.* a space, esp. an enclosure, around a building (also in *pl.*): a limit: a district or division within certain boundaries: (in *pl.*) environs.—**shopping precinct**, a shopping centre, often free of vehicular traffic. [L.L. *praecinctum,* neut. pa.p. of *praecingĕre—prae,* before, *cingĕre,* to gird.]

precious, *presh'us, adj.* of great price or worth: cherished: worthless (in irony): over-refined in language, &c.—(*coll.*) extremely.—*ns.* **prec'iousness; precios'ity**, over-refinement in language, &c.—*adv.* **prec'iously.—precious metals**, metals of great value, esp. gold or silver; **precious stone**, a gem or jewel. [O.Fr.

precios — L. *pretiōsus* — *pretium*, price.]
precipice, *pres'i-pis, n.* a high vertical, or nearly vertical cliff.—*v.t.* **precip'itāte,** to hurl headlong: to force (into hasty action): to bring on suddenly or prematurely: (*chem.*) to separate from a state of solution or suspension.—*v.i.* to condense and fall as rain, hail, &c.: (*chem.*) to come out of solution or suspension.—*adj.* (*-ăt*) headlong: hasty.—*n.* (*chem.*) a substance separated from solution or suspension.—*adv.* **precip'itately.**—*n.* **precipitā'tion,** act of precipitating: great hurry: rash haste: rainfall.—*adj.* **precip'itant,** falling headlong: rushing down with too great velocity: hasty.—*n.* anything that brings down a precipitate.—*adv.* **precip'itantly.**—*ns.* **precip'itance, precip'itancy,** quality of being precipitate: headlong haste or rashness.—*adj.* **precip'itable** (*chem.*), that may be precipitated.—*n.* **precipitabil'ity.**—*adj.* **precip'itous,** like a precipice: sheer.—*adv.* **precip'itously.**—*n.* **precip'itousness.** [L. *praeceps, praecipitis,* headlong— *prae,* before, *caput,* head.]
précis, *prā'sē, n.* an abstract, a summary:—*pl.* **précis** (*-sēz*). [Fr.]
precise, *pri-sīs', adj.* definite, exact: very accurate: scrupulous: formal, prim.—*adv.* **precise'ly.**—*ns.* **precise'ness; preci'sian,** a too precise person; **preci'sion,** quality of being precise: exactness: minute accuracy.—*adj.* adapted to produce minutely accurate results: characterised by great accuracy. [Fr. *précis, -e* — L. *praecīsus,* pa.p. of *praecīdĕre* — *prae,* before, *caedĕre,* to cut.]
preclude, *pri-klōōd', v.t.* to hinder by anticipation: to prevent (from): to make out of the question (e.g. a possibility, doubt).—*n.* **preclusion** (*pri-klōō'zh(ó)n*).—*adj.* **preclusive** (*pri-klōō'siv*), tending to preclude: hindering beforehand. [L. *praeclūdĕre, -clūsum* — *prae,* before, *claudĕre,* to shut.]
precocious, *pri-kō'shús, adj.* early in reaching some stage of development, e.g. flowering, ripening, mental maturity: premature (e.g. of action).—*adv.* **preco'ciously.**—*ns.* **preco'ciousness, precoc'ity** (*-kos'-*), state or quality of being precocious: too early ripeness of the mind. [L. *praecox, praecōcis* — *prae,* before, *coquĕre,* to cook, to ripen.]
precognition, *prē-kog-nish'(ó)n, n.* knowledge beforehand: (*Scots law*) a preliminary examination of witnesses.—*v.t.* **precognosce** (*prē-kog-nos'*), to take a precognition of. [L. *prae-cognoscĕre* — *prae,* before, and *cognoscere.* See **cognition.**]
preconceive, *prē-kon-sēv', v.t.* to conceive or form a notion of before having actual knowledge.—*ns.* **preconceit',** a preconceived notion; **preconcep'tion,** act of preconceiving: previous opinion formed without actual knowledge. [L. *prae,* before, *concipĕre.* See **conceive.**]
precondition, *prē-kón-dish'ón, n.* a condition that must be satisfied beforehand.—*v.t.* to prepare beforehand.
preconcert, *prē-kon-sûrt', v.t.* to settle, arrange beforehand. [L. *prae,* before, and **concert.**]
precursor, *prē-kûr'sór, n.* a forerunner: one who, or that which, indicates the approach of an event.—*adj.* **precur'sory.** [L.,—*prae,* before, *cursor* — *currĕre, cursum,* to run.]

predacious, *pri-dā'shús, adj.* living by prey: predatory.—*n.* **pred'ator,** an animal that preys on other animals: a creature that plunders, e.g. crops: a human being who figuratively plunders others.—*adj.* **pred'atory,** plundering: of, relating to, or characterised by plundering: living by plunder. [L. *praeda,* booty.]
predate, *prē-dāt', v.t.* to date before the true date: to be earlier than. [Pfx. **prē-,** and **date** (1).]
predecease, *prē-di-sēs', n.* decease or death before another's death, or before another event.—*v.t.* to die before. [Pfx. **pre-,** and **decease.**]
predecessor, *prē-di-ses'ór, n.* one who has been before another in any office: a thing that has been supplanted or succeeded: an ancestor. [L. *prae,* before, *dĕcessor,* a retiring officer— *dēcēdĕre, dēcessum,* to withdraw— *dē,* away, *cēdĕre,* to go.]
predestine, *prē-* (or *pri-*) *des'tin, v.t.* to destine or decree beforehand, to fore-ordain.—*v.t.* **predes'tinate,** to determine beforehand: to preordain by an unchangeable purpose.—*adj.* (*-ăt*) fore-ordained: fated.—*n.* **predestinā'tion,** act of predestinating: (*theology*) God's decree fixing unalterably from all eternity whatever is to happen, esp. the eternal happiness or misery of men.—*adj.* **predestinā'rian,** pertaining to predestination.—*n.* one who holds the doctrine of predestination.—*n.* **predestinā'rianism.** [L. *praedestināre* — *prae,* before, *destināre.* See **destine.**]
predetermine, *prē-di-tûr'min, v.t.* to determine or settle beforehand.—*adjs.* **predeter'minable; predeter'minate** (*-ăt*), determined beforehand.—*n.* **predetermină'tion.** [L. *prae,* before, and *dētermināre.* See **determine.**]
predicable, *pred'i-kä-bl, adj.* that may be predicated or affirmed of something.—*n.* anything that can be predicated or asserted.—*n.* **predicabil'ity.** [Fr. *prédicable* — L. *praedicābilis,* praiseworthy— *praedicāre.* See **predicate.**]
predicament, *pri-dik'ä-mént, n.* (*logic*) any one of the categories in which predicables are arranged: an unfortunate or trying position. [Low L. *praedicāmentum,* something predicated or asserted.]
predicant, *pred'i-kánt, adj.* predicating: preaching.—*n.* one who affirms anything: a preacher, a preaching friar or Dominican. [L. *praedicans, -antis,* pr.p. of *praedicāre.* See **predicate.**]
predicate, *pred'i-kāt, v.t.* to affirm: (*logic*) to state as a property or attribute of the subject.—*n.* (*-ăt; logic, gram.*) that which is stated of the subject.—*n.* **predicā'tion,** act of predicating: assertion, affirmation.—*adj.* **predicative** (*pri-dik'ä-tiv,* or *pred'i-kā-tiv*), expressing predication or affirmation: forming part of the predicate (e.g. in '*he is foolish*' we have the predicative use of '*foolish*').—*adv.* **predic'atively.** [L. *praedicāre, -ātum,* to proclaim.]
predict, *pri-dikt', v.t.* to foretell (esp. after a study of facts).—*adj.* **predic'table.**—*n.* **predic'tion,** act of predicting: that which is foretold: prophecy.—*adj.* **predic'tive,** foretelling: prophetic.—*n.* **predic'tor,** one who, or that which, predicts: a device used in anti-aircraft defence

Neutral vowels in unaccented syllables: *em'pér-ór*; for certain sounds in foreign words see p. ix.

which transmits information automatically to the gun crew. [L. *praedictus*, pa.p. of *praedīcĕre—prae*, before, *dīcĕre*, to say.]

predilection, *prē-di-lek'sh(ó)n*, *n.* favourable prepossession of mind: preference. [L. *prae*, before, *dīlectiō, -ōnis*, choice—*dīligĕre*, *dīlectum*, to love—*dis*, apart, *legĕre*, to choose.]

predispose,*prē-dis-pōz'*, *v.t.* to dispose or incline beforehand: to render favourable (towards): to render liable (to).—*n.* **predisposi'tion**. [L. *prae*, before, and **dispose**.]

predominate, *pri-dom'in-āt*, *v.i.* to be dominant, to surpass in strength or authority: to prevail, be most obvious because most numerous or in greatest quantity.—*adj.* **predom'inant**, ruling: ascendant: preponderating, prevailing.—*adv.* **predom'inantly.**—*ns.* **predom'inance**, **predom'inancy**. [L. *prae*, before, *dominārī*. See **dominate**.]

pre-eminent, *prē-em'in-ént*, *adj.* eminent above others: surpassing others in good or bad qualities: outstanding.—*n.* **prē-em'inence.**—*adv.* **prē-em'inently.** [L. *praeēminens*, pr.p. of *praeēminēre—prae*, before, *ēminēre* See **eminent.**]

pre-emption, *prē-em(p)'sh(ó)n*, *n.* act or right of purchasing in preference to others: act of attacking first to forestall hostile acts.—*v.t.* **prē-empt'**, to acquire by pre-emption.—*adj.* **prē-emp'tive**, having the power to pre-empt: pre-empting. [L. *prae*, before, *ēmptiō, -ōnis*, a buying—*emĕre*, to buy.]

preen, *prēn*, *v.t.* to arrange as birds do their feathers: to trim: to plume or pride (oneself). [App. **prune** (1).]

pre-engage, *prē-én-gāj'*, *v.t.* to engage beforehand.—*n.* **prē-engage'ment**. [L. *prae*, before, and **engage.**]

pre-establish, *prē-és-tab'lish*, *v.t.* to establish beforehand.—*n.* **prē-estab'lishment**. [L. *prae*, before, and **establish.**]

pre-exist, *prē-ég-zist'*, *v.i.* to exist beforehand.—*n.* **prē-exist'ence**, previous existence.—*adj.* **prē-exist'ent**, existent or existing beforehand. [L. *prae*, before, and **exist.**]

prefabricate, *prē-fab'ri-kā-tid*, *adj.* made of parts manufactured beforehand and ready to be fitted together.—*n.* **prefabricā'tion**.[L.*prac*, before, and *fabricārī*. See **fabricate.**]

preface,*pref'is*, *n.* something said or written by way of introduction or preliminary explanation: anything preliminary or immediately antecedent.—*v.t.* to introduce by a preface: to precede (with *with*).—*adj.* **pref'atory**, pertaining to a preface: introductory.—*adv.* **pref'atorily.** [Fr. *préface*—L. *praefātiō—prae*, before, *farī, fātus*, to speak.]

prefect, *prē'fekt*, *n.* one set in authority over others: in a school, a pupil charged with disciplinary powers: in France, the governor of a department.—*ns.* **prē'fectship**, **prē'fecture**, the office or district of a prefect. [Fr. *préfet*—L. *praefectus*, pa.p. of *praeficĕre*, to set over—*prae*, before, *facĕre*, to make.]

prefer,*pri-fûr'*, *v.t.* (*arch.*) to put forward, submit for acceptance or consideration: to promote, advance: to regard or hold in higher estimation: to like better (with *to* or *rather than*, not with *than* alone):—*pr.p.* **prefer'ring**; *pa.t.* and *pa.p.* **preferred'**.—*adj.* **pref'erable** (*pref'-*), to

be preferred, more desirable.—*n.* **preferabil'ity.**—*adv.* **pref'erably**, by choice, in preference.—*n.* **pref'erence**, the act of choosing, liking, or favouring one above another: higher estimation: the state of being preferred: that which is preferred: priority. —*adj.* **preferential** (*pref-ér-en'shl*), having, or giving, allowing, a preference.—*adv.* **preferentially.**—*n.* **prefer'ment**, advancement: promotion.—**preference shares**, or **stock**, shares or stock on which the dividends must be paid before those on ordinary shares. [Fr. *préférer*—L. *praeferre—prae*, before, *ferre*, to bear.]

prefigure, *prē-fig'ûr*, *v.t.* to imagine beforehand: to represent beforehand (e.g. *these types or symbols prefigured Christ*): (*loosely*) to foreshadow.—*ns.* **prefigūrā'tion**, **prefig'urement** (*-fig'ûr-*).—*adj.* **prefig'ūrātive**. [L.L. *praefigūrāre—prae*, before, and *figūrāre*—L. *figūra*. See **figure.**]

prefix, *prē-fiks'*, *v.t.* to put before, or at the beginning. *n.* **prē'fix**, a particle in a word put before a word to affect its meaning (usu. joined to it). [L. *praefigĕre—prae*, before, and *figĕre*. See **fix.**]

pregnant,*preg'nánt*, *adj.* having a child or young in the womb: fruitful in results: (with *with*) about to produce: momentous, significant: implying more than is actually expressed: full of promise.—*n.* **preg'nancy.**—*adv.* **preg'nantly.** [O.Fr.—L. *praegnans*, *-antis*—earlier *praegnās*, *-ātis*, app.—*prae*, before, and the root *gnāscī*, to be born.]

prehensile, *pri-hen'sīl*, *adj.* capable of grasping. [L. *praehendĕre*, *-hensum*, to seize.]

prehistoric, -al,*prē-his-tor'ik, -ál*, *adj.* of a time before extant historical records.—*n.* **prē-his'tory**. [L. *prae*, before, and **historic.**]

prejudge, *prē-juj'*, *v.t.* to judge or decide upon before hearing the whole case: to condemn unheard.—*n.* **prejudg(e)'ment**. [L. *praejūdicāre*, *-ātum—prae*, before, *jūdicāre*, to judge.]

prejudice, *prej'ŏŏ-dis*, *n.* a judgment or opinion formed beforehand or without due examination: prepossession for or against anything, bias: injury, disadvantage (*to the prejudice of*).—*v.t.* to fill with prejudice, to bias the mind of: to injure, hurt, or to impair the validity of.—*adj.* **prejudicial** (*-dish'ál*), causing prejudice or injury, detrimental.—*adv.* **prejudi'cially.** [Fr. *préjudice*, wrong, and L. *praejūdicium—prae*, before, *jūdicium*, judgment.]

prelate, *prel'at*, *n.* an ecclesiastic of high rank.—*n.* **prel'acy**, the office of a prelate: the order of bishops or the bishops collectively: episcopacy.—*adjs.* **prelat'ic, -al**, pertaining to prelates or prelacy.—*n.* **prel'atist**, an upholder of prelacy. [Fr. *prélat*—L. *praelātus—prae*, before, *lātus*, borne.]

prelect, *pri-lekt'*, *v.i.* to lecture (esp. in a university).—*ns.* **prelec'tion**, a lecture; **prelec'tor**, a public reader or lecturer. [L. *praelegĕre—prae*, before, *legĕre*, *lectum*, to read.]

prelibation, *prē-lī-bā'sh(ó)n*, *n.* a foretaste. [L. *praelībātiō*, *-ōnis—prae*, before, *lībāre*, to taste.]

preliminary, *pri-lim'in-àr-i*, *adj.* introductory: preparatory.—*n.* that which precedes or pre-

---

fāte, fär; mē, hûr (her); *mīne; mōte, för; mūte, mōōn, fŏŏt;* ᴛʜen (then) pares for—used mostly in *pl.*: a preliminary or entrance examination: (in *pl.*) preliminary pages—preface, contents, &c. [L. *prae*, before, *līmināris*, relating to a threshold—*līmen*, *līminis*, a threshold.]

prelude, *prel′ūd*, *n.* a preliminary performance: an event preceding and leading up to another of greater importance: (*mus.*) an introductory passage or movement: a short independent composition such as might be the introduction to another.—*v.t.* (*prel′ūd*, formerly, and still by some, *pri-lūd′*, *-lōōd′*) to precede as a prelude.—*adjs.* **prelu′sive** (*-lōō′-* or *-lū′-*), **prelu′sory**, introductory. [Fr. *prélude*—L.L. *praelūdium*—L. *prae*, before, *lūdĕre*, to play.]

premature, *prem′a-tūr*, *prēm′-*, or *-tūr′*, *adj.* unduly early: over-hasty.—*adv.* **premature′ly** (or *prem′-*, *prēm′-*).—*ns.* **premature′ness** (or *prem′-*, *prēm′-*), **prematur′ity**. [L. *praemātūris—prae*, before, *mātūrus*, ripe.]

premeditate, *prē-med′i-tāt*, *v.t.* to meditate upon beforehand: to design, intend, beforehand.—*n.* **premeditā′tion**. [L. *praemeditārī*, *-ātus—prae*, before, *meditārī*, to meditate.]

premier, *prem′i-ér*, *prem′yér*, *prēm′i-ér*, formerly also *pri-mēr′*, *adj.* prime or first: chief: (*her.*) most ancient.—*n.* the first or chief: the prime minister.—*ns.* **prem′iership**; **première** (*pré-myer′*; Fr. *fem.*), a leading actress, dancer. &c.: first performance of a play, &c.—*v.t.* to give a first performance of. [Fr.,—L. *prīmārius*, of the first rank—*prīmus*, first.]

premise, **premiss**, *prem′is*, *n.* (*logic*) a proposition stated or assumed, for after-reasoning, esp. one of the two propositions in a syllogism from which the conclusion is drawn: (in the form **premise** only, usu. in *pl.* **prem′ises**) the thing set forth in the beginning of a deed: (*pl.*) a building and adjuncts.—*v.t.* **premise** (*pri-mīz′*), to mention or state by way of introduction. [Fr. *prémisse*—L. (*sententia*) praemissa, (a sentence) put before—*prae*, before, *mittĕre*, *missum*, to send.]

premium, *prē′mi-um*, *n.* a reward, a prize: a bounty: payment made for insurance: a fee for admission as a pupil for a profession: excess over the original price or par of stock—opp. to *discount*: anything asked or given as an incentive.—**Premium Bond**, a Government bond, the holder of which gains no interest but is eligible for a money prize allotted by draw held at stated intervals.—**at a premium**, above par. [L. *praemium—prae*, above, *emĕre*, to buy.]

premolar, *prē-mō′lár*, *n.* a tooth between the canine and the molars, a bicuspid. [L. *prae*, before, and **molar**.]

premonition, *prē-mŏn-ish′(ŏ)n*, *n.* a forewarning: a feeling that something is going to happen.—*adjs.* **premonitive** (*pri-mon′-*), **prēmon′itory**, giving warning or notice beforehand.—*n.* **prēmon′itor**, one who, or that which, gives warning beforehand.—*adv.* **prēmon′itorily**. [Through Fr. from L.L. *praemonitiō—praemonēre*, to forewarn—*prae*, before, *monēre*, to warn.]

prentice, *pren′tis*, *n.*, *adj.* and *v.t.* (*arch.*). Short for **apprentice**.

preoccupy, *prē-ok′ū-pī*, *v.t.* to occupy or fill beforehand or before others: to take or keep exclusive possession of: to fill the mind of: (*arch.*) to prejudice.—*n.* **prēocc′upancy**, the act or the right of occupying beforehand.—*adj.* **prēocc′upied**, already occupied: lost in thought, abstracted: having one's attention wholly taken up by (with *with*).—*n.* **prēoccupā′tion**. [L. *praeoccupāre*, *-ātum—prae*, before, and *occupāre*. See **occupy**.]

preordain, *prē-ör-dān′*, *v.t.* to ordain, appoint, determine, beforehand. [L. *prae*, before, *ordināre*. See **ordain**.]

prepaid. See **prepay**.

prepare, *pri-pār′*, *v.t.* to make ready: to equip, train: to make (someone) ready or fit (to bear a shock, &c.).—*v.i.* to make oneself ready.—*n.* **preparation** (*prep-a-rā′sh(ŏ)n*), the act or process of preparing: preliminary study of prescribed class-work (abbrev. **prep**): the time allotted for this: the state of being prepared: that which has been prepared: an anatomical specimen.—*adj.* **preparative** (*pri-par′á-tiv*), serving to prepare: preliminary.—*n.* that which prepares: a preparation.—*adjs.* **prepar′atory**, preparing for something coming: introductory; **prepared′**, made ready: ready: willing.—*ns.* **prepā′redness**; **prepā′rer**.—**preparatory** (abbrev. **prep**) **school**, one which prepares pupils for a higher school, esp. for a public school; **preparatory to**, before and in the intention of (doing something). [Fr. *préparer*—L. *praeparāre—prae*, before, *parāre*, to make ready.]

prepay, *prē′pā′*, *v.t.* to pay before or in advance:—*pa.t.* and *pa.p.* pre′paid′.—*n.* **prepay′ment**. [L. *prae*, before, and **pay**.]

prepense, *pri-pens′*, *adj.* premeditated, intentional, chiefly in the phrase 'malice prepense' = malice aforethought. [Fr.,—L. *prae*, before, *pensāre—pendĕre*, *pensum*, to weigh.]

preponderate, *pri-pon′dér-āt*, *v.i.* to weigh more, to turn the balance: (of a scale) to sink: (*fig.*) to prevail or exceed in any respect, as number, quantity, importance, influence.—*adj.* **prepon′derant**, superior in number, weight, influence, &c.—*n.* **prepon′derance**.—*adv.* **prepon′derantly**. [L. *praeponderāre*, *-ātum—prae*, before, *pondus*, a weight.]

preposition, *prep-ŏ-zish′(ŏ)n*, *n.* a word placed before a noun or its equivalent to show its relation to another word.—*adj.* **preposi′tional**.—*adv.* **preposi′tionally**.—*ns.* **prepos′itor**, **praeposit′or**, a school prefect. [Fr.,—L. *praepositiō*, *-ōnis—prae*, before, *pōnĕre*, *positum*, to place.]

prepossess, *prē-poz-es′*, *v.t.* (*rare*) to take possession of beforehand: to preoccupy, as the mind with some opinion (e.g. *he sought to prepossess them with the idea that* . . .; *prepossessed by, with, the notion*): to bias or prejudice, esp. favourably (e.g. *I was not prepossessed by, with, her*).—*adj.* **prepossess′ing**, tending to prepossess: making a favourable impression.—*adv.* **prepossess′ingly**.—*n.* **prepossess′ion**, an impression or opinion formed beforehand, usu. favourable. [Pfx. **pre-**, and **possess**.]

preposterous, *pri-pos′tér-us*, *adj.* contrary to the order of nature or reason, utterly absurd.—*adv.* **prepos′terously**.—*n.* **prepos′terousness**.

Neutral vowels in unaccented syllables: *em′pér-ŏr*; for certain sounds in foreign words see p. ix.

[L. *praeposterus—prae*, before, *posterus*, after—*post*, after.]

pre-Raphaelite, *prē-raf'ā-ēl-īt, n.* one of a school of English artists, formed about 1850, who sought inspiration in the works of painters *before Raphael* (1483-1520).—Also *adj.*

prerequisite, *prē-rek'wi-zit, n.* a condition or requirement that must be fulfilled beforehand.—*adj.* required as a condition of something else. [L. *prae*, before, *requīrere, requisītum*, to need.]

prerogative, *pri-rog'ā-tiv, n.* a special right or privilege belonging to a particular rank or station. [L. *praerogātīvus*, asked first for his vote, as a richer Roman citizen in an assembly consisting of both patricians and plebeians— *prae*, before, *rogāre, -ātum*, to ask.]

presage, *pres'ij*, formerly also *pri-sāj', n.* an omen, an indication of the future: a presentiment.—*v.t.* **presage** (*pri-sāj'*), to portend, to forebode: to predict.—*adj.* **presage'ful.**—*n.* **presag'er.** [L. *praesāgium*, a foreboding—*prae*, before, and *sāgus*, prophetic.]

presbyopia, *pres-bi-ō'pi-a, n.* long-sightedness, difficulty in accommodating the eye to near vision (common in old age). [Gr. *presbys*, old, *ōps*, gen. *ōpos*, the eye.]

presbyter, *prez'bi-tér, n.* an *elder* or pastor of the early Christian church: a minister or priest in rank between a bishop and a deacon: a member of a presbytery.—*adjs.* **presbytē'rial** (*-tē'ri-ál*), of a presbytery; **presbytē'rian**, pertaining to, or consisting of presbyters: pertaining to presbytery or that form of church government in which no higher office than that of presbyter is admitted—opp. to *episcopacy.*—*ns.* **Presbytē'rian**, a member or adherent of such a church; **Presbytē'rianism**, the form of church government by presbyters; **pres'bytery**, a church court ranking next above the kirk-session (q.v.), consisting of the ministers and one ruling elder from each church within a certain district: the district so represented: the Presbyterian system: that part of a church reserved for the officiating priests, the eastern extremity: (*R.C.*) a priest's house. [L.,—Gr. *presbyteros*, comp. of *presbys*, old; cf. **priest.**]

prescience, *prē'sh(y)ens, -shi-ens,* also *pre'-, n.* knowledge of events beforehand: foresight.— *adj.* **pre'scient.**—*adv.* **pre'sciently.** [L. *praesciens, -entis,* pr.p. of *praescīre—prae,* before, *scīre,* to know.]

prescribe, *pri-skrīb', v.t.* to lay down as a rule or direction: (*med.*) to order, advise, the use of (a remedy).—*ns.* **prescrib'er; pré'script,** an ordinance or rule: a remedy or treatment prescribed; **prescrip'tion,** act of prescribing or directing: (*med.*) a written direction for the preparation of a medicine: (*law*) custom continued until it becomes a right or has the force of law.—*adj.* **prescrip'tive,** prescribing, laying down rules: consisting in, or acquired by, custom or long-continued use, customary. [L. *praescrībēre, -scrīptum—prae,* before, *scrībēre,* to write.]

preselect, *prē-si-lekt', v.t.* to select beforehand.—*n.* **preselec'tion.**—*adj.* **preselect'ive.**— **preselector gearbox,** a gearbox in which the gear ratio is selected before it is actually required. [**pre-, select.**]

presence, *prez'ens, n.* fact or state of being present—opp. of *absence*: immediate neighbourhood: a presence-chamber or other place where a great personage is: an assembly, esp. of great persons: personal appearance and manner.—*n.* **pres'ence-chām'ber,** the room in which a great personage receives company.— **presence of mind,** coolness and readiness in emergency, danger, or surprise.—**real presence,** a doctrine or belief that the body and blood of Christ are really and substantially present in the eucharist. [O.Fr.,— L. *praesentia—praesens.* See following word.]

present, *prez'ent, adj.* in the place in question or implied—opposed to *absent*: (*arch.*) ready (with help): now under consideration: before the mind of (with *to*): now existing, not past or future: (*gram.*) denoting time just now, or making a general statement.—*n.* the present time: the present tense: (*pl.*) documents.— *adv.* **pres'ently,** (*obs.* or *Scot.*) now, without delay: soon. [O.Fr.,—L. *praesens, -sentis.*]

present, *prez'ent, n.* a gift. [O.Fr. *present*, orig. presence, hence gift (from the phrase *mettre en present à,* put into the presence of, hence offer as a gift to).]

present, *pri-zent', v.t.* to set before, to introduce into the presence of: to introduce at court: to put on the stage: to exhibit to view: to put something into the possession of (esp. in the form of a presentation) or put something before (a person—e.g. *presented her with a silver teapot; this presented him with a problem*): to make a gift of: to appoint to a benefice: to put forward for consideration: to have as a characteristic: to point, as a gun before firing.—*adj.* **present'able,** fit to be presented: fit to be seen: passable.—*ns.* **presentation** (*prez-en-tā'sh(ö)n*), act of presenting: an exhibition, display; a setting forth: manner of presenting: a formal, ceremonious giving of a gift by a number of persons to mark an occasion, e.g. retirement from office or employment: the gift itself: (*psych.*) anything that affects the consciousness, either in the form of a real sensation or in the form of a memory image of a sensation: the act or the right of presenting to a benefice; **presentee** (*prez-en-tē'*), one who is presented to a benefice; **present'er; present'ment,** act of presenting: the thing presented or represented: (*law*) a statement presented to a court by a jury from their own knowledge or observation.—**present arms,** to bring a firearm to the salute. [O.Fr. *presenter—*L. *praesentāre, -ātum—praesens, present.*]

presentiment, *pri-zent'i-ment,* sometimes *-sent', n.* a vague foreboding, esp. of evil. [Obs. Fr.,—*pre-* (L. *prae,* before), and **sentiment.**]

preserve, *pri-zūrv', v.t.* to keep safe from injury: to save from danger: to keep from decay: to keep in existence: to guard from intrusion: to maintain (e.g. silence): to retain (a quality). —*n.* that which is preserved, as fruit, &c.: that which preserves: a place for the protection of animals, as game: (*fig.*) anything regarded as closed or forbidden to outsiders.—*n.* **preservā'tion,** act of preserving or keeping safe: state of being preserved: safety.—*adjs.* **pre-**

ser'vative, preser'vatory, tending to preserve: having the quality of preserving.—*n.* that which preserves: a preventive of injury or decay.—*n.* preserv'er. [Fr. *préserver*—L. *prae*, beforehand, *servāre*, to keep.]

preses, *prē'sēz, n.* (*Scot.*) a president or chairman. [L. *praeses.*]

preside, *pri-zīd', v.i.* to sit in the chair or chief seat (e.g. at a meeting, at table): to exercise authority or control (over): (with *at*) to play on (e.g. the organ), esp. as director of a musical performance.—*ns.* presidency (*prez'i-dĕn-si*), the office of a president, or his dignity, term of office, jurisdiction, or residence; pres'ident, one who presides: a chairman: the head of a board, council, or department of government: the chief executive officer of a republic.—*adj.* presiden'tial (*-sh(á)l*), pertaining to a president.—*n.* pres'identship.—presiding officer, a person in charge of a polling-place at an election. [Fr. *présider*—L. *praesidēre*—*prae*, before, *sedēre*, to sit.]

presidium, *pre-sid'i-um, n.* in the Soviet Union, an administrative committee, usu. permanent. [L. *presidium*, a presiding over.]

press, *pres, v.t.* to exert a pushing force upon: to thrust: to squeeze: to clasp: to harass, weigh down: to beset (e.g. *hard pressed*): to urge strongly.—*v.i.* to exert pressure: to push with force: to crowd: to force a way (forward): to be urgent.—*n.* an act of pressing: a crowd: stress: a cupboard or shelved closet: an apparatus for pressing: a printing machine: the journalistic profession: newspapers and periodicals collectively.—*ns.* press'-agent, one who arranges for newspaper advertising and publicity, esp. for an actor or theatre; press'-box, an erection for the accommodation of reporters at sports, &c.; press'-button (see push-button); press'-cutt'ing, an extract cut from a newspaper or magazine; press'er; press'fat (*B.*), the vat for collecting the liquor from an olive or wine press; press-gall'ery, a gallery for reporters.—*p.adj.* press'ing, urgent: importunate.—*adv.* press'ingly.—press conference, a meeting of a public personage with the press for the purpose of making an announcement or in order to answer questions.—in the press, in course of printing, about to be published; press of sail, as much sail as can be spread. [Fr. *presser*—L. *pressāre*—*premĕre*, *pressum*, to squeeze.]

press, *pres, v.t.* (*hist.*) to carry off and force into service in the navy: to commandeer: to compel, force (a person or thing into the service of).—*n.* press'gang (*hist.*), a gang or body of sailors under an officer empowered to impress men into the navy. [From obs. *prest*, to engage by paying earnest—O.Fr. *prester*—L. *praestāre*, to offer, &c.]

pressure, *presh'úr, n.* act of pressing: the state of being pressed: constraining force: that which presses or afflicts: urgency: strong demand: a force directed over a surface measured by so much weight on a unit of area.—*ns.* press'ure-ca'bin, a pressurised cabin in an aircraft; press'ure-cooker, a strong container from which little steam escapes and in which food can be cooked quickly and at a temperature above the boiling-

point of water.—*v.t.* press'urise, to fit (an aeroplane, &c.) with a device that maintains nearly normal atmospheric pressure.—*n.* press'ure-suit, an automatically inflating suit worn by airmen as a protection against the effects of pressure-cabin failure, if this should occur at high altitudes.—pressure group, a group of people who put pressure on a government in order to obtain a particular end. [L. *pressura*—*premĕre*, to press.]

prestidigitation, *pres-ti-dij-i-tā'sh(ó)n, n.* sleight of hand.—*n.* prestidig'itātor. [Fr.,—*preste*, nimble, and L. *digitus*, a finger.]

prestige, *pres-tēzh', n.* (*orig.*) illusion: glamour: influence arising from rank or reputation. [Fr.—L. *praestigium*, delusion—*praestin-guĕre*, to dazzle.]

presto, *pres'tō, adv.* quickly: at once. [It.,—L. *praestō*, at hand.]

presume, *pri-zūm', v.t.* to take as true without examination or proof: to take for granted.—*v.i.* to venture without right (to do): to count unduly (on, upon), take advantage of (with *on, upon*): to act without due regard to the claims of others.—*adj.* presūm'able, that may be presumed or supposed to be true.—*adv.* presūm'ably.—*adj.* presūm'ing, venturing without permission, unreasonably bold.—*adv.* presūm'ingly.—*n.* presumption (-*zum'sh(ó)n, -zump'sh(ó)n*), act of presuming: a supposition: strong probability: conduct going beyond proper bounds: (*law*) an assumption made from known facts: an assumption made failing evidence to the contrary.—*adj.* presump'tive, grounded on probable evidence: that may be assumed as true, accurate, &c.: giving grounds for presuming.—*adv.* presump'tively.—*adj.* presumptuous (-*zump'tū-ùs*), presuming: rash, wilful.—*adv.* presump'tuously.—*n.* presump'tuousness. [Fr. *présumer*—L. *praesūmĕre*, -*sumptum*—*prae*, before, *sūmĕre*, to take—*sub*, under, *emĕre*, to buy.]

presuppose, *prē-sù-pōz', v.t.* to assume or take for granted: to involve as a necessary antecedent.—*n.* presupposi'tion. [Fr. *présupposer*—L. *prae*, before, and *suppōnĕre*. See suppose.]

pretend, *pri-tend', v.t.* to profess falsely that: to feign, to sham: (*arch.*) to aspire, attempt (to do).—*v.i.* to put forward a claim (to e.g. the crown), to aspire (to): to profess to have (e.g. *he did not pretend to genius*): to make believe.—*ns.* pretence', an act of pretending: a claim: a pretext: something pretended: appearance or show to hide reality: sham: make-believe; preten'der, one who pretends: a claimant; preten'sion, claim: aspiration: show: pretentiousness.—*adj.* preten'tious (-*shús*), claiming more than is warranted: showy, ostentatious.—*adv.* preten'tiously.—*n.* preten'tiousness. [Fr. *prétendre*—L. *praetendĕre*—*prae*, before, *tendĕre*, *tentum*, *tensum*, to stretch.]

preter-, *prē'tér-*, in composition, beyond, as *adj.* preterhuman, more than human. [L. *praeter.*]

preterit(e), *pret'ér-it, adj.* past.—*n.* the simplest form of the past tense (e.g. *he went, I hid the money*)—also called *aorist.*—preterite-present, said of certain Gmc. verbs whose

Neutral vowels in unaccented syllables: *em'pér-òr*; for certain sounds in foreign words see p. ix.

572

pretermit

present tense was orig. a past form (see **can may, shall**). [L. *praeteritus—praeter*, beyond, *ire, ĭtum*, to go.]

pretermit, prē-tér-mit', *v.t.* to omit: to desist from for a time:—*pr.p.* prētermitt'ing;*pa.t.* and *pa.p.* prētermitt'ed.—*n.* **pretermiss'ion**. [L. *praetermittĕre—praeter*, past, *mittĕre, missum*, to send.]

preternatural, prē-tér-nat'ū-rál, or -na'chùr-ál, *adj.* beyond what is natural, abnormal: supernatural.—*adv.* **preternat'urally**. [L. *praeter*, beyond, and *nātūra*, nature.]

pretext, prē'tekst, or prē-tekst', *n.* an ostensible motive or reason put forward to conceal the real one, or as an excuse. [L. *praetextum—praetexĕre—prae*, before, *texĕre*, to weave.]

pretor, &c. Same as **praetor**, &c.

pretty, prit'i, *adj.* (*orig.*) tricky: ingenious: neat: (esp. ironically) fine: (*arch.*) stalwart: attractive, but not strikingly beautiful, beautiful without dignity: considerable in amount.—*adv.* in some degree: moderately.—*adv.* **prett'ily**, pleasingly: neatly.—*n.* **prett'iness**.—*adj.* **prett'y-prett'y**, namby-pamby: insipidly pretty, pretty much, very nearly. [O.E. *prættig*, tricky—*prætt*, trickery.]

prevail, pri-vāl', *v.i.* to gain the mastery (with *over, against*): to succeed: to urge successfully (with *on, upon*—e.g. *she prevailed on Mary to say nothing*): to be usual or customary: to predominate.—*adjs.* **prevail'ing**, having great power: controlling: very general or common, most common: prevalent, prevailing.—*ns.* **prevalence** (*prev'ál-éns*), **prev'alency**, the state of being prevalent: wide-spread diffusion: superior strength or influence [L. *praevalēre prae*, before, *valēre*, to be powerful.]

prevaricate, pri-var'i-kāt, *v.i.* to evade the truth, to quibble.—*ns.* **prevarica'tion**; **prevar'icator**. [L. *praevāricārī, -ātus*, to walk crookedly—*prae*, inten., *vāricus*, straddling—*vārus*, bent.]

prevent, pri-vent', *v.t.* (*arch.*) to anticipate, forestall: to hinder: to keep from coming to pass, make impossible: (*orig.*) to go before, to be earlier than.—*adj.* **prevent'able** (also, **-ible**)—*n.* **preven'tion**, act of preventing: (*obs.*) anticipation.—*adjs.* **preven'tive** (also, irregularly **preven'tative**), tending to prevent or hinder: prophylactic: concerned with the prevention of smuggling.—*n.* that which prevents or averts.—**preventive detention**, specially prolonged imprisonment for persistent offenders of 30 or over for periods of from 5 to 14 years. [L. *praevenīre, -ventum—prae*, before, *venīre*, to come.]

preview, prē'vū, *n.* a view of a performance, exhibition, &c., before it is open to the public.—Also *v.t.* (*prē-vū'*). [**pre-, view**.]

previous, prē'vi-ùs, *adj.* going before in time: former: (*facetiously*) premature.—*adv.* previously (with *to*).—*adv.* **prē'viously**, beforehand: at an earlier time.—*n.* **prē'viousness**.— **Previous Examination**, little-go (q.v.); **previous question**, in parliament, motion 'that the question' (i.e. the main question) 'be not now put'. The device of 'moving the previous question' enables the House to postpone discussion of the main question. In public meetings the carrying of the 'previous question' means that the meeting passes on to the next

priest

business. [L. *praevius—prae*, before, *via*, a way.]

prevision, prē-vizh'(ó)n, *n.* foresight: foreknowledge. [Through Fr.*prévision*, or direct from L. *praevidēre, -vīsum*, to foresee—*prae*, before, *vidēre*, to see.]

prey, prā, *n.* booty, plunder: an animal that is, or may be, killed and eaten by another: a victim.—*v.i.* (commonly with *on, upon*) to make depredations: to take plunder: to live (on a victim): to waste or distress (body or mind). —**beast, bird, of prey**, one that devours other animals. [O.Fr. *preie* (Fr. *proie*) L. *praeda*, booty.]

price, prīs, *n.* the amount, usually in money, for which a thing is sold or offered: that which one gives up or suffers in order to gain something: (*arch.*) value.—*v.t.* to fix the price of: (*coll.*) to ask the price of.—*adjs.* **price'less**, beyond price, invaluable: (*coll.*) absurd; **pric'ey** (*coll.*), expensive.—**price of money**, the rate of discount in lending or borrowing capital; **price on one's head**, a reward offered for one's capture or slaughter.—**of price**, of great value; **one's price**, the sum of money, &c., for which one's connivance at, or help in, something nefarious may be obtained; **the price of one** (*coll.*), one's natural or just reward for folly or iniquity; **what price?** what about (this or that) now? what do you think of (this or that)?; **without price**, priceless: without payment. [O.Fr. *pris*—L. *pretium*, price.]

prick, prik, *n.* a sharp point: the act or experience of piercing or puncturing with a small sharp point: the wound or mark so made: centre of an archery target: penis (*coll.*): (*arch.*) a goad (whence **kick against the pricks**—see **kick**): (usu.*pl.*) remorse (of conscience): (*obs.*) a note in written music.—*v.t.* to pierce with a fine point: to indicate by a prick or dot: to spur or goad, to incite: to stick up (the ears).—*v.i.* to ride with spurs—*pa.t.* and *pa.p.* pricked.—*adj.* **prick'-eared**, having pointed ears.—*ns.* **prick'er**, that which pricks: sharp-pointed instrument: a light-horseman: a priming wire; **prickle** (prik'l), a little prick: a sharp point growing from the bark of a plant or from the skin of an animal.—*adj.* **prick'ly**, full of prickles, easily annoyed.—*ns.* **prick'liness**; **prick'ly-pear**, a genus of plants with clusters of prickles and pear-shaped fruit. [O.E. *prica*, point; cf. Du. *prik*.]

pride, prīd, *n.* state or feeling of being proud: too great self-esteem: haughtiness: a proper sense of what is becoming to oneself: a feeling of pleasure in achievement: that of which one is proud: splendour, magnificence: a group, herd (of lions).—*v.t.* (*reflex.*) to feel proud (foll. by *on, upon*).—**pride of place**, distinction of holding the highest position. [O.E. *prýde—prúd*, proud.]

priest, prēst, *n.* one who offers sacrifices or performs sacred rites (*fem.* **priest'ess**): a minister above a deacon and below a bishop: a clergyman.—*ns.* **priest'craft**, priestly policy directed towards worldly ends; **priest'hood**, the office or character of a priest: the priestly order.—*adjs.* **priest'-like**, **priest'ly**, pertaining to or like a priest.—*n.* **priest'liness**.—*adj.* **priest'-ridd'en**, controlled by priests.—**high**

priest (see **high**). [O.E. *prēost*—L. *presbyter* —Gr. *presbyteros,* elder.]

prig, *prig, n.* a person whose smug and scrupulous behaviour offends others.—*adj.* **prigg'ish.**

prig, *prig, n.* (*slang*) a thief.—*v.t.* to filch, to steal. [Origin unknown.]

prim, *prim, adj.* exact and precise in manner: demure.—*v.t.* to deck with great nicety: to form, purse, with affected propriety:—*pr.p.* primm'ing; *pa.t.* and *pa.p.* primmed.—*adv.* **prim'ly.**—*n.* **prim'ness.** [Late 17th century slang.]

prima ballerina, *prē'mä bal-ėr-ēn'ä, n.* the leading ballerina. [It.]

primacy, *prī'mä-si, n.* state of being first: the chief place: the office or dignity of a primate (q.v.). [L. *prīmus,* first.]

prima donna, *prē'mä don'(n)ä, n.* the leading lady in opera:—*pl.* **pri'ma donn'as, prime donne** (*prē'mä don'nä*). [It.,—L. *prīma domina.*]

prima facie, *prī'ma fā'shi-ē,* at first view or sight.—**prima facie case,** (*law*) a case established by sufficient evidence: a case consisting of evidence sufficient to go to a jury. [L. *prīmā,* abl. fem. of *prīmus,* first, *faciē,* abl. of *faciēs,* a face.]

primage, *prīm'ij, n.* a payment, in addition to freight, made by shippers for loading. [Anglo-L. *primāgium.*]

primary, *prī'mär-i, adj.* first: original: fundamental: chief: primitive: elementary: (*cap.*— *geol.*) Palaeozoic.—*n.* that which is highest in rank or importance.—*adv.* **prī'marily.**—**primary colours,** those from which all others can be derived—red, blue, yellow: the colours of the rainbow—red, orange, yellow, green, blue, indigo, and violet; **primary department, school,** a department, school, in which children are given the earliest stages of their book-education. [L. *prīmārius*—*prīmus,* first.]

primate, *prī'māt, -mät, n.* one who is first: an archbishop: (*zool.*) a member of the order Primates.—*n.pl.* **Primates** (*prī-māt'ēz*) the highest order of mammals, including man, the anthropoid apes, monkeys, and lemurs.—*n.* **pri'mateship.** [L. *prīmās, -ātis*—*primus,* first.]

prime, *prīm, adj.* first in order of time, rank, or importance: chief: of the highest quality: (*arith.*) divisible by no whole number except unity and itself.—*n.* the beginning: the spring: the height of perfection: full health and strength.—*adj.* **prī'mal,** first: original: fundamental.—**prime minister,** the chief minister of state; **prime mover,** a natural source of energy: a machine that transforms energy from such a source into motive power. [L. *prīmus,* first.]

prime, *prīm, v.t.* to charge, fill: to supply (a firearm) with powder: to bring into activity or working order by a preliminary charge (as an internal-combustion engine by injecting gas or oil): to fill (a person with liquor): to prepare for painting by laying on a first coat of paint or oil: to post up, instruct, prepare beforehand.—*ns.* **prī'mer; prī'ming; prī'ming-pow'der,** detonating powder: a train of powder. [Ety. obscure.]

primer, *prī'mér, prim'ér, n.* (*hist.*) small prayer-book for laymen, used for teaching reading: a

first reading-book: an elementary introduction to any subject. [L. *prīmārius,* primary.]

primeval, *prī-mē'väl, adj.* belonging to the first ages.—*adv.* **prime'vally.** [L. *prīmaevus*— *prīmus,* first, *aevum,* an age.]

primitive, *prim'i-tiv, adj.* belonging to the beginning, or to the first times: original: ancient: antiquated, old-fashioned: crude: not derivative.—*n.* that from which other things are derived: a root-word: a 19th- and 20th-century school of painting, characterised by a complete simplicity of approach to subject and technique.—*adv.* **prim'itively.**—*n.* **prim'itiveness.** [Fr.,—L. *prīmitīvus,* an extension of *prīmus,* first.]

primogenitor, *prī-mō-jen'i-tór, n.* earliest ancestor: (*loosely*) a forefather.—*n.* **primogen'iture,** the state or fact of being first-born: inheritance by the first-born child. [L. *prīmō,* first (adv.), *genitor,* begetter.]

primordial, *prī-mör'di-äl, adj.* existing from the beginning: original: rudimentary: first-formed.—*n.* first principle or element. [L. *prīmus,* first, *ordīrī,* to begin.]

primrose, *prim'rōz, n.* a species of plant of the genus *Primula,* or its flower, common in woods and meadows: extended to other flowers.—*adj.* pale yellow like a primrose: flowery, gay.—**Primrose League,** an association for Conservative propaganda—formed in 1883 in memory of Lord Beaconsfield, named from his supposed favourite flower. [O.Fr. *primerose,* as if—L. *prīma rosa*; perh. really through M.E. and O.Fr. *primerole*— Low L. *prīmula*—*prīmus,* first.]

primula, *prim'ū-la, n.* the genus of plants to which the primrose belongs. [L. *prīmus,* first.]

Primus, *prī'mus, n.* the presiding bishop in the Scottish Episcopal Church.

Primus, *prī'mus, n.* a portable cooking stove burning vaporised oil. [Trademark.]

prince, *prins, n.* one of the highest rank: a sovereign: son of a king or emperor: a title of nobility, as formerly in Germany: one eminent in any class of men (e.g. *a prince of poets, of liars*):—*fem.* **princess** (usu. *prin-ses',* but with Christian name, *prin'ses*).—*ns.* **Prince'-Con'sort,** the husband of a reigning queen; **prince'dom,** the estate, jurisdiction, sovereignty, or rank of a prince; **Prince'-Impē'rial,** the eldest son of an emperor; **prince'ling,** a petty prince.—*adj.* **prince'ly,** becoming a prince: splendid.—*ns.* **prince'-liness; Prin'cess-Roy'al,** the eldest daughter of a sovereign.—**Prince of Wales,** the eldest son of the British sovereign. [Fr.,—L. *princeps*—*prīmus,* first, *capĕre,* to take.]

principal, *prin'si-pl, adj.* highest in rank, character, or importance: chief.—*n.* a principal person: the head of a college or university or sometimes of a school: one who takes a leading part: money on which interest is paid: (*archit.*) a main beam or timber: (*law*) the perpetrator of a crime, or an abettor: one for whom another acts as agent: challenger or challenged in a duel: (*mus.*) a type of organ-stop.—*n.* **principal'ity,** the territory of a prince or the country that gives him title: (*B.*) a prince.—*adv.* **prin'cipally,** chiefly, for the most part.—*n.* **prin'cipalship,** position of a princi-

Neutral vowels in unaccented syllables: *em'pėr-ór*; for certain sounds in foreign words see p. ix.

574

pal.—**principal boy**, an actress (now often an actor) who plays the role of the hero in pantomime. [L. *principālis*—*princeps, -ipis*, chief.]

principate, *prin′si-pāt, n.* the Roman Empire in its earlier form in which something of republican theory remained: a principality. [L. *principātus*—the emperor's title *princeps* (*cīvitātis*), chief (of the city or state).]

principia, *prin-sip′i-a, n. pl.* first principles: elements. [L., pl. of *principium.*]

principle, *prin′si-pl, n.* a fundamental truth on which others are founded or from which they spring: a law or doctrine from which others are derived: a settled rule or action: consistent regulation of behaviour according to moral law: a constituent part: fundamental substance: manner of working.—*adj.* **prin′cipled**, holding specified principles: having, or behaving in accordance with, good principles.—**first principles**, fundamental principles, not deduced from others; **in principle**, so far as general character or theory is concerned, without respect to details; **on principle**, for the sake of obeying or asserting a principle. [L. *principium*, beginning—*princeps.*]

prink, *pringk, v.t.* and *v.i.* to deck up, smarten. [App. conn. with **prank** (2).]

print, *print, n.* an impression: a mould or stamp: printed characters or lettering: a copy: an engraving: a newspaper: printed state: a printed cotton cloth: a positive photograph made from a negative: (*archit.*) a plaster-cast in low relief.—*v.t.* to impress: to stamp a pattern on or transfer it to: to impress on paper, &c., by types, plates, or blocks: to publish: to write in imitation of type.—*v.i.* to practise the art of printing: to publish a book.—*ns.* **print′er**, one who prints, esp. books, newspapers, &c.; **print′ing**, act, art, or practice of printing; **print′ing-press**, a machine by which impressions are taken in ink on paper from types; **print′-works**, an establishment where cloth is printed.—**printed circuit**, a wiring circuit, free of loose wiring, formed by printing the design of the wire on copper foil bonded to a flat base and etching away the unprinted foil.—**out of print**, sold out and not procurable from the publisher. [M.E. *print, prent*—O.Fr. *preinte, priente*—*preindre*—L. *premĕre*, to press.]

prior, *prī′or, adj.* previous: previous (to).—*n.* the head of a priory (*fem.* **prī′oress**): (formerly, in Italy) a chief magistrate.—*ns.* **prī′orate**, **prī′orship**, the government or office of a prior; **prior′ity**, state of being prior or first in time, place, or rank: preference: a person, thing, entitled to preferential treatment or requiring early attention; **prī′ory**, a convent of either sex, under a prior or prioress, and next in rank below an abbey. [L. *prior*, former.]

prise. See **prize** (1).

prism, *prizm, n.* (*geom.*) a solid whose ends are similar, equal, and parallel polygons, and whose sides are parallelograms: a triangular prism of glass or the like for resolving light into separate colours or, in optical instruments, for other purposes.—*adjs.* **prismat′ic**, **-al**, resembling or pertaining to a prism: formed by a prism.—*adv.* **prismat′ically.**—*n.* **pris′moid**, a figure like a prism but with simi-

lar unequal ends.—**prismatic colours**, the seven colours into which a ray of white light is refracted by a prism—red, orange, yellow, green, blue, indigo, and violet. [Gr. *prīsma, -atos*, a piece sawn off—*prīein*, to saw.]

prison, *priz′n, n.* a building for the confinement of criminals or others, a jail: any place of confinement: confinement.—*ns.* **pris′oner**, one under arrest or confined in prison: a captive: anyone involuntarily kept under restraint; **pris′on-break′er**, one who escapes out of prison; **pris′on-van**, a closed conveyance for carrying prisoners.—**prison officer**, official title of warder (still so-called unofficially) in prison. [O.Fr. *prisun*—L. *prensiō, -ōnis*, for *praehensiō*, a seizing—*praehendĕre, -hensum*, to seize.]

pristine, *pris′tīn, adj.* original: former: belonging to the earliest time. [L. *pristinus*; cf. *priscus*, antique, *prior*, former.]

prithee, *priTH′ē*, a corruption of *I pray thee.*

privacy, *priv′-ă-si, priv′-, n.* seclusion: avoidance of notice or display: a place of seclusion: secrecy. [From **private.**]

private, *prī′vāt, adj.* apart from the state: not invested with public office: (of a member of parliament) not in the ministry: (of a soldier) not an officer or non-commissioned officer: peculiar to oneself, own: belonging to or concerning an individual person or company: not open to the public: not made generally known: confidential.—*n.* a common soldier.—*adv.* **prī′vately.**—*n.* **privateness.**—**private company**, a company whose shares may not be offered to the general public; **private enterprise**, economic system in which individual private firms operate and compete freely; **private eye** (*coll.*), a private detective; **private judgment**, the judgment of an individual, esp. on the meaning of a passage or doctrine of Scripture, as distinguished from the interpretation of the church.—**in private**, privately, in secret. [L. *prīvātus*, pa.p. of *prīvāre*, to separate.]

privateer, *prī-vă-tēr′, n.* a private vessel commissioned to seize and plunder an enemy's ships. [From **private.**]

privation, *prī-vā′sh(ŏ)n, n.* state of being deprived of something, esp. of what is necessary for comfort: (*logic*) absence (of any quality). —*adj.* **privative** (*priv′ă-tiv*), causing privation: expressing privation, absence, or negation (e.g. the 'be-' in 'behead' is a privative pfx.; Gr. *alpha privative* is seen in 'atermōn', without bounds, from 'termōn', a boundary).—*n.* that which is privative or depends on the absence of something else: (*logic*) a term denoting the absence of a quality: (*gram.*) a privative prefix, suffix, or word.—*adv.* **priv′atively.** [L. *prīvātiō, -ōnis, prīvātīvus*—*prīvāre*, to deprive.]

privet, *priv′et, n.* a half-evergreen European shrub used for hedges. [Origin unknown.]

privilege, *priv′i-lij, n.* an advantage granted to or enjoyed by an individual or a few: prerogative.—*v.t.* to grant a privilege to: to authorise: to exempt (from). [Fr.,—L. *prīvilēgium*—*prīvus*, private, *lex, lēgis*, a law.]

privy, *priv′i, adj.* private: pertaining to one person: secret: secluded: (with *to*) sharing the knowledge of (something secret).—*n.* (*law*) a person having an interest in an action: a room set apart with a container in which to evacuate body waste products (esp. one in an outhouse).—*adv.* **priv′ily**, privately, secretly. —*n.* **priv′ity**, knowledge, shared with another, of something private or confidential: knowledge implying concurrence: any legally recognised relation between two parties.— **privy council**, originally the private council of a sovereign to advise in the administration of government—its functions are now mainly formal or performed by committees, &c.; **privy councillor**; **privy purse**, an allowance for the private or personal use of the sovereign; **privy seal**, the seal used by or for the king in subordinate matters, or those which are not to pass the great seal.—**Lord Privy Seal**, a cabinet minister whose nominal duty is to affix the privy seal to documents. [Fr. *privé*—L. *prīvātus*, private.]

prize, **prise**, *prīz*, *v.t.* to force (esp. up or open) with a lever. [Fr. *prise*, hold, grip.]

prize, *prīz*, *n.* anything taken from an enemy in war, esp. a ship.—*ns.* **prize′-court**, a court for judging regarding prizes made on the high seas; **prize′-mon′ey**, share of the money or proceeds from any prizes taken from an enemy. [Fr. *prise*, capture, thing captured—L. *prehendĕre*, to seize.]

prize, *prīz*, *n.* a reward or symbol of success offered or won in competition by contest or by chance: anything well worth striving for: a highly valued acquisition.—*adj.* awarded, or worthy of, a prize.—*v.t.* to set a prize on, to value: to value highly.—*ns.* **prize′(-)fight**, a public boxing-match for money; **prize′(-)fighting**; **prize′(-)fighter**, a professional pugilist; **prize′(-)list**, a list of winners of a prize; **prize′man**, a winner of a prize; **prize′(-)ring**, an enclosure for a prize-fight. [O.Fr. *pris* (n.), *prisier* (vb.)—L. *pretium*, price.]

pro-, *prō*, *pfx.* from Latin prep. meaning before (as in *proceed*, *proposition*, q.v.), in place of or as the substitute of, in favour of, for:—e.g. **procathedral**, a church used temporarily as a cathedral; **proproctor**, a deputy proctor; **pro-German**, favouring, a partisan of, the Germans.—**pro and con** (L. *prō et contrā*), for and against.—*n.pl.* **pros and cons**, arguments for and against an opinion, a plan, &c.

pro. Abbrev. for **professional** (q.v.).

proa, *prō′a*, *n.* a small Malay sailing-vessel. [Malay *prau.*]

probable, *prob′á-bl*, *adj.* having more evidence for than against: that may be expected, likely.—*n.* one that has a good chance, or is likely to become the thing in question.—*n.* **probabil′ity**, quality of being probable: appearance of truth: likelihood: likelihood estimated mathematically: that which is probable.—*adv.* **prob′ably**. [Fr.,—L. *probābilis*—*probāre*, *-ātum*, to prove.]

probate, *prō′bāt*, *-bát*, *n.* the proof before a competent court that a written paper purporting to be the will of a person who has died is indeed his lawful act: the official copy of a will, with the certificate of its having been proved. —**Probate Court**, a court created in 1858 to exercise jurisdiction in matters touching the succession to personal estate in England—

now the **Probate Division** of the High Court of Justice. [L. *probātus*, tested—*probāre*. See **probable.**]

probation, *prō-bā′sh(ó)n*, *n.* testing: proof: a preliminary time or condition appointed to allow fitness or unfitness to appear: noviciate: suspension of sentence with liberty (depending on good behaviour) under supervision. —*adjs.* **probā′tional**, relating to, or serving the purpose of, probation or trial; **probā′tionary**, probational: on probation.—*n.* **probā′tioner**, one who is undergoing probation: (*Scot.*) one licensed to preach, but not ordained to a pastorate.—*adj.* **probative** (*prō′bá-tiv*), testing: affording proof. [L. *probātiō*, *-ōnis*, trial—*probāre*, *-ātum*, to test, prove.]

probe, *prōb*, *n.* an instrument for exploring a wound, locating a bullet, &c: an investigation: any of various instruments used for investigation in space-research, electronics, &c.—*v.t.* to examine with, or as with, a probe: to examine searchingly. [L. *proba*, a proof—*probāre*, to test.]

probity, *prob′i-ti*, or *prōb′-*, *n.* uprightness, moral integrity. [L. *probitās*—*probus*, good.]

problem, *prob′lém*, *n.* a matter difficult to arrange, or in which it is difficult to decide the best course of action: a person difficult to deal with (esp. a **problem child**): a question propounded for solution: (*geom.*) a proposition in which something is required to be constructed, not merely proved as in a theorem.—*adjs.* **problemat′ic**, **-al**, of the nature of a problem: questionable, doubtful.—*adv.* **problemat′ically**. [Gr. *problēma*, *-atos*—*pro*, before, *ballein*, to throw.]

pro bono publico, *prō bo′nō pub′li-kō*, *bō′nō poŏ′bli-kō*, for the public good. [L.]

proboscis, *prō-bos′is*, *n.* the snout or trunk of some animals, as the elephant. [L.,—Gr. *proboskis*, a trunk—*pro*, in front, *boskein*, to feed.]

proceed, *prō-sēd′*, *v.i.* to go on: to continue (with): to advance to (a higher degree): to come forth, issue: to result: to take measures or action: to take legal action.—*v.t.* to say (in continuation).—*n.* **prō′ceed** (usu. in *pl.*), money, &c., acquired by any action.—*adj.* **procedural** (*-sēd′yŭ-rál*).—*ns.* **procē′dure**, method of conducting business, esp. in a law case or in a meeting: course of action: a step taken or an act performed; **proceed′ing**, a going forward, continuance, advance: an action: (*pl.*) steps in a legal action: (in *pl.*) a record of the transactions of a society. [Fr. *procéder*—L. *prōcēdĕre*—*prō*, before, *cēdĕre*, *cessum*, to go.]

process, *prō′ses*, sometimes *pros′es*, *n.* state of being in progress or of being carried on: course (e.g. of time): a series of actions or events: a sequence of operations, or of changes undergone: a lawsuit: (*biol.*) a projecting part, esp. on a bone.—*v.t.* to subject to a special process, e.g. in manufacturing food: to arrange (documents) systematically: to examine and analyse: to test the suitability (of a person) for some purpose: (of a computer) to perform operations of adding, subtracting, &c., or other operations on (data supplied): to subject (data) to such opera-

Neutral vowels in unaccented syllables: *em′pér-ór*; for certain sounds in foreign words see p. ix.

576

tions.—**data processing**, the handling and processing of information by computer. [Fr. *procès*—L. *prōcessus*—*prōcēdĕre*. See **proceed**.]

procession, *prō-sesh'(ó)n*, *n*. the act of proceeding: a large company advancing in order.—*adj.* **process'ional**, pertaining to a procession.—*n.* a hymn sung during a procession. [L. *prōcessiō, -ōnis*—*prōcēdĕre*. See **proceed**.]

proclaim, *prō-klām'*, *v.t.* to publish abroad: to announce or declare officially: to place under restrictions by proclamation.—*ns.* **proclaim'er**; **proclamation** (*prok-la-mā'sh(ó)n*), the act of proclaiming: official notice given to the public. [Fr. *proclamer*—L. *prōclāmāre*—*prō*, out, *clāmāre*, to cry.]

proclivity, *prō-klivi-ti*, *n*. inclination, propensity (to, towards). [L. *prōclīvis*—*prō*, forward, *clīvus*, a slope.]

proconsul, *prō-kon'sul*, *n*. a Roman magistrate having the authority of a consul outside the city: the governor of a province.—*adj.* **procon'sular** (*-sū-làr*).—*ns.* **procon'sulate**, **procon'sulship**, the office, or term of office, of a proconsul. [L.]

procrastinate, *prō-kras'ti-nāt*, *v.i.* to put off action, to delay.—*ns.* **procrastinā'tion**, a putting off till a future time: dilatoriness; **procras'tinātor**. [L. *prōcrastināre*—*prō*, onward, *crastinus*—*crās*, tomorrow.]

procreate, *prō'krē-āt*, *v.t.* to bring into being, to beget.—*n.* **procrea'tion**, generation: production.—*adj.* **prō'creative**, having the power to procreate: generative: productive.—*ns.* **prō'creativeness**; **prō'creātor**, a parent. [L. *prōcreāre, -ātum*—*prō*, forth, *creāre*, to produce.]

Procrustean, *prō-krus'té-àn*, *adj.* violently making conformable to a standard—from *Procrustes*, a robber who by lopping or stretching fitted his victims to the same bed.

proctor, *prok'tór*, *n*. a procurator or manager for another: an attorney in the spiritual courts: a representative of the clergy in Convocation: an official in the English universities whose duties include the enforcement of university regulations.—*n.* **proc'torship**.—**King's**, **Queen's**, **Proctor**, an official who intervenes in divorce cases in England if collusion or fraud is suspected. [Syncopated form of **procurator**.]

procumbent, *prō-kum'bént*, *adj.* lying or leaning forward: prone, prostrate: (*bot.*) lying along the ground. [L. *prōcumbens, -entis*, pr.p. of *prōcumbĕre*—*prō*, forward, *cumbĕre*, to lie down.]

procurator, *prok'ū-rā-tór*, *n*. a financial agent in a Roman imperial province: one who manages affairs for another.—*ns.* **procurator-fiscal** (see **fiscal**); **proc'uratorship**. [L. *prōcūrātor*—*prōcūrāre*. See **procure**.]

procure, *prō-kūr'*, *v.t.* to contrive to obtain: (*arch.*) to contrive to bring about (e.g. *steps to procure the tyrant's downfall*).—*adj.* **procur'able**.—*ns.* **prō'curacy**, office of a procurator; **procurā'tion**, management of another's affairs: the instrument giving power to do so: a sum paid by incumbents to the bishop or archdeacon on visitations; **procure'ment**, the act of procuring: management: agency; **procur'er**, one who procures: a pander (*fem.* pro-

cur'ess). [Fr. *procurer*—L. *prōcūrāre*, to manage—*prō*, for, *cūrāre, -ātum*, to care for.]

prod, *prod*, *v.t.* to poke, goad into activity (*lit.* and *fig.*).—*pa.p.* prodd'ed.—*n.* an act of prodding: a sharp instrument. [Origin unknown.]

prodigal, *prod'i-g(à)l*, *adj.* wasteful: lavish.—*n.* a waster: a spendthrift.—*n.* **prodigal'ity**, state or quality of being prodigal: extravagance: profusion.—*adv.* **prod'igally**, profusely: wastefully. [Fr.,—*prōdigĕre*, to squander—pfx. *prōd-* (early form of *prō*), away, *agĕre*, to drive.]

prodigy, *prod'i-ji*, *n*. a portent: a wonder: a child of precocious genius or virtuosity: a monster.—*adj.* **prodig'ious**, astonishing: enormous: monstrous.—*adv.* **prodig'iously**.—*n.* **prodig'iousness**. [Fr. *prodige*—L. *prōdigium*, a prophetic sign.]

produce, *prō-dūs'*, *v.t.* to bring forward or out: to bring into being, to yield: to bring about, cause: to make, manufacture: to put on the stage: to prepare for exhibition to the public: to extend.—*ns.* **produce** (*prod'ūs*), that which is produced, product, proceeds, crops: **producer**, one who produces: a farmer or a manufacturer: one who is in general charge of the presentation of a play or motion picture: an apparatus that makes gas by the partial combustion of coal, coke, or anthracite, in a mixed air-steam blast.—*adj.* **produc'ible**.—*ns.* **product** (*prod'ukt*), a thing produced: a result: a work: (*arith.*) the result of multiplication: (*chem.*) a substance obtained from another by chemical change; **produc'tion**, act or process of producing: that which is produced: a product: a work, esp. of art: a representation (of a play).—*adj.* **produc'tive**, having the power to produce: generative: fertile, producing richly.—*n.* **productiv'ity**.—**producer gas**, a low-grade gas, used chiefly for furnaces and the production of power, made in a producer; **producer(s') goods**, goods, such as tools and raw materials, used in the production of *consumer(s') goods* (q.v.). [L. *prōdūcĕre, -ductum*—*prō*, forward, *dūcĕre*, to lead.]

proem, *prō'em*, *n*. an introduction, preface: a prelude.—*adj.* **proē'mial**. [Fr. *proème* L. *prooemium*—Gr. *prooimion*—*pro*, before, *oime*, a song.]

profane, *prō-fān'*, *adj.* not sacred, secular: heathen: showing contempt of sacred things, impious: uninitiated (*e g. the profane and vulgar*).—*v.t.* to violate, desecrate: to put to an unworthy use.—*adv.* **profane'ly**.—*ns.* **profane'ness**; **profān'er**; **profanation** (*prof-á-nā'sh(ó)n*), desecration: irreverence to what is holy; **profan'ity**, irreverence: that which is profane: profane language or conduct. [L. *profānus*, outside the temple, not sacred—*prō*, before, *fānum*, a temple.]

profess, *prō-fes'*, *v.t.* to make open declaration of: to declare in strong terms: to pretend to be expert in.—*adj.* **professed'**, openly avowed, acknowledged: alleged, pretended.—*adv.* **profess'edly**.—*n.* **profession** (*-fesh'(ó)n*), the act of professing: open declaration: religious belief: avowal: pretence: an employment not mechanical and requiring some degree of learning: the collective body of persons engaged in any profession: entrance into a religious order.—*adj.* **profess'ional**, pertaining to a profession: competing for money prizes or against those who sometimes do so: showing the skill, behaviour or standards appropriate in a member of a profession.—*n.* one who makes his living by an art, game, &c., as opp. to an amateur who practises it merely as a pastime (abbrev. **pro**).—*adv.* **profess′ion-ally.**—*n.* **profess′or,** one who professes: a teacher of the highest grade in a university.—*adj.* **professō′rial.**—*ns.* **professō′riāte,** office of a professor: his period of office: body of professors; **profess′orship.** [L. *professus,* perf.p. of *profitērī—prō,* publicly, *fatērī,* to confess.]

proffer, *prof′ėr, v.t.* to tender, to offer for acceptance:—*pr.p.* proff′ering; *pa.t.* and *pa.p.* proff′ered.—*n.* an offer made.—*n.* **proff′erer.** [Anglo-Fr. *proffrir—*L. *prō,* forward, *offerre.* See **offer.**]

proficient, *prō-fish′ėnt, adj.* competent, well-skilled, thoroughly qualified (in, at).—*n.* an adept, an expert.—*n.* **profi′ciency.**—*adv.* **profi′-ciently.** [L. *prōficiens, -entis,* pr.p. of *prōficĕre,* to make progress.]

profile, *prō′fīl, -fēl, -fil, n.* a head or portrait in a side-view: the side-face: the outline of any object without foreshortening: outline of the course of an operation: (orig. *U.S.*) a short sketch of character and career.—*v.t.* to draw in profile. [It. *profilo—*L. *prō,* before, *filum,* a thread.]

profit, *prof′it, n.* gain: the gain resulting from the employment of capital: advantage, benefit.—*v.t.* to benefit or to be of advantage to.—*v.i.* to gain advantage: to be of advantage.—*adj.* **prof′itable,** yielding or bringing profit or gain: advantageous.—*n.* **prof′itableness.**—*adv.* **prof′itably.**—*n.* **profiteer′,** one who exacts exorbitant profits.—Also *v.i.*—*adj.* **prof′itless,** without profit.—*adv.* **prof′itlessly.**—*n.* **prof′it-shār′ing,** a voluntary agreement under which the employee receives a share, fixed beforehand, in the profits of a business. [Fr.,—L. *prōfectus,* progress—*prōficĕre, prōfectum,* to make progress.]

profligate, *prof′li-gāt, -gát, adj.* abandoned to vice, dissolute: prodigal, extravagant.—*n.* one leading a profligate life.—*n.* **prof′ligacy** (*-ás-i*), state or quality of being profligate: a vicious course of life.—*adv.* **prof′ligately.** [L. *prō-flīgatus,* pa.p. of *prōfligāre—prō,* forward, *fligĕre,* to dash.]

pro forma, *prō för′ma,* as a matter of form, as an illustration or specimen made up to show prices, &c. (used of an invoice, account, &c.). [L.]

profound, *prō-fownd′, adj.* deep: far below the surface: intense: penetrating deeply into knowledge: abstruse.—*n.* the sea or ocean: an abyss.—*adv.* **profound′ly.**—*ns.* **profound′ness, profund′ity,** the state or quality of being profound: depth of place, of knowledge, &c.: that which is profound. [Fr. *profond—*L. *pro-fundus—prō,* forward, *fundus,* bottom.]

profuse, *prō-fūs′, adj.* liberal to excess, lavish (with *in, of*): excessively abundant (e.g. *profuse thanks*).—*adv.* **profūse′ly.**—*ns.* **profūse′-ness, profusion** (*-fū′zh(ó)n*), state of being profuse: extravagance: prodigality. [L. *prō-fūsus,* pa.p. of *prōfundĕre—prō,* forth, *fundĕre,*

to pour.]

progenitor, *prō-jen′i-tòr, n.* a forefather, an ancestor.—*n.* **prog′eny,** that which is brought forth: descendants: children. [L. *prōgenitor—prō,* before, *gignĕre, genitum,* to beget.]

progesterone, *prō-jes′tér-ōn, n.* one of the female sex hormones.

prognosis, *prog-nō′sis, n.* a forecast, esp. of the course of a disease.—*n.* **prognost′ic,** a foretelling: an indication, a presage.—*adj.* indicating what is to happen by signs or symptoms.—*v.t.* **prognos′ticate,** to foretell: to indicate (what is to come).—*ns.* **prognosticā′tion; prognos′ticātor,** one who predicts the future, esp. a weather prophet. [Gr. *prognōsis—pro,* before, *gignōskein,* to know.]

programme, program, *prō′gram, n.* a sheet or booklet giving the details of proceedings arranged for any occasion or ceremony: the items of an entertainment, &c.: a scheme or plan: the sequence of actions to be performed by an electronic computer in dealing with data of a certain kind: course of instruction (by book or teaching machine) in which subject-matter is broken down into a logical sequence of short items of information.—*v.t.* to provide with, enter in, a programme: to prepare a program for (an electronic computer, &c.).—*adj.* **pro′grammed.—programme music,** music that seeks to depict a scene or tell a story. [Gr. *programma,* proclamation—*pro,* before, *graphein,* to write.]

progress, *prō′gres,* also *prog′res, n.* forward movement: advance: improvement, gain in proficiency: course (e.g. of a narrative, an event): (*rare*) passage from place to place: (*arch.*) a journey of state, or a circuit.—*v.i.* **progress′,** to go forward: to go on, continue: to advance: to improve: to travel in state.—*n.* **progression** (*gresh′(ó)n*), motion onward: progress: movements by successive stages: a series of numbers or magnitudes increasing or decreasing according to a fixed law: (*mus.*) a regular succession of chords: the movements of the parts in harmony.—*adjs.* **progress′ional; progress′ive,** moving forward: advancing by successive stages: tending to improvement: favouring reforms, or encouraging the adoption of new methods and inventions.—*adv.* **progress′ively.**—*n.* **progress′iveness.—progressive whist,** &c., whist, or other game, played by several sets of players, some of whom move from table to table after each hand.—**arithmetical, geometrical, harmonic progression** (see the adjectives); **in progress,** going on, taking place. [Fr. *progresse* (now *progrés*)—L. *prōgressus—prō,* forward, *gradī,* to step.]

prohibit, *prō-hib′it, v.t.* to forbid: to prevent.—*n.* **prohibition** (*prō-hi-bi′sh(ó)n,* or *prō-i-*), the act of prohibiting, forbidding, or interdicting: an interdict: the forbidding by law of the manufacture and sale of alcoholic drinks.—*adj.* **prohibitive** (*-hib′-*), prohibitory: having the effect of restricting the sale, use, &c., of something (e.g. *prohibitive price, tax*).—*adv.* **prohib′itively.**—*adj.* **prohib′itory,** that prohibits or forbids: forbidding. [L. *prohibēre, prohibitum—prō,* before, *habēre,* to have.]

project, *proj′ekt, n.* a scheme, plan, proposal for

Neutral vowels in unaccented syllables: *em′pér-ór*; for certain sounds in foreign words see p. ix.

578

an undertaking: an undertaking: a task, problem, piece of research.—*v.t.* **project** (*projekt'*), to throw, impel, out or forward: to contrive or plan: to cast (as a light, a shadow, an image) upon a surface or into space: to throw an image of (*lit.*; also *fig.* to externalise, make objective): to show outlined against a background: (*theat.*) to speak or sing in such a way as to aim the voice at the back of the auditorium: (*geom.*) to derive a new figure from, such that each point corresponds to a point of the original figure in accordance with a definite rule.—*v.i.* to jut out.—*adj.* **projec'tile**, projecting or throwing forward: impelling: capable of being thrown forward.—*n.* a body projected by force: a missile.—*ns.* **projec'tion**, an act or method of projecting: the fact or state of being projected: that which is projected: planning: a jutting out: a method of representing geographical detail on a plane: a projected image (*lit.*; also *fig.*, e.g. *his picture of the character and reactions of Evans was a projection of his own soul and emotions*): (*psych.*) the reading of one's own emotions and experience into a particular situation: a person's unconscious attributing to other people of certain attitudes towards himself: (*geom.*) a figure formed by projection; **projec'tor**, one who projects enterprises: an apparatus for projecting, esp. an image or a beam of light. [L. *prōicĕre, projectum—prō,* forth, *jacĕre,* to throw.]

prolate, *prō'lāt, adj.* (of a spheroid) drawn out along the polar diameter—opp. to *oblate*. [L. *prōlātus,* pa.p. of *prōferre—prō,* forth, *ferre,* to bear.]

prolegomena, *prō-leg-om'en-a, n.pl.* an introduction, esp. to a treatise. [Gr. *prolegomenon,* pl. *-a,* pa.p. neut. of *prolegein—pro,* before, *legein,* to say.]

prolepsis, *prō lop'sis, or -lep-, n.* a rhetorical figure of anticipation, use of a word, such as an adjective, not literally applicable till a later time: a figure of speech by which objections are anticipated and answered.—*adjs.* **prolep'tic, -al.**—*adv.* **prolep'tically.** [Gr.,—*pro,* before, *lambanein,* to take.]

proletarian, *prō-le-tā'ri-án, adj.* of the lower wage-earning class: having little or no property.—*n.* a member of the proletariat.—*n.* **proletā'riat** (*-āt*), **-ate**, the wage-earning class, esp. those without capital. [L. *prōlētārius,* (in ancient Rome) citizen of sixth and lowest class, who served the state not with property, but with his *prōles* (children).]

prolicide, *prō'li-sīd, n.* the killing of offspring: the killing off of the human race.—*adj.* **prolicīd'al.** [L. *prōlēs,* offspring, *caedĕre,* to kill.]

prolific, *prō-lif'ik, adj.* bringing forth much offspring: fruitful, fertile: abounding (in).—*v.i.* **prolif'erate**, to grow by multiplication of parts (cells, buds, &c.); increase rapidly and abundantly.—*n.* **proliferā'tion.** [L. *prōles,* offspring, *facĕre,* to make.]

prolix, *prō'liks, or -liks', adj.* long and wordy: long-winded (e.g. of a writer).—*ns.* **prolix'ity, prolix'ness.**—*adv.* **prolix'ly.** [L. *prōlixus—prō,* forward, *līquī,* to flow.]

prolocutor, *prō-lok'ū-tor, n.* a spokesman: the

chairman of the lower house of the Convocation of Canterbury. [L. *prō,* before, *loquī, locūtus,* to speak.]

prologue, *prō'log, n.* in a Greek play, the part before the entry of the chorus: an introduction to a poem, &c.: an introductory event or action. [Fr.,—L. *prologus*—Gr. *prologos—pro,* before, *logos,* speech.]

prolong, *prō-long', v.t.* to lengthen out, extend.—*n.* **prolongā'tion** (*prō-long-gā'sh(ō)n*), act of prolonging in space or time: a piece added in continuation. [L. *prōlongāre—prō,* forward, *longus,* long.]

promenade, *prom-ė nād', or -näd', n.* a walk ride, or drive, for pleasure, show, or gentle exercise: an esplanade.—*v.i.* to walk, ride, or drive in promenade.—**promenade concert,** one in which part of the audience stand throughout the performance and can move about. [Fr., from (*se*) *promener,* to walk—L. *prōmināre,* to drive forwards—*prō,* forward, *mināre,* to drive (with threats).]

Promethean, *prō-mē'thē-án, adj.* pertaining to or resembling *Prometheus,* who made a man of clay and put life into him by fire stolen from heaven.

promethium, *prō-mēth'i-um, n.* a rare-earth element (atomic number 61; symbol Pm). [*Prometheus*; see above.]

prominent, *prom'i-nent, adj.* projecting: conspicuous: in the public eye: distinguished.—*ns.* **prom'inence, prom'inency,** state or quality of being prominent: a prominent point or thing.—*adv.* **prom'inently.** [L. *prōminens, -entis,* pr.p. of *prōminēre,* to jut forth.]

promiscuous, *prō-mis'kū-us, adj.* confusedly or indiscriminately mixed: collected together without order: indiscriminate (now usu. referring to one indulging in indiscriminate sexual intercourse). (*coll.*) casual.—*ns.* **promiscū'ity** (*prom-*), **promis'cuousness.**—*adv.* **promis'cuously** [L. *prōmiscuus—prō-,* pfx. (of obscure force here), *miscēre,* to mix.]

promise, *prom'is, n.* an engagement to do or keep from doing something: a thing promised: a ground for hope of future excellence (e.g. *a young man of promise*).—*v.t.* to make an engagement (to do or not to do something): to afford reason to expect: to assure: to engage to bestow.—*v.i.* to make a promise: to afford hopes or expectations.—*ns.* **prom'iser,** (*law*) **prom'isor.**—*adj.* **prom'ising,** affording ground for hope or expectation of good results.—*adv.* **prom'isingly.**—*adj.* **prom'issory,** containing a promise of some engagement, to be fulfilled.—**promissory note,** a written promise to pay a sum of money to another, or to bearer, at a certain date, or at sight, or on demand. [L. *prōmissum,* neut. pa.p. of *prōmittĕre,* to send forward—*prō,* forward, *mittĕre,* to send.]

promontory, *prom'on-tor-i, or -tri, n.* a headland or high cape. [L.L. *prōmontōrium* (L. *prōmuntūrium*)—*prō,* forward, *mons, montis,* a mountain.]

promote, *prō-mōt', v.t.* to help forward: to further the growth or improvement of, to encourage: to take steps for passing of (an act): to raise to a higher position: to encourage the sales of by advertising.—*ns.* **promo'ter,** one who promotes: one who takes part in the setting up of companies (**company promoter**) or in other business projects; **promō'tion**, the act of promoting: advancement in rank or in honour; encouragement.—*adj.* **promō'tive**. [L. *prŏmovēre, -mōtum—prō*, forward, *movēre*, to move.]

prompt, *prom(p)t, adj.* ready in action: performed at once: immediate, unhesitating: pertaining to a prompter.—*v.t.* to incite: to inspire (e.g. an action): to supply forgotten words, or elusive words, facts, or ideas, to.—*ns.* **prompt'er**, one who prompts, esp. actors; **prompt'itūde, prompt'ness**, quickness, immediateness: quickness in decision and action. —*adv.* **prompt'ly**.—**prompt side**, the side of the stage from which prompting is done — usu. to the actor's left. [L. *promptus—prōmĕre*, to bring forward.]

promulgate, *prom'ul-gāt, v.t.* to proclaim, publish abroad, make widely known: to put in execution by proclamation (as a law).—*ns.* **promulgā'tion; prom'ulgātor**. [L. *prōmulgāre, -ātum.*]

prone, *prōn, adj.* with the face, ventral surface, or palm of the hand downward: prostrate: disposed, inclined (to).—*adv.* **prone'ly**.—*n.* **prone'ness**. [L. *prōnus.*]

prong, *prong, n.* the spike of a fork or forked object.—*adj.* **pronged**, having prongs. [M.E. *prange*; origin obscure.]

pronominal. See pronoun.

pronoun, *prō'nown, n.* a word used instead of a noun, to indicate without naming.—*adj.* **pronom'inal**, belonging to, or of the nature of, a pronoun.—*adv.* **pronom'inally**. [L. *prō*, before, (hence) instead of, and **noun**.]

pronounce, *prō-nowns', v.t.* to utter formally (e.g. a sentence, judgment): to declare (e.g. a decision): to utter: to articulate.—*adjs.* **pronounce'able**, capable of being pronounced; **pronounced'**, marked, decided, noticeable.—*adv.* **pronoun'cedly**.—*ns.* **pronounce'ment**, a confident or authoritative assertion: proclamation; **pronoun'cer**.—*adj.* **pronoun'cing**, giving or marking pronunciation. [Fr. *prononcer*—L. *prōnuntiāre—prō*, forth, *nuntiāre*, to announce—*nuntius*, a messenger.]

pronucleus, *prō-nū'klē-ús, n.* the nucleus of a germ cell after the maturation divisions. [Pfx. **pro-**, and **nucleus**.]

pronunciamento, *prō-nun-si-ä-men'tō, n.* a manifesto, a formal proclamation. [Sp.]

pronunciation, *pro-nun-si-ā'sh(ó)n, n.* mode of pronouncing: articulation. [L. *pronuntiātiō, -ōnis—pronuntiāre*. See **pronounce**.]

proof, *prōōf, n.* that which proves: evidence that convinces the mind: the fact, act, or process of proving or showing to be true: test: demonstration: ability to stand a test: (*print.*) an impression taken for correction: (*photography*) the first print from a negative.—*adj.* impervious, invulnerable (often with *against*, or as suffix, as in **fireproof**).—*ns.* **proof'ing**, the process of making waterproof, fireproof, &c.: material used for the purpose; **proof'(-) read'er**, one who reads printed proofs to discover and correct errors; **proof'-spir'it**, a mixture containing fixed proportions of alcohol and water.—**proof strength**, the strength of proof-spirit. [O.Fr. *prove* (Fr. *preuve*)—L.

probāre, to prove.]

prop, *prop, n.* a rigid support: a pit-prop (q.v.): (*fig.*) a supporter, upholder, on whom one depends.—*v.t.* to hold up by means of something placed under or against: to sustain:—*pr.p.* propp'ing; *pa.t.* and *pa.p.* propped. [M.E. *proppe*; cf. Du. *proppe*, wine-prop.]

prop, *prop, n.* abbrev. for **propeller** as in **propjet**, a name for **turboprop** (see **jet**).

propagate, *prop'a-gāt, v.t.* to cause to increase by natural process, to multiply: to pass on: to transmit (e.g. sound): to spread from one to another (e.g. a belief, knowledge).—*v.i.* to breed: to multiply.—*ns.* **propagan'da**, a committee (*congregatio de propaganda fide*) at Rome charged with the management of the R.C. missions: any concerted action for the spread of opinions and principles: action done, statement made, purely for the purpose of inculcating an idea or belief; **propagand'ist**, one engaged in propaganda.—Also *adj.*—*ns.* **propagā'tion**, act of propagating: the spreading or extension of anything; **prop'agātor**. [L. *propāgāre, -ātum*, conn. with *propāgō*, a layer.]

propane, *prō'pān, n.* a colourless inflammable gas occurring naturally or obtained from petroleum, used for heating.

propel, *prō-pel', v.t.* to drive forward:—*pr.p.* propell'ing; *pa.t.* and *pa.p.* propelled'.—*n.* **propell'er**, one who, or that which, propels: a driving mechanism: a shaft with helical blades (*screw-propeller*) for driving a ship, aeroplane, &c. [L. *prōpellĕre—prō*, forward, *pellĕre*, to drive.]

propensity, *pro-pens'i-ti, n.* inclination, tendency, disposition (with *to, for*). [L. *prōpensus*, inclined, pa.p. of *prōpendēre, -pensum— prō*, forward, *pendēre*, to hang.]

proper, *prop'ér, adj.* (*arch.*) own: natural, characteristic, appropriate: pertaining characteristically (to): fitting: suitable (to): correct: strictly so-called: decorous, conforming strictly to convention: (*arch.*) handsome, comely: (*coll.*) thorough.—*adv.* **prop'erly**, in a proper manner: strictly: (*coll.*) thoroughly.— **proper fraction**, a fraction that is less than 1 in value; **proper noun, name**, a noun, name, designating a particular person, animal, town, &c. [Fr. *propre*—L. *prōprius*, own.]

property, *prop'ér-ti, n.* a quality that is always present, a characteristic: any quality: that which is one's own: land or buildings: ownership: an article required by actors in a play or a motion picture (see **props**).—*adj.* **prop'er-tied**, possessed of property.—*n.* **prop'erty-tax**, a tax levied on property, at the rate of so much per cent. on its value. [O.Fr. *properte*— L. *proprietās*. See **propriety**.]

prophecy, *prof'é-si, n.* inspired utterance: prediction: (*obs.*) public interpretation of Scripture. [O.Fr. *prophecie*—L. *prophētīa*—Gr. *prophēteiā—prophētēs*, prophet.]

prophesy, *prof'é-sī, v.i.* to utter prophecies: to foretell the future: to expound the Scriptures.—*v.t.* to foretell:—*pa.t.* and *pa.p.* proph'esīed. [A variant of **prophecy**.]

prophet, *prof'ét, n.* one who proclaims or interprets the will of God: an inspired teacher, preacher, or poet: one who foretells events: (*cap.—pl.*) a division of the Old Testament,

Neutral vowels in unaccented syllables: *em'pér-ór*; for certain sounds in foreign words see p. ix.

the writings concerned with the prophets, Isaiah, Jeremiah, &c.: (cap.) Mohammed: (cap.) Joseph Smith, founder of the Mormon religion.—n. fem. **proph'etess.**—adjs. **prophet'ic, -al,** pertaining to a prophet: containing prophecy: foreseeing or foretelling events.—adv. **prophet'ically.** [Fr. prophète—L. prophēta—Gr. prophētēs—pro, for (another), phanai, to speak.]

prophylactic, prof-i-lak'tik, adj. guarding against disease.—n. a prophylactic medicine or other preventive of infection.—n. **prophylax'is** (not a Greek word), preventive treatment. [Gr. propylaktikos—pro, before, phylax, a guard.]

propinquity, prō-ping'kwi-ti, n. nearness in place, time, blood relationship, quality—proximity, similarity. [L. propinquitās—propinquus, near—prope, near.]

propitiate, prō-pish'i-āt, v.t. to render (a person) favourable: to appease (one who is angry or resentful).—adj. **propitiable** (prō-pish'i-ä-bl), that may be propitiated. —ns. **propitiā'tion,** act of propitiating: atonement: atoning sacrifice: **propi'tiator,** one propitiatory, having power to, or intended to, propitiate.—n. the Jewish mercy-seat.—adv. **propi'tiatorily.**—adj. **propi'tious,** favourable, of good omen: favourable (for, to): disposed to be gracious.—adv. **propi'tiously.**—n. **propi'tiousness.** [L. propitiāre, -ātum, to make favourable—propitius, well-disposed.]

proportion, prō-pōr'sh(ò)n, -pōr'-, n. the relation of one thing to another, or of a part to the whole, in regard to magnitude: ratio: (math.) the identity or equality of ratios: due relation (in respect of accuracy, or of harmony or rhythm): an equal or just share: (coll.) a part or portion: (pl.) dimensions.—v.t. to adjust or fashion in due proportion (to).—adjs. **proportionable,** that may be proportioned: having a due or definite relation (to): **proportional,** having a due proportion: relating to proportion: (math.) having the same or a constant ratio.—n. (math.) a number or quantity in a proportion —n. **proportional'ity.**—adv. **propor'tionally.**—adj. **propor'tionate,** in fit proportion, proportional.—adv. **propor'tionately.—proportional representation,** a system intended to give parties in an elected body a representation as nearly as possible proportional to their voting strength: often loosely applied to the system by which a vote can be transferred to the system by which a vote can be transferred to an elector's second choice. [L. prōportiō, -ōnis—prō, in comparison with, portiō, part, share.]

propose, prō-pōz', v.t. to put forward for consideration, to propound: to suggest: to put before one as an aim: to nominate (a person): to invite the company to drink (a health): to purpose or intend.—v.i. to form or put forward an intention: to make an offer, especially of marriage.—ns. **propo'sal,** an act of proposing: anything proposed: an offer, esp. of marriage; **propo'ser.** [Fr.,—pfx. pro- (L. prō) and poser, to place.]

proposition, prop-o-zish'(ò)n, n. an act of propounding or (more rarely) proposing: the thing propounded: a proposal: (logic) a form of statement in which a predicate is affirmed

or denied of a subject: (math.) a statement of a theorem or problem for (or with) solution or demonstration: (orig. U.S.) any situation, thing, or person considered as something to be coped with.—v.t. to make a proposition to someone.—adj. **proposi'tional,** pertaining to a proposition: considered as a proposition. [Fr.,—L. prōpositiō, -ōnis—prō, before. See **position.**]

propound, prō-pownd', v.t. to offer for consideration, to state.—n. **propound'er.** [Orig. propone—L. prō, forth, ponĕre, to place.]

proprietor, prō-prī'e-tór, n. an owner:—fem. **propri'etress,** propri'etrix.—n. **propri'etary,** an owner: a body of owners.—adj. owning property: legally made only by a person or body of persons having special rights (e.g. a medicine).—n. **propri'etorship.** [L.L. proprietārius—proprius, own.]

propriety, prō-prī'e-ti, n. (obs.) ownership: conformity with accepted standards of conduct: appropriateness: rightness, as in the use of words.—**the proprieties,** conventional standards of social behaviour. [Fr., propriété—L. proprietās—proprius, own.]

props, props, n.pl. theatrical properties: the man who looks after them. [**properties.**]

propulsion, prō-pul'sh(ò)n, n. act of propelling.—adj. **propul'sive,** tending or having power to propel. [L. prōpellĕre, prōpulsum, to push forward. See **propel.**]

pro rata, prō rā'ta, rä'ta, in proportion. [L.]

prorogue, prō-rōg', v.t. to discontinue the meetings of (parliament) for a time:—pr.p. **prorog'uing:** pa.t. and pa.p. prorogued'.—n **proroga'tion,** act of proroguing. [L. prōrogāre, -ātum—prō, forward, rogāre, to ask.]

prosaic, -al, prō-zā'ik, -äl, adj. like prose: commonplace: dull.—adv. **prosā'ically.** [**prose.**]

proscenium, prō-sē'ni-um, n. the front part of the stage: the curtain and its framework, esp the arch that frames the more traditional type of stage [L.,—Gr. proskēnion—pro, before, skēnē, the stage.]

proscribe, prō-skrīb', v.t. (Roman hist.) to put on the list, posted in a public place, of those who may be put to death: to outlaw: to refuse to tolerate, to prohibit.—ns. **proscrib'er;** **proscrip'tion.**—adj. **proscrip'tive.** [L. prōscrībĕre—prō, before, publicly,scrībĕre, scriptum, to write.]

prose, prōz, n. ordinary spoken and written language with words in direct straightforward arrangement: all writings not in verse.—adj. of or in prose: not poetical: plain: dull.—v.i. to write prose: to speak or write tediously.—adj. **prōs'y,** dull, tedious.—adv. **prōs'ily.**—n. **prōs'iness.** [Fr.,—L. prōsa—prorsus, straightforward—prō, forward, vetĕre, versum, to turn.]

prosecute, pros'e-kūt, v.t. to engage in, practise (e.g. a trade): to follow up (e.g. an inquiry): to pursue by litigation.—v.i. to be prosecutor in a lawsuit.—ns. **prosecū'tion,** the act of prosecuting or pursuing, esp. by litigation: pursuit: the prosecuting party in legal proceedings; **pros'ecūtor,** one who prosecutes or pursues any plan or business: one instituting a lawsuit:—fem **pros'ecūtrix.** [L.prōsequī—prō, onwards, sequī, secūtus, to follow.]

proselyte, *pros'e-līt, n.* one who has come over from one religion or opinion to another: a convert, esp. from paganism to Judaism.—*v.t.* **pros'elytīse,** to make proselytes.—*n.* **pros'elytism.** [Gr. *prosēlytos,* a new-comer—*pros-,* towards, and the stem *elyth-,* used to form aorists for *erchesthai,* to go.]

prosody, *pros'o-di, n.* the study of versification.—*adjs.* **prosō'dial, prosod'ic, -al.**—*n.* **pros'odist,** one skilled in prosody. [L. *prosōdia,* Gr. *prosōidia*—*pros,* to, *ōidē,* a song.]

prosopopoeia, *pros-ō-po-pē'ya, n.* personification. [Gr. *prosōpopoiiā*—*prosōpon,* a person, *poieein,* to make.]

prospect, *pros'pekt, n.* a wide view: a scene: (*fig.*) outlook for the future, (in *pl.,* with possessive *pron.*) measure of success to be expected by one: expectation: a probable source of profit.—*v.i.* **prospect',** to look around: to make a search, esp. for chances of mining.—*n.* **prospec'tor.**—*adj.* **prospec'tive,** looking forward: relating to the future: expected.—*adv.* **prospec'tively.**—*n.* **prospec'tus,** the outline of any plan submitted for public approval, particularly of a literary work or of a joint-stock concern: a booklet giving details about a school or other place of education. [L. *prōspectus*—*prōspicĕre, prōspectum*—*prō,* forward, *specĕre,* to look.]

prosper, *pros'pér, v.i.* to thrive, to succeed: to turn out well.—*v.t.* to cause to thrive or succeed.—*n.* **prosper'ity,** the state of being prosperous: success, good fortune.—*adj.* **pros'perous,** thriving: successful.—*adv.* **pros'perously.** [L. *prosper,* or *prosperus,* successful.]

prostate, *pros'tāt, n.* a gland in males at the neck of the bladder. [Fr. *prostatēs*—*pro,* before, *sta,* root of *histanai,* to set up.]

prosthesis, *pros'thé-sis, n.* the fitting of artificial parts to the body.—*n.* **prosthet'ics,** the surgery or dentistry involved in supplying artificial parts to the body. [Gr.—*pros,* to, *thesis,* putting.]

prostitute, *pros'ti-tūt, v.t.* to offer or sell for evil or base use: to degrade by improper use (e.g. *to prostitute one's talents*).—*adj.* openly devoted to vice.—*n.* a woman who offers herself to indiscriminate sexual intercourse for money: a base hireling.—*ns.* **prostitū'tion,** the act or practice of prostituting: lewdness for hire: devotion to base purpose; **pros'titūtor.** [L. *prōstituĕre, -ūtum,* to set up for sale—*prō,* before, *statuĕre,* to place.]

prostrate, *pros'trāt, adj.* lying with face on the ground: reduced to helplessness: completely exhausted.—*v.t.* (*-āt*) to throw forwards on the ground: to lay flat: to overthrow: to reduce to impotence or exhaustion: to bow (oneself) in humble reverence.—*n.* **prostrā'tion.** [L. *prōstrātus,* pa.p. of *prōsternĕre*—*prō,* forwards, *sternĕre, strātum,* to spread.]

prosy. See **prose.**

protactinium, *prōt-ak-tin'i-ùm, n.* a radioactive element (symbol Pa; atomic no. 91), which, on disintegration, yields *actinium.*—Also **protoactinium.** [Pfx. **prot(o)-,** and **actinium.**]

protagonist, *prō-tag'on-ist, n.* the chief actor or character: a champion (of a cause). [Gr. *prōtos,* first, *agōnistēs,* a combatant.]

protasis, *prot'a-sis, n.* the subordinate clause of a conditional sentence—opp. to *apodosis.* [Gr.,—*pro,* before, *tasis,* a stretching—*teinein,* to stretch.]

Protean, protean, *prō'té-án, prō-tē'án, adj.* readily assuming different shapes: variable, inconstant. [**Proteus,** sea-god who assumed any form he pleased.]

protect, *prō-tekt', v.t.* to shield from danger, injury, capture, loss, change: to defend: to shelter: to provide (e.g. machinery) with devices designed to prevent accidents: to seek to foster by import duties.—*ns.* **protec'tion,** act of protecting: state of being protected: defence: that which protects: a guard, shield: encouragement of home produce and manufactures by taxing imported goods; **protec'tionist,** one who favours the protection of trade by taxing imports.—Also *adj.*—*adj.* **protec'tive,** affording protection, defensive, sheltering: intended to protect.—*n.* **protec'tor,** one who protects from injury or oppression: a guard, shield: a regent:—*fem.* **protec'tress, protec'trix.**—*adjs.* **protec'toral, protectō'rial,** pertaining to a protector or a regent.—*n.* **protec'torate,** the rule of a protector: authority over a vassal state: relation assumed by a state over territory which it governs without annexing it; **protec'torship.**—**protected state,** a state under the protection of another state but less subject to the control of that state than a protectorate; **protection money,** money extorted from shopkeepers, &c. as a bribe for leaving their property, &c. unharmed; **protective custody,** detention of a person for his personal safety or from doubt as to his possible actions. [L. *prōtegĕre, -tectum*—*prō,* in front, *tegĕre,* to cover.]

protégé, *prō'-,* or *pro'tā-zhā, n.* one under the protection or patronage of another:—*fem.* **protégée.** [Fr., p.p. of *protéger,* to protect—L. *prōtegĕre.*]

protein, *prō'tēn, n.* any one of a group of complex nitrogenous substances that play an important part in the bodies of plants and animals.—*n.* **pro'teid** (*-tē-id*), a less scientific name for protein. [Gr. *prōteus,* primary—*prōtos,* first.]

pro tempore, *prō tem'po-rē,* for the time being: temporarily.—Abbrev. **pro tem.** [L.]

protest, *prō-test', v.i.* to express or record dissent or objection (often with *against*).—*v.t.* to make a solemn declaration of: to note, as a bill of exchange, on account of non-acceptance or non-payment.—*ns.* **prō'test,** a declaration of objection or dissent: remonstrance: affirmation, protestation: the noting by a notary-public of an unpaid or unaccepted bill; **prot'estant,** one who protests: (*cap.*) one of those who, in 1529, protested against an edict of Charles V and the Diet of Spires denouncing the Reformation: a member of one of the churches founded by the Reformers.—*adj.* pertaining to Protestants or their doctrine.—*ns.* **Prot'estantism,** the Protestant religion: state of being a Protestant; **protestation** (*pro-tes-tā'sh(ó)n*), an affirmation, asseveration (of) a protest (against): a declaration in pleading; **protest'er.** [Fr.,—L. *prōtestāri, -ātus,* to bear witness in public—*prō,* before, *testārī*—*testis,* a witness.]

Neutral vowels in unaccented syllables: *em'pér-ór* ; for certain sounds in foreign words see p. ix.

protium, *prō′ti-ŭm, -shi-ŭm, n.* ordinary hydrogen of atomic weight 1. [Gr. *prōtos,* first.]

proto-, *prō-tō-,* **prot-,** in composition, first in time, most primitive or earliest, chief [Gr. *prōtos,* first]:—e.g. **protomartyr** (see below); **proto-Germanic,** primitive Germanic; **prototraitor.**

protoactinium. See **protactinium.**

protocol, *prō′tō-kol, n.* an original note, minute, or draft of an instrument or transaction: etiquette. [Fr. *protocole,* through L.L.—Late Gr. *prōtokollon,* the glued-on descriptive first leaf of a MS.—Gr. *prōtos,* first, *kolla,* glue.]

protomartyr, *prō′tō-mär-tér, n* the first martyr in any cause, esp. St Stephen. [Gr. *prōtos,* first, and **martyr.**]

proton, *prō′ton, n.* an elementary particle of unit positive charge and unit atomic mass—the atom of the lightest isotope of hydrogen without its electron. [Gr., neut. of *prōtos,* first.]

protoplasm, *prō′tō-plazm, n.* the material basis of all living matter, a greyish semi-transparent, semi-fluid substance of complex chemical composition [fr. *prōtos,* first, *plasma,* form—*plassein,* to form.]

prototype, *prō′tō-tīp, n.* the first or original type or model from which anything is copied. [Fr.—Gr. *prōtos,* first, *typos,* a type.]

Protozoa, *prō-tō-zō′ä, n.pl.* the lowest and simplest type of animals, unicellular forms or colonies, multiplying by fission:—*sing.* **protozō′on.**—*n.* and *adj.* **protozō′an**—*adj.* **protoz′oic,** pertaining to the Protozoa. (*obs.*) containing remains of the earliest life of the globe. [Gr. *prōtos,* first, *zōion,* an animal.]

protract, *prō-trakt′, v.t.* to draw out or lengthen in time, to prolong: to draw to a scale.—*n.* **protrac′tion.**—*adj.* **protrac′tive,** drawing out in time, prolonging, delaying.—*n.* **protrac′tor,** one who, or that which, protracts: an instrument for laying down angles on paper, used in surveying &c: a muscle whose contraction draws a part forward or away from the body. [L. *prōtrahēre, -tractum—prō,* forth, *trahēre,* to draw.]

protrude, *prō-trōōd′, v.t.* to thrust or push on or forward: to obtrude.—*v.i.* to stick out, project.—*n.* **protru′sion,** the act of protruding: the state of being protruded: that which protrudes.—*adj.* **protru′sive,** thrusting or impelling forward: protruding. [L. *prōtrūdĕre, -trūsum—prō,* forward, *trūdĕre,* to thrust.]

protuberance, *prō-tūb′ér-äns, n.* a bulging out: a swelling.—*adj.* **protū′berant.**—*adv.* **protū′berantly.** [L. *prōtūberāre, -ātum—prō,* forward, *tūber,* a swelling.]

proud, *prowd, adj.* having excessive self-esteem: haughty: ostentatious: having a proper sense of self-respect: having an exultant sense of credit or gratification: giving reason for pride or boasting.—*n.* **proud′-flesh,** a growth or excrescence of flesh in a wound. —*adv.* **proud′ly.** [O.E. *prūd.*]

Proustian, *prōōs′ti-än, adj.* pertaining to Marcel Proust (1871-1922), French novelist.—*n.* an admirer of Proust.

prove, *prōōv, v.t.* to test: to experience, suffer: to establish or ascertain as true or genuine: to demonstrate (the correctness of any result): to cause or allow (dough) to rise. —*v.i.* to turn

out, to be shown by the event.—*n.* **prov′er.**—*adj.* **prov′able.**—*adv.* **provably.**—**proving ground,** a place for testing scientifically (*lit.* and *fig.*). [O.Fr. *prover*—L. *probāre—probus,* excellent; perh. partly O.E. *prōfian,* to assume to be.]

proven, *prōv′n, prōōv′n, p.adj.* (*dial.* and *Scots law*) proved. [Pa.p. of M.E. *preve,* an alternative form of *prove.*]

provenance, *prov′é-näns, n.* source. [Fr.,—L. *prō,* forth, *venīre,* to come.]

Provençal, *prov-ä-säl, adj.* of or pertaining to Provence in France.

provender, *prov′in-dér, -en-dér, n.* food: dry food for beasts, as hay or corn—esp. a mixture of meal and cut straw or hay. [L.L. *praebenda,* later *provenda,* a daily allowance of food; cf. **prebend.**]

proverb, *prov′érb, n.* a short familiar sentence expressing a supposed truth or moral lesson: a byword: (*cap.—pl.*) a book of maxims in the Old Testament.—*adj.* **prover′bial,** like or of the nature of a proverb, mentioned in a proverb: widely known.—*adv.* **prover′bially.** [Fr. *proverbe*—L. *prōverbium prō,* before, publicly, *verbum,* a word.]

provide, *prō-vīd′, v.t.* to make ready beforehand: to supply: to furnish (a person with).—*v.i.* to procure supplies, means, &c.: to make provision (for, against): to prescribe as a necessary condition (that).—*conj.* **provi′ded,** (often with *that*) on condition.—*n.* **provi′der.**—**provided school,** in England and Wales, a school maintained by, and under the management of, the local education authority. [L. *prōvidēre—prō,* before, *vidēre,* to see.]

providence, *prov′i-déns, n.* foresight: timely preparation: prudent management and thrift: (*theology*) foresight and benevolent care of God: God, considered in this relation: an event in which God's care is clearly shown.—*adj.* **prov′ident,** seeing beforehand, and providing for the future: prudent: thrifty.—*adv.* **prov′idently.**—*adj.* **providential** (*-den′sh(ä)l*), effected by, or proceeding from, divine providence: fortunate.—*adv.* **providen′tially.** [L. *prōvidens, -entis,* pr.p. of *prōvidēre—prō,* before, *vidēre,* to see.]

province, *prov′ins, n.* a portion of an empire or a state marked off for purposes of government: the district over which an archbishop has jurisdiction: a region vaguely: a sphere of duty, activity, or knowledge: (*pl.*) all parts of the country except the capital.—*adj.* **provincial** (*prō-vin′sh(ä)l*), relating to a province: characteristic of the inhabitants of a province, unpolished, narrow.—*n.* an inhabitant of a province or country district: (*R.C.*) the superintendent of the heads of the religious houses in a province.—*n.* **provin′cialism,** a manner, a turn of thought, or a word or idiom peculiar to a province or a country district: state or quality of being provincial: ignorance and narrowness of interests shown by one who gives his attention entirely to local affairs.—*adv.* **provin′cially.** [Fr.,—L. *prōvincia,* a province.]

provision, *prō-vizh′(ŏ)n, n.* act of providing (for, against): measures taken beforehand: preparation: a stipulation, previous agreement: a clause in a law or a deed: a store or stock:

(commonly in *pl.*) a store of food, food.—*v.t.* to supply with provisions or food.—*n.* **provi'sion-mer'chant,** a general dealer in articles of food.—*adj.* **provi'sional,** provided for the occasion to meet necessity: temporary, not final, subject to alteration in altered circumstances: containing a provision.—*adv.* **provi'sionally.—provisional order,** an order granted by a secretary of state, which, when confirmed by the legislature, has the force of an act of parliament. [Fr.,—L. *prōvīsiō, -ōnis—prōvidēre.* See **provide.**]

proviso, *prō-vī'zō, n.* a provision or condition in a deed or other writing: the clause containing it: any condition:—*pl.* **provi'sos** (*-zōz*).—*adj.* **provi'sory,** containing a proviso or condition, conditional: making provision for the time. [From the L. law phrase *prōvīsō quod,* it being provided that.]

provoke, *prō-vōk', v.t.* to call forth, give rise to, result in (e.g. a protest, laughter, an attack): to excite (a person) to action: to excite with anger: to annoy, exasperate.—*n.* **prŏvoca'tion,** act of provoking: incitement: that which provokes.—*adj.* **provŏc'ative,** tending or designed to provoke or excite (often with *of*): such as to stimulate thought or discussion.—*n.* anything that stirs up or provokes.—*adj.* **provō'king,** irritating.—*adv.* **provō'kingly.** [L. *prōvocāre, -ātum—prō,* forth, *vocāre,* to call.]

provost, *prov'ost, n.* the dignitary set over a cathedral or collegiate church: the head of a college: (*Scotland*) until 1975, chief magistrate of a burgh (*mayor* in England).—*ns.* **prov'ost-mar'shal,** (*army*—pronounced *prō-vō'*) an officer with special powers for enforcing discipline and securing prisoners till brought to trial: (*navy*) an officer (master-at-arms) having charge of prisoners; **prov'ostship,** the office of a provost.—**Lord Provost,** the chief magistrate of Edinburgh, Glasgow, Perth, Aberdeen, and Dundee. [O.E. *profast* and O.Fr. *provost*—L. *praepositus,* pa.p. of *praepōnĕre—prae,* over, *pōnĕre,* to place.]

prow, *prow, n.* the forepart of a ship. [Fr. *proue*—L. *prōra.*]

prowess, *prow'es, n.* bravery, esp. in war: achievement through valour: skill. [From O.Fr. *prou* (Fr. *preux*), valiant.]

prowl, *prowl, v.i.* to move about stealthily: to rove in search of prey or plunder.—*n.* (*coll.*) the act of prowling: a roving for prey.—*n.* **prowl'er.—on the prowl,** engaged in prowling. [M.E. *prollen*; origin unknown.]

proximate, *proks'i-māt* or *-māt, adj.* nearest or next (often with *to*): without anything between, immediate (of a cause and its effect).—*adv.* **prox'imately.**—*n.* **proxim'ity,** immediate nearness in time, place, relationship, &c.—*adv.* **prox'imo,** next month—often written *prox.* (for L. *proximō mense*).—**proximity fuse,** a device for activating an explosive device when it comes near the object. [L. *proximus,* next, superl.—*prope,* near.]

proxime accessit, *prok'si-mi ak-ses'it,* he came very near (the winner of the prize, &c.): (used as noun) a place next the winner, &c. [L.]

proxy, *prok'si, n.* the agency of one who acts for another: one who acts or votes for another: the writing by which he is authorised to do so.

[Contr. form of **procuracy.** See **procure.**]

prude, *prōōd, n.* a woman who prides herself on her strict modesty and propriety.—*n.* **pru'dery,** manners of a prude.—*adj.* **pru'dish.**—*adv.* **pru'dishly.** [O.Fr. *prode,* fem. of *prou, prod,* excellent.]

prudent, *prōō'dént, adj.* cautious and wise in conduct: discreet, dictated by forethought.—*adv.* **pru'dently.**—*n.* **pru'dence,** quality of being prudent: wisdom applied to practice, caution.—*adj.* **pruden'tial,** using or practising prudence.—*adv.* **pruden'tially.** [Fr.,—L. *prūdens, prūdentis,* contr. of *prōvidens,* p.r.p. of *prōvidēre,* to foresee.]

prune, *prōōn, v.t.* to trim by lopping off superfluous shoots or parts: to divest of anything superfluous: to remove by pruning.—*ns.* **pru'ner; pru'ning-hook,** a hooked bill for pruning. [O.Fr. *proignier*; origin unknown.]

prune, *prōōn, n.* (*obs.*) a plum: a dried plum. [Fr.,—L. *prūnum*; cf. Gr. *prou(m)non.*]

prunella, *prōō-nel'a, n.* sore throat: quinsy. [Latinised from Ger. *bräune,* quinsy.]

prunella, *prōō-nel'a, n.* a genus of plants, the best known of which is *self-heal,* once reputed to cure *prunella* (see above).

prunella, *prōō-nel'a, n.* a strong silk or woollen stuff, generally black—also **prunell'o.** [App. from Fr. *prunelle,* a sloe, dim. of Fr. *prune,* a plum.]

prurient, *prōō'ri-ént, adj.* itching: morbidly curious: having lascivious thoughts.—*ns.* **pru'rience, pru'riency**—*adv.* **pru'riently.** [L. *prūriens,* pr.p. of *prūrīre,* to itch.]

Prussian, *prush'án, adj.* of or pertaining to Prussia.—**Prussian blue,** a cyanide of iron, used as a pigment, first discovered in Berlin; **prussic acid,** a deadly poison, an acid first obtained from Prussian blue.

pry, *prī, v.i.* to peer or peep (into what is closed or—*fig.*—into what is not divulged): to try curiously or impertinently to find out about other people's affairs:—*pa.t.* and *pa.p.* pried.—*adv.* **pry'ingly.** [M.E. *prien*; origin unknown.]

psalm, *säm, n.* a devotional song or hymn, esp. one of those included in the Old Testament *Book of Psalms.*—*ns.* **psalmist** (*säm'ist*), a composer of psalms, applied to David and to the writers of the Scriptural psalms; **psalmody** (*sal'mo-di,* or *säm'o-di*), the singing of psalms, esp. in public worship: psalms collectively.—*adjs.* **psalmodic** (*sal-mod'ik*), **-al,** pertaining to psalmody.—*n.* **psalmodist** (*sal'mo-dist, säm'o-dist*), a singer of psalms. [O.E. (*p*)*salm,* (*p*)*sealm*—Low L. *psalmus*—Gr. *psalmos,* music of or to a stringed instrument—*psallein,* to pluck.]

psalter, *söl'tér, n.* the Book of Psalms, esp. when separately printed.—*n.* **psal'tery,** an ancient and mediaeval stringed instrument used by the Jews. [O.E. *saltere*—L. *psaltērium*—Gr. *psaltērion,* a psaltery.]

psephology, *sē-fol'ó-ji, n.* sociological and statistical study of election results and trends.—*n.* **psephol'ogist.** [Gr. *psēphos,* a pebble (used in the same way as a voting paper), *logos,* discourse.]

pseudo-, *sū-dō-,* in composition, false or spurious: deceptively resembling. [Gr. *pseudo-,* false, seeming, pretended], e.g. **pseu'do-**

Neutral vowels in unaccented syllables: *em'pér-ór*; for certain sounds in foreign words see p. ix.

class'icism, false or affected classicism.—As a separate word, *adj.* **pseudo**, false, sham.—*n.* a pretender.

pseudomorph, *sū'dō-mörf, n.* a portion of a mineral showing the outward form of another which it has replaced by molecular substitution or otherwise. [Gr. *pseudo-*, false, *morphē*, form.]

pseudonym, *sū'dō-nim, n.* a fictitious name assumed, as by an author.—*adj.* **pseudon'ymous**, bearing a fictitious name,—*adv.* **pseudon'ymously**. [Gr. *pseudo-*, false, *onoma*, name.]

pshaw, *shö, interj.* expressing contempt. [Imit.]

psyche, *sī'kē, n.* the soul, spirit, mind: the principle of mental and emotional life.—*adjs.* **psych'ic, -al**, pertaining to the soul or mind: spiritual: sensitive to, or in touch with, that which cannot be explained physically.—*n.* (**psych'ic**), that which is of the mind or psyche: a spiritualistic medium.—*adj.* **psychedel'ic** (see **psychodelic**).—*ns.* **psychi'atrist**, one who treats diseases of the mind; **psychi'atry**, the treatment of mental diseases; **psych'o-anal'ysis**, a method whereby nervous diseases or mental ailments are traced to forgotten hidden concepts in the patient's mind and are treated by bringing these to light; **psych'o-an'alyst**.—*v.t.* **psych'o-an'alyse**.—*adjs.* **psychodel'ic** (the irregularly formed **psychedelic** is commoner), pertaining to a state of relaxation and pleasure, with heightened perception and increase of mental powers: pertaining to drugs which cause, or are believed to cause, such a state: pertaining to visual and/or sound effects whose action on the mind resembles slightly that of psychedelic drugs, dazzling in pattern: loosely very upto-date; **psychogen'ic**, having origin in the mind or a mental condition.—*n.* **psychol'ogy**, the science that investigates the phenomena of mental and emotional life.—*adjs.* **psycholog'ic, -al**, pertaining to psychology.—*adv.* **psycholog'ically**.—*ns.* **psychol'ogist**, one who studies psychology; **psychonut'rics**, the branch of psychology dealing with measurable factors: statistical treatment of mental test results; **psy'chopath**, one suffering from a behavioural disorder resulting in indifference to or ignorance of his obligations to society, often shown in anti-social behaviour, as acts of violence.—*adj.* **psychopath'ic**, pertaining to psychopathy or psychopath.—*ns.* **psychopathol'ogy**, the branch of psychology that deals with the abnormal workings of the mind; **psychopathol'ogist**; **psychop'athy**, derangement of mental functions; **psychoprophylax'is**, a method of training for childbirth aimed at making labour painless; **psychōs'is**, a serious mental disorder.—*adj.* **psychosomat'ic**, of mind and body as a unit: concerned with physical diseases that have an emotional origin.—*ns.* **psychother'apy, -therapeut'ics**, the treatment of disease by hypnosis, psychoanalysis and similar means.—*adj.* **psychot'ic**, pertaining to a psychosis.—*n.* one suffering from a psychosis.—**psychological moment**, the best, most appropriate, moment: (*loosely*) the nick of time; **psychological warfare**, the use of propaganda to influence enemy opinion

or morale. [Gr. *psychē*, the soul.]

ptarmigan, *tär'mi-gan, n.* a mountain-dwelling grouse, white in winter. [Gael. *tàrmachan*.]

pterodactyl, *ter-ō-dak'til, n.* an order of fossil flying reptiles with a flying-membrane attached to an elongated finger. [Gr. *pteron*, wing, *daktylos*, finger.]

Ptolemaic, *tol-e-mā'ik, adj.* pertaining to the *Ptolemies*, Greek kings of Egypt, or to *Ptolemy* the astronomer (of the 2nd century A.D.).—**Ptolemaic system**, the theory by which Ptolemy explained the motions of the heavenly bodies on the assumption that the earth is the centre of the solar system.

ptomaine, *to-mān', or tō'mā-īn, n.* a loosely used name for substances, often poisonous, formed from putrefying animal tissues. [Gr. *ptōma*, a corpse—*piptein*, to fall.]

pub, *pub, n.* (*coll.*) short for **public-house.**

puberty, *pū'bėr-ti, n.* the beginning of sexual maturity.—*n.* **pūbescence** (*-es'ėns*), puberty: a soft downy covering, esp. in plants, of fine short hairs,—*adj.* **pūbes'cent, pubic**. [Fr. *puberté*—L. *pūbertās*—*pūbēs*, grown up.]

public, *pub'lik, adj.* of, belonging to, or concerning, the people: pertaining to a community or a nation: engaged in the affairs of the community: common to, or shared in by, all: generally known: not private, unconcealed. *n.* the general body of mankind: the people, indefinitely: a specified section of the community (e.g. *an author's public*): public view, or a public place, society, or the open.—*adv.* **pub'licly**.—*ns.* **pub'lican**, the keeper of an inn or public-house: (*orig.*) a farmer of Roman taxes, a tax-collector; **publica'tion**, the act of making public: the act of sending out for sale, as a book: that which is published, as a book, &c.; **pub'lic(-)house**, a house where alcoholic liquors are sold to the public: an inn or tavern; **pub'licist** (*-sist*), one who writes on or is skilled in public law, or on current political topics. (esp. *U.S.*) an advertising agent; **publicity** (*-lis'i-ti*), quality or state of being public or open to the knowledge of all: (chiefly *U.S.*) advertising.—*adj.* **public-spirited**, actuated by public spirit, an unselfish concern for the welfare of the community. **public company**, one whose shares can be purchased on the stock market by members of the public; **public corporation**, one owned by the government and run on business principles, being for the most part self-ruling; **public enemy**, someone whose behaviour is considered to be a menace to a community; **public funds**, government funded debt; **public image**, the picture in the minds of most people of what e.g. a political party stands for; **publicity agent**, a person employed, e.g. by an actor, to make the public familiar with his name and talents; **public relations**, (used adjectivally) directing relations with the public, e.g. by promoting knowledge through advertisement (**public relations officer**, an official in charge of public relations); **public school**, a school maintained by a local education authority: one of a class of endowed schools, such as Eton and Harrow,—**public address system**, a system that enables groups of people, including large crowds, to be addressed clearly, con-

fāte, fär; mē, hûr (her); mīne; mōte, fŏr; mūte; mōōn, fŏŏt; тнen (then)

sisting of some or all of the following—microphones, amplifiers, loudspeakers, sound projectors; **public opinion poll**, a testing of public opinion by questioning representative sample members of the community.—**in public**, in open view: among people, in society. [L. *pūblicus—populus*, the people.]

publish, *pub′lish*, *v.t.* to make public, to divulge: to announce formally, to proclaim: to put forth and offer for sale (as a book).—*n.* **pub′lisher**, one who makes public: one who publishes books. [Fr. *publier*—L. *pūblicāre*.]

puce, *pūs*, *n.* and *adj.* brownish-purple. [Fr. *puce*—L. *pūlex, -icis*, a flea.]

puck, *puk*, *n.* a goblin or mischievous sprite: (*cap.*) a merry fairy in *Midsummer Night's Dream*. [O.E. *pūca*; cf. O.N. *pūki*, Ir. *puca*, W. *pwca*.]

pucker, *puk′er*, *v.t.* and *v.i.* to wrinkle.—*n.* a fold or wrinkle. [Prob. from the same root as *poke*, a bag.]

pudding, *pŏŏd′ing*, *n.* a skin or gut filled with meat and other materials, a sausage: a soft kind of dessert food, usually farinaceous, commonly with sugar, milk, eggs, &c.: meat, fruit, &c. cooked in a casing of flour.—*n.* **pudding′-stone**, conglomerate (q.v.). [M.E. *poding*; origin unknown.]

puddle, *pud′l*, *n.* a small muddy pool: a mixture of clay and sand.—*v.t.* to make muddy: to make water-tight by means of clay: to convert from pig-iron into wrought iron by stirring in a molten state.—*v.i.* to dabble.—*n.* **pudd′ler**. [App. dim. of O.E. *pudd*, ditch.]

pueblo, *pweb′lō*, *n.* a town or settlement (in Spanish-speaking countries): a communal habitation of the Indians of New Mexico, &c. [Sp., town—L. *populus*, people.]

puerile, *pū′er-īl*, *adj.* (*rare*) pertaining to children: childish, trifling, silly.—*n.* **pūeril′ity**, quality of being puerile: a childish expression: an instance of childishness or foolish triviality. [L. *puerīlis—puer*, a boy.]

puerperal, *pū-ûr′pér-ál*, *adj.* relating to childbirth.—**puerperal fever, insanity**, fever, insanity, occurring in connection with childbirth. [L. *puerpera*, a woman in labour—*puer*, a child, *parĕre*, to bear.]

puff, *puf*, *v.i.* to blow or issue in whiffs: to breathe with vehemence, to pant: to swell (up, out).—*v.t.* to drive with a puff: to inflate: to praise in exaggerated terms (esp. by way of advertisement).—*n.* a sudden, forcible breath: a gust or whiff: anything light and porous, or swollen and light: a downy pad for dusting powder on the skin, &c.: an exaggerated expression of praise intended as, or serving as, advertisement.—*ns.* **puff′-add′er**, a thick, venomous African snake that distends its body when irritated; **puff′-ball**, any fungus with ball-shaped fructification filled when ripe with a snuff-like mass of spores; **puff′er**, one who puffs: a steam-engine, a steamboat: one employed to bid at an auction to incite others to run up prices; **puff′ery**, advertisement disguised as honest praise: puffs generally.—*adj.* **puff′y**, puffed out with air or any soft matter: swollen: out of breath.—*adv.* **puff′ily**.—*ns.* **puff′iness**; **puff′-paste**, a rich flaky paste for pastry: the pastry itself.—

puffed up, swollen with pride. [O.E. *pyffan*; cf. Ger. *puffen*, &c.]

puffin, *puf′in*, *n.* any of several sea-birds of the auk family with parrot-like beak.

pug, *pug*, *n.* a monkey: a fox: a pug-dog: a pug-engine: a pug-nose.—*ns.* **pug′-dog**, a small, short-haired dog with wrinkled face, upturned nose, and short curled tail; **pug′-engine**, a small locomotive used for shunting.—*adj.* **pug′-faced**, monkey-faced.—*n.* **pug′-nose**, a short, thick nose with the tip turned up.

pug, *pug*, *v.t.* to line or pack with **pugging**, clay, sawdust, plaster, &c., put between floors to deaden sound. [Origin unknown.]

pugilism, *pū′jil-izm*, *n.* the art or practice of boxing: prize-fighting.—*n.* **pū′gilist**, one who fights with his fists.—*adj.* **pūgilist′ic**. [L. *pugil*, a boxer.]

pugnacious, *pug-nā′shús*, *adj.* fond of fighting, combative, quarrelsome.—*adv.* **pugnā′ciously**.—*n.* **pugnacity** (*-nas′-*). [L. *pugnax, -ācis*, fond of fighting—*pugnāre*, to fight.]

Pugwash, *pug′wosh*, *n.* a conference held at intervals by scientists from many countries to discuss the dangers and difficulties into which the world is running. [Name of village in Nova Scotia.]

puisne, *pū′ni*, *adj.* an obsolete form of *puny*, surviving as applied to certain judges—junior. [O.Fr., from *puis* (L. *posteā*), after, *né* (L. *nātus*), born.]

puissant, *pwis′ánt*, *pū′is-ánt*, *adj.* powerful.—*n.* **puiss′ance**, power.—*adv.* **puiss′antly**. [Fr., apparently from a vulgar Latin substitute for L. *potens*, powerful.]

puke, *pūk*, *v.i.* to vomit. [Perh. conn. with Flemish *spukken*, Ger. *spucken*.]

pukka, *puk′a*, *adj.* good: genuine, real. [Hindustani *pakkā*, ripe.]

pulchritude, *pul′kri-tūd*, *n.* beauty.—*adj.* **pulchritud′inous**. [L. *pulchritudiō, -inis—pulcher*, beautiful.]

pule, *pūl*, *v.i.* to whimper or whine.—*n.* **pū′ler**. [Imit.; cf. Fr. *piauler*.]

pull, *pŏŏl*, *v.t.* to pluck, to cull: to move, or try or tend to move, towards oneself (or in a direction so thought of): to draw: to drag: to attract: to extract: to stretch: to row: to hold back (esp. a horse to prevent his winning): (*cricket*, *golf*) to strike to the left (or right for the left-handed): (*U.S.*) to draw or fire (a weapon).—*v.i.* to perform the action of pulling anything.—*n.* the act of pulling: a pulling force: a struggle or effort: an apparatus for pulling: a draught of liquor: an advantage.—*ns.* **pull′-in**, a stopping-place: a transport café; **pull′over**, a jersey, a jumper, a body garment put on over the head.—**pull a face**, to grimace; **pull a fast one** (*coll.*), to take advantage of by a sudden trick; **pull down**, to take down or apart: to demolish; **pull off**, to gain or achieve by effort; **pull oneself together**, to regain one's self-control: to collect oneself, preparing to think or act; **pull one's weight**, to take one's full share of exertion, to co-operate heartily; **pull out**, to draw out: to leave: to abandon a place or situation which has become too difficult to cope with; **pull round**, to bring, or come, back to good health or condition; **pull the long bow**, to exaggerate; **pull through**, to

Neutral vowels in unaccented syllables: *em′pér-ór*; for certain sounds in foreign words see p. ix.

586

get safely to the end of a difficult or dangerous experience; **pull up**, to tighten the reins: to bring to a stop: to halt. [O.E. *pullian*, to pluck, draw.]

pullet, *pōōl'et, n.* a young hen. [Fr. *poulette*, dim. of *poule*, a hen—Low L. *pulla*, a hen, fem. of L. *pullus*, a young animal.]

pulley, *pōōl'i, n.* a wheel turning about an axis, and having a groove on its rim in which runs a rope, chain, or band—used for raising weights, changing direction of pull, &c.:—*pl.* **pull'eys**. [M.E. *poley, puly*—O.Fr. *polie*.]

Pullman (car), *pōōl'mán (kär), n.* a railway saloon or sleeping-car, first made by George M. *Pullman* (1831-97) in America.

pulmonary, *pul'món-ár-i, adj.* pertaining to, or affecting, the lungs.—*n.pl.* **Pulmona'ta**, an air-breathing order of Gasteropoda, to which snails, &c., belong. [L. *pulmōnārius*—*pulmō, pulmōnis*, a lung.]

pulp, *pulp, n.* any soft fleshy part of an animal, esp. the tissue in the cavity of a tooth: the soft part of plants, esp. of fruits: any soft structureless mass: (*fig.*) sentimentality: a cheap magazine printed on wood-pulp paper, esp. as characterised by paltriness, sentimentality or sensationalism (also **pulp magazine**).—*v.t.* to reduce to pulp: to deprive of pulp.—*adjs.* **pulpous, pulp'y**—*n.* **pulp'iness**. [L. *pulpa*, flesh, pulp.]

pulpit, *pōōl'pit, n.* a raised structure, esp. in a church, occupied by a preacher: an auctioneer's desk: preachers or preaching collectively.—*adj.* belonging to the pulpit.—*n.* **pulpiteer'**, one who speaks from a pulpit: a preacher. [L. *pulpitum*, a stage.]

pulsate, *pul'sāt, v.i.* to beat, throb.—*n.* **pulsā'tion**.—*adjs.* **pul'satile**, capable of pulsation: played by beating, as a drum: acting by pulsation; **pul'sative, pul'satory**, beating or throbbing. [L. *pulsāre, -ātum*, to beat, freq. of *pellēre, pulsum*, to drive.]

pulse, *puls, n.* a measured beat or throb: the beating of the heart and the arteries: (*radio*) a signal of very short duration.—*v.t.* to drive by pulsation: to produce or cause to be emitted, in the form of pulses.—**feel the pulse**, to test or measure the heart-beat, usually by holding the patient's wrist: to explore (a person's) feelings or inclinations in a tentative way. [L. *pulsus*—*pellēre, pulsum*, to drive.]

pulse, *puls, n.* grain or seed of beans, pease, and other leguminous plants: the plants bearing them. [L. *puls*, porridge; cf. Gr. *poltos*, pap.]

pulverise, *pul'vér-īz, v.t.* to reduce to dust or fine powder.—*adj.* **pul'verisable**.—*ns.* **pulverisā'tion; pul'veriser**, one who pulverises: a machine for pulverising. [L. *pulvis, pulveris*, powder.]

puma, *pū'ma, n.* a carnivorous animal, of the cat kind, reddish-brown without spots, the cougar. [Peruvian *puma*.]

pumice, *pum'is, pū'mis* (also **pum'ice-stone**), *n.* the hardened froth of certain glassy lavas, so full of minute gas-cavities as to float in water: a piece of such lava, used for smoothing or cleaning.—*adj.* **pumiceous** (*pū-mish'ús*), of or like pumice. [M.E. *pomis*, pumice—L. *pūmex, icis*—*spuma*, foam.]

pummel, *pum'l, n.* a less usual spelling of **pommel**.—*v.t.* to beat, pound, thump, esp. with the fists:—*pr.p.* pumm'elling; *pa.p.* pumm'elled. [**pommel**.]

pump, *pump, n.* a machine for raising fluids, or for compressing, rarefying, or transferring gases.—*v.t.* to raise or force with a pump: to draw information from (a person) by artful questions.—Also *v.i.*—*n.* **pump'-room**, the apartment at a mineral spring in which the waters are drunk. [Origin obscure.]

pump, *pump, n.* a light dancing shoe without fastening. [Origin unknown.]

pumpkin, *pum(p)'kin, n.* a plant of the gourd family or its fruit. [O.Fr. *pompon*—L. *pepō*—Gr. *pepōn*, ripe.]

pun, *pun, v.i.* to play upon words alike or nearly alike in sound but different in meaning:—*pr.p.* punn'ing; *pa.t.* and *pa.p.* punned.—*n.* a play upon words. [Origin unknown.]

Punch, *punch* or *-sh, n.* a hook-nosed hunchback, chief character in the street puppet show 'Punch and Judy'; **Punch**, or the **London Charivari**, the chief illustrated English comic journal (begun July 17, 1841). [Shortened from **Punchinello**.]

punch, *punch* or *-sh, n.* a drink ordinarily of spirit, water, sugar, lemon-juice, and spice (with variations). [Traditionally from the five original ingredients—Hindi *pāc*, five—Sans. *pañcha*.]

punch, *punch* or *-sh, v.t.* to prod: to strike with a forward thrust: to stamp, pierce by a thrust of a tool (or with a machine): (*U.S.*) to drive (cattle).—*n.* a vigorous thrust: (*coll.—lit.* and *fig.*) striking power, vigour: a tool or machine for punching.—*n.* **punch'-card**, a card with perforations representing data, used in the operation of automatic computers.—*adj.* **punch-drunk**, (of a boxer) stupefied with blows.—*ns.* **punch'-line**, the last line of conclusion of a joke, in which the point lies: the last part of a story giving it meaning or an unexpected twist; **punch'-up**, a fight with fists.—**pull one's punches**, to hold back one's blows (also *fig.*). [**pounce**; or shortened from **puncheon** (1); possibly in some senses for **punish**.]

puncheon, *pun'ch(ō)n*, or *-sh(ō)n, n.* a tool for piercing or stamping metal plates. [O.Fr. *poinçon*—L. *pungēre, punctum*, to prick.]

puncheon, *pun'ch(ō)n*, or *-sh(ō)n, n.* a cask: a liquid measure of from 70 to 120 gallons. [O.Fr. *poinçon*, a cask.]

Punchinello, *punch-i-nel'ō, punsh-, n.* a hook-nosed character in an Italian puppet-show: a buffoon. [From It.]

punctate(d), *pungk'tāt(id), adj.* dotted: pitted. [L. *punctum*, point—*pungēre, punctum*, to prick.]

punctilio, *pungk-til'i-ō, -yō, n.* a nice point in behaviour or ceremony: nicety in forms: exact observance of forms:—*pl.* **punctilios**.—*adj.* **punctil'ious**, attentive to punctilios, scrupulous and exact.—*adv.* **punctil'iously**.—*n.* **punctil'iousness**. [It. *puntiglio*, Sp. *puntillo*, dims. of *punto*—L. *punctum*, a point.]

punctual, *pungk'tū-ál, adj.* of or pertaining to a point: (*arch.*) punctilious: exact in keeping time and appointments: done at the exact time: up to time.—*n.* **punctual′ity.**—*adv.* **punc′tually.** [L.L. *punctuālis—punctum,* a point.]

punctuate, *pungk′tū-āt, v.t.* to mark with points: to divide into sentences, clauses, and phrases by punctuation marks: to intersperse (with): (*loosely*) to emphasise.—*n.* **punctua′tion,** the act or art of dividing by points or marks.— **punctuation marks,** the comma, semi-colon, colon, period, &c. [L.L. *punctuāre, -ātum,* to prick—L. *punctum,* a point.]

puncture, *pungk′tyur, -chur, n.* a pricking: a small hole made with a sharp point: perforation of a pneumatic tyre.—*v.t.* to prick: to pierce with a sharp point.—*v.i.* to suffer perforation. [L. *punctūra—pungĕre, punctum,* to prick.]

pundit, *pun′dit, n.* a Hindu scholar: any learned man: an authority. [Hindi *paṇḍit*—Sans. *paṇḍita.*]

pungent, *pun′jent, adj.* pricking or acrid to taste or smell: keen, sarcastic (e.g. of a comment). —*n.* **pun′gency.**—*adv.* **pun′gently.** [L. *pungens, -entis,* pr.p. of *pungĕre,* to prick.]

Punic, *pū′nik, adj.* of ancient Carthage: of, pertaining to, characteristic of, the Carthaginians: faithless, treacherous, deceitful (as the Romans alleged the Carthaginians to be).—*n.* the Semitic language of ancient Carthage. [L. *Pūnicus—Poenī,* the Carthaginians.]

punish, *pun′ish, v.t.* to cause (a person) to suffer for an offence: to cause one to suffer for (e.g. *to punish one's carelessness*): to chastise: to treat severely.—*adj.* **pun′ishable,** that may be punished—said both of persons and of crimes.—*n.* **pun′isher.**—*adj.* **pun′ishing,** causing suffering or retribution: (*coll.*) severe, testing.—*n.* **pun′ishment,** act or method of punishing: penalty imposed for an offence: severe treatment.—*adj.* **punitive** (*pū′ni-tiv*), pertaining to punishment: inflicting, or with the purpose of inflicting, punishment (e.g. measures, an expedition). [Fr. *punir, punissant*—L. *pūnīre,* to punish—*poena,* penalty.]

punka, punkah, *pung′kä, n.* a large mechanical fan for cooling a room. [Hindi *pākhā,* a fan.]

punnet, *pun′et, n.* a small shallow chip-basket, as for strawberries. [Origin unknown.]

punster, *pun′ster, n.* one who makes puns. [**pun.**]

punt, *punt, n.* a flat-bottomed boat with square ends.—*v.t.* to propel by pushing a pole against the bottom of a river. [O.E. *punt*—L. *pontō, -ōnis,* punt, pontoon.]

punt, *punt, v.i.* to bet on a horse.—*n.* **punt′er,** a habitual gambler. [Fr. *ponter.*]

punt, *punt, n.* the act of kicking a dropped football before it touches the ground.—*v.t.* to kick in this manner. [Origin obscure.]

puny, *pū′ni, adj.* stunted: feeble.—*n.* **pun′iness.** [**puisne.**]

pup, *pup, n.* a shortened form of **puppy.**—*v.t.* and *v.i.* to whelp:—*pr.p.* pupp′ing.— **buy a pup,** to be swindled.

pupa, *pū′pa, n.* the stage that intervenes between the larva (e.g. caterpillar) and the imago (e.g. butterfly) in the life-history of certain insects: a chrysalis (q.v.):—*pl.* **pupae** (*pū′pē*). [L. *pūpa,* a girl, a doll.]

pupil, *pū′pil, n.* (*Rom.* and *Scots law*) a boy up

to the age of 14, or a girl up to 12: a ward: one who is being taught: one who is being, or has been, taught by a particular teacher.—*adj.* under age.—*n.* **pū′pilage, pū′pillage,** state of being a pupil: the time during which one is a pupil.—*adj.* **pū′pilary, pū′pillary,** pertaining to a pupil or ward.—**pupil teacher,** one who is both a pupil and a teacher. [Fr. *pupille*—L. *pūpillus, pūpilla,* dims. of *pūpus,* boy, *pūpa,* girl.]

pupil, *pū′pil, n.* the round opening in the middle of the eye through which the light passes.— *adj.* **pū′pilary, pū′pillary.** [L. *pūpilla,* pupil of the eye, orig. the same as the preceding, from the small image to be seen in the eye.]

puppet, *pup′et, n.* a doll or image moved by wires or hands in a show: one who acts just as another tells him.—*adj.* behaving like a puppet: actuated by others.—*ns.* **pupp′etry,** puppets collectively: the art of producing puppetshows; **pupp′et-show, -play,** a drama performed by puppets. [O.Fr. *poupette,* dim. from L. *pūpa,* a girl, doll.]

puppy, *pup′i, n.* (*dial.*) a puppet: a young dog: a conceited young man.—*ns.* **pupp′y-fat,** temporary fatness in childhood or adolescence; **pupp′yism,** conceit in men. [Fr. *poupée,* a doll or puppet—L. *pūpa.*]

pur. See **purr.**

purblind, *pûr′blind, adj.* (*orig.*) wholly blind: nearly blind: dim-sighted, esp. spiritually.— *adv.* **pur′blindly.**—*n.* **pur′blindness.** [**pure** (or perh. O.Fr. intensive pfx. *pur-*), and **blind.**]

purchase, *pûr′chas, v.t.* to buy: to obtain by labour, danger, &c.: (*law*) to get in any way other than by inheritance.—*n.* act of purchasing: that which is purchased: any mechanical advantage in raising or moving bodies: means of exerting force advantageously.—*adj.* **pur′chasable,** that may be purchased.—*n.* **pur′chaser.**—**purchase tax,** a British form of sales tax levied on specified goods sold within the country, replaced by **value-added tax** (1973). —**at so many years′ purchase,** at a price (for a house, &c.), equal to the amount of so many years′ rent or income. [O.Fr. *porchacier,* to seek eagerly, pursue—*pur* (L. *prō*), for, *chacier, chasser,* to chase.]

purdah, *pûr′dä, n.* a curtain, esp. for screening women′s apartments: the seclusion of women. [Hindi and Pers. *pardah,* a curtain.]

pure, *pūr, adj.* clean, unsoiled: unmixed: not adulterated: free from guilt or defilement: chaste, modest: mere: that and that only: utter: (*mus.*) clear and smooth in tone: perfectly in tune: monophthongal, not diphthongal.—*adv.* **pure′ly,** chastely: unmixedly: wholly, entirely: solely.—*n.* **pure′ness.**—**pure mathematics, science,** theoretical mathematics, science, considered apart from practical applications. [Fr. *pur*—L. *pūrus,* pure.]

purée, *pū-rā, n.* food material reduced to pulp and passed through a sieve, or reduced to pulp by a blending machine: a soup in which there are no solid pieces. [Fr.]

purfle, *pûr′fl, v.t.* to ornament the edge of, as with embroidery or inlay.—*n.* a decorated border.—*n.* **pur′fling,** a purfle, esp. around the edges of a fiddle. [Fr. *pourfiler*—L. *prō,* before, *fīlum,* a thread.]

Neutral vowels in unaccented syllables: *em′pér-ór*; for certain sounds in foreign words see p. ix.

purge, *pûrj*, *v.t.* to purify, to cleanse: to clear of undesirable elements or persons: to remove (an impurity): to clarify (liquor): to clear from accusation: to evacuate (bowels).—*v.i.* to become pure by clarifying: to have frequent evacuations.—*n.* act of purging: a medicine that purges: (*fig.*) act of ridding a political party by violent means of rebellious or half-hearted members.—*n.* **purga′tion**, a purging: spiritual purification: (*law*) the act of clearing from imputation of guilt.—*adj.* **pur′gative**, cleansing: having the power of evacuating the intestines.—*n.* a medicine that evacuates.—*adjs.* **purgatō′rial**, pertaining to purgatory; **pur′gatory**, purging or cleansing: expiatory.—*n.* (*R.C.*) a place or state in which souls are after death purified from venial sins: any kind or state of suffering for a time. [Fr. *purger*—L. *purgāre, -ātum*—*pūrus*, pure, *agĕre*, to do.]

purify, *pu′ri-fī*, *v.t.* to make pure: to cleanse from foreign or hurtful matter: to free from guilt or ritual uncleanness: to free from improprieties or barbarisms in language.—*v.i.* to become pure:—*pr.p.* pu′rifying; *pa.t.* and *pa.p.* pu′rified.—*n.* **purifica′tion**, act of purifying: (*B.*) the act of cleansing ceremonially according to Jewish law.—*adj.* **pū′rificātory**, tending to purify or cleanse.—*n.* **pū′rifier**. [Fr. *purifier*—L. *pūrificāre*—*pūrus*, pure, *facĕre*, to make.]

purism, *pūr′izm*, *n.* fastidious insistence upon purity of language in vocabulary or idiom.—*n.* **pūr′ist**. [L. *pūrus*, pure.]

Puritan, *pūr′i-tán*, *n.* one of a religious and political party in the time of Elizabeth and the Stuarts which desired greater purity and simplicity of doctrine and ceremony in the Church of England: any person of like views, in sympathy with the historical Puritans: a person professing strict (often narrow) morality in conduct and opinions.—*adj.* in sympathy with the Puritans.—*adjs.* **pūritan′ic, -al.**—*adv.* **pūritan′ically.**—*n.* **Pūr′itanism.** [L. *pūrus*, pure.]

purity, *pūr′i-ti*, *n.* condition of being pure: freedom from stain, fault, or taint: chastity. [L. *pūrus*, pure.]

purl, *pûrl*, *v.i.* to flow with a murmuring sound: to flow in eddies.—*n.* a soft murmuring sound, as of a stream. [Cf. Norw. *purla*, to babble; Swed. *porla*, to ripple.]

purl, *pûrl*, *v.t.* to fringe with a waved edging, as lace: to knit with inverted stitches.—*n.* an embroidered border: knitting with inverted stitches.—Also **pearl**. [Origin unknown.]

purl, *pûrl*, *n.* ale warmed and spiced.

purlieu, *pûr′lū*, *n.* (*pl.*) borders or outskirts: (*pl.*) environs, neighbourhood: locality: (*orig.*) an area on the borders of a royal forest, wrongly added to the forest, but afterwards restored and marked out by a new perambulation. [Anglo-Fr. *puralee*, land severed by perambulation—O.Fr. *pur* (L. *prō*), *allee*, a going; app. influenced by Fr. *lieu*, place.]

purloin, *pûr-loin′*, *v.t.* to filch, steal.—*n.* **purloin′er**. [Anglo-Fr. *purloigner*, to remove to a distance—*pur-* (L. *prō*), for, *loin* (L. *longē*), far.]

purple, *pûr′pl*, *n.* a colour formed by the mixture of blue and red: in ancient times used for a variety of shades, including purple and crim-

son: a purple dress or robe, originally worn only by royalty: royal rank or (*fig.*) exalted position in any sphere (as *born in the purple*).—*adj.* of the colour purple: blood-red.—*v.t.* or *v.i.* to make, or to turn, purple.—**purple patch**, a passage of fire or (often) over-ornate writing. [L. *purpura*—Gr. *porphȳrā*, a shellfish yielding purple dye.]

purport, *pûr′pōrt*, *n.* meaning conveyed: substance, gist.—*v.t.* (*pûr-port′*) to signify: to seem, profess, be alleged—with an infinitive as object (e.g. *a letter purporting to come from you; purporting to act in the public interest*). [O.Fr. from *pur* (L. *prō*), forward, *porter* (L. *portāre*), to carry.]

purpose, *pûr′pus*, *n.* the end or object towards which effort is directed: intention: function.—*v.t.* to intend.—*v.i.* to have an intention.—*adj.* **pur′poseful**, directed towards, serving, a purpose: actuated by purpose, conscious of a purpose, determined.—*adv.* **pur′posefully.**—*adj.* **pur′poseless.**—*adv.* **pur′poselessly.**—*adj.* **pur′pose-like**, (*Scot.*) purposeful, efficient.—*adv.* **pur′posely**, with purpose: intentionally.—*adj.* **pur′posive**, having an aim.—**on purpose**, purposely; **to good purpose**, effectively; **to the purpose**, to the point: relevant. [O.Fr. *pourpos, propos*—L. *prōpositum*, a thing intended—*prō*, forward, *pōnĕre, positum*, to place. Cf. **propose**.]

purr, pur, *pûr*, *v.i.* to utter a low, murmuring sound, as a cat when pleased. *ns.* **purr**; **purr′ing**. [Imit.]

purse, *pûrs*, *n.* a small bag for carrying money, orig. made of skin, the mouth being closed by means of thongs: a sum of money: funds.—*v.t.* to put into a purse: to contract as the mouth of a purse (esp. lips): to draw into folds.—*n.* **purse′ful**, as much as a purse can hold: enough to fill a purse.—*adj.* **purse′proud**, proud of one's wealth.—*ns.* **purs′er**, formerly, a naval paymaster: a ship's officer in charge of cabins, stewards, &c.; **purs′ership.**—*n.pl.* **purse′-strings**, the strings, thongs, fastening a purse (usu. *fig.*).—**privy purse** (see **privy**). [Low L. *bursa*—Gr. *byrsa*, a hide.]

purslane, *pûrs′lin*, *n.* an annual plant, used in salads. [O.Fr. *porcelaine*—L. *porcilāca, portulāca*.]

pursue, *pûr-s(y)ōō′*, *v.t.* to harass, persecute: (*Scots law*) to prosecute: to follow in order to overtake and capture: to seek to attain: to be engaged in: to proceed with.—*v.i.* to go in pursuit: to continue what one is saying.—*n.* **pursū′ance**, act of following, or of carrying out.—*adj.* **pursū′ant**, (with *to*) following: (approaching an *adv.*) according (to).—*n.* **pursū′er**, one who pursues: (*Scots law*) a plaintiff. [Anglo-Fr. *pursuer, pursiwer*—L. *prōsequī, persequī*—*prō-, per-*, and *sequī*, to follow.]

pursuit, *pûr-s(y)ōōt′*, *n.* the act of pursuing: occupation, employment. [Anglo-Fr. *purseute*, fem. pa.p. of *pursuer*. See **pursue**.]

pursuivant, *pûr′s(w)i-vänt*, *n.* an attendant or follower: a state messenger: an officer ranking below a herald. [Fr. *poursuivant*, pr.p. of *poursuivre*, to pursue.]

pursy, *pûrs′i*, *adj.* short-winded: fat and short.—*n.* **purs′iness.** [O.Fr. *poulsif*, broken-winded—O.Fr. *poulser*—L. *pulsāre*, to drive.]

purtenance, *pûr'tën-áns, n.* that which pertains or belongs to: (*B.*) the inwards of an animal. [Earlier form of **pertinence.**]

purulent, *pū'r(y)ŏŏ-lént, adj.* consisting of, full of, or resembling pus.—*ns.* **pū'rulence, pū'rulency.**—*adv.* **pū'rulently.** [L. *pūrulentus—pūs, pūris*, pus.]

purvey, *pûr-vā', v.t.* to provide, furnish, supply.—*v.i.* to furnish provisions or meals as one's business.—*ns.* **purvey'ance,** the act of purveying: that which is supplied: the former royal prerogative of pre-emption of necessaries; **purvey'or,** one whose business is to provide victuals: an officer who formerly exacted provisions for the use of the king's household. [Anglo-Fr. *purveier*—L. *prōvidēre.* See **provide.**]

purview, *pûr'vū, n.* the body or enacting part of a statute: scope: (*lit.* and *fig.*) range of vision. [Anglo-Fr. *purveu*, provided, pa.p. of *purveier.* See **purvey.**]

pus, *pus, n.* a thick yellowish fluid exuded from inflamed tissues. [L. *pūs, pūris*, matter; cf. Gr. *pyon.*]

push, *pŏŏsh, v.t.* to thrust or press against: to drive by pressure: to thrust (out): to advance, carry to a further point: to press forward (with *on*): to urge (to): to promote vigorously: to peddle (drugs): (*coll.*) to come near an age or number.—*v.i.* to make a thrust: to make an effort: to press forward.—*n.* a thrust: an impulse: effort: enterprising or aggressive pertinacity: exigence: an offensive (esp. in trench warfare): (*Austr. slang*) a gang of convicts: (*slang*) a gang of roughs, a company: (*slang*) dismissal.—*adj.* **pushed,** having been pushed: (*coll.*) in a hurry: (*coll.*) short of money.—*ns.* **push'er,** one who, or that which, pushes: (*coll.*) an ambitious and self-assertive person: an implement (or an attachment to a plate) to help a child to use a spoon: a dope pedlar; **push'-bicycle, -bike,** a bicycle, propelled by foot not a motor-bicycle; **push'-button,** a knob which when pressed puts on or cuts off an electric current, as for bells, &c.—*adjs.* **push'ful,** energetically or aggressively enterprising; **push'ing,** pressing forward in business, enterprising, vigorous: self-assertive.—*n.* **push'-over** (*coll.*), an easy task: a person or side easily overcome: a person easily persuaded.—*adj.* **push-pull,** of any piece of apparatus in which two electrical or electronic devices act in opposition to each other, as, e.g. of an amplifier in which two thermionic valves so acting serve to reduce distortion.—**push-button war,** one carried on by guided missiles, released by push-button (also **press-button war).** [Fr. *pousser*—L. *pulsāre,* freq. of *pellĕre, pulsum,* to beat.]

pusillanimous, *pū-si-lan'i-mus, adj.* lacking firmness of mind, mean-spirited, cowardly.—*adv.* **pusillan'imously.**—*n.* **pusillanim'ity.** [L. *pusillanimis—pūsillus,* very little, *animus,* mind.]

puss, *pŏŏs, n.* a familiar name for a cat or a hare.—*n.* **puss'y,** a dim. of **puss**—also **puss'y-cat.**—*v.i.* **puss'yfoot,** to go stealthily: to act timidly or cautiously. [Cf. Du. *poes,* puss; Ir. and Gael. *pus,* a cat.]

pustule, *pus'tūl, n.* a pimple containing pus.—*adjs.* **pus'tular, pus'tūlous.** [L. *pustula.*]

put, *pŏŏt, v.t.* to push or thrust: to cast, throw: to constrain (to a specified action), to compel to go (to): to set, lay, or deposit: to apply (to): to add (to): to bring into any state or position: to propose (a question): to express, state.—*v.i.* (*naut.*) to proceed, make one's way:—*pr.p.* putting (*pŏŏt'-*); *pa.t.* and *pa.p.* put.—**put about,** to change the course, as of a ship: to inconvenience, trouble: to publish (e.g. an item of news, a rumour): (also *adj.*; see **about**); **put across,** to transport across: (*slang*) to bring off (e.g. a deception): to explain convincingly: to perform in such a way as to gain the appreciation and sympathy of the audience; **put down,** to crush, quell: to kill: to write down on paper: to attribute: of an aeroplane, to land; **put in for,** to make a claim for: to become a candidate for; **put in mind,** to remind; **put it across (someone),** to defeat (someone) by ingenuity; **put it on,** to pretend (to be ill, &c.); **put off,** to lay aside: to appease by evasive pretexts: to delay; **put out,** to expel: to extinguish: to publish: to expend: to disconcert; **put through,** to bring to an end: to accomplish: to put in telephonic communication; **put two and two together,** to draw a conclusion from certain circumstances; **put up to,** to incite to: to supply with useful information; **put up with,** to endure.—**a put-up job,** a preconcerted affair; **(hard) put to it,** hard pressed: experiencing very great difficulty in (with infinitive; e.g. *hard put to it to find the necessary money*). [M.E. *puten*; cf. Dan. *putte,* Swed. *putta.*]

putative, *pū'ta-tiv, adj.* supposed, reputed. [L. *putātīvus—putāre, -ātum,* to suppose.]

putrefy, *pū'tre-fī, v.t.* to cause to rot, to corrupt.—*v.i.* to rot:—*pa.t.* and *pa.p.* pu'trefied.—*n.* **putrefac'tion,** rotting.—*adjs.* **putrefac'tive; putres'cent** (*-tres'ént*), rotting.—*n.* **putres'cence** (*-tres'éns*), incipient rottenness.—*adj.* **pū'trid,** rotten: (*slang*) wretchedly bad.—*ns.* **pūtrid'ity, pū'tridness.** [L. *putrefacĕre, putrescĕre, putridus—puter, putris,* rotten.]

putsch, *pŏŏch, n.* a sudden revolutionary outbreak. [Swiss Ger. dialect.]

putt, also **put,** *put, v.t.* (*Scot.*) to hurl (as a weight): (*golf*) to strike in making a putt.—*v.i.* to make a putt:—*pr.p.* putt'ing (*put'-*); *pa.t.* and *pa.p.* putt'ed.—*n.* (Scot.) a throw or cast: (*golf*) a gentle stroke intended to make the ball roll into the hole.—*n.* **putter** (*put'ér*), one who putts: a club used in putting. [A Scottish form of **put.**]

puttee, puttie, *put'ī, n.* a cloth strip wound round the legs from ankle to knee, as a legging. [Hindi *paṭṭī.*]

putty, *put'i, n.* powder used in polishing glass, &c.—*polishers'* or *jewellers' putty:* a cement of whiting and linseed-oil—*glaziers'* or *painters' putty:* a fine cement of lime only—*plasterers' putty.*—*v.t.* to fix or fill with putty:—*pa.t.* and *pa.p.* putt'ied. [Fr. *potée,* potful—*pot.*]

put-up, *adj.* See **put.**

puzzle, *puz'l, v.t.* (of a situation, person) to be difficult for (one) to understand: to perplex (with a difficult question or exercise).—*v.i.* to

Neutral vowels in unaccented syllables: *em'pér-ór*; for certain sounds in foreign words see p. ix.

be bewildered: to labour at solution.—*n.* perplexity: a cause of perplexity: a riddle or exercise that tests ingenuity.—*n.* **puzz'ler.**—*adj.* **puzzling,** baffling, perplexing.—**puzzle out,** to discover, by persevering mental effort. [Ety. obscure.]

pyaemia, *pī-ē'mi-a, n.* poisoning of the blood by bacteria from a part of the body that has become septic, resulting in the formation of abscesses in other parts. [Gr. *pyon,* pus, *haima,* blood.]

pyebald. See **piebald.**

pye-dog, *pī-dog, n.* an ownerless or pariah dog. [From Hindi *pāhī,* outsider.]

pygmy, pigmy, *pig'mi, n.* a member of a dwarf human race, fabulous or actual: a dwarf: any diminutive thing.—*adj.* diminutive, insignificant. [Gr. *pygmaios,* measuring a *pygmē* ($13^{1}/_{2}$ inches, distance from elbow to knuckles).]

pyjamas, *pi-* or *pī-jä'máz, n.pl.* loose trousers tied round the waist, worn by Moslems: (in European use) a sleeping-suit.—*ns.* **pyja'majacket, -trousers.** [Hindi *pāëjāmah—pāë,* leg, *jāmah,* clothing.]

pylon, *pī'lon, n.* a gateway to an Egyptian temple: a guiding mark at an aerodrome: a structure for supporting electric power-cables. [Gr.*pylōn—pylē,* a gate.]

pylorus, *pi-lō'rus, n.* the lower opening from the stomach to the intestines.—*adj.* **pylor'ic.** [L.,—Gr. *pylōros—pylē,* an entrance, *ouros,* a guardian.]

pyorrhoea, *pī-ō-rē'a, n.* discharge of pus: now, suppuration in the sockets of the teeth. [Gr. *pyon,* pus, *rheein,* to flow.]

pyramid, *pir'a-mid, n.* a solid figure on a triangular, square, or polygonal base, with triangular sides meeting in a point: any similar structure, esp. one of the great Egyptian monuments: (*pl.*) a game played on a billiard-table in which the balls are arranged in pyramid shape. *adjs.* **pyram'idal, pyramid'ic, -al,** having the form of a pyramid.— *advs.* **pyram'idally, pyramid'ically.** [Gr *pyra mis, idos.*]

pyre, *pīr, n.* a pile of wood, &c., for burning a dead body. [L. *pyra* – Gr. *pȳr,* fire.]

pyretic, *pī-ret'ik, adj.* of, of the nature of, for the cure of, fever.—*n.* **pyrex'ia,** fever. [Gr. *pȳretikos—pȳretos,* fever—*pȳr,* fire.]

Pyrex,*pī'reks, n.* (often, but incorrectly, without *cap.*) a registered trademark applied to glassware resistant to heat. [Gr. *pȳr,* fire, and

L. *rex,* king.]

pyrexia. See **pyretic.**

pyrites, *pī-rī'tēz, n.* a yellow mineral compound of iron and sulphur (also **iron pyrites**), so called because it strikes fire like a flint: extended to a large class of mineral compounds of metals with sulphur or arsenic.—*adjs.* **pyrit'ic, -al.** [Gr. *pȳrītēs—pȳr,* fire.]

pyro-, *pīr-o-,* in composition, fire: also (*chem.*) obtained by, or as if by, heating [Gr. *pȳr,* fire]:—e.g. **pyrolatry** (*-ol'-á-tri*), *n.* fireworship (Gr. *latreiā,* worship); **pyrogenic** (*-jen'-*), **pyrogenetic** (*-jén-et'ik*), *adjs.* produced by or producing fire or fever (see **genetic**).

pyro-electric, *pī-rō-el-ek'trik, adj.* becoming positively and negatively electrified at opposite poles on heating or cooling. [Gr. *pȳr,* fire, and **electric.**]

pyrolysis,*pī-rol'is-is, n.* decomposition of a substance by means of great heat. [Gr. *pȳr,* fire, *lysis,* loosing—*lyein,* to loose.]

pyrometer, *pī-rom'e-tér, n.* an instrument for measuring high temperatures.—*adjs.* **pyromet'ric, -al.** [Gr.*pȳr,* fire, *metron,* a measure.]

pyrotechnics, *pī-rō-tek'niks, n.* the art of making fireworks: display of fireworks: showy display in talk, music, &c.—also **py'rotechny.**—*adjs.* **pyrotech'nic, -al.** [Gr. *pȳr,* fire, *technikos,* skilled—*technē,* art.]

Pyrrhic victory, *pir'ik vik'tór-i,* a victory gained at too great a cost, such as those gained (esp. 279 B.C.) by King *Pyrrhus* of Epirus (Greece) over the Romans.

Pythagorean, *pī-thag-ó-rē'án, adj.* pertaining to *Pythagoras* (6th cent. B.C.), a celebrated Greek philosopher, or to his philosophy.—*n.* a follower of Pythagoras.

Pythian, *pith'i-án, adj.* pertaining to the *Pythia* or priestess of Apollo at Delphi, or to the Delphic oracles, or to the national games held there.

python,*pī'thón, n.* (*cap.*) a great snake killed by Apollo at Delphi in Greece: a genus of snakes of the boa family, all natives of the Old World.—*n.* **py'thoness,** the priestess of the oracle of Apollo at Delphi: a witch. [Gr. *pȳthōn.*]

pyx, *piks, n.* a box. (*R.C.*) a vessel in which the host is kept after consecration, now usually that in which it is carried to the sick: a box at the Mint containing sample coins for testing.—*v.t.* to test the weight and fineness of. [L. *pȳxis* a box—Gr. *pȳxis—pȳxos,* a box-tree.]

---

fate, tär; mē, hûr (her); *mīne; mōte, fôr; mūte; mōōn, fŏŏt;* THen (then)

Q

quack, *kwak, n.* the cry of a duck.—*v.i.* to make such a sound. [Imit.]

quack, *kwak, n.* a shortened form of **quack′-salver,** a charlatan.—Also *adj.*—*ns.* **quack′-ery,** the pretensions or practice of a quack, esp. in medicine; **quack′salver,** a boastful pretender to knowledge and skill (esp. in medicine) that he does not possess. [Du. *quacksalver* (now *kwakzalver*), perh. one who quacks about his salves.]

Quadragesima, *kwod-ra-jes′i-ma, n.* (*obs.*) the forty days of Lent: (also **Quadragesima Sunday**) the first Sunday in Lent.—*adj.* **quadrages′imal,** of the number forty: of Lent. [L. *quadrāgēsimus, -a, -um,* fortieth—*quadrāgintā,* forty—*quattuor,* four.]

quadrangle, *kwod-rang′gl,* also *kwod′-, n.* (*geom.*) a plane figure with four angles (and therefore four sides): an object or space of that form: an open space, usually rectangular, enclosed by buildings (as in a college)—abbrev. **quad.**—*adj.* **quadrang′ular.** [Fr.,—L. *quadrangulum*—*quattuor,* four, *angulus,* an angle.]

quadrant, *kwod′rant, n.* (*geom.*) the fourth part of the circumference of a circle, an arc of 90°: an area or street of that form: a sector bounded by a quadrant and two radii, the fourth part of the area of a circle: any of the four regions marked off on a surface by rectangular axes: an instrument with an arc of 90° for taking altitudes. [L. *quadrāns, -antis,* a fourth part—*quattuor,* four.]

quadrate, *kwod′rāt, adj.* square: rectangular: square as a power or root.—*v.i.* to square or agree (with).—*adj.* **quadrat′ic,** of or like a quadrate: (*alg.*) involving the square but no higher power.—*n.* a quadratic equation.—*n.* **quad′rature,** squareness: a squaring: the finding of a square equal to a given figure of some other shape: an angular distance of 90°: the position of a heavenly body at such an angular distance from another, or the time of its being there. [L. *quadrātus,* pa.p. of *quadrāre,* to square—*quattuor,* four.]

quadrennial, *kwod-ren′yál, adj.* comprising four years: once in four years.—*adv.* **quadrenn′ially.** [L. *quadrennis*—*quattuor,* four, *annus,* a year.]

quadri-, *kwod-ri-,* in composition, of or with four, as in **quadrisyllable** (*kwod-ri-sil′ä-bl*), *n.* a word of four syllables. [L. *quadri-*—*quattuor,* four.]

quadriga, *kwod-rī′ga, n.* in Greek and Roman times a two-wheeled car drawn by four horses abreast: a statue of such a car. [L., a later singular form from *quadrīgae,* a contr. of *quadrijugae*—*quattuor,* four, *jugum,* a yoke.]

quadrilateral, *kwod-ri-lat′ér-ál, adj.* four-sided.—*n.* (*geom.*) a plane figure bounded by four straight lines: an area so bounded. [L. *quadrilaterus*—*quattuor,* four, *latus, lateris,* a side.]

quadrille, *kwó-dril′,* or *kä-, n.* a square dance for four couples: music for such a dance. [Fr.,—Sp. *cuadrilla,* a troop, app.—L. *quadra,* a square.]

quadrillion, *kwod-ril′yón, n.* a million raised to the fourth power, represented by a unit with 24 ciphers: (*U.S.*) a thousand to the fifth power, a unit with 15 ciphers. [Modelled on **million**—L. *quarter,* four times.]

quadrinomial, *kwod-ri-nō′mi-ál, adj.* (*alg.*) of four terms.—Also *n.* [L. *quattuor,* four, *nōmen,* a name.]

quadrivium, *kwod-riv′i-um, n.* in mediaeval times, the more advanced part of the university course of seven liberal arts, namely, the four subjects of *arithmetic, music, geometry,* and *astronomy.* Cf. **trivium.** [L. cross-roads.]

quadroon, *kwod-rōōn′, n.* the offspring of a mulatto and a white, one whose blood is one quarter Negro. [Sp. *cuarterón*—*cuarto,* a fourth.]

quadrumanous, *kwod-rōō′mán-us, adj.* four-handed: of the **Quadru′mana,** a group of mammals with four feet that can be used as hands, the primates other than man. [L. *quattuor,* four, *manus,* a hand.]

quadruped, *kwod′rōō-ped, n.* a four-footed animal. [L. *quattuor,* four, *pēs, pedis,* a foot.]

quadruple, *kwod′rōō-pl, adj.* fourfold: consisting of four: having four parts or divisions.—*v.t.* to increase fourfold.—*v.i.* to become four times as much or as many.—*n.* **quad′ruplet,** a set of four things: one of four born at a birth (also *kwod-rōō′plet*)—abbrev. **quad.** [L. *quadruplus*—*quattuor,* four.]

quadruplex, *kwod′rōō-pleks, adj.* fourfold, esp. of a telegraphic system capable of sending four messages, two each way, over one pair of wires at the same time—*n.* an instrument of this kind.—*adj.* **quadru′plicate,** fourfold.—*v.t.* to make fourfold.—**in quadruplicate,** in four identical copies. [L. *quadruplex, -icis,* fourfold—*quattuor,* four, *plicāre, -ātum,* to fold.]

quaestor, *kwēs′tór, n.* a Roman magistrate with financial responsibilities and judicial functions: a treasurer. [L.,—*quaerēre, quaesītum,* to seek.]

quaff, *kwäf, kwof, v.t.* and *v.i.* to drink in large draughts.—*n.* **quaff′er.** [Origin obscure.]

quag, *kwag, n.* a boggy place, esp. one that quakes underfoot.—*adj.* **quagg′y,** spongy, boggy. [Prob. from the root of **quake.**]

quagga, *kwag′a, n.* an extinct S. African wild ass, less fully striped than the zebra. [Hottentot.]

quagmire, *kwag′mīr, n.* wet, muddy ground in which one sinks. [App. **quag, mire.**]

quaich, quaigh, *quā*H, *n.* a shallow drinking cup, usu. made of wood. [Gael. *cuach,* cup.]

Quai d'Orsay, *kā dör-sā,* the French Foreign Office. [Name of a quay on the Seine faced by

---

Neutral vowels in unaccented syllables: *em′pér-ór*; for certain sounds in foreign words see p. ix.

592

the French Ministry of Foreign Affairs.]

quail, *kwāl, v.i.* to cower, to flinch. [M.E. *quayle.*]

quail, *kwāl, n.* a genus of small birds of the partridge family. [O.Fr. *quaille* ; prob. Gmc.]

quaint, *kwānt, adj.* (*obs.*) ingenious, skilful: odd, whimsical (e.g. *a quaint conceit*): pleasantly odd or strange, esp. because old-fashioned— *adv.* **quaint′ly.**—*n.* **quaint′ness.** [O.Fr. *cointe*— L. *cognitus,* known; perh. confused with *comptus,* neat.]

quake, *kwāk, v.i.* to tremble, esp. with cold or fear: to quiver: —*pr.p.* quā′king; *pa.t.* and *pa.p.* quāked.—*n.* a shake: a shudder, esp. of the earth's surface. [O.E. *cwacian* ; perh. allied to *quick.*]

Quaker, *kwā′kėr, n.* one of the Society of Friends, founded by George Fox (1624-91):—*fem.* **Quā′keress.**—*n.* **Quā′kerism,** the tenets of the Quakers. [The nickname Quakers was given them because Fox bade a judge before whom he was summoned *quake* at the word of the Lord.]

qualify, *kwol′i-fī, v.t.* to ascribe a quality to (e.g. *an adjective qualifies a noun*): to describe (as—e.g. *he qualified his rival's action as dishonest*): to render capable or suitable: to furnish with legal power: to limit by modifications (e.g. *he now qualified his first statement*; *qualified appproval*): to mitigate.—*v.i.* to prove oneself fit for a certain position, or activity: to reach an accepted standard of attainment, esp. academic: —*pr.p.* qual′ifying; *pa.t.* and *pa.p.* qual′ified.—*ns.* **qualificā′tion,** that which qualifies: a quality or attainment that fits a person for a place, &c.: limitation; **qual′ifier.** [Fr.,—Low L. *quālificāre*—L. *quālis,* of what sort, *facĕre,* to make.]

quality, *kwol′i-ti, n.* that which makes a thing what it is, nature: kind or degree of goodness or worth: attribute: social rank: the upper class collectively: (*logic*) the character of a proposition as affirmative or negative.—*adj.* **qual′itātive,** relating to quality: (*chem.*) determining the nature of components. **quality newspaper,** one seeking to provide material that will interest educated readers. [O.Fr. *qualité*—L. *quālitās,* *-ātis*—*quālis,* of what kind.]

qualm, *kwäm, n.* a sensation of faintness or sickness: an uneasiness, as of conscience. [Perh. O.E. *cwealm,* death, pain.]

quandary, *kwon′da-ri,* also *kwon-dā′ri, n.* a state of perplexity, a predicament.

quantity, *kwon′ti-ti, n.* an amount that can be counted or measured: an indefinite amount: a large amount: bulk: a sum: the length or shortness of the duration of a sound or syllable: (*logic*) the character of a proposition as universal or particular.—*adj.* **quan′titātive,** measurable in quantity: (*chem.*) determining the relative proportions of components.— **quantity surveyor,** one who estimates quantities required, obtains materials, evaluates work done, &c.—**unknown quantity,** a quantity whose mathematical value is not known: (*fig.*) fact, person or thing whose importance or influence cannot be foreseen. [O.Fr. *quantité*—L. *quantitās,* *-ātis*—*quantus,* how much.]

quantum, *kwon′tum, n.* quantity: amount: a fixed minimum: in atomic physics, indivisible

quantity of any form of energy, equal to the frequency of the particular radiation multiplied by a constant.—*pl.* **quan′ta.**—**quantum number,** any of a set of integers or half-integers which together describe the state of a particle or system of particles; the **principal quantum number** specifies the shell an electron occupies; **quantum theory,** a theory in physics to explain the discontinuous nature of energy within the atom. [L. *quantum,* neut. of *quantus,* how great.]

quarantine, *kwor′ăn-tēn, n.* a period (orig. for a ship forty days) of compulsory isolation or detention to prevent contagion or infection: isolation or detention for such a purpose: the place in which the period is spent.—*v.t.* to put in quarantine. [It. *quarantina*—*quaranta,* forty—L. *quadrāgintā,* forty—*quattuor,* four.]

quarrel, *kwor′ĕl, n.* a square-headed arrow for a cross-bow. [O.Fr.,—Low L. *quadrellus*—*quadrus,* a square—L. *quattuor,* four.]

quarrel, *kwor′ĕl, n.* a dispute: a breach of friendship: a ground of dispute.—*v.i.* to dispute violently: to disagree: to find fault (with):—*pr.p.* quarr′elling; *pa.t.* and *pa.p.* quarr′elled.—*n.* **quarr′eller.**—*adj.* **quarr′elsome,** disposed to quarrel.—*n.* **quarr′elsomeness.** [O.Fr. *querele*—L. *querēla*—*queri,* *questus,* to complain.]

quarry, *kwor′i, n.* an excavation from which stone is taken, by cutting, blasting, &c.—*v.t.* to dig from a quarry: to cut into or cut away— *v.i.* to make, or to dig in, a quarry:—*pr.p.* quarr′ying; *pa.t.* and *pa.p.* quarr′ied.—*n.* **quarr′y-man,** a man who works in a quarry. [L.L. *quareia,* for *quadrāria*—L. *quadrāre,* to square.]

quarry, *kwor′i, n.* (*obs.*) a deer's entrails given to the dogs after the chase: a hunted animal: a prey, victim. [O.Fr. *cuirée,* *ourée*—*cuir*—L. *corium,* hide.]

quart, quarte, *kärt, n.* one of the eight thrusts and parries in fencing.—**quart and tierce,** practice between fencers. [Fr. *quarte.*]

quart, *kwört, n.* the fourth part of a gallon, or two pints: a vessel containing two pints. [Fr. *quarte*—L. *quartus,* fourth—*quattuor,* four.]

quartan, *kwör′tăn, adj.* occurring every third (by Roman reckoning fourth) day, as a fever. [Fr. *quartaine*—L. *quārtānus,* of the fourth.]

quarter, *kwör′ter, n.* a fourth part: the fourth part of a cwt.—28 lb. avoirdupois (abbrev. *qr.*): 8 bushels, as a measure of capacity: the fourth part of the year, or of the moon's period: three-monthly period for reckoning bills, rents, &c.: (*her.*) one of four divisions of a shield: one of four sections of a dismembered corpse: a haunch (as in *hindquarters*): a cardinal point, or any point of the compass: a direction: a district: lodging, as for soldiers, esp. in *pl.*: mercy granted to an antagonist (perh. from sending him as prisoner to quarters): (*naut.*) the after part of a ship's side.— *v.t.* to divide into four equal parts: to divide into parts: to dismember: to lodge in quarters: to lodge with (with *on, upon*): (*her.*) to bear, place, or divide quarterly.—*n.* **quar′tering** (*her.*), the bearing of two or more coats-of-arms on a shield divided by horizontal and perpendicular lines: one of the divisions so formed.—*adj.* **quar′terly,** relating to a quarter, esp. of a year: recurring, or published, once a quarter.—*adv.* once a quarter: (*her.*) in quarters or quarterings.—*n.* a periodical published every quarter of a year.—*adj.* **quar′ter-bound,** bound in leather or cloth on the back only.— *ns.* **quar′ter-day,** the first or last day of a quarter, on which rent or interest is paid; **quar′ter-deck,** the after deck of a ship—used by cabin passengers and by superior officers; **quar′termaster,** an officer who looks after the quarters of the soldiers, and attends to the supplies: (*naut.*) a petty officer who attends to the helm, signals, &c.; **quar′termaster-gen′eral,** a staff-officer of high rank who deals with questions of transport, marches, quarters, fuel, clothing, &c.; **quar′ter-sess′ions,** a court held quarterly by Justices of the Peace; **quar′ter-staff,** a long staff or weapon of defence, grasped at a quarter of its length from the end, and at the middle.—**at close quarters,** very near: hand to hand. [O.Fr. *quarter*—L. *quartārius,* a fourth part—*quārtus,* fourth.]

quartern, *kwör′térn, n.* a quarter, esp. of a peck, a stone, a pound (weight), a pint, or a hundred.—*n.* **quartern-loaf,** a four-pound loaf, as if made from a quarter of a stone of flour. [Anglo-Fr. *quartrun,* O.Fr. *quarteron—quart(e),* fourth part.]

quartet, quartette, *kwör-tet′, n.* a set of four: a composition for four voices or instruments: a set of performers for such compositions: a group of four persons or things. [It. *quartetto,* dim.—*quarto*—L. *quārtus,* fourth.]

quartier, *kär-tē-ā, n.* a particular district in a French town or city. [Fr.]

quarto, *kwör′tō, adj.* folded into four leaves or eight pages (often written 4to).—*n.* a book of sheets so folded in one of three standard sizes, or of such a size. [L. (*in*) *quarto,* (in) one-fourth.]

quartz, *kwörts, n.* the commonest rock-forming mineral, crystalline silica. [Ger. *quarz.*]

quasar, *kwā′sár, n.* a *quasi-star,* a point (star-like) source of radiation (usu. light) outside our galaxy, claimed by some to be merely an optical effect.

quash, *kwosh, v.t.* to crush: to annul. [O.Fr. *quasser* (Fr. *casser*)—L. *quassāre,* inten. of *quatĕre,* to shake.]

quasi, *kwā′sī, kwā′sē, adv.* as if: in composition, **quasi-,** in a certain manner or sense: in appearance only, as *quasi-historical,* &c. [L.]

quassia, *kwosh′(y)a, n.* a South American tree, whose bitter wood and bark are used as a tonic: the drug extracted from this and other tropical American trees. [Named from *Quassi,* a Negro, who discovered its value against fever.]

quatercentenary, *kwot-, kwat-er-sen-tēn′ár-i, -sin-ten′ár-i, -sen′tin-ár-i, n.* a 400th anniversary. [L. *quater,* four times, and **centenary.**]

quaternary, *kwo-tûr′nár-i, adj.* consisting of four: by fours: (*cap.*) pertaining to the geological era which followed the Tertiary and includes the Pleistocene and Recent periods.—*n.* a group of four: (*cap.*) the Quaternary era.—*n.* **quater′nion,** a set or group of four: (*pl.*) in mathematics, a calculus invented by Sir W.R. Hamilton (1805-1865), primarily concerned with the operations by which one

directed quantity or vector is changed into another. [L. *quaternī,* four by four.]

quatrain, *kwot′rān, n.* a stanza of four lines usually rhyming alternately. [Fr.]

quattrocento, *kwät-rō-chen′tō, n.* the 15th century in Italian art and literature. [It. 'four-hundred', used for dates beginning with fourteen hundred.]

quaver, *kwā′vér, v.i.* to tremble, quiver: to speak or sing with tremulous modulations.—*n.* a trembling, esp. of the voice: (*mus.*) half a crotchet. [Frequentative—obs. or dial. *quave,* M.E. *cwavien,* to shake; akin to **quake.**]

quay, *kē, n.* a landing-place, a wharf for the loading or unloading of vessels.—*n.* **quay′age,** payment for use of a quay: provision or space of quays. [O.Fr. *kay, cay,* perh. Celtic; assimilated to mod. Fr. spelling *quai.*]

quean, *kwēn, n.* a saucy girl: a woman of worthless character: (*Scot.*) a girl. [O.E. *cwene,* woman; cf. **queen** (O.E. *cwēn*).]

queasy, *kwē′zi, adj.* sick, squeamish: overfastidious: causing nausea.—*adv.* **quea′sily.**— *n.* **quea′siness.** [Perh. O.Fr. *coisier,* to hurt; or O.N. *kveisa,* a boil.]

quebracho, *kā-brä′chō, n.* the name of several South American trees yielding very hard wood. [Sp. *quebrar,* to break, *hacha,* axe.]

queen, *kwēn, n.* the wife of a king: a female monarch: a woman, or (*fig.*) anything, of surpassing beauty, excellence, &c.: the sexually functional (egg-laying) female of bees and other social insects: in chess, the piece that has the greatest freedom of movement.—*v.t.* to make a queen of: (with *it*) to play the queen.—*n.* **queen′-con′sort,** the wife of the reigning sovereign.—*adj.* **queen′ly,** like a queen: becoming or suitable to a queen.—*ns.* **queen′-moth′er,** the mother of the reigning king or queen; **queen′-of-the-mead′ows,** the meadow-sweet; **queen′-reg′nant,** a queen reigning as monarch.—For **Queen's Bench, Queen's Counsel,** &c. (so-called during the reign of a queen), see **King's.** [O.E. *cwēn,* O.N. *kvæn, kvän.*]

Queensberry Rules, *kwēnz′ber-i rōōlz,* rules applied to boxing, originally drawn up in 1867 and named after the Marquess of *Queensberry,* who took a keen interest in the sport.

queer, *kwēr, adj.* odd, strange: eccentric: arousing suspicion: sick or faint (e.g. *to feel queer*): (*slang*) homosexual.—*adv.* **queer′ly.**—*n.* **queer′ness.—Queer Street,** embarrassment, esp. financial; **queer the pitch,** to spoil the plans of a rival (or other person). [Perh. Ger. *quer,* across.]

quell, *kwel, v.t.* to crush, subdue.—*n.* **quell′er.** [O.E. *cwellan,* to kill, causal of *cwelan,* to die.]

quench, *kwench,* or *-sh, v.t.* to put out, extinguish, as a flame: to cool: to slake (thirst): to subdue, suppress (e.g. enthusiasm): to put (a person) to silence.—*adjs.* **quench′able; quench′less,** unquenchable. [O.E. *cwencan,* found only in the compound *ācwencan,* to quench.]

querist, *kwē′rist, n.* one who puts questions. [**query.**]

quern, *kwûrn, n.* a stone handmill. [O.E. *cwyrn, cweorn*; O.N. *kwern.*]

querulous, *kwer′ū-lús, -ōō-lús, adj.* complaining,

Neutral vowels in unaccented syllables: *em′pér-ôr*; for certain sounds in foreign words see p. ix.

peevish.—*adv.* **quer'ulously.**—*n.* **quer'ulousness.** [Low L. *querulōsus*—L. *querī*, to complain.]

query, *kwē'ri, n.* a question: the mark of interrogation: doubt.—*v.t.* to inquire into: to question, to doubt: to mark with a query.—*v.i.* to question:—*pa.t.* and *pa.p.* quē'ried. [L. *quaere*, imper. of *quaerĕre, quaesītum,* to seek, ask.]

quest, *kwest, n.* the act of seeking: search, pursuit: the object pursued.—*v.i.* to go in search. [O.Fr. *queste*—L. (*rēs*) *quaesīta,* a thing sought—*quaerĕre, quaesītum,* to seek.]

question, *kwes'ch(ŏ)n, n.* an enquiry: an interrogative sentence: a problem: a subject of doubt or controversy: a subject of discussion, esp. the particular point actually before the meeting, &c.: an individual part of a test of knowledge.—*v.t.* to ask questions of: to examine by questions: to regard as doubtful: to object to.—*adj.* **quest'ionable,** doubtful: suspicious: morally unjustifiable.—*n.* **quest'ionableness.**—*adv.* **quest'ionably.**—*ns.* **quest'ionmark,** a point of interrogation; **quest'ionmaster,** a quiz-master; **questionnaire** (*kes-tē-on-ār', kwes-tyón ār'*), a prepared set of written questions to obtain data on which to base a report or account (e.g. of industrial conditions).—**in question,** under consideration: in dispute, open to question; **out of the question,** not to be regarded as feasible. [O.Fr.,—L. *quaestiō, -onis*—*quaerĕre,* to ask.]

queue, *kū, n.* a pendent braid of hair at the back of the head, a pigtail; a line of persons awaiting their turn.—*v.t.* and *v.i.* to arrange, or to stand, in a queue. [Fr.,—L. *cauda,* a tail.]

quibble, *kwib'l, n.* an evasive turning away from the point in question: a merely verbal argument: a pun: a petty conceit.—*v.i.* to evade a question by a play upon words: to trifle in argument: to pun: to cavil.—*n.* **quibb'ler.** [Perh. dim. of obs. *quib,* quibble; or a variant of *quip.*]

quiche, *kēsh, n.* a shell of unsweetened pastry filled with egg custard, cheese, &c. [Fr.]

quick, *kwik, adj.* living: speedy: nimble: readily responsive: prompt in perception, learning, or repartee: hasty.—*adv.* without delay: rapidly: soon.—*n.* the living: the living flesh: the sensitive parts.—*adv.* **quick'ly.**—*v.t.* **quick'en,** to make quick or alive: to invigorate, reinvigorate: to excite: to sharpen: to accelerate.—*v.i.* to become alive or lively: to move faster.—*ns.* **quick'ener; quick'ening,** the period in pregnancy when the mother first becomes conscious of the movement of the child; **quick'hedge,** a hedge of living plants; **quick'lime,** recently burnt lime, unslaked; **quick'march** (same as **quick'step**); **quick'ness; quick'sand,** a tract of apparently firm sand which engulfs those who set foot on it: anything treacherous; **quick'set,** a living plant set to grow for a hedge, particularly the hawthorn.—*adj.* consisting of living plants.—*n.* **quick'silver,** mercury, so called from its great mobility and its silvery colour; **quick'step,** a march, step, dance, or tune in quick time.—*adjs.* **quick'tem'pered,** irascible; **quick'-witt'ed,** alert and quick in mind: quick in repartee.—**a quick one** (*coll.*), a quick drink. [O.E. *cwic;* O.N. *kvikr,* living.]

quid, *kwid, n.* something chewed or kept in the mouth, esp. a piece of tobacco. [A variant of **cud.**]

quid, *kwid, n.* (*slang*) a pound (100p): formerly a guinea:—*pl.* **quid.** [Origin unknown.]

quiddity, *kwid'i-ti, n.* the essence of anything: any trifling nicety, a subtle or captious distinction. [Schoolmen's L. *quidditās, -tātis.*]

quidnunc, *kwid'nungk, n.* a gossiping busybody. [L. *quid nunc?* what now?]

quid pro quo, *kwid prō quō, n.* something given, or taken, as equivalent to, a just return for, something else. [L., something for something.]

quiescent, *kwī-es'ént, adj.* resting: dormant: inactive: not sounded, as a letter.—*ns.* **quies'cence, quies'cency.**—*adv.* **quies'cently.** [L. *quiēscēns, -entis,* pr.p. of *quiēscĕre,* to rest.]

quiet, *kwī'ét, adj.* at rest, calm: peaceable: gentle, unobtrusive, inoffensive: silent: undisturbed.—*n.* rest, repose, calm, stillness, peace.—*v.t.* and *v.i.* to make or become quiet.—*v.t.* and *v.i.* **qui'eten,** to quiet.—*ns.* **qui'etism,** mental tranquillity: the doctrine that religious perfection consists in passive and uninterrupted contemplation of the Deity; **qui'etist,** one who believes in this doctrine.—*adv.* **qui'etly.**—*ns.* **qui'etness, qui'etude.** [L. *quiētus*—*quiēscĕre,* to rest.]

quietus, *kwī-ē'tùs, n.* an acquittance: release from office or from life: final discomfiture. [L. *quiētus est,* he is quit.]

quiff, *kwif, n.* a heavy forelock, usu. combed up and back from the forehead. [Poss. **coif.**]

quill, *kwil, n.* the hollow basal part of a feather: a spine, e.g. of a porcupine: a goose or other feather used as a pen, hence a pen: anything made from a quill-feather: a prong for plucking the strings of certain musical instruments: a weaver's bobbin.—*v.t.* to plait with small ridges like quills: to wind on a quill.—*n.* **quill'-driv'er** (used disparagingly), a clerk: an author. [Ety. obscure.]

quilt, *kwilt, n.* a bed-cover of two thicknesses of material, with padding between held in place by stitching, any material so treated.—*v.t.* to pad, cover, or line with a quilt: to form into a quilt: to flog with a rope's end. [O.Fr. *cuilte*—L. *culcita,* a cushion.]

quinary, *kwī'nár i, adj.* fivefold: by or in fives. [L. *quīnī,* five each—*quinque,* five.]

quince, *kwins, n.* a fruit with an acid taste and pleasant flavour, used in making preserves and tarts. [Pl. of *quine*—O.Fr. *coin*—L. *cotōneum*—Gr. *kydōnion*—*Kydōnia,* in Crete.]

quincentenary, *kwin-sin-tēn'ar-i, -sin-ten'ar-i,* or *-sen'tin-ār-i, adj.* relating to five hundred, especially five hundred years.—*n.* a five hundredth anniversary. [L. *quinque,* five, and **centenary.**]

quincunx, *kwin'kungks, n.* an arrangement of five things (e.g. trees) in the positions of the pips for five on a die or a domino. [L., five-twelfths of a pound—*quinque,* five, *uncia,* ounce.]

quinine, *kwin-ēn', kwin'ēn,* or *kwī'nīn, n.* a colourless, inodorous, very bitter alkaloid (obtained from cinchona tree bark), or one of its salts, used against malaria and fevers. [Fr.,—Sp. *quina*—Peruvian *kina, kinakina,* bark.]

fāte, fär; mē, hûr (her); *mīne; mōte, för; mūte; mōōn, fŏŏt;* тнen (then)

Quinquagesima (Sunday), *kwin-kwä-jes'ï-ma* (*sun'dä*), the Sunday before Lent, being the fiftieth day before Easter. [L. *quinquāgēsimus, -a, -um,* fiftieth.]

quinquennial, *kwin-kwen'yál, adj.* occurring once in five years: lasting five years.—*n.* a fifth anniversary or its celebration. [L. *quinquennium,* a period of five years—*quinque,* five, *annus,* a year.]

quinquereme, *kwin'kwi-rēm, n.* an ancient ship, usu. described as having five banks of oars, but the actual arrangement is uncertain. [L.,—*quinque,* five, *rēmus,* an oar.]

quinsy, *kwin'zi, n.* an inflammatory affection of the tonsils, attended by suppuration. [L.L. *quinancia*—Gr. *kynanchē*—*kyōn,* a dog, *anchein,* to throttle.]

quintain, *kwin'tin, -tán, n.* a post for tilting at, often with a revolving cross-piece to strike the unskilful tilter. [Fr.,—L. *quintāna via,* the place of recreation in the Roman camp.]

quintal, *kwin't(á)l, n.* a hundredweight: 100 kilograms. [Fr. and Sp. *quintal*—Ar. *qintār*—L. *centum,* a hundred.]

quintessence, *kwin-tes'éns, n.* the pure concentrated essence (of anything, esp. of something immaterial): the most essential part or most typical example (of anything).—*adj.* **quintessen'tial** (*-shál*). [Fr.,—L. *quinta essentia,* fifth essence, orig. a fifth entity (esp. that considered as composing the heavenly bodies) in addition to the four ancient elements (q.v.).]

quintet, quintette, *kwin-tet', n.* a musical composition for five voices or instruments: a set of performers or instruments for such compositions: a group of five persons or things. [It. *quintetto,* dim. of *quinto*—L. *quintus,* fifth.]

quintillion, *kwin-til'yón, n.* the fifth power of a million, represented by a unit and thirty ciphers: (*U.S.*) the sixth power of one thousand—a unit with eighteen ciphers. [Modelled on **million**—L. *quintus,* fifth.]

quintuple, *kwin'tū-pl, adj.* fivefold: having five parts or divisions.—*v.t.* and *v.i.* to increase fivefold.—*n.* **quin'tūplet,** a set of five things: one of five born at a birth (also *kwin-tōō'-plet*)—abbrev. **quin.** [L. *quintus,* fifth, on the model of **quadruple.**]

quip, *kwip, n.* a short, clever remark: a repartee: a gibe: a fanciful jest or action. [Perh. L. *quippe,* forsooth.]

quire, *kwīr, n.* formerly, eight sheets of paper or parchment folded in eight leaves: now, the twentieth part of a ream, twenty-four sheets, each having a single fold: (*obs.*; also **quair,** *kwär*) a (quire-filling) book or poem. [O.Fr. *quaier* (Fr. *cahier*), prob. from Low L. *quaternum,* a set of four sheets—L. *quattuor,* four.]

quire, *kwīr, n.* obs. spelling of **choir.**

Quirites, *kwi-rī'tēz, n.pl.* the citizens of ancient Rome in their civil capacity. [L.]

quirk, *kwûrk, n.* a quick turn: an artful evasion: a quibble: a quip: an oddity of character. or behaviour.—*adjs.* **quirk'ish; quirk'y,** inclined to trickery: having sudden turns, hence (*fig.*) tricky, difficult. [Origin unknown.]

quisling, *kwiz'ling, n.* a traitor who takes office under a government formed by an enemy who has occupied his country.—Also *adj.* [Vidkun *Quisling,* who thus acted during the German occupation of Norway (1940-45).]

quit, *kwit, v.t.* to pay, requite: to release from obligation: to acquit: to depart from: to cease to occupy: to rid (oneself of): (*slang*) to leave off: (*reflex.*) to behave.—*v.i.* to cease: to depart: (*coll.*) to desert one's job or task:—*pr.p.* quitt'ing; *pa.t.* and *pa.p.* quitt'ed.—*adjs.* quit, set free: acquitted: rid (of); **quits,** even: neither debtor nor creditor.—*ns.* **quit'-rent,** a rent by which the tenants are discharged from all other services; **quitt'ance,** a release, discharge: acquittance; **quitt'er,** one who gives up easily, a shirker.—**double or quits,** in gambling, a hazard, often the toss of a coin, to decide whether the loser of a previous bet shall pay *double* the sum originally staked or recover his loss and so be *quits.* [O.Fr. *quiter*—Low L. *quiētāre,* to pay—L. *quiētāre,* to make quiet—*quiētus,* quiet.]

quite, *kwīt, adv.* completely: exactly: enough to justify the use of the word so modified: indeed, yes. [A form of **quit.**]

quiver, *kwiv'ér, n.* a case for arrows.—*n.* **quiv'erful,** (*fig.*) a large family (Psalm cxxvii. 5). [O.Fr. *cuivre*; prob. Gmc.; cf. O.H.G. *kohhar* (Ger. *köcher*), O.E. *cocer.*]

quiver, *kwiv'ér, v.i.* to shake with slight and tremulous motion: to tremble, to shiver.—*n.* **quiv'er,** a tremulous motion, shiver. [Perh. O.E. *cwifer,* seen in adv. *cwiferlīce,* eagerly.]

qui vive, *kē vēv, n.* alert. [From the French sentry's challenge, meaning (long) live who? i.e. whose side are you on?]

quixotic, *kwiks-ot'ik, adj.* like Don *Quixote,* the knight-errant in the romance of Cervantes (1547-1616), extravagantly chivalrous: idealistic but impracticable (e.g. a project).—*adv.* **quixot'ically.**—*n.* **quix'otism,** absurdly romantic or magnanimous notions or conduct.

quiz, *kwiz, n.* an odd-looking person: a piece of banter or mockery: a public testing of knowledge, often competitive, for the amusement or edification of an audience.—*v.t.* to make fun of: to tease: to eye with mockery: to interrogate.—*v.i.* to practise derisive joking:—*pr.p.* quizz'ing; *pa.t.* and *pa.p.* quizzed.—*adj.* **quizz'ical.**—*n.* **quiz'-master,** a person who presides at a quiz. [Origin obscure.]

quoad sacra, *kwō'ad sak'ra,* as far as concerns sacred matters, as a parish formed for ecclesiastical purposes only. [L.]

quod, *kwod, n.* (*slang*) prison. [Origin unknown.]

quod vide, *kwod vī'dē, vi'de,* which see.—Abbrev. **q.v.** [L.]

quoif, *koif, n.* Same as **coif.**

quoin, *koin, n.* a wedge, esp. for locking type in a forme, or for raising a gun: an angle, esp. of a building: a cornerstone: a keystone.—*v.t.* to wedge. [See **coin.**]

quoit, *koit, n.* a heavy flat ring for throwing as near as possible to a *hob* or pin: (*pl.*) the game played with such rings.—*v.i.* to play at quoits.

quondam, *kwon'dam, adj.* former. [L., formerly.]

quorum, *kwō'rum, kwō'-, n.* the fixed minimum attendance necessary for the transaction of business at a meeting. [The first word of a commission formerly issued in Latin to certain magistrates.]

quota, *kwō'ta, n.* a proportional share: a part or number assigned. [L. *quota* (*pars*), the how-

---

Neutral vowels in unaccented syllables: *em'pêr-ór*; for certain sounds in foreign words see p. ix.

manieth (part)—*quŏtus*, of what number?—*quŏt*, how many?]

quote, *kwōt, v.t.* (*orig.*) to divide into numbered chapters, verses, &c.: to refer to: to cite: to give the actual words of: to adduce for authority or illustration: to give the current price of (shares, a commodity, &c.—e.g. *Kaffirs were quoted*; *he quoted wheat at so much a bushel*).—*n.* a quotation: a quotation mark.—*v.i.* to make a quotation: word used to indicate that what follows immediately is a quotation.—*adj.* **quō′table**.—*ns.* **quōtā′tion**, act of quoting: that which is quoted: a price quoted; **quōtā′tion(-)mark**, one of the marks used to note the beginning and the end of a written or printed quotation. [O.Fr. *quoter*, to number—Low L. *quotāre*, to divide into chap-

ters and verses—L. *quŏtus*, of what number?—*quŏt*, how many?]

quoth, *kwōth, v.t.* said (1st and 3rd persons sing. past tense of the otherwise obs. verb *quethe*), followed by its subject. [O.E. *cwæthan*, pa.t. *cwæth*, to say.]

quotidian, *kwō-tid′i-ăn, adj.* everyday: daily.—*n.* a fever or ague that recurs daily. [L. *quotīdiānus*—*quotīdiē*, daily—*quot*, how many, *diēs*, a day.]

quotient, *kwō′shĕnt, n.* (*math.*) the number of times one quantity is contained in another: a ratio, usu. multiplied by 100, used in giving a numerical value to ability, &c. [L. *quotiens*, *quoties*, how often?—*quot*, how many?]

quotum, *kwō′tum, n.* a quota. [L., neut. of *quŏtus*; cf. **quota**.]

fāte, fär; *mē, hûr* (her); *mīne*; *mōte, för*; *mūte, mōōn, fŏŏt*; THen (then)

R

R, *är,* abbrev. for **röntgen unit.**

rabbet, *rab'ét, n.* a groove cut to receive an edge.—*v.t.* to groove: to join by a rabbet:—*pr.p.* rabb'eting; *pa.p.* rabb'eted. [Fr. *rabat—rabattre,* to beat back.]

rabbi, *rab'i,* or *rab'ī,* **rabbin,** *rab'in, n.* a Jewish expounder of the law:—*pl.* **rabb'is, rabb'ins.** —*adjs.* **rabbin'ic, -al,** pertaining to the rabbis or to their opinions, learning, and language. [Heb. *rabbi,* my great one—*rabh,* great, master.]

rabbit, *rab'it, n.* a small burrowing animal of the hare family: its flesh (as food): its fur: (*slang*) a timid, contemptible person: (*slang*) an incurably inferior performer in games or sport.—*ns.* **rabb'it-hutch,** a box for housing rabbits; **rabb'it-warr'en,** a place where rabbits are bred or abound: an overpopulated or confusingly intricate building or place. [M.E. *rabet.*]

rabble, *rab'l, n.* a disorderly, noisy crowd, a mob: the lowest class of people.—Also *adj.*—*v.t.* to assault by a mob.—*ns.* **rabb'lement,** a rabble: tumult; **rabb'ling,** esp. (*Scot. hist.*) the mobbing and ousting of the Episcopal 'curates' at the Revolution (1688). [Cf. Old Du. *rabbelen,* to gabble, Ger. *rabbeln.*]

Rabelaisian, *rab-é-lā'zi-án, adj.* marked by the broad humour and indecency in which the writings of *Rabelais* (d. 1553) abound.

rabid, *rab'id, adj.* violent (of a feeling): fanatical (of a person or opinion): affected with rabies, as a dog.—*adv.* **rab'idly.**—*ns.* **rab'idness; rabies** (*rā'-* or *ra'bi-ez*), a disease of dogs, wolves, &c., also called hydrophobia, due to a virus transmitted by the bite of an infected animal. [L. *rabidus* (adj.), *rabiēs* (n).—*rabēre,* to rave.]

raccoon, racoon, *ra-kōōn', n.* an American animal related to the bears: its fur. [Amer. Indian.]

race, *rās, n.* the descendants of a common ancestor: a tribal or national stock: a breed or variety: a division of mankind, a distinct variety of the genus *Homo*: peculiar flavour as of wine, by which its origin may be recognised.—*adj.* **racial** (*rā'sh(i-á)l*), of, relating to race.—*n.* **ra'cialism,** hatred, rivalry or prejudice accompanying difference of race: belief in inherent superiority of some races over others, usu. with implication of right to rule: discriminative treatment based on that belief; **ra'cialist; rac'ism,** racialism; **rac'ist.**—*adj.* **rac'y** (see separate article).—**race hatred,** animosity towards people of different race; **race suicide,** voluntary limitation of reproduction, causing the birth-rate to fall lower than the death-rate, and thus leading to extinction of the race. [Fr.,—Ital. *razza*; of doubtful origin.]

race, *rās, n.* (*arch.* and *Scot.*) a rush: a strong

and rapid current: a channel to or from a water-wheel: a competitive trial of speed: a horse-race: a fixed course, esp. of life.—*v.i.* to run swiftly: to compete in a trial of speed: to run wildly (as an engine, a propeller) when resistance is removed.—*v.t.* to cause to race: to oppose in a race: to rush: to run (e.g. an engine) wildly.—*ns.* **race'-card,** a programme of horse-races; **race'-course, -track,** the course over which races are run; **race'horse,** a horse bred for racing; **ra'cer,** one who or that which races. [O.N. *rās*; O.E. *ræs.*]

raceme, *ra-sēm', rā-sēm', ras'ēm, n.* a cluster of flowers attached by stalks to a central stem.—*adj.* **racemed',** having racemes. [L. *racēmus,* a cluster of grapes.]

Rachmanism, *rak'man-izm, n.* conduct of a landlord who charges extortionate rents for property in which very bad slum conditions prevail. [From name of landlord exposed in 1963.]

racial, racialism. See race.

rack, *rak, n.* an instrument for racking or stretching, esp. an instrument of torture: hence (*fig.*) extreme pain, anxiety, or doubt: a framework on which articles are arranged, as plate-rack, &c.: (*mech.*) the grating above a manger for hay: a bar with teeth to work into those of a wheel pinion, or endless screw.—*v.t.* to stretch forcibly: to strain (e.g. *to rack one's brains*): to torture, torment.—*ns.* **rack'-rail,** a railway having cogs into which similar cogs on a locomotive work; **rack'-rent,** the utmost rent that can be extorted. [The radical sense is to stretch, closely allied to **reach.**]

rack, *rak, n.* same as **wrack,** destruction.—**rack and ruin,** a state of neglect and collapse.

rack, *rak, n.* flying cloud: driving mist. [App. O.N. *rek,* drifting wreckage; cf. **wrack, wreck**; O.E. *wrecan,* to drive.]

racket, *rak'ét, n.* a bat strung with catgut or nylon, for playing tennis, &c.: a snowshoe of like design: (*pl.*) a modern variety of the old game of tennis, played against a wall.—Also **racquet** (*rak'ét*). [Fr. *raquette* perh.—Ar. *rāhat,* coll. form of *rāha,* the palm of the hand.]

racket, *rak'ét, n.* din, clamour: disorderly conduct: a fraudulent activity.—*n.* **racketeer',** one who extorts money by threats or makes profit by illegal action. [Prob. imit.]

raconteur, *ra-kõ-tœr, n.* a story-teller. [Fr.]

racoon. See raccoon.

racy, *rā'si, adj.* having a distinctive flavour imparted by the soil, as wine: spirited: piquant: risqué.—*adv.* **rā'cily.**—*n.* **rā'ciness.** [race (1).]

rad, *rad, n.* a unit of dosage of *rad*iation.

radar, *rā'där, n.* (*radio*) the technique of using reflection of radio waves for locating objects (aircraft, ships, landmarks, &c.). A short radio impulse is transmitted and the reflected impulse received is examined electrically for

Neutral vowels in unaccented syllables: *em'pér-ór*; for certain sounds in foreign words see p. ix.

direction of arrival and delay. Formerly known as *radiolocation* (a more general term).—**radar altimeter,** a high altitude radio altimeter. [American code-word, from *ra*dio *d*etecting *a*nd *r*anging.]

raddle, *rad'l, n.* a hedge formed by interweaving the branches of trees: a hurdle.—*v.t.* to interweave. [Anglo-Fr. *reidele,* rail.]

raddle, *rad'l, n.* red ochre.—*v.t.* to plaster with rouge. [Akin to **red.**]

radial, *rā'di-ál, adj.* pertaining to or like a ray or radius: arranged like spokes or radii: pertaining to the radius of the forearm. [L.L. *radiālis*—L. *radius.* See **radius.**]

radian, *rā'di-án, n.* the SI unit of circular measure, the angle subtended at the centre of a circle by an arc equal to the radius, nearly 57·3°.—Abbrev. **rad.** [L. *radius.* See **radius.**]

radiant, *rā'di-ánt, rā'dyánt, adj.* emitting rays: issuing in rays: glowing: shining: beaming with joy.—*n.* luminous point from which rays emanate: the centre from which meteoric showers seem to proceed: (*geom.*) a straight line from a point about which it is conceived in radiation as **ra'diance, ra'diancy,** quality of being radiant: brilliancy: splendour.—*adv.* **ra'diantly.** [L. *radians, -antis,* pr.p. of *radiāre, -ātum,* to radiate—*radius.* See **radius.**]

radiate, *rā'di-āt, v.t.* to emit rays: to shine: to issue in rays: to proceed in divergent lines from any central point or surface.—*adj.* (*-āt*) having ray florets: spreading like a ray or rays: having a form showing symmetrical divergence from a centre.—*v.t.* to send out in or by rays.—*ns.* **rādia'tion,** act of radiating: the emission and diffusion of rays: that which is radiated, esp. energy emitted in the form of electromagnetic waves (as light, radio, waves); **rādiator,** an apparatus for emitting heat, as for warming a room, or cooling an engine: a wireless transmitting aerial. **radiation sickness,** an illness caused by excessive exposure to the rays from radioactive substances. [L. *radiātus,* rayed.]

radical, *rad'i-k(á)l, adj.* pertaining to the root or origin: original: intrinsic: inherent: thorough: (*bot.*) proceeding from near the root: (*politics,* usually with *cap.*) bent on drastic but constitutional reform.—*n.* a root in any sense: (*chem.*) a group of atoms behaving like a single atom and passing unchanged from one compound to another: (*with cap.*) an advocate of drastic political reform.—*n.* **Rad'icalism,** the principles or spirit of a Radical.—*adv.* **rad'ically.** [L. *rādīx, -īcis,* a root.]

radicle, *rad'i-kl, n.* a little root: the part of a seed that becomes the root: (*chem.*) a radical. [L. *rādicula,* a little root; dim. of *rādīx.*]

radio-, *rā'di-ō, -o,* in composition (most terms can be spelt as one word, a hyphenated word, or two words), denotes rays, radiation, radium, radius: radio, wireless: (of product or isotope) radio-active, as **radio-tho'rium,** isotope of thorium.—*ns.* **ra'dio,** wireless communication: a wireless message or broadcast; **radioactiv'ity,** spontaneous disintegration, first observed in certain naturally occurring heavy elements (e.g. radium and uranium) accompanied by the emission of α-rays (alpha rays

or particles, q.v.), β-rays (beta rays or particles) and γ-rays (gamma rays).—*adj.* **radioact'ive.**—*ns.* **radio amateur,** a person licensed to send and receive wireless messages privately on certain VHF, short-wave bands.—Also **radio ham; radio-astron'omy,** astronomical study by means of radar: study of radio waves generated in space; **radiobiol'ogy,** the study of the effects of radiation on living tissue; **radiocar'bon,** a radioactive isotope of carbon, specifically carbon-14, used as a tracer element and in carbon-dating; **ra'dioele'ment, -is'otope** (see **isotope**); **radio frequency,** a frequency suitable for radio transmission.—*adj.* **radiogen'ic,** produced by radioactive disintegration: suitable for broadcasting.—*ns.* **ra'diogram,** an X-ray photograph: a wireless telegram: (for **radiogram'ophone**) a combined wireless receiver and gramophone; **ra'diograph,** an instrument for recording radiation: an X-ray, etc. photograph; **rādiog'raphy,** the technique, or practice, of making photographs of interior of body or specimen by radiations other than light, as X-rays, &c.; **radio ham** (see **radio amateur**); **rādioloca'tion,** position-finding by wireless signals; **rādiol'ogy,** the study of radiation and radioactivity: their application to medicine; **radiol'ogist; radio sonde** (Fr. *sonde,* plummet, probe), apparatus for ascertaining atmospheric conditions at great heights, consisting of a hydrogen-filled balloon, radio transmitters, &c.; **radio star,** a discrete (i.e. separate and distinct) source of radio waves in outer space corresponding to no visible object; **radiostrontium,** strontium-90, a radioactive isotope of strontium; **radiotelegraph, radiotelephone,** wireless telegraph, telephone; **radio telescope** (*radio-astronomy*), an apparatus for the reception of radio waves from outer space; **rādiotherapeut'ics, rādiother'apy,** treatment of disease by radiation esp by X rays, or by radioactive substances; **radio wave,** an electromagnetic wave of radio frequency. [L. *radius,* a spoke, radius, ray.]

radish, *rad'ish, n.* a plant whose pungent root is eaten as a salad. [Fr. *radis*—Provençal *raditz*—L. *rādīx, rādicis,* a root.]

radium, *rā'di-um, n.* a radioactive metallic element (symbol Ra; atomic no. 88) discovered in 1898, remarkable for its active, spontaneous disintegration. [L. *radius,* a ray.]

radius, *rā'di-us, n.* (*geom.*) a straight line from the centre to the circumference of a circle: anything like a radius, as the spoke of a wheel: (*anat.*) the exterior bone of the forearm: the movable arm of a sextant:—*pl.* **rād'iī.** [L. *radius,* a spoke, radius, ray.]

radix, *rā'diks, n.* a root: (*rare*) a source: the quantity on which a system of numeration or of logarithms is based: a word from which other words are formed:—*pl.* **radices** (*rā'disēz*). [L. *rādīx, rādicis.*]

radon, *rā'don, n.* a radioactive element, a colourless gas (symbol Rn; atomic number 86). [*Radium,* with suffx. *-on.*]

Raf, *raf, n.* the *R.A.F.*—Royal Air Force.

raff, *raf, n.* riff-raff.—*adj.* **raff'ish,** disreputable, rakish: flashy.—*adv.* **raff'ishly.**—*n.* **raff'ishness.** [See **riff-raff.**]

raffia, *raf'i-a, n.* strips of the pliant fibre of the bark or leaves of the raffia palm (genus *Raphia*). [Malagasy (q.v.).]

raffle, *raf'l, n.* an old dicing game: a lottery to decide which of the subscribers shall receive a certain article.—*v.t.* to sell by raffle. [Fr. *rafle*, a winning throw of the dice.]

raft, *räft, n.* a floating mass of logs or other objects: a flat structure of logs or planks for support or conveyance on water. [O.N. *raptr*, a rafter.]

rafter, *räft'ér, n.* an inclined beam supporting the roof of a house.—*v.t.* to furnish with rafters. [O.E. *ræfter*, a beam.]

rag, *rag, n.* worn, torn, or waste scrap of cloth: a tatter or shred: a worthless piece of any material: (in *pl.*) tattered clothing: ragtime or a piece of ragtime music: (*coll.*) a person in a state of exhaustion.—*adj.* made of rags.—*n.* **rag'-fair**, a market for old clothes, &c.: (*mil. slang*) a kit inspection.—*adj.* **ragg'ed**, shaggy: jagged: uneven: irregular: torn into rags: wearing ragged clothes.—*adv.* **ragg'edly.**—*ns.* **ragg'edness**; **rag'man**, a man who deals in rags; **rag'time**, music of American Negro origin, having more or less continuous syncopation in the melody.—**ragtag and bobtail**, riffraff; **the rag trade**, the trade concerned with designing, making and selling clothes. [O.E. *ragg*, inferred from the adj. *raggig*, shaggy.]

rag, *rag, v.t.* to torment with persistent ridicule, often with horseplay.—*n.* a boisterous frolic, esp. and orig. of undergraduates—now in British Universities associated with the raising of money for charity. [Perh. shortened from **bullyrag**; perh. from **rag** (1).]

ragamuffin,*rag'a-muf-in,* or *-muf'-, n.* an ill-clad dirty man or boy. [Perh. **rag** (1).]

rage, *räj, n.* overmastering passion of any kind, as desire or (esp.) anger: frenzy: vogue: a thing in the vogue: violence (e.g. of the wind).—*v.i.* to behave with passion, esp. with furious anger: to storm: to be prevalent and violent.—*adj.* **rä'ging**, violent, furious.—*adv.* **rä'gingly.** [Fr.,—L. *rabiēs—rabĕre*, to rave.]

raglan,*rag'lán, n.* an overcoat, with the sleeve in one piece with the shoulder.—*adj.* of a sleeve, in one piece with the shoulder. [From Lord *Raglan* (1788-1855).]

ragout, *ra-gōō', n.* a highly seasoned stew of meat and vegetables. [Fr. *ragoût—ragoûter,* to restore the appetite.]

ragtime. See **rag** (1).

ragwort,*rag'wúrt, n.* a large coarse weed with a yellow flower. [**rag** (1), and O.E. *wyrt,* a plant.]

raid, *räd, n.* a sudden swift inroad, orig. of horsemen, for assault or seizure: an air attack.—*v.t.* to make a raid on: (*coll.*) to help oneself to things from.—*v.i.* to go on a raid.—*n.* **raid'er**, one who raids: an aircraft over enemy territory. [O.E. *räd,* a riding.]

rail,*räl, n.* a bar extending from one support to another, as in fences, staircases, &c.: one of the steel bars used to form a track for wheeled vehicles: the railway as a means of travel or transport.—*v.t.* to enclose or separate by rails.—*ns.* **rail'bus**, a smaller version of the railcar; **rail'car**, a single railway coach operating as a unit with a light engine; **rail'-chair**, an iron block by which the rails are secured to

the sleepers; **rail'head,** the farthest point reached by a railway under construction: (*loosely*) a station serving a large rural area: the end of railway transport; **rail'ing,** a fence of posts and rails: material for rails; **rail'road** (chiefly *U.S.*), a railway.—*v.t.* to push forward unduly: to get rid of, esp. by sending to prison on a false charge.—*ns.* **rail'-splitt'er** (*U.S.*), one who splits logs into rails for a fence; **rail'way,** a track laid with rails on which wheeled vehicles, esp. locomotive engines and wagons, run: the system of rail transport. [O.Fr. *reille*—L. *rēgula,* ruler.]

rail,*räl, v.i.* to utter angry taunts or reproaches (at, against, or *arch.* upon, on): (*obs.*) to banter.—*n.* **railery** (*rāl'ér-i*), railing or mockery, banter, playful satire. [Fr. *railler.*]

rail, *räl, n.* any of the family of birds—many of them water birds—to which the corncrake or landrail belongs. [O.Fr. *rasle* (Fr. *râle*).]

raiment, *rā'mént, n.* clothing. [Contr. of obs. *arrayment*—**array.**]

rain, *rān, n.* water from the clouds in drops: a shower: a fall of anything in the manner of rain: (in *pl.*) the rainy season.—*v.i.* and *v.t.* to fall, or send down, like rain.—*ns.* **rain'bow,** the brilliant-coloured bow or arch seen when rain is falling opposite the sun (see **primary colours**): a similar bow (called *lunar rainbow*) formed by the moon; **rain'-check** (*U.S.*), a ticket for future use given to spectators when a sports meeting, &c. is cancelled or stopped because of bad weather: a token for future use given by some supermarkets when they are temporarily out of a special offer: a request or promise to accept an invitation at a later date; **rain'-coat,** a light waterproof overcoat; **rain'fall,** a fall of rain: the amount of rain that falls in a given time; **rain'-gauge,** an instrument for measuring rainfall.—*adjs.* **rain'less,** without rain; **rain'-proof,** impervious to rain; **rain'y,** characterised by rain.—**rain cats and dogs,** to rain very heavily.—**a rainy day** (*fig.*), a future time of need. [O.E. *regn*; Du. and Ger. *regen,* O.N. *regn.*]

raise,*rāz, v.t.* to cause to rise: to lift up: to set up or upright: to make higher or greater: to rear, grow, or breed: to give rise to, to create: to bring to life: to cause to swell, as by fermentation: to put prominently forward (e.g. an objection, a question): to get, collect, or levy: to discontinue (e.g. *to raise the siege*): (*phonet.*) to pronounce (a vowel sound) with some part of the tongue closer to the palate (e.g. *to raise 'a' as in 'hat', to 'e', as in 'bell'*).—*n.* a rising road: (*coll.*) an increase in wages or salary.— **raised beach** (*geol.*), a terrace of gravel, &c., marking a former sea-level; **raise the wind,** to procure the necessary money. [M.E. *reisen*— O.N. *reisa,* causative of *rīsa,* to rise. Cf. **rise, rear.**]

raisin, *rā'z(i)n, n.* a dried grape. [Fr., grape—L. *racēmus,* a bunch of grapes.]

raison d'être, *rā-zɔ̃ detr',* justification for being, purpose of existence. [Fr.]

raj, *räj, n.* rule, sovereignty.—*n.* **ra'ja(h),** an Indian prince or king. [Hindustani *rāj, rājā.*]

rake, *rāk, n.* a toothed bar on a handle for scraping, gathering together, smoothing, &c.—*v.t.* to draw a rake over: to gather as with

Neutral vowels in unaccented syllables: *em'pér-ór*; for certain sounds in foreign words see p. ix.

600

a rake: (*naut.* and *mil.*) to sweep with gun-fire from stem to stern, or in the direction of the length: (*lit.* and *fig.*) to scrape, gather (together): (*lit.* and *fig.*) to search minutely.—*v.i.* to work with a rake: to make close search.—*n.* **rake-off,** pecuniary gain, esp. a commission illegally exacted.—**rake up,** to detect and bring to notice (usu. something scandalous). [O.E. *raca*; Ger. *rechen,* rake, O.N. *reka,* shove.]

rake, *rāk, n.* a dissolute person, esp. a man of fashion.—*adj.* **rak′ish.**—*adv.* **rak′ishly.** [**rakehell.**]

rake, *rāk, n.* (*naut.*) the projection of the stem and stern of a ship beyond the extremities of the keel: the slope or slant (of a mast): the slope of a stage, auditorium, &c.—*adj.* **rā′kish,** having a rake: dashing, jaunty.—*adv.* **rā′kishly.**

rakehell, *rāk′hel, n.* an utterly vicious character. [Prob. **rake** (1) and **hell**—i.e. one such as might be found by searching hell.]

rallentando, *ral-én-tan′do, adj.* and *adv.* (*mus.*) becoming slower. *n.* a passage or movement so played [It. pa.p. of *rallentare,* to slacken.]

rally, *ral′i, v.t.* to reassemble: to gather for renewed and united effort: to muster by an effort (as the faculties).—*v.i.* to come together: to renew concerted effort in a common cause: to recover some degree of health or vigour: to take part in a rally:—*pr.p.* **rall′ying;** *pa.t.* and *pa.p.* **rallied** (*ral′id*).—*n.* act of rallying: a gathering to promote a common purpose: a temporary or partial recovery: (*tennis,* &c.) a sustained exchange of strokes: a competition to test skill in driving and ability to follow an unknown route, or to test the quality of a motor vehicle. [O.Fr. *rallier*—pfx. *re-* and *allier.* See **ally.**]

rally, *ral′i, v.t.* to tease or banter:—*pr.p.* **rall′ying;** *pa.t.* and *pa.p.* **rall′ied.** [Fr. *railler;* cf. **rail** (2).]

ram, *ram, n.* a male sheep: (*cap.*) Aries: a battering-ram: a hydraulic (q.v.) ram or water-ram: (*hist.*) an iron beak on the stem of a warship for piercing the hull of a hostile vessel.—*v.t.* to push or press hard, to cram: to drive by hard blows: to strike, batter, pierce, with a ram: to strike (esp. a ship) head-on:—*pr.p.* **ramm′ing;** *pa.t.* and *pa.p.* **rammed.** [O.E. *ram, rom;* Ger. *ramm.*]

Ramadan, Ramadhan, *ram-a-dän, n.* the month throughout which Moslems are required to fast from dawn to sunset. [Ar. *Ramadān.*]

ramble, *ram′bl, v.i.* to wander at will for pleasure: to straggle: to wander in mind or discourse: to be incoherent.—*n.* a leisurely walk with no fixed goal.—*n.* **ram′bler,** one who rambles: a trailing climbing plant.—*adj.* **ram′bling,** desultory: incoherent. [M.E. *romblen;* app. conn. with **roam.**]

ramie, ramee, rami, *ram′ē, n.* a plant of the nettle family long cultivated in China: its fibre, used for cloth, banknote paper, gas mantles, &c. [Malay *rami.*]

ramify, *ram′i-fī, v.t.* and *v.i.* to divide into branches:—*pr.p.* **ram′ifying;** *pa.t., pa.p.* **ram′ified.**—*n.* **ramification** (*ram-i-fi-kā′sh(ò)n*), division into branches: (*lit.* and *fig.*) a branch, esp. a remote branch, offshoot, or link (*fig* of a division or part of a subject, a plot, a con-

sequence that must be taken into account, &c.). [Fr. *ramifier*—L. *rāmus,* a branch, *facĕre,* to make.]

ramjet. See **jet.**

ramose, *rā′mōs, adj.* branched. [L. *rāmōsus*—*rāmus,* a branch.]

ramp, *ramp, v.i.* to climb: to grow rankly: to rear on the hind-legs: to slope from one level to another: to rage.—*n.* an inclined plane: (*slang*) a swindle, a scheme by which public excitement (a craze or a panic) is worked up as a means of private gain.—*n.* **rampāge′,** aggressively agitated behaviour or rushing about.—*v.i.* to storm: to rush about wildly.—*adjs.* **rampā′geous,** unruly: boisterous; **ram′p′ant,** unrestrained: prevalent: (*her.*) standing on the left hind-leg.—*n.* **rampancy.**—*adv.* **ramp′antly.** [Fr. *ramper,* to creep, to clamber.]

rampart, *ram′pärt, n.* a flat-topped defensive mound: that which defends.—*v.t.* to fortify or surround with ramparts. [Fr. *rempart*—O.Fr. *rempar*—*remparer,* to defend—L. pfx, *re-,* again, *anto, before, parare,* to prepare.]

ramrod, *ram′rod, n.* a rod for ramming down the charge in a gun-barrel: (*fig.*) a stern, inflexible person: a strict disciplinarian.—*adj.* rigid: stern. [**ram, rod.**]

ramshackle, *ram′shak′l, adj.* tumble-down: rickety. [Ety. doubtful.]

ran, *pa.t.* of **run.**

ranch, *ränch or ränsh, n.* a stock farm, as in western N. America, with its buildings and persons employed.—*v.i.* to manage or work upon a ranch.—*ns.* **ranch′er, ranchero** (*rän chā′ro*), **ranch′man,** one employed in ranching; **ran′cho,** in S. America, a roughly built house or hut: a ranch. [Sp. *rancho,* mess, mess-room.]

rancid, *ran′sid, adj.* rank in smell and taste, as putrid butter or oil.—*ns.* **rancid′ity, ran′cidness.** [L. *rancidus.*]

rancour, *rang′kur, n.* deep-seated enmity, spite.—*adj.* **ran′corous.**—*adv.* **ran′corously.** [L. *rancor,* old grudge—*rancēre,* to be rancid.]

rand, *rand, n.* a border, margin: a strip, esp. of flesh or of leather: (*S. Africa*) a ridge overlooking a valley: (*S. Africa*) coin (= 100 cents) worth about 60p.—**the Rand,** Witwatersrand goldfield. [O.E., Du.]

random, *ran′dom, n.* and *adj.* haphazard, chance.—**random access,** in computers, direct access to any data required from a large store of information, bypassing other data.—**at random,** aimlessly: haphazardly. [O.Fr *randon*—*randir,* to gallop.]

ranee. See **rani.**

rang, *rang, pa.t.* of **ring.**

range, *rānj, v.t.* to set in a row: to place in proper order: to make level (with): to traverse in all directions: to sail along: to determine the range of.—*v.i.* to lie in a certain direction: to extend: to take or have position in line or alongside: to move freely: to vary (within limits).—*n.* a system of points in a straight line: anything extending in line, as a chain of mountains: variety: area within which movement takes place: position in relation to a person taking aim: distance to which a projectile can be thrown: ground on which shooting is practised: an enclosed kitchen fireplace.—

fāte, fär; mē, hûr (her); *mīne; mōte, för; mūte; mōōn, fŏŏt;* ᴛʜen (then)

ns. **range'-find'er,** an instrument for finding the range of a target: a camera attachment serving a similar purpose; **rang'er,** officer who superintends a forest or park: a member of a body of mounted troops policing an area: a soldier specially trained for raiding combat: a member of a senior branch of the Girl Guide organisation.—**to range oneself with,** to side, to take sides, with. [Fr. *ranger,* to range—*rang,* a rank.]

rani, ranee, *rän′ē, n. fem.* of **raja.** [Hindustani *rānī*—Sans. *rājñī,* queen, fem of *rājan.*]

rank, *rangk, n.* a row or line: a line of soldiers standing side by side: order, grade, or degree: high standing: (in *pl.*) persons of ordinary grade, esp. private soldiers.—*v.t.* to place in a line: to assign to a definite class or grade (*U.S.*) to take higher rank than.—*v.i.* to have a specified place in a scale, or a place in a specified class.—*n.* **rank'er,** one who serves or has served as a private soldier: an officer promoted from the ranks.—**rank and file,** common soldiers: ordinary people. [O.Fr. *renc* perh.—O.H.G. *hring, hrinc,* ring.]

rank, *rangk, adj.* growing high and luxuriantly: coarsely overgrown: excessive: strong-scented or strong-tasted: arrant, utter.—*adv.* **rank'ly.** —*n.* **rank'ness.** [O.E. *ranc,* proud, strong.]

rankle, *rangk′l, v.i.* to fester: to cause persistent pain, vexation, or bitterness. [O.Fr. *rancler, raoncler—draoncler,* app.—L.L. *dra(cu)nculus,* an ulcer, dim. of L. *dracō*—Gr. *drakōn,* dragon.]

ransack, *ran′sak,* or *-sak′, v.t.* to search thoroughly: to piunder, to pillage. [O.N. *rannsaka—rann,* house, *sœkja,* seek.]

ransom, *ran′sóm, n.* redemption from captivity: price of redemption: a huge sum.—*v.t.* to pay, demand, or accept ransom.—*n.* **ran'somer.**— *adj.* **ran'somless.** [Fr. *rançon*—L. *redemptiō, -ōnis,* redemption.]

rant, *rant, v.i.* to use vehement or extravagant language.—*n.* empty declamation, bombast.— *n.* **rant'er,** one who rants: a bombastic preacher: a member of a sect in which such preachers are admired. [Obs. Du. *ranten,* to rave; Low Ger. *randen,* Ger. *ranzen.*]

ranunculus, *rä-nung′kū-lus, n.* (*cap.*) the buttercup (q.v.) genus of plants: any plant of this genus:—*pl.* **ranun'culī, ranun'culuses.** [L., a dim. of *rāna,* a frog—name for a medicinal plant, perh. a buttercup.]

rap, *rap, n.* a sharp blow: a sound made by knocking.—*v.t.* to hit sharply: to utter hastily. —*v.i.* to knock or tap:—*pr.p.* rapp'ing;*pa.t.* and *pa.p.* rapped.—**take the rap** (*slang*), to take the blame or punishment, esp. in place of another. [Imit.]

rap, *rap, v.t.* to snatch away: to transport with rapture:—*pr.p.* rapp'ing; *pa.p.* rapped or rapt. [Partly akin to Middle Low Ger.*rappen,* Swed. *rappa,* to snatch; influenced by **rapt.**]

rap, *rap, n.* a counterfeit halfpenny current in Ireland in 18th century: any worthless coin: a whit. [Origin obscure.]

rapacious, *ra-pā′shús, adj.* given to plunder: ravenous: greedy of gain.—*adv.* **rapā'ciously.**— *ns.* **rapā'ciousness, rapac'ity.** [L. *rapāx, rapācis—rapēre,* to seize and carry otf.]

rape, *rāp, n.* the act of seizing by force: sexual

intercourse with a woman without her consent.—*v.t.* to commit rape upon. [Prob. L. *rapēre,* to snatch, confused with **rap** (2).]

rape, *rāp, n.* a plant akin to the turnip, cultivated for its leaves and oil-producing seeds.—*n.* **rape'-cake,** refuse of rape-seed after the oil has been expressed. [L. *rāpa, rāpum,* a turnip.]

rapid, *rap′id, adj.* swift: quickly accomplished: steeply sloping.—*n.* a swift-flowing, steeply-descending part of a river, often with broken water (usu. in *pl.*).—*ns.* **rapid'ity, rap'idness.**—*adv.* **rap'idly.** [L. *rapidus—rapēre,* to seize.]

rapier, *rā′pi-èr, n.* a long slender sword, suitable for thrusting. [Fr. *rapière.*]

rapine, *rap′in, n.* act of seizing forcibly: plunder, robbery. [L. *rapīna—rapēre,* to seize.]

rapparee, *rap-a-rē′, n.* a wild Irish plunderer.[Ir. *rapaire,* a robber.]

rapper, *rap′ér, n.* one who raps: a door-knocker. [**rap** (1).]

rapport, *rä-pōr′, n.* relation, connection, sympathy, accord.—**en rapport** (**with**), in sympathy (with). [Fr.]

rapprochement, *rä-prosh′mä, n.* a drawing together: establishment or renewal of cordial relations. [Fr.]

rapscallion, *rap-skal′yón, n.* a rascal, a ne'er-do-well. [From *rascallion*—**rascal.**]

rapt, *rapt, adj.* carried away: transported, enraptured: wholly engrossed. [L.*raptus,* pa.p. of *rapēre,* to seize and carry off; but partly also pa.p. of **rap** (2).]

raptorial, *rap-tō′ri-ál, adj.* predatory: adapted to predatory life. [L. *raptor, -ōris,* a plunderer— *rapēre,* to seize.]

rapture, *rap′tyúr, -chùr, n.* (orig.) a seizing and carrying away: extreme delight, transport, ecstasy.—*adj.* **rap'tūrous.**—*adv.* **rap'tūrously.** [L. *rapēre, raptum,* to seize.]

rare, *rār, adj.* thin, not dense: uncommon: excellent.—*adv.* **rāre'ly,** seldom: remarkably well.—*ns.* **rāre'ness; rarity** (*rār′-* or *rar′i-ti*), state of being rare: thinness: uncommonness: something valued for its scarcity.—*v.t.* and *v.i.* **rarefy** (*rār′-* or *rar′i-fī*), to make or become less dense: to refine:—*pa.t.* and *pa.p.* **rar'efied.**—*ns.* **rarefac'tion** (*rār-i-* or *rar-i-*), rarefying; **rāre'bit,** a would-be correction of (*Welsh*) *rabbit.*—**rare earth,** an oxide of a **rare-earth element,** a group of metallic elements closely similar in chemical properties and very difficult to separate: now more usu. a rare-earth element itself. [Fr.,—L. *rārus.*]

rare, *rār, adj.* of meat, lightly cooked. [O.E. *hrēr.*]

raree-show, *rār′ē-shō, n.* a show carried about in a box: a spectacle. [App. a Savoyard showman's pron. of **rare show.**]

raring, *rā′ring, adj.* eager (for), full of enthusiasm and sense of urgency (with *infin.*). [**rear** (2).]

rascal, *räs′kál, n.* a knave, rogue, scamp.—*ns.* **ras'caldom,** the world, or the conduct, of rascals; **rascality** (*-kal′-*), the rabble: the character or conduct of rascals.—*adj.* **ras'cally.** [O.Fr. *rascaille,* scum of the people.]

rase, *rāz.* Same as **raze.**

rash, *rash, adj.* over-hasty, wanting in caution.—*adv.* **rash'ly.**—*n.* **rash'ness.** [Cognate

Neutral vowels in unaccented syllables: *em′pér-ór*; for certain sounds in foreign words see p. ix.

602

with Dan. and Swed. *rask*; Du. and Ger. *rasch*, rapid.]

rash, *rash, n.* a slight eruption on the skin: a large number of instances at the same time or in the same place. [Perh. O.Fr. *rasche*.]

rasher, *rash'ėr, n.* a thin slice (of bacon). [Perh. from *rash,* to slash, a variant of *raze*.]

rasp, *räsp, n.* a coarse file: a grating sound or feeling.—*v.t.* to grate as with a rasp: to utter gratingly.—*v.i.* to have a grating effect.—*ns.* **rasp'atory,** a surgeon's rasp; **rasper.**—*adj.* **ras'py,** rough. [O.Fr. *raspe*; perh. Gmc.]

raspberry, *räz'bėr-i,* (*Scot.*) *rasp'bėr-i, n.* a fruit consisting of small drupes, of the same genus as the blackberry. (*slang*) a sign of disapproval, esp. a noise produced by blowing hard with the tongue between the lips.—Also (now *coll.* and *Scot.*) **rasp.**—**raspberry vinegar,** a drink of raspberry juice, vinegar, and sugar. [*rasp,* earlier *raspis* (origin unknown), and **berry.**]

raster, *ras'tėr, n.* a complete set of television scanning lines appearing at the receiver as a rectangular patch of light on which the image is produced [Perh. L. *rāstrum* rake.]

rasure, razure, *rä'zh(y)ūr, n.* the act of scraping or shaving: erasure: obliteration. [L. *rāsūra*.]

rat, *rat, n.* a genus of animals closely allied to mice (formerly included in the same genus), but larger: a renegade, turncoat (from the rat's alleged desertion of a doomed ship): a strike-breaker: a worker for less than recognised wages.—*v.i.* to hunt or catch rats: to desert one's associates for unworthy motives:—*pr.p.* **rat'ting;** *pa.t.* and *pa.p.* **rat'ted.**—*ns.* **rat'-race,** the scramble to get on in the world by fair means or foul; **rats'bane, rat's'-bane,** poison for rats, esp. white arsenic; **rat'ter,** a killer of rats, esp. a dog.—*adj.* **ratt'y,** of a rat, like a rat: full of rats' (*slang* of a person) mean, rather despicable: (see also separate article).—**rat on** (*coll.*), to inform against: **smell a rat,** have a suspicion of something afoot. [O.E. *ræt*; cf. Ger. *ratte*.]

rat(e)able, *rā'tá-bl, adj.* See **rate.**

ratafia, *rat-ä-fē'ä, n.* a flavouring essence made with the essential oil of almonds: a cordial or liqueur flavoured with fruit: an almond biscuit or cake. [Fr.; origin unknown.]

rataplan, *rat-a-plan', n.* the beat of a drum. [Fr.]

ratch, *rach, n.* a ratchet: a ratched wheel.—**ratch'er,** a click, a catch, a pawl; **ratch'et-wheel,** a wheel with inclined teeth with which a pawl engages. [History obscure; cf. Ger. *ratsche,* Fr. *rochet*.]

rate, *rāt, n.* price or cost: ratio, esp. time-ratio, speed: a standard: a class or rank, esp. of ships or of seamen: (often *pl.*) a tax levied by a local authority according to the annual value of property.—*v.t.* to estimate the value of: to settle the relative rank, scale, or position of: to value for purpose of rate-paying: to esteem, regard as: to deserve, to be worthy of.—*v.i.* to be classed (as).—*adj.* **rat(e)'able.**—*ns.* **rat(e)-abil'ity; rāte'-cutting,** a lowering of charges to obtain traffic; **rāte'payer,** one who pays a local rate; **rāt'ing,** a fixing of rates: classification according to grade: a sailor's grade in the ship's crew: a member of the British Navy below the rank of commissioned officer.—**at**

any rate, in any case, anyhow; **at that rate,** if that is so: under those conditions; **first (second,** &c.) **rate,** of the highest (or, less than the highest) quality. [O.Fr.—L.L. (*pro*) *ratā* (*parte*), according to a calculated part—*rērī, rătus,* to think, judge.]

rate, *rāt, v.t.* to scold, to chide, to reprove.—*n.* **rat'ing.** [M.E. *raten*; origin obscure.]

rath, räth, rathe, *rāᴛн, adj.* eager, early.—Also *adv.* [O.E. *hræd* (rarely *hræth*), quick; O.N. *hrathr*.]

rath, *rath, n.* an Irish hill fort. [Ir. *ráth*.]

rather, *rä'ᴛнėr, adv.* more willingly: in preference: somewhat, in some degree: more properly.—*interj.* **ra'ther** (sometimes affectedly *rä-*ᴛнėr'), I should think so, yes, indeed. [Comp. of **rath,** adv.; O.E. *hrathor*.]

ratify, *rat'i-fī, v.t.* to approve and sanction, esp. by signature: to give validity to:—*pr.p.* **rat'i-fying;** *pa.t.* and *pa.p.* **rat'ified.**—*n.* **ratifica'tion.** [Fr. *ratifier*—L. *rătus,* pa.p. of *rērī* (see **rate**), *facēre,* to make.]

ratio, *rā'shi-ō, n.* the measurable relation of one thing to another: the relation of quantities as shown by their quotient: proportion. [L. *rătiō, -ōnis,* reason—*rērī, rătus,* to think.]

ratiocination, *rat-* or *rash-i-os-i-nā'sh(ó)n, n.* the process of reasoning: deduction from premises.—*adj.* **ratioc'inative** (*-os'-*). [L. *ratiōcinārī, -ātus,* to reason.]

ration, *ra'sh(ó)n,* sometimes *rā'-, n.* a fixed allowance or portion: (in *pl., coll.*) food.—*v.t.* to put on an allowance: to restrict the supply of to so much for each.—*ns.* **ra'tion-book, -card,** a book, card, of coupons or vouchers for rationed commodities. [Fr.—L. *ratiō, ōnis,* reckoning, reason, &c.]

rational, *ra'shón-ál, adj.* of the reason: endowed with reason: agreeable to reason: sane. (*arith., alg.*) noting a quantity which can be exactly expressed by numbers without a root sign.—*n.* **rationale** (*ra-shi-ō-nä'li, -y-nā'li*), underlying principle, basis, reason (of): a theoretical explanation or solution.—*v.t.* **ra'tionalise,** to make rational, to conform to reason: to explain or justify by reason (thoughts or actions motivated by emotion): (*math.*) to clear from irrational quantities: to reorganise scientifically (e.g. an industry) so as to reduce cost or effort.—*v.i.* to think or argue rationally.—*ns.* **rationalisa'tion; ra'tionalism,** (*phil.*) a system which regards reasoning as the source of knowledge—opp. to *empiricism, sensationalism*: a disposition to apply to religious doctrines the same critical methods as to science and history, and to attribute all phenomena to natural rather than miraculous causes; **ra'tionalist.**—*adj.* **rationalist'ic.**—*adv.* **rationalist'ically.**—*n.* **rationality** (*ra-shón-al'i-ti*), quality of being rational: the possession, or due exercise, of reason: reasonableness.—*adv.* **ra'tionally.**—**rational number,** a number expressed as the ratio of two integers. [L. *ratiōnālis, -e*—*ratiō,* reason.]

ratlin, rattlin, -line, -ling, *rat'lin, n.* one of the small lines or ropes forming steps of the rigging of ships. [Origin obscure.]

rattan, ratan, *ra-tan', n.* any of a number of climbing palms with very long thin stem: a cane made from part of a stem. [Malay *rōtan*.]

---

fāte, fär; mē, hûr (her); *mīne; mōte, för; mūte, mōōn, fŏŏt;* ᴛнen (then)

rat-tat, *rat′tat′, n.* a knocking sound. [Imit.]

rattle, *rat′l, v.i.* to clatter: to move along rapidly with a clatter: to chatter briskly and emptily.—*v.t.* to cause to rattle: to utter glibly, as by rote: (*coll.*) to disturb the equanimity of.—*n.* the sound of rattling: a sound in the throat of a dying person: an instrument or toy for rattling: a vivacious prattler: two wild-flowers—*yellow-rattle* and *red-rattle*—whose seeds rattle in the capsule: the rings of a rattlesnake's tail.—*ns.* **ratt′le-brain, -head, -pate,** a shallow, voluble, volatile person; **ratt′ler** (*coll.*), a rattlesnake; **ratt′le-snake,** any of several venomous American snakes with rattling bony rings on the tail.—*p.adj.* **ratt′ling,** lively, vigorous: (*coll.*) excellent (or as *adv.,* e.g. *a rattling good story*). [M.E. *ratelen*; cf. Ger. *rasseln,* Du. *ratelen,* to rattle.]

ratty, *rat′i, adj.* (*slang*) angry, ill-tempered: (see also under **rat**). [Prob. from **rat.**]

raucous, *rö′kus, adj.* hoarse, harsh.—*adv.* **rauc′ously.** [L. *raucus,* hoarse.]

ravage, *rav′ij, v.t.* to lay waste, to pillage: to despoil (of).—*n.* devastation: ruin.—*n.* **rav′-ager.** [Fr. *ravager*—*ravir,* to carry off by force—L. *rapĕre.*]

rave, *rāv, v.i.* to rage: to talk as if mad, delirious, or enraptured.—*n.* (*slang*) infatuation: extravagant praise.—*adj.* (*coll.*) wildly enthusiastic (as *rave* notices of a book).—*n.* and *adj.* **rā′ving.** [Perh. O.Fr. *raver,* which may be—L. *rabĕre,* to rave.]

ravel, *rav′l, v.t.* to entangle: to disentangle, untwist, unweave, unravel (usually with *out*).—*v.i.* to become entangled: to be untwisted or unwoven:—*pr.p.* rav′elling; *pa.t.* and *pa.p.* rav′elled.—*n.* a tangle: confusion. [App. Du. *ravelen.*]

ravelin, *rav′lin, n.* a defensive fortification forming a salient angle built beyond the main ditch. [Fr.]

raven, *rā′vén, n.* a large glossy black species of crow.—*adj.* black as a raven. [O.E. *hræfn*; O.N. *hrafn,* Du. *raaf.*]

raven, *rav′én, v.t.* to devour hungrily or greedily.—*v.i.* to prey rapaciously: to be intensely hungry.—*adj.* **rav′enous,** rapacious: voracious: intensely hungry.—*adv.* **rav′enously.**—*n.* **rav′-enousness.** [O.Fr. *ravine,* plunder—L. *rapīna,* plunder.]

ravin, also **raven, ravine,** *rav′in, n.* rapine: preying.—*v.t.* and *v.i.* (see **raven,** *vb.*). [Same as foregoing.]

ravine, *ra-vēn′, n.* a deep, narrow gorge. [Fr.,—L. *rapīna,* rapine, violence.]

ravioli, *rav-i-ōl′ē, n.* small pieces of noodle paste with savoury filling. [It.]

ravish, *rav′ish, v.t.* to seize or carry away by violence: to snatch away from sight or from the world: to rape: to enrapture.—*n.* **rav′isher.**—*p.adj.* **rav′ishing,** charming, enrapturing.—*n.* **rav′ishment.** [Fr. *ravir*—L. *rapĕre,* to seize and carry off.]

raw, *rö, adj.* not altered from its natural state —not cooked or dressed, not prepared or manufactured: not mixed: having the skin abraded or removed: unrefined: untrained, immature, inexperienced: chilly and damp.—*adjs.* **raw′boned,** with little flesh on the bones,

gaunt; **raw′hide,** of untanned leather.—*n.* a rope or whip of untanned leather.—*adv.* **raw′ly.**—*n.* **raw′ness.**—**raw material** (see **material**).—**a raw deal,** harsh, inequitable treatment. [O.E. *hrēaw*; Du. *rauw,* O.N. *hrār,* Ger. *roh.*]

ray, *rā, n.* a line along which light or heat is propagated: a narrow beam: a gleam (of intellectual light): a radiating line or part: fringing outer part of a composite flower-cluster: (or **ray floret**) one of the small flowers forming this. [O.Fr. *rais* (acc. *rai*)—L. *radius.* See **radius.**]

ray, *rā, n.* a class or order of fishes including the skates and torpedoes. [Fr. *raie*—L. *raia.*]

rayah, *rī′ä, n.* a non-Mohammedan subject of Turkey. [Ar. *ra′īyah*—*ra′ā,* to pasture.]

rayon, *rā′on, n.* artificial silk. [From **ray** (1).]

raze, *rāz, v.t.* (*rare*) to graze, scrape: (usu. *fig.*) to erase: to lay level with the ground. [Fr. *raser*—L. *rādĕre, rāsum,* to scrape.]

razor, *rā′zór, n.* a keen-edged implement for shaving.—*ns.* **rā′zor-bill,** a species of auk, with compressed bill; **rā′zor-blade; rā′zor-strop** (see **strop**). [O.Fr. *rasour*—*raser.* See **raze.**]

re, *rē, prep.* (commercial jargon) in the matter of, concerning. [L. *in rē* (abl. of *rēs,* thing), in the matter.]

re-, *rē-,* again, or back: again and in a different way—used so freely, esp. with verbs, that it is impossible to give a full list; see also separate articles following. In words borrowed from French and Latin as compounds, **re-** is usu. pronounced *ri-,* and sometimes two forms, used differently, arise, e.g. **reform** (*ri-*), from L. *reformāre,* and **re-form** (*rē-*), from *pfx.* **re-** and **form** (see article on **reform**). In the latter class of words a hyphen is generally used. In some words a hyphen is necessary to avoid misunderstanding, e.g. in **re-sign,** to sign again, which could be confused with **resign,** to give up office or employment.

reach, *rēch, v.t.* to stretch forth: to hand, pass: to succeed in touching or getting: to arrive at: to extend to: to attain to.—*v.i.* to stretch out the hand: to extend: to amount to: to attain: to arrive at (usu. with *to*).—*n.* act or power of reaching: extent of stretch: range, scope: a stretch or portion between defined limits, as of a stream between bends.—*adj.* **reach-me-down,** ready-made.—*n.* a cheap, ready-made garment. [O.E. *rǣcan,* Ger. *reichen,* to reach.]

reach. Same as **retch.**

react, re-act, *rē-akt′, rē′akt′, v.t.* to act anew.—*v.i.* (**react,** *ri-akt′,* in this sense) to return an impulse: to respond to a stimulus: to have a reciprocatory effect: to undergo chemical change produced by a reagent: (*loosely*) to behave, or to feel, in specified circumstances.—*ns.* **reac′tance** (*elect.*), the component of impedance due to inductance or capacitance; **reac′tion,** action resisting other action: backward tendency from revolution, reform, or progress: response to stimulus: loosely, feeling or thought aroused by, in response to, a statement, situation, person, &c.: mutual effect: a chemical change: a transformation within the nucleus of an atom.—*adj.* **reac′tionary,** of, or favouring, reaction.—*n.* one who attempts to revert to past political condi-

Neutral vowels in unaccented syllables: *em′pêr-ór*; for certain sounds in foreign words see p. ix.

604

tions.—*adj.* **reac'tive,** of, pertaining to, reaction: responsive to stimulus: produced by emotional stress.—*n.* **reac'tor,** one who or that which undergoes a reaction: a container in which a chemical reaction takes place: a nuclear reactor (see **nucleus**). [L.L. *reagĕre, -actum—agĕre,* to do.]

read, *rēd, v.t.* to utter aloud, or go over with silent understanding (written or printed words): to observe and interpret (signs, or from signs, other than letters (*lit.* e.g. *to read the clock, the time*; *fig.* e.g. *to read one, one's face, one's thoughts, meaning*)): to study.—*v.i.* to perform the act of reading: to practise much reading: to study:—*pa.t.* and *pa.p.* read (*red*).—*adjs.* **read** (*red*), versed in books, learned; **read'able** (*rēd'-*), legible: interesting and attractively written (often implying lack of enduring literary quality).—*ns.* **readabil'ity, read'ableness.**—*adv.* **read'ably.**—*ns.* **read'er,** one who reads or reads much: one who reads prayers in church: a lecturer, esp. a higher grade of university lecturer: a proof-corrector: one who reads and reports on MSS for a publisher: a reading-book; **read'ership.**—*adj.* **read'ing,** addicted to reading.—*n.* the action of the verb *read:* perusal: study or knowledge of books: public or formal recital, esp. of a bill before Parliament: the actual words that may be read in a passage of a text: an interpretation: a performer's conception of the meaning, rendering: the figure indicated on the scale of a measuring instrument, as a thermometer.—*ns.* **read'ing-book,** a book of exercises in reading; **read'ing-desk,** a desk for holding a book or paper while it is read: a lectern; **read'ing-lamp,** a lamp for reading by; **read'ing-room,** a room for consultation, study, or investigation of books in a library: a room with papers, periodicals, &c., resorted to for reading; **read'-out,** output unit of a computer: data from it, printed, or registered on magnetic tape or punched paper tape: data from a radio transmitter.—**read between the lines,** to detect a meaning not expressed; **read up,** to amass knowledge of by reading. [O.E. *rǣdan,* to discern, read—*rǣd,* counsel; Ger. *raten,* to advise.]

readdress, *rē-a-dres', v.t.* to change the address on. [Pfx. **re-,** and **address.**]

readjust, *rē-a-just', v.t.* to adjust or put in order again, or in a new way.—*n.* **readjust'ment,** [Pfx. **re-,** and **adjust.**]

readmit, *rē-ad-mit', v.t.* to admit again.—*ns.* **readmiss'ion, readmitt'ance,** act of readmitting: state of being readmitted. [Pfx. **re-,** and **admit.**]

ready, *red'i, adj.* prepared: willing: inclined: liable: dexterous: prompt: quick, esp. in repartee: handy: immediately available.—*n.* (*mil.*) the position of a fire-arm ready to be fired.—*adv.* **read'ily.**—*n.* **read'iness.**—*adj.* **read'y-made,** made before sale, not made to order.—*n.* a ready-made article, esp. a garment.—*adjs.* **read'y-money,** paying, or for payment, in money on the spot; **read'y-witt'ed,** having ready wit, clever, sharp.—**make ready,** to prepare; **ready money,** money ready at hand: cash; **ready reckoner,** a book of tables giving the value of so many things at so much each,

and interest on any sum of money for periods from a day upwards. [O.E. *(ge)rǣde;* cf. Ger. *bereit.*]

reafforest, *rē-a-fŏr'est, v.t.* to convert anew into a forest.—*n.* **reafforesta'tion.** [Pfx. **re-,** and **forest.**]

reagent, *rē-ā'jent, n.* a substance with a characteristic reaction, used as a chemical test. [From same root as **react.**]

real, *rē'ál, adj.* actually existing: not counterfeit or assumed—true, genuine, sincere: (*law*) consisting of fixed property, as lands or houses (*real estate*).—*v.t.* **rē'alise,** to make real or as if real: to bring into being or fact, to accomplish, achieve: to convert into money: to obtain, bring (a specified price): to feel strongly, or to comprehend completely.—*adj.* **reāli'sable** (or *rē'-*).—*ns.* **realisā'tion** (or *-li-*); **rē'alism,** the mediaeval doctrine that general terms stand for real existences (opp. to *nominalism*): the tendency to look at, to accept, or to represent, things as they really are—now often taken to mean things in their most ignoble and uninspiring aspect: precision in representing the details of actual life, or the most sordid details of life, in art or literature: the tendency to take a practical view in human problems, planning chiefly to deal with immediate difficulties; **realist.**—*adj.* **rēalist'ic,** pertaining to the realists or to realism: lifelike.—*n.* **reality,** (*re-al'i-ti,* or *rē-*), the state or fact of being real: truth: (*law*) the fixed, permanent nature of real property.—*adv.* **rē'ally,** in reality: actually: in truth.—*n.* **rē'alty** (same as **reality**—*law*).—**real estate,** land, houses, trees, minerals, &c.; **real presence** (see **presence**). [Low L. *reālis*—L. *rēs,* a thing.]

real, *rā-al', rē'ál, n.* a former Spanish coin, one-eighth of a dollar. [Sp., L. *rēgālis,* royal.]

realign, *rē-a-līn', v.t.* to align afresh: to group or divide on a new basis.—*n.* **realign'ment.** [Pfx. **re-,** and **align.**]

realm, *relm, n.* a kingdom: a domain, province, region: (*fig.*) sphere (of action), or scope (of subject). [O.Fr. *realme*—hypothetical L.L. *rēgālimen*—L. *rēgālis,* royal.]

ream, *rēm, n.* 20 quires of paper—**printer's ream,** 516 sheets: (*coll.,* in *pl.*) large quantities (of written matter, e.g. of verse). [Ar. *rizmah,* a bundle.]

reanimate, *rē-an'i māt, v.t.* to restore to life: to infuse new life or spirit into.—*v.i.* to revive.—*n.* **reanimā'tion.** [Pfx. **re-,** and **animate.**]

reap, *rēp, v.t.* to cut down, as grain: to clear by cutting a crop: to derive (an advantage or reward).—*ns.* **reap'er,** one who reaps: a reaping machine; **reap'ing-hook,** a sickle; **reap'ing-machine',** a machine for cutting grain. [O.E. *rīpan,* or *ripan.*]

reappear, *rē-a-pēr', v.i.* to appear again or a second time.—*n.* **reappear'ance.** [Pfx. **re-,** and **appear.**]

rear, *rēr, n.* the back or hindmost part or position: a position behind.—*ns.* **rear-ad'miral,** an officer next below a vice-admiral—orig. one in command of the rear; **rear'-guard,** the rear of an army: troops protecting it; **rear'most,** last of all; **rear'ward, rere'ward,** the rear (with *to, in the*): (*arch.*) the part of an army or fleet in the rear.—*adv.* backward: at the back. [Contracted from **arrear;** also partly from O.Fr. *rere* (Fr. *arrière*).]

rear, *rēr, v.t.* to raise: to bring up, breed and foster: to set up.—*v.i.* to rise on the hind-legs. [O.E. *rǣran,* to raise, causative of *rīsan,* to rise.]

reason, *rē'zn, n.* ground, support, or justification (of an act or belief): a motive or inducement: the mind's power of drawing conclusions and determining truth: the exercise of this power: conformity to what is fairly to be expected or called for: moderation: sanity.—*v.i.* to exercise the faculty of reason: to deduce inferences from premises: to argue.—*v.t.* to examine or discuss: to think (out) logically.—*adj.* **rea'sonable,** endowed with reason, rational: acting according to reason: agreeable to reason: just, not excessive, moderate.—*n.* **rea'sonableness.**—*adv.* **rea'sonably.**—*p.adj.* **rea'soned,** argued out, logical.—*ns.* **rea'soner; rea'soning.**—**by reason of,** on account of, in consequence of; **in reason,** within limits; **listen to reason,** allow oneself to be convinced or talked round. [Fr. *raison*—L. *ratiō, -ōnis*—*rērī, rātus,* to think.]

reassemble, *rē-a-sem'bl, v.t.* and *v.i.* to assemble or collect again: to put the parts of together again. [Pfx. **re-,** and **assemble.**]

reassure, *rē-a-shōōr', v.t.* to assure anew: to reinsure: to give confidence to.—*n.* **reassur'ance.** [Pfx. **re-,** and **assure.**]

Réaumur, *rā-ō-mür, adj.* of a thermometer or thermometer scale, having the freezing point of water marked 0° and the boiling point 80°. [R. A. F. de *Réaumur* (1683-1757).]

reave, also (orig. *Scot.*) **reive,** *rēv, v.t.* and *v.i.* to plunder: to rob:—*pa.t.* and *pa.p.* reft.—*n.* **reav'er, reiv'er.** [O.E. *rēafian,* to rob; cf. Ger. *rauben,* to rob.]

rebate, *ri-bāt', v.t.* (*arch.*) to reduce, abate: to dull, to blunt.—*n.* discount, deduction: repayment.—*n.* **rēbāte'ment,** rebate: diminution in amount. [Fr. *rabattre,* to beat back—pfx. *re-,* and *abattre,* to abate.]

rebeck, rebec, *rē'bek, n.* a medieval instrument of the viol class. [O.Fr. *rebec*—Ar. *rabāb, rebāb.*]

rebel, *reb'(é)l, n.* one who rebels.—*adj.* rebellious.—*v.i.* (*ri-bel'*) to renounce the authority of the laws and government, or to take up arms and openly oppose them: to oppose any authority:—*pr.p.* rebell'ing; *pa.t.* and *pa.p.* rebelled'.—*n.* **rebell'ion** (*-yón*), act of rebelling: revolt.—*adj.* **rebell'ious** (*-yús*), engaged in rebellion: characteristic of a rebel or rebellion: inclined to rebel: refractory.—*adv.* **rebell'iously.**—*n.* **rebell'iousness.** [Fr. *rebelle*—L. *rebellis,* insurgent—pfx. *re-,* against, *bellum,* war.]

rebind, *rē-bind', v.t.* to bind again, put a new binding on:—*pa.t.* and *pa.p.* rebound'. [Pfx. **re-,** and **bind.**]

rebound, *ri-bownd', v.i.* to bound or start back from collision: (*lit.* and *fig.*) to spring back: to recover quickly after a setback.—*n.* act of rebounding: recoil.—**on the rebound,** after bouncing: while reacting against a setback, disappointment, &c. [Fr. *rebondir.*]

rebroadcast, *rē-bröd'kāst, v.t.* to broadcast a second or additional time.—Also *n.* [Pfx. **re-,** and **broadcast.**]

rebuff, *ri-buf', n.* a repulse, unexpected refusal, snub.—*v.t.* to repulse, to snub. [O.Fr. *rebuffe*—It. *ribuffo,* a reproof—It. *ri-* (= L. *re-*), back, *buffo,* puff.]

rebuke, *ri-būk', v.t.* (*rare*) to check, beat back: to put to shame: to reprove sternly.—*n.* a reproach: stern reproof, reprimand.—*n.* **rebūk'er.** [Anglo-Fr. *rebuker* (O.Fr. *rebucher*) —pfx. *re-, bucher,* to strike.]

rebus, *rē'bus, n.* an enigmatical representation of a name, &c., by pictures or signs punningly representing parts of a word or phrase, as in a puzzle, or a coat of arms:—*pl.* **re'buses.** [L. *rēbus,* by things, abl. pl. of *rēs,* thing.]

rebut, *ri-but', v.t.* to drive back: to repel: to refute.—*v.i.* (*law*) to return an answer:—*pr.p.* rebutt'ing; *pa.t.* and *pa.p.* rebutt'ed.—*ns.* **rebutt'al, rebutt'er.** [O.Fr. *reboter, rebouter, rebuter,* to repulse.]

recalcitrate, *ri-kal'si-trāt, v.i.* to show repugnance or opposition (with *against, at*): to be refractory.—*n.* **recal'citrance,** repugnance or opposition: refractoriness.—*adj.* **recal'citrant,** refractory, obstinate in opposition. [L. *recalcitrāre, -ātum,* to kick back—*calx, calcis,* the heel.]

recall, *ri-köl', v.t.* to call back: to command to return: to revoke: to call back to mind.—*n.* act, power, or possibility of recalling or revoking: remembrance of things learned or experienced. [Pfx. **re-,** and **call.**]

recant, *ri-kant', v.t.* to retract.—*v.i.* to revoke a former declaration: to declare one's renunciation of one's former religious or political belief or adherence.—*n.* **recanta'tion.** [L. *recantāre,* to revoke—*cantāre,* to sing, to charm.]

recap, *rē-kap'.* Abbrev. for **recapitulate** and **recapitulation.**

recapitulate, *rē-ka-pit'ū-lāt, v.t.* to go over again the chief points of: to repeat in one's own life-history (the process of development of the species).—*n.* **recapitūlā'tion.**—*adjs.* **recapi'tūlātive, recapit'ulatory.** [L. *recapitulāre, -ātum*—*re-,* again, *capitulum,* heading, chapter—*caput,* head.]

recapture, *rē-kap'tyúr, -chúr, v.t.* to capture back or retake, as a prize from a captor: (*fig.*) to regain, or to bring back to memory.—*n.* act of retaking: a thing recaptured. [Pfx. **re-,** and **capture.**]

recast, *rē-käst', v.t.* to cast or mould anew: to reconstruct: to compute anew:—*pa.t.* and *pa.p.* recast'. [Pfx. **re-,** and **cast.**]

recede, *ri-sēd', v.i.* to go, draw, or fall back, or to appear to do so: to bend or slope backward: (*fig.*) to withdraw (from): to grow less, decline.—*v.t.* recede (*rē'-sēd'*), to yield back.—*adj.* **reced'ing,** sloping backward. [L. *recēdere, recessum*—*re-,* back, *cēdere,* to go, yield.]

receipt, *ri-sēt', n.* receiving: place of receiving: a written acknowledgment of anything received: that which is received: a recipe esp. in cookery: (*pl.*) amount of money received from business transactions.—*v.t.* to mark as paid. [O.Fr. *receite, recete* (Fr. *recette*)—L. (*rē*) *recepta,* fem. pa.p. of *recipěre,* to receive.]

receive, *ri-sēv', v.t.* to take, get, or catch, usu. more or less passively: to have given or delivered to one: to admit, take in, or serve as receptacle of: to meet or welcome on entrance:

Neutral vowels in unaccented syllables: *em'pér-ór;* for certain sounds in foreign words see p. ix.

606

to give audience to, or acknowledge socially: to give a specified reception to: to accept as authority or as truth: to be acted upon by, and transform, electrical signals.—*v.i.* to be a recipient: to hold a reception of visitors.—*adj.* **receiv′able.**—*p.adj.* **received′,** generally accepted.—*ns.* **receiv′er,** one who receives: one who knowingly accepts stolen goods: (*chem.*) a vessel for receiving the products of distillation, or for containing gases: the glass vessel of an air-pump in which the vacuum is formed: an instrument which transforms electrical signals into audible or visual form, as a telephone receiver: a receiving-set. (also **offi- cial receiver**) a person to whom a debtor's estate or a disputed property, &c., is given in trust until a decision about its disposal is reached; **receiv′er-gen′eral,** an officer who receives revenues; **receiv′ing-office,** a branch post-office for receipt of letters, &c.; **receiv′ing-or′der,** an order putting a receiver in temporary possession of a debtor's estate; pending bankruptcy proceedings, **receiv′ing- set,** apparatus for receiving wireless communications, **receiv′ing-ship,** a stationary ship for naval recruits. [Anglo-Fr. *receivre*—L. *re- cipĕre, receptum*—re-, back, *capĕre,* to take.]

recension, *ri-sen′sh(ó)n, n.* a critical revision of a text: a text established by critical revision: a review. [L. *recēnsēre*—re-, *cēnsēre,* to value.]

recent, *rē′sént, adj.* of late origin or occurrence: relatively near in past time: modern: (*cap.*) of the present geological epoch—Post-Glacial. *adv.* **rē′cently.**—*ns.* **rē′centness, re′cency.** [L. *recēns, recentis.*]

receptacle, *ri-sep′tä-kl, n.* that in which anything is or may be received or stored: the enlarged end of an axis bearing the parts of a flower or the crowded flowers of an inflorescence. [L. *recipĕre, receptum,* to receive.]

reception, *ri-sep′sh(ó)n, n.* the act, fact, or manner of receiving or of being received: a formal receiving, as of guests: treatment on arrival: (*radio*) act or manner of receiving signals.—*n.* **recep′tionist,** a woman employed, e.g. in an office, to greet callers.—*adj.* **recept′ive,** quick to receive impression, able to take in and absorb.—*ns.* **recept′iveness, receptiv′ity;** **recep′tion-order,** an order for the reception and detention of a person in a mental hospital; **recep′tion-róom,** a room for formal receptions: any public room in a house. [L, *re- cipĕre, receptum,* to receive.]

recess, *ri-ses′, n.* a going back or withdrawing: a short remission of business: vacation (esp. of Parliament): an indentation: a niche or alcove.—*ns.* **recession** (*ri-sesh′ón*), act of receding: withdrawal: the state of being set back: in trade, a temporary decline: (*chem.*) a ceding back; **recessional** (*ri-sesh′ón-ál*), a hymn sung during recession or retirement of clergy and choir.—*adj.* **recess′ive,** tending to recede: of an ancestral character, apparently suppressed in cross-bred offspring in favour of the alternative contrasted character from the other parent, though it may be transmitted to later generations.—Also *n.* [See **recede.**]

Rechabite, *rek′a bīt, n.* one of the descendants of Jonadab, son of Rechab, who, following

Jonadab's injunction, did not drink wine or live in houses: a total abstainer: a tent-dweller.

réchauffé, *rā-shō′fā, n.* a warmed-up dish: a fresh concoction of old material. [Fr.]

recherché, *ré-sher′shā, adj.* carefully chosen: particularly choice, select, peculiar and refined, rare. [Fr.]

recidivism, *ri-sid′i-vizm, n.* the habit of relapsing into crime.—*n.* **recid′ivist.** [Fr. *récidi- visme*—L. *recidīvus,* falling back.]

recipe, *res′i-pi, n.* directions for making something, esp. a food or drink: a method laid down for achieving a desired end:—*pl.* **rec′ipes.** [L. *recipe,* take, imper, of *recipĕre.*]

recipient, *ri-sip′i-ént, adj.* receiving.—*n.* one who or that which receives. [L. *recipiēns, -entis,* pr.p. of *recipĕre,* to receive.]

reciprocal, *ri-sip′ro-k(á)l, adj.* acting in return: mutual: giving and receiving or given and received: related inversely, complementary: (*gram.*) expressing mutual action or relation (e.g. the pronouns *each other* and *one another*).—*n.* that which is reciprocal: (*math.*) the multiplier that gives unity (e.g. *b/a is the reciprocal of a/b*): unity divided by any quantity (e.g. *1/a*).—*adv.* **recip′rocally.**—*v.t.* **recip′rocate,** to give and receive mutually: to return, repay in kind.—*v.i.* to make a return: (*mech.*) to move alternately to and fro.—*ns.* **recip′rocating-en′gine,** an engine in which the piston moves to and fro in a straight line; **reciproca′tion.**—*adj.* **recip′rocative,** characterised by or inclined to reciprocation.—*ns.* **recip′- rocator,** one who or that which reciprocates: a double-acting steam-engine; **reciprocity** (*res-i-pros′it-i*), mutual relation: concession of mutual privileges or advantages, esp. mutual tariff concessions. [L. *reciprocus.*]

recision, *ri-sizh′(ó)n, n.* (*rare*) cutting back: rescinding or cancelling [L *recīsĭō, ōnis recīdĕre,* to cut off.]

recite, *ri-sīt′, v.t.* to repeat from memory: to declaim: (*rare*) to read aloud: to narrate, to give the particulars of.—*v.i.* to give a recitation.—*ns.* **reci′tal,** act of reciting, setting forth: enumeration, narration: a public performance of music, usu. by one performer, or one composer, or of one class of composition; **recita- tion** (*res-i-tā′sh(ó)n*), a poem or passage for repeating from memory before an audience: the act of repeating it; **recitative** (*-tä-tēv′*), a style of song resembling speech in its succession of tones and freedom from melodic form.—*adj.* in the style of recitative.—*n.* **recit′er.** [L. *recitāre*—*citāre, -ātum,* to call.]

reck, *rek, v.t.* (*arch.*) to care for, heed: (*impers.*) to matter.—*v.i.* (with *of*) to care for.—*adj.* **reck′less,** careless, rash: heedless (of consequences).—*adv.* **reck′lessly.**—*n.* **reck′less- ness.** [O.E. *reccan, rēcan;* cf O.H.G. *ruoh,* care, Ger. *ruchlos,* regardless.]

reckon, *rek′n, -ón, v.t.* to count, compute: to include (in an account): to place or class (with, among): to estimate, judge to be: to think, believe, suppose or expect.—*v.i.* to calculate: (*lit. and fig.*) to go over, or settle, accounts (with): to count or rely (on, upon).—*ns.* **reck′oner, reck′oning.—day of reckoning,** day of settling accounts (*lit. and fig.*): the

Judgment Day. [O.E. *gerecenian*, to explain; Ger. *rechnen*.]

reclaim, *ri-klām′, v.t.* orig. to call back (as a hawk): to win back: to win from evil, wildness: to make (waste land) fit for cultivation: to drain and use (land submerged by the sea, &c.): to obtain from waste material or from by-products: (*rē-klām′*) to claim back.—*v.i.* (*arch.*) to exclaim in protest.—*adj.* **reclaim′able.**—*adv.* **reclaim′ably.** [O.Fr. *reclamer*—L. *reclāmāre.*]

reclamation, *rek-lá-mā′sh(ó)n, n.* act of reclaiming: state of being reclaimed. [L. *reclāmātiō, -ōnis*—*reclāmāre*—*clāmāre*, to cry out.]

recline, *ri-klīn′, v.t.* to incline or bend (properly backwards).—*v.i.* to lean in a recumbent position, on back or side. [L. *reclīnāre, -ātum*—*clīnāre*, to bend.]

recluse, *ri-klōōs′, adj.* enclosed, as an anchorite: secluded, retired, solitary.—*n.* a religious devotee who lives shut up in a cell: one who lives retired from the world. [L. *reclūsus*, pa.p. of *reclūdĕre*, to open, in later Latin, shut away—*re-*, back, away, *claudĕre*, to shut.]

recognise, *rek′og-nīz, v.t.* to know again, to identify by means of characteristics, or as known or experienced before: to show signs of knowing (a person): to acknowledge, admit, realise (e.g. *to recognise one's obligations*; *recognised as the ablest surgeon*; *to recognise that it was necessary*): to acknowledge formally: to acknowledge the status or legality of (e.g. a government): to show appreciation of, reward.—*adj.* **recognīs′able** (or *rek′-*).—*n.* **recognisance, recognizance** (*ri-kog′ni-záns*), acknowledgment: (*ri-kon′i-záns*) a legal obligation entered into before a magistrate to do, or not do, some particular act. [O.Fr. *reconiss-*, stem of *reconoistre*—L. *recognoscĕre*, with *g* restored from L. and ending assimilated to the suffx. *-ise, -ize.*]

recognition, *rek-og-nish′(ó)n, n.* act of recognising: state of being recognised: acknowledgment: acknowledgment of status: sign of recognising: (*Scots law*) a return of the feu to the superior.—*adjs.* **recog′nitive, recog′nitory.** [L. *recognoscĕre*—*re-*, again, *cognoscĕre, -nitum*, to know.]

recoil, *ri-koil′, v.t.* (*obs.*) to beat back.—*v.i.* (*arch.*) to retreat: to rebound: to shrink (in horror, &c.): to kick, as a gun.—*n.* a starting or springing back, rebound: the kick of a gun: in nucleonics, the change in motion of a particle caused by ejection of another particle or sometimes by a collision. [Fr. *reculer*—*cul*—L. *cūlus*, the hinder parts.]

recollect, *rek-ól-ekt′, v.t.* to remember: to recover composure or resolution (with reflex. pron.).—*n.* **recollec′tion,** act or power of recollecting: a memory, reminiscence: a thing remembered. [L. *re-*, again, and **collect.**]

recommend, *rek-o-mend′, v.t.* to commend, commit (e.g. *to God's care*): to introduce as worthy of confidence or favour: to advise: to make acceptable.—*adj.* **recommend′able.**—*n.* **recommendā′tion.**—*adj.* **recommend′atory.** [L. *re-*, again, and **commend.**]

recommit, *rē-kom-it′, v.t.* to commit again: to send back (e.g. a bill) to a committee.—*n.* **recommit′ment, recommitt′al.** [L. *re-*, again,

and **commit.**]

recompense, *rek′om-pens, v.t.* to return an equivalent for—to repay or to reward (e.g. *to recompense one's losses, one's efforts*; also *a person*—often foll. by *for*).—*n.* that which is so returned—repayment, reward. [O.Fr. *récompenser*—L. *re-*, again, *compensāre*, to compensate.]

recompose, *rē-kom-pōz′, v.t.* to compose again or anew: to form anew: to soothe or quiet.—*n.* **recomposi′tion.** [L. *re-*, again, and **compose.**]

reconcile, *rek′on-sīl, v.t.* to restore to friendship or union (persons; also a person to, with, another): to bring to regard with resignation or submission (e.g. *to reconcile one to shorter holidays*): to make or prove consistent: to adjust, settle (e.g. *differences*).—*adj.* **reconcilable** (or *-sīl′-*).—*ns.* **rec′onciler; reconcilia′tion** (*-sil-*), **rec′oncilement** (or *-sīl′-*), act of reconciling: state of being reconciled: agreement after discord. [Fr. *réconcilier*—L. *re-*, again, *conciliāre, -ātum*, to call together.]

recondite, *rek′on-dīt, ri-kon′dīt, adj.* obscure, abstruse, profound (of subject, style, author). [L. *recondĕre, -itum*, to put away—*re-*, again, *condĕre*, to establish, store.]

recondition, *rē-con-dish′(ó)n, v.t.* to repair and refit: to restore to sound condition. [L. *re-*, again, and **condition.**]

reconnaissance, *ri-kon′i-sáns, n.* the act of reconnoitring: a preliminary survey.—**reconnaissance in force,** an attack by a large force to discover the position and strength of the enemy. [Fr.]

reconnoitre, *rek-ó-noi′tér, v.t.* to survey or examine with a view to military or other operations.—*v.i.* to make preliminary examination:—*pr.p.* reconnoi′tring (*-tér-*); *pa.t.* and *pa.p.* reconnoi′tred (*-térd*). [Fr. *reconnoître* (now *reconnaître*)—L. *recognoscĕre*, to recognise.]

reconsider, *rē-kon-sid′ér, v.t.* to consider again with a view to altering (e.g. a decision): hence, to alter.—*n.* **reconsiderā′tion.** [L. *re-*, again, and **consider.**]

reconstitute, *rē-kon′sti-tūt, v.t.* to constitute anew: to restore the constitution of (esp. of dried foods).—*adj.* **reconstit′uent.**—*n.* **reconstitu′tion.** [L. *re-*, again, and **constitute.**]

reconstruct, *rē-kon-strukt′, v.t.* to construct again, to rebuild: to restore in imagination or theory.—*n.* **reconstruc′tion.** [L. *re-*, again, and **construct.**]

record, *ri-körd′, v.t.* (*obs.*) to get by heart: to set down in writing for future reference: (of an instrument) to indicate, show as a reading: to register, as a vote or verdict: to put in permanent form on a sensitive disk or cylinder, as sounds for reproduction on a gramophone.—*n.* **record** (*rek′örd,* formerly *ri-körd′*), a register: a formal account in writing of any fact or proceedings: a memorial: a performance or event that surpasses all others previously noted: a disk or cylinder on which sounds are recorded for reproduction by an instrument such as a gramophone: the sounds so recorded.—*ns.* **record′er,** one who records or registers: a judge of a city or borough court of quarter-sessions: a flute of the earlier style blown through a mouthpiece at the upper end,

Neutral vowels in unaccented syllables: *em′pér-ór*; for certain sounds in foreign words see p. ix.

not through a hole on the side; **record′ership**; **record′ing**, a record of sound or images made for later reproduction, e.g. on magnetic tape, film, or gramophone disk.—**recording angel**, an angel supposed to keep a book in which every misdeed is recorded against the doer; **record office**, a place where public records are kept; **record player**, a small portable instrument for playing gramophone records, run on batteries or mains electricity, not spring-driven as the older-fashioned gramophone.—**beat**, or **break, the record**, to outdo the highest achievement yet recorded; **off the record**, not for publication in the press, &c.; **on record**, recorded in a document, &c.: publicly known. [O.Fr. *recorder*—L. *recordārī*, to call to mind, get by heart.]

recount, *ri-kownt′*, *v.t.* to narrate the particulars of: to detail: (**recount, re-count**—*rē-kownt′*), to count over again.—*n.* a second count. [O.Fr. *reconter*—*re-*, again, *conter*, to tell.]

recoup, *ri-kōōp′*, *v.t.* to make good (losses): (usu. *reflex.*) to recover expenses or losses: to compensate. [Fr. *recouper*, to cut again—*re-*, again, *couper*, to cut.]

recourse, *ri-kōrs′*, *-körs′*, *n.* resort for aid or protection. [Fr. *recours*—L. *recursus*—*re-*, back, *currĕre*, *cursum*, to run.]

recover, re-cover, *rē-kuv′ér*, *v.t.* to cover again. [Pfx. *re-*, and **cover**.]

recover, *ri-kuv′ér*, *v.t.* to get or find again: to retrieve: (*arch.*) to cure, to revive: (*reflex.*) to bring back to normal condition, as after stumbling, losing control of feelings, &c.: to obtain as compensation.—*v.i.* to regain health or any former state or position.—*adj.* **recov′erable.** *n.* **recov′ery,** the act, fact, process, possibility, or power of recovering, or state of having recovered, in any sense. [O.Fr. *recovrer*—L. *recuperāre.* See **recuperate**.]

recreant, *rek′ri-ánt*, *adj.* surrendering, craven: false, apostate.—*n.* a craven, a mean-spirited wretch: a renegade.—*n.* **rec′reancy** [O.Fr. pr.p. of *recroire*, to yield in combat—LL. *re credĕre*, to surrender—L. *crēdĕre*, to entrust.]

recreate, *rek′rē-āt*, *v.t.* to reinvigorate, to refresh, esp. to indulge, gratify, or amuse by sport or pastime.—*v.i.* to take recreation, amuse oneself.—*v.t.* (*rē-*) to create again, anew, esp. (*fig.*) in the mind. *n.* **recrea′tion**, refreshment after toil, sorrow, &c.: a daily interval for rest between lessons at school: pleasurable occupation of leisure time: an amusement or sport: (*rē-*) a new creation.—*adjs.* **recrea′tional** (*rek-*), **rec′reative** (and *rē-*) [L. *re-*, again, and **create**.]

recriminate, *ri-krim′in-āt*, *v.i.* to charge an accuser.—*n.* **recrimina′tion.**—*adjs.* **recrim′inative, recrim′inatory.** [Through Low L.—L. *re-*, again, *crīmināri*, to accuse.]

recrudesce, *rē-krōō-des′*, *v.i.* to break out afresh.—*n.* **recrudes′cence.**—*adj.* **recrudes′cent** [L. *recrūdēscens, -entis*, pr.p. of *recrūdēscĕre*—*crūdus*, raw.]

recruit, *ri-krōōt′*, *n.* a newly enlisted soldier or member.—*v.i.* to obtain fresh supplies: to enlist new soldiers: to recover in health, pocket, &c.—*v.t.* to reinforce: to restore, to reinvigorate: to enlist or raise.—*n.* **recruit′er.**—*adj.* **recruit′ing.**—*n.* **recruit′ment**, recruiting. [Obs.

Fr. *recrute*, reinforcement, dial. pa.p. fem. of *recroître*—L. *recrēscĕre*, to grow again.]

rectangle, *rek′tang-gl*, or *-tang′-*, *n.* a four-sided plane figure with all its angles right angles.—*adjs.* **rec′tangled**, having a right angle; **rec-tang′ular**, of the form of a rectangle: at right angles: right-angled. [L.L. *rēct(i)angulum*—L. *angulus*, an angle.]

rect(i)-, *rekt(i)-*, in composition, right: straight. [L. *rēctus*, straight, right.]

rectify, *rek′ti-fī*, *v.t.* to set right, to correct, to adjust: (*chem.*) to purify by distillation: to change (an electric current) from alternating to direct: to determine the length of (an arc):—*pr.p.* **rec′tifying**; *pa.t.* and *pa.p.* **rec′tified.**—*adj.* **rec′tifiable.**—*ns.* **rectifica′tion; rec′tifier**, one who rectifies (esp. alcohol): apparatus for rectifying (esp. spirit, or an alternating current). [Fr. *rectifier*—L.L. *rēctificāre*—L. *rēctus*, straight, *facĕre*, to make.]

rectilineal, *rek-ti-lin′ē-ál*, *adj.* rectilinear.—*adj.* **rectilin′ear** (*-ē-ár*), in a straight line or lines: straight: bounded by straight lines. [L. *rēctus*, straight, *līnĕa*, a line.]

rectitude, *rek′ti-tūd*, *n.* rightness: uprightness: integrity. [Fr.,—L.L. *rēctitūdō*—L. *rēctus*, straight.]

rector, *rek′tor*, *n.* in the Church of England, the parson of a parish where tithes are paid to the incumbent: in the United States, or (since 1890) in Scotland, an Episcopal clergyman with charge of a parish: the headmaster of certain secondary schools in Scotland: elective head of a University (in Scotland, honorary—Lord Rector; in France, executive): a college head (as at Lincoln and Exeter Colleges, Oxford, &c.): the head of a Jesuit seminary.—*adj.* **rec′toral**, of God as a ruler.—*n.* **rec′torate**, a rector's office or term of office.—*adj.* **rectorial** (*-tō′ri-al*), of a rector.—*n.* an election of a Lord Rector.—*ns.* **rec′torship; rec′tory**, the province or residence of a rector. [L. *rēctor, -ōris*—*regĕre, rēctum*, to rule.]

rectum, *rek′tum*, *n.* the terminal part of the large intestine:—*pl.* **rec′ta.** [L. neut. of *rēctus*, straight.]

recumbent, *ri-kum′bent*, *adj.* reclining.—*ns.* **recum′bence, recum′bency.**—*adv.* **recum′bently.** [L. *recumbĕre*—*re-*, back, *cubāre*, to lie down.]

recuperate, *ri-kū′pér-āt*, *v.t.* and *v.i.* to recover.—*n.* **recupera′tion.**—*adjs.* **recu′perative, recu′peratory.** [L. *recuperāre*, to recover.]

recur, *ri-kûr′*, *v.i.* to revert (to): to come back (to the mind): to occur again: to come up or come round again, or at intervals:—*pr.p.* **recurr′ing**; *pa.t.* and *pa.p.* **recurred′.**—*ns.* **recurr′ence, recurr′ency.**—*adjs.* **recurr′ent**, returning at intervals; **recur′sion**, of a mathematical formula, enabling a term in a sequence to be computed from one or more of the preceding terms; **recur′sive**, of a mathematical definition, consisting of rules which allow values or meaning to be determined with certainty.—**recurring decimal**, a decimal fraction in which after a certain place one figure (*repeating decimal*), or a group of figures (*circulating*), is repeated to infinity. [L. *recurrĕre*—*re-*, back, *currĕre*, to run.]

recusant, *rek′ū-zánt*, or *ri-kū′zánt*, *n.* one (esp. a Roman Catholic) who refused to attend the

Church of England when it was legally compulsory: a dissenter: one who refuses, esp. to submit to authority.—*adj.* refusing or neglecting to attend the Church of England: refusing generally. [L. *recūsāre*—*re-*, against, *causa*, a cause.]

recycle, *rē-sī′kl, v.t.* to pass again through a series of changes or treatment: to cause (material) to be broken down by bacteria and then reconstitute it: to turn scrap, &c. into raw material for re-use. [L. *re-*, **cycle**.]

red, *red, adj.* (*comp.* **redd′er;** *superl.* **redd′est**) of a colour like blood: revolutionary: (*cap.*) pertaining to the U.S.S.R. (e.g. *Red Army*).—*n.* one of the primary colours, of several shades, as scarlet, pink, &c.—*v.t.* **redd′en,** to make red.—*v.i.* to grow red: to blush.—*adj.* **red′-d′ish.**—*n.* **red′ness.**—*ns.* **red′-ad′miral,** a common butterfly with reddish-banded wings; **red′-bidd′y,** a drink made of red wine and methylated spirit; **red′breast,** the robin; **red brick,** brick made from clay containing iron compounds which are converted into ferric oxide (**redbrick university,** a general name for the later type of English university, as opposed to Oxford or Cambridge); **red′-cabb′age,** a purplish cabbage, often used for pickling; **red′cap,** a gold-finch: a goblin said to haunt Scottish castles: (*slang*) a military policeman; **red carpet,** a strip of red carpet put out for the highly favoured to walk on (*adj.* **red-carpet,** as in **red-carpet treatment,** with special honour or ceremony); **Red Cross,** a red cross on a white ground, the old national flag of England (as in Spenser's **Redcross Knight,** representing holiness and the Church of England), or the Swiss flag with the colours reversed (also **Geneva Cross**), hence an organisation for tending sick and wounded in war and large-scale disaster, &c., enjoying privileges under Convention of Geneva (1864); **red deer,** the common stag or hind, reddish-brown in summer; **Red Devils,** the Parachute Regiment; **red flag,** a flag used as a danger-signal: the banner of socialism, or of revolution: (*caps.*) a socialist song, sung to an old tune.—*adj.* **red′-hand′ed,** in the very act, or immediately after, as if with bloody hands.—*ns.* **red′-hat,** a cardinal: (*army slang*) a staff officer; **red heat,** the temperature at which a thing is red-hot.—*adj.* **red′hot,** heated to redness: (*fig.*) extreme.—*ns.* **red herring,** a cured herring: a subject introduced to divert discussion, as a herring drawn across a track would throw hounds off the scent; **Red Indian,** an American Indian—called 'Indian' because America was at first thought to be eastern Asia, and 'Red' because some tribes have coppery-brown skins: often restricted to a North American Indian; **red′-lead,** an oxide of lead of a fine red colour, used in paint-making.—*adj.* **red′-letter,** marked with red letters, as holidays or saints' days in the old calendars: joyful and deserving to be so marked.—*ns.* **red light,** a traffic signal meaning 'stop': a warning or danger signal: (*coll.*) a brothel (*adj.* **red′-light,** disreputable); **red man,** an American Indian; **red rag,** a cause of infuriation (as red is said to be to a bull); **red′-shank,** a wading bird with red legs, of the

same family as the sandpipers; **red′skin,** a Red Indian; **red′start,** bird with a conspicuous chestnut-coloured tail; **red tape,** the tape used in government offices: rigid formality of intricate official routine.—*adj.* **red′-tape′.**—*ns.* **red-tāp′ism, red-tāp′ist; red wine,** wine coloured by (red) grape skins during fermentation; **red′wood,** Californian timber-tree of great height.—**red out,** to experience a red hazy field of vision, &c., as a result of aerobatics; **see red,** to grow furiously angry: to thirst for blood. [O.E. *rēad*; cf. Ger. *rot,* L. *ruber, rūfus,* Gr. *erythros,* Gael. *ruadh.*]

redact, *ri-dakt′, v.t.* to edit, work into shape, to frame.—*ns.* **redac′tion, redac′tor.** [L. *redigĕre, redactum,* to bring back—pfx. *red-, re-,* back, *agĕre,* to drive.]

redan, *ri-dan′, n.* (*fort.*) a fieldwork of two faces forming a salient. [O.Fr. *redan*—L. *re-, dēns, dentis,* a tooth.]

reddle, redd′leman. See **ruddle.**

redeem, *ri-dēm′, v.t.* to buy back, recover by payment, &c.: to ransom: to rescue: to pay the penalty of: to atone for: to compensate for: to fulfil (a promise).—*adj.* **redeem′able.**—*ns.* **redeem′ableness, redeem′er.** [L. *redimĕre—red-, re-,* back, *emĕre,* to buy.]

redemption, *ri-dem(p)′sh(ŏ)n, n.* act of redeeming: atonement.—*adjs.* **redemp′tive, redemp′tory.** [L. *redimĕre, redemptum*; cf. **redeem.**]

redeploy, *rē-di-ploi′, v.t.* to transfer (e.g. military forces, supplies, industrial workers) from one area to another.—Also *v.i.*—*n.* **redeployment.** [L. *re-,* again, and **deploy.**]

redingote, *red′ing-gōt, n.* a long double-breasted overcoat. [Fr.,—Eng. *riding-coat.*]

redintegrate, *red-in′tē-grāt, v.t.* to restore to wholeness: to renew.—*n.* **redintegrā′tion.** [L. *redintegrāre, -ātum—red-, re-,* again, *integrāre,* to make whole—*integer.*]

redirect, *rē-di-rekt′, v.t.* to direct again or anew, esp. to put a new address on (a letter, &c.). [L. *re-,* again, and **direct.**]

redolent, *red′ō-lĕnt, adj.* fragrant: smelling of: suggestive (of).—*ns.* **red′olence, red′olency.** [L. *redolēns, -entis—red-, re-,* again, *olēre,* to emit smell.]

redouble, *ri-dub′l, v.t.* and *v.i.* to double: to intensify (e.g. efforts): to increase: (*rē-dub′l*) to double after previous doubling, esp. in playing bridge. [Fr. *redoubler.* See **double.**]

redoubt, *ri-dowt′, n.* a fieldwork enclosed on all sides, its ditch not flanked from the parapet: an inner last retreat. [Fr. *redoute*—It. *ridotto*—L. *reductus,* retired—*redūcĕre*; the *b* from confusion with **redoubt** (2).]

redoubt, *ri-dowt′, v.t.* (*arch.*) to fear.—*adj.* **redoubt′able,** formidable: valiant. [O.Fr. *redouter,* to fear greatly—L. *re-,* back, *dubitāre,* to doubt.]

redound, *ri-downd′, v.i.* (*obs.*) to flow back, or to rebound: to contribute as a consequence (to one's credit, discredit, advantage, &c.). [O.Fr. *redonder*—L. *redundāre—red-, re-,* back, *undāre,* to surge—*unda,* a wave.]

redraft, *rē-drāft′, n.* a new draft or copy: a new bill of exchange which the holder of a protested bill draws on the drawer or endorsers, for the amount of the bill, with costs and charges.—Also *v.t.* [L. *re-,* again, and **draft.**]

Neutral vowels in unaccented syllables: *em′pėr-ŏr*; for certain sounds in foreign words see p. ix.

redress, ri-dres', v.t. to set right (a wrong, a grievance): to reform (an abuse, a fault): to readjust (the balance—fig.): to remedy.—n. relief: reparation.—v.t. and v.i. **re-dress** (rē'dres'), to dress anew. [Fr. redresser. See **dress**.]

reduce, ri-dūs', v.t. to change (to another form): to express in other terms (with to): to range in order or classification: to put into (e.g. to reduce to writing, practice): to degrade: to impoverish: to subdue: to lessen: to diminish in weight or girth: to weaken: to drive to (e.g. reduce to tears): to extract (a metal from ore): to change (a substance) by removing oxygen from the molecule, &c.: to add an electro-negative atom or group to, or remove an electro-positive atom or group from, a molecule.—v.i. to resolve itself: to slim.—p.adj. **reduced'**, in a state of reduction: weakened: impoverished: diminished: simplified.—adj. **reduc'ible**.—n. **reduction** (-duk'sh(ò)n), act of reducing or state of being reduced: diminution: subjugation: (arith.) changing of numbers or quantities from one denomination to another.—**reduce to the ranks**, to degrade to the condition of a private soldier; **reducing agent**, a substance capable of bringing about chemical reduction, esp. of removing oxygen; **reductio ad absurdum**, proof of the falsity of an assumption by pointing out its logical, but obviously false, inferences: carrying the application of a principle to absurd lengths. [L. redūcĕre, reductum—re-, back, dūcĕre, to lead.]

redundant, ri-dun'dánt, adj. copious: overcopious: superfluous: of workers, no longer needed and therefore dismissed.—ns. **redun'dance, redun'dancy,—adv. redun'dantly**. [L. redundans, -antis, pr.p. of redundāre, to overflow.]

reduplicate, ri-dū'pli-kāt, v.t. to double: to repeat: (gram.) to show, have, reduplication—adj. **doubled**.—n. **reduplicā'tion**, a folding or doubling: the repetition of the initial part in grammatical inflection and word-formation (as in L. fefellī, perf. of fallō, I deceive).—adj. **redu'plicātive**. [L. reduplicāre, -ātum—dupli-cāre, to double.]

re-echo, rē-ek'ō, v.t. to echo back: to repeat as or like an echo.—v.i. to give back echoes: to resound.—n. a re-echoing. [L. re-, back, and **echo**.]

reed, rēd, n. a tall stiff hard-culmed marsh or water grass of various kinds: a thing made, or formerly made, of a reed or reeds—a pen, an arrow, a music pipe, the vibrating tongue of an organ pipe or wood-wind instrument, the part of a loom by which the threads are separated: a reed instrument: a narrow moulding.—adjs. **reed'ed; reed'en**, of reed.—ns. **reed'(-)instrument**, a wood-wind with reed—as clarinet, oboe, bassoon; **reed'(-)or'gan**, a keyboard instrument with free reeds, as the harmonium; **reed'(-)pipe**, a pipe, esp. of an organ, whose tone is produced by the vibration of a reed (cf. **flue pipe**); **reed'(-)stop**, in an organ, a set of reed-pipes controlled by a single stop-knob; **reed'(-)war'bler**, a warbler that frequents marshy places, and builds its nest on reeds—also called **reed'(-)wren**, the

reed'(-)thrush being a larger species (great reed-warbler).—adj. **reed'y**, abounding with reeds: resembling a reed. having the tone quality of a reed instrument. [O.E. hrēod; cf. Du. and Ger. riet.]

reef, rēf, n. a chain of rocks at or near the surface of water. [Du. rif—O.N. rif.]

reef, rēf, n. a portion of a sail that may be rolled or folded up.—v.t. to reduce the exposed surface of, as a sail: to gather up in a similar way.—ns. **reef'er**, one who reefs: a short jacket worn by sailors: any similar close-fitting, double-breasted coat: an oyster found on reefs: (coll.) a cigarette containing marijuana; **reef-knot**, a square knot. [O.N. rif.]

reek, rēk, n. smoke: vapour: fume.—v.i. emit smoke, fumes, or (esp. evil) smell (lit. and fig.).—adj. **reek'y** (Scot. **reek'ie**), smoky.— **Auld Reekie**, Edinburgh. [O.E. rēc; O.N. reykr, Ger. rauch, Du. rook, smoke.]

reel, rēl, n. a cylinder, drum, spool, bobbin, or frame on which yarn, wire, cables, films, &c., may be wound: a lively dance, esp. Highland or Irish: a tune for it: a length of material wound on a reel—of cinematograph film, 1000 feet.—v.t. to wind on a reel: to take off by or from a reel.—v.i. to dance the reel: to stagger: to waver.—(**right**) **off the reel**, without stop or hesitation; **reel off**, to repeat with rapidity or fluency. [O.E. hrēol, but possibly partly of other origin; Gael. righil (the dance) may be from English.]

re-elect, rē-ē-lekt', v.t. to elect again.—n. **re-elec'tion**. [L. re-, again, and **elect**.]

re-eligible, rē-el'i-ji-bl, adj. capable of re-election.—n. **re-eligibil'ity**. [L. re-, again, and **eligible**.]

re-embark, rē-im-bärk', v.t. and v.i. to go or put on board again.—n. **re-embarka'tion**. [L. re-, again, and **embark**.]

re-enact, rē-en-akt', v.t. to enact again.—n. **re-enact'ment**. [L. re-, again, and **enact**.]

re-enter, re-en'tér, v.t. and v.i. to enter again or anew: in engraving, to cut deeper.—adj. **re-en'trant**, pointing inwards (opp. to salient).—n. a re-entering angle.—n. **re-en'try**, an entering again: resumption of possession.—**re-entering angle**, (geom.) an angle cutting into a plane figure: also a reflex angle: (mil.) an angle, e.g. in a fortification, with its apex away from the enemy. [L. re-, again, and **enter**.]

re-establish, rē-es-tab'lish, v.t. to establish again, to restore.—n. **re-estab'lishment**. [L. re-, again, and **establish**.]

reeve, rēv, n. (hist.) a high official, chief magistrate of a district: a bailiff or steward. [O.E. gerēfa.]

reeve, rēv, v.t. to pass the end of a rope through any hole, as the channel of a block:—pa.t. and pa.p. reeved, rove. [Origin obscure.]

re-examine, rē-eg-zam'in, v.t. to examine again or anew.—n. **re-examina'tion**. [L. re-, again, and **examine**.]

refection, ri-fek'sh(ò)n, n. refreshment: a meal or repast.—n. **refectory** (ri-fek'tór-i), a dining-hall, esp. monastic.—**refectory table**, a long narrow dining-table supported on two shaped pillars each set in a base. [L. reficĕre, refectum—re-, again, facĕre, to make.]

refer, ri-fúr, v.t. to assign (to a class, a cause or

source, &c.): to hand over for consideration: to direct for information (to a person or place). —*v.i.* to have recourse (to, e.g., a dictionary) for information: to make mention or allusion (with *to*):—*pr.p.* referr'ing; *pa.t.* and *pa.p.* referred'.—*adj.* **referable** (*ref'ér-ä-bl*; sometimes **referrible**, *ri-ferʹi-bl*), to be referred or assigned.—*ns.* **referee** (*ref-é-rēʹ*), one to whom anything is referred: an arbitrator, umpire, or judge; **ref'erence**, the act of referring: a submitting for information or decision: (*law*) the act of submitting a dispute for investigation or decision: relation: allusion: (*loosely*) one who is referred to: a testimonial: a book or passage referred to; **ref'erence Bi'ble**, a Bible having references to parallel passages; **ref'erence book**, a book to be consulted on occasion, not for consecutive reading; **ref'erence li'brary**, a library containing books to be consulted only in the building; **referen'dum**, the principle or practice of submitting a question directly to the vote of the entire electorate; **ref'erent**, the object of reference or discussion: the first term in a proposition; **referr'al**, act or instance of referring or being referred, esp. to another person, &c. for e.g. consideration, treatment.—**terms of reference**, the scope of an investigation or similar piece of work: (more accurately) a guiding statement defining this. [L. *referre*, to carry back—*re-*, back, *ferre*, to carry.]

refill, *rē-filʹ*, *v.t.* to fill again.—*n.* (*rēʹ-* or *-filʹ*) a fresh fill: a duplicate for refilling purposes. [L. *re-*, again, and **fill**.]

refine, *ri-fīnʹ*, *v.t.* to purify: to clarify: to free from coarseness, vulgarity, crudity: to make more cultured.—*v.i.* to become more fine, pure, subtle, or cultured: to affect nicety: to improve by adding refinement or subtlety (with *on* or *upon*).—*p.adj.* **refined'**, polished, well-mannered: cultured: affectedly well-bred.—*ns.* **refine'ment**, act or practice of refining: state of being refined: culture in feelings, taste, and manners: an improvement: a subtlety; **refin'er**; **refin'ery**, a place for refining e.g. sugar, oil; **refin'ing**. [L. *re-*, denoting change of state, and **fine** (1).]

refit, *rē-fitʹ*, *v.t.* to fit out afresh and repair.—*v.i.* to undergo refitting.—*ns.* **refit'**, **refit'ment**, **refitt'ing**. [L. *re-*, again, and **fit** (1).]

reflation, *rē-flāʹshŏn*, *n.* inflation, increase in the amount of currency, after deflation.—*v.t.* (back-formation from *n.*) **rēflate'**.—*adj.* **reflā'tionary**. [L. *re-*, again, and **inflation**.]

reflect, *ri-flektʹ*, *v.t.* to bend back or aside: to throw back after striking: to give an image of in the manner of a mirror: (*fig.*) to cast, shed (as credit, discredit): to express, exemplify.—*v.i.* to bend or turn back or aside: to mirror: to meditate: to consider meditatively (with *upon*): to cast reproach (with *on*, *upon*).—*p.adj.* **reflect'ed**, cast or thrown back: turned or folded back: mirrored.—*adj.* **reflect'ing**.—*n.* **reflection**, also (now chiefly in scientific use) **reflexion** (*ri-flekʹsh(ŏ)n*), a turning, bending, or folding aside, back or downwards: change of direction when a ray strikes upon a surface and is thrown back: reflected light, colour, heat, &c.: an image in a mirror: the action of the mind by which it is conscious of

its own operations: attentive consideration: contemplation: a thought or utterance resulting from contemplation: censure or reproach.—*adj.* **reflect'ive**, reflecting: reflected: meditative.—*adv.* **reflect'ively.**—*ns.* **reflect'iveness**; **reflect'or**, a reflecting surface, instrument, or body.—*adj.* **reflex** (*rēʹfleks*, formerly *ri-fleksʹ*), bent or turned back: reflected: reactive: of an angle, more than 180°: involuntary—produced by, or concerned with, the response from a nerve-centre to a stimulus from without.—*n.* a reflection, reflected image: reflected light: a reflex action.—*adj.* **reflex'ible.**—*n.* **reflexibil'ity.**—*adj.* **reflex'ive** (*gram.*), referring back to the subject.—*adv.* **reflex'ively.**—**reflecting telescope**, one in which the principal means of focusing the light is a mirror. [L. *reflectĕre, reflexum*—*flectĕre*, to bend.]

refluent, *refʹlŏŏ-ént*, *adj.* flowing back, ebbing.—*ns.* **ref'luence**, **reflux** (*rēʹfluks*), flowing back, ebb. [L. *refluens, -entis*, pr.p. of *refluĕre*—*re-*, back, *fluĕre, fluxum*, to flow.]

reform, **re-form**, *rē'fōrmʹ*, *v.t.* and *v.i.* to form again or anew.—*v.t.* **reform'** (*ri-*), to remove defects from (e.g. a political institution, a practice): to put an end to (e.g. an abuse): to bring (a person) to a better way of life.—*v.i.* to abandon evil ways.—*n.* amendment or transformation, esp. of a system or institution: removal of political or social abuses.—*ns.* **reformation** (*rēʹfŏr-māʹsh(ŏ)n*), the act of forming again; **reformation** (*ref-ŏr-māʹsh(ŏ)n*), the act of reforming: amendment, improvement; **Reformation**, the great religious revolution of the 16th century, which gave rise to the various evangelical or Protestant organisations of Christendom.—*adjs.* **reformative** (*ri-fōrmʹa-tiv*), tending to produce reform; **refor'matory**, reforming: tending to produce reform.—*n.* (in U.K., formerly) an institution for reclaiming young delinquents or women.—*adjs.* **rē'formed'**, **rē'-formed'**, formed again, anew; **reformed** (*ri-formdʹ*), amended, improved; **Reformed'**, Protestant, esp. Calvinistic in doctrine or polity.—*ns.* **reform'er**, one who reforms: one who advocates political reform; **Reform'er**, one of those who took part in the Reformation of the 16th century; **Reform Bill**, an act (esp. that of 1832) to reform the distribution of Parliamentary seats and to extend the franchise. [L. *refōrmāre, -ātum*—*fōrmāre*, to shape—*fōrma*, form; partly from *re-*, and **form**.]

refract, *ri-fraktʹ*, *v.t.* (of a medium—as glass, water, a layer of air of different density) to deflect (rays of light, sound, &c. passing into it from another medium).—*n.* **refrac'tion.**—*adj.* **refrac'tive.**—**refracting telescope**, one in which the principal means of focusing the light is a lens. [L. *refringĕre, refractum*—*re-*, back, *frangĕre*, to break.]

refractory, *ri-frakʹtŏr-i*, *adj.* unruly, unmanageable, obstinate, perverse: not yielding to treatment: difficult of fusion.—*n.* a material suitable for lining furnaces.—*n.* **refrac'toriness**. [L. *refractārius*, stubborn.]

refrain, *ri-frānʹ*, *n.* a burden, a line or phrase recurring, esp. at the end of a stanza: the music of such a burden. [O.Fr. *refrain*—*re-*

Neutral vowels in unaccented syllables: *em'pér-ŏr*; for certain sounds in foreign words see p. ix.

612

fraindre—L. *refringĕre*—*frangĕre*, to break.]

refrain, ri-frān′, *v.t.* (*arch.*) to curb, restrain.—*v.i.* to keep from action: to abstain (from). [O.Fr. *refrener*—Low L. *refrēnāre*—*re-*, back, *frēnum*, a bridle.]

refrangible, ri-fran′ji-bl, *adj.* that may be refracted.—*n.* **refrangibil′ity**. [For *refringible*—root of **refract.**]

refresh, ri-fresh′, *v.t.* to make fresh again: to give new vigour, spirit, brightness, &c., to.—*v.i.* to become fresh again: (*coll.*) to take refreshment, esp. drink.—*p.adj.* **refresh′ing**, reviving, invigorating: pleasing or stimulating by a lack of sophistication.—*n.* and *adj.* **refresh′er**, a course of study or training to maintain the standard of one's knowledge or skill.—*n.* **refresh′ment**, the act of refreshing: state of being refreshed: renewed strength or spirit: that which refreshes, as food or rest. [L. *re-*, again, and **fresh.**]

refrigerate, ri-frij′er-āt, *v.t.* to make cold: to expose to great cold, as (food) for preservation.—*n.* **refrigera′tion.**—*adj.* **refrig′erative** (*-ėr-ā-tiv*), cooling.—*n.* **refrig′erator** (*-ėr-ā-tör*), an apparatus for producing and maintaining a low temperature.—*adj.* **refrig′eratory** (*-ėr-ā-tór-i*), cooling.—*n.* a refrigerator, [L. *refrigerāre*, *-ātum*—*re-*, denoting change of state, *frīgerāre*—*frīgus*, cold.]

reft, reft, *pa.t.* and *pa.p.* of **reave.**

refuge, ref′ūj, *n.* a shelter or protection from danger or trouble: an asylum or retreat: a street island for foot-passengers.—*n.* **refugee′**, one who flees for refuge to another country, esp. from religious or political persecution: a fugitive. [Fr.,—L. *refugium*—*re-*, back, *fugĕre*, to flee.]

refulgent, ri-ful′jent, *adj.* casting a flood of light, radiant, beaming.—*ns.* **reful′gence**, **reful′gency**. [L. *refulgens*, *-entis*, pr.p. of *refulgēre*—*re-*, inten., *fulgēre*, to shine.]

refund, ri- or rē-fund′, *v.t.* to repay.—*v.i.* to restore what was taken. [L. *refundĕre*—*re-*, back, *fundĕre*, to pour.]

refuse, ri-fūz′, *v.t.* to decline to take or accept: to renounce: to decline to give.—*v.i.* to make refusal.—*v.t.* **re-fuse** (rē-fūz′), to fuse again.—*n.* **refu′sal**, the act of refusing: the option of taking or refusing. [Fr. *refuser*—L. *refundĕre*—*refūsum*—*fundĕre*, to pour.]

refuse, ref′ūs, *adj.* rejected as worthless.—*n.* that which is rejected or left as worthless. [Prob. O.Fr. *refus*, refusal—*refuser*; see foregoing.]

refute, ri-fūt′, *v.t.* to disprove.—*adj.* **refutable** (ref′ūt-á-bl, or ri-fūt′-).—*adv.* **ref′utably** (or ri-fūt′-).—*n.* **refuta′tion** (ref′-). [L. *refutāre*.]

regain, rē-gān′, *v.t.* to gain back: to get back to (e.g. *to regain the shore*). [Fr. *regaigner* (now *regagner*).]

regal, rē′gál, *adj.* royal: kingly.—*n.* **regality** (rē-gal′i-ti), state of being regal: royalty: sovereignty: (*Scot.*) a territorial jurisdiction formerly conferred by the king.—*adv.* **re′gally.** [L. *rēgālis*—*rex*, a king—*regĕre*, to rule.]

regal, rē′gál, *n.* a small portable organ. [Fr. *régale.*]

regale, ri-gāl′, *v.t.* to feast, to entertain (*lit.* and *fig.*)—*v.i.* to feast.—*n.* (*arch.*) a feast, or a choice dish.—*n.* **regale′ment.** [Fr. *régaler*—It. *regalare*, perh.—*gala*, a piece of finery.]

regalia, ri-gā′li-a, *n.pl.* royal privileges or powers: the insignia of royalty—crown, sceptre, &c., esp. those used at a coronation: (*loosely*) insignia or special garb generally, as of the Freemasons. [Neut. pl. of L. *rēgālis*, royal.]

regard, ri-gärd′, *v.t.* to look at, to observe: (*fig.*) to look on (with e.g. affection): to esteem highly, to respect: to consider (as): (with *neg.*) not to heed: to take into account.—*n.* (*orig.*) look: attention with interest: concern (for): esteem, respect: relation: reference: (*pl.*) in messages of greeting, respectful good will.—*n.* **regar′der.**—*adj.* **regard′ful**, heedful: respectful.—*prep.* **regar′ding**, concerning.—*adj.* **regard′less**, heedless: inconsiderate.—*adv.* (*slang*) despite expense: without regard to consequences.—**as regards, with regard to**, with respect to, as far as (the thing specified) is concerned; **in this regard**, in this respect. [Fr. *regarder*—*re-*, *garder*, to keep watch.]

regatta, ri-gat′a, *n.* a yacht or boat race-meeting. [It. (Venetian) *regata*.]

regelation, rē-jē-lā′sh(ò)n, *n.* (of ice melted under pressure) the act of freezing anew when pressure is removed. [L. *re-*, again, *gelāre*, to freeze.]

regency, rē′jėn-si, *n.* the office, term of office, jurisdiction, or dominion of a regent.—**the Regency**, in Eng. hist., 1810-1820, when the Prince of Wales (later George IV) was Prince Regent. [Formed from **regent.**]

regenerate, ri-jen′er-āt, *v.t.* to produce anew: to renew spiritually: to reform completely: to reproduce (a part anew: the body): to produce again in the original form (*chem.*, *nucleonics*, &c.).—*v.i.* to be regenerated.—*adj.* (*-āt*) regenerated, renewed: changed from a natural to a spiritual state.—*ns.* **regen′eracy** (*-á-si*); **regenera′tion**, renewal of lost parts: spiritual rebirth: reformation.—*adj.* **regen′erative.**—*adv.* **regen′eratively.** [L. *regenerāre*, *-ātum*, to bring forth again *re-*, again, *generāre*, to generate.]

regent, rē′jėnt, *adj.* ruling: invested with interim or vicarious sovereign authority.—*n.* a ruler: one invested with interim authority on behalf of another. [L. *regens*, *-entis*, pr.p. of *regĕre*, to rule.]

regicide, rej′i-sīd, *n.* the killing or killer of a king.—*adj.* **regici′dal.** [L. *rēx*, *rēgis*, a king. *caedĕre*, to kill.]

régime, regime, rā-zhēm′, *n.* regimen: administration. [Fr.,—L. *regimen.*]

regimen, rej′i-men, *n.* government: system of government: (*med.*) course of treatment, as diet: grammatical government. [L. *regimen*, *-inis*—*regĕre*, to rule.]

regiment, rej′mėnt, *n.* government, rule, regimen: (usu. *rej′mént*) a body of soldiers constituting the largest permanent unit, commanded by a colonel.—*v.t.* (rej′i-mėnt, or *-mėnt′*) to form into a regiment or regiments: to systematise, organise: to subject to excessive control.—*n.* **regimentation** (*-i-mėn-tā′sh(ò)n*).—*adj.* **regimental** (*-i-ment′(á)l*), of a regiment.—*n.* (in *pl.*) the uniform of a regiment. [L.L. *regimentum*—L. *regĕre*, to rule.]

region, rē′jon, *n.* a tract of country: any area of earth, air, or sea (also *fig.*): in Scotland, the largest local govt. unit: a part of the body.—

adj. **rē′gional.—in the region of,** near: about, approximately. [Anglo-Fr. *regiun*—L. *rēgiō, -ōnis*—*regĕre*, to rule.]

register, *rej′is-tér, n.* a written record, regularly kept: the book containing such a record: an entry in it: a recording apparatus: apparatus for regulating a draught: an organ stop or stop-knob: the set of pipes controlled by an organ stop: the compass of a voice or instrument: the range of tones produced by a particular adjustment of the vocal cords, namely, the lower or *chest register,* and the upper or *head register*: exact correspondence in position.—*v.t.* to enter in a register: (of an instrument) to record: (*coll.*) to indicate by bodily expression (e.g. *to register astonishment*): to pay a special fee for (a letter, &c.) in order that it may have special care in transit.—*v.i.* to enter one's name (esp. as a hotel guest): to correspond: (*slang*) to make an impression.—*p.adj.* **reg′istered,** recorded, entered, or enrolled, e.g. as a voter: recorded as to ownership or designation, as of luggage or a letter requiring special precautions for security, &c.—*ns.* **Register House,** the building in Edinburgh where Scottish records are kept; **reg′istrar** (*-trär,* or *-trär′*), one who keeps a register or official record: one who makes an official record of births, deaths, and marriages locally; **Reg′istrar-Gen′eral,** an officer having the superintendence of the registration of all births, deaths, and marriages; **registrā′tion,** act of registering: record of having registered: the act or art of combining stops in organ-playing; **reg′istry,** registration: an office or place where a register is kept; **reg′istry-office,** an office for putting domestic servants in touch with employers: a registrar's office where births, &c., are recorded and civil marriages are celebrated.—**parish register,** the parish record of births, deaths, and marriages; **ship's register,** a document showing the ownership of a vessel. [O.Fr. *registre,* or Low L. *registrum,* for L. pl. *regesta,* things recorded—*re-,* back, *gerĕre,* to carry.]

Regius, *rē′ji-ŭs* (L. *rā′gi-ŏŏs*), *adj.* royal, as **Rē′gius professor,** one whose chair was founded by Henry VIII or, in Scotland, by the Crown. [L. *rēgius*—*rex,* king.]

regnant, *reg′nánt, adj.* reigning (often after the noun, as **queen regnant,** a reigning queen, not a *queen consort*): prevalent. [L. *rēgnāns, -antis,* pr.p. of *rēgnāre,* to reign.]

regress, *rē′gres, n.* passage back: return: right or power of returning.—*v.i.* (*ri-gres′*) to go back: to return to a former place or state.—*n.* **regression** (*ri-gresh(ó)n*), act of regressing: reversion: return towards the mean: return to an earlier stage of development.—*adj.* **regressive** (*ri-gres′iv*). [L. *regressus, -ūs*—*regredī, regressus*—*re-,* back, *gradī, grĕssus,* to go.]

regret, *ri-gret′, v.t.* to remember with sense of loss or of having done amiss: to feel sorrow or dissatisfaction because (with *that*), or because of:—*pr.p.* regrett′ing; *pa.t.* and *pa.p.* regrett′ed.—*n.* sorrowful wish that something had been otherwise: compunction: an intimation of regret or refusal.—*adjs.* **regret′ful,** feeling regret; **regret′able,** to be regretted.—*advs.* **regret′fully, regrett′ably.** [O.Fr. *regreter, re-*

grater; perh. conn. with **greet** (2).]

regular, *reg′ū-lár, adj.* subject to a monastic rule (opp. to *secular*): governed by or according to rule, law, order, habit, custom, established practice, mode prescribed, or the ordinary course of things: uniform: periodical: (*gram.*) inflected in the usual way (esp. of weak verbs): (*geom.*) having all the sides and angles equal: (of soldier, army) permanent, professional, or standing (opp. to belonging to, forming, a volunteer, or temporary force).—*n.* a soldier of the regular army.—*v.t.* **reg′ularise,** to make regular.—*n.* **regularity** (*-ar′i-ti*), state, character, or fact of being regular.—*adv.* **reg′ularly.—*v.t.* **reg′ulāte,** to control: to adapt or adjust continuously: to adjust by rule.—*n.* **regulā′tion,** act of regulating: state of being regulated: a rule prescribed, esp. in the interests of order or discipline.—*adj.* prescribed by regulation (e.g. *regulation dress*).—*adj.* **reg′ulātive,** tending to regulate.—*n.* **reg′ulātor,** one who, or that which, regulates: a controlling device, esp. for the speed of a clock or watch. [L. *rēgula,* a rule—*regĕre,* to rule.]

regulus, *reg′ū-lus, n.* an impure metal, an intermediate product in smelting of ores: antimony in this intermediate form. [L. *rēgulus,* dim. of *rex,* king.]

regurgitate, *rē-gûr′ji-tāt, v.t.* to cast out again, to pour back: to bring back into the mouth after swallowing.—*v.i.* to gush back.—*n.* **regurgitā′tion.** [Low L. *regurgitāre, -ātum*—*re-,* back, *gurges, gurgitis,* a whirlpool, gulf.]

rehabilitate, *rē-(h)a-bil′i-tāt, v.t.* to reinstate, restore to former privileges, rights, &c.: to clear the character of: to restore, by opportunity for gradual adjustment or specialised training (after illness or absence), fitness for living or making a living in normal or contemporary conditions.—*n.* **rehabilitā′tion.** [L.L. *rehabilitāre, -ātum*—*habilitāre,* to enable—L. *habilis,* able.]

rehash, *rē-hash′, n.* something (esp. a book or an article) made up of materials formerly used.—Also *v.t.* [L. *re-,* again, and **hash.**]

rehearse, *ri-hûrs′, v.t.* to repeat, to recount, narrate in order: to practice beforehand.—*v.i.* to take part in rehearsal.—*ns.* **rehears′al,** the act of rehearsing: repetition: narration: enumeration: a performance for trial or practice; **rehear′ser.—dress rehearsal,** a formal, usu. final, rehearsal with all costumes and properties. [O.Fr. *rehercer, reherser*—*re-,* again, *hercer,* to harrow—*herce* (Fr. *herse*)—L. *hirpex, -icis,* a rake, a harrow.]

reheat, *rē-hēt′, v.t.* to heat again.—*n.* (the use of) a device to inject fuel into the hot exhaust gases of a turbojet in order to obtain increased thrust. [L. *re-,* again, and **heat.**]

rehouse, *rē-howz′, v.t.* to provide with a new or substitute house or houses.—*n.* **rehous′ing.** [L. *re-,* and **house.**]

Reich, *rīн, n.* Germany as an empire, federal republic, or unitary republic.—*n.* **Reichstag** (*-täн*), parliament of the German Reich. [Ger.; O.E. *rīce,* kingdom, as in 'bishopric'.]

reign, *rān, n.* (*arch.*) realm: rule of a monarch: predominating influence: time of reigning.—*v.i.* to be a monarch: to be predominant. [O.Fr. *regne*—L.*rēgnum*—*regĕre,* to rule.]

Neutral vowels in unaccented syllables: *em′pér-ór*; for certain sounds in foreign words see p. ix.

reimburse, rē-im-bûrs′, v.t. to repay: to pay an equivalent to (for loss or expense).—n. **reimburse′ment**. [L.L. imbursāre—in, in, bursa, purse.]

rein, rān, n. the strap of a bridle: (fig.) any means of curbing or governing.—v.t. to govern with the rein: to restrain or control.—adj. **rein′less**, without rein or restraint.—**draw rein**, to pull up, stop riding; **give rein** (or **the reins**) **to**, to leave unchecked; **take the reins**, to take control. [O.Fr. reine, resne, rene, perh. from L. retinēre, to hold back.]

reindeer, rān′dēr, n. any of several large deer, wild and domesticated, of northern regions, antlered in both sexes.—n. **rein′deer-moss**, a lichen, the winter food of the reindeer. [O.N. hreinndȳri, or O.N. hreinn (O.E. hrān), and **deer**.]

reinforce, rē-in-fōrs′, -fōrs′, v.t. to enforce again: to strengthen with new force or support.—n. **reinforce′ment**, the act of reinforcing: additional force or assistance, esp. (pl.) of troops.—**reinforced concrete**, concrete strengthened by embedded steel bars [L. re-, again, and **enforce**.]

reins, rānz, n.pl. the kidneys, now esp. as the formerly supposed seat of emotion: the loins. [O.Fr. reins—L. rēnēs.]

reinstate, rē-in-stāt′, v.t. to restore or re-establish in a former station, condition, or employment.—n. **reinstate′ment**. [L. re-, again, and obs. instate, to install.]

reinvest, rē-in-vest′, v.t. to clothe again: to endow again: to invest again.—n. **reinvest′ment**. [L. re-, again, and **invest**.]

reinvigorate, rē-in-vig′ór-āt, v.t. to put new vigour into. [L. re-, again, and **invigorate**.]

reissue, rē-ish′(y)ōō, is′ū, v.t. to issue again.—n. a second or subsequent issue. [L. re-, again, and **issue**.]

reiterate, rē-it′é-rāt, v.t. to repeat: to repeat again and again.—n. **reitera′tion**.—adj. **reit′erative**. [L. re-, again, and **iterate**.]

reject, ri-jekt′, v.t. to throw out: to refuse to adopt, to have, to believe, to grant (e.g. a request), &c.—n. (rē′jekt), a person or thing put aside as unsatisfactory.—n. **rejec′tion**. [L. rejicĕre, rejectum—re-, back, jacĕre, to throw.]

rejoice, ri-jois′, v.t. to make joyful, to gladden.—v.i. to feel joy, to exult: to make merry.—n. **rejoic′ing**, act of being joyful: expression, subject, or experience of joy: (in pl.) festivities, celebrations, merrymaking.—**rejoice in**, to feel joy in the possession of: (facetiously) to have. [O.Fr. resjoir, resjoiss- (Fr. réjouir)—L. re-, ex, gaudēre, to rejoice.]

rejoin, ri-join′, v.i. (law) to reply to a charge or pleading.—v.t. to say in answer: (rē-) to join again.—n. **rejoin′der** (ri-), (law) the defendant′s answer to a plaintiff′s replication: an answer to a reply, an answer [L. re-, again, and **join**.]

rejuvenate, ri-jōō′vé-nāt, v.t. to make young again.—n. **rejuvena′tion**.—v.i. **rejuvenesce** (-es′), to grow young again.—n. **rejuvenes′cence**.—adj. **rejuvenes′cent**. [L. re-, again, juvenis, young, juvenēscĕre, to become young.]

rekindle, rē-kin′dl, v.t. to kindle again: to set on fire, or arouse, anew. [L. re-, again, **kindle**.]

relapse, ri-laps′, v.i. to slide, sink or fall back: to return to a former state or practice, to backslide.—n. a falling back into a former bad state: return of an illness after partial recovery. [L. relābī, relapsus—re-, back, lābī, to slide.]

relate, ri-lāt′, v.t. to recount, narrate, tell: to ally by connection or kindred.—v.i. to have reference or relation.—adj. **rela′ted**, recounted: referred: connected: allied by kindred or marriage.—n. **rela′tion**, act of relating: recital: a narrative: state or mode of being related: way in which one thing is connected with another: (pl.) mutual behaviour or attitude: a relative by birth or marriage.—adj. **rela′tional**, expressing relation: of the nature of relation.—n. **rela′tionship**, state or mode of being related: relations.—adj. **relative** (rel′a-tiv), in or having relation: corresponding: relevant: comparative, not absolute or independent: having reference: (gram.) referring to an antecedent.—n. that which is relative: a relative word, esp. a relative pronoun: one who is related by blood or marriage.—adv. **rel′atively**.—n. **relativ′ity**, state or fact of being relative: a principle which asserts that only relative, not absolute, motion can be detected in the universe.—**relative density**, the ratio of the mass of a given volume of a substance to the mass of an equal volume of water at a temperature of 4°C.—**relative atomic mass**, the ratio between the average mass of an atom of an element and 1/12 the mass of a Carbon-12 atom; **relative molecular mass**, molecular weight (q.v.). [L. relātus, -a, -um, used as a p.p. of referre, to bring back—re-, ferre.]

relax, ri-laks′, v.t. and v.i. to loosen (e.g. one′s hold): to make or become less close, tense, rigid, strict or severe.—n. **relaxa′tion**, act of relaxing: state of being relaxed: recreation: remission.—adj. **relax′ing**, (of weather, climate) tending to deprive people of energy, enervating. [L. rolaxāre, ātum—laxus, loose.]

relay, ri-lā′, also rē′lā, rē′lā′, n. a fresh set of dogs, horses, &c., to relieve others: a relieving shift of men: a device whereby a weak electric current can control or operate one or more currents: simultaneous reception and transmission of a broadcast message or programme.—v.t. to operate a relay of, esp. to broadcast anew.—v.i. to get a fresh relay.—pa.t. and pa.p. relayed. [O.Fr. relais, relay of dogs or horses.]

release, ri-lēs′, v.t. to let loose: to set free: to relieve (from): to give up to another (e.g. a legal right): to make available, permit the publication of (e.g. news) or public exhibition of (e.g. a film).—n. a setting free: discharge or acquittance: the giving up of a claim: authorisation to make available. [O.Fr. relaissier—L. relaxāre. See **relax**.]

re-lease, **release**, rē′-lēs′, v.t. to lease again.—Also n. Cf. previous article. [Pfx. **re-**, and **lease**.]

relegate, rel′é-gāt, v.t. to banish: to consign (usu. to an inferior position): to assign (e.g. to a class): to refer (to an authority for decision): to delegate (e.g. a duty).—n. **relega′tion**. [L.

relēgāre, -ātum—*re-*, away, *lēgāre*, to send.]

relent, *ri-lent´, v.i.* to soften or grow less severe.—*adj.* **relent´less,** without relenting: without tenderness or compassion, merciless.—*adv.* **relent´lessly.**—*n.* **relent´lessness.** [L. *re-*, back, *lentus*, sticky, sluggish, pliant.]

relevant, *rel´é-vánt, adj.* bearing upon, or applying to, the matter in question, pertinent: (*Scots law*) sufficient legally.—*ns.* **rel´evance, rel´evancy.** [L. *relevāns, -antis*, pr.p. of *relevāre*, to raise up, relieve; from the notion of helping.]

reliable, &c. See **rely.**

relic, *rel´ik, n.* that which is left after loss or decay of the rest: a corpse (usu. in *pl.*): (*R.C.*) any personal memorial of a saint: a memorial of antiquity: a souvenir: a survival (e.g. of a custom) from the past. [Fr. *relique*—L. *reliquiae*—*relinquĕre, relictum*, to leave behind.]

relict, *rel´ikt, n.* a survivor or surviving trace: (*arch.*) widow. [L. *relictus, -a, -um*, left, pa.p. of *relinquĕre*, to leave.]

relief, *ri-lēf´, n.* the lightening or removal of any discomfort, stress, or evil: release from a post or duty: one who releases another by taking his place: that which relieves or mitigates: aid: assistance to the poor: projection or standing out from the general surface: a sculpture, carving, or impression so made: appearance of standing out solidly: distinctness by contrast.—*adj.* providing relief in cases of distress, danger, or difficulty.—*ns.* **relief´map,** a map in which the form of the country is shown by elevations and depressions of the material used, or by the illusion of such elevations and depressions, or (*loosely*) by other means.—**comic relief** (see **comic**). [O.Fr. *relef*—*relever*. See **relieve**; cf. **relievo.**]

relieve, *ri-lēv´, v.t.* to bring, give, or afford relief to: to release: to ease, to mitigate: to raise the siege of: to set off by contrast.—*adj.* **reliev´ing.**—**relieving officer,** an official formerly in charge of relief of the poor.—**relieve one of,** to take from one's possession, with or without one's approval: to steal from one: to free one from (a necessity, restriction, &c.). [O.Fr. *relever*—L. *relevāre*, to lift, relieve—*re-*, again, *levāre*, to raise—*levis*, light.]

relievo, *ri-lē´vō*, also (*It.*) **rilievo,** *rē-lyā´vō, n.* (in art) relief: a work in relief. [It. *rilievo.*]

religion, *ri-lij´ón, n.* belief in, acceptance of, or non-rational sense of, a superhuman unseen controlling power or powers, with the emotion and morality connected therewith: rites or worship: any system of such belief or worship.—*ns.* **relig´ionist,** one attached to a religion: a bigot; **religiosity** (*-i-os´i-ti*), spurious or sentimental religious feeling or observance.—*adj.* **relig´ious** (*-us*), of, concerned with, devoted to, or imbued with, religion: scrupulous: (*R.C.*) bound to a monastic life: strict.—*n.* one bound by monastic vows.—*adv.* **relig´iously.** [L. *religiō, -ōnis*, n., *religiōsus*, adj., perh. conn. with *religāre*, to bind, perh. with *relegĕre*, to read again.]

relinquish, *ri-ling´kwish, v.t.* to give up: to let go.—*n.* **relin´quishment.** [O.Fr. *relinquir, relinquissant*—L. *relinquĕre, relictum*—*re-*, *linquĕre*, to leave.]

relique, *rel´ik, ri-lēk´, n.* an old form of **relic.**—*n.*

reliquary (*rel´i-kwár-i*), a receptacle for relics. [Fr. *reliquaire.*]

relish, *rel´ish, n.* a flavour: enough to give a flavour: a condiment: zest-giving quality: zestful enjoyment.—*v.t.* to like the taste of: to be pleased with: to appreciate discriminatingly. —*v.i.* to have an agreeable taste: to give pleasure. [O.Fr. *reles, relais*, remainder—*relaisser*, to leave behind; perh. with idea of after-taste.]

reluctance, *ri-lukt´áns, n.* unwillingness: magneto-motive force applied to whole or part of a magnetic circuit divided by the flux in it.—Also **reluct´ancy.**—*adj.* **reluct´ant,** unwilling: resisting. [L. *reluctans, -antis*, pr.p. of *reluctāri*—*re-*, against, *luctāri*, to struggle.]

rely, *ri-lī´, v.i.* to depend confidently:—*pr.p.* re-ly´ing; *pa.t.* and *pa.p.* relied´.—*adj.* **reli´able,** to be relied on, trustworthy.—*ns.* **reliabil´ity, reli´ableness.**—*adv.* **reli´ably.**—*n.* **reli´ance,** trust: (*arch.*) that in which one trusts: dependence.—*adj.* **reli´ant.**—**reliability test, trial,** a public test of the qualities of motor vehicles. [O.Fr. *relier*—L. *religāre*, to bind back.]

rem, *rem, n.* a unit of radiation dosage, the amount which has the same effect as one rad of X-radiation. [*r*öntgen *e*quivalent *m*an or *m*ammal.]

remain, *ri-mān´, v.i.* to stay or be left behind: to continue in the same place: to be left after or out of a greater number: to continue in one's possession, mind: to continue unchanged.—*n.* (esp. in *pl.* **remains´**) what is left: relics: a corpse: literary productions unpublished at the author's death.—*n.* **remain´der,** that which remains after the removal of a part: an interest in an estate to come into effect after a certain other event happens: right of succession to a post or title: residue of an edition when the sale of a book has fallen off.—*v.t.* to sell (book) as a remainder. [O.Fr. *remaindre*—L. *remanēre*—*re-*, back, *manēre*, to stay.]

remake, *rē´māk´, v.t.* to make again, anew. [Pfx. **re-,** and **make.**]

remand, *ri-mand´, v.t.* to send back (esp. a prisoner into custody to await further evidence). **remand home,** a home to which a child or young person may be committed by a magistrate for restraint or protection. [O.Fr. *remander*, or L.L. *remandāre*—*re-*, back, *mandāre*, to order, commit.]

remark, *ri-märk´, v.t.* to notice: to comment, utter as an observation, say incidentally (that): (*rē´-märk´*) to mark again.—*v.i.* (*ri-*) to comment (on).—*n.* noteworthiness: comment.—*adj.* **remark´able,** noteworthy—unusual, strange, or distinguished.—*n.* **remark´ableness.**—*adv.* **remark´ably.** [O.Fr. *remarquer*—*re-*, inten., *marquer*, to mark.]

remedy, *rem´é-di, n.* any means of curing a disease, redressing, counteracting, or repairing any evil or loss.—*v.t.* to put right, repair, counteract:—*pr.p.* rem´edying; *pa.t.* and *pa.p.* rem´edied.—*adjs.* **remē´diable,** that may be remedied, curable; **remē´dial,** tending or intended to remedy. [Anglo-Fr. *remedie*, O.Fr. *remede*—L. *remedium*—*re-*, back, *medēri*, to restore.]

remember, *ri-mem´bér, v.t.* to keep in, or recall to, memory or mind: to bear in mind with

Neutral vowels in unaccented syllables: *em´pér-ór*; for certain sounds in foreign words see p. ix.

616

gratitude or honour or as one to be rewarded.—*ns.* **remem′brance,** memory: that which serves to bring to or keep in mind—a souvenir, a memorial: the reach of memory: (in *pl.*) a message of friendly greeting; **remem′brancer,** one who or that which reminds: a recorder: an officer of exchequer **(King's Remembrancer)** whose duty it is to collect debts due to the King. [O.Fr. *remembrer* —L. *re-,* again, *memor,* mindful.]

remind, *ri-mīnd′, v.t.* to put in mind (of), to cause to remember.—*n.* **remind′er,** that which reminds. [Pfx. **re-,** and **mind.**]

reminiscence, *rem-i-nis′ens, n.* the recurrence to the mind of the past: a recollection: a suggestion (of), a feature suggestive (of): an account of something remembered (*often pl.*).—*v.i.* **reminisce** (*-nis′*), (*coll.*) to recount reminiscences.—*adj.* **reminis′cent.** [L. *reminiscens, -entis,* pr.p. of *reminiscī,* to remember.]

remiss, *ri-mis′, adj.* negligent, slack, lax (of a person or action).—*adv.* **remiss′ly.**—*n.* **remiss′ness.**—*adj.* **remiss′ible,** that may be remitted.—*ns.* **remissibil′ity.**—*n.* **remission** (*ri-mish′(ō)n*), act of remitting: slackening, abatement: relinquishment (of a claim): cancellation: forgiveness.—*adj.* **remiss′ive,** remitting: forgiving. [L. *remittĕre, remissum. See* **remit.**]

remit, *ri-mit′, v.t.* to relax: to pardon: to refrain from exacting or inflicting: to transmit, as money, &c.: to put again in custody: to refer for decision (to another committee, court, &c.).—*v.i.* to abate, to relax:—*pr.p.* remitt′ing; *pa.t.* and *pa.p.* remitt′ed.—*n.* the act, or an instance, of referring for decision, to another authority.—*ns.* **remitt′ance,** the sending of money, &c., to a distance: a sum or thing sent; **remitt′ance-man,** one dependent upon remittances from home.—*adj.* **remitt′ent,** remitting at intervals, as **remittent fever,** a severe type of malaria in which the temperature falls slightly from time to time.—*n.* **remitt′er,** one who makes a remittance. [L. *remittĕre, remissum* re-, back, *mittĕre,* to send.]

remnant, *rem′nant, n.* a fragment or a small number remaining after destruction, removal, sale, &c., of the greater part: esp. a remaining piece of cloth. [L. *re*-, back, *manēre,* to remain.]

remonstrance, *ri-mon′strans, n.* a strong or formal protest: expostulation.—*adj.* **remon′strant,** remonstrating.—*n.* one who remonstrates.—*v.i.* **remon′strate** (or *rem′*), to make a remonstrance: to expostulate (with). [L. *re-,* again, *monstrāre,* to point out.]

remorse, *ri-mörs′, n.* the gnawing pain of conscience: compunction.—*adj.* **remorse′ful,** penitent: compassionate.—*adv.* **remorse′fully.**—*adj.* **remorse′less,** without remorse: cruel, relentless.—*adv.* **remorse′lessly.**—*n.* **remorse′lessness.** [O.Fr. *remors* (Fr. *remords*)—Low L. *remorsus*—L. *remordēre, remorsum,* to bite again.]

remote, *ri-mōt′, adj.* far removed in place, or time: widely separated (from): out-of-theway, not quickly reached: (*fig.*) slight (e.g. *a remote resemblance*): very indirect: aloof in manner.—*adv.* **remote′ly.**—*n.* **remote′ness.**— **remote control,** control of a device from a

distance by the making or breaking of an electric circuit or by means of radio waves. [L. *remōtus,* pa.p. of *removēre.* See **remove.**]

remount, *rē-mownt′, v.t.* and *v.i.* to mount again.—*n.* a fresh horse, or supply of horses. [L. *re-,* again, and **mount** (2).]

remove, *ri-mōōv′, v.t.* to put or take away: to transfer (to): to withdraw (from).—*v.i.* to go away: to change abode.—*n.* a step in any scale of gradation: promotion: in some schools, an intermediate class.—*adj.* **remov′able.**—*ns.* **removabil′ity; remov′al,** the act of taking away: displacement: going away: change of abode: a euphemism for murder.—*adj.* **removed′,** remote: distant by specified degrees, as in descent. [O.Fr. *remouvoir*—L. *removēre, remōtum*—*re,* away, *movēre,* to move.]

remunerate, *ri-mū′ne-rāt, v.t.* to recompense: to pay.—*adj.* **remū′nerable.**—*n.* **remunera′tion,** recompense: payment.—*adj.* **remū′nerative,** profitable. [L. *remūnerārī* (late *-āre*), *-ātus*— *mūnus, -ĕris,* a gift.]

renaissance, *ri-nā′sāns, ren′i-sāns, n.* a new birth or revival: (*cap.*) revival of arts and letters, under classical influence, marking the transition from the Middle Ages to the modern world: period of this revival (about 15th century). *adj.* of the period, or in the style, of the Renaissance. [Fr.,—L. *renascī.* See **renascent.**]

renal, *rē′n(a)l, adj.* of the kidneys. [L. *rēnālis* — *rēnēs* (sing. *rēn,* rare), the kidneys.]

renascent, *ri-nas′ent,* also *-nās′-, adj.* coming into renewed life or vitality.—*n.* **renas′cence,** being born anew: **Renas′cence,** Renaissance. [L. *renāscēns, -entis,* pr.p. of *renāscī*—*re-,* again, *nāscī,* to be born.]

rencounter, *ren-kownt′er,* **rencontre,** *rä-kō-tr′,* (Fr.) *n.* a chance meeting: a casual combat: a collision.—*v.t.* to meet. [Fr. *rencontre.*]

rend, *rend, v.t.* to tear asunder with force: to split:—*pa.t.* and *pa.p.* rent.—*v.i.* to become torn. [O.E. *rendan,* to tear.]

render, *ren′der, v.t.* to give up: to give back: to give in return: to pay: to represent or reproduce (esp. artistically): to translate: to cause to be: to melt, or clarify by melting.—*ns.* **ren′dering,** the act of rendering: version: translation: performance; **rendi′tion,** surrender: rendering. [O.Fr. *rendre*—L.L. *rendĕre,* app. formed by influence of *prendĕre,* to take—L. *reddĕre*—*re-,* back, *dăre,* to give.]

rendezvous, *rä′dā-vōō, ren′di-, n.* an appointed meeting-place: a meeting by appointment: a general resort.—*v.i.* to assemble at any appointed place. [Fr. *rendez-vous,* render yourselves—*rendre,* to render.]

renegade, *ren′e-gād, n.* one faithless to principle or party, an apostate, a turncoat.—Also **renegā′do.** [L.L. *renegātus*—L. *re-,* inten., *negāre, -ātum,* to deny; partly through Sp *renegado.*]

reneg(u)e. See **renig.**

renew, *ri-nū′, v.t.* to renovate: to transform to new life, revive: to begin again: to repeat: to grant or obtain an extension of (e.g. a lease).—*v.i.* to become new: to begin again.—*adj.* **renew′able.**—*n.* **renew′al,** renewing. [L. *re-,* again, and **new.**]

reniform, *ren′i-förm, adj.* kidney-shaped. [L. *rēnēs* (sing. *rēn*), the kidneys, *forma,* form.]

---

fāte, fär; mē, hûr (her); *mīne; mōte, för; mūte; mōōn, fŏŏt;* THen (then)

renig, *ri-nig'*, **renegue, renege**, *ri-nēg', v.t.* to renounce: to apostatise from.—*v.i.* (*obs.*) to deny: to revoke at cards: to go back on one's word (with *on*):—*pa.t.* and *pa.p.* renigg'ed. [L. *re-*, inten., *negāre, -ātum,* to deny.]

rennet, *ren'it, n.* any means of curdling milk, esp. a preparation of calf's stomach.—*n.* **rennin**, the enzyme (q.v.) in the gastric juice that causes curdling of milk. [O.E. *rinnan,* to run.]

rennet, *ren'it, n.* an apple of certain old varieties. [Fr.*reinette, rainette* ;origin uncertain.]

renounce, *ri-nowns', v.t.* to disclaim, repudiate: to reject publicly and finally: to abandon (e.g. one's faith).—*v.i.* to fail to follow suit at cards.—*n.* **renounce'ment.** [O.Fr. *renuncer*—L. *renuntiāre*—*re-,* away, *nuntiāre, -ātum,* to announce.]

renovate, *ren'ō-vāt, v.t.* to make new again: to make as if new.—*ns.* **renovā'tion; ren'ovātor.** [L. *re-,* again, *novāre, -ātum,* to make new— *novus,* new.]

renown, *ri-nown', n.* fame.—*adj.* **renowned',** famous. [O.Fr. *renoun* (Fr. *renom*)—L. *re-,* again, *nōmen,* a name.]

rent, *rent, n.* an opening made by rending: fissure.—Also *pa.t.* and *pa.p.* of **rend.**

rent, *rent, n.* periodical payment for use of another's property, esp. houses and lands: revenue.—*v.t.* to hold or occupy by paying rent: to let or hire out for a rent.—*v.i.* to be let at a rent.—*ns.* **ren'tal,** a rent-roll: rent: annual value; **rent'er,** a tenant who pays rent; **rentier** (*rä-tyā*), one who has a fixed income from land, bonds, stocks and the like; **rent-restric'tion,** restriction of landlord's right to raise rent; **rent'-roll,** a list of tenements and rents: total income from property. [Fr. *rente*— L. *reddita* (*pecūnia*), money paid—*reddĕre,* to pay.]

renunciation, *ri-nun-si-ā'sh(ò)n, n.* act of renouncing: self-denial. [L. *renūntiāre,* to proclaim.]

renvoi, *ren-voi', Fr. rä-vwä, n.* sending back by a government of an alien to his own country: a referring or relegation. [Fr.]

reorient, *rē-ō'ri-ént, -ō', v.t.* to orient again.—*v.t* **reo'rientate,** reorient. [L. *re-,* again and **orient.**]

rep, repp, *rep, n.* a corded cloth. [Fr. *reps,* perh.—Eng. **ribs.**]

rep, *rep, n.* an abbreviation for **repertory** (theatre), **repetition,** and **reputation.**

repaid, *rē-pād', pa.t.* and *pa.p.* of **repay.**

repair, *ri-pār', v.i.* to betake oneself, to go, to resort.—*n.* a resort, haunt. [O.Fr. *repairer,* to return to a haunt—L. *re-,* back, *patria,* native country.]

repair, *ri-pār', v.t.* to mend: to remedy: to make amends for.—*n.* (often *pl.*) restoration after injury, decay, or loss: sound condition.—*n.* **repair'er.**—*adj.* **reparable** (*rep'ár-a-bl*), capable of being made good.—*adv.* **rep'arably.**—*n.* **reparā'tion,** repair: supply of what is wasted: amends: compensation.—*adj.* **reparative** (*ri-par'a-tiv*). [O.Fr. *reparer*—L. *reparāre*—*re-,* again, *parāre,* to prepare.]

repartee, *rep-är-tē', n.* a ready and witty retort: skill in making such retorts. [O.Fr. *repartie*— *repartir*—*re-,* back, *partir,* to set out—L. *partīrī,* to divide.]

repartition, *rep-är-tish'(ò)n, n.* distribution: (*rē-pär-*) a second partition: a division into smaller parts. [L. *re-,* and **partition.**]

repast, *ri-päst', n.* a meal. [O.Fr. *repast* (Fr. *repas*)—L.L. *repastus*—L. *re-,* inten., *pascĕre, pastum,* to feed.]

repatriate, *rē-pāt'ri-āt,* or *-pat'-, v.t.* to restore or send back to one's country.—*n.* **repatriā'tion.** [L.L. *repatriāre, -ātum,* to return to one's country—L. *patria.*]

repay, *rē-pā', v.t.* to pay back: to make return for: to recompense:—*pr.p.* repay'ing;*pa.t.* and *pa.p.* repaid'.—*adj.* **repay'able,** that is to be repaid.—*n.* **repay'ment.** [L. *re-,* back, and **pay.**]

repeal, *ri-pēl', v.t.* to revoke, to annul.—*n.* abrogation, annulment.—*adj.* **repeal'able.**—*n.* **repeal'er,** one who repeals: an advocate of repeal. [O.Fr. *rapeler*—pfx. *re-, appeler,* to appeal.]

repeat, *ri-pēt', v.t.* to say, do, perform, again: to quote from memory: to recount: to divulge: to say or do after another.—*v.i.* to recur: to make a repetition: to strike the last hour, quarter, &c., when required: to fire several shots without reloading: to rise so as to be tasted after swallowing.—*n.* a repetition: (*mus.*) a passage repeated or marked for repetition: the sign directing repetition.—*adjs.* **repeat'able,** fit, sufficiently decent, to be repeated; **repeat'ed,** done, appearing, &c., again.—*adv.* **repeat'edly,** many times, again and again.—*n.* **repeat'er,** one who, or that which, repeats: a repeating decimal (see **recur**): a watch or clock, or a fire-arm, that repeats.—*n.* and *adj.* **repeat'ing.**—**repeat oneself,** to say again what one has said already. [Fr.*répéter*—L. *repetĕre, -ītum*—*re-,* again, *petĕre,* to seek.]

repel, *ri-pel', v.t.* to drive back: to repulse: to hold off: to be repulsive or distasteful to:—*pr.p.* repell'ing;*pa.t.* and *pa.p.* repelled'.—*adj.* **repell'ent,** driving back: able or tending to repel: distasteful.—*n.* that which repels.—*n.* **repell'er.** [L. *repellĕre*—*re-,* back, *pellĕre,* to drive.]

repent, *ri-pent', v.i.* to regret, sorrow for, or wish to have been otherwise, what one has done or left undone (with *of*): to change from past evil: to feel contrition.—*v.t.* to regret.—*n.* **repent'ance,** act of repenting: penitent state of mind.—*adj.* **repent'ant,** experiencing or expressing repentance. [O.Fr. *repentir*—L. *paenitēre,* to cause to repent.]

repercussion, *rē-pér-kush'(ò)n, n.* driving back: reverberation, echo: a return stroke, a reaction or consequence, esp. one that is unexpected and embarrassing.—*adj.* **repercussive** (*-kus'iv*), driving back: reverberating, echoing.—*v.t.* **repercuss'** (*obs.* and now *coll.*), to drive back, reflect, reverberate, or have consequences. [L. *repercutĕre, -cussum*—*re-, per, quatĕre,* to shake.]

repertory, *rep'ér-tór-i, n.* a storehouse, repository: a stock of pieces that a person or company is prepared to perform.—*n.* **repertoire** (*rep'ér-twär* ; Fr. *répertoire*), a performer's or company's repertory.—**repertory theatre,** a theatre with a repertoire of plays and a stock or permanent company. [L.L. *repertōrium* —L. *reperīre,* to find again—*parēre,* to bring forth.]

repetition, *rep-i-tish'(ò)n, n.* act of repeating:

Neutral vowels in unaccented syllables: *em'pér-ór* ; for certain sounds in foreign words see p. ix.

recital from memory.—*adj.* **repetitive** (*ri-pet'-i-tiv*), overmuch given to repetition. [L. re-, *petēre*, *-ītum*, to seek again, repeat—*petēre*, to seek.]

repine, *ri-pīn'*, *v.i.* to fret (with *at* or *against*): to feel discontent: to murmur.—*n.* **repī'ner.**—*n.* and *adj.* **repī'ning.** [App. from **pine** (2).]

replace, *ri-* or *rē-plās'*, *v.t.* to put back: to provide a substitute for: to take the place of.—*adj.* **replace'able.**—*n.* **replace'ment**, act of replacing: person or thing that replaces another. [L. re-, back, again, **place.**]

replenish, *ri-plen'ish*, *v.t.* to fill again: to fill completely: to stock abundantly.—*n.* **replen'ishment.** [O.Fr. *replenir*, *-issant*, from *replein*, full—L. re-, again, *plēnus*, full.]

replete, *ri-plēt'*, *adj.* full, well stored (*lit.* and *fig.*—with *with*): completely filled: filled to satiety.—*n.* **replē'tion**, superabundant fullness: (*med.*) fullness of blood. [L. *replētus*, pa.p. of *replēre*—re-, again, *plēre*, to fill.]

replica, *rep'li-ka*, *n.* a duplicate, properly one by the original artist: a facsimile. [I[..—L. *re-plicāre*, to repeat.]

replicate, *rep'li-kāt*, *v.t.* to fold back: to repeat: to make a replica of.—*v.i.* of molecules of living material, to reproduce molecules identical with themselves.—Also *adj.* (*-āt*).—*n.* **replicā'tion**, a reply: (*law*) the plaintiff's reply to the defendant's counterstatement of facts (plea, answer, defence): doubling back: reproduction [L. *replicāre*, *-ātum*, to fold back—*plicāre*, to fold.]

reply, *ri-plī'*, *v.t.* and *v.i.* to say or write in answer:—*pr.p.* reply'ing; *pa.t.* and *pa.p.* replied'.—*n.* an answer.—*n.* **replī'er.** [O.Fr. *re-plier*—L. *replicāre*, to repeat.]

report, *ri-pōrt'*, *v.t.* to bring back, as an answer, news, or account of anything: to announce: to give a formal statement of: to circulate publicly: to write down or take notes of, esp. for a newspaper: to make a complaint about, against.—*v.i.* to make a formal statement (on): to write an account of occurrences: to present oneself (for duty).—*n.* a statement of facts: a newspaper account of an event or the words of a speech: a formal or official statement, as of results of an investigation: written statement on a pupil's work and behaviour: rumour, hearsay: repute: explosive noise.—*ns.* **report'age** (*-ij*), accurately observed and vividly written account of contemporary events (e.g. *a piece of brilliant reportage*): journalistic style of writing: gossip; **report'er**, one who reports, esp. for a newspaper.—*n.* and *adj.* **report'ing.** [O.Fr. *reporter*—L. *reportāre*—re-, back, *portāre*, to carry.]

repose, *ri-pōz'*, *v.t.* to lay at rest: to place (e.g. confidence): to refresh by rest.—*v.i.* to rest: to rely (on): to rest or (*fig.*) be based (on).—*n.* rest: stillness: ease of manner: serenity.—*adj.* **repōsed'**, calm: settled. [Fr. *reposer*—Low L. *repausāre*—re-, and *pausāre*. See **pose** (1).]

repository, *ri-poz'i-tōr-i*, *n.* place or receptacle in which anything is stored (*lit.* and *fig.*): a confidant. [L. *repōnĕre*, *repositum*, to put back, lay aside—*pōnĕre*, to put; confused with foregoing.]

repossess, *rē-poz-es'*, *v.t.* to regain possession of: to take back because payment has not been

made.—*n.* **repossession** (*-esh'(ó)n*). [L. re-, again, and **possess.**]

repoussé, *ré-pōō-sā'*, or *-pōō'-*, *adj.* raised in relief by hammering from behind or within.—*n.* repoussé work.—*n.* **repoussage'** (*-äzh*). [Fr.]

repp. Same as **rep** (1).

reprehend, *rep-ré-hend'*, *v.t.* to find fault with, to reprove.—*adj.* **reprehen'sible**, blameworthy.—*adv.* **reprehen'sibly.**—*n.* **reprehen'sion**, reproof, censure.—*adjs.* **reprehen'sive**, **reprehen'sory**, containing reproof: given in reproof. [L. *reprehendĕre*, *-hensum*—re-, inten., *prehendĕre*, to lay hold of.]

represent, *rep-re-zent'*, *v.t.* to present to, bring before, the mind: to point out (e.g. *he represented to him the danger of this course*): to make to appear (as), to allege (to be): to depict: to act the rôle of on the stage: to serve as a symbol for: to correspond to: to be a substitute, agent, or delegate for: to be a parliamentary delegate for.—*v.t.* **re-present'** (*rē-*), to present again, anew.—*adj.* **representable.**—*n.* **representation** (*zen-tā'sh(ó)n*), act of representing or being represented: that which represents: an image, picture: dramatic performance: a remonstrance, petition: a presentation of a view of facts or arguments.—*adj.* **representative** (*rep-ré-zent'a-tiv*), representing: consisting of, or carried on by, elected deputies: typical, typical (of).—*n.* one who represents another or others, as a deputy, delegate, agent, ambassador, heir.—**representative government**, government by representatives chosen by the electorate; **representative peers**, Scottish and Irish peers chosen by their fellows to sit in the House of Lords; **House of Representatives**, the lower branch of the United States Congress, consisting of members chosen biennially by the people: also of various state and other legislatures. [L. *repraesentāre*, *-ātum*—re-, again, *praesentāre*, to place before.]

repress, *ri-pres'*, *v.t.* to restrain: to keep under: to confine to the unconscious mind: (*rē-*) to press again.—*adj.* **repress'ible.**—*n.* **repression** (*-presh'(ó)n*).—*adj.* **repress'ive.** [L. *reprimĕre*, *repressum*—premĕre, to press back.]

reprieve, *ri-prēv'*, *v.t.* to delay or commute the execution of: to give a respite to: to rescue, redeem.—*n.* a suspension of a criminal sentence: interval of ease or relief. [Supposed to be from Anglo-Fr. *repris*, pa.p. of *reprendre*, to take back (see **reprisal**); the *v* app. by confusion.]

reprimand, *rep'ri-mänd*, *n.* a severe reproof.—*v.t.* (also *-mänd'*) to reprove severely, esp. publicly or officially. [Fr. *réprimande*—L. *re-primĕre*, *repressum*, to press back—re-, back, *premĕre*, to press.]

reprint, *rē-print'*, *v.t.* to print again: to print a new impression of.—*n.* **rē'print**, a later impression. [L. re-, again, and **print.**]

reprisal, *ri-prī'zàl*, *n.* seizure in retaliation: an act of retaliation. [Fr. *reprise*—*reprendre*—L. *reprehendĕre*. See **reprehend.**]

reproach, *ri-prōch'*, *v.t.* to lay to the charge of (with *with*): to censure, upbraid: to reprove gently: to bring into discredit.—*n.* upbraiding, reproof, censure: a source or matter of disgrace or shame.—*adjs.* **reproach'able; reproach'ful,** reproving.—*adv.* **reproach'fully.** [Fr. *reprocher,* perh. from L. *prope,* near; cf. **approach.**]

reprobate, *rep'rō-bāt, -āt, adj.* rejected by God, given over to sin, depraved, unprincipled: condemnatory.—*n.* an abandoned or profligate person: (often playfully) a scamp.—*v.t.* (-*āt*) to reject: to disapprove, express disapproval, of: to exclude from salvation.—*n.* **reprobā'tion,** the act of reprobating: disapproval: rejection: predestination to eternal punishment. [L. *reprobāre, -ātum,* to reprove, contrary of *approbāre—probāre,* to prove.]

reproduce, *rē-prō-dūs', v.t.* to produce a copy of: to form anew: to propagate.—*v.i.* to produce offspring: to turn out (well, ill, &c.) when reproduced or copied.—*n.* **reproduction** (*-duk'sh(ó)n*), the act of reproducing: the act of producing new organisms: a copy, facsimile: a representation.—*adj.* **reproduc'tive.** [L. *re-,* again, and **produce.**]

reproof, *ri-prōōf', n.* a reproving: rebuke, censure, reprehension.—*v.t.* (*rē-*) to make waterproof again.—*n.* **reproval** (*ri-prōō'v(à)l*), reproof.—*v.t.* **reprove',** to rebuke, to censure.—*n.* **repro'ver.**—*adv.* **repro'vingly.** [O.Fr. *reprover* (Fr. *réprouver*)—L. *reprobāre.* See **reprobate.**]

reptile, *rep'tīl, adj.* creeping: like a reptile in nature.—*n.* an animal that moves or crawls on its belly or with short legs—one of the **Reptil'ia,** a class of vertebrate, cold-blooded animals including alligators and crocodiles, lizards, snakes, &c.: a base, malignant, abject, or treacherous person.—*adj.* **reptilian** (*-til'i-án*). [L.L. *reptilis, -e—repēre,* to creep.]

republic, *ri-pub'lik, n.* (*arch.*) the state: a form of government without a monarch, in which the supreme power is vested in the people and their elected representatives: a state or country so governed.—*adj.* **repub'lican,** of or favouring a republic.—*n.* one who advocates a republican form of government: of the Republican party (in the U.S., now opposed to the *Democratic* party, and favouring a strong federal government).—*n.* **repub'licanism.**—**republic of letters,** the world of books and authors. [L. *rēspublica,* commonwealth—*rēs,* affair, *publica* (fem.) public.]

republish, *rē-pub'lish, v.t.* to publish again.—*n.* **republicā'tion.** [L. *re-,* again, and **publish.**]

repudiate, *ri-pū'di-āt, v.t.* to divorce: to disown: to refuse to recognise (e.g. authority), believe (e.g. a suggestion), acknowledge or pay (e.g. a debt): to deny as unfounded (a charge, &c.).—*ns.* **repudiā'tion; repū'diātor.** [L. *repudiāre, -ātum—repudium,* divorce—*re-,* away, and the root of *pudēre,* to be ashamed.]

repugnance, *ri-pug'náns, n.* inconsistency: aversion.—*adj.* **repug'nant,** inconsistent: incompatible: distasteful, disgusting: opposing, resisting. [L. *repugnāre,—re-, against, pugnāre,* to fight.]

repulse, *ri-puls', v.t.* to drive back, to beat off (e.g. an attack): to rebuff (an overture, a person).—*n.* a driving back, a beating off: a check: a refusal, a rebuff.—*n.* **repulsion** (*-pul'sh(ó)n*), driving off: a repelling force, action, or influence: strong distaste.—*adj.* **repul'sive,** that repulses or drives off: repelling:

cold, reserved, forbidding: causing aversion and disgust.—*adv.* **repul'sively.**—*n.* **repul'siveness.** [L. *repulsus,* pa.p. of *repellēre—re-,* back, *pellēre,* to drive.]

repurchase, *rē-pûr'chás, v.t.* to purchase or buy back or again.—*n.* the act of buying again: that which is bought again. [L. *re-,* again, and **purchase.**]

repute, *ri-pūt', v.t.* to consider, deem.—*n.* general opinion or impression: attributed character: widespread or high estimation.—*adj.* **reputable** (*rep'ūt-á-bl*), in good repute, respectable.—*adv.* **rep'ūtably.**—*n.* **repūtā'tion** (*rep-*), repute: estimation, character generally ascribed: good report, fame: good name.—*p.adj.* **reputed** (*ri-pūt'id*), supposed: of high repute.—*adv.* **repūt'edly,** in common repute or estimation.—**reputed owner,** a person who has to all appearance the title to the property. [L. *reputāre, -ātum—re-,* again, *putāre,* to reckon.]

request, *ri-kwest', n.* the asking of a favour: a petition: a favour asked for: the state of being sought after.—*v.t.* to ask as a favour: to ask politely: to ask for.—**request note,** an application for a permit to remove excisable goods. [O.Fr. *requeste* (Fr. *requête*)—L. *requisītum,* pa.p. of *requīrēre—re-,* away, *quaerēre,* to seek.]

requiem, *rek'wi-em, n.* a mass for the rest of the soul of the dead: music for it: any music of similar character. [L. acc. of *requiēs*—(*re-, inten., quiēs,* rest): first word of the mass.]

requiescat in pace, *re-kwi-es'kät in pä'chä, pä'sē, pä'ke,* abbrev. **R.I.P.,** may he (or she) rest in peace.

require, *ri-kwīr', v.t.* to demand, to exact: to direct, order: to need.—*adj.* **requir'able.**—*n.* **require'ment,** a need: a thing needed: a necessary condition: a demand. [L. *requīrēre*; partly through O.Fr. *requerre,* later assimilated to L.]

requisite, *rek'wi-zit, adj.* required, needful, indispensable.—*n.* that which is required, necessary, or indispensable.—*n.* **requisi'tion,** the act of requiring: a formal demand, request, or order, as for the supply of anything for military purposes.—*v.t.* to demand or take by requisition: to make such a demand upon (for).—*n.* **requisi'tionist,** one who makes a requisition. [L. *requīsītus,* pa.p. of *requīrēre.* See **require.**]

requite, *ri-kwīt', v.t.* to repay (an action): to avenge: to repay (a person, for).—*n.* **requī'tal,** the act of requiting: payment in return, retribution, recompense, reward. [Pfx. **re-,** and **quit.**]

reredos, *rēr'dos, n.* a screen or panelling behind an altar: (*loosely*) a choir-screen. [O.Fr., *rere,* rear, *dos*—L. *dorsum,* back.]

reremouse, *rēr'mows, n.* a bat:—*pl.* **rere'mice.** [O.E. *hrēremūs,* app.—*hrēran,* to move, *mūs,* a mouse.]

rescind, *ri-sind', v.t.* (*rare*) to cut away: to annul, abrogate.—*n.* **rescission** (*-sizh'(ó)n*), abrogation.—*adj.* **rescissory** (*-sis'ór-i*), annulling. [L. *rescindēre, rescissum—re-,* back, *scindēre,* to cut.]

rescript, *rē'skript, n.* the official answer of a pope or an emperor to any legal question: an

Neutral vowels in unaccented syllables: *em'pér-ór*; for certain sounds in foreign words see p. ix.

620

edict or decree: a rewriting. [L. *rescriptum*—*re*-, back, *scrībēre*, *scrīptum*, to write.]

rescue, *res′kū*, *v.t.* to free from danger, captivity, or evil plight: to deliver forcibly from legal custody:—*pr.p.* res′cūing; *pa.t.* and *pa.p.* res′cūed.—*n.* the act of rescuing: deliverance from danger or evil: forcible recovery (of property): forcible release from arrest or imprisonment.—*n.* res′cuer. [O.Fr. *rescourre*—L. *re*-, away, *excutĕre*—*ex*, out, *quatĕre*, to shake.]

research, *ri-sérch′*, *n.* a careful search or investigation: systematic investigation towards increasing the sum of knowledge.—*v.i.* to make researches.—*n.* research′er. [O.Fr. *recerche*. See **search**.]

resect, *ri-sekt′*, *v.t.* to cut away part of, esp. the end of a bone.—*n.* resect′ion. [L. *resecāre*, *-sectum*, to cut off—*secāre*, to cut.]

resemble, *ri-zem′bl*, *v.t.* to be like: (*arch.*) to compare.—*n.* resem′blance, likeness. [O.Fr. *resembler* (Fr. *ressembler*)—*re*-, again, *sembler*, to seem—L. *simulāre*, to make like.]

resent, *ri-zent′*, *v.t.* to take badly, to consider as an injury or affront.—*adj.* resent′ful.—*adv.* resent′fully.—*n.* resent′ment. [O.Fr. *ressentir*—L. *re*-, in return, *sentīre*, to feel.]

reserve, *ri-zûrv′*, *v.t.* to hold back, to save up for future use or emergency: to retain (for one's own use): to set apart or destine (for): (*reflex.*) to save one's energies (for): to book, engage.—*n.* that which is reserved: a reservation: (esp. in *pl.*) a military force kept out of action till occasion serves: (esp. in *pl.*) a force not usually serving but liable to be called up when required: (often *pl.*) resources of physical or spiritual nature available in abnormal circumstances: part of assets kept readily available for ordinary demands: restrained manner: reticence: a mental reservation.—*adj.* reserv′able.—*n.* reserva′tion (*rez-*), the act of reserving or keeping back or keeping for oneself: an expressed, or tacit, proviso, limiting condition, or exception: something withheld: safe keeping: a tract of public land reserved for some special purpose, as for Indians, schools, game, &c.: the booking of a seat, room, passage, &c.: a booked seat, room, &c.—*p.adj.* reserved′, reticent, uncommunicative: aloof in manner.—*adv.* reservedly (*-id-li*).—*ns.* reservedness (*ri-zervd′nés*); reser′vist, a member of a reserve force.—reserved occupation, an employment that exempts from service in the armed forces.—mental reservation, the tacit withholding of some word or proviso whose inclusion would change the import of an expressed agreement: the proviso so withheld. [O.Fr. *reserver*—L. *reservāre*—*re*-, back, *servāre*, to save.]

reservoir, *rez′ér-vwär, -vwör*, *n.* a receptacle: a store: a receptacle for fluids, esp. an artificial lake or tank for storing water. [Fr.]

reset, *ri-set′*, *v.t.* (*Scot.*) to receive (stolen goods) with the intention of profiting from them.—Also *v.i.* and *n.* [O.Fr. *receter*.]

reset, *rē-set′*, *v.t.* to set again: to set up in type again. [Pfx. **re-**, and **set**.]

reside, *ri-zīd′*, *v.i.* to dwell permanently: to be vested (in): to inhere (in).—*ns.* residence (*rez′i-déns*), act of dwelling in a place: period of dwelling: a dwelling-house, esp. of some

size and style: that in which anything permanently inheres or has its seat; res′idency, the official abode of a Resident or governor of a protected state: an administrative district under a Resident.—*adj.* res′ident, dwelling in a place for some time: residing on one's own estate or the place of one's duties: not migratory.—*n.* one who resides: a public minister at a foreign court: (*cap.*) a representative of a governor in a protected state: a junior doctor residing in a hospital. *adjs.* residential (*-den′shál*), of, for, connected with, residence: (of a quarter) suitable for, occupied by residences; residentiary (*-den′-shä-ri*), resident: officially bound to reside.—*n.* an inhabitant: one bound to reside, as a canon.—in residence, at official abode. [L. *residēre*—*re*-, back, *sedēre*, to sit.]

residue, *rez′i-dū*, *n.* that which is left, remainder.—*adjs.* resid′ual, remaining as residue; resid′uary, of, or of the nature of, a residue, esp. of an estate: to whom the residue of an estate is willed (e.g. *residuary legatee*).—*n.* resid′uum (L.), a residue. [L. *residuum*—*residēre*, to remain behind.]

resign, *ri-zīn′*, *v.t.* to yield up, to relinquish: (*reflex.*) to submit calmly: to entrust (to).—*v.i.* to give up office, employment, &c.—*n.* resignation (*rez-ig-nā′sh(ó)n*), act of giving up: formal statement that one is giving up (a post): the document conveying it: state of being resigned or quietly submissive.—*p.adj.* resigned (*ri-zīnd′*), calmly submissive. [O.Fr. *resigner*—L. *resignāre*, *-ātum*, to unseal, annul—*re*-, signifying reversal, *signāre*, to seal—*signum*, a mark.]

re-sign. See **re-**.

resile, *ri-zīl′*, *v.i.* to recoil, to rebound, to spring back into shape or position: (esp. *Scots*) to back out.—*ns.* resilience (*ri-zil′i-éns*), recoil: elasticity: physical or mental: the stored energy of a strained material, or the work done per unit volume of an elastic material by any force in producing strain: resil′iency, (*lit.* and *fig.*) elasticity.—*adj.* resil′ient, elastic, buoyant (physically or in spirits). [L. *resilīre*, to leap back—*re*-, back, *salīre*, to leap.]

resin, *rez′in*, *n.* any of a number of substances, products obtained from the sap of certain plants and trees (*natural resins*), used in plastics, &c.: any of a large number of substances made by polymerisation or condensation (*synthetic resins*) which, though not related chemically to natural resins, have some of their physical properties, very important in the plastics industry, &c.—*adj.* res′inous, of, like, containing, of the nature of, resin.—*adv.* res′inously. [Fr. *résine*—L. *rēsīna*.]

resist, *ri-zist′*, *v.t.* to strive against: to oppose with success: to be little affected by.—Also *v.i.*—*ns.* resis′tance, act or power of resisting: opposition: (in full, **resistance movement**) opposition, or a party continuing opposition to a foreign occupying power after the country has nominally capitulated: the opposition of a body to the motion of another: that property of a substance in virtue of which the passage of an electric current through it is accompanied with dissipation of energy; resis′tance-box, a box containing resistors; resis′tance-coil, a coil of wire used to offer resistance to the passage of electricity.—*adj.* **resis′tant**, making resistance: (with *to*) habitually unaffected by.—*adj.* **resis′tible**.—*n.* **resistibil′ity**.—*advs.* **resis′tibly**; **resis′tingly**.—*adj.* **resis′tive**.—*n.* **resistiv′ity**, · capacity for resisting: (also, now *obs.*, **specific resistance**) a property of a conducting material expressed as resistance × cross-sectional area over length.—*adj.* **resist′less**, irresistible: unresisting, unable to resist.—*adv.* **resist′lessly**.—*ns.* **resist′lessness**; **resist′or**, a piece of apparatus used to offer electric resistance.—**resistance thermometer** (or **resistance pyrometer**), a device for taking very high temperatures very accurately by means of the variation in the electrical resistance of a wire as the temperature changes.—**line of least resistance**, the easiest course of action. [L. *resistĕre*—*re*-, against, *sistĕre*, to make to stand.]

resoluble, *rez′ol-ū-bl, adj.* that may be resolved, dissolved, analysed.—*adj.* **resolute** (*rez′ol-ūt, -ōōt*), having a fixed purpose, constant in pursuing a purpose, determined.—*adv.* **res′olutely**.—*ns.* **res′oluteness**; **resolution** (*rez-ol-ū′sh(ȯ)n, -ōō′sh(ȯ)n*), act of resolving: analysis: solution: state of being resolved: fixed determination: that which is resolved: (*mus.*) progression from discord to concord: formal proposal in a public assembly: the definition of a picture in TV or facsimile: (*phys., electronics*) the smallest measurable difference, or separation, or time interval: **re-solution** (*rē-sol-*), renewed or repeated solution.—*v.t.* **resolve** (*ri-zolv′*), to separate (into components), to analyse: to solve, to free from doubt or difficulty: to explain: to determine: to pass as a resolution: to disperse, as a tumour: (*mus.*) to make to pass into a concord.—*v.i.* to undergo resolution: to melt: to come to a decision (with *on*).—*n.* anything resolved or determined: resolution, fixed purpose.—*adj.* **resol′vable**.—*n.* **resolvabil′ity**.—*adj.* **resolved′**, fixed in purpose.—*adv.* **resolvedly** (*ri-zol′vid-li*), resolutely.—*n.* **resol′vedness**. [L. *resolvĕre, resolūtum*—*re*-, inten., *solvĕre*, to loose.]

resonance, *rez′on-áns, n.* resounding: sympathetic vibration: sonority: the sound heard in auscultation: (*phys.*) (the state of a system in which) a large vibration (is) produced by a small stimulus of approx. the same frequency as that of the system.—*adj.* **res′onant**, resounding, ringing: vibrating. [L. *resonāre, -ātum*—*re*-, back, *sonāre*, to sound.]

resort, *ri-zört′, v.i.* to go, to betake oneself: to have recourse (to—usu. some action, e.g. violence) in difficulty.—*n.* act of resorting: a place much frequented: a haunt.—**in the last resort**, as a last expedient. [O.Fr. *resortir* (Fr. *ressortir*), to rebound, retire—*sortir*, to go out.]

resound, *ri-zownd′, v.t.* to echo: to sound with reverberation: to sound or spread (the praises of).—*v.i.* to echo: to re-echo, reverberate: to sound sonorously.—*p.adj.* **resound′ing**, echoing: thorough, decisive. [Pfx. **re-**, and **sound**.]

resource, *ri-sōrs′, -sörs′, n.* source or possibility of help: an expedient: (*pl.*) means of raising money, means of support: means of self-occupation: resourcefulness.—*adj.* **resource′-**

ful, rich in expedients.—*n.* **resource′fulness**. [O.Fr. *ressource*—*resourdre*—L. *resurgĕre*, to rise again.]

respect, *ri-spekt′, v.t.* to relate to, to refer to: to feel or show esteem, deference or honour to: to refrain from violating, treat with consideration (e.g. a person's privacy, innocence, desire not to discuss).—*n.* a particular: reference: regard: esteem: deferential behaviour: (often in *pl.*) a greeting or message of esteem.—*adj.* **respec′table**, worthy of respect: considerable: passable, mediocre: fairly well-to-do: decent and well-behaved, reputable.—*adv.* **respec′tably**.—*n.* **respectabil′ity**.—*adj.* **respect′ful**, showing or feeling respect.—*adv.* **respect′fully**.—*prep.* **respec′ting**, concerning.—*adj.* **respec′tive**, particular or several, relating to each distributively (e.g. *in their respective places*; *the respective claims, merits, of*).—*adv.* **respec′tively**, in the order indĭcated (e.g. *Books I, II, and III have respectively yellow, red, and blue covers*).—**respect of persons**, undue favour, as for wealth, &c.—**in respect of**, in the matter of; **with respect to**, with regard to. [L. *respicĕre, respectum*—*re*-, back, *specĕre*, to look.]

respire, *ri-spīr′, v.i.* to breathe: to take breath.—*v.t.* to breathe in and out: (*rare*) to exhale.—*adj.* **respirable** (*res′pir-á-bl, ri-spīr′á-bl*).—*ns.* **respiration** (*res-pir-ā′sh(ȯ)n*), breathing: a breath; **res′pirător**, an appliance worn on the mouth or nose to filter and warm the air breathed: a gas-mask.—*adj.* **respiratory** (*ri-spir′a-tör-i, res′pir-ā-tör-i, ri-spīr′a-tör-i*), of or for respiration. [L. *respīrāre, -ātum*—*re*-, signifying repetition, *spīrāre*, to breathe.]

respite, *res′pīt, -pit, n.* temporary cessation of something that is tiring or painful: postponement requested or granted: (*law*) temporary suspension of the execution of a criminal.—*v.t.* to grant a respite to: to relieve by a pause: to delay, postpone (something disagreeable, e.g. punishment): to grant postponement to. [O.Fr. *respit* (Fr. *répit*)—L. *respectus*, respect.]

resplendent, *ri-splen′dént, adj.* very splendid, gorgeous, shining ·brilliantly.—*ns.* **resplen′dence, resplen′dency**.—*adv.* **resplen′dently**. [L. *resplendēre*—*re*-, inten., *splendēre*, to shine.]

respond, *ri-spond′, v.i.* to answer: to utter liturgical responses: to act in answer: to react.—*adj.* **respon′dent**, answering: corresponding: responsive.—*n.* one who answers: one who refutes objections: a defendant, esp. in a divorce suit: (*math.*) the quantity dependent on the argument (q.v.).—*ns.* **respond′er**, one who or that which responds: the part of a transponder which replies automatically to the correct interrogation signal; **response′**, an answer: oracular answer: answer made by the congregation to the priest during divine service: a reaction to stimulus: an action or feeling incited by the request, action, &c., of another person or by an occurrence.—*adj.* **respon′sible**, liable to be called upon to answer (to): answerable (for): deserving the blame or credit of (with for): morally answerable (for): governed by a sense of responsibility: trustworthy: involving responsibility.—*n.* **responsibil′ity**, state of being responsible: what one is responsible for.—*adv.* **respon′-**

Neutral vowels in unaccented syllables: *em′pér-ór*; for certain sounds in foreign words see p. ix.

622

sibly.—*n.pl.* **respon'sions** (-*shónz*), the first of the three examinations for the B.A. degree at Oxford, 'smalls'.—*adj.* **respon'sive**, ready to respond: answering: correspondent.—*adv.* **respon'sively.** [L. *respondēre*, *responsum*—*re*-, back, *spondēre*, to promise.]

rest, *rest*, *n.* repose, refreshing inactivity: intermission of, or freedom from, motion: tranquillity: a place for resting (e.g. a *travellers' rest*): a prop or support (e.g. for a musket, a billiard cue, &c.): a pause in speaking or reading: an interval of silence in music, or a mark indicating it.—*v.i.* to repose: to be at ease: to be still: to be supported, to lean (on): to put trust (in): to have foundation (in, on): to remain: (*theatrical slang*), to be unemployed.—*v.t.* to give rest to: to place or hold in support: to lean: to base.—*ns.* **rest'-centre**, a place of shelter for numbers of people driven from their homes by an emergency; **rest'(-)cure**, treatment consisting of inactivity and quiet.—*adj.* **rest'ful**, at rest: rest-giving: tranquil.—*adv.* **rest'fully.**—*ns.* **rest'fulness**; **rest'-home**, an establishment for those who need special care and attention, e.g. invalids, old people, &c.; **rest'house**, a house of rest for travellers; **rest'ing-place**, a place where rest may be taken, esp. the grave.—*adj.* **rest'less**, without rest, unresting: uneasily active, impatient of inactivity.—*adv.* **rest'lessly.**—*n.* **rest'lessness.—at rest**, stationary, motionless: free from disquiet. [O.E. *rest*, *ræst*; Ger. *rast*, Du *rust*: converging and merging in meaning with the following word.]

rest, *rest*, *n.* remainder: all others.—*v.i.* to remain.—**for the rest**, as regards other matters. [Fr. *reste*—L. *restāre*, to remain—*re*-, back, *stāre*, to stand.]

restaurant, *res'tó-rā*, *-ront*, *-rong*, *n.* a house where meals may be had.—*n.* **restaurateur** (*res-tór-a-tœr'*), the keeper of a restaurant. [Fr.—*restaurer*, to restore.]

rest-harrow, *rest'-har'ō*, *n.* a common wildflower with pink, butterfly-shaped flowers and long, tough roots which tend to *arrest* the *harrow* on neglected land; hence its name.

restitution, *res-ti-tū'sh(ó)n*, *n.* act of restoring what was lost or taken away: amends: restoration: (of an elastic body) return to former shape. [L. *restituěre*, *-ūtum*—*re*-, again, *statuěre*, to make to stand.]

restive, *res'tiv*, *adj.* unwilling to go forward: obstinate, refractory, uneasy, as if ready to break from control.—*adv.* **res'tively.**—*n.* **res'tiveness.** [O.Fr. *restif*—L. *restāre*, to rest.]

restore, *ri-stōr'*, *-stör'*, *v.t.* to bring, put, or give back: to re-establish (e.g. peace): to reinstate (e.g. a ruler): to repair: to bring back to a known or conjectured former state: to supply (a part) by conjecture: to cure (a person).—*n.* **restoration** (*res-tō-rā'sh(ó)n*), act of restoring: renovation and reconstruction of a building, painting, &c.: a model, &c., of a conjectured original form.—*adj.* **restorative** (*ris-tōr'-a-tiv*, or *-tor'-*), tending to restore, esp. to strength and vigour.—*n.* a medicine that restores.—*adv.* **restor'atively.**—*n.* **restor'er.** [O.Fr. *restorer*—L. *restaurāre*, *-ātum.*]

restrain, *ri-strān'*, *v.t.* to hold back (from): to control: to subject to forcible repression.—*adj.*

restrained', controlled: self-controlled: free from excess.—*ns.* **restrain'edness**; **restraint'**, act of restraining: state of being restrained: a restraining influence: want of liberty: artistic control or reticence: reserve.—**restraint of trade**, interference with freedom of trade, e.g. by means of monopolies. [O.Fr. *restraindre*, *restrai(g)nant*—L. *restringěre*, *restrictum*—*re*-, back, *stringěre*, to draw tightly.]

restrict, *ri-strikt'*, *v.t.* to limit.—*p.adj.* **restrict'ed.**—*n.* **restric'tion**, act of restricting: limitation: confinement: a limiting or restraining regulation.—*adj.* **restric'tive**, restricting: tending to restrict.—*adv.* **restric'tively.** **—restricted area**, one from which certain classes of people are excluded: one in which there is a speed limit; **restrictive practice**, a trade practice that is against the public interest, as e.g. an agreement to sell only to certain buyers or to keep up resale prices: used also of certain trade union practices, as the closed shop, demarcation, working to rule. [L. *restringěre*, *restrictum*.]

result, *ri-zult'*, *v.i.* to issue (with *in*): to follow as a consequence.—*n.* consequence: effect: quantity obtained by calculation: decision, resolution, as of a council.—*adj.* **resul'tant**, resulting.—*n.* a force compounded of two or more forces. [L. *resultāre*, to leap back—*saltāre*, to leap.]

resume, *ri-zūm'*, *-zōōm'*, *v.t.* to take back: to put on again: to take up again: to summarise: (also *v.i.*) to begin again, continue after an interruption.—*adj.* **resum'able.**—*ns.* **résumé** (*rā-zū-mā*, *rez'ū-mā*; Fr. *pa.p.*), a summary, **resumption** (*ri-zump'sh(ó)n*, or *-zum'-*), act of resuming.—*adj.* **resump'tive.**—*adv.* **resump'tively.** [L. *resūmĕre*, *-sumptum*—*re*-, back, *sumĕre*, to take.]

resurge, *ri-sûrj'*, *v.i.* to rise again.—*n.* **resur'gence.**—*adj.* **resur'gent**, in a robel, esp. against political oppression. [L. *resurgěre*, *resurrectum*—*re*-, again, *surgěre*, to rise.]

resurrect, *rez-ûr-ekt'*, *v.t.* to restore to life.—*ns.* **resurrec'tion**, rising from the dead: resuscitation; **resurrectionist**, **resurrection-man**, (*hist.*) one who stole dead bodies for dissection; **resurrection-pie**, a dish compounded of remnants of former meals. [Same root as **resurge**.]

resuscitate, *ri-sus'i-tat*, *v.t.* and *v.i.* to revive.—*n.* **resuscita'tion.**—*adj.* **resus'citative**, tending to resuscitate, reviving, revivifying, reanimating.—*n.* **resusc'itātor**, one who, or that which resuscitates: an oxygen-administering apparatus used to induce breathing after asphyxiation. [L. *resuscitāre*, *-ātum*—*re*-, *sus-* (*sub-*), from beneath, *citāre*, to put into quick motion—*ciēre*, to make to go.]

ret, *ret*, *v.t.* to expose to moisture.—*v.t.* and *v.i.* to soften, spoil, or rot by soaking:—*pr.p.* **rett'ing**; *pa.t.* and *pa.p.* **rett'ed.** [App. akin to **rot.**]

retail, *rē'tāl*, *n.* sale to consumer, or in small quantities.—*adj.* pertaining to such sale.—*v.t.* (*ri-*, *rē-tāl'*), to sell by retail: to repeat in detail: to pass on by report.—*n.* **retail'er.** [O.Fr. *retail*, piece cut off—*re*-, again, *tailler*, to cut.]

retain, *ri-tān'*, *v.t.* to keep: to hold back: to continue to keep, to hold secure: to reserve the services of, by a preliminary fee.—*adj.* **re-**

tain'able.—n. **retain'er,** one who or that which retains: a person attached to, and owing service to, a family: a retaining fee.—**retaining fee,** the advance fee paid to a lawyer to defend a cause; **retaining wall,** a wall to hold back solid material, as earth or (loosely) water. [Fr. retenir—L. retinēre—re-, back, tenēre, to hold.]

retaliate, ri-tal'i-āt, v.t. to repay in kind (now usu. an injury).—v.i. to return like for like.—n. **retaliā'tion,** return of like for like: imposition of counter-tariffs.—adjs. **retal'iātive, retal'iatory** (-āt-ór-i, -at-ór-i). [L. retāliāre, -ātum—re-, in return, tālio, -ōnis, like for like—tālis, such.]

retard, ri-tärd', v.t. to slow, to delay.—Also v.i.—n. **retardā'tion** (rē-), slowing: delay: lag.—adj. **retar'ded,** slow in development, mental or physical, or having made less than normal progress in learning. [L. retardāre, -ātum—re-, inten., tardāre, to slow.]

retch, rech, v.i. to strain as if to vomit. [O.E. hrǣcan.]

retention, ri-ten'sh(ó)n, n. act or power of retaining: memory: custody: (med.) abnormal retaining in the body.—adj. **reten'tive,** retaining: tenacious.—adv. **reten'tively.**—n. **reten'tiveness.** [L. retentiō, -ōnis; Fr. retentif. See **retain.**]

retexture, rē-teks'chér, v.t. to treat (a material) so as to restore firmness lost through the action of spirit in process of dry-cleaning. [L. re-, again, and **texture.**]

rethink, rē-thingk', v.t. to consider again and come to a different decision about.—Also n. [L. re-, again, and **think.**]

reticent, ret'i-sént, adj. reserved or sparing in communication.—ns. **ret'icence, ret'icency.** [L. reticēns, -entis, pr.p. of reticēre—re-, tacēre, to be silent.]

reticle, ret'i-kl, n. an attachment to an optical instrument consisting of a network of lines of reference.—adj. **reticular** (ré-tik'ū-lár), netted: netlike: reticulated.—v.t. **retic'ulate,** to form into, or mark with, a network: to distribute (e.g. water, electricity) by a network.—adj. netted: marked with network: net-veined.—p.adj. **retic'ulated,** reticulate.—ns. **reticulā'tion,** network: netlike structure; **reticule** (ret'i-kūl), a reticle: a small bag, orig. and properly of network, formerly carried by ladies. [L. rēticulum, dim. of rēte, net.]

retiform, rē'ti-förm, adj. having the form of a net. [L. rēte, net, förma, form.]

retina, ret'i-na, n. the layer of the eye that is sensitive to light and receives the image formed by the lens. [L.L. rētina, app.—L. rēte, net.]

retinue, ret'i-nū, n. a body of retainers: a suite or train. [Fr. retenue, pa.p. of retenir. See **retain.**]

retire, ri-tīr', v.i. to withdraw: to retreat: to recede: to withdraw from office, business, profession, &c. (esp. on reaching a certain age): to go to bed.—v.t. to withdraw: to draw back: to cause to retire.—n. **reti'ral,** giving up of office, business, &c. (more usu. **retirement**): withdrawal (e.g. from the market).—adj. **retired',** withdrawn: reserved in manner: secluded: withdrawn from business.—n.

retire'ment, act of retiring: state of being retired: solitude: privacy.—p.adj. **reti'ring,** retreating: reserved, unobtrusive, modest.—**retired list,** a list of officers who are relieved from active service but receive a certain amount of pay (**retired pay**). [Fr. retirer—re-, back, tirer, to draw.]

retort, ri-tört', v.t. to throw back (fig., e.g. a charge, an incivility—obs. in literal sense): to return upon an assailant or opponent: to answer in retaliation, sharply, or wittily.—v.i. to make a sharp reply.—n. retaliation: a ready and sharp or witty answer: a vessel used in distillation, typically a flask with long bent-back neck. [L. retorquēre, retortum—re-, back, torquēre, to twist.]

retouch, rē-tuch', v.t. to touch again: to touch up, seek to improve by new touches.—n. an act of touching up.—n. **retouch'er.** [L. re-, again, and **touch.**]

retrace, rē-trās', v.t. to trace back: to go back upon: to renew the outline of. [L. re-, back, and **trace** (1).]

retract, ri-trakt', v.t. to draw back: to withdraw, to revoke, to unsay.—v.i. to take back, or draw back from, what has been said or granted.—adj. **retrac'table,** able to be drawn back or withdrawn: of an aeroplane undercarriage, that can be drawn up into the body or wings: that can be drawn up towards the body of a vehicle.—n. **retractā'tion** (rē-), revoking, recantation.—adj. **retrac'tile** (-tīl), that may be drawn back.—n. **retrac'tion,** drawing back: retractation.—adj. **retrac'tive,** tending to retract.—adv. **retrac'tively.** [Mainly from L. retrahēre, retractum; partly from retractāre, retractātum; both from re-, back, trahēre, to draw.]

retread, rē-tred', v.t. to tread again: to make a new tread on (a worn pneumatic tyre). [Pfx. re-, and **tread.**]

retreat, ri-trēt', n. withdrawal: an orderly withdrawal before an enemy, or from a position of danger or difficulty: a signal for withdrawal or retirement: seclusion: place of privacy, seclusion, refuge, or quiet.—v.i. to draw back: to retire: to recede.—**beat a retreat** (see **beat**). [O.Fr. retret, -e, pa.p. of retraire—L. retrahēre; to draw back.]

retrench, rē-trench', -sh', v.t. to cut off, out, down: to protect by a retrenchment.—v.i. to cut down expenses.—n. **retrench'ment,** an act of retrenching: economy: a work within another for prolonging defence. [O.Fr. retrencher (Fr. retrancher)—re-, off, trencher, to cut. See **trench.**]

retribution, ret-ri-bū'sh(ó)n, n. requital (now esp. of evil).—adj. **retrib'utive** (ri-), involving retribution, punishing suitably. [L. retribuĕre, -būtum, to give back—re-, back, tribuĕre, to give.]

retrieve, ri-trēv', v.t. to search for and fetch, as a dog does game: to recover, repossess: to rescue (from, out of): to restore (e.g. one's fortunes, credit): to make good, repair (e.g. a loss, a disaster).—adj. **retriev'able.**—adv. **retriev'ably.**—ns. **retriev'al,** retrieving; **retriev'er,** a dog trained to find and fetch game that has been shot. [O.Fr. retrover-, retreuv-, stressed stem of retrover (Fr. retrouver)—re-,

Neutral vowels in unaccented syllables: em'pér-ór; for certain sounds in foreign words see p. ix.

624

again, *trouver*, to find.]

retro-, *ret'ro-*, *pfx.* backwards: behind. [L. *retrō*, backward.]

retroact, *ret-rō-akt'*, or *rē-tro-akt'*, *v.i.* to act backward on, take effect in the case of, something past or preceding.—*n.* **retroac'tion.**—*adj.* **retroac'tive**, having efficacy in a time prior to enactment, imposition, &c.—*adv.* **retroac'-tively.** [L. *retroagĕre*, *-actum*—*retrō*, backward, *agĕre*, to do.]

retrocession, *ret-rō-sesh'(ò)n*, *n.* a moving back: a giving back. [L. *retrōcēdĕre*, *-cessum* cēdĕre, to go, yield; partly from *retrō*, backward, and **cede** or Fr. *céder*.]

retrograde, *ret'rō-grād*, or *rē'trō-*, *adj.* going backward: falling from better to worse: reverting.—*n.* one who degenerates.—*v.i.* to go back or backwards.—*ns.* **retrogradation** (*-grā-dā'sh(ò)n*); **retrogression** (*-gresh'(ò)n*), a going backward: a decline in quality or merit.—*adj.* **retrogress'ive.**—*adv.* **retrogress'-ively.** [L. *retrōgradus*, going backward, *retrō-gressus*, retrogression—*retrō*, backward, *gradī, gressus*, to go.]

retro-rocket, *ret-*, *ret'rō-rok'et*, *n.* a rocket whose function is to slow down, fired in a direction opposite to that in which a body, e.g. a spacecraft, an artificial satellite, is travelling. [L. *retrō*, back, and **rocket.**]

retrospect, *ret'rō-spekt*, or *rē'trō-*, *n.* a looking back: a contemplation of the past.—*n.* **retro-spec'tion.**—*adj.* **retrospec'tive**, looking back in time: retroactive: characterised by, addicted to, the habit of looking back to the past.—*adv.* **retrospec'tively.** [L. *retrō*, back, *specĕre, spectum*, to look.]

retroussé, *ré-trōōs'ā*, *rè-trōōs-ā'*, *adj.* turned up (esp. of the nose). [Fr. *retrousser* (p.p. *re-troussé*), to turn up.]

retry, *rē-trī'*, *v.t.* to try again (judicially).—*pr.p.* **retry'ing**; *pa.t.* and *pa.p.* **retried'.**—*n.* **retri'al.** [L. *re-*, again, and **try.**]

return, *ri-tûrn'*, *v.i.* to come or go back: to revert: to recur.—*v.t.* to give, put, cast, bring or send back: to answer, to retort: to report officially to give in return: to render (e.g. thanks).—*n.* the act of returning: something returned (often in *pl.*): a recurrence: reversion: that which comes in exchange: proceeds, profit, yield: recompense: requital: an answer: an official report: (*pl.*) a light-coloured mild tobacco (orig. refuse): a return ticket.—*adj.* **retur'nable.**—**returning officer,** the officer who presides at an election; **return match,** a second match played by the same set of players, **return ticket,** a ticket entitling a passenger to travel to a place and back to his starting-point.—**by return (of post),** by the next post leaving in the return direction. [Fr. *retourner*—*re-*, back, *tourner*, to turn.]

reunion, *rē-ūn'yòn*, *n.* a union or a meeting after separation: a social gathering [Fr. *réunion*—*re-*, again, *union*, union.]

reunite, *rē-ū-nīt'*, *v.t.* and *v.i.* to join after separation. [L. *re-*, again, and **unite.**]

rev, *rev*, *v.t.* to increase the speed of revolution in (often with *up*).—*v.i.* to revolve: to increase in speed of revolution:—*pr.p.* **revv'ing**; *pa.t.* and *pa.p.* **revved.** [From **revolution.**]

revanche, *ri-vänch'*, *n.* revenge: policy directed

towards recovery of territory lost to an enemy.—*ns.* **revanch'ism, revanch'ist.** [Fr.]

reveal, *ri-vēl'*, *v.t.* to make known by divine agency or inspiration: to disclose: to make visible.—*n.* and *adj.* **reveal'ing.** [O.Fr. *reveler* (Fr. *révéler*)—L. *revēlāre*—*re-*, the reverse of, *vēlāre*, to veil.]

reveille, *ri-val'i*, *ri-vel'i*, *ri-vāl'yi*, *n.* the sound of the drum or bugle at daybreak to awaken soldiers. [Fr. *réveillez*, awake, imper. of *ré-veiller*—L. *re-*, *vigilāre*, to watch.]

revel, *rev'l*, *v.i.* to feast or make merry in a riotous or noisy manner: to take intense delight (with *in*):—*pr.p.* **rev'elling**; *pa.t.* and *pa.p.* **rev'elled.**—*n.* a riotous feast: (often in *pl.*) merry-making.—*ns.* **rev'eller; rev'elry,** revelling. [O.Fr. *reveler*—L. *rebellāre*, to rebel.]

revelation, *rev-é-lā'sh(ò)n*, *n.* the act or experience of revealing: that which is revealed: an illuminating experience: divine or supernatural communication: (*cap.*) the Apocalypse or last book of the New Testament. [L. *re-vēlāre*, *-ātum*. See **reveal**.]

revenant, *rev'nä*, *rev'é-nänt*, *n.* one who returns from the dead, a ghost. [Fr.]

revenge, *ri-venj'*, *-venzh'*, *v.t.* to inflict injury in retribution for: (*esp. reflex.*) to avenge.—*n.* (act of inflicting) a malicious injury in return for an injury received: the desire for retaliation: its satisfaction.—*adj.* **revenge'ful,** ready to seek revenge.—*adv.* **revenge'fully.**—*ns.* **revenge'fulness; reveng'er.** [O.Fr. *revenger, revencher* (Fr. *revancher*)—L. *re-*, in return, *vindicāre*, to lay claim to.]

revenue, *rev'én-ū*, *n.* receipts or return from any source, as income: the income of a state.—*n.* **rev'enue-cutt'er,** an armed vessel employed in preventing smuggling.—**Inland Revenue,** revenue from stamps, excise, income-tax, &c. [Fr. *revenue*, pa.p. of *revenir*, to return—L. *revenīre*—*re-*, back, *venīre*, to come.]

reverberate, *ri-vûr'bér-āt*, *v.t.* to send back, to reflect (light, heat, esp. sound): to heat in a reverberatory furnace.—*v.i.* to recoil, rebound, be reflected: to re-echo, resound.—*adj.* **re-ver'berant**, reverberating.—*n.* **reverbera'tion.**—*adj.* **rever'beratory** (*-āt-òr-i*, or *-āt-*).—**reverberatory furnace,** a furnace in which the flame is turned back over the substance to be heated. [L. *reverberāre*, *-ātum*—*re-*, back, *verberāre*, to beat—*verber*, a lash.]

revere, *ri-vēr'*, *v.t.* to regard with high respect, to venerate.—*n.* **reverence** (*rev'ér-éns*), high respect: respectful awe: state of being held in high respect: a gesture or observance of respect: Irish title of respect for a cleric.—*v.t.* to venerate, regard with respect: to treat with respect.—*adjs.* **rev'erend,** worthy of reverence: clerical; **Reverend** (usu. written Rev.), a title prefixed to a clergyman's name; **rev'er-ent,** feeling or showing reverence; **reverential** (*-en'sh(à)l*), proceeding from reverence: reverent: respectful.—*advs.* **reveren'tially, rev'-erently.** [O.Fr. *reverer* (Fr. *révérer*)—L. *rev-erērī*—*re-*, inten., *verērī*, to feel awe.]

reverie, revery, *rev'é-ri*, *n.* an undirected train of thoughts or fancies in meditation: mental abstraction: a waking dream, a brown study. [Fr. *rêverie*—*rêver*, to dream.]

revers, *ri-vēr'*, *n.* any part of a garment that is

turned back, as a lapel:—*pl.* **revers** (-*vērz'*). [Fr.,—L. *reversus.*]

reverse, ri-vûrs', *v.t.* to turn the other way about, as upside down, outside in, &c.: to invert: to set moving backwards: to annul.—*v.i.* to move backwards: to set an engine moving backwards.—*n.* the contrary, opposite: the back, esp. of a coin or medal (opp. to *obverse*): a set-back, misfortune, defeat: a reversing gear, &c.—*adj.* contrary, opposite: turned about: reversing (e.g. *a reverse gear*).—*n.* **rever'sal**, act or fact of reversing or being reversed.—*adj.* **rever'sible.**—*n.* a fabric having both sides well finished.—*n.* **rever'sion**, the act or fact of reverting or of returning: that which reverts or returns: the return, or the future possession (of any property) after some particular event: the right to future possession.—*adj.* **rever'sionary**, of the nature of a reversion: involving reversion.—**reverse the charges**, to charge a telephone call to the one who receives it instead of to the caller. [L. *reversāre*, to turn round, and *reversus*, turned round; partly through Fr.]

revert, ri-vûrt', *v.t.* to turn (the eyes) back.—*v.i.* to return: to fall back (to a former state): to recur (to a former subject): to return (to the original owner or his heirs).—*adj.* **rever'tible.** [L. *re-*, *vertĕre*, to turn.]

review, ri-vū', *n.* a viewing again, a reconsideration: a general survey (*to take a review of*, *pass in review*): (*law*) a revision: a descriptive and critical account (of e.g. a book, play), a critique: a periodical with critiques of books, &c.: a display and inspection of troops or ships.—*v.t.* to re-examine: to examine critically: to write a critique on: to inspect, as troops.—*n.* **review'er**, a writer of critiques: a writer in a review. [Partly pfx. **re-**, and **view**; partly Fr. *revue*, fem. of *revu*, pa.p. of *revoir*—L. *revidēre*—*vidēre*, to see.]

revile, ri-vīl', *v.t.* to assail with bitter abuse.—*ns.* **revile'ment**; **revil'er**. [O.Fr. *reviler*—L. *re-*, inten., *vīlis*, worthless.]

revise, ri-vīz', *v.t.* to examine and correct: to make a new, improved version of: to study anew.—*n.* review: a later proof-sheet embodying previous corrections.—*ns.* **revī'sal**, revision; **revī'ser** (also **-or**); **revision** (-*vizh'-* (*ò*)*n*), act, or product, of revising; **revī'sionist**, an advocate of revision (e.g. of a treaty): a Communist favouring modification of stricter orthodox Communism, and evolution, rather than revolution, as a means of achieving world domination: a reviser of the Bible.—**Revised Version**, an English translation of the Bible, issued 1881-5. [Fr. *reviser* and L. *revīsĕre*—*re-*, *vīsĕre*, inten. of *vidēre*, to see.]

revive, ri-vīv', *v.t.* to bring back to life, vigour, memory, notice, use, the stage, &c.—*v.i.* to come back to life, good spirits, &c.—*ns.* **revī'val**, act or fact of reviving: recovery from languor, neglect, depression, &c.: renewed performance of, as of a play: renewed interest or attention: a time of extraordinary religious awakening; **revī'valist**, one who promotes religious or other revivals; **revī'valism**; **revī'ver**, one who, or that which, revives: a renovating preparation.—**Gothic Revival**, the resuscitation of Gothic architecture in (and before) the

19th century; **Revival of Learning**, the Renaissance. [L. *revīvĕre*, to live again—*vīvĕre*, to live.]

revivify, ri-viv'i-fī, *v.t.* to restore to life: to put new life into:—*pr.p.* reviv'ifying; *pa.t.* and *pa.p.* reviv'ified.—*n.* **revivifica'tion**. [L.L. *revivificāre*—*re-*, *vīvus*, alive, *facĕre*, to make.]

revoke, ri-vōk', *v.t.* to annul: to retract.—*v.i.* to make revocations, to rescind one's authority, permission, &c.: to neglect to follow suit (at cards).—*n.* revocation, recall: act of revoking at cards.—*adj.* **revocable** (*rev'ō-kà-bl*).—*ns.* **rev'ocableness**, **revocabil'ity**.—*adv.* **rev'ocably**.—*n.* **revoca'tion**, act of revoking: repeal, reversal. [L. *revocāre*—*re-*, back, *vocāre*, to call.]

revolt, ri-vōlt', *v.t.* to renounce allegiance, to rise in opposition: to go over (to): to rise in disgust or loathing (at, against).—*v.t.* to disgust.—*n.* rebellion: insurrection: secession.—*n.* **revol'ter**.—*adj.* **revol'ting**, repulsive.—*adv.* **revol'tingly**. [Fr. *révolter*—L. *re-*, *volūtāre*, freq. of *volvĕre*, *volūtum*, to turn.]

revolution, rev-ol-ōō'sh(ò)n, or -*ū'*-, *n.* act or condition of revolving: motion round a centre: a complete turn by an object or figure, through four right angles, about an axis: a cycle of phenomena or of time: a great upheaval: a complete change, e.g. in outlook, social habits or circumstances: a radical change, often accompanied by violence, esp. in government.—*adj.* **revolu'tionary**, of, favouring, or of the nature of, revolution, esp. in government or conditions.—*v.t.* **revolu'tionise**, to cause radical change in.—*n.* **revolu'tionist**, one who favours revolution. [L.L. *revolūtiō, -ōnis*—L. *revolvĕre*; see **revolt**.]

revolve, ri-volv', *v.t.* and *v.i.* to ponder: to move about a centre, to rotate.—*adj.* **revolute** (*rev'-ol-ūt*), rolled backward.—*n.* **revol'ver**, a revolving device of various kinds: a pistol with a rotating magazine. [L. *revolvĕre*, *revolūtum*—*re-*, back, *volvĕre*, to roll.]

revue, ri-vū', *n.* a loosely constructed theatrical show, more or less topical and musical. [Fr.]

revulsion, ri-vul'sh(ò)n, *n.* disgust: a sudden change or reversal, esp. of feeling: (*med.*) diversion to another part, esp. by counter-irritation.—*adj.* **revul'sive**. [L. *revellĕre*, *revulsum*, to pluck back, *vellĕre*, to pluck.]

reward, ri-wörd', *n.* that which is given in return for good (sometimes evil), or in recognition of merit, or for performance of a service.—*v.t.* to give or be a reward to or for: (*B.*) to give as a reward.—*adj.* **reward'ing**, of an activity, study, &c., giving pleasure or profit. [O.Fr. *rewarder*, *regarder*—*re-*, again, *warder*, *garder*, to guard; cf. **regard**, **guard**, **ward**.]

Reynard, **reynard**, *rān'-* or *ren'ärd*, -*ärd*, *n.* a fox, from the name given to the fox in the famous beast epic of Low Ger. origin, *Reynard the Fox*. [Middle Du. *Reynaerd*—O.H.G. *Reginhart*, lit. strong in counsel.]

rhabdomancy, *rab'dō-man-si*, *n.* divination by rod, esp. the finding of water, &c., by means of the divining-rod. [Gr. *rhabdos*, rod, *manteiā*, divination.]

rhadamanthine, *rad-a-man'thīn*, *adj.* rigorously just and severe, like *Rhadamanthus* (Gr. *-os*), a judge of the lower world.

Neutral vowels in unaccented syllables: *em'pér-òr*; for certain sounds in foreign words see p. ix.

Rhaeto-Romanic, *rē'tō-rō-man'ik*, *n.* a general name for a group of Romance dialects spoken from south-eastern Switzerland to Friuli (a district north of the Gulf of Venice). [From L. *Rhaetia*, a province of the Roman Empire, and *Rōmānicus*, Roman.]

rhapsody, *raps'o-di*, *n.* (*Gr. hist.*) an epic or instalment of an epic recited at one time: any wild or unconnected composition: an ecstatic utterance of feeling: an irregular emotional piece of music.—*adjs.* **rhapsodic** (*-od'ik*), of the nature of rhapsody: **rhapsod'ical**, rhapsodic: emotionally enthusiastic.—*adv.* **rhapsod'ically**.—*v.t.* **rhap'sodise**, to recite in rhapsodies.—*v.i.* to write or utter rhapsodies.—*n.* **rhap'sodist**. [Gr. *rhapsōidiā*, an epic, a rigmarole—*rhaptein*, to sew, *ōide*, a song.]

rhea, *rē'a*, *n.* a genus of S. American ostriches. [Gr. *Rhēā*, mother of Zeus.]

Rhenish, *ren'ish*, *adj.* of the river *Rhine*.—*n.* Rhine wine. [L. *Rhēnus*, the Rhine.]

rhenium, *rē'ni-ùm*, *n.* a very rare metallic element (symbol Re; at. no. 75). [L. *Rhēnus*, Rhine.]

rheology, *rē-ol'o-ji*, *n.* the science of flow of matter—the critical study of elasticity, viscosity, and plasticity. [From Gr. *rheos*, flow, *logos*, discourse.]

rhesus (monkey), *rē'sùs*, *n.* an Indian monkey, used in blood-tests, and giving its name to the **Rh-factor** (Rhesus factor), a blood group factor in the red blood cells of rhesus monkeys and those of the majority of human beings (said to be Rh-positive); a small percentage of human beings lack this factor and are said to be Rh-negative.

rhetoric, *ret'ór-ik*, *n.* the theory and practice of eloquence, whether spoken or written: the art of literary expression, esp. in prose: false, showy, or declamatory expression.—*adj.* **rhetor'ical**, pertaining to rhetoric: oratorical: ornate or insincere in style.—*adv.* **rhetor'ically**.—*n.* **rhetorician** (*ret-ór-ish'(á)n*), one who teaches the art of rhetoric: an orator.—**rhetorical question**, a question in form, for rhetorical effect, not calling for an answer. [Gr. *rhētōr*, a public speaker.]

rheum, *rōōm*, *n.* mucous discharge.—*adj.* **rheumat'ic**, of the nature of, pertaining to, affected with, rheumatism.—*n.* one who suffers from rheumatism.—*n.* **rheum'atism**, diseases causing inflammation and pain in muscles, joints.—*adj.* **rheum'atoid**, resembling rheumatism.—*n.* **rheumatol'ogy**, the study of rheumatism.—*adj.* **rheum'y**, **rheumatic fever**, an acute disease characterised by fever, multiple arthritis, and liability of the heart to be inflamed, and which is caused by a streptococcal infection. [Gr. *rheuma*, gen. *-atos*—*rheein*, to flow.]

rhinal, *rī'nàl*, *adj.* of the nose.—*n.* **rhini'tis**, inflammation of the mucous membrane of the nose. [Gr. *rhīs*, gen. *rhīnos*, nose.]

rhinoceros, *rī-nos'ér-os*, *n.* a family of large animals in Africa and southern Asia, having a very thick skin, and one or two horns on the nose:—*pl.* **rhinoc'eroses**. [Gr. *rhīnokerōs*, gen. *-ōtos*—*keras*, horn, *rhīs*, gen. *rhīnos*, nose.]

rhizome, *rī'zōm*, *n.* a rootstock, an underground stem producing roots and leafy shoots. [Gr.

rhizōma, a root mass—*rhizā*, root.]

rhodium, *rō'di-ùm*, *n.* a metallic element (symbol Rh; atomic no. 45), resembling platinum. [From Gr. *rhodon*, rose—some of its salts are rose-coloured.]

rhododendron, *rō-dō-den'dron* or *rod-*, *n.* a genus of trees and shrubs of the heath family, with evergreen leaves and large, beautiful flowers. [Gr. *rhodon*, rose, *dendron*, tree.]

rhodomontade. Same as **rodomontade**.

rhomb, *rom(b)*, *n.* a parallelogram having its sides equal but its angles usu. not right angles.—*adjs.* **rhombic** (*rom'bik*), shaped like a rhombus; **rhom'boid**, like a rhombus.—*n.* a parallelogram whose adjacent sides are unequal and whose angles are not right angles.—*adj.* **rhomboid'al**, more or less like a rhomboid.—*n.* **rhom'bus**, (*geom.*) a rhomb: an object shaped like a rhomb:—*pl.* **rhombi** (*-bī*). [Gr. *rhombos*, bull-roarer, magic wheel, rhombus.]

rhubarb, *rōō'bärb*, *n.* a genus of plants, the leaf-stalks of which are much used in cooking, and (*chiefly in medicine*) (*slang*) a row, squabble. (*slang*) nonsense. [O.Fr. *reubarbe*, through Low L.—Gr. *rhā*, rhubarb (*Rhā*, the Volga), and L. *barbarum* (neut.; Gr. *barbaron*), foreign.]

rhumb, *rum*, *n.* any point of the compass.—*n.* **rhumb'line**, a line which cuts all the meridians at the same angle. [Fr. *rumb*, or Sp. or Port. *rumbo*—L. *rhombus*—Gr. *rhombos*. See **rhomb**.]

rhyme, rime, *rīm*, *n.* the correspondence of sounds at the ends of verses: poetry: a short poem: a word that corresponds in its accented vowel and succeeding sounds with a specified word (e.g. *mean, sincere', sen'sible*, are rhymes respectively for *screen, revere', reprehen'sible*).—*v.i.* to correspond in sound in such a way (with, to): to make rhymes or verses.—*v.t.* to put into rhyme.—*ns.* **rhy'mer**, a versifier, a poetaster: a minstrel; **rhyme'-roy'al**, a seven-line stanza borrowed by Chaucer from the French—its formula *a b a b b c c*; **rhyme'ster**, a poetaster, a would-be poet.—**without rhyme or reason**, without either pleasant sound or good sense: without reasonable or sensible purpose or explanation. [O.Fr. *rime*—L. *rhythmus*—Gr. *rhythmos*. See **rhythm**; associated and confused with O.E. *rīm*, number.]

rhythm, *riTHm*, *n.* regular recurrence, esp. of stresses or of long and short sounds: pattern of recurring stresses in music, or correlated shapes, colours, &c., in art: syncopated music for dancing: movement, course of change, showing regular recurrence of features or phenomena.—*adjs.* **rhyth'mic, -al**.—*adv.* **rhyth'mically**.—**rhythm method**, a method of birth control requiring the avoidance of sexual intercourse during the time in which conception is most likely to occur. [L. *rhythmus*—Gr. *rhythmos*—*rheein*, to flow; cf. **rhyme**.]

rib, *rib*, *n.* one of the bones that curve round and forward from the backbone: a curved member of the side of a ship running from keel to deck: a vein of a leaf: a member supporting the fabric of an aeroplane wing or of an umbrella: a ridge: a moulding or projecting band on a ceiling.—*v.t.* to furnish, form, cover, or enclose with ribs:—*pr.p.* ribb'ing; *pa.t.* and *pa.p.* ribbed.—*n.* **ribb'ing**, an arrangement of ribs. [O.E. *ribb*, rib; Ger. *rippe*, rib.]

rib, rib, *v.t.* (*slang*) to tease, ridicule, make fun of. [Perh. **rib**(1).]

ribald, rib'áld, *n.* a loose, low character.—*adj.* low, licentious, foul-mouthed (e.g. *a ribald jest*).—*n.* **rib'aldry**, obscenity, scurrility. [O.Fr. *ribald, ribaut* (Fr. *ribaud*); origin doubtful.]

riband, ribband, rib'án(d), spellings of **ribbon**, now rare except in heraldic use and in sporting language, e.g. the **Blue Riband**, the distinction of winning the Derby race.

ribbon, rib'ón, *n.* material woven in narrow bands or strips: a strip of such or other material.—*v.t.* to adorn with ribbons.—*ns.* **ribb'on-building,** **-development**, building, growth of towns, in long strips along the main roads. [O.Fr. *riban*; origin obscure.]

ribonucleic acids, rī'bō-nū-klē'ik as'ids, nucleic acids containing **ribose**, a pentose, $C_5 H_{10} O_5$, present in living cells, where they play an important part in the development of proteins—abbrev. **RNA**.

rice, rīs, *n.* a grass grown in warm climates: its grain, a valuable food.—*ns.* **rice'-bis'cuit**, a sweet biscuit made of flour mixed with rice; **rice'-pā'per**, 'sliced and flattened pith of a Formosan tree. [O.Fr. *ris*—L. *oryza*—Gr. *oryza*, a word of Oriental origin.]

rich, rich, *adj.* abounding in possessions, wealthy: abounding (in, with): costly, splendid, elaborately decorated: sumptuous: abundant: fertile: deep in colour: full-toned: full-flavoured: abounding in oily ingredients: full of absurdities, ridiculous, very amusing.—*adv.* **rich'ly**.—*n.* **rich'ness**. [O.E. *rīce*, great, powerful; Ger. *reich*, Du. *rijk*.]

riches, rich'iz, *n.* (now usu. treated as *pl.*) wealth. [O.Fr. *richesse*—*riche*, rich, powerful; of Gmc. origin.]

rick, rik, *n.* a stack: a heap. [O.E. *hrēac*; O.N. *hraukr*.]

rickets, rik'éts, *n. sing.* a disease of children, characterised by softness of the bones.—*adj.* **rick'ety**, **rick'etty**, affected with rickets: feeble: tottery, unsteady. [First recorded in S.W. England in the 17th cent., perh. M.E. *wrikken*, to twist; or Gr. *rhachītis*.]

rickshaw, ricksha, rik'shö, *n.* a small, two-wheeled, hooded vehicle drawn by a man or men, much used in Japan and China. [Abbrev. of **jinricksha(w), jinrik'isha**; Jap. *jin*, man, *riki*, power, *sha*, a vehicle.]

ricochet, rik-ō-shā', -shet', or rik'-, *n.* a glancing rebound or skip, as of a projectile flying low.—*v.i.* to glance, to skip along the ground:—*pr.p.* ricocheting (-shā'ing), ricochetting (-shet'ing); pa.t. and pa.p. ricocheted (-shād'), ricochetted (-shet'id). [Fr.]

rid, rid, *v.t.* to free from, clear of, disencumber (of): (*rare*) to deliver (from, out of): (*rare*) to expel:—*pr.p.* ridd'ing; *pa.t.* and *pa.p.* rid or ridd'ed.—*n.* **ridd'ance**, clearance: deliverance.—**a good riddance**, a welcome relief; **get rid of**, to disencumber oneself of. [O.N. *rythja*, to clear.]

riddle, rid'l, *n.* an obscure description of something which the hearer is asked to name: a puzzling question: anything puzzling.—*v.t.* to solve as a riddle.—*v.i.* to make riddles: to speak obscurely. [O.E. *rǣdelse*—*rǣdan*, to guess, to read—*rǣd*, counsel.]

riddle, rid'l, *n.* a large coarse sieve.—*v.t.* to separate with a riddle: to make full of holes like a riddle, as with shot.—*n.pl.* **ridd'lings**, refuse. [O.E. *hriddel*, earlier *hridder*.]

ride, rīd, *v.i.* to travel or be borne on the back of an animal, on a bicycle, or in a (usu. public) vehicle: to float buoyantly (*lit.* and *fig.*): to lie at anchor: to be supported, or to grate (upon something): to work up out of position (as a collar).—*v.t.* to traverse on horseback, on bicycle, &c.: to perform on horseback, bicycle, &c. (e.g. a race): to sit on and control (e.g. a horse): to control at will or oppressively: to torment, harass:—*pa.t.* rōde; *pa.p.* ridd'en.—*n.* a journey on horseback, on bicycle, or in a vehicle: a spell of riding: a road for horse-riding, a glade: an excise-officer's district.—*n.* **rī'der**, one who rides or can ride: an added clause or corollary: (*hist.*) a moss-trooper.—*n.* and *adj.* **rī'ding**.—*ns.* **rī'ding-hab'it**, a dress for riding, esp. one with a long skirt for riding side-saddle; **rī'ding-light**, a light hung out in the rigging at night when a vessel is riding at anchor.—**let it ride**, let it alone, do not interfere; **ride for a fall**, to court disaster; **ride out**, to keep afloat throughout (a storm); **ride to hounds**, to take part in fox-hunting; **take for a ride**, to give (someone) a lift in a car, often with the object of murdering him in some remote place: to play a trick on, dupe. [O.E. *rīdan*; Du. *rijden*, Ger. *reiten*.]

ridge, rij, *n.* (orig.) the back of an animal: the earth thrown up by the plough between the furrows: a long narrow top or crest: the horizontal line of a roof-top: a narrow elevation: a hill range.—*v.t.* and *v.i.* to form into ridges: to wrinkle.—*adj.* **ridg'y**, having ridges. [O.E. *hrycg*; O.N. *hryggr*, Ger. *rücken*, back.]

ridicule, rid'i-kūl, *n.* derision, mockery.—*v.t.* to laugh at, to expose to merriment, to mock.—*adj.* **ridic'ulous**, deserving or exciting ridicule, absurd.—*adv.* **ridic'ulously**.—*n.* **ridic'ulousness**. [L. *rīdiculus*—*rīdēre*, to laugh.]

riding, rī'ding, *n.* formerly one of the divisions of Yorkshire (North, East, and West Riding). [For *thriding*—O.N. *thrithi*, third.]

riding. See **ride**.

rife, rīf, *adj.* prevalent: abounding.—*adv.* **rife'ly**.—*n.* **rife'ness**. [O.E. *rȳfe, rīfe*; Du. *rijf*, O.N. *rīfr*.]

riff-raff, rif'-raf, *n.* the scum of the people: rubbish. [M.E. *rif and raf*—O.Fr. *rif et raf*.]

rifle, rī'fl, *v.t.* to plunder thoroughly (a person, place): to steal, carry away.—*n.* **rī'fler**. [O.Fr. *rifler*.]

rifle, rī'fl, *v.t.* to groove spirally.—*n.* a firearm with spirally grooved barrel.—*ns.* **rī'fle-corps**, a body of soldiers armed with rifles; **rī'fle-grenade'**, a grenade or bomb fired from a rifle, by means of a rod; **rī'fleman**, a soldier armed with a rifle; **rī'fle-pit**, a pit to shelter riflemen; **rī'fle-range**, the range of a rifle: a place for rifle practice; **rī'fling**, the spiral grooving of a gun-bore. [O.Fr. *rifler*, to scratch; cf. Ger. *riefeln*, and preceding word.]

Neutral vowels in unaccented syllables: em'pér-ór; for certain sounds in foreign words see p. ix.

rift, *rift, n.* a cleft; a fissure.—*v.t.* and *v.i.* to cleave, split.—*n.* **rift'-valley**, valley formed by subsidence of a portion of the earth's crust between two faults;—**rift within the lute**, beginning of disagreement or discord (because a crack in a musical instrument makes it discordant). [Cf. Dan. and Norw. *rift*, a cleft.]

rig, *rig, v.t.* (*naut.*) to fit with sails and tackling: to fit up or fit out: to set in working order:—*pr.p.* rigg'ing; *pa.t.* and *pa.p.* rigged.—*n.* masts, sails, and tackling: well-boring plant (esp. that used in boring and pumping oil-wells).—*ns.* **rigg'ing**, tackle: the system of cordage which supports a ship's masts and extends the sails: form and arrangement of masts, sails, and tackling; **rig'-out**, an outfit.—**rig out**, to furnish with complete dress, &c.: to put up quickly from available, rather inadequate, materials. [Origin obscure; perh. conn. with Norw. *rigga*, to bind.]

rig, *rig, n.* the northern form of **ridge**.

rig, *rig, n.* a frolic, prank, trick.—*v.t.* to manipulate fraudulently. [Origin obscure.]

right, *rīt, adj.* straight, direct: perpendicular: forming one-fourth of a revolution: (*arch.*) true, genuine: truly judged or judging: in accordance, or identical, with what is true and fitting: not mistaken: just, normal, sane: at or towards that side at which, in most normal persons, is the better developed hand (ōt a river, as referred to a person going downstream): conservative.—*adv.* straight: straightway: exactly: in a right manner: justly: correctly: (*arch.* and *dial.*) very: to or on the right side.—*n.* that which is right or correct: equity: truth: justice: just or legal claim: what one has a just claim to: due: the right side: the right wing: (*cap.*) those members of certain of the legislative assemblies of Europe (e.g. France) who have seats to the right of the presiding officer—conservatives, monarchists, &c.—*v.t.* to set right: to set in order: to do justice to: (*reflex.*) to recover balance or upright position.—*v.i.* to recover an erect position.—*adv.* and *n.* **right'about**, (in) the opposite direction.—*n.* **right'(-)angle**, an angle equal to a fourth of a revolution.—*adj.* and *adv.* **right'-down**, out and out.—*adj.* **right'ful**, having a just claim: according to justice: belonging by right.—*adv.* **right'fully**.—*n.* **right'fulness**, righteousness: justice.—*adv.* **right'ly**.—*n.* **right'ness**.—*interj.* **right'-oh!** (*coll.*) expressing acquiescence.—*adj.* **right'-wing**, of or on the right wing: conservative.—**Right Honourable**, a title of distinction given to peers below the rank of marquis, privy councillors, present and past cabinet ministers, certain Lord Mayors and Lord Provosts, &c.; **right of entry**, a legal right to enter a place; **right off**, right away, without delay; **right of way**, the right of the public to pass over a piece of ground: a track over which there is such a right: precedence in passing other traffic.—**all right** (see **all**); **by rights**, rightfully; **in one's own right**, by absolute and personal right, not through another; **in the right**, maintaining a justifiable position. [O.E. *riht* (n. and adj.), *rihte* (adv.), *rihtan* (vb.); cf. Ger. *recht*, L. *rēctus*.]

righteous, *rī'chùs, -tyùs, adj.* just, upright.—*adv.*

right'eously.—*n.* **right'eousness**, rectitude: a righteous act. [O.E. *rihtwīs—riht*, right, *wīs*, wise, prudent, or *wīse*, wise, manner.]

rigid, *rij'id, adj.* stiff, unbending: rigorous, strict: of an airship, having a rigid structure to maintain shape.—*adv.* **rig'idly**.—*ns.* **rig'idness**, **rigid'ity**. [L. *rigidus—rigēre*, to be stiff.]

rigmarole, *rig'ma-rōl, n.* a long rambling discourse. [A corr. of *ragman-roll*, a document with a long list of names, or with numerous seals pendent.]

rigor, *rī'gor, n.* (*med.*) a sense of chilliness with contraction of the skin, a preliminary symptom of many diseases.—*adj.* **rigorous** (*rig'or-us*), rigidly strict or scrupulous: exact: very harsh, severe.—*adv.* **rig'orously**.—*ns.* **rig'orousness; rigour** (*rig'ór*), stiffness: rigor: unswerving enforcement of law, rule or principle: strict exactitude: harshness, cruelty, or an instance of it: severity (of weather or climate).—**rigor mortis** (L.), stiffening of the body after death. [L. *rigor—rigēre*, to be stiff.]

rile, *rīl, v.t.* to irritate, make angry. [A form of obs. and U.S. *roil*, to make turbid.]

rilievo, *rēl-yā'vō, n.* (*sculpture, archit.*) relief. [It.]

rill, *ril, n.* a very small brook: a runnel.—*v.i.* to flow in a rill or rills. [Cf. Du. *ril*, Ger. (orig. Low Ger.) *rille*, channel, furrow.]

rim, *rim, n.* a border, brim, edge, or margin, esp. when raised and curved.—*v.t.* to form or furnish a rim to:—*pr.p.* rimm'ing; *pa.t.* and *pa.p.* rimmed.—*adj.* **rim'less**. [O.E. *rima* (found in compounds).]

rime, *rīm, n.* hoar-frost or frozen dew: (*meteorology*) ice formed by freezing of fog.—*adj.* **rī'my**. [O.E. *hrīm*; Du. *rijm*, Ger. *reif*.]

rime. Same as **rhyme**.

rind, *rīnd, n.* bark: peel: crust: skin. [O.E. *rinde*; Du. and Ger. *rinde*.]

rinderpest, *rin'dér-pest, n.* a contagious disease of cattle. [Ger., cattle-plague.]

ring, *ring, n.* a circlet or small hoop, esp. one of metal, worn on the finger, in the ear, nose, or elsewhere: any object, mark, group, &c., circular but hollow in form: a space set apart for sport, as boxing, wrestling, amusement, display, &c.: a clique organised to control the market or for other gain: (*math.*) a system of elements in which addition is associative and commutative and multiplication is associative and distributive with respect to addition.—*v.t.* to encircle: to put a ring on or in.—*v.i.* to move in rings: to gather or be in a ring:—*pa.t.* and *pa.p.* ringed.—*n.* **ring'dove**, the wood-pigeon, from the broken white ring or line on its neck.—*adj.* **ringed**, surrounded by, or marked with, a ring or rings: ring-shaped.—*ns.* **ring'-finger**, the third finger, esp. of the left hand, on which the wedding-ring is worn; **ring'-leader**, one who takes the lead in mischief; **ring'let**, a little ring: a fairy ring: a long curl of hair; **ring'-master**, one who has charge of performances in a circus-ring; **ring'-road**, a road or boulevard encircling a town or its inner part; **ring'worm**, a contagious skin disease characterised by ring-shaped patches, caused by infection with certain fungi.—**a ringside seat**, a position which allows one to have a clear view (also *fig.*); **run rings round**, to be markedly superior to. [O.E. *hring*; O.N. *hringr*, Ger., Dan., and Swed. *ring*.]

ring, *ring*, *v.i.* to give a metallic or bell-like sound: to sound aloud and clearly: to resound, re-echo: to be filled (with sound, or a sensation like sound, or report, or renown): (*fig.*) to have a sound suggestive of a quality indicated (e.g. *his words ring true*).—*v.t.* to cause to give a metallic or bell-like sound: to summon or announce by a bell or bells: to re-echo, resound, proclaim: to call on the telephone:—*pa.t.* rang (now rarely 'rung'); *pa.p.* rung.—*n.* a sounding of a bell: a characteristic sound or tone: a set of bells.—*n.* **ring'er.**—*n.* and *adj.* **ring'ing.—ring a bell**, to begin to arouse a memory; **ring down**, or **up (the curtain)**, to give the signal for lowering or raising; **ring in**, **out**, to usher in, out (esp. the year) with bell-ringing; **ring off**, to signal the ending of a telephone conversation; **ring up**, to summon by bell, esp. to the telephone; **ring the bell**, to achieve a success; **ring the changes**, to proceed through all the permutations in ringing a chime of bells: to do a limited number of things repeatedly in varying order: to run through all possible variations. [O.E. *hringan*; O.N. *hringja*; Ger. *ringen*; Dan. *ringe*.]

rink, *ringk*, *n.* a portion of a bowling-green, curling-pond, &c., allotted to one set of players: a team of bowlers, &c.: a piece of ice, or a floor, prepared for skating: a building enclosing a floor for skating. [Orig. Scots.]

rinse, *rins*, *v.t.* to wash lightly by pouring, shaking, or dipping: to wash in clean water to remove soap traces.—*n.* an act of rinsing: liquid used for rinsing: a solution used in hairdressing, esp. one to tint the hair slightly and impermanently. [O.Fr. *rinser* (Fr. *rincer*).]

riot, *rī'ŏt*, *n.* wild revelry, debauchery: tumult: a disturbance of the peace by a crowd (legally three or more): an exuberance (e.g. of colour, emotion): a great, usu. boisterous, success. —*v.i.* to take part or indulge in riot: to revel. —*ns.* **rī'oter**, **rī'oting.**—*adj.* **rī'otous.**—*adv.* **rī'otously.**—*n.* **rī'otousness.—run riot**, to act or grow without restraint or control. [O.Fr. *riot, riotte.*]

rip, *rip*, *v.t.* to slash or tear open, apart, off, or out: to reopen (with *up*): to utter explosively (with *out*).—*v.i.* to part in rents: to break out violently (*coll.*): to move very fast:—*pr.p.* rip'ping; *pa.t.* and *pa.p.* ripped.—*n.* a tear: a rent: a rakish fellow.—*ns.* **rip'-cord**, a cord for opening a parachute or a balloon's gas-bag; **rip'per**, (*slang*) an especially admirable person or thing.—*adj.* **rip'ping**, (*slang*) excellent.—*n.* **rip'saw**, a saw for cutting along the grain.—**let rip**, to express oneself, or to act, violently and with abandon: to increase speed in greatly: (**let it rip**), to refrain from trying to check an action or process. [Precise origin uncertain; cf. Frisian *rippe*, Flemish *rippen*, Norw. *rippa*.]

riparian, *rī-pā'ri-ăn*, *adj.* of, or inhabiting, a river bank. [L. *rīpārius—rīpa*, a river bank.]

ripe, *rīp*, *adj.* ready for harvest: fully developed: mature: arrived at perfection, consummate (e.g. scholarship, wisdom): in best condition for use (e.g. *a ripe cheese*): maturated.—*adv.* **ripe'ly.**—*v.t.* **rī'pen**, to make or grow ripe or

riper.—*n.* **ripe'ness.** [O.E. *rīpe*, ripe, *rīpian*, to ripen; conn. with *rīp*, harvest, and perh. **reap.**]

riposte, *ri-pōst'*, *n.* a quick return thrust after a parry: a repartee. [Fr.,—It. *risposta*, reply.]

ripple, *rip'l*, *n.* light fretting of the surface of a liquid: a little wave: a sound as of rippling water.—*v.t.* to cause a ripple in.—*v.i.* to move or run in ripples. [Origin obscure.]

ripple, *rip'l*, *n.* a toothed implement for removing seeds, &c., from flax or hemp.—*v.t.* to clear of seeds by drawing through a ripple.—*n.* **ripp'ler.** [Cf. Ger. and Du. *repel*, a ripple, hoe, Ger. *riffel*.]

rise, *rīz*, *v.i.* to get up: to stand up: to come back to life: to become excited or hostile: to revolt: to close a session: to move upward (*lit.* and *fig.*): to come up to the surface: to come above the horizon: to come (into view, notice, or consciousness): to grow upward: to attain (to): to advance in rank, fortune, &c.: to swell: to increase in price: to become more acute in pitch: to take origin: to tower: to slope up: to respond as to provocation, or to a situation calling forth one's powers:—*pa.t.* rose (*rōz*); *pa.p.* risen (*riz'n*).—*n.* rising: ascent: vertical difference or amount of elevation: origin: an increase of salary, price, &c.: (*fig.*) progress upward: a sharpening of pitch.—*ns.* **rī'ser**, one who rises, esp. from bed: that which rises: the upright portion of a step; **rī'sing**, act of rising: a revolt: a prominence: a swelling: a hill.—*p.adj.* and *pr.p.* ascending: increasing: coming above the horizon.—**rise to it** (*fig.*, from fishing), to take the lure. [O.E. *rīsan*, allied to O.N. *rīsa*.]

risible, *riz'i-bl*, *adj.* able or inclined to laugh: of laughter: ludicrous.—*n.* **risibil'ity**, laughter: inclination to laugh: (often in *pl.*) faculty of laughter. [L. *rīsibilis—rīdēre, rīsum*, to laugh.]

risk, *risk*, *n.* hazard: chance of loss or injury: degree of probability of loss: person, thing, or factor likely to cause loss or danger.—*v.t.* to expose to hazard: to venture.—*adj.* **risk'y**, dangerous.—**run a risk**, to expose oneself to, or to involve, the possibility of loss, injury, or failure. [Fr. *risque*—It. *risco*.]

risotto, *ri-sot'to*, *n.* dish of rice mixed with savoury ingredients, as chicken, onions. [It.]

risqué, *rēs'kā*, *adj.* bordering on the improper. [Fr., risky.]

rissole, *ris'ōl*, *rēs-ōl'*, *n.* a fried ball or cake of minced food. [Fr.]

ritardando, *rē-tär-dan'dō*, *adj.* and *adv.* with diminishing speed. [It.]

rite, *rīt*, *n.* a ceremonial form or observance, esp. religious: a liturgy. [L. *rītus*.]

ritual, *rit'ū-ăl*, *adj.* relating to, or of the nature of, rites.—*n.* manner of performing divine service, or a book containing it: a body or code of ceremonies: performance of rites.—*ns.* **rit'-ūalism**, attachment of importance to ritual, esp. with the implication of undue importance; **rit'ūalist**, one skilled in or devoted to a ritual: one of the High Church party in the Church of England.—*adj.* **ritūalist'ic.**—*advs.* **ritūalist'ically, rit'ūally.—ritual murder**, the killing of a human being as part of a tribal ceremony. [L. *rītuālis—rītus*, rite.]

ritzy, *rit'zi*, *adj.* (*slang*) stylish, elegant, ostentatiously rich. [The *Ritz* hotels.]

Neutral vowels in unaccented syllables: *em'pér-ór*; for certain sounds in foreign words see p. ix.

rival, *rī'vàl, n.* one pursuing an object in competition with another, one who strives to equal or excel another: one for whom, or that for which, a claim to equality might be made.—*adj.* standing in competition: of like pretensions or comparable claims.—*v.t.* to try to gain the same object as: to try to equal or excel: to be worthy of comparison with:—*pr.p.* rī'valling; *pa.t.* and *pa.p.* rī'valled.—*n.* rī'valry, state of being a rival: competition, emulation. [L. *rīvālis*, said to be from *rīvus*, river, as one who draws water from the same river.]

rive, *rīv, v.t.* to tear asunder: to split.—*v.i.* to tug, tear: to split:—*pa.t.* rīved; *pa.p.* riven (*riv'n*), rived (*rivd*). [O.N. *rīfa*.]

river, *riv'ér, n.* a large stream of water flowing across country.—*adj.* riv'erain (-*ān*), of a river or its neighbourhood.—*ns.* riv'er-basin, the whole region drained by a river with its affluents; riv'er-bed, the channel in which a river flows; riv'er-front, land, quays, buildings, &c., facing a river; riv'er-head, the source of a river; riv'er-horse, a hippopotamus.—*adj.* riv'erine (-*īn*, -*ēn*), of, on, or dwelling near or in a river.—*ns.* riv'er-tide, the current of a river: the tide from the sea rising or ebbing in a river; riv'er-wall, a wall confining a river within bounds.—river novel, a novel in a series of self-contained narratives telling the story of a family or other social group over successive generations (trans. of Fr. *roman fleuve*). [O.Fr. *rivere* (Fr. *rivière*)—L. *rīpārius, adj.—rīpa*, bank; cf. It. *riviera.*]

rivet, *riv'et, n.* a bolt fastened by hammering the end.—*v.t.* to fasten with rivets: to fix immovably:—*pr.p.* riv'eting; *pa.t.* and *pa.p.* riv'eted.—*ns.* riv'eter, one who rivets: a machine for riveting; riv'eting. [O.Fr. *rivet river*, to clinch.]

rivulet, *riv'ū-let, n.* a small river. [L. *rīvulus*, dim. of *rīvus*, a stream, perh. through It. *rivoletto—rivolo—rivo.*]

roach, *rōch, n.* a silvery fresh-water fish. [O.Fr. *roche.*]

road, *rōd, n.* a highway: a roadway: (often in *pl.*) a roadstead: (*fig.*) a path (e.g. *the road to ruin*).—*ns.* road'-block, an obstruction set up across a road: a coach-driver or other traveller by road; road'-hog (see hog); road'house, a roadside public-house, or refreshment-room, or inn, catering for motorists, cyclists, &c.; road'man, one who keeps a road in repair; road'-met'al, broken stones for roads; road'rail'er, a container for transporting goods that can run on road and on rails, the wheels for road use being retractable; road'-sense, aptitude for doing the right thing in driving or using a road; road'side, border of a road (also *adj.*); road'stead, a place near a shore where ships may ride at anchor; road'-ster, a horse, cycle, or car suitable for ordinary use on the road: a coach-driver or other traveller by road; road'-survey'or, one who supervises making and maintenance of roads; road'way, the part of a road or street used by horses and vehicles.—*adj.* road'worthy, fit for the road.—road up, road surface being repaired; rule of the road (see rule). [O.E. *rād*, a riding, raid; cf. raid, ride.]

roam, *rōm, v.i.* to rove about: to ramble.—*v.t.* to wander over.—*n.* roam'er. [M.E. *romen.*]

roan, *rōn, adj.* bay or dark, with spots of grey and white: of a mixed colour, with a decided shade of red (also red-roan, strawberry roan).—*n.* a roan colour: a roan animal, esp. a horse. [O.Fr. *roan* (Fr. *rouan*).]

roar, *rōr, rōr, v.i.* to make a full, loud, hoarse, low-pitched sound, as a lion, fire, wind, the sea: to bellow: to bawl: to guffaw.—*v.t.* to utter, say, very loudly.—*n.* a sound of roaring.—*n.* roar'ing.—roaring forties, the tract of stormy west winds south of 40° S. latitude (also, occasionally, that north of 40° N.).—the roaring game, curling. [O.E. *rārian*; but partly from Middle Du. *roer,* stir, disturbance.]

roast, *rōst, v.t.* to cook before a fire: to bake in fat: to parch by heat: to heat strongly: to dissipate the volatile parts of (esp. sulphur) by heat: to criticise harshly:—*pa.p.* roast'ed; *p.adj.* roast.—*v.i.* to undergo roasting.—*n.* a joint, esp. of beef, roasted or to be roasted.—*n.* roast'ing-jack, an apparatus for turning a joint in roasting.—rule the roast (mistakenly *roost*), to lord it, predominate. [O.Fr. *rostir* (Fr. *rôtir*); of Gmc. origin.]

rob, *rob, v.t.* to deprive (of), esp. wrongfully and forcibly: to steal from (a person): to plunder (a place): (*rare*) to take as plunder:—*pr.p.* robb'ing; *pa.t.* and *pa.p.* robbed.—*ns.* robb'er, one who robs; robb'ery, (*law*) theft from the person, aggravated by violence or intimidation: plundering.—rob Peter to pay Paul, to satisfy or benefit one person by depriving another. [O.Fr. *rober*, of Gmc. origin; cf. reave, O.H.G. *roubōn,* Ger. *rauben.*]

robe, *rōb, n.* a gown or loose outer garment: a dress of office, dignity, or state: a rich dress.—*v.t.* to dress: to invest in robes.—*v.i.* to assume official vestments. [Fr. *robe,* orig. booty; cf. rob.]

robin, *rob'in, n.* the rob'in-red'breast, a singing bird with a reddish-orange breast.—*n.* Robin-run-in-the-hedge, cleavers or goosegrass. [A familiar form of Robert; cf. Jackdaw, Magpie.]

robot, *rō'bot, n.* a mechanical man: a more than humanly efficient automaton: an automatic traffic signal. [Name of artificially made persons in Karel Capek's play *R.U.R.* (1920)—Czech *robota,* statute labour.]

robust, *rō-bust', adj.* stout, strong, and sturdy—constitutionally healthy: requiring strength and vigour: (*fig.*—e.g. of style, humour, intelligence) vigorous, sane, not inclined to subtlety.—*adv.* robust'ly.—*n.* robust'ness. [L. *rōbustus—rōbur,* strength, oak.]

roc, *rok, n.* a fabulous bird, able to carry off an elephant—also rok, ruc, rukh (*rŏŏk*). [Pers. *rukh.*]

rochet, *roch'et, n.* a close-fitting surplice-like vestment proper to bishops and abbots. [O.Fr.; of Gmc. origin; cf. Ger. *rock,* O.E. *rocc.*]

rock, *rok, n.* a large outstanding natural mass of stone: (*geol.*) a natural mass of one or more minerals, consolidated or loose: (*slang*) a diamond or other precious stone: a hard sweetmeat made in sticks: (*fig.*) a sure foundation or support.—*n.* rock'-bott'om, bedrock: the very bottom, esp. of poverty or despair.—*adj.* the lowest possible.—*ns.* rock'cake, a small hard bun with irregular top; rock'-crys'tal, colourless quartz, esp. when well crystallised; **rock'-dove,** a pigeon that nests on rocks, source of the domestic varieties; **rock'ery,** a heap of rock-fragments in a garden for growing rock-plants; **rock garden,** a garden of rockery, for rock-plants; **rock'-oil,** petroleum; **rock'-pi'geon,** the rock-dove; **rock'-plant,** a plant adapted to growing on or among rocks; **rock'(-)salt,** salt as a mineral; **rock'-tar,** petroleum; **rock'work** (*archit.*), masonry in imitation of rock: rockery.—*adj.* **rock'y,** full of rocks: like rock.—**on the rocks,** penniless: (of whisky, &c.) on ice; **the Rock,** Gibraltar. [O.Fr. *roke*—Low L. *rocca.*]

rock, *rok, n.* a distaff. [M.E. *roc*; cf. O.N. *rokkr*; Ger. *rocken.*]

rock, *rok, v.t.* and *v.i.* to sway to and fro, tilt from side to side: (*fig.*) to startle, stagger.—*n.* (see **rock 'n' roll**).—*ns.* **rock'er,** one who rocks: apparatus that rocks; a curved support on which anything rocks: (*cap.*) a member of a teenage faction in the 1960s who wore leather jackets and rode motor bicycles; **rock'ing,** a swaying backward and forward; **rock'ing-chair,** a chair mounted on rockers; **rock'ing-horse,** the figure of a horse mounted on rockers.—*adj.* **rock'y,** disposed to rock: shaky: unsteady: (*slang*) unsatisfactory, unpleasant.—**rock 'n' roll, rock and roll** (now usu. **rock**), a simple form of jazz music, two-beat, strongly accented: dancing done to this music; **rock the boat,** to make things difficult for one's colleagues. [O.E. *roccian.*]

rocket, *rok'ét, n.* any of a number of types of power-plant (q.v.), cylindrical in shape, in which combustion of a fuel or fuels produces an exhaust or jet of hot gas—used in simple form to send up fireworks, signalling lights, &c., in more elaborate form to propel aircraft, &c.: a projectile propelled by rocket apparatus: (*slang*) a reprimand.—*v.i.* to fly like a rocket: of e.g. prices, to become higher very rapidly: (*fig.*) to come to an important position, with remarkable speed.—*n.* **rock'etry,** the scientific study of rockets.—**rocket propulsion,** propulsion by the reaction of a jet of high-velocity gas expelled backwards from a rocket; **rock'et-range,** a place for experimentation with rocket projectiles. [It. *rocchetta*; of Gmc. origin.]

rococo, *rō-kō'kō, rō-kō-kō', n.* a debased style of architecture, decoration, and furniture-making, prevailing in Louis XV's time, marked by endless multiplication of ornamental details unrelated to structure (a lighter, freer, frivolous development of the baroque): any art in this style.—Also *adj.* [Fr., prob.—*rocaille,* rockwork.]

rod, *rod, n.* a long straight shoot: a slender stick: a slender bar of metal or other matter: an emblem of authority: an instrument of correction: a wand for magic, divination: a fishing-rod: a pole or perch ($5\frac{1}{2}$ yards): (*B.*) race or tribe.—**a rod in pickle,** punishment in reserve; **kiss the rod,** accept punishment with submission. [O.E. *rodd*; cf. O.N. *rudda,* club.]

rode, *rōd, pa.t.* of **ride.**

rodent, *rō'dént, adj.* gnawing.—*n.* a rodent mammal, such as a rabbit, a squirrel, a rat. [L. *rōdēns, -entis,* pr.p. of *rōdère,* to gnaw.]

rodeo, *rō-dā'ō, n.* a round-up of cattle: an exhibition of cowboy skill: a contest suggestive of a cowboy rodeo involving e.g. motor-bicycles. [Sp.—*rodear,* to go round—L. *rotāre,* to wheel.]

rodomontade, *rod-ō-mon-tād', n.* extravagant boasting, like that of *Rodomonte* in Ariosto's *Orlando Furioso* (1516).—*v.i.* to bluster or brag.

roe, *rō, n.* the eggs or spawn of fishes. [M.E. *rowe*; cf. O.N. *hrogn,* Ger. *rogen.*]

roe, *rō, n.* a species of small deer of Europe and Asia, very graceful and agile: sometimes applied to the female red deer.—*ns.* **roe'buck,** the male roe; **roe'-deer,** a roe. [O.E. *rā, rāha*; Ger. *reh,* Du. *ree.*]

rogation, *rō-gā'sh(ò)n, n.* an asking: supplication.—**Rogation days,** the three days before Ascension Day, when (R.C. Church) supplications are recited in procession. [L. *rogātiō, -ōnis—rogāre,* to ask.]

rogue, *rōg, n.* a vagrant: a rascal: a wag, a mischievous person (often playfully or affectionately): a sport, or variation from type.—*v.t.* to cheat: to eliminate rogues from.—*n.* **roguery** (*rōg'ér-i*), knavish tricks: fraud: mischievousness, waggery.—*adj.* **roguish** (*rōg'ish*), knavish: mischievous, waggish.—*adv.* **rog'uishly.**—*n.* **rog'uishness.**—**rogue elephant,** a savage elephant cast out or withdrawn from the herd; **rogues' gallery,** a police collection of photographs of criminals; **rogues' march,** derisive music played when a soldier is drummed out of a regiment. [Cant.]

roister, royster, *rois'tér, v.i.* to bluster, swagger, revel noisily.—*n.* **rois'terer, roys'terer.** [O.Fr. *rustre,* a rough, rude fellow—O.Fr. *ruste*—L. *rusticus,* rustic.]

rôle, role, *rōl, n.* a part played by an actor or other: a function. [Fr.]

roll, *rōl, n.* a scroll: a sheet of paper or other material wound upon itself into cylindrical form: a revolving cylinder: a register: a list, esp. of names: a small loaf: a part turned over in a curve: act of rolling: a swaying or rotary motion about an axis in the direction of advance (e.g. of a ship, aircraft): a continuous reverberatory sound (e.g. of drums, cannon, thunder): a trill of some birds, esp. a canary. —*v.i.* to move like a ball, a wheel, a wheeled vehicle, or a passenger in one: to turn on an axis: to turn over or from side to side: to move in, on, or like waves: to flow: to sound with a roll: to undulate: to curl.—*v.t.* to cause to roll: to turn on an axis: to wrap round on itself: to enwrap: to drive forward: to move upon wheels: to press or smooth with a roller or between rollers: to beat rapidly, as a drum.—*ns.* **roll'-call,** the calling of a list of names to ascertain attendance; **roll'er,** one who or that which rolls: a revolving or rolling cylinder used for grinding, rolling, &c.: a long, coiled-up bandage: a long heavy wave; **roll'er-coast'er,** a circular switchback railway ridden in open coasting cars for amusement; **roll'er-skate,** a skate with wheels instead of a blade; **roll'er-skating; roll'er-towel,** a towel with joined ends hung over a roller.—*n.* and *p.adj.* **roll'ing.**—*ns.* **roll'ing-pin,** a cylinder for rolling dough; **roll'ing-stock,** the stock or store of engines and vehicles that run upon a

Neutral vowels in unaccented syllables: *em'pér-òr*; for certain sounds see p. ix.

railway.—*adjs.* **roll-on'-roll-off'**, (of a ferry-boat or ferry-service) designed to allow goods vehicles to embark and disembark without unloading; **roll'-top**, having a flexible cover of slats that rolls up.—**be rolling in**, to have large amounts of (e.g. money); **rolled gold**, metal coated with gold and rolled very thin; **roll one's r's**, to trill or otherwise pronounce the letter *r*, esp. strongly or where it is not pronounced in standard Eng. (e.g. finally, as in *pear, father*). [O.Fr. *rolle*, n., *roller*, vb.—L. *rotula*, dim. of *rota*, a wheel.]

rollicking, *rol'ik-ing, adj.* careless, swaggering, exuberantly gay or jovial. [Origin unknown.]

roly-poly, *rōl'i-pōl'i, n.* a pudding made of a sheet of paste, covered with jam or fruit, and rolled up: a round podgy person. [Prob. **roll**.]

rom, *rom, n.* a gypsy man. [Romany, man, husband.]

Romaic, *rō-mā'ik, n.* and *adj.* modern Greek. [Modern Gr. *Rhōmaikos*, Roman (i.e. of the Eastern Roman Empire)—*Rhōmē*, Rome.]

Roman, *rō'màn, adj.* pertaining to Rome, esp. ancient Rome, its people, or the empire founded by them: pertaining to the Roman Catholic religion, papal: (of type) of the ordinary upright kind, as opposed to *italics*: (of numerals) written in letters (as IV, iv), opposed to Arabic.—*n.* a native or citizen of Rome: a Roman Catholic. *adj.* **Ro'man'ic**, of Roman, Latin origin, Romance.—*v.t.* **Ro'manise**, to make Roman or Roman Catholic.—*v.i.* to accept Roman or Roman Catholic ways, laws, doctrines, &c.—*ns.* **Ro'manism**, Roman Catholicism, **Rō'manist**, a Roman Catholic: one versed in Romance philology or in Roman law or antiquities.—*adj.* Roman Catholic.—**Roman candle**, a firework discharging a succession of white or coloured stars: bad landing by aeroplane or parachute; **Roman Catholic**, recognising the spiritual supremacy of the Pope or Bishop of Rome: a member of the Roman Catholic Church; **Roman Catholicism**, doctrines and polity of the Roman Catholic Church; **Roman nose**, one with a high bridge, aquiline. [L. *Rōmānus*—*Rōma*, Rome.]

roman, *ro-mā, n.* a mediaeval romance, tale of chivalry: novel.—**roman à clef** (*nä klā*; lit. novel with a key), a novel in which the characters are real persons more or less disguised; **roman fleuve** (*flœv*), a river novel (q.v.).

Romance, *rō-mans', n.* a general name for the vernaculars that developed out of popular Latin—French, Provençal, Italian, Spanish, Portuguese, Rumanian, Romansch, with their various dialects.—Also *adj.*—*n.* **romance'**, a tale of chivalry, orig. one in verse, written in one of the Romance tongues: any fictitious and wonderful tale: a fictitious narrative in prose or verse which passes beyond the limits of ordinary life: a love-story, romantic fiction as a branch of literature: a love-affair or a career involving social difficulties or other vicissitudes successfully overcome: a love-affair: a romantic habit of mind: romantic quality: an imaginative lie.—*v.i.* to write or tell romances: to talk extravagantly: to lie.—*n.* **roman'cer**. [O.Fr. *romanz*—(hypothetical) L.L. *rōmānicē* (adv.), in (popular) Roman language.]

Romanesque, *rō-màn-esk', adj.* of the transition from Roman to Gothic architecture, characterised by round arches and vaults.—*n.* the Romanesque style, art, or architecture. [Fr.]

Romansch, *rō-mansh', n.* and *adj.* Rhaeto-Romanic (q.v.): sometimes confined to the Upper Rhine dialects. [Romansch.]

romantic, *rō-man'tik, adj.* pertaining to, inclining towards, or suggesting, romance: fictitious: extravagant, fantastic.—Also *n.*—*adj.* **roman'tical**.—*adv.* **roman'tically**.—*v.t.* **roman'ticise**, to make seem romantic.—*v.i.* to have or express romantic ideas.—*ns.* **roman'ticism**, (-*sizm*), romantic quality, tendency, or spirit; **roman'ticist**.—**Romantic Revival**, the late 18th-century and early 19th-century revolt from classicism to a freer, more imaginative style, a more appreciative interest in wild nature, and the inspiration of mediaeval literature and Gothic architecture. [Fr. *romantique*—O.Fr. *romant*, romance.]

Romany, Rommany, *rom'à-ni, n.* a gypsy: the language of the gypsies.—*adj.* gypsy.—**Romany rye** (*rī*), a gentleman who affects the society of gypsies. [Romany, *rom*, man.]

Romeo, *rōm'i-ō, n.* a young man very much in love: a Don Juan (q.v.) in the making. [Shakespearian character.]

Romish, *rōm'ish, adj.* (used hostilely) Roman Catholic. [L. *Rōma*, Rome.]

romp, *romp, v.i.* to frolic actively: to move (along, home) easily and quickly.—*n.* a child or girl who romps: a vigorous frolic: a swift, easy run.—*n.* **rom'per**, one who romps: (usu. in *pl.*) a child's all-over garment with legs, for play—*adj.* **romp'ish**.—*adv.* **romp'ishly**.—*n.* **romp'ishness**. [ramp.]

rondeau, *ron'dō, rõ-dō, n.* a (usu.) thirteen-lined poem of two rhymes, in three parts, the first two or three words of the first part being repeated at the end of the second and third parts, so that the poem ends as it began:—*pl.* **ron'deaux** (*-dōz*).—*ns.* **ron'del**, a similar form of French verse, earlier than the rondeau; **ron'do**, a musical composition whose principal subject recurs. [Fr. *rondeau*, earlier *rondel*—*rond*, round.]

rone, roan, rhone, *rōn, n.* (*Scot.*) the gutter which collects rain from a roof.

röntgen, roentgen, *rœnt'yen,* also *ront'-, runt'-,* (sometimes *cap.*), *adj.* of Konrad von Röntgen (1845-1923), discoverer of the **Röntgen (roentgen) rays** or X-rays (see **X-**).—*n.* the international unit of dose of X-rays or gamma rays.

rood, *rōōd, n.* (*obs.*) Christ's cross: a cross or crucifix, esp. at the entrance to a church chancel: (locally) a rod, pole, or perch, linear or square (with variations in value).—*ns.* **rood'-beam**, beam for supporting the rood; **rood'-loft**, a gallery over the rood-screen; **rood'-screen**, an ornamental partition separating choir from nave; **rood'-steeple, -tower,** that over the crossing of a church. [O.E. *rōd*, gallows, cross.]

roof, *rōōf, n.* the top covering of a building or vehicle: a ceiling: the upper covering of any cavity: a dwelling: an upper limit:—*pl.* **roofs**.—*v.t.* to cover with a roof: to be the roof of.—*n.* **roof'ing**, covering with a roof: materials for a roof: a roof.—*adj.* for roofing.—

---

fāte, fär; mē, hûr (her); mīne; mōte, för; mūte; mōōn, fōōt; тнen (then)

adj. **roof'less.**—*ns.* **roof'-garden,** a garden on a flat roof; **roof'-tree,** the beam at the peak of a roof.—**roof of the world,** the Pamir, a very lofty plateau in central Asia. [O.E. *hrōf*; Du *roef.*]

rook, *rŏŏk, n.* a gregarious species of crow: a sharper.—*v.t.* to fleece.—*n.* **rook'ery,** a breeding-place of rooks in a group of trees: a breeding-place of penguins or other gregarious birds, or of seals: a crowded cluster of mean tenements. [O.E. *hrōc.*]

rook, *rŏŏk, n.* a castle in chess. [O.Fr. *roc*—Pers. *rukh.*]

rookie, rooky, *rŏŏk'i, n.* (*slang*) a raw beginner, a callow recruit. [App. from **recruit.**]

room, *rŏŏm, n.* space: necessary or available space: space unoccupied: opportunity, scope, or occasion: stead: (*B.*) a seat: a compartment of a house, a chamber: the people in a room: (*pl.*) lodgings.—*adj.* **room'y,** having ample room, wide, spacious.—*adv.* **room'ily.**—*n.* **room'iness.** [O.E. *rūm*; Ger. *raum,* Du. *ruim.*]

roost, *rŏŏst, n.* a perch or place for a sleeping bird: a hen-house: a sleeping-place: a set of fowls resting together.—*v.i.* to settle or sleep on a roost or perch.—*n.* **roost'er,** a domestic cock.—**come home to roost,** recoil upon oneself: to return to a place (usu. after travel) in order to settle down; **rule the roost** (see **roast**). [O.E. *hrōst*; Du. *roest.*]

roost, *rŏŏst, ,n.* (Orkney and Shetland) a tidal race. [O.N. *röst.*]

root, *rŏŏt, n.* ordinarily and popularly, the underground part of a plant, esp. when edible: (*bot.*) that part of a higher plant, usu. underground and descending, which never bears leaves or reproductive organs, and which serves to absorb salts in solution: the cause, origin, or basis of anything, as an ancestor, an embedded or basal part, as of a tooth: a growing plant with its root: (*math.*) the factor of a quantity which multiplied by itself a specified number of times produces that quantity: any value of the unknown quantity for which an equation is true.—*v.i.* to fix the root: to be firmly established.—*v.t.* to plant in the earth: to implant deeply.—*adj.* and *adv.* **root'-and-branch',** without leaving any part, completely.—*adj.* **root'ed,** firmly planted: fixed by roots: deep-seated (e.g. a *rooted dislike*).—*ns.* **root'let,** a little root; **root'stock,** (*bot.*) a rhizome or underground creeping stem.—**root up, out,** (*fig.*) to tear up by the root, eradicate.—**take root,** to become established. [Late O.E. *rōt*—O.N. *rōt*; Dan. *rod*; O.E. *wyrt.*]

root, *rŏŏt, v.t.* to turn up with the snout.—*v.i.* to grub: to poke about.—See **rout** (3). [O.E. *wrōtan*—*wrōt,* a snout.]

rooty, *rŏŏt'i, n.* (*mil. slang*) bread. [Hindustani *roti,* loaf.]

rope, *rōp, n.* a thick twisted cord: a string of pearls, onions, &c.: a climbing party roped together.—*v.t.* to fasten, enclose, or mark off, with a rope.—*ns.* **rope'-danc'er,** a tight-rope performer; **rope'-ladd'er,** a ladder of ropes; **rō'per,** a rope-maker; **rō'pery,** a rope-work; **rope'-trick,** a disappearing trick with a rope; **rope'-walk,** a long narrow shed or alley for rope-spinning; **rope'-walker,** a tight-rope per-

former; **rop'ing-down,** abseiling.—*adj.* **rō'py,** stringy: glutinous: wrinkled: (*slang*) bad of its kind.—*n.* **rō'piness.**—**rope in,** bring in, enlist as (reluctant) supporter; **rope's end,** the end of a rope used for flogging.—**give one rope,** to allow a person full scope to defeat his own ends; **know the ropes** (see **know**). [O.E. *rāp*; cf. O.N. *reip,* Du. *reep,* Ger. *reif.*]

rorqual, *rör'kwäl, n.* a genus of whales of the largest size. [Fr.,—Norw. *röyrkval,* lit. red whale.]

rosaceous, *rō-zā'shŭs, adj.* of the rose family: roselike. [L. *rosāceus*—*rösa,* a rose.]

rosary, *rō'zår-i, n.* a rose-garden or rose-bed (also **ro'sery**): a series of prayers: a string of beads used by Roman Catholics as a guide to devotions. [L. *rosārium,* rose-garden—*rösa,* a rose.]

rose, *pa.t.* of **rise.**

rose, *rōz, n.* the flower of a plant of many species (genus *Rosa,* family *Rosaceae*), emblem of England, white, yellow, pink, or red, with five petals in the wild state but double or semi-double in many cultivated forms: the shrub bearing it, generally prickly: a rosette: a perforated nozzle: light crimson.—*adjs.* **roseāte** (*rō'zė-āt*), rosy: of roses: rose-scented; **rose'-col'oured,** pink: seeing or representing things in too favourable a light, optimistic.—*ns.* **rō'sery,** a rose-garden (see **rosary**); **rose'-wa'ter,** water distilled from rose-leaves.—*adj.* sentimental: superfine.—*ns.* **rose'-win'dow,** a circular window with radiating compartments; **rose'wood,** valuable heavy dark-coloured wood of certain Brazilian and other trees, said to smell of roses when fresh-cut.—*adj.* **rō'sy,** of or abounding in roses: rose-red: blooming: blushing: bright, hopeful.—*n.* **rō'siness.**—**under the rose** (emblem of secrecy, hung up at Roman banquets), in confidence: secretly. [O.E. *rōse*—L. *rōsa.*]

rosé, *rō-zā, n.* a pinkish table wine in making which grape skins are removed early in fermentation. [Fr. lit., pink.]

rosemary, *rōz'má-ri, n.* a small fragrant evergreen Mediterranean shrub of a pungent taste—an ancient emblem of fidelity. [L. *rōs marīnus,* sea dew.]

rosette, *rō-zet', n.* a knot of radiating loops of ribbon or the like: (*archit.*) a rose-shaped ornament. [Fr., dim. of *rose.*]

rosin, *roz'in, n.* a resin obtained e.g. when turpentine is prepared from dead pine wood.—*v.t.* to rub with rosin: to add rosin to.—*adj.* **ros'iny.** [Formed from **resin.**]

roster, *rōs'tér, ros'-, n.* a list showing order of rotation, as for army duties. [Du. *rooster,* orig. gridiron (from the ruled lines)—*roosten,* to roast.]

rostrum, *ros'trum, n.* a beak: (properly in *pl.,* **rostra**) a platform for public speaking (from the *rostra* in the Roman forum, adorned with beaks of captured ships).—*adjs.* **ros'tral,** of or like a rostrum; **ros'trāte, -d,** beaked. [L. *rōstrum,* beak—*rōdēre, rōsum,* to gnaw.]

rot, *rot, v.i.* to putrefy: to decay.—*v.t.* to cause to rot: (*slang*) to banter, make fun of (also *v.i.*):—*pr.p.* **rott'ing;** *pa.t.* and *pa.p.* **rott'ed.**—*n.* decay: putrefaction: corruption: applied to various diseases of sheep, timber, &c.: (*coll.*)

Neutral vowels in unaccented syllables: *em'pér-ór*; for certain sounds in foreign words see p. ix.

nonsense. [O.E. *rotian,* pa.p. *rotod*; cf. **rotten.**]

rota, *rō′ta, n.* a roster: a course or round of duty, &c.: the Roman Catholic supreme ecclesiastical tribunal.—*ns.* **Rotarian** (*rō-tā′ri-ån*), a member of a Rotary club; **Rōtā′rianism.**—*adj.* **rotary** (*rō′tår-i*), turning like a wheel: having parts that rotate: resembling the motion of a wheel: (*cap.*) belonging to an international system of clubs with a wheel as badge, each member being of a different occupation from the rest of his club.—*v.t.* and *v.i.* **rōtāte′,** to turn like a wheel: to put, take, go, or succeed in rotation.—*ns.* **rotā′tion,** a turning round like a wheel: succession in definite order, as of crops; **rotā′tor.**—*adj.* **rotatory** (*rō′tā-tór-i, rō-tāt′ór-i*), rotary. [L. *rota,* a wheel—*rotāre, -ātum,* to turn, roll.]

rote, *rōt, n.* in the phrase **by rote,** by mechanical memory, repeating or performing without regard to the meaning. [Origin obscure; L. *rota,* wheel, and O.Fr. *rote,* road, have been conjectured.]

rotor, *rō′tór, n.* a rotating part, esp. of a dynamo, motor, or turbine: a system of rotating aerofoils producing lift, as in a helicopter. [For **rotator.**]

rotten, *rot′n, adj.* putrefied: decaying: corrupt: unsound: disintegrating.—*ns.* **rott′enness;** **rott′enstone,** a decomposed silicious limestone, used for polishing metals.—**rotten borough (see borough).** [O.N. *rotinn*; cf. **rot.**]

rotter, *rot′ér, n.* a thoroughly depraved or worthless person. [*rot.*]

rotund, *rō-tund′, adj.* round: rounded: nearly spherical.—*ns.* **rotund′a,** a round (esp. domed) building or hall; **rotund′ity,** roundness: a round mass. [L. *rotundus—rota,* a wheel.]

rouble, *rōō′bl, n.* the Russian monetary unit, 100 kopecks. [Russ. *rubl′,* perh.—*rubit′,* to cut; or Pers. *rūpīya,* a rupee.]

roué, *rōō′ā, n.* a profligate, rake, debauchee. [A name given by Philippe, Duke of Orléans, Regent of France 1715-23, to his dissolute companions—Fr. *roué,* broken on the wheel—pa.p. of *rouer—roue,* a wheel—L. *rota.*]

rouge, *rōōzh, n.* a powder used to colour the cheeks or lips: a red polishing powder for plate.—*v.t.* to colour with rouge.—*v.i.* to use rouge: to blush.—*n.* **rouge-et-noir** *rōōzh-ā-nwär*), a gambling card game played on a table with two red and two black diamond marks—also called *trente-et-quarante.* [Fr. *rouge—*L. *rubeus,* red.]

rough, *ruf, adj.* uneven: rugged: unshorn: unpolished: harsh: crude: unfinished: unbroken (as a horse): coarse in texture: unrefined: ungentle: turbulent.—*n.* untended ground (e.g. on a golf-course): difficulty, hardship: a rowdy, violent person of the lowest social class: a crude preliminary sketch.—*v.t.* to make rough: to shape or depict roughly.—*n.* **rough′age,** refuse of grain or crops: bran, fibre, &c., in food.—*adjs.* **rough-and-read′y,** easily improvised, and serving the purpose well enough; **rough-and-tum′ble,** haphazard and scrambling.—*n.* a scuffle.—*v.t.* **rough′cast,** to shape roughly: to cover with roughcast.—*n.* plaster mixed with small stones, used to coat walls.—*vs.t.* **rough′-draft, -draw,** to draft roughly; **rough′en,** to make rough.—*v.i.* to be-

come rough.—*n.* **rough-house (rough house),** a disturbance, a brawl.—*v.i.* to brawl.—*v.t.* to maltreat.—*adv.* **rough′ly.**—*ns.* **rough′-neck** (*slang*), an unmannerly lout: a hooligan; **rough′ness,** the quality of being rough; **rough′-rid′er,** a rider of untrained horses: a horse-breaker.—*adj.* **rough′-shod,** provided with roughened horseshoes (i.e. horse-shoes armed with calks).—**rough breathing,** in Greek, the mark (′) over an initial vowel or over ρ, indicating aspiration; **rough it,** to live without the ordinary comforts of civilisation, to take whatever hardships come; **rough justice,** approximate justice, hastily assessed and carried out; **rough on,** hard luck for: pressing hard upon; **rough shooting,** shooting over moorland (mainly for grouse).—**cut up rough** (see **cut**); **ride rough-shod over,** to set at nought (e.g. a person's feelings); **sleep rough,** to sleep out-of-doors. [O.E. *rūh,* rough; Ger. *rauch, rauh,* Du. *ruig.*]

rouleau, *rōō-lō′, n.* a roll (e.g. of coins) or a coil: a cylindrical pile of coins, blood-corpuscles, or other disks. [Fr.]

roulette, *rōōl-et′, n.* a little roller: a game of chance in which a ball rolls from a rotating disk into one or other of a set of compartments answering to those on which the players place their stakes. [Fr.]

round, *rownd, adj.* having a curved outline or surface: circular, globular, or cylindrical in form: plump: smooth and full-sounding: full: considerable (e.g. of a sum of money): approximate (number), in whole tens, hundreds, &c.: unqualified: without mincing: pronounced with lips contracted to a circle.—*adv.* about: on all sides: in a ring: from one to another successively.—*prep.* around: on every side of: all over.—*n.* a round thing or part: a ring, circumference, circle, or globe: a ladder rung: a dance in a ring, or its tune: a canon sung in unison: a complete revolution: a recurring series of events or doings: an accustomed walk: a prescribed circuit: a slice of toast: a cut of beef across the thigh-bone: a sandwich consisting of two whole slices: a portion dealt around to each: a volley, as a shot or of applause: a unit of ammunition: a successive or simultaneous action of each member of a company or player in a game: a part of a competition complete in itself: a bout, part of a contest of prearranged duration, as in boxing: (*golf*) play over the whole course once: (*sculpture*) the condition of being visible from all sides, not merely in relief.—*v.t.* to make round: to go round.—*v.i.* to become round.—*adj.* **round′-about,** circuitous: indirect.—*n.* a merry-go-round: a place at a road junction where traffic circulates in one direction.—*adjs.* **round′-arm,** (of bowling) with nearly horizontal swing of the arm; **round′ed,** round: finished, complete, developed to perfection.—*ns.* **round′ers,** a bat-and-ball game in which players run from station to station; **round game,** a game to be played by any number of players, each for himself; **Round′head,** a Puritan (from the close-cut hair); **round′-house,** a cabin on the afterpart of the quarter-deck.—*adj.* **round′ish.**—*adv.* **round′ly.**—*ns.* **round′ness;**

rounds′man, one who goes round, esp. one sent to by a shopkeeper to take orders and deliver goods.—*adj.* **round′-ta′ble,** meeting on equal terms, like the inner circle of King Arthur's knights who sat at a round table.—*n.* **round′-up,** a driving together, as all the cattle in a ranch, a set of persons wanted by the police, &c.—**get round to,** to have the time or inclination to do (something) after delay; **round off,** to finish off neatly; **round on,** to turn upon in anger, to assail with reproaches: to betray; **round robin (Robin),** a paper with signatures in a circle, that no one may seem to be a ringleader; **round the clock,** for twenty-four hours on end; **round up,** gather in, collect. [O.Fr. *rund-, rond-* (Fr. *rond*)—L. *rotundus*—*rota,* a wheel.]

roundel, *rown′dl, n.* anything circular: a circle: a rondeau, a rondel.—*n.* **roun′delay,** a song with a refrain: a dance in a ring. [O.Fr. *rondel, rondele, rondelet,* dims. of *rond,* round.]

roup, *rowp, n.* (*Scot.*) sale by auction.—*v.t.* to sell by auction. [Scand.]

rouse, *rowz, v.t.* to start (as game from cover or lair): to stir up: to awaken: to excite, to anger: to put in action.—*v.i.* to awake: to be excited to action.—*adj.* **rous′ing,** awakening: stirring, vigorous, violent.—*v.t.* **roust,** to stir up: to rout out.—*n.* **roustabout,** (*U.S.*) a wharf labourer: one who does odd jobs. [Origin obscure.]

rouse, *rowz, n.* a carousal: a bumper. [Prob. shortened form of **carouse.**]

rout, *rowt, n.* a tumultuous crowd, a rabble: a pack, herd, flock: (*arch.*) a large party, a fashionable evening assembly: a defeated body: an utter defeat: disorderly flight: disturbance.—*v.t.* to defeat utterly: to put to disorderly flight. [O.Fr. *route,* from the pa.p. of L. *rumpĕre, ruptum,* to break.]

rout, *rowt, v.i.* to snore. [O.E. *hrūtan.*]

rout, *rowt, v.t.* to grub up, as a pig: to scoop out.—*v.i.* to grub: to poke about. [An irregular variant of **root** (2).]

route, *rōōt* (in the army, *rowt*), *n.* a course to be traversed: marching orders.—*v.t.* to fix the route of: to send (by a particular route).—*n.* **route′-march,** a long march of troops in training. [Fr.,—L. *rupta (via),* broken way.]

routine, *rōō-tēn′, n.* regular, unvarying, or mechanical course of action or round: the set series of movements gone through in a dancing, skating, or other performance.—*adj.* (usu. *rōō′tēn*). [Fr.]

rove, *rōv, v.t.* to wander over or through.—*v.i.* to wander about: to ramble: to change about inconstantly.—*n.* **rō′ver,** a pirate, a privateer: a wanderer: an inconstant person: (formerly) a senior grade of Boy Scout.—*n.* and *adj.* **rō′ving.** [Partly at least from Du. *rooven,* to rob, *roofer,* robber.]

rove, *rōv, v.t.* to twist slightly in preparation for spinning. [Origin obscure.]

row, *rō, n.* a line or rank of persons or things as spectators, houses, turnips: a series in line, or in ordered succession.—**in a row,** in unbroken sequence. [O.E. *rāw*; Ger. *reihe,* Du. *rij.*]

row, *rō, v.t.* to impel with an oar: to transport by rowing.—*v.i.* to work with the oar: to be moved by oars.—*n.* an outing in a rowing-boat.—*ns.* **row′er; row′ing-boat.** [O.E. *rōwan.*]

row, *row, n.* a noisy squabble, a brawl: a din, hubbub: a chiding. [A late 18th-century word; possibly a back-formation from **rouse** (2).]

rowan, *row′ăn,* also *rō′ăn, n.* the mountain-ash, a tree of the rose family: its small red berry-like fruit. [Cf. Norw. *raun,* Swed. *rönn.*]

rowdy, *row′él, n.* a noisy turbulent person.—Also *adj.*—*ns.* **rowd′iness; rowd′yism.**

rowel, *row′él, n.* a little spiked wheel on a spur: a knob, ring, or disk on a horse's bit. [Fr. *rouelle*—Low L. *rotella,* dim. of L. *rota,* a wheel.]

rowlock, *rul′ók, n.* a contrivance serving as fulcrum for an oar. [Prob. for **oarlock**—O.E. *ārloc.*]

Roxburghe, *roks′b(ü)r-ŭ, n.* style of binding for books, with cloth or paper sides, plain leather back, gilt-top, other edges untrimmed, named from the Duke of *Roxburghe* (1740-1804), book-collector.

royal, *roi′ál, adj.* of a king or queen: kingly: magnificent: founded, chartered, or patronised by a king or queen.—*n.* a large size of paper: (also **royal sail**) a sail immediately above the top-gallant sail: a stag having antlers with twelve points.—*ns.* **roy′alism,** attachment to monarchy; **roy′alist,** an adherent of royalism.—*adv.* **roy′ally.**—*n.* **roy′alty,** kingship: the character, state, or office of a king: kingliness: the person of the sovereign: a royal family or its individual members: kingdom: a right or prerogative granted by a king or queen, esp. a right over minerals: payment to an author, composer, &c., for every copy sold or every public performance.—**royal blue,** a bright, deep-coloured blue; **Royal Commission,** a body of persons nominated by the Crown to inquire into and report on a specified matter; **royal road,** a short and easy way of circumventing difficulties.—**the Royals,** formerly the first regiment of foot in the British army (the Royal Scots). [Fr.,—L. *rēgālis,* regal.]

royster. Same as **roister.**

rozzer, *roz′ér, n.* (*slang*) a policeman.

rub, *rub, v.t.* to move something with pressure along the surface of: to clean, polish, or smooth, by friction: to remove, erase, or obliterate by friction (usu. with *away, off, out*): to irritate, fret.—*v.i.* to move with friction, to chafe, to grate: to make shift to get along somehow (with *along*):—*pr.p.* **rubb′ing:** *pa.t.* and *pa.p.* **rubbed.**—*n.* process or act of rubbing: a difficulty, a hitch, an irritating experience.—*n.* **rubb′er,** one who, or that which, rubs or massages: an eraser: an article for rubbing with, as a hard brush, a file, &c.: india-rubber (q.v.), or a substitute: a piece of india-rubber for erasing: a rubber overshoe.—*n.* **rubb′er-neck,** one who cranes or twists his neck in curiosity: a sight-seer.—*v.i.* to behave as a rubber-neck.—*n.* **rubb′erstamp,** an instrument for stamping by hand with ink, the characters being in flexible vulcanised rubber: a conventional person or one unquestioningly devoted to routine or officialdom.—*adj.* routine, official.—*n.* **rubb′ing,** application of friction: an impression of an inscribed surface (esp. a church brass) produced by rubbing heel-ball or plumbago upon

Neutral vowels in unaccented syllables: *em′pér-ór*; for certain sounds in foreign words see p. ix.

636

paper laid over it.—**rub along,** to make shift to get along somehow; **rub down,** to rub from head to foot; **rub in,** to force into the pores by friction: to be unpleasantly insistent in emphasising; **rub the wrong way,** to irritate by tactless handling; **rub shoulders,** to come into social contact; **rub up,** to polish: to freshen one's memory of. [Cf. Low Ger. *rubben.*]

rub-a-dub(-dub), *rub'a-dub(-dub'), n.* the sound of a drum. [Imit.]

rubato, *rōō-bä'tō, adj.* and *adv.* (*mus.*) in modified or distorted rhythm.—*n.* a passage so played. [It., pa.p. of *rubare,* to steal.]

rubber. See under **rub.**

rubber, *rub'ér, n.* chiefly in bridge and whist, the winning of, or play for, the best of three games (sometimes five). [Origin obscure.]

rubbish, *rub'ish, n.* fragments of ruinous buildings: waste matter: litter: trash: nonsense.—*adj.* **rubb'ishy,** worthless. [Origin obscure; app. conn. with **rubble.**]

rubble, *rub'l, n.* loose fragments of rock or ruined buildings: undressed irregular stones used in rough masonry: masonry of such a kind.—*n.* **rubb'le-work** coarse masonry. [Origin obscure; cf. **rubbish.**]

rubella, *rōō-bel'a n.* German measles. [Dim. from L. *rubeus,* red.]

Rubicon, *rōōb'i-kon, n.* a stream of Central Italy, separating Caesar's province of Gallia Cisalpina from Italia proper—its crossing by Caesar (49 B.C.) being thus a virtual declaration of war against the republic.—**cross the Rubicon,** take a decisive, irrevocable step. [L. *Rubicō, -ōnis.*]

rubicund, *rōō'bi-kund, adj.* ruddy.—*n.* **rubicun'dity.** [L. *rubicundus—rubēre,* to be red.]

rubidium, *rōō-bid'i-úm, n.* a metallic element (symbol Rb; atomic no. 37), widely distributed in nature in small amounts. [Formed from L. *rubidus,* red.]

ruble. Same as **rouble.**

rubric, *rōō'brik, n.* a heading, entry, or liturgical direction, orig. one in red: a flourish after a signature: a thing definitely settled.—*adj.* in red: ruddy.—*adj.* **ru'brical.** [L. *rubrīca,* red ochre—*ruber,* red.]

ruby, *rōō'bi, n.* a highly-prized precious stone of a red colour: applied to various red things (lip, pimple, wine): a small printing type.—*adj.* red as a ruby.—*v.t.* to redden:—*pr.p.* ru'bying; *pa.t.* and *pa.p.* ru'bied. [O.Fr. *rubi* and *rubin*—L. *rubeus—ruber,* red.]

ruche, *rōōsh, n.* a pleated frilling.—*v.t.* to trim with a ruche.—*n.* **ruch'ing.** [Fr.; prob. Celt.]

ruck, *ruk, n.* a wrinkle, fold, or crease.—*v.t.* and *v.i.* to wrinkle.—*n.* **ruck'le,** a pucker. [O.N. *hrukka,* a wrinkle.]

ruck, *ruk, n.* a heap, stack, or rick, as of fuel, hay, &c.: the common run of people. [Probably Scand.]

rucksack, *rōōk'-, ruk'-sak, -zäk, n.* a bag carried on the back by tourists. [Ger. dial. *ruck* (Ger. *rucken*), back, and Ger. *sack,* bag.]

ruction, *ruk'sh(ó)n, n.* (*slang*) a disturbance, a rumpus. [Perh. for **insurrection.**]

rudder, *rud'ér, n.* a steering apparatus: a flat structure hinged to the stern of a ship or boat for steering: a similar movable surface in a vertical plane for steering an aeroplane left or

right: (*fig.*) something, as a principle, that guides a person in life. [O.E. *rōthor,* oar; Ger. *ruder,* oar.]

ruddle, *rud'l, n.* red ochre.—*v.t.* to mark with ruddle: to rouge coarsely.—*n.* **rudd'leman,** one who digs or deals in ruddle.—Also **redd'le, redd'leman.** [Prob. from obs. *rud,* red.]

ruddy, *rud'i* (*comp.* **rudd'ier,** *superl.* **rudd'iest**), *adj.* red: reddish: of the colour of the skin in high health.—*adv.* **rudd'ily.**—*n.* **rudd'iness.** [O.E. *rudig;* cf. **red.**]

rude, *rōōd, adj.* uncultured: unskilled: discourteously unmannerly: ungentle, harsh: crude, coarse.—*adv.* **rude'ly.**—*n.* **rude'ness.** [L. *rudis,* rough.]

rudiment, *rōōd'i-mént, n.* (usu. in *pl.*) a first principle or element: anything in a rude or first state.—*adjs.* **rudimental** (*-ment'ál*), rudimentary; **rudiment'ary,** of rudiments: elementary: in an early or arrested stage of development. [L. *rudīmentum—rudis,* rough, raw.]

rue, *rōō, n.* a strong-smelling Mediterranean shrub, with bitter leaves and greenish-yellow flowers. [Fr. *rue*—L. *rūta*—Peloponnesian Gr. *rhytē.*]

rue, *rōō, n.* (*arch.*) repentance, regret: sorrow: pity.—*v.t.* to be sorry for, to repent of: to contemplate backing out of:—*pr.p.* rue'ing, ru'ing; *pa.t.* and *pa.p.* rued.—*adj.* **rue'ful,** sorrowful: (facetiously) piteous.—*adv.* **rue'fully.**—*n.* **rue'fulness.** [O.E. *hrēow,* n., *hrēowan,* vb.; cf. Ger. *reue,* O.H.G. *hriuwa,* mourning.]

ruff, *ruf, n.* a frill, usually starched and pleated, worn round the neck, esp. in the reigns of Elizabeth and James I: a frilled appearance on the neck of a bird or animal.—*v.t.* to furnish with a ruff. [Perh. from **ruffle.**]

ruff, *ruf, n.* a kind of sandpiper, the male with a ruff during the breeding season:—*fem.* **reeve, ree.** [Perh. **ruff** (1), but the fem. is a difficulty.]

ruff, *ruf, n.* an old card game: an act of trumping. *v.t.* and *v.i.* to trump. [Perh. conn. with O.Fr. *roffle,* It. *ronfa,* a card game.]

ruffian, *ruf'i-án, -yän, n.* a brutal, violent person: a bully.—*adj.* brutal: violent.—*n.* **ruff'ianism.**—*adj.* **ruff'ianly.** [O.Fr. *ruffian.*]

ruffle, *ruf'l, v.t.* to make uneven, disturb the smoothness of: to wrinkle: to disorder: to agitate, to disturb the equanimity of.—*v.i.* to grow rough: to flutter.—*n.* a frill, esp. at the wrist or neck: annoyance: a quarrel: agitation. [Origin uncertain. Cf. Low Ger. *ruffelen.*]

rufous, *rōō'fus, adj.* reddish or brownish-red. [L. *rūfus,* akin to *ruber,* red.]

rug, *rug, n.* a thick heavy floor-mat, esp. for the hearth: a thick covering or wrap, as for travelling. [Cf. Norw. dial. *rugga, rogga,* coarse coverlet, Swed. *rugg,* coarse hair.]

Rugby, rugby, *rug'bi, n.* the form of football using an oval ball which (unlike *Association*) permits carrying the ball—(*coll.*) **rugg'er.**—**Rugby (Union) football,** the original form of the game, with 15 players; **Rugby League football,** a modified form of the game subject to professional rules, with 13 players. [From *Rugby* school.]

rugged, *rug'id, adj.* rough: uneven: massively irregular: unpolished (e.g. verse): strong, unbending (e.g. character, honesty).—*adv.* **rugg'edly.**—*n.* **rugg'edness.** [Prob. rel. to **rug.**]

rugose **run**

rugose, rōō′gōs′, adj. wrinkled, covered with sunken lines.—Also **ru′gous.** [L. rūgōsus—rūga, a wrinkle.]

ruin, rōō′in, n. downfall, collapse, overthrow: complete destruction: bankruptcy: irrevocable loss of position or reputation: cause of ruin: broken-down remains, esp. of a building (often in pl.).—v.t. to reduce or bring to ruin.—n. **ruina′tion,** act of ruining: state of being ruined.—adj. **ru′inous,** fallen to ruins, decayed: bringing ruin. [L. ruīna—ruěre, to tumble down.]

rule, rōōl, n. an instrument used in drawing straight lines: a measuring-rod: government: a principle, a standard, maxim or formula: a straight line: that which is normal: a regulation, an order.—v.t. to mark with straight lines: to draw with a rule: to govern, to manage: to determine or declare authoritatively to be: to determine, decree (that).—v.i. to exercise power (with over): to be prevalent: to stand or range in price.—n. **ru′ler,** a strip or roller for ruling lines: one who rules.—adj. **ru′ling,** predominant: prevailing: reigning.—n. an authoritative decision.—**as a rule,** usually; **be ruled,** take advice; **rule of the road,** the regulations to be observed in traffic by land, water, or air—thus in Britain drivers, riders and cyclists take the left side in meeting, and the right in overtaking; **rule of three,** the method of finding the fourth term of a proportion when three are given; **rule of thumb,** any rough-and-ready practical method; **rule out,** to exclude as a choice or possibility; **slide-rule,** see **slide.** [O.Fr. reule (Fr. règle)—L. rēgula—regěre, to rule.]

rum, rum, n. a spirit distilled from fermented sugar-cane juice or from molasses. [Perh. from rumbullion; or kindred form.]

rum, rum, adj. (slang) queer, droll, odd.—Also **rumm′y.**—advs. **rumm′ly, rumm′ily.**—n. **rumm′iness.** [16th-century slang.]

rumba, rōōm′ba, rum′ba, n. a violent Cuban Negro dance: a civilised imitation of it. [Sp.]

rumble, rum′bl, v.i. to make a low heavy grumbling or rolling noise.—v.t. (slang) to guess (a secret) correctly or discover it accidentally.—n. a sound of rumbling: a seat, as for servants, behind a carriage: a quarrel, disturbance.—n. **rum′bling.—rum′ble seat,** a folding seat at the back of a car. [Perh. Low Ger.; cf. Du. rommelen, Ger. rummeln.]

rumbullion, rum-bul′yon, n. (obs.) rum.

rumbustious, rum-bust′yús, adj. (coll.) boisterous. [Prob. robust.]

ruminant, rōō′mi-nánt, n. an animal that chews the cud.—adj. cud-chewing: meditative.—v.i. **ru′mināte,** to chew the cud: to meditate.—v.t. to chew over again: to muse on.—n. **ruminā′tion.** [L. rūmināre, -ātum—rūmen, -inis, the gullet.]

rummage, rum′ij, n. a thorough search: a search creating disorder.—v.t. to ransack.—v.i. to make a search.—**rummage sale,** a sale of unclaimed goods: a jumble sale. [Fr. arrumage (now arrimage), stowage.]

rummer, rum′ér, n. a large drinking-glass. [Du. roemer; Ger. römer.]

rummy, rum′i, n. a card game for two or more.

rumour, rōō′mór, n. hearsay, general talk: a current story.—v.t. to put about by report. [O.Fr.,—L. rūmor, -ōris, a noise.]

rump, rump, n. the hinder part of an animal's body, the root of the tail with parts adjoining. [Scand.]

rumple, rum′pl, n. a fold or wrinkle.—v.t. to crush out of shape, crumple, crease. [Du. rompel; cf. O.E. hrimpan, to wrinkle.]

rumpus, rum′pus, n. an uproar, a disturbance.

run, run, v.i. to go swiftly: to go at a running pace: to hurry: to ply (from, to, between): to proceed through a sequence of operations, or go, as a machine: to follow a course: to flow: to spread, diffuse: to discharge: to have a course, stretch, or extent: to average: to be current: to be valid: to stand as a candidate: to recur repeatedly or remain persistently (in the mind).—v.t. to cause to run: to hunt: to drive forward: to thrust: to enter, promote, put forward: to incur:—pr.p. runn′ing; pa.t. ran; pa.p. run.—n. an act, spell, or manner of running: a trip: distance or time of running: a continuous stretch or series: a rush for payment, as upon a bank: flow or discharge: a ladder, e.g. in a stocking: course: prevalence: the usual kind: a spell of being in general demand: a unit of scoring in cricket, the batsmen's passage between the wickets: an enclosure for chickens, &c.: freedom of access to all parts.—ns. **run′about,** a gadabout: a vagabond: a small light vehicle or aeroplane; **run′away,** a fugitive: a horse that bolts: a flight.—adj. fleeing: done by or in flight.—adj. **run′-down′,** in weakened health.—n. a reduction in numbers: a statement bringing together all the main items.—adj. **runn′able,** of a stag, fit for hunting.—ns. **runn′er,** one who, or that which, runs: a racer: a messenger: a rooting stem that runs along the ground: (hist.) a police officer: a rope to increase the power of a tackle: a blade of a skate or sledge; **runn′er-up,** the competitor next after the winner or winners.—adj. **runn′ing,** kept for the race: done at or with a run: continuous: flowing: easy: discharging: hasty: (used adverbially) successively (three days running).—n. action of the verb: the pace: management, control.—ns. **runn′ing-board,** a footboard along the side of a motor-car or engine; **runn′ing comm′entary,** commentary accompanying a text: a broadcast description of a game or other event in progress; **runn′ing-fight,** a fight between pursuer and pursued; **runn′ing-fire** (mil.) a rapid succession of firing; **runn′ing-gear,** wheels and axles of a vehicle; **runn′ing knot,** one that slips along a string or rope and increases or decreases the size of a loop or noose.—n.pl. **runn′ing-lights,** the lights shown by vessels between sunset and sunrise.—**running mate,** a runner who makes the pace for another: a horse teamed with another, or making the pace for another: in U.S., the candidate for the less important of two associated offices, esp. the candidate for the vice-presidency considered in relation to the presidential candidate.—adj. **run-of-the-mill,** constituting an ordinary fair sample, not selected: mediocre.—n. **run′way,** track or passage-way: path for aircraft to take off from or land on.—**run down,** pursue to exhaustion

Neutral vowels in unaccented syllables: em′pér-ór; for certain sounds in foreign words see p. ix.

638

or capture: collide with and knock over or sink: to disparage: to become unwound or exhausted: to find after searching; **run in**, to go in: to arrest and take to a lock-up: to bring (new machinery) into good condition by preliminary working; **run off**, to cause to flow out: to print impressions of: to repeat rapidly; **run on**, to continue without a break; **run out**, to leak: to run short (of): to put out (a batsman) by striking with the ball the wicket to which he is running; **run over**, to overflow: to run down: to go over cursorily: of a vehicle, to knock down a person or animal; **run short**, to exhaust supplies; **run it fine**, to allow very little margin; **run to**, to be sufficient for; **run to seed**, to produce seed rather than vegetation: to go to waste; **run up**, to make or mend hastily: to build hurriedly: to string up, hang: to incur increasingly.—**a run for one's money**, a spell of fun or gain for expense or effort; **in the running**, on the list of candidates having a chance of success; **make the running**, to set the pace. [O.E. *rinnan, irnan, iernan,* to run.]

runagate, *run'ā-gāt, n.* a vagabond. [renegade, influenced by **run,** and adv. *agate,* away.]

rune, *rōōn, n.* a letter of the ancient Germanic alphabet: a secret, a mystic symbol, sentence, spell, or song: a song or canto.—*adj.* **ru'nic.** [O.E. and O.N. *rūn,* mystery, rune.]

rung, *rung, n.* a spoke: a cross-bar or rail: a ladder round or step. [O.E. *hrung*; Ger. *runge.*]

rung, *pa.p.* of **ring** (2).

runnel, *run'l, n.* a little brook: a gutter. [O.E. *rynel,* dim. of *ryne,* a stream—*rinnan,* to run.]

runner, running. See **run.**

runt, *runt, n.* small, stunted, or old ox or cow: a small pig, esp. the smallest of a litter: anything undersized: a breed of pigeons: a dead tree-stump: a cabbage stem: a vague term of abuse. [Origin obscure.]

rupee, *rōō-pē', n.* a monetary unit and nickel (orig. silver) coin; in new Indian coinage, 100 new pice (see **pice**). [Hindustani *rupīyah.*]

rupture, *rup'tyur, -chŭr, n.* a breach, breaking, or bursting: the state of being broken: breach of harmony, relations, or negotiations: hernia (q.v.).—*v.t.* and *v.i.* to break or burst. [L.L. *ruptūra*—L. *rumpĕre, ruptum,* to break.]

rural, *rōō'rål, adj.* of the country (as opposed to the town).—*v.t.* **ru'ralise,** to render rural.—*v.i.* to become rural: to rusticate.—*adv.* **ru'rally.** [L. *rūrālis*—*rūs, rūris,* the country.]

ruse, *rōōz, n.* a trick, stratagem, artifice. [O.Fr. *ruse*—*ruser,* to get out of the way, double on one's tracks; cf. **rush** (1).]

rush, *rush, v.i.* to move forward with haste, impetuosity, or rashness.—*v.t.* to force out of place: to hasten or hustle forward, or into any action.—*n.* a swift impetuous forward movement: (*fig.*) haste suggesting this: a hurry: an unedited print of a motion picture scene or series of scenes for immediate viewing by the film-makers.—**rush hour,** a time of maximum activity or traffic.—**rush one's fences,** to act over-hastily. [Anglo-Fr. *russher,* O.Fr. *ruser* (Fr. *ruser*); cf. **ruse.**]

rush, *rush, n.* a grasslike marsh-growing plant: a stalk of such a plant: a rush wick: a valueless trifle.—*adj.* **rush'-bott'omed,** having a seat made with rushes.—*ns.* **rush'-cand'le, rush'-**

light, a candle or night-light having a wick of rush-pith: a small, feeble light.—*adjs.* **rush'en,** made of rushes; **rush'y,** rush-like: abounding in, or made of, rushes.[O.E. *risce*; Ger. *risch.*]

rusk, *rusk, n.* a small cake like a piece of very hard toast. [Sp. *rosca,* a roll; origin unknown.]

russet, *rus'ét, n.* a coarse homespun cloth or dress: a reddish brown colour: a reddish brown variety of apple.—*adj.* made of russet: reddish brown.—*adj.* **russ'ety.** [O.Fr. *rousset*—rare L. *russus,* red.]

Russian boots, *rush'yån bōōts,* high boots, with pliable leather uppers round the calves of the legs, and without laces or buttons in front.

Russian tea, tea with lemon instead of milk.

Russo-, *rus'ō-, adj.* (in composition) Russian, as **Russ'ophile** (*n.* and *adj.*), favouring or friendly towards Russia; **Russ'ophobe,** afraid of or hostile towards Russia.

rust, *rust, n.* the reddish-brown coating on iron exposed to moisture: any similar coating or appearance: any plant disease characterised by a rusty appearance, caused by fungi: the colour of rust.—*v.i.* to become rusty: to become dull by inaction.—*v.t.* to make rusty: to impair by time and inactivity.—*adj.* **rust'y,** covered with rust: impaired by inactivity or disuse: discoloured through age.—*n.* **rust'iness.**—*adjs.* **rust'less; rust'-proof.** [O.E. *rūst*; Ger. *rost.*]

rustic, *rus'tik, adj.* of, or characteristic of, the country or country-dwellers: simple: awkward, unrefined.—*adv.* **rus'tically.**—*v.t.* **rus'ticate,** to send into the country: to banish for a time from town or college.—*v.i.* to live in the country.—*ns.* **rustica'tion; rusticity** (*-tis'i-ti*), rustic manner: simplicity: rudeness. [L. *rūsticus*—*rūs,* the country.]

rustle, *rus'l, v.i.* to make a soft, whispering sound, as of dry leaves.—*n.* a quick succession of small sounds, as that of dry leaves.—*n.* and *adj.* **rus'tling.** [Imit.; cf. Flemish *ruysselen.*]

rustle, *rus'l, v.i* to act energetically.—*v.t.* to steal, esp. cattle.—*n.* **rust'ler,** a hustler: a cattle thief.—**rustle up,** to gather together, arrange. [rustle (1).]

rut, *rut, n.* a furrow made by wheels: a fixed course difficult to depart from.—*v.t.* to furrow with ruts:—*pr.p.* rutt'ing; *pa.t.* and *pa.p.* rutt'ed.

rut, *rut, n.* sexual excitement in male deer: also in other animals.—*v.i.* to be in heat. [O.Fr. *ruit, rut*—L. *rugītus*—*rugīre,* to roar.]

ruth—*rōōth, n.* pity, sorrow, remorse.—*adj.* **ruth'ful.**—*adv.* **ruth'fully.**—*adj.* **ruth'less,** pitiless: unsparing.—*adv.* **ruth'lessly.**—*n.* **ruth'lessness.** [M.E. *ruthe, reuth.* From **rue** (2); with ending *-th.*]

ruthenium, *rōō-thē'ni-ùm, n.* a metallic element (symbol Ru; atomic no. 44). [From Low L. *Ruthenia,* Russia.]

rutherfordium. See **kurchatovium.**

rye, *rī, n.* a grass allied to wheat and barley: its grain, used for making bread, &c.: rye-whisky.—*ns.* **rye'-grass,** a variety of grass cultivated for pasture and fodder; **rye'-whisky,** whisky made from rye. [O.E. *ryge*; O.N. *rugr,* Ger. *roggen.*]

rye, *rī, n.* a gypsy word for gentleman. [Romany *rei, rai,* lord.]

ryot, *raiyat, rī'ōt, n.* an Indian peasant [Hindustani *raiyat*—Ar. *ra'iyah,* a subject.]

---

fāte, fär; mē, hûr (her); *mīne; mōte, för; mūte; mōōn, fŏŏt;* ᴛʜᴇɴ (then)

S

Sabaoth, *sa-bā'oth, n.pl.* armies, used only in the B. phrase, 'the Lord of Sabaoth': erroneously for Sabbath. [Heb. *tsebāōth, tseboāth,* pl. of *tsābā,* an army.]

Sabbath, *sab'ath, n.* among the Jews, Saturday, set apart for rest from work: among most Christians, Sunday: a sabbatical year of the Jews: a time of rest: (also **sabb'at**) witches' midnight meeting.—*adj.* of, or appropriate to, the Sabbath.—*n.* **Sabbatā'rian,** a very strict observer of the Sabbath, Saturday or Sunday.—*adj.* pertaining to the Sabbath or to Sabbatarians.—*ns.* **Sabbatā'rianism; Sabb'ath-break'er,** one who profanes the Sabbath; **Sabb'ath-break'ing,** profanation of the Sabbath.—*adjs.* **sabbat'ic, -al** (or *cap.*), pertaining to, or resembling, the Sabbath: enjoying or bringing rest.—**sabbatical year,** (*hist.*) among the Jews, every seventh year, in which the ground was left untilled, &c.: a year's vacation, e.g. from a university post. [Heb. *Shabbāth.*]

sable, *sā'bl, n.* a marten found in arctic regions, valued for its glossy fur: its fur.—*adj.* made of sable fur. [O.Fr. *sable*; prob. from Slav.]

sable, *sā'bl, n.* and *adj.* black: dark: the heraldic tincture (colour) black, represented by horizontal and vertical lines crossing each other. [Fr. *sable*; perh. the same as the foregoing.]

sabot, *sab'ō, n.* a wooden shoe, worn by the peasantry in France and elsewhere.—*n.* **sabotage** (-*täzh'*), deliberate destruction of machinery, &c., in the course of a dispute with an employer: similar destruction intended to slow down production for political or other reasons: action taken to prevent the achievement of any aim.—*v.t.* and *v.i.* to destroy or do damage in this way: (*fig.*) deliberately to destroy the chances of success of (an undertaking).—*n.* **saboteur** (-*tœr'*), one who sabotages. [Fr. *sabot.*]

sabre, *sā'bér, n.* a heavy one-edged sword, slightly curved towards the point, used by cavalry.—*v.t.* to wound or kill with a sabre.—*n.* **sā'bre-ratt'ling,** military bluster. [Fr. *sabre*—Ger. *Säbel.*]

sac, *sak, n.* (*biol.*) a pouch. [Fr.,—L.*saccus,* a bag.]

saccharine, *sak'a-rin, -rēn, adj.* pertaining to, or having the qualities of, sugar: (*fig.*) sickly-sweet (e.g. *a saccharine smile*).—*adjs.* **sacchar'ic,** pertaining to, or obtained from, sugar and allied substances; **saccharif'erous,** yielding sugar.—*v.t.* **sacchar'ify,** to convert into sugar.—*ns.* **saccharom'eter,** an instrument for measuring the quantity of saccharine matter in a liquid; **sacch'arin,** an intensely sweet crystalline solid, used as a substitute for sugar. [Fr. *saccharin*—L. *saccharum,* sugar.]

sacerdotal, *sas-ér-dō'tál, adj.* priestly.—*ns.* **sacerdō'talism,** the spirit of the priesthood: devotion to priestly interests, priestcraft; **sacerdō'talist,** a supporter of sacerdotalism.

—*adv.* **sacerdō'tally.** [L. *sacerdōs, -ōtis,* a priest—*sacer,* sacred, *dăre,* to give.]

sachem, *sā'chem, n.* a North American Indian chief. [Native word.]

sachet, *sa'shā, n.* a small, usu. perfumed, bag: a small paper or plastic envelope for holding shampoo, &c. [Fr.]

sack, *sak, n.* a large bag of coarse cloth material for holding grain, flour, &c.: the contents of a sack: a woman's gown, loose at the back: a short coat fitting loosely: a woman's loose-fitting waistless dress.—*v.t.* to put into a sack: (*coll.*) to dismiss.—*ns.* **sack'cloth,** cloth for sacks: coarse cloth formerly worn in mourning or penance; **sack'ing,** coarse cloth or canvas for sacks, &c.; **sack'-race,** a race in which the legs of each competitor are confined by a sack.—**get the sack,** to be dismissed or rejected; **give the sack,** to dismiss. [O.E. *sacc*—L. *saccus*—Gr. *sakkos.*]

sack, *sak, n.* the plunder or devastation of a town.—*v.t.* to plunder: to strip of valuables.—*n.* **sack'ing,** the storming and pillaging of a town. [Fr. *sac,* a sack, plunder (*saccager,* to sack)—L. *saccus,* a sack.]

sack, *sak, n.* the old name of a dry Spanish wine. [Fr. *sec*—L. *siccus,* dry.]

sackbut, *sak'but, n.* an early form of the trombone (q.v.): (*B.*) a stringed instrument resembling the guitar. [Fr. *saquebute.*]

sacrament, *sak'rá-mént, n.* a religious rite variously regarded as a channel, or as a sign, of grace: the Lord's Supper.—*adj.* **sacramen'tal,** belonging to or constituting a sacrament.—*adv.* **sacramen'tally.**—*n.* **sacramentā'rian,** one who holds a high or extreme view of the efficacy of the sacraments.—*adj.* **sacramen'tary,** pertaining to the sacrament of the Lord's Supper, or to the sacramentarians. [L. *sacrāmentum,* an oath, pledge—*sacrāre,* to consecrate—*sacer,* sacred.]

sacred, *sā'krid, adj.* dedicated (esp. to God): appropriated (to a specified person) for his sole use: made holy by dedication, or by association with a holy person: proceeding from God: religious: not to be violated: (*rare*) accursed.—*adv.* **sā'credly.**—*n.* **sā'credness.**—**sacred college,** the cardinals, to whom pertains the right of electing a new pope; **sacred cow,** an institution, custom, &c. so venerated that it is above criticism. [O.Fr. *sacrer*—L. *sacrāre*—L. *sacer,* sacred.]

sacrifice, *sak'ri-fīs, n.* the fundamental institution of all natural religions, primarily a sacramental meal at which the communicants are a deity and his worshippers: the act of sacrificing or offering to a deity, esp. a victim on an altar: that which is sacrificed or offered: destruction or surrender of anything to gain an important end: that which is surrendered or destroyed for such an end: loss of profit.—

Neutral vowels in unaccented syllables: *em'pér-ór*; for certain sounds in foreign words see p. ix.

640

v.t. (*-fīs*, or *-fīz*) to offer up in sacrifice: to make a sacrifice of: to give up for a higher good or for mere advantage: to disregard or neglect the interests of.—*v.i.* to offer sacrifice.—*n.* **sac′rificer.**—*adj.* **sacrifi′cial** (*-fish′ál*), relating to, or consisting in, sacrifice: performing sacrifice.—*adv.* **sacrifi′cially.** [L. *sacrificium*—*sacer*, sacred, *facĕre*, to make.]

sacrilege, *sak′ri-léj, n.* profanation of anything holy: the breaking into a place of worship and stealing therefrom.—*adj.* **sacrilegious** (*-léj′ús*, or *-lij′-*), guilty of sacrilege: profane.—*adv.* **sacrileg′iously.**—*n.* **sacrileg′iousness.** [Fr. *sacrilège*—L. *sacrilegium*—*sacer*, sacred, *legĕre*, to gather.]

sacrist, *sā′krist, n.* a sacristan: a person in a cathedral who copies out music for the choir and takes care of the books.—*ns.* **sac′ristan** (*sak′-*), an officer in a church who has charge of the sacred vessels and other movables: a sexton; **săc′risty,** an apartment in a church where the sacred utensils, vestments, &c., are kept: a vestry. [Low L. *sacrista, sacristānus,* a sacristan, *sacristia,* a vestry—L. *sacer,* sacred.]

sacrosanct, *sak′rō-sangt′, adj.* inviolable, that must not be profaned: holy and worthy of reverence. [L. *sacrōsanctus*—*sacer,* sacred, *sanctus,* pa.p. of *sancīre,* to hallow.]

sacrum, *sā′krum, n.* a triangular bone situated at the lower part of the vertebral column. [L. (*os*) *sacrum,* holy (bone).]

sad, *sad* (*comp.* **sadd′er,** *superl.* **sadd′est**), *adj.* (*orig.*) sated: serious, earnest, grave: sorrowful, dejected: regrettable, calamitous: deplorable (often playfully): sober-coloured: not properly risen (e.g. bread).—*v.t.* **sadd′en,** to make sad.—*v.i.* to grow sad.—*adv.* **sad′ly.**—*n.* **sad′ness.** [O.E. *sæd,* sated, weary; cf. Du. *zat,* Ger. *satt*; L. *sat, satis.*]

saddle, *sad′l, n.* a seat for a rider: a pad for the back of a draught animal: anything of like shape: a col: a butcher's cut, including a part of the backbone with the ribs.—*v.t.* to put a saddle on, to load: to encumber (with): to fix the responsibility for (something, upon a person).—*n.* **sadd′le-bag,** a bag carried at or attached to the saddle.—*adj.* upholstered in cloth in imitation of camels' saddle-bags.—*ns.* **sadd′le-bow** (*-bō*), the arched front of a saddle-tree or saddle from which weapons, &c., were often hung; **sadd′le-girth,** a band passing round the body of a horse to hold the saddle in its place; **sadd′le-horse,** a horse suitable for riding; **sadd′ler,** a maker or seller of saddles; **sadd′lery,** occupation of a saddler: his shop or stock in trade: materials for saddlery **sadd′le-tree,** the frame of a saddle. [O.E. *sadol, sadel*; cf. Du. *zadel,* Ger. *sattel.*]

Sadducee, *sad′ū-sē, n.* one of a Jewish sceptical school or party of priestly aristocrats, in opposition to whom a class of lay teachers, later called Pharisees, arose.—*adj.* **Saddūcē′an,** of or relating to the Sadducees. [Gr. *Saddoukaios*—Heb. *Tsaddūqīm* (pl.).]

sadism, *sād′-, sad′-,* or *sād′izm, n.* a perversion in which pleasure is obtained by torturing the loved one: pleasure in inflicting or watching cruelty.—*n.* **sad′ist.**—*adj.* **sadis′tic.**—*ns.* **sad′omas′ochism,** obtaining pleasure by inflicting pain on oneself or another; **sado-masochist.**

—*adj.* **sado-masochistic.** [Marquis de *Sade,* 1740–1814, who died insane, depicted this perversion in his novels.]

safari, *sa-fä′ri, n.* an expedition, esp. of hunting: a caravan, esp. for such a purpose: a long expedition involving difficulty or danger and/or requiring planning. [Swahili (q.v.).]

safe, *sāf, adj.* unharmed: free from danger: secure (from): not involving risk: trustworthy: cautious (e.g. *a safe driver*).—*n.* a chest or closet for money, &c., safe against fire, thieves, &c., generally of iron: a chest or cupboard for meats.—*ns.* **safe′-blow′ing,** forcing safes using explosives; **safe′-break′ing,** illegal opening of safes; **safe′-con′duct,** a writing, passport, or guard granted to a person to enable him to travel with safety; **safe′guard,** anything that increases security or averts danger: a guard, passport, or warrant to protect a traveller.—*v.t.* to protect.—*n.* **safe′-keep′ing,** protection: custody.—*adv.* **safe′ly.**—*ns.* **safe′ness; safe′ty,** freedom from danger or loss; **safe′ty-belt,** a belt for fastening a workman, &c., to a fixed object while he carries out a dangerous operation: a belt for fastening a passenger to his seat as a precaution against injury in a crash; **safe′ty-cur′tain,** fireproof curtain in a theatre; **safe′ty(-)glass,** a sandwich of plastic material between sheets of glass: glass toughened by heating and cooling in a particular way: glass reinforced with wire; **safe′ty(-)lamp,** a lamp, used in mines, that will not ignite inflammable gases; **safe′ty(-)match,** a match which can be ignited only on a surface specially prepared for the purpose; **safe′ty(-)pin,** a pin in the form of a clasp with a guard covering its point; **safe′ty(-)razor,** a razor with a detachable blade held in a guard or guards; **safe′ty (-)valve,** a valve that opens when pressure becomes too great for safety; (*fig.*) any outlet that gives relief.—**safe and sound,** unharmed, uninjured; **safety first,** a slogan advocating a policy of taking no risks.—**a safe seat,** a seat that the political party or politician under consideration will certainly win; **err** (or **be**) **on the safe side,** to choose the safer alternative; **play for safety,** (*lit.* and *fig.*) to avoid risks in a game, &c. [O.Fr. *sauf*—L. *salvus*: prob. allied to *sōlus,* alone.]

saffron, *saf′rón, n.* a species of crocus: a colouring substance prepared from its yellow stigmas.—*adj.* orange-yellow. [O.Fr. *safran*—Ar. *za′farān.*]

sag, *sag, v.i* to bend, sink, or droop: to yield or give way as from weight or pressure:—*pr.p.* **sagging;** *pa.t.* and *pa.p.* **sagged.**—*n.* a droop. [Cf. Swed. *sacka,* to sink down; Low Ger. *sacken,* to sink.]

saga, *sä′ga, n.* a prose tale in the old literature of Iceland: (*coll.*) a long, detailed story—**saga novel,** a river novel. [O.N.]

sagacious, *sa-gā′shús, adj.* keen in perception or thought, discerning and judicious: shrewd, having practical wisdom: arising from or showing judiciousness or shrewdness: (of animals) intelligent.—*adv.* **sagā′ciously.**—*ns.* **sagā′ciousness, sagacity** (*sa-ga′si-ti*) [L. *sagāx, sagācis.*]

sage, *sāj, n.* a genus of plants of the same family

as the mints, one of which is used as stuffing for goose, &c.—*ns.* **sage′-brush**, a growth of undershrubs, with scent resembling sage, on dry American plains: any of the plants forming it; **sage′-green**, a greyish green.—*adj.* **sā′gy**, full of, or seasoned with, sage. [O.Fr. *sauge* (It. *salvia*)—L. *salvia—salvus*, safe.]

sage, *sāj, adj.* wise.—*n.* a man of great wisdom, esp. one of seven famous wise men of ancient Greece or a wise man of later times supposed to resemble them.—*adv.* **sage′ly.**—*n.* **sage′-ness.** [Fr. *sage*—L. *sapĕre*, to be wise.]

Sagittarius, *saj-i-tār′i-us, n.* the Archer, a constellation and sign of the zodiac. [L. *sagittārius—sagitta*, an arrow.]

sago, *sā′gō, n.* a nutritive farinaceous substance produced from the pith of several East Indian palms. [Malay *sāgū*.]

Sahara, *sa-hä′ra, n.* the great desert in N. Africa: any desert place (*lit.* and *fig.*). [Ar. *çahra*, desert.]

sahib, *sä′ib, n.* a term of respect given in India to persons of rank and formerly to Europeans. [Ar., friend.]

said, *sed, pa.t.* and *pa.p.* of **say**: the beforementioned (e.g. *the said witness*).

sail, *sāl, n.* a sheet of canvas, &c., spread to catch the wind, by which a ship is driven forward: a ship or ships: a trip in a vessel: an arm of a windmill.—*v.i.* to be moved by sails: to go by water: to begin a voyage: to glide or float smoothly along.—*v.t.* to navigate: to move upon, cross, in a ship (e.g. the sea): to fly through.—*ns.* **sail′-cloth**, a strong cloth for sails; **sail′er**, a boat or ship with respect to its mode of sailing, or its speed; **sail′ing**, act of sailing: motion of a vessel on water: act of directing a ship's course; **sail′ing-ship**, a ship driven by sails; **sail′or**, one who sails in a ship: a mariner: a navigator: a seaman; **sail(-)yard**, a yard on which a sail is spread.—**fore-and-aft sails**, those set parallel to the keel of a ship, as opp. to **square sails**, those set across the ship; **full sail**, with all sails set; **make sail**, to spread more sails; **set sail**, to spread the sails: to set out on a voyage; **shorten sail**, to reduce the extent of sails spread; **strike sail**, to lower the sail or sails; **under sail**, having the sails spread. [O.E. *segel*; cf. Du. *zeil*, Ger. *segel*.]

sain, *sān, v.t.* (*arch.*) to make the sign of the cross over: (by association with L. *sānāre*) to heal. [O.E. *segnian*—L. *signāre—signum*, mark.]

sainfoin, *sān′foin, n.* a leguminous fodder-plant.—Also **saint′foin.** [Fr., prob. *sain*, wholesome, *foin*, hay—L. *sānum fēnum.*]

saint, *sānt,* (when prefixed to a name) *sint, n.* a holy person, one eminent for virtue: one of the blessed dead: one canonised by the R.C. Church: (*pl.*) Christians generally.—*adjs.* **saint′ed**, holy, virtuous: sacred: gone to heaven: canonised; **saint′-like, saint′ly**, like or becoming a saint.—*n.* **saint′liness.**—**St. Bernard's dog** or (**Great**) **St Bernard**, a large dog, perh. a cross between the short-haired Newfoundland and the mastiff, kept, esp. formerly, at the hospice of the Great St Bernard pass in the Swiss Alps to rescue travellers lost in the snow; **St Elmo's fire**, a glow that appears at the end of masts and spars of ships during thunderstorms at night; **Saint's day**, a day set apart for the commemoration of a particular saint, as **St Andrew's Day**, 30th November, **St David's Day**, 1st March, **St George's Day**, 23rd April, **St Patrick's Day**, 17th March, **St Swithin's Day**, 15th July; **St Luke's summer**, a spell of pleasant weather about the middle of October; **St Martin's summer**, a spell of mild damp weather in late autumn.—**Latterday saints**, the Mormons' name for themselves. [Fr.,—L. *sanctus*, holy.]

saith, *seth, v.t.* and *v.i.* 3rd pers. sing. pres. indic. of **say**.

sake, *sāk, n.* purpose, motive (e.g. *for the sake of peace, argument*): behalf, advantage (e.g. *for my, pity's, sake*). [O.E. *sacu*, strife, a lawsuit; Du. *zaak*, Ger. *sache*; O.E. *sacan*, to strive. **seek** is a doublet.]

sake, *sä′ki, n.* a kind of beer made by the Japanese from fermented rice. [Jap.]

sal, *sal, n.* (*chem., pharmacy*) salt.—*ns.* **sal(-)ammo′niac**, ammonium chloride; **sal(-)vola-tile** (*vol-at′i-li*), ammonium carbonate. [L.]

salaam, *sä-läm′, n.* a word and gesture of salutation in the East, chiefly among Moslems: obeisance: greeting. [Ar. *salām*, peace; Heb. *shālōm.*]

salacious, *sal-ā′shùs, adj.* lustful, lecherous. [L. *salax, -ācis—salīre*, to leap.]

salad, *sal′ad, n.* a cold dish of vegetables or herbs (either raw or pre-cooked) generally seasoned with salt, vinegar, &c.—*ns.* **sal′ad-dress′ing, -oil**, sauce, olive-oil, used in dressing salads.—**salad days**, days of youthful inexperience. [Fr. *salade*—L. *sāl,* salt.]

salamander, *sal′a-man-dėr,* or *-man′-, n.* a genus of tailed amphibians, nearly related to the newts, harmless, but long dreaded as poisonous, once supposed able to live in fire: a spirit inhabiting the element fire (cf. **gnome, sylph**).—*adj.* **salaman′drine**, like a salamander: enduring fire. [Fr. *salamandre*—L.,—Gr. *salamandra*; prob. of Eastern origin.]

salami, *sa-lä′mi,* **salame**, *-mä, n.* a highly seasoned Italian sausage. [It.]

sal(-)ammoniac. See **sal**.

salary, *sal′a-ri, n.* periodical payment for services other than mechanical.—*adj.* **sal′aried**, receiving a salary. [O.Fr. *salarie*—L. *salārium,* salt-money (which formed a part of the Roman soldier's pay)—*sal,* salt.]

sale, *sāl, n.* act of selling: the exchange of anything for money: power or opportunity of selling: demand: a public offer of goods to be sold, esp. at reduced prices or by auction.—*adj.* **sāl(e)′able**, fit to be sold: easy to sell: in good demand.—*n.* **sal(e)′ableness.**—*ns.* **sale′-room**, an auction-room; **sales′man**, a man who sells goods:—*fem.* **sales′woman.**—*ns.* **sales′manship**, the art of selling: skill in presenting wares in the most attractive light or in persuading purchasers to buy; **sales′-talk**, talk designed to persuade the listener to buy; **sales′-tax**, a tax on the sale of goods and services, esp. one that is general in character and flat-rate.—**sale of work**, a sale of things made by members of a church congregation or other association to raise money. [Late O.E. *sala,* perh.—O.N. *′sala.*]

salep, *sal′ep, n.* the dried tubers of various

Neutral vowels in unaccented syllables: *em′pėr-ór*; for certain sounds in foreign words see p. ix.

642

orchids: the food prepared from them. [Ar.]

Salic Law, *sal'ik lö*, a very early code of laws that included some of those of the *Salian* Franks: a rule limiting succession to males, originally applied to certain of the Frankish territories, but later extended to the crowns of France (14th century) and of Spain (15th and 19th centuries).

salicin, *sal'i-sin*, *n.* a bitter crystalline substance with medicinal properties, obtained from the bark of willows.—**salicylic** (*sal-i-sil'ik*) **acid**, a colourless crystalline acid occurring in many plants and fruits, formerly obtained from salicin, it is used as an antiseptic and has important derivatives, e.g. aspirin. [L. *salix, salicis,* a willow.]

salient, *sā'li-ént*, *adj.* leaping or springing: (*fort.*) projecting outwards, as an angle: outstanding, prominent, striking.—*n.* an outward pointing angle, esp. in a line of defences.—*adv.* **sā'liently.** [Fr.,—L. *saliēns, -entis,* pr.p. of *salīre,* to leap.]

salify, *sal'i-fī, v.t.* to combine with an acid or base to form a salt:—*pa.t.* and *pa.p. sal'ified. adj.* **salifi'able.** [L. *sal,* salt, *facĕre* to make.]

saline, *sā'līn, or sā-līn', adj.* consisting of, or containing, salt: partaking of the qualities of salt.—*n.* an effervescing aperient. [Fr.,—L. *salīnus—sāl,* salt.]

saliva, *sa-lī'va, n.* the spittle—one of the digestive fluids, mainly the product of the **salivary glands.**—*adjs.* **sali'val, sa'livary,** pertaining to, secreting or conveying saliva.—*v.t.* **sal'ivāte,** to produce, or discharge, saliva, esp. in excess.—*n.* **salivā'tion,** a flow of saliva, esp. in excess. [L. *salīva.*]

sallow, *sal'ō, n.* a willow, esp. of the broader-leaved kinds with comparatively brittle twigs. [O.E. *salh, sealh*; cf. L., *salix.*]

sallow, *sal'ō, adj.* of a pale, yellowish colour.—*n.* **sall'owness.** [O.E. *salo, salu*; cf. Du. *zaluw,* and O.H.G. *salo.*]

sally, *sal'i, n.* (*arch.*) a leap: a sudden rush forth to attack besiegers: excursion: outburst (of fancy, wit, &c.)—*v.i.* to rush out suddenly: to set forth, issue:—*pa.t.* and *pa.p.* sall'ied.—*n.* **sall'y-port,** a passage by which a garrison may make a sally. [Fr. *saillie—saillir* (It. *salire*)—L. *salīre,* to leap.]

sally-lunn, *sal'i-lun', n.* a sweet spongy teacake. [From the name of a girl who sold them in the streets of Bath about the close of the 18th century.]

salmon, *sam'ón, n.* a large fish (*Salmo salar*), noted for its gameness, with silvery sides and delicate flesh, that ascends rivers to spawn.—*ns.* **salm'on-col'our,** an orange-pink; **salm'on-fly,** any artificial fly for taking salmon; **salm'on-leap,** a waterfall ascended by salmon leaping; **salm'on-trout,** a fish like the salmon, but smaller and thicker in proportion. [O.Fr. *saumon*—L. *salmō, -ōnis—salīre,* to leap.]

Salmonella, *sal-mó-nel'á, n.* a large genus of bacteria many of which are associated with poisoning by contaminated food. [Daniel *Salmon,* veterinarian.]

salon, *sal'ɔ̃, n.* a drawing-room: a fashionable reception, esp. a periodic gathering of notable persons, in the house of an eminent hostess: a great annual exhibition of works by living artists: a rather elegant shop or business establishment (e.g. *beauty salon*). [Fr.]

saloon, *sa-lōōn', n.* a spacious apartment: a large public room: a public cabin or dining-room for passengers: a railway carriage not divided into compartments: a motor-car with a closed-in body of one compartment: a drinking-bar.—*n.* **saloon'-pass'enger,** a steamer passenger entitled to use the principal cabin. [Fr. *salon.*]

saloop, *sa-lōōp', n.* salep: a drink made of salep, later of sassafras. [salep.]

Salopian, *sal-ō'pi-án, adj.* of Shropshire.—*n.* a native or inhabitant of Shropshire. [From *Salop,* Shropshire—an Anglo-Fr. corruption of the O.E. name for Shrewsbury.]

salsify, *sal'si-fi, n.* a biennial plant whose long and tapering root has a flavour resembling asparagus—also **sal'safy.** [Fr. *salsifis,* prob. It. *sassefrica,* goat's-beard—L. *saxum,* a rock, *fricāre,* to rub.]

salt, *sölt, n.* sodium chloride, or common salt, used for seasoning, either mined from the earth (**rock salt**) or obtained by evaporation from brine, &c.: seasoning: piquancy: that which preserves from corruption: (*chem.*) a compound formed by the replacement of one or more hydrogen atoms of an acid by metal atoms or radicals: (*pl.*) a mixture of salts used as a medicine: a sailor, esp. an old sailor.—*adj.* containing salt: seasoned or cured with salt: overflowed with, or growing in, salt-water: pungent: (*slang*) expensive, more than one ought to be expected to pay.—*v.t.* to sprinkle, season, cure, impregnate with salt: (*fig.*) to overcharge (a person) for goods.—*adj.* **salt'ish,** somewhat salt.—*adv.* **salt'ly.**—*ns.* **salt(-) lick,** a place where salt is found and to which animals go to lick it up: an artificial salt preparation given to cattle and sheep; **salt'-pan,** a pan, basin, or pit where salt is obtained by evaporation.—*adjs.* **salt-wat'er,** of, pertaining to, or living or growing in, salt water; **salt'y,** saltish: (*fig.*) piquant, racy, witty.—**salt away,** to store away, to hoard; **salt(s) of sorrel,** a mixture of the oxalates of potassium, used for removing ink-stains and iron-mould (see **wood sorrel**); **salt of the earth,** the most worthy people.—**above, below, the salt,** among those of high, or low, social rank, the saltcellar marking the boundary when all dined at the same table; **lay, put, salt on the tail of,** to catch; **take with a grain of salt,** to believe with some reserve; **worth one's salt,** worth at least the value of the salt one consumes. [O.E. *salt, sealt*; cf. Ger. *salz,* also L. *sāl,* Gr. *hals.*]

saltcellar, *sölt'sel-ār, n.* a small table vessel for holding salt: a depression behind the collarbone. [salt, and O.Fr. *saliere*—L. *salārium—sāl,* salt; spelling influenced by **cellar.**]

saltire, saltier, *sal'tīr, söl'-, n.* a diagonal cross, also called a St Andrew's Cross. [O.Fr. *sautoir, sautoir*—Low L. *saltātōrium,* a stirrup—L. *saltāre,* to leap.]

saltpetre, *sölt-pē'tér, n.* potassium nitrate, nitre. [O.Fr. *salpetre*—Low L. *salpetra*—L. *sāl,* salt, *petra,* a rock.]

salubrious, *sa-lōō'bri-ús, or -lū'-, adj.* healthful, health-giving.—*adv.* **salu'briously.**—*ns.* **salu'-**

briousness, salu′brity. [L. *salūbris—salūs, salūtis,* health.]

salutary, *sal′ū-tár-i, adj.* promoting health or safety: wholesome.—*adv.* **sal′ūtarily.**—*n.* **sal′ūtariness.** [L. *salūtāris—salūs,* health.]

salute, *sal-ūt′, v.t.* to greet with words or (now esp.) a gesture (e.g. of the hand), or with a bow or kiss: to honour formally by a discharge of cannon, striking colours, &c.—*v.i.* to perform the act of saluting.—*n.* act or attitude of saluting: a complimentary discharge of cannon, dipping colours, presenting arms, &c.—*n.* **salūta′tion,** act, or words, of greeting. [L. *salūtāre, -ātum—salūs, salūtis.*]

salvage, *sal′vij, n.* reward paid for saving or rescuing a ship or cargo from danger or loss: the act of saving a ship or cargo, or of saving goods from fire, &c.: goods so saved: waste material saved for further use.—*v.t.* to save from loss or destruction: to recover (wreckage). [Fr.,—Low L. *salvāre,* to save.]

salvation, *sal-vā′sh(ó)n, n.* act of saving: means of preservation from evil: (*theol.*) the saving of man from the power and penalty of sin.—*n.* **Salvā′tionist,** a member of the Salvation Army.—**Salvation Army,** an organisation for the spread of religion among the masses, founded by Wm. Booth about 1865. [Low L. *salvāre,* to save.]

salve, *salv, v.t.* to preserve unhurt: to salvage. [Low L. *salvāre,* to save.]

salve, *säv,* also *salv, n.* an ointment: a remedy: anything to soothe the feelings or conscience.—*v.t.* to anoint: to heal: to soothe. [O.E. *sealf;* Ger. *salbe,* Du. *zalf.*]

salver, *sal′vér, n.* a tray on which anything is presented. [Sp. *salva,* a salver—*salvar,* to save—Low L. *salvāre.*]

salvo, *sal′vō, n.* a saving clause: an expedient for saving appearances, avoiding offence, &c. [L., in phrase, *salvo jure,* one's right being safe.]

salvo, *sal′vō, n.* a simultaneous discharge of artillery, or of bombs: a round of applause:—*pl.* **salvo(e)s** (*sal′vōz*). [It. *salva,* salute—L. *salvē,* hail!]

sal(-)volatile. See **sal.**

samara, *sam′ár-a, sa-mä′ra, n.* a dry, indehiscent, usually one-sided, fruit with a wing. [L. *samara, samera,* elm seed.]

Samaritan, *sa-mar′i-tán, adj.* pertaining to *Samaria* in Palestine.—*n.* an inhabitant of Samaria: the language of Samaria.—**a good Samaritan,** a friend in need (Luke x. 30-37).

samarium, *sa-mā′ri-ùm, n.* a metallic element (symbol Sm; atomic no. 62), a member of the rare-earth group. [From *samarskite* (named after a Russian mine official), the mineral in which it was first observed.]

samba, *sam′ba, n.* a Brazilian Negro dance in duple time with syncopation: a ballroom development of this: a tune for it.

Sam Browne, *sam brown, n.* a military officer's leather belt with shoulder-strap. [General Sir *Samuel Browne* (1824-1901).]

same, *sām, adj.* identical: not different: unchanged: mentioned before.—*pron.* the person, thing, just mentioned (e.g. in commercial jargon, *to acknowledge same*).—*n.* **same′ness,** the being the same: tedious monotony.—**all the same,** for all that; **at the same time,** still,

nevertheless. [O.E. *same*; L. *similis,* like, Gr. *homos.*]

samite, *sam′īt, n.* a heavy silken fabric. [O.Fr. *samit*—Low L. *examitum*—Gr. *hexamiton—hex,* six, *mitos,* thread.]

samovar, *sam′ō-vär, -vär′, n.* a Russian tea-urn. [Russ.]

Samoyed(e), *sam-ō-yed′,* or *sam′-, n.* a people of north-west Siberia: their language: a dog of a breed used by them.—Also *adj.* [Russ.]

sampan, *sam′pan, n.* a Chinese boat. [Chinese *san,* three, *pan,* board.]

samphire, *sam′fīr,* or *sam′fer, n.* a plant found chiefly on rocky cliffs near the sea, used in pickles and salads. [Fr. (*herbe de*) *Saint Pierre,* Saint Peter's herb.]

sample, *säm′pl, n.* a specimen: a small portion to show the quality of the whole: an example.—*v.t.* to make up samples of: to test or estimate by taking a sample.—*n.* **sam′pler,** one who makes up samples (in compounds, as *wool-sampler*). [Short for M.E. *essample*—O.Fr.—L. *exemplum,* example.]

sampler, *säm′plér, n.* a piece of ornamental embroidery, worsted-work, &c., containing names, figures, texts, &c. [O.Fr. *essemplaire*—L. *exemplar,* a pattern.]

samurai, *sam′ōō-rī, n. sing.* (also *pl.*) a member of the military class in the old feudal system of Japan, including both territorial nobles and their military retainers. [Jap.]

sanative, *san′ä-tiv, adj.* tending, or able, to heal, healing.—*n.* **sanatō′rium,** a hospital, esp. for consumptives or convalescents: a health station:—*pl.* **sanator′ia, -iums.**—*adj.* **san′atory,** healing: conducive to health. [L. *sānāre, -ātum,* to heal.]

sanctify, *sang(k)′ti-fī, v.t.* to make sacred or holy, to set apart to sacred use: to free from sin or evil: to make efficient as the means of holiness:—*pa.t.* and *pa.p.* **sanc′tified.**—*ns.* **sanctifica′tion,** act of sanctifying: state of being sanctified; **sanc′tifier.**—*adj.* **sanctimō′nious,** simulating or pretending holiness. —*adv.* **sanctimō′niously.**—*ns.* **sanctimō′niousness,** **sanc′timony,** affected devoutness, show of sanctity; **sanctity** (*sang(k)′ti-ti*), quality of being sacred or holy, purity, godliness: inviolability (e.g. of an oath): (*pl.* **sanc′tities**) holy feelings, obligations, or objects; **sanc′tuary,** a sacred place: a place of worship: the most sacred part of a temple or church: a consecrated place which affords immunity from arrest or violence: the privilege of refuge therein: an animal or plant reserve; **sanc′tum,** a sacred place: a private room.—**odour of sanctity,** a sweet odour once said to have been exhaled by some saints before or after death: hence, obvious signs of, reputation for, saintliness. [Fr.,—L. *sanctificāre, -ātum—sanctus,* sacred, *facēre,* to make.]

sanction, *sang(k)′sh(ó)n, n.* (*hist.*) a law, decree: act of ratifying, or giving authority to: permission, countenance (e.g. of a person in authority, or—*fig.*—of social custom): (*ethics*) motive for obedience to any moral or religious law: penalty expressly attached to breach of a law or treaty: (usu. in *pl.*) a coercive measure applied e.g. to a nation taking a course of action disapproved by others.—*v.t.* to give val-

Neutral vowels in unaccented syllables: *em′pér-ór*; for certain sounds in foreign words see p. ix.

644

idity to: to authorise: to countenance. [L. *sanctiō, -ōnis—sancīre, sanctum*, to hallow, ratify.]

sanctus, *sang(k)'tus, n.* the hymn *Holy, holy, holy* from Isa. vi.: music for it. [L., holy.]

sand, *sand, n.* a mass of fine particles of crushed or worn rocks: (*pl.*) lands covered with sand: a sandy beach: moments (of time), from the use of sand in the hour-glass.—*v.t.* to sprinkle with sand.—*n.* **sand'(-)bag**, a bag filled with sand.—*v.t.* to protect with sandbags: to stun with a sandbag.—*ns.* **sand'-bank**, a bank of sand formed by tides and currents; **sand'-eel**, any of several small eel-like fishes, which bury themselves in the sand when the tide retires; **sand'erling**, a small wading-bird that seeks its food in the sea-sand; **sand'-glass**, a glass instrument for measuring time by the running out of sand; **sand'man**, a fairy who throws sand in children's eyes towards bedtime; **sand'-mar'tin**, a species of swallow that nests in sandy banks; **sand'-pā'per**, paper covered with sand for smoothing and polishing; **sand'pīper**, any of numerous wading-birds which frequent sandy shores and riverbanks, distinguished by their clear piping note; **sand'shoe**, a shoe for walking or playing on the sands, usually with canvas upper and rubber sole; **sand'stone**, any of a number of compacted and cemented sedimentary rocks consisting essentially of rounded grains of quartz, with variable content of other minerals, e.g. silica, or iron oxide.—*adj.* **sand'y**, consisting of, or covered with, sand: gritty: loose in grain: of the colour of sand.—*ns.* **sand'iness**; **sand'-yacht**, a wheeled boat with sails, for running on the sea-beach; **sand'-yacht'ing**. [O.E. *sand*; Du. *zand*, Ger. *sand*, O.N. *sandr*.]

sandal, *san'd(à)l, n.* a sole bound to the foot by straps: an ornate shoe or slipper.—*adj.* **san'-dalled**, wearing sandals. [L. *sandalium*—Gr. *sandalion*, dim. of *sandalon*.]

sandalwood, *san'd(à)l-wōōd, n.* a compact and fine-grained tropical wood, remarkable for its fragrance. [Low L. *santalum*; cf. Late Gr. *sandanon*.]

sandwich, *san(d)'wij, -wich, n.* two slices of bread with any sort of food between, said to be named the Earl of *Sandwich* (1718-1792) who ate a snack of this kind in order not to have to leave the gaming-table: anything in like arrangement.—*v.t.* to lay or place (between two layers or between two things of another kind).—*n.* **sand'wichman**, a man who walks about carrying two boards (**sand'wich-boards**) with advertisements, one before him and one behind.

sane, *sān, adj.* sound in mind: rational, sensible.—*adv.* **sane'ly**. [L. *sānus*, healthy.]

sang, *sang, pa.t.* of **sing**.

sangfroid, **sang-froid**, *sä-frwä', n.* coolness, composure, absence of excitement. [Fr., *sang*, blood, *froid*, cold.]

sangraal, **-grail**, **-greal**, *san(g)-grāl', san(g)'-grāl, n.* the holy grail (q.v.). [**saint**, **grail**.]

sanguinary, *sang'gwin-àr-i, adj.* attended with much bloodshed: bloodthirsty. [L. *sanguinārius—sanguis, sanguinis*, blood.]

sanguine, *sang'gwin, adj.* blood-red: ruddy: ardent, hopeful, confident.—*adv.* **san'guinely**, hopefully, confidently.—*n.* **san'guineness.—**

adj. **sanguin'eous**, sanguine: resembling or constituting blood. [Fr.,—L. *sanguineus—sanguis, sanguinis*, blood.]

sanhedrim, **sanhedrin**, *san'i-drim, -drin, n.* the supreme ecclesiastical and judicial tribunal of the ancient Jews. [Heb. *sanhedrīn*—Gr. *synedrion—syn*, together, *hedra*, a seat.]

sanitary, *san'i-tàr-i, adj.* pertaining to the promotion of health, esp. by drainage and sewage-disposal.—*ns.* **sanitary-towel**, an absorbent cotton pad for use in menstruation; **san'itary-ware**, coarse glazed earthenware for sewer-pipes, &c.; **sanitā'tion**, sanitary condition: methods and apparatus for making and maintaining houses healthy; **sanitā'rium**, (*U.S.*) a sanatorium. [Fr. *sanitaire*—L. *sānitās*, health.]

sanity, *san'i-ti, n.* state of being sane, soundness of mind. [L. *sānitās—sānus*, sane.]

sank, *sangk, pa.t.* of **sink**.

Sanskrit, *sans'krit, n.* the ancient Indo-Germanic literary language of India (consisting of *Vedic*—q.v.,—*Sanskrit*, from about 1500 B.C. and *Classical Sanskrit*, from about the 4th or 5th century B.C.).—*adj.* **Sanskrit'ic**. [Sans. *saṁskrta*, perfected—*sam*, together, *karoti*, he makes, cog. with L. *creāre*, to create.]

Santa Claus, *san'ta klöz, n.* a fat rosy old fellow who brings children Christmas presents, Father Christmas: an improbable source of benefits. [U.S. modification of Du. dial. *Sante Klaas*, St. Nicholas.]

sap, *sap, n.* juice, esp. the vital juice of plants, an aqueous solution of mineral salts, sugars and other organic substances (also *fig.*): sapwood: (*slang*) a weakling, a dupe.—*v.t.* to drain or withdraw the sap from: (*fig.*) to exhaust, weaken (e.g. energy).—*n.* **sap'-green**, a green paint made from the juice of buckthorn berries: its colour.—*adj.* **sap'less**, wanting sap: lacking vitality or worth.—*n.* **sap'ling**, a young tree, so called from being full of sap.—*adj.* **sapp'y**, abounding with sap: juicy: (*fig.*) vital, pithy.—*ns.* **sapp'iness**; **sap'-wood**, alburnum (q.v.), [O.E. *sæp*; Low Ger. *sap*, juice, Ger. *saft*.]

sap, *sap, n.* a trench (usually covered or zigzag) by which approach is made towards a hostile position.—*v.t.* to undermine (*lit.* and *fig.*)—in *fig.* sense, very close to **sap** (1).—*v.i.* to make a sap: to proceed insidiously:—*pr.p.* sapp'ing; *pa.t.* and *pa.p.* sapped.—*n.* **sapp'er**, one who saps: a private in the Royal Engineers. [It. *zappa* and Fr. *sappe* (now *sape*); cf. L.L. *sapa*, a pick.]

sapid, *sap'id, adj.* perceptible by taste: well-tasted, savoury.—*n.* **sapid'ity**, savouriness. [L. *sapidus—sapĕre*, to taste.]

sapience, *sā'pi-éns, n.* discernment, judgment, wisdom (often ironical).—*adj.* **sā'pient**, wise, sagacious (often ironical).—*adv.* **sā'piently**. [L. *sapientia—sapiens, sapientis*, pr.p. of *sapĕre*, to be wise.]

sapling, *sap'ling, n.* See **sap** (1).

sapodilla, *sap-ō-dil'a, n.* a large evergreen tree, native of tropical America, yielding chicle: its edible fruit. [Sp. *zapotilla*.]

saponaceous, *sap-o-nā'shŭs, adj.* soapy: soaplike. [L. *sāpō, sāpōnis*, soap.]

sapper, *sap'ér, n.* See **sap** (2).

Sapphic, *saf'ik, adj.* pertaining to *Sappho*, a

---

fāte, fär; mē, hûr (her); *mīne; mōte, för; mūte; mōōn, fŏŏt;* ᴛʜen (then)

Greek lyric poetess (*c.* 600 B.C.), or to her poetry.—*n.* one of the metres said to have been invented by Sappho.—*n.* **Sapph'ism,** lesbianism, of which she was accused.

sapphire, *saf'īr,* or *saf'ir, n.* a brilliant precious stone, a variety of corundum, generally of beautiful blue colour: the colour of sapphire.—*adj.* of sapphire: deep pure blue. [Fr.,—L. *sapphīrus*—Gr. *sappheiros.*]

saprophagous, *sap-rof'a-gus, adj.* feeding on decaying organic matter. [Gr. *sapros,* rotten, and *phagein,* to eat.]

saprophyte, *sap'rō-fīt, n.* a plant that feeds upon decaying organic matter.—*adj.* **saprophytic** (*sap-ro-fit'ik*).—*adv.* **saprophyt'ically.** [Gr. *sapros,* rotten, *phyton,* a plant.]

saraband, *sar'a-band, n.* a slow Spanish dance or its music. [Sp. *zarabanda.*]

Saracen, *sar'a-sén, n.* (orig.) a Syrian or Arab nomad: a Mohammedan: an opponent of the Crusaders. [L. *Saracēnus*—Late Gr. *Sarakēnos.*]

Saratoga (trunk), *sar-a-tōg'a* (*trungk*), *n.* a large travelling trunk. [Prob. from *Saratoga* Springs, N.Y. State.]

sarcasm, *sär'kazm, n.* a satirical remark in scorn or contempt, esp. one worded ironically: the tone or language of such sayings: the use of such.—*adjs.* **sarcas'tic, -al,** containing sarcasm: given to sarcasm.—*adv.* **sarcas'tically.** [L. *sarcasmus*—G. *sarkasmos*—*sarkazein,* to tear flesh like dogs, to speak bitterly—*sarx,* gen. *sarkos,* flesh.]

sarcenet. Same as **sarsenet.**

sarcoma, *sär-kō'ma, n.* a tumour, or group of tumours, derived from connective tissue:—*pl.* **sarcō'mata.** [Gr. *sarkōma*—*sarx,* flesh.]

sarcophagus, *sär-kof'a-gus, n.* a limestone used by the Greeks for coffins, thought to consume the flesh of corpses: a stone coffin: a tomb:—*pl.* **sarcoph'agī, sarcoph'aguses.** [L.,—Gr. *sarkophagos*—*sarx,* flesh, *phagein* (aor.), to eat.]

sard, *särd, n.* a deep-red chalcedony.—Also **sard'ius.** [Gr. *sardios* (*lithos*), the Sardian (stone)—*Sardeis,* Sardis, in Lydia.]

sardine, *sär-dēn', n.* a young pilchard commonly tinned in oil. [Fr., (It. *sardina*)—L. *sardīna*—Gr. *sardīnē.*]

sardonic, *sär-don'ik, adj.* forced, heartless, or bitter (said of a laugh, smile, &c.).—*adv.* **sardon'ically.** [Fr. *sardonique*—L. *sardonius*—Late Gr. *sardonios,* doubtfully referred to *sardonion,* a plant of Sardinia (Gr. *Sardō*), which was said to screw up the face of the eater.]

sardonyx, *sär'do-niks, n.* an onyx with layers of cornelian or sard. [Gr.]

sargasso, *sär-gas'ō, n.* gulf-weed, a seaweed found floating in immense quantities in a part of the North Atlantic Ocean called the **Sargasso Sea.** [Port. *sargaço.*]

sari, *sär'ē, n.* a Hindu woman's chief garment, wrapped round the waist and passed over the shoulder and head. [Hindustani.]

sarong, *sä-rong', n.* a Malay skirt-like garment for man or woman. [Malay.]

sarsaparilla, *sär-sä-pár-il'a, n.* any tropical American species of *Smilax*: its dried root: a medicinal preparation from it. [Sp. *zarzaparilla*—*zarza,* bramble (prob. Basque, *sartzia*),

parilla, a dim. of *parra,* a vine.]

sarsenet, *särs'nit, -net, n.* a thin tissue of fine silk. [Anglo-Fr. *sarzinett,* prob.—*Sarzin,* Saracen.]

sartorial, *sär-tō', -tō', ri-äl, adj.* pertaining to a tailor or tailoring. [L. *sartor,* a patcher.]

sash, *sash, n.* a band or scarf worn round the waist or over the shoulder. [Ar. *shāsh.*]

sash, *sash, n.* a frame, esp. a sliding frame, for panes of glass. [Fr. *châsse*—L. *capsa,* a case.]

sasine, *sä'sin, n.* (*Scots law*) the act of giving legal possession of feudal property. [Variant of **seisin.**]

sassafras, *sas'ä-fras, n.* a tree of the laurel family, common in North America: the bark, esp. of the root. [Sp. *sasafrás.*]

Sassenach, *sas'é-nach, n.* a Saxon: an Englishman: (*Scott,* etc.) a Lowlander. [Gael. *Sasunnach.*]

sat, *sat, pa.t.* and *pa.p.* of **sit.**

Satan, *sä'tán, n.* the enemy of mankind: the devil: the chief of the fallen angels.—*adjs.* **Sătan'ic, -al** (or without *cap.*), pertaining to, or like, Satan: devilish.—*adv.* **satan'ically.** [O.Fr.,—Heb. *sātān,* enemy—*sātan,* to be adverse.]

satchel, *sach'él, n.* a small sack or bag, esp. for school-books, &c. [O.Fr. *sachel*—L. *saccellus,* dim. of *saccus,* a sack.]

sate, *sāt, v.t.* to satisfy fully: to glut. [M.E. *sade*—O.E. *sadian,* to become satisfied, influenced by L. *satis,* enough.]

sate, *sat, sāt,* a poetical archaism for **sat** (see **sit**).

sateen, *sa-tēn', n.* a glossy fabric of cotton or wool. [**satin.**]

satellite, *sat'él-īt, n.* an obsequious follower: a small member of the solar system, a planet revolving round one of the larger planets: anything controlled by a more powerful associate: an artificial or earth satellite.—**satellite state, country,** one which relies on and obeys the dictates of a larger, more powerful state; **satellite town,** a garden city, limited in size, built near a great town to check overgrowth.—**artificial, earth, satellite,** any manmade body, including spacecraft, launched by rocket into space and put into orbit round the earth. [Fr.,—L. *satelles, satellitis,* an attendant.]

satiate, *sä'shi-āt, v.t.* to gratify fully: to glut.—*adj.* **sä'tiable,** that may be satiated.—*n.* **satiety** (*sa-tī'et-i*), state of being satiated: surfeit. [L. *satiāre, -ātum*—*satis,* enough.]

satin, *sat'in, n.* a closely woven silk with a lustrous and unbroken surface.—*adj.* made of satin: resembling satin.—*ns.* **sat'inet, satinette',** a thin species of satin: a cloth with a cotton warp and woollen weft; **sat'in-stitch,** an embroidery stitch, flat or raised, repeated in parallel lines, giving a satiny appearance and making both sides alike; **sat'inwood,** a beautiful ornamental wood from East and West Indies, having a smooth, satiny texture.—*adj.* **sat'iny,** like, or composed of, satin. [Fr. *satin,* app.—L.L. *sēta,* silk.]

satire, *sat'īr, n.* a literary composition, orig. in verse, essentially a criticism of folly or vice, which it holds up to ridicule or scorn: cutting comment: ridicule.—*adjs.* **satir'ic, -al,** pertain-

Neutral vowels in unaccented syllables: *em'pér-ór*; for certain sounds in foreign words see p. ix.

ing to, or conveying, satire: (**satirical**) using, or given to using, satire.—*adv.* **satir′ically.**—*v.t.* **sat′irīse**, to make the object of satire, to ridicule by sarcasm.—*n.* **sat′irist**, a writer of satire. [Fr.,—L. *satira, satura* (*lanx*), a dish of mixed fruit, a poem dealing with various subjects, or a poem in which vices and follies are ridiculed or denounced.]

satisfy, *sat′is-fī*, *v.t.* to give enough to: to supply fully and hence appease (e.g. hunger, a desire, curiosity): to pay (a creditor) in full: to meet (a claim) in full: to atone for (e.g. *to satisfy guilt*): to answer (a question) adequately, or dispel (a doubt): to be in accordance with (a hypothesis), or to fulfil (a condition): to come up to (an idea, preconception): to convince (e.g. oneself) by investigation or production of evidence.—*v.i.* to give content, leave nothing to be desired:—*pa.t.* and *pa.p.* sat′isfīed.—*n.* **satisfac′tion**, the act of satisfying: state of being satisfied: gratification, comfort: that which satisfies: amends, atonement, payment.—*adj.* **satisfactory**, satisfying, giving contentment: making amends or payment: atoning: convincing: adj. satisfac′torily.—*n.* **satisfac′toriness.** [O.Fr. *satisfier*—L. *satisfacĕre*—*satis*, enough, *facĕre*, to make.]

satrap, *sat′rap*, or *sā′trap*, *n.* a viceroy or governor of an ancient Persian province: a despot: a provincial governor, esp. if powerful and ostentatiously rich.—*n.* **sat′rapy**, a satrap's province, office, or period of office. [Gr. *satrapēs*, from Pers. *khshatrapā* or Zend (q.v.) *shōithra-paiti*—lit. 'chief of a district'.]

satsuma (orange), *sat′sōō-ma, sat-sōō′ma* (*or′-inj*), *n.* a thin-skinned seedless type of man darin orange or its tree; **Satsuma (ware)** (*wār*), *n,* a hard-glazed yellow Japanese pottery. [*Satsuma*, name of a former province in south-west Japan.]

saturate, *sat′ū-rāt*, *v.t.* to impregnate (with): to unite with till no more can be absorbed: to soak: to charge with a maximum quantity of magnetism, electricity, heat, &c.: to fill completely: to pervade: to surfeit: to cover (a target) completely with aerial bombs.—*adjs.* **sat′urable**, that may be saturated; **sat′urate, sat′urated**, charged to the fullest extent: pure in colour, free from white.—*n.* **satūrā′tion**, act of saturating: state of being saturated: the purity of a colour, its degree of freedom from mixture with white or grey—also used as *adj.*, meaning of very great, or greatest possible, intensity (e.g. *saturation bombing*).—**saturated compound**, (*chem.*) a compound which does not contain any free valencies and which, therefore, does not tend to form new compounds by an *additive reaction* (i.e. by direct combination with hydrogen atoms or their equivalent); **saturation point**, the point at which saturation is reached: the limit in numbers that can be accommodated, used, &c.; the limit of emotional response, endurance, &c. [L. *saturāre, -ātum—satur*, full, akin to *satis*, enough.]

Saturday, *sat′ur-dā*, *n.* the seventh day of the week, dedicated by the Romans to Saturn. [O.E. *Sæterdæg, Sætern(es)dæg,* Saturn's day—L. *Sāturnus*.]

Saturn, *sat′urn*, *n.* the ancient Roman god of agriculture: one of the major planets.—*n.pl.* **Saturnā′lia**, the annual festival in honour of Saturn, a time of unrestrained licence with suspension of class distinctions.—*adjs.* **Saturnā′lian**, pertaining to the Saturnalia: riotously merry: dissolute; **Satur′nian**, pertaining to Saturn, whose fabulous reign was called 'the golden age'—happy, pure, simple: denoting the verse in which the oldest Latin poems were written; **sat′urnine**, grave, gloomy, phlegmatic—those born under the planet Saturn being said to be so disposed. [L. *Sāturnus—serēre, setum,* to sow.]

satyr, *sat′ėr*, *n.* a silvan deity, represented as part man and part goat, and extremely wanton: a very lustful person: (*B.*) a desert demon.—*adjs.* **satyr′ic, -al,** pertaining to satyrs. [L. *satyrus*—Gr. *satyros*.]

sauce, *sôs*, *n.* a dressing poured over food: (*fig.*) anything that gives relish: (*coll.*) impudence.—*v.t.* to add or give sauce to: to make piquant or pleasant.—*ns.* **sauce′-boat**, a vessel for sauce; **sauce′pan**, a handled and usu. lidded metal pan in which sauce and other foods are boiled, stewed, &c. [Fr. *sauce*—L. *salsa—sallēre, salsum,* to salt—*sāl,* salt.]

saucer, *sô′sėr*, *n.* (*orig.*) a dish for salt or sauce: a shallow dish, esp. one placed under a tea or coffee cup: anything of like shape. [O.Fr. *saussiere*—Low L. *salsārium*—L. *salsa,* sauce.]

saucy, *sô′si*, *adj.* (*comp.* **sau′cier,** *superl.* **sau′ciest**) pert, bold, forward: smart and trim.—*adv.* **sau′cily.**—*n.* **sau′ciness.** [sauce.]

sauerkraut, *sowr′krowt*, *n.* a German dish of cabbage allowed to ferment with salt, &c. [Ger. 'sour cabbage'.]

sauna, *sow′na, sô′na, n.* (a building or room equipped for) a Finnish form of steam bath. [Finn.]

saunter, *sôn′ter*, *v.i.* to wander about idly, to loiter, to stroll.—*n.* a sauntering gait: a leisurely stroll.—*n.* **saun′terer.**

saurian, *sô′ri-ân*, *n.* a group of scaly reptiles including the lizards: formerly including the crocodile and certain extinct reptiles, as the dinosaur.—*adj.* pertaining to, or of the nature of a saurian. [Gr. *sauros,* a lizard.]

sausage, *sos′ij*, *n.* chopped meat seasoned and stuffed in a tube of gut or formed into the shape of a tube: anything of like shape.—*n.* **sau′sage-roll**, minced meat cooked in a roll of pastry. [Fr. *saucisse*—Low L. *salsīcia*—L. *salsus,* salted.]

sauté, *sô′tā, adj.* fried lightly and quickly. [Fr.]

sauterne (or with *cap.*), *sō-tûrn′, -tern′, n.* a white wine produced at *Sauternes,* in France.

savage, *sav′ij, adj.* in a state of nature: wild (of an animal): (*arch.*) uncivilised: ferocious, furious.—*n.* a human being in an uncivilised state: a brutal, fierce, or cruel person.—*adv.* **sav′agely.**—*ns.* **sav′ageness; sav′agery,** the condition or behaviour of a savage: ferocity. [O.Fr. *salvage*—L. *silvāticus,* pertaining to the woods—*silva,* a wood.]

savanna, savannah, *sa-van′a, n.* a tract of level land, covered with low vegetation, treeless, or dotted with trees or patches of wood. [Sp. *zavana* (now *sabana*).]

savant, *sa′vä, n.* a learned man. [Fr., obs. pr.p. of *savoir,* to know.]

save, *sāv, v.t.* to bring safe out of evil or danger, to rescue: to rescue (from): to protect, prevent the loss of: to keep, preserve (from): to deliver from the power of sin and from its consequences: to prevent waste of (e.g. time, energy): to use thriftily with a view to future need: to set aside for future use: to obviate the necessity of.—*v.i.* to be economical.—*prep.* except.—*n.* **sā'ver,** one who saves.—*adj.* **sā'ving,** thrifty: making a reservation: redeeming: (*theol.*) securing salvation.—*prep.* excepting.—*n.* that which is saved: (*pl.*) money kept for future use.—*adv.* **sā'vingly,** so as to save.—*ns.* **sā'vingness; Sā'vings-bank,** a bank for the receipt of small deposits, and their accumulation at compound interest.—**save up,** to amass by thrift. [Fr. *sauver*—Low L. *salvāre*—L. *salvus,* safe.]

saveloy, *savé-loi, n.* a highly seasoned sausage, orig. of brains. [Fr. *cervelat, cervelas*—It. *cervellata*—*cervello,* brain—L. *cerebellum,* dim. of *cerebrum,* the brain.]

saviour, *sā'vyór, n.* one who saves from evil or danger: (*cap.*) a title applied by Christians to Jesus Christ. [M.E. *sauveur*—O.Fr. *sauvéour*—L. *salvātor*—*salūs, -ūtis,* health, well-being, safety.]

savoir-faire, *sav-wär-fer', n.* the faculty of knowing just what to do and how to do it, tact. [Fr.]

savoir-vivre, *sav-wär-vē'vr', n.* good breeding, knowledge of polite usages. [Fr.]

savour, *sā'vór, n.* taste: (*rare*) odour: characteristic flavour: (*fig.*) quality suggestive (of): relish, or (*fig.*) zest: (*arch.*) repute.—*v.i.* to have the taste, smell, or quality (of—*lit.* or *fig.*).—*v.t.* to discern or appreciate the distinctive quality of.—*adj.* **sā'voury,** having savour, of good savour or relish.—*n.* a course or dish by way of relish, usu. at the end of a dinner.—*n.* **sā'vouriness.** [Fr. *saveur*—L. *sapor*—*sapēre,* to taste.]

savoy, *sa-voi', n.* a winter cabbage, with large close head and wrinkled leaves—originally from *Savoy.*—*n.* **Savoyard** (*sav'oi-ärd*), a native or inhabitant of Savoy (many itinerant organ-grinders in Europe were Savoyards): a native or inhabitant of the part of London where the Savoy Palace once stood: a performer in the Gilbert and Sullivan operas produced at the Savoy theatre.—Also *adj.* [Fr. *Savoie, Savoyard.*]

saw, *sö, pa.t.* of **see.**

saw, *sö, n.* an instrument for cutting, formed of a blade, band, or disk of thin steel, with a toothed edge.—*v.t.* to cut with a saw.—*v.i.* to use a saw:—*pa.t.* sawed; *pa.p.* sawed or sawn.—*ns.* **saw'dust,** dust or small pieces of wood, &c., made in sawing; **saw'-fish,** any of several rays with a flattened bony beak toothed on the edges; **saw'-horse,** a support for wood while it is being sawn; **saw'-mill,** a mill for sawing timber.—*adj.* **sawn'-off** (or **sawed'-off**), shortened by cutting with a saw (as **sawn-off shotgun**).—*ns.* **saw'pit,** a pit where wood is sawed, one sawyer standing above the timber and the other below it; **saw'yer,** one who saws timber. [O.E. *saga*; Ger. *säge.*]

saw, *sö, n.* a saying: a proverb. [O.E. *sagu*—sec-

gan, to say.]

saxe (blue), *saks* (*blōō*), *n.* a deep shade of light blue. [Fr. *Saxe,* Saxony.]

saxhorn, *saks'hörn, n.* a brass wind-instrument having a long winding tube with bell opening, invented by Antoine or Adolphe *Sax* (1814-1894)—esp. the bass saxhorn or tuba.

saxifrage, *sak'si-frij, n.* a genus of rock plants many with basal, tufted leaves. [L. *saxifraga,* spleenwort—*saxum,* a stone, *frangēre,* to break.]

Saxon, *saks'ón, n.* one of a North German people that conquered part of Britain in the 5th and 6th centuries.—*adj.* pertaining to the Saxons. [L. *Saxōnēs* (pl.), of Gmc. origin; cf. O.E. *Seaxe*; Ger. *Sachsen.*]

saxophone, *sak'sö-fōn, n.* a military and dance band wind-instrument with reed, metal tube, and about twenty finger-keys. [*Sax* (see **saxhorn**), the inventor, Gr. *phōnē,* the voice.]

say, *sā, v.t.* to utter (a word, &c., e.g. *to say Yes*): to state in words: to assert, affirm, declare: to tell (e.g. *to say one's mind*): to go through in recitation or repetition (e.g. prayers).—*v.i.* to make a statement: to affirm:—*pa.t.* and *pa.p.* said (*sed*); 2nd sing. pr. indic. sayst (*sāst*), sayest (*sā'ist*); 3rd sing. says (*sez*), (*arch.*) saith (*seth*).—*n.* a remark: a speech: what one wants to say: opportunity of speech: a voice, part, or influence, in decision.—*n.* **say'ing,** an expression: a maxim.—**say a person nay,** to refuse his request.—**I say!***interj.* calling attention, or expressing surprise or protest; **that is to say,** in other words. [O.E. *secgan* (*sægde, gesægd*); O.N. *segja,* Ger. *sagen.*]

scab, *skab, n.* a crust formed over a sore: any of various diseases of plants, as *potato scab,* any of several diseases characterised by scab-like spots on the potato tubers: a mange (q.v.), esp. of sheep: a scoundrel: a blackleg.—*adj.* **scabb'ed,** affected or covered with scabs: diseased with the scab.—*n.* **scabb'edness.**—*adj.* **scabb'y,** scabbed.—*n.* **scabb'iness.** [App. from an O.N. equivalent of O.E. *sceabb,* influenced by association with L. *scabiēs*—*scabēre,* to scratch.]

scabbard, *skab'ärd, n.* the case in which the blade of a sword is kept: a sheath. [M.E. *scauberc,* prob. through O.Fr.—O.H.G. *scala,* a scale, *bergan,* to protect.]

scabies, *skā'bi-ēz, n.* (*med.*) the itch (q.v.). [L. *scabiēs*—*scabēre,* to scratch.]

scabious, *skā'bi-ús, n.* any plant of a genus of the teasel family, some of which were long thought to cure scaly eruptions. [L. *scabiōsus*—*scabiēs,* the itch.]

scabrous, *skab'rús, adj.* bristly, rough: (*fig.*) indecent. [L. *scaber,* rough.]

scaffold, *skaf'old, n.* a temporary erection for men at work on a building: a raised platform, esp. for the execution of a criminal: (*fig.*) capital punishment: a raised framework.—*v.t.* to furnish with a scaffold: to sustain.—*n.* **scaff'olding,** a framework for supporting workmen on a building: materials for scaffolds: (*fig.*) a frame, framework. [O.Fr. *escadafault* (Fr. *échafaud*).]

scalar. See **scale** (1).

scal(l)awag. Same as **scallywag.**

scald, *sköld, v.t.* to injure with hot liquid: to cook

Neutral vowels in unaccented syllables: *em'pér-ór*; for certain sounds in foreign words see p. ix.

648

or heat short of boiling.—*n.* a burn caused by hot liquid. [O.Fr. *escalder* (Fr. *échauder*)— Low L.*excaldāre*, to bathe in warm water—*ex*, from, *calidus*, warm, hot.]

scald, skald, *sköld, n.* in ancient Scandinavia, one who composed and recited poems in honour of great men. [O.N. *skáld.*]

scale, *skāl, n.* a ladder (now only *fig.*): a graduated measure: (*mus.*) the selected system or sequence of notes adhered to in a musical composition: a succession of these performed in ascending or descending order of pitch through an octave or more: compass or range of a voice or instrument: relative dimensions: relative scope of an activity or size, grandeur, of a production: a system or scheme of relative values: a numeral system.—*v.t.* to mount, as by a ladder, to ascend: to change in fixed ratio or proportion (often with *up* or *down*).—*adj.* **scā'lable,** that can be scaled or climbed.—*ns.* **scāl'ar (quan'tity),** a quantity that is completely specified by its magnitude (e.g. temperature or energy), as distinct from a vector quantity (see **vector**); **scal'ing-ladd'er,** a ladder used for climbing the walls of a fortress: a fireman's ladder. [L. *scāla*, a ladder—*scandĕre*, to mount.]

scale, *skāl, n.* a small, thin plate on a fish or reptile: a thin layer.—*v.t.* to clear of scales: to peel off in thin layers.—*v.i.* to come off in thin layers or flakes.—*adjs.* **scaled,** having scales: covered with scales; **scale'less,** without scales; **scal'y,** covered with scales: like scales: formed of scales.—*n.* **scal'iness.** [M.E. *scāle*—O.Fr. *escale*, husk, of Gmc. origin.]

scale, *skāl, n.* the dish of a balance: a balance—chiefly in *pl.*: (*cap., pl.*) Libra, one of the signs of the zodiac.—*v.t.* and *v.i.* to weigh, as in scales: to show (a specified weight) in scales.—*n.* **scale'-beam,** the beam or lever of a balance. [O.N. *skāl,* bowl; cf. O.E. *sceale,* shell, Du. *schaal,* Ger. *schale.*]

scalene, *skā'lēn, skal-ēn', adj.* (*geom.*) having three unequal sides.—*n.* a **scalene** triangle. [Gr. *skalēnos,* uneven.]

scall, *skōl, n.* (*B.*) a scabbiness. [O.N. *skalli,* bald head.]

scallop, *skol'óp, skal'óp, n.* a bivalve having the edge of its shell in the form of a series of curves: one of a series of curves in the edge of anything.—*v.t.* to cut into scallops or curves: to cook (esp oysters) by baking in a scallop shell, or utensil of comparable shape, with breadcrumbs, &c.—*n.* **scall'op-shell,** a scallop, or the shell of one, the badge of a pilgrim [O.Fr. *escalope*; of Gmc. origin.]

scallywag, *skal'i-wag, n.* a good for nothing, a scamp. [Ety. uncertain.]

scalp, *skalp, n.* the outer covering of the skull: the skin on which the hair of the head grows: the skin and hair on the top of the head, torn or cut off as a token of victory by the North American Indians.—*v.t.* to cut the scalp from.—*n.* **scal'ping-knife,** a knife for scalping enemies.—*adj.* **scalp'less,** having no scalp.—*n.* **scalp'-lock,** a long tuft of hair left unshorn by the North American Indians as a challenge. [M.E. *scalp*; perh. Scand.; cf. O.N. *skálpr,* sheath.]

scalpel, *skalp'él, n.* a small surgical knife for

dissecting or operating. [L. *scalpellum,* dim. of *scalprum,* a knife—*scalpĕre,* to engrave.]

scaly. See **scale** (2).

scamp, *skamp, n.* a rascal: a lively tricky fellow.—*v.i.* **scam'per,** to run in alarm or haste: to run gaily.—*n.* a hurried, often undignified, flight: a gallop on horseback for pleasure: a romp.—*adj.* **scam'pish,** rascally. [O.Fr. *escamper,* or It. *scampare,* to decamp—L. *ex,* from, *campus,* field; cf. **decamp.**]

scamp, *skamp, v.t.* to do, execute, perfunctorily, over-hastily, without thoroughness. [Perh. O.N. *skemma,* to shorten.]

scampi, *skam'pē, n.* Norway lobsters (lobsters of European seas) when considered as food. [It., pl. of *scampo.*]

scan, *skan, v.t.* to analyse the metrical structure of (a line, verse): to examine carefully, to scrutinise: (*coll.*) to cast an eye quickly over: (*television*) to pass a beam over every part of in turn: (*radar*) to detect by rotating the beam.—*v.i.* to agree with the rules of metre:—*pr.p.* scann'ing; *pa.t.* and *pa.p.* scanned.—*ns.* **scann'ing** (*television*) the repeated traversing of the surface of a television picture by a beam of light or electrons for the purpose of transmitting or reproducing the image; **scan'sion,** act, art, or mode, of scanning verse. [Fr. *scander,* to scan—L. *scandĕre, scansum,* to climb.]

scandal, *skan'd(à)l, n.* a stumbling-block to faith: anything that brings discredit on the agent or agents by offending the moral feelings of the community: a feeling of moral outrage, or the talk it gives rise to: ignominy, disgrace: malicious gossip, slander.—*v.t.* **scan'dalise,** to give scandal or offence to, to shock: to disgrace: to slander.—*v.i.* to talk scandal.—*ns.* **scan'dal-mong'er,** one who spreads stories of scandal; **scan'dal-mongering.**—*adj.* **scan'dalous,** giving offence, calling forth condemnation, openly vile: defamatory.—*adv.* **scan'dalously.**—*n.* **scan'dalousness.** [L. *scandalum*—Gr. *skandalon,* a stumbling-block.]

Scandinavian, *skan-di-nā'vi-án, adj.* of *Scandinavia,* the peninsula divided into Norway and Sweden, but, in a historical sense, applying also to Denmark and Iceland: (*philol.*) North Germanic.—*n.* a native of Scandinavia. [L. *Scandinavia,* (from Gmc, word which did not have *n* before *d*), applied to the southern part of the peninsula and its shortened form *Scandia.*]

scandium, *skan'di-ùm, n.* a rare metallic element (symbol Sc; atomic no. 21) discovered in 1879 in the Scandinavian mineral euxenite. [L. *Scandia*; see **Scandinavian.**]

scansion. See **scan.**

scant, *skant, adj.* not full or plentiful, scarcely sufficient, deficient.—*adj* **scant'y,** scant: meagre, deficient, inadequate.—*adv.* **scant'ily.** —*n.* **scant'iness.** [O.N. *skamt,* neut. of *skammr,* short.]

scape, 'scape, *skāp, v.t.* and *v.i.* to escape. [A contr. of **escape.**]

scape, *skāp, n.* a peduncle, quite or nearly leafless, arising from the middle of a rosette of leaves, and bearing a flower, several flowers, or a crowded inflorescence.—*adj.* **scāp'ose,**

bearing a scape: like a scape. [L. *scāpus*, a shaft.]

scapegoat, *skāp'gōt*, *n.* a goat on which, once a year, the Jewish high-priest laid symbolically the sins of the people, and which was then allowed to escape into the wilderness (Levit. xvi.): one who is made to bear the misdeeds of another. [**scape** (1), and **goat.**]

scapegrace, *skāp'grās*, *n.* one whose conduct shows no respect for grace or virtue—often used playfully. [**scape** (1), and **grace.**]

scapula, *skap'ū-la*, *n.* the shoulder-blade.—*adj.* **scap'ular**, pertaining to the shoulder.—*n.* originally an ordinary working garb, now the mark of the monastic orders, a long strip of cloth with an opening for the head, worn hanging before and behind over the habit.— *adj.* **scap'ulary**, in form like a scapular.—*n.* a scapular. [L. *scapulae*, the shoulder-blades.]

scar, *skär*, *n.* the mark left by a wound, sore or injury (also *fig.*): any mark or blemish.—*v.t.* to mark with a scar.—*v.i.* to become scarred:—*pr.p.* scarr'ing; *pa.t.* and *pa.p.* scarred. [O.Fr. *escare*—L. *eschara*—Gr. *eschara*, a scar produced by burning.]

scar, *skär*, *n.* a precipitous bank or rock. [App. O.N. *sker*—*skera*, to cut.]

scarab, *skar'ab*, *n.* a dung-beetle, esp. the sacred beetle of the ancient Egyptians: a gem, cut in the form of a beetle. [L. *scarabaeus*; cf. Gr. *kārabos.*]

scaramouch, *skar'ä-mowch*, *n.* a bragging, cowardly buffoon. [Fr.,—It. *Scaramuccia,* a stock character in Italian comedy.]

scarce, *skārs*, *adj.* not plentiful, not equal to the demand (used predicatively): rare, not common.—*advs.* **scarce'ly**, **scarce** (*B.*), hardly, barely.—*ns.* **scarce'ness**; **scarc'ity**, state of being scarce: deficiency: rareness: want, famine.—**make oneself scarce**, to go, run away unobtrusively for reasons of prudence, tact, &c. [O.Fr. *escars*, niggardly—L. *excerptus*, pa.p. of *excerpĕre*—*ex*, out of,*carpĕre*, to pick.]

scare, *skär*, *v.t.* to startle, to affright: to drive or keep (off) by frightening.—*n.* a panic, a baseless alarm.—*ns.* **scare'crow**, a figure set up to scare away birds: a cause of needless fear: a person meanly and tastelessly dressed: a person very thin or very odd-looking; **scare'-monger**, one who habitually causes panic by spreading or initiating alarming rumours. [M.E. *skerre*—O.N. *skirra*, to avoid—*skiar*, shy.]

scarf, *skärf*, *n.* a light piece of material worn loosely on the shoulders or about the neck or head: a necktie:—*pl.* **scarves**, **scarfs**. [Perh. O.Fr. *escarpe* (Fr. *écharpe*), sash.]

scarf, *skärf*, *v.t.* to join two pieces of timber endwise, so that they may appear to be used as one. [Perh. Scand.]

scarfskin, *skärf'skin*, *n.* the surface skin.

scarify, *skar'i-fī*, *v.t.* (*surgery*) to make a number of scratches or slight cuts in: to lacerate: to criticise severely: to break up the surface of (ground):—*pa.t.* and *pa.p.* scar'ifīed.—*n.* **scar-ificā'tion**, act of scarifying. [L. *scarīficāre*, *-ātum*—Gr. *skarīphaesthai*—*skarīphos*, an etching tool.]

scarlatina, *skär-lä-tē'na*, *n.* scarlet fever. [It. *scarlattina.*]

scarlet, *skär'lĕt*, *n.* orig. a fine cloth, not always red: a brilliant red: a brilliant red cloth or garb.—*adj.* of the colour called scarlet: dressed in scarlet.—*ns.* **scar'let(-)fē'ver**, an infectious fever usually marked by sore throat and a scarlet rash; **scar'let-hat**, a cardinal's hat; **scar'let-runn'er**, a bean with scarlet flowers which runs up any support. [O.Fr. *escarlate* (Fr. *écarlate*), thought to be from Pers. *saqalāt*, scarlet cloth.]

scarp, *skärp*, *n.* an escarp (q.v.): an escarpment.—*v.t.* to cut into a scarp. [It. *scarpa.*]

scarper, *skär'pėr*, *v.i.* (*slang*) to run away, escape, leave without notice. [It. *scappare.*]

scathe, **scath**, *skāTH*, *n.* damage, injury.—*v.t.* to injure.—*adj.* **scā'thing**, damaging: vehement, bitter (e.g. of criticism).—*adv.* **scā'thingly.**— *adj.* **scāthe'less**. [O.N. *skathe*; cf. O.E. *sceatha*, an injurer; Ger. *schade*, injury.]

scatter, *skat'ér*, *v.t.* to disperse widely: to throw loosely about, to strew, to sprinkle: to dispel: to reflect or disperse irregularly (waves or particles).—*v.i.* to disperse.—*n.* scattering: a sprinkling: extent of scattering.—*p.adj.* **scat't'ered**, dispersed irregularly, widely, or here and there.—*ns.* **scatt'ering**, dispersion: radiation afresh of wave-energy when a ray is incident on an obstacle, or when it enters an irregularly ionised region: the deflection of particles as a result of collisions with other particles: a small proportion occurring sporadically; **scatt'erbrain**, a thoughtless, unreliable person, one incapable of sustained attention or thought.—*adj.* **scatt'er-brained**, erratic.

scatty, *skat'i*, *adj.* (*coll.*) slightly crazy and unpredictable in conduct.—*n.* **scatt'iness**. [Poss. *scatter*brain.]

scavenger, *skav'en-jér*, *n.* one who cleans the streets: an animal who feeds on waste: one who deals in or delights in filth. [Orig. *scav-ager*, an inspector of goods for sale, and also of the streets: from *scavage*, duty on goods for sale.]

scenario, *shā-nä'ri-ō*, *sē-nä'ri-ō*, or *-nā'*, *n.* a skeleton of a dramatic work, film, &c., scene by scene: an outline of future development or of a plan to be followed. [It.,—L. *scēna*, Gr. *skēnē*, a tent, a background.]

scene, *sēn*, *n.* (*orig.*) the stage of a theatre: the place of action in a play, or a story, or that of an actual occurrence: a division of a play marked by change of place, by the fall of the curtain, or by the entry or exit of an important character: an episode: a dramatic or stagy incident, esp. an uncomfortable, untimely, or unseemly display of hot feelings: a landscape, picture of a place or action: a view, spectacle.—*ns.* **scē'nery**, theatrical flats, hangings, &c., collectively: prospects of beautiful, picturesque, or impressive country: general aspect of a landscape; **scene'-shift'er**, one employed to set and remove the scenery in a theatre.— *adj.* **scenic** (*sē'nik*, *sen'ik*), pertaining to scenery: dramatic, theatrical.—*n.* **scenog'raphy**, the art of perspective: representation in perspective.—*adjs.* **scēnograph'ic**, **-al**, drawn in perspective.—*adv.* **scēnograph'ically.**—**scenic railway**, a railway on a small scale, running through artificial representations of picturesque scenery.—**behind the scenes**, at the

Neutral vowels in unaccented syllables: *em'pėr-ŏr*; for certain sounds in foreign words see p. ix.

650

back of the visible stage: (*fig.*) hidden from public view: in private: in a position to know what is going on. [L. *scēna* – Gr. *skēnē*, a tent, a stage.]

scent, *sent*, *v.t.* to discern by the sense of smell: to have some suspicion of: to perfume. – *n.* a perfume: odour: guidance afforded to pursuers by the sense of smell: scraps of paper dropped to mark the trail of the pursued in the game of hare-and-hounds. – *n.* **scent'-bott'le**, a small bottle for holding perfume. – *adjs.* **scent'ed**, perfumed; **scent'less**, having no scent or smell. – **on the scent**, (*lit.* and *fig.*) on the trail that will lead to the hunted animal or to the information, explanation, &c., that the investigator is seeking. [Fr. *sentir* – L. *sentīre*, to feel, perceive.]

sceptic, (*U.S.*) **skeptic**, *skep'tik*, *adj.* (*rare*) sceptical: pertaining to the sceptics or their doctrine. – *n.* an adherent of any of the schools of Greek philosophers who doubted the possibility of certain knowledge: one inclined to question commonly received opinions: one who withholds belief from prevailing opinions, esp. in religion. – *adj.* **scep'tical**, unwilling to believe without conclusive evidence: inclined to incredulity: doubtful, unconvinced – *adv.* **scep'tically**. – *n.* **scep'ticism** (*-ti-sizm*), state of the mind before it has formed a decided opinion: doubt: the doctrine of the sceptics: doubt of the existence of God or the truth of revelation. [L. *scepticus* – Gr. *skeptikos*, thoughtful – *skeptesthai*, to consider.]

sceptre, *sep'tér*, *n.* the staff or baton borne by kings as an emblem of authority: royal power. – *adj.* **scep'tred**, bearing a sceptre: regal. [L. *scēptrum* – Gr. *skēptron* – *skēptein*, to lean.]

schedule, *shed'ūl*, (*U.S.*) *sked'ūl*, *n.* a slip or scroll with writing: a list, inventory, or table: a supplementary, explanatory, or appended document: a form for filling in particulars, or such a form filled in: a time-table, plan, programme, or scheme. – *v.t.* to form into, or place in, a schedule or list: to plan, appoint, arrange. – *p.adj.* **sched'uled**, (orig. *U.S.*) planned, appointed, arranged (for, to happen at, a specified time). [O.Fr. *cedule* – L.L. *sc(h)edula*, dim. of *scheda*, a strip of papyrus – Gr. *schedē*.]

scheme, *skēm*, *n.* a diagram of positions, esp. (*astrol.*) of planets: a diagram: a system: a plan of proposed action, a project: a plan for building operations of various kinds, or the buildings, &c., constructed (e.g. *housing-scheme, irrigation scheme*): a plan pursued secretly, insidiously, by intrigue, or for private ends. – *v.t.* to plan: to lay schemes for. – *v.i.* to lay schemes. – *n.* **sche'mer**, one who forms schemes, esp. a habitual plotter, intriguer. – *adj.* **sche'ming**, given to forming schemes, intriguing. [Gr. *schēma*, form, from root of *echein* (fut. *schēsein*), to have.]

scherzo, *skér'tsō*, *n.* (*mus.*) a lively busy movement in triple time, now generally filling the place of the minuet in a sonata or symphony. [It., – Gmc.; cf. Ger. *scherz*, jest.]

schipperke, *ship'ér-ké*, *n.* a breed of dogs with almost no tail, orig. watchdogs on barges. [Du.,

'little boatman'.]

schism, *'sizm*, *n.* a breach or division, esp. in the unity of a church: the contentious temper or conduct that leads to such disunity: a body or faction formed by breach or division. – *n.* **schismat'ic**, one who separates from a church on account of difference of opinion. – *adjs.* **schismat'ic**, **-al**, tending to, or of the nature of, schism. – *adv.* **schismat'ically**. [Gr. *schisma*, a cleft – *schizein*, to split.]

schist, *shist*, *n.* a term applied to a group of rocks which have a tendency to split on account of the presence of layers of flaky minerals, such as mica and talc. – *adj.* **schist'ose**, like schist. [Fr. *schiste* – Gr. *schistos* – *schizein*, to split.]

schizocarp, *ski'-*, *ski'zō-kärp*, *n.* a dry fruit, formed from more than one carpel, and separating when ripe into a number of one-seeded parts which do not dehisce (q.v.). [Gr. *schizein*, to split, *karpos*, fruit.]

schizoid, *skit'soid*, *skid'*, *adj.* showing qualities of a schizophrenic personality, [Gr. *schizein*, to cleave, *eidos*, form.]

schizophrenia, *skī-*, *ski-zō-frē'ni-a* or *skidz-*, *n.* a psychosis marked by introversion, loss of connection between thoughts, feelings and actions, and by delusions. – *adj.* and *n.* **schizophrenic** (*-fren'ik*). [Gr. *schizein*, to split, *phrēn*, mind.]

schmaltz, *shmolts*, *n.* (*slang*) mush: sentimentality: a production in music, art, &c. that is sentimental. – *adj.* **schmaltz'y**, old-fashioned, old-style, outmoded: sentimental. [Yiddish – Ger. *schmalz*, cooking fat, grease.]

schnapps, **schnaps**, *shnaps*, *n.* Holland gin, Hollands. [Ger. *schnapps*, a dram.]

schnorkel, *shnör'kél*, *n.* a tube with a float for bringing air to a submarine or an underwater swimmer. – Anglicised as **snor'kel**, **snort**. [Ger. *schnörkel*, a spiral ornament.]

scholar, *skol'ár*, *n.* a pupil, a disciple, a student: an educated person: one whose learning is extensive and exact: the holder of a scholarship. – *adj.* **schol'arly**, of, natural to, a mature scholar: having the learning of a careful and diligent scholar. – *ns.* **schol'arliness**; **schol'arship**, scholarly learning: a foundation grant for the maintenance of a pupil or student: the status and emoluments of such a pupil or student. [O.E. *scōlere* – L.L. *scholāris* – L. *schōla*; see **school** (1).]

scholastic, *skol-as'tik*, *adj.* pertaining to schools, universities or to their staffs or teaching or to schoolmen (q.v.): excessively subtle: pedantic. – *n.* a schoolman: one who adheres to the method or subtleties of the schools of the Middle Ages: a university teacher (often suggesting pedantry). – *n.* **scholas'ticism** (*-tis-izm*), the aims, methods, and doctrines of the schoolmen. [Gr. *scholastikos* – *schōlē*, leisure, school.]

scholium, *skō'li-um*, *n.* an explanatory note such as grammarians wrote in ancient manuscripts: a note added to a mathematical problem: – *pl.* **scho'lia**, **scho'liums**. – *n.* **scho'liast**, a writer of scholia, an annotator, a commentator. – *adj.* **scholias'tic**. [Gr. *scholion*, *scholiastes* – *schōlē*, leisure, school.]

school, *skōōl*, *n.* a place for instruction and

education, esp. of children: the pupils of a school: a method of instruction: the disciples of a particular teacher, or those who hold a common doctrine or tradition: the body of instructors and students in a university, college, faculty, or department: a group of studies in which honours may be taken.—*v.t.* to educate in a school: to send to school: to subdue, train by repressive methods (e.g. *to school oneself to patience, to show no sign of emotion*), to train.—*ns.* **school'-board,** formerly, an elected board of school managers for a parish; **school'(-)boy,** a boy attending a school: one learning the rudiments of a subject.—*n.pl.* **school'(-)days,** the time of life during which one goes to school.—*ns.* **school'-fell'ow,** one taught at the same school: an associate at school; **school(-)girl,** a girl attending school; **school'-house,** a building used as a school: a house provided for a school-teacher; **school house,** a headmaster's or headmistress's boarding-house: its boarders; **school'ing,** instruction at school: maintenance at school: tuition: training, discipline; **school'man,** a philosopher or theologian of the Middle Ages; **school'master,** a master or teacher of a school, a pedagogue:—*fem.* **school'mistress; school'-mate,** one who attends the same school; **school'(-)room,** a room for teaching in. [O.E. *scōl*—L. *schŏla*—Gr. *schŏlē,* leisure, school.]

school, *skōōl, n.* a shoal of fish, whales, or other swimming animals. [Du. *school*; cf. **shoal** (1).]

schooner, *skōōn'ėr, n.* a sharp-built, swift-sailing vessel, generally two-masted, rigged either with fore-and-aft sails on both masts, or with square top and top-gallant sails on the foremast: a large beer-glass: a large sherry-glass: (**prairie schooner**) a covered emigrant wagon in America. [Early 18th century (Massachusetts) *skooner, scooner,* said to be from a dial. Eng. word *scoon,* to skim.]

schottische, *sho-tēsh', shot'ish, n.* a dance, or dance-tune, like the polka. [Ger. (*der*) *schottische (tanz*), (the) Scottish (dance).]

schuss, *shŏŏs, n.* in skiing, a straight slope on which it is possible to make a fast run: such a run.—*v.i.* to make such a run. [Ger.]

sciatic, *sī-at'ik, adj.* of, or in the region of, the hip.—*n.* **sciat'ica,** neuritis of the great sciatic nerve, which passes down the back of the thigh. [Low L. *sciaticus*—Gr. *ischion,* hipjoint.]

science, *sī'ens, n.* knowledge: knowledge ascertained by observation and experiment, critically tested, systematised, and brought under general principles: a department of such knowledge, esp. now *natural science* (q.v.).—*adj.* **scientif'ic,** according to, or versed in, science: used in science: systematic: accurate.—*adv.* **scientif'ically.**—*n.* **sci'entist,** one who studies science, esp. natural science.— **science fiction,** fiction dealing with life on the earth in the future, with space travel and with life on other planets and the like. [Fr.,—L. *scientia*—*sciēns, -entis,* pr.p. of *scīre,* to know.]

scilicet, *sīl'i-set, adv.* to wit, namely—often contracted to **sc.** [L. =*scīre licet,* it is permitted to know.]

scilla, *sil'a, n.* a genus of the lily family, includ-

ing the wood-hyacinth. [Gr. *skilla,* a sea-onion, squill (q.v.).]

scimitar, *sim'i-tár, n.* a short, single-edged curved sword, broadset at the point end, used by the Turks and Persians. [Perh. through Fr. *cimeterre* or It. *scimitarra*—Pers. *shamshīr.*]

scintilla, *sin-til'a, n.* a spark: (*fig.*) a trace.—*v.i.* **scin'tillate,** to spark: to sparkle, twinkle (*lit.* and *fig.*): to talk wittily: to emit characteristic light when subjected to radioactivity.—*ns.* **scintillā'tion; scin'tillātor,** an instrument for detecting radioactivity by using the fact that phosphors scintillate. [L., a spark.]

sciolism, *sī'ō-lizm, n.* superficial pretentious knowledge.—*n.* **sci'olist,** a pretender to science. [L. *sciolus,* dim. of *scius,* knowing—*scīre,* to know.]

scion, *sī'ón, n.* a cutting. or twig for grafting: a young member of a family: a descendant. [O.Fr. *sion, cion.*]

scirrhus, *skir'us,* or *sir'us, n.* (*med.*) a hard swelling: a hard cancer.—*adj.* **scirr'hous.** [Gr. *skirros, skīros,* a tumour, *skīros,* hard.]

scissors, *siz'órz, n.pl.* a cutting instrument with two blades: shears: a style of high jump in which the leg nearest the bar leads through. [O.Fr. *cisoires*—L.L. *cīsōrium,* a cutting instrument—L. *caedĕre, caesum,* to cut.]

sclerosis, *sklér-ō'sis, n.* (*med.*) hardening, as of the arteries: (*bot.*) hardening of cell walls or of tissues.—*adj.* **scleröt'ic,** hard, firm, applied esp. to the outer membrane of the eye-ball: pertaining to sclerosis.—*n.* the outermost membrane of the eye-ball. [Gr. *sklēros,* hard.]

scoff, *skof, v.i.* to mock, jeer (at): to show contempt or scorn.—*n.* an expression of scorn: mockery: an object of derision.—*n.* **scoff'er.**—*adv.* **scoff'ingly.** [Cf. obs. Dan. *skof,* jest.]

scoff, skoff, *skof, v.t.* (*dial.* and *slang*) to devour: to plunder. [App. from Scot. *scaff,* food, riffraff.]

scold, *skōld, n.* a rude, clamorous person, esp. a woman.—*v.i.* to vituperate: to find fault.—*v.t.* to chide.—*ns.* **scold'er; scold'ing,** a reprimand. [App. O.N. *skáld,* poet (through an intermediate sense, lampooner). See **scald** (2).]

scollop. Same as **scallop.**

sconce, *skons, n.* a small fort or earthwork: (*arch.*) a shelter.—*v.t.* to entrench: to screen. [Du. *schans.*]

sconce, *skons, n.* a candlestick with a handle or on a bracket fixed to a wall. [O.Fr. *esconse*—Low L. *absconsa,* a dark-lantern—*abscondĕre,* to hide.]

sconce, *skons, n.* the head: the crown of the head: brains, wits. [Origin obscure.]

sconce, *skons, n.* (in Oxford colleges) a fine, a forfeit.—*v.t.* to fine. [Origin obscure.]

scone, *skon,* in England often pronounced *skōn, n.* (*Scot.*) a flattish plain cake baked on a girdle or in an oven. [Perh. from Du. *schoon* (*brot*), fine (bread).]

scoop, *skōōp, n.* a hollow vessel or concave utensil, in which water or loose material can be raised and removed: the material so removed: an unexpected gain, a haul: the forestalling of other newspapers in obtaining a piece of news: a place hollowed out.—*v.t.* to bail until dry: to raise and remove in a concave utensil: to dig (out): to secure in advance

Neutral vowels in unaccented syllables: *em'pėr-ór*; for certain sounds in foreign words see p. ix.

652

of, or to the exclusion of, a rival. [Prob. partly Middle Du. *schôpe*, bailing-vessel, partly Middle Du. *schoppe*, shovel.]

scoot, *skōōt, v.i. (dial.)* to squirt forth: (*coll.*) to move or go swiftly.—Also *v.t.—interj.* off you go!—*n.* **scoot′er**, a toy, wheeled footboard and steering handle, propelled by kicking the ground: a development of it driven by a motor (also **motor-scooter**). [Prob. conn. **shoot.**]

scope, *skōp, n. (rare)* point aimed at: (*fig.*) range, field of activity, extent of field covered (e.g. *outside my scope, within the scope of the enquiry*): room (for action) or opportunity (for activity—e.g. *his instructions gave him no scope, gave no scope for originality*): spaciousness: length of cable at which a vessel rides at liberty. [Gr. *skopeein,* to look at.]

scopolamine, *sko-pol′ă-mēn* (also *-min, -mēn′, -lam′in*),*n.* an alkaloid used as an anaesthetic, obtained from various plants. Because of its sedative effects on the central nervous system scopolamine was once used to obtain criminal confessions: hence the popular name 'truth drug'. [*Scopoli* (1723–88), Italian naturalist.]

scorbutic, *al.*, ol. *ba′tik, -ăl, adj.* pertaining to, resembling, or affected by, scurvy. [Low L. *scorbūticus—scorbūtus,* scurvy; of Gmc. origin.]

scorch, *skörch, v.t.* to burn slightly: to parch: to singe: to wither with scorn, censure, &c.—*v.i.* to be burned on the surface: to be dried up: to cycle or drive furiously.—*n.* **scorch′er**, a very caustic rebuke, criticism, &c.: one who rides furiously: a very hot day.—*p.adj.* **scorch′ing**, burning superficially: bitterly sarcastic, scathing.—**scorched earth**, devastation of a region, for the purpose of hindering an enemy advance—also used adjectively, as in *scorched earth policy*. [Perh.—M.E. *skorken*; cf. O.N. *skorpna,* to shrivel; prob. affected by O.Fr. *escorcher,* to flay.]

score, *skōr, skör, n.* a notch: an incised line: a line drawn to indicate deletion or to define a position: an arrangement of music on a number of staves: a composition so arranged: an account of charges, orig. reckoned by notches in a tally: the total or record of points in a game or examination: a point gained: a set of twenty: applied also to an indefinitely large number: account, ground (e.g. *declined on the score of lack of practice*): matter (*don't worry on that score*).—*v.t.* to mark with notches or lines: to furrow: to gain, or record, as points in a game (*mus.*) to orchestrate.—*v.i.* to gain a point: to achieve a success.—*n.* **scor′er,** one who makes or keeps a score.—**know the score,** to know the hard facts of a situation. [Late O.E. *scoru*—O.N. *skor, skora*; cf. O.E. *scor—sceran* (pa.p. *scoren*), to shear.]

scoria, *skō′ri-a, n.* dross or slag left after smelting ore: a piece of lava with steam holes:—*pl.* **sco′riae.** [L.,—Gr. *skōriā—skōr,* dung.]

scorn, *skörn, n.* extreme contempt: object of contempt.—*v.t.* to feel or express scorn for: to refuse with scorn.—*n.* **scorn′er.**—*adj.* **scorn′ful**—*adv.* **scorn′fully.** [O.Fr. *escarn,* mockery; of Gmc. orig.; cf. O.H.G. *skern,* mockery.]

scorpion, *skör′pi-ón, n.* any one of an order of animals belonging to the same class as

spiders, with head and thorax united, pincers, four pairs of legs, and a segmented abdomen including a tail with a sting: (*B.*) a whip with points like a scorpion's tail: (*cap.*) Scorpio.—*n.* **Scor′pio,** a constellation and a sign of the zodiac. [L. *scorpiō, -ōnis*—Gr. *skorpios.*]

scot, *skot, n.* a payment: a share of a reckoning (also **shot**).—*adj.* **scot′-free′,** free from payment, penalty, or loss. [O.E. *scot, sceot—scēo-tan,* to shoot.]

Scot, *skot, n.* a native of Scotland: one of the Scoti or Scots, a Celtic race who migrated from Ireland (the original *Scotia*) before the end of the 5th century.—*n.* **Scotia** (*skō′sha*), Scotland. [O.E. *Scottas,* the Scots—L.L. *Scottus.*]

Scotch, *skoch, adj.* a form of **Scottish**, or **Scots**, in common use though disapproved by many Scotsmen: the generally accepted form when applied to certain products or articles associated with Scotland, as *Scotch whisky.—n.* Scotch whisky.—**Scotch mist,** a fine rain; **Scotch pebble,** an agate or similar stone. [From **Scottish.**]

scotch, *skoch, v.t.* to cut or wound slightly: to render harmless (e.g. a snake), stamp out (e.g. a rumour). [Origin unknown.]

Scotland Yard, *skot′lánd yärd, n.* (strictly, *New* Scotland Yard) the headquarters of the Metropolitan Police: hence the London Criminal Investigation Department.

Scots, *skots, adj.* Scottish (almost always used of money, manners, and law; preferably also of language).—*n.* the dialect of Lowland Scotland developed from the northern form of Middle English.—*n.* **Scots′man.**—**Scots Greys,** a famous regiment of dragoons, established in 1683, amalgamated (1971) with 3rd Carabiniers; **Scots pine,** the only native British pine. [Shortened form of M.E. *Scottis,* Scottish.]

Scot(t)ice, *skot′i-sē, adv.* in Scots dialect.—*n.* **Scott′icism,** a Scottish idiom. [L.L. *Scot(t)icus,* Scottish.]

Scottish (obs. **Scotish**), *skot′ish, adj.* of Scotland, its people, or its English dialect.

scoundrel, *skown′drėl, n.* a low mean blackguard, an utter rascal.—*n.* **scoun′drelism,** rascality.—*adj.* **scoun′drelly,** fit for or like a scoundrel. [Origin unknown.]

scour, *skowr, v.t.* to clean by hard rubbing: to scrub: to cleanse, clear out (e.g. a harbour, a pipe) by a current of water: to purge.—*n.* the action of a strong current in a narrow channel.—*n.* **scour′er.** [O.Fr. *escurer*—L. *ex,* inten., and *cūrāre,* to take care of.]

scour, *skowr, v.t.* to rush along: to move quickly, esp. in search or pursuit.—*v.t.* to traverse in search or pursuit: to search thoroughly. [Perh. O.N. *skūr,* storm; cf. **shower.**]

scourge, *skūrj, n.* a whip made of leather thongs: an instrument of punishment: a punishment, an affliction.—*v.t.* to whip severely: to afflict.—*n.* **scour′ger.** [O.Fr. *escorge*—L. *excoriāre,* to flog—*corium,* leather.]

scouse, *skows, n.* a native of Liverpool: the northern English dialect spoken in and around Liverpool. [Short for *lobscouse.*]

scout, *skowt, n.* one sent out to bring in tidings, observe the enemy, &c.: a Scout (orig. *Boy*

fāte, fär; mē, hûr (her); *mīne; mōte, för; mūte; mōōn, fŏŏt;* ᴛʜᴇɴ (then)

Scout; see **boy**): a college servant at Oxford: a road patrolman to help motorists.—*v.t.* to watch closely: to reconnoitre (often with *about* or *around*).—*v.i.* to act as a scout.—*n.* **scout′master**, formerly, the leader of a band of Scouts. [O.Fr. *escoute*—*escouter*—L. *auscultāre*, to listen—*auris*, the ear.]

scout, *skowt, v.t.* to reject with disdain. [Cf. O.N. *skūta*, a taunt.]

scow, *skow, n.* a flat-bottomed boat. [Du. *schouw*.]

scowl, *skowl, v.i.* to contract the brows in displeasure: to look gloomy.—*n.* the contraction of the brows in displeasure. [Cf. Dan. *skule*, to cast down the eyes, look sidelong.]

scrabble, *skrab′l, v.t.* and *v.i.* to scratch, to scrape: to scrawl. [Du. *schrabbelen*, freq. of *schrabben*, to scratch.]

Scrabble, *skrab′l, n.* a word-building game. [Trademark.]

scrag, *skrag, n,* anything thin or lean and rough: the bony part of the neck.—*v.t.* to put to death by hanging: to throttle.—*adjs.* **scragg′ed**, **scragg′y**, lean and gaunt.—*ns.* **scragg′edness**, **scragg′iness**.—*adv.* **scragg′ily**. [Cf. Du. *kraag*, Ger. *kragen*, the neck.]

scramble, *skram′bl, v.i.* to make one's way by hasty and awkward effort: to clamber (*lit.* or *fig.*) to dash or struggle for what one can get before others.—*v.t.* to put, make, get together, scramblingly: to jumble up (a message) so that it can be read only after decoding: to make (a radiotelephone conversation) unintelligible to all except the two speakers by a device that alters frequencies.—*n.* act of scrambling: a struggle for what can be had: a form of motor or motor-cycle trial.—*n.* **scram′bler**, one who or that which scrambles, esp. a telephone device.—*adj.* **scram′bling**, confused and irregular.—**scrambled eggs**, eggs beaten up and mixed with milk, butter, salt, and pepper, and heated till they thicken. [Cf. the dialect word *scramb*, to rake together with the hands.]

scrap, *skrap, n.* a small piece: a remnant: a picture or a piece of printed matter suited for preservation in a scrap-book: parts, or articles, discarded because unusable for their original purpose. refuse.—*v.t.* to consign to the scrap-heap (*fig.*) to discard:—*pr.p.* scrapp′ing; *pa.p.* and *pa.t.* scrapped.—*ns.* **scrap′-book**, a blank book for extracts, prints, &c.; **scrap′-heap**, a place where old iron is collected: rubbish-heap (*lit.* and *fig.*); **scrap′-ī′ron**, **scrap′-met′al**, scraps of iron or other metal, of use only for remelting; **scrap′-mer′chant**, one who deals in scrap metal.—*adj.* **scrapp′y**, fragmentary: disconnected.—*n.* **scrapp′iness.**—**not a scrap**, not in the least. [O.N. *skrap*, scraps.]

scrap, *skrap, n.* (*slang*) a fight, scrimmage.—Also *v.i.* [Origin unknown.]

scrape, *skrāp, v.t.* to rub with something sharp: to remove by drawing a sharp edge over: to gain or collect by laborious effort: to save penuriously.—*v.i.* to scratch the ground or floor.—*n.* an act or process of scraping: a mark made by scraping: backward movement of one foot in making a bow: a predicament that threatens disgrace or penalty.—*ns.* **scrap′er**, an instrument used for scraping, esp. the soles of shoes; **scrap′ing**, a piece scraped off.—**bow and scrape**, to be obsequious; **scrape through**, to avoid failure by a narrow margin. [O.E. *scrapian*, or O.N. *skrapa*.]

scratch, *skrach, v.t.* to draw a sharp point over the surface of: to leave a mark on by so doing: to tear or to dig with the claws: to write hurriedly: to withdraw from a competition.—*v.i.* to use the claws or nails in tearing or digging: to retire from a contest.—*n.* a mark or tear made by scratching: a slight wound: the line from which competitors start in a race (hence **start from scratch**, to start from nothing—*lit.* and *fig.*): the line in a prize-ring up to which boxers are led—hence test, trial (as in **come up to the scratch**, (*fig.*) not to back out or shirk, to act or be as desired or expected).—*adj.* improvised (as a *scratch crew*): receiving no handicap.—*n.* **scratch′er.**—*adj.* **scratch′y**, like scratches: likely to scratch: uneven: grating. [Perh. M.E. *cracchen*, to scratch.]

scrawl, *skröl, v.t.* and *v.i.* to mark or write irregularly or hastily, to scribble.—*n.* irregular, hasty, or bad writing: a letter, &c., written thus.—*n.* **scrawl′er.** [Origin obscure.]

scrawny, *skrö′ni, adj.* gaunt and lean. [Cf. Norw. *skran*, lean.]

scream, *skrēm, v.i.* and *v.t.* to cry out in a loud shrill voice, as in fear, pain, or immoderate mirth, to shriek.—*v.i.* (*coll.*) of colours, to be so acutely inharmonious as to suggest shrieking.—*n.* a shrill, sudden cry, as in fear or pain, a shriek. [M.E. *scræmen*.]

scree, *skrē, n.* loose debris on a rocky slope. [O.N. *skritha*, a landslip—*skrītha*, to slide.]

screech, *skrēch, v.i.* to utter a harsh, shrill, and sudden cry.—*n.* a harsh, shrill, and sudden cry.—*n.* **screech′-owl**, a screeching owl, esp. the barn-owl. [M.E. *scrichen*.]

screed, *skrēd, n.* a piece torn off: a shred: a long and tedious discourse. [O.E. *scrēade*.]

screen, *skrēn, n.* that which shelters from danger or observation, that which protects from heat, cold, or the sun: an enclosure or partition in churches: a surface on which cinematograph (or other) pictures are projected: motion pictures collectively: the motion-picture profession: surface on which a television picture appears: a coarse riddle for sifting coal, &c.—Also *adj.*—*v.t.* to shelter or conceal: to sift through a coarse riddle: to subject (e.g. persons in the armed forces) to tests to determine what kind of work their abilities best fit them for: to subject (e.g. the political records of a number of persons, persons boarding an aircraft, &c.) to close examination in order to separate the desirable from the undesirable: to project on a screen: to make a motion picture of.—*n.pl.* **screen′ings**, the refuse matter after sifting.—*ns.* **screen′-play**, the written text for a film, with dialogue, stage-directions, and descriptions of characters and setting; **screen′-writer**, a writer of screenplays. [App. related to O.Fr. *escren* (Fr. *écran*); cf. Ger. *schirm*.]

screw, *skrōō, n.* a cylinder with a helical groove or thread (q.v.) (**male screw**), or a cylindrical hole with a thread or groove on the inward surface (**female screw**), used as fastenings: any mechanical device for applying pressure

Neutral vowels in unaccented syllables: *em′pėr-ȯr*; for certain sounds in foreign words see p. ix.

654

having a helical thread or groove: a screw-propeller: a twisted cone of paper: a turn of a screw: a twist: a spin imparted to a ball: (*fig.*) pressure: a stingy fellow, an extortioner: (*coll.*) salary, wages: (*coll.*) a worn-out horse.—*v.t.* to fasten, tighten, compress, force, adjust, extort, by a screw, a screwing motion, or as if by a screw: to summon up (courage, &c.; with *up*): to turn in the manner of a screw: to pucker.—*v.i.* to admit of screwing: to wind, to worm.—*ns.* **screw'-driv'er,** an instrument for driving or turning screw nails; **screw'-nail,** a nail made in the form of a screw; **screw'-propell'er,** a propeller with helical blades, used in steamships and aircraft; **screw'-steam'er,** a steamer propelled by a screw; **screw'-wrench,** a tool for gripping and turning nuts and the heads of large screws.—*adj.* **screw'y** (*coll.*), eccentric, slightly mad: not quite honest.—**a screw loose,** something defective; **put the screws on,** to coerce. [Earlier *scrue*; app.—O.Fr. *escroue*, of obscure origin.]

scribble, *skrib'l, v.t.* to scrawl, to write badly or carelessly (as regards handwriting or substance): to fill with worthless writing.—*v.i.* to write carelessly: to make meaningless marks suggestive of writing.—*n.* careless writing: marks suggestive of writing: a hastily written letter, &c.—*n.* **scribb'ler,** a petty author. [A freq. of **scribe.**]

scribe, *skrīb, n.* a public or official writer: (*hist.*) a clerk, amanuensis, secretary: (*B.*) an expounder and teacher of the Mosaic and traditional law: a pointed instrument to mark lines on wood, &c.—*v.t.* to mark or score. [L. *scrība—scrībĕre,* to write.]

scrim, *skrim, n.* a cloth used in upholstery, &c.

scrimmage, *skrim'ij,* **scrummage,** *skrum'ij, n.* a tussle.—*v.i.* to take part in a scrimmage. [Prob. corr. of **skirmish.**]

scrimp, *skrimp, adj.* (also **scrimp'y**) meagre, scanty.—*v.t.* to make meagre or scanty: to stint, to limit rigidly.—*v.i.* to be sparing or niggardly. [Cf. Swed. and Dan. *skrumpen,* O.E. *scrimman,* to shrink.]

scrip, *skrip, n.* that which is written: a piece of paper containing writing: a preliminary certificate of stock or shares subscribed, or partly subscribed, or allotted. [A variant of **script,** but partly perh. from **scrap.**]

scrip, *skrip, n.* a small bag, a satchel, a pilgrim's pouch. [Cf. O.N. *skreppa,* a bag.]

script, *skript, n.* (*law*) an original document: a manuscript: the text of a talk, play, &c., often for broadcasting: handwriting in imitation of print: print in imitation of handwriting: a set of characters used in writing a language.—*v.t.* to write a script, esp. for broadcasting or the theatre or cinema.—*n.* **script'-writer.** [L. *scrīptum—scrībĕre,* to write.]

scriptorium, *skrip-tō', -tō', ri-ŭm, n.* a writing-room, esp. in a monastery. [L. *scrīptōrium—scrībĕre,* to write.]

scripture, *skrip'tyúr, -chúr, n.* (*arch.*) hand-writing: (*arch.*) something written: (in *sing.* or *pl.*) sacred writings of a religion, esp. (**Scripture, -s**) the Bible.—Also *adj.—adj.* **scrip'tural,** contained in, or according to, Scripture, biblical. [L. *scrīptūra—scrībĕre.*]

scrivener, *skriv'nér, n.* a scribe, a copyist: one

who draws up contracts, &c.: one who lays out money at interest for others. [O.Fr. *escrivain* (Fr. *écrivain*)—L.L. *scrībānus*—L. *scrība,* a scribe.]

scrofula, *skrof'ū-la, n.* tuberculosis, esp. of the lymphatic glands, called also the king's evil.—*adj.* **scrof'ulous.** [L. *scrōfulae—scrōfa,* a sow.]

scroll, *skrōl, n.* a roll of paper or parchment: a writing in the form of a roll: a rough draft: a schedule: a ribbon-like strip, partly coiled or curved, often bearing a motto: (*mach.*) any of various parts shaped more or less like a scroll: (*archit.*) a spiral ornament.—*adj.* **scrolled,** formed into a scroll: ornamented with scrolls. [Earlier *scrowl(e)*—M.E. *scrow*—Anglo-Fr. *escrowe.*]

scrub, *skrub, v.t.* and *v.i.* to rub hard in order to cleanse: (*slang*) to cancel:—*pr.p.* **scrubb'ing;** *pa.t.* and *pa.p.* **scrubbed.**—*n.* act or process of scrubbing: a brush with short, stiff bristles.—*n.* **scrubb'er.** [Perh. obs. Du. *schrubben.*]

scrub, *skrub, n.* a stunted tree: stunted trees and shrubs collectively: country covered with bushes or low trees: an undersized or inferior animal: an insignificant person: a player in an inferior team: a team of inferior players or one with too few players.—*adj.* mean, insignificant: (of a team) improvised, hastily got together for the occasion.—*n.* **scrubb'er** (*Australia*), an animal that has run wild.—*adj.* **scrubb'y,** stunted: covered with scrub: mean.—*n.* **scrub'-rider,** one who looks for cattle that stray into the scrub. [A variant of **shrub.**]

scruff, *skruf, n.* the nape of the neck. [Perh. O.N. *skopt, skoft,* the hair.]

scruff, *skruf, n.* (*coll.*) an untidy, dirty person.—*n.* **scruff'iness.**—*adj.* **scruff'y** (*coll.*), untidy, dirty. [**scurf.**]

scrum, *skrum, n.* a scrimmage: (*Rugby football*) a closing-in of rival forwards round the ball on the ground, or in readiness for its being inserted (by the scrum-half) between the two compact, pushing masses.—*v.i.* to form a scrum.—*n.* **scrum'-half** (*Rugby football*), a half-back whose duty it is to put the ball into the scrum and secure it as soon as it emerges. [Abbreviation of **scrummage.** See **scrimmage.**]

scruple, *skrōō'pl, n.* a small weight—in apothecaries' weight, 20 grains: a very small quantity: a difficulty or consideration, usu. moral, restraining one from action—esp. a difficulty turning on a fine point of right or wrong.—*v.t.* to hesitate (to do) on account of a scruple.—*adj.* **scru'pulous,** influenced by scruples, conscientious: exact, very careful (e.g. *scrupulous honesty, cleanliness*).—*adv.* **scru'pulously.**—*ns.* **scru'pulousness,** **scrupulos'ity,** state of being scrupulous. [L. *scrūpulus,* dim. of *scrūpus,* a sharp stone, anxiety.]

scrutiny, *skrōō'ti-ni, n.* a vote by poll: close, careful, or minute investigation: a searching look: official examination of votes: (*R.C.*) a public catechising, &c., before baptism, &c.—*n.* **scrutineer',** one who makes a scrutiny.—*v.t.* **scru'tinise,** to examine carefully or critically: to investigate. [O.Fr. *scrutine*—L. *scrūtinium—scrūtārī,* to search even to the rags—*scrūta,* rags, trash.]

scud, *skud, v.i.* to move or run swiftly: (*naut.*) to

run before the wind in a gale:—*pr.p.* scudd'ing; *pa.t.* and *pa.p.* scudd'ed.—*n.* act of moving quickly: driving cloud, shower, or spray. [Origin obscure.]

scuffle, *skuf'l, v.i.* to struggle closely: to fight confusedly.—*n.* a struggle in which the combatants grapple closely: any confused contest. [Cf. Swed. *skuffa,* to shove, Du. *schoffelen* ; cf. **shove, shovel, shuffle.**]

sculk. Same as **skulk.**

scull, *skul, n.* a short, light oar for one hand.—*v.t.* to propel with a pair of sculls, or with one oar worked like a screw over the stern.—*v.i.* to use sculls.—*n.* **scull'er,** one who sculls: a small boat rowed by one man.

scullery, *skul'ér-i, n.* a room for rough kitchen work, as cleansing of utensils. [O.Fr. *escuelerie* — Low L. *scutellārius* — L. *scutella,* a tray.]

scullion, *skul'yón, n.* a servant for drudgery, a menial—*adj.* base. [O.Fr. *escouillon,* a dishclout — L. *scōpa,* a broom.]

sculpt, *skulpt, v.t.* and *v.i.* to sculpture: to carve. [Fr. *sculpter* — L. *sculpĕre,* to carve.]

sculptor, *skulp'tór, n.* an artist in carving:—*fem.* **sculp'tress.**—*adj.* **sculp'tural,** pertaining to sculpture: resembling, having the quality of, sculpture.—*n.* **sculp'ture,** the act or art of carving figures, esp. in stone: the work of a sculptor.—*v.t.* to carve: to shape in relief: to mould or form so as to have the appearance, or (*fig.*) other quality, of sculpture: to modify the form of (the earth's surface).—*adj.* **sculp'tured,** carved: engraved: (of features), fine and regular. [L. *sculptor, sculptūra*—*sculpĕre, sculptum,* to carve.]

scum, *skum, n.* foam or froth: matter rising to, and floating on, the surface: anything superfluous or worthless.—*v.t.* to take the scum from, to skim:—*pr.p.* scumm'ing;*pa.t.* and*pa.p.* scummed.—*n.* **scumm'er.** [Cf. Dan. *skum,* Ger. *schaum,* foam.]

scunner, *skun'ér, (dial.) v.t.* to nauseate.—*v.i.* to feel disgust (at).—*n.* disgust: cause of disgust. [O.E. *scunian,* to shun.]

scupper, *skup'ér, n.* a hole in a ship's side to drain the deck. [Ety. uncertain.]

scupper, *skup'ér, v.t.* to do for: to ruin.

scurf, *skûrf, n.* small flakes or scales of dead skin, esp. on the scalp: a crust of flaky scales: an incrustation.—*adj.* **scurf'y.**—*n.* **scurf'iness.** [O.E. *scurf, sceorf.*]

scurrilous, *skur'il-ùs, adj.* befitting a vulgar buffoon, indecent: opprobrious, grossly abusive.—*adjs.* **scurr'il, scurr'ile,** (*arch.*) scurrilous.—*n.* **scurril'ity,** buffoonery, low or obscene jesting: indecency of language: vulgar abuse.—*adv.* **scurr'ilously.**—*n.* **scurr'ilousness.** [L. *scurrīlis—scurra,* a buffoon.]

scurry, *skur'i, v.i.* to hurry along, to scamper.—*n.* a flurry, bustle. [From **hurry-scurry,** reduplication of **hurry,** or from **scour** (2).]

scurvy, *skûr'vi, adj.* scurfy: shabby: vile, contemptible.—*n.* a disease marked by general debility, due to a lack of fresh vegetables and consequently of vitamin C.—*adv.* **scur'vily,** in a scurvy manner: meanly, basely.—*n.* **scur'viness,** state of being scurvy: meanness. [**scurf.**]

scut, *skut, n.* a short erect tail, like a hare's: a hare. [Origin obscure.]

scutage, *skū'tij, n.* (*hist.*) a tax paid instead of

the personal service which a vassal or tenant owed to his lord. [L.L. *scūtāgium* — L. *scūtum,* shield.]

scutcheon, *skuch'ón, n.* a shortened form of **escutcheon.**

scutiform, *skū'ti-förm, adj.* having the form of a shield. [L. *scūtum,* a shield, and suffx. *-form.*]

scuttle, *skut'l, n.* a shallow basket: (also **coal-scuttle**) a vessel for holding coal. [O.E. *scutel* — L. *scutella,* a tray.]

scuttle, *skut'l, n.* an opening in a ship's deck or side: its lid.—*v.t.* to make a hole in, esp. in order to sink: to destroy, ruin. [O.Fr. *escoutille,* a hatchway.]

scuttle, *skut'l, v.i.* to hurry: to withdraw in haste.—*n.* hurry: hasty retreat.

scythe, *sīth, n.* an instrument with a large curved blade for mowing grass, &c.—*v.t.* and *v.i.* to mow with a scythe.—*adj.* **scythed,** armed with scythes. [O.E. *sīthe* ; cf. O.N. *sigthr,* Ger. *sense.*]

sea, *sē, n.* the great mass of salt water covering the greater part of the earth's surface: any great expanse of salt water less than an ocean: a rough or agitated surface: a wave: the tide: a flood: any wide expanse.—*adj.* (in composition) of the sea, marine.—*ns.* **sea'-anem'one,** any of numerous, usu. solitary, soft-bodied, often beautiful, polyps preying on small animals found on rocks on the sea-coast; **sea'-board,** the border or shore of the sea.—*adj.* **sea'-borne,** carried on the sea.—*ns.* **sea'-breeze,** a breeze blowing from the sea towards the land, esp. in the daytime; **sea'-calf,** the common seal; **sea'-change,** a change effected by the sea: a transformation; **sea'-coal,** (*arch.*) coal in the ordinary sense, not charcoal; **sea'coast,** the land adjacent to the sea; **sea'-dog,** the common seal: a dogfish: an old sailor: a pirate; **sea'-el'ephant,** the elephant seal, a very large member of the seal family, found in the southern seas; **sea'fārer,** a traveller by sea, usu. a sailor.—*adj.* **sea'fāring.**—*ns.* **sea'-fight,** a naval battle; **sea'food,** food obtained from the sea, esp. shellfish; **sea'-front,** the side of an area, or of a building, that looks towards the sea: a promenade with its buildings facing the sea.—*adjs.* **sea'-girt,** surrounded by seas; **sea'-going,** (of a ship) sailing on the deep sea, as opposed to coasting or river vessels; **sea'-green,** green like the sea.—*ns.* **sea'-gull,** a gull (q.v.); **sea'-hedge'hog,** a sea-urchin; **sea'horse,** a hippocampus or kindred fish: the walrus; **sea'kale,** a cabbage-like seaside plant cultivated for its sprouts; **sea'-king',** a leader of the Vikings; **sea'-law'yer,** a captious, verbose amateur lawyer, esp. if a sailor; **Sea Lord,** a naval member of the Board of Admiralty.—*n.pl.* **sea'-legs,** ability to walk on a ship's deck when it is pitching or rolling: resistance to seasickness.—*ns.* **sea'-lev'el,** the mean level of the surface of the sea; **sea'-lī'on,** any of several large seals of the Pacific Ocean with external ears, so called from their roar and the mane of the male; **sea'man,** a sailor: one of a ship's crew other than an officer or apprentice; **sea'manship,** the art of handling ships at sea; **sea'mark,** a mark of tidal limit: an object serving as a guide to those at sea; **sea'-mew,** any gull; **sea'-mile,** a geographical

Neutral vowels in unaccented syllables: *em'pér-ór* ; for certain sounds in foreign words see p. ix.

656

or nautical mile (see **mile**); **sea′-pie**, a sailor's dish made of salt-meat, vegetables, and dumplings baked: the oyster-catcher; **sea′-piece**, a picture representing a scene at sea; **sea′plane**, an aeroplane that can alight on, or rise from, the sea; **sea′port**, a port or harbour on the seashore: a town with such a harbour; **sea power**, national strength in naval armaments: a nation with a notably strong navy; **sea′-room**, space within which a ship can be safely manoeuvred; **sea′-rō′ver**, a pirate; **sea′-salt**, salt obtained from sea-water; **sea′scape**, a sea-piece (q.v.); **sea′-ser′pent**, an enormous marine animal of serpent-like form, whose existence is frequently alleged but has never been proved; **sea′shore′**, the land immediately adjacent to the sea: the foreshore.—*adj.* **sea′sick′**, affected with sickness through the rolling of a vessel at sea.—*ns.* **sea′sickness**; **sea′side**, the neighbourhood of the sea; **sea′-swall′ow**, a tern, esp. the common tern: the stormy petrel; **sea′-trout**, the salmon trout: any of certain other trout that live in the sea but ascend rivers to spawn; **sea′-ur′chin**, any of a class of marine animals, with globular, ovoid, or sometimes heart-shaped body, walled in by continuous calcareous plates, without arms; **sea′-wall**, a wall to keep out the sea.—*adj.* **sea′ward**, towards the sea.—*adv.* (also **sea′wards**) towards or in the direction of the sea.—*ns.* **sea′ware**, seaweed, esp. when used as manure; **sea′-way**, (often **sea′way**), a way by sea: a heavy sea: a regular route taken by ocean traffic: an inland waterway on which ocean-going vessels can sail; **sea′weed**, marine algae collectively: any one of the lower plant-forms growing in the sea near the shore; **sea′-wolf**, a viking, a pirate.—*adj.* **sea′worthy**, fit for sea, able to endure stormy weather.—*ns.* **sea′worthiness**; **sea′wrack**, coarse sea-weeds of any kind.—**all at sea**, out of one's reckoning, completely at a loss; **at sea**, away from land: on the ocean: astray; **go to sea**, to become a sailor; **half-seas over**, half-drunk; **heavy sea**, a sea in which the waves run high; **ship a sea**, of a vessel, to have a wave wash over the side. [O.E. *sǣ*; Du. *zee*, Ger. *see*, O.N. *sær*.]

seal, *sēl*, *n.* a piece of wax, lead, or other material, stamped with a device and attached as a means of authentication or attestation: a piece of wax, &c., used as a means of keeping closed a letter, door, &c.: an engraved stone or other stamp for impressing a device: a significant mark: an act done as an assurance, guarantee.—*v.t.* to attach a seal to: to mark, fasten, or close with a seal: to attest, authenticate, confirm: to close (*lit.* and *fig.*) securely, keep closed: to decide irrevocably (e.g. *this sealed his fate*).—*ns.* **seal′ant**, something that seals a place where there is a leak; **seal′ing-wax**, wax for sealing letters, &c.—**a sealed book**, something beyond one's knowledge or understanding; **seal off**, to isolate completely.—**Great Seal**, the state seal of the United Kingdom; **Privy Seal**, the seal appended to grants, and in Scotland authenticating royal grants of personal rights; **set one's seal to**, to give one's authority or assent to. [O.Fr. *seel*—L. *sigillum*, dim. of *signum*, a mark.]

seal, *sēl*, *n.* the name commonly applied to two families of carnivorous mammals, one of which has no external ears, adapted to a marine existence and valuable for their skin and oil.—*v.i.* to hunt seals.—*ns.* **seal′er**, a man, or a ship, engaged in the seal-fishery; **seal′rook′ery**, a place where seals breed; **seal′skin**, the prepared fur of the fur-seal or an imitation: a garment made of this. [O.E. *seolh*; O.N. *selr*.]

Sealyham, *sē′li-(h)ăm*, *n.* a white terrier with short legs. [*Sealyham*, in Pembrokeshire.]

seam, *sēm*, *n.* a piece of sewing-work: the line formed by the sewing together of two pieces: a line of union: a wrinkle, furrow: (*geol.*) a thin layer between thicker strata.—*v.t.* to unite by a seam: to sew: to make a seam in.—*n.* **seam′-bowl′ing** (*cricket*), bowling in which the seam of the ball is used in delivery to make the ball swerve in flight or first to swerve and then to break in the opposite direction on pitching.—*adj.* **seam′less**, without a seam: woven throughout.—*n.* **seamstress** (*sēm′stres, sem′stres*), **sempstress** (*sem′-stres*), one who sews, a needlewoman.—*adj.* **seamy** (*sēm′i*), having or showing a seam or seams.—*n.* **seam′y-side**, the under or inner side of a garment; hence (*fig.*) the disreputable side or aspect. [O.E. *sēam*—*sīwian*, to sew; Du. *zoom*, Ger. *saum*.]

sean, *sēn.* Same as **seine**.

séance, *sā′ās*, *n.* a sitting or session, esp. of psychical researchers or of spiritualists. [Fr.—L. *sedēre*, to sit.]

sear, *sēr*, *adj.* (usu. **sere**) dry and withered.—*v.t.* (rarely **sere**) to dry up: to scorch: to cauterise: to render callous or insensible. [O.E. *sēar*, dry, *sēarian*, to dry up; Low Ger. *soor*, Du. *zoor*.]

search, *sûrch*, *v.t.* to survey inquiringly, to examine or inspect closely: to probe.—*v.i.* to make search or inquisition.—*n.* inquisition: investigation: quest.—*n.* **search′er**, one who searches: one appointed to search, as a custom-house officer.—*adj.* **search′ing**, penetrating: severe.—*adv.* **search′ingly.**—*ns.* **search′-light**, a strong beam of electric light for picking out objects by night; **search′-warr′ant**, a warrant authorising the searching of a house, &c.—**right of search**, the right of a belligerent to search neutral vessels for contraband of war; **search me** (*slang*), I don't know. [O.Fr. *cerchier*—L. *circāre*, to go about—*circus*, a circle.]

season, *sē′z(ó)n*, *n.* one of the four divisions of the year: the usual or appropriate time: any particular time: any brief period of time: seasoning, relish.—*v.t.* to mature: to accustom, inure (to): to give relish, or (*fig.*) zest, to: to moderate by admixture (e.g. *to season justice with mercy*): to dry (timber) until the moisture content is brought down to a suitable amount.—*v.i.* to become seasoned.—*adj.* **sea′sonable**, happening in due season: timely, opportune.—*n.* **sea′sonableness.**—*adv.* **sea′sonably.**—*adj.* **sea′sonal**, belonging to a particular season.—*n.* **sea′soning**, that which is added to food to give relish: the process by which anything is seasoned.—**in season**, ripe, fit and ready for use: opportune; **out of season**, not in season: inopportune; **season**

ticket, a ticket valid for repeated use during a specified period. [O.Fr. *seson* — L. *satiō, -ōnis,* a sowing.]

seat, *sēt, n.* a chair, bench, &c.: the part of a chair on which the body rests: that part of the body or of a garment on which one sits: the manner in which one sits: a place where anything is settled or established: a mansion: the right to sit: membership: a constituency. — *v.t.* to place on a seat: to cause to sit down: to assign a seat to: to place in any situation, site, &c.: to establish, to fix: to furnish with a seat, or with seats: to have seats for (a specified number). — *p.adj.* **seat'ed,** fixed, confirmed: situated, located: furnished with a seat or seats. — *ns.* **seat'-belt,** a belt which can be fastened to hold a person in his seat in a car or aircraft; **seat'ing,** provision or arrangement of seats. — **take a seat,** to sit down; **take a back seat** (see **back**). [O.N. *sæti,* seat; cf. O.E. *sæt,* ambush.]

sebaceous, *se-bā'shus, adj.* pertaining to, producing, or containing fatty material. [L.L. *sēbāceus — sēbum,* tallow.]

secant, *sē'kant, sek'ant, adj.* cutting, dividing. — *n.* a line that cuts another: one of the six trigonometrical functions of an angle, the reciprocal of the cosine (q.v.), identical with the cosecant of the complementary angle. — *abbrev.* **sec** (*sek*). [L. *secāns, -antis,* pr.p. of *secāre,* to cut.]

secateurs, *sek-a-tûrz', n.* clippers for pruning with one hand. [Fr., — L. *secāre,* to cut.]

secede, *si-sēd', v.i.* to withdraw, esp. from a society or federation. — *ns.* **secē'der,** one who secedes: (*cap.*) one of a body of Presbyterians who seceded from the Church of Scotland about 1733; **secess'ion,** the act of seceding: the party that secedes. [L. *sēcēdĕre, sēcessum — sē-,* apart, *cēdĕre,* to go.]

seclude, *si-klōōd', v.i.* to shut off, esp. from association or influence (with *from*). — *adj.* **seclud'ed,** withdrawn from observation· or society. — *adv.* **seclud'edly.** — *n.* **seclusion** (*si-klōō'zh(ó)n*), the act of secluding: the state of being secluded: retirement, privacy, solitude. [L. *sēclūdĕre, sēclūsum — sē-,* apart, *claudĕre,* to shut.]

second, *sek'ónd, adj.* next after the first in time, place, power, quality, &c.: other, alternate (e.g. *every second day*): additional: comparable to (the person or thing specified — e.g. *a second Nero*). — *n.* one who, or that which, is second: one who attends another in a duel or a prizefight: a supporter: 1/60th of a minute of time (SI unit), or of angular measure: (*mus.*) the part next to the highest in part-singing: second gear: (*pl.*) articles inferior to the best. — *v.t.* to act as second (to): to support, back up: to further, encourage: to make the second speech in support of (a motion): (*sé-kond'*) to transfer temporarily to special employment. — *adj.* **sec'ondary,** subordinate: of a second stage: of a second order in importance (e.g. *a secondary consideration*): of education, between primary and higher: derivative: (*cap.*; *geol.*) Mesozoic, between Primary or Palaeozoic and Tertiary or Cainozoic. — *n.* that which is secondary: a subordinate. — *adv.* **sec'ondarily.** — *adjs.* **sec'ond-best,** next to the

best: not the best — (**come off second-best,** to get the worst of a contest); **sec'ond-class,** of the class next to the first: inferior (**second-class citizen,** a member of a group in the community not accorded the full rights and privileges enjoyed by the community as a whole; **second-class mail,** mail sent at a cheaper rate because the sender accepts slower delivery). — *n.* **sec'onder,** one who seconds or supports. — *adj.* **sec'ond-hand',** derived from another: not new, that has been used by another. — *adv.* **sec'ondly,** in the second place. — *adj.* **sec'ond-rate,** inferior, mediocre. — **Second Advent, Coming,** a second coming of Christ; **secondary school,** a school for secondary education; **second childhood,** mental weakness in old age; **second cousin** (see **cousin**); **second lieutenant,** a military officer of lowest commissioned rank, next below a lieutenant; **second nature,** ingrained habit, tendency that has become instinctive; **second self,** a person with whom one has the closest possible ties and understanding; **second sight,** a gift of prophetic vision, attributed to certain persons, esp. Highlanders; **second thoughts,** reconsideration. [Fr., — L. *secundus — sequī, secūtus,* to follow.]

secret, *sē'kret, adj.* concealed from others, guarded against discovery or observation: not avowed: constructed, carried out, so as to escape discovery or notice (e.g. *secret drawer, secret nailing*): recondite: secluded: keeping secrets, secretive. — *n.* a fact, purpose, or method that is kept undivulged: anything unrevealed or unknown: privacy: the explanation (of — e.g. *the secret of his success*), the method by which something is attained (e.g. *the secret of good health*). — *n.* **sē'crecy,** the state of being secret: concealment: privacy: the power or habit of keeping secrets. — *adj.* **secretive** (*sē'kré-tiv, si-krē'tiv*), given to secrecy, very reticent: indicative of secrecy. — *adv.* **sē'cretly,** in a secret manner: unknown to others: inwardly. — *n.* **sē'cretness,** the state of being secret. — **secret agent,** one employed in secret service; **Secret Service,** a department of government service whose operations are kept secret. [L. *sēcrētus — sēcernĕre, sēcrētum — sē-,* apart, *cernĕre,* to separate.]

secretary, *sek're-ta-ri, n.* one employed to conduct correspondence and transact business for an individual, society, &c.: the minister in charge of certain departments of state: an ambassador's or minister's assistant: a secretaire. — *n.* **secretaire** (*sek-ré-tār'*), a secret repository: a writing desk. — *adj.* **secretā'rial,** pertaining to a secretary or his duties. — *ns.* **secretariat(e)** (*sek-ré-tā'ri-át*), secretaryship: a secretary's rooms: a body of secretaries; **sec'retary-bird,** a long-legged snake-eating bird of prey — said to be named from the tufts of feathers at the back of its head like pens stuck behind the ear; **sec'retaryship,** the office or duties of a secretary. — **Secretary of State,** a cabinet minister holding one of the more important portfolios (in U.S. the Foreign Secretary). [L.L. *sēcrētārius,* a confidential officer, from same root as **secret**.]

secrete, *si-krēt', v.t.* to appropriate secretly: to hide: to form and separate by the activity of

Neutral vowels in unaccented syllables: *em'pér-òr*; for certain sounds in foreign words see p. ix.

658

living matter.—*n.* **secrē'tion**, the act, or process, of secreting: that which is secreted, esp. a substance elaborated, collected, and discharged by a gland or gland-cell.—*adj.* **secrē'tive**, tending to, or causing, secretion.—*adv.* **secrē'tively.**—*adj.* **secrē'tory**, performing the office of secretion. [L. *sēcernēre, sēcrētum.* See **secret.**]

sect, *sekt, n.* a body of men who unite in holding some particular views, esp. in religion and philosophy: those who dissent from an established creed or system: a party: faction.—*adj.* **sectā'rian,** of a sect: devoted to a sect: narrow, exclusive.—*n.* a member of a sect: one strongly imbued with the characteristics of a sect.—*ns.* **sectā'rianism,** excessive devotion to a sect; **sec'tary,** a member of a sect: a dissenter. [L. *secta,* a school of philosophy—*sequī, secūtus,* to follow; influenced by *secāre,* to cut.]

section, *sek'sh(ó)n, n.* act of cutting: a division: a portion: one of the parts into which anything may be considered as divided, or of which it may be built up: a thin slice for microscopic examination: the plan of any object cut through, as it were, to show its interior: the line of intersection of two surfaces: the surface formed when a solid is cut by a plane: a fourth part of a company, platoon, battery, &c.: a district or a community having separate interests or characteristics.—*adjs.* **sec'tile,** capable of being cut with a knife; **sec'tional,** of a section: in section: built up by sections: local, or pertaining to a limited part of the community (e.g. *sectional interests*).—*n.* **sec'tionalism,** class spirit.—*adv.* **sec'tionally.** [L. *sectiō, -ōnis—secāre,* to cut.]

sector, *sek'tór, n.* a plane figure bounded by two radii and an arc: a length or section of a fortified line or army front: (*fig.*) a division, section: a mathematical instrument consisting of two graduated rulers hinged together. [L. *secāre, sectum,* to cut.]

secular, *sek'ū-lár, adj.* pertaining to an age or generation: occurring or observed only once in a century or similar period: becoming appreciable only in the course of ages: agelong: pertaining to the present world, or to things not spiritual: lay or civil, as opposed to clerical: not bound by monastic rules.—*n.* a layman: an ecclesiastic not bound by monastic rules.—*v.t.* **sec'ularise,** to make secular.—*ns.* **secularisā'tion,** the state or process of being secularised; **sec'ularism,** the belief that politics, morals, education, &c., should be independent of religion; **sec'ularist,** one who believes in secularism; **secular'ity,** state of being secular: worldliness. [L. *saeculāris—saeculum,* an age, a generation.]

secure, *si-kūr', adj.* (*arch.*) without care or anxiety, confident or over-confident: confident in expectation (of), assured (of): free from danger, safe: affording safety: firmly fixed or held: certain (e.g. *a secure victory*).—*v.t.* to make safe (from, against): to guarantee against loss: to make it certain (that such-and-such will happen): to make (a person) sure in possession of (e.g. *to secure him,* or *to secure him in, of, his due reward*): to make (something) certain for a person (with *to*; e.g. *to secure this office to Jones*): to

fasten: to seize and guard: to gain possession of, to obtain.—*adj.* **secūr'able,** that may be secured.—*adv.* **secūre'ly.**—*ns.* **secūre'ness;** **secūr'ity,** state of being secure: freedom from fear or anxiety: certainty: a pledge: a guarantor: (*pl.*) bonds or certificates in evidence of debt or property.—**Security Council,** a body of the United Nations consisting of five permanent members (China, France, U.K., U.S.A., U.S.S.R.—each with the right of veto) and six elected two-yearly members, charged with the maintenance of international peace and security; **security measures,** measures to prevent espionage or leakage of information; **security police,** police whose duty it is to prevent espionage: police whose function it is to detect and stamp out any opposition to the existing régime; **security risk,** a person considered to be unsafe for state service because of his political leanings. [L. *sēcūrus—sē-,* without, *cūra,* care.]

sedan, *si-dan', n.* a covered chair for one, carried on two poles (also **sedan'-chair**).

sedate, *si-dāt', adj.* quiet: composed: staid.—*adv.* **sedāte'ly.**—*ns.* **sedāte'ness;** **sedā'tion,** act of calming, or state of being calmed, by means of sedatives: use of sedatives to calm a patient.—*adj.* **sed'ative,** tending to calm, soothe: allaying excitement or pain.—*n.* a soothing medicine. [L. *sedātus,* pa.p. of *sedāre,* to still.]

sedentary, *sed'(é)n-tä-ri, adj.* sitting (e.g. of a posture): stationary: passed chiefly in sitting, requiring much sitting (e.g. of occupation).—*n.* **sed'entariness.** [L. *sedentārius—sedēre,* to sit.]

sederunt, *si-dē'runt, n.* in Scotland, a sitting, as of a court: those, or the list of those, present. [L., 'they sat'—*sedēre,* to sit.]

sedge, *sej, n.* any of several coarse grasses growing in swamps and rivers.—*adj.* **sedg'y,** overgrown with sedge. [O.E. *secg;* cf. Low Ger. *segge.*]

sediment, *sed'i-mént, n.* what settles at the bottom of a liquid, dregs.—*adj.* **sedimen'tary,** pertaining to, consisting of, or formed by sediment. **sedimentary rocks,** rocks resulting from the wastage of pre-existing rocks, or from deposits consisting of the hard parts of organisms, &c. [L. *sedimentum—sedēre,* to sit.]

sedition, *si-dish'(ó)n, n.* stirring up of discontent against the government: any offence against the State short of treason.—*adj.* **sedi'tious,** pertaining to, or exciting, sedition.—*adv.* **sedi'tiously.**—*n.* **sedi'tiousness.** [Fr.,—L. *sēditiō, -ōnis—sēd-,* away, *īre, itum,* to go.]

seduce, *si-dūs', v.t.* to draw aside from right conduct or belief, to entice, to corrupt: to lead astray, esp. from chastity.—*ns.* **sedūce'ment,** act of seducing: allurement; **sedū'cer; seduc'tion,** act of enticing from virtue by promises: allurement, attraction.—*adj.* **seduc'tive,** tending to seduce: attractive. [L. *sēdūcēre—sē-,* apart, *dūcēre, ductum,* to lead.]

sedulous, *sed'ū-lùs, adj.* diligent, assiduous.—*n.* **sed'ulousness.**—*adv.* **sed'ulously.** [L. *sēdulus—sedēre,* to sit.]

sedum, *sē'dum, n.* a large genus of plants, often with tufted stems, the stonecrops. [L. *sēdum,* house-leek.]

see, *sē, n.* (*obs.*) a throne or seat of dignity: the seat or jurisdiction of a bishop or archbishop.—**Holy See**, the papal court: the papacy. [O.Fr. *se, siet*—L. *sēdēs*—*sedēre,* to sit.]

see, *sē, v.t.* to perceive by the eye: to observe, to discern: (*fig.*) to perceive with the understanding: to ascertain (e.g. *I'll see what has been arranged*): to ensure (e.g. *see that he does what he has promised*): to deem (e.g. *as she sees fit*): to inspect (a document, &c.): to watch, look at, visit (e.g. a race, the sights): to escort (a person to a specified place): to meet: to visit: to consult: to undergo, experience (e.g. *to see trouble*).—*v.i.* to have power of vision: to look, inquire (into): to consider (e.g. *let me see*): to understand:—*pa.t.* saw; *pa.p.* seen.—*interj.* look! behold!—*n.* **see'ing,** sight, vision.—*adj.* having sight or insight: observant.—*conj.* since, in view of the fact that.—**see about,** consider: attend to; **see off,** to accompany (a person) when he is departing: to make certain (a person) leaves a particular place, or (*fig.*) ceases to play a part in a particular affair; **see out,** to conduct to the door: to see to the end: to outlast; **see over,** to be conducted all through; **see things,** to have hallucinations; **see through,** to participate in to the end: to support to the very end: to discern the secret of; **see to,** to attend to: to make sure about; **have seen better days,** to be on the decline. [O.E. *sēon*; Ger. *sehen,* Du. *zien.*]

seed, *sēd, n.* a cellular structure containing the embryo of a flowering plant together with stored food, the whole protected by a seedcoat: a quantity of these used for sowing: a small, hard fruit or part in a fruit, as a pip in an orange: semen: race: progeny: condition of having or proceeding to form seed: germ: first principle: a seeded tournament player.—*v.i.* to produce seed: to shed seed.—*v.t.* to sow: to remove the seeds from: to cause to form granules or crystals: to arrange (the draw for a tournament) in such a way that the best players will not meet in the early rounds: to scatter (clouds) with a chemical in order to produce rain.—*adj.* **seed'y,** abounding in seed: having the flavour of seeds: run to seed: unwell: shabby.—*adv.* **seed'ily.**—*ns.* **seed'iness,** the state of being seedy; **seed'bed,** a piece of ground for receiving seed; **seed'-cake,** a sweet cake containing aromatic seeds; **seed'-coat,** the outer covering of a seed; **seed'-leaf, seed'-lobe,** a cotyledon (q.v.); **seed'ling,** a plant reared from the seed; **seed'-pearl,** a very small pearl; **seeds'man,** one who deals in seeds:—*pl.* **seeds'men; seed'-vessel,** a dry fruit: the ovary of a flower.—**run to seed** (see **run**). [O.E. *sǣd*; cf. *sāwan,* to sow, O.N. *sath,* Ger. *saat.*]

seek, *sēk, v.t.* to look for: to try to find, get, or achieve: to attempt (to do): (*arch.*) to ask (of a person): to resort to (e.g. *to seek the shade*).—*v.i.* to make search: to try:—*pa.t.* and *pa.p.* sought.—*n.* **seek'er.**—**seek after,** to go in quest of; **sought after,** in demand.—**is, was, to seek,** is, was, wanting. [O.E. *sēcan* (pa.t. *sōhte,* pa.p. *gesōht*); cf. Du. *zoeken,* Ger. *suchen.*]

seem, *sēm, v.i.* to appear to be: to appear (to be, or to do): (*impers.; it seems, it seemed*) the evidence shows, showed, or suggests, suggested, that: (*impers.*) it is, was, said that.—*n.* **seem'er.**—*adj.* **seem'ing,** apparent: ostensible.—*n.* appearance: semblance.—*adv.* **seem'ingly.**—*n.* **seem'ingness.**—*adj.* **seem'ly** (*comp.* **seem'lier,** *superl.* **seem'liest**), becoming: suitable: decent: handsome.—*n.* **seem'liness.** [O.E. *sēman,* to satisfy, to suit; or prob. direct from O.N. *scema,* to conform to.]

seen, *sēn, pa.p.* of **see.**

seep, *sēp, v.i.* to ooze gently, to percolate.—*n.* **seep'age,** act or process of seeping: liquid that has percolated: the quantity of liquid that has done so. [O.E. *sipian,* to soak.]

seer, *sē'er, n.* one who sees: (*sēr*) one who sees into the future, a prophet. [see (2).]

seesaw, *sē'sö,* or *-sö', n.* alternate up-and-down motion: repeated alternation: a plank balanced so that its ends may move up and down alternately: the sport of rising and sinking on it.—*adj.* and *adv.* like a seesaw.—*v.i.* to move like a seesaw. [Prob. a reduplication of **saw,** from a sawyer's jingle.]

seethe, *sēTH, v.t.* to boil: to soak.—*v.i.* to boil: (*lit.* or *fig.*) to surge (e.g. with anger):—*pa.t.* seethed or (*obs.*) sod; *pa.p.* seethed or sodd'en (q.v.). [O.E. *sēothan*; O.N. *sjōtha,* Ger. *sieden.*]

segment, *seg'mént, n.* a part cut off: a portion: the part of a circle or ellipse cut off by a straight line: the part of a sphere cut off by a plane: any one of the more or less distinct sections into which the bodies of many animals are divided.—*v.t.* and *v.i.* (also *-ment'*), to divide into segments.—*n.* **segmenta'tion,** the act or process of dividing into segments: the state of being divided thus: the early divisions of the nucleus of a fertilised ovum. [L. *segmentum*—*secāre,* to cut.]

segregate, *seg'ré-gāt, v.t.* to separate from others, to group apart: to isolate (from).—*v.i.* to separate out in a group or groups or mass.—*n.* **segrega'tion,** act of segregation: state of being segregated: a segregated group: separation of one particular class of persons from another, as on grounds of race. [L. *sēgregāre, -ātum*—*sē-,* apart, *grex, gregis,* a flock.]

seguidilla, *seg-i-dēl'ya, n.* a Spanish dance: a tune for it in triple time. [Sp.,—L. *sequī,* to follow.]

seidlitz, *sed'lits, adj.* applied to an aperient medicine consisting of an effervescent solution of two powders—totally different from the mineral water of *Se(i)dlitz* in Bohemia, though named from a fancied resemblance.

seignior, *sē'nyér,* **seigneur,** *sen'yér, n.* a title of respectful address: a feudal lord.—*adjs.* **seigniorial** (*sē-nyō'ri-ál*), **seigneu'rial** (*sē-nū'-*), manorial.—*n.* **seign'iory,** the power or authority of a seignior: the council in a mediaeval Italian city-state.—**Grand Seignior,** the Sultan of Turkey. [Fr. *seigneur*—L. *senior,* comp. of *senex,* old. In Late L. *senior* is sometimes equivalent to *dominus,* lord.]

seine, *sān,* or *sēn, n.* a large vertical fishing-net whose ends are brought together and hauled. [O.E. *segne*—L. *sagēna*—Gr. *sagēnē,* a fishing-net.]

seise, *sēz, v.t.* an old spelling of **seize,** still used legally in the sense of to put in possession

Neutral vowels in unaccented syllables: *em'pér-ór*; for certain sounds in foreign words see p. ix.

660

(of).—*n.* **seis′in**, legal possession of feudal property: evidence of such.

seismograph, *sīs′mō-gräf, n.* an instrument for registering the shock of earthquakes.—*adj.* **seis′mic**, belonging to an earthquake.—*n.* **seismol′ogy**, the science of earthquakes and volcanoes. [Gr. *seismos*, an earthquake, *graphein*, to write, *logos*, discourse.]

seize, *sēz, v.t.* (*law*) to put in legal possession (of): to take possession of suddenly, eagerly, or forcibly: to snatch, to grasp: to take prisoner.—*v.t.* (of machinery) to jam, become stuck.—*adj.* **seiz′able.—***ns.* **seiz′er; seiz′in** (same as **seisin**); **seiz′ure**, the act of seizing: capture: grasp: the thing seized: a fit or attack of illness, e.g. of apoplexy.—**seize up**, to jam, seize. [O.Fr. *saisir*—L.L. *sacīre*; cf. O.H.G. *sazzan*, to set, Ger. *setzen*, Eng. *set*.]

selah, *sē′lä, n.* in the Psalms, a Hebrew word, probably meaning 'pause'.

seldom, *sel′dóm, adv.* rarely, not often. [O.E. *seldum*, altered (on the analogy of *hwīlum*, whilom) from *seldan.*]

select, *si-lekt′, v.t.* to pick out from a number by preference, to choose. *adj.* picked out: choice. (of a society) intolusive.—*n.* **selec′tion**, not of selecting: thing, or a collection of things, selected: (*mus.*) a pot-pourri: a horse selected as likely to win a race.—*adj.* **selec′tive**, exercising power of selection: (*radio*—of a circuit or apparatus) able, in a specified or implied degree, to respond to a desired frequency and not to others: characterised by selection.—*ns.* **selectiv′ity**, quality of being selective: ability to discriminate, **select′or.—select committee**, a number of members of parliament chosen to report and advise on some matter; **selective weedkiller**, a weedkiller that does not destroy garden plants.—**natural selection** (see **natural**). [L. *sēlĭgĕre, sēlectum—sē* , aside, *legĕre*, to choose.]

selenium, *se-lē′ni-úm, n.* semi-metallic element (symbol Se; atomic no. 34) similar to sulphur. [Coined from Gr. *selēnē*, the moon, as *tellurium* is from L. *tellūs*, earth.]

selenography, *se-lēn-og′raf-i, n.* delineation or description of the moon, study of the moon's physical features. [Gr. *selēnē*, moon, *graphein*, to write.]

self, *self, n.* an identical person, personality: an aspect of one's personality: personality: what one is: personal advantage:—*pl.* **selves** (*selvz*).—*adj.* (*arch.*) very same: uniform in colour or material—*adj.* **self′ish**, chiefly or wholly regarding oneself, heedless of others.—*adv.* **self′ishly.—***n.* **self′ishness.—***adj.* **self′less**, regardless of self, utterly unselfish. [O.E. *self*; Du. *zelf*; Ger. *selbe*.]

self-, *self-*, in composition, indicating that the agent is also the object of the action: by, of, for, in, in relation to, oneself or itself: automatic:—e.g. **self′-pleas′ing**, pleasing oneself; **self′-condemned′**, condemned by oneself; **self′-pit′y**, pity for oneself; **self′-trust**, trust in oneself; **self′-sat′isfied**, satisfied with oneself; **self′-right′eous**, righteous in one's own esteem; **self′-clo′sing**, closing of itself.—*adj.* **self′-absorbed′**, wrapped up in one's own thoughts or affairs.—*n.* **self-advert′isement**, calling, or a means of calling, public attention to oneself.—*adjs.* **self′-assert′ing, self′-assert′ive**, given to asserting one's opinion, or to putting oneself forward.—*ns.* **self′-bind′er**, a reaping-machine with automatic binding apparatus; **self′-col′our**, uniform colour: natural colour.—*adj.* **self′-col′oured.—***n.* **self′-conceit′**, an over-high opinion of one's merits, abilities, &c., vanity.—*adj.* **self′-conceit′ed.—***n.* **self′-con′fidence**, confidence in one's own powers: self-reliance.—*adjs.* **self′-con′fident; self′-con′scious**, conscious of one's own mind and its acts and states: embarrassed by a morbid sense of personal inferiority, real or imaginary.—*n.* **self′-con′sciousness.—***adjs.* **self′-con′-stituted**, constituted or appointed by oneself; **self′-contained′**, absorbed in oneself, reserved: of a house, not approached by an entrance common to others: complete in itself.—*n.* **self′-control′**, power of controlling oneself.— *adj.* **self′-defeat′ing**, that defeats its own purpose.—*ns.* **self′-defence′**, the act of defending one's own person, rights, &c. (art of self defence, boxing) **self′-deni′al**, refusal to yield to one's natural appetites or desires.—*adj.* **self′-deny′ing.—***n.* **self′-determina′tion**, decision without extraneous impulse: power of a community to decide its own form of government and political relations, or of an individual to live his own life.—*adjs.* **self′-drive′**, of a motor vehicle, to be driven by the hirer; **self′-ed′ucated**, educated by one's own efforts.—*n.* **self′-efface′ment**, keeping oneself in the background out of sight: (*fig.*) refraining from claiming one's rights.—*adjs.* **self′-effac′ing**, given to self-effacement; **self′-employed′**, working independently in one's own business; **self′-ev′ident**, evident without proof; **self′-exist′ent**, existing of or by oneself or itself, independent of any other cause.—*n.* **self′-expression** (*-presh′(ó)n*), a giving expression to one's personality, as in art.—*adjs.* **self′-fill′ing**, (of a fountain pen) that can be filled without a dropping-tube; **self′-gov′erning.—***ns.* **self′-gov′ernment**, self-control: government without external interference: government administered and controlled by citizens; **self-help′**, providing for one's needs by personal effort without help from others; **self′-import′ance**, an absurdly high sense of one's own importance: pomposity.—*adj.* **self′-import′ant.—***n.* **self′-indul′gence**, undue gratification of one's appetites or desires.—*adj.* **self′-indul′gent.—***n.* **self′-int′erest**, personal advantage: selfish concern for one's own private aims.—*adjs.* **self-made′**, made by one's own effort: risen to a high position from poverty or obscurity by unaided personal exertions; **self′-possessed′**, calm or collected in mind or manner.—*ns.* **self′-possess′ion**, ability to use one's faculties in a crisis, presence of mind: calm, composure; **self′-realisa′tion**, the attainment of such development as one's mental and moral nature is capable of.—*adj.* **self′-regard′ing**, concerned with one's own self, or with the promotion of one's own interests.—*n.* **self′-reli′ance**, healthy confidence in one's own abilities.—*adj.* **self′-reli′ant.—***n.* **self′-respect′**, due regard and concern for one's character and reputation.—*adjs.* **self′-respect′ing;**

self′-right′eous, righteous in one's own estimation: pharisaical.—*ns.* **self′-right′eousness; self′-sac′rifice,** the act of seeking the welfare of others at the cost of one's own.—*adjs.* **self′-sac′rificing; self′-same,** the very same.—*n.* **self′-seek′er,** one who pursues only selfish aims.—*adj.* **self′-ser′vice,** of restaurants, shops, &c., in which goods are displayed on shelves for customers to help themselves, paying at a cash-desk at the exit.—*ns.* **self′-ser′vice; self′-start′er,** a small electric motor, fed from the lighting battery, for starting an automobile.—*adjs.* **self-styled′,** so called by oneself, pretended; **self′-suffi′cient,** requiring nothing from without: excessively confident in oneself.—*ns.* **self′-suffi′ciency; self′-support′,** support or maintenance without outside help.—*adj.* **self′-support′ing.**—*n.* **self-will′,** one's own will: persistence in attempts to do as one chooses.—*adj.* **self-willed′,** governed by self-will, obstinate.—**self-raising flour,** flour so prepared that it rises into dough without the addition during cooking of baking-powder or similar agents. [**self** (1).]

sell, *sel, v.t.* to give or give up for money or other equivalent: (*pass.*) to be imposed upon, cheated: to make acceptable to buyers: (*fig.*) to make (an idea, a course of action, &c.) seem desirable (to a person).—*v.i.* to make sales: to be sold, to be in demand for sale:—*pa.t.* and *pa.p.* sōld.—*n.* a fraud.—*ns.* **sell′er; sell-out,** a show for which all seats are sold: a betrayal.—**be sold on,** to be keen on, in favour of; **sell down the river,** to play false, betray; **sellers′ market,** one in which sellers control the price, demand exceeding supply; **sell off,** to sell cheaply in order to dispose of; **sell out,** to sell the whole stock: to betray for profit; **sell short,** to belittle, disparage: to betray; **sell up,** to sell a debtor's goods for the creditors' benefit. [O.E. *sellan,* to hand over; O.N. *selja.*]

seltzer, *selt′zėr, n.* a mineral water from Nieder-*Seltsers* in Prussia, or an imitation.

selvage, selvedge, *sel′vij, n.* the firm edge of a woven piece of cloth: a border. [**self, edge.**]

selves, *selvz, pl.* of **self.**

semantic, *si-man′tik, adj.* pertaining to meaning, esp. of words.—*n.* (in *sing.* or *pl.*) the science of the development of the meaning of words. [Gr. *sēmantikos.*]

semaphore, *sem′à-fōr, -fōr, n.* a signalling apparatus, consisting of an upright with arms that can be turned up and down—often the signaller's own body and arms with flags. [Gr. *sēma,* a sign, *pherein,* to bear.]

semblance, *sem′blàns, n.* likeness, image, guise: a deceptive appearance: a faint indication. [Fr.—*sembler,* to seem, resemble—L. *similis,* like.]

semen, *sē′men, n.* the liquid that carries spermatozoa. [L. *sēmen,* seed.]

semester, *si-mes′tėr, n.* one of the half-year courses, esp. in German universities: a term of six months. [L. *sēmestris—sex,* six, *mēnsis,* a month.]

semi-, *sem′i-, pfx.* half: (*loosely*) nearly, partly incompletely.—*adj.* **sem′i-ann′ual,** half-yearly. —*ns.* **sem′ibrēve,** musical note, half a breve— 2 minims or 4 crotchets; **sem′icircle,** half a circle: the figure bounded by the diameter and half the circumference.—*adj.* **semicir′cular.**— *n.* **sem′icōlon,** the point (;) marking a division more strongly than the comma.—*adj.* **sem′i-detached′,** partly separated: of house, joined to an adjacent house by a mutual wall, but detached from other buildings.—*n.* **sem′i-diam′eter,** half the diameter of a circle, a radius.—*adj.* **semi-fīn′al,** immediately before the final: last but one.—*n.* the last stage but one, esp. of a competition.—*adj.* **sem′i-offic′ial,** partly official: having some official authority, emanating from official sources but not formally made public.—*ns.* **sem′iquāver,** a musical note, half the length of a quaver; **sem′i-tone,** half a tone—one of the lesser intervals of the musical scale, as from E to F.—*adj.* **sem′i-transpa′rent,** imperfectly transparent. [L. *sēmi-,* half-.]

semiconductor, *sem-i-kon-dukt′ór, n.* orig. any material whose conductivity was intermediate between that of good conductors (e.g. metals) and insulators: now, certain semi-metals (e.g. germanium, silicon) in which conductivity can be modified by the controlled addition of impurities, and exploited for use in electronic circuits. [**semi-.**]

seminal, *sem′in-ál, adj.* pertaining to, or of the nature of, seed or of semen: (*lit.* and *fig.*) generative, originative.—*v.t.* **sem′ināte,** to sow: to propagate.—*n.* **semină′tion,** act of sowing: natural dispersion of seed. [L. *sēmen, sēminis,* seed—*serēre,* to sow.]

seminar, *sem′in-är, n.* a group of advanced students working under a teacher in some specific branch of study: a class at which a group of students and a tutor discuss a particular topic.—*n.* **sem′inary,** a seed-plot: a nursery: formerly, a school: a college, esp. for theology. [L.*sēminārium,* a seed-plot—*sēmen.*]

Semite, *sem′- or sēm′īt, n.* a member of any of the peoples said (Gen. x.) to be descended from Shem, or speaking a Semitic language, as Hebrew or Arabic.—*adj.* **Semit′ic,** pertaining to the Semites. [Gr. *Sēm,* Shem.]

semolina, *sem-o-lē′na, n.* the particles of fine, hard wheat that do not pass into flour in milling: an article of food consisting of granules of the floury part of wheat. [It. *semolino,* dim. of *semola,* bran—L. *simila,* fine flour.]

sempiternal, *sem-pi-tûr′nál, adj.* everlasting. [L. *sempiternus—semper,* ever, always.]

sempstress. See **seamstress.**

senary, *sēn′-, sen′ár-i, adj.* of, involving, based on, six. [L. *sēnārius—sēnī,* six each—*sex,* six.]

senate, *sen′át, n.* a legislative or deliberative body, esp. the upper house of a national legislature—as in the United States, Australia, Canada, South Africa: the governing body of certain British universities.—*n.* **sen′ator,** a member of a senate.—*adj.* **senatō′rial,** pertaining to, or becoming, a senate or a senator.—*adv.* **senatō′rially,** with senatorial dignity.—*n.* **sen′atorship.** [L. *senātus—senex, senis,* an old man.]

send, *send, v.t.* to cause or direct to go: to cause to be conveyed, to dispatch, to forward: to propel: to commission (to do): to bestow, inflict (of God, providence): orig. of jazz, to rouse (a person) to ecstasy.—*v.i.* to dispatch a message or messenger:—*pa.t.* and *pa.p.*

Neutral vowels in unaccented syllables: *em′pėr-ór*; for certain sounds in foreign words see p. ix.

662

sent.—*ns.* **sen′der**, one who sends: an instrument by which a message is transmitted; **send′-off**, a farewell demonstration; **send-up**, a process of making fun of someone.—**send down**, to rusticate or to expel from a university or college; **send up**, to send to prison: to make fun of. [O.E. *sendan*; O.N. *senda*, Ger. *senden*.]

sendal, *sen′dál*, *n.* a thin silk or linen. [O.Fr. *cendal*, prob. Gr. *sindōn*.]

senescent, *sen-es′ént*, *adj.* growing old.—*n.* **sene′scence**. [L. *senēscēns*, -*entis*, pr.p. of *senēscēre*, to grow old.]

seneschal, *sen′é-shál*, *n.* a steward: a majordomo.—*n.* **sen′eschalship** [O.Fr. (Fr. *sénéchal*), of Gmc. origin, lit. old servant.]

senile, *sē′nīl*, *adj.* pertaining to, or attendant on, old age: showing the feebleness or imbecility of old age.—*n.* **senility** (*se-nil′i-ti*). [L. *senīlis*—*senex*, *senis*, old.]

senior, *sēn′yór*, *adj.* elder: older in office or higher in standing: more advanced.—*n.* one who is senior.—*n.* **seniority** (*sē-ni-or′i-ti*), state or fact of being senior. [L., comp. of *senex*, old.]

senna, *sen′a*, *n.* the purgative dried leaflets of several species of cassia.—**senna tea**, a drink made from these [Ar. *sanā*.]

sennight, *sen′īt*, *n.* a week. [**seven**, **night**.]

señor, *se-nyōr′*, -*nyōr′*, *n.* a gentleman: prefixed to a name, Mr:—*fem.* **señora** (*se-nyō′ra*), a lady. [Sp.]

sensation, *sen-sā′sh(ó)n*, *n.* awareness of a physical experience: awareness by the senses generally: an effect on the senses: a thrill: a state, or matter, of general and excited interest: melodramatic quality or method.—*adj.* **sensa′tional**, pertaining to sensation: tending to excite violent emotions: melodramatic.—*ns.* **sensa′tionalism**, the doctrine that our ideas originate solely in sensation: a striving after wild excitement and melodramatic effects; **sensa′tionalist**, a believer in sensationalism: a sensational writer. [L.L. *sensātiō*, -*ōnis*—L. *sensus*. See **sense**.]

sense, *sens*, *n.* a faculty by which objects are perceived (sight, hearing, smell, taste, or touch): immediate consciousness: consciousness (of—e.g. shame, responsibility): impression (of—e.g. strangeness): appreciation (of—e.g. the ridiculous, the fitness of things): quality of intellect or character expressed in such appreciation (e.g. *sense of humour*, *honour*): soundness of judgment: (usu. in *pl.*) one's right wits: that which is reasonable: meaning, purport: general feeling, opinion (*the sense of the meeting*).—*v.t.* to have a sensation of: to perceive, grasp, understand.—*adj.* **sense′less**, unconscious: deficient in good sense, foolish.—*adv.* **sense′lessly.**—*n.* **sense′lessness.**—*adj.* **sen′sible**, perceptible by sense: easily perceived: appreciable: cognisant, aware (of): prudent, judicious: having power of sensation.—*ns.* **sen′sibleness**; **sensibil′ity**, state or quality of being perceptible by sense, or of feeling readily: readiness and delicacy of emotional response, sensitiveness: sentimentality.—Also in *pl.* (**sensibil′ities**) those feelings most readily wounded, oversensitive feelings.—*adv.* **sen′sibly**, prudently:

appreciably.—*v.t.* **sen′sitise**, to render sensitive, esp. to rays of light.—*ns.* **sensitisā′tion**; **sen′sitiser.**—*adj.* **sen′sitive**, having power of sensation: ready and delicate in response to outside influences: feeling readily, acutely, or painfully: susceptible to action of light.—*adv.* **sen′sitively.**—*ns.* **sen′sitiveness**; **sensit′vity**, state of being sensitive: ability to register minute changes or differences: degree of responsiveness to stimuli: abnormal responsiveness.—*adj.* **sensō′rial**, sensory.—*ns.* **sensō′rium**, the seat of sensation in the brain: the brain: the mind: the nervous system; **sen′sory**, **sensorium.**—*adj.* of the sensorium: of sensation.—*adj.* **sensual** (*sens′ū-ál*, *sen′shōō-ál*), of the senses, as distinct from the mind, not intellectual or spiritual: given to the pleasures of sense, carnal, voluptuous.—*v.t.* **sen′sualise**, to make sensual: to debase by carnal gratification.—*ns.* **sen′sualism**, sensual indulgence: the doctrine that all our knowledge is derived originally from sensation; **sen′sualist**, a debauchee: a believer in the doctrine of sensualism; **sensual′ity**, indulgence in sensual pleasures: lewdness.—*adv.* **sen′sually.**—*n.* **sen′sualness.**—*adj.* **sen′suous**, pertaining to sense: connected with sensible objects: easily affected through the medium of the senses.—*adv.* **sen′suously.**—*n.* **sen′suousness.**—**sensitive plant**, any of certain species of *Mimosa* that show more than usual irritability when touched or shaken.—**make sense**, to be understandable or sensible; **make sense of**, to understand; **sixth sense**, an ability to perceive that which is beyond the powers of the five senses. [Fr.,—L. *sēnsus*—*sentīre*, to feel.]

sent, *sent*, *pa.t.* and *pa.p.* of **send**.

sentence, *sen′téns*, *n.* (*arch.*) opinion: a judgment: determination of punishment pronounced by a court or judge: a maxim: (*gram.*) a number of words making a complete grammatical structure.—*v.t.* to pronounce judgment on: to condemn.—*adj.* **senten′tious** (-*shús*), terse and pithy (e.g. *a sententious style*): abounding (often superabounding) in maxims: fond of moralising.—*adv.* **senten′tiously.**—*n.* **senten′tiousness.** [Fr.,—L. *sententia*—*sentīre*, to feel.]

sentient, *sen′sh(y)ént*, *adj.* conscious, capable of sensation, responsive to stimulus.—*ns.* **sen′tience**, **sen′tiency.**—*adv.* **sen′tiently**, in a sentient or perceptive manner. [L. *sentiēns*, -*entis*, pr.p. of *sentīre*, to feel.]

sentiment, *sen′ti-mént*, *n.* a thought, or body of thought, tinged with emotion: an opinion: a thought expressed in words: a maxim: a thought or wish propounded to be ratified by drinking: feeling bound up with some object or ideal (e.g. *patriotic sentiment*): regard to ideal considerations (e.g. *influenced by sentiment rather than by expediency*): sensibility, refined feelings: consciously worked up or partly insincere feeling, sentimentality.—*adj.* **sentimen′tal**, having an excess of sentiment or feeling (usu. worked up or partly insincere): affectedly tender.—*ns.* **sentimen′talism**, **sentimental′ity**, quality of being sentimental: affectation of fine feeling; **sentimen′talist**, one who delights in sentiment or fine feeling: one

---

fāte, *fär*; *mē*, *hûr* (her); *mīne*; *mōte*, *för*; *mūte*; *mōōn*, *fŏŏt*; THEN (then)

who regards sentiment as more important than reason.—*adv.* **sentimen′tally.** [Fr.,—L.L. *sentīmentum*—L. *sentīre*, to feel.]

sentinel, *sen′ti-nèl*, *n.* one posted on guard, a sentry.—**stand sentinel**, to keep watch. [Fr. *sentinelle*—It. *sentinella*, a watch, sentinel.]

sentry,*sen′tri*, *n.* a sentinel, a soldier on guard to prevent or announce the approach of an enemy.—*ns.* **sen′try-box,** a box to shelter a sentry; **sen′try-go,** a sentry's beat or duty.

sepal, *sep′ál*, or *sē′pál*, *n.* one of the leaf-like members forming the calyx of a flower. [Fr. *sépale.*]

separate, *sep′á-rāt*, *v.t.* to divide, part: to sever: to disconnect: to set apart: to keep apart: to sort into different sizes, divide into different constituents, &c.—*v.i.* to part, go different ways: (of husband and wife) to live apart by consent: to become disunited.—*adj.* (*sep′á-rát*) divided: apart from another: distinct.—*adj.* **sep′arable,** that may be separated or disjoined.—*n.* **separabil′ity.**—*advs.* **sep′arably; sep′arately.**—*n. pl.* **separates,** two items of dress, e.g. blouse and skirt, worn together as an outfit.—*ns.* **separā′tion,** act of separating or disjoining: state of being separate; **sep′arat-ism,** the action or policy of a separatist: withdrawing, esp. from an established church; **sep′aratist,** one who withdraws or advocates separation, esp. from an established church, federation, organisation, &c.: a dissenter.—*adj.* **sep′arative,** tending to separate.—*n.* **sep′-arātor,** one who, or that which, separates: a machine for separating cream from milk.—**separation allowance,** government allowance to a soldier's wife and dependants. [L. *sē-parāre, -ātum*—*sē-*, aside, *parāre,* to put.]

sepia, *sē′pi-a*, *n.* a cuttle-fish: the ink of a cuttle-fish: a pigment made from it: its colour, a fine brown. [L.,—Gr. *sēpiā*, the cuttle-fish.]

sepoy, *sē′poi*, *n.* an Indian soldier in European service. [Hindustani and Pers. *sipāhī*, a horseman.]

sepsis, *sep′sis*, *n.* putrefaction. [Gr.]

sept, *sept*, *n.* in ancient Ireland, a division of a tribe: a similar division elsewhere, as a division of a Scottish clan. [Prob. for **sect**; influenced by **septum.**]

September, *sep-tem′bér*, *n.* the ninth, orig. the seventh, month of the year. [L.,—*septem,* seven.]

septenary, *sep-tēn′á-ri, sep′té-ná-ri*, *adj.* numbering or based on seven. [L. *septēnārius,* consisting of seven.]

septennial, *sep-ten′i-ál*, *adj.* lasting seven years: happening every seven years.—*adv.* **septen-n′ially.** [L. *septennis*—*septem*, seven, *annus*, a year.]

septet, septette, *sep-tet′*, *n.* a work for seven voices or instruments: a company of seven (*esp.* musicians). [L. *septem*, seven.]

septic, *sep′tik*, *adj.* putrefactive: suppurating.—**septic tank,** a tank in which sewage is partially purified by the action of certain bacteria. [Gr. *sēptikos*—*sēpein*, to rot.]

septicaemia, *sep-ti-sē′mi-a*, *n.* presence of poisonous bacteria in the blood. [**septic**, and Gr. *haima*, blood.]

septuagenarian, *sep-tū-á-je-nā′ri-án*, *n.* a person over seventy and under eighty years of

age.—*adj.* **septūagēn′ary,** consisting of or relating to seventy. [L. *septuāgēnārius*—*septuā-gēni*, seventy each—*septum*, seven.]

Septuagesima (Sunday), *sep-tū-á-jes′i-ma* (*sun′dā*), *n.* the third Sunday before Lent. [L. *septuāgēsimus,* seventieth.]

septuagint,*sep′tū-á-jint*, *n.* the Greek version of the Old Testament, said to have been made by 72 translators at Alexandria in the 3rd century B.C. [L. *septuāgintā*, seventy—*septum*, seven.]

septum, *sep′tum*, *n.* (*biol.*) partition separating two cells or cavities:—*pl.* **sep′ta.** [L.,—*saepīre, sēpīre*, to enclose.]

sepulchre, *sep′ul-kér*, *n.* a place of burial, tomb.—*adj.* **sepul′chral,** pertaining to a sepulchre: funereal, dismal: deep, hollow in tone.—*n.* **sep′ulture,** interment, burial.—**whited sepulchre** (see under **white**). [L. *sepul-crum*—*sepelīre, sepultum,* to bury.]

sequel, *sē′kwél*, *n.* that which follows, the succeeding part: result, consequence: a resumption of a story already complete in itself.—*n.* **sequela** (*si-kwē′la*), morbid affection following a disease:—*pl.* **sequē′lae** (*-lē*). [L. *sequēla*—*sequī*, to follow.]

sequence, *sē′kwéns*, *n.* state of being sequent or following: order of succession: a series of things following in order: (*mus.*) a regular succession of similar chords: in cinematography, a division of a film.—*adjs.* **sē′quent,** following: successive; **sequen′tial.—sequential access,** (of a computer) finding a required item of information by going through the information store till that item is reached (see also **random access**). [L. *sequēns, -entis*, pr.p. of *sequī*, to follow.]

sequester, *si-kwes′tér*, *v.t.* to set aside: to seclude (e.g.*sequester oneself*; usu. in *pa.p.* or as *p.adj.*, e.g. *sequestered from society or from scenes of activity; a sequestered life*): (law) to confiscate: to remove from one's possession until a dispute be settled, creditors satisfied, or the like.—*adj.* **seques′tered,** retired, secluded.—*v.t.* **seques′trate** (*law*), to sequester: to make bankrupt.—*ns.* **sequestrā′tion,** the act of sequestering: (*Scots law*) bankruptcy; **sequestrā′tor.** [Low L. *sequestrāre, -ātum*—L. *sequester*, a depositary—*secus,* apart.]

sequin, *sē′kwin*, *n.* an old Italian gold coin, worth about 47p: a spangle. [Fr.,—It. *zec-chino*—*zecca*, the mint; of Ar. origin.]

sequoia,*si-kwoi′a*, *n.* either species of a genus of gigantic conifers consisting of the Californian 'big tree' and the redwood—sometimes called Wellingtonia. [After the name of an American Indian scholar.]

seraglio, *se-ral′yō*, *n.* formerly, a palace or residence of the Sultan of Turkey, esp. (*cap.*) the chief palace at Constantinople (Istanbul): a harem: its occupants. [It. *serraglio*—L. *sera*, a door-bar. The word was confused with Turk. *serāī*, a palace.]

seraph, *ser′áf*, *n.* an angel of the highest rank:—*pl.* **seraphs** (*ser′afs*), **seraphim** (*ser′-af-im*).—*adjs.* **seraph′ic, -al,** like a seraph, angelic, pure, sublime.—*adv.* **seraph′ically.** [Heb. *Serāphīm* (pl.).]

Serb, *sûrb*, *n.* a native or citizen of Serbia, formerly a kingdom, now part of Yugoslavia.—*adj.* **Serbian,** of Serbia, its people, or their

Neutral vowels in unaccented syllables: *em′pér-ór*; for certain sounds in foreign words see p. ix.

language.—*n.* a Serb: the language of the Serbs. [Serbian *Srb*.]

sere. See **sear.**

serenade, *ser-ė-nād', n.* evening music in the open air: music played or sung by a lover under his lady's window at night: a piece of music suitable for such an occasion.—*v.t.* to entertain with a serenade. [Fr. *sérénade*, and It. *serenata*—*sereno*, serene—L. *serēnus*, clear; meaning influenced by L. *sērus*, late.]

serendipity, *ser-ėn-dip'i-ti, n.* the faculty of making happy chance finds. [*Serendip*, a former name for Ceylon. Horace Walpole coined the word (1754) from title of fairy tale, 'Three Princes of Serendip', whose heroes 'were always making discoveries, by accidents and sagacity, of things they were not in quest of'.]

serene, *si-rēn', adj.* calm (e.g. of sea): unclouded (e.g. of sky): (*fig.*) tranquil: an adjunct to the titles of some princes (a translation of German *Durchlaucht*).—*adv.* **serēne'ly,** calmly, tranquilly.—*n.* **seren'ity,** state or quality of being serene, calmness, tranquillity. [L. *serēnus*, clear.]

serf, *sûrf, n.* a person in modified slavery, esp. one attached to the soil:—*pl.* **serfs.**—*n.* **serf'dom,** condition of a serf. [Fr.,—L. *servus*, a slave.]

serge, *sûrj, n.* a strong twilled fabric, now usually of worsted. [Fr.,—L. *sērica*, silk—*Sēres*, the Chinese.]

sergeant, serjeant, *sär'jänt, n.* (usu. with *g*) a non-commissioned officer next above a corporal: (with *g*) an officer of police: (usu. with *g*) alone, or as a prefix, designating certain officials: (with *j*) formerly a barrister of the highest rank (in full, **serjeant-at-law**).—*ns.* **ser'gean(t)cy, serjean(t)cy,** office or rank of sergeant, serjeant; **ser'geant-** (or **serjeant-) at-arms,** an officer of a legislative body for making arrests, &c.; **ser'geant-mā'jor,** the highest non-commissioned officer; formerly, an officer of rank varying from major to major-general; **ser'geantship, ser'jeantship.** [Fr. *sergent*—L. *serviēns, -entis,* pr.p. of *servīre*, to serve.]

seriatim. See **series.**

series, *sē'ri-ēz, sē'rēz, n. sing.* and *pl.* a set of things in line or succession or so thought of: a set of things having something in common: a set of things differing progressively: a succession of quantities each derivable from its predecessor by a law: (*geol.*) the rocks formed during an epoch: (*music*) a set of notes in a definite order used instead of a traditional scale as the basis of a composition.—*adj.* **sē'rial,** forming a series: in series: in a row: of publications, films, or broadcasts, in instalments.—*n.* a publication, film, or broadcast, in instalments.—*v.t.* **se'rialise,** to arrange in series: to publish serially.—*n.* **serialisa'tion.**—*adv.* **sē'rially.**—*adj.* **sē'riate,** arranged in rows.—*adv.* **sēriātim,** one after another. [L. *seriēs*—*serēre*, to join.]

serin, *ser'in, n.* a small bird of the same genus as the canary. [Fr., canary.]

serious, *sē'ri-ùs, adj.* solemn, grave: in earnest: demanding close attention: approaching the critical or dangerous.—*adjs.* **sē'rio-com'ic, -al,** partly serious and partly comic.—*adv.*

sē'riously.—*n.* **sē'riousness.** [L.L. *sēriōsus*—L. *sērius*, earnest.]

serjeant. See **sergeant.**

sermon, *sûr'món, n.* a discourse, esp. one preached from the pulpit, on a text of Scripture: any serious admonition or reproof.—*v.i.* **ser'monise,** to compose sermons: to preach. [L. *sermō, -ōnis*—*serēre*, to join.]

serous. See **serum.**

serpent, *sûr'pént, n.* formerly, any reptile or creeping thing, esp. if venomous: now, a snake: a treacherous or malicious person: (*cap.*) a northern constellation.—*adj.* **ser'pentine,** resembling a serpent: winding, tortuous.—*n.* a soft, usually green, mineral, some forms of which are fibrous, composed of silica and manganese, occurring in winding veins, and sometimes spotted like a serpent's skin. [L. *serpēns, -entis,* pr.p. of *serpēre*, to creep: akin to Gr. *herpein*.]

serrate, *ser'āt, adj.* notched like a saw.—*v.t.* (*-āt*) to notch.—*n.* **serrā'tion,** state of being serrated: (usu. in *pl.*) a sawlike tooth. [L. *serrātus*—*serra*, a saw.]

serried, *ser'id, adj.* crowded, dense, set close together (e.g. *serried ranks, serried shields*). [Fr. *serrer*, to crowd—L. *sera*, a door-bar.]

serum, *sē'rum, n.* a watery fluid, esp. that which separates from coagulating blood: blood serum used for serum-therapy:—*pl.* **sēr'a, sēr'ums.**—*adj.* **sē'rous,** resembling serum: thin, watery.—*n.* **sē'rum-ther'apy,** treatment by injecting immune blood serum, e.g. serum that has been infected with the bacteria of a disease or their toxin and has developed the appropriate anti-toxin. [L. *sērum*, whey.]

servant, *sûr'vánt, n.* one hired to work for another: a labourer: a domestic: one who is in the service of the state or a public body: (*B.*) a slave: one who endeavours to please another: a term of civility, as 'your humble servant.'—**servants' hall,** a servants' sitting-and dining-room. [Fr., pr.p. of *servir*—L. *servīre*, to serve.]

serve, *sûrv, v.t.* to be a servant to, to work for: to attend or wait upon: to obey: to worship: to treat, behave towards: to be of use to or for: to suffice for: to help to food, &c.: to distribute (food) at table: (*law*) to deliver or present formally: to undergo (a prison sentence): to operate (a machine, a gun): to strike (a ball) to begin a rally in tennis, &c.: (of male animals) to copulate with.—*v.i.* to be employed as a servant: to perform appointed duties: to be used (for): to suffice, to avail.—*n.* the act of serving in tennis, &c.—*n.* **ser'ver,** one who serves, esp. at meals, mass, or tennis: a salver: a fork, spoon, or other instrument for distributing or helping at table.—**serve as,** to act as: to take the place of; **serve one out,** to take revenge on some one; **serve one right,** to be no worse than one deserves; **serve up,** to bring to table. [Fr. *servir*—L. *servīre*, to serve.]

service, *sûr'vis, n.* condition or occupation of a servant: employ: employment in one of the armed forces: work: duty required in any office: (in *pl.*) the armed forces: a public administrative department or its personnel: public religious worship or ceremonial: a musical composition for devotional purposes:

assistance to another: supplementary activities for the advantage of customers: use: hard usage: disposal: profession of respect: supply, as of water, railway-trains: waiting at table: order of dishes at table: a set, as of dishes for a particular meal: act or mode of serving a ball.—*v.t.* to keep (a machine, e.g. a car) in good running order by periodical repairs and other attention: to distribute supplies to regularly.—*adj.* **ser′viceable**, durable: useful: durable or useful, implying 'not ornamental': (with *to*) serving to promote: (*arch.*) obliging.—*adv.* **ser′viceably.**—*ns.* **serviceabil′ity, ser′viceableness; ser′vice-book**, a book of forms of religious service: a prayer-book; **service-flat**, a flat in which domestic service is provided and its cost included in the rent; **ser′vice-hatch**, one connecting dining-room to kitchen, &c., through which dishes, &c., may be passed; **service industry**, one providing services rather than manufactured goods; **ser′vice-pipe, -wire**, a branch-pipe, -wire, from a main-pipe, -wire, to a dwelling; **service road**, a minor road parallel to a main road and serving local traffic without obstructing the main road; **service station**, an establishment providing general services for motorists.— **active service**, service of a soldier, &c., in the field; **have seen service**, to have been in active military service: to have been put to hard use. [Fr.,—L. *servitium*—*servus*, slave.]

service, *sûr′vis, n.* a tree very like the rowan. [O.E. *syrfe*—L. *sorbus.*]

serviette, *sér-vi-et′, n.* a table-napkin. [Fr.]

servile, *sûr′vīl, adj.* pertaining to slaves or servants: suitable to a slave: meanly submissive, cringing.—*adv.* **ser′vilely.**—*n.* **servil′ity**, state or quality of being servile: slavery: obsequiousness. [L. *servīlis*—*servus.*]

servitor, *sûr′vi-tôr, n.* one who serves, a servant. [L., *servīre*, to serve.]

servitude, *sûr′vi-tūd, n.* state of being a slave: slavery: state of slavish dependence: menial service. [L. *servitūdō*—*servus*, slave.]

servo(-)mechanism, *sûr′vō(-)mek′ăn-izm, n.* a system providing for remote control and/or manual control of heavy machinery. [L. *servus*, slave.]

sesame, *ses′ă-me, n.* annual herb of Southern Asia, whose seed yields valuable oil.—**open sesame**, charm by which door of robbers' cave flew open in 'Ali Baba and the Forty Thieves': (*fig.*) a magic key. [Fr.—L.—Gr.]

sesquipedalian, *ses-kwi-pé-dā′li-án, adj.* containing a foot and a half: often humourously said of a very long word.—*ns.* **sesquipedálity, sesquipedāl′ianism.** [L. *sēsquipedālis*—*sēsqui*, one-half more, *pēs, pedis*, a foot.]

sessile, *ses′īl, adj.* having no stalk or peduncle, attached directly (as a leaf without petiole to a branch, or certain marine animals to rock, mud, &c.). [L. *sessilis*, low, dwarf.]

session, *sesh′(ó)n, n.* an act of sitting: the sitting of a court or public body: the time it sits: the time between the meeting and prorogation of Parliament: period of the year during which classes are held in a school or college: (*Scot.*) the kirk-session: a period of time spent engaged in any one activity.—**Court of Session**, supreme civil court of Scotland. [Fr.,—L. *ses-*

siō, -ōnis—*sedēre, sessum*, to sit.]

sesspool. Same as **cesspool.**

sestet, sestette, *ses-tet′, n.* a group of six: the last six lines of a sonnet: (*mus.*) a composition for six performers. [It. *sestetto*—*sesto*—L. *sextus*, sixth.]

set, *set, v.t.* to seat: (*lit.* and *fig.*) to place, to put, to fix: to put and fix in its proper place, as a broken limb: to dispose, arrange: to regulate: to plant: to compose, put together (type) for printing: to embed: to frame: to stud, dot, sprinkle, variegate (with): to render coagulated, rigid, fixed, or motionless: to propound (e.g. a problem, an examination question, an examination): to present for imitation: to start (a person, e.g. *this set him complaining*): to direct (a person to do something): to prescribe (e.g. a task for a person): to appoint (e.g. a limit): to rate, value: to pitch, as a tune: to compose music for (words—*to set, to set to music*): to incite to hostility (against): to sharpen, as a razor: to put on eggs: to put under a hen: to indicate by crouching, as a dog: to arrange (hair) in waves or curls.—*v.i.* to go down towards or below the horizon: to become rigid, fixed, hard, solid, or permanent: to coagulate: of a bone, to knit: to develop, as fruit: to have or take a course or direction: to begin to go: to dance in a facing position: to point out game:—*pr.p.* set′ting; *pa.t.* and *pa.p.* set.—*p.adj.* fixed: settled: deliberate, intentional: regular, established: rigid: of mature habit of body.—*n.* a group of persons or things such as associate, occur, or are used together: a clique, coterie: a complete series or collection: a series of dance movements or figures: a complete apparatus, esp. for wireless reception: complete scenery for a scene in a play or motion picture: a part of a film studio prepared for a scene: a fixing of hair waves, &c.: an act, process, mode, or time of setting: build, carriage, pose: the hang of a garment: a young plant, slip, &c.: an inclination: direction of flow: a dog's indication of game: (*math.*) any collection of objects, called 'elements', defined by specifying the elements: for the following senses **set** or **sett**—a badger's burrow: (*tennis*) a group of games in which the winning side wins six, with such additional games as may be required in case of deuce: a street-paving block.—*ns.* **set′-back**, a check, reverse, or relapse; **set′-off**, a claim set against another: a counterbalance: an ornament; **set′-piece**, a performance elaborately arranged in advance: a picture in fireworks: a piece of theatrical scenery with a supporting framework; **sett′er**, one who or that which sets: a breed of dog trained to point game; **sett′ing**, act of one who sets: direction of current: fixation: scene: environment: adaptation to music: music composed for a song, &c.; **set′-to′**, a bout, a hot contest; **set′-up**, bodily carriage and physique: configuration: arrangement of apparatus, or of properties on a motion picture set, &c., or (*coll.*) structure of an organisation, &c.—**set about**, to begin: to attack (a person): to spread (a rumour); **set agoing**, to put in motion; **set at nought** (see **nought**); **set fair**, of weather, steadily fair; **set forth**, to exhibit, display: to start on a journey; **set free**, to

Neutral vowels in unaccented syllables: *em′pér-ör*; for certain sounds in foreign words see p. ix.

666

release, put at liberty; **set in**, to become prevalent: to begin; **set off**, to mark off: to show to advantage: to counterbalance: to depart; **set on**, to attack: to incite to attack; **set one's face** (against, to, &c.), to oppose, or support, resolutely; **set one's hand to**, to sign: to begin; **set oneself**, to bend one's energies; **set one's teeth**, to clench teeth together, as in a strong resolution; **set on foot**, to set agoing, to start; **set out**, start, to begin a journey: to begin, with an intention (to): to display: to expound; **set sail** (see **sail**); **set speech**, a studied oration; **set square**, a right-angled, triangular drawing instrument; **set terms**, terms deliberately thought out, definite, prescribed; **set up**, to erect: to begin: to enable to begin (e.g. *to set him up in business*): (*print.*) to put in type. [O.E. *settan*; cog. with Ger. *setzen*, O.N. *setja*; *settan* is the weak causative of *sittan*, to sit.]

settee, *se-tē'*, *n.* a long seat with a back. esp. a sofa for two. [Prob. **settle**.]

setter, **setting**. See under **set**.

settle, *set'l*, *n.* a long high-backed bench: (*B.*) a ledge—*v.t.* to place at rest or in comfort: to establish, install: to colonise: to restore to order: to quiet, compose: to determine, decide: to put beyond doubt or dispute: to secure by gift or legal act: to make final payment of—*v.i.* to come to rest: to subside: to sink to the bottom: to take up permanent abode: to adopt fixed habits: to grow calm or clear: to come to a decision or agreement: to adjust claims or accounts.—*ns.* **settle'ment**, act of settling: state of being settled: payment: arrangement: a local community: an establishment of social workers aiming at benefit to the surrounding population: a colony newly established: a subsidence or sinking: a settling of property, an instrument by which it is settled, or the property settled, esp. on a woman at marriage; **sett'ler**, one who settles: a colonist.—**settle for**, to agree to accept (usu. as a compromise); **settle in**, to adapt to a new environment. [O.E. *setl*, seat, *setlan*, to place; the vb. may be partly from, or influenced by, late O.E. *saht lian*, to reconcile.]

seven, *sev'n*, *adj.* and *n.* the cardinal number next above six. *n.* a figure denoting seven units (7, or vii).—*adjs.* **sev'enfold**, folded seven times: multiplied seven times; **sev'enth**, last of seven: being one of seven equal parts.—*n.* one of seven equal parts.—*adv.* **sev'enthly.** [O.E. *seofon*; Du. *zeven*, Ger. *sieben*, Gr. *hepta*, L. *septem*.]

seventeen, *sev'n-tēn* (when used absolutely *sev-n-ten'*), *adj.* and *n.* seven and ten.—*adj.* **seventeenth**, the seventh after the tenth.—*n.* one of seventeen equal parts. [O.E. *seofontēne*, *seofontīene*.]

seventy, *sev'n-ti*, *adj.* and *n.* seven times ten.—*adj.* **sev'entieth**, last of seventy.—*n.* one of seventy equal parts. *n.* **sev'enty-eight**, a seventy-eight revolutions per minute gramophone record, standard before the introduction of long-playing microgroove records—usu. written 78. [O.E. *seofontig*—*seofon*, seven.]

sever, *sev'ér*, *v.t.* and *v.i.* to separate, to divide: to cut or break, or be broken, off, away from.—*n.* **sev'erance**, act of severing: separation. [Fr.

sevrer, to wean—L. *sēparāre*, to separate.]

several, *sev'ér-ál*, *adj.* particular, distinct: respective: various: more than one (usu. more than three) but not very many.—*adv.* **sev'erally**, separately. [O.Fr.,—L. *sēparāre*, to separate.]

severe, *sé-vēr'*, *adj.* rigorous, very strict: unsparing: inclement: hard to endure: austerely restrained or simple (e.g. style): rigidly exact (e.g. reasoning).—*adv.* **severe'ly.**—*n.* **severity** (*sé-ver'i-ti*), quality of being severe. [L. *sevērus.*]

sew, *sō*, *v.t.* to join or fasten together with a needle and thread.—*v.t.* to ply the needle:—*pa.t.* sewed (*sōd*); pa.p. sewn (*sōn*) or sewed (*sōd*).—*ns.* **sew'er**; **sew'ing**, act of sewing: what is sewn; **sew'ing-machine.** [O.E. *sīwian*, *sēowian.*]

sewer, *sū'ér*, *n.* a channel for receiving the drainage of house-drains and streets.—*ns.* **sew'age**, refuse carried off by sewers; **sew'erage**, system or provision of sewers: sewage. [O.Fr. *sewiere*, a canal to carry off, aqua, water.]

sex, *seks*, *n.* the sum-total of the characteristics, structural and functional, which distinguish male and female organisms, esp. with regard to the part played in reproduction: either of the divisions of organisms according to this distinction, or its members collectively: all matters involving this distinction: sexual intercourse.—*adjs.* **sex'less**, of neither sex: without sex: without sexual feelings; **sex'ual**, pertaining to sex: distinguished by, founded on, sex: relating to the distinct organs of the sexes.—*n.* **sexual'ity.**—*adv.* **sex'ually.**—*ns.* **sex'-appeal'**, power of attracting the other sex; **sex'-chro'mosome**, a chromosome that determines sex; **sex'-determina'tion**, the settling of what the sex of a new organism is to be.—*adjs.* **sexed** (*sekst*), having sex: having sexual character or feelings: to a specified degree (as in **over-, under-, highly sexed**); **sex'-link'ed**, inherited along with sex, that is by a factor located in the sex-chromosome; **sexy**, over-concerned with sex: of a person, very attractive to the opposite sex.—**the sex**, (*arch.*) womankind. [Fr. *sexe*—L. *sexus.*]

sex-, *seks-*, **sexi-**, *seks-i-*, in composition, six [L. *sex*, six]:—e.g. **sex'foil**, a window, design, &c., with six lobes or leaves (L. *folium*, leaf).

sexagenarian, *seks-sà-je-nā'ri-án*, *n.* a person over sixty and under seventy years of age.—*adj.* **sexagen'ary**, of or relating to sixty. [L. *sexāgēnārius sexāgintā*, sixty.]

Sexagesima (Sunday), *sek-sà jes'i-ma* (*sun'dà*), *n.* the second Sunday before Lent; the reason for the name was prob. that the day came before *Quinquagesima* (q.v.) *Sunday*, which in turn preceded *Quadragesima* (q.v.) *Sunday*, but it cannot be justified numerically. [*sexāgesimus, -a, -um*, sixtieth.]

sexcentenary, *sek-sin-tēn'ár-i, -sin-ten'*, or *-sen'tin-ár-i*, *adj.* relating to six hundred, esp. to six hundred years.—*n.* a six hundredth anniversary. [L. *sex*, six, and **centenary**.]

sexennial, *seks-en'yál*, *adj.* lasting six years: recurring every six years.—*adv.* **sexenn'ially.** [L. *sex*, six, *annus*, a year.]

sextant, *seks'tánt*, *n.* an instrument with an arc

of a sixth part of a circle, used for measuring angular distances. [L. *sextāns, -antis*, the sixth part.]

sextet, sextette, *seks-tet', n.* (*mus.*) a work for six voices or instruments: a company of six. [Variant of **sestet**.]

sexton, *seks'tón, n.* an officer who rings a church bell, attends the clergyman, digs graves, &c.—*n.* **sex'tonship**. [Through O.Fr. from root of **sacristan**.]

sextuple, *seks'tū-pl, adj.* sixfold. [L.L. *sextuplus*—L. *sex,* six.]

sforzando, *sför-tsän'dō, adj.* and *adv.* (*mus.*) forced, with sudden emphasis. Abbrevs. *sf., fz.* and *sfz.,* or marked >, ∧. [It., pr.p. and pa.p. of *sforzare,* to force.]

shabby, *shab'i, adj.* threadbare or worn, as clothes: having a look of poverty: mean in appearance or conduct: low, paltry.—*adv.* **shabb'ily.**—*n.* **shabb'iness.**—*adj.* **shabb'y-genteel'**, keeping up or affecting an appearance of gentility, though really shabby. [From obs. or dial, *shab,* scab.]

shack, *shak, n.* a roughly built hut. [Amer.]

shackle, *shak'l, n.* a prisoner's or slave's ankle-ring or wrist-ring, or the chain connecting a pair: a coupling of various kinds: (*pl.*) fetters, manacles: a hindrance.—*v.t.* to fetter: to join or couple by a shackle: to impede. [O.E. *sc(e)acul.*]

shad, *shad, n.* a genus of fish of the herring kind. [O.E. *sceadd.*]

shaddock, *shad'ók, n.* an Oriental citrus fruit like a very large orange, esp. the larger pear-shaped variety as distinguished from the finer *grape-fruit* (q.v.). [Introduced to the W. Indies, *c.* 1700, by Captain *Shaddock.*]

shade, *shād, n.* a partial or relative darkness: interception of light: obscurity: a shady place: (in *pl.*) the abode of the dead, Hades: shelter from light or heat: a screen: degree of colour: a hue mixed with black: the dark part of a picture: a very minute amount (of difference): the disembodied soul: a ghost.—*v.t.* to screen: to overshadow: to mark with gradations of colour or shadow: to darken.—*n.* **shā'ding**, the act of making a shade, or of marking shadows or a shadow-like appearance: the effect of light and shade, as in a picture: fine gradations, nuances: toning down, modification.—*adj.* **shā'dy**, having, or in, shade: sheltered from light or heat: (*coll.*) not fit to bear the light, disreputable.—*adv.* **shā'dily.**—*n.* **shā'diness.**—**put in the shade**, to outdo completely. [O.E. *sceadu*. See **shadow**.]

shadoof, shaduf, *sha-dōōf', n.* a contrivance for raising water by a bucket on a counterpoised pivoted rod. [Egyptian Ar. *shādūf.*]

shadow, *shad'ō, n.* shade due to interception of light by an object: the dark shape of that object so projected on a surface: protective shade: the dark part, e.g. of a picture: gloom, affliction: a mere appearance, a semblance: an extremely emaciated person: an inseparable companion: a ghost, spirit.—*v.t.* to shade: to cloud or darken: to represent as by a shadow: to hide: to follow closely and watch, to dog.—*adj.* unreal: feigned: existing only in skeleton (e.g. *a shadow factory*): inactive but ready for the time when opportunity or need arises.—

adj. **shad'owy,** shady: like a shadow: dim, vague: unsubstantial.—**shadow boxing,** sparring practice with an imaginary opponent: making a show of opposition or other action, as a cover for inactivity. [O.E. *sceadwe,* gen., dat., acc. of *sceadu* (**shade** representing the nom.).]

shaft, *shäft, n.* anything long and straight: a stem: a narrow beam (of light): an arrow: a missile (esp. *fig.*; e.g. *shafts of wit*): a bar, usu. cylindrical, used to support rotating parts of machinery: a pole: the part of a column between the base and capital: the main upright part of anything: a long handle: a well-like excavation: the entrance to a mine.—*adj.* **shaft'ed,** having a shaft or handle.—*n.* **shaft'ing** (*mach.*), the system of shafts connecting machinery with the prime mover. [O.E. *sceaft*; perh. partly Ger. *schacht,* pit.]

shag, *shag, n.* a ragged mass of hair, or the like: a long coarse nap: a kind of tobacco cut into shreds: the green cormorant.—*adj.* **shagg'y,** covered with rough hair, wool, or other growth: rough, rugged: untidy.—*n.* **shagg'iness.**—**shaggy dog story** (from the shaggy dog featured in many), a whimsical story humorous from its length and the inconsequence of its ending. [O.E. *sceaga.*]

shagreen, *sha-grēn, n.* a granular leather made from horse's or ass's skin: the skin of shark, ray, &c., covered with small nodules.—*adj.* (also **shagreened'**) of, or covered with, sha-green. [Fr. *chagrin*—Turk. *saghrī,* &c., horse's rump, shagreen.]

Shah, *shä, n.* the monarch of Persia. [Pers.]

shake, *shāk, v.t.* to move with quick, short motions, to agitate: to brandish: to disturb the stability of: to upset the composure of: to make to tremble or totter: to cause to waver.—*v.i.* to be agitated: to tremble: to trill:—*pa.t.* shook, (*B.*) shaked; *pa.p.* shāk'en.—*n.* a shaking: a tremulous motion: (*lit.* or *fig.*) a damaging or disconcerting blow: (*mus.*) a rapid alternation of two notes, a tone or semitone apart: a drink made by shaking ingredients together.—*n.* **shake'down**, a temporary bed, originally made by shaking down straw.—*adj.* **shāk'y**, shaking or inclined to shake: loose: tremulous: precarious: unreliable.—*adv.* **shāk'ily.**—*n.* **shāk'iness.**—**shake hands**, to salute by grasping the hand and moving it up and down; **shake off**, to get rid of; **shake off the dust from one's feet**, used *lit.* and symbolically in Matthew x. 14, (*B.*): (*fig.*) to leave hurriedly or gladly; **shake the head**, to move the head from side to side in token of reluctance, disapproval, &c.—**(no) great shakes**, (*coll.*) of (no) great account. [O.E. *sc(e)acan.*]

Shakespearian, *shāk-spē'ri-ân, adj.* of or relating to, or in the style of, *Shakespeare,* or his works—also **Shakespē'rian, Shakspear'ean, Shakspē'rian.**

shako, *shak'ō, n.* a military cap of cylindrical shape. [Hungarian *csákó.*]

shale, *shāl, n.* clay-rock, splitting readily into thin laminae, some varieties of which yield paraffin and other mineral oils. [Ger. *schale,* a scale.]

shall, *sh(a)l, v.t.* originally expressing a debt or

Neutral vowels in unaccented syllables: *em'pér-ór*; for certain sounds in foreign words see p. ix.

moral obligation, now used with the infinitive of a verb (without *to*) to form a future tense denoting, in the first person, mere futurity (as *wilt, will* in the second and third), or in the second and third, implying promise, decree, or control on the part of the speaker:—*infin.* obsolete; no participles; 2nd pers. sing. (*arch.*) shalt; 3rd shall; *pa.t.* should (*shŏŏd*). [O.E. *sculan*, pr.t. (orig. a preterite) *sceal, scealt, sceal*; pa.t.*sceolde*; cf. Ger.*soll*, O.N.*skal*, to be in duty bound.]

shallop, *shal′op, n.* formerly a heavy fore-and-aft-rigged boat: a small or light boat. [O.Fr. *chalupe*; cf. **sloop.**]

shallot, *shă-lot′, n.* a species of onion with a flavour like that of garlic.—Also **shalot′.** [O.Fr. *eschalote.*]

shallow, *shal′ō, adj.* not deep: not profound: not wise: superficial.—*n.* a place where the water is not deep: a shoal.—*adjs.* **shall′ow-heart′ed,** not capable of deep feelings; **shall′ow-pā′ted,** weak in intellect.—*n.* **shall′owness.—the shallows,** the shallow part. [M.E. *schalowe*, perh. related to **shoal** (2).]

shalt, *shalt,* 2nd pers. sing. of **shall.**

sham, *sham, n.* a pretence: that which gives a false impression.—*adj.* not real, pretended, false.—*v.t.* to pretend, to feign.—*v.i.* to make false pretences: *pr.p.* shamm′ing; *pa.t.* and *pa.p.* shammed. [First found as slang, late 17th cent.]

shamble, *sham′bl, v.i.* to walk with an awkward, unsteady gait.—*n.* a shambling gait. [Perh. from next word, in allusion to trestle-like legs.]

shamble, *sham′bl, n.* a stall on which butchers exposed their meat for sale: (in *pl.*) a flesh-market, a slaughter-house. (*pl.* as *sing.*) a scene of blood and slaughter: (*coll.*) mess, muddle, scene of confusion.—*adj.* **shambol′ic** (*coll.*), chaotic. [O.E. *scamel*, a stool—Low L. *scammellum*, dim. of *scamnum*, a bench.]

shame, *shām, n.* the sense of humiliation due to fault or failure: modesty: dishonour, disgrace: a cause or source of disgrace: a thing to be ashamed of: (*coll.*) an instance, a case of bad luck.—*v.t.* to make ashamed: to disgrace: to put to shame by greater excellence: to drive by shame (into doing).—*adj.* **shame′faced** (orig. **shame′fast**), very modest or bashful: abashed.—*adv.* **shame′facedly.**—*ns.* **shame′facedness, shame′fastness.**—*adj.* **shame′ful,** disgraceful.—*adv.* **shame′fully.**—*n.* **shame′fulness.**—*adj.* **shame′less,** immodest: brazen: done without shame or compunction.—*adv.* **shame′lessly.**—*n.* **shame′lessness.—for shame,** an interjectional phrase, signifying 'you should be ashamed!'—**put to shame,** to cause to feel shame; **think shame,** to be ashamed. [O.E. *sc(e)amu*; Ger. *scham.*]

shammy, *sham′i, n.* a soft leather, originally made from chamois-skin. Also *adj.* [**chamois.**]

shampoo, *sham-pōō′, v.t.* to massage: to wash and rub (the scalp and hair): to clean (carpet, &c.) by rubbing with a special preparation:—*pa.t.* and *pa.p.* shampooed′.—*n.* **shampoo′,** act of shampooing: a soap or other preparation for this purpose. [Hindustani *cāpna*, to squeeze.]

shamrock, *sham′rok, n.* a trifoliate leaf or plant, the national emblem of Ireland: various suggestions have been made as to the identity of the original shamrock, but in living popular tradition it is usu. accepted to be one of the clovers, the lesser yellow trefoil. [Ir. *seamróg*, Gael. *seamrag*, dim. of *seamar*, trefoil.]

shandy, *shan′di, n.* a mixture of bitter ale or beer with ginger-beer or lemonade.

shanghai, *shang-hī′, v.t.* to drug or make drunk and ship as a sailor: to trick into performing an unpleasant task:—*pa.p.* shanghai′ing; *pa.t.* and *pa.p.* shanghaied′. [*Shanghai* in China.]

Shangri-la, *shang′gri-lä, n.* an imaginary pass in the Himalayas, an earthly paradise, described in James Hilton's novel, *Lost Horizon* (1933).

shank, *shangk, n.* the leg from knee to foot: the straight or long part: a shaft, stem. [O.E. *sc(e)anca*, leg; Du.*schonk*, Low Ger.*schanke.*]

shan't, *shänt* (*coll.*), a contraction of **shall not.**

Shantung, *shan-tung′, n.* a plain rough cloth of wild silk. [*Shantung*, province of China.]

shanty, *shan′ti, n.* a roughly built hut: a ramshackle dwelling-house.—*n.* **shant′y-town,** a town, or an area of one, where housing is makeshift and ramshackle. [App. Fr.*chantier*, a timber-yard.]

shanty, *chant′i, n.* a song with chorus, sung by sailors while heaving at the capstan, or the like.—Also **chant′y, chant′ie.** [Said to be from Fr. *chanter*, to sing.]

shape, *shāp, v.t.* to form, to fashion, to frame: to model, to mould (*lit.* and *fig.*): to regulate, direct, to determine.—*v.i.* to take shape, to develop: to show promise of acquitting oneself (e.g. *he shapes well at English*);—*pa.p.* shāped, (*B.*) shāp′en.—*n.* form or figure: external appearance: condition (e.g. *in good shape*; *in no shape to do it*): that which has form or figure: an apparition: a pattern: (*cookery*) a jelly, or the like, turned out of a mould.—*adjs.* **sha′pable, shape′able; shape′less,** having no shape or regular form: lacking symmetry.—*n.* **shape′lessness.**—*adj.* **shape′ly,** having shape or regular form: well-proportioned.—*n.* **shape′liness.—shape up,** to develop: to be promising.—**take shape,** to assume a definite form or plan. [O.E. *scieppan*, to form, make; O.N.*skapa*, Ger.*schaffen.*]

shard, *shärd, n.* a fragment, as of an earthen vessel: the wing-case of a beetle. [O.E. *sceard.*]

share, *shār, n.* a part shorn or cut off: a division, section, portion: a fixed and indivisible section of the capital of a company.—*v.t.* to divide into shares: to apportion: to give or take a share of: to have in common.—*v.i.* to have a share.—*n.* **share′holder,** one who owns a share, esp. in a company. [O.E. *scearu*; cf. **shear.**]

share, *shār, n.* the iron blade of a plough which cuts the ground. [O.E. *scear*; cf. foregoing word, and **shear.**]

shark, *shärk, n.* any of a class of large voracious fishes, some of which are dangerous to man: an extortioner, a swindler, a sponging parasite.—**basking shark,** one of the largest species but harmless unless attacked, noted for its habit of lying at the surface and basking in the sun. [Origin doubtful.]

sharp, *shärp, adj.* cutting, piercing: having a

thin edge or fine point: affecting the senses as if pointed or cutting: severe: harsh: pungent: astringent: shrill: high in pitch or too high: raised a semitone: sarcastic: alive to one's own interests: barely honest: of keen or quick perception: alert: abrupt: clear-cut, well-defined: (*coll.*) stylish.—*adv.* high or too high in pitch: punctually, precisely: abruptly.—*n.* a note raised a semitone: the symbol for it.—*v.t.* shar'pen, to make sharp.—*v.i.* to grow sharp.—*n.* sharp'er, a trickster, a swindler.—*adv.* sharp'ly.—*n.* sharp'ness.—*adj.* sharp'-set, hungry.—*n.* sharp'-shoot'er, a good marksman.—*adjs.* sharp'-sight'ed, having acute sight: shrewd; sharp'-witt'ed, having an acute wit.—**look sharp,** be quick. [O.E. *scearp*; O.N. *skarpr*, Ger. *scharf*.]

shatter, *shat'ėr, v.t.* to dash to pieces: (*fig.*) to wreck, ruin, derange.—*v.i.* to break into fragments. [Perh. Low Ger.; cf. **scatter.**]

shave, *shāv, v.t.* to scrape or pare off a superficial slice, hair (esp. of the face), or other surface material from: to graze the surface of.—*v.i.* to remove hair by a razor:—*pa.p.* shāved or (*arch.*) shā'ven.—*n.* the act or process of shaving: a paring: a narrow miss or escape (especially *close shave*).—*ns.* shave'ling, a monk or friar, from his shaven crown; shā'ver, one who shaves: a barber: a sharp or extortionate dealer: (*coll.*) a youngster; shā'ving, the act of scraping or using a razor: a thin slice, esp. a curled piece of wood planed off. [O.E. *sc(e)afan*; Du. *schaven*, Ger. *schaben*.]

Shavian, *shā'vi-ān, adj.* pertaining to the dramatist George Bernard *Shaw* (1856-1950).

shaw, *shö, n.* a thicket, a small wood. [O.E. *sc(e)aga*; O.N. *skōgr*, Dan. *skov*.]

shawl, *shöl, n.* a wrap or loose covering for the shoulders.—*v.t.* to wrap in a shawl. [Pers. *shāl*.]

shawm, shalm, *shöwm, n.* an obsolete musical instrument of the oboe class. [O.Fr. *chalemie*—L. *calamus*, a reed-pipe.]

shay, *shā, n.* (*arch.* or *coll.*) a chaise. [Formed from *chaise*, mistaken as a pl.]

she, *shē, pron. fem.* the female (or thing spoken of as a female) named before, indicated or understood:—*pl.* **they.**—*n.* a woman or other female.—*adj.* female. [O.E. *sēo*, orig. the fem. of the definite article; in the 12th century it began to replace *hēo*, the old fem. pron.]

sheaf, *shēf, n.* a bundle of things bound side by side, esp. stalks of corn: a bundle of (usually 24) arrows:—*pl.* **sheaves** (*shēvz*).—*vs.t.* sheaf, sheave, to bind in sheaves.—*v.i.* to make sheaves.—*adj.* sheaf'y. [O.E. *scēaf*); cf. Ger. *schaub*, Du. *schoof*.]

shear, *shēr, v.t.* to cut, esp. to clip with shears: (*Scot.*) to reap with a sickle.—*v.i.* to separate:—*pa.t.* sheared, (*arch.*) shore; *pa.p.* sheared or shorn.—*n.* a type of deformation in which parallel planes in a body remain parallel but are relatively displaced in a direction parallel to themselves (also **shearing stress**).—*ns.* shear'er; shear'ling, a sheep only once sheared.—*n.pl.* shears, (*orig.* and *Scot.*) scissors: now usu. a larger implement of similar kind, with pivot or spring: a hoisting apparatus (same as **sheers**). [O.E. *sceran*; O.N. *skera*, to clip, Ger. *scheren*, to shave.]

sheath, *shēth, n.* a case for a sword or blade: a covering (esp. tubular or long): the wing-case of an insect:—*pl.* **sheaths** (*shēᴛʜz*).—*v.t.* **sheathe** (*shēᴛʜ*), to put into, or cover with, a sheath or case.—*ns.* **sheath'ing** (ᴛʜ), that which sheathes: casing: the covering of a ship's bottom; **sheath'-knife,** a knife encased in a sheath. [O.E. *scēath, scǣth*; Ger. *scheide,* O.N. *skeithir.*]

sheave, *shēv, n.* the wheel of a pulley over which the rope runs. [M.E. *shefe, shive*; cf. Ger. *scheibe,* a flat thin piece.]

shebeen, *she-bēn', n.* an illicit liquor shop. [Ir.]

shed, *shed, v.t.* (*dial.*) to part, separate: to cast off (e.g. clothing, skin, leaves): to pour forth (tears, blood): to diffuse (e.g. light, *lit.* and *fig.*):—*pr.p.* shedd'ing; *pa.t.* and *pa.p.* shed.—*n.* a division, parting (as in *watershed*). [O.E. *scēadan,* to separate; Ger. *scheiden.*]

shed, *shed, n.* a structure, often open-fronted, for storing or shelter: an outhouse. [App. a variant of **shade.**]

sheen, *shēn, n.* shine, lustre, radiance. [O.E. *scēne,* beautiful; Du. *schoon,* Ger. *schön.*]

sheep, *shēp, n.* a genus of beardless, woolly, wild or domesticated, animals closely allied to goats: (*fig.*) a silly, helpless creature:—*pl.* **sheep.**—*ns.* **sheep'-cote,** an enclosure for sheep; **sheep'-dip,** a liquid preparation for disinfecting sheep; **sheep'-dog,** a dog trained to watch sheep, or of a breed used for that purpose; **sheep'-fold,** a fold or enclosure for sheep.—*adj.* **sheep'ish,** like a sheep: bashful, foolishly diffident or embarrassed.—*adv.* **sheep'ishly.**—*ns.* **sheep'ishness; sheep'-run,** a tract of grazing country for sheep; **sheep'-shank,** a knot for temporarily shortening a rope; **sheep'-shearer,** one who shears sheep; **sheep'-shearing; sheep'-skin,** the skin of a sheep: leather or parchment prepared from it; **sheep'-walk,** a range of pasture for sheep.—**the sheep and the goats,** the good and the bad (Matt. xxv. 33). [O.E. *scēap;* Ger. *schaf.*]

sheer, *shēr, adj.* pure, unmingled: mere, downright: vertical or very nearly so: very thin, diaphanous (of fabric).—*adv.* vertically: outright. [M.E. *schere,* perh. from a lost O.E. equivalent of O.N. *skærr,* bright.]

sheer, *shēr, v.i.* to deviate, swerve.—*n.* deviation: oblique position: the fore-and-aft upward curve of a ship's deck or sides.—*n.pl.* sheers, an apparatus for hoisting heavy weights, having legs or spars spread apart at their lower ends, and bearing at their tops, where they are joined, hoisting-tackle.—*n.* sheer'-hulk, an old dismasted ship with sheers mounted on it: popularly, a mere hulk, as if from sheer (1).—**sheer off,** (*trans.* and *intrans.*) to turn aside: to move away, take oneself off. [Partly at least another spelling of **shear;** perh. partly from the Low Ger. or Du. equivalent, *scheren,* to cut, withdraw.]

sheet, *shēt, n.* a large, thin piece: a large, broad piece of cloth, esp. for a bed: a large, broad piece of paper, &c.: a piece of notepaper, foolscap, &c.: a wide expanse: a sail.—*v.t.* to cover with, or as with, a sheet: to furnish with sheets: to form into sheets.—*ns.* **sheet'-copp'er, -i'ron, -lead, -met'al,** copper, iron, lead, metal in thin sheets; **sheet'-glass,** a kind

Neutral vowels in unaccented syllables: *em'pėr-ŏr;* for certain sounds in foreign words see p. ix.

sheet

sheet

of crown-glass made in a cylinder, and flattened out; **sheet'ing**, cloth for sheets: protective boarding or metal covering; **sheet'-lightning**, diffused appearance of distant lightning. [O.E. *scēte*; cf. next word.]

sheet, *shēt*, *n.* a rope attached to the lower corner of a sail. [O.E. *scēata*, corner; akin to **sheet** (1).]

sheet-anchor, *shēt'-angk'ôr*, *n.* an anchor for an emergency: chief support, last refuge. [Formerly, *shut-*, *shot-*, *shoot-anchor*.]

sheik, sheikh, *shāk*, *shēk*, *n.* an Arab chief: a Hindu convert to Islam: (*slang*) a young man considered by girls to be irresistibly fascinating. [Ar. *shaikh—shākha*, to be old.]

sheiling. Same as **shieling.**

shekel, *shek'l*, *n.* a Jewish weight (about half an ounce) and coin (about 14p): (*pl.—slang*) money. [Heb. *shequel—shāgal*, to weigh.]

Shekinah, Schechinah, *shē-kī'na*, *n.* the Divine presence which rested like a cloud or visible light over the mercy-seat. [Heb.,—*shākan*, to dwell.]

sheldrake, *shel'drāk*, *n.* a genus of birds of the duck family. [Prob. dial. *sheld*, variegated, and **drake.**]

shelf, *shelf*, *n.* a board fixed in a cupboard, on a wall, &c., for laying things on: a flat layer of rock, a ledge: a shoal, a sandbank:—*pl.* **shelves** (*shelvz*).—*adj.* **shelf'y.**—*n.* **shelf'-mark**, indication on a book of its place in a library.—**on the shelf**, shelved: laid aside from duty or service: without prospects of marriage. [O.E. *scylf*, shelf, ledge.]

shell, *shel*, *n.* a hard outer covering, esp. of a shellfish, a tortoise, an egg, or a nut: the external ear: a husk, pod, or rind: any framework, as of an uncompleted or gutted building, &c.: any frail structure: a frail boat: a light coffin: an explosive projectile shot from a cannon: in some schools, an intermediate class.—*adj.* of, with or like, shell or shells.—*v.t.* to separate from the shell: to bombard with shells.—*ns.* **shellac** (see under **lac**); **shell'-back**, an old sailor; **shell'-fish**, a shelled aquatic invertebrate, esp. a mollusc (e.g. an oyster) or crustacean (e.g. a crab), or such animals collectively; **shell'-heap**, a heap of shells: a prehistoric accumulation of shells, &c.; **shell'-lime**, lime made from sea-shells.—*adj.* **shell'proof**, able to resist shells or bombs.—*n.* **shell'-shock**, former name for nervous or mental disturbance due to war experiences, once supposed to be caused by bursting of shells.—*adj.* **shell'y**, composed of shells: abounding in shells.—**come out of one's shell**, to cease to be shy and reticent; **shell out** (*slang*), to pay out. [O.E. *scel*; Du. *schel*, O.N. *skel*.]

shelter, *shel'tér*, *n.* a structure that shields or protects, esp. against weather: a place of refuge, retreat, or temporary lodging in distress: protection.—*v.t.* to cover or shield: to conceal.—*v.i.* to take shelter. [Orig. *sheltron*—O.E. *scyld-truma*, shield-troop.]

shelve, *shelv*, *v.t.* to furnish with shelves: to place on a shelf: to put aside.—*v.i.* to slope, incline.—*n.* a ledge: a shelf.—*n.pl.* **shelves**, pl. of **shelf** and of **shelve.**—*n.* **shelv'ing**, provision of, or material for, shelves: act of putting on a

shift

shift

shelf.—*adj.* shallowing: sloping. [See **shelf.**]

Shemitic. Same as **Semitic.**

shepherd, *shep'érd*, *n.* one who tends sheep: a pastor:—*fem.* **shep'herdess.**—*v.t.* to tend, or to guide, as a shepherd.—*ns.* **shepherd's check, tartan**, a small black and white checked pattern; **shepherd's pie**, a dish of meat cooked with potatoes on the top. [O.E. *scēaphirde.* See **sheep, herd.**]

Sheraton, *sher'á-tón*, *adj.* applied to a style of furniture characterised by delicate curves, designed by Thomas *Sheraton* (1751-1806).

sherbet, *shûr'bét*, *n.* fruit juice: an effervescent drink, or powder for making it: a kind of water-ice. [Turk. and Pers. *sherbet*, from Ar.]

sheriff, *sher'if*, *n.* (*hist.*) the king's representative in a shire, with wide judicial and executive powers: now in England, the chief officer of the crown in the shire: in Scotland, the chief judge of the county (also **sheriff-principal**): (*U.S.*) elected officer who enforces law in a county, &c.—*ns.* **sher'iffalty, sher'iffdom, sher'iffship**, shrievalty (*q.v.*); **sher'iff-sub'stitute**, the acting-sheriff in a Scottish county or city, appointed by the crown:—*pl.* **sher'iffs-substitute.** [O.E. *scīrgerēfa—scīr*, shire, *gerēfa*, a reeve.]

Sherlock Holmes, *shûr'lok homz*, one who shows highly developed powers of observation and deduction, as did the detective, Sherlock Holmes, in the stories of Conan Doyle (1859-1930).

Sherpa, *shûr'pä*, *n. sing.* and *pl.* one or more of an Eastern Tibetan people living high on the south side of the Himalayas. [Tibetan *shar*, east, *pa*, inhabitant.]

sherry, *sher'i*, *n.* a fortified wine made in the neighbourhood of Jerez de la Frontera in Spain. [*Xeres*, earlier form of *Jerez*.]

Shetland pony, *shet'land pō'ni*, a small sturdy and shaggy horse, originally bred in the *Shetland* Islands.—**Shetland wool**, a thin but strong undyed worsted, spun from the wool of the sheep in the Shetland Islands.

shew, *shō.* Same as **show.**—*n.* **shew'bread**, the twelve loaves offered weekly in the sanctuary by the Jews.

shibboleth, *shib'ó-leth*, *n.* (*B.*) a test-word used by the Gileadites to detect the fleeing Ephraimites, who could not pronounce *sh* (Judges, xii. 4-6): any such test: the criterion or catchword of a group. [Heb. *shibbōleth*, an ear of corn, or a stream.]

shield, *shēld*, *n.* a broad plate carried for defence against weapons and missiles: anything that protects: a person who protects: defence: the escutcheon used for displaying arms: a trophy shaped like a shield.—*v.t.* to protect by shelter.—*adj.* **shield'less**, defenceless. [O.E. *sceld*; Ger. *schild*; O.N. *skjöldr*, protection.]

shieling, *shēl'ing*, *n.* a small cottage, esp. in the Scottish Highlands. [Ety. uncertain.]

shift, *shift*, *v.i.* to manage, get on, do as one can: to change one's clothes: to change position: to fluctuate: to go away.—*v.t.* to change (clothes): (*arch.*) to change the clothes of: to change the position of: to transfer (to): to dislodge.—*n.* (*arch.*) a smock, chemise: a loose dress: provision of clothes: an expedient: an artifice: a set of persons taking turns with

fāte, fär; mē, hûr (her); *mīne; mōte, för; mūte; mōōn, fōōt;* THen (then)

another set: time worked by such a set: a change of position:—e.g. (geol.) the displacement of masses of rock on either side of a fault: a change in position of the left hand in a violin, &c., or any position except that nearest the nut (q.v.): a phonetic change affecting a considerable class, or classes, of sounds.—*n.* **shift′er**, one who shifts: a trickster.—*adj.* **shift′less**, without resource: inefficient, feckless.—*adv.* **shift′lessly.**—*n.* **shift′lessness.**—*adj.* **shift′y**, full of, or ready with, shifts or expedients, esp. evasive, tricky: indicating evasiveness or trickery (e.g. *shifty eyes*): tending to shift.—*n.* **shift′iness.**—**make shift**, to manage somehow; **make shift to**, to contrive to; (for **makeshift,** *adj.* and *n.,* see **make**). [O.E. *sciftan,* to divide, O.N. *skipta.*]

shillelah, shi-lā′la, *n.* the oak or blackthorn cudgel of the conventional Irishman. [*Shillelagh*, an oak-wood in County Wicklow.]

shilling, shil′ing, *n.* a coin at first silver, later cupronickel, worth £$^1/_{20}$: its value.—**shilling shocker,** a sensational story (orig. one published at a shilling).—**take the king's (queen's) shilling,** to enlist as a soldier by accepting the recruiting officer's shilling —discontinued 1879. [O.E. *scilling*; Ger. *schilling.*]

shilly-shally, shil′i-shal′i, *n.* vacillation, indecision.—*v.i.* to hesitate feebly. [A reduplication of **shall I?**]

shimmer, shim′ér, *v.i.* to gleam tremulously, to glisten.—*n.* **shimm′er,** a tremulous gleam. [O.E. *scimerian*—*scīmian,* to shine; Ger. *schimmern.*]

shimmy, shim′i, *n.* a shivering dance. [From **chemise.**]

shin, shin, *n.* the forepart of the leg below the knee.—*n.* **shin′-bone,** the tibia. [O.E. *scin,* the shin (*scin-bān,* shin-bone); Du. *scheen,* Ger. *schiene.*]

shindig, shin′dig, *n.* (*slang*) a lively celebration: a row. [Cf. **shindy.**]

shindy, shin′di, *n.* (*slang*) a row, disturbance. [Perh. **shinty.**]

shine, shīn, *v.i.* to give or reflect light: to beam with steady radiance, to glow, to be bright: to excel, or to appear pre-eminent.—*v.t.* to cause to shine:—*pa.t.* and *pa.p.* shone (*shon*), (*B*) shīned.—*n.* brightness, lustre, sheen: sunshine: an act or process of polishing: (*slang*) a shindy.—*adj.* **shī′ny,** clear, unclouded: glossy.—**shine at,** to be very good at; **take a shine to** (*slang*), to take a liking to; **take the shine out of** (*slang*), to outshine, eclipse: to take the brilliance or pleasure-giving quality out of. [O.E. *scīnan*; Ger. *scheinen.*]

shingle, shing′gl, *n.* a wooden slab used like a roofing slate: a board: a mode of haircutting showing the form of the head at the back.—*v.t.* to cover with shingles: to cut in the manner of a shingle. [Low L. *scindula,* a wooden tile—L. *scindĕre,* to split.]

shingle, shing′gl, *n.* coarse gravel: a large pebble: a bank or bed of large rounded stones.—*adj.* **shing′ly.** [Origin obscure.]

shingles, shing′glz, *n.pl.* a painful eruption of clusters of firm vesicles along the course of a nerve, sometimes, though rarely, spreading round the body like a belt. [L. *cingulum,* a

belt—*cingĕre,* to gird.]

Shinto, shin′tō, *n.* the system of nature- and hero-worship forming the indigenous religion of Japan. [Jap., = Chinese *shin tao*—*shin,* god, *tao,* way, doctrine.]

shinty, shin′ti, *n.* a game like hockey, played chiefly in the Scottish Highlands.

ship, ship, *n.* a large vessel, esp. a three-masted square-rigged sailing vessel: sometimes any floating craft: an aircraft.—*v.t.* to put, receive, or take on board: to send or convey by ship: to dispatch by land or air: to send off: to engage for service on board a ship.—*v.i.* to embark: to engage for service on shipboard:—*pr.p.* ship′p′ing; *pa.t.* and *pa.p.* shipped.—*ns.* **ship′-bis′cuit,** hard biscuit for use on shipboard; **ship′board,** a ship's side: hence, a ship; **ship′-break′er,** one who breaks up vessels no longer fit for sea; **ship′-brok′er,** a broker who effects sales, insurance, &c., of ships; **ship′builder; ship′building; ship′-canal′,** a canal large enough for sea-going vessels; **ship′-chand′ler,** a dealer in cordage, canvas, and other ship furniture or stores; **ship′master,** the captain of a ship; **ship′mate,** a companion in the same ship; **ship′ment,** act of putting on board ship; consignment by ship: that which is shipped; **ship′-mon′ey,** a tax imposed by the king on seaports, revived without authorisation of parliament by Charles I. in 1634-37; **ship′-of-the-line,** before steam navigation, a man-of-war large enough to take a place in a line of battle; **ship′-owner,** the owner of, or owner of a share in, a ship or ships; **shipp′er; shipp′ing,** ships collectively: putting aboard ship: transport by ship.—*adj.* **ship′-shape,** in a seamanlike condition—trim, neat, orderly.—*ns.* **ship′way,** a sliding-way for launching ships: a support for ships under examination or repair: a ship-canal; **ship′wreck,** the wreck or destruction (esp. by accident) of a ship: ruin, disaster.—*v.t.* to wreck.—*ns.* **ship′wright,** a wright or carpenter employed in shipbuilding; **ship′yard,** a yard where ships are built or repaired.—**ship a sea** (see **sea**); **ship's husband** (see **husband**); **when one's ship comes home,** when one becomes rich. [O.E. *scip*; O.N. *skip,* Ger. *schiff.*]

shire, shīr (in composition, -*shér*), *n.* a county: applied also to certain smaller districts in England, as Richmondshire, Hallamshire.— *ns.* **shire′-horse,** a large, strong draughthorse, once bred chiefly in the Midland shires; **shire′-moot** (O.E. *scīrgemōt*), (*hist.*) the court of the shire.—**the Shires** (often *shērz*), those English counties whose names end in -*shire*, esp. (for hunting) Leicestershire, Rutland-(shire), Northamptonshire, and part of Lincolnshire. [O.E. *scīr,* office, authority.]

shirk, shûrk, *v.t.* to evade, to slink out of facing or shouldering.—*v.i.* to evade duties or obligations.—*n.* **shir′ker.** [shark.]

shirr, shir, *shûr,* *n.* a puckering or gathering.—*v.t.* to make gathers in (cloth): to bake (eggs broken into a dish).

shirt, shûrt, *n.* a man's loose sleeved garment, typically with fitted collar and cuffs: an undershirt: a woman's tailored blouse.—*v.t.* to cover with a shirt.—*ns.* **shirt′-band,** the neckband of a shirt; **shirt′ing,** cloth for shirts;

Neutral vowels in unaccented syllables: em′pér-ór; for certain sounds in foreign words see p. ix.

672

shirts collectively; **shirt'-waist,** (*U.S.*) a tailored blouse having ends that are tucked in under the skirt; **shirt'waist'er,** a tailored dress with shirtwaist top.—*adj.* **shirt'y,** (*slang*) ruffled in temper.—**boiled shirt,** a white shirt (with starched front); **in one's shirt-sleeves,** with coat off; **keep one's shirt on,** (*slang*) to keep calm; **put one's shirt on,** (*slang*) to bet one's all on. [O.E. *scyrte*; cf. **short.**]

shist, &c. Same as **schist,** &c.

shittim, *shit'im, n.* in full **shitt'im wood,** (*B.*) the wood of the **shittah-tree,** believed to be an acacia. [Heb. *shittāh,* pl. *shittim.*]

shiver, *shiv'ér, n.* a splinter, a chip, a small fragment.—*v.t.* and*v.i.* to shatter.—*adj.* **shiv'ery,** brittle. [Early M.E. *scifre*; cf. **sheave;** Ger. *schiefer.*]

shiver, *shiv'ér, v.i.* to quiver or tremble, to make an involuntary movement as with cold or fear.—*v.t.* to cause to quiver.—*n.* a shivering movement or feeling.—*adj.* **shiv'ery,** inclined to shiver or tremble. [M.E. *chivere.*]

shoal, *shōl, n.* a multitude of fishes swimming together.—*v.i.* to crowd. [O.E. *scolu,* troop; cf. **school** (2).]

shoal, *shōl, adj.* shallow.—*n.* a shallow: a sand-bank.—*v.i.* to become shallow.—*adj.* **shoal'y,** full of shoals or shallows. [O.E. *sceald,* shallow.]

shock, *shok, n.* a violent impact, a collision: a sudden jarring or shaking as if by a blow: an alarming and disconcerting experience: a convulsive excitation of nerves, as by electricity: an earthquake: prostration of voluntary and involuntary functions caused by pain or excessive sudden emotional disturbance: (*coll.*) a stroke of paralysis.—*v.t.* to give a shock to: to startle: to dismay, to horrify.—*v.i.* to be horrified: to collide.—*n.* **shock'er** (*coll.*), a very sensational tale: a very unpleasant person or thing.—*adj.* **shock'ing,** causing horror or dismay, highly offensive. *adv.* **shock'ingly.**—*ns.* **shock'-absorber,** a contrivance for diminishing shocks, as in an aeroplane or motor car; **shock'(-)troops,** troops trained or selected for attacks demanding exceptional physique and bravery; **shock'-wave,** a wave of the same nature as a sound wave but of very great intensity, caused e.g. by an atomic explosion.—**shock tactics,** (*orig.*) tactics of cavalry attacking in masses and depending for their effect on the force of impact: (*fig.*) any action that seeks to achieve its object by means of suddenness and force; **shock treatment,** **shock therapy,** use of electric shocks in treatment of mental disorders: (*fig.*) use of violent measures to change one's way of thinking. [App. Fr. n. *choq,* vb. *choquer,* or perh. directly from a Gmc. source.]

shock, *shok, n.* a stook or propped-up pile of sheaves. [M.E. *schokke.*]

shock, *shok, n.* a shaggy mass (of hair).—*adjs.* **shock-head, -ed,** having a thick and bushy head of hair. [Perh. a variant of **shag.**]

shod, *shod, pa.t.* and *pa.p.* of **shoe.**

shoddy, *shod'i, n.* wool from shredded rags: cloth made of it, alone or mixed: any inferior article seeking to pass for better than it is.—*adj.* of shoddy: cheap and nasty: sham.

shoe, *shōō, n.* a stiff outer covering for the foot,

not coming above the ankle: a rim of iron nailed to the hoof of an animal: anything in form, position, or use like a shoe, as a metal tip or ferrule, a piece attached where there is friction, the touching part of a brake:—*pl.* **shoes** (*shōōz*), also (*arch.* and *dial.*) **shoon** (*shōōn*).—*v.t.* to furnish with shoes: to cover at the bottom: to fit with an iron tyre:—*pr.p.* shoe'ing; *pa.t.* and *pa.p.* shod.—*ns.* **shoe'black,** one who blacks shoes or boots; **shoe'horn,** a curved piece of horn or metal used to help the heel into a shoe; **shoe-lace,** a string passed through the eyelet holes to fasten a shoe; **shoe'-leather,** leather for shoes: shoes generally; **shoe'maker,** one who makes, or now often one who sells and repairs, shoes or boots; **shoe'making; shoe'string** (*U.S.*), a shoe-lace: anything paltry: a very small amount of capital.—**another pair of shoes,** (*coll.*) quite a different matter; **in someone's shoes,** in his place, circumstances; **on a shoestring,** with an extremely small amount of capital. [O.E. *scōh* (pl. *scōs*—weak pl. in *-n* appears in M.E.); Ger. *schuh.*]

shone, *shon, pa.t.* and *pa.p.* of **shine.**

shook, *shōōk, pa.t.* of **shake.**

shoon, *shōōn,* an old *pl.* of **shoe.**

shoot, *shōōt, v.t.* to dart, to let fly with force: to discharge (a gun): to hit, wound, or kill with a shot: to thrust forward (with *out, forth*): to eject suddenly, to dump: to utter suddenly and rapidly: to move swiftly over, under, &c. (e.g. *to shoot a rapid, a bridge*): to slide along (e.g. a bolt): to put forth in growth: to crystallise: to variegate, to produce play of colour in (usu. in *pa.p.*): to photograph, esp. for motion pictures.—*v.i.* to dart forth or forward: 'to discharge a shot or a weapon: to use a gun habitually, esp. for sport: to jut out: to sprout: to advance or grow rapidly: (*slang*; usu. in *imper.*) to begin, esp. to tell what one knows or thinks:—*pa.t.* and *pa.p.* shot.—*n.* act of shooting: a shooting-party: a new growth, sprout: a chute.—*ns.* **shoot'er,** one who, or that which, shoots; **shoot'ing,** act of discharging firearms or an arrow: a twinge of quick pain: killing game with firearms on a certain area: the district so limited; **shoot'ing-box,** a small house in the country for use in the shooting season; **shoot'ing-gall'ery,** a long room used for practice in the use of firearms; **shoot'ing-range,** a place for shooting at targets; **shoot'ing-star,** a meteor; **shoot'ing-stick,** a walking-stick with a head that opens out into a seat.—**shoot home,** to hit the target (also *fig.*); **shoot up,** to attack, injure or kill by shooting: (*fig.*) to grow very rapidly; **the whole shoot** (*coll.*), the whole lot. [O.E. *scēotan*; Du. *schieten,* Ger. *schiessen,* to dart.]

shop, *shop, n.* a building or room in which goods are sold: a place where mechanics work, or where any kind of industry is carried on: details of one's own work, business, or profession, or talk about these: (*slang*) an institution.—*v.i.* to visit shops, esp. for the purpose of buying.—*v.t.* (*slang*) to imprison: to betray or inform against.:—*pr.p.* shopp'ing; *pa.p.* shopped.—*ns.* **shop'keeper,** one who keeps a shop of his own; **shop'keeping; shop'-lift'ing,**

lifting or stealing anything from a shop; **shop'-lift'er; shop'man,** one who serves in a shop.—*adjs.* **shop'-soiled, shop'-worn,** somewhat tarnished by being exposed in a shop.—*ns.* **shop'-stew'ard,** a representative of factory or workshop employees elected from their own number; **shop'-walk'er,** one who walks about in a shop to see the customers attended to.—**shopping centre,** a place where there is a concentration of shops selling various goods.—**all over the shop,** scattered all around; **on the shop floor,** among the workers in a factory or workshop (*adj.* **shop'-floor**); **shop around,** to compare prices and quality of goods at various shops before making a purchase; **talk shop** (*coll.*), to converse (esp. at an inappropriate time) about one's own trade or profession. [O.E. *sceoppa,* a treasury, perh. booth.]

shore, *shōr, pa.t.* of **shear.**

shore, *shōr, shōr, n.* land bordering on the sea or an expanse of water.—*adj.* **shore'less,** having no coast: indefinite or unlimited.—*adv.* **shore'-ward,** towards the shore. [M.E. *schore*; cf. Du. *schoor, schor.*]

shore, *shōr, shōr, n.* a prop to support a building, or to keep a vessel in dock steady on the slips.—*v.t.* to prop. [Cf. Du. *schoor.*]

shorn, *shōrn, shōrn, pa.p.* of **shear.**

short, *shört, adj.* (*comp.* **short'er,** *superl.* **short'est**) not long: not tall: (radio waves) of wavelength 50 metres or less: of brief duration: less than a given standard: scanty, insufficient: brittle, friable: brusque, uncivil: (in accentual verse, *loosely*) unaccented.—*adv.* briefly: abruptly: on the near side, not far enough.—*n.* a short film subordinate to the main film in a programme: (*coll.*) a short alcoholic drink.—*n.pl.* **shorts,** short trousers as for football.—*adv.* **short'ly,** in a short time, soon: briefly: curtly.—*ns.* **short'ness; short'age,** deficiency; **short'bread,** a crisp, brittle cake of flour and butter; **short'-cake,** shortbread or other friable cake.—*v.t.* **short'-change',** to give less than the correct change to: to deal dishonestly with.—*n.* **short'-cir'cuit** (*elect.*), a new path of comparatively low resistance between two points of a circuit: a deviation of current by path of low resistance.—*v.t.* to establish a short-circuit in: to interconnect where there was an obstruction between: (*fig.*) to provide with a short cut or a more direct method.—*v.i.* to cut off current by a short circuit: to save a roundabout passage.—*n.* **short'-coming,** act of falling short: neglect of, or failure in, duty: defect.—*adj.* **short'-dat'ed,** having little time to run from its date, as a bill.—*v.t.* **short'en,** to make shorter: to make to seem short: to reduce the amount of (sail) spread: to draw in or back: to make friable.—*v.i.* to become shorter.—*ns.* **short'ening** (*shört'ning*), act of making, or becoming, short, or shorter: fat suitable for making pastry, &c., friable; **short'hand,** a method of swift writing (by signs for sounds and groups of sounds) to keep pace with speaking: writing of such a kind.—Also *adj.*—*adj.* **short'-hand'ed,** not having the proper number of work-people, &c.—*ns.* **short'-horn,** one of a breed of cattle having very short horns;

short'-leg, (*cricket*) the fielder, or the field, near the batsman on the left side behind the wicket; **short'-list,** a selected list of candidates for an office.—*v.t.* **short'-list,** to include (someone) in a short-list.—*adjs.* **short'-lived,** living or lasting only for a short time; **short'-sight'ed,** having clear sight only of near objects: lacking foresight.—*n.* **short'sight'ed-ness.**—*adjs.* **short'-tem'pered,** easily put into a rage; **short'-term,** extending over a short time: of a policy, concerned with the immediate, as distinct from time ahead; **short-wave,** of, or using wavelengths 50 metres or less; **short'-wind'ed,** soon becoming breathless.—**at short sight,** (of a bill) payable soon after being presented; **in short,** in a few words; **make short work of,** to settle or dispose of promptly; **short of,** less than: poorly provided with (also **short on;** *coll.*): (*fig.*) without going so far as (e.g. *every means to mislead, short of telling a direct lie*).—**stop short,** to come to a sudden standstill; **take up short,** to interrupt curtly. [O.E. *sc(e)ort*; cf. O.H.G. *scurz.*]

shot, *pa.t.* and *pa.p.* of **shoot.**—*p.adj.* hit or killed by shooting: elongated by rapid growth.

shot, *shot, n.* the act of shooting: a single sound of shooting: a projectile, esp. one that is solid or spherical without bursting charge—e.g. a cannon-ball, a bullet, a small pellet of which several are shot together, such pellets collectively: a marksman: flight of a missile, or its distance: an explosive charge: an injection: a photographic exposure, esp. for a motion picture: a unit in film-production: the action or method of making this: in games, a stroke: an attempt: an aggressive remark: a guess: a spell, turn: (also **scot**) a payment, esp. of a tavern reckoning: a contribution.—*v.t.* to load with shot:—*pr.p.* **shot'ting;** *pa.p.* **shot'ted.**—*n.* **shot'gun,** a smooth-bore gun for small shot.—*adj.* pertaining to a shotgun: involving force (e.g. *shotgun marriage*).—**a big shot** (*coll.*), an important person; **a shot in the arm** (*fig.*), a reviving injection, as of money, fresh talent; **a shot in the dark,** a random guess; **shot of,** rid of.—**a shot in the locker,** something still in reserve. [O.E. *sc(e)ot*; cf. **shoot.**]

should, *shŏŏd, pa.t.* of **shall.** [O.E. *sceolde.*]

shoulder, *shōl'dér, n.* the part of the trunk between the neck and the free portion of the fore-limb: the upper joint of a foreleg of an animal cut for the table: a bulge, a prominence: either edge of a road.—*v.t.* to thrust with the shoulder: to take upon the shoulder, to sustain: to undertake: to take responsibility for.—*ns.* **shoul'der-belt,** a belt that passes across the shoulder; **shoul'der-blade, -bone,** the broad, flat, blade-like bone of the shoulder.—*adj.* **shoul'dered,** having a shoulder or shoulders (esp. of a specified kind).—*n.* **shoul'der-knot,** a knot worn as an ornament on the shoulder.—**cold shoulder** (see **cold**); **put,** or **set, one's shoulder to the wheel,** to make a vigorous effort. [O.E. *sculdor*; Ger. *schulter,* Du. *schouder.*]

shout, *showt, n.* a loud cry: a call.—*v.i.* to utter a shout.—*v.t.* to utter with a shout.—*n.* **shout'er.**—**shout down,** to make another's speech inaudible by shouting or talking loudly. [Origin unknown.]

Neutral vowels in unaccented syllables: *em'pér-ór*; for certain sounds in foreign words see p. ix.

shove, *shuv*, *v.t.* and *v.i.* to thrust: to push along: to jostle.—*n.* act of shoving: a push. [O.E. *scūfan*; Du. *schuiven*, Ger. *schieben*.]

shovel, *shuv'l*, *n.* a broad spade-like tool: a scoop.—*v.t.* to move with, or as if with, a shovel.—*v.i.* to use a shovel:—*pr.p.* shov'el-ling; *pa.t.* and *pa.p.* shov'elled.—*n.* **shov'el-hat**, a hat with a broad brim, turned up at the sides, and projecting in front. [O.E. *scofl*, from *scūfan*, to shove.]

show, (now rarely **shew**), *shō*, *v.t.* to exhibit, to display: to cause or allow to be seen or known: to prove: to manifest: to usher or conduct (in, out, over, round, &c.).—*v.i.* to appear: to come into sight: to be visible:—*pa.p.* shŏwn or shōwed.—*n.* act of showing: display: a spectacle, an entertainment: (*coll.*) a theatrical performance: (*coll.*) a social gathering: appearance: parade, pretence.—*ns.* **show'-bill**, a bill announcing a show; **show'bread** (see **shewbread**); **show'-business**, the entertainment business, esp. the branch of the theatrical profession concerned with variety entertainments. Also (*coll.*) **show'-biz**; **show'-down**, exposure of playing cards, or (*fig.*) of intentions: open conflict; **show'er**; **show'man**, one who exhibits, or owns, a show: one who is skilled in showing off things (e.g. his own merits) so as to arouse public interest; **show'manship**, skilful display, or a talent for it; **show'-room**, a room where goods or samples are displayed to the best advantage.—*adj.* **showy** (*shō'i*), making a show, ostentatious, gaudy: given to show.—*adv.* **show'-ily**.—*n.* **show'iness**.—**show fight**, to show readiness to resist; **show off**, to display or behave ostentatiously: to try to make an impression by one's possessions or talents; **show up**, to expose to blame or ridicule: to be present: to appear to advantage or disadvantage.—**a show of hands**, a vote indicated by raising hands; **good**, **bad**, **show**, well not well done, fortunate, unfortunate, occurrences. [O.E. *scēawian*; Du. *schouwen*, Ger. *schauen*, to behold.]

shower, *show'ér*, *showr*, *n.* a short fall, as of rain or hail: a fall, flight of many things together, as of meteors, arrows, &c.: a copious supply: a shower-bath: quantities of fast particles arising from a high-energy particle.—*v.t.* to wet with rain: (*fig.*) to pour, bestow (upon): to gift liberally (with).—*v.i.* to drop in showers: to take a shower-bath.—*n.* **shower'-bath**, a bath in which water is showered from above.—*adjs.* **shower'-proof**, impervious to showers; **showers**, marked by showers: raining intermittently. [O.E. *scūr*; O.N. *skūr*, Ger. *schauer*.]

shrank, *shrangk*, *pa.t.* of **shrink**.

shrapnel, *shrap'n(é)l*, *n.* a shell filled with musket-balls with a bursting charge, invented by General *Shrapnel* (1761-1842): fragments scattered by such a shell on explosion: any later improved version of the orig. shell.

shred, *shred*, *n.* a strip: a scrap, fragment.—*v.t.* to cut or tear into shreds. [O.E. *scrēad*; cf. **screed**.]

shrew, *shrōō*, *n.* any of numerous small mouse-like animals of the Insectivora, formerly thought venomous: a brawling, troublesome woman, a scold.—*adj.* **shrewd**, (*arch.*) ill-natured: having, or showing, an acute judgment: biting, keen (e.g. pain, cold).—*adv.* **shrewd'ly**.—*n.* **shrewd'ness.**—*adj.* **shrew'ish**, having the qualities of a shrew or scold, ill-natured and troublesome.—*adv.* **shrew'ishly**.—*n.* **shrew'ishness**. [O.E. *scrēawa*.]

shriek, *shrēk*, *v.i.* to utter a shrill scream.—*v.t.* to utter with a shriek.—*n.* a shrill outcry: a wild, piercing scream. [Cf. **screech**.]

shrieval, *shrē'vál*, *adj.* pertaining to a sheriff.—*n.* **shriev'alty**, office, term of office, or area of jurisdiction, of a sheriff. [From *shrieve*, obs. form of *sheriff*.]

shrift, *shrift*, *n.* a confession made to a priest: time granted to a condemned criminal to make such a confession before execution (as in *short shrift*—usu. *fig.* meaning summary treatment of a person or matter). [O.E. *scrift—scrīftan*, to shrive.]

shrike, *shrīk*, *n.* any of numerous passerine birds, some kinds of which impale small animals on thorns—hence called butcher-birds [App. O.E. *scrīc*, perh. thrush.]

shrill, *shril*, *adj.* high pitched and piercing: sounding so through impatience or insistence.—*v.i.* and *v.t.* to sound or cry shrilly.—*n.* **shrill'ness.**—*adv.* **shrill'y**. [Cf. Low Ger. *schrell*, whence prob. Ger. *schrill*.]

shrimp, *shrimp*, *n.* any of numerous small edible crustaceans: any unduly small or contemptible person or thing.—*v.i.* to catch shrimps. [Cf. **scrimp** and O.E. *scrimman*, to shrink.]

shrine, *shrīn*, *n.* a case for relics or an erection over it: a place hallowed by its associations. [O.E. *scrīn*—L. *scrīnium*, a case for paper: *scrībēre*, to write.]

shrink, *shringk*, *v.i.* to contract: to give way, to draw back, to recoil (from).—*v.t.* to cause to shrink or contract:—*pa.t.* shrank, shrunk; *pa.p.* shrunk.—*n.* **shrink'age**, a contraction into a less compass: the extent of such diminution.—*adjs.* **shrink'-proof**, **-resis'tant**, that will not shrink on washing; **shrunk'en**, contracted, reduced: shrivelled. [O.E. *scrincan*.]

shrive, *shrīv*, *v.t.* to hear a confession from and give absolution to.—*v.i.* to receive, or make, confession:—*pa.t.* shrōve or shrīved; *pa.p.* shriv'en. [O.E. *scrīfan*, to write, to prescribe penance—L. *scrībēre*.]

shrivel, *shriv'l*, *v.i.* and *v.t.* to contract into wrinkles:—*pr.p.* shriv'elling; *pa.t.* and *pa.p.* shriv'elled. [Ety. uncertain.]

shroud, *shrowd*, *n.* the dress of the dead: that which clothes or covers: (*pl.*) a set of ropes from the mast-head, to a ship's sides, to support the mast.—*v.t.* to enclose in a shroud: to cover: to hide: to shelter. [O.E. *scrūd*; O.N. *skrūth*, clothing.]

Shrove-tide, *shrōv'-tīd*, *n.* the season at which confession is made, the days immediately preceding Ash-Wednesday. [Of obscure origin; related to O.E. *scrīfan*, to shrive.]

shrub, *shrub*, *n.* a low woody plant, a bush.—*n.* **shrubb'ery**, a plantation of shrubs.—*adj.* **shrubb'y**, full of shrubs: like a shrub: consisting of shrubs. [O.E. *scrybb*, scrub.]

shrub, *shrub*, *n.* a drink prepared from the juice of lemons, or other acid fruit, with spirits, esp. rum. [Ar. *sharab* for *shurb*, drink.]

shrug, *shrug*, *v.i.* to draw up the shoulders as an

expression of doubt, indifference, contempt, &c.—*v.t.* to raise (the shoulders) expressively:—*pr.p.* shrug'ging; *pa.t.* and *pa.p.* shrugged.—*n.* an expressive drawing up of the shoulders.—**shrug off,** to shake off: (*fig.*) to show indifference to, unwillingness to tackle (e.g. responsibility, a difficulty).

shrunk, shrunken. See **shrink.**

shudder, *shud'ér, v.i.* to shiver from cold or horror: to vibrate.—*n.* a tremor as from cold or horror: a vibration. [Cf. Ger. *schaudern.*]

shuffle, *shuf'l, v.t.* to mix at random, as playing cards: to shove (the feet) along without lifting them: to slip or move surreptitiously or evasively.—*v.i.* to mix cards in a pack: to shift ground: to evade fair questions: to move by shoving the feet along.—*n.* act of shuffling: a shuffling gait: an evasion or artifice.—*n.* **shuff'ler.—to shuffle off,** to thrust aside, put off, wriggle out of. [A byform of *scuffle.*]

shun, *shun, v.t.* to avoid, to keep clear of:—*pr.p.* shunn'ing; *pa.t.* and *pa.p.* shunned. [O.E. *scunian.*]

shunt, *shunt, v.t.* to turn aside, to divert upon a side-track (e.g. a train, an electric current).—*v.i.* to be diverted by a shunt.—*n.* an act of shunting: a switch.—*n.* **shunt'er.** [Perh. conn. with **shun.**]

shut, *shut, v.t.* to close the opening of: to lock, bar, fasten: to forbid entrance into: to confine: to catch or pinch (in a fastening).—*v.i.* to become closed: to admit of closing:—*pr.p.* shutt'ing; *pa.t.* and *pa.p.* shut.—*n.* **shutt'er,** one who, or that which, shuts: a close cover for a window or aperture.—**shut down,** to stop working; **shut up,** to close firmly or completely: to confine: (*coll.*) to cease speaking: (*coll.*) to silence. [O.E. *scyttan,* to bar; cf. *scēotan,* to shoot.]

shuttle, *shut'l, n.* an instrument used for shooting the thread of the woof between the threads of the warp in weaving, or through the loop of thread in a sewing-machine: anything that makes similar back-and-forward movements.—*adj.* running, or run, backwards and forwards (e.g. *shuttle service, race*).—*n.* **shutt'lecock,** a cork stuck with feathers, driven to and fro with battledores or badminton rackets: the game played with battledores.—**shuttle service,** a transport service moving constantly between two points. [O.E. *scytel,* bolt, *scēotan,* to shoot; Dan. and Swed. *skyttel.*]

shy, *shī, adj.* timid, shrinking from notice or approach: bashful: warily reluctant to (e.g. *shy of committing himself*): doubtful, suspicious (of):—*compar.* **shy'er** (or **shi'er**);*superl.* **shy'est** (or **shi'est**).—*v.i.* to start aside, as a horse from fear: to boggle (at):—*pa.t.* and *pa.p.* shīed.—*advs.* **shy'ly, shi'ly.**—*ns.* **shy'ness; shy'ster,** one who resorts to petty sharp practices: a shady lawyer.—**fight shy of** (see **fight**). [O.E. *scēoh*; Ger. *scheu,* Dan. *sky.*]

shy, *shī, v.t.* to fling, toss.—*n.* a throw, a fling: a shot, trial: a thing to shy at: a cock-shy.

Shylock, *shī'lok, n.* a ruthless creditor, or a grasping person. [From Shylock in *The Merchant of Venice.*]

Siamese, *sī-am-ez', adj.* of Siam.—**Siamese cat,** a domestic fawn-coloured cat, with blue eyes

and a small head; **Siamese twins,** Chinese twins (1811-74), born in Siam, joined from birth by a fleshy ligature: any pair of twins similarly joined.

sib, *sib, adj.* related (to).—*n.* **sib'ling,** one who has a parent, or parents, in common with another. [O.E. *sibb,* relationship.]

sibilate, *sib'i-lāt, v.t.* and *v.i.* to hiss.—*adj.* **sib'i-lant,** hissing.—*n.* hissing consonant sound, as of *s* or *z.—ns.* **sib'ilance, sib'ilancy;** **sibilā'tion,** a hissing sound. [L. *sībilāre,* -*ātum,* to hiss.]

Sibyl, *sib'il, n.* (*myth.*) one of several ancient prophetesses: (**sibyl**) a prophetess, sorceress, or witch, or an old crone.—*adj.* **sibylline** (*sib'-i-līn,* or *si-bil'īn*), pertaining to sibyls: prophetical: oracular. [Gr. *Sybylla.*]

sic, *sik, adv.* so, thus—printed within brackets in quoted matter to show that the original is being faithfully reproduced, even though incorrect or seemingly incorrect or seemingly so.—**sic passim,** so throughout. [L.]

siccative, *sik'ā-tiv, adj.* drying.—*n.* a drying agent. [Through L.L.—L. *siccus,* dry.]

sick, *sik, adj.* unwell, ill: vomiting, or inclined to vomit: out of condition: suffering the effects (of): thoroughly wearied (of): disgusted: of or for the sick: of humour, comedy, macabre, gruesome.—*n.* **sick'ness.**—*adj.* **sick'ly,** inclined to be ailing: feeble: pallid: suggestive of sickness (e.g. a *smile*): slightly sickening: mawkish.—*ns.* **sick'liness; sick'-bay, sick'-berth,** a compartment for sick and wounded on a ship; **sick'-bed,** a bed on which one lies sick.—*v.t.* **sick'en,** to make sick: to disgust: to make weary (of).—*v.i.* to become sick: to be disgusted: to become disgusting or tedious.—*adj.* **sick'ening.**—*adv.* **sick'eningly.**—*ns.* **sick'leave,** leave of absence because of sickness; **sick'-list,** a list containing the names of the sick; **sick'-room,** a room to which one is confined by sickness. [O.E. *sēoc*; Ger. *siech,* Du. *ziek.*]

sickle, *sik'l, n.* a hooked instrument for cutting grain. [O.E. *sicol, sicel,* perh. L. *secula,* a sickle—*secāre,* to cut.]

side, *sīd, n.* a line or surface forming part of a boundary: the part near such a boundary: the margin: a surface or part turned in a certain direction, esp. one more or less upright, or one regarded as right or left (not front or back, top or bottom): the part of the body between armpit and hip: half of a carcase divided along the backbone: a direction: an aspect: the slope (of a hill): the wall (of a vessel or cavity): either of the extended surfaces of anything in the form of a sheet: a department or division (e.g. of a school, a prison): the father's or the mother's line in a genealogy: part (e.g. *on my side,* for my part): any party, team, interest, or opinion opp. to another: a spin given to a billiard ball: (*slang*) pretentious behaviour.—*adj.* at or towards the side: indirect: subsidiary.—*v.i.* to embrace the opinion or cause of one party against another.—*adj.* **sid'ed,** having sides (of a specified kind).—*n.pl.* **side'-arms,** weapons worn at the side, as a sword or bayonet.—*ns.* **side'board,** a piece of dining-room furniture for holding dishes, &c.; **side'burns,** short side-whiskers worn without beard; **side'car,** a small car attached to the

Neutral vowels in unaccented syllables: *em'pér-ór*; for certain sounds in foreign words see p. ix.

676

side of a motor-cycle: a kind of cocktail; **side'-effect,** a subsidiary effect: effect, (often undesirable) additional to that sought; **side'glance,** a sidelong glance: a passing allusion; **side'-iss'ue,** a subordinate issue apart from the main business; **side'-kick,** partner, deputy: a special friend; **side'light,** light coming from the side: a light carried on the side of a vessel or vehicle: any incidental illustration; **side'-line,** a branch route or track: a subsidiary activity.—*adj.* **side'long,** oblique, not straight.—*adv.* in the direction of the side: obliquely: on the side.—*ns.* **side'-sadd'le,** a saddle for riding with both feet on one side; **side'-show,** an exhibition, show, attached to and subordinate to a larger one: any subsidiary or incidental activities or happenings; **side'-slip,** a skid.—*v.i.* to skid.—*n.* **sides'man,** a deputy churchwarden.—*adj.* **side'-splitting,** effecting the sides convulsively, esp. by provoking uncontrollable laughter.—*n.* **side'-step,** a step taken to one side.—*v.i.* to step aside.—*v.t.* to avoid as by a step aside.—*n.* **side'-track,** a siding.—*v.t.* to divert into a siding: *(coll.)* to divert (a person) from his purpose: to turn (a subject) as it were out of the path of attention and abandon discussion of it.—*n.* **side'-walk** *(U.S.),* pavement or foot-walk.—*advs.* **side'ways, side'wise,** toward or on one side.—*ns.* **side'-wind,** a wind blowing laterally: any indirect influence or means; **sid'ing,** a short line of rails on which wagons are shunted from the main line,—**take sides,** to range oneself with one party or other. [O.E. *sīde*; Ger. *seite,* Du. *zijde.*]

sidereal, sī-dē'ri-ăl, *adj.* relative to a star or stars: of, like, or measured by, the apparent motion of the stars *(sidereal year).* [L. *sīdus, sīderis,* a star.]

sidesman, siding. See **side.**

sidle, sī'dl, *v.i.* to move side-foremost, to edge along. [Back-formation from obs. adv. *sidling,* now **sidelong.**]

siege, sēj, *n.* (arch.) a seat, throne: an attempt to take a fortified place by keeping it surrounded by an armed force: *(fig.)* a persistent attempt to gain possession or control (of).—*n.* **siege'-train,** men, artillery, &c., for laying siege to a place.—**lay siege to,** *(lit.* and *fig.)* to besiege, beleaguer, invest, to surround with armed forces in order to force to surrender; **raise the siege** (see **raise**); **state of siege,** a condition of suspension of civil law or its subordination to military law. [O.Fr. *sege* (Fr. *siège*), seat—L. *sēdēs,* seat.]

siemens, sē'menz, *n.* unit of electrical conductance, that of a body with a resistance of one ohm. Abbrev. **S.** [William *Siemens,* 1823-83.]

sienna, sē-en'a, *n.* a fine pigment—brownyellow when *raw,* warm reddish-brown when *burnt* (i.e. roasted). [It. *terra di Siena,* Sienna earth.]

sierra, si-er'a, *n.* a jagged ridge of mountain peaks. [Sp.,—L. *serra,* a saw.]

siesta, si-es'ta, *n.* a short sleep or rest usually taken in the afternoon. [Sp.,—L. *sexta (hōra),* the *sixth* (hour) after sunrise, the hour of noon.]

sieve, siv, *n.* a vessel with a meshed or perforated bottom to separate the fine part of any-

thing from the coarse. [O.E. *sife*; Ger. *sieb.*]

sift, sift, *v.t.* to separate as by passing through a sieve: to examine closely.—*n.* **sift'er.** [O.E. *siftan—sife,* a sieve.]

sigh, sī, *v.i.* to inhale and respire with a sigh: to yearn (for): to grieve: to sound like a sigh.—*v.t.* to express by sighs: to spend in sighing.—*n.* a long, deep, audible respiration, expressive of yearning, dejection, relief, &c. [Prob. from the weak pa.t. of M.E. *sichen*—O.E. (strong) *sīcan.*]

sight, sīt, *n.* act of seeing: faculty of seeing: an opportunity of seeing, view: that which is seen: a spectacle: an unusual object: an unsightly object: space within vision: a small opening for observing objects: a device in a gun, or optical or other instrument, to guide the eye: mental view, estimation.—*v.t.* to descry, discern: to look at through a sight: to adjust the sights of (a gun, &c.).—*adjs.* **sight'ed,** having sight of a specified character (e.g. *short-sighted*); **sight'less,** wanting sight: blind.—*n* **sight'lessness.**—*adj.* **sight'ly,** pleasing to the sight or eye, comely.—*ns.* **sight'liness; sight'-read'er,** one who can read or perform music at first sight of the notes; **sight'-read'ing; sight'-see'ing,** visiting scenes or objects of interest; **sight'-se'er.—at sight,** without previous study or practice; **at sight, after sight,** terms applied to bills or notes payable on, or after, presentation. [O.E. *siht, gesiht*—*gesegen,* pa.p. of *sēon,* to see; Ger. *sicht.*]

sign, sīn, *n.* a gesture expressing a meaning, a signal: a mark with a meaning: a symbol, an emblem: a token, proof, outward evidence: a portent: a miracle: (*math.*) a conventional mark used as part of the description of a quantity (e.g. $\sqrt{}$, +, −), or to indicate an operation to be performed (e.g. +, ÷, Σ, $\int$): a device marking an inn, &c.: a board or panel giving a shopkeeper's name or trade &c. *(ustron.)* one of the twelve parts of the zodiac bearing the name of, but not coincident with, a constellation.—*v.t.* to mark with a sign: to indicate, convey, communicate (a meaning or message), or direct (a person), by a sign or signs: to attach a signature to: to write as a signature.—*v.i.* to make a sign: to sign one's name.—*ns.* **sign'-board,** a board bearing a sign, esp. of a shop or inn; **sign'er; signet** *(sig'-),* a small seal: the impression of such a seal: one of the royal seals for authenticating grants; **sign'-man'ual,** a signature, esp. a king's; **sign'post,** a post on which a sign is hung: a direction-post.—*v.t.* to furnish with a signpost: to point out as a signpost does.—*n.* **sign-writer,** an expert in lettering for shop signs.—**sign away,** to transfer by signing; **sign of the cross,** a gesture of tracing the form of a cross; **sign in, out,** to sign one's name on coming in, going out; **sign on,** to engage *(v.t* or *v.i.)* by signature: to record arrival at work; **sign off,** to record departure from work: to stop work, &c.: to discharge from employment: to leave off broadcasting. [Fr. *signe*—L. *signum.*]

signal, sig'n(ă)l, *n.* a, usu. visible or audible, intimation, e.g. of warning, conveyed to a distance: apparatus used for the purpose: an effect transmitted by telephone, or wireless, constituting or conveying a message: an intimation of, or event taken as marking, the moment (for action).—*v.t.* to make signals to (a person): to convey (information) by signals.—Also *v.i.*:—*pr.p.* sig′nalling; *pa.t.* and *pa.p.* sig′nalled.—*adj.* remarkable, notable.—*adv.* sig′nally.—*ns.* sig′nal-box, -cab′in, &c., a railway signalman's cabin.—*v.t.* sig′nalise, to mark or distinguish.—*ns.* sig′nalling; sig′nalman, one who transmits signals: one who works railway signals. [Fr.,—through L.L.—L., *signum.*]

signature, *sig′na-tyùr, -chùr, n.* a signing: a signed name: an indication of key, also of time, at the beginning of a line of music, or where a change occurs: a letter or numeral at the foot of a page to indicate sequence of sheets.—*n.* sig′natory, one bound by signature to an agreement.—*n.* sig′nature-tune′, a tune heralding the broadcast of some particular person or group. [L.L. *signātūra*—L. *signāre, -ātum,* to sign.]

signet. See sign.

signify, *sig′ni-fī, v.t.* to be a sign of: to mean: to indicate or declare (e.g. *to signify one's approval*).—*v.i.* to have importance (with much, little, &c.):—*pa.t.* and *pa.p.* sig′nified.—*n.* significance (*sig-nif′ik-àns*), meaning (esp. disguised or implicit): import: importance.—*adj.* significant, having, or conveying, meaning: expressive of much: important: indicative (of).—*adv.* signif′icantly.—*n.* significā′tion, act of signifying: accepted meaning.—*adj.* significative, indicative· (of): significant.—signif′icant figures, (*arith.*) the figures 1 to 9, or ciphers occurring medially; the following numbers are expressed to three significant figures:—3·15, 0·0127, 1·01, 10 700. [L. *significāre, -ātum—signum,* a sign, *facĕre,* to make.]

Signor, *sē′nyor, n.* an Italian word of address equivalent to *Mr* or *Sir.*—*ns.* Signora (*sē-nyō′ra*), feminine of *signor*; Signorina (*sē-nyō-rē′na*), the Italian equivalent of *Miss.* [It. *signore.*]

Sikh, *sēk, sik, n.* one of a North Indian monotheistic sect founded about 1500, later a military confederacy: a Sikh soldier in the Indian army. [Hindustani, 'disciple'.]

silage, *sī′lij, n.* fodder preserved by ensilage in a silo. [ensilage.]

silence, *sī′lens, n.* absence of sound: forbearance from sounding, or from speech: abstention from mentioning or divulging something: a time characterised by absence of sound: a time of abstention from communication by speech or other means: taciturnity.—*v.t.* to cause to be silent.—*interj.* be silent!—*n.* sī′lencer, a mechanism for reducing noise in the exhaust pipe of an internal-combustion engine, or for silencing a gun, telegraph wires, &c.—*adj.* sī′lent, noiseless: unaccompanied by sound: refraining from speech, or from mentioning or divulging: taciturn: not pronounced.—*adv.* sī′lently. [L. *silēre,* to be silent.]

silhouette, *sil-ōō-et′, n.* a shadow-outline filled in with black or other colour: an outline showing against a contrasting background: the outline of a clothed figure,—*v.t.* to represent or display in silhouette. [Etienne de *Silhouette*

(1709-67), French minister of finance in 1759, after whom, because of his injudicious parsimony, anything cheap was named.]

silica, *sil′i-ka, n.* a compound of silicon and oxygen, a white or colourless substance, the most abundant solid constituent of our globe, existing both in the crystalline and in the amorphous form, the best examples of the former being rock-crystal, quartz, chalcedony, flint and sandstone, of the latter, opal.—*ns.* sil′icate, a salt of silicic acid; silicōs′is, a disease (due to the inhalation of silica dust) contracted by masons, and by miners who work in the presence of silica.—*adj.* silic′ic (*-is′ik*), pertaining to, or obtained from, silica; silic′ious, -eous (*-ish′ùs*), pertaining to, containing, or resembling, silica.—*v.t.* silic′ify (*-is′-*), to render silicious, to impregnate with, or turn into, silica.—*v.i.* to become silicified.—*ns.* sil′icon (*-kon*), a non-metallic element (symbol Si; atomic no. 14); sil′icone, any organic derivative of silicon (used esp. as heat-resisting plastics, lubricants, polishes, &c.). [L. *sīlex, sīlicis,* flint.]

silicle, *sil′i-kl, n.* (*bot.*) a seed-vessel similar to, but shorter than, a silique.—Also sil′icule, silic′ula.—*ns.* (*bot.*) silique (*si-lēk′*) siliqua (*sil′i-kwa*), a two-valved elongated seed-vessel. [L. *silicula,* dim. of *siliqua,* a pod.]

silicon, silicone, silicosis. See silica.

silk, *silk, n.* a fibre produced by the larvae of silkworm moths, formed by the hardening of liquid emitted from spinning-glands: a similar fibre from another insect or a spider: an imitation (artificial silk) made by forcing a viscous solution of modified cellulose through small holes: a thread, cloth, or garment, or attire, made from silk fibres: the silk gown, or the rank, of a King's or Queen's Counsel.—*adj.* pertaining to, or consisting of, silk.—*adj.* silk′en, made of silk: dressed in silk: resembling silk: soft, delicate.—*n.* silk′worm, the larva of any of certain moths (esp. a species long domesticated) which spins silk to construct a cocoon before changing to the pupa stage.—*adj.* silk′y, like silk in texture, soft, smooth: glossy.—*n.* silk′iness.—take silk, to become a King's or Queen's Counsel. [O.E. *seolc*—L. *sēricum*—Gr. *sērikon,* neut. of adj. *sērikos,* silken, (*cap.*) pertaining to the *Sēres* —*Sēr,* prob. a native of China.]

sill, *sil, n.* the timber, stone, &c., at the foot of an opening, as for a door or window. [O.E. *syl*; O.N. *sylla,* Ger. *schwelle.*]

sillabub, syllabub, *sil′a-bub, n.* a drink or dish made of wine or cider mixed with cream: anything frothy or insubstantial. [Origin obscure.]

silly, *sil′i, adj.* harmless: innocent: simple: witless: feeble-minded: foolish: (*cricket*) qualifying the name of a position on the field, indicates that it is closer to the wicket than when unqualified (e.g. *silly point* is closer-in than *point*).—*n.* a silly person.—*adv.* sill′ily.—*n.* sill′iness.—silly season, a season, usu. late summer, when newspapers fill up with trivial matter for want of more newsworthy material. [Orig. 'blessed', and so 'innocent', 'simple', O.E. *sǣlig, gesǣlig,* happy, prosperous—*sǣl,*· time, due time, happiness; Ger. *selig,* blest, happy.]

silo, *sī′lō, n.* a pit or air-tight chamber for stor-

Neutral vowels in unaccented syllables: *em′pér-ór*; for certain sounds in foreign words see p. ix.

silt, *silt, n.* fine sediment.—*v.t.* and *v.i.* to fill (up) with sediment. [M.E. *sylt*; cf. Dan. and Norw. *sylt*, salt-marsh.]

Silurian, *sil-(y)ōō′ri-án, adj.* of the *Silures*, a British tribe of South Wales.—*n.* the period of the primary geological era between the Cambrian and the Devonian: the system of rocks formed during this period.

silvan, sylvan, *sil′ván, adj.* abounding in woods, woody: concerned with, or suggestive of, woods: inhabiting woods: located in woods.—*n.* **silvicul′ture**, forestry. [Fr.,—L. *silva.*]

silver, *sil′vér, n.* a white metallic element (symbol Ag—for L. *argentum*; atomic no. 47), capable of a high polish: money made of silver: silver ware: anything having the appearance of silver.—*adj.* made of silver: resembling silver: silver-coloured: clear and ringing in tone—*v.t.* to cover with silver: to make silvery.—*v.i.* to become silvery.—*ns.* **sil′ver-bath**, a solution of a silver salt for sensitising photographic plates; **sil′ver-beat′er**, one who beats silver into foil; **sil′ver-fish**, a whitish goldfish, or other white fish: a wingless, silvery insect sometimes found in houses; **sil′ver-foil′, -leaf′**, silver beaten into thin leaves; **sil′ver-fox**, an American fox with white-tipped black fur; **sil′ver-gilt′**, gilded silver.—Also *adj.*—*n.* **sil′vering**, the operation of covering with silver or quicksilver: the metal so used.—*v.t.* **sil′verise**, to coat with silver;—*pr.p.* sil′ver-ising; *pa.p.* sil′verised.—*n.* **sil′verling** (*B.*), a small silver coin.—*adj.* **sil′vern**, made of silver.—*ns.* **sil′ver-pap′er**, tinfoil (q.v.); **sil′ver-plate′**, utensils of silver: electroplate; **sil′ver-side**, the top of a round (q.v.) of beef; **sil′ver-smith**, a smith who works in silver; **sil′ver-stick**, an officer of the royal palace—from his silvered wand. *adj.* **sil′ver-tongued**, eloquent, persuasive.—*n.* **sil′ver-wedd′ing**, (see **wedding**), *adj.* **sil′very**, covered with silver: resembling silver in colour: clear and musical in tone.—*n.* **sil′veriness**. [O.E. *silfer, seolfor*; O.N. *silfr*, Ger. *silber.*]

simian, *sim′i-án, adj.* of the apes: apelike.—Also *n.* [L. *sīmia*, ape.]

similar, *sim′i-lár, adj.* somewhat like, resembling: having resemblance (to): (*geom.*) exactly corresponding in shape, without regard to size.—*n.* **similar′ity**.—*adv.* **sim′ilarly**. [Fr, *similaire*—L. *similis*, like.]

simile, *sim′i-le, n.* an explicit likening of one thing to another resembling it only in a certain characteristic, or certain characteristics (e.g. *in controversy he is like a tiger*)—cf. *metaphor*:—*pl.* **sim′iles**.—*n.* **simil′itude**, the state of being similar or like: semblance, likeness. comparison: (*B.*) a parable. [Fr. *similaire*—L., neut. of *similis*, like.]

simmer, *sim′ér, v.i.* to make a gentle, hissing sound, as heated liquids approaching the boiling point: to be on the point of boiling out: (*fig.*) of emotions, to be ready to break out: of persons, to be in a state of suppressed indignation, &c.—*v.t.* to cause to simmer.—*n.* a gentle heating. [Imit.]

simnel, *sim′n(é)l, n.* a sweet cake for Christmas, Easter, &c.—Also **sim′nel-bread′, -cake′**. [O.Fr. *simenel*—L. *simila*, fine flour.]

simony, *sī′món-i, sim′ón-i, n.* the buying or selling of a benefice.—*n.* **simō′niac**, one guilty of simony.—*adj.* **simoni′acal**, pertaining to, guilty of, or involving simony. [*Simon* Magus (Acts viii. 18, 19).]

simoom, *si-mōōm′, n.* a hot suffocating wind which blows in northern Africa and Arabia and the adjacent countries from the interior deserts. Also **simoon′**. [Ar. *samùm*—*samm*, to poison.]

simper, *sim′pér, v.i.* to smile in a silly, affected manner.—*n.* a silly or affected smile. [Norw. *semper*, smart.]

simple, *sim′pl, adj.* consisting of one thing or element: not complex or compound: (*bot.*) not divided into leaflets: easy: plain, unornate: unpretentious: mere, sheer: ordinary: of humble rank or origin: unlearned or unskilled: unaffected, artless: unsuspecting, credulous: weak in intellect, silly.—*n.* a simple person (also collectively): a medicine of one constituent: hence a medicinal herb.—*adjs.* **sim′ple-heart′ed**, guileless; **sim′ple-mind′ed**, having a mind of less than normal ability: unsuspecting, undesigning.—*ns.* **sim′pleness**; **sim′pleton**, a weak or foolish person: one easily imposed on; **simplic′ity**, the state or quality of being simple: lack of complication: easiness: freedom from excessive adornment, plainness: artlessness: credulity, silliness, folly; **simplifica′tion**, the act, or result, of making simple.—*v.t.* **sim′plify**, to make simple, simpler, less difficult:—*pr.p.* sim′plifying; *pa.t.* and *pa.p.* sim′plified.—*adv.* **sim′ply**, in a simple manner: considered by itself: merely: veritably, absolutely (e.g. *simply magnificent*).—**simple sentence**, sentence with one predicate. [Fr., L. *simplex*—*semel*, once, *plicāre*, to fold.]

simulacrum, *sim-ū-lā′krum, n.* an image, semblance;—*pl.* **simulā′cra** [L.]

simulate, *sim′ū-lāt, v.t.* to feign: to have or assume a false appearance of.—*adj.* **sim′ulant**, simulating.—*n.* **simulā′tion**, the act of simulating or putting on a character or appearance which is not true.—*adj.* **sim′ulative**.—*n.* **sim′ulator**, one who simulates. [L. *simulāre, -ātum*, to make (something) similar to (another thing)—*similis*, like.]

simultaneous, *sim-ul-tā′nyús, adj.* being, or happening, at the same time: (*math.*) of equations, satisfied by the same values of the variables.—*adv.* **simultā′neously.—simultaneous translation**, at a meeting of people of different nationalities, translation of a speaker's words into other languages at the same time as he is speaking. [Formed from L. *simul*, at the same time.]

sin, *sin, n.* moral offence or shortcoming, esp. from the point of view of religion: condition of so offending: an offence generally: (*coll.*) a shame, a pity.—*v.i.* to commit sin.—*v.t.* to commit (with cognate object): to burden with sin (as, *to sin one's soul*):—*pr.p.* sinn′ing; *pa.t.* and *pa.p.* sinned.—*adj.* **sin′ful**, tainted with sin: wicked.—*adv.* **sin′fully**.—*n.* **sin′fulness**.—*adj.* **sin′less**.—*adv.* **sin′lessly**.—*ns.* **sin′lessness**;

sinn'er; sin'-off'ering, sacrifice in expiation of sin.—**mortal,** or **deadly, sin,** such as wilfully violates the divine law and separates the soul from God—the seven deadly sins are *pride, covetousness, lust, anger, gluttony, envy,* and *sloth*—opp. to *venial* (q.v.) *sin*; **original sin,** the innate depravity and corruption of human nature due to the sin of Adam.—**live in sin,** to cohabit in an unmarried state; **sin one's mercies,** to be ungrateful. [O.E. *syn, sinn*; Ger. *sünde*; perh. L. *sons, sontis,* guilty.]

Sinaitic, *sī-na-it'ik, adj.* pertaining to, made, or given at Mount *Sinai.*—Also **Sinā'ic.**

since, *sins, adv.* past, ago.—*prep.* after: from the time of.—*conj.* from the time that: seeing that, because. [M.E. *sins, sithens*—O.E. *sīth-thām,* lit. 'after that'—*sīth,* late, *thām,* dat. of *thæt,* that.]

sincere, *sin-sēr', adj.* (*arch.*) pure, unadulterated, unmixed: unfeigned, genuine, the same in reality as in appearance.—*adv.* **sincēre'ly.**—*n.* **sincer'ity** (-*ser'*-), state or quality of being sincere: honesty of mind: freedom from pretence. [Fr.,—L. *sincērus,* clean.]

sinciput, *sin'si-put, n.* the forepart of the head from the forehead to the vertex. [L.,—*sēmi-,* half, *caput,* the head.]

sine, *sīn, n.* (*math.*) one of the six trigonometrical functions of an angle, the ratio of the perpendicular to the hypotenuse—identical with the cosine of the complementary angle—*abbrev.* **sin** (*sīn*). [L. *sinus,* a bay.]

sine, *sī'ne, prep.* without, as in:—**sine die** (*dī'ē*), without an appointed day, i.e. indefinitely; **sine qua non** (*quā non*), an indispensable condition: a necessity. [L. *sine,* without, *diē,* abl. sing. of *diēs,* day, *quā* (*causā*), fem. abl. sing. of *qui,* which (*causa,* cause, circumstance), *nōn,* not.]

sinecure, *sī'né-kūr* (or *sin'-*), *n.* benefice without the cure or care of souls: an office with salary but without work.—*n.* **si'necurist,** one who holds a sinecure. [L. *sine,* without, *cūra,* care.]

sinew, *sin'ū, n.* that which joins a muscle to a bone, a tendon: muscle, nerve: (*fig.*) strength, or that which it depends on.—*adjs.* **sin'ewed; sin'ewless; sin'ewy, sinewous** (*sin'ū-us*), having sinews, esp. well-developed sinews: consisting of, belonging to, or resembling sinews: strong, vigorous.—*n.* **sin'ewiness.**—**sinews of war,** money. [O.E. *sinu,* gen. *sinwe.*]

sing, *sing, v.i.* to utter melodious sounds in successive musical notes: to emit songlike sounds: to compose poetry: to give a cantabile or lyrical effect: to ring (as the ears).—*v.t.* to utter, perform by voice, musically: to celebrate: to relate in verse:—*pa.t.* **sang** or (now rarely) **sung;** *pa.p.* **sung.**—*ns.* **sing'er;** **sing'ing,** the act or art of singing; **sing'ing-gall'ery,** a gallery occupied by singers; **sing'ing-mas'ter,** a master who teaches singing; **sing'ing-voice,** the voice as used in singing; **sing'song** (see separate article).—**sing another song,** or **tune,** to change one's tone or attitude, esp. to a humbler manner; **sing dumb,** to say nothing; **sing out,** to call out distinctly, to shout; **sing small,** to assume a humble tone. [O.E. *singan*; Ger. *singen.*]

singe, *sinj, v.t.* and *v.i.* to burn on the surface, to scorch:—*pr.p.* **singe'ing;** *pa.t.* and *pa.p.* **singed.**—*n.* a burning of the surface, a slight burn. [O.E. *sen(c)gan.*]

Singhalese. See Sinhalese.

single, *sing'gl, adj.* consisting of one only, individual, unique: uncombined: unmarried: for one person: consisting of one part, undivided: man to man (e.g. *single combat*): having one player only on each side (in a game): for one direction of a journey (*single ticket*): sincere.—*n.* anything single: a gramophone record with one tune, or other short recording on each side.—*v.t.* to select, pick (out).—*n.* **sin'gle-en'try,** a system of book-keeping in which each entry appears only once on one side or other of an account.—*adjs.* **sin'glehand'ed,** by oneself, unassisted; **sing'leheart'ed,** sincere, without duplicity; **sing'lemind'ed,** sincere: bent upon one sole purpose.—*ns.* **sing'leness; sing'lestick,** a fighting stick for one hand: a fight or game with singlesticks; **sing'let,** an undershirt; **sing'leton,** a single card of its suit.—*adv.* **sing'ly,** one by one: alone. [O.Fr.—L. *singulī,* one by one.]

single-tree. See swingle-tree.

singsong, *sing'song, n.* monotonous up-and-down intonation: jingly verse: (*coll.*) a convivial meeting where every one should sing.—*adj.* of the nature of singsong. [sing, song.]

singular, *sing'gū-lár, adj.* (*gram.*) denoting one person or thing: unique: pre-eminent, exceptional: unusual, extraordinary, strange, odd.—*n.* (*logic*) of, or applied to, a single individual or instance (e.g. *singular term, proposition*)—opp. to *universal.*—*n.* **singular'ity,** the state of being singular: peculiarity: anything curious or remarkable.—*adv.* **sing'ularly,** unusually: strangely: so as to express one or the singular number. [Fr.,—L. *singulāris.*]

Sinhalese, *sin'há-lēz, -lēz', Singhalese, Cingalese,* *sing'gá-lēz, -lēz', adj.* of Ceylon (Sri Lanka): of the most numerous of its peoples: of, or in, their language, akin to Pali.—*n.* a native or citizen of Ceylon: a member of the Sinhalese people: their language. [Sans. *Sinhalam,* Ceylon.]

sinicise, Sinicism. See Sino-.

sinister, *sin'is-tér, adj.* left: on the left side (e.g. of the bearer of a shield): unlucky, inauspicious, suggestive of threatened evil.—*adj.* **sin'istral,** turning to the left: (of a shell) coiled contrary to the normal way.—*adv.* **sin'istrally.** [L.]

sink, *singk, v.i.* to become submerged, wholly or partly: to subside: to fall slowly: to pass to a lower level or state: to expire, perish: to slope away, dip: to penetrate (into).—*v.t.* to cause or allow to sink: to lower: to keep out of sight, to suppress: to make by digging or delving: to invest, usually at a loss:—*pa.t.* **sank,** (now rarely) **sunk;** *pa.p.* **sunk, sunk'en** (*obs.* except as *p.adj.*).—*n.* a drain to carry off dirty water: a cesspool: a place into which vice and iniquity flow: a kitchen or scullery trough or basin with a drain: a depression in a surface: an area without surface drainage.—*ns.* **sink'er,** anything that causes sinking, esp. a weight fixed to a fishing-line (**hook, line**

Neutral vowels in unaccented syllables: *em'pér-ór*; for certain sounds in foreign words see p. ix.

680

and sinker, with foolish credulity); **sink'ing; sink'ing-fund,** a fund formed by setting aside income every year to accumulate at interest for the purpose of paying off debt.—**sink unit,** a fitting consisting of sink, draining board, and cupboards, &c. underneath.—**sink in,** to be absorbed: to be understood. [O.E. *sincan* (intrans.); Ger. *sinken*, Du. *zinken.*]

Sinn Fein, *shin fān,* an Irish Society formed in 1905 to promote economic prosperity in Ireland: the revolutionary movement that led to the establishment of the Irish Free State (later Eire, later again Irish Republic) in 1921.—*n.* **Sinn Fein'er,** a supporter of Sinn Fein. [Ir., 'ourselves'.]

Sino- (also **Sin-**), *sin'ō-, sīn'ō,* in composition, Chinese.—*ns.* **sinol'ogy,** knowledge of Chinese history, customs, language, &c.; **sinol'ogist, sin'ologue.**—*v.t.* and *v.i.* **sin'icise** (*sīz*); to make, or become, Chinese.—*n.* **Sin'icism** (*-sizm*), a Chinese custom, idiom, &c. [Gr. *Sīnai,* Chinese (*pl.*).]

sinter, *sin'tėr, n.* a name given to rocks precipitated from hot springs.—*v.i.* to coalesce into a single mass under heat without actually liquefying.—*v.t.* to heat a mixture of powdered metals to the melting-point of the metal in the mixture which has the lowest melting-point; the melted metal then binds together the harder particles. [Ger.]

sinus, *sī'nus, n.* an indentation, a notch: a cavity:—*pl.* **sīn'uses.**—*adjs.* **sinuate** (*sin'ū-āt*), **d** (*-id*), wavy-edged: winding.—*adv.* **sin'uately.**—*ns.* **sinuā'tion,** winding; **sīnusī'tis,** inflammation of any one of the air-containing cavities of the skull which communicate with the nose.—*adj.* **sin'uous,** wavy: winding: bending with suppleness.—*adv.* **sin'uously.**—*n.* **sinuos'ity.** [L. *sinus, -ūs,* a bend, fold, bay.]

sip, *sip, v.t.* and *v.i.* to drink in small quantities.—*pr.p.* **sipp'ing;** *pa.t.* and *pa.p.* **sipped.**—*n.* an act of sipping: the quantity sipped at once. [Cf. **sup;** O.E. *sypian.*]

siphon, *sī'fon, n.* a pipe line full of water, connecting two reservoirs so that flow can take place over an intervening barrier under atmospheric pressure: a tube on this principle for drawing off fluids.—*n.* **sī'phon-(bottle),** a glass bottle for containing and discharging aerated liquid, fitted with a glass tube reaching nearly to the bottom and bent like a siphon at the outlet. [Fr.,—Gr., *sīphōn.*]

sippet, *sip'et, n.* a morsel, esp. of bread with soup. [App. dim. of **sop;** cf. **sip, sup.**]

sir, *sûr, n.* a word of respect (or disapprobation) used in addressing a man: a word of address to a man in a formal letter: (*cap.*) prefixed to the Christian name of a knight or baronet (hence a knight or baronet) and formerly of a priest.—*v.t.* to address as 'sir'. [O.Fr. *sire,* from L. *senior,* an elder.]

sirdar, *sėr-där',* or *sėr', n.* a military head: a commander-in-chief. [Hindustani *sardār.*]

sire, *sīr, n.* (*arch.*) a term of address to a king: a male parent, esp. of a horse: (*pl.*) ancestors.—*v.t.* to beget, used esp. of animals. [**sir.**]

siren, *sī'ren, n.* (*Gr. myth.; cap.*) one of certain fabulous nymphs in south Italy who lured sailors to destruction by their sweet music: a charming temptress: a ship's fog-horn: a fac-

tory hooter: a similar instrument for sounding an air-raid warning: a genus of eel-like, amphibious animals with only one pair of feet. [L. *sīrēn*—Gr. *seirēn,* prob.—*seira,* a cord.]

Sirius, *sir'i-us, n.* the Dogstar. [L.,—Gr. *Seirios.*]

sirloin, *sûr'loin, n.* the loin, or upper part of a loin, of beef. [Fr. *surlonge—sur,* over, and *longe* (O.Fr. *loigne;* cf. **loin**).]

sirname, *sûr'nām, n.* Same as **surname.**

sirocco, *si-rok'ō, n.* a name given in Italy to dust-laden dry (becoming moist farther north) wind from Africa. [It. *s(c)irocco*—Ar. *sharq,* the east.]

sirrah, *sir'a, n.* sir, used in anger or contempt. [**sir.**]

sirup. See **syrup.**

sisal, *sis'-, sis'(á)l, n.* prepared fibre of West Indian species of agave, supplying cordage, &c.: similar fibre from related plants, as *henequen.* [From *Sisal,* a Yucatan port.]

siskin, *sis'kin, n.* a yellowish-green perching bird belonging to the finch family. [Ger. dial. *sischen,* app. Slav.]

sister, *sis'tėr, n.* the name applied to a female by other children of the same parents: a female fellow-member: a member of a sisterhood: a nun: a nurse, esp. one in charge of a hospital ward.—*adj.* closely related, akin.—*ns.* **sis'terhood,** fact or state of being a sister: the relationship of sister: a society, esp. a religious community, of women: a set or class of women; **sis'ter-in-law,** a husband's or wife's sister, or a brother's wife.—*adjs.* **sis'ter-like, sis'terly,** like or befitting a sister, kind, affectionate.—*n.* **sis'terliness.** [O.N. *systir;* O.E. *sweostor;* Du. *zuster,* Ger. *schwester.*]

sit, *sit, v.i.* to rest on the haunches, to be seated: to perch, as birds: to brood: to have a seat, esp. officially: to be in session: to reside: to be located, have station or (as the wind) direction: to pose, be a model: to weigh, bear, press: to hang, fit (e.g. *the coat sits well*).—*v.t.* to seat: to have a seat on, ride: undergo (an examination), or be examined in (a subject):—*pr.p.* **sitt'ing;** *pa.t.* and *pa.p.* **sat.**—*ns.* **sitt'er,** one who poses: a sitting bird: an easy target; a baby-sitter; **sitt'ing,** state of resting on a seat: a seat: a seat in a church pew, &c.; brooding on eggs: a clutch: a continuous meeting of a body of persons: a spell of posing for an artist.—*adj.* seated: brooding: actually in parliament at the time.—*n.* **sitt'ing-room,** an apartment in which one can sit comfortably.—**sit back,** to give up taking active part; **sit down,** to take a seat: to pause, rest: to begin a siege (*adj.* **sit'-down,** that one sits down to); **sit'-down, sit'-down strike,** a strike in which workers down tools but remain in occupation of the plant, workshop, &c.; **sit down under,** to accept, to submit to; **sit in,** to act as a baby-sitter: to be present as a visitor (e.g. at a conference), not being an official member; **sit on,** or **upon,** to hold an official inquiry regarding: (*slang*) to repress, check; **sit out,** to sit apart without participating: to sit to the end of; **sit tight,** to refuse to move; **sit up,** to raise the body from a recumbent to a sitting position: to keep watch during the night (*with*). [O.E. *sittan;* Ger. *sitzen,* L. *sedēre.*]

sit(t)ar, *si-tär′, n.* a Hindu plucked-string instrument with a long neck. [Hind. *sitār.*]

site, *sīt, n.* situation, esp. of a building: ground occupied by, or set apart for, a building, &c.—*v.t.* to locate. [Fr.,—L. *situs—sinĕre, situm,* to set down.]

situated, *sit′ū-āt-id,* (arch. **situate,** *sit′ū-át*), *adj.* set, placed, located: placed with respect to other objects or conditions, circumstanced.—*n.* **situā′tion,** position: temporary state: condition: a set of circumstances, a juncture: office, employment. [Low L. *situātus*—L. *situs,* site.]

sitz-bath, *sits-bäth, n.* a hip-bath: a tub adapted for such. [Ger. *sitz-bad.*]

SI units, *es ī ūnits,* the modern international system of units. [Système International d'Unités.]

Siva, *sē′va, shē′va,* **Shiva,** *shē′va, n.* the destroyer and restorer, one of the triad of Hindu gods (see **Vishnu**). [Sans. *śiva,* happy.]

six, *siks, adj.* and *n.* the cardinal number next above five.—*n.* the figure 6 or vi denoting this.—*adj.* **six′fold,** repeated six times: consisting of six.—*n.* **six′pence,** a coin, orig. of silver, later of cupronickel, worth six old pennies (2½p): its value.—*adj.* **six′penny,** worth sixpence.—*n.* **six′-shoot′er,** a revolver with six chambers.—*adj.* **sixth,** the last of six: being one of six equal parts.—*n.* one of six equal parts: (*mus.*) an interval of five (conventionally six) diatonic degrees (e.g. C to A).—*adv.* **sixth′ly,** in the sixth place.—**be at sixes and sevens,** to be in disorder; **hit for six,** to overcome completely: to take by surprise. [O.E. *siex*; Ger. *sechs,* Gael. *sé*; also L. *sex,* Gr. *hex,* Sans. *ṣaṣ.*]

sixteen, *six′tēn* (when used absolutely, *sixtēn′*), *adj.* and *n.* six and ten.—*adj.* **six′teenth,** the last of sixteen: being one of sixteen equal parts.—Also *n.* [O.E. *sixtēne, sixtīene.*]

sixty, *siks′ti, adj.* and *n.* six times ten.—*adj.* **six′tieth,** the last of sixty: being one of sixty equal parts.—Also *n.*—**sixty-four dollar question** (*fig.*), from a U.S. quiz game, a hard question to answer, the supreme or crucial question. [O.E. *sixtig.*]

sizar, *sī′zár, n.* at Cambridge and Dublin, a student receiving an allowance from his college towards his expenses.—*n.* **sī′zarship.** [*size,* orig. a fixed quantity.]

size, *sīz, n.* magnitude: (*obs.*) a portion of food and drink: an allotted portion: one, or belonging to one, of a series of classes according to standard dimensions.—*v.t.* to arrange according to size: to measure.—*adjs.* **sī′zable, size′able,** of considerable size; **sized,** having a size of specified kind (e.g. *middle-sized*).— **size up,** (*fig.*) to take mental measure of, estimate the worth of. [Contr. of **assize** (q.v.).]

size, *sīz,* **sizing,** *sī′zing, ns.* weak glue, or gluey material.—*v.t.* to cover with size. [Perh. same as **size** (1).]

sizzle, *siz′l, v.i.* to make a hissing sound of frying.—*v.t.* and *v.i.* to fry, scorch, sear.—*n.* a hissing sound: extreme heat. [Imit.]

sjambok, *sham′bok, n.* a strip of hippopotamus or other hide, used as a whip.—Also **jambok** (*jam′bok*). [S. African.]

skald, *n.* See **scald** (2).

skate, *skāt, n.* a sole or sandal mounted on a blade or on rollers for moving over ice, &c.—*v.i.* to move on skates.—*ns.* **skā′ter; skā′ting.**—**skate over** (*fig.*), to hurry over lightly. [Du. *schaats*; Low Ger. *schake,* shank, bone (skates orig. being made of bones).]

skate, *skāt, n.* any one of several species of large flat fish of the ray order. [O.N. *skata.*]

skathe. Same as **scathe.**

skean-dhu, *skēn′dōō, n.* a dirk, dagger, stuck in the stocking.—Also **skene-dhu.** [Gael. *sgian,* knife, *dhu,* black.]

skein, *skān, n.* a loosely tied coil or standard length of thread or yarn: anything suggesting such a coil: a flight of geese. [O.Fr. *escagne.*]

skeleton, *skel′e-tón, n.* the bony framework of an animal: the framework or outline of anything: a very lean and emaciated person or animal.—*adj.* (of a set of persons, e.g. a staff) reduced to lowest strength.—**skeleton in the cupboard, closet, house,** &c., a closely kept secret, the disclosure of which would distress the family concerned; **skeleton-key,** a key made in outline for opening varied locks—a form of master key. [Gr. *skeleton* (*sōma*), a dried (body)—*skellein,* to dry.]

skep, *skep, n.* a basket: a beehive, esp. one made of straw. [O.N. *skeppa.*]

skeptic. See **sceptic.**

skerry, *sker′i, n.* a reef of rock. [O.N. *sker.*]

sketch, *skech, n.* a drawing, slight, rough, or without detail, esp. as a study towards a more finished work: an outline or short account: a short and slightly constructed play, dramatic scene, musical entertainment, &c.: a short descriptive essay.—*v.t.* to make a rough draft of: to draw the outline of: to give the principal points of.—*v.i.* to practise sketching.—*adj.* **sketch′y,** like a sketch: incomplete, slight: imperfect, inadequate.—*adv.* **sketch′ily.**—*n.* **sketch′iness.** [Du. *schets,* prob.—It. *schizzo*— L. *schedium,* an extempore—Gr. *schedios,* off-hand.]

skew, *skū, adj.* oblique.—*adv.* awry.—*v.t.* and *v.i.* to set, go, or look, obliquely.—*adj.* **skewed,** distorted. [Prob. O. Norman Fr. *eskiu(w)er*— O.Fr. *eschiver, eschever.* See **eschew.**]

skewbald, *skū′bóld, adj.* marked in white and another colour (not black).—*n.* a skewbald horse. [Origin obscure.]

skewer, *skū′ér, n.* a long pin of wood or metal, esp. for keeping meat together while roasting.—*v.t.* to fasten with a skewer: to transfix or pierce. [**shiver** (1).]

ski, *skē, shē, n.* a long narrow runner orig. of wood, now also of metal, &c., fastened to the foot to enable the wearer to slide across snow, &c.:—*pl.* **ski,** or **skis.**—*v.i.* to travel on skis:—*pa.t.* skied, ski′d.—*ns.* **ski′er; ski′ing.**—*ns.* **ski′-lift, -tow,** devices for taking skiers uphill. [Norw.]

skid, *skid, n.* a support on which something rests, is brought to the desired level, or slides: a ship's wooden fender: a shoe or other device to check a wheel on a down-slope: an aeroplane runner: a side-slip.—*v.t.* to check with a skid: to cause to slip or slide sideways.—*v.i.* to slide without revolving: to slip (esp. sideways).—**skid row,** a street of squalid, dilapidated buildings where chronic drunks and other derelicts live. [Of Scand. origin.]

Neutral vowels in unaccented syllables: *em′pér-ór*; for certain sounds in foreign words see p. ix.

skiff, *skif*, *n.* a small light boat. [Akin to **ship**.]
skiffle, *skif'l*, *n.* strongly accented jazz type of folk-music played by guitars, drums, wash-boards, &c., popular about 1957.
skill, *skil*, *n.* expertness: (*arch.*) expert knowledge: a craft accomplishment (e.g. *manual skills*): a complex movement or action carried out with facility as a result of practice.—*adj.* **skil'ful.**—*adv.* **skil'fully.**—*n.* **skil'fulness.**—*adj.* **skilled**, expert. [O.N. *skil*, a distinction, *skilja*, to separate.]
skillet, *skil'et*, *n.* a small metal vessel with a long handle, used in cooking, &c. [Origin doubtful.]
skim, *skim*, *v.t.* to remove floating matter from the surface of: to take off by skimming: to glide lightly over: to read superficially, skipping portions.—*v.i.* to pass over lightly: to glide along close above the surface:—*pr.p.* skimm'ing; *pa.t.* and *pa.p.* skimmed.—*ns.* **skimm'er**, a utensil for skimming milk; **skim'-milk**, milk from which the cream has been skimmed. [App. related to **scum**.]
skimp, *skimp*, *v.t.* to give (a person) scanty measure (in): to stint.—*v.i.* to be parsimonious.—*adj.* scanty, spare.—*adj.* **skim'py**.—*adv.* **skim'pily**. [Perh. **scamp** combined with **scrimp**.]
skin, *skin*, *n.* the natural outer covering of an animal: a hide: an integument: a thin outer layer or covering: a vessel for containing wine or water made of an animal's skin.—*v.t.* to cover with a skin: to strip the skin from: (*fig.—slang*) to fleece.—*v.i.* to become covered with skin: (*slang*) to slip through or away: —*pr.p.* skinn'ing; *pa.t.* and *pa.p.* skinned. —*adj.* **skin'-deep**, no deeper than the skin: superficial.—*ns.* **skin'-diving**, orig., diving naked, as a pearl diver: diving with simple equipment, not connected with a boat at the surface and not wearing the traditional diver's helmet and suit; **skin'flint**, one who meanly seeks gain by every possible method: a very niggardly person; **skin'head**, any member of certain gangs of young people (1969) wearing simple, severe, clothes and having closely cropped hair; **skinn'er**.—*adj.* **skinn'y**, of or like skin: emaciated.—*n.* **skinn'iness.**—*adj.* **skin'-tight**, fitting close to the skin.—**by**, or **with, the skin of one's teeth**, very narrowly; **get under one's skin**, to annoy one greatly: to interest one deeply; **save one's skin**, to escape without injury, esp. by cowardly means. [O.E. *scinn*; O.N. *skinn*, skin, Ger. *schinden*, to flay.]
skip, *skip*, *v.i.* to spring or hop: to bound lightly and joyfully: to make jumps over a whirling rope: to omit portions.—*v.t.* to leap over: to omit:—*pr.p.* skip'ping; *pa.t., pa.p.* skipped. —*n.* an act of skipping.—*n.* **skipp'ing rope**, a rope used in skipping. [M.E. *skippen*; perh. of Scand. origin.]
skipper, *skip'ér*, *n.* the captain of a merchantship or of an aircraft, &c.: the captain of a team. [Du. *schipper*; Dan. *skipper*.]
skirmish, *skûr'mish*, *n.* an irregular fight between small parties.—*v.i.* to fight slightly or irregularly.—*n.* **skir'misher**. [O.Fr. *escarmouche*.]
skirt, *skûrt*, *n.* a garment, or part of a garment, generally a woman's, that hangs from the waist: the lower part of a gown, coat, or other garment: a midriff of an animal: a rim, border, margin.—*v.t.* to border: to pass along the edge of.—*v.i.* to be (on the border): to move (along the border).—*ns.* **skir'ting**, material for skirts: skirting board; **skir'ting board**, the narrow board next the floor round the walls of a room.—**divided skirt**, trousers made to look like a skirt. [O.N. *skyrta*, a shirt, kirtle; cf. **shirt**.]
skit, *skit*, *n.* a piece of banter or burlesque, esp. in dramatic or literary form. [Perh. related to O.N. *skjōta*, to shoot.]
skittish, *skit'ish*, *adj.* (of a horse) shy, nervous, easily frightened: frivolous, frisky: lively: coquettish, coy: wanton.—*adv.* **skitt'ishly.**—*n.* **skitt'ishness**. [Dial. *skit*, to caper.]
skittle, *skit'l*, *n.* a pin, or wooden object set on end, for the game of **skittles**, a wooden ball being used to knock the pins down.—*v.t.* **skitt'le**, to knock down.
skrimshank, **scrimshank**, *skrim'shangk*, *v.i.* (*mil. slang*) to evade work or duty.
skua, *skū'a*, *n.* any one of several species of rapacious gulls which rob weaker birds of their prey, esp. the Great Skua, breeding in the Shetlands. [Norw.]
skulk, *skulk*, *v.i.* to sneak out of the way: to lurk: to malinger.—*n.* **skulk'er**. [Scand., as in Dan. *skulke*, to sneak.]
skull, *skul*, *n.* the bony case that encloses the brain: the head.—*n.* **skull'cap**, a cap that fits closely to the head.—**skull and crossbones**, a symbolic emblem of death and decay. [M.E. *scolle*; perh. Scand.]
skunk, *skungk*, *n.* a genus of small North American carnivorous quadrupeds of the same family as otters and weasels, defending themselves by emitting an offensive fluid: a low fellow. [North Amer. Indian *segonku*.]
sky, *skī* (often used in the *pl.*, **skies**), *n.* the apparent canopy over our heads: the heavens: the weather: (*fig.*) the prospect.—*v.t.* to raise aloft: to hit high into the air: to hang (pictures) above the line of sight.—*adj.* **sky'blue**, blue like the sky (also *n.*).—*ns.* **sky'-diving**, **-jumping**, jumping by parachute as a sport.— *adjs.* **sky'ey**, like the sky: ethereal; **sky'-high**, very high.—*n.* **sky'lark**, the common lark, which mounts high towards the sky and sings on the wing.—*v.i.* to frolic boisterously.—*ns.* **sky'larking**, running about the rigging of a ship in sport: frolicking; **sky'light**, a window in a roof or ceiling; **sky'line**, the horizon; **sky'-rock'et**, a rocket that ascends high towards the sky and flares as it flies; **sky'sail**, the sail above the royal; **sky'scraper**, a lofty building of many storeys.—*adv.* **sky'ward**, toward the sky. [O.N. *skȳ*, a cloud.]
Skye (terrier), *skī* (*ter'i-ér*), *n.* a small long-haired Scotch terrier. [*Skye* in the Inner Hebrides.]
slab, *slab*, *n.* a plane-sided plate: a flat piece of stone, &c., as for a table top: a large thick slice of cake: an outside piece sawed from a log. [M.E. Origin obscure.]
slabber, *slab'ér*, *v.i.* to slaver, to drivel.—*v.t.* to beslobber: to gobble sloppily and grossly.—*n.* **slabb'erer**. [Allied to Low Ger. and Du. *slabberen*.]
slack, *slak*, *adj.* loose, not firmly extended or

drawn out: not holding fast: not strict: not eager or diligent: remiss, negligent: not busy (as *the slack season*): not brisk or active: (of a vowel) pronounced with the muscles of the tongue relaxed (also *open, wide*)—opp. to *tense.—adv.* **slackly.**—*n.* the slack part of a rope, belt, &c.: a time, occasion, or place, of relaxed movement or activity: (in *pl.*) trousers.—*vs.i.* **slack, slack′en,** to become loose or less tight: to abate: to become slower: to fail or flag: to idle, shirk work.—*vs.t.* to make less tight, to loosen: to relax: to abate: (*B.*) to delay.—*n.* **slack′er,** an idler, shirker.—*adv.* **slack′ly.**—*n.* **slack′ness.**—*n.* and *adj.* **slack′ening.**—*n.* **slack′-wa′ter,** the turn of the tide: a stretch of still water, slow-moving water. [O.E. *sleac*; Swed. *slak,* O.N. *slakr.*]

slack, *slak, n.* coal dross. [Cf. Ger. *schlacke,* dross.]

slag, *slag, n.* vitrified cinders from smelting-works, &c.: scoriae from a volcano.—*adj.* **slagg′y,** pertaining to, or like slag. [Cf. Ger. *schlacke,* dross.]

slain, *slān, pa.p.* of **slay.**

slake, *slāk, v.t.* to quench, satisfy (e.g. thirst): to extinguish (a fire): to hydrate (lime).—*v.i.* to become slaked: to die down. [O.E. *sleacian,* to grow slack—*slæc, sleac,* slack.]

slalom, *slä′lom, n.* a race in which tactical skill is required, esp. a downhill or zig-zag ski-run among posts or trees: an obstacle race in canoes. [Norw.]

slam, *slam, v.t.* or *v.i.* to shut with violence and noise, to bang: to put forcibly, noisily, hurriedly (down, on, against, &c.): to censure, criticise:—*prp.* slamm′ing; *pa.t.* and *pa.p.* slammed.—*n.* the act or sound of slamming.—*adv.* with a slam. [Cf. Norw. *slemma.*]

slam, *slam, n.* the winning of every trick (in bridge called *grand slam,* all but one being known as *little slam*). [Perh. same as preceding word.]

slander, *slän′dèr, n.* a false or malicious report: injurious defamation by spoken words.—*v.t.* to defame, to calumniate.—*n.* **slan′derer.**—*adj.* **slan′derous,** given to, or containing, slander: calumnious.—*adv.* **slan′derously.**—*n.* **slan′derousness.** [O.Fr. *esclandre*—L. *scandalum*—Gr. *skandalon.* See **scandal.**]

slang, *slang, n.* cant, jargon peculiar to a class, as thieves, gypsies, &c.: words or phrases common in colloquial speech (e.g. new coinages, abbreviations, fantastic or violent metaphors) which are not accepted for dignified use—though they may be later (see **donkey**) —and which are usually ephemeral.—*adj.* pertaining to slang.—*v.t.* (*coll.*) to revile.—*adj.* **slang′y.**—*n.* **slang′iness.**—**slanging match,** a bitter verbal quarrel, usu. involving an exchange of insults. [Ety. uncertain.]

slant, *slänt, v.t.* and *v.i.* to slope: to turn, strike, fall, obliquely.—*v.t.* to incline in a certain direction (esp. with a view to one's own advantage) when presenting facts.—*n.* a slope: obliquity: a sloping surface, line, ray, or movement: a divergence from a direct line: a point of view, way of looking at a thing (with *on*).—*adj.* sloping, oblique, inclined from a direct line.—*adj.* **slanted,** sloping: biassed, prejudiced.—*advs.* **slant′ly, slant′wise.** [M.E.

slent; cf. Norw. *slenta,* Swed. *slinta,* to slope, slip.]

slap, *slap, n.* a blow with the hand or anything flat: (*fig.*) a snub.—*v.t.* to give a slap to:—*prp.* slapp′ing; *pa.t.* and *pa.p.* slapped.—*adv.* with a slap: suddenly, violently.—*adv.* **slap′-dash,** in a bold, careless way.—*adj.* off-hand, rash.—*n.* **slap′stick,** a harlequin's double lath that makes a noise like a slap: (in full, **slap′stick comedy**) knock-about low comedy or farce. [Allied to Low Ger. *slapp,* Ger. *schlappe*; imit.]

slash, *slash, v.t.* to cut by striking with violence and at random: to make long cuts in: to slit so as to show lining or material underneath: (*fig.*) to criticise very harshly: to reduce drastically or suddenly.—*v.i.* to strike violently and at random with an edged instrument: to strike right and left.—*n.* a long cut: a cut at random: a cut in cloth to show colours underneath. [Perh. O.Fr. *eslachier,* to break.]

slat, *slat, n.* a thin strip of wood, &c.—*adj.* **slatt′ed,** having slats. [O.Fr. *esclat.*]

slate, *slāt, n.* an argillaceous rock, easily split, usu. dull blue, grey, purple or green: a slab of this material (or a substitute) for roofing or for writing on: slate-colour.—*adj.* of slate: slate-coloured.—*v.t.* to cover with slate.—*adj.* **slate′-coloured,** dull bluish-grey approaching black.—*ns.* **slate′-pen′cil,** a stick of soft slate, compressed slate-powder, or pyrophyllite (a hydrous aluminium silicate), for writing on slate; **slā′ter,** one who covers roofs with slates: (*dial.*) a wood-louse; **slā′ting,** the act of covering with slates: a covering of slates: materials for slating.—*adj.* **slā′ty,** of, or like, slate. [O.Fr. *esclate*; cf. **slat.**]

slate, *slāt, v.t.* to criticise, or reprimand, severely.—*n.* **slā′ting,** a severe criticism. [From the O.N. word corresponding to O.E. *slǣtan,* to bait.]

slattern, *slat′ėrn, n.* a slut, a dirty woman.—*adj.* **slatt′ernly,** sluttish.—*n.* **slatt′ernliness.** [App. obs. *slat,* to strike, splash.]

slaughter, *slö′tėr, n.* killing of animals, esp. for food: killing of great numbers, carnage, butchery: wanton or inexcusable killing, esp. of the helpless.—*v.t.* to slay in large numbers or ruthlessly.—*ns.* **slaugh′terer; slaugh′terhouse,** a place where beasts are killed for the market; **slaugh′terman,** a man employed in killing or butchering animals.—*adj.* **slaugh′terous,** given to slaughter, destructive, murderous. [O.N. *slātr,* butchers' meat, whence *slātra,* to slaughter cattle.]

Slav, *släv, n.* one whose language is Slavonic, i.e. belongs to the division of the Indo-Germanic tongues that includes Russian, Polish, Czech, Serbian, Bulgarian, &c.—*adjs.* **Slav, Slavic, Slavonic** (-*von′ik*), of the group of languages indicated above, or the peoples speaking them. [Mediaeval L. *Sclavus*—Late Gr. *Sklabos,* from the stem of the Slavonic words *slovo,* word, *sloviti,* to speak.]

slave, *släv, n.* a person held as property: one who is submissive under domination: one who is submissively devoted: one whose will has lost power of resistance (to): one who works like a slave, a drudge: a mechanism controlled by another mechanism.—*v.i.* to work like a slave, to drudge.—*ns.* **slave′-dri′ver,** one who

Neutral vowels in unaccented syllables: *em′pér-ór*; for certain sounds in foreign words see p. ix.

superintends slaves at their work: a cruel taskmaster; **slave'-hold'er**, an owner of slaves; **slā'ver**, a slave-trader: a slave-ship; **slā'very**, the state of being a slave: the institution of ownership of slaves: drudgery; **slave'-ship**, a ship used for transporting slaves; **slave'-trade**, the trade of buying and selling slaves.—*adj.* **slā'vish**, of or belonging to slaves: befitting a slave, servile, abject: servilely following guidance or conforming to pattern or rule (e.g. *slavish adherence to the text*): laborious.—*adv.* **slā'vishly.**—*n.* **slā'vishness.** [O.Fr. *esclave*, orig. a Slav, the slaves of the Germanic races being usually captive Slavs.]

slaver, *slav'ér*, or *slāv'ér*, *n.* saliva running from the mouth.—*v.i.* to let the saliva run out of the mouth: to drivel: to fawn.—*v.t.* to smear with saliva.—*n.* **slav'erer.** [Allied to **slabber.**]

slay, *slā*, *v.t.* (*obs.*) to strike: to kill:—*pa.t.* slew (*slōō*); *pa.p.* slain (*slān*).—*n.* **slay'er.** [O.E. *slēn*; O.N. *slā*, Ger. *schlagen*, to strike.]

sled, *sled*, **sledge**, *slej*, *n.* a vehicle with runners made for sliding upon snow: a framework without wheels for dragging goods along the ground.—*v.t.* and *v.i.* to convey, or to travel, in a sled. [Middle Du. *sleedse.*]

sledge, *slej*, *n.* a large heavy hammer.—Also **sledge' hammer.** [O.E. *slecg*—*slēan*, to strike, slay.]

sleek, *slēk*, *adj.* smooth, glossy, and soft: having an oily plastered-down look: insinuating, plausible.—*v.t.* to make sleek.—*adv.* **sleek'ly.** —*n.* **sleek'ness.** [A later form of **slick.**]

sleep, *slēp*, *v.i.* to take rest by relaxation of consciousness: to slumber: to be motionless, inactive, or dormant: to be dead: to rest in the grave: (of limbs) to be numb: (of a top) to spin steadily, appearing to stand still.—Also *v.t.* (with cognate object):—*pa.t.* and *pa.p.* slept.—*n.* the state of being asleep: a spell of sleeping: dormancy.—*n.* **sleep'er**, one who sleeps: a horizontal beam supporting and spreading a weight: a support for railway lines: a sleeping car: a berth in a sleeping-car.—*ns.* **sleep'ing-bag**, a bag for sleeping in, used by travellers, campers, &c.; **sleep'ing-car**, a railway-carriage with berths for sleeping in; **sleep'ing-draught, -pill**, a drink, pill to induce sleep; **sleep'ing-part'ner**, a partner who has money invested in a business but takes no share in its management; **sleep'ing-sick'ness**, a deadly disease of tropical Africa, caused by a parasite conveyed to the blood by the bite of several species of tsetse fly, producing great drowsiness; **sleep'y-sickness**, an epidemic disease, inflammation of the brain, causing an abnormal tendency to sleep.—*adj.* **sleep'less**, without sleep: unable to sleep.—*adv.* **sleep'lessly.**—*ns.* **sleep'lessness; sleep'-walk'er**, one who walks in sleep, a somnambulist; **sleep'-walk'ing.** *adj.* **sleep'y**, inclined to sleep: drowsy: inducing, or suggesting, sleep.—*adv.* **sleep'ily.**—*n.* **sleep'iness.**—*n.* **sleep'yhead**, a lazy person.—**on sleep** (*B.*), asleep; **sleep off**, to recover from by sleeping; **sleep on**, to consider overnight; **sleep with**, to have sexual relations with. [O.E. *slǽpan*; Ger. *schlafen*.]

sleet, *slēt*, *n.* rain mingled with snow or hail.—*v.i.* to hail or snow with rain mingled.—*adj.*

sleet'y.—*n.* **sleet'iness.** [M.E.; prob. conn. with Ger. *schlosse*, hail.]

sleeve, *slēv*, *n.* the part of a garment which covers the arm: (*mach.*) a contrivance acting as a covering like a sleeve: a thin covering, container for a gramophone record.—*v.t.* to furnish with sleeves—*adj.* **sleeve'less**, without sleeves.—*n.* **sleeve'-link**, two buttons, &c., joined by a link for fastening a shirt-cuff.—**have up one's sleeve**, to keep hidden for use in an emergency; **laugh in, up, one's sleeve**, to laugh secretly. [O.E. (Anglian) *slēfe*, a sleeve.]

sleigh, *slā*, *n.* (esp. in U.S. and Canada) a sledge.—*n.* **sleigh'ing**, the act of riding in a sleigh. [Du. *slee.*]

sleight, *slīt*, *n.* cunning, dexterity: an artful trick.—*n.* **sleight-of-hand'**, legerdemain: expert manipulation: skill in tricks depending on such. [O.N. *slægth*, cunning, *slægr*, sly.]

slender, *slen'dér*, *adj.* thin or narrow: slim: slight.—*adv.* **slen'derly.**—*n.* **slen'derness.**

slept, *slept*, *pa.t.* and *pa.p.* of **sleep.**

sleuth, *slōōth*, *n.* a track or trail: a bloodhound: (*coll.*) a detective.—*n.* **sleuth'-hound**, a bloodhound: a detective. [O.N. *slōth*, track.]

slew, *slōō*, *pa.t.* of **slay.**

slew, *slōō*, *v.t.*, *v.i.* to turn, swing, round.

slice, *slīs*, *n.* a thin broad piece: a flat or broad-bladed instrument of various kinds, esp. a broad knife for serving fish: a slash: (*golf*) a sliced stroke: (*coll.*) a share: a representative section.—*v.t.* to cut into slices: to cut a slice from: to cut as a slice: (*golf*) to strike or play so as to impart a right-hand spin sending the ball to the right (left-hand spin and left in left-handed play).—Also *v.t.*—*n.* **slic'er.**—*n.* and *adj.* **slic'ing.** [O.Fr. *esclice*—O.H.G. *slīzan*, to split.]

slick, *slik*, *adj.* sleek, smooth, trim: smooth-tongued, glib: adroit, dexterous: smoothly skilful.—*n.* a smooth surface: a film of spilt oil.—*adv.* smoothly: glibly: deftly: quickly: exactly.—*v.t.* to polish, make glossy: to tidy up.—*ns.* **slick'er**, a smoothing tool: a shifty person: a sophisticated city-dweller (**city-slicker**); **slick'ing.**—*adv.* **slick'ly.**—*n.* **slick'ness.** [O.E. *slīcian* (in composition), to smooth.]

slid, slidden. See **slide.**

slide, *slīd*, *v.i.* to slip or glide: to pass along smoothly: to glide in a standing position (without skates or snow-shoes) over ice or other slippery surface: (*fig.*) to pass quietly, imperceptibly, gradually: to lapse: to take its own course.—*v.t.* to push smoothly along: to slip:—*pa.t.* slid; *pa.p.* slid, (*rare*) slidd'en.—*n.* a polished slippery track (on ice): a chute: a bed, groove, rail, &c., on which a thing slides: a sliding part, e.g. of a trombone: a sliding clasp: a slip for mounting objects for the microscope: a picture for projection on a screen: a landslip: a gliding from one note to another.—*n.* **slī'der**, one who, or that which, slides: the part of an instrument or machine that slides: (*coll.*) ice-cream between wafers.—*n.* and *adj.* **slīd'ing.**—*ns.* **slīde'-, slī'ding-rule**, mechanical device for multiplying, dividing, &c., consisting of two logarithmic graduated rules sliding one against the other; **slide-valve**, a valve in which openings are covered and uncovered by a sliding part; **slī′ding-scale**, a scale of duties, wages, or charges, varying according to variation in something else: a slide-rule.—**let slide**, to take no action over. [O.E. *slīdan*, to slide.]

slight, *slīt*, *adj.* frail, flimsy—lacking solidity, massiveness, weight: slim: trifling, insignificant.—*v.t.* to ignore or overlook disrespectfully.—*n.* discourteous disregard: an affront by showing neglect or want of respect.—*adv.* **slight′ly**, slenderly, flimsily: in a small degree.—*n.* **slight′ness**, slenderness or frailness: inadequacy, lack of thoroughness: small degree (of).—*adv.* **slight′ingly**, in a neglectful, discourteous, or disparaging, manner. [Cf. O.E. *eorthslihtes*, close to the ground.]

slily, *slī′li*, *adv.* See under **sly**.

slim, *slim*, *adj.* (*comp.* **slimm′er**, *superl.* **slimm′est**) very thin, slender, slight: crafty.—*v.t.* to make slim.—*v.i.* to practise rules for making the figure more slender.—*ns.* **slim′ness; slimm′ing**. [Low Ger. *slim*, crafty; Ger. *schlimm*, bad; reintroduced from South African Du.]

slime, *slīm*, *n.* ooze, very fine, thin, slippery, or gluey mud: bitumen: any viscous organic secretion, as mucus: moral filth: obsequiousness.—*adj.* **slīm′y**, viscous: covered with slime: disgusting: meanly ingratiating.—*n.* **slim′iness**. [O.E. *slīm*; Ger. *schleim*.]

sliness, *slī′nes*, *n.* Same as **slyness**.

sling, *sling*, *n.* a strap or pocket with a string attached to each end, for hurling a stone—a catapult, a ballista: a loop for hoisting, lowering, or carrying, a weight: a hanging support for an injured arm or foot.—*v.t.* to throw with a sling: to hang so as to swing: to move or swing by means of a rope: (*coll.*) to hurl, toss:—*pa.t.* and *pa.p.* slung.—*adj.* **slingback(ed)**, of a shoe, having the back absent except for a strap representing the top edge.—*n.* **sling′er.—sling ink**, to write for the press. [Prob. from several sources: cf. O.N. *slyngva*, to fling, O.E. *slingan*, to wind, twist.]

sling, *sling*, *n.* an American drink, spirits and water sweetened and flavoured. [Perh. **sling** (1) in sense of toss off; perh. Ger. *schlingen*, to swallow.]

slink, *slingk*, *v.i.* to move stealthily, to sneak:—*pa.t.* and *pa.p.* slunk.—*adj.* **slink′y**, slinking: sinuous: close-fitting. [O.E. *slincan*, to creep; Low Ger. *slinken*, Ger. *schleichen*.]

slip, *slip*, *v.i.* to slide or glide along: to move out of position: to lose foothold: to excape: to slink: to move unobserved: to make a slight mistake: to lapse morally: to lose one's grip on things, one's control of the situation.—*v.t.* to cause to slide: to convey quietly or secretly: to let pass: to let slip: to let loose: to escape from, to elude:—*pr.p.* slipp′ing; *pa.t.* and *pa.p.* slipped.—*n.* act of slipping: a mistake from inadvertence: a slight error or transgression: an escape: a cutting from a plant, a young shoot: a slim young person: a garment easily slipped on, esp. one worn under a dress: a pillow or bolster cover: a strip, a narrow piece of anything: a leash: an inclined plane, sloping down to the water: (*print.*—also **slip′-proof**) a galley-proof (q.v.): (*cricket*) a fielder, or (often *pl.*) position on the offside, somewhat behind the batsman.—*ns.* **slip-coach**, a

carriage detachable from the rear of a train in motion; **slip′-knot**, a knot that slips along rope; **slipp′er**, a loose shoe easily slipped on: a skid for a wheel.—*adjs.* **slipp′ered**, wearing slippers; **slipp′ery, slipp′y**, so smooth or slimy as to allow, or cause, slipping: elusive, evasive: unstable, uncertain.—*ns.* **slipp′eriness, slipp′iness; slip′-road**, a local bypass.—*adj.* **slip′shod**, shod with slippers, or shoes, down at the heel: (*fig.*) slovenly, careless, negligent (of method of speaking, writing, working, or of person).—*ns.* **slip′stream**, the stream of air driven back by an aircraft propeller; **slip′-up**, (*coll.*) an error or failure; **slip′way**, a slope in a dock or shipyard.—**slip off**, to take off, or (*v.t.* and *v.i.*) to move away, noiselessly or hastily.—**give the slip to**, to escape stealthily from; **let slip**, to reveal by accident. [Perh. Low Ger. or Du.; O.E. has *slipor*, slippery.]

slip, *slip*, *v.t.* to take cuttings from (a plant): (*her.*) to tear obliquely. [M.E. *slippen*.]

slit, *slit*, *v.t.* to cut lengthwise: to cut into strips.—*v.i.* to tear lengthwise:—*pr.p.* slitt′ing; *pa.t.* and *pa.p.* slit.—*n.* a long cut: a narrow opening.—**slit trench**, a deep narrow trench. [O.E. *slītan*; Ger. *schlitzen*.]

slither, *sli′ᴛʜér*, *v.i.* to slide, esp. interruptedly, as on mud or scree: to slip about: to crawl, wriggle. [O.E. *slidderian*, to slide.]

sliver, *sliv′ér*, *v.t.* and *v.i.* to split, to tear off lengthwise.—*n.* a long thin piece cut or rent off. [O.E. (*tō-*)*slīfan*, to cleave.]

slobber, *slob′ér*, same as **slabber**.—*adj.* **slobb′ery**, moist, wet.

sloe, *slō*, *n.* a small sour plum, the fruit of the blackthorn: the blackthorn. [O.E. *slā*; Du. *slee*.]

slog, *slog*, *v.i.* to hit, or work, hard: to walk, or work, doggedly.—*v.t.* to hit hard: to obtain by hard hitting: to make (one's way) laboriously.—*n.* a hard blow (usu. without regard to direction): a strenuous spell of work.—*n.* **slog′er**, a hard hitter or worker.

slogan, *slō′gán*, *n.* a war-cry among the ancient Highlanders of Scotland: a party catchword: an advertising catch-phrase. [Gael. *sluagh*, army, *gairm*, cry.]

sloop, *slōōp*, *n.* a light boat: a one-masted vessel, differing little from a cutter. [Du. *sloep.*]

slop, *slop*, *n.* slush: spilled liquid: a puddle: (in *pl.*) liquid refuse: (in *pl.*) weak or insipid liquor or semi-liquid food: gush, wishy-washy sentiment.—*v.t.* and *v.i.* to spill: to splash with slops.—*v.t.* to wash away:—*v.i.* to walk in slush:—*pr.p.* slopp′ing; *pa.p.* slopped.—*adj.* **slopp′y**, wet: muddy: wishy-washy: slipshod (of work or language): sentimental, maudlin.—*n.* **slopp′iness**. [O.E. (*cu-*)*sloppe*, (cow-)droppings.]

slop, *slop*, *n.* a loose garment: (in *pl.*) wide baggy trousers or breeches: (in *pl.*) ready-made clothing. [Cf. O.E. *oferslop*, loose outer garment.]

slope, *slōp*, *n.* an incline: an inclined surface: an inclined position: an inclination, upward or downward slant.—*v.t.* to form with a slope, or put in a sloping position.—*v.i.* to have a slope or slant: (*slang*) to decamp.—**at the slope**, (of a rifle) on the shoulder with the barrel sloping back and up; **slope arms**, place or hold a rifle in this position. [From **aslope**.]

Neutral vowels in unaccented syllables: *em′pér-ȯr*; for certain sounds in foreign words see p. ix.

slot, *slot, n.* a bar or bolt: a cross piece that holds other parts together. [Low Ger. or Du. *slot,* a lock.]

slot, *slot, n.* a long narrow depression or opening to receive a coin, or part of a mechanism, &c.: a slit: a niche in an organisation, &c.—*ns.* **slot′-machine, -meter,** one operated by inserting a coin in a slot. [O.Fr. *esclot.*]

sloth, *slōth,* or *sloth, n.* laziness, sluggishness: any of several sluggish arboreal quadrupeds of tropical America. *adj.* **sloth′ful,** given to sloth, inactive, lazy.—*adv.* **sloth′fully.**—*n.* **sloth′fulness.** [M.E. *slawthe,* altered from O.E. *slǽwth*—*slāw,* slow.]

slouch, *slowch, n.* a loose, ungainly, stooping gait: a clown.—*v.i.* to go or bear oneself with a slouch.—*v.t.* to turn down the brim of.—*n.* **slouch′-hat,** a soft hat with broad brim turned down. [Cf. O.N. *slōkr,* a slouching fellow.]

slough, *slow, n.* a hollow filled with mud: a marsh. [O.E. *slōh.*]

slough, *sluf, n.* cast-off skin: dead tissue in a sore—*v.i.* to come away as a slough (with *off*). to cast the skin.—*v.t.* to cast off, as a slough. [M.E. *sloh*; origin uncertain.]

sloven, *sluv′n, n.* a person carelessly or dirtily dressed, or slipshod in work.—Also *adj.*—*adj.* **slov′enly.**—*n.* **slov′enliness.** [Cf. O.Du. *slof, sloef,* Low Ger. *sluf,* slow, indolent.]

slow, *slō, adj.* not swift: not hasty: not progressive: dull: behind in time.—*adv.* slowly (also in compounds).—*v.t.* to delay, retard, slacken the speed of.—*v.i.* to slacken in speed.—*n.* **slow′coach,** a laggard: a sluggish person.—*adv.* **slow′ly.** *n., adj., adv.* **slow′-mo′tion,** much slower than normal or (*cinematograph*) actual motion.—*n.* **slow′ness.**—*adjs.* **slow′-mov′ing, slow′-go′ing,** moving slowly (*lit.* and *fig.*).—*n.* **slow′-worm,** a blindworm (q.v.).—**slow down,** to go more slowly.—**go slow** (see **go**). [O.E. *slāw*; Du. *sleе,* O.N. *sljōr.*]

sludge, *sluj, n.* soft mud or mire: half-melted snow: a slimy precipitate as from sewage. [Cf. **slush.**]

slug, *slug, n.* a heavy, lazy fellow: a name for several families of land molluscs, with shell rudimentary or absent, very destructive to garden crops: anything slow-moving.—*n.* **slugg′ard,** one habitually idle or inactive.—*adj.* **slugg′ish,** habitually lazy: having little motion: having little or no power.—*adv.* **slugg′ishly.**—*n.* **slugg′ishness.** [Prob. of Scand. origin.]

slug, *slug, n.* a lump of metal, esp. one for firing from a gun (*print.*) a solid line of type cast by a composing machine: (*engineering*) unit of mass, approx. 32 lb.: a quantity of liquor that can be swallowed in one gulp. [Perh. from **slug** (1).]

sluice, *slōōs, n.* a structure with a gate for stopping or regulating the flow of water: a drain, channel: a regulated outlet or inlet: a trough for washing gold from sand, &c.: a sluicing, quick wash.—*v.t.* to flood with water: to flush or clean out by flinging water.—*v.i.* (of water) to pour, as from a sluice. [O.Fr. *escluse*—Low L. *exclūsa* (*aqua*), a sluice, i.e. (water) shut out—pa.p. of L. *exclūdĕre,* to shut out.]

slum, *slum, n.* an overcrowded squalid street or (usu in *pl.*) neighbourhood.—*v.i.* to visit slums, esp. for pleasure. [Cant (q.v.)]

slumber, *slum′bér, v.i.* to sleep, esp. lightly: to be negligent or inactive.—*n.* (often in *pl.*) light sleep: repose.—*n.* **slum′berer.**—*adjs.* **slum′-berous, slum′brous,** inviting or causing slumber: sleepy. [M.E. *slūmeren*—O.E. *slūma,* slumber.]

slump, *slump, v.i.* to fall or sink suddenly into water or mud: to flop, clump, plump: (of stocks, trade, &c.) to lose value suddenly or heavily.—*n.* a sudden or serious fall of prices, business, &c.—opp. to *boom.* [Prob. imit.]

slung, *pa.t.* and *pa.p.* of **sling.**

slunk, *pa.t.* and *pa.p.* of **slink.**

slur, *slûr, v.t.* (*dial.*) to smear, besmirch: to disparage, asperse: to sing or play legato: to sound indistinctly: to glide (over) slyly so as to mask or to avert attention from:—*pr.p.* slur′ring; *pa.t.* and *pa.p.* slurred.—*n.* (*dial.*) thin mud: an aspersion, stain, imputation of blame: (*mus.*) a smooth or legato effect: a curved line indicating that notes are to be sung to one syllable, or played with one bow, or with a smooth gliding effect: a running together resulting in indistinctness in writing or speech.—*n.* **slurr′y,** a thin watery mixture, e.g. of cement. [Origin obscure.]

slush, *slush, n.* liquid mud: melting snow: worthless sentimental drivel—*v.t.* to wash by throwing water upon.—*adj.* **slush′y.**

slut, *slut, n.* a dirty, untidy woman.—*adj.* **slut′ish,** resembling a slut, dirty, careless.—*adv.* **slutt′ishly.**—*n.* **slutt′ishness.** [Ety. uncertain.]

sly, *slī, adj.* skilful in doing anything so as to be unobserved: cunning, wily, secretive: done with artful dexterity: with hidden meaning.—*n.* **sly′boots,** a sly or cunning person or animal.—*adv.* **sly′ly** (or **sli′ly**).—*n.* **sly′ness** (or **sli′ness**).—**on the sly,** surreptitiously. [O.N. *slǽgr*; cf. **sleight.**]

slype, *slīp, n.* a passage between walls, esp. a covered passage between transept and chapter-house. [Perh. **slip.**]

smack, *smak, n.* taste: a distinctive or distinguishable flavour: small quantity, enough to taste: a trace, tinge.—*v.i.* to have a taste (of), savour (of). [O.E. *smæc.*]

smack, *smak, n.* a small coaster or fishing-vessel with one mast. [Du. *smak*; Ger. *schmacke.*]

smack, *smak, v.t.* to strike smartly, to slap loudly: to kiss roughly and noisily: to make a sharp noise with, as the lips by separation.—*n.* a sharp sound: a loud slap or blow: a hearty kiss.—*adv.* with sudden violence. [Prob. imit.; Du. *smakken,* to smite, Ger. *schmatzen,* to smack.]

small, *smöl, adj.* little in size, extent, quantity, or degree: fine in grain, texture, gauge, &c.: of little value, power, or importance: operating on no great scale: unimposing, humble: petty (e.g. *it was small of him to do that*): dilute: soft or gentle (e.g. *in a small voice*).—*adv.* in a low tone, gently: in small pieces.—*n.* the slenderest part, esp. of the back: (in *pl.*) small clothes: (in *pl.*) responsions (q.v.)—*ns.* **small ads,** classified advertisements; **small′-arm,** (usu. in *pl.*) any weapon, esp. a firearm, that can be carried by a man; **small′-beer,** a kind of weak beer: trivial matters.—*n.pl.* **small′-**

clothes, knee-breeches, esp. those of the close-fitting eighteenth-century kind.—*n.* **small'holding,** a holding of land smaller than an ordinary farm: the working of such.—*n.pl.* **small'-hours,** the hours immediately following midnight.—*adj.* **small'ish,** somewhat small.—*ns.* **small'ness; small'pox,** a contagious, febrile disease, characterised by small pocks or eruptions on the skin; **small'-sword,** a light thrusting sword for fencing or duelling; **small'-talk,** light or trifling conversation.—*adj.* **small'-time** (*coll.*), unimportant.—*n.* **small'-tooth comb,** a comb with a row of fine teeth on each side: (*fig.*) any means of minute investigation.—**feel small,** to feel humiliated, feel that one has appeared, or been made to appear, petty or dishonourable; **in a small way,** with little capital or stock: unostentatiously; **the small screen,** television. [O.E. *smæl*; Ger. *schmal*.]

smarm, *smärm, v.t.* and *v.i.* to smear, plaster, sleek.—*v.i.* to fawn ingratiatingly and fulsomely.—*adj.* **smarm'y.** [Origin obscure.]

smart, *smärt, n.* quick, stinging pain of body or mind.—*v.i.* to feel a smart: to be punished.—*adj.* sharp and stinging: vigorous, brisk: acute, witty: vivacious: keen, quick, and efficient in business: trim, spruce, fine: fashionable, stylish: belonging to, or characteristic of, society, the fashionable world.—*v.t.* **smart'en,** to make smart, to brighten (up).—*adv.* **smart'ly.**—*n.* **smart'ness.** [O.E. *smeortan*; Du. *smarten,* Ger. *schmerzen.*]

smash, *smash, v.t.* to shatter: to strike with great force: to dash violently: (*fig.*) to ruin.—*v.i.* to fly into pieces: to be ruined, to fail: to dash violently (into).—*n.* an act or occasion of smashing, destruction, ruin, bankruptcy.—*n.* and *adj.* **smash-and-grab',** (a raid) effected by smashing a shop-window and grabbing goods.—*n.* **smash'-hit',** overwhelming success. [Imit.; cf. Swed. dial. *smaske,* to smack.]

smattering, *smat'ér-ing, n.* a scrappy superficial knowledge. [M.E. *smateren,* to rattle, to chatter.]

smear, *smēr, v.t.* to overspread with anything sticky and oily, as grease: to rub in such a way as to make a smear: to defame, slander (a person): to sully (a person's reputation).—*v.i.* to smudge, become smeared.—*n.* a rub with, or a mark or patch of, anything sticky or oily: a small quantity of something smeared on a slide for examination under the microscope.—*adj.* **smear'y,** ready to smear: showing smears.—**smear campaign,** a determined attempt, by various means, to ruin a reputation. [O.E. *smeru,* fat, grease; Ger. *schmeer,* grease, O.N. *smjör,* butter.]

smell, *smel, n.* the sense by which gases, vapours, substances very finely divided, are perceived—a sense located, in the case of the higher animals, in olfactory cells in the mucous membrane of the nose: the specific sensation excited by such a substance: the property of exciting it: a perfume, scent, odour, or stench: an act or instance of exercising the sense: (*fig.*) a smack, savour, suggestion, intimation.—*v.i.* to affect the sense of smell: to have odour (esp. unpleasant) or an odour (of): to have or use the sense of smell.—*v.t.* to

perceive, detect, find, by smell: to take a smell at: (*arch.*) to emit a smell of:—*pa.t.* and *pa.p.* smelled, smelt.—*ns.* **smell'ing-bott'le,** a bottle containing smelling-salts, or the like; **smell'ing-salts,** a preparation of ammonium carbonate with lavender, &c., used as a stimulant in faintness, &c.—*adj.* **smell'y,** having a bad smell.—**smell out,** to detect by prying. [Very early M.E. *smel,* prob. O.E. but not recorded.]

smelt, *smelt, n.* a fish of, or akin to, the salmon family, with a cucumber-like smell. [O.E.]

smelt, *smelt, v.t.* to melt (ore) in order to separate metal.—*ns.* **smel'ter; smel'tery,** a place for smelting. [Swed. *smälta.*]

smew, *smū, n.* a small species of merganser.

smilax, *smī'laks, n.* a genus of plants of the lily order, tropical American species of which yield sarsaparilla: a South African plant of the asparagus genus, used for decoration. [L.,—Gr. *smīlax,* bindweed.]

smile, *smīl, v.i.* to express amusement, slight contempt, favour, pleasure, &c., by a slight drawing up of the corners of the lips: to look joyous: to be favourable.—*v.t.* to indicate by smiling: also with cognate object.—*n.* act of smiling: the expression of the features in smiling: favour. [M.E. *smīlen*; perh. from Low Ger.]

smirch, *smûrch, v.t.* (*lit.* and *fig.*) soil, stain, sully.—*n.* a stain. [Earlier *smorch,* prob.—O.Fr. *esmorcher,* to hurt; influenced by **smear.**]

smirk, *smûrk, v.i.* to put on a complacent, conceited, or foolish smile.—*n.* an affected or foolish smile. [O.E. *smercian.*]

smite, *smīt, v.t.* to strike, to beat: to overthrow in battle: (*fig.*) to strike, affect suddenly (e.g. of pain, an idea, charms): (*B.*) to afflict.—*v.i.* to strike:—*pa.t.* smōte; *pa.p.* smitt'en, (*arch.*) smit, (*rare*) smōte.—*n.* **smī'ter.** [O.E. *smītan,* to smear.]

smith, *smith, n.* one who forges with the hammer: a worker in metals: one who makes anything.—*n.* **smith'y,** the workshop of a smith. [O.E. *smith*; Ger. *schmied.*]

smithereens, *smiTH-ér-ēnz', n.pl.* (*coll.*) small fragments. [Ir. *smidirīn.*]

smitten, *smit'n, pa.p.* of **smite.**

smock, *smok, n.* (*arch.*) a chemise: a smock-frock: a similar loose garment of any material.—*ns.* **smock'-frock,** a shirtlike outer garment of coarse white linen with smocking; **smock'ing,** ornamental gathering or honeycombing, as on the yoke and cuffs of a smock. [O.E. *smoc.*]

smog, *smog, n.* smoky fog.

smoke, *smōk, n.* the gases, vapours, and small particles that come off from a burning substance: any similar vapour: (*coll.*) a cigar or cigarette: a spell of smoking.—*v.i.* to send up smoke: to diffuse smoke by reason of imperfect draught: to smoulder: to draw in and puff out the smoke of tobacco, &c.—*v.t.* to fumigate: to dry or cure by smoke: to draw in and puff out the smoke from.—*adj.* **smoke'less,** having or producing no smoke.—*ns.* **smō'ker,** one who smokes tobacco: a smoking-carriage: a smoking-concert; **smoke'-screen,** a dense cloud of smoke raised to conceal movements; **smoke'-stack,** a ship's funnel.—*ns.* **smō'king-**

Neutral vowels in unaccented syllables: *em'pér-ór*; for certain sounds in foreign words see p. ix.

carr'iage, -compart'ment, -room, a railway-carriage, -compartment, or a room, in which smoking is permitted; **smō'king-con'cert,** a concert at which smoking is allowed.—*adj.* **smō'ky,** giving out smoke: like smoke: coloured like or by smoke: filled, or subject to be filled, with smoke: tarnished or noisome with smoke.—*adv.* **smō'kily.**—*n.* **smō'kiness.** —**smokeless fuel,** that authorised for use in a smokeless zone; **smokeless zone,** an area in which the emission of smoke from chimneys is prohibited.— **smoke out,** to destroy or expel by diffusion of smoke.— **go up in smoke,** to vanish, to come to nothing. [O.E. *smoca* (n.), *smocian* (vb.); Ger. *schmauch.*]

smolt, *smōlt, n.* a young river salmon at the stage when it emigrates to the sea.

smooch, *smōōch, v.i.* (*coll.*) to kiss, to pet.

smooth, *smōōTH, adj.* having an even surface: not rough: evenly spread: glossy: slippery: hairless: of even consistency: gently flowing: easy: bland, agreeable: fair-spoken, plausible (also **smooth'-spoken, smooth'-tongued**)—*v.t* to make smooth: to free from obstruction, difficulty, harshness: to reduce from diphthong to single vowel: to remove by smoothing: to calm, soothe: to gloss (over).—*v.i.* to become smooth: to flatter, behave ingratiatingly.—*n.* the smooth part.—*adj.* **smooth'-bore,** not rifled.—*n.* a gun with smooth-bored barrel.—*adj.* **smooth'faced,** having a smooth face or surface: beardless: unwrinkled: plausible.—*n.* **smooth'ing i'ron,** a flat-iron. —*adv.* **smooth'ly.**—*n.* **smooth'ness.**—**smooth breathing,** in Greek, the mark (') over an initial vowel indicating absence of aspiration. [O.E. *smōth,* usually *smēthe.*]

smörbröd, smørrebrød, *smør'brōō, smœr'brō, smœr'ė-brœth, smōr'ė-brōd, n* lit, bread and butter: hors d'oeuvres served on slices of buttered bread. [Norw, and Dan.]

smörgåsbord, *smör'gås-börd,* Sw. *smœr'gōs-bōōrd n* a Swedish style table assortment of hors d'oeuvres and many other dishes to which one helps oneself. [Sw.]

smote, *smōt, pa.t.* (and rare *pa.p.*) of **smite.**

smother, *smuTH'ér, v.t.* to suffocate by excluding the air, esp. by means of a thick covering: to suppress.—*v.i.* to undergo suffocation.—*n.* smoke: thick floating dust. [M.E. *smorther*— O.E. *smorian,* to smother.]

smoulder, *smōl'dér, v.i.* to burn slowly or without flame: (*fig.*) to persist, linger on, in a suppressed state (e.g. *his resentment smouldered*): to show suppressed feeling, as anger, jealousy (e.g. *his eyes smouldered*). [M.E. *smolderen;* origin obscure.]

smudge, *smuj, n.* a smear, a blur: a choking smoke.—*v.t.* and *v.i.* to blot, blur.—*adj.* **smud'gy,** stained with smoke: blotted, blurred. [Scand., Swed. *smuts,* dirt, Dan. *smuds,* smut; Ger. *schmutz.*]

smug, *smug, adj.* (*arch.*) neat, spruce: complacent, self-satisfied.—*adv.* **smug'ly.**—*n.* **smug'ness.** [Low Ger.; cf. Ger. *schmuck,* fine.]

smuggle, *smug'l, v.t.* to import or export illegally or without paying duty: to convey secretly. —*p.adj.* **smug'gled.**—*ns.* **smug'gler,** one who smuggles: a vessel used in smuggling; **smug'gling.** [Low Ger. *smuggeln;* Ger. *schmuggeln.*]

smut, *smut, n.* soot: a flake or spot of dirt, soot, &c.: the popular name of certain small fungi with numerous black spores, which infest flowering land-plants, esp. the grasses: the disease caused by any of these: obscene discourse.—*v.t.* to soil, spot, or affect with smut:—*pr.p.* smutt'ing; *pa.t.* and *pa.p.* smutt'ed.—*adj.* **smutt'y,** stained with smut: obscene, filthy.—*adv.* **smutt'ily.**—*n.* **smutt'iness.** [Cf. Low Ger. *schmutt,* Ger. *schmutz,* dirt.]

smutch, *smuch, v.t.* to smut, to sully.—*n.* a dirty mark: soot: grime. [Cf. **smudge.**]

snack, *snak, n.* a share: a slight, hasty meal.—*n.* **snack'-bar, snack'-counter,** a counter in a restaurant where snacks are served promptly. [**snatch.**]

snaffle, *snaf'l, n.* a jointed bit (less severe than the curb).—*v.t.* to put a snaffle on: the control by the snaffle: (*coll.*) to get possession of, purloin. [Origin doubtful, but cf. Du. *snavel,* the muzzle.]

snag, *snag, n* a stump, as of a branch or tooth: an embedded tree, dangerous for boats: hence a catch, a hidden obstacle or drawback.—*v.t.* to catch on a snag: to tear on a snag: to clear of snags. [Cf. O.N. *snagi,* peg.]

snail, *snāl, n.* a term for certain molluscs, esp. land molluscs, having well-formed coiled shells.—*v.i.* to crawl, go very slowly.—**snail's pace,** a very slow pace. [O.E. *snegl, snægl;* Ger. *schnecke.*]

snake, *snāk, n.* a class of limbless and much elongated reptiles: anything snakelike in form or movement: an ungrateful or treacherous person.—*v.i.* to wind, to creep —**snake in the grass,** (*fig.*) a person who furtively does one an injury. [O.E. *snaca.*]

snap, *snap, v.t.* to bite suddenly: to seize, secure promptly (usu. with *up*): to interrupt sharply (often with *up*): to utter impatiently (with *out*): to make (a swift and sharp retort): to shut with a sharp sound: to cause to make a sharp sound: to send or put with a sharp sound: to break suddenly: to take an instantaneous photograph of, esp. with a hand-camera.—*v.i.* to make a bite (often with *at*): to grasp (with *at*): to speak tartly in sudden irritation: to shut suddenly, as by a spring: to make a sharp noise: to go off with a sharp noise: to break suddenly:—*pr.p.* snapp'ing; *pa.t.* and *pa.p.* snapped.—*n.* act of snapping, or the noise made by it: a small catch or lock: a sudden onset of cold weather: a crisp kind of gingerbread biscuit: vigour, energy: a quick, crisp, incisive, epigrammatic quality in style: a snapshot: a card game.—*adj.* sudden, unexpected, without preparation (e.g. *a snap debate, decision, vote*).—*n.* **snap'dragon,** any garden species of antirrhinum, whose flower when pinched and released snaps like a dragon: a Christmas game of snatching raisins from a dish of burning brandy.—*adj.* **snapp'ish,** inclined to snap: eager to bite: sharp in reply.—*adv.* **snapp'ishly.**—*n.* **snappishness.**— *adj.* **snapp'y,** snappish: brisk: smart.—*n.* **snap'shot,** a hasty shot: an instantaneous photograph.—**snap out of it,** to give up (mood, habit, &c.) at once.— **look snappy** (*coll.*) to hurry. [Du. *snappen,* to snap; Ger. *schappen.*]

snare, *snār, n.* a running noose of string or wire, &c., for catching an animal: a trap: (*fig.*) an allurement, temptation, moral danger, entanglement.—*v.t.* to catch. [O.E. *sneare,* or O.N. *snara.*]

snarl, *snärl, v.i.* to make a surly resentful noise with show of teeth: to speak in a surly manner.—*v.t.* to utter snarlingly.—*n.* an unnatural growl: a surly malicious utterance.—*n.* **snar′ler.** [Prob. imit.; Low Ger. *snarren.*]

snarl, *snärl, v.t.* (*arch.*) to twist, entangle.—*n.* a knot: a complication. [**snare.**]

snatch, *snach, v.t.* to seize suddenly: to pluck away quickly: to take as opportunity occurs.—Also *v.i.*—*n.* an attempt to seize: a seizure: a spell: a fragment. [Perh. related to **snack.**]

snazzy, *snaz′i, adj.* (*slang*) very attractive or fashionable: flashy.

sneak, *snēk, v.i.* to go furtively or meanly, slink, skulk: to behave meanly: to tell tales, to inform.—*v.t.* (*slang*) to steal.—*n.* a mean fellow: a mean thief: a tell-tale: (*cricket*) a ball bowled along the ground.—*n.* **sneak′er,** one who, or that which, sneaks: a soft-soled shoe: a sandshoe.—*adj.* **sneak′ing,** mean: underhand, not openly avowed: lurking under other feelings.—*n.* **sneak′-thief,** a thief who steals through open doors or windows without breaking in. [Connection with O.E. *snīcan,* to crawl, is obscure.]

sneer, *snēr, v.i.* to show cynical contempt by the expression of the face, as by drawing up the lip: to show harsh derision and contempt in speech or writing.—*v.t.* to utter sneeringly.—*n.* a sneering expression of face: a remark conveying contemptuous ridicule: an act of sneering.—*n.* **sneer′er.**—*n. and adj.* **sneer′ing.**—*adv.* **sneer′ingly.** [Perh. related to Frisian *sneere,* to scorn.]

sneeze, *snēz, v.i.* to eject air violently through the nose with an explosive sound.—*n.* an act of sneezing.—**not to be sneezed at,** not to be treated as unimportant. [M.E. *snesen, fnesen*—O.E. *fnēosan,* to sneeze; Du. *fniezen.*]

snick, *snik, v.t.* to cut, snip, nick: (*cricket*) to deflect (the ball) slightly by a touch of the bat.—*n.* a small cut or nick: a glancing stroke in cricket.—*n.* **snick′ersnee,** a large knife for fighting. [Orig. uncertain.]

snicker, *snik′ér.* Same as **snigger.**

snide, *snīd, adj.* base, mean, cheap: sham, insincere: superior in attitude: sneering: derogatory in an insinuating manner.

sniff, *snif, v.t.* to draw in by the nose with the breath: to smell.—*v.i.* to draw in air sharply through the nose: to do so inquisitively, suspiciously, or scornfully.—*n.* an act of sniffing: the sound of sniffing: a slight smell.—*v.i.* **sniffle,** to snuffle slightly, to sniff.—*adj.* **sniffy,** disdainful. [Imit.; cf. **snuff.**]

snigger, *snig′ér, v.i.* to laugh in a half-suppressed, broken manner, usu. implying that the subject of mirth is unworthy, as another's discomfiture, an indecency, &c.—*v.t.* to say with a snigger.—*n.* a half-suppressed laugh. [Imit.]

snip, *snip, v.t.* to sever instantaneously, esp. by a single cut with scissors:—*pr.p.* **snipp′ing;** *pa.t.* and *pa.p.* **snipped.**—*n.* a single cut with scissors: a small shred: a notch: a share: a

certainty: a bargain.—*n.* **snipp′et,** a little piece snipped off: a scrap (e.g. of news). [Du. *snippen*; Ger. *schnippen.*]

snipe, *snīp, n.* a genus of birds with long straight flexible bills, frequenting marshy places.—*v.i.* to go snipe-shooting: to shoot at single men from cover.—*v.t.* to pick off by rifle from (usually distant) cover.—*n.* **snip′er.** [Prob. Scand.; O.N. *snīpa.*]

snivel, *sniv′l, v.i.* to run at the nose: to whimper: to whine tearfully: to talk sanctimoniously and insincerely:—*pr.p.* **sniv′elling;** *pa.t.* and *pa.p.* **sniv′elled.**—*n.* mucus of the nose: an affected tearful state: cant.—*n.* **sniv′eller.**—*adj.* **sniv′elling.** [O.E. *snofl,* mucus.]

snob, *snob, n.* (*obs.*) a person of ordinary or low rank: one animated by obsequious admiration for those of higher social rank or by a desire to dissociate himself from those whom he regards as inferior.—*n.* **snobb′ery,** the quality of being snobbish.—*adj.* **snobb′ish,** having the feelings of, or acting like, a snob: characteristic of, or befitting, a snob.—*adv.* **snobb′ishly.**—*n.* **snobb′ishness.** [Origin slang.]

snoek, *snōōk, n.* a large voracious edible fish common on the coasts of South Africa, Australia, &c. [Du.]

snog, *snog, v.t.* (*slang*) to embrace, kiss.—Also *n.*

snood, *snōōd, n.* a fillet for the hair, once in Scotland the badge of virginity: revived in the sense of a conspicuous net supporting the back hair: the hair-line, gut, &c., by which a fish-hook is fixed to the line. [O.E. *snōd.*]

snooker, *snōōk′ér, n.* (also **snooker pool**) a variety of pool (see **pool** (2)). [Ety. unknown.]

snoop, *snōōp, v.i.* to act as a mean spy.—*n.* **snoop′er.** [Du. *snoepen.*]

snooze, *snōōz, v.i.* to doze.—*n.* a nap.—*n.* **snooz′er.** [Origin obscure; perh. orig. slang.]

snore, *snōr, snōr, v.i.* to breathe roughly and hoarsely in sleep with vibration of uvula and soft palate or of the vocal chords.—*n.* a noisy breathing of this kind.—*ns.* **snōr′er; snōr′ing.** [Imit.; cf. **snort.**]

snort, *snört, v.i.* to force the air with violence and noise through the nostrils, as horses: to make a like noise, esp. as a token of displeasure.—*v.t.* to express by a snort: to utter with a snort.—*n.* an act of snorting: a sound of snorting.—*n.* **snort′er,** (*coll.*) anything characterised by extreme force. [Imit.]

snot, *snot, n.* mucus of the nose.—*adj.* **snott′y,** like, or foul with, snot: superciliously stand-offish, with nose in air: of no importance.—*n.* (*slang*) a midshipman. [M.E. *snotte*; cf. Du. *snot*; allied to **snout.**]

snout, *snowt, n.* the projecting nose of a beast, as of a swine: any similar projection.—*v.t.* to furnish with a snout. [M.E. *snūte*; cf. Swed. *snut*; Ger. *schnauze,* Du. *snuit.*]

snow, *snō, n.* the frozen atmospheric vapour, in crystalline form, which falls as light, white flakes: a snowfall: a mass or expanse of snow: snowlike specks on a television screen caused by electrical interference: (*slang*) cocaine, morphine, heroin.—*v.i.* to fall in snow-flakes.—*v.t.* to pour abundantly, as if snow.—*n.* **snow′ball,** a ball made of snow pressed hard together: the guelder-rose: a round white pudding, cake, or sweetmeat:

Neutral vowels in unaccented syllables: *em′pér-ór*; for certain sounds in foreign words see p. ix.

something that grows like a snowball rolled in snow, esp. a distribution of begging letters, each recipient being asked to send out so many copies.—*v.t.* to pelt with snowballs.—*v.i.* to throw snowballs: to go on becoming greater more and more quickly.—*ns.* **snow'-blind'-ness**, impaired eyesight caused by the reflection of light from snow; **snow'-boot**, a boot or overshoe made to protect the feet while walking in snow.—*adjs.* **snow'bound**, confined to a restricted space by snow; **snow'-capped, -capt**, crowned with snow.—*ns.* **snow'drift**, a bank of snow drifted together by the wind; **snow'drop**, a bulbous plant with drooping bell-shaped flower, often seen while snow still lies on the ground; **snow'fall**, a fall of snow: the amount falling in a given time; **snow'field**, a wide expanse of snow, esp. where permanent; **snow'flake**, a feathery flake of snow; **snow'line**, the line upon a mountain that marks the limit of perpetual snow; **snow'-man**, a human figure shaped from a mass of snow; **snow'mobile**, a motorised sleigh; **snow'plough**, a machine for clearing snow from roads and railways; **snow'-shoe**, a strung frame or other contrivance attached to the feet for walking on the surface of snow; **snow'-storm**, a storm accompanied with falling snow.—*adjs.* **snow'-white**, as white as snow; **snow'y**, abounding or covered with snow: white, like snow: pure.—**snowed under with**, overwhelmed with the rapid accumulation of; **snowed up**, blocked by, or isolated by, snow. [O.E. *snāw*; Ger. *schnee*, L. *nix, nivis.*]

snub, *snub*, *v.t.* to check, curb: to humiliate by an intentional rebuff or crushing retort:—*pr.p.* **snubb'ing**; *pa.t.* and *pa.p.* **snubbed.**—*n.* an act of snubbing.—*adj.* flat and broad, with end slightly turned up.—*n.* **snub'-nose**, a short or flat nose.—*adj.* **snub'-nosed**, [O.N. *snubba*, to chide, snub.]

snuff, *snuf*, *v.i.* to draw in air violently and noisily through the nose: to sniff, smell (at anything) doubtfully: to use snuff.—*v.t.* to draw into the nose: to smell, to examine, suspect, or detect, by smelling.—*n.* a powdered preparation of tobacco or other substance for snuffing: a pinch of such: a sniff.—*ns.* **snuff'box**, a box for snuff; **snuff'er**, one who snuffs.—*adj.* **snuff'y**, soiled with, or smelling of, snuff. [Du. *snutten*; Ger. *schnaufen*, to snuff.]

snuff, *snuf*, *n.* the charred portion of a candle or lamp-wick.—*v.t.* to crop or pinch the snuff from, as a burning candle.—*n.pl.* **snuff'ers**, an instrument for taking the snuff off a candle. —**snuff it** (*slang*), to die; **snuff out**, to extinguish: to put a sudden end to: to come suddenly to an end. [M.E. *snoffe*; connection with **snuff** (1) is obscure.]

snuffle, *snuf'l*, *v.i.* to breathe hard or in an obstructed manner through the nose: to sniff: to speak through the nose.—Also *v.t.*—*n.* an act or sound of snuffling: a snuffling tone: cant: (in *pl.*) an obstructed condition of the nose. [Frequentative of **snuff** (1).]

snug, *snug*, *adj.* lying close and warm: comfortable (e.g. *a snug dinner*): sheltered: not exposed to view or notice: in good order: moderate, enough to produce comfort (as, *a snug income*).—*n.* **snugg'ery**, a cosy little room.—*v.i.* **snugg'le**, to cuddle, nestle.—*adv.* **snug'ly.** —*n.* **snug'ness.** [Origin obscure.]

so, *sō*, *adv.* merging in *conj.* or *interj.*, in this, that, or such manner, degree, or condition: thus: as indicated: to such an extent: to a great extent or high degree indicated or implied: likewise: accordingly, therefore: thereupon, thereafter: (*arch.*) provided (that): (*coll.*) in order (e.g. *he liked everything just so*): an abbrev. for is it so? be it so.—*n.* **so'-and-so**, this or that person or thing: such-and-such a person or thing: sometimes used as a substitute for an opprobrious term.—*adjs.* **so'-called**, styled thus—usually implying doubt; **so-so**, neither very good nor very bad, tolerable, indifferent.—*adv.* indifferently.—**so as**, in such a manner as, or that: in order (to): (*arch.*) if only, on condition that; **so far**, to that, or such an, extent, degree, or point; **so forth**, more of the same or a like kind; **so much**, as much as is implied or mentioned: an amount implied but not stated: such an amount (of); **so much as**, as much as: even (e.g. *she did not so much as say 'thank you'*); **so much for**, that disposes of, that is the end of; **so on, so forth**; **so that**, with the purpose that: with the result that: (*arch.*) if only; **so to say**, or **speak**, if one may use that expression.—**or so**, or thereabouts: approximately; **quite so**, just as you have said. [O.E. *swā*; O.N. *svā*, Ger. *so.*]

soak, *sōk*, *v.t.* to steep in a fluid: to drench, saturate (with): to draw in through pores (*lit.* and *fig.*): (*slang*) to beat, pummel: (*slang*) to overcharge.—*v.i.* to be steeped in a liquid: to pass (through pores): to drink to excess.—*n.* **soak'er**, a habitual drunkard.—*p.adj.* **soak'ing**, drenching: drenched.—**soaking wet**, extremely wet. [M.E. *soke*—O.E. *socian*, a weak verb, related to *sūcan*, to suck.]

soap, *sop*, *n.* a compound of oils or fats with salts of sodium (*hard soaps*) or of potassium (*soft soaps*), used in washing.—*v.t.* to rub with soap.—*ns.* **soap'-boil'er**, one whose occupation is to make soap; **soap'-boil'ing**, the occupation of making soap; **soap'-box**, a box for packing soap: a street orator's improvised platform; **soap'-bubb'le**, a globe of air enclosed in a film of soap-suds; **soap-opera**, a broadcast serial chiefly concerned with the emotional involvement of the characters, orig. American and often sponsored by soap manufacturers; **soap'-stone**, steatite (q.v.).—*n.pl.* **soap-suds**, soapy water, esp. when worked into a foam.—*adj.* **soap'y**, like soap: covered with soap: containing soap: (*coll.*) unctuous.—*n.* **soap'iness.** [O.E. *sāpe*; Du. *zeep*, Ger. *seife.*]

soar, *sōr, sör*, *v.i.* to mount high in the air: to rise high (*lit.* and *fig.*). [O.Fr. *essorer*, to expose to air—L. *ex*, out, *aura*, air.]

sob, *sob*, *v.i.* to catch the breath convulsively in distress or other emotion: to make a similar sound.—*v.t.* to utter with sobs:—*pr.p.* **sobb'ing**; *pa.t.* and *pa.p.* **sobbed.**—*n.* a convulsive catch of the breath: any similar sound.—*ns.* **sob'-story**, a pitiful story told to arouse sympathy; **sob'stuff**, cheap and extravagant pathos calculated to draw tears. [Imit.]

fāte, fär; mē, hûr (her); *mīne; mōte, för; mūte; mōōn, fŏŏt;* тнen (then)

sober, *sō′bėr, adj.* not drunk: temperate, esp. in use of intoxicants: moderate: without excess or extravagance: serious: sedate: quiet in colour.—*v.t.* to make sober.—*v.i.* to become sober.—*adv.* **sō′berly.**—*ns.* **sō′berness; sō′bersides,** a sedate and solemn person; **sōbrī′ety,** state or habit of being sober: calmness: gravity. [Fr. *sobre*—L. *sōbrius*—*sē-*, apart, not, *ēbrius,* drunk.]

sobriquet, *sō′brē-kā, n.* a nickname.—Also **sou′briquet** (*sōō′*). [Fr.]

socage, soccage, *sok′ij, n.* tenure of lands by service fixed and determinate in quality. [O.E. *sōc,* a right of holding a court.]

soccer, *sok′ėr, n.* football under the laws of the Football Association. [Abbrev. of **association.**]

sociable, *sō′sha-bl, adj.* inclined to society: companionable: favourable to social intercourse.—*ns.* **sōciabil′ity, sō′ciableness,** quality of being sociable.—*adv.* **sō′ciably.**—*adv.* **sō′cial,** pertaining to society or companionship: pertaining to an organised community, or to fashionable circles: growing or living in communities or societies (e.g. *social insects*): gregarious: convivial.—*adv.* **sō′cially.**—*v.t.* **sō′cialise,** to train or adapt to fit social environment: to make (e.g. the organisation of a state) conformable to the principles of socialism.—*v.i.* (*coll.*) to behave in a sociable manner.—**sō′cialism,** a theory, principle, or scheme of social organisation which places the means of production and distribution in the hands of the community; **sō′cialist,** an adherent of socialism.—*adj.* **sōcialist′ic.**—*ns.* **sō′cialite,** a person who has a place in fashionable society; **society** (*sō-sī′it-i*), fellowship, companionship: company: a corporate body: any organised association: a community: the body of mankind: the fashionable world generally.—*adj.* of fashionable society.—**social stience,** sociology; **social security,** security for all against financial difficulties arising from sickness, unemployment or old age; **social service,** welfare work.—**the alternative society,** a better, more humane form of society as envisaged by those who reject the values of present-day society. [Fr.—L. *sociabilis*—*sociāre,* to associate—*socius,* a companion.]

Socinian, *sō-sin′i-ân, adj.* pertaining to *Socinus,* who in the 16th century denied the doctrine of the Trinity, the deity of Christ, &c.—*n.* a follower of Socinus: a Unitarian.—*n.* **Socin′ianism,** the doctrines of Socinus.

sociology, *sō-shi-ol′o-ji, n.* the science that treats of man as a social being and of human society and culture.—*adjs.* **sociolog′ic, -al.**—*adv.* **sociolog′ically.**—*n.* **sociol′ogist.** [A hybrid from L. *socius,* a companion, and Gr. *logos,* discourse—*legein,* to speak.]

sock, *sok, n.* a light shoe worn by Greek and Roman actors of comedy (cf. **buskin**): a kind of short-legged stocking. [O.E. *socc*—L. *soccus.*]

sock, *sok, v.t.* to strike hard: (with *it*) to give a blow (to a person).—*n.* a violent blow.

socket, *sok′et, n.* a cavity into which something is inserted, as the receptacle of the eye, of a bone, a tooth, the shaft of an iron golf-club.—*adj.* **sock′eted,** provided with, placed in, or

received in a socket: (*golf*) hit with the socket, not the club face. [O.Fr. *soket.*]

Socratic, -al, *sō-krat′ik, -âl, adj.* pertaining to *Socrates* (469-399 B.C.), to his philosophy, or to his method of teaching, which was to elicit and test the opinions of others by a series of questions.—*adv.* **Socrat′ically.**

sod, *sod, n.* any surface of earth grown with grass, &c.: a turf.—*adj.* consisting of sod.—*v.t.* to cover with sod. [Low Ger. *sode*; Ger. *sode.*]

soda, *sō′da, n.* an inclusive name for various alkaline compounds of sodium: most frequently applied to sodium carbonate, the ash of certain marine plants, and crystallised as washing-soda: extended to sodium bicarbonate (baking-soda), an effervescent agent used to leaven flour and also in the manufacture of aerated waters, and to sodium hydroxide (caustic soda), a powerful cleansing agent used in the manufacture of soap: in chemical compounds, a synonym for sodium, as in nitrate of soda (sodium nitrate): soda-water.—*ns.* **sō′da-fount′ain,** a vessel for holding soda-water: apparatus for preparing soda-water and iced refreshments: a counter where these are sold; **sō′da-wa′ter,** orig. a weak solution of sodium bicarbonate with an admixture of acid to cause effervescence: a beverage consisting of water highly charged under pressure with carbonic acid gas. [It. and L.L. *soda.*]

sodality, *sō-dal′i-ti, n.* a fellowship or fraternity. [L. *sodālitās*—*sodālis,* a comrade.]

sodden, *sod′n, pa.p.* of **seethe,** boiled: soaked thoroughly: boggy: doughy, not well baked.

sodium, *sō′di-um, n.* a metallic element (atomic no. 11; symbol Na—abbrev. of *nātrium,* alternative name of sodium, from *nātron,* native sodium carbonate).—**sodium light,** a street lamp using sodium vapour and giving yellow light. [Latinised from **soda.**]

sodomy, *sod′om-i, n.* unnatural sexuality, as male homosexuality, so called because imputed to the inhabitants of *Sodom* (Genesis xix).—*n.* **sod′omite,** an inhabitant of Sodom: one guilty of sodomy.—*adj.* **sodomit′ical.**—*adv.* **sodomit′ically.**

soever, *sō-ev′ėr, adv.* or *suffx.* generally used to extend or render indefinite the sense of *who, what, where, how,* &c.

sofa, *sō′fa, n.* long upholstered seat with back and arms. [Ar. *suffah.*]

soft, *soft, adj.* easily yielding to pressure: easily cut: (*min.*) easily scratched: (*fig.*) not firm enough, yielding: not rigorous enough: weak in mind: weak in muscle, out of training: pleasing to the touch: not loud: not glaring: not hard in outline: gentle: tender: of water, free from calcium or magnesium salts: of coal, bituminous: wet, rainy: (*phonet.*) of *c, g,* as pronounced in *cell, germ*: of drug, not habit-forming.—*adv.* gently: quietly.—*interj.* hold! not so fast!—*v.t.* **soften** (*sof′n*), to make soft or softer: to mitigate.—*v.i.* to grow soft or softer.—*n.* **soft′ener.**—*n.pl.* **soft′-goods,** cloth, and cloth articles, as opposed to *hard-ware,* &c.—*adj.* **soft′-heart′ed,** kind-hearted, gentle.—*adv.* **soft′ly.**—*n.* **soft′ness.**—*adj.* **soft′-spō′ken,** having a mild or gentle voice: affable: suave, plausible in speech.—*ns.* **soft′-**

Neutral vowels in unaccented syllables: *em′pėr-ȯr*; for certain sounds in foreign words see p. ix.

ware (*computers*), programs, &c.; **soft′wood**, timber of a coniferous tree (also *adj.*).—**soft drink**, a non-alcoholic beverage; **soft option**, an alternative that is easy to carry out; **soft palate**, the back part of the palate; **soft pedal**, a pedal for reducing tone in the piano, esp. by causing the hammer to strike only one string (*v.t.* and *v.i.* **soft′-ped′al**, to play with the soft pedal down: (*fig.*) to tone down); **soft sell**, selling or sale by preliminary softening up or other indirect method; **soft soap**, potassium soap: flattery, blarney (*v.t.* to rub or cover with ′soft soap: to flatter).—**soften up**, to lessen resistance in; **a soft thing**, an easy task or situation. [O.E. *sŏfte*, *sēfte*; Du. *zacht*, Ger. *sanft*.]

soggy, *sog′i*, *adj.* soaked with water.—*n.* **sog**, a bog. [Origin unknown.]

soi-disant, *swä-dē-zä*, *adj.* self-styled, pretended, would-be. [Fr.]

soigné, *swä-nyā′*, **soignée** (*fem.*), *adj.* very well groomed. [Fr.]

soil, *soil*, *n.* the mould on the surface of the earth in which plants grow, country. [O.Fr. *soel*, *suel*, *sueil*—L. *solum*, ground.]

soil, *soil*, *n.* dirt: dung: sewage: a spot or stain: a watery place where a hunted animal takes refuge.—*v.t.* to make dirty: to stain: to manure.—*v.i.* to become dirty.—*n.* **soil′-pipe**, an upright discharge-pipe which receives the general refuse from water-closets, &c., in a building. [O.Fr. *soil*, *souil*, wallowing-place.]

soirée, *swär-ā′*, *swor′ā*, *n.* an evening social meeting with tea, &c. [Fr.,—*soir*, evening—L. *sērus*, late.]

sojourn, *sō′-*, *so′-*, *su′júrn*, *v.i.* to stay for a short time.—*n.* a stay, a temporary residence.—*n.* **so′journer**. [O.Fr. *sojourner*—L. *sub*, under, and Low L. *jornus*—L. *diurnus*, of a day—*diēs*, a day.]

Sol, *sol*, *n.* the sun. [L. *sōl*.]

sola, *sō′lä*, *n.* an Indian plant of the pea family, or its pith-like stems, used for making topees, &c. [Hindustani *sholā*.]

solace, *sol′ás*, *n.* consolation, comfort in distress: a source of comfort or pleasure.—*v.t.* to comfort in distress: to divert, amuse (oneself): to allay (e.g. *to solace grief*). [O.Fr. *solas*—L. *sōlātium*—*sōlārī*, *-ātus*, to comfort in distress.]

solan (**goose**), *sō′lan* (*goōs*), *n.* the common gannet. [O.N. *sula*.]

solar, *sō′lár*, *adj.* of, from, like, or pertaining to, the sun: measured by the progress of the sun: influenced by the sun: powered by energy from the sun's rays.—*n.* **sōlā′rium**, a sun-dial: a place, e.g. in a hospital, for sunning or sun-bathing.—**solar plexus**, in higher mammals a central network of nerves, situated in the pit of the stomach, from which nerves regulating involuntary motions radiate in all directions; **solar system**, the sun and the attendant bodies moving about it under the attraction of gravity. [L. *sōl*, the sun, *sōlāris*, pertaining to the sun.]

solatium, *sō-lā′shi-um*, *n.* compensation for disappointment, inconvenience, or wounded feelings. [L. *sōlātium*. See **solace**.]

sold, *sōld*, *pa.t.* and *pa.p.* of **sell.**—**sold on** (see **sell**).

solder, *sol′dér*, or *sod′ér* (sometimes *sōl′dér*,

sōd′ér), *v.t.* to make fast with solder: (*fig.*) to join (together): to mend, patch (up).—*n.* a fusible alloy for uniting metals. [O.Fr. *soud-*, *souldure*—*souder*, *soulder*, to consolidate—L. *solidāre*, to make solid.]

soldier, *sōl′jér*, *n.* a man engaged in military service: a private, as distinguished from an officer: a man of military skill.—*v.i.* to serve as a soldier.—*n.* **sol′diering.**—*adjs.* **sol′dier-like**, **sol′dierly**, like a soldier: martial: brave.—*ns.* **sol′dier-of-for′tune**, one ready to serve under any flag if there is good prospect of pay or advancement; **sol′diership**, state or quality of being a soldier: military qualities: martial skill; **sol′diery**, soldiers collectively: a body of military men.—**soldier on**, to continue doggedly in the face of difficulty. [O.Fr. *soldier*—L. *solidus*, a piece of money, the pay of a soldier.]

sole, *sōl*, *n.* the underside of the foot: the bottom of a boot or shoe: the bottom, understructure, floor, or undersurface of various things.—*v.t.* to put a sole on. [O.E. *sole*—L. *solea*, a sandal, a sole (fish).]

sole, *sōl*, *n.* any of various elliptical flat-fish with small twisted mouth and teeth on the underside only, esp. the common sole. [Fr. *sole*—L. *solea*. See **sole** (1).]

sole, *sōl*, *adj.* (*arch.*) alone: only (e.g. *the sole heir*): acting without another (e.g. *the sole author*): belonging to one person, or group exclusively (e.g. *his sole responsibility*, *the sole rights*): alone: only: exclusively.—*n.* **sole′ness**. [Fr.,—L. *sōlus*, alone.]

solecism, *sol′ē-sizm*, *n.* a flagrant grammatical error: any conspicuous breach of the rules of good taste and conduct.—*n.* **sol′ecist**, one who commits solecisms.—*adjs.* **solecist′ic**, **-al**, pertaining to, or involving, a solecism: incorrect: incongruous. [Gr. *soloikismos*, said to come from the corruption of the Attic dialect among the Athenian colonists (*oikizein*, to colonise) of *Soloi* in Cilicia (in Turkey).]

solemn, *sol′em*, *adj.* attended with, or marked by, special (esp. religious) ceremonies, pomp, or gravity: attended with an appeal to God, as an oath: in serious earnestness: awed, grave: glum: awe-inspiring: sombre: stately: pompous.—*v.t.* **sol′emnise**, to perform religiously or solemnly: to celebrate with rites: to make grave or serious.—*ns.* **solemnisā′tion**; **sol′emniser**; **solem′nity**, a solemn ceremony: seriousness: affected gravity.—*adv.* **sol′emnly.**—*n.* **sol′emnness**. [O.Fr. *solempne*, *solemne* (Fr. *solennel*)—L. *sollemnis*, *sollennis*, *perh.*—*sollus*, all, every, *annus*, a year.]

sol-fa, *sol-fä*, *n.* (*mus.*) a system of syllables (*do* or *ut*, *re*, *mi*, *fa*, *sol* or *so*, *la*, *si* or *ti*) representing and sung to the notes of the scale.—*adj.* belonging to this system.—*v.t.* and *v.i.* to sing to sol-fa syllables:—*pr.p.* sol-faing (*fä′ing*); pa.p. sol-faed (*-fäd*).—**tonic solfa** (see **tonic**). [It.]

solicit, *sō-lis′it*, *v.t.* (*rare*) to disquiet: (*rare*) to incite: to petition, importune (a person for something): to plead for (something): to call for, require, invite: (esp. of a prostitute) to invite to immorality.—*v.i.* to petition: to act as a solicitor: (of a prostitute) to make advances: (of a beggar) to importune for alms.—*ns.* **sol-**

ic′itant, one who solicits; solicita′tion, act of soliciting: earnest request: invitation; solic′itor, one who asks earnestly: one who is legally qualified to act for another in a court of law—a lawyer who prepares deeds, manages cases, instructs counsel in the superior courts, and acts as an advocate in the inferior courts; Solic′itor-Gen′eral, in England, the law-officer of the crown next in rank to the Attorney-General—in Scotland, to the Lord Advocate; solic′itorship.—adj. solic′itous, soliciting or earnestly asking or desiring: very desirous (to): anxious (about, for, of).—adv. solic′itously.—n. solic′itude, state of being solicitous: anxiety or uneasiness of mind. [Fr.,—L. sōlicitāre, sollicitāre—sō-, sollicitus —sollus, whole, citus, aroused—ciēre, to cite.]

solid, sol′id, adj. resisting change of shape, having the parts firmly cohering (opp. to fluid; distinguished from liquid and gaseous): hard: compact: full of matter, not hollow: strong, strongly constructed: having three dimensions: of uniform undivided substance (e.g. solid silver): unanimous, standing together in close union: well-grounded, weighty (e.g. a solid argument): financially sound (e.g. a solid business man): sensible: genuine (e.g. solid comfort): concerned with solids (e.g. solid geometry).—n. a substance, body, or figure, that is solid: a solid mass or part.—n. solidar′ity, firm union in sentiment and action.—v.t. solid′ify, to make solid or compact.—v.i. to grow solid: (fig.) to harden:—pa.p. solid′ified.—ns. solidifica′tion, act of making, becoming, solid; solid′ity, the state of being solid: fullness of matter: strength or firmness, moral or physical: soundness: volume.—adv. sol′idly.—n. sol′idness.—solid-state physics, branch of physics which covers all properties of solid materials; solid with, packed tight with: supporting fully. [L. solidus, solid.]

soliloquy, so-, sō-, só-lil′ó-kwi, n. talking to oneself when no one else is present: a discourse uttered with none to hear: a speech of this nature made by a character in a play, &c.—v.i. solil′oquise, to speak to oneself, to utter a soliloquy. [L. sōliloquium—sōlus, alone, loquī, to speak.]

soliped, sol′i-ped, n. an animal with uncloven hoofs. [L. sōlus, alone, pēs, pedis, a foot.]

solitaire, sol-i-tār′, n. a recluse: a game played by one person with balls on a board: a card game for one, patience: a gem, esp. a diamond, set by itself. [Fr.]

solitary, sol′i-tár-i, adj. alone: without company: only: single (e.g. not a solitary example): (bot.) growing singly: (zool.) living alone, not social or gregarious: lonely: remote from society, retired.—n. one who lives alone: a hermit.—adv. sol′itarily.—n. sol′itariness. [Fr. solitaire—L. sōlitārius—sōlus, alone.]

solitude, sol′i-tūd, n. a being alone: a lonely life: want of company: a lonely place or desert. [Fr.,—L. sōlitūdō—sōlus, alone.]

solmisation, sol-mi-zā′sh(ó)n, n. sol-faing: a recital of the notes of the gamut, do, re, mi, &c. [sol (or so), mi. See sol-fa.]

solo, sō′lō, n. a piece or passage for one voice or instrument (pl. sō′lōs, soli, sō′lē): any performance, e.g. a song, an aeroplane flight, in

which no other person or instrument participates: a motor-bicycle without sidecar: a card game (solo whist) based on whist.—adj. performed, or for performance, as a solo: for one: performing a solo.—v.i. to fly solo.—n. sō′lōist. [It.,—L. sōlus, alone.]

Solomon's seal, sol′ó-món′s sēl, n. any one of several species of perennial herbs akin to lily of the valley—so named because of the scars on the rootstock. [King Solomon (1 Kings).]

solstice, sol′stis, n. either of the two points in the ecliptic (the first points of the signs Cancer and Capricorn respectively) at which the sun is farthest from the equator and consequently appears to pause and turn in its course: the time when the sun reaches these two points in its orbit, about 21st June and about 21st December.—adj. solstitial (-sti′sh(á)l), pertaining to, or happening at, a solstice, esp. at the north one. [Fr.,—L. solstitium—sōl, the sun, sistĕre, to make to stand—stāre, to stand.]

soluble, sol′ū-bl, adj. capable of being dissolved in a fluid: (fig.) capable of being solved, or resolved.—n. solubil′ity. [L. solūbilis—solvĕre, to loosen.]

solus, sō′lus, adj. alone (in dramatic directions): —fem. sōla. [L. sōlus, -a, -um.]

solution, sol-ū′sh(ò)n, n. act of dissolving: condition of being dissolved: the liquid resulting therefrom: the act or process of discovering the answer to a problem: the answer discovered: a breach (as of continuity): a solution of rubber.—n. sol′ute, a substance which is dissolved in another.—solution of triangles (trig.), finding the values of the remaining sides and angles, some being given. [L. solūtiō—solvĕre, solūtum, to loosen.]

solve, solv, v.t. (obs.) to unbind, free: to discover the answer to: to clear up, explain: to remove (a difficulty).—adj. sol′vable, capable of being solved or explained.—n. sol′vency, state of being solvent, or able to pay all debts.—adj. sol′vent, able to solve or to dissolve: able to pay all debts.—n. anything that dissolves another.—n. sol′ver, one who solves. [L. solvĕre, to loosen, prob. from sē-, aside, luĕre, to loosen.]

sombre, som′bér, adj. dark and gloomy (lit. and fig.).—Also som′brous.—adv. som′brely.—n. som′breness. [Fr. sombre—L. sub, under, umbra, a shade.]

sombrero, som-brā′rō, n. a broad-brimmed hat, generally of felt. [Sp.,—sombra, a shade.]

some, sum, indef. pron. an indefinite part of a whole number or quantity: certain (undetermined) ones: (U.S.) a great deal: (U.S.) a good deal more.—adj. in an indefinite number or quantity: several, a few: a little: a certain: (coll., esp. U.S.) remarkable, no ordinary.—n. and pron. some′body, someone.—adv. some′how, in some way or other.—n. and pron. some′one, some person: a person of importance.—n. some′thing, a thing undefined: a thing of some importance: a measure of truth or relevancy: a portion (of): some of the character or quality (of).—Also used as substitute for any word, or component of a word, forgotten or avoided.—adv. (arch.) in some degree.—adv. some′time, (arch.) formerly: at a

Neutral vowels in unaccented syllables: em′pér-ór; for certain sounds in foreign words see p. ix.

694

time not definitely known (e.g. *sometime in the autumn*): on some future occasion not specified.—*adj.* former, late (e.g. *sometime Professor of French*).—*adv.* **some'times**, at times, now and then.—*n.* **some'what**, an unfixed quantity or degree (of): something (e.g. *somewhat of importance to tell you*; *he is somewhat of a bore*).—*adv.* in some degree.—*adv.* **some'where**, in some place. [O.E. *sum*; O.N. *sumr.*]

somersault, *sum'ér-sölt*, *n.* a leap in which a person turns with his heels over his head.—*v.i.* to turn a somersault.—Also **som'erset**, **sum'merset**. [O.Fr. *sombre saut* (Fr. *soubresaut*)—L. *supra*, over, *saltus*, a leap—*salīre*, to leap.]

somnambulate, *som-nam'bū-lāt*, *v.i.* to walk in sleep.—*ns.* **somnambūlā'tion**; **somnam'bulism**, act or practice of walking in sleep; **somnam'būlist**, a sleep-walker. [L. *somnus*, sleep, *ambulāre*, *-ātum*, to walk.]

somniferous, *som-nif'ér-us*, *adj.* bringing or causing sleep. [L. *somnus*, sleep, *ferre*, to bring.]

somnolence, *som'nō-lens*, *n.* sleepiness: inclination to sleep.—Also **som'nolency**.—*adj.* **som'nolent**, sleepy: drowsy.—*adv.* **som'nolently**. [L. *somnolentia*—*somnus*, sleep.]

son, *sun*, *n.* a male child or offspring, or a descendant, or one so treated: a disciple: a native or inhabitant.—*ns.* **son'-in-law**, a daughter's husband: formerly, a stepson:—*pl.* **sons'-in-law**; **sonn'y**, a little son: a familiar mode of address to a boy; **son'ship**, state or character of a son. [O.E. *sunu*; Du. *zoon*, Ger. *sohn.*]

sonant, *sō'nänt*, *adj.* (*phonet.*) voiced (q.v.).—*n.* a voiced sound. [L. *sonāns*, *-antis*, pr.p. of *sonāre*, to sound.]

sonata, *sō-*, *sō-nä'ta*, *n.* (*orig.*) an instrumental composition: a composition usually of three or more movements designed chiefly for a solo instrument.—*n.* **sonatina** (*sō-nä-tē'na*), a short or simplified sonata. [It.,—L. *sonāre*, to sound.]

sonde, *sond*, *n.* any device for obtaining information about atmospheric and weather conditions at high altitudes. [Fr.]

son et lumière, *son ā lüm-yér*, a dramatic spectacle presented after dark, involving lighting effects on natural features of the country or on a chosen building, and an appropriate theme illustrated by spoken words and by music. [Fr.]

song, *song*, *n.* that which is sung: a short poem or ballad for singing, or set to music: the melody to which it is sung: an instrumental composition of like form and character: singing: the melodious outburst of a bird: any characteristic sound: a poem, or poetry in general: a mere trifle: (*coll.*) a fuss.—*ns.* **song'-bird**, a bird that sings; **song'-book**, a collection of songs; **song'-cy'cle**, a sequence of songs connected in subject; **song'hit**, a popular song and dance tune; **song'ster**, a singer:—*fem.* **song'stress**.—**old song** (see old). [O.E. *sang*—*singan*, to sing; Du. *zang*, Ger. *gesang*, O.N. *söngr.*]

sonic, *son'ik*, *adj.* pertaining to, or using, sound-waves.—**sonic bang**, **sonic boom**, shock-waves projected from an aircraft travelling at supersonic speed, and heard as a loud double report. [L. *sonus*, sound, and suffx. *-ic.*]

sonnet, *son'et*, *n.* a poem in which one thought is developed in a single stanza of fourteen lines, usually iambic pentameters rhyming according to a fixed pattern.—*ns.* **sonneteer'**, a composer of sonnets; **sonn'et-se'quence**, a connected series of sonnets. [It. *sonetto*, dim of *suono*—L. *sonus*, a sound.]

sonorous, *sō-nō'rus*, *so'nō rus*, *adj.* sounding or ringing when struck (e.g. *sonorous metal*): giving a clear, loud sound: high-sounding (e.g. *sonorous phrases*).—*adv.* **sonō'rously**.—*n.* **sonō'rousness**, sonorous quality or character. [L. *sonōrus*—*sonor*, *-ōris*, a sound—*sonāre*, to sound.]

soon, *sōōn*, *adv.* immediately or in a short time: without delay: early (e.g. *can you come as soon as that?*): readily, willingly (implying comparison—e.g. *I would as soon go, sooner go*). [O.E. *sōna.*]

soot, *sŏŏt*, *n.* a black deposit from imperfect combustion of carbonaceous matter: a smut.—*adj.* **soot'y**, of, foul with, or like, soot.—*n.* **soot'iness**. [O.E. *sōt*; Dan. *sod.*]

sooth, *sōōth*, *n.* (*arch.*) truth, reality.—*adj.* (*arch.*) true: (*poet.*) pleasant.—*ns.* **sooth'sayer**, one who divines or foretells events, esp. a pretender to the power; **sooth'saying**, divination, prediction. [O.E. *sōth*, true; O.N. *sannr.*]

soothe, *sōōth*, *v.t.* to calm, comfort, compose, tranquillise: to appease: to allay, soften.—*adj.* **sooth'ing**.—*adv.* **sooth'ingly**. [O.E. *(ge)sōthian*, to confirm as true—*sōth*, true.]

sop, *sop*, *n.* bread or other food dipped or soaked in liquid: a puddle: a soaking: a gift or concession made to propitiate (from the drugged sop the Sibyl gave to Cerberus to gain passage for Aeneas to Hades, *Aen.* vi. 420).—*v.t.* to steep in liquor: to take (up) by absorption:—*pr.p.* **sopp'ing**; *pa.t.* and *pa.p.* sopped.—*n.*, *adj.*, and *adv.* **sopp'ing**.—*adj.* **sopp'y**, drenched, thoroughly wet: sloppily sentimental.—*adv.* **sopp'ily**.—*n.* **sopp'iness**. [O.E. *sopp* (n.), *soppian* (vb.); prob. conn. with *sūpan*, to sup.]

sophism, *sof'izm*, *n.* specious fallacy.—*n.* **soph'ist**, (*cap.*) one of a class of public teachers of rhetoric, philosophy, &c., in ancient Greece: a captious or fallacious reasoner.—*adjs.* **sophis'tic**, **-al**, pertaining to a sophist or to sophistry: fallaciously subtle.—*adv.* **sophis'tically**.—*v.t.* **sophis'ticate**, to render sophistical or unsound: to falsify (e.g. a text) so as to support a line of argument: to imbue (a person) with superficial knowledge and subtlety, or make dissatisfied with simplicity of thought and manners: to give a fashionable air of worldly wisdom to.—*n.* a sophisticated person.—*adj.* **sophis'ticāted**, adulterated, falsified: not simple or natural: worldly-wise and disillusioned: very refined and subtle: with the most up-to-date skill or devices.—*ns.* **sophisticā'tion**, act of sophisticating: state of being sophisticated; **soph'istry**, specious but fallacious reasoning. [Fr. *sophisme*—Gr. *sophisma*—*sophizein*, to make wise—*sophos*, wise.]

---

fāte, fär; mē, hûr (her); *mīne; mōte, för; mūte; mōōn, fŏŏt;* THen (then)

sophomore, *sof'ō-mōr, -mör, n.* (*U.S.*) a second-year student.—Also *adj.* [Prob. from *sophom* (obs. form of *sophism*) and *-or*, as if from *sophos*, wise, *mōros*, foolish.]

soporific, *sōp-, sop-or-if'ik, adj.* inducing sleep.—*n.* anything that causes sleep.—*adj.* **soporif'erous**, soporific. [L. *sopor*, deep sleep, and *facĕre*, to make, *ferre*, to bring.]

soprano, *sō-, sō-prä'no, n.* the highest variety of voice, treble: a singer with such a voice: a part for such a voice:—*pl.* **sopra'nos, sopra'ni.** [It. from *sopra*—L. *suprā*, or *super*, above.]

sorcery, *sōr'ser-i, n.* divination by the assistance of evil spirits: enchantment: magic.—*n.* **sor'cerer**, one who practises sorcery:—*fem.* **sor'ceress**. [O.Fr. *sorcerie*—L. *sors, sortis*, a lot.]

sordid, *sōr'did, adj.* dirty, squalid: meanly avaricious, mercenary: of low or unworthy ideals, ignoble.—*adv.* **sor'didly.**—*n.* **sor'didness**. [L. *sordidus*, dirty.]

sore, *sōr, sör, n.* a painful or tender injured or diseased spot: an ulcer or boil: grief: an affliction.—*adj.* wounded: tender: painful: grievous: irritable, touchy, vexed: aggrieved: intense.—*adv.* **sore'ly**, painfully: grievously: very much.—*n.* **sore'ness**, a feeling of discomfort, pain, or grievance; **sore point**, subject provoking bitter feelings.—**like a sore thumb**, too obtrusive, painful or awkward to be ignored. [O.E. *sār*; Ger. *sehr*, very, O.N. *sārr*, sore.]

sorghum, *sōr'gum, n.* a tropical Old World genus of grasses, including durra (q.v.). [It. *sorgo*, prob. from an East Indian word.]

sorites, *sō-rī'tēz, n.* (*logic*) a string of propositions in which the predicate of one is the subject of the next, the conclusion consisting of the subject of the first and the predicate of the last. [From Gr. *sōros*, a heap.]

Soroptimist, *sor-opt'i-mist, adj.* of an international organisation of women's clubs.—*n.* a member of one of these clubs. [L. *soror*, sister, and **optimist**.]

sorosis, *sō-, sō-rō'sis, n.* a fleshy fruit resulting from many flowers, as the pineapple. [From Gr. *sōros*, a heap.]

sorrel, *sor'él, n.* any of several species of plants with a sour taste belonging to the dock genus: any wood-sorrel (see **wood**).—**salts of sorrel** (see **salt**). [O.Fr. *sorele, surele*—*sur*, sour—O.H.G. *sūr* (Ger. *sauer*).]

sorrel, *sor'él, adj.* reddish-brown.—*n.* a reddish-brown colour: a sorrel horse. [O.Fr. *sorel*; perh. from Low Ger.]

sorrow, *sor'ō, n.* pain of mind, grief: an affliction, misfortune: (*arch.*) an expression of grief.—*v.i.* to feel sorrow or pain of mind, grieve.—*adj.* **sorr'owful**, causing or expressing sorrow: sad, dejected.—*adv.* **sorr'owfully.**—*n.* **sorr'owfulness**. [O.E. *sorg, sorh*; Ger. *sorge*, O.N. *sorg*.]

sorry, *sor'i, adj.* regretful: often merely formally apologetic: regretful in sympathy with another (e.g. *sorry for her, for her disappointment*): poor, worthless, contemptible.—*adv.* **sorr'ily.**—*n.* **sorr'iness**. [O.E. *sārig*, wounded—*sār*, pain; Du. *zeerig*.]

sort, *sört, n.* (*obs.*) a company, group: a class, kind, or species (e.g. *people of this sort, this sort of person*; also—ungrammatically—*these, those sort of people*): something of the nature

but not quite worthy of the name (e.g. *wearing a sort of tiara*): (*arch.*) way, fashion.—*v.t.* to separate into lots or classes, to group, classify: to pick (out), select: (*Scot.*) to adjust, put to rights: (*Scot.*) to deal effectively with (esp. in a vague threat).—*v.i.* to be joined (with others of the same sort): to associate: to harmonise, agree (with).—*n.* **sort'er**, one who separates and arranges, as letters.—**in some sort**, in a way: to some extent; **of a sort, of sorts**, inferior; **out of sorts**, out of order, slightly unwell; **sort of**, (*coll.* or *vulg.*), used adverbially and parenthetically) as it were: rather. [Partly through O.Fr., from L. *sors, sortis*, a lot—*sortīrī*, to draw lots.]

sortie, *sōr'tē, n.* a sally of besieged to attack the besiegers: a raiding excursion.—Also *v.i.* [Fr.,—*sortir*, to go out, to issue.]

S O S, *es-ō-es'*, a code signal (in Morse ···— —···) calling for help.—*n.* a distress signal, an urgent summons.—*v.t.* to send out an urgent summons or request to.—Also *v.i.*

sostenuto, *sos-te-nōō'tō, adj.* (*mus.*) sustained.—*adv.* with full time allowed for each note. [It.]

sot, *sot, n.* (*obs.*) a dolt, dullard: a habitual drunkard.—*adj.* **sott'ish**, foolish: stupid with drink.—*adv.* **sott'ishly.**—*n.* **sott'ishness**. [O.Fr. *sot*.]

sotto voce, *sot'tō vō'chē, adv.* in an undertone, aside. [It., 'below the voice'.]

sou, *sōō, n.* a French five-centime piece. [Fr.,—L. *solidus*, a piece of money.]

soubrette, *sōō-bret', n.* a pert, intriguing, coquettish maid-servant in comedy. [Fr.]

soubriquet. See **sobriquet**.

souchong, *sōō-shong', -chong', n.* a fine black tea. [Chinese *siao*, small, *chung*, sort.]

soufflé, *sōō'flā, n.* a light dish, properly one with white of eggs whisked into a froth.—*adj.* prepared thus. [Fr. pa.p.of *souffler*—L. *sufflāre*, to blow.]

sough, *sow, suf*, or (*Scot.*) *sōōн, v.i.* to sigh, as the wind in trees.—*n.* a murmur, rustle. [O.E. *swōgan*, to rustle.]

sought, *söt, pa.t.* and *pa.p.* of **seek**.

soul, *sōl, n.* that which thinks, feels, desires, &c.: a spirit, embodied or disembodied: innermost being or nature: nobleness of spirit or its sincere expression: embodiment or exemplification: essence: the moving spirit, inspirer, leader: a person, a human being.—*adjs.* **souled**, having a soul (esp. in compounds—e.g. *high-souled*); **soul'ful**, having, or expressive of, elevated feeling or yearning sentiment; **soul'less**, without nobleness of mind, mean: spiritless. [O.E. *sāwol*; Ger. *seele*.]

sound, *sownd, adj.* healthy: uninjured, unimpaired, in good condition: deep (as sleep): solid: thorough (as a thrashing): well-founded, well-grounded (e.g. of reasoning): trustworthy, dependable: of the right way of thinking, orthodox.—*adv.* soundly.—*adv.* **sound'ly**, deeply: thoroughly: in a manner accordant with logic or common sense.—*n.* **sound'ness**. [O.E. *gesund*; Ger. *gesund*.]

sound, *sownd, n.* a narrow passage of water connecting two seas: the swimming bladder of a fish. [O.E. *sund*, swimming.]

sound, *sownd, n.* sensation of hearing: a trans-

Neutral vowels in unaccented syllables: *em'pér-ór*; for certain sounds in foreign words see p. ix.

696

mitted disturbance perceived by, or perceptible by, the ear: esp. a tone produced by regular vibrations (opp. to *noise*): mere noise without meaning (as distinguished from *sense*): a noise, report: range of audibility.—*v.i.* to give out a sound: to resound: to be audible: to give an impression on hearing that it is, to seem to be (*lit.* and *fig.*—e.g. *that sounds like the train*; *it sounds like Mary*; *it sounds like an attempt to blackmail you*).—*v.t.* to cause to make a sound: to produce, utter, make, the sound of: to pronounce: to announce, publish, proclaim (e.g. *to sound his praises*): to examine by percussion and listening.—*p.adj.* **sound′ing,** sonorous, resounding.—*ns.* **sound′-board,** a thin plate of wood or metal which increases the sound in a musical instrument; **sound′ing-board,** a sound-board: the horizontal board or structure over a pulpit, reading-desk, &c., carrying the speaker's voice towards the audience.—*adj.* **sound′proof,** impenetrable by sound.—*ns.* **sound′-track,** on a cinematograph film the strip on which sounds are recorded; **sound′ wave,** a longitudinal disturbance propagated through air or other medium.—**sound barrier** (*aero.*), difficulty met about the speed of sound when power required to increase speed rises steeply; **sound effects,** sounds other than dialogue or music used in films, radio and television. [M.E. *sound* (n.), *sounen* (vb.)—L. *sonāre,* to sound.]

sound, *sownd, v.t.* to measure the depth of: to probe: to try to discover the thoughts and intentions of.—*v.i.* to take soundings: to dive deep (of a whale).—*ns.* **sound′ing,** the action of the verb *sound*; an ascertained depth; **sound′ing-lead,** the weight at the end of a sounding-line, a plummet; **sound′ing-line,** a line with a plummet at the end for soundings.—**sound off** (**about, on**), to speak loudly and freely, esp. in complaint: to boast. [O.E. *sund-* (in compounds), or perh.—O.Fr. *sonder,* to sound.]

soup, *sōōp, n.* the nutritious liquid obtained by boiling meat, vegetables, &c., in stock (q.v.): (*slang*) a photographic developer.—*n.* **soup′-kitch′en,** a place for supplying soup gratis or at a nominal price.—**in the soup,** (*slang*) in difficulties or trouble. [O.Fr. *soupe*; cf. **sop.**]

soupçon, *sōōp-sŏ, n.* a hardly perceptible quantity. [Fr., suspicion, a trace.]

sour, *sowr, adj.* having an acid taste or smell: turned, as milk: rancid, morose, embittered, discontented: crabbed or peevish: cold and wet, as soil.—*v.t.* to make sour: to embitter, to make peevish or discontented.—*v.i.* to become sour: to become peevish or crabbed.—*adv.* **sour′ly.**—*n.* **sour′ness.** [O.E. *sūr*; Ger. *sauer,* O.N. *sūrr.*]

source, *sōrs, sörs, n.* a spring: the head of a stream: that from which anything rises or originates. [O.Fr. *sorse* (Fr. *source*), from *sourdre*—L. *surgĕre,* to rise.]

souse, *sows, n.* pickled meat, esp. pig's feet or ears: pickling liquid: a plunge in pickling or other liquid: a ducking: (*slang*) a drunkard: a heavy blow or fall.—*v.t.* to pickle: to plunge, immerse, duck: to smite.—*v.i.* to wash

thoroughly: (*slang*) to be a drunkard. [Partly O.Fr. *sous, souce,* from the root of salt; partly imit.; partly **source.**]

south, *sowth, n.* the direction in which the sun appears at noon to people north of the Tropic of Cancer: the region lying in that direction: a part of a country, continent, &c., lying relatively in that direction: (*cap.*) in U.S., the Southern States.—*adj.* situated in, facing towards, the south: blowing from the south: south-seeking (of a pole of a magnet).—Also *adv.*—*v.i.* (*sowth*) to veer towards the south: to cross the meridian.—*adjs.* **south′erly** (*suth′*ėr-li—also *adv.*); **south′ern** (*suth′-*); **south′er(n)most** (*suth′-*); **south′ward** (*sowth′-,* also *adv.*), towards the south.—*adv.* **south′wards,** southward.—*adj.* **south′-bound,** travelling southwards.—*ns.* **south′erner** (*suth′-*), a native of, or resident in, the south; **south′ing** (*sowth′-*), southward progress or deviation in sailing.—Compounds such as:—*n.* **south-east′,** the direction midway between south and east: the region lying in that direction: (*poet.*) the wind blowing from that direction.—Also *adj.* and *adv.*—*ns.* **south′west′**; **south′er** (*sowth′-*), **south-east′er, south-west′er** (*sou′west′er*—see also below), winds blowing from these directions.—*adjs.* **south-east′ern; south-west′ern.**—*advs.* **south-east′-ward(s); south-west′ward(s).**—*n.* **southern-wood** (*suth′-*), an aromatic plant of southern Europe, of the wormwood genus.—*adj.* **south-ron** (*suth′-*), southern, esp. English.—*n.* a native or inhabitant of a southern region: an Englishman.—*n.* **south-west′er,** usu. **sou′-west′er,** a waterproof hat with flap at the back of the neck: see also above.—**Southern Cross** (see **cross**); **south pole,** the end of the earth's axis in Antarctica: its projection on the celestial sphere: the south-seeking pole of a magnet; **South Sea,** the Pacific Ocean. [O.E. *sūth*; Ger. *süd,* O.N. *sudhr.*]

Southdown, *sowth′down, n.* a breed of hornless sheep yielding excellent mutton, originally reared on the *South Downs* in Hampshire: their mutton.

souvenir, *sōō-vė-nēr′, n.* a memento, a keepsake. [Fr.,—L. *subvenīre,* to come up, to come to mind—*sub,* under, *venīre,* to come.]

sovereign, *sov′(ė)rin,* or *suv′-, adj.* supreme, possessing absolute authority within a given sphere: superior to all rivals: invariably efficacious: extreme, utter (e.g. *sovereign contempt*).—*n.* a supreme ruler: a monarch: a gold coin = £1.—*n.* **sov′ereignty,** supreme power: dominion. [O.Fr. *sovrain*—L. *super,* above.]

soviet, *sō′vi-et,* or *sō′-, n.* a council, esp. one of those forming (since 1917) the machinery of local and national government in Russia (the Union of Soviet Socialist Republics). [Russ. *sovet.*]

sow, *sow, n.* a female pig: a female badger, &c.: a main channel for molten iron, leading to *pigs* (q.v.): metal solidified there: (*hist.*) a movable shed for protecting besiegers. [O.E. *sū, sugu*; Ger. *sau,* O.N. *sȳr*; L. *sūs,* Gr. *hȳs.*]

sow, *sō, v.t.* to scatter or put in the ground, as seed: to plant by strewing: to scatter seed over: to spread, disseminate.—*v.i.* to scatter seed for growth:—*pa.t.* sowed (*sōd*); *pa.p.* sown (*sōn*) or sowed (*sōd*).—*n.* sow′er. [O.E. *sāwan*; Ger. *säen*, O.N. *sā*.]

soya, *sō′yä, soi′a,* soya bean, soybean, *n.* a leguminous plant, native to China and Japan, now largely cultivated elsewhere, the nutritious beans of which are used for fodder and human consumption and yield an oil which has many important uses.—soya sauce, a thick, piquant sauce made from the soya bean. [Jap. *shō-yu.*]

spa, *spä, n.* a resort where there is a mineral spring. [From *Spa* in Belgium.]

space, *spās, n.* that in which material bodies have extension: extension in one, two, or three dimensions: room: an intervening distance: an open or empty place: regions remote from the earth: an interval between lines or words: an interval between the lines of the stave: a portion or interval of time: opportunity, leisure.—*v.t.* to make or arrange intervals between.—*ns.* space′craft, vehicle, manned or unmanned, designed for putting into space, orbiting the earth or reaching other planets; space′man, -woman, a traveller in interplanetary space; space probe, a spacecraft designed to obtain, and usu. transmit, information about the environment into which it is sent; space′ship, a spacecraft; space′-suit, a suit devised for use in space-travel; space′-travel, travel in interplanetary space; spā′cing.—*adjs.* spā′cial (see spatial); spā′cious (*spā′shŭs*), large in extent: roomy, wide.—*adv.* spā′ciously.—*n.* spā′ciousness.—space age, the present time when exploration of, and ability to travel in, space are increasing; space out, to set wide apart or wider apart; spacious times, days of expansion (in knowledge, trade, &c.) and scope (for discovery, adventure, and the like), as in the reign of Queen Elizabeth. [Fr. *espace*—L. *spatium*; Gr. *spaein,* to draw.]

spade, *spād, n.* a broad-bladed tool with a handle, used for digging.—*v.t.* to dig, work, or to remove, with a spade.—*ns.* spade′ful, as much as a spade will hold; spade′-work, toilsome preparation for a projected operation: drudgery.—call a spade a spade, to speak out plainly without euphemism. [O.E. *spadu, spædu*; akin to Gr. *spathē.* See spade (2).]

spade, *spād, n.* a playing-card with black leaf-shaped pips: (on Spanish cards sword-shaped pips): (*slang*) derogatorily, a Negro or other coloured person. [Sp. *espada,* sword—L. *spatha*—Gr. *spathe,* a broad blade.]

spadix, *spā′diks, n.* (*bot.*) a spike with a swollen fleshy axis, enclosed in a spathe:—*pl.* spadices (*spā-dī′sēz*). [Gr. *spādix, -īkos,* a torn-off (palm) branch.]

spaghetti, *spa-get′i, n.* an Italian paste in solid cords intermediate in size between the type commonly known as macaroni (q.v.) and vermicelli. [It., pl. of *spaghetto,* dim. of *spago,* a cord.]

spahi, *spä′hē, n.* formerly a Turkish, now a French Algerian, cavalryman. [Turk. (from Pers.) *sipāhī*.]

spake, *spāk,* old *pa.t.* of speak.

spalpeen, *spal′pēn, n.* a rascal, a mischievous fellow. [Ir. *spailpín,* a (migratory) labourer.]

span, *span, n.* the space from the end of the thumb to the end of the little finger when the fingers are extended: nine inches: the distance from wing-tip to wing-tip in an aeroplane: distance between abutments, piers, supports, &c., or the portion of a structure (e.g. a bridge) between: total spread or stretch: a stretch of time, esp. a life-time.—*v.t.* to measure by spans or otherwise: to form an arch or bridge across:—*pr.p.* spann′ing; *pa.t., pa.p.* spanned. [O.E. *spann*; cf. Ger. *spanne*.]

span, *span, n.* a pair of horses or a team of oxen.—*v.t.* to yoke. [Du. and Low Ger. *span*.]

spandrel, *span′drel, n.* the space between the curve of an arch and the enclosing mouldings, or the like. [Poss. connected with expand.]

spangle, *spang′gl, n.* a thin glittering plate of metal: a sparkling speck, flake, or spot.—*v.t.* to adorn with spangles.—*v.i.* to glitter. [O.E. *spange*; cf. Ger. *spange, spängel*.]

Spaniard, *span′yärd, n.* a native or citizen of *Spain*.

spaniel, *span′yel, n.* any of several breeds of dogs with large pendent ears, of *Spanish* origin, comprising gun dogs (e.g. field spaniels, springers, clumbers, cockers), water spaniels, and toy dogs (e.g. King Charles and Blenheim spaniels): one who fawns. [O.Fr. *espaigneul* (Fr. *épagneul*)—Sp. *español,* Spanish.]

Spanish, *span′ish, adj.* of or pertaining to *Spain*.—*n.* the language of Spain.—Spanish fly, a green blister beetle (q.v.); Spanish grass, esparto; Spanish juice, liquorice; Spanish Main (i.e. mainland), the mainland coasts of the Caribbean Sea dominated by Spain in the 16th and 17th centuries: (*popularly*) the Caribbean Sea itself.

spank, *spangk, v.i.* and *v.t.* to move, or drive, with speed or spirit.—*n.* spank′er, one who walks with long vigorous strides: a fast-going horse: any person or thing particularly dashing or striking: a fore-and-aft sail on the aftermost mast.—*adj.* span′king, spirited, speedy: striking. [Poss. back-formation from spanking.]

spank, *spangk, v.t.* to strike with the flat of the hand, to smack.—*n.* a loud slap, esp. on the buttocks.—*n.* spank′ing. [Imit.]

spanner, *span′er, n.* a wrench for tightening or loosening nuts, screws, &c.—throw a spanner in the works, to introduce confusion. [Ger.; cf. span (1).]

spar, *spär, n.* a rafter: a pole: (*chiefly Scot.*) a bar or rail: a general term for masts, yards, booms, gaffs, &c. [O.E. *gesparrian,* to bar; cf. O.N. *sparri,* Du. *spar*.]

spar, *spär, n.* any bright non-metallic mineral with a good cleavage (esp. in compounds, as *fluorspar*). [Middle Low Ger. *spar,* related, to O.E. *spærstān,* gypsum.]

spar, *spär, v.i.* to fight with spurs, as cocks: to box, or make the motions of boxing: to exchange provocative remarks:—*pr.p.* sparr′ing; *pa.t.* and *pa.p.* sparred.—sparring partner, one with whom a boxer practises: a person with whom one enjoys lively arguments. [O.Fr. *esparer,* to kick out; prob. Gmc.]

sparable, *spar′a-bl, n.* a small headless shoe-nail, shaped like a sparrow's bill. [sparrow, bill.]

Neutral vowels in unaccented syllables: *em′pér-ór*; for certain sounds in foreign words see p. ix.

spare, *spār, v.t.* to use frugally: to refrain from using: to do without or afford (e.g. *I cannot spare her, spare the time*): (*arch.*) to refrain from (with *to*): to forbear to hurt, injure, kill, &c: to treat mercifully: to forbear to inflict (something) on (a person).—*v.i.* to be frugal: to forbear, to be merciful.—*adj.* sparing, frugal, scanty: lean: extra, not in actual use: kept or available for others or for such purposes as may occur.—*n.* a spare man: a spare part: a duplicate kept or carried for emergencies.—*adv.* **spare'ly.**—*ns.* **spare'ness; spare'rib,** a piece of pork consisting of ribs with a little meat adhering to them.—*adj.* **spä'ring,** scanty: frugal, economical.—*adv.* **spä'ringly,** frugally: not abundantly or frequently.—**spare part,** a duplicate part of a vehicle or machine carried or kept for an emergency; **spare room,** a bedroom for visitors.—**to spare,** over and above what is required. [O.E. *sparian,* to spare—*spær,* sparing.]

spark, *spärk, n.* a glittering or glowing particle of matter thrown off by an incandescent substance: anything of like appearance or (esp. *fig.*) character, as anything easily extinguished, ready to cause explosion, burning hot: a flash: an electric discharge across a gap: a gay sprightly person: (*arch.*) a lover, beau.—*v.i.* to emit sparks.—*ns.* **sparking-plug,** a plug screwed into the cylinder head of an internal-combustion engine and carrying wires between which an electric spark passes and fires the explosive mixture of gases; **spark-gap,** space between electrodes across which electric sparks pass.—**spark (off),** to cause to begin, kindle.—**(not) a spark of,** (not even) a very small amount of (esp. a quality —e.g. imagination). [O.E. *spearca*; Du. *spark.*]

sparkle, *spärk'l, n.* a little spark: emission of sparks: bright effervescence, as in wines: vivacity: coruscation of wit.—*v.i.* to emit sparks: to shine, glitter: to effervesce with glittering bubbles, as certain wines: to be bright, animated, vivacious, or witty.—*n.* **spark'ler,** one who, or that which, sparkles: a sparkling gem: a small firework which can be held in the hand.—*n.* and *adj.* **spark'ling.** [Inten. and freq. of **spark.**]

sparrow, *spar'ō, n.* an Old World genus of birds of the finch family, one very common species of which, the house-sparrow, is remarkable for the boldness of its approach to man.—*ns.* **sparr'ow-grass,** asparagus; **sparr'ow-hawk,** a genus of small hawks. [O.E. *spearwa*; O.N. *spörr,* Ger. *sperling.*]

sparse, *spärs, adj.* thinly scattered: scanty.—*adv.* **sparse'ly.**—*n.* **sparse'ness.** [L. *sparsus,* pa.p. of *spargĕre,* to scatter; Gr. *speirein,* to sow.]

Spartan, *spär'tán, adj.* of or pertaining to *Sparta* in ancient Greece: rigorously severe: trained to endure privation or hardship.

spasm, *spazm, n.* an involuntary and irregular contraction of muscles, less violent than a convulsion: a strong short burst (of feeling or activity).—*n.* **spasmod'ic,** a medicine for relieving spasms.—*adjs.* **spasmod'ic, -al,** relating to, or consisting in, spasms: convulsive: intermittent.—*adv.* **spasmod'ically.**—*adj.* **spastic** (*spas'-*), of the nature of, character-

ised by, spasm: spasmodic.—*n.* one suffering from spastic paralysis.—**spastic paralysis,** a form of paralysis in which the patient suffers from permanent muscle constriction or involuntary jerky muscle movement. [Gr. *spasma, -atos,* convulsion, and *spastikos—spaein,* to draw, pull, convulse.]

spat, *spat, pa.t.* of **spit** (2).

spat, *spat, n.* the spawn of shellfish.—*v.i.* to shed spawn. [Perh. from root of **spit** (2).]

spat, *spat, n.* a short gaiter. [**spatterdash.**]

spate, *spāt, n.* (orig. *Scot.*) a flood.

spathe, *spāтн, n.* (*bot.*) a sheathing bract, usu. one enclosing a spadix (e.g. the white part of the arum lily). [Gr. *spathē,* a broad blade.]

spatial, *spā'sh(á)l, adj.* relating to space.—Also (*rare*) **spä'cial.**—*adv.* **spä'tially.** [L. *spatium,* space.]

spatter, *spat'ér, v.t.* to scatter, sprinkle (something about): to sprinkle (a thing) with dirt or anything moist: to cast a slur on the reputation of, sully.—*v.i.* to fly or fall in drops: to let drops fall or fly about.—*n.* the act of spattering: what is spattered.—*n.* **spatt'erdash,** a long gaiter or legging. [Cf. Du. and Low Ger. *spatten.*]

spatula, *spat'ū-la, n.* a broad blunt blade or flattened spoon: a similar instrument made of wood, plastic or rubber. (*med.*) an instrument for holding down the tongue.—*adj.* **spat'ulate,** shaped like a spatula: broad and rounded at the tips and tapering at the base. [L. *spatula, spathula,* dim. of *spatha*—Gr. *spathē,* a broad blade.]

spavin, *spav'in, n.* chronic inflammation of the hock joint of a horse.—*adj.* **spav'ined,** affected with spavin. [O.Fr. *espa(r)vain.*]

spawn, *spön, n.* a mass of eggs, as of fishes or frogs, laid in water: brood: (*contemptuously*) offspring: mushroom mycelium.—*adj.* containing spawn.—*v.t.* to produce (spawn): (*contemptuously*) to generate, esp. in mass (*lit.* and *fig.*).—*v.i.* to produce or deposit spawn: (*fig.*) to put forth any worthless production in large quantities: to come forth as or like spawn. [O.Fr. *espandre,* to shed—L. *expandĕre,* to spread out.]

speak, *spēk, v.i.* to utter words: to talk: to hold a conversation (with—or with *to*): to make a speech: to sound: to convey an impression (of), to be evidence (of).—*v.t.* to pronounce: to converse, or be able to converse, in (a specified language): to voice, to make known (e.g. *to speak one's thoughts, the truth*): to utter (e.g. *to speak sense*): (*arch.*) to declare (one) to be (e.g. *that speaks him a patrician*): to hail, or to communicate with:—*pa.t.* **spōke,** (*arch.*) **spāke;** *pa.p.* **spōken.**—*ns.* **speak'-eas'y** (*U.S.*) an illicit dram-shop, shebeen; **speak'er,** one who speaks or proclaims: (*cap.*) the person who presides in a deliberative or legislative body, as the House of Commons, of Representatives: short for *loudspeaker;* **Speak'ership,** the office of Speaker.—*adj.* **speak'ing,** seeming to speak—expressive, or lifelike: used to assist the voice.—*ns.* **speak'ing-trum'pet,** an instrument for intensifying the sound of the voice; **speak'ing-tube,** a tube for speaking through, communicating from one room to another.—**speak one fair,** to

address one in conciliatory terms; **speak out,
up,** to speak clearly and audibly: to speak
boldly and unreservedly; **speak to,** to talk
with: to reprove: to attest, testify to; **speak
well for,** to be creditable to. [O.E. *specan* (for
sprecan); Du. *spreken*, Ger. *sprechen*.]

spear, *spēr, n.* a weapon used in war and hunting, having a long shaft pointed with iron: a
lance with barbed prongs used for catching
fish: a spearsman: a shoot (e.g. of a
grass).—*v.t.* to pierce or kill with a spear.—*ns.*
spear'-head, the iron point of a spear: the
foremost and most effective element in an
attacking force (*lit.* and *fig.*); **spear(s)'man,** a
man armed with a spear; **spear'mint,** the common garden mint.—**spear side,** the male line
of a family. [O.E. *spere*; Ger. *speer.*]

spec, *spek, n.* a coll. abbrev. of **specification,** and
of **speculation.—on spec,** on the chance of
achieving something.

special, *spesh'(ä)l, adj.* especial—i.e. (*a*) exceptional, uncommon, marked, or (*b*) peculiar to
one person or thing: limited (to one person or
thing): designed—appointed, arranged, run,
&c.—for a particular purpose (e.g. *special envoy, performance, train*): additional to ordinary.—*n.* any person or thing set apart for a
particular duty or purpose.—*adv.* **specially**
(*spesh'äl-i*).—*v.t.* **spec'ialise,** to narrow and
intensify (e.g. one's studies): to become or be
a specialist in (with *in*): to differentiate: to
develop (a part of an organism) in such a way
that it becomes adapted for a particular function: to specify, particularise.—*v.i.* to give particular attention to a single branch of study or
business: to go into details or particulars: to
become differentiated.—*adj.* **spec'ialised,** adapted to a particular function, or limited purpose: restricted and made more exact (e.g.
specialised meaning): appropriate to a specialist (e.g. *specialised knowledge*).—*ns.* **spec-
ialisa'tion,** the act or process of specialising;
spec'ialist, one who applies himself to a special business or pursuit; **speciality** (*spesh-i-
al'-i-ti*), the particular quality which distinguishes a person or thing from others: a specialty; **specialty** (*spesh'äl-ti*), a special activity
or object of attention: a special product.—
special correspondent, a person employed
to send reports to a particular newspaper,
agency, &c.; **special offer,** an article offered
for sale at a reduced price for a fixed period.
[L. *speciālis,* particular—*speciēs.* See **species.**]

specie, *spē'shi, n.* gold and silver coin. [L. *in
speciē,* in (the required) kind.]

species, *spē'shēz, spē'shēz, spē'shi-ēz, n.* a group
of individuals having common characteristics,
specialised from others of the *genus*: a kind or
sort:—*pl.* **spe'cies.** [L. *speciēs,* kind or sort.]

specify, *spes'i-fī, v.t.* to mention particularly: to
mention in detail: to set down as a requis-
ite:—*pa.t.* and *pa.p.* spec'ified.—*n.* specif'ic, a
remedy regarded as a certain cure for a particular disease (also *fig.*).—*adjs.* **specif'ic, -al,**
pertaining to or constituting a species: distinctive, peculiar: precise.—*n.* **specifica'tion,**
the act of specifying: any point or particular
specified: a comprehensive statement of details.—**specific gravity,** now more usu. *relative
density* (q.v.). [O.Fr. *specifier*—L.L. *specifi-*

cāre—L. *speciēs,* kind, *facĕre,* to make.]

specimen, *spes'i-mĕn, n.* an object or portion
serving as a sample, esp. for purposes of study
or collection: (*coll.*) an individual, person. [L.
specimen—*specĕre,* to see.]

specious, *spē'shüs, adj.* that looks well at first
sight: deceptively attractive: plausible.—*ns.*
speciosity (*spē-shi-os'i-ti*), **spē'ciousness.**—
adv. **spē'ciously.** [L. *speciōsus,* showy, plausible—*speciēs,* form, kind—*specĕre,* to look at.]

speck, *spek, n.* a small spot: the least morsel or
quantity.—*v.t.* to spot. [O.E. *specca.*]

speckle, *spek'l, n.* a little spot, esp. of colour.—
v.t. to mark with speckles.—*adjs.* **speck'led;
speck'less,** spotless, perfectly clean.—*adv.*
speck'lessly. [**speck.**]

spectacle, *spek'tä-kl, n.* a sight: a pageant, exhibition: (in *pl.*) a pair of lenses (with nose
piece, and supports passing over the ears) to
help vision.—*adjs.* **spec'tacled,** wearing spectacles; **spectacular** (*-tak'ū-lär*), of the nature
of, or marked by, unusual display: remarkable, extraordinary.—*n.* a theatrical show, esp.
on television, or any display, that is large-
scale and elaborate.—*adv.* **spectac'ularly.** [L.
spectāculum—*spectāre, -ātum,* intensive of
specĕre, to look at.]

spectator, *spek-tā'tor, n.* one who looks on.
[L.,—*spectāre.* See **spectacle.**]

spectre, *spek'tĕr, n.* a ghost.—*adj.* **spec'tral,** relating to, or like, a spectre.—*adv.* **spec'trally.**
[L. *spectrum,* a vision—*specĕre,* to look at.]

spectrum, *spek'trum, n.* the image of something
seen continued after the eyes are closed:
(**optical spectrum**) the range of colour produced by a prism or by any form of the device
known as a diffraction (q.v.) grating—violet,
indigo, blue, green, yellow, orange, red (the
colours of the rainbow): any analogous range
of radiations in order of wavelength:—*pl.*
spec'tra.—*ns.* **spectrom'eter,** an instrument
for measuring refractive indices: one used for
measurement of wavelength or energy distribution in a beam of radiation; **spec'troscope,**
an instrument for obtaining and observing
spectra.—*adjs.* **spectroscop'ic, -al.**—*adv.* **spectroscop'ically.—spectrum analysis,** determination of chemical composition by observing
the spectrum of rays coming from or through
the substance. [L.,—*specĕre,* to look at.]

speculate, *spek'ū-lāt, v.i.* to reflect (on): to
theorise, make conjectures or guesses
(about): to engage in business transactions
that offer profits at the risk of loss.—*n.* **specu-
lā'tion,** act of speculating: meditation: conjecture: any more or less risky investment of
money for the sake of profits.—*adj.* **spec'ulative,** of the nature of, based on, speculation:
given to speculation or theory: engaging in
speculation in business, &c.—*adv.* **spec'ula-
tively.**—*n.* **spec'ulator.**—*adj.* **spec'ulatory,** exercising speculation: adapted for spying or
viewing. [L. *speculātus,* pa.p. of *speculārī*—
specula, a lookout—*specĕre,* to look at.]

speculum, *spek'ū-lum, n.* (*opt.*) a reflector
usually made of polished metal: (*surg.*) an
instrument for bringing into view parts otherwise hidden:—*pl.* **spec'ula.** [L.,—*specĕre,* to
look at.]

sped, *pa.t.* and *pa.p.* of **speed** (also *p.adj.*).

Neutral vowels in unaccented syllables: *em'pér-ör*; for certain sounds in foreign words see p. ix.

speech, *spēch, n.* that which is spoken: language: the power of speaking: manner of speaking: oration, discourse.—*v.i.* **speech′ify,** (implying contempt) to make speeches, harangue.—*ns.* **speechifica′tion,** (*coll.*); **speech′-ifier.**—*adj.* **speech′less,** unable to speak.—*adv.* **speech′lessly.**—*ns.* **speech′lessness; speech′-day,** a day at the close of a school year when the public are admitted to a ceremony at which recitations and/or speeches are made and prizes are distributed; **speech′-read′ing,** lip-reading; **speech′-therapy,** treatment of speech defects. [O.E. *spǣc, sprǣc*; Ger. *sprache.*]

speed, *spēd, n.* quickness, velocity: good progress.—*v.i.* to move quickly, to hurry: (*arch.*) to succeed, fare: to drive at high, or at dangerously or illegally high, speed.—*v.t.* to further, help: to send forth with good wishes: to push forward: to regulate the speed of:—*pr.p.* **speed′ing;** *pa.t.* and *pa.p.* **sped.**—*p.adj.* **sped,** (*arch.*) gone: slain.—*n.* **speedom′eter,** an instrument for measuring speed.—*adj.* **speed′y,** swift: prompt: soon achieved.—*adv.* **speed′ily.**—*ns.* **speed′iness; speed′-boat,** a swift motor-boat; **speed′-limit,** the maximum speed at which motor vehicles may be driven legally on certain roads; **speed′way,** a road for fast traffic: a motorcycle racing track.—**speed up,** to quicken the rate of (*n* **speed′-up,** an acceleration, esp. in work). [O.E. *spēd*; Du. *spoed.*]

speedwell, *spēd′wel, n.* a genus (also called *veronica*) of herbaceous plants and small shrubs with beautiful blue, white, or pink flowers. [**speed, well.**]

spell, *spel, n.* (*arch.*) a tale, news: any form of words supposed to possess magical power: fascination. [O.E. *spell,* a narrative; O.N. *spjall,* a tale.]

spell, *spel, v.t.* to name or set down in order the letters of: to represent in letters (e.g. *ç-a-t* *spells cat*): (*fig.*) to import, amount to: to read laboriously, letter by letter: to make out, decipher, laboriously.—*v.i.* to spell words, esp. correctly:—*pr.p.* **spell′ing;** *pa.t.* and *pa.p.* **spelled, spelt.**—*n.* **spell′binder,** (*U.S.*) an orator, usu. political or evangelical, who holds his audience spell-bound.—*adj.* **spell′bound,** entranced, fascinated.—*ns.* **spell′er; spell′ing; spell′ing-bee,** a competition in spelling; **spell′ing-book,** a book for teaching to spell.—**spell (it) out,** to be specific in explaining something. [O.Fr. *espeller* (Fr. *épeler*), of Gmc. origin. See **spell** (1).]

spell, *spel, v.t.* (*rare*) to take the place of (another) at work:—*pr.p.* **spell′ing;** *pa.t.* and *pa.p.* **spelled.**—*n.* a turn at work: a bout, turn: a short time: a stretch of time. [O.E. *spelian,* to act for another; cf. Du. *spelen,* Ger. *spielen,* to play.]

spelt, *spelt, n.* a species of wheat, the grains of which are firmly enclosed in the chaff, widely cultivated in Europe in ancient times and still grown in mountainous regions. [O.E. *spelt* — L.L. *spelta.*]

spelter, *spel′tėr, n.* crude commercial zinc: a soldering alloy (also **spelter solder**). [Low Ger. *spialter.*]

spencer, *spens′ėr, n.* (late 18th, early 19th cen-

tury) a short double-breasted overcoat: also a woman's short over-jacket: now, a knitted woollen jacket. [After Earl *Spencer.*]

spend, *spend, v.t.* to expend, pay out (money): to give, bestow, employ (e.g. one's energies) for any purpose. to exhaust: to pass, as time.—*v.i.* to expend money:—*pr.p.* **spend′ing;** *pa.t.* and *pa.p.* **spent.**—*n.* **spen′der.**—*p.adj.* **spent,** exhausted: having little force left (e.g. of a bullet, a storm): (of fish) exhausted by spawning. [O.E. *spendan* — L. *expendĕre* or *dispendĕre,* to weigh out.]

spendthrift, *spend′thrift, n.* one who spends the savings of thrift: a prodigal.—*adj.* excessively lavish. [**spend** and **thrift.**]

Spenserian, *spen-sē′ri-án, adj.* pertaining to Edmund *Spenser* (1552–99), esp. to his stanza in *The Faerie Queene,* of eight decasyllabic lines and an Alexandrine, rhyming according to the scheme *a b a b b c b c c.*

spent, *spent, pa.t.* and *pa.p.* of **spend.**

sperm, *spûrm, n.* semen: a spermatozoon: (*fig.*) generative substance: spermaceti.—*adjs.* **spermat′ic, -al,** pertaining to, consisting of, conveying, sperm: generative; **sper′matoid,** sperm-like.—*ns.* **spermatozo′on,** one of the male reproductive cells of animals, a male gamete:—*pl.* **spermatozo′a; sperm′-oil,** oil from the sperm-whale; **sperm′-whale,** the cachalot, a species of whale from which spermaceti is obtained. [Fr.—L. *sperma,* seed—Gr. *sperma, -atos—speirein,* to sow.]

spermaceti, *spèr-ma-set′i,* or *-sē′ti, n.* a waxy matter obtained mixed with oil from the head of the sperm-whale and others, used for candles and ointment. Also *adj.* [L. *sperma,* seed, *cētī,* gen. of *cētus,* a whale—Gr. *kētos.*]

spew, spue, *spū, v.t.* and *v.i.* to vomit: to eject with loathing. [O.E. *spīwan*; Du. *spuwen,* Ger. *speien*; also L. *spuĕre,* Gr. *ptyein.*]

sphagnum, *sfag′num, n.* a genus of mosses—peat- or bog-moss—used for dressing wounds.—*adj.* **sphag′nous.** [Gr. *sphagnos,* moss.]

sphenoid, *sfē′noid, -oid′al, adj.* wedge-shaped—esp. of a set of bones at base of the skull. [Gr. *sphēn, sphēnos,* wedge, *eidos,* form.]

sphere, *sfēr, n.* a solid body bounded by a surface of which all points are equidistant from a centre: its bounding surface: a ball or other spherical object: the apparent sphere of the heavens in which the stars seem to be placed: any one of the concentric spherical shells once supposed to carry the planets in their revolutions: a circle of society, orig. of the higher ranks: domain, scope, range: field of activity: any one of the celestial bodies.—*adjs.* **spher′al; spheric** (*sfer′ik*)**, -al,** of a sphere or spheres: having the form of a sphere.—*adv.* **spher′ically.**—*ns.* **spher′icalness, sphericity** (*sfer-is′i-ti*), state or quality of being spherical; **sphē′roid,** a body or figure of a form differing very slightly from that of a sphere esp. an ellipsoid of revolution.—*adj.* **sphē-roi′dal,** having the form of a spheroid.—*n.* **spher′ūle,** a little sphere.—*adj.* **sphē′ry,** spherical, round: belonging to the celestial spheres.—**spherical triangle,** a triangle on a sphere formed by the intersection of three arcs of great circles (q.v.). [Fr.—L. *sphaera* — Gr. *sphaira.*]

fāte, fär; mē, hûr (her); *mīne; mōte, fõr; mūte; mōōn, fõõt;* тнen (then)

sphincter, *sfingk'tėr, n.* (*anat.*) a muscle whose contraction narrows or shuts an orifice. [Gr. *sphinktēr—sphingein,* to bind tight.]

Sphinx, *sfingks, n.* a monster of Greek mythology, with the head of a woman and the body of a lioness, that strangled all wayfarers who could not solve the riddle she proposed: the gigantic image of the Sphinx near the Pyramids in Egypt: (**sphinx**) an enigmatic or inscrutable person. [Gr.,—*sphingein,* to bind tight, throttle.]

spica, *spī'ka, n.* a spiral bandage with reversed turns.—*adjs.* **spī'cāte, -d,** in, or having, forming, a spike: spike-like. [L. *spīca,* an ear of corn.]

spice, *spīs, n.* an aromatic and pungent vegetable substance used as a condiment and for seasoning food (e.g. pepper, ginger, nutmeg, cinnamon): such substances collectively or generally: (*fig.*) anything that adds piquancy or interest: (*fig.*) a smack, flavour, tincture.—*v.t.* to season with spice: to impart variety to, to flavour.—*n.* **spī'cery,** spices in general: a repository of spices. [O.Fr. *espice*—Late L. *speciēs,* kinds of goods, spices—L. *speciēs,* a kind.]

spick, *spik, n.* (*arch.*) a nail, a spike.—*adj.* **spick'-and-span** (orig. **spick-and-span new,** perfectly new), trim and speckless, like a spike new cut and a chip new split. [**spike,** a nail.]

spicy, *spī'si, adj.* producing or abounding with spices: fragrant: pungent: piquant, pointed, racy, sometimes with a touch of indecency.—*adv.* **spī'cily.**—*n.* **spī'ciness.** [**spice.**]

spider, *spī'dėr, n.* one of an order of small predaceous creatures, resembling insects but differing structurally from them, furnished with spinnerets from which issues a viscous fluid hardening into a silken thread and used to spin the cobweb or **spider-web** in which flies and other victims are ensnared.—*adj.* **spī'dery,** spider-like: sprawling and thin (e.g. *spidery handwriting*): abounding in spiders.—*n.* **spi'der-man,** an erector of steel building structures. [M.E. *spither*—O.E. *spinnan,* to spin; cf. Dan. *spinder,* Ger. *spinne.*]

spiel, *spēl, n.* eloquent talk: sales talk: a long story.—*v.i.* to talk glibly.—*n.* **spiel'er,** one who talks glibly and persuasively. [Ger., play, game.]

spigot, *spig'ŏt, n.* a small pointed peg or bung. [Conn. with root of **spike,** a nail.]

spike, *spīk, n.* an ear of corn: (*bot.*) an inflorescence in which sessile (q.v.) flowers, or spikelets are arranged on a long axis.—*n.* **spike'let,** in grasses, &c., a small spike itself forming part of a greater inflorescence. [L. *spīca,* an ear of corn.]

spike, *spīk, n.* a hard, thin, pointed object: a large nail: (in *pl.*) spiked shoes.—*v.t.* to fasten, set, or pierce with a spike or spikes: to make (a gun) useless, orig. by driving a spike into the vent.—*p.adj.* **spiked,** furnished, fastened, or stopped with spikes.—*adj.* **spī'ky,** furnished with spikes: having a sharp point.—**spiked shoes,** shoes with projecting pieces of metal on the soles, to prevent runners, &c., from slipping; **spike heel,** a very narrow metal heel on a woman's shoe; **spike nail,** a large,

small-headed nail. [O.E. *spīcing,* a spike, nail; perh.—L. *spīca,* an ear of corn.]

spikenard, *spīk'närd, n.* an aromatic oil or balsam yielded by an Indian plant, the *nardus,* or a substitute: the plant itself. [L. *spīca nardī.* See **nard.**]

spill, *spil, v.t.* to allow to run out of a vessel: to shed (blood): to pour: to cause or allow to fall to the ground.—*v.i.* to be shed: to be allowed to fall, be lost, or wasted:—*pa.t.* and *pa.p.* spilled, spilt.—*n.* a fall, a tumble.—*ns.* **spill'age,** the act of spilling: that which is spilt; **spill'way,** a passage for overflow-water from a dam.—**spill the beans,** (*coll.*) to divulge information, esp. unintentionally. [O.E. *spillan*; Du. *spillen,* O.N. *spilla,* to destroy.]

spill, *spil, n.* a small peg or pin to stop a hole: a thin strip of wood or twisted paper for lighting a pipe, &c. [Ety. uncertain.]

spin, *spin, v.t.* to draw out and twist into threads: to shape into threadlike form (usu. in *pa.p.*—e.g. *spun glass*): to draw out as a thread, as spiders do: to form by spinning: to twirl, revolving rapidly: to send hurtling.—*v.i.* to practise the art or trade of spinning: to perform the act of spinning: to whirl: to go swiftly, esp. on wheels:—*pr.p.* spinn'ing; *pa.t.* and *pa.p.* spun.—*n.* a rotatory motion: a cycle ride: a short trip in a motor-car: a spurt at high speed: the movement of an aircraft in a steep continuous helical (q.v.) dive: a spiral descent (*lit.* and *fig.*): confused excitement.—*ns.* **spin'-drier,** a device that dries washed clothes without wringing, by forcing the water out of them by means of the centrifugal force in a rapidly revolving drum (*v.t.* **spin'-dry**); **spinn'er; spinn'eret,** a spinning organ in spiders, &c.; **spinn'ing-jenn'y,** a machine by which a number of threads can be spun at once; **spinn'ing-mill,** a factory where thread is spun; **spinn'ing-wheel,** a machine for spinning yarn, consisting of a wheel driven by the hand or by a treadle, which drives one or two spindles; **spin'-off,** a by-product that proves profitable on its own account.—**spin a yarn,** to tell a yarn (q.v.); **spin out,** to prolong: to make to last. [O.E. *spinnan*; Ger. *spinnen.*]

spinach, *spin'ij, n.* a plant whose young leaves are eaten as a vegetable: the leaves. [O.Fr. *espinage, espinache*; of doubtful origin.]

spinal, *spīn'ál, adj.* See **spine.**

spindle, *spin'dl, n.* the pin by which thread is twisted in spinning: a pin on which anything turns: the fusee of a watch: anything very slender.—*v.i.* to grow long and slender.—*ns.pl.* **spin'dle-legs, -shanks,** long slim legs—hence an unusually tall and slender person.—*adjs.* **spin'dle-legged, -shanked; spin'dly,** disproportionally long and slender.—**spindle side,** the female line of a family, the *distaff side.* [O.E. *spinel—spinnan,* to spin; Ger. *spindel.*]

spindrift, *spin'drift, n.* the spray blown from the crests of waves.—Also **spoon'drift.** [Scot. form of *spoon* (arch. and of uncertain ety.), to scud, and **drift.**]

spine, *spīn, n.* a thorn: a thin, pointed spike, esp. in fishes: the backbone of an animal: any like ridge.—*adj.* **spīn'al,** of the backbone.—*n.* **spine'-chiller,** a frightening story, happening, &c.—*adjs.* **spine'less,** having no spine: unable

Neutral vowels in unaccented syllables: *em'pėr-ór*; for certain sounds in foreign words see p. ix.

to make a firm stand: irresolute; **spī′nose** (or
-*nos′*), **spī′nous**, full of spines: thorny; **spī′ny**,
full of spines: thorny: troublesome, per-
plexed.—**spina bifida**, (*bif′i-da*), a condition in
which two parts of the bony spinal canal fail
to unite perfectly at the embryo stage; **spinal
column**, the backbone; **spinal cord**, a cord of
nervous tissue, contained in the **spinal canal**
(a passage running through the vertebrae),
and forming the most important part of the
central nervous system. [O.Fr. *espine*—L.
spīna, a thorn.]

spinet, *spin′et, spin-et′, n.* (*mus.*) an instrument
like a small harpsichord. [It. *spinetta*.]

spinnaker, *spin′á-kėr, n.* a jib-shaped sail sometimes carried by racing yachts. [Said to be
from a yacht, the *Sphinx*, that carried it.]

spinneret, &c. See **spin**.

spinney, also **spinny**, *spin′i, n.* a small clump of
trees, a copse:—*pl.* **spinn′eys** (**spinn′ies**).
[O.Fr. *espinei*—L. *spīnētum*, a thorn-hedge,
thicket—*spīna*, a thorn.]

spinster, *spin′stėr, n.* an unmarried woman: an
old maid.—*ns.* **spin′sterhood; spin′stress**, a
woman who spins a spinster. [**spin**, and suffix
-*ster*.]

spiracle, *spīr′á-kl, n.* an air-hole or air-shaft: a
vent, passage: (*zool.*) a breathing aperture,
ranging from the minute orifices of members
of the Arthropoda (q.v.) to the blow-hole or
nostril of whales, &c. [L. *spīrāculum* *spīrāre*,
to breathe.]

spiraea, *spī′ rē′a, n.* the genus of plants of which
meadow-sweet is a species. [L.,—Gr. *speiraiā*,
meadow-sweet—*speira*, a coil.]

spiral, *spīr′ál, adj.* See **spire** (1) and (2).

spirant, *spī′ránt, n.* any of certain open (q.v.)
consonants, esp. *f* and *v, th,* тн; sometimes
made to include the sibilants, *s, sh, z, zh.* [L.
spīrans, -*antis*, pr.p. of *spīrāre*, to breathe.]

spire, *spīr, n.* (*arch.*) a shoot, sprout: a tapering
or conical body, esp. a tree-top: a tall, slender
architectural structure tapering to a point.
v.i. to sprout: to shoot up.—*adjs.* **spir′al**, towering and tapering; **spī′ry**, tapering like a spire
or a pyramid: abounding in spires. [O.E. *spīr*,
shoot, sprout.]

spire, *spīr, n.* a coil: a spiral: the spiral part of a
shell, excluding the body whorl.—*v.i.* to wind,
mount, or proceed, in spirals.—*adj.* **spī′ral**,
winding like the spring of a watch: winding
like the thread of a screw.— *n.* a spiral line,
course, or object: (*geom.*) a curve (usu.
plane), the locus of a point whose distance
from a fixed point round which it moves increases or decreases according to a rule: (incorrectly) a helix: a progressively more rapid
increase or decrease, rise or fall (e.g. in prices
or in the value of money).—*v.i.* to go, or move,
in a spiral.—*v.t.* to make into a spiral.—*adv.*
spir′ally.—*n.* **spir′ochaete** (-*kēt;* Gr. *chaitē,*
hair, mane), any of a number of spirally coiled
bacteria, the cause of various diseases. [Gr.
speira, a coil.]

spirit, *spir′it, n.* vital principle: the soul: a disembodied soul: a ghost: an incorporeal being:
actuating emotion, disposition, frame of mind
(e.g. *in a spirit of rivalry;* *in the right spirit*)
—often in *pl.* (e.g. *in good, low, spirits*): animation, verve: courage: (in *pl.*) cheerful or

exuberant vivacity: a leading, independent, or
lively, person: a distilled liquid (e.g. *motor
spirit, wood spirits*): (usu. in *pl.*) distilled
liquor (e.g. whisky, brandy): the essence,
chief quality: the real meaning, intent (e.g. *the
spirit of the law in preference to the letter*).—
v.t. to convey away secretly, as if by magic.—
adj. **spir′ited**, full of spirit, life, or fire: animated.—*adv.* **spir′itedly.**—*ns.* **spir′itedness;
spir′it-lamp**, a lamp in which an inflammable
spirit is burned to give heat.—*adj.* **spir′itless**,
without spirit, cheerfulness, or courage:
dead.—*adv.* **spir′itlessly.**—*ns.* **spir′it-lev′el**, a
glass tube nearly filled with alcohol, and containing a small bubble of air which indicates
by its position variation from perfect level;
spir′it-rapp′er, one who claims that spirits
convey intelligence to him by raps or
knocks.—*adj.* **spir′itual**, of, of the nature of,
relating to, a spirit or spirits: of, of the nature
of, relating to, spirit or the soul: highly refined
in thought and feeling, habitually or naturally
looking to things of the spirit: ecclesiastical.—*n.* an American Negro hymn, sometimes
with syncopated rhythm.—*v.t.* **spir′itūalise**, to
imbue with spirituality: to free from sensuality: to give a spiritual meaning to.—*ns.* **spiri-
tualisā′tion; spir′itualism**, a being spiritual:
the philosophical doctrine that nothing is real
but soul or spirit: the doctrine that spirit has
a real existence apart from matter: the belief
that certain abnormal phenomena (as rap-
ping, table-turning, &c.) are directly due to
the influence of departed spirits invoked by
specially sensitive persons or mediums; **spir′i-
tūalist**, one who holds any doctrine of spiritualism.—*adj.* **spiritūalist′ic**, relating to, or
connected with, spiritualism.—*n.* **spiritūal′ity**,
state of being spiritual: essence distinct from
matter.—*adv.* **spir′itūally.**—*adjs.* **spiritual,
fem.** (used indiscriminately for either sex)
spirituelle (Fr *spē-rē-tü-el′; coll. spir it ū el′*),
showing refined, witty, grace and delicacy;
spir′ituous, alcoholic.—**spirit(s) of wine**, alcohol; **spiritual court**, an ecclesiastical
court.—**in spirits**, cheerfully vivacious; **out of
spirits**, depressed; **the Spirit**, the Holy Spirit.
[L. *spīritus,* a breath—*spīrāre*, to breathe.]

spirochaete. See **spire** (2).

spirt, *spûrt, v.i.* and *v.t.* to shoot out forcibly, or
in a strong, fine jet.—*n.* a sudden fine jet.
[Origin uncertain; cf. **spurt**.]

spit, *spit, n.* a prong, usu. iron, on which meat is
roasted: a long narrow strip of land or sand
jutting into the sea.—*v.t.* to pierce with a spit:
to impale, transfix:—*pr.p.* spitt′ing; *pa.t.* and
pa.p. spitt′ed. [O.E. *spitu*; Du. *spit*, Ger. *spiess*.]

spit, *spit, v.t.* to throw out from the mouth: to
eject with violence: to utter with hate, scorn
or violence.—*v.i.* to throw out saliva from the
mouth: to rain in scattered drops: to make a
spitting sound, like an angry cat:—*pr.p.* spit-
t′ing; *pa.t.* and *pa.p.* spit, spat; *pa.p.* (*B.*)
spitt′ed.—*n.* saliva: a light fall of rain or snow:
(*coll.*) an exact replica (e.g. *the dead, very,
spit of him*).—*ns.* **spit′fire**, that which emits
fire: a type of fighting aeroplane: a hot-
tempered person; **spittle**, spit, saliva; **spittoon′**,
receptacle for spittle.—**spit and polish**, futile
and burdensome efforts after military smart-

ness. [Northern O.E. *spittan*; O.N. *spȳta*.]

spite, *spīt, n.* grudge, lasting ill-will: a cause of vexation.—*v.t.* to annoy spitefully, to thwart out of hatred.—*adj.* **spite'ful**, showing spite, desirous to vex or injure: arising from spite, malignant.—*adv.* **spite'fully.**—*n.* **spite'fulness.**—**in spite of**, notwithstanding: in defiance of, in contempt of. [Short for **despite**.]

spitz, *spits, n.* a Pomeranian dog. [Ger.]

spiv, *spiv, n.* (*slang*) a slacker, usu. flashily dressed, who makes easy money by dubious or dishonest means. [Perh. a variant of earlier slang *spiff* (n. a toff, adj. dandified) and/or *spiffs*, a percentage allowed, according to the *spiff system*, for selling undesirable stock; or perh. Romany *spivic*, sparrow.]

splash, *splash, v.t.* to spatter with liquid or mud: to throw (about), as liquid: to dash liquid on or over: to variegate as if by splashing: to display, print very prominently.—*v.i.* to dabble: to dash liquid about: to fall into liquid with a splash.—*n.* a dispersion of liquid suddenly disturbed, as by throwing something into it or throwing it about: a wet or dirty mark: a bright patch: a little soda-water: ostentation, display, publicity: a sensation.—**splash'-board**, a mud-guard: a dash-board; **splash'down**, (moment of) the landing of a spacecraft on the sea.—*adj.* **splash'y**, splashing: likely to splash: wet and muddy. [**plash**.]

splatter, *splat'ér, v.t.* and *v.i.* to spatter, splash, sputter. [**spatter**.]

splay, *splā, v.t.* (*archit.*) to slope, slant or bevel: to turn out at an angle.—*n.* a slant or bevel, as of the side of a doorway, window, &c.—*adj.* with a splay.—*n.* **splay'-foot**, a flat foot turned outward.—*adj.* **splay'-footed.** [Short for **display**.]

spleen, *splēn, n.* a spongy, wide-mouthed organ close to the stomach, once thought to be the seat of anger and melancholy, hence various meanings, mostly in *Shak.* and more or less *obs.*, e.g. spite, ill-humour, melancholy, mirth, caprice.—*adjs.* **splĕnet'ic, -al** (formerly *splēn'-*), affected with spleen: peevish: melancholy.—*n.* a splenetic person.—*adv.* **splenet'ically.**—*adj.* **splĕn'ic**, pertaining to the spleen.—*n.* **splēnī'tis**, inflammation of the spleen.—**splenic fever**, anthrax. [L. *splēn*—Gr. *splēn.*]

splendid, *splen'did, adj.* brilliant: magnificent: (*coll.*) excellent.—*adj.* **splen'dent**, brightly shining.—*adv.* **splen'didly.**—*ns.* **splen'didness**, **splen'dour**, brilliance: magnificence. [L. *splendidus*—*splendēre*, to shine.]

splice, *splīs, v.t.* to unite (two ends of a rope) by separating and interweaving the strands: to join together (two pieces of timber) by overlapping: to unite: (*slang*) to unite in marriage.—*n.* act of splicing: joint made by splicing: the part of the handle of a cricket bat or the like that fits into the blade.—**splice the main brace** (*nautical slang*) to serve out an allowance of spirits, to fall to drinking. [Du. (now dial.) *splissen.*]

splint, *splint, n.* a small piece of wood split off: a thin piece of padded wood, &c., for keeping a fractured limb in its proper position: a hard excrescence on the shank-bone of a horse.—*v.t.* to put in splints.—*n.* **splint'er**, a piece of wood, &c., split off, esp. a needle-like piece.—

v.t. and *v.i.* to split into splinters.—*adj.* **splin't'ery**, made of, or like, splinters: apt to splinter.—**splinter group, party**, a group, party, formed by breaking away from a larger party. [Middle Du. or (Middle) Low Ger. *splinte.*]

split, *split, v.t.* to cleave lengthwise: to break in pieces, asunder: to divide: to disunite.—*v.i.* to divide or part asunder: to be dashed to pieces: to divulge secrets:—*pr.p.* splitt'ing; *pa.t.* and *pa.p.* split.—*n.* a crack or rent lengthwise: a schism: a half glass of spirits: a small bottle of aerated water: (in *pl.*) the acrobatic feat of going down to the floor with the legs spread out laterally, or one forward and one back.—*adj.* **splitt'ing**, rending: cleaving: (of a headache) very severe.—**split hairs**, to make exceedingly fine distinctions; **split infinitive**, an infinitive in which an adverb separates 'to' from the verb (e.g. *be sure to carefully place it in position*); **split-level house**, a house of one storey but having rooms on more than one level; **split mind**, schizophrenia; **split personality**, a tendency towards schizophrenia; **split second**, a fraction of a second; **split one's sides**, to laugh immoderately; **split the difference**, to divide equally the sum or matter in dispute, to take the mean. [Du. *splitten*; related to Ger. *spleissen.*]

splurge, *splûrj, n.* a boisterous display, esp. of wealth.—*v.i.* to make such a display.

splutter, *splut'ér, v.i.* to eject drops of liquid with spitting noises: to articulate confusedly, as in rage: to scatter ink upon a paper, as a bad pen.—*v.t.* to utter in a spluttering manner.—*n.* bustle.—*n.* **splutt'erer**, one who splutters. [Variant of **sputter**.]

spode, *spōd, n.* a kind of porcelain made with addition of bone ash by Josiah *Spode* (1754-1827).

spoil, *spoil, v.t.* to take spoil from, to plunder.—*v.i.* to practise robbery.—*n.* plunder: (in *pl.*) profits, esp. public offices, or their emoluments: pillage, robbery: a prey.—*n.* **spoil'er.**—**spoils system**, (*U.S.*) the system by which a political party coming into office replaces the civil servants of the previous régime by nominees of its own. [O.Fr. *espoille*—L. *spolium*, plunder.]

spoil, *spoil, v.t.* to mar, to impair: to impair the disposition of (a child) by indulgence.—*v.i.* to deteriorate, decay:—*pa.t.* and *pa.p.* spoiled, spoilt.—*n.* **spoil'er**, a corrupter.—**spoiling for**, eager for, impatient for, ripe for. [Same as **spoil** (1).]

spoke, *spōk, pa.t.* of **speak**.

spoke, *spōk, n.* one of the radiating bars of a wheel.—**put a spoke in one's wheel**, to thwart one. [O.E. *spāca*; Du. *speek*, Ger. *speiche*.]

spoken, *spōk'n, pa.p.* of **speak**, used as adj. in **smooth-spoken**, &c.

spokeshave, *spōk'shāv, n.* a carpenter's plane for dressing the spokes of wheels, &c. [**spoke** (2) and **shave**.]

spokesman, *spōks'mán, n.* one who speaks for another, or for others:—*pl.* **spok'esmen**:—*fem.* **spok'eswoman**. [**spoke** (1) and **man**.]

spoliate, *spō'li-āt, v.t.* and *v.i.* to despoil, to plunder.—*n.* **spōliā'tion**, act of despoiling: robbery. [L. *spoliāre, -ātum*—*spolium*, spoil.]

spondee, *spon'dē, n.* in classical poetry, a foot of

Neutral vowels in unaccented syllables: *em'pér-ór*; for certain sounds in foreign words see p. ix.

two long syllables, as *ōrīs*: in English verse, a foot of two accented syllables, as *sea'-king'.—adjs.* **spondā'ic, -al.** [Fr.,—L. *spondēus* (*pēs*)—Gr. *spondeios* (*pous*), (a foot) used in the slow solemn hymns sung at a *spondē* or drink-offering.]

sponge, *spunj, n.* any member of a phylum of sessile aquatic animals with a single cavity in the body, with many pores: the fibrous skeleton of such an animal, remarkable for its power of sucking up water: a piece of such a skeleton, or a substitute, used for washing, obliterating, absorbing, &c.: any sponge-like substance, as leavened dough, a pudding or a sponge-cake: a hanger-on or parasite: a drunkard: an application of a sponge.—*v.t.* to wipe, wipe out, soak up, remove, with a sponge: to obtain by the mean devices of the parasite.—*v.i.* to suck in, as a sponge: to be meanly dependent on others, as a parasite.—*ns.* **sponge'(-)cake,** a very light cake of flour, eggs, and sugar; **spong'er,** one who uses a sponge: a sponge or parasite; **sponge'-rubber,** rubber processed into sponge-like form; **spong'ing-house,** (*hist.*) a bailiff's lodging-house for debtors in his custody before their committal to prison.—*adj.* **spongy** (*spun'ji*), like a sponge, absorptive: of open texture, porous: wet and soft.—*n.* **spong'iness.—throw up the sponge,** to acknowledge defeat by throwing into the air the sponge with which a boxer is rubbed down between rounds: to give up any struggle. [O.Fr. *esponge*—L. *spongia*—Gr. *spongiā*.]

sponsal, *spon'sal, adj.* pertaining to a betrothal, a marriage, or a spouse. [L. *sponsālis*—*spondēre, sponsum,* to promise.]

sponsor, *spon'sŏr, n.* one who promises solemnly for another, a surety: a godfather or godmother: one who assumes responsibility for (e.g. the introduction of legislation): one who finances a radio programme on condition that part of the time allotted to it is devoted to advertising a specified product.—*v.t.* to act as sponsor for.—*adj.* **sponso'rial.—*n.* spon'sorship.** [L.,—*spondēre, sponsum,* to promise.]

spontaneous, *spon-tā'né-ús, adj.* uttered, offered, done, &c., of one's free-will: natural, unforced: involuntary: acting by its own impulse or natural law: produced of itself or without interference.—*ns.* **spontané'ity, spontā'neousness,** the state or quality of being spontaneous: naturalness, unforced quality. —*adv.* **spontā'neously.—spontaneous combustion,** combustion due to heat caused by chemical action within an inflammable substance, mineral or organic; **spontaneous generation,** also known as *abiogenesis,* the origination of living by from non-living matter. [L. *spontāneus*—*sponte,* of one's own accord.]

spoof, *spōōf, n.* (*slang*) a hoaxing game invented and named by Arthur Roberts (1852-1933), a comedian.—*adj.* bogus.—*v.t.* and *v.i.* to hoax.

spook, *spōōk, n.* a ghost.—*adjs.* **spook'ish, spook'y.** [App. Low Ger.; cf. Ger. *spuk,* Du. *spook.*]

spool, *spōōl, n.* a cylinder, bobbin, or reel, for winding thread, photographic film, &c., upon.—*v.t.* to wind on spools. [Low Ger. *spôle,* Du. *spoel;* Ger. *spule.*]

spoon, *spōōn, n.* an instrument, with a shallow bowl and a handle, for supping food (see **dessertspoon, tablespoon, teaspoon**): a wooden-headed golf club with considerable loft.—*v.t.* to scoop (up): to transfer with, or as with, a spoon.—*v.i.* to court in an excessive and ridiculous manner.—*n.* **spoon'-bill,** a family of birds with long, flat, broad bill, spoon-shaped at the tip.—*adj.* **spoon'-fed,** fed with a spoon: (*fig.*) artificially fostered: taught by doled-out doses of cut-and-dried information.—*ns.* **spoon'ful,** as much as fills a spoon: a small quantity:—*pl.* **spoon'fuls; spoon'meat,** food taken with a spoon, such as is given to young children.—*adjs.* **spoon'y,** **spoon'ey,** foolishly and demonstratively fond. [O.E. *spōn,* sliver, chip, shaving; Ger. *span,* chip, O.N. *spānn,* chip, spoon.]

spoonerism, *spōōn'ér-izm, n.* transposition of the initial sounds of spoken words—e.g. 'shoving leopard' for 'loving shepherd'. [Rev. W. A. *Spooner* (1844-1930), who was prone to this error.]

spoor, *spōōr, n.* track, esp. of a hunted animal. [Du. *spoor,* a track; cf. O.E. and O.N. *spor.*]

sporadic, *spo-rad'ik, adj.* occurring here and there and now and then: occurring casually.—Also (*rare*) **sporad'ical.—*adv.* sporad'ically.** [Gr. *sporadikos*—*sporas, -ados,* scattered—*speirein,* to sow.]

spore, *spōr, spŏr, n.* a unicellular asexual reproductive body in flowerless plants like ferns: a seed-like stage in the life-cycle of *Protozoa.—n.* **sporangium** (*spor-an'ji-úm*) a spore-case, a sac in which spores are produced:—*pl.* **sporan'gia.—*adj.* sporan'gial.—*n.* spo'rophyte** (*-fīt*), the spore-bearing or asexual generation in the life-cycle of a plant.—*adj.* **sporophyt'ic** (*-fitik*). [Gr. *sporos,* a sowing, a seed—*speirein,* to sow.]

sporran, *spor'án, n.* an ornamental pouch worn in front of the kilt by the Highlanders of Scotland. [Gael. *sporan.*]

sport, *spōrt, spŏrt, v.i.* to play, to frolic: to practise field diversions: to trifle: to deviate from the normal.—*v.t.* to display, flaunt.—*n.* a pastime, amusement: a game, esp. one involving bodily exercise: a field diversion (e.g. hunting, fishing, athletics): such games or field diversions collectively: (esp. *fig.*) a plaything: a laughing-stock: mirth, contemptuous mirth: a sportsman (*fig.*), a good companion: (*biol.*) an individual differing markedly from the normal.—*adj.* **sport'ful,** merry: full of jesting.—*adv.* **sport'fully.—*n.* sport'fulness.—*adj.* sport'-ing,** relating to, or engaging in, sports.—*adv.* **sport'ingly.—*adj.* sport'ive,** inclined to sport, playful: merry.—*adv.* **sport'ively.—*ns.* sport'-iveness; sports'man,** one who practises, or one skilled in, field-sports: one who shows a good spirit in sport, hence (*fig.*) one ready to accept all chances happily:—*fem.* **sports'-woman.—*adj.* sports'manlike.—*n.* sports'manship,** practice, skill, or spirit, of a sportsman.—**sporting chance,** a chance or possibility involving such a risk as attracts a sportsman—an off-chance; **sports jacket,** a man's jacket, usu. tweed, for casual wear. [Shortened from *disport.*]

spot, *spot, n.* a mark made by a drop of wet

matter: a blot: a discoloured place: a small part of a different colour: a locality, place of limited area: the precise place: (*coll.*) a small quantity (of food, liquor, bother): a spotlight: a place on e.g. a television or radio programme: a turn, performance, esp. a short one.—*v.t.* to mark with spots: to tarnish (reputation): (*slang*) to recognise, identify, to espy, detect:—*pr.p.* spott'ing; *pa.t.* and *pa.p.* spott'ed.—*adj.* spot'less, without a spot: untainted, pure.—*adv.* spot'lessly.—*n.* spot'lessness.—*adjs.* spott'ed, spott'y, marked with spots.—*ns.* spot-check, a check on the spot without warning: a check of random samples to serve in place of a general check; spot'light, a circle of light thrown upon one actor or a small part of the stage (also *fig.*): apparatus for projecting it (*v.t.* to turn the spotlight on); spott'er, one who spots or detects.—spot cash, money down.—have a soft spot for, to be fond of; in a spot, in a difficult situation; on the spot, at once: in the place required: alert, equal to any emergency: (*slang*) in a position of extreme difficulty or danger; put on the spot, to get rid of (a rival or a disloyal associate) by murder. [Cf. obs. Du., Low Ger. *spot*, O.N. *spotti*.]

spouse, *spowz*, *n.* a husband or wife.—*adj.* spous'al, nuptial: matrimonial.—*n.* usually in *pl.* nuptials: marriage. [O.Fr. *espous*, fem. *espouse* (Fr. *époux*, fem. *épouse*)—*espouser.* See espouse.]

spout, *spowt*, *v.t.* to throw out in a jet: to blow as a whale: to declaim: (*slang*) to pawn.—*v.i.*·to issue in a jet: to blow as a whale: to declaim.—*n.* a projecting lip or tube for discharging liquid from a vessel, a roof, &c.: a gush, discharge, or jet: an undivided waterfall: a waterspout: the blowing, or the blow-hole, of a whale: a lift in a pawnshop, hence a pawnshop.—*ns.* spout'er, one who, or that which, spouts; spout'-hole, a blow-hole. [M.E. *spouten*; cf. Du. *spuiten*, to spout, O.N. *spȳta*, to spit.]

sprag, *sprag*, *n.* a prop used by miners: a bar inserted to stop a wheel: a device to prevent a vehicle from running backwards.

sprain, *sprān*, *n.* a wrenching of a joint with tearing or stretching of ligaments.—*v.t.* to wrench so as to cause a sprain. [Connection with O.Fr. *espreindre*, to squeeze out, is disputed.]

sprang, *pa.t.* of spring.

sprat, *sprat*, *n.* a small fish of the same genus as the herring and the pilchard. [O.E. *sprot*; Ger. *sprotte.*]

sprawl, *spröl*, *v.i.* to stretch the body carelessly when lying: to spread ungracefully, to straggle.—*n.* sprawling posture.—*n.* sprawl'er. [O.E. *sprēawlian*, to move convulsively.]

spray, *sprā*, *n.* a cloud of small flying drops: such a cloud applied as a disinfectant, insecticide, &c.: an atomiser or other apparatus for dispersing it.—*v.t.* to sprinkle or squirt in fine mist-like jets.—*n.* spray'-gun, a device for applying paint, &c. [Middle Du. *sprayen.*]

spray, *sprā*, *n.* a shoot or twig, esp. one spreading out in branches or flowers: an ornament, casting, &c., of similar form.—*v.i.* to spread or branch in a spray. [Perh. conn. with sprig, or

with O.E. *spræc*, twig.]

spread, *spred*, *v.t.* to cause to extend more widely or more thinly: to scatter abroad or in all directions: to extend (over time, or over a surface): to overlay: to shoot out (branches): to circulate (news): to convey to others, as a disease: to set with provisions, as a table.—*v.i.* to extend or expand in all directions: to be extended or stretched: to be propagated or circulated:—*pa.t.* and *pa.p.* spread.—*n.* act or process of spreading: extent, compass, expansion: a feast: a cover for a bed or a table.—*n.* spread'-ea'gle, a heraldic eagle with wings and legs stretched out.—*adj.* bombastic, boastful, esp. noisily patriotic.—*v.t.* to tie up with outstretched limbs: (*coll.*) to throw or to knock down (a person, wickets) so that (he, they) assume such a position, or a similar position: to spread out.—*v.i.* to lie, fall, &c., with outstretched arms.—*n.* spread'-over, an arrangement by which the total of working hours for a week may be made up of spells longer or shorter than the usual average. [O.E. *sprǣdan*; Du. *spreiden*, Ger. *spreiten.*]

spree, *sprē*, *n.* a merry frolic: a drunken bout. [Orig. slang.]

sprig, *sprig*, *n.* a small shoot or twig: a scion, a young person: a small nail with little or no head.—*v.t.* to pattern with representations of twigs:—*pr.p.* sprigg'ing; *pa.t.* and *pa.p.* sprigged. [Origin obscure.]

spright, *sprīt*, *n.* (*Spens., Shak.*) a spelling of sprite.—*adj.* spright'ful (*Shak.*), spirited.—*adv.* spright'fully (*Shak.*).—*n.* spright'fulness.—*adjs.* spright'less, destitute of spirit or life; spright'ly, vivacious, animated: lively: brisk.—*n.* spright'liness.

spring, *spring*, *v.i.* to move suddenly, as by elastic force: to bound, to leap: to start up suddenly, to break forth: to appear, to issue: to take origin: to sprout.—*v.t.* to cause to spring up, to start: to release the elastic force of: to let off, allow to spring: to cause (a mine) to explode: to produce suddenly (e.g. a surprise), to make known suddenly (with *on, upon,* a person): to open, as a leak: to crack, as a mast: to bend by force, strain: to leap over: to set with springs: (*slang*) to procure the escape of from jail:—*pa.t.* sprang (now rarely sprung); *pa.p.* sprung.—*n.* a leap: a sudden movement: a recoil or rebound: elasticity: an elastic device or appliance used e.g. for setting in motion, or for reducing shocks: a source (of action or life): a motive: rise, beginning: cause or origin: a source: an outflow of water from the earth: (*B.*) the dawn: (often Spring) the season when plants spring up and grow—in North temperate regions roughly February or March to April or May, astronomically from the spring equinox to the summer solstice: (now *Scot.*) a lively dance tune: a crack in a mast.—*adj.* having, or operated by, a spring: of the season of spring: sown, appearing, or used in, spring.—*ns.* spring'ald, an active sprightly young man, a youth; spring'-bal'ance, an instrument for weighing by the elasticity of a spiral spring; spring'-bed, a spring-mattress; spring'bok (*Du.*), a beautiful South African antelope, larger than a roebuck: (*slang*) a South African, esp. a footballer; spring'-

Neutral vowels in unaccented syllables: *em'pêr-ór*; for certain sounds in foreign words see p. ix.

706

clean′ing, a thorough house-cleaning, usu. in spring.—*v.t.* **spring′-clean′**.—*ns.* **spring′er**, a kind of spaniel useful in copses: one who springs; **spring′-gun**, a gun set to go off like a trap; **spring′-halt**, a jerking lameness in a horse; **spring′-house**, (*U.S.*) a larder, dairy, &c., built for coolness over a spring or brook; **spring′-matt′ress**, a mattress of spiral springs in a frame; **spring′(-)tide**, the very high (and very low) tide occurring about new and full moon, when sun and moon pull together; **spring′tide**, the season of spring; **spring′time**, the season of spring; **spring′-wa′ter**, water of or from a spring; **spring′-wheat**, wheat sown in the spring, rather than autumn or winter.—*adj.* **spring′y**, elastic: resilient.—*n.* **spring′iness.—spring a leak**, to begin to leak. [O.E. *springan*; Ger. *springen*.]

springe, *sprinj*, *n.* a snare with a spring-noose.—*v.t.* to catch in a springe. [Earlier *sprenge*, from a prob. O.E. *sprencg*.]

sprinkle, *spring′kl*, *v.t.* to scatter in small drops or particles (on something): to scatter (something with something): to baptize with a few drops of water: to strew, dot, diversify. *v.i.* to scatter in drops.—*ns.* **sprin′kle, sprin′kling**, a small quantity sprinkled; **sprin′kler**. [Frequentative from O.E. *sprengan*, the causative of *springan*, to spring; cf. Ger. *sprenkeln*.]

sprint, *sprint*, *n.* a short run, row, or race, at full speed.—*v.i.* to run at full speed.—*n.* **sprin′ter**. [Scand.]

sprit, *sprit*, *n.* (*naut.*) a spar set diagonally to extend a fore-and-aft sail. [O.E. *sprēot*, a pole; Du. and Ger. *spriet*, sprit.]

sprite, *sprīt*, *n.* a spirit—*obs.* except in the senses of goblin, elf, imp, impish or implike person. [O.Fr. *esprit*, cf. **spright, spirit**.]

sprocket, *sprok′et*, *n.* a tooth on the rim of a wheel or capstan for engaging the chain.—*n.* **sprock′et (wheel)**, a toothed wheel used for a chain drive, as on the pedal shaft and rear hub of a bicycle. [Origin unknown.]

sprout, *sprowt*, *n.* a new growth: a young shoot: a side bud, as in **Brussels-sprouts** (q.v.): a scion, descendant: a sprouting condition.—*v.i.* to push out new shoots: to begin to grow.—*v.t.* to cause to sprout: to put forth, grow (a sprout, a bud, &c.). [O.E. *sprūtan* (found in compounds); cf. Du. *spruiten*, Ger. *spriessen*.]

spruce, *sprōōs*, *adj.* smart, neat, dapper: over-fastidious, finical.—*v.t.* to smarten.—*v.i.* to become spruce or smart (often with *up*).—*adv.* **spruce′ly.—*n.* **spruce′ness**. [Prob. from **spruce** (2), from the vogue of Spruce (i.e. Prussian) leather in the 16th century.]

spruce, *sprōōs*, *n.* (*cap.—obs.*) Prussia: a spruce fir or its wood: spruce-beer.—*adj.* (*cap.*) brought from Prussia: of spruce or its wood.—*ns.* **spruce′-beer′**, a drink made from a solution of sugar or treacle and green tops of spruce; **spruce′-fir′**, a genus of conifers with long shoots only, four-angled needles, and pendulous cones: extended to some other trees. [M.E. *Spruce*, Prussia—O.Fr. *Pruce*.]

spruit, *sprü′it*, *sprīt*, *n.* a small, deepish watercourse, dry except during and after rains. [Du. *sprout*.]

sprung, *pa.t.* and *pa.p.* of **spring**.—*adj.* cracked (e.g. a bat, a mast), strained: fitted with springs: (*coll.*) tipsy.—**sprung rhythm**, a term used by the poet Gerard Manley Hopkins (1844–1889) for a rhythm (closer to that of ordinary speech than is the 'running rhythm' of classical English poetry) consisting of mixed feet, each stressed on the first syllable; occasional examples can be found in the older poets.

spry, *sprī*, *adj.* nimble, agile. [Origin uncertain.]

spud, *spud*, *n.* a small narrow digging tool: a stumpy person or thing: (*slang*) a potato.

spue. Same as **spew**.

spume, *spūm*, *n.* foam: scum.—*v.i.* to foam.—Also *v.t.*—*adjs.* **spū′mous, spū′my**. [L. *spūma*—*spuēre*, to spew.]

spun, *pa.t.* and *pa.p.* of **spin**.—**spun sugar**, sugar spun into fine fluffy threads, as in candy floss.

spunk, *spungk*, *n.* touchwood, tinder: a match: esp. (*Scot.*) a spark: a spirited, usu. small or weak, person: spirit, mettle, courage.—*adj.* **spunk′y**. [Cf. Ir. *sponc*, tinder, sponge—L. *spongia*, a sponge—Gr. *spongiā*.]

spur, *spûr*, *n.* an instrument on a rider's heel, with sharp point for goading the horse: incitement, stimulus: a hard sharp projection: a claw-like projection at the back of a cock's or other bird's leg: an artificial substitute on a game-cock: a short, usu. flowering or fruit-bearing, branch: a lateral root: a tubular pouch at the base of a petal: a small range of mountains extending laterally from a larger range.—*v.t.* to apply the spur to: to urge on: to put spurs on.—*v.i.* to press forward with the spur: to hasten:—*pr.p.* spurr′ing;*pa.t.* and *pa.p.* **spurred.—win one's spurs** (see **win**). [O.E. *spora*; O.N. *spori*, Ger. *sporn*.]

spurge, *spûrj*, *n.* a genus of plants with a resinous milky juice, generally poisonous. [O.Fr. *espurge*—L. *expurgāre*, to purge—*ex*, off, *purgāre*, to clear.]

spurious, *spūr′i us*, *adj.* bastard, illegitimate: not genuine, sham: forged: (*bot.*) simulating but essentially different.—*adv.* **spur′iously.—*n.* **spūr′iousness**. [L. *spurius*, false.]

spurn, *spûrn*, *v.t.* to kick, esp. in contempt: to reject with contempt.—*v.i.* to kick (often with *at, against*).—*n.* a kick: disdainful rejection. [O.E. *spornan, spurnan*, related to **spur**.]

spurt, *spûrt*, *v.t.* to spout, or send out in a sudden stream or jet.—*v.i.* to gush out suddenly: to flow out forcibly or at intervals: to make a sudden, short, intense effort.—*n.* a sudden or violent gush: a jet: a short spell of intensified effort, speed, &c. [Variant of **spirt**.]

sputnik, *spŏŏt′nik*, *n.* a man-made earth satellite. [After the Russian *Sputnik* ('travelling companion') 1, the first such satellite, put in orbit in 1957.]

sputter, *sput′er*, *v.i.* to spit or throw out moisture in scattered drops: to speak rapidly and indistinctly: to make a noise of sputtering.—*v.t.* to spit out or throw out in or with small drops: to utter hastily and indistinctly.—*n.* sputtering: matter sputtered out. [Imit.; cf. Du. *sputteren*.]

sputum, *spū′tum*, *n.* matter composed of secretions from the nose, throat, bronchi, lungs, which is spat out:—*pl.* **spū′ta**. [L. *spūtum*—*spuēre*, to spit, spat.]

spy, *spī*, *n.* a secret agent employed to watch

others or to collect information, esp. of a military nature: act of spying.—*v.t.* to descry, make out: to discover by close search: to inspect secretly.—*v.i.* to play the spy:—*pa.t.* and *pa.p.* spied (*spīd*).—*n.* **spy′glass**, a small hand-telescope. [O.Fr. *espie* (n.), *espier* (vb.); cf. **espy**.]

squab, *skwob*, *adj.* fat, clumsy: newly hatched.—*n.* a young pigeon or rook. [Poss. Scand.]

squabble, *skwob′l*, *v.i.* to dispute noisily, to wrangle.—*n.* a noisy, petty quarrel, a brawl.—*n.* **squabb′ler**. [Scand.; prob. imit.]

squad, *skwod*, *n.* a small group of soldiers drilled or working together: any working party: a set or group.—**awkward squad**, a body of recruits not yet competent in drill, &c.; **flying squad**, a group of highly móbile detectives. [Fr. *escouade*.]

squadron, *skwod′rón*, *n.* (*obs.*) a body of soldiers drawn up in a square: a detachment, body, group: a division of a cavalry regiment under a major or captain: a section of a fleet under a flag-officer: a group of aeroplanes acting as a unit under one commander.—*n.* **squad′ron-lead′er**, a Royal Air Force officer corresponding in rank to a lieut.-commander or a major. [It. *squadrone*—*squadra*, a square.]

squalid, *skwol′id*, *adj.* filthy, foul: neglected, uncared-for: sordid and dingy.—*adv.* **squal′idly.**—*ns.* **squal′idness; squal′or**, state of being squalid: dirtiness. [L. *squālidus* (adj.), stiff, rough, dirty, *squālor*, *-ōris* (n.).]

squall, *skwöl*, *v.i.* to cry out violently: to sing loudly and unmusically.—*n.* a loud cry or scream: a violent gust of wind.—*n.* **squall′er.**—*adj.* **squall′y**, abounding with, or disturbed with, squalls or gusts of wind: gusty.—**white squall**, a tropical whirlwind, preceded by a small white cloud. [Prob. imit.]

squama, *skwā′ma* (L. *skwä′ma*), *n.* a scale: a scale-like structure:—*pl.* **squä′mae** (-*ē*).—*adjs.* **squä′mous**, **squä′mose**, covered with, or consisting of, scales: scaly. [L. *squāmōsus*—*squāma*, a scale.]

squander, *skwon′dér*, *v.t.* to spend lavishly or wastefully.—*ns.* **squan′derer; squander-mā′nia**, (*slang*) a spirit of reckless expenditure (in a government). [Origin obscure.]

square, *skwār*, *n.* an equilateral rectangle: an object, piece, space, figure of approximately that shape: an open space—commonly but not necessarily of that shape—in a town, with its surrounding buildings: a body of troops drawn up in that form: an instrument for drawing or testing right angles: the product of a number or quantity multiplied by itself: one of square tastes or outlook.—*adj.* having the form of a square: approaching the form of a square: squared: relatively broad: thick-set: right-angled: fair, honest: even, leaving no balance, settled, as accounts: equal in score: unequivocal, uncompromising (e.g. *a square denial*): solid, satisfying (e.g. *a square meal*): (*coll.*) of taste in music, &c., traditional and orthodox (*coll.*) bourgeois in outlook.—*v.t.* to make square or rectangular, esp. in cross-section: to straighten (the shoulders), bend (the elbows) to form right angles: to form into squares: to convert into an equivalent square: to multiply

by itself: to regulate (by, according to—also with *on*) any given standard: to adjust (to), harmonise (with): (*naut.*) to place at right angles with the mast or keel: (*coll.*) to bribe.—*v.i.* to suit, fit: to accord or agree: to adopt the posture of a boxer.—*adv.* at right angles: solidly: directly: fairly, honestly.—*adv.* **square′ly.**—*n.* **square′ness.**—*adj.* **square′-rigged**, rigged chiefly with square-sails.—*ns.* **square′-root**, that number or quantity which being multiplied by itself produces the given quantity (e.g. 4 is √16, i.e. the square root of 16); **square′-sail**, a four-sided sail extended by yards suspended by the middle at right angles to the mast (see also **sail**); **square′-toes**, an old-fashioned, puritanical, punctilious person.—**square foot, inch,** &c., an area equal to that of a square whose side measures one foot, inch, &c.; **square measure**, a system of measure for surfaces, its units being square inch, square foot, &c.; **square leg**, (*cricket*) the position of a fielder to the left of, and in line with, the batsman: that fielder.—**square up**, to settle accounts: to adopt the posture of a boxer; **square up to**, to face up to, adopt an attitude of defiance to.—**back to square one**, back to the original position with the problem, &c., unchanged; **on the square**, honestly. [O.Fr. *esquarre*—L. *ex* and *quadra*, a square.]

squarrose, *skwar′ōs*, *skwor′ōs*, *adj.* rough, with many scales, bracts, hairs, &c., standing out at right angles. [L. *squarrōsus*, scurfy.]

squash, *skwosh*, *v.t.* to press into pulp: to crush flat: to put down, suppress: to snub.—*v.i.* to form a soft mass as from a fall: to become crushed or pulpy: to squelch: to crowd.—*n.* anything soft and easily crushed: anything soft or unripe: a beverage containing the juice of crushed fruit.—*adj.* **squash′y**, like a squash: muddy.—**squash rack′ets**, a form of the game of rackets played with a soft ball. [O.Fr. *esquacer*, *esquasser*—*es-* (L. *ex-*) and *quasser.* See **quash**.]

squash, *skwosh*, *n.* any of several species of gourd. [From Amer. Indian name.]

squat, *skwot*, *v.i.* to sit down upon the hams or heels: to sit close, as an animal: to settle on land or in property, without title, or (*Austr.*) with a view to acquiring a title:—*pr.p.* squat′-t′ing; *pa.t.* and *pa.p.* squatt′ed.—*adj.* short and thick, dumpy.—*n.* **squatt′er**, a settler without title, or one who has not yet acquired a title. [O.Fr. *esquatir*, to crush; allied to **squash** (1).]

squaw, *skwö*, *n.* an American Indian woman, esp. a wife. [Amer. Indian word.]

squawk, *skwök*, *n.* a croaky call or cry: (*coll.*) a complaint, protest.—*v.i.* and *v.t.* to utter a squawk or with a squawk. [Imit.]

squeak, *skwēk*, *v.i.* to utter, or to give forth, a high-pitched nasal-sounding cry, or note: (*slang*) to peach, be an informer, or to confess.—*n.* a squeaky sound: a narrow escape or bare chance.—*n.* **squeak′er.**—*adj.* **squeak′y**; squeaking or given to squeaking: of the nature of a squeak.—*adv.* **squeak′ily.**—*n.* **squeak′iness.**—**a narrow squeak**, a narrow escape. [Imit.; cf. Swed.*sqväka*, to croak, Ger.*quieken*, to squeak.]

squeal, *skwēl*, *v.i.* to utter a shrill and prolonged sound: (*coll.*) to be an informer.—*v.t.* to utter,

Neutral vowels in unaccented syllables: *em′pér-ór*; for certain sounds in foreign words see p. ix.

708

express, &c., with squealing.—*n.* a shrill loud cry. [Imit.; cf. Swed. dial. *sqväla*, to cry out.]

squeamish, *skwēm'ish, adj.* inclined to nausea: easily shocked or disgusted: fastidious: reluctant from scruples or compunction.—*adv.* **squeam'ishly.**—*n.* **squeam'ishness.** [M.E. *scoymous*—Anglo-Fr. *escoymous*; origin obscure.]

squeegee, *skwē'jē* or -*jē', n.* a wooden implement edged with rubber for clearing water away from decks, floors, windows, &c.: a photographer's roller for squeezing the moisture from a print. [Perh. **squeeze.**]

squeeze, *skwēz, v.t.* to crush, press hard, compress: to grasp tightly: to embrace: to force (through, into) by pressing: to force liquid, juice, from by pressure: to force to discard winning cards: to fleece, extort from.—*v.i.* to press: to force a way.—*n.* act of squeezing: pressure: an embrace: a close grasp: a portion withheld and appropriated: a few drops got by squeezing: an impression of an object taken e.g. in wax: a restriction or time of restriction (usually financial or commercial).—*n.* **squeez'er.** [M.E. *queisen* O.E. *cwīsan.*]

squelch, *skwel(t)sh, n.* a heavy blow on, or fall of, a soft and moist body: the sound of such an impact: the sound made by wet mud under pressure: a pulpy mass.—*v.t.* to crush down.—*v.i.* to take heavy steps in water or on moist ground. [Imit.]

squib, *skwib, n.* a paper tube filled with combustibles, used as firework: a petty lampoon. [Perh. imit.]

squid, *skwid, n.* any of various ten-armed cephalopods, often, but not always, confined to those (as opp. to *cuttle-fishes*) in which the internal shell, the *pen*, is not calcified and is hence flexible; also called *calamary* (L. *calamus,* a reed pen—Gr. *kalamos*).

squill, *skwil, n.* any flower of the genus *Scilla,* esp. the sea-onion, a Mediterranean species which is used as a diuretic. [Fr. *squille*—L. *squilla, scilla*—Gr. *skilla.*]

squint, *skwint, adj.* looking obliquely: squinting: oblique.—*v.i.* to look obliquely: to be strabismic: to have a side reference or allusion to (with *at,* &c.): to hint disapprobation of (with *at, on*).—*v.t.* to cause to squint: to direct or divert obliquely.—*n.* act or habit of squinting: an oblique look: a glance, a peep: an oblique reference, hint, tendency: a hagioscope (q.v.): strabismus, distortion of vision due to an infirmity whereby the line of vision of the eye affected is not parallel to that of the other. [Shortened from **asquint.**]

squire, *skwīr, n.* an esquire, an aspirant to knighthood attending a knight: one who escorts a lady: an English landed gentleman, esp. of old family: (*U.S.*) one who has been a justice of the peace, &c.—*v.t.* (of a man) to escort or attend (a woman).—*n.* **squir(e)'archy,** the rule of squires: squires as a body. [Shortened from **esquire.**]

squirm, *skwûrm, v.i.* to writhe: to go writhing: to feel humiliated. [Prob. imit.]

squirrel, *skwir'él, n.* any of a family of rodents, esp. those of arboreal habit, which have a bushy tail and strong hind legs: the pelt of such an animal. [O.Fr. *escurel*—Low L. *scu-*

rellus, dim. of L. *sciūrus*—Gr. *skiouros*—*skia,* shade, *oura,* tail.]

squirt, *skwûrt, v.t.* to throw out liquid in a jet.—*v.i.* to spurt.—*n.* an instrument for squirting: a jet: (*coll.*) a contemptible creature. [Cf. Low Ger. *swirtjen.*]

stab, *stab, v.t.* to wound or pierce with a pointed weapon: (*fig.*) to pain suddenly and deeply: to injure secretly, or by slander: (*lit.* and *fig.*) to aim (at).—Also *v.i.*:—*pr.p.* stabb'ing; *pa.t.* and *pa.p.* stabbed.—*n.* an act of stabbing: a wound, as with a pointed weapon: (*slang*) an attempt, a go (at something).—*n.* **stabb'er.—stab in the back** (*lit.* and *fig.*), to injure in a treacherous manner. [Perh. variant of *stob,* a stake.]

Stabat Mater, *stā'bät mā'tér,* or *stä'bat mä'tér, n.* a mediaeval Latin hymn on the seven dolours of the Virgin: a musical setting of it. [Its opening words, 'the mother stood'.]

stable, *stā'bl, adj.* standing firm: firmly established: durable: firm in purpose or character, constant: not decomposing readily: not radioactive (e.g. *stable isotopes*).—*ns.* **stabil'ity,** state of being stable: steadiness: **sta'bleness.**—*adv.* **stā'bly.**—*v.t* **stab'ilise** (*stab'-,* or *stāb'-*), to render stable or steady: to fix the value of (the currency): to fix, make steady (e.g. *to stabilise prices*): to establish, maintain, or regulate, the equilibrium of (e.g. an aircraft).—*ns.* **stabilisation** (*stab-,* or *stāb-il-īz-ā'sh(ó)n*), **stab'iliser.** [Fr.,—L. *stabilis—stāre,* to stand.]

stable, *stā'bl, n.* a building for housing horses, or sometimes other animals: a group of horses under one ownership: a horse-keeping establishment, organisation, or staff.—*v.t.* to put or keep in a stable.—*v.i.* to be accommodated in a stable or as in a stable.—*n.* **stā'bling,** act of putting into a stable: accommodation for horses, &c.—**stable companion** (*fig*), one who lodges in the same place or is a member of the same club, &c.—**out of the same stable,** having the same social background, esp. a privileged one. [O.Fr. *estable*—L. *stabulum—stāre,* to stand.]

stablish, *stab'lish, v.t.* old form of **establish.**

staccato, *stä-kä'tō, stäk-ka'to, adj.* and *adv.* (*mus.*) with each note detached: marked by jerkiness, in a jerky manner. [It., pa.p. of *staccare,* for *distaccare,* to separate.]

stack, *stak, n.* a large built-up pile of hay, corn, wood, &c.: a group or cluster of chimneys or flues: the funnel of a steamer, steam-engine, &c.: (*Scot.*) an isolated pillar of rock: a pyramidal group or pile: (*coll.*—often in *pl.*) a large quantity.—*v.t.* to pile into a stack: to shuffle (cards) for cheating.—*n.* **stack'yard,** a yard for stacks.—**stack against, in favour of,** to arrange (circumstances) to the disadvantage, advantage, of. [O.N. *stakkr,* a stack of hay.]

stadium, *stā'di-úm, n.* a Greek measure of length, 600 Greek, or 606³/₄ English, feet: a race-course, sports-ground: a stage in development:—*pl.* **stā'dia.** [L.,—Gr. *stadion.*]

staff, *stäf, n.* a stick carried in the hand: a prop: a pole: a flagstaff: the long handle of an instrument: a stick or ensign of authority: lines and spaces on which music is written or printed: a body of officers who help a commanding officer, or perform special duties: a body of persons employed in an establishment—business, professional, or domestic:—*pl.* **staffs** (the older plural was **staves,** *stāvz,* and this gave rise to a singular **stave;** see this as separate entry).—*v.t.* to provide with a staff.—*ns.* **staff'-coll'ege,** a college that trains officers; **staff'-dū'ty,** the occupation of an officer who serves on a staff, having been detached from his regiment; **staff-notā'tion,** musical notation in which a staff is used, as opposed to the tonic-solfa system; **staff'-off'icer,** an officer serving on a staff; **staff'-room,** a room for the use of a staff, esp. the teaching staff of a school; **staff'-ser'geant,** a non-commissioned officer serving on a regimental staff.—**staff of life,** staple food, esp. bread. [O.E. *stæf;* O.N. *stafr,* Ger. *stab.*]

stag, *stag, n.* a male deer, esp. a red deer over four years old.—*ns.* **stag'-beetle,** any of a family of beetles, the males of which have large antler-like mandibles; **stag'hound,** a hound formerly used in hunting deer; **stag'-party,** a party without women. [O.E. *stagga;* cf. O.N. *steggr,* cock-bird, gander.]

stage, *stāj, n.* a tier, shelf, floor, storey: a tiered structure for plants: a scaffold: an elevated platform, esp. for acting on: the theatre: theatrical representation: the theatrical calling: any field of action, scene: a place of rest on a journey or road: the portion of a journey between two such places: a point reached in, or a section of, life, development, or any process: a subdivision of a geological series or formation: in a microscope, &c., the support for an object to be examined: a stagecoach.—*v.t.* to represent, or to put, on the stage: to contrive dramatically, organise and bring off.—*ns.* **stage'-coach,** a coach that ran regularly with passengers from stage to stage; **stage'-craft,** skill in, knowledge of, the technicalities of the dramatist's and of the actor's art; **stage'-direc'tion,** in a copy of a play, an instruction to the actor to do this or that; **stage'-door,** the actors' entrance to a theatre; **stage'-fē'ver,** a passion to go on the stage; **stage'-fright,** nervousness before an audience, esp. for the first time; **stage'-hand,** a workman employed about the stage; **stage'-man'ager,** one who superintends the production of plays, with general charge behind the curtain.—*v.t.* **stage'-man'age** (back-formation—*q.v.*), used *lit.*; also *fig.,* meaning to arrange (an event) effectively as if it were a stage scene.—*ns.* **stage'-play,** a play played, or intended to be played, on a stage; **stā'ger,** a horse that draws a stage-coach: one long engaged in any occupation (*old stager*).—*adj.* **stage'-struck,** sorely smitten with stagefever.—*ns.* **stage'-whis'per,** audible utterance conventionally understood by the audience to represent a whisper: a loud whisper meant to be heard by people other than the person addressed; **stā'ging,** a scaffold-like structure, e.g. for workmen: putting on the stage.—*adj.* **stagy** (*stā'ji;* also **stagey**), savouring of the stage: theatrical, artificial, melodramatic.—*n.* **stā'giness.** [O.Fr. *estage,* a storey of a house, through L.L. from L. *stāre,* to stand.]

stagger, *stag'ér, v.i.* to reel: to go reeling or tottering: to waver.—*v.t.* to cause to reel: to

give a shock to: to nonplus, confound: to cause to waver: to arrange on each side of a line, at equal distances and symmetrically, or otherwise: to arrange (opening of businesses, hours of work, holidays, &c.) so that sets of workers alternate with each other on the job, or are free at different times.—*n.* a staggering: a wavering: a staggered arrangement: (in *pl.* form, often treated as *sing.*) giddiness—also a disease of various kinds causing horses, &c., to stagger.—*adj.* **stagg'ering,** disconcerting, overwhelming.—*adv.* **stagg'eringly.** [O.N. *stakra,* to push, freq. of *staka,* to push.]

stagnant, *stag'nánt, adj.* not flowing, motionless: impure through lack of inflow and outflow: (*fig.*) inactive, dull.—*ns.* **stag'nancy, stagnā'tion.**—*adv.* **stag'nantly.**—*v.i.* **stag'nate,** to be, or become, stagnant: to exist, pass one's time, in dullness and inactivity. [L. *stagnans, -antis,* pr.p. of *stagnāre—stagnum,* a pool, swamp.]

staid, *stād, adj.* steady, sober, grave: sedate.—*adv.* **staid'ly.**—*n.* **staid'ness.** [Archaic pa.p. of **stay.**]

stain, *stān, v.t.* to impart a new colour to: to tinge, to discolour, spot, sully (*lit.* and *fig.*): in microscopy, to impregnate (plant or animal material) with a substance that colours some parts, so as to pick out certain tissue elements, or to make transparent tissues visible, &c.—*v.i.* to take or impart a stain.—*n.* a dye or colouring matter: a discoloration, a spot: taint of guilt: cause of reproach or shame.—*adj.* **stain'less,** free from stain: not liable to stain, rust, or tarnish.—**stained glass,** glass painted with certain pigments fused into its surface; **stain'less steel,** an alloy of steel and chromium which does not rust. [Short for *distain* (*arch.* and *obs.*), to take away the colour; through O.Fr.—L. *dis-,* private, and *tingĕre,* to colour.]

stair, *stār, n.* a series of steps (in Scotland, the whole series from floor to floor, elsewhere—usu. in *pl.*—a flight from landing to landing): one of such steps.—*ns.* **stair'case, stairway,** the structure enclosing a stair: stairs with banisters, &c.; **stair'-rod,** one of a number of rods for holding a stair-carpet in place.—*n.* and *adj.* **back'stairs** (see **back**).—**below stairs,** in the basement: among the servants. [O.E. *stæger—stīgan,* to ascend.]

stake, *stāk, n.* a strong stick pointed at one end: one of the upright pieces of a fence: a post to which one condemned to be burned was tied, hence, death or martyrdom by burning.—*v.t.* to fasten to or with, to protect, shut, support with, a stake or stakes: to pierce with a stake: to mark the bounds of with stakes (often with *off, out*).—**stake a claim (for, to),** to intimate one's right or desire to possess. [O.E. *staca,* a stake.]

stake, *stāk, v.t.* to deposit as a wager: to risk, hazard.—*n.* anything pledged as a wager: anything to gain or lose: an interest, concern: the condition of being at hazard: (in *pl.*) a race for money staked or contributed.—**at stake,** hazarded, in danger, at issue. [Perh. Middle Du. *staken,* to place.]

stakhanovite, *stá-kan'ō-vīt, n.* a worker who has received recognition for his part in increasing the rate of production in the factory, &c.,

Neutral vowels in unaccented syllables: *em'pér-ór;* for certain sounds in foreign words see p. ix.

710

where he works. [*Stakhanov*, a Russian worker.]

stalactite, *stal'ak-tīt* (also *sta-lak'tīt*), *n.* an icicle-like pendant of calcium carbonate (carbonate of lime), formed by evaporation of water percolating through limestone, as on a cave roof: the material it is composed of: anything of similar form.—*adjs.* **stalac'tic, -al, stalactit'ic, -al; stalac'tiform.** [Gr. *stalaktos* (p.adj.)—*stalassein*, to drip.]

stalag, *stä'läg, -läн*, *n.* a German prisoner-of-war camp for non-commissioned officers and men. [Ger.—*stamm*, base, *lager*, camp.]

stalagmite, *stal'äg-mīt* (also *sta-lag'mīt*), *n.* a deposit on the floor of a cavern, usually cylindrical or conical in form, caused by the dripping from the roof, or from a stalactite (q.v.), of water holding calcium carbonate in solution.—*adjs.* **stalagmit'ic, -al.** [Gr. *stalagmos* (n.), dropping—*stalassein*, to drip.]

stale, *stāl, adj.* altered for the worse by age: tainted: vapid or tasteless from age: (*fig.*) having lost its novelty or piquancy through repetition, trite: out of condition by overtraining or over-study: *ref.* and *v.i.* to make or become stale, over-familiar, or insipid.—*n.* **stale'ness.** [Perh. from the root *sta-*, as in **stand**.]

stale, *stāl, n.* urine, now esp. of horses.—*v.i.* to urinate. [Cf. Du. *stalle*, Ger. *stall*, O.Fr. vb. *estaler*.]

stalemate, *stāl'māt, n.* (*chess*) a situation in which the person to play, while not actually in check, cannot move without getting into check—result, an unsatisfactory draw: a deadlock. [Anglo Fr. *estale*, with the addition of *mate* as in **checkmate**.]

stalk, *stök, n.* the stem of a plant: the stem on which a flower or fruit grows: anything resembling the stem of a plant, as the stem of a quill: a tall chimney.—*adj.* **stalk'less,** having no stalk. [Dim. from the root of O.E. *stæla, stala, stalk.*]

stalk, *stök, v.i.* to stride stiffly or haughtily: to go after game, keeping under cover.—*v.t.* to approach under cover: to walk stiffly or haughtily over or through (often *fig.* with a personification, e.g. famine, disease, as subject).—*n.* an act of stalking: stalking gait.—*n.* **stalk'er.** —*n.* and *adj.* **stalk'ing.**—*n.* **stalk'ing-horse,** a horse, or substitute, behind which a sportsman hides while stalking game: a person, thing, or ostensible motive, used to divert attention from one's doings or real aims. [O.E. *(bi)stealcian*, frequentative of **steal**.]

stall, *stöl, n.* (*obs.*) a standing-place: a stable, cowshed, or the like: a compartment for one animal: a bench, table, booth, or stand, for display or sale of goods: a church-seat with arms, usu. one of those lining the choir or chancel on both sides, reserved for cathedral clergy, for choir, for monks, or for knights of an order: a doorless pew: a superior armed seat in a theatre, usually one of those in the front division of the ground floor (**orchestra stall**): a covering for a finger: loss of flying-speed in aircraft: a standstill.—*v.t.* to put or keep in a stall: to bring to a standstill.—*v.i.* (of aircraft) to lose flying speed and so fall temporarily out of control: (of an engine) to stop

owing to a too sudden application of a load or brake.—*n.* **stall'age,** rent for liberty of erecting a stall in a fair or market.—*adj.* **stalled,** kept or fed in a stall: fatted.—*v.t.* **stall'-feed,** to feed and fatten in a stall or stable. [O.E. *stall*, *steall*; O.N. *stallr*, Ger. *stall*.]

stall, *stöl, v.i.* (*slang*) to play for time, avoid a decision or decisive action.—Also used with force of *v.t.* in **stall off**. [From obs. *stale*, a decoy—root of **stall** (1).]

stallion, *stal'yón, n.* an uncastrated male horse, esp. one kept for breeding. [O.Fr. *estalon*— O.H.G. *stal*, stall.]

stalwart, *stöl'wärt, adj* stout, sturdy: staunch, resolute.—*n.* a resolute person.—*n.* **stal'wartness.** [Orig. Scot. form (popularised by Sir Walter Scott) of *stalworth*—O.E. *stælwierthe*—*stæl*, place, *wierthe*, worth.]

stamen, *stā'mén, n.* the pollen-producing part of a flower, consisting of anther and filament:— *pl.* **stā'mens.**—*n.pl.* (generally treated as *sing.*) **stam'ina** (*stam'-*), constitutional strength: staying power.—*adjs.* **stam'inal,** of stamens or stamina; **stam'inate,** having stamens but no carpels. [L. *stāmen* (pl. *stāmina*), a warp thread (upright in an old loom)—*stāre*, to stand.]

stammer, *stam'ér, v.i.* to falter in speaking: to stutter.—*v.t.* to utter falteringly or with a stutter.—*n.* hesitation in speech: a stammering mode of utterance.—*n.* **stamm'erer.** *adv.* **stamm'eringly.** [O.E. *stamerian*; Du. *stameren*.]

stamp, *stamp, v.t.* (*dial.*) to pound, crush: to bring the foot forcibly down upon: to trample: to bring (the foot) forcibly down: to impress, imprint, or cut with a downward blow, as with a die or cutter: to mint, make, shape, by such a blow: to fix or mark (both on—*lit.* and *fig.*): to impress with a mark attesting official approval, ratification, payment, &c.: to affix an adhesive stamp to: (*fig.*) to mark (as), to declare, prove, to be: *v.i.* to step or set down the foot forcibly and noisily.—*n.* the act of stamping: an impression: a stamped device, mark, imprint: an adhesive paper with a device used as a substitute for stamping: attestation: authorisation: kind, form, character: distinguishing mark, imprint, sign, evidence: an instrument or machine for stamping.—*ns.* **stamp'-album,** a book for keeping a collection of postage-stamps in; **stamp'-collec'tor,** a receiver of stamp-duties: one who makes a hobby of collecting postage or other stamps; **stamp'-dū'ty,** a tax imposed e.g. on legal documents, paid by using paper marked with a government revenue stamp or by affixing adhesive stamps; **stamp'er; stamping-ground,** an animal's or person's usual place of resort; **stamp'-off'ice,** an office where stamp-duties are received and stamps issued.— **stamp out,** to put out by trampling: to extirpate: to make by stamping from a sheet with a cutter. [From an inferred O.E. *stampian*, from the same root as O.E. *stempan*; Ger. *stampfen.*]

stampede, *stam-pēd', n.* a sudden rush of a panic-stricken herd: any impulsive action of a large number of people.—*v.i.* to rush in a stampede.—*v.t.* to send rushing in a stampede. [Sp. *estampido*, a crash—*estampar*, to stamp.]

stance, *stans, n.* manner of standing, posture in

fāte, fär; mē, hûr (her); *mīne; mōte, för; mūte, mōōn, fŏŏt; тнen* (then) playing golf, cricket, &c.: (*Scot.*) position, site, stand. [Fr. *stance,* now meaning only 'stanza'.]

stanch, *stän(t)sh,* **staunch,** *stön(t)sh, v.t.* to stop the flow of, as blood: to allay.—*v.i.* (*B.*) to cease to flow.—*n.* a styptic: a flood-gate. [O.Fr. *estanchier,* perh.—L. *stagnāre,* to be or make stagnant.]

stanch (*adj.*) **stanchly, stanchness.** See **staunch.**

stanchion, *stan'sh(ò)n, n.* an upright iron bar of a window or screen: (*naut.*) an upright beam used as a support. [O.Fr. *estançon—estance,* prop—L. *stāre,* to stand.]

stand, *stand, v.i.* to be, become, or remain, upright, erect, rigid, or still: to be on, or rise to one's feet: to have or take a position: to be or remain: to be set or situated: to come from a specified direction (*the wind stands in the east*): to endure, continue: to hold good: to scruple, to hesitate (at): to act as (e.g. sponsor): to be a candidate.—*v.t.* to set upright: (*arch.*) to withstand: to endure, bear, tolerate: to endure the presence of (a person): to offer and pay for:—*pa.t.* and *pa.p.* stood.—*n.* an act, manner, or place, of standing: a taking up of a position for resistance: resistance: a standing position: a standstill: a post, station: a place for vehicles awaiting hire: an erection for spectators: (*U.S.*) a witness-box: a base or structure for setting things on: a piece of furniture for hanging things from: a stop on tour to give one or more theatrical performances, or the place where it is made.—*ns.* **stand'by,** that which, or one whom, one relies on or readily resorts to; **stand'er; stand'-in,** a substitute.—*adj.* **stand'ing,** erect, on one's feet: established, accepted (e.g. *a standing rule, objection, joke*): permanent (e.g. *standing army*): stagnant.—*n.* the action of the verb: duration: place to stand in: position or grade in a profession, university, society: a right or capacity to bring a legal action.—*n.* **stand'ing-ground,** a place on which to stand: any basis or principle on which rest rests.—*n.pl.* **stand'ing-or'ders** (see **order**).—*ns.* **stand'ing-room,** room for standing, without a seat; **stand'ing-stone,** a great stone set erect in the ground; **stand'ish,** an inkstand; **stand'-off,** a Rugby half-back who stands away from the scrum as a link between scrum-half and the three-quarters.—*adj.* **stand'off,** aloof, reserved—also **stand'off'ish.**—*ns.* **stand'off'ishness; stand'point,** viewpoint; **stand'still,** a complete stop.—*v.i.* **stand'-to',** to take post in readiness for orders.—*n.* a precautionary parade or taking of posts.—*adj.* **stand'-up,** erect: done or taken in a standing position: of a fight, in earnest.— **stand by,** to stand close to: to adhere to, to abide by (e.g. a decision): to support: to hold oneself in readiness; **stand down,** to leave the witness-box: to go off duty: to withdraw from a contest or from a controlling position; **stand fast,** to be unmoved; **stand fire,** to remain steady under the fire of an enemy—also *fig.*; **stand for,** to be a candidate for: to be a sponsor for: to champion: to represent, symbolise: (*slang*) to put up with, endure, to countenance: (*naut.*) to direct the course towards; **stand from,** to direct the course away from; **stand in,** to become a party to an under-

taking: to give assistance in case of need. to substitute, (*orig.* for a motion-picture actor during preparations for scenes): to cost (e.g. *the upkeep stands him in £200 a year*); **stand in with,** to have a secret understanding with; **stand off,** to remain at a distance: to direct the course away from: to suspend temporarily from employment; **stand off and on,** to sail away from shore and then towards it; **stand one's ground,** to maintain one's position; **stand on one's own feet,** to manage one's own affairs unaided; **stand out,** to project, to be prominent: to refuse to comply or yield; **stand pat,** (*U.S.*—in poker) to play one's hand as it was dealt without drawing any cards: (*fig.*) to adhere to an established political or other policy, resisting all compromise or change; **stand to,** to fall to, set to work: to stick to (e.g. one's guns): to adhere to, abide by (e.g. one's promise): to be likely to: to take up position in readiness for orders; **to stand to reason,** to be in accordance with reason, logic, or probability; **stand up,** to get to one's feet: to take position for a dance: to be clad (in): (*coll.*) to fail to keep an appointment with; **stand up for,** to support or attempt to defend; **stand up to,** to face boldly: to fulfil manfully; **stand up with,** to dance with as a partner; **stand well,** to be in favour (with); **stand with,** to be consistent. [O.E. *standan*; Ger. *stehen*; cf. Gr. *histanai,* to place, L. *stāre,* to stand.]

standard, *stand'ärd, n.* a flag or military symbolic figure on a pole, marking a rallying-point: a flag generally: a rallying-point (also *fig.*): the uppermost petal of a papilionaceous flower: that which stands or is fixed: an upright post, pillar: a standing shrub or tree not trained on an espalier or a wall: a basis of measurement, esp. a specimen weight or measure preserved for reference (see **pound, yard** (1)): the legally fixed fineness of coinage metal, or weight of a new coin: the metal with reference to which the values of a monetary system are fixed (e.g. *the gold standard*): a criterion: an established or accepted model: in schools (formerly), a grade of classification: a definite level of excellence or adequacy required, aimed at, or possible.—*adj.* serving as a standard, or conforming to, a standard: growing as a standard.—*ns.* **stand'ard-bear'er,** one who carries a standard or banner; **stand'ard-gauge** (see **gauge**).—*v.t.* **stand'ardise,** to make, or keep, of uniform size, shape, &c.—*n.* **standard-isā'tion.—Standard English,** the form of English used (with minor variations) by the majority of cultured English speakers; **standard lamp,** a lamp on a tall support. [O.Fr. *estandart*; prob. connected either with **extend** or with **stand.**]

stank, *stangk, pa.t.* of **stink.**

stannary, *stan'är-i, n.* a tin-mining district.—*n.* **stann'ate,** a salt of stannic acid.—*adjs.* **stann'ic,** denoting a compound in which tin has a valency of 4; **stann'ous,** denoting a compound in which tin has a valency of 2 (e.g. *stannic chloride,* Sn Cl_4; *stannous chloride,* Sn Cl_2); **stannif'erous,** tin-bearing.—**stannic acid,** any of various acids of two types of which tin forms an element. [L. *stannum,* tin.]

stanza, *stan'za, n.* a series of lines or verses

Neutral vowels in unaccented syllables: *em'pér-ór*; for certain sounds in foreign words see p. ix.

(following a definite pattern as regards lengths of line, accentuation, and rhyme scheme) forming a unit of a poem.—*adj.* **stanzā'ic**. [It. *stanza*, a stop—L. *stāre*, stand.]

staple, *stā'pl*, *n.* a settled mart or market: a leading commodity of trade or industry, main element (e.g. of diet, reading, conversation): unmanufactured wool or other raw material: textile fibre or its length or quality.—*adj.* constituting a staple: leading, main.—*v.t.* to grade according to staple.—*n.* **stā'pler**, a merchant of a staple: one who grades and deals in wool. [O.Fr. *estaple*—Low Ger. *stapel*, a heap, mart.]

staple, *stā'pl*, *n.* a bent rod or wire, both ends of which are driven into a wall, post, &c., to form a fastening: the part that passes through the slot of a hasp, receives a bolt, &c.—*v.t.* to fasten with a staple. [O.E. *stapol*, a prop.]

star, *stär*, *n.* any one of the heavenly bodies, esp. of those visible by night whose places in the firmament are relatively fixed (**fixed stars**), sometimes (*loosely*) including planets, comets, meteors, less commonly the sun and moon, or even the earth: a planet as a supposed influence, hence (usu. in *pl.*) one's luck or destiny: an object or figure with pointed rays, most commonly five: a representation of a star worn as a badge of rank or honour: (*print.*) an asterisk (*): a pre-eminent or exceptionally brilliant person: a leading performer, or one supposed to draw the public.—*adj.* of stars: marked by a star: leading, pre-eminent, brilliant.—*v.t.* to mark with a star: to set with stars, to bespangle: to make a star of: (*coll.*) to have (a specified person) as a star performer.—*v.i.* to shine, as a star: to appear as a star performer;—*pr.p.* **starr'ing**; *pa.t.* and *pa.p.* **starred**.—*ns.* **star'-cat'alogue**, a list of stars, with their places, magnitudes, &c.; **star'dom**, the state of being, the status of, a star or leading performer on stage or screen; **star'-dust**, cosmic dust, meteoric matter in fine particles: distant stars seen like dust grains; **star'fish**, a class of invertebrate marine animals, often found on the seashore, so named because the body consists of a central disk, from which the arms, most commonly five in number, radiate; **star'-gāz'er**, an astrologer: an astronomer: an absent-minded person, a wool-gatherer; **star'-gāz'ing**; **star'-shell**, a shell that explodes high in the air scattering burning chemicals to illuminate the scene.—*adj.* **star'less**, having no stars visible: having no light from stars.—*n.* **star'light**, light from the stars.—*adj.* **star'lit**, lighted by the stars.—*n.* **star'-of-Beth'lehem**, a plant of the lily family, with starlike flowers.—*adjs.* **starr'ed**, adorned or studded with stars: marked with a star, as specially distinguished; **starr'y**, abounding or adorned with stars: consisting of, or proceeding from, the stars: like, or shining like, the stars; **starr'y-eyed**, innocently idealistic: out of touch with reality: radiantly happy.—*n.* **starr'iness**.—*adjs.* **star'-shaped**, shaped like a conventional star, with pointed rays; **star'-spang'led**, spangled or studded with stars.—*n.* **star'-turn**, (*coll.*) the chief item in an entertainment: a pre-eminent performer.—**Stars and Stripes**, the flag of the United States of America, with thirteen horizontal stripes alternately red and white, and a blue field containing as many stars as there are states. [O.E. *steorra*; Ger. *stern*, L. *stella* (for *sterula*), Gr. *astēr*.]

starboard, *stär'bō(r)d, -bōrd*, *n.* the right-hand side of a ship, when one is looking towards the bow.—*adj.* of, to, towards, on, the right side of a ship. [O.E. *stēorbord*—*stēor*, steering, *bord*, a board, the side of a ship.]

starch, *stärch*, *n.* the principal reserve food-material stored in plants, chemically a carbohydrate, used in the laundry as a stiffener: stiffness, formality.—*v.t.* to stiffen with starch.—*adj.* **starched**, stiffened with starch: stiff, formal.—*ns.* **starch'edness**; **starch'er**.—*adj.* **starch'y**, of, or like, starch: stiff, precise.—*n.* **starch'iness**. [O.E. *stercan*, to stiffen (inferred from *stercedferhth*, stiff-spirited); cf. **stark**.]

Star Chamber, *stär' chām'bèr*, *n.* a tribunal with a civil and criminal jurisdiction which met in the old council chamber of Westminster, abolished in the reign of Charles I. [Prob. named from the gilt stars on the ceiling.]

stare, *stār*, *v.i.* to look with a fixed gaze, as in horror, astonishment, &c.: to glare: to be insistently or obtrusively conspicuous, or obvious to (e.g. *to stare one in the face*): (*Shak.*) to stand on end.—*v.t.* to bring (a person, &c., into a specified condition, action) by staring.—*n.* a fixed look.—*n.* **stā'rer**. [O.E. *starian*, from a Gmc. root seen in Ger. *starr*, rigid: also in Eng. **stern**.]

stark, *stärk*, *adj.* stiff: (*arch.*) strong: harsh: sheer, out-and-out: stark-naked: unadorned (of style).—*adv.* utterly.—*adv.* **stark'ly**.—*n.* **stark'ness**. [O.E. *stearc*, hard, strong; cog. with O.N. *sterkr*, Ger. *stark*.]

stark-naked, *stärk'-nā'kid*, *adj.* utterly naked, quite bare—sometimes shortened to **stark**.—Earlier (now *dial.*) **start'-na'ked**. [M.E. *start-naked*, O.E. *steort*, tail, *nacod*, naked; influenced by foregoing word.]

starling, *stär'ling*, *n.* a black, brown-spotted bird with purple or green reflections, a good mimic: any other member of its genus. [O.E. *stærling*, dim of *stær*, a starling.]

start, *stärt*, *v.i.* to shoot, dart, move, suddenly forth or out: to spring up or forward: to break away, become displaced: to make a sudden involuntary movement, as of surprise or becoming aware: to begin: to set forth on a journey, race, career.—*v.t.* to begin: to set going: to set on foot: to set up (e.g. in business): to drive from lair or hiding-place: to cause, or to undergo, displacement or loosening of (e.g. a tooth, a nail, a bolt, timbers).—*n.* a sudden involuntary motion of the body: a startled feeling: a spurt: an outburst or fit: a beginning of movement, esp. of a journey, race, or career: a beginning: a setting in motion: a help in, or opportunity of, beginning: an advantage in being early or ahead: the extent of such an advantage in time or distance.—*ns.* **start'er**, one who, or which, sets out on a race or journey: one who gives the signal to begin a race or game: that which sets machinery in motion; **start'ing-point**, the point from which motion or (*fig.*) action begins; **start'ing-post**, the post or barrier from which competitors begin a race.—**start up,** to rise suddenly: to come suddenly into notice or being: to set in motion. [M.E. *sterten*; closely akin to Du. *storten,* to plunge, Ger. *stürzen.*]

startle, *stärt'l, v.i.* to start, to feel sudden alarm.—*v.t.* to cause (a person) surprise mingled with alarm, outrage to sense of propriety or fitness, or similar emotion: to cause (a person) to start with surprise and alarm. [O.E. *steartlian,* to stumble, struggle, kick; or from **start.**]

starve, *stärv, v.i.* to die, now only of hunger or (chiefly *Scot.* or *North*) cold: to suffer extreme hunger (or cold): (*fig.*) to be in want: to feel a great longing (for).—*v.t.* to cause to starve: to force (into) by want of food: to cure (e.g. a fever) by starving: to deprive (of) anything needful.—*n.* **starvā'tion.**—*adjs.* **starving;** **starve'ling,** hungry, lean, weak.—*n.* a thin, weak, pining person, animal, or plant. [O.E. *steorfan,* to die; Du. *sterven,* Ger. *sterben,* to die.]

stash, *stash, v.t.,* to stow in hiding.

stasis, *stas'is, n.* stoppage, esp. of growth, of blood-circulation, or of the contents of the bowels. [Gr.]

state, *stāt, n.* condition: circumstances at any time: a phase or stage: station in life: high station: pomp, display, ceremonial dignity: an estate, order, or class in society or the body politic: hence (*hist.* in *pl.*) the legislature: the civil power: any body of people politically organised and independent: any of the members of a federation: the territory of such: high politics.—*adj.* of, belonging to, relating to, the state or a federal state: public: ceremonial.—*v.t.* to set forth, express the details of: to set down fully and formally: to assert, affirm: to fix, settle.—*adj.* **state'-aid'ed,** receiving contributions from the state.—*n.* **state'-craft,** the art of managing state affairs.—*adjs.* **stāt'ed,** settled, fixed, regular; **stāte'ly,** showing state or dignity: majestic, very impressive.—*ns.* **state'liness; state'ment,** the act of stating: that which is stated: a formal account: a financial record; **state'-pā'per,** an official paper or document relating to affairs of state; **state'-pris'oner,** a prisoner confined for offence against the state; **state'room,** a room of state in a palace or mansion: a private cabin or railway compartment; **states'man,** one skilled in government: one who takes an important part in governing the state, esp. with wisdom and broad-mindedness.—*adj.* **states'manlike,** befitting a statesman—judicious, sagacious.—*ns.* **states'manship; state'-trī'al,** a trial for an offence against the state.—**State Department,** the U.S. Foreign Office; **stately home,** a large, fine old house in private ownership but usu. open to the public.—**lie in state,** of a corpse, to be laid out in a place of honour before being buried. [L. *status, -ūs*—*stāre, statum,* to stand; partly through O.Fr.]

static, -al, *stat'ik, -ál, adj.* pertaining to statics: pertaining to bodies, forces, charges, &c., in equilibrium: stationary: stable: acting by mere weight.—*n.* statics: atmospheric disturbances in wireless or television reception.—*n.* **stat'ics,** the science of forces in equilibrium. [Gr.

statikē (fem. of adj.), bringing to a standstill—*histanai,* to cause to stand.]

station, *stā'sh(ó)n, n.* (*surveying*) a fixed point from which measurements are made: a standing place, fixed stopping place, esp. now one on a railway with associated buildings and structures: a local office, headquarters, or depôt (e.g. *police station*): (*R.C.*) a holy place visited as one of a series, esp. one of (usu.) fourteen representative of stages in Christ's way to Calvary, disposed around a church interior or elsewhere: (*bot.* and *zool.*) a habitat: an actual place where a species has been found: an assigned place or post: a position: an assigned region for naval duty: a place in India where officials and officers reside: the people residing there: an Australian stock farm: position in life, or in the scale of nature: exalted position or status.—*adj.* of a station.—*v.t.* to assign a station to: to appoint to a post, place, of office.—*adj.* **stā'tionary,** standing, not moving: fixed: permanently located.—*n.* **stā'tioner,** (*obs.*) a bookseller or publisher: one who sells paper and other articles used in writing (L.*stātiōnārius,* a shopkeeper, in the Middle Ages a university bookseller as distinguished from an itinerant).—*adj.* **stā'-tionery,** belonging to a stationer.—*n.* goods sold by a stationer.—*n.* **stā'tion-mas'ter,** one in charge of a railway station.—**Stationers' Hall,** the hall in London belonging to the Company of the Stationers, who, until the passing of the Copyright Act in 1842, enjoyed an absolute monopoly of printing and publishing; **Stationery Office,** an office for providing books, stationery, &c., to government offices and for arranging for the printing of government reports and other public papers. [Fr.,—L. *statiō, -ōnis*—*stāre,* to stand.]

statist, *stā'tist, n.* (*obs.*) a politician: a statistician.—*n.* **statis'tic,** a statistician: (in *pl.*) tabulated numerical facts, orig. those relating to a state: (in *pl.* form, treated as *sing.*) the classification, tabulation, and study of such facts.—*adj.* **statist'ical,** of, concerned with, of the nature of, statistics.—*adv.* **statist'ically.**—*n.* **statistician** (*stat-is-tish'án*), one skilled in statistics: a compiler or student of statistics. [It.*statista* and Ger.*statistik*—L.*status,* state.]

stator, *stā'tór, n.* a stationary part within which a part rotates, as the fixed part of an electrical machine. [L. *stātor,* stander.]

statue, *stat'ū, n.* a representation (usu. near or above life-size) of a human or animal form in the round.—*adj.* **stat'ūary,** of, or suitable for, sculpture: sculptured.—*n.* **statuary:** a sculptor.—*adj.* **statuesque** (*stat-ū-esk'*), like a statue.—*adv.* **statuesquely.**—*n.* **statuette',** a small statue, figurine. [L. *statua*—*statuĕre,* to cause to stand—*stāre.*]

stature, *stat'yur, n.* height of body.—Also *fig.*—*adj.* **stat'ured,** of a specified stature (e.g. *low statured*). [L. *statūra.*]

status, *stā'tus, n.* social position: standing in profession, in society, or in any organisation of persons: condition, description from the point of view of the law, determining capacity to sue, &c.: position of affairs.—**status symbol,** a possession or a privilege considered to mark a person out as having a high position in his

Neutral vowels in unaccented syllables: *em'pér-ór*; for certain sounds in foreign words see p. ix.

714

social group.—**status (in) quo**, the state, condition of affairs, existing before a certain event, date. [L. *status*.]

statute, *stat'ūt*, *n.* a law expressly enacted by the legislature (as distinguished from a customary law or law of use and wont): a written law: the act of a corporation or its founder, intended as a permanent rule or law.—*adj.* **stat'-ūtable**, prescribed, permitted, recognised by, or according to, statute.—*adv.* **stat'ūtably.**—*ns.* **stat'ute-book**, a record of statutes or enacted laws; **stat'ute-law**, law in the form of statutes.—*adj.* **stat'ūtory**, enacted by statute: required by statute: depending on statute for its authority. [L. *statutum*, that which is set up—*statuere*.]

staunch, *stönch*, *-sh*, **stanch**, *stanch*, *-sh*, *adj.* water-tight: firm in principle: trusty, constant, zealous. [O.Fr. *estanche*—*estanchier*. See **stanch** (1).]

stave, *stāv*, *n.* one of the side pieces of a cask or tub: a staff, rod, bar, shaft: (*mus.*) a staff: a stanza, verse of a song.—*v.t.* to break a stave or the staves of, to break, to burst (often with *in*): to drive (off), keep at bay, as with a staff: to delay (e.g. *to stave off the evil day*): to put together, or repair, with staves:—*pa.t.* and *pa.p.* **stāved** or **stōve**. [By-form of **staff**.]

staves, *stāvz*, plural of **staff** and of **stave**.

stay, *stā*, *n.* a rope supporting a mast: a guy: a prop, support: a brace, connecting piece to resist tension: (in *pl.*) a stiff corset (also **pair of stays**): a stopping, bringing or coming to a standstill: a suspension of legal proceedings: delay: a sojourn: staying power.—*v.t.* to support or incline with a stay or stays: (*fig.*) to support, prop, sustain: to endure: to endure to the end: to stop: to detain: to hold, restrain, check the action of: to allay: (*arch.*) to await.—*v.i.* to stop: to remain, to tarry: to wait (for): to sojourn: (*Scot.*) to dwell: to hold out, last, endure:—*pa.t.* and *pa.p.* **stayed**, (*arch.*) **staid** (see **staid**, *adj.*).—*ns.* **stay**, one who, or that which, stops or that holds or supports a competitor whose strength does not flag in a contest; **stay'ing-power**, ability to go on long without flagging; **stay'lace**, a lace for fastening a corset; **staysail** (*stā'sl*), a sail extended on a stay.—**stay-in strike**, a strike in which employees are in their places but do no work; **stay put** (*coll.*) to stay where one is put, to remain in the same place, to remain in the required position; **stay the course**, to endure until the end of the race (*lit.* and *fig.*). [Partly O.E. *stæg*, stay (rope); partly O.Fr. *estayer*, to prop, from the same Gmc. root; partly O.Fr. *ester*—*stāre*, to stand.]

stead, *sted*, *n.* a place (now chiefly in compounds and idiomatic phrases): esp. the place which another had, or might have: service, advantage.—*v.t.* to avail, help:—*pa.t.* and *pa.p.* **stead'ed**, **stead** (*sted*).—*n.* **stead'ing**, (*Scot.*) farm buildings including, or without, the farm-house.—**stand one in good stead**, prove of good service to one in time of need. [O.E. *stede*, place; cf. Ger. *stadt*, town, *statt*, place.]

steadfast, *sted'fast*, *adj.* firmly fixed or established: firm, constant, resolute.—*adv.* **stead'fastly.**—*n.* **stead'fastness**. [O.E. *stede-fæst*—*stede*, a place (see **stead**), *fæst*, firm.]

steady, *sted'i*, *adj.* (*comp.* **stead'ier**, *superl.* **stead'iest**) firm in standing or in place: (*fig.*) stable: unshaking, unfaltering: constant, consistent (e.g. a *steady supporter*): regular (e.g. *steady work*): uniform (e.g. *steady flow*): sober, industrious.—*v.t.* to make steady, to make or keep firm:—*pr.p.* stead'ying; *pa.t.* and *pa.p.* stead'ied.—*n.* (*coll.*) a regular boy friend or girl friend.—*adv.* **stead'ily.**—*n.* **stead'iness.**—*adj.* **stead'y-gō'ing**, of steady habits or action.—**go steady**, (*coll.*) to go about regularly and exclusively with one person of the opposite sex. [**stead**, and suffx. *-y*.]

steak, *stāk*, *n.* a slice of meat (esp. hindquarters of beef) or fish. [O.N. *steik*; *steikja*, to roast on a spit.]

steal, *stēl*, *v.t.* to take by theft, esp. secretly: to take, gain, or win, by address, by contrivance, unexpectedly, insidiously, or gradually: to snatch.—*v.i.* to practise theft: to take feloniously: to pass quietly, unobtrusively, gradually, or surreptitiously:—*pa.t.* stōle; *pa.p.* stōl'en.—*n.* **steal'er.**—**steal a march on**, to gain an advantage over unperceived. [O.E. *stelan*; Ger. *stehlen*, Du. *stelen*.]

stealth, *stelth*, *n.* secret procedure or manner, furtiveness.—*adj.* **stealth'y**, acting, or acted, with stealth, furtive.—*n.* **stealth'iness.**—*adv.* **stealth'ily**. [**steal**.]

steam, *stēm*, *n.* the dry, invisible and transparent vapour into which water is converted by boiling: (*loosely*) the moist, visible cloud formed by the condensation of this vapour in contact with cold air: any vapour, or mist, or film of liquid drops: steam-power: a spell of travel by steam-power: (*fig.*) energy, force, spirit.—*v.i.* to rise or pass off in steam or vapour: to emit or generate steam, vapour, or smell: to become dimmed with condensed vapour: to move by steam.—*v.t.* to expose to steam: to cook by means of steam: to dim with vapour.—*adj.* in composition, propelled or operated by steam-power, as **steam'ship**, **steam'hamm'er.**—*ns.* **steam'-boil'er**, a boiler for generating steam; **steam'-chest**, a chamber above a steam-boiler serving as a reservoir for steam; **steam'-coal**, coal suitable for raising steam; **steam'er**, a ship propelled by steam, a steamship: formerly, an engine or machine worked by steam: a vessel in which things are steamed; **steam'-gauge**, an instrument for measuring the pressure of steam in a boiler; **steam'-iron**, an electric iron having a compartment in which water is heated to provide steam to damp material; **steam'-jack'et**, a hollow casing, filled with steam, surrounding the cylinder of a steam-engine, or the like, to maintain a high temperature; **steam'-navv'y**, an excavator operated by steam; **steam'-pipe**, a pipe for conveying steam; **steam'-pow'er**, the force, or agency, of steam when applied to machinery; **steam'-radio**, sound radio as distinct from the more modern television; **steam'-roll'er**, a locomotive engine with a heavy roller in place of front wheels, used for crushing metal into a road surface: (*fig.*) any weighty crushing force; **steam'-whis'tle**, a whistle sounded by the passage of steam.—*adj.* **steam'y**, of, like, full of, covered with, as if covered with, emitting, steam or vapour.—*n.* **steam′iness.**—**steamed up,** (*coll.*) indignant; **steam open,** to open by softening gum by exposure to steam.—**full steam ahead,** at the greatest speed possible to the engine: (*fig.*) with maximum effort; **get up steam,** to build up steam pressure: to collect one's forces: to become excited; **let off steam,** to release steam into the atmosphere: (*fig.*) to work off energy, or to give vent to anger or annoyance; **under one's own steam,** (*fig.*) by one's own unaided efforts. [O.E. *stēam*; Du. *stoom.*]

stearin, *stē′a-rin, n.* an ester of stearic acid, being a white crystalline solid found in many vegetable and animal fats, esp. hard fats: (also **stearine**) the solid part of any fat: (also **stearine**) a mixture of stearic acid and another fatty acid, palmitic acid.—**stearic acid,** a fatty acid obtained e.g. from mutton suet. [Gr. *stěār*, gen. *stěātos*, suet.]

steatite, *stē′a-tīt, n.* a coarse, massive, or granular variety of talc, soft and greasy to the touch. [Gr. *steatitēs—stěār*, gen. *stěātos*, suet.]

stedfast. Same as **steadfast.**

steed, *stēd, n.* a horse, esp. a spirited horse. [O.E. *stēda*, stallion; cf. O.E. *stōd*, stud.]

steel, *stēl, n.* iron containing a little carbon, with or without other substances: a cutting tool or weapon: an instrument, object, or part, made of steel, e.g. a steel knife-sharpener, a skate: a piece of steel as for stiffening a corset, striking fire from a flint: (*fig.*) extreme hardness, staying-power, trustworthiness.—*adj.* of, or like, steel.—*v.t.* to cover or edge with steel: to harden, make obdurate: to nerve (oneself).—*adj.* **steel′-clad,** clad in armour.—*n.* **steel′engrav′ing,** engraving on steel plates: an impression or print so obtained.—*adj.* **steel′y,** of, or like, steel. [O.E. *stēle* (W.S. *stīele*); Ger. *stahl.*]

steelyard, *stēl′yärd, n.* a weighing machine, in using which a single weight is moved along a graduated beam. [From the *Steelyard* or *Stālhof* (Low Ger. 'sample yard'—*stāl*, sample), the headquarters of Hanseatic traders in London.]

steep, *stēp, adj.* rising or descending with great inclination, precipitous, headlong: (*coll.*) difficult: (*coll.*) excessive, exorbitant.—*n.* a precipitous place.—*v.t.* and *v.i.* **steep′en,** to make or become steep.—*n.* **steep′ness.**—*adv.* **steep′ly.** [O.E. *stēap*; cf. **stoop.**]

steep, *stēp, v.t.* to dip or soak in a liquid: to wet thoroughly: to saturate: to imbue.—*v.i.* to undergo soaking or thorough wetting.—*n.* a soaking process: a liquid, for steeping anything in.—*n.* **steep′er,** a vessel in which articles are steeped. [M.E. *stepen*; perh. conn. with **stoup.**]

steeple, *stēp′l, n.* a tower of a church or other building, with or without, including or excluding, a spire: the spire alone.—*adj.* **steep′led,** having a steeple or steeples, or appearance of steeples.—*ns.* **steep′lechase,** orig. an impromptu horse-race with a visible church-steeple as goal: a horse-race across country: one over a course with artificial obstacles: a foot-race of like kind; **steeple′-hat,** a high and narrow-crowned hat; **steep′le-jack,** one who climbs steeples and chimneystalks to make

repairs. [O.E. *stēpel, stўpel*; from root of *stēap*, steep.]

steer, *stēr, n.* a young ox, esp. a castrated one from two to four years old. [O.E. *stēor*; Ger. *stier.*]

steer, *stēr, v.t.* to direct with, or as with, the helm: to guide: to direct (one's course).—*v.i.* to direct a ship, cycle, &c., in its course: to be directed or guided: to move (for, towards).—*n.* **steer′age,** act or practice of steering: the effect of a rudder on the ship: accommodation (usually in the bow) for passengers paying the lowest rate of fare.—Also *adj.—ns.* **steer′age-way,** sufficient rate of progress to bring a vessel under the control of the helm; **steer′ing-wheel,** the wheel by which a ship's rudder is turned, or a motorcar, &c., guided; **steers′man,** one who steers.—**steering committee,** (*U.S.*) a group of members of the majority party in a legislative assembly who decide what measures shall be brought forward and in what order: any similar unofficial committee of management. [O.E. *stēoran, stўran,* to steer.]

stele, *stē′lē, n.* an upright stone slab or tablet:—*pl.* **stē′lae** (*-ē*). [Gr. *stēlē—histanai,* to set, stand.]

stellar, *stel′är, adj.* of the stars: of the nature of a star, starry.—*adjs.* **stell′āte, -d,** star-shaped: radiating from a centre: (*geom.*) with sides that intersect one another, giving a star-like effect; **stell′ular,** like a little star or stars: set with stars or star-like marks. [L. *stellāris—stella,* a star.]

stem, *stem, n.* the leaf-bearing axis of a plant, a stalk: anything stalk-like, as the upright slender part of a note, of a wine-glass, &c.: the main line (or sometimes a branch) of a family: a curved timber at the prow of a ship: the forepart of a ship: (*philol.*) the base of a word, to which inflectional suffixes are added.—*v.t.* to provide with a stem: to deprive of stalk or stem: (of a ship) to oppose the stem to: hence, to make way against, breast.—*v.i.* to grow in stem: to spring, take rise (from):—*pr.p.* stemm′ing; *pa.t.* and *pa.p.* stemmed.—*adj.* **stem′less.**—**from stem to stern,** from one end of a vessel to the other: completely, throughout. [O.E. *stefn, stemn;* Ger. *stamm;* perh. conn. with **stand.**]

stem, *stem, v.t.* to stop, check, to dam, to staunch: to tamp:—*pr.p.* stemm′ing; *pa.t.* and *pa.p.* stemmed. [O.N. *stemma.*]

stench, *stench, -sh, n.* stink.—*adj.* **stench′y.** [O.E. *stenc,* smell (good or bad); Ger. *stank.*]

stencil, *sten′s(i)l, v.t.* and *v.i.* to paint by brushing over a perforated plate or sheet: to make a stencil for producing copies of typewriting or writing (see below):—*pr.p.* sten′cilling; *pa.t.* and *pa.p.* sten′cilled.—*n.* the plate or the colouring-matter used to paint as described above: the lettering or design so produced: a piece of waxed paper, &c., on which letters are cut by means of a typewriter or a stylus in such a way that ink will pass through and produce a facsimile of them.—*ns.* **sten′ciller; sten′cilling.** [O.Fr. *estinceller,* to spangle—*estincelle*—L. *scintilla,* a spark.]

sten gun, *n.* a small automatic gun. [*ST* (designers' initials) and *En*field, cf. **bren. gun.**]

Neutral vowels in unaccented syllables: *em′pér-ór*; for certain sounds in foreign words see p. ix.

stenography, *sten-og'rá-fi*, *n.* the art, or any method, of writing very quickly, shorthand.— *n.* **sten'ograph**, a shorthand character or report: a machine for writing in shorthand characters.—*v.t.* to write in shorthand.—*ns.* **sten-og'rapher, stenog'raphist**.—*adjs.* **stenograph'ic, -al**. [Gr. *stenos*, narrow, *graphein*, to write.]

stentorian, *sten-tō', -tō'ri-án, adj.* very loud or powerful, like the voice of *Stentor*, a herald celebrated by Homer.

step, *step*, *n.* a pace: a movement of the leg in walking, running, or dancing: the distance so covered: a footstep—a footfall, a footprint: gait: a small space: a short journey: a degree: a degree of a scale: a stage upward or downward: one tread of a stair, rung of a ladder: a door-step: a move towards an end or in the course of proceeding: coincidence in speed or phase: a support for the end of a mast, pivot, or the like: (in *pl.*) walk: (in *pl.*; also **step'-ladder, pair of steps**) a self-supporting ladder with flat treads.—*v.i.* to advance, retire, mount, or descend, by taking a step or steps: to pace: to walk: to walk slowly or gravely.— *v.t.* to perform by stepping: to measure by pacing: to arrange or shape stepwise: (now *U.S.*) to place (the foot): to fix (a mast):—*pr.p.* **stepp'ing**, *pa.t.* and *pa.p.* **stepped** (also **stept**).—*ns.* **step'-dance**, a dance involving an effective display of steps by an individual dancer; **step'-dancer; step'-dancing; step'-in**, a garment that needs no fastening; **stepp'ing-stone**, a stone rising above water or mud to afford a passage. (*fig.*) a means to gradual progress.—*adv.* **step'wise**, in the manner of steps.—**step in**, or **into**, to enter easily or unexpectedly; **step out**, to go out a little way: to increase the length of the step and so the speed; **step up**, to come forward: to build up into steps; to raise by a step or steps: to increase the voltage of: to increase the rate of (production).—**step on it**, (*coll.*) hurry, increase the speed.—**in step**, simultaneously putting forward of the right (or left) feet in marching, &c.; **out of step**, not in step; **keep step**, to continue in step; **break step**, to get out of step. [O.E. (Mercian) *steppe* (W.S. *stæpe*); Du. *stap*, Ger. *stapfe*.]

step-, *step-*, in composition denotes the mutual relationship between children who, in consequence of a second marriage, have only one parent in common (as **step'-sister**) or between such children and the second husband or wife of the mother or father (as **step'-mother, step'-son**). [O.E. *stēop* (as in *stēopmōdor*), orig. meaning orphan.]

steppe, *step*, *n.* a dry, grassy, generally treeless and uncultivated, and sometimes salt, plain, as in the south-east of Europe and in Asia. [Russ. *step*.]

steradian, *sti-rā'di-än*, *n.* a unit of measurement for solid angles, the angle subtended at the centre of a sphere by an area on its surface numerically equal to the square of the radius. [Gr. *stereos*, solid, and **radian**.]

stercoral, *stûr'kó-rál*, **stercoraceous**, *stêrk-ó-rā'shús, adj.* of, of the nature of, dung. [L. *stercus, -ŏris*, dung.]

stere, *stēr*, *n.* a cubic metre. [Fr. *stère*—Gr. *stereos*, solid.]

stereo. See **stereophonic**.

stereograph, *stēr'i-ō-gräf, ster'i-ō-gräf, n.* a double photograph for viewing in a stereoscope: a picture, diagram suggestive of solidity.—Also **ste'reogram**.—*adjs.* **stereograph'ic, -al**.—*adv.* **stereograph'ically**.—*n.* **stereog'raphy**, the art of showing solids on a plane. [Gr. *stereos*, solid, *graphein*, to write.]

stereophonic, *stēr-, ster-i-ō-fon'ik, adj.* giving the effect of sound coming from different directions.—*n.* **ster'eo**, stereophonic reproduction of sound. [Gr. *stereos*, solid, *phōnē*, sound.]

stereoscope, *stēr'i-ō-skōp, ster'i-ō-skōp, n.* an instrument by which the images of two pictures differing slightly in point of view are seen one by each eye and so give an effect of solidity.—*adjs.* **stereoscop'ic, -al**, pertaining to the stereoscope: producing such an effect (e.g. *stereoscopic television*).—*n.* **stereos'copy**. [Gr. *stereos*, solid, *skopeein*, to look at.]

stereotype, *stē'ri-ō-tīp, ster'i-ō-tīp, n.* a solid metallic plate for printing, cast from a mould (of papier-mâché or other substance) from movable types: the art, method, or process, of making such plates: a fixed conventionalised representation.—*adj.* pertaining to, or done with, stereotypes.—*v.t.* to make a stereotype of; to print with stereotypes: to make in one unchangeable form.—*p.adj.* **ste'reotyped**, fixed, unchangeable (e.g. patterns, opinions): conventionalised.—*ns.* **ste'reotyper**, one who makes stereotype plates for printing; **stereotypog'rapher**, a stereotype printer. [Gr. *stereos*, solid, and **type**.]

sterile, *ster'īl, adj.* unfruitful, barren: not producing or unable to produce, offspring, fruit, seeds, or spores: (of a flower) without pistils: sterilised: destitute of ideas or results.—*v.t.* **ster'ilise**, to cause to be fruitless: to deprive of power of reproduction: to destroy micro-organisms in.—*ns.* **sterilisā'tion; ster'iliser**, anything which sterilises: an apparatus for sterilising objects by boiling water, steam, or dry heat; **steril'ity**, quality of being sterile. [L. *sterilis*, barren.]

sterling, *stûr'ling, n.* (*obs.*) an old English silver penny: (*hist.*) English, Scottish, (now) British, money of standard value.—*adj.* of standard British money: genuine: of thoroughly good character, thoroughly good: (of silver) of standard quality.—**sterling area**, a group of countries with currencies tied to sterling and freely settling transactions among themselves through London. [Prob. a coin with a star— O.E. *steorra*, a star.]

stern, *stûrn, adj.* severe of countenance, manner, or feeling—austere, harsh, unrelenting: rigorous.—*adv.* **stern'ly**.—*n.* **stern'ness**. [O.E. *styrne*.]

stern, *stûrn, n.* the hind-part of a vessel: the rump or tail.—*n.* **stern'-chase**, a chase in which one ship follows directly in the wake of another.—*adj.* **stern'most**, farthest astern.— *ns.* **stern'post**, the aftermost timber of a ship, supporting the rudder; **stern'sheet**, (usu. in *pl.*) the part of a boat between the stern and the rowers.—*advs.* **stern'ward** (also *adj.*), **stern'wards**. [O.N. *stjōrn*, a steering; cog. with **steer** (2).]

---

fāte, *fär*; *mē*, *hûr* (her); *mīne*; *mōte*, *för*; *mūte*; *mōōn*, *fŏŏt*; *тнen* (then)

sternum, *stûr'num, n.* the breast-bone.—*adj.* **ster'nal.** [Gr. *sternon,* chest.]

sternutation, *stûr-nū-tā'sh(ŏ)n, n.* sneezing.—*adj.* **sternū'tatory,** that causes sneezing.—*n.* a substance that causes sneezing. [L. *sternūtātiō, -ōnis—sternūtāre, -ātum,* inten. of *sternuĕre,* to sneeze.]

stertorous, *stûr'tŏ-rus, adj.* with a snoring sound.—*adv.* **ster'torously.** [L. *stertĕre,* to snore.]

stet, *stet, v.t.* to restore after marking for deletion:—*pr.p.* stett'ing; *pa.t.* and *pa.p.* stett'ed. [L., 'let it stand', 3rd sing. pres. subj. of *stāre,* to stand; written on a proofsheet with dots under the words to be retained.]

stethoscope, *steth'ō-skōp, n.* an instrument used in auscultation.—*adjs.* **stethoscop'ic, -al** (*-skop'ik-ál*). [Gr. *stēthos,* chest, *skopeein,* to look at, examine.]

stevedore, *stēv'e-dōr, -dör, n.* one who loads and unloads vessels. [Sp. *estivador,* packer—*estivar,* to stow—L. *stīpāre,* to press.]

stew, *stū, n.* (*Shak.*) a boiling pot: a room for hot-air baths: an overheated or sweaty state: mental agitation: (usu. in *pl.* form with *sing.* or collective sense) a brothel, or a prostitutes' quarter: (*slang*) one who studies hard, esp. unintelligently: a dish of stewed food, esp. meat with vegetables.—*v.t.* to bathe in hot air or water: to bathe in sweat: to keep in a swelter or narrow confinement: to simmer or boil slowly with some moisture: to over-infuse (tea).—*v.i.* to swelter: to undergo stewing: to be in a state of worry or agitation: (*slang*) to study strenuously: **stew in one's own juice,** to reap the consequences of one's actions. [O.Fr. *estuve,* stove; prob. conn. with **stove.**]

steward, *stū'árd, n.* one who manages the domestic concerns of a family or institution: one who superintends another's affairs, esp. on an estate or farm: the manager of the provision department, or an attendant on passengers, in a ship, aircraft: a college caterer: one who helps in arrangements, marshalling, &c., at races, a dance, a wedding, an entertainment: an overseer, a foreman:—*fem.* **stewardess.**—*n.* **stew'ardship,** office of a steward: management. [O.E. *stigweard—stig,* a hall (cog. with **sty**), *weard,* a ward.]

stibium, *stib'i-ùm, n.* antimony. [L.,—Gr. *stibi, stimmi.*]

stick, *stik, v.t.* to pierce, transfix: to stab: to spear: to thrust: to fasten by piercing: to insert: to set in position: to set or cover (with things fastened on): to cause to adhere: (*coll.*) to bear, endure: to bring to a standstill: to nonplus.—*v.i.* to be fixed by means of something inserted: to adhere: to become or remain fixed (*lit.* and *fig.*): to remain: to be detained by an impediment: to jam: to fail to proceed or advance: to hold fast, keep resolutely (to):—*pa.t.* and *pa.p.* stuck.—*ns.* **stick'er,** one who kills pigs, &c.: one who perseveres: an adhesive label; **stick'ing-plas'ter,** an adhesive plaster for wounds; **stick'-in-the-mud,** an absolutely unprogressive person.—*adj.* **stick'y,** adhesive: tenacious: gluey: over scrupulous.—*v.t.* to make sticky.—*n.* **stick'iness.**—**stick around,** (*slang*) to wait about; **stick at,** to hesitate or scruple at: to persist at; **stick by,**

to be firm in supporting, to adhere closely to; **stick out,** to project: to continue to resist; **stick out a mile,** to be extremely obvious; **stick out for,** to insist on; **stick to,** to adhere to: to persevere in; **stick up for,** to speak or act in defence of; **stick with,** to remain with: to force (a person) to cope with (something unpleasant)—usu. in passive, *to be stuck with*; **sticky end,** an unpleasant end, disaster; **sticky wicket,** a difficult situation to cope with. [O.E. *stician*; cf. **stick** (2).]

stick, *stik, n.* a small shoot or branch of a tree: a walking-stick: a piece of firewood: an instrument for beating a percussion instrument: an instrument for playing hockey or other game: a control rod of an aeroplane: a composing-stick (q.v.): the amount of type a composing-stick will hold: anything in the form of a stick or rod: a support for a candle: a group of bombs, or of paratroops, released at one time from an aeroplane: a person of stiff or wooden manner, or wanting in enterprise.—*n.* **stick'-lac** (see **lac**).—**in a cleft stick,** in a dilemma; **the sticks,** remote areas, backwoods. [O.E. *sticca*; O.N. *stika.*]

stickle, *stik'l, v.i.* (*obs.*) to interpose between combatants: to be scrupulous or obstinately punctilious.—*n.* a sharp point, a spine.—*n.* **stick'ler,** (*obs.*) a second in a duel, an umpire, or a mediator: one who insists on scrupulous exactness, punctilious observance of rules, &c. (with *for*). [Prob. M.E. *stightle*—O.E. *stihtan,* to set in order.]

stickleback, *stik'l-bak, n.* any of a family of small spiny-backed river-fish. [O.E. *sticel,* sting, prick, and **back.**]

stiff, *stif, adj.* not easily bent: rigid: wanting in suppleness: moved or moving with difficulty or friction: dead: approaching solidity: dense, difficult to mould or cut: difficult, toilsome: stubborn, pertinaceous (e.g. *a stiff resistance*): strong (e.g. *a stiff breeze*): concentrated and strong (e.g. *a stiff drink*): (*coll.*—of price) high or excessive: not natural and easy, constrained, formal.—*adv.* stiffly: stark: (*coll.*) extremely.—*n.* (*slang*) a corpse: (*slang*) one having not much more sense, or skill, or graciousness, &c., than a corpse.—*v.t.* **stiff'en,** to make stiff.—*v.i.* to become stiff: to become less impressible or more obstinate.—*ns.* **stiff'ener,** one who, or that which, stiffens; **stiff'ening,** something used to make a substance stiff.—*adv.* **stiff'ly.**—*adj.* **stiff'-necked,** obstinate, hard to move: haughty: formal and unnatural.—*n.* **stiff'ness.** [O.E. *stīf,* stiff; Du. *stijf,* Ger. *steif.*]

stifle, *stī'fl, v.t.* to stop the breath of by foul air or other means: to suffocate: to make breathing difficult for: to smother or extinguish (*lit.* as cries, flames; *fig.* as a rumour, anger): to make stifling.—*v.i.* to suffocate.—*adj.* **stī'fling,** impeding respiration, close, oppressive.

stigma, *stig'ma, n.* a brand, a mark of infamy: any special mark: a place on the skin which bleeds periodically: the part of a carpel that receives pollen:—*pl.* **stig'mas** or **stig'mata.** —*n.pl.* **stig'mata,** the marks of the wounds on Christ's body, or marks resembling them, claimed to have been miraculously impressed on the bodies of certain persons, as Francis of Assisi in 1224.—*adj.* **stig'matic,** of, pertaining

Neutral vowels in unaccented syllables: *em'pér-ŏr*; for certain sounds in foreign words see p. ix.

to, of the nature of, a stigma: marked or branded with a stigma: giving infamy or reproach.—*adv.* **stigmat′ically.**—*v.t.* **stig′matise,** to mark with a stigma or with stigmata: to describe abusively (as). [Gr. *stigma, -atos,* tattoo-mark, brand, *stigmē,* a point.]

stile, *stīl, n.* a step, or set of steps, for climbing over a wall or fence. [O.E. *stigel*; *cf.* O.E. *stīgan,* Ger. *steigen,* to mount.]

stile, *stīl, n.* an upright member in framing or panelling. [Origin uncertain.]

stile, *stīl, n.* Older spelling of **style.**

stiletto, *sti-let′ō, n.* a dagger with a narrow blade: a pointed instrument for making eyelet-holes:—*pl.* **stilett′os.**—*v.t.* to stab with a stiletto:—*pr.p.* stilett′oing; *pa.t.* and *pa.p.* stilett′oed—**stiletto heel,** a high, thin heel on a woman's shoe. [It., dim. of *stilo,* a dagger—L. *stilus,* a stake.]

still, *stil, adj.* motionless: silent: calm: not sparkling or effervescent.—*v.t.* to quiet, to silence, to appease, to restrain.—*v.i.* (*rare*) to become still.—*adv.* always, constantly: up to the present time or time in question: nevertheless, for all that: yet, even (usu. with comparative). —*n.* calm: an ordinary photograph, esp. one of a part of a motion picture.—*n.* **still′-birth,** birth of the already dead or very nearly dead: publication not followed by sales: anything born without life.—*adj.* **still′-born,** dead, or in suspended animation, when born.—*ns.* **still′(-)life′,** the class of pictures representing inanimate objects (also *adj.*); **still′ness,** silence: calm.—*adj.* **still′y,** still, quiet, calm. [O.E. *stille,* quiet, calm, stable; Du. *stil,* Ger. *still.*]

still, *stil, v.t.* (*arch.*) to exude, or cause to fall, by drops: to distil.—*n.* an apparatus for distilling liquids.—*n.* **still′-room,** an apartment where liquors, preserves, and the like are kept, and where tea, &c., is prepared for the table, a housekeeper's pantry. [From **distil.**]

stilt, *stilt, n.* one of a pair of props or poles with a rest for the foot mounted on which a man can walk with longer strides.—*v.t.* to raise on stilts: to elevate by unnatural means.—*adj.* **stilt′ed,** elevated as if on stilts: stiff and pompous. [M.E. *stilte*; *cf.* Du. *stelt,* Ger. *stelze.*]

Stilton, *stil′ton, n.* a rich white cheese, often blue-veined. [*Stilton* in Huntingdonshire.]

stimulant, *stim′ū-lànt, adj.* stimulating: increasing or exciting vital action.—*n.* anything that stimulates or excites: a stimulating drug: alcoholic liquor.—*v.t.* **stim′ulate,** to incite: to produce increased action in: to excite.—*n.* **stimula′tion,** act of stimulating, or condition of being stimulated.—*adj.* **stim′ulative,** tending to stimulate.—*n.* that which stimulates or excites.—*ns.* **stim′ulism,** the practice of treating diseases by stimulation; **stim′ulus,** a sting or stinging hair: an action, influence, or agency, that produces a response in a living organism: anything that rouses to action or increased action:—*pl.* **stim′uli.** [L. *stimulāre, -ātum,* to goad—*stimulus* (for *stigmulus*)—Gr. *stizein,* to prick.]

sting, *sting, n.* in some plants and animals a weapon (hair, modified ovipositor, tooth, &c.) that pierces and injects poison: the act of inserting a sting: the pain or the wound

caused: any sharp tingling or irritating pain or its cause (also *fig.*): the point of an epigram: stinging power, pungency: a goad, an incitement.—*v.t.* to pierce, wound, with a sting: to pain or incite as if with a sting (*lit.* e.g. *the wind stung his face; fig.* e.g. *remorse stings him; stung with remorse, by reproaches*): (*slang*) to rob, cheat, or to involve in expense (e.g. *to sting him for a dollar*).—*v.i.* to have a sting: to give pain: to have a stinging feeling:—*pa.t.* and *pa.p.* stung.—*n.* **sting′er,** one who, or that which, stings.—*adj.* **sting′less,** having no sting.—*n.* **sting′-ray,** any of a large number of cartilaginous fishes, of the ray order, with tail bearing a long spine capable of giving an ugly wound. [O.E. *stingan*; O.N. *stinga.*]

stingy, *stin′ji, adj.* niggardly, parsimonious.—*adv.* **stin′gily.**—*n.* **stin′giness.** [sting and adj. suffx. *-y.*]

stink, *stingk, v.i.* to give out a smell, now only a strong and usu. offensive smell: to be of bad repute.—*v.t.* to fill, impregnate with a strong smell:—*pa.t.* stank; *pa.p.* stunk.—*n.* a disagreeable smell.—*ns.* **stink′-ball, -pot,** a ball or jar filled with a stinking, combustible mixture, formerly used in boarding an enemy's vessel; **stink′er,** one who, or that which, stinks: (*coll.*) a disagreeable person or thing; **stink′-trap,** a contrivance to prevent rise of gases in drains.—**cry stinking fish,** to miscall one's own wares or possessions, to speak libellously about one's own concerns. [O.E. *stincan.*]

stint, *stint, v.t.* (*arch.*) to cease (to do): to give (a person) a niggardly allowance (e.g. *to stint him in food and drink*): to supply (something) in a niggardly manner.—*v.i.* (*arch.*) to cease, stop: to be saving.—*n.* limitation, restriction (e.g. *praised him without stint; worked without stint*): task, share of task, allotted.—*adj.* **stint′less.** [O.E. *styntan*—*stunt,* stupid.]

stipe, *stīp, n.* (*bot.*) the stalk of a mushroom or similar fungus: the petiole of a fern-frond up to the lowest leaflet. [Fr.,—L. *stīpes,* a stem.]

stipend, *stī′pénd, n.* a salary paid for services, esp. to a clergyman in Scotland: settled pay.—*adj.* **stipend′iary,** receiving stipend.—*n.* one who performs services for a salary, esp. a paid magistrate. [L. *stipendium*—*stips,* donation, *pendĕre,* weight.]

stipple, *stip′l, v.t.* to engrave, paint, draw, &c., in dots or separate touches:—*pr.p.* stipp′ling; *pa.p.* stipp′led.—*n.* any process in which an effect (e.g. of shade or of gradation of colour) is produced by separate touches: the effect itself: the process of breaking up the smoothness of a painted or plastered surface by dabbing it repeatedly with a special brush, or the effect so produced.—*ns.* **stipp′ler,** one who stipples: a coarse brush for stippling; **stipp′ling,** stippled work of any kind. [Du. *stippelen,* dim. of *stippen,* to dot.]

stipulate, *stip′ū-lāt, v.t.* and *v.i.* (often with *for*) to specify or require as a condition or essential part of an agreement.—*ns.* **stipulā′tion,** act of stipulating: a condition of agreement; **stip′ulātor.** [L. *stipulārī, -ātus,* conn. with *stīpāre,* to press firm.]

stipule, *stip′ūl, n.* (*bot.*) one of the two appendages, usually leaf-like, often present at the base of the petiole of a leaf. [L. *stipula,* a stalk, dim. of *stīpes.*]

stir, *stûr, v.t.* to change the position of: to set in motion: to move ar ᵛ ᵕ .d: to rouse, to move to activity, to excite.—*v.i.* to move oneself: to be active:—*pr.p.* stirr'ing; *pa.p.* and *pa.t.* stirred.—*n.* tumult: bustle: sensation.—*n.* **stirr'er.**—*p.adj.* **stirr'ing,** putting in motion: active: bustling: exciting.—**stir up,** to mix by stirring: to rouse, incite: to provoke. [O.E. *styrian*; Du. *storen,* Ger. *stören,* to disturb.]

stir, *stûr, n.* (*slang*) prison. [Perh. O.E. *stēor, stȳr,* punishment.]

stirrup, *stir'ŭp, n.* a ring or hoop (**stirr'up-iron**) suspended by a rope or strap (**stirr'up-leath'er**) from the saddle, for a horseman's foot while mounting or riding.—*ns.* **stirr'up-cup,** a cup drunk by a guest who is departing (or arriving) on horseback; **stirr'up-pump,** a portable hand-pump, held in position by pressing the foot on the stirrup-shaped rest at its base. [O.E. *stigrāp—stīgan,* to mount, *rāp,* a rope.]

stitch, *stich, n.* one of series of loops made by drawing a thread through a fabric or body tissue by means of a needle: a loop made in knitting: the kind of work produced by stitching: a sharp spasmodic pain, esp. between the ribs: a bit of clothing, a rag.—*v.t.* to sew so as to show a regular line of stitches: to sew.—*v.i.* to practise stitching.—*ns.* **stitch'ing,** a regular line of stitches; **stitch'wort,** a genus of slender plants, including the chickweed, so called because once believed to cure 'stitch' in the side. [O.E. *stice,* a prick; Ger. *sticken,* to embroider.]

stithy, *stiᴛʜ'i, stith'i, n.* an anvil: a smith's shop. [O.N. *stethi*; Swed. *städ,* an anvil.]

stiver, *stī'vér, n.* a Dutch coin: any small coin. [Du. *stuiver.*]

stoat, *stōt, n.* a kind of weasel, called the ermine when in its winter dress. [M.E. *stote.*]

stoccade, *stok-ad',* **stoccado,** *stok-ä'do, n.* a thrust in fencing. [It. *stoccata,* a thrust—*stocco,* a rapier—Ger. *stock,* a stick.]

stock, *stok, n.* a post, a log, a block of wood: a stupid person: the trunk or main stem of a plant: a plant into which a graft is inserted: a part into which another is fixed, as the handle of a whip, the wood holding the barrel of a firearm: the original progenitor: family, race: a fund, capital, shares of a public debt: a store, supply (e.g. of goods): the cattle, horses, &c., kept on a farm: the liquor obtained by boiling meat or bones, the foundation for soup: a stiff band worn as a cravat, often fastened with a buckle at the back: (*pl.*) an instrument in which the legs of offenders were confined: (*pl.*) the frame for a ship while building.—*v.t.* to store: to keep for sale: to fill: to supply with domestic animals or stock: to fit with a stock.—*adj.* kept in stock: usual, trite.—*ns.* **stock'-breed'er,** one who raises live-stock; **stock'broker,** a broker who deals in stocks or shares; **stock company,** a permanent repertory company attached to a theatre; **stock'(-) dove,** the common wild pigeon of Europe; **stock exchange,** premises where stocks are bought and sold: an association of share-

brokers and dealers; **stock'-farm'er,** a farmer who rears live-stock, as cattle, &c.; **stock'-feed'er,** one who feeds or fattens live-stock; **stock'holder,** one who holds stocks in the public funds, or in a company; **stock'-in-trade,** all the goods a shopkeeper keeps for sale: a person's equipment for any enterprise: (*fig.*) a person's basic intellectual and emotional resources; **stock'-jobb'ing,** speculating in stocks; **stock'-jobb'er;** **stock'-jobb'ery;** **stock'-list,** a list of stocks and current prices regularly issued; **stock'man,** a stock-farmer's herdsman; **stock'-mar'ket,** a market for the sale of stocks, the stock exchange; **stock'pile,** a heap of road-metal, ore, &c.: a reserve supply (*v.t.* to accumulate reserve supplies); **stock'-pot,** the pot in which the stock for soup is kept (also used *fig.*); **stock'-raising,** the breeding of live-stock; **stock'-rīd'er,** a mounted herdsman; **stock'-room,** a room in which goods are stored or kept in reserve.—*adj.* **stock'-still,** perfectly motionless.—*ns.* **stock'-tak'ing,** a periodical inventory made of the stock or goods in a shop or warehouse; **stock'-whip,** a whip with short handle and long lash for use in herding; **stock'-yard,** a large yard with pens, stables, &c., where cattle are kept for slaughter, market, &c.—**stock-car racing,** motor-racing in which old ordinary cars are used, not cars specially built for racing.—**off, on, the stocks,** (of a ship) launched, in process of building: hence (*fig.* of a piece of work) finished, in the course of being done; **take stock,** to make an inventory of goods on hand: (*fig.*) to make an estimate (of); **take stock in,** to trust to, attach importance to. [O.E. *stocc,* a stick; Ger. *stock.*]

stock, *stok, n.* Same as **stock-gillyflower.**

stockade, *stok-ād', n.* a palisade formed of stakes fixed in the ground.—*v.t.* to fortify with such. [Fr. *estocade—estoc*—Ger. *stock,* stick.]

stockfish, *stok'fish, n.* a commercial name of dried but unsalted cod and other fish of the same family. [Du. *stokvisch,* Ger. *stockfisch.*]

stock-gillyflower, *stok'-jil'i-flow(é)r, n.* a genus of herbaceous or half-shrubby plants, having their flowers in racemes, generally fragrant. —Now more usu. **stock.** [**stock,** stem, and **gillyflower.**]

stocking, *stok'ing, n.* a close covering for the foot and lower leg.—*n.* **stockinet(te),** an elastic knitted fabric for undergarments. [From (*arch.*) **stock,** hose, the stockings being the *nether-stocks* when the long hose (q.v.) came to be cut at the knee.]

stocky, *stok'i, adj.* short and stout, thick-set: having a strong stem.—*adv.* **stock'ily.** [**stock** (1) and adj. suffx. *-y.*]

stodgy, *stoj'i, adj.* heavy and indigestible: heavy and uninteresting.—*v.t.* and *v.i.* **stodge,** to stuff, cram.—*n.* a heavy uninteresting meal.—*n.* **stodg'iness.** [Perh. imit.]

stoep, *stōōp, n.* the raised platform or veranda at the entrance of a South African house. [Du. *stoep,* step.]

stoic, *stō'ik, n.* a disciple of the school founded by the philosopher Zeno (died c. 261 B.C.), who taught in the *Stoa Poikilē* ('painted porch') at Athens: one indifferent to pleasure or pain.— *adjs.* **stō'ic, -al,** pertaining to the Stoics, or to their opinions: indifferent to pleasure or

Neutral vowels in unaccented syllables: *em'pér-ór*; for certain sounds in foreign words see p. ix.

720

pain.—*adv.* **stō'ically.**—*ns.* **stō'icalness; stō'icism** (-*sizm*), the doctrines of the Stoics strongly opposed to Epicureanism in its views of life and duty: limitation of wants: austere impassivity. [Gr. *Stōikos—stoa*, a porch.]

stoke, *stōk*, *v.t.* to feed with fuel.—*ns.* **stoke'hold,** the hold containing the boilers of a ship; **stoke'hole,** the space about the mouth of a furnace: the space allotted to the stokers; **stōk'er,** one who, or that which, feeds a furnace with fuel. [Du. *stoker*, stoker—*stōken*, to stoke.]

stole, *stōl*, *pa.t.* and *obs. pa.p.* of **steal.**

stole, *stōl*, *n.* a long robe: a narrow vestment worn on the shoulders, hanging down in front: a woman's outer garment, esp. of fur, of similar form: (*loosely*) a gown, a surplice. [L. *stōla*, a Roman matron's long robe—Gr. *stolē*, equipment, garment—*stellein*, to array.]

stolen, *stōl'ĕn*, *pa.p.* of **steal.**

stolid, *stol'id*, *adj.* dull, heavy, impassive: unemotional.—*ns.* **stolid'ity, stol'idness.**—*adv.* **stol'idly.** [L. *stolidus*.]

stolon, *stō'lon*, *n.* a shoot from the root of a plant, a sucker—*adjs.* **sto'lonate, stolonif'erous.** [L. *stolō*, *-ōnis*, a sucker, twig.]

stoma, *stō'ma*, *n.* (*bot.*) a mouth-like opening, esp. one (including or excluding its guard-cells) by which gases pass through the epidermis or green parts of a plant: (*zool.*) a small aperture:—*pl.* **stō'mata.** [Gr. *stoma*, *-atos*, a mouth.]

stomach, *stum'ăk*, *n.* the strong muscular bag into which the food passes when swallowed, and where it is principally digested: (in ruminants, &c.) one of several digestive cavities: (*loosely* or *euphemistically*) the belly: appetite, or (*fig.*) inclination generally: (*arch.*) courage, pride.—*v.t.* to brook or put up with: to digest.—*n.* **stomacher** (*stum'ak-ĕr*, *-ach-ĕr*; *hist.*), a part of a woman's dress covering the front of the body, generally forming the lower part of the bodice in front, sometimes richly ornamented: a large brooch. *adjs.* **stomach'ic, -al,** pertaining to the stomach: strengthening or promoting the action of the stomach.—*n.* a medicine for this purpose.—*n.* **stom'ach-pump,** a syringe with a flexible tube for withdrawing fluids from the stomach, or injecting them into it. [O.Fr. *estomac*—L. *stomachus*—Gr. *stomachos*, the throat, later stomach—*stoma*, a mouth.]

stomp, *stomp*, *v.i.* (*coll.*) to stamp: to dance.—*n.* an early jazz composition with heavily accented rhythm: lively dance with foot stamping: (*coll.*) a stamp. [Variant of **stamp.**]

-stomy, *stóm-i*, in composition, indicating a new opening into an organ. [Gr. *stoma*, a mouth.]

stone, *stōn*, *n.* a detached piece of rock: a piece of such material fashioned for a particular purpose, as a *grindstone*: a precious stone or gem: a tombstone: a concretion formed in the bladder: a hard shell containing the seed, e.g. of a drupe (q.v.): a seed of a grape: a standard weight of 14 lb. avoirdupois (in *pl.* **stone**).—*adj.* made of, consisting of, containing, stone: made of stoneware: of the Stone Age.—*v.t.* to pelt with stones: to free from stones: to wall with stones.—*n.* **Stone Age,** an early period of history when the use of metals was unknown

and tools and weapons were made of stone—divided into the *Old Stone Age* (before the last Ice Age; see **palaeolithic**) and the *New Stone Age* (see **neolithic**).—*adj.* **stone'-blind,** completely blind.—*ns.* **stone'-cast, stone's'-cast, stone'-shot, stone's'-throw,** the distance which a stone may be thrown by the hand: a short distance; **stone'-chat, stone'chatter,** a small bird of the chat genus, so named because its monotonous note resembles the sound of a hammer striking stones; **stone'-crop,** any of several plants that grow in rocky or stony places; **stone'-cutt'ing,** the business of hewing and carving stones for walls, monuments, &c.; **stone'-cutt'er.**—*adjs.* **stone'-dead,** lifeless; **stone'-deaf,** quite deaf.—*ns.* **stone'-dress'er,** one who prepares stones for building; **stone'-fruit,** a fruit whose seeds are enclosed in a stone or hard shell; **stone'-hamm'er,** a hammer for breaking stones (**stone hammer,** a hammer with a stone head); **stone'-mill,** a machine for breaking stone.—*v.t.* and *v.i.* **stone'wall,** to obstruct: to offer unyielding resistance: (*cricket*) to bat extremely cautiously.—*ns.* **stone'waller, stone'walling; stone'ware,** a coarse kind of potter's ware baked hard and glazed.—*adj.* **stō'ny,** made of, or resembling, stone: abounding with stones: hard, pitiless, obdurate.—*adv.* **stōn'ily,** in a cold, hard, unrelenting manner.—*adj.* **sto'ny(-broke),** (*coll.*) penniless.— **leave no stone unturned,** to try every possible expedient; **rolling stone,** a person who does not settle in any place, or to any job. [O.E. *stān*; Ger. *stein*, Du. *steen*.]

stood, *stōōd*, *pa.t.* and *pa.p.* of **stand.**

stooge, *stōōj*, *n.* a comedian's assistant and foil: a foil, dupe, the minion and scapegoat, e.g. of a gangster.—*v.i.* to act as a stooge. [Slang; origin uncertain.]

stook, *stōōk*, *n.* (*Scot.*) a full shock of cornsheaves, generally twelve, as set up in the field.—*v.t.* and *v.i.* to set up in stooks, as sheaves. [Cf. Low Ger. *stuke*, a bundle.]

stool, *stōōl*, *n.* a seat without a back: a low support for the feet when sitting, or the knees when kneeling: the seat used in evacuating the bowels: the act of evacuating the bowels: faeces: a portable piece of wood to which a pigeon is fastened as a decoy for wild birds.—*n.* **stool'-pigeon,** a decoy pigeon: a decoy, informer.—**stool of repentance,** (*Scot.*) a place in church where delinquents, esp. fornicators, were seated to receive censure. [O.E. *stōl*; Ger. *stuhl*; cf. Ger. *stellen*, to place.]

stoop, *stōōp*, *v.i.* to bend the body forward: to lean forward: to submit: to descend from rank or dignity (to do something), to condescend: (*rare*) to swoop down on the wing, as a bird of prey.—*v.t.* to cause to incline downward.—*n.* the act of stooping: inclination forward: condescension: (*rare*) a swoop. *adj.* **stooped,** having a stoop, bent. [O.E. *stūpian*; O.N. *stūpa*.]

stop, *stop*, *v.t.* to stuff up and so close or partially close (also **stop up**): to obstruct, to render impassable, to close: to bring to a standstill, prevent the motion of: to prevent (from): to put an end to: to discontinue: to keep back (e.g. *to stop payment of a cheque*): (*mus.*) to alter the pitch of by means of a stop.—*v.t.* to cease going forward, halt: to cease from any motion: to leave off, desist: to come to an end: (*coll.*) to stay:—*pr.p.* stopp′ing; *pa.t.* and *pa.p.* stopped.—*n.* act of stopping: state of being stopped: a cessation: a halt: a stopping-place: (*coll.*) a stay: an obstacle: in machinery, a device for arresting movement or for limiting scope of action: a screen having a circular aperture, used e.g. to limit the effective aperture of a lens in a camera: (*mus.*) a method of, or device for, altering pitch, as pressing a string with the fingers, closing a vent-hole: a set of organ pipes of like tone-quality graduated in pitch, or a knob operating a lever for bringing them into use: (*phonet.*) a sound requiring complete closure of the breath passage, as *k, p, t*: a mark used in punctuation: a full-stop (q.v.).—*ns.* **stop′-cock**, a short pipe in a cask, &c., opened and stopped by turning a key or handle: loosely, the key or handle; **stop′-gap**, that which fills a gap or supplies a deficiency, esp. an expedient of emergency.— *adj.* **stop-go**, of policy, alternately discouraging and encouraging forward movement.—*ns.* **stop′-off, stop′-over**, a break in journey (*vs.i.* **stop off, stop over**); **stopp′age**, act of stopping: state of being stopped: a cessation: an obstruction; **stopp′er**, one who stops: that which closes a vent or hole, as the cork or glass mouthpiece for a bottle: (*naut.*) a short rope for making something fast.—*v.t.* to close or secure with a stopper.—*ns.* **stopp′ing**, that which fills up—material for filling up cracks, &c., filling material for teeth; **stopple** (*stop′l*), that which stops or closes the mouth of a vessel, a cork or plug.—*v.t.* to close with a stopple; **stop′-press**, brief late news inserted in a newspaper, after printing has begun: space for it; **stop′-watch**, a watch with hands that can be started and stopped, used in timing a race, &c.—**pull out all the stops**, to express with maximum emotion: to act with as much energy as possible, to do everything in one's power. [O.E. *stoppian*, found in the compound *forstoppian*, to stop up, from L. *stūpa*, tow.]

store, *stōr, stōr, n.* a hoard or quantity gathered (*lit.* and *fig.*): (in *pl.*) supplies of food, ammunition, &c.: abundance: a storehouse: a shop, esp. one with many departments or branches, or one run on a co-operative system: a computer memory unit, in which program and data are stored.—*v.t.* to accumulate and put in a place for keeping: to put in a storehouse, warehouse, &c.: to furnish (with supplies): to put (data) into a computer memory.—*ns.* **stō′rage**, the act of placing in a store: the safe-keeping of goods in a store: the price paid or charged for keeping goods in a store; **stō′rage batt′ery**, (*elect.*) an accumulator; **store′house**, a house for storing goods of any kind, a repository: (*fig.*) a place—e.g. book, mind—where things of value are stored, a treasury; **store′-keep′er**, a man who manages or owns a store; **stō′rer**, one who stores; **store′room**, a room in which things are stored; **store′-ship**, a vessel used for transporting naval stores.—**in store**, (*fig.*) destined, about to come: in readiness (for a person); **set (great) store by**, to value greatly. [O.Fr. *estor,*

estoire—L. *instaurāre*, to provide.]

storey, story, *stō′ri, stō′-, n.* a set of rooms on the same floor: a floor, or the distance between one floor and the next.—*adj.* **storeyed, storied** (*stōr′id*), having storeys.—**first storey**, the ground floor. [Prob. same word orig. as **story** below.]

storied. See under **storey** and **story.**

stork, *stôrk, n.* any of various long-necked and long-legged wading-birds allied to the herons.—*n.* **stork's′-bill**, a pelargonium (q.v.) or related plant. [O.E. *storc*; Ger. *storch.*]

storm, *stôrm, n.* a violent commotion of the atmosphere producing wind, rain, &c., a tempest: a violent commotion or outbreak of any kind: a paroxysm: (*fig.*) a violent shower (of): (*mil.*) an assault.—*v.i.* to blow, rain, &c., with violence (e.g. *it stormed all night*): to be in, show, a violent passion: to rage (at).—*v.t.* to attack and take by a storming-party, or by force.—*adjs.* **storm′-beat, -beat′en**, beaten or injured by storms.—*n.* **storm′-belt**, a region in which storms are particularly frequent.—*adj.* **storm′bound**, delayed by storms: cut off by storm from communication with the outside.—*ns.* **storm′-cen′tre**, the position of lowest pressure in a cyclonic storm; **storm′-cone**, a cone hoisted as a storm signal; **storm′ing-par′ty**, the party of men who first enter the breach or scale the walls in storming a fortress; **storm′-pet′rel**, or (popularly) **stor′my-pet′rel**, kinds of petrel (q.v.) supposed to be much in evidence before a storm: hence, a person frequently involved in conflict, whose presence foretells strife; **storm′-sail**, a sail of the strongest canvas, for stormy weather; **storm′-sig′nal**, a signal displayed on seacoasts, &c., to intimate the approach of a storm.—*adjs.* **storm′-stayed**, hindered from proceeding by storms; **storm′-tossed**, tossed about by storms: much agitated by conflicting passions.—*ns.* **storm′-troops**, shock-troops (q.v.); **storm′-win′dow**, a window raised above the roof, slated above and at the sides: an additional outer casement.—*adj.* **storm′y**, having many storms: agitated with furious winds: boisterous: violent: passionate.—*n.* **storm′iness.—take by storm**, to take by assault: (*fig.*) to captivate totally and instantly. [O.E. *storm*; O.N. *stormr*; from root of **stir**.]

story, *stō′ri, stō′-, n.* a narrative of consecutive events: an anecdote: an account, allegation: a fictitious narrative: the plot of a novel, &c.: an untruth: a news article.—*adj.* **stō′ried**, told or celebrated in a story: having a history: interesting from the stories belonging to it: adorned with scenes from history.—*n.* **stō′ry-book**, a book of tales true or fictitious.—*adj.* luckier or happier than is usual in real life. [Anglo-Fr. *estorie*—L. *historia.*]

stoup, *stōōp, n.* a flagon, or its contents: a small measure for liquids: a basin for holy water. [Cf. O.N. *staup*, Du. *stoop*; O.E. *stēap.*]

stout, *stowt, adj.* strong, robust: corpulent: of strong material: resolute, staunch: forceful: (*B.*) stubborn.—*n.* type of strong dark beer.— *adj.* **stout-heart′ed**, having a brave heart. —*adv.* **stout′ly.**—*n.* **stout′ness.** [O.Fr. *estout*, bold— Old Du. *stolt, stout*; Ger. *stolz*, bold.]

Neutral vowels in unaccented syllables: *em′pėr-ôr*; for certain sounds in foreign words see p. ix.

stovaine, *stōv′ān, n.* a synthetic alkaloid, used as an anaesthetic, esp. for spinal purposes. [From **stove** (1), Eng. translation of the name of Professor Furneau, who first prepared it.]

stove, *stōv, n.* a heated room or chamber: a closed heating or cooking apparatus: a fire-grate: a kiln.—*v.t.* to heat or keep warm.—*n.* **stove′-pipe**, a metal pipe for carrying smoke and gases from a stove to a chimney-flue. [O.E. *stofa*, a hot air bath; cf. Ger. *stube*.]

stove, *stōv, pa.t.* and *pa.p.* of **stave**.

stow, *stō, v.t.* to place, arrange, pack, out of the way, or in a convenient place: to fill by packing things in (e.g. *to stow the case with boxes*): (*slang*) to cease, abstain from.—*ns.* **stow′age**, act of placing in order: state of being stowed: room for articles to be laid away: money paid for stowing goods; **stow′away**, one who hides himself in an outward-bound vessel in order to get a passage for nothing. [M.E. *stowen*, to place—O.E. *stōw*, a place; cf. Du. *stuwen*, to stow, to push, Ger. *stauen*, to pack.]

strabismus, *stra-biz′mus, n.* a squint (q.v.) in the eye [(τ. *strabos* and *strabismos*, squinting: cf. *strephein*, to twist.]

straddle, *strad′l, v.i.* to part the legs wide: to stand or walk with the legs far apart: (of legs) to spread apart.—*v.t.* to stand or sit astride of: to shoot a missile beyond and another short of (a target) in order to determine the range: to cover the area containing (a target) with bombs.—*n.* act or posture of straddling. [Freq. of O.E. *stræd*, pa.t. of *strīdan*, stride.]

Stradivarius, *strad-i-vā′ri-us, n.* a violin, esp. one made by Antonio *Stradivari* (1644-1737) of Cremona.

straggle, *strag′l, v.i.* to stray from the course or line of march: to wander beyond, or to escape from, proper limits: to move in an irregular way, not as a compact body (e.g. *the crowd straggled over the park*): to grow irregularly and untidily.—*n.* **strag′gler**, one who strays from, or is left behind by, the body of persons or animals to which he, she, belongs: a plant, &c., out of its proper place or required position.

straight, *strāt, adj.* (of a line) invariable in direction, determined by the position of two points: not curved or bent: direct (e.g. *the straight way to the churchyard*): (*fig.*) going directly and honestly to the point (as in *a straight talk, straight thinking*): honest, fair (e.g. *straight dealings, a straight race*): placed levelly or symmetrically (e.g. *the pictures, mats, are not straight*): in order (*put the room, your accounts, straight*): unmixed, undiluted (e.g. *a straight whisky*).—*adv.* in the most direct line or manner (*lit.* and *fig.*): (*arch.*) without delay: honestly, fairly.—*ns.* **straight angle**, an angle of 180° or two right-angles; **straight′-edge**, a narrow board or piece of metal having one edge perfectly straight for applying to a surface to ascertain whether it is exactly even.—*v.t.* **straight′en**, to make straight.—*ns.* **straight face**, a sober, unsmiling face; **straight fight**, a contest, esp. in politics, in which only two persons or sides take part.—*adj.* **straightfor′ward**, going forward in a straight course: honest, open, downright.—*advs.* **straightfor′wardly**; **straight′ly**,

evenly: tightly: closely.—*ns.* **straight′ness**, evenness: narrowness: tightness; **straight part**, a part portraying a man or woman without emphasis on eccentricities of manner, &c.—opp. to *character part*; **straight play**, one without music; **straight talk**, a candid outspoken talk; **straight thinking**, clear, logical, thinking not confused by emotion, predispositions, or preconceived ideas; **straight tip**, a racing tip that comes straight from the owner: inside information that can be relied on.—*adv.* **straight′way**, directly, without loss of time.—**go straight**, to give up criminal activities. [O.E. *streht*, pa.p. of *streccan*, to stretch.]

strain, *strān, v.t.* to stretch tight: to make tight: (*fig.*) to stretch beyond due limits, make cover too much (e.g. *to strain credulity, the meaning, the law*): to exert to the utmost (e.g. *to strain every nerve*): to injure by overtasking: to constrain, make uneasy or unnatural: to separate the solid from the liquid part of by a filter.—*v.i.* to make violent efforts: to trickle through a filter.—*n.* the act of straining over-stretching, over-exertion, tension (*lit.* and *fig.*): a violent effort: an injury inflicted by straining, esp. a wrenching of the muscles: (*mech.*) any change in form or in volume of a portion of matter either solid or fluid due to a system of forces (see **stress**).—*adj.* **strained**, having been strained: forced or unnatural.—*n.* **strain′er**, one who, or that which, strains, esp. a utensil to separate solid from liquid.—**strain a point**, to make a special effort or concession; **strain at**, to strive after: to balk at. [O.Fr. *straindre*—L. *stringère*, to stretch tight.]

strain, *strān, n.* race, stock, generation: (in domestic animals) individuals of common descent: hereditary character: natural tendency, element in character: a passage of a song, a poem, a flight of the imagination: mood, temper, prevailing note. [App. O.E. *(ge)streon*, gain, getting, begetting, with altered vowel by confusion with **strain** (1).]

strait, *strāt, adj.* difficult: distressful: (*arch.*) strict, rigorous: (*arch.*) narrow.—*n.* a narrow pass in a mountain (*arch.*), or in the ocean (often in *pl.*) between two portions of land: (usu. *pl.*) difficulty, distress.—*v.t.* **strait′en**, to make strait, narrow, difficult (*fig.*—esp. in *pa.p.*, as **straitened circumstances, means**): to hem in, distress, put into difficulties (e.g. *he was straitened in circumstances*).—*adj.* **strait′-laced**, orig., laced tightly, in tightly laced stays, &c.: now, rigid in adherence to a narrow code of morals and manners.—*adv.* **strait′ly**, narrowly: (*arch.*) strictly.—*ns.* **strait′ness**, state of being strait or narrow: strictness: (*arch.*) distress or difficulty; **strait′-waist′coat**, **strait′-jack′et**, a garment made with long sleeves which can be tied behind, so that the arms are restrained. (*fig.*) anything which inhibits freedom of movement or initiative. [O.Fr. *estreit, estrait* (Fr. *étroit*)—L. *strictus*, pa.p. of *stringère*, to draw tight.]

strand, *strand, n.* the margin or beach of the sea or of a lake.—*v.t.* to run aground.—*v.i.* to drift or be driven ashore. *pa.adj.* **strand′ed**, driven on shore: (*fig.*) friendless and helpless. [O.E.

fāte, fär; mē, hûr (her); *mīne; mōte, för; mūte; mōōn, fōōt;* THen (then)

strand; Ger. *strand*, O.N. *strönd*, border.]

strand, *strand, n.* one of the strings or parts that compose a rope: a tress of hair.—*v.t.* to break a strand: to form by uniting strands, compose of strands. [Origin obscure.]

strange, *stränj, adj.* foreign: alien: from elsewhere: not of one's own place, family, or circle: not one's own: not formerly known or experienced: unfamiliar: interestingly unusual: odd: estranged: distant or reserved: unacquainted, unversed.—*adv.* **strange′ly.**—*ns.* **strange′ness; strän′ger,** a foreigner: one whose home is elsewhere: one unknown or unacquainted: a guest or visitor: one not admitted to communion or fellowship: one ignorant of, or with no experience of (e.g. *a stranger to your thoughts, to truth, to fear*). [O.Fr. *estrange*—L. *extrāneus*—*extrā,* beyond.]

strangle, *strang′gl, v.t.* to kill by compressing the throat, to choke: to suppress, stifle.—*ns.* **strangle′hold,** a choking hold in wrestling: an influence strongly repressing development or freedom of action or expression; **strang′ler.** [O.Fr. *estrangler*—L. *strangulāre*; see next word.]

strangulate, *strang′gū-lāt, v.t.* to strangle: to compress so as to suppress or suspend the function of.—*n.* **strangulā′tion,** act of strangling: compression of the throat and partial suffocation: the state of an organ abnormally constricted. [L. *strangulāre, -ātum*—Gr. *strangalaein,* to strangle, *strangos,* twisted.]

strap, *strap, n.* a narrow strip of leather or cloth, esp. one with a buckle or other fastening: a razor-strop: an iron plate secured by screwbolts, for connecting two or more timbers.—*v.t.* to beat with a strap: to bind with a strap: to strop, as a razor:—*pr.p.* strapp′ing;*pa.t.* and *pa.p.* strapped.—*ns.* **strap′-hang′er,** a passenger in a crowded vehicle who stands and steadies himself by holding a strap suspended from the roof; **strapp′ing,** the act of fastening with a strap: materials for straps: a thrashing.—*adj.* tall, handsome. [Northern form of **strop.**]

strata, *strā′ta, pl.* of **stratum.**

stratagem, *strat′a-jem, n.* action planned to outwit an enemy: an artifice.—*adjs.* **strategic** (*strat-ē′jik*), **-al,** pertaining to strategy: dictated by strategy (e.g. *strategic withdrawal*): of value for strategy.—*n.* **strat′egy,** generalship, the art of managing armed forces in a campaign (cf. **tactics**): artifice or finesse generally.—*adv.* **strateg′ically.**—*n.* **strat′egist,** one skilled in strategy.—**strategic position,** in a campaign or battle, a position, the possession of which gives the combatant who occupies it a decisive advantage over the enemy (also *fig.*). [Gr. *stratēgēma*—*stratēgos,* a general—*stratos,* an army, *agein,* to lead.]

strath, *sträth, strath, n.* in the Highlands of Scotland, a broad valley. [Gael. *srath,* a valley; cog. with L. *strāta,* a street.]

strathspey, *sträth-spā′, n.* a Scottish dance, allied to the reel. [*Strathspey,* valley of the *Spey.*]

stratify, *strat′i-fī, v.t.* to form or lay in strata or layers:—*pr.p.* strat′ifying;*pa.t.* and *pa.p.* strat′ified.—*n.* **stratifica′tion,** act of stratifying: state of being stratified: process of being ar-

ranged in layers. [Fr. *stratifier*—L. *strātum* (see **stratum**) and *facĕre,* to make.]

stratosphere, *strat′-* or *strat′ō-sfēr, n.* a layer of the earth's atmosphere, beginning about $4^{1}/_{2}$ to 10 miles up, in which temperature does not fall as height increases. [**stratum** and **sphere.**]

stratum, *strā′tum, n.* a bed of earth or sedimentary rock, consisting usually of a series of layers: any bed or layer: (*fig.*) level (of society):—*pl.* **strā′ta.**—*adj.* **strat′iform,** formed like strata: in layers. [L. *strātum,* a bed-cover, a horse-cloth, a pavement—*sternĕre, strātum,* to spread out.]

stratus, *strā′tus, n.* low clouds, in a widely-extended horizontal sheet, of varied thickness:—*pl.* **strā′tī.** [L. *strātus,* a coverlet—*sternĕre, strātum,*. to spread out.]

straw, *strö, n.* the stalk on which grain grows, and from which it is thrashed: a quantity of dried stalks of corn. &c.: a tube for sucking up a beverage: a straw hat: a trifle, a whit.—*ns.* **straw′berry,** the fruit (botanically, the enlarged receptacle) of a genus of perennial plants of the rose family, with long creeping shoots: the plant itself; **straw′berry-mark,** a soft reddish birth-mark; **straw′-plait,** a narrow band of plaited wheat-straw, used in making straw hats, &c.—*adj.* **straw′y,** made of, or like, straw.—**straw hat,** a hat made of plaited straw; **straw vote,** an unofficial vote taken to get some idea of the general trend of opinion.—**man of straw** (see under **man**); **straw in the wind,** a sign of possible future developments. [O.E. *strēaw*; Ger. *stroh.*]

strawed (*B.*), for strewed, *pa.t.* and *pa.p.* of **strew.**

stray, *strā, v.i.* to wander: to wander (from e.g. the proper place, the company to which one belongs): to deviate from duty or rectitude.—*n.* a domestic animal that has strayed or is lost: a waif, a truant: anything occurring casually, isolatedly, out of place.—*adj.* wandering, lost: casual (e.g. *a stray remark*), isolated (e.g. *a stray example*). [O.Fr. *estraier,* to wander—L. *extrā,* beyond, *vagārī,* to wander.]

streak, *strēk, n.* a line or long mark different in colour from the surface on which it is traced: a stripe: a flash: a· slight characteristic, a trace: (*min.*) the appearance presented by the surface of a mineral when scratched.—*v.t.* to form streaks in: to mark with streaks.—*v.i.* (*coll.*) to run swiftly.—*adj.* **streak′y,** marked with streaks, striped: (of bacon) fat and lean in alternate layers: uneven in quality. [O.E. *strica,* a stroke—*strīcan,* to go, Ger. *strich.*]

stream, *strēm, n.* a current (of water, air, light, &c.): running water: a river, brook, &c.: anything flowing out from a source: anything flowing and continuous: a large quantity coming continuously: a division of pupils in a school consisting of those of roughly equal ability or those following a particular course of study: drift, tendency.—*v.i.* to flow in a stream: to gush abundantly: to be covered with a flow of (with *with*): to issue in rays: to stretch in a long line.—*v.t.* to discharge in a stream: to wave (e.g. a pennant): to divide (pupils) into streams.—*ns.* **stream′er,** an ensign or flag streaming or flowing in the wind: a long ribbon for decorative purposes: a lumi-

Neutral vowels in unaccented syllables: *em′pėr-ôr*; for certain sounds in foreign words see p. ix.

724

nous beam shooting upward from the horizon: a headline: a narrow roll of coloured paper; **stream'let**, a little stream; **stream-line**, the line followed by a streaming fluid.—Also *v.t.* to make streamlined.—*adjs.* **stream'lined**, shaped so as to offer least possible resistance to air or water: (general term of approval) graceful, efficient, up-to-the-minute, &c.; **streamy.—stream of consciousness**, the continuous succession of thoughts, emotions, and feelings, both vague and well-defined, that forms an individual's conscious experience. [O.E. *strēam*; Ger. *strom*, O.N. *straumr*.]

street, *strēt*, *n.* a road in a town lined with houses, broader than a lane: a Roman road.—*ns.* **street'-car** (*U.S.*, &c.), a public transport vehicle running along a regular street route; **street'-door**, a door of a house that opens on a street; **street'-sweep'er**, one who, or that which, sweeps the streets clean; **street'-walker**, anyone who walks the streets, esp. a prostitute.—**streets ahead of**, very much better, more skilful, &c., than,—**not in the same street**, not comparable, of an entirely different (usu. inferior) quality: **on the street**, homeless, destitute; **on the streets**, practising prostitution; **up one's street**, in the region in which one's tastes, knowledge, abilities, &c. lie. [O.E. *strēt* (Du. *straat*, Ger. *strasse*, It. *strada*)—L. *strāta* (*via*), a paved (way), from *sternēre*, *strātum*, to spread out, level.]

strength, *strength*, *n.* quality of being strong: power of any kind, active or passive—force, vigour, solidity or toughness, power to resist: degree in which a person or thing is strong (e.g. *he has the strength of a horse*; *the enemy's strength*): intensity (e.g. *the strength of his hatred*): the proportion of the essential ingredient in any compound or mixture: vigour (of style or expression): validity (of an argument): a source of power or firmness.—*vt.* **strength'en**, to make strong or stronger: to confirm: to encourage: to increase the power or security of.—*v.i.* to become stronger.—**go from strength to strength**, to move forward successfully, having one triumph after another; **on the strength**, on the muster-rolls of the organisation in question; **on the strength of**, in reliance on, encouraged by. [O.E. *strengthu*—*strang*, strong.]

strenuous, *stren'ū-ŭs*, *adj.* vigorous, urgent, zealous: necessitating exertion.—*adv.* **stren'uously.**—*n.* **stren'uousness.** [L. *strēnuus*, akin to Gr. *strēnēs*, strong.]

streptococcus, *strep'tō-kok'ŭs*, *n.* a group of bacteria that form bent chains, some species of which are associated with diseases such as scarlet fever:—*pl.* **streptococci** (-*kok'sī*). [Gr. *streptos*, pliant, twisted, *kokkos*, a grain.]

stress, *stres*, *n.* pressure, urgency, strain, violence (e.g. *stress of circumstance, weather*), emphasis: (*mech.*) a system of forces operating over an area, esp. a combination producing or sustaining a *strain* (q.v.).—*v.t.* to put pressure on: to emphasise. [Abbrev. for **distress**; prob. also partly from O.Fr. *estrece*—L. *strictus*—*stringēre*, *strictum*, to draw tight.]

stretch, *strech*, *v.t.* to extend, to draw out: to lay at full length: to reach out: to exaggerate,

strain, or carry further than is right.—*v.i.* to be drawn out: to extend, reach: to be extensible without breaking: to straighten and extend fully one's body and limbs.—*n.* act of stretching: state of being stretched: reach: extension: utmost extent: strain: undue straining: exaggeration: extensibility: a single spell: a continuous journey: a straight part of a course: (*slang*) a term of imprisonment.—*adj.* capable of being stretched.—*n.* **stretch'er**, anything for stretching (e.g. *a glove-stretcher*): a frame on which anything is stretched: a frame for carrying the sick or wounded: a rower's footboard: a brick or stone laid along a wall lengthwise.—**at a stretch**, without interruption, continuously. [O.E. *streccan*.]

strew, *strōō* (or *strō*), *v.t.* to scatter loosely: to cover by scattering (with):—*pa.p.* strewed or strewn. [O.E. *strewian*, *streowian*.]

stria, *strī'a*, *strē'a*, *n.* a fine streak, furrow, or threadlike line usu. parallel to others:—*pl.* **stri'ae** (-*ē*).—*adjs.* **stri'ate**, **-d**, marked with striae or small parallel channels.—*n.* **striā'tion**, [L. *stria*, a furrow, flute of a column.]

stricken, *strik'n* (*B.*), *pa.p.* of **strike** and *p.adj.* struck, now chiefly *poet.* or in special senses and phrases: wounded in the chase: afflicted: advanced (*stricken in years*): (*U.S.*) expunged. —**stricken field**, a pitched battle, or the scene of it; **stricken hour**, an hour as marked by the clock.

strict, *strikt*, *adj.* exact (e.g. *in the strict meaning of the term*): allowing of no exception, irregularity, laxity (e.g. *strict confidence, orders, obedience, honesty*): rigorous, severe (e.g. *strict laws, regulations*): enforcing rigorous discipline, usu. in conformity with a narrow code of behaviour (e.g. *their parents were very strict*).—*adv.* **strict'ly**, narrowly, closely, rigorously, exclusively.—*ns.* **strict'ness**; **stric'ture** (-*tyŭr*, -*chŭr*), an abnormal contraction of a duct or passage in the body: an unfavourable criticism. [L. *strictus*, pa.p. of *stringēre*, to draw tight.]

stride, *strīd*, *v.i.* to walk with long steps: to take a long step.—*v.t.* to stride over: to bestride:—*pa.t.* **strōde** (*obs.* **strid**); *pa.p.* **stridden** (*strid'n*).—*n.* a long step: the space stepped over.—**make great strides**, to make rapid progress; **take in one's stride**, to accomplish without undue effort or difficulty. [O.E. *strīdan*.]

strident, *strī'dènt*, *adj.* loud and grating.—*adv.* **strī'dently.**—*ns.* **strī'dence**, **-cy.** [L. *strīdens*, *entis*, pr.p. of *strīdēre*, to creak.]

stridulate, *strid'ū-lāt*, *v.i.* (of insects) to make a chirping or scraping sound (e.g. as a grasshopper does by rubbing its forewings).—*ns.* **stridulā'tion**; **strid'ulātor**, an insect that makes a sound by scraping: the organ it uses. [L. *strīdēre*. See **strident**.]

strife, *strīf*, *n.* contention: contest: striving. [O.Fr. *estrif*. See **strive**.]

strike, *strīk*, *v.t.* to hit with force, to smite: to stab, pierce (e.g. to the heart): to move in a specified direction by hitting: to dash (against, on): to cause to pierce: to collide with, knock against: (of a ship) to ground (upon): to attack, punish: to hook (a fish) by a quick turn of the wrist: to give (a blow): to ignite (a match) by friction: to produce by friction (e.g. a light, sparks): to cause to sound: to mint: (of a tree, &c.) to thrust (roots) down in the earth: to lower, let down (a flag, sail, or tent): (*theat.*) to dismantle a stage set, &c., (also *n.*): various *fig.* meanings, including the following:—to impress, or to affect in a specified way, with force or suddenness like that of a blow (e.g. *I was struck by the resemblance*; *a thought struck me*; *it strikes one with astonishment; to strike dumb; to strike terror into*): to light upon, to come upon, esp. unexpectedly: to make (a compact or agreement): to assume (e.g. an attitude): to cancel, erase (with *off, out, from*): to arrive at by calculation (e.g. an average): to cause (a cutting) to take root: to propagate by cuttings.—*v.i.* to give a quick or sudden blow: to stab, penetrate (to—*lit.* and *fig.*): to make an attack: to fight: (of a fish) to seize the bait: to knock (against): (*fig.*) to fall (e.g. *the light strikes on her hair*): (of a clock) to sound: to take a course (e.g. *to strike across the field, through the wood*; also—*coll.*—*to strike for home*): to happen (on) suddenly: to take root: to cease work in support of a demand for higher wages or improved conditions of service, or as a protest against a grievance:—*pa.t.* struck; *pa.p.* struck (*arch.* strick'en. q.v.).—*n.* act of striking for higher wages, &c.: (*geol.*) the direction of a horizontal line at right angles to the dip of a bed: a find (as of oil, ore, &c.): rooting (of cuttings): an attack, esp. by aircraft.—*n.* strīk'er. —*adj.* strīk'ing, that strikes: for hitting, smiting, attacking: surprising: impressive.— *adv.* strīk'ingly.—*n.* strike-break'er, one who works during a strike, esp. one brought in with a view to defeating it.—on strike, taking part in a strike; strike a balance, to calculate the difference between the debtor and creditor sides of an account; strike camp, to dismantle a camp and continue the march; strike hands, to join or slap hands together in confirmation of an agreement; strike home, to strike right to the point aimed at, or to the vulnerable or sensitive point; strike in, to enter suddenly: to interpose; strike into, to enter upon suddenly: to break into (e.g. *to strike into song*); strike off, to erase, to deduct: to sever by a blow; strike oil, (*fig.*) to make a lucky hit; strike out, to efface: to force out by a blow: to form by sudden effort: to direct one's course boldly outwards: to strike from the shoulder; strike up, to begin to beat, sing, or play: (*coll.*) to form (e.g. an acquaintance) suddenly; strike work, to cease work; striking distance, distance short enough to allow a blow, attack, &c., to be delivered effectively; struck on, enamoured of. [O.E. *strīcan*, to stroke, go, move.]

Strine, *strīn, n.* Australian speech. [Alleged pron. of *Australian*.]

string, *string, n.* coarse material in very narrow and relatively long pieces, made by twisting threads, used for tying, fastening, &c.: a portion of this: a piece of anything for tying: anything of like character as a nerve, tendon, fibre: a stretched piece of catgut, silk, wire, or other material in a musical instrument: (in

pl.) the stringed instruments played by a bow in an orchestra or other combination: their players: a cord on which things are filed (e.g. a string of beads): a line or (*fig.*) series of things.—*v.t.* to supply with strings: to put the strings of in tune: to make tense: to put on a string: to remove the strings from, as beans: to stretch out in a long line.—*v.i.* to stretch out or move in a long line:—*pa.t.* and *pa.p.* strung.—*n.* string'-band, a band composed chiefly of stringed instruments.—*adjs.* stringed, having strings; string'less, having no strings; string'y, consisting of strings or small threads: fibrous: capable of being drawn into strings.—harp upon one string (see harp); have strings attached, (*coll.*—of a gift or benefit) to be limited by an obligation of some kind; have two strings to one's bow (see bow); pull the strings, to control the actions of others, be the real instigator of an action; string along, to fool: to give false expectations to; strung up, nervously tensed. [O.E. *streng*; cf. Ger. *strang*, O.N. *strengr.*]

stringent, *strin'jént, adj.* binding strongly, exact and strictly enforced (e.g. *stringent regulations*).—*n.* strin'gency, state or quality of being stringent: severe pressure.—*adv.* strin'gently.—*n.* strin'gentness. [L. *stringens, -entis,* pr.p. of *stringĕre,* to draw tight.]

strip, *strip, v.t.* to pull off in strips: to tear off: to deprive of a covering—to skin, to peel, to remove fruit or leaves from: to make bare (*lit.* and *fig.*): to deprive (of).—*v.i.* to undress: to come off (e.g. leaves):—*pr.p.* stripp'ing; *pa.t.* and *pa.p.* stripped.—*n.* a long narrow piece of anything (cf. stripe).—*n.pl.* stripp'ings, the last milk drawn from a cow at a milking.—*n.* strip'tease, an act of undressing slowly and seductively in a place of entertainment.—strip lighting, lighting by means of long fluorescent tubes.—comic strip (see comic). [O.E. *strȳpan*; Ger. *streifen.*]

stripe, *strīp, n.* (*arch.*; usu. in *pl.*) a blow, esp. one made with a lash, rod, &c.: a weal or discoloured mark made by a lash or rod: a line, or long narrow division of a different colour from the ground: a chevron on a sleeve, indicating non-commissioned rank or good behaviour.—*v.t.* to make stripes on: to form with lines of different colours. [Old Du. *strijpe*, a stripe in cloth; Low Ger. *stripe*, Ger. *streif.*]

stripling, *strip'ling, n.* a lad who has not reached full growth. [Dim. of strip.]

strive, *strīv, v.i.* to endeavour earnestly, labour hard (to do, for): to struggle, contend (with, against):—*pa.t.* strōve; *pa.p.* strīven.—*n.* strīv'er. [O.Fr. *estriver*; perh. of Gmc. origin.]

strode, *strōd, pa.t.* of stride.

stroke, *strōk, n.* an act of striking: a blow (*lit.* and *fig.*): an attempt to hit: a sudden attack of apoplexy or paralysis: the sound of a clock: a dash in writing: the sweep of an oar in rowing: the stroke-oar of a rowing boat: one complete movement, e.g. of the piston of a steam-engine: a movement in one direction of a pen, pencil, or paint-brush: a method of striking in games, &c.: an effective action, a feat, achievement.—*v.t.* and *v.i.* to act as stroke for, to row the stroke-oar of a boat.—*n.* stroke'-oar, the sternmost oar in a rowing boat, or its rower,

Neutral vowels in unaccented syllables: *em'pér-ŏr*; for certain sounds in foreign words see p. ix.

726

stroke   stud

whose stroke the crew imitate. [O.E. (inferred) *strāc*; cf. Ger. *streich*.]

stroke, *strōk*, *v.t.* to rub gently in one direction: to do so as a sign of affection. [O.E. *strācian*; cf. Ger. *streichen*, to rub.]

stroll, *strōl*, *v.i.* to ramble idly, to saunter: to wander on foot.—*n.* a leisurely walk: a ramble on foot.—*n.* **stroll′er**. [Origin unknown; perh. conn. with Ger. *strolch*, a vagrant.]

strong, *strong*, *adj.* able to endure—e.g. firm, solid, well fortified, having wealth or resources: hale, healthy: having great physical power: having great vigour, as the mind: forcible: energetic: convincing (e.g. *a strong argument*): powerfully affecting the sense of smell or taste, pungent: having a quality in a great degree—e.g. very bright, loud, intense, rich in alcohol: (*gram.*) inflecting by a change of radical vowel, as *sing*, *sang*, *sung*, instead of by syllabic addition.—*adv.* **strong′ly**.—*adj.* **strong′arm**, by, having, or using physical force.—*n.* **strong′hold**, a place strong to hold out against attack, a fastness: a fortress: a place where a doctrine is strongly held or a cause strongly supported.—*adj.* **strong′-mind′ed**, having a vigorous mind, strong powers of reasoning: determined to make one's views known and effective.—*ns.* **strong language**, forcible, emphatic language: language made emphatic by blasphemous expressions, swearing; **strong point**, that in which one excels; **strong′ room**, **box**, a room, case, of great strength, used as a safe for the storage of valuables. [O.E. *strang*, strong; O.N. *strangr*, Ger. *streng*, tight.]

strontium, *stron′shi-ùm*, *n.* a metallic element (symbol Sr; atomic no. 38), existing as a carbonate in the mineral *strontianite* (first found in 1790 near *Strontian*—*stron-tē′àn*—in Argyllshire).—**strontium 90**, a radioactive isotope of strontium, an important element in nuclear fall-out.

strop, *strop*, *n.* a strip of leather, or of wood covered with leather, &c., for sharpening razors.—*v.t.* to sharpen on a strop:—*pr.p.* stropp′ing; *pa.t.* and *pa.p.* stropped. [Older form of **strap**.]

strophe, *strōf′e*, *n.* in ancient Greek drama, a stanza of an ode sung by the chorus while dancing towards one side of the orchestra (cf. **antistrophe**).—*adj.* **stroph′ic**. [Gr. *strŏphē*, a turn.]

strove, *strōv*, *pa.t.* of **strive**.

strow, *strō*, *v.t.* same as **strew**:—*pa.p.* strōwed or strōwn.

struck. See **strike**.

structure, *struk′tyùr*, *-chùr*, *n.* manner of building, or putting together, construction (*lit.* and *fig.*): arrangement of parts or of particles in a substance, or of atoms in a molecule: manner of organisation (e.g. *the structure of society*): an erection: a building. esp. one of large size: an organic form.—*v.t.* to organise, build up: to construct a framework for.—*adj.* **struc′tural**, of, pertaining to, affecting, produced by, structure.—*adv.* **struc′turally**, in, as regards, structure. [L. *structūra*—*struĕre*, *structum*, to build.]

strudel, *s(h)trŏŏdl*, *n.* very thin pastry enclosing fruit, or cheese, &c. [Ger.]

struggle, *strug′l*, *v.i.* to make great efforts with contortions of the body: to make great exertions (to): to contend (with, for, against): (*lit.* and *fig.*) to make one's way (along, through, up, &c.) with difficulty.—*n.* a violent effort with contortions of the body: great labour: agony.—*n.* **strugg′ler**. [M.E. *strogelen*.]

strum, *strum*, *v.t.* to play on (a musical instrument), or to play (a tune, &c.), in an inexpert, noisy manner.—Also *v.i.*:—*pr.p.* strumm′ing; *pa.t.* and *pa.p.* strummed. [Imit.; cf. **thrum**.]

strumpet, *strum′pet*, *n.* a prostitute. [O.Fr. *strupe*, *stupre*—L. *stuprum*, dishonour, *stuprāre*, to debauch.]

strung, *strung*, *pa.t.* and *pa.p.* of **string**.

strut, *strut*, *v.i.* to walk in a pompous manner, with affected dignity:—*pr.p.* strutt′ing; *pa.t.* and *pa.p.* strutt′ed.—*n.* a step or walk suggesting vanity or affected dignity. [O.E. *strūtian* or kindred form.]

strut, *strut*, *n.* any light structural part or long column that resists pressure in the direction of its length: a prop. *v.t.* to brace.

strychnine, *strik′nin*, *-nēn*, *n.* a poisonous alkaloid obtained from the seeds of nux vomica—also **strych′nia**. [Gr. *strychnos*, a kind of nightshade.]

stub, *stub*, *n.* the stump left after a tree is cut down: a short piece left after the larger part has been used (as a cigarette, pencil, &c.): a counterfoil. anything short and thick. *v.t.* to take the stubs or roots of from the ground: to grub (up): to strike (e.g. the toe) against a stub or other object: to put (out), to extinguish (a cigarette) by pressure on the end:—*pr.p.* stubb′ing; *pa.t.* and *pa.p.* stubbed.—*adjs.* **stubbed**, short and thick like a stump, blunt, obtuse; **stubb′y**, abounding with stubs: short, thick and strong.—*n.* **stubb′iness**. [O.E. *stubb*, *stybb*.]

stubble, *stub′l*, *n.* the stubs or stumps of corn left in the ground when the stalks are cut: an ill shaven beard.—*adj.* **stubb′ly**. [O.Fr. *estuble*—L. *stipula*, dim. of *stīpes*, a stalk.]

stubborn, *stub′órn*, *adj.* immovably fixed in opinion, obstinate: persevering: stiff, inflexible.—*adv.* **stubb′ornly**.—*n.* **stubb′ornness**. [Connection with **stub** is obscure.]

stucco, *stuk′ō*, *n.* a plaster of lime and fine sand, &c., used as a coating for walls, for decorations, &c.: work done in stucco.—*v.t.* to face or overlay with stucco: to form in stucco. [It. *stucco*; from O.H.G. *stucchi*, a crust, a shell.]

stuck, *stuk*, *pa.t.* and *pa.p.* of **stick**.—*adj.* **stuck′-up′**, self-importantly aloof.

stud, *stud*, *n.* a collection of breeding horses and mares, also the place where they are kept: a number of horses kept for racing or hunting: a stud-horse.—*ns.* **stud′-book**, a record of the pedigrees of famous animals, esp. horses; **stud′-farm**, a farm where horses are bred; **stud′-groom**, a groom at a stud; **stud′-horse**, a stallion kept for breeding. [O.E. *stōd*; Ger. *gestüt*.]

stud, *stud*, *n.* a nail with a large head: a headless bolt: a double-headed button worn e.g. in a shirt: an ornamental knob or boss.—*v.t.* to adorn with knobs: to set thickly, as with studs:—*pr.p.* stud′ing; *pa.t.* and *pa.p.* stud′ed. [O.E. *studu*, a post.]

fāte, fär; mē, hûr (her); *mīne; mōte, för; mūte; mōōn, fŏŏt;* тнen (then)

student, *stū'dėnt, n.* one who studies at a higher school, college, or university: one devoted to study or to books.—*n.* **stū'dentship**, an endowment for a student in a college. [L. *studens, -entis,* pr.p. of *studēre,* to be zealous.]

studio, *stū'di-ō, n.* the workshop of a painter, sculptor, or of a photographer: a building or (also in *pl.*) place where motion pictures are made: a room or rooms from which radio or television programmes are broadcast.—Also *adj.*:—*pl.* **stūdios.**—**studio couch,** a couch, usu. without a back, that can be converted into a bed. [It.]

studious, *stū'di-ùs, adj.* fond of study: careful (to do, of): studied, deliberately planned or consistently carried out: (*arch.*) suitable for, conducive to, study.—*adv.* **stū'diously.**—*n.* **stū'diousness.** [L. *studiōsus,* assiduous—*studium,* zeal.]

study, *stud'i, v.t.* to observe (e.g. phenomena) closely: to examine (information) thoroughly so as to understand, interpret, select data from, &c.: to memorise: to give attention to (a branch of learning—e.g. *to study mathematics*): to ascertain and act in accordance with (e.g. *to study his wishes, convenience*; hence, *to study him,* to consult, consider, indulge his wishes, convenience, &c.): to aim at achieving, producing (e.g. *you should study variety in the menu*).—*v.i.* to apply the mind closely to a subject, to books: (*arch.*) to meditate: to try hard, take pains (e.g. *study to be quiet, to avoid controversy*):—*pa.t.* and *pa.p.* stud'ied. —*n.* application of the mind to a subject, to books: any object of attentive consideration: a branch of learning: earnest endeavour (e.g. *to make it his study to please*): a brown study (see **brown**): a room devoted to study: an artist's preliminary sketch from nature, a student's exercise in painting or sculpture: a composition in music intended to help in acquiring mechanical facility: in theatrical language, one who commits a part to memory.—*adj.* **stud'ied,** deliberate, premeditated (e.g. *a studied insult*), over-carefully sustained (e.g. *with studied politeness*).—**study out,** to think out.—**make a study of,** to examine, investigate: to treat as a subject for study. [O.Fr. *estudie* (Fr. *étude*) — L. *studium,* zeal.]

stuff, *stuf, n.* material of which anything is made: essence, elemental part: textile fabrics: cloth, esp. when woollen: a medicinal mixture: worthless matter: possessions generally, esp. household furniture, &c.: (*slang*) way of behaving or talking, esp. characteristic way (e.g. *rough stuff, gangster's stuff*).—*v.t.* to fill by crowding: to cram: to cause to bulge (out) by filling: to fill with seasoning, as a fowl: to fill the skin of, as in taxidermy.—*v.i.* to feed gluttonously.—*ns.* **stuff'-gown,** a gown of material other than silk, esp. that of a junior barrister; **stuff'ing,** material used to stuff or fill anything.—**do one's stuff,** to do what is expected of one; **know one's stuff,** to have a thorough knowledge of the field in which one is concerned; **that's the stuff!** that's what (i.e. the substance, object, action, attitude, &c., that) is wanted. [O.Fr. *estoffe,* prob.—L. *stuppa,* tow.]

stuffy, *stuf'i, adj.* badly ventilated, musty: causing difficulty in breathing: (*coll.*) obstinate, ungracious, sulky.—*n.* **stuff'iness.** [O.Fr. *estouffer,* to choke—*estoffe,* stuff.]

stultify, *stul'ti-fī, v.t.* to cause to appear foolish, or absurd: hence, to make of no effect, value, or weight (e.g. *to stultify oneself by inconsistent actions, one's argument by self-contradiction, one's efforts by an ill-judged step*): to dull the mind:—*pa.t.* and *pa.p.* stul'tified.—*n.* **stultifica'tion,** act of stultifying, showing in a foolish light, depriving of weight or effect: state of being stultified. [L. *stultus,* foolish, *facĕre,* to make.]

stumble, *stum'bl, v.i.* to strike the feet against something and trip or lose balance: to falter: to light (on) by chance: to slide into crime or error.—*v.t.* to cause to trip or stop: to puzzle.—*n.* a trip in walking or running: a faltering: a blunder, a failure.—*ns.* **stum'bling-block, -stone,** a block or stone over which one would be likely to stumble: a cause of error: an obstacle, impediment. [M.E. *stomblen, stomelen, stumlen*; cf. **stammer.**]

stump, *stump, n.* the part of a tree left in the ground after the trunk is cut down: the part of a limb, tooth, remaining after a part is cut off or destroyed: a similar remnant, e.g. of a pencil: (*cricket*) one of the three sticks forming a wicket.—*v.t.* to reduce to a stump, to truncate, to cut off a part of: (*cricket*) to put out (a batsman who is not in his ground) by striking the stumps with the ball: to baffle, thwart, make helpless: to make stump-speeches throughout (a district): (*slang*) to pay (up; also *v.i.*).—*v.i.* to walk along heavily: to make stump-speeches.—*ns.* **stump'er**; **stump'-or'ator,** one who makes stump-speeches; **stump'-speech,** a speech delivered on any improvised platform, as the stump of a tree: a speech intended to excite popular enthusiasm and support.—*adj.* **stump'y,** full of stumps: short and thick. [Late M.E. *stompe*; Du. *stomp,* Ger. *stumpf.*]

stun, *stun, v.t.* to stupefy with a loud noise, or with a blow: to surprise completely, to amaze:—*pr.p.* **stunn'ing**; *pa.t.* and *pa.p.* stunned.—*n.* **stunn'er,** a person or an action that strikes with amazement or admiration: a very attractive person. [O.Fr. *estoner,* to astonish; cf. Ger. *staunen.*]

stung, *stung, pa.t.* and *pa.p.* of **sting.**

stunk, *stungk, pa.p.* of **stink.**

stunt, *stunt, v.t.* to check the growth of, to dwarf, check.—*adj.* **stunt'ed,** dwarfed, checked in development. [O.E. *stunt,* dull, stupid; O.N. *stuttr,* short.]

stunt, *stunt, n.* a spectacular feat: a project designed to attract attention.—*v.i.* to perform stunts.—*n.* **stunt'man,** one paid to perform dangerous and showy feats (esp. a stand-in for a film actor). [U.S. slang.]

stupefy, *stū'pe-fī, v.t.* to make stupid or insensible (with drink, drugs, misery, &c.), to deaden the perceptive faculties of:—*pa.t.* and *pa.p.* stū'pefied.—*n.* **stūpefac'tion,** the act of making stupid or senseless: insensibility: (*coll.*) dazed condition caused by astonishment and intense disapproval. [L. *stupēre,* to be struck senseless, *facĕre,* to make.]

stupendous, *stū-pen'dùs, adj.* wonderful, amaz-

Neutral vowels in unaccented syllables: *em'pėr-ôr*; for certain sounds in foreign words see p. ix.

728

ing, astonishing for its magnitude: often used loosely as a coll. term of approbation or admiration.—*adv.* **stūpen′dously.**—*n.* **stūpen′dousness.** [L. *stupendus*—*stupēre.* See **stupefy.**]

stupid, *stū′pid, adj.* struck senseless: deficient or dull in understanding: formed or done without reason or judgment, foolish.—*ns.* **stūpid′ity, stū′pidness.**—*adv.* **stū′pidly.** [Fr.,—L. *stupidus*—*stupēre.* See **stupefy.**]

stupor, *stu′por, n.* suspension of sense either complete or partial, dazed condition: excessive amazement or astonishment. [L.,— *stupēre.* See **stupefy.**]

sturdy, *stûr′di, adj.* (*comp.* **stur′dier,** *superl.* **stur′diest**) resolute, firm, forcible: strong, robust.—*adv.* **stur′dily.**—*n.* **stur′diness.** [O.Fr. *estourdi,* pa.p. of *estourdir,* to stun.]

sturgeon, *stûr′jōn, n.* a genus of large fishes with head and body partly covered by cartilaginous shields, esteemed for its palatable flesh, and for the caviare and isinglass which it yields. [O.Fr. *esturgeon.*]

stutter, *stut′ėr, v.i.* to hesitate in utterance, repeating initial consonants, to stammer.—*v.t.* to say or utter in this way.—*n.* the act of stuttering: a hesitation in utterance.—*n.* **stutt′erer,** one who stutters.—*adv.* **stutt′eringly.** [A frequentative of obs. *stut,* to stutter.]

sty, stye, *stī, n.* a small inflamed swelling on the eyelid. [Obs. or dial.*stian, styan*—O.E.*stigend,* perh. *stīgan,* to rise.]

sty, *stī, n.* a pen for swine: any extremely filthy place:—*pl.* **sties.** [O.E. *stī*; cog. with *stig,* hall. See **steward.**]

Stygian, *stij′i-ăn, adj.* relating to *Styx,* a river of the lower world: hellish, infernal (e.g.*Stygian darkness*). [L.*Stygius* Gr.*Stygios stygeein,* to hate.]

style, *stīl, n.* anything long and pointed, esp. an ancient pointed tool for engraving or writing on wax: mode of expressing thought in language (e.g. *the matter was excellent but the style was poor*): ideas in the visual arts, &c.: manner of performing an action or of playing a game (e.g. *he got the results he wanted, but his style was ugly*): the distinctive manner peculiar to an author, painter, &c. or to a period: manner, method, form (*good style, bad style*): fashion: air of fashion, elegance, consequence: mode of reckoning time: title, mode of address: the pin of a sun-dial: (*bot.*) the middle portion of the pistil, between the ovary and the stigma.—*v.t.* to entitle in addressing or speaking of: to name or designate: to arrange, dictate the fashion or style of.— *adjs.* **sty′lar,** pertaining to the pin of a dial; **sty′lish,** (*coll.*) displaying style, fashionable, showy: pretending to style.—*adv.* **sty′lishly.**— *ns.* **sty′lishness; sty′list,** one with a distinctive and fine literary style: one who arranges a style, esp. in hair-dressing.—*adj.* **stylist′ic.**— *adv.* **stylist′ically.**—**in style,** in a grand manner; **new, old, style,** (see **new, old**). [Partly from L. *stilus*; perhaps some meanings from Gr. *stylos,* a pillar, (erroneously) a style.]

stylite, *stī′līt, n.* any of an early class of ascetics who lived unsheltered on the tops of pillars— St Simeon Stylites (*stī-lī′tēz*; c. 390-459) is said to have lived thirty years on one. [Gr.

stylītēs—*stylos,* pillar.]

stylus, *stī′lus, n.* stile in senses of writing tool, pin of sundial, part of pistil: a cutting tool used in making gramophone records: a gramophone needle. [Root as **style.**]

stymie, *stī′mi, n.* in golf, a position on the putting-green when an opponent's ball lies on the direct line between the player's ball and the hole, and blocks the line of play.—Also *v.t.* (*lit.* and *fig.*). [Ety. obscure.]

styptic, *stip′tik, adj.* astringent, that stops bleeding.—*n.* an astringent agent for application to a bleeding surface. [Fr.,—L. *stypticus*—Gr. *styptikos*—*styphein,* to contract.]

suasion, *swā′zh(ŏ)n, n.* the act of persuading, persuasion.—*adj.* **suā′sive,** tending to persuade. [Fr.,—L. *suāsiō, -ōnis*—*suādēre,* to advise.]

suave, *swāv,* or *swäv, adj.* pleasant, agreeable, polite: bland, mollifying.—*adv.* **suave′ly.**—*n.* **suav′ity** (*swav´-*). [Fr.,—L. *suāvis,* sweet.]

sub-, *sub-, pfx.* (by assimilation before *c, f, g, m, p, r, s,* **suc-,** as suc*ceed,* **suf-,** as suf*fuse,* **sug-,** as sug*gest,* **sum-,** as sum*mon,* **sup-,** as sup*port,* **sur-,** as sur*reptitious,* **sus-,** as sus*pend*—also as **s-** in *s*ombre and **so-** in *so*journ) denotes:—

(1) under, below, as **subterranean,** *sub*stratum, substructure, subway;

(2) below the level of, less than, as **subconscious,** subhuman, subnormal;

(3) slightly less than, almost, as **subacute,** subarctic, subtemperate, subtorrid, subtropical;

(4) formed by subdivision, as **subtype,** subphylum, subclass, suborder, subfamily, subgenus, subspecies, subgrade, subgroup, subsection, subvariety;

(5) under the control of, subordinate, as **subagent,** subcontract, suboffice, substation;

(6) next in rank to, under (*fig.*) as **subdeacon,** subdean, subinspector, sublibrarian. [L. *sub,* under (which in O.Fr. became *so-*).]

sub, *sub, n.* (*coll.*) a subordinate: used as an abbreviation for many compounds of **sub-,** as subaltern, subeditor, subsistence (money), substitute, subscription, &c.—*v.i.* to act as a substitute: to work as a newspaper editor.— *v.t.* to subedit.

subacid, *sub-as′id, adj.* moderately acid: somewhat sharp or biting (e.g. *a subacid manner*). [L. *subacidus*—*sub,* under, somewhat, *acidus,* sour.]

subacute, *sub-a-kūt′, adj.* (of a disease) between acute and chronic, moderately acute. [**sub-,** less than, and **acute.**]

subagent, *sub-āj′ėnt, n.* one employed by an agent to transact business in his stead. [**sub-,** subordinate, and **agent.**]

subaltern, *sub′al-tėrn,* (*U.S.*) *sub-öl′tėrn, adj.* inferior, subordinate.—*n.* a subordinate: an officer in the army under the rank of captain. [Fr.,—L. *sub,* under, *alternus,* one after the other—*alter,* the other.]

subapostolic, *sub-ap-os-tol′ik, adj.* pertaining to the period just after that of the apostles [L. *sub,* under, and **apostolic.**]

subaqueous, *sub-ā′kwe-us, adj.* lying under water: formed under water: living under water.—*adj.* **subaquat′ic,** subaqueous: partially aquatic. [sub-, and **aqueous, aquatic.**]

subatomic, *sub-á-tom′ik, adj.* smaller than an atom: occurring within an atom. [**sub-**, less than, and **atom.**]

subclinical, *sub-klin′i-kal, adj.* of a slightness not detectable by usual clinical means. [**sub-**, below the level of, and **clinical.**]

subcommittee, *sub′ko-mit′i, n.* a committee exercising powers delegated to it by a larger committee by which it is appointed. [**sub-**, subordinate, and **committee.**]

subconscious, *sub-kon′shŭs, adj.* of, pertaining to, mental operations just below the level of consciousness: active beneath consciousness.—*n.* subconscious mental operations.—*adv.* **subcon′sciously.**—*n.* **subcon′sciousness.** [**sub-**, below the level of, and **conscious.**]

subcontinent, *sub-con′tinent, n.* a portion of a continent having many of the characteristics of a continent and sometimes regarded as such. [**sub-**, almost, and **continent.**]

subcutaneous, *sub-kū-tā′ne-ŭs, adj.* under the skin. [**sub-**, under, **cutaneous** (see **cutis**.)]

subdeacon, *sub-dē′kŏn, n.* a member of the order of the ministry next below that of deacon. [**sub-**, under, and **deacon.**]

subdivide, *sub-di-vīd′, v.t.* to divide into smaller divisions, to divide again.—*v.i.* to be subdivided: to separate into smaller divisons.—*n.* **subdivi′sion,** the act of subdividing: a part made by subdividing. [**sub-**, under, and **divide.**]

subdominant, *sub-dom′i-nánt, n.* (*mus.*) the tone next below the dominant. [**sub-**, under, and **dominant.**]

subdue, *sub-dū′, v.t.* to conquer: to render submissive, to tame: to overcome (e.g. a desire, impulse), discipline (e.g. the flesh): to soften, tone down (often in *pa.p.*—e.g. colour, light, mood or manner, emotion or feeling).—*adj.* **subdū′able.**—*ns.* **subdū′al,** the act of subduing: **subdū′er.** [M.E. *soduen*—O.Fr. *so(u)duire*—L. *sēdūcere,* to seduce; meaning influenced by confusion with L. *subdĕre,* to put under—*sub,* under, *dăre,* to put.]

subedit, *sub-ed′it, v.t.* and *v.i.* to edit under the control of an editor.—*n.* **subed′itor,** a subordinate editor. [**sub-**, under (*fig.*), and **edit.**]

subinspector, *sub-in-spek′tŏr, n.* a subordinate or assistant inspector. [**sub-**, subordinate, and **inspector.**]

subjacent, *sub-jā′sént, adj.* lying under or below, being in a lower situation. [L. *subjacēns, -entis,* pr.p. of *subjacēre*—*sub,* under, *jacēre,* to lie.]

subject, *sub′jekt, adj.* (*obs.*) subjacent: under the power of, owing allegiance to, another: not independent: liable, prone (to—e.g. *subject to temptation, to colds*): dependent on (a condition) for validity, being put into effect, &c. (e.g. *the treaty is subject to ratification*; *this plan is subject to your approval*).—*n.* one under the power of another: one under allegiance to a sovereign: the person or thing on which any operation or experiment is performed: (*anat.*) a dead body for dissection: a person (used critically, with a suggestion of the laboratory attitude—e.g. a *nervous subject, a touchy subject*): that which the artist is trying to express, the scheme or idea of a

work of art, as a painting, poem, &c.: a principal theme of a piece of music: the topic or theme of a discourse, &c.: hence, material (e.g. circumstances) suitable for specified treatment (e.g. *not a subject for mirth, a subject for congratulation*): an organised body of knowledge (e.g. *studied three subjects*—*history, French, and chemistry*): the mind, regarded as the thinking power, in contrast with the *object,* that about which it thinks: (*gram.*) the noun or noun-equivalent about which something is predicated.—*v.t.* **subject′,** to bring under the power of: (with *to*) to expose or make liable (to—e.g. *such an indiscretion would subject you to widespread criticism*): to cause to undergo (e.g. *to subject to great pressure*—lit. or *fig.*).—*n.* **subjec′tion,** the act of subjecting: the state of being subjected.—*adj.* **subject′ive,** relating to the subject (e.g. *the nominative or subjective case*): determined by, derived from, one's own mind or consciousness (e.g. *subjective reality*—see **objective**): (in literature and other arts) showing clearly the individual tastes, views, prejudices, of the artist (e.g. *subjective treatment*; cf. *objective*).—*adv.* **subject′ively.**—*ns.* **subject′iveness; subjectiv′ity,** state of being subjective: that which is treated subjectively.—**subjective genitive** (see **genitive**); **sub′ject-matter,** the material (facts, ideas) dealt with in a book, &c. [Fr. *sujet*—L. *subjectus*—*subjicĕre, -jectum*—*sub,* under, *jacĕre,* to throw.]

subjoin, *sub-join′, v.t.* to add at the end or afterwards. [Through Fr.—L. *subjungĕre*—*sub,* under, *jungĕre,* to join.]

subjugate, *sub′jŏŏ-gāt, v.t.* to bring under the yoke, under power or dominion: to conquer.—*ns.* **subjugā′tion; sub′jugātor.** [L. *subjugāre, -ātum*—*sub,* under, *jugum,* a yoke.]

subjunctive, *sub-jungk′tiv, adj.* denoting that mood of a verb which expresses condition, hypothesis, or contingency.—*n.* the subjunctive mood. [L. *subjunctīvus*—*sub,* under, *jungĕre, junctum,* to join.]

subkingdom, *sub-king′dŏm, n.* a subordinate kingdom: (*bot.* and *zool.*) a primary division of a kingdom. [**sub-**, under, and **kingdom.**]

sublease, *sub-lēs′, n,* a lease by a tenant to another, the subtenant.—Also *v.t.* [**sub-**, under, and **lease.**]

sublet, *sub-let′, v.t.* (of one who is himself a tenant of the property concerned) to lease to another.—Also *n.* [**sub-**, under, and **let.**]

sublieutenant, *sub-lé-ten′ánt,* or *-lŏŏ-, n.* (*navy*) a junior officer next below a lieutenant: (*army*—*obs.* **sub-léf-ten′ánt**) a second lieutenant.—**acting sublieutenant,** an officer entrant to the navy since the discontinuance of midshipmen in 1957. [**sub-**, next in rank to, and **lieutenant.**]

sublimate, *sub′lim-āt, v.t.* to refine and exalt: to purify by turning into vapour through the action of heat and allowing the vapour to solidify again: (*psych.*) to use the energy of (a primitive impulse) for purposes of a high nature such as artistic creation.—*n.* (*-át*), the product of sublimation.—*n.* **sublimā′tion,** the act or process of sublimating. [L. *sublīmāre, -ātum,* to lift up.]

Neutral vowels in unaccented syllables: *em′pér-ór*; for certain sounds in foreign words see p. ix.

sublime, *sub-līm'*, *adj.* lofty, majestic, awakening feelings of awe or veneration: (ironically) great in a degree that would befit worthier conduct, a finer feeling, &c. (e.g. *sublime indifference*).—*n.* that which is sublime: the lofty or grand in thought or style.—*v.t.* to exalt, dignify, ennoble: to sublimate (a substance).—*v.i.* to be sublimed or sublimated.—*adv.* **sublime'ly.**—*ns.* **sublime'ness, sublim'ity,** loftiness, elevation, grandeur. [L. *sublīmis,* high; origin uncertain.]

subliminal, *sub-lim'i-nál, adj.* beneath the level of consciousness: too weak or small to produce a conscious sensation or perceptible effect.—**subliminal advertising,** advertising in the cinema, &c., flashed too quickly and briefly to make a conscious impression. [L. *sub,* under, *līmen, līminis,* the threshold.]

sublunar, *sub-lū'när, adj.* under the moon, earthly, belonging to this world—also **sub'lunary.** [**sub-,** under, and **lunar.**]

submachine-gun, *sub-ma-shēn'-gun, n.* a lightweight type of machine-gun, usu. one for firing from the shoulder. [**sub-,** slightly less than, and **machine-gun.**]

submarine, *sub-má-rēn', adj.* under, or in, the sea.—*n. (sub'-)* a submersible boat, capable of being propelled under water, esp. for firing torpedoes. [**sub-,** under, and **marine.**]

submediant. Same as **superdominant.**

submerge, *sub-merj', submerse, sub-mers', v.t.* to plunge under water: to flood with water.—*v.i.* to sink under water.—*ns.* **submerg'ence, submer'sion.**—*adj.* **submers'ible.** [L. *submergĕre, -mersum—sub,* under, *mergĕre,* to plunge.]

submit, *sub-mit', v.t.* to surrender (oneself) to another: to offer to another for consideration or criticism (e.g. *he submitted the manuscript to a friend; I have only one suggestion to submit*): to offer (a thought) diffidently for consideration (e.g. *I submit that it would have been better to follow the second course*).—*v.i.* to yield, surrender: to yield one's opinion: to be resigned: to consent:—*pr.p.* **submit'ting;** *pa.t.* and *pa.p.* **submit'ted.**—*n.* **submission** (*sub-mish'(ó)n*), act of submitting: that which is submitted: acknowledgment of inferiority or of a fault: humble behaviour: resignation.—*adj.* **submiss'ive,** willing or ready to submit, yielding: humble, obedient.—*adv.* **submiss'ively,** humbly.—*n.* **submiss'iveness.** [L. *submittĕre—sub,* under, *mittĕre, missum,* to send.]

submultiple, *sub-mul'ti-pl, n.* a number or quantity which is contained in another an exact number of times, an aliquot part. [**sub-,** under, and **multiple.**]

subnormal, *sub-nör'mál, adj.* less than normal, esp. medically of a person with a low range of intelligence. [**sub-,** below the level of, and **normal.**]

subordinate, *sub-ör'di-nät, adj.* lower in order, rank, nature, power, &c.: of less authority, weight, or importance than (with *to*).—*n.* one in a lower order or rank: an inferior.—*v.t.* (*-āt*) to consider, treat, as of less importance than (with *to*): to make subject (to).—*adv.* **subor'dinately.**—*n.* **subordinā'tion,** act of subordinating: state of being subordinate: in-

feriority of rank or importance. [L. *sub,* under, *ordŏ, ordĭnis,* order.]

suborn, *sub-örn', v.t.* to procure, persuade (a person) e.g. by bribery, to commit a perjury or other unlawful act.—*ns.* **subornā'tion; subborn'er.** [L. *subornāre—sub,* under, *ornāre,* to fit out.]

subpoena, subpena *sub-pē'na, n.* a writ commanding the attendance of a person in court under a penalty.—*v.t.* to summon by a writ of subpoena:—*pa.t.* and *pa.p.* **subpoe'na'd.** [L. *sub,* under, *poena,* punishment.]

subscribe, *sub-skrīb', v.t.* to write (usu. one's name) underneath, e.g. a document: to give consent to (something written) by writing one's name underneath: to authenticate (a document) officially in this way: to sign: to promise to give or pay by attaching one's name to a list: to contribute.—*v.i.* to promise a certain sum by signature: to contribute (to, for): (with *for*) to promise before publication to buy (a copy or copies of a book, or a newspaper or periodical for a certain time): to indicate one's acceptance of, agreement with (with *to*—e.g. *I refuse to subscribe to that statement, opinion*).—*n.* **subscrīb'er.**—*adj.* **sub'script,** written underneath (e.g. *iota subscript,* the Greek letter ι—iōta—written below *ā, ē,* and *ō,* i.e. *ạ, η, ῳ*).—*n.* **subscript'ion,** act of subscribing: a name subscribed: consent as by signature: sum subscribed. [L. *subscrībĕre—sub,* under, *scrībĕre, scriptum,* to write.]

subsequent, *sub'sé-kwént, adj.* following or coming after.—*adv.* **sub'sequently.** [L. *subsequens, -entis,* pr.p. of *subsequī—sub,* under, after, *sequī,* to follow.]

subserve, *sub-surv', v.t.* to serve subordinately or instrumentally, to help forward (e.g. a purpose, plan).—*ns.* **subser'vience, subser'viency,** state of being subservient: undue deference.—*adj.* **subser'vient,** subserving, serving to promote: submissive, obsequious.—*adv.* **subser'viently.** [L. *subservīre—sub,* under, *servīre,* to serve.]

subside, *sub-sīd', v.i.* to settle at the bottom, as lees: to sink in level, as the ground, floodwater, &c.: to become gradually more deeply submerged: (*coll.*) to collapse (into a chair): to fall into a state of quiet (*lit.* and *fig.*—e.g. *the storm, the fever, subsided*).—*n.* **subsī'dence** (or *sub'si-déns*), act or process of subsiding, settling, or sinking, esp. the sinking or caving-in of the ground or the settling down of a structure to a lower level. [L. *subsīdĕre—sub,* down, *sīdĕre,* to settle.]

subsidy, *sub'si-di, n.* aid in money or property: (*hist.*) a sum of money formerly granted by parliament to the sovereign for state purposes: a sum of money paid by one state to another for assistance in war: money granted by the state to a commercial undertaking (such as a transportation service) considered to be of public benefit, to growers of an important product (such as wheat) in order to keep down the price to the consumer, &c.—*adj.* **subsid'iary,** of, pertaining to, constituting, a subsidy: furnishing help or additional supplies: aiding but secondary: subordinate.—*n.* one who, or that which, aids or supplies: an assistant: a subordinate.—*adv.*

subsid′iarily.—*v.t.* **sub′sidīse,** to furnish with a subsidy: to purchase the aid of, to buy over. —**subsidiary company,** a company the majority of whose shares are held by a related larger company. [Fr.,—L. *subsidium,* orig. troops stationed behind in reserve, aid—*sub,* under, *sīdĕre,* to settle.]

subsist, *sub-sist′, v.i.* to have existence: to remain, continue: to keep oneself alive (on).—*v.t.* to provide food for.—*n.* **subsist′ence,** state of being subsistent: (*philos.*) real being: inherence: means of supporting life, livelihood.—*adj.* of wage, allowance, &c., providing the bare necessities of living.—*adj.* **subsist′ent,** subsisting: having real being: inherent. [Fr.,—L. *subsistĕre,* to stand still—*sub,* under, *sistĕre,* to stand.]

subsoil, *sub′soil, n.* the under soil, the bed or stratum of earth lying immediately beneath the surface soil. [**sub-,** under, and **soil** (1).]

subsonic, *sub-son′ik, adj.* of speed, less than that of sound. [**sub-,** below the level of, and **sonic.**]

substance, *sub′stáns, n.* that which underlies outward manifestation, the essential nature: the essential part, purport, meaning (e.g. *the substance of his discourse was as follows*): material: a material object: solidity, worth (e.g. *this cloth has no substance*): property, possessions (e.g. *a man of substance, to waste one's substance*): a particular kind of matter—an element, compound, or mixture [L. *substantia*—*substāre,* to stand under—*sub,* under, *stāre,* to stand.]

substantial, *sub-stan′sh(á)l, adj.* consisting of, of the nature of, substance: real, not merely seeming: virtual, in total effect though not in all details (e.g. *this is the substantial truth; in substantial agreement*): considerable, important (e.g. *a substantial sum, argument*): strong, stout, bulky: having property or estate.—*n.* an essential part (usu. in *pl.*).—*n.* **substantial′ity.**—*adv.* **substan′tially,** in essence, in total effect, to all intents and purposes.—*v.t.* **substantiate** (-*stan′shi-āt*), to make substantial: to prove, to show the validity of, grounds for (e.g. *a statement, a charge, a claim*).—*n.* **substantiā′tion.**—*adj.* **sub′stantive,** expressing existence: real: of real, independent importance.—*n.* (*gram.*) the part of speech denoting something that exists, a noun.—*adv.* **sub′stantively.** [Fr. *substantiel*—L. *substantiālis*—*substantia.* See **substance.**]

substitute, *sub′sti-tūt, v.t.* to put in place of another person or thing (with *for*): to replace (by).—*n.* one who, or that which, is put in place of, or used instead of, for want of, another.—*adj.* put instead of another.—*ns.* **substit′uent,** something that may be, or is, substituted: an atom or radical taking the place of an atom or radical removed from a molecule; **substitū′tion,** act of substituting: (*alg.*) the replacing of one quantity by another which is equal to it but expressed differently, or of a variable by one of its values: (*chem.*) the act or process of replacing an atom or radical in a molecule by another atom or radical.—*adj.* **substitū′tional.** [L. *substituĕre, -ūtum*—*sub,* under, *statuĕre,* to set.]

subsume, *sub-sūm′, v.t.* to include (e.g. a particular, an instance) under a universal, a rule,

class.—*n.* **subsump′tion.** [L. *sub,* under, *sumĕre,* to take.]

subtenant, *sub-ten′ánt, n.* a tenant who leases from one who is also a tenant. [**sub-,** under, and **tenant.**]

subtend, *sub-tend′, v.t.* to extend under or be opposite to, as a hypotenuse a right-angle, or a chord an arc. [L. *subtendĕre*—*sub,* under, *tendĕre,* to stretch.]

subterfuge, *sub′tér-fūj, n.* an artifice to escape censure or the force of an argument, evasion. [Fr.,—L. *subterfugĕre*—*subter,* under, *fugĕre,* to flee.]

subterranean, *sub-te-rā′né-àn, adj.* under the earth or ground—also **subterrā′neous:** hidden, secret. [L. *subterrāneus*—*sub,* under, *terra,* the earth.]

subtile, *sub′til* or *sut′il, adj.* (*arch.* in all meanings) delicately constructed, fine, thin or rare: piercing or penetrating: shrewd, discerning: cunning.—*adv.* **sub′tilely.**—*ns.* **sub′tileness; subtilty** (*sub′til-ti* or *sut′il-ti*). See **subtle.** [L. *subtīlis*—*sub,* under, *tēla,* a web.]

subtitle, *sub′tī-tl, n.* an additional or second title to a book, a half-title: a film caption, esp. a printed translation (at the foot of the screen) of foreign dialogue. [**sub-,** subordinate, and **title.**]

subtle, *sut′l* (*B.* **sub′til**)*, adj.* subtile (q.v.), esp. in figurative senses, as:—pervasive but difficult to describe (e.g. *a subtle perfume, a subtle feeling of horror*): difficult to define, put into words (e.g. *a subtle distinction, subtle variations*): acute (of mind): showing acuteness of mind (e.g. *a subtle analysis of the situation*): insinuating, sly, artful.—*n.* **subt′leness, subt′lety,** quality of being subtle: tenuousness, indefinableness: acuteness (of mind): quality of being discerning and penetrative (e.g. *the subtlety of the analysis*): a fine distinction.—*adv.* **subt′ly** (*B.* **sub′tilly**). [Contr. of **subtile.**]

subtopia, *sub-tō′pi-a, n.* a region where the city has sprawled into the country. [L. *sub,* under, Gr. *topos,* a place.]

subtract, *sub-trakt′, v.t.* to take away (a part from—*lit.* and *fig.*): to take (one number or quantity from another) in order to find their difference.—Also *v.i.*—*n.* **subtrac′tion.**—*adj.* **subtract′ive,** subtracting: tending to subtract or lessen.—*n.* **sub′trahend,** the sum or number to be subtracted from another. [L. *subtrahĕre, -tractum*—*sub,* under, *trahĕre,* to draw away.]

subtype, *sub′tīp, n.* a type included in another and more general one. [**sub-,** under, and **type.**]

suburb, *sub′úrb, n.* (orig.) a district near but beyond the walls of a city: an area (esp. residential) in the outskirts of a large town.—*adj.* **subur′ban,** of a suburb: (*fig.*) conventional, narrow in outlook.—*n.* **subur′bia,** dwellers in suburbs collectively. [L. *suburbium*—*sub,* under, near, *urbs,* a city.]

subvention, *sub-ven′sh(ó)n, n.* act of coming to relief, support: a government aid or subsidy. [L. *sub,* under, *venīre, ventum,* to come.]

subvert, *sub-vûrt′, v.t.* (*fig.*) to turn upside down, to overthrow, to ruin utterly (e.g. morality, principles, arguments): to corrupt (a person). —*n.* **subver′sion,** act of subverting: entire overthrow, ruin.—*adj.* **subver′sive,** tending to subvert (e.g. *subversive of morality*).—*n.* **sub-**

Neutral vowels in unaccented syllables: *em′pér-ór*; for certain sounds in foreign words see p. ix.

732

vert'er. [L. *subvertĕre*—*sub*, under, *vertĕre*, *versum*, to turn.]

subway, *sub'wā, n.* a tunnel for foot-passengers: an underground passage for water-pipes, gas-pipes, &c.: an underground railway. [**sub-**, under and **way.**]

succeed, *suk-sēd', v.t.* to come after, to follow in order (e.g. *spring succeeds winter*): to follow, take the place of (e.g. *Henry III succeeded John*; *he succeeded him in office*).—*v.i.* to follow in order: to take the place of: to accomplish one's aim: to prosper.—*n.* **success'** (or *suk'-*), act of succeeding or state of having succeeded: the prosperous termination (of anything attempted): a successful person or affair.—*adj.* **success'ful,** having, achieving, the desired end or effect, gaining the prize aimed at: prosperous.—*adv.* **success'fully.**—*n.* **success'ion,** act of following after: series (of persons or things following each other in time or place): right of succeeding: series of persons having this:order of succeeding.—*adj.* **success'-ive,** following in succession or in order.—*adv.* **success'ively.**—*n.* **success'or,** one who succeeds or comes after: one who takes the place of another.—**in succession,** one after another, running. [L. *succēdĕre*—*sub*, up, *cēdĕre*, to go.]

succès d'estime, *sük-se des-tēm, n.* a good reception given to a work because of its author's reputation, not its own merits; **succès fou** (*foo*), success with wild enthusiasm; **succès de scandale** (*dé skä-dal*), success of a book, play, &c. due not to merit but to its connection with or reference to a topical scandal [Fr.]

succinct, *suk-singkt', adj.* short, concise.—*adv.* **succinct'ly.**—*n.* **succinct'ness.** [L. *succinctus*—*sub*, up, *cingĕre*, to gird.]

succory, *suk'ŏr-i, n.* a variant of **chicory.**

succour, *suk'ŏr, v.t.* to assist, to relieve.—*n.* aid, relief: one who gives such. [L. *succurrĕre*, to run up to—*sub*, up, *currĕre*, to run.]

succulent, *suk'ū-lent, adj.* full of juice or moisture, not dry or barren.—*ns.* **succ'ulence,** **succ'ulency.**—*adv.* **succ'ulently.** [L. *succulentus*—*succus*, juice *sūgĕre*, to suck.]

succumb, *su-kum', v.i.* (*fig.*) to lie down under, to sink under (with *to*): to yield: to die. [L. *succumbĕre*—*sub*, under, *-cumbĕre* (found only in compounds), to lie down.]

such, *such, adj.* of this or that kind (e.g. *such people, such a man*): of the quality or character mentioned or implied: used to give emphasis (as in *such a fine day!*): of the kind (that, as—followed by explanatory clause or infinitive; e.g. *his absorption was such that he lost all sense of time, such as to make him unconscious of time*).—**such and such,** a demonstrative phrase vaguely indicating a person or thing not named—some (e.g. *such and such a person may say*); **such as,** of the same kind as: for example: (*arch.*) those who; **such like,** things like those mentioned (usu. *vulg.*).—**as such,** in that capacity (e.g. *he was the heir and, as such, had certain duties to perform*): in the character, or for the quality, implied by the name (e.g. *the poems are of little worth as such, but they are valuable to the philologist and the historian*). [O.E. *swylc*—*swa*, so, *līc*, like.]

suck, *suk, v.t.* to draw into the mouth: to draw milk or other liquid from with the mouth: to lick, squeeze, and roll about in the mouth: to draw in as if by sucking (with *in, up,* &c.): to drain, exhaust (e.g. *to suck dry*): (*fig.*) to imbibe (e.g. knowledge).—Also *v.i.*—*n.* act of sucking: a sucking movement: what is drawn in by such a movement: milk drawn from the breast.—*n.* **suck'er,** one who, or that which, sucks: the organ by which an animal adheres to other bodies: the piston of a suction-pump: a shoot rising from a subterranean stem: a leather disk to the middle of which a string is attached, used as a toy: (*slang*) a gullible person.—*adj.* **suck'ing,** still nourished by milk: young and inexperienced.—**suck in, up,** to absorb (*lit.* and *fig.*); **suck up to** (*slang*), to truckle to, toady to, seek to ingratiate oneself with. [O.E. *sūcan, sūgan*; Ger. *saugen.*]

suckle, *suk'l, v.t.* to give suck to, to nurse at the breast.—*n.* **suck'ling,** a young child or animal still being fed on its mother's milk.—*adj.* **suck'ling.** [Dim. of **suck.**]

sucrose, *sū'krōs, n.* the form of sugar obtained from sugar-cane, sugar-beet, &c. [Fr. *sucre*, sugar, and suffix. *-ose.*]

suction, *suk'sh(ŏ)n, n.* act, or power, of sucking: act or process of exhausting the air and creating a vacuum into which fluids are pushed by atmospheric pressure or, more generally, of exerting a force on a body (solid, liquid, or gas) by reducing the air pressure on part of its surface.—*n.* **suc'tion-pump,** the common pump, in which liquid rises to fill a partial vacuum produced by a simple mechanism of piston and valves. [L. *suctiō, -ōnis*—*sūgĕre*, *suctum*, to suck.]

sudatory, *sū'da-tŏr-i, adj.* sweating.—*n.* a sweating-bath. [L. *sūdatōrius*—*sūdāre, -ātum.*]

sudd, *sud, n.* floating plants which hinder navigation on the river Nile. [Ar., barrier.]

sudden, *sud'én, adj.* unexpected (e.g. *a sudden call*; *sudden death*), hasty (e.g. *a sudden departure*), abrupt (e.g. *a sudden bend in the road*).—*adv.* **sudd'enly**—*n.* **sudd'enness.**—**on, of, a sudden,** suddenly. [O.Fr. *sodain*—L. *subitāneus*, sudden—*subitus*, coming stealthily—*sub*, up, *īre, ĭtum*, to go.]

sudorific, *sū-dor-if'ik, adj.* causing sweat.—*n.* a medicine producing sweat, a diaphoretic.—*n.* **sū'dor,** sweat.—*adjs.* **sū'doral;** **sūdorif'erous.** [L. *sūdor*, sweat, *facĕre*, to make.]

suds, *sudz, n.pl.* soapy water: the froth and bubbles of stirred soapy water. [O.E. *soden*, pa.p. of *sēothan*, to seethe; cog. with Ger. *sod*—*sieden.*]

sue, *sū* or *sōō, v.t.* (*obs.*) to follow, pursue: to entreat, make petition to: to prosecute at law.—*v.i.* to make legal claim: to petition, to entreat, to demand (*to* a person *for* a thing).—**sue out,** (*law*) to apply or petition for and obtain (e.g. a writ, a pardon). [M.E. *suen*—O.Fr. (*il*) *siut, suit,* 3rd sing. pres. indic. of *sevre* (Fr. *suivre*)—L. *sequī, secūtus,* to follow.]

suède, suede, *swād, swed, n.* skins used for gloves and shoe uppers, made from sheep or lamb skins dressed on the flesh side and finished without glaze.—Also *adj.* [Fr. *Suède*, Sweden.]

suet

suet, *sū'ét, sōō'ét, n.* a solid fatty tissue, accumulating about the kidneys of the ox, sheep, &c.—*adj.* **su'ety.**—**suet pudding,** a boiled pudding made with suet. [O.Fr. *seu* (Fr. *suif*)—L. *sēbum,* fat.]

suffer, *suf'ér, v.t.* to undergo (e.g. *to suffer a change*): to endure (e.g. pain, martyrdom): to permit (to do): to tolerate (e.g. *he would not suffer any interference*).—*v.i.* to feel pain: to undergo punishment (for): to sustain loss or injury.—*adj.* **suff'erable,** that may be suffered: endurable: allowable.—*ns.* **suff'erance,** (*arch.*) state of suffering: (*arch.*) endurance: permission, esp. when tacit or unwilling, tolerance (usu. in phrase **on sufferance**—e.g. *he was there on sufferance,* his presence was tolerated but not desired or approved, or, *he was there subject to good behaviour*); **suff'erer;** **suff'ering,** distress, pain, loss, or injury. [L. *sufferre*—*sub,* under, *ferre,* to bear.]

suffice, *su-fīs', v.i.* to be enough: to be equal (to do), adequate (for the end in view).—*v.t.* to satisfy.—*adj.* **suffi'cient** (*-fi'shént*), enough: equal to any end or purpose.—*adv.* **suffi'ciently.** —*n.* **sufficiency** (*sù-fi'shén-si*), an adequate quantity (of): adequate resources: state of being sufficient: competence, ability, capacity. [Fr.,—L. *sufficĕre,* to put in the place of—*sub,* under, *facĕre,* to make.]

suffix, *suf'iks, n.* a particle placed after the root of a word to form an oblique case of a noun, &c., a tense of a verb, a derivative adjective, adverb, &c.—*v.t.* **suffix',** to add a letter or syllable at the end of a word for such a purpose. [L. *suffixus*—*sub,* under, *fīgĕre,* to fix.]

suffocate, *suf'ō-kāt, v.t.* to kill by stopping the breath, to stifle: to cause to feel unable to breathe freely: (*fig.*) to deprive of conditions necessary for growth or expression, to destroy (e.g. aspirations).—*p.adj.* **suff'ocāting,** choking, hindering respiration: hindering self-expression.—*adv.* **suff'ocātingly.**—*n.* **suffocā'tion,** act of suffocating: state of being suffocated. [L. *suffōcāre, -ātum*—*sub,* under, *fauces,* the throat.]

suffragan, *suf'ra-gán, n.* orig. a bishop who might be required by his metropolitan to attend a synod and give a vote: a coadjutor-bishop. [O.Fr. *suffragan*—L. *suffrāgans,* pr.p. of *suffrāgāri,* to vote for—*suffrāgium,* a vote.]

suffrage, *suf'rij, n.* a vote: a vote in approbation or assent: the right to vote.—*n.* **suffragette',** a woman who took part in the vehement, and ultimately successful, agitation for votes for women (1908-1918). [L. *suffrāgium,* a vote.]

suffuse, *su-fūz', v.t.* to overspread or cover, as with a fluid (e.g. *eyes suffused with tears*), or with colour or light.—*n.* **suffū'sion,** act or operation of suffusing: state of being suffused: that which suffuses. [L. *suffundĕre*—*sub,* underneath, *fundĕre, fūsum,* to pour.]

sugar, *shŏŏg'ár, n.* a sweet substance obtained chiefly from the sugar-cane and the sugar-beet, and also from maple and palm trees, &c.: any of a number of similar sweet soluble carbohydrates, e.g. fructose, glucose, lactose: excessive flattery or compliment: (*slang*) money: (*coll.*) a term of endearment.—*v.t.* to sprinkle or mix with sugar: to compliment.—*ns.* **sug'ar-beet,** any one of several varieties of

suit

the common garden beet, grown for sugar; **sug'ar-can'dy,** sugar candied or in large crystals; **sug'ar-cane,** the saccharine grass from which sugar is obtained.—*adj.* **sug'ar-coat'ed,** coated with sugar.—*n.* **sug'ar-daddy,** an elderly man who spends much money on girls.—*p.adj.* **sug'ared,** sweetened with sugar: (*fig.*) delightful, charming: (*fig.*) too sweet.—*ns.* **sug'ar-loaf,** a loaf or mass of sugar, usually in the form of a truncated cone (also *adj.*); **su'gar-plum,** a species of sweetmeat made up in small lumps like a plum: a pleasing bit of flattery; **sug'ar-refi'ner,** one who refines raw sugar; **sug'ar-refi'nery.**—*n.pl.* **sug'ar-tongs,** an implement for lifting pieces of sugar at table.—*adj.* **sug'ary,** sweetened with, tasting of, or like, sugar: sickly sweet.—*n.* **sug'ariness.**—**sugar of lead,** an acetate (q.v.) of lead, used as a mordant in dyeing, &c. [Fr. *sucre*—Sp. *azucar*—Ar. *sukkar*—Pers. *shakar*—Sans. *śarkarā,* sugar, orig. grains of sand, applied to sugar because occurring in grains.]

suggest, *suj-est', sug-jest', v.t.* to put into one's mind: to bring to one's mind by association of ideas: to imply or seem to imply: to propose: to hint (to).—*adj.* **suggest'ible,** that may be suggested: easily influenced by, susceptible to, suggestion.—*n.* **suggestion** (*su-jes'ch(ó)n*), act of suggesting: the mental process by which one thought or idea calls up another: the process by which an individual accepts an idea presented by another person or thing and acts in accordance with it: (*psycho-analysis*) such acceptance of an idea or attitude induced by an unconscious emotional tie with another person—used as a method of treatment in psychotherapy: a proposal: an indecent proposal: a hint: a slight trace.—*adj.* **sugges'tive,** containing a hint: fitted to bring to one's mind the idea (of): of, pertaining to, suggestion: rather indecent.—*adv.* **sugges'tively.**—*n.* **sugges'tiveness.** [L. *suggerĕre*—*sub,* under, *gerĕre, gestum,* to carry.]

suicide, *sū'i-sīd,* or *sōō'-, n.* one who dies by his own hand: self-murder: a self-inflicted disaster.—*adj.* **sūici'dal,** of, pertaining to, suicide: directed towards, or with an impulse towards, suicide: (*fig.*) giving a death-blow, e.g. to one's career.—*adv.* **sūici'dally.** [Coined from L. *sui,* of himself, *caedĕre,* to kill.]

suit, *sūt, sōōt, n.* act of suing: an action at law: petition: courtship of a particular woman: a series: a sequence: a set: a set of cards of one kind (e.g. of hearts): a number of things made to be worn together, as pieces of clothing or armour.—*v.t.* to fit, accommodate (to, e.g. *he suited his views to his audience*): to become (e.g. *the hat, sarcasm, does not suit you*): to please (e.g. *suit yourself*): to be convenient to (e.g. *the hour chosen did not suit him*): to agree with (e.g. *the climate did not suit her*).—*v.i.* to go well (with).—*pa.p.* **suit'ed,** fitted (to, for).—*adj.* **suit'able,** fitting: agreeable (to), convenient (to, for).—*ns.* **suitabil'ity, suit'ableness.**—*adv.* **suit'ably.**—*ns.* **suit'-case,** an easily portable oblong travelling-case for carrying suits and clothes. &c.; **suit'ing,** material for suits of clothes; **suit'or,** one who sues in love or (*arch.*) law.—**follow suit,** to play a card of the

Neutral vowels in unaccented syllables: *em'pér-ôr;* for certain sounds in foreign words see p. ix.

734

suit led: to do the same; **strong suit**, one's forte. [Through O.Fr.,—L. *sequī, secūtus,* to follow.]

suite, *swēt, n.* a train of followers or attendants: a regular set, esp. of rooms, furniture, pieces of music. [Fr. **suit.**]

sukiyaki, *sōō'kē-yä-kē, n.* beef, vegetables, sauce, &c., cooked together, often at table. [Jap.]

sulcate, -d, *sul'kāt, -id, adj.* furrowed, grooved. [L. *sulcāre, -ātum—sulcus,* a furrow.]

sulk, *sulk, v.i.* to be sulky.—*n.pl.* **sulks,** a fit of sulkiness.—*adj.* **sulk'y,** silently sullen, withdrawn and unresponsive because of (usu. petty) resentment.—*n.* a light vehicle, consisting of a single seat, mounted on two wheels.—*n.* **sulk'iness,** quality or state of being sulky.—*adv.* **sulk'ily,** in a morose, sullen manner. [O.E. *solcen,* slow—*seolcan,* to be slow.]

sullen, *sul'én, adj.* gloomily angry and silent: dark, dull (e.g. *a sullen sky*).—*adv.* **sull'enly** —*n.* **sull'enness.** [O.Fr. *solain*—L. *sōlus,* alone.]

sully, *sul'i, v.t.* to soil, to spot, to tarnish.—*v.i.* to be soiled:—*pa.t.* and *pa.p.* sull'ied. [Fr. *souiller.*]

sulphonamide. See **sulphur.**

sulphur, *sul'fúr, n.* **a** yellow non-metallic element (symbol S; atomic no. 16), very brittle, fusible, and inflammable.—*ns.* **sul'phate,** a salt of sulphuric acid; **sul'phide,** a compound of sulphur with another element or radical; **sul'phite,** a salt of sulphurous acid.—*v.t.* **sul'phūrate,** to combine with, or subject to the action of sulphur.—*adj.* **sulphū'reous,** consisting of, containing, or having the qualities of, sulphur.—*n.* **sul'phūret,** a sulphide.—*adjs.* **sul'phūretted,** having sulphur in combination; **sul'phūrous,** sulphureous: see also below; **sulphū'ric** and **sul'phūrous** are used for compounds in which sulphur has respectively a higher and a lower valency or combining power, e.g. *sulphuric acid* (H_2SO_4); *sulphurous acid* (H_2SO_3—known only as an aqueous solution of sulphur dioxide, but forming sulphites); **sulphonic** denotes compounds containing an acid group ($SO_2\cdot OH$) of valency 1, and appears in composition as **sulphon-,** e.g. **sulphon'amide,** any of a group of drugs with powerful anti-bacterial action.—**sulphur dioxide,** (SO_2) a colourless gas formed when sulphur burns in air; **sulphuretted hydrogen,** a poisonous inflammable gas with an odour like that of bad eggs.—**flowers of sulphur,** a yellow powder obtained by distilling other forms of sulphur; **roll sulphur,** brimstone, sulphur liquefied and cast into sticks. [L. *sulphur.*]

sultan, *sul'tan, n.* a Mohammedan sovereign, esp. the former head of the Ottoman empire:—*fem.* **sultana** *(sul-tä'na),* the mother, a wife, or a daughter of a sultan (also **sul'taness**): a king's mistress: a small kind of raisin.—*n.* **sul'tanship.** [Ar. *sultān,* victorious, a ruler.]

sultry, *sul'tri, adj.* sweltering, very hot and oppressive, close: hot with rage: passionate.—*adv.* **sul'trily.**—*n.* **sul'triness.** [Earlier **sweltry**; see **swelter.**]

sum, *sum, n.* the amount of two or more things taken together: the whole amount, aggregate: a quantity of money: a problem in arithmetic or algebra: the substance or result of reason-

ing: summary, gist (also **sum and substance**). —*v.t.* to collect into one amount or whole: to add: (usu. **sum up**) to give the gist of:—*pr.p.* summ'ing; *pa.t.* and *pa.p.* summed.—*ns.* **sum'mand** (or *-and'*), an addend: part of a sum; **summ'ing-up,** a recapitulation or review: a judge's summary survey of the evidence for the information and guidance of the jury; **sum total,** emphatic form of *sum,* strictly the aggregate of various smaller sums: the essential point, total effect.—**in sum,** in short. [O.Fr. *summe*—L. *summa*—*summus, suprēmus,* highest, superl. of *superus,* on high—*super,* above.]

sumac, sumach, *sū'mak, n.* any of a number of small trees and shrubs, the leaves and shoots of which yield tannin and are used in dyeing. [Fr. *sumac*—Sp. *zumaque*—Ar. *summāq.*]

Sumerian, *sū-mē'ri-án, adj.* pertaining to *Sumer,* one of the two divisions of ancient Babylonia (the plain watered by the lower streams of the Tigris and Euphrates).

summary, *sum'á-ri, adj.* short, brief, compendious: quick, without waste of time or words, without formalities (e.g. *a summary dismissal, summary jurisdiction*).—*n.* an abstract, abridgment, or compendium.—*adv.* **summ'arily.** *v.t.* **summ'arise,** to present in a summary, to state briefly: to be a summary of. [L. *summārium*—*summa.* See **sum.**]

summation, *sum-ā'sh(ó)n, n.* act of forming a total or sum: an aggregate. [**sum.**]

summer, *sum'ér, n.* the second and warmest season of the year—in northern temperate regions from May or June to July or August; astronomically, from the summer solstice to the autumn equinox.—*v.i.* to pass the summer.—*adj.* of or like summer.—*ns.* **summ'erhouse,** a structure in a garden for sitting in: a summer residence; **summ'er-time,** the summer season: (also **summer time**) time one hour in advance of Greenwich time, adopted (since 1916; see British Standard Time) for the purpose of daylight-saving (q.v.) during summer months.—*adj.* **sum'mery,** like summer: suitable for summer. [O.E. *sumer, sumor*; Du. *zomer,* Ger. *sommer.*]

summerset. Same as **somersault.**

summit, *sum't, n.* the highest point, the top (*lit.* and *fig.*).—*n.* **summ'itry,** the practice or technique of holding summit conferences.—**summit conference,** a conference between heads of states: extended to mean a conference between heads of any group of organisations. [O.Fr. *sommette,* dim. of *som,* the top of a hill—L. *summum,* highest.]

summon, *sum'ón, v.t.* to call with authority: to command to appear, esp. in court: (also **summon up**) to rouse to activity (e.g. *to summon energy, courage to do this*).—*ns.* **summ'oner; summ'ons,** an authoritative call; a call to appear, esp. in court: a call to surrender.—*v.t.* to serve with a legal summons. [O.Fr. *somoner*— L. *summonēre*—*sub,* secretly, *monēre,* to warn.]

sump, *sump, n.* a small pit at the lowest point of a mine or excavation into which water can drain and out of which it can be pumped: a pit for used metal: the oil container in a motor vehicle. [Du. *somp*; Ger. *sumpf.*]

fāte, fär; mē, hûr (her); *mīne; mōte, för; mūte, mōōn, fŏŏt*; ᴛнen (then)

sumpter, *sump'tėr, n.* (*arch.*) a horse for carrying burdens: its driver. [O.Fr. *sommetier,* a pack-horse driver — L. *sagmārius* — Gr. *sagma,* a pack-saddle, *sattein,* to pack.]

sumptuary, *sumpt'ū-ár-i, adj.* pertaining to or regulating expense, as in **Sumptuary Laws,** which sought to prevent extravagance in banquets, dress, &c. [L. *sumptuārius* — *sumptus,* cost.]

sumptuous, *sumpt'ū-ús, adj.* costly, magnificent. — *n.* **sumpt'ūousness.** — *adv.* **sumpt'ūously.** [L. *sumptuōsus,* costly — *sumptus,* cost.]

sun, *sun, n.* the star which gives light and heat to the solar system: a body which, like the earth's sun, forms the centre of a system of orbs: that which resembles the sun in position of importance or in brightness: the sunshine. — *v.t.* to expose (e.g. oneself) to the sun's rays: (*fig.*) to enjoy (oneself in a person's company) as if in warmth and brightness. — *v.i.* to bask in sunshine: — *pr.p.* sunn'ing; *pa.t.* and *pa.p.* sunned. — *n.* **sun'-bath,** exposure of the body to the sun's rays. — *v.i.* **sun'-bathe,** to take a sun-bath. — *ns.* **sun'bather; sun'beam,** a ray of the sun; **sun'-bird,** a family of small tropical birds, the males with resplendent metallic plumage; **sun'-bonn'et,** a sun-hat to enclose the face and neck; **sun'burn,** a burning or scorching by the sun, esp. the browning of the skin by exposure to the sun. — *adj.* **sun'burned, sun'burnt,** burned or coloured by the sun. — *ns.* **sun'dew,** a genus of small insectivorous plants, found in bogs and moist heathy ground; **sun'-dī'al,** an instrument for measuring time by means of the motion of the sun's shadow cast by a style or gnomon erected on its surface; **sun'down,** sunset; **sun'-downer,** (*Austr.*) a vagrant who habitually arrives at a remote station about sundown in the hope of getting free rations and lodging for the night: (*slang*) an alcoholic drink served in the evening. — *adj.* **sun'-drīed,** dried by exposure to the sun. — *ns.* **sun'-fish,** a fish whose body resembles the forepart of a larger fish cut short off, supposed to be so called from its nearly circular form; **sun'-flower,** any of a genus of plants whose seeds yield oil — so called from their flower, which is a large disk with yellow rays; **sun'-glasses,** dark-lensed spectacles used against strong light; **sun'hat,** a light hat with wide brim to shade the face from the sun; **sun'-lamp,** a lamp that gives out ultraviolet rays curatively or to induce artificial sunburn. — *adj.* **sun'less,** without sun: without happiness or cheerfulness. — *n.* **sun'light,** the light of the sun. — *adjs.* **sun'lit,** lighted up by the sun; **sunn'y,** exposed to, filled with, warmed by, the sun's rays: like the sun or sunshine, esp. in brightness: cheerful. — *ns.* **sunn'iness; sun'rise, sun'rising,** the rising or first appearance of the sun above the horizon: the time of this rising: the east; **sun'set, sun'setting,** the setting or going down of the sun: the west; **sun'shade,** a parasol, a kind of umbrella used as protection against the sun: an awning; **sun'shine,** bright sunlight: (*fig.*) warmth and brightness. — *adjs.* **sun'shine, sun'shiny,** bright with sunshine: pleasant: bright like the sun. — *ns.* **sunshineroof,** a car-roof that can be pushed open;

sun'spot, one of the dark irregular spots appearing on the surface of the sun; **sun'-stroke,** a condition of fever, convulsions, coma, caused by exposure to blazing sunshine; **sun'tan,** a browning of the skin as a result of exposure to the sun. — *adj.* **sun'-tanned.** — *n.* **sun'-time,** time as reckoned by taking the highest position of the sun as 12 noon or midday. — *adv.* **sun'ward,** toward the sun. — **a place in the sun,** a place or opportunity for attaining prosperity or good living; **take the sun,** to ascertain the latitude from the sun; **under the sun,** in the world, on earth. [O.E. *sunne;* O.N. *sunna,* Old Ger. *sunne.*]

sundae, *sun'dā, n.* an ice-cream with fruits in syrup. [**Sunday.**]

Sunday, *sun'dā, n.* the first day of the week, so called because anciently dedicated to the *sun* or its worship, now regarded as the Sabbath by most Christians. — *ns.* **Sun'day-best,** one's best clothes; **Sun'day-school,** a school for religious instruction of children, held on Sunday. — **a month of Sundays,** a very long time. [O.E. *sunnan dæg;* Ger. *sonntag.*]

sunder, *sun'dér, v.t.* and *v.i.* (*poet.*) to separate, to divide. — **in sunder** (*B.*), asunder. [O.E. *syndrian,* to separate — *sundor,* separate; O.N. *sundr,* asunder.]

sundry, *sun'dri, adj.* (*obs.*) separate: more than one or two, several, divers. — *n.pl.* **sun'dries,** various small things. — **all and sundry,** one and all. [O.E. *syndrig* — *syndrian,* to separate.]

sung, *sung, pa.p.* of **sing.**

sunk, *sungk,* **sunken,** *sungk'n. pa.p.* of **sink.**

sup, *sup, v.t.* to take into the mouth in small quantities, as with a spoon: to provide with supper. — *v.i.* to eat the evening meal: (*B.*) to sip: — *pr.p.* supp'ing; *pa.t.* and *pa.p.* supped. — *n.* a small mouthful, as of a liquid. [O.E. *sūpan;* O.N. *sūpa,* Ger. *saufen,* to drink.]

super-, *s(y)ōō'pér-, pfx.* [L. *super,* prep. and pfx., above, &c.] conveys meanings such as the following: — (1) (*lit.*) above, on the top of, e.g. **superstructure,** *superhumeral,* **superimpose;** (2) in addition, e.g. **supertax,** *superadd;* (3) beyond, beyond the normal, e.g. *supernormal,* **supersaturate;** (4) of higher quality than, e.g. **superman, superhuman;** (5) excessively, e.g. **supersensitive,** *supersubtle;* (6) other shades of meaning in words from L. or Low L., e.g. (*fig.*) over, from above, as in **supervise.**

super, *s(y)ōō'pér, n.* a supernumerary actor. [Contr. of **supernumerary.**]

superable, *s(y)ōō'pér-á-bl, adj.* able to be surmounted. [L. *superāre,* to overcome — *super,* above.]

superabundant, *s(y)ōō-pér-ab-und'ánt, adj.* abundant to excess, more than enough. — *v.i.* **superabound',** to abound exceedingly, to be more than enough. — *n.* **superabund'ance.** — *adv.* **superabund'antly.** [L. *superabundans, -antis,* pr.p. of *superabundāre.* See **super,** and **abound.**]

superannuate, *s(y)ōō-pér-an'ū-āt, v.t.* to discharge from service or employment on account of age: to pension on account of old age or infirmity. — *n.* **superannuā'tion,** state of being superannuated: the allowance granted in consideration of such. [L. *super,* above, *annus,* a year.]

Neutral vowels in unaccented syllables: *em'pér-ór;* for certain sounds in foreign words see p. ix.

736

superb, *s(y)ōō-pûrb',* *adj.* proud, magnificent, stately: of the highest, most impressive, quality.—*adv.* **superb'ly.** [L. *superbus,* proud—*super,* above.]

supercalender,*s(y)ōō-pér-kal'én-dér, v.t.* to give (paper) an extra smooth surface by means of calenders (q.v.). [**super-,** beyond the normal, and **calender.**]

supercargo, *s(y)ōō'pér-kär'go, n.* a person in a merchant ship placed in charge of the cargo and superintending all the commercial transactions of the voyage. [**super-,** over, **cargo.**]

supercharger,*s(y)ōō'pér-chär'jér, n.* a compressor used to supply air or combustible mixture to an internal-combustion engine at a pressure greater than atmospheric.—*v.t.* **supercharge',** to supply air, &c., to by means of a supercharger: to give an additional charge to, or to charge in excess. [**super-,** beyond the normal, and **charger** (see **charge**).]

supercilious, *s(y)ōō-pér-sil'i-us, adj.* prone to despise others: haughty, disdainful.—*adv.* **supercil'iously.** *n.* **supercil'iousness.** [L. *superciliōsus—supercilium,* an eyebrow—*super,* above, *cilium,* eyelid.]

superconductivity, *s(y)ōō'pér-kon-duk-tiv'i-ti, n.* the property possessed by many metals at extremely low temperatures of having no resistance to the flow of electricity. [**super-,** beyond the normal, and **conductivity.**]

supercool,*s(y)ōō pér-kōōl', v.t.* to cool below the freezing-point without solidification. [**super-,** beyond the normal, and **cool.**]

superdominant,*s(y)ōō-pér-dom'i-nánt, adj.* the tone next above the dominant; same as *submediant.* [**super-,** above, and **dominant.**]

supereminent, *s(y)ōō-pér-em'i-nént, adj.* eminent beyond others.—*n.* **superem'inence.**—*adv.* **superem'inently.** [**super-,** beyond the normal, and **eminent.**]

supererogation, *s(y)ōō'pér-er-ō-gā'sh(ó)n, n.* performance of good deeds beyond those which the Church requires as necessary for salvation, hence anything superfluous or uncalled for.—*adj.* **supererog'atory.** [L. *super,* above, *ērogāre, -ātum,* to pay out.]

superexcellent, *s(y)ōō-pér-ek'sel-ént, adj.* excellent in an uncommon degree.—*n.* **superex'cellence.** [**super-,** beyond the normal, and **excellent.**]

superfatted,*s(y)ōō'pér-fat'id, adj.* (of soap) containing more fat than usual. [**super-,** beyond the normal, and **fat.**]

superficies, *s(y)ōō-pér-fish-i-ēz, n.* the upper surface, outer face: the external area: external features, appearance.—*adj.* **superficial** (*-fi'sh(á)l*), of, or near, the surface: not going deeper than the surface: slight, not thorough: (of a person) shallow in nature or knowledge.—*adv.* **superfi'cially.**—*ns.* **superfi'cialness, superficial'ity.** [L. *superficiēs—super,* above, *faciēs,* face.]

superfine, *s(y)ōō'pér-fīn, adj.* finer than ordinary. [**super-,** beyond the normal, and **fine** (1).]

superfluous, *s(y)ōō-pér'flōō-ùs, adj.* beyond what is enough: unnecessary.—*n.* **superflu'ity,** a superfluous quantity or more than enough, superabundance: state of being superfluous: something unnecessary.—*adv.* **super'fluously.**

[L. *superfluus—super,* above, *fluĕre,* to flow.]

superheat, *s(y)ōō-pér-hēt', v.t.* to overheat: to heat (a liquid) beyond its boiling-point without converting it into vapour: to heat (steam, &c.) out of contact with the liquid from which it was formed. [**super-,** above the normal, and **heat.**]

superhighway, *s(y)ōō'pér-hī'wā, n.* (*U.S.*) a wide road for fast motor-traffic with no crossings on the same level. [**super-,** beyond the normal, and **highway.**]

superhuman, *s(y)ōō-pér-hū'mán, adj.* above what is human: divine. [**super-,** of higher quality than, and **human.**]

superimpose, *s(y)ōō-pér-im-pōz', v.t.* to impose or lay above (often something not in keeping; with *on, upon*—e.g. *a Victorian upper storey superimposed on a Georgian ground floor*; *to superimpose new customs on old*). [**super-,** above, and **impose.**]

superincumbent, *s(y)ōō-pér-in-kum'bént, adj.* lying, esp. heavily (on a person or thing). [**super-,** above, and **incumbent.**]

superinduce, *s(y)ōō-pér-in-dūs', v.t.* to bring in over and above, in addition to, something else (e.g. a disease, beliefs, in addition to that or those already existing). [L. *superindūcĕre,* to draw over—*super,* above, *in,* on, *dūcĕre,* to lead.]

superintend, *s(y)ōō-pér-in-tend', v.t.* to have the oversight or charge of, to control, manage.—*v.i.* to exercise supervision.—*ns.* **superinten'dence, superinten'dency,** oversight, direction, management.—*adj.* **superinten'dent.**—*n.* one who superintends: a police officer above an inspector. [L. *superintendĕre—super,* above, *in,* on, *tendĕre,* to stretch.]

superior, *s(y)ōō-pē'ri-ór, adj.* upper: higher in place: higher in rank: higher in excellence: greater in number, power: above the common in quality or rank (e.g. *a superior article, person*): implying a sense of greater importance, knowledge, &c. (e.g. *a superior air, smile*): beyond the influence of: too courageous, self-controlled, &c., to yield (to—e.g. *superior to temptation*): supercilious or uppish.—*n.* one superior to others: the chief of a monastery, &c., and of certain churches and colleges: the feudal lord of a vassal: (*Scots law*) one to whom feu-duty is paid.—*n.* **supérior'ity,** quality or state of being superior.—**superiority complex,** overvaluation of one's worth, often affected to cover a sense of inferiority. [L., comp. of *superus,* high—*super,* above.]

superlative, *s(y)ōō-pér'lá-tiv, adj.* of the highest degree or quality (e.g. *a superlative example, superlative insolence, skill*).—*n.* (*gram.*) the superlative or highest degree of adjectives and adverbs (e.g. kindest, best, most beautiful; most readily, worst): an adjective or adverb in the superlative degree.—*adv.* **super'latively.** [L. *superlātīvus—superlātus,* pa.p. of *superferre—super,* above, *ferre,* to carry.]

superman, *s(y)ōō'pér-man, n.* a being of a higher type than man: Nietzsche's overman (q.v.): a man of extraordinary powers. [**super-,** of higher quality than, and **man.**]

supermarket,*s(y)ōō'pér-mär-két, n.* (orig. *U.S.*) a large, usu. self-service, retail store selling food and other domestic goods. [**super-**, beyond the normal, and **market**.]

supernal, _s(y)ōō-pûr'nál, adj._ (_poet._) that is above or in a higher place or region: celestial. [L. _supernus—super_, above.]

supernatural, _s(y)ōō-pér-nat'ū-rál, adj._ not according to the usual course of nature, miraculous: spiritual.—_adv._ **supernat'urally.** [**super-**, beyond, and **natural**.]

supernova, _s(y)ōō-pér-nōv'á, n._ a very brilliant new star that flares up, resulting from an explosion. [**super-**, above, and L. _nova_ (_stella_), new (star).]

supernumerary, _s(y)ōō-pér-nūm'ér-ár-i, adj._ over and above the number stated, or which is usual or necessary.—_n._ a person or thing beyond the usual, necessary, or stated number: one who appears on stage or screen without a speaking part. [L. _supernūmerārius—super_, over, _nūmerus_, a number.]

superphosphate, _s(y)ōō-pér-fos'fāt, n._ an acid phosphate (see **acid salt**): a fertiliser of which the main ingredient is acid calcium phosphate. [**super-**, beyond the normal, and **phosphate**.]

superpose, _s(y)ōō-pér-pōz', v.t._ to place over or upon. [L. _super_, over, and Fr. _poser_ (see **pose**, n.).]

supersaturation, _s(y)ōō-pér-sat-ū-rā'sh(ó)n, n._ a metastable (q.v.) state in which the concentration of a solution or a vapour is greater than that corresponding to saturation.—_v.t._ **supersat'urate.** [**super-**, beyond the normal, and **saturation**.]

superscribe, _s(y)ōō-pér-skrīb', v.t._ to write or engrave (an inscription) on the outside or top: to write the name on the outside or cover of.—_n._ **superscrip'tion,** act of superscribing: that which is written or engraved above or on the outside. [L. _superscrībĕre—super_, above, _scrībĕre, scriptum_, to write.]

supersede, _s(y)ōō-pér-sēd', v.t._ to take the place of by reason of superior right, power, &c.: to displace, set aside, render unnecessary: to put in the room of, to replace (by). [L. _supersedēre_, to desist—_super_, above, _sedēre_, to sit.]

supersensitive, _s(y)ōō-pér-sen'si-tiv, adj._ extremely, or unduly, sensitive. [**super-**, beyond the normal, and **sensitive**.]

supersonic, _s(y)ōō-pér-son'ik, adj._ faster than the speed of sound: (of vibrations and radiations) often erroneously used to mean _ultrasonic_ (q.v.): (_aero._) faster than sound in air—an important milestone in the development of speed because of new aerodynamical problems that arise as this speed is approached.—_n._ (in _pl._; erroneously) supersonic vibrations, or the science that deals with them. [**super-**, beyond, and **sonic**.]

superstition, _s(y)ōō-pér-sti'sh(ó)n, n._ excessive reverence or fear, based on ignorance: false worship or religion: an ignorant and irrational belief in supernatural agency: belief in what is absurd or without evidence.—_adj._ **supersti'tious,** pertaining to, or proceeding from, superstition: holding, influenced by, superstitions.—_adv._ **supersti'tiously.** [L. _superstitiō, -ōnis,_ excessive religious belief—_super_, over, above, _sistĕre—stāre_, to stand.]

superstratum, _s(y)ōō-pér-strā'tum, n._ a stratum or layer situated above another. [**super-**, above, and **stratum**.]

superstructure, _s(y)ōō-pér-struk'tyùr, -chùr, n._ a structure above or on something else: anything erected on a foundation. [**super-**, above, and **structure**.]

supertax, _s(y)ōō'pér-taks, n._ an extra or additional tax on large incomes. [**super-**, in addition, and **tax**.]

supertonic, _s(y)ōō-pér-ton'ik, n._ (_mus._) the note next above the keynote. [**super-**, above, and **tonic**.]

supervene, _s(y)ōō-pér-vēn', v.i._ to come in addition, or closely after: (_loosely_) to occur, take place.—_n._ **superven'tion,** act of supervening or taking place. [L. _supervenīre_, to follow—_super_, above, _venīre, ventum_, come.]

supervise, _s(y)ōō'pér-vīz, v.i._ and _v.t._ to oversee, to superintend.—_ns._ **supervī'sal, supervī'sion,** act of supervising: inspection, control; **supervī'sor,** one who supervises, an overseer, an inspector. [L. _super_, over, _vidēre, vīsum_, to see.]

supine, _s(y)ōō-pīn',_ or _s(y)ōō'-, adj._ lying on the back: negligent, indolent, lacking in energy and initiative.—_n._ **sū'pine,** one of two parts of the Latin verb, really verbal nouns, ending in -_um_ and -_u_.—_adv._ **sūpine'ly.**—_n._ **sūpine'ness.** [L. _supīnus—sub_, under.]

supper, _sup'ér, n._ a meal taken at the close of the day.—_adj._ **supp'erless,** without supper. [O.Fr. _soper_—Low Ger. _supen_, to sup.]

supplant, _su-plänt', v.t._ to displace by guile: to take the place of.—_n._ **supplant'er.** [L. _supplantāre_, to trip up one's heels—_sub_, under, _planta_, the sole of the foot.]

supple, _sup'l, adj._ pliant: lithe: yielding to the humour of others, fawning.—_v.t._ to make supple: to make soft or compliant.—_v.i._ to become supple.—_n._ **supp'leness.**—_adv._ **supp'ly.** [Fr. _souple_—L. _supplex_, bending the knees—_sub_, under, _plicāre_, to fold.]

supplement, _sup'lé-mént, n._ any addition by which defects are made good: that which completes or brings closer to completion: a special part of a periodical publication accompanying an ordinary part: the quantity by which an angle or an arc falls short of 180° or a semicircle.—_v.t._ **supplement'** (also _sup'-_), to add to (with _with_).—_adjs._ **supplemen'tal, supplement'ary,** added to supply what is wanting, additional. [L. _supplēmentum—supplēre_, to fill up.]

suppliant, _sup'li-ánt, adj._ supplicating, asking earnestly, entreating.—_n._ a humble petitioner.—_adv._ **supp'liantly.** [Fr. _suppliant_, pr.p. of _supplier_—L. _supplicāre_. See **supplicate**.]

supplicate, _sup'li-kāt, v.t._ to entreat earnestly: to address in prayer.—_n._ **supplicā'tion,** act of supplicating: earnest prayer or entreaty.—_adj._ **supp'licātory,** containing supplication or entreaty, imploring. [L. _supplicāre, -ātum,_ to beseech—_supplex_, bending the knee—_sub_, under, _plicāre_, to fold.]

supply, _su-plī', v.t._ to fill up, meet (a deficiency, a need): to furnish: to fill (a vacant place):—_pa.t._ and _pa.p._ **supplīed'.**—_n._ act of supplying: that which is supplied, or which supplies a want: amount of food or money provided (usu. in _pl._): grant provided by a legislature for the expenses of government: a

---

Neutral vowels in unaccented syllables: _em'pér-ór_; for certain sounds in foreign words see p. ix.

person who fills another's place. [Fr.,—L. *sup-plēre*—*sub,* up, *plēre,* to fill.]

support, *su-pōrt', -pört', v.t.* to hold up, bear part of the weight of: (*fig.*) to give power of resistance, enable to endure: to supply with means of living: to subscribe to: to uphold by countenance, patronise (a cause, policy): to take the side of: to defend, speak in favour of (e.g. a motion, contention): to endure, tolerate: to tend to confirm (e.g. a statement): to keep up (a part or character).—*n.* act of supporting or upholding: that which supports, sustains, or maintains: maintenance.—*adj.* **support'able,** capable of being supported: endurable: capable of being maintained.—*adv.* **support'ably.**—*n.* **support'er,** one who, or that which, supports: an adherent: a backer, a defender: (*her.*) a figure, usu. animal, on each side of an escutcheon. [L. *supportāre*—*sub,* up, *portāre,* to bear.]

suppose, *su-pōz', v.t.* to assume, state as true, for the sake of argument: to presume, think probable: to believe without sufficient proof: to require as a condition, presuppose: in the imper. followed by a clause, without conj., conveying a suggestion or a veiled command (e.g. *suppose we give it to her, suppose you go now*).—*adjs.* **suppō'sable,** that may be supposed; **supposed',** believed on insufficient evidence to exist or have reality (e.g. *the once supposed indestructibility of the atom*): wrongly believed to be, bear the character specified (*his supposed partner, interests, benevolence*).—*adv.* **suppō'sedly,** according to supposition.—*ns.* **suppō'ser; supposi'tion,** act of supposing: that which is supposed, assumption. [Fr. *supposer*—L. *suppōnĕre, -positum sub,* under, *pōnĕre,* to place.]

supposititious, *su-poz i tish'us, adj.* put by trick in the place of another, spurious: of the nature of a supposition.—*adv.* **supposti'tiously.** [L. *supposititius*—*suppōnĕre, suppositum,* to put in the place of another—*sub,* under,*pōnĕre,* to place.]

suppository, *su-poz'i-tôr-i, n.* a conical or cylindrical plug of medicated soluble material for insertion into the rectum, vagina, or urethra. [L.L. *suppositōrium* (neut.), that is placed underneath—L. *suppōnĕre.* See **suppose.**]

suppress, *su-pres', v.t.* to crush, put down (e.g. a rebellion, rebels, freedom of speech): to restrain (a person): to keep in (e.g. a sigh, an angry retort): to keep from publication or circulation or from being known (e.g. a book, a name, evidence, the truth).—*ns.* **suppress'er; suppress'or,** one who suppresses: a device for suppressing anything, e.g. electrical interference with television reception; **suppress'ion,** act of suppressing: stoppage: concealment.—*adj.* **suppress'ive,** tending to suppress. [L. *supprimĕre, suppressum*—*sub,* under, *premĕre,* to press.]

suppurate, *sup'ū-rāt, v.i.* to gather pus or matter.—*n.* **suppura'tion,** the softening and liquefaction of inflamed tissue, with the production of pus.—*adj.* **supp'urative,** tending to suppurate: promoting suppuration.—*n.* a medicine which promotes suppuration. [L. *suppūrāre, -ātum*—*sub,* under, *pūs, pūris, pus.*]

supra-, *s(y)ōō'pra-, pfx.* above, situated above:

upper [L. *supra,* above]:—e.g. **supramundane, supranasal, supramaxilla.**

supramundane, *s(y)ōō-pra-mun'dān, adj.* above the world. [**supra-,** above, and **mundane.**]

supranational, *s(y)ōō-prä-nash'ŏn-āl, adj.* overriding national sovereignty. [**supra-,** above, and **national.**]

supreme, *s(y)ōō-prēm', adj.* highest: greatest: most excellent.—*n.* **suprēm'acy,** state of being supreme: highest authority or power.—*adv.* **suprēme'ly.** [L. *suprēmus,* superl. of *superus,* high—*super,* above.]

supremo, *s(y)ōō-prā'mō, n.* a supreme head. [Sp.—L. *suprēmus,* highest.]

surcease, *sûr-sēs', (arch.) v.i.* and *v.t.* to cease, cause to cease.—*n.* (*arch.*) cessation. [O.Fr. *sursis,* pa.p. of *surseoir*—L. *supersedēre,* to refrain from.]

surcharge, *sûr-chärj', v.t.* to overcharge (a person): to charge in addition: to overload: to fill excessively (with): to mark (a postage stamp) with a surcharge.—*n.* **sur'charge,** an additional or abnormal tax or charge: an excessive load: an imprint on a postage stamp altering its original value. [Fr. *sur*—L. *super,* over, and **charge.**]

surcoat, *sûr'kōt, n.* an overcoat (generally applied to the tunic-like robe worn by knights over their armour). [O.Fr. *surcote, surcot*—*sur,* over, *cote,* a garment.]

surd, *sûrd, adj.* (*alg.*) involving surds: irrational: (*phonet.*) voiceless (q.v.).—*n.* (*alg.*) a quantity inexpressible by rational numbers, or which has no root. [L. *surdus,* deaf.]

sure, *shōōr, adj.* secure, safe: firm, strong: reliable, to be depended on, certain: certain (to do): certain, having apparently adequate grounds for belief, or for expectation: convinced (of, that).—*advs.* **sure,** firmly: safely: certainly; **surely,** firmly, safely: certainly, assuredly: as it would seem (often ironically).—*adjs.* **sure'-fire,** infallible; **sure'footed,** not liable to slip or stumble.—*adv.* **surefoot'edly.** —*ns.* **surefoot'edness; sure'ness.—sure enough,** in very fact. **be sure,** see to it that, **make sure,** to make certain; **to be sure,** (adverbial phrase) certainly: I admit. [O.Fr. *seur* (Fr. *sûr*)—L. *sēcūrus*—*se-,* apart from, *cūra,* care.]

Sûreté, *sûr-tā, n.* the French criminal investigation department. [Fr.]

surety, *shōōr'ti, n.* sureness, certainty: security against loss or for payment: a guarantee: one who undertakes responsibility for the default of another.—*n.* **sure'tyship,** state of being surety: obligation of one person to answer for another. [Doublet **security.**]

surf, *sûrf, n.* the foam made by the dashing of waves.—*adj.* **surf'y.**—*ns.* **surf'board,** a board on which a bather allows himself to be carried inshore by the surf; **surf'-riding,** riding on a surfboard. [Earlier *suffe.* Origin unknown.]

surface, *sûr'fis, n.* the exterior part of anything.—*adj.* of, on, or near a surface.—*v.t.* put a surface or finish on.—*v.t.* and *v.i.* bring, or rise, to surface, esp. of water: (*coll.*) to regain consciousness.—*ns.* **sur'face-man,** a miner employed in open-air working: a workman keeping a railway-track in repair: a repairer of road surfaces; **sur'face-ten'sion,** in liquids, that property in virtue of which a liquid surface behaves as if it were a stretched membrane. [Fr. *sur*, above, *face*, face.]

surfeit, *sûr'fit*, *v.t.* to fill to satiety and disgust.—*n.* excess in eating and drinking: sickness or satiety caused by such excess: excess.—*n.* **sur'feiting**, eating overmuch: gluttony. [O.Fr. *surfait*, excess—*sur-*, *sorfaire*, to augment—L. *super*, above, *facĕre*, *factum*, to make.]

surge, *sûrj*, *n.* the rising or swelling of a large wave: (*fig.*) a rising wave (e.g. of emotion, pain, sound, colour): of spacecraft, movement in the direction of travel.—*v.i.* to rise high: to move (forward) like a wave. [L. *surgĕre*, to rise.]

surgeon, *sûr'jŏn*, *n.* one who treats injuries or diseases by operations on the living body, e.g. by excision of injured or diseased parts: a naval doctor: a ship's doctor.—*ns.* **sur'geoncy**, **sur'geonship**, office or employment of a surgeon in one of the armed forces; **sur'gery**, act and art of treating diseases or injuries by operations: a doctor's or dentist's consulting room.—*adj.* **sur'gical**, pertaining to surgeons, or to surgery: done by surgery.—*adv.* **sur'gically.**—**surgical boot**, **shoe**, a boot, shoe designed to correct deformities of the foot. [A doublet of **chirurgeon** (q.v.).]

surloin. Same as **sirloin.**

surly, *sûr'li*, *adj.* ill-natured, growling, morose, uncivil: gloomy, angry.—*adv.* **sur'lily.**—*n.* **sur'liness.** [Earlier *sirly*, for **sir**, **like**—like a domineering or ungracious master.]

surmise, *sûr-mīz'*, *sûr'-*, *n.* (*rare*) a suspicion: conjecture: a conjecture.—*v.t.* to infer the existence of from slight evidence: to suppose, conjecture: to guess (e.g. the truth). [O.Fr.—*surmettre*, to accuse—L. *super*, upon, *mittĕre*, *missum*, to send.]

surmount, *sûr-mownt'*, *v.t.* (*rare*) to mount above, surpass: to top, be the top of: to climb over: (*fig.*) get past, to get the better of (e.g. a difficulty, temptation).—*adj.* **surmount'able**, that may be surmounted. [Fr.—*sur* (L. *super*), above, *monter*, to mount.]

surname, *sûr'nām*, *n.* a name over and above the Christian name: the family name.—*v.t.* to call by a surname. [Formed from Fr. *sur* (L. *super*), over and above, and Eng. **name**, on the analogy of Fr. *surnom*.]

surpass, *sûr-pas'*, *v.t.* (*arch.*) to pass beyond: to exceed, to excel, outdo: to be beyond the reach or capacity of (e.g. *to surpass understanding*, *description*, *one's skill*).—*adj.* **surpass'able**, that may be surpassed. [Fr.*surpasser*—*sur* (L. *super*), beyond, *passer*, to pass.]

surplice, *sûr'plis*, *n.* a white linen garment worn over the cassock by the clergy. [Fr. *surplis*—Low L. *superpellicium*, an over-garment—*pellis*, skin.]

surplus, *sûr'plus*, *n.* the overplus, excess above what is required. [Fr., from *sur* (L. *super*), over, *plus*, more.]

surprise, *sûr-prīz'*, *n.* act of taking unawares: the emotion caused by anything sudden and/or unexpected—a less strong word than *astonishment* or *amazement*.—*v.t.* to come upon suddenly or unawares: to lead or bring unawares, to betray (with *into*, *out of*—e.g. *to*

surprise him into an admission; *to surprise an admission out of him*): to strike with wonder or astonishment.—*adj.* **surpris'ing.**—*adv.* **surpris'ingly.** [Fr.,—*surpris*, pa.p. of *surprendre*—L. *super*, over,*prehendĕre*, to catch.]

surrealism, *su-rē'ál-izm*, *n.* a form of art claiming to express activities of the unconscious mind, escaping the control of reason and all preconceptions.—*n.* and *adj.* **surrē'alist.** [Fr. *surréalisme*—*sur*, above, *réalisme*, realism.]

surrender, *su-ren'dér*, *v.t.* to deliver over, yield (to another): to give up, relinquish (e.g. a right a claim): to abandon (oneself to, e.g. grief).—*v.i.* to yield up oneself to another.—*n.* act or fact of surrendering. [O.Fr. *surrendre*, from *sur* (L.*super*), over,*rendre* (L.*reddĕre*), to render.]

surreptitious, *sûr-ep-ti'shús*, *adj.* done by stealth or fraud: enjoyed secretly.—*adv.* **surrepti'tiously.** [L., from *surripĕre*, *surreptum*, to take away secretly—*sub*, under, *rapĕre*, to seize.]

surrogate, *sûr'ō-gāt*, *n.* a substitute, deputy: a person or thing standing for another person or thing: the deputy of a bishop or his chancellor: a thing, substance used as a substitute. [L. *surrogāre*, *-ātum*—*sub*, in the place of, *rogāre*, to ask.]

surround,*su-rownd'*, *v.t.* to come round about: to come round about in order to cut off communications or to lay siege to: to lie round about, encompass, encircle (*lit.* and *fig.*).—*n.* a border, esp. the floor or floor-covering round a carpet.—*adj.* **surround'ing**, encompassing: neighbouring.—*n.* an encompassing: (*pl.*) things which surround, external circumstances, environment. [O.Fr. *suronder*—L. *superundāre*, to overflow; meaning influenced by confusion with **round.**]

surtax, *sûr'taks*, *n.* an additional tax. [Fr. *sur*, over, and **tax.**]

surtout, *sûr-tōō'*, *-tōōt'*, *n.* a close-bodied frockcoat. [Fr.,—*sur*, over, *tout*, all.]

surveillance, *sûr-vāl'(y)áns*, *n.* a being vigilant or watchful: supervision. [Fr.,—*surveiller*—*sur* (L.*super*), over,*veiller* (L.*vigilāre*), to watch.]

survey, *sûr-vā'*, *v.t.* to see or look over: (*fig.*) to take a general view of: to inspect, examine: to measure and estimate the position, extent, contours of (e.g. a piece of land).—*ns.* **sur'vey**, oversight: a view: an examination: the measuring of land, or of a country; **survey'or**, an overseer, superintendent: one who examines the condition e.g. of roads: a measurer of land surfaces, &c.; **survey'orship.** [O.Fr. *surveoir*—L. *super*, over, *vidēre*, to see.]

survive, *sûr-vīv'*, *v.t.* to live longer than, to outlive: to come through alive.—*v.i.* to remain alive.—*n.* **survī'val**, the state of surviving: anything that survives: a relic.—*adj.* designed to help one to survive exposure or other dangerous condition.—*n.* **survī'vor**, one who lives on after another's death: one who survives (e.g. a disaster).—**survī'vorship.—survival of the fittest** (see under **natural selection**). [Fr.,—L. *super*, beyond, *vīvĕre*, to live.]

susceptible, *su-sep'ti-bl*, *adj.* liable to be affected by (with *to*; e.g. *susceptible to colds, flattery, feminine charm*): easily affected, impressionable: capable (of), admitting (of—e.g. *suscep-*

Neutral vowels in unaccented syllables: *em'pér-ór*; for certain sounds in foreign words see p. ix.

740

tible of proof, of a specified interpretation).— *n.* **susceptibil'ity,** quality of being susceptible: sensibility: (in *pl.*) feelings.—*adv.* **suscep'tibly.**—*adj.* **suscep'tive,** receptive of emotional impressions: susceptible. [Fr.,—L. *suscipĕre, susceptum,* to take up—*sub,* up, *capĕre,* to take.]

suspect, *sus-pekt', v.t.* to mistrust (e.g. *to suspect one's motives*): to imagine to be guilty: to conjecture, be inclined to think (that).—*n.* (*sus'pekt* or *-pekt'*) a person suspected.—*adj.* suspected, open to suspicion. [L. *suspicĕre, suspectum,* to look at secretly—*sub,* up, *specĕre,* to look.]

suspend, *sus-pend', v.t.* to hang: to hold floating in a fluid, hold in suspension (q.v.): to discontinue, or discontinue the operation of, for a time (e.g. *to suspend publication, a law*): to debar for a time from a privilege, &c.: to defer, postpone.—*ns.* **suspen'ded-anima'tion,** the temporary cessation of the outward signs and of some of the functions of life—due to asphyxia, drowning, strangulation; **suspen'der,** one who, or that which, suspends: one of a pair of straps to support socks, stockings, or trousers; **suspense',** state of being suspended: temporary cessation: anxious uncertainty; **suspen'sion,** act of suspending: state of being suspended: a system in which denser particles, which are at least microscopically visible, are distributed through a less dense liquid or gas, settling being hindered either by the viscosity of the fluid or by the impact of its molecules on the particles: temporary privation of office or privilege: in a motor vehicle or railway carriage, the system of springs, &c., supporting the chassis on the axles; **suspen'sion-bridge,** a bridge in which the road way is supported from chains or cables stretched between elevated piers; **suspension-building,** building round a concrete core and from the top downward—*adj.* **suspen'sory,** that suspends.—*n.* that which suspends: a supporting bandage.—**suspend payment,** to discontinue payments due to creditors and thus to incur bankruptcy. [L. *suspendĕre—sub,* beneath, *pendĕre, pensum,* to hang.]

suspicion, *sus-pish(ŏ)n, n.* act of suspecting: an opinion formed or entertained on slender evidence: mistrust: (*coll.*) a very slight amount.—*adj.* **suspi'cious,** showing suspicion: inclined to suspect: exciting suspicion (e.g. *actions*).—*adv.* **suspi'ciously.**—*n.* **suspi'ciousness.** [Through O.Fr. from L.L. *suspectiō*—L. *suspicĕre* (see **suspect**): influenced by L. *suspicio, -onis,* distrust.]

sustain, *sus-tān', v.t.* to hold up, bear the weight of, support: to maintain (e.g. *to sustain the deception*; *a sustained effort*): to prolong (e.g. a musical note): to give strength to, enable to endure (e.g. *sustained by the belief that*): to nourish: to endure, bear up under (an affliction of any kind): to uphold the legality or rightness of: to corroborate, confirm: to act (a character, part).—*adjs.* **sustain'able,** that may be sustained; **sustained',** kept up at one uniform pitch.—*ns.* **sustain'er,** one who, or that which, sustains: the main motor in a rocket, continuing with it throughout its flight; **sus'tenance,** that which sustains: maintenance:

nourishment (*lit.* and *fig.*): food and drink; **sustenta'tion,** support, maintenance. [L. *sustinēre—sub,* up, *tenēre,* to hold.]

sutler, *sut'lér, n.* a person who followed an army and sold liquor or provisions, a camphawker.—*adj.* **sut'ling,** pertaining to sutlers: engaged in the occupation of a sutler. [O.Du. *soeteler,* (now *zoetelaar*), a small trader—*soetelen,* to do mean work.]

suttee, *sut'ē, sut-ē', n.* a usage long prevalent in India, in accordance with which the faithful widow burned herself on the funeral pyre along with her husband's body: a Hindu widow who died thus. [Sans. *satī,* a true wife.]

suture, *s(y)ōō'tyúr, n.* a line of junction of two structures: an immovable articulation between bones as between the various bones of the cranium and face: (*bot.*) a line of union between two adjacent edges, or of dehiscence: (*surg.*) the sewing up of a wound.—*adj.* **su'tured,** having, or united by, sutures. [L. *sūtūra—suĕre,* to sew.]

suzerain, *s(y)ōō'ze-rān, n.* a feudal lord: supreme or paramount ruler.—*n.* **su'zerainty** the dominion of a suzerain: paramount authority: nominal sovereignty. [O.Fr.,—L. *sursum* (*sub-vorsum*), on high.]

svelte, *svelt, adj.* slender, supple and graceful. [Fr.]

swab, *swob, n.* a mop for cleaning or drying floors or decks, or for cleaning out the bore of a cannon: (*med.*) an absorbent pad, as of cotton-wool: a specimen of a morbid secretion taken on a swab for bacteriological examination.—*v.t.* to clean or dry with a mop or swab: to coat (with) by means of a swab:—*pr.p.* **swabb'ing;** *pa.t.* and *pa.p.* **swabbed.**—*n.* **swabb'er,** one who, or that which, swabs. [Du. *zwabber,* a swabber, *zwabberen,* to swab; Ger. *schwabber.*]

swaddle, *swod'l, v.t.* to swathe or bind tight with clothes, as an infant.—*n.pl.* **swadd'ling-clothes,** bands of cloth, or clothes, swathed round an infant: (*fig.*) the condition of being very young and immature. [O.E. *cwæthel, swethel,* a bandage; cf. **swathe.**]

swag, *swag, v.i.* to sway: to sag.—*n.* (*slang*) a bundle, pack, or booty: booty obtained by theft or plunder. [Related to **sway**]

swagger, *swag'ér, v.i.* to swing the body proudly or defiantly: to brag noisily, to bully.—*n.* boastfulness: insolence of manner: a self confident, swinging gait.—*adj.* (*slang*) very fashionable.—*n.* **swagg'erer.** [A frequentative of **swag.**]

Swahili, *swä-hē'li, n.* (a member of) a people of Zanzibar and the opposite coast, belonging to the Bantu stock, with an infusion of Arab blood: the language of this people:—*pl.* **Swahili,** also **-lis.**

swain, *swān, n.* (*obs.*) a young man: a peasant: an admirer, suitor. [O.N. *sveinn,* young man, servant, Dan. *svend,* servant.]

swallow, *swol'ō, n.* any of numerous migratory birds with long wings, which seize their insect food on the wing.—*ns.* **swall'ow-dive,** a dive during which one's arms are outstretched to the sides (also *v.i.*); **swall'ow-tail,** a forked and tapering tail: a tailed dress coat: any of numerous butterflies having a tail-like process on each of the hind wings. [O.E. *swalewe*; Ger. *schwalbe*.]

swallow, *swol'ō*, *v.t.* to receive through the gullet into the stomach: to engulf: to absorb: (*fig.*) to retract: to accept without protest: to accept as true. [O.E. *swelgan*, to swallow; cog. with Ger. *schwelgen.*]

swam, *swam*, *pa.t.* of **swim**.

swamp, *swomp*, *n.* wet, spongy land, low ground saturated with water.—*v.t.* to sink in, or (*fig.*) as in, a swamp: to overset, or cause to fill with water, as a boat.—*adj.* **swamp'y**, consisting of swamp: wet and spongy. [Prob. of Low German origin.]

swan, *swon*, *n.* a group of birds constituting a distinct section of the duck family, having a very long neck and noted for grace and stateliness of movement on the water.—*ns.* **swann'- ery**, a place where swans are kept and tended; **swan's'-down**, the down or under-plumage of a swan: (usu. **swans'down**) a cotton of the fustian type, bleached and with a raised surface, or piece-dyed; **swan'-shot**, a shot of large size, like buck-shot; **swan'-song**, the fabled song of a swan just before its death: a poet's or musician's last work: last work of any kind: final appearance.—**swan around** (*coll.*), to move about aimlessly. [O.E. *swan*; Ger. *schwan*, Du. *zwaan*.]

swank, *swangk*, *n.* (*slang*) bragging or ostentation.—*v.i.* to show off.—*adj.* **swank'y**, boastful, ostentatious: stylish. [O.E. *swancer*, pliant; Ger. *schwank.*]

swap, *swop*. Same as **swop**.

sward, *swörd*, *n.* the grassy surface of land: green turf.—*v.t.* to cover with sward.—*adjs.* **sward'ed**, **sward'y**, covered with sward. [O.E. *sweard*, skin, rind; Du. *zwoord*, Ger. *schwarte.*]

sware, *swār* (*B.*), pa.t. of **swear**.

swarm, *swörm*, *n.* a large number of small animals in movement together, esp. a number of bees migrating under the guidance of a queen to establish a new colony: a great number, throng.—*v.i.* to gather as bees: to appear in a crowd, to throng: to abound (with), teem (with). [O.E. *swearm*; Ger. *schwarm.*]

swarm, *swörm*, *v.t.* and *v.i.* to climb by scrambling up by means of arms and legs (often with *up*). [Origin uncertain.]

swarthy, *swörтнi*, *adj.* of a blackish complexion, dark-skinned—also **swart**, **swarth**.—*adv.* **swarth'ily**.—*n.* **swarth'iness**. [O.E. *sweart*; O.N. *svartr*, Ger. *schwarz*, black.]

swash, *swosh*, *v.t.* to dash or splash.—*n.* **swash'buck'ler**, literally, one who clashes his shield (buckler) defiantly—a bully, a blusterer.—*v.i.* (back formation) **swash'buckle**, most commonly used as *p.adj.* **swash'buckling** (also *n.*). [Imit.]

swastika, **swastica**, *swas'ti-ka*, *swos'-*, *n.* a widespread religious symbol of the form of a cross with equal arms and a limb of the same length projecting (clockwise or counterclockwise) from the end of each arm, adopted as the badge of the Nazi party under Adolf Hitler. [Sans. *svastika*, fortunate.]

swat, *swot*, *v.t.* to hit smartly or heavily.—*n.* a sharp or heavy blow.—*n.* **swatt'er**, a flexible fly-killer. [**squat**.]

swath, *swöth*, *n.* a line of grass or corn cut by the

scythe: a strip: the sweep of a scythe.—Also **swathe** (*swāтн*). [O.E. *swathu*, a track.]

swathe, *swāтн*, *v.t.* to bind, wrap round, with a band or bandage, or with loose material: also *fig.*—*n.* a bandage. [O.E. *swethian*; cf. **swaddle**.]

sway, *swā*, *v.t.* to swing, cause to oscillate, with the hand: to incline to one side, esp. *fig.* to influence by power or moral force: to govern.—*v.i.* to incline to one side: to oscillate: to have weight or influence.—*n.* the motion of swaying: the power that moves: controlling influence: jurisdiction. [M.E. *sweyen*, from Scand. or Low Ger.]

swear, *swār*, *v.i.* to make a solemn declaration, promise, &c., calling God to witness: to give evidence on oath: to utter the name of God or of sacred things profanely.—*v.t.* to utter (an oath), calling God to witness: to administer an oath to: to declare on oath:—*pa.t.* swōre; *pa.p.* sworn.—*n.* **swear'er**.—**swear away**, to bring about the loss of by swearing; **swear by**, to put complete confidence in; **swear in**, to inaugurate by oath; **swear off**, to renounce, abstain from; **swear to**, to identify, or to affirm the truth or accuracy of, with certainty. [O.E. *swerian*; Du. *zweren*, Ger. *schwören.*]

sweat, *swet*, *n.* the moisture from the skin, perspiration: moisture in drops on any surface: the state of one who sweats: a spell of sweating induced for curative purposes: (*coll.*) labour, drudgery: a state of fidgety anxiety: (*slang*) a soldier.—*v.i.* to give out sweat or moisture: to toil, drudge: to suffer penalty, smart.—*v.t.* to give out (sweat or other moisture): to cause to sweat or give out moisture: to get rid of by sweating (with *out*, *away*): (*fig.*) to produce laboriously (with *out*): to squeeze money or extortionate interest from: to oppress by exacting incessant and unhealthy labour for shamefully inadequate wages.—*ns.* **sweat'er**, one who sweats, or that which causes sweating: a jersey (*orig.* heavy, used by athletes); **sweat'-shirt**, a shortsleeved sweater; **sweat'-shop**, a factory or shop where the workers are oppressed.—*adj.* **sweat'y**, wet with sweat: consisting of sweat: laborious.—*n.* **sweat'iness**. [O.E. *swāt*, sweat, *swǽtan*, to sweat; Du. *zweet*; Low Ger. *sweet*, Ger. *schweiss.*]

Swede, *swēd*, *n.* a native of *Sweden*: (without *cap.*) a Swedish turnip.—*adj.* **Swed'ish**, pertaining to Sweden.—*n.* the Scandinavian language of Sweden.

sweep, *swēp*, *v.t.* to remove dirt, &c., from with a brush or broom: to drag over (e.g. a river bottom): to gather together by sweeping: to carry (away, down, off, along) by a long brushing stroke: to strike with a long, esp. light, stroke: (*fig.*) to rid of, make free from, by vigorous action (e.g. *he swept the seas of enemy ships*): (*fig.*—with *off*) to remove by force, or by strong measures, or in a highhanded manner: to traverse (e.g. the seas): to pass rapidly (over), or to pass rapidly over (with e.g. one's eyes, a telescope).—*v.i.* to pass swiftly and forcibly: to pass with pomp: to move with a long reach: to curve widely:—*pa.t.* and *pa.p.* swept.—*n.* act of sweeping: extent of a stroke, or of anything turning or in motion: a sweeping movement: compass, range: a

Neutral vowels in unaccented syllables: *em'pėr-ŏr*; for certain sounds in foreign words see p. ix.

curve: a chimney-sweeper: a very long oar: (*coll.*) a sweepstake: (*coll.*) a dirty scoundrel.—*adj.* sweep'ing, that sweeps: comprehensive, complete (e.g. changes, victory): taking no account of exceptions, or insufficient account of facts or evidence (e.g. statements, charges).—*n.* sweep'er.—*adv.* sweep'ingly, in a sweeping manner.—*n.pl.* sweep'ings, things collected by sweeping: rubbish.—*n.* sweep'-stake(s), a method of gambling or competition by which the total amount staked by the entrants is divided among the winners.
sweep off one's feet, (*fig.*) to inspire one with such enthusiasm, or fill one with such rapturous emotion, that one no longer consults judgment or common sense.—make a clean sweep, to clear away, get rid of, everything that may be regarded as rubbish (*fig.* to turn all the hide-bound or incompetent, or all those of a different party, out of office). [O.E. *swāpan*; Ger. *schweifen*; cf. swoop.]
sweet, *swēt, adj.* pleasing to the taste: tasting like sugar: pleasing to other senses—fragrant, melodious, beautiful: fresh, as opposed to salt or to sour: fresh, not stale, sour, or putrid: amiable, kindly, gracious.—*n.* a sweet substance: a term of endearment: (*pl.*) sweetmeats, confections.—*n.* sweet'ness.—*adj.* sweet'-and-sour', cooked with sugar, and vinegar or lemon juice, soya sauce, &c.—*ns.* sweet'bread, the pancreas of an animal used for food; sweet'-bri'er, -bri'ar, a rose with many prickles, having a single flower and scented leaves.—*v.t.* sweet'en, to make sweet: to make pleasing, mild, or kind: to make pure, free from sourness.—*v.i.* to become sweet.—*ns.* sweet'ener; sweet'ening, act of sweetening: that which sweetens; sweet'-gale (see gale (2)), sweet'heart, a lover, darling.—*n.pl.* sweet'ies, confections. *adj.* sweet'ish, somewhat sweet to the taste.—*adv.* sweet'ly.—*ns.* sweet'meat, a confection made wholly or chiefly of sugar; sweet'-pea, a pea cultivated for its fragrance and beauty, sweet'-pota'to, also called batata, a twining plant in tropical and subtropical countries, having large sweetish edible tubers; sweet'-will'iam, a species of pink of many colours and varieties. sweet on, enamoured of. [O.E. *swēte*; Ger. *süss*, Gr. *hēdys*, L. *suāvis*, Sans. *svādu*, sweet.]
swell, *swel, v.i.* to expand, to be inflated: to rise into waves: to heave: to bulge out: to become elated, arrogant, or angry: to grow louder.—*v.t.* to increase the size of, or number of: to increase the sound of: to raise to arrogance:—*pa.p.* swelled or swollen (*swōln, swōl'ēn*).—*n.* act of swelling: a bulge: increase in size: an increase and a succeeding decrease in the volume of a tone: a gradual rise of ground: a wave or succession of waves rolling in one direction, as after a storm: a piece of mechanism in an organ for producing a swell of tone: (*slang*) a dandy, one elaborately and fashionably dressed, an important person.—*adj.* (*slang*) befitting a swell: (*slang*) a vague term of commendation.—*n.* swell'ing, a protuberance: a tumour: a rising, as of passion.—swelled head, self-conceit. [O.E. *swellan*; Ger. *schwellen.*]
swelter, *swelt'er, v.i.* to be faint or oppressed

with heat.—*n.* a condition of oppressive heat.—*p.adj.* swelt'ering, oppressively hot.—Also swelt'ry.—*adv.* swelt'eringly. [O.E. *sweltan*, to die.]
swept, *swept, pa.t.* and *pa.p.* of sweep.
swerve, *swûrv, v.i.* to turn, deviate (from a line or course): (*fig.*) to turn aside (from the right course of action or conduct).—*n.* an act of swerving. [M.E.; origin uncertain.]
swift, *swift, adj.* moving, or able to move, quickly—fleet or fast: rapid, taking only a short time: not long delayed, speedy: quick in action.—*n.* a family of birds with long pointed wings, a short tail, and remarkable powers of rapid and prolonged flight—superficially resembling swallows.—*adv.* swift'ly.—*n.* swift'ness. [O.E. *swift*, from same root as swoop.]
swig, *swig, n.* a large draught.—*v.t.* to drink by large draughts, to gulp down.
swill, *swil, v.t.* or *v.i.* to drink greedily or copiously: to wash, rinse.—*n.* a large draught of liquor: semi-liquid food from kitchen-waste, &c., given esp. to pigs.—*n.* swill'er. [O.E. *swilian*, to wash.]
swim, *swim, v.i.* to float, not to sink: to move on or in water by using limbs or fins: to glide along, or simply to move with a gliding motion: to be dizzy: to be drenched, overflow, abound (with).—*v.t.* to cross by swimming: to make to swim or float:—*pr.p.* swimm'ing; *pa.t.* swam; *pa.p.* swum.—*n.* act of swimming: any motion like swimming: a dizziness: the swim-bladder of a fish.—*ns.* swimm'er, one who swims: a web-footed aquatic bird; swimbladder, a fish's air-bladder (q.v.); swimm'ing, the act of floating or moving on or in the water: gliding motion: dizziness; swimm'ing-bath, a bath large enough for swimming in.—*adv.* swimm'ingly, in a gliding manner, as if swimming: smoothly, successfully.—*ns.* swimm'ing-pond, -pool, artificial pond, pool adapted for swimming in, swim'suit, a garment for bathing in.—in the swim, in the main current of affairs, business, fashion, &c. [O.E. *swimman*; Gr. *schwimmen.*]
swindle, *swin'dl, v.t.* and *v.i.* to cheat.—*n.* the act of swindling or defrauding: a fraud: anything not what it appears to be.—*n.* swin'dler. [Ger. *schwindler*, a cheat—*schwindeln*, to be giddy.]
swine, *swīn, n.sing.* and *pl.* a quadruped with bristly skin and long snout, reared for its flesh—a pig: pigs collectively: (*coll.*) a low person.—*n.* swine'herd, a herd or keeper of swine. [O.E. *swīn*, a pig; Ger. *schwein*, L. (adj.) *suīnus—sūs*, Gr. *hȳs.*]
swing, *swing, v.i.* to sway or wave to and fro, as a body hanging in air: to oscillate (*lit.* and *fig.*): to hang (from): to move forward with swaying rhythmical gait: to turn round on some fixed centre, as a ship at anchor, a door on its hinges: to turn quickly: to move to and fro on a swinging seat: to be hanged: to attract, excite: (*coll.*) to be perfectly appropriate to place or mood: (*coll.*) to be full of vitality: (*coll.*) to be up-to-date: (*coll.*) to be thoroughly responsive (to jazz, any of the arts, any aspect of living).—*v.t.* to move to and fro, to cause to wave or vibrate: to whirl, to brandish: to cause to wheel or turn as about some point: to influence the result of (e.g. a doubtful elec-

tion) in favour of an individual or party: to play (music) as swing:—*pa.t.* and *pa.p.* swung.—*n.* the act of swinging: motion to and fro: a vigorous swinging motion: a seat suspended for swinging in: the sweep or compass of a swinging body: influence or force of anything put in motion: vigorous sweeping rhythm: jazz music in which the basic melody and rhythm are overlaid with impromptu variations &c.—*ns.* **swing′boat,** a boat-shaped carriage swung from a frame, in use at fairs, &c.; **swing′-bridge,** a bridge that may be moved aside by swinging, at the mouth of docks, &c.; **swing-door,** a door which swings freely on special hinges, so that it can be pushed (or pulled) open from either side; **swing′ing,** the act of moving back and forth, esp. the pastime of moving in a swing.—*adj.* having a free easy motion: (*coll.*) fully alive to, and appreciative of, the most recent trends and fashions in living: (*coll.*) up-to-date: (*coll.*) gay.—**in full swing,** in mid career, in fully active operation; **swing the lead,** to malinger, to lie to avoid work. [O.E. *swingan*; Ger. *schwingen,* to swing.]

swinge, *swinj, v.t.* (*arch.*) to beat, chastise.—*adj.* **swinge′ing,** tremendous (of a blow or a lie). [O.E. *swengan,* to shake, a causal form of *swingan,* to swing.]

swingle, swingel, *swing′gl, n.* a wooden instrument for beating flax: the part of the flail which falls on the grain in threshing.—*ns.* **swing′le-tree, sing′le-tree,** the cross-piece of a carriage, plough, &c., to which the traces of a harnessed horse are fixed. [**swing.**]

swinish, *swī′nish, adj.* like or befitting swine: gross, sensual, bestial.—*adv.* **swin′ishly.**—*n.* **swin′ishness.** [**swine.**]

swipe, *swīp, n.* a wild blow.—*v.t.* and *v.i.* to hit hard and somewhat wildly.—*n.* **swī′per.** [O.E. *swipe,* a whip.]

swirl, *swûrl, v.t.* and *v.i.* to sweep along with a whirling motion.—*n.* whirling motion, as of wind or water: an eddy. [Orig. Scot.; cf. Norw. *svirla,* to whirl round.]

swish, *swish, v.t.* to brandish, or to strike, with a whistling sound: to flog.—*v.i.* to move with a hissing sound.—*n.* a swishing sound. [Imit.]

swish, *swish, adj.* (*coll.*) smart.

Swiss, *swis, adj.* of or belonging to *Switzerland.*—*n.* a native of Switzerland: a High German dialect, spoken by most of the natives of Switzerland. [Middle High Ger. *swiz.*]

switch, *swich, n.* a small flexible twig: a whip: a separate tail of hair attached to supplement the wearer's own hair: a device which, by means of movable sections of rails, transfers rolling stock from one track to another: a mechanical device for opening or closing an electric circuit: an act of switching, a changing, change (-over).—*v.t.* to strike with a switch: to swing, whisk: to transfer from one line of rails to another by a switch: (*fig.*) to divert (e.g. the conversation—with *to*): to change over: to divert (on to another circuit) by means of a switch: to turn (off, on, e.g. current, light) by means of a switch.—*v.i.* to change over (from, to).—*ns.* **switch′back,** (*orig.*) a zigzag railway, so arranged that a train making a steep ascent runs into a siding,

from which it passes out along another line at an acute angle to the first: a short length of undulating railway, along which a car runs by its own weight: up-and-down road; **switch′-board,** (*elect.*) an assembly of switch-panels: a board with the apparatus necessary for making temporary connections between telephones, &c.; **switch′(board)-pan′el,** a sheet of slate, marble, or other material on which instruments, switches, relays, &c., are mounted; **switch′-over,** changeover.—**switched on,** (*coll.*) aware of and responsive to recent trends and fashions: (*slang*) under the influence of drugs. [Old Du. *swick,* a whip.]

swivel, *swiv′l, n.* something fixed in another body so as to turn round it: a ring or link that turns round on a pin or neck.—*v.i.* to turn on a pin or pivot. [O.E. *swīfan,* to move quickly, to turn round.]

swiz, *swiz′,* **swizzle,** *swiz′l, ns.* (*slang*) fraud: great disappointment. [Poss. from **swindle.**]

swollen, *pa.p.* of **swell.**

swoon, *swōōn, v.t.* to faint, fall into a fainting-fit.—*n.* the act of swooning: a fainting-fit. [O.E. *geswōgen,* fainted, pa.p. of a lost verb.]

swoop, *swōōp, v.t.* to sweep down upon and seize (often with *up*).—*v.i.* to descend with a sweep.—*n.* the act of swooping: a seizing, as of its prey by a bird.—**at one (fell) swoop,** (*fig.*) all at once, at one stroke. [O.E. *swāpan,* to sweep.]

swop, swop, *v.t.* to exchange, to barter.—*pr.p.* swopp′ing; *pa.t.* and *pa.p.* swopped.—*n.* an exchange.—Also **swap.** [Perh. connected with obs. *swap,* a blow.]

sword, *sōrd, sōrd, n.* an offensive weapon with a long blade, sharp on one or both edges, for cutting or thrusting: destruction by the sword or by war: military force: the emblem of vengeance or justice, or of authority and power. —*ns.* **sword′-arm, -hand,** the arm, hand, that wields the sword; **sword′-bear′er,** a public officer who carries the sword of state; **sword′-belt,** a military belt from which the sword is hung; **sword′-cane, -stick,** a cane or stick containing a sword; **sword′craft,** skill with the sword; **sword′-dance,** a dance over and between crossed swords, or one in which there is a display of naked swords; **sword′fish,** a large fish, with a sword-like prolongation of the upper jaw; **sword′-guard,** the part of a sword-hilt that protects the user's hand; **sword′-knot,** a ribbon tied to the hilt of a sword; **sword′-play,** fencing: skilful repartee or argument; **swords′man,** a man skilled in the use of a sword; **swords′manship.** [O.E. *sweord*; Ger. *schwert.*]

swore, sworn. See **swear.**

sworn, *swōrn, swōrn, adj.* that has taken an oath: attested by oath.—**sworn enemy, friend,** &c., one who has vowed to treat another as an enemy, friend, &c.—an inveterate enemy, devoted friend, &c.

swot, *swot,* (*coll.*) *v.t.* and *v.i.* to study hard, esp. by memorising for an examination.—*n.* (often contemptuously) one who swots. [A form of **sweat.**]

swum, *swum, pa.p.* of **swim.**

swung, *swung, pa.t.* and *pa.p.* of **swing.**

Sybarite, *sib′a-rīt, n.* an inhabitant of *Sybaris,* a

Neutral vowels in unaccented syllables: *em′pér-ór*; for certain sounds in foreign words see p. ix.

Greek city in ancient Italy, noted for the effeminacy and luxury of its inhabitants: one devoted to luxury.—*adjs.* **sybarit′ic, -al.**

sycamine, *sik′a-mīn, n.* (*B.*) supposed to be the black mulberry-tree. [Gr. *sȳkamīnos.*]

sycamore, *sik′a-mōr, -mōr, n.* a fruit-tree of the fig family, common in Palestine, &c.—the sycamore of the Bible: a species of maple, in Scotland usually called *plane-tree*: in America, any of the plane trees. [Gr. *sȳkomoros—sȳkon,* a fig, *moron, black mulberry.*]

sycophant, *sik′ō-fant, n.* a servile flatterer.—*n.* **syc′ophancy,** the behaviour of a sycophant: obsequious flattery.—Also **sycophant′ism.**— *adjs.* **sycophant′ic, -al, sycophant′ish,** like a sycophant, obsequiously flattering, parasitic. [Gr. *sȳkophantēs,* usually said to mean one who informed against persons exporting figs from Attica or plundering the sacred fig-trees; but more prob. one who brings figs to light by shaking the tree, hence one who makes rich men yield up their fruit—*sȳkon,* a fig, *phainein,* to show.]

syllable, *sil′a-bl, n.* a word or part of a word uttered by a single effort of the voice.—*v.t.* to pronounce syllable by syllable: to utter.—*adjs.* **syllab′ic, -al,** consisting of, constituting, a syllable: articulated in syllables.—*adv.* **syllab′ically.**—*vs.t.* **syllab′icate, syllab′ify** (*pa.t.* and *pa.p.* syllab′ified), to form into syllables.—*ns.* **syllabica′tion, syllabifica′tion.** [L. *syllaba*—Gr. *syllabē*—*syn,* with, *lambanein,* to take.]

syllabub, *sil′a-bub, n.* Same as **sillabub.**

syllabus, *sil′a-bus, n.* an abstract: a table of contents: a programme, e.g. of a course of lectures.—*pl.* **syll′abuses, syll′abī.** [L.]

syllogism, *sil′ō-jizm, n.* a logical form of argument, consisting of three propositions, of which the first two are called the premises (major and minor), and the last, which follows from them, the conclusion, e.g. 'all men are fallible', James is a man, therefore James is fallible'. The truth of the conclusion depends on the truth of the premises; for instance, an argument having as major premise 'all dogs bark', or one having as minor premise 'Gelert was a wolf', might lead to a conclusion not in accordance with fact.—*v.i.* **syll′ogise,** to reason by syllogisms.—*adjs.* **syllogis′tic, -al,** pertaining to a syllogism: in the form of a syllogism.—*adv.* **syllogis′tically.** [Gr. *syllogismos—syllogizesthai—syn,* together, *logizesthai,* to reckon—*logos,* speech.]

sylph, *silf, n.* according to the system or view of the universe set forth by Paracelsus (1493-1541), one of the elemental spirits of the air, intermediate between immaterial and material beings, occasionally holding intercourse with human creatures: a slender woman. [Fr. *sylphe,* of Celtic origin.]

sylvan. Same as **silvan.**

symbiosis, *sim-bī ō′sis, n.* the living together in close association or union of two organisms of different kinds, e.g. the union of algae and fungi to form lichen. Cf. *commensalism,* which, as its derivation implies, is a much less intimate connection.—*n.* **sym′biōn(t),** an organism living with another in symbiosis.—*adj.* **symbiot′ic.** [Gr. *symbioein—syn,* together, *bioein,* to live—*bios,* life.]

symbol, *sim′bol, n.* a thing accepted as representing another because it in some way suggests the essential quality of the other—in many cases interchangeable with *emblem,* but implying more strongly that the thing represented is worthy of reverence or cannot readily be expressed (e.g. *scales are an emblem of justice* ; *the cross is the symbol of Christianity* ; *white is the symbol of purity, purple of royalty*) : any of the conventional signs used for brevity of scientific expression, as in algebra, and esp. chemistry: (*theology*) a creed, compendium of doctrine, or a typical religious rite, as the Eucharist.—*adjs.* **symbol′ic, -al,** pertaining to, or of the nature of, a symbol: representing by signs: figurative: serving as a symbol (of).—*adv.* **symbol′ically.**—*v.i.* **sym′bolise,** to use symbols or symbolism.—*v.t.* to represent by symbols: to serve as symbol of.—*ns.* **sym′bolist,** one who uses symbols: one of a school of French writers in the late 19th and early 20th century who reacted against what had come to be known as realism in favour of idealism and the mystical (treating the actual as an expression of something underlying), and sought to make verse more subtle and musical; **sym′bolism,** representation by symbols or signs: a system of symbols: use of symbols in literature or art: the theory or practice of the symbolists: (*theology*) the study of the history and contents of Christian creeds. [Gr. *symbolon,* from *symballein—syn,* together, *ballein,* to throw.]

symmetry, *sim′e-tri, n.* the state in which one part exactly corresponds to another in size, shape, and position: harmony or adaptation of parts to each other.—*adjs.* **symmet′ric, -al,** having symmetry or due proportion in its parts.—*adv.* **symmet′rically,** with symmetry.—*v.t.* **symm′etrīse,** to make symmetrical. [L. and Ger. *symmetria—syn,* together, *metron,* a measure.]

sympathy, *sim′pa-thi, n.* a state of conformity of tastes and inclinations, or of understanding of one another's tastes and inclinations, or the goodwill based on such conformity or understanding: an association or relationship which produces the same or a similar reaction or response to a particular phenomenon: compassion, pity: condolences: conformity of parts in the fine arts.—*adjs.* **sympathet′ic, -al,** showing, or inclined to, sympathy: compassionate: produced by sympathy: congenial: inclined to support or favour (with *to, towards,* e.g. a scheme).—*adv.* **sympathet′ically.**—*v.i.* **sym′pathīse,** to feel with or for another: to express sympathy (with).—*n.* **sym′pathiser.** [Gr. *sympatheia—syn,* with, *pathos,* suffering.]

symphony, *sim′fō-ni, n.* (*arch.*) a consonance or harmony of sound: (*mus.*) a composition for a full orchestra in several movements: an instrumental movement in the midst of a choral work: harmony of any kind (e.g. of colour, emotion): something which, by its harmony and/or grandeur, suggests a symphony.—*adjs.* **symphon′ic,** relating to, or resembling, a symphony: symphonious; **sympho′nious,** agreeing or harmonising in sound, accordant, harmonious.—*n.* **sym′phonist,** a composer of

---

fāte, fär; mē, hûr (her); *mīne; mōte, för; mūte; mōōn, fōōt;* ᴛнen (then)

symphonies.—**symphonic poem**, a large orchestral composition, a form of programme (q.v.) music, usu. not divided into separate movements.—**choral symphony**, a symphony containing a movement for a chorus of singers. [Gr. *symphōnia—syn*, together, *phōnē*, a sound.]

symposium, *sim-pō'zi-um*, *n.* a drinking together: a banquet with philosophic conversation: an account of such conversation: a collection of essays on a single subject by various writers. [L.,—Gr. *symposion—syn*, together, *posis*, a drinking—*pīnein*, to drink.]

symptom, *sim(p)'tóm*, *n.* that which attends and indicates the existence of something else, not as a cause, but as a constant effect: (*med.*) that which indicates disease.—*adjs.* **symptomat'ic, -al**, pertaining to symptoms: indicating the existence (of something else): (*med.*) proceeding from some prior disorder.—*adv.* **symptomat'ically**. [Gr. *symptōma—sympiptein*, to coincide—*syn*, with, *piptein*, to fall.]

synagogue, *sin'a-gog*, *n.* an assembly of Jews for worship: a Jewish place of worship.—*adjs.* **syn'agogal, synagogical** (*-goj'-*). [Fr.,—Gr. *synagōgē—synagein*, to assemble—*syn*, together, *agein*, to lead.]

syncarpous, *sin-kär'pus*, *adj.* (*bot.*—of a gynaeceum) consisting of two or more united carpels.—*n.* **syn'carp**, a collective fruit. [Gr. *syn*, together, *karpos*, a fruit.]

synchromesh gear, *sing'krō-mesh gēr*, a gear in which the speeds of the driving and the driven members which it is desired to couple are first automatically synchronised so as to avoid shock and noise in gear changing. [**synchronous**, and **mesh**.]

synchronous, *sing'krō-nus*, *adj.* happening or being at the same time, simultaneous: having the same period, or period and phase.—Also **syn'chronal**.—*v.i.* **syn'chronīse**, to be simultaneous (e.g. *B's arrival synchronised with A's departure*): to agree in time (e.g. *the movements of the lips in the picture did not synchronise with the sound of the words*).—*v.t.* to cause to happen at the same time: to tabulate (e.g. events) so as to show coincidence in time: to cause (clocks) to agree in time: to adjust two alternating current machines so that their speeds of rotation are such as to make their electrical frequencies identical: to add (sound, dialogue, &c) in time with the action to a motion picture: to provide (a picture) with sound effects.—*ns.* **synchronīsā'tion; synchronīser; syn'chronism**, concurrence of events in time: the tabular arrangement of contemporary events, &c., in history: the state of being synchronous: synchronised operation.—*adj.* **synchronis'tic**, showing synchronism.—*adv.* **synchronis'tically**. [Gr. *synchronismos—synchronizein*, to agree in time—*syn*, together, *chronos*, time.]

syncopate, *sing'kō-pāt*, *v.t.* to contract a word by taking away letters from the middle: (*mus.*) to alter rhythm by transferring the accent to a normally unaccented beat.—*ns.* **syncopā'tion**, act of syncopating: state of being syncopated; **syn'cope**, the omission of letters from the middle of a word (e.g. *ne'er* for *never*): (*med.*) a fainting-fit, an attack in which the breath-

ing and circulation become faint: (*mus.*) syncopation. [Low L. *syncopāre, -ātum*—L. *syncopē*—Gr. *syn*, together, *koptein*, to cut off.]

syndic, *sin'dik*, *n.* formerly a magistrate in certain continental cities: the accredited agent of a city, or company: a member of the special committee of the Senate of Cambridge University.—*n.* **syn'dicāte**, a body of syndics, a council: the office of a syndic: the managers of a company or of a bankrupt's property: an association of merchants or others for the purpose of carrying through some important enterprise, or for securing a monopoly in the production or supply of some commodity, as material for publication: a combination of persons for some common purpose or interest: a group of newspapers under the same management.—*v.t.* (*U.S.*) to form a syndicate: to sell for simultaneous publication in a number of newspapers.—*ns.* **syn'dicalism**, a form of trade-unionism that arose in France in the late 19th century; its aim was to get economic and political power away from the capitalists and politicians into the hands of unions (*syndicats*) of workers: the theory or practice of this form of government; **syn'dicalist**.—*adj.* **syndicalist'ic**. [L. *syndicus*—Gr. *syndikos—syn*, with, *dikē*, justice.]

syndrome, *sin'drōm*, *n.* a characteristic pattern or group of symptoms of a disease. [Gr. *syndromē—syn*, together, *dramein*, to run.]

synecdoche, *sin-ek'do-kē*, *n.* a figure of speech by which a part is made to comprehend the whole, or the whole is put for a part, as *sail* for *ship*, *steel* for *sword*. [Gr. *synekdochē—syn*, together, *ekdechesthai*, to receive.]

synod, *sin'od*, *n.* an ecclesiastical council: among Presbyterians, a church court consisting of several presbyteries, to which these presbyteries are subordinate and which is subordinate to the General Assembly. [L. *synodus*—Gr. *synodos—syn*, together, *hodos*, a way.]

synonym, *sin'o-nim*, *n.* a word having the same, or very nearly the same, meaning as another or others (e.g. ass, donkey; brave, courageous; to hide, to conceal). Synonyms are not often identical in meaning and use; the following are some common differences:—(1) they may differ in shade of meaning or in implications (e.g. *terror* is stronger than *fear*; *opulent* implies adverse criticism while *rich* does not; *strabismus* is the technical word, *squint* the word in everyday use); (2) they may coincide in one sense, or a few senses, only (e.g. *ask*, *inquire*—both mean to put a question, but inquire does not mean to request, beg, or to invite); (3) one of them may be customary in a particular idiom (e.g. *to set at liberty*, not *freedom*).—*adj.* **synon'ymous**, pertaining to synonyms: expressing the same thing: having the same meaning as (with *with*).—*adv.* **synon'ymously**.—**be a synonym for, be synonymous with** (*fig.*), to seem to personify, to suggest very strongly (e.g. *the name of Nero has become a synonym for cruelty and profligacy*). [Gr. *synōnymon—syn*, with, *onoma*, a name.]

synopsis, *si-nop'sis*, *n.* a collective or general view of any subject, a summary:—*pl.* **syn-**

Neutral vowels in unaccented syllables: *em'pér-ór*; for certain sounds in foreign words see p. ix.

op'sēs.—*adjs.* synop'tic, -al, affording a general view of the whole.—*adv.* synop'tically.—
the synoptic gospels, the gospels of Matthew, Mark, and Luke, which have such a similarity in matter and form that they readily admit of being brought under one and the same combined view or *synopsis*. [Gr. *synopsis—syn*, with, together, *opsis*, a view.]

synovial, *sin-ō'vi-ål, adj.* of, pertaining to, syn-ō'via, a lubricating fluid occurring typically within tendon sheaths and the capsular ligaments surrounding movable joints.—*n.* synovī'tis, inflammation of the membrane lining a tendon sheath or a capsular ligament.

syntax, *sin'taks, n.* (*gram.*) the grammatical arrangement of words in a sentence: the rules governing this.—*adjs.* syntac'tic, -al, pertaining to syntax: according to the rules of syntax.—*adv.* syntac'tically. [Gr. *syntaxis—syn*, together, *taxein*, fut. of *tassein*, to put in order.]

synthesis, *sin'the-sis, n.* the process of making a whole by putting together its separate component parts: the combination of separate elements of thought into a whole, as opposed to *analysis*: reasoning from principles to a conclusion: (*med.*) the reunion of parts that have been divided: (*chem.*) the uniting of elements to form a compound, the building-up (of a compound) from elements:—*pl.* syn'-theses (*-sēz*).—*adjs.* synthet'ic, -al, pertaining to synthesis: consisting in, or formed by, synthesis: artificially produced, and usu. of like nature with, but not identical with, the natural product: (*loosely—lit.* and *fig.*) not genuine, not natural: not sincere.—*adv.* synthet'i-cally.—synthetic resin, any of a large number of compounds, produced artificially by the condensation and polymerisation of other substances, which have most of the physical properties of natural resins. [Gr. *synthesis—syn*, with together, *thesis*, a placing *thōvein*, fut. of *tithenai*, to place.]

syphilis, *sif'i-lis, n.* a hereditary or markedly infective venereal disease.—*adj.* syphilit'ic, [Fr.—the title of a Latin poem by Fracastoro, an Italian physician and astronomer (1483-1553).]

syphon, syren. Same as siphon, siren.

Syriac, *sir'i-ak, adj.* relating to *Syria*, or to its language.—*n.* the language, esp. the ancient language of Syria, a western dialect of Aramaic (q.v.).

syringa, *si-ring'gä, n.* a genus of Old World plants, the lilacs: commonly applied to various shrubs of a different genus (whose stems were formerly used for pipe-stems), including the mock-orange. [Gr. *syrinx*, gen. *syringos*, a musical pipe.]

syringe, *sir-inj', n.* a tube with a piston or a rubber bulb, by which liquids are sucked up and ejected: a tube used by surgeons for injecting, &c.—*v.t.* to inject, or to clean, with a syringe. [L. *syrinx*—Gr. *syrinx*, gen. *syringos*, a musical pipe.]

syrup, *sir'up, n.* water or the juice of fruits saturated with sugar, with or without other ingredients: treacle (q.v.), molasses, esp. when refined and decolourised for table use: (*fig.*) cloying sweetness.—Also sir'up.—*adj.* syr'upy. [Fr. *syrop*—Ar. *sharāb*.]

system, *sis'tēm, n.* anything formed of parts placed together to make a regular and connected whole working as if one machine (e.g. *a system of pulleys, the solar system*): the body regarded as functioning as one whole: a set of organs that together perform a particular function (e.g. *digestive system*): the universe: a succession of rocks formed during a geological *period*: a method of organisation (e.g. *the feudal system*): a customary plan, method of procedure: regular method or order: a method or scheme of classification: a full and connected view of some department of knowledge.—*adjs.* systemat'ic, -al, pertaining to, or consisting of, system: formed or done according to system, methodical.—*adv.* systemat'ically.—*v.t.* sys'tematise, to reduce to a system.—system building, building using standardised factory-produced components (*adj.* sys'tem-built), systems analyst, one who plans the work of a large organisation to ensure maximum efficiency from equipment, &c [Gr. *systēma syn*, together, and the root of *histanai*, to set.]

systole, *sis'to-lē, n.* rhythmical contraction, esp. of the heart.—*adj.* systol'ic (*-tol'ik*). [Gr. *systolē—syn*, together, *stellein*, to place.]

T

T′-square, a ruler shaped like the letter T, used in mechanical and architectural drawing; **T′-junction,** a road junction in the shape of the letter T.—**to a T,** with perfect exactness.

Taal, *tǟl,* (**the**) *n.* Afrikaans (q.v.). [Du., 'speech'.]

tab, *tab, n.* a small tag, flap, or strap: (*U.S.*) reckoning, check—*v.t.* to fix a tab on: to tabulate.—**keep tabs on,** to keep under observation.

tabard, *tab′ärd, n.* a short outer garment of the 15th and 16th centuries, worn by knights often over armour: a loose short-sleeved or sleeveless coat worn by heralds: a sleeveless tunic. [O.Fr.,—L.L. *tabardum*; perh. conn. with L. *tapēte,* tapestry.]

tabasco, *tá-bas′kō, n.* a hot pepper sauce. [From trademark—*Tabasco* state in Mexico.]

tabby, *tab′i, n.* a coarse kind of waved or watered silk: a brindled cat, esp. a female, or (*fig.*) a spiteful gossiping woman—also **tabb′y-cat.**—*adj.* brindled, or similarly diversified in colour.—*v.t.* to water or cause to look wavy:—*pa.t.* and *pa.p.* tabb′ied. [Fr. *tabis*—Ar.*′attābiy,* a quarter in Baghdad where it was made.]

tabernacle, *tab′ér-na-kl, n.* (*B.*—*cap.*) the movable tent carried by the Jews through the desert, and used as a temple: a tent: the human body as the abode of the soul: a place of worship: (*R.C.*) the place in which the consecrated elements of the Eucharist are kept. [L.*tabernāculum,* double dim. of *taberna,* a hut, shed of boards.]

tabid, *tab′id, adj.* wasted by disease. [L. *tabidus*—*tabēre,* to waste away.]

table, *tā′bl, n.* a smooth, flat slab or board, with legs, used as an article of furniture: supply of food, entertainment: the company at a table: the board or table on which a game is played, as billiards, backgammon, draughts: a surface on which something is written or inscribed: that which is cut or written on a flat surface (*the tables of the law*): a syllabus or index: a list of facts, figures, reckonings, &c., systematically arranged, esp. in columns: (*B.*) a writing tablet.—*adj.* of, on, at, a table.—*v.t.* to make into a table or catalogue: to lay on the table: to submit (a proposal) for discussion: to postpone indefinitely (esp. a Parliamentary measure, by laying it on the presiding officer's table).—*n.* **table d'hôte** (*tab′l-dōt*) a common table for guests in a hotel: a meal at a fixed total price, not paid for according to the dishes or items (cf. *à la carte*).—Also *adj.*—*ns.* **tā′ble-cloth,** a cloth for covering a table; **tā′bleland,** an extensive region of elevated land with a plain-like or undulating surface, a plateau; **tā′ble-leaf,** a board attached to, or inserted in, a table to increase its size; **tā′blelin′en,** table-cloths, napkins, &c.; **tā′ble-manners,** social behaviour during meals; **tā′ble-rapp′ing,** production of raps on tables

by alleged spiritual agency; **tā′ble-spoon,** **tā′blespoon,** a large serving spoon with three times the capacity of a tea-spoon, often used as a measure in cooking; **tā′ble-spoon′ful,** as much as will fill a table-spoon; **tā′ble-talk,** familiar conversation, as that round a table, during and after meals; **tā′ble tennis,** a game like tennis played on a table with small bats and light balls; **tā′ble-turn′ing,** movements of tables (or other objects) attributed to spiritualists to the agency of spirits—similarly **tā′ble-lift′ing; tā′ble-wine,** an unfortified wine usually drunk with a meal.—**turn the tables (on someone),** to seize the position of advantage previously held by him. [O.Fr. *table*—L. *tabula,* a board.]

tableau, *tab′lō, n.* a picture: a striking and vivid scene or representation:—*pl.* **tableaux** (*tab′-lōz*).—**tableau vivant** (*tab′lō vē′vä*), a 'living picture', a motionless representation of a well-known character, painting, scene, &c., by one or more living persons in costume:—*pl.* **tableaux vivants** (as *sing.*). [Fr.,—L. *tabula,* a board, painting.]

tablet, *tab′let, n.* a small flat surface: something flat on which to write, paint, &c.: a confection in a flat, usu. rectangular, form. [Dim. of **table.**]

tabloid, *tab′loid, n.* proprietary name for a small tablet containing a certain portion of some drug, &c.: loosely applied to a drug or anything else in concentrated form: a newspaper of halfsize sheets, consisting mostly of pictures, and often sensational.—*adj.* in the form of tabloids: concentrated. [**table,** and -*oid*; cf. **tablet.**]

taboo, tabu, *tá-bōō′, n.* an institution among the Polynesians, whose penal system is based on religious sanctions, the use of certain things held sacred or consecrated being prohibited: any prohibition, interdict, restraint, ban, exclusion, ostracism.—*adj.* prohibited (orig. because sacred): (by transference of ideas) unholy.—*v.t.* to forbid approach to: to forbid the use of:—*pr.p.* tabōō′ing; *pa.t.* and *pa.p.* tabōōed′. [Polynesian *tapu*—prob. *ta,* to mark, *pu,* expressing intensity.]

tabour, tabor, *tā′bór, n.* a small drum, usually played with one stick.—*ns.* **tab′ouret, tab′ret,** a small tabour or drum: a low stool. [O.Fr. *tabour* (Fr. *tambour*); an Oriental word.]

tabu. Same as **taboo.**

tabular, *tab′ū-lär, adj.* of the form of a table: having a flat surface: having the form of laminae or plates: arranged in a table or schedule: computed from tables.—*v.t.* **tab′ulate,** to reduce to tables or synopses: to shape with a flat surface.—*n.* **tabulā′tion.** [L. *tabulāris*—*tabula,* a board.]

tache, *tash, n.* (*B.*) a fastening or catch. [**tack** (1).]

Neutral vowels in unaccented syllables: *em′pér-ór*; for certain sounds in foreign words see p. ix.

748

tacheometer, *tak'i-om'ét-ér, n.* a surveying instrument for rapid measurement of distances. [Gr. *tachys,* swift, *metron,* measurement.]

tacit, *tas'it, adj.* implied, but not expressed by words: silent.—*adv.* **tac'itly.**—*adj.* **tac'iturn,** habitually reserved in speech.—*n.* **taciturn'ity.**—*adv.* **tac'iturnly.** [L. *tacitus,* silent—*tacēre,* to be silent.]

tack, *tak, n.* a short, sharp nail with a broad head: in sewing, a long temporary stitch: the course of a ship in reference to the position of her sails: a temporary change of course: a course of policy: a strategical move: adhesiveness, sticky condition, as of varnish, &c.: (*dial.*) a strong, distinctive flavour.—*v.t.* to attach or fasten, esp. in a slight manner, as by tacks.—*v.i.* to change the course or tack of a ship, orig. by shifting the position of the sails: to shift one's position, to veer.—*adj.* **tack'y,** adhesive, sticky, not yet dry. [O.Fr. *tache, taque,* a nail, a stain.]

tack, *tak, n.* stuff, substance: food, fare, as *hardtack* (q.v.). [App. from **tackle.**]

tacket, *tak'ét, n.* (*Scot.*) a hobnail for boots and shoes: a pimple. *adj.* **tack'ety.** [Dim. of **tack** (1).]

tackle, *tak'l (naut. tāk'l), n.* ropes, rigging, &c., of a ship: tools, gear, weapons, equipment (for fishing, &c.): ropes, &c., for raising heavy weights: a pulley: the act of grasping and stopping, or of obstructing and depriving of the ball (an opponent in football, &c.): a grasp.—*v.t.* to grapple with (*lit.* and *fig.*—e.g. a heavier man, a problem).—*v.i.* to make a tackle in football. [M.E. *takel*—Low Ger.]

tact, *takt, n.* adroitness in managing the feelings of persons dealt with: nice perception in seeing and doing exactly what is best in the circumstances: (*mus.*) the stroke in keeping time.—*adjs.* **tact'ful; tact'less.**—*ns.* **tact'fulness; tact'lessness.** [L. *tactus*—*tangĕre, tactum,* to touch.]

tactics, *tak'tiks, n.sing.* the science or art of manoeuvring fighting forces in the presence of the enemy (cf. *strategy*): way or method of proceeding.—*adjs.* **tac'tic, -al,** pertaining to tactics.—*adv.* **tac'tically.**—*n.* **tactician** (*tak-tish'án*), one skilled in tactics. [Gr. *taktikē (technē)* (art of) arranging men in a field of battle—*tassein,* to arrange.]

tactile, *tak'tīl, adj.* capable of being touched or felt: concerned with touching or the sense of touch.—*adj.* **tact'ual,** concerned with touch. [L. *tactilis*—*tangĕre, tactum,* to touch.]

tadpole, *tad'pōl, n.* a young toad or frog in its first state, during which the poll or head is prominent. [**toad, poll.**]

tael, *tāl, n.* a small Chinese measure of weight: a money of account (but not normally a coin) formerly in China, orig. a tael weight of pure silver. [Port.,—Malay *tail,* weight.]

taffeta, *taf'e-ta, n.* a thin glossy silk-stuff having a wavy lustre: (*orig.*) silk-stuff plainly woven. [It. *taffetà*—Pers. *tāftah,* woven—*tāftan,* to twist.]

taffrail, *taf'rāl, tafferel, taf'ér-él, n.* the upper part of a ship's timbers: the rail round the stern of a vessel. [Du. *tafereel,* a panel—*tafel,* a table—L. *tabula,* a table.]

Taffy, *taf'i, n.* (*coll.*) Welshman. [Welsh pronun-

ciation of *Davy.*]

tag, *tag, n.* a tack or point of metal at the end of a string or lace: any small thing tacked or attached to another—e.g. a luggage-label: a trite quotation.—*v.t.* to fit a tag or point to, to furnish with tags: to tack, fasten, or hang (to).—*v.i.* to string words or ideas together: to attach oneself to (a person—with *on to, after*):—*pr.p.* **tag'ging;** *pa.t.* and *pa.p.* **tagged.** —*n.* **tag'-end,** a fag-end.—*n.* and *adj.* **tag'rag, ragtag.**—**tagged atom,** an atom of a tracer element. [A weaker form of **tack** (1).]

tag, *tag, n.* a children's game in which one player chases the rest till he touches one, who then takes his place—also **tig.** [Ety. obscure; may be connected with **tack** (1).]

tail, *tāl, n.* the prolonged hindmost extremity of an animal, generally hanging loose: anything resembling a tail in appearance, position, &c.: the back, lower, or hinder part of anything: a queue or body of persons in single file: anything long and hanging, as a catkin, train of a comet, long curl of hair, &c.: (*slang*) one who follows another and keeps constant watch on him: (*pl.*) a tail-coat, full evening dress for a man.—*v.t.* to furnish with a tail: to follow like a tail: (*slang*) to shadow: (*slang*) to drive close behind (another vehicle): to take the tail or tails off (e.g. turnips, gooseberries).—*n.* **tail'-end,** the end or finish of anything—a position sometimes indicating weakness and unimportance.—*n.pl.* **tail'ings,** refuse, dregs. —*adj.* **tail'less,** having no tail.—*ns.* **tail'-light,** a light carried at the end of a train, a tram, or other vehicle; **tail'piece,** a piece at the end, esp. of a series, as of engravings: an ornamental design at the end of a chapter in a book.—**tail off,** to fall behind in a scattered order: to deteriorate or diminish towards the end.—**make neither head nor tail of** (see **head**); **turn tail,** to run away, to shirk a combat: **with the tail between the legs,** in a subdued way, after the manner of a beaten cur when he sneaks off. [O.E. *tægel.*]

tail, *tāl, n.* (*law*) entail.—*adj.* limited (e.g. *fee tail*): entailed (e.g. *estate tail*). [Fr. *taille,* cutting.]

tailor, *tāl'ór, n.* one whose business is to cut out and make outer garments, as coats, suits:—*fem.* **tail'oress.**—*v.i.* to work as a tailor.—*v.t.* to fit with clothes (esp. in passive—e.g. *he was well tailored*): to fashion by tailor's work: to make or adapt so as to fit a special need.—*p.adj.* **tail'ored,** tailor-made.—*n.* **tail'oring,** the business or work of a tailor.—*adj.* **tail'or made,** made by a tailor (esp. of plain, close-fitting garments for women): (*fig.*) exactly adapted (for a purpose). [Fr. *tailleur*—*tailler,* to cut.]

taint, *tānt, v.t.* to tinge, moisten, or impregnate with anything noxious, to infect (*lit.* and *fig.*)—*v.i.* to be affected with something corrupting: to begin to putrefy (of meat).—*n.* (*obs.*) a stain or tincture: infection or corruption: a source of corruption: a blemish in nature, character, or morals. [O.Fr. *taint,* pa.p. of *teindre,* to dye—L. *tingĕre, tinctum,* to wet.]

take, *tāk, v.t.* to lay hold of: to get into one's possession: to capture: to receive (e.g. a prize): to choose: to accept: to captivate:

fāte, fär; mē, hûr (her); *mīne; mōte, för; mūte, mōōn, fŏŏt;* THen (then)

to lead or carry with one: to lead or carry hence (opp. to *bring*): to subtract (from): to appropriate and use (e.g. *to take a chair*): to use or require (e.g. *that takes time*): to deprive one of, steal from one: to employ (e.g. *to take pains, strong measures*): to choose and range oneself on (a side): to feel, experience (e.g. *to take umbrage*): to experience, enjoy (e.g. *to take a rest, a holiday*): to understand: to assume, take *on* (q.v.): to have room for: to swallow: to eat or drink habitually: to allow, agree to, accept: to infer (with *it*): to become infected with: to endure calmly.—*v.i.* to root, begin to grow: to become effective: (of fish) to bite: to gain reception, to please: to become (*to take ill*): to betake oneself (to; e.g. *he took to the hills*): to have recourse to:—*pa.t.* took; *pa.p.* tā′ken.—*n.* quantity of fish taken or captured at one time: (*cinematography*) the filming of one scene.—*n.* tā′ker.—*adj.* tā′king, captivating, alluring.—*adv.* tā′kingly.—*n.* take′-over, assumption of control of: acquirement of control of a business by purchase of a majority of its shares.—Also *adj.* (e.g. take-over bid).—take advantage of, to employ to advantage: to make use of circumstances to the prejudice of (someone else); take after, to resemble; take breath, to stop in order to breathe or be refreshed; take care of (see care); take down, to reduce: to bring down from a higher place, to humble: to pull down: to write down; take for, to mistake for; take French leave (see French); take from, to derogate or detract from; take heed, to be careful; take heed to, to attend to with care; take in, to enclose, to embrace: to receive: to contract, to furl, as a sail: to comprehend: to accept as true: to cheat; take in hand, to undertake: to impose authority on; take into one's head, to be seized with a sudden notion (that, to do); take it, to endure punishment or misfortune without giving way; take it out on, to vent one's anger, spite on; take it out of, to extort reparation from: to exhaust the strength or energy of; take leave (see leave); take notice, to observe, take cognisance of one's surroundings; take off, to remove: to begin flight: to swallow: to mimic or imitate (*n.* take-off, the spot from which jumpers, divers, aircraft, &c., leave the ground: the act, or the manner, of leaping or rising: a ridiculing imitation); take on, to take aboard: to challenge or accept as an opponent: to undertake: to assume (a new meaning, dignity): (*coll.*) to grieve: (of ideas, &c.) to gain acceptance; take one up on (something), to accept a person's (challenge or offer): to put a person's statement to the test; take orders, to receive ordination; take over, to assume control of: to acquire control of (a business) by purchase of a majority of its shares; take part, to share (in): assist (in); take place, to happen; take root, to strike out roots, to live and grow, as a plant: to be established; take the field, to begin military operations; take to, to resort to (esp. as a habit): to be immediately attracted by; take to heart, to feel deeply; take up, to lift, to raise: to occupy, fill (e.g. time, energy): to arrest: to adopt, begin to follow (e.g. an occupation): to try to further (e.g. a

cause): to bestow patronage and help upon (a person); take up arms, to prepare for combat; take upon, to assume; take up with, to form a connection with, to fall in love with; taken with, pleased with. [Scand.; O.N. *taka* (pa.t. *tōk*, pa.p. *tekinn*).]

talc, *talk, n.* a mineral occurring in thin flakes, of a white or green colour and a soapy feel (also **talc′um**): also used for one of the micas.—*adjs.* **talck′y, talc′ous,** containing, consisting of, or like, talc. [Fr. *talc*—Sp. *talco*—Ar. *talq*.]

tale, *tāl, n.* a narrative or story: an invented account, a lie: what is counted off, number, reckoning.—*n.* **tale′-bear′er,** one who maliciously and officiously gives information about others.—*adj.* and *n.* **tale′-bear′ing.—old wives′ tale,** any marvellous story that makes demands on one's credulity; **tell tales,** to play the informer; **tell tales out of school,** to reveal confidential matters. [O.E. *talu,* a reckoning, a tale, also speech.]

talent, *tal′ent, n.* an ancient weight for money and commodities—in the Attic (q.v.) system of money (*N.T.*) the talent weighed 58 lb. avoirdupois: any natural or special gift or aptitude: eminent ability.—*adj.* **tal′ented,** possessing mental gifts.—**talent scout,** one whose business is to discover and recruit talented people esp. on behalf of the entertainment industry. [L. *talentum*—Gr. *talanton,* a weight, a talent.]

talisman, *tal′iz-man,* or *-is-, n.* a species of charm, engraved on metal or stone, supposed to exert some protective influence over the wearer: an amulet.—Also *fig.*:—*pl.* **tal′ismans.** [Fr.,—Ar. *tilsam*—Late Gr. *telesma,* consecration, incantation.]

talk, *tōk, v.i.* to speak: to converse: to communicate ideas (e.g. by signs): to speak to little purpose: to gossip: (*coll.*) to divulge information.—*v.t.* to utter, express (e.g. nonsense, treason): to use in communication (e.g. *to talk German*).—*n.* familiar conversation: a discussion: a lecture: subject of discourse (e.g. *she is the talk of the town*): rumour.—*adjs.* **talk′ing,** given to talking: able to speak: with synchronised reproduction of speech; **talk′ative,** given to much talking, prating.—*adv.* **talk′atively.**—*ns.* **talk′ativeness; talk′er; talk′ing-point,** a matter of or for talk; **talk′ing-to,** a scolding.—**talk big,** to talk boastfully; **talk down,** to silence by much talk: to bring (aircraft) to a landing by radioed instructions from the ground; **talk into,** to persuade; **talk out,** to defeat (a parliamentary bill or motion) by going on speaking until it is too late to vote on it; **talk over,** to persuade, convince: to discuss, consider together; **talk round,** to discuss at length without getting to the point, or without reaching a conclusion: to persuade; **talk shop** (see **shop**.). [M.E. *talken,* freq. of **tell**.]

talkies, *tō′kiz, n.pl.* (*coll.*) talking films, moving pictures with mechanical reproduction of speech. [From **talk**.]

tall, *tōl, adj.* high, esp. in stature: lofty: (*arch.*) sturdy: hardly to be believed (*a tall story*).—*ns.* **tall′ness; tall′boy,** a long narrow top for a smoky chimney: a high chest of drawers.

Neutral vowels in unaccented syllables: *em′pér-ôr*; for certain sounds in foreign words see p. ix.

tallow, *tal′ō, n.* the fat of animals melted: any coarse, hard fat.—*ns.* **tal′ow-can′dle,** a candle made of tallow; **tall′ow-chand′ler,** a dealer in tallow, candles, &c. [Old Du. *talgh, talch,* O.N. *tōlgr, tolg.*]

tally, *tal′i, n.* a stick cut or notched to match another stick, used to mark numbers or keep accounts by: anything made to correspond with, duplicate another: a score or account: a label:—*pl.* **tall′ies.**—*v.t.* to score with corresponding notches: to make to fit, agree: to estimate, count (up).—*v.i.* to correspond: to agree (with):—*pa.t.* and *pa.p.* tall′ied. [Fr. *taille*—L. *talea,* a cutting.]

tally-ho, *tal′i-hō, interj.* the huntsman's cry betokening that a fox has gone away.

Talmud, *tal′mŏŏd, n.* the fundamental code of the Jewish civil and canonical law, comprising the written law and the traditions and comments of the Jewish doctors.—*adj.* **Talmud′ic.**—*n.* the language of the Talmud. [Heb. *talmūd,* instruction—*lāmad,* to learn.]

talon, *tal′on, n.* the claw of a bird of prey. [Fr. *talon,* through L.L.,—L. *tālus,* the heel.]

tamarind, *tam′a-rind, n.* a tropical tree, with edible leaves and flowers, and pods filled with pulp used to make a cooling drink, &c. [*tamarindus,* Latinised from Ar. *tamr Hindī,* 'date of India'.]

tamarisk, *tam′är-isk, n.* a genus of Mediterranean evergreen shrubs with small white or pink flowers. [L. *tamariscus.*]

tambour, *tam′bŏŏr, n.* a small, shallow drum: a frame on which muslin or other material is stretched for embroidering: a rich kind of gold and silver embroidery: a flexible top or front (as of a cabinet) made of narrow strips of wood fixed closely together on canvas, the whole sliding in grooves. [Fr. *tambour*; cf. **tabour.**]

tambourine, *tam-bŏŏ-rēn′, n.* a shallow drum (with one skin and jingles) played with the hand. [Fr. *tambourin,* dim. of *tambour.* See **tabour.**]

tame, *tām, adj.* having lost native wildness and shyness, domesticated: gentle: spiritless, without vigour: dull.—*v.t.* to reduce to a domestic state: to make gentle, to humble (e.g. spirit, pride).—*adv.* **tame′ly.**—*ns.* **tame′ness;** **tā′mer,** one who tames.—*adjs.* **tām′able, tāme′able,** that may be tamed; **tāme′less,** untamable.—*n.* **tāme′lessness.** [O.E. *tam.*]

Tamil, *tam′il, n.* a Dravidian language of southeast India, and north, east and central Ceylon (Sri Lanka): one of the people speaking it.

tam-o′-shanter, *tam-ō-shan′tér, n.* a broad bonnet.—*contr.* **tamm′y.** [From the hero of Burns's poem of that name.]

tamper, *tam′pér, v.i.* to meddle (with): to make changes in without necessity or authority (with *with*): to practise upon, influence secretly and unfairly (with *with*). [A byform of **temper.**]

tampon, *tam′pon, n.* a plug of cotton or other material inserted in a wound or orifice to control haemorrhage, &c. [Fr.]

tan, *tan, n.* bark of the oak, &c., bruised and broken for tanning hides: a yellowish-brown colour: sunburn.—*v.t.* to convert skins and hides into leather by steeping in vegetable solutions containing tannin or by impregnation with various mineral salts, or by treatment with oils and fats: to make brown, to sunburn: (*coll.*) to beat.—*v.i.* to become tanned:—*pr.p.* tann′ing: *pa.t.* and *pa.p.* tanned. —*ns.* **tann′er,** one whose occupation is tanning; **tann′ery,** a place for tanning; **tan′yard,** a yard or enclosure where leather is tanned. [O.E. *tannian*; cf. Du. *tanen,* or prob. O.Fr. *tan*—Breton *tann,* an oak.]

tandem, *tan′dem, adv.* applied to the position of horses harnessed singly one before the other instead of abreast.—*n.* a team of horses (usually two) so harnessed: a bicycle or tricycle on which two ride one before the other. [Orig. university slang, a play on the L. adv. *tandem,* at length.]

tang, *tang, n.* a prong or tapering part of a knife or tool that goes into the haft: a strong or offensive taste, esp. of something extraneous: specific flavour. [O.N. *tange*; cog. with **tongs.**]

tangent, *tan′jént, n.* a line which touches a curve: one of the six trigonometrical functions of an angle, the ratio of the perpendicular to the base—identical with the cotangent of the complementary angle.—*abbrev.* **tan.**—*n.* **tan′gency,** state of being tangent: a contact or touching.—*adj.* **tangential** (-*jen′shál*) of or pertaining to, of the nature of, a tangent: in the direction of a tangent: digressive.—*adv.* **tangen′tially.—go off,** or **fly off, at a tangent,** to break off suddenly into a different line of thought, &c. [L. *tangēns, -entis,* pr.p. of *tangěre,* to touch.]

Tangerine, *tan-je-rēn′, adj.* relating or belonging to *Tangier* on the Morocco coast.—*n.* (**tangerine**) a Tangerine orange, a small, flattish, loose-skinned variety.

tangible, *tan′ji-bl, adj.* perceptible by the touch: capable of being realised by the mind (e.g. a distinction): real, substantial (e.g. tangible *benefits*).—*n.* **tangibil′ity.**—*adv.* **tan′gibly.** [L. *tangibilis*—*tangěre,* to touch.]

tangle, *tang′gl, n.* a knot of things united confusedly: any of various large seaweeds, some of them edible: (*fig.*) a complication: conflict.—*v.t.* to unite together confusedly: to ensnare, entangle (*fig.*) to make complicated.—*v.i.* to become tangled or complicated (*lit.* and *fig.*): to become involved in conflict or argument (with *with*). [Scand.; Dan. *tang,* O.N. *thang,* seaweed.]

tango, *tang′gō, n.* a dance of Argentine origin, music in tango rhythm.—Also *v.i.* [Sp.]

tank, *tangk, n.* a large basin or cistern: a reservoir of water, oil, &c.: an armoured motor vehicle, with caterpillar wheels, mounted with guns.—*ns.* **tank′age,** the act of storing oil, &c., in tanks: the price charged for such storage: the capacity of a tank or series of tanks; **tank′er,** a ship, or heavy vehicle, for carrying oil or other liquids in bulk: an aircraft that refuels others. [Port. *tanque* (Sp. *estanque,* O.Fr. *estang*)—L. *stagnum,* a stagnant pool.]

tankard, *tangk′ärd, n.* a large vessel for holding liquors: a drinking-vessel, often with a hinged lid. [O.Fr. *tanquard.*]

tanner, tannery. See **tan.**

tanner, *tan′ér, n.* (*coll.*) a sixpence (2½p)

tannin, *tan′in, n.* an astringent substance found

largely in oak-bark or gall-nuts, of great use in tanning.—*adj.* **tann′ic**, of or from tannin. [Fr. *tannin*.]

Tannoy, *tan′oi, n.* a sound-reproducing and amplifying system. [Proprietary name.]

tansy, *tan′zi, n.* a bitter, aromatic plant with small yellow flowers, common on old pasture. [O.Fr. *tanasie*, through Late L.—Gr. *athanasia*, immortality.]

tantalise, *tan′ta-līz, v.t.* to torment by presenting something to excite desire, but keeping it out of reach.—*n.* **tan′talus,** a case for wines, &c., that locks. [*Tantalus*, who was punished by having to stand up to his chin in water, with branches of fruit hung over his head, the water receding when he wished to drink, and the fruit when he desired to eat.]

tantalum, *tan′tal-ùm, n.* a metallic element (symbol Ta; atomic no. 73). [*Tantalus*. See **tantalise.**]

tantalus. See **tantalise.**

tantamount, *tan′ta-mownt, adj.* amounting (to), equivalent (to), in effect or meaning. [O.Fr. *tant* (L. *tantum*, so much, so great), and *amunter*, to amount.]

tantivy, *tan-tiv′i, n.* a hunting cry: a rapid movement, a rush. [Imit.]

tantrum, *tan′trùm, n.* a capricious fit of ill-temper. [Prob. W. *tant*, a passion.]

Tâoism, *tä′ō-izm,* or *tow′izm, n.* a Chinese liberal philosophy and religion, founded by Lâo-tsze (born 604 B.C.).—*n.* **Tâ′oist,** an adherent of this system.—*adj.* **Tâoist′ic.** [Chin. *tao*, a road.]

tap, *tap, n.* a gentle blow or touch, esp. with something small.—*v.t.* to strike lightly, touch gently.—*v.i.* to give a gentle knock:—*pr.p.* tap′p′ing; *pa.t., pa.p.* tapped—*n.* **tap′-dance,** a step dance in syncopated rhythm in which the rapid tapping of the dancer's toes or heels on the floor is made clearly audible by the use of special shoes. [O.Fr. *tapper*—Low Ger. *tappen*]

tap, *tap, n.* a hole or short pipe through which fluid is drawn: a plug or spigot: a cock for regulating the flow of liquid from a pipe or cask: a place where liquor is drawn: liquor of a particular brewing and hence of a particular quality.—*v.t.* to open (a cask) and draw off liquor, to broach: to pierce, so as to let out fluid (e.g. an organ of the body, a tree): *(fig.)* to draw on (any source of wealth or profit): *(slang)* to ask for a loan or gift of money from: secretly to attach a receiver to telephone wire in order to overhear a conversation:—*pr.p.* tapp′ing; *pa.t., pa.p.* tapped.—*ns.* **tap′room,** a room where beer is served from the tap or cask; **tap′root,** a root of a plant striking directly downward without dividing, and tapering towards the end, as that of the carrot; **tap′ster,** one who taps or draws off liquor, a publican, barman.—**on tap,** kept in cask—opp. to bottled: ready to be drawn upon *(lit.* and *fig.).* [O.E. *tæppa,* seen in *tæppere,* one who taps casks.]

tape, *tāp, n.* a narrow fillet or band of woven work, used for strings, &c.: such a band stretched between the winning posts on a race track: a ribbon of paper, &c., printed by a recording instrument as in telegraphy: a tape recording.—*v.t.* to furnish, or tie up, with tape: to tape-record.—*adj.* **taped** *(slang),* measured,

summed up: arranged to one's liking.—*ns.* **tape′-line, -meas′ure,** a measuring-line of tape, marked with inches, &c.; **tape′-machine,** a telegraphic instrument by which messages received are automatically printed on a tape; **tape′-recorder,** an instrument for recording sound on magnetic tape and subsequently reproducing it; **tape′-recording,** a magnetic tape on which sound has been recorded *(v.t.* **tape′record).—have (something** or **someone) taped,** to have a thorough understanding (of something or someone). [O.E. *tæppe,* a fillet—L. *tapēte.* See **tapestry.**]

taper, *tā′pėr, n.* a long, thin wax-candle or light.—*adj.* narrowed towards the point, like a taper: long and slender.—*v.i.* to become gradually smaller towards one end.—*v.t.* to make to taper.—*adj.* **tā′pering,** growing gradually thinner. [O.E. *tapor.*]

tapestry, *tap′es-tri, n.* a woven fabric with wrought figures, used for the covering of walls and furniture, and for curtains and hangings. [O.Fr. *tapisserie*—*tapis,* a carpet—L. *tapētium* Gr. *tapēs, -ētos*—prob. Iranian.]

tapeworm, *tāp′wûrm, n.* any one of numerous tape-like parasitic worms, often of great length, found in the intestines of men and animals. [**tape,** worm.]

tapioca, *tap-i-ō′ka, n.* a glutinous, granular, farinaceous substance obtained from roots of the cassava.—*n.* **pearl-tapioca,** tapioca granulated and graded according to size. [Brazilian *tipioka*—*tipi,* residue, *ok,* to press out.]

tapir, *tā′pėr, n.* a family of thick-skinned, short-necked quadrupeds with a short flexible proboscis, all but one species of which are found in South America. [Brazilian.]

tapis, *tap′is,* or *tap′ē, n.* tapestry, carpeting: formerly, the cover of a council-table.—**on the tapis,** on the table, under consideration. [Fr. See **tapestry.**]

tar, *tär, n.* a dark, viscous, resinous mixture obtained from wood, coal, peat, &c. (varying in constituents according to source and method used): a natural bituminous substance of like appearance (*mineral tar*): a sailor, so called from his tarred clothes.—*v.t.* to smear with tar:—*pr.p.* tarr′ing; *pa.t.* and *pa.p.* tarred.—**tar and feather,** to humiliate and punish by smearing with tar and then covering with feathers.—**be tarred with the same brush,** or **stick,** to have the same faults (as another); **have a touch, dash, lick, of the tar-brush,** to have an infusion of Negro or Indian blood in the veins. [O.E. *teoro, teru.*]

tarantella, *tar-an-tel′a, n.* a lively Neapolitan dance for one couple, once believed to cure the effects of a tarantula's bite: music for such a dance. [From **tarantula.**]

tarantula, *tar-an′tū-la, n.* a species of poisonous spider found in South Italy. [It. *tarantola*—*Taranto*—L. *Tarentum,* a town in South Italy where the spider abounds.]

taraxacum, *tar-aks′a-kum, n.* the root of the dandelion, used in medicine. [A botanical Latin word, prob. of Ar. origin.]

tarboosh, tarboush, tarbush, *tär-bōōsh′, n.* a cap (usually red) with dark tassel worn by Moslem men—the *fez* is the Turkish form. [Ar. *tarbūsh.*]

Neutral vowels in unaccented syllables: *em′pėr-òr*; for certain sounds in foreign words see p. ix.

tardy, *tär'di, adj.* slow, late, sluggish: out of season.—*adv.* **tar'dily.**—*n.* **tar'diness.** [Fr. *tardif—tard*—L. *tardus,* slow.]

tare, *tār, n.* any one of several species of vetch: (*B.*) an unidentified weed, prob. darnel.

tare, *tār, n.* the weight of the vessel or package in which goods are contained: an allowance made for it, the remainder being the *net* weight. [Fr.,—Sp. *tara*—Ar. *tarhah,* thrown away.]

target, *tär'gét, n.* a small buckler or shield (also **targe,** *tärj; arch.*): a mark to aim at: any object of desire or ambition: a standard of quantity set for output, &c.: an object against which marks of hostile feeling (e.g. of scorn) are directed. [O.E. *targe;* O.H.G. *zarga,* a frame, wall; Fr. *targe* is of Gmc. origin.]

tariff, *tar'if, n.* a list of the duties, &c., fixed by law on merchandise: a list of charges, fees, or prices. [Fr.,—Sp.,—Ar. *ta'rīf,* giving information, from *'arafa,* to explain.]

tarlatan, *tär'lá-tán, n.* a kind of transparent muslin.—Also **tar'letan.** [Ety. uncertain.]

tarmacadam, *tär-mak-ad'ám, n.* a road surfacing formed of broken stone which has been covered with tar and rolled.—Also **tar'mac.** [**tar,** and **macadam** (see **macadamise**).]

tarn, *tärn, n.* a small lake among mountains. [O.N. *tjörn.*]

tarnish, *tär'nish, v.t.* to diminish the lustre or purity of (a metal) by exposure to the air, &c.: to stain, sully (e.g. one's reputation). *v.i.* to become dull, to lose lustre. [Fr. *ternir* (pr.p. *ternissant*)—*terne,* dull, wan.]

tarpaulin, *tär-pö'lin, n.* strong linen or hempen cloth coated with tar, pitch, etc. to render it waterproof: a sailor's wide-brimmed storm-hat.—Also **tarpau'ling.** [From **tar,** and dial. Eng *pauling,* a curt cover.]

tar(r)adiddle, *tar-a-did'l, n.* (*coll.*) a fib, a trifling lie. [App. a coined word, connected with **diddle.**]

tarragon, *tar'a-gon, n.* a bitter herb used for flavouring vinegar, sauces, &c. [Sp. *tara gona*—Ar. *tarkhun*—Gr. *drakōn,* a dragon.]

tarry, *tär'i, adj.* consisting of, covered with, or like tar. [**tar.**]

tarry, *tar'i, v.i.* to be tardy or slow: to stay, lodge: to wait (for): to delay:—*pa.t.* and *pa.p.* **tarr'ied.** [M.E. *targen,* to delay (confused in form with *tarien,* to irritate)—O.Fr. *targer*—L. *tardus,* slow.]

tarsus, *tär'sus, n.* the ankle:—*pl.* **tar'sī.**—*adj.* **tar'sal.** [Gr. *tarsos,* the flat part of the foot.]

tart, *tärt, adj.* sharp or sour to the taste: (*fig.*) sharp, severe.—*adv.* **tart'ly.**—*n.* **tart'ness.** [O.E. *teart*—*teran,* to tear.]

tart, *tärt, n.* a fruit pie: a small, uncovered pastry cup, containing fruit or jelly: (*coll.*) a prostitute.—*n.* **tart'let,** a small tart.—*adj.* **tart'y** (*coll.*), like a prostitute. [O.Fr. *tarte.*]

tartan, *tär'tán, n.* a woollen or worsted stuff checked with various colours, once the distinctive dress of the Scottish Highlanders, each clan having its own pattern. [Perh. conn. with Fr. *tiretaine,* linsey-woolsey.]

tartar, *tär'tár, n.* a salt formed on the sides of wine-casks: a concretion which sometimes forms on the teeth.—*adjs.* **tartā'reous, tar'tarous,** consisting of, or resembling, tartar: **tar-**

tar'ic, pertaining to, or obtained from, tartar.—**cream of tartar** (see **cream**). [Fr. *tartre*—L.L. *tartarum*—Ar. *durd,* dregs.]

Tartar, *tär'tár, n.* a native of *Tartary* or *Tatary*—in the Middle Ages a belt of territory extending from eastern Europe right across central Asia—noted for their ferocity as invaders of mediaeval Europe (properly **Tatar,** *tä'tär*): one too strong for his assailant (*to catch a Tartar*): a person of irritable or intractable temper.—Also *adj.*

tartar(e) (sauce), *tär'tär (sös), n.* a mayonnaise dressing with chopped pickles, olives, capers, &c., added, usu. served with fish. [Fr *sauce tartare.*]

Tartarus, *tar'tá-rús, n.* the lower world, esp. the place of punishment for the wicked.—*adj.* **Tartā'rean.** [L.,—Gr. *Tartaros.*]

Tarzan, *tär'zan, n.* a man of great strength and agility. [From hero of stories by Edgar Rice Burroughs about a man brought up by apes.]

task, *täsk, n.* a set amount of work, esp. of study, given by another: work: drudgery.—*v.t.* to impose a task on: to burden with severe work, to tax, strain.—*n.* **task'master,** one who imposes a task: an overseer.—**task force,** (*U.S.*) a combined force of land, sea, and air elements, under one commander, to which is assigned a particular exactly defined operation: a working party for a civilian purpose.—**take to task,** to reprove. [O. Norman Fr. *tasque*—L.L. *tasca, taxa*—L. *taxāre.* See **taste.**]

Tasmanian devil. See **devil.**

tassel, *tas'l, n.* a hanging ornament consisting of a bunch of silk or other material.—*adj.* **tass'elled,** adorned with tassels. [O.Fr. *tassel,* an ornament of a square shape, attached to the dress—L. *taxillus,* dim. of *tālus,* a die.]

taste, *tāst, v.t.* to perceive (a flavour) by the touch of the tongue or palate: to try by eating or drinking a little: to eat or drink a little of: to experience.—*v.i.* to try or perceive by the mouth: to have a flavour (of).—*n.* the act or sense of tasting: the particular sensation caused by a substance on the tongue: the quality or flavour of anything: a small portion: intellectual relish or discernment: the faculty of recognising what is seemly, fitting, beautiful, excellent in its kind: arrangement or choice resulting from the exercise of that faculty: liking, predilection.—*adjs.* **tāst'able,** that may be tasted; **taste'ful,** having a high relish: showing good taste.—*adv.* **taste'fully.** —*n.* **taste'fulness.**—*adj.* **taste'less,** without taste, insipid: unsuitable: ugly.—*adv.* **taste'lessly.**—*ns.* **taste'lessness; tāst'er,** one skilful in distinguishing flavours by the taste, esp. one employed in judging tea, wine, &c.: (*hist.*) one whose duty it was to test the quality of food by tasting it before serving it to his master: a publisher's reader: a sample.—*adj.* **tāst'y,** having a good taste, highly flavoured.—**to one's taste,** to one's liking. [O.Fr. *taster,* prob.—L. *taxāre,* to touch repeatedly, to estimate—*tangēre,* to touch.]

Tatar. See **Tartar.**

tatt, *tat, n.* a rag, esp. an old one: pretentious odds and ends of little value.—*adj.* **tatt'y,** (of clothes or ornament) fussy: cheap, of poor quality: untidy. [**tatter.**]

tatter, *tat'ėr, n.* a torn piece: a loose hanging rag.—*adj.* **tatt'ered,** in tatters or rags: torn. [Cf. Icel. *tóturr,* rags, a torn garment.]

tatting, *tat'ing, n.* knotted thread-work used for trimmings: the act of making it.—*v.i.* **tat,** to do tatting. [Prob. Icel. *tæta,* shreds, *tæta,* to tease or pick wool.]

tattle, *tat'l, n.* trifling talk or chat.—*v.i.* to talk idly or triflingly: to tell tales or secrets.—*n.* **tatt'ler.** [M.E. *tatelen*; Low Ger. *tateln,* to gabble; an imit. word.]

tattoo, *ta-tōō', n.* a beat of drum and a bugle-call to call soldiers to quarters, originally to shut the taps or drinking-houses against them: a military fête by night.—**the devil's tattoo,** drumming absent-mindedly or impatiently with the fingers on a table, &c. [Du. *taptoe*—*tap,* a tap, and *toe,* which is the prep., Eng. *to,* Ger. *zu,* in the sense of 'shut'.]

tattoo, *ta-tōō', v.t.* to mark permanently (as the skin) with figures, by pricking in colouring-matter, or by making symmetrical scars.—*n.* marks or figures made on the skin in these ways. [*tatu,* native word in Tahiti.]

taught, *töt, pa.t.* and *pa.p.* of **teach.**

taunt, *tönt, v.t.* to reproach or upbraid jeeringly or contemptuously.—*n.* upbraiding, sarcastic, or insulting words.—*n.* **taunt'er.**—*adv.* **taunt'ingly.** [O.Fr. *tanter*—L. *tentāre,* to assail.]

Taurus, *tö'rus, n.* the Bull, one of the signs of the zodiac.—*adjs.* **Tau'rine; tau'rine,** bull-like, bovine. [L.,—Gr. *tauros.*]

taut, taught, *töt, adj.* tightly drawn: shipshape: tense.—*v.t.* **taut'en,** to draw tightly.—*v.i.* to become tight or tense. [A form of **tight.**]

tautology, *tö-tol'o-ji, n.* needless repetition of the same thing in different words.—*adjs.* **tautolog'ic, -al,** containing tautology.—*adv.* **tautolog'ically.**—*n.* **tautol'ogist.** [Gr. *tautologia*—*tauto,* the same, *legein,* to speak.]

tavern, *tav'ėrn, n.* a licensed house for the sale of liquors, with accommodation for travellers—an inn. [Fr. *taverne*—L. *taberna.*]

taw, *tö, n.* a special marble chosen to be aimed with: a game at marbles: the line from which to play. [Origin obscure.]

taw, *tö, v.t.* to prepare and dress, as skins into white leather. [O.E. *tawian,* to prepare; O.H.G. *zoujan,* make, Du. *touwen,* curry.]

tawdry, *tö'dri, adj.* showy, cheap, and tasteless: gaudily dressed.—*adv.* **taw'drily.**—*n.* **taw'driness.** [Said to be corr. from *St Awdrey*=*St Ethelreda,* at whose fair, at Ely, laces and gay toys were sold.]

tawny, *tö'ni, adj.* of the colour of things tanned, a yellowish brown.—*n.* **taw'niness.** [Fr. *tanné,* pa.p. of *tanner,* to tan.]

tax, *taks, n.* a rate imposed on property or persons for the benefit of the state: a strain, a burdensome duty.—*v.t.* to lay a tax on: to burden, strain: to accuse of (with *with*): (*law*) to assess (costs).—*adj.* **tax'able,** capable of being, or liable to be, taxed.—*n.* **taxā'tion,** act of taxing.—*adj.* **tax'-free,** exempt from taxation.—*ns.* **tax'-gath'erer; tax'-pay'er.** [Fr. *taxe,* a tax—L. *taxāre.* See **task.**]

taxi, *tak'si, n.* (also **taxi'-cab**) a motor-driven vehicle, usu. fitted with a taximeter, licensed to ply for hire.—*v.i.* to go by taxi: (of an aeroplane) to run along the ground under its own power:—*pr.p.* tax'iing; *pa.t.* and *pa.p.* tax'ied. [Contr. of **taximeter.**]

taxidermy, *taks'i-dėr-mi, n.* the art of preparing and stuffing the skins of animals.—*n.* **tax'idermist.** [Fr.,—Gr. *taxis,* arrangement, *derma,* skin.]

taximeter, *tak-sim'e-tėr, n.* an instrument fitted to cabs to indicate the fare due for the distance travelled. [Fr. *taxe,* price, and Gr. *metron,* a measure.]

taxis, *tak'sis, n.* arrangement: (*biol.*) movement of a whole organism in response to a stimulus. [Gr.—*tassein,* to arrange.]

tea, *tē, n.* a shrub (of which there are two main varieties, China and Assam) of the same family as camellias, growing in China, India, Ceylon, &c.: its dried leaves: an infusion of the leaves in boiling water: any vegetable infusion (e.g. *senna tea*): an afternoon meal at which tea is generally served: (*slang*) marijuana.—*ns.* **tea'-break,** a rest-period during the working day when tea is drunk; **tea-cadd'y, tea-can'ister,** an air-tight box or jar for holding tea; **tea'-cō'sy** (see **cosy**); **tea'cup; tea'gar'den, -room,** a public garden, restaurant, where tea and other refreshments are served; **tea'-gown,** a loose gown for wearing at afternoon tea at home; **tea'-kett'le,** a kettle in which to boil water for making tea; **tea'-par'ty,** a social gathering at which tea is served: also the persons present; **tea'-plant,** the shrub from which tea is obtained; **tea'-pot,** a vessel in which the beverage tea is made; **tea'-rose,** any of many tea-scented roses; **tea'-ser'vice, -set,** the utensils necessary for a tea-table; **tea'-spoon,** a small spoon used with a teacup, &c., holding about 5 millilitres; **tea'-tāst'er,** one whose profession it is to ascertain the quality of tea by tasting it.—*n.pl.* **tea'-things,** the tea-pot, cups, &c.—*ns.* **tea'-towel,** a cloth for drying crockery, &c.; **tea'-urn,** a vessel for boiling water or keeping it hot, used to make tea.—**black tea, green tea,** tea that has, or has not, been fermented between the process of rolling and that of 'firing' or drying; **(not) to be one's cup of tea,** (*slang*) (not) to be to one's taste, (not) to appeal to one. [From South Chinese *te* (pron. *tā*).]

teach, *tēch, v.t.* to impart knowledge to: to impart knowledge of (e.g. *to teach arithmetic*): to explain, show (that, how to): train in, show the desirability of (e.g. *experience teaches patience*): to make aware of the penalty attached (to an action—e.g. *that'll teach you to meddle*).—*v.i.* to give instruction, esp. as a profession:—*pa.t.* and *pa.p.* taught (*tawt*).—*adj.* **teach'able,** capable of being taught: apt or willing to learn.—*ns.* **teach'er,** one who teaches or instructs, esp. as an occupation: one who instructs skilfully; **teach'ing,** the act, practice, or profession of giving instruction.—**teach'-in,** long public debate consisting of a succession of speeches by well-informed persons holding different views on a matter of general importance; **teaching machine,** any mechanical device capable of presenting an instructional programme. [O.E. *tǣcan,* to show, teach.]

teak, *tēk, n.* a tree in the East Indies and also trees of Africa, &c.: their very hard wood. [Dravidian (q.v.) *tēkka.*]

Neutral vowels in unaccented syllables: *em'pér-ör*; for certain sounds in foreign words see p. ix.

teal, *tēl*, *n.* any of several web-footed waterfowl allied to the ducks, but smaller. [Du. *teling*, *taling*.]

team, *tēm*, *n.* a number of animals moving together or in order: two or more oxen or other animals harnessed to the same vehicle: a number of persons associated for doing anything conjointly, playing a game, &c.—*v.i.* and *v.t.* of clothes, &c. to match.—*ns.* **team'ster**, one who drives a team; **team'work**, the subordination of the individual's task to the common purpose of the team: the ability of a team so to work together.—**team up with**, to join forces with. [O.E. *tēam*, offspring; prob. *tēon*, to draw.]

tear, *tēr*, *n.* a drop of the fluid secreted by the lachrymal gland, appearing in the eyes: anything like a tear.—*adj.* **tear'ful**, shedding tears: mournful.—*adv.* **tear'fully.**—*ns.* **tear'fulness**; **tear'-gas**, a gas that temporarily blinds the eyes with tears; **tear'-jerk'er**, an extravagantly sentimental song, book, &c., inviting pity, sorrow.—*adjs.* **tear'less**; **tear'-stained** [O.E. *tēar*.]

tear, *tār*, *v.t.* to draw asunder with violence: to make a violent rent in: to lacerate (*lit.* and *fig.*): to pull violently (away from) or separate violently (from).—*v.i.* to move or act with speed or impetuosity: to rage:—*pa.t.* tōre, (*B.*) tāre; *pa.p.* tōrn (or *tōrn*).—*n.* act of tearing: a rent.—*n.* **tear'away**, an impetuous, often violent person.—Also *adj.* [O.E. *teran.*]

tease, *tēz*, *v.t.* to separate into single fibres: to comb or card, as wool: to scratch, raise a nap on with a teasel, as cloth: to vex with importunity, jests, &c., esp. playfully: to torment, irritate.—*n.* one who teases or torments. [O.E. *tǣsan*, to pluck.]

teasel, *tēz'l*, *n.* a plant with large burs or heads covered with stiff, hooked awns, used, attached to a revolving cylinder, in raising a nap on cloth (**fuller's teasel**): any other plant of the same genus. Also **teaz'le**. [O.E. *tǣsel*, *tǣsl*—*tǣsan*, to pluck.]

teat, *tēt*, *n.* the nipple of the female breast through which the young suck the milk: a valve on a baby's feeding-bottle. [O.E. *tit*; or perh. through O.Fr. *tete*, from Gmc.]

teazle, *tēz'l* Same as **teasel**.

technetium, *tek-nē'shi-üm*, *n.* the chemical element of atomic number 43 (symbol Tc), the first element to be made artificially. [Gr. *technētos*, artificial—*technē*, art.]

technical, *tek'nik-ál*, *adj.* pertaining to skill in the arts: concerned with the mechanical or applied arts: belonging to, peculiar to, a particular art or profession (e.g. of a term or expression): concerned with, or abounding in, terms, methods, fine distinctions, &c., important to the expert practitioner of an art: so called in strict legal or technical language: (sometimes) technological.—*n.* **technical'ity**, state or quality of being technical: a technical expression or its strict interpretation.—*adv.* **tech'nically.**—*n.* **technician** (*tek-nish'án*), one skilled in the practical arts or in the practice of any art.—*n.pl.* **tech'nics**, the doctrine of arts in general: the branches of learning that relate to the arts.—*n.* **Technicolor**, a proprietary name of a process of colour

photography in motion-pictures.—*adj.* **technicolour** (modelled on above), in bright, artificial colours: cheaply romantic.—*ns.* **technique** (*tek-nēk'*), method of performance, manipulation, or execution, as in music or art: individualised execution: formal construction (e.g. of poetry); **technoc'racy** (*-nok'*), government by technical experts: a state, &c. so governed: a body of ruling technical experts; **tech'nocrat**, a member of a technocracy: a believer in technocracy; **technol'ogy**, the practice of any or all of the applied sciences that have practical value and/or industrial use: technical method(s) in a particular field of industry or art: technical means and skills characteristic of a particular group, period, &c.: technical nomenclature.—*adjs.* **technolog'ic**, **-al**, relating to technology.—*n.* **technol'ogist**, one skilled in technology. [Gr. *technikos*—*technē*, art, akin to *tiktein*, to produce.]

ted, *ted*, *v.t.* to spread or turn, as new-mown grass, for drying:—*pr.p.* **tedd'ing**; *pa.t.* and *pa.p.* **tedd'ed**.—*n.* **tedd'er**, an implement for spreading hay. [Scand.; O.N. *tedhja*, spread manure.]

teddy-bear, *ted'i-bār*, *n.* a stuffed toy bear, usu. of yellow plush—often abbreviated to **tedd'y**. [Named in allusion to the fondness of Theodore (popularly *Teddy*) Roosevelt, President of the U.S. 1901-09, for hunting big game.]

Teddy boy, *ted'i-boi*, an unruly adolescent (1950s) wearing clothes reminiscent of those worn by dandies in *Edward* VII's time.—Also **Ted.**

Te Deum, *tē dē'um*, *n.* a famous Latin hymn of the Western Church, beginning with the words *Te Deum laudamus*, 'We praise thee, O God'.—**sing the Te Deum**, (*fig.*) exult, rejoice.

tedious, *tē'di-üs*, *adj.* wearisome, tiresome.—*n.* **tē'diousness.**—*adv.* **tē'diously.**—*n.* **tē'dium**, wearisomeness, irksomeness. [L. *taedium*—*taedet*, it wearies.]

tee, *tē*, *n.* a mark for quoits, curling-stones, &c.: (*golf*) the tiny sand-heap or other contrivance from which the ball is first played at each hole: the strip of level ground (also **tee'ing-ground**) where this may be placed.—*v.t.* to place (the golf-ball) on the tee. [Prob. from *T.*]

teem, *tēm*, *v.i.* to be pregnant: to be full or prolific of (with *with*). [O.E. *tēam*, offspring.]

teem, *tēm*, *v.t.* (*dial.*) to pour out.—*v.i.* (*dial.*) to rain heavily. [O.N. *tœma*, to empty.]

teens, *tēnz*, *n.pl.* the years of one's age from thir*teen* to nine*teen*.—*adj.* **teen'age**, suitable for people between these ages.—*n.* any age within the teens: (in *pl.*) people in the teens.—*n.* **teen'ager**, (*coll.*) a person in the teens.

tee-shirt, *tē'shûrt*, *n.* a slip-on shirt usu. with short sleeves, no collar, and no buttons. [From *T.*]

teeth. See **tooth.**

teething, *tēтн'ing*, *n.* the first growth of teeth, or the process by which they make their way through the gums.—*v.i.* **teethe**, to grow or cut the teeth.—**teething troubles**, pain caused by cutting of teeth: (*fig.*) difficulties encountered in the early stages of any undertaking or when first using a new machine, &c. [**teeth.**]

teetotal(l)er, *tē-tō'tal-ėr, n.* one pledged to entire abstinence from intoxicating drinks.—*adj.* **teetō'tal.**—*n.* **teetō'talism.** [Prob. from a stammering pronunciation of the word **total**.]

teetotum, *tē-tō'tum, n.* a small top, orig. four-sided and marked with letters for use in a game of chance. [From *T.* the letter on one side, standing for L. *totum*, all (the stakes).]

teg, *teg, n.* a young sheep. [Origin obscure.]

tegument, *teg'ū-mėnt, n.* an integument, skin.— *adjs.* **tegumen'tal, tegumen'tary.** [L. *tegumentum—tegĕre,* to cover.]

teinds, *tēndz, n.pl.* the name given in Scotland to that part of the estates of the laity which is liable to be assessed for the stipend of the clergy of the established church. [O.N. *tīund,* tenth.]

tele-, *tel'i-,* in composition, distant: television. [Gr. *tēle,* at a distance.]

telecast, *tel'i-käst, n.* a television broad*cast.* — Also *v.t.* and *v.i.*

telecommunication, *tel'i-kȯ-mū-ni-kā'shȯn, n.* communication of information, in verbal, written, coded, or pictorial form, by telephone, telegraph, cable, radio, television: (in *pl.*) the science of such communication. [Gr. *tēle,* at a distance, and **communication.**]

telecontrol, *tel-i-kon-trōl', n.* control of mechanical devices remotely, e.g. by radio. [Gr. *tēle,* at a distance and **control.**]

telegram, *tel'e-gram, n.* a message sent by telegraph.—*n.* **tel'egraph**, an apparatus for transmitting, or means of transmitting, coded messages to a distance, formerly applied to any kind of signals (e.g. **bush telegraph**, a system of signals used by primitive peoples in the bush, now the obscure and rapid transmission of news through a population), now confined to communication using electricity, wires, and a code.—*v.t.* to convey or announce by telegraph, to signal.—*n.* **teleg'raphist**, one who works a telegraph.—*adj.* **telegraph'ic**, pertaining to, or communicated by, a telegraph: shortened.—*n.* **teleg'raphy**, the science or art of constructing or using telegraphs. — **telegraphic address**, a shortened address (e.g. of a business firm) registered for use in telegraphing. [Gr. *tēle,* at a distance, *graphein,* to write.]

teleology, *tel-e-ol'ȯ-ji, n.* the doctrine that natural processes are determined by an end to which they are directed—which seeks to explain the universe in the light of final purposes.—*adjs.* **teleolog'ic, -al.**—*adv.* **teleolog'ically.** [Gr. *telos,* issue, *logos,* a discourse.]

telepathy, *te-lep'a-thi, n.* communication between mind and mind otherwise than through the senses, the persons concerned in the communication being not necessarily in the same place.—*adj.* **telepath'ic**.—*adv.* **telepath'ically.** [Gr. *tēle,* at a distance, *pathos,* feeling.]

telephone, *tel'e-fōn, n.* an instrument for reproducing sound, esp. speech, at a distance, esp. by means of electricity.—*v.t.* and *v.i.* to communicate by telephone.—*adj.* **telephon'ic**.—*ns.* **telephonist** (*tel-ef'-*), one who operates the telephone, a switchboard operator; **teleph'ony**, the use of a telephone system for transmitting sounds. [Gr. *tēle,* far, *phōnē,* a sound.]

telephotography, *tel-e-fō-tog'ra-fi, n.* a branch

of photography which involves the use of a camera with a lens analogous to a telescope, so that very distant views can be registered, either on plates or on cinematograph films: also used (*wrongly*) for phototelegraphy.— **telephoto lens**, a lens of long focal length for obtaining large images of distant objects. [Gr. *tēle,* at a distance, and **photography.**]

teleprinter, *tel'e-print-ėr, n.* a form of telegraph transmitter having a typewriter keyboard and a type-printing telegraph receiver. [Gr. *tēle,* at a distance, and **printer.**]

telerecording, *tel-i-rė-kör'ding, n.* recording for broadcasting by television: a television transmission from a recording. [*tele*vision and **recording.**]

telescope, *tel'e-skōp, n.* an optical instrument for viewing objects at a distance.—*v.t.* to drive or slide one into another like the movable joints of a spyglass—*v.i.* to be forced into each other in such a way.—*adj.* **telescop'ic**, pertaining to, performed by, or like a telescope: seen only by a telescope.—*adv.* **telescop'ically.** [Fr.—Gr. *tēle,* at a distance, *skopeein,* to look at.]

television, *tel-e-vizh'(ȯ)n, n.* the wireless transmission and reproduction on a screen of a view of objects, &c. at a place distant from the beholder: a television receiving set.—*v.t.* **tel'evise**, to transmit by television. [Gr. *tēle,* at a distance, and **vision.**]

telex, *tel'eks, n.* a Post Office service whereby subscribers hire teleprinters which are connected by telephone lines through automatic exchanges. [*tele*typewriter (teleprinter) *ex*change.]

tell, *tel, v.t.* to number, count: to utter (e.g. a lie): to narrate: to disclose: to inform: to discern (e.g. *I can't tell what it is*): to distinguish (e.g. *to tell one from the other*).—*v.i.* to produce or have a marked effect: to tell tales, play the informer:—*pa.t.* and *pa.p.* tōld.—*n.* **tell'er**, one who tells: a clerk whose duty it is to receive and pay money: one who counts votes in a legislative body.—*p.adj.* **tell'ing**, having great effect.—*n.* **tell'tale**, one who officiously tells the private concerns of others, or matters to the detriment of others.—*adj.* giving clear and unexpected evidence.—**tell on**, to affect obviously (e.g. *the strain told on him*); **tell off**, to count off: to detach on some special duty: (*coll.*) to rebuke. [O.E. *tellan.*]

tellurium, *te-lū'ri-um, n.* a metallic element (symbol Te; atomic no. 52).—*adj.* **tellū'ric**, pertaining to, or proceeding from, the earth: of or from tellurium. [L. *tellūs, tellūris,* the earth.]

telly, *tel'i, n.* (*coll.*) television.

Telugu, *tel'ŏŏ-gŏŏ, n.* a Dravidian language of south-east India: one of the people speaking it.—Also *adj.*

temerity, *te-mer'i-ti, n.* rashness. [Fr. *témérité*—L. *temeritās*—*temere,* by chance, rashly.]

temper, *tem'pėr, v.t.* (*arch.*) to mix in due proportion: to bring to a proper degree of hardness and elasticity by repeated heating and cooling, as steel: to moderate: to moderate by blending (*fig.*): to tune (a piano) in such a way that it can be used to play a scale in any key (see **temperament**).—*n.* due mixture or

---

Neutral vowels in unaccented syllables: *em'pėr-ȯr*; for certain sounds in foreign words see p. ix.

756

balance of different or contrary qualities: state of a metal as to hardness, &c.: constitutional state of mind, esp. with regard to feelings, disposition, mood: passion, irritation: in disposition, proneness, to anger.—*adj.* **tem′-pered,** having a certain specified disposition or temper (e.g. *even-tempered*): brought to a certain temper, as steel.—**to keep one's temper,** to restrain oneself from showing one's anger or losing one's temper; **to lose one's temper,** to lose one's equanimity, show anger. [L. *temperāre,* to combine properly, allied to *tempus,* time.]

tempera, *tem′pe-ra, n.* distemper (q.v.), esp. as used in the fine arts. [It.]

temperament, *tem′pér-a-mént, n.* in ancient physiology, the combination of the four humours (q.v.) by the relative proportions of which a man's natural disposition was determined: disposition, characteristic mental and emotional reactions as a whole: passionate disposition: (*mus.*) the adjustment of the intervals between the notes of a piano (which does not contain a large enough number of notes to allow a sufficient number of exact distinctions of pitch) so that it is possible to modulate from one key to another—the inaccuracies of pitch being distributed according to a definite plan: the system on which this is done: the act of tempering.—*adj.* **temperamen′tal,** pertaining to temperament: displaying alternation of moods, inclined to be swayed by emotion.—*adv.* **temperamen′tally.** [L. *temperāmentum—temperāre.* See **temper.**]

temperance, *tem′pér-áns, n.* moderation, esp. in the indulgence of the natural appetites and passions; moderation in the use of alcoholic liquors, and even entire abstinence from such.—**temperance hotel,** one which professes to supply no alcoholic liquors. [L. *temperantia.*]

temperate, *tem′pér-āt, adj.* moderate in degree of any quality, esp. in the appetites and passions, self-restrained: calm: cool, mild, moderate in temperature: abstemious.—*adv.* **tem′perately.—***ns.* **tem′perateness; tem′perature,** degree of any quality, esp. of hotness or coldness measured with respect to an arbitrary zero: measured degree of the heat of a body or of the atmosphere, recorded on a thermometer: body heat above the normal. [L. *temperātus,* pa.p. of *temperāre.* See **temper.**]

tempest, *tem′pest, n.* wind rushing with great velocity, usually with rain or snow, a violent storm: any violent commotion.—*adj.* **tempes′tuous,** resembling, or pertaining to, a tempest: very stormy: turbulent.—*adv.* **tempes′tuously.—***n.* **tempes′tuousness.** [O.Fr. *tempeste*—L. *tempestās,* a season, tempest—*tempus,* time.]

Templar, *tem′plär, n.* one of a religious military order, the **Knights Templars,** founded in 1119 for the protection of the Holy Sepulchre and pilgrims going thither: a student or lawyer living in the Temple, London.—**Good Templar,** a member of a teetotal society whose organisation is modelled on that of the Freemasons. [Orig. called 'Poor fellow-soldiers of Christ and of the *Temple* of Solomon', from their first headquarters in Jerusalem, on the

site of the temple of Solomon.]

template, *tem′plāt, n.* a pattern, in the form of a thin plate cut to the shape required, by which a surface of an article being made is marked out.—Also **tem′plet.** [L. *templum,* small timber.]

temple, *tem′pl, n.* an edifice erected to a deity: a place of worship: anything regarded as sanctified by divine presence.—**the Temple,** in London, two inns of court, once occupied by the Knights Templars. [L. *templum.*]

temple, *tem′pl, n.* the flat portion of either side of the head above the cheekbone.—*adj.* **tem′-poral.** [O.Fr. *temple*—L. *tempora,* the temples, pl. of *tempus,* time.]

templet. See **template.**

tempo, *tem′pō, n.* (*mus.*) time, rhythmic speed: (*fig.*) rate of any activity. [It.]

temporal, *tem′por-ál, adj.* pertaining to time, esp. to the period of the history of this world, hence to this life or world—opp. to *eternal*: secular or civil—opp. to *sacred* or *ecclesiastical*.—*n.* **temporal′ity,** temporalness or temporariness: (in *pl.*—**temporal′ities**) secular possessions, revenues of an ecclesiastic from lands, tithes, and the like.—*adj.* **tem′porary,** lasting, used, for a time only: transient.—*n.* a person employed temporarily.—*adv.* **tem′porarily.—***n.* **tem′porariness.—***v.i.* **tem′porise,** to act according to expediency: to yield temporarily to circumstances: to play for time, avoid committing oneself definitely.—*ns.* **tem′poriser; tem′porising.** [Fr.,—L. *temporālis—tempus,* time.]

temporal. See **temple** (2).

tempt, *temt, v.t.* (*arch.*) to test: to try to persuade, esp. ,to evil: to attract, pull strongly towards a course of action: to entice, induce.—*ns.* **tempta′tion,** act of tempting: state of being tempted: that which tempts: enticement to evil: trial; **temp′ter,** one who tempts, esp. (with 'the') the devil;—*fem.* **temp′tress.** *adj.* **tempt′ing,** adapted to tempt or entice, attractive. *adv.* **tempt′ingly.** [O.Fr. *tempter, tenter*—L. *tentāre,* to feel, test, try, inten. of *tendĕre,* to stretch.]

ten, *ten, adj.* and *n.* the cardinal number next above nine: a round number, several (as *ten times more useful*).—*n.* a figure denoting ten units, as 10 or x. —*adjs.* **ten′fold,** ten times: ten times more; **tenth** (see below).—**upper ten** (see **upper**). [M.E. *ten,* shortened form of *tēne*—O.E. *tēn,* earlier *tīen*; Ger. *zehn,* W. *deg,* L. *decem,* Gr. *deka,* Sans. *daśa.*]

tenable, *ten′a-bl, adj.* capable of being retained, held, or defended against attack (*lit.* and *fig.*)—*ns.* **tenabil′ity, ten′ableness.** [Fr. *tenable,* from *tenir*—L. *tenēre,* to hold.]

tenacious, *ten-ā′shús, adj.* retaining or holding fast (*lit.* and *fig.*): sticky: retentive: stubborn: persevering.—*adv.* **tenā′ciously.—***ns.* **tenā′ciousness, tenac′ity** (*-as′-*), quality of being tenacious: the quality of bodies which makes them stick to others. [L. *tenāx, -ācis—tenēre,* to hold.]

tenant, *ten′ánt, n.* one who holds or possesses land or property under another: one who has, on certain conditions, temporary possession of any place: an occupant.—*v.t.* (usu. in *pa.p.*) to hold as a tenant.—*n.* **ten′ancy,** a temporary

---

fāte, fär; mē, hûr (her); *mīne; mōte, fōr; mūte; mōōn, fŏŏt;* ᴛнen (then) holding or occupying of land or buildings by a tenant: the period of this.—*adjs.* **ten′antable,** fit to be tenanted: in a state of repair suitable for a tenant; **ten′antless,** without a tenant.—*n.* **ten′antry,** the body of tenants on an estate. [Fr. *tenant*—L. *tenēns, -entis,* pr.p. of *tenēre,* to hold.]

tench, *tench, -sh, n.* a fresh-water fish, of the same family as the carp, very tenacious of life. [O.Fr. *tenche*—L. *tinca.*]

tend, *tend, v.t.* to take care of, look after.—*n.* **ten′der,** a small craft that attends a larger with stores, &c.: one plying between a larger vessel and the shore: a vehicle attached to locomotives to carry fuel and water. [Contracted from **attend.**]

tend, *tend, v.i.* to be directed, move, or incline, in a specified direction: (*fig.*) to be directed (to any end or purpose): to contribute or conduce (to a result).—*n.* **ten′dency,** direction, object, or result to which anything tends: inclination: drift.—*adj.* **tenden′tious** (-*shús*), having a deliberate tendency or bias, written or uttered with set purpose. [L. *tendēre;* Gr. *teinein,* to stretch.]

tender, *ten′dér, v.t.* to offer for acceptance: to offer as payment.—*v.i.* to make an offer (for a contract—e.g. to offer to supply certain commodities for a certain period at rates specified).—*n.* an offer or proposal, esp. of some service: the thing offered, esp. money offered —payment.—**legal tender,** currency which the creditor may not refuse to accept in payment. [L. *tendēre,* to stretch.]

tender, *ten′dér, adj.* soft, delicate: succulent: not hardy, fragile: easily moved to pity, love, &c.: careful not to injure (with *of*): unwilling to cause pain: apt to feel pain, sensitive: expressive of the softer passions: young and inexperienced: delicate, requiring careful handling: apt to lean over under sail.—*n.* **ten′derfoot,** one not yet hardened to life in the prairie, mining-camp, &c.: a newcomer: (*obs.*) a (Boy) Scout or Girl Guide who has passed only the first test.—*adj.* **ten′der-heart′ed,** full of feeling.—*v.t.* **ten′derise,** to break down the connective tissue (of meat) by pounding or by applying a chemical.—*adv.* **ten′derly.**—*n.* **ten′derness.** [Fr. *tendre*—L. *tener.*]

tendon, *ten′dón, n.* a cord, band, or sheet of fibrous tissue by which a muscle is attached to a bone or to another muscle. [Fr. *tendon*—L. *tendēre,* to stretch; cf. Gr. *tenōn*—*teinein,* to stretch.]

tendril, *ten′dril, n.* a slender, spiral shoot of a plant by which it attaches itself for support.—*adj.* clasping or climbing. [App. L. *tendēre,* to stretch.]

tenebrous, *ten′e-brus, adj.* dark, gloomy.—Also **ten′ebrose.** [L. *tenebrōsus*—*tenebrae,* darkness.]

tenement, *ten′e-ment, n.* (*law*) anything held, or that may be held, by a tenant, in the widest sense of the word: a dwelling or habitation, or part of it: a building divided into flats or apartments, each occupied by a separate tenant, but with certain communal facilities—esp. such buildings occupied by poorer people. [L.L. *tenementum*—L. *tenēre,* to hold.]

tenet, *ten′et, tēn′-, n.* any opinion, principle, or doctrine that a person holds or maintains as true. [L. *tenet,* he holds—*tenēre,* to hold.]

tenner, *ten′ér, n.* (*coll.*) a ten-pound note. [**ten.**]

tennis, *ten′is, n.* an ancient game for two to four persons, played with ball and rackets within a building specially constructed for the purpose: lawn-tennis (q.v.).—*n.* **tenn′is-court,** a place or court for playing tennis. [Prob. Fr. *tenez,* imper. of *tenir,* take, receive.]

tenon, *ten′ón, n.* a projection at the end of a piece of wood inserted into the socket or mortise of another, to hold the two together. —*v.t.* to fit with tenons. [Fr.,—*tenir,* to hold —L. *tenēre.*]

tenor, *ten′ór, n.* general run or course, prevailing direction: purport: the highest kind of adult male voice, except falsetto (app. because the melody was assigned to it): the part next above the bass in a vocal quartet: one who sings tenor.—*adj.* pertaining to the tenor in music. [L.,—*tenēre,* to hold.]

tense, *tens, n.* time in grammar, the form of a verb which indicates the time of the action. [O.Fr. *tens* (Fr. *temps*)—L. *tempus,* time.]

tense, *tens, adj.* tightly strained, hence rigid: critical, exciting: nervous and highly strained (e.g. *he was tense with emotion*): (of a vowel) pronounced with the muscles of the tongue tense—opp. to *slack.*—*adv.* **tense′ly.**—*n.* **tense′ness.**—*adjs.* **ten′sible, ten′sile,** capable of being stretched.—*ns.* **ten′sion,** act of stretching: state of being stretched or strained: strain, effort: mental strain: a state of barely suppressed emotion, as excitement, suspense, anxiety: strained relations (between persons): opposition (between conflicting ideas or forces); **ten′sor,** a muscle that tightens a part. [L. *tensus,* pa.p. of *tendēre,* to stretch.]

tent, *tent, n.* a plug or roll of lint, &c., used to dilate a wound or a natural opening.—*v.t.* to probe: to keep open with a tent. [O.Fr. *tente*—*tenter, tempter.* See **tempt.**]

tent, *tent, n.* a portable lodge or shelter, generally of canvas stretched on poles: anything like a tent.—*ns.* **tent′-bed,** a bed having a canopy hanging from a central point overhead; **tent′-cloth,** canvas, duck, &c., suitable for tents.—*adj.* **ten′ted,** covered with tents.—*ns.* **tent′-guy,** an additional rope for securing a tent against a storm; **tent′-peg, -pin,** a strong peg of notched wood, or of iron, driven into the ground to fasten one of the ropes of a tent to; **tent′-pole,** one of the poles used in pitching a tent. [Fr. *tente*—L.L. *tenta*—L. *tendēre,* to stretch.]

tentacle, *ten′ta-kl, n.* a thread-like organ of certain animals for feeling or motion, &c.—*adj.* **tentac′ular.** [Fr. *tentacule*—L. *tentāre,* to feel—*tendēre,* to stretch.]

tentative, *ten′ta-tiv, adj.* of the nature of an attempt: experimental: provisional.—*adv.* **ten′tatively.** [Fr.,—L. *tentāre,* to feel, try—*tendēre,* to stretch.]

tenter, *ten′tér, n.* a machine on which cloth is extended or stretched by hooks.—*v.t.* to stretch on hooks.—*n.* **ten′ter-hook,** a sharp, hooked nail.—**be on tenter-hooks,** to be tortured by suspense or anxiety. [Fr. *tenture*—L. *tendēre, tentum,* to stretch.]

Neutral vowels in unaccented syllables: *em′pér-ôr*; for certain sounds in foreign words see p. ix.

tenter   terra-cotta

tenter, *ten'tér*, *n.* one who looks after something (e.g. a machine in a factory). [From dial. vb. *tent* — **intent**.]

tenth, *tenth*, *adj.* the last of ten: being one of ten equal parts.—*n.* one of ten equal parts.—*adv.* **tenth'ly**, in the tenth place. [**ten.**]

tenue, *té-nü*, *n.* bearing, carriage: manner of dress. [Fr.]

tenuity, *te-nū'i-ti*, *n.* thinness: slenderness: rarity: meagreness: faintness.—*adj.* **ten'uous.** —*n.* **ten'uousness.** [L. *tenuitās*—*tenuis*, thin, slender; cf. *tendēre*, to stretch.]

tenure, *ten'ūr*, *n.* act or conditions of holding property or office: a tenant's rights, duties, &c.: the period during which office or property is held. [Fr. *tenure*—L.L. *tenura*—L. *tenēre*, to hold.]

tepee, *té'pē, tep'ē*, *n.* an American Indian tent formed of skins, &c., stretched over a frame of converging poles. [Amer. Indian.]

tepefy, *tep'é-fī*, *v.t.* to make tepid or moderately warm:—*pa.t.* and *pa.p.* tep'efied.—*n.* **tepefac'-tion**, act of making tepid or lukewarm. [L. *tepefacĕre*—*tepēre*, to be warm, *facĕre*, to make.]

tepid, *tep'id*, *adj.* moderately warm, lukewarm.—*ns.* **tepid'ity**, **tep'idness**, lukewarmness. [L. *tepidus*—*tepēre*, to be warm.]

teraphim, *ter'ā-fim*, *n.pl.* images of some sort used in ancient Jewish religion and divination:—*sing.* **ter'aph.** [Heb.]

teratogen, *tér-at'ō-gén*, *n.* an agent that raises the incidence of congenital malformations.—*adj.* **terat'ogenic**, producing monsters. [Gr. *teras*, *-atos*, a monster.]

terbium, *tûr'bi-ùm*, *n.* a metallic element (symbol **Tb**; atomic no. 65). [*Ytterby*, a Swedish quarry.]

terce, *tûrs*, *n.* (*Scots law*) a widow's right, where she has no conventional provision, to a life-rent of a third of the husband's heritable property: the office of the third hour, which should be said between sunrise and noon. [Same as **tierce.**]

tercentenary, *tér-sen-tē'nā-ri*, or *tér-sen'te-nā-ri*, *adj.* including or relating to an interval of three hundred years.—*n.* the 300th anniversary of anything.—*adj.* **tercentenn'ial.** [L. *ter*, thrice, and **centenary.**]

tercet, *tûr'set*, *n.* a group of three lines of verse. [Fr.,—L. *tertius*, third.]

terebinth, *ter'e-binth*, *n.* the tree from which turpentine (q.v.) was obtained in early times.—*adj.* **terebinth'ine.** [L.,—Gr. *terebinthos.*]

teredo, *té-rē'dō*, *n.* any of the ship-worms, worms that bore into wood and are very destructive of it. [L.,—Gr. *terēdōn*, from *teirein*, to wear away.]

tergiversation, *ter-ji-ver-sā'sh(o)n*, *n.* a shuffling or shifting, subterfuge: fickleness of conduct: flight, desertion.—*v.i.* **ter'giversate**, to use evasion: to desert one's party or principles.—*n.* **ter'giversātor.** [L. *tergum*, the back, *versārī*, to turn.]

term, *tûrm*, *n.* a limit: any limited period: the time for which anything lasts: the time during which the courts of law are open: certain days on which rent is paid: a division of the school year: that by which a thought is expressed, a word or expression: (usu. *pl.*) a condition, arrangement: (*pl.*) fixed charges: one of the three elements in a syllogism: (*alg.*) a member of a compound quantity.—*v.t.* to apply a term to, to name or call.—*n.* **terminol'ogy**, doctrine of terms: the terms used in any art, science, &c.—*adj.* **terminolog'ical.**—*advs.* **terminolog'ically; term'ly**, term by term.—**terms of reference** (see **reference**).—**be on good, bad**, &c., **terms with**, to have friendly, unfriendly, &c., relations with; **bring to terms**, to compel to the acceptance of conditions (with); **come to terms** (*with*), to come to an agreement: to submit (to): (*fig.*) to find a way of living (with some personal trouble or difficulty); **in terms of**, in the language peculiar to: (*math.*) by an expression containing (e.g. *express x in terms of y*); **make terms**, to come to an agreement; **set terms** (see **set**). [Fr. *terme*—L. *terminus*, a boundary.]

termagant, *tûr'ma-gänt*, *n.* a boisterous, bold woman: a scold.—*adj.* boisterous, brawling, quarrelsome, scolding. [*Termagant* or *Tervagant*, a supposed Mohammedan idol, represented in mediaeval plays and moralities as of a violent character.]

terminate, *tûr'min-āt*, *v.t.* to set a limit to: to set the boundary to: to put an end to, to finish.— *v.i.* to be limited: to come to end either in space or in time.—*adjs.* **ter'minable**, that may be, or is liable to be, terminated: limitable; **ter'minal**, pertaining to, or growing at, the end or extremity: ending a series or part, occurring in every term.—*n.* an end: a point of connection in an electric circuit: a point where the supply to an electrical machine is taken: a railway terminus: an airport when considered as the terminus of a long-distance flight.—*n.* **terminā'tion**, act of terminating or ending: limit: end: the ending of words as varied by their signification. *adjs.* **terminā'-tional**, pertaining to, or forming, a termination; **ter'minative**, tending to terminate, or to determine.—**terminal illness**, a fatal disease in its final stages. [L. *terminus*, a boundary.]

terminus, *tûr'min-nus*, *n.* the end or extreme point: one of the extreme points of a railway, &c.:—*pl.* **ter'mini** (*-ī*). [L., a boundary.]

termite, *tûr'mīt*, *n.* an order of social insects, pale in colour and superficially resembling the ants—hence known as *white ants.* [L. *termes*, *-itis*, a wood-worm.]

tern, *tûrn*, *n.* a long-winged aquatic bird allied to the gulls. [O.N. *therna*; O.E. *tearn.*]

ternary, *tûr'nā-ri*, *adj.* proceeding by, or consisting of, threes.—*n.* the number three.—*adj.* **ter'nāte**, threefold, or arranged in threes. [L. *ternī*, three each—*trēs*, three.]

terpsichorean, *tûrp-sik-ō-rē'án*, *adj.* concerned with dancing. [Gr. *Terpsichorē*, the muse of dancing.]

terrace, *ter'ás*, *n.* a raised level bank of earth: any raised flat place: the flat roof of a house: a row of houses.—*v.t.* to form into a terrace, or terraces. [Fr. *terrasse*—It. *terrazza*—L. *terra*, the earth.]

terra-cotta, *ter'a-cot'a*, *n.* a composition of clay and sand used for statues, hardened like bricks by fire: the colour of terra-cotta. [I. *terra*, earth, *cocta*, pa.p. of *coquĕre*, to cook.]

fāte, fär; mē, hûr (her); *mīne; mōte, för; mūte; mōōn, fŏŏt; ᴛʜen* (then)

759

terra firma, *ter'a fûr'ma, n.* land as opposed to water. [L.]

terrain, *ter'ān, n.* a tract of land: any tract considered in relation to its fitness for some purpose: field of activity. [Fr.,—L. *terrēnum*—*terra,* the earth.]

terrapin, *ter'a-pin, n.* any of several edible tortoises, living in fresh or brackish water. [Prob. Amer. Indian.]

terraqueous, *ter-ā'kwē-us, adj.* consisting of land and water. [L. *terra,* earth, *aqua,* water.]

terrene, *te-rēn', adj.* pertaining to the earth: earthy: earthly. [L. *terrēnus*—*terra,* the earth.]

terrestrial, *te-res'tri-ál, adj.* (opp. to *celestial*) pertaining to, or existing on, the earth: earthly: living on the ground: representing the earth. [L. *terrestris*—*terra,* the earth.]

terrible, *ter'i-bl, adj.* fitted to excite terror or awe, awful, dreadful: (*coll.*) very bad.—*n.* **terr'ibleness,** state of being terrible: dreadfulness.—*adv.* **terr'ibly,** frighteningly: (*coll.*) extremely. [L. *terribilis*—*terrēre,* to frighten.]

terrier, *ter'i-ér, n.* a name originally applied to any breed of dog used to burrow underground, but now applied to any small dog: (*coll.*) a member of a territorial army. [Fr. *terrier*—*terre,* the earth—L. *terra.*]

terrier, *ter'i-ér, n.* a roll or register of landed property and its tenantry. [O.Fr.,—Low L. *terrārius* (adj.)—L. *terra,* land.]

terrify, *ter'i-fī, v.t.* to cause terror in, to frighten greatly, to alarm:—*pa.t.* and *pa.p.* **terr'ified.**—*adj.* **terrif'ic,** creating or causing terror, dreadful: (*coll.*) huge, impressive: (*coll.*) loosely, very good, enjoyable, attractive, &c.—*adv.* **terrif'ically.** [L. *terrēre,* to terrify, *facēre,* to make.]

territory, *ter'i-tó-ri, n.* the extent of land around or under the jurisdiction of a city or state: domain: (*U.S.*) a portion of the country not yet admitted as a State into the Union, and still under a provisional government: a wide tract of land: scope: (*lit.* and *fig.*) field of activity.—*adj.* **territó'rial,** pertaining to territory: limited to a district.—*n.* a soldier in the Territorial and Army Reserve, a voluntary military force on a territorial basis, the successor (1967) of the Territorial Force (1908) and the Territorial Army (1920).—*adv.* **territó'rially.**—**territorial waters,** that part of the sea reckoned as part of the adjacent state— orig. within a three-mile limit. [L. *territō-rium*—*terra,* the earth.]

terror, *ter'ór, n.* extreme fear: an object of fear or dread.—*v.t.* **terr'orise,** to terrify: to govern by terror.—*ns.* **terrorisā'tion; terr'orism,** a state of terror: an organised system of intimidation; **terr'orist,** one who practises terrorism.—*adjs.* **terr'or-smitt'en, -strick'en, -struck,** seized with terror, terrified. [L.,— *terrēre,* to frighten.]

terse, *tûrs, adj.* compact or concise, with smoothness or elegance (e.g. of style).—*adv.* **terse'ly.**—*n.* **terse'ness.** [L. *tersus*—*tergēre, tersum,* to rub clean.]

tertian, *tûr'shi-àn, adj.* occurring every other day (*lit.* on the *third* day, reckoning both first and last days).—*n.* an ague or fever with paroxysms every other day. [L. *tertiānus*— *tertius,* third—*trēs,* three.]

tertiary, *tûr'shi-àr-i, adj.* of the third degree, order, or formation.—*n.* (*cap.*) the geological era following the Mesozoic or Secondary era.—*adj.* pertaining to the series of sedimentary rocks or strata formed during this period, lying above the chalk and other Mesozoic strata, and abounding in organic remains: (of education) post secondary school, i.e. university, college of education, &c. [L. *tertiārius*— *tertius.*]

terza-rima, *ter'tsa-rē'ma, n.* a form of Italian triplet in iambic decasyllables, in which the middle line of the first triplet rhymes with the first and third lines of the next triplet, as in Dante's *Divina Commedia* and Longfellow's translation of it. [It., *terza,* fem. of *terzo,* third, *rima,* rhyme.]

tesla, *tes'lá, n.* SI unit of magnetic flux density, equal to one weber per sq. metre. Abbrev. T. [N. *Tesla,* U.S. inventor.]

tessera, *tes'e-ra, n.* one of the small square tiles or cut stones used in forming tessellated pavements:—*pl.* **tess'erae** (*-ē*).—*v.t.* **tess'ellate,** to form into squares or lay with chequered work.—*n.* **tessellā'tion,** tessellated or mosaic work: the operation of making it. [L. *tessella,* dim. of *tessera,* a square piece.]

test, *test, n.* a pot in which metals are tried and refined: any critical trial: means of trial: (*chem.*) anything used to distinguish substances or detect their presence, a reagent: a standard: a series of questions or exercises.— *v.t.* to put to proof: to examine critically.—*ns.* **test'er; test'-case,** a legal case whose decision may serve as an example for others of the same kind; **test'-flight,** trial flight of new aeroplane; **test'-match,** in cricket, &c., one of a series of international matches (esp. between England and Australia); **test pilot,** one whose job it is to take up new types of aircraft to test their quality; **test'-tube,** a cylinder of thin glass closed at one end, used in testing substances chemically.—**test-tube baby,** a child born as the result of artificial insemination: a baby, part of whose development takes place in the laboratory. [O.Fr. *test*—L. *testa,* an earthen pot, a broken piece of earthenware, a skull, a shell.]

testa, *tes'ta, n.* the seed coat, several layers of cells in thickness. [L. See **test.**]

testaceous, *tes-tā'shùs, adj.* consisting of, or having, a hard shell. [L. *testāceus*—*testa.* See **test.**]

testament, *tes'ta-mént, n.* that which testifies, or in which an attestation is made: the solemn declaration in writing of one's will: a will: a covenant made by God with men: (*cap.*) one of the two great divisions of the Bible, **Old Testament** and **New Testament,** dealing respectively with the covenant made by God with Moses and that made by God through Christ.—*adjs.* **testamen'tal, testamen'tary,** pertaining to a testament or will: bequeathed or done by will; **tes'tāte,** having made and left a will.—*n.* **testā'tor,** one who leaves a will:— *fem.* **testā'trix.** [L. *testāmentum*—*testārī,* to be a witness—*testis,* a witness.]

tester, *tes'tér, n.* a flat canopy, esp. over the head of a bed. [O.Fr. *teste,* the head—L. *testa.* See **test.**]

Neutral vowels in unaccented syllables: *em'pér-ór*; for certain sounds in foreign words see p. ix.

testicle, *tes'ti-kl, n.* a gland that secretes spermatozoa in males.—Also **testis.**—*adjs.* **testic'ulate, -d,** shaped like a testicle. [L. *testiculus,* dim. of *testis,* a testicle.]

testify, *tes'ti-fī, v.i.* to give evidence: to bear witness (to): to protest or declare a charge (against): (with *to*) to be evidence of.—*v.t.* to affirm or declare solemnly or on oath (e.g. one's determination that): to be evidence of:—*pa.t.* and *pa.p.* tes'tified.—*n.* **tes'tifier.** [L. *testificārī—testis,* a witness, *facĕre,* to make.]

testimony, *tes'ti-mō-ni, n.* evidence: declaration to prove some fact: (*B.*) the two tables of the law: the whole divine revelation.—*adj.* **testimō'nial,** containing testimony —*n.* a writing or certificate bearing testimony to one's character or abilities: a sum of money raised by subscription and presented in any form to a person as a token of respect. [L. *testimōnium—testārī,* to witness.]

testudo, *tes-tū'dō, n.* a cover for the protection of Roman soldiers attacking a fortified place, formed by overlapping their oblong shields above their heads, or consisting of a fixed or movable shed of various kinds. [L. a tortoise, testudo, tortoise.]

testy, *tes'ti, adj.* touchy, easily irritated, peevish.—*adv.* **tes'tily.**—*n.* **tes'tiness.** [O.Fr. *teste,* head, shell, cf. **test.**]

tetanus, *tet'a-nus, n.* an intense and painful spasm of more or less extensive groups of the voluntary muscles caused by poison due to a bacillus often introduced through a wound: lockjaw (q.v.).—*adj.* **tetan'ic.** [L.,—Gr., *tetanos—teinein,* to stretch.]

tête-à-tête, *tet'-a-tet', n.* a private confidential interview.—*adj.* confidential, secret.—*adv.* in private conversation: face to face. [Fr. *tête,* head.]

tether, *teTH'ér, n.* a rope or chain for tying an animal, while feeding, within certain limits.—*v.t.* to confine with a tether: to restrain within certain limits—**at the end of one's tether,** desperate, having no further strength, resources, &c. [App. O.N. *tjōthr.*]

tetragon, *tet'ra-gon, n.* a figure of four angles.—*adj.* **tetrag'onal.** [Gr. *tetragōnon—tetra-,* four, *gōnia,* an angle.]

tetrahedron, *tet-ra-hē'dron, n.* a solid figure enclosed by four bases or triangles.—*adj.* **tetrahē'dral,** having four sides: bounded by four triangles. [Gr. *tetra-,* four, *hedrā,* a base.]

tetralogy, *te-tral'o-ji, n.* a group of four related dramatic or literary works. [Gr. *tetralogia—tetra-,* four, *logos,* discourse.]

tetrameter, *te-tram'e-ter, n.* a verse line of four measures. [Gr. *tetrametros—tetra-,* four, *metron,* measure.]

tetrarch, *tet'rärk, tē'trärk, n.* under the Romans, the ruler of the fourth part of a province: a subordinate prince.—*ns.* **tet'rarchate, tet'rarchy,** office or jurisdiction of a tetrarch: the fourth part of a province. [Gr. *tetrarchēs—tetra-,* four, *archēs,* a ruler.]

tetrasyllable, *tet-ra-sil'a-bl, n.* a word of four syllables.—*adjs.* **tetrasyllab'ic, -al,** consisting of four syllables. [Gr. *tetra-,* four, **syllable.**]

tetter, *tet'ér, n.* a popular name for several eruptive diseases of the skin.—*v.t.* to affect with such. [O.E. *teter.*]

Teuton, *tū'ton, n.* one of a race, typically tall and blonde, a division of the Indo-Gmc. peoples including Germans and Scandinavians.—*adj.* **Teuton'ic,** belonging to the race called Teutons, or to the Germanic (q.v.) language. [L. *Teutones;* from the same root as Ger. *Deutsch,* German, and Eng. *Dutch.*]

text, *tekst, n.* the original words of an author: a passage of Scripture on which a sermon is based: a short quotation from the Bible used as a motto or a moral maxim: any concise phrase or statement on which a written or spoken discourse is based: a theme: the main printed part of a book as distinguished from preliminaries, index, illustrations.—*ns.* **text'book,** a book containing the leading principles of a subject (*adj.* of operation, exactly as planned, in perfect accordance with theory or calculation); **text'-hand,** a large hand in writing—so called because it was the practice to write the text of a book in large hand.—*adj.* **tex'tual,** pertaining to, or contained in, the text: serving for a text.—*adv.* **tex'tually.**—**textual criticism,** criticism with a view to establishing the actual words of a book as originally written. [L. *textus—texĕre, textum,* to weave.]

textile, *teks'tīl, -til, adj.* woven, or capable of being woven: pertaining to weaving.—*n.* a woven fabric. [L. *textilis—texĕre, textum,* to weave.]

texture, *teks'tyúr, -chúr, n.* anything woven, a web: the manner in which threads, &c., in a material, &c., are interwoven or combined: the manner of arrangement of particles in a substance: structural impression resulting from the manner of combining or interrelating the parts of a whole, as in music, art, &c.: the quality conveyed to the touch by woven fabrics, &c. *adj.* **tex'tural.** [L. *textura—texĕre, textum,* to weave.]

thaler, taler, *tä'ler, n.* any of various large silver coins formerly used in Germany and Austria. [Ger. See **dollar.**]

thalidomide, *tha-lid'ō-mīd, n.* a sedative discovered to cause malformation in the foetus if taken during pregnancy.—**thalidomide baby,** an infant with malformation caused by thalidomide.

thallium, *thal'i-úm, n.* a metallic element (symbol Tl; atomic no. 81). [Gr. *thallos,* a green shoot (from the bright green line in its spectrum).]

thallus, *thal'ús, n.* a plant body that is not differentiated into root, stem, leaves—whether a single cell, a filament of cells, or a complicated branching multicellular structure. [Gr. *thallos,* a young shoot.]

than, *THan, conj.* a word placed after the comparative of an adjective or adverb to introduce the second part of a comparison. [O.E. *thonne,* used after comparatives to introduce the standard of comparison; closely allied to *thone,* acc. masc. of definite article.]

thane, *thān, n.* a member of a class in the old English community that stood below the old nobility, but above the ordinary freeman.—*n.* **thane'dom,** the jurisdiction or the dignity of a thane. [O.E. *thegen, thegn,* a servant, nobleman *thīhan,* to grow.]

---

fāte, fär; mē, hûr (her); *mīne; mōte, för; mūte; mōōn, fŏŏt;* THen (then)

thank, *thangk, v.t.* to express gratitude to (someone) for a favour: to acknowledge indebtedness to (e.g. *he has to thank the calm weather for his safe return*; often ironically, meaning to blame).—*n.* (usually in *pl.*) expression of gratitude, often used elliptically, meaning 'My thanks to you'.—*adj.* **thank′ful,** full of thanks: grateful.—*adv.* **thank′fully.**—*n.* **thank′fulness.**—*adj.* **thank′less,** unthankful: not expressing thanks for favours: not winning thanks.—*adv.* **thank′lessly.**—*ns.* **thank′-lessness,** state of being thankless: ingratitude; **thank′-off′ering,** an offering made to express thanks for mercies received; **thanks′giver,** one who gives thanks, or acknowledges a favour; **thanks′giving,** act of giving thanks: a public acknowledgment of divine goodness and mercy: the form of words used for this: a day set apart for this, esp. that in the United States on the last Thursday of November.—*adj.* **thank′worthy,** worthy of, or deserving, thanks.—**thank you,** polite formula to express thanks. [O.E. *thanc, thonc,* will, thanks; akin to **think.**]

that, THα*t,* as a *demons. pron.* or *adj.* (*pl.* **those**), points out a person or thing—the former or more distant thing, not this but the other.—*rel. pron.,* who or which.—*conj.* used to introduce a noun clause, and various types of adverbial clauses, expressing the following:—because (e.g. *it is not that I mind*): in order that: that as a result (following *so* and *such*).—*conj.* **now that** (see **now**).—**and that's that,** and that is the end of that matter. [O.E. *thæt,* neut. of the article *the.* Cf. **the.**]

thatch, *thach, v.t.* to cover, as a roof, with straw, reeds, &c.—*n.* straw, &c., used to cover the roofs of buildings and stacks.—*ns.* **thatch′er,** **thatch′ing,** the act or art of covering with thatch: the materials used for thatching. [O.E. *thæc,* thatch, whence *theccan,* to cover.]

thaumaturgy, *thō′ma-tûr-ji, n.* the art of working wonders or miracles.—*adjs.* **thaumatur′gic, -al,** wonder-working. [Gr. *thaumatourgia—thauma, -atos,* a wonder, *ergon,* work.]

thaw, *thö, v.i.* to melt or grow liquid, as ice: to become so warm as to melt ice: to relax stiffness or unfriendly reserve.—*v.t.* to cause to melt.—*n.* the melting of ice or snow by heat: the change of weather which causes it. [O.E. *thawian.*]

the, THε, or (when emphatic) THḖ, *demons. adj.* usually called the definite article, used to denote a particular person or thing: also to denote a species. [O.E. *the,* rarely used as nom. masc. of definite article, but common as an indeclinable relative; cf. **that.**]

the, THḖ, *adv.* used before comparatives, as, 'the more the better'. [O.E. *thȳ,* by that, by that much, the instrumental case of the definite article.]

theatre, *thē′a-tėr, n.* a place where public representations, chiefly dramatic or musical, are seen, a play-house: any place rising by steps like the seats of a theatre: a room so arranged for lectures, demonstrations, or surgical operations: any room for surgical operations: scene of action, field of operations: dramatic literature: the stage: dramatic effect: material lending itself to effective production on the stage.—*adjs.* **theat′ric, -al,** relating to, or suitable to, a theatre, or to actors: pompous: melodramatic, affected.—*adv.* **theat′rically.**—*n.pl.* **theat′ricals,** (esp. amateur) dramatic performances.—**theatre-in-the-round,** a theatre with central stage and audience on all sides: the style of staging plays in such a theatre; **theatre of the absurd,** branch of drama dealing with fantastic deliberately unreal situations, in reaction against the tragedy and irrationality of life. [Gr. *theātron—theaesthai,* to see.]

thee, THḖ, *pron.* objective case (*acc.* or *dat.*) of **thou.** [O.E. *the,* dat., acc. of *thu* (cf. **thou**).]

theft, *theft, n.* act of thieving. [O.E. *thēofth, thȳfth—thēof,* thief.]

theine, *thē′in, n.* caffeine (q.v.). [Fr.,—*thé,* tea.]

their, THār, THεr, *possessive adj.* (also called *possessive pron.*) of or belonging to them. [O.N. *theirra*; O.E. *thǣra,* gen. pl. of the definite article.]

theirs, THārz, THεrs, *pron.* the possessive (*gen.*) case of **they** (e.g. *the furniture is theirs*).—Also *possessive adj.* (used without noun—e.g. *that is my car at the door, not theirs*). [Like **hers, ours, yours,** a double genitive containing a plural suffix *-r* + a sing. *-s.* These forms were confined in the 13th and 14th centuries to the Northern dialects, and are probably due to Scandinavian influence.]

theism, *thē′izm, n.* belief in the existence of God with or without a belief in a special revelation.—*n.* **the′ist,** one who believes in God.—*adjs.* **theist′ic, -al,** pertaining to theism, or to a theist: according to the doctrines of theists. [Gr. *theos,* God.]

them, THεm, *pron.* the objective case (*accusative* or *dative*) of **they.** [O.N. *theim*; O.E. *thǣm,* dat. pl. of the definite article (this replaced the older *heom, hem*).]

theme, *thēm, n.* a subject set or proposed for discussion, or on which a person speaks or writes: (*mus.*) subject, a short melody developed with variations or otherwise.—*adj.* **themat′ic,** (*mus.*) pertaining to a theme: (*gram.*) pertaining to a word stem.—**theme song,** a melody that is repeated often in a musical drama, film, or radio or television series, and is associated with a certain character, idea, emotion, &c.: a person's characteristic, often repeated, complaint, &c. [Fr. *thème*—L. *thēma*—Gr. *thēma—tithēnai,* to place, set.]

themselves, THεm-selvz′, *pron. pl.* of **himself, herself,** and **itself.** [**them** and **self.**]

then, THεn, *adv.* at that time: afterwards: immediately: at another time.—*conj.* for that reason, therefore: in that case. [O.E. *thanne, thonne, thænne,* acc. sing. from stem of definite article *the.* Doublet of **than.**]

thence, THεns, *adv.* from that time or place: for that reason.—*advs.* **thence′forth, thence-for′ward,** from that time forward. [M.E. *thennes* (*thenne* with the gen. ending *-s*)—O.E. *thanon.* Cf. **hence** and **whence.**]

theocracy, *thē-ok′rȧ-si, n.* a state, usu. controlled by priests, in which God is regarded as the sole sovereign, and the laws of the realm as divine commands rather than human ordinances.—*adjs.* **theocrat′ic, -al.** [Gr. *theokratiā—theos,* a god, *krateein,* to rule.]

Neutral vowels in unaccented syllables: *em′pér-ór*; for certain sounds in foreign words see p. ix.

theodicy, *thē-od'i-si, n.* an exposition of Divine Providence, designed to vindicate the holiness and justice of God in creating a world in which evil seems so largely to prevail. [Gr. *theos*, a god, *dikē*, justice.]

theodolite, *thē-od'ō-līt, n.* an instrument used in land-surveying for the measurement of angles horizontal and vertical. [Ety. unknown.]

theogony, *thē-og'o-ni, n.* the birth and genealogy of the gods, esp. as told in ancient poetry.—*n.* **theog'onist**, a writer on theogony. [Gr. *theogoniā—theos*, a god, *gonē*, race.]

theology, *thē-ol'o-ji, n.* the science which treats of God, and of man's duty to Him.—*n.* **theolō'gian**, one well versed in theology: a divine, a professor of divinity.—*adjs.* **theolog'ic, -al**, pertaining to theology or divinity.—*adv.* **theolog'ically.**—*v.t.* **theol'ogise**, to render theological.—*v.i.* to make a system of theology.—*n.* **theol'ogist**, a student in the science of theology: a theologian. [Gr. *theologiā—theos*, a god, *logos*, a treatise.]

theorem, *thē'o-rem, n.* a proposition never yet disproved.—*adjs.* **theoret'ic, -al**, (opp. to *prac-tical*) concerned with theory, not with its applications: not derived from experience: speculative: arrived at by calculation, not by experiment (e.g. of a result).—*adv.* **theoret'ically.**—*v.i.* **thē'orise**, to form a theory: to form opinions solely by theories: to speculate.—*ns.* **thē'oriser; thē'orist**, a theoriser: one given to theory and speculation; **thē'ory**, an explanation or system of anything: an exposition of the abstract principles of a science or art: speculation as opposed to proof: a hypothesis: reasoned expectation as opposed to practice. [Gr. *theōrēma—theoreein*, to view—*theaesthai*, to see.]

theosophy, *the-os'o-fi, n.* immediate divine illumination or inspiration claimed to be possessed by specially gifted men, who are also held to possess abnormal control over natural forces: the doctrines of various sects, including a modern school founded in 1875, which profess to attain knowledge of God by inspiration.—*adjs.* **theosoph'ic, -al**, pertaining to theosophy.—*n.* **theos'ophist**, one who believes in theosophy. [Gr. *theosophia—theos*, a god, *sophiā*, wisdom.]

therapeutic, *ther-a-pū'tik, adj.* pertaining to healing, curative.—*adv.* **therapeu'tically.**—*n.sing.* **therapeu'tics**, that part of medicine concerned with the treatment and cure of diseases.—*ns.* **therapeu'tist; ther'apy**, the curative and preventive treatment of disease or an abnormal condition. [Gr. *therapeuein*, to take care of, to heal.]

there, *THār, THēr, adv.* in that place: at that point: to that place or point—opp. to *here*: in that respect: in that matter.—Also used pronominally as an anticipatory subject when the real subject follows the verb (e.g. *there is no one at home*).—*n.* that place: that point.—*advs.* **thereabout'** or **-abouts'**, about or near that place: near that number, quantity, or degree; **thereaft'er**, after, or according to that; **thereat'**, at that place or occurrence: on that account; **thereby'**, by that means: in consequence of that; **therefor'**, for that, this, or it; **therefore** (*THār'för*), for that or this reason:

consequently; **therefrom'**, from that or this; **therein'**, in that or this place, time, or thing; **thereof'**, of that or this; **thereon'**, on that or this; **thereto', thereun'to**, to that or this; **thereupon'**, upon, or in consequence of, that or this: immediately; **therewith'**, with that or this: thereupon; **there'withal**, with that or this: at the same time, over and above. [O.E. *thǽr, thēr*; conn. with the stem of definite article *the*.]

therm, *thûrm, n.* usu. of gas, a unit of energy, equal to 100,000 British thermal units (105·5 megajoules), that unit being the amount of heat necessary to raise the temperature of 1 lb. of water at maximum density 1° Fahrenheit.—*adjs.* **ther'mal, ther'mic**, pertaining to heat: warm: due to heat.—*ns.* **ther'mal**, an ascending column of air; **ther'modynam'ics**, the branch of physics concerned with energy utilisation and transfer, esp. by means of heat; **ther'mo-electric'ity**, electricity developed by the unequal heating of bodies.—*adj.* **ther'monuc'lear**, pertaining to the fusion of atomic nuclei as seen in a **thermonuclear reaction**, a reaction produced by the fusion of nuclei at extremely high temperatures, as in the hydrogen bomb.—*n.* **ther'mopile**, an apparatus for the direct conversion of heat into electrical energy.—*adj.* **thermoplastic** (*thēr-mō-plas'tik*) becoming plastic on heating.—*n.* any resin that can be melted by heat and then cooled, an unlimited number of times, without appreciable change in properties.—*n.* **ther'mostat**, an automatic device for regulating temperatures.—*adj.* **thermostat'ic.**—*adv.* **thermostat'ically.**—**thermal springs**, natural springs of hot water. [Gr. *thermos*, hot—*therme*, heat—*therein*, to heat.]

thermionics, *thûr-mi-on'iks, n.sing.* the science dealing with the emission of electrons from hot bodies.—**thermion'ic valve**, or **tube**, a vacuum tube containing a heated cathode from which electrons are emitted, an anode for collecting some or all of these electrons, and generally, additional electrodes for controlling their flow to the anode. [*therm* and *ion* (q.v.), with *-ics* on the analogy of *mathematics*, &c.]

thermometer, *thûr-mom'e-tėr, n.* an instrument for measuring temperature.—*adjs.* **thermomet'ric, -al**, pertaining to a thermometer: ascertained by means of a thermometer.—*adv.* **thermomet'ically.**—**maximum thermometer**, one that registers the maximum temperature to which it is exposed; **minimum thermometer**, one that registers the minimum temperature to which it is exposed. [Gr. *thermē*, heat, *metron*, a measure.]

thermoplastic. See **therm.**

thermosetting compositions, *thûr'mō-set'ing kom-po-zish'(ō)nz*, compositions in which a chemical reaction takes place while they are being moulded under heat and pressure, the appearance and chemical and physical properties being entirely changed, and the product being resistant to further applications of heat (up to charring point). [*thermo-*, combining form of **therm** (q.v.), **setting**, **composition**.]

Thermos flask, *thûr'mos fläsk, n.* a flask or

bottle with a vacuum jacket, for keeping liquids hot or cold (often, but incorrectly, spelt without *cap.*). [Trade mark—Gr. *thermos*, hot, and **flask.**]

thermostat. See **therm.**

thesaurus, *thē-sō'rus, n.* a treasury or repository, esp. of knowledge, words, quotations, &c., a lexicon or cyclopaedia. [L.,—Gr. *thēsauros—tithenai,* to place.]

these, THēz, *demons. adj.* and *pron., pl.* of **this.** [O.E. *thǽs,* pl. of *thes,* this. Doublet **those.**]

thesis, *thē'sis, n.* a position, or that which is set down or advanced for argument: a subject for a scholastic exercise: an essay on a theme:—*pl.* **theses** (*thē'sēz*). [L.,—Gr. *tithenai,* to set, place.]

Thespian, *thes'pi-àn, adj.* pertaining to tragedy: tragic. [Gr. *Thespis,* founder of Greek tragedy.]

theurgy, *thē'úr-ji, n.* that kind of magic which claims to work by supernatural agency, as distinguished from natural magic and necromancy.—*adjs.* **theur'gic, -al.** [Gr. *theourgiā—theos,* a god, *ergein,* to work.]

thew, *thū, n.* (used chiefly in *pl.*) muscle or sinews: strength: resolution. [O.E. *thēaw,* manner.]

they, THā, *pers. pron., pl.* of **he, she,** or **it.** [The form *thei, tha* (meaning 'that') came into use in the north of England in the 13th cent., replacing the older *hī, hīe.* It is the O.E. *thā,* nom. pl. of the definite article, prob. modified by Scandinavian influence.]

thick, *thik, adj.* dense: firm (of a paste): crowded: closely set, abundant: frequent, in quick succession: having considerable depth or circumference, usu. solid: not transparent or clear: misty: dull, stupid: indistinct (of speech): (*coll.*) intimate.—*n.* the thickest or densest part of anything (esp. *fig.*—e.g. *in the thick of the fight*).—*adv.* closely: frequently: fast: to a great depth.—*v.t.* **thick'en,** to make thick or close: to strengthen.—*v.i.* to become thick or obscure: to crowd or press.—*ns.* **thick'-ening,** something put into a liquid or mass to make it thick; **thick'et,** a collection of trees or shrubs thickly or closely set, a close wood or copse.—*adjs.* **thick'-head'ed,** having a thick head or skull: stupid; **thick'ish,** somewhat thick.—*adv.* **thick'ly.**—*n.* **thick'ness.**—*adjs.* **thick'-set,** closely planted: having a short, thick body; **thick'-skinned,** having a thick skin: wanting sensibility, insensitive.—**a bit thick** (*coll.*), more than one can be expected to endure or accept, inconsiderate, going too far; **lay it on thick,** to praise extravagantly: to exaggerate; **through thick and thin,** in spite of all obstacles, without wavering. [O.E. *thicce.*]

thief, *thēf, n.* one who steals or takes unlawfully what is not his own:—*pl.* **thieves.** [O.E. *thēof;* O.N. *thjófr,* Ger. *dieb.*]

thieve, *thēv, v.i.* to practise theft, to steal.—*n.* **thiev'ery,** the practice of thieving.—*adj.* **thiev'ish,** addicted to theft: like theft: characteristic of a thief.—*adv.* **thiev'ishly.**—*n.* **thiev'ishness.** [O.E. *thēofian.*]

thigh, *thī, n.* the thick fleshy part of the leg from the knee to the trunk. [O.E. *thēo, thēoh;* O.N. *thjō,* O.H.G. *dioh.*]

thimble, *thim'bl, n.* a cap or cover to protect the finger and push the needle in sewing.—*ns.*

thim'bleful, as much as a thimble will hold: a small quantity; **thim'ble-rig,** a sleight-of-hand trick in which the performer conceals, or pretends to conceal, a pea or small ball under one of three thimble-like cups.—*v.i.* to cheat by such means. [O.E. *thȳmel,* a thumbstall—*thūma,* a thumb.]

thin, *thin, adj.* having little thickness: slim: lean: (of material) fine or transparent: lacking strength or substance (e.g. *thin soup*): rarefied: not dense: not close or crowded: inadequate, flimsy: not full or well grown, meagre: lacking in volume or resonance: unduly full of hardships or misfortunes.—*adv.* not thickly, not closely, in a scattered state.—*v.t.* to make thin: to make less close or crowded (with *away, out,* &c.): to make rare or less thick or dense.—*v.i.* to grow or become thin;—*pr.p.* thinn'ing; *pa.t.* and *pa.p.* thinned.—*adv.* **thin'ly.** —*n.* **thin'ness.**—*adjs.* **thinn'ish,** somewhat thin; **thin'-skinned,** having a thin skin: sensitive.—**into thin air,** into nothing or nothingness; **thin on the ground,** present in very small, inadequate numbers. [O.E. *thynne.*]

thine, THīn, *pron.,* (*arch.*) possessive (*gen.*) case of **thy** (e.g. *the fault is thine*).—Also *possessive adj.* (now used without noun—e.g. *that was my responsibility, but this is thine*): (*arch.*) thy, used before a following vowel. [O.E. *thīn,* thy—*thīn,* gen. of *thū,* thou.]

thing, *thing, n.* an inanimate object: a living being (in tenderness or in contempt): whatever may exist independently in space and time, as opposed to an idea: an event: an action: a production of hand or brain, esp. spoken or written: (*pl.*) possessions, esp. clothes or wraps: any distinct and individual object, fact, action, event, series, quality, or idea of which one may think or to which one may refer: (*coll.*) that which is wanted or is appropriate: (*coll.*) a slight obsession or phobia: (*coll.*) a liking or dislike.—**do one's (own) thing** (*coll.*), to behave as is natural to or characteristic of oneself: to do something in which one specialises; **have a thing about,** to have an unaccountable feeling about, as of fear, &c.; **just one of those things,** a happening one cannot account for or do anything to prevent; **make a thing of,** to make an issue of, to make a fuss about; **see things,** to imagine one sees things that are not there; **the thing,** the proper or right thing: in a normal state of health. [O.E. *thing, thinc.*]

thing, *ting, n.* a parliament, or a court of law, in Scandinavian countries. [O.N. *thing,* an assembly.]

think, *thingk, v.i.* to exercise the mind: to revolve ideas in the mind: to consider: to purpose or design (with *of*).—*v.t.* to imagine: to judge, to believe or consider:—*pa.t.* and *pa.p.* thought (*thawt*).—*n.* **think'er,** esp. one who is capable of deep and fruitful thought.—*p.adj.* **think'ing,** having the faculty of thought.— **think fit to,** to choose to (do something inadvisable, &c.); **think little, nothing, of,** to have a poor opinion of: not to regard as difficult or laborious; **think out,** to devise in detail (a plan): to solve by a process of thought; **think up,** to concoct, devise. [O.E. *thencan,* pa.t. *thōhte;* cog. with Ger. *denken.*]

Neutral vowels in unaccented syllables: *em'pér-ór;* for certain sounds in foreign words see p. ix.

third, *thûrd, adj.* the last of three: being one of three equal parts.—*n.* one of three equal parts: (*mus.*) a note two (conventionally, three) diatonic degrees above or below a given note, or the interval between the two notes (e.g. C to E).—*adv.* **third′ly,** in the third place.—*adjs.* **third-par′ty,** of, involving, a third person or party (e.g. *third-party risks,* those incurred by a third party—the insured person, i.e. the owner of vehicle, &c., being the first party, and the insurance company the second party); **third′-pro′gramme,** highbrow, in allusion to the Third Programme (1946-70) of the B.B.C.; **third′-rate,** of the third order: inferior.—**third degree** (see **degree**); **third man** (*cricket*), a fielder on the offside between point and slip but further out; **Third Reich,** Germany as a totalitarian state from 1933-45 (see **Reich**); **Third World,** the developing countries. [O.E. *thridda—thrēo,* three.]

thirst, *thûrst, n.* the uneasiness caused by want of drink: vehement desire for drink: eager desire (for anything).—*v.i.* to feel thirst: to have vehement desire.—*adj.* **thirst′y,** suffering from thirst: dry, parched: vehemently desirous.—*adv.* **thirst′ily.**—*n.* **thirst′iness.** [O.E. *thurst, thyrst.*]

thirteen, *thûr′tēn* (when used absolutely, *thûr-tēn′), adj.* and *n.* three and ten.—*adj.* **thir′teenth,** the last of thirteen: being one of thirteen equal parts.—Also *n.* [O.E. *thrēotēne—thrēo,* three, *ten,* ten.]

thirty, *thûr′ti, adj.* and *n.* three times ten.—*adj.* **thir′tieth,** the last of thirty: being one of thirty equal parts.—Also *n.* [O.E. *thrītig—thrī,* three, *tig,* ten, related to *tīen, tēn.*]

this, *THis, demons. pron.* or *adj.* denoting a person or thing near, just mentioned, or about to be mentioned:—*pl.* **these.** [O.E., the neut. of the demons. pron. *thes* (masc.), *thēos, thīos* (fem.); pl. *thās,* which gave **those**; later pl. *thǣs,* which gave **these**; O.N. *thessi,* Ger. *dieser.*]

thistle, *this′l, n.* a genus of prickly plants.—*n.* **this′tle-down,** the tufted feathery bristles of the seeds of a thistle.—*adj.* **this′tly,** overgrown with thistles. [O.E. *thistel.*]

thither, *THiTH′ér, adv.* to that place: to that end or result.—*adv.* **thith′erward,** toward that place. [O.E. *thider.*]

tho′, THO, abbreviation for **though.**

thole, *thōl, n.* a pin in the side of a boat to keep the oar in place.—Also **thole′-pin, thowl, thowel.** [O.E. *thol.*]

Thomism, *tō′mizm, n.* the doctrines of the scholastic theologian, *Thomas Aquinas* (1226-1274), esp. as these are set forth in his *Summa Theologiae,* which still represent, with few exceptions, the general teaching of the R.C. Church.—*n.* **Thō′mist,** a follower of Aquinas.

thong, *thong, n.* a piece or strap of leather to fasten anything: the lash of a whip. [O.E. *thwang.*]

thorax, *thō′-, thō′raks, n.* the part of the body between the neck and belly, the chest: in insects, the middle one of the three chief divisions of the body.—*adj.* **thoracic** (-*ras′-*).—**thoracic duct,** the main trunk of the vessels conveying lymph in the body. [L.,—Gr.]

thorium, *thō′ri-um, n.* a radioactive metallic el

ement (symbol Th; atomic no. 90). [*Thor,* the Norse deity.]

thorn, *thörn, n.* a sharp, woody projection (a sharp-pointed, leafless branch) on the stem of a plant: (*loosely*) a prickle (as on roses) or a spine: a shrub or small tree having thorns, esp. hawthorn and blackthorn: anything prickly or troublesome: (also **thorn letter**) þ, an early English symbol for *th,* orig. a rune (q.v.)—used by the scribes both for *th* in *thin* and for TH in THen, interchangeable with another symbol, ð, a crossed *d*; these signs are distinguished by modern phoneticians and used for the breath and the voiced consonant respectively.—*adj.* **thorn′y,** full of thorns: prickly: troublesome: harassing.—**thorn in the flesh,** any cause of constant irritation, from 2 Cor. xii. 7. [O.E. *thorn.*]

thorough, *thûr′ō, adj.* (*rare*) passing through from end to end: complete, consummate (e.g. *a thorough rogue, master of his art*): very exact and painstaking (of a person, his methods, or his work)—whole-hearted, or exhaustive. *prep.* (*obs.*) through.—*n.* **thor′ough-bass** (*mus.*), a bass line throughout a piece, to which harmonies, &c., have to be added (harmonies often being indicated by numbers).—*adj.* **thor′oughbred,** bred from a dam and sire of the best blood, as a horse: (*fig.*) aristocratic—well-bred, spirited, having distinction—*n.* an animal, esp. a horse, of pure blood: a thoroughbred person.—*n.* **thor′oughfare,** a place or passage for going through: a public way or street: right of passing through.—*adj.* **thor′ough-gō′ing,** going all lengths, complete, out-and-out, uncompromising.—*adv.* **thor′oughly,** completely, entirely.—*n.* **thor′oughness.**—*adj.* **thor′ough-paced,** thoroughly or perfectly paced or trained: complete, thorough-going. [A longer form of **through.**]

thorp, thorpe, *thörp, n.* a hamlet. [O.E. *thorp: Ger. dorf.*]

those, *THōz, adj.* and *pron., pl.* of **that.** [O.E. *thās,* the old pl. of *thes,* this. Cf. **this.** Doublet **these.**]

thou, *THow, pron.* of the second person sing., the person spoken to (now generally used only in solemn address). [O.E. *thū*; cog. with Gr. *ty,* L. *tu,* Sans. *tvam.*]

thou, *thow, n.* (*coll.*) ¹⁄₁₀₀₀ in. [**thousand.**]

though, *THō, conj.* admitting, allowing, even if: (used absolutely) however. [O.N. *thauh, thō*; O.E. *thēah, thēh.*]

thought, *thôt, pa.t.* and *pa.p.* of **think.** [O.E. *thoht—thencan,* to think.]

thought, *thôt, n.* the act of thinking: power of reasoning: conception: deliberation: that which one thinks: an idea: opinions collectively: consideration: meditation: design, intention (often *pl.*): care.—*adj.* **thought′ful,** full of thought: employed in meditation: marked by or showing thought: attentive, considerate.—*adv.* **thought′fully.**—*n.* **thought′fulness.**—*adj.* **thought′less,** without thought or care: careless: inconsiderate: inattentive: stupid.—*adv.* **thought′lessly.**—*ns.* **thought lessness; thought-reading,** discerning what is passing in another's mind by observing his expressions, or by telepathy; **thought-transference,** transference of thought from one mind to another—telepathy at close quarters.—**on second thoughts,** after further consideration. [O.E. *gethōht*; cf. **think.**]

thousand, *thow'zănd, adj.* ten hundred: denoting any great number.—*n.* the number ten hundred: any large number.—*adjs.* **thou'sandfold,** repeated a thousand times: multiplied by a thousand; **thou'sandth,** the last of a thousand or of any great number.—*n.* one of a thousand equal parts of a whole.—**one in a thousand,** rare and excellent. [O.E. *thūsend*; Ger. *tausend.*]

thowel, thowl. See **thole.**

thrall, *thrōl, n.* a slave, serf: slavery, servitude.—*v.t.* to enslave.—*n.* **thral'dom, thrall'dom,** the condition of a thrall or slave: slavery, bondage. [O.N. *thræll,* a slave; akin to O.E. *thrǣgan,* to run.]

thrash, *thrash, v.t.* to beat out grain from the straw by means of e.g. a flail or machinery (more often **thresh**): to beat soundly: (with *out*) to discuss thoroughly, so as to reach agreement.—*v.i.* to thresh grain: to move, stir, or toss violently (with *about*). *ns.* **thrash'er, thresh'er; thrash'ing, thresh'ing; thrash'ingfloor, thresh'ing-floor,** a floor on which grain is thrashed. [From a northern form of O.E. (W.S.) *therscan.*]

thrawn, *thrön, adj.* twisted: perverse, intractable, obstinate. [Scots form of *thrawn*—see **throw.**]

thread, *thred, n.* a very thin line of any substance twisted and drawn out: a filament of any fibrous substance: a fine line of yarn: anything resembling a thread: the prominent helical part of a screw: a line (of reasoning): sequence (of ideas).—*v.t.* to pass a thread through the eye of (as a needle): to pass or pierce through, as a narrow way: to furnish with a thread.—*adjs.* **thread'bare,** worn to the bare thread, having the nap worn off: hackneyed; **thread'y,** like thread: slender: containing, or consisting of, thread. [O.E. *thrǣd—thrāwan,* to wind, to twist.]

threat, *thret, n.* a declaration of an intention to inflict punishment or other evil upon another: a menace (to).—*v.t.* and *v.i.* **threat'en,** to declare an intention (to do, of doing): to declare the intention of inflicting (punishment or other evil upon another): to terrify by menaces: to suggest the approach of (evil or something unpleasant).—*n.* **threat'ener.**—*adj.* **threat'ening,** indicating a threat or menace: indicating something approaching or impending.—*adv.* **threat'eningly.** [O.E. *thrēat—thrēotan,* to afflict.]

three, *thrē, adj.* and *n.* the cardinal number next above two.—*n.* the figure 3 or iii denoting this.—*adjs.* **third** (see separate article); **three'fold,** thrice repeated: consisting of three; **three'-foot,** measuring three feet.—*ns.* **threepence** (*thrip'ens, threp'ens*), three pennies; **threepenny bit** (*thrip'-, threp'-*; now *obs.*) a coin of the value of three old pence (3d.)—*adjs.* **three'-ply,** having three plies or strands; **three'-score,** three times a score, sixty (also *n*). [O.E. *thrēo,* fem. and neut. of *thrī*; O.N. *thrīr.* Gael. *tri,* Ger. *drei,* L. *trēs,* Gr. *treis,* Sans. *tri.*]

threnody, *thren'ö-di* or *thrēn'ö-di, n.* an ode or song of lamentation. [Gr. *thrēnōidiā—thrēnos,* a lament, *ōidē,* a song.]

thresh, *thresh. See* **thrash.**

threshold, *thresh'ōld, -hōld, n.* the piece of timber or stone under the door of a building: doorway, entrance: (*fig.*) the place or point of entering or beginning: the point, limit at which a physiological or psychological experience begins (e.g. the *threshold of consciousness, threshold of pain*). [O.E. *therscwald—therscan,* to thresh, *wald,* wood.]

threw, *thrōō, pa.t.* of **throw.**

thrice, *thrīs, adv.* three times. [O.E. *thrīwa,* thrice—*thrī,* three.]

thrift, *thrift, n.* careful management, frugality: (*obs.*) prosperity: a plant of several species, esp. sea-pink.—*adj.* **thrift'y,** showing thrift or economy: thriving by frugality.—*adv.* **thrift'ily.**—*n.* **thrift'iness.**—*adj.* **thrift'less,** not thrifty, extravagant: not thriving.—*adv.* **thrift'lessly.**—*n.* **thrift'lessness.** [Same root as **thrive.**]

thrill, *thril, v.t.* (*obs.*) to pierce: to excite.—*v.i.* to tingle with excitement: to throb or pulse.—*n.* a thrilling sensation: vibration.—*n.* **thrill'er,** an exciting (usu. detective) novel or play.—*adj.* **thrill'ing,** exciting. [O.E. *thyrlian,* to bore a hole—*thyrel,* a hole.]

thrive, *thrīv, v.i.* to prosper, to increase in goods: to be successful: to grow vigorously, to flourish:—*pa.t.* **thrōve** and **thrived**; *pa.p.* **thriv'en.**—*p.adj.* **thrī'ving,** flourishing, successful.—*adj.* [O.N. *thrīfa,* to grasp.]

throat, *thrōt, n.* the forepart of the neck, in which are the gullet and windpipe: an entrance: a narrow part of anything.—*adj.* **throat'y,** formed in the throat, guttural in sound: hoarse. [O.E. *throte.*]

throb, *throb, v.i.* to beat, as the heart or pulse, with more than usual force: to vibrate:—*pr.p.* **throbb'ing;** *pa.t.* and *pa.p.* **throbbed.**—*n.* a beat or strong pulsation. [Imit.]

throe, *thrō, n.* (usu. *pl.*) suffering, pain: the pains of childbirth: distressing effort or struggle. [O.E. *thrēa, thrēaw,* suffering—*thrēowan,* to suffer.]

thrombosis, *throm-bō'sis, n.* a coagulation of blood, forming a clot in a blood-vessel. [Gr. *thrombos,* a clot.]

throne, *thrōn, n.* a chair of state richly ornamented and raised: seat of a bishop in the cathedral-church of his diocese: sovereign power: the sovereign.—*v.t.* to place on a royal seat: to exalt:—*pr.p.* **thrōn'ing;** *pa.t.* and *pa.p.* **thrōned.** [O.Fr.,—L. *thronus*—Gr. *thronos,* a seat.]

throng, *throng, n.* a crowd: a great multitude.—*v.t.* to press or crowd upon (a person): to fill with a crowd: (of a crowd) to fill very full.—*v.i.* to crowd (together): to come in multitudes. [O.E. *gethrang—thringan,* to press.]

throstle, *thros'l, n.* the song-thrush or mavis. [O.E. *throstle*; Ger. *drossel.*]

throttle, *throt'l, n.* the throat or windpipe: a valve controlling the flow of steam or other gas to an engine.—*v.t.* to choke by pressure on the windpipe: to shut off the steam from a steam-pipe, engine, &c. [Dim. of **throat.**]

through, *thrōō, prep.* from end to end, or from side to side, of: into and then out of: over the

Neutral vowels in unaccented syllables: *em'pėr-ŏr*; certain sounds in foreign words see p. ix.

766

whole extent of: (*fig.*) from beginning to end of: by means of: in consequence of: (*U.S.*) up to and including.—*adv.* from one end or side to the other: from beginning to end.—*adj.* clear, unobstructed: going from starting-point to destination without break or change.—*adv.* **through'-and-through,** thoroughly.—*prep.* **throughout'**, in every part of: from one end to the other of.—*adv.* in every part, everywhere: from beginning to end.—*n.* **through'-put,** the amount of material put through a process.— **through with,** finished with. [O.E. *thurh.*]

throve, *throv,* pa.t. of **thrive.**

throw, *thrō, v.t.* to hurl, to fling: to wind or twist together, as yarn: to form on a wheel, as pottery: to venture at dice: to shed, cast off: (*coll.*) to lose (a contest) deliberately: to put on or spread carelessly (with *on*): to cast down in wrestling: to put in position, or to offer, in such a way as to suggest throwing (e.g. *to throw a bridge across a river*; *to throw a word*): (*coll.*) to hold, give (a party).—*v.i.* to cast or hurl: to cast dice:—*pa.t.* threw (*thrōō*); *pa.p.* thrōwn.—*n.* the act of throwing: a cast, esp. of dice: the distance to which anything may be thrown.—*ns.* **throw'-away,** a contest without serious competition: a line or joke that an actor purposely delivers without emphasis or dramatic effect: very cheap, as if being thrown away); **throw'er; throw'back,** a set-back: a reversion to an ancestral or more primitive type; (in a film) a flash-back; **throw'-in,** (*football*) a throw from the touchline to put the ball back into play.—**throw in,** to add, give, gratuitously: to make (a comment) casually, to interpose; **throw off,** to cast off hastily, abruptly: get rid of (e.g. a disease, depression): to produce extempore (e.g. *to throw off epigrams*); **throw oneself at,** to make a determined and obvious attempt to captivate; **throw oneself into,** to engage heartily in, **throw oneself (up)on the mercy of,** to appeal to, rely on, for leniency; **throw up (something) against someone,** to reproach him with (something). [O.E. *thrāwan,* to turn, to twist.]

thrum, *thrum, n.* the end of a weaver's thread: any loose thread or fringe: coarse yarn.—*v.t.* to furnish with thrums: to fringe: to insert short pieces of rope-yarn in a mat or piece of canvas:—*pr.p.* thrumm'ing; *pa.t.* and *pa.p.* thrummed.—*adj.* **thrumm'y,** made of, or like, thrums. [O.E. *thrōmr,* the edge; Ger. *trumm,* a fragment.]

thrum, *thrum, v.i.* to play crudely or monotonously on an instrument with the fingers. [Imit.]

thrush, *thrush, n.* a genus (in a wider sense, a family) of passerine birds, specifically the throstle, song-thrush, or mavis of Europe. [O.E. *thrysce,* a thrush.]

thrush, *thrush, n.* an inflammatory and suppurating affection of the sensitive surfaces within the frog of the horse: a disease of the mouth and throat, usu. affecting infants. [Scand., O.N. *thurr,* dry.]

thrust, *thrust, v.t.* to push or drive with force: to press (in): to stab, pierce: to force (oneself, one's company, on). *v.i.* to make a push, esp.

with a pointed weapon: to squeeze (in), to intrude:—*pa.t.* and *pa.p.* thrust.—*n.* a stab: pressure: stress between two parts of a structure, esp. the equal horizontal forces acting on the abutments of an arch, due to the loading carried by it: the propulsive force developed by a motor. [O.N. *thrȳsta,* to press.]

thud, *thud, n.* a dull, hollow sound, caused by a blow or 'a heavy body falling.—*v.i.* to make such a sound. [O.E. *thōden,* noise.]

thug, *thug, n.* one of a class of professional robbers and assassins in India (extirpated 1826-35) whose violent deeds had a religious motive: a man who lives by violence.—*ns.* **thuggee', thugg'ism,** the practice and superstition of the thugs; **thugg'ery,** organised robbery and violence. [Hindustani *thag,* cheat.]

Thule, *thū'lē, n.* the name given by the ancients to the most northerly part of Europe of which they had heard—perh. Scandinavia, or Iceland, or the Orkney and Shetland groups.— Also **Ultima** (*ul'ti-ma*) **Thule.** [L. *Thūlē.*]

thulium, *thū'li-um, n.* a rare metallic element (symbol Tm; atomic no. 69) [L. *Thūlē.* See **Thule.**]

thumb, *thum, n.* the short, thick finger of the human hand: the corresponding member in other animals. *v.t.* to handle awkwardly: to turn over, or to soil, with the thumb or fingers: (*slang*) to make a signal to (a person, vehicle) by means of the thumb.—*adj.* **thumbed,** having thumbs: marked by the thumb, worn by use.—*ns.* **thumb'-index,** one arranged as indentations on the outer margins of pages of books; **thumb'kin, thumb'-screw,** an old instrument of torture for compressing the thumb by means of a screw; **thumb'(-)nail,** the nail of the thumb (*adj.* small but complete—e.g. *a thumbnail sketch*); **thumb'-stall,** a stall or sheath for the thumb.—**rule of thumb,** a rough-and-ready practical method, found by experience to be convenient; **thumb a lift (ride)** (*coll.*), to beg a lift from passing motorists by signalling from the side of the road with the thumb; **under one's thumb,** completely under one's influence. [With intrusive *b,* O.E. *thuma.*]

thump, *thump, n.* a heavy blow.—*v.t.* to beat with something heavy.—*v.i.* to strike or fall with a dull, heavy blow.—*n.* **thump'er,** one who, or that which, thumps: (*coll.*) anything very big, a big lie, &c.—*adj.* **thump'ing** (*coll.*), unusually big. [Prob. imit., like O.N. *dumpa,* to thump.]

thunder, *thun'dér, n.* the deep rumbling sound after a flash of lightning: thunder and lightning: any loud noise.—*v.i.* to make thunder: to sound as thunder: to storm, threaten.—*v.t.* to utter loudly and emphatically.—*ns.* **thun'derbolt,** a bolt or shaft of lightning and a peal of thunder: anything sudden and irresistible: an unexpected threat or disaster; **thun'derer,** esp. (*cap.*) Jupiter: (once popularly) the London *Times.*—*adjs.* **thun'dering,** unusually big, tremendous; **thun'derous,** giving forth a sound like thunder: angry-looking; **thun'derstruck,** struck by lightning: astonished, struck dumb; **thun'dery,** indicative of thunder, or attended by it.—**steal one's thunder,** to deprive one of the chance to make an im-

fāte, fär; mē, hûr (her); *mīne; mōte, för; mūte; mōōn, fŏŏt;* ᴛʜᴇɴ (then)

pression or produce a startling effect by appropriating one's idea or material and using it first—a method of representing thunder invented by John Dennis (1657-1734) was used first in a rival's play. [With intrusive *d*, O.E. *thunor*, thunder, *Thunor*, thunder-god, Thor.]

thurible, *thū'ri-bl, n.* a censer.—*n.* **thū'rifer,** the server who carries the thurible. [L. *thūri-bulum*—*thūs*, gen. *thūris*, frankincense; akin to Gr. *thyos*, a sacrifice.]

Thursday, *thûrz'dā, n.* the fifth day of the week, so called because originally sacred to *Thunor*, the English god of thunder. [O.E. *Thunres dæg*, Thunor's day; O.N. *Thōrsdagr*, Thor's day.]

thus, ᴛʜᴜs, *adv.* in this or that manner: to this degree or extent.—*adv.* **thus'wise,** in this manner. [O.E. *thus*, prob. *thȳs*, instrumental case of *thes*, this.]

thwack, *thwak, v.t.* to strike with something blunt and heavy, to thrash.—*n.* a heavy blow. [Perh. **whack,** or O.E. *thaccian*, to smack.]

thwart, *thwört, adj.* cross, lying crosswise.—*v t.* to baffle, to frustrate (e.g. a purpose, a person).—*n.* the bench for rowers placed athwart the boat. [O.N. *thvert*, neut. of *thverr*, perverse.]

thy, ᴛʜɪ, *possessive adj.* (also called *possessive pron.*) of or pertaining to thee. [Short for *thine*, O.E. *thīn*, gen. of *thū*, thou.]

thyme, *tīm, n.* a genus of aromatic herbs.—the common garden-thyme, used for seasoning, wild-thyme, &c.—*adj.* **thy'my.** [Fr.,—L. *thymum*—Gr. *thyein*, to fill with sweet smells, to burn in sacrifice.]

thymus, *thī-mùs, n.* a ductless gland near the root of the neck.—*n.* **thymine** (*thī'mēn*), one of the four bases in deoxyribo-nucleic acids. [Gr. *thymos*, thymus gland.]

thyroid, *thī'roid, adj.* in the form of a shield: denoting a ductless gland that arises in the earlier human embryo as an ingrowth from the lower part of the pharynx and has a profound influence on development and growth. [Gr. *thyreos*, a shield, *eidos*, form.]

thyself, ᴛʜɪ-*self', pron.* thou or thee in person—used for emphasis. [**thy, self.**]

tiara, *ti-ä'ra, n.* the lofty ornamental headdress of the ancient Persians: the mitre of the Jewish high-priest: the pope's triple crown: a circular or semi-circular head-ornament, often of jewels. [Fr.—L. *tiare*—L. *tiāra*—Gr. *tiāra.*]

tibia, *tib'i-a, n.* the larger of the two bones between the knee and the ankle: an ancient flute: one of several organ-stops. [L., the shin-bone, hence a flute, originally made from it.]

tic, *tik, n.* a convulsive motion of certain muscles, esp. of the face: (*fig.*) an involuntary habitual response.—*n.* **tic'-doul'oureux** (-*dol-ŏ-rōō'*; Fr. *tek dōō-lōō-rø*), painful convulsive motion of a nerve, usually in the face. [Fr. *tic*, a twitching.]

tick, *tik, n.* the popular name for numerous large mites that infest men and animals: (*coll.*) a small objectionable person. [M.E. *teke*; Du. *teek.*]

tick, *tik, n.* the cover in which feathers, &c., are put for bedding.—*n.* **tick'ing,** the cloth of which ticks are made. [L. *thēca*—Gr. *thēkē*, a case.]

tick, *tik, v.i.* to make a small, quick noise: to beat, as a watch: (*coll.*) to work, function.—*n.* the sound of a watch: a moment.—*n.* **tick'er,** anything which ticks, as a watch: a telegraphic receiving machine.—**tick'er-tape,** tape, paper ribbon used on an automatic machine which prints telegraphically the latest news, stock exchange prices, &c.; **tick'ing-off,** a reprimand. [Imit.]

tick, *tik, n.* credit, trust. [**ticket.**]

tick, *tik, v.t.* (often with *off*) to mark off lightly, as items in a list.—*n.* a light mark.—**tick off,** (*coll.*) to rebuke sharply. [M.E. *tek*, a touch; Du. *tik.*]

ticket, *tik'et, n.* a marked card: a token of any right or debt, as for admission, penalty for some offence (esp. motoring), &c.: (*slang*) release from the armed forces: (*U.S.*) a list of candidates put forward by a party for election: the principles associated with a particular political party.—*v.t.* to mark by a ticket.—*n.* **tick'et-of-leave,** a licence to be at large, granted to a convict for good conduct (also *adj.*).—**season ticket** (see **season**); **the ticket,** the correct thing. [Short for O.Fr. *e(s)tiquet(te)*, a label (Fr. *étiquette*), from Gmc.; Ger. *stecken*, to stick.]

tickle, *tik'l, v.t.* to touch lightly and provoke to laughter: to please or amuse: to puzzle.—*n.* **tick'ler,** something difficult, a puzzle.—*adj.* **tick'lish,** easily tickled: easily affected: nice, critical, difficult to handle (e.g. a problem).—*adv.* **tick'lishly.**—*n.* **tick'lishness.**—*adj.* **tick'ly,** ticklish.—**tickle pink,** to please, amuse, very much. [Freq. of **tick** (5).]

tiddly, *tid'li, n.* (*coll.*) slightly drunk.

tide, *tīd, n.* time, season: a feast-day, festival: the regular ebb and flow of the sea: turning-point: (*poet.*) a stream, flood: trend.—*v.t.* to cause to float with the tide: to pass over (e.g. *this tides over the first few years*), or to surmount (with *over*): to help to pass through or surmount (with *over*—e.g. *to tide a person over a difficulty*).—*v.i.* to work in or out of a river or harbour with the tide.—*adj.* **ti'dal,** pertaining to, or having, tides: flowing and ebbing periodically.—*ns.* **tide'-gate,** a gate through which the water flows into a basin or dock with the tide, and which is shut to keep it from flowing out again when the tide ebbs: a place where the tide runs with great velocity; **tide'-gauge,** an instrument for registering the state of the tide continuously.—*adj.* **tide'less,** having no tides.—*ns.* **tide'-lock,** a lock placed between an entrance-basin and a harbour, canal, or river, and furnished with double gates, so that vessels can pass either out or in at all times of the tide; **tide'mark,** high-water mark: (*coll.*) rim of dirt where washing has been perfunctory; **tide'-mill,** mill moved by tide-water; **tide'-tā'ble,** a table giving the time of high-tide at any place; **tide'-wa'ter,** the water of the portion of a river affected by the tide: the seaboard; **tide'-way,** the channel in which the tide sets.—**tidal wave,** a great wave caused by the tide or an earthquake. [O.E. *tīd*, time, tide.]

tidings, *tī'dingz, n.pl.* news, intelligence. [O.N. *tīthindi*—*tīth*, time; cf. Ger. *zeitung*, news, from *zeit*, time.]

Neutral vowels in unaccented syllables: *em'pér-òr*; for certain sounds in foreign words see p. ix.

tidy, *tī′di, adj.* neat: in good order: (*coll.*) considerable (e.g. *a tidy sum of money*).—*n.* a cover for chairs, &c.: a child's pinafore: a receptacle for small odds and ends.—*v.t.* to make neat: to put in good order;—*pa.t.* and *pa.p.* ti′died.—*adv.* ti′dily.—*n.* ti′diness. [M.E. *tidy*, seasonable—O.E. *tīd*, time, tide.]

tie, *tī, v.t.* to bind: to fasten with a cord: to make a bow or knot in: to unite: to constrain, bind (a person to): (*mus.*) to unite (notes) with a tie.—*v.i.* to score the same number of points:—*pr.p.* ty′ing; *pa.t.* and *pa.p.* tied (*tīd*).—*n.* a knot, bow, &c.; a bond: something for tying: necktie: a beam, &c., fastening parts together: an equality in numbers, as of votes, or of points in a game: one of a series of matches or games in a competition: (*mus.*) a curved line drawn over two or more consecutive notes of the same pitch to show they are to be played continuously.—*ns.* tie′-beam, a beam resting on the walls and stretching across, keeping the rafters fast; tie′-dye′ing, a method of hand-dyeing textiles in which parts of the material are bound or knotted so as to resist the dye; tie′-wig, a wig tied with ribbon at the back.—tie in (up) with, to be closely associated with; tie up, parcel up: to tether: to secure against squandering, alienation, &c.: to restrict the use of, by conditions. [O.E. *tēag*, *tēah*, *tȳge*, a rope.]

tier, *tēr, n.* a row or rank, especially when several rows are placed one above another. [O.Fr. *tire*, sequence—*tirer*, to draw.]

tierce, *ters, n.* a cask containing one-third of a pipe—that is, 42 gallons: a sequence of three cards of the same suit: (*mus.*) a third: a position in fencing. [O.Fr. *tiers*, *tierce*—L. *tertia* (*pars*), a third (part)—*trēs*, three.]

tiff, *tif, n.* a slight quarrel or disagreement. [Perh. orig. a *sniff*; cf. Norw. *tev*, a drawing in of the breath, *teva*, to sniff.]

tiffin, *tif′in, n.* an Anglo-Indian name for luncheon. [From (*dial.*) Eng. *tiff*, a draught of beer.]

tig, *tig.* See **tag** (2).

tiger, *tī′gėr, n.* a large, fierce Asiatic quadruped of the cat genus:—*fem.* tī′gress.—*ns.* tī′ger-cat, any of several wild-cats; tī′ger-lily, a Mexican plant cultivated in gardens for its streaked flowers. [Fr. *tigre*—L. *tigris*—Gr. *tigris*—O. Pers. *tighri*, an arrow, whence the river Tigris.]

tight, *tīt, adj.* close: compact: rigid: taut: not loose: fitting closely: snug, trim: (*fig.*) allowing little space or time for deviation from plan: not leaky: concise: strict: of a contest, close: (*coll.*) tipsy: scarce, not easy to obtain (as money): difficult (e.g. *a tight place*): (*coll.*) stingy.—*v.t.* tight′en, to make tight or tighter: to straiten.—*v.i.* to grow tight or tighter.—*adv.* tight′ly.—*ns.* tight′ness; tight′-rope, a tightly-stretched rope on which rope-dancers perform.—*n.pl.* tights, a close fitting garment covering the lower part of the body and the legs. [Scand.,—O.N. *théttr*.]

tika, *tē′ka, n.* red mark on forehead of Hindu women, formerly with religious significance.

tilde, *til′de, n.* in Spanish, a mark over *n* when pronounced *ny*, as in *señor*. [Sp. *titulo*—L. *titulus*. See **title**.]

tile, *tīl, n.* a piece of baked clay used for covering roofs, floors, &c.: a tube or pipe of baked clay used in drains: (*slang*) a tall cylindrical silk hat.—*v.t.* to cover with tiles.—*ns.* ti′ler, one who makes or who lays tiles; ti′lery, a place where tiles are made; ti′ling, a roof of tiles: tiles in general.—on the tiles, on the spree. [O.E. *tigele*—L. *tegula*—*tegĕre*, to cover.]

till, *til, n.* a money-box or drawer in a desk counter, or trunk. [M.E. *tillen*, to draw out—O.E. *tyllan*, seen in *fortyllan*, to draw aside.]

till, *til, prep.* to the time of. *conj.* to the time when. [O.N. *til.*]

till, *til, v.t.* to cultivate.—*ns.* till′age, act or practice of tilling: cultivation: a place tilled; till′er. [O.E. *tilian*, to till.]

till, *til, n.* boulder-clay. [Ety. obscure.]

tiller, *til′ėr, n.* the handle or lever for turning a rudder. [O.E. *tyllan*, to draw.]

tilt, *tilt, n.* the canvas covering of a cart or wagon: an awning in a boat.—*v.t.* to cover with an awning. [O.E. *teld*—*teldan*, to cover.]

tilt, *tilt, v.i.* to ride against another and thrust with a lance (often with *at*): to attack (*lit.* and *fig.* —with *at*): to fall into a sloping posture, to heel over: to be raised at an angle.—*v.t.* to slant: to raise one end of: to forge with a tilt-hammer.—*n.* a thrust: in the Middle Ages, an exercise in which combatants rode against each other with lances: any comparable encounter: an altercation (with): inclination, dip, slant.—*ns.* tilt′er; tilt′-hamm′er, a heavy hammer used in ironworks, which is tilted or lifted by means of projections on the axis of a wheel.—full tilt, at full speed, with full force. [O.E. *tealt*, tottering; O.N. *tölta*, to trot.]

tilth, *tilth, n.* cultivation: cultivated land: the depth of soil turned up in cultivation. [From **till** (3).]

timber, *tim′bėr, n.* wood for building purposes: trees suitable for building: woods. one of the larger pieces of the framework of a house, ship, &c.—*v.t.* to furnish with timber or beams.—*adj.* tim′bered, built of wood: (of country) wooded.—*ns.* timber line, on a mountain or in cold regions, the line beyond which there are no trees; tim′ber-toes, a person with a wooden leg. [O.E. *timber*, building, wood.]

timbre, *tēbr′,* or *tim′bėr, n.* character or quality of a musical sound. [O.Fr., L. *tympanum*, a drum.]

timbrel, *tim′brėl, n.* an ancient musical instrument, carried in the hand, apparently like a tambourine. [O.Fr. *timbre*—L. *tympanum*, a drum.]

time, *tīm, n.* a point at which, or period during which, things happen: hour of the day (e.g. *what time is it?*): an appropriate season or moment: an opportunity: duration: an interval: a period in the past: the duration of one's life: allotted or measured period or its completion: occasion: a repeated instance of anything or mention with reference to repetition: musical measure, or rate of movement: period of gestation: hour of travail: hour of death: the state of things at any period, usually in *pl.*: the history of the world, as opposed to eternity: system of reckoning the passage of time.—*v.t* to do at the proper season: to regulate as to time: to measure or record the duration of: to measure rate of movement.—*ns.* **time′-ball,** a ball arranged to drop from the summit of a pole at a particular time; **time′-bomb,** a bomb exploded by a time-fuse; **time′-fuse,** a fuse calculated to burn a definite length of time; **time′-gun,** a gun which is fired by means of a mechanical contrivance and a current of electricity at a particular time.—*adj.* **time′-hon′oured,** honoured a long time: venerable on account of antiquity.—*ns.* **time′-keep′er,** a clock, watch, or other instrument for keeping or marking time: one who keeps the time of workmen, &c.; **time′-lag,** the interval of delay between two connected phenomena; **time′-lim′it,** a fixed period within which something must be completed.—*adj.* **time′ly,** in good time: opportune.—*adv.* (*arch.*) early.—*ns.* **time′liness; time′piece,** a clock, watch, chronometer; **time′-serv′er,** one who meanly suits his opinions to the occasion or circumstances; **time′-switch,** a switch working automatically at a set time; **time′-tā′ble,** a table or list showing the times of certain things, as arrival or departure of trains, steamers, &c.— *adj.* **time′-worn,** worn or decayed by time. —*n.* **time′-zone,** one of the 24 longitudinal divisions of the globe each having a standard time throughout its area.—*adj.* **tim′(e)ous** (chiefly *Scot.*), timely.—**against time** with the aim or necessity of finishing by a certain time; **all in good time,** in due course: soon enough; **at times,** at distinct intervals: occasionally; **do time** (*coll.*), serve a prison sentence; **have little, no, time for,** to have little, no interest in or patience with; **in time,** in good season, sufficiently early; **mean time** (see **mean**) **take time off,** to find time to do something, for an activity; **the time being,** the present time; **time and again,** repeatedly; **time and motion study,** an investigation of the motions performed and the time taken in industrial &c., work with a view to increased efficiency and production; **time out of mind,** from time immemorial. [O.E. *tīma*; cf. O.N. *tīmī.*]

timid, *tim′id, adj.* timorous, shy: wanting courage, faint-hearted.—*n.* **timid′ity,** quality or state of being timid.—*adv.* **tim′idly.** [Fr.,—L. *timidus—timēre,* to fear.]

timorous, *tim′ör-ùs, adj.* timid, easily frightened.—*adv.* **tim′orously.**—*n.* **tim′orousness.** [L.L. *timorōrus*—L. *timor,* fear.]

timpani, tympani, *tim′pán-ē, n.pl.* kettledrums: the set of kettledrums used in an orchestra and usu. played by one performer.—*n.* **tim′panist, tympanist.** [It.]

tin, *tin, n.* a silvery-white, non-elastic, easily fusible, and malleable metal (atomic no. 50; symbol Sn—see **stannic, stannous**): a vessel of tin or tinplate, a can, &c.—*adj.* made of tin or tinplate.—*v.t.* to cover or overlay with tin, tinfoil, or solder: to pack in tins:—*pr.p.* **tin′ning;** *pa.t.* and *pa.p.* **tinned.**—*ns.* **tin′-plate,** thin sheet-steel coated with tin; **tin′-smith,** a manufacturer of tin vessels: a worker in tin: a dealer in tin-ware; **tin′-ware,** articles made of tin.—**tin foil,** tin (alloy) or aluminium in thin leaves for wrapping articles; **Tin Pan Alley,** the realm of popular music production, the

world of its composers, publishers, recordmakers, &c. [O.E.]

tincture, *tingk′tyùr, -chùr, n.* a tinge, shade (of colour): a slight taste added to anything: (*med.*) a solution of any substance in or by means of spirit of wine.—*v.t.* to tinge: to imbue. [L. *tinctūra—tingēre,* to tinge.]

tinder, *tin′dèr, n.* anything used for kindling fire from a spark. [O.E. *tynder.*]

tine, *tīn, n.* a spike of a fork or harrow, or of a deer's antler.—*adj.* **tīned,** furnished with spikes. [O.E. *tind,* a point; O.N. *tindr,* a tooth, a prickle.]

tinge, *tinj, v.t.* to tint or colour: to modify by admixture:—*pr.p.* ting(e)′ing.—*n.* a slight tint or flavour. [L. *tingère, tinctum.*]

tingle, *ting′gl, v.i.* to feel a thrilling sensation, as in hearing a shrill sound: to feel a prickling or stinging sensation.—*v.t.* to cause to tingle.—*n.* a tingling sensation. [M.E. *tinglen,* a variant of *tinklen,* itself a freq. of *tinken,* to tinkle.]

tinker, *tingk′èr, n.* a mender of brazen or tin kettles, pans, &c.—*v.i.* to do tinker's work: to work ineffectively: to meddle (with). [M.E. *tinkere—tinken,* to tinkle, to make a sharp, shrill sound.]

tinkle, *tingk′l, v.i.* to make small, sharp sounds, to clink, to jingle: to tinkle repeatedly or continously.—*v.t.* to cause to clink to make quick, sharp sounds.—*n.* a sharp, clinking sound. [A freq. of M.E. *tinken.*]

tinsel, *tin′sel, n.* a stuff for ornamental dresses &c., consisting of cloth overlaid with a thin coating of glittering metal: anything showy, but of little value.—*adj.* like tinsel: gaudy: superficial.—*v.t.* to adorn with, or as with, tinsel:—*pr.p.* tin′selling; *pa.t.* and *pa.p.* tin′selled.—*adj.* **tin′selly,** like tinsel, gaudy, showy. [O.Fr. *estincelle*—L. *scintilla,* a spark.]

tint, *tint, n.* a variety of any colour, esp. diluted: a slight admixture of colour other than the main one, a tinge.—*v.t.* to give a slight colouring to: to tinge. [L. *tinctus—tinguēre,* to tinge.]

tintinnabulation, *tin-tin-ab-ū-lā′sh(ò)n, n.* the tinkling sound of bells. [L. *tintinnābulum,* a bell—*tintinnāre,* to jingle, reduplicated from *tinnīre,* to jingle.]

tiny, *tī′ni, adj.* (*comp.* **tī′nier,** *superl.* **tī′niest**) very small. [Ety. uncertain.]

tip, *tip, n.* the small top or point of anything: the end, as of a billiard-cue, &c.—*v.t.* to form a point to: to cover the tip or end of:—*pr.p.* tipp′ing; *pa.t.* and *pa.p.* tipped. [A variant of **top.**]

tip, *tip, v.t.* to strike lightly: to cause to slant: to overturn: to empty (out, into, &c.): to give private information to, about betting, &c.: to give a hint to: to give a small gift of money to.—*v.i.* to slant: to give tips.—*n.* a tap or light stroke: a place for tipping refuse into, a dump: private information about horse-racing, stock speculations, &c.: a small gratuity.—*n.* **tip-and-run,** a form of cricket in which a batsman must run whenever he strikes the ball.—*adj.* of an action whose author flees immediately on its completion, as **tip-and-run** (*air*)*raid* (also *hit-and-run*; phrase from baseball).—*ns.* **tip′-cat,** a game in which a pointed piece of wood called a cat is made to spring up from

---

Neutral vowels in unaccented syllables: *em′pér-òr*; for certain sounds in foreign words see p. ix.

the ground by being struck on the tip with a stick, and is then driven as far as possible; **tip'-off,** a hint or warning in advance; **tip'ster,** one whose business is to give private hints about racing, the rise and fall of stocks, &c.—*adj.* **tip'-tilt'ed,** having the tip tilted up.—**tip off,** to give a tip-off to; **tip the scale,** to depress one end of the scales: to prove the decisive factor.—**straight tip,** a reliable hint about betting, &c. [Scand.,—Swed. *tippa,* to tap.]

tippet, *tip'et, n* the cape of a coat: a cape of fur, &c. [O.E. *tæppet*—L. *tapēte,* cloth—Gr. *tapēs, -ētos,* a carpet.]

tipple, *tip'l, v.i.* to drink in small quantities. to drink strong liquors often or habitually.—*v.t.* to drink (strong liquors) to excess.—*n.* **tip'p'ler,** a constant toper. [Cf. Norw. dial. *tipla.*]

tipstaff, *tip'stäf, n.* a staff tipped with metal, or an officer who carries it: a constable. [**tip** (1), **staff.**]

tipsy, *tip'si, adj.* partially intoxicated.—*ns.* **tip'siness; tipsy-cake,** sponge-cake soaked in wine, served in custard sauce. [**tipple.**]

tiptoe, *tip'tō, n.* the end of the toe.—*adv.* on tiptoe, literally or figuratively, through excitement, expectation, &c.—*v.i.* to walk on tiptoe, to go lightly and slyly. [**tip** (1), **toe.**]

tiptop, *tip'top, adj.* first-rate. [**tip** (1), **top** (1).]

tirade, *ti-rād' or ti-, n.* a long vehement speech of censure or reproof. [Fr.,—It. *tirata,* a volley—*tirare,* to pull, to fire.]

tire, *tīr, n.* (*arch.*) attire, apparel: (*arch.*) a head dress.—*v.t.* to dress, as the head.—*n.* **tire'-wom'an,** a lady's-maid. [Short for **attire.**]

tire, *tir, n.* (*U.S.,* not now usu. British) **tyre.**

tire, *tīr, v.t.* to exhaust the strength of, to weary.—*v.i.* to become weary: to have the patience exhausted.—*adj.* **tired,** wearied: (with *of*) bored with.—*n.* **tired'ness** (*tīrd'-*). *adj.* **tire'less,** unwearying, indefatigable.—*n.* **tire'lessness.**—*adj.* **tire'some,** fatiguing: tedious: annoying. *adv.* **tire'somely.**—*n.* **tire'someness.** [App. O.E. *tēorian,* to be tired.]

tiro, See **tyro.**

Tirolese, Tyrolese, *tir-ol-ēz', of,* pertaining to, the *Tirol* or *Tyrol,* or its inhabitants.—*n.* a native or inhabitant of the Tirol.—Also *adj.* and *n.* **Tyrolē'an.**

tissue, *tish'ū or tis'ū, n.* cloth interwoven with gold or silver, or with figured colours: a very finely woven fabric: the substance of which the organs of the body are composed: a connected series: a handkerchief made of soft, thick tissue-paper.—*n.* **tiss'ue-pā'per,** a thin, soft, semi-transparent kind of paper. [Fr. *tissu,* woven—L. *texĕre,* to weave.]

tit, *tit, n.* any of various small birds, esp. a titmouse or titlark. [O.N. *tittr,* a little bird, Norw. *tita.*]

tit, *tit, n.* in phrase **tit for tat,** properly *tip for tap,* blow for blow (esp. *fig.*)—an equivalent of any kind in retaliation.

tit, *tit, n.* female breast. [M.E. *titte;* variant of **teat.**]

Titan, *tī'tàn, n.* one of the giants of Greek mythology: the sun, son of one of these giants: (without *cap.*) a person of great power or ability.—*adj.* **titan'ic,** enormous in size and strength. [Gr.]

titanium, *tī-tā'ni-ùm, n.* a strong light-weight metallic element (symbol Ti; atomic no. 22). [From **Titan.**]

titbit, *tit'bit, n.* a choice little bit. [Obs. Eng. *tit,* anything small, and **bit.**]

tithe, *tīth, n.* a tenth part, hence any indefinitely small part: the tenth of the produce of land and stock, allotted for the maintenance of the clergy and other church purposes.—*ns.* **tithe-barn,** a barn for storing tithes in corn; **ti'ther,** one who collects tithes; **ti'thing,** (*hist.*) a district containing ten householders, each responsible for the behaviour of the rest. [O.E. *tēotha,* tenth; cog. with *tīen, tēn,* ten.]

Titian, titian, *tish'àn, n.* a red-yellow colour used by *Titian,* Venetian painter (1477-1576).—*adj.* (chiefly of hair) of this colour, or (*loosely*) of other shade of red or reddish-brown.

titillate, *tit'il-lāt, v.t.* to tickle: to excite pleasurably.—*n.* **titilla'tion,** act of titillating: state of being titillated: a pleasant feeling. [L. *titillāre, -ātum.*]

titlark, *tit'lärk, n.* a song-bird, a species of the pipit genus, found in marshes and moors. [**tit, lark.**]

title, *tī'tl, n.* an inscription placed over, or at the beginning of a thing, by which that thing is known: a title-page: a credit title: a name denoting nobility or rank, or office held, or formally attached to personal name without implying any distinction (Mr, Mrs, Miss): that which gives a just right (to possession): the writing that proves a right: (*B.*) a sign.—*adj.* **ti'tled,** having a title.—*ns.* **ti'tle-deed,** a deed or document that proves a title or right to exclusive possession; **ti'tle-page,** the page of a book containing its title and usually the author's and publisher's names; **ti'tle-rôle,** the part in a play which gives its name to it, as 'Macbeth'. [O.Fr. *title* (Fr. *titre*)—L. *titulus.*]

titmouse, *tit'mous, n.* a genus of little birds that feed on insects. &c.:—*pl.* **titmice** (*tit'mīs*). [Obs. Eng. *tit,* anything small; O.E. *māsc,* a titmouse.]

titrate, *tīt'-, tit'rāt, v.t.* to subject to titration.—*ns.* **titra'tion,** the addition of a solution from a graduated vessel (burette) to a known volume of a second solution, until the chemical reaction between the two is just completed—a knowledge of the volume of liquid added, and of the strength of one of the solutions, enabling that of the other to be calculated; **titre** (*tī'tér, tē'-*) the concentration of a substance in a solution as determined by titration. [Fr. *titrer*—*titre,* title.]

titter, *tit'èr, v.i.* to giggle or laugh with the tongue striking the teeth: to laugh restrainedly.—*n.* a restrained laugh. [Prob. imit.]

tittle, *tit'l, n.* a small mark, point or sign, as the dot over *i* or *j,* or a vowel point in Hebrew or Arabic: a small particle. [O.Fr. *title*—*titulus,* a title.]

tittle, *tit'l, v.t.* to chatter.—*n.* **titt'le-tatt'le,** idle, empty gossip.—*v.i.* to prate idly.—*ns.* **titt'le-tatt'ler; titt'le-tatt'ling,** the act of talking idly. [Variant of **tattle.**]

tittup, *tit'ùp, v.i.* to walk springily or jerkily. [Imit.]

titular, *tit'ū-lár, adj.* held by virtue of a title: existing in name of title only: having the title

fāte, fär; mē, hûr (her); *mīne; mōte, fôr; mūte, mōōn, fŏŏt;* тнen (then) without the duties of an office.—*adv.* **tit'u-larly.**—*adj.* **tit'ulary,** consisting in, or pertaining to, a title.—*n.* one having the title of an office whether he performs its duties or not. [From L. *titulus,* as **title.**]

tizzy, *tiz'i, n.* state of agitation, nervousness, confusion, dither.

T.N.T. Abbrev. for **trinitrotoluene.**

to, *tōō, tó,* or *tōō* (according to word or sentence stress), *prep.* in the direction of: as far as: expressing the end or purpose of an action, as in many uses of the gerundial infinitive: the sign of the infinitive mood: introducing the indirect object of a verb: in comparison with, with reference to, &c. (*this is nothing to what he has done already*; *true to life, &c.*—*adv.* to a place or condition required, or understood (e.g. *to lie to, come to.*)—**to and fro,** backwards and forwards. [O.E. *tō*; Ger. *zu.*]

toad, *tōd, n.* a family of amphibious reptiles, like the frogs, once wrongly believed to emit poison.—*ns.* **toad'-eat'er,** a fawning sycophant—originally a mountebank's assistant, whose duty was to swallow, or pretend to swallow, any kind of garbage; **toad-in-the-hole,** sausage baked in batter; **toad'stool,** any of various umbrella-shaped and other fungi, particularly (esp. in pop. usage) the poisonous kinds of mushroom; **toad'y,** a mean hanger-on and flatterer.—*v.t.* to fawn upon as a sycophant.—*v.i.* to fawn upon (usu. with *to*):—*pa.t.* and *pa.p.* toad'ied.—*n.* **toad'yism,** the practice of a toady. [O.E. *tādige, tādie,* a toad.]

toast, *tōst, v.t.* to brown by means of the heat of fire, gas flame, or electricity: to warm: to name when a health is drunk: to drink to the health of.—*v.i.* to drink toasts.—*n.* bread toasted: (*arch.*) a slice of it dipped in liquor: the person or thing whose health is drunk: (*arch.*) much-admired young woman: a proposal of health.—*ns.* **toast'er,** one who, or that which, toasts; **toast'ing-fork,** a long-handled fork for toasting bread; **toast'-master,** the announcer of toasts at public dinners; **toast'-rack,** a stand with partitions for slices of toast.—**on toast** (*coll.*), at a disadvantage. [O.Fr. *toster*—L. *tostus,* roasted, pa.p. of *tor-rēre.*]

tobacco,. *to-bak'ō, n.* any plant of the genus *Nicotiana,* native to America, the dried leaves of which are used for smoking, chewing, or as snuff.—*ns.* **tobacc'onist,** one who sells or manufactures tobacco; **tobacc'o-pipe,** a pipe used for smoking tobacco. [Through Sp. *tabaco,* from native word in Haiti.]

toboggan, *tó-bog'án, n.* a kind of sled turned up at the front for sliding down snow-covered slopes.—*v.i.* to slide down over snow on such a sled:—*pr.p.* tobogg'aning; *pa.t.* and *pa.p.* tobogg'aned. [Amer. Indian.]

toccata, *to-kä'tä, n.* (*mus.*) a work for keyboard instrument primarily intended to display the performer's touch. [It.,—*toccare,* to touch.]

Toc H, *tok äch,* signallers' rendering of T H, the initials of Talbot House, a rest and recreation centre at Poperinghe in Belgium during the First World War, and subsequently the name of a Christian organisation for social service all over the British Commonwealth.

tocsin, *tok'sin, n.* an alarm-bell, or the ringing of it. [O.Fr. *toquesin*—*toquer,* to strike, *sing,* a sign, signal.]

today, to-day, *tōō-dā', tó-, n.* this day: the present time.—*adv.* on the present day: nowadays. [O.E. *tōdæge.*]

toddle, *tod'l, v.i.* to walk with short feeble steps, as a child.—*n.* **todd'ler,** a young child. [Prob. a by-form of **totter.**]

toddy, *tod'i, n.* the fermented juice of various palms of the East Indies: a mixture of spirits, sugar, and hot water. [Hindustani *tāṛī—tāṛ,* a palm-tree.]

to-do, *tōō-dōō', n.* bustle, stir, commotion, ado. [Infin. of **do.**]

toe, *tō, n.* one of the five small members at the point of the foot: the corresponding member of an animal's foot: the front of an animal's hoof, of a shoe, a golf-club, &c.—*v.t.* to touch or strike with the toe(s): to provide with a toe or toes.—*n.* **toe'-cap,** a cap of leather, &c., covering the toe of a shoe.—*adj.* **toed** (*tōd*), having toes, usu. of a specified kind (e.g. *square-toed.*)—*n.* **toe'-hold,** a place to fix the toes in: a small established position.—**on one's toes,** poised for a quick start: alert, eager; **toe the line,** come into rank: to accept a rule, standard, or convention: to fulfil one's obligations; **tread on the toes of** (*fig.*), to offend. [O.E. *tā* (pl. *tān*).]

toff, *tof, n.* (*coll.*) a person of the better classes: swell.

toffee, toffy, *tof'i, n.* a hard-baked sweetmeat, made of sugar and butter.—Also **taff'y.**

tog, *tog, n.* (*slang*) a garment—generally in *pl.*—*v.t.* to dress. [Prob. L. *tŏga,* a robe.]

toga, *tō'ga, n.* the mantle or outer garment of a Roman citizen. [L. *tŏga*—*tegĕre,* to cover.]

together, *tōō-geTH'ér, tó-, adv.* gathered to one place: in the same place, time, or company: in or into union: in concert.—*n.* **togeth'erness,** unity: closeness. [O.E. *tōgædere*—*tō,* to, *geador,* together.]

toil, *toil, n.* a net or snare (esp. in *pl.*; *fig.*). [O.Fr. *toile,* cloth—L. *tēla,* from *texĕre,* to weave.]

toil, *toil, v.i.* to labour: to work with fatigue: to move with great effort.—*n.* labour, esp. of a fatiguing kind.—*n.* **toil'er.**—*adj.* **toil'some,** causing fatigue, wearisome.—*adv.* **toil'some-ly.**—*n.* **toil'someness.**—*adj.* **toil'-worn,** worn, or worn out, with toil [O.Fr. *touiller,* to entangle; of uncertain origin.]

toilet, *toil'et, n.* (*orig.*) a cloth or towel worn while dressing: mode or process of dressing: any particular costume: a lavatory.—*ns.* **toil'et-cloth, -cov'er,** a cover for a dressing-table; **toil'etry,** any article or preparation used in washing and dressing oneself; **toilet-set,** the utensils collectively used in dressing; **toil'et-table,** a dressing-table; **toilette** (*twa-let'*), a toilet performed with special care: an elaborate costume.—**make one's toilet,** to dress. [Fr. *toilette,* dim. of *toile,* cloth.]

Tokay, *tō-kā', n.* a white wine with an aromatic flavour, produced at *Tokay* in Hungary.

token, *tō'kén, n.* something representing another thing or event: a symbol, sign: a memorial (of friendship, &c.): a coin or voucher, issued privately, redeemable in current money or goods (as *gift token*).—*adj.* serving

---

Neutral vowels in unaccented syllables: *em'pér-òr*; for certain sounds in foreign words see p. ix.

as a symbol, hence being a mere show or semblance, not effective reality (e.g. *token raid, resistance*).—**by the same token, more by token,** as further corroboration. [O.E. *tācen*.]

told, *tōld, pa.t.* and *pa.p.* of **tell.**

tolerable, *tol'ér-ȧ-bl, adj.* that may be endured: moderately good or agreeable.—*n.* **tolerabil'ity.**—*adv.* **tol'erably.**—*n.* **tol'erance,** endurance of, or permitting liberty to, uncongenial persons, or opinions differing from one's own: (*biol.*) the quality of being tolerant: ability to resist the action of a poison, &c.: allowable variation in dimension of a machine or part.—*adj.* **tol'erant,** showing tolerance, indulgent (of): favouring toleration: (*biol.*) able to endure adverse environmental and other conditions.—*adv.* **tol'erantly.**—*v.t.* **tol'erāte,** to endure: to allow by not hindering.—*n.* **tolerā'tion,** act or practice of tolerating: allowance of what is not approved: liberty given to a minority to hold and express their own political or religious opinions, and to be admitted to the same civil privileges as the majority. [L. *tolerāre, -ātum*—*tollēre,* to lift up.]

toll, *tōl, n.* a tax for the liberty of passing over a bridge or road, selling goods in a market, &c.: grain taken by a miller as payment for grinding: (*Scot.*) a place where toll is, or was, taken: any exaction, esp. of human lives.—*ns.* **toll'bar,** a movable bar across a road, &c., to stop passengers liable to toll; **toll'booth, tol'booth,** (*Scot.*) a booth where tolls are collected: (*Scot.*) a town jail; **toll'bridge, toll'gate, toll'-house,** a bridge, gate, house, where toll is taken.—**take toll of,** to inflict loss, hardship, pain, &c. on. [O.E. *tol, toll*; allied to *tell,* to count.]

toll, *tōl, v.i.* to sound, as a large bell, esp. with a measured sound, as a funeral bell.—*v.t.* to cause (a bell) to sound: to ring a bell with measured strokes in mourning for (a person, a person's death) —*n.* the sound of a bell when tolling. [M.E. *tollen,* to pull—O.E. *tyllan,* seen in *fortyllan,* to allure.]

tomahawk, *tom'a-hŏk, n.* a light war-hatchet of the North American Indians, either wielded or thrown.—*v.t.* to cut or kill with a tomahawk. [Amer. Indian.]

tomato, *tō-mä'tō, n.* a plant with red (or yellow) pulpy edible fruit, native to South America— earlier called the 'love-apple':—*pl.* **toma'toes.** [Sp. *tomate*—Aztec (q.v.) *tomatl.*]

tomb, *tōōm, n.* a pit or vault in the earth, in which a dead body is placed: a memorial sarcophagus: (with *the*) death.—*n.* **tomb'-stone,** a stone erected over a tomb to preserve the memory of the dead. [Fr. *tombe*—L. *tumba*— Gr. *tymbos.*]

tomboy, *tom'boi, n.* a girl who prefers boyish games and activities to those generally considered more suitable for her sex. [*Tom* (dim. of Thomas), a common male name, and **boy.**]

tomcat, *tom'kat, n.* a full-grown male cat. [*Tom* (see **tomboy**) and **cat.**]

Tom, Dick, and Harry, any persons taken at random—ordinary men or citizens.

tome, *tōm, n.* a book, a volume, esp. a large, heavy one: a book, esp. a learned one. [Fr.,—L. *tomus*—Gr. *tomos*—*temnein,* to cut.]

tomfool, *tom'fōōl', n.* a great fool: a trifling fellow.—*adj.* foolish.—*n.* **tomfool'ery,** foolish trifling or jesting: buffoonery. [*Tom* (see **tomboy**) and **fool.**]

tommy, *tom'i, n.* (*coll.*) a British private soldier. [*Thomas Atkins,* the fictitious name used as a model in army forms.]

tommy gun, *tom'i gun,* a submachine-gun (q.v.) invented by U.S. General John Thompson (1860-1940).

tomography, *tō-mog'rȧ-fi, n.* radiography of a layer in the body by moving the X-ray tube and photoplate in such a way that only the chosen plane appears in clear detail.—*ns.* **tom'ogram,** a radiogram produced by tomography; **tom'ograph,** a machine for making tomograms. [Gr. *tomos,* slice, *graphein,* to draw.]

tomorrow, to-morrow, *tōō-mor'ō, tȯ-, n.* and *adv.* the day after today. [O.E. *tō morgen.*]

tomtit, *tom'tit, n.* same as titmouse. [*Tom* (see **tomboy**) and **tit** (1).]

tom-tom, *tom'-tom, n.* the drum used in India by musicians, jugglers, &c.: a gong. [Imit.]

-tomy, *-tō-mi,* in composition used to denote surgical incision in an organ. [Gr. adj. *tomos,* cutting, sharp.]

ton, *tun, n.* a unit of mass = 20 cwt. = (usu.) 2240 lb.: (usu. **tonne**) 1000 kilograms: (*pl.*) a lot: (*slang*) 100 miles per hour.—*adj.* **ton'-up,** orig. of a motor-cyclist, having done a ton: noisy and reckless: travelling at 100 m.p.h. [O.E. *tunne,* a vat, tub.]

tone, *tōn, n.* the character of a sound: quality of the voice: inflection of the voice which conveys the speaker's feeling or attitude: harmony of the colours of a painting, also its prevailing effect as due to the combination of light and shade: tint, shade of colour: character or style: stylishness: state of mind: mood: a healthy state of the body.—*v.t.* to give tone to: to alter or modify the colour of.—*v.i.* to harmonise (with): *n.* **tonal'ity,** the type of scale and key in which a musical work is written: the principle of having a key: the colour scheme, or the tone quality, of a picture.—**tone down,** to give a lower tone to, to moderate, to soften; **tone poem,** (*mus.*) a variety of the symphonic poem, a piece of programme music, not divided into movements, conveying a poetical idea or translating a literary theme. [L. *tonus*—Gr. *tonos,* a sound—*teinein,* to stretch.]

tonga, *tong'ga, n.* a light two-wheeled cart or carriage, in use in India. [Hindustani.]

tongs, *tongz, n.pl.* a domestic instrument, consisting of two shafts of metal jointed, pivoted, or sprung, used for grasping and lifting. [O.E. *tange.*]

tongue, *tung, n.* the fleshy organ in the mouth, used in tasting, swallowing, and speech: power of speech: manner of speaking: a language: an animal's tongue served as food: anything like a tongue in shape: a jet of flame: a strip of leather under the lacing in a boot or shoe: the catch of a buckle: the pointer of a balance: a point of land.—*adjs.* **tongued,** having a tongue; **tongue'less,** having no tongue: mute; **tongue'-tied,** having an impediment, as if the tongue were tied: unable to speak free-

fāte, fär; mē, hûr (her); *mīne; mōte, för; mūte, mōōn, fŏŏt;* THEN (then)

ly.—*n.* **tongue'-twister,** a word, phrase, or sentence difficult to enunciate clearly because of a sequence of similar consonants.—**hold one's tongue** (see **hold**); **lose one's tongue,** to become speechless; **with tongue in cheek,** ironically or whimsically, not sincerely or seriously. [O.E. *tunge.*]

tonic, *ton'ik, adj.* relating to tones or sounds: (*med.*) giving tone and vigour to the system: (*fig.*) giving or increasing strength.—*n.* a medicine that gives tone and vigour to the system: (*music*) a keynote, the first note of a scale.—**tonic solfa** (*sol-fä'*), a system of musical notation, in which the notes are indicated by letters, and time and accent by dashes and colons. [Fr. *tonique*—Gr. *tonikos*—*tonos.* See **tone.**]

tonight, to-night, *too-nīt', tó-, n.* and *adv.* this night: the night after the present day. [O.E. *tō niht.*]

tonnage, *tun'ij, n.* total weight in tons: the cubic capacity of a ship measured by a scale in which 100 cubic feet = 1 ton: ships collectively, esp. merchant ships: a duty on ships, estimated per ton. [**ton.**]

tonne. See **ton.**

tonneau, *ton'ō, n.* the body of a motor-car open at the back. [Fr.]

tonsil, *ton'sil, n.* either of two bodies, of uncertain function, consisting of lymphoid tissue and situated one on each side of the throat.—*n.* **tonsilli'tis,** inflammation of the tonsils. [L. *tonsilla,* a stake, a tonsil, dim. of *tonsa,* an oar.]

tonsure, *ton'shùr,* or *-sūr, n.* act of clipping the hair, or of shaving the head: the shaving of the head as a sign of dedication to the special service of God: the part of the head so shaven.—*adj.* **ton'sured,** having the crown of the head shaven as a priest: shaven: bald. [L. *tonsūra,* a shearing—*tondēre,* to shave.]

tontine, *ton-tēn', n.* a kind of life annuity increasing as the subscribers die: a loan raised with the benefit of survivorship.—Also *adj.*—*n.* **tontin'er.** [From Lorenzo *Tonti,* its inventor.]

too, *too, adv.* over, extremely: also, likewise.—*adj.* **too-too,** quite too: extreme, superlative: (*slang*) extravagantly and affectedly sentimental, gushing. [A form of *to,* signifying lit. 'added to'.]

took, *took, pa.t.* and obsolete *pa.p.* of **take.**

tool, *tool, n.* an implement for manual work: an instrument for achieving any purpose: one who acts as the mere instrument of another: (*slang*) penis.—*v.t.* to mark with a tool, esp. (of bookbinders) to ornament or imprint designs upon.—**machine tool** (see **machine**).—*v.i.* (*coll.*) to travel (along) in a vehicle esp. smoothly and at a moderate speed. [O.E. *tōl, tohl.*]

toot, *toot, v.i.* to make short unmusical sounds on a flute or horn: to sound a motor-horn.—Also *v.t.*—*n.* a sound, as of a horn, a blast: the sound of a motor-horn. [Prob. imit.]

tooth, *tooth, n.* one of the hard bodies in the mouth, attached to the skeleton but not forming part of it, used in biting and chewing: the taste or palate: anything toothlike: a prong: one of the projections on a saw or wheel:—*pl.* **teeth.**—*v.t.* to furnish with teeth: to cut into

teeth.—*n.* **tooth'-ache,** an ache or pain in a tooth.—*adjs.* **toothed,** having teeth: (*bot.*) having toothlike projections on the edge, as a leaf; **tooth'less,** having no teeth.—*n.* **tooth'pick,** an instrument for picking out anything in or between the teeth.—*adj.* **tooth'some,** pleasant to the taste.—**tooth and nail,** with all possible vigour and fury.—**a sweet tooth,** a relish for sweet things; **in the teeth of,** in defiant opposition to; **show one's teeth,** to threaten, to show one's anger and power to injure; **take the teeth out of,** to render harmless or powerless; **throw, cast, in one's teeth,** to fling at one, as a taunt, or in challenge. [O.E. *tōth* (pl. *tēth*).]

tootle, *toot'l, v.i.* to make a series of feeble sounds, as a poor player on the flute.—*v.t.* play (a tune) in such a way. [Freq. **toot.**]

top, *top, n.* the highest part of anything: the upper end or surface: the part of a plant above ground: the crown of the head: the highest place, rank, or crown, consummation: the chief or highest person: (*naut.*) a small platform at the head of the lower mast: a circus tent: the end-piece of a jointed fishing rod: (in *pl.*) top-boots.—*adj.* highest, foremost, chief: good, capital.—*v.t.* to cover on the top: to rise above: to surpass: to reach the top of: to take off the top of:—*pr.p.* topp'ing; *pa.t.* and *pa.p.* topped.—*n.pl.* **top'-boots,** long-legged boots with a showy band of leather round the top.—*ns.* **top'-coat,** an overcoat; **top'-dress'ing,** a dressing of manure laid on the surface of land: (*fig.*) any superficial covering.—*adj.* **top'gallant** (see **mast**).—*n.* **top'(-)hat',** a tall silk hat (*adj.* upper class: designed to benefit high executives or the rich, as *top-hat budget*).—*adj.* **top'-heav'y,** having the upper part too heavy for the lower: tipsy.—*ns.* **top'-knot,** a crest, tuft of hair, or knot of ribbons, &c., on the top of the head; **top'mast** (see **mast**).—*adj.* **top'most,** next the top, highest.—*n.* **topsail** (*top'sāl,* or *-sl*), a sail across the topmast.—*adj.* **top'-sec'ret,** of information, very secret, because of the highest importance.—**top dog,** the winner: the leader or dominant person (*adj.* (used predicatively) in the dominant position, most favourably placed); **top drawer,** the highest level, esp. of society.—**top up,** to fill up, as with fuel oil.—**go over the top,** to take sudden action after hesitation; **in the top flight,** among those of the highest quality or eminence. [O.E. *top.*]

top, *top, n.* a child's toy, with a point on which to spin, set whirling by means of a string, a whip, or a spring.

topaz, *tō'paz, n.* a mineral, ranked among gems, found generally in primitive rocks in great variety of shades, the most prized being the yellow from Brazil: in ancient times, a yellow sapphire (now called **oriental topaz**). [O.Fr. *topase, topaze*—Gr. *topazion,* also *topazos.*]

tope, *tōp, n.* a Buddhist tumulus for the preservation of relics. [Corr. from Sans. *stūpa,* a heap.]

tope, *tōp, v.i.* to drink hard.—*n.* **top'er,** a drunkard.

topee, *tō-pē', n.* a pith-helmet worn by Europeans in India—also **topi** (*tō'pē*). [Hindustani *topī,* hat.]

Neutral vowels in unaccented syllables: *em'pêr-ór*; for certain sounds in foreign words see p. ix.

topiary, tō'pi-a-ri, n. the art and practice of clipping trees and shrubs into ornamental shapes. [L. topia (opera), mural decorations depicting landscapes—Gr. topos, a place.]

topic, top'ik, n. a subject of discourse or argument.—adj. **top'ical,** relating to a topic or subject: of current interest: (med.) for local application.—adv. **top'ically.** [Fr.,—Gr. ta topika, the general principles of argument—topos, a place.]

topographer, to-pog'raf-ér, n. one who describes a place, &c.: one skilled in topography.—n. **topog'raphy,** the description of a place: a detailed account of the superficial features of a tract of country: the art of describing places.—adjs. **topograph'ic, -al,** pertaining to topography.—adv. **topograph'ically.** [Gr. topos, a place, graphein, to describe.]

topple, top'l, v.i. to fall forward, to tumble (down, over).—v.t. to cause to overbalance and fall. [Freq. of **top.**]

topsyturvy, top'si-tûr'vi, adv. bottom upwards.—adj. turned upside down: disordered, in confusion. [Prob. top + sy (adv.) + tervy, overturned—M.E. terven, to roll—O.E. torfian, to throw.]

toque, tōk, n. a close-fitting brimless hat or bonnet for women. [Fr., prob. Celt.; Breton tok, W. toc, a hat.]

tor, tör, n. a hill, rocky hill-top, esp. on Dartmoor. [O.E. torr; W. tor, a knob.]

torch, torch, n. a light formed of twisted tow dipped in pitch or other inflammable material: a large candle or a small flambeau: a small light, with switch and electric battery, for carrying in the hand.—**carry the torch (for),** to suffer unrequited love (for). [Fr. torche—L. tortum, pa.p. of torquēre, to twist.]

tore, tōr, pa.t. of **tear.**

toreador, tor'e-a-dör, or -dör', n. a bull-fighter, esp. on horseback. [Sp.]

to-rights, tōō-rīts', adv. (coll.) straight, in order (lit. and fig.). [to, right.]

torment, tör'ment, n. torture, anguish: that which causes pain.—v.t. **torment',** to torture, to put to extreme pain, physical or mental: to distress, to afflict: to tease.—adv. **tormen'tingly,** in a tormenting manner.—n. **tormen'tor, -er,** one who, or that which, torments. [O.Fr.,—L. tormentum, an engine for hurling stones—L. torquēre, to twist.]

torn, törn, törn, pa.p. of **tear.**

tornado, tor-nā'dō, n. an intensely destructive advancing whirlwind formed from strongly ascending currents of air:—pl. **torna'does.**—adj. **tornad'ic.** [Prob. Sp. tronada, thunderstorm, altered as if from tornada, a turning.]

torpedo, tör-pē'dō, n. (cap.) genus of fishes of the same order as skates and rays, with organs on the head that give an electric shock: self-propelled submarine offensive weapon (usu. cigar-shaped), carrying explosive charge:—pl. **torpe'does.**—v.t. to attack, hit or destroy, with torpedo(es): (fig.) to wreck (a plan).—ns. **torpe'do-boat,** a small swift warship, designed to attack by discharging torpedoes; **torpe'do-boat destroy'er** (now usu. **destroyer**), a swifter and more powerful type of torpedo-boat; **torpe'do-tube,** a tube from which torpedoes are discharged. [L. torpēre, to be stiff.]

torpid, tör'pid, adj. stiff, numb, having lost the power of motion and feeling: sluggish.—adv. **tor'pidly.**—ns. **torpid'ity, tor'pidness, tor'pitude,** state of being torpid: numbness: inactivity: dullness. [L. torpidus—torpēre, to be stiff.]

torque, törk, n. a necklace of metal rings interlaced: the turning effect of a tangential force acting at a distance from the axis of rotation or twist (expressed in lbf. ft. or newton metres). [L. torquēs, necklace, and torquēre, to twist.]

torr, tör, n. the pressure which will support 1 millimetre of mercury—a unit used in expressing very low pressures. [E. Torricelli (1608-47), Italian mathematician.]

torrefy, tor'e-fi, v.t. to parch: to dry, roast.:—pa.t. and pa.p. torr'efied.—n. **torrefac'tion,** act of torrefying: state of being torrefied. [L. torrēre, to dry, to burn, facēre, to make.]

torrent, tor'ént, n. a rushing stream (of water, lava, &c.): (fig.) a violent and copious flow (e.g. of abuse, words, rain).—adj. **torren'tial,** like a torrent. [L. torrēns, -entis, burning, boiling, rushing, pr.p. of torrēre, to burn.]

torrid, tor'id, adj. burning hot: dried with heat.—ns. **torrid'ity, torr'idness.—torrid zone,** the broad belt round the earth between the tropics of Cancer and Capricorn, on either side of the equator. [L. torridus—torrēre, to burn.]

torsion, tör'sh(ò)n, n. act of twisting or turning a body: the force with which a thread or wire tends to return when twisted.—n. **tor'sion-bal'ance,** an instrument for measuring very small forces, such as those due to gravitation, magnetism, or electric charges, by a delicate horizontal bar or needle suspended by a very fine thread or wire. [L. torsiō, -ōnis—torquēre, tortum, to twist.]

torso, tör'sō, n. the trunk of a statue without head or limbs: the trunk of the body:—pl. **tor'sos.**—Also **torse.** [It.]

tortoise, tör'tùs, or -toiz, n. an order of reptiles, distinguished especially by the dorsal and ventral shields which protect the body—sometimes synonymous with turtle, sometimes restricted to land species.—n. **tor'toise-shell** (tör'tò-shel), the shell of a species of turtle.—adj. of the colour of this shell, mottled in yellow, red, and black. [O.Fr. tortis—L. tortus, twisted.]

tortuous, tör'tu-us, adj. twisting, winding: not straightforward: (fig.) deceitful.—adj. **tor'tuōse,** twisted: wreathed: winding.—ns. **tor'tuousness, tortuos'ity.**—adv. **tor'tuously.** [Fr.,—L. tortuōsus—torquēre, tortum, to twist.]

torture, tör'tyúr, -chúr, n. subjection to the rack or severe pain to extort a confession, or as a punishment: anguish of body or mind.—v.t. to put to torture: to pain excessively: to torment: to twist or wrench out of the natural shape, position, meaning, &c.—n. **tor'turer.**—adv. **tor'turingly.**—adj. **tor'turous,** causing torture. [L.L. tortūra—torquēre, to twist.]

Tory, tō'ri, tö'ri, n. a Conservative (q.v.) in English politics: often applied derogatorily to an extreme Conservative.—n. **Tō'ryism,** the principles of the Tories. [Ir. toiridhe, a pursuer; first applied to the 17th century Irish highway robbers: next, about 1680, to the most hot-headed supporters of James II, and, after the Revolution, to one of the two great political parties.]

toss, *tos, v.t.* to throw up, esp. suddenly or violently: to throw back (one's head): to throw (e.g. oneself) restlessly about: to pass (from one to another) lightly: to toss up with (someone; e.g. *I'll toss you for the seat*).—*v.i.* to be tossed, to be agitated violently: to tumble about.—*n.* act of throwing upward: a throwing up (of the head): a toss-up.—*ns.* **toss'er; toss'pot**, (*arch.*) a drunkard; **toss'-up**, the throwing up of a coin to decide anything: an even chance or hazard.—**toss off**, to drink off: to produce rapidly and easily (e.g. verses); **toss up**, to throw up a coin and stake money or a choice on which side will fall uppermost.—**argue the toss**, to dispute a decision. [Celt., as W. *tosio*, to jerk, *tos*, a quick jerk.]

tot, *tot, n.* anything little, esp. a child: a small dram. [Cf. O.N. *tottr*, a dwarf.]

tot, *tot, v.t.* to add or sum up (usu. **tot up**).—*n.* an addition of a long column. [Coll. abbrev. of **total**.]

total, *tō'tál, adj.* whole, complete: unqualified, absolute.—*n.* the sum: the entire amount.—*v.t.* to bring to a total, add up: to amount to.—*n.* **tō'talisātor**, an automatic betting-machine.—*adj.* **totalitā'rian**, belonging to a system of government by one party that allows no rivals.—*n.* **tōtal'ity**, the whole sum, quantity, or amount.—*adv.* **tō'tally—total abstinence**, abstinence from all alcoholic beverages; **total theatre**, dramatic entertainment comprising in one performance all or most of the following—acting, dancing, gymnastics, singing, instrumental music, elaborate costumes and visual effects; **total war**, war with every weapon at the combatants' disposal—war that sticks at nothing, and spares nobody. [Fr.,—L.L. *tōtālis*—L. *tōtus*, whole.]

tote, *tōt, n.* a familiar abbreviation for **totalisator.**

tote, *tōt, v.t.* (orig. *U.S.*) to carry.

totem, *tō'tem, n.* a type of animal, plant, or object chosen as the badge of a primitive clan or group and treated with superstitious respect as the symbol of an intimate and mysterious relationship.—*adj.* **totem'ic.**—*n.* **tō'-temism**, the use of totems as the foundation of a vast social system of alternate obligation and restriction.—*adj.* **tō'temistic—totem pole, post**, a pole, set up by the Indians in the north-west of North America, on which totems were carved and painted. [Amer. Indian.]

totter, *tot'ér, v.i.* to walk unsteadily: (*lit.* and *fig.*) to be unsteady, to shake as if about to fall.—*n.* **tott'erer.**—*adv.* **tott'eringly**, in a tottering manner.—*adj.* **tott'ery**, shaky. [For *tolter*—O.E. *tealtrian*, to totter, *tealt*, unsteady.]

toucan, *tōō-kan', or tōō'-, n.* a genus of South American birds, with an immense beak. [Fr.,—Brazilian.]

touch, *tuch, v.t.* to be, or to come, in contact with: to strike, handle, gently or slightly: to reach: to take, taste: (*fig.*) to approach in some good quality: (with *neg.*) to take nothing to do with: to treat of (a subject) in passing: to relate to: to concern: to affect slightly: to

move or soften: (*coll.*) to persuade to a gift or loan of money.—*v.i.* to be in contact: to make a passing call (at): to speak of (usu. with *on*).—*n.* act of touching: any impression conveyed by contact: sense of feeling or contact: sympathy, understanding (e.g. *out of touch with*): a slight degree of a thing: distinctive handling of a musical instrument, skill or nicety in such: (*football*) either side of the field outside the bounds (**touch-lines**) of play.—*adj.* **touch'ing**, affecting, moving, pathetic.—*prep.* concerning, with regard to.—*adv.* **touch'ingly.**—*adj.* **touch'y**, irritable, sensitive, apt to take offence.—*adv.* **touch'ily.**—*n.* **touch'iness.**—*n.* **touch and go**, a precarious situation or condition.—*adj.* **touch'-and-go.**—*n.* **touch'-down**, (*Rugby football*) the touching to the ground behind the goal-line of a ball by a player: of aircraft, act of alighting.—*adj.* **touched**, (*coll.*) mentally disturbed or unsound.—*ns.* **touch'(-)hole**, in older cannons, &c., a hole through which fire was passed to the powder; **touch judge**, (*Rugby*) either of two officials whose duty it is to observe when and where the ball goes into touch, &c.; **touch'-nee'dle**, a small bar or needle of gold for testing articles of the same metal by comparing the streaks they make on a touchstone with those made by the needle; **touch'stone**, a compact silicious or other stone for testing gold or silver by the streak of the touch-needle: any test.—*v.t.* and *v.i.* **touch'-type**, to type without looking at the keys of the typewriter.—*n.* **touch'wood**, soft combustible material, used as tinder.—**touch down**, of aircraft, to alight; **touch off**, to cause to explode, or (*fig.*) burst forth or become active: to sketch, describe, in a few quick strokes but effectively; **touch up**, to improve by a series of small touches, to embellish: to sting somewhat by whip or sarcasm; **touch wood**, to put one's fingers on something made of wood as a supposed means of averting evil when one has spoken boastfully of one's good fortune.—**in touch with**, in direct relation with (by personal intercourse, correspondence, sympathy). [Fr. *toucher* O.H.G. *zucchen*, to move, to draw.]

touché, *tōō-shā', adj.* (*fencing*) touched by the opponent's weapon: (*fig.*) scored against in argument, having received an effective thrust. [Fr.]

tough, *tuf, adj.* not easily broken: stiff, viscous, tenacious: difficult: (*coll.* —of luck) hard: stubborn: able to endure hardship, physical or spiritual: (*U.S.*) hardened in wrong-doing, brutal and criminal: (of a locality) inhabited by toughs.—*n.* a rough, a bully—*v.t.* or *v.i.* **tough'en**, to make or become tough.—*adj.* **tough'ish**, rather tough.—*adv.* **tough'ly.**—*n.* **tough'ness.** [O.E. *tōh.*]

toupee, *tōō-pā', n.* a little tuft or lock of hair: (*hist.*) a wig with a top-knot: a small wig. [Fr. *toupet.*]

tour, *tōōr', n.* a going round: a journey in a circuit: a prolonged journey: a ramble.—*v.t.* to travel round or through.—*v.i.* to travel, to make a tour.—*ns.* **tour'ism**, touring, travelling for pleasure: tourists collectively: business of catering for them; **tour'ist**, one who makes a

Neutral vowels in unaccented syllables: *em'pér-ór*; for certain sounds see p. ix.

tour, a sight-seeing traveller.—Also *adj.* —**tourist class,** a type of less expensive accommodation in a boat or aeroplane.—**grand tour,** a journey through Western Europe, once fashionable as completing a youth's education. [Fr.,—L. *tornus,* a turn.]

tour de force, *tōōr de fōrs, n.* a feat of strength or of skill. [Fr.]

tourmalin, -line, *tōōr'ma-lin, n.* a beautiful mineral, some varieties of which are used as gems. [Fr.—Sinhalese *tòramalli,* carnelian.]

tournament, *tōōr'na-mėnt, n.* a military sport of the Middle Ages in which combatants engaged one another to display their courage and skill in arms: any contest in skill involving a number of competitors and a series of games.—*n.* **tour'ney** (*tōōr'-,* or *tûr'-*), a mediaeval tournament. [O.Fr. *tournoiement, tornoi—torner*—L. *tornāre,* to turn.]

tournedos, *tōōr-nė-dō, n.* small beef fillet served with some kind of garnish. [Fr.]

tourniquet, *tōōr'ni-ket, -kā, n.* an instrument for compressing the main artery of the thigh or arm, to prevent great loss of blood. [Fr.,—L. *tornāre,* to turn.]

tousle, *tow'zl, v.t.* to make untidy, disarrange, make tangled (esp. hair). [M.E. *tusen;* cf. dog's name, Towzer.]

tout, *towt, v.i.* to solicit custom in an obtrusive way.—*n.* one who does so: one who (esp. improperly) obtains and purveys racing information for betting purposes. [O.E. *tōtian,* to look out.]

tout ensemble. See **ensemble.**

tow, *tō, n.* the coarse part of flax or hemp.—*adj.* **tow'-headed,** flaxen-haired. [O.E. *tow,* spinning; O.N. *to,* a tuft or wool for spinning.]

tow, *tō, v.t.* to pull (a vessel) through the water with a rope: to pull along with a rope.—*n.* a rope for towing with: the act of towing: two vessels or vehicles joined for towing.—*ns.* **tow'age,** act of towing: money for towing: **tow'-boat,** a boat that is towed, or one used for towing others; **tow'ing path, tow' path,** a path alongside a canal, &c., for horses towing barges; **tow'line,** a line used in towing.—**have, take, in tow,** have, take, under one's guidance or protection: to be accompanied by. [O.E. *togian,* to pull.]

toward(s), *tōrd(z), t(w)örd(z), tōō-wörd(z)', prep.* in the direction of: with a tendency to: for, as a help to (e.g. *towards the price, purchase, of*): near, about.—*adv.* (usu. **toward;** *arch.*) in a state of preparation, just coming. [O.E. *tōweard,* adj.—*tō,* to, *ward,* signifying direction.]

towel, *tow'ėl, n.* a cloth for wiping the skin after it is washed, and for other purposes.—*ns.* **tow'el-horse, -rack,** a frame for hanging towels on; **tow'elling,** cloth for towels: a rubbing with a towel. [Fr. *touaille*—O.H.G. *twahilla—twahan,* to wash.]

tower, *tow'ėr, n.* a lofty building, standing alone or forming part of another: a fortress.—*v.i.* to rise into the air, to be lofty: (*lit.* and *fig.*) to overtop the surrounding things or people (with *over, above*).—*adjs.* **tow'ered,** having towers; **tow'ering,** very high: very violent (*a towering rage*); **tow'ery,** having towers: lofty.—**tower of strength,** a stable, reliable

person. [O.Fr. *tur*—L. *turris,* a tower.]

town, *town, n.* a place larger than a village (incl. a city): the inhabitants of a town: (without *a* or *the*) London, or the nearest town or city habitually visited (e.g. *to go up to town*).—*ns.* **town centre,** the most important shopping and business area of a town; **town'-clerk,** an official who keeps the records of a town; **town'-coun'cil,** the governing body in a town, elected by the ratepayers; **town'-coun'cillor,** a member of a town-council; **town'-crī'er,** one who makes public proclamations in a town; **town'-hall,** a public hall for the official business of a town; **town house,** one's house in town as opposed to one's house in the country.—*n.pl.* **towns'folk,** the folk or people of a town.—*ns.* **town'ship,** the territory or district of a town: the corporation of a town: a district; **towns'man,** an inhabitant, or fellow-inhabitant, of a town.—*n.pl.* **towns'people,** townsfolk.—*n.* **town talk,** the general talk of a town: the subject of common conversation.— **go to town** (*coll.*), to let oneself go, act without restraint, spend freely; **take to town,** to mystify, bewilder. [O.E. *tūn,* an enclosure, town.]

toxicology, *tok-si-kol'ò-ji, n.* the science of poisons—*n.* **toxē'mia, toxae'mia,** a type of blood-poisoning, a condition caused by the absorption into the tissues and blood of toxins formed by micro-organisms at the site of infection.—*adjs.* **tox'ic, -al,** pertaining to poisons, toxicological: caused by, acting as, or affected by, a poison, **toxicolog'ical,** pertaining to toxicology.—*ns.* **toxicol'ogist,** one versed in toxicology; **tox'in, -e,** any of numerous poisons elaborated by micro-organisms, as well as by certain plants and insects, and by snakes, which induce the formation of antitoxins, (q.v.). [Gr. *toxikon,* arrow-poison (*toxikos,* for the bow—*toxon,* a bow), and *logica* (*legein,* to say).]

toy, *toi, n.* a child's plaything: a trifle: a thing only for amusement: an occupation of no importance: (*obs.*) amorous sport. *v.i.* to trifle: to dally amorously.—*ns.* **toy-dog,** a very small pet dog; **toy-shop,** a shop where toys are sold. [Du. *tuig,* tools.]

trace, *trās, n.* a mark left: footprint: a small quantity: (*mil.*) the ground-plan of a defensive work.—*v.t.* to follow by tracks: to discover the whereabouts of: to follow with exactness: to sketch: to copy (a map or drawing) by going over the lines on transparent paper and transferring it (usu. by carbon-paper) onto another sheet—*adj.* **trace'able,** that may be traced.—*adv.* **trace'ably.**—*ns.* **trace element,** a substance whose presence in the soil in minute quantities is necessary for plant growth or animal health; **trā'cer,** an attachment to the base of a small projectile, which, by emitting smoke or flame, makes the projectile's path visible; hence, e.g. **trā'cer bull'et,** a bullet which leaves a trail of smoke to mark its course; **tracer element,** any of the radioisotopes (or of certain stable isotopes) used for experiments in which its properties enable its location to be determined and followed; **trā'cery,** ornamentation traced in flowing outline: the beautiful forms in stone with which the arches of Gothic windows are filled for the support of the glass; **tra'cing,** a copy made by tracing; **tra'cing-paper,** paper for tracing made translucent (e.g. with oil of turpentine). [Fr.,—L. *tractus,* pa.p. of *trahēre,* to draw.]

trace, *trās, n.* one of the straps by which a vehicle is drawn.—*n.* **trace'-horse,** a horse drawing in traces, not in shafts.—**kick over the traces,** to throw off restraint. [O.Fr. *trays, trais,* same as *traits,* pl. of *trait;* cf. **trait.**]

trachea, *tra-kē'a, trā'ke-a, n.* the windpipe (q.v.):—*pl.* **trachē'ae** (*-ē'ē*).—*adj.* **trā'cheal,** pertaining to the trachea.—*ns.* **tracheo'stomy,** surgical formation of an opening into the trachea; **trāchēot'omy,** cutting into the trachea. [L. *trāchīa*—Gr. *trācheia (artēriā),* rough (artery; because formed of rings of gristle).]

track, *trak, v.t.* to follow by marks or footsteps: to find by so doing: to tread (a path, &c.): to follow the movement of (satellite, &c.) by radar, &c. and record its position.—*n.* a mark left: footprint: a beaten path: course laid out for races: a line of rails: the endless band on which the wheels of a caterpillar tractor or tank move: the groove cut in a gramophone record by the recording instrument: sound-track: one of several items recorded on a gramophone record.—*adj.* **track'less,** without a path: untrodden: without tracks (e.g. *a trackless trolley*).—*ns.* **track'-event,** in a sports competition, a race of any kind; **track'-suit,** a type of garment worn by athletes before and after e.g. a race or when training.—**make tracks for,** to go off towards, esp. hastily; **the beaten track,** frequented roads: (*fig.*) the normal conventional routine. [Fr. *trac*—Du. *trek,* draught, *trekken,* to draw.]

tract, *trakt, n.* a region, area: a part of a bodily system or organ: (*arch.*) a period of time: a short treatise, esp. on a religious subject.—*adj.* **trac'table,** easily worked or managed: easily taught: docile.—*ns.* **trac'tableness, tractabil'ity,** quality or state of being tractable: docility.—*adj.* **trac'tile,** that may be drawn out, ductile.—*ns.* **trac'tion,** act of drawing or state of being drawn: (*med.*) pulling on a muscle, organ, &c. by means e.g. of weights to correct an abnormal condition; **trac'tion-en'gine,** a steam vehicle for hauling heavy weights along a road, &c.; **trac'tor,** a motor vehicle used for haulage or for working ploughs and other agricultural implements. [L. *tractus,* pa.p. of *trahēre,* to draw.]

tractarian, *trakt-ār'i-án, n.* one of the writers of the famous *Tracts for the Times,* published at Oxford during the years 1833-41 to assert the authority and dignity of the Anglican Church (see **Oxford Movement**).—*n.* **tractar'ianism.** [**tract.**]

trad, *trad, adj.* abbrev. of *traditional,* used esp. of a rhythmically monotonous style of jazz, which became popular about 1960.

trade, *trād, n.* buying and selling: commerce: occupation, craft: men engaged in the same occupation.—*v.i.* to buy and sell: to traffic (with a person, for something): to carry goods (to a place): to deal (in).—*v.t.* to barter.—*ns.* **trade'-mark, trade'mark,** name or distinctive device warranting goods for sale as the production of any individual or firm; **trade'-price,** the price at which goods are sold to members

of the same trade, or are sold by wholesale to retail dealers; **trā'der,** one who trades: a merchant vessel; **trades'man,** a shopkeeper: a mechanic.—*n.pl.* **trades'-peo'ple,** people employed in various trades, esp. shop-keeping, &c.—*ns.* **trade'(-)un'ion,** (rarely, **trades'-**) an organised association of workmen of any trade or industry for the protection of their common interests; **trade'-un'ionism; trade'-un'ionist; trade'-wind,** a wind blowing steadily towards the equator and deflected westwardly by the rotation of the earth; **trading stamp,** a stamp which may be exchanged without payment for articles provided by the trading stamp firm.—**trade in,** to give in part payment (*n.* **trade'-in**); **trade on,** to take advantage of, presume on unscrupulously. [M.E., a trodden path; akin to O.E. *tredan,* to tread.]

tradition, *tra-dish'(ó)n, n.* the handing down in unwritten form of opinions or practices to posterity: a belief or practice thus handed down: a convention established by habitual practice.—*adjs.* **tradi'tional, tradi'tionary,** delivered by tradition.—*adv.* **tradi'tionally.**—*n.* **tradi'tionist,** one who adheres to tradition. [L. *trāditiō, -ōnis*—*trāns,* over, *dăre,* to give.]

traduce, *tra-dūs', v.t.* to calumniate, to defame.—*n.* **tradū'cer.** [L. *trādūcĕre,* to lead along—*trāns,* across, *dūcĕre,* to lead.]

traffic, *traf'ik, n.* trade: dealings, intercourse (esp. when involving dishonesty or evil): the business done on a railway, &c.: the vehicles, pedestrians, &c. (collectively) using a road, railway, water-way: passing to and fro.—*v.i.* to trade: to trade meanly.—*v.t.* to exchange: —*pr.p.* **traff'icking;** *pa.t.* and *pa.p.* **traff'icked.**—*ns.* **traff'icator,** a movable pointer by means of which the driver of a vehicle can give warning of a change of direction; **traff'icker; traffic-lights,** lights of changing colour to regulate traffic at street crossings; **traff'ic-man'ager,** the manager of the traffic on a railway, &c. [O.Fr. *trafique;* origin obscure.]

tragedy, *traj'e-di, n.* a species of drama in which the action and language are elevated, and the climax a catastrophe: one such drama: any mournful and dreadful event.—*ns.* **tragē'dian,** a writer of tragedy: an actor in tragedy; **tragēdienne',** an actress of tragic rôles.—*adjs.* **trag'ic, -al,** pertaining to tragedy: sorrowful: calamitous.—*adv.* **trag'ically.**—*n.* **trag'icom'edy,** a dramatic piece in which grave and comic scenes are blended: a play in the manner of a tragedy but with a happy ending.—*adjs.* **trag'i-com'ic, -al.**—*adv.* **trag'i-com'ically.** [Lit. 'goat-song' (explanation of name uncertain)—L. *tragoedia*—Gr. *tragōidiā*—*tragos,* a he-goat, *aoidos, ōidos,* a singer—*aeidein, āidein,* to sing.]

trail, *trāl, v.t.* to draw along the ground: to have in one's, its, wake: to carry (arms, a rifle) with barrel parallel to the ground, or (**short trail**) butt close to the ground and barrel about 30 degrees from the vertical: to hunt by tracking.—*v.i.* to hang or drag loosely behind: to lag: to run or climb as a plant.—*n.* anything drawn out in length: something long left stretching in the wake of anything (e.g. *a trail of smoke*): a continuous track left by some-

---

Neutral vowels in unaccented syllables: *em'pér-òr;* for certain sounds in foreign words see p. ix.

thing drawn or moving over a surface: a track
followed by the hunter: a beaten path in unsettled country: a tedious journey.—*n.* **trail'er,**
one who trails: a climbing plant: a vehicle
dragged behind another which supplies the
motive power: a strip of film shown in a cinema to advertise a forthcoming motion picture.—**trailing edge,** the rear edge (e.g. of an
aeroplane wing). [Ety. dub.; poss. O.Fr. *trail-
lier,* to tow—L. *tragula,* sledge.]

train, *trān, v.t.* to draw along: to educate, to
discipline: to tame for use, as animals: to
cause to grow properly: to prepare men for
athletic feats, or horses for racing: to aim,
point at (with *on*), bring to bear (on).—*v.i.* to
undergo systematic exercise or preparation:
(*coll.*) to make a journey by rail.—*n.* that
which is drawn along after something else:
the part of a dress that trails behind the
wearer: a retinue: a line of gunpowder to fire
a charge: a line of linked carriages behind a
railway engine: a number of baggage animals
or of vehicles moving in a file: a series.—*ns.*
train'-band (*hist.*), band of citizens trained to
bear arms; **train'-bear'er,** one who holds up a
train, as of a robe or gown.—*adj.* **trained,**
disciplined by training: skilled.—*ns.* **trainee',**
one who is being trained; **train(-)ferry,** a
ferry-boat that carries a railway train across a
stretch of water; **train'er,** one who prepares
men for athletic feats, horses for a race, or the
like; **train'ing,** practical instruction in any
profession, art, or handicraft: a course of systematic physical exercise in preparation for
an athletic event; **train'ing-college,** former
name for college of education; **train'ing-ship,**
a ship equipped with instructors, &c., to train
boys for the sea.—**in train,** in order, ready. [Fr.
train, trainer—L. *trahĕre,* to draw.]

train-oil, *trān'-oil, n.* whale-oil extracted from
the blubber by boiling. [Old Du. *traen,* whale-
oil.]

trait, *trā, or trāt, n.* a feature, lineament: a distinguishing feature of character or mind: a
touch (of a quality). [Fr.,—L. *tractus*—*trahĕre,*
to draw.]

traitor, *trā'tor, n.* one who, being trusted,
betrays: one guilty of treason:—*fem.*
trait'ress.—*adj.* **trait'orous,** like a traitor, perfidious, treasonable.—*adv.* **trait'orously.** [Fr.
traître—L. *trāditor*—*trādĕre,* to give up.]

trajectory, *tra-jek'tō-ri, n.* the curve described
by a body (as a planet or a projectile) under
the action of given forces. [From L. *trājicĕre,*
-jectum—*trāns,* across, *jacĕre,* to throw.]

tram, *tram,* **tram -car,** *-kär, n.* a carriage for
conveying passengers along the public streets,
running on rails, at first drawn by horses,
later worked by cable, now impelled by electrical power.—*v.i.* to go by tram.—*ns.*
tram'way, rails for tram-cars: the system of
tram-car transport; **tram'line(s),** tram rails.
[Dial. Eng. *tram,* a beam, a coal wagon, is prob.
cog. with Swed. dial. *tromm,* a log, Low Ger.
traam, a beam, &c.]

trammel, *tram'l, n.* a net used in fowling and
fishing: shackles for making a horse amble:
anything that hampers movement.—*v.t.* to
shackle, hamper:—*pr.p.* tramm'elling;*pa.t.* and
pa.p. tramm'elled.[O.Fr.*tramail,* a net—Low L.

tramacula—L. *tres,* three, *macula,* a mesh.]

tramp, *tramp, v.t.* to travel over on foot: to tread
heavily.—*v.i.* to walk, to go on foot: to wander
about as a vagrant: to tread heavily.—*n.* a
journey on foot: a heavy tread: a vagrant: a
cargo-boat with no fixed trade route. [Ger.
trampen.]

trample, *tramp'l, v.t.* to tread under foot: to treat
arrogantly or unfeelingly.—*v.i.* to tread in contempt (on, over): to tread forcibly and rapidly.—*n.* **tramp'ler.** [A freq. of **tramp.**]

trampoline, *tram'pō-lin, n.* an elastic mattress-
like contrivance on which acrobats, gymnasts,
&c. leap. [It. *trampolino,* springboard.]

trance, *träns, n.* a state of unconsciousness, as
under hypnosis, in which some of the powers
of the waking body may be retained: complete
abstraction from one's surroundings, ecstasy:
the unconscious state into which spiritualistic
mediums relapse. [Fr. *transe*—L. *transitum*—
transīre, to go across, in Late L. to die.]

tranquil, *trang'kwil, adj.* quiet, serene, peaceful.—*v.t.* **tran'quillise,** to make tranquil.—*ns.*
tran'quilliser, a sedative drug; **tranquil'lity,**
tran'quilness, state of being tranquil.—*adv.*
tran'quilly. [Fr.,—L. *tranquillus.*]

trans-, *tranz-, trans-, tränz-, träns-,* (the latter
two pronunciations are common but are not
given in the list of words beginning with
trans- for space reasons),*pfx.* across, through,
on the other side of [L.].—e.g. *adj.* **trans-
Andean,** across, or beyond, the Andes.

transact, *tranz-akt', trans-akt', v.t.* to carry
through, perform.—*v.i.* to carry through a
piece of business (with someone).—*ns.* **transac'tion,** act of transacting: management of
any affair: a mutual arrangement, a deal: (*pl.*)
report on the work of certain societies, esp.
the Royal Society; **transac'tor.** [L. *transactum,*
pa.p. of *transigĕre*—*trāns,* through, *agĕre,*
carry on.]

transalpine, *tranz-, trans-al'nin or -pīn adj.*
beyond the *Alps* (considered from the point of
view of Rome) [L. *transalpinus trans,*
beyond, *Alpīnus,* pertaining to the Alps.]

transatlantic, *tranz-, trans-at-lan'tik, adj.*
beyond, or across, the Atlantic Ocean. [L.
trāns, across, and **Atlantic.**]

transceiver, *tran-sēv'ér, n.* a radio *trans*mitter
and re*ceiver* in one.

transcend, *tran-send', v.t.* to rise above, to surpass: to be outside the range of.—*adj.* **transcen'dent,** supreme in excellence: surpassing
others: beyond human knowledge.—*adv.* **transcen'dently.**—*ns.* **transcen'dence, transcen'-
dency.**—*adj.* **transcenden'tal,** concerned with
what is independent of experience, intuitive:
highly abstract: vague, visionary.—*ns.* **transcenden'talism,** the investigation of what, in
human knowledge, is known by reasoning
alone, independent of experience: that which
is vague and illusive in philosophy; **transcenden'talist.**—*adv.* **transcenden'tally.** [L. *trāns,*
beyond, *scandĕre,* to climb.]

transcribe, *tran-skrīb', v.t.* to write over from
one book into another, to copy: to write, type
(shorthand notes) in full in ordinary letters:
to make an arrangement (q.v.) of (a musical
composition): to record for future broadcasting or the like: to broadcast a transcrip-

tion of.—*ns.* **transcrib′er; trans′cript**, that which is transcribed, a copy: a written or printed copy of proceedings, &c.; **transcrip′tion**, the act of copying: a transcript. [L. *transcrībĕre, -scriptum—trāns*, over, *scrībĕre*, to write.]

transducer, *trans-dū′sér*, *n.* a device that transforms power from one system to another in the same or in different form. [L. *transdūcĕre, -ductum*, to lead across.]

transept, *tran′sept, n.* one of the wings or crossaisles of a church, at right angles to the nave. [L. *trāns*, across, *saeptum*, an enclosure.]

transfer, *trans-fûr′, v.t.* to carry, convey, to another place: to give, hand over, to another person, esp. legally: to convey (e.g. a picture) to another surface.—*v.i.* to change over:—*pr.p.* transferr′ing; *pa.t.* and *pa.p.* transferred′.—*n.* **trans′fer**, the act of transferring: the conveyance of anything from one person or place to another: that which is transferred: a child's toy consisting of coloured pictures to be cut out, moistened, and transferred by pressure to another surface.—*adj.* **trans′ferable** (or *-fer′-*), that may be transferred from one place or person to another.—*ns.* **transferabil′ity; transferee′**, the person to whom a thing is transferred; **trans′ference**, the act of conveying from one person or place to another; **transfer′or, -ferr′er.** [L. *trāns*, across, *ferre*, to carry.]

transfiguration, *trans-fig-ūr-ā′sh(ó)n, n.* a change of form or appearance: glorifying: idealisation.—*v.t.* **transfig′ure** (*-fig′ér*), to change the form of: to change the appearance of: to glorify.—**the Transfiguration**, the supernatural change in the appearance of Christ, described in Matt. xvii.: a festival on 6th August, in commemoration of it. [L. *trāns*, across, and **figure.**]

transfix, *trans-fiks′, v.t.* to pierce through: to paralyse with emotion. [L. *trāns*, through.]

transform, *trans-förm′, v.t.* to change the shape, appearance, character, or disposition of: to change the form of an algebraic expression or geometrical figure.—*v.i.* to be changed in form or substance.—*adj.* **transform′able.**—*ns.* **transformā′tion**, change of form or substance; **transform′er**, a device for converting electrical energy received at one voltage to electrical energy sent out at a different voltage. [L. *trāns*, across, and **form.**]

transfuse, *trans-fūz′, v.t.* to pour out into another vessel: to transfer blood from one to another. —*n.* **transfū′sion**, the act of transfusing, esp. blood from the veins of one living being into another. [L. *trāns*, over, *fundĕre, fūsum*, to pour.]

transgress, *tranz-gres′, trans-, v.t.* to pass beyond (a boundary, limit): to break (e.g. a law, commandment).—Also *v.i.*—*ns.* **transgress′ion**, the act of transgressing: violation of a law or command: fault: sin; **transgress′or**, one who transgresses: one who violates a law or command: a sinner. [L. *trāns*, across, *gradī, gressus*, to step.]

tranship, *tran-ship′, v.t.* to convey from one ship or conveyance to another.—*n.* **tranship′ment.** [L. *trāns*, across, and **ship.**]

transient, *tranz′i-ént, tran′si-ént, tran′shént*, &c., *adj.* passing, not lasting: of short duration,

momentary.—*adv.* **tran′siently.**—*n.* **transience** (*tranz′-, trans′i-éns, tran′shéns*, &c.). [L. *transiēns, -entis*, pr.p. of *transīre—trāns*, across, *īre, itum*, to go.]

transistor, *tran-sis′tór, n.* piece of semiconductor material so treated with impurities that a small current flowing from one electrode to another causes a large change in current between one of those electrodes and a third one, thus amplifying the current. Used frequently to replace thermionic valves.—*v.t.* **transis′torise**, to fit with a transistor.—**transistor (radio)**, small portable radio. [*transfer* and *resistor*.]

transit, *tran′zit* or *-sit, n.* a passing over: act or duration of conveyance: (*astron.*) the passage of a heavenly body over the meridian of a place: the passage of a planet over the sun's disk.—*ns.* **trans′it-dū′ty**, a duty chargeable on goods passing through a country; **transi′tion**, passage from one place or state to another: change: (*mus.*) a change of key.—*adjs.* **transi′tional**, characterised by or denoting transition; **trans′itive**, passing over: having the power of passing: (*gram.*) denoting a verb that has a direct object.—*adv.* **trans′itively.**—*n.* **trans′itiveness.**—*adj.* **trans′itory**, going or passing away: lasting for a short time.—*adv.* **trans′itorily.**—*ns.* **trans′itoriness; trans′it-trade**, the trade of carrying foreign goods through a country. [L., 3rd sing. pres. indic. of *transīre*, to cross over—*trāns*, across, *īre*, to go.]

translate, *trans-lāt′, v.t.* to remove to another place or office: to convey to heaven, esp. without death: to render into another language: to express (an idea) in a different artistic medium from that in which it was originally expressed: to explain, interpret (e.g. a gesture, a remark).—*ns.* **translā′tion**, the act of translating: removal to another place: the rendering into another language: a version; **translā′tor.** [O.Fr. *translater*—L. *trāns*, over, *ferre, lātum*, to carry.]

transliterate, *trans-lit′e-rāt, v.t.* to express the words of one language in the alphabetic characters of another.—*ns.* **transliterā′tion; translit′erātor.** [L. *trāns*, across, *lītera, littera*, a letter.]

translucent, *trans-lū′sént, adj.* allowing light to pass, but not transparent: clear.—*ns.* **translū′cence, translū′cency.**—*adv.* **translū′cently.** [L. *translūcēns, -entis—trāns*, across, *lūcēre*, to shine—*lux, lūcis*, light.]

transmarine, *tranz-ma-rēn′, adj.* across or beyond the sea. [L. *trāns*, across, and **marine.**]

transmigrate, *tranz′mī-grāt*, or *trans′-* or *-mī′-, v.i.* to migrate across, esp. to another country: (of a soul) to pass into another body.—*ns.* **transmigrā′tion**, the act of removing to another country: the passage of the soul after death into another body; **trans′migrātor.**—*adj.* **transmī′grātory**, passing to another place, body, or state. [L. *trāns*, across, and **migrate.**]

transmit, *tranz-mit′, trans-, v.t.* to pass on to another person or place: to cause (e.g. heat, electricity, news) to pass through:—*pr.p.* transmitt′ing; *pa.t.* and *pa.p.* transmitt′ed.— *adj.* **transmiss′ible**, that may be transmitted from one to another, or through any body or

Neutral vowels in unaccented syllables: *em′pér-ór*; for certain sounds in foreign words see p. ix.

780

substance.—*ns.* **transmissibil'ity; transmis-s'ion, transmitt'al,** act of transmitting: the sending from one place or person to another: passage through; **transmitt'er,** one who transmits: an apparatus for converting sound waves into electrical waves and thus transmitting a message or signal: (*radio*) a set or station sending out radio waves. [L. *trāns,* across, *mittĕre, missum,* to send.]

transmute, *tranz-mūt',* *trans-, v.t.* to change to another form or substance.—*adj.* **transmū'table,** that may be transmuted.—*ns.* **transmū'ableness, transmūtabil'ity.**—*adv.* **transmū'tably.**—*n.* **transmūtā'tion,** a changing into a different form, nature, or substance: (*chem.*) the conversion of one element into another, either spontaneously or artificially. [L. *trāns,* over, *mūtāre, -ātum,* to change.]

transoceanic, *tranz-ō-shē-an'ik, adj.* crossing the ocean. [L. *trāns,* across, and **ocean.**]

transom, *tran'sóm, n.* a horizontal beam or lintel across a window or the top of a door: in ships, a beam across the stern-post.—*n.* **trans'omwin'dow,** a window divided into two parts by a transom. [App. L. *transtrum,* a cross-beam.]

transparency, *trans-pär'en-si, tranz-,* or *-pär'-, n.* quality of being transparent: that which is transparent: a picture on semi-transparent material seen by means of light shining through.—*adj.* **transpar'ent,** (*lit.* and *fig.*) that may be distinctly and easily seen through: clear.—*adv.* **transpar'ently.**—*n.* **transpar'entness** [L. *trāns,* through, *pārēre,* to appear.]

transpierce, *trans-pērs', v.t.* to pierce through. [L. *trāns,* through, and **pierce.**]

transpire, *tran-spīr', v.t.* to breathe out or pass through the pores of the skin.—*v.i.* to exhale: (*bot.*) to exhale watery vapour through the stomata: to become public, to come to light: (*wrongly*) to occur.—*n.* **transpirā'tion,** act or process of transpiring: an exhalation through pores or stomata. [L. *trāns,* through, *spīrāre,* to breathe.]

transplant, *trans-plänt', v.t.* to remove and plant in another place: to remove and resettle: to remove (skin, a part, an organ) from its normal place in an individual and graft it into another position in the same or another individual.—*ns.* **trans'plant,** a part, &c., so grafted; **transplantā'tion.** [L. *trāns,* across, and **plant.**]

transponder, *tranz-pon'dér, trans-, n.* a radio or radar device which, on receiving a signal, transmits a signal of its own. [*trans*mitter res*ponder.*]

transport, *trans-pōrt', -pört', v.t.* to carry from one place to another: to banish overseas, esp. to a convict station: (of strong emotion) to carry (one) away.—*n.* **trans'port,** carriage from one place to another: the conveyance of troops and their necessaries by sea or land: a ship, truck, &c., for this purpose: the system organised for transporting goods or passengers: ecstasy.—*adj.* **transport'able,** that may be carried across.—*n.* **transportā'tion,** removal: banishment of convicts beyond seas: means of transport. [L. *trāns,* across, *portāre,* to carry.]

transpose, *tranz-pōz', v.t.* to put each in the place of the other: (*mus.*) to change the key

of.—*ns.* **transpō'sal,** a change of place or order; **transposi'tion,** act of putting one thing in place of another: state of being transposed: a change of the order of words: (*mus.*) a change of key. [Fr.,—L. *transpōnēre—trāns,* across, *pōnĕre, positum,* to place.]

trans-ship. Same as **tranship.**

transubstantiation, *tran-sub-stan-shi-ā'sh(ó)n, n.* a change into another substance: (*R.C.*) the conversion, in the consecration of the elements of the Eucharist, of the whole substance of the bread and wine into Christ's body and blood, only the appearances of bread and wine remaining. [L. *trāns,* across, *substantia,* a substance.]

transuranic, or **transuranium, element,** *tranz-ū-ran'ik, tranz-ū-rā'ni-úm el'e-mént,* an element (as neptunium, plutonium) of atomic number greater than uranium (92), the last of the series of elements occurring naturally. (See **element.**) [*trans-,* beyond, and **uranium.**]

transverse, *tranz-vûrs', adj.* turned, or lying, or acting, crosswise.—*v.t.* to cross: to thwart: to reverse: to transform.—*n.* **transver'sal,** a line drawn across several others so as to cut them all.—*adv.* **transverse'ly,** in a transverse or cross direction. [L. *trāns,* across, *vertĕre, versum,* to turn.]

transvest, *tranz-vest', v.t.* and *v.i.* to dress oneself in the clothes of another, esp. of the opposite sex.—*n.* and *adj.* **transvestite** (*-vest'īt*), one given to the practice of this. [L. *trāns,* across, *vestīre, vestītum,* to dress.]

trap, *trap, n.* an instrument for snaring animals: an ambush: a trick to catch someone out: a bend in a pipe so arranged as to be always full of water, in order to imprison air within the pipe: a trap-door: a carriage, a gig.—*v.t.* (*lit.* and *fig.*) to catch in a trap:—*pr.p.* **trapp'ing;** *pa.t.* and *pa.p.* **trapped.**—*ns.* **trap'-door,** a door in a floor shutting like the catch of a trap; **trapp'er,** one who traps animals for their fur, &c. [O.E. *træppe;* O.H.G. *trapa,* a snare (whence Fr. *trappe,* by which the Eng. word has been modified).]

trap, *trap, n.* a term loosely applied to many rocks of volcanic origin, so called because lying often in steps or terraces.—*adj.* **trap-pe'an.** [Swed. *trapp—trappa,* a stair.]

trap, *trap, v.t.* to drape or adorn with gay clothes:—*pr.p.* **trapp'ing;** *pa.t.* and *pa.p.* **trapped.**—*ns.pl.* **traps,** personal luggage; **trapp'ings,** gay clothes: ornaments, esp. those put on horses. [Fr. *drap*—L.L. *drappus,* cloth.]

trapan, *tra-pan', v.t.* to ensnare, beguile:—*pr.p.* **trapann'ing;** *pa.t.* and *pa.p.* **trapanned'.** *n.* a snare: a stratagem: a trapanner.—*n.* **trapann'er.** [From **trap,** instrument for snaring.]

trapes, *trāps, n.* a slattern.—*v.i.* to gad about idly.

trapezium, *tra-pē'zi-um, n.* (*orig.*) any quadrilateral that is not a parallelogram: (*now rarely*) quadrilateral with no sides parallel, (*now*) one with only one pair parallel (first two meanings now *erron.*):—*pl.* **trapē'zia, -ziums.**—*n.* **trapēze',** a swing of one or more cross-bars used in gymnastics.—*adj.* **trapē'ziform,** having the form of a trapezium.—*n.* **trapē'zoid,** a quadrilateral with no sides parallel: (*obs.*) one with two sides parallel.—*adj.* **trapezoid'al,** having the form of a trapezoid. [Gr.

trapezion, dim. of *trapeza,* a table—*tetra,* four, *pous,* gen. *podos,* a foot.]

Trappist, *trap'ist, n.* a member of a monastic body, a branch of the Cistercians, noted for the extreme austerity of the rule—so named from the abbey of La *Trappe* in France.

trash, *trash, v.t. (arch.)* to crop, to strip off superfluous leaves.—*n.* refuse, matter unfit for food: rubbish.—*adj.* **trash'y,** like trash: worthless.—*n.* **trash'iness.** [Prob. Scand.; O.N. *tros,* fallen twigs.]

trass, *tras, n.* a volcanic earth used to give additional strength to lime mortars and plasters. [Du. *tras.*]

trauma, *trö'ma, n.* bodily condition arising from physical injury: disturbing experience that may be the origin of a neurosis.—*adj.* **traumat'ic,** pertaining to, or caused by, a physical injury or emotional shock (often used loosely). [Gr., a wound.]

travail, *trav'āl, n.* excessive labour, toil: labour in childbirth.—*v.i.* to labour: to suffer the pains of childbirth. [O.Fr. *travailler.*]

trave, *trāv, n.* a beam: a wooden frame to confine unruly horses while being shod. [O.Fr. *traf, tref*—L. *trabs,* a beam.]

travel, *trav'él, v.i.* to walk: to journey: to move: to offer (a commodity) for sale in various places (with *in*).—*v.t.* to journey along, through: —*pr.p.* trav'elling; *pa.t.* and *pa.p.* trav'elled. —*n.* act of passing from place to place: journey: (*often pl.*) distant journeys in foreign lands: written account of such journeys.— *p.adj.* **trav'elled,** experienced in travelling.— *ns.* **trav'eller,** one who travels: a wayfarer: one who travels for a mercantile house: a ring that slides along a rope or spar; **trav'eller's-tale,** a strange and incredible story; **travelogue** (*trav'é-log*), a talk, lecture, or article about travels, esp. one in the form of a motion picture with commentary.—*p.adjs.* **trav'el-soiled, -stained,** showing the marks of travel.—**travel agency,** an agency providing information, brochures, tickets, &c. relating to travel; **traveller's cheque,** a cheque which can be cashed at any foreign bank or specified agent of the bank issuing it; **travelling-wave tube,** a device used in communications for increasing signal power. [A form of **travail.**]

traverse, *trav'érs, adj. (arch.)* turned or lying across: denoting a method of cross-sailing.—*n.* anything laid or built across: (*law*) a plea containing a denial of some fact alleged by an opponent: a work for protection from the fire of an enemy: sideways course in rock-climbing: the place where this is done: a journey over or across (usu. a mountain): (also **traverse survey**) a survey consisting of a set of connected lines whose lengths and directions are measured.—*v.t.* to cross: to pass over, across, or through: to survey: to travel over sideways in rock-climbing: (*law*) to deny an opponent's allegation.—*v.i.* (*fencing*) to use the motions of opposition or counteraction: to direct a gun to the right or left of its position.—*adv.* athwart, crosswise.—*adj.* **trav'ersable,** that may be traversed or denied.—*n.* **trav'erser.** [L. *trāns, vertĕre, versum,* to turn.]

travesty, *trav'es-ti, n.* a kind of burlesque in which the original characters are preserved,

the situations parodied: any grotesque or misrepresentative imitation.—*v.t.* to turn into burlesque: to imitate badly or grotesquely. [Fr. *travestir,* to disguise—L. *trāns,* over, *vestīre,* to clothe.]

trawl, *tröl, v.i.* to fish (for sole, &c., which frequent the bottom of the sea) by dragging a trawl along.—*v.t.* to catch with a trawl.—*n.* any of several types of wide-mouthed bag-net.— *ns.* **traw'ler,** one who trawls: a vessel used in trawling; **trawl-fish,** fish caught with a trawl. [Cf. **trail,** and M.Du. *traghel,* drag-net.]

tray, *trā, n.* a flat board, or sheet of metal, &c., surrounded by a rim, used for carrying or containing sundry articles: a salver. [O.E. *trēg.*]

treachery, *trech'ér-i, n.* faithlessness, betrayal of trust.—*adj.* **treach'erous,** faithless: liable to deceive, betray confidence (e.g. of friend, memory, ice, bog).—*adv.* **treach'erously.**—*n.* **treach'erousness.** [O.Fr. *tricherie*—*tricher.* **Trick** is a doublet.]

treacle, *trē'kl, n.* the dark, viscous liquid that drains from sugar at various stages in the process of manufacture, molasses.—*adj.* **trea'cly,** composed of, or like, treacle (*lit.* and *fig.*). [O.Fr. *triacle*—L. *thēriacum*—Gr. *thēriaka (pharmaka),* antidotes against the bites of wild beasts—*thērion,* a wild beast.]

tread, *tred, v.i.* to set the foot down: to walk or go: to copulate, as fowls.—*v.t.* to walk on: to press with the foot: to trample (under foot) in contempt: to step in dancing (e.g. *to tread a measure*):—*pa.t.* trod; *pa.p.* trod or trodden.—*n.* pressure with the foot: a step, way of stepping: the part of a shoe, wheel, or tyre, that touches the ground.—*ns.* **tread'er; tread'le, tread'le,** the part of any machine which the foot moves; **tread'mill,** a mill in which a rotary motion is produced by the weight of a person or persons treading or stepping from one to another of the steps of a cylindrical wheel, formerly used as an instrument of prison discipline: any monotonous routine.—**tread in one's steps,** to follow one's example; **tread on one's toes,** to give offence to one; **tread on the heels of,** to follow close after; **tread water,** to maintain upright position in deep water. [O.E. *tredan.*]

treason, *trē'zn, n.* betraying of the government or an attempt to overthrow it: disloyalty.—*adj.* **trea'sonable,** pertaining to, consisting of, or involving treason.—*n.* **trea'sonableness.**—*adv.* **trea'sonably.**—**high treason,** treason against the sovereign or the state, the highest civil offence. [O.Fr. *traïson* (Fr. *trahison*)—*trahir*—L. *trādĕre,* to betray.]

treasure, *trezh'úr, n.* wealth stored up: riches: anything much valued.—*v.t.* to hoard up: to value greatly.—*ns.* **treas'ure-chest,** a box for keeping articles of value; **treas'urer,** one who has the care of a treasure or treasury: one who has charge of collected funds; **treas'urership; treas'ury,** a place where treasure is deposited: (*cap.*) a department of a government which has charge of the finances; **Treas'urybench,** the first row of seats on the Speaker's right hand in the House of Commons, occupied by the members of the government; **Treasury notes,** currency notes for £1 and 10s. issued between 1914 and 1928 by the Treasury

Neutral vowels in unaccented syllables: *em'pér-ör*; for certain sounds in foreign words see p. ix.

782

to replace gold coinage. [Fr. *trésor* — L. *thēsaurus* — Gr. *thēsauros*.]

treasure-trove, *trezh'ŭr-trōv, n.* treasure or money found in the earth, the owner unknown. [**treasure** and O.Fr. *trové,* pa.p. of *trover,* to find.]

treat, *trēt, v.t.* to handle, use, deal with, act towards (in a specified manner — e.g. *to treat unkindly*): to apply remedies to, prescribe remedies for (a person for an ailment): to subject to the action of a chemical: to discourse on: to entertain, as with food or drink, &c., take one's turn at being host. — *v.i.* to negotiate: to entertain, act as host: (*fig.*) to deal with (with *of*). *n.* an entertainment: turn at being host: a pleasure seldom indulged: an unusual cause of enjoyment. — *ns.* **treat'ise** (*-is*), a written composition in which a subject is treated systematically, a formal essay; **treat'ment,** act, or manner, of treating: behaviour to (anyone — with *of*): remedies and manner of applying them; **treat'y,** a formal agreement between states: (*Shak.,* same as **entreaty**). — **Dutch treat,** a treat at which each is his own host and pays his own expenses. [O.Fr. *traitier* — L. *tractare,* to manage — *trahĕre, tractum,* to draw.]

treble, *treb'l, adj.* triple, threefold: (*mus.*) denoting the treble: that plays or sings the treble. — *n.* the highest of the four principal parts in singing, soprano: a shrill, high-pitched voice: a singer or instrument taking the soprano part. — *v.t.* to make three times as much. — *v.i.* to become threefold: — pa.p. treb'led (-ld). — *adv.* **treb'ly. — treble chance,** a mode of competing in football pools in which, in a selection of matches made from a list, the aim is to pick all score draws, they counting more than the away and home wins, and non-score draws. [O.Fr., — L. *triplus.*]

treddle. See **tread.**

tree, *tre, n.* a perennial plant having a single trunk, woody, branched, and of a large size: anything like a tree: piece of wood for specified purpose, as in *saddle-tree* (q.v.): a gibbet, cross. — *v.t.* to drive into or up a tree: to force into a hopeless situation. — *adj.* **tree'less. — ns. tree'nail, tre'nail** (*trē'nāl, tren'l*), a long wooden pin or nail to fasten the planks of a ship to the timbers. — **at the top of the tree,** in the highest position in e.g. a profession; **family, genealogical tree** (see **genealogy**); **up a tree,** in a predicament. [O.E. *trēo, trēow.*]

trefoil, *trē'foil, tre'-, n.* any plant of the genus *Trifolium* (the clovers), whose leaves are divided into three leaflets: (*archit.*) an ornament like trefoil. [L. *trifolium* — *trēs,* three, *folium,* a leaf.]

trek, *trek, v.i.* to journey by ox-wagon: to migrate: (*coll.*) to make a laborious journey (to). — *n.* a journey by ox-wagon or stage of it: a migration: (*loosely*) a long or wearisome journey. *n.* **trekk'er.** [Du. *trekken,* to draw.]

trellis, *trel'is, n.* a structure of cross-barred or lattice work, for supporting plants, &c. — *adj.* **trell'ised,** having a trellis, or formed as a trellis. [O.Fr. *treillis*; origin obscure.]

tremble, *trem'bl, v.i.* to shake, shiver, as from fear, cold, or weakness: (*fig.*) to be alarmed, fear greatly (to think, for a person, at some-

thing): to quiver, vibrate (e.g. of sound, leaves, and *fig.* one's fate). — *n.* the act of trembling: a fit of trembling. — *n.* **trem'bler.** — *adv.* **trem'blingly.** — *adj.* **trem'ulous,** trembling, affected with fear: quivering. — *adv.* **trem'ulously.** — *n.* **trem'ulousness.** [O.Fr. *trembler* — L. *tremulus,* trembling — *trĕmĕre,* to shake.]

tremendous, *trē-men'dŭs, adj.* such as astonishes or terrifies by its force or greatness: very large or great — often used loosely with exaggeration. — *adv.* **tremen'dously,** (*coll.*) very. [L. *tremendus,* fit to be trembled at — *tremĕre,* to tremble.]

tremolo, *trem'o-lō, n.* (*mus.*) a tremulous effect suggesting passion: the device in an organ by which this is produced. [It.]

tremor, *trem'ôr, n.* a quivering: a vibration: an involuntary shaking. [L., — *tremĕre,* to shake.]

trench, *trench* or *-sh, v.t.* to dig a ditch in: to dig deeply with the spade or plough: to cut a groove in. — *v.i.* to make a trench: to encroach (on). — *n.* a long narrow cut in the earth: such an excavation made for military purposes: a wrinkle — *n.* **tren'cher. — trench coat,** a lined waterproof overcoat, originally military; **trench feet,** a painful, sometimes gangrenous, affection of the feet suffered by soldiers in wet, cold trenches; **trench fever,** a fever, spread by lice, to which soldiers serving in trenches are subject; **trench-mortar** a small, portable short-range mortar or cannon; **trench'-plough,** a plough for trenching or turning up the land more deeply than usual. — *v.t.* to plough with a trench-plough. [O.Fr. *trenchier* (Fr. *trancher*), prob — L. *truncāre,* to maim — *truncus,* maimed.]

trenchant, *tren'chänt* or *-shänt, adj.* (*lit. — rare*) sharp, cutting. (*fig.* — e.g. of style) incisive, vigorous, to the point. — *n.* **tren'chancy,** [O.Fr., pr.p. of *trenchier,* to cut.]

trencher, *tren'cher,* or *-shèr, n.* a wooden plate formerly used for cutting meat on at meals: the table. food. pleasures of the table: a trencher-cap. — *ns.* **tren'cher-cap,** a style of college-cap resembling an inverted trencher; **tren'cher-man,** a hearty eater. [O.Fr. *trencheor — trenchier,* to cut.]

trend, *trend, v.i.* to tend, to run, to go in a particular direction (with e.g. *towards, away from, southward*): (*fig.*) to show a drift or tendency (towards, &c.). — *n.* tendency. — *n.* **trend'-sett'er,** one who helps to give a new direction to follow. *adj.* **trend'y** (*coll.*), in the forefront of fashion in any sphere. [O.E. *trendan.*]

trental, *tren't(ä)l, n.* a service of thirty masses for thirty days, one each day, for a deceased person. [L.L. *trentāle* — L. *trīgintā,* thirty.]

trepan, *tri-pan'.* [Same as **trapan.**]

trepan, *tri-pan', n.* (*surg.*) a small cylindrical saw used in perforating the skull: a powerful rock-boring tool. — *v.t.* to remove a circular piece of the skull with a trepan, in order to relieve the brain from pressure or irritation. [Fr., — Low L. *trepanum* — Gr. *trypănon — trȳpaein,* to bore.]

trephine, *trē-fēn',* or *tre-fīn', n.* the modern trepan, having a little sharp borer called the centre-pin. — *v.t.* to perforate with the trephine. [Dim. of **trepan** (2).]

fāte, fär; mē, hûr (her); *mīne; mōte, fôr; mūte; mōōn, fŏŏt;* ᴛнen (then)

trepidation, *trep-i-dā'sh(ó)n, n.* a state of confused hurry or alarm: an involuntary trembling. [L. *trepidāre, -ātum,* to hurry with alarm—*trepidus,* restless.]

trespass, *tres'pás, v.i.* to enter unlawfully upon another's land: to encroach upon another's rights: to make too great a claim (on, e.g. another's generosity): to injure or annoy another: to sin.—*n.* act of trespassing: any injury to another's person or property: a sin.—*ns.* **tres'passer; tres'pass-off'ering,** an offering in expiation of a trespass or sin (see Lev. xiv. 12ff.). [O.Fr. *trespasser*—L. *trāns,* across, *passus,* a step.]

tress, *tres, n.* a lock, braid, or ringlet of hair, esp. a woman's or girl's: (*pl.*) hair, usu. long.—*v.t.* to form into tresses, to braid.—*adj.* **tressed,** having tresses. [Fr. *tresse,* through Low L. *tricia, trica,* from Gr. *tricha,* threefold—*treis,* three.]

trestle, *tres'l, n.* a movable support (e.g. for a platform): the under-frame of a table—also **tress'el.** [O.Fr. *trestel;* ety. uncertain; perh. through Low L.—L. *transtrum,* a beam.]

tret, *tret, n.* an allowance to purchasers of 4 lb. on every 104 lb. for waste. [Norman Fr. *trett,* deduction—*traire*—L. *trahēre,* to draw.]

trews, *trōōz, n.pl.* trousers, esp. of tartan cloth. [Ir. *trius,* Gael. *triubhas.*]

tri-, *trī-, pfx.* having, consisting of, three or three parts: every third [Gr. and L.]:—e.g. **tricycle, triad; triennial.**

triad, *trī'ad, n.* a group or union of three: a group of three short aphorisms, a common Welsh literary form: (*mus.*) the three fundamental notes of a consonance. [Gr. *trias, -ados*—*treis,* three.]

trial, *trī'ál, n.* the act of trying: the state of being tried: examination by a test: experimental use: judicial examination: an attempt: a preliminary race, game, &c.: suffering, hardship: a source of suffering or of annoyance.—**trial run,** a test drive in a motor vehicle to ascertain its efficiency: any introductory test, rehearsal, &c.; **trial trip,** a short voyage to test the sailing-powers, &c., of a new vessel: any experiment.—**by trial and error,** by trying out several methods and discarding those which prove unsuccessful; **on trial,** undergoing proceedings in a court of law: on probation, as an experiment. [From **try.**]

triangle, *trī'ang-gl, n.* (*math.*) a plane figure with three angles and three sides: a spherical (q.v.) triangle: a musical instrument of percussion, formed of a steel rod bent in the shape of a triangle: (*fig.*) an emotional situation in which three people (usu. man and wife and another man or another woman) are involved.—*adjs.* **tri'angled, triang'ular,** having three angles.—*adv.* **triang'ularly.**—*v.t.* **triang'ulāte,** to survey by means of a series of triangles.—*n.* **triangulā'tion,** act of triangulating: the series of triangles so used.—**the eternal triangle,** an emotional situation involving two men and a woman or two women and a man. [Fr.,—L. *triangulum*—*trēs,* three, *angulus,* an angle.]

Trias, *trī'as, n.* (*geol.*) the oldest system of the Mesozoic or Secondary rocks, largely composed of red sandstone, or the period during which they were formed.—Also **Triass'ic** (*adj.*

and *n.*). [So called by the German geologists, from their threefold grouping of the system, from Gr. *trias,* union of three.]

tribe, *trīb, n.* a race or family descended from the same ancestor: an aggregate of families, forming a community usually under the government of a chief: a political division in ancient Rome: a number of things having certain common qualities: a set of people associated in some way (often used contemptuously).—*adj.* **trīb'al.**—*n.* **trib'alism,** condition of existing as a separate tribe: tribal life or organisation: tribal feeling.—*adv.* **trib'ally.** —*n.* **tribes'man.** [L. *tribus,* one of the three (later increased to as many as thirty-five) tribes of Rome.]

tribology, *trib-ol'ó-ji, n.* a science and technology embracing all subjects involved when surfaces in contact move in relation to each other. [Gr. *tribein,* to rub, *logos,* a discourse.]

tribrach, *tri'brak,* or *trī'-, n.* (*poet.*) a foot of three short syllables, e.g. *rĕgĕre.* [L.,—Gr. *tribrachys*—*tri-,* root of *treis,* three, *brachys,* short.]

tribulation, *trib-ū-lā'sh(ó)n, n.* severe affliction, distress, trial, hardship. [L. *trībulātiō, -ōnis*—*trībulāre, -ātum,* to afflict—*trībulum,* a sledge for rubbing out corn—*terĕre,* to rub.]

tribunal, *trī-bū'nál, n.* the bench on which a judge and his associates sit to administer justice: a court of justice: a body authorised to decide cases of dispute, esp. appeals against conforming with state regulations, or to enquire into some disputed question. [L.]

tribune, *trib'ūn, n.* a magistrate elected by the Roman plebeians to defend their rights: a champion of popular rights: the raised platform from which speeches were delivered.—*n.* **trib'uneship.** [L. *tribūnus*—*tribus,* a tribe.]

tribute, *trib'ūt, n.* a fixed amount paid at certain intervals by one nation to another for peace or protection: (*hist.*) a tax paid to a superior or to the state: an expression of respect or gratitude.—*adj.* **trib'ūtary,** paying tribute: subject: yielding supplies of anything, subsidiary: paid in tribute.—*n.* one who pays tribute: a stream that flows into another. [L. *tribūtum*—*tribuĕre,* to give, assign—*tribus,* a tribe.]

trice, *trīs, v.t.* (*naut.*) to haul or lift up by means of a rope:—*pr.p.* trīc'ing; *pa.p.* triced.—*n.* a haul or tug (*obs.*): hence a single effort: an instant. [Middle Low Ger. *trissen.*]

tricennial, *trī-sen'i-ál, adj.* pertaining to thirty years: occurring every thirty years. [L. *trīcennium,* thirty years—*trīgintā,* thirty, *annus,* a year.]

trichina, *tri-kī'na, n.* a parasitic worm, which in its mature state infests the intestinal canal, and in its larval state the muscular tissue of man and certain animals, esp. the hog:—*pl.* **trichī'nae** (*-ē*).—*ns.* **trichinī'asis,** (makes usu.) **trichinō'sis,** the disease caused by the presence of trichinae in the body. [Gr. *trichinos,* small like a hair—*thrix,* gen. *trichos,* hair.]

trick, *trik, v.t.* to dress, to decorate (with *out, up*). [Same as **trick** (2).]

trick, *trik, n.* any fraud or stratagem to deceive: an illusion (e.g. *a trick of the imagination*): a clever contrivance to puzzle, amuse, or annoy: skill, knack: a habit, mannerism: a parcel of

Neutral vowels in unaccented syllables: *em'pêr-ór*; for certain sounds in foreign words see p. ix.

784

cards falling to a winner at one turn: a turn, as at the helm.—*adj.* using fraud or clever contrivance to deceive (e.g. the eye—as in *trick photography*).—*v.t.* to deceive, to cheat.—*ns.* **trick'er; trick'ery,** act or practice of playing fraudulent tricks: artifice, stratagem.—*adj.* **trick'y,** given to trickery: (*lit.* and *fig.*) requiring skill or dexterity, difficult to handle or do successfully.—*adv.* **trick'ily.**—*n.* **trick'iness.**—*adj.* **trick'ish,** addicted to tricks: artful in making bargains: tricky, difficult.—*n.* **trick'ster,** one given to trickery, a cheat. **trick cyclist** (*slang*), a psychiatrist.—**do the trick,** bring something about. [O.Fr. *trichier,* to beguile.]

trickle, *trik'l, v.i.* to flow gently or in a small stream: to drip: to come or go very gradually or in very small quantities.—*n.* a trickling flow. [M.E. *triklen,* prob. for *striklen,* freq. of *striken,* to go.]

tricolour, tricolor, *trī'kŭl-ŏr, trī'-, n.* the national flag of France, adopted in 1789, of three colours, red, white, and blue, in vertical stripes.—*adj.* **tri'coloured,** having three colours. [Fr. *tricolore*—L. *trēs,* three, *color,* colour.]

tricycle, *trī'si-kl, n.* a vehicle with three wheels, ridden by one or more persons. [Gr. *tri-,* root of *treis,* three, *kyklos,* circle, wheel.]

trident, *trī'dėnt, n.* the three-pronged spear or sceptre of Neptune, god of the ocean: any three-toothed instrument.—*adjs.* **tri'dent, tri'dented,** having three teeth or prongs. [Fr.,—L. *trēs,* three, *dēns, dentis,* tooth.]

tridimensional, *trī-di-men'shŏn-ȧl, adj.* having three dimensions—length, breadth, thickness. [L. *tri-, trēs,* three, and **dimension.**]

tried. See **try.**

triennial, *trī-en'yȧl, adj.* continuing three years: happening every third year.—*adv.* **trienn'ially.** [L. *triennis*—*trēs,* three, *annus,* a year.]

trier, *trī'ėr, n.* one who tests by experiment: one who tries, as a judge: (*coll.*) one who perseveres. [From **try.**]

trifle, *trī'fl, v.i.* to act, or to talk, lightly, without seriousness: to toy, play, dally (with).—*n.* anything of little value: a light confection of whipped cream or white of egg, sponge-cake, wine, &c.—*n.* **tri'fler.**—*adj.* **tri'fling,** of small value or importance: acting or talking without seriousness.—*adv.* **tri'flingly.** [O.Fr. *trufle,* mockery, deception.]

trifocal, *trī-fōk'ȧl, adj.* of a spectacle lens, giving separately near, intermediate, and far vision. [L. *tri-,* three, and **focal.**]

trifoliate, -d, *trī-fō'li-āt, -id, adjs.* having three leaflets. [L. *trēs,* three, *folium,* leaf.]

triforium, *trī-fō'ri-um, n.* an arcaded gallery above nave, choir, or transept arches of a church. [L. *tri-, trēs,* three, *foris,* a door.]

triform, *trī'förm, adj.* having a triple form. [L. *triformis*—*trēs,* three, *förma,* form.]

trig, *trig, adj.* trim, neat: tight, sound. [Prob. Scand., *tryggr,* fine.]

trigger, *trig'ėr, n.* a catch which when pulled looses the hammer of a gun in firing.—*v.t.* (usu. with *off*), to set off (something violent). —*adj.* **trigg'er-happy** (*lit.* and *fig.*), over-ready to shoot or begin a fight. [Du. *trekker*—*trekken,* to pull.]

triglyph, *trī'glif* or *tri'-, n.* three-grooved tablet repeated at equal distances along the frieze in Doric architecture. [L. *trīglyphus*—Gr. *triglyphos*—*treis,* three, *glyphein,* to carve.]

trigonometry, *trig-o-nom'ė-tri, n.* the branch of mathematics which treats of the relations between the sides and angles of triangles—*adjs.* **trigonomet'ric, -al,** pertaining to trigonometry: done by the rules of trigonometry.—*adv.* **trigonomet'rically.—trigonometric(al) function** or **ratio,** any of six ratios determining, and determined by, the size of an angle—each ratio expressing the relation between a pair of sides in a right-angled triangle (see **sine, cosine, tangent, cotangent, secant, cosecant**); **trigonometrical survey,** the survey of a country by triangulation and trigonometrical calculation using a single base. [Gr. *trigōnon,* a triangle, *metron,* a measure.]

trihedral, *trī-hē'drȧl, adj.* having three faces.—*n.* **trihē'dron,** a solid having three bases or sides. [Gr. *treis,* three, *hedrȧ,* a seat.]

trilateral, *trī-lat'ėr-ȧl, adj.* having three sides.—*adv.* **trilat'erally.** [L. *trēs,* three, *latus, lateris,* side.]

trilinear, *trī-lin'ė-ȧr, adj.* consisting of three lines. [L. *trēs,* three, and **linear** (see **line**).]

trilingual, *trī-ling'gwȧl, adj.* consisting of, or using, three tongues or languages. [L. *trēs,* three, *lingua,* tongue.]

trill, *tril, v.t.* and *v.i.* to utter with a tremulous vibration: to pronounce with a quick vibration of one speech organ against another.—*n.* (*mus.*) a shake (q.v.): a sound suggestive of tongue against the teeth ridge: a letter (e.g. a trilled *r*) so made. [It. *trillare,* to shake; imit.]

trillion, *tril'yŏn, n.* a million raised to the third power, or multiplied twice by itself—represented by a unit and 18 ciphers: in U.S., ten thousand raised to the third power, represented by a unit and 12 ciphers.—*adj.* **trill'ionth** [Fr.,—L. *trēs,* three, L.L. *millio,* a million.]

trilobite, *trī'lō-bīt, n.* any of a group of fossil marine animals generally considered as belonging to the Crustacea. [Gr. *tri-,* three, and *lobos,* a lobe.]

trilogy, *tril'o-ji, n.* the name given by the Greeks to a group of three tragedies, each complete in itself, yet mutually related as parts of a larger whole: any series of three related dramatic or literary works. [Gr. *trilogiā*—*tri-, tris,* thrice, *logos,* discourse.]

trim, *trim, adj.* in good order, tidy, neat.—*v.t.* to make trim: to put in due order: to decorate: to clip: to arrange (sails, a ship in regard to disposition of cargo) for sailing.—*v.i.* to balance or fluctuate between parties:—*pr.p.* **trimm'ing;** *pa.t.* and *pa.p.* **trimmed.**—*n.* dress (e.g. *hunting trim*): state of a ship as to readiness for sailing: (*fig.*) state, degree of readiness or fitness.—*adv.* **trim'ly.**—*ns.* **trimm'er,** one who trims: one who fluctuates between parties, a time-server; **trimm'ing,** that which trims: ornamental parts, esp. of a garment, dish, &c.: (*pl.*) fittings; **trim'ness.** [O.E. *trymian,* to strengthen, set in order—*trum,* firm.]

trimeter, *trim'ė-tér, n.* a verse line consisting of three measures.—*adjs.* **trim'eter, trimet'ric, -al.** [Gr. *trimetros*—*metron,* measure.]

fāte, fär; mē, hûr (her); *mīne; mōte, för; mūte; mōōn, fŏŏt;* THen (then)

785

trinitrotoluene, trī-nī-trō-tol'ū-ēn, n. a highly explosive agent, commonly known as T.N.T. [Named from its chemical constituents.]

trinity, trin'i-ti, n. a group of three: (cap.) the union of three in one Godhead: the persons of the Godhead.—adj. **Trinitā'rian,** pertaining to the Trinity, or to the doctrine of the Trinity.—n. one who holds the doctrine of the Trinity.—ns. **Trinitā'rianism,** the tenets of Trinitarians; **Trin'ity House,** a corporation entrusted with the regulation and management of the lighthouses and buoys of the shores and rivers of England, and with the licensing and appointing of pilots for the English coast, founded at Deptford in 1518; **Trin'ity Sun'day,** the Sunday next after Whitsunday, the Festival of the Holy Trinity. [L. trīnitās, a triad—trīnī, three each.]

trinket, tring'kėt, n. a small ornament for the person: anything of little value.

trinomial, trī-nō'mi-ál, adj. (math.) consisting of three terms (as a−b+c).—n. a trinomial quantity. [L. trēs, three, nōmen, name.]

trio, tre'o, trī'o, n. a set of three: (mus.) a composition for, or company of, three performers: a composition performed in triple time:—pl. **tri'os.** [It.]

triode, trī'ōd, adj. with three electrodes.—n. a three-electrode valve. [Gr. hodos, way.]

triolet, trī'ō-let, or trē'-, n. a stanza of eight lines on two rhymes—viz., a, b, a, a, a, b, a, b; lines 1, 4, 7 are identical, and 8 is the same as 2. [Fr.]

trip, trip, v.i. to move with short, light steps: to stumble and fall: to err.—v.t. to cause (a person) to stumble by impeding his feet (often with up): to catch in a fault:—pr.p. tripp'ing; pa.t. and pa.p. tripped.—n. a light, short step: a catch by which an antagonist is thrown: a false step, a mistake: a short voyage or journey, an excursion: (slang) a hallucinatory experience under the influence of a drug, or the quantity of a drug that will produce such an experience.—ns. **tripp'er,** one who makes a popular trip or excursion; **tripp'ing,** the act of tripping: a light kind of dance.—adv. **tripp'ingly,** with a light, quick step: in a quick, gay manner.—n. **trip'-wire,** a wire which releases some mechanism when pulled, e.g. by being tripped over. [O.Fr. treper, trip(p)er; akin to O.E. treppan, to tread.]

tripartite, trī-pär'tīt, or trip'är-tīt, adj. divided into three parts: having three corresponding parts: relating to, or binding, three parties (as a tripartite agreement).—adv. **tripar'titely.**—n. **triparti'tion.** [L. ter, thrice, partītus, pa.p. of partīrī, to divide—pars, a part.]

tripe, trīp, n. (pl.) entrails: parts of compound stomach of a ruminant, esp. of sheep or horned cattle, prepared as food: (coll.) rubbish, poor stuff. [Fr.; ety. uncertain.]

triple, trip'l, adj. consisting of three united: three times repeated.—v.t. and v.i. to treble.—n. **trip'let,** three of a kind, or three united: three lines rhyming together: (mus.) a group of three notes occupying the time of two, indicated by a slur and the figure 3: one of three children born at one birth.—adjs. **trip'lex,** consisting of three parts: threefold; **trip'licate** (-át), threefold: made thrice as much.—n. a third copy or thing corresponding

to two others of the same kind.—v.t. to make threefold.—n. **triplicā'tion,** act of making threefold or adding three together.—adv. **trip'ly.—triple time** (mus.), time or rhythm of three beats, or of three times three beats, in a bar; **Triplex glass,** a patented form of laminated safety glass, composed of three layers, the middle one of which is a plastic material.—**in triplicate,** in three identical copies. [Fr.,—L. triplus, triplex, threefold—trēs, three.]

tripod, trī'pod, n. anything on three feet or legs, as a stool, &c. [Gr. tripous, -podos—tri-, treis, three, pous, foot.]

tripoli, trip'o-li, n. a mineral substance employed in polishing metals, marble, glass, &c. [Orig. brought from Tripoli in Africa.]

tripos, trī'pos, n. an examination for honours at Cambridge University: the list of successful candidates in the examination: a tripod. [Prob. traceable to the custom by which a B.A., known as Mr Tripos, sat on a three-legged stool and disputed in the Philosophy School at Cambridge on Ash Wednesday.]

triptych, trip'tik, n. a set of tablets consisting of three leaves, each painted with a distinct but related subject, joined together by hinges, the smaller outside leaves folding over the centre one: a set of three hinged writing tablets. [Gr. tri-, thrice, ptyx, gen. ptychos, a fold, a leaf—ptyssein, to fold.]

trireme, trī'rēm, n. an ancient galley—esp. a war-galley—having three banks of oars (cf. **quinquereme**). [Fr.,—L. trirēmis—tri-, trēs, three, rēmus, an oar.]

trisect, trī-sekt', v.t. to cut or divide into three, esp. equal, parts.—n. **trisec'tion,** the division of anything, as an angle, into three (equal) parts. [L. tri-, thrice, secāre, sectum, to cut.]

trisyllable, trī-, or tri-sil'á-bl, n. a word of three syllables.—adjs. **trisyllab'ic, -al,** pertaining to a trisyllable: consisting of three syllables.—adv. **trisyllab'ically.** [Gr. treis, three, syllabē, syllable.]

trite, trīt, adj. (obs.) worn by use: used till novelty and interest are lost, hackneyed (e.g. of a figure of speech, a remark).—adv. **trite'ly.**—n. **trite'ness.** [It. trito—L. trītus, rubbed, pa.p. of terēre, to rub.]

tritium, trit'i-um, trish'-, n. a heavy isotope of hydrogen, radioactive, of mass number 3.—n. **trīt'on,** the nucleus of tritium. [Gr. tritos, third.]

triturate, trit'ū-rāt, v.t. to rub or grind to a fine powder.—adj. **trit'urable,** that may be reduced to a fine powder by grinding.—n. **triturā'tion.** [L.L. trītūrāre, -ātum—L. terēre, to rub.]

triumph, trī'umf, n. in ancient Rome, a solemn procession in honour of a victorious general: victory: success: a great achievement: joy for success.—v.i. to celebrate a victory with pomp: to obtain victory or success: to rejoice for victory: to boast: to exult (over a rival).—adjs. **trium'phal,** pertaining to triumph: used in celebrating victory or success; **trium'phant,** celebrating, or rejoicing for, a triumph, expressing joy for success: victorious.—adv. **trium'phantly.**—n. **trī'umpher.** [L. triumphus—Gr. thriambos, a hymn to Bacchus.]

triumvir, trī-um'vėr, n. one of three men in the same office or with the same authority:—pl.

Neutral vowels in unaccented syllables: em'pėr-ór; for certain sounds in foreign words see p. ix.

trium′virī, trium′virs.—*n.* **trium′virate**, an association of three men in office or government, or for any political ends. [L. *trium*- (from *trēs*), three, *vir*, a man.]

triune, *trī′ūn, adj.* being three in one. [Coined from L. *tri*-, root of *trēs*, three, *ūnus*, one.]

trivet, *triv′ét, n.* a stool or the like supported on three feet: a movable iron frame for hooking to a grate for supporting kettles, &c.—**right as a trivet** (*coll.*), standing steadily like a tripod, perfectly right. [O.Fr. *trepied*—L. *tripēs*, *tripedis*—*trēs*, three, *pēs*, a foot.]

trivia, *tri′vi-á, n. pl.* trifles, trivialities, unimportant details.—*adj.* **tri′vial**, of little importance: trifling: commonplace: (of a name) popular, not scientific.—*n.* **trivial′ity**, the state or quality of being trivial: that which is trivial, a trifle.—*adv.* **triv′ially.**—*n.* **triv′ialness.** [L. *triviālis*, (lit.) 'at the crossroads or in public streets'—*trivium*, a place where three ways meet—*trēs*, three, *via*, a way.]

trivium, *tri′vi-úm, n.* in mediaeval schools, the name given to the first three liberal arts—grammar, rhetoric, and logic—which combined with the *quadrivium* (q.v.) to make up a complete system of education. [L. *tri*-, three, *via*, a way.]

trochee, *trō′kē, n.* a metrical foot of two syllables, so called from its tripping or joyous character—in Latin verse, consisting of a long and a short, as *dŭlcĕ*: in English verse, of an accented and unaccented syllable, as *laughing wa′ter*, a trochaic verse or measure.—*adjs.* **trochā′ic, -al**, consisting of trochees. [Gr., *trochaios* (*pous*), running, tripping (foot)—*trochos*, a running—*trechein*, to run.]

trod, *trod, pa.t.* of **tread.**

trodden, *trod′n, pa.p.* of **tread.**

troglodyte, *trog′lō-dīt, n.* a cave dweller: a genus of anthropoid apes, a gorilla or a chimpanzee: (*fig.*) a hermit. [Fr.,—Gr. *trōglodytēs*—*trōglē*, a cave, *dyein*, to enter.]

Trojan, *trō′jän, adj.* pertaining to ancient Troy.—*n.* an inhabitant of ancient Troy: (*coll.*) one who shows pluck and endurance.—**Trojan horse**, the gigantic wooden horse inside which the Greeks entered Troy: a person, organisation, placed within a country, group, &c., with the purpose of destroying it.

troll, *trōl, n.* a supernatural being, sometimes a giant, sometimes a dwarf, dwelling in a cave, hill, &c. [O.N. *troll.*]

troll, *trōl, v.t.* (*obs.* or *arch.*) to move circularly: to sing the parts of in succession, as of a catch or round: to sing loudly and light-heartedly: to fish for in a certain way: to fish (water).—*v.i.* (*arch*) to roll, to move, stroll, ramble: to sing a catch: to fish.—*n.* a moving round, repetition: a round song.—*ns.* **troll′er; trolley** (*trol′i*), **troll′y**, a costermonger's cart: an overhead current collector for tramway cars, trolleybuses, &c., having a small grooved wheel running under the contact wire: a small truck or wheel-barrow; **troll′ey-bus**, a bus that receives power from an overhead wire by a trolley.—*n.* **tea-trolley**, a small tiered table on wheels, used for serving afternoon tea or other light refreshments. [O.Fr. *troller, trauler*, to stroll; O.H.G. *trollen*, to run.]

trollop, *trol′op, n.* a loitering, slatternly woman: a prostitute. [From **troll** (2), in the sense of 'to run about'.]

trombone, *trom′bōn,* or *trom-bōn′, n.* a deeptoned brass musical wind instrument of the trumpet kind, consisting of a tube bent twice on itself. [It.; augmentative of *tromba*, a trumpet.]

troop, *trōōp, n.* a crowd or collection of people: (usually in *pl.*) soldiers taken collectively: a small body of cavalry corresponding to a company of infantry.—*v.i.* to collect in numbers: to go in a crowd, or in haste.—*ns.* **troop′er**, a private cavalry soldier; **troop′-ship**, a vessel for conveying soldiers.—**trooping the colour**, a ceremony performed at the public mounting of garrison guards. [Fr. *troupe.*]

trope, *trōp, n.* a figurative use of a word or expression, a figure of speech. [Fr.,—L. *tropus*—Gr. *tropos*—*trepein*, to turn.]

trophy, *trō′fi, n.* (Gr. *hist.*) a memorial of a victory, consisting of a pile of arms erected on the field of battle: anything taken from an enemy and preserved as a memorial of victory: a possession that is evidence of achievement in any sphere.—*adj.* **trō′phied**, adorned with trophies. [Fr. *trophée*—L. *tropaeum*—Gr. *tropaion*—*tropē*, a rout—*trepein*, to turn.]

tropic, *trop′ik, n.* one of the two imaginary circles on the celestial sphere, 23° 28′ on each side of the celestial equator, where the sun turns, as it were, after reaching its greatest declination north or south: one of two imaginary circles on the terrestrial globe corresponding to these—the tropics of Cancer and Capricorn: (*pl.*) the regions lying between these circles.—*adjs.* **trop′ic, -al**, pertaining to the tropics: within or near the tropics: very hot: luxuriant.—*adv.* **trop′ically.** [L. *tropicus*—Gr. *tropikos*, relating to a turning—*tropos*, a turning.]

tropism, *trō′pizm, n.* (*bot.* and *zool.*) a reflex response to an external stimulus that involves movements of the whole body. [Gr. *tropos*, a turning, and suffx. *-ism.*]

troposphere, *trop′ō-sfēr, n.* the lowest layer of the atmosphere, in which temperature falls as height increases. [Gr. *tropos*, a turning, *sphaira*, a sphere.]

trot, *trot, v.i.* (of a horse) to go, lifting the feet quicker and higher than in walking, moving them in diagonal pairs: to walk or move fast, esp. with small steps: to run.—*v.t.* to ride at a trot:—*pr.p.* trott′ing;*pa.t.* and *pa.p.* trott′ed.—*n.* the pace of a horse, &c., when trotting.—*n.* **trott′er**, one that trots: a trotting-horse: the foot of an animal, esp. when used for food.—**trot out**, to exhibit the paces of: to display for admiration: to bring forward, adduce: to tell for applause (often an already familiar story). [O.Fr. *trotter, troter.*]

troth, *troth,* or *trōth, n.* (*arch.*) truth, veracity (*by my troth*): faith, fidelity (*to plight one's troth*). [O.E. *trēowth.* Doublet **truth.**]

troubadour, *trōō′ba-dōōr, n.* one of a class of poets and poet-musicians of chivalric love, who first appeared in Provence, and flourished from the 11th to the 13th century. [Fr.,—Provençal *trobador*—*trobar* (Fr. *trouver*), to find, compose.]

fāte, fär; mē, hûr (her); *mīne; mōte, för; mūte; mōōn, fŏŏt;* тнen (then)

trouble, *trubl*, *v.t.* to agitate (e.g. water): (*fig.*) to disturb: to worry: to pain, afflict: to put to inconvenience.—*v.i.* to take pains (to).—*n.* disturbance: uneasiness: affliction: disease: that which disturbs or · afflicts: the taking of pains.—*n.* **troub′ler.**—*adj.* **troub′lesome,** causing or giving trouble or inconvenience: vexatious: importunate.—*adv.* **troub′lesomely.** —*n.* **troub′lesomeness.**—*adj.* **troub′lous,** full of trouble or disorder, agitated, tumultuous. —*n.* **troub′le-shooter,** an expert detector and mender of any trouble, mechanical or other. [O.Fr. *tourbler* — Low L. *turbulāre* — L. *turbāre*, to disturb — *turba*, a crowd.]

trough, *trof*, or *tröf*, *n.* a long, hollow vessel for water or other liquid: a long tray: a long narrow channel: a hollow: an elongated area of low barometric pressure. [O.E. *trog*; Ger. *trog*.]

trounce, *trowns*, *v.t.* to punish or beat severely.

troupe, *trōōp*, *n.* a company, esp. of actors, dancers, or acrobats. [Fr. See **troop.**]

trousers, *trow′zèrs*, *n.pl.* a two-legged garment worn on the lower limbs and trussed or fastened up at the waist by braces or belt. The sing. is used in **trous′er-butt′on, -stretch′er,** &c.—*adj.* **trou′sered,** wearing trousers.—**wear the trousers,** of a wife, to be the dominant partner in marriage. [O.Fr. *trousses,* breeches worn by pages; allied to **trews.**]

trousseau, *trōō′sō*, or *-sō′*, *n.* a bride's outfit:—*pl.* **-seaux** (*-sōz*). [Fr., a dim. of *trousse,* a bundle.]

trout, *trowt*, *n.* a common name for certain fish of the salmon genus, smaller than salmon and in most cases living practically exclusively in fresh water: (*coll.*) an unpleasant interfering old woman. [O.E. *truht* — L. *tructa, tructus* — Gr. *trōktēs,* a sea-fish with sharp teeth — *trōgein,* to gnaw.]

trouvère, *trōō-ver′*, *n.* one of a school of mediaeval French poets (11th-14th century) whose works were chiefly narrative. [Same root as **troubadour.**]

trove. See treasure-trove.

trover, *trō′vèr*, *n.* (*law*) the gaining possession of goods: an action to recover goods wrongfully detained. [O.Fr. *trover,* to find.]

trow, *trō, trow, v.i.* (*B.*) to trust: (*arch.*) to believe, to think. [O.E. *trēowian,* to trust.]

trowel, *trow′el, n.* a tool used in spreading mortar, paint, &c., and in gardening.—**lay it on with a trowel,** to spread thickly: to flatter grossly. [O.Fr. *truelle* — L. *trulla,* dim of *trua,* a ladle.]

trowsers. Same as **trousers.**

troy-weight, *troi′-wāt, n.* the system of weights traditionally used in England for gold, silver, and precious stones. [From *Troyes,* in France, the pound weight of which was adopted in England in the 14th century.]

truant, *trōō′ant, n.* pupil who, without excuse, absents himself from school: anyone who absents himself from his work without reason. —*adj.* wandering from duty: loitering, idle.— *ns.* **tru′ancy, tru′antship.**—**play truant,** to stay from school or work without leave. [O.Fr. *truand* — Celt; W. *truan,* wretched, Breton *truek,* a beggar.]

truce, *trōōs, n.* a suspension of hostilities between two armies, states, or disputants for a period specially agreed upon: a temporary cessation.—*n.* **truce′-break′er,** one who violates a truce or engagement. [M.E. *trewes, treowes,* pl. of *trewe,* a truce—O.E. *trēow,* faith; allied to *trēowe,* true.]

truck, *truk, v.t.* to exchange or barter.—*v.i.* to traffic by exchange.—*n.* exchange of goods, barter: (*coll.*) small goods, rubbish: business dealings, association: (*U.S.*) market-garden produce.—*ns.* **truck′age,** the practice of exchanging or bartering goods; **truck′-sys′tem,** the practice of paying workmen in goods instead of money.—**Truck Act,** a statute of 1831, extended in 1887, requiring workmen's wages to be paid in money instead of goods.—**have no truck with,** to have nothing to do with. [O.Fr. *troquer.*]

truck, *truk, n.* a wheel: a railway goods-wagon: a porter's wheeled hand-barrow for luggage: a transport motor-vehicle: a small wooden cap at the top of a mast or flag-staff.—*n.* **truck′age,** conveyance by trucks: charge for carrying articles on a truck. [L. *trochus,* a wheel—Gr. *trochos*—*trechein,* to run.]

truckle, *trukl, v.i.* to submit slavishly.—*n.* **truckle-bed,** a low bed on wheels that could be pushed under another, such as servants formerly used. [Gr. *trochlea,* a pulley.]

truculent, *truk′ū-lent,* or *trōōk′-, adj.* very fierce: threatening and overbearing in manner.—*ns.* **truc′ulence, truc′ulency.**—*adv.* **truc′ulently.** [L. *truculentus* — *trux,* wild, fierce.]

trudge, *truj, v.i.* and *v.t.* to′travel on foot, esp. with labour or weariness.—*n.* a weary walk.

trudgen, (*incorrectly*) **trudgeon**, *truj′én, n.* a swimming stroke in which each hand alternately is raised above the surface, thrust forward, and pulled back through the water. [John *Trudgen,* who popularised the stroke in England.]

true, *trōō, adj.* agreeing with fact (e.g. *a true story*): correct, accurate (e.g. *a true estimate, idea*): properly so called, genuine (e.g. *a true reptile*): placed, fitted accurately: perfectly in tune: rightful (e.g. *the true heir*): (*arch.*) honest: (of persons—*rare*) in the habit of telling the truth, truthful: sincere: faithful, loyal.— *adjs.* **true′-bred,** of good breeding or manners; **true′-heart′ed,** sincere: loyal.—*ns.* **true′-love,** a sweetheart; **true′-love′-knot, true′-lov′er's-knot,** lines interwoven with many involutions, fancifully held as an emblem of interwoven affection; **true′ness.**—*adv.* **tru′ly.—true bill,** a bill of indictment endorsed, after investigation, by a grand (q.v.) jury, as containing a well-founded charge; **true rib,** a rib attached to spine and sternum—opp. to *floating rib.*— **come true** (see **come**). [O.E. *trēowe*; O.N. *tryggr,* Ger. *treu.*]

truffle, *trufl,* *trōōfl, n.* a round underground fungus used in cookery.—*adj.* **truff′led,** cooked with truffles. [O.Fr. *truffle* — prob. L. *tūber.*]

truism, *trōō′izm, n.* a plain or self-evident truth. [**true,** and suffx. *-ism.*]

trump, *trump, v.t.* (*obs.*) to deceive.—*n.* **trum′pery,** something showy but worthless: nonsense, idle talk.—*adj.* showy and worthless.— **trump up,** to devise falsely, to fabricate. [Fr. *tromper,* to deceive, orig. to play on the trump.]

trump, *trump, n.* a trumpet: a Jew's-harp. [O.Fr.

Neutral vowels in unaccented syllables: *em′pér-ôr*; for certain sounds in foreign words see p. ix.

trompe (It. *tromba*); cf. Ger. *tromme*, Eng. *drum.*]

trump, *trump, n.* a card of the suit (determined each deal by chance or by choice) which takes precedence of any card of any other suit: (*coll.*) a good, trusty fellow.—*v.t.* to play a trump card upon.—Also *v.i.*—*n.* **trump-card,** (*fig.*) a means of triumph, a victorious expedient. [From **triumph,** confused with **trump,** to deceive.]

trumpet, *trum'pet, n.* a brass wind instrument with a clear ringing tone, consisting of a long narrow tube usu. bent once or twice upon itself and tapering into a bell at the end: in organs, a powerful reed-stop with a trumpet-like sound: (*fig.*) one who praises.—*v.t.* to publish by trumpet, to proclaim: to sound the praises of.—*v.i.* to sound a trumpet, or to make a sound suggestive of one.—*ns.* **trum'pet-call,** a call or summons on the trumpet: any resounding call to action; **trum'peter,** one who sounds on the trumpet the regimental calls and signals: one who proclaims, praises, or denounces: a loud-voiced, crane-like South American bird: a kind of domestic pigeon: any of several large Australian or New Zealand food-fishes.—*adj.* **trum'pet-tongued,** (*lit.* and *fig.*) having a voice loud as a trumpet.—*n.* **speaking'-trum'pet** (see **speak**).—**blow one's own trumpet,** to sound one's-own praises. [O.Fr. *trompette,* dim. of *trompe.*]

truncate, *trungk-āt', v.t.* to cut the top or end off, to lop, to maim.—*n.* **trunca'tion.—truncated cone, pyramid,** a cone, pyramid, having the vertex cut off by plane. [L. *truncāre, -ātum—truncus,* maimed.]

truncheon, *trun'ch(o)n, -sh(o)n, n.* a cudgel: a baton or staff of authority. [O.Fr. *tronçon.*]

trundle, *trun'dl, n.* a wheel: a truck.—*v.t.* to roll, as on wheels.—*v.i.* to roll, bowl along.—*n.* **trun'dle-bed,** a bed moving on trundles or low wheels, a truckle-bed. [O.E. *trendel,* a circle, wheel.]

trunk, *trungk, n.* the stem of a tree: the body of a man or an animal apart from the limbs: the main body of anything: anything long and hollow: the proboscis of an elephant: the shaft of a column: a portable box or chest for clothes, &c., esp. on a journey: (*pl.*) short, light pants, e.g. for running, swimming: (*pl.*) system of telephone trunk-lines.—*ns.* **trunkcall,** a telephone message sent or received by a main or trunk-line; **trunk'hose, -breech'es,** wide hose or breeches formerly worn over the lower part of the body and the upper part of the thigh; **trunk'-line,** the main-line of a railway, canal, telephone system, &c.; **trunk'-road,** a main-road. [O.Fr. *tronc*—L. *truncus,* a stock—*truncus,* maimed.]

trunnion, *trun'yon, n.* (formerly) a knob on each side of a cannon, on which it rested on the carriage: similar pivots, supported in bearings, forming part of machinery. [Fr. *trognon,* a stalk—*tronc,* a stump—L. *truncus,* maimed.]

truss, *trus, n.* a bundle: timbers fastened together for binding a beam or supporting a roof: in ships, the rope or iron for keeping the lower yard to the mast: a bandage or apparatus used in ruptures.—*v.t.* to bind (up): to skewer in cooking: to support with a truss.

[O.Fr. *trosser,* orig. *torser,* to bind together—L. *tortus,* pa.p. of *torquēre,* to twist.]

trust, *trust, n.* confidence in the truth of anything, as in the integrity, friendship, &c., of another: faith: confident expectation: credit (esp. sale on credit or on promise to pay): he who, or that which, is the ground of confidence: that which is given or received in confidence: charge, keeping: an arrangement by which property is transferred to a person, in the trust or confidence that he will use and dispose of it for a specified purpose: the property so transferred: in modern commerce, an arrangement for the control of several companies under one direction.—*adj.* held in trust.—*v.t.* to place confidence in: to give credit to, to sell to on credit: to commit (to) the care of: to believe: to expect confidently.—*v.i.* to be confident or confiding.—*ns.* **trust'-deed,** a deed conveying property to a trustee; **trustee',** one to whom anything is entrusted: one to whom the management of a property is committed in trust for the benefit of others; **trustee'ship: trust'er; trust'-estate,** an estate held by trustees.—*adj.* **trust'ful,** trusting.—*adv.* **trust'fully.**—*ns.* **trust'fulness; trust'-house,** a public-house owned by a trust company, not privately or by liquor manufacturers.—*adj.* **trust'worthy,** worthy of trust or confidence, dependable.—*n.* **trust'worthiness.**—*adj.* **trust'y,** deserving confidence: honest: strong, firm.—*adv.* **trust'ily.**—*n.* **trust'iness.—investment trust,** an organisation which invests its stockholder's money and distributes the net return among them; **unit trust,** a type of investment trust in which given amounts of different securities form a unit, and a number of units made up of different selections of securities are available to investors. [Scand., O N. *traust,* trust; Ger. *trost,* consolation.]

truth, *trōōth, n.* that which is true or according to the facts of the case: agreement with reality: practice of saying or telling, or disposition to say or tell, what is in accordance with the facts: fidelity: a true statement: an established principle:—*pl.* **truths** (*trōōTHz, trōōths*).—*adj.* **truth'ful,** according to, or adhering to, truth, veracious.—*adv.* **truth'fully.**—*n.* **truth'fulness.**—**truth drug,** scopolamine or other drug which makes subjects under questioning less wary in their replies.—**of a truth** (*B.*), truly. [O.E. *trēowthu*—*trēowe,* true. Doublet **troth.**]

try, *trī, v.t.* to put to the test or proof, to test by experiment: to examine judicially: to examine carefully: to experiment with, use experimentally, or seek to use as means: to attempt: to put to severe trial, cause suffering to: to subject to strain: to annoy greatly.—*v.i.* to endeavour, attempt: to make an effort:—*pa.t.* and *pa.p.* tried (*trīd*).—*n.* a trial: effort: a score in Rugby football, or the action that gains it.—*adjs.* **tried,** proved, experienced; **try'ing,** testing: causing strain or suffering.—**try on,** to put on for trial, as a garment: (*slang*) to attempt (an action or a course of action) in the hope that it will be permitted or tolerated (*n.* **try'-on**); **try out,** to test (*n.* **try'-out**).—**try it on,** to attempt to do something risky or aud-

acious to see how far one can go unscathed.
[O.Fr. *trier,* to pick out, to cull (grain from
straw); origin obscure.]

trypanosome, *trip'á-nō-sōm, n.* any of the **Try-
panosom'a,** a genus of protozoan (q.v.) parasites, some of which cause serious or deadly
disease (e.g. sleeping sickness). [Formed from
Gr. *trypanon,* an auger, *sōma,* a body.]

trysail, *trī'sāl,* or *trī'sl, n.* a reduced sail used by
small craft, instead of their mainsail, in a
storm: a small fore-and-aft sail set with a
boom and gaff. [**try, sail.**]

tryst, *trīst,* or *trist* (all uses *arch., Scot.,* or *dial.*),
n. an appointment to meet: an appointed place
of meeting.—*v.t.* to make an appointment
with.—*v.i.* to agree to meet.—*ns.* **trys'ting-day,**
a fixed day of meeting; **trys'ting-place,** an
arranged meeting-place. [A variant of **trust.**]

tsar, tzar, czar, *tsär, n.* the title of the former
emperors of Russia:—*fem.* **tsarina** (*tsär-ē'na*),
the empress.—*adj.* **tsar'ist,** (of a period when)
governed by a tsar: of the nature of government by a tsar, autocratic: in favour of government by a tsar (also *n.*). [Russ.,—L.
Caesar.]

tsetse, *tset'si, n.* a dipterous insect, found in
Southern and Central Africa, whose bite conveys a protozoan (q.v.) parasite that causes a
fatal disease to domesticated animals: a
closely related insect which transmits the
parasite causing sleeping sickness to man.
[Native word.]

tub, *tub, n.* a two-handed open wooden vessel: a
vessel, made of staves and hoops, to hold
water: a wide, deep, fixed basin for washing
clothes: a small cask: a bath: a clumsy boat: a
clumsy vehicle.—*v.t.* and *v.i.* to give, take, a
bath, a wash.—*adj.* **tubb'y,** like a tub, plump.
[Low Ger. *tubbe.*]

tuba, *tū'ba, n.* a large, low-pitched, brass wind-
instrument: in organs, a reed-stop of large
scale:—*pl.* **tūbae** (*-ē*), **tū'bas.** [L.]

tube, *tūb, n.* a pipe, a long hollow cylinder for
the conveyance of fluids, &c.: a cylindrical
receptacle for holding semi-fluid substances,
as pigments: (chiefly *U.S.*) thermionic valve
(q.v.): the body of a musical instrument: an
underground electric railway, especially in
London.—*v.t.* to furnish with, enclose in, a
tube.—*n.* **tū'bing,** the act of making tubes:
tubes collectively: material for tubes.—*adjs.*
tū'bular, having the form of a tube; **tū'bulate,
-d, tū'bulous,** formed like a tube: formed of
tubes.—*n.* **tū'būle,** a small tube. [Fr.,—L. *tubus,*
a pipe.]

tuber, *tū'bér, n.* a swelling in the stem or root of
a plant where reserves of food are stored up:
a swelling.—*adjs.* **tū'berous, tū'berōse,** having,
or consisting of, tubers: knobbed. [L. *tūber,* a
swelling—*tumēre,* to swell.]

tubercle, *tū'bér-kl, n.* a small swelling: a small
tuber: a small mass or nodule of cells resulting from infection with the bacillus of tuberculosis.—*adjs.* **tū'bercled,** having tubercles;
tuber'cular, of, pertaining to, resembling, or
affected with tubercles or nodules: (less correctly) tuberculous; **tuber'culous,** affected
with, or caused by, tuberculosis.—*ns.* **tuber'-
culin, -e,** any one of a number of preparations
from a culture of the tubercle bacillus for use

in the diagnosis and treatment of tuberculosis; **tuberculō'sis,** a wasting disease, esp. of
the lungs, induced by the invasion of a bacillus, and characterised by the presence of
tubercles or other tubercular formations.—
tubercle bacillus, the micro-organism that
causes tuberculosis.—*adj.* **tuber'culin-tested,**
tested with tuberculin to make sure that no
tubercle bacilli are present. [L. *tūberculum,*
dim. of *tūber.* See **tuber.**]

tuberose, *tū'be-rōs, tūb'rōz, n.* a bulbous plant
with creamy white, fragrant flowers. [From
tūberōsa, fem of *tūberōsus,* tuberous.]

tuck, *tuk, v.t.* to draw or press (in or together):
to fold (under): to gather (up): to enclose by
pressing clothes closely around (with *in* or
up): (*slang*) to eat greedily or with enjoyment
(with *in*; also *v.i.*).—*n.* a horizontal or vertical
fold stitched in a garment: (*slang*) eatables,
esp. pastry and sweets.—*n.* **tuck'er,** a piece of
cloth tucked or drawn over the bosom, formerly worn by women and children. [O.E.
tucian, to pull.]

tucket, *tuk'et, n.* (*arch.*) a flourish of trumpets.
[It. *toccata;* see **toccata.**]

Tudor, *tū'dôr, adj.* pertaining to the royal line of
the *Tudors* (1485–1603), or to that historical
period, or to the style of architecture common
in that period.]

Tuesday, *tūz'dā, n.* the third day of the week.
[O.E. *Tīwes dæg,* the day of Tiw (the god of
war); Ger. *dienstag;* cf. L. *dies Martis.*]

tufa, *tū'fa, n.* a porous rock, a form of calcium
carbonate, usually deposited from springs. [It.
tufa—L. *tōfus,* a soft stone.]

tuff, *tuf, n.* a rock formed of compacted volcanic
fragments. [Fr. *tuf, tuffe*—It. *tufo, tufa*—L.
tōfus.]

tuft, *tuft, n.* a crest of hair or feathers: a small
bunch or knot of fragments, wool, &c.: a cluster: a dense head of flowers.—*v.t.* to separate
into tufts: to adorn with tufts.—*adjs.* **tuft'ed,
tuft'y.** [O.Fr. *tuffe*—Gmc.; cf. Low Ger. *topp,*
Ger. *zopf.*]

tug, *tug, v.t.* to pull with effort: to drag along.—
v.i. to pull with great effort:—*pr.p.* **tugg'ing;**
pa.t. and *pa.p.* **tugged.**—*n.* a strong pull: a
steam-vessel for towing ships: an aeroplane
towing a glider.—*ns.* **tug'-boat,** a strongly-
built steamship for towing vessels; **tug'-of-
war,** a contest in which opposing teams tug at
the ends of a rope in an effort to pull one
another over a line marked on the ground
between them. [Closely conn. with **tuck** and
tow (vb.).]

tuition, *tū-ish'(ô)n, n.* (*rare*) care over a young
person: teaching, private coaching: instruction. [L. *tuitiō, -ōnis*—*tuērī.* See **tutor.**]

tulip, *tū'lip, n.* a genus of bulbous plants with
highly-coloured bell-shaped flowers. [O.Fr.
tulipe, tulippe, tulipan—Turk. *tulbend,* a
turban.]

tulle, *tūl,* or *tōōl, n.* a delicate kind of thin silk
network used for the trimmings of ladies'
dresses, and also for veils. [Fr., from *Tulle,* in
south central France.]

tumble, *tumb'l, v.i.* to fall, to come down suddenly and violently: to roll: to move in a blun-
dering manner: to twist the body, as a
mountebank.—*v.t.* to throw headlong: to turn

Neutral vowels in unaccented syllables: *em'pér-ôr*; for certain sounds in foreign words see p. ix.

over: to throw carelessly: to toss about while examining: to disorder, dishevel.—*n.* a fall: a rolling over, a somersault.—*adj.* **tum′ble-down**, dilapidated.—*n.* **tum′bler**, one who performs any feats or tricks of the acrobat or contortionist: a large drinking-glass, so called because formerly, having a pointed base, it could not be set down without tumbling: a kind of domestic pigeon, so called from its tumbling on the wing; **tum′ble-drier**, a machine which dries (clothes, &c.) by tumbling them in a strong current of hot air.—**tumble to**, (*slang*) to grasp, realise, understand without explanation. [Freq. from O.E. *tumbian*.]

tumbrel, *tum′brel*, **tumbril**, *tum′bril*, *n.* a cart with two wheels for conveying the tools of pioneers, artillery stores, &c.: the name given to the carts which conveyed victims to the guillotine during the French Revolution. [O.Fr. *tomberel—tomber*, to fall, because the body of the cart could be tipped up without unyoking.]

tumefy, *tū′me-fī*, *v.t.* to cause to swell.—*v.i.* to swell: to rise in a tumour:—*pa.t.* and *pa.p.* **tū′mefied.**—*n.* **tumefac′tion**, tumour: swelling. [L. *tumefacĕre—tumēre*, to swell, *facĕre*, to make.]

tumid, *tū′mid*, *adj.* swollen or enlarged, inflated: falsely sublime, bombastic.—*ns.* **tūmid′ity**, **tū′midness**;—*adv.* **tū′midly.** [L. *tumidus—tumēre*, to swell.]

tummy, *tum′i*, *n.* childish form of the word **stomach.**

tumour, *tū′mór*, *n.* a morbid swelling in any part of the body, of independent growth. [L. *tumor—tumēre*, to swell.]

tumult, *tū′mult*, *n.* uproar of a multitude, violent agitation with confused sounds: high excitement.—*adjs.* **tumult′uary**, acted by, or acting in, a mob or a disorderly multitude: chaotic: haphazard; **tumult′üous**, disorderly: agitated: noisy.—*adv.* **tumult′uously.**—*n.* **tumult′uousness.** [L. *tumultus—tumēre*, to swell.]

tumulus, *tū′mū-lus*, *n.* a mound of earth over a grave, a barrow:—*pl.* **tū′mūlī.**—*adjs.* **tū′mūlar**, formed in a heap; **tū′mūlous**, full of mounds. [L.,—*tumēre*, to swell.]

tun, *tun*, *n.* a large cask: an obsolete liquid measure of capacity.—*n.* **tunn′age** (*hist.*) a duty on imported wines. [O.E. *tunne.*]

tuna, *tōō′na*, *lū′na*, *n.* species of tunny. [Sp.]

tundra, *tōōn′dra*, or *tun′-*, *n.* a level treeless plain of arctic or sub-arctic regions, with lichens, mosses, and dwarfed vegetation. [Lapp.]

tune, *tūn*, *n.* a melodious succession of notes or chords, a melody: state of giving a sound or sounds of the correct pitch (e.g. *to be in tune*): state of giving a sound or sounds of exactly the same pitch: exact correspondence of vibrations other than sound vibrations: harmony (*in tune with*): frame of mind, temper (e.g. *not in good tune*).—*v.t.* to adjust the tones of, as a musical instrument: to adjust the resonant frequency of a circuit or circuits to a particular value.—*adjs.* **tūn′able** and **tune′ful**, melodious.—*adv.* **tune′fully.**—*n.* **tune′fulness.**—*adj.* **tune′less**, without tune: silent.—*ns.* **tū′ner**, one who tunes instruments; **tū′ning-fork**, a steel two-pronged instrument, designed when set in vibration to give a musical sound of a certain pitch.—**tune in**, (*radio*) to

adjust the circuit settings of a radio receiver so as to produce maximum response to a particular signal.—**change one's tune**, to alter one's attitude, or way of talking; **in tune**, true in pitch: (*fig.*) in accord; **out of tune**, not true in pitch: (*fig.*) not agreeing; **to the tune of**, to the amount of. [A doublet of **tone.**]

tungsten, *tung′sten*, *n.* dense metal (atomic no. 74; symbol W, from older name *wolframium*), chiefly derived from wolfram. [Swed.—*tung*, heavy, *sten*, stone.]

tunic, *tū′nik*, *n.* a short, loose, usu. belted, coat or coat-blouse: a sleeveless frock, cut wide at the neck, for wear over a blouse: a loose frock worn by schoolgirls: an ecclesiastical short-sleeved vestment: a close body-coat worn by soldiers and policemen: (*anat.*) a membrane that covers an organ: (*bot.*) a covering, as of a seed.—*adjs.* **tū′nicate, -d**, (*bot.*), covered with a tunic or with layers. [Fr. *tunique*—L. *tunica*, an undergarment worn by both sexes.]

tunnel, *tun′él*, *n.* an underground passage, esp. one by which a road or railway is carried under an obstacle.—*v.i.* to make a passage through.—*v.i.* to make a tunnel. [O.Fr. *tonnel* (Fr. *tonneau*), a cask; also O.Fr. *tonnelle*, an arched vault.]

tunny, *tun′i*, *n.* any of several large fish of same order as the mackerels, fished chiefly off the Mediterranean coasts. [L. *thunnus*—Gr. *thynnos—thynein*, to dart along.]

tup, *tup*, *n.* a ram. [M.E. *tuppe*; origin obscure.]

turban, *tûr′bán*, *n.* a head-covering worn by Eastern nations, consisting of a cap with a sash wound round it: a head-dress worn by ladies: the whole whorls of a shell.—*adj.* **tur′baned**, wearing a turban. [Earlier forms *turbant, tulipant* (Fr. *turban*)—Pers. *dulband.*]

turbid, *tûr′bid*, *adj.* muddy, thick: disordered, muddled.—*adv.* **tur′bidly.**—*n.* **tur′bidness.** [L. *turbidus—turba*, tumult.]

turbine, *tûr′bīn*, or *tûr′bin*, *n.* a machine in which the forced passage of a fluid through a tube containing a close-fitting rotor with shaped vanes causes the rotor to rotate. Fluids used include compressed air (dentist's drill), gas (jet aero-engine), water (hydro-electric generator) and steam (coal, oil, or nuclear power station).—*n.* **turb′ine-steam′er**, a vessel impelled by a steam-turbine. [Fr.,—L. *turbō, turbinis*, a whirl—*turbāre*, to disturb—*turba*, disorder.]

turbojet, turboprop. See **jet.**

turbot, *tûr′bot*, *n.* a large, flat, round fish, highly esteemed, and abundant in the North Sea. [O.Fr., *turbot*, prob.—L. *turbō*, a whirl, a spinning-top.]

turbulent, *tûr′bū-lént*, *adj.* tumultuous, disturbed, in violent commotion: producing commotion: having an exciting, disturbing effect: inclined to insubordination or unrest.—*n.* **tur′bulence**, disturbed state (also esp. formerly **tur′bulency**): irregular movement of large volumes of air: irregular eddying motion of particles in a fluid.—*adv.* **tur′bulently.** [Fr.,—L. *turbulentus—turba*, a crowd.]

tureen, *tū-rēn′, tu-rēn′*, *n.* a large dish for holding soup at table. [Fr. *terrine*—L. *terra*, earth.]

turf, *tûrf*, *n.* the surface of land matted with the roots of grass, &c.: a cake of turf cut off, a sod:

fāte, fär; mē, hûr (her); *mīne; mōte, för; mūte; mōōn, fŏŏt;* ᴛʜen (then)

in Ireland, peat: horse-racing, the race-course:—*pl.* **turfs.**—*v.t.* to cover with sod.—*adj.* **turf'y,** resembling or abounding in turf.—*n.* **turf'iness.**—**turf out** (*slang*), forcibly to throw out. [O.E. *turf*; O.N. *torf.*]

turgent, *tûr'jėnt, adj.* (*rare*) swelling: bombastic.—*adj.* **turges'cent,** swelling.—*n.* **turges'cence.**—*adj.* **tur'gid,** swollen: extended beyond the natural size: pompous, bombastic.—*ns.* **turgid'ity, tur'gidness.**—*adv.* **tur'-gidly.**—*n.* **turgor** (*tûr'gór*), state of being full, the normal condition of the capillaries. [L. *turgēns, -entis,* pr.p. of *turgēre,* to swell.]

Turk, *tûrk, n.* a native of *Turkey,* an Ottoman: a savage person: an unmanageable child.—*ns.* **Turk'ey-car'pet,** a soft thick kind of carpet; **Turk'ey-red,** a fine durable red dye, obtained from madder, but now mostly prepared chemically.—*adj.* **Turk'ish,** pertaining to the Turks or to Turkey, Ottoman.—*n.* the language of the Turks.—*ns.* **Turk'ish-bath,** a kind of hot-air bath, the patient being sweated, rubbed down, massaged, and gradually cooled; **Turk'ish-delight',** a gelatinous sweetmeat, orig. Turkish.

turkey, *tûrk'i, n.* a large gallinaceous bird, a native of America, orig. confused with the guinea fowl supposed to have come from *Turkey.*—*n.* **turk'ey-buzz'ard,** an American vulture.

Turki, *tŏŏr'kē, n.* the group of languages to which the chief language of Turkey belongs.

Turkoman, *tûrk'ō-mán, n.* a member of a group of tribes, speaking a Turki language, found in Asiatic Russia north-east of Persia. [Pers. *Turkmān,* Turk-like.]

turmeric, *tûr'mėr-ik, n.* the rootstock or rhizome of a herbaceous plant cultivated all over India, used as a yellow dye, in curry-powder, and as a chemical test for the presence of alkalis. [Cf. Fr. *terre-mérite*—as if from L. *terra,* earth, and *merita,* deserved; both prob. corr. from an Oriental name.]

turmoil, *tûr'moil, n.* physical or mental agitation: disturbance, confusion.

turn, *tûrn, v.i.* to revolve: to move through an arc of a circle: to go in the opposite direction: to turn one's head: to take a different direction (*lit.* and *fig.*—e.g. *his thoughts then turned to supper*): to become by a change, to change (to, into—e.g. *the ice turned to water*): to hinge (on), or (*fig.*) to depend on: to be shaped on the lathe: (of milk, &c.) to sour: (of head, brain) to become giddy: to change from ebb to flow or from flow to ebb.—*v.t.* to cause to revolve: to reverse: to change the position or direction of: to reach and go round: to direct, apply: to transfer: to convert (into): to transform: to translate (into): to sour: to make giddy: to nauseate: to form in a lathe: to shape: to have just passed (a certain age, hour, &c.).—*n.* act of turning: new direction or tendency: a walk to and fro: a turning-point, crisis: a spell of work: performer's act, or performer: opportunity, alternating with that of others: requirement of the moment (e.g. *this will serve our turn*): (with *good* or *ill*) act of kindness or of malice: form, style, fashion: a natural aptitude (for): (*coll.*) a nervous shock: a winding: a bend: (*mus.*) an ornament

of the form EDCD (where D is the principal note).—*ns.* **turn'coat,** one who abandons his principles or party; **turn'er,** one who uses a lathe; **turn'ery,** art of shaping by a lathe: things made by a turner; **turn'ing,** a winding: deviation from the proper course: a street corner: turnery: (*pl.*) chips: act or manner of shaping or fashioning (*lit.* and *fig.*); **turn'ing-point,** the point at which anything turns in its course: a maximum or minimum point on a graph: a critical point; **turn'ing-saw,** a thin-bladed saw contrived for cutting curved wood for chair-backs, &c.; **turn'key,** one who turns the keys in a prison, a warder; **turn'-out,** a crowd, a large gathering for a special purpose: a carriage and its horses: clothes, manner of dress: general appearance produced: output or production; **turn'over,** act of turning over, upset, overthrow: a fruit or meat pasty: the total amount of the sales in a business for a specified time; **turn'pike,** a gate set across a road to stop those liable to toll: a turnpike-road; **turn'pike-road,** a road on which turnpikes or toll-gates were (or are; *U.S.*) established; **turn'spit,** one who turns a spit: a person engaged in some menial occupation: a dog employed to drive a wheel by which roasting-spits were turned; **turn'stile,** a revolving frame across a footpath or entrance which admits only one person at a time, and can be used to register the number admitted; **turn'-tä'ble,** a circular revolving platform for turning a railway engine round; **turn'-up,** the cuff at the bottom of a trouser-leg: (*coll.*) a disturbance, commotion: (*coll.*) a dramatically unexpected result in racing: a piece of material folded up.—**turn about, turn and turn about,** alternately; **turn adrift,** to unmoor and let float away: to cast off; **turn an enemy's flank, line,** or **position,** to manoeuvre so as to attack an enemy in the rear: to outwit; **turn around one's finger,** to make subservient to one's will; **turn away,** to dismiss from service, to discharge: to avert (one's eyes), to look in another direction: to deviate, to depart (from); **turn down,** to double or fold down: to reject; **turn in,** bend inward: enter: to surrender, hand over voluntarily: (*coll.*) to go to bed; **turn off,** to deviate: to dismiss: to divert: to shut off: to make (a person) unenthusiastic, less aware and less vital; **turn on,** to set running (as water): to hinge, depend on: to confront angrily: (*slang*) to excite, to give (a person) a sense of heightened awareness and vitality as do psychedelic drugs; **turn one's hand to,** to apply oneself to; **turn one's head,** or **brain,** to make one giddy: to fill with pride or conceit; **turn out,** to drive out, to expel: to make for market or for use: to prove in the result: to muster: (*coll.*) to get out of bed: to extinguish (a light): to clean thoroughly (a room): to dress elaborately; **turn the edge of,** to blunt; **turn the scale,** to prove decisive; **turn the stomach,** to nauseate; **turn to,** to have recourse to: to change to: to set to work; **turn turtle** (see turtle (2)); **turn up,** to appear: to happen: to refer to in a book: (*coll.*) to disgust, nauseate; **turn up for the book,** a totally unexpected occurrence.—**by turns,** one after another: alternately; **have turned, be turned,**

Neutral vowels in unaccented syllables: *em'pér-ór*; for certain sounds in foreign words see p. ix.

792

to have gone, or to be, beyond (e.g. *he has turned* 30); **in turn,** in order of succession; **not to turn a hair,** to be quite undisturbed or unaffected; **on the turn,** at the turning-point, changing; **take one's turn,** to take one's part, alternately with others, e.g. in a task; **take turns,** to do (e.g. to work) in rotation; **to a turn,** exactly, perfectly. [O.E. *tyrnan*; Ger. *turnen*; Fr. *tourner*; all from L. *tornāre*, to turn in a lathe.]

turnip, *tûr′nip, n.* a plant with swollen and fleshy root—cultivated as a vegetable and for feeding cattle and sheep. [Perh. orig. *turn-nep*—*turn*, implying something round, and *nep*—O.E. *nǣp*, a turnip.]

turpentine, *tûr′pen-tīn, n.* a semi-solid resinous substance secreted by the terebinth and other coniferous trees: the oil or spirit of turpentine, used for making paint and varnish, and in medicine. [O.Fr. *terbentine*—L. *terebinthina* (*rēsīna*), (the resin) of the terebinth—Gr. *terebinthos.*]

turpitude, *tûr′pi-tūd, n.* baseness, extreme depravity or wickedness. [L. *turpitūdō*—*turpis,* base.]

turquoise, *tûr′koiz,* or *tûr′kwoiz, n.* an opaque greenish-blue mineral, a phosphate of aluminium and copper, valued as a gem. [O.Fr.; because first brought through *Turkey* or from *Turkestan.*]

turret, *tûr′et, n.* a small tower on a building or structure, rising above it: a tower, often revolving, for offensive purposes.—*adj.* **turr′eted,** furnished with turrets. [O.Fr. *touret,* dim. of *tour,* a tower.]

turtle, *tûr′tl,* **turtle-dove,** *tûr′tl-duv, n.* a genus of doves noted for their soft cooing and their affection towards each other and their young. [O.E. *turtle*; Ger. *turtel,* Fr. *tourtereau, tourterelle*—L. *turtur.*]

turtle, *tûr′tl, n.* sometimes synonymous with *tortoise* (q.v.), but usu. restricted to aquatic (esp. marine) species: the flesh of certain turtles, as the *green turtle,* used for making soup.—*ns.* **tur′tleback,** a turtle-shaped projection on the bows or stern of a ship for the purpose of keeping off heavy seas; **tur′tleneck,** (a garment having) a high close-fitting neckline (*adj.* **tur′tle-necked**).—**mock turtle** (see **mock**); **turn turtle,** to capsize as a boat. [A corr. of *tortoise,* or of Sp. *tortuga,* or Port. *tartaruga,* a tortoise.]

Tuscan, *tus′kán, adj.* of or belonging to *Tuscany* in Italy: denoting the simplest of the five classic orders of architecture. [L. *Tuscānus.*]

tusk, *tusk, n.* a long, protruding tooth on either side of the mouth of certain animals.—*adjs.* **tusked, tusk′y.** [O.E. *tusc, tux*; O.N. *toskr.*]

tussle, *tus′l, n.* a struggle.—*v.i.* to struggle. [Frequentative of M.E. *tusen,* to treat roughly.]

tussock, *tus′ók, n.* a tuft of grass or twigs. [Perh. conn. with Swed. dial, *tuss,* a wisp of hay.]

tussore, tusser, *tus′ōr, tus′ór, n.* a silkworm that spins fawn-coloured silk: the silk itself. [Hind. *tasar,* shuttle—Sans. *tasara,* silkworm.]

tutelage, *tū′te-lij, n.* guardianship: state of being under a guardian.—*adjs.* **tū′telar, tū′telary,** protecting: having the charge of a person or place. [L. *tūtēla*—*tūtārī,* to guard—*tuērī,* to look at; cf. **tutor.**]

tutor, *tū′tór, n.* one who has charge of the education of another: one who directs the studies of, and examines, students: a book of instructions or lessons (esp. in a branch of music): (*Scots law*) a guardian of the person and estate of a boy or girl.—*v.t.* to instruct: to treat with authority or sternness: to direct the studies of.—*adj.* **tutō′rial,** belonging to, or exercised by, a tutor.—*n.* a meeting for study between a tutor and a student or students.—*n.* **tū′torship.** [L. *tūtor,* a guardian—*tuērī, tuitus,* to look at, to watch, guard.]

tutti, *tōō′ti, adj.* (*mus.*) for all voices or instruments playing together.—*n.* a passage so sung or played. [It.]

tutu, *tōō′tōō, n.* a ballet dancer's short, stiff, spreading skirt. [Fr.]

tuum. See **meum.**

twaddle, *twod′l, v.i.* to talk in a silly manner.—*n.* silly talk.—*n.* **twadd′ler.** [Earlier form *twattle,* a variant of **tattle.**]

twain, *twān, n.* two, a couple, pair.—**in twain,** asunder. [O.E. *twēgen* (masc.), two.]

twang, *twang, n.* a sharp, quick sound, as of a tight string, when pulled and let go: a nasal tone of voice: (*coll.*) a local accent.—*v.i.* to sound as a tight string pulled and let go: to have a nasal sound.—*v.t.* to make to sound with a twang. [Imit.]

twayblade, *twā′blād, n.* one of several kinds of orchid with green or purple flowers and a single pair of leaves. [Obs. *tway,* two, and **blade.**]

tweak, *twēk, v.t.* to twitch, to pull, to pull with sudden jerks.—*n.* a sharp pinch or twitch. [A by-form of **twitch.**]

twee, *twē, adj.* (*coll.*) small and sweet: sentimentally pretty. [*tweet* for 'sweet' and later *tiny* and *wee.*]

tweed, *twēd, n.* a kind of woollen twilled cloth of various patterns.—*adj.* made of tweed. [From a mistaken reading of *'tweels'* (see **twill**) on an invoice; not, as supposed, from the *Tweed* valley.]

'tween. Abbreviation for **between.**

tweezers, *twēz′èrz, n.sing.* nippers: small pincers for pulling out hairs, &c. [Obs. *tweeze,* a surgeon's case of instruments—*etuis,* pl. of *etui*—Fr. *étui,* a case.]

twelfth, *twelfth, adj.* the last of twelve: being one of twelve equal parts.—Also *n.*—*ns.* **Twelfth′-day, -tide,** the twelfth day after Christmas, the Epiphany; **Twelfth′-night,** the eve of Twelfth-day or evening before Epiphany.—**twelve tone** (or **note**) **music,** music based on a pattern formed from the twelve notes of the chromatic scale, esp. as developed by Arnold Schönberg (1874-1951) and his pupils. [O.E. *twelfta; th* on the analogy of *fourth.*]

twelve, *twelv, adj.* and *n.* the cardinal number next after eleven.—*n.* the figures 12 or xii denoting this.—*adj.* **twelfth** (see separate article).—*n.* **twelve′-month,** twelve months, a year.—**the Twelve,** the twelve apostles. [M.E. inflected form *twelve*—O.E. *twelf;* Ger. *zwölf.*]

twenty, *twen′ti, adj.* and *n.* two times ten.—*adj.* **twen′tieth,** the last of twenty: being one of twenty equal parts.—Also *n.* [O.E. *twēntig*—*twēn* (-*twēgen*), two, and *tig,* ten, related to *tīen, tēn.*]

fāte, fär; mē, hûr (her); *mīne; mōte, för; mūte; mōōn, fōōt;* тнen (then)

twerp, *twûrp, n.* (*coll.*) a contemptible person, either stupid or a cad, or both.

twice, *twīs, adv.* two times, once and again: doubly.—**twice over,** twice (emphatically). [O.E. *twiges—twiwa—twā*; see **two.**]

twiddle, *twid'l, v.t.* to twirl idly, to play with.—**twiddle one's thumbs,** to be idle.

twig, *twig, n.* a small shoot or branch of a tree.—*adj.* **twigg'y,** abounding in twigs. [O.E. *twig—twī-,* double.]

twig, *twig, v.t.* and *v.i.* (*slang*) to notice: to understand, grasp the meaning.

twilight, *twī'līt, n.* the faint light after sunset and before sunrise: partial darkness: (*fig.*) a period of decay following a period of success, greatness, &c.—*adj.* of twilight: faintly illuminated, obscure.—**twilight sleep,** partial anaesthesia sometimes used in childbirth. [Lit. "tween light", O.E. *twi—twā* (see **two**), and **light.**]

twill, *twil,* or **tweel,** *twēl, ns.* woven fabric, in which the warp is raised one thread, and depressed two or more threads for the passage of the weft—thus giving a curious appearance of diagonal lines: a fabric with a twill.—*v.t.* to weave in this way. [Low Ger. *twillen,* to make double, *twill,* a forked branch.]

twin, *twin, n.* one of a pair: one of two born at a birth: one very like another.—*adj.* twofold, double: being one of two born at a birth: very like another: consisting of two parts nearly alike.—*ns.* **twin'-bed,** one of a matching pair of single beds; **twin'-screw,** a steam-vessel with two propellers on separate shafts; **twin'-set,** matching cardigan and jumper.—**the Twins,** the constellation Gemini. [O.E. *getwinn, twinn,* double—*twī,* two.]

twine, *twīn, n.* a cord composed of two or more threads twisted together: an intertwining.—*v.t.* to twist together: to form by twisting together: to wind (about something), encircle.—*v.i.* to unite closely: to make turns (e.g. of a river): to ascend spirally round a support. [O.E. *twīn,* double-thread. (Du. *twijn*)—*twi-,* double.]

twinge, *twinj, v.t.* (*rare*) to affect with a sharp, sudden pain.—*n.* a sudden, sharp pain. [O.E. *twengan.*]

twinkle, *twing'kl, v.i.* to shine with a trembling, sparkling light, to sparkle: to move rapidly (as toes or eyes).—*ns.* **twink'le, twink'ling,** a quick motion of the eye: the time occupied by a wink, an instant: the scintillation of the fixed stars; **twink'ler.** [O.E. *twinclian.*]

twirl, *twûrl, v.t.* to turn round rapidly, esp. with the fingers.—*v.i.* to turn round rapidly: to be whirled round.—*n.* a whirl, a rapid circular motion: a flourish, a coil, or an eddy.—**twirl one's thumbs,** to be idle. [O.E. *thwirel,* a whisk for whipping milk—*thweran,* to churn, stir.]

twist, *twist, v.t.* to ⸢wine: to unite or form by winding together: to encircle (with): to wreathe: to wind spirally: to bend: to wrest, wrench: to turn from the true form or meaning, to distort.—*v.i.* to be united by winding: to be bent or to move spirally, to revolve, to writhe: to turn deviously: to behave with dishonesty.—*n.* that which is twisted: a cord: a single thread: manner of twisting: a con-

tortion: a roll of tobacco or bread: a wrench, strain: a peculiar bent, perversion.—*n.* **twist'er,** one who, or that which, twists: a prevaricator, one who avoids unpleasantness by dishonest means.—**the twist,** a dance which became popular in the sixties in which the dancer constantly twists his body. [O.E. *twist,* a rope—*twi,* two; Ger. *zwist,* discord.]

twit, *twit, v.t.* to remind of some fault, &c., to tease:—*pr.p.* **twitt'ing;** *pa.t.* and *pa.p.* **twitt'ed.**—*n.* **twitt'er.** [O.E. *ætwītan,* to reproach—*æt,* against, *wītan,* to blame.]

twit, *twit, n.* (*coll.*) a fool.

twitch, *twich, v.t.* to pull with a sudden jerk, to pluck, to snatch.—*v.i.* to be suddenly jerked: to move spasmodically.—*n.* a sudden, quick pull: a spasmodic contraction of the muscles. [O.E. *twiccian,* to pluck.]

twitter, *twit'ér, n.* a chirp, as of a bird: a tremulous broken sound: nervous excitement.—*v.i.* to make a succession of small tremulous noises, to chirp: to be excited, to palpitate.—*n.* **twitt'ering,** act of twittering: the sound of twittering: nervous excitement. [Imit.]

'twixt. Abbreviation for **betwixt.**

two, *tōō, adj.* and *n.* the cardinal number next above one.—*n.* the figure 2 or ii denoting this.—*adjs.* **two'-edged,** having two edges; **two'-faced** (see **face**), having two faces: multiplied by two: double.—*adv.* doubly.—*adj.* **two'-hand'ed,** having, or used with, two hands: ambidextrous: to be used, played, by two persons.—*n.* **twopence** (*tup'éns*), the sum of two pennies.—*adj.* **twopenny** (*tup'én-i*), of the value of twopence: cheap, worthless.—*adj.* **two'-ply,** consisting of two thicknesses: woven double.—*n.* **two'some,** a tête-à-tête: (*loosely*) in golf, a single, a match between two players.—*v.t.* **two'-time,** to deceive: to double-cross (*n.* **two-tim'er**).—**in two,** asunder. [O.E. *twā,* fem. and neut. of *twēgen*; cf. **twain.**]

tycoon, *tī-kōōn', n.* (*orig.*) used mistakenly by foreigners in the 19th century as a Japanese title: (*coll.*) a business magnate. [Jap. *taikun,* a great prince.]

tympanum, *tim'pan-um, n.* (*anat.*) the membrane that separates the external from the internal ear—the drum of the ear: (*archit.*) the triangular space between sloping and horizontal cornices, or in the corners or sides of an arch: the panel of a door:—*pl.* **tym'-pana.**—*adjs.* **tym'panal, tym'panic,** like a drum: pertaining to the tympanum.—*n.* **tympanī'tis,** inflammation of the membrane of the ear. [L.,—Gr. *tympanon, typanon,* a kettledrum—*typtein,* to strike.]

tympanum. *Sing.* of **tympani,** q.v. at **timpani.**

Tynewald, Tinewald, *tin'wold, n.* the parliament of the Isle of Man. [O.N. *thing-völlr—thing,* a parliament, *völlr,* a wood.]

type, *tīp, n.* a mark or figure struck or stamped upon something: an emblem or figure of something to come (the *antitype*): an exemplar, pattern: (*bot., zool.*) that which combines best the characteristics of a group: a particular kind, sort (of anything): a rectangular piece of metal or of wood on one end of which is cast or engraved a character, sign, &c., used in printing: a set of these: the general effect of

Neutral vowels in unaccented syllables: *em'pér-ór*; for certain sounds in foreign words see p. ix.

794

printing in one set of types or of the types chosen: loosely and derogatorily, a person.— *v.t.* to reproduce by means of a typewriter: (*coll.*) to make (e.g. an actor) conform to a type.—*v.t.* **type′-cast**, to cast (an actor) for a part in accord with his own real character: to cast (an actor) repeatedly for the same kind of part.—*ns.* **type′-found′er**, one who founds or casts printers' type; **type′-met′al**, metal used for making types, various alloys of tin, antimony, and lead; **type′script**, a copy of a book, document, &c., produced by means of a typewriter: typewriting; **type′(-)sett′er**, a compositor: a machine that combines types in proper order for printing; **type′(-)sett′ing**, the act or process of setting type (also *adj.*).—*v.t.* and *v.i.* **type′write**, to produce by means of a typewriter: to practise typewriting.—*ns.* **type′writer**, a machine for producing legible characters on paper by mechanical means; **type′writing**.—*adj.* **typ′ical** (*tip′-*), pertaining to, or constituting, a type: emblematic: characteristic: (*biol.*) combining the characteristics of a group.—*adv.* **typ′ically**.—*v.t.* **typ′ify** (*tip′-*), to serve as a type of: to represent by an image or resemblance: to prefigure:—*pa.p.* and *pa.t.* **typ′ified**.—*ns.* **typ′ist**, one who uses a typewriter; **typog′rapher**, a printer; **typog′raphy**, the art of printing: the general appearance of printed matter.—*adjs.* **typograph′ic**, **-al**, pertaining to typography or printing.—*adv.* **typograph′ically**. [Fr. *type*—L. *typus*—Gr. *typos*—*typtein*, to strike.]

typhoid, *tī′foid*, *adj.* pertaining to a widely-spread form of enteric or intestinal fever, caused by a bacillus conveyed in tainted food or drinking water.—*n.* enteric fever. [Gr. *typhōdēs*—*typhos*, smoke (see **typhus**), *eidos*, likeness.]

typhoon, *tī-fōōn′*, *n.* a violent cyclone that occurs in the Chinese seas.—*adj.* **typhon′ic**. [Perh. Ar., Pers., Hindustani *tūfān*, a cyclone—Gr. *typhōn*, *typhōs*, a whirlwind; or Chinese *t′ai fung*, a great wind, *pao fung*, fierce wind.]

typhus, *tī′fus*, *n.* an extremely contagious and often fatal fever, transmitted by lice and by rat fleas, and specially associated with filth and overcrowding. [L.L.,—Gr. *typhos*, smoke, hence stupor arising from fever—*typhein*, to smoke.]

typical, typify, typist, &c. See **type**.

tyrant, *tī′rant*, *n.* one who uses his power arbitrarily and oppressively: (*orig.*) an absolute monarch or a magistrate with unlimited powers.—*adjs.* **tyrann′ic**, **-al**, **tyr′annous** (*tir′-*), pertaining to or suiting a tyrant: unjustly severe: despotic.—*advs.* **tyrann′ically**, **tyr′annously** (*tir′-*).—*n.* **tyrann′icide**, act of killing a tyrant: one who kills a tyrant.—*v.i.* **tyr′annise** (*tir′-*), to act as a tyrant: to rule (over) with oppressive severity.—*n.* **tyr′anny** (*tir′-*), the government or authority of a tyrant: absolute monarchy cruelly administered: oppression, harshness. [O.Fr. *tirant* (Fr. *tyran*)—L. *tyrannus*—Gr. *tyrannos*.]

tyre, tire, *tīr*, *n.* the hoop of iron that ties or binds the fellies of a wheel: a rubber band, cushion or tube round a wheel rim. [Prob. **attire**.]

Tyrian, *tir′i-án*, *adj.* of, pertaining to, ancient Tyre or its people: of **Tyrian purple**, a crimson or purple dye made by the ancients (see **murex**). [L. *Tyrius*—*Tyrus*, Tyre—Gr. *Tyros*.]

tyro, tiro, *tī′rō*, *n.* one learning an art or skill: one not yet well acquainted with a subject:—*pl.* **ty′ros**, **ti′ros**. [L. *tīrō*, a young recruit.]

Tyrolean, Tyrolese. See **Tirolese**.

U

U, $\bar{u}$, *adj.* (esp. of words, phrases, customs) ordinarily used by, found in, the *u*pper classes:—opp. **non'-U.**—*ns.* **U-boat,** $\bar{u}'b\bar{o}t$, a German submarine or *Untersee-boat*; **U'-turn,** a turn made by a vehicle which reverses its direction of travel, crossing into the path of oncoming traffic on the other side of the road.

ubiquity, $\bar{u}$-*bi'kwi-ti, n.* existence everywhere at the same time, omnipresence.—*adj.* **ubi'quitous,** present everywhere. [Fr. *ubiquité*—L. *ubīque,* everywhere—*ubi,* where.]

udder, *ud'ér, n.* the organ in which cows and some other female animals accumulate milk and from which they yield it. [O.E. *ūder*; cog. with Ger. *euter*; L. *ūber,* Gr. *outhar.*]

ugli, *ug'li, n.* a cross between the grape-fruit and the tangerine, or its fruit. [From the fruit's unattractive appearance.]

ugly, *ug'li, adj.* offensive to the eye: hateful to refined taste or to moral feeling: illnatured: very discreditable: dangerous.—*n.* **ug'liness.**—*v.t.* **ug'lify,** to make ugly.—*n.* **uglificā'tion.**—**ugly duckling,** despised member of family or group who later proves the most successful. [O.N. *uggligr,* frightful, *uggr,* fear; akin to O.E. *ōga,* terror.]

uhlan, $\bar{u}'l\acute{a}n, n.$ a mounted lancer in the Polish, later in the Prussian. army. [Polish *ulan,* orig. a light Tatar (q.v.) horseman—Turk. *oğlān,* a young man.]

Uitlander, *éit'land-ér, oit'lān-dér, n.* in S. Africa a name given to British and other residents in the Transvaal who had not been enfranchised. [Du. *uit,* out, *land,* land.]

ukase, $\bar{u}$-*kās', -kāz', n.* a Russian imperial decree having the force of law: any comparable edict. [Russ. *ukaz,* an edict.]

ukelele, $\bar{u}$-*ku-lā'lé, n.* a small, usually four-stringed guitar. [Hawaiian = flea, from the movement of the fingers.]

ulcer, *ul'sér, n.* an open sore due to localised destruction of the surface of skin or mucous membrane—usu. a result of infection: (*fig.*) a continuing source of evil.—*v.i.* **ul'cerate,** to be formed into an ulcer.—*v.t.* to affect with an ulcer or ulcers.—*n.* **ulcerā'tion,** the inflammatory process by which an ulcer is formed: an ulcer.—*adj.* **ul'cerous.** [Fr. *ulcère*—L. *ulcus, ulcēris*; Gr. *helkos,* a wound.]

ulna, *ul'na, n.* the inner and larger of the two bones of the forearm:—*pl.* **ul'nae** (-*ē*).—*adj.* **ul'nar.** [L. *ulna.* See **ell.**]

ulster, *ul'stér, n.* a long and loose kind of overcoat worn by men and women, sometimes having a hood and belt. [*Ulster,* in Ireland.]

ulterior, *ul-tē'ri-ór, adj.* situated on the further side: in the future: remoter, beyond what is seen or avowed (e.g. *ulterior motives*). [L. *ulterior,* comp. adj. *ultrā,* beyond.]

ultimate, *ul'ti-mát, adj.* furthest: final: fundamental (e.g. *ultimate truths*): maximum.—*adv.*

ul'timately.—*n.* **ultima'tum,** the final proposition or terms whose rejection will end a negotiation:—*pl.* **ultima'ta.**—*adj.* **ul'timo,** in the last (month).—**ultimus haeres** (*last heir*), the crown or the state, which succeeds to the property of those who die intestate without leaving next of kin. [L. *ultimus,* the last—*ultrā,* beyond.]

Ultima Thule. See **Thule.**

ultra-, *ul'trá-, pfx.* beyond, as *ultramontane*: beyond in degree, as *ultramicroscopic* (too small to be seen with an ordinary microscope): extreme, as *ultra-conservative, ultra-high.* [L. *ultrā,* beyond.]

ultramarine, *ul-trä-ma-rēn', · adj.* situated beyond the sea.—*n.* the most beautiful and durable sky-blue colour, so called either from its intense blue, or from the bringing of *lapis lazuli* (its former source) from Asia, beyond the sea. [L. *ultrā,* beyond, and **marine.**]

ultramontane, *ul-trä-mon'tān, adj.* being beyond the mountains (i.e. the Alps): originally used in Italy of the French, Germans, &c.; afterwards applied by the northern nations to the Italians: hence, holding or denoting extreme views as to the Pope's supremacy.—*ns.* **ultramon'tanism,** extreme support of the Pope's supremacy; **ultramon'tanist.** [L. *ultrā,* beyond, *montānus*—*mons, montis,* a mountain.]

ultra-short waves, *ul'trä-shört wāvz, n. pl.* electro-magnetic waves of wavelength less than 10 metres.

ultrasonic, *ul-trä-son'ik, adj.* applied to mechanical vibrations and radiations in solids, liquids, and gases, which have frequencies in excess of those which, in a sound-wave, are normally perceivable by the ear.—*n.* **ultrason'ics,** the science of these vibrations and radiations. [Pfx. **ultra-,** and **sonic.**]

ultra sound, *ul'trä sound, n.* sound vibrations too rapid to be audible. [Pfx. **ultra-,** and **sound.**]

ultraviolet, *ul'trä-vī'o-let, adj.* beyond the violet end of the visible spectrum.—**ultraviolet rays, radiations,** radiations of wavelengths less than those of visible light; **ultraviolet microscope** (see **microscope**). [**ultra-,** and **violet.**]

ululate, *ul'ū-lāt, v.i.* to hoot or screech: to wail in lamentation.—*n.* **ululā'tion,** howling, wailing. [L. *ululāre,* to hoot.]

umbel, *um'bél, um'bl, n.* an inflorescence in which a number of stalks, each bearing a flower, radiate from one centre.—*adj.* **umbel'liferous,** bearing or producing umbels. [L. *umbella,* dim. of *umbra,* a shade.]

umber, *um'bér, n.* a brown pigment. [*Umbria,* in Italy.]

umbilic, -al, *um-bil'ik, -i-kål, adj.* pertaining to the navel.—**umbilical cord,** the vascular cord connecting the foetus with the placenta. [L. *umbilīcus,* the navel; Gr. *omphalos.*]

umbles. See under **humble-pie.**

Neutral vowels in unaccented syllables: *em'pér-ór*; for certain sounds in foreign words see p. ix.

umbra
unbend

umbra, *um′bra, n.* a shadow: (*astron.*) the dark cone projected from a planet or satellite on the side opposite to the sun. [L.]

umbrage, *um′brij, n.* suspicion of injury, sense of injury, offence (*take, give, umbrage*): (*poet.*) shade.—*adj.* **umbrā′geous,** shady or forming a shade.—*adv.* **umbrā′geously.** [Fr. *ombrage*—L. *umbra,* a shadow.]

umbrella, *um-brel′a, n.* a covered collapsible frame carried in the hand, as a screen from rain or sun: a protective force of aircraft covering land or sea operations: (*fig.*) a protection, a general cover.—*ns.* **umbrell′a-bird,** a fruit-crow of South America, so called from its radiating crest; **umbrell′a-grass,** an Australian grass with millet-like seeds; **umbrell′a-tree,** a small magnolia of the United States. [It. *ombrella,* dim. of *ombra,* a shade—L. *umbra.*]

umiak, *ōōm′yak, n.* a large skin boat of the Eskimo. [Eskimo.]

umlaut, *ōōm′lowt, n.* vowel mutation, esp. the change of vowel sound brought about by the influence of an *i* (or *j*) in the following syllable; examples are:—Ger. *gänse,* pl. of *gans,* Eng. *mice* from *mouse, men* from *man,* &c. (the syllable containing *i* has been modified or lost). [Ger. *um,* about, *laut,* sound.]

umpire, *um′pīr, n.* a third person called in to decide a matter on which arbitrators disagree: (*cricket,* &c.) an impartial person chosen to enforce the rules, and decide disputes.—Also *v.i.* and *v.t.* [For *numpire*; M.E. *nompere*—O.Fr. *nompair—non,* not, *pair,* a peer. From the sense of 'unequal' the meaning passes to an odd man, an arbitrator.]

un-, *un-, pfx.* attached to verbs to denote reversal of an action implied by the simple verb, as **unfasten, unpack, unwind,** and to nouns to denote release from, removal or deprivation of, as **unchain, uncork, unfrock.** Occasionally, as in **unbare, unloose,** 'un-' serves to intensify the sense of deprivation implied by the word to which it is prefixed. [O.E. *un-, on-,* cf. Ger. *ent-.*]

un-, *un-, negative pfx.* denoting the opposite of the word to which it is attached, as **unbleached** (not bleached), **unconsciousness** (lack of consciousness). The new word formed with *un* often means something more than the simple reverse of the original word. Thus, the sense of **unkind** is stronger than 'not showing gentleness or sympathy'; it is 'harsh, cruel'. [O.E. *un-*; cf. L. *in-.*]

unable, *un-ā′bl, adj.* without sufficient strength, power, skill, or opportunity. [O.E. *un-,* negative, and **able.**]

unaccountable, *un-a-kown′ta-bl, adj.* not to be explained or accounted for: not responsible: of a person, puzzling in character.—*adv.* **unaccount′ably,** inexplicably. [O.E. *un-,* negative, and **accountable.**]

unadopted, *un-a-dop′ted, adj.* not adopted.—**unadopted road,** a road for the repairing, maintenance, &c., of which the local authority is not responsible. [O.E. *un-,* negative, and **adopted.**]

unadulterated, *un-ad-ul′tér-ā-tid, adj.* unmixed: without reservation. [O.E. *un-,* negative, and **adulterated.**]

unadvisable. Same as **inadvisable.**

unadvised, *un-ăd-vīzd′, adj.* not advised: not prudent or discreet, rash.—*adv.* **unadvīs′edly.** [O.E. *un-,* negative, and **advised.**]

unaffected, *un-á-fek′tid, adj.* not affected or influenced: without affectation, simple, direct: genuine, sincere.—*adv.* **unaffect′edly.** [O.E. *un-,* negative, and **affected.** See **affect** (2).]

unalloyed, *un-á-loid′, adj.* not alloyed or mixed: pure. [O.E. *un-,* negative, and **alloyed.**]

unanimity, *ū-nă-nim′i-ti, n.* state of being unanimous.—*adj.* **unan′imous,** agreeing, one and all, in opinion or will: having the agreement, support, consent, of all.—*adv.* **unan′imously.** [L. *unus,* one, *animus,* mind.]

unanswerable, *un-an′ser-á-bl, adj.* that cannot be refuted, conclusive. [O.E. *un-,* negative, and **answer.**]

unapproachable, *un-á-prōch′á-bl, adj.* inaccessible: forbidding intimacy: that cannot be rivalled. [O.E. *un-,* negative, and **approach.**]

unarmed, *un-ärmd′, adj.* without weapons, defenceless. [O.E. *un-,* deprivation of, and **arm** (2).]

unassuming, *un-á-sūm′ing,* or *-sōōm′-, adj.* not forward or arrogant, modest. [O.E. *un-,* negative, and **assuming.**]

unattached, *un-á-tacht′, adj.* not attached, as of a student not living in college: not seized for debt: not assigned to a particular regiment or company, on half-pay: not engaged to be married or not married. [O.E. *un-,* negative, and **attached.**]

unattended, *un-á-tend′id, adj.* not accompanied: not attended to: without occupier and not in the care of an attendant. [O.E. *un-,* negative, and **attended.**]

unauthorised, *un-öth′ór-īzd, adj.* not sanctioned by authority. [O.E. *un-,* negative, and **authorised.**]

unavailing, *un-á-vāl′ing, adj.* of no avail or effect, useless. [O.E. *un-,* negative, and **availing.**]

unaware, *un-á-wār′, adj.* not aware, ignorant (usu. with *of*) —*adv.* (also **unawares**′) without warning: unexpectedly. [O.E. *un-,* negative, and **aware.**]

unbalanced, *un-bal′ánst, adj.* not in a state of equipoise: mentally unstable: (*book-keeping*) not adjusted so as to show debtor and creditor: of e.g. a view, judgement, not giving due weight to all features of the situation. [O.E. *un-,* negative, and **balance.**]

unbar, *un-bär′, v.t.* to remove a bar or hindrance from: to unfasten, to open. [O.E. *un-,* release from, and **bar.**]

unbecoming, *un-bi-kum′ing, adj.* not suited to the wearer or not showing him, her, to advantage: of behaviour, &c., inappropriate, unseemly, improper. [O.E. *un-,* negative, and **becoming.**]

unbeknown, *un-bē-nōn′, adv.* without the knowledge of (with *to*).—Also (*coll.*) **unbeknown′st.** [O.E. *un-,* negative, *be-,* about, and **known.**]

unbelief, *un-bi-lef′, n.* want of belief, or disbelief, esp. in divine revelation.—*n.* **unbeliev′er,** one who does not believe, esp. in divine revelation: an incredulous person. [O.E. *un-,* lack of, and **belief** (see **believe**).]

unbend, *un-bend′, v.t.* to free from being in a bent state, to make straight: to free from strain or exertion.—*v.i.* to become relaxed: to

fāte, fär; mē, hûr (her); *mīne; mōte, fōr; mūte; mōōn, fŏŏt;* THen (then)

behave without formality or constraint.—
p.adj. **unbend'ing,** that unbends: becoming
relaxed or informal.—Also *n.* See also next
article. [O.E. *un-,* reversing action, and **bend.**]

unbending, *un-bend'ing, adj.* not bending: unyielding, resolute.—*adv.* **unbend'ingly.** See
also above. [O.E. *un-,* negative, and **bending**
(see **bend**).]

unbias(s)ed, *un-bī'ast, adj.* free from bias or
prejudice, impartial. [O.E. *un-,* negative, and
bias(s)ed.]

unbidden, *un-bid'n, adj.* not commanded: uninvited. [O.E. *un-,* negative, and **bidden** (see
bid).]

unbind, *un-bīnd', v.t.* to remove a binding from:
to set free. [O.E. *un-,* reversing action, and
bind.]

unblessed, *un-blest', adj.* having received no
blessing: wretched: evil.—Also **unblest'.** [O.E.
un-, not, and **blessed.**]

unblushing, *un-blush'ing, adj.* without shame,
impudent. [O.E. *un-,* negative, and **blush.**]

unbolt, *un-bōlt', v.t.* to remove a bolt from: to
open.—*p.adj.* **unbolt'ed.** See also next article.
[O.E. *un-,* release from, and **bolt** (1).]

unbolted, *un-bōlt'id, adj.* not separated by bolt-
ing (see **bolt** (2)), coarse (e.g. *unbolted flour*).
See also above.

unbosom, *un-bōōz'ŏm, v.t.* to disclose (one's
thoughts or secrets): to talk freely (usu. *reflexive*).—Also *v.i.* [O.E. *un-,* removal from,
and **bosom.**]

unbound, *un-bownd', adj.* not bound: loose,
wanting a cover. [O.E. *un-,* negative, and
bound (see **bind**).]

unbounded, *un-bown'did, adj.* not limited,
boundless: having no check or control. [O.E.
un-, negative, and **bound** (2).]

unbridle, *un-brī'dl, v.t.* to free from the bridle: to
free from restraint.—*adj.* **unbri'dled,** unrestrained: licentious. [O.E. *un-,* removal of, and
bridle.]

unbuckle, *un-buk'l, v.t.* to undo the buckle or
buckles of, to unfasten.—*v.i.* (*fig.*) to relax, or
become slack. [O.E. *un-,* release from, and
buckle.]

unburden, *un-bûr'dn, v.t.* to take a burden off: to
free from any weight or anxiety: (*reflexive*) to
tell one's secrets or anxieties freely. [O.E. *un-,*
removal of, and **burden** (1).]

unbutton, *un-but'n, v.t.* to loose the buttons of.
[O.E. *un-,* release from, and **button.**]

uncalled-for, *un-köld'-för, adj.* quite unnecessary, gratuitous: gratuitously rude, impudent.
[O.E. *un-,* negative, **called,** and **for.**]

uncanny, *un-kan'i, adj.* weird, unearthly: suggestive of supernatural powers, inexplicable
on rational grounds. [O.E. *un-,* negative, and
canny, in sense of 'safe to meddle with,
of good omen'.]

uncertain, *un-sûr't(i)n, adj.* not knowing with
certainty, doubtful: not definitely known:
such as cannot be definitely forecast: subject
to chance: not to be depended on: changeable.
[O.E. *un-,* negative, and **certain.**]

unchain, *un-chān', v.t.* to free from chains, or
from slavery. [O.E. *un-,* release from, and
chain.]

uncharted, *un-chärt'id, adj.* not marked on a
chart or map: of which a detailed chart has

not been prepared. [O.E. *un-,* negative, and
charted.]

unchurch, *un-chûrch', v.t.* to deprive of the
rights of membership in a church: to refuse
the name of church to. [O.E. *un-,* deprivation
of, and **church.**]

uncial, *un'shäl, adj.* written in the large round
characters used in ancient MSS. (before the
10th century). [Lit. 'an *inch* long'—L., from
uncia, a twelfth part, an inch.]

unciform, *un'si-förm, adj.* hook-shaped.—*adj.*
un'cinate, hooked at the end. [L. *uncus,* a
hook, and suffx. *-form.*]

uncircumcision, *un-sėr-kum-sizh'(ŏ)n, n.* want
of circumcision: (*B.*) those who are not cir-
cumcised. [O.E. *un-,* lack of, and **circumcision.**]

uncivil, *un-siv'il, adj.* not courteous, rude. [O.E.
un-, negative, and **civil.**]

unclasp, *un-kläsp', v.t.* to loose the clasp of (e.g.
a necklace, the hands). [O.E. *un-,* release from,
and **clasp.**]

unclassified, *un-klas'i-fīd, p. adj.* not on the
security list.—**unclassified road,** a road not in
a class entitled to receive a government grant.
[O.E. *un-,* negative, and **classified.**]

uncle, *ung'kl, n.* the brother of one's father or
mother: an aunt's husband: (*slang*) a pawnbroker.—**Uncle Sam,** the personification of
the United States or its people. [O.Fr. (Fr.
oncle)—L. *avunculus.*]

unclean, *un-klēn', adj.* not clean, foul: (*B.*) ceremonially impure: sinful, lewd. [O.E. *un-,*
negative, and **clean.**]

unclose, *un-klōz', v.t.* to open: to disclose, reveal.
[O.E. *un-,* reversing action, and **close,** vb.]

unclothe, *un-klōᴛʜ', v.t.* to take the clothes off:
to make naked. [O.E. *un-,* reversing action,
and **clothe** (see **cloth**).]

uncoil, *un-koil', v.t.* and *v.i.* to open out from
being coiled, to unwind. [O.E. *un-,* reversing
action, and **coil** (1).]

uncoloured, *un-kul'örd, adj.* not coloured, undyed: truthful, not exaggerated. [O.E. *un-,*
negative, and **coloured.**]

uncommitted, *un-kom-it'id, adj.* not pledged to
support any party, policy or action: impartial.
[O.E. *un-,* negative, and **committed.**]

uncommon, *un-kom'ŏn, adj.* rare: exceptional,
remarkable in quality.—*adv.* (*coll.*) very.—*adv.*
uncomm'only. [O.E. *un-,* negative, and **common.**]

uncompromising, *un-kom'prō-mīz-ing, adj.* not
willing to compromise, intractable, unyielding. [O.E. *un-,* negative, and **compromise.**]

unconcern, *un-kon-sùrn', n.* absence of concern
or anxiety: indifference.—*adj.* **unconcerned',**
not affected: indifferent: untroubled. [O.E. *un-,*
lack of, and *concern.*]

unconditional, *un-kon-di'sh(ŏ)n-ál, adj.* unqualified, unreserved, made without conditions,
absolute.—*adv.* **uncondi'tionally.** [O.E. *un-,*
negative, and **conditional.**]

unconfirmed, *un-kon-fûrmd', adj.* without final
proof or ratification: not yet having received
the rite of confirmation. [O.E. *un-,*
negative, and **confirm.**]

unconscionable, *un-kon'sh(ŏ)n-ä-bl, adj.* not
conformable to conscience—conscienceless,
or unscrupulous: unreasonable (e.g. of de-

Neutral vowels in unaccented syllables: *em'pér-ör*; for certain sounds in foreign words see p. ix.

798

mands): inordinate—used as intensive with derogatory terms. [O.E. *un-*, negative, and *conscionable* (rare), regulated by **conscience**.]

unconscious, *un-kon'shús, adj.* not aware (of): deprived of perception by the senses, insensible: not present to, or a part of, the conscious mind, esp. (*psych.*) prevented by repression from rising to the conscious mind.—*n.* the deepest level of mind, frequently providing motives for conscious action otherwise inexplicable.—*adv.* **uncon'sciously.**—*n.* **uncon'sciousness.** [O.E. *un-*, negative, and **conscious.**]

uncork, *un-körk', v.t.* to draw the cork from. [O.E. *un-*, removal of, and **cork.**]

uncouple, *un-kup'l, v.t.* to loose from being coupled, to disjoin, to set loose. [O.E. *un-*, reversing action, and **couple.**]

uncouth, *un-kōōth', adj.* awkward, ungraceful, esp. in manners or language, grotesque, odd.—*n.* **uncouth'ness.** [O.E. *uncúth*—*un-*, not, *cúth, gecúth,* known—*cunnan,* to know.]

unco-ordinated, *un-kō-ör'di-nāt-id, adj.* not coordinated: having clumsy movements. [O.E. *un-*, negative, and **co-ordinated.**]

uncover, *un-kuv'ér, v.t.* to remove the cover of: to lay open.—*v.i.* to take off the hat.—*adj.* **uncov'ered,** having no covering, esp. on the head. [O.E. *un-*, removal of, and **cover.**]

uncrown, *un-krown', v.t.* to deprive of a crown.—*adj.* **uncrowned',** possessing kingly power without the actual title and dignity. [O.E. *un-*, deprivation of, and **crown.**]

unction, *ungk'sh(ó)n, n.* an anointing: that which is used for anointing: ointment: that quality in language which raises emotion or devotion: warmth of address: divine or sanctifying grace: religious glibness: exaggerated fervour—*adj.* **unctuous** (*ungk'tū-ús*), oily, greasy: ostentatiously holy or fervent: offensively smug. *adv.* **unc'tuously.**—*ns.* **unc'tuousness, unctuos'ity,** state or quality of being unctuous—**extreme unction** (*R.C. Church*), the sacrament of anointing persons with consecrated oil in their last hours. [L. *unctiō*, *-ōnis*—*unguĕre, unctum,* to anoint.]

uncurl, *un-kûrl', v.t.* to straighten out, free from curls or ringlets.—*v.i.* to relax, unwind, from a curled state. [O.E. *un-*, reversing action, and **curl.**]

undated, *un-dā'tid, adj.* having no date. [O.E. *un-*, negative, and **date** (1).]

undaunted, *un-dön'tid, adj.* (*obs.*) untamed: unsubdued: intrepid.—*adv.* **undaun'tedly.**—*n.* **undaun'tedness.** [O.E. *un-*, negative, and **daunt.**]

undeceive, *un-di-sēv', v.t.* to free from deception or mistake: to inform of the truth. [O.E. *un-*, reversing action, and **deceive.**]

undecided, *un-di-sī'did, adj.* not having the mind made up, irresolute: not yet settled or determined. [O.E. *un-*, negative, and **decided.**]

undefiled, *un-di-fīld', adj.* unstained, pure, innocent. [O.E. *un-*, negative, and **defile** (2).]

undenominational, *un-di-nom-i-nā'sh(ó)n-ál, adj.* not conveying or teaching the doctrines or using the rites of any particular religious sect. [O.E. *un-*, negative, and **denominational.**]

under, *un'dér, prep.* in a lower position than: beneath, below: less than, falling short of: in subjection, subordination to: during the time of: undergoing: subject to, bound by, in accordance with (e.g. *under this agreement*): in (e.g. *occurring under different forms*).—*adv.* in, or to, a lower place or condition: below, lower down, in subjection.—*adj.* lower in position, rank, or degree: subject, subordinate.—**under age,** still a minor: not yet of the age prescribed for some action or undertaking; **under arms,** armed and ready for combat; **under canvas,** in tents; **under fire,** exposed to the fire or shot of any enemy; **under one's nose,** so near as to be easily detected; **under sail,** moved by sails: in motion; **under the breath,** with low voice, very softly; **under way** (sometimes, *wrongly,* **weigh**), moving: having commenced a voyage. [O.E. *under* ; O.N. *undir,* Ger. *unter,* L. *infrā.*]

under-, *un'dér-, pfx.* beneath, below, as **underlie:** too little, as **underfed:** lower in position, as **undercurrent, underclothes:** less in rank or attainments, as **undergraduate:** subordinate, as **underplot.** [**under.**]

underbid, *un-dér-bid', v.t.* to bid or offer less than, as at an auction: to bid less than the value of (a hand at bridge). [**under-, bid.**]

underbred, *un-dér-bred', adj.* of inferior breeding or manners [**under-, breed.**]

undercarriage, *un'dér-kar-ij, n.* the supporting framework, e.g. of a gun, wagon, motor-car: the landing-gear of an aircraft. [**under-, carriage.**]

underclay, *un'dér-klā, n.* the bed of clay almost always found under coal seams.

underclothes, *un'dér-klōTHz, n.pl.* clothes worn under the outer garments.—Also —**clothing.**

undercover, *un'dér-kuv'ér, adj.* working, or done, in secret.

undercurrent, *un'dér-kur-ént, n.* a current under the surface of the water: any hidden influence or tendency, esp. of feeling contrary to that shown on the surface. [**under-, current.**]

undercut, *un-dér-kut', v.t.* to cut under: to strike a heavy blow upward: to sell at a price lower than (a competitor): to accept (prices) lower than the standard.—*n.* **un'dercut,** a blow dealt upward: the under side of a sirloin. [**under-, cut.**]

underdeveloped, *un-dér-dé-vel'opt, adj.* insufficiently developed: of a country, with resources inadequately used, having a low standard of living, and backward in education. [**under-, developed.**]

underdo, *un-dér-dōō', v.t.* to do less than is requisite, esp. to cook insufficiently.—*adj.* **underdone** (when used absolutely, *un-dér-dun'*; with noun, *un'dér-dun*), incompletely cooked. [**under-, do.**]

underdog, *un'dér-dog, n.* the loser in a struggle, esp. a person always at the mercy of others having superior power and privilege. [**under-, dog.**]

underestimate, *un-dér-es'ti-māt, v.t.* to estimate at less than the real value or amount.—*n.* an estimate that is too low. [**under-, estimate.**]

underexposed, *un-dér-eks-pōzd', adj.* (*photography*) not exposed to the light long enough to make a good negative. [**under-, expose.**]

underfeed, *un'dér-fēd', v.t.* to feed inadequately.—*adj.* **underfed'.**—*n.* **underfeed'ing.** [under-, feed.]

underfoot, *un-dėr-fŏŏt'*, *adv.* under the feet: on the ground. [under, foot.]

undergarment, *un'dėr-gär-mėnt*, *n.* any article of clothing habitually worn under others. [under-, garment.]

undergo, *un-dėr-gō'*, *v.t.* to be subjected to: to endure or suffer: to pass through without loss of courage. [under-, go.]

undergraduate, *un-dėr-grad'ū-āt*, *n.* a student who has not taken his first degree. [under-, graduate.]

underground, *un'dėr-grownd*, *adj.* under the surface of the ground: secret.—*n.* a secret movement working for the overthrow and expulsion of a foreign power in control of the country: a group whose activities are partly concerned with resisting things they disapprove of in social, artistic, and political life.—*adv.* **underground'**, beneath the surface of the earth. [under, ground.]

undergrowth, *un'dėr-grōth*, *n.* shrubs or low woody plants growing among trees, copsewood. [under-, growth.]

underhand, *un-dėr-hand'* (with noun, *un'dėr-hand*), *adj.* sly, mean: dishonest: in cricket, (bowled) with the hand under the ball and below the level of the shoulder.—*adv.* secretly, by secret means: by fraud: in cricket, with underhand motion. [under, hand.]

underhung, *un-dėr-hung'*, *adj.* (of the lower jaw) protruding beyond the upper: supported from below, as a sliding door. [under-, hung.]

underlay, *un-dėr-lā'*, *v.t.* to lay under: to support by something laid under.—*n.* **un'derlay**, a piece of felt, rubber, etc. laid under a carpet or mattress. [under-, lay (2).]

underlie, *un-dėr-lī'*, *v.t.* to lie under or beneath: to be the foundation of: to be the hidden or unacknowledged cause or source of.—*adj.* **underly'ing**, lying under or lower in position: supporting, fundamental: present though not immediately obvious. [under-, lie (2).]

underline, *un-dėr-līn'*, *v.t.* to draw a line under or below: to emphasise.—*n.* a caption, legend. [under-, line (2)]

underling, *un'dėr-ling*, *n.* an agent of inferior rank: a subordinate, esp. one of servile character. [under, and suffx. -*ling.*]

undermentioned, *un-dėr-men'sh(ó)nd*, *adj.* mentioned underneath or hereafter. [under-, mention.]

undermine, *un-dėr-mīn'*, *v.t.* to make a passage under: to render insecure by secret operations (*lit.* and *fig.*—e.g. *to undermine his authority*). [under-, mine (2).]

undermost, *un'dėr-most*, *adj.* lowest in place or condition. [under, and suffx. -*most.*]

underneath, *un-dėr-nēth'*, *adv.* beneath, below, in a lower place.—*prep.* under, beneath. [under, and O.E. *neothan*, beneath.]

underpass, *un'dėr-päs*, *n.* a road passing under another road, a railway, &c. [under, pass.]

underpay, *un-dėr-pā'*, *v.t.* to pay insufficiently. —*p.adj.* **underpaid'.**—*n.* **underpay'ment.** [under-, pay (1).]

underpin, *un-dėr-pin'*, *v.t.* to lay pins, props, or stones under for support. [under-, pin.]

underplot, *un'dėr-plot*, *n.* a plot under or subor-

dinate to the main plot in a play or tale: secret scheme. [under-, plot (2).]

underprivileged, *un-dėr-priv'i-lijd*, *adj.* not enjoying normal social and economic rights. [under, privileged.]

underprop, *un-dėr-prop'*, *v.t.* to prop from beneath: to support. [under-, prop.]

underrate, *un-dėr-rāt'*, *v.t.* to rate at less than the real value. [under-, rate (1).]

undersecretary, *un-dėr-sek'rē-tä-ri*, *n.* an assistant secretary, esp. (*cap.*) an official next below a Secretary of State.—Also **under(-) secretary.** [under-, secretary.]

undersell, *un-dėr-sel'*, *v.t.* to sell at lower prices than: to defeat fair trade by selling (goods) for too small a price. [under-, sell.]

underset, *un'dėr-set*, *n.* a current of water below the surface.—*ns.* **un'dersetter** (*B.*), prop, support; **un'dersetting**, underpinning. [under-, set (1).]

undershoot, *un-dėr-shŏŏt'*, *v.t.* to fail to reach by falling short.—*n.* (*aero.*), a falling short of the mark in landing.—*adj.* **un'dershot**, having been undershot: having the lower teeth protruding beyond the upper, underhung: (of a wheel) moved by the impulse of water, passing under, on vanes projecting from the outer rim. [under-, shoot.]

undershrub, *un'dėr-shrub*, *n.* a low, shrubby growth. [under-, shrub (1).]

undersign, *un-dėr-sīn'*, *v.t.* to sign or write one's name under or at the foot of.—*the* **undersigned**, the person or persons whose signatures are below, at the end of the document. [under-, sign.]

undersized, *un'dėr-sīzed*, *adj.* below the usual size. [under-, size (1).]

understand, *un-dėr-stand'*, *v.t.* to comprehend, to have just ideas of: to grasp without explanation: to know thoroughly: to be informed, or, more usually, to gather (that): to take as the meaning of (e.g. *what are we to understand by that remark?*): to take for granted as part of an agreement: to take as meant though not expressed (e.g. *in 'the more, the merrier', parts of the verb 'to be' are understood*): to stand beneath.—*v.i.* to have the use of the intellectual faculties: to be informed: to learn:—*pa.t.* and *pa.p.* understood'.—*n.* **understan'ding**, the act of comprehending: the faculty of the mind by which it understands or thinks: the power to understand: exact comprehension: agreement of minds, harmony: informal arrangement for mutual convenience: conditional agreement: implicit bond.—*adj.* knowing, skilful: sympathetically discerning.—**to understand each other**, to have a secret or tacit agreement. [O.E. *understandan*, to perceive, &c.]

understate, *un-dėr-stāt'*, *v.t.* to state or represent less than the whole truth concerning: to state or describe or to use artistically without emphasis or embellishment.—*n.* **understate'ment.** [under-, state.]

understock, *un-dėr-stok'*, *v.t.* to supply with an insufficient amount of stock (e.g. a farm). [under-, stock (1).]

understood, *un-dėr-stŏŏd'*, *pa.t.* and *pa.p.* of **understand.**

understrapper, *un'dėr-strap-ėr*, *n.* an inferior

Neutral vowels in unaccented syllables: *em'pėr-ór*; for certain sounds in foreign words see p. ix.

agent, an underling, a petty fellow. [under-, strap (vb.).]

understudy, un'dér-stud-i, v.t. and v.i. to study a dramatic part so as to be able to take the place of (the actor playing it): to prepare to act as a substitute for.—n. an actor who prepares a part in the above way: one who is ready to act as a substitute. [under-, study.]

undertake, un-dér-tāk', v.t. to attempt, enter upon, engage in: to take upon oneself: to promise: to guarantee.—v.i. to take upon oneself: to manage funerals.—ns. un'dertaker, one who undertakes: a surety: one who manages funerals, undertā'king, that which is undertaken: any business or project engaged in: a pledge: conducting of funerals. [under, take.]

undertone, un'dér-tōn, n. a low tone of voice: (fig.) hidden or suppressed feeling, an undercurrent of feeling: subdued colour. [under-, tone.]

undertook, un-dér-tŏŏk', pa.t of undertake.

undertow, un'dér-tō, n. an undercurrent in a different direction from that at the surface. [under-, tow, (2).]

undervalue, un-dér-val'ū, v.t. to value below the real worth: to esteem too lightly.—n. a value or price under the real worth.—n. undervaluā'tion, an undervaluing: rate below the worth. [under-, value.]

underwater, un-dér-wô'tér, adj. existing, acting, carried out, &c., below the surface of the water: below the water-line. [under-, water.]

underwear, un'dér-wār, n undercloting. [under-, wear.]

underwent, un-dér-went', pa.t of undergo.

underwood, un'dér-wŏŏd, n. low wood or trees growing under large ones, coppice. [under-, wood.]

underworld, un'dér-wûrld, n. Hades: the criminal poor and those who exploit their poverty in anti-social or illegal activities. [under-, world.]

underwrite, un dér rīt', v.t. to write under something else: to sign one's name under: to accept for insurance: to accept liability for: to guarantee (money or shares).—v.i. to practise insuring.—n. un'derwriter, one who insures, as shipping, so called because he underwrites his name for a certain amount to the conditions of the policy. [under, write.]

undesirable, un-di-zī'rá-bl, adj. not to be wished for: reprehensible.—ns. undesir'abil'ity, undesir'ableness.—adv. undesir'ably.—adjs. undesired'; undesir'ing; undesir'ous. [O.E. un-, negative, and desire.]

undid, un-did', pa.t. of undo.

undies, un'diz, n.pl. (coll.) women's (usu. dainty) undergarments. [Abbreviation for under-clothes.]

undistinguished, un-dis-ting'gwisht, adj. not distinguished: without conspicuous qualities: ordinary, commonplace. [O.E. un-, negative, and distinguished.]

undistributed, un-dis-trib'ūt-id, adj. not distributed: not the subject of a universal (q.v.) statement.—undistributed middle, a minor premise or middle term of a syllogism which does not make a universal statement about the predicate of the major premise, and therefore leads to an unsound conclusion,

e.g. that in the syllogism
    all men are liars,
    all fishermen are liars,
therefore all men are fishermen—where 'liars' is undistributed. [O.E. un-, negative, and distributed.]

undo, un-dōō', v.t. to reverse (what has been done): to open: to loose: to unravel: to bring to naught: to ruin.—n. undo'ing, the reversal of what has been done: ruin.—adj. undone', not done: ruined: untied, unfastened.—come undone, to go wrong [O.E. un-, reversing action, and do.]

undoubted, un-dowt'id, adj. not doubted: unquestioned: certainly genuine. [O.E. un-, negative, and doubted.]

undress, un-dres', v.t. to take the dress or clothes off: to bare.—v.i. to take off one's clothes.—n. (also un'dress) incomplete dress: informal dress: the plain dress worn by soldiers when off duty.—adj. pertaining to ordinary dress, as opposed to uniform, &c.—adj. undressed', not dressed: informally dressed: not trimmed or tidied: not bandaged: not prepared for serving: not arranged for display (as a shop-window). [O.E. un-, removal of, and dress.]

undue, un-dū', adj. not due or owing: improper, immoderate, excessive. [O.E. un-, negative, and due.]

undulate, un'dū-lāt, v.t. to wave, or to move like waves: to cause to vibrate:—v.i. to wave: to vibrate: to present a rolling appearance, as of waves.—adjs. un'dulant, un'dulating.—n. undulā'tion, a waving motion or vibration: a wavy appearance.—adj. un'dulatory, moving like waves: relating to the theory of light which considers its transmission as wave-motion in a medium filling space. [L.L. undulāre, -ātum —L. unda, a wave.]

unduly, un-dū'li, adv. in undue measure, too, excessively: improperly. [O.E. un-, negative and duly.]

unearned, un-ûrnd', adj. not gained by labour.—unearned income, income, e.g. dividends, that is not remuneration for work done; unearned increment (see increment). [O.E. un-, negative, and earn.]

unearth, un-ûrth', v.t. to take out of, drive or draw from, the earth or a burrow, as a fox or badger: to discover, to disclose. [O.E. un-, removal from, and earth.]

unearthly, un-ûrth'li, adj. supernatural, weird: unreasonable, absurd (e.g. an unearthly hour, an unduly early hour). [O.E. un-, negative, and earthly.]

uneasy, un-ē'zi, adj. not at ease: restless: feeling pain: feeling anxiety, disquieted: not comfortable—constraining, or precarious.—n. uneas'iness.—adv. uneas'ily. [O.E. un-, negative, and easy.]

unemployed, un-em-ploid', adj. not put to use or profit: out of work, without a job.—n. (collectively) those without jobs.—n. unemploy'ment. [O.E. un-, negative, and employed.]

unequal, un-ē'kwál, adj. not equal or alike in quality, extent, duration, &c.: unfair, unjust: varying, not uniform: having insufficient strength, ability, &c., for (e.g. unequal to the task).—adj. une'qualled, unrivalled: unpar-

unequivocal / unholy

unequivocal, *un-é-kwiv'o-kál, adj.* unambiguous: explicit: clear and emphatic. [O.E. *un-*, negative, **equivocal.**]

Unesco, *ū-nes'kō, n.* the United Nations Educational Scientific and Cultural Organisation.

unestablished, *un-es-tab'lisht, adj.* (of a post) not on the establishment or permanent staff. [O.E. *un-*, negative, and **established.**]

uneven, *un-ē'vn, adj.* not even, smooth, straight, or uniform: odd, not divisible by two without remainder.—*adv.* **unē'venly.** [O.E. *un-*, negative, and **even.**]

unexceptionable, *un-ek-sep'sh(ó)n-á-bl, adj.* not liable to exception or objection: faultless. [O.E. *un-*, negative, and **exceptionable.**]

unfailing, *un-fāl'ing, adj.* never running short or giving out (e.g. supplies): unceasing: unflagging (e.g. efforts): certain.—*adv.* **unfail'ingly.** [O.E. *un-*, negative, and **failing.**]

unfair, *un-fār', adj.* not fair: not just: dishonest: inequitable.—*adv.* **unfair'ly.**—*n.* **unfair'ness.** [O.E. *un* , negative, and **fair** (1).]

unfaithful, *un-fāth'fool, -fl, adj.* not-holding the true faith, infidel (esp., not a Mohammedan): disloyal: treacherous: inexact, not true to the original: guilty of adultery.—*n.* **unfaith'fulness,** disloyalty: often signifying adultery. [O.E. *un-*, negative, and **faithful.**]

unfasten, *un-fäs'n, v.t.* to loose, as from a fastening: to unfix. [O.E. *un-*, reversing action, and **fasten.**]

unfathomable, *un-faтн'om-á-bl, adj.* too deep to be fathomed or to be understood.—*adj.* **unfath'omed,** not plumbed. [O.E. *un-*, negative, and **fathom.**]

unfeeling, *un-fē'ling, adj.* without feeling: without kind feelings, hard-hearted. [O.E. *un-*, negative, and **feeling.**]

unfetter, *un-fet'ér, v.t.* to take the fetters from: to set at liberty.—*adj.* **unfett'ered,** unrestrained. [O.E. *un-*, removal of, and **fetter.**]

unfilial, *un-fil'yál, adj.* not becoming a child, undutiful. [O.E. *un-*, negative, and **filial.**]

unfinished, *un-fin'isht, adj.* not finished or completed: showing lack of finish. [O.E. *un-*, negative, and **finished.**]

unfit, *un-fit', adj.* unsuitable, improper.—*v.t.* to make unsuitable (for): to make unable (to, for).—*n.* **unfit'ness.** [O.E. *un-*, negative, and **fit** (1).]

unfix, *un-fiks', v.t.* to make not fixed, to loose the fixing of: to unsettle. [O.E. *un-*, reversing action, and **fix.**]

unflagging, *un-flag'ing, adj.* not flagging or drooping: untiring. [O.E. *un-*, negative, and **flag** (1).]

unflappable, *un-flap'á-bl, adj.* (*coll.*) imperturbable, never agitated or alarmed. [O.E. *un-*, negative, and **flap.**]

unfold, *un-fōld', v.t.* to open the folds of: to spread out: to tell.—*v.i.* to spread open, expand, develop. [O.E. *un-*, reversing action, and **fold** (1).]

unformed, *un-förmd', adj.* structureless, amorphous: not fully formed, immature: not arranged in order. [O.E. *un-*, negative, and **formed.**]

unfortunate, *un-för'tū-nát, adj.* not fortunate, auspicious, or successful—unlucky.—*n.* one

who is unfortunate.—*adv.* **unfor'tunately,** unhappily, unluckily. [O.E. *un-*, negative, and **fortunate.**]

unfounded, *un-fown'did, adj.* not founded: (*fig.*) baseless, without foundation in reality (e.g. of fears, hopes). [O.E. *un-*, negative, and **founded.** See **found** (2).]

unfreeze, *un-frēz', v.t.* to thaw: to free (prices, wages, &c.) from the control imposed by a standstill order. [O.E. *un-*, reversing action, and **freeze.**]

unfrock, *un-frok', v.t.* to strip of the frock or gown worn by ecclesiastics, to deprive of priestly office. [O.E. *un-*, removal of, and **frock.**]

unfurl, *un-fûrl', v.t.* to loose from being furled: to unfold, display: to spread.—*v.i.* to spread out. [O.E. *un-*, reversing action, and **furl.**]

ungainly, *un-gān'li, adj.* awkward, clumsy, uncouth.—*n.* **ungain'liness.** [M.E. *ungein,* inconvenient—O.E. *un-*, negative, O.N. *gegn,* ready, serviceable.]

ungetatable, *un-get-at'a-bl, adj.* inaccessible. [O.E. *un-*, negative, **get at,** and suffx. *-able.*]

ungirt, *un-gûrt', adj.* not wearing a girdle: not ready for action. [O.E. *un-*, negative, and **girt,** pa.p. of **gird** (2).]

ungodly, *un-god'li, adj.* not godly, neglecting God: sinful, impious: (*coll.*) outrageous, unholy, unearthly.—*n.* **ungod'liness,** the quality of being ungodly: wickedness. [O.E. *un-*, negative, and **godly.**]

ungrammatical, *un-gra-mat'i-kál, adj.* not according to the rules of grammar. [O.E. *un-*, negative, and **grammatical.**]

ungrounded, *un-grown'did, adj.* without basis, unfounded: uninstructed: (*elect.*) not earthed. [O.E. *un-*, negative, and **grounded;** see **ground** (2).]

ungual, *ung'gwál, adj.* relating to, like, or having a nail, claw, or hoof. [L. *unguis,* a nail.]

unguarded, *un-gär'did, adj.* without guard or protection: unscreened: not on one's guard, incautious: careless, inadvertent.—*adv.* **unguar'dedly.**—*n.* **unguar'dedness.** [O.E. *un-*, negative, and **guarded.**]

unguent, *ung'gwént, n.* ointment. [L. *unguentum*—*unguēre,* to anoint.]

ungulate, *ung'gū-lāt, adj.* having hoofs: shaped like a hoof.—*n.* one of the **Ungulā'ta,** a large group of hoofed animals. [L. *ungula,* a hoof.]

unhallowed, *un-hal'ōd, adj.* unholy: profane: very wicked. [O.E. *un-*, negative, and **hallow.**]

unhand, *un-hand', v.t.* to take the hands off, to let go. [O.E. *un-*, release from, and **hand.**]

unhappy, *un-hap'i, adj.* not happy, miserable: not fortunate, fraught with evil, disastrous.—*adv.* **unhapp'ily.**—*n.* **unhapp'iness.** [O.E. *un-*, negative, and **happy.**]

unharness, *un-här'nes, v.t.* to take the harness off: to remove armour from. [O.E. *un-*, removal of, and **harness.**]

unhealthy, *un-hel'thi, adj.* not healthy, weak, sickly: morally harmful or undesirable: (*coll.*) unsafe.—*n.* **unhealth'iness.**—*adv.* **unhealth'ily.** [O.E. *un-*, negative, and **healthy.**]

unhinge, *un-hinj', v.t.* to take from the hinges: to render unstable, to upset, to derange (the mind). [O.E. *un-*, removal from, and **hinge.**]

unholy, *un-hō'li, adj.* not sacred or hallowed:

Neutral vowels in unaccented syllables: *em'pér-ór*; for certain sounds in foreign words see p. ix.

wicked, sinful: mischievous: (*coll.*) excessive (esp. of noise). [O.E. *un-*, negative, and **holy**.]

unhook, *un-hŏŏk'*, *v.t.* to loose from a hook: to unfasten the hooks of (e.g. a dress). [O.E. *un-*, release from, and **hook**.]

unhorse, *un-hörs'*, *v.t.* to cause to come off, or to throw from, a horse. [O.E. *un-*, removal from, and **horse**.]

unhouse, *un-howz'*, *v.t.* to deprive of or drive from a house or shelter. [O.E. *un-*, removal from, and **house**.]

Uniat, *ū'ni-ât*, *n.* a member of any community of Oriental Christians that acknowledges the papal supremacy but adheres to the discipline, rites, and liturgy of the Greek Church.—Also **U'niate**. [Russian *uniyat*—*uniya*, union—L. *ūnus*, one.]

unicameral, *ū-ni-kam'ér-ál*, *adj.* of a legislature, consisting of one chamber. [L. *ūnus*, one, *camera*, a vault; see **chamber**.]

Unicef, *ū'ni-sef*, *n.* United Nations International Children's Emergency Fund.

unicellular, *ū-ni-sel'ū-lár*, *adj.* having but one cell. [L. *ūnus*, one, and **cellular**.]

unicorn, *ū'ni-korn*, *n.* a fabulous animal with a body like that of a horse and one straight horn on the forehead: (*B.*) an animal conjectured to be the rhinoceros or the wild ox. [L. *ūnus*, one, *cornu*, a horn.]

uniform, *ū'ni-förm*, *adj.* having one or the same form: not varying, always of the same quality, character, degree, &c. (e.g. *a uniform temperature*): undiversified in appearance: consistent: agreeing, conforming to the same standard.—*n.* a dress or livery of the same kind for persons (e.g. soldiers) who belong to the same organisation.—*n.* **uniform'ity**, state of being uniform: agreement with a pattern or rule: sameness: likeness between the parts of a whole.—*adv.* **u'niformly**. [L. *unus*, one, and suffix *-form*.]

unify, *ū'ni-fī*, *v.t.* to make into one: to make consistent.—*n.* **unifica'tion**. [L. *ūnus*, one, *faćēro*, to make.]

unilateral, *u-ni-lat'é-rál*, *adj.* one-sided: on one side only: (*law*—of an obligation) affecting one party only.—*adv.* **unilat'erally**. [L. *ūnus*, one, and **lateral**.]

unimpeachable, *un-im-pēch'á-bl*, *adj.* not liable to be doubted or discredited: blameless. [O.E. *un-*, negative, and **impeachable**.]

uninhibited, *un-in-hib'i-tid*, *adj.* not repressed, natural, unrestrained: not inhibited (q.v.). [O.E. *un-*, negative, and **inhibited**.]

uninterrupted, *un-in-tér-rup'tid*, *adj.* not interrupted, incessant.—*adv.* **uninterrup'tedly**. [O.E. *un-*, negative, and **interrupted**.]

union, *ūn'yón*, *n.* act of uniting or state of being united: a whole formed by the combination of individual parts or persons: concord, agreement: marriage: an association between those in the same or kindred employment to safeguard wages and conditions: (formerly) several parishes united for joint support and management of their poor, also the workhouse for such: (*pl.*) textile fabrics made up of more than one kind of fibre, as of wool and cotton: (*math.*) the set formed from all the elements present in two (or more) sets.—*ns.* **Un'ionist**, originally one opposed to granting Home Rule

to Ireland: a Conservative in politics; **Union Jack**, the national flag of the United Kingdom, consisting of a union of the crosses of St George, St Andrew, and St Patrick (properly Union Flag; see **jack**). [Fr. *union*—L. *ūniō*, *-ōnis*—*ūnus*, one.]

unique, *ū-nēk'*, *adj.* single or alone in any quality, without a like or equal. [Fr.,—L. *ūnicus*—*ūnus*.]

unisex, *ū'ni-seks*, of a style adopted by both sexes. [L. *unus*, one, and **sex**.]

unison, *ū'ni-són*, *n.* identity of pitch: (*fig.*) agreement. [L. *ūnus*, one, *sonus*, a sound—*sonāre*, to sound.]

unit, *ū'nit*, *n.* one: a single thing or person: a known determinate quantity by which other quantities of the same kind are measured (e.g. the metre, 1 650 763·73 wavelengths of the orange radiation of the krypton-86 atom, serves as a unit of length): a group forming a constituent part of a larger body divided e.g. for administrative purposes: a single complete domestic fixture combining what are sometimes separate parts. *adj.* **u'nitary**, pertaining to unity: of or to a unit.—**unit trust** (see **trust**). [L. *ūnus*, one.]

unite, *ū-nīt'*, *v.t.* to join (two or more parts, &c.): into one: to make to agree, feel as one, or act in concert.—*v.i.* to become one: to grow or act together.—*adj.* **uni'ted**, joined, made one: acting in concert: harmonious *adv.* **uni'tedly**. —**United Kingdom**, the kingdom consisting of England, Wales, Scotland and Northern Ireland; **United Nations Organisation**, post-war organisation for discussion of problems by the nations. [L. *ūnīre*, *ūnītum*.]

unity, *ū'ni-ti*, *n.* oneness, state of being one or at one: the arrangement of all the parts to one purpose or effect (e.g. *there was no unity of idea in the picture*): harmony: (*math.*) any quantity taken as one.—*n.* **Unita'rian**, one who asserts the *unity* of the Godhead as opposed to the Trinity, and ascribes divinity to God the Father only. *adj.* pertaining to Unitarians or their doctrine.—*n.* **Unita'rianism**, the doctrines or principles of a Unitarian.—**dramatic unities**, unity of time (period covered not more than twenty-four hours), place (no change of scene), and action (a single plot, without underplot or irrelevancies). [L. *ūnitās*—*ūnus*, one.]

univalent, *ū-ni-vāl'ént*, *adj.* (*chem.*) having a valency of one, capable of combining with one atom of hydrogen or its equivalent. [L. *unus*, one, **valent** (see **valency**).]

univalve, *ū'ni-valv*, *adj.* having one valve or shell only.—*n.* a shell of one valve only: a mollusc whose shell is composed of a single piece.—*adj.* **unival'vular**. [L. *ūnus*, one, and **valve**.]

universal, *ū-ni-vûr'sál*, *adj.* comprehending, affecting, or extending to the whole: comprising all the particulars: applied to a great variety of uses: affecting, including, or applicable to all mankind: (*logic*) affirming or denying something of every member of a class (e.g. *all horses are herbivorous*).—*n.* a universal proposition, a general concept, or that in reality to which it corresponds.—*ns.* **univer'salism**, the doctrine or belief of universal salvation, or the ultimate salvation of all mankind; **uni-**

ver′salist, a believer in universalism; **universal′ity,** state or quality of being universal.—*adv.* **univer′sally.** [L. *ūniversālis*—*ūniversus.* See **universe.**]

universe, *ū′ni-vûrs, n.* the whole system of existing things: all existing things viewed as one whole: the world. [L. *ūniversum,* neut. sing. of *ūniversus,* whole—*ūnus,* one, *vertĕre, versum,* to turn.] .

university, *ū-ni-vûr′si-ti, n.* a corporation of teachers, or assemblage of colleges, for teaching the higher branches of learning, and having power to confer degrees. [L. *ūniversitās,* a corporation—*ūniversus.* See **universe.**]

unjust, *un-just′, adj.* not just or controlled by justice: addicted to injustice. [O.E. *un-,* negative, and **just.**]

unkempt, *un-kemt′, adj.* uncombed: untidy, rough. [O.E. *un-,* negative, *cemban,* to comb—*camb,* a comb.]

unkind, *un-kīnd′, adj.* wanting in kindness or sympathy: harsh, inflicting pain deliberately or through indifference.—*n.* **unkind′ness.**—*adj.* **unkind′ly,** (*obs.*) unnatural: not kind: (*dial.*) not kindly, uncomfortable, inclement.—*adv.* in an unkindly manner, cruelly.—*n.* **unkind′liness.** [O.E. *un-,* negative, and **kind.**]

unknot, *un-not′, v.t.* to free from knots: to untie. [O.E. *un-,* removal of, and **knot.**]

unlace, *un-lās′, v.t.* to undo the lace in (a boot, shoe, corset): to loose the corsets of. [O.E. *un-,* reversing action, and **lace.**]

unlade, *un-lād′, v.i.* to unload: to take out the cargo of. [O.E. *un-,* reversing action, and **lade.**]

unlatch, *un-lach′, v.t.* to open by lifting the latch. [O.E. *un-,* release from, and **latch.**]

unlearn, *un-lûrn′, v.t.* to learn or accustom oneself to the opposite of: to forget or lose acquaintance with. [O.E. *un-,* reversing action, and **learn.**]

unlearned, *un-lûr′nid, adj.* having no learning: ignorant. [O.E. *un-,* negative, and **learned.**]

unleash, *un-lēsh′, v.t.* to free from a leash: to allow uncontrolled action to. [O.E. *un-,* release from, and **leash.**]

unless, *un-les′, conj.* if not, supposing that not.—*prep.* (*rare*) save, except. [Formerly *on les, on lesse,* in phrase *on lesse that* (followed by clause), in a less case than.]

unlettered, *un-let′érd, adj.* unlearned, illiterate. [O.E. *un-,* negative, and **letter.**]

unlike, *un-līk′, adj.* not like or similar, different: not characteristic of. [O.E. *un-,* negative, and **like.**]

unlikely, *un-līk′li, adj.* not likely, improbable. [O.E. *un-,* negative, and **likely.**]

unload, *un-lōd′, v.t.* to take the load or cargo from, to discharge, to disburden: to get rid of: to dump. [O.E. *un-,* removal of, and **load.**]

unlock, *un-lok′, v.t.* to unfasten what is locked, to open (*lit.* and *fig.*). [O.E. *un-,* release from, and **lock.**]

unlooked-for, *un-lŏŏkt′-för, adj.* not anticipated.—Also, as predicate, **unlooked for.** [O.E. *un-,* negative, and **look.**]

unloose, *un-lŏŏs′, v.t.* to make loose: to set free.—*v.t.* **unloos′en,** to unloose. [O.E. *un-,* intensive, and **loose.**]

unlucky, *un-luk′i, adj.* not lucky or fortunate: ill-omened.—*adv.* **unluck′ily.** [O.E. *un-,* negative, and **lucky.**]

unmake, *un-māk′, v.t.* to destroy the form and qualities of: to annul: to separate into its component parts.—*adj.* **unmade′,** not made: reduced to its original form. [O.E. *un-,* reversing action, and **make.**]

unman, *un-man′, v.t.* to deprive of the powers of a man, as courage, virility, &c.: to remove men from.—*adj.* **unmanned′,** overcome or incapacitated by emotion: not manned or furnished with men. [O.E. *un-,* deprivation of, and **man.**]

unmanly, *un-man′li, adj.* not becoming to a man—weak, base, cowardly. [O.E. *un-,* negative, and **manly.**]

unmask, *un-mäsk′, v.t.* to take a mask or disguise off, to expose.—*v.i.* to put off a mask. [O.E. *un-,* removal of, and **mask.**]

unmeaning, *un-mē′ning, adj.* having no meaning, not intelligible: unintentional. — *adv.* **unmean′ingly.** [O.E. *un-,* negative, and **mean** (3).]

unmeasured, *un-mezh′ürd, adj.* boundless: unrestrained. [O.E. *un-,* negative, and **measure.**]

unmentionable, *un-men′sh(ó)n-à-bl, adj.* unfit to be mentioned in polite conversation; scandalous:indecent.—*n.pl.* **unmen′tionables,** (*coll.*) articles of underclothing: (*obs. coll.*) trousers.

unmitigated, *un-miti′-gā-tid, adj.* not mitigated: unqualified, out-and-out. [O.E. *un-,* negative, and **mitigate.**]

unmoor, *un-mōōr′, v.t.* to loose from being moored or anchored.—*v.i.* to weigh anchor. [O.E. *un-,* reversing action, and **moor** (2).]

unmoved, *un-mōōvd′, adj.* not moved, firm: not affected by emotion, calm. [O.E. *un-,* negative, and **move.**]

unmuffle, *un-muf′l, v.t.* to take' a muffler or covering from.—*v.i.* to throw off concealments. [O.E. *un-,* reversing action, and **muffle.**]

unnatural, *un-nat′ū-rál, -na′chûr-ál, adj.* not following the course of nature: artificial: strange: cruel, wicked, without natural affection. [O.E. *un-,* negative, and **natural.**]

unnerve, *un-nûrv′, v.t.* to deprive of courage, strength, or vigour, to weaken, to frighten. [O.E. *un-,* deprivation of, and **nerve.**]

unnumbered, *un-num′bérd, adj.* not to be counted, innumerable: not provided with a number. [O.E. *un-,* negative, and **number.**]

unobtrusive, *un-ob-trōō′siv, adj.* not obvious: modest, unassuming.—*adv.* **unobtru′sively.**—*n.* **unobtru′siveness.** [O.E. *un-,* negative, and **obtrusive.**]

unpack, *un-pak′, v.t.* to take out of packing: to open (luggage) and take out the contents.—*v.i.* to unpack luggage. [O.E. *un-,* reversing action, and **pack.**]

unparalleled, *un-par′á-leld, adj.* without precedent or equal. [O.E. *un-,* negative, and **parallel.**]

unparliamentary, *un-pär-li-men′tàr-i, adj.* inconsistent with the standards of polite speech and behaviour observed in Parliament. [O.E. *un-,* negative, and **parliamentary.**]

unperson, *un-pûr′són, n.* an individual whose influence has ceased so completely that he might never have existed. [O.E. *un-,* negative, and **person.**]

unpick, *un-pik′, v.t.* to take out the stitches of (e.g. a garment): to unfasten, undo (stitches). [O.E. *un-,* intensive, and **pick.**]

Neutral vowels in unaccented syllables: *em′pér-ór*; for certain sounds in foreign words see p. ix.

unpin, *un-pin′, v.t.* to take pins out of. [O.E. *un-*, removal of, and **pin**.]

unpleasant, *un-plez′ănt, adj.* not pleasant, disagreeable.—*adv.* **unpleas′antly.**—*n.* **unpleas′antness,** quality of being unpleasant: a disagreeable experience or situation, as an outburst, or a state, of anger or ill-feeling. [O.E. *un-*, negative, and **pleasant.**]

unpopular, *un-pop′ū-lȧr, adj.* disliked: not winning general approval.—*n.* **unpopular′ity.** [O.E. *un-*, negative, and **popular.**]

unprecedented, *un-pres′i-den-tid,* or *-prēs′-,* or *-den′-, adj.* having no precedent—novel: unique. [O.E. *un-*, negative, and **precedent.**]

unprepossessing, *un-prē-pȯ-zes′ing, adj.* unattractive, not enlisting favour by its appearance. [O.E. *un-*, negative, and **prepossess.**]

unpretending, *un-pri-ten′ding, adj.* not making undue claims, modest. [O.E. *un-*, negative, and **pretend.**]

unprincipled, *un-prin′si-pld, adj.* without settled principles: not restrained by conscience, profligate. [O.E. *un-*, negative, and **principled.**]

unprofessional, *un-prȯ-fesh′ȯn-ȧl, adj.* not having a profession: not being a member of a particular profession: not according to the standards or etiquette of some particular profession.—*adv.* **unprofess′ionally.** [O.E. *un-*, negative, and **professional.**]

unpromising, *un-prom′i-sing, adj.* affording little prospect of success, &c. [O.E. *un-*, negative, and **promise.**]

unqualified, *un-kwol′i-fīd, adj.* not possessing recognised qualifications: not competent: not modified, complete (e.g. *unqualified praise, support*). [O.E. *un-*, negative, and **qualify.**]

unquestionable, *un-kwes′tyȯn ȧ bl,* or *-ch(ȯ)n-, adj.* that cannot be questioned, indisputable: not doubtful, certain.—*adv.* **unques′tionably.** [O.E. *un-*, negative, and **question.**]

unquiet, *un-kwī′ét, adj.* not at rest, disturbed, restless: anxious. [O.E. *un-*, negative, and **quiet.**]

unquote, *un-kwōt′, v.i.* to close the inverted commas, because it is the end of the quotation. [O.E. *un-*, release from, and **quote.**]

unravel, *un rav′él, v.t.* to take out of a ravelled state, to disentangle: to elucidate.—*v.i.* to become untwisted or unknitted. [O.E. *un-*, reversing action, and **ravel,** to entangle.]

unread, *un-red′, adj.* not read: not well educated: not experienced.—*adj.* **unreadable** (*un-rē′dȧ-bl*), illegible: too boring or too ill-composed to read. [O.E. *un-*, negative, and **read.**]

unreasonable, *un-rē′zȯn-ȧ-bl, adj.* not agreeable to reason: exceeding the bounds of reason, immoderate: not influenced by reason.—*ns.* **unrea′son,** lack of reason; **unrea′sonableness.**—*adv.* **unrea′sonably.**—*adjs.* **unrea′soned,** not based on reason; **unreasoning,** not using reason. [O.E. *un-*, negative, and **reasonable.**]

unredeemed, *un-ri-dēmd′, adj.* unregenerate: not ransomed or recovered: not fulfilled: unmitigated: not taken out of pawn. [O.E. *un-*, negative, and **redeem.**]

unregenerate, *un-ri-jen′é-rȧt, adj.* not having repented: not having undergone religious conversion: wicked.—*n.* an unregenerate person. [O.E. *un-*, negative, and **regenerate.**]

unremitting, *un-ri-mit′ing, adj.* not relaxing or lessening: incessant. [O.E. *un-*, negative, and **remit.**]

unrequited, *un-rē-kwīt-éd, adj.* not repaid, not returned. [O.E. *un-*, negative, and **requited.**]

unreserved, *un-ri-zûrvd′, adj.* not reserved: not booked in advance: withholding nothing, frank, open: complete, entire (e.g. *unreserved approval*).—*adv.* **unreser′vedly** (*-vid-li*), without reservation: frankly. [O.E. *un-*, negative, and **reserved.**]

unrest, *un-rest′, n.* want of rest: disquiet of mind or body: disturbance affecting a group. [O.E. *un-*, negative, and **rest.**]

unriddle, *un-rid′l, v.t.* to explain the riddle of: to interpret. [O.E. *un-*, removal of, and **riddle.**]

unrip, *un-rip′, v.t.* rip, tear, open or apart. [O.E. *un-*, intensive, and **rip.**]

unrivalled, *un-rī′vȧld, adj.* surpassing the efforts of any rival: matchless. [O.E. *un-*, negative, and **rival.**]

unrobe, *un-rōb′, v.t.* to strip of a robe, to undress.—*v.i.* to take off a robe, esp. a robe of state. [O.E. *un-*, removal of, and **robe.**]

unroll, *un-rōl′, v.t.* to roll down, to open out.—*v.i.* to become uncoiled or opened out. [O.E. *un-*, reversing action, and **roll.**]

unroof, *un-rōōf′, v.t.* to strip the roof off. [O.E. *un-*, removal of, and **roof.**]

unrope, *un-rōp′, v.t.* to loosen from ropes: to unharness. [O.E. *un-*, removal of, and **rope.**]

unruly, *un-rōō′li, adj.* regardless of restraint or law: disorderly. [O.E. *un-*, negative, and **rule.**]

unsaddle, *un-sad′l, v.t.* to take the saddle off: to throw from the saddle. [O.E. *un-*, removal of or from, and **saddle.**]

unsaid, *un-sed′, adj.* not said. [O.E. *un-*, negative, and **say.**]

unsavoury, *un-sā′vȯr-i, adj.* not savoury, tasteless: unpleasant, disgusting: immoral. [O.E. *un-*, negative, and **savoury.**]

unsay, *un-sā′, v.t.* to withdraw, retract. [O.E. *un-*, reversing action, and **say.**]

unscathed, *un-skā*ᴛʜ*d, adj.* not harmed or injured. [O.E. *un-*, negative, and **scathe.**]

unscramble, *un-skram′bl, v.t.* to decode (a message) or make (a telephone message) intelligible. [O.E. *un-*, reversing action, and **scramble.**]

unscrew, *un-skrōō′, v.t.* to unfasten by loosening screws: to loosen and take off by turning. [O.E. *un-*, removal of, and **screw.**]

unseal, *un-sēl′, v.t.* to remove the seal of: to open. [O.E. *un-*, removal of, and **seal** (1).]

unseasonable, *un-sē′z(ȯ)n-ȧ-bl, adj.* not at the proper season: not suitable for the time of year: inopportune. [O.E. *un-*, negative, and **seasonable.**]

unseat, *un-sēt′, v.t.* to throw from or deprive of a seat: to remove or oust from an official position. [O.E. *un-*, removal from, and **seat.**]

unseeded, *un-sēd′éd, adj.* not seeded: in lawn-tennis tournaments, &c., not placed in the draw of top players. [O.E. *un-*, negative, and **seeded.**]

unseen, *un-sēn′, adj.* not seen: invisible: not previously read or studied.—*n.* an unfamiliar passage for translation: (with *the*) the spiritual world. [O.E. *un-*, negative, and **see** (2).]

unsettle, *un-set′l, v.t.* to move from being settled:

to disturb: to make insecure or uncertain.—
adj. **unsett′led,** changeable: undecided: unpaid
(e.g. of a bill, score). [O.E. *un-,* reversing
action, and **settle.**]

unsex, *un-seks′, v.t.* to deprive of sex: to make
unmanly or unwomanly. [O.E. *un-,* deprivation
of, and **sex.**]

unshackle, *un-shak′l, v.t.* to loose from shackles:
to set free. [O.E. *un-,* removal of, and **shackle.**]

unsheathe, *un-shē*TH′*, v.t.* to draw from the
sheath or scabbard. [O.E. *un-,* removal from,
and **sheathe.**]

unship, *un-ship′, v.t.* to take out of a ship or
other vessel: to remove from the place where
it is fixed or fitted. [O.E. *un-,* removal from,
and **ship.**]

unsightly, *un-sīt′li,′ adj.* not pleasing to the eye,
ugly. [O.E. *un-,* negative, and **sightly.**]

unsophisticated, *un-sō-fis′ti-kā-tid, adj.* genuine: artless, simple, not worldly-wise. [O.E.
un-, negative, and **sophisticated.**]

unsound, *un-sownd′, adj.* not in perfect condition: not solid or firm: not correct: not clearly
reasoned: (of mind) not functioning normally,
not sane. [O.E. *un-,* negative, and **sound**(1).]

unsparing, *un-spār′ing, adj.* not sparing: liberal,
profuse: relentless.—*adv.* ,**unspar′ingly.** [O.E.
un-, negative, and **spare.**]

unspeakable, *un-spē′kā-bl, adj.* incapable of
being spoken, uttered, or described: inde-
scribably objectionable.—*adv.* **unspea′kably,**
in an unspeakable or inexpressible manner.
[O.E. *un-,* negative, **speak,** and suffx. -*able.*]

unstop, *un-stop′, v.t.* to free from a stopper: to
free from hindrance. [O.E. *un-,* removal of, and
stop.]

unstring, *un-string′, v.t.* to free from a string: to
take the strings off: to relax or loosen.—*adj.*
unstrung′, unnerved. [O.E. *un-,* removal of,
and **string.**]

unstuck, *un-stuk′, adj.* detached, loosened from
sticking.—**come unstuck,** (*slang*) of a plan, to
go wrong. [O.E. *un-,* negative, and **stuck.**]

unstudied, *un-stud′id, adj.* done without pre-
meditation, natural, easy: not acquired by
study. [O.E. *un-,* negative, and **study.**]

unsung, *un-sung′, adj.* not celebrated in song:
not yet sung. [O.E. *un-,* negative, and **sing.**]

unsuspected, *un-sus-pek′tid, adj.* not suspected:
not known or supposed to exist. [O.E. *un-,*
negative, and **suspect.**]

unthinkable, *un-thingk′ā-bl, adj.* inconceivable:
improbable in the highest degree: (of an occurrence) very painful to imagine. [O.E. *un-,*
negative, **think,** and suffx. -*able.*]

untie, *un-tī′, v.t.* to loose from being tied: to
unbind: to loosen.—*adj.* **untied′.** [O.E. *un-,*
reversing action, and **tie.**]

until, *un-til′, prep.* and *conj.* Same as **till**(2).
[M.E. *untill*—**unto,** and **till** (prep.).]

untimely, *un-tīm′li, adj.* premature: immature:
inopportune.—Also *adv.* [O.E. *un-,* negative,
and **timely.**]

untiring, *un-tīr′ing, adj.* not interrupted by
weariness: diligent, assiduous.—*adv.* **untir′-
ingly.** [O.E. *un-,* negative, and **tire**(3).]

unto, *un′tŏŏ, prep.* (*arch.*) to. [Modelled on **until.**]

untold, *un-tōld′, adj.* not told or related: too
great to be counted or told. [O.E. *un-,* negative,
and **tell.**]

untouchable, *un-tuch′ā-bl, adj.* not to be touched
or equalled.—*n.* one whose excellence in some
respect cannot be rivalled: (esp. formerly) a
Hindu of very low caste, carrying out menial
tasks. [O.E. *un-,* negative, and **touchable.**]

untoward, *un-tō′ārd, un-tō-*:*wörd′, adj.* not easily
guided, perverse: unseemly: inconvenient.
[O.E. *un-,* negative, and **toward.**]

untried, *un-trīd′, adj.* not attempted: not tested
by experience. [O.E. *un-,* negative, and **try.**]

untrodden, *un-trod′n, adj.* seldom or never trodden, unfrequented. [O.E. *un-,* negative, and
trodden.]

untroubled, *un-trub′ld, adj.* not troubled or
anxious: not rising in waves, not agitated.
[O.E. *un-,* negative, and **troubled.**]

untrue, *un-trōō′, adj.* not true, false: not faithful,
disloyal: not in accordance with a standard:
not level, not straight.—*n.* **untruth′,** falsehood:
one's lie. [O.E. *un-,* negative, and **truth.**]

untutored, *un-tū′tórd, adj.* uninstructed: lacking
refinement or elegance, rough. [O.E. *un-,*
negative, and **tutor.**]

untwine, *un-twīn′, v.t.* to untwist, unwind.—*v.i.*
to become untwisted. [O.E. *un-,* reversing
action, and **twine.**]

untwist, *un-twist′, v.t.* to open what is twisted, to
unravel.—*v.i.* to become loosened out. [O.E.
un-, reversing action, and **twist.**]

unutterable, *un-ut′ér-ā-bl, adj.* incapable of
being uttered or expressed: too horrible to be
expressed or described: (*coll.*) very great (used
with a noun implying a bad quality; e.g. *an
unutterable cad*). [O.E. *un-,* negative, **utter**(2),
and suffx. -*able.*]

unvarnished, *un-vär′nisht, adj.* not varnished:
plain: straightforward, truthful. [O.E. *un-,*
negative, and **varnish.**]

unveil, *un-vāl′, v.t.* to remove a veil from: to
disclose, reveal, esp. a statue or monument
displayed to the public for the first time.—*v.i.*
to become unveiled, to reveal oneself. [O.E.
un-, removal of, and **veil.**]

unwary, *un-wā′ri, adj.* not cautious, not on one's
guard: not characterised by caution.—*adv.* **un-
wā′rily.** [O.E. *un-,* negative, and **wary.**]

unweave, *un-wēv′, v.t.* to undo what is woven.
[O.E. *un-,* reversing action, and **weave.**]

unwelcome, *un-wel′kóm, adj.* received with regret: causing grief or disappointment. [O.E.
un-, negative, and **welcome.**]

unwell, *un-wel′, adj.* not in perfect health: temporarily indisposed. [O.E. *un-,* negative, and
well(2).]

unwept, *un-wept′, adj.* not mourned. [O.E. *un-,*
negative, and **weep.**]

unwieldy, *un-wēl′di, adj.* not easily moved or
handled, awkward, clumsy.—*adv.* **unwield′-
ily.**—*n.* **unwield′iness.** [O.E. *un-,* negative, and
obs. *wieldy,* manageable—**wield.**]

unwilling, *un-wil′ing, adj.* not willing, disinclined, reluctant: reluctantly done or said.—
adv. **unwill′ingly.**—*n.* **unwill′ingness.** [O.E. *un-,*
negative, and **willing.**]

unwind, *un-wīnd′, v.t.* to wind down or off.—*v.i.*
to become unwound: (*coll.*) to relax. [O.E. *un-,*
reversing action, and **wind**(2).]

unwise, *un-wīz′, adj.* not wise: injudicious: foolish. [O.E. *un-,* negative, and **wise**(1).]

unwitting, *un-wit′ing, adj.* not aware, ignorant:

Neutral vowels in unaccented syllables: *em′pér-ŏr*; for certain sounds in foreign words see p. ix.

806

unintentional, unconscious (e.g. *gave him un-willing aid*).—*adv.* **unwitt'ingly.** [O.E. *un-*, negative, and **wit**(1).]

unwonted, *un-wōn'tĕd, adj.* unaccustomed: unusual. [O.E. *un-*, negative, and **wonted.**]

unworthy, *un-wûr'THi, adj.* not worthy: not deserving (of): not in keeping with, unbecoming to (e.g. *unworthy of your high talents*): contemptible (e.g. *an unworthy act*). [O.E. *un-*, negative, and **worthy.**]

unwrap, *un-rap', v.t.* to open what is wrapped or folded.—*v.i.* to become unwrapped. [O.E. *un-*, reversing action, and **wrap.**]

unwritten, *un-rit'n, adj.* not written: not committed to writing or record, traditional: oral.—**unwritten law,** the supposed right to take revenge for certain injuries, esp. for the seduction of one's wife. [O.E. *un-*, negative, and **written** (see **write**).]

unyoke, *un-yōk', v.t.* to loose from a yoke: to disjoin. [O.E. *un-*, removal of, and **yoke.**]

up, *up, adv.* towards a higher place: aloft, on high: from a lower to a higher position, as out of bed, above the horizon, &c.: towards a more important place, esp. London (with *to*): in or to the north: in a higher position: at a college or university: (*coll.*) before a magistrate or court: as far as, abreast of, a place or person understood (*e.g. then the bus came up*): (of a jockey) in the saddle: in or into a condition of activity or excitement (e.g. *the hunt is up*; *my blood was up*—I was angry and on my mettle): completely: at an end, over.—*prep.* from a lower to a higher place on or along.—*adj.* inclining up, upward.—*v.t.* to raise: to lift or haul up: to move up.—*v.i.* to set up: to move up: to intervene boldly, to start into activity or speech.—*n.* in phrase **ups and downs,** rises and falls, vicissitudes.—*adjs.* **up'-and-com'ing,** alert and pushful: likely to succeed (in a career, &c.).—**up against,** confronting (**up against it,** in great difficulty); **up in,** having a knowledge of; **up to** (*coll.*), about, engaged in doing: capable of and ready for: incumbent upon (*it is up to you*); **up to date,** to the present time: in touch with or in possession of the latest ideas, practices or devices; **up to the minute,** right up to the present time: right up to date.—**on the up and up,** in a state of continuous progression towards ever greater success; **what's up,** (*coll.*) what's the matter, what's wrong? [O.E. *up, upp*; Ger. *auf*; L. *sub*, Gr. *hypo*.]

upas, *ū'pas, n.* the juice of the upas-tree of Java, &c., a powerful vegetable poison, used for arrows. [Malay, *ūpas,* poison.]

upbear, *up-bār', v.t.* to bear up: to raise aloft.—*pa.p.* **upborne** (*up-bōrn', -bŏrn'*), sustained. [**up, bear**(1).]

upbraid, *up-brād', v.t.* to charge (with something wrong or disgraceful—also with *for*): to reproach. [O.E. *upbregdan, upgebrēdan.*]

upbringing, *up'bring-ing, n.* the process of nourishing and training (a child). [**up, bring.**]

upcast, *up'käst, n.* a shaft for the upward passage of air from a mine (also **up'cast-shaft**): a current of air passing along a shaft of this kind. [**up, cast.**]

up-country, *up-kun'tri, adv.* towards the interior, inland.—*adj.* (*up'kun-tri*) belonging to the interior of a country. [**up, country.**]

update, *up-dāt', v.t.* to bring up to date. [**up, date.**]

up-grade, *up'grād, n.* a rising slope.—**on the up-grade,** improving, progressing, achieving success.—*v.t.* (*up-grād'*; *coll.*) to promote, advance. [**up, grade.**]

upheave, *up-hēv', v.t.* to heave or lift up.—*n.* **upheav'al,** the raising of surface formations by the action of internal forces: a commotion, convulsion. [**up, heave.**]

upheld, *up-held', pa.t.* and *pa.p.* of **uphold.**

uphill, *up'hil, adj.* ascending: difficult.—*adv.* (*up-hil'*) up a hill: against difficulties. [**up, hill.**]

uphold, *up-hōld', v.t.* to hold up: to sustain: to countenance: to defend: to maintain, confirm (a decision).—*n.* **uphōl'der.** [**up, hold.**]

upholster, *up-hōl'stér, v.t.* to furnish (furniture) with stuffing, springs, &c.: to provide with curtains, &c.—*ns.* **uphōl'sterer,** one who does this: one who sells furniture, curtains, &c.; **uphōl'stery,** furniture, &c., supplied by upholsters: the trade of an upholsterer. [**up, hold,** and suffix. *-ster.*]

upkeep, *up'kēp, n.* maintenance, cost of support. [**up, keep.**]

upland, *up'länd, n.* upper or high land, as opposed to meadows, river-sides, &c.—*adj.* high in situation: pertaining to uplands. [**up, land.**]

uplift, *up-lift', v.t.* to raise: to elate: to collect (dues).—*n.* (*up'lift*) a raising or upheaval of strata: elevation: exhilaration, mental or moral stimulus: (*coll.*) something intended to elevate morally or mentally, esp. through an appeal to the emotions. [**up, lift.**]

upmost. See **upper.**

upon, *up-on', prep.* on, on the top of. [**up, on.**]

upper, *up'ér, adj.* (*comp.* of **up**) farther up: higher in position, dignity, &c.: superior:—*superl.* **upp'ermost, up'most.**—*ns.* **upp'er,** the part of a boot or shoe above the sole and welt; **upp'erhand,** superiority, advantage, control, **upper atmosphere,** the region of the atmosphere above about 20 miles from the earth; **upper class,** the people of highest social rank (*adj.* **upp'er-class'**); **upper crust,** the top of the loaf: (*coll.*) the aristocracy; **upper house** (or with *caps.*), in a two-chamber legislature, the house with greater (or *originally* with greater) dignity or importance (e.g. the House of Lords, or the U.S. Senate); **upper ten (thousand),** the aristocracy.—*adj.* **upp'ish,** (*coll.*) presumptuous, over-confident, affecting superiority.—*n.* **upp'ishness.**—*adj.* **upp'ity,** uppish.

upright, *up'rit, adj.* straight up, in an erect position: possessing moral integrity—honest, just.—*n.* a vertical post or support.—*adv.* vertically.—*adv.* **up'rightly.**—*n.* **up'rightness.**—**upright piano,** one with vertical strings. [**up, right.**]

uprising, *up'riz-ing, n.* an insurrection, revolt. [**up, rising.**]

uproar, *up'rōr, -rŏr, n.* noise and tumult, bustle and clamour.—*adj.* **uproar'ious,** making or accompanied by great uproar.—*adv.* **uproar'iously.** [Du. *oproer,* revolt—*op,* up, and *roeren* (Ger. *rühren,* O.E. *hrēran*), to stir; the form due to confusion with **roar.**]

uproot, *up-rōōt', v.t.* (*lit.* and *fig.*) to tear up by the roots.—*n.* **uproot'al,** act of uprooting. [up, root (1).]

upset, *up-set', v.t.* to turn upside down: to overthrow: to put out of order: to distress: to affect temporarily the health of.—*n.* **up'set,** an overturning: distress or its cause.—*adj.* relating to what is set up for sale, in phrase **upset price,** the minimum sum fixed for a bid at a sale by auction. [up, set.]

upshot, *up'shot, n.* (*orig.*) the last shot in an archery match: the final issue, end. [up, shot (2).]

upside, *up'sīd, n.* the upper side.—*adv.* **up'side-down,** with the upper part undermost: in complete confusion. [up, side.]

upstage, *up'stāj', adv.* away from or at a distance from the footlights: (*coll.*) superior, disdainful. [up, stage.]

upstairs, *up-stārz', adv.* in or towards an upper storey.—*adj.* **up'stairs,** pertaining to an upper storey or flat. [up, stair.]

upstanding, *up-stan'ding, adj.* robust, healthy: worthy, honest. [up, stand.]

upstart, *up'stärt, n.* one who has suddenly risen from poverty or obscurity to wealth or power but who does not appear to have the appropriate dignity or ability. [up, start.]

upstream, *up'strēm', adv.* towards the upper part of a stream. [up, stream.]

upstroke, *up'strōk, n.* an upward line made by the pen in writing. [up, stroke (1).]

uptake, *up'tāk, n.* (*dial.*) power, or act, of comprehension. [up, take.]

upthrust, *up'thrust, n.* a thrust upward: an upheaval of a mass of rock. [up, thrust.]

uptight, *up'tīt, adj.* (*coll.*) tense, nervous. [up, tight.]

upward, *up'wärd, adj.* directed up or to a higher place.—*advs.* **up'ward, up'wards,** in a higher direction. [up, and suffx. *-ward.*]

uranium, *ū-rā'ni-úm, n.* a radioactive metallic element (symbol U; atomic no. 92). One of the isotopes of uranium, U-235, was used to make the first atomic bomb. [Gr. *ouranos,* heaven.]

Uranus, *ū-rā'nus, n.* a Greek god, grandfather of Zeus: one of the most distant of the major planets. [Gr. *ouranos,* heaven.]

urban, *ûr'bán, adj.* of or belonging to a city.—*adj.* **urbāne',** pertaining to, or influenced by, city life, civilised, polished, suave.—*adv.* **urbāne'ly.**—*v.t.* **ur'banise,** to make (a district) town-like as opposed to rural in character.—*n.* **urbanisā'tion.**—*n.* **urbăn'ity,** the quality of being urbane.—**urban district,** a thickly-populated district: formerly, a subdivision of a county, administered by an Urban District Council. [L. *urbānus—urbs,* a city.]

urchin, *ûr'chin, n.* a hedgehog: a pert or mischievous child. [O.Fr. *(h)eriçun,* &c. (Fr. *hérisson*)—L. *ēricius,* a hedgehog.]

Urdu, *ōōr'dōō, n.* Hindustani, esp. in the form (containing a large admixture of Persian and Arabic) spoken by Moslems in India. [Hindustani, 'camp (language)'.]

urea, *ū-rē'á, n.* a substance found in mammalian urine, the chief form in which nitrogenous waste is carried off. [Gr. *ouron,* urine.]

ureter, *ū-rē'tér, n.* the duct which conveys the urine from the kidneys to the bladder.

[Gr.,—*ouron,* urine.]

urethra, *ū-rē'thra, n.* the canal by which the urine is discharged from the bladder:—*pl.* **urē'thrae** (*-ē*). [Gr.,—*ouron,* urine.]

urge, *ûrj, v.t.* to drive forward, make to move faster: to press, entreat (a person) earnestly: to advocate earnestly (an action, course).—*v.i.* to insist: to press (on, &c.).—*n.* an impulse, inner prompting.—*n.* **ur'gency,** quality of being urgent: insistence: pressing necessity.—*adj.* **ur'gent,** impelling: pressing with importunity: calling for immediate attention.—*adv.* **ur'gently.** [L. *urgēre,* to press.]

urine, *ū'rin, n.* the fluid which is secreted or separated by the kidneys from the blood and conveyed to the bladder.—*n.* **u'rinal,** a vessel for urine: accommodation provided for discharging urine.—*adjs.* **u'rinary,** pertaining to, or like, urine; **urinogen'ital,** pertaining to the urinary and genital systems. [Fr.,—L. *ūrīna;* Gr. *ouron,* Sans. *vāri,* water.]

urn, *ûrn, n.* a vessel or jar of earthenware or metal with a circular base, used to hold liquids, or as a ballot-box, &c.: such a vessel used for preserving the ashes of the dead: a vessel with a tap and a heating apparatus, esp. one for tea. [L. *urna,* an urn—*urēre,* to burn.]

ursine, *ûr'sin, ûr'sīn, adj.* of or resembling a bear: clothed with bristles, as certain caterpillars.—*n.* **Ur'sa** (see Bear). [L. *ursus,* a bear.]

us, *us, pron.* the objective (accusative or dative) case of we.—*adv.* **us'ward,** toward us. [O.E.]

usage, *ū'zij, n.* act of using: mode of using, treatment: customary use: practice, custom. [Fr.,—L. *usūs.*]

use, *ūz, v.i.* to put to some purpose: to avail oneself of: to employ as an instrument: make use of (a person): to speak, converse in: to engage in: to make use of (see below): to habituate (chiefly in *pa.p.*; e.g. *a person used to living frugally*; *arch.—as he had once been used to do*): to treat or behave towards (e.g. *to use him well, ill*).—*v.i.* to be accustomed (used only in the past, and pronounced *ūst*; before vowels *ūsd*).—**use up,** to consume, use completely: (*coll.*) to exhaust (a person). [Fr. *user*—L. *ūtī, ūsus,* to use.]

use, *ūs, n.* act of using or putting to a purpose: usage (e.g. *this book has seen much use*): employment: need (for), opportunity of employing: advantage, suitability, effectiveness: practice, custom.—*adj.* **use'ful,** convenient, advantageous, serviceable, helpful, able to do good.—*adv.* **use'fully.**—*n.* **use'fulness.**—*adj.* **use'less,** having no use: answering no good purpose: ineffective.—*adv.* **use'lessly.**—*n.* **use'lessness.**—**use and wont,** the customary practice.—**have no use for,** (*fig.*) have no admiration or liking for; **in use,** in employment or practice; **make use of,** to use, to employ: to treat (another) as a means to one's own gain; **of no use,** useless; **of use,** useful. [L. *ūsus—ūtī,* to use.]

usher, *ush'ér, n.* one whose business it is to introduce and direct strangers, or to walk before a person of rank: (*hist.*) an under-teacher.—*v.t.* to introduce or conduct: to escort.—*n.* **usherette',** a female usher in a cinema. [O.Fr. *ussier* (Fr. *huissier*)—L. *ostiārius,* a door-keeper—*ostium,* a door.]

Neutral vowels in unaccented syllables: *em'pér-ór*; for certain sounds in foreign words see p. ix.

usquebaugh, *us'kwe-bö, n.* whisky. [Ir. and Gael. *uisgebeatha—uisge,* water, *beatha,* life; cf. L. *vīta,* life, Gr. *bios.*]

usual, *ū'zhū-ál,* or *ū'zū-ál, adj.* customary: occurring in ordinary use, common, most frequent.—*adv.* **u'sually.** [L. *ūsuālis.*]

usufruct, *ū'zū-frukt, n.* the use and profit, but not the property, of a thing: liferent. [L. *ūsusfructus—ūsus,* use, *fructus,* fruit.]

usurp, *ū-zūrp', v.t.* to take possession of by force without right: to assume (e.g. a right) that properly belongs to another.—*ns.* **usurpā'tion,** act of usurping: unlawful seizure and possession; **usur'per.** [Fr.,—L. *ūsurpāre, -ātum.*]

usury, *ū'zhū-ri,* or *ū'zū-ri, n.* the taking of iniquitous or illegal interest on a loan: formerly, interest of any kind on money lent.—*n.* **u'surer,** (*orig.* and *B.*) any moneylender for interest: one who practises usury. [L. *ūsūra —ūtī, ūsus,* to use.]

ut, *ŏŏt, n.* (*mus.*) do, the keynote. [From the initial syllable of the first line of a mediaeval Latin hymn, successive phrases of which began on successive notes of the major scale.]

utensil, *ū-ten'sil, n.* an instrument or vessel used in common life. [Fr. *utensile*—L. *ūtensilis,* fit for use—*ūtī,* to use.]

uterine, *ū'te-rin, -rīn, adj.* pertaining to the womb: born of the same mother by a different father.—*n.* **u'terus,** a womb. [Fr. *uterin*—L. *uterīnus—uterus,* the womb.]

utilise, *ū'ti līz, v.t.* to make useful, put to profitable use: to use as an expedient (something not wholly suitable or not primarily intended for the purpose).—*n.* **utilisā'tion.** [Fr. *utiliser*—L. *ūtī,* to use.]

utility, *u-til'i-ti, n.* usefulness, profit: a useful thing: (*esp. U.S.*) public service: fitness to produce happiness: ability to satisfy human wants.—*adj.* used of a serviceable type of (orig. wartime) article (e.g. clothing) under government control in price and quality: (*disparagingly*) good enough, of rather inferior quality.—*adj.* **ūtilitā'rian,** consisting in, or

pertaining to, utility or to utilitarianism.—*n.* one who holds utilitarianism.—*n.* **utilitā'rianism,** the ethical theory which finds the basis of moral distinctions in the utility of actions, i.e. their fitness to produce happiness.—**utility man,** an actor of miscellaneous minor parts. [L. *ūtilitās, -ātis—ūtī,* to use.]

utmost, *ut'mōst,* or *-móst, adj.* outermost: most distant: last: in the greatest degree: highest.—*n.* the greatest that can be: the greatest effort. [O.E. *ūtemest,* formed with double superlative suffix. *-m-est* from *ūt,* out.]

Utopian, *u-tō'pi-án, adj.* ideally perfect.—*n.* one who advocates impracticable reforms or who expects an impossible state of perfection in society. [From *Utopia,* lit. 'nowhere' (Gr. *ou,* not, *topos,* place), an imaginary island represented by Sir T. More (1478-1535) as enjoying perfection in politics, laws, &c.]

utricle, *ū'tri-kl, n.* a cell or bladder: a more or less inflated, bladder-like envelope surrounding the fruits of various plants. [L. *ūtriculus,* dim. of *ūter,* a bag.]

utter, *ut'ér, adj.* (*obs.*) farthest out: extreme: complete (in an utter unforeseenness).—*adv.* **utt'erly,** completely. [O.E. *ūtor,* outer—*ūt,* out.]

utter, *ut'ér, v.t.* to emit: to put into circulation: to speak, give voice to.—*adj.* **utt'erable,** that may be uttered or expressed.—*ns.* **utt'erance,** act of uttering: manner of speaking: expression in speech, or in other sound, of a thought or emotion: words spoken, a saying; **utt'erer.** [O.E. *ūtian,* to put out—*ūt,* out.]

uttermost, *ut'ér-mōst,* or *-móst, adj.* farthest out: utmost.—*n.* the greatest degree. [Same as *utmost,* the *r* being intrusive, and *t* being doubled on the analogy of *utter.*]

uvula, *ū'vū-la, n.* the fleshy conical body suspended from the palate over the back part of the tongue.—*adj.* **u'vūlar.** [L. *ūva,* a bunch of grapes.]

uxorious, *uk-sō'ri-ús, adj.* excessively or submissively fond of a wife.—*adv.* **uxō'riously.**—*n.* **uxō'riousness.** [L. *uxōrius—uxor,* a wife.]

V

V-sign, *vē′sīn, n.* a sign made with the index and middle fingers in the form of a V, with palm turned outwards in token of victory, with palm inwards as a sign of derision.

vacant, *vā′kánt, adj.* empty: free, unoccupied: unreflecting (e.g. *vacant mood*): inane.—*n.* **vā′cancy,** emptiness: empty space, gap between bodies: an unoccupied situation or office: (*rare*) idleness.—*adv.* **vā′cantly.**—*v.t.* **vā′cāte′,** to leave empty: to quit possession of.—*n.* **vācā′tion,** a vacating or making void: (time of) freedom from regular duties and engagements: a holiday, esp. from academic or legal duties. [Fr.,—L. *vacāns, -antis,* pr.p. of *vacāre, -ātum,* to be empty.]

vaccinate, *vak′si-nāt, v.t.* to inoculate with *vaccine* as a preventive against smallpox or other infectious disease.—*n.* **vaccinā′tion.**—*adj.* **vaccine** (*vak′sēn*), pertaining to, derived from, cows: of, relating to, vaccination.—*n.* lymph containing the virus of cowpox used in the process of vaccination: any virus prepared for inoculation purposes. [L. *vaccīnus—vacca,* a cow.]

vacillate, *vas′i-lāt, v.i.* to sway to and fro: to waver, show indecision.—*n.* **vacillā′tion.** [L. *vacillāre, -ātum.*]

vacuous, *vak′ū-us, adj.* empty, void: lacking intelligence, inane.—*ns.* **vacū′ity,** emptiness: an unoccupied space: idleness, listlessness: **vac′-uōle,** a very small cavity in the tissue of organisms; **vac′ūum,** (theoretically—*perfect vacuum*) a space empty or devoid of all matter: (in practice) a region in which the gas pressure is considerably lower than atmospheric: a vacuum-cleaner:—*pl.* **vac′ūa; vac′uum-brake,** a brake system in which a vacuum, maintained in reservoirs by exhausters, is simultaneously applied to brake cylinders throughout a train: a brake on the same principle in a motor-car; **vac′uum(-)clean′er,** an apparatus for removing dust from carpets, &c., by suction; **vac′uum(-)flask,** a flask or bottle made of silvered glass, with double walls, the space between them being exhausted of air—used for keeping liquids, &c., hot or cold.—*adj.* **vac′uum-packed′,** sealed in a container from which most of the air has been removed.—*n.* **vac′ūum-tube,** a sealed glass tube in which a vacuum has been made, e.g. a thermionic (q.v.) valve. [L. *vacuus,* empty.]

vade-mecum, *vā′di-mē′kum, n.* a handbook carried for reference. [L. 'go with me'—*vādere,* to go, *me,* abl. of *ego,* I, *cum,* with.]

vagabond, *vag′á-bond, adj.* wandering: having no settled home: driven to and fro: unsettled.—*n.* one who has no settled abode: a vagrant: a rascal.—*n.* **vag′abondage.** [Fr., —L.L.,—L. *vagārī,* to wander—*vagus,* wandering.]

vagary, *vā′gá-ri, vá-gā′ri, n.* a wandering of the thoughts: a whim: an aberration:—*pl.* **vagaries.** [Prob. L. *vagārī,* to stray.]

vagina, *vá-jī′na, n. (anat.)* the canal or passage which leads from the external orifice to the uterus: (*bot.*) a leaf-base surrounding the stem and forming a sheath, as in grasses:—*pl.* **-as, -ae** (*-ē*). [L. *vāgīna,* a sheath.]

vagrant, *vā′gránt, adj.* without a settled abode: wandering, erratic.—*n.* one who has no settled home: an idle and disorderly person, as one who has no means of livelihood but begging or stealing.—*n.* **va′grancy,** the act of wandering: the condition of a vagrant: (*law*) the offence of being a vagrant. [M.E. *vagraunt,* perh. Anglo-Fr. *wackerant,* influenced by L. *vāgārī,* to wander.]

vague, *vāg, adj.* indefinite (e.g. *vague statements*): indistinct, lacking precision (e.g. *he saw a vague figure*): (of a person) lacking character and purpose, or addicted to haziness of thought.—*adv.* **vague′ly.**—*n.* **vague′ness.** [Fr.,—L. *vagus,* wandering.]

vail, *vāl, v.t. (arch.)* to lower, let fall (e.g. crest, pride).—*v.i.* to yield. [Contr. from obs. v.b. *avale* —Fr. *avaler;* cf. **avalanche.**]

vails, *vālz, n.pl.* money given to servants by guests or others: a bribe. [A contr. of **avail,** to profit.]

vain, *vān, adj.* unsatisfying: fruitless, unavailing, ineffectual: empty, worthless (e.g. threats, boasts, promises): conceited: showy.—*adv.* **vain′ly.**—*ns.* **vain′ness; van′ity,** worthlessness, futility: empty pride or ostentation: idle show, or empty pleasure.—**Vanity Fair,** the world depicted as a scene of vanity and folly in Bunyan's *Pilgrim's Progress.*—**in vain,** ineffectually, to no end; **take in vain,** to use (one's name) in an irreverent or profane manner. [Fr.,—L. *vānus,* empty.]

vainglory, *vān-glō′ri, -glō′-, n.* boastful pride.—*adj.* **vainglō′rious,** given to vainglory: proceeding from vanity.—*adv.* **vainglō′riously.** [**vain, glory.**]

valance, *val′áns, n.* hanging drapery for a bed, &c.—Also **val′ence.**—*v.t.* to decorate with such. [Poss. A. Fr. *valer,* to descend.]

vale, *vāl, n.* a tract of low ground, esp. between hills, a valley. [Fr. *val* —L. *vallis,* a vale.]

valediction, *val-e-dik′sh(ó)n, n.* a farewell.—*adj.* **valedic′tory,** saying farewell: taking leave.—*n.* a farewell speech. [L. *valedīcĕre, -dictum—valē,* farewell, *dīcĕre,* to say.]

valency, *vā′len-si, n. (chem.)* the combining power of an atom or group in terms of hydrogen atoms or their equivalent.—Also **vā′lence. -vāl′ent,** in composition, having a (specified) valence. [From L. *valēre,* to be strong.]

valentine, *val′en-tīn, n.* a lover or sweetheart chosen on St *Valentine's* Day, 14th February: a love-letter or other token sent on that day.

Neutral vowels in unaccented syllables: *em′pér-ór;* for certain sounds in foreign words see p. ix.

[So named from the notion that birds choose their mates on that day.]

valerian, *va-lē′ri-ån*, *n.* a genus of dicotyledons, certain species of which have an edible root with medicinal properties. [O.Fr.,—L. *valēre*, to be strong.]

valet, *val′et*, or *val′ā*, *n.* a man-servant, esp. one who attends on a gentleman's person.—*v.t.* to act as a valet to:—*pr.p.* val′eting; *pa.t.* and *pa.p.* val′eted (or *val′ād*). [O.Fr.,—*vaslet*, later also *varlet*. See **varlet, vassal.**]

valetudinarian, *val-e-tū-di-nā′ri-ån*, *adj.* pertaining to ill-health: sickly, weak.—Also **valetū′dinary.**—n. a person of weak health: a person preoccupied with his health.—*n.* **valetūdinā′rianism**, weak health: pre-occupation with health. [L. *valētūdinārius*—*valētūdō*, state of health—*valēre*, to be strong.]

valiant, *val′yånt*, *adj.* (*obs.*) strong: brave, heroic (of a deed, &c.): intrepid in danger.—*adv.* **val′iantly.**—*n.* **val′iantness**, valour, courage. [Fr. *vaillant*—L. *valēns, valentis*, pr.p. of *valēre*, to be strong.]

valid, *val′id*, *adj.* (*arch.*) strong: having sufficient strength or force, founded in truth, sound (e.g. of an argument, objection): fulfilling all the necessary conditions: (*law*) executed with the proper formalities, legal.—*n.* **valid′ity.** *adv.* **val′idly.** [Fr.,—L. *validus*—*valēre*, to be strong.]

valise, *va-lēs′*, *n.* a travelling-bag, generally of leather, opening at the side. [Fr.,—L.L. *valisia*; origin uncertain.]

valley, *val′i*, *n.* low land between hills or mountains: a low, extended plain, usually watered by a river:—*pl.* **vall′eys.** [O.Fr. *valee*—*val*, a vale.]

valour, *val′ór*, *n.* stoutness of heart, intrepidity: prowess.—*adj.* **val′orous**, intrepid, valiant.—*adv.* **val′orously.** [O.Fr. *valour*—Low L. *valor*—L. *valēre*, to be strong.]

valse, *völs, vals, n.* a waltz [Fr.]

value, *val′ū*, *n.* worth, that which renders anything useful or estimable: efficacy, importance, excellence: relative worth (e.g. *a sense of values*): estimated worth (e.g. *a high value*): price: purchasing power: an equivalent, fair return (e.g. *value for one's money*): precise meaning (of a word): quality of sound (as expressed by a phonetic symbol): duration (of a musical note): (*painting*) relation of one part of a picture to the others with reference to light and shade: amount indicated by an algebraic term or expression.—*v.t.* to estimate the worth of: to rate (at a price): to esteem: to prize.—*adj.* **val′uable**, having considerable value or worth.—*n.* a thing of value (esp. an article of small bulk)—often in *pl.*—*ns.* **val′uableness, valuā′tion**, the act of valuing: estimated worth; **val′uātor**, one who sets a value on goods, esp. one licensed to do so, an appraiser.—Also **val′uer.**—*adj.* **val′ueless.**—**valuation roll**, a list of properties and their assessed values for local taxation purposes; **value-added tax**, a tax on the rise in value of a product due to the manufacturing and marketing processes; **value judgement**, a personal estimate of merit in a particular respect. [O.Fr. *value*, properly fem. of Fr. *valu*, pa.p. of *valoir*, to be worth—L. *valēre*.]

valve, *valv*, *n.* one of the leaves of a folding-door: a lid that opens in one direction and not in the other for controlling the flow of liquid or gas in a pipe: a membranous fold or other structure that performs the same function in a tube or organ of the body: one of the separable pieces forming a mollusc shell: a term used in electronics and thermionics, strictly applicable to a *rectifier* (q.v.) but generally applied to all forms of thermionic and gas discharge tubes.—*adj.* **val′vūlar.** [Fr.,—L. *valva*, a folding door.]

vamp, *vamp*, *n.* front upper part of a boot or shoe: a patch: (*mus.*) a simple and uninspired accompaniment.—*v.t.* to repair with a new vamp: to patch old with new: give a new appearance to: (*mus.*) to improvise a crude accompaniment to: to play (such an accompaniment).—**vamp up**, to patch up, concoct, improvise. [Corr. of Fr. *avant-pied*, the forepart of the foot—*avant*, before, *pied*—L. *pēs, pedis*, foot.]

vamp, *vamp*, *n.* (*slang*) a seductive type of woman who allures and exploits men.—*v.t.* to allure. [Abbrev. of **vampire.**]

vampire, *vam′pīr*, *n.* in the superstition of eastern Europe, a corpse which by night leaves its grave to suck the blood of sleeping men: an extortioner: a vampire-bat.—*n.* **vam′pire-bat**, species of bats found in Central and South America which suck the blood of sleeping men and animals: other species erroneously believed to do so. [*vampir* is common in the Slavonic tongues.]

van, *van*, *n.* the front: the front of an army or a fleet: the pioneers of any movement. [Abbrev. of **vanguard.**]

van, *van*, *n.* a fan for grain, &c.—Also *v.t.* [Fr.—L. *vannus*.]

van, *van*, *n.* covered wagon for conveying goods, &c., by road or rail. [Short for **caravan.**]

vanadium, *van ā′di üm*, *n.* a rare metallic element (symbol V; atomic no. 23). [*Vanadis*, a Scandinavian goddess.]

Van Allen radiation belts, zones of intense particle radiation surrounding the earth at a distance of from 2000 to 12000 miles. [J. A. *Van Allen*, American physicist, born 1914.]

vandal, *van′dål*, *n.* (*cap.*) one of a fierce race who overran and barbarously devastated provinces of the Roman Empire in the 5th century: (without *cap.*) one who wantonly damages property: one who destroys what is beautiful.—*n.* **van′dalism**, behaviour of a vandal [L.L. *Vandali, Vinduli* Gmc.]

Vandyke, *van-dīk′*, *n.* a painting by *Vandyke*; a small round cape, an elaborately bordered lace collar, or a pointed beard, as seen in paintings by Vandyke.—*n.* **Vandyke′-brown**, a reddish-brown pigment. [Anthony *Van Dyck* or *Vandyke*, a great Flemish painter (1599-1641).]

vane, *vān*, *n.* (*obs.*) a flag or banner: a thin slip of wood or metal at the top of a spire, &c., to show which way the wind blows, a weathercock: the thin web of a feather: one of the blades of a windmill or propeller, &c. [Older form *fane*—O.E. *fana*; Ger. *fahne*; akin to L. *pannus*, Gr. *pēnos*, a cloth.]

vanguard, *van′gärd, n.* the part of an army

vanilla

preceding the main body: the front line. [Formerly *vantgard*—Fr. *avant-garde*—*avant*, before, *garde*, guard.]

vanilla, *va-nil′a, n.* the-dried aromatic sheathlike pod or fruit of a tropical orchid, used in confectionery, &c. [Latinised from Fr. *vanille*— Sp. *vainilla*—*vaina*—L. *vāgīna,* a sheath.]

vanish, *van′ish, v.i.* to pass suddenly out of sight, to disappear: to become gradually less, to fade away: (*math.*) to become zero.—**vanishing cream,** cosmetic cream that, when rubbed over the skin, virtually disappears; **vanishing point,** the point at which a diminishing object or quantity disappears. [Through Fr. from L. *vānescĕre,* to pass away—*vānus,* empty.]

vanity. See **vain.**

vanquish, *vangk′wish, v.t.* to conquer, to defeat in any contest (*lit.* and *fig.*).—*n.* **vanq′uisher.** [Late O.Fr. *vainquir* (Fr. *vaincre,* pa.t. *vainquis*)—L. *vincĕre,* to conquer.]

vantage, *vän′tij, n.* advantage (q.v.).—*ns.* **van′tage-ground, -point,** advantageous place, position that gives one superiority in a contest (*lit.* and *fig.*). [M.E.,—O.Fr. *avantage.* See **advantage.**]

vapid, *vap′id, adj.* flat, insipid, without zest (e.g. of wine, beer, conversation).—*adv.* **vap′idly.**— *ns.* **vap′idness, vapid′ity.** [L. *vapidus.*]

vapour, vapor, *vā′pŏr, n.* the gaseous state of a substance normally liquid or solid: water or other matter (e.g. smoke) suspended in the atmosphere: an exhalation: anything vain or transitory: (*pl.*; often with *the*) hysterical fainting fits, or temporary depression of spirits: a fanciful idea: (*obs.*; *pl.*) bragging, blustering.—*v.i.* to pass off in vapour: to emit vapours: to indulge in vapours—i.e. express oneself extravagantly or utter empty boasts.—*v.t.* **vā′porise,** to convert into vapours.—i.e. to pass off in vapour.—*adj.* **vā′porisable,** capable of being converted into vapour.—*ns.* **vāporisā′tion; vāp′orīser** (or *-īz′-*), an apparatus for discharging liquid in a fine spray.—*adjs.* **vā′porish,** full of vapours: hypochondriacal: peevish; **vā′porous,** full of or like vapour: affected with the vapours: unsubstantial, vainly imaginative.—*ns.* **vā′pourbath,** an apparatus for bathing the body in vapour; **vā′pourer,** one who vapours, a boaster.—*n.* **vapour-trail,** a white trail of condensed vapour left in the sky from the exhaust of an aircraft.—*adj.* **vā′poury,** full of vapour: affected with the vapours: peevish. [Fr.,—L. *vapor.*]

variable, *vā′ri-ä-bl, adj.* that may be varied: liable to change, unsteady.—*n.* (*math.*) a quantity that may have an infinite number of values in the same expression.—*ns.* **variabil′ity, vā′riableness.**—*adv.* **vā′riably.**—*ns.* **vāriā′tion,** act or process of varying or being varied: an instance of it: extent to which a thing varies: (*gram.*) change of termination: (*mus.*) a transformation of a melody by-melodic, harmonic, contrapuntal, and rhythmic changes: (*astron.*) deviation from the mean orbit of a heavenly body; **vā′riance,** state of being varied: a change of condition: discrepancy: difference that arises from, or produces, dispute; **vā′riant,** a different form or version.— *adj.* diverse.—**at variance,** in disagreement. [L.

vase

variābilis—*variāre,* *-ātum,* to vary—*varius,* various.]

varicose, *var′i-kōs, adj.* permanently dilated.— **varicose veins,** a condition in which the superficial veins, usually of the leg, are swollen. [L. *varicōsus,* full of dilated veins—*varix,* a dilated vein—*vārus,* bent, crooked.]

variegate, *vā′ri-e-gāt, v.t.* to mark with different colours: to diversify.—*n.* **variegā′tion.** [L. *variegātus*—*varius,* various, *agĕre,* to make.]

variety, *va-rī′e-ti, n.* the quality of being various: absence of uniformity or monotony: many-sidedness: a collection (of different things, or of similar things differing slightly): one or more individuals of a species, which, owing to accidental causes, differ from the normal form in minor points: variety-shows collectively, vaudeville:—*pl.* **varī′eties.**—*ns.* **varī′ety-show,** a mixed entertainment comprising dances, songs, farces, &c.; **varī′ety-thē′atre,** a theatre for variety-shows. [L. *varietās*—*varius,* various.]

variorum, *vā-ri-ō′rŭm, -ō′,- adj.* a term applied to an edition in which the notes of various commentators are inserted. [From Latin 'editio cum notis *variōrum*', an edition with annotations of various persons.]

various, *vā′ri-ŭs, adj.* varied, different, unlike each other: changeable, uncertain: several (e.g. *various people said it*).—*adv.* **vā′riously.**—*n.* **vā′riousness.** [L. *varius.*]

varlet, *vär′let, n.* (*obs.*) a footman: a low fellow, a scoundrel. [O.Fr. *varlet,* formerly *vaslet,* from a dim. of Low L. *vassālis.* See **vassal.**]

varnish, *vär′nish, v.t.* to cover with a liquid so as to give a glossy surface to: to give a fair appearance to.—*n.* a sticky liquid which dries and forms a hard, lustrous coating: a glossy, lustrous appearance: an attractive surface which serves to hide blemishes: gloss or palliation. [Fr. *vernis*—L.L. *vitrinus,* glassy—L. *vitrum,* glass.]

varsity, *vär′si-ti, n.* (*coll.*) university. [**university;** spelling and pronunciation are due to the 18th-century pronunciation of *e* before *r*; cf. **clerk, parson** (*orig.* same as **person**).]

varve, *värv, n.* a seasonal layer of clay deposited in still water, of service in fixing Ice Age chronology. [Sw. *varv,* layer.]

vary, *vā′ri, v.t.* to make different, to diversify, modify: to free from monotony.—*v.i.* to alter, to be or become different: to deviate (from): to differ (from):—*pa.t.* and *pa.p.* vā′ried.—**vary directly, or inversely, as,** to increase, or to decrease, in proportion to increase in—or the other way round. [Fr. *varier*—L. *variāre*— *varius.*]

vas, *vas, n.* (*zool.*) a vessel, duct, or tube for carrying fluid:—*pl.* **va′sa.**—*adj.* **vas′cūlar,** pertaining to, or provided with, such vessels.—*ns.* **vascular′ity; vasectomy,** excision of the vas deferens or part of it, esp. in order to produce sterility.—**vascular bundle,** (*bot.*) a strand of conducting tissue, consisting chiefly of xylem and phloem; **vas deferens,** a sperm-carrying duct. [L. *vās.*]

vasculum, *vas′kū-lŭm, n.* a botanist's specimen-box. [L. dim. of *vās,* a vessel.]

vase, *väz,* or *vāz, n.* a vessel of greater height than width, anciently used for domestic pur-

---

Neutral vowels in unaccented syllables: *em′pér-ŏr*; for certain sounds in foreign words see p. ix.

812

poses and in sacrifices: an ornamental vessel: a sculptured, vase-like ornament. [Fr.,—L. *vāsum* or *vās.*]

Vaseline, *vas'i-lēn, n.* (usually, but incorrectly, spelt without *cap.*) a registered trade-mark applied to certain petroleum products and emollient preparations of them. [Ger. *wasser*, water, and Gr. *elaion*, oil.]

vassal, *vas'ál, n.* one who holds land from, and renders homage to, a superior: a dependant, retainer.—*n.* **vass'alāge**, state of being a vassal, dependence, subjection. [Fr.,—Low L. *vassālis*—Breton *gwaz*, a servant; cf. W. *gwas*, a youth.]

vast, *väst, adj.* of great extent: very great in amount or degree.—*adv.* **vast'ly.**—*n.* **vast'ness.** L. *vastus*, waste, vast; cf. O.E. *wēste*, waste.]

vat, *vat, n.* a large vessel or tank, esp. one for holding liquors. [Older form *fat*—O.E. *fæt*; Du. *vat*, O.N. *fat*, Ger. *fass.*]

VAT. Abbrev. for **value-added tax.**

Vatican, *vat'i-kan, n.* the part of Rome, built on the Vatican hill, in which the Pope resides and which is an independent city under his temporal jurisdiction: the papal authority. [Fr.,—It. *Vaticano*—L. *Mons Vāticānus*, Vatican hill.]

vaticinate, *va-tis'i-nāt, v.t.* to prophesy.—*n.* **vaticinā'tion.** [L. *vāticinārī, -ātus*, to prophesy —*vātes*, a seer, *canĕre*, to prophesy.]

vaudeville, *vōd'vil, n.* originally a popular song with topical allusions: (*rare*) a play interspersed with dances and such songs: variety entertainment. [From *vau (val) de Vire*, the valley of the Vire, in Normandy, where such songs were composed about 1400 A.D.]

vault, *völt, n.* an arched roof: a chamber with an arched roof, esp. one underground: a cellar: anything vault-like: a leap or spring in which the weight of the body is supported by the hands, or by a pole: the bound of a horse.—*v.t.* to arch: to roof with an arch: to form vaults in: to leap over by performing a vault.—*v.i.* to curvet or leap, as a horse: to leap (over).—*adj.* **vault'ed**, arched: covered with a vault.—*ns.* **vaul'ter**, one who vaults or leaps; **vaul'ting-horse**, a wooden horse used in a gymnasium for vaulting over. [O.Fr. *volte*—L. *volvĕre, volūtum*, to roll.]

vaunt, *vönt, v.i.* and *v.t.* to make a vain display, or display of: to boast.—*n.* vain display: a boast. [O.Fr. *vanter*—L.L. *vanitāre*—L. *vānitās*, vanity—*vānus*, vain.]

veal, *vēl, n.* the flesh of a calf. [O.Fr. *veël*—L. *vitellus*, dim. of *vitulus*, a calf.]

vector, *vek'tor, n.* (*math.*) a straight line or definite length drawn from a given point in a given direction, usu. representing a quantity (as a velocity or a force) that has both magnitude and direction: the course of an aircraft, missile, &c.—*adj.* **vecto'rial.**—**vector quantity**, one that has direction as well as magnitude. [L.,—*vehĕre, vectum*, to convey.]

Veda, *vā'dä, vē'dä, n.* one or all of the four holy books, collections of hymns, prayers, &c., of the Hindus—written in ancient Sanskrit:—*pl.* **Vedas.**—*adj.* **Ve'dic.**—*n.* the Sanskrit of the Vedas. [Sans. *veda*, knowledge—*vid*, to know.]

vedette, *ve-det', n.* a mounted sentry stationed at the outposts of an army to watch an enemy.

[Fr.,—It. *vedetta*—*vedere*, to see—L. *vidēre*, to see.]

veer, *vēr, v.i.* (of the wind) to change direction clockwise: (loosely) to change direction: to change course, as a ship: (*fig.*) to pass from one mood or opinion to another.—*v.t.* to turn (a ship's head) away from the wind. [Fr. *virer*—L.L. *virāre*, to turn.]

veer, *vēr, v.t.* to slacken, let out (as a rope). [Middle Du. *vieren*, to slacken.]

vegetable, *vej'e-tä-bl, n.* an organised body without sensation and voluntary motion, nourished by roots fixed in the ground: a plant grown for food—*adj.* belonging to plants: consisting of or having the nature of plants: derived from vegetables.—*adjs.* **veg'etal**, of the nature of a vegetable: pertaining to the vital functions of plants and animals, as growth, reproduction, &c.; **vegetā'rian**, consisting of vegetables: pertaining to a diet confined to vegetables.—*n.* one who holds that vegetables are the only proper food for man and abstains from animal food.—*n.* **vegetā'rianism.**—*v.i.* **veg'etāte**, to grow by roots and leaves: to sprout: to lead an idle, aimless life.—*n.* **vegetā'tion**, process of growing, as a plant: vegetable growth: plants in general.—*adj.* **veg'etative**, growing, as plants: having power to produce growth: pertaining to unconscious or involuntary bodily functions (e.g. digestion): without intellectual activity, unprogressive (e.g. of a manner of life).—*adv.* **veg'etatively.**—*n.* **veg'etativeness.**—**vegetable marrow**, the fruit of a species of gourd. [O.Fr.,—L.L. *vegetābilis*, animating—L. *vegetāre*, to quicken.]

vehement, *vē'(h)e-mént, adj.* passionate: very eager or urgent: violent, furious.—*ns.* **vē'hemence**, **vē'hemency**, the quality of being vehement: violence: great ardour or fervour.—*adv.* **vē'hemently.** [O.Fr.,—L. *vehemens, -entis.*]

vehicle, *vē'i-kl, n.* any kind of carriage or conveyance: (*lit.* and *fig.*) that which is used to convey: (**space vehicle**) a structure for carrying burdens through air or space, or a rocket used to launch a spacecraft: (*med.*) a substance in which a medicine is taken: the liquid substance which, when mixed with pigments, forms a paint.—*adj.* **vehicular** (*vé-hik'ū-lár*), pertaining to, or serving as, a vehicle. [L. *vehiculum*—*vehĕre*, to carry.]

veil, *vāl, n.* a curtain: anything that hides an object: a piece of fabric worn by ladies to shade or hide the face: the head-dress of a nun: a disguise, mask—*v.t.* to cover with a veil: to cover: to conceal.—*n.* **veil'ing**, the act of concealing with a veil: material for making veils.—**take the veil**, to become a nun. [O.Fr. *veíle* (Fr. *voile*)—L. *vēlum*, a curtain—*vehĕre*, to carry.]

vein, *vān, n.* one of the vessels or tubes that convey the blood back to the heart: loosely, any blood vessel: one of the horny tubes forming the framework of an insect's wings: (*bot.*) one of the small branching ribs in a leaf: a seam of mineral through a rock of different formation: a streak of different quality, e.g. of different colour, in wood, stone, &c.: mood or humour (e.g. *he was not in the vein* *for jesting*): a recurrent characteristic, streak, strain (*a vein of irony runs throughout the story*):—*v.t.* to form veins or the appearance of veins in.—*n.* **vein'ing**, formation or disposition of veins: streaking. [Fr. *veine*—L. *vēna*, perh. from *vehĕre*, to carry.]

veld, *felt, velt, n.* in S. Africa, open, unforested, or thinly-forested grass-country.—Also **veldt**, but never so written in S. Africa. [Du. *veld*, field.]

vellum, *vel'ŭm, n.* a superior kind of parchment prepared from the skins of calves, kids, or lambs. [O.Fr. *velin*—L.L. *(c(h)arta) vitulina* (writing material—see **chart**), of a calf—L. *vitulus*.]

velocipede, *ve-los'i-pēd, n.* a vehicle propelled by the feet of the rider, of which the bicycle is a development. [Fr.,—L. *vēlox, vēlōcis*, swift, *pēs, pedis*, foot.]

velocity, *ve-los'i-ti, n.* (popularly) swiftness, speed: rate of change of position of a point per unit of time—for complete specification, direction as well as magnitude must be stated. [L. *vēlōcitas*—*velox*, swift.]

velodrome, *vel'ō-drōm, n.* a building containing a cycle-racing track. [Fr. *vélodrome*.]

velour(s), *ve-lōōr', n.* any of several velvet-like materials: a hat of such material.—Also **velure** (*vel'yŭr, vel-ūr'*).—*adj.* **velū'tinous**, velvety. [O.Fr. *velours, velous*—L. *villōsus*, shaggy.]

velvet, *vel'vét, n.* a cloth made from silk, with a close shaggy pile: a similar cloth made of cotton.—*adj.* made of velvet: soft like velvet.—*n.* **velveteen'**, a fustian made of twilled cotton with a pile of the same material: a kind of velvet made of silk and cotton mixed throughout.—*adj.* **vel'vety**, made of or like velvet: soft in taste or touch.—**on velvet**, in a safe or advantageous position; **the velvet glove**, gentleness concealing strength. [From L.L. *velluetum*—L.L. *villutus*—L. *villus*, shaggy hair.]

vena, *vē'na, n.* a vein.—**vena cava**, in man, either of the large veins entering the right auricle of the heart. [L., *vēna*.]

venal, *vē'nál, adj.* (of a person or his services) that may be sold or got for a price: (of conduct) mercenary, corrupt.—*n.* **ven'der, -dor**, one who sells.—*adj.* **vend'ible**, that may be sold: that may be disposed of as an object of trade. —*n.* **vendibil'ity**.—*adv.* **ven'dibly**.—**vending machine**, a slot-machine. [Fr. *vendre*—L. *vendĕre*—*vēnus*, sale, *dăre*, to give.]

vendage, *ven'dij, n.* a harvest of grapes. [M.E.—(O.) Fr. *vendange*.]

vendetta, *ven-det'a, n.* a sanguinary feud in pursuit of private vengeance for the death of a kinsman: inveterate hostility. [It.,—L. *vindicta*, revenge—*vindicāre*, to claim.]

vendeuse, *vā-dœz, n.* a saleswoman. [Fr.]

veneer, *ve-nēr', v.t.* to overlay or face with another and superior wood, or with a thin coating

of another substance: (*fig.*) to disguise with superficial polish.—*n.* a thin coating, as of wood: false show or charm.—*n.* **veneer'ing**, the act or art of overlaying an inferior wood with thin leaves of a more valuable kind: the thin leaf thus laid on. [Formerly *fineer*; corruption of Ger. *furniren*—O.Fr. *fornir*, It. *fornire*, to furnish.]

venerate, *ven'e-rāt, v.t.* to honour or reverence with religious awe: to reverence, to regard with the greatest respect.—*n.* **venerā'tion**, the act of venerating: the state of being venerated: the highest degree of reverence, respect mingled with awe.—*adj.* **ven'erable**, that may be venerated, rendered sacred by religious or other associations: aged.—*n.* **ven'erableness**.—*adv.* **ven'erably**. [L. *venerārī, -ātus*.]

venereal, *ve-nē're-ál, adj.* pertaining to, or arising from, sexual intercourse: exciting desire for sexual intercourse: curing venereal diseases.—*n.* **ven'ery**, sexual intercourse.—**venereal disease**, a contagious disease characteristically transmitted by sexual intercourse. [L. *venereus*—*Venus, Venĕris*, the goddess of love: conn. with L. *venerārī*.]

venery, *ven'er-i, n.* (arch.) hunting. [O.Fr. *venerie*—L. *vēnārī*, to hunt.]

venesection, *ve-ne-sek'sh(ŏ)n, n.* the cutting open of a vein for letting blood: bloodletting. [L. *vēna*, a vein, *sectio*, cutting.]

Venetian, *ve-nē'sh(á)n, adj.* of or belonging to *Venice*.—*n.* a native or inhabitant of Venice.—*n.* **Venē'tian-blind**, a window-blind formed of thin slips of wood or other material, so hung as to admit of being set either edgewise or overlapping. [L. *Venetia*, Venice.]

venge, *venj, v.t.* (*Shak.*) to avenge.—*n.* **vengeance** (*venj'áns*), the infliction of punishment upon another in return for an injury or offence, retribution.—*adj.* **venge'ful**, vindictive, revengeful.—*adv.* **venge'fully**.—**with a vengeance** (*coll.*), with excessive force, in excessive measure. [O.Fr. *venger*—L. *vindicāre*.]

venial, *vē'ni-ál, adj.* pardonable, excusable: opp. to *mortal* or *deadly* (see **sin**.).—*adv.* **vē'nially**.—*ns.* **vē'nialness, vēnial'ity**. [Fr.,—L. *veniālis*, pardonable—*venia*, pardon.]

venison, *ven'zn, ven'i-zn,* or *ven'i-sn, n.* the flesh of animals taken in hunting, esp. the deer. [Fr. *venaison*—L. *vēnātio*, a hunting, game—*vēnārī*, to hunt.]

venom, *ven'ŏm, n.* any drink, juice, or liquid injurious or fatal to life, poison: spite, malice.—*adj.* **ven'omous**, poisonous: spiteful, malignant.—*adv.* **ven'omously**.—*n.* **ven'omousness**. [Fr. *venin* (It. *veneno*)—L. *venēnum*.]

venous, *vē'nŭs, adj.* pertaining to, or contained in, veins: veined. [L. *vēnōsus*—*vēna*, a vein.]

vent, *vent, n.* a small opening, slit, or outlet: the flue of a chimney: the anus of birds and fishes: (*hist.*) touch-hole: (*fig.*) outlet, expression.—*v.t.* to provide with vent or opening: to give vent to: to utter.—**give vent to**, to allow to break out, give outlet or utterance to. [Altered form of *fent*, M.E. *fente*—O.Fr. *fente*, a slit; confused with Fr. *vent*—L. *ventus*, wind.]

ventilate, *ven'ti-lāt, v.t.* to fan with wind: to admit fresh air to: to provide with duct(s) for circulating air, or for escape of air: to cause

Neutral vowels in unaccented syllables: *em'pér-ŏr*; for certain sounds in foreign words see p. ix.

(blood) to take up oxygen, by supply of air: to supply air to (lungs): to expose to examination and discussion.—*n.* **ventilā'tion,** act or art of ventilating: state of being ventilated.—*adj.* **ven'tilătive.**—*n.* **ven'tilātor,** that which ventilates: a contrivance for introducing fresh air. [L. *ventilāre, -ātum*—*ventulus,* dim. of *ventus,* the wind.]

ventral, *ven'trăl, adj.* belonging to the belly: on the anterior surface.—*n.* in fishes, one of the pelvic fins.—*n.* **ventricle** (*ven'tri-kl*), a small cavity within an animal body, as in the heart or brain.—*adj.* **ventric'ūlar.** [L. *ventrālis—venter,* the belly.]

ventriloquism, *ven-tril'o-kwizm, n.* the act or art of speaking in such a way that the hearer imagines the voice to come from a source other than the actual speaker—also **ventril'o-quy.**—*v.i.* **ventril'oquise,** to practise ventriloquism.—*n.* **ventril'oquist,** one who practises ventriloquism.—*adj.* **ventrilo'quial.** [L. *ventriloquus,* speaking from the belly—*venter,* the belly, *loquī,* to speak.]

venture, *ven'tyūr, chūr, n.* (*rare*) chance, luck, hazard: that which is put to hazard (esp. goods sent by sea at the sender's risk): an undertaking whose issue is uncertain or dangerous.—*v.t.* to send on a venture: to expose to hazard, to risk.—*v.i.* to run a risk: to dare.—*adjs.* **ven'turous, ven'tūresome.**—*advs.* **ven'turously, ven'tūresomely.**—*ns.* **ven'tū-rousness, ven'tūresomeness.**—**at a venture,** at random.—**Venture Scout,** a member of a senior branch of the Scout organisation, formerly called Rover (Scout). [Short for **adventure.**]

venturi (tube), *ven-tōōr'ē (tūb),* a tube or duct, wasp-waisted and expanding at the ends, used in e.g. measuring flow rate of fluids. [G.B. *Venturi,* Italian physicist.]

venue, *ven'ū, n.* the scene of an action or event: (*law*) the area within which a crime is alleged to have been committed and from which a jury is summoned to try a question of fact: an appointed place of meeting. [O.Fr.,—L. *venīre,* to come, but confused with O.Fr. *visne, neigh-*bourhood—L. *vīcīnia,* neighbourhood.]

Venus, *vē'nus, n.* Roman goddess of beauty and love: the most brilliant of the planets, second in order from the sun. [L. *Venus.*]

veracious, *ve-rā'shŭs, adj.* truthful: true.—*adv.* **verā'ciously.**—*n.***veracity** (*ve-ras'i-ti*), truthfulness, esp. habitual: truth, conformity with truth or fact. [L. *vērax, vērācis—vērus,* true.]

veranda, verandah, *ve-ran'da, n.* a kind of covered balcony or open portico, with a roof sloping beyond the main building, supported by light pillars. [Hindustani *varandā.*]

verb, *vûrb, n.* (*gram.*) the part of speech which asserts or predicates something.—*adj.* **ver'bal,** relating to or consisting in words: spoken (as opposed to *written*): literal, word for word: derived directly from a verb.—*n.* a part of speech, a noun derived from a verb.—*v.t.* **ver'balise,** to turn (another part of speech) into a verb.—*advs.* **ver'bally; verbā'tim,** word for word.—*n.* **ver'biāge,** abundance of words, wordiness, verbosity.—*adj.* **verbōse',** containing more words than are necessary, wordy: (of a person) prolix.—*adv.* **verbōse'ly.**—*ns.*

verbōse'ness, verbos'ity.—**verbal inspiration,** literal inspiration—used in speaking of the view that every word of the Scriptures was inspired by God; **verbal note,** in diplomacy, an unsigned memorandum calling attention to a matter that might otherwise be forgotten or neglected; **verbal noun,** a form of a verb, e.g. infinitive or gerund, functioning as a noun. [Fr. *verbe*—L. *verbum.*]

verbatim. See **verb.**

verbena, *vêr-bē'na, n.* a genus of tropical or subtropical plants, of which the vervain is common in the south of England is a species: the lemon-scented verbena, a plant of another genus of the same family. [L. *verbenae,* leaves, twigs, &c.]

verbiage, verbose, &c. See **verb.**

verdant, *vûr'dănt, adj.* green: fresh (as grass or foliage): flourishing: (*fig.*) inexperienced.—*n.* **ver'dancy.**—*adv.* **ver'dantly.**—*n.* **ver'dūre,** greenness, freshness of growth: green vegetation. [Fr. *verdoyant*—L. *viridāns, -antis,* pr.p. of *viridāre,* to grow green.]

verdict, *vûr'dikt, n.* the finding of a jury on a trial: decision, opinion pronounced.—**open verdict** (see **open**). [O.Fr. *verdit*—Low L. *vere-dictum*—L. *vērē,* truly, *dictum,* a saying.]

verdigris, *vûr'di-grēs, n.* the greenish rust of copper, brass, or bronze: a bluish-green paint got artificially from copper-plates.—Also **ver'degris.** [M.E. *verdegrese,* &c.—O.Fr. *verd* (*vert*) *de gris—verd,* green, *de,* of, *Grèce,* Greece; cf. Low L. *viride Grecum.*]

Verey light. See **Very light.**

verge, *vûrj, n.* a rod, staff, or mace, or the like, used as an emblem of authority: extent of jurisdiction: the brink, extreme edge (*lit.* and *fig.*): grass edging of a garden bed or of a road.—*n.* **ver'ger,** one who carries a verge or emblem of authority: the beadle of a cathedral church: a pew-opener or attendant in church: one who looks after the interior of the church building, &c.—**on the verge of,** on the point of. [L. *virga,* a slender branch.]

verge, *vûrj, v.i.* to slope: to approach closely to (with *on*): to border. [L. *vergere,* to incline.]

veriest. See **very.**

verify, *ver'i-fī, v.t.* to establish as true by evidence: to confirm as true by research:—*pa.t.* and *pa.p.* **ver'ifīed.** *adj.* **ver'ifīable,** that may be verified, proved, or confirmed.—*n.* **verifi-cā'tion,** the process of verifying: the state of being verified. [L. *vērus,* true, *facēre,* to make.]

verily, *ver'i-li, adv.* truly, certainly, really. [L. *vērus,* true. See **very.**]

verisimilar, *ver-i-sim'i-lar, adj.* truth-like, likely, probable.—*n.* **verisimil'itude,** similitude or likeness to truth, appearance of truth: a thing probably true. [L. *vērisimilis—vērus,* true, *similis,* like.]

verity, *ver'i-ti, n.* the quality of being true or real: truth: a true assertion or tenet:—*pl.* **ver'-ities.**—*adj.* **ver'itable,** true, real, actual.—*adv.* **ver'itably.** [L. *vēritās—vērus,* true.]

verjuice, *vûr'jōōs, n.* the expressed juice of green or unripe fruit, used in cooking. [Fr. *verjus—vert,* green, *jus,* juice.]

vermicelli, *ver-mi-chel'i,* or *-sel'i, n.* stiff paste or dough of fine wheat-flour made into small worm-like or thread-like rolls. [It., *pl.* of *vermicello* — L. *vermiculus*, dim. of *vermis*, worm.]

vermicide, *vûr′mi-sīd, n.* a worm-killer.—*adjs.* **vermic′ular**, **vermic′ūlate, -d,** pertaining to, or like, a worm (esp. in its motion).—*v.t.* **vermic′ūlate**, to decorate with inlaid work like the motion or track of worms.—*n.* **vermiculā′-tion.**—*adj.* **ver′miform,** having the form of a worm.—*n.* **ver′mifuge** (*med.*), a substance that destroys intestinal worms or expels them from the digestive canal. [L. *vermis*, a worm.]

vermilion, *vėr-mil′yón, n.* a bright-red pigment obtained from cinnabar, but generally made artificially from mercury and sulphur: any beautiful red colour.—*adj.* of the colour of vermilion.—*v.t.* to dye vermilion: to colour a delicate red. [O.Fr. *vermilion*—*vermeil*—L. *vermiculus* (in L.L. a scarlet colour, from an insect or a berry used in dyeing), dim. of *vermis*, a worm.]

vermin, *vûr′min, n.* (*orig.*) a reptile or other repulsive creature: (*collectively*) loathsome parasites on the body, as fleas, lice, bedbugs: domestic pests, as rats, mice: birds or animals destructive to preserved game: any contemptible and obnoxious person or persons.—*adj.* **ver′minous**, consisting of vermin: like vermin: infested with parasitic or other vermin. [Fr. *vermine*—L. *vermis*, a worm.]

vermuth, -mouth, *vûr′mŭth, -mŏŏt(h), n.* a cordial containing white wine flavoured with wormwood, &c., used as a stimulant for the appetite, or in mixed drinks. [Ger. *wermut(h)*, wormwood; cf. O.E. *wermōd*.]

vernacular, *vėr-nak′ū-lár, adj.* native, belonging to the country of one's birth.—*n.* mothertongue: native dialect.—*adv.* **vernac′ularly.** [L. *vernāculus*—*verna*, a home-born slave.]

vernal, *vûr′nál, adj.* belonging to the spring: appearing in spring: belonging to youth.—*adv.* **ver′nally.**—*n.* **vernā′tion**, the particular manner of arrangement of leaves in the bud.— **vernal equinox**, the spring equinox (see **equinox**). [L. *vernālis*—*vēr*, spring.]

vernier, *vėr′ni-ér, n.* a contrivance consisting of a short scale made to slide along a graduated instrument and measure very small intervals. [So called from Pierre *Vernier* (1580-1637) of Brussels, its inventor.]

Veronal, *ver′o-nál, n.* (often, but incorrectly, without *cap.*) registered trade-mark for a drug with hypnotic properties. See **barbital**.

veronica, *ve-ron′ik-a, n.* (or with *cap.*) a portrait of Christ's face on a handkerchief—from the legend that, on the way to Calvary, St *Veronica* wiped the sweat from His face with her handkerchief, whereupon His features were impressed on the cloth: speedwell (q.v.).

verruca, *ve-rŏŏ′ka, n.* a wart. [L.]

versatile, *vûr′sa-tīl,* or *-til, adj.* capable of moving or turning freely: able to turn easily and successfully to new tasks, &c.: (*rare*) changeable: of a material, capable of being used for many purposes.—*n.* **versatil′ity.** [Fr.,—L. *versātilis*—*versāre*, freq. of *vertĕre*, to turn.]

verse, *vûrs, n.* a line of poetry: a metrical arrangement and language: poetry: a short division of any composition, esp. of the chapters of the Bible—originally confined to the metrical books: (*mus.*) a portion of an anthem

to be performed by a single voice to each part.—*ns.* **ver′sicle**, a little verse: in liturgy, the verse said by the officiant; **versificā′tion**, the act, art, or practise of composing metrical verses: prosody: metrical scheme: individual metrical style.—*v.i.* **ver′sify**, to make verses.— *v.t.* to relate in verse: to turn into verse:—*pa.t.* and *pa.p.* ver′sified.—*ns.* **ver′sifier; ver′sion**, the act of translating or turning from one language into another: that which is translated from one language into another: a school or college exercise in prose translation from English into Latin (*Scot.; obs.*): account from one point of view (e.g. *A. gave his version of what had occurred*). [O.E. *fers*—L. *versus, vorsus,* a line, furrow, turning—*vertĕre,* to turn; influenced by O.Fr. *vers.*]

versed, *vûrst, adj.* thoroughly acquainted with, skilled in (with *in*): (*math.*) reversed. [Fr. *versé*—L. *versātus,* pa.p. of *versārī,* to turn round.]

versicle, versify, version, &c. See **verse**.

vers-libre, *ver′lē′br, n.* free verse—verse defying usual metrical rules, rhythmic prose arranged as irregular verse. [Fr.]

verso, *vûr′sō, n.* a left-hand page: the reverse of a coin or medal. [L. *verso (folio)*, with the page turned—*versus,* pa.p. of *vertĕre,* to turn, *folium,* a leaf or page.]

verst, *vûrst, n.* a Russian mile, 3500 feet in length, or about two-thirds of an English mile. [Russ. *versta.*]

versus, *vûr′sús, prep.* (in law and in games) against—abbreviated *v.* and *vs.* [L.]

vertebra, *vûr′te-bra, n.* one of the segmented portions of the spinal column:—*pl.* vertebrae (*vér′te-brē*).—*adj.* **ver′tebral.**—*n.* **ver′tebrate,** an animal having an internal skeleton with a backbone.—*adjs.* **ver′tebrāte, -d,** furnished with joints: having a backbone.—*n.pl.* **Vertebrā′ta,** a division of the animal kingdom containing all vertebrates. [L.,—*vertĕre,* to turn.]

vertex, *vûr′teks, n.* the top or summit: the point of a cone, pyramid, or angle: (*astron.*) the zenith: (*anat.*) the crown of the head:—*pl.* vertices (*vûr′ti-sēz*).—*adj.* **ver′tical,** pertaining to the vertex: placed in the zenith: perpendicular to the plane of the horizon.—*n.* a vertical line.—*adv.* **ver′tically.**—*n.* **vertical′ity,** quality of being vertical.—**vertical scanning,** (*TV*) scanning in which the lines are vertical, not, as normally, horizontal; **vertical take-off,** (*aero.*) immediate take-off without preliminary run (also *adj.*). [L., eddy, summit—*vertĕre,* to turn.]

vertigo, *vûr′ti-gō,* or *vėr-tī′gō, n.* (*lit.* and *fig.*) a sensation of giddiness, dizziness.—*adj.* **vertig′inous** (*-tij′-*), causing, or tending to cause, dizziness: like vertigo. [L.,—*vertĕre,* to turn.]

vertu. Same as **virtu.**

vervain, *vûr′vān, n.* any of several plants of the genus *Verbena,* esp. one formerly used in love-philtres, and as a charm against witchcraft. [O.Fr. *verveine*—L. *verbēna.*]

verve, *vûrv, n.* the enthusiasm that animates a poet or artist: animation, energy. [Fr.]

very, *ver′i, adj.* (*obs.*) the true (e.g. *very God*): (*arch.*) true, real (e.g. *my very son Esau*): in the fullest sense of the word (often in superlative, **ver′iest**; e.g. *for very shame*; *a very*

Neutral vowels in unaccented syllables: *em′pér-ór*; for certain sounds in foreign words see p. ix.

816

knave: *the veriest novice*): exact, same (e.g. *the very person I want*): used as equivalent to 'even the' (e.g. *the very children saw the absurdity*).—*adv.* in a high degree.—**in very deed**, of a truth, certainly; **the very thing**, precisely what is wanted or needed. [Older form *veray*—O.Fr. *verai*—L. *vērax, vērācis*, speaking truly—*vērus*, true.]

Very light, *ver'i līt, n.* a small coloured flare fired from a pistol—used for signalling. [From Samuel *Very*, the inventor.]

vesica, *ve-sī'ka, n.* (*anat.*) a bladder, sac, esp. the urinary bladder:—*pl.* **vesicae** (*ve-sī'sē*).—*v.t.* **ves'icāte**, to raise blisters on:—*pr.p.* ves'icāting; *pa.p.* ves'icated.—*ns.* **vesica'tion**; **ves'i-cant**, a substance that vesicates, esp. a war gas causing blistering and destruction of tissues, e.g. mustard gas; **ves'icle**, a small bladder or blister: a small cavity in an animal body: (*bot.*) a bladder-like cell.—*adjs.* **vesic'ular**, having the structure of a vesicle; **vesic'ulose**, full of vesicles or interstices. [L. *vēsīca*, bladder.]

vesper, *ves'pėr, n.* the evening star, Venus: the evening: (*pl.*) evensong, evening service generally. [Fr.,—L.; Gr. *hesperos.*]

vessel, *ves'ėl, n.* a vase or utensil for holding something: a hollow structure made to float on water, used for navigation: a tube in which fluids, as blood, &c., are contained: a person considered as an agent of God: **the weaker vessel**, woman—from 1 Pet. iii. 7. [O.Fr. *vessel* (Fr. *vaisseau*)—L. *vascellum*, dim. of *vas*, a vase.]

vest, *vest, n.* (*arch.*) a dress, garment: a waist-coat: a detachable front for a dress: a knitted or woven undergarment.—*v.t.* to clothe: to invest (with—e.g. authority): to grant to or confer on (with *in*—e.g. *power is vested in him*).—*v.i.* to descend or to take effect, as a right.—**vested interest**, a particular interest in the continuance of an existing system, institution, &c., for personal reasons, often financial: (in *pl.*) rights or possessions conferred absolutely: (in *pl.*) the class of persons who have acquired rights, possessions, or powers in any sphere of a country's activity. [Fr. *veste*—L. *vestis.*]

Vesta, *ves'ta, n.* the fourth asteroid, discovered in 1807.—*n.* **ves'ta**, a match or waxlight:—*pl.* **ves'tas**.—*adj.* **Ves'tal**, pertaining to or consecrated to the service of Vesta: chaste, pure.—*n.* a chaste virgin. [L. *Vesta*, goddess of household fire and domestic life.]

vestibule, *ves'ti-būl, n.* formerly an open court before a house: a hall next the entrance to a building: (*anat.*) a small bony cavity forming part of the ear. [Fr.,—L. *vestibulum.*]

vestige, *ves'tij, n.* (*orig.*) a track or footprint: a trace, esp. one that serves as a clue: (loosely) a scrap, particle: (*biol.*) an organ or tissue which survives without performing the function it fulfils in an organism of lower type.—*adj.* **vestig'ial** (*-tij'-*). [Fr.,—L. *vestīgium*—*vestīgāre*, to track.]

vestment, *vest'ment, n.* a garment: a long outer robe: (*pl.*) articles of dress worn by the clergy during divine service. [L. *vestīmentum*—*vestīre*, to clothe—*vestis*, a garment.]

vestry, *ves'tri, n.* a room adjoining a church in which the vestments are kept and parochial meetings held, any small room attached to a church: in English parishes, a meeting of the parishioners entitled to share in the management of the ecclesiastical affairs of the parish.—*n.* **ves'tryman**, a member of a vestry. [Fr.,—L. *vestiārium*—*vestiārius*, belonging to clothes—*vestis*, a garment.]

vesture, *ves'tyūr, n.* clothing, dress: a robe: a covering. [O.Fr. *vêture*)—L. *vestīre*, to clothe—*vestis*, a garment.]

vet, *vet, n.* (*coll.*) an abbreviation for *veterinary* (*surgeon*).—*v.t.* to subject to veterinary treatment, or (*coll.*; *fig.*) thorough scrutiny.

vetch, *vech, n.* a genus of plants, mostly climbing, some cultivated for fodder, esp. a tare. [O.Fr. *veche* (Fr. *vesce*)—L. *vicia*, akin to *vincīre*, to bind.]

veteran, *vet'é-ràn, adj.* old, experienced, long exercised, esp. in military life: pertaining to a veteran: consisting of veterans.—*n.* one long exercised in any service, esp. in war.—**veteran car**, an old motor-car, specif. one made before 1916. [L. *veterānus*—*vetus, veteris*, old.]

veterinary, *vet'e-ri-na-ri, adj.* pertaining to the art of treating the diseases of domestic animals: professing or practising this art.—*n.* one skilled in the diseases of domestic animals.— Also **veterinary surgeon**, **veterinā'rian**. [L. *veterīnārius*—*veterīnae*, beasts of burden.]

veto, *vē'tō, n.* any authoritative prohibition: the power of rejecting or forbidding, specif., the right of any of one of the five permanent members of the Security Council of the United Nations to prevent the Council taking action on any matter other than purely procedural:—*pl.* **vetoes** (*vē'tōz*).—*v.t.* to reject by a veto: to withhold assent to. [L. *vetāre*, to forbid.]

vex, *veks, v.t.* to irritate by small provocations, to annoy: to pain, grieve: to disturb, trouble. —*n.* **vexā'tion**, act of vexing: state of being vexed: something causing vexation.—*adj.* **vexā'tious**, causing annoyance: full of trouble: harassing.—*adv.* **vexā'tiously.**—*n.* **vexā'tiousness.**—**vexed question**, a matter frequently and hotly debated. [Fr. *vexer*—L. *vexāre*, to shake, annoy—*vehēre*, to carry.]

via, *vī'a, prep.* by way of.—**via media** (*mēd'i-a*), a middle course. [L.]

viable, *vī'á-bl, adj.* capable of living: capable of growing or developing: of plan, project, of such a kind that it has a prospect of success. [Fr.,—*vie*, life—L. *vīta.*]

viaduct, *vī'a-dukt, n.* a road or railway carried by a structure over a valley, river, &c.: the high, bridge-like structure that carries it. [L. *via*, a way, *dūcēre, ductum*, to lead, bring.]

vial, *vī'al, n.* Same as **phial.**

viand, *vī'ànd, n.* food, articles for food—usually in *pl.* [Fr. *viande*—L.L. *vivanda* (for *vivenda*), food necessary for life—L. *vīvēre*, to live.]

viaticum, *vī-at'ik-ùm, n.* (*orig.*) provisions for the way: (*R.C. Church*) the eucharist given to persons in danger of death. [L.,—*via*, a way.]

vibrate, *vī'brāt, -brāt', v.i.* to shake: to move, swing, backwards and forwards: to oscillate: to produce an oscillating effect: (*fig.*) to thrill.—*v.t.* to cause to shake: to move to and fro: (of a pendulum) to measure (e.g. seconds)

fāte, fär; mē, hûr (her); *mīne; mōte, fôr; mūte; mōōn, fŏŏt;* ᴛнen (then)

817

by moving to and fro.—*adj.* **vi′brant**, vibrating: sonorous.—*n.* **vibrā′tion**, act of vibrating: state of being vibrated: tremulousness, quivering motion.—*adj.* **vī′brātory**, vibrating: consisting in vibrations: causing vibrations.—*n.* **vī′brātor**. [L. *vibrāre, -ātum,* to tremble.]

vicar, *vik′ár, n.* one who holds authority as the delegate or substitute of another: the clergyman of an impropriated (*q.v.*) benefice: (*R.C. Church*) a bishop's assistant who exercises jurisdiction in his name.—*ns.* **vic′arage**, the benefice, or residence, of a vicar; **vic′ar-apostol′ic**, a titular bishop appointed by the Pope; **vic′ar-gen′eral**, an official performing the work of an archdeacon under the bishop: in the English Church, an officer, lay or clerical, assisting the bishop in administrative business.—*adjs.* **vicā′rial**, pertaining to a vicar: substituted; **vicā′riāte**, having vicarious or delegated power.—*n.* delegated power. —*adj.* **vicā′rious**, filling the place of another: performed or suffered in place of or for the sake of another: (*loosely*) imagined through the experiences of others.—*adv.* **vicā′riously**. —**Vicar of Christ**, a title assumed by the Pope. [L. *vicārius,* supplying the place of another—*vicis* (genitive), change, alternation.]

vice, vise, *vīs, n.* an iron or wooden clamping device, usu. consisting of two jaws that can be brought together by means of a screw, lever, &c., for holding work that is to be operated on. [Fr. *vis* (It. *vite,* screw)—L. *vītis,* tendril of a vine.]

vice, *vīs, n.* a blemish or fault: immoral conduct, depravity: a bad trick or habit e.g. in a horse: (*cap.*; *hist.*) the buffoon in a morality (*q.v.*).—*adj.* **vicious** (*vish′ús*), having a vice or defect: depraved: faulty, incorrect (e.g. of style): unsound (e.g. of argument): fierce, refractory (e.g. of a horse): malicious (e.g. *vicious remarks*).—*adv.* **vic′iously.**—*n.* **vic′iousness.**—**vice squad,** a police squad whose task is to see that the laws dealing with prostitution, gambling, &c., are observed; **vicious circle,** reasoning that begs the question, assumes as true something that is to be proved: a chain of actions in which every step taken to improve the situation creates new difficulties which in the end aggravate the difficulty of the original situation: reciprocal aggravation. [Fr.,—L. *vitium,* a blemish.]

vice-, *vīs-, pfx.* forming compounds denoting one who acts in place of, or ranks second to, another, e.g. *vice′-ad′miral, vice′-pres′ident.* —*prep.* (*vī′se*) in place of.—**vice versa** (*vī′se vúr′sa*), the terms being exchanged the other way round. [L., 'in place of', abl. of *vicis* (gen.), change.]

vicegerent, *vīs-je′rént, n.* one acting in place of a superior.—*n.* **viceger′ency.** [L. *vice,* in place of, *gerens, -entis,* pr.p. of *gerĕre,* to act.]

viceroy, *vīs′roi, n.* a deputy ruling a province in name of his sovereign. [L. *vice,* in place of, Fr. *roi,* a king.]

vicinage, *vis′i-nij, n.* neighbourhood: the places near.—*n.* **vicin′ity,** neighbourhood: nearness. [O.Fr. *veisinage—veisin*—L. *vīcīnus,* neighbouring—*vīcus,* a row of houses.]

vicious. See vice.

vicissitude, *vi-sis′i-tūd, n.* change from one state

to another: (*pl.*) successive changes of fortune. [L. *viscissitūdō—vicis* (gen.), change.]

victim, *vik′tim, n.* a living creature offered as a sacrifice: one injured by others who pursue selfish aims, or by lack of self-control: anyone who incurs loss or harm (e.g. by mischance): a dupe.—*v.t.* **vic′timise,** to make a victim: to cause to suffer for something that is not essentially a fault: to cheat.—*n.* **victimīsā′tion.** [Fr.,—L. *victima,* a beast for sacrifice, adorned with the fillet—*vincīre,* to bind.]

victor, *vik′tór, n.* one who conquers in battle or other contest, a winner.—*adjs.* **vic′tor, victō′rious,** relating to victory: superior in contest: successful, triumphant.—*adv.* **victō′riously.**— *n.* **vic′tory,** success in battle or other contest: a battle gained. [L.,—*vincĕre, victum,* to conquer.]

Victoria Cross, *vik-tō′ri-a, -tō′-, kros, n.* decoration, consisting of a bronze Maltese cross, founded by Queen *Victoria* in 1856, and awarded for conspicuous bravery on the field.

Victorian, *vik-tō′ri-án, -tō′-, adj.* pertaining to Queen *Victoria,* or to her reign: conventional, prudish, sentimental, and narrow—like the fashion in social conduct of Queen Victoria's time.

victual, *vit′l, n.* food for human beings (usu. in *pl.*).—*v.t.* to supply with food: to store with provisions:—*pr.p.* victualling (*vit′l-ing*); *pa.t.* and *pa.p.* victualled (*vit′ld*).—*n.* **victualler** (*vit′lér*), one who supplies provisions. [O.Fr. *vitaille*—L.L. *victualia*—L. *victuālis,* relating to living—*vivĕre, victum,* to live.]

vicuña, vicugna, *vi-kōō′nya,* or *vi-kū′na, n.* an undomesticated South American quadruped, resembling a deer but of the same genus (allied to the camels) as the llama.—*n.* **vicu′nacloth,** cloth made from the fine silky wool of the vicuña: a trade name for a mixture of wool and cotton. [Sp., from Quechua.]

video, *vid′i-ō, adj.* pertaining to television, to the television signal or to the television image.— **video signal,** that part of a television signal which conveys all the information required for establishing the visual image; **video (tape) recording,** recording both television picture and sound on magnetic tape (**videotape**) so that the programme can be rebroadcast. [L. *vidēre,* to see.]

vidette. Same as **vedette.**

vidimus, *vīd′i-mùs,* or *vid′-, n.* an inspection, as of accounts, &c. [L., 'we have seen'—*vidēre,* to see.]

vie, *vī, v.i.* to strive for superiority (followed by *with*):—*pr.p.* vy′ing; *pa.t.* and *pa.p.* vied. [M.E. *vien,* by aphaeresis from *envien,* to vie, through Fr. from L. *invītāre,* to invite.]

Viennese, *vē-e-nēz′,* or *-nēs′, adj.* pertaining to *Vienna.*—*n.* an inhabitant, or the inhabitants, of Vienna.

view, *vū, n.* sight: reach of the sight: whole extent seen: direction in which a thing is seen: scene, natural prospect: the picture of a scene: a sketch: inspection, examination: a mental survey: mode of looking at: opinion: intention, object (*with a view to, of*).—*v.t.* to see: look at attentively: look at on television: examine intellectually.—Also *v.i.—ns.* **view′er,** one who views: one who watches television:

Neutral vowels in unaccented syllables: *em′pér-ór*; for certain sounds in foreign words see p. ix.

an apparatus used to project film for purposes of editing: a device with magnifying lens, &c., for viewing transparencies, or one for viewing photographic slides; **view'-finder**, a camera attachment or part for determining the field of view; **view'-halloo'**, huntsman's cry when the fox breaks cover.—*adj.* **view'less**, invisible: having no view.—*n.* **view'point**, point of view (*lit.* and *fig.*).—**in view of**, having regard to; **on view**, open to inspection; **take a dim view of**, to regard unfavourably. [Fr. *vue*—*vu*, pa.p. of *voir*, to see.]

vigil, *vij'il*, *n.* watching: keeping awake for religious exercises: the eve before a feast or fast day, originally kept by watching through the night.—*n.* **vig'ilance**, wakefulness, watchfulness, circumspection.—*adj.* **vig'ilant**, watchful, on the lookout for danger, circumspect.—*n.* **vigilan'te**, a member of an organisation to look after the interests, threatened in some way, of a group: a member of a vigilance committee.—*adv.* **vig'ilantly.**—**vigilance committee**, a body of people whose aim is to control an unsettled country or to scrutinise the moral behaviour of a locality. [Fr.,—L. *vigilia*—*vigil*, awake, watchful—*vigēre*, to be lively.]

vignette, *vin-yet'*, *n.* any small ornamental engraving, design, or photograph, not enclosed by a definite border: (*orig.*) an ornamental flourish of vine leaves and tendrils on manuscripts and books: a portrait with background shaded off: character sketch. [Fr., *vigne*—L. *vīnea*, a vine.]

vigour, *vig'ór*, *n.* active strength, physical force: vital strength in animals or plants: strength of mind: energy.—*adj.* **vig'orous**, strong, either in mind or in body: showing such strength, energetic, forceful.—*adv.* **vig'orously.**—*n.* **vig'orousness.** [Fr.,—L. *vigor*—*vigēre*, to be strong.]

viking, *vī'king* (also *vik'ing*), *n.* one of the Norse invaders who in the 8th, 9th, and 10th centuries ravaged the coasts of western Europe. [O.N. *vīkingr*, prob from O.E. *wīcing*—*wīc*, a camp.]

vile, *vīl*, *adj.* worthless, mean: morally impure, wicked: (*coll.*) very objectionable.—*adv.* **vile'ly.** —*n.* **vile'ness.**—*v.t.* **vil'ify** (*vil'-*), (*orig.*) to make vile: to slander, to defame:—*pa.t.* and *pa.p.* vil'ified.—*ns.* **vilifica'tion** (*vil-*), act of vilifying: defamatory speech: abuse; **vil'ifier** (*vil'-*). [Fr.,—L. *vīlis*.]

villa, *vil'a*, *n.* (*orig.*) a country residence or seat: a detached or semi-detached suburban house. *ns.* **vill'adom**, villas collectively, or people living in them; **vill'age** (*-ij*), any small assemblage of houses, less than a town: (*orig.*) a number of inhabited houses near the residence of a proprietor or farmer; **vill'ager**, an inhabitant of a village. [O.Fr. *ville*—L. *villa*, a country-house, prob. reduced from *vicla*, dim. of *vīcus*, a village; Gr. *oikos*, a house.]

villain, *vil'ān*, *n.* (*orig.*) a serf attached to a *villa* or farm: a man of base or evil character.—*adj.* **vill'ainous**, like or suited to a villain, base, depraved, infamous: (*coll.*) ugly, in exceedingly bad style.—*adv.* **vill'ainously.**—*n.* **vill'ainy**, extreme depravity: atrocious misconduct. [O.Fr. *villain* Low L. *villānus*—L. *villa*.]

villein, another spelling of **villain** (only in its original meaning).—*n.* **vill'e(i)nage**, in feudal times, the tenure of land (by a villein) by base or menial services.

villi, *vil'ī*, *n.pl.* (*anat.*) fine small fibres covering certain membranes: (*bot.*) fine soft hairs on fruits, flowers, and other parts of plants:—*sing.* **vill'us.** [L., pl. of *villus*, hair, wool.]

vim, *vim*, *n.* (*slang*) energy, force. [Acc. of L. *vis*, strength.]

vinaigrette, *vin-ā-gret'*, *n.* a small box of silver or gold for holding aromatic vinegar, used as a smelling-bottle: a mixture of oil, vinegar and seasoning used as a salad dressing. [Fr.,—*vinaigre*, vinegar.]

vinculum, *ving'kū-lum*, *n.* a bond: (*math.*) a horizontal line placed over several quantities to show that they are to be treated as one compound quantity. [L.,—*vincīre*, to bind.]

vindicate, *vin'di-kāt*, *v.t.* to justify, to defend with success: to clear from blame.—*adj.* **vin'dicable.**—*n.* **vindica'tion**, act of vindicating: defence: justification.—*adj.* **vin'dicative**, vindicating: tending to vindicate.—*n.* **vin'dicator**, one who vindicates.—*adjs.* **vin'dicatory**, tending to vindicate: (of laws) inflicting punishment; **vindic'tive**, revengeful.—*adv.* **vindic'tively.** —*n.* **vindic'tiveness.** [L. *vindicāre*, *ātum.*]

vine, *vīn*, *n.* a **grape-vine**, any plant of either of two genera of woody, climbing plants, whose smooth, juicy berries are used to make wine, &c.: any climbing or trailing plant, or its stem.—*ns.* **vine'-dress'er**, one who dresses or trims and cultivates vines; **vi'nery**, a glasshouse for rearing vines; **vine'-yard** (*vin'yärd*), a plantation of grape vines; **vin'iculture**, the cultivation of the vine.—*adj.* **vi'nous**, pertaining to wine: wine coloured: caused by wine. [O.Fr.,—L. *vīnea*, a vine—*vīnum*, wine; Gr. *oinos*.]

vinegar, *vin'e-gár*, *n.* a liquor containing acetic acid, made by fermentation from malt, or from fruit juices.—*adjs.* **vin'egary**, **vin'egarish**, sour (also *fig.*). [Fr. *vinaigre*—*vin* (L. *vinum*), wine, *aigre* (L. *ācer*) sour.]

vingt-et-un, *vē̃-tā-ũ'* *n.* a game of cards the aim in which is to hold cards the sum of whose pips is nearest to, but not exceeding, twenty-one. Also **pontoon.** [Fr., twenty-one.]

vintage, *vin'tij*, *n.* the gathering of grapes: the time of grape gathering: the produce of grapes, or of wine, for one season: wine, esp. of good quality: a wine of a particular season or region: the product of a particular period: a period of origin.—*adj.* pertaining to the grape vintage: of wine, of a specified year and of good quality: generally, e.g. of a play by an author, among the best and most characteristic: old-fashioned and out of date and no longer admired.—**vintage car**, an old-fashioned one (specif. built between 1916 and 1930); **vintage year**, one in which a particular product (usu. wine) reaches an exceptionally high standard. [Fr. *vendange*—L. *vindēmia*—*vīnum*, wine, grapes, *dēmēre*, to remove—*dē*, out of, *emēre*, to take, buy.]

vintner, *vint'nér*, *n.* a wine-seller. [O.Fr. *vinetier*, through L.L.—L. *vīnētum*, a vineyard—*vīnum*, wine.]

vinyl, *vīn'il, n.* an organic radical CH_2CH: loosely, polymerised vinyl chloride.—**vinyl chloride,** CH_2CHCl, a substance which, when polymerised, produces a widely used plastic—abbrev. **PVC; vinyl resins, plastics,** thermoplastic resins, polymers or co-polymers of vinyl compounds.

viol, *vī'ol, n.* a musical instrument which was the immediate precursor of the violin, having from three to six strings, and played by means of a bow.—*n.* **vi'olist,** a player on the viol or the viola.—**bass viol,** the violoncello. [O.Fr. *viole*—L.L. *vīdula*—L. *vītulārī*, to make merry.]

viola, *vē-ō'la, vī'ō-la, n.* a larger description of violin, having four strings tuned in fifths, to which the part between the second violin and violoncello is generally assigned. [Same as **viol.**]

viola, *vī'ō-la, n.* the genus of plants of which the pansy is a species: a plant, common in garden beds, resembling the pansy but of another species. [L. *vīŏla.*]

violate, *vī'ō-lāt, v.t.* to profane, treat with disrespect: to break, to transgress (e.g. a promise, a law): to abuse: to rape, ravish.—*adj.* **vi'olable,** that may be violated.—*ns.* **viōlā'tion,** the act of violating: profanation: infringement, transgression: rape; **vī'olātor.** [L. *violāre, -ātum—vīs,* strength.]

violent, *vī'ō-lént, adj.* acting with, or characterised by, physical force or strength: forcible, esp. unlawfully so: produced by force (e.g. a death, end): moved by strong feeling: passionate: intense (e.g. of pain, a contrast).—*n.* **vi'olence,** quality of being violent: force, intensity, vehemence: unjust force: outrage, profanation, injury: rape.—*adv.* **vi'olently.** [Fr.,—L. *violentus—vīs,* force.]

violet, *vī'ō-let, n.* any plant of genus *Viola,* of many species, with a flower, generally blue, sometimes white or yellow, and most often fragrant: the colour of the violet, a bluish or light purple.—Also *adj.* [Fr. *violette,* dim. of O.Fr. *viole*—L. *vĭŏla.*]

violin, *vī-ō-lin'* (or *vī'-*), *n.* a musical instrument of four strings played with a bow, a fiddle.—*n.* **vi'olinist,** a player on the violin. [It. *violino—viola.* Same root as **viol.**]

violoncello, *vē-ō-lon-chel'ō,* or *vī-, n.* a large four-stringed musical instrument of the violin class, held between the knees in playing:—*pl.* **violoncell'os.**—abbrev. **cello.**—*n.* **violoncell'ist,** a player on the violoncello. [It., dim. of *violone,* a bass violin.]

VIP. Abbrev. for **very important person.**

viper, *vī'pér, n.* a genus of venomous snakes, once believed to be the only viviparous serpents: the common viper or adder, the only poisonous snake indigenous to Britain: any base, malicious person.—*adjs.* **vi'perish, vi'perous,** having the qualities of a viper: venomous, malignant. [Fr.,—L. *vīpera* (contr. of *vīvipara*)—*vīvus,* living, *parĕre,* to bring forth.]

virago, *vi-rā'gō,* or *vi-rä'gō, n.* a masculine woman: a bold, shrewish woman, a termagant. [L.,—*vir,* a man.]

virelay, *vir'e-lā, n.* ancient kinds of poem, esp. French, in short lines, often with only two rhymes to the stanza. [Fr. *virelai—virer,* to turn, *lai,* a song.]

virgin, *vûr'jin, n.* a maiden, a woman who has had no sexual intercourse with man: a person of either sex who has not known sexual intercourse: (*cap.*) **Virgo** (*vûr'gō*), one of the signs of the zodiac.—*adj.* (also **vir'ginal**) becoming a maiden, maidenly, pure, chaste, unsullied, undefiled: fresh, new, unused (e.g. *virgin soil*).—*n.* **virgin'ity,** the state of a virgin.—**the Virgin,** the Virgin Mary, the mother of Christ. [O.Fr.,—L. *virgō, virginis.*]

virginal, *vûr'jin-ál, n.* an old keyed musical instrument, oblong in shape, one of the three forms of harpsichord. [O.Fr.,—L. *virginālis —virgō, -inis,* a maiden. Perh. as played by young ladies.]

viridity, *vi-rid'i-ti, n.* greenness: freshness. [L. *viridis,* green—*virēre,* to be green.]

virile, *vir'īl,* or *-il, adj.* having the qualities of, or belonging to, a man or to the male sex: of a man, sexually potent: (of style, &c.) manly, forceful.—*n.* **viril'ity,** state or quality of being a man: the power of procreation: manhood: manly vigour. [L. *virīlis—vir,* a man.]

virtu, *vûr'tōō,* or *-tōō', n.* a love of the fine arts: taste for curiosities: objects of art or antiquity: the artistic quality they show.—*ns.* **virtuos'ity** (*-tū-*), exceptional technical skill in the fine arts; **virtuō'sō,** one skilled in the fine arts, in antiquities, curiosities, and the like: a skilful musician, painter, &c.:—*pl.* **virtuō'sōs, virtuō'sī.** [It.; a doublet of *virtue.*]

virtual. See **virtue.**

virtue, *vûr'tū, n.* worth: moral excellence: the practice of duty: a moral excellence: sexual purity, esp. female chastity: inherent power, efficacy.—*adj.* **vir'tual,** (*arch.*) having virtue or efficacy: in effect, though not in fact or strict definition.—*adv.* **vir'tually,** in effect, though not in fact: loosely, almost, nearly.—*adj.* **vir'tuous,** animated by virtue, obedient to the moral law (of person or action): chaste (of a woman): (*rare*) efficacious, potent.—*adv.* **vir'tuously.—by, in, virtue of,** through the power inherent in: on the ground of. [O.Fr.,—L. *virtūs,* bravery, moral excellence—*vir,* a man; cf. Gr. *hērōs,* Sans. *vīra,* a hero.]

virulent, *vir'ū-lent, adj.* full of poison: very active in injury, deadly: bitter in enmity, malignant.—*ns.* **vir'ulence, vir'ulency.**—*adv.* **vir'ulently.** [L. *vīrulentus—vīrus,* poison.]

virus, *vī'rus, n.* the smallest living organism capable of reproducing itself: the transmitted cause of infection: a disease agent which is capable of increasing rapidly inside a living cell: (*fig.*) anything that poisons mind or soul.—*n.* **virol'ogy,** the study of viruses and virus diseases.—**filterpassing** or **filterable virus, filter-passer,** terms used formerly for virus in sense of submicroscopic disease agent. [L. *vīrus*; cog. with Gr. *ios,* Sans. *visha,* poison.]

visa, *vēz'a, n.* an endorsement on a passport denoting that it has been officially examined, and that the bearer may proceed on his journey. [Fr.,—L.L. *visāre,* freq. of L. *vidēre, vīsum,* to see.]

visage, *viz'ij, n.* the face or look.—*adj.* **vis'aged.** [Fr.,—L. *vīsus,* seen—*vidēre,* to see.]

vis-à-vis, *vēz'-a-vē', adj.* face to face, opposite.— Also *adv.* and *prep.—n.* a person facing an-

---

Neutral vowels in unaccented syllables: *em'pér-ôr*; for certain sounds in foreign words see p. ix.

viscera   vitriol

other (e.g. *at table B. was his vis-á-vis*):
opposite number. [Fr.,—*vis* (L. *vīsus*; see
visage), face, à, to, *vis*, face.]

viscera, *vis'e-ra, n.pl.* the inner parts of the
animal body, the entrails:—*sing.* **viscus**
(*vis'kŭs*). [L. *viscera* pl., *viscus* sing.]

viscount, *vī'kownt, n.* an officer (the *vice-
comes*) who formerly acted as deputy to an
earl: a title of nobility next below an earl:—
fem. **viscountess** (*vī'kownt-es*). [O.Fr. *vis-
comte*—L. *vice*, in place of, *comes*, a companion. See **count**.]

viscous, *vis'kŭs, adj.* sticky, tenacious.—*n.* **vis-
cos'ity**, the property of being viscous: (*phys.*)
internal friction due to molecular cohesion in
fluids.—*adj.* **viscid** (*vis'id*), sticky, viscous.—
ns. **viscid'ity; viscose** (*vis'kōs*), a solution obtained by treating a certain salt of cellulose
with sodium hydroxide and dissolving in carbon disulphide—used in the manufacture of
rayon, &c. [L.L. *viscōsus*, sticky—L. *viscum*,
bird-lime, mistletoe; cog. with Gr. *ixos*, mistletoe.]

vise. See **vice** (1).

visé, *vē-zā', n.* Same as **visa**.

Vishnu, *vish'nōō, n.* 'the Preserver', who with
Brahma and Siva makes up the triad or trinity of Hindu gods; in his numerous avatars
(e.g. as Krishna) he showed himself the
friend and benefactor of men. [Sans. *Visnu.*]

visible, *viz'i-bl, adj.* that may be seen: obvious.—*ns.* **visibil'ity**, state or quality of being
visible, or perceivable by the eye: clearness of
the atmosphere: range of vision in the atmospheric conditions at a particular time;
vis'ibleness.—*adv.* **vis'ibly**. [L. *vīsibilis*—
vidēre, vīsum, to see.]

vision, *vizh'(ó)n, n.* the act or sense of seeing,
sight: anything seen: anything imagined to be
seen: a supernatural appearance, an apparition: anything imaginary: imaginative perception: foresight.—*adj.* **vis'ionary**, affected by
visions: imaginative: unpractical: existing in
imagination only, not real.—*n.* one who sees
visions: one who forms schemes that are impracticable or difficult to put into effect.
[Fr.,—L. *vīsiō, vīsiōnis*—*vidēre, vīsum,* to see.]

visit, *viz'it, v.t.* to go to see or inspect: to pay a
call upon: to go to see professio-
sionally: to enter, appear in: (*B.*) to punish, or
reward, bless: (*B.*) to punish or reward
(with): to afflict (with).—*v.i.* to be in the habit
of seeing or meeting each other at home.—*n.*
act of going to see.—*adj.* **vis'itant**, paying
visits, visiting.—*n.* one who visits.—*ns.* **visi-
tā'tion**, act of visiting: a formal visit by a superior: a dispensation of divine favour or displeasure; **vis'iting-card**, a small card bearing
the name and address, left in paying visits,
and sometimes sent as an act of courtesy or in
token of sympathy; **vis'itor**, one who visits,
calls on, or makes a stay with a person: a
person authorised to visit for purposes of inspection or supervision.—*adj.* **visitō'rial**, pertaining to an authorised visitor. [Fr. *visiter*—L.
vīsitāre, freq. of *vīsĕre,* to go to see, visit—
vidēre, to see.]

visor, *vīz'ŏr, n.* a part of a helmet covering the
face, movable, and with openings through
which the wearer can see: a mask: the peak of

a cap: a movable flap on a motorcar windscreen, used as a shade against the sun.—*adj.*
vis'ored, wearing a visor: masked. [Fr.
visière—*vis*, countenance.]

vista, *vis'ta, n.* a view or prospect through or as
through an avenue: the trees, &c., that form
the avenue. [It. *vista*, sight, view—L. *vidēre,* to
see.]

visual, *viz'ū-ál, adj.* belonging to vision or sight:
produced by sight: used in sight.—*v.t.* **vis'ual-
ise**, to make visible: to picture, call up a clear
mental image of.—Also *v.i.*—*n.* **visualisā'-
tion**.—*adv.* **vis'ually**.—**visual aid**, a picture,
photograph, film, diagram, &c., used as an aid
in teaching. [L. *vīsuālis*—*vidēre, vīsum,* to see.]

Vita glass, *vī'ta gläs,* (often, but incorrectly,
without *cap.*) trade-mark for a glass that
transmits ultraviolet light.

vital, *vī'tál, adj.* contributing to, or necessary to,
life: manifesting or containing life: fatal (e.g.
a vital wound): essential, in the highest degree important.—*v.t.* **vī'talīse**, to make alive, to
give life to: to animate, give vigour to (*lit.* and
fig.).—*ns.* **vītalisā'tion; vītal'ity**, quality of
being vital: capacity to endure and flourish.—
adv. **vī'tally**.—*n.pl.* **vī'tals**, the interior organs
essential for life: the part of any whole necessary for its existence.—**vital statistics**, statistics dealing with population, esp. the number
of births, deaths, and marriages: woman's
bust, waist, and hip measurements. [L.
vītālis—*vīta,* life—*vīvĕre,* to live; cog. with Gr.
bios, life.]

vitamin, *vī't'a-min, vit'a-min, n.* any one of numerous organic substances, present in minute
quantities in nutritive foods, which are essential for the health of the animal organism—
accessory food factors, named provisionally
Vitamin A, B, B$_2$, C, &c., but later given
names as their chemical nature was determined (e.g. Vitamin C—see **scurvy**—is known
as *ascorbic acid*). [Coined in 1906 from L.
vīta, life, and (inappropriately) Eng. *amine*
(which denotes a class of compounds formed
from ammonia).]

vitiate, *vish'i-āt, v.t.* to render faulty or defective: to make less pure, to deprave, to taint.—*n.*
vitiā'tion. [L. *vitiāre, -ātum*—*vitium.* See **vice**
(2).]

viticulture, *vit'i-kul-tyŭr, -chŭr, n.* cultivation of
the vine. [L. *vītis,* a vine, *colēre, cultum,* to
cultivate.]

vitreous, *vit'ri-ŭs, adj.* glassy: pertaining to, consisting of, or like glass.—*adj.* **vitres'cent**, tending to become glass.—*ns.* **vitres'cence, vitri-
fac'tion**.—*v.t.* **vit'rify**, to make into glass.—*v.i.*
to become glass.—*n.* **vitrificā'tion**, act, process,
or operation of converting into glass.—*adj.*
vit'rifiable, that may be vitrified or turned
into glass.—*ns.pl.* **vit'rified-forts, -walls**, certain ancient forts or walls in which the stone
appears to be vitrified by fire. [L. *vitrum,*
glass—*vidēre,* to see.]

vitriol, *vit'ri-ól, n.* the popular name of sulphuric
acid: a soluble sulphate of a metal—*green
vitriol* = sulphate of iron, *blue vitriol* = sulphate of copper, *white vitriol* = sulphate of
zinc.—*adj.* **vitriol'ic**, pertaining to or having
the qualities of vitriol: biting, scathing.
[Fr.,—Low L. *vitriolum*—L. *vitreus,* of glass.]

fāte, fär; mē, hûr (her); *mīne; mōte, fŏr; mūte; mōōn, fŏŏt;* ᴛʜᴇn (then)

vituperate   volition

vituperate, *vī-tū′pé-rāt,* or *vi- v.t.* to assail with abusive reproaches, revile.—*v.i.* to use abusive language.—*n.* **vitüperā′tion,** act of vituperating: censure, abuse.—*adj.* **vitü′perätive,** containing vituperation or censure.—*adv.* **vitü′perätively.** [L. *vituperāre,* *-ātum*—*vitium,* a fault, *parāre,* to prepare, furnish.]

vivace, *vē-vä′che, adj.* lively.—Also *adv.* [It.]

vivacious, *vī-vā′shŭs* (or *vi-*)*, adj.* lively or full of vitality, sportive—*adv.* **vivā′ciously.**—*ns.* **vivā′ciousness, vivacity** (*vi-vas′i-ti*), state of being vivacious: animation, liveliness or sprightliness of temper or behaviour. [L. *vīvax, vīvācis*—*vīvĕre,* to live.]

vivarium, *vī-vā′ri-ŭm, n.* an artificial enclosure for keeping or raising living animals, as a park, &c.[L. *vīvārium*—*vīvus,* alive—*vīvĕre,* to live.]

viva voce, *vī′va vō′sē, adv.* by word of mouth, orally.—Also *adj.*—*n.* (often **viva** alone) an oral examination:—*v.t.* (often **viva**) to examine orally. [L., with living voice—*vīvus,* living, *vox, vōcis,* voice.]

vive, *vēv,* long live. [Fr.]

vivid, *viv′id, adj.* lively or life-like, having the appearance of life: forming brilliant images (e.g. *a vivid imagination*): striking: intense.—*adv.* **viv′idly.**—*n.* **viv′idness.**—*v.t.* **viv′ify,** to make vivid, endue with life. [L. *vīvidus*—*vīvĕre,* to live.]

viviparous, *vī-vip′á-rus, adj.* producing young alive. [L., *vīvus,* alive, *parĕre,* to produce.]

vivisection, *viv-i-sek′sh(ŏ)n, n.* the practice of performing surgical operations on living animals, for the purposes of research or demonstration. [L. *vīvus,* alive, *sectiō, -ōnis*—*secāre,* to cut.]

vixen, *vik′sn, n.* a she-fox: an ill-tempered woman.—*adj.* **vix′enish,** ill-tempered, shrewish. [A form of *fixen* O.E. *fyxon,* a she-fox.]

viz., *viz, adv.* namely (usu. so read). [Contr. for *vidēlicet* L. *vidēre licet,* it is permissible to see.]

vizard, *viz′árd,* **vizor,** *vīz′ór.* Same as **visor.**

vizir, vizier, *vi-zēr′, viz′i-ér, n.* an oriental minister or councillor of state. [Ar. *wazīr,* a porter.]

vocable, *vō′ká-bl, n.* a word: a name.—*n.* **vocab′ulary,** a list of words explained in alphabetical order: the words of a language: any list of words: the words known to or used by a particular person (e.g. *his vocabulary is very limited*): the words used in a (particular) science or art: the signs or symbols used in any nonverbal type of communication, e.g. in computer technology. [L. *vocābulum*—*vocāre,* to call.]

vocal, *vō′kál, adj.* having a voice: uttered or modulated by the voice: talkative: having a vowel function.—*v.t.* **vō′calise,** to give utterance to: to form into voice, sing: to use as a vowel: (*phonet.*) to voice, make voiced.—*ns.* **vōcalisā′tion; vō′calist,** a vocal musician, a singer.—*adv.* **vō′cally.**—**vocal cords,** two elastic membranous folds of the larynx which vibrate and produce sound. [L. *vōcālis*—*vox, vōcis,* the voice.]

vocation, *vō-kā′sh(ŏ)n, n.* call or act of calling (e.g. to a religious mission): talent: calling, occupation.—*adj.* **vocā′tional,** pertaining to a trade or occupation: in preparation for a trade

or occupation: pertaining to the act of calling.—*n.* **vōc′ative,** the case of a word when a person or thing is addressed—also *adj.* [L. *vocātiō, -ōnis, vocātīvus*—*vocāre,* to call.]

vociferate, *vō-sif′e-rāt, v.i.* to cry with a loud voice.—*v.t.* to utter with a loud voice.—*n.* **vociferā′tion.**—*adj.* **vocif′erous,** making a loud outcry, noisy.—*adv.* **vocif′erously.** [L.,—*vox, vōcis,* voice, *ferre,* to carry.]

vodka, *vod′ka, n.* a Russian spirit, properly distilled from rye, but sometimes from potatoes. [Russ., 'brandy', dim. of *voda,* water.]

vogue, *vōg, n.* the prevalent mode or fashion: prevalency, popularity. [Fr. *vogue,* course of a ship—*voguer,* to row, from O.H.G.]

voice, *vois, n.* sound from the mouth: sound given out by anything: power of, or mode of, utterance: medium of expression: expressed opinion, vote: mode of inflecting verbs, as being active, passive or middle.—*v.t.* to give utterance to: to regulate the tone of (organ pipes): to utter with voice, as distinguished from breath only (e.g. as *b, d, v,* TH, in contrast to *p, t, f, th*). *adj.* **voice′less,** having no voice, having no vote: (*phonet.*) not voiced.—**in voice,** in good condition for singing or speaking; **give voice to,** to express. [Fr. *voix*—L. *vox, vōcis.*]

void, *void, adj.* unoccupied, empty: not valid or binding: nullified: lacking in (with *of*).—*n.* an empty space.—*v.t.* to make vacant: to quit: to emit: to render of no effect, to nullify.—*adj.* **void′able,** that may be voided or evacuated.—*n.* **void′ance,** act of voiding or emptying: state of being void: ejection. [O.Fr. *voide, void.*]

voile, *voil, n.* a thin semi-transparent dress material. [Fr., veil.]

volant, *vō′lánt, adj.* flying, able to fly: nimble.—*adj.* **vōl′atile,** evaporating very quickly: gay or capricious in emotion.—*ns.* **vol′atileness, volatil′ity,** quality of being volatile: tendency to evaporate rapidly: sprightliness: fickleness.—*v.t.* **vol′atilise** (ŏr *-āt-*), to make volatile, to cause to evaporate. *n.* **volatilisā′tion.**—**volatile oils** (see **essential oils**). [Fr.,—L. *volans, -antis,* pr.p. of *volāre,* to fly.]

Volapük, *vō-la-pük′, n.* a language devised by a German in 1879 for international use, but not generally adopted (cf. **Esperanto**). [Lit. 'world-speech'—*vol,* shortened from Eng. *world, pük,* for Eng. *speak.*]

volcano, *vol-kā′no, n.* a conical hill or mountain with a crater on the summit, from which issue hot vapours and gases, and streams of molten rock: (*fig.*) a state suggestive of a volcano because an upheaval or outburst seems imminent.—*adj.* **volcan′ic,** pertaining to, produced or affected by, a volcano. [It. *volcano*—L. *Volcānus, Vulcānus,* god of fire.]

vole, *vōl, n.* a subfamily of rodent quadrupeds of the same family as rats and mice, including the **bank vole,** also called the *red field mouse,* the **field vole,** called the *short-tailed field mouse* and the **water vole,** often known as the *water rat.* [For *vole-mouse,* field-mouse; *vole* from the same root as **wold.**]

volitant, *vol′i-tánt, adj.* having the power of flight, volant. [L. *volitāre, -ātum,* freq. of *volāre,* to fly.]

volition, *vō-li′sh(ŏ)n, n.* act of willing or choos-

Neutral vowels in unaccented syllables: *em′pér-ór*; for certain sounds in foreign words see p. ix.

ing, the exercise of the will: the power of determining. [Low L. *volitō*—L. *volo, velle*, to will, be willing.]

volkslied, *folks′lēt, n.* a folk-song. [Ger.]

volley, *vol′i, n.* a flight of missiles: the discharge of many missiles or small-arms at once: a vehement outburst: (*tennis, cricket*, &c.) a hard stroke to return the ball before it reaches the ground:—*pl.* **voll′eys.**—*v.t.* to discharge in a volley: to return (a ball) before it bounces.—*v.i.* to fly in a volley, as missiles: to sound loudly, as firearms. [Fr. *volée*, a flight—*voler*—L. *volare*, to fly.]

volt, *vŏlt, n.* (*fencing*) a sudden movement or leap to avoid a thrust: the gait of a horse going sideways round a centre.—Also **volte.** [Fr. *volte*—It. *volta*—L. *volvĕre*; see **voluble.**]

volt, *vōlt, n.* the SI unit of potential difference.—*n.* **vōl′tage,** potential difference reckoned in volts.—*adj.* **voltā′ic,** pertaining to Alessandro *Volta* (1745-1827), who developed the theory of current electricity, or to his discoveries and inventions.—*n.* **vŏlt′meter,** an instrument for measuring potential difference directly, calibrated in volts.—**voltaic electricity,** current electricity, galvanism.

volte-face, *volt-fas, n.* a turning round: (*fig.*) a sudden and complete change in opinion or in views expressed. [Fr.]

voluble, *vol′ū-bl, adj.* (*orig.*) easy to roll or move: overwhelmingly fluent in speech.—*n.* **volubil′ity,** excessive fluency of speech.—*adv.* **vol′ubly.** [L. *volūbilis*—*volvĕre, volūtum*, to roll, turn.]

volume, *vol′ūm, n.* a roll or scroll of papyrus or the like, on which ancient books were written: any book: cubical content: dimensions: fullness (of voice or other sound).—*adjs.* **volumet′ric, -al,** pertaining to the measurement of volume; **volū′minous,** consisting of many volumes or books: of great bulk: copious: producing many books, as an author.—*adv.* **volū′minously.**—*n.* **volū′minousness.—speak, tell, volumes,** to signify much. [Fr.,—L. *volūmen*, a roll—*volvĕre, volūtum*, to roll.]

voluntary, *vol′un-ta-ri, adj.* acting by choice: proceeding from the will: subject to the will: done by design or without compulsion: brought about by, proceeding from, free action.—*n.* one who does anything of his own free-will: a piece of music to be played at will on a church organ: an upholder of voluntaryism.—*adv.* **vol′untarily.**—*ns.* **vol′untariness; vol′untaryism,** the system of maintaining the Church by voluntary offerings without the aid of the State.—**voluntary school,** a school built mainly by voluntary contributions, in England now called a 'non-provided' school—i.e. not provided by the local authority. [L. *voluntārius*—*voluntās*, choice—*volo*, I am willing.]

volunteer, *vol-un-ter′, n.* one who enters any service, or undertakes any task, esp. military, voluntarily.—*adj.* entering into service voluntarily.—*v.t.* to offer voluntarily.—*v.i.* to enter into any service of one's own free-will or without being asked. [Fr. *volontaire*—L. *voluntārius.* See **voluntary.**]

voluptuary, *vo-lup′tū-ā-ri, n.* a person excessively given to bodily enjoyments or luxury, a sensualist.—*adj.* **volup′tuous,** inducing, or

filled with, pleasure: given to excess of pleasure, esp. sensual.—*adv.* **volup′tuously.**—*n.* **volup′tuousness.** [L. *voluptuārius, voluptuōsus*—*voluptās*, pleasure.]

volute, *vo-lūt′, n.* in Greek architecture, a spiral scroll used in capitals: a kind of spiral shell, chiefly tropical: whorl of a spiral shell.—*adj.* (*bot.*) rolled up in any direction.—*adj.* **volū′ted,** having a volute.—*n.* **volū′tion,** a convolution: a whorl. [Fr.,—L. *volvĕre, volūtum*, to roll.]

vomit, *vom′it, v.i.* to throw up the contents of the stomach by the mouth, to spew.—*v.t.* to throw out with violence.—*n.* matter ejected from the stomach: something that excites vomiting.—*adj.* **vom′itory,** causing to vomit.—*n.* a vomit or emetic: (*hist.*) a door of a large building by which the crowd is let out. [L. *vomĕre, -itum*, to throw up; Gr. *emein.*]

voodoo, voudou, *vōō′dōō, -dōō′, n.* in the southern U.S. one who practises witchcraft, especially when tinctured with African rites or superstitions: the supreme evil spirit of the voodoos.—*n.* **voo′dooism** (or *doo′*), voodoo superstitions. [Creole (q.v.) Fr. *vaudoux*, a Negro sorcerer.]

voracious, *vo-rā′shus, adj.* eager to devour: very greedy.—*adv.* **vorā′ciously.**—*n.* **vorac′ity** (-*as′*). [L. *vorax, vorācis*—*vorāre*, to devour.]

vortex, *vor′teks, n.* a whirling motion of a fluid forming a cavity in the centre—a whirlpool, a whirlwind: (*fig.*) a pursuit, way of life, &c., which, by its attraction or power, irresistibly engulfs one, taking up all one's attention or energies:—*pl.* **vor′tices** (-*tis-ēz*), **vor′texes.**—*adj.* **vor′tical,** whirling.—*ns.* **vor′ticism** (-*ti-sizm*), a British movement in painting, a development from futurism, blending cubism and expressionism; **vor′ticist.** [L. *vortex, vertox*—*vortĕre, vertĕre*, to turn.]

votary, *vō′ta-ri, adj.* bound or consecrated by a vow.—*n.* one devoted as by a vow to some service, worship, or way of life: one enthusiastically addicted to a pursuit, study, &c.:—*fem.* **vō′taress.** [L.L. *votārius*—L. *vōtum*, a vow.]

vote, *vōt, n.* expression of a wish or opinion as to a matter on which one has a right to be consulted: the token by which a choice is expressed, as a ballot: decision by a majority: something granted by the will of the majority.—*v.i.* to express choice by a vote.—*v.t.* to resolve (that), express a desire (that): (*coll.*) to suggest (that): to pronounce, adjudge to be (e.g. *it was voted a great success*): to grant by a vote: to bring about a result by voting (e.g. *they had voted him into power*).—*n.* **vo′ter.**—**vote in,** to elect. [L. *vōtum*, a vow, wish—*vovēre, vōtum*, to vow.]

votive, *vō′tiv, adj.* given by vow: vowed.—*adv.* **vō′tively.** [L. *vōtīvus*—*vōtum*, a vow, wish.]

vouch, *vowch, v.t.* (*arch.*) to call upon to witness: to maintain by repeated affirmations, to warrant.—*v.i.* to bear witness (for), answer (for).—*n.* **vouch′er,** one who vouches or gives witness: a paper that vouches or confirms the truth of anything, as of accounts, or that money has been paid. [O.Fr. *voucher, vocher*, to call to defend—L. *vocāre*, to call.]

vouchsafe, *vowch-sāf′, v.t.* to condescend to grant (e.g. a reply): to condescend (to).—*v.i.* to condescend. [**vouch, safe.**]

vow, *vow, n.* a voluntary promise solemnly made to God: a solemn or formal promise.—*v.t.* to give by solemn promise: to devote: to threaten solemnly (e.g. vengeance): to maintain solemnly (e.g. *he vowed he had done so*). [O.Fr. *vou* (Fr. *vœu*)—L. *vōtum*—*vovēre,* to vow.]

vowel, *vow′él, n.* a simple vocal sound produced by continuous passage of the breath: a letter representing such a sound, as *a, e, i, o, u* (in English, each of these letters is used to represent more than one vowel sound).—*adj.* vocal: pertaining to a vowel. [Fr. *voyelle*—L. *vōcālis*—*vox, vōcis,* the voice.]

vox, *voks, n.* voice.—**vox humana,** in organ-building, a reed-stop producing tones resembling those of the human voice. [L.]

voyage, *voi′ij, n.* a journey, esp. a passage by water or by air.—*v.i.* to make a voyage.—*n.* **voy′ager.**—*n.pl.* **voyageurs** (*vwä-ya-zhœr′*), name given to the boatmen who kept up communication between the trading stations on the rivers and lakes of Canada. [Fr.,—L. *viāticum,* travelling-money—L. *via,* a way.]

voyeur, *vwä-yœr, n.* a sexual pervert who derives pleasure from secretly watching sexual acts or objects: a peeping Tom. [Fr., one who sees.]

vulcanise, *vul′kan-īz, v.t.* to combine with sulphur by heat, as rubber.—*n.* **vul′canite,** vulcanised rubber. [L. *Vulcānus,* Vulcan, the Roman god of fire.]

vulgar, *vul′går, adj.* pertaining to the common people: vernacular (*the vulgar tongue*): public: common, usual: prevalent: low, unrefined: coarse.—*v.t.* **vul′garise,** to make vulgar.—*ns.*

vul′garism, a vulgar phrase: coarseness; **vulgar′ity,** quality of being vulgar: crudity of manner or language: an instance of this.—*adv.* **vul′garly.**—*n.* **Vul′gate,** an ancient Latin version of the Scriptures, made by St Jerome and others in the 4th century, and later twice revised—so called from its common use in the R.C. Church.—**vulgar fraction,** a common, as distinguished from a decimal, fraction.—**the vulgar,** the common people. [L. *vulgāris*—*vulgus,* the people.]

vulnerable, *vul′né-ra-bl, adj.* capable of being wounded, liable to injury or hurt (*lit.* and *fig.*): exposed to attack: (*contract bridge*—of a side that has won a game) liable to have doubled the points scored against it.—*ns.* **vulnerabil′ity, vul′nerableness.**—*adj.* **vul′nerary,** useful in healing wounds.—Also *n.* [L. *vulnerābilis*—*vulnerāre,* to wound—*vulnus, vulneris,* a wound.]

vulpine, *vul′pin, vul′pīn, adj.* relating to or like the fox: cunning. [L. *vulpes,* a fox.]

vulture, *vul′tyur, -chŭr, n.* any of a number of large rapacious birds of prey, temperate and tropical, living chiefly or entirely on carrion, constituting two families and allied to the hawks and eagles: one who or that which resembles or behaves like a vulture.—*adjs.* **vul′tūrine, vul′tūrish,** like the vulture: rapacious. [O.Fr. *voutour*—L. *vultur;* perh. from *vellēre,* to pluck, to tear.]

vulva, *vul′va, n.* the external genital opening of a female mammal. [L. *volva, vulva,* integument, womb.]

vying, *vī′ing, pr.p.* of **vie.**

Neutral vowels in unaccented syllables: *em′pér-ór*; for certain sounds in foreign words see p. ix.

W

Waaf, *waf, n.* (a member of) the Women's Auxiliary (earlier and later Royal) Air Force.

wad, *wod, n.* a pad of loose material, as hay, tow, &c., thrust in to aid packing, &c.: formerly a little mass of paper, tow, or the like, now a disk of felt or paper, to keep the charge in a gun: a bundle (of bank notes).—*v.t.* to form into a wad: to pad, stuff out: to stuff a wad into:—*pr.p.* **wadd′ing;** *pa.t.* and *pa.p.* **wadd′ed.**—*n.* **wadd′ing,** a wad: materials for wads: a soft stuff, as sheets of carded (see **card** (2)) cotton, for stuffing garments, &c.: cotton-wool. [Cf. Swed. *vadd,* wadding; Ger. *watte.*]

waddle, *wod′l, v.i.* to take short steps and move from side to side in walking.—*n.* a clumsy, rocking gait. *n.* **wadd′ler.** [Perh. freq. of **wade.**]

wade, *wād, v.i.* to walk through any substance that yields to the feet, as water: to pass (through) with difficulty or labour (*lit.* and *fig.*).—*v.t.* to cross by wading.—*n.* **wa′der,** one who wades: a bird that wades, e.g. the heron: (*pl.*) high waterproof boots used by anglers. [O.E. *wadan,* to move; Ger. *waten.*]

wadi, wady, *wod′i, n.* the dry bed of a torrent. [Ar. *wādī,* a ravine (Sp. *guad-,* first syllable of many river-names).]

wafer, *wā′fėr, n.* a thin crisp biscuit: a thin round cake of unleavened bread, used in the Eucharist: a thin leaf of coloured paste for sealing letters, &c.—*v.t.* to close with a wafer. [O Fr *waufre* (Fr.*gaufre*)—Old Du. *waefel,* a cake of wax; Ger. *wabe,* a honeycomb.]

waffle, *wof′l, n.* a kind of batter-cake cooked in a **waff′le-iron,** a metal utensil with hinged halves having projecting studs on the insides. [Du. *wafel,* wafer.]

waffle, *wof′l, v.i.* (*coll.*) to talk incessantly or nonsensically: to waver, vacillate.—Also *n.*

waft, *wäft, v.t.* to bear lightly through a fluid medium, as air or water.—*v.i.* to float or drift lightly.—*n.* a signal made by moving something in the air, esp. a flag: a breath, puff, slight odour. [From the same root as **wave.**]

wag, *wag, v.t.* and *v.i.* to move from side to side, to shake to and fro or up and down:—*pr.p.* **wagg′ing;** *pa.t.* and *pa.p.* **wagged.**—*n.* a single wagging movement. [O.E. *wagian,* to wag, *wegan,* to carry, move; conn. with **weigh** and **wagon.**]

wag, *wag, n.* a droll, mischievous fellow, a habitual joker, a wit.—*n.* **wagg′ery,** mischievous merriment.—*adj.* **wagg′ish,** characteristic of a wag: roguish.—*adv.* **wagg′ishly.**—*n.* **wagg′ishness.** [Prob. Eng. (*obs.*) *waghalter,* one who deserves hanging.]

wage, *wāj, v.t.* (*arch.*) to pledge: to carry on (esp. war).—*n.* (*obs.*) a gage or stake: payment for work, wages.—*n.pl.* **wā′ges** (also used as *sing.*), that which is paid for services.—*n.*

wā′ger, (*obs.*) a pledge: something staked on the issue of anything, a bet: that on which bets are laid: (*law*) an offer to make oath.—*v.t.* to hazard on the issue of anything.—*v.i.* to lay a wager.—*n.* **wage′-freeze,** a fixing of wages at a certain level for some time ahead. [O.Fr. *wager* (Fr. *gager*), to pledge. A doublet of **gage.**]

waggle, *wag′l, v.i.* and *v.t.* to wag, esp. in an uncertain or unrhythmical way. [Freq. of **wag** (1).]

Wagnerian, *väg-nē′ri-àn, adj.* pertaining to, or characterised by, the ideas or style of Richard *Wagner* (1813–83), German composer of operas.—*n.* **Wag′nerite,** an adherent of Wagner's musical methods, or an admirer of his work.

wagon, waggon, *wag′òn, n.* a four-wheeled vehicle for carrying heavy goods: an open railway truck or a closed railway van.—*ns.* **wag′oner, wagg′oner,** one who drives a wagon; **wagonette′,** a kind of open carriage with one or two seats crosswise in front and two back seats arranged lengthwise and facing inwards. [Du. *wagen;* O.E. *wægn;* cf. **wain.**]

wagtail, *wag′tāl, n.* any of numerous small birds of a family that also includes the pipits; they have very long tails which they constantly move up and down. [wag (1), **tail.**]

waif, *wāf, n.* (*law*) anything found astray without an owner: a homeless wanderer, esp. a child without guardians.—**waifs and strays,** homeless destitute persons [O Fr *waif, wef*—O.N. *veif,* any flapping or waving thing.]

wail, *wāl, v.i.* to lament or sorrow audibly.—*v.t.* to bemoan, to grieve over.—*n.* a cry of woe: loud weeping.—*n.* **wail′ing.**—*adv.* **wailingly.** [M.E. *weilen*—O.N. *vaela, väla,* to wail—*væ, vei,* woe.]

wain, *wān, n.* a wagon. [O.E. *wægen, wæn—wegen,* to carry; Ger. *wagen,* L. *vehère.*]

wainscot, *wān′skôt, n.* a wooden lining, usually panelled, applied to the walls of rooms.—*v.t.* to line with, or as if with, boards or panels.—*n.* **wain′scoting, wain′scotting,** the act of lining with boards or panels: materials for making a wainscot. [App. Du. *wagenschot,* oakwood, beechwood.]

waist, *wāst, n.* the smallest part of the human trunk, between the ribs and the hips: the middle part, as of a ship.—*ns.* **waist′band,** the band or part of a garment that encircles the waist; **waist′coat** (also, esp. formerly, *wes′két*), a short coat, usu. sleeveless, worn immediately under the coat, and fitting the waist tightly.—*adj.* **waist′ed,** having a waist, often of specified type.—*n.* **waist′line,** a line thought of as marking the waist: the measurement of a waist. [M.E. *wast;* conn. with O.E. *wæstm,* growth, *weaxan,* to grow.]

wait, *wāt, v.i.* to stay, or to be, in expectation (often with *for*): to tarry, remain: to attend (with *on*).—*v.t.* to stay for, to await: to serve, as a waiter or waitress (*to wait table*).—*n.* ambush, now used only in such phrases as **to lie in wait, to lay wait:** delay: (*pl.*) itinerant musicians who welcome Christmas.—*ns.* **wait′er,** one who waits: an attending servant, now usu. one who serves at table: a salver or tray; **wait′ing-list, wait′-list,** a list of people waiting for something, as a list of candidates awaiting a vacancy; **wait′ing-room,** a room for the convenience of persons waiting; **wait′ress,** a female waiter.—**wait upon, on,** to pay a formal visit to: to serve as attendant to: to serve (a person) at table: to follow as a consequence. [O.Fr. *waiter* (Fr.*guetter*), to watch, attend—O.H.G. *wahta* (Ger. *wacht*), a watch-man.]

waive, *wāv, v.t.* to give up, not insist upon (e.g. a claim, a right): (*law*) to relinquish voluntarily: to neglect, disregard (e.g. an opportunity, scruples). [O.Fr. *guever,* to refuse, resign, perh.—O.N. *veifa,* to move to and fro; cf. L. *vibrāre.*]

wake, *wāk, v.i.* to cease from sleep: to be awake: to be roused up, active, or vigilant.—*v.t.* to rouse from sleep: to revive: to reanimate:—*pa.t.* waked (*wākt*) or woke (*wōk*), pa.p. waked, wo′ken, (*rare*) woke.—*n.* (*obs.*) act of waking: feast of the dedication of a church, formerly kept by watching all night: a watch or vigil beside a corpse, sometimes with revelry: annual holiday (North of England).—*adj.* **wake′ful,** not asleep: indisposed to sleep: vigilant.—*adv.* **wake′fully.**—*n.* **wake′fulness.** —*v.t.* and *v.i.* **wā′ken,** to wake or awake: to be awake.—**wake up to,** to become conscious of, alive to. [O.E. has verbs *wacan,* to be born, *wacian, wæcnan, wæcnian,* to waken.]

wake, *wāk, n.* the streak of smooth-looking or foamy water left in the track of a ship: hence (*fig.*) **in the wake of,** in the train of, immediately after. [Cf. O.N. *vök,* a hole in the ice, *vökr,* moist. The root is seen in L. *humēre,* to be moist, Gr. *hygros,* moist.]

wale,*wāl, n.* a ridge on the surface of cloth: **weal:** (*pl.*) planks along the outer timbers of ships.— *v.t.* to make or furnish with wales. [O.E. *walu,* the mark of a stripe; O.N. *völr,* a rod.]

walk, *wök, v.i.* to move along on foot with alternate steps: to travel on foot: (of animals) to move with slow gait: to go: to conduct oneself, behave.—*v.t.* to pass through or upon: to pace: to cause to walk.—*n.* act of walking: gait: distance walked over: place for walking, path, &c.: regular beat: high pasture ground: conduct: sphere of action (**walk of life**).—*adv.* **walk′about,** (orig. *Austr. slang*) on the move. —*n.* a journey, a walk around.—*ns.* **walk′er;** **walk′ie-talk′ie,** wireless set for sending out and receiving messages, carried on the person; **walk′ing-stick, -cane, -staff,** a stick, cane, or staff used in walking; **walk′-out,** the act of leaving, usu. as a gesture of disapproval: a sudden industrial strike; **walk′-ŏ′ver,** a race where only one competitor appears and wins the prize by walking over the course, or where one competitor far excels the others: an easy victory; **walk′way,** road, path, &c., constructed for pedestrians only.—**walk away with,** to win with ease; **walk into** (*coll.*), to beat: to storm

at: to eat heartily of; **walk out with,** to take a walk with as a stage of courtship.—**charity walk, sponsored walk,** an organised walk undertaken in aid of charity, sponsors paying a certain amount of money according to distance covered by the participators. [O.E. *wealcan,* to roll, turn.]

wall, *wöl, n.* an erection of brick, stone, &c. for a fence or security: the side of a building: (*fig.*) a defence, means of security: (*pl.*) fortifications.—*v.t.* to enclose with, or as with, a wall: to defend with walls.—*ns.* **wall′flower,** a plant of the *Cruciferae,* with fragrant flowers, yellow when wild, found on old walls: any other plant of the same genus: (*coll.*) a person who remains a spectator at a dance, usu. a woman who cannot obtain partners; **wall′-pā′per,** paper, usually coloured or decorated, for pasting on the walls of a room.—**go to the wall,** to be hard pressed: to be forced to give way: to fail, go under; **turn one's face to the wall,** to resign oneself to death or despair; **up the wall,** (*coll.*) mad, distracted; **with one's back to the wall,** in desperate straits, at bay. [O.E. *weall, wall*; Ger. *wall,* both from L. *vallum,* a rampart.]

wallaby, *wol′ab-i, n.* any of various small kangaroos. [From Australian native name.]

wallah, *wol′a, n.* (often in combination) one employed in, or concerned with, a specific type of work: one who occupies an eminent position in an organisation, &c. [Hindi -*wālā.*]

wallaroo, *wol-å-rōō′, n.* a name for various kinds of large kangaroos. [From Australian native name.]

wallet, *wol′ét, n.* a bag for carrying necessaries (*arch.* personal necessaries on a journey): a pocket-book. [M.E. *walet,* possibly from *watel,* a bag.]

wall-eye, *wöl′-ī, n.* an eye in which the white part is very large: the popular name for the disease of the eye called glaucoma (*glö-kō′-ma*).—*adj.* **wall′-eyed,** very light grey in the eyes, esp. of horses: squinting outwards: staring-eyed. [The adj. is the earlier, prob. from O.N. *vagleygr*—*vagl,* a disease of the eye, and *eygr,* eyed—*auga,* an eye.]

Walloon, *wal-ōōn′, adj.* of or pertaining to a population of mixed Celtic and Romanic stock akin to the French, occupying the tract along the frontiers of France and Belgium.—*n.* a native or inhabitant of that region: the language of the Walloons, a popular dialect of northern French, with a considerable infusion both of Old Celtic and Low German elements. [O.Fr. *Wallon*; cog. with **Welsh.**]

wallop, *wol′op, v.t.* (*slang*) to beat, flog.—*n.* a blow. [Orig. uncertain.]

wallow, *wol′ō, v.i.* (*lit.* and *fig.*) to roll about in mud, &c., as an animal (implying enjoyment): (in a bad sense) to live in filth or gross vice. [O.E. *wealwian*—L. *volvĕre.*]

Wall Street, *wöl strēt,* a street in New York, the chief financial centre in the United States: hence American financial interests.

walnut, *wöl′nut, n.* a genus, comprising seven or eight species of beautiful trees, the wood of which is much used for furniture: its nut or fruit. [O.E. *wealh,* foreign, *hnut,* a nut.]

walrus, *wöl′rus,* or *wol′-, n.* a large aquatic ani-

Neutral vowels in unaccented syllables: *em′pér-ŏr*; for certain sounds in foreign words see p. ix.

mal, allied to the seals, having long canine teeth—also called the *morse* or the *seahorse*. [Du.,—Swed. *vallross* (O.N. *hross-hvalr*)—*vall*, a whale, O.N. *hross*, a horse.]

waltz, *wöl(t)s*, *n.* a whirling or slowly circling dance performed by couples: music for such: a piece of instrumental music in triple time.— *v.i.* to dance a waltz.—*v.i.* and *v.t.* to move as in a waltz. [Ger. *walzer*—*walzen*, to roll.]

wampum, *wom'pum*, *n.* the North American Indian name for shells or beads used as money.

wan, *won*, *adj.* faint, wanting colour, dark, pale and sickly: languid: (*arch.*) gloomy.—*adv.* **wan'ly.**—*n.* **wan'ness.** [O.E. *wann*, dark, lurid.]

wand, *wond*, *n.* a long slender rod: a rod of authority, or of conjurers. [O.N. *vöndr*, a shoot of a tree.]

wander, *won'dèr*, *v.i.* to ramble with no definite object: (*lit.* or *fig.*) to go astray: to leave home: to depart from the subject: to be delirious: (*coll.*) to lose one's way.—*v.t.* to traverse: (*coll.*) to lead astray.—*n.* **wan'derer.**—**Wandering Jew**, a legendary Jew who must wander till the Day of Judgment, for an insult offered to Christ on the way to the Crucifixion. [O.E. *wandrian*; Ger. *wandern*; allied to **wend**, and to **wind** (*wind*).]

wanderlust, *won'dèr-lust*, *vän'der-lŏost*, *n.* a craving for change of place, thirst for travel. [Ger.]

wane, *wān*, *v.i.* to decrease, esp. of the moon— opp. to *wax*: to decline, to fail.—*n.* decline, decrease. [O.E. *wanian* (O.N. *vana*), to decrease—*wan*, deficient, lacking.]

wangle, *wang'gl*, (*coll.*) *v.t.* and *v.i.* to achieve (something) by trickery.—Also *n.*

want, *wont*, *n.* state of privation: lack of what is needful or desired: poverty: scarcity: need.— *v.t.* to be destitute of: to lack: to feel need of: to wish for.—*v.i.* (*arch.*) to be deficient or lacking: to be in need: to be without something desired or necessary (e.g. *never to want for help*).—*adjs.* **want'ed**, sought after: desired; **want'ing**, absent: deficient. [Scand., O.N. *vant*, neut. of *vanr*, lacking; cog. with **wane.**]

wanton, *won'ton*, *adj.* sportive: licentious: wilful: running to excess, or unrestrained (e.g. of vegetation): motiveless (e.g. destruction): unprovoked (e.g. an assault).—*n.* a wanton or lewd person, esp. a female.—*v.i.* to frolic: to play lasciviously.—*adv.* **wan'tonly.**—*n.* **wan'tonness.** [M.E. *wantowen*, from pfx. *wan-*, signifying want, O.E. *togen*, educated, pa.p. of *tēon*, to draw, lead.]

wapenshaw, *wap'n-shö*, *n.* in ancient Scottish usage, a periodical review of the people within an area for the purpose of seeing that each man was armed in accordance with his rank. [Lit. 'weapon-show'.]

wapentake, *wap'n-tāk*, *n.* a name given in Yorkshire to the territorial divisions of the county (similar to the *hundreds* of southern counties), so called from the inhabitants being formerly taught the use of arms. [O.E. *wæpen-getæc*, lit. 'weapon-taking'.]

wapiti, *wop'i-ti*, *n.* the North American elk. [N. American Indian.]

war, *wör*, *n.* a state of opposition or contest: a contest between states carried on by arms: open hostility: the profession of arms.—*v.i.* to

make war: to contend, fight (against):—*pr.p.* **warr'ing**; *pa.t.* and *pa.p.* **warred.**—*ns.* **war'crime**, crime associated with war, esp. one that violates the code of war; **war'-cry**, a cry or signal used in war; **war'-dance**, a dance engaged in by some savage tribes before going to war; **war'fare**, armed contest, hostilities: conflict, struggle; **war'-head**, section of torpedo, or other missile, containing the explosive; **war'-horse**, horse used in battle.—*adj.* **war'like**, fond of war: pertaining to or threatening war: martial, military.—*ns.* **war-monger** (*wör'-mung-gèr*), one who encourages war, esp. for personal gain; **war neurosis**, a better term for shell shock; **War Office**, the British military Department of State, since 1964 absorbed in the Ministry of Defence; **war'-paint**, paint applied to the face and person by savages, indicating that they are going to war: (*slang*) full-dress; **war'-path**, the path followed on a Red Indian military expedition: the expedition itself: also *fig.*; **warr'ior**, a veteran soldier: a fighting man: a redoubtable person; **war'ship**, a vessel for war; **war'time**, time of war (also *adj.*).—**war of nerves**, systematic attempts to undermine morale by means of threats, rumours, and counter-rumours, &c.—**cold war**, an intense and remorseless struggle for the upper hand by all means short of actual fighting. [O.E. *werre*, influenced by O.Fr. *werre* (Fr. *guerre*), which is from O.H.G. *werra*, quarrel.]

warble, *wör'bl*, *v.i.* to sing in a quavering way, or with variations: to sing sweetly as birds do.— Also *v.t.*—*n.* a quavering modulation of the voice: a song.—*n.* **war'bler**, a songster: a singing-bird: any of various kinds of small birds, not all fine singers, e.g. the **reed-warbler** (q.v.). [O. Norman Fr. *werbler*— O.Fr. *guerbler*; of Gmc. origin.]

ward, *wörd*, *v.t.* to guard or take care of: to keep away, fend off (with *off*).—*n.* act of warding: state of being guarded: means of guarding: one who is under a guardian: a division of a city: a room with several beds in a hospital, &c.: a part of a lock of special configuration to prevent its being turned by any except a particular key, or the part of the key of corresponding configuration: (*B.*) guard, prison. —*ns.* **ward'en**, one who wards or guards: a keeper, especially a public officer appointed for the naval or military protection of some particular district of country: the head of certain institutions, as colleges, hostels, &c.: one appointed for duties among the civil population in cases of fire or air-raids or to control traffic circulation and parking of motor vehicles; **ward'er**, one who guards, esp. (formerly) one in charge of prisoners:—*fem.* **ward'ress**; **ward'robe**, a cupboard or piece of furniture for clothes: wearing apparel; **ward'-room**, a room used as a messroom by the officers of a warship; **ward'ship**, the office of a ward or guardian: state of being under a guardian.—**Ward in Chancery**, a minor under the protection of the Court of Chancery (q.v.). [O.E. *weardian*; Ger. *warten*, to watch in order to protect; doublet of **guard.**]

Wardour Street English, *wör'dòr strēt ing'glish*, sham-antique diction. [*Wardour Street*, Lond-

fāte, fär; mē, hûr (her); *mīne, mōte, för; mūte, mōōn, fŏŏt;* тнen (then) on, once noted for antique and sham-antique furniture, now for entertainment business.]

ware, *wār, n.* manufactured articles, esp. earthenware: (*pl.*) merchandise, commodities, goods.—*n.* ware′house, a house or store for wares or goods.—*v.t.* to deposit in a warehouse. [O.E. *waru*; Ger. *ware.*]

ware, *wār, adj.* aware. [See **wary.**]

ware, *wār,* in *B. pa.t.* of **wear.**

warily, wariness. See **wary.**

warlock, *wŏr′lok, n.* a sorcerer, a wizard. [O.E. *wærloga,* a breaker of an agreement—*wǣr,* a compact, *lēogan,* to lie.]

warm, *wŏrm, adj.* having moderate heat, hot: violent: zealous, enthusiastic, ardent: excited: angry: having a warm colour (see below).—*v.t.* to make warm: to interest: to excite.—*v.i.* to become warm or ardent.—*n.* war′ming-pan, (*hist.*) covered pan, with long handle, for holding live coals to warm a bed.—*adv.* warm′ly.—*ns.* warm′ness, warmth, moderate heat: geniality: earnestness: growing anger: the bright effect of warm colours.—*adj.* warm′-blood′ed, having body temperature constantly maintained at a point usually above the environmental temperature: generous, passionate.—*n.* war′mer.—*adj.* warm′-heart′ed, having warm affections: affectionate: hearty.—*n.* warm′-up, a practice exercise before an event.—**warm colour** (*paint*), any colour of which the basis is yellow or red; **warm front,** the advancing front of a mass of warm air. [O.E. *wearm*; Ger. *warm.*]

warn, *wŏrn, v.t.* to give notice of danger to: to caution (against): to admonish.—*v.i.* to give warning (that).—*ns.* war′ner; war′ning, caution against danger, &c.: admonition: previous notice.—**warn off,** to advise, instruct to go, keep away. [O.E. *warnian*; cf. O.N. *varna,* to warn, forbid, Ger. *warnen*; allied to **ward, beware, wary.**]

warp, *wŏrp, v.t.* to twist out of shape: to pervert: to haul (a ship) by warps or ropes attached to posts on a wharf, &c.—*v.i.* to be twisted out of the straight: to swerve.—*n.* the threads stretched out lengthwise in a loom to be crossed by a weft or woof: a rope used in towing.—*adj.* warped, twisted by shrinking: perverted, embittered and biased in outlook (e.g. *he had a warped nature*). [O.E. *weorpan, werpan*; Ger. *werfen,* to cast.]

warrant, *wor′ant, v.t.* to guarantee: to justify, constitute adequate grounds for.—*n.* that which warrants or authorises, esp. a document: a commission giving authority: a writ for arresting a person or for carrying a judgment into execution: justification: in the armed forces, certificate of appointment inferior to a commission.—*adj.* warr′antable, authorised by warrant or right: justifiable.—*n.* warr′antableness.—*adv.* warr′antably.—*ns.* warr′anter, -or, one who warrants; warr′ant-off′icer, an officer holding a warrant (see above; see also **branch-officer**); warr′anty, a legal warrant or deed of security: a guarantee: authority. [O.Fr. *warant* (Fr. *garant*)—O.H.G. *weren.*]

warren, *wor′en, n.* a piece of ground kept for breeding game or rabbits: rabbit burrows in waste ground: a dwelling resembling

these. [O.Fr. *warenne* (Fr. *garenne*)—*warir,* to defend.]

warrior. See under **war.**

wart, *wŏrt, n.* a small, hard excrescence on the skin: a small protuberance.—*adj.* wart′y, like a wart: overgrown with warts. [O.E. *wearte*; Ger. *warze*; prob. allied to L. *verrūca.*]

wary, *wā′ri, adj.* warding or guarding against deception, &c.: cautious.—*adv.* wā′rily.—*n.* wā′riness. [Longer form of **ware** (2)—O.E. *wær,* cautious.]

was, *woz,* used as *pa.t.* of **be.** [O.E. *wæs, wære—wesan,* to remain, be; O.N. *vera,* pa.t. *var.*]

wash, *wosh, v.t.* to cleanse with water or other liquid: to overflow: to flow against: to waste (away), or to sweep (along, &c.), by the action of water: to cover with a thin coat of metal or paint: in mining, to separate from earth by means of water.—*v.i.* to be engaged in cleansing with water: (*coll.*) to stand the test.—*n.* a washing: the break of waves on the shore: the rough water left behind by a boat: the shallow part of a river or arm of the sea: a marsh or fen: alluvial matter: waste liquor, refuse of food, &c.: that with which anything is washed: a lotion: a thin coat of paint, metal; &c.—*ns.* wash′-bowl, -bā′sin, a bowl, basin, in which to wash dishes, &c.; wash′hand bā′sin, a bowl in which to wash face and hands; wash′er, one who washes: a washing-machine: a flat ring of metal, rubber, &c., to keep joints or nuts secure; wash′er-woman, a woman whose job is to wash clothes; wash′-house, wash′ing-house, a room or building for washing clothes in; wash′ing, the act of cleansing by water: clothes washed, or to be washed; wash′ing-machine, machine for washing clothes; wash′ing-so′da, sodium carbonate in crystals; wash′-out, an erosion of earth by the action of water: the hole made by such: (*coll.*) an utter failure.—**wash out,** to cancel; **washed out,** cancelled: pale: exhausted; **wash up,** to wash the dishes and cutlery after a meal: to sweep up (something, e.g. on to a shore); **washed up,** (*slang*) exhausted, at the end of one's resources: spoiled, finished.—**come out in the wash,** of a situation, to work out satisfactorily. [O.E. *wascan*; O.N. *vaska,* Ger. *waschen.*]

wasp, *wosp, n.* any of a large number of winged insects with biting mouth parts, slender waist, and usu. (in the case of females and workers) a sting—(of the same order as ants and bees.—*adj.* was′pish, like a wasp: spiteful.—*adv.* was′pishly.—*n.* was′pishness. [O.E. *wæsp, wæps*; Ger. *wespe,* L. *vespa.*]

wassail, *wos′(ā)l, n.* a festive occasion: a drunken bout: the ale used on such occasions.—*v.i.* to hold a wassail or merry drinking-meeting.—*n.* wass′ailer, a reveller. [O.N. *ves heill,* 'be in health', the salutation used in pledging another, which the Normans transferred to mean 'a carousal'.]

wast, *wost, pa.t.* 2nd pers. sing. of the verb **be.**

waste, *wāst, adj.* empty, desert, desolate: uncultivated (e.g. ground): lying unused: rejected, discarded, useless (e.g. *waste products of manufacture*).—*v.t.* to lay waste or make desolate: to destroy: to wear out gradually: to squander: to impair.—*v.i.* to be diminished, to dwindle, to be consumed.—*n.* act of wasting:

Neutral vowels in unaccented syllables: *em′pér-ór*; for certain sounds in foreign words see p. ix.

useless expenditure: extravagant use: loss, destruction: that which is wasted or waste: uncultivated country: a desert: an unbroken expanse (e.g. of water, snow).—*n.* **wās′tage**, loss by use, natural decay.—*adj.* **waste′ful**, characterised by, leading to, waste: given to waste, very extravagant.—*adv.* **waste′fully.—** *ns.* **waste′fulness; wās′ter**, a ne′er-do-well; **wās′trel**, a waif: a profligate. [O.Fr. *wast, gaste* — L. *vastus*, waste; cf. O.N. *wēste*, Ger. *wüst*, desolate.]

watch, *woch*, *n.* act of looking out: close observation: guard: one who watches or those who watch: a sentry: the place where a guard is kept: a division of the night: time of watching, esp. in a ship: a small time-piece for carrying in a pocket, wearing on the wrist, &c.—*v.i.* to look with attention: to be awake, to keep vigil: to be on one's guard, be vigilant: to keep guard.—*v.t.* to keep one's eyes fixed on: to observe closely: to follow and note the movements of (a person): to wait for (e.g. one's opportunity, chance).—*n.* **watch′er.—***adj.* **watch′ful**, careful to watch or observe: on the alert to further or to prevent (with *for*): circumspect, cautious.—*adv.* **watch′fully.—***ns.* **watch′fulness; watch′-glass**, the glass covering the face of a watch: a glass of similar shape for other purposes; **watch′-guard**, a watch-chain of any material; **watch′māk′er**, one who makes and repairs watches; **watch′man**, a man who watches or guards, esp. premises; **watch′-tow′er**, a tower on which a sentinel keeps watch; **watch′word**, formerly, the password to be given to a watch or sentry: a maxim, rallying-cry.—**watch and ward**, uninterrupted vigilance; **watching brief**, instructions to a lawyer to watch a case on behalf of someone who is not directly involved in it; **watch′-night service**, a religious service held to usher in the New Year; **watch over**, to keep guard over, care for and protect; **watch out**, to look out, be careful. [O.E. *wæcce* — *wacan*, to wake.]

water, *wö′tėr*, *n.* a clear transparent liquid, perfectly neutral in its reaction, and devoid of taste or smell: any collection of it, as the ocean, a lake, river, &c.: mineral water: tears: saliva: urine: lustre, as of a diamond.—*v.t.* to wet, overflow, or supply with water: to dilute with water.—*v.i.* to shed water: to gather saliva: to take in water.—*ns.* **wa′ter-bail′iff**, (*obs.*) a custom-house officer for ships: an official who guards the fish in protected waters; **wa′ter-bed**, an India-rubber mattress filled with water, sometimes used by invalids to prevent bed-sores and now more generally used; **wa′ter-butt**, a large barrel for rain-water; **wa′ter-cannon**, a high-pressure hose pipe used to disperse crowds; **wa′ter-clock**, a clock which is made to go by the fall of water; **wa′ter-clos′et**, a closet used as a lavatory, in which the discharges are carried off by water; **wa′ter-col′our**, a colour or pigment diluted with water and gum, instead of oil: a painting in such a colour or colours; **wa′tercourse**, a course or channel for water; **wa′ter-cress**, a small plant growing in watery places, much esteemed as a salad, **wa′terfall**, a fall or perpendicular descent of a body of water—a cata-

ract or cascade; **wa′terfowl**, birds, esp. game birds, that live on and beside water; **wa′terga(u)ge**, an instrument for measuring the quantity or height of water; **wa′terglass**, a silicate of sodium or potassium, soluble in hot water, and impervious to air; **wa′ter-hen**, also called *moorhen*, any of various birds of the rail subfamily including the coots; **wa′tering-can, -pot**, a vessel used for watering plants; **wa′tering-place**, a place where water may be obtained: a place to which people resort to drink mineral water, for bathing, &c.—*adjs.* **wa′terish**, resembling, abounding in, water: somewhat watery, thin, **wa′terless**, lacking water.—*ns.* **wa′ter-lev′el**, the level formed by the surface of still water: a level-testing instrument in which water is used; **wa′ter-lil′y**, any of a genus of aquatic plants, with showy flowers and floating leaves; **wa′ter-line**, the line on a ship to which the water rises.—*adj.* **wa′ter-logged**, rendered log-like or unmanageable from being filled with water.—*ns.* **wa′ter-main**, a large subterranean pipe carrying a public water-supply; **wa′terman**, a man who plies a boat on water for hire, a boatman, a ferryman; **wa′ter-mark**, a mark showing the height to which water has risen: a tide-mark: a mark wrought into paper, denoting its size or its manufacturer: a design of this type on postage stamps; **wa′ter-mead′ow**, a meadow kept fertile by flooding from a stream; **wa′ter-melon**, often called **melon** (q.v.) in the U.S., a native of the warm parts of the Old World, a plant having large round fruits with dark green spotted rind, pink or white flesh, and much juice; **wa′ter-mill**, a mill driven by water; **wa′ter-part′ing** (same as **watershed**); **wa′ter-pō′lo**, an aquatic game played by swimmers; **wa′ter-pow′er**, the power of water, employed to move machinery, &c.—*adj.* **wa′terproof**, proof against water.—*n.* a garment of some waterproof substance.—*v.t.* to make impervious to water.—*ns.* **wa′ter rat**, water vole (see **vole**); **wa′tershed**, the line that separates two river-basins: a district from which several rivers rise: (*fig.*) a crucial point or dividing line between two phases, conditions, &c.; **wa′ter-skiing**, the sport of being towed at speed on skis behind a motor-boat; **wa′terspout**, a pipe from which water spouts: a moving spout or column of water, often seen at sea, and sometimes on land; **wa′ter-supply′**, the obtaining of quantities of water and distribution of it to consumers: the amount of water so supplied. *adj.* **wa′tertight**, so tight as not to let water pass through: (*fig.*) completely separate: such that no flaw or weakness can be found in it.—*ns.* **wa′ter-way**, a navigable channel; **wa′terwheel**, a wheel moved by water: an engine for raising water; **wa′terwork** (mostly in *pl.*), any apparatus or plant by which water is supplied, e.g. to a town.—*adj.* **wa′tery**, pertaining to or like water: thin, containing too much water: promising rain (e.g. *a watery sunset*): (*fig.*) feeble, pale, tasteless, uninteresting.—*ns.* **high(-)wa′ter** (see **high**); **low(-)wa′ter** (see **low**).—**water down**, (*lit.* and *fig.*) to make less strong; **water of crystallisation**, the water present in crystalline compounds, e.g. the five molecules of water in

fāte, fär; mē, hûr (her); *mīne; mōte, fŏr; mūte; mōōn, fŏŏt;* ᴛʜen (then)

hydrated copper sulphate, $CuSO_4 \cdot 5H_2O$; **water of life,** spiritual refreshment or enlightenment: (*Scot.*) whisky; **watered silk,** silk on which a changeable pattern has been worked by means of pressing and moistening; **watered stocks,** shares whose nominal amount has been increased without any corresponding payment in cash.—**first water** (see **first**); **heavy water** (see **heavy**); **hold water,** to be correct or well-grounded, to bear examination; **like water,** copiously. [O.E. *wæter*; Du. *water,* Ger. *wasser*; Gr. *hydōr,* L. *ūdus,* wet, *unda,* a wave, Sans. *udan,* water.]

watt, *wot, n.* the SI unit of power—equal to a rate of working of 1 joule per sec. [James *Watt* (1736-1819).]

wattle, *wot'l, n.* a twig or flexible rod: a hurdle: the fleshy excrescence under the throat of a cock or turkey: any Australian species of acacia.—*v.t.* to bind with wattles or twigs: to form by plaiting twigs. [O.E. *watel,* a hurdle.]

waul, wawl, *wöl, v.t.* to cry as a cat. [Imit.]

wave, *wāv, n.* a surge travelling on the surface of water: (*poet.*) the sea: a state of vibration propagated through a system of particles: inequality of surface: a line or streak like a wave: an undulation: one of an undulating succession of curves in hair: a rush of anything (*lit.* and *fig.*—e.g. of prosperity): a gesture: a movement of the raised hand, expressing greeting, farewell. &c.—*v.i.* to move like a wave: to move backwards and forwards: to flutter, as a signal: to undulate: to move the raised hand in greeting, farewell, &c.—*v.t.* to move backwards and forwards, to brandish, to flourish: to direct by, or to express by, a wave of the hand: to raise into inequalities of surface: to give an undulating appearance to (hair).—*ns.* **wave'-band,** a range of wavelengths occupied by transmission of a particular type; **wave'-length,** the distance between the crests (or other corresponding points) of successive waves (including electro-magnetic and sound waves): (*fig.*) level of understanding, knowledge, feeling, &c.—*adj.* **wave'less,** free from waves: undisturbed.—*n.* **wave'let,** a little wave.—*v.i.* **wā'ver,** to move uncertainly or unsteadily to and fro, to shake: to falter, to be irresolute.—*n.* **wā'verer.**—*adj.* **wā'vy,** full of, or rising in, waves: undulating.—*n.* **wā'viness.** [O.E. *wafian,* to wave; cf. O.N. *vafra,* to waver.]

wax, *waks, n.* beeswax (q.v.): this substance used to make candles, &c.: any substance like it in some respect, as that in the ear: the substance used to seal letters, sealing-wax: that used by shoemakers to rub their thread.—*v.t.* to smear or rub with wax.—*n.* **wax'-cloth,** cloth covered with a coating of wax, used for table-covers, &c.: colloquial name for all oil floorcloths.—*adjs.* **wax,** made of wax; **wax'en,** made of wax (now *rare*): like wax: (*fig.*) impressible.—*ns.* **wax'-light,** a candle or taper made of wax; **wax'work,** work made of wax, esp. figures or models formed of wax: (*pl.*) an exhibition of wax figures.—*adj.* **wax'y,** resembling wax: soft: pallid, pasty: adhesive.—*n.* **wax'iness.** [O.E. *weax*; O.N. *vax,* Du. *was,* Ger. *wachs.*]

wax, *waks, v.i.* to grow or increase, esp. of the moon, as opposed to *wane*: to become,

grow:—*pa.p.* wax'en (*B.*), grown. [O.E. *weaxan*; O.N. *vaxa,* Ger. *wachsen,* L. *augēre,* to increase, Gr. *auxanein.*]

way, *wā, n.* passage: road: length of space, distance: room to advance: direction: condition, state (e.g. *he is in a bad way*): general manner of acting (e.g. *as is his way*; also in *pl.*): means: manner: (*naut.*) progress or motion through the water, headway.—*ns.* **way'-bill,** list of passengers and goods carried by a conveyance; **way'farer,** a traveller or passenger, esp. on foot.—*adj.* and *n.* **way'faring.**—*v.t.* **way'lay,** to watch or lie in ambush for (a person)—now usu. (*fig.*) in order to converse with him against his inclination.—*ns.* **way'leave,** permission to pass over another's ground or property; **way'side,** the side of a way, path, or highway.—*adj.* growing or lying near the wayside.—*adj.* **way'ward,** wilful, capricious: perverse: irregular.—*n.* **way'wardness.**—*adj.* **way'worn,** worn-out by travel.—**ways and means,** resources: methods e.g. of raising money for the carrying on of government.—**be under way,** to be in motion, as a vessel; **by the way,** incidentally, in passing: while travelling; **by way of,** as a kind of (e.g. *he said this by way of apology*): as for the purpose of (*by way of making matters better*); **be by way of,** to be supposed, alleged (inaccurately) to be, do (e.g. *she was by way of tidying the room*); **get one's own way,** to get what one wants; **give way** (see **give**); **have a way with one,** to have a fascinating or a persuasive manner; **have one's way,** to get what one wants; **in a small way,** on a small scale; **in the way,** on the way: impeding, obstructing; **make one's way,** to push forward; **make way,** to give place: to advance; **out of the way,** so as not to hinder or obstruct: unusual; **take one's way,** to proceed: to follow one's own inclination or plan. [O.E. *weg*; Ger. *weg,* L. *via,* Sans. *vaha,* akin to L. *vehēre,* to carry, draw.]

way, 'way, *wā, adv.* abbrev. form of **away,** far: at a considerable distance or interval of time.—*adj.* **way'-out,** (*slang*) lost in what one is doing: eccentric, unusual: excellent.

we, *wē, pron. pl.* of I: I and others. [O.E. *wē,* cog. with Ger. *wir.*]

weak, *wēk, adj.* wanting strength: not able to sustain a great weight: easily overcome or subdued: wanting health: frail: having little of the important ingredient (e.g. *weak tea*; *a weak solution*): impressible, easily led: inconclusive (e.g. *a weak argument*): (*gram.*) of a verb which forms *pa.t.* and *pa.p.* by addition of **-ed.**—*v.t.* **weak'en,** to make weak: to reduce in strength or spirit.—*v.i.* to grow weak or weaker.—*adj.* **weak'-kneed,** having weak knees: lacking firm will.—*n.* **weak'ling,** a weak or feeble creature.—*adv.* **weak'ly.**—*adj.* **weak'-mind'ed,** having feeble intelligence: having, or showing, lack of resolution—too easily convinced or persuaded.—*n.* **weak'ness,** state of being weak: infirmity: inability to resist.—**weaker sex,** women. [O.E. *wāc,* pliant—*wīcan,* to yield; Du. *week, veikr,* Ger. *weich.*]

weal, *wēl, n.* (*arch.*) state of being well, a sound or prosperous state: welfare. [O.E. *wela,* wealth, bliss; Ger. *wohl.*]

Neutral vowels in unaccented syllables: *em'pėr-ŏr*; for certain sounds in foreign words see p. ix.

830

weal, *wēl*, *n.* a raised streak left by a blow with a lash, etc. [**wale.**]

weald, *wēld*, *n.* any open country.—**the Weald**, a district comprising portions of Kent and Sussex. [O.E. *weald*, a forest, wold. There has been some confusion with **wild**. Cf. **wold.**]

wealth, *welth*, *n.* possessions of any kind: riches: (*fig.*) an abundance (of).—*adj.* **wealth'y**, rich: prosperous.—*adv.* **wealth'ily.**—*n.* **wealth'iness.** [**weal**(1).]

wean, *wēn*, *v.t.* to accustom to nourishment other than the mother's milk: to estrange the affections of (a person from any object or habit).—*n.* **wean'ling**, a child or animal newly weaned. [O.E. *wenian*; O.N. *venja*, Ger. *gewöhnen*, to accustom, *entwöhnen*, to wean.]

weapon, *wep'on*, *n.* any instrument or organ of offence or defence. [O.E. *wæpen*; Ger. *waffen* and *wappen.*]

wear, *wār*, *v.t.* to carry on the body: to arrange (clothes, hair) in a specified way: to have, show, display (e.g. *she wears a pleased expression*): (of a ship) to fly (e.g. a flag): to consume, waste, damage, by use or exposure: to make by friction (e.g. a hole, a path): to exhaust, tire (out): to tolerate—*v.i.* to be wasted by use or time: to be spent tediously: to consume slowly: to last under use (e.g. *corduroy is a material that wears well*):—*pa.t.* wōre; *pa.p.* wōrn.—*n.* act of wearing: lessening or injury by use or friction: articles worn.—*adj.* **wear'able**, fit to be worn.—*n.* **wear'er.**—*p.adj.* **wear'ing**, made or designed for wear: consuming, exhausting.—**wear and tear**, damage by wear or use. [O.E. *werian*, to wear; O.N. *verja*, to cover.]

wear, *wār*, *v.t.* and *v.i.* (*naut.*) to bring, or be brought, to another course by turning the helm to windward:—*pa.t.* and *pa.p.* wore. [Prob. **veer**(1).]

wear, *wēr*, *n.* another spelling of **weir.**

weary, *wē'ri*, *adj.* tired, having the strength or patience exhausted: tedious.—*v.t.* to wear out or make weary, to reduce the strength or patience of: to harass.—*v.i.* to become weary or impatient.—*n.* **wea'riness.**—*adj.* **wea'risome**, making weary, tedious.—*adv.* **wea'risomely.** *n.* **wea'risomeness.** [O.E. *wērig*, weary.]

weasand, *wē'zānd*, *n.* the windpipe: the throat. [O.E. *wǣsend*, *wāsend.*]

weasel, *wē'zl*, *n.* a genus of small carnivores with long slender body, active, furtive, and blood-thirsty, eating frogs, birds, mice, &c. [O.E. *wesle*; Ger. *wiesel.*]

weather, *weTH'ér*, *n.* atmospheric conditions as to heat or cold, wetness, cloudiness, &c.: season.—*v.t.* to affect by exposing to the air: to sail to the windward of: to gain or pass, as a cape: (*lit.* and *fig.*) to come safely through (a storm).—*v.i.* to become discoloured, disintegrated (as rocks), &c., by exposure.—*adj.* (*naut.*) toward the wind, windward.—*adjs.* **weath'er-beat'en**, distressed by, or seasoned by, the weather; **weath'er-bound**, delayed by bad weather.—*ns.* **weath'ercock**, a vane (often in the form of a cock) to show the direction of the wind: (*fig.*) one who changes his opinions, allegiance, &c., easily and often; **weath'erglass**, a barometer; **weath'ering** (*archit.*), a slight inclination given to the top of a cornice or moulding, to prevent water from lodging on it: (*geol.*) the action of the elements in altering the form, colour, texture, or composition of rocks; **weath'er-sat'ellite**, a satellite used for the study of cloud formations and other meteorological conditions; **weath'er-ship**, a ship engaged on meteorological work; **weath'er-side**, the windward side.—**keep one's weather eye open**, to be alert; **make heavy weather of**, to find excessive difficulty in; **under the weather**, indisposed, seedy. [O.E. *weder*; O.N. *vedhr*, Ger. *wetter.*]

weave, *wēv*, *v.t.* to twine threads together: to interlace threads in a loom to form cloth: to work (into a fabric, story, &c.): to construct, contrive.—*v.i.* to practise weaving:—*pa.t.* wōve, (rarely) weaved; *pa.p.* wōv'en.—*ns.* **weav'er**; **weav'ing**, the act or the art of forming a web or cloth by the intersecting of two distinct sets of fibres, threads, or yarns—the *warp* and the *weft* or *woof.* [O.E. *wefan*; O.N. *vefa*, Ger. *weben.*]

weave, *wēv*, *v.i.* to move to and fro, or in and out: (in boxing) to move back or forward with sinuous movements of the body: (in flying) to fly with a weaving motion.—**get weaving**, (*slang*) get on the move. [M.E. *weve*; ety. dub.]

web, *web*, *n.* that which is woven: a roll of cloth, paper, &c.: the fine texture spun by the spider as a snare for flies: a film over the eye: the skin between the toes of waterfowl.—*ns.* **webb'ing**, a woven fabric of hemp, used for belts, &c.; **web'-foot**, a foot the toes of which are united with a web or membrane. [O.E. *webb*; O.N. *vefr*, Ger. *gewebe*; from root of **weave.**]

weber, *vā'bér*, *wē'bér*, *n.* the SI unit of magnetic flux. [Wilhelm *Weber*, German physicist (1804–91).]

wed, *wed*, *v.t.* to marry: to join in marriage: to unite closely.—*v.i.* to marry:—*pr.p.* wedd'ing; *pa.t.* and *pa.p.* wedd'ed or wed.—*ns.* **wedd'ing**, marriage: marriage ceremony; **wedd'ing-fa'vour**, a white rosette, &c., worn at a wedding.—**silver, golden, diamond wedding**, the 25th, 50th, and 60th anniversaries of a wedding. [O.E. *weddian*, to engage, to marry (Ger. *wetten*, to wager)—*wedd*, a pledge; Ger. *wette*, a bet.]

wedge, *wej*, *n.* a piece of wood or metal, thick at one end and sloping to a thin edge at the other, used in splitting or in fixing tightly: anything shaped like a wedge: a wedge-soled golf-club: a shoe in which the heel and sole together form a wedge and there is no gap under the instep (also **wedge-heeled shoe**).—*v.t.* to fasten, or to fix, with a wedge or wedges: to press, thrust (in), tightly (a person, e.g. oneself, or a thing).—*v.i.* to become fixed or jammed by, or as if by, a wedge.—**the thin**, or **small, end of the wedge**, a small beginning that is bound to be followed by important developments and results. [O.E. *wecg*; O.N. *veggr*, Ger. *weck*, a wedge; prob. from the root of **weigh.**]

Wedgwood ware, *wej'wŏŏd wār*, a superior kind of pottery invented by Josiah *Wedgwood* (1730–1795).

wedlock, *wed'lok*, *n.* matrimony: married state,

esp. in the phrase **born in**, or **out of, wedlock,** i.e. legitimate, or illegitimate. [O.E. *wedlāc—wedd, lāc,* a gift.]

Wednesday, *wenz′dā* (in the North, *wednz′dā*), *n.* fourth day of the week. [O.E. *Wōdenes dæg,* the day of *Woden* or *Odin,* the king of gods and men in Scandinavian myth.]

wee, *wē, adj.* small, tiny. [M.E. *we,* a bit.]

weed, *wēd, n.* any useless troublesome plant: a worthless fellow or horse: (*coll.*) tobacco, a cigarette, a cigar.—*v.t.* to free from weeds: to remove (anything troublesome or useless; often **weed out**).—*v.i.* to remove weeds.—*ns.* **weed′er; weed′killer,** anything, esp. a chemical preparation, for killing weeds.—*adj.* **weed′y,** weed-like, consisting of weeds: full of weeds: lanky, ungainly. [O.E. *wēod,* a herb.]

weed, *wēd, n.* (used in *pl.*) a widow's mourning apparel. [O.E. *wæd,* clothing.]

week, *wēk, n.* the space of seven days, esp. from Sunday to Sunday: the working days of the week.—*ns.* **week′day,** any day of the week except Sunday; **week-end,** a period including the end of one week and the beginning of the next.—*adj.* **week′ly,** coming, happening, or done once a week.—*adv.* once a week.—*n.* a publication appearing once a week.—**this day week,** a week from today. [O.E. *wice;* Du. *week,* Ger. *woche.*]

ween, *wēn, v.i.* to think or fancy (*poet.*). [O.E. *wēnan—wēn* (Ger. *wahn*), expectation, hope.]

weep, *wēp, v.i.* to express grief by shedding tears: to wail or lament: to drip, ooze.—*v.t.* to lament: to pour forth (e.g. *to weep bitter tears*): to express while or by weeping: to exude—*pa.t.* and *pa.p.* wept.—*n.* **weep′er,** one who weeps: (*hist.*) a long black hat-band worn by a mourner, or a white border round the sleeve of a mourning dress.—*adj.* **weep′ing,** of trees, drooping the branches. [O.E. *wēpan—wēp,* clamour.]

weevil, *wēv′il n.* a pop. name for any of a large number of beetles injurious to stored grain.—*adjs.* **weev′iled, weev′illed, weev′ily,** infested by weevils. [Conn. with O.E. *wifel,* beetle.]

weft, *weft, n.* the threads woven into and crossing the warp.—Also **woof.** [O.E. *weft—wefan,* to weave.]

weigh, *wā, v.t.* to compare by, or as by, the balance (with, against): to find the heaviness of: to be equal to in heaviness (e.g. *to weigh 1 lb.*): to bear up, to raise, esp. a ship's anchor: to ponder, consider (e.g. arguments, probabilities).—*v.i.* to have weight: to be considered of importance: to press heavily.—*ns.* **weigh′bridge,** a machine for weighing vehicles with their loads; **weight,** the heaviness of a thing when weighed, or the amount which anything weighs: the force with which a body is attracted to the earth, measured by product of mass and acceleration: a mass of metal adjusted to a standard and used for finding weight: anything heavy: a ponderous mass: pressure: importance: power: impressiveness.—*v.t.* to attach or add a weight or weights to: to hold down in this way: to make more heavy (*lit.* and *fig.*).—*n.* **weight′lessness,** the condition where little or no reaction to the force due to gravity is experienced, as e.g. in free fall

through thin air at high altitude, or in space travel.—*adj.* **weigh′ty,** heavy: important: being the fruit of judicious consideration and hence worthy of attention.—*adv.* **weigh′tily.**—*n.* **weigh′tiness.—weigh in,** to ascertain one's weight before a fight, after a horse-race (**weigh out,** before): to join in a project; **weigh in with,** (*fig.*) to produce (a new argument) in a discussion.—**throw one's weight about,** to use one's authority in an ostentatious, domineering manner. [O.E. *wegan,* to carry; Ger. *wiegen;* L. *vehĕre,* to carry.]

weigh, *wā, n.* a very common misspelling of *way* in the phrase 'under way', through confusion with the phrase 'to weigh anchor'.

weir, *wēr, n.* a dam across a river: a fence of stakes set in a stream for catching fish. [O.E. *wer,* an enclosure, allied to *werian,* to protect.]

weird, *wērd, n.* fate: that which comes to pass.—*adj.* skilled in witchcraft: unearthly, mysterious: odd, very queer.—*n.* **weirdie,** (*coll.*) an eccentric: someone unconventional in dress, &c.—**the weird sisters,** the Fates. [O.E. *wyrd,* fate—*weorthan,* to become; Ger. *werden.*]

welcome, *wel′kóm, adj.* received with gladness, admitted willingly: causing gladness: free to enjoy.—*n.* (kindly) reception.—*v.t.* to receive with kindness: to receive (anything) with pleasure or enthusiasm. [O.E. *wilcuma,* influenced by O.N. *velkominn.*]

weld, *weld, v.t.* to join together, as metal by pressure, with or without heat: to join closely.—*n.* a welded joint. [Conn. with O.E. *weallan,* to boil; Ger. *wallen.*]

welfare, *wel′fār, n.* state of faring or doing well: satisfactory standard of living.—**welfare state,** a country with a public health service, pensions, insurance against unemployment, &c.; **welfare work,** efforts to improve conditions of living for a class (e.g. the very poor) or group (e.g. employees or workers). [**well, fare.**]

welkin, *wel′kin, n.* the sky or region of clouds. [O.E. *wolcnu,* pl. of *wolcen,* cloud, air, sky; Ger. *wolke,* cloud.]

well, *wel, n.* a spring: (*fig.*) a source: a lined shaft made in the earth whence a supply of water, oil, &c., is obtained: any similar walled space, e.g. the open space in the middle of a staircase or court-room, a lift-shaft.—*v.i.* to issue forth, as water from the earth (*lit.* and *fig.*).—*n.* **well′-spring,** a fountain. [O.E. *wella—weallan,* to boil; cf. O.N. *vella,* to boil.]

well, *wel, adj.* (usu. predicative) fortunate: comfortable: in health.—*adv.* in a proper manner: thoroughly: favourably, successfully: conveniently.—*interj.* expressing surprise, &c., or introducing resumed narrative, &c.—*adjs.* **well′-advised′,** wise, prudent; **well′-appoint′ed,** finely equipped.—*n.* **well′-bē′ing,** state of being well, welfare.—*adjs.* **well′-born,** born of a good or respectable family; **well′-bred,** of polished manners: of good stock; **well′-conduct′ed,** properly managed: behaving properly; **well′-disposed′,** favourable.—*n.* **well′-do′ing,** virtuous conduct, doing good deeds.—*adjs.* **well′-earned,** thoroughly deserved; **well′-fāv′oured** (see **favour**); **well′-heeled,** (*coll.*) prosperous; **well′-informed′,** having, or based on, varied information; **well′-knit,**

Neutral vowels in unaccented syllables: *em′pér-ór*; for certain sounds in foreign words see p. ix.

832

strongly framed; **well′-known,** familiar: celebrated; **well′-marked,** obvious, decided; **well′-mean′ing,** having good intentions; **well′-meant,** rightly intended.—*adv.* **well′-nigh,** nearly, almost.—*adjs.* **well′-off,** in good circumstances; **well′-read′,** widely acquainted with books; **well′-timed′,** opportune; **well′-to-do,** prosperous; **well′-worn′,** worn threadbare.—**well away,** progressing rapidly: (*slang*) drunk; **well up in,** well versed in.—**as well,** in addition; **as well as,** 'both ...and'. [O.E. *wel*; cog. with Ger. *wohl*.]

wellingtons, *wel′ing-tónz, n.* a kind of ridingboot: rubber boots loosely covering the calves. [Named after the Duke of *Wellington* (1769-1852).]

Welsh, (*obs.*) **Welch,** *welsh, adj.* pertaining to *Wales* or its inhabitants.—*n.pl.* the inhabitants of Wales:—*sing.* their language.—*n.* **Welsh′man,** a native of Wales.—**Welsh rabbit,** (also *rarebit*), cheese melted on toasted bread. [O.E. *wealas,* foreigners; Anglo-Saxon invaders' name for Welsh and native Britons.]

welsh, *welsh, v.i.* to run off from a racecourse without settling or paying one's bets: to dodge fulfilling an obligation.—*v.t.* to cheat (a person) in such a way.—Also **welch.**—*n.* **welsh′er, welch′er.** [Perh. in allusion to the alleged bad faith of Welshmen.]

welt, *welt, n.* a band or strip fastened to an edge to give strength or for ornament: a narrow strip of leather used in one method of sewing the upper to the sole of a shoe: a blow.—*v.t.* to furnish with a welt: (*coll.*) to lash, beat. [W. *gwald,* a hem.]

welter, *wel′tér, v.i.* to roll or wallow, esp. in dirt.—*n.* a turmoil.—*adj.* **wel′tering.** [M.E. *walten,* to roll over.—O.E. *wealtan,* to roll.]

welter(-)weight, *wel′tér-wāt, n.* (*boxing*) a weight between *light* (9 st. 9 lb.) and *middle* (10 st. 7 lb.): such a boxer: an amateur boxer of not less than 10 st. and not more than 10 st. 8 lb.: an unusually heavy weight, carried mostly in steeplechases and hurdle-races.

wen, *won, n.* a fleshy, pulpy tumour, most commonly on the scalp. [O.E. *wen,* a swelling, a wart; Du. *wen.*]

wench, *wench, -sh, n.* a girl: a maid-servant: a harlot.—*v.i.* to frequent the company of harlots: to go courting. [O.E. *wencel,* a child.]

wend, *wend, v.i.* to go, to wind or turn.—*v.t.* in **wend one's way,** follow the road in a leisurely fashion. [O.E. *wendan,* the causative of *windan,* to turn round.]

went, *went,* properly *pa.t.* of **wend,** but now used as *pa.t.* of **go.**

wept, *wept, pa.t.* and *pa.p.* of **weep.**

were, *wûr, v.i.* the *pl.* of **was,** used as *pa.t.* of **be.** [O.E. *wære*; Ger. *war,* O.N. *vera,* to be. Cf. **was.**]

weregild, wergild, *wér′gild, n.* (among Germanic races) a fine by which homicide and other heinous crimes against the person were expiated. [O.E. *wergield,* from *wer,* man, *gield—gieldan,* to pay.]

werewolf, werwolf, *wér′woolf, n.* a person supposed to be able to change himself for a time into a wolf: member of an underground Nazi organisation. [O.E. *werwulf—wer,* man (L. *vir*), *wulf,* a wolf.]

wert, *wûrt,* the 2nd pers. sing. of **were,** used as

2nd pers. sing. of past subjunctive of **be.**

Wesleyan, *wes′le-ăn, adj.* pertaining to Wesleyanism.—*n.* adherent of Wesleyanism.—*n.* **Wes′leyanism,** the system of doctrine and church polity of the Wesleyan Methodists. [Named from John *Wesley* (1703-91).]

west, *west, n.* the quarter where the sun sets: one of the four chief points of the compass: the region in the west of any country: (*cap.*) Europe or Europe and America, as opposed to Asia, the East.—*adj.* situated towards, or (of wind) coming from, the west.—*adv.* towards the west.—*adjs.* **wes′tering,** passing to the west; **wes′terly,** lying or moving towards the west: from the west.—*adv.* towards the west.—*adj.* **wes′tern,** situated in the west: belonging to the west: moving towards, or coming from, the west.—*n.* a film or novel whose scene is the western United States, esp. the former Wild West.—*n.* **wes′terner,** a person belonging to the west.—*adj.* **west′most,** most westerly.—*adj.* and *adv.* **west′ward,** towards the west.—*advs.* **west′wardly, west′wards,** towards the west.—**West End,** the fashionable quarter in the west of London: a similar district in other large towns; **West Saxon,** a southern dialect of Old English, the chief literary dialect before the Norman Conquest. **to go west,** to die: to be lost: to become useless; **Wild West,** the western United States in the days of the first settlers, chiefly cattlemen and goldminers, before the establishment of law and order. [O.E. *west* (Fr. *ouest,* O.N. *vestr*).]

wet, *wet, adj.* containing water: having water on the surface: rainy.—*n.* water or wetness: moisture.—*v.t.* to make wet: to soak with water: to sprinkle:—*pr.p.* **wet′ting;** *pa.t.* and *pa.p.* **wet,** (rarely) **wet′ted.** *ns.* **wet′-dock,** a dock or basin for floating vessels at all states of the tide; **wet′ness; wet′-nurse,** a nurse who suckles a child for its mother; **wet suit,** a suit for wearing in cold water, which allows water to pass through but retains body heat.—*adj.* **wet′ish,** somewhat wet.—**a wet blanket,** (*fig.*) any cause of discouragement or depression: a depressing companion; **wet behind the ears,** very young, immature, gullible. [O.E. *wǣt*; O.N. *vātr*; from root of **water.**]

wether, *weTH′ér, n.* a castrated ram. [O.E. *wither*; Ger. *widder.*]

whack, *hwak, v.t.* and *v.i.* to strike smartly, esp. making a sound.—*n.* a blow: a stroke: an attempt: a share.—*adjs.* **whacked,** (*coll.*) exhausted; **whack′ing,** very large, astounding.—*n.* a beating (*lit.* and *fig.*). All meanings of 'whack' and 'whacking' are *coll.* or *slang.* [**thwack.**]

whale, *hwāl, n.* any of numerous cetaceous (q.v.) mammals, esp. the larger kinds as opp. to dolphins and porpoises: (*slang*) something very large or impressive of its kind.—*v.i.* to catch whales.—*ns.* **whale-back,** kind of steamboat used on the Great Lakes to carry grain, &c., having rounded upper deck, &c.; **whale′-bone,** a light flexible substance from the upper jaw of certain whales.—*adj.* made of whalebone.—*ns.* **whale′-calf,** a young whale—also **whale′-calf; whale′-oil,** oil obtained from the blubber of a whale; **whāler,** a ship or a person

---

fāte, fär; mē, hûr (her); mīne; mōte, för; mūte; mōōn, fŏŏt; THen (then)

employed in whale-fishing: (*slang*) something very large of its kind.—**bull, cow, whale,** an adult male, female, whale. [O.E. *hwæl* (O.N. *hvalr,* Ger. *walfisch*); orig. unknown.]

wharf, *hwörf, n.* a landing-stage, for loading and unloading ships:—*pl.* **wharfs, wharves.**—*v.t.* to secure beside a wharf: to place on a wharf.—*ns.* **wharf´age,** the dues paid for using a wharf: accommodation at a wharf; **wharfin-ger** (*hwörf´in-jér*) one who has the care of, or owns, a wharf. [O.E. *hwerf,* a dam; prob. conn. with *hweorfan* (O.N. *hverfa*), to turn.]

what, *hwot, interrog. pron.* neuter of **who**—also used elliptically and as an interjection of astonishment.—*interrog. adj.* of what sort, how much, how great.—*rel. pron.* that which (e.g. *give me what you have*).—*rel. adj.* such ... as (e.g. *give me what money you have*).—*prons.* **whatev´er, whate´er´,** anything which.—*adj.* any or all that, no matter what.—*adjs.* **whatsoev´er, whatsoe´er´,** of whatever kind.—**what have you,** (*coll.*) anything else of the kind; **what's-his, -its, -name,** the person or thing indicated or understood; **what's what,** the true position of affairs; **what time,** at the very time when. [O.E. *hwæt,* neut. of *hwā,* who; Ger. *was,* L. *quid.*]

whatnot, *hwot´not, n.* a piece of furniture with shelves for books, &c., so called because used to hold anything. [**what, not.**]

wheat, *hwēt, n.* a cereal grass, the grain furnishing a nutritious flour for bread.—*adj.* **wheat´en,** made of wheat. [O.E. *hwǣte*—*hwīt,* white; Ger. *weizen*; allied to *white,* its colour.]

wheatear, *hwēt´ēr, n.* a small bird of the chat genus, a common summer visitant of Britain. [Corr. from *white-arse,* white-rump.]

wheedle, *hwēd´l, v.t.* to entice by soft words, flatter, cajole (into): to coax (something out of a person): to cheat (a person out of something) by cajolery.—*n.* **wheed´ler.** [Perh. from O.E. *wǣdlian,* to be in want, to beg.]

wheel, *hwēl, n.* a circular frame turning on an axle: an old instrument of torture: a steering-wheel.—*v.t.* to cause to whirl: to convey on wheels.—*v.i.* to turn round or on an axis: to be provided with wheels on which to be propelled: to change direction.—*ns.* **wheel´-bar-row,** a barrow with one wheel in front and two handles and legs behind: (loosely) any other hand cart; **wheel´base,** the distance between the front and rear axles of a vehicle.—*p.adj.* **wheeled,** having wheels.—*ns.* **wheel´er,** one who wheels: a horse nearest the wheels of a carriage: a maker of wheels; **wheel´-house,** the shelter in which a ship's steering-wheel is placed; **wheel´wright,** a craftsman who makes wheels and wheel-carriages.—**wheels within wheels,** a situation in which a complication of influences are at work. [O.E. *hwēol;* O.N. *hjōl.*]

wheeze, *hwēz, v.i.* to breathe with a hissing sound: to breathe audibly or with difficulty.—*n.* the act of wheezing.—*adj.* **wheez´y.** [O.E. *hwēsan;* O.N. *hvǣsa,* to wheeze, to hiss.]

whelk, *hwelk, n.* any of numerous edible molluscs with spiral shell. [O.E. *wiloc, weoluc.*]

whelm, *hwelm, v.t.* to cover completely, to submerge: to overpower. [M.E. *whelmen.*]

whelp, *hwelp, n.* the young of the dog and of lions, &c.—a puppy, a cub: a young man (in contempt).—*v.i.* and *v.t.* to bring forth young. [O.E. *hwelp;* O.N. *hvelpr.*]

when, *hwen, adv.* and *conj.* at what time? at which time? at or after the time that: while: even though.—*rel. pron.* at which (e.g. *at the time when I said that I believed it was so*).—*adv.* and *conj.* **whence** (also **from whence**), from what place: from which things: wherefore.—*conjs.* **whencesoev´er,** from what place, cause, or source soever; **whenev´er,** at every time when; **whensoev´er,** at what time soever: whenever. [O.E. *hwænne, hwonne* (Ger. *wann, wenn*); orig. acc. of interrog. pron. *hwā,* who.]

where, *hwār, adv.* and *conj.* at which place: at what place? to which place: to what place?—*rel. pron.* in which, to which (e.g. *he could not find the place where he had left it*).—*adv.* and *conj.* **whereabout´,** about where: near what?—also **where´abouts.**—*n.* **where´-abouts,** situation, location, esp. approximate. —*conj.* **whereas´,** when in fact: but, on the other hand.—*advs.* and *conjs.* **whereat´,** at which: at what? **whereby´,** by which (?); **where´fore,** for which reason: for what reason? why?—*n.* the cause.—*advs.* and *conjs.* **wherein´,** in which respect: in what? **whereof´,** of which: of what? **whereon´,** on which: on what? **wheresoev´er,** in or to what place soever; **whereto´,** to which: to what? **where-un´to** (or *-un´tōō´*), whereto: for what purpose? **whereupon´,** upon or in consequence of which; **wherev´er,** at, to, whatever place; **where-with´, wherewithal´,** with which: with what? —*n.* (usu. **wherewithal**) the means. **whereat, whereby,** &c., may also be used as *rel. prons.* [O.E. *hwǣr, hwār;* from stem of **who.**]

wherry, *hwer´i, n.* a shallow, light boat, sharp at both ends for speed: a sailing barge.

whet, *hwet, v.t.* to sharpen by rubbing: to make keen: to excite:—*pr.p.* **whet´ting;** *pa.t.* and *pa.p.* **whett´ed.**—*n.* act of sharpening: something that sharpens the appetite.—*ns.* **whet´-stone,** a stone for sharpening edged instruments; **whett´er.** [O.E. *hwettan*—*hwæt,* sharp; Ger. *wetzen.*]

whether, *hweTH´ér, rel.* and *interrog. pron.* (*arch.*) which (of two).—*conj.* introducing the first of two alternative words, phrases, clauses, the second being introduced by *or,* or (in the case of clauses) sometimes by *or* or *whether*—used similarly as *interrog. adv.* [O.E. *hwæther,* from *hwā,* who, with the old comp. suffx. *-ther;* cog. with Ger. *weder;* also with L. *uter,* Sans. *katara.* Cf. **other** and **alter.**]

whew, *hwū, interj.* expressing wonder or dismay.

whey, *hwā, n.* the watery part of milk, separated from the curd, esp. in making cheese.—*adj.* **whey´-faced,** pale with terror. [O.E. *hwæg;* Low Ger. *wey.*]

which, *hwich, interrog. pron.* what one of a number?—also used adjectively.—*rel. pron.* (*obs.*) who, whom: now used of things only.—*prons.* **whichev´er, whichsoev´er,** every one which: any one, no matter which.—**which is which?** which is the one, which is the other? [O.E. *hwilc, hwelc,* from *hwī,* instrumental case of *hwā,* who, and *līc,* like; Ger. *welch, welcher;* L. *quālis.* Cf. **such** and **each.**]

whiff, *hwif, n.* a sudden puff of air or smoke

Neutral vowels in unaccented syllables: *em´pér-ór;* for certain sounds in foreign words see p. ix.

from the mouth: a slight blast: a slight inhalation: a puff of smell.—*v.t.* to throw out in whiffs: to puff (along, away).—Also *v.i.*—*v.i.* **whiff'le**, to veer about, blow in gusts: to be fickle: to prevaricate. [Imit.]

whig, *hwig, n.* (usu. *cap.*) the name of one of the great English political parties—applied in the late 17th century to the party upholding popular rights and opposed to the King; after 1830 almost superseded by 'Liberal' (q.v.): a Scottish Presbyterian, first so called in the middle of the 17th century.—*adj.* composed of Whigs—also **whigg'ish**.—*ns.* **whigg'ism**, **whigg'ery**, whig principles. [Prob. short for **whiggamore**.]

whiggamore, *hwig'a-mōr, -mör, n.* originally a person who came from the west and southwest of Scotland to Leith to buy corn: a Scottish Presbyterian, a whig. [Origin disputed; most prob. *whig*, to urge forward, *mere*, mare.]

while, *hwīl, n.* space of time: time and trouble spent (only in **worth (one's) while**).—*conj.* (also **whilst**) during the time that: at the same time that: although: (erroneously) whereas.—*v.i.* to cause to pass without irksomeness (with *away*).—*adv.* **whī'lom**, formerly, once.—*adj.* former.—**the while**, (*arch.*) while: meantime. [O.E. *hwīl*; Ger. *weile*.]

whim, *hwim, n.* a caprice: a fancy.—*adj.* **whim'sical**, full of whims, odd, fantastical. — *ns.* **whimsical'ity**, **whim'sicalness**.—*adv.* **whim'sically**.—*n.* **whim'sy**, **whim'sey**, a whim, freak: whimsical behaviour. [O.N. *hvima*, to have the eyes wandering.]

whimper, *hwim'pér, v.i.* to cry with a low, whining voice.—*n.* a peevish cry. [From *whimmer*; Ger. *wimmern*; perh. from the root of **whine**.]

whin, *hwin, n.* gorse, furze.—*adj.* **whinn'y**, covered with whins. [Prob. of Scand. origin.]

whine, *hwīn, v.i.* to utter a plaintive cry: to complain in an unmanly way.—*n.* a plaintive cry: an affected nasal tone of utterance.—*n.* **whī'ner**.—*adv.* **whī'ningly**. [O.E. *hwīnan*, to whine; O.N *hvína*, to whistle through the air.]

whinger, *hwing'ér, n.* a kind of sword. [Prob. conn. with **whine**.]

whinny, *hwin'i, v.t.* to neigh:—*pa.t.* and *pa.p.* whinn'ied.—*n.* a neigh. [Freq. of **whine**.]

whinstone, *hwin'stŏn, n.* a popular name for any hard and compact kind of stone. [**whin** (ety. uncertain), **stone**.]

whinyard. Same as **whinger**.

whip, *hwip, n.* that which whips: a lash with a handle for punishing or driving: a stroke administered as by a whip: a driver, coachman: a whipper-in: in parliament, a member chosen by his party to make sure that they do not fail to vote in important divisions: a notice issued by a parliamentary whip.—*v.t.* to lash: to drive or punish with lashes: (*coll.*) to beat, outdo: to beat into a froth, as eggs, cream, &c.: to sew or bind round: to snatch (with *up, away, out*).—*v.i.* to move nimbly: to move in the manner of a whip lash:—*pr.p.* whipp'ing; *pa.t.* and *pa.p.* whipped, whipt.—*ns.* **whip'cord**, cord for making whips: a strong worsted material with ribs; **whip'-hand**, the hand that holds the whip: the advantage; **whipp'er**; **whipp'er-in**, one who whips the hounds to keep them to

the line of chase; **whipp'er-snapp'er**, a pretentious but insignificant person; **whipp'ing**, act of whipping: punishment with the whip or lash: a defeat; **whipp'ing-boy**, a boy who was educated with a prince and whipped for the royal pupil's faults—also *fig.*; **whipp'ing-post**, a post to which offenders are tied to be whipped; **whipp'ing-top**, a top kept spinning with a whip; **whip'-round**, an appeal for contributions.—**whiplash injury**, a neck injury caused by the sudden jerking forwards and backwards of the head, common in motor-vehicle accidents involving collision from the rear; **whip up**, to rouse, raise to greater intensity. [M.E. *whippen*; prob. a form of *wippen*—Old Du. *wippen*, to shake.]

whippet, *hwip'et, n.* a racing-dog, like a greyhound but smaller. [Perh. **whip**.]

whippoorwill, *hwip-pŏŏr-wil', or -pŏr-, n.* a nocturnal bird of N. America. [From its notes.]

whir(r), *hwûr, n.* a sound from rapid whirling.—*v.t.* and *v.i.* to whirl round with a noise:—*pr.p.* whirr'ing, *pa.t.* and *pa.p.* whirred. [Imit., cf. Dan *hvirre*, to whirl.]

whirl, *hwûrl, n.* a turning which suddenly: anything that turns with velocity: a great or confusing degree (of activity or emotion): commotion, agitation.—*v.i.* to revolve rapidly.—*v.t.* to turn (round) rapidly: to carry (away) rapidly, as on wheels.—*n.* **whirl'igig**, a child's toy which is spun or whirled rapidly round: anything whirling (*lit.* and *fig.*); **whirl'pool**, a circular current in a river or sea, produced by opposing tides, winds, or currents: an eddy; **whirl'wind**, a violent aerial current, with a whirling, rotary, or spiral motion—also *fig.*; **whir'lybird**, (*slang*) a helicopter. [Cf. O.N. *hvirfla*, freq. of *hverfa*, to turn round; Ger. *wirbeln.*]

whisk, *hwisk, v.t.* to move with a quick motion: to sweep, or stir, rapidly.—*v.i.* to move nimbly and rapidly.—*n.* a rapid sweeping motion: a small bunch of anything used for a brush: a small instrument for beating or whisking, esp. eggs.—*n.* **whis'ker**, he who, or that which, whisks: formerly, hair on the upper lip, now usu. hair on the side of the face, side-whiskers (esp. in *pl.*): a long bristle on the face of a cat, &c.—*adj.* **whis'kered**. [Scand., O.N. *visk*, a wisp of hay; Swed. *viska*, to wipe, Ger. *wischen*; prob. conn. with **wash**.]

whisky, **whiskey**, *hwis'ki, n.* an alcoholic beverage distilled from grain. [Gael. *uisge beatha*; see **usquebaugh**.]

whisper, *hwis'pér, v.i.* to speak with a low sound: to speak covertly, spread rumours: to make a sound like soft speech.—*v.t.* to utter in a low voice or under the breath, or covertly, or by way of gossip.—*n.* a low hissing voice or sound: cautious or timorous speaking: a secret hint: a rumour.—*ns.* **whis'perer**, one who whispers: (*B.*) a secret informer; **whis'peringgall'ery**, a gallery or dome so constructed that a whisper or slight sound is carried to an unusual distance.—**whispering campaign**, an attack by means of furtively spread rumours. [O.E. *hwisprian*; Ger. *wispern*, O.N. *hvīskra*, allied to **whistle**.]

whist, *hwist, n.* a game at cards, played by two against two.—*n.* **whist'-drive**, a progressive whist party. [Orig. *whisk*; ety. uncertain.]

whistle, *hwis'l, v.i.* to make a sound by forcing the breath through the lips or teeth: to make a like sound with an instrument: to sound shrill: to whizz (through the air).—*v.t.* to form or utter by whistling: to call by a whistle.—*n.* the sound made in whistling: an instrument for whistling.—*ns.* **whis'tler; whis'tle-stop,** (*U.S.*) a small town or railway station, where trains stop only by signal (**whistle-stop speech,** an electioneering speech made on tour (orig. at railway stations)).—*v.i.* of a political candidate, to make an electioneering tour with many brief personal appearances.—**boatswain's whistle** (also **pipe, call**), a whistle of special shape used by a boatswain or boatswain's-mate to summon sailors to various duties. [O.E. *hwistlian.*]

whit, *hwit, n.* the smallest particle imaginable: a bit. [By-form of **wight,** a creature.]

white, *hwīt, adj.* able to reflect all wavelengths of light equally: of the colour of pure snow: stainless: pure: bright: light-coloured, as of wine: pallid: of the light complexion characteristic of Europeans.—*n.* the colour of snow: anything white, as a white man, the centre of a target, the albuminous part of an egg, a pigment.—*v.t.* to make white.—*ns.* **white'-alloy',** a cheap alloy used to imitate silver; **white(-)ant,** a termite (q.v.).—*adj.* **white'-backed,** having the back white or marked with white.—*n.* **white'bait,** the fry of the herring and sprat.—*adj.* **white'-coll'ar,** pertaining to, or designating the class of workers, as clerks, &c., who are not engaged in manual labour.—*n.* **white'-lead,** a carbonate of lead used in painting white.—*adj.* **white'-liv'ered,** having a pale look, so called because thought to be caused by a white liver: cowardly: malicious.—*ns.* **white'-meat,** the flesh of poultry, rabbits, veal, pork; **white'-met'al,** a general name for alloys of light colour.—*v.t.* **whi'ten,** to make white: to bleach.—*v.i.* to become or turn white.—*ns.* **white'ness; white'wash,** a mixture of whiting or lime and water, used for whitening walls and as a disinfectant: anything that conceals a stain.—*v.t.* to cover with whitewash: to give a fair appearance to: to attempt to clear (a stained reputation).—*n.* **whi'ting,** a small sea-fish allied to the cod, so called from its white colour: ground chalk free from stony matter (also **white'ning**).—*adj.* **whi'tish,** somewhat white.—**white coal,** water-power; **white corpuscle,** a leucocyte, one of the colourless amoeba-like cells occurring in suspension in the blood plasma of many animals, in lymph, &c.; **whited sepulchre,** one professedly righteous but inwardly wicked, a hypocrite (Matt. xxiii 27); **white elephant, feather** (see **elephant, feather**); **white flag,** an emblem of truce or of surrender; **White Friar,** one of the carmelite order of friars, so called from their white dress; **white heat,** the degree of heat at which bodies become white (*adj.* **white-hot**); **white horse,** a white-topped wave; **White House,** official residence of the President of the U.S.A. at Washington; **white light,** light containing all wavelengths in the visible range at the same intensity; **white night,** a sleepless night; **white noise,** a mixture of sound waves covering a wide frequency range; **white paper,** a statement, printed on white paper, issued by government for the information of parliament; **white sale,** a sale of linen goods at reduced prices; **white slave,** a white girl exported or transported to live as a prostitute; **white spirit,** a petroleum distillate used as a substitute for turpentine in mixing paints, &c. [O.E. *hwīt*; O.N. *hvitr,* Ger. *weiss.*]

whither, *hwiTH'ér, adv.* to what place? to which place: to what.—*adv.* **whithersoev'er,** to whatever place. [O.E. *hwider,* from the stem of **who.**]

whitlow, *hwit'lō, n.* a painful inflammation of a finger or toe, esp. near the nail, tending to suppurate. [A corr, of *whick-flaw,* quick-flaw. Cf. **quick,** living flesh, and **flaw** (2).]

Whitsun, *hwit'sun, adj.* pertaining to, or observed at, Whitsuntide.—*ns.* **Whit'sunday,** the seventh *Sunday* after Easter, commemorating the day of Pentecost, when the converts in the primitive Church wore white robes; **Whit'sun(tide),** the season of Pentecost. [white, Sunday.]

whittle, *hwit'l, v.t.* to pare or cut with a knife: to shape with a knife: to diminish gradually (with *away, down*). [M.E. *thwitel*—O.E. *thwītan,* to cut.]

whiz, whizz, *hwiz, v.i.* to make a hissing sound, like an arrow or ball flying through the air: to move rapidly:—*pr.p.* whizz'ing; *pa.t.* and *pa.p.* whizzed.—*n.* a hissing sound.—*ns.* **whizz'bang,** (*slang*) a light shell of high velocity which is heard arriving before the sound of the gun's report: a firework suggestive of this; **whizz-kid,** (*slang*) one who achieves success rapidly: one who has progressive ideas. [Imit.; cf. **wheeze, hiss.**]

who, *hōō, pron.* (both *rel.* and *interrog.*) what person? which person.—*pron.* **whoev'er,** every one who: whatever person.—Also **whoso', whosoev'er.—whom, whose** (see separate articles). [O.E. *hwā*; cog. with O.N. *hver,* Ger. *wer*; also with Sans. *ka,* L. *quis.*]

whodun(n)it, *hōō-dun'it, n.* a story concerned with a crime mystery.

whole, *hōl, adj.* not broken, unimpaired: containing the total amount, number, &c.: all complete: sound, as in health (*B.*).—*n.* the entire thing: a system or combination of parts.—*adj.* **whole'-heart'ed,** zealous and sincere.—*ns.* **whole'-meal,** unbolted flour, containing bran; **whole'ness; whole'sale,** sale of goods, usually by the whole piece or large quantity, to a retailer.—*adj.* buying and selling thus: extensive.—*adj.* **whole'some,** healthy: sound: salutary.—*adv.* **whole'somely.**—*n.* **whole'someness.**—*adv.* **wholly** (*hōl'li, hōl'i*), completely, altogether.—**upon, on, the whole,** taking everything into account; **go the whole hog,** (*slang*) to do completely, to the limit; **with whole skin,** safe, unharmed. [O.E. *hāl,* healthy; O.N. *heill,* Ger. *heil.* By-form **hale** (1).]

whom, *hōōm, pron.* objective case (*acc.* or *dat.*) of **who.**—*pron.* **whomsoev'er,** objective case of **whoever, whosoever.** [O.E. *hwām,* which was orig. dat. of *hwā,* who, and replaced as acc. the older acc. *hwone.*]

Neutral vowels in unaccented syllables: *em'pér-ór*; for certain sounds in foreign words see p. ix.

whoop, hoop, *hwōōp*, or *hōōp*, *n.* a loud eager cry: the long noisy inspiration heard in whooping-cough.—*v.i.* to give a loud cry of triumph or scorn.—*ns.* **whoop'er,** a species of swan; **whoop'ing-cough, hoop'ing-cough,** an infectious and epidemic disease of children, causing a convulsive cough. [O.Fr. *houper,* to shout.]

whoopee, *hwōōp'ē, interj.,* an exclamation of delight.—**make whoopee,** (*slang*) to indulge in hilarious amusements or dissipation. [whoop.]

whore, *hōr, hôr, n.* a prostitute: any unchaste woman.—*v.i.* to practise lewdness.—*ns.* **whore'dom,** unlawful sexual intercourse: idolatry; **whore'monger,** a lecher: a pander.—*adj.* **whō'rish.**—*adv.* **whō'rishly.**—*n.* **whō'rishness.** [O.N. *hōra,* an adulteress.]

whorl, *hwôrl, hwûrl, n.* a number of leaves in a circle round the stem: a turn in a spiral shell.—*adj.* **whorled,** having whorls. [By-form of **whirl.**]

whortleberry, *hwûr'tl-ber-i, n.* a widely-spread heath plant with a dark blue edible berry, called also the **bilberry.** [Earlier *hurtleberry*; cf. O.E. *hortan,* whortleberries.]

whose, *hōōz, pron.* the possessive case of **who** or **which.**—*pron.* **whosesoev'er** (*B.*), of whomsoever. [M.E. *hwas*—O.E. *hwæs,* gen. of *hwā,* who.]

why, *hwī, adv.* and *conj.* for what cause or reason (?).—*rel. pron.* on account of which (e.g. *the reason why I came*).—*interj.* expressing sudden realisation, or protest, or marking resumption after a question or a slight pause.—**the why and wherefore,** the whole reason. [O.E. *hwī, hwȳ,* instrumental case of *hwā,* who.]

wick, *wik, n.* the twisted threads of cotton or other substance in a candle, lamp, &c., which draw up the inflammable liquid. [O.E. *wēoce.*]

wicked, *wik'id, adj.* evil in principle or practice, deviating from morality, sinful, ungodly: mischievous, spiteful: (*coll.*) very bad: (*coll.*) roguish.—*n.* (*B.*) a wicked person, (*pl.*) wicked persons collectively.—*adv.* **wick'edly.** —*n.* **wick'edness.** [M.E. *wicked, wikked*; perh. conn. with O.E. *wicca,* wizard.]

wicker, *wik'ér, n.* a small pliant twig or osier.—*adj.* made of twigs or osiers.—*n.* **wick'erwork,** basketwork of any kind. [M.E. *wiker*—O.E. *wīcen,* pa.p. of *wīcan,* to bend.]

wicket, *wik'et, n.* a small gate: a small door or gate forming part of a larger one: (*cricket*) a set of three upright stumps at which the bowler aims the ball: one of these stumps: the ground between the bowler and the batsman: a batsman's innings.—*ns.* **wick'et-door, -gate,** a wicket; **wick'et-keep'er,** in cricket, the fieldsman who stands immediately behind the wicket. [O.Fr. *wiket* (Fr. *guichet*); of Germanic origin.]

wide, *wīd, adj.* extending far: having a considerable distance between the sides: broad: opened as far as possible: far apart: far from the point aimed at (with *of*): astute: (*fig.*) of large scope, comprehending or considering much.—*n.* in cricket, a ball bowled beyond the batsman's reach: a penalty run allowed for such a bowl.—*advs.* **wide, wide'ly.**—*adjs.*

wide'-angle, (*phot.*) pertaining to a lens having an angle of view of 60° or more and a short focal length; **wide'-awake',** fully awake: on the alert: ready.—*n.* a kind of soft felt hat. —*v.t.* and *v.i.* **wi'den,** to make or grow wide or wider.—*ns.* **wide'ness; wide screen,** a wide curved cinema screen designed to give the viewer a greater sense of actuality in the picture.—*adjs.* **wide'-spectrum,** of an antibiotic, &c., active against a wide range of micro-organisms; **wide'-spread,** widely extended or diffused.—*n.* **width,** wideness, breadth.—**to the wide,** (*coll.*) completely, utterly. [O.E. *wīd*; O.N. *vīthr,* Ger. *weit.*]

widgeon, *wij'ŏn, n.* a genus of wild ducks, feet rather small, wings long and pointed, and the tail wedge-shaped: a fool (*obs.*). [O.Fr. *vigeon*—L. *vipiō, vipiōnis,* a small crane.]

widow, *wid'ō, n.* a woman who has lost her husband by death.—*v.t.* to bereave of a husband: to strip of anything valued.—*ns.* **wid'ower,** a man whose wife is dead; **wid'owhood,** state of being a widow, or (rarely) of being a widower.—**widow's weeds,** the mourning dress of a widow. [O.E. *widewe, wuduwe*; Ger. *witwe,* L. *vidua.*]

wield, *wēld, v.t.* to use with full command: to manage, to use.—*n.* **wiel'der.**—*adj.* **wiel'dy,** capable of being wielded, manageable. [O.E. *geweldan*—*wealdan*; Ger. *walten.*]

wiener schnitzel, *ve'ner shnit'sél,* a veal cutlet dressed with egg and breadcrumbs. [Ger.]

wife, *wīf, n.* a married woman: the woman to whom one is married: a woman:—*pl.* **wives.**—*adjs.* **wife'less,** without a wife; **wife'-like, wife'ly.** [O.E. *wīf*; O.N. *vīf,* Ger. *weib.*]

wig, *wig, n.* an artificial covering of hair for the head.—*adj.* **wigged,** wearing a wig. [Short for **periwig.**]

wig, *wig, v.t.* (*coll.*) to scold.—*n.* **wigg'ing,** (*coll.*) a scolding. [Ety. obscure.]

wight, *wit, n.* a creature or a person—used chiefly in sport or irony. [O.E. *wiht,* a creature, prob. from *wegan,* to move, carry; Ger. *wicht*; cf. **whit.**]

wigwam, *wig'wom, -wam, n.* an Indian hut. [Eng. corr. of American Indian word.]

wild, *wīld, adj.* being in a state of nature, not tamed or cultivated: uncivilised: lawless: violent: distracted: licentious: tempestuous (e.g. *a wild night*): haphazard: rash: wide of the mark.—*n.* an uncultivated region: such regions collectively.—*adj.* **wild'-cat,** of business, scheme, &c. unreliable, unsound: of a strike, not authorised by union officials.—*v.t.* **wilder** (*wil'dér*), to bewilder.—*ns.* **wil'derness,** a wild or waste place: an uncultivated part of a garden: (*fig.*) a vast dreary extent, a large number, a confused collection; **wild'-fire,** a composition of inflammable materials: a kind of lightning flitting at intervals; **wild-goose chase** (see **chase**).—*adv.* **wild'ly.**—*n.* **wild'ness.**—**sow wild oats** (see **oat**). [O.E. *wild*; Ger. *wild.*]

wile, *wīl, n.* a trick, a sly artifice.—*v.t.* to beguile, inveigle. [O.E. *wīl, wīle*; O.N. *vēl, væl,* a trick. Prob. same root as **guile.**]

will, *wil, n.* power (also called *faculty*) of choosing or determining: act of using this power, volition: choice or determination: pleasure:

arbitrary disposal: feeling towards, as in *good* or *ill will*: disposition of one's effects at death: the written document containing such.—*v.i.* to be accustomed, ready, or sure to (do, &c.): used as an auxiliary in future constructions in 2nd and 3rd persons: to exercise the will: to decree: (*B.*) to be willing:—*pa.t.* **would** (*wŏŏd*).—*v.t.* to desire: to be resolved: to command: to seek to force, influence (oneself or another to perform a specified action) by silent exertion of the will: to dispose of by will, to bequeath:—*pa.t.* **willed** (*wild*).—*adj.* **wil'ful**, governed only by one's will: obstinate: done intentionally.—*adv.* **wil'fully.**—*n.* **wil'fulness.**—*adj.* **will'ing**, not reluctant (to), disposed (to): eager.—*adv.* **will'ingly.**—*n.* **will'ingness; will'-power,** the ability to control one's impulses, emotions, actions, &c.—**at will,** as one chooses; **with a will,** heartily. [O.E. *willa*, will—*willan*, to wish; Ger. *wollen*, L. *velle*.]

will-o'-the-wisp, *wil'-o-the-wisp'*, *n.* a luminous marsh gas, the ignis-fatuus: an elusive person or thing.

willow, *wil'ō*, *n.* a genus of trees with slender, pliant branches: the wood of the willow: a cricket bat.—*adj.* **will'owy**, abounding in willows: flexible, graceful.—**willow pattern,** a blue design of Chinese character used on china made in England from the late 18th century onwards. [O.E. *welig*; Low Ger. *wilge*, Du. *wilg*.]

willy-nilly, *wil'i-nil'i, adv.* whether one wishes it or not. [**will** (vb.) and obs. *nill* (neg. of **will**).]

wilt, *wilt, v.i.* to droop, lose energy. [Cf. Ger. *welk*, withered.]

wilt, *wilt,* 2nd pers. sing of **will.**

wily, *wī'li, adj.* full of *wiles* or tricks: using craft or stratagem, artful, sly.—*adv.* **wī'lily.**—*n.* **wī'liness,** cunning.

wimple, *wim'pl, n.* (*hist.*) a wrapping folded round neck and face (still part of a nun's dress): a flag. [O.E. *wimpel*, a neck-covering; cf. Ger. *wimpel*, a pennon, Fr. *guimpe*, a nun's veil, Eng. **gimp.**]

Wimpy, *wim'pi, n.* a kind of hamburger. [Trademark; name of hamburger-loving character in a comic strip.]

win, *win, v.t.* to get by effort: to gain in contest: to gain e.g. by luck: to gain influence over: to induce (to): to obtain the favour of.—*v.i.* to gain the victory: to gain favour: to make one's way:—*pr.p.* **winn'ing**; *pa.t.* and *pa.p.* **won** (*wun*).—*n.* a victory, success.—*ns.* **winn'er; winn'ing,** the act of one who wins: that which is won (usually in *pl.*).—*adj.* prepossessing, persuasive, attractive.—*adv.* **winn'ingly.**—*n.* **winn'ing-post,** the goal of a race-course.—**win by a head,** to win very narrowly; **win in a canter,** to win easily; **win,** or **gain, one's spurs,** to earn one's knighthood by valour on the field, hence to gain recognition or reputation by merit of any kind; **win over,** to bring over to one's opinion or party; **win through,** to be successful after overcoming difficulties. [O.E. *winnan*, to suffer, to struggle; O.N. *vinna*, to accomplish, Ger. *gewinnen*, to win.]

wince, *wins, v.i.* to shrink or start back: to make an involuntary movement (e.g. in pain): to be affected acutely, as by a sarcasm. [O.Fr. *guin-*

c(h)ir, to wince—Gmc.; cf. O.H.G. *wenken* (Ger. *wanken*), to wince. Allied to Eng. **wink,** and Ger. *winken,* to nod.]

wincey, winsey, *win'si, n.* a cloth, plain or twilled, usually with a linen or cotton warp and woollen woof.—*n.* **winceyette',** an imitation of wincey. [From **linsey-woolsey** (q.v.).]

winch, *winch, -sh, n.* the crank of a wheel or axle: a kind of hoisting machine. [O.E. *wince*, prob. orig. 'a bent handle'.]

wind, *wind* (*poet. wīnd*), *n.* air in motion: a current of air: air bearing the scent e.g. of game: breath: flatulence: empty, insignificant words.—*v.t.* (*wīnd*) to sound or signal by blowing: (*wind*) to expose to the wind: to drive hard, so as to put out of breath: to allow to recover wind: to perceive by the scent:—*pr.p.* wīnd'ing and wind'ing; *pa.p.* wound (*wownd*), winded (in each case the first form belongs with wīnd).—*ns.* **wind'age,** the difference between the size of the bore of a gun and that of the ball or shell: the influence of the wind in deflecting a missile; **wind'bag,** an excessively talkative person.—*adj.* **wind'-bound,** hindered from sailing by a contrary wind.—*ns.* **wind'cheater,** a closeknitted pullover: an anorak; **wind'-fall,** fruit blown off a tree: any unexpected gain or advantage; **wind'(-)flower,** (*poet.*) an anemone; **wind'-gauge,** an instrument for gauging or measuring the velocity of the wind (anemometer); **wind'-in'strument,** musical instrument sounded by means of wind or by the breath; **wind'jammer,** a large sailing vessel: (*coll.*) a wind-resisting golf blouse; **wind'mill,** a mill driven by the force of the wind acting on a set of sails; **wind'pipe,** the passage for the breath between the mouth and lungs, the trachea; **wind'-screen,** a transparent screen on motorcars, &c., to shelter the interior from the wind.—*adj.* **wind'-swept,** exposed to, or swept by, the wind.—*n.* **wind tunnel,** an experimental apparatus for producing a uniform steady air-stream past a model for aerodynamic investigation work.—*adv.* and *adj.* **wind'ward,** towards where the wind blows from.—*n.* the point from which the wind blows.—*adj.* **wind'y,** consisting of or resembling wind: exposed to the winds: tempestuous: (*fig.*) empty, pretentious: (*coll.*) frightened, nervous.—**get the wind up,** (*slang*) to become nervous, apprehensive; **get wind of,** to get a hint or intimation of; **in the wind,** astir, afoot; **in the wind's eye, in the teeth of the wind,** right against the wind; **like the wind,** very rapidly; **sail close to the wind,** to keep the boat's head so near to the wind as to fill but not shake the sails: to be in danger of transgressing an approved limit; **second wind,** power of respiration recovered after breathlessness: (*fig.*) the energy necessary for a renewal of effort. [O.E. *wind*; O.N. *vindr*, Ger. *wind*, L. *ventus*, Gr. *aētēs*, Sans. *vāta*, wind.]

wind, *wīnd, v.t.* to turn, to twist, to coil: to haul or hoist, as by a winch: to encircle: to screw the mechanism of (e.g. a timepiece): to wind (one's way) by turning and twisting.—*v.i.* to turn completely or often: to turn round something, to twist, to move spirally: to meander:

Neutral vowels in unaccented syllables: *em'pėr-ȯr*; for certain sounds in foreign words see p. ix.

838

—pr.p. wind′ing; *pa.t.* and *pa.p.* wound (*wownd*).—*n.* **wind′er**, one who winds: an instrument for winding: a twisting plant.—*adj.* **wind′ing**, curving, full of bends: spiral.—*n.* a turning: a twist.—*ns.* **wind′ing-en′gine**, a machine for hoisting; **wind′ing-sheet**, a sheet enwrapping a corpse; **wind′-up**, the close.—**wind up**, to coil completely: to wind the spring or the mechanism of tightly: to excite very much (e.g. *wound up*, excited): to bring or come to a conclusion: to adjust for final settlement. [O.E. *windan*; Ger. *winden*, O.N. *vinda*; cf. **wend, wander**.]

windlass, *wind′las*, *n.* a machine for raising weights by winding a rope round a revolving cylinder. [M.E. *windas*, a windlass—O.N. *vindāss*—*vinda*, to wind, *āss*, pole.]

window, *win′dō*, *n.* an opening in a wall of a building, &c., for air and light: the frame in the opening: any opening, or any enclosed area consisting of a different material, that suggests a window.—*adj.* **win′dowed**, having a window or windows.—**window dressing**, the art of arranging effectively, or the arrangement of, goods in a shop-window: (*fig.*) the art of giving a specious attractiveness to a cause, or an unduly favourable appearance to a situation (e.g. political); **window envelope**, an envelope with an opening or a transparent panel that allows the name and address on the communication to show through; **window shopping**, considering the goods in shop windows without intending to buy. [M.E. *windowe*—O.N.*vindauga*—*vindr*, wind, *auga*, eye.]

Windsor, *win′zor*, *adj.* pertaining to *Windsor*, as in **Wind′sor-chair**, a kind of strong, plain, polished chair, made entirely of wood.

wine, *wīn*, *n.* the fermented juice of grapes: a liquor made from other fruits: a rich red colour.—*ns.* **wine′-bibb′er**, a continual drinker of wine: a drunkard; **wine′-press**, a machine in which grapes are pressed in the manufacture of wine; **wine′-skin**, a bottle made of skin for holding wine. [O.E. *wīn*, Ger. *wein*—L. *vīnum*; cog. with Gr. *oinos.*]

wing, *wing*, *n.* the organ of a bird, or other animal or insect, by which it flies: flight: any side-piece on a stage, aeroplane, building, &c.: the flank of an army: a player on either extreme of the forward line in football, &c.: a group of three squadrons in the Royal Air Force: (*pl.*) a badge worn by flying members of the R.A.F.—*v.t.* to furnish or transport with wings: to lend speed to: to traverse by flying: to wound in the wing, or in the arm or shoulder.—*v.i.* to soar.—*adj.* **winged** (*wingd* or *wing′id*), furnished with wings: swift: (*wingd*) wounded in the wing, shoulder, or arm.—*n.* **wing-commander**, a Royal Air Force officer corresponding in rank to a naval commander or to a lieutenant-colonel.—**flying wing** (see **flying**); **on, upon, the wing**, flying, in motion: departing; **in the wings**, waiting in reserve; **on the wings of the wind**, with the utmost speed; **take wing**, to fly off, flee, depart; **under one's wing**, under one's protection, guidance. [O.N. *vœngr*, a wing; Swed. *vinge*.]

wink, *wingk*, *v.i.* to move the eyelids quickly: to give a hint by winking: to seem not to see, connive at (usu. with *at*): to flicker,

twinkle.—*v.t.* to close and open quickly.—*n.* act of winking: a hint given by winking.—**forty winks** (*coll.*), a short nap. [O.E. *wincian* (Ger. *winken*).]

winkle, *wing′kl*. Same as **periwinkle** (2).—**winkle out**, (*fig.*) to force out gradually and with difficulty (perh. derived from Ger. *winkel*, corner).

winning, winner. See **win**.

winnow, *win′ō*, *v.t.* to separate the chaff from (the grain) by wind: to fan: (*fig.*) to sift.—Also *v.i.*—*n.* **winn′ower**. [O.E.*windwian*, to winnow.]

winsome, *win′sòm*, *adj.* cheerful: pleasant, attractive.—*adv.* **win′somely**.—*n.* **win′someness**. [O.E. *wynsum*, pleasant—*wyn*, joy (Ger. *wonne*).]

winter, *win′tér*, *n.* the cold season of the year—in northern temperate regions, from November or December to January or February; astronomically, from the winter solstice to the vernal equinox: any season of cheerlessness.—*adj.* pertaining to winter.—*v.i.* to pass the winter.—*v.t.* to feed, or to detain, during winter.—*ns.* **win′ter-gar′den**, an ornamental conservatory; **win′ter-green**, any of a genus of plants of temperate regions, esp. *common winter-green*, which has smooth stiff evergreen leaves close to the root and a small head of white or reddish flowers; a low evergreen herb of a different family, one source of an oil used in medicine and confectionery.—*n.pl.* **win′ter-quar′ters**, the quarters of an army during winter: a winter residence.—*n.* **win′ter-wheat**, wheat sown in autumn.—*adj.* **win′try**, **win′tery**, resembling, or suitable to, winter: stormy.—**winter sports**, open-air sports practised on snow and ice, as skiing, &c. [O.E. *winter*; Ger. *winter*; of uncertain origin; not conn. with **wind**.]

wipe, *wīp*, *v.t.* to clean or dry by rubbing: (with *away, off, out, up*) to clear away.—*n.* act of cleaning by rubbing: a blow.—*ns.* **wi′per**, one who, or that which, wipes: a moving arm, electrically operated, for removing raindrops, &c. from the windscreen of a motor vehicle; **wī′ping**, the act of wiping: a thrashing. [O.E. *wīpian.*]

wire, *wīr*, *n.* a thread of metal: the metal thread used in telegraphy, &c.: the string of an instrument: a telegram: a telegram.—*adj.* formed of wire.—*v.t.* to fasten with wire: to supply (e.g. a building) with wires necessary for carrying an electric current: to send by, or to inform by, telegraph.—*v.i.* to telegraph.—*adjs.* **wire′-drawn**, spun out into needless fine distinctions; **wire′less**, without a wire or wires, esp. in telegraphy and telephony.—*n.* wireless telegraphy or telephony: a message thereby: radio programmes: radio apparatus: broadcasting generally.—*v.t.* and *v.i.* to communicate by radio.—*ns.* **wire′less sta′tion**, a station for wireless transmission; **wire′less teleg′raphy**, **teleph′ony**, telegraphy, telephony, by means of electric waves without the use of conducting wires between transmitter and receiver; **wire′-pull′er**, one who exercises an influence felt but not seen, as if the actors were his puppets and he pulled the wires that move them: an intriguer; **wire′-pull′ing**.—*adjs.* **wire′-wove**, denoting a fine quality of writing-paper (see **wove**); **wī′ry**, made of, or like, wire: flexible and strong: (of a person) strong and able to endure.—**wire in**, to act with vigour. [O.E. *wīr*; O.N. *vīrr*; perh. conn. with L. *viriae*, bracelets.]

wis, *wis, v.* (in the form *I wis*) erroneously used as 'I know'; the *pr.t.* of O.E. *witan*, to know, was *wāt* (a preterite form). [*I wis* is the M.E. adv. *i-wis*, certainly—O.E. p.adj. *gewis*, certain; cf. Ger. *gewiss.*]

wisdom, *wiz′dóm, n.* quality of being wise: ability to make right use of knowledge: (*B.*) spiritual perception.—*n.* **wis′dom-tooth**, one of the four teeth cut after childhood, usually about the age of twenty. [O.E. *wīsdōm*, wisdom; cf. **wise.**]

wise, *wīz, adj.* having knowledge: learned: able to use knowledge well, judging rightly, discreet: skilful, dictated by wisdom: containing wisdom.—*adv.* **wise′ly.**—**wise guy**, a conceited, over-confident person; **wise woman**, a witch. [O.E. *wīs*; Ger. *weise*; from root of **wit** (1) and (2).]

wise, *wīz, n.* way, manner.—**in any wise**, **in no wise**, in any way, in no way; **on this wise**, in this way. [O.E. *wīse*, orig. wiseness; Ger. *weise*; akin to **wise** and **wit** (1) and (2). Doublet **guise.**]

wiseacre, *wīz′ā-kér, n.* one who unduly assumes an air of superior wisdom: a simpleton quite unconscious of being such. [Perh. through the medium of Middle Du. from O.H.G. *wīzago*, a prophet.]

wish, *wish, v.i.* to have a desire (for): to long (so in *B.*): to express a desire.—*v.t.* to desire or long for: to express a desire (that, to do, &c.): to pray or hope for on behalf of (someone).—*n.* desire, longing: thing desired: expression of desire.—*n.* **wish′er.**—*adj.* **wish′ful**, having a wish or desire: eager.—*adv.* **wish′fully.**—*n.* **wish′fulness.**—**wishful thinking**, a belief that a particular thing will happen, engendered by desire that it should: (loosely) thinking about and wishing for an event or turn of fortune that may not take place; **wish fulfilment**, (*psych.*) the satisfaction of a desire in dreams, day-dreams, &c.—**wish one joy of,** (usu. ironical) to hope that possession of may be a benefit to one. [O.E. *wȳscan—wūsc*, a wish; Ger. *wünschen*, Swed. *önska.*]

wishy-washy, *wish′i-wosh′i, adj.* thin and weak, diluted, feeble. [Formed from **wash.**]

wisp, *wisp, n.* a small tuft or thin strand. [M.E. *wisp*; of doubtful origin.]

wist, *wist, v.i.* (arch.) to know—really *pa.t.* and *pa.p.* of **wit** (1).

wistful, *wist′fŏŏl, -fl, adj.* pensive: yearning with little hope.—*adv.* **wist′fully.**—*n.* **wist′fulness.** [Most prob. for *wistly*, intently—*whistly*, silently; and not conn. with **wish.**]

wit, *wit, v.t.* and *v.i.* to know (obs.):—*pr.t.* 1st pers. sing. **wot**; 2nd, **wost** (erroneously **wot′t′est**); 3rd, **wot** (erroneously **wott′eth**):—*pl.* 1st, 2nd, 3rd, **wot**; *pa.t.* **wist** (erroneously **wott′ed**); *pr.p.* **witt′ing**, **weet′ing** (erroneously **wott′ing**); *pa.p.* **wist**.—**to wit**, that is to say—the O.E. gerund *tō witanne*. [O.E. *witan*, to know; Ger. *wissen*; cf. L. *vidēre*, Gr. *idein* (aor.), to see.]

wit, *wit, n.* understanding: a mental faculty (chiefly in *pl.*): common sense: facility in combining ideas with a pointed verbal effect: the product of this power: a person endowed with such power.—*adj.* **wit′less**, without wit or understanding: thoughtless.—*adv.* **wit′lessly.** —*ns.* **wit′lessness; wit′ling**, one who has little wit: a pretender to wit.—*adj.* **witt′ed**, having wit or understanding—usu. in composition, as *quick-witted* (q.v.).—*n.* **witticism** (*wit′i-sizm*), a witty remark.—*adv.* **witt′ingly**, knowingly, by design.—*adj.* **witt′y**, possessed of wit—amusing, droll, sarcastic: (*B.*) ingenious.—*adv.* **witt′ily.**—*n.* **witt′iness—at one′s wits′ end,** utterly perplexed; **live by one′s wits,** to gain a livelihood by ingenious expedients rather than by honest labour. [O.E. (*ge*)*wit*—**wit** (1).]

witch, *wich, n.* a woman regarded as having supernatural or magical power and knowledge through compact with the devil: a hag, crone: (*fig.*) a fascinating woman.—*v.t.* to bewitch.— *ns.* **witch′craft**, the craft or practice of witches, sorcery, supernatural power; **witch′ery**, witchcraft: fascination; **witch′-hunt**, (orig. *U.S.*) the searching out of political opponents for exposure on grounds of alleged disloyalty to the state, &c.: also applied to any similar non-political search. [M.E. *wicche* (both masc. and fem.)—O.E. *wicca* (masc.), *wicce* (fem.), wizard, witch.]

witch, **witch-elm**, *wich, wich′-elm, n.* a common wild elm—also called *Scotch elm* or *witch hazel.—n.* **witch′-hā′zel**, any of a number of different trees and shrubs, one of which, a North American shrub, supplies bark for making a supposed remedy for bruises, &c. [O.E. *wice*, the service-tree—*wican*, to bend.]

witenagemot, *wit′e-na-ge-mōt′, n.* the supreme council of England in Anglo-Saxon times. [O.E. *witena gemōt—wita*, a wise man, *gemōt*, a meeting.]

with, *n.* Same as **withe.**

with, *with, with, prep.* denoting nearness, agreement, or connection—e.g. in competition: in contrast: on the side of: in the same direction as: in company with: among: possessing: in respect of, in the regard of: by, by means of, through.—*adv.* **withal′** (*obs.*), with all or the rest: likewise: moreover.—*prep.* an emphatic form of **with** (used after its object).—**feel**, or **be**, or **think, with,** to feel as, or be of the same opinion as, the other person specified; **in with**, (*coll.*) friendly with; **with it**, (*slang*) aware of and abreast of current trends in popular taste. [O.E. *with*, against; O.N. *vith*, Ger. *wider*. It ousted the O.E. *mid*, with (Ger. *mit*).]

withdraw, *with-dró′* (or *-th*), *v.t.* to draw back or away: to take back or away: to recall, retract, unsay.—*v.i.* to retire: to go away.—*ns.* **withdraw′al, withdraw′ment.**—*adj.* **withdrawn′**, secluded (of place): remote, detached (of manner). [Pfx. *with-*, against, and **draw.**]

withe, *with, with,* or *wīth, withy, with′i, n.* a flexible twig, esp. of willow: a band of twisted twigs. [O.E. *withthe*, or *wīthig*; O.N. *vithir*, Ger. *weide*, willow.]

wither, *with′ér, v.i.* to fade or become dry: to lose freshness: to decay, waste.—*v.t.* to cause to dry up, fade, or decay: (*fig.*) to blight: to cause to feel very unimportant or despicable (e.g. *withered her with a look*). [O.E. *wederen* to expose to weather.]

Neutral vowels in unaccented syllables: *em′pér-ór*; for certain sounds in foreign words see p. ix.

withers, wiᴛн′érz, *n.pl.* the ridge between the shoulder-bones of a horse. [O.E. *wither*, against, an extension of *with*, against.]

withhold, wiᴛн-hōld′ (or *with*-), *v.t.* to restrain: refuse to give:—*pa.t.* and *pa.p.* **withheld′**. [Pfx. *with*-, against, and **hold**.]

within, wiᴛн-in′, *prep.* in the inner part of, inside: in the limits of, not going beyond.—*adv.* in the inner part: inwardly.—**within reach**, obtainable without difficulty. [O.E. *withinnan*—*with*, against, with, *innan*, in.]

without, wiᴛн-owt′, *prep.* outside or out of, beyond: not with, in absence of, not having, free from.—*adv.* on the outside: (*arch.*) out of doors. [O.E. *withūtan*—*with*, against, *ūtan*, outside.]

withstand, wiᴛн-stand′ (or *with*-), *v.t.* to stand against, to oppose or resist:—*pa.t.* and *pa.p.* **withstood′**. [Pfx. *with*-, against, and **stand**.]

withy. Same as **withe**.

witness, wit′nes, *n.* knowledge brought in proof: testimony (of a fact): that which furnishes proof: one who sees or has personal knowledge of a thing: one who gives evidence or attests, —*v.t* to have direct knowledge of: to see: to be the scene of: to testify to, or (that): to show.—*v.i.* to give evidence: to attest.—*n.* **wit′ness-box**, the enclosure in which a witness stands when giving evidence in a court of law. —**bear witness**, to provide evidence or proof, give testimony. [O.E. *witnes*, testimony—*witan*, to know.]

wivern, wī′vérn, *n.* (*her.*) a fictitious monster, winged and two-legged, allied to the dragon and the griffin. [O. Norman Fr. *wivre*, a viper—L. *vīpera*.]

wives, wīvz, *pl.* of **wife**.

wizard, wiz′árd, *n.* one (usually a man) who practises witchcraft or magic: one who works wonders, —*adj.* (*slang*) wonderful, very good. [M.E. *wysard*—*wys*, *wis*, wise, and suffx. -*ard*.]

wizen, wiz′n, **wizened**, wiz′nd, *adj.* dried up, thin, shrivelled.—*v.i.* and *v.t.* to become or make dry. [O.E. *wisnian*, to wither; cog. with O.N. *visinn*, wizened, *visna*, to wither.]

woad, wōd, *n.* a genus of plants yielding a blue dye: the dyestuff made from their leaves. [O.E. *wād*; Ger. *waid*.]

wobble, wob′l, *v.i.* to rock unsteadily from side to side: (*fig.*) to waver, to vacillate.—*n.* **wob′b′ler**.—*adj.* **wobb′ly**. [Low Ger. *wabbeln*; cog. with **waver**.]

woe, wō, *n.* grief, misery: a heavy calamity: a curse: an exclamation of grief.—*adjs.* **woe′begone**, beset with woe (*begone* is *pa.p.* of O.E. *begān*, to go round, beset); **woe′ful**, sorrowful; bringing calamity: wretched.—*adv.* **woe′fully.**—*n.* **woe′fulness.**—**woe worth the day** (see **worth** (2)). [O.E. (interj.) *wā*; Ger. *weh*; L. *vae*; cf. **wail**.]

wog, wog, *n.* a disrespectful name for an Arab, an Egyptian, &c.: also for a foreigner generally, usu. coloured. [Perh. from (golly)**wog**.]

woke, *pa.t.* and (*rare*) *pa.p.* of **wake**; **woken**, *pa.p.* of **wake**.

wold, wōld, *n.* By-form of **weald**.

wolf, wŏŏlf, *n.* a gregarious beast of prey of the dog genus: anything very ravenous: a greedy and cruel person: (*slang*) a philanderer without restraint or conscience:—*pl.* **wolves**.—*v.t.*

(*slang*) to devour ravenously.—*ns.* **Wolf Cub** (former name for **Cub Scout**), a member of a division of the Scouts organisation for boys from eight years of age to eleven; **wŏlf′-dog**, a dog of large breed kept to guard sheep, esp. against wolves.—*adjs.* **wolf′fish**, **wol′vish**, like a wolf either in form or quality: rapacious.—*adv.* **wolf′ishly.**—*ns.* **wolf′s′bane** (**wolf′s′-bane**), an aconite; **wolf′-skin**, the skin or pelt of a wolf; **wolf′-whistle**, a two-note male whistle emitted at the sight of a woman.—**a wolf in sheep's clothing**, someone, seemingly gentle and harmless, who is really fierce and dangerous; **cry wolf**, to give a false alarm; **keep the wolf from the door**, to keep hunger or want from the home. [O.E. *wulf*; Ger. *wolf*; L. *lupus*; Gr. *lykos*.]

wolfram, wŏŏl′fram, *n.* an ore containing iron, manganese, and tungsten, from which tungsten is obtained: tungsten. [Ger.]

wolverene, **wolverine**, wŏŏl-ve-rēn′, *n.* a carnivorous quadruped of N. America, of the same genus as the glutton. [Extension of **wolf**.]

woman, wŏŏm′án, *n.* the female of man, an adult female of the human race: the female sex, women collectively: a female attendant:—*pl.* **women** (wim′én),—*ns.* **wom′an-hāt′er**, a misogynist; **wom′anhood**, the state, character or qualities of a woman.—*adj.* **wom′anish**, like or befitting a woman (used disparagingly): effeminate.— *adv.* **wom′anishly.**—*ns.* **wom′anishness**; **wom′ankind**, **wom′enkind**, women taken together, the female sex.—*adj.* and *adv.* **wom′an-like.**—*adj.* **wom′anly**, (of conduct, feelings) like or befitting a woman (a more flattering epithet than 'womanish').—*n.* **wom′anliness.**—**women's liberation movement**, **women's lib.**, a movement (begun in the late 1960's) advocating the complete equality of men and women in all fields; **women's rights movement**, an earlier movement aiming at (mainly political) equality of men and women. [O.E. *wimman*, *wifman*, a compound of *wíf*, a woman, *man*, man.]

womb, wŏŏm, *n.* the organ in which the young of mammals are developed and kept till birth: the place where anything is produced: any deep cavity. [O.E. *wamb*; Ger. *wamme*, paunch.]

wombat, wom′bat, *n.* a genus of Australian marsupial mammals of the same order as opossums. [Native name.]

won, wun, *pa.t.* and *pa.p.* of **win**.

wonder, wun′dér, *n.* the state of mind produced by something new, unexpected, or extraordinary: a strange thing: a prodigy: quality of being strange, unexpected.—*v.i.* to feel wonder: to be amazed (with *at*): to speculate: to feel doubt.—*v.t.* to speculate (with noun clause or direct quotation).—*adj.* **won′derful**, full of wonder, exciting wonder, strange: (*B.*) wonderfully.—*adv.* **won′derfully.**—*n.* **won′derfulness.**—*adv.* **won′deringly**, with wonder.—*n.* **won′derland**, a land of wonders.—*adj.* **won′drous**, such as may excite wonder, strange.—*adv.* **won′drously.**—*n.* **won′drousness.**—**Seven Wonders of the World**, the Pyramids, the Hanging Gardens of Babylon, the Temple of Artemis at Ephesus, Phidias's statue of Zeus at Olympia, the Mausoleum at Halicarnassus, the Colossus of Rhodes, and the Pharos of Alexandria; **nine-days' wonder**, something that astonishes everybody for a short time. [O.E. *wundor*; Ger. *wunder*, O.N. *undr*.]

wonky, *wong′ki*, *adj*. (*coll*.) unsound: shaky: amiss.

wont, *wŏnt*, *wunt*, *adj*. accustomed.—*n*. habit.—*v.i.* to be accustomed.—*adj.* **won′ted**, accustomed: usual.—*n*. **won′tedness**. [Orig. pa.p. of *won*, to dwell—O.E. *wunian*; Ger. *wohnen*.]

won't, *wŏnt*, will not. [Contr. of M.E. *wol not*.]

woo, *wōō*, *v.t.* to ask in marriage: to court: to solicit eagerly: to seek to gain.—Also *v.i.*—*n*. **woo′er**. [O.E. *wōgian*, to woo—*wōg*, *wōh*, bent.]

wood, *wŏŏd*, *n.* the hard part of trees: trees cut or sawed, timber: a kind of timber: a collection of growing trees (also used in *pl.*): a cask, barrel.—*v.t.* to cover with trees.—*ns*. **wood′bine**, **wood′bind**, the honeysuckle, applied also to other climbers, such as some kinds of ivy, the Virginia-creeper, &c.; **wood′-coal**, coal like wood in texture, lignite or brown coal: charcoal; **wood′cock**, a genus of bird allied to the snipes; **wood′craft**, skill in the chase and everything pertaining to life in the forests; **wood′cut**, an engraving cut on wood: an impression from it; **wood′-cutter**.—*adjs.* **wood′ed**, covered with trees; **wood′en**, made of, or like, wood: (of golf-club) with head made of wood: dull, stupid, lacking animation or grace of manner or execution: clumsy.—*ns*. **wood′-engra′ving**, the art of engraving designs on wood: an engraving on or print from wood; **wood′-engra′ver**; **wood′-fi′bre**, fibre derived from wood; **wood′-hy′acinth**, the wild hyacinth or English bluebell, a flower of the genus *Scilla*; **wood′land**, land covered with wood; **wood′lark**, a species of lark, found in or near woods, singing chiefly on the wing; **wood(-)louse** (*pl.* **wood(-)lice**), any of numerous small crustaceans (q.v.), usu. greyish or brownish, and usu. living under stones, &c.; **wood′-man**, a man who cuts down trees: a forest officer; **wood′pecker**, any of a family of birds that peck holes in the wood or bark of trees and extract the insects on which they feed; **wood′-pig′eon**, the cushat or ringdove; **wood′-pulp**, wood-fibre reduced to a pulp, used in making paper; **wood′ruff**, a genus of plants with whorled leaves and a funnel-shaped corolla; **wood sorrel**, a genus of plants with delicate white flowers, growing in woods—a source of acid potassium oxalate and hence of oxalic acid (see **salts of sorrel**); **wood spirit**, a spirit living among trees: methanol, wood alcohol, an alcohol obtained from wood or synthetically, used as a solvent, &c.; **wood′ward**, an officer to guard the woods; **wood-wind**, section of an orchestra in which wind-instruments of wood are played; **wood′work**, the wooden part of any structure; carpentry; **wood′-worm**, a larva that bores in wood.—*adj.* **wood′y**, abounding with woods: pertaining to woods: consisting of, or resembling, wood. [O.E. *wudu*; cog. with O.N. *vithr*, wood; akin to Ir. *fiodh*, timber.]

woodchuck, *wŏŏd′chuk*, *n.* the marmot (q.v.). [Corr. of an Amer. Indian name.]

wooer, **wooing**, &c. See **woo**.

woof, *wŏŏf*, *n.* same as **weft**. [O.E. *ōwef*, *ōwebb*—*āwefan*, to weave—*ā-*, inten; *wefan*, to weave.]

wool, *wŏŏl*, *n.* the soft hair of sheep and other animals: thread or yarn made of wool: fabric of wool: short, thick hair: any light, fleecy substance resembling wool: any substance with a fibrous texture resembling wool.—*n*. **wool′gath′ering**, absent-minded dreaming.—*adj.* dreamy.—*n*. **wool′-grow′er**, one who raises sheep for the production of wool.—*adj.* **wool′len**, made of, or pertaining to, wool.—*n*. cloth made of wool.—*adj.* **wool′ly**, consisting of, or like, wool: clothed with wool: (*fig.*) vague, hazy.—*ns*. **wool′liness**; **wool′-pack**, a bale of wool weighing 240 lb.: fleecy cloud; **wool′sack**, the seat of the Lord Chancellor in the House of Lords, a large square sack covered with scarlet: the office of Lord Chancellor. [O.E. *wull*; Ger. *wolle*.]

woozy, *wōō′zi*, *adj.* fuddled: dazed: blurred, vague.

wop, *wop*, *n.* a derogatory term for an Italian or other foreigner of olive complexion. [It. (dial.) *guappo*.]

word, *wûrd*, *n.* an oral or written sign denoting a thing or an idea: talk, discourse: a message: a promise: a declaration: a password: a watchword: a signal or sign: a brief conversation: a rumour: (*pl.*) verbal quarrel.—*v.t.* to express in words.—*ns*. **word′-book**, a book with a collection of words, a vocabulary; **wor′ding**, act or manner of expressing in words: choice of words, phrasing.—*adjs.* **word-perfect**, having memorised exactly; **wor′dy**, using or containing many words.—*adv.* **wor′dily**.—*n*. **wor′diness**.—**word for word**, literally, verbatim.—**a word in one's ear**, a confidential conversation; **break one's word**, to fail to fulfil a promise; **by word of mouth**, orally; **get a word in edgeways**, get a word into a conversation with difficulty; **good word**, favourable mention, praise; **hard words**, angry, hot words; **have a word with**, to have some conversation with; **have words with**, to quarrel, dispute with; **in a word**, **in one word**, in short, to sum up; **in word**, in speech only, in profession only; **pass one's word**, to make a promise; **take at one's word**, to accept one's statements as being literally true; **the Word**, the Scripture: (*theology*) second person in the Trinity. [O.E. *word*; O.N. *orth*, Ger. *wort*; also conn. with L. *verbum*, a word, Gr. *eirein*, to speak.]

wore, *wōr*, *wŏr*, *pa.t.* of **wear**.

work, *wûrk*, *n.* effort directed to an end: employment: that on which one works: the product of work, anything made or done: needlework: deed: doings: a literary composition: a book: management, manner of working (as good, skilful, bad, &c.): (in *pl.*) walls, trenches, &c.: (*pl.*) a manufactory, workshop: (*pl.*) mechanism, e.g. of a watch: (*phys.*) the act of producing an effect by means of a force (F) whose point of application moves through a distance (s) in its own line of action—measured by the product of the force and the distance $(W = Fs)$.—*v.i.* to make efforts (to achieve or attain anything): to be in action: to be occupied in business or labour: to produce effects: to make one's way slowly and labori-

Neutral vowels in unaccented syllables: *em′pėr-ŏr*; for certain sounds in foreign words see p. ix.

842

ously: to strain or labour: to ferment, to seethe.—*v.t.* to make by labour: to bring (into any state) by action: to effect: to solve, e.g. an equation in algebra: to fashion: to manipulate: to cause to ferment: to keep going, e.g. a machine: to embroider:—*pa.t.* and *pa.p.* worked or **wrought** (q.v.).—*adjs.* **work'able**, that may be worked; **work'aday**, fit for a working day: dull, prosaic.—*ns.* **work'-bag**, **-bas'ket**, a bag, basket, for holding materials for work, esp. needlework; **work'-box**, a lady's box for holding materials for work; **work'er**; **work'house**, a house of shelter for the poor, who were made to work; **work'-in**, of workers, a continuation at work in protest against e.g. proposed dismissal or proposed closure of works; **work'ing**, action, operation: (*pl.*) the parts of a mine, &c., where work is, or has been, carried on; **work'ing-class**, manual workers (often in *pl.*); **work'ing-day**, a day on which work is done, as distinguished from a holiday: the period of actual work each day; **working majority**, a majority sufficient to enable the political party in office to carry on without accidental defeats; **work(ing) party**, a group of persons who carry out a specially assigned task: a group appointed to investigate a subject, as methods of attaining maximum efficiency in an industry; **work'man**, a man who works, esp. manually.—*adj.* **work'man-like**, befitting a skilful workman: well performed.—*ns.* **work'manship**, the skill of a workman: manner of making: that which is made or produced by one's hands (also *fig.*); **work'-out**, a practice trial or exercise; **work'room**, **work'shop**, a room or shop where work is done.—*adj.* **work'-shy**, hating, avoiding work, lazy. *n.* **work study**, a time and motion study.—**work in**, to intermix, to introduce, **work into**, to make way gradually into; **work off**, to get rid of; **work on**, or **upon**, to act or operate upon, to influence; **work one's passage**, to earn one's passage by service; **work out**, to effect by continued labour: to solve or study fully: to come out by degrees: to turn out in the end; **work to rule**, to observe all the regulations scrupulously for the express purpose of slowing down work (*n.* **work-to-rule**); **work up**, to excite, rouse: to create by degrees.—**give (someone) the works**, to give (someone) everything available, every service possible: to inflict on (someone) all possible abuse or punishment (often to kill him); **have one's work cut out**, to be faced with a difficult task; **out of work**, without employment. [O.E. *weorc*; O.N. *verk*, Ger. *werk*; further conn. with Gr. *ergon*.]

world, *wûrld, n.* the earth and its inhabitants: the universe: present state of existence: any planet or heavenly body: public life or society: sphere of interest or activity: the public: a secular life: course of life: very much or a great deal, as 'a world of good': time, as in the phrase 'world without end' = eternally: possibility, as in 'nothing in the world': (*B.*) the ungodly.—*n.* **world'ling**, one who is devoted to worldly pursuits and temporal possessions.—*adj.* **world'ly**, pertaining to the world, esp as distinguished from the world to come: devoted to this life and its enjoyments: bent on

gain.—Also *adv.* in compounds, as **world'ly-mind'ed**, having the mind set on the present world, **world'ly-wise**, sophisticated, showing the earthly wisdom of those experienced in, and affected by, the ways of the world.—*ns.* **world'liness; World War**, a war of world-wide scope, esp. the Great War of 1914-18 (First World War) and that of 1939-45 (Second World War).—*adj.* **world'-wide**, extending over, or found everywhere in, the world.—**all the world**, everybody: everything; **for all the world**, precisely, entirely; **in the world**, an intensive phrase, usually following an interrogative pronoun or adverb; **on top of the world**, in a state of great elation or happiness; **out of this world**, wonderful, good beyond all experience; **the best (worst) of both worlds**, to have the advantage (disadvantage) of both alternatives when a choice is presented; **the New World**, the western hemisphere, the Americas; **the Old World**, the eastern hemisphere, comprising Europe, Africa, and Asia; **the other world**, the non-material sphere, the spiritual world; **the world is his oyster**, the world lies before him, ready to yield him profit or success; **the world's end**, the most distant point possible. [O.E. *woruld, world, weorold*, (lit.) 'a generation of men', from *wer*, a man, and *yldo*, signifying an age; O.N. *veröld*, O.H.G. *weralt* (Ger. *welt*).]

worm, *wûrm, n.* an earthworm (q.v.), loosely applied to invertebrate animals which more or less resemble the earthworm: anything helical: the thread of a screw: anything that corrupts, or that torments: remorse: a mean, grovelling creature: (*pl.*) any intestinal disease arising from the presence of parasitic worms.—*v.i.* to make one's way like a worm: to work slowly or secretly.—*v.t.* to treat for, rid of, worms: to work (oneself into a position) slowly or secretly: to elicit by slow and indirect means (e.g. *to worm the information out of him*).—*n.* **worm'-cast**, the earth voided by the earthworm.—*adjs.* **worm'-eat'en**, eaten into by wood-worms: old: worn-out; **worm'-hole**, a hole made by a wood-worm; **worm'y**, like a worm: having many worms. [O.E. *wyrm*, dragon, snake, creeping animal; cog. with O.N. *ormr*, Ger. *wurm*; also with L. *vermis*.]

wormwood, *wûrm'wood, n.* a plant (of the southernwood genus, *Artemisia*) with a bitter taste, formerly used as a vermifuge, with which absinth is flavoured: bitterness. [O.E. *wermōd* (Ger. *wermuth*), wormwood; of doubtful origin but influenced by **worm**, **wood**.]

worn, *wōrn, wōrn, pa.p.* of **wear**.

worn-out, *wōrn'-, wōrn'-owt*, (when used predicatively, *-owt'*) *adj.* much injured or rendered useless by wear: wearied. [**worn, out**.]

worry, *wur'i, v.t.* to tear with the teeth: to harass: to tease.—*v.i.* to be unduly anxious: to fret:—*pa.t.* and *pa.p.* worr'ied.—*n.* trouble, perplexity, vexation. [O.E. *wyrgan*, found in compound *āwyrgan*, to harm; cf. Du. *worgen*, Ger. *würgen*, to choke.]

worse, *wûrs, adj.* (used as *comp.* of **bad**) bad or evil in a greater degree: not so well as before.—*adv.* badly in a higher degree.—*v.i.* and *v.t.* **wor'sen**, to grow, make, worse.—**none the**

worse for, not harmed by. [O.E. *wyrsa*, from *wirsiza*, formed with comp. suffx. *-iz* from a Gmc. root *wers*, found in Ger. *verwirren*, to confuse.]

worship, *wûr'ship, n.* religious service: fervent esteem: adoration paid to God: a title of honour: submissive respect.—*v.t.* to pay divine honours to: to adore or idolise.—*v.i.* to perform acts of adoration: to take part in religious service:—*pr.p.* wor'shipping: *pa.t.* and *pa.p.* wor'shipped.—*adj.* **wor'shipful,** worthy of worship or honour, used as a term of respect.—*n.* **wor'shipper.** [O.E. *weorthscipe*—*weorth, wurth,* worth, *-scipe,* -ship.]

worst, *wûrst, adj.* (used as *superl.* of **bad;** see also **worse**) bad or evil in the highest degree.—*adv.* to a very bad or very evil degree.—*n.* the highest degree of badness: the least good part (esp. of news): one's utmost in evil or mischief (e.g. *to do one's worst*).—*v.t.* to get the advantage over in a contest, to defeat. [O.E. *wyrst, wyrrest, wyrresta,* from the same source as **worse.**]

worsted, *wŏŏst'id,* or *wōōrst'id, n.* twisted thread or yarn spun out of long, combed wool.—*adj.* made of worsted yarn. [From *Worsted,* a village near Norwich in England.]

worsted, *wûrst'id, pa.t.* and *pa.p.* of *v.t.* **worst.**

wort, *wûrt, n.* a herb: a plant of the cabbage kind. [O.E. *wyrt;* Ger. *wurz, wurzel,* a root.]

wort, *wûrt, n.* new beer unfermented or in the act of fermentation: the sweet infusion of malt: malt extract used as a medium for the culture of micro-organisms. [O.E. *wyrte,* new beer—*wyrt,* root.]

worth, *wûrth, n.* value: that quality which renders a thing valuable: price: moral excellence: importance.—*adj.* equal in value to (e.g. *worth a penny*): deserving of.—*adj.* **worth'less,** of no value, virtue, excellence.—*adv.* **worth'lessly.** —*n.* **worth'lessness.**—*adjs.* **worthwhile',** such as to repay trouble and time spent on it: good: estimable; **worthy** (*wûr'тнi*), having worth: valuable: estimable (used patronisingly): deserving (of): deserving of: suited to, in keeping with: of sufficient merit (to do).— *n.* a notability, esp. local:—*pl.* **wor'thies.**—*adv.* **worth'ily** (тн), in a worthy manner.—*n.* **worth'iness** (тн).— **for all one's worth,** with all one's might or energy; **for what it is worth,** a phrase implying that the speaker is doubtful of the truth of what he has reported or unwilling to be responsible for its accuracy. [O.E. *weorth, wurth* (Ger. *wert*), value.]

worth, *wûrth, v.i.* to be, happen, as in the phrase **woe worth** =*woe be to* (with the noun in the dative). [O.E. *weorthan,* to become; cf. Ger. *werden.*]

wot, *wot,* **wotteth,** *wot'eth,* &c. See **wit** (1).

would, *wŏŏd, pa.t.* of **will.**—*adj.* **would'-be,** aspiring, trying, or merely professing, to be. [O.E. *wolde,* pa.t. of *willan.*]

wound, *wownd, pa.t.* and *pa.p.* of **wind** (*wīnd*), (1) and (2).

wound, *wōōnd, n.* any cut, bruise, hurt, or injury caused by external force.—*v.t.* to make a wound in: (*lit.* and *fig.*) to injure. [O.E. *wund* (Ger. *wunde,* O.N. *und*).]

wove, woven, *pa.t.* and *pa.p.* of **weave.** In the form **wove** used of the surface of paper, mean-

ing marked in manufacture by a wire gauze (cf. **laid**).

wrack, *rak, n.* seaweed cast up on the shore, kelp (q.v.): destruction (see **rack** (2)). [Doublet of **wreck.**]

wraith, *rāth, n.* a spectre, an apparition, esp. of a living person: (*fig.*) a thin, pale person.

wrangle, *rang'gl, v.i.* (*arch.*) to dispute: to dispute noisily or peevishly.—Also *v.t.*—*n.* a noisy dispute.—*ns.* **wrang'ler,** one who disputes angrily: in the University of Cambridge, one of those who have attained the first class in the examinations for mathematical honours; **wrang'lership.** [A freq. of **wring.**]

wrap, *rap, v.t.* to roll or fold together: to enfold (*lit.* and *fig.*): to cover by folding or winding something round (often with *up*):—*pr.p.* wrapp'ing; *pa.t.* and *pa.p.* wrapped.—*n.* a covering, as a shawl, &c.—*n.* **wrapp'er,** one who, or that which, wraps: a garment like a dressing-gown: a loose paper bookcover: a paper band, e.g. on a newspaper for the post.—**wrap up,** (*coll.*) to settle completely: to have completely in hand: (as *interj.; slang*) be quiet!; **wrapped up in,** comprised in: devoted to, engrossed in. [M.E. *wrappen,* also *wlappen.* Cf. **lap** (v.t. to wrap) and **envelop.**]

wrath, *rōth, rath, n.* violent anger: holy indignation.—*adj.* **wrath'ful,** full of wrath, very angry: springing from, or expressing, wrath.—*adv.* **wrath'fully.**—*n.* **wrath'fulness.** [Old Northumbrian *wrǣththu*—O.E. *wrāth,* adj. wroth; O.N. *reithi.*]

wreak, *rēk, v.t.* to give full play or effect to (anger, resentment, &c.): inflict or execute (e.g. vengeance). [O.E. *wrecan,* orig. to drive, and so to punish, avenge; O.N. *reka,* to drive, pursue, Ger. *rächen;* conn. with L. *urgēre.*]

wreath, *rēth, n.* a chaplet: a garland: a drift or curl of vapour: a snowdrift: a defect in glass:—*pl.* **wreaths** (*rē*тнz)—*v.t.* **wreathe** (*rē*тн), to form into a wreath: to twine about or encircle.—*v.i.* to twine. [O.E. *writha;* allied to *wrīthan,* to writhe.]

wreck, *rek, n.* destruction: destruction of a ship: a badly damaged ship: remains of anything ruined: a person ruined mentally or physically.—*v.t.* to destroy or disable: to ruin.—*v.i.* to suffer wreck or ruin.—*ns.* **wreck'age,** the act of wrecking: wrecked material; **wreck'er,** a person who purposely causes a wreck or who plunders wreckage. [O.E. *wrǣc,* expulsion—*wrecan,* to drive, Low Ger. *wrak,* Du. *wrak,* O.N. *reki,* a thing drifted ashore; a doublet of **wrack.**]

wren, *ren, n.* a family of small passerine songbirds. [O.E. *wrenna, wrænna.*]

Wren, *ren, n.* a member of the W.R.N.S., Women's Royal Naval Services.

wrench, *rench,* or *-sh, v.t.* to wring or pull with a twist: to force by violence: to sprain.—*v.i.* to undergo a violent wrenching.—*n.* a violent twist: a sprain: an instrument for turning nuts, &c.: emotional pain at parting. [O.E. *wrencan* (Ger. *renken*)—*wrenc,* fraud; root of **wring.**]

wrest, *rest, v.t.* to twist by force (from): to get by toil: to twist from truth or from its natural meaning.—*n.* **wrest'er.** [O.E. *wrǣstan*—*wrǣst,* firm—*wrāth,* pa.t. of *wrīthan,* to writhe.]

Neutral vowels in unaccented syllables: *em'pér-òr;* for certain sounds in foreign words see p. ix.

wrestle, *res'l*, *v.t.* and *v.i.* to contend with another by grappling and trying to throw him down: to struggle (with—*lit.* and *fig.*).—*n.* a bout of wrestling: a struggle between two to throw each other down.—*n.* **wrest'ler**. [O.E. *wræstlian*; a freq. of *wræstan*, to wrest.]

wretch, *rech*, *n.* a most miserable person: one sunk in vice: a worthless person.—*adj.* **wretch'ed**, very miserable: distressingly bad: despicable, worthless.—*adv.* **wretch'edly.**—*n.* **wretch'edness**. [O.E. *wrecca*, an outcast—*wræc*, pa.t. of *wrecan*, to drive, punish, exile.]

wriggle, *rig'l*, *v.i.* to twist to and fro: to move with a twisting or sinuous motion: (*fig.*) to use evasive tricks.—*v.t.* to cause to wriggle.—*n.* the motion of wriggling.—*n.* **wrigg'ler**. [A freq. of obs. *wrig*, to move about, itself a variant of *wrick*, M.E. *wrikken*, to twist; cf. Du. *wriggelen*, to wriggle.]

wright, *rīt*, *n.* a maker (chiefly used in compounds, as *shipwright* &c.). [O.E. *wyrhta—wyrht*, a work—*wyrcan*, to work.]

wring, *ring*, *v.t.* to twist: to force by twisting: (*lit.* and *fig.*) to expel moisture from material by hand twisting or roller pressure: to pain: to extort:—*pa.t.* and *pa.p.* **wrung**, (*B.*) **wringed.**—*n.* **wring'er**, one who wrings: a machine for forcing water from wet clothes.—*adj.* **wring'ing-wet**, so wet that water can be wrung out. [O.E. *wringan*, to twist; Du. *wringen*, Ger. *ringen*; cf. **wreak**, **wry**.]

wrinkle, *ring'kl*, *n.* (*coll.*) a tip, valuable hint. [Perh. from O.E. *wrenc*, a trick; cf. **wrench**.]

wrinkle, *ring'kl*, *n.* a small crease or furrow on a surface: unevenness.—*v.t.* to contract into wrinkles or furrows: to make uneven.—*v.i.* to shrink into ridges.—*adj.* **wrink'ly**, full of wrinkles: liable to be wrinkled. [M.E. *wrinkel*, conn. with O.E. *wringan*, to twist.]

wrist, *rist*, *n.* the joint by which the hand is united to the arm.—*ns.* **wrist'band**, the band or part of a sleeve that covers the wrist; **wrist'let**, a band or strap on the wrist: a bracelet: a wrist-watch on a bracelet or strap. [O.E. *wrist—wríthan*, to twist.]

writ, *rit*, obsolete pa.t. and pa.p. of **write**.

writ, *rit*, *n.* a writing: (*law*) a written document by which one is summoned or required to do something.—**Holy Writ**, the Scriptures. [**write**.]

write, *rīt*, *v.t.* to form letters as with a pen or pencil: to express in writing: to compose (e.g. a poem): to record: to communicate by letter.—*v.i.* to perform the act of writing: to compose: to send a letter (to a person):—*pr.p.* **wrī'ting**;*pa.t.* **wrōte**;*pa.p.* **writt'en.**—*ns.* **wrī'ter**, one who writes: a professional scribe or clerk: an ordinary legal practitioner in Scottish country towns: an author; **wrī'ter's-cramp**, cramp of the muscles of the hand caused by much writing; **wrī'tership**, the office of a writer; **wrī'ting**, the act of forming letters as with a pen: that which is written: literary production; **wrī'ting-case**, a portable case containing materials for writing.—*adj.* **writt'en**, expressed in writing—opposed to *oral*. —**Writers to the Signet**, an ancient society of solicitors in Scotland who formerly had the exclusive right to prepare all writs issued under the royal signet.—**write down**, to set down in writing: to depreciate, to write disparagingly of: to write so as to be intelligible (to), or attractive (to), people of lower intelligence or inferior taste—esp. to do so condescendingly or contemptuously; **write (in) for**, to apply for: to send away for; **write off**, to cancel, esp., in book-keeping, to take (e.g. a bad debt) off the books: (*fig.*) to regard, accept, as an irredeemable loss (*n.* **write'-off**; *adj.* **writt'en-off**); **write out**, to transcribe; **write up**, to bring (a writing) up to date: to write a full description of: to write in praise of. [O.E. *wrītan*; O.N. *rita*; the original meaning being 'to scratch'; cf. the cog. Ger. *reissen*, to tear.]

writhe, *rīTH*, *v.t.* to twist violently.—*v.i.* to twist this way and that: to squirm (under, at). [O.E. *wríthan*, to twist; O.N. *rítha*; cf. **wreath**, **wrest**, **wrist**.]

wrong, *rong*, *adj.* not according to rule, incorrect: not in accordance with moral law, wicked: not that (thing) which is required, intended, advisable, or suitable: amiss: mistaken, misinformed.—*n.* whatever is not right or just: any injury done to another.—*adv.* not correctly: not in the right way; astray (*to go wrong*; *lit.* or *fig.*).—*v.t.* to do wrong to, to deprive of some right: to impute fault to unjustly.—*ns.* **wrong'-do'er**, an offender, transgressor; **wrong'-do'ing.**—*adj.* **wrong'ful**, wrong: unjust: unlawful.—*adv.* **wrong'fully.**—*n.* **wrong'fulness.**—*adj.* **wrong'head'ed**, obstinate and perverse, adhering stubbornly to wrong principles or policy.—*n.* **wrong'head'edness.**—*adv.* **wrong'ly**, in a wrong manner.—*adj.* **wrong'ous**, unjust, illegal.—*adv.* **wrong'ously.**—**get on the wrong side of (someone)**, to arouse dislike or antagonism in (someone); **in the wrong**, guilty of error or injustice; **put in the wrong**, to cause to appear in the wrong. [O.E. *wrang*, a wrong; most prob. O.N. *rangr*, unjust; allied to O.E. *wringan*, to wring, like Fr. *tort*, from L. *tortus*, twisted.]

wrote, *rōt*, pa.t. of **write**.

wroth, *rōth*, *roth*, *adj.* (used predicatively) wrathful. [O.E. *wrāth*, angry; cf. O.N. *reithr*.]

wrought, *rōt*, pa.t. and pa.p. of **work** (q.v.), (*arch.*) except in certain senses:—e.g. fashioned: ornamented: manufactured: beaten into shape.—*n.* **wrought'-ī'ron**, iron containing only a small amount of other elements. [O.E. *worhte*, *geworht*, pa.t. and pa.p. of *wyrcan*, *wircan*, to work.]

wrung, *rung*, pa.t. and pa.p. of **wring**.

wry, *rī*, *adj.* twisted or turned to one side: (*fig.*) expressing displeasure.—*ns.* **wry'-neck**, a twisted or distorted neck: a genus of small birds, allied to the woodpeckers, that twist round their heads strangely when surprised; **wry'ness**. [O.E. *wrīgian*, to drive, bend. Conn. with **wriggle** and **writhe**.]

wych-elm, *n.* Same as **witch-elm**.

wynd, *wīnd*, *n.* (*Scot.* and *N. Eng.*) a lane, narrow alley in a town. [Same as **wind** (2).]

wyvern. Same as **wivern**.

fāte, fär; mē, hûr (her); *mīne; mōte, for; mūte; mōōn, fōōt;* ᴛʜen (then)

X

X-chromosome, *ex-krō'mō-sōm,* a chromosome associated with sex-determination, usually occurring paired in the female zygote and cell and alone in the male zygote and cell.—*n. pl.* **X-rays,** *ex-rāz,* electromagnetic rays of very short wavelength which can penetrate matter opaque to light-rays, produced when cathode rays impinge on matter—discovered by Röntgen in 1895.—*n. sing.* a photograph taken by X-rays.—*v.t.* to photograph or treat by, or otherwise expose to, X-rays.

xenon, *zen'on, n.* a gaseous element (symbol Xe; at. no. 54) present in the atmosphere in minute quantities. [Gr. *xenos,* a stranger.]

xenophobia, *zen-ō-fō'bi-ä, n.* fear or hatred of strangers or things foreign. [Gr. *xenos,* guest, stranger, *phobos,* fear.]

xerography, *zē-rog'rá-fi, n.* a non-chemical reprographic process in which the plate is sensitised electrically and developed by dusting with electrically-charged fine powder. [Gr. *xēros,* dry, *graphein,* to write.]

xylem, *zī'lem, n.* the woody part of vegetable tissue—opposed to the *phloem.* [Gr. *xylon,* wood.]

xylography, *zī-log'rá-fi, n.* the art of engraving on wood.—*n.* **xylog'rapher.**—*adjs.* **xylograph'-ic, -al.** [Gr. *xylon,* wood, *graphein,* to write.]

Xylonite, *zī'lon-īt, n.* a thermoplastic, a form of cellulose. [Gr. *xylon,* wood, and suffx. *-ite.*]

xylophone, *zī'lo-fōn, n.* a musical instrument consisting of a series of bars, each sounding a different note when struck by wooden hand-hammers. [Gr. *xylon,* wood, *phōnē,* sound.]

Neutral vowels in unaccented syllables: *em'pér-ór;* for certain sounds in foreign words see p. ix.

Y

yacht, *yot*, *n.* a vessel, generally of light tonnage, fitted for pleasure-trips or racing.—*v.i.* to sail in a yacht.—*ns.* **yacht'-club**, a club of yachtsmen; **yachts'man**, one who keeps or sails a yacht.—**land'-**, **sand'-yacht**, a wheeled boat with sails, for running on land, usu. seabeaches. [Du. *jacht* (formerly *jaght*), from *jagen*, to chase; Ger. *jagen*, to hunt.]

yahoo, *ya-hōō'*, *n.* a name given by Swift in *Gulliver's Travels* to a class of animals which have the forms of men but the understanding and passions of the lowest brutes: a despicable character.

yak, *yak*, *n.* a species of ox found in Tibet, and domesticated there. [Tibetan.]

yam, *yam*, *n.* the potato-like tuber of various tropical plants: the plants themselves. [Port. *inhame.*]

yank, *yangk*, *v.t.* to remove with a jerk (with *out*, *over*). [Origin uncertain.]

Yankee, *yang'ki*, *n.* in America, a citizen of the New England States, or an inhabitant of the northern United States, as opposed to the southern: in British usage, generally an inhabitant of the United States. [Prob. *Janke*, a diminutive of Dutch *Jan*, John.]

yap, *yap*, *v.i.* to yelp, bark sharply: (*coll.*) to speak constantly, esp. in a noisy or foolish manner. [Imit.]

yapp, *yap*, *n.* a limp leather binding in which the cover overlaps the edges of the book. [*Yapp*, a bookseller.]

yard, *yärd*, *n.* an English measure of 3 feet or 36 inches, and equivalent to 0.9144 metre, formerly the distance at 62° F. between two lines crossing two gold studs on a standard bar of gun-metal, in 1963 re-defined by Act of Parliament as 0·9144 metre: a piece (e.g. of material) this length: a long beam on a mast for spreading sails.—*n.* **yard'-arm**, either end of a ship's yard (right or left). [O.E. *gyrd*, *gierd*, a rod, measure; Du. *gardo*, Ger. *gerte*; further conn. with L. *hasta*, a spear.]

yard, *yärd*, *n.* an enclosed place, esp. near a building: an enclosure for a special purpose, as *dockyard*, *railway yard*, *wood yard.*—**The Yard**, Scotland Yard, the London Metropolitan Police headquarters. [O.E. *geard*, hedge, enclosure; Ger. *garten*; conn. with L. *hortus*, Gr. *chortos.*]

yarn, *yärn*, *n.* spun thread: one of the threads of a rope: a sailor's story (spun out to some length), a story generally.—*v.i.* to tell stories. [O.E. *gearn*, thread; O.N. and Ger. *garn.*]

yarrow, *yar'ō*, *n.* a strongly scented plant with finely dissected leaves and a nearly flat-topped cluster of small, usu. white, flowers. [O.E. *gearwe*; Ger. *garbe.*]

yashmak, *yash'mak*, or *-mak'*, *n.* the veil worn by Mohammedan women, covering the face below the eyes. [Ar. *yashmaq.*]

yataghan, *yat'a-gan*, *n.* a long Turkish dagger, without guard, usually curved. [Turk.]

yaw, *yö*, *v.i.* (*orig. naut.*) to deviate from a set course.—Also *v.t.* [Origin obscure.]

yawl, *yöl*, *n.* a ship's small boat, generally with four or six oars: a small fishing or sailing-boat. [Du. *jol.*]

yawn, *yön*, *v.i.* to open the jaws involuntarily from drowsiness: to gape.—*n.* the opening of the mouth from drowsiness.—*adj.* **yawn'ing**, gaping: opening wide: drowsy. [O.E. *gānian*, to yawn—*gīnan*, pa.t. *gān*, to gape widely; O.N. *gīna*, to gape, Gr. *chainein*, to gape.]

yaws, *yöz*, *n.* a tropical contagious skin disease.

yclept, or **ycleped**, *i-klept'*, *pa.p.* (*obs.*) called. [O.E. *clipian*, to call.]

ye, *yē*, *pron.* the nom. pl. of the 2nd person. [O.E. *gē* (nom.), *ye*; *ēower* (gen.); *ēow* (dat. and acc.). See **you**.]

ye, archaic script for 'the', arising from the thorn (q.v.) letter.

yea, *yā*, *adv.* yes: verily. [O.E. *gēa*; Du. and Ger. *ja*, O.N. *jā*; cf. **yes**.]

year, *yēr*, *n.* a period of time determined by the revolution of the earth in its orbit: the period beginning with 1st January and ending with 31st December, consisting of 365 days (except in 'leap-year', when one day is added to February, making the number 366): a space of twelve calendar months: (*pl.*) period of life, esp. age or old age.—*ns.* **year' book**, an annual review of the events of the past year; **year'ling**, an animal a year old.—*adj.* **year'ly**, happening every year: lasting a year.—*adv.* once a year: from year to year.—**year in, year out**, happening every year: happening with monotonous regularity. [O.E. *gēar*, *gēr*; Ger. *jahr*, O.N. *ār*, Gr. *hōrā*, season.]

yearn, *yûrn*, *v.i.* to feel earnest desire (for): to feel uneasiness, from longing or pity.—*n.* **yearn'ing**, earnest desire, tenderness, or pity.—*adj.* longing.—*adv.* **yearn'ingly**, eager.] [O.E. *giernan*, *giernian*, to desire—*georn*, desirous, eager.]

yeast, *yēst*, *n.* a substance, consisting of certain minute fungi, which causes alcoholic fermentation, used in brewing and baking (see **enzyme**).—*adj.* **yeast'y**, like yeast: frothy, foamy. [O.E. *gist*, *gyst*; Ger. *gäscht*, *gischt.*]

yelk. Same as **yolk**.

yell, *yel*, *v.i.* to howl or cry out with a sharp noise: to scream from pain or terror.—*v.t.* to utter with a yell.—*n.* a sharp outcry. [O.E. *gellan*; Ger. *gellen*; conn. with O.E. *galan*, to sing.]

yellow, *yel'ō*, *adj.* of the colour of gold or of the primrose: of Mongolian race: (*coll.*) cowardly: sensational.—*n.* the colour of the rainbow between orange and green.—*v.i.* to become yellow(ish), e.g. with age.—*ns.* **yellow fever**, a pestilential tropical fever—also known as yellow jack; **yellow flag,** a flag of a yellow colour, displayed by a vessel in quarantine or over a military hospital or ambulance; **yell′ow-hamm′er,** a finch, so named from its yellow colour, also called **yell′ow-bunt′ing.**—*adj.* **yel′-l′owish,** somewhat yellow.—*ns.* **yell′owish-ness; yell′owness.**—**yellow peril,** the threat that the yellow-skinned races may overrun the world: derogatorily the Chinese or Japanese. [O.E. *geolo*; Ger. *gelb*; cog. with L. *helvus,* light bay.]

yelp, *yelp, v.i.* to utter a sharp bark.—*n.* a sharp, quick cry or bark. [O.E. *gilpan,* to boast, exult; O.N. *giālpa,* to yelp.]

yen, *yen, n.* a Japanese gold or silver coin, used as the monetary unit since 1871. [Jap.,—Chinese *yüan,* round, a dollar.]

yen, *yen, n.* (*slang*) an intense desire, longing, urge.—*v.i.* to desire, yearn. [Chinese *yeen,* craving, addiction.]

yeoman, *yō′mán, n.* in early English history, a common menial attendant: after the fifteenth century, one of a class of small farmers, the next grade below gentlemen: a man of small estate, any countryman above the grade of labourer: an officer of the royal household: a member of the yeomanry cavalry:—*pl.* **yeo′-men.**—*n.* **yeo′manry,** the collective body of yeomen or smaller freeholders: a cavalry volunteer force in Great Britain, formed during the wars of the French Revolution.—**yeomen of the guard,** a veteran company of picked soldiers, employed in conjunction with the gentlemen-at-arms on special occasions as the sovereign's bodyguard; **yeoman('s) service,** powerful aid, such as came from the yeomen in the English armies of early times. [M.E. *yoman, yeman,* doubtless from an O.E. *gāman,* not found, but seen in Old Frisian *gāman,* villager—*gā,* a village (Ger. *gau,* district), *man,* man.]

yerba, *yûr′ba, n.* a herb, esp. **yerba maté,** or Paraguay tea. [Sp.,—L. *herba.* See also **maté.**]

yes, *yes, adv.* ay: a word of affirmation or consent.—*n.* **yes′-man,** (*coll.*) one who agrees with everything that is said to him, an obedient follower with no initiative. [O.E. *gīse, gēse*—*gēa,* yea, *sȳ,* let it be.]

yester, *yes′tér, adj.* relating to yesterday last.—*n.* **yes′terday,** the day last past.—*adv.* on the day last past.—*ns.* **yes′ternight,** the night last past; **yestreen,** (*Scot.* and *poet.*) yesterday evening. [O.E. *geostran-, giestran-* (only in compounds); Ger. *gestern*; cf. L. *hesternus,* Gr. *chthes.*]

yet, *yet, adv.* in addition, besides: still: up to the present time: before the matter is finished (e.g. *will get even with him yet*): even (e.g. a *yet more terrible experience*).—*conj.* nevertheless: however.—**as yet,** up to the time under consideration. [O.E. *gīet, gīeta*; Ger. *jetzt.*]

yeti, *yet′i, n.* the abominable snowman. [Native Tibetan name.]

yew, *ū, n.* an evergreen tree, allied to the pine, long planted in graveyards, yielding an elastic wood good for bows: any other tree of the same genus. [O.E. *īw, ēow, ēoh*; Ger. *eibe.*]

Yiddish, *yid′ish, n.* a compound of very corrupt Hebrew and ancient or provincial German

spoken by Jews. [Ger. *jüdisch,* Jewish.]

yield, *yēld, v.t.* to resign: to grant: to give out, to produce.—*v.i.* to submit: to give place.—*n.* amount yielded: the return on a financial investment.—*adj.* **yield′ing,** inclined to give or to give way: compliant.—*adv.* **yield′ingly.** [O.E. *gieldan, gildan,* to pay; Ger. *gelten*; O.N. *gjalda.*]

Yin, Yang, *yin, yang, ns.* the two opposing principles of Chinese philosophy and religion influencing destiny, the former negative, feminine and dark, the latter positive, masculine and light.

yob, *yob, n.* (*slang*) a raw recruit: a lout.—Also **yobbo.** [Back-slang for **boy.**]

yodel, yodle, *yō′dl, v.t.* and *v.i.* to sing, changing frequently from the ordinary voice to falsetto and back again after the manner of the mountaineers of the Tirol.—*n.* a song sung in this fashion.—Also **jō′del.**—*n.* **yō′deler, yō′dler.** [Ger. dial. *jodeln.*]

yoga, *yō′ga, n.* a meditative Hindu philosophy showing the means of emancipation of the soul from further migrations.—*ns.* **yō′gi,** a Hindu ascetic who practises the *yoga* system; **yō′gism.** [Hindustani—Sans. *yoga,* union.]

yogh, *yoн, n.* the obsolete English letter ʒ. [M.E.; origin unknown; contains the two chief sounds of the letter.]

yoghourt, yoghurt, *yōg′oŏrt, yog′ért, n.* a semi-liquid food made from fermented milk.—Also **yaourt** (*yä′oōrt*). [Turk. *yōghurt.*]

yoke, *yōk, n.* that which joins together: the frame of wood joining oxen for drawing together: any similar frame, as one for carrying pails: a mark of servitude: slavery: a pair or couple: part of a garment which fits the shoulders.—*v.t.* to put a yoke on: to join together: to enslave.—*ns.* **yoke′-fell′ow, -mate,** a comrade, partner. [O.E. *geoc, iuc, ioc*; Ger. *joch*; L. *jugum,* Gr. *zygon.*]

yokel, *yō′kl, n.* a country bumpkin.

yolk, *yōk,* (*rare*) **yelk,** *yelk, n.* the yellow part of an egg. [O.E. *geolca, geoleca—geolo,* yellow.]

yon, *yon, yonder, yon′dér, advs.* in that place (referring to somewhere at a distance within view).—*adj.* that (referring to something at a distance within view). [O.E. *geon*; Ger. *jener,* that.]

yore, *yōr, yŏr, n.* old time, time long past.—**of yore,** formerly. [O.E. *geāra,* formerly, apparently connected with *gēar,* a year.]

yorker, *yōr′kér, n.* (*cricket*) a ball pitching just under the bat. [Orig. unknown.]

you, *ū, pron.* 2nd pers. pl., but also used as singular: anyone. [O.E. *ēow* (perh. through a later form *ēōw*), orig. only dat. and acc.; cf. **ye.**]

young, *yung, adj.* not long born: in early life: in the first part of growth: the offspring of animals.—*adj.* **young′ish,** somewhat young.—*ns.* **young′ling,** a young person or animal; **young′ster,** a young person: a lad.—**with young,** pregnant. [O.E. *geong*; Ger. *jung*; also conn. with L. *juvenis,* Sans. *yuvan,* young.]

younker, *yung′kér, n.* a young person. [Old Du. *joncker* (Du. *jonker*), from *jonk-heer,* 'young master' or 'lord'; Ger. *junker.*]

your, *ūr, possessive adj.* (also called *possessive pron.*) of or belonging to you: the ordinary

Neutral vowels in unaccented syllables: *em′pér-ór*; for certain sounds in foreign words see p. ix.

(e.g. *your enthusiast will maintain*). [O.E. *ēower*; cf. **ye.**]

yours, *ūrz, pron.* the possessive (*gen.*) case of **you.**—Also *possessive adj.* (used without noun); cf. **theirs** for uses and derivation.

yourself, *ūr-self', pron.* the emphatic form of **you**: in your real character: having command of your faculties: sane: in good form: the reflexive form of **you** (objective):—*pl.* **yourselves'**.

youth, *yōōth, n.* state of being young: early life: a young person, esp. a young man: young persons collectively.—*adj.* **youth'ful**, pertaining to youth or early life: young: suitable to youth: fresh: buoyant, vigorous.—*adv.* **youth'fully.**—*n.* **youth'fulness.**—**youth hostel**, a hostel (q.v.) for hikers, &c., provided by the Youth Hostels Association.—*v.i.* to stay in youth hostels.—*n.* **youth hosteller.** [O.E. *geogoth*—*geong*, young; Ger. *jugend.*]

yowl, *yowl, v.i.* to cry mournfully, as a dog: to yell, bawl.—*n.* a distressed cry. [M.E. *yowlen.*]

ytterbium, *i-tûr'bi-ùm, n.* a rare metallic element (symbol Yb; at. no. 70).—Also called **neo-ytterbium** to distinguish it from the substance, consisting of a mixture of ytterbium and lutetium, originally given the name ytterbium. [*Ytterby*, a Swedish quarry.]

yttrium, *it'ri-ùm, n.* a rare metallic element (symbol Y; atomic no. 39). [*Ytterby*, a Swedish quarry.]

yucca, *yuk'a, n.* a large garden plant of the lily family, familiarly called Adam's needle, native to subtropical America: other species of the same genus. [W. Indian name.]

yule, *yōōl, n.* the season or feast of Christmas.—*n.* **yule'tide**, the Christmas season. [O.E. *gēol*; O.N. *jōl.*]

yurt, yourt, *yŏŏrt, n.* a light tent of skins, &c., used by nomads in Siberia. [From Russ.]

ywis. Same as **iwis.**

fāte, fär; mē, hûr (her); mīne; mōte, för; mūte; mōōn, fŏŏt; ᴛʜen (then)

Z

zany, *zā′ni, n.* (*obs.*) a merry-andrew, a buffoon: an idiot, a fool.—*adj.* crazy, clownish. [Fr. *zani*—It. *zani*, a corr. of *Giovanni*, John.]

Zarathustrian, *zar-a-thōōs′tri-án, adj.* and *n.* Same as **Zoroastrian** (q.v.).

zareba, *za-rē′ba, n.* a stockade: a camp protected by a stockade. [Ar. *zarībah.*]

zeal, *zēl, n.* intense or passionate ardour, enthusiasm.—*n.* **zealot** (*zel′ot*), one full of zeal, an enthusiast, a fanatic.—*adj.* **zealous** (*zel′-*), full of zeal, warmly engaged or ardent in anything.—*adv.* **zealously** (*zel′-*). [O.Fr. *zele*—L. *zēlus*—Gr. *zēlos*—*zeein*, to boil.]

zebra, *zē′bra, n.* any of several beautifully striped animals of the horse kind, peculiar to the African continent.—**zebra crossing**, a street-crossing marked with stripes, where pedestrians have priority. [Of African origin.]

zebu, *zē′bū, n.* the humped domestic ox, found in many parts of India, China, the east coast of Africa, &c. [Fr. *zébu*, ultimately of Asiatic origin.]

zeitgeist, *tsīt′gīst, n.* the spirit of the age. [Ger.]

zemindar, *zem-in-dar′, n.* in India, a native land-holder paying revenue to the Government. [Pers. *zamīndār*, a land-holder.]

Zen, *zen, n.* a Japanese Buddhist sect which holds that the truth is not in scriptures but in man's own heart if he will but strive to find it by meditation and self-mastery. [Jap.—Chin. *ch′an*, Sans. *dhyāna*, religious contemplation.]

zenana, *ze-nä′na, n.* the apartments in which Indian women are secluded. [Pers. *zanāna*—*zan*, a woman.]

Zend, *zend, n.* the ancient Aryan (q.v.) language of Persia, closely related to Sanskrit.—**Zend-Avesta**, the ancient sacred writings of the Parsees (q.v.). [Pers. *zend, zand*, commentary.]

zenith, *zen′ith, n.* that point of the heavens which is exactly overhead: greatest height, summit of ambition, &c. [Fr., through Sp. *zenit*, from Ar. *samt*, short for *samt-ar-ras*, lit. 'way, direction, of the head'.]

zephyr, *zef′ir, n.* the west wind: a soft, gentle breeze. [Gr. *zephyros*—*zophos*, darkness, the west.]

Zeppelin, *zep′el-in, n.* a dirigible, cigar-shaped airship of the type designed by Count *Zeppelin* (about 1900).

zero, *zē′ro, n.* cipher: nothing: the point from which the reckoning begins in scales, such as those of the barometer, &c.: zero hour.—**zero hour**, exact time (hour, minute, and second) fixed for launching an attack or beginning an operation. [Fr.,—Ar. *sifr.* Doublet **cipher**.]

zest, *zest, n.* skin of an orange or lemon used to give flavour: something that gives a relish: relish, enthusiasm. [Fr. *zeste*—Gr. *schizein*, to cleave.]

zeugma, *zūg′ma, n.* a figure of speech by which an adjective or verb is applied to two nouns, though strictly appropriate to only one of them. [Gr.,—*zeugnynai*, to yoke.]

zigzag, *zig′zag, n.* a sharp turning: a line or road with sharp angles.—*adj.* having sharp turns.—*v.i.* to proceed in sharp turns:—*pr.p.* zig′zagging; *pa.p.* zig′zagged.—*adv.* with frequent sharp turns. [Fr. *zigzag*—Ger. *zick-zack.*]

zinc, *zingk, n.* a bluish-white metallic element (symbol Zn; atomic no. 30). [Ger. *zink*, prob. allied to *zinn*, tin.]

zincography, *zing-kog′ra-fi, n.* a process of etching on zinc (or copper) by which black and white pictures can be reproduced as blocks for printing by the ordinary process. [*zinc*, Gr. *graphein*, to write.]

Zingaro, *zing′ga-rō, n.* a name in Italy for the Gypsies:—*pl.* **Zing′ari.**—Also **Zing′ano**:—*pl.* **Zing′ane.** [Cf. Ger. *Zigeuner.*]

zinnia, *zin′i-a, n.* a tropical American plant of the thistle family. [From J.G. *Zinn* (1727-59).]

Zion, *zī′on, n.* a hill in Jerusalem: Jerusalem: Judaism: Christianity: heaven.—*ns.* **Zi′onism**, (before 1948) a movement for securing national privileges and territory for the Jews; **Zi′onist.** [Heb. *Tsīyōn.*]

zip, *zip, n.* a whizzing sound: a zip-fastener.—*v.i.* and *v.t.* to whizz: to fasten with a zip.—*n.* **zip-fastener** (*zip-fäsn′ér*), a fastening device for clothes, &c., on which two sets of teeth are operated by pulling a slide. [From the sound.]

zirconium, *zér-kō′ni-úm, n.* a rare metallic element (symbol Zr; at. no. 40). [Ar. *zarqūn*, vermilion—Pers. *zargūn*, gold-coloured.]

zither, *zith′ér, n.* a flat many-stringed musical instrument popular in the Tirol. [Ger.; allied to **cithara**.]

zodiac, *zō′di-ak, n.* an imaginary belt in the heavens, containing the twelve constellations, each constellation now (through not in ancient times) lying in the sign (q.v.) next to that which bears its name. [Fr. *zodiaque*—L. *zōdiacus*—Gr. *zōidiakos*, of figures—*zōidion*, a small carved or painted figure—*zōion*, an animal.]

zoic, *zō′ik, adj.* pertaining to animals: (of rocks) containing evidences of life in fossils. [Gr. *zōikos*, of animals—*zōion*, an animal.]

zombi, zombie, *zombi, n.* orig. in Africa, the deity of the python: in American voodooism, the snake deity: a corpse reanimated by sorcery: a stupid or useless person. [W. African *zumbi*, fetish.]

zone, *zōn, n.* (*arch.*) a girdle, a belt: one of the five great belts into which the surface of the earth is divided: any continuous area of belt-like form: a region.—*v.t.* to encircle as with a zone: to divide into zones: to assign to a zone.—*adj.* **zoned**, wearing a zone, having zones. [L. *zōna*—Gr. *zōnē*, a girdle—*zōnnynai*, to gird.]

Neutral vowels in unaccented syllables: *em′pér-ôr*; for certain sounds in foreign words see p. ix.